MAJOR 20th-CENTURY WRITERS

KT-160-549

MAJOR 20th-CENTURY WRITERS

♦
♦
♦
♦

A Selection of Sketches from
Contemporary Authors

Contains more than one thousand entries on the most widely studied twentieth-century writers, all originally written or updated for this set.

First Edition

Bryan Ryan, Editor

♦

Volume 4: R–Z/Indexes

 Gale Research Inc. · DETROIT · LONDON

STAFF

Bryan Ryan, **Editor**

Marilyn K. Basel, Barbara Carlisle Bigelow, Christa Brelin, Carol Lynn DeKane, Janice E. Drane,
Kevin S. Hile, Thomas Kozikowski, Sharon Malinowski, Emily J. McMurray,
Michael E. Mueller, Kenneth R. Shepherd, Les Stone, Diane Telgen,
Polly A. Vedder, and Thomas Wiloch, **Associate Editors**

Marian Gonsior, Katherine Huebl, James F. Kamp, Margaret Mazurkiewicz,
Jani Prescott, and Neil R. Schlager, **Assistant Editors**

Anne Janette Johnson, Donna Olendorf, and Curtis Skinner, **Contributing Sketchwriters**

Hal May, **Senior Editor,** *Contemporary Authors*

Mary Rose Bonk, **Research Supervisor, Biography Division**

Jane Cousins, Andrew Guy Malonis, and Norma Sawaya, **Editorial Associates**

Reginald A. Carlton, Shirley Gates, Sharon McGilvray,
Diane Linda Sevigny, and Tracey Head Turbett, **Editorial Assistants**

Mary Beth Trimper, **Production Manager**
Evi Seoud, **Assistant Production Manager**

Arthur Chartow, **Art Director**
Kathleen A. Mouzakis, **Graphic Designer**
C. J. Jonik, **Keyliner**

While every effort has been made to ensure the reliability of the information presented in this publication, Gale Research Inc. does not guarantee the accuracy of the data contained herein. Gale accepts no payment for listing; and inclusion in the publication of any organization, agency, institution, publication, service, or individual does not imply endorsement of the editors or publisher. Errors brought to the attention of the publisher and verified to the satisfaction of the publisher will be corrected in future editions.

∞™ This book is printed on acid-free paper that meets the minimum requirements of American National Standard for Information Sciences Permanence Paper for Printed Library Materials, ANSI Z39.48-1984.

♲ This book is printed on recycled paper that meets Environmental Protection Agency standards.

This publication is a creative work copyrighted by Gale Research Inc. and fully protected by all applicable copyright laws, as well as by misappropriation, trade secret, unfair competition, and other applicable laws. The authors and editors of this work have added value to the underlying factual material herein through one or more of the following: unique and original selection, coordination, expression, arrangement, and classification of the information.
Gale Research Inc. will vigorously defend all of its rights in this publication.

Copyright © 1991 by Gale Research Inc.
835 Penobscot Building
Detroit, MI 48226-4094
All rights reserved including the right of reproduction in whole or in part in any form.

Library of Congress Catalog Card Number: 90-84380
ISBN 0-8103-7766-7 (Set)
ISBN 0-8103-7915-5 (Volume 4)

No part of this book may be reproduced in any form without permission in writing from the publisher, except by a reviewer who wishes to quote brief passages or entries in connection with a review written for inclusion in a magazine or newspaper.

Printed in the United States of America.

Published simultaneously in the United Kingdom
by Gale Research International Limited
(An affiliated company of Gale Research Inc.)

CONTENTS

INTRODUCTION

An Important Information Source on 20th-Century Literature and Culture

Major 20th-Century Writers provides students, educators, librarians, researchers, and general readers with an affordable and comprehensive source of biographical and bibliographical information on more than 1,000 of the most influential authors of our time. Of primary focus are novelists, short story writers, poets, and dramatists from the United States and the United Kingdom, but prominent writers from over sixty other nations have also been included. Important figures from beyond the literary realm, nonfiction writers who have influenced twentieth-century thought, are also found here.

The vast majority of the entries in *Major 20th-Century Writers* were selected from Gale's acclaimed *Contemporary Authors* series and completely updated for this publication. About 40 sketches on important authors not already in *CA* were written especially for this four−volume set to furnish readers with the most comprehensive coverage possible. These newly written entries will also appear in future volumes of *Contemporary Authors*.

International Advisory Board

Before preparing *Major 20th-Century Writers*, the editors of *Contemporary Authors* conducted a telephone survey of librarians and mailed a print survey to more than four thousand libraries to help determine the kind of reference tool libraries wanted. Once it was clear that a comprehensive, yet affordable source of information on the best 20th-century writers was needed to serve small and medium-sized libraries, a wide range of resources was consulted: national surveys of books taught in American high schools and universities; British secondary school syllabi; reference works such as the *New York Public Library Desk Reference*, *Reading Lists for College-Bound Students: The Books Most Recommended by America's Top Colleges*, *The List of Books*, E. D. Hirsch's *Cultural Literacy*, and volumes in Gale's Literary Criticism series and *Dictionary of Literary Biography*.

A preliminary list of authors drawn from these sources was then sent to an advisory board of librarians and teaching professionals in both the United States and Great Britain. The recommendations made by these advisors helped define the scope of the project and the final list of authors to be included in the four-volume set. Stephen T. Willis, Social Sciences Librarian at the Manchester Central Library in Manchester, England, focused on the literary and nonliterary writers of most interest to British school libraries and public libraries, with special consideration for those authors who are relevant to the GCSE and A-level public examinations. Jacqueline G. Morris of the Indiana Department of Education provided input from an American secondary school perspective; Tim LaBorie of St. Joseph University in Philadelphia and Rev. John P. Schlegel, S.J., the Executive and Academic Vice President of John Carroll University in Cleveland, reviewed the list with college students in mind.

Broad Coverage in a Single Source

Built upon these suggestions, *Major 20th-Century Writers* provides single-source coverage of the most influential writers of our time, including:

- *Novelists and short story writers*: James Baldwin, Saul Bellow, Willa Cather, James Joyce, Franz Kafka, Thomas Mann, Flannery O'Connor, George Orwell, Eudora Welty, and Edith Wharton.

- *Dramatists*: Samuel Beckett, Bertolt Brecht, Eugene O'Neill, and Tennessee Williams.

- *Poets*: W. H. Auden, T. S. Eliot, Robert Frost, Ezra Pound, and William Butler Yeats.

- *Contemporary literary figures*: Chinua Achebe, Don DeLillo, Gabriel Garcia Marquez, Nadine Gordimer, Guenter Grass, John Irving, Toni Morrison, V. S. Naipaul, Joyce Carol Oates, and Thomas Pynchon.

- *Genre writers*: Isaac Asimov, Agatha Christie, Tom Clancy, Stephen King, Louis L'Amour, John le Carre, Ursula K. Le Guin, Danielle Steel, and J. R. R. Tolkien.

- *20th-Century thinkers*: Hannah Arendt, Bruno Bettelheim, Joseph Campbell, Albert Einstein, Sigmund Freud, Mohandas Gandhi, Margaret Mead, Jean Piaget, Bertrand Russell, and Jean-Paul Sartre.

Easy Access to Information

Both the newly written and the completely updated entries in *Major 20th-Century Writers* provide in-depth information in a format designed for ease of use. Individual paragraphs within each entry, labeled with descriptive rubrics, ensure that a reader seeking specific information can quickly focus on the pertinent portion of an entry.

A typical entry in *Major 20th-Century Writers* contains the following, clearly labeled information sections:

- *PERSONAL:* dates and places of birth and death; parents' names and occupations; name(s) of spouse(s), date(s) of marriage(s); names of children; colleges attended and degrees earned; political and religious affiliation when known.

- *ADDRESSES:* complete home, office, and agent's addresses.

- *CAREER:* name of employer, position, and dates for each career post; résumé of other vocational achievements; military service.

- *MEMBER:* memberships and offices held in professional and civic organizations.

- *AWARDS, HONORS:* literary and professional awards received and dates.

- *WRITINGS:* title-by-title chronological bibliography of books written and edited, listed by genre when known; list of other notable publications, such as plays, screenplays, and periodical contributions.

- *WORK IN PROGRESS:* description of projects in progress.

- *SIDELIGHTS:* a biographical portrait of the author's development; information about the critical reception of the author's works; revealing comments, often by the author, on personal interests, aspirations, motivations, and thoughts on writing.

- *BIOGRAPHICAL/CRITICAL SOURCES:* books, feature articles, and reviews in which the writer's work has been treated.

Nationality Index Reveals International Scope

Authors included in *Major 20th-Century Writers* appear alphabetically in an index organized by country of birth and/or citizenship. More than 60 nations are represented, reflecting the international scope of this set.

Genre/Subject Index Indicates Range of Writers' Works

The written works composed by the authors collected in this four-volume set represent not only literary novels, short stories, plays, and poems, but also over 25 other genres and subject areas of fiction and nonfiction.

Acknowledgments

The editor wishes to thank: Barbara Carlisle Bigelow for her editorial assistance; Kenneth R. Shepherd for his technical assistance; and James G. Lesniak and Susan M. Trosky, editors of the *Contemporary Authors* series, for their cooperation and assistance, and for that of their staffs.

Comments Are Appreciated

Major 20th-Century Writers is intended to serve as a useful reference tool for a wide audience, so your comments about this work are encouraged. Suggestions of authors to include in future editions of *Major 20th-Century Writers* are also welcome. Send comments and suggestions to: The Editor, *Major 20th-Century Writers*, Gale Research Inc., 835 Penobscot Bldg., Detroit, MI 48226-4094. Or, call toll-free at 1-800-347-GALE.

MAJOR 20th-CENTURY WRITERS

VOLUME 1: A-D

Abe, Kobo 1924-
Abrahams, Peter 1919-
Achebe, Chinua 1930-
Adamov, Arthur 1908-1970
Adams, Alice 1926-
Adams, Richard 1920-
Adamson, Joy 1910-1980
Adler, Mortimer J. 1902-
Adler, Renata 1938-
Agnon, S. Y. 1888-1970
Aiken, Conrad 1889-1973
Aiken, Joan 1924-
Aitmatov, Chingiz 1928-
Akhmatova, Anna 1888-1966
Albee, Edward 1928-
Alcayaga, Lucila Godoy
    See Godoy Alcayaga, Lucila
Aldiss, Brian W. 1925-
Aleixandre, Vicente 1898-1984
Alexander, Lloyd 1924-
Algren, Nelson 1909-1981
Allen, Woody 1935-
Allende, Isabel 1942-
Allingham, Margery 1904-1966
Alther, Lisa 1944-
Amado, Jorge 1912-
Ambler, Eric 1909-
Amichai, Yehuda 1924-
Amis, Kingsley 1922-
Ammons, A. R. 1926-
Anand, Mulk Raj 1905-
Anaya, Rudolfo A. 1937-
Andersch, Alfred 1914-1980
Anderson, Poul 1926-
Anderson, Sherwood 1876-1941
Andrews, V. C. ?-1986
Andric, Ivo 1892-1975
Angelou, Maya 1928-
Anouilh, Jean 1910-1987
Anthony, Piers 1934-
Antschel, Paul 1920-1970
Aragon, Louis 1897-1982
Arden, John 1930-
Arendt, Hannah 1906-1975
Armah, Ayi Kwei 1939-
Arnow, Harriette Simpson 1908-
    1986
Ashbery, John 1927-
Ashton-Warner, Sylvia 1908-1984
Asimov, Isaac 1920-

Asturias, Miguel Angel 1899-1974
Atwood, Margaret 1939-
Auchincloss, Louis 1917-
Auden, W. H. 1907-1973
Avison, Margaret 1918-
Ayckbourn, Alan 1939-
Azuela, Mariano 1873-1952
Bach, Richard 1936-
Bachman, Richard
    See King, Stephen
Bainbridge, Beryl 1933-
Baker, Russell 1925-
Baldwin, James 1924-1987
Ballard, J. G. 1930-
Bambara, Toni Cade 1939-
Baraka, Amiri 1934-
Barker, Clive 1952-
Barker, George Granville 1913-
Barnes, Djuna 1892-1982
Barnes, Peter 1931-
Barth, John 1930-
Barthelme, Donald 1931-1989
Barthes, Roland 1915-1980
Bashevis, Isaac
    See Singer, Isaac Bashevis
Bassani, Giorgio 1916-
Bates, H. E. 1905-1974
Baum, L. Frank 1856-1919
Baumbach, Jonathan 1933-
Beattie, Ann 1947-
Beauvoir, Simone de 1908-1986
Beckett, Samuel 1906-1989
Behan, Brendan 1923-1964
Bell, Clive 1881-1964
Bell, Marvin 1937-
Bellow, Saul 1915-
Benavente, Jacinto 1866-1954
Benchley, Peter 1940-
Bennett, Alan 1934-
Berger, Thomas 1924-
Berne, Eric 1910-1970
Bernhard, Thomas 1931-1989
Berryman, John 1914-1972
Bester, Alfred 1913-1987
Beti, Mongo
    See Biyidi, Alexandre
Betjeman, John 1906-1984
Bettelheim, Bruno 1903-1990
Bioy Casares, Adolfo 1914-
Birney, Earle 1904-

Bishop, Elizabeth 1911-1979
bissett, bill 1939-
Biyidi, Alexandre 1932-
Blackwood, Caroline 1931-
Blair, Eric 1903-1950
Blais, Marie-Claire 1939-
Blasco Ibanez, Vicente 1867-1928
Blish, James 1921-1975
Blixen, Karen 1885-1962
Blount, Roy, Jr. 1941-
Blume, Judy 1938-
Blunden, Edmund 1896-1974
Bly, Robert 1926-
Bodet, Jaime Torres
    See Torres Bodet, Jaime
Boell, Heinrich 1917-1985
Bogan, Louise 1897-1970
Boll, Heinrich
    See Boell, Heinrich
Bolt, Robert 1924-
Bombeck, Erma 1927-
Bond, Edward 1934-
Bonnefoy, Yves 1923-
Bontemps, Arna 1902-1973
Borges, Jorge Luis 1899-1986
Bova, Ben 1932-
Bowen, Elizabeth 1899-1973
Bowles, Paul 1910-
Boyle, Kay 1902-
Bradbury, Malcolm 1932-
Bradbury, Ray 1920-
Bradford, Barbara Taylor 1933-
Bradley, Marion Zimmer 1930-
Braine, John 1922-1986
Brautigan, Richard 1935-1984
Brecht, Bertolt 1898-1956
Brenton, Howard 1942-
Breslin, James 1930-
Breslin, Jimmy
    See Breslin, James
Breton, Andre 1896-1966
Brink, Andre 1935-
Brittain, Vera 1893(?)-1970
Brodsky, Iosif Alexandrovich 1940-
Brodsky, Joseph
    See Brodsky, Iosif Alexandrovich
Brook, Peter 1925-
Brooke, Rupert 1887-1915
Brookner, Anita 1938-
Brooks, Cleanth 1906-

Brooks, Gwendolyn 1917-
Brophy, Brigid 1929-
Brother Antoninus
    See Everson, William
Brown, Dee 1908-
Brown, George Mackay 1921-
Brown, Rita Mae 1944-
Brown, Sterling Allen 1901-1989
Brownmiller, Susan 1935-
Brunner, John 1934-
Buber, Martin 1878-1965
Buchwald, Art 1925-
Buck, Pearl S. 1892-1973
Buckley, William F., Jr. 1925-
Buechner, Frederick 1926-
Buero Vallejo, Antonio 1916-
Bukowski, Charles 1920-
Bullins, Ed 1935-
Bultmann, Rudolf Karl 1884-1976
Burgess, Anthony
    See Wilson, John Burgess
Burke, Kenneth 1897-
Burroughs, Edgar Rice 1875-1950
Burroughs, William S. 1914-
Bustos Domecq, H.
    See Bioy Casares, Adolfo
    and Borges, Jorge Luis
Butler, Octavia E. 1947-
Butor, Michel 1926-
Byars, Betsy 1928-
Byatt, A. S. 1936-
Cabrera Infante, G. 1929-
Cade, Toni
    See Bambara, Toni Cade
Cain, Guillermo
    See Cabrera Infante, G.
Cain, James M. 1892-1977
Calder, Nigel 1931-
Caldicott, Helen 1938-
Caldwell, Erskine 1903-1987
Calisher, Hortense 1911-
Callaghan, Morley Edward 1903-
    1990
Calvino, Italo 1923-1985
Cameron, Eleanor 1912-
Campbell, John W. 1910-1971
Campbell, Joseph 1904-1987
Camus, Albert 1913-1960
Canetti, Elias 1905-
Capote, Truman 1924-1984
Card, Orson Scott 1951-
Cardenal, Ernesto 1925-
Carey, Peter 1943-
Carr, John Dickson 1906-1977
Carruth, Hayden 1921-
Carson, Rachel Louise 1907-1964
Carter, Angela 1940-
Carter, James Earl, Jr. 1924-
Carter, Jimmy
    See Carter, James Earl, Jr.
Cartland, Barbara 1901-

Carver, Raymond 1938-1988
Casares, Adolfo Bioy
    See Bioy Casares, Adolfo
Castaneda, Carlos 1931(?)-
Cather, Willa
    See Cather, Willa Sibert
Cather, Willa Sibert 1873-1947
Causley, Charles 1917-
Cela, Camilo Jose 1916-
Celan, Paul
    See Antschel, Paul
Celine, Louis-Ferdinand
    See Destouches, Louis-Ferdinand
Cendrars, Blaise
    See Sauser-Hall, Frederic
Cesaire, Aime 1913-
Chandler, Raymond 1888-1959
Char, Rene 1907-1988
Charyn, Jerome 1937-
Cheever, John 1912-1982
Chesnutt, Charles W. 1858-1932
Chesterton, G. K. 1874-1936
Ch'ien Chung-shu 1910-
Childress, Alice 1920-
Chomsky, Noam 1928-
Christie, Agatha 1890-1976
Churchill, Caryl 1938-
Churchill, Winston 1874-1965
Ciardi, John 1916-1986
Cixous, Helene 1937-
Clancy, Thomas L., Jr. 1947-
Clancy, Tom
    See Clancy, Thomas L., Jr.
Clark, Kenneth 1903-1983
Clark, Mary Higgins 1929-
Clarke, Arthur C. 1917-
Clavell, James 1925-
Cleary, Beverly 1916-
Cleese, John 1939-
Clifton, Lucille 1936-
Clutha, Janet Paterson Frame 1924-
Cocteau, Jean 1889-1963
Coetzee, J. M. 1940-
Cohen, Leonard 1934-
Colegate, Isabel 1931-
Colette 1873-1954
Colum, Padraic 1881-1972
Colwin, Laurie 1944-
Commager, Henry Steele 1902-
Commoner, Barry 1917-
Compton-Burnett, I. 1884(?)-1969
Condon, Richard 1915-
Connell, Evan S., Jr. 1924-
Connolly, Cyril 1903-1974
Conrad, Joseph 1857-1924
Conran, Shirley 1932-
Conroy, Pat 1945-
Cookson, Catherine 1906-
Coover, Robert 1932-
Cormier, Robert 1925-
Cornwell, David 1931-

Corso, Gregory 1930-
Cortazar, Julio 1914-1984
Cousins, Norman 1915-
Cousteau, Jacques-Yves 1910-
Coward, Noel 1899-1973
Cowley, Malcolm 1898-1989
Cox, William Trevor 1928-
Cozzens, James Gould 1903-1978
Crane, Hart 1899-1932
Creasey, John 1908-1973
Creeley, Robert 1926-
Crews, Harry 1935-
Crichton, Michael 1942-
Cullen, Countee 1903-1946
Cummings, E. E. 1894-1962
Dahl, Roald 1916-
Dahlberg, Edward 1900-1977
Dailey, Janet 1944-
Daly, Mary 1928-
Dannay, Frederic 1905-1982
Dario, Ruben 1867-1916
Davie, Donald 1922-
Davies, Robertson 1913-
Day Lewis, C. 1904-1972
de Beauvoir, Simone
    See Beauvoir, Simone de
de Bono, Edward 1933-
de Filippo, Eduardo 1900-1984
Deighton, Len
    See Deighton, Leonard Cyril
Deighton, Leonard Cyril 1929-
Delaney, Shelagh 1939-
Delany, Samuel R. 1942-
Delibes, Miguel
    See Delibes Setien, Miguel
Delibes Setien, Miguel 1920-
DeLillo, Don 1936-
Deloria, Vine, Jr. 1933-
del Rey, Lester 1915-
de Man, Paul 1919-1983
de Montherlant, Henry
    See Montherlant, Henry de
Dennis, Nigel 1912-
Desai, Anita 1937-
Destouches, Louis-
    Ferdinand 1894-1961
De Vries, Peter 1910-
Dexter, Pete 1943-
Dick, Philip K. 1928-1982
Dickey, James 1923-
Dickson, Carter
    See Carr, John Dickson
Didion, Joan 1934-
Dillard, Annie 1945-
Dinesen, Isak
    See Blixen, Karen
Diop, Birago 1906-1989
Disch, Thomas M. 1940-
Doctorow, E. L. 1931-
Donleavy, J. P. 1926-
Donoso, Jose 1924-

Doolittle, Hilda 1886-1961
Dos Passos, John 1896-1970
Doyle, Arthur Conan 1859-1930
Drabble, Margaret 1939-
Dreiser, Theodore 1871-1945
Du Bois, W. E. B. 1868-1963
Duerrenmatt, Friedrich 1921-
Duffy, Maureen 1933-
Duhamel, Georges 1884-1966

du Maurier, Daphne 1907-1989
Dunbar, Alice
  See Nelson, Alice Ruth Moore
  Dunbar
Dunbar-Nelson, Alice
  See Nelson, Alice Ruth Moore
  Dunbar
Duncan, Robert 1919-1988

Dunn, Douglas 1942-
Durant, Will 1885-1981
Duras, Marguerite 1914-
Durrell, Gerald 1925-
Durrell, Lawrence 1912-
Durrenmatt, Friedrich
  See Duerrenmatt, Friedrich
Dworkin, Andrea 1946-

VOLUME 2: E-K

Eagleton, Terence 1943-
Eagleton, Terry
  See Eagleton, Terence
Eberhart, Richard 1904-
Echegaray, Jose 1832-1916
Eco, Umberto 1932-
Edgar, David 1948-
Ehrenreich, Barbara 1941-
Einstein, Albert 1879-1955
Ekwensi, Cyprian 1921-
Eliade, Mircea 1907-1986
Eliot, T. S. 1888-1965
Elkin, Stanley L. 1930-
Ellin, Stanley 1916-1986
Ellison, Harlan 1934-
Ellison, Ralph 1914-
Ellmann, Richard 1918-1987
Elytis, Odysseus 1911-
Emecheta, Buchi 1944-
Empson, William 1906-1984
Endo, Shusaku 1923-
Erdrich, Louise 1954-
Erikson, Erik H. 1902-
Esslin, Martin 1918-
Estleman, Loren D. 1952-
Everson, William 1912-
Ewart, Gavin 1916-
Fallaci, Oriana 1930-
Farmer, Philip Jose 1918-
Farrell, J. G. 1935-1979
Farrell, James T. 1904-1979
Faulkner, William 1897-1962
Feiffer, Jules 1929-
Feinstein, Elaine 1930-
Ferber, Edna 1887-1968
Ferlinghetti, Lawrence 1919(?)-
Fermor, Patrick Leigh
  See Leigh Fermor, Patrick
Feynman, Richard Phillips 1918-
  1988
Fiedler, Leslie A. 1917-
Filippo, Eduardo de
  See de Filippo, Eduardo
Fitzgerald, F. Scott 1896-1940
Flanagan, Thomas 1923-
Fleming, Ian 1908-1964
Fo, Dario 1926-
Follett, Ken 1949-
Ford, Ford Madox 1873-1939

Fornes, Maria Irene 1930-
Forster, E. M. 1879-1970
Forsyth, Frederick 1938-
Fossey, Dian 1932-1985
Foucault, Michel 1926-1984
Fowles, John 1926-
Fox, Paula 1923-
Frame, Janet
  See Clutha, Janet Paterson
  Frame
France, Anatole
  See Thibault, Jacques Anatole
  Francois
Francis, Dick 1920-
Frank, Anne 1929-1945
Fraser, Antonia 1932-
Frayn, Michael 1933-
French, Marilyn 1929-
Freud, Anna 1895-1982
Freud, Sigmund 1856-1939
Friday, Nancy 1937-
Friedan, Betty 1921-
Friedman, Milton 1912-
Friel, Brian 1929-
Frisch, Max 1911-
Fromm, Erich 1900-1980
Frost, Robert 1874-1963
Fry, Christopher 1907-
Frye, Northrop 1912-
Fuentes, Carlos 1928-
Fugard, Athol 1932-
Fuller, Buckminster
  See Fuller, R. Buckminster
Fuller, Charles 1939-
Fuller, R. Buckminster 1895-1983
Fussell, Paul 1924-
Gaddis, William 1922-
Gaines, Ernest J. 1933-
Galbraith, John Kenneth 1908-
Gallant, Mavis 1922-
Gallegos, Romulo 1884-1969
Gandhi, Mahatma
  See Gandhi, Mohandas Karam-
  chand
Gandhi, Mohandas Karamchand
  1869-1948
Garcia Lorca, Federico 1898-1936
Garcia Marquez, Gabriel 1928-
Gardam, Jane 1928-

Gardner, Erle Stanley 1889-1970
Gardner, John 1926-
Gardner, John, Jr. 1933-1982
Garner, Alan 1934-
Gascoyne, David 1916-
Gass, William H. 1924-
Gasset, Jose Ortega y
  See Ortega y Gasset, Jose
Geisel, Theodor Seuss 1904-
Genet, Jean 1910-1986
Gide, Andre 1869-1951
Gilbert, Sandra M. 1936-
Gilchrist, Ellen 1935-
Gill, Brendan 1914-
Ginsberg, Allen 1926-
Ginzburg, Natalia 1916-
Giono, Jean 1895-1970
Giovanni, Nikki 1943-
Godoy Alcayaga, Lucila 1889-1957
Godwin, Gail 1937-
Golding, William 1911-
Goodall, Jane 1934-
Goodman, Paul 1911-1972
Gorbachev, Mikhail 1931-
Gordimer, Nadine 1923-
Gordon, Caroline 1895-1981
Gordon, Mary 1949-
Gordone, Charles 1925-
Gould, Lois
Gould, Stephen Jay 1941-
Gouldner, Alvin W. 1920-1980
Goytisolo, Juan 1931-
Grass, Guenter 1927-
Grau, Shirley Ann 1929-
Graves, Robert 1895-1985
Gray, Alasdair 1934-
Gray, Francine du Plessix 1930-
Gray, Simon 1936-
Greeley, Andrew M. 1928-
Green, Julien 1900-
Greene, Graham 1904-
Greer, Germaine 1939-
Grey, Zane 1872-1939
Grieve, C. M. 1892-1978
Grigson, Geoffrey 1905-1985
Grimes, Martha
Grizzard, Lewis 1946-
Grossman, Vasily 1905-1964
Guare, John 1938-

Gubar, Susan 1944-
Guest, Judith 1936-
Guiraldes, Ricardo 1886-1927
Gunn, Thom 1929-
H. D.
    See Doolittle, Hilda
Hailey, Arthur 1920-
Haley, Alex 1921-
Hall, Willis 1929-
Hamilton, Virginia 1936-
Hammett, Dashiell 1894-1961
Hampton, Christopher 1946-
Hamsun, Knut
    See Pedersen, Knut
Handke, Peter 1942-
Hanley, James 1901-1985
Hannah, Barry 1942-
Hansberry, Lorraine 1930-1965
Hardwick, Elizabeth 1916-
Hardy, Thomas 1840-1928
Hare, David 1947-
Harris, Wilson 1921-
Harrison, Tony 1937-
Hartley, L. P. 1895-1972
Hasek, Jaroslav 1883-1923
Havel, Vaclav 1936-
Hawkes, John 1925-
Hayden, Robert E. 1913-1980
Hayek, F. A. 1899-
Hazzard, Shirley 1931-
Head, Bessie 1937-1986
Heaney, Seamus 1939-
Hearne, John 1926-
Heath, Roy A. K. 1926-
Hebert, Anne 1916-
Heidegger, Martin 1889-1976
Heinlein, Robert A. 1907-1988
Heller, Joseph 1923-
Hellman, Lillian 1906-1984
Helprin, Mark 1947-
Hemingway, Ernest 1899-1961
Henley, Beth
    See Henley, Elizabeth Becker
Henley, Elizabeth Becker 1952-
Henri, Adrian 1932-
Henry, O.
    See Porter, William Sydney
Herbert, Frank 1920-1986
Herbert, Zbigniew 1924-
Herr, Michael 1940(?)-
Hersey, John 1914-
Hesse, Hermann 1877-1962
Heyer, Georgette 1902-1974
Heyerdahl, Thor 1914-
Higgins, George V. 1939-
Higgins, Jack
    See Patterson, Harry
Highsmith, Patricia 1921-
Hill, Geoffrey 1932-
Hill, Susan 1942-
Himes, Chester 1909-1984

Hinton, S. E. 1950-
Hiraoka, Kimitake 1925-1970
Hirsch, E. D., Jr. 1928-
Hite, Shere 1942-
Hoban, Russell 1925-
Hochhuth, Rolf 1931-
Hochwaelder, Fritz 1911-1986
Hoffman, Abbie 1936-1989
Hoffman, Alice 1952-
Hofstadter, Douglas R. 1945-
Holroyd, Michael 1935-
Hope, A. D. 1907-
Horgan, Paul 1903-
Housman, A. E. 1859-1936
Howard, Maureen 1930-
Howe, Irving 1920-
Hoyle, Fred 1915-
Hughes, Langston 1902-1967
Hughes, Richard 1900-1976
Hughes, Ted 1930-
Hunter, Evan 1926-
Hurston, Zora Neale 1903-1960
Huxley, Aldous 1894-1963
Huxley, Julian 1887-1975
Ibanez, Vicente Blasco
    See Blasco Ibanez, Vicente
Illich, Ivan 1926-
Infante, G. Cabrera
    See Cabrera Infante, G.
Inge, William Motter 1913-1973
Innes, Michael
    See Stewart, J.I.M.
Ionesco, Eugene 1912-
Irving, John 1942-
Isaacs, Susan 1943-
Isherwood, Christopher 1904-1986
Ishiguro, Kazuo 1954-
Jacobson, Dan 1929-
Jaffe, Rona 1932-
Jakes, John 1932-
James, C. L. R. 1901-1989
James, Clive 1939-
James, Henry 1843-1916
James, P. D.
    See White, Phyllis Dorothy
    James
Jarrell, Randall 1914-1965
Jeffers, Robinson 1887-1962
Jennings, Elizabeth 1926-
Jhabvala, Ruth Prawer 1927-
Jimenez, Juan Ramon 1881-1958
Johnson, Diane 1934-
Johnson, James Weldon 1871-1938
Johnson, Pamela Hansford 1912-
    1981
Johnson, Uwe 1934-1984
Jones, David 1895-1974
Jones, Gayl 1949-
Jones, James 1921-1977
Jones, LeRoi
    See Baraka, Amiri

Jones, Mervyn 1922-
Jong, Erica 1942-
Jordan, June 1936-
Joyce, James 1882-1941
Jung, C. G. 1875-1961
Kafka, Franz 1883-1924
Kammen, Michael G. 1936-
Karnow, Stanley 1925-
Kavan, Anna 1901-1968
Kavanagh, Patrick 1904-1967
Kaye, M. M. 1909-
Kazakov, Yuri Pavlovich 1927-
Kazantzakis, Nikos 1883(?)-1957
Keating, H. R. F. 1926-
Keillor, Garrison
    See Keillor, Gary
Keillor, Gary 1942-
Keller, Helen 1880-1968
Keneally, Thomas 1935-
Kennedy, John Fitzgerald 1917-
    1963
Kennedy, William 1928-
Kenyatta, Jomo 1891(?)-1978
Kerouac, Jack
    See Kerouac, Jean-Louis Lebrid
    de
Kerouac, Jean-Louis Lebrid de
    1922-1969
Kerr, M. E.
    See Meaker, Marijane
Kesey, Ken 1935-
Kidder, Tracy 1945-
Kienzle, William X. 1928-
King, Francis 1923-
King, Larry L. 1929-
King, Martin Luther, Jr. 1929-
    1968
King, Stephen 1947-
Kingston, Maxine Hong 1940-
Kinnell, Galway 1927-
Kinsella, Thomas 1928-
Kinsella, W. P. 1935-
Kipling, Rudyard 1865-1936
Kirk, Russell 1918-
Kis, Danilo 1935-
Kissinger, Henry A. 1923-
Knowles, John 1926-
Koestler, Arthur 1905-1983
Konigsburg, E. L. 1930-
Konwicki, Tadeusz 1926-
Koontz, Dean R. 1945-
Kopit, Arthur 1937-
Kosinski, Jerzy 1933-
Krantz, Judith 1927-
Kroetsch, Robert 1927-
Kueng, Hans 1928-
Kumin, Maxine 1925-
Kundera, Milan 1929-
Kung, Hans
    See Kueng, Hans
Kunitz, Stanley 1905-

VOLUME 3: L-Q

Lagerkvist, Paer 1891-1974
La Guma, Alex 1925-1985
Laing, R. D. 1927-1989
Lamming, George 1927-
L'Amour, Louis 1908-1988
Langer, Susanne K. 1895-1985
Lardner, Ring
    See Lardner, Ring W.
Lardner, Ring W. 1885-1933
Larkin, Philip 1922-1985
Lasch, Christopher 1932-
Laurence, Margaret 1926-1987
Lavin, Mary 1912-
Lawrence, D. H. 1885-1930
Laye, Camara 1928-1980
Layton, Irving 1912-
Leakey, Louis S. B. 1903-1972
Leary, Timothy 1920-
Leavis, F. R. 1895-1978
Lebowitz, Fran 1951(?)-
le Carre, John
    See Cornwell, David
Lee, Harper 1926-
Lee, Laurie 1914-
Leger, Alexis Saint-Leger 1887-
    1975
Le Guin, Ursula K. 1929-
Leiber, Fritz 1910-
Leigh Fermor, Patrick 1915-
Lem, Stanislaw 1921-
L'Engle, Madeleine 1918-
Leonard, Elmore 1925-
Leonov, Leonid 1899-
Lessing, Doris 1919-
Levertov, Denise 1923-
Levi, Primo 1919-1987
Levin, Ira 1929-
Levi-Strauss, Claude 1908-
Lewis, C. S. 1898-1963
Lewis, Norman 1918-
Lewis, Sinclair 1885-1951
Lindbergh, Anne Morrow 1906-
Lippmann, Walter 1889-1974
Little, Malcolm 1925-1965
Lively, Penelope 1933-
Livesay, Dorothy 1909-
Llosa, Mario Vargas
    See Vargas Llosa, Mario
Lodge, David 1935-
London, Jack
    See London, John Griffith
London, John Griffith 1876-1916
Lopez, Barry Holstun 1945-
Lorca, Federico Garcia
    See Garcia Lorca, Federico
Lorde, Audre 1934-
Lorenz, Konrad Zacharias 1903-
Lovecraft, H. P. 1890-1937
Lovelace, Earl 1935-

Lovesey, Peter 1936-
Lowell, Robert 1917-1977
Lowry, Malcolm 1909-1957
Luce, Henry R. 1898-1967
Ludlum, Robert 1927-
Lukacs, George
    See Lukacs, Gyorgy
Lukacs, Gyorgy 1885-1971
Lukas, J. Anthony 1933-
Luria, Alexander R. 1902-1977
Lurie, Alison 1926-
MacBeth, George 1932-
MacDiarmid, Hugh
    See Grieve, C. M.
MacDonald, John D. 1916-1986
Macdonald, Ross
    See Millar, Kenneth
MacInnes, Colin 1914-1976
MacInnes, Helen 1907-1985
MacLean, Alistair 1922(?)-1987
MacLeish, Archibald 1892-1982
MacLennan, Hugh 1907-
MacNeice, Louis 1907-1963
Madden, David 1933-
Mahfouz, Naguib 1911(?)-
Mahfuz, Najib
    See Mahfouz, Naguib
Mailer, Norman 1923-
Mais, Roger 1905-1955
Malamud, Bernard 1914-1986
Malcolm X
    See Little, Malcolm
Malraux, Andre 1901-1976
Mamet, David 1947-
Manchester, William 1922-
Mann, Thomas 1875-1955
Manning, Olivia 1915-1980
Mao Tse-tung 1893-1976
Marcel, Gabriel Honore 1889-1973
Marsh, Ngaio 1899-1982
Marshall, Paule 1929-
Martin, Steve 1945-
Masefield, John 1878-1967
Maslow, Abraham H. 1908-1970
Mason, Bobbie Ann 1940-
Masters, Edgar Lee 1868-1950
Matthews, Patricia 1927-
Matthiessen, Peter 1927-
Matute, Ana Maria 1925-
Maugham, W. Somerset
    See Maugham, William Somerset
Maugham, William Somerset 1874-
    1965
Mauriac, Francois 1885-1970
Maurois, Andre 1885-1967
Maxwell, Gavin 1914-1969
McBain, Ed
    See Hunter, Evan
McCaffrey, Anne 1926-

McCarthy, Mary 1912-1989
McCullers, Carson 1917-1967
McCullough, Colleen 1938(?)-
McEwan, Ian 1948-
McGahern, John 1934-
McGrath, Thomas 1916-
McGuane, Thomas 1939-
McIntyre, Vonda N. 1948-
McKay, Claude
    See McKay, Festus Claudius
McKay, Festus Claudius 1889-1948
McKillip, Patricia A. 1948-
McLuhan, Marshall 1911-1980
McMurtry, Larry 1936-
McPhee, John 1931-
McPherson, James Alan 1943-
McPherson, James M. 1936-
Mead, Margaret 1901-1978
Meaker, Marijane 1927-
Mehta, Ved 1934-
Mencken, H. L. 1880-1956
Menninger, Karl 1893-1990
Mercer, David 1928-1980
Merril, Judith 1923-
Merrill, James 1926-
Merton, Thomas 1915-1968
Merwin, W. S. 1927-
Michaels, Leonard 1933-
Michener, James A. 1907(?)-
Millar, Kenneth 1915-1983
Millay, Edna St. Vincent 1892-
    1950
Miller, Arthur 1915-
Miller, Henry 1891-1980
Millett, Kate 1934-
Milligan, Spike
    See Milligan, Terence Alan
Milligan, Terence Alan 1918-
Milne, A. A. 1882-1956
Milner, Ron 1938-
Milosz, Czeslaw 1911-
Mishima, Yukio
    See Hiraoka, Kimitake
Mistral, Gabriela
    See Godoy Alcayaga, Lucila
Mitchell, Margaret 1900-1949
Mo, Timothy 1950(?)-
Momaday, N. Scott 1934-
Montague, John 1929-
Montale, Eugenio 1896-1981
Montherlant, Henry de 1896-1972
Moorcock, Michael 1939-
Moore, Brian 1921-
Moore, Marianne 1887-1972
Morante, Elsa 1918-1985
Moravia, Alberto
    See Pincherle, Alberto
Morgan, Robin 1941-
Morris, Desmond 1928-

Morris, James
   See Morris, Jan
Morris, Jan 1926-
Morris, Wright 1910-
Morrison, Toni 1931-
Mortimer, John 1923-
Mowat, Farley 1921-
Mrozek, Slawomir 1930-
Muggeridge, Malcolm 1903-
Mukherjee, Bharati 1940-
Munro, Alice 1931-
Munro, H. H. 1870-1916
Murdoch, Iris 1919-
Nabokov, Vladimir 1899-1977
Naipaul, Shiva 1945-1985
Naipaul, V. S. 1932-
Narayan, R. K. 1906-
Nash, Ogden 1902-1971
Naughton, Bill 1910-
Naylor, Gloria 1950-
Nehru, Jawaharlal 1889-1964
Nelson, Alice Ruth Moore Dunbar
   1875-1935
Nemerov, Howard 1920-
Neruda, Pablo 1904-1973
Newby, P. H. 1918-
Ngugi, James T.
   See Ngugi wa Thiong'o
Ngugi wa Thiong'o 1938-
Nichols, Peter 1927-
Nin, Anais 1903-1977
Niven, Larry
   See Niven, Laurence Van Cott
Niven, Laurence Van Cott 1938-
Nixon, Richard M. 1913-
Norton, Andre 1912-
Nye, Robert 1939-
Oates, Joyce Carol 1938-
O'Brien, Edna 1936-
O'Casey, Sean 1880-1964
O'Cathasaigh, Sean
   See O'Casey, Sean
O'Connor, Flannery 1925-1964
Odets, Clifford 1906-1963
Oe, Kenzaburo 1935-
O'Faolain, Julia 1932-
O'Faolain, Sean 1900-
O'Flaherty, Liam 1896-1984
O'Hara, Frank 1926-1966
O'Hara, John 1905-1970

Okigbo, Christopher 1932-1967
Olsen, Tillie 1913-
Olson, Charles 1910-1970
O'Neill, Eugene 1888-1953
Onetti, Juan Carlos 1909-
Oppenheimer, J. Robert 1904-1967
Ortega y Gasset, Jose 1883-1955
Orton, Joe
   See Orton, John Kingsley
Orton, John Kingsley 1933-1967
Orwell, George
   See Blair, Eric
Osborne, John 1929-
Ousmane, Sembene 1923-
Oz, Amos 1939-
Ozick, Cynthia 1928-
Page, P. K. 1916-
Pagnol, Marcel 1895-1974
Paley, Grace 1922-
Panova, Vera 1905-1973
Pargeter, Edith Mary 1913-
Parker, Dorothy 1893-1967
Parker, Robert B. 1932-
Parra, Nicanor 1914-
Parsons, Talcott 1902-1979
Pasolini, Pier Paolo 1922-1975
Pasternak, Boris 1890-1960
Patchen, Kenneth 1911-1972
Paterson, Katherine 1932-
Paton, Alan 1903-1988
Patterson, Harry 1929-
Pauling, Linus 1901-
Paz, Octavio 1914-
p'Bitek, Okot 1931-1982
Peake, Mervyn 1911-1968
Peale, Norman Vincent 1898-
Pearson, Andrew Russell 1897-
   1969
Pearson, Drew
   See Pearson, Andrew Russell
Pedersen, Knut 1859-1952
Percy, Walker 1916-1990
Perelman, S. J. 1904-1979
Perse, Saint-John
   See Leger, Alexis Saint-Leger
Peters, Ellis
   See Pargeter, Edith Mary
Petry, Ann 1908-
Pevsner, Nikolaus 1902-1983

Phillips, Jayne Anne 1952-
Piaget, Jean 1896-1980
Piercy, Marge 1936-
Pilcher, Rosamunde 1924-
Pincherle, Alberto 1907-
Pinter, Harold 1930-
Pirsig, Robert M. 1928-
Plante, David 1940-
Plath, Sylvia 1932-1963
Plimpton, George 1927-
Plomer, William Charles Franklin
   1903-1973
Plowman, Piers
   See Kavanagh, Patrick
Pohl, Frederik 1919-
Pollitt, Katha 1949-
Popper, Karl R. 1902-
Porter, Katherine Anne 1890-1980
Porter, William Sydney 1862-1910
Potok, Chaim 1929-
Potter, Dennis 1935-
Potter, Stephen 1900-1969
Pound, Ezra 1885-1972
Powell, Anthony 1905-
Powers, J. F. 1917-
Powys, John Cowper 1872-1963
Prevert, Jacques 1900-1977
Prichard, Katharine Susannah
   1883-1969
Priestley, J. B. 1894-1984
Pritchett, V. S. 1900-
Proust, Marcel 1871-1922
Puig, Manuel 1932-1990
Purdy, James 1923-
Puzo, Mario 1920-
Pym, Barbara 1913-1980
Pynchon, Thomas 1937-
Python, Monty
   See Cleese, John
Qian Zhongshu
   See Ch'ien Chung-shu
Quasimodo, Salvatore 1901-1968
Queen, Ellery
   See Dannay, Frederic
   and Sturgeon, Theodore
   and Vance, John Holbrook
Queneau, Raymond 1903-1976
Quiroga, Horacio 1878-1937
Quoirez, Francoise 1935-

VOLUME 4: R-Z

Raine, Kathleen 1908-
Rand, Ayn 1905-1982
Ransom, John Crowe 1888-1974
Rao, Raja 1909-
Rattigan, Terence 1911-1977
Ravitch, Diane 1938-
Reed, Ishmael 1938-
Remarque, Erich Maria 1898-1970

Rendell, Ruth 1930-
Rexroth, Kenneth 1905-1982
Rhys, Jean 1894-1979
Rice, Elmer 1892-1967
Rich, Adrienne 1929-
Richler, Mordecai 1931-
Richter, Conrad 1890-1968
Rilke, Rainer Maria 1875-1926

Ritsos, Giannes
   See Ritsos, Yannis
Ritsos, Yannis 1909-
Robbe-Grillet, Alain 1922-
Robbins, Harold 1916-
Robbins, Thomas Eugene 1936-
Robbins, Tom
   See Robbins, Thomas Eugene

Robinson, Edwin Arlington 1869–
1935
Robinson, Joan 1903–1983
Rodd, Kylie Tennant 1912–1988
Roethke, Theodore 1908–1963
Rogers, Carl R. 1902–1987
Rogers, Rosemary 1932–
Romains, Jules 1885–1972
Rooney, Andrew A. 1919–
Rooney, Andy
    See Rooney, Andrew A.
Rossner, Judith 1935–
Rostand, Edmond 1868–1918
Roth, Henry 1906–
Roth, Philip 1933–
Roy, Gabrielle 1909–1983
Rozewicz, Tadeusz 1921–
Rubens, Bernice 1923–
Rukeyser, Muriel 1913–1980
Rulfo, Juan 1918–1986
Rushdie, Salman 1947–
Russ, Joanna 1937–
Russell, Bertrand 1872–1970
Sabato, Ernesto 1911–
Saberhagen, Fred 1930–
Sacks, Oliver 1933–
Sackville-West, V. 1892–1962
Sagan, Carl 1934–
Sagan, Francoise
    See Quoirez, Francoise
Saint-Exupery, Antoine de 1900–
1944
Saki
    See Munro, H. H.
Salinger, J. D. 1919–
Salisbury, Harrison E. 1908–
Sanchez, Sonia 1934–
Sandburg, Carl 1878–1967
Sanders, Lawrence 1920–
Sandoz, Mari 1896–1966
Sansom, William 1912–1976
Santmyer, Helen Hooven 1895–
1986
Saroyan, William 1908–1981
Sarraute, Nathalie 1900–
Sarton, May 1912–
Sartre, Jean-Paul 1905–1980
Sassoon, Siegfried 1886–1967
Sauser-Hall, Frederic 1887–1961
Sayers, Dorothy L. 1893–1957
Schaeffer, Susan Fromberg 1941–
Schlafly, Phyllis 1924–
Schlesinger, Arthur M., Jr. 1917–
Schmitz, Aron Hector 1861–1928
Schwartz, Delmore 1913–1966
Sciascia, Leonardo 1921–1989
Scott, Paul 1920–1978
Seferiades, Giorgos
Stylianou 1900–1971
Seferis, George
    See Seferiades, Giorgos
    Stylianou

Segal, Erich 1937–
Seifert, Jaroslav 1901–1986
Selvon, Samuel 1923–
Sendak, Maurice 1928–
Sender, Ramon 1902–1982
Senghor, Leopold Sedar 1906–
Sepheriades, Georgios
    See Seferiades, Giorgos
    Stylianou
Setien, Miguel Delibes
    See Delibes Setien, Miguel
Seuss, Dr.
    See Geisel, Theodor Seuss
Sexton, Anne 1928–1974
Shaffer, Peter 1926–
Shange, Ntozake 1948–
Shapiro, Karl 1913–
Shaw, George Bernard 1856–1950
Shaw, Irwin 1913–1984
Sheed, Wilfrid 1930–
Sheehy, Gail 1936(?)–
Sheen, Fulton J. 1895–1979
Sheldon, Alice Hastings Bradley
    1915–1987
Sheldon, Sidney 1917–
Shepard, Sam 1943–
Shirer, William L. 1904–
Sholokhov, Mikhail 1905–1984
Siddons, Anne Rivers 1936–
Sillanpaa, Frans Eemil 1888–1964
Sillitoe, Alan 1928–
Silone, Ignazio 1900–1978
Silverberg, Robert 1935–
Simak, Clifford D. 1904–1988
Simenon, Georges 1903–1989
Simon, Claude 1913–
Simon, Kate 1912–1990
Simon, Neil 1927–
Simpson, Dorothy 1933–
Simpson, George Gaylord 1902–
1984
Simpson, Harriette
    See Arnow, Harriette Simpson
Simpson, Louis 1923–
Sinclair, Andrew 1935–
Sinclair, Upton 1878–1968
Singer, Isaac Bashevis 1904–
Sitwell, Dame Edith 1887–1964
Skinner, B. F. 1904–1990
Skvorecky, Josef 1924–
Smith, Florence Margaret 1902–
1971
Smith, Stevie
    See Smith, Florence Margaret
Smith, Wilbur 1933–
Snodgrass, William D. 1926–
Snow, C. P. 1905–1980
Solzhenitsyn, Aleksandr I. 1918–
Sontag, Susan 1933–
Soyinka, Wole 1934–
Spark, Muriel 1918–

Spencer, Elizabeth 1921–
Spender, Stephen 1909–
Spillane, Frank Morrison 1918–
Spillane, Mickey
    See Spillane, Frank Morrison
Spock, Benjamin 1903–
Stafford, Jean 1915–1979
Stead, Christina 1902–1983
Steel, Danielle 1947–
Stegner, Wallace 1909–
Stein, Gertrude 1874–1946
Steinbeck, John 1902–1968
Steinem, Gloria 1934–
Steiner, George 1929–
Stevens, Wallace 1879–1955
Stevenson, Anne 1933–
Stewart, J. I. M. 1906–
Stone, Irving 1903–1989
Stone, Robert 1937–
Stoppard, Tom 1937–
Storey, David 1933–
Stow, Randolph 1935–
Straub, Peter 1943–
Sturgeon, Theodore 1918–1985
Styron, William 1925–
Susann, Jacqueline 1921–1974
Suzuki, D. T.
    See Suzuki, Daisetz Teitaro
Suzuki, Daisetz Teitaro 1870–1966
Svevo, Italo
    See Schmitz, Aron Hector
Swenson, May 1919–1989
Symons, Julian 1912–
Tagore, Rabindranath 1861–1941
Talese, Gay 1932–
Tate, Allen 1899–1979
Taylor, A. J. P. 1906–
Taylor, Elizabeth 1912–1975
Taylor, Peter 1917–
Taylor, Telford 1908–
Teller, Edward 1908–
Tennant, Kylie
    See Rodd, Kylie Tennant
Terkel, Louis 1912–
Terkel, Studs
    See Terkel, Louis
Theroux, Paul 1941–
Thibault, Jacques Anatole Francois
1844–1924
Thomas, Audrey 1935–
Thomas, D. M. 1935–
Thomas, Dylan 1914–1953
Thomas, Joyce Carol 1938–
Thomas, Lewis 1913–
Thomas, R. S. 1913–
Thompson, Hunter S. 1939–
Thurber, James 1894–1961
Tillich, Paul 1886–1965
Tiptree, James, Jr.
    See Sheldon, Alice Hastings
    Bradley

Toffler, Alvin 1928-
Toland, John 1912-
Tolkien, J. R. R. 1892-1973
Toomer, Jean 1894-1967
Torres Bodet, Jaime 1902-1974
Torsvan, Ben Traven
    See Traven, B.
Tournier, Michel 1924-
Townsend, Sue 1946-
Traven, B. ?-1969
Tremblay, Michel 1942-
Trevor, William
    See Cox, William Trevor
Trifonov, Yuri 1925-1981
Trillin, Calvin 1935-
Trilling, Diane 1905-
Trilling, Lionel 1905-1975
Troyat, Henri 1911-
Truman, Margaret 1924-
Tryon, Thomas 1926-
Tsvetaeva, Marina 1892-1941
Tuchman, Barbara W. 1912-1989
Tutuola, Amos 1920-
Tyler, Anne 1941-
Tynan, Kenneth 1927-1980
Uchida, Yoshiko 1921-
Unamuno, Miguel de 1864-1936
Undset, Sigrid 1882-1949
Updike, John 1932-
Uris, Leon 1924-
Valery, Paul 1871-1945
Vallejo, Antonio Buero
    See Buero Vallejo, Antonio
Vance, Jack
    See Vance, John Holbrook
Vance, John Holbrook 1916-
Van Doren, Mark 1894-1972
van Lawick-Goodall, Jane
    See Goodall, Jane
Vargas Llosa, Mario 1936-
Vendler, Helen 1933-
Vidal, Gore 1925-
Vine, Barbara
    See Rendell, Ruth
Voinovich, Vladimir 1932-

von Hayek, Friedrich August
    See Hayek, F. A.
Vonnegut, Kurt, Jr. 1922-
Voznesensky, Andrei 1933-
Wain, John 1925-
Walcott, Derek 1930-
Walker, Alice 1944-
Walker, Margaret 1915-
Wallace, Irving 1916-1990
Wallant, Edward Lewis 1926-1962
Wambaugh, Joseph 1937-
Warner, Sylvia Ashton
    See Ashton-Warner, Sylvia
Warner, Sylvia Townsend 1893-1978
Warren, Robert Penn 1905-1989
Waruk, Kona
    See Harris, Wilson
Waterhouse, Keith 1929-
Waugh, Evelyn 1903-1966
Wedgwood, C. V. 1910-
Weinstein, Nathan
    See West, Nathanael
Weldon, Fay 1933(?)-
Wells, H. G. 1866-1946
Welty, Eudora 1909-
Wesker, Arnold 1932-
Wesley, Mary 1912-
West, Jessamyn 1902-1984
West, Morris L. 1916-
West, Nathanael 1903-1940
West, Rebecca 1892-1983
Wharton, Edith 1862-1937
Wheatley, Dennis 1897-1977
White, E. B. 1899-1985
White, Edmund 1940-
White, Patrick 1912-
White, Phyllis Dorothy James 1920-
White, Theodore H. 1915-1986
Wiesel, Elie 1928-
Wilbur, Richard 1921-
Wilder, Thornton 1897-1975
Wilhelm, Kate
    See Wilhelm, Katie Gertrude

Wilhelm, Katie Gertrude 1928-
Will, George F. 1941-
Willard, Nancy 1936-
Williams, Emlyn 1905-1987
Williams, Raymond 1921-1988
Williams, Tennessee 1911-1983
Williams, William Carlos 1883-1963
Williamson, Henry 1895-1977
Willingham, Calder 1922-
Wilson, Angus 1913-
Wilson, August 1945-
Wilson, Colin 1931-
Wilson, Edmund 1895-1972
Wilson, Edward O. 1929-
Wilson, Ethel Davis 1888(?)-1980
Wilson, John Burgess 1917-
Wilson, Robert M. 1944-
Winters, Yvor 1900-1968
Wodehouse, P. G. 1881-1975
Wolf, Christa 1929-
Wolfe, Thomas 1900-1938
Wolfe, Thomas Kennerly, Jr. 1931-
Wolfe, Tom
    See Wolfe, Thomas Kennerly, Jr.
Woodiwiss, Kathleen E. 1939-
Woodward, Bob
    See Woodward, Robert Upshur
Woodward, Robert Upshur 1943-
Woolf, Virginia 1882-1941
Wouk, Herman 1915-
Wright, Charles 1935-
Wright, James 1927-1980
Wright, Judith 1915-
Wright, Richard 1908-1960
Yeats, William Butler 1865-1939
Yerby, Frank G. 1916-
Yevtushenko, Yevgeny 1933-
Yezierska, Anzia 1885(?)-1970
Yglesias, Helen 1915-
Yourcenar, Marguerite 1903-1987
Zelazny, Roger 1937-
Zindel, Paul 1936-
Zukofsky, Louis 1904-1978

MAJOR ◆
20th- ◆
CENTURY ◆
WRITERS ◆

Volume 4: R–Z/Indexes

R

RAINE, Kathleen (Jessie) 1908-

PERSONAL: Born June 14, 1908, in London, England; daughter of George (a schoolmaster) and Jessie (a teacher) Raine; married Hugh Sykes Davies (a Cambridge don; divorced); married Charles Madge (a poet and professor; divorced); children: (second marriage) one daughter, one son. *Education:* Girton College, Cambridge, M.A., 1929.

ADDRESSES: Home—47 Paultons Sq., London S.W.3, England.

CAREER: Poet, critic, editor, and translator. Lecturer at Morley College, London; Andrew Mellon lecturer at National Gallery of Art, Washington, D.C., 1962.

MEMBER: University Women's Club.

AWARDS, HONORS: Harriet Monroe Memorial Prize, 1952; Arts Council award, 1953; Oscar Blumenthal Prize, 1961; Cholmondeley Award, 1970; W. H. Smith & Son Literary Award, 1972, for *The Lost Country;* D. Litt., Leicester University, 1974; Foreign Book Prize (France), 1979; Chapelbrook Award.

WRITINGS:

Stone and Flower: Poems, 1935, Nicholson & Watson, 1943.
(Translator) Denis de Rougemont, *Talk of the Devil,* Eyre & Spottiswoode, 1945.
Living in Time (poems), Editions Poetry, 1946.
(Compiler with Max-Pol Fouchet) *Aspects de la litterature anglaise,* Fountaine, 1947.
(Translator) Honore de Balzac, *Cousin Bette,* Hamish Hamilton, 1948.
(Translator) Paul Foulquie, *Existentialism,* Dobson, 1948.
The Pythoness and Other Poems, Hamish Hamilton, 1948, Farrar, Straus, 1952.
(Translator) Balzac, *Lost Illusions,* Lehmann Books, 1951, Modern Library, 1985.
(Editor and author of introduction) Samuel Taylor Coleridge, *The Letters of Samuel Taylor Coleridge,* Grey Walls Press, 1952.
Selected Poems, Weekend Press, 1952, Inner Traditions, 1989.
The Year One (poems), Farrar, Straus, 1953.
Collected Poems, Hamish Hamilton, 1956, Random House, 1957.
(Editor and author of introduction) Coleridge, *Selected Poems and Prose of Coleridge,* Penguin (London), 1957.

Christmas: An Acrostic (poem), privately printed, 1960.
(Author of introduction) William Butler Yeats, *Letters on Poetry From W. B. Yeats to Dorothy Wellesley,* Oxford University Press, 1964.
The Hollow Hill and Other Poems, 1960-1964, Hamish Hamilton, 1965.
Defending Ancient Springs, Oxford University Press, 1967, Inner Traditions, 1985.
Blake and Tradition, two volumes, Princeton University Press, 1968.
Ninfa Revisited (poems) Enitharmon, 1968.
Six Dreams and Other Poems, Enitharmon, 1968.
(Translator with R. M. Nadal) Pedro Calderon de la Barca, *Life's a Dream,* Hamish Hamilton, 1968, Theatre Arts, 1969.
(Editor) Coleridge, *Letters,* Folcroft, 1969.
(Editor with George Mills Harper) *Thomas Taylor the Platonist: Selected Writings,* Princeton University Press, 1969.
William Blake, Thames & Hudson, 1970, Praeger, 1971.
The Lost Country (poems), Dolmen Press, 1971.
Faces of Day and Night (autobiography), Enitharmon, 1972.
Yeats, the Tarot, and the Golden Dawn, Dolmen Press, 1972, revised edition, Humanities Press, 1976.
Farewell Happy Fields: Memories of Childhood (autobiography), Hamish Hamilton, 1973, Braziller, 1977.
On a Deserted Shore (poems), Hamish Hamilton, 1973.
Death-in-Life and Life-in-Death: "Cuchulain Comforted" and "News for the Delphic Oracle," Oxford University Press, 1974.
(Editor) William Blake, *A Choice of Blake's Verse,* Faber, 1974.
(Editor) Percy Bysshe Shelley, *Shelley,* Penguin (London), 1974.
The Land Unknown (autobiography), Braziller, 1975.
The Oval Portrait and Other Poems, Enitharmon, 1977.
The Lion's Mouth: Concluding Chapters of Autobiography, Hamish Hamilton, 1977.
Blake and Antiquity, Princeton University Press, 1978.
Fifteen Short Poems, Enitharmon, 1978.
From Blake to "A Vision," Dolmen Press, 1978.
Blake and the New Age, Allen & Unwin, 1979.
The Oracle in the Heart, and Other Poems, 1975-1978, Allen & Unwin, 1980.
Collected Poems, 1935-1980, Allen & Unwin, 1981.
The Human Face of God: William Blake and the Book of Job, Thames & Hudson, 1982.

The Inner Journey of the Poet, and Other Papers, edited by Brian Keeble, Braziller, 1982.

Yeats to Initiate: Essays on Certain Themes in the Writings of W. B. Yeats, Dolmen Press, 1984, Allen & Unwin, 1985.

The Presence: Poems, 1984-1987, Inner Traditions, 1988.

SIDELIGHTS: Though she was born in London and has lived there much of her life, Raine has said she stills feels exiled from the Northumberland countryside where she spent her youth. At the outset of World War I, Raine's parents sent her to live with her maternal grandmother and an aunt in a northern England hamlet. There she spent the years she claims to be the epitome of all she's ever loved. A return to her parents' home in an "ugly" London suburb at the age of ten only heightened her longing for the bucolic north; but she remained in the city until she left for Cambridge on a scholarship. Two short-lived marriages followed her college career, the second of which haunted her deeply: "That I hurt a man so fine by marrying him for inadequate, indeed for deeply neurotic, reasons, lies heavily on my conscience." Helen Bevington reported that "at this point of distress she began to write poems, 'a few grains of gold calcinated from all that dross of life in the fires of an overwhelming physical passion.' " In addition, Bevington believed Raine's impulse to devote many years to the study of William Blake was rooted in a personal searching. Together, her poems, her criticism, and her autobiographies form the essence of Raine's written work.

Raine's attraction to the natural world and her introspective nature are reflected in her poetry. Babette Deutsch observed from Raine's verse that she "is a woman whose pity tends to lapse into self-pity. But, she holds with [Edwin] Muir that 'the ever-recurring forms of nature mirror an eternal reality.'. . . Raine's poems gain in depth and subtlety because they keep returning to the actualities that embody the mystery of the physical universe and of conscious selfhood." This response to nature also impressed Ralph J. Mills: "She is, first of all, gifted with an intuitive sense of the relationship existing between human beings and the surrounding world of nature, a relationship so foreign to our habitual modern ways of thinking about ourselves and the urbanized, technological environment in which most of us live that its very simplicity jars us. . . . Like Blake, Wordsworth, and Coleridge, she is concerned with deciphering the secret hints of the larger scheme of being embodied in the visible surface of the natural world."

Many critics feel Raine's poetry is closely associated with the romantic tradition in another way, language. A *Spectator* reviewer questioned the "resolutely archaic diction" in *The Lost Country:* "Who else could offer us so many examples of a vocabulary long since fossilised. . . . There's only the occasional hint to suggest that English poetry has progressed at all since the Georgians." A *Listener* critic, meanwhile, heard a similar "slightly dated" diction in *The Oval Portrait* but found it effective: "Miss Raine writes of old age, its losses and memories, without making concessions to modernism other than to use a free-flowing verse form which gives her poems a dream-like quality." Howard Nemerov also felt Raine quite consciously instills her work with the language of the past: "Kathleen Raine's poems are unfashionable on purpose, unworldly, traditional, meditative, belonging to memory and dream, to solitude and silence." A key influence on Raine's poetry has been the literary tradition to which she closely associates herself. As Nemerov noted, Raine "is one of the great poetic inheritors" in a tradition "given intellectual form by Plato and mediated to us chiefly . . . by Blake and his contemporary Thomas Taylor." Raine has been variously called a Wordsworthian, a Shelleyan Platonist, and a Christian Metaphysical, but she holds her closest alliance with Blake. Mills

cited "certain spiritual affinities" she has with Blake, and Deutsch said "close as she seems to Blake, she appears to have escaped his confusions." Her devotion to Blake, though prevalent in her poetry, can be more accurately measured in her critical work, *Blake and Tradition.*

The purpose behind *Blake and Tradition* was to establish "that Blake's thought, including much of his symbolic imagery, belongs to the classical tradition of anti-materialist philosophy since Plotinus," declared J. Bronowski. *Books Abroad* reviewer John E. Rexine defined the work more specifically, claiming it to be a demonstration of "how much he owes to Jewish mysticism, alchemy, and mythology, particularly classical, as well as to show the relation of Blake's work to Orphic, Neoplatonic, Gnostic, and Hermetic writings, and to Swedenborgian theology, to mention only the most obvious." Ants Oras described the amount of scholarship entailed by this monumental task: "Twenty years of labor involving an examination of everything Blake is known or supposed to have read, a meticulous scrutiny of his engravings as to their bearing on his thought, and of nearly everything written about him, are embodied in more than eight hundred pages of lucid, closely reasoned text." Not surprisingly, Rexine cautioned that "this is not a book for the masses but for the serious scholar and student."

This one aspect, the "examination of everything Blake is known or supposed to have read," has posed a problem for reviewers of *Blake and Tradition.* "Raine is at constant pains to try to establish Blake's detailed knowledge of specific texts," argued Robert F. Gleckner. Bronowski voiced a similar reservation, arguing "not everything in Blake is an echo or an analogue of old beliefs and symbols; and when Kathleen Raine seems to labor to find it so, she must make many wonder whether she really is sensitive to Blake's endlessly springing originality." And, Oras stated simply, "Reading Miss Raine, one occasionally feels that Blake cannot have been so completely immersed in what he read in Boehme, Porphyry, Plotinus and the others . . . as not to respond in a more impulsively personal, eruptive fashion." Jerome McGann, on the other hand, felt Raine did not overestimate the need to establish Blake's tradition so completely. He insisted "she hardly exaggerates when she says that we must recover the sources of his special symbolic language in order to understand much of his poetry."

Aside from this problem, many critics heralded the undeniable significance of Raine's *magnum opus.* This product of an obvious "labor of love" helped Kathleen Nott understand Blake's "curious" and formerly "deeply boring" "Prophetic Books." "Now, with Miss Raine's intricate and efficient key, I shall find out what they really mean and will never permit myself to be bored by them again." Oras was also lured to this "epic feat" by a personal awareness of Blake made possible by Raine's efforts. "The skill with which Kathleen Raine unravels these threads of traditions, and yet manages to reconstitute them in our minds as components of very living, very personal art, is remarkable from the start," he said. Others raised *Blake and Tradition* to an eminent position in the realm of Blake scholarship. McGann, for example, included Raine's work as "certainly one of the four most important books yet written on Blake's ideas" (along with those by Northrop Frye, David Erdman, and Peter Fisher).

Raine again concentrated on the importance of a writer's literary tradition in another major work, *Defending Ancient Springs.* In this book, "Miss Raine argues that the authentic poet draws his inspiration from such a source as Plato's world of Ideas, or Yeats's *Anima Mundi,*" summarized Wallace Fowlie. M. L. Rosenthal shared this view: "Miss Raine's whole argument, in fact revolves around the idea of 'the learning of the poets,' a traditional symbolic language in which they are expert that is the key to 'the beautiful order of "eternity"' as grasped by Blake, Shelley, Yeats, St. John Perse, Muir, and others." Though *Defending Ancient Springs* has been criticized for being dogmatic and having a narrowly focused vision, Rosenthal contended that, overall, it instructs with a voice "warmly engaged with its subject." "When Miss Raine writes in this way we can only be grateful, and forgive her efforts elsewhere to disdain the opposition out of existence, and rebuke ourselves for any impatience with the merely local and petulant side of her argument."

A highlight of Raine's more recent work has been the three-volume publication of her autobiography. The first volume, *Farewell Happy Fields,* covers the years before her entrance to Cambridge. One striking aspect of the book is the early sense of isolation felt by Raine. Despite her idyllic love for Northumberland, she still longed for something more—Scotland, "the place of poetry." She was, in Bevington's terms, "happy in paradise, yet unhappy in exile." One specific incident, reported V. S. Pritchett, intensified this sense of isolation and marked a turning point in a predominantly happy childhood. Pritchett recalled an early love affair broken when Raine's father threatened to kill the boy and forced the young couple to separate: "The dazed girl accepted her situation without question. But from this date begins the open war with her father about his politics, and a hatred of the timidity and meanness of suburban life." Such experiences, evidently, were as crucial to Raine's development as were her fond childhood memories. For Victor Howes, they symbolized a universal meaning: "Her twin themes of innocence and experience, of a magical world almost carelessly thrown aside in exchange for an asphalt jungle, seem not merely to recapitulate the story of a single life, they seem in some Proustian way to encapsulate the history of our time."

The second segment of Raine's autobiography, *The Land Unknown,* examined the literary and social culture of the twenties and thirties while continuing to explore her developing sensibilities. Jane Larkin Crain found some "marvelous moments here: a sketch of William Empson, a poet's description of English landscape, [and] clear-headed speculation on matters literary and philosophical." Though Crain did object to "all the self-absorption" in the autobiography, others welcomed Raine's explanation of "where she went wrong in her life." Without self-pity but in penitential tones, the chronicle includes reflections on her two marriages, the World War II years, her brief conversion to Roman Catholicism, and her longing for what Bevington called "some higher vision of radiance and joy"—a void eventually filled by Blake. Robert Nye appreciated Raine's candor: "What is beautiful and remarkable about 'The Land Unknown' is the way in which a great deal of messy material is given shape and substance by Miss Raine's truthfulness."

In the last segment of her autobiography, *The Lion's Mouth,* Raine described the "central event" of her life, her relationship with writer and artist Gavin Maxwell. The *New Yorker* explained the intensity of the relationship: "Whether they saw one another or not, wherever they went (she lectured and taught), whatever they did (he married briefly and disastrously), they could not break off, and they remained the most important, terrifying, and beloved figures in each other's lives until his death in 1971."

With the varied publication of poetry, criticism, editings, and autobiographies, Raine in her sixties and seventies was more productive than ever, showing no sign of abating her lifelong devotion to literature and writing.

BIOGRAPHICAL/CRITICAL SOURCES:

BOOKS

Contemporary Literary Criticism, Gale, Volume 7, 1977, Volume 45, 1987.
Deutsch, Babette, *Poetry in Our Time,* Doubleday, 1963.
Dictionary of Literary Biography, Volume 20: *British Poets, 1914-1945,* Gale, 1983.
Mills, Ralph J., *Kathleen Raine: A Critical Essay,* Eerdmans, 1967.

PERIODICALS

American Literature, May, 1970.
Books Abroad, winter, 1970.
Books and Bookmen, February, 1971, February, 1974, July, 1977, November, 1977.
Christian Science Monitor, October 23, 1975, May 18, 1977.
Guardian Weekly, December 12, 1970, January 8, 1973, July 19, 1975.
Hudson Review, spring, 1970.
Journal of Aesthetics and Art Criticism, spring, 1971.
Listener, January 4, 1968, January 3, 1974, September 29, 1977, October 13, 1977.
Los Angeles Times, September 9, 1982, February 6, 1983.
Modern Philology, August, 1970.
Nation, December 22, 1969.
New Statesman, July 18, 1969, October 1, 1971, November 23, 1973, February 15, 1974, July 11, 1975, October 21, 1977.
New Yorker, October 13, 1975, April 18, 1977, April 17, 1978.
New York Review of Books, October 23, 1969, December 13, 1973.
New York Times Book Review, October 12, 1975, May 1, 1977.
Observer, December 13, 1970, November 18, 1973, May 5, 1974, August 3, 1974, July 27, 1975, October 2, 1977.
Observer Review, August 17, 1969.
Philological Quarterly, July, 1971.
Poetry, May, 1969, October, 1970.
Review of English Studies, February, 1971.
Saturday Review, November 1, 1975, March 19, 1977.
Sewanee Review, July, 1968, January, 1972, July, 1972.
Spectator, December 25, 1971, October 22, 1977.
Times Literary Supplement, January 29, 1970, December 10, 1971, January 7, 1972, June 1, 1973, December 14, 1973, May 3, 1974, February 14, 1975, August 8, 1975, July 29, 1977, October 21, 1977, September 12, 1980, August 14, 1981, April 16, 1982, October 22, 1982.
Virginia Quarterly Review, autumn, 1968, summer, 1969.

*　　*　　*

RALEIGH, Richard
  See LOVECRAFT, H(oward) P(hillips)

*　　*　　*

RALLENTANDO, H. P.
  See SAYERS, Dorothy L(eigh)

*　　*　　*

RAMON, Juan
  See JIMENEZ (MANTECON), Juan Ramon

RAND, Ayn 1905-1982

PERSONAL: First name rhymes with "pine"; original name Alice Rosenbaum; born February 2, 1905, in St. Petersburg, Russia (now Leningrad, U.S.S.R.); came to United States, 1926, naturalized, 1931; died March 6, 1982, in New York, N.Y.; buried in Kensico Cemetery, Valhalla, N.Y.; daughter of Fronz (a chemist) and Anna Rosenbaum; married Charles Francis "Frank" O'Connor (an artist), April 15, 1929. *Education:* University of Petrograd (now University of Leningrad), graduated with highest honors in history, 1924. *Politics:* Radical for capitalism. *Religion:* Atheist.

ADDRESSES: Office—The Ayn Rand Letter, P.O. Box 177, Murray Hill Station, New York, N.Y. 10016. *Agent*—Curtis Brown Ltd., 10 Astor Place, New York, N.Y. 10003.

CAREER: Worked as tour guide at Peter and Paul Fortress; Cecil B. DeMille Studio, Hollywood, Calif., movie extra and junior screenwriter, 1926-32, began as filing clerk, became office head in wardrobe department; worked as screenwriter for Universal Pictures, Paramount Pictures, and Metro-Goldwyn-Mayer, 1932-34; worked as free-lance script reader for RKO Pictures, then for Metro-Goldwyn-Mayer, both New York City, 1934-35; worked without pay as a typist for Eli Jacques Kahn, an architect in New York City, doing research work for *The Fountainhead,* 1937; Paramount Pictures, New York City, script reader, 1941-43; Hal Wallis Productions, Hollywood, Calif., screenwriter (worked under special contract which committed her to work only six months of each year; during the other six months she pursued her own writing), 1944-49; full-time writer and lecturer, 1951-82.

Visiting lecturer at Yale University, 1960, Princeton University, 1960, Columbia University, 1960 and 1962, University of Wisconsin, 1961, Johns Hopkins University, 1961, Harvard University, 1962, Massachusetts Institute of Technology, 1962. Presenter of annual Ford Hall Forum, Boston, Mass., beginning 1963.

AWARDS, HONORS: Doctor of Humane Letters, Lewis and Clark College, 1963.

WRITINGS:

NOVELS

We the Living (also see below), Macmillan, 1936, reprinted, Random House, 1959.
Anthem, Cassell, 1938, revised edition, Pamphleteers, Inc., 1946.
The Fountainhead (also see below), Bobbs-Merrill, 1943, reprinted with special introduction by Rand, 1968.
Atlas Shrugged, Random House, 1957.

NONFICTION

For the New Intellectual: The Philosophy of Ayn Rand, Random House, 1961.
The Virtue of Selfishness: A New Concept of Egoism, with additional articles by Nathaniel Branden, New American Library, 1964.
Capitalism: The Unknown Ideal, with additional articles by Branden and others, New American Library, 1966.
Introduction to Objectivist Epistemology, Objectivist, 1967.
The Romantic Manifesto: A Philosophy of Literature, World Publishing, 1969.
The New Left: The Anti-Industrial Revolution, New American Library, 1982.
Philosophy: Who Needs It, with introduction by Leonard Peikoff, Bobbs-Merrill, 1971.

The Ayn Rand Lexicon: Objectivism from A to Z, with introduction and notes by Peikoff, New American Library, 1984.

PLAYS

Night of January 16th (produced as "Woman on Trial" at Hollywood Playhouse, October, 1934, first produced on Broadway under the title "Night of January 16th," at Ambassador Theater, September 16, 1935; produced under the title "Penthouse Legend," 1973), Longmans, Green, 1936, reprinted, New American Library, 1971.
"The Unconquered" (adaptation by Rand of *We the Living*), first produced on Broadway, February 14, 1940.

OTHER

"Love Letters" (screenplay; adapted from the novel of the same title by Chris Massie), Paramount, 1945.
"You Came Along" (screenplay), Paramount, 1945.
"The Fountainhead" (filmscript; adaptation by Rand of the novel), Warner Bros., 1949.
The Early Ayn Rand: A Selection from Her Unpublished Fiction, with introduction and notes by Peikoff, New American Library, 1984.

Co-editor and contributor, *The Objectivist Newsletter,* 1962-65, and its successor, *The Objectivist* (monthly journal), 1966-71; writer and publisher, *The Ayn Rand Letter,* 1971-76. Columnist for *Los Angeles Times.*

SIDELIGHTS: "Ayn Rand is dead. So, incidentally, is the philosophy she sought to launch dead; it was in fact stillborn." William F. Buckley's derogatory obituary in the *National Review* sounded a note of wishful thinking on the part of Ayn Rand's persistent critics. More objective observers of the contemporary political and publishing scenes, however, might be moved to remark, as Mark Twain did upon hearing rumors of his own demise, that the news of that death was greatly exaggerated. Rather than quelling interest in her or her philosophy, Rand's death, in March of 1982, initiated a new era of academic interest and fueled the continued promotion of her philosophies by her followers. In the five years following her death there were as many books published about Rand as there were during all the years of her life. Some of her writing is also being published posthumously: *Philosophy: Who Needs It,* a volume of essays she had planned but did not complete, came out the year of her death; and *The Early Ayn Rand: A Selection from Her Unpublished Fiction,* was issued in 1984. Her novels continue to sell well as do some of her nonfiction works, and further publishing ventures are planned by her literary executor, Leonard Peikoff.

Ayn Rand, born Alice Rosenbaum in St. Petersburg, Russia, in 1905, occupies a unique position in the history of American literature. In many ways she was a paradox: a writer of popular romances whose ideas were taken seriously, a fierce individualist who collected many followers. Politically and aesthetically, she defied the cultural currents of her times.

Rand's lifelong enmity to collectivist political systems was engendered by her personal experiences growing up in Russia and living through the Bolshevik revolution and the beginnings of the Soviet system. In 1979 when Phil Donahue asked her about her feelings for Russia, Rand described them as "complete loathing." Russia, she said, is "the ugliest, and incidentally, most mystical country on earth." She was an American patriot in the manner that only one who has emigrated from a totalitarian regime can be.

Capitalism was the system she championed; one of her best-known novels, *Atlas Shrugged,* is described as, among other things, a theodicy of capitalism. A rugged individualist and a believer in rational self-interest, Rand was a proponent of laissez-faire capitalism, a system she defined as the only social system based on the recognition of individual rights, the only system that bans force from social relationship, and the only system that fundamentally opposes war. Rand's defense of capitalism on moral grounds is unique. She based this defense on her view that only capitalism is consonant with man's rational nature, protective of his survival as man, and fundamentally just.

Rand's championing of individual rights and minimal government is part of her appeal to the Libertarian political movement, although she herself denounced Libertarians, calling them hippies of the right and advocates of anarchism. Neither, however, would she ally herself with most Conservatives because of what she called their mysticism, their staunch support of religion. Among her most persistent concerns about America was her belief that capitalism was being sold out by the very people who should be its strongest advocates. Rand felt that rather than supporting capitalism for the morality of its central vision, most capitalists defended it only on practical bases.

In "Global Balkanization" Rand pointed out the following paradoxes: "Capitalism has been called a system of greed—yet it is the system that raised the standard of living of its poorest citizens to heights no collectivist system has ever begun to equal, and no tribal gang can conceive of. Capitalism has been called nationalistic—yet it is the only system that banished ethnicity, and made it possible, in the United States, for men of various, formerly antagonistic nationalities to live together in peace. Capitalism has been called cruel—yet it brought such hope, progress and general good will that the young people of today, who have not seen it, find it hard to believe. As to pride, dignity, self-confidence, self-esteem—these are characteristics that mark a man for martyrdom in a tribal society and under any social system except capitalism."

Tibor Machan explained in the *Occasional Review* that "for Rand, as for Aristotle, the question How should a human community be organized? can only be answered after the question How should I, a human being, live my life? has been answered. Rand follows the Greek tradition of regarding politics as a subfield of ethics."

Rand's firsthand experience of Communism determined her politics for life. Her family lived through the privations of World War I and then struggled to adapt themselves to the new Communist regime. For her, life in Russia at that time was dreary, and the future held little hope, particularly for one who rejected the system in power. Rand wanted to write about a world as it could be, to show life as she felt it was meant to be lived. As a young girl, she had decided to become a writer. Still, she chose to major in history at the University of Petrograd (now the University of Leningrad). She dismissed literature and philosophy, the fields in which she would later make her mark, because she had rejected the majority of what the academic world valued in both of those fields. Aristotle is the only philosopher to whom she acknowledges any intellectual debt; early in her life, she had been attracted to the theories of Friedrich Wilhelm Nietzsche, but she discarded his writing when she encountered his *The Birth of Tragedy* with its antirational stance. Barbara Branden notes in *The Passion of Ayn Rand* that Nietzsche, according to Rand, "said that reason is an inferior faculty, that drunken-orgy emotions were superior. That finished him as a spiritual ally." Her favorite novelists were Victor Hugo and Fyodor Dostoevsky, her favorite playwrights, Friedrich Schiller and Edmond Rostand.

After graduating with highest honors from the university, Alice Rosenbaum found work as a tour guide in the Peter and Paul Fortress. Dreadfully unhappy in Soviet Russia, she was rescued from her dead-end job by a letter from relatives in America. An invitation from the Portnoy family to visit them in Chicago was her passage to freedom. She left Russia in 1926 and never saw members of her immediate family again, except for a sister with whom she was reunited briefly in the early 1970s.

In the United States Alice Rosenbaum became Ayn Rand. Her unique personality and insistent individuality are reflected in her name choice. Her first name, which should be pronounced to sound like the German number one, "ein," rhymes with "pine." The last name she adopted from the Remington-Rand typewriter she used to write her first movie scenarios in America.

Despite her raw language skills, Rand left Chicago after a brief stay and headed for Hollywood where she hoped to make her living writing for the movies. On her second day in town she was befriended by her favorite American director, Cecil B. DeMille, who took her to watch the shooting of "The King of Kings" and then gave her work first as an extra and then as a junior writer. Rand's April 15, 1929, marriage to Charles Francis "Frank" O'Connor, also an extra in "The King of Kings," insured that she would be allowed to stay in America.

Shortly after her marriage, Rand got a job in the wardrobe department of RKO. She hated the work, but it provided sustenance while she improved her English and perfected her craft. Her progress was remarkable, and she was one of a very few writers—Joseph Conrad and Vladimir Nabokov come to mind—to attain artistic success in a language nonnative to them. It is possible that one of Ayn Rand's few childhood friends was Nabokov's sister. Barbara Branden tells of the relationship, based on common intellectual interests, in her biography of Rand.

Rand's first novel was written in response to a promise she had made to a friend of her family at a farewell party given for her before she left Russia. Her friend had implored her to tell Americans that Russia was a huge cemetery and that its citizens were slowly dying; and in *We the Living* Rand details the deterioration of spirit and body under the Communist system. In particular, she wanted to show that Communism wreaks havoc not only on average people but particularly on the best and the brightest. All three of the major characters are destroyed. The heroine loses her life; the anti-Communist hero loses his spirit; and the Communist hero's faith and life are so undermined by the excesses he sees in the system that he takes his own life. By making one of her major characters a hero of the revolution, one who had believed fervently in the Communist cause, Rand was able to communicate basic flaws in the system. In the foreword to the 1959 edition, Rand warned her readers not to dismiss the story of Russia of the 1920s as inapplicable to the Russia of their own day: "*We the Living* is not a story about Soviet Russia in 1925. It is a story about Dictatorship, any dictatorship, anywhere, at any time, whether it be Soviet Russia, Nazi Germany, or—which this novel might do its share in helping to prevent—a socialist America." Rand continually emphasized that her opposition to Communism was based on the evil of its essential principle, that Man should exist for the sake of the state. She warned Americans against accepting the myth that the Communist ideal was noble, although its methods might be evil.

The publishing world was not taken with Rand's accomplishments in *We the Living,* which was rejected by many publishing houses as either too intellectual or too anti-Soviet. It was not until after Rand had achieved some success as a playwright that *We the Living* finally appeared in 1936. Macmillan, the publisher, had so little faith in the novel that they did little promotion and issued only one edition of three thousand copies. The reviews were not enthusiastic. Although Lee E. Cannon in the *Christian Century* called it "vigorous" and emotionally intense, Ben Belitt in the *Nation* questioned the accuracy of Rand's depiction of the U.S.S.R., claiming that she was out "to puncture a bubble—with a bludgeon." Rand was often subsequently accused of overkill.

Though neither her publisher nor her reviewers expected much from the book, *We the Living* earned word-of-mouth recommendation and sold more copies in its second year than just after publication. However, Macmillan had destroyed the type and *We the Living* was not published again in the United States until it was reissued by Random House in 1959. It has since sold more than two million copies.

Rand's primary reputation is as a novelist, but her first professional success was as a playwright. In all, Rand wrote four plays, two of which were produced on Broadway. She originally called her first play "Penthouse Legend," but its title was changed twice. Under the title "Woman on Trial" it opened in October, 1934, at the Hollywood Playhouse under the direction of E. E. Clive. Al Woods then purchased the rights, and under the title "Night of January 16th" it began a seven-month run on Broadway in September of 1935. A 1973 revival bearing Rand's original title "Penthouse Legend" was not so successful.

Night of January 16th is significant for dramatic ingenuity as well as for historical sidelights. Rand developed the innovative theatrical device of using audience members at each performance to serve as the jury in this courtroom drama. (A number of celebrities acted as jurors for the play: Jack Dempsey served on the opening night jury; Helen Keller was foreman for an all-blind jury.) Rand wrote alternative endings for the cast to use in response to either the guilty or the not guilty verdict. Moreover, the Broadway production provided actor Walter Pidgeon in the role of "Guts" Regan with a vehicle to revive his flagging career. The play also inspired Gertrude M. Moffat, Chair of the New York League of Women Voters, to write to the *New York Times* to complain of the all-male juries who were initially selected to judge Karen Andre, the defendant in the play. Moffat used the play to question a New York law that specified "male" jurors; women should be judged by their peers, which include women, she argued. The New York law was subsequently changed.

Anthem, a novella, first published in England in 1938, is Rand's shortest work. A parable-like dystopian tale, it portrays a totally collectivized world after some great war or holocaust. Originally titled "Ego," the work illustrates the negative effects on society of the suppression of individual ego and talent for the supposed good of all: When, in the name of all, no individual is allowed to stand above the others, then all stand in darkness. *Anthem* was republished in 1946 and 1953, and in 1961 the New American Library issued a paperback edition that continues to go through new printings. In a 1966 issue of the *New York Times Book Review* Gerald Raftery called the work "a surprising favorite among high-school taste-makers." Larry M. Arnoldson reported in the *Journal of Reading* that his reading of *Anthem* to his high school class created a log jam for the school librarian who had only one copy of each of Rand's novels and over fifty students on a waiting list for the books.

The Fountainhead might not have been published at all were it not for the faith of Archibald G. Ogden, who was at that time a new young editor for Bobbs-Merrill. He wired the head of the company, who had told him to reject it, "If this is not the book for you, then I am not the editor for you." At that point it had already been refused by some dozen other publishers.

Rand had done extensive research before she began writing *The Fountainhead,* which was originally titled "Secondhand Lives." Although she worked for some time in the office of Eli Jacques Kahn, a famous New York architect, Rand's main purpose was not to extol the profession of architecture. The central theme in this novel, as in the ones before it, is individualism versus collectivism, the difference being that in *The Fountainhead* the focus is not on the political system, as it was in *We the Living,* but on what Rand called collectivism in the soul. *The Fountainhead* is a defense of egoism, a positive rational egoism. Protagonist Howard Roark explains to Dominique Fracon at one point in the book, "To say 'I love you' one must know first how to say the 'I.' " The egoism Rand defined in this novel is an integral part of the individualism she championed, just as the selfishness she described is a virtue as opposed to the selflessness she abhorred.

In *The Fountainhead* Rand moved closer to her goal of creating the ideal man. Because of the resemblance in their professions and architectural styles, it was generally assumed that Howard Roark was modeled after Frank Lloyd Wright. Barbara Branden asserted in *Who Is Ayn Rand?: An Analysis of the Novels of Ayn Rand,* however, that Rand insisted, "The only resemblance is in their basic architectural principles and in the fact that Wright was an innovator fighting for modern architecture against tradition. There is no similarity in their respective characters, nor in their philosophical convictions, nor in the events in their lives." Rand had tried unsuccessfully to interview Wright while she was writing her novel. It was only after the success of *The Fountainhead* that they established an amicable relationship. Eventually he designed a home for her; it was never built.

Asked about the models for her other main characters, Rand remarked that Wynand could have been William Randolph Hearst or Henry Luce or Joseph Pulitzer. Harold Laski, the British Socialist, was the main model for Ellsworth Toohey. Other lesser sources for Toohey were Heywood Broun, Lewis Mumford, and Clifton Fadiman, although when Rand met Fadiman some years later, they liked each other. A young woman Rand had met in Hollywood, whose main goal was not to have things because she wanted them but only so that she would have more than her neighbors, was the inspiration for Peter Keating. Ayn Rand characterized the book's heroine, Dominique Francon, as herself in a bad mood.

In *The Fountainhead* Rand declares that Howard Roark's success progresses "as if an underground stream flowed through the country and broke out in sudden springs that shot to the surface at random, in unpredictable places." She might have been discussing the publishing history of her novel. Although D.L. Chambers, the head of Bobbs-Merrill, had ultimately supported his editor Archie Ogden's dedication to the book, he did not give *The Fountainhead* his wholehearted support once it was published. Rather than print significant numbers of new editions as the book gained popularity, he kept issuing small editions that quickly went out of print. When Bobbs-Merrill decided to produce a twenty-fifth anniversary deluxe edition in 1968, Nora Ephron, not an admirer of Rand's theories or writing abilities, noted in the *New York Times Book Review* that *The Fountainhead* was "one of the most astonishing phenomena in publishing history." At that date it had sold over two and one-half million copies. By the 1980s the number of copies sold was closer to four and one-half million.

Positive reviewers appreciated the powerful writing, intensity, and dramatic plot of *The Fountainhead*. Rand's favorite review was by Lorine Pruette in a May, 1943, *New York Times Book Review.* Pruette correctly identified *The Fountainhead* as a novel of ideas, pointing out that a novel of ideas by an American woman was a rarity. She lauded the quality of Rand's intellect, calling her "a writer of great power" with "a subtle and ingenious mind and the capacity of writing brilliantly, beautifully, bitterly."

The success of *The Fountainhead* brought Rand to the attention of her kind of reader, individuals who shared her perception of life. It also precipitated a lucrative movie sale, which necessitated a move back to Hollywood from New York, where Rand and her husband had moved for the Broadway production of "Night of January 16th." In California they bought a house of steel and glass in very modern design, a house which might have been designed by Howard Roark. There Rand wrote the screenplay for *The Fountainhead* and major parts of *Atlas Shrugged.*

In 1950 Nathaniel Branden (born Nathaniel Blumenthal) wrote a fan letter to Rand which so impressed her that she did something quite uncharacteristic: she answered his letter. Their meeting set in motion a series of events that would profoundly affect many lives. By the time Rand's next book was published, Branden had joined Frank O'Connor on the dedication page. Her afterword describes Branden as her "ideal reader" and "intellectual heir." Nathaniel Branden and his wife, Barbara Weidman Branden, became more than fans and students; they became close friends and intellectual allies. The Brandens' move to New York was followed shortly by a similar move by Rand and Frank O'Connor.

The Brandens introduced many of their friends and relatives to Rand and these people formed a close group called by Rand "the class of '43" because of their shared interest in *The Fountainhead,* which had been published in that year. She also called them "the children," by which she meant that they were the children of her brain. Members of this group included Alan Greenspan, who became head of the Federal Reserve System and economic advisor to three presidents; Leonard Peikoff, Barbara Branden's cousin and Rand's literary executor; Nathaniel Branden's sister, Elayne Kalberman, the circulation manager for *The Objectivist Newsletter,* and her husband, Harry Kalberman; Allan Blumenthal; Edith Efron; Mary Ann Rukavina; and Robert and Beatrice Hessen. They were privy to prepublication reading of *Atlas Shrugged,* and from their ranks the philosophical movement that Rand called Objectivism was born.

Atlas Shrugged was to be Rand's last novel, but it initiated her career as a well-known philosopher and public figure. She became a popular campus speaker in the 1960s, a regular at the Ford Hall Forum, and a columnist for the *Los Angeles Times.* She was interviewed by Johnny Carson, Tom Snyder, Phil Donahue, and *Playboy.* Nathaniel Branden began teaching her basic philosophical principles through a twenty-lecture course of study offered by Nathaniel Branden Lectures. Nathaniel Branden Lectures developed into the Nathaniel Branden Institute, which began to offer taped courses on Objectivism in cities throughout the United States. A publication branch of the Institute printed essays and monographs; a book service sold approved books. The first issue of *The Objectivist Newsletter,* which was published from 1962-65, contained articles by Rand, both Brandens, and Greenspan. *The Objectivist Newsletter* was replaced in 1966 by *The Objectivist.* In 1971 the format was changed to a simple typewritten letter called *The Ayn Rand Letter.* Rand continued issuing numbers of this letter until February of 1976.

In *Atlas Shrugged* Ayn Rand accomplished her goal of creating the ideal man. His name is John Galt, and he and a number of like-minded followers succeed in stopping the motor of the world by removing themselves and their productive capacities from exploitation by those forces they regard as looters and leeches. All of Rand's novels dramatize the primacy of the individual. The unique and precious individual human life is the standard by which good is judged. If something nourishes and sustains life, it is good; if it negates or impoverishes the individual's pursuit of happiness, then it is evil. The secondary themes in Rand's fiction unfold as the logical consequence of her major theme, but it was not until *Atlas Shrugged,* the fullest explication in fiction of her philosophy, that Rand worked out all the political, economic, and metaphysical implications of that theme.

Critical calumny greeted the publication of *Atlas Shrugged,* especially from the battlements of the conservative establishment. Whittaker Chambers in the *National Review* called it "remarkably silly," "bumptious," and "preposterous." He remarked, "Out of a lifetime of reading, I can recall no other book in which a tone of overriding arrogance was so implacably sustained. Its shrillness is without reprieve. Its dogmatism is without appeal." *Catholic World*'s Riley Hughes called it a "shrill diatribe against 'non-productive' people." Hughes claimed that though Rand decried mysticism, her book is full of parallels to Christianity: "Her John Galt is offered as a secular savior (Dagny is his Magdalene); and his disciples find him at his place of torture." In the *Saturday Review,* Helen Beal Woodward, who conceded that "Ayn Rand is a writer of dazzling virtuosity," reacted negatively to the "stylized vice-and-virtue characters" and "prolixity." Woodward found *Atlas Shrugged* a book "shot through with hatred." Such critical attacks had no effect on the reading public who have made *Atlas Shrugged* a multi-million selling phenomenon. *Atlas Shrugged,* like *Uncle Tom's Cabin,* is a book that fueled a movement. Its publication established Rand as a thinker whose influence extended to such diverse locales as Parliament (Margaret Thatcher is an admirer); tennis courts (Billie Jean King acknowledges Rand's effect on her); the Federal Reserve System (Alan Greenspan calls her instrumental in forming his thinking); and the Alaskan legislature (it issued a citation in memoriam of Rand at the request of Dick Randolph, a Libertarian legislator).

Rand was fifty-two when she published her last novel, but the end of her career as a fiction writer launched the beginning of her career as a public philosopher, speaker, and cult figure. The publication of *For the New Intellectual: The Philosophy of Ayn Rand* in 1961 began a series of nonfiction books that anthologized her essays on such diverse subjects as the American public school system, Romanticism, and racism. In her nonfiction writings as well as in her fiction, she characterized the main areas of conflict in the field of human rights: (1) individualism versus collectivism, (2) egoism versus altruism, (3) reason versus mysticism. In Rand's philosophy all of these areas are interconnected. Reason is the tool by which the individual discerns that which is life-sustaining and ego-nourishing. Collectivism, altruism, and mysticism work against individual freedom, a healthy ego, and rationality.

Rand's career as the leader of an intellectual movement had two phases. Until 1968 Nathaniel Branden was her chief spokesperson and teacher of her philosophies. In that year Rand broke with both Brandens, who had separated by then. The rupture, with its public response, established divisions between friends and relatives that never healed. It also established divisions among her other admirers: some remained purists, continuing to call themselves Objectivists and publishing only that which was sanctioned by Rand or which did not deviate from her dictums; others acknowledged influence, but moved from the letter of Rand's philosophy to other interpretations and permutations.

Leonard Peikoff became Rand's associate editor for *The Objectivist.*

To the end of her life, Rand's appearance on a television program or at a Ford Hall Forum would create controversy and inordinate audience response. She possessed great charisma and an intense intellectuality that affected both admirers and detractors. Her last years were clouded by ill health (she lost a lung to cancer) and grief (her husband, who she called her greatest value, died in 1979). Yet she made an appearance on a Phil Donahue show in 1979, affirming her love of life and her belief that there is no hereafter. If she believed in a hereafter, she explained, her desire to be with her husband would necessitate her committing suicide so as to join him. Some four months before her death, she delivered a speech at the conference of the National Committee for Monetary Reform. Thus until her death alone in her apartment on March 6, 1982, Ayn Rand's unquenchable spirit continued to assert itself.

MEDIA ADAPTATIONS: Night of January 16th was filmed by Paramount and released in 1941. A year later, *We the Living* was filmed in Italy; a revised and abridged version of the Italian film was released in the United States in 1988.

BIOGRAPHICAL/CRITICAL SOURCES:

BOOKS

Baker, James T., *Ayn Rand,* Twayne, 1987.
Barnes, Hazel Estella, *An Existential Ethics,* Knopf, 1967.
Branden, Barbara, *The Passion of Ayn Rand,* Doubleday, 1986.
Branden, Nathaniel, *Who Is Ayn Rand?: An Analysis of the Novels of Ayn Rand,* with biographical essay by Barbara Branden, Random House, 1977.
Cerf, Bennett, *At Random,* Random House, 1977.
Contempory Literary Criticism, Gale, Volume 3, 1975, Volume 30, 1984, Volume 44, 1987.
Den Uyl, Douglas and Douglas Rasmussen, editors, *The Philosophical Thought of Ayn Rand,* University of Illinois Press, 1984.
Ellis, Albert, *Is Objectivism a Religion?,* Lyle Stuart, 1968.
Gladstein, Mimi Reisel, *The Ayn Rand Companion,* Greenwood Press, 1984.
Haydn, Hiram, *Words and Faces,* Harcourt, 1974.
O'Neill, William, *With Charity Toward None: An Analysis of Ayn Rand's Philosophy,* Philosophical Library, 1971.
Peary, Gerald and Roget Shatzkin, editors, *The Modern American Novel and the Movies,* Unger, 1978.
Rand, Ayn, *We the Living,* Random House, 1959.
Rand, Ayn, *The Fountainhead,* Bobbs-Merrill, 1968.
Schwartz, Peter, editor, *The Battle for Laissez-Faire Capitalism,* Intellectual Activist, 1983.
Slusser, George E., Eric S. Rabkin, and Robert Scholes, editors, *Coordinates: Placing Science Fiction and Fantasy, Alternative Series,* Southern Illinois University Press, 1984.
Tuccille, Jerome, *It Usually Begins with Ayn Rand,* Stein & Day, 1972.

PERIODICALS

Atlantic, November, 1957.
Boston Review, December, 1984.
Catholic World, January, 1958.
Chicago Sunday Tribune, October 13, 1957.
Christian Century, July 1, 1936, December 13, 1961.
Christian Science Monitor, October 10, 1957.
Christianity Today, July 18, 1982.
College English, February, 1978.
Commonweal, November 8, 1957.

English Journal, February, 1983.
House and Garden, August, 1949.
Journal of Reading, March, 1982.
Journal of Thought, January, 1969.
Life, April 7, 1967.
Los Angeles Times, November 12, 1988.
Los Angeles Times Book Review, September 2, 1984.
Ms., September, 1978.
Nation, April 22, 1936.
National Review, December 28, 1957, October 3, 1967, April 2, 1982.
New Republic, April 24, 1961, December 10, 1966, February 21, 1970.
New Statesman, March 11, 1966.
Newsweek, March 27, 1961.
New Yorker, October 26, 1957.
New York Herald Tribune Book Review, October 6, 1957.
New York Herald Tribune Books, April 19, 1936.
New York Times, April 19, 1936, May 16, 1943, October 13, 1957, March 9, 1966, March 10, 1982, September 13, 1987.
New York Times Book Review, May 16, 1943, April 9, 1961, February 27, 1966, December 22, 1967, May 5, 1968.
Objectivist Forum, June, 1982, August, 1982, October, 1982, December, 1982.
Occasional Review, winter, 1976.
Personalist, spring, 1971.
Playboy, March, 1964.
Rampart Journal of Individualist Thought, spring, 1968.
Reason, November, 1973, May, 1978, December, 1982.
Religious Humanism, winter, 1970.
San Francisco Chronicle, April 9, 1961.
Saturday Evening Post, November 11, 1961.
Saturday Review, October 12, 1957.
Saturday Review of Literature, April 18, 1936.
Time, October 14, 1957, September 30, 1974.
Washington Post Book World, December 12, 1982.
West Coast Review of Books, November, 1984.

OTHER

"Donahue," WGN-TV, Chicago, Illinois, April 29, 1979.

OBITUARIES:

PERIODICALS

A B Bookman, March 29, 1982.
Detroit Free Press, March 7, 1982.
Los Angeles Times, March 7, 1982.
Newsweek, March 15, 1982.
New York Times, March 8, 1982.
Publishers Weekly, March 19, 1982.
Time, March 15, 1982.
Times (London), March 8, 1982.

*   *   *

RANDALL, Robert
See SILVERBERG, Robert

*   *   *

RANGER, Ken
See CREASEY, John

RANSOM, John Crowe 1888-1974

PERSONAL: Born April 30, 1888, in Pulaski, Tenn.; died July 3, 1974, in Gambier, Ohio; son of John James (a Methodist minister) and Ella (Crowe) Ransom; married Robb Reavill, December 22, 1920; children: Helen (Mrs. O. D. Forman), David Reavill, John James. *Education:* Vanderbilt University, A.B., 1909; Christ Church College, Oxford, B.A. in Lit.Hum., 1913; attended University of Grenoble, briefly, after World War I.

ADDRESSES: Home—Gambier, Ohio.

CAREER: Taught Latin in a preparatory school for one year; Harvard University, Cambridge, Mass., assistant in English, 1914; Vanderbilt University, Nashville, Tenn., 1914-37, professor of English, 1927-37; Kenyon College, Gambier, Ohio, Carnegie Professor of Poetry, 1937-58, professor emeritus, 1958-74. Summer lecturer, Colorado State Teachers College (now University of Northern Colorado), George Peabody College for Teachers (now George Peabody College for Teachers of Vanderbilt University), University of New Mexico, University of Florida, University of Kentucky, University of Texas, University of Chattanooga, Women's College of the University of North Carolina (now University of North Carolina at Greensboro), West Tennessee Teachers College (now Memphis State University), Harvard University, and Bread Loaf School of English. Honorary consultant in American letters, Library of Congress. *Military service:* U.S. Army, 1917-19; served with 5th Field Artillery; became first lieutenant.

MEMBER: American Academy of Arts and Letters, American Academy of Arts and Sciences, Phi Beta Kappa, Kappa Sigma.

AWARDS, HONORS: Rhodes scholar, Oxford University; Guggenheim fellow, 1931; Bollingen Prize for poetry, 1951; Russell Loines Prize for poetry, 1951; honored at Chicago Poetry Day, 1957; Brandeis University Creative Arts Award, 1958-59; Academy of American Poets fellow, 1962; National Book Award, 1964, for *Selected Poems;* National Endowment for the Arts award), 1967; Emerson-Thoreau Medal, American Academy of Arts and Sciences, 1968; Gold Medal, National Institute of Arts and Letters, 1973.

WRITINGS:

Poems about God, Holt, 1919, reprinted, Folcroft, 1972.
Armageddon (poem; bound with *A Fragment* by William Alexander Percy and *Avalon* by Donald Davidson), Poetry Society of South Carolina, 1923.
Chills and Fever (poems), Knopf, 1924, reprinted, Folcroft, 1972.
Grace after Meat (poems), introduction by Robert Graves, L. & V. Woolf, 1924.
Two Gentlemen in Bonds (poems), Knopf, 1927.
God without Thunder: An Unorthodox Defense of Orthodoxy (essays), Harcourt, 1930, reprinted, Shoe String, 1965.
(With others) *I'll Take My Stand* (essays), Harper, 1930.
(Editor) *Topics for Freshman Writing,* Holt, 1935.
The World's Body (essays), Scribner, 1938, reprinted, Louisiana State University Press, 1968.
The New Criticism (essays), New Directions, 1941, reprinted, Greenwood Press, 1979.
(Contributor) Donald A. Stuffer, editor, *The Intent of the Critic,* Princeton University Press, 1941, reprinted, Peter Smith, 1963.
Poetics (essays), New Directions, 1942.
A College Primer of Writing, Holt, 1943.
Selected Poems, Knopf, 1945, reprinted, Richard West, 1977, 3rd revised edition, Knopf, 1969.

(Editor) *The Kenyon Critics: Studies in Modern Literature from the "Kenyon Review,"* World Publishing, 1951, reprinted, Kennikat, 1967.
Poems and Essays, Vintage Books, 1955.
Exercises on the Occasion of the Dedication of the New Phi Beta Kappa Memorial Hall, the College of William and Mary in Virginia (an address), College of William and Mary, 1958.
(With Delmore Schwartz and John Hall Wheelock) *American Poetry at Mid-Century* (lectures), Library of Congress, 1958, reprinted, Norwood, 1977.
(Editor) Thomas Hardy, *Selected Poems,* Macmillan, 1961.
(With others) *Symposium on Formalist Criticism,* University of Texas, 1967.
Beating the Bushes: Selected Essays, 1941-1970, New Directions, 1972.
Selected Essays of John Crowe Ransom, edited by Thomas D. Young and John Hindle, Louisiana State University Press, 1984.
Selected Letters of John Crowe Ransom, edited by Young and George Core, Louisiana State University Press, 1985.

Also author of an unpublished book on aesthetics, 1926. Cofounder, editor, and publisher, *Fugitive,* 1922-25. *Kenyon Review,* founder and editor, 1939-59, editor emeritus, 1959-71.

SIDELIGHTS: Around the year 1915, a group of fifteen or so Vanderbilt University teachers and students began meeting informally to discuss trends in American life and literature. Led by John Crowe Ransom, a member of the university's English faculty, these young "Fugitives," as they called themselves, opposed both the traditional sentimentality of Southern writing and the increasingly frantic pace of life as the turbulent war years gave way to the Roaring Twenties. They recorded their concerns in a magazine of verse entitled the *Fugitive,* which, though it appeared little more than a dozen times after the first issue was published in 1922, proved to be in the vanguard of a new literary movement—Agrarianism—and a new way of analyzing works of art—the New Criticism. As one of the group's major spokesmen (along with fellow members Allen Tate, Robert Penn Warren, and Donald Davidson), John Crowe Ransom eventually came to be known as the dean of twentieth-century American poets and critics.

Agrarianism was a direct descendent of the Fugitive philosophy; the Agrarians, in fact, were former Fugitives (the original group drifted apart around 1925) who banded together again in the late 1920s to extol the virtues of the rural South and to promote the establishment of an agrarian as opposed to an industrial economy. As far as Ransom and his fellow Agrarians were concerned, noted John L. Stewart in his study of the poet and critic, "poetry, the arts, ritual, tradition, and the mythic way of looking at nature thrive best in an agrarian culture based on an economy dominated by small subsistence farms. Working directly and closely with nature man finds aesthetic satisfaction and is kept from conceitedness and greed by the many reminders of the limits of his power and understanding. But in an industrial culture he is cut off from nature. He gets into the way of thinking that machinery can give him limitless control over it, and he is denied the little indulgences of the sensibility. His arts and religions wither and he lives miserably in a rectilinear jungle of factories and efficiency apartments." In short, explained Louis D. Rubin, Jr., in *Writers of the Modern South,* "for Ransom the agrarian image is of the kind of life in which leisure, grace, civility can exist in harmony with thought and action, making the individual's life a wholesome, harmonious experience. . . . His agrarianism is of the old Southern plantation, the gentle, mannered life of leisure and refinement without the need or inclination to pioneer."

Though the rustic dream of the Agrarians more or less evaporated with the coming of the Depression, it left its philosophical imprint on Ransom's later work. As Richard Gray observed in his book *The Literature of Memory,* "the thesis that nearly all of [Ransom's] writing sets out to prove, in one way or another, is that only in a traditional and rural society—the kind of society that is epitomized for Ransom by the antebellum South—can the human being achieve the completeness that comes from exercising the sensibility and the reason with equal ease."

Ransom's poems, written primarily between 1915 and 1927 but revised several times during the following years, reflected this preoccupation with regionalism and the struggle between reason and sensibility from a thematic as well as a stylistic standpoint. Ransom's "poetic world," for instance, reported the *Washington Post Book World*'s Chad Walsh, "is mostly the South, not the South as it actually was when cotton and slavery were crowned heads, not the empirical South that the sociologists study today, but a might-have-been South, a vision of gentleness in all senses of that Chaucerian word." Stewart agreed that Ransom was "truly a Southern writer," but he attributed this less to the poet's choice of themes and backgrounds than to "his style and his vision." Explained the critic: "[Regional] qualities, violence coupled with elegance, affinity for unusual diction, concern with the insignia of feudalism and the chevalier as the embodiment of its values, mockery of the man of ideas, and so forth, are transformed by Ransom's double vision and irony into a poetry so conspicuously his own that his individuality rather than any regionalism first impresses the reader. . . . Yet it is difficult to conceive of such poetry being written in twentieth-century American by anyone not from the South."

Besides being unmistakably Southern in character, Ransom's world is a world of fundamental opposites, a world where man is constantly made aware of "the inexhaustible ambiguities, the paradoxes and tensions, the dichotomies and ironies that make up [modern] life," wrote Thomas Daniel Young in a study of the poet. His themes, continued Young, emphasized "man's dual nature and the inevitable misery and disaster that always accompany the failure to recognize and accept this basic truth; mortality and the fleetingness of youthful vigor and grace, the inevitable decay of feminine beauty; the disparity between the world as man would have it and as it actually is, between what people want and need emotionally and what is available for them, between what man desires and what he can get; man's divided sensibilities and the wars constantly raging within him, the inevitable clash between body and mind, between reason and sensibility; the necessity of man's simultaneous apprehension of nature's indifference and mystery and his appreciation of her sensory beauties; the inability of modern man, in his incomplete and fragmentary state, to experience love."

These various dualisms in Ransom's poetry could best be described in terms of a debate between the head and the heart—that is, as Young noted, between reason and aesthetic sensibility. Ransom continually sought a balance between the two, a balance which, however precarious it might have been, tried to give equal time to both logic and sentiment. He detested extremes of either kind and deliberately strived for a certain detachment in his poetry that struck some critics as being rather cold and academic. By establishing such an "aesthetic distance," however, Ransom felt that he could provide the reader with a better view of his subject than those poets who imbued their work with sentimentalism and other distracting personal attitudes. Thus, the typical

Ransom poem was never autobiographical or didactic, for, as Wesley Morris pointed out in his book *Towards a New Historicism,* "[Ransom's] dualistic theory demands that in the realm of poetic discourse the artist must never assert his own personality; he must remain as 'nearly anonymous' as possible." As a result, Thornton H. Parsons observed in his critical study, "a proper appreciation of Ransom's poetry calls for a modest cultivation of literary asceticism. The reader must accustom himself to the idea that he will encounter no portrayal of strong personalities, no highly emotional drama, and (except very faintly and indirectly) little sense of a poet's dreadful self-discovery. He must tune himself to register elusive subtleties of perception and elegances of rhyme, wit, and rhetoric. He must be somewhat willing to forgive Ransom for the acute esthetic self-consciousness that made him habitually subordinate passion to tonal control. He must be indulgent of Ransom's addictions to pale or paralyzing irony and to refined whimsicality. In brief, he should accept the limitations inherent in a civilized poetry and try to savor the fragile excellences."

In Ransom's case, as Parsons suggested, these "fragile excellences" had more to do with actual poetic technique than with the creation of a particular mood. Many critics, in fact, felt Ransom was one of the greatest stylists of modern American poetry due to what Stewart described as the "unabashed elegance and artifice [of his work], both carried at times to the edge of affectation and preciousness. This poetry is made and proudly exhibits its technical ingenuity." Randall Jarrell, among others, regarded this obsession with what he called "rhetorical machinery" as Ransom's "way of handling sentiment or emotion without ever seeming sentimental or over-emotional; as a way of keeping the poem at the proper aesthetic distance from its subject; and as a way for the poem to extract from its subject, no matter how unpleasant or embarrassing, an unembarrassed pleasure."

Stylistically, Ransom maintained a "proper aesthetic distance" through wit (primarily irony), tone, and diction. His humor, noted Karl F. Knight in *The Poetry of John Crowe Ransom,* is similar to that of Voltaire, Rabelais, Swift, and Twain in that "it is based upon a sense of far-reaching incongruity. The times are out of joint, Ransom seems to say, but we can still take an objective look at things. And a good way to keep one's balance is to look at things through a witty and ironic style."

For the most part, stated Robert Buffington in his book *The Equilibrist,* this irony stemmed from a particular use of the language and "a subtle, and gentle, irony of tone." Rueful, wry, and often whimsical, Ransom's poetry was "detached, mock-pedantic, [and] wittily complicated," according to Jarrell, and displayed, said Parsons, a "peculiar kind of self-indulgence" and a certain "archaism and grandiloquence." His speech, wrote Buffington, "is that of the Gentleman, rather than that of the Common Man. . . . His sentences have the effect of an ease that can indulge itself in the direction of elegance. He is learned enough and assured enough to range in his words from the colloquial to the archaic or pedantic. Or to play a Latinate vocabulary off against an Anglo-Saxon." The *Sewanee Review*'s George Core also identified a certain dualism in Ransom's writing, describing it as "deliberately archaic yet timeless, occasionally eccentric but never obscure, at once quiet and nervous, pedantic and plain, formal and idiomatic, mannered and colloquial." A *Times Literary Supplement* critic once remarked that "the language of Ransom's people suggests the old-fashioned speech of pious Southern farmers in his boyhood; and it is not without a parodical trace of Southern oratory. The words are often Biblical in flavour or otherwise archaic; the phrasing is angular or enigmatically concise. Mixed with rarities are coarse words and slang. Often an obsolete or etymological sense is preferred to the normal meaning." In short, concluded the critic, Ransom "has invented an idiom that both connects him with and separates him from the situations he describes. His language implies a judgment on the people around him, a distance between present and past, speaker and story. But it also implies an ironic depreciation of the poet; for this is only his judgment."

Many of these same qualities and attitudes eventually found their way into the new philosophy of criticism developed by Ransom and others in the 1930s. Using the *Kenyon Review* (founded by Ransom in 1939) as their principal forum, he and his fellow proponents of the "New Criticism" rejected the romanticists' commitment to self-expression and perfectability as well as the naturalists' insistence on fact (mostly scientific fact) and inference from fact as the basis of evaluating a work of art. Instead, the New Critics focused their attention on the work of art as an object in and of itself, independent of outside influences (including the circumstances of its composition, the reality it creates, the author's intention, and the effect it has on readers). The New Critics also tended to downplay the study of genre, plot, and character in favor of detailed textual examinations of image, symbol, and meaning. As far as they were concerned, the ultimate value (in both a moral and an artistic sense) of a work of art was a function of its own inner qualities. In short, explained James E. Magner, Jr., in the book *John Crowe Ransom: Critical Principles and Preoccupations,* "[Ransom] wishes the world and the poem to be perceived as what they are and not as someone would have them to be. . . . [He] is a critic who wishes to be faithful to the reality of 'the world's body,' who wishes the poem aesthetically to reveal that reality, and wishes criticism to show the poem as revealing or distorting it. . . . [He is] bent on letting the poem be itself and not something else; not, for example, a means of moral propaganda or psychic therapy. . . . Ransom believes that in knowing this aesthetic being, the poem, we will more surely and deeply know its correlative—the world, in the fullness and realness of its 'body.' "

Ransom's interest in the conflict between reason and aesthetic sensibility, so prominent in his own poetry, was also reflected in his "structure/texture" approach to poetry criticism. As interpreted by Young, this time commenting in the *Georgia Review,* Ransom's theory required a poem "to perform a dual role with words. On the one hand they must be arranged in such a manner as 'to conduct a logical sequence with their meaning,' and on the other they must 'realize an objective pattern with their sounds.' " The actual process of creating a poem, wrote Magner, is therefore "a movement from simple realization in the mind [the structure or theme] to a phrase that textures the realization and stimulates the creative mind into spinning further texture and further poetic suspension, until the original realization has been textured into the web of poetic existence." According to John Paul Pritchard in his book *Criticism in America,* Ransom believed that since this "texture"—sounds, imagery, and other details meant to enhance the poem's basic meaning—overwhelms the structure, "the critic should devote his most careful attention to the texture, realizing that he is analyzing an ontology, an order of existence which cannot be treated by scientific modes of thought."

Ransom's theories were not greeted with universal enthusiasm. Magner, for example, comparing his style to that of T. S. Eliot, pointed out that "neither Ransom nor Eliot is particularly logical in his critical progression. They lack the order which the mind urges when reading them. They do not define, divide, and discuss very systematically. Both critics intimate a part of a definition, make somewhat arbitrary divisions, and then discuss

what they are interested in, with a casual unpredictability." Core, echoing the views of those who felt Ransom's own poetry was too cool, subdued, and philosophical, cited Ransom's "neglect of the emotive dimension of the poem" as "the most serious possible deficiency in [his] theoretical formulations about poetry." Despite these and other reservations, however, most critics agreed with Magner that "Ransom has given the world a redirection. . . . He has made the pragmatists clear their vision again and again, and made them focus upon the poem, whose reason for existence, he thinks, is to catch up the world beautifully in the texture of its worded being."

The debate continues as to whether Ransom will be remembered in the years to come primarily as a poet or as a critic. Although Pritchard contended that "of all the American New Critics, Ransom is the most significant figure," Stewart was of the opinion that "inevitably his reputation in criticism will decline. The theories are too insubstantial and the criticism itself (of which there is surprisingly little, considering how much he wrote about it) is too occasional. But his reputation as a poet, which is high, will continue to rise." Stewart based this conclusion on his belief that Ransom's "conception of the mind and fury against abstraction which . . . served his poetry well when qualified by narrative and image . . . served his poetics ill. To the poems they gave a unique vision; to the criticism they brought myopia."

Hyatt H. Waggoner, commenting in his *American Poets from the Puritans to the Present,* concurred with Stewart that "Ransom's poetry will outlast his critical theory. His influence has been enormous, . . . all out of proportion, really, to his actual accomplishments as a critic. He taught a generation how to write poems and how to criticize them. . . . [But] he will be remembered as a distinguished minor poet who, chiefly in his early youth, wrote a small number of perfectly wrought, finely textured poems that are likely to be remembered a long time." On the other hand, Robert D. Jacobs stated in the *South Atlantic Quarterly* that "John Crowe Ransom may be called a minor poet, and by some an eccentric critic, but within his special province he is unique." Core, impressed by both Ransom the poet *and* Ransom the critic, agreed that his contributions to literature should not be minimized. He concluded: "The present fame of John Crowe Ransom is very great, perhaps greater than it will be in a few decades when the fires are banked down but continuing to throw forth radiant light and steady warmth, but this much is clear: the essential reputation is certain and will endure."

BIOGRAPHICAL/CRITICAL SOURCES:

BOOKS

Buffington, Robert, *The Equilibrist: A Study of John Crowe Ransom's Poems, 1916-1963,* Vanderbilt University Press, 1967.

Contemporary Literary Criticism, Gale, Volume 2, 1974, Volume 4, 1975, Volume 5, 1976, Volume 6, 1979, Volume 11, 1979, Volume 24, 1983.

Dictionary of Literary Biography, Gale, Volume 45: *American Poets, 1880-1945, First Series,* 1986, Volume 63: *Modern American Critics, 1920-1955,* 1988.

Gray, Richard, *The Literature of Memory: Modern Writers of the American South,* Johns Hopkins Press, 1978.

Jarrell, Randall, *Poetry and the Age,* Knopf, 1953.

Knight, Karl F., *The Poetry of John Crowe Ransom: A Study of Diction, Metaphor, and Symbol,* Mouton, 1964.

Magner, James E., Jr., *John Crowe Ransom: Critical Principles and Preoccupations,* Mouton, 1971.

Morris, Wesley, *Towards a New Historicism,* Princeton University Press, 1972.

Nemerov, Howard, *Poetry and Fiction,* Rutgers University Press, 1963.
Parsons, Thornton H., *John Crowe Ransom,* Twayne, 1969.
Pritchard, John Paul, *Criticism in America,* University of Oklahoma Press, 1956.
Rubin, Louis D., Jr., *Writers of the Modern South: The Faraway Country,* University of Washington Press, 1963.
Stewart, John L., *John Crowe Ransom,* University of Minnesota Press, 1962.
Untermeyer, Louis, *Lives of the Poets,* Simon & Schuster, 1959.
Waggoner, Hyatt H., *American Poets from the Puritans to the Present,* Houghton, 1968.
Young, Thomas Daniel, *John Crowe Ransom,* Steck, 1971.

PERIODICALS

Books, May 8, 1938.
Christian Science Monitor, August 1, 1963, December 18, 1969.
Georgia Review, summer, 1968, fall, 1968, spring, 1969, spring, 1971, summer, 1973.
Kenyon Review, Volume 39, number 120, issue 3, 1968.
Life, May 10, 1968.
Nation, July 12, 1941.
New Republic, August 10, 1938.
New Yorker, July 7, 1945.
New York Times, December 18, 1938, July 8, 1945.
New York Times Book Review, May 20, 1984.
Poetry, February, 1969.
Saturday Review of Literature, May 21, 1938, July 5, 1941, July 14, 1945.
Sewanee Review, summer, 1948, summer, 1968, summer, 1969, fall, 1974.
South Atlantic Quarterly, spring, 1969.
Spectator, February 14, 1970.
Time, May 9, 1938.
Times Literary Supplement, April 23, 1970.
Washington Post Book World, September 7, 1969.
Yale Review, autumn, 1938.

OBITUARIES:

PERIODICALS

Antiquarian Bookman, October 14, 1974.
Newsweek, July 15, 1974.
New York Times, July 4, 1974.
Publishers Weekly, July 29, 1974.
Time, July 15, 1974.
Washington Post, July 5, 1974.

*   *   *

RAO, Raja   1909-

PERSONAL: Born November 21, 1909 (some sources list 1908), in Hassan, Mysore, India; son of H. V. (a professor) and Srimathi (Gauramma) Krishnaswamy; married Camille Mouly, 1931; married Katherine Jones (a playwright), April, 1966; children: (second marriage) Christopher. *Education:* Attended Aligarh Muslim University, 1926-27; Nizam College, Hyderabad, University of Madras, B.A., 1929; attended University of Montpellier, 1929-30, and the Sorbonne, 1930-33.

ADDRESSES: Home—1808 Pearl, Austin, Tex. 78701. *Agent*—William Morris Agency, 1350 Avenue of the Americas, New York, N.Y. 10019.

CAREER: University of Texas at Austin, professor of philosophy, 1966-80.

AWARDS, HONORS: Sahitya Academy Award, 1964, for *The Serpent and the Rope;* Padma Bhushan, Government of India, 1970; Neustadt International Prize for Literature, 1988.

WRITINGS:

Kanthapura (novel), Allen and Unwin, 1938, New Directions, 1938, reprinted, 1976.
(Editor with Iqbal Singh) *Changing India,* Allen and Unwin, 1939.
The Cow of the Barricades and Other Stories (short stories), Oxford University Press, 1947.
(Editor with Singh) *Whither India?,* Padmaja (Baroda), 1948.
(Editor) Jawaharlal Nehru, *Soviet Russia: Some Random Sketches and Impressions,* Chetana (Bombay), 1949.
The Serpent and the Rope (novel), Murray, 1960, Pantheon, 1963, reprinted, Overlook Press, 1988.
The Cat and Shakespeare: A Tale of India (novel), Macmillan, 1965.
Comrade Kirillov (novel), Orient, 1976.
The Policeman and the Rose (short stories), Oxford University Press, 1978.
The Chess Master and His Moves (novel), Vision, 1978.

Contributor to *Pacific Spectator.* Editor, *Tomorrow* (Bombay), 1943-44.

SIDELIGHTS: A novelist, short story writer, essayist, and philosopher, "Raja Rao is perhaps the most brilliant—and certainly the most interesting—writer of modern India," states Santha Rama Rau in the *New York Times Book Review.* Rao's writings frequently the explore philosophical significance of Indian religions, traditions, and values—especially as they contrast with those of Western society. He is also considered a writer of the metaphysical, in that many of his novels abound with symbolism, and displays a broad knowledge of history and Indian dialects. Born a Brahmin in South India, Rao was educated in Europe as well as India and taught philosophy in the United States. While a number of critics recognize him as the finest English writer to come out of India, "Raja Rao is a man of great literary cultures being equally at home in the knowledge of classical Sanskrit and modern European literature, [yet] is basically an Indian," remarks Harish Raizada in *Indo-English Literature: A Collection of Critical Essays.* "His whole approach to life and literature has been outlined against the broad perspective of Indian philosophy and tradition." In 1988, Rao received the prestigious Neustadt International Prize for Literature, awarded every two years to a living writer for outstanding contributions in poetry, fiction, or drama.

One of Rao's most famous works is his first novel, *Kanthapura,* written when he was only twenty-one and published eight years later in England in 1938. Considered by E. M. Forster as the best novel in English about India, *Kanthapura* describes a small Indian village influenced by a young Brahmin to turn from their old ways of acceptance and conformity to become involved in the Mahatma Gandhi's nonviolence movement for Indian independence from Great Britain. Narrated by a woman of the village, *Kanthapura,* according to Geoffrey Godsell in the *Christian Science Monitor* is "a story fascinatingly told, building up . . . to a crashing climax that well-nigh shatters the little village and its traditional organization of society." A number of critics praised Rao's depiction—in English—of Indian speech patterns and idioms, while weaving various elements of Indian culture and lore. "Written in an elegant style verging on poetry," according to Rama Rau, *Kanthapura* "has all the content of an ancient Indian classic, combined with a sharp, satirical wit and a clear understanding of the present," while Lois Harley notes in *America* that "it is a book of extraordinary veracity in its details of village life in India."

BIOGRAPHICAL/CRITICAL SOURCES:

BOOKS

Contemporary Literary Criticism, Gale, Volume 25, 1983, Volume 56, 1989.
Contemporary Novelists, St. James Press/St. Martin's, 1986.
Naik, M. K., *Raja Rao,* Twayne, 1972.
Narasimhaiah, C. D., *Raja Rao: A Critical Study of His Work,* Heinemann, 1973.
Rao, K. R., *The Fiction of Raja Rao,* Parimal (Aurangabad), 1980.
Sharma, K. K., editor, *Indo-English Literature: A Collection of Critical Essays,* Vimal Prakashan, 1977.
Sharma, K. K., editor, *Perspectives on Raja Rao,* Vimal (Ghaziabad), 1980.

PERIODICALS

America, February 29, 1964.
Christian Science Monitor, January 16, 1964.
Los Angeles Times Book Review, August 24, 1986.
New York Times Book Review, January 5, 1964.

*   *   *

RATCLIFFE, James P.
See MENCKEN, H(enry) L(ouis)

*   *   *

RATTIGAN, Terence (Mervyn) 1911-1977

PERSONAL: Born June 10, 1911, in London, England; died November 30, 1977, in Hamilton, Bermuda; son of William Frank Arthur (a diplomat) and Vera (Houston) Rattigan. *Education:* Attended Trinity College, Oxford, 1930-1933.

CAREER: Playwright and screenwriter, 1934-77. *Military service:* Royal Air Force, Coastal Command, 1940-45; became flight lieutenant.

AWARDS, HONORS: Ellen Terry Award, 1947, and New York Drama Critics' Circle Award, 1948, both for "The Winslow Boy"; Ellen Terry Award, 1948, for "The Browning Version"; named Commander of the Order of the British Empire (C.B.E.), 1958; knighted, 1971.

WRITINGS:

PLAYS

(With Philip Heimann) "First Episode," first produced in London, 1933, produced in New York City, 1934.
French Without Tears (first produced in London, 1939; produced in New York City, 1934; revised version produced as "Joie de vivre" in London, 1960), Hamish Hamilton, 1937, Farrar & Rinehart, 1938.
After the Dance (produced in London, 1939), Hamish Hamilton, 1939.
(With Anthony Maurice) "Follow My Leader," produced in London, 1940.
(With Hector Bolitho) "Grey Farm," produced in New York City, 1940, produced in London, 1942.
Flare Path (first produced in London, 1942; produced in New York City, 1942), Hamish Hamilton, 1942.
While the Sun Shines (first produced in London, 1943; produced in New York City, 1944), Samuel French, 1945.

Love in Idleness (produced in London, 1944), Hamish Hamilton, 1945, revised version published as *O Mistress Mine* (produced in New York City, 1946), Samuel French, 1949.
The Winslow Boy (first produced in London, 1946; produced in New York City, 1947), Dramatists Play Service, 1946.
Playbill: "The Browning Version" and "Harlequinade" (first produced in London, 1948; produced in New York City, 1949), Hamish Hamilton, 1949, published in two volumes by Samuel French, 1950.
Adventure Story (produced in London, 1949), Samuel French, 1950.
Who Is Sylvia? (produced in London, 1950), Hamish Hamilton, 1951.
The Deep Blue Sea (produced in London, 1952; produced in New York City, 1952), Hamish Hamilton, 1952, Random House, 1953.
The Sleeping Prince (two-act; produced in London, 1953; produced in New York City, 1956), Hamish Hamilton, 1954, Random House, 1957.
Separate Tables: Two Plays (produced in London, 1954; produced in New York City, 1956), Hamish Hamilton, 1955, Random House, 1957.
"The Prince and the Showgirl": The Script for the Film, New American Library, 1957.
Variation on a Theme (produced in London, 1958), Hamish Hamilton, 1958.
Ross: A Dramatic Portrait (produced in London, 1960; produced in New York City, 1961), Hamish Hamilton, 1960, Random House, 1962.
Man and Boy (produced in London, 1963; produced in New York City, 1963), Samuel French, 1963.
Collected Plays, 3 volumes, Hamish Hamilton, 1964.
A Bequest to the Nation (televised as "Nelson," 1966; revised version produced in London at the Haymarket Theatre on September 23, 1970, as "A Bequest to the Nation"), Hamish Hamilton, 1970.
"All on Her Own" (televised, 1968; produced in London, 1974; produced in London as "Duologue," 1976), published in *The Best Short Plays 1970,* edited by Stanley Richards, Chilton, 1970.
"High Summer" (televised, 1972), published in *The Best Short Plays 1973,* edited by Richards, Chilton, 1973.
In Praise of Love: "Before Dawn" and "After Lydia" (produced in London, 1973; "After Lydia" produced as "In Praise of Love" on Broadway at Morosco Theatre, 1974), Hamish Hamilton, 1973, Samuel French, 1975.
"Cause Celebre," first produced on the West End at Her Majesty's Theatre, July 14, 1977.

SCREENPLAYS

(With Anatole de Grunwald and Ian Dalrymple) "French Without Tears" (based on Rattigan's play of the same name), Paramount, 1939.
(With de Grunwald) "Quiet Wedding," Universal, 1941.
(With Rodney Ackland) "Uncensored," Twentieth Century-Fox, 1943.
(With de Grunwald) "Johnny in the Clouds," United Artists, 1946.
(With de Grunwald) "Her Man Gilbey," Universal, 1949.
(With de Grunwald and Anthony Asquith) "The Winslow Boy" (based on Rattigan's play of the same name), Eagle Lion, 1950.
(With Graham Greene) "Young Scarface" (based on Greene's novel *Brighton Rock*), Mayer-Kingsley, 1952.

"The Browning Version" (based on Rattigan's play of the same name), Universal, 1952.

"Breaking the Sound Barrier," United Artists, 1952.

"The Final Test," J. Arthur Rank Organisation, 1954.

"The Deep Blue Sea" (based on Rattigan's play of the same name), Twentieth Century-Fox, 1955.

"The Man Who Loved Redheads," United Artists, 1955.

"The Prince and the Showgirl" (based on Rattigan's play "The Sleeping Prince"), Warner Bros., 1957.

(With John Gay) "Separate Tables" (based on Rattigan's play of the same name), United Artists, 1958.

"The V.I.P.s," Metro-Goldwyn-Mayer, 1963.

"The Yellow Rolls Royce," Metro-Goldwyn-Mayer, 1965.

"Goodbye, Mr. Chips" (based on James Hilton's novel of the same name), Metro-Goldwyn-Mayer, 1969.

Also author or coauthor of other screenplays, including "The Day Will Dawn," 1941; "The Avengers," 1942; "English Without Tears," 1944; "Journey Together," 1946; "While the Sun Shines" (based on Rattigan's play of the same name), 1947; "Bond Street," 1950; "A Bequest to the Nation" (based on Rattigan's play of the same name), 1973; "Conduct Unbecoming"; and "Mr. Burke and Mr. Wills."

Author of television plays, including "The Final Test," 1951; "Heart to Heart"; 1962; "Ninety Years On," 1964.

Author of radio plays, including "A Tale of Two Cities" (based on Charles Dickens's novel of the same name), 1950, and "Cause Celebre," 1975.

SIDELIGHTS: Stagestruck as a youngster, Terence Rattigan decided at an early age that he wanted to be a dramatist. While he was still in college, Rattigan wrote a play, "First Episode," that had brief and disastrous runs in London and New York City. Rattigan was undaunted by the failure and quit college to pursue a career in the theatre. His father disapproved of his career plans but agreed to finance the aspiring playwright for two years. As his part of the bargain, Rattigan promised his father that if he was still unsuccessful after the two years had elapsed he would begin a career in diplomacy or banking. Shortly before the probationary period expired, Rattigan's "French Without Tears" became a smash hit in London. More success was to follow. Rattigan is the only dramatist to have written two plays that ran for more than one thousand performances apiece in London. In addition to his popular plays, he wrote a number of original movie scripts, including "The V.I.P.s," "The Yellow Rolls Royce," and "Conduct Unbecoming."

Rattigan's predilection for bourgeois characters and middle class values aroused the disdain of some critics and the approbation of others. Reviewing productions of "The Winslow Boy" and "A Bequest to the Nation," Hilary Spurling noted that "both plays are designed to take one back . . . to the days when one was proud to be an Englishman. . . . Pain and fear are discreetly underplayed in favour of the soothing virtues, courage, loyalty and perseverance in face of frightful odds." Ronald Bryden also remarked upon the traditional values espoused in "The Winslow Boy": "Rattigan's surface self-congratulation is part of an argument that British society is strong enough to tolerate questioning, dissent, individuality. Today we can see that the quantity of reassurance was a measure of British insecurity in those post-war years. . . . But it's possible to envy the confidence still underlying the play that tolerance is something we can afford, that our sameness is sufficient to permit differences."

Characters rather than ideas are emphasized in Rattigan's plays. "I rejoice," he wrote in an article for the *New York Herald Tri-*

bune in 1956, "in the death of the cult of the play of ideas and [in] the re-emergence since the war, in Europe as in America, of the play that unashamedly says nothing except possibly that human beings are strange creatures, and worth putting on the stage where they can be laughed at or cried over, as our pleasure takes us." Rattigan contended that "character makes the play" not only in serious plays but also in farce. John Russell Taylor observed that "French Without Tears" "is under the bright, bustling surface, a gentle comedy of character, in which each seems for a moment to be faced with what he has most desired and finds that it is in fact what he most fears." While granting the effectiveness of farces like "French Without Tears," Frederick Lumley asserted that Rattigan failed in his serious plays of character: "In his farces we do not ask that his characters should be complete individuals, whereas in a serious play that character must be a creation. The main criticism of Rattigan's work, then, is a fundamental criticism, namely, that his characters are wishy-washy creatures with neither nobility in their thoughts nor individuality in their actions. They are types we know exist, and though we might recognise them, they are certainly not people we would want as our friends."

Whatever the defects in Rattigan's characterization, virtually all commentators concede that he was a master craftsman. "Terence Rattigan has been turning out neatly turned-out comedies and dramas since the 1930s, and is still writing 1930s plays," Stanley Kauffmann wrote in 1975. "He finds his little idea, for comedy or poignance, and he stitches his little script about it with considerable craft and no unnecessary nuisance." In *The Rise and Fall of the Well-Made Play,* John Russell Taylor examined in detail the quality of Rattigan's craftsmanship. Taylor offered "The Winslow Boy" and "The Browning Version" as examples of plays that were expertly constructed, but he regarded "The Deep Blue Sea" as the play in which Rattigan "most happily constructed a fully articulated plot according to well-made principles without too obviously showing his hand." After viewing a performance of "A Bequest to the Nation," Spurling also paid tribute to Rattigan's craftsmanship: "Mr Rattigan's lightness of touch belongs with much else—his knack of smuggling serviceable information in small, discreetly wrapped and easily assimilated packages; his manner of sewing a scene together and finishing off with an exit line, which snaps it shut like a pressstud; his habit, when approaching troubled emotional waters, of quoting Shakespeare—all these belong to a style of playwriting long neglected, but by no means to be sneezed at."

Rattigan's style of playwriting has indeed been long neglected. Although he had exulted in 1956 that the play of ideas was dead, later that same year the showing of John Osborne's "Look Back in Anger" ushered in a new era in British theatre, one in which plays of craftsmanship and character were distinctly unfashionable. Rattigan took this turn of events philosophically. "Fashion is ephemeral," he once told an interviewer. "Someday we'll get back to the state in which a curtain goes up on a sitting room where the maid is on the phone saying 'Lady Silversmith is out.'" Although drawing-room drama has not yet come back into vogue, Rattigan's reputation has gained considerable luster in recent years. A reviewer for *Newsweek* remarked in 1974: "The plays of Terence Rattigan are precisely the kind of thing that Britain's Angry Young Men were supposed to have swept off the stage in the '50s, led by John Osborne on first broom. . . . But how would history judge between Rattigan and Osborne right now? Angry shmangry. Rattigan the 'drawing-room dramatist' has almost certainly written more good plays . . . than Osborne."

AVOCATIONAL INTERESTS: Golf and squash, watching cricket games.

BIOGRAPHICAL/CRITICAL SOURCES:

BOOKS

Contemporary Literary Criticism, Volume 7, Gale, 1977.
Dictionary of Literary Biography, Volume 13: *British Dramatists Since World War II,* Gale, 1982.
Lumley, Frederick, *New Trends in 20th Century Drama: A Survey Since Ibsen and Shaw,* Oxford University Press, 1967.
Nathan, George Jean, *The Theatre Book of the Year 1944: A Record and an Interpretation,* Knopf, 1945.
Taylor, John Russell, *The Rise and Fall of the Well-Made Play,* Methuen, 1967.

PERIODICALS

Christian Science Monitor, November 29, 1969.
Nation, December 28, 1974.
New Republic, January 4, 1975, January 11, 1975.
New Statesman and Nation, March 4, 1950.
Newsweek, December 23, 1974.
New Yorker, April 1, 1974.
New York Herald Tribune, September 23, 1956.
New York Times, September 25, 1970, October 29, 1980, April 23, 1982, August 31, 1989.
Observer Review, September 27, 1970, November 8, 1970.
Plays and Players, November, 1970, December, 1970, November, 1973.
Variety, October 14, 1970.

OBITUARIES:

PERIODICALS

AB Bookman's Weekly, February 6, 1978.
Newsweek, December 12, 1977.
New York Times, December 1, 1977.
Time, December 12, 1977.
Washington Post, December 1, 1977.

*   *   *

RAVITCH, Diane   1938-

PERSONAL: Born July 1, 1938, in Houston, Tex.; daughter of Walter Cracker (a businessman) and Ann Celia (Katz) Silvers; married Richard Ravitch (a lawyer and businessman), June 26, 1960 (divorced December, 1986); children: Joseph, Steven (deceased), Michael. *Education:* Wellesley College, B.A., 1960; Columbia University, Ph.D., 1975.

ADDRESSES: Office—Teachers College, Columbia University, Box 177, New York, N.Y. 10027.

CAREER: Columbia University, Teachers College, New York, N.Y., assistant professor, 1975-78, adjunct associate professor, 1978-84, adjunct professor of history and education, 1984—. Director, Educational Excellence Network, 1982—, and Encyclopaedia Britannica Corporation, 1985—. Chairman, Secretary of Education's Research Priorities Panel, 1985. Member, Second Circuit Judicial Nominating Commission, as appointed by President Carter, 1978-79, 1980; member, Secretary of Education's Study Group on the Elementary School, 1985-86. Delegate, International Seminar on Educational Reform, Tokyo and Kyoto, Japan, 1985. Lifetime trustee of New York Public Library. Consultant to several university presses, including Princeton University Press, Harvard University Press, and Johns Hopkins University Press.

MEMBER: PEN International, National Academy of Education, American Educational Research Association, American Academy of Arts and Sciences, American Historical Association, Society of American Historians, Organization of American Historians, Woodrow Wilson National Fellowship Foundation (trustee, 1988—), Council for Basic Education (director, 1989—).

AWARDS, HONORS: Delta Kappa Gamma Educators' Award, 1975, for *The Great School Wars, New York City, 1805-1973,* and 1984, for *The Troubled Crusade: American Education, 1945-1980;* Doctor of Humane Letters, Williams College, 1984, Reed College, 1985, Amherst College, 1986, and State University of New York, 1988; Phi Beta Kappa visiting scholar, 1984-85; Ambassador of Honor Award from English-Speaking Union, 1984, for *The Troubled Crusade,* and 1985, for *The Schools We Deserve: Reflections on the Educational Crises of Our Times;* Phi Beta Kappa visiting scholar, 1984-85; Henry Allen Moe Prize from American Philosophical Society, 1986; designated honorary citizen by State of California Senate Rules Committee, 1988, for work on state curriculum; Alumnae Achievement Award from Wellesley College, 1989.

WRITINGS:

The Great School Wars, New York City, 1805-1973, Basic Books, 1974.
The Revisionists Revised: A Critique of the Radical Attack on the Schools, Basic Books, 1978.
(Editor with Ronald Goodenow) *Educating an Urban People: The New York City Experience,* Holmes & Meier, 1981.
The Troubled Crusade: American Education, 1945-1980, Basic Books, 1983.
(Editor with Goodenow) *The School and the City: Community Studies in the History of American Education,* Holmes & Meier, 1983.
(Editor with Chester E. Finn, Jr., and Robert Fancher) *Against Mediocrity: The Humanities in America's High Schools,* Holmes & Meier, 1984.
The Schools We Deserve: Reflections on the Educational Crises of Our Times (essays), Basic Books, 1985.
(Editor with Finn and Holley Roberts) *Challenges to the Humanities,* Holmes & Meier, 1985.
(With Finn) *What Do Our Seventeen-Year-Olds Know?: A Report on the First National Assessment of History and Literature,* foreword by Lynne V. Cheney, Harper, 1987.

Also author, with Charlotte Crabtree, of *California K-12 History: A Social Science Framework.*

CONTRIBUTOR

Jane Newitt, editor, *Future Trends in Education,* D. C. Heath, 1979.
Derrick A. Bell, Jr., editor, *Shades of Brown: New Perspectives on School Desegregation,* Teachers College Press, Columbia University, 1980.
Adam Yarmolinsky and Lance Leibman, editors, *Race and Schooling in the City,* Harvard University Press, 1981.
John H. Bunzel, editor, *Challenge to American Schools: The Case for Standards and Values,* Oxford University Press, 1985.
Winthrop Knowlton and Richard Zeckhauser, editors, *American Society: Public and Private Responsibility,* Harvard University Press, 1986.

OTHER

Contributor of more than a hundred articles and reviews to such periodicals as *New York Times Magazine, American Scholar,* and

Harvard Educational Review. Editor, *Notes on Education,* 1974-75.

SIDELIGHTS: As an historian of American education, Diane Ravitch has authored a number of reputable historiographies that explore the successes and failures played out in the American school system through the years. The widely reviewed *The Troubled Crusade: American Education, 1945-1980,* for instance, is considered by *Los Angeles Times Book Review* critic David Savage to be "a fascinating history of 35 years of conflict and turmoil in the nation's schools and universities. Whether the issue was the McCarthy crusades (Joe's or Gene's), racial desegregation, rights for women and the handicapped, bilingual education or affirmative action, each has been fought out, to a greater or lesser degree, on school and college campuses."

According to Savage, the underlying theme of *The Troubled Crusade* is that "social scientists, political activists and compliant educators have often combined to lead the schools astray. If educational history does resemble a pendulum swinging, it has swung further right or left . . . because educators have been too willing to follow any fad, Ravitch says." In support of this theme, Ravitch addresses the issue of education for all. Immediately after World War II, teachers and administrators were adamant about providing equal opportunity education for all students and they hoped to do this through federal financial aid. According to reviewer Stanley Aronowitz for the *Village Voice Literary Supplement,* this effort was, "as Ravitch sees it, derailed by reformers' meddling in the educational process. . . . Things went wrong, according to Ravitch, when the simple claim that local taxes were not sufficient to deliver first-class education to millions of blacks and rural whites got tangled up with the idea that the federal government should use its financial clout to regulate curriculum, college entrance requirements, and other matters of policy. Rank amateurs—civil rights groups, radical students, militant feminists—began to demand a say in decisions best left to professionals; the inevitable result was mediocrity." *New York Times* critic Christopher Lehmann-Haupt believes that, on the whole, "what is recounted in 'The Troubled Crusade' is every conservative's fear of what befalls a freely functioning community system when Big Government gets its hands on it. For in the 35-year history that Mrs. Ravitch covers, the long-deferred dream of Federal aid to education could be said to have been corrupted into a nightmare of bureaucratic meddling and muddling." Apart from her critique of the federal government's expanding influence on school policy matters, Ravitch analyzes the damaging effects other faddish ideas, from both the political left and right, have had on students. Because she has viewed such issues from both political perspectives, Ravitch objects to the neo-conservative label some critics have given her. She told *CA,* "I find that I am conservative in some matters, liberal in some others, and radical in a few more. Therefore it is obnoxious to me to have one or several people hang a political label on me which does not reflect my own thinking about my views and life."

With regard to critical acceptance, Hechinger claims *The Troubled Crusade* "does what American historiography usually does not: it places education near the center of national affairs instead of near the periphery. It is thus indispensable for a full understanding of the critical postwar period. . . . One may argue with Mrs. Ravitch's less than enthusiastic view of the federal and judicial role in education; but she is surely justified, in the light of past history, in her suspicion of panaceas and her ardent and intelligent defense of 'piecemeal change'. . . . This . . . holds a lesson for today. The air is crowded with calls for school reform, and generally such a mood is cause for celebration. But once

again, there is a temptation for politicians to demand miracles." Aronowitz, in contrast, faults what he sees as Ravitch's limited view of the role of the American education system: "She really wants to persuade us that there's only one royal road to success—acquiring the skills and values of the dominant culture while learning the three Rs. Within those bounds, Ravitch supports piecemeal reform, but her perspective is profoundly antiutopian. . . . *The Troubled Crusade* could serve as the autobiography of a generation of former social critics and disillusioned radicals convinced by the turbulent struggle of the postwar era that profound social change inevitably leads to totalitarianism." In his *Newsweek* assessment, Gene Lyons is similarly harsh, for he feels *The Troubled Crusade* "is less a history of American schools than of intellectual fashion, government studies, federal court decisions and the sorts of books and periodicals mentioned regularly in The New York Times. If Ravitch has so much as entered an elementary classroom, a junior-high teachers' lounge or attended a high-school football game in the course of her studies, there's no sign of it here." As for Lehmann-Haupt, his is a mixed analysis. Accordingly, he writes that "at times her narrative assumes the aspect of a very dark comedy, and one fully expects her to pronounce some dire moral at the end. But she never does. . . . She discovered that there really are no villains. Everyone behaved with the best of motives, she seems to be saying. . . . It was just that the winds of history kept shifting and changing the landscape." In his conclusion, Lehmann-Haupt notes that *The Troubled Crusade* "leaves the reader with a refreshingly clear and objective review that lends valuable perspective to a confusing period in the very recent past."

Two additional works by Ravitch that address the troubles of American education are *The Schools We Deserve: Reflections on the Educational Crises of Our Time* and, with Chester E. Finn, Jr., *What Do Our Seventeen-Year-Olds Know?: A Report on the First National Assessment of History and Literature.* Regarding the former, *New York Times Book Review* critic Philip W. Jackson explains that whereas *The Troubled Crusade* "offered a panoramic view of education in the United States[,] . . . in 'The Schools We Deserve,' [Ravitch] concentrates with equal skill on more sharply defined issues, ranging from the . . . debate over tuition tax credits to the place of history in today's elementary schools, from aspects of school desegregation to the uses and misuses of tests. No matter what the focus of her concern, Mrs. Ravitch brings to bear a keen intelligence working in the service of a neoconservative educational outlook." Jackson continues that "even though its central message has been sounded many times before . . . , 'The Schools We Deserve' demands to be read all the same by every citizen who cares about our schools and would like to see them better than they are."

In the *Washington Post,* Paul Piazza calls *What Do Our Seventeen-Year-Olds Know?* "a statistical description of a generation, a 'snapshot in time.'" The book, more specifically, is an analysis of how nearly eight thousand high school juniors fared on a multiple choice examination on American history and English literature that the National Assessment of Educational Progress, a major testing organization, devised and distributed in 1986. Cleverly put by Piazza, "the results are, as one might expect, abysmal. Mediocrity has been quantified. We have met ignorance, Ravitch and Finn might declare, and it is ourselves." Although both Piazza and the authors admit that multiple-choice examinations have shortcomings, overall Piazza is encouraged by the undertaking: "Recognizing one's ignorance is the beginning of wisdom. To Ravitch and Finn we owe a great deal for starting us down the road, if not to wisdom, at least to a knowledge of our failure." Alternately, Deborah Meier and Florence

Miller for *Nation* sense that Ravitch and Finn's "view of ignorance is familiar and fruitless. They miss the vital connection between knowing and not knowing, and because they do so, not knowing is failure, or bad schooling. . . . Given the influence of Ravitch and Finn, new curriculums are probably already in the making. If so, we will have foreclosed on the real debate and be witness to one more cycle of alarm and reform, swinging from fad to fad and never digging deep." Even though *New York Times* critic John Gross detects that "none of their conclusions are particularly earthshaking . . . they do make a lengthy series of recommendations on how to improve things. . . . A few are fairly vague, but others could in principle be acted on quite quickly. . . . The chief value," continues Gross, "of 'What Do Our 17-Year-Olds Know?' lies in its documentation of existing conditions," and he concludes that the same type of study should be conducted in Western Europe for the sake of comparison.

BIOGRAPHICAL/CRITICAL SOURCES:

BOOKS

Finn, Chester E., Jr., and Diane Ravitch, *What Do Our Seventeen-Year-Olds Know?: A Report on the First National Assessment of History and Literature,* Harper, 1987.
Ravitch, Diane, *The Troubled Crusade: American Education, 1945-1980,* Basic Books, 1983.

PERIODICALS

Chicago Tribune, October 13, 1983.
Harper's, June, 1985.
Los Angeles Times Book Review, September 11, 1983, November 29, 1987.
Nation, September 2, 1978, January 9, 1988.
New Republic, June 1, 1974, October 17, 1983.
Newsweek, November 28, 1983.
New York Times, July 6, 1978, September 7, 1983, October 2, 1987.
New York Times Book Review, May 12, 1974, June 18, 1978, September 18, 1983.
Times Literary Supplement, July 6, 1984.
Village Voice Literary Supplement, May, 1985.

*   *   *

READE, Hamish
   See GRAY, Simon (James Holliday)

*   *   *

REED, Eliot
   See AMBLER, Eric

*   *   *

REED, Ishmael 1938-
   (Emmett Coleman)

PERSONAL: Born February 22, 1938, in Chattanooga, Tenn.; son of Henry Lenoir (a fundraiser for YMCA) and Thelma Coleman (a homemaker and salesperson); stepfather, Bennie Stephen Reed (an auto worker); married Priscilla Rose, September, 1960 (divorced, 1970); married Carla Blank (a modern dancer); children: (first marriage) Timothy, Brett (daughter); (second marriage) Tennessee Maria (daughter). *Education:* Attended State University of New York at Buffalo, 1956-60. *Politics:* Independent.

ADDRESSES: Home—2140 Shattuck Ave., No. 311, Berkeley, Calif. 94704. *Agent*—Ellis J. Freedman, 415 Madison Ave., New York, N.Y. 10017.

CAREER: Writer. Yardbird Publishing Co., Inc., Berkeley, Calif., co-founder, 1971, editorial director, 1971-75; Reed, Cannon & Johnson Communications Co. (a publisher and producer of video cassettes), Berkeley, co-founder, 1973—; Before Columbus Foundation (a producer and distributor of work of unknown ethnic writers), Berkeley, co-founder, 1976—; Ishmael Reed and Al Young's *Quilt* (magazine), Berkeley, co-founder, 1980—. Teacher at St. Mark's in the Bowery prose workshop, 1966; guest lecturer, University of California, Berkeley, 1968—, University of Washington, 1969-70, State University of New York at Buffalo, summer, 1975, and fall, 1979, Yale University, fall, 1979, Dartmouth College, summers, 1980-81, Sitka Community Association, summer, 1982, Columbia University, 1983, University of Arkansas at Fayetteville, 1982, Harvard University, 1987, and Regents lecturer, University of California, Santa Barbara, 1988. Judge of National Poetry Competition, 1980, King's County Literary Award, 1980, University of Michigan Hopwood Award, 1981. Chair of Berkeley Arts Commission, 1980 and 1981. Coordinating Council of Literary Magazines, chairman of board of directors, 1975-79, advisory board chair, 1977-79.

AWARDS, HONORS: Certificate of Merit, California Association of English Teachers, 1972, for *19 Necromancers from Now;* nominations for National Book Award in fiction and poetry, 1973, for *Mumbo Jumbo* and *Conjure: Selected Poems, 1963-1970;* nomination for Pulitzer Prize in poetry, 1973, for *Conjure;* Richard and Hinda Rosenthal Foundation Award, National Institute of Arts and Letters, 1975, for *The Last Days of Louisiana Red;* John Simon Guggenheim Memorial Foundation award for fiction, 1974; Poetry in Public Places winner (New York City), 1976, for poem "From the Files of Agent 22," and for a bicentennial mystery play, *The Lost State of Franklin,* written in collaboration with Carla Blank and Suzushi Hanayagi; Lewis Michaux Award, 1978; American Civil Liberties Award, 1978; Pushcart Prize for essay "American Poetry: Is There a Center?," 1979; Wisconsin Arts Board fellowship, 1982; associate fellow of Calhoun College, Yale University, 1982; A.C.L.U. publishing fellowship; three New York State publishing grants for merit; three National Endowment for the Arts publishing grants for merit; California Arts Council grant; associate fellow, Harvard Signet Society, 1987—.

WRITINGS:

FICTION

The Free-Lance Pallbearers, Doubleday, 1967, Avon, 1985.
Yellow Back Radio Broke-Down, Doubleday, 1969, reprinted, Bantam, 1987.
Mumbo Jumbo, Doubleday, 1972, reprinted, Bantam, 1987.
The Last Days of Louisiana Red (Book-of-the-Month Club alternate selection), Random House, 1974.
Flight to Canada, Random House, 1976.
The Terrible Twos, St. Martin's/Marek, 1982.
Reckless Eyeballing, St. Martin's, 1986.
The Terrible Threes, Macmillan, 1989.

NONFICTION

Shrovetide in Old New Orleans (essays; original manuscript entitled *This One's on Me*), Doubleday, 1978.

God Made Alaska for the Indians: Selected Essays, Garland, 1982.

Contributor to numerous volumes, including *Armistad I: Writings on Black History and Culture,* Vintage Books, 1970; *The Black Aesthetic,* Doubleday, 1971; *Nommo: An Anthology of Modern Black African and Black American Literature,* Macmillan, 1972; *Cutting Edges: Young American Fiction for the 70s,* Holt, 1973; *Superfiction; or, The American Story Transformed: An Anthology,* Vintage Books, 1975; and *American Poets in 1976,* Bobbs Merrill, 1976.

EDITOR

(Under pseudonym Emmett Coleman) *The Rise, Fall, and . . .? of Adam Clayton Powell,* Bee-Line Books, 1967.
(And author of introduction, and contributor) *19 Necromancers from Now,* Doubleday, 1970.
(With Al Young) *Yardbird Lives!,* Grove Press, 1978.
(And contributor) *Calafia: The California Poetry,* Y-Bird Books, 1979.
Writin' Is Fightin': Thirty-seven Years of Boxing on Paper, Atheneum, 1988.

POETRY

catechism of d neoamerican hoodoo church, Paul Breman (London), 1970, Broadside Press, 1971.
Conjure: Selected Poems, 1963-1970, University of Massachusetts Press, 1972.
Chattanooga: Poems, Random House, 1973.
A Secretary to the Spirits, illustrations by Betye Saar, NOK Publishers, 1977.
New and Collected Poems, Atheneum, 1990.

Poetry also represented in anthologies, including *Where Is Vietnam? American Poets Respond: An Anthology of Contemporary Poems,* Doubleday, 1967; *The New Black Poetry,* International Publishers, 1969; *The Norton Anthology of Poetry,* Norton, 1970; *The Poetry of the Negro, 1746-1970,* Doubleday, 1970; *Afro-American Literature: An Introduction,* Harcourt, 1971; *The Writing on the Wall: 108 American Poems of Protest,* Doubleday, 1971; *Major Black Writers,* Scholastic Book Services, 1971; *The Black Poets,* Bantam, 1971; *The Poetry of Black America: Anthology of the 20th Century,* Harper, 1972; and *Giant Talk: An Anthology of Third World Writings,* Random House, 1975.

OTHER

"Ishmael Reed Reading His Poetry" (cassette), Temple of Zeus, Cornell University, 1976.
"Ishmael Reed and Michael Harper Reading in the UCSD New Poetry Series" (reel), University of California, San Diego, 1977.
(Author of introduction) Elizabeth A. Settle and Thomas A. Settle, *Ishmael Reed: A Primary and Secondary Bibliography,* G. K. Hall, 1982.
Cab Calloway Stands In for the Moon, Bamberger, 1986.

Also author, with wife, Carla Blank, and Suzushi Hanayagi, of a bicentennial mystery play, *The Lost State of Franklin.* Executive producer of pilot episode of soap opera *Personal Problems* and co-publisher of *The Steve Cannon Show: A Quarterly Audio-Cassette Radio Show Magazine. Mumbo Jumbo* was translated into French and Spanish, 1975.

Contributor of fiction to such periodicals as *Fiction, Iowa Review, Nimrod, Players, Ramparts, Seattle Review,* and *Spokane Natural;* contributor of articles and reviews to numerous periodicals, including *Black World, Confrontation: Journal of Third*

World Literature, Essence, Le Monde, Los Angeles Times, New York Times, Playgirl, Rolling Stone, Village Voice, Washington Post, and *Yale Review;* and contributor of poetry to periodicals, including *American Poetry Review, Black Scholar, Black World, Essence, Liberator, Negro Digest, Noose, San Francisco Examiner, Oakland Tribune, Life, Connoisseur,* and *Umbra.* Co-founder of periodicals, *East Village Other* and *Advance* (Newark community newspaper), both 1965. Editor of *Yardbird Reader,* 1972-76, editor-in-chief, *Y'Bird* magazine, 1978-80, and co-editor of *Quilt* magazine, 1981.

SIDELIGHTS: The novels of contemporary black American writer Ishmael Reed "are meant to provoke," writes *New York Times* contributor Darryl Pickney. "Though variously described as a writer in whose work the black picaresque tradition has been extended, as a misogynist or an heir to both [Zora Neale] Hurston's folk lyricism and [Ralph] Ellison's irony, he is, perhaps because of this, one of the most underrated writers in America. Certainly no other contemporary black writer, male or female, has used the language and beliefs of folk culture so imaginatively, and few have been so stinging about the absurdity of American racism." Yet this novelist and poet is not simply a voice of black protest against racial and social injustices but instead a confronter of even more universal evils, a purveyor of even more universal truths.

Reed's first novel, *The Free-Lance Pallbearers,* introduces several thematic and stylistic devices that reappear throughout his canon. In this novel, as in his later works, Reed's first satirical jab is at the oppressive, stress-filled, Western/European/Christian tradition. But in *The Free-Lance Pallbearers,* the oppressor/oppressed, evil/good dichotomy is not as simple as it first appears. While Reed blames whites, called HARRY SAM in the novel, for present world conditions, he also viciously attacks culpable individuals from different strata in the black community and satirizes various kinds of black leaders in the twentieth century. Reed implies that many such leaders argue against white control by saying they want to improve conditions, to "help the people," but that in reality they are only waiting for the chance to betray and exploit poor blacks and to appropriate power.

Leaders of the black movement at the time of the novel's publication regarded as permissible the ridiculing of the white, Christian Bible, as in this grotesque caricature of St. John's vision and the Four Horsemen of the Apocalypse: "I saw an object atop the fragments of dead clippings. I waded up to my knees through grassy film and the phlegm-covered flags and picked up an ivory music box. On the cover done in mother-of-pearl was a picture of Lenore in her Bickford's uniform. I opened the music box and heard the tape of the familiar voice: ROGER YOUNG IN THE FIRST AT SARATOGA / ROGER YOUNG IN THE NINTH AT CHURCHILL DOWNS / ROGER YOUNG IN THE FOURTH AT BATAVIA / ROGER YOUNG IN THE FIFTH AT AQUEDUCT / ANNOUNCED BY RAPUNZEL." But the inclusion of negative black characters was thought by critics such as Houston Baker, Amiri Baraka, and Addison Gayle to be the wrong subject matter for the times. Reed, however, could never agree to rigid guidelines for including or excluding material from the novel form. As he would say later in *Shrovetide in Old New Orleans* concerning his battle with the critics, "The mainstream aspiration of Afro-Americans is for more freedom—and not slavery—including freedom of artistic expression."

Among the black characters whom Reed puts into a negative light in *The Free-Lance Pallbearers* are Elijah Raven, the Muslim/Black Nationalist whose ideas of cultural and racial separation in the United States are exposed as lies; Eclair Pockchop, the minister fronting as an advocate of the people's causes, later discovered performing an unspeakable sex act on SAM; the black cop who protects white people from the blacks in the projects and who idiotically allows a cow-bell to be put around his neck for "meritorious service"; Doopeyduk's neighbors in the projects who, too stupid to remember their own names, answer to "M/Neighbor" and "F/Neighbor"; and finally Doopeyduk himself, whose pretentions of being a black intellectual render all his statements and actions absurd. Yet Reed reserves his most scathing satire for the black leaders who cater to SAM in his palace: "who mounted the circuitous steps leading to SAM'S, assuring the boss dat: 'Wasn't us boss. 'Twas Stokely and Malcolm. Not us, boss. No indeed. We put dat ad in da *Times* repudiating dem, boss? Look, boss. We can prove it to you, dat we loves you. Would you like for us to cook up some strange recipes for ya, boss? Or tell some jokes? Did you hear the one about da nigger in the woodpile? Well, seems dere was this nigger, boss. . . .' "

The rhetoric of popular black literature in the 1960s is also satirized in *The Free-Lance Pallbearers*. The polemics of the time, characterized by colloquial diction, emotionalism, direct threats, automatic writing, and blueprints for a better society, are portrayed by Reed as representing the negative kind of literature required of blacks by the reading public. Reed's point is that while literature by blacks might have been saying that blacks would no longer subscribe to white dictates, in fact the converse was true, manifested in the very literature that the publishing houses generally were printing at the time.

Furthermore, *The Free-Lance Pallbearers* fully exemplifies Reed's orthographic, stylistic, and rhetorical techniques. He prefers phonetic spellings to standard spellings, thus drawing special attention to subjects otherwise mundane. He also uses capitalization for emphasis, substitutes numerals for words (1 for one) when including number references in the text, borrows Afro-American oral folklore as a source for his characters (as when Doopeyduk acts the part of "Shine" of the old crafty black tale), and utilizes newsflashes and radio voice-overs to comment on the book's action.

In his second novel, *Yellow Back Radio Broke-Dawn,* Reed begins to use at length Hoodoo (or Voodoo) methods and folklore as a basis for his work. Underlying all of the components of Hoodoo are two precepts: 1) the Hoodoo idea of syncretism, or the combination of beliefs and practices with divergent cultural origins, and 2) the Hoodoo concept of time. Even before the exportation of slaves to the Caribbean, Hoodoo was a syncretic religion, absorbing all that it considered useful from other West African religious practices. As a religion formed to combat degrading social conditions by dignifying and connecting man with helpful supernatural forces, Hoodoo thrives because of its syncretic flexibility, its ability to take even ostensibly negative influences and transfigure them into that which helps the "horse," or the one possessed by the attributes of a Hoodoo god. Hoodoo is bound by certain dogma or rites, but such rules are easily changed when they become oppressive, myopic, or no longer useful.

Reed turns this concept of syncretism into a literary method that combines aspects of "standard" English, including dialect, slang, argot, neologisms, or rhyme, with less "standard" language, whose principal rules of discourse are taken from the streets, popular music, and television. By purposely mixing language from different sources in popular culture, Reed employs expressions that both evoke interest and humor through seeming incon-

gruities and create the illusion of real speech. In *Black American Literature Forum,* Michel Fabre draws a connection between Reed's use of language and his vision of the world, suggesting that "his so-called nonsense words raise disturbing questions . . . about the very nature of language." Often, "the semantic implications are disturbing because opposite meanings co-exist." Thus Reed emphasizes "the dangerous interchangeability of words and of the questionable identity of things and people" and "poses anguishing questions about self-identity, about the mechanism of meaning and about the nature of language and communication."

The historical sense of time in Reed's discourse, based on the African concept of time, is not linear; dates are not generally ascribed to the past, and past events overlap with those in the present. Berndt Ostendorf in *Black Literature in White America* notes that the African time sense is "telescoped," that it contains no concept of a future, only the certainty that man's existence will never end. Reed's version of this concept of synchronicity or simultaneity incorporates a future by positing a time cycle of revolving and re-evolving events but maintains an essentially African concept of the past/present relationship, as characters treat past and present matters as though they were simultaneous.

Syncretism and synchronicity, along with other facets of Hoodoo as literary method, are central to *Yellow Back Radio Broke-Down.* The title is street-talk for the elucidation of a problem, in this case the racial and oligarchical difficulties of an Old West town, *Yellow Back Radio;* these difficulties are explained, or "broke down," for the reader. The novel opens with a description of the Hoodoo fetish, or mythical cult figure, Loop Garoo, whose name means "change into." Loop is a truly syncretic character who embodies diverse ethnic backgrounds and a history and power derived from several religions.

At least one of Reed's themes from *The Free-Lance Pallbearers* is reworked in *Yellow Back Radio Broke-Down,* as Christianity is again unmercifully attacked. Three Horsemen of the Apocalypse are represented by the Barber, Marshall, and Doctor, criminals, hypocrites, and upholders of the one-and-only-way-of-doing-things, that is, the way which materially benefits them; and the fourth Horseman is embodied in the Preacher Reverend Boyd, who will make a profit on guilt with the volume of poetry he is putting together, *Stomp Me O Lord.* Loop calls his own betrayal by other blacks—Alcibiades and Jeff—and his resurrection a parody of "His Passion." The Pope, who appears in Yellow Back Radio in the 1880s, is revealed as a corrupt defender of the white tradition, concerned only with preventing Loop's magic from becoming stronger than his own.

The year 1972 saw the publication of Reed's first major volume of poetry, *Conjure: Selected Poems, 1963-1970,* followed in 1973 by his second collection, *Chattanooga: Poems,* and in 1977 by *A Secretary to the Spirits.* It is really in *Conjure* that Reed fully develops his literary method. Although the poem beginning "I am a cowboy in the boat of Ra" continues an earlier Reed interest in Egyptian symbolism, after this work he lyrically draws his symbols from Afro-American and Anglo-American historical and popular traditions—two distinct, but intertwined sources for the Afro-American aesthetic. "Black Power Poem" succinctly states the Hoodoo stance in the West: "may the best church win. / shake hands now and come out conjuring"; a longer poem "Neo-Hoodoo Manifesto" defines all that Hoodoo is, and thus sheds light on the ways Reed uses its principles in writing, primarily through his absorption of material from every available source and his expansive originality in treating that material.

The theme of *Mumbo Jumbo,* Reed's 1972 novel, is the origin and composition of the "true Afro-American aesthetic." Testifying to the novel's success in fulfilling this theme, Houston Baker in *Black World* calls *Mumbo Jumbo* "the first black American novel of the last ten years that gives one a sense of the broader vision and the careful, painful, and laborious 'fundamental brainwork' that are needed if we are to define the eternal dilemma of the Black Arts and work fruitfully toward its melioration. . . . [The novel's] overall effect is that of amazing talent and flourishing genius." *Mumbo Jumbo*'s first chapter is crucial in that it presents the details of the highly complex plot in synopsis or news-flash form. Reed has a Hoodoo detective named Papa LaBas (representing the Hoodoo god Legba) search out and reconstruct a black aesthetic from remnants of literary and cultural history. To lend the narrative authenticity, Reed inserts favorite scholarly devices: facts from nonfictional, published works; photographs and historical drawings; and a bibliography. The unstated subtext throughout the book is "My aesthetic is just as good as yours maybe better and certainly is founded on no more ridiculous a set of premises than yours."

At the opening of *Mumbo Jumbo,* set in New Orleans in the 1920s, white municipal officials are trying to respond to "Jes Grew," an outbreak of behavior outside of socially conditioned roles; white people are "acting black" by dancing half-dressed in the streets to an intoxicating new loa (the spiritual essence of a fetish) called jazz. Speaking in tongues, people also abandon racist and other oppressive endeavors because it is more fun to "shake that thing." One of the doctors assigned to treat the pandemic of Jes Grew comments, "There are no isolated cases in this thing. It knows no class no race no consciousness. It is self-propagating and you can never tell when it will hit." No one knows where the germ has come from; it "jes grew." In the synoptic first chapter, the omniscient narrator says Jes Grew is actually "an anti-plague. Some plagues caused the body to waste away. Jes Grew enlivened the host. Other plagues were accompanied by bad air (malaria). Jes Grew victims said the air was as clear as they had ever seen it and that there was the aroma of roses and perfumes which had never before enticed their nostrils. Some plagues arise from decomposing animals, but Jes Grew is electric as life and is characterized by ebullience and ecstasy. Terrible plagues were due to the wrath of God; But Jes Grew is the delight of the gods." Jes Grew also is reflected in Reed's writing style, which may take on any number of guises, but is intended both to illuminate and enliven the reader.

In the novel, Christianity is called "Atonism," a word with its origin in the worship of the sun-god, Aton, of ancient Egypt. Atonists are forever at war to stamp out Jes Grew, as it threatens their traditions and their power. The word *Atonism* is also a cognate of the word *atone,* with its connotations of guilt. The Atonists do not simply wage war against nonwhites and non-Christians. Anyone who opposes their beliefs is attacked. When a white member of a multi-ethnic gang, Thor Wintergreen, sides with nonwhites, he is first duped and then killed by Atonist Biff Musclewhite. Though Musclewhite is initially being held captive by Wintergreen, the prisoner persuades Wintergreen to release him by giving the following explanation of the Atonist cause: "Son, this is a nigger closing in our mysteries and soon he will be asking our civilization to 'come quietly.' This man is talking about Judeo-Christian culture, Christianity, Atonism, whatever you want to call it. . . . I've seen them, son, in Africa, China, they're not like us, son, the Herronvolk. Europe. This place. They are lagging behind, son, and you know in your heart this is true. Son, these niggers writing. Profaning our sacred words. Taking them from us and beating them on the anvil of Boogie-Woogie, putting their black hands on them so that they shine like burnished amulets. Taking our words, son, these filthy niggers and using them. . . . Why 1 of them dared to interpret, critically mind you, the great Herman Melville's *Moby Dick!!*'" *Mumbo Jumbo* thus presents a battle for supremacy between powers that see the world in two distinct, opposed ways, with the separate visions endemic to the human types involved: one, expansive and syncretic; the other, impermeable and myopic.

Hoodoo time resurfaces in *Mumbo Jumbo* through a stylistic technique that produces a synchronic effect. Certain chapters which have detailed past events in the past tense are immediately followed by chapters that begin with present-tense verbs and present-day situations; this effect introduces simultaneity to the text, and elicits from the reader a response that mirrors the feeling of the Hoodoo/oral culture. That is, the reader feels that all of the actions are thematically and rhetorically related, because they all seem to be happening in the same narrative time frame. Commenting on his use both of time and of fiction-filled newsflashes, Reed says in *Shrovetide in Old New Orleans* that in writing *Mumbo Jumbo,* he "wanted to write about a time like the present or to use the past to prophesy about the future—a process our ancestors called necromancy. I chose the twenties because they are very similar to what's happening right now. This is a valid method and has been used by writers from time immemorial. Nobody ever accused James Joyce of making up things. Using a past event of one's country or culture to comment on the present."

The close of *Mumbo Jumbo* finds Jes Grew withering with the burning of its text, the Book of Thoth, which lists the sacred spells and dances of the Egyptian god Osiris. LaBas says Jes Grew will reappear some day to make its own text: "A future generation of young artists will accomplish this," says LaBas, referring to the writers, painters, politicians, and musicians of the 1960s, "the decade that screamed," as Reed termed it in *Chattanooga.*

In the course of the narrative, Reed constructs his history of the true Afro-American aesthetic and parallels the uniting of Afro-American oral tradition, folklore, art, and history, with a written code, a text, a literate recapitulation of history and practice. By calling for a unification of text and tradition, Reed equates the Text (the Afro-American aesthetic) with the Vedas, the Pentateuch, the Koran, the Latin Vulgate, the Book of Mormon, and all "Holy" codifications of faith. *Mumbo Jumbo,* which itself becomes the Text, appears as a direct, written response to the assertion that there is no "black" aesthetic, that black contributions to the world culture have been insignificant at best.

As seen in *Mumbo Jumbo,* Reed equates his own aesthetic with other systems based on different myths. Then he insists that his notion of an aesthetic is more humanistic than others, especially those based on Americanized, Christian dogma. Finding its spiritual corollary in Hoodoo, Reed's method achieves a manual of codification in *Mumbo Jumbo.* This code also is used in his next two novels, *The Last Days of Louisiana Red* and *Flight to Canada,* to reaffirm his belief that Hoodoo, now understood as a spiritual part of the Afro-American aesthetic, can be used as a basis for literary response.

The Last Days of Louisiana Red consists of three major story lines that coalesce toward the close of the novel to form its theme. The first and main plot is the tale of Ed Yellings, an industrious, middle-class black involved in "The Business," an insider's term for the propagation of Hoodoo. Through experimentation in his business, Solid Gumbo Works, Yellings discovers a cure for cancer and is hard at work to refine and market this remedy and other remedies for the various aspects of Louisiana Red, the Hoodoo name for all evil. When he is mysteriously murdered, Hoodoo detective Papa LaBas appears, and the stage is set for the major part of the action. This action involves participants in the novel's second and third story lines, the tale of the Chorus and the recounting of the mythical Antigone's decisions to oppose the dictates of the state. Antigone is clearly heroic in her actions, but the Chorus also fulfills a significant function by symbolizing black Americans who will not disappear, even though they are relegated by more powerful forces to minor roles. Never satisfied with this position, black Americans want to be placed where they believe they belong: in the forefront of the action, where they can succeed or fail depending upon their merits. Therein lies Reed's theme in *The Last Days of Louisiana Red.*

In *Flight to Canada* Reed most effectively explores Hoodoo as a force that gives his black protagonists the strength to be hopeful and courageous in the face of seemingly hopeless situations. Canada has, in this novel, at least two levels of meaning. It is, first of all, a literal, historical region where slaves might flee to freedom. Second, it becomes a metaphor for happiness; that is, anything that makes an individual character happy may be referred to as "Canada."

The major plot of *Flight to Canada* involves the escape of Raven Quickskill from his owner, Massa Arthur Swille, and Swille's efforts to return Quickskill to captivity. The historical Canada is the eventual destination where Quickskill and other slaves wish to arrive when they flee from Swille in Virginia, but this historical Canada is not the heaven slaves think, and pray, it will be. Yet in the face of the depressing stories about Canada from his friends Leechfield, Carpenter, Cato, and 40s, Quickskill will not relinquish his dream. For him, Canada is personified beyond the physical plane. Refuting those who would deny or degrade the existence of the Canada that his reading tours have allowed him to see as well as the Canada that he must invent to live in peace, Quickskill reflects: "He was so much against slavery that he had begun to include prose and poetry in the same book, so that there would be no arbitrary boundaries between them. He preferred Canada to slavery, whether Canada was exile, death, art, liberation, or a woman. Each man to his own Canada. There was much avian imagery in the poetry of slaves. Poetry about dreams and flight. They wanted to cross that Black Rock Ferry to freedom even though they had different notions as to what freedom was. They often disagreed about it, Leechfield, 40s. But it was his writing that got him to Canada. 'Flight to Canada' was responsible for getting him to Canada. And so for him, freedom was his writing. His writing was his Hoodoo. Others had their way of Hoodoo, but his was his writing. It fascinated him, it possessed him; his typewriter was his drum he danced to."

In *Flight to Canada* Hoodoo becomes a kind of faith that sustains and uplifts without necessarily degrading those to whom it is opposed. Unable to explain how he has attained success, Quickskill can only attribute his freedom to things unseen. Ultimately, all of the black characters turn to this transcendent vision as their shield against the harsher aspects of reality. As is true with Quickskill when he is confronted with the truth about Canada, the black characters' ability to rely upon the metaphysical saves their lives as well as their dreams.

In *The Terrible Twos,* Reed maintains the implicit notions of Hoodoo, while using his main story line to resurrect another apocryphal tale: the legend of Santa Claus and his assistant/boss, Black Peter. The time frame of the novel is roughly Christmas 1980 to Christmases of the 1990s, and the novel is clearly an alle-

gory on Ronald Reagan's presidency and its consequences, as Reed sees them, in the 1990s. The evil of *The Terrible Twos* is the type that comes from selfishness fed by an exclusive monetary system, such as capitalism. Yet Reed does not endorse any other sort of government now in existence but criticizes any person or system that ignores what is humanly right in favor of what is economically profitable. Santa Claus (actually an out-of-work television personality) exemplifies the way Hoodoo fights this selfish evil: by putting those who were prosperous onto the level of those who have nothing and are abandoned. Santa characterizes American capitalists, those with material advantages, as infantile, selfish and exclusionary because their class station does not allow them to empathize with those who are different: "'Two years old, that's what we are, emotionally—Americans, always wanting someone to hand us some ice cream, always complaining, Santa didn't bring me this and why didn't Santa bring me that.' People in the crowd chuckle. 'Nobody can reason with us. Nobody can tell us anything. Millions of people staggering about passing out in the snow and we say that's tough. We say too bad to the children who don't have milk. I weep as I read these letters the poor children send me at my temporary home in Alaska.'"

In *The Terrible Twos* Reed leaves overt Hoodoo references as a subtext and focuses on the Rasta and Nicolaite myths, two conflicting quasi-religious cults revitalized by Black Power. He also concentrates on the myths of power and privilege created by "the vital people," those who are white and wealthy. However, the racist policies of the Nicolaites are eventually thwarted by inexplicable circumstances that stem from the supernatural powers of Hoodoo and from the Hoodoo notion that time is circular and that therefore the mighty will possibly—even probably—fall.

One device used in the novel is perhaps central in conveying Reed's vision. The first chapter is almost all factual reportage about Christmas and related matters, thus laying the foundation of belief for the fantastic Christmas Reed is about to construct. Yet, in comparison, the facts of Christmas seem as preposterous as the fiction of Christmas: Is it fact or fantasy that around Christmas of 1980 the *Buffalo Evening News* put under the headline "The Wild West is Back in the Saddle Again" the story of "First Actor" campaigning in cowboy attire in the West and a Confederate uniform in the South; is it fact or fantasy that a 6,000-pound ice sculpture of Santa and his reindeer carved by Andrew Young appears in a San Francisco Christmas parade? As John Leonard declares in his *New York Times* review of the book: "Mr. Reed is as close as we are likely to get to a Garcia Marquez, elaborating his own mythology even as he trashes ours. . . . *The Terrible Twos* tells many jokes before it kills, almost as if it had been written with barbed wire."

Reckless Eyeballing is a bitingly satiric allegory. Ian Ball, a black male writer, responds to the poor reception of his earlier play, *Suzanna,* by writing *Reckless Eyeballing,* a play sure to please those in power with its vicious attacks against black men. ("Reckless eyeballing" was one of the accusations against Emmett Till, the young Chicago black who was murdered in Mississippi in 1953 for "looking and whistling at a white woman.") Tremonisha Smarts, a black female writer whose first name is drawn from a Scott Joplin opera of that title, is alternately popular and unpopular with the white women who are promoting her books. The battle for whose vision will dominate in the literary market and popular culture is fierce, and those critics who have seen in the portrait of Tremonisha a thinly veiled response to the current popularity of feminist writers are probably correct.

In Joplin's opera, the character Tremonisha represents the powers of assimilation into American culture in opposition to the "powers of the Hoodoo men." Thus, not only does Reed's version of the Tremonisha character allude to the original Tremonisha's disagreement with early African-American currents, but she also becomes one of the critical forces that Reed has long opposed. More ironically, this allusive connection may be merely a feint, a trick leading critics to believe that Reed is covering the same, familiar Hoodoo ground covered before; actually, he moves in this novel toward unearthing the truly universal structures of Hoodoo, which are rooted in the apocryphal rites of other religions.

For example, the name of the character Abiahus in *Reckless Eyeballing* is a variant of the Hebrew "Lilith," and the name helps to remind the reader of the legend of the amulet used when Hebrew women gave birth to ward off child-stealers. Reed found the connections between the shared traditions of Judaism and Hoodoo in *The Legends of Genesis* by Hermann Gunkel, in David Meltzer's magazine *TREE,* and in Mike Gold's *Jews without Money,* the last of which includes a description of a Jewish woman similar to the Mambos and Conjure Women of Hoodoo origin. Reed thus reminds readers that Hoodoo is ever-changing by constantly absorbing materials from diverse cultures. He also warns his readers that he, too, is ever-changing and that a sure way to be misled is to believe that one has Hoodoo's concepts (and Reed's) pinned down as to their "one true" meaning.

Syncretic and synchronic in form, Reed's novels focus most often on social circumstances that inhibit the development of blacks in American society. As satire is usually based on real types, the writer draws in part from history and the news to satirize America's cultural arrogance and the terrible price paid by those who are not "vital people," members of the dominant culture or the moneyed class. His assertion, in a *Review of Contemporary Fiction* interview with Reginald Martin, that Hoodoo is "solidly in the American tradition" is supported by his collation of myth, fact, and apocryphal data into a history; from that history, a method or aesthetic is drawn not only for formulating art and multi-ethnic cultural standards but also for developing a different and more humane way of experiencing and influencing the world.

MEDIA ADAPTATIONS: Some of Reed's poetry has been scored and recorded on *New Jazz Poets;* a dramatic episode from *The Last Days of Louisiana Red* appears on *The Steve Cannon Show: A Quarterly Audio-Cassette Radio Show Magazine,* produced by Reed, Cannon & Johnson Communications.

BIOGRAPHICAL/CRITICAL SOURCES:

BOOKS

Bellamy, Joe David, editor, *The New Fiction: Interviews with Innovative American Writers,* University of Illinois Press, 1974.

Bruck, Peter, and Wolfgang Karrer, editors, *The Afro-American Novel since 1960,* B. R. Bruener (Amsterdam), 1982.

Chesi, Gert, *Voodoo: Africa's Secret Power,* Perlinger-Verlag (Austria), 1979.

Contemporary Literary Criticism, Gale, Volume 2, 1974, Volume 3, 1975, Volume 5, 1976, Volume 6, 1976, Volume 8, 1980, Volume 32, 1985.

Conversations with Writers, Volume 2, Gale, 1978.

Dictionary of Literary Biography, Gale, Volume 2: *American Novelists since World War II,* 1978, Volume 5: *American Poets since World War II,* 1980, Volume 33: *Afro-American Fiction Writers after 1955,* 1984.

Klinkowitz, Jerome, *Literary Subversions: New American Fiction and the Practice of Criticism,* Southern Illinois University Press, 1985.

Martin, Reginald, *Ishmael Reed and the New Black Aesthetic Critics,* Macmillan (London), 1987.

O'Brien, John, *Interviews with Black Writers,* Liveright, 1973.

Ostendorf, Berndt, *Black Literature in White America,* Noble, 1982.

Reed, Ishmael, *The Free-Lance Pallbearers,* Doubleday, 1967.

Reed, Ishmael, *Yellow Back Radio Broke-Down,* Doubleday, 1969.

Reed, Ishmael, *Conjure: Selected Poems, 1963-1970,* University of Massachusetts Press, 1972.

Reed, Ishmael, *Mumbo Jumbo,* Doubleday, 1972.

Reed, Ishmael, *Chattanooga: Poems,* Random House, 1973.

Reed, Ishmael, *The Last Days of Louisiana Red,* Random House, 1974.

Reed, Ishmael, *Flight to Canada,* Random House, 1976.

Reed, Ishmael, *A Secretary to the Spirits,* NOK Publishers, 1977.

Reed, Ishmael, *Shrovetide in Old New Orleans,* Doubleday, 1978.

Reed, Ishmael, *The Terrible Twos,* St. Martin's/Marek, 1982.

Reed, Ishmael, *Reckless Eyeballing,* St. Martin's, 1986.

Rush, Theresa Gunnels, Carol Fairbanks Myers, and Ester Spring Arata, *Black American Writers Past and Present: A Biographical and Bibliographical Dictionary,* Scarecrow, 1975.

Settle, Elizabeth A., and Thomas A. Settle, *Ishmael Reed: A Primary and Secondary Bibliography,* G. K. Hall, 1982.

Stebich, Ute, *Haitian Art,* Abrams, 1978.

PERIODICALS

Afriscope, May, 1977.

American Book Review, May/June, 1983.

American Poetry Review, May/June, 1976, January/February, 1978.

Arizona Quarterly, autumn, 1979.

Arts Magazine, May, 1967.

Berkeley News, April 10, 1975.

Black American Literature Forum, Volume 12, 1978, spring, 1979, spring, 1980, fall, 1984.

Black Books Bulletin, winter, 1976.

Black Creation, fall, 1972, winter, 1973.

Black Enterprise, January, 1973, December, 1982, April, 1983.

Black History Museum Newsletter, Volume 4, number 3/4, 1975.

Black Scholar, March, 1981.

Black Times, September, 1975.

Black World, October, 1971, December, 1972, January, 1974, June, 1974, June, 1975, July, 1975.

Changes in the Arts, November, 1972, December/January, 1973.

Chicago Review, fall, 1976.

Chicago Tribune Book World, April 27, 1986.

Critical Inquiry, June, 1983.

Essence, July, 1986.

Fiction International, summer, 1973.

Harper's, December, 1969.

Journal of Black Poetry, summer/fall, 1969.

Journal of Black Studies, December, 1979.

Journal of Negro History, January, 1978.

Los Angeles Free Press, September 18, 1970.

Los Angeles Times, April 29, 1975.

Los Angeles Times Book Review, April 20, 1986, June 4, 1989.

MELUS, spring, 1984.

Modern Fiction Studies, summer, 1976.

Modern Poetry Studies, autumn, 1973, autumn, 1974.

Nation, September 18, 1976, May 22, 1982.

Negro American Literature Forum, winter, 1967, winter, 1972.
Negro Digest, February, 1969, December, 1969.
New Republic, November 23, 1974.
New Yorker, October 11, 1969.
New York Review of Books, October 5, 1972, December 12, 1974, August 12, 1982, January 29, 1987.
New York Times, August 1, 1969, June 17, 1982, August 9, 1972, April 5, 1986.
New York Times Book Review, August 6, 1972, November 10, 1974, September 19, 1976, July 18, 1982, March 23, 1986, May 7, 1989.
Nickel Review, August 28-September 10, 1968.
Obsidian: Black Literature in Review, spring/summer, 1979.
Parnassus: Poetry in Review, spring/summer, 1976.
Partisan Review, spring, 1975.
People, December 16, 1974.
PHYLON: The Atlanta University Review of Race and Culture, December, 1968, June, 1975.
Review of Contemporary Fiction, summer, 1984, spring, 1987.
San Francisco Review of Books, November, 1975, January/ February, 1983.
Saturday Review, October 14, 1972, November 11, 1978.
Southern Review, July, 1985.
Studies in American Fiction, Volume 5, 1977.
Studies in the Novel, summer, 1971.
Twentieth Century Literature, April, 1974.
Village Voice, January 22, 1979.
Virginia Quarterly Review, winter, 1973.
Washington Post Book World, March 16, 1986, June 25, 1989.
World Literature Today, autumn, 1978, autumn, 1986.

* * *

REID, Desmond
See MOORCOCK, Michael (John)

* * *

REILLY, William K.
See CREASEY, John

* * *

REMARQUE, Erich Maria   1898-1970

PERSONAL: Born June 22, 1898, in Osnabrueck, Germany; came to the United States in 1939; naturalized U.S. citizen, 1947; died September 25, 1970, in Locarno, Switzerland; son of Peter Maria (a bookbinder) and Anna Maria Remarque; married first wife, 1923 (divorced, 1932); married Ilsa Intta Zambota, 1938 (divorced); married Paulette Goddard, February 25, 1958. *Education:* Attended University of Munster.

ADDRESSES: Home—New York, NY.

CAREER: Novelist and playwright. Worked variously as a teacher, stonecutter, drama critic, salesman for a tombstone company, test driver for a Berlin tire company, advertising copywriter for an automobile company, and organist at an insane asylum. *Military service:* Germany Army, served on Western front during World War I.

MEMBER: German Academy of Speech and Poetry.

AWARDS, HONORS: German Grand Cross of Merit.

WRITINGS:

NOVELS

Die Traumbude: Ein Kuenstlerroman, Schoenheit, 1920.
Im Westen nichts Neues, Kiepenheuer & Witsch, 1928, reprinted, 1968, translation by A. W. Wheen published as *All Quiet on the Western Front,* Little, Brown, 1929, reprinted, Fawcett, 1987.
Der Weg zurueck, Im Propylaen-verlag, 1931, translation by Wheen published as *The Road Back,* Little, Brown, 1931.
Drei Kameraden, Querido Verlag, 1937, abridged edition, American Book Co., 1941, complete original edition reprinted, Desch, 1969, original edition translated by Wheen published as *Three Comrades,* Little, Brown, 1937.
Liebe deinen Naechsten, Querido Verlag, 1941, translation by Denver Lindley published as *Flotsam,* Little, Brown, 1941.
Arc de Triomphe, F. G. Micha, 1946, translation by Walter Sorell and Lindley published as *Arch of Triumph,* Appleton-Century, 1945, reprinted, New American Library, 1985.
Der Funke Leben, Kiepenheuer & Witsch, 1952, 6th edition, 1972, original edition translated by James Stern published as *Spark of Life,* Appleton-Century, 1952, reprinted, Granada, 1981.
Zeit zu Leben und Zeit zu Sterben, Kiepenheuer & Witsch, 1954, translation by Lindley published as *A Time to Live and a Time to Die,* Harcourt, 1954, published as *Bobby Deerfield,* Fawcett, 1961.
Der Schwarze Obelisk: Geschichte einer verspaeteten Jugend, Kiepenheuer & Witsch, 1956, translation by Lindley published as *The Black Obelisk,* Harcourt, 1957.
Der Himmel kennt keine Guenstlinge, Kiepenheuer & Witsch, 1961, translation by Richard Winston and Clara Winston published as *Heaven Has No Favorites,* Harcourt, 1961.
Die Nacht von Lissabon, Robin Productions, 1961, translation by Ralph Manheim published as *The Night in Lisbon,* Harcourt, 1964.
Schatten im Paradies, Droemer Knaur, 1971, translation by Manheim published as *Shadows in Paradise,* Harcourt, 1972.

OTHER

Die lezte Station (play; title means "The Last Station"; first produced in 1956), adaptation by Peter Stone published as *Full Circle,* Harcourt, 1974.

Also author of film script *The Last Act,* 1955. Assistant editor of *Sportbild* (illustrated sports magazine).

MEDIA ADAPTATIONS: Three film adaptations of *All Quiet on the Western Front* have been produced, one of them with a screenplay by F. Scott Fitzgerald; an audio cassette edition of *All Quiet on the Western Front* was produced by Cram Cassettes, 1988.

SIDELIGHTS: All Quiet on the Western Front is unquestionably Remarque's best known and most enduring work. Originally written in German, it has been translated into more than forty languages and made into three separate film versions. Its antimilitary tone led to its censorship by the Nazis, who also exiled its author. When this semi-autobiographical novel was published in English, it met nearly unequivocal praise. T. R. Ybarra wrote, "To the best of my knowledge, nothing written about the War while it was still being fought or since the armistice, in any one of the countries engaged in it or in any neutral land, has done to readers what this book has done." Herbert Read called it "the Bible of the common soldier, the Tommy in the front-line who month after month endured the mess and stink of death, and all the loud riot of killing, the testament of the only man who is competent and worthy to speak of the war."

An example of neo-realism, *All Quiet on the Western Front* has been appreciated for its directness and simplicity. "The book is starkly simple, thoroughly lacking in all bugle calls, all flag waving, all false patriotism," observed K. Schriftgiesser. "It is just War." F. F. Hill found Remarque's narrative to have "the lean savagery of an Ibsen tragedy," and *Catholic World* added: "The author's style is unfurbished, unapologetic, unemotional. In its masterful directness, it transmits with almost equal force the whole range of the war's reverberating hell-tones of agony and horror; the dreadful intimacy of the men with fiendish reality, their gleeless, death-dodging humor; their ominous, half-courageous, half-indifferent comradeship." Joseph W. Krutch concluded: "Remarque tells his plain tale with a sort of naivete which is the result, not of too little experience, but of too much. He has given up rhetoric because it is inadequate and given up analysis because he has gone through more than can ever be analyzed."

BIOGRAPHICAL/CRITICAL SOURCES:

BOOKS

Contemporary Literary Criticism, Volume 21, Gale, 1982.
Dictionary of Literary Biography, Volume 56: *German Fiction Writers, 1914-1945*, Gale, 1987.

PERIODICALS

Boston Transcript, June 1, 1929.
Catholic World, November, 1929.
Nation, July 10, 1929.
Nation and Atheneum, April 27, 1929.
Newsweek, April 1, 1957.
New York Herald Tribune, June 2, 1929.
Outlook, July 31, 1929.
Saturday Review, May 22, 1954.

*   *   *

RENDELL, Ruth (Barbara) 1930-
(Barbara Vine)

PERSONAL: Born February 17, 1930, in London, England; daughter of Arthur Grasemann (a teacher) and Ebba (a teacher) Kruse; married Donald Rendell, 1950 (divorced, 1975; remarried, 1977); children: one son. *Education:* Educated in Essex, England.

ADDRESSES: Home—Nussteads, Polstead, Colchester, Suffolk CO6 5DN, England. *Agent*—Sterling Lord Agency, 660 Madison Ave., New York, N.Y. 10021.

CAREER: Writer. Express and Independent Newspapers, West Essex, England, reporter and subeditor for the Chigwell *Times*, 1948-52.

AWARDS, HONORS: Edgar Allan Poe Award, Mystery Writers of America, 1974, for story "The Fallen Curtain," 1976, for collection *The Fallen Curtain and Other Stories*, 1984, for story "The New Girlfriend," and 1986, for novel *A Dark-Adapted Eye*; Gold Dagger Award, Crime Writers Association, 1977, for *A Demon in My View*, 1986, for *Live Flesh*, and 1987, for *A Fatal Inversion*; Silver Dagger Award, Crime Writers Association, 1984, for *The Tree of Hands*; British Arts Council bursary, 1981; British National Book Award, 1981, for *The Lake of Darkness*; Popular Culture Association Award, 1983.

WRITINGS:

MYSTERY NOVELS

From Doon with Death (also see below), John Long, 1964, Doubleday, 1965.
To Fear a Painted Devil, Doubleday, 1965.
Vanity Dies Hard, John Long, 1965, reprinted, Beagle, 1970, published as *In Sickness and in Health*, Doubleday, 1966.
A New Lease of Death (also see below), Doubleday, 1967, published as *Sins of the Fathers*, Ballantine, 1970.
Wolf to the Slaughter, John Long, 1967, Doubleday, 1968.
The Secret House of Death, John Long, 1968, Doubleday, 1969.
The Best Man to Die (also see below), John Long, 1969, Doubleday, 1970.
A Guilty Thing Surprised, Doubleday, 1970.
No More Dying Then, Hutchinson, 1971, Doubleday, 1972.
One Across, Two Down, Doubleday, 1971.
Murder Being Once Done, Doubleday, 1972.
Some Lie and Some Die, Doubleday, 1973.
The Face of Trespass, Doubleday, 1974.
Shake Hands Forever, Doubleday, 1975.
A Demon in My View, Hutchinson, 1976, Doubleday, 1977.
A Judgment in Stone, Hutchinson, 1977, Doubleday, 1978.
A Sleeping Life, Doubleday, 1978.
Make Death Love Me, Doubleday, 1979.
The Lake of Darkness, Doubleday, 1980.
Put on by Cunning, Hutchinson, 1981, published as *Death Notes*, Pantheon, 1981.
Master of the Moor, Pantheon, 1982.
The Speaker of Mandarin, Pantheon, 1983.
The Killing Doll, Pantheon, 1984.
The Tree of Hands, Hutchinson, 1984, Pantheon, 1985.
An Unkindness of Ravens, Pantheon, 1985.
Live Flesh, Hutchinson, 1986.
Heartstones, Harper, 1987.
Talking to Strange Men, Pantheon, 1987.
The Veiled One, Hutchinson, 1988.
The Bridesmaid, Mysterious Press, 1989.

STORY COLLECTIONS

The Fallen Curtain: Eleven Mystery Stories by an Edgar Award-Winning Writer, Doubleday, 1976, (published in England as *The Fallen Curtain and Other Stories*, Hutchinson, 1976).
Means of Evil and Other Stories, Hutchinson, 1979, published as *Five Mystery Stories by an Edgar Award-Winning Writer*, Doubleday, 1980.
The Fever Tree and Other Stories, Hutchinson, 1982, Pantheon, 1983, published as *The Fever Tree and Other Stories of Suspense*, Ballantine, 1984.
The New Girlfriend and Other Stories, Pantheon, 1985.
Collected Short Stories, Hutchinson, 1987, published as *Collected Stories*, Pantheon, 1988.

OTHER

(Editor) *A Warning to the Curious: The Ghost Stories of M. R. James*, Hutchinson, 1986.
Wexford: An Omnibus (contains *From Doon with Death*, *A New Lease of Death*, and *The Best Man to Die*), Hutchinson, 1988.

Contributor of short stories to *Ellery Queen's Mystery Magazine*.

UNDER PSEUDONYM BARBARA VINE

A Dark-Adapted Eye, Viking, 1985.
A Fatal Inversion, Viking, 1987.

(With others) *Yes, Prime Minister: The Diaries of the Right Honorable James Hacker,* Salem House Publishers, 1988.
The House of Stairs, Harmony Books, 1989.

MEDIA ADAPTATIONS: A Judgment in Stone was filmed as "The Housekeeper," Rawfilm/Schulz Productions, 1987.

SIDELIGHTS: "It's infuriating to see Ruth Rendell consistently referred to as the new Agatha Christie," writes Cryptus in the *Detroit News.* "The fact is that Rendell . . . is incomparably better, attempting more and achieving more." Indeed, since issuing her first novel, *From Doon with Death,* in which she introduced her popular sleuth Chief Inspector Reginald Wexford of murder-plagued Kingsmarkham, Sussex, England, Rendell has been applauded by critics for her deftness of characterization, ingenious plots, and surprising conclusions. Francis Wyndham of the *Times Literary Supplement* praised Rendell's "masterly grasp of plot construction [and] highly developed faculty for social observation." David Lehman of *Newsweek* reports that "few detective writers are as good at pulling such last-second rabbits out of their top hats—the last page making us see everything before it in a strange, new glare."

Rendell writes two different kinds of mystery novels. In her Wexford books, she creates traditional "police procedural" stories, while her non-series books are psychological thrillers, "energized by the startling, disturbing, seductive notion that all psychology is abnormal psychology and that the criminal mind isn't all that different from our own," as Lehman notes. Wyndham remarks on Rendell's agility in both areas of mystery fiction: "Ruth Rendell's remarkable talent has been able to accomodate the rigid rules of the reassuring mystery story (where a superficial logic conceals a basic fantasy) as well as the wider range of the disturbing psychological thriller (where an appearance of nightmare overlays a scrupulous realism)."

Rendell's popular character Chief Inspector Wexford is middle-aged, married, and the father of two grown daughters. His extensive reading allows him to quote from a wide range of literature during his murder investigations. "Wexford is quite witty, I think," Rendell tells Marilyn Stasio of the *New York Times.* "He is also a big, solid type, very cool and calm. He also likes women very much and always has time for them. What more could you want in a man?" Along with his assistant, Michael Burden, Wexford solves mysterious murders in the town of Kings Markham in rural Sussex, a gritty and rather glum setting. "I don't want people to see Kings Markham as a pretty village," Rendell explains to Stasio.

Rendell's adroitness at building suspense in all her mystery books is admired by reviewers. In a *New York Times Book Review* critique of *A Demon in My View,* Newgate Callender writes: "Nothing much seems to happen, but a bit here, a bit there, a telling thrust, and suddenly we are in a sustained mood of horror. Rendell is awfully good at this kind of psycho-suspense." Writing in the *Los Angeles Times Book Review* about *The Lake of Darkness,* Charles Champlin calls the book "a cleverly plotted story whose several strands, seemingly only tentatively connected at the start, move toward a last, violent knotting (the sort of construction Alfred Hitchcock, who preferred suspense to the classic timetable mystery, might well have enjoyed)." Commenting on *Master of the Moor,* T. J. Binyon of the *Times Literary Supplement* finds it "immaculately written and constructed, . . . another of Ruth Rendell's skillful studies in abnormal psychology; a powerful, intriguing, if ultimately depressing novel." Speaking of *The Bridesmaid,* Carol Kleiman of the *Chicago Tribune* remarks that "it is a fine, psychological novel that holds its own as good literature." Similarly, John Gross of the *New York*

Times claims that "Rendell's work . . . is equally notable for subtle psychological tension and sharp social observation."

BIOGRAPHICAL/CRITICAL SOURCES:

BOOKS

Contemporary Literary Criticism, Gale, Volume 28, 1984, Volume 48, 1988, Volume 50, 1988.

PERIODICALS

Chicago Tribune, August 29, 1989.
Chicago Tribune Book World, December 19, 1982.
Detroit News, August 12, 1979.
Globe and Mail (Toronto), May 31, 1986, September 16, 1989.
Los Angeles Times Book Review, August 3, 1980, May 8, 1983.
Maclean's, May 19, 1986.
Newsweek, September 21, 1987.
New York Times, September 9, 1988, February 4, 1990.
New York Times Book Review, June 25, 1967, June 23, 1968, August 24, 1969, February 26, 1974, June 2, 1974, December 1, 1974, April 27, 1975, November 23, 1975, February 27, 1977, January 23, 1979, October 14, 1979, February 24, 1980.
Saturday Review, January 30, 1971.
Times (London), December 11, 1987.
Times Literary Supplement, February 23, 1967, December 21, 1967, April 23, 1970, October 1, 1976, June 5, 1981, July 23, 1982.
Washington Post Book World, September 20, 1981.

* * *

REXROTH, Kenneth 1905-1982

PERSONAL: Born December 22, 1905, in South Bend, Ind.; moved to Chicago, Ill., at the age of twelve; died June 6, 1982, in Montecito, Calif., of a heart ailment; son of Charles Marion (a wholesale druggist) and Delia (Reed) Rexroth; married Andre Deutcher, 1927 (died, 1940); married Marie Kass, 1940 (divorced, 1948); married Marthe Larsen, 1949 (divorced, 1961); married Carol Tinker (a poet), 1974; children: (by third marriage) Mary, Katharine. *Education:* Attended the Chicago Art Institute and the Art Students League, New York, N.Y.; largely self-educated. *Politics:* None.

CAREER: Poet, translator, playwright, essayist, and painter. Worked as mucker, harvest hand, packer, fruit picker, forest patrolman, factory hand, and attendant in a mental institution. Held one-man art shows in Los Angeles, Santa Monica, New York, Chicago, Paris, and San Francisco. *The Nation,* San Francisco correspondent, beginning 1953. Co-founder of the San Francisco Poetry Center; columnist for the *San Francisco Examiner.* Taught at various universities, including San Francisco State University, University of California, Santa Barbara, and University of Wisconsin—Milwaukee. Lectured and gave poetry readings throughout the world. *Military service:* Conscientious objector.

MEMBER: National Institute of Arts and Letters.

AWARDS, HONORS: California Literature Silver Medal Award for poetry, 1941, for *In What Hour,* 1945, for *The Phoenix and the Tortoise,* and 1980, for *The Morning Star;* Guggenheim fellowship in poetry, 1948 and 1949; Eunice Teitjens Award, 1957; Shelley Memorial Award, 1958; Amy Lowell fellowship, 1958; Longview Award; Chapelbrook Award; National Institute of Arts and Letters grant, 1964; Rockefeller grant, 1967; Akademische Austausdienfp, 1967; Academy of American Poets' Copernicus Award, 1975.

WRITINGS:

In What Hour (poetry), Macmillan, 1940.
The Phoenix and the Tortoise (poetry), New Directions, 1944.
The Art of Wordly Wisdom (poetry), Decker Press, 1949.
The Signature of All Things: Poems, Songs, Elegies, Translations, and Epigrams, New Directions, 1950.
Beyond the Mountains (verse plays; produced in New York at Cherry Lane Theatre, December 30, 1951), New Directions, 1951, reprinted, 1974.
The Dragon and the Unicorn (poetry; originally published in part in *New Directions Annual,* 1950-51), New Directions, 1952.
Thou Shalt Not Kill (poetry), Good Press, c. 1955.
In Defense of the Earth (poetry), New Directions, 1956.
The Homestead Called Damascus (poem), New Directions, 1963.
Natural Numbers: New and Selected Poems, New Directions, 1963.
An Autobiographical Novel, Doubleday, 1966.
The Collected Shorter Poems of Kenneth Rexroth, New Directions, 1967.
The Heart's Garden, the Garden's Heart (poems and calligraphic designs), Pym-Randall Press, 1967.
Collected Longer Poems of Kenneth Rexroth, New Directions, 1968.
The Spark in the Tender of Knowing (poetry), Pym-Randall, 1968.
Sky Sea Birds Tree Earth House Beasts Flowers, Unicorn Press, 1971.
American Poetry: In the Twentieth Century (essays), Herder, 1971.
The Rexroth Reader, edited and with a foreword by Eric Mottram, Cape, 1972.
New Poems, New Directions, 1974.
The Silver Swan: Poems Written in Kyoto, 1974-75 (also see below), Copper Canyon Press, 1976.
On Flower Wreath Hill (poem; also see below), Blackfish Press, 1976.
The Morning Star (includes *The Silver Swan, On Flower Wreath Hill,* and *The Love Songs of Marichiko*), New Directions, 1979.
Saucy Limericks and Christmas Cheer, Bradford-Morrow, 1980.
Selected Poems, New Directions, 1984.

ESSAYS

Bird in the Bush: Obvious Essays, New Directions, 1959.
Assays, New Directions, 1962.
Classics Revisited, Quadrangle Books, 1968.
The Alternative Society: Essays from the Other World, Herder, 1970.
With Eye and Ear, Herder, 1970.
The Elastic Retort: Essays in Literature and Ideas, Seabury, 1973.
Communalism: From Its Origin to the Twentieth Century, Seabury, 1974.
World Outside the Window: The Selected Essays of Kenneth Rexroth, edited by Bradford Morrow, New Directions, 1987.
More Classics Revisited, edited by Bradford Morrow, New Directions, 1989.

EDITOR

(And author of introduction) D. H. Lawrence, *Selected Poems,* New Directions, 1948.
New British Poets: An Anthology, New Directions, 1949.
Fourteen Poems of O. V. de Lubicz-Milosz, Peregrine Press, 1952.

(And translator) *One Hundred Poems from the Japanese,* New Directions, 1955.
(And translator with Ling O. Chung) *The Orchid Boat: Women Poets of China,* Herder, 1972.
Czeslav Milosz, *The Selected Poems of Czeslav Milosz,* Seabury, 1973.
David Meltzer, *Tens: Selected Poems, 1961-71,* McGraw, 1973.
(And author of introduction) Jessica Tarahata Hagedorn and others, *Four Young Women: Poems,* McGraw, 1973.
(And translator) *One Hundred More Poems from the Japanese,* New Directions, 1974.
The Buddhist Writings of Lafcadio Hearn, Ross-Erikson, 1977.
(And translator with Ikuko Atsumi) *The Burning Heart: The Women Poets of Japan,* Seabury, 1977.
(And author of introduction and translator with Atsumi) Kazuko Shiraishi, *Seasons of Sacred Lust—Selected Poems,* New Directions, 1978.

TRANSLATOR

One Hundred Poems from the French, Jargon, 1955, reprinted, Pym-Randall, 1970.
One Hundred Poems from the Chinese, New Directions, 1956.
Thirty Spanish Poems of Love and Exile, City Lights, 1956, reprinted, Kraus Reprint, 1973.
(And author of introduction) *Poems from the Greek Anthology,* University of Michigan Press, 1962.
Pierre Reverdy, *Selected Poems,* New Directions, 1969.
Love and the Turning Year: One Hundred More Chinese Poems, New Directions, 1970.
(With Chung) *Li Ch'ing Chao: The Complete Poems,* New Directions, 1979.
Tu Fu, *Tu Fu, Kenneth Rexroth, Brice Marden,* Blumarts, 1987.

Also author of shorter works of poetry, including broadsides and "Lament for Dylan Thomas," c. 1955, and "As the Full Moon Rises," published by Old Marble Press; author of autobiographical work *Excerpts from a Short Life,* 1981. Contributor of poetry, translations, essays, and criticism to numerous popular and academic periodicals.

SIDELIGHTS: In a reminiscence written for the *Los Angeles Times Book Review,* Kenneth Rexroth's friend and former student Thomas Sanchez portrayed the author as a "longtime iconoclast, onetime radical, Roman Catholic, Communist fellow traveler, jazz scholar, I.W.W. anarchist, translator, philosopher, playwright, librettist, orientalist, critical essayist, radio personality, newspaper columnist, painter, poet and longtime Buddhist." While Rexroth played all these roles, he is best recognized for his contributions to modern American poetry. The length and breadth of his career resulted in a body of work that not only chronicles his personal search for visionary transcendence but also reflects the artistic, cultural, and political vicissitudes of more than half a century. Commented John Unterecker in a 1967 *New York Times Book Review:* "Reading through all of Kenneth Rexroth's shorter poems is a little like immersing oneself in the literary history of the last forty years; for Rexroth experimented with almost all of the poetic techniques of the time, dealt, at least in passing, with all of its favorite themes."

A prolific painter and poet by age seventeen, Rexroth traveled through a succession of avant-garde and modernist artistic movements, gaining a reputation as a radical by associating with labor groups and anarchist political communities. He experimented amid Chicago's "second renaissance" in the early 1920s, explored modernist techniques derived from the European-born "revolution of the word," played an integral part in the anarchist-pacifist politics and poetic mysticism that pervaded San

Francisco's Bay Area in the 1940s, and affiliated himself with the "Beat Generation" in the mid-1950s. Intellectually as well as artistically eclectic, Rexroth scorned institutionalized education and criticism, calling American academics "corn belt Metaphysicals and country gentlemen," as M. L. Rosenthal noted in *The Modern Poets.* After quitting school in his early teens, the poet pursued a curriculum of self-education that included not only literature from diverse cultures and times but encompassed science, philosophy, theology, anthropology, Oriental thought and culture, and half a dozen languages. William R. McKaye of the *Washington Post* emphasized: "In an era in which American colleges crank out graduates who seemingly have never read anything, Rexroth . . . [appeared] well on the way to having read everything. And 'everything' is not just the standard European classics in translation: it is the Latins and Greeks in the original; it is the Japanese and Chinese; it is poetry of all kinds; finally, as a sort of spicy sauce over all, it is such . . . curiosities as the literature of alchemy, the writings of 18th and 19th century Anglican divines and the 'Religio Medici' of Sir Thomas Browne."

James Laughlin, founder of the New Directions Publishing Corporation which published and kept in print most of Rexroth's books, agreed that the poet found his mature style in *The Phoenix and the Tortoise* and *The Signature of All Things* (1950). "When he hit his true vein, a poetry of nature mixed with contemplation and philosophy, it was magnificent," Laughlin claimed in a tribute written for *Dictionary of Literary Biography Yearbook: 1982.* Published in 1944, *The Phoenix and the Tortoise* was called by Morgan Gibson in his book *Kenneth Rexroth,* "much more coherent in style and theme" than Rexroth's earlier work while focusing less on experimentation and politics. Instead, the book initiated a study of "the 'integral person' who, through love, discovers his responsibility for all in a world of war, cold war, and nuclear terror." The true achievement of *The Phoenix and the Tortoise* and Rexroth's next book, *The Signature of All Things,* was the emergence of "poems that affirm more convincingly than ever the transcendent power of personal love," Gibson stated. "Read 'The Signature of All Things,'" Laughlin urged. "It, how shall I put it, pulls everything in human life together. It is all there, all the things we cherish, all our aspirations, and over it all a kind of Buddhist calm." Reviewing *The Signature of All Things* in the *New York Times,* Richard Eberhart outlined both Rexroth's intent and his accomplishment: "Mr. Rexroth's purpose is to make a particular kind of poem which will be classical in its restraint, but without severity; personal, revealing, and confessional, without being sentimental; and it must, according to his bent, eschew symbolism and any kind of ambiguous imagery for a narrative or statement strength based on noun and verb, but not weakened by adjectives."

The form Rexroth adopted in his mature work, which he called "natural numbers," was unrhymed and syllabic rather than metrically regular. Generally varying from seven to nine syllables per line, the structure allowed him to emphasize the "natural cadences of speech," which Gibson pointed out had been important to the poet from the days of his earliest Cubist experiments. Looking back to the 1950s, Karl Malkoff remarked in a 1970 *Southern Review:* "Rexroth . . . never stopped experimenting with rhythms, which not surprisingly are crucial to the success of his poems. Here his work is most vulnerable; here his successes, when they come, are most striking. When . . . Rexroth hit upon the seven syllable line as a temporary resolution, he was accused of writing prose broken up into lines. . . . Actually, on rereading, Rexroth's ear proves reasonably reliable." When he published his first collection of selected work in 1963, the poet entitled it *Natural Numbers: New and Selected Poems,* thus reaf-

firming the importance of an element critics had dismissed earlier as ineffective or unimportant.

Rexroth's tetralogy of verse plays in "natural numbers," *Beyond the Mountains* (1951), proves not only his devotion to the natural patterns of speech but indicates his knowledge of classical Greek and Oriental literature. Gibson claimed in his study that the author's "poetic, philosophical, and visionary powers [reached] their epitome" in the four dramas "Phaedra," "Iphigenia at Aulis," "Hermaios," and "Berenike." While the characters were based in Greek tragedy, Rexroth's style reflected Japanese *Noh* drama. As Gibson related, an "important quality of *Noh* found in Rexroth's plays is *yugen,* a term derived from Zen Buddhism and defined by Arthur Waley as 'what lies beneath the surface'; the subtle, as opposed to the obvious; the hint, as opposed to the statement." Although several commentators felt *Beyond the Mountains* suffered from obscurity or was more complex than necessary—including R. W. Flint, who wrote in *Poetry* that the "plotting has been just a shade too ambitious for [Rexroth's] poetic gift"—the renowned poet William Carlos Williams applauded both the work's language and its form. "Rexroth is one of the leading craftsmen of the day," proclaimed Williams in the *New York Times.* "There is in him no compromise with the decayed line of past experience. His work is cleanly straightforward. The reek of polluted Shakespeare just isn't in it, or him. I don't know any Greek, but I can imagine that a Greek, if he knew our language as we ought to but don't, would like the athletic freshness of the words."

A common concern for poetry as straightforward, spoken language was only one of the links between Rexroth and the Beat Generation. Quoting Jack Kerouac's definition found in *Random House Dictionary,* Charters defined the term Beat Generation as "'members of the generation that came of age after World War II who, supposedly as a result of disillusionment stemming from the Cold War, [espoused] mystical detachment and relaxation of social and sexual tension.' Emerging at a time of great postwar change, the Beat Generation was more than a literary movement, but at its heart was its literature." Charters and Miller explained how Rexroth came to be connected with the movement: "By the mid-1950s many of the poets who were to become famous as Beat writers—Lawrence Ferlinghetti, Allen Ginsberg, Jack Kerouac, Michael McClure, Gary Snyder, Philip Whalen—had moved to San Francisco, attracted by the climate of radical poetry and politics, and they were soon part of Rexroth's circle. . . . Considering the diverse aspects of Rexroth's interests in avant-garde art, radical politics, and Eastern philosophy, one can understand why he seemed the perfect mentor for the Beats."

Rexroth occupied a central position in the Bay Area's literary community at the time. Characterized as "anarchopacifist in politics, mystical-personalist in religions, and experimental in esthetic theory and practice" by Gibson, the community revolved around the Pacifica Foundation, with its public arts radio station, and the Poetry Center at San Francisco State College, both of which Rexroth helped establish. As a contributor to *Nation,* the *San Francisco Chronicle,* and the *New York Times,* he also wielded a certain critical power across the country. Rexroth used these forums to champion the younger poets' work in articles like his February, 1957, *Nation* review entitled "San Francisco's Mature Bohemians." Most instrumental in linking Rexroth with the Beats, however, may have been the frequent poetry readings—often to jazz accompaniment—that Rexroth attended or helped organize from 1955 to 1957.

Rexroth considered the readings essential to foment "poetry as voice, not as printing," as he told readers in his *American Poetry: In the Twentieth Century* (1971). Supporting the Beats morally with reviews and with his presence at their events, including his series of readings at the Cellar jazz club, Rexroth earned the title "Godfather of the Beats." "Kenneth Rexroth seemed to appear everywhere at their side like the shade of Virgil guiding Dante through the underworld," Alfred Kazin wrote in *Contemporaries*. "Rexroth . . . suddenly became a public figure."

Undoubtedly influencing the Beats more than they influenced him, the poet nonetheless was considered part of the school he instructed by many conservative or academic critics. As such, he often was dismissed or opposed as being part of a nonconformist craze. Some reviewers looked beyond the image, however, to assess the poet's work itself. "Rexroth's *In Defense of the Earth* [1956] showed him the strongest of West Coast anarchist poets because he is a good deal more than a West Coast anarchist poet," emphasized Rosenthal. "He is a man of wide cultivation and, when not too busy shocking the bourgeois reader (who would like nothing better), a genuine poet." Added Gibson: "Rexroth's book of the Beat period, *In Defense of the Earth*, . . . is no period piece. . . . These poems of love and protest, of meditation and remembrance, stand out as some of his most deeply felt poems."

Despite the vehement support Rexroth expressed for the birth of the Beat Generation, he became disillusioned when he saw the movement's more prominent members become "hipsters." Miller and Charters state that the poet "seemed to have become jealous of [the Beats'] success and widespread attention from the national press. He had fought for many years for his own recognition as a Poet," they pointed out, "and as [the Beats'] popularity increased, his growing hostility toward [them] was expressed in a series of articles over the next several years." Nevertheless, Rexroth remained supportive of certain aspects of some Beat writers' works while condemning the movement as a whole. Several critics now note this point, attributing both Rexroth's animosities and his preferences to an individual integrity not influenced by blind allegiance—or enmity—to any literary collective.

Rexroth's position as a central yet independent figure in American literature was further strengthened by a personal account of his youth, entitled *An Autobiographical Novel*. According to Dean Stewart, writing in the *Los Angeles Times Book Review,* the 1966 work "did most to enhance [Rexroth's] image as a living historical personality; his essays in book form and spreading reputation as a keen social critic and insightful philosopher also helped." Yet, while his role as the "outsider's insider" in the literary world became widely acknowledged, serious attention to his own poetry seemed to receive secondary consideration. Commented Stewart: "For a poet who has constantly said he 'only writes prose for money,' Rexroth rivals H. L. Mencken as a terse and cogent critic. But like Mencken, the largely forgotten lexicographer, little-read essayist and much remembered personality, Rexroth may share a similar descending fame from poet to translator to essayist to personality."

Gibson emphasized that in order to appreciate the importance of what Rexroth presents in *An Autobiographical Novel* the reader must understand Rexroth's world view as it evolves through all his works. Integral to the development of the poet's vision were his translation of foreign verse (both contemporary and ancient) and his study of Oriental thought. Rexroth felt an artistic kinship with the Greeks and Romans of classical times and with Japanese and Chinese writers. As Peter Clothier pointed out in a *Los Angeles Times* review of Rexroth's last Japa-

nese translations: "The sharpness of focus and the directly experiential quality of . . . [Oriental] poets are close to Rexroth's own aesthetic. . . . Rexroth has long championed this directness and simplicity of diction in poetry, a clarity of image and emotion clearly compatible with the Japanese aesthetic." Although, as Gibson commented, literary critics have yet to explore the relationships between Rexroth's translations and his own poetry, it has been generally recognized that his later poems are characterized by a serenity and quiet intensity that reflect Oriental art and philosophy.

The Heart's Garden, the Garden's Heart (1968), *New Poems* (1974), and *The Morning Star* (1979)—Rexroth's major poetry collections published after his autobiography—illustrate both his involvement with Oriental culture and his final resolutions of philosophical and technical concerns. Rexroth was, stated Victor Howes in the *Christian Science Monitor,* looking "for a sort of day-to-day mysticism." It was "a poetry of direct statement and simple clear ideas," the critic continued. "A poetry free of superfluous rhetoric. One might call it a poetry of moments." Agreed Richard Eberhart in *Nation,* "Rexroth . . . settled down to the universal validity of stating simple and deep truths in a natural way." "Though he [had] always been a visionary, he spent more than three decades searching for a philosophical rationale for his experience, for history, and for nature. In the 1960s he seems to have abandoned that kind of quest in favor of pure visionary experience," Gibson summarized. "[*The Heart's Garden, the Garden's Heart*], an extended Buddhist-Taoist meditation written in Japan, shows the depths of his resignation and enlightenment."

Written as Rexroth celebrated his sixtieth birthday, *The Heart's Garden, the Garden's Heart* did not "aim at giving answers to final questions that have none," explained Luis Ellicott Yglesias in the *New Boston Review.* "Instead it is a meditation on a handful of central images that have been treasured for centuries because they have the virtue of clarifying experience to the points of making it possible to relinquish life with the facility of a ripe apple dropping from its branch." Woodcock, who recognized in Rexroth's earlier works a dialogue between the poet's "conceptualizing mind" and his "experiencing sensibility," felt the two were reconciled in the volume. Out of the fusion "there appears a unique contemplative intensity," the critic stated in *New Leader.* "What has been forged is a supercharged imagism in which every physical object, every scene, every picture the poet creates, is loaded with burdens of meaning that cannot otherwise be expressed." This reconciliation of the immediate and the enduring continued in *New Poems,* which Herbert Leibowitz said were composed "of a flash or revelatory image and silent metamorphoses." Describing what he saw as Rexroth's achievement, Leibowitz continued in the *New York Times Book Review:* "Syntax is cleared of the clutter of subordinate clauses, that contingent grammar of a mind hesitating, debating with itself, raging against death and old age. The dynamics of his poems are marked *piano*—even storms are luminous rather than noisy." The quietness, as well as a vital eroticism, carried over to Rexroth's volume of verse *The Morning Star.* Containing three previously published collections, including the sequence that Rexroth pretended was translated from the Japanese ("The Love Songs of Marichiko"), the book offers a "directness and clarity" not usually associated with Western art, according to David Kirby in the *Times Literary Supplement.* "How different this is from the Rexroth of *The Phoenix and the Tortoise* (1944), who sounds like Lawrence and Pound and Whitman, or the one who wrote ["Thou Shalt Not Kill"] in *In Defense of the Earth*. . . . Now he appears to belong, or to want to belong, at least as much as a publishing writer can, to the Buddhist bodhisattvas [or other Eastern religions]."

"Revolutionary and conservative, worldly and spiritual, Asian and western ideas from traditions that may seem irreconcilable were uniquely harmonized in Rexroth's world view as expressed [throughout] his philosophical poetry and essays," Gibson wrote in his study *Kenneth Rexroth*. Concluded Douglas Dunn in *Listener:* "Insufficient credit has been granted to Rexroth's identity as an old-fashioned, honest-to-God man of letters of downright independence of mind. . . . His temper [was] too independent, too scholarly, for cut-and-dried allegiances. He [turned] his back on Eliot and Pound. He [had] the irritating habit—for the mediocre, that is, the literary side-takers—of liking some but not all of certain poets or movements. Like all good examples in modern poetry, he has been seen as a figure instead of as a creator; as a representative rather than as a participant. That he is all four of these persons at once comes as a sweet discovery from a reading of his work instead of from side-glances at other people's estimates of his reputation."

BIOGRAPHICAL/CRITICAL SOURCES:

BOOKS

Concise Dictionary of American Literary Biography: The New Consciousness, 1941-1968, Gale, 1987.
Contemporary Literary Criticism, Gale, Volume 1, 1973, Volume 2, 1974, Volume 6, 1976, Volume 11, 1976, Volume 22, 1982, Volume 49, 1988.
Dictionary of Literary Biography, Gale, Volume 16: *The Beats: Literary Bohemians in Postwar America,* 1983, Volume 48: *American Poets, 1880-1945, Second Series,* 1986.
Dictionary of Literary Biography Yearbook: 1982, Gale, 1983.
Gardner, Geoffrey, editor, *For Rexroth,* Ark, 1980.
Gibson, Morgan, *Kenneth Rexroth,* Twayne, 1972.
Kazin, Alfred, *Contemporaries,* Little, Brown, 1962.
Kerouac, Jack, *The Dharma Bums,* Signet Books, 1958.
Lipton, Lawrence, *The Holy Barbarians,* Messner, 1959.
Rexroth, Kenneth, *Bird in the Bush: Obvious Essays,* New Directions, 1959.
Rexroth, Kenneth, *Assays,* New Directions, 1962.
Rexroth, Kenneth, *An Autobiographical Novel,* Doubleday, 1966.
Rexroth, Kenneth, *American Poetry: In the Twentieth Century,* Herder, 1971.
Rosenthal, M. L., *The Modern Poets: A Critical Introduction,* Oxford University Press, 1960.

PERIODICALS

America, August 4, 1973, December 20, 1975.
American Association of Political and Social Science Annals, September, 1975.
American Literature, March, 1972.
American Poetry Review, November, 1978.
Antioch Review, number 3, 1971.
Best Sellers, August 1, 1971, February, 1980.
Booklist, March 1, 1949, April 1, 1969, November 1, 1973, February 1, 1975, February 15, 1975, October 15, 1976, July 1, 1978, October 1, 1979.
Book Review, March, 1971.
Books, December 22, 1940.
Book Week, December 24, 1944.
Choice, November, 1969, October, 1971, October, 1972, January, 1974, April, 1974, March, 1975, June, 1975, May, 1977, March, 1978, July/August, 1978.

Christian Century, September 4, 1940, July 1, 1970, May 19, 1971.
Christian Science Monitor, August 31, 1940, July 11, 1967, January 9, 1969, September 14, 1970, February 6, 1980.
Commentary, December, 1957.
Commonweal, December 6, 1974.
Comparative Literature, Volume 10, 1958.
Harper's, August, 1967.
Hudson Review, spring, 1960, summer, 1967, summer, 1968, autumn, 1968, summer, 1971, autumn, 1974.
Journal of Asian Studies, November, 1973, May, 1978.
Kirkus Reviews, February 1, 1949, April 1, 1970, May 15, 1971, November 1, 1972, February 1, 1973, September 1, 1974, November 1, 1974, November 1, 1979.
Kyoto Review, Volume 15, fall, 1982.
Library Journal, June 15, 1949, July, 1970, August, 1971, July, 1972, September 15, 1972, December 15, 1972, October 15, 1974, January 15, 1975, September 1, 1976, September 15, 1977, October 15, 1979, November 15, 1979.
Library Review, autumn, 1977.
Life, September 9, 1957.
Listener, June 16, 1977.
London Magazine, April/May, 1974.
Los Angeles Free Press, January 10, 1969.
Los Angeles Times, October 3, 1978, February 5, 1980.
Los Angeles Times Book Review, August 3, 1980, June 20, 1982.
Minnesota Review, spring, 1962, fall, 1962.
Nation, February 12, 1949, June 10, 1950, September 28, 1957, June 6, 1966, March 18, 1968, April 22, 1968, March 24, 1969, December 31, 1973.
National Observer, December 9, 1968.
New Boston Review, Volume 3, number 3, December, 1977.
New Leader, April 24, 1967, February 17, 1969, October 27, 1969, September 21, 1970.
New Republic, August 12, 1940, August 8, 1949, February 9, 1953, February 18, 1957, September 16, 1957.
New Statesman, January 2, 1976.
New York Herald Tribune, May 7, 1950, February 1, 1953.
New York Herald Tribune [Weekly] Book Review, June 12, 1949, October 2, 1949, May 7, 1950, February 19, 1956.
New York Times, December 19, 1948, August 6, 1950, January 28, 1951, February 15, 1953, January 1, 1956, November 22, 1964, July 23, 1967, August 17, 1968, July 10, 1970.
New York Times Book Review, July 23, 1967, November 16, 1969, February 15, 1970, October 4, 1970, March 23, 1975, November 23, 1980.
New Yorker, December 30, 1944, March 26, 1949, May 20, 1950, February 4, 1956, May 3, 1958.
Ohio Review, winter, 1976.
Parnassus, spring, 1981.
Poetry, November, 1940, June, 1950, May, 1956, June, 1957, July, 1963, December, 1967, April, 1969.
Prairie Schooner, winter, 1971-72.
Progressive, June, 1975.
Psychology Today, July, 1975.
Publishers Weekly, September 1, 1969, April 13, 1970, September 28, 1970, January 1, 1973, October 8, 1979.
Quarterly Review of Literature, Volume 9, number 2, 1957.
Reporter, April 3, 1958, March 3, 1960, May 19, 1966.
sagetrieb, Volume 2, number 3, winter, 1983.
San Francisco Chronicle, May 29, 1949, March 12, 1950, January 29, 1956, February 10, 1957.
Saturday Review, June 16, 1956, November 9, 1957, February 12, 1966, March 15, 1969.

Saturday Review of Literature, June 4, 1949, September 17, 1949, May 20, 1950.
Southern Review, spring, 1970.
Spectator, March 13, 1959.
Sydney Southerly (Sydney, Australia), Volume 28, 1968.
Time, December 2, 1957, February 25, 1966.
Times Literary Supplement, April 30, 1971, June 16, 1972, March 25, 1977, May 30, 1980.
U.S. Quarterly Booklist, June, 1950.
Virginia Quarterly Review, summer, 1973, spring, 1975.
Voice Literary Supplement, December, 1984.
Washington Post, August 29, 1968, February 1, 1971.
Washington Post Book World, January 6, 1974, June 29, 1975, March 12, 1978.
Weekly Book Review, January 14, 1945.
World Literature Today, winter, 1978, spring, 1978, autumn, 1978, winter, 1981.

OBITUARIES:

PERIODICALS

AB Bookman's Weekly, September 6, 1982.
Detroit Free Press, June 9, 1982.
Los Angeles Times, June 8, 1982, August 13, 1987.
Newsweek, June 21, 1982.
New York Times, June 8, 1982.
Publishers Weekly, June 25, 1982.
Times (London), June 12, 1982.
Washington Post, June 9, 1982.

*   *   *

RHYS, Jean   1894-1979

PERSONAL: Original name Ella Gwendolen Rhys Williams; born August 24, 1894, in Roseau, Dominica, West Indies; died May 14, 1979, in Exeter, England; daughter of William Rhys (a doctor) and Minna (Lockhart) Williams; married Jean Lenglet (a poet, journalist, and singer; divorced); married Leslie Tilden Smith (a literary agent and reader for a publishing company; deceased, 1945), 1934; married Max Hamer (a poet and retired naval officer; deceased), 1947; children: Maryvonne (Mrs. Moerman). *Education:* Attended The Convent, Roseau; studied for one term at the Royal Academy of Dramatic Art, London.

CAREER: Writer. Moved to England at the age of sixteen; after leaving drama school, toured England as a chorus-girl in musical comedy during World War I; went to live in Paris, and spent a number of years traveling around the European continent; worked in Juan-les-Pins, France, as ghost-writer of a book about eighteenth-century furniture and decoration; returned to England.

MEMBER: Royal Society of Literature (fellow).

AWARDS, HONORS: W. H. Smith Award and Heinemann Award, both 1967, for *Wide Sargasso Sea;* Arts Council of Great Britain Award for Writers, 1967; named Commander of the British Empire, c. 1979, for service to literature.

WRITINGS:

The Left Bank, and Other Stories, preface by Ford Madox Ford, J. Cape, 1927, reprinted, Harper, 1971.
Postures (novel), Chatto & Windus, 1928, published as *Quartet,* Simon & Schuster, 1929, reprinted, Harper, 1971.
After Leaving Mr. Mackenzie (novel), J. Cape, 1930, Knopf, 1931, reprinted, Harper, 1972.
Voyage in the Dark (novel), Constable, 1934, Morrow, 1935, reprinted, Popular Library, 1975.

Good Morning, Midnight (novel), Constable, 1939, Harper, 1970.
Wide Sargasso Sea (novel), introduction by Francis Wyndham, Deutsch, 1966, Norton, 1967.
Tigers Better-Looking (stories, including selections from *The Left Bank, and Other Stories*), Deutsch, 1968, reprinted, Popular Library, 1974.
(With William Sansom, Bernard Malamud, and David Plante) *Penguin Modern Stories I,* Penguin, 1969.
My Day, F. Hallman, 1975.
Sleep it Off, Lady, Harper, 1976.
Smile Please: An Unfinished Autobiography, Harper, 1980.
The Letters of Jean Rhys, edited by Francis Wyndham and Diana Melly, Viking, 1984 (published in England as *Jean Rhys Letters 1931-1966,* Deutsch, 1984).
Jean Rhys: The Complete Novels, Norton, 1985.
The Collected Short Stories, Norton, 1987.

Contributor to *Art and Literature* and *London Magazine.*

MEDIA ADAPTATIONS: Good Morning, Midnight was adapted into a radio play by Selma Vaz Dias and broadcast in 1957; *Quartet* was adapted into a motion picture by James Ivory and Ruth Prawer Jhabvala and released in 1981.

SIDELIGHTS: Jean Rhys, the author of five novels, three collections of short stories, and an unfinished autobiography, was neglected critically until late in her life when she was called by Alfred Alvarez in the *New York Times Book Review* "one of the finest British writers of this century." This claim may be somewhat exaggerated since Rhys's work is often uneven, raw, sometimes more in control of her than she of it. "When she wrote a novel," says her former editor, Diana Athill, in the foreword to *Smile Please,* "it was because she had no choice, and she did it—or 'it happened to her'—for herself, not for others." Frequently, however, she wrote with powerful insistence and control, drawing the reader relentlessly into her startling language that according to David Plante in *Difficult Women: A Memoir of Three,* consists of "intense events which occur in space and silence."

Born Ella Gwendolen Rhys (sometimes spelled Rees) Williams in Roseau, Dominica, on August 24, 1890, she was the daughter of Rhys Williams, a Welsh doctor trained in London, and Minna Lockhart, a third-generation Dominican Creole. Although she was the fourth of five children, Rhys spent a rather lonely childhood. According to her unfinished autobiography *Smile Please,* her two older brothers were sent to school abroad, her older sister went to live with an aunt in St. Kitts, and a baby sister born seven years after Rhys "supplanted" her; she had few friends, finding herself "alone except for books" and voices that, as she later reported to Plante, " 'had nothing to do with me. I sometimes didn't even know the words. But they wanted to be written down, so I wrote them down.' "

At the Catholic convent school she attended, Rhys experienced what she described in *Smile Please* as a "religious fit." Immersed in and fascinated by the "movements," "sounds," and "smells" of the service, she wished for a time to convert from Anglicanism to Catholicism and become a nun. Rhys's early impulses may help explain why her fiction, despite its strange, severed, empty, schizophrenic quality, is highly attuned to both ritual and the rhythms of the senses. The convent school also influenced Rhys's writing through her exposure to a particular nun, Mother Sacred Heart: "I date all my love of words, especially beautiful words, to her half-ironical lessons."

Smile Please documents yet another appeal of Catholicism to Rhys: "Instead of the black people sitting in a different part of the church, they were all mixed up with the white and this pleased me very much." The split between black and white preoccupied Rhys, who was herself of mixed heritage; although her feelings about the racial division of her native island were often ambivalent, she always felt a nostalgia for the blacks of her homeland. Part of that longing resulted from her affinity with native nurses and servants. Despite the racial strife on the island, including riots and violence, the black women in particular offered Rhys access to a mysterious sphere of sorcery and patois that, both frightening and seductive, recurs throughout her novels. Her attraction to both the ritual of Catholicism and the subversiveness of island magic is an example of the polarities caught in her work. There is always a double language going on in Rhys—the bourgeois, white, English discourse of survival and control, and the secret, private, primitive subtext of incantation, sexuality, and madness.

Another appeal of the black women in Rhys's life was perhaps the contrast they provided to her own mother, who was distant and distracted. "She drifted away from me," Rhys recalled in her autobiography, "and when I tried to interest her she was indifferent." Her mother, however, seemed to love babies, and Rhys once heard her remark that black ones were prettier than white ones: "Was this the reason why I prayed so ardently to be black, and would run to the looking-glass in the morning to see if the miracle had happened?" Although the "My Mother" chapter of *Smile Please* concludes with the dismissive statement "Gradually I came to wonder about my mother less and less until at last she was almost a stranger and I stopped imagining what she felt or what she thought," the motif of the indifferent mother permeates much of Rhys's work. As Ronnie Scharfman has noted in an article appearing in *Yale French Studies,* there is great damage caused in Rhys's fiction by the "distant, inaccessible, depressed, rejecting mother" and by the "yearning, . . . [the] desire for this present-absent figure." This motif is developed most clearly in the maternal deathbed scene in *After Leaving Mr. Mackenzie* and in the figure of the mad mother in *Wide Sargasso Sea.*

In 1907 Rhys (still known as Gwen Williams) left her native island for England where she was to be under the care of her aunt, Clarice Williams. At first drawn by the promise of adventure, Rhys soon discovered that England was cold, alien, and hostile and that she was an outsider. As Thomas Staley has pointed out in *Jean Rhys: A Critical Study,* "The drastic climatic change becomes a constant metaphor in her work to dramatise the parallel, chilling psychological effects of England," which often leave transplanted women like Julia Martin's mother in *After Leaving Mr. Mackenzie* "sickening for the sun." In the autumn of 1907 Rhys was enrolled in the Perse School where she was tormented by English girls who, according to Carole Angier's *Jean Rhys,* appreciated neither her Creole background nor her "flashing, instinctive . . . mind." Although she was incompetent in many aspects of English life, Rhys's early affinity for language stood her in good stead: the *Persean Magazine,* Angier reports, wrote that "she expressed her views fearlessly" against a debate resolution "that 'The popularity of modern literature, to the exclusion of standard works, is unreasonable and deplorable.'" Rhys was still years from discovering herself to be a writer, but this anecdote presages both the intensity and the style of her later work, described by Francis Wyndham in the introduction to *Wide Sargasso Sea* as a "mixture of quivering immediacy and glassy objectivity." Rhys's unhappy time at Perse reinforced impulses that would later become motifs in her writing; as Staley observes, "Her sense of displacement and cultural rift created a . . . racial identity with blacks and an affinity for the exile."

After Rhys left the Perse school, she entered the Academy of Dramatic Art in 1909 to become an actress. There, too, she met with disappointment, and when her father died, she found herself, with little money, forced to drop out. Shortly afterwards she found a job in a musical chorus and for two years, under the stage name Ella (sometimes Emma) Gray, toured the provinces while living in shabby hotels, eating meagerly, and beginning the heavy drinking with which she struggled until her death. Between runs she took odd jobs, working as an artist's model and posing for advertisements. As Staley has observed, her early experiences provided "scenes she was later to recreate so well in her novels."

During this period Rhys lived with women who eventually served as prototypes for characters in her books: disenfranchised women who depended financially on men, fatalistic and satiric "tarts," as Angier reports, whose slang drew Rhys to them. According to Angier, they spoke a "secret language, like the ones at home—the servants' patois, or the Carib women's language, which the men didn't know." It is clear that long before Rhys thought of herself as a writer, language compelled her, particularly private, female language, the subtext in a world where, as *After Leaving Mr. Mackenzie* records, women are "for sleeping with—not for talking to."

Despite the rats in the dressing room, her almost paralyzing shyness, and her pervasive sense of herself as an outsider, Rhys had not yet succumbed to the depression and rage that would ultimately permeate her novels and her life. In 1910 she began an affair with a distinguished and respectable Englishman named Lancelot Hugh Smith who seemed to engage her not just through love but through language, "a secret language . . . a male language of upper-class cliche," Angier writes. When the affair ended, Rhys was devastated—desperate, disillusioned, and suicidal. However, as Staley has observed, "It was in the aftermath of this loss that she began to record her experiences and feelings in a notebook. This was the first writing she had done since childhood, and as she painfully recorded her feelings, she was, unknowingly, embarking on another career which would allow her to transform the bitter experiences of her life into art." The transformation was still a long time coming, however; after the initial purging, as Athill reports in her introduction to *Jean Rhys: The Complete Novels,* Rhys buried her notebooks in the bottom of a suitcase where they remained untouched for years although she continued writing diaries and lived on an allowance from Smith.

In 1917 she met the half-French, half-Dutch, Jean Lenglet in the London boarding house where she lived. Within a few weeks she was engaged to a man she barely knew, a singer, painter, and sometimes author who wrote under the name Edouard de Neve. By 1919 Rhys and Lenglet were married and living in Holland where she worked in a pensions office. Shortly afterwards they moved to Paris, reinforcing the pattern of transit and upheaval that was to mark Rhys's life. In Paris, Rhys became an English tutor while Lenglet pursued clandestine espionage activities of which Rhys apparently knew little if anything. In late December 1919, Rhys gave birth to a son, William Owen, who died within a few weeks. Accounts of his birth and death appear in thinly veiled autobiographical sections of *After Leaving Mr. Mackenzie* and *Good Morning, Midnight.* When she was able, Rhys joined Lenglet in Vienna, where he had taken a post as secretary-interpreter but was also dealing in the black-market currency exchange. This was a time of relative wealth followed by a transfer to Budapest where Rhys found herself pregnant again with her daughter, Maryvonne, who was born in 1922 in Brussels after the Lenglets fled Budapest, in Angier's words, "like hunted animals" following revelation of Lenglet's illegal activities.

Leaving the baby at a clinic in Brussels (she was later cared for by a family in Paris), Rhys and Lenglet returned to Paris where he attempted a career as a journalist. Rhys, working in a dress shop, tried to help her husband sell his rejected articles, which she translated into English, by calling on an old acquaintance, Pearl Adam, the wife of a London *Times* correspondent in Paris. Adam, who was more interested in Rhys's language than in Lenglet's ideas, asked whether Rhys had written anything herself. Reluctantly, Rhys gave her access to the old notebooks, which Adam tried to unify into a narrative she called "Triple Sec." Although the two women never succeeded as author and editor and the work was abandoned, Pearl Adam effected a turning point in Rhys's life by introducing her to Ford Madox Ford, then editor of the *Transatlantic Review.*

Ford became Rhys's mentor, helping her with her writing, exposing her to contemporary literature, introducing her to writers, and publishing some of the stories she began to write. When they were collected in 1927 as her first book, *The Left Bank, and Other Stories,* Ford wrote the introduction in which he described her "terrifying insight and a terrific—an almost lurid!—passion for stating the case of the underdog." Ironically, while Ford launched Jean Rhys the writer, he also exploited Jean Rhys the woman. In 1923, after the police finally arrested and extradited Lenglet, Rhys, desperate and penniless, turned to Ford who drew her into a short-lived menage a trois with his live-in mistress, Stella Bowen. In *Drawn from Life: Reminiscences* Bowen later described Rhys as a "tragic person" with a "gift for prose" and a "personal attractiveness," which, however, "were not enough to ensure her any reasonable life, for on the other side of the balance were bad health, destitution, shattered nerves, an undesirable husband, lack of nationality, and a complete absence of any desire for independence." With the exception of the last observation, Bowen probably accurately reports the state in which she and Ford found Rhys, who thought she had discovered in Ford a patron and protector but found instead, as Staley declares, confirmation of "her deepest suspicions about her own feminine vulnerability and male exploitation." Lenglet, who returned to Paris about the time Ford was disentangling himself from Rhys, harbored suspicions about the nature of the Ford-Rhys relationship, suspicions that led to the breakup of the Lenglet-Rhys marriage. Nonetheless, the couple returned for a time to Amsterdam where they lived again with Maryvonne, and Rhys translated Francis Carco's *Perversite,* a translation that was later attributed to Ford, who had negotiated with its American publisher, Pascal Covici. In Amsterdam Rhys also completed the final version of her first published novel, *Quartet.* By the time Rhys left Lenglet and Maryvonne together in Holland and returned to England as the writer now known as Jean Rhys, all the central plots and motifs—the divisions, disappointments, and conflicts—of her future work had been irrevocably established.

The abusive, shattering relationship with Ford, which reinforced the bitterness and despair Rhys felt after the breakup with Lancelot Smith, is the basis of *Quartet* (1928), which details the involvement of art-dealer H. J. Heidler and his wife with the young Marya Zelli, whose husband is in prison. Jonathan Cape, the first publisher to whom Rhys submitted the barely disguised roman a clef, was afraid of a libel suit from Ford. Chatto and Windus eventually published the book, requiring first that Rhys change the title to *Postures* (her original title—and the one by which the novel is generally known—was restored in the 1929 American edition). Although there were some encouraging reviews, neither

The Left Bank nor *Postures* was a financial success. Staley states, "Her work . . . would seem relentlessly depressing. . . . However well-wrought and deeply felt, her subject matter would seem narrow, confining, and even suffocating."

Critics for many years have tended to focus on Rhys's subject matter and to judge—rather than attempt to understand—her characters from psychological, economic, racial, or feminist perspectives. In his Twayne study Peter Wolfe, for example, writes of *Voyage in the Dark,* "Single women who live alone do not always become prostitutes or drunkards. Anna might have supported herself honorably. Somebody with more fiber would not have slid so easily into her groove of sameness." This kind of moralizing, along with extended plot summary, represents Rhys criticism at its weakest. Plante feels that Rhys herself failed to understand the women about whom she wrote: "There is about [Rhys's female characters] a great dark space in which they do not ask themselves, removing themselves from themselves in the world in which they live: Why do I suffer?"

The most interesting critics deal with the admittedly problematic aspects of Rhys's work, but they do so in ways that interrogate the issues underlying the disintegration of women's lives, and they question the texts, not the women. Accordingly, Elizabeth Abel asks in her *Contemporary Literature* essay, "Does Rhys's unremitting pessimism become an artistic failure that drives us to dismiss her vision despite her insight and control?" This question is a crucial one; however, in assessing Rhys's work, it is important not to focus on a particular event or even a particular novel but instead to examine her entire canon, for her novels intersect and engender each other, especially the four earliest ones, which might themselves be read as a "quartet." As Dennis Porter has suggested in the *Massachusetts Review,* "To read the first four novels is to be aware that the stories they tell concern a fundamentally similar woman at different stages on the journey from early womanhood into middle age. But beyond that, one comes to perceive the existence of an itinerary which, since she returns to it with an obsessive insistence, seems to be deeply rooted in Jean Rhys's own experience. Yet, through the objectifying power of her art, it achieves an almost mythic generality. Nowhere completely written-up in a single novel, the itinerary exists as a kind of structural model that can be abstracted from the novels taken together and that reflects back revealingly on any given novel."

Quartet, Rhys's first major attempt to manipulate material for a reading audience, is clearly the least polished, the least aesthetically distanced of her novels, betraying "uncertainties," as Wyndham writes, "that were later eliminated from her style" as she gained a sense of the shape of her work. According to Plante, "Jean often talked of the 'shape' of her books: she imagined a shape, and everything that fit into the shape she put in, everything that didn't she left out, and she left out a lot." Forged during the modernist period, Rhys's art, as Staley suggests, "shares many of [the] characteristics and impulses of literary modernism, but she was unaware of or removed from many of its preoccupations. . . . [H]er work was never very closely attuned to the technical innovations of modernism; her art developed out of an intensely private world—a world whose sources of inspiration were neither literary nor intellectual." Rhys's isolation from the intellectual and literary sources of modernism, along with her position as an economically and culturally disenfranchised woman, may partially explain the longtime critical neglect of her work.

Despite its technical weaknesses, *Quartet* introduces at least two devices characteristic of all of Rhys's work: her style, described by Staley as "carefully modulated, terse, frequently flat, always understated," and interior monologues resulting from her female protagonists' inability to posit themselves as speaking selves, particularly to men who, according to Judith Kegan Gardiner, in her *boundary 2* essay, deny Rhys's women "the freedom of language and therefore the freedom to define [themselves]" and then despise them for their failures. But Judith Thurman argues in *Ms.* that "one of the strongest impressions . . . one gets from *Quartet* is that Jean Rhys mistrusts other women." Thurman perceives Rhys's otherness as genderless in a world where women, as exemplified by Heidler's mistress Lois, are "even more treacherous than men." Although many feminist critics have been drawn to Rhys, she herself did not embrace feminism; Rhys, in fact, was impatient with and pessimistic about most -isms, including those associated with the women's movement: according to Angier, "Whenever she read a review that was even mildly feminist, she laughed and tore it up." Her novels are not feminist tracts but rather records of the alienation that results when women have no cultural context out of which to speak or write.

Another important aspect of *Quartet* is its blending of realism with what Staley call "open-ended images and dreamlike flights" that initially are "rigidly controlled by the direct and simple style" and then give way to the protagonist's "horror, fear, dislocation, and desperation," producing a "stylisation of consciousness." In later works this control vanishes, and much of the language and behavior of Rhys's characters exhibits qualities of schizophrenia, as Elizabeth Abel describes it in her *Contemporary Literature* essay: "impoverished affect, apathy, obsessive thought and behavior coupled with the inability to take real initiative, a sense of the unreality of both the world and self, and a feeling of detachment from the body." Accordingly, Rhys's second novel, *After Leaving Mr. Mackenzie,* has been labeled by Thurman "a vision, in slow motion, of a woman coming apart." Again taking up the story of a woman abandoned by a lover, it also draws material from Rhys's Caribbean childhood and her ambivalent relationship to her dying mother. Moreover, *After Leaving Mr. Mackenzie* features a shift in language coincident with the island—a rhythmic, maternally connoted subtext which reveals to protagonist Julia Martin "the feeling that she was so close to seeing the thing that was behind all this talking and posturing, and that the talking and the posturing were there to prevent her from seeing it."

Between the publication of *Quartet* and *After Leaving Mr. Mackenzie,* Rhys had met Leslie Tilden Smith, a literary agent who was instrumental in placing her novels; Rhys moved in with him in 1929, and they married in 1934. The years of their relationship, during which Rhys wrote virtually all of her early work were, however, far from happy. Smith apparently indulged Rhys with great kindness, took on most of the household chores, endured her drinking and her periodic rages, but according to Angier, "He had come too late. Instead, she went over and over the loss of love, the loss of hope." Nonetheless, Smith supported her in her work, typing and reading manuscripts, and borrowing money (which he mismanaged) to subsidize her trips to Paris, the setting of so much of her work. For Rhys writing was apparently an arduous process during which she seemed to need to relive her own pain, bitterness, and desperation through that of the women about whom she wrote. She also was unable to end work on a book; as Angier reports, "she wrote and rewrote, in an obsessive search for perfection that would not allow her to let anything go. When Leslie knew that a manuscript was finished, he simply took it away from her. There would be a terrible row, but

at least it was done; and soon Jean would forget her anguish and feel relieved."

In 1934, *Voyage in the Dark* was completed and published: derived from notebooks written more than a decade before *Quartet,* this third novel combined the immediacy and urgency of a journal with the now more developed craft of an experienced writer, and it remained for Rhys, despite years of critical neglect, her favorite work. *Voyage in the Dark* reworks the familiar Rhysian plot of a destitute, powerless chorus girl, abandoned by lovers and left alone and pregnant; stylistically, however, it develops more fully the strategies and preoccupations established in her earlier published work: flashbacks to Dominica, floating memories that disrupt the text, syntactical aberrations, and finally, following Anna Morgan's abortion, a kind of delirious discourse in which all boundaries between past and present, hallucination and reality, disappear. Rhys's publishers insisted she change the "morbid" ending in which Anna died. In a June 1934 letter printed in Francis Wyndham and Diana Melly's collection of Rhys's correspondence, Rhys confided: "I minded more than I would have believed possible. . . . I suppose I shall have to give in and cut the book and I'm afraid it will make it meaningless. The worst is that it is precisely the last part which I am most certain of that will have to be mutilated." She was haunted by this revision for more than thirty years.

The last of Rhys's early novels, *Good Morning, Midnight,* which appeared in 1939, confirmed, as Staley has observed, that "her fiction was not a literature of social engagement. . . . [H]er writing seemed untouched by the devastating political and military events which had occurred and by the even more horrendous ones which were on the horizon." *Good Morning, Midnight* centers on the oldest of Rhys's protagonists, Sasha Jansen, wandering the streets of Paris and trying just to keep control, to avoid the psychological and physical traps and threats in a "combination of paranoia and insight," as Staley says. Critics disagree just what the book is "about." Gardiner, for example, claims in her *boundary 2* essay that the novel is "a sustained critique of polarizations about sex, class and moral value that oppress women and the poor" and that the alienation is not private, as Staley believes, or schizophrenic, as Abel maintains, but rather "the specific historical result" of women being "female, poor, and sexually active" and "misdefined by a language and literary heritage that belong primarily to propertied men."

If the earlier novels are marked by a kind of defeated passivity, *Good Morning, Midnight* is characterized by fear and violence. "I'm very much afraid of men," Sasha says. "And I'm even more afraid of women. And I'm very much afraid of the whole bloody human race." At another moment, when she feels a woman is staring at her in a bar, she declares, "One day, quite suddenly, when you're not expecting it, I'll take a hammer from the folds of my dark cloak and crack your little skull like an egg-shell. Crack it will go, the egg-shell; out they will stream, the blood, the brains. One day, one day. . . . One day the fierce wolf that walks by my side will spring on you and rip your abominable guts out. One day, one day. . . . Now, now, gently, quietly, quietly. . . ." The elliptical style is characteristic of Rhys's novels, as Gardiner observes in her *boundary 2* essay: "She uses [ellipses] often, as through she is quoting herself incompletely, deliberately leaving gaps that we must fill in." More important than the technique, however, are the strange, haunted, unexpected shifts, particularly in *Good Morning, Midnight,* between engagement and dissociation, desire and loss, and power and exploitation. Sasha herself summarizes the effect of the novel when she thinks, "You imagine the carefully-pruned, shaped thing that is presented to you is truth. That is just what it isn't. The truth is improbable, the truth is fantastic; it's in what you think is a distorting mirror that you see the truth." The ending of the novel involves a rather sadistic, surreal sexual encounter with a traveling salesman whose presence and function for Sasha, as she both seduces and submits to him, remain complex and ambiguous. Whether her final affirmation "Yes—yes—yes . . ." is masochistic or enlightened remains unclear, reflecting the precarious state of consciousness that structures this last novel before Rhys "disappeared" into years of heavy drinking and emotional instability.

After *Good Morning, Midnight,* Rhys became depressed and unsettled. According to Angier, Leslie Smith gave his wife a copy of Charlotte Bronte's nineteenth-century novel *Jane Eyre,* and by the end of 1939, by which time Smith had volunteered for the war effort and was traveling a great deal, Rhys had finished part if not all of a version of *Wide Sargasso Sea,* called at the time "Le Revenant" and based on *Jane Eyre.* Apparently, however, in one of the rages to which she was increasingly prone, she burned the typescript and, during a move, lost most of the manuscript. Angier reports that "many years later [Rhys] found 'two chapters (in another suitcase)', and used them for *Wide Sargasso Sea.* But she had to undergo much more suffering before she could create the final version of Antoinette," the novel's protagonist.

During the war, with her husband gone much of the time, Rhys did, in Angier's words, "cross a line between anguish and breakdown." Stories such as "The Insect World" reflect her wartime paranoia and her sense that "almost any book was better than life," as she declared in *Sleep It Off, Lady,* her final collection of short stories; the suicidal Teresa of "A Solid House" confirms, as does much of the writing of this period, Rhys's own precarious state. As Angier notes, Rhys struggled to transform her own fragile and violent states into art, but the emotions became again "too raw, too close to breakdown and delusion. Her notebooks and drafts for the stories show how close they were. They are wild, obsessive, almost illegible. . . ." When *Tigers Are Better-Looking* finally appeared in 1968, two of its most disturbing stories had been removed and were printed separately in *Penguin Modern Stories 1.*

Leslie Smith died suddenly in 1945, and Rhys's condition worsened. In 1947 she married Max Hamer, Smith's cousin and estate executor, who, like Rhys's first husband, was apparently involved in illegal financial dealings. In 1949 she "cracked" and was prosecuted for having raged at and assaulted a neighbor. She spent almost a week in the hospital wing of Holloway Prison and then was sent home on probation. She began to write the story "Let Them Call it Jazz," with which she struggled for over a decade; her fears that she was losing her ability to sustain either herself or her work seemed well founded. In 1950 Max Hamer was arrested for stealing checks and Rhys, supported anonymously during Hamer's imprisonment, was truly desperate and incapacitated. When she began to work again, Angier reports, "it was return to the very first form she had used, to lift the blackness of her first big 'smash': a diary. . . . The part of it she kept (for later she tore out most of its pages) was published in her autobiography, *Smile Please,*" after she died.

By now all of Rhys's books were out of print, and she had been virtually forgotten. She wrote erratically, more concerned with her health and finances than with her work; her novel based on *Jane Eyre* had been abandoned. In November 1949, however, an advertisement had appeared in the *New Statesman* seeking Jean Rhys or anyone who knew her whereabouts. It had been placed by Selma Vaz Dias, an actress who was familiar with Rhys's work and who wanted permission to adapt *Good Morning, Midnight* for a radio monologue. Vaz Dias and Rhys, who had seen

the ad, corresponded, and the actress gave an initial performance at the Anglo-French Art Centre in London. The production was rejected by the BBC, but Vaz Dias had initiated a kind of resurrection of Rhys. In 1957 the adaptation was finally broadcast and well received, starting a chain of events that would change the direction of Rhys's last years.

Francis Wyndham, an editor with Andre Deutsch, had long been an admirer of Rhys's work but had, like many others, presumed her dead. Wyndham and another Deutsch editor, Diana Athill, secured for Rhys an option on the novel that would become *Wide Sargasso Sea.* However, her depression, ill health, continued heavy drinking, and sporadic attention to the stories that would later comprise *Sleep It Off, Lady* delayed her completion of the novel. It took her eight years to finish a manuscript she had promised to have done in six to nine months. Moreover, *Wide Sargasso Sea* was more demanding than her other work had been. Structurally it was complicated because it was written in the context of another novel, *Jane Eyre,* retelling the story from the madwoman Bertha Mason's point of view and creating a history for the inarticulate Creole locked in the attic of an English mansion; psychologically it was complicated because of the obvious similarities between Rhys's own life and that of Antoinette/Bertha.

In 1936 Rhys and Leslie Smith had visited Dominica, the only time she returned to her homeland. Despite the troubling nature of Rhys's journey, Staley credits it with "enabl[ing] her to integrate the experience of her childhood with a mature sensibility in order to inform [*Wide Sargasso Sea*] with the deep and complex feelings that arose within her." But the problem involved more than coming to terms with one's past; as Athill declares in her introduction to *Jean Rhys: The Complete Novels,* "Nowhere else did [Rhys] write with more poignancy about what it is like to be rejected, and nowhere else did she go so deeply into something which filled her with a special terror because . . . there had been times when she felt it happening to herself: what it is like to be driven beyond your psychic strength, and go mad. At a hidden level the story of Antoinette and her mother is that of Jean and her own mother, and the story of Antoinette and Mr. Rochester is that of Jean and England; and it is from this hidden level that its vibrancy springs." In a sense, Rhys comes full cycle in *Wide Sargasso Sea,* defending the transplanted Creole woman locked away in England and searching for the voice to tell her story through a kind of hidden, primal language that is silenced by the white patriarchy in all the earlier novels. It is as if her earlier female protagonists are all somehow exonerated through the attempted revenge on Rochester who embodies all the English male betrayers of Rhys from Lancelot Smith onward.

Narratively, *Wide Sargasso Sea* is constructed around Antoinette's and Rochester's alternating voices, his discourse punctuated by a strange section in the middle of the novel where Antoinette returns to her old nurse; as Angier observes, "Whenever she was hurled most low, Jean found a black woman from her islands to speak for her." What is important in this last novel is not that Christophine speaks for Rhys and Antoinette, but that it is through the black woman that Rhys can speak with the most power, can disturb and disrupt the control Rochester has over her protagonist economically, physically, and linguistically. The end of the novel is somewhat problematic as the two stories merge, Antoinette having been taken to England where she replays in the last section Bertha Mason's suicide as she leaps from the burning roof of Thornfield. In Rhys's version, however, the conclusion is more open-ended than some critics allow; Antoinette/Bertha dreams Bronte's ending and then takes off down a dark passageway thinking, "Now at last I know why I was brought here and what I have to do." Whether or not she acts out the dream is left unclear; in either case, Rhys has transformed the madwoman into a woman who has taken control of her own narrative despite the presumably predetermined outcome. As Staley has pointed out, working within the framework of an already written story allowed Rhys to concentrate on "the tale of the telling rather than the telling of the tale."

Wide Sargasso Sea, which in 1967 won the W. H. Smith literary award and an award from the Royal Society of Literature, brought Rhys the success that had eluded her for so long. Yet despite moderate fame and the reissuance of all her earlier novels, Rhys was uncertain, unhappy, and ill; scholars and students plagued her, she was helpless when faced with legal or financial decisions, and she signed away artistic control and fifty percent of her profits to Vaz Dias, who began to exploit her. According to Angier, Rhys "retreated further and further into self-absorption, self-pity, and anger. She had always remembered feelings more than facts: now that she was old, and ill, and dying, she confused them utterly."

The years following *Wide Sargasso Sea* saw the publication of three more volumes of Rhys' work. In 1968 appeared the short story collection *Tigers Are Better-Looking,* which includes nine pieces from *The Left Bank* and eight previously published but theretofore uncollected pieces. In 1975, *My Day,* a trio of autobiographical sketches, was privately printed, followed in 1976 by *Sleep It Off, Lady,* mostly unpublished work, much of which predates the newer stories of *Tigers Are Better-Looking.* Staley considers this third volume "a kind of thematic code, or retrospective chorus, to all of Rhys's previous work" with a "clarity of focus" and "certainty of feeling within that narrow world she draws upon for her subject matter." Rhys herself, however, confessed that she regarded these last pieces "no good, no good, magazine stories."

In the last years before her death, Rhys worked with Plante on compiling her autobiography from scribbles, abandoned fragments of novels, diaries, and an increasingly unreliable memory. As described in *Difficult Women,* this was a grueling process during which Rhys despaired of the project, her life, and her previous work. Plante reports that Rhys saw writing as "a way of getting rid of something, something unpleasant especially" and that she considered herself " 'a pen . . . nothing but a pen' " through which a story told itself: " 'I think and think for a sentence, and every sentence I think for is wrong, I know it. Then, all at once, the illuminating sentence comes to me. Everything clicks into place.' " By the time Rhys was putting together her last work, the autobiography, which she felt compelled to do to set the record straight—"everything they say about me is wrong"—fewer and fewer illuminations were coming to her. She never did finish *Smile Please,* which is rather abruptly divided into two major sections: the first, reflections on her early life in Dominica, and the second, pre-1923 "first major drafts, or notes towards first drafts" dealing with her life in England, which Athill arranged and entitled "It began to grow cold." The volume also contains an appendix, "From a diary," drawn from entries Rhys had made over a period of some thirty years.

Six months before the publication of *Smile Please* in 1979, Rhys died, a lonely, angry woman who, despite receiving shortly before her death the CBE for her service to literature, saw herself finally only as part of something much greater than her own work. " 'All of writing is a huge lake,' " she had told Plante. " 'There are great rivers that feed the lake, like Tolstoy and Dostoevsky. And there are trickles, like Jean Rhys. All that matters is feeding the lake. I don't matter. The lake matters. You must keep feeding the lake.' "

BIOGRAPHICAL/CRITICAL SOURCES:

BOOKS

Angier, Carole, *Jean Rhys,* Penguin, 1985.
Bowen, Stella, *Drawn From Life: Reminiscences,* Collins, 1941.
Contemporary Literary Criticism, Gale, Volume 2, 1974, Volume 4, 1975, Volume 6, 1976, Volume 14, 1980, Volume 19, 1981, Volume 51, 1989.
Dictionary of Literary Biography, Volume 36: *British Novelists, 1890-1929: Modernists,* Gale, 1985.
Jacobs, Fred Rue, *Jean Rhys—Bibliography,* Loop Press, 1978.
Nebeker, Helen, *Jean Rhys: Woman in Passage,* Eden Press, 1981.
Plante, David, *Difficult Women: A Memoir of Three,* Atheneum, 1983.
Staley, Thomas F., *Jean Rhys: A Critical Study,* University of Texas Press, 1979.
Wolfe, Peter, *Jean Rhys,* Twayne, 1980.

PERIODICALS

Arizona Quarterly, autumn, 1976.
Bookseller, August 20, 1966.
Book World, April 5, 1970.
boundary 2, autumn/winter, 1982-83.
Caribbean Quarterly, September, 1973.
Chicago Tribune, September 9, 1987.
Contemporary Literature, autumn, 1972, spring, 1979, winter, 1985.
Critical Inquiry, winter, 1981.
Feminist Studies, June, 1978.
Globe and Mail (Toronto), August 11, 1984.
Los Angeles Times Book Review, November 4, 1984.
Massachusetts Review, autumn, 1976.
Ms., January, 1976.
Nation, October 2, 1967.
Newsweek, June 1, 1970, March 6, 1972.
New York Times, May 28, 1980, October 25, 1981, September 10, 1984, August 14, 1985.
New York Times Book Review, June 18, 1967, March 17, 1974, May 25, 1980, September 30, 1984.
Observer Review, June 11, 1967.
Punch, August 16, 1967.
Studies in the Literary Imagination, autumn, 1978.
Studies in the Novel, summer, 1984.
Sunday Times (London), December 17, 1967.
Times (London), May 17, 1984, May 21, 1984.
Times Literary Supplement, July 20, 1967.
Times Saturday Review (London), December 16, 1967.
Transatlantic Review, summer, 1970.
Twentieth-Century Literature, winter, 1982.
Washington Post Book World, June 8, 1980, October 30, 1983, June 28, 1987.
World Literature Written in English, autumn, 1985.
Yale French Studies, 1981.

*   *   *

RICE, Elmer (Leopold) 1892-1967

PERSONAL: Surname originally Reizenstein; born September 28, 1892, in New York, N.Y.; died of a heart attack, May 8, 1967, in Southampton, England; son of Jacob and Fanny (Lion)

Reizenstein; married Hazel Levy, June 16, 1915 (divorced January 10, 1942); married Betty Field (actress), January 12, 1942 (divorced, 1955); married Barbara A. Marshall; children: (first marriage) Robert, Margaret; (second marriage) John, Judith, Paul. *Education:* New York Law School, LL.B. (cum laude), 1912; attended Columbia University. *Politics:* Liberal. *Religion:* "I could never bring myself to an acceptance of ritual, dogma, and denominationalism; nor was I ever willing to submit to the authority of self-appointed spiritual guides."

ADDRESSES: Home—815 Long Ridge Rd., Stamford, Conn.

CAREER: Samstag and Hilder Bros., New York City, claims clerk, 1907; law clerk, 1908-12, admitted to New York Bar, 1913; dramatic director, University Settlement, and chairman, Inter-Settlement Dramatic Society, New York City; Samuel Goldwyn Pictures Corp., Hollywood, Calif., scenarist, 1918-20; Famous Players-Lasky Corp. and Real Art Films, Hollywood, free-lance writer, 1920; organized the Morningside Players with Hatcher Hughes, New York City; purchased and operated David Belasco Theatre, New York City, 1934-c. 1937; Works Progress Administration, Federal Theatre Project, regional director, New York City, 1935-36; Playwright's Producing Co., director and co-founder with Robert E. Sherwood, Maxwell Anderson, S. N. Behrman and Sidney Howard, 1937-59. University of Michigan, Ann Arbor, lecturer in English, 1954; New York University, New York City, adjunct professor, 1957-58. Directed numerous plays, including: Robert E. Sherwood's "Abe Lincoln in Illinois" (produced on Broadway at Plymouth Theatre, October 15, 1938, starring Raymond Massey); Maxwell Anderson's "Journey to Jerusalem" (produced on Broadway at National Theatre [now Billy Rose Theatre], October 5, 1940); S. N. Behrman's "The Talley Method" (produced on Broadway at Henry Miller's Theatre, February 24, 1941); "Second Fiddle" for Theatre Guild (closed out of town, 1953).

MEMBER: Dramatists Guild (founding member; contract committee, president, 1939-43), Authors League of America (Dramatists Guild representative on council; president, 1945-46), P.E.N. (former international vice-president, New York), American National Theatre and Academy (executive committee member), League of British Dramatists, National Council on Freedom from Censorship (chairman), National Institute of Arts and Letters, American Civil Liberties Union (board member), American Arbitration Association, Writer's War Board (advisory council member).

AWARDS, HONORS: Pulitzer Prize, 1929, for *Street Scene;* Canada Lee Foundation Award, 1954, for *The Winner;* Litt.D., University of Michigan, 1961.

WRITINGS:

PLAYS

On Trial (first produced in New York at Candler Theatre, August 19, 1914; produced in London's West End at Lyric Theatre, April 29, 1915), Samuel French, 1919.

The Adding Machine (first produced Off-Broadway at Garrick Theatre, March 19, 1923), Doubleday, Page & Co., 1923.

(With Hatcher Hughes) *Wake Up, Jonathan* (three-act comedy; first produced on Broadway at Henry Miller's Theatre, January 17, 1920), Samuel French, 1928.

(With Dorothy Parker) *Close Harmony, or The Lady Next Door* (first produced in New York at Gaiety Theatre, December 1, 1924), Samuel French, 1929.

(With Philip Barry) Cock Robin (three-act; first produced on Broadway at Forty Eighth Street Theatre, January 12, 1928), Samuel French, 1929.

(And director) *Street Scene* (three-act; first produced on Broadway at Plymouth Theatre, January 10, 1929), Samuel French, 1929 (adapted as musical with music by Kurt Weill, libretto by Rice, and lyrics by Langston Hughes; first produced in London's West End at Adelphi Theatre, January 9, 1947), Chappell, 1948.

The Subway (first produced Off-Broadway at Cherry Lane Theatre, January 25, 1929; later produced on Broadway), Samuel French, 1929.

See Naples and Die (three-act comedy; first produced in New York at Vanderbilt Theatre, September 24, 1929), Samuel French, 1930.

The Left Bank (first produced by Rice on Broadway at Little Theatre, October 5, 1931), Samuel French, 1931.

Counsellor-at-Law (three-act; first produced on Broadway at Plymouth Theatre, November 6, 1931, and at Royale Theatre, November 24, 1942), Samuel French, 1931.

House in Blind Alley (three-act comedy), Samuel French, 1932.

We, the People (first produced in New York at Empire Theatre, January 21, 1933), Coward, 1933.

The Home of the Free (first produced in repertory by the Washington Square Players in New York at Comedy Theatre, 1917), Samuel French, 1934.

Judgment Day (three-act melodrama; first produced on Broadway at Belasco Theatre, September 12, 1934; produced in London's West End at Strand Theatre, 1935), Coward, 1934.

The Passing of Chow-Chow (one-act comedy written in 1913 for Columbia University one-act play contest), Samuel French, 1935.

Between Two Worlds (first produced on Broadway at Belasco Theatre, October 25, 1934), published with "Not for Children," as *Not for Children* [and] *Between Two Worlds,* Coward, 1935.

"Life is Real" (first produced in San Francisco, 1937; produced under title "Not for Children," directed by Rice, on Broadway at Coronet Theatre [now Eugene O'Neill Theatre], February 13, 1951), published with "Between Two Worlds" as *Not for Children* [and] *Between Two Worlds,* Coward, 1935, published as *Not for Children,* Samuel French, 1951.

Black Sheep (three-act comedy; first produced on Broadway at Morosco Theatre, October 13, 1932), Dramatists Play Service, 1938.

(And director) *American Landscape* (three-act; first produced on Broadway at Cort Theatre, December 3, 1938), Coward, 1939.

(And director) *Two on an Island* (first produced on Broadway at Broadhurst Theatre, January 22, 1940), Coward, 1940.

(And director) *Flight to the West* (first produced on Broadway at Guild Theatre [now American National Theatre & Academy, ANTA], December 30, 1940), Coward, 1941.

(And director) *A New Life* (first produced on Broadway at Royale Theatre, September 9, 1943), Coward, 1944.

(And director) *Dream Girl* (comedy; first produced on Broadway at Coronet Theatre [now Eugene O'Neill Theatre], December 14, 1945), Coward, 1946, final script, Feuer & Martin Productions, 1965.

(And director) *The Grand Tour* (two-act; first produced on Broadway at Martin Beck Theatre, December 10, 1951), Dramatists Play Service, 1952.

(And director) *The Winner* (first produced on Broadway at Plymouth Theatre, February 17, 1954), Dramatists Play Service, 1954.

(And director) *Cue for Passion* (first produced on Broadway at Henry Miller's Theatre, November 25, 1958), Dramatists Play Service, 1959.

Love Among the Ruins (two-act; first produced at University of Rochester, 1963), Dramatists Play Service, 1963.

The Iron Cross (first produced in New York at Comedy Theatre, February 13, 1917), Proscenium Press, 1965.

Also author of "A Diadem of Show" (one-act), published in *The Liberator,* 1918, and of unpublished and unproduced play "Find the Woman," c. 1918. Work represented in anthologies, including *Famous American Plays of the Nineteen Twenties,* edited by Kenneth MacGowan, Dell, 1980.

PLAYS PRODUCED ONLY

"For the Defense," first produced on Broadway at Playhouse Theatre, December 19, 1919.

"It Is the Law" (dramatization of Hayden Talbot's unpublished novel), first produced in New York at Ritz Theatre, November 19, 1922.

"The Mongrel" (adaptation of play by Hermann Bahr), first produced on Broadway at Longacre Theatre, December 15, 1924.

"Is He Guilty?" (adaptation of play "The Blue Hawaii" by Rudolph Lothar), closed in Boston, Mass., September, 1927.

OTHER

(Editor) *One Act Plays for Stage and Study,* fifth series, Samuel French, 1929.

A Voyage to Purilia (novel; serialized in *New Yorker*), Cosmopolitan Book, 1930.

Imperial City (novel), Coward, 1937.

The Show Must Go On (novel), Viking, 1949.

Supreme Freedom, Graphics Group, 1949.

The Living Theatre, Harper, 1959.

Minority Report (autobiography), Simon & Schuster, 1963.

Also author or co-author of screenplays, including "Help Yourself," Goldwyn Pictures Corp., 1920; "Doubling for Romeo," Goldwyn Pictures Corp., 1921; "Street Scene," United Artists, 1931; and "Counsellor-at-Law," Universal Pictures, 1933. Author of unpublished novel "Papa Looks for Something," c. 1926.

Contributor of articles and stories to *Collier's, New Yorker,* and other periodicals. Rice's works have also appeared in omnibus volumes.

SIDELIGHTS: "There have always been at least three Rice's to keep track of," wrote a reviewer in *Newsweek.* "One is the professional Rice—prolific, erratic, a restless innovator, a superb craftsman, winner of the Pulitzer Prize. The second is the public Rice—unselfish, bold, a socialist who has held fast to principles. . . . Finally, there is the private Rice—cool, casual, emotionally uncommitted. His life was often dictated by happenstance, and he sometimes seems, in his autobiography, hardly to exist at all."

The public Rice regarded the Broadway theatre as a platform to express his views. "Justice was the subject to which he was most passionately devoted," commented Brooks Atkinson, "and he wrote for a theatre that believed in taking sides and making partisan statements." He began championing causes early in his career. "I had been one of a small male contingent that had marched up Fifth Avenue in a woman-suffrage parade headed by the beautiful Inez Milholland astride a white horse," wrote Rice in his autobiography, *Minority Report.* He fought child labor with his play, "The House in Blind Alley."

Along with the American Civil Liberties Union he was instrumental in instituting a screening process by which many Japanese internees were released from West Coast concentration camps during World War II. His longest battle, perhaps, was against blacklisting and the "new wave of anti-liberalism" that swept the country in the 1940s and 1950s. Because of his left wing views (established in youth through the writings of George Bernard Shaw and H. G. Wells), Rice was constantly on everyone's "red" or "front" list. He insisted, however, that his penchant for socialism did not include Marxism or Leninism, or "any historical or economic dogma, but the development of a society in which the implements of production are employed primarily for the satisfaction of human needs, rather than for the enrichment and aggrandizement of a few individuals. There is no greater fallacy than the identification of the imperialism and totalitarianism of the Soviet Union with true socialism." He was never a member of the Socialist or any other party and claimed his socialism was of the "utopian variety." The many right-wing booklets and exposes released in that period placed Rice in excellent company, however, for among others named as possible dupes of the Kremlin were Clifford Odets, Lillian Hellman, Garson Kanin, Arthur Miller, Oscar Hammerstein II, and Gypsy Rose Lee. Rice was incredulous that "Freud and Gandhi were not included."

Rice has been praised for his role in opposing censorship throughout his lifetime. When Albert Deutsch, a New York columnist, called the film version of *Oliver Twist* flagrantly anti-Semitic and caused delay in the American opening, Rice became active in the campaign to release the picture. He convinced the Jewish organizations "that it was one thing to criticize and condemn the picture, to urge people not to see it, even to picket the theatres in which it might be shown, but quite another to prevent it from being shown at all. In a democratic society there should be no sacred cows; no one should claim immunity from criticism or even from ridicule." Rice also encountered censorship with his own works. While filming "Street Scene" he was notified that Miss Simpson would not be characterized as a social worker "unless she is shown as a kindly and tolerant person." With his views on censorship it is ironic that Rice felt that the highest honor ever paid him was the Nazis' inclusion of his published works in a book-burning.

Although his political plays, *We, the People, Judgment Day, Between Two Worlds,* and *Flight to the West,* were powerful advocates for social change, he is more apt to be remembered for his expressionism and theatrical innovations. His play *On Trial* presented the first attempt at the flashback technique on the stage. Louis Sherwin of the *New York Globe* wrote: "Can you imagine the wickedness of a play that has the sheer audacity to be original? A play that breaks well-nigh every rule of construction that has been dinned into our ears by the professors? A play that has the impertinence to be a good play instead of a well-made play? . . . 'On Trial' contains the most radical innovation in play construction, the most striking novelty that has been seen for years. Undoubtedly, it will bring about important changes in the technique of the theatre."

Rice, however, was not entirely impressed with his success, noting that "a good theatrical craftsman is not necessarily a worthy dramatist, a distinction that the reviewers failed to make." After a few failures, Rice began to take his writing seriously with *The Adding Machine,* which, he recalled, "flashed into my mind—characters, plot, incidents, title, and some of the dialogue." The play, which concerns a man who is replaced by a machine and subsequently kills his boss, was written in the stylized, intensified form of expressionism. An allegation has persisted that he borrowed liberally from the German expressionists, but Rice insisted that, although he had heard of expressionism, he had not read any of the German plays until after the play was written. Since its inception, *The Adding Machine* has had innumerable productions.

His most notable success (601 consecutive performances on Broadway), however, was *Street Scene,* a panoramic impression of New York. The set, designed by Jo Mielzner (as were many other sets for Rice's plays), contained a typical Manhattan brownstone walk-up apartment house that was an integral part of the play. "I was excited by the concept of a large number of diverse individuals whose behavior and relationships were largely conditioned by their accidental common occupancy of a looming architectural pile," wrote Rice. "To some extent, the play adhered to the classical unities. The single setting was analogous to the traditional temple or palace; the elapsed time was less than a day. There even the superficial resemblance ended, for instead of unity of action there was a multitude of varied and seemingly irrelevant incidents. Blending and arranging these unrelated elements into a patterned mosaic and introducing the many characters in a seemingly natural way posed technical problems of the greatest difficulty. The play is, by all odds, the most experimental I have ever attempted, a fact not readily apparent to the reader or spectator, for its construction depends not upon novel or striking technological devices, but upon concealed architectonics." *Street Scene* was originally rejected by the Theatre Guild for lack of content, and, after numerous other rejections, William A. Brady, a one-time leading producer who had not had a success for twelve years, agreed to take on the play. The critics, although praising the play themselves, expressed doubts concerning its popular appeal. For example, a *Variety* reviewer wrote: "Whether this play which starts so interestingly will catch high public favor is questionable," but the line in front of the box office did not break for six months.

Because of his caustic remarks and one unfortunate speech at Columbia University, Rice was often regarded as a chronic critic-baiter. At Columbia, Rice had remarked that "the critics were fostering the theatre of sterile entertainment" and were "discouraging innovators and rebels. With a few honorable exceptions, they were stupid and illiterate." The private Rice, however, was a modest man who wrote in his autobiography: "Since I became aware early of my artistic limitations, I have not essayed to scale unattainable heights or attempted Icarian flights. If it is true that a man's reach should exceed his grasp, I deserve commendation, for my aspirations have always exceeded my achievements."

MEDIA ADAPTATIONS: On Trial was made into a motion picture by Essanay Film Manufacturing Co., 1917, by Warner Bros., 1928, and remade by Warner Bros., 1939; "For the Defense" was filmed by Famous Players-Lasky Corp., 1922, by Paramount, 1930; *It Is the Law* was filmed by Fox Film Corp., 1924; *See Naples and Die* was made into a movie by Warner Bros. under the title "Oh! Sailor, Behave," 1930; *Dream Girl* was filmed by Paramount Pictures, 1948, and was the basis for the musical "Skyscraper," 1966; *The Adding Machine* was filmed by Universal Pictures, 1969. *The Grand Tour* was adapted for television on the "U.S. Steel Hour," August 17, 1954. The Theatre Guild presented many of Rice's best known plays on radio, 1949-54.

BIOGRAPHICAL/CRITICAL SOURCES:

BOOKS

Contemporary Literary Criticism, Gale, Volume 7, 1977, Volume 49, 1988.

Dictionary of Literary Biography, Gale, Volume 4: *American Writers in Paris, 1920-1939,* 1980, Volume 7: *Twentieth-Century American Dramatists,* 1981.
Lumley, Frederick, *New Trends in Twentieth Century Drama,* Oxford University Press, 1967.

PERIODICALS

Chicago Tribune, November 25, 1985.
Newsweek, August 26, 1963.
Time, August 30, 1963.

OBITUARIES:

PERIODICALS

Newsweek, May 22, 1967.
New York Times, May 9, 1967.
Time, May 19, 1967.
Village Voice, May 11, 1967.

*   *   *

RICH, Adrienne (Cecile) 1929-

PERSONAL: Born May 16, 1929, in Baltimore, Md.; daughter of Arnold Rice (a physician) and Helen Elizabeth (Jones) Rich; married Alfred Haskell Conrad (an economist), June 26, 1953 (died, 1970); children: David, Paul, Jacob. *Education:* Radcliffe College, A.B. (cum laude), 1951.

ADDRESSES: Office—Department of English, Stanford University, Stanford, Calif. 94305.

CAREER: Poet. Conductor of workshop, YM-YWHA Poetry Center, New York City, 1966-67; visiting lecturer, Swarthmore College, Swarthmore, Penn., 1967-69; adjunct professor in writing division, Columbia University, Graduate School of the Arts, New York City, 1967-69; City College of the City University of New York, New York City, lecturer in SEEK English program, 1968-70, instructor in creative writing program, 1970-71, assistant professor of English, 1971-72, and 1974-75; Fannie Hurst Visiting Professor of Creative Literature, Brandeis University, Waltham, Mass., 1972-73; Lucy Martin Donelly fellow, Bryn Mawr College, 1975; professor of English, Douglass College, Rutgers University, New Brunswick, N.J., 1976-78; A. D. White Professor-at-Large, Cornell University, 1981-86; Clark Lecturer and distinguished visiting professor, Scripps College, Claremont, Calif., 1983; Burgess Lecturer, Pacific Oaks College, Pasadena, Calif., 1986; professor of English and feminist studies, Stanford University, Stanford, Calif., 1986—. Member of advisory board, Boston Woman's Fund and New Jewish Agenda.

MEMBER: P.E.N., Modern Language Association (honorary fellow, 1985—), Authors Guild, Authors League of America, Phi Beta Kappa.

AWARDS, HONORS: Yale Series of Younger Poets award, 1951, for *A Change of World;* Guggenheim fellowships, 1952 and 1961; Ridgely Torrence Memorial Award of the Poetry Society of America, 1955; Grace Thayer Bradley Award, Friends of Literature (Chicago), 1956, for *The Diamond Cutters and Other Poems;* Phi Beta Kappa Poet, College of William and Mary, 1960, Swarthmore College, 1965, and Harvard University, 1966; National Institute of Arts and Letters award for poetry, 1961; Amy Lowell travelling fellowship, 1962; Bollingen Foundation translation grant, 1962; Bess Hokin Prize of *Poetry* magazine, 1963; Litt.D., Wheaton College, 1967; National Translation Center grant, 1968; Eunice Tietjens Memorial Prize of *Poetry* magazine, 1968; National Endowment for the Arts grant, 1970, for poems in *American Literary Anthology: 3;* Shelley Memorial Award of Poetry Society of America, 1971; Ingram Merrill Foundation grant, 1973-74; National Book Award, 1974, for *Diving into the Wreck: Poems, 1971-1972;* National Book Critics Circle Award in Poetry nomination, 1978, for *The Dream of a Common Language: Poems, 1974-1977;* Litt.D., Smith College, 1979; Fund for Human Dignity Award, National Gay Task Force, 1981; *Los Angeles Times* Book Prize nomination, 1982, for *A Wild Patience Has Taken Me This Far: Poems, 197&-1981;* Ruth Lilly Poetry Prize, Modern Poetry Association and American Council for the Arts, 1986.

WRITINGS:

POETRY

A Change of World, with foreword by W. H. Auden, Yale University Press, 1951, reprinted, AMS Press, 1971.

Poems, Fantasy Press/Oxford University Poetry Society, 1952.

The Diamond Cutters and Other Poems, Harper, 1955, reprinted, University Microfilms, 1978.

The Knight, after Rilke, privately printed, 1957.

Snapshots of a Daughter-in-Law: Poems, 1954-1962, Harper, 1963, revised edition, Norton, 1967.

Focus, [Cambridge, Mass.], 1966.

Necessities of Life, Norton, 1966.

Selected Poems, Chatto & Windus, 1967.

Leaflets: Poems, 1965-1968, Norton, 1969.

The Will to Change: Poems, 1968-1970 (also see below), Norton, 1971.

Diving into the Wreck: Poems, 1971-1972, Norton, 1973.

Poems: Selected and New, 1950-1974, Norton, 1974.

Adrienne Rich's Poetry: Texts of the Poems, The Poet on Her Work, Reviews and Criticism, edited by Barbara Charlesworth Gelpi and Albert Gelpi, Norton, 1975.

Pieces (poem; previously published in *The Will to Change: Poems, 1968-1970*), Poythress Press (San Francisco), 1977.

Twenty-One Love Poems (also see below), Effie's Press (Emeryville, Calif.), 1977.

The Dream of a Common Language: Poems, 1974-1977 [bound with *Twenty-One Love Poems*], Norton, 1978.

A Wild Patience Has Taken Me This Far: Poems, 1978-1981, Norton, 1981.

Sources, Heyeck Press (Woodside, Calif.), 1983.

The Fact of a Doorframe: Poems Selected and New, 1950-1984, Norton, 1984.

Your Native Land, Your Life, Norton, 1986.

Time's Power: Poems, 1985-1988, Norton, 1989.

PROSE

Of Woman Born: Motherhood as Experience and Institution, Norton, 1976.

Women and Honor: Some Notes on Lying (monograph), Motheroot Publishing, Pittsburgh Women Writers, 1977.

On Lies, Secrets and Silence: Selected Prose, 1966-1978, Norton, 1979.

Compulsory Heterosexuality and Lesbian Existence (mongraph), Onlywomen Press, 1981, Antelope Publications (Denver, Colo.), 1982.

Blood, Bread and Poetry: Selected Prose, 1979-1986, Norton, 1986.

PLAYS

Ariadne: A Play in Three Acts and Poems, J. H. Furst (Baltimore), 1939.

Not I, But Death, A Play in One Act, J. H. Furst, 1941.

CONTRIBUTOR

Anthony Ostroff, editor, *The Poet As Critic,* Little, Brown, 1965.

Janine Hensley, editor, *The Works of Anne Bradstreet,* Harvard University Press, 1967.

Robert Lowell, Peter Taylor, and Robert Penn Warren, editors, *Randall Jarrell, 1914-1965,* Farrrr, Straus, 1967.

TRANSLATOR

(With Aijaz Ahmad and William Stafford) Ahmad, editor, *Poems by Ghalib,* Hudson Review, 1969.

Mark Insingel, *Reflections,* Red Dust, 1973.

CONTRIBUTOR OF TRANSLATIONS

Olga Carlisle, editor, *Poets on Street Corners: Portraits of 15 Russian Poets,* Random House, 1968.

Irving Howe and Eliezer Greenberg, editors, *A Treasury of Yiddish Poetry,* Holt 1969.

Ahmad, editor, *Selected Poems of Mirza Ghalib,* Columbia University Press, 1971.

CONTRIBUTOR TO ANTHOLOGIES

Donald Hall, editor, *Contemporary American Poetry,* Penguin, 1962.

New Poets of England and America, Meridian, 1962.

P. Leary and Robert Kelly, editors, *A Controversy of Poets,* Doubleday, 1965.

John Hollander, editor, *Poems of Our Moment,* Pegasus, 1968.

Mark Strand, editor, *The Contemporary American Poets: American Poetry since 1940,* New American Library, 1969.

Hayden Carruth, editor, *The Voice That Is Great Within Us: American Poetry of the Twentieth Century,* Bantam, 1970.

Oscar Williams, editor, *A Little Treasury of Modern Poetry, English and American,* Scribner, 1970.

George Plimpton and Peter Ardery, editors, *American Literary Anthology: 3,* Viking, 1970.

Robert Vas Dias, editor, *Inside Outer Space: New Poems of the Space Age,* Anchor Books, 1970.

Florence Howe and Ellen Bass, editors, *No More Masks!: An Anthology of Poems by Women,* Anchor Press, 1973.

Barbara Segnitz and Carol Rainey, editors, *Psyche—The Feminine Poetic Consciousness: An Anthology of Modern American Women Poets,* Dial, 1973.

Richard Ellmann, editor, *The New Oxford Book of American Verse,* Oxford University Press, 1976.

Carol Konek and Dorothy Walters, editors, *I Hear My Sisters Saying: Poems by Twentieth-Century Women,* Crowell, 1976.

A. Poulin, Jr., editor, *Contemporary American Poetry,* 3rd edition, Houghton, 1980.

RECORDINGS

"Adrienne Rich Reading at Stanford," Stanford, 1973.

(With others) "A Sign I Was Not Alone," Out and Out, 1978.

Also recorded, with others, "Today's Poets Four," Folkways.

OTHER

Contributor of reviews and critical articles to *Poetry, Nation, New York Review of Books, Partisan Review, Boston Review, Women's Review of Books, Freedomways, New York Times Book Review, Village Voice,* and other publications. Columnist, *American Poetry Review,* 1972-73. Co-editor, *Sinister Wisdom,* 1981-84; contributing editor, *Chrysalis: A Magazine of Women's Culture.*

SIDELIGHTS: "Adrienne Rich is not just one of America's best feminist poets," writes Margaret Atwood in *Second Words: Selected Critical Prose,* "or one of America's best woman poets, she is one of America's best poets." Rich's poetry has not always been described as "feminist." She "began as [a] poet-ingenue," according to Carol Muske in the *New York Times Book Review,* "polite copyist of Yeats and Auden, wife and mother. She has progressed in life (and in her poems . . .) from young widow and disenchanted formalist, to spiritual and rhetorical convalescent, to feminist leader . . . and *doyenne* of a newly-defined female literature." In *Poet and Critic* David Zuger describes a similar metamorphosis in Rich's work. He writes, "The 20-year-old author of painstaking, decorous poems that are eager to 'maturely' accept the world they are given becomes a . . . poet of prophetic intensity and 'visionary anger' bitterly unable to feel at home in a world 'that gives no room to be what we dreamt of being.'"

Albert Gelpi observes that Rich's stance in her early poems is far from feminist. In *American Poetry since 1960* Gelpi notes that in W. H. Auden's foreword to *A Change of World,* Rich's introductory book of poetry, Auden said her poems "are neatly and modestly dressed, speak quietly but do not mumble, respect their elders but are not cowed by them, and do not tell fibs." "In other words," Gelpi comments, "[the poems reflect] the stereotype— prim, fussy and schoolmarmish—that has corseted and straitlaced women-poets into 'poetesses' whom men could deprecate with admiration." In *Writing Like a Woman,* Alicia Ostriker states, "Rich at this point [was] a cautious good poet in the sense of being a good girl, a quality noted with approval by her early reviewers."

Critics Ruth Whitman and Le Anne Schrieber see Rich's development as a reflection of the changing consciousness of women in general during the last half of the twentieth century. In *Harvard Magazine* Whitman observes, "Rich's process of transformation over the years has been an astonishing phenomenon to watch: in one woman the history of women in our country, from careful and traditional obedience (that was Auden's description of her) to cosmic awareness." Schrieber notes in the *New York Times:* "[Rich] has written through youth, fame, marriage, motherhood, separation, solitude, political rage, [and] feminist awakening. In its broad outlines . . . her progress through the decades has paralleled that of her generation of women."

The evolution in Rich's work is a result of the poet's growth from imitation to personal discovery and disclosure. In the *Dictionary of Literary Biography,* Anne Newman observes that Rich's first book contains "many echoes of her masters" but only "muted notes of her personal voice," while in the *Michigan Quarterly Review,* Laurence Goldstein declares, "Rich's career really began when she emerged from the shadow of influence and began to speak in the impassioned rhythms of her own reveries."

Many critics find in Rich's book *Snapshots of a Daughter-in Law: Poems, 1954-1962* the first indication of both the end of Rich's imitative efforts and the beginning of her concern with feminist issues. In *Southwest Review,* Willard Spiegelman calls *Snapshots* "the liminal volume, attempting a journey from one self, world, poetic form, to another." Spiegelman notes that the poem, "Roof-walker" articulates Rich's precarious position as a poet balancing between two modes of writing: "exposed, larger than life, / and due to break my neck." Ostriker also comments on the change in Rich's poetry evident in *Snapshots.* Calling the collection "Rich's break-through volume," Ostriker notes that the book's title poem "consists of fragmentary and odd-shaped sections instead of stanzas, and has the immediacy and force which Rich did not attempt earlier."

Snapshots offers the reader a change in the form of Rich's poetry, as Ostriker observes. This change, according to Newman, includes "dropping the initial capital letter in each line, increasing enjambment, using speech cadences in place of formal meters, limiting the use of rhyme, and varying stanza length." The content of Rich's poetry changes also. Her work begins to reflect her personal confrontation with what it means to be female in a male dominated society. In Rich's 1971 essay, "When We Dead Awaken: Writing as Re-vision," quoted by Newman, the poet comments: "In the late fifties I was able to write, for the first time, directly about experiencing myself as a woman—Until then I had tried very hard not to identify myself as a female poet. Over two years I wrote . . . 'Snapshots of a Daughter-in-Law' (1958-60), in a longer, looser mode than I'd ever trusted myself with before. It was an extraordinary relief to write that poem."

The happiness that Rich felt upon writing "Snapshots" was not echoed by all readers of the book in which it was published. Negative criticism crept into the reviews of previously enthusiastic critics. In "Blood, Bread and Poetry," an essay which first appeared in the *Massachusetts Review,* Rich explains what happened: "In the fifties and early sixties there was much shaking of heads if an artist was found meddling in politics; art was mystical and universal but the artist was also, apparently irresponsible and emotional, and politically naive. . . . In my own case, as soon as I published . . . a book of poems which was informed by any conscious sexual politics [Snapshots], I was told, in print, that this work was 'bitter,' 'personal'; and I had sacrificed the sweetly flowing measures of my earlier books for a ragged line and a coarsened voice."

"Snapshots," Wendy Martin notes in *American Triptych: Ann Bradstreet, Emily Dickinson, Adrienne Rich,* "marks the beginning of a personal and political pilgrimage; subsequent works describe the stages of the journey." Rich's journey through greater and greater degrees of personal and political awareness has alienated some critics while pleasing others. A *Times Literary Supplement* reviewer states, for example, that while the poet "began as an elegant American," she has since "lost a great deal of her intensity." In the *New York Review of Books,* Rosemary Tonks writes: "In . . . Rich's work, the moral proportions are valid, the protagonists are sane, responsible persons, and the themes are moving on their courses. Why is it then that we are still waiting for the poetry? . . . She has taken on too much, and the imagination is exhausted by the effort required to familiarize itself with all the burdens of the modern world." And, in the *New Republic,* Barbara Grizzuti Harrison calls Rich "a polemicist . . . [whose] respect and love for the written word [is] betrayed by her ideology."

Frequently, Rich is criticized for the harsh depictions of males in her poetry. This is especially true in reviews of *Diving into the Wreck: Poems, 1971-1972* and *A Wild Patience Has Taken Me This Far: Poems, 1978-1981.* Ostriker comments on what she calls Rich's "partisanship" and observes, "Men in [*Diving into the Wreck*] are depicted universally and exclusively as parasitic on women, emotionally threatened by them, brutal . . . and undeserving of pity." In *Parnassus: Poetry in Review,* Helen Vendler notes that the poem "Rape" from *Diving into the Wreck,* seems to bestow on all men the image of the sadistic rapist portrayed in the work. "This poem," she writes, "like some others [in the volume], is a deliberate refusal of the modulations of intelligence in favor of . . . propaganda." Similarly, in the *Voice Literary Supplement,* Kathryn Kilgore calls *A Wild Patience* "a ritual of man-hatred" while in the *Times Literary Supplement* Jay Parini states that in some of the poems in the volume Rich "wilfully misrepresents men, committing the same act of distortions that she complains about elsewhere."

On the other hand, *Diving into the Wreck* was granted the prestigious National Book Award (Rich declined the award as an individual but accepted it on behalf of all women and donated the cash award to a charitable organization) and praised by many critics. Goldstein, for example, believes it is "Rich's finest single volume," and observes that the title poem is "a modern classic." In *Harvard Magazine,* Ruth Whitman calls the same piece "one of the great poems of our time."

In her *Ms.* review of the book, Erica Jong declares that Rich handles political issues well in her poetry. "Rich is one of the few poets," she states, "who can deal with political issues in her poems without letting them degenerate into social realism." Focusing on the title poem, Jong also denies that Rich is anti-male. A portion of the poem reads: "And I am here, the mermaid whose dark hair / streams black, the merman in his armored body. / We circle silently / about the wreck. / We dive into the hold. / I am she: I am he." Jong comments, "This stranger-poet-survivor carries 'a book of myths' in which her/his 'names do not appear.' These are the old myths . . . that perpetuate the battle between the sexes. Implicit in Rich's image of the androgyne is the idea that we must write new myths, create new definitions of humanity which will not glorify this angry chasm but heal it." *A Wild Patience* received similar if not as abundant praise. For instance, Sara Mandlebaum notes in *Ms.* that in the volume "the radicalism of [Rich's] vision . . . remains strong and invigorating: the writing as lyrical . . . and moving as ever—and even more honest."

Rich's prose has caused as much controversy as her poetry. Newman discusses the reception of *Of Woman Born: Motherhood as Experience and Institution,* Rich's study of the concept of motherhood. "Some critical reactions to the book," Newman observes, "are almost vehement, claiming Rich's perspective has been clouded by a rage that has led her into biased statements and a strident style. Others, who have read it with more sympathy, call it scholarly and well researched and insist that it should not be read . . . for polemics." In her *New York Times Book Review* critique of the volume, for example, Francine du Plessix Gray writes, "It is vexing to see such a dedicated feminist playing the dangerous game of using the oppressor's tactics. Going from mythologization of history to remythologization of male and female character traits, Rich indulges in stereotypes throughout the book." Speaking of the same book, but representative of the other half of the critics, Laura E. Casari comments in *Prairie Schooner:* "[In *Of Woman Born* Rich] thoroughly documents the powerlessness of women in a patriarchal culture and vividly depicts its results."

Rich's recent prose and poetry appear to be far removed from the poems that spoke quietly to W. H. Auden more than thirty years ago. Rich's recent work seems more in line with the description of her recorded in *The Journals of Sylvia Plath.* After Plath's first meeting with Rich, Plath wrote: "Adrienne Cecile Rich: little, round and dumpy, all vibrant short black hair; great sparkling black eyes and a tulip-red umbrella: honest, frank, forthright and even opinionated." Despite criticism, Rich refuses to keep her opinions to herself and, according to Martin, by doing so "establishes a coherent point of view, a feminist identity and poetic vision which becomes part of the composite reality of a community. Her poetry, then, like all good poetry changes the way we perceive and experience the world."

BIOGRAPHICAL/CRITICAL SOURCES:

BOOKS

Altieri, Charles, *Self and Sensibility in Contemporary American Poetry,* Cambridge University Press, 1984.

Atwood, Margaret, *Second Words: Selected Critical Prose,* House of Anansi Press, 1982.

Contemporary Literary Criticism, Gale, Volume 3, 1975, Volume 6, 1976, Volume 7, 1977, Volume 9, 1979, Volume 18, 1981, Volume 36, 1986.

Cooper, Jane Roberta, editor, *Reading Adrienne Rich: Reviews and Re-Visions, 1951-81,* University of Michigan Press, 1984.

Dictionary of Literary Biography, Gale, Volume 5: *American Poets since World War II,* 1980, Volume 67: *Modern American Critics since 1955,* 1988.

Gelpi, Barbara Charlesworth and Albert Gelpi, editors, *Adrienne Rich's Poetry: Texts of the Poems, the Poet on Her Work, Reviews and Criticism,* Norton, 1975.

Kalstone, David, *Five Temperaments: Elizabeth Bishop, Robert Lowell, James Merrill, Adrienne Rich, John Ashbery,* Oxford University Press, 1977.

Martin, Wendy, *An American Triptych: Anne Bradstreet, Emily Dickinson, Adrienne Rich,* University of North Carolina Press, 1984.

McDaniel, Judith, *Reconstituting the World: The Poetry and Vision of Adrienne Rich,* Spinsters Ink (Argyle, N.Y.), 1979.

Ostriker, Alicia, *Writing Like a Woman,* University of Michigan Press, 1983.

Plath, Sylvia, *The Journals of Sylvia Plath,* edited by Ted Hughes and Frances McCullough, Dial Press, 1982.

Rich, Adrienne, *A Change of World,* foreword by W. H. Auden, Yale University Press, 1951.

Rich, Adrienne, *Snapshots of a Daughter-in-Law: Poems, 1954-1962,* Harper, 1963.

Rich, Andrienne, *Diving into the Wreck: Poems, 1971-1972,* Norton, 1973.

Shaw, Robert B., editor, *American Poetry since 1960: Some Critical Perspectives,* Carcanet, 1973.

Vendler, Helen, *Part of Nature, Part of Us: Modern American Poets,* Harvard University Press, 1980.

Wagner, Linda W., *American Modern: Essays in Fiction and Poetry,* Kennikat, 1980.

PERIODICALS

America, February 26, 1977.

American Poetry Review, September/October 1973, March/April, 1975, July/August, 1979.

Atlantic, June, 1978.

Christian Science Monitor, August 18, 1966, July 24, 1969, January 26, 1977.

Contemporary Literature, winter, 1975.

Harper's, December, 1973, November, 1978.

Harvard Magazine, July-August, 1975, January-February, 1977.

Hudson Review, autumn, 1971, autumn, 1975.

Los Angeles Times, April 23, 1986, June 7, 1986.

Los Angeles Times Book Review, October 17, 1982, March 25, 1984, August 10, 1986, March 1, 1987.

Massachusetts Review, autumn, 1983.

Michigan Quarterly Review, summer, 1976, winter, 1983.

Modern Poetry Studies, autumn, 1977.

Ms., July, 1973, December, 1981.

Nation, July 28, 1951, October 8, 1973, July 1, 1978, December 23, 1978.

New Leader, May 26, 1975.

New Republic, November 6, 1976, December 9, 1978, June 2, 1979, January 7-14, 1985.

Newsweek, October 18, 1976.

New Yorker, November 3, 1951.

New York Review of Books, May 7, 1970, October 4, 1973, September 30, 1976, December 17, 1981.

New York Times, May 13, 1951, August 25, 1973.

New York Times Book Review, July 17, 1966, May 23, 1971, December 30, 1973, April 27, 1975, October 10, 1976, June 11, 1978, April 22, 1979, December 9, 1981, December 20, 1981, January 7, 1985, January 20, 1985, December 14, 1986, January 18, 1987, March 15, 1987, October 22, 1989.

Parnassus: Poetry in Review, fall-winter, 1973, spring-summer, 1979.

Partisan Review, winter, 1978.

Poet and Critic, Volume 9, number 2, 1976, Volume 10, number 2, 1978.

Poetry, February, 1955, July, 1963, March, 1970, February, 1976.

Prairie Schooner, summer, 1978.

Salmagundi, spring-summer, 1973, spring-summer, 1979.

Saturday Review, December 18, 1971, November 13, 1976.

Southern Review, April, 1969.

Southwest Review, autumn, 1975.

Times Literary Supplement, November 23, 1967, June 9, 1972, April 20, 1973, November 12, 1982, July 20, 1984, July 10, 1987, September 15-21, 1989.

Tribune Books (Chicago), July 9, 1989.

Village Voice, November 8, 1976.

Voice Literary Supplement, December, 1981.

Washington Post Book World, December 23, 1973, November 14, 1976, December 5, 1976, December 3, 1978, May 6, 1979, May 20, 1982.

Western Humanities Review, autumn, 1975.

Women's Review of Books, December, 1983.

World Literature Today, winter, 1979.

Yale Review, autumn, 1956, autumn, 1978.

*   *   *

RICH, Barbara
See GRAVES, Robert (von Ranke)

*   *   *

RICHLER, Mordecai 1931-

PERSONAL: Born January 27, 1931, in Montreal, Quebec, Canada; son of Moses Isaac and Lily (Rosenberg) Richler; married Florence Wood, July 27, 1960; children: Daniel, Noah, Emma, Martha, Jacob. *Education:* Attended Sir George Williams University, 1949-51. *Religion:* Jewish.

ADDRESSES: Home and office—1321 Sherbroake St. W., Apt. 80C, Montreal, Quebec, Canada H3G 1J4. *Agent*—Lynn Nesbit, International Creative Management, 40 West 57th St., New York, N.Y. 10019; (for films) William Morris Agency, 1350 Avenue of the Americas, New York, N.Y. 10019.

CAREER: Author and screenwriter. Left Canada in 1951 to become free-lance writer in Paris, France, 1952-53, and London, England, 1954-72; returned to Canada, 1972. Writer in residence, Sir George Williams University, 1968-69; visiting professor, Carleton University, 1972-74. Member of editorial board, Book-of-the-Month Club, 1972—.

AWARDS, HONORS: President's medal for nonfiction, University of Western Ontario, 1959; Canadian Council junior art fellowships, 1959 and 1960, senior arts fellowship, 1967; Guggenheim Foundation creative writing fellowship, 1961; *Paris Review* humor prize, 1967, for section from *Cocksure;* Canadian Governor-General's award for literature and London Jewish Chronicle literature award, both 1972, both for *St. Urbain's Horseman;* Berlin Film Festival Golden Bear, Academy Award nomination, and Screenwriters Guild of America award, all 1974, all for the screenplay, "The Apprenticeship of Duddy Kravitz"; Canadian Bookseller's award for best children's book and Canadian Librarian's medal, both 1976, both for *Jacob Two-Two Meets the Hooded Fang;* London *Jewish Chronicle*/H. H. Wingate award for fiction, 1981, for *Joshua Then and Now.*

WRITINGS:

The Acrobats (novel; also see below), Putnam, 1954, published as *Wicked We Love,* Popular Library, 1955.

Son of a Smaller Hero (novel), Collins (Toronto), 1955, Paperback Library, 1965.

A Choice of Enemies (novel), Collins, 1957.

The Apprenticeship of Duddy Kravitz (novel; also see below), Little, Brown, 1959.

The Incomparable Atuk (novel), McClelland & Stewart, 1963, published as *Stick Your Neck Out,* Simon & Schuster, 1963.

Cocksure (novel), Simon & Schuster, 1968.

Hunting Tigers under Glass: Essays and Reports, McClelland & Stewart, 1969.

The Street: Stories, McClelland & Stewart, 1969, New Republic, 1975.

(Editor) *Canadian Writing Today* (anthology), Peter Smith, 1970.

St. Urbain's Horseman (novel; Literary Guild featured alternate), Knopf, 1971.

Shoveling Trouble (essays), McClelland & Stewart, 1973.

Notes on an Endangered Species and Others (essays), Knopf, 1974.

Jacob Two-Two Meets the Hooded Fang (juvenile), Knopf, 1975.

Images of Spain, photographs by Peter Christopher, Norton, 1977.

The Great Comic Book Heroes and Other Essays, McClelland & Steward, 1978.

Joshua Then and Now (novel; also see below), Knopf, 1980.

(Editor) *The Best of Modern Humor,* Knopf, 1984.

Home Sweet Home: My Canadian Album (nonfiction), Knopf, 1984, published in paperback as *Home Sweet Home,* Penguin, 1985.

Jacob Two-Two and the Dinosaur (juvenile), Knopf, 1987.

Solomon Gursky Was Here (novel), Knopf, 1990.

SCREENPLAYS

(With Nicholas Phipps) "No Love for Johnnie," Embassy, 1962.

(With Geoffrey Cotterell and Ivan Foxwell) "Tiara Tahiti," Rank, 1962.

(With Phipps) "The Wild and the Willing," Rank, 1962, released in United States as "Young and Willing," Universal, 1965.

"Life at the Top," Royal International, 1965.

"The Apprenticeship of Duddy Kravitz" (adapted from his novel), Paramount, 1974.

(With David Giler and Jerry Belson) "Fun with Dick and Jane," Bart/Palevsky, 1977.

"Joshua Then and Now" (adapted from his novel), Twentieth Century-Fox, 1985.

TELEVISION AND RADIO SCRIPTS

"The Acrobats" (based on his novel), Canadian Broadcasting Corp. (CBC), 1956 (radio), 1957 (television).

"Friend of the People," CBC-TV, 1957.

"Paid in Full," ATV (England), 1958.

"Benny, the War in Europe, and Myerson's Daughter Bella," CBC-Radio, 1958. "The Trouble with Benny" (based on his short story), ABC (England), 1959.

"The Apprenticeship of Duddy Kravitz" (based on his novel), CBC-TV, 1960.

"The Spare Room," CBC-Radio, 1961.

"Q for Quest" (excerpts from his fiction), CBC-Radio, 1963.

"The Fall of Mendel Krick," British Broadcasting Corp. (BBC-TV), 1963.

"It's Harder to Be Anybody," CBC-Radio, 1965.

"Such Was St. Urbain Street," CBC-Radio, 1966.

"The Wordsmith" (based on his short story), CBC-Radio, 1979.

OTHER

"The Suit" (animated filmstrip), National Film Board of Canada, 1976.

(Author of Book) "Duddy" (play; based on his novel *The Apprenticeship of Duddy Kravitz*), first produced in Edmonton, Alberta, at the Citadel Theatre, April, 1984.

Contributor to Canadian, U.S., and British periodicals. Richler's papers are collected at the University of Calgary Library in Alberta.

SIDELIGHTS: "To be a Canadian and a Jew," as Mordecai Richler wrote in his book *Hunting Tigers under Glass: Essays and Reports,* "is to emerge from the ghetto twice." He refers to the double pressures of being in both a religious minority and the cultural enigma that is Canada. Yet in his decades as a novelist, screenwriter, and essayist, Richler has established himself as one of the few representatives of Canadian Jewry known outside his native country.

That many of his fictional works feature Jewish-Canadian protagonists in general (most notably in his best-known book *The Apprenticeship of Duddy Kravitz*), and natives of Montreal in particular, denotes the author's strong attachment to his early years. Richler was born in the Jewish ghetto of Montreal to a religious family of Russian emigres. "In his teens, however, he abandoned Orthodox customs, gradually becoming more interested both in a wider world and in writing," relates R. H. Ramsey in a *Dictionary of Literary Biography* article on Richler. After a stint at a university, Richler cashed in an insurance policy and used the money to sail to Liverpool, England. Eventually he found his way to Paris, where he spent some years emulating such expatriate authors as Ernest Hemingway and Henry Miller, then moved on to London, where he worked as a news correspondent.

During those early years, Richler produced his first novel, *The Acrobats,* a book he now characterizes as "more political than anything I've done since, and humorless," as he tells Walter Goodman in a *New York Times* interview, adding that the volume, published when he was twenty-three, "was just a very young man's novel. Hopelessly derivative. Like some unfortunate collision of [Jean-Paul] Sartre and Hemingway and [Louis-Ferdinand] Celine, all unabsorbed and undigested. I wasn't writing in my own voice at all. I was imitating people." But Richler found his voice soon after, with novels like *Son of a Smaller Hero, A Choice of Enemies,* and *The Incomparable Atuk.* Ramsey finds that from these efforts on, "two tendencies dominate Richler's fiction: realism and satire. [Much of the early work is] realistic, their plots basically traditional in form, their settings accurately detailed, their characters motivated in psychologically familiar ways." At the other extreme, Ramsey continues,

there is "pure satiric fantasy, [with] concessions to realism slight. In [such works] Richler indulges the strong comic vein in his writing as he attacks Canadian provincialism and the spurious gratifications of the entertainment medium."

Richler gained further notice with three of his best-known titles, *The Apprenticeship of Duddy Kravitz, St. Urbain's Horseman,* and *Joshua Then and Now.* These books share a common theme—that of a Jewish-Canadian protagonist at odds with society—and all three novels revolve around the idea of the way greed can taint success. *The Apprenticeship of Duddy Kravitz* presents its eponymous hero as a ghetto-reared youth on a never-ending quest to make a name for himself in business. It is also "the first of Richler's novels to exhibit fully his considerable comic talents, a strain that includes much black humor and a racy, colloquial, ironic idiom that becomes a characteristic feature of Richler's subsequent style," according to Ramsey.

Comparing *The Apprenticeship of Duddy Kravitz* to other such coming-of-age stories as James Joyce's *Portrait of the Artist as a Young Man* and D. H. Lawrence's *Sons and Lovers,* A. R. Bevan, in a new introduction to Richler's novel, finds that the book, "in spite of its superficial affinity with the two novels mentioned above, ends with [none of their] affirmation." The character of Duddy, "who has never weighted the consequences of his actions in any but material terms, is less alone in the physical sense than the earlier young men, but he is also much less of a man. . . . He is a modern 'anti-hero' (something like the protagonist in Anthony Burgess's *A Clockwork Orange*) who lives in a largely deterministic world, a world where decisions are not decisions and where choice is not really choice." In *Modern Fiction Studies,* John Ower sees *The Apprenticeship of Duddy Kravitz* as "a 'Jewish' novel [with] both a pungent ethnic flavor and the convincingness that arises when a writer deals with a milieu with which he is completely familiar." For the author, Ower continues, "the destructive psychological effects of the ghetto mentality are equalled and to some extent paralleled by those of the Jewish family. Like the society from which it springs, this tends to be close and exclusive, clinging together in spite of its intense quarrels. The best aspect of such clannishness, the feeling of kinship which transcends all personal differences, is exemplified by Duddy. Although he is in varying degrees put down and rejected by all of his relatives except his grandfather, Duddy sticks up for them and protects them."

For all its success, *The Apprenticeship of Duddy Kravitz* was still categorized by most scholars as among Richler's early works. By the time *St. Urbain's Horseman* was published in 1971, the author had all but sealed his reputation as a sharp cultural critic. In this work, a character named Jacob Hersh, a Canadian writer living in London, questions "not only how he rose to prominence but also the very nature and quality of success and why, having made it, [he] is dissatisfied," as Ramsey puts it. Hersh's success as a writer "brings with it a guilt, a sense of responsibility, and an overwhelming paranoia, a belief that his good fortune is largely undeserved and that sooner or later he will be called to account," Ramsey adds. In his guilt-based fantasies, Hersh dreams that he is a figure of vengeance protecting the downtrodden, a character based on the Horseman, a shadowy figure from Hersh's past. "Richler prefaces *St. Urbain's Horseman* with a quotation from [British poet W. H.] Auden which suggests that he does not wish to be read as a mere entertainer, a fanciful farceur," notes David Myers in *Ariel.* "What is there in the *Horseman* that would justify us as regarding it as such a[n affirming] flame? Certainly the despair that we find there is serious enough; the world around Jake Hersh is sordid and vile." The author accords sympathy "to only two characters in his novel, Jake and his wife Nancy," Myers says. "They are shown to feel a very deep love for one another and the loyalty of this love under duress provides the ethical counterbalance to the sordidness, instability, lack of integrity, injustice, and grasping materialism that Richler is satirizing in this book."

In the opinion of Kerry McSweeney, writing in *Studies in Canadian Literature,* the novel "gives evidence everywhere of technical maturity and full stylistic control, and combines the subjects, themes and modes of Richler's earlier novels in ways that suggest—as does the high seriousness of its epigraph—that Richler was attempting a cumulative fictional statement of his view on the mores and values of contemporary man. But while *St. Urbain's Horseman* is a solid success on the level of superior fictional entertainment, on the level of serious fiction it must be reckoned a considerable disappointment. It doesn't deliver the goods and simply does not merit the kind of detailed exegesis it has been given by some Canadian critics." Elaborating on this thesis, McSweeney adds that everything in the novel "depends on the presentation of Jake, especially of his mental life and the deeper reaches of his character, and on the intensity of the reader's sympathetic involvement with him. Unfortunately, Jake is characterized rather too superficially. One is told, for example, but never shown, that he is charged with contradictions concerning his professional life; and for all the time devoted to what is going on in his head he doesn't really seem to have much of a mental life. Despite the big issues he is said to be struggling with, *St. Urbain's Horseman* can hardly claim serious attention as a novel of ideas."

Robert Fulford offers a different view. In his *Saturday Night* article, Fulford lauds *St. Urbain's Horseman* as "the triumphant and miraculous bringing-together of all those varied Mordecai Richlers who have so densely populated our literary landscape for so many years. From this perspective it becomes clear that all those Richlers have a clear purpose in mind—they've all been waiting out there, working separately, honing their talents, waiting for the moment when they could arrive at the same place and join up in the creation of a magnificent *tour de force,* the best Canadian book in a long time."

The third of Richler's later novels, *Joshua Then and Now,* again explores a Jewish-Canadian's moral crises. Joshua Shapiro, a prominent author married to a gentile daughter of a senator, veers between religious and social classes, and withstands family conflicts, especially as they concern his father Reuben. It is also a novel full of mysteries. Why, asks *Village Voice* critic Barry Yourgrau, "does the book open in the present with this 47-year-old Joshua a rumple of fractures in a hospital bed, his name unfairly linked to a scandalous faggotry, his wife doped groggy in a nuthouse and he himself being watched over by his two elderly fathers?" The reason, Yourgrau continues, "is Time. The cruelest of fathers is committing physical violence on Joshua's dearest friends (and crucial enemies)."

Joshua, sometimes shown in flashback as the son of the ever-on-the-make Reuben and his somewhat exhibitionist mother (she performed a striptease at Joshua's bar mitzvah), "is another one of Richler's Jewish *arrivistes,* like Duddy Kravitz [and] Jacob Hersh," says *New Republic* critic Mark Shechner. After noting Joshua's unrepentant bragging, Shechner finds the character "a fairly unpleasant fellow, and indeed, though his exploits are unfailingly vivid and engaging—even fun—they rarely elicit from us much enthusiasm for Joshua himself. He is as callow as he is clever, and, one suspects, Richler means him to be an anti-type, to stand against the more common brands of self-congratulation that are endemic to Jewish fiction. From Sholom Aleichem and his Tevye to [Saul] Bellow and [Bernard] Malamud, . . . Jewish fiction has repeatedly thrown up figures of wisdom and endurance, observance and rectitude. . . . Richler, by contrast, adheres to a tradition of dissent that runs from Isaac Babel's Odessa stories through Daniel Fuchs's *Williamsburg Trilogy* and Budd Schulberg's *What Makes Sammy Run?,* which finds more color, more life, and more fidelity to the facts of Jewish existence in the demimonde of hustlers, heavies, strong-arm types and men on the make than in the heroes of *menschlichkeit* [Yiddish slang for the quality of goodness]."

But whatever message *Joshua Then and Now* might deliver, the lasting appeal of the novel, to John Lahr, is that "Richler writes funny. Laughter, not chicken soup, is the real Jewish penicillin. . . . Richler's characters enter as philosophers and exit as stand-up comics, firing zingers as they go," as Lahr explains in a *New York* article. On the other hand, *New York Times Book Review* writer Thomas R. Edwards, while acknowledging the novel's humor, finds it "dangerously similar in theme, situation and personnel to a number of Mordecai Richler's other novels—'Son of a Smaller Hero,' 'The Apprenticeship of Duddy Kravitz,' 'Cocksure' and 'St. Urbain's Horseman.' It's as if a rich and unusual body of fictional material had become a kind of prison for a writer who is condemned to repeat himself ever more vehemently and inflexibly." *Joshua Then and Now* brought much more critical debate. Mark Harris, on one hand, faults the novel for its style, "resplendent with every imaginable failure of characterization, relevance, style or grammar," in his *Washington Post Book World* review. An *Atlantic* critic, on the other hand, saw the book as "good enough to last, perhaps Richler's best novel to date."

Among his nonfiction works, Richler's *Home Sweet Home: My Canadian Album* drew some attention. It's "a different sort of book, but no less direct and pungent in its observations about what makes a society tick," according to a Toronto *Globe and Mail* writer. In this volume the author uses essays to examine Canadian culture, addressing subjects from nationalism to hockey. In another *Globe and Mail* article, Joy Fielding sees the book as "a cross-country tour like no other, penetrating the Eastern soul, the Western angst, and the French-Canadian spirit." *Home Sweet Home* drew admiring glances from American as well as Canadian critics. Peter Ross, of the *Detroit News,* writes, "Wit and warmth are constants and though Richler can temper his fondness with bursts of uncompromising acerbity, no reader can fail to perceive the depth of his feelings as well as the complexities of Canada." And *Time*'s Stefan Kanfer observes that "even as he celebrates [Canada's] beauties, the author never loses sight of his country's insularity: when Playboy Films wanted to produce adult erotica in Toronto, he reports, officials wanted to know how much Canadian content there would be in the features. But Richler also knows that the very tugs and pulls of opposing cultures give the country its alternately appealing and discordant character."

"Throughout his career Richler has spanned an intriguing gulf," concludes Ramsey in his *Dictionary of Literary Biography* piece. "While ridiculing popular tastes and never catering to popular appeal, he has nevertheless maintained a wide general audience. Though drawing constantly on his own experience, he rejects the writer as personality, wishing instead to find acceptance not because of some personal characteristic or because of the familiarity of his subject matter to a Canadian reading public but because he has something fresh to say about humanity and says it in a well-crafted form, which even with its comic exuberance, stands firmly in the tradition of moral and intellectual fiction."

MEDIA ADAPTATIONS: Richler's children's book *Jacob Two-Two Meets the Hooded Fang* was filmed in 1977 by Cinema Shares International. Film rights have been sold for both *Stick Your Neck Out* and *Cocksure.* A reading by Christopher Plummer of *Jacob Two-Two Meets the Hooded Fang* was recorded by Caedmon Records in 1977.

BIOGRAPHICAL/CRITICAL SOURCES:

BOOKS

Authors in the News, Volume 1, Gale, 1976.
Contemporary Literary Criticism, Gale, Volume 3, 1975, Volume 5, 1976, Volume 9, 1978, Volume 13, 1980, Volume 18, 1981, Volume 46, 1987.
Dictionary of Literary Biography, Volume 53: *Canadian Writers since 1960, First Series,* Gale, 1986.
Klinck, Carl F., and others, editors, *Literary History of Canada: Canadian Literature in English,* University of Toronto Press, 1965.
New, W. H., *Articulating West,* New Press, 1972.
Northey, Margot, *The Haunted Wilderness: The Gothic and Grotesque in Canadian Fiction,* University of Toronto Press, 1976.
Ramraj, Victor J., *Mordecai Richler,* Twayne, 1983.
Richler, Mordecai, *The Apprenticeship of Duddy Kravitz,* introduction by A. R. Bevan, McClelland & Stewart, 1969.
Richler, Mordecai, *Hunting Tigers under Glass: Essays and Reports,* McClelland & Stewart, 1969.
Sheps, G. David, editor, *Mordecai Richler,* McGraw-Hill/Ryerson, 1971.
Woodcock, George, *Mordecai Richler,* McClelland & Stewart, 1970.

PERIODICALS

Ariel, January, 1973.
Atlantic, July, 1980.
Books in Canada, August-September, 1984.
Canadian Literature, spring, 1973, summer, 1973.
Commentary, October, 1980.
Detroit News, July 29, 1984.
Esquire, August, 1982.
Globe and Mail (Toronto), May 5, 1984, June 24, 1985, June 13, 1987.
Los Angeles Times Book Review, August 19, 1984.
Maclean's, May 7, 1984.
Modern Fiction Studies, autumn, 1976.
Nation, July 5, 1980.
New Republic, May 18, 1974, June 14, 1980, December 5, 1983.
Newsweek, June 16, 1980, February 3, 1986.
New York, June 16, 1980.
New York Review of Books, July 17, 1980.
New York Times, June 22, 1980.
New York Times Book Review, May 4, 1975, October 5, 1975, June 22, 1980, September 11, 1983, February 5, 1984, June 3, 1984, October 18, 1987.
Saturday Night, June, 1971, March, 1974.
Spectator, August 25, 1981.
Studies in Canadian Literature, summer, 1979.
Time, June 16, 1980, November 7, 1983, April 30, 1984.
Times Literary Supplement, April 2, 1976, September 26, 1980, August 3, 1984, December 21, 1984.
Village Voice, June 2, 1980, May 1, 1984.
Washington Post, November 9, 1983.
Washington Post Book World, June 29, 1980.

RICHTER, Conrad (Michael) 1890-1968

PERSONAL: Born October 13, 1890, in Pine Grove, Pa.; died of a heart attack, October 30, 1968, in Pottsville, Pa.; son of John Absalom (a minister) and Charlotte Esther (Henry) Richter; married Harvena M. Achenbach, 1915; children: Harvena. *Education:* Attended public schools in Pennsylvania.

ADDRESSES: Home—11 Maple St., Pine Grove, Pa. *Agent*—Paul R. Reynolds & Son, 599 Fifth Ave., New York, N.Y.

CAREER: Editor and journalist for newspapers in Patton, Pa., Johnstown, Pa., and Pittsburgh, Pa., and private secretary in Cleveland, Ohio, 1910-24; writer, 1924-68.

MEMBER: National Institute of Arts and Letters, Authors League, PEN.

AWARDS, HONORS: National Book Award nomination, 1937, for *The Sea of Grass;* Gold Medal for Literature from Society of Libraries of New York University, 1942, for *The Sea of Grass* and *The Trees;* Ohioana Library Medal, 1947; Pulitzer Prize for Fiction, 1951, for *The Town;* National Institute of Arts and Letters grant in literature, 1959; Maggie Award, 1959, for *The Lady;* National Book Award, 1961, for *The Waters of Kronos;* Litt.D., Susquehanna University, 1944, University of New Mexico, 1958, Lafayette College, 1966; LL.D., Temple University, 1966; L.H.D., Lebanon Valley College, 1966.

WRITINGS:

Brothers of No Kin and Other Stories, Hinds, Hayden & Eldredge, 1924, reprinted, Books for Libraries Press, 1973.
Human Vibration, Handy Book, 1925.
Principles in Bio-Physics, Good Books, 1927.
Early Americana and Other Stories, Knopf, 1936, reprinted, Gregg, 1978.
The Sea of Grass, Knopf, 1937, reprinted, Ballantine, 1984.
The Trees (first volume in trilogy; also see below), Knopf, 1940, reprinted, Bantam, 1975.
Tacey Cromwell, Knopf, 1942, reprinted, University of New Mexico Press, 1974.
The Free Man, Knopf, 1943, reprinted, 1966.
The Fields (second volume in trilogy; also see below), Knopf, 1946, reprinted, 1964.
Smoke over the Prairie and Other Stories, Boardman, 1947.
Always Young and Fair, Knopf, 1947.
The Town (third volume in trilogy; also see below), Knopf, 1950, reprinted, Harmony Raine, 1981.
The Light in the Forest, Knopf, 1953, Bantam, 1984.
The Mountain on the Desert: A Philosophical Journey, Knopf, 1955.
The Lady, Knopf, 1957, reprinted, University of Nebraska Press, 1985.
Dona Ellen, Rauch, 1959.
The Waters of Kronos, Knopf, 1960.
A Simple, Honorable Man, Knopf, 1962.
Over the Blue Mountain (juvenile), Knopf, 1962.
Individualists under the Shade Trees in a Vanishing America, Holt, 1964.
The Grandfathers, Knopf, 1964.
A Country of Strangers, Knopf, 1966, Schocken, 1982.
The Awakening Land: I. The Trees, II. The Fields, III. The Town, Knopf, 1966.
The Wanderer, Knopf, 1966.
The Aristocrat, Knopf, 1968.
The Rawhide Knot and Other Stories, Knopf, 1978, reprinted, University of Nebraska Press, 1985.

Also author of monograph, *Life Energy.* Contributor to anthologies and magazines.

SIDELIGHTS: The late Conrad Richter brought the American past to life with his historical novels celebrating the hardy pioneer spirit. While many of his literary contemporaries bemoaned the malaise engendered by an industrial-technological society, Richter explored the world of his forebears, an era when seas of forest and grassland challenged a whole generation. A dedicated researcher, Richter took care to infuse his work with realistic dialogue, settings, and events, while creating a story the general reader could relish. The resulting novels and short stories were popular with the public but were also treated as serious fiction by the critics. Over the forty years of his writing career, Richter received several of the most prestigious awards the literary community bestows. He earned a Pulitzer Prize in 1951 for *The Town,* the final volume of his highly successful trilogy collected as *The Awakening Land,* and in 1961 he was given the National Book Award for *The Waters of Kronos. New York Herald Tribune Weekly Book Review* contributor Louis Bromfield observes that Richter's fiction not only reflects scholarly attention and sympathetic interpretation, but also creates for the reader "a world as real as the one in which he lives, a world which the reader enters on reading the first page and in which he remains until the last."

According to Marvin J. LaHood in *University Review,* Richter belonged "to that group of writers who are impressed with the strength and perseverance of the pioneer, and feel that this strength was a direct result of having dealt with the rigors of the frontier." In *The Trees, The Fields,* and *The Town,* brought together in *The Awakening Land,* Richter's frontier is the Ohio valley, once an uncharted wilderness of pines. In *Early Americana and Other Stories* and *The Sea of Grass,* among others, the author wrote about the American West from the perspective of its first white settlers. "Painstaking research underlies these books," Dayton Kohler declares in *College English,* "but they illustrate the fact that the more a novelist knows about a region or a period the less his atmosphere depends on local color for its effect. . . . There is no surface decoration here—merely the facts of pioneer existence springing from a background of simple necessity. The remarkable fact is that [Richter] has accomplished so much with so little reference to actual history. . . . There are no novels quite like Richter's in the whole range of historical fiction. Together they probably give us our truest picture of the everyday realities of frontier life." LaHood draws a similar conclusion: "Conrad Richter's greatest contribution to American letters [was] his tireless effort to put into fiction the setting and the people of an important moment in our nation's history. In the best of his novels and stories that moment lives again."

The son of a minister, Richter was deeply interested in philosophical issues. As Edwin W. Gaston, Jr., notes in the *Dictionary of Literary Biography,* Richter began his fiction-writing career with a "reasonably complete" philosophical system, a world view he explained in two works, *Human Vibration* and *Principles in Bio-Physics.* These books, and the 1955 title *The Mountain on the Desert,* "hold that man functions in response to bodily cellular vibrations which are regulated by the availability of physical and psychical energy," according to Gaston, who adds: "If the energy is plentiful, man is in harmony with life. . . . On the other hand, if energy is low, man is out of sorts with life. . . . To satisfy his energy hunger, man must engage in intense activity. Activity causes the strong cells in one's body to overflow, revitalizing the weak cells." Richter found this unscientific view quite satisfying; he felt the early American pioneers served as clear examples of people who achieved harmony with the envi-

ronment through strenuous work and cooperation. As civilization advanced, however, the pioneers' children and grandchildren endured fewer hardships and therefore often suffered a resulting loss of character. In *The Old Northwest,* Dawn Wilson writes: "The major message of Richter's philosophy is that hard times have their own rewards; they provide the energy people need to grow. . . . Richter was so intrigued by the land and its settlers that he set out to portray in his fiction the courage and strength of the people, and the causes of the early settlers' enormous strength—causes which his own philosophy, by coincidence, so aptly explained. At last Richter had found the ideal topic for his fiction. He began writing tales of the frontier, authentic stories of danger and adventure on the early plains, which were in themselves both instances and examples of Richter's energy theories."

Richter was born in 1890 in Pine Grove, Pennsylvania, and grew up in a series of tiny coal mining towns through which his father moved as a Lutheran minister. The family always struggled to make ends meet; Richter's own formal schooling ended when he graduated from high school at the age of fifteen. For four years thereafter, Richter tried his hand at numerous jobs. He drove teams, worked on farms, cut timber, sold subscription magazines door-to-door, served as a bank teller, and clerked. Then, at nineteen, he became editor of a weekly newspaper called the Patton (Pennsylvania) *Courier* and discovered that he enjoyed journalism. He left Patton for reporting jobs first in Johnstown and then in Pittsburgh, learning how to write "plain sentences against the discipline of a deadline," in the words of *Saturday Review* contributor John K. Hutchens. "Of his early jobs," claims Gaston, "reporting and editing most affected [Richter's] belletristic writing. As it had for Hemingway, journalism taught Richter concision of expression." Eventually Richter succumbed to wanderlust and took a job as private secretary to a wealthy Cleveland family who provided the means for wider travel. It was during this period that one of his first short stories was accepted. The work, entitled "Brothers of No Kin," was first published in *Forum* magazine and then was reprinted several times. Despite the piece's success, Richter had a very difficult time getting payment for it—and when the twenty-five-dollar check arrived, he was still disappointed. He told the *Saturday Review:* "I thought to myself, if that's all I get for the kind of story I want to write, why go on?"

Though convinced he would never be able to support his wife and daughter on a writer's salary, Richter persevered. In 1924 he published a collection of short fiction, *Brothers of No Kin and Other Stories. New Mexico Quarterly* essayist Bruce Sutherland characterizes these tales as "well-made" and "tailored for the trade." Some of them, the critic continues, "have elements of nativism and local color, some have a glimmer of characterization, but for the most part they give the impression of assembly-line mass production which at best gave the author practice in the art of writing." A major turning point in Richter's career occurred in 1928, when his wife's ill health forced him to move his family from Pennsylvania to Albuquerque, New Mexico. There, in the rugged terrain of the American Southwest, Richter "came upon a new world that he was to make his own," according to Hutchens. Poring through old newspapers and scrapbooks, and interviewing the oldest residents of the area, Richter became immersed in the folklore and history of his adopted state. "There was nothing new or startling about the Richter stories which began to appear in the magazines early in 1934," Sutherland writes. "On the surface they were Western stories of a high order, authentic, carefully conceived, and skillfully narrated. Closer scrutiny reveals how vastly different they are from the type of Western to which Americans have become accustomed. These are stories of pioneer fortitude aimed at a depression-ridden world; and the contemporary soul, battered and bewildered by life, through them is brought into closer contact with people of another age who also lived, loved, struggled, and died but whose lives form a pattern out of which emerges completeness and serenity." Richter's 1936 publication *Early Americana and Other Stories* is a collection of these Southwestern tales. It was followed in 1937 by *The Sea of Grass,* a novel that brought the author national recognition.

The Sea of Grass chronicles the nineteenth-century conflict between the free-ranging Western ranchers and the "nesters" who settled, fenced, and farmed. Sutherland describes the novel as the story "of change which destroys and builds at the same time, of the past which succumbs to the present and of the personal tragedy which attends the tide of progress." Kohler suggests that the Western theme caused critics to overlook the work at first, even though it transcends genre fiction. *The Sea of Grass,* writes Kohler, "is first a book about people. . . . We are not reading a local colorist. The surface decoration of most Western fiction—night herding, the roundup, cowboy sprees—is lacking here." Sutherland also finds *The Sea of Grass* "a completely successful short novel which meets even the most exacting literary standards." In all, Richter wrote three novels about the Southwest—*The Sea of Grass, Tacey Cromwell,* and *The Lady.* His main goal, Wilson contends, "was to recapture the essence of life in the past. All three Southwestern novels thus emphasize the idea that men and women of the past were of greater stature than the people of the present. . . . Thematically, he depicts the conflict between the old and the new in these novels, the lyrical quality of which is a result of the captivating power of the Southwestern landscape over his imagination."

Even as he labored on his book about the West, Richter continued to feel drawn toward the Pennsylvania Dutch country of his youth. His best-known and most highly regarded work, the trilogy *The Awakening Land,* gives a microcosmic overview of the settlement of the Ohio valley. According to Orville Prescott in his book *In My Opinion: An Inquiry into the Contemporary Novel,* the three segments of the trilogy "are certain to rank among the fine novels of our time. Taken together as a vast epic of the American frontier seen in terms of one family they are a majestic achievement. . . . There is a rare quality in these glowing pages—the most finished yet unobtrusive artistry, and a profound understanding of the pioneer character as it was manifested in and affected by a way of life now vanished from the earth." Through the character of Sayward Luckett Wheeler—widely considered one of the most sensitively drawn pioneer women in fiction—Richter portrayed the gradual replacement of the gloomy and dangerous forest wilderness by farming communities and then a thriving town. Most of the work is indebted to folklore; Richter took care to detail daily activities, superstitions, social mores, and special ceremonies, and his characters speak a dialect that has all but disappeared in modern America. In a *Midwest Folklore* essay, John T. Flanagan concludes that Richter's fiction "is the richer and the more convincing because he has seen fit to incorporate such material in his dialogue, action, and characterization." Individually and collectively, the three novels united in *The Awakening Land* have drawn critical acclaim. *Chicago Sunday Tribune* contributor Edward Wagenknecht finds the trilogy "unified in its design, sustained in its inspiration. It pulses from beginning to end with the passion of the land, this flesh, and the spirit. It has the American heartbeat in it. Cut it and it bleeds American."

In addition to the major works of his middle years and later life, Richter wrote a number of minor novels. These include *The Free Man,* a story of a German indentured servant who fights in the Revolutionary War, *Always Young and Fair,* the psychological portrait of a woman robbed of her fiance by war, *The Light in the Forest,* an account of a white child raised by Indians, and *The Grandfathers,* a comic tale of western Maryland hill folk. In his book *Conrad Richter,* Gaston observes that although such works created the impression of being interludes, they performed useful fictional functions for the author. They enabled Richter "to explore topics anterior to the subjects of his Ohio trilogy and thus to fill gaps helpful to greater appreciation of the larger novels." *Saturday Review* contributor Granville Hicks finds even these lesser works successful because Richter "has been a careful student of the relevant documents and because he has a deep sympathy with the life of earlier times." Hicks notes that Richter's prose is "direct and unpretentious," and his stories are capable of amusing and instructing without sentimentality. "Although his books have often been popular," the critic observes, "[Richter] has never written down to the masses. He has gone his own way, and he has no reason to regret it."

Two very personal, autobiographical novels—*The Waters of Kronos* and *A Simple, Honorable Man*—brought Richter further critical plaudits late in his career. Both books are set in Pennsylvania; in *The Waters of Kronos,* an aging writer named John Donner mystically visits his birthplace—a town submerged beneath the waters of the dammed-up Kronos River—and in *A Simple, Honorable Man,* Donner's father becomes a Lutheran minister and dedicates himself to serving his poorest and most needy parishioners. "Richter's nostalgia for the American past, so obvious in his carefully researched novels, brought him at seventy to an exact rendering of his relatives as he remembered them," LaHood explains in *University Review.* "It is an undertaking with few equals in American literature. But it is more than just a nostalgic family history, for in the two novels Richter wrestled with his own metaphysical problems." Most critics have praised the National Book Award-winning *Waters of Kronos* and its prequel *A Simple, Honorable Man* for their dignified exploration of a nostalgic theme. "Seldom has a man written more candidly of himself and his relatives than has Richter," LaHood contends in *Conrad Richter's America.* "Richter honestly attempted to portray his struggles with life's most teasing intellectual and spiritual problems: man's existence before and after this life, the tenets of organized religion, the differences in character from person to person, the father-son relationship, and the old problem of fate versus free will. He also exhibited in these two novels a great pride in various ancestors from whom he received what he considered a priceless legacy."

Richter spent most of the last twenty years of his life in Pennsylvania, his ancestral home. He died on October 30, 1968, within a few miles of his birthplace. According to Bruce Sutherland, the author's chief contribution to Americana "is a restrained realism which depends greatly on brevity and understatement for its effect. This, combined with an understanding of people, a feeling for historical things which transcends mere knowledge, and the ability to think and write in terms of his characters and their environment places him among the chosen few who have made the past of America come alive." In his *Saturday Review* piece, Granville Hicks observes that Richter's name is not likely to come to mind as an important novelist of his period, but "no careful history of American fiction in the twentieth century could ignore his work." Hicks concludes that Richter's career illustrates the notion "that a man of talent and integrity may, with a little luck, thumb his nose at fashion and write the kind of books he wants to write."

BIOGRAPHICAL/CRITICAL SOURCES:

BOOKS

Barnes, Robert J., *Conrad Richter,* Steck-Vaughn, 1968.
Contemporary Literary Criticism, Volume 30, Gale, 1984.
Dictionary of Literary Biography, Volume 9: *American Novelists, 1910-1945,* Gale, 1981.
Edwards, Clifford Duane, *Conrad Richter's Ohio Trilogy: Its Ideas, Themes, and Relationships to Literary Tradition,* Mouton, 1971.
Gaston, Edwin W., Jr., *Conrad Richter,* Twayne, 1965.
LaHood, Marvin J., *Conrad Richter's America,* Mouton, 1975.
Lee, L. L., and Merrill Lewis, *Women, Women Writers, and the West,* Whitston, 1979.
Prescott, Orville, *In My Opinion: An Inquiry into the Contemporary Novel,* Bobbs-Merrill, 1952.
Stuckey, W. L., *The Pulitzer Prize Novels,* University of Oklahoma Press, 1966.

PERIODICALS

American Review, April, 1937.
Atlantic, November, 1943, June, 1946, April, 1947, August, 1950, June, 1964.
Books, February 7, 1937, March 3, 1940, November 1, 1942.
Book Week, August 22, 1943, March 31, 1946, June 7, 1964, May 22, 1966.
Boston Transcript, March 2, 1940.
Chicago Sunday Tribune, April 23, 1950, May 26, 1957.
Christian Science Monitor, March 10, 1937, June 1, 1940, May 4, 1946, November 5, 1968, October 23, 1978.
College English, February, 1947, November, 1950.
Commonweal, November 10, 1967.
Critic, June-July, 1964.
English Journal, September, 1946.
Midwest Folklore, spring, 1952.
New Mexico Quarterly, winter, 1945.
New Republic, March 18, 1940, December 9, 1978.
New York Herald Tribune Book Review, March 30, 1947, April 23, 1950, May 17, 1953, July 3, 1955, May 19, 1957, April 17, 1960.
New York Herald Tribune Books, August 2, 1936, February 7, 1937, April 22, 1962.
New York Herald Tribune Weekly Book Review, August 22, 1943, March 31, 1946.
New York Times, March 3, 1940, August 8, 1943, March 31, 1946, March 30, 1947, April 23, 1950, June 5, 1955, May 1, 1960, October 10, 1968.
New York Times Book Review, August 2, 1936, October 25, 1942, May 1, 1960, May 6, 1962, May 24, 1964, July 10, 1966, September 18, 1966, October 6, 1968, December 24, 1978.
Northwest Ohio Quarterly, autumn, 1957.
Old Northwest, December, 1975.
San Francisco Chronicle, May 1, 1950, May 15, 1953, June 22, 1955, April 18, 1960.
Saturday Evening Post, October 12, 1946.
Saturday Review, May 16, 1953, May 25, 1957, April 16, 1960, April 28, 1962, May 14, 1966, December 21, 1968.
Saturday Review of Literature, February 27, 1937, April 22, 1950.
Southwest Review, summer, 1958.
Spectator, May 17, 1940.
Springfield Republican, March 14, 1937, November 8, 1942, June 23, 1957.

Time, May 1, 1950, April 18, 1960, September 27, 1968.
University Review, summer, 1964.
Yale Review, June, 1946.

OBITUARIES:

PERIODICALS

New York Times, October 31, 1968.

*   *   *

RILEY, Tex
See CREASEY, John

*   *   *

RILKE, Rainer Maria   1875-1926

PERSONAL: Birth name Rene Karl Wilhelm Johann Josef Maria Rilke; born December 4, 1875, in Prague, Austria (now Czechoslovakia); changed his name to Rainer Maria Rilke, 1897; died of leukemia (some sources cite blood poisoning resulting from rose thorn prick), December 29, 1926, in Montreaux, Switzerland; buried in Raron, Valais, Switzerland, in graveyard of village church; son of Josef (a railway official) and Sophie Entz Rilke; married Clara Westhoff (a sculptress), 1901 (separated, 1902); children: Ruth. *Education:* Attended Handelsakademie, Linz, Austria, 1891-92, and University of Prague, 1895-96. *Religion:* Raised Roman Catholic.

CAREER: Poet, novelist, short story writer, and translator. Traveled extensively throughout Europe. Joined the Worpswede artists' colony, 1900-02; worked as a secretary for sculptor Auguste Rodin in Paris, France, 1905-06. *Military service:* Austro-Hungary Army, First Infantry Regiment; served in the War Department, 1916.

WRITINGS:

Leben und Lieder: Bilder und Tagebuchblaetter (poems; main title means "Life and Songs"), Kattentidt, 1894.
Larenopfer (poems; title means "Offering to the Lares"), Dominicus (Prague), 1896.
Todtentaenze: Zwielicht-Skizzen aus unseren Tagen, Loewit & Lamberg (Prague), 1896.
Traumgekroent: Neue Gedichte (poems; main title means "Crowned with Dreams"), Friesenhahn (Leipzig), 1896.
Wegwarten (poems), Selbstverlag (Prague), 1896.
In Fruehfrost: Ein Stueck Daemmerung, Drei Vorgaenge (play), Theaterverlag O. R. Eirich (Vienna), 1897.
Advent (poems), Friesenhahn, 1898.
Ohne Gegenwart: Drama in zwei Akten, Entsch (Berlin), 1898.
Am Leben hin: Novellen und Skizzen, Bonz (Stuttgart), 1898.
Zwei Prager Geschichten, Bonz, 1899.
Mir zur Feier: Gedichte (poems), Meyer (Berlin), 1899, reprinted as *Die fruehen Gedichte,* Insel (Germany), 1909, Ungar, 1943.
Vom lieben Gott und Anderes: An Grosse fuer Kinder erzaehlt (short stories), Schuster & Loeffler, 1900, published as *Geschichten vom lieben Gott,* Insel, 1904, Ungar, 1942, translation by Nora Purtscher-Wydenbruck and M. D. Herter Norton published as *Stories of God,* Norton, 1932, revised edition, 1963.
Das taegliche Leben: Drama in zwei Akten (play; first produced in Berlin at the Residenz Theater, December, 1901), Langen (Munich), 1902.
Zur Einweihung der Kunsthalle am 15. Februar 1902: Festspielszene, [Bremen], 1902.

Buch der Bilder (poems), Juncker (Berlin), 1902, enlarged edition, 1906, Ungar, 1943.

Die Letzten, Juncker, 1902.

Worpswede: Fritz Mackensen, Otto Modersohn, Fritz Overbeck, Hans am Ende, Heinrich Vogeler, Velhagen & Klasing, 1903.

Auguste Rodin (biography), Bard (Berlin), 1903, translation by Jesse Lemont and Hans Trausil published as *Auguste Rodin,* Sunwise Turn (New York), 1919, published as *Rodin,* Haskell Booksellers, 1974.

Das Stundenbuch enthaltend die drei Buecher: Vom moenchischen Leben; Von der Pilgerschaft; Von der Armuth und vom Tode (poems), Insel, 1905, translation by Babette Deutsch published as *Poems from the Book of Hours,* New Directions, 1941, reprinted, 1975, translation by A. L. Peck published as *The Book of Hours; Comprising the Three Books: Of the Monastic Life, Of Pilgrimage, Of Poverty and Death,* Hogarth, 1961.

Die Weise von Liebe und Tod des Cornets Christoph Rilke (prose poem), Juncker, 1906, translation by B. J. Morse published as *The Story of the Love and Death of Cornet Christopher Rilke,* Osnabrueck, 1927, translation by Herter Norton published as *The Tale of the Love and Death of Cornet Christopher Rilke,* Norton, 1932, translation by Stephen Mitchell published as *The Lay of the Love and Death of Cornet Christopher Rilke,* Arion, 1983, new edition, Graywolf Press, 1985.

Neue Gedichte (poems), two volumes, Insel, 1907-08, translation by J. B. Leishman published as *New Poems,* New Directions, 1964, translation by Edward Snow, North Point Press, Volume 1: *New Poems (1907),* 1984, Volume 2: *New Poems: The Other Part (1908),* 1987.

Requiem (poems), Insel, 1909.

Die Aufzeichnungen des Malte Laurids Brigge (novel), Insel, 1910, translation by John Linton published as *The Journal of My Other Self,* Norton, 1930, translation by Norton published as *The Notebooks of Malte Laurids Brigge,* Norton, 1964, translation by Mitchell published as *The Notebooks of Malte Laurids Brigge,* Random House, 1983.

Erste Gedichten, Insel, 1913, Ungar, 1947.

Das Marien-Leben, Insel, 1913, translation by R. G. L. Barrett published as *The Life of the Virgin Mary,* Triltsch (Wuerzburg), 1921, translation by Stephen Spender published as *The Life of the Virgin Mary,* Philosophical Library, 1951.

Poems, translation by Lemont, Wright, 1918.

Aus der Fruehzeit Rainer Maria Rilke: Vers, Prosa, Drama (1894-1899), edited by Fritz Adolf Huenich, Bibliophilenabend (Leipzig), 1921.

Mitsou: Quarante images par Baltusz, Rotapfel, 1921.

Puppen, Hyperion (Munich), 1921.

Duineser Elegien (poems; also see below), Insel, 1923, Ungar, 1944, translation by V. Sackville-West and Edward Sackville-West published as *Duineser Elegien: Elegies from the Castle of Duino,* Hogarth, 1931, translation by Leishman and Spender published as *Duino Elegies,* Norton, 1939, translation by Robert Hunter and Gary Miranda published as *Duino Elegies,* Breitenbush, 1981.

Die Sonette an Orpheus: Geschrieben als ein Grab-Mal fuer Wera Ouckama Knoop (poems; also see below), Insel, 1923, Ungar, 1945, translation by Leishman published as *Sonnets to Orpheus, Written as a Monument for Wera Ouckama Knoop,* Hogarth, 1936, translation by Norton published as *Sonnets to Orpheus,* Norton, 1942, translation by Mitchell published as *The Sonnets to Orpheus,* Simon & Schuster, 1986.

Vergers suivi des Quatrains Valaisans, Editions de la Nouvelle Revue Francaise (Paris), 1926, translation by Alfred Poulin, Jr., published as *Orchards,* Graywolf Press (Port Townsend, Wash.), 1982.

Gesammelte Werke, six volumes, Insel, 1927.

Les Fenetres: Dix Poemes, Officina Sanctandreana (Paris), 1927, translation by Poulin published as "The Windows" in *The Roses and the Windows,* Graywolf Press, 1979.

Les Roses, Stols (Bussum, Netherlands), 1927, translation by Poulin published as "The Roses" in *The Roses and the Windows,* Graywolf Press, 1979.

Erzaehlungen und Skizzen aus der Fruehzeit, Insel, 1928.

Ewald Tragy: Erzaehlung, Heller (Munich), 1929, Johannespresse (New York), 1944, translation by Lola Gruenthal published as *Ewald Tragy,* Twayne, 1958.

Verse und Prosa aus dem Nachlass, Gesellschaft der Freunde der Deutschen Buecherei (Leipzig), 1929.

Gesammelte Gedichte, four volumes, Insel, 1930-33.

Ueber den jungen Dichter, [Hamburg], 1931.

Gedichte, edited by Katharina Kippenberg, Insel, 1931, Ungar, 1947.

Rainer Maria Rilke auf Capri: Gespraeche, edited by Leopold von Schloezer, Jess (Dresden), 1931.

Spaete Gedichte, Insel, 1934.

Buecher, Theater, Kunst, edited by Richard von Mises, Jahoda & Siegel (Vienna), 1934.

Der ausgewaehlten Gedichten anderer Teil, edited by Kippenberg, Insel, 1935.

Ausgewaehlte Werke, two volumes, edited by Ruth Sieber-Rilke, Carl Sieber, and Ernst Zinn, Insel, 1938.

Translations from the Poetry of Rainer Maria Rilke, translation by Norton, Norton, 1938, reprinted, 1962.

Fifty Selected Poems with English Translations, translation by C. F. MacIntyre, University of California Press, 1940.

Selected Poems, translation by Leishman, Hogarth, 1941.

Tagebuecher aus der Fruehzeit, edited by Sieber-Rilke, Insel, 1942.

Briefe, Verse und Prosa aus dem Jahre 1896, two volumes, Johannespresse, 1946.

Thirty-one Poems, translation by Ludwig Lewisohn, Ackerman, 1946.

Freundschaft mit Rainer Maria Rilke: Begegnungen, Gespraeche, Briefe und Aufzeichnungen mitgeteilt durch Elga Maria Nevar, Zuest (Buempliz), 1946.

Five Prose Pieces, translation by Carl Niemeyer, Cummington Press (Cummington, Mass.), 1947.

Gedichte, edited by Hermann Kunisch, Vandenhoeck & Ruprecht (Goettingen), 1947.

Gedichte in franzoesicher Sprache, edited by Thankmar von Muenchhausen, Insel, 1949.

Aus Rainer Maria Rilkes Nachlass, four volumes, Insel, 1950, Volume 1: *Aus dem Nachlass des Grafen C. W.,* translation by Leishman as *From the Remains of Count C. W.,* Hogarth, 1952.

Werke: Auswahl in zwei Baenden, two volumes, Insel, 1953.

Gedichte, 1909-26: Sammlung der verstreuten und nachgelassenen Gedichte aus den mittleren und spaeteren Jahren, translation, with additions, by Leishman published as *Poems 1906 to 1926,* Laughlin (Norfolk, Conn.), 1953.

Selected Works, two volumes, translation by G. Craig Houston and Leishman, Hogarth, 1954, New Directions, 1960.

Saemtliche Werke, six volumes, edited by Zinn, Insel, 1955-66.

Angel Songs/Engellieder (bilingual), translation by Rhoda Coghill, Dolmen Press (Dublin), 1958.

Die Turmstunde und andere Novellen (novella collection), edited by Fritz Froehling, Hyperion, 1959.

Selected Works: Prose and Poetry, two volumes, 1960.

Poems, edited by G. W. McKay, Oxford University Press, 1965.

Werke in drei Baenden, three volumes, Insel, 1966.

Gedichte: Eine Auswahl, Reclam (Stuttgart), 1966.

Visions of Christ: A Posthumous Cycle of Poems, translation by Aaron Kramer, edited by Siegfried Mandel, University of Colorado Press, 1967.

Das Testament, edited by Zinn, Insel, 1975.

Holding Out: Poems, translation by Rika Lesser, Abbatoir Editions (Omaha, Neb.), 1975.

Possibility of Being: A Selection of Poems, translation by Leishman, New Directions, 1977.

The Voices, translation by Robert Bly, Ally Press, 1977.

Duino Elegies [and] *The Sonnets to Orpheus,* translation by Poulin, Houghton, 1977.

Werke: In 3 Baenden, three volumes, edited by Horst Nalewski, Insel, 1978.

Where Silence Reigns: Selected Prose, New Directions, 1978.

Nine Plays, translation by Klaus Phillips and John Locke, Ungar, 1979.

I Am Too Alone in the World: Ten Poems, translation by Bly, Silver Hands Press, 1980.

Selected Poems of Rainer Maria Rilke, translation by Bly, Harper, 1980.

Requiem for a Woman, and Selected Lyric Poems, translation by Andy Gaus, Threshold Books (Putney, Vt.), 1981.

An Unofficial Rilke: Poems 1912-1926, edited and with translation by Michael Hamburger, Anvil Press, 1981.

Selected Poetry of Rainer Maria Rilke, edited and with translation by Mitchell, Random House, 1982.

The Astonishment of Origins: French Sequences, translation from the French by Poulin, Graywolf Press, 1982.

Selected Poems, translation by A. E. Flemming, Golden Smith (St. Petersburg, Fla.), 1983.

The Unknown Rilke: Selected Poems, translation by Franz Wright, Oberlin College, 1983.

The Migration of Powers: French Poems, translation by Poulin, Graywolf Press, 1984.

Between Roots: Selected Poems, translation by Lesser, Princeton University Press, 1986.

The Complete French Poems of Rainer Maria Rilke, translation by Poulin, Graywolf Press, 1986.

Rodin and Other Prose Pieces, translation by G. Craig Houston, Salem House, 1987.

Shadows on the Sundial (selected poems), edited by Stanley H. Barkan, translation by Norbert Krapf, Cross-Cultural Communications, 1989.

The Best of Rilke, translation by Walter Arndt, University Press of New England, 1989.

TRANSLATOR

Elizabeth Barrett Browning, *Sonette nach dem Portugiesischen,* Insel, 1908.

Maurice de Guerin, *Der Kentaur,* Insel, 1911.

Die Liebe der Magdalena: Ein franzoesischer Sermon, gezogen durch den Abbe Joseph Bonnet aus dem Ms. Q I 14 der Kaiserlichen Bibliothek zu St. Petersburg, Insel, 1912.

Marianna Alcoforado, *Portugiesische Briefe,* Insel, 1913.

Andre Gide, *Die Rueckkehr des verlorenen Sohnes,* Insel, 1914.

Die vierundzwanzig Sonette der Louise Labe, Lyoneserin, 1555, Insel, 1918.

Paul Valery, *Gedichte,* Insel, 1925.

Valery, *Eupalinos oder Ueber die Architektur,* Insel, 1927.

Uebertragungen, Insel, 1927.

Dichtungen des Michelangelo, Insel, 1936.

Gedichte aus fremden Sprachen, Ungar, 1947.

Maurice Maeterlinck, *Die sieben Jungfrauen von Orlamuende,* Dynamo (Liege), 1967.

LETTERS

Briefe an Auguste Rodin, Insel, 1928.

Briefe aus den Jahren 1902 bis 1906, edited by Sieber-Rilke and Sieber, Insel, 1929.

Briefe an einen jungen Dichter, Insel, 1929, translation by Norton published as *Letters to a Young Poet,* Norton, 1934, translation by K. W. Maurer published as *Letters to a Young Poet,* Langley (London), 1943, revised edition, Norton, 1963, translation by Mitchell, Random House, 1984.

Briefe an eine junge Frau, Insel, 1930, translation by Maurer published as *Letters to a Young Woman,* Langley, 1945.

Briefe aus den Jahren 1906 bis 1907, edited by Sieber-Rilke and Sieber, Insel, 1930.

Briefe und Tagebuecher aus der Fruehzeit, edited by Sieber-Rilke and Sieber, Insel, 1931.

Briefe aus den Jahren 1907 bis 1914, edited by Sieber-Rilke and Sieber, Insel, 1933.

Ueber Gott: Zwei Briefe, Insel, 1933.

Briefe an seinen Verleger 1906 bis 1926, edited by Sieber-Rilke and Sieber, Insel, 1934.

Briefe aus Muzot 1921 bis 1926, edited by Sieber-Rilke and Sieber, Insel, 1935.

Gesammelte Briefe, six volumes, edited by Sieber-Rilke and Sieber, Insel, 1936-39.

Lettres a une Amie Venitienne, Asmus, 1941.

Briefe an eine Freundin, edited by Herbert Steiner, Wells College Press, 1944.

Briefe, Oltener Buecherfreunde (Olten), 1945.

Briefe an Baronesse von Oe, edited by von Mises, Johannespresse, 1945.

Letters of Rainer Maria Rilke, translation by Jane Bannard Greene and Norton, Norton, Volume 1: *1892-1910,* 1945, reprinted, 1969, Volume 2: *1910-1926,* 1948, reprinted, 1969.

Briefe an eine Reisegefaehrtin: Eine Begegnung mit Rainer Maria Rilke, Ibach (Vienna), 1947.

Briefe an das Ehepaar S. Fischer, edited by Hedwig Fischer, Classen (Zurich), 1947.

La derniere amitie de Rainer Maria Rilke: Lettres inedites de Rilke a Madame Eloui Bey, edited by Edmond Jaloux, Laffont (Paris), 1949, translation by William H. Kennedy published as *Rainer Maria Rilke: His Last Friendship; Unpublished Letters to Mrs. Eloui Bey,* Philosophical Library, 1952.

"So lass ich mich zu traeumen gehen," Mader, 1949, translation by Heinz Norden published as *Letters to Benvenuta,* Philosophical Library, 1951.

Briefe an seinen Verleger, two volumes, edited by Sieber-Rilke and Sieber, Insel, 1949.

Briefe, two volumes, edited by Sieber-Rilke and Karl Altheim, Insel, 1950.

Die Briefe an Graefin Sizzo, 1921 bis 1926, Insel, 1950, enlarged edition, edited by Ingeborg Schnack, Insel, 1977.

Briefwechsel in Gedichten mit Erika Mitterer 1924 bis 1926, Insel, 1950, translation by N. K. Cruickshank published as *Correspondence in Verse with Erika Mitterer,* Hogarth, 1953.

Lettres francaise a Merline 1919-1922, du Seuil (Paris), 1950, translation by Violet M. Macdonald published as *Letters to Merline, 1919-1922,* Methuen, 1951.

Rainer Maria Rilke/Marie von Thurn und Taxis: Briefwechsel, two volumes, edited by Zinn, Niehans & Rokitansky (Zurich), 1951, translation by Nora Wydenbruck published as *The Letters of Rainer Maria Rilke and Princess Marie von Thurn and Taxis,* New Directions, 1958.

Rainer Maria Rilke/Lou Andreas-Salome, Briefwechsel, edited by Ernst Pfeiffer, Insel, 1952, revised and enlarged edition, 1975.

Rainer Maria Rilke/Andre Gide: Correspondance 1909-1926, edited by Renee Lang, Correa (Paris), 1952.

Briefe ueber Cezanne, edited by Clara Rilke, Insel, 1952, translation by Joel Agee published as *Letters on Cezanne,* Fromm, 1985.

Die Briefe an Frau Gudi Noelke aus Rilkes Schweizer Jahren, edited by Paul Obermueller, Insel, 1953, translation by Macdonald published as *Letters to Frau Gudi Noelke during His Life in Switzerland,* Hogarth, 1955.

Rainer Maria Rilke/Katharina Kippenberg: Briefwechsel, edited by Bettina von Bomhard, Insel, 1954.

Briefwechsel mit Benvenuta, edited by Kurt Leonhard, Bechtle (Esslingen), 1954, translation by Agee published as *Rilke and Benvenuta: An Intimate Correspondence,* Fromm, 1987.

Rainer Maria Rilke et Merline: Correspondace 1920-1926, edited by Dieter Basserman, Niehans (Zurich), 1954, reprinted, Paragon House, 1988.

Lettres milanaises 1921-1926, edited by Lang, Plon (Paris), 1956.

Rainer Maria Rilke/Inge Junghanns: Briefwechsel, edited by Wolfgang Herwig, Insel, 1959.

Selected Letters, edited by Harry T. Moore, Doubleday, 1960.

Wartime Letters of Rainer Maria Rilke, 1914-1921, translation by Norton, Norton, 1964.

Briefe an Sidonie Nadherny von Borutin, edited by Bernhard Blume, Insel, 1973.

Ueber Dichtung und Kunst, edited by Hartmut Engelhardt, Suhrkamp (Frankfurt), 1974.

Rainer Maria Rilke on Love and Other Difficulties: Translations and Considerations of Rainer Maria Rilke, edited by John J. L. Mood, Norton, 1975.

Rainer Maria Rilke/Helene von Nostitz: Briefwechsel, edited by Oswalt von Nostitz, Insel, 1976.

Briefe an Nanny Wunderly-Volkart, two volumes, edited by Niklaus Bigler and Raetus Luck, Insel, 1977.

Lettres autour d'un jardin, La Delirante (Paris), 1977.

Hugo von Hofmannsthal/Rainer Maria Rilke: Briefwechsel, edited by Rudolph Hirsch and Schnack, Suhrkamp, 1978.

Briefe an Axel Juncker, edited by Renate Scharffenberg, Insel, 1979.

Briefwechsel mit Rolf Freiherrn von Ungern-Sternberg, edited by Knorad Kratzsch, Insel Verlag Anton Kippenberg (Leipzig), 1980.

Rainer Maria Rilke/Anita Forrer: Briefwechsel, edited by Magda Kerenyi, Leipzig (Frankfurt am Main), 1982.

Rainer Maria Rilke/Marina Zwetajewa/Boris Pasternak: Briefwechsel, edited by Jewgenij Pasternak, Jelena Pasternak, and Konstantin M. Asadowski, Insel, 1983, translation by Margaret Wettlin and Walter Arndt published as *Letters Summer 1926,* Harcourt, 1985.

Rainer Maria Rilke: Briefe an Ernst Norlind, edited by Paul Astroem, Paul Astroems Forlag (Partille), 1986.

Rilke und Russland: Briefe, Erinnerungen, Gedichte, edited by Asadowski, Russian text translation by Ulrike Hirschberg, Insel, 1986.

Rainer Maria Rilke: Briefwechsel mit Regina Ullman und Ellen Delp, edited by Walter Simon, Insel, 1987.

Rainer Maria Rilke/Stefan Zweig: Briefe und Dokumente, edited by Donald Prater, Insel, 1987.

SIDELIGHTS: Of the poetry composed by the three majors German poets writing during the early twentieth century—Stefan George, Hugo von Hofmannsthal, and Rainer Maria Rilke—the lyrical intensity of Rilke's verses is generally considered to represent the highest artistic achievement. Rilke is unique in his efforts to expand the realm of poetry through new uses in syntax and imagery and in the philosophy that his poems explored. With regard to the former, W. H. Auden declared in *New Republic,* "Rilke's most immediate and obvious influence has been upon diction and imagery." Rilke expressed ideas with "physical rather than intellectual symbols. While Shakespeare, for example, thought of the non-human world in terms of the human, Rilke thinks of the human in terms of the non-human, of what he calls Things (Dinge)." Besides this technique, the other important aspect of Rilke's writings is the evolution of his philosophy, which reached a climax in *Duineser Elegien (Duino Elegies)* and *Die Sonette an Orpheus (Sonnets to Orpheus).* Rejecting the Catholic beliefs of his parents as well as Christianity in general, the poet strove throughout his life to reconcile beauty and suffering, life and death into one philosophy. As C. M. Bowra observed in *Rainer Maria Rilke: Aspects of His Mind and Poetry,* "Where others have found a unifying principle for themselves in religion or morality or the search for truth, Rilke found his in the search for impressions and the hope these could be turned into poetry. . . . For him Art was what mattered most in life."

Rilke's writing can be separated into several phases. His early work included not only verse, but a number of short stories and plays as well, all of which were characterized by their romanticism. His poems of this period show the influence of the German folk song tradition and have been compared to the lyrical work of Heinrich Heine. *Dictionary of Literary Biography* contributor George C. Schoolfield called Rilke's first poetry collection, *Leben und Lieder* ("Life and Songs"), "unbearably sentimental," but later works such as *Larenopfer* ("Offering to the Lares") and *Traumgekroent,* ("Crowned with Dreams") demonstrate "considerably better proof of his lyric talent." Although none of Rilke's plays are considered major works and his short stories, according to Schoolfield, demonstrate the author's immaturity, the latter do show "his awareness of language and a certain psychological refinement," as well as "flashes of brilliant satiric gift" and "evidence of a keen insight into human relations." The most popular poetry collections of Rilke's during this period were *Vom lieben Gott und Anderes (Stories of God)* and the romantic cycle *Die Weise von Liebe und Tod des Cornets Christoph Rilke (The Story of the Love and Death of Cornet Christoph Rilke),* which remained the poet's most widely recognize book during his lifetime.

A turning point came in Rilke's career as a result of several sojourns to Russia at the turn of the century. Inspired by the lives of the Russian people, whom the poet considered more devoutly spiritual than other Europeans, Rilke became convinced that he could live a fulfilling life only by seeking to love and understand God. Soon after his return from Russia in 1900, he began writing *Das Stundenbuch enthaltend die drei Buecher: Vom moenchischen Leben; Von der Pilgerschaft; Von der Armuth und vom Tode,* a collection that "marked for him the end of an epoch," according to Bowra and others. This book, translated as *The Book of Hours; Comprising the Three Books: Of the Monastic Life, Of Pilgrimage, Of Poverty and Death,* consists of a series of prayers about the search for God. Because of this concern, *Hound and Horn* critic Hester Pickman noted that the book "might have fallen out of the writings of Christian contemplatives," except that "the essential pattern is an inversion of theirs. God is not light but darkness—not a father, but a son, not the creator but the created. He and not man is our neighbor for men are infinitely far from each other. They must seek God, not where one or two are gathered in His name, but alone."

Whenever Rilke writes about God, however, he is not referring to the deity in the traditional sense, but rather uses the term to refer to the life force, or nature, or an all-embodying, pantheistic consciousness that is only slowly coming to realize its existence. "Extending the idea of evolution," Eudo C. Mason explained in an introduction to *The Book of Hours,* "and inspired probably also in some measure by Nietzsche's idea of the Superman, Rilke arrives at the paradoxical conception of God as the final result instead of the first cause of the cosmic process." Holding in contempt "all other more traditional forms of devoutness, which . . . merely 'accept God as a given fact,'" Rilke did not deny God's existence, but insisted that all possibilities about the nature of life be given equal consideration.

The real theme of *The Book of Hours,* concluded Mason, is the poet's "own inner life," his struggles toward comprehension, and, "above all . . . his perils *as a poet*"; the second major concept in *The Book of Hours,* then, is Rilke's apotheosis of art. "Religion is the art of those who are uncreative," Mason quoted Rilke as having said; the poet's work is often concerned with the artist's—especially poet's—role in society and with his inner doubts about his belief in poetry's superiority. Because of the firm establishment of these two themes in *The Book of Hours,* the collection "is essential to the understanding of what comes afterwards" in Rilke's writing, attests Pickman. *The Book of Hours* was also another of the poet's most popular works, second only to *The Story of the Love and Death of Cornet Christoph Rilke* during his lifetime. But despite being a "very beautiful" book, it also "remains too constantly abstract. It lacks the solid reality of great poetry," according to Pickman.

Rilke fixed his verse more firmly in reality in his next major poetry collection, *Neue Gedichte* (*New Poems*). The major influence behind this work was Rilke's association with the famous French sculptor, Auguste Rodin. Working as Rodin's secretary from 1905 to 1906, Rilke gained a greater appreciation of the work ethic. More importantly, however, the poet's verses became objective, evolving from an impressionistic, personal vision to the representation of this vision with impersonal symbolism. He referred to this type of poetry as *Dinggedichte* (thing poems). These verses employed a simple vocabulary to describe concrete subjects experienced in everyday life. Having learned the skill of perceptive observation from Rodin, and, later, from the French painter Paul Cezanne, Rilke "sustained for a little while the ability to write without inspiration, to transform his observations—indeed his whole life—into art," according to Nancy Willard, author of *Testimony of the Invisible Man.* The " 'thingness' of these poems," explained Erich Heller in his *The Artist's Journey into the Interior and Other Essays,* "reflects not the harmony in which an inner self lives with its 'objects'; it reflects a troubled inner self immersing itself in 'the things.' " But although this objective approach innovatively addressed subjects never before recognized by other poets and created "dazzling poems," Rilke realized, reported Willard, that it "did not really open the secret of living things."

By this point in his career, Rilke was reaching a crisis in his art that reveals itself both in *New Poems* and his only major prose work, the novel *Die Aufzeichnungen des Malte Laurids Brigge* (*The Notebooks of Malte Laurids Brigge*). These works express the poet's growing doubts about whether anything existed that was superior to mankind and his world. This, in turn, brought into question Rilke's very reason for writing poetry: the search for deeper meanings in life through art. E. M. Butler elucidated in her *Rainer Maria Rilke:* "[*The Notebooks of Malte Laurids Brigge*] marks a crisis in Rilke's attitude to God, a crisis which might be hailed as the loss of a delusion, or deplored as the loss of an ideal. [His concept of the] future artist-god had never been more than a sublime hypothesis, deriving from Rilke's belief in the creative and transforming powers of art." Having failed, in his mind, to accurately represent God in his poetry, Rilke attempted to "transform life into art" in his *New Poems.* "What he learnt," Butler continued, ". . . is what every artist has to face sooner or later, the realisation that life is much more creative than art. So that his mythological dream, the apotheosis of art, appeared to be founded on delusion. Either art was not as creative as he had thought, or he was not such a great artist. Both these doubts were paralyzing, and quite sufficient to account for the terrible apprehension present in every line of *Malte Laurids Brigge.* For this skepticism struck at the roots of his reason and justification for existence. Either he was the prophet of a new religion, or he was nobody."

Some critics, however, felt that Butler's interpretation overanalyzed Rilke's novel. In *Rainer Maria Rilke: The Ring of Forms,* for example, author Frank Wood granted that Butler had devised an "ingenious theory," but added that her interpretation "does less than justice to its artistic importance. Though no one would claim the *Notebooks* to be a completely achieved work of art, Malte's story nonetheless provides a valuable commentary on [Rilke's] Paris poetry and that yet to come, interpreting and enlarging still nuclear ideas. More than that, Malte allows us an inside view, as the poetry itself rarely does, into the poetic mind in process, with all its variety and even confusion."

"*The Notebooks of Malte Laurids Brigge* were supposed to be the coherent formulation of the insights which were formulated disjointly in the *New Poems,*" wrote *Phases of Rilke* author Norbert Fuerst. The book is a loosely autobiographical novel about a student who is the last descendant of a noble Danish family (Rilke believed, erroneously according to his biographers, that he was distantly related to Carinthian nobility), and follows his life from birth to a grim, poverty-stricken life as a student in Paris. Images of death and decay (especially in the Paris scenes) and Malte's fear of death are a continuous presence throughout the narrative. The novel concludes with a retelling of the story of the Prodigal Son that represents, according to a number of critics like Schoolfield, "Rilke's long search for the freedom that would enable him to apply his artistic will to the fullest."

Because Rilke never finished *The Notebooks of Malte Laurids Brigge* (in one of his letters, the author told a friend he ended the book "out of exhaustion," reported Schoolfield) Malte's ultimate fate is left ambiguous. Ronald Gray commented in his *The German Tradition in Literature: 1871-1945:* "Malte seems to have come to terms with suffering not so much by enduring it as by cutting himself off from contact with all others. But does Rilke present this as an ideal or as a deplored end? His own comments . . . are inconclusive, and in part this was due to his own uncertainty as to the extent to which Malte's life could be identified with his own." In one of Rilke's letters translated in the collection *Letters of Rainer Maria Rilke: 1910-1926,* the author remarked that the most significant question in *The Notebooks of Malte Laurids Brigge* is: "[How] is it possible to live when after all the elements of this life are utterly incomprehensible to us?"

Some authorities, summarized Wood, concluded that the answer to this question is that it is not possible to live; therefore, Malte is doomed. Others believed that Malte's answer lies in finding God. Wood, however, held that both these interpretations are too extreme. The solution, he proposed, can instead be found in Rilke's poetry collection, *Requiem,* which was written about the same time as his novel and "emphasizes that not victory but surviving is everything." As William Rose determined in *Rainer Maria Rilke: Aspects of His Mind and Poetry, The Notebooks of Malte Laurids Brigge* actually was kind of a catharsis for the author in which "Rilke gave full vent . . . to the fears which haunted him." "Without the *Notebooks* behind him," Wood concluded, "the poet would hardly have ventured to" write the *Duino Elegies* in 1912.

Duino Elegies "might well be called the greatest set of poems of modern times," averred Colin Wilson, author of *Religion and the Rebel.* Wilson added, "They have had as much influence in German-speaking countries as [T. S. Eliot's] *The Waste Land* has in England and America." Having discovered a dead end in the objective poetry with which he experimented in *New Poems,* Rilke once again turned to his own personal vision to find solutions to the questions about the purpose of human life and the poet's role in society. *Duino Elegies* finally resolved these puzzles to Rilke's own satisfaction. Called *Duino Elegies* because Rilke began writing them in 1912 while staying at Duino Castle on the Italian Adriatic coast, the collection took ten years to complete due to a depression the poet suffered during and after World War I. When his inspiration returned, however, the poet wrote a total of eleven lengthy poems for the book.

The unifying poetic image that Rilke employs throughout *Duino Elegies* is that of angels, which carry a variety of meanings except for the usual Christian denotation. The angels represent a higher force in life, both beautiful and terrible, completely indifferent to mankind; they represent the power of poetic vision, as well as Rilke's personal struggle to reconcile art and life. Butler elaborates: "[The] Duino angels are truly a poetical creation to be completely susceptible of rational interpretation, and too complex to stand for any one idea. Rilke's idolatry of art as the supreme creative power became incarnate in them; a more mysterious and less ambiguous piece of symbolism than his previous use of the word God to represent an emergent aesthetic creator. These angels had more of the protean nature of the God of *The Book of Hours;* they were far more arresting and terrible in their utter aloofness, and self-sufficiency, as befitting beings who were not in a state of becoming but of eternal and immortal existence. Their absolute beauty annihilated human standards; and Rilke could only avert his personal destruction as a poet by accepting the challenge implicit in their very being. This is the drama inherent in *Duino Elegies.*" The Duino angels thus allowed Rilke to objectify abstract ideas as he had done in *New Poems,* while not limiting him to the mundane materialism that was incapable of thoroughly illustrating philosophical issues.

Duino Elegies, according to E. L. Stahl, a contributor to *Rainer Maria Rilke: Aspects of His Mind and Poetry,* "begin with lament, but end with praise." Beginning in the first elegy with what Butler called "a bitter confession of poetical and emotional bankruptcy," Rilke steadily develops his reasons for lamenting our existence, until the seventh elegy, where the discovery of a means to solving life's puzzles first turns lament into praise. The "lesson of the seventh elegy," wrote Butler, is "that the only real world is within us, and that life is one long transformation. Rilke had at last found the formula for his cosmic mission and a connecting link between himself and the angel." However, it is not until the ninth elegy that this formula is used. "We exist," said

Stahl in his clarification of Rilke's revelation, "because existence is in itself of value and because everything which exists apparently appeals to us and depends on us for its future existence, though in this world we are the most fleeting creatures of all. But we pass on into another world, and it is our task to ensure for other beings a form of continued existence. We accomplish this task by expressing their hidden and inner meaning and by taking this possession 'across' with us. The purpose of our existence is to praise and extol the simple things of existence."

This conclusion allowed Rilke to accept life's suffering and death because he realized the purpose of life was not to avoid these destructive forces in favor of happiness. Instead, as the poet explains in the tenth elegy, the "principle of the whole of our life, in this world and the next, is sorrow." Having reconciled himself to the belief that man's existence by necessity involves suffering, Rilke concluded, according to Stahl, that the poet's function is to project "the world into the angel, where it becomes invisible." "Then the angels," Butler finished, "who can only apprehend what is invisible, will marvel at this hymn of praise to humble, simple things. They will receive them and rescue them from oblivion." This complex explanation of life's purpose, which Rilke developed slowly over many years, is not one that lends itself to a "rational explanation," Stahl pointed out. "It is a matter of Rilke's personal belief."

Nevertheless, the revolutionary poetic philosophy that Rilke proposes in *Duino Elegies* is considered significant to many literary scholars. "No poet before him had been brave enough to accept the *whole* of [the dark side of the] world, as if it were unquestionably valid and potentially universal," asserted Conrad Aiken in his *Collected Criticism.* Like the German philosopher Friedrich Nietzsche, who lived about the same time as Rilke, the poet determined his objective to be "[praise] and celebration in the face of and in full consciousness of the facts that had caused other minds to assume an attitude of negativity," wrote *Emergence from Chaos* author Stuart Holroyd. But even though the final purpose of *Duino Elegies* is to praise existence, the "predominant note . . . is one of lament." But by overcoming his quandaries in this collection, Rilke was completely free to devote his poetry to praise in his *Sonnets to Orpheus.*

"The Sonnets are the songs of his victory," affirmed Bowra in his *The Heritage of Symbolism.* "In the Sonnets," Bowra also wrote, "Rilke shows what poetry meant to him, what he got from it and what he hoped for it. The dominating mood is joy. It is a complement to the distress and anxiety of the Elegies, and in Rilke's whole performance the two books must be taken together." Aiken similarly commented that the "*Sonnets to Orpheus* . . . is, with the *Elegies,* Rilke's finest work—the two books really belong together, shine the better for each other's presence."

In the last few years of his life, Rilke was inspired by such French poets as Paul Valery and Jean Cocteau, and wrote most of his last verses in French. Always a sickly man, the poet succumbed to leukemia in 1926 while staying at the Valmont sanatorium near Lake Geneva. On his deathbed, he remained true to his anti-Christian beliefs and refused the company of a priest. Hermann Hesse summed up Rilke's evolution as a poet in his book, *My Belief: Essays on Life and Art:* "Remarkable, this journey from the youthful music of Bohemian folk poetry . . . to *Orpheus,* remarkable how . . . his mastery of form increases, penetrates deeper and deeper into his problems! And at each stage now and again the miracle occurs, his delicate, hesitant, anxiety-prone person withdraws, and through him resounds the music of the universe; like the basin of a fountain he becomes at once instrument and ear." Without his parents' religious ideals to comfort him, Rilke found peace in his art. As Holroyd concluded, the "poetry which Rilke wrote to express and extend his experience . . . is one of the most successful attempts a modern man has made to orientate himself within his chaotic world."

BIOGRAPHICAL/CRITICAL SOURCES:

BOOKS

Aiken, Conrad, *Collected Criticism,* Oxford University Press, 1968.
Baron, Frank, Ernst S. Dick, and Warren R. Maurer, editors, *Rilke: The Alchemy of Alienation,* Regents Press of Kansas, 1980.
Bowra, C. M., *The Heritage of Symbolism,* Macmillan, 1943.
Burnshaw, Stanley, editor, *The Poem Itself,* Holt, 1960.
Butler, E. M., *Rainer Maria Rilke,* Macmillan, 1941.
Dictionary of Literary Biography, Volume 81: *Austrian Fiction Writers, 1875-1913,* Gale, 1989.
Feste-McCormick, Diana, *The City as Catalyst: A Study of Ten Novels,* Fairleigh Dickinson University Press, 1979.
Fuerst, Norbert, *Phases of Rilke,* Indiana University Press, 1958.
Graff, W. L., *Rainer Maria Rilke: Creative Anguish of a Modern Poet,* Princeton University Press, 1956.
Gray, Ronald, *The German Tradition in Literature: 1871-1945,* Cambridge at the University Press, 1965.
Heller, Erich, *The Artist's Journey into the Interior and Other Essays,* Random House, 1965.
Hesse, Herman, *My Belief: Essays on Life and Art,* Farrar, Straus, 1974.
Holroyd, Stuart, *Emergence from Chaos,* Houghton, 1957.
Lewisohn, Ludwig, *Cities and Men,* Harper & Brothers, 1927.
Olivero, Federico, *Rainer Maria Rilke: A Study in Poetry and Mysticism,* W. Heffer & Sons, 1931.
Peters, H. F., *Rainer Maria Rilke: Masks and the Man,* University of Washington Press, 1960.
Pollard, Percival, *Masks and Minstrels of New Germany,* John W. Luce and Company, 1911.
Rilke, Rainer Maria, *Letters of Rainer Maria Rilke: 1910-1926,* Volume 2, Norton, 1948.
Rilke, Rainer Maria, *The Book of Hours: Comprising the Three Books, Of the Monastic Life, Of Pilgrimage, Of Poverty and Death,* Hogarth Press, 1961.
Rilke, Rainer Maria, *Nine Plays,* Ungar, 1979.
Rilke, Rainer Maria, *The Notebooks of Malte Laurids Brigge,* Vintage Book, 1985.
Rose, William, and G. Craig Houston, editors, *Rainer Maria Rilke: Aspects of His Mind and His Poetry,* Gordian, 1970.
Twentieth Century Literary Criticism, Gale, Volume 1, 1978, Volume 6, 1982, Volume 19, 1986.
Willard, Nancy, *Testimony of the Invisible Man,* University of Missouri Press, 1970.
Wilson, Colin, *Religion and the Rebel,* Houghton, 1957.
Wood, Frank, *Rainer Maria Rilke: The Ring of Forms,* University of Minnesota Press, 1958.
Ziolkowski, Theodore, *Dimensions of the Modern Novel: German Texts and European Contexts,* Princeton University Press, 1969.

PERIODICALS

Hound and Horn, April-June, 1931.
Listener, December 18, 1975.
Modern Language Review, April, 1979.
Nation, December 17, 1930.
New Republic, September 6, 1939.
New York Herald Tribune Books, December 14, 1930.
PMLA, October, 1974.
Times Literary Supplement, December 12, 1975.
University of Dayton Review, spring, 1981.

—*Sketch by Kevin S. Hile*

*   *   *

RINGMASTER, The
  See MENCKEN, H(enry) L(ouis)

*   *   *

RITSOS, Giannes
  See RITSOS, Yannis

*   *   *

RITSOS, Yannis 1909-
(Giannes Ritsos)

PERSONAL: Born May 1, 1909, in Monemvasia, Greece; son of Eleftherios (a land-owner) and Eleftheria (Vouzounara) Ritsos; married Fallitasa Georgiades (a medical doctor), 1954; children: Erie. *Education:* Educated in Greece. *Religion:* Greek Orthodox.

ADDRESSES: Home—39 M. Koraka St., Athens 219, Greece.

CAREER: Poet. Angelopoulos (law firm), Athens, Greece, law clerk, 1925; Mitzopoulos-Oeconomopoulos (notaries for National Bank of Greece), Athens, clerk, 1925-26; Lawyer's Association, Athens, assistant librarian, 1926; confined to a sanatorium because of tuberculosis, 1927-31; employed by a music theatre during the 1930s; National Theatre of Greece, Athens, member of Chorus of Ancient Tragedies, 1938-45; Govostis (publisher), Athens, editor and proofreader, 1945-48, 1952-56; full-time writer, 1956—. Former actor and dancer for Lyriki Skini (Athens Opera House).

MEMBER: European Community of Writers, Society of Greek Writers, Society of Greek Dramatists, Comite des Gens des Lettres, Societe des Ecrivains et Compositeurs Dramatiques Francais, Academy of Meinz, Academy Mallarme.

AWARDS, HONORS: State Prize Award for Poetry (Greece), 1956; Grand Prix International de la Biennale de Poesie de Knokke (Belgium), 1972; International Prize "Georgi Dimitroff" (Bulgaria), 1974; honorary doctorate from Salonica University (Greece), 1975, and from University of Birmingham, 1978; Grand Prix Francais de la Poesie "Alfred de Vigny," 1975; International Prize for Poetry "Etna-Taormina" (Italy), 1976; International Prize for Poetry "Seregno-Brianza" (Italy), 1976; Lenin Prize for Peace, 1977; Mondello Prize (Italy), 1978.

WRITINGS:

POETRY IN ENGLISH

Romiosyne, Kedros, 1966, translation by O. Laos published as *Romiossyni,* Dustbooks, 1969.
Poems of Yannis Ritsos, translated by Alan Page, Oxonian Press, 1969.
Romiossini and Other Poems, translated by Dan Georgakas and Eleni Paidoussi, Quixote Press, 1969.
Gestures and Other Poems, 1968-1970, translated by Nikos Stangos, Cape Golliard, 1971.
Contradictions, translated by John Stathatos, Sceptre Press, 1973.
Dekaochto lianotragouda tes pikres patridas, Kedros, 1973, translation by Amy Mims published as *Eighteen Short*

Songs of the Bitter Motherland, North Central Publishing, 1974.

Diadromos kai skala, Kedros, 1973, translation by Nicos Germanacos published as *Corridor and Stairs,* Goldsmith Press (Ireland), 1976.

Yannis Ritsos: Selected Poems, translated by Stangos, Penguin, 1974.

The Fourth Dimensions: Selected Poems of Yannis Ritsos, translated and introduced by Rae Dalven, David R. Godine, 1977.

Chronicle of Exile, translated and introduced by Minas Savvas, Wire Press, 1977.

Ritsos in Parenthesis, translated by Kimon Friar, Princeton University Press, 1979.

Grafe tyflou, Kedros, 1979, translated by Friar and Kostas Myrsiades as *Scripture of the Blind,* Ohio State University Press, 1979.

Subterranean Horses, translated by Savvas, Ohio State University Press, 1980.

Erotica: Small Suite in Red Major, Naked Body, Carnal Word, translated by Friar, Sachem Press, 1982.

Selected Poems, translated by Edmund Keely, Ecco Press, 1983.

Exile and Return, translated by Keely, Ecco Press, 1985.

Monovasia and the Women of Monemvasia, translated by Friar and Myrsiades, Nostos Books, 1988.

POETRY IN GREEK

Trakter (title means "Tractors"), Govostis, 1934.

Pyramides (title means "Pyramids"), Govostis, 1935.

Epitaphios, Rizospastis, 1936.

To tragoudi tes adelphes mou (title means "The Song of My Sister"), Govostis, 1937.

Earini Symphonia (title means "Spring Symphony"), Govostis, 1938.

To emvatirio tou okeanou (title means "The March of the Ocean"), Govostis, 1940.

Palia Mazurka se rythmo vrohis (title means "An Old Mazurka in the Rhythm of the Rain"), Govostis, 1942.

Dokimasia (title means "Trial"), Govostis, 1943.

O syntrofos mas (title means "Our Comrade"), Govostis, 1945.

O anthropos me to gary fallo (title means "The Man with the Carnation"), Politikes Ke Logotechnikes Ekdoseis, 1952.

Agrypnia (title means "Vigil"), Pyxida, 1954.

Proino astro (title means "Morning Star"), [Athens], 1955.

He sonata tou selenophotos (title means "Moonlight Sonata"), Kedros, 1956.

Croniko (title means "Chronicle"), Kedros, 1957.

Apochairetisnos (title means "Farewell"), Kedros, 1957.

Hydria (title means "The Urn"), Kedros, 1957.

Cheimerinediaugeia (title means "Winter Limpidity"), Kedros, 1957.

Petrinos Chronos (title means "Stony Time"), P.L.E., 1957.

He Geitonies tou Kosmou (title means "The Neighborhood of the World"), P.L.E., 1957.

Otan erchetai ho xenos (title means "When the Stranger Comes"), Kedros, 1958.

Any potachti Politeia (title means "Unsubjugated City"), P.L.E., 1958.

He architectoniki ton dentron (title means "The Architecture of the Trees"), P.L.E., 1958.

Hoi gerontisses k'he thalassa (title means "The Old Woman and the Sea"), Kedros, 1959.

To parathyro (title means "The Window"), Kedros, 1960.

He gephyra (title means "The Bridge"), Kedros, 1960.

Ho mavros Hagios (title means "The Black Saint"), Kedros, 1961.

Pieimata Tomos I (title means "Poems Volume I"), Kedros, 1961.

Pieimata Tomos II (title means "Poems Volume II"), Kedros, 1961.

To nekro spiti (title means "The Dead House"), Kedros, 1962.

Kato ap' ton iskio tou vounou (title means "Beneath the Shadow of the Mountain"), Kedros, 1962.

To dentro tis phylakis Kai he gynaikes (title means "The Prison Tree and the Women"), Kedros, 1963.

Martyries (title means "Testimonies"), Kedros, 1963.

Dodeka pieimata gia ton Kavaphe (title means "12 Poems for Cavafy"), Kedros, 1963.

Pieimata Tomos III (title means "Poems Volume III"), Kedros, 1964.

Paichnidia t'ouranou kai tou nerou (title means "Playful Games of the Sky and the Water"), Kedros, 1964.

Philoktetes, Kedros, 1964.

Orestes, Kedros, 1966.

Martyries (title means "Testimonies II"), Kedros, 1966.

Ostrava, Kedros, 1967.

Petres, Epanalepseis, Kinklidoma (title means "Stones, Repetitions, Railings"), Kedros, 1972.

He epistrophe tes Iphigeneias (title means "The Return of Iphigenia"), Kedros, 1972.

He Helene (title means "Helen"), Kedros, 1972.

Cheironomies (title means "Gestures"), Kedros, 1972.

Tetarte distase (title means "Fourth Dimension"), Kedros, 1972.

Chrysothemis, Kedros, 1972.

Ismene, Kedros, 1972.

Graganda, Kedros, 1973.

Ho aphanismos tis Milos (title means "The Annihilation of Milos"), Kedros, 1974.

Hymnos kai threnos gia tin Kypro (title means "Hymn and Lament for Cyprus"), Kedros, 1974.

To Kapnismeno tsoukali (title means "The Soot-Black Pot"), Kedros, 1974.

To kodonostasio (title means "Belfry"), Kedros, 1974.

Ho tichos mesa ston Kathrephti (title means "The Wall in the Mirror"), Kedros, 1974.

Chartina (title means "Papermade"), Kedros, 1974.

He Kyra ton Ambelion (title means "The Lady of the Vineyards"), Kedros, 1975.

He teleftaia pro Anthropou ekatontaeteia (title means "The Last Century before Humanity"), Kedros, 1975.

Epikairika (title means "Circumstantial Verse"), Kedros, 1975.

Ho hysterographo tis doxas (title means "The Postscript of Glory"), Kedros, 1975.

Hemerologia exorias (title means "Diaries in Exile"), Kedros, 1975.

Mantatofores, Kedros, 1975.

Pieimata Tomos IV (title means "Poems Volume IV"), Kedros, 1976.

To makrino (title means "Remote"), Kedros, 1977.

Gignesthai (title means "Becoming"), Kedros, 1977.

Epitome, Kedros, 1977.

Loipon?, Kedros, 1978.

Volidoskopos, Kedros, 1978.

Toichokollettes, Kedros, 1978.

To soma kai to haima, Kedros, 1978.

Trochonomos, Kedros, 1978.

He pyle, Kedros, 1978.

Monemvassiotisses, Kedros, 1978.

To teratodes aristioorghima, Kedros, 1978.

Phaedra, Kedros, 1978.
To roptro, Kedros, 1978.
Mia pygolampida fotizei ti nychta, Kedros, 1978.
Oneiro kalokerinou messimeriou, Kedros, 1980.
Diafaneia, Kedros, 1980.
Parodos, Kedros, 1980.
Monochorda, Kedros, 1980.
Ta erotica, Kedros, 1981.
Syntrofica tragoudia, Synchroni Epochi, 1981.
Hypokofa, Kedros, 1982.
Italiko triptycho, Kedros, 1982.
Moyovassia, Kedros, 1982.
To choriko ton sfougarhadon, Kedros, 1983.
Teiresias, Kedros, 1983.

OTHER

Pera ap'ton iskio ton Kyparission (title means "Beyond the Shadow of the Cypress Trees"; three-act play; first produced in Bucharest at the National Theatre, January, 1959), P.L.E., 1958.
Mia gynaika plai sti thalassa (title means "A Woman by the Sea"; three-act play; first produced in Bucharest, 1959), Politikes Ke Logotechnikes Ekdoseis, 1959.
Meletimata (title means "Essays"), Kedros, 1974.
Ariostos ho prosechtikos afhighite stigmes tou viou tou ke tou hypnou tou, Kedros, 1982.
Ti paraxena pragmata, Kedros, 1983.

Also author of works under name Giannes Ritsos.

SIDELIGHTS: "Yannis Ritsos," writes Peter Levi in the *Times Literary Supplement,* "is the old-fashioned kind of great poet. His output has been enormous, his life heroic and eventful, his voice is an embodiment of national courage, his mind is tirelessly active." At their best, Ritsos's poems, "in their directness and with their sense of anguish, are moving, and testify to the courage of at least one human soul in conditions which few of us have faced or would have triumphed over had we faced them," as Philip Sherrard notes in the *Washington Post Book World.*

The hardship and misfortunes of Yannis Ritsos's early life play a large role in all of his later writings. His wealthy family suffered financial ruin during his childhood, and soon afterward his father and sister went insane. Tuberculosis claimed his mother and an older brother, and later confined Ritsos himself to a sanatorium in Athens for several years. Poetry and the Greek communist movement became the sustaining forces in his life. But because his writing was often political in nature, Ritsos also endured persecution from his political foes. One of his most celebrated works, the "Epitaphios," a lament inspired by the assassination of a worker in a large general strike in Salonica, was burned by the Metaxas dictatorship, along with other books, in a ceremony enacted in front of the Temple of Zeus in 1936. After the Second World War and the annihilation of the National Resistance Movement, Ritsos was exiled for four years to the islands of Lemnos, Makronisos, and Ayios Efstratios. His books were banned until 1954. In 1967, when army colonels staged a coup and took over Greece, Ritsos was again deported, then held under house arrest until 1970. His works were again banned.

BIOGRAPHICAL/CRITICAL SOURCES:

BOOKS

Contemporary Literary Criticism, Gale, Volume 6, 1976, Volume 13, 1980, Volume 31, 1985.
Papandreou, Chrysa, *Ritsos: Etude, choix de texte, et bibliographie,* Seghers (Paris), 1968.

PERIODICALS

American Poetry Review, September-October, 1973.
Times Literary Supplement, July 18, 1975.
Washington Post Book World, May 8, 1977.

* * *

RIVERS, Elfrida
    See BRADLEY, Marion Zimmer

* * *

RIVERSIDE, John
    See HEINLEIN, Robert A(nson)

* * *

ROBBE-GRILLET, Alain 1922-

PERSONAL: Born August 18, 1922, in Brest, France; son of Gaston (a manufacturer) and Yvonne (Canu) Robbe-Grillet; married Catherine Rstakian, October 23, 1957. *Education:* Institut National Agronomique, ingenieur agronome. *Religion:* Not religious.

ADDRESSES: *Home*—18 Boulevard Maillot, 92200 Neuilly-sur-Seine, France. *Office*—Editions de Minuit, 7 rue Bernard-Palissy, 75006 Paris, France. *Agent*—Georges Borchardt, 136 East 57th St., New York, N.Y. 10022.

CAREER: Institut National des Statistiques, Paris, France, charge de mission, 1945-50; engineer with the Institut des Fruits et Agrumes Coloniaux in Morocco, French Guinea, Martinique, and Guadeloupe, 1949-51; Editions de Minuit, Paris, France, literary advisor, beginning 1954. Has travelled and lectured in Europe, Asia, and North and South America. Visiting professor, New York University and University of California, Los Angeles.

MEMBER: Legion d'Honneur (Officier du Merite, Officier des Arts et Lettres).

AWARDS, HONORS: Prix Feneon, 1954, for *Les Gommes;* Prix des Critiques, 1955, for *Le Voyeur;* Prix Louis Delluc, 1963, for *L'Immortelle;* best screenplay, Berlin Festival, 1969, for "L'Homme qui mont"; Premio Internazionale Mondello, 1982, for *Djinn.*

WRITINGS:

Les Gommes (novel), Editions de Minuit, 1953, translation by Richard Howard published as *The Erasers,* Grove, 1964, edited by J. S. Wood, Prentice-Hall, 1970.
Le Voyeur (novel), Editions de Minuit, 1955, translation by Howard published as *The Voyeur,* Grove, 1958, published under original French title, edited and with an introduction by Oreste F. Pucciani, Ginn-Blaisdell, 1970.
La Jalousie (novel), Editions de Minuit, 1957, translation by Howard published as *Jealousy,* Grove, 1959 (also see below), and as *Jealousy: Rhythmic Themes by Alain Robbe-Grillet* (limited edition with pen and ink drawings by Michele Forgeois), Allen Press, 1971, published under original French title, edited by Germaine Bree and Eric Schoenfeld, Macmillan, 1963 (published in England under original French title, edited by B. G. Garnham, Methuen, 1969).
Dans le labyrinthe (novel), Editions de Minuit, 1959, translation by Howard published as *In the Labyrinth,* Grove, 1960 (also see below), also published as *Dans le labyrinthe* [and] *Dans les couloirs du Metropolitain* [and] *Le Chambre secrete,* with

an essay on Robbe-Grillet by Gerard Genette, Union Generale D'Editions, 1964.

L'Annee derniere a Marienbad: Cine-roman (screenplay with photo extracts), Editions de Minuit, 1961, translation by Howard published as *Last Year at Marienbad,* Grove, 1962 (published in England as *Last Year at Marienbad: A Cine-Novel,* J. Calder, 1962).

Instantanes (short stories; also see below), Editions de Minuit, 1962, translation by Bruce Morissette published as *Snapshots,* Grove, 1968, new edition, 1972.

L'Immortelle: Cine-roman (screenplay with photo extracts from the film produced in 1963), Editions de Minuit, 1963, translation by A. M. Sheridan Smith published as *The Immortal One,* Calder & Boyars, 1971.

Pour un nouveau roman (essays), Editions de Minuit, 1963, new edition, Gallimard, 1970, translation by Barbara Wright published as *Snapshots* [and] *Towards a New Novel,* Calder & Boyars, 1965, translation by Howard published as *For a New Novel: Essays on Fiction,* Grove, 1966.

La Maison de rendezvous (novel), Editions de Minuit, 1965, translation by Howard published by Grove, 1966 (translation by Sheridan Smith published in England as *The House of Assignation: A Novel,* Calder & Boyars, 1970).

Two Novels by Robbe-Grillet (contains *Jealousy* and *In the Labyrinth,* with introductory essays by Morrissette and Roland Barthes), translated by Howard, Grove, 1965.

Projet pour le revolution a New York (novel), Editions de Minuit, 1970, translation by Howard published as *Project for a Revolution in New York,* Grove, 1972.

(With David Hamilton) *Reves de jeunes filles,* Montel, 1971, published in the United States as *Dreams of a Young Girl,* Morrow, 1971 (translation by Elizabeth Walter published in England as *Dreams of Young Girls,* Collins, 1971).

(With Hamilton) *Les Demoiselles d'Hamilton,* Laffont, 1972.

Glissements progressifs du plaisir (cine-roman; also see below), Editions de Minuit, 1974.

Construction d'un temple en ruines a la deesse Vanada, Bateau-Lavoir, 1975.

La Belle captive (novel; also see below), Bibliotheque des Arts, 1976.

Topologie d'une cite fantome (novel), Editions de Minuit, 1976, translation by J. A. Underwood published as *Topology of a Phantom City,* Grove, 1976.

Un regicide (novel), Editions de Minuit, 1978.

Souvenirs du triangle d'or (novel), Editions de Minuit, 1978, translation by Underwood published as *Recollections of the Golden Triangle,* Calder, 1984, Grove, 1986.

Temple aux miroirs, Seghers, 1979.

Djinn: Un trou rouge entre les paves disjoints (novel; also see below), Editions de Minuit, 1981, translation by Yvone Lenard and Walter Wells published as *Djinn,* Grove, 1982.

(Contributor) *Le Rendez-vous* (textbook; includes *Djinn*), Holt, 1981.

Le Miroir qui revient (novel) Editions de Minuit, 1985, translation by Jo Levy published as *Ghosts in the Mirror,* Calder, 1988, Grove, 1989.

Angelique; ou, L'Enchantement, Editions de Minuit, 1988.

SCREENPLAYS

"L'Annee derniere a Marienbad," Cocinor, 1961.
"L'Immortelle," Cocinor, 1963.
"Trans-Europ-Express," Lux-C.C.F., 1966.
"L'Homme qui ment," Lux-C.C.F., 1968.

"L'Eden et apres," Plan Films, 1970, adapted for French television and produced as "N'a pris les des," broadcast on Channel 3, 1975.
"Glissements progressifs du plaisir," Fox, 1974.
"Le Jeu avec le feu," U.G.C., 1975.
"La Belle captive," Argos Films, 1983.

OTHER

Also author of *Traces suspectes en surfaces,* with lithographs by Robert Rauschenberg. Contributor to *L'Express, Evergreen Review, New Statesman, Nouvelle Revue Francaise, Critique* (Paris), and *Revue de Paris.*

SIDELIGHTS: As the acknowledged leader and spokesman of the avant-garde New Novelists in France, Alain Robbe-Grillet has denounced those who talk of the novelist's social responsibility; for him the novel is not a tool and probably has little effect on society. "For us," he writes, "literature is not a means of expression, but a search. And it does not even know for what it searches. . . . [But] we prefer our searches, our doubts, our contradictions, our joy of having yet invented something." The New Novelists under Robbe-Grillet's fiction introduced new, experimental concepts into the French novel. Occasionally described as "the school of sight" or "the pen camera," the form of writing Robbe-Grillet expounds concentrates on vision and gives minute descriptions of matter-of-fact objects.

For the New Novelists, phenomenology replaced traditional psychology; personality was rendered indefinable and fluid; and objective description became the primary goal. Moral judgments are avoided: "The world is neither significant nor absurd," says Robbe-Grillet. "It simply is." Furthermore, "our concept of the world around us is now only fragmentary, temporary, contradictory even, and always disputable. How can a work of art presume to illustrate a preordained concept, whatever it might be?" Robbe-Grillet's preoccupation with inanimate objects has led critics, notably Francois Mauriac, to suggest that the author dehumanizes literature. Moreover, confusion for many readers results from the lack of distinction between a seen object and one that is imagined; reality for Robbe-Grillet is always flowing from one state to another. Descriptions are repeated with slight variations, leading to charges of obscurity and tedium.

Robbe-Grillet's style is to a great extent borrowed from the cinema. According to critic Peter Cortland this style "concentrates on distorted visual images because it is representing mental life, which is of necessity different from the physical 'life,' or arrangement, of things in the material world." John Weightman believes Robbe-Grillet wants his books to have "the solidity and independent existence of a statue or a picture, which resists any anecdotal or intellectual summary." Robbe-Grillet once noted: "It seems that the conventions of photography (its two-dimensional character, black and white coloring, the limitations of the frame, the differences in scale according to the type of shot) help to free us from our own conventions."

BIOGRAPHICAL/CRITICAL SOURCES:

BOOKS

Contemporary Literary Criticism, Gale, Volume 1, 1973, Volume 2, 1974, Volume 4, 1975, Volume 6, 1976, Volume 8, 1978, Volume 10, 1979, Volume 14, 1980, Volume 43, 1987.

Cruickshank, John, editor, *The Novelist as Philosopher,* Oxford University Press, 1962.

Dictionary of Literary Biography, Volume 83: *French Novelists since 1960,* Gale, 1989.

Le Sage, Laurent, *The French New Novel*, Pennsylvania State University Press, 1962.

Mauriac, Claude, *The New Literature*, Braziller, 1959.

Moore, Henry T., *French Literature Since World War II*, Southern Illinois University Press, 1966.

Peyre, Henri, *French Novelists of Today*, Oxford University Press, 1967.

Stoltzfus, Ben Frank, *Alain Robbe-Grillet and the New French Novel*, Southern Illinois University Press, 1961.

Sturrock, I., *The French New Novel*, Oxford University Press, 1969.

Szanto, G. H., *Narrative Consciousness*, University of Texas Press, 1972.

PERIODICALS

Critique (Paris), August, 1954, September-October, 1955, July, 1959.

Critique: Studies in Modern Fiction, winter, 1963-64.

Evergreen Review, Volume 2, number 5, 1956, Volume 3, number 10, 1959.

Film Quarterly, fall, 1963.

Hudson Review, winter, 1972-73.

Les Temps Modernes, June, 1957, July, 1960.

Listener, February 15, 1968.

Modern Language Notes, May, 1962, May, 1963.

Modern Language Quarterly, September, 1962.

Nation, April 25, 1959.

New Statesman, February 17, 1961.

New York Review of Books, June 1, 1972.

New York Times Book Review, November 22, 1959, May 28, 1972.

Nouvelle Revue Francaise, November, 1960.

PMLA, September, 1962.

Spectator, December 16, 1960.

Time, July 20, 1962.

Vogue, January 1, 1963.

Wisconsin Studies in Contemporary Literature, Volume 1, number 3, 1960.

Yale French Studies, summer, 1959.

*   *   *

ROBBINS, Harold 1916-

PERSONAL: Original name, Francis Kane; took name Harold Rubin (some sources list as Rubins) when adopted in 1927; name legally changed to Harold Robbins; born May 21, 1916, in New York, N.Y.; married Lillian Machnivitz, 1937 (divorced, 1962); married Grace Palermo; children: Caryn, Adreana. *Education:* Attended public high school in New York City.

ADDRESSES: Home—Le Cannet, Cannes, France. *Office*—c/o Simon & Schuster, 1230 Avenue of the Americas, New York, N.Y. 10020.

CAREER: Novelist. Worked as a grocery clerk, cook, cashier, errand boy, and bookies' runner, 1927-31; in food factoring business during 1930s; Universal Pictures, New York City, shipping clerk in warehouse, 1940-41, executive director of budget and planning, 1942-57.

WRITINGS:

NOVELS

Never Love a Stranger, Knopf, 1948, reprinted, Pocket Books, 1985.

The Dream Merchants, Knopf, 1949, reprinted, Pocket Books, 1987.

A Stone for Danny Fisher, Knopf, 1952, reprinted, Pocket Books, 1985.

Never Leave Me, Knopf, 1953, reprinted, Pocket Books, 1978.

79 Park Avenue, Knopf, 1953, reprinted, Pocket Books, 1982.

Stiletto, Dell, 1960, reprinted, 1982.

The Carpetbaggers, Trident Press, 1961, reprinted, Pocket Books, 1987.

Where Love Has Gone, Trident Press, 1962, reprinted, Pocket Books, 1987.

The Adventurers, Simon & Schuster, 1966, reprinted, Pocket Books, 1987.

The Inheritors, Trident Press, 1969, reprinted, Pocket Books, 1985.

The Betsy, Trident Press, 1971.

The Pirate, Simon & Schuster, 1974.

The Lonely Lady, Simon & Schuster, 1976.

Dreams Die First, Simon & Schuster, 1977.

Memories of Another Day, Simon & Schuster, 1979.

Goodbye, Janette, Simon & Schuster, 1981.

Spellbinder, Simon & Schuster, 1982.

Descent from Xanadu, Simon & Schuster, 1984.

The Storyteller, Simon & Schuster, 1985.

Piranha, Simon & Schuster, 1986.

OTHER

Also author of "The Survivors," a television series for American Broadcasting Co., 1969-70.

SIDELIGHTS: Each day, some 40,000 people buy a Harold Robbins novel, while total sales of his twenty books is over 250 million copies worldwide. Sales figures for individual titles are also phenomenal. *The Carpetbaggers* has gone through more than seventy printings and sold over eight million copies; *79 Park Avenue* has sold more than five and a half million copies; *Never Love a Stranger* and *Dreams Die First* have each topped three million in sales. None of Robbins's novels have sold less than 600,000 copies. The books have also been translated into thirty-nine languages and are on sale in sixty-three countries around the world. Many have been made into popular films as well.

Because of these impressive statistics, Robbins calls himself the best novelist alive. "There's not another writer being published today," he tells Leslie Hanscom of the *Pittsburgh Press*, "whose every book—every book he's ever written—is always on sale everywhere, and that's gotta mean something. . . . You can find my books anywhere in the world in any language."

The typical Robbins novel is a long, intricately-plotted story loaded with illicit sex, graphic violence, and powerful conflicts between members of the international jet set. Often they are also exposes of a sort, taking the reader behind the scenes of a glamorous and respected industry to reveal the secret corruption there. Often, too, the characters are thinly veiled versions of famous people in business and high society. The best of Robbins's novels are "fun to read, full of outrageous people and complicated plot lines, not to mention lots of supposedly sizzling sex," as Joy Fielding writes in the Toronto *Globe and Mail*.

Robbins divides his books into two categories. The first are the adventure novels like *The Carpetbaggers* which focus on the Machiavellian power plays of unscrupulous captains of industry. The second type is what Robbins calls his Depression novels. These are, Dick Lochte explains in the *Los Angeles Times Book Review*, "close in style and substance to the hardboiled novels of the '30s in which tough street kids fight their way out of the proletarian jungle to achieve wealth and power." These latter books are largely based on Robbins's own life story, which in many ways sounds fantastic enough to be fiction.

Robbins began life as Francis Kane, an abandoned infant whose parents were unknown. Raised in a Roman Catholic orphanage in New York's tough Hell's Kitchen area, Robbins was placed in a series of foster homes as a youth. When the last of his foster parents, a Manhattan pharmacist, adopted him in 1927, he was given the name of Harold Rubin. He used the name of Harold Robbins when he turned to writing in the 1940s and has since made it his legal name.

At the age of fifteen, Robbins left home to begin a series of low-paying jobs in New York City. He worked as a bookies' runner, a cook, a clerk, and an errand boy, yet none of these jobs in the Depression years of the 1930s provided much opportunity for the ambitious Robbins. But while working as an inventory clerk in a grocery store, Robbins noted that fresh produce was difficult to find. The food distribution system of the time was so bad that some crops were rotting in the fields while store shelves were empty. Robbins got into the food factoring business, buying options on farmers' crops that were in demand in the city and selling the options to canning companies and wholesale grocers. By the time he was twenty, Robbins was a millionaire.

But in 1939, with war looming in the public mind, Robbins speculated in crop futures and lost. Reasoning that a major war would cut off or sharply reduce shipments of sugar, thus sending prices upward, Robbins invested his fortune in sugar at $4.85 per hundred pounds. Unfortunately, the Roosevelt administration chose to freeze food prices, and sugar was frozen at $4.65 per hundred pounds. Robbins went bankrupt. He took a job with the Universal Pictures warehouse in New York City as a shipping clerk. When he uncovered overcharges made to the company in excess of $30,000, Robbins was promoted, eventually becoming the executive director of budget and planning.

It was while working for Universal Pictures that Robbins first began to write. A vice-president of the company overheard Robbins complain about a novel that the studio had bought for filming. He challenged him to write a better book himself, and Robbins took him up on it. The resulting six-hundred-page novel was sent to an agent and within three weeks, the publishing house of Alfred Knopf accepted the book for publication.

Never Love a Stranger, still Robbins's personal favorite of his novels, appeared in 1948. Although the book's candid approach to sex caused the police in Philadelphia to confiscate copies, many reviewers found it a realistic portrayal of a tough New York City orphan coming of age. Drawing heavily on Robbins's own experiences on the streets of Manhattan, the story revolves around the hustlers and racketeers of that city and recounts the protagonist's efforts to find his place in the world. N. L. Rothman of the *Saturday Review of Literature* notes that "Robbins' writing is strong, his pace varied, and his invention admirable."

Robbins followed his initial success with *The Dream Merchants,* a novel set in the Hollywood film world and telling of the rise of Johnny Edge, a movie entrepreneur. The novel also traces the rise of Hollywood itself. Budd Schulberg of the *Saturday Review of Literature* finds that "the upward climb of immigrant shopkeepers to positions of power in the industry of mass entertainment makes colorful history and entertaining reading, [but] Mr. Robbins never quite succeeds in re-creating them as vital fictional characters." Citing Robbins's daring sex scenes, the reviewer for the *Christian Science Monitor,* M. W. Stoer, complains that "it is regrettable that a book with so much in it that is otherwise entertaining and tempered with warm humanity should

have been allowed to lapse into such tastelessness." But the *New York Post*'s Lewis Gannett judges the novel more favorably. "Robbins," Gannett writes, "knows the great Hollywood art: he keeps his story moving, shifting expertly from tears to laughter and from desperation to triumph."

Perhaps the most critically praised of Robbins's novels is *A Stone for Danny Fisher,* the story of a poor Jewish boy's struggle to succeed in the New York of the 1930s and 1940s. James B. Lane, writing in the *Journal of Popular Culture,* claims that the book "recorded the epic battle of ethnic groups against inconsequentialness, and the disintegration of their rigid moral, ethical, and cultural standards under the stress and strain of survival." James Kelly of the *New York Times,* despite some reservations about the novel's believability, praises Robbins's "vivid characterization" and "feeling for individual scenes." Thomas Thompson of *Life* speculates that had Robbins ended his career with *A Stone for Danny Fisher,* the novel "would have reserved him a small place in literature."

Unfortunately, Robbins went on to write many more best-selling novels, few of which have received a sympathetic hearing from the critics. Evan Hunter of the *New York Times Book Review,* for instance, argues that "in true pulp style Mr. Robbins never tries to evoke anything except through cliche. . . . His people never simply say anything. They say it 'shortly' or 'darkly,' or they 'growl' or 'grunt' it." Reviewing *Spellbinder* for the *Chicago Tribune Book World,* Frederick Busch states that "the book is the paginated equivalent of television: shallow, semiliterate, made of cliches and stereotypes, full of violence and heavy breathing. People who love TV love such books." Reviewing *The Betsy* for *Books and Bookmen,* Roger Baker calls it "about as realistic and pungent as Batman. . . . The superficiality of the characters is beyond belief; the mechanical setting-up of the sexual bouts is crude; and the fact that everyone in the saga seems either vicious or bats or both doesn't help at all." Fielding even claims that Robbins's work has gotten worse over time: "Robbins keeps churning them out, seemingly oblivious to the fact that his already cardboard characters have turned to paper, that his plots have virtually disappeared, and that . . . his sex scenes [are] not only silly but downright pathetic."

But not all critics are so harsh with Robbins. In his review of *The Storyteller,* for instance, Lochte admits that "in describing the art of economic survival in the 1940s—how deals were cut with Brooklyn crime bosses, Manhattan publishers and Hollywood studio heads—Robbins shows how good a writer he is. His prose is lean and straightforward, with a keen, cynical edge." Robert Graecen of *Books and Bookmen* points out that "nobody can accuse Harold Robbins of not telling a story. He knows how to handle narrative and keep the novel on the move." Lane argues that "Robbins, the bestselling American novelist, has been spurned and overlooked by literary critics because of the alleged mediocrity of his work. Nevertheless, he has won public affection by portraying identifiable life-situations in a realistic and titillating manner. His characters resemble the common man even as their bizarre exploits, fascinating sex lives and heroic struggles exude an air of Walter Mitty."

Despite the usual scorn his work receives from the critics, Robbins has fared quite well with the reading public. His books have set phenomenal sales records, while his *The Carpetbaggers* is estimated to be the fourth most-read book in history. The profits from such overwhelming popularity have assuaged some of the critical barbs. As a writer for the *Pittsburgh Press* notes, "all Robbins has to show for it is a style of living that might serve as a model for an oil sheik. His 85-foot yacht is moored in the

Mediterranean not far from his Riviera villa. In Beverly Hills, he lives in Gloria Swanson's old mansion." Robbins tells Hanscom how he feels about his success: "I know it hurts some of the others to admit I am the best. I couldn't care less about their feelings. I'll make it very simple. I've been writing books now for almost 30 years, and my books have lasted."

MEDIA ADAPTATIONS: Never Love a Stranger was filmed by Allied Artists in 1957; *A Stone for Danny Fisher* was filmed as "King Creole" by Paramount in 1958; *The Carpetbaggers* was filmed by Paramount in 1963; *Where Love Has Gone* was filmed by Paramount in 1964; "Nevada Smith," based on a character in *The Carpetbaggers,* was filmed by Paramount in 1966; *The Adventurers* was filmed by Paramount in 1968; *Stiletto* was filmed by Avco-Embassy in 1970; *The Betsy* was filmed by Allied Artists in 1978; *Dreams Die First* was filmed by American International in 1979.

BIOGRAPHICAL/CRITICAL SOURCES:

BOOKS

Biography News, Gale, 1975.
Contemporary Literary Criticism, Volume 5, Gale, 1976.

PERIODICALS

Books and Bookmen, April, 1971.
Chicago Tribune Book World, February 3, 1980, January 2, 1983.
Christian Science Monitor, October 28, 1949.
Coronet, February, 1970.
Globe and Mail (Toronto), January 25, 1986.
Journal of Popular Culture, fall, 1974.
Life, December 8, 1967.
Los Angeles Times Book Review, September 12, 1982, February 16, 1986.
Newsday, April 16, 1966.
Newsweek, June 6, 1966.
New Yorker, March 15, 1952, June 17, 1961, November 29, 1969.
New York Post, March 31, 1966, February 4, 1967, September 6, 1969, June 24, 1972.
New York Times, March 7, 1948, March 9, 1952, June 25, 1961, February 28, 1965.
New York Times Book Review, June 25, 1961, November 18, 1979, June 7, 1981, September 5, 1982, April 29, 1984, January 26, 1986.
People, July 19, 1976.
Pittsburgh Press, March 16, 1975.
Punch, June 12, 1974.
Saturday Review of Literature, May 22, 1948, October 29, 1949.
Time, December 13, 1971, November 11, 1974.
TV Guide, April 11, 1970.
Variety, November 5, 1969.
Washington Post, November 29, 1979, October 5, 1983.
Washington Post Book World, July 5, 1981.

OTHER

"I'm the World's Best Writer—There's Nothing More to Say" (television documentary), ITV Network, 1971.

*   *   *

ROBBINS, Thomas Eugene 1936-
(Tom Robbins)

PERSONAL: Born in 1936, in Blowing Rock, N.C.; son of Katherine (Robinson) Robbins; married second wife, Terrie (di-

vorced); children: (second marriage) Fleetwood Star (son). *Education:* Attended Washington and Lee University, 1950-52, Richmond Professional Institute (now Virginia Commonwealth University), and University of Washington.

ADDRESSES: Home—LaConner, Wash. *Agent*—Pheobe Larmore, 228 Main St., Venice, Calif. 90291.

CAREER: Writer. *Richmond Times-Dispatch,* Richmond, Va., copy editor, 1960-62; *Seattle Times* and *Seattle Post-Intelligence,* Seattle, Wash., copy editor, 1962-63; *Seattle Magazine,* Seattle, reviewer and art critic, 1964-68. Conducted research in New York City's East Village for an unwritten book on Jackson Pollock. *Military service:* U.S. Air Force; served in Korea.

WRITINGS:

UNDER NAME TOM ROBBINS

Guy Anderson (biography), Gear Works Press, 1965.
Another Roadside Attraction (novel), Doubleday, 1971.
Even Cowgirls Get the Blues (novel), Houghton, 1976.
Still Life with Woodpecker (novel), Bantam, 1980.
Jitterbug Perfume (novel), Bantam, 1984.
Skinny Legs and All (novel), Bantam, 1990.

SIDELIGHTS: Tom Robbins was a critically admired but low-selling novelist until the mid-1970s, when his first two works of fiction, *Another Roadside Attraction* and *Even Cowgirls Get the Blues,* went into paperback editions. Only then did the books become accessible to students, and they took to the novels with an enthusiasm that made the author "the biggest thing to hit the 'youth market' in years," according to *New York Times Magazine* reporter Mitchell S. Ross. Much of Robbins's popularity among young readers, most critics agree, can be attributed to the fact that his novels encompass the countercultural "California" or "West Coast" school of writing, whose practitioners also include the likes of Ken Kesey and Richard Braughtigan. In the words of R. H. Miller, writing in a *Dictionary of Literary Biography Yearbook* piece, the West Coast school emphasizes "the themes of personal freedom, the pursuit of higher states of being through Eastern mysticism, the escape from the confining life of urban California to the openness of the pastoral Pacific Northwest. Like the writings of his mentors, Robbins's own novels exhibit an elaborate style, a delight in words for their own sake, and an open, at times anarchical, attitude toward strict narrative form."

All of these qualities are evident in the author's first novel, *Another Roadside Attraction.* In this story, a collection of eccentrics with names like Plucky Purcell and Marx Marvelous gets involved with the mummified body of Jesus Christ, which somehow ends up at the Capt. Kendrick Memorial Hot Dog Wildlife Preserve, formerly Mom's Little Dixie Diner. As Ross sees it, the novel's plot "is secondary to the characters and tertiary to the style. [These characters] are nothing like your next-door neighbors, even if you lived in Haight-Ashbury in the middle '60s." Jerome Klinkowitz, digging deeper into the novel's meaning, declares in his book *The Practice of Fiction in America: Writers from Hawthorne to the Present* taht in *Another Roadside Attraction* Robbins "feels that the excessive rationalization of Western culture since [17th-century philosopher Rene] Descartes has severed man from his roots in nature. Organized religion has in like manner become more of a tool of logic and control than of spirit. Robbins' heroine, Amanda, would reconnect mankind with the benign chaos of the natural world, substituting magic for logic, style for substance, and poetry for the analytical measure of authority." Klinkowitz also finds the author is "a master of plain

American speech . . . and his greatest trick is to use its flat style to defuse the most sacred objects."

Robbins followed *Another Roadside Attraction* with what would become his best-known novel to date. In *Even Cowgirls Get the Blues,* the author "shows the same zest of his earlier book, but the plot is focused and disciplined, mostly because Robbins had learned by this time to use the structure of the journey as a major organizing principle in the narrative," according to Miller. This tale concerns one Sissy Hankshaw, an extraordinary hitchhiker due mainly to the fact that she was born with oversized thumbs. One of her rides takes her to the Rubber Rose Ranch, run by Bonanza Jellybean and her cowgirls, "whom Sissy joins in an attempt to find freedom from herself, as she participates in their communal search for that same freedom," as Miller relates. "They yearn for an open, sexual, unchauvinistic world, much like that of the Chink, a wizened hermit who lives near the ranch and who has absorbed his philosophy of living from the Clock people, a tribe of Indians, and from Eastern philosophy."

Again, plot takes a backseat to the intellectual forces that drive the characters on. To *Nation* critic Ann Cameron, *Even Cowgirls Get the Blues* shows "a brilliant affirmation of private visions and private wishes and the power to transform life and death. A tall tale and a parable of essential humanness, it is a work of extraordinary playfulness, style and wit." In his study *Tom Robbins,* author Mark Siegel sees two "major paradoxes in [the author's] ideas." One is the emphasis he places on individual fulfillment while he simultaneously castigates egotism. The second is his apparent devotion to Eastern philosophies in *Another Roadside Attraction,* although he warns against adopting Eastern religions in *Cowgirls.* Actually the two issues are closely related, both stemming from Robbins's notion that any truly fulfilling way of life must evolve from the individual's recognition of his true, personal relationship to the world. Thus, although Americans can learn from Oriental philosophies much about liberation from the ego, Western man must nevertheless find a way of liberation that is natural to him in his own world."

"Robbins has an old trunk of a mind," says Thomas LeClair in a *New York Times Book Review* piece on *Cowgirls.* "[He] knows the atmosphere on Venus, cow diseases, hitchhiking manuals, herbs, the brain's circuitry, whooping cranes, circles, parades, Nisei internment" adding that these visions "add up to a primitivism just pragmatic enough to be attractive and fanciful enough to measure the straight society." In Ross's opinion, the author's style "generates its own head of steam and dances past the plot, characters and clockwork philosophy. . . . Oddly, it is a style without a single voice. At times, Robbins booms out like a bard; the next instant he forces us to mourn the loss of the next Bob Hope to beautiful letters." Ross notes too that "a piling on of wisecracks is made to substitute for description."

Robbins's penchant for cracking wise reperesents a sore point in his next novel, *Still Life with Woodpecker,* according to Julie B. Peters. A *Saturday Review* writer, Peters states that in this tale of a princess's romance with an outlaw, the prose "is marbled with limping puns heavily splattered with recurrent motifs and a boyish zeal for the scatalogical." Taking a similar tack, *Commonweal* critic Frank McConnell points out that "a large part of the problem in reading Robbins [is that] he's so *cute:* his books are full of cute lines populated by unrelentingly cute people, even teeming with cute animals—frogs, chipmunks and chihuahuas in *Still Life with Woodpecker.* No one ever gets hurt very badly . . ., and although the world is threatened by the same dark, soulless business cartels that threaten the worlds of [Thomas] Pynchon, [Norman] Mailer, and our century, in Robbins it

doesn't seem, finally, to matter. Love or something like it really does conquer all in his parables, with a mixture of stoned gaiety, positive thinking, and Sunday Supplement Taoism."

In telling the story of the unusual relationship between Princess Leigh-Cheri, heiress of the Pacific island of Mu, and good-hearted terrorist Bernard Micky Wrangle, alias Woodpecker, the author also frames the tale by a monologue "having to do with his [Robbins's] efforts to type out his narrative on a Remington SL-3 typewriter, which at the end fails him, and he has to complete the novel in longhand," says Miller, who also finds that the moral of *Still Life with Woodpecker* "is not as strong as that of the earlier two [novels], and while the plot seems more intricately interlaced, it has the complexity and exoticism of grand opera but little of its brilliance."

The generally disappointed reaction of critics to *Still Life with Woodpecker* left some writers wondering whether Robbins, with his free-form style, was addressing the needs of fiction readers in the upwardly mobile 1980s. The author answered his critics with *Jitterbug Perfume,* published in 1984. In this novel, Seattle waitress Priscilla devotes her life to inventing the ultimate perfume. The challenge is taken up in locales as varied as New Orleans and Paris, while back in Seattle, Wiggs Dannyboy, described by *Washington Post Book World* reviewer Rudy Rucker as "a Timothy Leary work-alike who's given up acid for immortality research" enters the scene to provide insights on the 1960s.

Comparing *Jitterbug Perfume* to the author's other works, Rucker notes that the first two novels were '60s creations— "filled with mushrooms and visions, radicals and police. *Still Life with Woodpecker* is about the '70s viewed as the aftermath of the '60s." And in *Jitterbug Perfume,* "Robbins is still very much his old Pan-worshipping self, yet his new book is lovingly plotted, with every conceivable loose end nailed down tight. Although the ideas are the same as ever, the form is contemporary, new-realistic craftsmanship. Robbins toys with the 1980s' peculiar love/hate for the 60s through his invention of the character Wiggs Dannyboy." To John House, the work "is not so much a novel as an inspirational fable, full of Hallmark sweetness, good examples and hope springing eternal." House, in a *New York Times Book Review* article, goes on to say that he finds Robbins's style "unmistakable—oblique, florid, willing to sacrifice everything for an old joke or corny pun." While *Jitterbug Perfume* "is still less exuberant than 'Cowgirls,' " according to Don Strachan in the *Los Angeles Times Book Review,* the former is still "less diminished than honed. The author may still occasionally stick his foot in the door of his mouth, as he would say in one of those metaphors he loves to mix with wordplay salads, but then he'll unfurl a phrase that will bring your critical mind to its knees."

"Robbins's contribution to the West Coast novel lies in his athletic style and iconoclastic attitude toward form," concludes Miller. "He refuses to be disciplined by the critics. His message is like the dying call of the whooping cranes in *Even Cowgirls Get the Blues,* a plea for freedom, naturalness, and peace, but it is a rather lonely voice echoing the concerns of an earlier decade, even an earlier generation." The author himself summed up his appeal in a *Detroit News* interview conducted by Randy Sue Coburn. "I'm an ordinary, sweet, witty guy who happens to possess a luminous cosmic vision and a passionate appreciation of fine sentences," Robbins says. "There. Now let's talk about books. Let's talk about life, death and goofiness. Best of all, let's talk about lunch."

BIOGRAPHICAL/CRITICAL SOURCES:

BOOKS

Contemporary Literary Criticism, Gale, Volume 9, 1978, Volume 32, 1985.
Dictionary of Literary Biography Yearbook: 1980, Gale, 1981.
Klinkowitz, Jerome, *The Practice of Fiction in America: Writers from Hawthorne to the Present,* Iowa State University Press, 1980.
Nadeau, Robert, *Readings from the New Book on Nature: Physics and Metaphysics in the Modern Novel,* University of Massachusetts Press, 1981.
Siegel, Mark, *Tom Robbins,* Boise State University Press, 1980.

PERIODICALS

Chicago Review, autumn, 1980.
Commonweal, March 13, 1981.
Detroit News, October 5, 1980, Janaury 6, 1985.
Los Angeles Times Book Review, December 16, 1984.
Nation, August 28, 1976, October 25, 1980.
New Boston Review, December, 1977.
New Republic, June 26, 1971.
New Statesman, August 12, 1977.
Newsweek, September 29, 1980.
New York Times Book Review, May 23, 1976, September 28, 1980, December 9, 1984.
New York Times Magazine, February 12, 1978.
Saturday Review, September, 1980.
Times Literary Supplement, October 31, 1980.
Washington Post Book World, October 25, 1980.

*   *   *

ROBBINS, Tom
See ROBBINS, Thomas Eugene

*   *   *

ROBERTSON, Ellis
See ELLISON, Harlan and SILVERBERG, Robert

*   *   *

ROBINSON, Edwin Arlington   1869-1935

PERSONAL: Born December 22, 1869, in Head Tide, Me.; died of cancer, April 6, 1935, in New York, N.Y.; son of Edward (a merchant) and Mary Elizabeth (Palmer) Robinson. *Education:* Attended Harvard University, 1891-93.

CAREER: Poet. Held various intermittent jobs, 1899-1905, including office assistant at Harvard University, Cambridge, Mass., time-checker for IRT Subway in New York, N.Y., and advertising editor, Boston, Mass. Held sinecure in New York Customs House under the patronage of Theodore Roosevelt, 1905-09. Guest writer at MacDowell Colony, Peterborough, N.H., 1911-35.

AWARDS, HONORS: Pulitzer Prize, 1922, for *Collected Poems,* 1925, for *The Man Who Died Twice,* and 1928, for *Tristram;* D.Litt., Yale University, 1922, Bowdoin College, 1925; Levinson Prize, *Poetry,* 1923; Gold Medal, National Institute and American Academy of Arts and Letters, 1929.

WRITINGS:

POETRY

The Torrent and The Night Before, Riverside Press, 1896.
The Children of the Night: A Book of Poems, Richard C. Badger, 1897.
Captain Craig: A Book of Poems, Houghton, 1902, revised and enlarged edition, Macmillan, 1915.
The Town down the River: A Book of Poems, Scribner, 1910.
The Man against the Sky: A Book of Poems, Scribner, 1916.
Merlin: A Poem, Macmillan, 1917.
Lancelot: A Poem, Thomas Seltzer, 1920.
The Three Taverns: A Book of Poems, Macmillan, 1920.
Avon's Harvest, Macmillan, 1921.
Collected Poems, Macmillan, 1921.
Roman Bartholow, Macmillan, 1923.
The Man Who Died Twice, Macmillan, 1924.
Dionysus in Doubt: A Book of Poems, Macmillan, 1925.
Tristram, Macmillan, 1927.
Collected Poems, 5 volumes, Dunster House, 1927, new edition in one volume published as *Collected Poems of Edwin Arlington Robinson,* Macmillan, 1929, enlarged edition, 1937.
Sonnets, 1889-1927, Crosby Gaige, 1928.
Fortunatus, Slide Mountain Press, 1928.
Modred: A Fragment, Brick Row Bookshop, 1929.
Cavender's House, Macmillan, 1929.
The Prodigal Son, Random House, 1929.
The Valley of the Shadow, Yerba Buena Press, 1930.
Collected Poems, Macmillan, 1930.
The Glory of the Nightingales, Macmillan, 1930.
Matthias at the Door, Macmillan, 1931.
(Contributor) Charles Cestre, *An Introduction to Edwin Arlington Robinson and Selected Poems,* preface by Bliss Perry, Macmillan, 1931.
Poems, selected and with a preface by Bliss Perry, Macmillan, 1931.
Nicodemus: A Book of Poems, Macmillan, 1932.
Talifer, Macmillan, 1933.
Amaranth, Macmillan, 1934.
King Jasper: A Poem, introduction by Robert Frost, Macmillan, 1935.
Collected Poems, Macmillan, 1937.
Tilbury Town: Selected Poems of Edwin Arlington Robinson, introduction and notes by Lawrence Thompson, Macmillan, 1953.
Selected Poems, edited by Morton Dauwen Zabel, introduction by James Dickey, Macmillan, 1965.
A Tilbury Score, Masterwork Press, 1969.
(Contributor) Bernard Grebanier, *Edwin Arlington Robinson: A Centenary Memoir-Anthology,* A. S. Barnes for the Poetry Society of America, 1971.

OTHER

Van Zorn: A Comedy in Three Acts (play), Macmillan, 1914.
The Porcupine: A Drama in Three Acts (play), Macmillan, 1915.
Selected Letters of Edwin Arlington Robinson, edited and with an introduction by Ridgely Torrence, Macmillan, 1940.
Letters from Edwin Arlington Robinson to Howard George Schmitt, edited by Carl J. Weber, Colby College Library, 1943.
Untriangulated Stars: Letters to Harry de Forest Smith 1890-1905, edited by Denham Sutcliffe, Harvard University Press, 1947.
Selected Early Poems and Letters, edited by Charles T. Davis, Holt, 1960.

Edwin Arlington Robinson's Letters to Edith Brower, edited by Richard Cary, Harvard University Press, 1968.

Uncollected Poems and Prose of Edwin Arlington Robinson, edited and compiled, and with an introduction and notes by Richard Cary, Colby College Press, 1975.

Edwin Arlington Robinson's papers are held in the collections of the Colby College Library in Waterville, Me,, the Houghton Library at Harvard University, Cambridge, Mass., the New York Public Library, and the Library of Congress.

SIDELIGHTS: "One of the most prolific major American poets of the twentieth century, Edwin Arlington Robinson is, ironically, best remembered for only a handful of short poems," stated Robert Gilbert in the *Concise Dictionary of American Literary Biography.* Fellow writer Amy Lowell declared in the *New York Times Book Review,* "Edwin Arlington Robinson is poetry. I can think of no other living writer who has so consistently dedicated his life to his work." Robinson is considered unique among American poets of his time for his devotion to his art; he published virtually nothing during his long career except poetry. "The expense of Robinson's single-mindedness," Gilbert explained, "was virtually everything else in life for which people strive, but it eventually won for him both fortune and fame, as well as a firm position in literary history as America's first important poet of the twentieth century."

Robinson seemed destined for a career in business or the sciences. He was the third son of a wealthy New England merchant, a man who had little use for the fine arts. He was, however, encouraged in his poetic pursuits by a neighbor and wrote copiously, experimenting with verse translations from Greek and Latin poets. In 1891 Edward Robinson provided the funds to send his son to Harvard partly because the aspiring writer required medical treatment that could best be performed in Boston. There Robinson published some poems in local newspapers and magazines and, as he later explained in a biographical piece published in *Colophon,* collected a pile of rejection slips "that must have been one of the largest and most comprehensive in literary history." Finally he decided to publish his poems himself, and contracted with Riverside, a vanity press, to produce *The Torrent and The Night Before,* named after the first and last poems in the collection.

In the poems of *The Torrent and The Night Before,* Robinson experimented with elaborate poetic forms and explored themes that would characterize much of his work—"themes of personal failure, artistic endeavor, materialism, and the inevitability of change," according to Gilbert. He also established a style recognizably his own: an adherence to traditional forms at a time when most poets were experimenting with the genre ("All his life Robinson strenuously objected to free verse," Gilbert remarked, "replying once when asked if he wrote it, 'No, I write badly enough as it is.' "), and laconic, everyday speech.

Robinson mailed copies of *The Torrent and The Night Before* out "to editors of journals and to writers who he thought might be sympathetic to his work," said Gilbert. The response was generally favorable, although perhaps the most significant review came from Harry Thurston Peck, who commented unfavorably in the *Bookman* on Robinson's bleak outlook and sense of humor. Peck found Robinson's tone too grim for his tastes, saying that "the world is not beautiful to [Robinson], but a prison-house." "I am sorry that I have painted myself in such lugubrious colours," Robinson wrote in the next issue of the *Bookman,* responding to this criticism. "The world is not a prison house, but a kind of spiritual kindergarten, where millions of bewildered infants are trying to spell God with the wrong blocks."

Encouraged by the largely positive critical reaction, Robinson quickly produced a second manuscript, *The Children of the Night,* which was also published by a vanity press, a friend providing the necessary funds. Unfortunately, reviewers largely ignored it; Gilbert suggests that they were put off by the vanity imprint. In 1902, two friends persuaded the publisher Houghton Mifflin to publish *Captain Craig,* another book of Robinson's verse, by promising to subsidize part of the publishing costs. *Captain Craig* was neither a popular nor a critical success, and for several years Robinson neglected poetry, drifting from job to job in New York City and the Northeast. He took to drinking heavily, and for a time it seemed that he would, as Gilbert put it, fall "into permanent dissolution, as both his brothers had done." "His whimsical 'Miniver Cheevy,' " Gilbert continued, "the poem about the malcontent modern who yearned for the past glories of the chivalric age and who finally 'coughed, and called it fate/And kept on drinking,' is presumably a comic self-portrait."

Robinson's luck changed in 1904, when Kermit Roosevelt brought *The Children of the Night* to the attention of his father, President Theodore Roosevelt. Roosevelt not only persuaded Random House to republish the book, but also reviewed it himself for the *Outlook* ("I am not sure I understand 'Luke Havergal,' " he said, "but I am entirely sure that I like it"), and obtained a sinecure for its author at the New York Customs House—a post Robinson held until 1909. The two thousand dollar annual stipend that went with the post provided Robinson with financial security. In 1910, he repaid his debt to Roosevelt in *The Town down the River,* a collection of poems dedicated to the former president.

Perhaps the best known of Robinson's poems are those now called the Tilbury Town cycle, named after the small town "that provides the setting for many of his poems and explicitly links him and his poetry with small-town New England, the repressive, utilitarian social climate customarily designated as the Puritan ethic," explained W. R. Robinson in *Edwin Arlington Robinson: A Poetry of the Act.* These poems also expound some of Robinson's most characteristic themes: "his curiosity," as Gerald DeWitt Sanders and his fellow editors put it in *Chief Modern Poets of Britain and America,* "about what lies behind the social mask of character, and . . . his dark hints about sexuality, loyalty, and man's terrible will to defeat himself."

Tilbury Town is first mentioned in "John Evereldown," a ballade collected in *The Torrent and The Night Before.* John Evereldown, out late at night, is called back to the house by his wife, who is wondering why he wants to walk the long cold miles into town. He responds, "God knows if I pray to be done with it all/But God's no friend of John Evereldown./So the clouds may come and the rain may fall,/the shadows may creep and the dead men crawl,—/But I follow the women wherever they call,/And that's why I'm going to Tilbury Town."

Tilbury Town reappears at intervals throughout Robinson's work. The title poem in *Captain Craig* concerns an old resident of the town whose life, believed wasted by his neighbors, proves to have been of value. *The Children of the Night* contains the story of Richard Cory, "a gentleman from sole to crown,/Clean favored, and imperially slim," who "one calm summer night,/Went home and put a bullet through his head," and Tilbury Town itself is personified in the lines "In fine, we thought that he was everything/To make us wish that we were in his place." *The Man against the Sky*—according to Gilbert, Robinson's "most important single volume," and probably his most critically acclaimed—includes the story of the man "Flammonde," one of the poet's most anthologized Tilbury verses.

Despite the fact that much of Robinson's verse dealt with failed lives, several critics see his work as life-affirming. May Sinclair, writing an early review of *Captain Craig* for the *Fortnightly Review,* said of the Captain, "He, ragged, old, and starved, challenges his friends to have courage and to rejoice in the sun." Amy Lowell, in her *Tendencies in Modern American Poetry,* stated, "I have spoken of Mr. Robinson's 'unconscious cynicism.' It is unconscious because he never dwells upon it as such, never delights in it, nor wraps it comfortably about him. It is hardly more than the reverse of the shield of pain, and in his later work, it gives place to a great, pitying tenderness. 'Success through Failure,' that is the motto on the other side of his banner of 'Courage.' " And Robert Frost, in his introduction to Robinson's *King Jasper,* declared, "His theme was unhappiness itself, but his skill was as happy as it was playful. There is that comforting thought for those who suffered to see him suffer."

Many Tilbury Town verses were among the poems Robinson included in his Pulitzer Prize-winning *Collected Poems* of 1922—the first Pulitzer ever awarded for poetry. He won his second poetry Pulitzer in 1924, this time for *The Man Who Died Twice,* the story of a street musician whose one musical masterpiece is lost when he collapses after a night of debauchery. Gilbert attributed the poem's success to its "combination of down-to-earth diction, classical allusion, and understated humor." In 1927, Robinson again won a Pulitzer for his long narrative poem *Tristram,* one in a series of poems based on Arthurian legends. *Tristram* proved to be Robinson's only true popular success—it was that rarity of twentieth-century literature, a best-selling book-length poem—and it received critical acclaim as well. "It may be said not only that 'Tristram' is the finest of Mr. Robinson's narrative poems," wrote Lloyd Morris in the *Nation,* "but that it is among the very few fine modern narrative poems in English."

Early in 1935, Robinson fell ill with cancer. He stayed hospitalized until his death, correcting galley proofs of his last poem, *King Jasper* only hours before slipping into a final coma. "Magazines and newspapers throughout the country took elaborate notice of Robinson's death," declared Gilbert, "reminding their readers that he had been considered America's foremost poet for nearly twenty years and praising his industry, integrity, and devotion to his art." "It may come to the notice of our posterity (and then again it may not)," wrote Robert Frost in his introduction to *King Jasper,* "that this, our age, ran wild in the quest of new ways to be new. . . . Robinson stayed content with the old-fashioned ways to be new." "Robinson has gone to his place in American literature and left his human place among us vacant," Frost concluded. "We mourn, but with the qualification that, after all, his life was a revel in the felicities of language."

BIOGRAPHICAL/CRITICAL SOURCES:

BOOKS

Barnard, Ellsworth, *Edwin Arlington Robinson,* Macmillan, 1952.
Brown, Rollo Walter, *Next Door to a Poet,* Appleton-Century, 1937.
Concise Dictionary of American Literary Biography: Realism, Naturalism, and Local Color, 1865-1917, Gale, 1988.
Coxe, Louis O., *Edwin Arlington Robinson: The Life of Poetry,* Pegasus, 1969.
Deutsch, Babette, *Poetry of Our Time,* Holt, 1952.

Dictionary of Literary Biography, Volume 54: *American Poets, 1880-1945,* Gale, 1987.
Hagedorn, Hermann, *Edwin Arlington Robinson: A Biography,* Macmillan, 1936.
Hogan, Charles Beecher, *A Bibliography of Edwin Arlington Robinson,* Yale University Press, 1936.
Joyner, Nancy Carol, *Edwin Arlington Robinson: A Reference Guide,* G. K. Hall, 1978.
Lowell, Amy, *Tendencies in Modern American Poetry,* Macmillan, 1917.
Murphy, Francis, *Edwin Arlington Robinson: A Collection of Critical Essays,* Prentice-Hall, 1970.
Neff, Emery, *Edwin Arlington Robinson,* Sloane, 1948.
Robinson, Edwin Arlington, *King Jasper,* introduction by Robert Frost, Macmillan, 1935.
Robinson, W. R., *Edwin Arlington Robinson: A Poetry of the Act,* Press of Western Reserve University, 1967.
Sanders, Gerald DeWitt, John Herbert Nelson, and M. L. Rosenthal, editors and compilers, *Chief Modern Poets of Britain and America,* 5th edition, Macmillan, 1970.
Smith, Chard Powers, *Where the Light Falls: A Portrait of Edwin Arlington Robinson,* Macmillan, 1965.
Twentieth-Century Literary Criticism, Volume 5, Gale, 1981.
Van Doren, Mark, *Edwin Arlington Robinson,* Literary Guild of America, 1927.
White, William, *Edwin Arlington Robinson: A Supplementary Bibliography,* Kent State University Press, 1971.
Winters, Yvor, *Edwin Arlington Robinson,* New Directions, 1946.

PERIODICALS

Bookman, February, 1897, March, 1897, May, 1921.
Boston Evening Transcript, February 26, 1916.
Boston Sunday Post, March 2, 1913.
Colophon, December, 1930.
Critic, March, 1903.
Dial, October 11, 1917.
Fortnightly Review, September 1, 1906.
Nation, June, 1898, May 25, 1927.
New Republic, May 27, 1916, October 25, 1933.
New York Times Book Review, September 8, 1912, December 21, 1919.
New York Times Magazine, April 9, 1916.
Personalist, January, 1962.
Poetry, April, 1916, July, 1917.
Reader, December, 1902.
Research Studies, June, 1968.

* * *

ROBINSON, Joan (Violet) 1903-1983

PERSONAL: Born October 31, 1903, in Camberley, Surrey, England; died August 5, 1983; daughter of Major General Sir Frederick Maurice; married E. A. G. Robinson (an economist), 1926; children: two daughters. *Education:* Girton College, Cambridge, economics tripos, 1925.

ADDRESSES: Home—62 Grange Rd., Cambridge, England.

CAREER: Cambridge University, Cambridge, England, assistant lecturer, 1931-37, university lecturer, 1937-49, reader, 1949-64, professor of economics, 1965-71. Special professor, Stanford University, spring, 1969.

MEMBER: British Academy (fellow).

WRITINGS:

The Economics of Imperfect Competition, Macmillan, 1933, 2nd edition, St. Martin's, 1969.

Essays in the Theory of Employment, Macmillan, 1937, 2nd edition, Basil Blackwell, 1947, Macmillan, 1948, reprinted, Hyperion Press, 1980, revised edition, Macmillan, 1969.

Introduction to the Theory of Employment, Macmillan, 1937, 2nd edition, St. Martin's, 1969.

An Essay on Marxian Economics, Macmillan, 1942, 2nd edition, St. Martin's, 1967.

(With others) *Can Planning Be Democratic?: A Collection of Essays Prepared for the Fabian Society,* G. Routledge & Sons, 1944.

Collected Economic Papers, Volume I, Basil Blackwell, 1951, Volume II, Basil Blackwell, 1960, Volume III, Humanities, 1966, Volume IV, Humanities, 1972, Volume V, Basil Blackwell, 1979, Volumes I-V reprinted, MIT Press, 1980.

The Rate of Interest, and Other Essays, Macmillan, 1952, reprinted, Hyperion Press, 1980, 2nd edition published as *The Generalisation of the General Theory, and Other Essays,* St. Martin's, 1979.

The Accumulation of Capital, Irwin, 1956, 3rd edition, Macmillan, 1969.

Exercises in Economic Analysis, Macmillan, 1960, St. Martin's, 1961.

Essays in the Theory of Economic Growth, Macmillan, 1962, St. Martin's, 1963.

Economic Philosophy, Aldine, 1962.

Economics: An Awkward Corner, Allen & Unwin, 1966, Pantheon, 1967.

(Compiler) *The Cultural Revolution in China,* Penguin, 1969.

Freedom and Necessity: An Introduction to the Study of Society, Pantheon, 1970.

Economic Heresies: Some Old-Fashioned Questions in Economic Theory, Basic Books, 1971.

(Contributor) Rendigs Fels, editor, *The Second Crisis of Economic Theory, and Other Selected Papers,* foreword by John Kenneth Galbraith, General Learning Press, 1972.

(Editor) *After Keynes,* Barnes & Noble, 1973.

(With John Eatwell) *An Introduction to Modern Economics,* McGraw, 1973, revised edition, 1974.

(With Michael Kalecki and P. A. Baran) *Aspetti politici della piena occupazione,* Celuc (Milan), 1975.

Joan Robinson Reports from China, 1953-76, Anglo-Chinese Educational Institute (London), 1977.

Contributions to Modern Economics, Academic Press, 1978.

Aspects of Development and Underdevelopment, Cambridge University Press, 1979.

What Are the Questions?, and Other Essays: Further Contributions to Modern Economics, M. E. Sharpe, 1981 (published in England as *Further Contributions to Modern Economics,* Basil Blackwell, 1981).

Author of numerous booklets on economics, 1932-74. Contributor to economics journals.

OBITUARIES:

PERIODICALS

Chicago Tribune, August 12, 1983.
New York Times, August 22, 1983.
Time, August 22, 1983.
Times (London), August 10, 1983.
Washington Post, August 12, 1983.

ROBINSON, Lloyd
See SILVERBERG, Robert

*   *   *

RODD, Kylie Tennant   1912-1988
(Kylie Tennant)

PERSONAL: First name originally Kathleen; born March 12, 1912, in Manly, New South Wales, Australia; died February 28, 1988, in Sydney, Australia; daughter of Thomas Walter and Kathleen (Tolhurst) Tennant; married Lewis Charles Rodd (a schoolteacher and headmaster), November 21, 1932 (died, 1979); children: Benison (daughter), John Laurence (died, 1978). *Education:* Attended Brighton College and University of Sydney. *Religion:* Church of England.

ADDRESSES: Home—Cliff View Orchard, Blackheath, New South Wales, Australia. *Agent*—Judy Barry, 25 Yarranabbe Rd., Darling Point, Sydney, New South Wales, Australia.

CAREER: Worked at various jobs, c. 1928-32; full-time writer, 1935-59; in addition to writing, worked as journalist, editor, and publishing adviser, 1959-69; full-time writer, 1969-88. Commonwealth Literary Fund, lecturer, 1957-58, member of advisory board, 1961-73. Member of board, Australian Aborigines Cooperatives. Australian literary advisor to Macmillan & Co., 1960-69. Made appearances on Australian television and radio.

MEMBER: Australian Fellowship of Writers (life patron), Australian Journalists Association.

AWARDS, HONORS: S. H. Prior Memorial Prize, 1935, for *Tiburon,* and 1941, for *The Battlers;* gold medal, Australian Literary Society, 1941, for *The Battlers;* fellowship from Commonwealth Literary Fund, 1951; Commonwealth Jubilee Stage Play Award, 1952, for *Tether a Dragon;* Children's Book of the Year Award, Australian Children's Book Council, 1960, for *All the Proud Tribesmen;* Officer of the Order of Australia, 1980.

WRITINGS:

FICTION; UNDER NAME KYLIE TENNANT

Tiburon (originally serialized in *Bulletin,* 1935), Endeavor Press, 1935.
Foveaux, Gollancz, 1939.
The Battlers, Macmillan, 1941.
Ride on, Stranger, Macmillan, 1943.
Time Enough Later, Macmillan, 1943.
Lost Haven, Macmillan, 1946.
The Joyful Condemned, St. Martin's, 1953, complete version published as *Tell Morning This,* Angus & Robertson, 1968.
The Honey Flow, St. Martin's, 1956.
Ma Jones and the Little White Cannibals (short stories), St. Martin's, 1967.
Tantavallon, Macmillan, 1983.

OTHER; UNDER NAME KYLIE TENNANT

John o' the Forest and Other Plays (juvenile), Macmillan, 1950.
Tether a Dragon (play), Associated General Publications, 1952.
Australia: Her Story; Notes on a Nation (history), St. Martin's, 1953, revised edition, Pan Books, 1964.
Long John Silver: The Story of the Film; Adapted by K. Tennant from the . . . Screenplay by Martin Rackin, Associated General Publications, 1954.
The Bells of the City and Other Plays (juvenile), Macmillan, 1955.
The Bushrangers' Christmas Eve and Other Plays (juvenile), Macmillan, 1959.

All the Proud Tribesmen (juvenile), illustrated by Clem Seale, St. Martin's, 1959.

Speak You So Gently (travelogue), Gollancz, 1959.

(General editor, and contributor) *Great Stories of Australia,* seven volumes, St. Martin's, 1963-66.

(General editor, and contributor) *Summer's Tales,* two volumes, St. Martin's, 1964-65.

Trail Blazers of the Air (juvenile stories), St. Martin's, 1966.

(With husband, Lewis C. Rodd) *The Australian Essay,* Cheshire, 1968.

Evatt: Politics and Justice (biography), Angus & Robertson, 1970.

The Man on the Headland (fictionalized biography), Angus Robertson, 1971.

The Missing Heir: The Autobiography of Kylie Tennant, Macmillan, 1986.

Contributor of short stories to numerous anthologies. Critic for *Sydney Morning Herald,* beginning 1953. A collection of Tennant's manuscripts is held at the Australian National Library in Canberra.

SIDELIGHTS: A noted Australian author of social-realist fiction, Kylie Tennant wrote novels offering spirited and authentic portrayals of Australian life. Her award-winning 1935 first novel *Tiburon,* profiling a small town during the Depression, launched a prolific writing career that, in addition to nine more novels, saw her produce short stories, nonfiction, plays, and criticism. Noted for emphasizing the externals of human experience, Tennant's fiction abounds with authentic place descriptions, colorful characters, and fast-paced, witty dialogue. Although she often emerges as a reformer—Tennant's writings display an affinity for characters besieged by modern social ills—at the same time she demonstrates a good-natured acceptance of some of life's harsher conditions. The obituary writer for the London *Times* noted that Tennant's "desire to improve society was at odds in her with her almost Brechtian celebration of its rougher elements and her conviction that human nature was not likely to change."

Originally named Kathleen, Tennant acquired the name "Kylie"—an Australian aborigine word for boomerang—during childhood, and kept it all of her life. Tennant left school at the age of sixteen, after which she took on a variety of jobs, including work for the Australian Broadcasting Commission, work as a salesgirl, and operating a chicken farm. For a year she attended the University of Sydney as a psychology student. In 1932, she hitchhiked and jumped trains throughout New South Wales, eventually ending up in the northern city of Coonabarabran where she married her husband. Three years later *Tiburon* appeared, garnering critical praise for its authentic and lively depiction of the residents of a small New South Wales village living on handouts during the Great Depression. *Tiburon* won for its twenty-three-year-old author the S. H. Prior Memorial Prize and, as the *Times* obituary writer notes, "a certain notoriety amongst the polite readership for its many swipes at things they held sacred, such as local politics and bureaucracy."

Throughout her writing career, Tennant was noted for the rigorous and thorough research invested in her novels—often gained through first-hand experience. For *The Battlers* she camped with vagabonds and migrant laborers, travelling across Australia in a cart. For *The Joyful Condemned,* Tennant lived among prostitutes and the slum inhabitants of Sydney—even managing to get herself thrown into jail. For other novels, she turned to technical tasks. Preparing for *Lost Haven,* she studied ship-building, and for *The Honey Flow,* accompanied beekeepers on their annual migrations through the blossoming eucalyptus trees of Australia.

Tennant once commented that her preference was for people who existed on the margins of modern industrial society.

Critics praised Tennant's ability to authentically portray, with understanding and honesty, a spectrum of unordinary characters, locales, and situations. Regarding *The Battlers,* which profiles the lives of hobos, vagrants, and migrant workers, Lionel Bridge commented in *Commonweal:* "Here is a combination of the most unusual events happening to the most original characters in the strangest setting the American fiction audience is likely to be offered again." J. S. Southron in the *New York Times* praised both Tennant's control of her subject matter and its integrity: "There are enough stories in 'The Battlers' to have filled a novel twice the size in the hands of a less concise, less artistic writer. And there is the curious affection aroused in us for characters as unglamorous and devoid of showmanship as they are genuine. It is a book whose outstanding feature is the sort of strength that compels admiration." Klaus Lambrecht in the *Saturday Review of Literature* called *The Battlers* "a most appealing book" in that "there is humor in it and a bitter realism, tragedy and love, warmth and cruelty, and sensitive conception of a peculiar form of life." Tennant's third novel won her another S. H. Prior Memorial Prize, in addition to a gold medal from the Australian Literary Society.

Like *The Battlers,* Tennant's other novels were noted for empathetic and vigorous characterizations. In *Ride on, Stranger,* she tells the story of an Australian girl who leaves her family of seven "on a career of moderately healthy disillusionment among faithhealers, occultists, left-wings, aesthetes and others," according to a reviewer for the *Times Literary Supplement.* John Hampon in *Spectator* called Tennant a "lively gifted writer," who, in *Ride on, Stranger,* "handles the seamy side of life with robust vigour." The *Times Literary Supplement* reviewer added: "There is a good deal of fun in this sprawling, crowded story of uncultivated types in the Australian wilds and of excessively cultivated or freakish types in Sydney, and with the fun goes a certain hard honesty of sentiment that is frequently telling." Regarding the 1946 novel *Lost Haven,* Robert Traver noted in *Book Week* that Tennant displayed "a remarkable facility for figurative expression, the evocative phrase." He added that, although such "occasionally gets a trifle out of hand" and that "at times she pelts the reader with words," when Tennant "wants to—which is most of the time—she can write like an inspired demon."

One of Tennant's most praised works is the 1953 novel *The Joyful Condemned,* initially published in abridged form due to a paper shortage and fears of censorship backlash, and reissued fifteen years later in its entirety as *Tell Morning This.* Tennant's longest novel, *The Joyful Condemned* traces the lives of several working-class girls in wartime Sydney who indulge themselves in the worlds of the slums. Tennant "is remarkably skilful in conveying the helpless ignorance of such girls in [the] face of authority and their eagerness to escape from the gentility of middle-class life into the riotous freedom of their own world," noted a reviewer for the *Times Literary Supplement.* Sylvia Stallings wrote in the *New York Herald Tribune Book Review* that Tennant's "quick ear and eye bring home both the raciness of underworld speech and the curious beauty of the city at night, the searchlights 'working through the clouds like the fingers of a wool-classer through fleeces.' Her novel comes as a great wash of fresh air after the thin-blooded elegance of so many of her peers." Upon the novel's reissue as *Tell Morning This,* a reviewer for the *Times Literary Supplement* commented that the book was "told with clarity and honesty, and even, despite the bumpiness of much of the writing, a degree of poetic sensitivity."

In addition to her celebrated fiction, Tennant wrote in other genres, continuing to demonstrate thorough and thoughtful treatment of subject matter. *Australia: Her Story; Notes on a Nation* was praised by Fritz Stern in the *Saturday Review* as an "excellent example of popular history, an art which nowadays is too often neglected in favor of specialized treatises or historical novels which mistake life for lust." Tennant's 1970 biography of Herbert Vere Evatt entitled *Evatt: Politics and Justice* "goes a long way towards doing justice to the most fascinating figure in the Australian labour movement since W. M. Hughes," according to a *Times Literary Supplement* reviewer, who singled out both Tennant's "control of complex material and events," in addition to "the insight into Evatt's character." And in her 1959 children's book *All the Proud Tribesmen,* Tennant relates the lifestyles and history of Australia's aborigines. P. D. Beard noted in *Library Journal* that Tennant's story "reveal[s] keen insight into the minds of a people and a fine sense of local atmosphere." Howard Boston likewise commented in the *New York Times Book Review* that in *All the Proud Tribesmen,* Tennant's "characterization is deft and sure, and she is adept at juggling several themes simultaneously." "The story's real strength, though," added Boston, "lies in its sensitive and appealing portrayal of the island folk."

Tennant's last novel *Tantavallon,* published in 1983, displays the complexion of her earlier novels, offering a panorama of varied characters and situations. Featured in *Tantavallon,* notes Ken Goodwin in *A History of Australian Literature,* are "Vietnamese migrants mining uranium, a churchwarden attempting suicide in Sydney Harbour, a fire, a suburban street battle, a spectacular car accident, and a cancer scare." *Tantavallon* "illustrates well [Tennant's] belief that life in general is 'a thin layer of ice over a raging human volcano', full of 'absurdity and chaos,' " according to Goodwin; however, as in Tennant's other novels, "there is always vigour, entertainment, and comedy in her depiction." The *Times* obituary writer comments on a lasting impression of Tennant's work: "Her often noted slapdash writing and lack of psychological penetration . . . are compensated for, in her best books, by her zest for life, humour and, above all, by her affection for the human race."

AVOCATIONAL INTERESTS: The welfare of Australian aborigines.

BIOGRAPHICAL/CRITICAL SOURCES:

BOOKS

Dick, Margaret, *The Novels of Kylie Tennant,* Rigby, 1966.
Goodwin, Ken, *A History of Australian Literature,* St. Martin's, 1986.
Tennant, Kylie, *The Joyful Condemned,* reissued as *Tell Morning This,* Angus & Robertson, 1968.
Tennant, Kylie, *The Missing Heir: The Autobiography of Kylie Tennant,* Macmillan, 1986.

PERIODICALS

Books, August 10, 1941.
Book Week, September 5, 1943, March 31, 1946.
Christian Science Monitor, November 5, 1953.
Commonweal, October 10, 1941.
Listener, March 23, 1943.
Meanjin Quarterly, number 4, 1953.
New Republic, August 25, 1941.
New Statesman and Nation, January 25, 1941.
New Yorker, August 28, 1943, March 30, 1946, October 2, 1954.
New York Herald Tribune Book Review, May 10, 1953.

New York Times, August 10, 1941, November 8, 1941, February 14, 1943, September 12, 1943, April 7, 1946, May 10, 1953.
New York Times Book Review, August 21, 1960.
Saturday Review, October 17, 1953.
Saturday Review of Literature, August 9, 1941, May 18, 1946.
Spectator, April 9, 1943.
Times Literary Supplement, January 4, 1941, March 20, 1943, February 27, 1953, June 26, 1953, February 8, 1968, July 30, 1971.
Weekly Book Review, April 4, 1943, September 12, 1943, March 31, 1946.
Yale Review, autumn, 1941.

OBITUARIES:

PERIODICALS

Times (London), March 10, 1988.

*   *   *

RODMAN, Eric
See SILVERBERG, Robert

*   *   *

ROETHKE, Theodore (Huebner) 1908-1963

PERSONAL: Born May 25, 1908, in Saginaw, Mich.; died August 1, 1963, on Bainbridge Island, Wash.; son of Otto Theodore (a floriculturalist and greenhouse owner) and Helen Marie (Huebner) Roethke; married Beatrice Heath O'Connell, January 3, 1953. *Education:* University of Michigan, A.B. (magna cum laude), 1929, M.A., 1936; graduate study at Harvard University, 1930-31.

CAREER: Lafayette College, Easton, Pa., instructor in English, 1931-35, director of public relations, 1934-35, also varsity tennis coach; Michigan State College (now University), East Lansing, instructor in English, 1935; Pennsylvania State University, University Park, instructor, 1936-39, assistant professor of English, 1939-43, 1947, also varsity tennis coach; Bennington College, Bennington, Vt., assistant professor of English, 1943-46; University of Washington, Seattle, associate professor, 1947-48, professor of English, 1948-62, poet-in-residence, 1962-63. Fulbright lecturer in Italy, 1955.

MEMBER: National Institute of Arts and Letters, Phi Beta Kappa, Phi Kappa Phi, Chi Phi.

AWARDS, HONORS: Guggenheim fellowship, 1945, 1950; Eunice Tietjens Memorial Prize, 1947; Levinson Prize, 1951, for poetry published in *Poetry;* Fund for the Advancement of Education fellowship, National Institute and American Academy Award in Literature, nomination for honorary membership in International Mark Twain Society, and National Institute of Arts and Letters grant, all 1952; Ford Foundation Grant, 1952, 1959; Pulitzer Prize in poetry, 1954, for *The Waking: Poems 1933-53;* Borestone Mountain Award, 1958; Bollingen Prize in poetry from Yale University Library, 1958 for *Words for the Wind;* National Book Award, 1959, for *Words for the Wind,* and 1965, for *The Far Field;* Edna St. Vincent Millay Award, Longview Award, and Pacific Northwest Writers Award, all 1959; D.Litt., University of Michigan, Shelley Memorial Award for poetry, and Poetry Society of America Prize, all 1962.

WRITINGS:

POEMS

Open House, Knopf, 1941.

The Lost Son and Other Poems, Doubleday, 1948.

Praise to the End!, Doubleday, 1951.

The Waking: Poems, 1933-1953, Doubleday, 1953.

Words for the Wind: The Collected Verse of Theodore Roethke, Secker & Warburg, 1957, Doubleday, 1958.

Sequence, Sometimes Metaphysical, Stone Wall Press, 1963.

The Far Field, Doubleday, 1964.

The Two Poems, [privately printed], 1965.

The Collected Poems of Theodore Roethke, Doubleday, 1966.

The Achievement of Theodore Roethke: A Comprehensive Selection of His Poems, edited by William J. Martz, Scott, Foresman, 1966.

Theodore Roethke: Selected Poems, selected by wife, Beatrice Roethke, Faber, 1969.

Dirty Dinkey and Other Creatures: Poems for Children, edited by B. Roethke and Stephen Lushington, Doubleday, 1973.

OTHER

I Am! Says the Lamb (juvenile), Doubleday, 1961.

Party at the Zoo (juvenile), Crowell, 1963.

(Contributor) Anthony Ostroff, editor, *The Contemporary Poet as Artist and Critic* (essays), Little, Brown, 1964.

On the Poet and His Craft: Selected Prose, edited by Ralph J. Mills, Jr., University of Washington Press, 1965.

Selected Letters of Theodore Roethke, edited by Mills, University of Washington Press, 1968.

Straw for the Fire (selections from notebooks), edited by David Wagoner, Doubleday, 1972.

SIDELIGHTS: "The motif of the journey," wrote Keen Butterworth in the *Concise Dictionary of American Literary Biography,* "is more crucial to the poetry of Theodore Roethke than to that of any other major American poet since Whitman." This journey took Roethke on an exploration of his own past, examining the events and characters of his life in minute and painful detail. Some critics believe this psychic exploration contributed to the poet's several nervous breakdowns. Despite his struggle for mental stability, Roethke nonetheless managed to create a body of poetry that placed him among the most important American poets of his time. According to Jay Parini in his *Theodore Roethke: An American Romantic,* "Roethke was a great poet, the successor to Frost and Stevens in modern American poetry."

Though as a child he read a great deal and as a high school freshman he had a Red Cross campaign speech translated into twenty-six languages, Roethke strove to be accepted by peers who felt "brains were sissys." The insecurity that led him to drink to be "in with the guys" continued at the University of Michigan, where he adopted a tough, bear-like image (he weighed well over 225 pounds) and even developed a fascination with gangsters. Eccentric and nonconformist—he later called himself "odious" and "unhappy"—Roethke yearned for a friend with whom he could talk and relate his ambitions. "His adolescence must have been a hell of a bright awareness," speculated Rolfe Humphries, "frustrated because he did not know what to do with it, and it was constantly sandpapered by those around him."

While attending college, Roethke decided to pursue teaching— and poetry—as a career. His fascination with nature compelled him to write in an undergraduate paper: "When I get alone under an open sky where man isn't too evident—then I'm tremendously exalted and a thousand vivid ideas and sweet visions flood my consciousness." In addition to the stories, essays, and criticism commonly expected of English students, Roethke began writing poetry at this time. "If I can't write, what can I do," he said, and though Richard Allen Blessing claimed he "wrote a reasonably good prose," it still would "have taken a

keen eye to detect the mature poet beneath the layers of undergraduate baby fat." The direction towards his eventual career cleared somewhat when Roethke dropped out "in disgust" after a brief stint as a University of Michigan law student: "I didn't wish to become a defender of property or a corporation lawyer as all my cousins on one side of the family had done." The attitude evident in this decision supported biographer Allan Seager's conclusion that it was more than an unsuppressible awareness of life that led him to choose poetry as a career: "It would be flattering to call it courage; more accurately it seems to have been an angry, defiant, Prussian pigheadedness that was leading him to his decision."

The first fifteen years of Roethke's writing career, from his beginnings as an undergraduate to the publication of *Open House,* formed a "lengthy and painful apprenticeship" for the young writer. In cultivating his poetic expression, Roethke relied heavily upon T. S. Eliot's belief that "the only way to manipulate any kind of English verse, [is] by assimilation and imitation." With this model in mind, Roethke himself once wrote "imitation, conscious imitation, is one of the great methods, perhaps THE method of learning to write. . . . The final triumph is what the language does, not what the poet can do, or display." In her book *The Echoing Wood of Theodore Roethke,* Jenijoy La Belle summarized Roethke's major challenge as a "conscious imitator": "The modern poet should move away from the Romantic concept of personal expression. . . . He must, in effect, march through the history of poetry—rewrite the poems of the past— that he may come out at the end of his journey a poet who has absorbed the tradition and who thus may take one step forward and add to that tradition."

Roethke's task was no easy one. In addition to debts to such contemporaries as W. H. Auden, Louise Bogan, Babette Deutsch, and William Carlos Williams, his extensive and varied poetic tradition included William Wordsworth, William Blake, Christopher Smart, John Donne, Sir John Davies, Walt Whitman, William Butler Yeats, T. S. Eliot, and Dante.

Along with these influences, the source of much of Roethke's poetry was the notes he dutifully kept throughout his life. A measure of the devotion given to his craft can be found in his statement "I'm always working," and indeed his pockets were seemingly always filled with jottings of striking thoughts and conversations. His less spontaneous reflections found a place in the workbench of his poetry—his notebooks. Though Roethke is not generally considered a prolific writer, a more accurate account of the time and effort spent developing his verse is apparent in this extensive accumulation of criticism (of himself and others), abstract thoughts, reflections on childhood, and, of course, poetry. In his biography of Roethke, *The Glass House,* Allan Seager estimated that only three percent of the lines of poetry in the more than two hundred notebooks was ever published.

The introspective Roethke announced his bold "intention to use himself as the material for his art" through the title of his first published volume, *Open House.* Not surprisingly, however, the book reflected the imitative and traditional elements of his "conscious imitation" apprenticeship. W. D. Snodgrass found it "old-fashioned and prerevolutionary. The poems are open and easily graspable; the metric quite regular and conventional." This "truly cautious" volume, remarked Blessing, is "a loose arrangement of poems . . . tacked together for the most part by the limitations of Roethke's early poetic techniques and by the shape of his personality. . . . At best, he achieves an effect something like that frigidly controlled hysteria that one often feels in Emily Dickinson.''

Regardless of the limitations evident in *Open House,* Seager pointed out that ''most of the reviews were good and those that contained adverse criticisms tacitly acknowledged that this was the work of a genuine poet and not a beginner.'' Marveling at Roethke's ''rare'' ability to ''remember and to transform the humiliation ['of feeling physically soiled and humiliated by life'] into something beautiful,'' W. H. Auden called *Open House* ''completely successful.'' In another review of the book, Elizabeth Drew felt ''his poems have a controlled grace of movement and his images the utmost precision; while in the expression of a kind of gnomic wisdom which is peculiar to him as he attains an austerity of contemplation and a pared, spare strictness of language very unusual in poets of today.''

Roethke kept both Auden's and Drew's reviews, along with other favorable reactions to his work. As he remained sensitive to how peers and others he respected should view his poetry, so too did he remain sensitive to his introspective drives as the source of his creativity. Understandably, critics picked up on the self as the predominant preoccupation in Roethke's poems. ''We have no other modern American poet of comparable reputation who has absorbed so little of the concerns of the age into his nerve-ends,'' said M. L. Rosenthal, and, as a result, many have cited this limited concern as a major weakness in his poetry. Others, however, interpreted Roethke's introspection more positively, claiming it is the essence of his work. Ralph J. Mills called this self-interest ''the primary matter of artistic exploration and knowledge, an interest which endows the poems with a sense of personal urgency, even necessity.'' Stanley Poss, too, heralded Roethke as ''a test case of the writer whose interest in himself is so continuous, so relentless, that it transforms itself and becomes in the end centrifugal. With hardly a social or political bone in his body he yet touches all our Ur-selves, our fear and love of our fathers, . . . our relish of the lives of plants and animals, our pleasures in women who have more sides than seals, our night fears, our apprehensions of Immanence.''

Whether or not this introspection is a weakness or the essence of his poetry, the intensity he devoted to teaching demonstrates an obvious concern outside the self. An immensely popular professor, Roethke succeeded in driving his students to share his enthusiasm for poetry. Not only was he well liked, often extending classroom sessions into the local bar, he was unique, as demonstrated by a popular anecdote from one of his classes at Michigan State: To stimulate his class in an assignment of the description of physical action, Boethke told his students to describe the act he was about to perform. He then crawled outside through a classroom window and inched himself along the ledge, making faces into each of the surrounding windows.

Such actions corresponded with what Roethke, a very demanding teacher, expected from his students' poetry. Oliver Everette recalled him exclaiming, ''You've got to have rhythm. If you want to dance naked in an open barndoor with a chalk in your navel, I don't care! You've got to have rhythm.'' Another student remembered him saying, ''Please let me see evidences of an active mind. Don't be so guarded—let your mind buzz around.'' And, Roethke impressed poet David Wagoner with the line ''motion is equal to emotion.'' Wagoner along with poets Richard Hugo and James Wright form an impressive trio of ex-Roethke students.

Despite his efforts, Roethke held no dream of developing his students into outstanding poets. In a 1943 letter to Leonie Adams he admitted ''one cannot be too grandiose about the results [of

teaching]: after all, there are only from five to fifteen with real talent for writing poetry in any one generation.'' Roethke's hopes for his students were much more practical: ''A bright student can be taught to write cleanly; he can learn—and this is most important—much about himself and his own time.''

This energetic pursuit of both a teaching and a writing career at times understandably affected his outlook. Part of his frustration stemmed from the amount of time teaching entailed. ''I'm teaching well,'' he wrote in 1947, ''—if I can judge by the response— but haven't done one damned thing on my own. It's no way to live—to go from exhaustion to exhaustion.'' Later, the fatigue seemed even more crucial to him. ''I think I can say there's a real need for me to get out of teaching for a time,'' he wrote William Carlos Williams in 1949. ''I'm getting caught up in it: too obsessed with making dents in these little bitches. The best ones keep urging me to quit: not worth it, etc. etc.''

There were times when Roethke was unable to maintain any semblance of balance. His well-publicized mental breakdowns were, at least in part, the result from his going ''from exhaustion to exhaustion.'' Allan Seager explained the apparent inevitability of the first attack in 1935: ''There was no great mystery about his going to the hospital—he had nearly ruined himself in a mad attempt to go without sleep, work hard on everything, eat only one or two meals a day because he was so intent on 'this experiment' he was making in his classes.'' Roethke himself told Rolfe Humphries (with what Seager noted is a ''perfectly rational'' explanation) that the reason for his illness, which eventually brought him to the Mercywood Sanitarium in Ann Arbor, ''was his own stupidity in trying to live 'a pure and industrious life all of a sudden.' ''

Though the second of his breakdowns did not occur until 1945, they became increasingly more frequent in the ensuing decade; by 1958, he was attending therapy sessions six times a week. In all probability he was dismissed from Michigan State because his breakdown was viewed as an unacceptable failing (the letter read ''we have decided that it will be better both for you and the College if your appointment for the coming year is not renewed''), but in later years his mental problems were recognized as an unfortunate but accepted part of his personality. When a perspiring Roethke entered the first class of the 1957-58 University of Washington school year by flinging ''himself against the blackboard in a kind of crucified pose, muttering incoherently,'' the plea to the police was a compassionate but urgent ''this is a very distinguished man and he is ill. All we want you to do is take him to a sanitarium.''

Despite some suspicions of his worth which followed such incidents, Roethke remained an invaluable and highly esteemed member of the Washington faculty. In 1959, a Washington state legislator concerned about Roethke's sick leaves approached university vice-president Frederick Thieme and asked, ''Who's this professor you've got down there that's some kind of nut?'' This prompted English Department chairman Robert Heilman's unequivocal defense of Professor Roethke, describing his illness, the university's obligation to its teachers, his distinguished writing, his teaching success, and his overall service to the university. It read, in part: ''Roethke has a nervous ailment of the 'manic-depressive' type. Periodically he goes into a 'high' or 'low' state in which he is incapable of teaching. . . . His illnesses are well-known throughout the University and the local community. I have always been pleased that they have been accepted as the terribly sad lot of an extraordinarily gifted man. . . . [In] teaching, developing interest in a great literary form, training writers who themselves go on to become known, and doing his own distinguished writing which has won all kinds of acclaim—Roethke is performing what I call a *continuing service to the University,* which goes on whether he is sick or well."

Although Seager admitted the cause of Roethke's problems "may have lain in the chemistries of his blood and nerves," some have claimed that they were attributable to his intense self-exploration and that he was able to see into himself more clearly because of his illnesses. Kenneth Burke has shown that by willingly immersing himself in the conflicts of his childhood Roethke precipitated his second breakdown; one psychiatrist has said "I think his troubles were merely the running expenses he paid for being his kind of poet." Not denying the personal tragedy of Roethke's illness, Rosemary Sullivan maintained "he was able to see in his experience a potential insight into other thresholds of consciousness." These views correspond with Roethke's premise on the search for truth: "To go forward (as a spiritual man) it is necessary first to go back." In *The Lost Son* he explored this pattern in the title poem and in its three companion pieces, as Sullivan explained: "They are desperate poems, each beginning in negative, life-denying solipsism which is gradually and painfully transcended until the poet achieves an exultant experience of wholeness and relation." In the same vein, Roethke probed the darkness of his childhood in "The Greenhouse Poems" of *The Lost Son.*

The roots of the greenhouse sequence lay in the extensive greenhouses owned by Roethke's father and uncle. For Roethke, whom Seager described as "thin, undersized and sickly as a boy, obviously intelligent but shy and diffident as well," the greenhouses became a source of ambivalence: "They were to me, I realize now, both heaven and hell, a kind of tropics created in the savage climate of Michigan, where austere German Americans turned their love of order and their terrifying efficiency into something beautiful."

Roethke's father, a German American, who died when Roethke was fourteen, was also a profound influence on the young boy. Sullivan explained the paradoxical father-son relationship: "Otto Roethke presented an exterior of authoritarian order and discipline [but] in the greenhouse he gave expression to a deep sensitivity to the beauty of nature." The apparent tendency of Otto to hide this "vulnerable core," Sullivan added, prevented Roethke from understanding his father. Feeling "angered and abandoned," Roethke implicated himself in his father's death, a death that prevented any gradual reconciliation between them. Sullivan further theorized that "from the consequent sense of his own inadequacy Roethke seems to have acquired the burdens of fears and guilts which haunted him all his life." Certainly his writings—from essays written at the University of Michigan to the poem "Otto" in *The Far Field*—uphold Seager's comment that "all his life the memory loomed over him."

By scrutinizing the plants, flowers, and creatures, Roethke attempted to tie the world of the greenhouse to the "inner world" of man. "The sensual world of the greenhouse is the first garden from which we have all emerged," explained Richard Blessing, "and the attempt to make meaning of it, to recall the energies of that place occupies us all in the lonely chill of our adult beds." James G. Southworth agreed that the search through the past is a painful one, as demonstrated in the opening lines of "Cuttings (later)": "This urge, wrestle, resurrection of dry sticks, / Cut stems struggling to put down feet, / What saint strained so much, / Rose on such lopped limbs to new life?" Ultimately the message of the greenhouse sequence, as interpreted by Blessing, "reads that life is dynamic, not static; that the energy of the moment from the past preserves it, in part, in the present; that experience is a continuum, not a collection of dead instants preserved and pinned on walls we have left behind."

While *The Lost Son* focused on a child's struggle for identity, Roethke made great advances in establishing his own identity as a poet during this time. Michael Harrington felt that "Roethke found his own voice and central themes in *The Lost Son*" and Stanley Kunitz saw a "confirmation that he was in full possession of his art and of his vision." Blessing echoed this praise when he wrote: "To my mind, the transformation of Theodore Roethke from a poet of 'lyric resourcefulness, technical proficiency and ordered sensibility' to a poet of 'indomitable creativeness and audacity . . . difficult, heroic, moving and profoundly disquieting' is one of the most remarkable in American literary history."

Praise to the End! followed much the same pattern set in *The Lost Son* by continuing "his most heroic enterprise," the sequence of interior monologues initiated in the title poem of *The Lost Son.* Roethke himself offered these suggestions on how to read the new book: "You will have no trouble if you approach these poems as a child would, naively, with your whole being awake, your faculties loose and alert. (A large order, I daresay!) Listen to them, for they are written to be heard, with the themes often coming alternately, as in music, and usually a partial resolution at the end. Each poem . . . is complete in itself; yet each in a sense is a stage in a kind of struggle out of the slime; part of a slow spiritual progress; an effort to be born, and later, to become something more."

Admittedly simplifying the two sections of *Praise to the End!,* Karl Malkoff classified the poems of the first section as concerning "the struggle to be born, [and] those of the second, the effort, perhaps even more strenuous, to become something more." In his article, "The Poetry of Theodore Roethke," Southworth traced the journey undergone in the second half and held that while Roethke does not resolve his personal problems in these poems, there is a pattern of emerging awareness for the subconscious probing poet. From the sequence's first poem, "The Lost Son," Southworth saw the confusion in the lines "Which is the way I take; / Out of what door do I go, / Where and to whom?" relieved by an awareness of the living plants and animals of the greenhouse. Roethke then, through introspection, leaves his past with a new awareness of the self and concludes the final section of the poem "Praise to the End!" with the lines "My ghosts are all gay. / The light becomes me." "From this point forward," observed Southworth, "the poems communicate a sense of restrained ecstasy that is unique in contemporary poetry. The poet has plumbed the depths of his subconciousness, has rid himself of concern for the dead, and has come to realize that excessive thinking without embracing life can be sterile. . . . In order to find the meaning in life, one must accept life to the full, not be too much concerned . . . by those who are not reaching upward. . . . [The book's final poems,] 'I cry Love! Love!' and 'O, Thou Opening, O' continue the achievement of the poet in his struggle to the point where he can face the past squarely and realize that the one true significance in life is in living and loving."

After the intense explorations of *The Lost Son* and *Praise to the End!* "it is not surprising," as W. D. Snodgrass pointed out, "that Roethke might at this point need to step back and regather his forces. He did just that in the group of 'New Poems' in *The Waking.* . . . Here Roethke returned to the more open lyricism of his earlier verse and gave us, again, several markedly successful poems."

Roethke's marriage, his readings in philosophy and religion, and his feelings of anxiety and illness are, according to Malkoff, the most important events projected in the "New Poems" of *Words for the Wind.* His love poems, which first appeared in *The Waking* and earned their own section in the new book, "were a distinct departure from the painful excavations of the monologues and in some respects a return to the strict stanzaic forms of the earliest work," said Stanley Kunitz. Ralph Mills described "the amatory verse" as a blend of "consideration of self with qualities of eroticism and sensuality; but more important, the poems introduce and maintain a fascination with something beyond the self, that is, with the figure of the other, or the beloved woman." Roethke's "surrender to sensualism," claimed Robert Boyers, is not permanent: "He eventually discovers that the love of woman is not the ultimate mode for him." James McMichael reasoned why: "The love poems stress that his simple biological attraction for women, both because it is mindless and because she seems to him more mindless than himself, is the most necessary step on the journey [out of the self]."

As Malkotf noted, Roethke is not a consistent poet. "He moves from utter despair, to resignation, to mystic faith beyond mysticism and back to despair. We shall not find in his poems the development of a systematic philosophy; there emerges rather the complex figure of a man directly confronting the limitations of his existence with none of life's possibilities . . . excluded." *Words for the Wind* wavers in this way when, in Kunitz's words, "the love poems gradually dissolve into the death poems." The book does conclude with "The Dying Man" and "Meditations of an Old Woman," but these poems are more than gloomy contemplations of death: Blessing believed "The Dying Man" (dedicated to Roethke's spiritual father, Yeats) "remains a poem about the creative possibilities inherent in the very shapelessness of death"; Malkoff thought "Meditations of an Old Woman" "provides a kind of frame of reference for the consideration of life, and which often reappearing, is never far from the poem's surface. . . . [Ultimately,] *Words for the Wind,* read from cover to cover, is the spiritual autobiography of a man whose excessive sensitivity to his experience magnifies rather than distorts man's universal condition."

Roethke earned much of this magnified vision with an understanding of the mysticism that pervades *Words for the Wind* and *The Far Field.* Heavily influenced by Evelyn Underhill's *Mysticism,* many of his later poems follow her psychological progression, as outlined by Sullivan: "They begin with the painful apprehension of personal insufficiency, aggravated by the awareness of the possibility of a deeper reality. This is followed by a desire for purification through self-castigation and mortification, which Underhill calls the painful descent into the 'cell of knowledge.' This leads to illumination, a sudden breakthrough to a heightened visionary joy in the awakening of transcendental consciousness. These are only the first three, as it were, secular stages of mystical insight; he never laid claim to the last stages which lead to union with Absolute Being."

William Heyen emphasized that Roethke was not one who dedicated "his life to educating himself to achieve union with God. Rather, Roethke was an artist who experienced moments of deep religious feeling and almost inexpressible illumination. His choice was not traditional Christianity or atheism, but a reliance upon the mystic perceptions of his own imagination." In "Sequence, Sometimes Metaphysical," for example, Roethke defined his focus as "a hunt, a drive toward God; an effort to break through the barrier of rational experience." McMichael, however, found a paradox involved in such an effort: "The more he thinks about that thing [something other than himself] the less likely he is to know it as it really is; for as soon as he begins to acquire for him any of the qualities that his conceptual faculty is ready to impose upon it, his intuition and love of it are lost." Roethke does reach points of ecstasy in his poems, though, and Heyen defended him against critics who have charged that his joy is superficial and too easily attained: "It is important to realize that the happiness achieved in any Roethke poem . . . is not one based on reason. . . . Armed with his study of Underhill and the mystics she discusses Roethke has found his rationale . . . he can rock irrationally between light and dark, can go by feeling where he has to go."

Admittedly in retrospect, Seager reflected on the years preceding *The Far Field* and Roethke's death: "The last years of Ted's life, as we look back on them knowing they were the last, seem to have a strange air of unconscious preparation. As the fabric of his body begins to give way, the best part of his mind, his poetry, . . . strives toward a mystical union with his Father. But this was unconscious. I don't think he was at all aware that he was getting ready to go. He had too much work in hand, too much projected, yet the last poems seem prophetic: they read like last poems." (Roethke told Ralph Mills, however, "a year before his death, that this might well be his final book.") Perceiving a similar pattern in *The Far Field,* W. D. Snodgrass wrote that "these poems, recording that withdrawal [as in 'The Longing'], also, I think suffer from it. The language grows imprecise with pain. . . . Metrically, too, one has a sense of discouragement and withdrawal. . . . More and more, Roethke's late poems seem to have lost their appetite, their tolerance for that anguish of concreteness." Why Roethke's poems might have lost their concreteness was interpreted by Sullivan, who believed the despair in Roethke's poetry to be rooted in his search for assurances. Since the mind cannot understand the mystery of being, Sullivan continued, Roethke learns to reject his self-destructive impulses and celebrates "the capacity to rest in mystery without feeling the need to reach after certainties."

The Far Field contained two sequences representing earlier themes and images, as well as "North American Sequence" and "Sequence, Sometimes Metaphysical." According to Sullivan, Roethke wished to be remembered by the last poems in the latter sequence. Roethke himself wrote that "in spite of all the muck and welter, the dreck of these poems [in 'Sequence, Sometimes Metaphysical'], I count myself among the happy poets: I proclaim once more a condition of joy." Indeed for those distressed by the tragic self-implications of his statement—"There is nothing more disconcerting than when a rich nature thins into despair"—these last poems, in celebrating the richness of nature and the poet's "capacity to face up to genuine mystery," erase the despair. His last lines read: "And everything comes to One, / As we dance on, dance on, dance on."

Roethke's death, of a heart attack while swimming in a friend's pool, was "an incalculable loss to American Literature," wrote Ralph Mills. While the poet was drinking much and suffering in his later years from a combination of ailments, including arthritis, bursitis, and periods of manic excitement, his poetry was reaching its peak and earned this praise from James Dickey: "Roethke seems to me the finest poet now writing in English. I [say] this with a certain fierceness, knowing that I have to put him up against Eliot, Pound, Graves, and a good many others of high rank. I do it cheerfully, however. . . . I think Roethke is the finest poet not so much because of his beautifully personal sense of form . . . but because of the way he sees and feels the aspects of life which are compelling to him."

The publication of *Collected Poems* in 1966 brought renewed interest in Roethke's work and prompted overviews of his career. David Ferry felt "there are many things wrong with the poetry of Theodore Roethke. . . . His seriousness is frequently too solemnly serious, his lyrical qualities too lyrically lyrical. His mystical vein often seems willed, forced. . . . And yet Roethke is a very interesting and important poet. For one thing there is . . . the brilliance there [in *Praise to the End!*] with which he uses imitations of children's voices, nursery rhymes, his beautiful sense of the lives of small creatures, the shifting rhythms and stanza forms. . . . [And, in *The Far Field*] there are signs of a new and promising expansiveness and tentativeness. . . . For the reader, the pity is not to be able to see where this would have taken him." In *Sewanee Review*, Karl Malkoff wrote: "Though not definite, *Roethke: Collected Poems* is a major book of poetry. It reveals the full extent of Roethke's achievement: his ability to perceive reality in terms of the tensions between inner and outer worlds, and to find a meaningful system of metaphor with which to communicate this perception. . . . It also points up his weaknesses: the derivative quality of his less successful verse, the limited areas of concern in even his best poems. The balance, it seems to me, is in Roethke's favor. . . . He is one of our finest poets, a human poet in a world that threatens to turn man into an object."

Roethke was altogether human, both in creating "the most exhaustive, vital, and vivid reports we have of a soul in the several agonies normally recorded in one human life," and in impressing "his friends and readers profoundly as a human being." His appreciation for all life is evident in his statement, "If I have a complex, it's a full-life complex." Roethke lived energetically, most notably through a devotion to his teaching and through the introspection necessary to his poetry. At the same time, it is generally acknowledged that he paid for his tremendous mental and physical energy with his breakdowns. Thus, as Snodgrass said, one can view Roethke's career "with an astonished awe, yet with sadness."

BIOGRAPHICAL/CRITICAL SOURCES:

BOOKS

Blessing, Richard Allen, *Theodore Roethke's Dynamic Vision,* Indiana University Press, 1974.
Concise Dictionary of American Literary Biography: The New Consciousness, 1941-1968, Gale, 1987.
Contemporary Authors Bibliograpical Series, Volume 2, Gale, 1986.
Contemporary Literary Criticism, Gale, Volume 1, 1973, Volume 3, 1975, Volume 8, 1978, Volume 11, 1979, Volume 19, 1981, Volume 46, 1988.
Deutsch, Babette, *Poetry in Our Time,* Doubleday, 1963.
Dickey, James, *Babel to Byzantium: Poets and Poetry Now,* Farrar, Strauss, 1968.
Dictionary of Literary Biography, Volume 5: *American Poets since World War II,* Gale, 1980.
French, Warren, editor, *The Fifties: Fiction, Poetry, Drama,* Everett/Edwards, 1971.
Heyen, William, compiler, *Profile of Theodore Roethke,* C. E. Merrill, 1971.
Hungerford, Edward Buell, editor, *Poets in Progress: Critical Prefaces to Ten Contemporary Americans,* Northwestern University Press, 1962.
Kostelanetz, Richard, editor, *On Contemporary Literature: An Anthology of Critical Essays,* Avon, 1964.
Kostelanetz, compiler, *The Young American Writers: Fiction, Poetry, Drama, and Criticism,* Funk, 1967.
LaBelle, Jenijoy, *The Echoing Wood of Theodore Roethke,* Princeton University Press, 1976.

Malkoff, Karl, *Theodore Roethke: An Introduction to the Poetry,* Columbia University Press, 1966.
Mazzaro, Jerome, editor, *Modern American Poetry: Essays in Criticism,* McKay, 1970.
McLeod, James R., *Roethke: A Manuscript Checklist,* Kent State University Press, 1971.
McLeod, *Theodore Roethke: A Bibliography,* Kent State University Press, 1973.
Mills, Ralph J., *Theodore Roethke,* University of Minnesota Press, 1963.
Mills, *Contemporary American Poetry,* Random House, 1965.
Nyron, Dorothy, editor, *A Library of Literary Criticism,* Ungar, 1960.
Parini, Jay, *Theodore Roethke: An American Romantic,* University of Massachusetts Press, 1979.
Rosenthal, M. L., *The New Poets: American and British Poetry Since World War II,* Oxford University Press, 1967.
Scott, Nathan A., *The Wild Cry of Longing,* Yale University Press, 1971.
Seager, Allan, *The Glass House: The Life of Theodore Roethke,* McGraw, 1968.
Stein, Arnold, editor, *Theodore Roethke: Essays on the Poetry,* University of Washington Press, 1966.
Sullivan, Rosemary, *Theodore Roethke: The Garden Master,* University of Washington Press, 1975.
Vernon, John, *The Garden and The Map: Schizophrenia in Twentieth Century Literature and Culture,* University of Illinois Press, 1973.
Waggoner, Hyatt H., *American Poets from the Puritans to the Present,* Houghton, 1968.
Walker, Ursula Genug, *Notes on Theodore Roethke,* University of North Carolina Press, 1968.

PERIODICALS

American Literature, May, 1964, November, 1974.
American Scholar, summer, 1959.
American Poetry Review, January/February, 1974.
Atlantic, November, 1968.
Chicago Review, winter, 1959.
College English, May, 1957, March, 1960, February, 1966.
Commonweal, February 21, 1969.
Earlham Review, spring, 1970.
Encounter, April, 1958.
Hudson Review, spring, 1959, winter, 1964-65, winter, 1966-67.
Journal of Modern Literature, July, 1974.
Kenyon Review, autumn, 1941, winter, 1954, autumn, 1965, November, 1966.
Listener, June 27, 1968, August 22, 1968.
Michigan Quarterly Review, fall, 1967.
Midwest Quarterly, autumn, 1965, January, 1966.
Minnesota Review, Volume 8, 1968.
Modern Poetry Studies, July, 1970.
Nation, March 22, 1952, November 14, 1953, March 21, 1959, September 28, 1964.
New Republic, July 14, 1941, July 16, 1956, August 10, 1959, January 23, 1965, August 27, 1966, September 21, 1968, March 4, 1972, February 9, 1974.
Newsweek, March 17, 1958, August 12, 1963.
New Yorker, May 15, 1948, February 16, 1952, September 24, 1966.
New York Herald Tribune Book Review, July 25, 1948, December 2, 1951.
New York Review of Books, September 22, 1966.

New York Times Book Review, December 16, 1951, May 16, 1954, November 9, 1958, August 5, 1964, July 18, 1965, July 17, 1966, September 29, 1968, April 9, 1972.

Northwest Review, summer, 1971.

Northwestern University Review, fall, 1958.

Poetry, January, 1949, June, 1959, October, 1960, April, 1962, November, 1964, March, 1966, January, 1967, August, 1969, March, 1973.

Saturday Review, April 5, 1941, August 19, 1949, August 31, 1963, January 2, 1965, July 31, 1965, December 31, 1966, June 22, 1968, March 11, 1972.

Sewanee Review, January, 1950, summer, 1967, summer, 1968, autumn, 1973.

Shenandoah, autumn, 1964.

Southern Review, summer, 1965, winter, 1967, winter, 1969, spring, 1965.

Speech Monographs, March, 1963.

Texas Studies in Literature and Language, winter, 1969, winter, 1973, winter, 1975.

Time, August 9, 1963.

Tulane Studies in English, Volume 20, 1972.

Virginia Quarterly Review, spring, 1959, winter, 1967, autumn, 1968, autumn, 1972.

Western Humanities Review, winter, 1966, autumn, 1975.

Western Review, winter, 1954.

Yale Review, June, 1959, winter, 1965, winter, 1967.

* * *

ROGERS, Carl R(ansom) 1902-1987

PERSONAL: Born January 8, 1902, in Oak Park, Ill.; died of a heart attack, February 4, 1987, in San Diego, Calif.; son of Walter Alexander and Julia (Cushing) Rogers; married Helen Elliott, 1928 (died March 29, 1979); children: David E., Natalie. *Education:* University of Wisconsin, B.A., 1924; graduate study at Union Theological Seminary, New York, N.Y., 1924-26; Columbia University, M.A., 1928, Ph.D., 1931.

ADDRESSES: Home—2311 Via Siena, La Jolla, Calif. 92037.

CAREER: Institute for Child Guidance, New York, N.Y., fellow in psychology, 1927-28; Society for the Prevention of Cruelty to Children, Rochester, N.Y., psychologist, 1928-30, director of child study department, 1930-38; Rochester Guidance Center, Rochester, director, 1939; Ohio State University, Columbus, professor of psychology, 1940-45; University of Chicago, Chicago, Ill., professor of psychology and executive secretary, Counseling Center, 1945-57; University of Wisconsin—Madison, Knapp Professor, 1957, professor in departments of psychology and psychiatry, 1957-63; Western Behavioral Sciences Institute, La Jolla, Calif., resident fellow, 1964-68; Center for Studies of the Person, La Jolla, resident fellow, 1968—. Lecturer, University of Rochester, 1935-40; visiting professor at Columbia University, University of California, Los Angeles, Harvard University, and other colleges, 1935-54. Fellow, Center for Advanced Study in the Behavioral Sciences, 1962-63. Member of executive committee, Wisconsin Psychiatric Institute, University of Wisconsin, 1960-63. Director of counseling services of United Service Organizations, 1944-45; psychological consultant to Army Air Forces, 1944.

MEMBER: American Association for Applied Psychology (charter member; fellow; chairman of clinical section, 1942-44; president, 1944-45), American Orthopsychiatric Association (fellow; vice-president, 1941-42), American Psychological Association (fellow; president, 1946-47; president of division of clinical and abnormal psychology, 1949-50), American Academy of Psychotherapists (charter member; first president, 1956-58), American Academy of Arts and Sciences (fellow), Phi Beta Kappa, Phi Kappa Alpha.

AWARDS, HONORS: Nicholas Murray Butler Silver Medal from Columbia University, 1955; special contribution award, American Psychological Association, 1956, for research in the field of psychotherapy; selected as humanist of the year, American Humanist Association, 1964; distinguished contribution award, American Pastoral Counselors Association, 1967; professional award, American Board of Professional Psychology, 1968; American Psychological Association, distinguished professional contribution award, 1972, and distinguished professional psychologist award from Division of Psychotherapy, 1972; D.H.L. from Lawrence College (now University), 1956, University of Santa Clara, 1971, and Union for Experimenting Colleges and Universities, Cincinnati, 1984; honorary doctorate from Gonzaga University, 1968; D.Sc. from University of Cincinnati, 1974, and Northwestern University, 1978; D.Ph. from University of Hamburg, 1975; DS.Sc. from University of Leiden, 1975; medal for distinguished service from Columbia University Teachers College, 1986.

WRITINGS:

Measuring Personality Adjustment in Children Nine to Thirteen Years of Age, Teachers College, Columbia University, 1931.

The Clinical Treatment of the Problem Child, Houghton, 1939.

Counseling and Psychotherapy, Houghton, 1942.

(With J. Wallen) *Counseling with Returned Servicemen,* McGraw, 1946.

Client-Centered Therapy: Its Current Practice, Implications, and Theory, Houghton, 1951

(Editor with Rosalind F. Dymond) *Psychotherapy and Personality Change,* University of Chicago Press, 1954.

(Contributor) Sigmund Koch, editor, *Psychology: A Study of Science,* Volume 3, McGraw, 1959.

On Becoming a Person, Houghton, 1961.

(Editor and co-author) *The Therapeutic Relationship and Its Impact: A Study of Psychotherapy with Schizophrenics,* University of Wisconsin Press, 1967.

Person to Person: The Problem of Being Human, Real People Press, 1967.

(Editor with William R. Coulson) *Man and the Science of Man,* C. E. Merrill, 1968.

Freedom to Learn: A View of What Education Might Become, C. E. Merrill, 1969.

Carl Rogers on Encounter Groups, Harper, 1970 (published in England as *Encounter Groups,* Lane, 1971).

Becoming Partners: Marriage and Its Alternatives, Delacorte, 1972.

(With B. F. Skinner) *A Dialogue on Education and the Control of Human Behavior* (includes six audio cassettes), edited by Gerald Gladstein, Jeffrey Norton, 1976.

Carl Rogers on Personal Power, Delacorte, 1977.

A Way of Being, Houghton, 1980.

Freedom to Learn for the 80s, C. E. Merrill, 1983.

Also author, with Barry Stevens, of *Person to Person: The Problem of Being Human.* Contributor of many articles in psychological, psychiatric, and educational journals.

SIDELIGHTS: A leading exponent of humanistic psychology, Carl R. Rogers is the author of a well-known theory of personality development and the father of client-centered therapy. Rogers revolutionized both the theory and practice of psychotherapy when he suggested that psychoanalytic, experimental, and behavioral clinicians direct their patients too much by imposing solutions on them, thereby diminishing the opportunity for self-directed growth. By expressing his ideas in numerous books, articles, lectures, recordings, films, and encounter sessions, Rogers has acquired a worldwide following, as well as some of psychology and psychotherapy's highest honors; yet he has also been branded by some as a rebel, a radical, and an iconoclast who is insufficiently scientific.

Evidence of Rogers's free spirit surfaced early in his career. He had originally intended to become a Protestant minister and accordingly entered Union Theological Seminary in 1924, after earning a bachelor's degree in history from the University of Wisconsin. But he soon realized that his interest lay more in spirituality than religion. In *On Becoming a Person* he traces the beginning of this realization back to a six-month visit to the Orient in 1922, which forced him to recognize "that sincere and honest people could believe in very divergent religious doctrines." After exploring his religious doubts in an independent seminar, he moved toward his own philosophy of life and decided to leave the seminary. "I felt that questions as to the meaning of life and of the improvement of life for individuals would probably always interest me," he recalls, "but could not work in a field where would be required to believe in some specified religious doctrine."

Rogers's development as an independent thinker in the field of clinical psychology followed a similar pattern. His training at Columbia University was a traditional one, emphasizing the objective, statistical approach common to the natural sciences. His professional horizons expanded when he encountered the Freudian psychoanalytic climate of the Institute for Child Guidance, the first of three centers where he diagnosed and treated mainly children over a twelve-year period. But during the latter half of the 1930s, Rogers began to question the authoritative theories and methodologies of psychotherapy, for his experience convinced him that he obtained better results when he listened to and followed his patients' lead rather than when he interpreted their problems and prescribed solutions based on external factors, such as early life experiences. "Unless I had a need to demonstrate my own cleverness and learning, I would do better to rely upon the client for the direction of movement," he says in *On Becoming a Person.*

Rogers began using the word 'client' instead of 'patient'—a practice that is now widespread in the field—because he felt that although they needed help and attention, his clients were not sick in the same sense as medical patients who must surrender power over themselves to a medical expert. He came to believe that success in the counseling process was primarily dependent upon the development of certain attitudes on the part of the therapist, rather than on technique, and that the relationship between clinician and client was paramount. New and different, his ideas sparked controversy, affecting even the conditions of his lectureship at the University of Rochester from 1935 to 1940. The psychology department there challenged the legitimacy of his clinical work and forced him, at first, to offer his courses through the departments of sociology and education.

Undaunted, Rogers continued to develop his theory of personality development and its concomitant approach to therapy in books such as *Counseling and Psychotherapy and Client-Centered Therapy,* as well as numerous articles and lectures. Each person, according to Rogers, has an inherent tendency to continually grow and develop in a way that enhances self-esteem and promotes self-actualization. This development however, can proceed only as long as the person receives unconditional accep-

tance from others, or what Rogers calls "unconditional positive regard." If praise and affection are not given unconditionally, the person begins to develop along the lines suggested by others, loses touch with himself or herself and may become neurotic.

In order to facilitate the emergence of self-actualizing forces the therapist must therefore demonstrate not only empathy and genuineness but also unconditional acceptance of the client as a person. One way this is achieved is through "reflection"—perhaps the best known aspect of Rogers's approach to therapy. Throughout the session the therapist restates, or reflects back, what the client says in an effort to both show acceptance of what is said and to help the client recognize possibly neglected feelings. The therapist may make interpretive remarks that clarify a problem and produce insight, but no formal guidance is given the client, who remains free to direct his or he own course.

Called "nondirective" and "client-centered" when first developed, Rogers's approach became known as "people-centered" as he carried it beyond psychotherapy to such areas a education, marriage, leadership, parent-child relationships, and the development of professional standards. In *On Becoming Person, Freedom to Learn, Becoming Partners* and other books he articulated his belief that personal growth is an ongoing process of becoming and that all healthy relationships are open and respectful struggles that foster growth. Rogers's radical ideas, coupled with those of Abraham Maslow and other humanistic psychologists, fostered a boom in therapy in America during the sixties and seventies. He became somewhat of a guru, acquiring such epithets as "Father of let-it-all-hang-out" and the "relisher of 'openness' as a thing in itself," to use the words of Benjamin DeMott in the *Atlantic.* Paperback sales of his 1967 book *Person to Person* surpassed eighty thousand copies in only six months, and by 1980 there were over half a million copies of *On Becoming a Person* in print.

Until his death in 1987 Rogers continued to exhort individuals, organizations, and even nations to be open and accepting in their dealings with one another. In his collection of essays *A Way of Being,* he advocates a person-centered approach to life, illustrates its effects on his own life, and suggests how the human potential for growth, creativity, and change can be nurtured in individuals, groups, communities, and other social settings. The book, writes Peter Gardner in *Psychology Today,* is "a recapitulation, reaffirmation, and updating of the beliefs and principles that have made Rogers famous."

BIOGRAPHICAL/CRITICAL SOURCES:

BOOKS

Evans, Richard Isadore, *Carl Rogers: The Man and His Ideas,* Dutton, 1975.
Kirschenbaum, Howard, *On Becoming Carl Rogers,* Delacorte, 1979.
Rogers, Carl R., *On Becoming a Person,* Houghton, 1961.
Rogers, Carl R., *A Way of Being,* Houghton, 1980.

PERIODICALS

America, April 7, 1973.
American Journal of Sociology, September, 1955.
American Sociological Review, June, 1955.
Atlantic, December, 1973.
Books and Bookmen, August, 1973, November, 1973.
Commonweal, November 5, 1971
New York Times Book Review, September 20, 1970, January 28, 1973.
Psychology Today, March, 1981.

Spectator, winter, 1972.
Time, July 1, 1957.
Times Literary Supplement, August 24, 1973.
U.S. Quarterly Book Review, December, 1954.

OBITUARIES:

PERIODICALS

Chicago Tribune, February 7, 1987.
Los Angeles Times, February 6, 1987.
New York Times, February 6, 1987.
Science News, February 21, 1987.
Times (London), February 10, 1987.
Washington Post, February 7, 1987.

*   *   *

ROGERS, Rosemary 1932-

PERSONAL: Born December 7, 1932, in Panadura, Ceylon (now Sri Lanka); came to United States in 1962, naturalized citizen; daughter of Cyril Allan (an owner and manager of a private school) and Barbara Jansze; married Summa Navaratnam (divorced); married Leroy Rogers (divorced); married Christopher Kadison (a poet); children: (first marriage) Rosanne, Sharon; (second marriage) Michael, Adam. *Education:* University of Ceylon, B.A. *Politics:* Democrat. *Religion:* Episcopalian.

ADDRESSES: Home—Carmel, Calif., and New York, N.Y.

CAREER: Associated Newspapers of Ceylon, Colombo, writer of features and public affairs information, 1959-62; Travis Air Force Base, Fairfield, Calif., secretary in billeting office, 1964-69; Solano County Parks Department, Fairfield, secretary, 1969-74; writer. Part-time reporter for *Fairfield Daily Republic.*

MEMBER: Authors Guild, Authors League of America, Writers Guild.

WRITINGS:

Sweet Savage Love, Avon, 1974.
The Wildest Heart, Avon, 1974.
Dark Fires, Avon, 1975.
Wicked Loving Lies, Avon, 1976.
The Crowd Pleasers, Avon, 1978.
The Insiders, Avon, 1979.
Lost Love, Last Love, Avon, 1980.
Love Play, Avon, 1981.
Surrender to Love, Avon, 1982.
The Wanton, Avon, 1985.
Bound by Desire, Avon, 1988.

SIDELIGHTS: Rosemary Rogers, who writes lengthy historical and contemporary romances, has helped change the course of the genre by adding a new element: explicit sex in the previously G-rated love scenes. Relates Kathryn Falk in *Love's Leading Ladies:* "When Rosemary used to read historical novels as a young girl she often wondered why they didn't say a little more in the love scenes. 'Not that you want to be clinical like a sex manual,' [Rogers] explains. 'But I always felt you can go into a bit of detail and at the same time you can leave a little to the imagination.' This is what she attempts to do."

Formerly, romance novels required a virginal heroine who remained chaste until she married the hero, which usually occurred at the novel's conclusion. The beginnings of Rogers's books generally follow the traditional format. But before long, the hero forcefully awakens the heroine to her dormant passions. "The difference between R. R. and most of her rivals is inten-

sity," writes Brad Darrach in *Time.* "Almost all the others write in pink ink about horse-and-carriage love and marriage; Rogers pumps out purple prose about red-blooded males and females living at white heat in electric-blue relationships." He adds that Rogers "perfected the soft-edge sex scene in which, just as the worst is about to happen, all the heavy breathing seems to steam the reader's glasses and the details fade discreetly into daydreams." Rogers's new formula has sold over fifty million copies of her books worldwide, disproving the theory that romances were "women's novels." Rogers includes men among her readers, some in unlikely places. "I have fan clubs in half the federal penitentiaries around the country!" she told *CA.*

"She's one author who looks and lives like one of her heroines," suggests Tom Huff, a romance writer quoted in *Love's Leading Ladies.* Rogers grew up in an environment similar to those depicted in her books. Her father owned and managed a group of private schools in Ceylon, and his eldest daughter was raised in a world of servants, chaperones, and European excursions. She wrote her first short story at the age of eight, read voraciously, and as a teenager wrote novels for pleasure. "At seventeen, initiating the pattern her heroines now follow, Rosemary rebelled against a feudal upbringing," writes a *Time* reporter. Rogers's rebellion took the form of being the first woman in her family to get a job. She became a feature writer for a Ceylon newspaper and worked there for three years. She also married a track star, who "often sprinted after other women," reports *Time.* A divorce followed, then another marriage, to Air Force Sergeant Leroy Rogers. The pair eventually moved to California, where she raised four children and continued to write. "Right through bringing up my own kids, through diaper time, instead of watching TV, I'd write stories," she told Falk.

But when her second marriage also ended, Rogers was left trying to support her family on a secretary's salary of $4,200 a year. About this time, her parents came to live with her after fleeing the Marxist rebellion in Ceylon. In order to survive economically, Rogers decided to market one of her old stories, eventually rewriting it twenty-four times before sending the 636-page manuscript to Avon Books, whose name her daughter had found on the first page of *Writer's Market.* It arrived on editor Nancy Coffey's desk in the wake of Avon's successful publishing of *The Flame and the Flower* by Kathleen Woodiwiss. Recognizing another potential bestseller, Avon immediately offered Rogers a contract.

The novel was called *Sweet Savage Love* and Rogers promptly followed it up with another bestseller, *Dark Fires.* The first two books, plus a third, *Lost Love, Last Love* relate the lengthy, passionate, and sometimes violent romance between Steven Morgan, a womanizing adventurer, and Virginia Brandon, the spirited, initially virginal, heroine. While the public reacted enthusiastically to the books, critics were often less pleased. Weeks says "*Dark Fires,* though promoted as an epic historical love story, is in fact crammed with violence, sexual perversion and sadomasochism. . . . The theory behind *Dark Fires* assumes that females groove on violence and that rape is a shortcut to the joy of sex." Charles Madigan comments on *Lost Love, Last Love* in the *Chicago Tribune:* "Basically, it's about sex. Almost everyone in this 378-page book is interested in sex. Steve and Ginny, for example, mate with regularity. . . . Steve also couples with many other women, too. They are his mistresses." The word romance does not always denote moonlight and chivalry, either. "[Steve] never kisses Ginny; he lays such a lip lock on her that he almost breaks her neck. And Ginny, hey. She loves it," Madigan continues. Some critics have even labeled her books as pornographic. Rogers disagrees. In a note to *CA* she explained that she does not write pornography. She says her novels "are more like morality plays—exposing life the way it is."

Rape is a common and recurring theme in Rogers's novels. To the criticism that her heroines are masochistic women with rape fantasies, Rogers told Carol Lawson, *New York Times Book Review* contributor: "Most women do have a rape fantasy. But there is a difference between actual rape, which is horrifying, and fantasy. In the rape fantasy, you pick the man and the circumstances. It's not at all scary." In an interview with Patricia Goldstone for the *Los Angeles Times* she says of her heroines, "They end up getting raped a lot because, historically speaking, that's what happened to any woman who went out on her own."

"My heroines are partly me, partly women I have known or read about," Rogers told Goldstone. "They are Woman." A *West Coast Review of Books* reviewer describes the heroine of *The Wanton* a little differently, as "a beautiful and highly intelligent young woman, who is nevertheless the prisoner of her base passions and desires."

Still, many critics agree that the books provide an escape from life's everyday monotony. Writes Madigan, describing a woman reading her Rogers novel at the laundromat, "You are carried from the drudgery of the Buck-a-wash, from the rhythmic pounding of that washing machine and the whirring of those dryers and that offensive smell of bleach to a world of magnolias and women who smell like flowers and men who are so dashing you would never expect to meet one in the laundromat." Darrach quotes an Avon executive who relates why Rogers's books are so popular with American women. "They identify with Rosemary's heroines because the heroines do everything the average housewife longs to do—they travel to exotic places, meet famous people, have passionate affairs with fascinating men, and in the end fall madly in love and live happily ever after." Darrach continues that those who read the books "are force-fed events as the action mounts to a terrific climax in which lust sprouts little pink wings and Beauty fetters Beast with a golden wedding band."

Rogers herself has undergone a Cinderella-type transformation with her books' successes. Elisabeth Busmiller of the *Washington Post* describes the now full-time author, who is also a grandmother: "She looks exactly as you would expect: Mink-wrapped (black, by Chloe) and jewelry-draped (one bracelet, two earrings, three necklaces and eight rings . . .). She is . . . tall, thin, olive-skinned, with cascading dark hair and full lips." Rogers now has two homes in California (one on Big Sur) and another home in Manhattan. She prefers to work at night, with music playing in the background.

Several elements, Rogers says, are necessary for a successful romance. "For me it has to have an element of adventure," she said in an interview with a *Chicago Tribune* reporter. Other requirements are "a strong male protagonist, a strong female who's a little bit feisty and rebellious, mystery, suspense, romance, and, above all, a happy ending. At the end, she's got to melt, but so does he." And while her readers want a happy ending, she continued, "They don't want sickening saccharine romance." She told Falk, "The basic thing is the chemistry. . . . If you have the attraction, then wherever you are becomes romantic. Society overdoes the candlelight, atmosphere bit. Love is a much abused word, nowadays. I believe in attraction at first sight, but love is precious and doesn't come too easily. It has a lot to do with liking. For love to last, it has to involve liking, friendship, and communication." What kind of book does she prefer to read? "I like something I can sink my teeth into," she added. "Something with action, mystery, and suspense."

Unfavorable critical reviews don't bother Rogers too much; she is content with her enthusiastic audience. "I could never do things to please critics or an intellectual coterie," she told a *Time* reporter. "I write to please ordinary people—I write the kinds of books *I* want to read." Madigan says of *Lost Love, Last Love,* "This book and its predecessors . . . never will be candidates for the Nobel Prize for Literature. Rogers knows that, too. . . . She says they are pure entertainment, nothing less, nothing more."

AVOCATIONAL INTERESTS: Reading, music, watching some sports (especially football), printing, cooking, opera, and disco dancing.

BIOGRAPHICAL/CRITICAL SOURCES:

BOOKS

Authors in the News, Volume 1, Gale, 1976.
Falk, Kathryn, *Love's Leading Ladies,* Pinnacle Books, 1982.

PERIODICALS

Booklist, July 15, 1981, May 15, 1982, February 15, 1985.
Book World, January 21, 1979.
Chicago Tribune, June 14, 1981.
Chicago Tribune Magazine, June 5, 1983.
Detroit News, May 31, 1979.
Fort Worth Star-Telegram, December 31, 1974.
Harper's Bazaar, August, 1985.
Los Angeles Times, February 12, 1981.
New York Times, March 25, 1979.
New York Times Book Review, March 18, 1979.
Savvy, July, 1985.
Time, January 17, 1977.
Washington Post, May 22, 1980.
Washington Post Book World, September 14, 1975, September 3, 1978, January 21, 1979.
West Coast Review of Books, July, 1985.

*   *   *

ROMAINS, Jules   1885-1972
(Louis Farigoule)

PERSONAL: Birth-given name Louis-Henri-Jean Farigoule; name legally changed in 1953; born August 26, 1885, in Cevannes, France; died August 14, 1972, in Paris, France; son of Henri (a teacher) and Marie (Richier) Farigoule; married Gabrielle Gaffe, 1912 (divorced, 1936); married Lisa Dreyfus, 1936. *Education:* Attended Lycee Condorcet, 1897-1905; Ecole Normale Superiure, agregation de philosophie, 1909.

ADDRESSES: Home—Paris, France.

CAREER: Writer, poet, dramatist, and essayist. Teacher of philosophy in Brest, France, 1909, Laon, France, 1910-17, and Nice, France, 1917-19; full-time writer, 1919-72. Member of Academie Francaise, beginning in 1946. *Military service:* French Army, 1914-15.

MEMBER: International PEN Club (president, 1938-41).

WRITINGS:

IN ENGLISH TRANSLATION

Mort de quelqu'un (novel), E. Figuiere, 1911, translation by Desmond McCarthy and Sydney Waterlow published as *The Death of a Nobody,* B. W. Huebsch, 1914, new edition, New American Library, 1961.

Les Copains, E. Figuiere, 1913, Gallimard, 1962, translation by Jacques Le Clercq published as *The Boys in the Back Room,* R. M. McBride, 1937.

Donogoo Tonka; ou, Les Miracles de la science (also see below; produced in Paris at Theatre Pigalle, October 25, 1930), Gallimard, 1920, translation and adaptation by Gilbert Seldes published as *Donogoo,* Federal Theatre Project, 1937.

(Under name Louis Farigoule) *La Vision extra-retinienne et le sens paraptique: recherches de psycho-psysiologie experimentale et de physiologie histologique,* Gallimard, 1920, new edition, 1964, translation by Charles Kay Ogden published as *Eyeless Sight: A Study of Extra-Retinal Vision and the Paroptic Sense,* Putnam, 1924.

Lucienne, Nouvelle Revue Francaise, 1922, translation by Waldo Frank, Boni & Liveright, 1925.

Psyche (contains "Lucienne," "Le Dieu des corps," and "Quand le navire"; also see below), three volumes, Gallimard, 1922-29, translation by John Rodker published as *The Body's Rapture* (contains "Lucienne's Story," "The Body's Rapture," and "Love's Questing"), Liveright, 1933.

Knock, ou Le Triomphe de la medecine [and] *Monsieur Le Trouhadec saisi par la debauche* (also see below; three-act comedy; former produced in Paris at La Comedie des Champs-Elysees, December 15, 1923; latter produced in Paris at Champs-Elysses, March 14, 1923), Gallimard, 1924, translation of *Knock, ou Le Triomphe de la medecine* by Harley Granville-Barker published as *Doctor Knock,* Benn, 1925, translation by James B. Gidney published as *Knock,* Barron's, 1962.

Le Dieu des corps, Gallimard, 1928, reprinted, 1966, translation by John Rodker published as *The Lord God of the Flesh,* Pocket Books, 1953.

Les Hommes de bonne volonte, 27 volumes, Flammarion, 1932-46, translations by W. B. Wells and Gerard Hopkins published as *Men of Good Will,* 14 volumes, Knopf, 1933-36, Volume 1: *Men of Good Will,* Volume 2: *Passion's Pilgrims,* Volume 3: *The Proud and the Meek,* Volume 4: *The World from Below,* Volume 5: *The Earth Trembles,* Volume 6: *The Depths and the Heights,* Volume 7: *Death of a World,* Volume 8: *Verdun,* Volume 9: *Aftermath,* Volume 10: *The New Day,* Volume 11: *Work and Play,* Volume 12: *The Wind Is Rising,* Volume 13: *Escape in Passion,* and Volume 14: *The Seventh of October.*

Sept mysteres du destin de l'Europe, Editions de la Maison Francaise (New York City), 1940, translation by Germaine Bree published as *Seven Mysteries of Europe,* Knopf, 1940.

Stefan Zweig: grand europeen, Editions de la Maison Francaise, 1941, translation by James Whitall published as *Stefan Zweig: Great European,* Viking, 1941.

Salsette decouvre l'Amerique (also see below), Editions de la Maison Francaise, 1942, translation by Lewis Galantiere published as *Salsette Discovers America,* Knopf, 1942.

Violation de frontieres, Flammarion, 1951, translation by Gerard Hopkins published as *Tussles with Time,* Sidgwick & Jackson, 1952.

Examen de conscience des Francais, Flammarion, 1954, translation by Cornelia Schaeffer published as *A Frenchman Examines His Conscience,* Essential Books, 1955.

Situation de la terre, Flammarion, 1954, translation by Richard Howard published as *As It Is on Earth,* Macmillan, 1962.

Une femme singuliere (novel), Flammarion, 1957, translation by A. Pomerans published as *The Adventuress,* Muller (London), 1958.

(Editor) *Napoleon I, Emperor of the French, 1769-1821: Napoleon par luimeme* (in English and French), Librairie Academique Perrin, 1963.

Lettre ouverte contre une vaste conspiration, A. Michel, 1966, translation by Harold J. Salemson published as *Open Letter against a Vast Conspiracy,* J. H. Heineman, 1967.

OTHER

Le Bourg regenere, petite legenude, L. Vanier, 1906.

La Vie unanime, L'Abbaye, 1908.

Un etre en marche (poetry; title means "Someone Walking"), Mercure de France, 1910, reprinted, Flammarion, 1967.

Manuel de deification, E. Sansot, 1910.

L'Armee dans la ville (play; produced in Paris at Theatre de L'Odeon, March 4, 1911), Mercure de France, 1911.

Puissances de Paris, E. Figuiere, 1911.

Odes et Prieres (poetry; title means "Odes and Prayers"), Mercure de France, 1913.

Sur les quais de la Villette, E. Figuiere, 1914, reprinted as *Le Vin blanc de la Villette,* Gallimard, 1923.

Europe (poetry), Gallimard, 1916, reprinted, 1960.

Le Voyage des amants (poetry), Gallimard, 1920.

Cromedeyre-le-Vieil (drama in verse; produced in Paris at Theatre du Vieux-Colombier, May 26, 1920), Gallimard, 1920.

Le Mariage de le Trouhadec [and] *La Scintillante* (former produced in Paris at Comedie des Champs-Elysees, January 31, 1925; latter produced in Paris at Comedie des Champs-Elysees, October 7, 1924), translation of *La Scintillante* by F. Vernon published as "The Peach," in *Modern One-Act Plays from the French,* Holt, 1933.

(Author of introduction) *La Fanconnier: vingt-deux reproductions de peintures,* [Amiens, France], 1921.

Amour couleur de Paris (poetry), Gallimard, 1921.

Monsieur le Trouhadec saisi par la debauche (five-act comedy; produced in Paris at Comedie des Champs-Elysees, March 14, 1923), Gallimard, 1921.

(With Georges Chenneviere) *Petit traite de versification,* Gallimard, 1923.

Theatre, [Paris], 1924-35.

Le Dictateur (four-act play; produced in Paris at Comedie des Champs-Elysees, October 5, 1926), Gallimard, 1925.

Demetrios (also see below; play), produced in Paris at Comedie des Champs-elysees, October 9, 1926.

Jean le Maufranc: mystere (five-act play; produced in Paris at Theatre des Arts, December 1, 1926), Gallimard, 1926, revised version (produced in Paris as *Musse, ou l'ecole de l'hypocrisie,* at Tjeatre de A'telier, November 21, 1930), published in *Musse: precede de la premiere version, Jean le Maufranc,* 1929.

Chants des dix annees, Gallimard, 1928.

Quand le navire, Gallimard, 1929.

Le Dejeuner morocain (also see below; play; produced in Paris at Theatre Saint-Georges, February 9, 1929), Gallimard, 1929.

(Adaptor with S. Zweig) Ben Jonson, *Volpone,* Gallimard, 1929.

Pieces en un acte (title means "One-Act Plays"; contains "La Scintillant," "Amedee et les messieurs en rang," "Demetrios," and "Le Dejeuner morocain"), Gallimard, 1930.

Boen, ou La Possession des biens (three-act comedy; produced in Paris at Theatre de l'Odeon, December 4, 1930), Gallimard, 1935.

Problemes d'aujourd'hui, Editions KRA, 1931, revised edition published as *Problemes europeens,* Flammarion, 1933.

Le Roi masque (three-act comedy; produced in Paris at Theatre Pigalle, December 19, 1931), [Paris], 1932.

Le Couple France-Allemagne, Flammarion, 1934.

Zola et son exemple: discours de Medan, Flammarion, 1935.

Visite aux Americains, Flammarion, 1936.

Pour l'esprit et la liberte, [Paris], 1937.

L'Homme blanc, Flammarion, 1937.

Cela depend de vous, Flammarion, 1939.

Une vue des choses, Editions de la Maison Francaise, 1941.

Grace encore pour la terre! (three-act play), Editions de la Maison Francaise, 1941.

Messages au francais, Editions de la Maison Francaise, 1941.

Mission ou demission de la France?, D. F. Ediciones Quetzal, 1942.

Retrouver la foi, Editions de la Maison Francaise, 1944.

Nomentanus le refugie (also see below), Editions de la Maison Francaise, 1944.

Bertrand de Ganges (also see below), Editions de la Maison Francaise, 1944, new edition edited by A. G. Lehman, G. G. Harrap (London), 1961.

Le Colloque de novembre: discours de Jules Romains a l'Academie francaise et response de Georges Duhamel de l'Academie Francaise, Flammarion, 1946.

L'An mil (play), produced in Paris at Theatre Sara-Bernhardt, March 5, 1947.

Bertrand de Ganges, suivi de Nomentames le refugie, Flammarion, 1947.

Le Probleme numero un, Plon, 1947.

Choix de poemes, [Paris], 1948.

Pierres levees (also see below), Flammarion, 1947.

Le Moulin et l'hospice, Flammarion, 1949.

Paris des hommes de bonne volonte, illustrations by Pierre Belves, Flammarion, 1949.

Salsette decouvre l'Amerique, suivi de Lettres de Salsette, Flammarion, 1950.

Portrait de Paris, Perrin, 1951.

Interviews avec Dieu, Flammarion, 1952.

Saints de notre calendrier: Goeth, Balzac, Hugo, Baudelaire, Gobineau, Zola, Strindberg, France, Zweig, Gide, Chenneviere, Fargue, Flammarion, 1952.

Pages choisies, edited by Pierre Toulze, Hachette, 1953.

Maisons (also see below), Seghers, 1953.

Passagers de cette planete, ou allons-nous?, B. Grasset, 1955.

Le Petit Charles, edited by Fernand Vial and Santina C. Vial, Dryden (Hinsdale, Ill.), 1956.

Le fils de Jerphanion (novel), Flammarion, 1956.

Pierres levees, suivi de Maisons (poetry), Flammarion, 1957.

(With others) *Le Roman des douze,* Julliard, 1957.

Souvenirs et confidences d'un ecrivain, Fayard, 1958.

Le Besoin de voir clair: deuxieme rapport Antonelli (novel), Flammarion, 1958.

Hommes, medecins, machines, Flammarion, 1959.

Memoires de Madame Chauverel (novel), two volumes, Flammarion, 1959-60.

Les Hauts et la bas de la liberte (also see below), Flammarion, 1960.

Les Hauts et les bas de la liberte [and] *Supremes avertissements* [and] *Retrouver la foi* [and] *Nouvelles inquietudes* (collection), [Paris], 1960.

Hommage a Alfonso Reyes, 1889-1959, [Cahors, France], 1960.

Les Hauts et les bas de la liberte, Flammarion, 1960.

Pour raison garder, three volumes, Flammarion, 1960-67.

Landowski: la main et l'esprit, photography by Pierre Berdoy, Biblioteque des Arts, 1961.

Un grand honnete homme, Flammarion, 1961, new edition, Harrap, 1963.

Portraits d'inconnus, Flammarion, 1962.

Recherche d'une eglise, Flammarion, 1962.

Alexandre le Grand, Hachette, 1962.

Ai-je fait ce que j'ai voulu?, Wesmael-Charlier (Namur, Belgium), 1964.

Lettres a un ami, Flammarion, Volume 1, 1964, Volume 2, 1965.

Marc-Aurele; ou, L'Empereur du bonne volonte, Flammarion, 1968.

Amities et rencontres (autobiography), Flammarion, 1970.

Richesses theatrales et knock la scintillante, [Paris], 1972.

Columnist in *Aurore.*

SIDELIGHTS: "The idea of a vast novel, composed of a great number of volumes, and in which I would try to present a sort of epic from the beginning of the 20th century all over the world, and especially in France . . . existed in my mind from earliest youth, from the very time when I began to write," Jules Romains once recalled. He was referring to the conception of his most extensive and notable work, the fourteen-volume "Les Hommes de bonne volonte" series ("Men of Good Will" series). Written in twenty-seven parts, the series has been compared to Honore de Balzac's "Comedie Humaine," Emile Zola's "Rougon-Macquart," and Marcel Proust's "A la recherche de temps perdu."

Described by Alden Whitman as "one of the most intricately designed and most majestic of modern novels," "Men of Good Will" encompasses twenty-five years of western European history. It chronicles the lives of four hundred characters caught up in the events of the time and in the lives of one another. "Their brilliant talk and [the] artful blend of imagination and history combine to create the illusion of reading the inside biography of an age in all its tortuosity," Whitman pointed out.

In setting the beginning and end of the novel on historically unexceptional days (October 6, 1908, and October 7, 1933), Romains underlines his belief that every day is in fact replete with action. He further emphasizes that all aspects of life, such as work, love, art, and politics, are intertwined. The protagonists of the novel, Jeraphanion and Jallez, both aspire to change the world, but through different means. The former is action-oriented while the latter promotes change through his writing. Regardless of the method, Romains asserts, good will alone can never overcome the power of fate. Andre Maurois concluded that Romains "has written an epic that, however pessimistic in its facts, remains inspiring in its love of freedom and its deep sympathy for the adventure of the human race."

Maurois has described Romains as a "great novelist, greater essayist and poet." But Romains was disappointed that he was not more widely known as a poet. Nevertheless, Georges Duhamel, who had known him for many years, assured him, "In your poems, you have painted the world, you have painted your own times, and your own self." In Europe, Romains's poetry reflects his defiance over World War I.

"Unanism" is the term Romains used to describe his belief in a single, universal spirit, a "tremendous conception of giving a picture of life that would encompass all classes of society and types of people, with emphasis on the group," O'Brien explained. Romains himself pointed out that *La Vie Unanime* reveals "a new vision of human groups in themselves and not, as was most often the case before them, of the individual elements that compose them."

Although Romains was considered aloof by his peers in France, he was revered for his storytelling talents in the United States, where he was exiled during World War II. He enjoyed talking with people, mainly as a means to obtain material for future writings. An acquaintance once accused him of "always sizing up people with the eye of a professional psychiatrist."

Romains was fluent in German, Italian, and Spanish, and could speak some English.

BIOGRAPHICAL/CRITICAL SOURCES:

BOOKS

Boak, Denis, *Jules Romains,* Twayne, 1974.
Bree, Germaine, and Otis Guiton, *The French Novel: From Gide to Camus,* Harcourt, 1962.
Contemporary Literary Criticism, Volume 7, Gale, 1977.
Dictionary of Literary Biography, Volume 65: *French Novelists, 1900-1930,* Gale, 1988.
Maurois, Andre, *From Proust to Camus: Profiles of Modern French Writers,* translated by Carl Morse and Renaud Bruce, Weidenfeld & Nicolson, 1967.
Peyre, Henri, *French Novelists of Today,* Oxford University Press, 1967.

OBITUARIES:

PERIODICALS

Newsweek, August 28, 1972.
New York Times, August 18, 1972.
Time, August 28, 1972.

*   *   *

ROONEY, Andrew A(itken) 1919-
   (Andy Rooney)

PERSONAL: Born January 14, 1919, in Albany, N.Y.; son of Walter Scott and Ellinor (Reynolds) Rooney; married Marguerite Howard (a teacher), April 21, 1942; children: Ellen, Martha, Emily, Brian. *Education:* Attended Albany Academy, Albany, N.Y., and Colgate University, 1942. *Politics:* "Vacillating."

ADDRESSES: Office—CBS News, 524 West 57th St., New York, N.Y. 10019.

CAREER: Writer, primarily for television. Worked for Metro-Goldwyn-Mayer, Inc., Hollywood, Calif., one year; free-lance magazine writer, 1947-49; wrote material for Arthur Godfrey, 1949-55, Sam Levenson, Herb Shriner, and Victor Borge, and for "Twentieth Century," and "Seven Lively Arts"; Columbia Broadcasting System, Inc. (CBS), New York City, writer for CBS Radio's "The Garry Moore Show," 1959-65, writer-producer of television essays, documentaries, and specials for CBS News, 1962-70; worked for public television, 1970-71, and for American Broadcasting Companies, Inc. (ABC-TV), 1971-72; CBS News, writer, producer, and narrator of television essays, documentaries, and specials, 1972—, regular commentator-essayist on CBS News program "60 Minutes," 1978—. *Military service:* U.S. Army, 1942-45, reporter for *Stars and Stripes;* became sergeant; received Air Medal and Bronze Star.

AWARDS, HONORS: Writers Guild of America Award for best television documentary, 1966 for "The Great Love Affair," 1968 for "Black History: Lost, Strayed, or Stolen," 1971 for "An Essay on War," 1975 for "Mr. Rooney Goes to Washington," 1976 for "Mr. Rooney Goes to Dinner," and 1979 for "Happiness: The Elusive Pursuit"; George Foster Peabody Award, University of Georgia, 1975, for "Mr. Rooney Goes to Washington"; recipient of three Emmy Awards, including two for "60 Minutes."

WRITINGS:

(With Oram C. Hutton) *Air Gunner,* Farrar & Rinehart, 1944.
(With Hutton) *The Story of the "Stars and Stripes,"* Farrar & Rinehart, 1946, reprinted, Greenwood Press, 1970.
(With Hutton) *Conquerors' Peace: A Report to the American Stockholders,* Doubleday, 1947.
(Editor and author of notes and comment with Dickson Hartwell) *Off the Record: The Best Stories of Foreign Correspondents,* collected by Overseas Press Club of America, Doubleday, 1952.
The Fortunes of War: Four Great Battles of World War II (History Book Club selection), Little, Brown, 1962.
A Few Minutes with Andy Rooney (collection of essays written for television; includes "Hotels," "In Praise of New York City," "Mr. Rooney Goes to Washington," "Mr. Rooney Goes to Dinner," "Mr. Rooney Goes to Work," and "An Essay on War"), Atheneum, 1981.
And More by Andy Rooney (essays originally published in his syndicated column), Atheneum, 1982.
Pieces of My Mind, Atheneum, 1984.
The Most of Andy Rooney, Macmillan, 1986.
Word for Word, Putnam, 1986.
Not That You Asked . . ., Random, 1989.

Author of television essays, documentaries, and specials for CBS-TV, including "An Essay on Doors"; "An Essay on Bridges"; (with Richard Ellison) "The Great Love Affair," broadcast 1966; "Hotels," broadcast June 28, 1966; "An Essay on Women," broadcast 1967; (with Perry Wolff) "Black History: Lost, Strayed, or Stolen," broadcast 1968; "In Praise of New York City," broadcast February 1, 1974; "Mr. Rooney Goes to Washington," broadcast January 26, 1975; "Mr. Rooney Goes to Dinner," broadcast April 20, 1976; "Mr. Rooney Goes to Work," broadcast July 5, 1977.

Author of documentary "An Essay on War," broadcast by WNET-TV, 1971, as part of "The Great American Dream Machine" series. Co-author of filmscript based on *The Story of the "Stars and Stripes,"* purchased by Metro-Goldwyn-Mayer. Writer, under name Andy Rooney, of column syndicated to more than 250 newspapers by Tribune Co. Syndicate, 1979—. Contributor to periodicals.

SIDELIGHTS: Andrew A. Rooney, more affectionately known as Andy, is "the homespun Homer whose celebrations of the commonplace and jeremiads against the degenerating twentieth century are cheered by 40 million viewers of one of the nation's top-rated TV shows," writes Elizabeth Peer in *Newsweek.* A longtime writer and producer for the Columbia Broadcasting System, Rooney became a regular essayist on the CBS newsmagazine "60 Minutes" in 1978 and has evolved into "a one-man institution," notes Anne Chamberlin in the *Washington Post Book World.* His observations on such everyday items as chairs, doors, jeans, and soap appear not only on television but also in a thrice-weekly column syndicated to more than 250 newspapers across the United States. Moreover, many of these essays have been compiled into two best-sellers, *A Few Minutes with Andy Rooney* and *And More by Andy Rooney.* The multimedia success of these wry, down-to-earth editorials, says Bruce Henstell in the *Los Angeles Times Book Review,* has made Rooney "the most listened-to curmudgeon in recent times."

Admitting in the *Detroit News* that it "makes me mad when people come up to me and don't know I lived before 1979," Rooney has been a writer all his working life. A reporter for the armed forces' *Stars and Stripes* during World War II, he and colleague Oram C. "Bud" Hutton co-authored two books while in the service and one after being discharged. *Air Gunner,* described by the late Edmund Wilson in the *New Yorker* as "an excellent piece of reporting," tells about the American boys who manned the guns on the flying fortresses over Europe, and *The Story of the "Stars and Stripes"* discusses the development of the GI newspaper and its staff over the course of World War II. *Conquerors' Peace* reports the findings of a postwar tour of Europe by Rooney and Hutton, who not only examined the landscape, the American cemeteries, and the displaced persons problem, but also probed into the inhabitants' feelings about the war and the occupation troops.

After being discharged from the army, Rooney went to Hollywood and co-wrote the filmscript of *The Story of the "Stars and Stripes"* for Metro-Goldwyn-Mayer. Then, having finished the script as well as other assignments with Hutton, he became a free-lance writer, publishing pieces in *Reader's Digest, Look, Life, Esquire,* and other magazines. But after spending six weeks on an article for *Harper's* and getting $350 for it, "I realized I was not going to make it as a magazine writer," Rooney says in *Time.* From 1949 to 1955, Rooney was Arthur Godfrey's radio and television writer, "at a more comfortable $625 a week" according to *Time,* and he later crafted clever lines for such personalities as Victor Borge, Sam Levenson, and Herb Shriner.

Rooney began his long affiliation with CBS in 1959, when the network hired him to write for "The Garry Moore Show." Three years later, he teamed up with veteran newsperson Harry Reasoner for the first in a series of television essays that focused mainly on such seemingly mundane subjects as bridges, doors, and hotels. During their six-year collaboration from 1962 to 1968, Rooney wrote the words and served as producer of the broadcasts, and Reasoner presented the reports on camera. Susan Slobojan of the *Detroit News* notes that in these specials, "observing life with both eyes open and tongue planted firmly in cheek became a sort of Rooney trademark." She cites the beginning of "An Essay on Women," produced in 1967, as indicative of the approach: "This broadcast was prepared by men, and makes no claim to be fair. Prejudice has saved us a great deal of time in preparation."

But Rooney did not take everything so lightly. In 1970, when CBS wanted to halve and rearrange his philosophical half-hour "An Essay on War," Rooney quit the network in protest and went over to public television—at lower pay, of course. He then bought the essay from CBS to air on "The Great American Dream Machine" series, broadcast by New York's WNET-TV. Unable to use Reasoner's voice for this work, Rooney had to read it himself. "It was the only practical thing to do," he explained to *New York*'s Lewis Grossberger. "We didn't have a star on the 'Dream Machine.' Everybody did their own pieces. So I read it. It wasn't very well read, but the piece was good." Indeed, "An Essay on War" was good enough to win Rooney one of his six Writers Guild of America Awards; perhaps a more important consequence, however, was that it launched him on a career as an on-camera commentator.

Lured back to CBS in 1972, Rooney wrote, produced, and narrated a series of television reports on American life that, like many of his previous essays, "were characterized by the same droll, stubborn sensibility," observes Slobojan. The finest of these reports, according to a *Time* writer, "was probably 'In Praise of New York City' (1974), a journalistic paean that anticipated parts of Woody Allen's 'Manhattan.'" In "Mr. Rooney Goes to Dinner," the commentator examined numerous facets of eating out, noting among other things that a tassel on the

menu "can add a couple of dollars per person" to the average bill.

"After traveling across the country and visiting more than a hundred factories and other places of business and after seeing a lot of people leaning on their shovels when they should have been shoveling and then hearing people testify that they don't work hard," he concluded in "Mr. Rooney Goes to Work," "I have still become convinced, to my great surprise, that Americans *are* working their tails off." And in the best-known of these reports, "Mr. Rooney Goes to Washington," he wittily surmised that the federal bureaucracy is not "being run by evil people; it's being run by people like you and me. And you know how we have to be watched."

Rooney's reports won several awards and garnered much public attention, but his role at CBS was still somewhat vague. "They have never known exactly what to do with me around here," he told Lewis Grossberger. Rooney felt there was a place for a short essay somewhere around the company, so he requested more air time. The network gave him a chance in 1978 as a summer replacement for the "Point Counterpoint" segment of the CBS newsmagazine "60 Minutes." The move was so successful that "A Few Minutes with Andy Rooney" became a regular feature of the show that fall, alternating with the mini-debates of Shana Alexander and Jack Kilpatrick. One year later, Alexander and Kilpatrick were gone for good, the frequency of Rooney's appearances increased, and Rooney's popularity soared. "Audiences began wondering where he'd been all these years," writes Slobojan.

Since joining "60 Minutes," Rooney's success has been phenomenal. In addition to prompting comparisons with humorists E. B. White, James Thurber, and Art Buchwald, his deadpan delivery and acerbic wit have made him as popular as Mike Wallace and the rest of the "60 Minutes" crew. A column syndicated to more than 250 newspapers, begun in 1979 out of frustration at not having a sufficient outlet for his ideas, earned Rooney $130,000 beyond his $125,000 salary from CBS in 1982, according to Elizabeth Peer. His $10,000 fee per speaking engagement rivals that of Henry Kissinger and William F. Buckley, Jr. Moreover, both his sampling of television essays published as *A Few Minutes with Andy Rooney* and a collection of 127 newspaper columns, *And More by Andy Rooney,* topped the *New York Times* best-seller list. "In a season when the book business tottered," writes Carolyn See in the *Los Angeles Times, A Few Minutes with Andy Rooney* "was one of the few titles that booksellers could not keep in stock."

Paradoxically, Rooney's overwhelming success "derives largely from his persona as an ordinary guy," explains Michael Dirda in the *Washington Post Book World.* Described by *Time* as "the Boswell of Stuff " and by CBS colleague Walter Cronkite as "Everyman, articulating all the frustrations with modern life that the rest of us Everymen . . . suffer with silence or mumbled oaths," Rooney told Slobojan he deliberately writes about "subjects of universal interest. Someone suggested I do a piece on telephone answering services. You know those and I know those, but everyone else doesn't. Telephone answering services are not a piece for me to do. Glue is. Doorknobs are." "Rooney appreciates such things," notes Lewis Grossberger, "[because] he believes that the mundane is more important than commonly thought. The pencil, for instance, ultimately has a greater effect on our existence, he figures, than, say, the Vietnam war." Carolyn See maintains that Rooney's attention to the commonplace "puts the rest of those '60 Minutes' in perspective: Crooked union bosses may be one thing, but making good vanilla ice cream, or getting strung out on what shampoo to buy—these are the issues that should, and do, preoccupy America."

Rooney claims to live a normal life and that this helps him in his work. "I'm the all-American consumer," he says in *A Few Minutes with Andy Rooney*. "My idea of a good time is to go out Saturday morning to buy something with some of the money I've made." His tastes, he maintains, are not extravagant. He lives in the same house he bought over thirty years ago, and though he acknowledges "I greatly enjoy the money I make," he adds in the *Detroit News:* "But I spend it on small things. Tools. I'll spend $27 for a chisel that will solve all my problems. It never does."

Though Rooney does not think of himself as a humorist, his wry wit must ultimately be considered part of his appeal. "Rooney's humor is dry," notes Grossberger. "He doesn't do many jokes as such. Instead of 'Ha!' he goes for the 'Huh!'—that grunt of recognition and pleasure evoked when you hit somebody with a homely truth." The preface to *A Few Minutes with Andy Rooney* typifies the Rooney wit. Having expressed an uneasiness over the fact that a book by anyone on a popular television broadcast "will probably sell whether it's any good or not," he deftly admits: "It wasn't hard to talk me into putting this book together. It is unsatisfactory for a writer to have his words said once and then disappear forever into the air. Seeing our names in print leads to the dream all of us have of immortality. You can't ask more from something than immortality and money next week."

BIOGRAPHICAL/CRITICAL SOURCES:

BOOKS

Rooney, Andrew A., *A Few Minutes with Andy Rooney,* Atheneum, 1981.

PERIODICALS

Detroit Free Press, January 19, 1983.
Detroit News, November 8, 1981.
Globe and Mail (Toronto), February 21, 1987.
Los Angeles Times, November 11, 1982, February 9, 1990, March 2, 1990.
Los Angeles Times Book Review, November 29, 1981.
Newsweek, December 6, 1982, October 15, 1984.
New York, March 17, 1980.
New Yorker, October 21, 1944, February 16, 1946.
New York Times, October 29, 1944, February 17, 1946, May 25, 1947, March 22, 1989, February 13, 1990.
New York Times Book Review, December 19, 1982.
Saturday Review of Literature, February 23, 1946, July 26, 1947.
Time, July 11, 1969, July 21, 1980, November 1, 1982.
TV Guide, December 24, 1983.
Virginia Quarterly Review, spring, 1982.
Washington Post, November 8, 1982, January 5, 1987, February 8, 1990.
Washington Post Book World, December 20, 1981, October 14, 1984.

*   *   *

ROONEY, Andy
   See ROONEY, Andrew A(itken)

*   *   *

ROSS, Barnaby
   See DANNAY, Frederic

ROSS, Bernard L.
   See FOLLETT, Ken(neth Martin)

*   *   *

ROSSNER, Judith (Perelman) 1935-

PERSONAL: Born March 1, 1935, in New York, N.Y.; daughter of Joseph George and Dorothy (Shapiro) Perelman; married Robert Rossner (a teacher and writer), June 3, 1954 (divorced); married Mort Persky (a magazine editor), January 9, 1979 (divorced, 1983); children: Jean, Daniel. *Education:* Attended City College (now of the City University of New York), New York, N.Y., 1952-55.

ADDRESSES: Home—New York City. *Agent*—Wendy Weil, Julian Bach Literary Agency, 747 Third Ave., New York, N.Y. 10017.

WRITINGS:

NOVELS

To the Precipice, Morrow, 1966.
Nine Months in the Life of an Old Maid, Dial, 1969.
Any Minute I Can Split, McGraw, 1972.
Looking for Mr. Goodbar, Simon & Schuster 1975.
Attachments, Simon & Schuster, 1977.
Emmeline, Simon & Schuster, 1980.
August, Houghton, 1983.
His Little Women, Summit Books, 1990.

OTHER

Also author of short stories published in *Ararat* and *Cosmopolitan.*

SIDELIGHTS: Since the publication of *To the Precipice* in 1966, Judith Rossner has produced several novels which concern themselves with women's lives, particularly in changing times. Featured prominently in her work is such subject matter as childbirth and childrearing, love and friendship, ambition, and sexual conflict. "My abiding theme is separations," Rossner told Curt Suplee in a *Washington Post* interview. Her novel *August,* which contrasts the psychoanalysis of a New England teenager with the imperfect life of her middle-aged Manhattan psychologist, has been particularly highly acclaimed, but she is best known for her best-seller *Looking for Mr. Goodbar,* a work that was inspired by the true-life murder of a teacher by a man she met in a singles' bar.

Looking for Mr. Goodbar is the work that provided Rossner with financial independence and a national reputation. According to Patricia Jewell McAlexander in the *Dictionary of Literary Biography,* the movie based on the book further advanced Rossner's standing and increased the sales of her earlier novels, which include *Nine Months in the Life of an Old Maid* and *Any Minute I Can Split.* Film rights to *Looking for Mr. Goodbar* were sold before the work even appeared in hardcover.

Rossner wrote *Looking for Mr. Goodbar* for money, although, at the time, she "never believed for a minute that I would be able to support myself just by writing for the rest of my life," the author told John Askins in a *Detroit Free Press* interview. Divorced, with two young children at home, Rossner used to rise early to work on the book every morning before going to her secretarial job. She hoped that the novel "might make $40,000 and enable her to quit," a *Time* reporter explains. Having received an advance and hoping for a paperback sale, "my idea was that I would make just enough money to not be a secretary for a year," Rossner told Suplee.

If Rossner never expected to realize the profits she eventually made from *Looking for Mr. Goodbar,* it was probably because she had always known she wanted to write whether she made a lot of money at it or not. As Rossner told Bruce Cook in a *Detroit News* interview, her mother was a schoolteacher who had always wanted to be a writer, and she was responsible for Rossner entering the field: "She kept encouraging me when I was young, and so I just accepted it—this was what I was going to do; I was going to write books. But she never said anything about money or success, so none of that was built into my expectations. Just writing and getting published was enough at first."

Although Rossner dropped out of New York City College at age nineteen to marry Robert Rossner, a teacher and writer, she was careful not to get side-tracked. She began working in the ad department of *Scientific American,* but started to enjoy the job so much that she found it difficult to devote any energy to writing. "I started to get all excited about it," she explained to Suplee, adding in an interview with Barbara A. Bannon in *Publishers Weekly* that, "right away knew I'd have to go to work in real estate or something else or could never finish my novel. Writers are the lunatic fringe of publishing, and they shouldn't be involved in it except as writers."

According to Suplee, Rossner took a speed-writing course and did get a job in a real estate office, and was "bored out of my mind." As she remarked to Cook, "I was efficient, and it took absolutely nothing out of me." And although she told Cook that she is a little hesitant about relating the experience, "because what works for me may not work for other people," she did a couple of chapters of her first novel the first month she was there: "For me, the more interesting the 9-to-5 work is, the more it takes away from my real work, which is writing." Rossner finished that manuscript, but never published it. She put it aside, had a daughter, and then completed her first published novel, *To the Precipice.*

To the Precipice is a naturalistic account of the coming of age of Ruth Kossoff, a Jewish woman who is raised in a New York City tenement building. The story takes place during the 1940s and 1950s, relating how the protagonist decides to marry and raise children with a wealthy gentile she uneasily grows to love, rather than commit herself to a self-made lawyer she grew up with and to whom she has formed a more passionate attachment.

Although some critics found the plot formulaic and melodramatic in parts, and others thought the heroine unsympathetic, some still praised the book. *Nation* critic Edward M. Potoker, who in 1976 called it Rossner's "most ambitious novel," indicates that *To the Precipice* "is a Bildungsroman, a psychological novel, a Jewish novel, a woman's novel, a luminous period piece, and a family chronicle with a large, complex canvas that displays many of the author's principle themes and preoccupations." According to McAlexander, *To the Precipice* is dominated by a theme that will be repeated throughout Rossner's books, "the conflict between selfishness and altruism."

After she had her second child, Rossner again took up this theme in *Nine Months in the Life of an Old Maid,* a story about a totally self-absorbed insane woman who lives in an isolated mansion with her sister. *Saturday Review* critic Cecile Shapiro characterizes it as a tale told "with quiet competence, that "many will read with quiet enjoyment." Neither *To the Precipice* nor *Nine Months in the Life of an Old Maid* sold particularly well when they were first published. Rossner related to Suplee that "my first [published] book took five years to write and I made $1,000 on it and I was in Heaven." *Nine Months in the Life of an Old Maid* "took three years and made $3,000." But during those

years Rossner also had the support of her husband: "I was very lucky—my husband wanted to write [full-time] but he couldn't afford to."

At the end of the 1960s, the Rossners left New York City to begin a free school in New Hampshire. And as Suplee reports, Rossner "found herself unsuited to living off the land and hungry for New Yorkers: 'Even the dropouts were from Boston! It was the end of the marriage,' " Rossner told Suplee. So Rossner returned to Manhattan in 1971 and began a job in a psychiatry department of a hospital. Her third book, *Any Minute I Can Split,* which was published in 1972, typifies the era.

Any Minute I Can Split is the wisecracking story of Margaret Adams, a woman who runs away from her husband while she is pregnant with twins and eventually stumbles into a 1960s-style commune. She later discovers that life with her wealthy husband is preferable to the uncertainty of the commune, even though he is verbally abusive. The book has a serious side, as it concerns itself with the nature of the nuclear and extended family. Potoker relates that "the farm, revealing much tension under superficial friendliness, is a repository for petty squabbles, money problems, lack of communication and lack of privacy. As the novel's title suggests, all relationships are uneasy and tentative. Margaret begins to recognize the commune as suburbia in disguise."

The book was generally well-received. In *Any Minute I Can Split,* says *New York Times Book Review* contributing critic Martin Levin, Rossner reveals "a sharp eye for the contradictions and paradoxes of her characters." J. D. O'Hara agrees in *Saturday Review* that Rossner "evokes the commune well," although he maintains that Rossner "is too willing to write about ideas; instead of being incited to thought, we are too often obliged to hear Margaret's expository thinking." O'Hara adds that Rossner's "unpleasant scenes are especially credible," while Thomas Lask indicates in the *New York Times* that the author "has a way of treating even the most outlandish of situations in a cool, almost clinical way. She lets the dialogue carry the nuances in the book." *Any Minute I Can Split* "refuses to exploit its theme for sensational purposes or easy victories," Lask concludes.

After *Any Minute I Can Split* was published, Rossner told Suplee, "I began to feel silly as a secretary. I was 37 years old—it was like being in drag. I wanted to support myself by writing. I started 'Attachments,' but thought of that as an entirely uncommercial hook and put it aside." Then Rossner was asked if she wanted to do a story for a women's issue of *Esquire,* and the author suggested a piece about Roseann Quinn, the 27-year-old schoolteacher who had recently been killed by a man she'd taken home from a singles' bar. Rossner was depressed from having burnt her leg in a car accident, according to Suplee, so she felt she was in the right mood to write the article. *Esquire*'s lawyers eventually killed the story, Rossner told Suplee, so she said, " 'Fine, I'm a lousy journalist anyway.' Which I am. I have the absolute urge to bend reality to my own needs. The facts are my enemy. So I figured I'd do it as a novel."

In the opinion of McAlexander, *Looking for Mr. Goodbar* is "not only the most popular of Rossner's novels but also the best, treating her dominant theme—the conflict between selfishness and altruism—most convincingly." The book opens with the actual recorded confession of the young drifter who killed the woman after meeting her in a bar and taking her back to her apartment for sexual intercourse. Rossner then relates Theresa Dunn's story from her lower-middle-class Irish-Catholic childhood in the Bronx, her recovery from poliomyelitus and her affair with a university professor, to her development into a promiscuous barhopper who chooses to seek only false forms of freedom. According to Caroline Blackwood in the *Times Literary Supplement,* "the real-life testimony that Miss Rossner has used is brutal, bleak and factual. Her imaginary report as she reconstructs a fictional account of the life of Theresa Dunn leading up to her sordid death, is equally brutal, bleak and factual."

The book reflects its times and can "be read as a long, flat piece of devastating testimony against the destructive and joyless hedonism of New York in the 1960s, the era when everyone realized they were meant to be swinging, to be 'turning on' to grass and acid, to be 'into' music like that of the Rolling Stones, the era when it was fashionable to say 'ciao' when you said goodbye, and all the girls had hair that was bouffant and teased to copy Jackie Kennedy," Blackwood writes. "Rossner's physical descriptions of New York are as desolate as the lives of their New York characters." In the opinion of McAlexander, *Looking for Mr. Goodbar* thus dramatizes the dilemma of many Americans of the time, who were beginning to be disillusioned by the wild sexual experimentation and rejection of past values, but were continuing to hold fast to the narcissistic ideal of sexual fulfillment."

As McAlexander explains, "In Theresa's fate there is an unmistakable moral: that the 1960s dream of complete sexual freedom and fulfillment—however much Rossner sympathizes with it—is ultimately an impossible, self-destructive one while traditional morality—however limiting—at least allows one to survive, even to be a credit to family and society." And while Christopher Lehmann-Haupt in the *New York Times* is uncomfortable with the fact that the third person narrator of the book knows so much, *Time* reviewer Martha Duffy refers to *Looking for Mr. Goodbar* as "both a compelling 'page turner' and a superior *roman a clef.*" The book is "a truly superior novel," McAlexander agrees. "It will have a place in American literary history because of its convincing, finely drawn portrait of the sexual and moral confusion of its time."

Rossner followed *Looking for Mr. Goodbar* with several novels about women caught in dramatic circumstances that reflect the conflicts of their gender and era. After completing the sensationally popular *Looking for Mr. Goodbar,* Rossner turned to *Attachments,* a black comedy about two good friends who marry siamese twins with whom they raise a family. It examines the tension between the need to maintain close, long-standing relationships and the need to establish individuality. And although Jerome Charyn in the *New York Times Book Review* considers the book "an extraordinary leap from the mundane, 'realistic' settings and sexual tableaux" of *Looking for Mr. Goodbar,* other critics objected to the graphic sexuality of the work and perceived it to be a commercial venture. Some simply found the subject matter freakish.

Discussing *Attachments* in the *New Yorker,* a reviewer writes that "though Miss Rossner's writing is fluid and easy to digest, she never fulfills the expectations raised by the oddity of her subject," while John Leonard in the *New York Times* is of the opinion that *Attachments* "is an ambitious, disturbing novel by a bestselling author who might have written a trashy book, but decided instead to mess up our minds." Charyn concludes that *Attachments* is "funny, sexy and sad . . . a crazy treatise on 'love' as the ultimate executioner."

Emmeline, a tragic literary period piece set in New England of the 1800s, is similar to *Looking for Mr. Goodbar,* since it is based on actual events. As Walter Clemons explains in *Newsweek,* in *Emmeline,* Rossner has again "chosen a bizarre catastrophe, which in this book she reveals only near the end and traced its origins with a steady attention to character and psychological

probability. The novel is constructed from a story told to Rossner about a woman who actually lived in New England in the mid-1800s. Rossner's version tells of a poor 13-year-old, sent from her farm by her family in Maine to work in the cotton mills of Lowell, Massachusetts, who is then seduced and impregnated by her overseer. Emmeline's pregnancy is hushed up, her child is taken from her for adoption, and she returns to her insular farming village. Many years later, around the time of the Civil War, she falls in love with and marries a younger man who is passing through town with a road crew. He is later revealed to be her son. When the knowledge of the true nature of the marriage is discovered, Emmeline is ostracized from her community and dies, impoverished and lonely.

According to Anthony Quinton of the London *Times, Emmeline* "is a low-keyed, unsensational book, written in pleasant, rather stately prose, that would have been fairly intelligible and even natural at the time of the events recorded." And true or not, points out Lindsay Duguid in the *Times Literary Supplement,* Rossner "has made the most of her material and produced a chilling saga. Her treatment is, in the main, stark; and Emmeline's early sufferings are particularly convincing."

Like *Looking for Mr. Goodbar,* which Blackwood describes as "a morality tale," *Emmeline* contains "themes of religion and punishment of sin," relates Duguid. And like the main character of that novel, Theresa Dunn, Emmeline "is doomed to repeat her worst mistakes," Nancy Yanes Hoffman says in the *Los Angeles Times.* However, *Village Voice* reviewer Eliot Fremont-Smith believes that no "moral" can be drawn from the book, that Emmeline is too much the victim. He also feels that the novel is too closely tied to the real-life story from which it is derived, and that neither the protagonist nor her son can be considered tragic characters, since they've been granted too little knowledge by the author to be able to affect their own fate. Julian Moynahan in the *New York Times Book Review* is of a similar opinion, indicating that the book may not even be a novel.

Marge Piercy argues in the *Washington Post Book World,* though, that "in *Emmeline,* Judith Rossner has taken on a plot of highly improbable melodrama and come so close to making it believable that the part we cannot swallow scarcely bothers our enjoyment." Piercy considers Emmeline "a fully realized character in her naivete, her courage, her failing piety, her stubborn will, her devotion to her mother and her desperate loneliness." And "only because Emmeline is well drawn and because we identify with her determination to survive difficulties and save her family, we are able to accept a story that is archaic and sensational," adds Piercy. As Susan Fromberg Schaeffer indicates in the *Chicago Tribune Book World,* "this is a novel of rare knowledge and great power, masterfully told, and its last lines descend on the reader with a great cosmic chill. 'Emmeline' does what all great novels should do." The book "is built to last," says Clemons, "and its muted ending has the power to haunt our imagination."

August, on the other hand, which examines the psychoanalysis of a teenager, has about the same resemblance to a real psychoanalysis as a novel does to life, according to Rossner in the book's preface. It also leaves more room for humor than did *Emmeline* or *Looking for Mr. Goodbar,* Rossner pointed out in a *Los Angeles Times* interview with Mary Schnack. The central character, Dawn Henley, was raised by a lesbian aunt and her lover after Dawn's mother killed herself and her homosexual father drowned in a boating accident. Her foster "parents" have since "divorced." Dawn is in psychoanalysis with Dr. Lulu Shinefeld, who has a daughter of her own. Dawn has no knowledge of Dr.

Shinefeld's life outside of her office, but she has a fear of abandonment and dreads each coming August, when Lulu, like many of her colleagues, will take her vacation. Dawn's psychoanalysis is examined against the backdrop of her psychoanalyst's imperfect life during the hours and Augusts she spends away from her patients.

In the words of William A. Henry III in *Time,* "the title refers to the month when, in Rossner's flippant vision, all the analysts go on vacation leaving the patients to fret or go crazy. . . . *August* is also a kind of wish fulfillment for patients who want to be the only person in the doctor's life yet long to find out where the analyst goes when the 50-minute-hour is over." *Washington Post Book World* reviewer Suzanne Freeman reports that "throughout the novel, Rossner allows us to shift focus from patient's story to doctor's story and back again. Over the course of five years, we follow the progress of Dawn's therapy and the interludes—Augusts, Christmas vacations—we tune back into Lulu Shinefeld's personal life." In *August,* Freeman says, "Lulu Shinefeld slips into a life that is almost as moving and messy as anything Dawn Henley has to offer."

Together, the lives of the two main characters comprise a compelling narrative, according to reviewers. Freeman writes that "the unraveling of Dawn's secrets and the ups and downs of Lulu's life are as absorbing as a good mystery story. Lulu Shinefeld "is a remarkably well-drawn character," Walter Kendrick relates in the *New York Times Book Review,* while Diane M. Ross points out in the *Chicago Tribune Book World* that "being female is itself a major subject of 'August.' As in her earlier novels, Judith Rossner here explores the complicated emotional lives of women."

At first, Christopher Lehmann-Haupt writes in the *New York Times,* he had a problem with Rossner's using a psychoanalysis as the basis for her plot: "Aside from being a rather hoary device . . ., it seemed gimmicky and mechanical in the author's handling." But in the opinion of Lehmann-Haupt, "the double focus of 'August' serves to establish psychoanalysis as a system of order by which to gauge contemporary American society, or at least the part of it that is being shaken by the sexual revolution in its various eruptions. Mind, I said 'a system of order,' not 'the system.' "

Discussing *August* in *Newsweek,* Jean Strouse reports that, "as she showed in 'Looking for Mr. Goodbar,' Rossner is a master of psychological truth in extremis. Here, she turns a nearly incredible scenario into a moving exploration of loss and loneliness, the byways of the psyche and the need for love—not to mention the art of psychoanalysis." According to Kendrick, "I know of no other account, imagined or factual, that gives such a vivid picture of the analytic experience on both sides of its intense, troubled, ambiguous relationship."

Reviewers tend to find that *August* represents an advance for Rossner. The novel "turns out to be more careful and more contemplative than any of [Rossner's] earlier works—and, ultimately, far more satisfying," Freeman relates. Kendrick points out that *August* "is absolutely true to its own design; it's a model of rigor and restraint, even when it must take risks." The book is about "pain and maturity," concludes Adam Mars-Jones in the *Times Literary Supplement.* "It also proposes affluence and self-obsession as necessary elements of modern life."

MEDIA ADAPTATIONS: Looking for Mr. Goodbar was filmed by Paramount, 1977.

BIOGRAPHICAL/CRITICAL SOURCES:

BOOKS

Authors in the News, Volume 2, Gale, 1976.
Contemporary Literary Criticism, Gale, Volume 6, 1976, Volume 9, 1978, Volume 29, 1984.
Dictionary of Literary Biography, Volume 6: *American Novelists since World War II,* Gale, 1980.

PERIODICALS

Atlantic, September, 1975.
Chicago Tribune Book World, September 21, 1980, September 11, 1983.
Detroit Free Press, April 25, 1976.
Detroit News, October 26, 1980, August 10, 1983, August 28, 1983.
Harper's, September, 1983.
Hudson Review, winter, 1975-76.
Los Angeles Times, October 5, 1980, August 21, 1983, September 7, 1983.
Los Angeles Times Book Review, August 21, 1983.
Ms., June, 1976, September, 1980.
Nation, May 29, 1976.
New Leader, October 6, 1980.
New Republic, October 1, 1980.
Newsweek, May 19, 1975, September 19, 1977, September 29, 1980, August 1, 1983.
New Yorker, July 14, 1975, October 3, 1977.
New York Times, December 22, 1972, May 21, 1975, September 12, 1977, September 25, 1980, July 21, 1983, April 13, 1990.
New York Times Book Review, October 26, 1969, July 30, 1972, June 8, 1975, September 18, 1977, September 14, 1980, July 24, 1983.
Publishers Weekly, August 22, 1980.
Saturday Review, November 22, 1969, August 5, 1972, October 1, 1977, September, 1980, October, 1983.
Spectator, November 2, 1977.
Time, July 7, 1975, August 22, 1983.
Times (London), January 8, 1981.
Times Literary Supplement, September 12, 1975, March 18, 1977, November 4, 1977, January 25, 1981, November 4, 1983.
Village Voice, September 24-30, 1980, September 6, 1983.
Washington Post, June 1, 1975, September 14, 1980, August 1, 1983.
Washington Post Book World, September 14, 1980, August 14, 1983.
Washington Star, July 8, 1975.

*   *   *

ROSTAND, Edmond (Eugene Alexis) 1868-1918

PERSONAL: Born April 1, 1868, in Marseilles, France; died December 2 (one source says December 22), 1918, in Paris, France; son of Eugene (a journalist, poet, and economist) Rostand; married Rosemonde Gerard (a poet) April 8, 1890; children: Maurice, Jean. *Education:* Attended the College Stanislas in Paris, beginning in 1884; briefly studied law.

CAREER: Poet and playwright.

MEMBER: Academie Francaise.

AWARDS, HONORS: Marseilles Academy prize, 1887, for "Deux Romanciers de Provence: Honore d'Urfe et Emile Zola"; Toirac prize from the Academie Francaise, 1894, for "Les Romanesques"; Ordre de Legion d'Honneur, 1900.

WRITINGS:

PLAYS

(With Henry Lee) "Le Gant rouge" (title means "The Red Glove"), first produced at the Cluny Theater, 1888.

Les Romanesques (three-act; first produced in Paris at the Comedie-Francaise, May 21, 1894), Charpentier et Fasquelle, 1900; translation by Mary Hendee published as *The Romancers,* Doubleday, 1899; translation by George Fleming published as *The Fantasticks,* R. H. Russell, 1900, reprinted, Fertig, 1987; edited by Henry Le Daum with preface, introduction, and notes, Ginn & Co., 1903, with vocabulary by Noelia Dubrule, 1924; translation by Barrett H. Clark published as *The Romancers,* Samuel French, 1915.

La Princesse lointaine (four-act; first produced in Paris at the Theatre de la Renaissance, April 5, 1895), edited by J. L. Borgerhoff with introduction and notes, Heath, 1909; translation and preface by Charles Renauld, F. A. Stokes, 1899; translation by Anna Emilia Bagstad published as *The Princess Far-away,* R. G. Badger, 1921; translation by John Heard, Jr., with introduction by Stark Young, published as *The Far Princess,* Holt, 1925, reprinted, Fertig, 1987; published by French & European Publications, 1947.

La Samaritaine (title means "The Woman of Samaria"; three-act; first produced in Paris at the Theatre de la Renaissance, April 14, 1897), Fasquelle, 1897; published by French & European Publications, 1953.

Cyrano de Bergerac (five-act; first produced in Paris at the Theatre de la Porte-Saint-Martin, December 28, 1897), Fasquelle, 1898; translation by Howard Thayer Kingsbury, Lamson, Wolfe & Co., 1898, edited and modernized by Oscar H. Fidell, Washington Square Press, 1966; translation by Gertrude Hall, Doubleday, 1898; translation by Gladys Thomas and Mary F. Guillemard, G. Munro's Sons, 1898; translation by Helen B. Dole with introduction by William P. Trent, Crowell, 1899, with illustrations by Nino Carbe, 1931; translation by Charles Renauld with introduction by Adolphe Cohn, Frederick A. Stokes Co., 1899; with introduction and notes by Oscar Kuhns, Holt, 1899; with introduction and notes by Reed Paige Clark, W. R. Jenkins, 1902; with introduction, notes, and vocabulary by Kuhns and Henry Ward Church, Holt, 1920; edited by A. G. H. Speirs with introduction, notes, and list of proper names and vocabulary, Oxford University Press, 1921, 2nd edition, 1938; translation by Brian Hooker with preface by Clayton Hamilton, Holt, 1923, with introduction by Hooker and illustrations by Sylvain Sauvage, Limited Editions, 1936, with introduction and notes by Elisabeth Hooker, Holt, 1937; adaptation by Erna Kruckemeyer, S. French, 1934; edited by Leslie Ross Meras, Harper, 1936; translation by Humbert Wolfe, Hutchinson & Co., 1937; edited by H. Aston, Blackwell, 1942; translation by Louis Untermeyer with illustrations by Pierre Brissaud, Limited Editions, 1954; translation by James Forsyth, Dramatic Publishing, 1968; edited by Edward A. Bird, Methuen, 1968; translation and adaptation by Anthony Burgess, Knopf, 1971; translation by Lowell Blair with an afterword by Henry Hanes, New American Library, 1972; translation by Christopher Fry, Oxford University Press, 1975; annotated by Patrick Besnier, Gallimard, 1983; edition with commentary by Jacques Truchet and illustrations by Jean-Denis Malcles, Imprimerie National, 1983.

L'Aiglon (title means "The Eaglet"; six-act; first produced in Paris at the Theatre Sarah-Bernhardt, March 15, 1900), Brentano's, 1900; translation by Louis N. Parker, R. H. Russell, 1900; translation by Basil Davenport, Yale University Press, 1927; translation and adaptation by Clemence Dane and Richard Addinsell published as *Edmond Rostand's L'Aiglon,* Doubleday, 1934; published as *Aiglon,* French & European Publications, 1964.

Chantecler (four-act; first produced in Paris at the Theatre de la Porte-Saint-Martin, February 7, 1910), Fasquelle, 1910, translation by Hall, Duffield & Co., 1910; translation by John Strong Newberry, Duffield & Co., 1911, translation by Kay Nolte Smith with drawings from original French edition adapted by Joan Mitchell Blumenthal, University Press of America, 1987.

La Derniere Nuit de don Juan (two-act; first produced in 1922), Charpentier et Fasquelle, 1921; translation by T. Lawrason Riggs with introduction by William Lyon Phelps published as *The Last Night of Don Juan,* Kahoe & Co., 1929.

Also author of play *Les Deux Pierrots; ou, Le Souper blanc* (title means "The Two Pierrots; or, The White Supper"), 1891, and of the unfinished, unpublished plays "Yorick" and "Les Petites Manies."

POETRY

Les Musardises (includes "Les Deux Cavaliers," "Nos Rires," "Le Cauchemar," "Le Contrebandier," "Priere d'un matin bleu," "La Fleur," "Le Mendiant fleuri," "Tout d'un coup," "Les Boeufs," "L'If," "La Brouette," "L'Eau," and "Ombres et fumees"), 1890, revised edition, Fasquelle, 1911, French & European Publications, 1955.

Le Vol de la Marseillaise (title means "The Flight of the Marseillaise"; includes "L'Etoile entre les peupliers"), Charpentier et Fasquelle, 1919.

Also author of *Le Cantique de l'aile* (title means "The Canticle of the Wing"; includes "Le Cantique de l'aile," "Un Soir a Hernani," "Les Mots," and "Le Bois Sacre"), 1910. Contributor of poetry to periodicals, including *Mireille.*

COLLECTED WORKS

Oevres completes illustrees de Edmond Rostand (contains "L'Aiglon," "Cyrano de Bergerac," "Les Romanesques," "La Samaritaine," "Chantecler," "La Princesse lointaine," "Les Musardises," and "Le Bois sacre"), seven volumes, P. Lafitte, 1910-11.

Plays of Edmond Rostand (contains "Romantics," "The Princess Far Away," "The Woman of Samaria," "Cyrano de Bergerac," "The Eaglet," "Chanticleer"), two volumes, translation by Henderson Daingerfield Norman, illustrations by Ivan Glidden, Macmillan, 1921.

Cyrano de Bergerac [and] *Chanticleer,* translation by Clifford Hershey Bissell and William Van Wyck, Ritchie, 1947.

OTHER

Also author of essay *Deux Romanciers de Provence: Honore d'Urfe et Emile Zola: Le Roman sentimental et le roman naturaliste,* E. Champion, 1921.

SIDELIGHTS: Edmond Rostand penned many plays and three volumes of poetry, but he is best remembered today for creating the romantic "Cyrano de Bergerac." The play, which combines comedy and heroic tragedy, has been continually revived since its first performance in Paris in 1897 and has been translated from its original French into many languages, including English, Spanish, Russian, and Hebrew, making its long-nosed title character beloved worldwide. In writing the role of Cyrano, Rostand provided a showcase for many great actors, starting with French theater star Constant Coquelin and including noted thespians

Ralph Richardson, Jose Ferrer, and Christopher Plummer. Especially with "Cyrano de Bergerac," but also with his dramas "The Far Princess," "The Eaglet," and "Chantecler," Rostand is credited with briefly reviving the popularity of romance and heroism on a turn-of-the-century French stage dominated by realism. Rostand is also known for his early comedic success "The Romancers," which continues to be performed in its 1960 adaptation as a popular Off-Broadway musical "The Fantasticks."

Rostand was born in 1868 in Marseilles, France, to wealthy parents. His father was the prominent economist Eugene Rostand, a member of the Academy of Moral and Political Sciences of Marseilles and the Institut de France, who wrote poems and translated the works of the ancient Roman lyric poet Gaius Valerius Catullus. One of Rostand's aunts, Victorine Rostand, was also a poet, and his uncle Alexis Rostand was a well-known composer of oratorios, pieces for piano, and an opera. As Alba della Fazia Amoia pointed out in her 1978 biography of the author, *Edmond Rostand,* "the cult of the arts was in the family tradition." Rostand's childhood in Marseilles also contains clues to his future career: his favorite activity was designing stage sets and costumes for his puppet theater, and one of his boyhood heroes was French emperor Napoleon Bonaparte, whose son Francois he would later bring to the stage as the subject of his "Eaglet." By his adolescence, according to Amoia, Rostand had been proclaimed the "school poet" of the Marseilles Lycee, and he had begun to publish his poetry in *Mireille* magazine.

After finishing secondary school in 1884, Rostand left Marseilles for Paris to attend classes at the College Stanislas. While studying law to please his father, he spent more of his concentration penning plays and poems, including the unfinished efforts "Yorick" and "Les Petites Manies." In 1888 Rostand's first play, "Le Gant rouge" (title means "The Red Glove"), written in collaboration with Henry Lee, was performed at the Cluny Theater, but it did not meet with much success. Though he won the Marseilles Academy prize in 1887 for his essay *Deux Romanciers de Provence* (title means "Two Provencal Novelists"), the French public was not aware of Rostand until 1890, the year in which he married poet Rosemonde Gerard, when his first volume of poems, *Les Musardises,* appeared.

Though *Musardises* was not critically acclaimed at its publication, Amoia asserted that the volume holds "a certain fascination." Dedicated to Rostand's wife, *Musardises* is divided into three sections: "La Chambre d'etudiant" (title means "The Student's Room"), "Incertitudes" (title means "Uncertainties"), and "La Maison des Pyrenees" (title means "Home in the Pyrenees"). Another section, criticized as "overly lyric and personal," according to Amoia, was taken out in the revised version of 1911. Besides containing some meritorious pieces, such as "Le Cauchemar" (title means "Nightmare"), which Amoia lauded as "an extremely well-constructed poem, vibrant with scorn," *Musardises* is interesting because many of the trademarks of Rostand's more famous works are already apparent in it. "The dedicatory poem which opens *Les Musardises,*" explained Amoia, "is, in fact, Rostand's declaration of love for 'les rates' (failures in life), whom the public scorns and insults because it cannot understand the dreams and ideals of the great poet's struggle for beauty and perfection." She continued: "To all Bohemian artists, painters, musicians—the lost children of society whose symphonies remain forever unfinished—Rostand declares his fraternity and friendship, joining with the outcast knights-errant to go out in search of Art." One of the poems in "Home in the Pyrenees," the section of *Musardises* inspired by the Rostand family vacation home in Cambo near the French-Spanish border, deals with Spanish author Miguel de Cervantes Saavedra's famous character Don Quixote and laments the fact that France no longer admires the spirit of the knight. This theme is picked up again in Rostand's *Cyrano de Bergerac.* Cyrano has often been compared to Don Quixote, and in a confrontational scene between Cyrano and the Comte de Guiche, de Guiche asks, "Have you read *Don Quixote?*" Cyrano returns, "I have—and found myself the hero."

Rostand's first taste of popular success came with the 1894 production of "The Romancers." Declared by novelist Henry James in *The Critic* "as charming an examination of the nature of the romantic, [and] as pleasant a contribution to any discussion, as can be imagined," the play concerns Sylvette and Percinet, a pair of young lovers who think they are comparable to playwright William Shakespeare's Romeo and Juliet in defying their mutually hostile fathers to become betrothed. In actuality, though, they have been tricked into falling in love. Their fathers, in reality the best of friends, have been feigning hostility and separating their adjoining properties by a stone wall because they believe their children will only marry each other if forbidden to do so. The fathers hire a group of men to stage a fake abduction of Sylvette so that Percinet can rescue her and thus provide an excuse for the pretended enemies' subsequent "reconciliation." When Sylvette and Percinet discover their respective danger and heroism were only contrived, they become disillusioned with their love, and separately seek true adventure. The lovers reunite, however, when they find that real adventure is not as appealing as their familiar, comfortable relationship.

James commented that in "The Romancers," the "action takes place in that happy land of nowhere—the land of poetry, comedy, drollery, delicacy, profuse literary association . . . and if the whole thing is the frankest of fantasies . . . it is the work of a man already conscious of all the values involved." Though he complained that "The Romancers" is "really too much made up of ribbons and flowers," James concluded that "we note as its especial charm the ease with which the author's fancy moves in his rococo world." Similarly, in the *Fortnightly Review,* G. Jean-Aubry saw "The Romancers" as a balanced example of both Rostand's writing talents and his deficiencies. There is in the play, he claimed, "the germ of all that is best and least good in Rostand; a very great technical cleverness, a facility for making his personages live and move, a tendency to complicate the simplest situations by play of words, and a real charm . . . in making his rhymes 'sing'. . . . Already he writes verses that are supple, natural, unforced, and others that are tortured and wrung out with difficulty." While most critics have concluded that "The Romancers," as a comedic satire on love, is lighter than Rostand's later plays, Amoia asserted that it "contain[s] a moral also: we must have faith in what we are doing and we must remain faithful to love." Rostand received the Toirac prize from the Academie Francaise for the play.

Encouraged by the success of "The Romancers," Rostand penned a more serious work, "The Far Princess," designed to showcase the talents of the famed French actress Sarah Bernhardt. Based on the medieval legend of troubadour prince Joffroy Rudel and Melissinde, princess of Tripoli, the play was produced in 1895. The action takes place on Rudel's ship—as he lies dying, his shipmates, inspired by the purity of his passion, row on in spite of hunger, thirst, and sickness in order that he might see before his death the princess he has long worshipped from afar—and in Melissinde's palace, where tales of Rudel's fervent love for her have kindled reciprocal feelings in the princess. Mistaking Bertrand, Rudel's faithful friend and messenger, for Rudel himself, Melissinde falls in love with him. Bertrand falls in love with the princess also, and the two of them almost ignore

Rudel's dying request that Melissinde come to his deathbed. The force of Melissinde's idealized love for Rudel, however, proves stronger than her more earthly attraction to Bertrand, and she reaches Rudel's ship in time for him to die in her arms, his vision realized.

Though "The Far Princess" was judged by author Stark Young in his preface to John Heard's translation of the play "the most completely achieved of Rostand's works" with the exception of "Cyrano de Bergerac," and even "the most perfect" and "the high-water mark of [Rostand's] literary achievement" by a critic for the *Edinburgh Review,* most others did not share this enthusiasm. Rostand's contemporary, playwright and critic George Bernard Shaw, commenting on the seriousness with which "The Far Princess" treats an unrealistic, ideal love, complained: "When the woman appears and plays up to the height of [Rudel and his companions'] folly, intoning her speeches to an accompaniment of harps and horns . . . always in the character which their ravings have ascribed to her, what can one feel except that an excellent opportunity for a good comedy is being thrown away?" Virginia M. Crawford in her 1899 *Studies in Foreign Literature* declared that "there is not a line that will live" in "The Far Princess." But while recognizing the unrealistic nature of the play, James announced that "the finest thing [in 'The Far Princess'] is the author's gallantry under fire of the extravagance involved in his subject; as to which . . . we can easily see that it would have been fatal to him to be timid." Amoia found the idealism of "The Far Princess" significant in its relation to the body of Rostand's work. "The reality of life for Rostand, the poet, is the dream," she asserted. "The dream in ['The Far Princess'] is incarnated in Melissinde, who symbolizes love." She concluded, however, that "the literary and artistic value" of the play "falls short of" Rostand's earlier "Romancers."

Regardless of its literary merit, "The Far Princess" was not very popular with Parisian theatergoers. This lack of public response disappointed Rostand and he went into a period of seclusion until he was inspired to write "La Samaritaine" (title means "The Woman of Samaria"). Another vehicle for Bernhardt, the play is based on a story from the Gospel of John, and was presented during the week before Easter of 1897. Rostand dramatizes the encounter between Jesus and the Samaritan woman of whom he asks a drink at the well. "La Samaritaine" depicts the transformation of the woman, Photine, from a devotee of sensual pleasure to a spiritually fulfilled follower of Christ who persuades her fellow Samaritans to listen to Jesus. Though "La Samaritaine" stresses the superiority of spiritual satisfaction over physical, like "The Far Princess," it also glorifies earthly love. Echoing the statement of Brother Trophimus, Joffroy Rudel's confessor, that "Love / is sanctified, and God hath willed it thus," and therefore that Rudel needs to make no last confession to gain heaven after death, Rostand's Jesus accepts Photine's erotic love song—the only kind she knows how to sing—as a sincere form of prayer. He even tells her, "The love of Me comes always to a heart / Where lesser, human loves have had a part."

"La Samaritaine" won high praise from an *Edinburgh Review* critic, who exclaimed, "With what precision is the situation put before us . . . with how few words, and yet how definitely, is the characterisation of the individual disciples . . . how swiftly and unconsciously we find ourselves informed of the political situation, the warring interests, all the complicated policy of the little inconspicuous mountain town!" Amoia, by contrast, lamented "the absence of a truly mystic sense," complaining that "the language and style of the play are too refined and . . . too affected." Though she felt that "La Samaritaine" lacked dramatic action, noting that Jesus remains seated throughout, Amoia conceded

the beauty of the work, saying "as a gospel in painting it is a composition worthy of admiration."

By the end of 1897, however, the curtain had risen on the drama that most critics agree eclipses the rest of Rostand's oeuvre: "Cyrano de Bergerac." Loosely based on the life of seventeenth-century French author and soldier Savinien de Cyrano de Bergerac, the play opens, significantly, in a theater. By threatening to display his fighting prowess, Cyrano, from the audience, stops the performance of Montfleury, a bad actor with an unsavory reputation who has dared to look amorously upon Cyrano's cousin and secret object of adoration, Roxane. When another spectator protests the closing, Cyrano challenges him to a duel. To emphasize his superior swordsmanship and demonstrate his proficiency at creating impromptu verse, Cyrano composes a ballad while fencing with his opponent, proposing to time his victory to coincide with the end of his poetic creation: "Then, as I end the refrain, thrust home!"

After wounding his adversary to end the duel, Cyrano confesses his love for Roxane to his friend Le Bret, explaining that his nose "that marches on / before me by a quarter of an hour" keeps him silent about his feelings: "I follow with my eyes / Where some boy, with a girl upon his arm / Passes a patch of silver . . . and I feel / Somehow, I wish I had a woman too, / Walking with little steps under the moon, / And holding my arm so, and smiling. Then / I dream—and I forget. . . . / And then I see / The shadow of my profile on the wall!" Le Bret tries to encourage Cyrano, pointing out that some women seem to overlook his oversized nose, and that Roxane herself seemed pale while watching his duel. Punctuating Le Bret's enthusiasm, Roxane's chaperon enters the scene to tell Cyrano that his cousin wishes to speak to him. Hopeful, Cyrano arranges for Roxane to meet him at his friend Ragueneau's pastry shop the next morning.

Roxane, however, has requested a meeting with Cyrano not to tell him that she loves him, but to ask her cousin to befriend the man she does love, the handsome Baron Christian de Neuvillette. Christian has just joined the same regiment that Cyrano serves in, and Roxane fears that as a Norman in a group of men predominantly Gascon he may be subject to bullying. Hiding his disappointment, Cyrano agrees to look out for Christian.

Cyrano continues to contain his feelings when the members of his regiment descend on the pastry shop demanding his account of his feat the night previous—in the height of his hope for Roxane's love, Cyrano had defeated a gang of one hundred men hired to ambush a fellow poet who had angered the Comte de Guiche. As he begins narrating, he is frequently interrupted by Christian, who turns each of Cyrano's phrases into a remark about his nose in order to prove to the Gascons that they do not have a monopoly on bravery. Cyrano is incensed until he learns the identity of his tormentor and remembers Roxane's request. Congratulating Christian on his courage, he tells him of his cousin's love for him. Christian has fallen in love with Roxane also, but he tells Cyrano that his love is hopeless because he does not have the gift of speaking or writing eloquently enough to a woman he loves, and he fears ridicule. Seeing an opportunity to express his fervent emotions without exposing himself to Roxane's indifference, Cyrano offers to coach Christian's speeches and write his letters to her for him.

Their scheme works well, and Roxane is greatly pleased at Christian's supposedly poetic nature, until Christian thinks Roxane loves him enough so that he no longer needs Cyrano's help. Alone with her without Cyrano's words, Christian fails utterly when Roxane asks him to rhapsodize upon the theme of his love for her—he can only extend his "I love you" to "I love you so!"

Angered at Christian's sudden lack of eloquence, Roxane retreats into her house, and Christian begs Cyrano for assistance. Initially Christian speaks to Roxane from beneath her balcony while Cyrano feeds him his lines, but the slowness of this process leads Cyrano to speak the words himself in a disguised voice, shadowed so that Roxane cannot see him. Intoxicated by the chance to tell Roxane of his love for her, Cyrano proclaims: "Love, I love beyond / Breath, beyond reason, beyond love's own power / Of loving! Your name is like a golden bell / Hung in my heart; and when I think of you, / I tremble, and the bell swings and rings—*Roxane!. . . / Roxane!*. . . along my veins, *Roxane!*" Knowing he has won her for Christian, Cyrano nevertheless is happy at the part he has played. "In my most sweet unreasonable dreams," he tells Roxane, "I have not hoped for this! . . ./ . . . It is my voice . . . / That makes you tremble there in the green gloom / Above me—for you do tremble . . ./ . . . and I can feel, / All the way down along these jasmine branches, / . . . the passion of you / Trembling. . . ." Christian demands that Cyrano ask Roxane for a kiss, and Cyrano, though disliking the idea, consents, saying to himself "Since it must be, I had rather be myself / The cause of . . . what must be."

After Christian obtains Roxane's kiss, a monk comes by her house with a message from the Comte de Guiche, who has been trying to force himself on Roxane despite the fact that he is married. Roxane intentionally misreads the message, which was to notify her that de Guiche would meet her that night, to the monk, tricking him into performing a marriage between herself and Christian. Meanwhile at Roxane's request, Cyrano—whom she assumes has just appeared on the scene, wrapped in his cloak and shading his face with his hat, distracts de Guiche by pretending to have fallen from the moon. When Cyrano gives up his charade and de Guiche finds that Roxane has married Christian, he sends Cyrano and Christian, with the rest of their regiment, to fight the Spanish at Arras. De Guiche, also going to fight, gloats, "The bridal night is not so near!" and Cyrano says to himself: "Somehow that news fails to disquiet me."

The fourth act opens on the siege of Arras. The Gascon regiment is hungry, their supplies having been cut off by the Spanish. Cyrano has been slipping through the enemy forces twice daily to carry his letters to Roxane, ostensibly written by Christian. After Cyrano casts aspersions on de Guiche's courage, de Guiche decides to use the Gascon regiment as a sacrifice; the men are almost certain to be killed. As they prepare for battle, Christian tells Cyrano that he wishes he could write Roxane a farewell letter; Cyrano has already composed one for him. In perusing it, Christian finds the water spots of Cyrano's tears, and finally realizes that Cyrano has loved Roxane all along.

Soon afterwards, Roxane arrives in her carriage, having smuggled food for the regiment through enemy territory. The Spanish, she claimed, because they were romantic, let her go through when she told them she was going to meet her lover. Refusing to leave when warned of the imminent battle, she tells Christian that she came because of his letters, which made her love him so much that she could not bear to be away from him. She begs his forgiveness for first loving him for his appearance, and says that because his letters have revealed his soul to her she would now love him even if he were ugly. Christian tells Cyrano about this and demands that he tell Roxane the truth so that she may choose between them. Cyrano is about to do this when Christian is mortally wounded by enemy fire. Feeling that he must now never reveal his secret because to do so would destroy Roxane's belief in Christian's perfect love for her, Cyrano comforts the dying Christian with a lie—that he has told Roxane, and that she still loves Christian.

In the fifth act, fifteen years have gone by. Both Cyrano and Roxane have survived Arras; Roxane lives among the nuns of a convent, still wearing mourning for Christian and keeping what she believes is his last letter over her heart. Cyrano, because of his proud refusal to submit to any rich man's patronage for his plays, has grown steadily poorer and made more enemies. He has visited Roxane at the convent every Saturday to give her the latest news of Paris, but this Saturday Cyrano is a few moments late for the first time. Giving his usual report, he struggles to hide from Roxane the fact that he has been severely hurt in an ambush prepared by his foes. Feeling his death approaching, Cyrano reminds Roxane that she once said he could read Christian's letter, and asks to do so. He reads it to her aloud, though the sky grows dark with the oncoming night. Roxane realizes that Cyrano could not possibly be reading it and that he must have it memorized; she also realizes that he is using the same voice that she remembered hearing beneath her window before her marriage to Christian. When Le Bret and Ragueneau rush in to exclaim over his foolhardiness in leaving his bed, Cyrano tells Roxane of the assault upon him. Roxane tells him that she loves him, lamenting, "I never loved but one man in my life, / And I have lost him—twice." Cyrano rises to face death on his feet, taking pride in the fact that he has remained true to his ideals throughout his life, symbolized by the white plume in his hat, or, in the original French, his "panache." His last words are: "There is one crown I bear away with me . . . / . . . One thing without stain, / Unspotted from the world, in spite of doom / Mine own! . . . / . . . My white plume."

Though "Cyrano de Bergerac" was to be Rostand's greatest success and was to win him lasting fame, before its debut the theater community had serious doubts about its value. Rostand had to pay for the play's costumes himself, and a few minutes before the curtain rose on "Cyrano" for the first time, he was begging forgiveness of its star, Constant Coquelin, for having involved him in such a fiasco. But when the curtain had fallen, Amoia reported, there was "overwhelming applause . . . for the poet who finally had dissipated the atmosphere of sadness and futility with which young Frenchmen had lived for so long. . . . *Cyrano* marked a complete reaction against the Realism of the problem plays then in vogue. It was a new and fresh Romantic poem, with a folk hero . . . whose identity was shared by all."

Not all critics agreed, however, on the importance or even on the theme of "Cyrano." Crawford felt that while nothing "could be more noble and beautiful . . . than Cyrano's love for his cousin Roxane . . . the whole *motif* of the play is . . . radically false, and consequently lacking in any permanent interest." A contemporary *Poet Lore* reviewer did not take the play's idealism seriously and saw it as a "satirical extravaganza," saying that it would be "naive . . . to take such double-edged fooling as all this for unvarnished tenderness and fresh-born romance." The critic also claimed that to do so would leave the work "bare of any literary distinction worth mentioning. If it is to be considered as a serious dramatic or poetic work, it must be perceived that its structure is of the slightest and most casual." But Hugh Allison Smith in his 1925 *Main Currents of Modern French Drama* pointed out that "Cyrano" should not "be judged . . . by realistic criterions. It is more proper to ask if it is artistic, beautiful, noble or poetic than it is to determine if it is practical, probable, typical or informative." Similarly, an *Edinburgh Review* critic found the play large enough to successfully explore many themes, declaring that to "say of 'Cyrano' that it is too elaborate is like objecting to some vigorous forest tree that its leafage is confusing. And the comparison holds good on this point—that 'Cyrano de Bergerac' is as structural and organic as a noble tree." He concluded: "In France, it is necessary to go back to Moliere and to [Pierre Augustin Caron de] Beaumarchais to find anything of equal dramatic fulness of conception, of equal reach and lightness of touch." Though many modern critics relegate Rostand to the position of minor literary figure, most would agree with Amoia's insistence that "*Cyrano [de] Bergerac* will continue to have meaning throughout the ages, will continue to move audiences everywhere, and probably will remain identified with the name of Edmond Rostand long after his other works have sunk into complete oblivion."

The success of "Cyrano" solidified Rostand's position in Parisian social circles, and he counted Bernhardt and Coquelin among his close friends. Like many other intellectuals of his time, Rostand risked his newfound status to become involved in the controversy surrounding the imprisonment for treason of French army captain Alfred Dreyfus, staunchly defending him as an innocent victim of anti-Semitism when new evidence suggested someone else had been responsible for giving secret documents to Germany. Dreyfus was eventually pardoned.

Rostand followed "Cyrano" with "L'Aiglon," or "The Eaglet," the story of Napoleon Bonaparte's son Francois and his vain efforts to win his rightful title of Emperor of France. Amoia posited that Rostand used this historical episode because in it "he found inspiration for the negative counterpart of the swashbuckling hero. . . . since no figure could possibly outdo Cyrano." Also, when Rostand was a child, a portrait of Francois, often called the Duke of Reichstadt or the King of Rome, hung over the author's bed. Haunted by the poignancy of the youth dying without realizing his dreams, Rostand found the sickly Francois, kept a virtual prisoner by his royal Austrian relatives because they feared he had inherited the ruthless strategical abilities of his father, a fit subject for tragedy. Rostand's version pits Francois (first played by Bernhardt) and his allies, including Seraphin Flambeau, a flamboyant old soldier of his father's who invites comparisons with Cyrano, against Prince Metternich, who as an Austrian administrator-spy must foil the young man's plots to return to France in triumph. Francois's daring plans, however, fail predominantly because of his own nature—a bold move on his part is too often followed by indecision or hesitation, and "The Eaglet" ends with Francois's deathbed scene. Despite being a failure, the twenty-year-old would-be emperor dies with royal dignity.

Edward Everett Hale, Jr., in his 1911 *Dramatists of Today* judged "The Eaglet" to be superior to "Cyrano," announcing, "This tragedy, with its poor, weak little hero . . . made a stronger effect than its wonderful predecessor—stronger, if less obvious." Not many agreed with his assessment; Jean-Aubry complained that "there is little action" in the play, though he felt that the third act—containing confrontations between Francois and his maternal grandfather the Austrian emperor, Flambeau and Metternich, and Metternich and Francois—"is amongst the best that Rostand ever wrote." Critic Max Beerbohm in his *Around Theaters* condemned "The Eaglet" for its length, saying that it "wearies us beyond measure" and should have been cut in half. Amoia saw the play in a more balanced light. Though she praised it as a "masterpiece," she labeled it a "defective" one, flawed by "too many details and excessive refinements, . . . too many superfluous literary allusions weighed down with alliterations." She also noted, however, that *The Eaglet* contains the great qualities of Rostand's art: lyricism and sincerity." The play was popular with French audiences, who shared Francois's reverence for his father, Napoleon.

In 1900, the same year that "The Eaglet" saw its first performance, Rostand began suffering from the lung problems that would plague him for the rest of his life; pulmonary congestion forced him to retire to his family home in the Pyrenees Mountains. He was elected to the Academie Francaise in 1901, the youngest writer to be so honored, but the formal reception celebrating the occasion had to be postponed until 1903 because of his ill health. Rostand's father died in 1907; setbacks such as these are probably a factor in the ten-year period between the premiere of "The Eaglet" and Rostand's next play, "Chantecler." An allegory about the pretentiousness of contemporary society and of the era's literary circles, "Chantecler" uses farm animals and creatures of the woods to make its statements. After the success of "Cyrano" and "The Eaglet," the play was eagerly awaited by Parisian theatergoers; according to translator Kay Nolte Smith in her preface to the work, the anticipation included "Chantecler fashions, toys, [and] floats." Smith reported further: "The advance [ticket] sale was an extraordinary (for the time) $200,000; people traveled from as far as America to attend; diplomats prolonged their stay to see it, making the French foreign minister complain that 'diplomatic relations between France and many a foreign power are being interrupted all because of a cock and a hen pheasant.'" A South American journalist attempted to steal part of the manuscript and was caught at Rostand's home.

Ironically, after all the prefatory excitement, "Chantecler" was something of a disappointment to audiences. Most critics now feel that while it is quality reading, "Chantecler" is not well-suited to performance; possibly the fact that the characters are animals makes it more difficult for the audience to identify with them. Chantecler, the rooster, believes that it is his pre-dawn song that brings the sun up, though he tells no one of this belief until he falls in love with a beautiful pheasant hen. The night animals—owls, cats, moles, etc.—know his secret anyway and plot to kill Chantecler so that the sun will not rise again, making night eternal. Aided by the faithful farm dog Patou, and mocked by the sarcastic caged blackbird, Chantecler nevertheless manages to defeat the vicious steel-spurred white pile rooster that allied itself with the forces of night and laid in wait for him at the pretentious gathering of the Guinea Hen. The conflict leaves the hero disillusioned and exhausted, and he seeks refuge in the forest with the Pheasant Hen. She is jealous of Chantecler's love for the dawn, and tricks him into not singing, proving to him that the morning will come without him. Chantecler is only temporarily daunted, however, and concludes that his song is still important because it wakes the other animals. He triumphs and follows his own ideal in spite of the cynicism, affectation, and pettiness of those around him.

Though "the play is too contrived, too far-fetched . . . and the language and style are too exaggerated," according to Amoia, "the invocation to the Sun, the ballads, and the dramatic, fast-paced dialogue of the Night Birds constitute examples of outstanding verse." Jean-Aubry felt "Chantecler" was evidence that Rostand's genius had run dry, noting that "one is conscious of the despairing efforts of an inspiration which seeks to keep itself alive, but no longer succeeds," and lamenting that Rostand had "no longer the strength to do justice to" his subject. By contrast, though admitting the difficulties in staging an animal allegory, Hale lauded "Chantecler" as "a play of very great beauty," and questioned "whether the judgment of time will not pronounce it Rostand's greatest."

In the same year that "Chantecler" was first performed, Rostand published a volume of twenty-four poems, *Le Cantique de l'aile* (title means "The Canticle of the Wing"). The first seven, reported Amoia, "reflecting the composite elements of the title, abound in personifications of song, winged images, expressions of flight, and a highly ethereal vocabulary." The title poem celebrates France's heroes and urges all people to help praise them. Another, perhaps the best known of Rostand's poems, "Les Mots" (title means "Words"), depicts a closet containing all the French words ever printed. The words protest at the way they are being mutilated by grammarians and bad writers. Amoia explained: "Rostand was in love with words, with each letter in each word. On them, he performed delicate vivisections to know and love them better." "Un Soir a Hernani" (title means "An Evening at Hernani") recognizes the centenary of the birth of French author Victor Hugo and takes its name from his drama "Hernani." The collection also contains "Le Bois Sacre," labeled by Amoia "a delightful blend of ancient mythology and modern technology" which concerns a young couple whose car is repaired by the Greek gods on Mount Olympus.

Rostand published a third volume of poems, *Le Vol de la Marseillaise* (title means "The Flight of the Marseillaise"), in 1914, but the work has been dismissed by most as unredeemed sentimental patriotism. Rostand probably saw writing these poems as his duty, since his health prevented him from serving France in World War I. He reportedly often visited the trenches, however, wanting to see the suffering and devastation even though it distressed him greatly and added to his decline in health. He died shortly after the war ended in 1918, leaving the unfinished play "The Last Night of Don Juan" to be published and performed posthumously.

"Don Juan" portrays the legendary lover conversing with the Devil before being dragged down to Hell. The Devil shows Don Juan the ghosts of all the women he has ever seduced—one thousand and three in number—and defies him to assign the correct name to any of them. He fails, and he also learns that he has had no real impact on the hearts of these women; the tears they have shed for him were all false. The White Ghost, though, has produced a sincere tear, but when she tells Don Juan her name, he does not remember her because he has not seduced her. Because of the White Ghost's tear Don Juan has an opportunity to save himself from Hell if he can learn to love, but he refuses to repent. The Devil traps him in the wooden body of a puppet—the appropriate version of Hell for a man who cannot love. Though Amoia claimed that "The Last Night of Don Juan" was a "complete fiasco" when it was first produced in 1922, other critics felt that the play showed a new direction in Rostand's creative thinking that would have brought forth even greater works if the playwright had lived longer.

MEDIA ADAPTATIONS: The Hooker translation of *Cyrano de Bergerac* was adapted for a film starring Jose Ferrer, Mala Powers, and William Prince, and released by United Artists in 1950; *The Romancers* was adapted as a musical titled "The Fantasticks," with book and lyrics by Tom Jones and music by Harvey Schmidt, in 1960; a loose, modern adaptation of *Cyrano de Bergerac,* titled "Roxanne" and starring Steve Martin, Daryl Hannah, and Rick Rossovich, was released by Columbia Pictures in 1987.

BIOGRAPHICAL/CRITICAL SOURCES:

BOOKS

Amoia, Alba della Fazia, *Edmond Rostand,* Twayne, 1978.
Beerbohm, Max, *Around Theatres,* Hart-Davis, 1953.
Chesterton, G. K., *Twelve Types,* Arthur L. Humphreys, 1906.
Chiari, Joseph, *The Contemporary French Theatre: The Flight From Naturalism,* Rockliff, 1958.

Clark, Barrett H., *Contemporary French Dramatists,* Stewart & Kidd Co., 1915.
Crawford, Virginia M., *Studies in Foreign Literature,* Duckworth, 1899.
Gerard, Rosemonde, *Edmond Rostand,* Fasquelle, 1935.
Hale, Edward Everett, Jr., *Dramatists of Today: Rostand, Hauptmann, Sudermann, Piner, Shaw, Phillips, Maeterlinck,* revised edition, Holt, 1911.
Hapgood, Norman, *The Stage in America 1897-1900,* Macmillan, 1901.
Rostand, Edmond, *Plays of Edmond Rostand,* translation by Henderson Daingerfield Norman, Macmillan, 1921.
Rostand, Edmond, *Cyrano de Bergerac,* translation by Brian Hooker, Holt, 1923.
Rostand, Edmond, *The Far Princess,* translation by John Heard, Jr., with introduction by Stark Young, Fertig, 1987.
Rostand, Edmond, *Chantecler,* translation and preface by Kay Nolte Smith, University Press of America, 1987.
Smith, Hugh Allison, *Main Currents of Modern French Drama,* Holt, 1925.
Twentieth Century Literary Criticism, Volume 6, Gale, 1982.

PERIODICALS

Arena, September, 1905.
Athenaeum, July 25, 1919.
Atlantic, January, 1972.
Chicago Tribune, June 19, 1987.
Critic, November, 1901.
Edinburgh Review, October, 1900.
Fortnightly Review, January 1, 1919.
New York Times, November 17, 1950, June 19, 1987.
New York Times Book Review, December 26, 1971.
Nineteenth-Century French Studies, February, 1973.
Poet Lore, winter, 1899.
Saturday Review, June 22, 1895.
Studies in Philology, October, 1949.
Times Literary Supplement, January 16, 1976.
Washington Post, February 1, 1985, February 10, 1985.

*   *   *

ROTH, Henry 1906-

PERSONAL: Born February 8, 1906, in Tysmenica, Galicia, Austria-Hungary (now part of U.S.S.R.); son of Herman (a waiter) and Leah (Farb) Roth; married Muriel Parker (an elementary school principal), October 7, 1939; children: Jeremy, Hugh. *Education:* College of the City of New York (now City College of the City University of New York), B.S., 1928. *Politics:* Unaffiliated. *Religion:* None.

ADDRESSES: Home—2600 New York Ave. N.W., Albuquerque, N.M. 87104. *Agent*—Roslyn Targ Literary Agency, 105 West 13th St., New York, N.Y. 10011.

CAREER: Roth says: "in writing and idleness [New York, N.Y.]," 1929-38; with Works Progress Administration (WPA), 1939; substitute high school teacher, Bronx, N.Y., 1939-41; precision metal grinder, New York, N.Y., 1941-45, Providence, R.I., and Boston, Mass., 1945-46; taught in a one-room school in Maine, 1947-48; Augusta State Hospital, Augusta, Me., attendant, 1949-53; waterfowl farmer, 1953-63; tutor in math, and occasionally Latin, 1956-65.

AWARDS, HONORS: Grant from National Institute of Arts and Letters, 1965; Townsend Harris Medal, City College of the City University New York, 1965; D. H. Lawrence fellowship, University of New Mexico, 1968.

WRITINGS:

Call It Sleep (novel), Ballou, 1934, 2nd edition with a history by Harold U. Ribalow, a critical introduction by Maxwell Geismar, and a personal appreciation by Meyer Levin, Pageant, 1960 (same edition published in England with a foreword by Walter Allen, M. Joseph, 1963).

(Contributor) *The Best American Short Stories, 1967,* Houghton, 1967.

Nature's First Green (memoir), Targ, 1979.

Shifting Landscape: A Composite, 1925-1987, Jewish Publication Society, 1987.

Contributor to *Atlantic, Commentary, Midstream,* and *New Yorker.* Boston University, which is starting a collection of manuscripts and materials on American Jewish literature, is beginning with a Henry Roth Collection.

SIDELIGHTS: First published in the 1930s, *Call It Sleep* received laudatory reviews, Alfred Hayes calling it "as brilliant as [James] Joyce's *Portrait of the Artist,* but with a wider scope, a richer emotion, a deeper realism." The book went into two printings (4,000 copies) and disappeared, leading an underground existence until republication by Pageant in 1960, as a result of the interest of the critic Harold Ribalow. In 1956, the *American Scholar* asked certain notable critics to list the most neglected books of the past twenty-five years. Alfred Kazin and Leslie Fiedler both chose *Call It Sleep,* making it the only book named twice. On October 25, 1961, Irving Howe's front-page review of *Call It Sleep* in the *New York Times Book Review* marked the first time such space was devoted to a paperback reprint. Howe described the book as "one of the few genuinely distinguished novels written by a 20th-century American, [one which] achieves an obbligato of lyricism such as few American novels can match. . . . Intensely Jewish in tone and setting, *Call It Sleep* rises above all the dangers that beset the usual ghetto novel: it does not deliquesce into nostalgia, nor sentimentalize poverty and parochialism. The Jewish immigrant milieu happens to be its locale, quite as Dublin is Joyce's and Mississippi [William] Faulkner's."

The novel concerns the slum life of a young boy. Haskel Frankel has written, however, that to offer *Call It Sleep* as a tale about "a period in the life of an immigrant Jewish boy in the slums of New York's Lower East Side . . . is to offer a synopsis on a par with Roz Russell's plot summation of [Herman Melville's novel] *Moby Dick* in the musical *Wonderful Town:* 'It's about this whale.'"

Howe believes that Roth is especially successful in the way he presents the mind of the young boy. "Yet the book is not at all the kind of precious or narrowing study of a child's sensibility that such a description might suggest. We are locked into the experience of a child, but are not limited to his grasp of it." Roth acknowledges the autobiographical qualities of the novel but emphasizes the methods he used in manipulating events remembered from his childhood. "I was working with characters, situations and events that had in part been taken from life, but which I molded to give expression to what was oppressing me. To a considerable extent I was drawing on the unconscious to give shape to remembered reality. Things which I could not fully understand but which filled me with apprehension played a critical role in determining the form of the novel."

Many critics disagree about the central theme or purpose of *Call It Sleep.* James Ferguson feels that it "is essentially the story of the development of a religious sensibility. Its implications are far more profoundly theological, even metaphysical, than they are

social." In *Proletarian Writers of the Thirties,* Gerald Green suggests that Roth did have some social motivation in writing the novel: "Unlike the fashionable terrorists, Roth never loses hope, even if salvation speaks to us through cracked lips." And Walter Allen sees the book as "the most powerful evocation of the terrors of childhood ever written. We are spared nothing of the rawness of cosmopolitan slum life."

Roth once said that "the man who wrote that book at the age of 27 is dead. I am a totally different man." Some years ago he started another novel. Maxwell Perkins at Scribner thought it was brilliant and gave him an advance, but Roth was dissatisfied and destroyed the manuscript. He has not yet finished another novel, although, he tells David Bronsen in *Partisan Review,* since the Israeli 1967 war he has begun to write again after many years. The war gave Roth "a place in the world and an origin. Having started to write, it seemed natural to go on from there, and I have been writing long hours every day since then. I am not yet sure what it is leading to, but it is necessary and is growing out of a new allegiance, an adhesion that comes from belonging." He said later: "The surge of partisanship awakened by the '67 war broke the hold of an ossified radicalism."

Despite his new commitment to writing fiction, Roth's commitment to his domestic life is of primary importance to him. He once said: "I find my greatest pleasure in matrimony, mathematics and puttering about the premises, in that order; I am daily compelled to admiration at the miracle of my wife."

BIOGRAPHICAL/CRITICAL SOURCES:

BOOKS

Allen, Walter, *The Modern Novel,* Dutton, 1965.

Contemporary Literary Criticism, Gale, Volume 2, 1974, Volume 6, 1976, Volume 11, 1979.

Dictionary of Literary Biography, Volume 28: *Twentieth-Century American-Jewish Fiction Writers,* Gale, 1984.

French, Warren, editor, *The Thirties: Fiction, Poetry, Drama,* Everett/Edwards, 1967.

Howe, Irving, *World of Our Fathers,* Harcourt, 1976.

Lyons, Bonnie, *Henry Roth,* Cooper Square, 1977.

Madden, Daniel, editor, *Proletarian Writers of the Thirties,* Southern Illinois University Press, 1968.

PERIODICALS

Centennial Review, spring, 1974.

Commentary, August, 1960, August, 1977, September, 1984.

Jewish Social Studies, July, 1966.

Life, January 8, 1965.

Los Angeles Times, December 8, 1987, December 11, 1987.

Modern Fiction Studies, winter, 1966.

New York Times, April 15, 1971.

New York Times Book Review, October 25, 1964.

Partisan Review, Volume 36, number 2, 1969.

Publishers Weekly, November 27, 1987.

Saturday Review, November 21, 1964.

Shenandoah, fall, 1973.

Studies in American Jewish Literature, spring, 1979.

Studies in the Novel, winter, 1975.

Twentieth Century Literature, October, 1966, January, 1969.

Washington Post, October 25, 1987.

* * *

ROTH, Philip (Milton) 1933-

PERSONAL: Born March 19, 1933, in Newark, N.J.; son of Herman (an insurance salesman) and Bess (Finkel) Roth; married

Margaret Martinson, February 22, 1959 (died, 1968). *Education:* Attended Rutgers University, 1950-51; Bucknell University, A.B., 1954; University of Chicago, M.A., 1955, additional study, 1956-57.

ADDRESSES: Home—Connecticut and London, England. *Office*—c/o Farrar, Straus & Giroux, 19 Union Square W., New York, N.Y. 10003.

CAREER: Novelist and short story writer. University of Chicago, Chicago, Ill., instructor, 1956-58; visiting lecturer, University of Iowa, Iowa City, 1960-62, and State University of New York at Stony Brook, 1967-68. Writer-in-residence, Princeton University, 1962-64, and University of Pennsylvania, 1965-80. *Military service:* U.S. Army, 1955-56.

MEMBER: National Institute of Arts and Letters, Phi Beta Kappa.

AWARDS, HONORS: Aga Khan Award, *Paris Review,* 1958; Houghton-Mifflin literary fellowship, 1959; National Institute of Arts and Letters grant, 1959; National Book Award for fiction, 1960, and Daroff Award, Jewish Book Council of America, both 1960, both for *Goodbye, Columbus, and Five Short Stories;* Guggenheim fellowship, 1960; received O. Henry second prize award, 1960; Ford Foundation grant in playwrighting, 1965; American Book Award nomination (declined), 1980, for *The Ghost Writer;* National Book Critics Circle nomination, 1983, and American Book Award nomination, 1984, both for *The Anatomy Lesson.*

WRITINGS:

Goodbye, Columbus, and Five Short Stories, Houghton, 1959, reprinted as *Goodbye, Columbus,* Houghton, 1989.
Letting Go (novel), Random House, 1962, reprinted, Farrar, Straus, 1982.
When She Was Good (novel), Random House, 1967, reprinted, Penguin Books, 1985.
On the Air (short stories), New American Library, 1969.
Portnoy's Complaint (novel), Random House, 1969, reprinted, Fawcett, 1984.
Our Gang (novel), Random House, 1971, published with a new preface and revised notes by the author, Bantam, 1973.
The Breast (novel), Holt, 1972, revised edition, Farrar, Straus, 1982.
The Great American Novel, Holt, 1973.
My Life as a Man (novel), Holt, 1974.
Reading Myself and Others (nonfiction), Farrar, Straus, 1975.
The Professor of Desire (novel), Farrar, Straus, 1977.
The Ghost Writer (novel; also see below), Farrar, Straus, 1979.
A Philip Roth Reader, Farrar, Straus, 1980.
Zuckerman Unbound (novel; also see below), Farrar, Straus, 1981.
The Anatomy Lesson (novel; also see below), Farrar, Straus, 1983.
Zuckerman Bound: A Trilogy and Epilogue (includes *The Ghost Writer, Zuckerman Unbound,* and *The Anatomy Lesson* with epilogue "The Prague Orgy"), Farrar, Straus, 1985 (published in England as *The Prague Orgy,* Cape, 1985).
(Contributor) *The American West's Acid Rain Test,* World Resources Institute, 1985.
The Counterlife (novel), Farrar, Straus, 1986.
(Author of foreword) *A Fanatic Heart,* New American Library, 1986.
(Editor) George Konrad, *The Case Worker,* translated by Paul Aston, Penguin Books, 1987.

(Editor) Milan Kundera, *The Farewell Party,* Penguin Books, 1987.
The Facts: A Novelist's Autobiography, Farrar, Straus, 1988.
Deception (novel), Simon & Schuster, 1990.

Also contributor of short stories to anthologies and articles to periodicals, including *Esquire, Harper's, New Yorker, Commentary,* and *Paris Review.*

SIDELIGHTS: "Can you honestly say," asks a character in Philip Roth's novel *The Ghost Writer,* "that there is anything in your short story that would not warm the heart of a Julius Streicher or a Joseph Goebbels?" The question is being posed to Roth's fictional alter ego, Nathan Zuckerman, and the accusation that a Jewish writer would produce work that would please an anti-Semite—even such Nazi figureheads as Streicher and Goebbels—is one that has often been leveled at Roth himself. Since the release of his first collection, *Goodbye, Columbus, and Five Short Stories,* the publication of the novel *Portnoy's Complaint,* and the series of presumed semiautobiographical volumes featuring novelist Nathan Zuckerman Roth has claimed a unique niche among contemporary fiction writers. And while he is often compared to other artists—including Anton Chekhov, Henry James, and especially Franz Kafka—Roth is one of a kind, most readers and critics ultimately agree.

Born in Depression-era Newark, New Jersey, Roth, the son of an insurance agent, grew up in relative affluence during World War II and eventually earned his M.A. from the University of Chicago. Yet his memories of the Jewish immigrant community of his childhood would be the inspiration of many of the author's plots and characters. This first became evident in *Goodbye, Columbus, and Five Short Stories;* the title piece, a novella, gained the most acclaim for the 26-year-old author. The story examines the relationship between Neil Klugman, a lower-middle-class Newark native, and Brenda Patimkin, a product of the burgeoning postwar Jewish nouveau riche. The depiction of the Patimkin family as boorish creatures of leisure infuriated some critics and impressed others with its candor. *Goodbye, Columbus* was in fact the first of many Roth books to be castigated from synagogue pulpits. "To be sure, Roth was hardly the first American-Jewish writer to cross verbal swords with the 'official' Jewish community," points out Sanford Pinsker in a *Dictionary of Literary Biography* article. "But Roth's book brought the antagonisms to a rapid boil. Granted, no social critic has an easy task. The 'glad tidings' he or she brings us about ourselves are never welcome, and, quite understandably, offended readers go to great lengths to prove that such writers are morbidly misanthropic, clearly immoral, merely insane—or, as in Roth's case, all of the above." The flood of criticism aimed at *Goodbye, Columbus* didn't stem the book's popularity, though. Several critics praised the new voice in American fiction, and the collection went on to win the National Book Award in 1960.

Two novels followed *Goodbye, Columbus*—*Letting Go* in 1962 and *When She Was Good* in 1967—but neither drew the kind of attention afforded Roth's debut in fiction. Yet any doubts about Roth's ability to both attract and shock his audience were quelled in 1969 with the publication of *Portnoy's Complaint.* Variously described as "the work of a virtuoso" (by Robert Fulford in *Saturday Night*) and as "a desperately dirty novel" (by Saul Maloff in *Commonweal*), *Portnoy's Complaint* so thoroughly divided its readers that to date it remains the work most closely associated with its author. Conflict and repression highlight the book's themes; a young Jewish man's infatuation with Gentile girls and his constant state of war with his overbearing mother comprise the plot. In another *Dictionary of Literary Biography* essay, Jeffrey Helterman compares protagonist Alex Portnoy with the hero of James Joyce's *Portrait of the Artist as a Young Man:* "Like Stephen Dedalus, Alexander Portnoy yearns for freedom from the repressive laws of his youth—and like Dedalus, Portnoy feels love as well as revulsion for that youth. In Portnoy's case, the laws are those of Jewish domesticity imposed by a mother whose domineering exterior hides a mass of guilt and fear. Her rules—eat your vegetables, beware of polio, don't fool around with shiksas [Yiddish slang for Gentile women], don't feel innocent when you can feel guilty—are the manifestation of a classic superego."

But the theme and plot of *Portnoy's Complaint* are perhaps not as memorable to most readers as are the book's sharply drawn characters—particularly the iconographic Jewish mother Sophie Portnoy, who, with a long bread knife in her hands, seems a castrating vision, and her son Alex, who manifests his frustrations with constant masturbation, described in graphic detail by Roth. The depiction of what some more demure critics called "onanism" was a major point of contention and helped earn the novel charges of pornography. And the author's continuing satiric examination of Jewish-American life sparked further debate. As Pinsker describes it, "the anti-Roth crusade that the rabbis began with *Goodbye, Columbus* turned into a full-scale suburban war."

Some of the criticism aimed at *Portnoy's Complaint* centered on the book's tone. As Fulford writes: "In one crucial way [the work] is a disappointment. On first reading I was caught up in Roth's brilliance and audacity. [But on further readings,] I discovered that the jokes were funny only once, that the situations quickly lost their freshness." "Though the satire in *Portnoy's Complaint* is generally first-rate, the book hardly ever rises to irony," notes Anatole Broyard in *The Critic as Artist: Essays on Books, 1920-1970.* "Irony requires dimension, the possibility of grandeur, and what we have here is a series of caricatures. Father, mother, sister, mistresses—even Portnoy himself—each has one act, one *shtik.*"

To Pinsker, *Portnoy's Complaint* "is simultaneously a confessional act and an attempt to exorcise lingering guilts. His is a complaint in the legalistic sense of an indictment handed down against those cultural forces that have wounded him; it is a complaint in the old-fashioned sense [of] an illness . . .; and, finally it is a complaint in the more ordinary, existential sense of the word." And in Helterman's view, Roth's book "is a hilariously funny novel which is significant for its use of obscenity as part of its intrinsic meaning."

The next few years brought a trio of Roth novels that ranged from the acerbic to the slapstick to the experimental. *Our Gang,* a biting indictment of the Nixon administration, features a president called Trick E. Dixon and a cabinet that is remarkable for its ability to use language to confound the citizens it is supposed to be serving. "Up to [a] point, Roth's material is fairly predictable; its episodic and topical nature will put you in mind of [columnist] Art Buchwald at best, a slew of stand-up comics at worst," says *Washington Post Book World* critic Michael Olmert. "Fortunately, in the last three chapters Roth's higher aspirations take over and his well-contained rage breaks loose." Olmert is not the only reviewer to see traces of George Orwell in Roth's political satire; he sees an Orwellian message in *Our Gang,* a warning "that people who begin to be lazy about the language that their leaders use can be told anything." Less impressed is Alvin B. Kernan, who writes in *Yale Review* that the stuff of *Our Gang* is not so much satire as it is parody. While the critic admires Roth's ear for dialogue—"he catches perfectly that strange mixture of jaunty self-assurance and desperate uncertainty"—

Kernan ultimately feels that Roth's use of principles are "the appropriate equipment for a man of a particular political and intellectual persuasion, rather than values so deeply felt that they inform the writing completely, the way that, say, [Jonathan] Swift's passionate commitment to good sense is everywhere in *Gulliver's Travels.*"

Despite its name, *The Great American Novel* is not about novel writing. It is about the great American game, baseball. Roth's 1973 book tells the tall tale of a long-ago baseball league, the Patriot, and the assembly of motley teams that played its season. One such remarkable team is "the hapless Ruppert Mundy's, a team of misfits created out of the few men who are left in America during World War II," says Helterman. Its members include "a fourteen-year-old second baseman who is so wet behind the ears that the only nickname he has earned is Nickname; a one-legged catcher, Hot Ptah, whose greatest achievement is his mastery of obscene behind-the-plate chatter; and Bud Parusha, the one-armed outfielder who takes the ball out of his glove with his teeth and who occasionally gets it stuck in his mouth, causing inside-the-park home runs."

The author's aggressive depiction of the 1940s and postwar era provoked the usual split critical reaction. For instance, in a *New York Times Book Review* article, Thomas R. Edwards finds that Roth's "talent for cruel and shameless comic extravagance gives us marvelously raunchy vignettes of the sporting life." But the author's "determination to get in every joke he can think of about our past and present follies—patriotic paranoia, racism, sexual infantilism, the vulgarity of the media—finally is exhausting and self-defeating." While *World* critic Dorothy Rabinowitz states that in *The Great American Novel* Roth's "considerable gifts are ill spent on parody in the service of an abstraction," *New York Review of Books* writer William H. Gass finds that the book is not so much about the game, but the society that surrounds baseball. In its rituals of "hymns, chants, [and] litanies" the game—and the novel—embody "the language of America: a manly, righteous, patriotic, and heroic tongue."

Franz Kafka's *The Metamorphosis,* the story of Gregor Samsa's discovery one morning that he had been transformed into a giant cockroach, found its influence in Roth's *The Breast,* an experimental work about a professor, David Kepesh, who is turned into a six-foot female breast. "What Roth has created is an elaborate literary joke," says Elizabeth Sabiston in an *International Fiction Review* piece. Kepesh, she adds, "is in quest of his identity, of reintegration and fusion of flesh and spirit in an overly cerebral, analytic age suffering from what T. S. Eliot called a 'dissociation of sensibility.'" Other critics weren't so admiring. Some thought that Roth's attempt to emulate Kafka and Nikolai Gogol (author of *The Nose,* a similar transformation story) was bold, but unsuccessful. As Helterman sees it, "the novel works only if the reader believes that Kepesh has indeed turned into a breast, and it is a tribute to Roth's skills that he can present the psychological portrait of a man in this state without resorting to teasing questions of whether this is dream or reality as does Gogol. . . . Kepesh may wonder if he is mad or dreaming, but the reader never does; he knows that the hero has become a breast."

For whatever critical and commercial response the author garnered from the post-Portnoy books, most scholars considered the volumes minor works, and called out for Roth's next major contribution to contemporary literature. The author responded in 1979 with *The Ghost Writer,* the first in a series of novels featuring Nathan Zuckerman, and a work that to this day many critics label his best.

While Roth himself has denied that the Zuckerman stories are autobiographical, "it may be fairly added that though *The Ghost Writer* is not in any literal sense a roman a clef, certain personal traits are unmistakably caught—not in full portrait, of course, but in broad strokes, a gesture here, a tone of voice there, a turn of mind everywhere," notes *Commonweal* critic Saul Maloff. Certainly some of the physical details parallel Roth's life. Nathan Zuckerman is in his mid-twenties when the book opens in the 1950s, as Roth was; he is a struggling writer from Newark, as Roth was. *The Ghost Writer* finds Zuckerman seeking an audience with the venerable, reclusive novelist E. I. Lonoff (who "strongly suggests Bernard Malamud," says Maloff). Given the rare privilege of an invitation to Lonoff's Berkshire farmhouse, Zuckerman meets Lonoff's neglected wife and another houseguest, the mysterious Amy Bellette.

Bellette, a young European, seems at first to be Lonoff's mistress, but their relationship also appears to be like that of a father and daughter. Zuckerman, increasingly attracted to the enigmatic woman and, at the same time, increasingly at odds with his family, concocts an existentialist fantasy. He imagines at first that Bellette is a survivor of the Nazi concentration camp at Belsen, and then decides that she is the actual Anne Frank, author of the memorable diary. Zuckerman reasons that Frank, having miraculously survived Belsen, is surprised to find that her memoirs have become the symbol of Jewish fortitude during the Holocaust. She changes her name in order to protect the reputation of the book, fearing if the world knew that Anne Frank lived, the diary would be just another adventure story.

Finally, Zuckerman fantasizes about asking Bellette/Anne Frank to marry him, and imagines the scene with his estranged father when he presents the preeminent Jewish woman as his bride. "Lonoff is a wonderfully parodic creature," remarks *New Republic* critic Jack Beatty, noting the character's Malamud-like characteristics. "As for Nathan, he is the familiar Rothian hero—confident, libidinous, and obsessively guilty." "*The Ghost Writer* is a curious book," adds Rhoda Koenig in *Saturday Review*. "Billed as a novel, it's really an anecdote with interruptions—a malicious character sketch of one of Nathan's (and Roth's) rivals; a summary of a Henry James story [*The Lesson of the Master*]; and two long digressions, one of them the chapter about Amy's past. The other—and the best part of the book—is Nathan's recollection of a terrible break with his father, who thinks Nathan's stories are not good for the Jews."

If Roth's Lonoff brings Henry James to mind in *The Ghost Writer,* says Mark Shechner, "that is intentional. In depicting him, Roth has been less interested in the sharp contrasts between Jewish and American cultural traits than in the blendings and overlappings of Old and New World versions of asceticism. Lonoff is one Jewish-American writer whose hyphen stands for a confluence, not a contradiction." Shechner, writing in *Nation,* continues that *The Ghost Writer* "is the least tendentious of Roth's books, far more the bemused slice of life than the anguished self-exculpation. Here, it is the other guy's marriage that is on the rocks."

In a *Village Voice* article, Eliot Fremont-Smith praises *The Ghost Writer* as Roth's "most controlled and elegant work. It is serious, intelligent, dramatic, acutely vivid, slyly and wickedly funny, almost formal in its respect for theme, almost daredevil in ambition, and almost wrenching so close it hurts. It is muscular and restrained, . . . quite marvelous in the strategic arrangements of its parts, and seductive beyond its [brief] efficiency." Yet *The Ghost Writer* "is also a strangely unsatisfying book. These days one is too decently in awe, too empathetic (maybe too sophisti-cated, or lazy) to demand [a level of catharsis] from every work of quality. . . . But Catharsis—or its modern impersonation, Insight, . . . is what *The Ghost Writer* seems to promise, seems to be rushing us toward, the grail of its endeavor, only we never get there. So at the end and afterward, one remains (not unhappily) in Roth's enticing grip, his thrall, but doesn't quite know why. Everything still impends, but the sense of purpose is diffused." *Commentary* critic Pearl K. Bell shares this view, noting that by the end of the story, the book "seems rather thin, . . . because it promises an intellectual and moral range which it does not wholly attain. Roth seems reluctant to engage himself fully with the demanding question he asks in many different ways throughout the novel: must life be sacrificed to art, in the uncompromising manner of a Lonoff?"

Still other reviewers find *The Ghost Writer* to be a work rich in meaning and value. The novel, says *Washington Post Book World* contributor Jonathan Penner, "provides further evidence that [the author] can do practically anything with fiction. His narrative power—the ability to delight the reader simultaneously with the telling and the tale, employing economy that looks like abundance, ornament that turns out to be structure—is superb. He is so good in this book that even when he's bad, he's good. *The Ghost Writer* is a thoroughly earned triumph. It is built not only with high craft but also with base craft, the laborious turning of sentences—what we would expect, not from a Lonoff fixed in the firmament, but from the most nervous, the least 'established,' the most sweatily hopeful, of Zuckermans." And to Maloff, *The Ghost Writer* is a novel "about the nature and risks—and limits—of art and the imagination, about the surprising uses of adversity, as subtle, intricate, serious, finely turned and deeply felt a fiction as Roth, in full voice, has wrought."

A "comedy about fame and its discontents," as James Wolcott describes it in *Esquire, Zuckerman Unbound* continues the young novelist's saga with Nathan Zuckerman, some years later, now famous (and infamous) for his "dirty" opus *Carnovsky,* a book that bears no small resemblance to Roth's own *Portnoy's Complaint.* "Not that the novel is at all straightforward autobiography," notes *Nation* reviewer Richard Gilman. "Roth is too much the artist for that. But there is something disingenuous about his attempt wholly to dissociate himself from his protagonist." *Zuckerman Unbound* "is in part an account of Nathan's struggle to accept the consequences of his eclat, to feel justified in having become so flashingly eminent," Gilman continues. "He's totally misunderstood, feels himself unreal. Strangers address him as Carnovsky, his book's protagonist."

Zuckerman faces another dilemma in this sequel: Alvin Pepler, a fellow Newark native, has latched himself onto Nathan and makes his life miserable. Pepler is a character who, in the 1950s, had gained fame as a contestant on a game show reminiscent of "$64,000 Question" until he was forced off the air by the producers and replaced with a more all-American—i.e., non-Jewish—type. Pepler's resulting bitterness and his obsession with his brief celebrity is harrowing for Nathan, who sees a parallel in his own life. "Pepler becomes Roth's outlandish personification of the creative mania set loose by our culture of democracy," Isa Kapp points out. "While their speech is different, victim [Zuckerman] and victimizer [Pepler] are psychological birds of a feather, preening their egos and brooding over their good name. Both hoard compliments, Alvin boasting about his embellishment of the Jewish image on prime time, Zuckerman recalling, with no small relish, praise from [a relative]. And both reason from paranoia, behaving as if they lived in a permanent state of siege," Kapp writes in *New Republic.*

Zuckerman's resentful father dies in the sequel, and his last word to his rebellious son is a mystery: "Vaster? Better? Faster? Could it have been bastard?," writes *Los Angeles Times Book Review* critic Elaine Kendall. Zuckerman's love life is also in a shambles. He breaks up with his first wife, and his girlfriend abandons him after one night to return to her one true love—Fidel Castro. "Zuckerman is almost a latter-day Emma Bovary, his life disrupted not by reading about desire, but by desiring to write," says Edward Rothstein in *New York Review of Books.* "He is a victim, bound by fictive yearnings. He could ask, 'Did fiction do this to me?' just as David Kepesh did after he turned into a giant breast in Roth's Kafkaesque fable. Does Zuckerman, only slightly less constricted by his desires, know how bound he is? How is Zuckerman unbound?"

Some critics, in praising *Zuckerman Unbound* for Roth's sense of dialogue and style, nevertheless feel that somehow the author hasn't worked up to his full potential. In a *New York Times Book Review* article, for instance, George Stade remarks that while the novel "is masterful, sure in every touch, clear and economical of line as a crystal vase, . . . there is something diminished about it, as about its immediate predecessors. The usual heartbreak and hilarity are there, but they no longer amplify each other; now both are muted." And Gilman feels that "in an important episode Roth inadvertently reveals how he's thrown away the opportunity to make *Zuckerman Unbound* a better book than it is." But to *Chicago Tribune Book World* reviewer Bernard Rodgers, *Zuckerman Unbound* "offers its readers the all too infrequent joy of watching a master storyteller at the height of his powers practice his craft; together with [*The Ghost Writer* and *The Professor of Desire, Zuckerman Unbound*] firmly establishes Roth as one of the small handful of contemporary American novelists who have created an oeuvre that deserves to be compared with those of today's Central European and South American writers in stylistic virtuosity, imagination, and moral intensity."

"When *Zuckerman Unbound* appeared, . . . it was widely assumed to be Nathan's farewell to his past and [Roth's] farewell to his alter ego Nathan. But Roth had [more] in mind," reports Gary Giddins of the *Village Voice.* And so 1983 saw the publication of *The Anatomy Lesson,* the third installment of the Zuckerman saga. The time is now the early 1970s and Zuckerman, forty years old and suffering from untreatable back pains, decides to give up the literary life and become a doctor. He enrolls in the University of Chicago medical school, but "the decision restores his creative urges in an unfortunate way," according to *Time*'s R. Z. Sheppard. "He buttonholes strangers with wildly obscene monologues describing himself as Milton Appel, a no-holds-barred pornographer. Appel is the name of Zuckerman's nemesis, a leading literary critic who once branded Carnovsky and its author vulgar and demeaning." (Those readers following the roman a clef elements in the Zuckerman books will remember that Irving Howe wrote a 1972 *Commentary* essay that is sharply critical of Roth's writings.)

Again the consequences of art on the artist's life is a theme of Roth's novel. *The Anatomy Lesson* "isn't necessarily dependent on the earlier novels for plot elements; it can be read—if not fully savored—on its own," as Giddens writes. "Yet the trilogy gains irony and gravity from the manifold ways in which the three volumes interlock. In *Zuckerman Unbound,* Roth succumbed to Walter Brennan Syndrome and gave the best and funniest part to a supporting character, . . . Alvin Pepler; Nathan's plight paled by comparison. *The Anatomy Lesson* redeems its predecessor, putting the middle volume and Nathan in perspective, and

highlighting themes only sketched the first and second times around. It clarifies Roth's ambivalence about Nathan."

"Zuckerman is not Philip Roth, of course; art is not to be confused with reality, as both the novelist and his hero have been insisting somewhat hysterically ever since the American reading public was philistine enough to confuse them with their fictional creations and to make them rich and famous into the bargain," points out Christopher Lehmann-Haupt in a *New York Times* article. "Still, we do get an awful lot of Zuckerman in 'The Anatomy Lesson.' He can be passionately articulate in his rage against his tormenters, and he can be a wildly funny black-comedian in his role as Milton Appel the purveyor of sex. But he can also be a little tedious in his endless self-absorption and scab-picking." To *New Republic* critic Michael Wood, "accomplished and enjoyable as the work is, the snag with *The Anatomy Lesson* is that Roth invites us to see the delusion in Zuckerman's altruism but then still gives him full marks for being decent enough to entertain it. Zuckerman wants to go to medical school in the way he wanted to marry Anne Frank: as an answer to the critics in his head. But this pathetic maneuver is so transparent that it won't carry the weight Roth placed on it."

"Roth has a genius for the comedy of entrapment. He is an uncompromising myth buster with a taste for bruising intimacy," observes Sheppard. The critic adds that in *The Ghost Writer, Zuckerman Unbound,* and *The Anatomy Lesson,* Roth has created his "most complex and structurally satisfying work. [The trilogy] is a disciplined string ensemble compared with *Portnoy's Complaint,* which had the primal power of a high school band. Yet Zuckerman and Portnoy have close ties. Both star in comedies of the unconscious, burlesques of psychoanalytic processes whose irreverence and shocking explicitness challenge the pieties that protect hidden feelings." In 1984 the novels were published together as *Zuckerman Bound: A Trilogy and Epilogue.* Here, Zuckerman is bound for Czechoslovakia, which is the setting for the epilogue "The Prague Orgy." This episode finds the novelist rediscovering his literary roots in the birthplace of Franz Kafka and trying to obtain a rare Yiddish manuscript in the process. What he finds is artistic and personal repression that makes him reevaluate his own priorities in life.

Zuckerman Bound "merits something reasonably close to the highest level of esthetic praise for tragicomedy, partly because as a formal totality it becomes much more than the sum of its parts," in the opinion of Harold Bloom. Commenting in the *New York Times Book Review,* Bloom goes on to say that what wins over the reader "is that both defense and definition are conveyed by the highest humor now being written. 'The Anatomy Lesson' and 'The Prague Orgy,' in particular, provoke a cleansing and continuous laughter, sometimes so intense that in itself it becomes astonishingly painful. One of the many esthetic gains of binding together the entire Zuckerman ordeal . . . is to let the reader experience the gradual acceleration of wit from the gentle Chekovian wistfulness of 'The Ghost Writer' on to the Gogolian sense of the ridiculous in 'Zuckerman Unbound' and then to the boisterous Westian farce of 'The Anatomy Lesson,' only to end in the merciless Kafkan irrealism of 'The Prague Orgy.' "

"Leave it to Philip Roth to make an ambitious business of pouring old wine into a new bottle," *Newsweek*'s Peter S. Prescott remarks. Prescott is referring to *The Counterlife,* Roth's 1986 release, a Zuckerman tale with an experimental twist. The reviewer acknowledges that the novel "isn't experimental fiction in the sense that the fiction of [Samuel] Beckett, [William] Gass and [Donald] Barthelme is experimental, but it's not conventional, either. There's no story that goes from here to there, no character who develops as characters do in novels, with each commitment closing doors to other opportunities, and the resulting patter effectively restricting what the author himself can do. Instead, Roth offers a sequence of alternatives: now change everything and try again."

Gass himself reviewed *The Counterlife* for the *New York Times Book Review* and found the book poses many questions—"the hedges, qualifications, objections entertained by critics—to which [the novel] gives a resounding answer. 'The Counterlife,' it seems to me, constitutes a fulfillment of tendencies, a successful integration of themes, and the final working through of obsessions that have previously troubled if not marred [Roth's] work. I hope it felt, as [the author] wrote it, like a triumph, because that is certainly how it reads to me."

In this story, the exploits of Nathan Zuckerman—now caught in the throes of critical self-examination—are contrasted to those of his brother, Henry Zuckerman (also known as Sherman Zuckerman in a previous incarnation). Henry, a solidly middle-class dentist, husband, and father, who has never forgiven Nathan for the sins of *Carnovsky,* faces the choice of heart-disease-related impotence or a life-threatening operation to cure the defect. In the first section of the novel, "Basel," Henry undergoes the operation, but does not survive it. However, in the second part of *The Counterlife,* "Judea," Henry has survived "and has fled his family and practice by going . . . to Israel and taking up with a Zionist zealot," according to a *New Yorker* piece by John Updike. "In the fourth chapter, it is Nathan who has the heart problem, the impotence, and the mistress called Maria. In pursuing these variations, the virtuoso imaginer rarely falters; satisfying details of place and costume, beautifully heard and knitted dialogues, astonishing diatribes unfold in chapters impeccably shaped, packed, and smoothed. No other writer combines such a surface of colloquial relaxation and even dishevelment with such a dense load of intelligence."

A bit more skeptical about *The Counterlife* is Lehmann-Haupt, who, in his *New York Times* review, notes that in the knockabout nature of the work and the shifting characters among the Zuckerman clan, "it's as if the novelist were saying, since I can make you believe in anything, the ultimate challenge is to make you believe in nothing. So we learn to count on nothing. Yet the novel pays a price for sabotaging its own reality. We become so aware of the narrative's duplicity that all that is left to us is the burden of the author's self-consciousness as an artist and a Jew. It's like being trapped between two funhouse mirrors that reflect each other's distortions unto a point that vanishes into absurdity."

But to Richard Stern, the plot twists in *The Counterlife* constitute an enjoyable look at a fiction writer at work, "an equivalent of action painting. Then there is the delight of liberation. . . . The claustrophobia which oppresses so many self-reflexive novels—novels about themselves—isn't here because Roth's worldly intelligence, satiric power, gift for portraiture, milieu, scene and action, are too strong to be mesmerized by technical discovery. If the writer has a measure of Tolstoyan worldliness in him, he will not have to pay the price of being caged by the techniques of exhibition," says Stern in the *Chicago Tribune Book World.* The critic concludes that in *The Counterlife,* the author "has made another remarkable advance in his illustrious career."

As with *The Counterlife,* Roth's best-selling novel, *Deception,* is also somewhat experimental. This time, the author explores the relationship between fiction and reality by writing an ambiguous tale about a struggling Jewish writer's diary. The journal recounts the protagonist's conversations with his lover, but when his wife discovers the diary and confronts him with it he tells her it is only a writing exercise. The problem of the novel then becomes a question of what is truth and what is falsehood, a subject that allows Roth to address the more general issue of the relationship between all authors and their work. Some critics, such as Lehmann-Haupt, feel that this point has already been discussed enough by other writers, as well as by Roth himself. He comments that *Deception* elaborates "the author's by now all-too-familiar point that in the act of committing any reality to paper, the writer is not only exercising his imagination, but also should be permitted absolute freedom to do so. . . . The argument is entertainingly made. . . . But it goes much too far: if the unenlightened don't understand by now, they never will." Many other reviewers, however, were more receptive to Roth's novel. For example, *Esquire* contributor Lee Eisenberg praises *Deception* as the latest successful effort by a talented author: "A good case, I think, can be made that Philip Roth will be one of those whose books will live well into the next century. . . . Some of [*Deception*] is funny, some of it is angry, some of it is wise. As always with Roth, the writing has perfect pitch."

Before he composed *Deception,* Roth spoke to Mervyn Rothstein in a *New York Times* interview about his life in fiction. "Twenty-seven years ago [when *Goodbye, Columbus* was released], I was just starting out, with all that implies about energy, confidence, innocence and ambition. I think I've put on plenty of pounds as a writer since then. And I would hope that most of those pounds are muscle. On the other hand, each book seems to me more of an ordeal than the one before. Up against those first books, you're a different kind of fighter from the kind of fighter you are later on. Certainly you lose your naive expectations. If the goal is to be innocent of all innocence, I'm getting there."

MEDIA ADAPTATIONS: Goodbye, Columbus was adapted as a film and released by Paramount in 1969; the film adaptation of *Letting Go* was released by Leon Mirell Productions, Inc., and Noblelight Productions in 1969; *Portnoy's Complaint* was filmed by Warner Bros. in 1972; *The Ghost Writer* was adapted for television and shown on the Public Broadcasting System in 1984. Three of Roth's short stories have been adapted for the theatre by Larry Arrick and produced under the title "Unlikely Heroes."

BIOGRAPHICAL/CRITICAL SOURCES:

BOOKS

Bestsellers 90, Issue 3, Gale, 1990.
Contemporary Literary Criticism, Gale, Volume 1, 1973, Volume 2, 1974, Volume 3, 1975, Volume 4, 1975, Volume 6, 1976, Volume 9, 1978, Volume 15, 1980, Volume 22, 1982, Volume 31, 1985.
Dictionary of Literary Biography, Gale, Volume 2: *American Novelists since World War II,* 1978, Volume 28: *Twentieth-Century American-Jewish Fiction Writers,* 1984.
Dictionary of Literary Biography Yearbook: 1982, Gale, 1983.
Gindin, James, *Harvest of a Quiet Eye: The Novel of Compassion,* Indiana University Press, 1971.
Guttman, Allen, *The Jewish Writer in America: Assimilation and the Crisis of Identity,* Oxford University Press, 1971.
Harrison, Gilbert A., editor, *The Critic as Artist: Essays on Books, 1920-1970,* Liveright, 1972.
Hoffman, Frederick J., *The Modern Novel in America,* revised edition, Regnery, 1963.
Howe, Irving, *The Critical Point,* Horizon, 1973.
Kazin, Alfred, *Contemporaries,* Little, Brown, 1962.
Malin, Irving, *Jews and Americans,* Southern Illinois University Press, 1965.

McDaniel, John, *The Fiction of Philip Roth,* Haddonfield House, 1974.

Pinsker, Sanford, *The Comedy That "Hoits": An Essay on the Fiction of Philip Roth,* University of Missouri Press, 1975.

Podhoretz, Norman, *Doings and Undoings,* Farrar, Straus, 1964.

Rogers, Bernard F., Jr., *Philip Roth,* Twayne, 1978.

Rogers, *Philip Roth: A Bibliography,* Scarecrow, 1974.

Roth, Philip, *Reading Myself and Others,* Farrar, Straus, 1975.

Roth, *The Ghost Writer,* Farrar, Straus, 1979.

Solotaroff, Theodore, *The Red Hot Vacuum and Other Pieces on the Writings of the Sixties,* Atheneum, 1970.

Weinberg, Helen, *The New Novel in America: The Kafkan Mode in Contemporary Fiction,* Cornell University Press, 1970.

Wisse, Ruth, *The Schlemiel as Modern Hero,* University of Chicago Press, 1971.

PERIODICALS

Atlantic, July, 1962, December, 1971, November, 1977.

Chicago Tribune Book World, May 31, 1981, November 6, 1983, June 23, 1985, January 11, 1987.

Commentary, December, 1972, September, 1974, December, 1979, September, 1981, January, 1984.

Commonweal, March 21, 1969, November 9, 1979.

Detroit Free Press, April 1, 1990.

Detroit News, April 4, 1990.

Esquire, May, 1970, June, 1981, February, 1990.

Harper's, July, 1974.

International Fiction Review, January, 1975.

Los Angeles Times Book Review, June 7, 1981, November 13, 1983, May 26, 1985, January 11, 1987.

Nation, December 27, 1975, September 15, 1979, June 13, 1981.

National Review, July 19, 1974, October 16, 1981.

New Republic, June 8, 1974, June 7, 1975, October 6, 1979, May 23, 1981, December 19, 1983, November 21, 1988.

New Statesman, September 21, 1973, November 9, 1978.

Newsweek, February 24, 1969, November 8, 1971, June 3, 1974, December 30, 1974, September 10, 1979, June 8, 1981, November 7, 1983, January 12, 1987.

New York, June 3, 1974.

New Yorker, March 2, 1987.

New York Review of Books, November 16, 1972, May 31, 1973, June 13, 1974, October 27, 1977, June 25, 1981, April 11, 1985.

New York Times, May 9, 1981, May 11, 1981, October 19, 1983, May 15, 1985, August 1, 1985, December 17, 1986, December 29, 1986, March 5, 1990.

New York Times Book Review, May 17, 1959, June 17, 1962, February 23, 1969, November 7, 1971, September 27, 1972, May 6, 1973, June 2, 1974, May 25, 1975, September 18, 1977, September 2, 1979, May 24, 1981, October 30, 1983, January 1, 1984, May 19, 1985, January 4, 1987.

Paris Review, fall, 1984.

Partisan Review, summer, 1973.

Saturday Night, April, 1969.

Saturday Review, April 11, 1959, June 16, 1962, November 6, 1971, December, 1979, June, 1981.

Time, May 11, 1959, June 15, 1962, June 10, 1974, September 3, 1979, May 25, 1981, November 7, 1983, January 19, 1987.

Times, March 5, 1987.

Times Literary Supplement, October 18, 1975, December 7, 1979, August 28, 1981, February 24, 1984, March 13, 1987.

Twentieth Century Literature, July, 1973.

Village Voice, June 20, 1974, October 8, 1979, November 1, 1983, January 27, 1987.

Virginia Quarterly Review, summer, 1969.

Washington Post, October 30, 1983, January 6, 1987.

Washington Post Book World, November 7, 1971, September 17, 1972, May 3, 1973, September 2, 1979, May 31, 1981, October 30, 1983, June 16, 1985, January 4, 1987.

World, May 8, 1983.

Yale Review, spring, 1972.

*   *   *

ROWLEY, Ames Dorrance
See LOVECRAFT, H(oward) P(hillips)

*   *   *

ROY, Gabrielle 1909-1983

PERSONAL: Born March 22, 1909, in St. Boniface, Manitoba, Canada; died of cardiac arrest, July 13, 1983, in Quebec City, Quebec; daughter of Leon and Melina (Landry) Roy; married Marcel Carbotte (a physician), August 30, 1947. *Education:* Educated in Canada. *Religion:* Roman Catholic.

ADDRESSES: Home—135 Grande Alice, Quebec City, Quebec, Canada G1R 2H1.

CAREER: Writer. Teacher in a Canadian prairie village school, 1928-29, and in St. Boniface, Manitoba, 1929-37.

MEMBER: Royal Society of Canada (fellow).

AWARDS, HONORS: Medaille of l'Academie Francaise, 1947; Prixfemina (France), 1947, for *Bonheur d'occasion;* received Canadian Governor General's Award four times; Duvernay Prix, 1955; Companion of the Order of Canada, 1967; Canadian Council of the Arts Award, 1968; Prix David, 1971; Knight of the Order of Mark Twain.

WRITINGS:

NOVELS

Bonheur d'occasion, Societe des Editions Pascal (Montreal), 1945, translation by Hannah Josephson published as *The Tin Flute* (Literary Guild selection), Reynal 1947.

La Petite Poule d'eau (also see below), Beauchemin (Montreal), 1950, translation by Harry L. Binsse published as *Where Nests the Water Hen: A Novel,* Harcourt, 1951, revised French language edition, Beauchemin, 1970.

Alexandre Chenevert, Caissier, Beauchemin, 1954, translation by Binsse published as *The Cashier,* Harcourt, 1955.

Rue Deschambault, Beauchemin, 1955, translation by Binsse published as *Streets of Riches,* Harcourt, 1957.

La Montagne secrete, Beauchemin, 1961, translation by Binsse published as *The Hidden Mountain,* Harcourt, 1962.

La Route d'Altamont, Editions HMH (Montreal), 1966, translation by Joyce Marshall published as *The Road past Altamont,* Harcourt, 1966.

(With others) *Canada. . .* (includes *La Petite Poule d'eau*), Editions du Burin (St. Cloud, France), 1967.

La Riviere sans repos, Beauchemin, 1970, translation by Marshall published as *Windflower,* McClelland & Stewart, 1970.

Cet ete qui chantait, Editions Francaises, 1972, translation by Marshall published as *Enchanted Summer,* McClelland & Stewart, 1976.

Un Jardin au bout du monde, Beauchemin, 1975, translation by Alan Brown published as *Garden in the Wind,* McClelland & Stewart, 1977.

Ces Enfants de ma vie, Stanke, 1977, translation by Brown published as *Children of My Heart,* McClelland & Stewart, 1979.

Fragiles Lumieres de la terre: Ecrits divers 1942-1970, Quinze, 1978.

Contributor to anthologies, including *Great Short Stories of the World,* Reader's Digest, 1972, and *The Penguin Book of Canadian Short Stories,* Penguin, 1980.

MEDIA ADAPTATIONS: Bonheur d'Occasion was made into a feature film, 1983.

WORK IN PROGRESS: Her memoirs.

SIDELIGHTS: Gabrielle Roy, who grew up in rural Manitoba, uses Montreal, St. Boniface, and the wilds of northern Canada as settings for her novels. *Saturday Night* critic George Woodcock believes that the complex mixture of cultures in rural Manitoba explains why Roy is "a Canadian writer of truly multicultural background and experience." Hugo McPherson, writing in *Canadian Literature,* comments: "Roy's experience has taught her that life offers an endless series of storms and mischances."

Roy fills her novels with people who are underprivileged, people of many origins, and minority people who have difficulty making the transition into the white man's world. "She records their plight with a tolerance and compassion that rests not on patriotism, humanism or religiosity, but on a deep love of mankind," McPherson states. "Gabrielle Roy *feels* rather than analyzes, and a sense of wonder and of mystery is always with her." Jeannette Urbas, writing in *Journal of Canadian Fiction,* presents a similar view: "Roy immerses us directly in the suffering of her characters: we feel, we think, we live with them. The appeal is directly to the heart."

Canadian Forum critic Paul Socken states that the link between all of Roy's writings is "people's lifelong struggle to understand the integrity of their own lives, to see their lives as a whole, and their need to create bridges of concern and understanding between themselves and others. . . . It is this very tension, and the success that she has demonstrated in dramatizing it, that makes Gabrielle Roy unique among Canadian writers."

BIOGRAPHICAL/CRITICAL SOURCES:

BOOKS

Contemporary Literary Criticism, Gale, Volume 10, 1979, Volume 14, 1980.

Dictionary of Literary Biography, Volume 68: *Canadian Writers, 1920-1959, First Series,* Gale, 1988.

Dossiers de Documentation de la litterature canadienne-francaise, Fides, 1967.

Gagne, Marc, *Visages de Gabrielle Roy,* Beauchemin, 1973.

Geniust, Monique, *La Creation romanesque chez Gabrielle Roy,* Cercle du Livre de France, 1966.

Ricard, Francois, *Gabrielle Roy,* Fides, 1975.

PERIODICALS

Canadian Forum, February, 1978.

Canadian Literature, summer, 1959.

Journal of Canadian Fiction, Volume I, number 2, 1972.

Maclean's, March 12, 1979.

Saturday Night, November, 1977.

OBITUARIES:

PERIODICALS

Chicago Tribune, July 16, 1983.

New York Times, July 15, 1983.

Times (London), July 18, 1983.

Washington Post, July 15, 1983.

*   *   *

ROZEWICZ, Tadeusz 1921-

PERSONAL: Born October 9, 1921, in Radomsko, Poland. *Education:* Studied art history at Jagellonian University, Krakow, 1945.

ADDRESSES: Home—Januszowicka 13/14, Wroclaw, Poland.

CAREER: Poet, playwright, and screenwriter. Worked as factory laborer and tutor during World War II. *Wartime service:* Served in home army of Polish Underground, 1943-44.

MEMBER: Bavarian Academy of Fine Arts, Academy of Fine Arts of East Germany.

AWARDS, HONORS: State Prize for poetry, 1955, 1962, and 1966; Krakow City Literary Prize, 1959; prize from minister of culture and art, 1962; Jurzykowski Foundation Prize (United States), 1966; Commander, Cross of Order, Polonia Restitula, 1970; prize from minister of foreign affairs, 1974 and 1987; Order of Banner of Labor, 2nd class, 1977; Austrian National Prize for European Literature, 1982; Golden Wreath, Struga Poetry Evening, 1987.

WRITINGS:

IN ENGLISH TRANSLATION

Rozmowa z ksieciem, Panstwowy Instytut Wydawniczy, 1960, translated by Adam Czerniawski as *Conversation With a Prince and Other Poems,* Anvil Poetry Press, 1982.

Faces of Anxiety (poems), translated by Czerniawski, Swallow Press, 1969.

"The Card Index" and Other Plays (contains "The Card Index," "Gone Out" [first produced as "Wyszedl z domu" in 1964], "Kartoteka" [first produced in Warsaw, March 25, 1960], and "The Interrupted Act" [first produced as "Akt przerwany" in 1964]), translated by Czerniawski, Grove Press, 1969.

"The Witnesses" and Other Plays (contains "The Witnesses" [first produced as "Swiadkowie, albo nasza mala stabilizacja," in 1962], "The Funny Old Man" [first produced as "Smieszny staruszek" in 1964], and "The Old Woman Broods" [first produced as "Stara kobieta wysiaduje" in 1968]), translated by Czerniawski, Calder & Boyars, 1970.

Selected Poems, translated by Czerniawski, Penguin, 1976.

"The Survivor" and Other Poems, translated by Magnus J. Krynski and Robert A. Maguire, Princeton University Press, 1976.

"Przyrost naturalny" (play; first published in Poland in *Dialog,* April, 1968), translation by Daniel Gerould published as "Birth Rate: The Biography of a Play for the Theatre" in *Twentieth-Century Polish Avant-Garde Drama,* edited by Gerould, Cornell University Press, 1977.

Unease, translated by Victor Contoski, New Rivers Press, 1980.

Green Rose, translated by Geoffrey Thurley, John Michael, 1982.

"Marriage Blanc" and "The Hunger Artist Departs," translated by Czerniawski, Marion Boyars, 1983.

IN POLISH; POETRY

Niepokoj (also see below; title means "Anxiety"), [Poland], 1947.

Czerwona rekawiczka (title means "The Red Glove"), [Poland], 1948.

W lyzce wody, [Poland], 1949.

Piec poematow (title means "Five Longer Poems"), [Poland], 1950.

Czas ktory idzie (title means "The Time to Come"), Czytelnik, 1951.

Wieraze i obrasy (title means "Poems and Images"), [Warsaw, Poland], 1952.

Kartki z Wegier, [Poland], 1953.

Wybor wierszy (also see below), Panstwowy Instytut Wydawniczy, 1953.

Rownina (title means "The Plain"), [Poland], 1954.

Usmiechy (title means "Smiles"), [Warsaw], 1955, 2nd edition, Czytelnik, 1957.

Srebrny klos (title means "Silver Ear of Grain"), [Poland], 1955.

Poemat otwarty (title means "The Open Poem"), [Krakow, Poland], 1956.

Poezje zebrane (title means "Collected Poetry"), Wydawnictwo Literackie, 1957.

Formy (poetry and prose; title means "Forms"), [Poland], 1958.

Rozmowa z ksieciem (title means "Conversation With the Prince"), Panstwowy Instytut Wydawniczy, 1960.

Zielona roza; Kartoteka (also see below; poetry and a play; first title means "The Green Rose"; second title means "The Card Index"), Panstwowy Instytut Wydawniczy, 1961.

Glos anonima (title means "Voice of an Anonymous Man"), Wydawnictwa Slask, 1961.

Nic w plaszczu Prospera (poetry and plays; title means "Nothing in Prospero Cloak"), Panstwowy Instytut Wydawniczy, 1963.

Niepoloj; Wybor wierszy, 1945-1961, Panstwowy Instytut Wydawniczy, 1963, 2nd edition, 1964.

Twarz (title means "Face"), Czytelnik, 1964, 2nd edition, 1966.

Wiersze poematy, Panstwowy Instytut Wydawniczy, 1967.

Poezje wybrane (title means "Selected Poems"), Ludowa Spoldzienia Wydawniczy, 1967.

Twarz trzecia (title means "The Third Face"), Czytelnik, 1968.

Regio, Panstwowy Instytut Wydawniczy, 1969.

Tadeusz Rozewicz, Czytelnik, 1969.

Wiersze (title means "Poems"), Czytelnik, 1969.

Wybor poezji, [Poland], 1969.

Wiersze Wstepem proprzedzil Stefan Lichanski, Panstwowy Instytut Wydawniczy, 1974.

Duszyczka (title means "Dear Spirit"), Wydawnictwo Literackie, 1977.

Na powienchni poematu i w srodku, Crytelnik, 1983.

Poezje wybrane, Ludowa Spoldzielnia Wydawnicra, 1984.

IN POLISH; PROSE

Opadly liscie z drzew (stories; title means "The Leaves Have Fallen From the Trees"), [Poland], 1955.

Przerwany egzamin (short stories; title means "The Interrupted Exam"), Panstwowy Instytut Wydawniczy, 1960, 2nd edition, 1965.

Wycieczka do muzeum (short stories; title means "Excursion to a Museum"), Czytelnik, 1966.

Opowiadania wybrane (title means "Selected Stories"), Czytelnik, 1968.

Smierc w starych dekoraoiach (novel; title means "Death Amidst Old Stage Props"), Panstwowy Instytut Wydawniczy, 1970.

Przygotowanie do wieczoru autorskiego (essays; title means "Preparation for an Author's Evening"), Panstwowy Instytut Wydawniczy, 1971, 2nd edition, 1977.

Proza (title means "Prose"), Zaklad Narodowy im Ossolinskich, 1972.

Proba rekonstrukcji, Ossolineum, 1979.

Echa lesne, Panstwowy Instytut Wydawniczy, 1985.

IN POLISH; PLAYS

"Grupa Laokoona" (title means "The Laocoon Group"), first produced in 1961.

"Spaghetti i miecz" (title means "Spaghetti and the Sword"), first produced in 1966.

Utwory dramatyczne, Wydawnictwo Literackie, 1966.

"Moja coreczka" (title means "My Little Daughter"), first produced in 1966.

Teatr niekonsekwneii (contains "Smierszny staruszek" and "Stara kobieta wysiaduje"), Panstwowy Instytut Wydawniczy, 1970.

Sztuki teatralne (title means "Pieces for the Theatre"), Zaklad Narodowy im Ossolinskich, 1972.

"Biale malzenstwo" (translated by Czerniawski as "White Marriage" and produced in New Haven, Conn., by Yale Repertory Co., April, 1977), published in *Biale Malzenstwo inn utowry sceniczne* (see below).

Biale Mtilzenstwo inn utowry sceniczne (contains "Biale Malzenstwo" [translation by Czerniawski as "White Marriage" produced in New Haven, Conn., by Yale Repertory Co., April, 1977], "Dzidzibobo czyli milosc romantyczna czeka juz pod drzwiami," "Sobowtor," "Dramat rozbienzny," and "Czego przbywa czego ubywa"), Wydawnictwo Literackie, 1975.

OTHER

(Editor) Leopold Staff, *Kto jest ten dziwny nieznajony* (poetry; title means "Who Is This Unusual Stranger"), [Warsaw], 1964.

Poezja, dramat, proza (collected works; title means "Poetry, Drama, Prose"), Zaklad Narodowy im Ossolinskich, 1973.

Work represented in numerous anthologies, including *The Broken Mirror: A Collection of Writing From Contemporary Poland,* edited by Pawel Mayewski, Random House, 1958; *The Modern Polish Mind,* edited by M. S. Kuncewiczowa, Little, Brown, 1962; *Introduction to Modern Polish Literature,* edited by Adam Gillon and Ludwik Kryzanowski, Twayne, 1964; *Polish Writing Today,* edited by Celina Wieniawska, 1967; *Postwar Polish Poetry,* edited and translated by Czeslaw Milosz, Penguin, 1970; and *The New Polish Poetry,* edited by Milne Holton and Paul Vangelisti, University of Pittsburgh Press, 1978.

SIDELIGHTS: Tadeusz Rozewicz is critically regarded as the most talented and influential poet and playwright of post-World War II Poland. In *World Literature Today,* E. J. Czerwinski called him "one of Poland's best writers, an innovator, a perpetual avant-gardist." After the cataclysm of World War II, which nearly leveled Poland and decimated one-fifth of its population, Rozewicz's poetry articulated the disillusionment, horror, and fear of those who endured. One of his colleagues explained: "We were all twenty-four then, and we all survived being led to the slaughter, but only Tadeusz Rozewicz expressed this experience on behalf of the entire generation so graphically, so brutally, and so simply. His 'I' became the voice of his generation."

The experience of the war motivates most of Rozewicz's poetry, which he began writing in the early 1940s, and his plays, which began to appear in the early 1960s. Before the war, Rozewicz was a member of the first generation of Poles to experience independence after more than one hundred fifty years of domination by various countries. "It was a self-assured and optimistic generation, which was coming to maturity when the Germans invaded in September, 1939," noted M. J. Krynski and R. A. Maguire in their introduction to *"The Survivor" and Other Poems*. The period of Nazi occupation overwhelmed the hopeful young author. The carnage of war undermined his faith in all things. Andrew Busza disclosed the writer's position in *Books Abroad:* "For Rozewicz, there is one overwhelming question: How to be, after the death of God, Man, and Art?" "I felt that something had forever ended for me and for mankind, something that neither religion nor science nor art had succeeded in protecting," Rozewicz related. "For me, a young poet who had revered the great poets, both living and dead, as gods, the words of Michiewicz that 'It is more difficult to live through a day well than to write a good book' became understandable all too early; all too early did I understand Tolstoy's statement that the writing of a primer was of greater significance to him than all the great novels."

As a result, Rozewicz came to suspect all abstractions and insubstantial ideology. "He regards the entire cultural heritage of the Western World as a construct of semblances and deceptions that conceals a colossal lie," contend Krynski and Maguire. "Spiritual values to him are illusions, or, at best, projections of idle yearnings." In his work, Rozewicz began to deal only in the concrete. He stripped his poetry of all pretense, which for him included metaphor and meter. Writing his poetry in a stark, unadorned style, Rozewicz endeavors to transmit "not verses but facts." Krynski and Maguire remarked that "the result is what critics have called a 'naked poem.' Rozewicz makes scant use of . . . hidden meanings: this is a deliberately anti-symbolic poetry, a poetry very much, as he put it, of the 'here and now.' "

In his renunciation of art, "Rozewicz has sought," asserted Daniel Gerould in his book *Twentieth-Century Polish Avant-Garde Drama,* "to destroy all distinctions and limitations of genre and form. Deliberately striving for maximum impurity, Rozewicz, antipoet and antiplaywright, creates 'junk art' out of scraps of quotations, clippings, lists, and documents." The artist believes "modern civilization's waste products are its only true art, its impermanent artifacts."

This philosophy, or lack of philosophy, is demonstrated in Rozewicz's plays. One of the most experimental playwrights of the Polish avant-garde theatre, Rozewicz writes dramas often compared by critics with those of Samuel Beckett. Combining elements of the theatre of the absurd and the avant-garde, his plays strive "to burst the bands of drama and break open its forms," asserted Gerould. For one such play, "The Old Woman Broods," Rozewicz "creates a score, an elastic scenario in which he invites the collaboration of a director and theatre; the playwright himself cannot complete the work. Rozewicz's stage directions, which constitute over a third of the printed play, are not descriptive or prescriptive, but offer the director suggestions and ideas that he is free to carry out as he wishes. The author does not tell the director how to produce his play, but once having posed the problem, deliberately leaves the work partly unfinished and open to different kinds of solutions."

"The Old Woman Broods" also reflects Rozewicz's thoughts about man and culture. In the play the principal character, an old woman, sits on a continually growing pile of garbage and tries to produce children. While she is thus occupied, other people work, play, and live in the rubbish surrounding her. Gerould described the scene as "the cemetery of the soul, where people are collected like garbage, yet where waiters and hairdressers

and the business of living survive the holocaust and persist. The end of the world seems a fraud—paper continues to pile up."

Rozewicz's nihilism is also amply illustrated in his well-known drama "The Card Index." The central figure of the work, a nameless man, lounges on his bed throughout the play, contemplating his body. Other characters walk by the man and ask him questions about what he thinks and believes, but they elicit no response from him. At one point, however, the man speaks. Gerould reported: "Lying in bed, looking at his own hand, and opening and closing his fingers, Rozewicz's everyman clutches at his own concrete humanness like a baby and hides from those forces outside himself that seek to fit him into restrictive categories. 'I like the little toe on my left foot better than I do all of humanity,' the inert protagonist asserts, rejecting all noble sentiments and big emotions. At least one's little toe is real—perhaps the only thing in the world that is." Rozewicz "mistrusts all words," explained Gerould, "and seeks truth in nakedness, in the bare biological facts of the human organism and the world of things that surrounds it."

The playwright's drama "Birth Rate" is the culmination of this belief and his efforts to create an antiplay. About human reproduction, "Birth Rate" features a train compartment that fills up with people until it is densely packed. Rozewicz invoked the scene in "Birth Rate": "All the while the pressure mounts from the inside, the walls start to buckle. The living mass is so tightly packed together that it begins to boil over. There are two or three explosions in close succession. Movement blends with shouting. Finally everything comes to a standstill. Out of the mass the young people come forward in silence. They sit down beside one another and start to flirt and exert mutual attraction. In the stillness their voices suggest the billing and cooing of pigeons."

But aside from this core idea, Rozewicz could not finish the play, and "Birth Rate" becomes the tale of his difficulties with his subject. "As in conceptual art," reflected Gerould, "the author's inability to write the play becomes the drama. . . . Rozewicz dramatizes his own hesitations in trying to write the play, his struggles with the 'living mass' out of which he had hoped to form a drama, but in the face of so much death, he wonders if he can write at all." Thus "Birth Rate," concluded Gerould, "describes the playwright's own inability to give birth."

BIOGRAPHICAL/CRITICAL SOURCES:

BOOKS

Contemporary Literary Criticism, Gale, Volume 9, 1978, Volume 23, 1983.
Milosz, Czeslaw, editor, *Postwar Polish Poetry,* Penguin, 1970.
Gerould, Daniel, editor, *Twentieth-Century Polish Avant-Garde Drama,* Cornell University Press, 1977.
Rozewicz, Tadeusz, *"The Survivor" and Other Poems,* translation and introduction by Magnus J. Krynski and Robert A. Maguire, Princeton University Press, 1976.

PERIODICALS

Books Abroad, summer, 1965, autumn, 1970, summer, 1972, winter, 1974.
Listener, July 22, 1971.
New Republic, March 19, 1979.
New Statesman, April 8, 1977.
Newsweek, May 9, 1977.
New York Times, April 18, 1977.
Performing Arts Journal, fall, 1976.
Polish Review, spring, 1967, summer, 1970.
Punch, October 1, 1969.

Tulane Drama Review, spring, 1967.
Virginia Quarterly Review, summer, 1977.
World Literature Today, summer, 1977, autumn, 1977, spring, 1978.

*　　　*　　　*

RUBENS, Bernice (Ruth) 1923-

PERSONAL: Born July 26, 1923, in Cardiff, Wales; daughter of Eli and Dorothy (Cohen) Rubens; married Rudi Nassauer (a novelist), December 29, 1947; children: Sharon, Rebecca. *Education:* University of Wales, B.A. (honors in English), 1944. *Politics:* Apolitical. *Religion:* Jewish.

ADDRESSES: Home—16A Belsize Park Gardens, London NW3 4LD, England. *Agent*—Robin Dalton, 18 Elm Tree Rd., London NW8, England.

CAREER: English teacher at grammar school for boys, Birmingham, England, 1948-49; free-lance film director and script writer, 1950—. Fellow, University of Wales, Cardiff, 1982.

AWARDS, HONORS: Blue Ribbon Award, American Documentary Film Festival, 1969, for *Stress;* Booker Prize, 1970, for *The Elected Member;* Welsh Arts Council award, 1976.

WRITINGS:

Set on Edge (novel), Eyre & Spottiswoode, 1960.
Madame Sousatzka (novel), Eyre & Spottiswoode, 1962.
Mate in Three (novel), Eyre & Spottiswoode, 1966.
Chosen People (novel), Atheneum, 1969 (published in England as *The Elected Member,* Eyre & Spottiswoode, 1969).
Sunday Best (novel), Eyre & Spottiswoode, 1971, Summit, 1981.
Go Tell the Lemming (novel), J. Cape, 1973.
I Sent a Letter to My Love (novel), W. H. Allen, 1975; play adaptation by author produced in New Haven, CT, 1978.
The Ponsonby Post (novel), W. H. Allen, 1977.
A Five-Year Sentence, W. H. Allen, 1978, published as *Favours,* Summit, 1979.
Spring Sonata, W. H. Allen, 1979.
Birds of Passage, Hamish Hamilton, 1981, Summit, 1982.
Brothers, Hamish Hamilton, 1983, Delacorte, 1984.
Mr. Wakefield's Crusade, Delacorte, 1985.
Our Father, Delacorte, 1987.
Kingdom Come, Hamish Hamilton, 1990.

Author of screenplays *One of the Family,* 1964, *Call Us by Name,* 1968, *Out of the Mouths,* 1970, *The Spastic Child, Stress,* and *Dear Mum and Dad;* author of television play *Third Party,* 1972.

MEDIA ADAPTATIONS: Madame Sousatzka was adapted as a film for Universal Pictures, 1988.

WORK IN PROGRESS: Adapting Olive Schreiner's *Story of an African Farm* for screen.

SIDELIGHTS: Chosen People, writes Julian Mitchell, "belongs to the familiar genre in which the loving unkindness of Jewish family life is explored with horrified affection. Its theme is peculiarly Jewish: the need for scapegoats and what happens to those 'cold and chosen ones' when the burden of other people's suffering becomes unbearable. But the novel goes beyond its particular Jewishness to say something about humanity at large. It is a remarkable achievement, easily the best of Miss Rubens' four novels so far." "Rubens," David Haworth says, "is one of our finest Jewish writers. She has a large compassion, and an intelligence which makes her compulsively readable. She is deeply committed, yet objectively truthful, about the Jewish world and people she describes." Mitchell faults Rubens for some clumsiness with flashbacks and a lack of conviction outside the home and hospital, "but for the most part she writes extremely well. . . . What most distinguishes this novel is Miss Rubens' touching respect for human weakness. . . . Above all, it is Miss Rubens' tenderness for the mad and broken which makes her book a grave pleasure to read."

Eileen Lottman feels that the story does not stand by itself because the story is "more B movie than Freud." She suggests that the book is "a parable, then—not so much a story of people as a cry of anguish for the human (Jewish) condition. We are all responsible for each other's pain, it says. And yet we cannot help it." Mitchell comments: "We all need scapegoats, she is saying, and we put them in what we genteelly call mental homes and asylums. But no hospital is ever a home and there is no asylum for such people except the imitation death of prolonged, drugged sleep. Everything is not better in the morning." Thomas Lask finds Rubens "a skilled, professional story teller, with a discerning eye for what is moving and effective." Harry Roskolenko writes: "Grecian-Judaic in its tragic inner spirit, the novel has special nuances of wit, irony and economy. You never doubt Rabbi Zweck's total existence, or Norman's—nor the Jewish traditions in another country." Concludes Haworth, "The plea and the uncertainty [of Norman] are Miss Rubens' underlying theme and she has made something excellent from it."

Rubens told *CA:* "I am interested primarily in noncommunication between people—the theme of all my novels. I have been something of a specialist in the making of documentary films about victims, the handicapped. Obviously there is some linkage here. I am interested in the links between sanity, madness, the ever-changing meaning of those terms. I inhabit that limbo, that no fixed abode, loitering there without intent."

BIOGRAPHICAL/CRITICAL SOURCES:

BOOKS

Contemporary Literary Criticism, Gale, Volume 19, 1981, Volume 31, 1985.
Dictionary of Literary Biography, Volume 14: *British Novelists since World War II,* Gale, 1982.

PERIODICALS

Chicago Tribune, December 11, 1987, October 14, 1988.
Chicago Tribune Book World, July 8, 1979, January 5, 1986.
Jewish Quarterly, summer, 1969.
Life, May 16, 1969.
Los Angeles Times, May 12, 1980, May 12, 1982, November 13, 1985, November 17, 1987, October 12, 1988.
Los Angeles Times Book Review, June 1, 1980.
New Statesman, February 14, 1969.
New York Times, May 27, 1969, December 6, 1978, May 10, 1979, November 28, 1987.
New York Times Book Review, May 18, 1969, May 6, 1979, June 20, 1982, March 25, 1984, November 17, 1985, December 27, 1987.
Publishers Weekly, March 16, 1984.
Saturday Review, July 26, 1969.
Times (London), September 24, 1981, March 23, 1989.
Times Literary Supplement, September 11, 1981, July 23, 1982, September 16, 1983, May 31, 1985, March 27, 1987, March 2-8, 1990.
Washington Post, May 8, 1979, December 14, 1987, October 14, 1988.
Washington Post Book World, June 15, 1980, April 8, 1984, January 12, 1986.

RUFFIAN, M.
See HASEK, Jaroslav (Matej Frantisek)

*   *   *

RUKEYSER, Muriel   1913-1980

PERSONAL: Born December 15, 1913, in New York, N.Y.; died February 12, 1980, in New York, N.Y.; daughter of Lawrence B. and Myra (Lyons) Rukeyser; married briefly; children: William L. *Education:* Attended Vassar College and Columbia University, 1930-32; briefly attended Roosevelt Aviation School.

CAREER: Poet, social activist, teacher, biographer, screenwriter, dramatist, translator, and author of children's books. Before World War II, worked for theaters and theater magazines and did office work; after the war, read poetry and taught; Sarah Lawrence College, Bronxville, N.Y., member of faculty, 1946 and 1956-67. House of Photography, vice-president, 1946-60. Co-founder, with Elizabeth Bishop, Mary McCarthy, and Eleanor Clark, of literary magazine *Student Review,* to protest the policies of the *Vassar Review,* c. early 1930s. (Later, the two magazines consolidated.)

MEMBER: PEN American Center (president, 1975-76), Society of American Historians, American Association of University Professors, National Institute of Arts and Letters, Teachers-Writers Collaborative (member of board of directors, 1967-80).

AWARDS, HONORS: Yale Younger Poets Prize, 1935, for *Theory of Flight;* Oscar Blumenthal Prize for poetry, 1940; Harriet Monroe Poetry Award, 1941; grant from National Institute of Arts and Letters, 1942; Guggenheim fellowship, 1943; Levinson Prize for poetry, 1947; D.Litt., Rutgers University, 1961; American Council of Learned Societies fellowship, 1963, for work on biography of Thomas Hariot; translation award (shared with Leif Sjoeberg) of the Swedish Academy in Stockholm, 1967, for *Selected Poems of Gunnar Ekeloef;* Copernicus Award, 1977, in recognition of lifetime contribution to poetry; Shelley Memorial Award, 1977; in 1979, Rukeyser was honored at the annual New York Quarterly Poetry Day for her outstanding contribution to contemporary poetry.

WRITINGS:

POETRY

Theory of Flight, foreword by Stephen Vincent Benet, Yale University Press, 1935, reprinted, AMS Press, 1971.
Mediterranean, Writers and Artists Committee, Medical Bureau to Aid Spanish Democracy, 1938.
U.S. One, Covici, Friede, 1938.
A Turning Wind: Poems, Viking, 1939.
The Soul and Body of John Brown, privately printed, 1940.
Wake Island, Doubleday, 1942.
Beast in View, Doubleday, 1944.
The Green Wave (contains a section of translated poems of Octavio Paz and Rari), Doubleday, 1948.
Orpheus (with the drawing "Orpheus," by Picasso), Centaur Press, 1949.
Elegies, New Directions, 1949.
Selected Poems, New Directions, 1951.
Body of Waking (contains a section of translated poems of Paz), Harper, 1958.
Waterlily Fire: Poems 1935-1962 (including the group of poems entitled "The Speaking Tree"), Macmillan, 1962.
The Outer Banks, Unicorn Press, 1967, 2nd revised edition, 1980.
The Speed of Darkness, Random House, 1968.

Mazes, photography by Milton Charles, Simon & Schuster, 1970.
Twenty-nine Poems, Rapp & Whiting, 1972.
Breaking Open: New Poems (contains translations of Eskimo songs), Random House, 1973.
The Gates: Poems, McGraw, 1976.
The Collected Poems of Muriel Rukeyser, McGraw, 1978.

OTHER

Willard Gibbs (biography), Doubleday, 1942.
"The Middle of the Air" (play), produced in Iowa City, 1945.
The Life of Poetry, Current Books, 1949, reprinted, Morrow, 1974.
(Self-illustrated) *Come Back, Paul* (for children), Harper, 1955.
One Life (biography of Wendell Willkie in poetry, prose, and documents), Simon & Schuster, 1957.
"The Colors of the Day" (play), produced in Poughkeepsie, N.Y., 1961.
I Go Out (for children), Harper, 1962.
(Translator with others) Paz, *Selected Poems of Octavio Paz,* Indiana University Press, 1963, revised edition published as *Early Poems 1935-1955,* New Directions, 1973.
(Translator) Paz, *Sun Stone,* New Directions, 1963.
The Orgy (a three-day journal), Coward, 1965.
Bubbles (for children), edited by Donald Barr, Harcourt, 1967.
(Translator with Leif Sjoeberg) Gunnar Ekeloef, *Selected Poems of Gunnar Ekeloef,* Twayne, 1967.
(Translator) Ekeloef, *Three Poems,* T. Williams, 1967.
The Traces of Thomas Hariot (biography), Random House, 1971.
"Houdini" (play), produced in Lenox, Mass., 1973.
The Poetry and Voice of Muriel Rukeyser (recording), Caedmon, 1977.
More Night (for children), Harper, 1981.
(Translator with Sjoeberg) Ekeloef, *A Molna Elegy: Metamorphoses,* two volumes, Unicorn Press, 1984.

Also author of film scripts "A Place to Live" and "All the Way Home." Translator of Bertolt Brecht's *Uncle Eddie's Moustache,* 1974. Contributor to periodicals, including *Nation, New Republic, Poetry,* and *Saturday Review.*

SIDELIGHTS: Although poet Muriel Rukeyser often provoked a varying critical response to her work, there was never any doubt during her five-decade literary career that a resounding passion was on display. Of her first book, the award-winning collection *Theory of Flight,* W. R. Benet remarked in the *Saturday Review of Literature:* "She is a radical politically, but she writes as a poet not a propagandist. When you hold this book in your hand you hold a living thing." Some forty-five years later, *Gramercy Review* contributor Jascha Kessler labeled Rukeyser "the heroic, the bardic, the romantic," and explained that "poets who are bardic . . . take on mankind and the whole cosmos as the field of their utterance, . . . [and] try to carry whole nations forward through the urgency of their message. . . . Wherever there are hot spots that journalists blow up on the front page—strikes, massacres, revolutions, tortures, wars, prisoners and marches—there is Rukeyser, in the very front line, a spokesperson, or spokespoet perhaps, speaking up loudly for freedom in the world." Though her outspoken nature obviously displeased certain critics, Rukeyser remained a "spokespoet" all of her adult life.

In the critical commentary on Rukeyser's several poetry collections, such phrases as "social activist" or "poet of social protest" are common. Alberta Turner notes in the *Dictionary of Literary Biography* that Rukeyser was a native of New York City and "by her own choice her life was not bland or sheltered." In the 1930s Rukeyser attended Vassar College and became literary editor of the leftist undergraduate journal *Student Review*. As a reporter for this journal, Rukeyser covered the 1932 Scottsboro trial in Alabama in which nine black youths were accused of raping two white girls. According to Wolfgang Saxon in his *New York Times* obituary of Rukeyser, the Scottsboro incident was the basis of Rukeyser's poem "The Trial" and "may have been the genesis of her commitment to the cause of the underdog and the unjustly condemned."

Following the Scottsboro trial, Rukeyser moved within very broad social circles for the remainder of her years. Among other things, she supported the Spanish Loyalists during the Spanish Civil War; she was once jailed in Washington for her protest of the Vietnam War; and, as president of the American Center for PEN, she travelled to South Korea in the 1970s to rally against the death sentence of poet Kim Chi-Ha, the incident which later became the framework of one of Rukeyser's last poems, "The Gates." Since she aligned her creative capacities so closely with the current events of her day, a number of reviewers believe the history of the United States for several decades can be culled from Rukeyser's poetry.

Though frequently incensed by worldly injustices—as is apparent in both the subject matter and tone of her writing—Rukeyser had an optimism that at times surprised her critics. According to Roy B. Hoffman in his *Village Voice* review of *The Collected Poems of Muriel Rukeyser*, Rukeyser's distress with injustice was "mingled with a romantic's belief in the perfectibility of the universe, and a young patriot's belief in the perfectibility of her nation. . . . Perhaps it is this belief of Rukeyser's—in a radiant epiphany behind the pain of conflict—that both dates her and makes her refreshing to read. Her idealism is unmarked by heavy irony, cynicism, or an intricacy of wit that characterizes much contemporary poetry." Because of her optimism, reviewers compared Rukeyser's style to that of nineteenth-century American poet Walt Whitman. In an assessment of *Waterlily Fire: Poems, 1935-1962*, a *Virginia Quarterly Review* critic explained that "like Whitman, Muriel Rukeyser has so much joy that it is not to be contained in regular verse but comes out in lines that are rugged and soaring." In much the same vein, *New York Times Book Review*'s Richard Eberhart judged Rukeyser's poems in general to be "primordial and torrential. They pour out excitements of a large emotional force, taking in a great deal of life and giving out profound realizations of the significance of being. . . . She belongs to the Whitman school of large confrontations and outpourings."

In opposition to those who appreciated the poet's ability to merge her outrage with hope, some reviewers considered Rukeyser's optimism a weakness or a mere posturing. For instance, Thomas Stumpf in the *Carolina Quarterly* found that Rukeyser's later collection *Breaking Open* contains an "indefatigable optimism, hand-clasping brotherhood, and love for all ethnic groups . . . [which] feed[s] a poetry that is without muscle. . . . It is poetry that is fatally in love with exhortations and public promises, with first person posturings." What Stumpf ultimately detected in this particular collection was "the stuff of bathos." In turn, Louise Bogan criticized Rukeyser for creating a world in her poetry that, in reality, "could not last overnight." In her book *Selected Criticism: Prose, Poetry*, Bogan described the world in Rukeyser's *A Turning Wind* as "deficient in a sense of human life. . . . Her world is at once too nightmare and too noble. . . . She does not realize that such a world could not last overnight, that the sense of injustice is only relevant when applied to living human beings. . . . [There] is something hid-

eously oversimplified in crude oppositions and blind idealism." Apart from complaints such as these, many reviewers fondly supported Rukeyser's optimism, an optimism grounded in what Kenneth Rexroth had labeled in a *Los Angeles Times* essay "the Community of Love."

In accordance with her impassioned nature, many of Rukeyser's earlier poems contain an intrepidness and exhortative voice that will surely be remembered. "Her intense tone, angry but also tender, jubilant, even exalted, which was to be dominant throughout her career, [was] already apparent in her first book," stated Turner; in it "she makes little use of silence." Some critics were inspired by this vigor. *Poetry* contributor John Malcolm Brinnin explained that with the publication of *Theory of Flight*, winner of the Yale Younger Poets Prize, "American poetry found its first full-blown expression of the rebellious temper that prevailed on American campuses and among the younger intellectuals. Its success was immediate. . . . Rukeyser was praised for the ruggedness of her technique, her experimentalism, and for the powerful utterance which, from a woman, seemed unique." Other critics could do without her brashness. "This passionate, innocent young woman . . . talks so noisily and so hurriedly that it never occurs to her that other people have seen these things before, and have learned to speak more calmly," wrote Michael Roberts in his *Spectator* review of *Theory of Flight*. When Turner remarked in her *Dictionary of Literary Biography* essay that Rukeyser would probably *not* be remembered as one of this century's greatest American poets, she based this statement, at least in part, on her belief that Rukeyser "wrote too much that was intense but fuzzy, trusting intensity to create a magic rather than selecting and juxtaposing fresh powerful words or images. But at times she was able to find the right image." Other critics of Rukeyser's early collections felt stimulated by her energy but, like Turner, professed that Rukeyser's methods needed perfecting. As one *Kirkus Reviews* contributor put it, "[Rukeyser] has achieved considerable reputation among those to whom lucidity is not a necessary factor."

Although Rukeyser's early poetic voice tended toward that of a sloganist, most critics sense that with time Rukeyser was able to develop greater sophistication and control in her poetry. Whereas Anne Stevenson commented in her *New York Times Book Review* critique of *The Collected Poems* that Rukeyser "seems to have been born poetically full-grown," others considered various developments in Rukeyser's craft important enough to analyze in their reviews. Brinnin, for instance, explains that "one of the most interesting phases of the transformation of the social poet in years of stress is the change in his use of language. In the case of Muriel Rukeyser, it moves from that of simple declarative exhortation, in the common phrases of the city man, to that of a gnarled, intellectual, almost private observation. In her earlier usage, images are apt to be simple and few; the whole approach is apt to be through the medium of urban speech. In the latter work, images become those of the psychologist, or of the surrealist, charged with meaning and prevalent everywhere." Nevertheless, her conviction was still strong, Brinnin added. Along the same lines, Turner found the later Rukeyser more relaxed, less rhetorical, "and though the poems still end firmly with clearly stated, strong opinions, they are less likely to pummel their readers."

Another change involved the movement toward shorter poems in contrast to the cluster poems, or collage poems, that were somewhat of a trademark for Rukeyser. These shorter poems centered on a single theme but developed in "separate, autonomous bits, [and] varied in line length and stanza form[,] . . . the parts of each book roll[ing] toward the reader in a series of waves, each of which crashes firmly," explained Turner. This movement toward more concrete images and shorter poems coincided rather closely with Rukeyser's increased devotion to the personal as well as to the political in her poetry.

Even though Rukeyser would continue to write poems that attempted to "carry whole nations forward through the urgency of their message," political poetry was not the be-all and end-all for Rukeyser, who explored a myriad of topics during her literary career. Many of her poems, particularly after her first few collections, were very personal, speaking on her role as a mother and daughter, speaking on sexuality, on creativity, on the poetic process, speaking also on illness and death. One of her poems from *The Gates,* "Resurrection of the Right Side," details the human body's slow recovery after a debilitating stroke: "I begin to climb the mountain on my mouth,/ word by stammer, walk stammered, the lurching deck of earth./ Left-right with none of my own rhythms." In her book *Beast in View,* the poem "Ajanta" is "purportedly" a poem about painted caves in India, "but when she wrote it," noted Rexroth, "Muriel had never been to India. . . . 'Ajanta' is an exploration . . . of her own interior—in every sense. It is the interior of her mind as a human being, as a poet, and as a woman. It is the interior of her self as her own flesh. It is her womb." Virginia R. Terris goes to some length in her *American Poetry Review* article to chronicle Rukeyser's movement from the social to the personal, or from theory to actual experience. Regarding Rukeyser's biography of business magnate Wendell Willkie entitled *One Life* and comprised partly of poems, Terris felt Rukeyser was "able to focus singlemindedly on what she [had] only tentatively explored in earlier volumes. . . . Although Rukeyser [was] exploring many of the themes she had earlier explored—family tensions, social and technological issues and women exploited—she [moved] into experiences that [were] hers uniquely."

In the same way that Rukeyser's poetry was one of variety—for it could be labeled many things: romantic, political, feminist, erotic, Whitmanesque—her oeuvre explored a variety of genres. Although known particularly for her poetry, Rukeyser wrote biographical material (which was sometimes in the form of poetry), children's books, plays, and television scripts, and she also translated poetry from the Swedish, French, German, Spanish, and Italian. In addition, she taught and read her poetry at institutions nationwide.

Poetry aside, Rukeyser's biographical work received the most critical attention. As Jane Cooper noted in the *Washington Post Book World,* Rukeyser "loved science and history and modern technology, enjoying their puzzles and solvings much as she enjoyed the puzzles and solvings of poetic form." Thus, the fact that Rukeyser wrote about individuals other than the literary and artistic should not be too surprising. While it is true that Rukeyser wrote memorable poems about the German lithographer Kaethe Kollwitz, American composer Charles Ives, and mythological figures like Orpheus, at the same time she profiled New England eccentric Lord Timothy Dexter; nineteenth-century mathematician Willard Gibbs; English mathematician and scientist Thomas Hariot; and, as previously noted, lawyer and business executive Wendell Willkie, who ran for president on the 1940 Republican party ticket. Additionally, Rukeyser wrote full-length biographies of the latter three men.

According to Terris, one of Rukeyser's intentions behind writing biographies of nonliterary persons was to find a meeting place between science and poetry. In an analysis of Rukeyser's expository work *The Life of Poetry,* Terris notes that Rukeyser was of the opinion that in the West, poetry and science are wrongly considered to be in opposition to one another. Thus, writes Terris, "Rukeyser [set] forth her theoretical acceptance of science . . . [and pointed] out the many parallels between [poetry and science]—unity within themselves, symbolic language, selectivity, the use of the imagination in formulating concepts and in execution. Both, she believe[d], ultimately contribute to one another."

Some critics were skeptical of the poet's attempts at interpreting history, but for others Rukeyser's poetic angle brought something more to the reader than could be expected from a biography in the strict sense. Regarding Rukeyser's account entitled *The Traces of Thomas Hariot, Washington Post Book World* critic Vincent Cronin stated: "By her carefully controlled imaginative sympathy, by the dazzling range of her learning, and above all by the poetry of her style she leads the reader further than he is ever likely to go into the speculative seventeenth century, where daring men were trying, on half-a-dozen fronts, to break through into what was to become the modern world. . . . From now on, thanks to this highly enjoyable trail-blazing book, Thomas Hariot will never be 'just another minor Elizabethan.' " *Commonweal* reviewer E. L. Keyes viewed Rukeyser's biography of Willard Gibbs as an "intelligible collation of a mountain of mysteries."

Impassioned, self-confident, eclectic, a poet of powerful expression, a poet of the political and the personal—these and similar phrases have characterized the life and work of Muriel Rukeyser for decades. Although the critics in Rukeyser's earlier, more prolific decades seldom agreed on the value of her achievements, a new generation of reviewers had come along by the time Rukeyser published *The Collected Poems;* and in looking at the totality of her accomplishments, these critics found cause for rejoicing. A year before Rukeyser's death, Hoffman concluded that "poems like 'The Poem as Mask' make me wonder if Muriel Rukeyser is not our greatest living American poet. *The Collected Poems* . . . enable us to see a breadth of history, energy, and experience rarely matched in American letters." As for Kessler, "any reading of [Rukeyser's] poems will excite the best and most ingenious impulses of . . . people everywhere, who want goodness and freedom and love in the world and in their own personal lives. Rukeyser remained faithful and consistent with her own youthful visions, and all this work [in *The Collected Poems*] . . . testifies to that."

BIOGRAPHICAL/CRITICAL SOURCES:

BOOKS

Bogan, Louise, *Selected Criticism: Prose, Poetry,* Noonday Press, 1955.
Contemporary Literary Criticism, Gale, Volume 6, 1976, Volume 10, 1979, Volume 15, 1980, Volume 27, 1986.
Dictionary of Literary Biography, Volume 48: *American Poets, 1880-1945, Second Series,* Gale, 1986.
Gould, Jean, *Modern American Women Poets,* Dodd, 1985.
Jarrell, Randall, *Poetry and the Age,* Knopf, 1953.
Kertesz, Louise, *The Poetic Vision of Muriel Rukeyser,* Louisiana State University Press, 1979.
Laughlin, James, editor, *New Directions in Prose and Poetry,* New Directions (Connecticut), 1953.
Rukeyser, Muriel, *The Gates: Poems,* McGraw, 1976.

PERIODICALS

American Poetry Review, May-June, 1974, May-June, 1978.
Best Sellers, April, 1977.
Books of the Times, August, 1979.
Book World, April 4, 1971.

Carolina Quarterly, spring, 1974.
Feminist Studies, fall, 1975.
Gramercy Review, autumn-winter, 1979-80.
Harper's, February, 1971.
Kirkus Reviews, December 15, 1947.
Los Angeles Times, March 2, 1980.
Ms., April, 1974.
Nation, February 23, 1963, March 15, 1965.
Newsweek, March 29, 1971.
New York Times, August 22, 1979.
New York Times Book Review, February 28, 1965, June 23, 1968, April 18, 1971, February 11, 1979.
Parnassus: Poetry in Review, spring-summer, 1979.
Partisan Review, Volume 47, number 4, 1980.
Poetry, May, 1936, January, 1943.
Saturday Review of Literature, December 7, 1935, August 10, 1940, March 11, 1950.
Spectator, May 1, 1936.
Times Literary Supplement, May 19, 1972.
Village Voice, November 22, 1976, February 26, 1979.
Virginia Quarterly Review, winter, 1963.
Washington Post Book World, January 21, 1979.

OBITUARIES:

PERIODICALS

Chicago Tribune, February 15, 1980.
Newsweek, February 25, 1980.
New York Times, February 14, 1980.
Time, February 25, 1980.

* * *

RULFO, Juan 1918-1986

PERSONAL: Born May 16, 1918, in Sayula, Jalisco, Mexico; died of a heart attack, January 7, 1986, in Mexico City, Mexico; married in 1948; wife's name, Clara; children: four.

ADDRESSES: Home—Mexico City, Mexico. *Office*—Centro Mexicano de Escritores, Luis G. Inclan, no. 2709, Col Villa de Cortes, 03130 Mexico 13, D.F., Mexico.

CAREER: Worked as an accountant and in several clerical positions; on staff of Mexican Immigration Department, beginning 1935, processed the crews of impounded German ships during World War II; member of sales staff, B. F. Goodrich Rubber Co., 1947-54; member of Papaloapan Commission, 1955; National Institute for Indigenous Studies, Mexico City, Mexico, beginning 1962, became director of editorial department. Adviser to writers at Centro Mexicano de Escritores.

MEMBER: Centro Mexicano de Escritores (fellow).

AWARDS, HONORS: Rockefeller grants, 1953 and 1954; Guggenheim fellowship, 1968; National Prize for Letters (Mexico), 1970; Principe de Asturias award (Spain), 1983.

WRITINGS:

FICTION

El llano en llamas y otros cuentos, Fondo de Cultura Economica, 1953, translation by George D. Schade published as *The Burning Plain and Other Stories,* University of Texas Press, 1967, 2nd Spanish edition, corrected and enlarged, Fondo de Cultura Economica, 1970.
Pedro Paramo (novel), Fondo de Cultura Economica, 1955, translation by Lysander Kemp published as *Pedro Paramo: A Novel of Mexico,* Grove, 1959.
El gallo de oro y otros textos para cine, Ediciones Era, 1980.

OMNIBUS VOLUMES

Obra completa, Biblioteca Ayacucho, 1977.
Antologia personal, Nueva Imagen, 1978.

CONTRIBUTOR

Aberlardo Gomez Benoit, editor, *Antologia contemporanea del cuento hispano-americano* (title means "A Contemporary Anthology of the Hispanic-American Story"), Instituto Latinoamericano de Vinculacion Cultural, 1964.
Cronicas de Latinoamericano, Editorial Jorge Alvarez, 1968.

OTHER

Juan Rulfo: Autobiografia armada, compiled by Reina Roffe, Ediciones Corregidor, 1973.
(With others) *Juan Rulfo: Homenaje nacional,* with photographs by Rulfo, Instituto Nacional de Bellas Artes (Mexico City), 1980, 2nd edition published as *Inframundo: El Mexico de Juan Rulfo,* edited by Juan J. Bremer, Ediciones del Norte (Hanover, N.H.), 1983, translation by Jo Anne Engelbert published as *Inframundo: The Mexico of Juan Rulfo,* Ediciones del Norte, 1983.

Also author of television scripts and film adaptations, beginning 1954. Collaborator with Juan Jose Arreola on the review *Pan.*

WORK IN PROGRESS: La cordillera (title means "The Mountain Range"), a novel.

SIDELIGHTS: The late Mexican novelist Juan Rulfo is included in what Alan Riding called in the *New York Times Magazine* "the contemporary Latin American literary boom." Rulfo and such writers as Jorge Luis Borges, Julio Cortazar, and Carlos Fuentes wrote imaginative fiction that was made available through translation to readers in the United States during the fifties, sixties, and early seventies. Unlike the other writers, who prolifically turned out stories and novels, Rulfo established his reputation with a solitary collection of stories, *El llano en llamas y otros cuentos*—translated as *The Burning Plain and Other Stories*—and one novel, *Pedro Paramo.*

Two characteristics of these Latin American writers were their special affinity for innovative narrative techniques and their style of interweaving the historical with the marvelous, called magic realism; both qualities are often mentioned by reviewers of Rulfo's work. In his introduction to *The Burning Plain and Other Stories,* George D. Schade used the story "Macario"—included in the collection—as an example of Rulfo's narrative style. "In 'Macario,'" Schade observed, "the past and present mingle chaotically, and frequently the most startling associations of ideas are juxtaposed, strung together by conjunctions which help to paralyze the action and stop the flow of time in the present." In *Into the Mainstream: Conversations with Latin-American Writers,* Luis Harss and Barbara Dohmann comment on the story "The Man," noting the multiple points of view and foreshadowing used to heighten the reader's identification with the protagonist.

The narrative devices mentioned by Schade, Harss and Dohmann are also found in Rulfo's *Pedro Paramo,* a novel which Schade called "a bold excursion into modern techniques of writing." Using flashbacks, interior monologues and dialogues, and atemporal time sequences, Rulfo creates what Enrique Anderson-Imbert claimed in *Spanish-American Literature: A History* is a "story . . . told in loops, forward, backward, [and] to the sides." The narrative technique demands a lot of the reader, and the story in itself is also difficult. Halfway through the novel, for example, the reader realizes that all the characters are dead; the story all along has been the remembered history of ghosts conversing from their graves.

Startling as this revelation is, the mingling of death and life is typical of Mexican culture. Commenting in a *Nation* essay, Earl Shorris noted: "Everywhere in the novel, death is present: not the hidden, feared death we know in the Unites States but Mexican death, the death that is neither the beginning nor the end, the death that comes and goes in the round of time." Shorris observed that the constant reminders of death in Mexican life destroy "the distinction between [this] life" and the next. This hazy line between life and death accentuates that author's deliberately ambiguous delineation of scenes, narrators, and past and present time. The technical difficulties with which Rulfo confronts the reader become the framework for what Kessel Schwartz called in *A New History of Spanish-American Fiction* "an ambiguous and magical world, a kind of timeless fable of life and death" where historical facts—references to actual events in Mexican history—and fictive details are fused.

In his analysis of *Pedro Paramo* appearing in *Tradition and Renewal: Essays on Twentieth-Century Latin American Literature and Culture,* Luis Leal observed that while Rulfo's style was experimental, it was also firmly rooted in the historical reality of Mexico. Leal wrote: "The scenes are juxtaposed, united only by the central theme and lyrical motifs. . . . The novel, a mixture of realism and fantasy . . . has been created through the use of images, which, although poetic, are structured in a language that is characteristic of the countryside."

Rulfo's sparse, dry prose reflects the parched, stark Mexican landscape. Harss and Dohmann remarked: "His language is as frugal as his world, reduced almost to pure heartbeat. . . . He sings the swan song of blighted regions gangrened by age, where misery has opened wounds that burn under an eternal midday sun, where a pestilent fate has turned areas that were once rolling meadows and grasslands into fetid open graves. . . . He writes with a sharp edge, carving each word out of hard rock, like an inscription on a tombstone." According to Irving A. Leonard in the *Saturday Review,* "the bleak, harsh surroundings" Rulfo described with his "bare phrases" reflected his "pessimistic view of man's condition. Murder, incest, adultery, death overpowering life, violence in varied forms are predominant themes, unrelieved by humor or love."

Although Rulfo published a collection of film scripts and worked on the manuscript for another novel, *La cordillera,* for the rest of his life, further success as a writer eluded him. While a London *Times* reporter noted that *Pedro Paramo* "will be remembered as a unique achievement," the same writer believed that Rulfo himself seemed content to be known merely as "the master who could not write a second masterpiece."

MEDIA ADAPTATIONS: Pedro Paramo was made into a film in the 1960s.

BIOGRAPHICAL/CRITICAL SOURCES:

BOOKS

Anderson-Imbert, Enrique, *Spanish-American Literature: A History,* Volume II: *1910-1961,* 2nd edition, revised and updated by Elaine Malley, Wayne State University Press, 1969.
Contemporary Literary Criticism, Volume 8, Gale, 1978.
Forster, Merlin H., editor, *Tradition and Renewal: Essays on Twentieth-Century Latin American Literature and Culture,* University of Illinois Press, 1975.

Harss, Luis, and Barbara Dohmann, *Into the Mainstream: Conversations with Latin-American Writers,* Harper, 1967.
Rulfo, Juan, *The Burning Plain and Other Stories,* translation by George D. Schade, University of Texas Press, 1967.
Schwartz, Kessel, *A New History of Spanish-American Fiction,* Volume II, University of Miami Press, 1971.

PERIODICALS

Christian Science Monitor, January 4, 1968.
English Journal, January, 1974.
Hispania, December, 1971, September, 1974, March, 1975.
Nation, May 15, 1982.
National Observer, March 24, 1973.
New York Herald Tribune Book Review, August 2, 1959.
New York Times Book Review, June 7, 1959.
New York Times Magazine, March 13, 1983.
San Francisco Chronicle, August 30, 1959.
Saturday Review, June 22, 1968.
Times (London), January 10, 1986.
Times Literary Supplement, February 5, 1960.

OBITUARIES:

PERIODICALS

AB Bookman's Weekly, February 17, 1986.
Los Angeles Times, January 9, 1986.
New York Times, January 9, 1986.
Times (London), January 10, 1986.
Washington Post, January 11, 1986.

*   *   *

RUSHDIE, (Ahmed) Salman 1947-

PERSONAL: Born June 19, 1947, in Bombay, India; son of Anis Ahmed (in business) and Negin (Butt) Rushdie; married Clarissa Luard (in publishing), May 22, 1976 (marriage dissolved, 1987); married Marianne Wiggins (an author), 1988; children: (first marriage) Zafar (son). *Education:* King's College, Cambridge, M.A. (history; with honors), 1968.

ADDRESSES: Agent—Deborah Rodgers Ltd., 49 Blenheim Crescent, London W11, England; and 19 Ravely St., London NW5 2HX, England.

CAREER: Actor with the Fringe Theatre, London, England, 1968-69; free-lance advertising copywriter, 1970-73, part-time, 1976-80; writer, 1975—. Executive member of Camden Committee for Community Relations, 1976-83; member of British Film Institute Production Board; member of advisory board, Institute of Contemporary Arts.

MEMBER: International PEN, Royal Society of Literature (fellow), Society of Authors, National Book League (member of executive committee).

AWARDS, HONORS: Booker McConnell Prize for Fiction from Booker McConnell Ltd., literary award from English Speaking Union, both 1981, and James Tait Black Memorial Prize, 1982, all for *Midnight's Children;* awarded Arts Council Literature bursary, 1981; Prix du Meilleur Livre Etranger, 1984; *The Satanic Verses* was named to the 1988 Booker Prize shortlist for fiction; Whitbread Prize, 1988, for *The Satanic Verses.*

WRITINGS:

Grimus (novel), Gollancz, 1975, Overlook Press, 1979.
Midnight's Children (novel), Knopf, 1981.
Shame (novel), Knopf, 1983.

The Jaguar Smile: A Nicaraguan Journey (nonfiction), Viking, 1987.
The Satanic Verses (novel), Viking, 1988.

Also author of television screenplays "The Painter and the Pest," 1985, and "The Riddle of Midnight," 1988. Contributor to magazines and newspapers, including *New Statesman, Atlantic Monthly, Granta, New York Times,* and *London Times.*

SIDELIGHTS: Salman Rushdie's first published novel, *Grimus,* tells the story of an American Indian who receives the gift of immortality and begins an odyssey to find life's meaning. The work initially attracted attention among science fiction readers and writers, including Mel Tilden, who called the book "engrossing and often wonderful" in a *Times Literary Supplement* review. Tilden determined the book to be "science of the word," recognizing at the same time that it "is one of those novels some people will say is too good to be science fiction, even though it contains other universes, dimensional doorways, alien creatures and more than one madman." Although many critics disagreed on the work's genre—calling it fable, fantasy, political satire, and magical realism—most agreed with David Wilson's assessment in *Times Literary Supplement* that *Grimus* was "an ambitious, strikingly confident first novel" and that Rushdie was an author to watch.

Rushdie turned to India, his birthplace, for the subject of his second book. An allegory, *Midnight's Children* chronicles the history of modern India throughout the lives of 1,001 children born within the country's first hour of independence from Great Britain on August 15, 1947. Saleem Sinai, the novel's protagonist-narrator, is one of two males born at the precise moment of India's independence—the stroke of midnight—in a Bombay nursing home. Moonfaced, stained with birthmarks, and possessed of a "huge cucumber of a nose," Sinai becomes by a twist of fate "the chosen child of midnight." He later explains to the reader that a nurse, in "her own revolutionary act," switched the newborn infants. The illegitimate son of a Hindu street singer's wife and a departing British colonist was given to a prosperous Muslim couple and raised as Saleem Sinai; his midnight twin, called Shiva, was given to an impoverished Hindu street clown who, first cuckolded and then widowed by childbirth, was left to raise a son—twice not his—on the streets of Bombay. Thus, in accordance with class privilege mistakenly bestowed, Sinai's birth was heralded by fireworks and celebrated in newspapers; a congratulatory letter from Jawaharlal Nehru portended his future. "You are the newest bearer of the ancient face of India which is also eternally young," wrote the prime minister. "We shall be watching over your life with the closest attention; it will be, in a sense, the mirror of our own."

The novel begins at a point more than thirty years after the simultaneous births of Sinai and independent India. Awaiting death in the corner of a Bombay pickle factory where he is employed, Sinai—prematurely aged, impotent, and mutilated by a personal history that parallels that of his country—tells his life story to Padma, an illiterate working girl who loves and tends him. Sinai begins his tale by relating thirty-two years of family history preceding his arrival into the world. He then reveals the circumstances and irony of his birth and includes an incredible account of his discovery, at age nine, of the extraordinary telepathic powers that enabled him to realize the events of his birth and to communicate with his multitudinous midnight siblings: the remaining 580 offspring (reduced from the original 1,001 by India's high child mortality rate) of the country's first hour of independence.

All of midnight's children, discloses Sinai, were possessed of magical gifts. "Among the children were infants with the powers of transmutation, flight, prophecy, wizardry." "The closer to midnight our birth-times were, the greater our gifts," he tells Padma. "To Shiva [destined to become India's most decorated war hero as well as Sinai's mortal enemy] the hour had given the gifts of war," he explains. "And to me, the greatest gift of all—the ability to look into the hearts and minds of men."

Sinai and the rest of midnight's children "incorporate the stupendous Indian past, with its pantheon, its epics, and its wealth of folklore," summarized *New York Times* critic Robert Towers, "while at the same time playing a role in the tumultuous Indian present." "The plot of this novel is complicated enough, and flexible enough, to smuggle Saleem into every major event in the subcontinent's past thirty years," agreed Clark Blaise in the *New York Times Book Review.* "It is . . . a novel of India's growing up; from its special, gifted infancy to its very ordinary, drained adulthood. It is a record of betrayal and corruption, the loss of ideals, culminating with 'the Widow's' Emergency rule." "Saleem . . . *lives* India," Bill Buford elaborated in a *New Statesman* review, "and his life chronicles the movement from the euphoric celebration of independence to . . . the dulled recognition of state repression."

Although *Midnight's Children* "spans the recent history, both told and untold, of both India and Pakistan as well as the birth of Bangladesh," commented Anita Desai in the *Washington Post Book World,* "one hesitates to call the novel 'historical' for Rushdie believes . . . that while individual history does not make sense unless seen against its national background, neither does national history make sense unless seen in the form of individual lives and histories." Rushdie "proceeds from his belief that 'to understand one life you have to swallow the whole world,' " Buford similarly observed. And Rushdie's "central point is clear: you cannot separate the individual from the environment." Describing Sinai in a *Commonweal* review, Una Chaudhuri carried Buford's assessment one step further. "Saleem Sinai is India," she ventured. "He has been handcuffed to history."

Midnight's Children was almost unanimously well received, claiming England's most exalted literary award, the Booker McConnell Prize for fiction, in 1981. It was variously praised as comic, exuberant, ambitious, and stylistically brilliant. Chaudhuri hailed it as "a literary event—a novel of international importance," and Towers called it "an extraordinary novel, . . . one of the most important to come out of the English-speaking world in this generation." "In this memorable novel, Rushdie pleases the senses and the heart," applauded Phyllis Bimbaum in *Saturday Review,* and *New Yorker* critic V. S. Pritchett deemed the book "irresistible." More than one critic described the book as a "tour de force."

The novel also elicited favorable comparisons to Laurence Sterne's *Tristram Shandy,* Gabriel Garcia Marquez's *One Hundred Years of Solitude,* Guenter Grass's *The Tin Drum,* Saul Bellow's *The Adventures of Augie March,* Louis-Ferdinand Celine's *Death on the Installment Plan,* and V. S. Naipaul's *India: A Wounded Civilization.* And yet, opined Clark Blaise, "It would be a disservice to Salman Rushdie's very original genius to dwell on literary analogues and ancestors. This is a book to accept on its own terms, and an author to welcome into world company."

Like *Midnight's Children,* Rushdie's third book, *Shame,* blends history, myth, politics, and fantasy in a novel at once serious and comic. "A sort of modern fairytale," describes the author, the novel is set in a country that "is not Pakistan, or not quite"; and it explores such issues as the uses and abuses of power and the relationship between shame and violence.

The idea for *Shame,* reported interviewer Ronald Hayman in *Books and Bookmen,* grew out of Rushdie's interest in the Pakistani concept of *sharam.* An Urdu word, *sharam* is apparently untranslatable, conveying a hybrid of sentiments including, according to the author, "embarrassment, discomfiture, decency, modesty, shyness, the sense of having an ordained place in the world." It speaks to a long tradition of honor that permits, and at times even insists upon, seemingly unconscionable acts. In developing this concept, Rushdie told Hayman, he began "seeing shame in places where [he] hadn't originally seen it." He explained: "I'd be thinking about Pakistani politics; and I'd find there were elements there that I could use. I had a feeling of stumbling on something quite central to the codes by which we live." Rushdie elaborated in a *New York Times Book Review* interview with Michael T. Kaufman: "There are two axes—honor and shame, which is the conventional axis, the one along which the culture moves, and this other axis of shame and shamelessness, which deals with morality and the lack of morality. 'Shame' is at the hub of both axes." He told Amanda Smith in *Publishers Weekly,* "Shame, honor, pride—those three [are] somewhere very close to the center of how we organize our experiences."

Shame and shamelessness are the roots of violence, concludes the novelist. He offers as an example the newspaper account of a Pakistani father who "murdered his only child, a daughter, because by making love to a white boy she had brought such dishonour upon her family that only her blood could wash away the stain." Rushdie comments that while he found the story shocking, equally shocking was the fact that he could understand it. "We who have grown up on a diet of honour and shame can still grasp what must seem unthinkable to peoples living in the aftermath of the death of God and of tragedy: that men will sacrifice their dearest love on the implacable altars of pride."

Rushdie develops his theme of shame and violence in a plot so complex and densely populated with characters that it caused Robert Towers to comment that "it is probably easier to play croquet (as in 'Alice in Wonderland') with flamingos as mallets and hedgehogs as balls than to give a coherent plot summary of 'Shame.' " The novel's storyline spans three generations and centers on the lives and families of two men—Raza Hyder, a celebrated general, and Iskander Harappa, a millionaire playboy. Their life-death struggle, played out against the political backdrop of their country, is based on recent Pakistani history. The two characters themselves are based on real-life Pakistani President Zia ul-Haq and former Prime Minister Zulfikar Ali Bhutto, who was deposed by Zia in 1977 and eventually executed.

Sufiya Zinobia, the novel's heroine, is the embodiment of both shame and violence. The daughter of Raza Hyder, a future military dictator who longed for a son, she is, explains Rushdie, the fictional reincarnation of the young girl who died to succor her father's shame. Sufiya's shame is born with her and is evidenced by the newborn baby's crimson blush. Later, as she absorbs the unfelt shame of others, Sufiya's blushes take on such intensity that they boil her bath water and burn the lips of those who kiss her. Eventually, the heat of her shame incubates violence, turning Sufiya into a monster capable of wrenching the heads off of grown men. The incarnation of an entire nation's shame, judged Una Chaudhuri, "Sufiya Zinobia is the utterly convincing and terrifying product of a culture lost in falsehood and corruption."

The novel's marginal hero is Sufiya Zinobia's husband, Omar Khayyam Shakil. Introduced at length at the beginning of the book, he disappears for long periods of time thereafter. "I am a peripheral man," he admits shamelessly; "other people have been the principal actors in my life story." The son of an unknown father and one of three sisters, all claiming to be his mother, Shakil was "scorned by the townspeople for his shameful origins," observed Margo Jefferson in the *Voice Literary Supplement,* and "he developed a defensive shamelessness." Omar Khayyam Shakil feels himself "a fellow who is not even the hero of his own life; a man born and raised in the condition of being out of things."

Rushdie's choice of a "not-quite hero" for a "not-quite country addresses an issue that Chaudhuri felt to be central to the book's theme. "Peripherality," she postulated, "is the essence of this land's deepest psychology and the novel's true hero: Shame. It is the doom of those who cannot exist except as reflections of other's perceptions, of those who are unable to credit the notion of individual moral autonomy." Shakil's peripherality is demonstrable throughout his life. He suffers from a debilitating fear of being on or near the edge of things. Convinced that he lives at the end of the world,' he is forever afraid of falling off into oblivion. "He grows dizzy whenever he approaches the border of his country," noted *New York Times's* Christopher Lehmann-Haupt. And Jefferson pointed out that even his name, Omar Khayyam, is that of "a poet unloved in his own land, and known largely in translation." Shakil also straddles two cultures and "embraces Western logic by becoming a medical doctor," added Lehmann-Haupt, who concluded that "the tragedy of 'Shame' lies both in the evasion of historical destiny and in embracing that destiny too violently."

Shame met with enthusiastic critical reception and was favorably compared to *Midnight's Children.* An achievement such as *Midnight's Children* "casts a long shadow from which its successor must struggle to escape if it is to find light and space for its own development," remarked Robert Towers. "Aware of this, Mr. Rushdie has moved the setting of his new novel from India proper . . . and has erected a less imposing, though equally fantastic edifice." Nominated for the 1983 Booker McConnell Prize, *Shame* "does for Pakistan what Mr. Rushdie's equally remarkable . . . 'Midnight's Children' did for India," applauded Lehmann-Haupt.

After the publication of *Shame* and the author's next book, *The Jaguar Smile: A Nicaraguan Journey,* a nonfiction account of the political and social conditions that Rushdie observed during his 1986 trip to Nicaragua, the author published a novel that caused such wide-spread furor as to make him a household word even to those unfamiliar with his earlier work. *The Satanic Verses* outraged Muslims around the world who were infuriated by what they believed to be insults to their religion. The book was banned in a dozen countries and caused demonstrations and riots in India, Pakistan, and South Africa, in which a number of people were killed or injured. Charging Rushdie with blasphemy, the late Iranian leader Ayatollah Ruhollah Khomeini proclaimed that the author and his publisher should be executed, and multimillion dollar bounties were offered to anyone who could carry out this decree. Western nations, supporting Rushdie's right to freedom of speech, were incensed by Iran's action and international relations were strained.

The objections to his novel regard sections of the book in which Rushdie writes about a religion that resembles Islam, whose prophet is named Mahound (a derisive epithet for Mohammed). Specifically, offense was taken to scenes in which a scribe named Salman alters the prophet's dictation, thus bringing into question the validity of the Koran, the holy book of the Muslims; and throughout the book many Muslims claim that Rushdie also repeatedly makes irreverent use of sacred names. *Observer* contributor Blake Morrison explains that to many Muslims Rushdie "has transgressed by treating the Holy Word as myth . . . not truth; by treating the Prophet as a fallible human rather than as a deity; and above all by bringing a skeptical, playful, punning intelligence to bear on a religion which, in these fundamentalist times, is not prepared to entertain doubts or jokes about itself."

However, Rushdie, himself a Muslim, argued that *The Satanic Verses* was not meant to be an attack on the Islamic religion, but that it has been interpreted as such by what he calls in the *Observer* "the contemporary Thought Police" of Islam who have erected taboos in which one "may not discuss Muhammed as if he were human, with human virtues and weaknesses. One may not discuss the growth of Islam as a historical phenomenon, as an ideology born out of its time." Contrary to this belief, Rushdie says that normally in the Islamic religion Muhammed, unlike Jesus in the Christian religion, "is not granted divine status, but the text is." A number of critics have pointed out that the whole controversy could be avoided if Rushdie's detractors took into consideration that all of the objectionable scenes take place in the character Gibreel Farishta's dreams, and are part of his insanity-inspired delusions. "It must be added," remarks *Time* critic Paul Gray, "that few of those outraged by *The Satanic Verses* have ever seen it, much less opened it."

The Satanic Verses is a complex narrative that tells several stories within a story in a manner that has been compared to the popular Arabic tales in *A Thousand and One Nights.* The central story concerns two men who miraculously survive a 29,000 foot fall after a terrorist attack on an Air India flight. One, Gibreel Farishta, a famous Indian actor, acquires a halo, while Saladin Chamcha, whose occupation involves providing voices for radio and television programs, metamorphoses into a satyr-like creature. Gibreel becomes deluded into thinking he is the archangel Gabriel and much of the novel is preoccupied with a number of his dreams which take on the form of "enigmatic and engrossing" parables, according to *Times Literary Supplement* contributor Robert Irwin. Each story, including the controversial tale concerning Mahound, comments on "the theme of religion and its inexorable, unwelcome and dubious demands." The novel concludes with a confrontation between Gibreel and Saladin on a movie set. By this time, the distinction between which character is good and which evil has been blurred beyond distinction. "Computation won't come up with an answer" to this puzzle, comments D. J. Enright in the *New York Review of Books.* "Both of them are both" good and evil. But if the inability to separate the two is the ultimate theme of *The Satanic Verses,* critics like *New York Times Book Review* writer A. G. Mojtabai wonder, "Does it require so much fantasia and fanfare to remind us that good and evil are deeply, subtly intermixed in humankind?"

Enright admits that the involved plotting of Rushdie's novel is "self-indulgent," but adds that "the reader is pleasured as well." In a comparable observation, Michael Wood remarks in *New Republic* that *The Satanic Verses* gives the reader the feeling that the writer is "trying to fill out a Big Book. But the pervading intelligence of the novel is so acute, the distress it explores so thoroughly understood, that the dullness doesn't settle, can't keep away the urgent questions and images that beset it. This is Rushdie's most bewildered book, but it is also his most thoughtful."

With *Midnight's Children* Rushdie "fulfilled his promise before we ever knew he had any," noted Cathleen Medwick in *Vogue.* And *Shame* "reveals the writer in sure control of his extravagant, mischievous, graceful, polemical imagination." Now, because Rushdie continued to pursue his art with *The Satanic*

Verses, which Enright calls "a fitting successor to *Midnight's Children* and *Shame,*" he has been forced into hiding, "living a nightmare, looking for words that will restore the rest of his days to him without compromising him as a writer," according to an article written by the editors of *New Republic.* "And we, the lucky ones, have been taught, at this late date in the history of infamy, when we still needed the lesson, that democracy can have its martyrs, too. May Salman Rushdie not become one of them."

For an earlier published interview, see *Contemporary Authors,* Volume 111.

BIOGRAPHICAL/CRITICAL SOURCES:

BOOKS

Contemporary Literary Criticism, Gale, Volume 23, 1983, Volume 31, 1985, Volume 55, *Yearbook 1988,* 1989.

PERIODICALS

Books and Bookmen, September, 1983.
Chicago Tribune, February 17, 1989.
Chicago Tribune Book World, March 15, 1981, April 26, 1981, January 22, 1984.
Christian Science Monitor, March 2, 1989.
Commonweal, September 25, 1981, December 4, 1981, November 4, 1983.
Encounter, February, 1982.
Illustrated London News, October, 1988.
India Today, September 15, 1988, October 31, 1988, March 15, 1989.
London Review of Books, September 29, 1988.
Los Angeles Times Book Review, August 26, 1979, December 25, 1983.
Mother Jones, April-May, 1990.
New Republic, May 23, 1981, March 6, 1989, March 13, 1989.
New Statesman, May 1, 1981.
New Statesman and Society, September 30, 1988.
Newsweek, April 20, 1981, February 12, 1990.
New Yorker, July 27, 1981, January 9, 1984.
New York Review of Books, September 24, 1981, March 2, 1989.
New York Times, April 23, 1981, November 2, 1983, January 27, 1989, February 13, 1989, February 15, 1989, February 16, 1989, February 17, 1989, February 18, 1989, February 20, 1989, February 21, 1989, February 22, 1989, February 23, 1989, February 24, 1989, February 25, 1989, March 1, 1989.
New York Times Book Review, April 19, 1981, March 28, 1982, November 13, 1983, January 29, 1989.
Observer, February 9, 1975, July 19, 1981, September 25, 1988, January 22, 1989, February 19, 1989.
Publishers Weekly, November 11, 1983.
Saturday Review, March, 1981.
Spectator, June 13, 1981.
Time, February 13, 1989, February 27, 1989.
Times Literary Supplement, February 21, 1975, May 15, 1981, September 9, 1983, September 30, 1988.
Vogue, November, 1983.
Voice Literary Supplement, November, 1983.
Washington Post, January 18, 1989, February 15, 1989, February 17, 1989, February 18, 1989.
Washington Post Book World, March 15, 1981, November 20, 1983, January 29, 1989.
World Literature Today, winter, 1982.

RUSS, Joanna 1937-

PERSONAL: Born February 22, 1937, in New York, N.Y.; daughter of Everett I. (a teacher) and Bertha (a teacher; maiden name, Zinner) Russ. *Education:* Cornell University, B.A., 1957; Yale University, M.F.A., 1960. *Politics:* Feminist. *Religion:* None.

CAREER: Queensborough Community College, Bayside, N.Y., lecturer in speech, 1966-67; Cornell University, Ithaca, N.Y., instructor, 1967-70, assistant professor of English, 1970-72; State University of New York at Binghamton, assistant professor of English, 1972-75; University of Colorado, Boulder, assistant professor of English, 1975-77; University of Washington, Seattle, associate professor, 1977-84, professor of English, 1984—. Member of New York University Hall of Fame Players, 1964-66.

MEMBER: Modern Language Association of America, Science Fiction Writers of America.

AWARDS, HONORS: Nebula Award, Science Fiction Writers of America, 1972, for short story "When It Changed"; National Endowment for the Humanities fellow, 1974-75; Hugo Award, World Science Fiction Convention, 1983, and Nebula Award, 1983, both for novella "Souls."

WRITINGS:

Picnic on Paradise (also see below), Ace Books, 1968.
And Chaos Died, Ace Books, 1970.
The Female Man, Bantam, 1975.
(Author of introduction) Mary Shelley, *Tales and Stories,* G. K. Hall, 1975.
Alyx (includes *Picnic on Paradise*), G. K. Hall, 1976.
We Who Are about To . . ., Dell, 1977.
The Two of Them, Berkeley, 1978.
Kittatinny: A Tale of Magic, Daughters Publishing, 1978.
On Strike against God: A Lesbian Love Story, Out & Out, 1979.
How to Suppress Women's Writing, University of Texas, 1983.
The Zanzibar Cat, Arkham, 1983.
Extra (Ordinary) People, (short story collection; includes "Souls"), St. Martin's, 1984.
(Contributor) Sandra Gilbert and Susan Gubar, editors, *The Norton Anthology of Literature by Women: The Tradition in English,* W. W. Norton, 1985.
Magic Mommas, Trembling Sisters, Puritans and Perverts: Feminist Essays, Crossing Press, 1985.
The Hidden Side of the Moon, St. Martin's, 1988.
Houston, Houston, Do You Read? [and] *Souls,* Tor Books, 1989.

Contributor of short stories, articles, and poetry to *Sinister Wisdom, Thirteenth Moon, Sojourner, Journal of Homosexuality, Ms.,* and other periodicals.

SIDELIGHTS: Joanna Russ combines a feminist perspective with a sophisticated style to write science fiction novels which, Marge Piercy states in the *American Poetry Review,* "are interesting beyond the ordinary. They ask nasty and necessary questions [and] offer a gallery of some of the most interesting female protagonists in current fiction." Gerald Jonas of the *New York Times Book Review* notes that in her early work, "Russ used science fiction as a vehicle for the most intelligent, hard-minded commentary on feminism that you are likely to find anywhere."

The Female Man is perhaps the novel in which Russ's feminist ideas are most completely expressed. The book's four heroines—each from a different time and place—represent different possibilities for women in society. "Each of these fictional realities," writes Barbara Garland in the *Dictionary of Literary Biography,* "makes a statement about the self versus society and about male

versus female: and each has a distinctive style." In their book *Science Fiction: History, Science, Vision,* Robert Scholes and Eric S. Rabkin find that in *The Female Man,* Russ "has used the visionary potential of science fiction to convey the contrast between life as it is presently lived by many women and life as it might be. Among other things, Russ has demonstrated the unique potential of science fiction for embodying radically different life styles, which can hardly be conveyed in fiction bound by the customs of present literature."

Not all critics judge *The Female Man* to have successfully presented its feminist ideas. Jonas, for example, thinks that Russ, "with her obvious grasp of the biological givens and her command of so many science-fictional weapons, . . . might have produced a truly provocative study of 'woman's fate.' Unfortunately, she keeps slipping into the easy rhetoric of mainstream feminist tracts." Michael Goodwin of *Mother Jones* claims that *The Female Man* "is not a novel—it's a scream of anger. . . . It's unfair, it's maddening, it's depressing. I hated it. . . . And yet, a year after reading it, *The Female Man* remains perfectly clear in my mind—seductive, disturbing and hateful. I'm not sure whether that makes it a good book or not, but I think it makes it an important one."

In an article for *Extrapolation,* Natalie M. Rosinsky analyzes *The Female Man* as "a model of the ways in which feminist humor can operate within a literary text" and sees Russ concerned primarily with "the ways in which humor has been used as a weapon against women." Although each female character in the novel comes from a different time and place, Rosinsky states, "all live in worlds in which humor is used as a weapon against women. Only Janet, the visitor from the all-female universe of Whileaway, has freely experienced and created a different kind of humor, one that does not wound or function to maintain a hierarchical status quo."

Rosinsky sees this difference in humor as pivotal to an understanding of the novel. "We can transcend and transform our lives," she states, "take what has been male-identified and make it female-identified or gender-free. Redefining what is or is not truly funny is one way to begin. And thus, humor in *The Female Man* is not peripheral to either its themes or structure, but is instead an integral, though often undervalued, component of its composition." Rosinsky calls the book "a classic of feminist polemical literature," while Ellen Morgan of *Radical Teacher* judges it "the truest, most complete account available of what it feels like to be alienated as a woman and a feminist."

The collection *The Hidden Side of the Moon* represents nearly thirty years of Russ's work in short fiction. Fred Pfeil, writing in the *Washington Post Book World,* says that in some of the stories, her "writing is incandescent, bordering on the visionary." The other pieces show the author reworking similar images and themes to heightened effect. *New York Times Book Review* contributor John Clute relates that all of the stories seem to directly address the reader with challenges about women's roles in contemporary society. "And because she is a writer of such energetic clarity," adds Clute, "Ms. Russ is very easy to read, which is to say very hard not to read, even though it may hurt. She lets no one off the hook. However hilarious, the pointed urgency of her anger can scathe." Russ excels when describing the complex relations between parents and children, he says of this "major writer within the science fiction genre, and beyond it."

Validating her status is her role as a pathfinder for women writers of science fiction, Pfeil observes. Her novel *The Female Man,* he explains, with its "dazzling play of points of view and narrative forms (from drama to fable and essay to epic) on the one hand, and its unapologetically explicit feminist politics and visions on the other, have helped to inspire a new generation of women writers within science fiction."

BIOGRAPHICAL/CRITICAL SOURCES:

BOOKS

Contemporary Literary Criticism, Volume 15, Gale, 1980.
Dictionary of Literary Biography, Volume 8: *Twentieth Century American Science Fiction Writers,* Gale, 1980.
Scholes, Robert and Eric S. Rabkin, *Science Fiction: History, Science, Vision,* Oxford University Press, 1977.
Walker, Paul, *Speaking of Science Fiction: The Paul Walker Interviews,* Luna Press, 1978.

PERIODICALS

Algol, summer, 1975.
American Poetry Review, May-June, 1977.
Booklist, November 1, 1977.
Extrapolation, spring, 1982.
Fantasy Newsletter, April, 1983.
Frontiers, spring, 1979.
Magazine of Fantasy and Science Fiction, August, 1975, February, 1978, April, 1979.
Mother Jones, August, 1976.
New York Times Book Review, May 4, 1975, September 25, 1977, June 25, 1978, January 31, 1988.
Radical Teacher, Number 10, 1978.
Science Fiction Review, May, 1975, May, 1978.
Washington Post Book World, February 28, 1988.

* * *

RUSSELL, Bertrand (Arthur William) 1872-1970

PERSONAL: Born May 18, 1872, in Trelleck, Monmouthshire, England; died February 2, 1970, in Penrhyndeudraeth, Merionethshire, Wales; son of Lord John (Viscount Amberley) and Katherine (Stanley) Russell; married Alys Whitall Pearsall Smith, 1894 (divorced, 1921; died, 1951); married Dora Winifred Black, 1921 (divorced, 1935); married Patricia Helen Spence, 1936 (divorced, 1952); married Edith Finch, 1952; children: (second marriage) John Conrad, Katharine Jane; (third marriage) Conrad Sebastian Robert. *Education:* Trinity College, Cambridge, M.A. (first class honors), 1894. *Politics:* Formerly member of Liberal Party, then of Labour Party for 5 years. *Religion:* Agnostic.

ADDRESSES: Home—Plas Penrhyn, Penrhyndeudraeth, Merionethshire, Wales.

CAREER: Succeeded brother as 3rd Earl of Russell, Viscount Amberley, 1931; honorary attache at British Embassy in Paris, 1894; fellow and lecturer at Trinity College, Cambridge University, 1894-1916 (dismissed for his opposition to World War I, and sentenced to four and one-half months in prison); Harvard University, Cambridge, Mass., temporary professor, 1914; National University of Peking, Peking, China, professor of philosophy, 1920-21; cofounder and director, with wife Dora Russell, of Beacon Hill School (an experimental school for children), Sussex, England, 1927-32; University of Chicago, Chicago, Ill., lecturer, 1938; University of California, Los Angeles, professor of philosophy, 1939-40; appointed William James Lecturer in Philosophy at Harvard University, and professor of philosophy at City College of New York (latter appointment withdrawn over controversy surrounding his beliefs); Barnes Foundation, Merion, Pa., lecturer on history of culture, 1941-42; stood for Parliament as Liberal candidate, 1907, and as Labour candidate, 1922 and 1923.

MEMBER: Royal Society of Literature (fellow, 1908), Athenaeum Club.

AWARDS, HONORS: Nicholas Murray Butler Medal, 1915; Sylvester Medal of Royal Society, 1934; British Order of Merit, 1949; Nobel Prize for Literature, 1950; Kalinga Prize, 1957; Sonning Foundation Prize (Denmark), 1960; Jerusalem Prize, 1963.

WRITINGS:

PHILOSOPHY AND SOCIAL COMMENT

German Social Democracy, Longmans, Green, 1896, reprinted, Simon & Schuster, 1966.
An Essay on the Foundations of Geometry, University Press (Cambridge), 1897, Dover, 1956.
A Critical Exposition of the Philosophy of Leibnitz, University Press (Cambridge), 1900, new edition, Allen & Unwin, 1937.
The Principles of Mathematics, Volume 1, University Press (Cambridge), 1903, 2nd edition, Norton, 1938, reprinted, 1964.
(With Alfred North Whitehead) *Principia Mathematica,* University Press (Cambridge), Volume 1, 1910, 2nd edition, 1935, Volume 2, 1912, 2nd edition, 1927, Volume 3, 1913, 2nd edition, 1927, 2nd edition in three volumes, 1950.
Philosophical Essays, Longmans, Green, 1910, reissued as *Mysticism and Logic and Other Essays,* 1918, revised edition published under original title, Allen & Unwin, 1966, Simon & Schuster, 1967.
Anti-Suffragist Anxieties, People's Suffrage Federation, 1910.
The Problems of Philosophy, H. Holt, 1912.
Our Knowledge of the External World as a Field for Scientific Method in Philosophy, Open Court, 1914, 2nd edition, Norton, 1929, reprinted, New American Library, 1960.
The Philosophy of Bergson, Macmillan, 1914.
Scientific Method in Philosophy (lecture), Clarendon, 1914.
War: The Offspring of Fear (pamphlet), Union of Democratic Control, 1915.
Why Men Fight, Century, 1916, reprinted, Books for Libraries, 1971 (published in England as *Principles of Social Reconstruction,* Allen & Unwin, 1916, reprinted, 1960).
The Policy of the Entente, 1904-1914, National Labour Press, 1916.
Justice in War-time, Open Court, 1916, reprinted, Haskell, 1974.
Political Ideals, Century, 1917, reprinted, Simon & Schuster, 1964.
Roads to Freedom: Socialism, Anarchism, and Syndicalism, Allen & Unwin, 1918, revised edition, 1919, published as *Proposed Roads to Freedom: Socialism, Anarchism, and Syndicalism,* H. Holt, 1919, reprinted under British title, Barnes & Noble, 1966.
Introduction to Mathematical Philosophy, Macmillan, 1919, Simon & Schuster, 1971.
Bolshevism: Practice and Theory, Harcourt, 1920, 2nd edition, Simon & Schuster, 1964 (published in England as *The Practice and Theory of Bolshevism,* Allen & Unwin, 1920, 2nd edition, 1949).
The Analysis of Mind, Macmillan, 1921, reprinted, Humanities, 1958.
The Problem of China, Century, 1922.
Free Thought and Official Propaganda, B. W. Huebsch, 1922.
A Free Man's Worship, T. B. Mosher, 1923.

MAJOR 20TH-CENTURY WRITERS

The ABC of Atoms, Dutton, 1923, 4th edition, Routledge & Kegan Paul, 1932.

Icarus; or, The Future of Science, Dutton, 1924.

How to Be Free and Happy, Rand School of Social Science, 1924.

The ABC of Relativity, Harper, 1925, 3rd revised edition, Allen & Unwin, 1969.

What I Believe, Dutton, 1925.

Education and the Good Life, Boni & Liveright, 1926, reprinted, 1970 (published in England as *On Education Especially in Early Childhood,* Allen & Unwin, 1926).

Why I Am Not a Christian (also see below), Watts, 1927, Freethought Press Association, 1940.

The Analysis of Matter, Harcourt, 1927, with new introduction by Lester E. Denonn, Dover, 1954.

Philosophy, Norton, 1927 (published in England as *An Outline of Philosophy,* Allen & Unwin, 1927), published under British title, World Publishing, 1961.

Selected Papers of Bertrand Russell, Modern Library, 1927.

Skeptical Essays, Norton, 1928, reprinted, Barnes & Noble, 1961.

Marriage and Morals, Liveright, 1929, 2nd edition, Unwin Books, 1961, reprinted, Liveright, 1970.

A Liberal View of Divorce, Haldeman-Julius, 1929.

The Conquest of Happiness, Book League of America, 1930, reprinted, Liveright, 1971.

Has Religion Made Useful Contributions to Civilization?, Haldeman-Julius, 1930.

The Scientific Outlook, Norton, 1931, 2nd edition, Allen & Unwin, 1962.

Education and the Modern World, Norton, 1932 (published in England as *Education and the Social Order,* Allen & Unwin, 1932).

Freedom Versus Organization, 1814-1914, Norton, 1934, reprinted, 1962 (published in England as *Freedom and Organization, 1814-1914,* Allen & Unwin, 1934, parts 1 and 2 reissued as *Legitimacy Versus Industrialism, 1814-1848,* 1965).

In Praise of Idleness and Other Essays, Norton, 1935, reprinted, Simon & Schuster, 1972.

Religion and Science, H. Holt, 1935, reprinted, Oxford University Press, 1961.

Determinism and Physics (Earl Grey Memorial Lecture), The Librarian, Armstrong College, 1936.

Which Way to Peace?, M. Joseph, 1936.

Power: A Social Analysis, Norton, 1938, reprinted, 1969.

An Inquiry Into Meaning and Truth, Norton, 1940, reprinted, Allen & Unwin, 1966.

Let the People Think: A Selection of Essays, Watts, 1941, 2nd edition, Rationalist Press Association, 1961.

How to Become a Philosopher: The Art of Rational Conjecture, Haldeman-Julius, 1942.

How to Become a Logician: The Art of Drawing Inferences, Haldeman-Julius, 1942.

How to Become a Mathematician: The Art of Reckoning, Haldeman-Julius, 1942.

An Outline of Intellectual Rubbish: A Hilarious Catalogue of Organized and Individual Stupidity, Haldeman-Julius, 1943.

How to Read and Understand History, Haldeman-Julius, 1943.

A History of Western Philosophy: Its Connection With Political and Social Circumstances from the Earliest Times to the Present Day, Simon & Schuster, 1945, new edition, Allen & Unwin, 1961.

Physics and Experience (Henry Sidgwick Lecture), Cambridge University Press, 1946.

Ideas That Have Harmed Mankind, Haldeman-Julius, 1946.

Ideas That Have Helped Mankind, Haldeman-Julius, 1946.

Is Materialism Bankrupt?, Haldeman-Julius, 1946.

Is Science Superstitious?, Haldeman-Julius, 1947.

Philosophy and Politics, Cambridge University Press, for National Book League, 1947.

Human Knowledge: Its Scope and Limits, Simon & Schuster, 1948.

Authority and the Individual, Simon & Schuster, 1949, reprinted, AMS Press, 1968.

Unpopular Essays, Allen & Unwin, 1950, Simon & Schuster, 1951, reprinted, Simon & Schuster, 1966.

New Hopes for a Changing World, Simon & Schuster, 1951, reprinted, Minerva Press, 1968.

The Impact of Science on Society, Columbia University Press, 1952, reprinted, AMS Press, 1968.

The Wit and Wisdom of Bertrand Russell, Beacon, 1951.

Bertrand Russell's Dictionary of Mind, Matter, and Morals, Philosophical Library, 1952, reprinted, 1965.

How Near is War?, D. Ridgway, 1952.

What Is Freedom?, Batchworth Press, 1952.

What Is Democracy?, Batchworth Press, 1953.

The Good Citizen's Alphabet (also see below), Gaberbocchus Press, 1953, Philosophical Library, 1958.

History as Art, Hand and Flower Press, 1954.

Human Society in Ethics and Politics, Allen & Unwin, 1954, Simon & Schuster, 1955, reprinted, New American Library, 1962.

John Stuart Mill, Oxford University Press, 1956.

Logic and Knowledge: Essays, 1901-1950, Macmillan, 1956.

Why I Am Not a Christian and Other Essays on Religion and Related Subjects, Simon & Schuster, 1957, 7th edition, 1963.

Understanding History and Other Essays, Philosophical Library, 1957.

The Will to Doubt, Philosophical Library, 1958.

Wisdom of the West: A Historical Survey of Western Philosophy in Its Social and Political Setting, Doubleday, 1959, reprinted, Fawcett, 1966.

The Philosophy of Logical Atomism (lectures), Department of Philosophy, University of Minnesota, 1959.

My Philosophical Development, Simon & Schuster, 1959.

The Future of Science, Philosophical Library, 1959.

Common Sense and Nuclear Warfare, Simon & Shuster, 1959, reprinted, AMS Press, 1968.

Bertrand Russell Speaks His Mind, World Publishing, 1960.

On Education, Allen & Unwin, 1960.

The Basic Writings of Bertrand Russell, 1903-1959, edited by Robert E. Egner and Lester E. Dennon, Simon & Schuster, 1961.

Education and Character, Philosophical Library, 1961.

Fact and Fiction, Allen & Unwin, 1961, Simon & Schuster, 1962.

Has Man a Future?, Simon & Schuster, 1962.

Unarmed Victory, Simon & Schuster, 1963.

War and Atrocity in Vietnam, Bertrand Russell Peace Foundation, 1965.

On the Philosophy of Science, Bobbs-Merrill, 1965.

Appeal to the American Conscience, Bertrand Russell Peace Foundation, 1966.

War Crimes in Vietnam, Monthly Review Press, 1967.

The Art of Philosophizing and Other Essays, Philosophical Library, 1968.

The Good Citizens Alphabet; and, History of the World in Epitome, Gaberbocchus Press, 1970.

Atheism: Collected Essays 1943-1949, Arno, 1972.

My Own Philosophy, McMaster University Press, 1972.

Russell's Logical Atomism, edited by David Pears, Collins, 1972.

Essays in Analysis, edited by Douglas Lackey, Simon & Schuster, 1973.

The Collected Papers of Bertrand Russell, edited by Kenneth Blackwell, 28 volumes, Allen & Unwin, 1983—.

Theory of Knowledge: The 1913 Manuscript, Allen & Unwin, 1984.

CONTRIBUTOR

Freda Kirchway, *Styles in Ethics,* A. & C. Boni, 1924.

J. H. Muirhead, editor, *British Philosophy,* Macmillan, Volume 1, 1924.

Frederich A. Lange, *The History of Materialism,* 3rd edition, Harcourt, 1925.

Charles A. Beard, editor, *Whither Mankind,* Longmans, Green, 1928.

Baker Brownell, editor, *Man and His World,* Van Nostrand, Volume 12, 1929.

N. A. Crawford and K. A. Menninger, *The Healthy-Minded Child,* Coward, 1930.

Charles W. Morris, *Six Theories of Mind,* University of Chicago Press, 1932.

Will Durant, editor, *On the Meaning of Life,* Ray Long & Richard R. Smith Inc., 1932.

M. Adams, editor, *Science in the Changing World,* Appleton, 1933.

Sidney Hook, editor, *The Meaning of Marx,* Farrar, Straus, 1934.

A. B. Brown, editor, *Great Democrats,* Nicholson, 1934.

R. S. Loomis and D. L. Clark, editors, *Modern English Readings,* Farrar, Straus, 1934.

E. A. Walter, editor, *Toward Today,* Scott, 1938.

Encyclopaedia and Unified Science, University of Chicago Press, Volume 1, 1938.

What Is Happiness?, H. C. Kinsey & Co., 1939.

Clifton Fadiman, editor, *I Believe: The Personal Philosophies of Certain Eminent Men and Women of Our Time,* Simon & Schuster, 1939.

Paul Arthur Schlipp, editor, *The Philosophy of John Dewey,* Northwestern University Press, 1939.

Calling America, Harper, 1939.

R. N. Anshen, editor, *Freedom: Its Meaning,* Harcourt, 1940.

Schilpp, editor, *The Philosophy of George Santayana,* Northwestern University Press, 1940.

Palestine: Jewish Commonwealth in Our Times, Zionist Organization of America, 1943.

Schilpp, *The Philosophy of Bertrand Russell,* Tudor, 1944.

Ben Raeburn, editor, *Treasury for the Free World,* Arco, 1945.

The Western Tradition, Beacon, 1951.

Worth Reading, New York Times Co., 1951.

Wallace Brockway, editor, *High Moment: Stories of Supreme Crisis in the Lives of Great Men,* Simon & Schuster, 1955.

Hugh Trevor-Roper, editor, *Why I Oppose Communism: A Symposium,* Phoenix House, 1956.

OTHER

(With wife Dora Russell) *The Prospects of Industrial Civilization,* Century, 1923, 2nd edition, Allen & Unwin, 1960.

(Debate with Scott Nearing) *Bolshevism and the West,* Macmillan, 1924.

(With others) *If I Could Preach Just Once,* Harper, 1929, reissued as *If I Had Only One Sermon to Preach,* 1932.

(With others) *Divorce,* Day, 1930 (published in England as *Divorce as I See It,* Douglas, 1930).

(Debate with John Cowper Powys) *Is Modern Marriage a Failure?,* Discussion Guild, 1930.

(Editor with wife Patricia Russell) *The Amberley Papers: The Letters and Diaries of Bertrand Russell's Parents,* two volumes, Norton, 1937, reprinted, Simon & Schuster, 1967.

(With others) *Dare We Look Ahead?* (Fabian Lectures), Macmillan, 1938.

(With others) *Invitation to Learning,* Random, 1941.

(With others) *New Invitation to Learning,* Random House, 1942.

(With others) *Among the Great,* N. M. Tripathi (Bombay), 1945.

(With others) *The Impact of America on European Culture,* Beacon, 1951.

Satan in the Suburbs and Other Stories, Simon & Schuster, 1953.

Nightmares of Eminent Persons and Other Stories, Bodley Head, 1954, Simon & Schuster, 1955.

Portraits From Memory and Other Essays, Simon & Schuster, 1956.

(Author of introduction) Ludwig Wittgenstein, *Logikofilosofskii traktat,* Izd-vo inostrannoi litry (Moscow), 1958.

Bertrand Russell's Best: Silhouettes in Satire, Allen & Unwin, 1958, New American Library, 1961.

The Vital Letters of Russell, Khrushchev, Dulles, MacGibbon & Kee, 1958.

Essays in Skepticism, Philosophical Library, 1963.

(With Stafford Cripps and Reinhold Niebuhr) *Que es, hoy, la democracia?,* Centro de Estudios y Documentacion Sociales (Mexico), 1964.

(Author of introduction) Harold Dicker, *The Bell of John Donne,* Intrepid Press, 1965.

The Autobiography of Bertrand Russell, Volume 1: *1872-1914,* Little, Brown, 1967, Volume 2: *1914-1944,* Little, Brown, 1968, Volume 3: *1944-1969,* Simon & Schuster, 1969.

(With others) *Nacionalidad Oprimida,* Ediciones Mordejai Anilevich (Montevideo, Uruguay), 1968.

Dear Bertrand Russell: A Selection of His Correspondence with the General Public, 1950-1968, edited by Barry Feinberg and Ronald Kasrils, Houghton, 1969.

(Editor with Jean-Paul Sartre) *Das Vietnam-Tribunal,* Rowohlt, 1970.

(With others) *Ladislas Reymont, Romain Rolland* [and] *Bertrand Russell,* A Gregory, 1971.

The Collected Stories of Bertrand Russell, Simon & Schuster, 1972.

Bertrand Russell's America: His Transatlantic Travels and Writings; A Socumented Account by B. Feinberg and R. Kasrils, Allen & Unwin, Volume 1: *1896-1945,* 1973, Volume 2, 1985, Volume 1 published in America as *Bertrand Russell's America,* Viking, 1974.

Mortals and Others: Bertrand Russell's American Essays 1931-1935, edited by Harry Ruja, Allen & Unwin, 1975.

Dewey and Russell: An Exchange, edited by Samuel Meyer, Philosophical Library, 1985.

Contributor to *Encyclopaedia Britannica,* and to *Mind, Independent Review, Edinburgh Review, American Journal of Mathematics, Hibbert Journal, Monist, Atlantic, Unpopular Review, International Journal of Ethics, American Scholar, Dial, New Republic, Nation, Saturday Review, Virginia Quarterly Review, Spectator, New Statesman, Esquire, American Mercury, Harper's, New Leader, Listener, New York Times Magazine, Science Digest, Look,* and other publications. McMaster University purchased Russell's collection of private papers in 1968.

SIDELIGHTS: Bertrand Russell's biographer, Alan Wood, wrote that "less than halfway through [Russell's] career he had already achieved immortality; his place was secure as a thinker who had made the greatest advances in logic since Greek times." Wood also wrote that Russell was "a philosopher without a philosophy. . . . He started by asking questions about mathematics and religion and philosophy, and he went on to question accepted ideas about war and politics and sex and education, setting the minds of men on the march, so that the world could never be quite the same as if he had not lived." Russell himself once declared: "Science is what you know, philosophy is what you don't know." In a letter (1918) he wrote: "I want to stand at the rim of the world and peer into the darkness beyond, and see a little more than others have seen, of the strange shapes of mystery that inhabit that unknown night. . . ." He later admitted the impossibility of definitely knowing very much at all: "I have been painfully forced to the belief that nine-tenths of what is regarded as philosophy is humbug. The only part that is at all definite is logic, and since it is logic, it is not philosophy."

Believing that "a philosophy which is to have any value should be built upon a wide and firm foundation of knowledge that is not specifically philosophical," Russell came to philosophy through other disciplines. He was an inquisitive child. Wood reports that at the age of five, "informed that the earth was round, he refused to believe it, but began digging a hole in the garden to see if he came out in Australia." At eleven he began to study Euclid and developed a passion for mathematics. Then he studied history ("History has always interested me more than anything else except philosophy and mathematics," Russell once remarked.), literature, and finally philosophy, always seeking some impersonal truth—examining the arguments favoring different religions, rejecting personal immortality, turning to Kant and Hegel, and by 1898 abandoning them both. "I wanted certainty," he wrote, "in the kind of way in which people want religious faith." "And yet I am unable to believe that, in the world as known, there is anything that I can value outside human beings, and, to a much lesser extent, animals. Not the starry heavens, but their effects on human percipients, have excellence; to admire the universe for its size is slavish and absurd; impersonal non-human truth appears to be a delusion." He came to realize, in effect, that "the non-human world is unworthy of worship."

Russell's best known works are *A History of Western Philosophy* and *Principia Mathematica.* The latter, written with Alfred North Whitehead, has become a classic in its field, though Wood wrote that "probably not more than twenty people have read it right through." Russell's output was prodigious, and his special gift was a lucid and witty style that makes him the most readable of philosophers. He once remarked: "I'm paid by the word so I always use the shortest words possible." He did do some potboiling, having, he said, no "lofty feelings" about it. But his work was always precise, having been thoroughly planned before he set it down on paper. In 1930 he said: "I dictate at full speed, just as fast as the stenographer can go. . . . I do three thousand words a day. I plan to work only in the morning. If I haven't done my stint, I sometimes go on working into the afternoon. . . . He claimed he never revised. To authors he offered this advice: 'Never alter anything you write—especially if someone else asks you to.' "

Russell's diminutive stature was likened to that of a gnome and to "a sophisticated koala bear" (the latter description particularly flattered him). Once, in China, he nearly died of pneumonia, and, as a result of the confusion in England about his condition, he had the unique pleasure of reading his own obituaries. (At the age of 70 he wrote his own obituary in which he said his life, "for all its waywardness, had a certain anachronistic consistency.") Beatrice Webb called him a dissector of persons and a demolisher of causes, and Jean Nichod once said that Russell's statements had "that slightly ludicrous quality which comes from being true." He espoused many unpopular causes, not the

least of these being free love. As for family relationships, he once wrote: "There is no greater reason for children to honour parents than for parents to honour children, except that while the children are young, the parents are stronger than the children. The same thing, of course, happened in the relations of men and women. It was the duty of wives to submit to husbands, not of husbands to submit to wives. The only basis for this view was that if wives could be induced to accept it, it saved trouble for their husbands."

Russell regarded the "good life" as one "inspired by love and guided by knowledge." And one that includes tobacco, he might have added. Some time ago he said: "When I was young I was told that smoking would shorten my life: after sixty years of smoking, it hasn't shortened much. . . . Anyway I get much more pleasure from smoking than I would from a few more years in decrepitude. I smoke heavily and only stop to sleep or eat."

As the grandson of Lord John Russell and of Lord Stanley of Alderly, Russell was long associated with notable people. He personally knew Henri Bergson, George Santayana, Aldous Huxley, John Maynard Keynes, and D. H. Lawrence, and was the teacher of Ludwig Wittgenstein and T. S. Eliot. He disagreed with many of his friends and acquaintances, especially with those philosophers who believe that the world is a unity. "The most fundamental of my intellectual beliefs," he wrote, "is that this is rubbish. I think the universe is all spots and jumps, without unity, without continuity, without coherence or orderliness or any of the other properties that governesses?? love. Indeed, there is little but prejudice and habit to be said for the view that there is a world at all."

Russell had always been involved with many things at any given time. At the age of 89 he was again jailed, this time for helping to plan a demonstration advocating unilateral disarmament and refusing to keep the Queen's peace. He said: "What I want is some assurance before I die that the human race will be allowed to continue."

Of the last volume of Russell's autobiography, Sidney Hook wrote in the *New York Times Book Review:* "Anyone who has spent more than a few hours in Russell's company during his prime will sense the failure of this autobiography to reflect his genius. He was without peer as a brilliant conversationalist. There was an unfailing play of common sense, profundity and puckish wit in his treatment of the most diverse themes. Others could have made careers out of the crumbs of his table talk. Here he appears as a figure of wooden virtue, violating by his dogmatism, self-righteousness and touches of malice key principles of his own decalogue of liberal commandments. . . . The greatness of Russell lies not in his political thought but in his contributions to philosophy and logic. There was a dramatic appropriateness in his envy of Socrates. Russell's life has been nobler than this portrait from memory suggests. Some day, let us hope, a proper biography will do justice to it."

BIOGRAPHICAL/CRITICAL SOURCES:

BOOKS

Aiken, L. W., *Bertrand Russell's Philosophy of Morals,* Humanities, 1963.
Ayer, A. J., *Russell and Moore,* Harvard University Press, 1971.
Dewey, John, and H. M. Kallen, editors, *The Bertrand Russell Case,* Viking, 1941.
Dorward, Alan, *Bertrand Russell: A Short Guide to His Philosophy,* Longmans, Green, for the British Council, 1951.
Fritz, C. A., *Bertrand Russell's Construction of the External World,* Humanities, 1952.

Jorgensen, J., *Bertrand Russell,* Levin, 1935.

Jourdain, P. E. B., editor, *The Philosophy of Mr. Bertrand Russell,* Open Court, 1918.

Klemke, E. D., editor, *Essays on Bertrand Russell,* University of Illinois Press, 1971.

Leggett, H. W., *Bertrand Russell,* Philosophical Library, 1950.

Pears, D. F., *Bertrand Russell and the British Tradition in Philosophy,* Vintage, 1971.

Santayana, George, *Winds of Doctrine,* Scribner, 1913.

Schilpp, P. A., editor, *The Philosophy of Bertrand Russell,* Tudor, 1944, 3rd edition, Harper, 1963.

Wood, Alan, *Bertrand Russell: The Passionate Skeptic,* Simon & Schuster, 1958.

OBITUARIES:

PERIODICALS

Antiquarian Bookman, February 16, 1970.
National Review, February 24, 1970.
New Statesman, February 6, 1970.
Newsweek, February 16, 1970.
New York Times, February 3, 1970.
Observer, February 8, 1970.
Publishers Weekly, February 16, 1970.
Time, February 16, 1970.

*   *   *

RYDER, Jonathan
See LUDLUM, Robert

S

S. S.
See SASSOON, Siegfried (Lorraine)

* * *

SABATO, Ernesto (R.) 1911-

PERSONAL: Born June 24, 1911, in Rojas, Argentina; son of Francisco Sabato (a mill owner) and Juana Ferrari; married Matilde Kusminsky-Richter, 1934; children: Jorge Federico, Mario. *Education:* National University of La Plata, Ph.D., 1937; additional study at Joliot-Curie Laboratory (Paris), 1938, and Massachusetts Institute of Technology, 1939.

ADDRESSES: Home—1676 Santos Lugares, Buenos Aires, Argentina.

CAREER: National University of La Plata, La Plata, Argentina, professor of theoretical physics, 1940-43; novelist and essayist, 1943—. Guest lecturer at universities throughout the United States and Europe. Chairman of National Commission on the Disappearance of Persons (Argentina), 1983.

AWARDS, HONORS: Argentine Association for the Progress of Science fellowship in Paris, 1937; sash of honor from Argentine Writers Society and Municipal Prose prize from the City of Buenos Aires, both 1945, both for *Uno y el universo;* prize from the Institute of Foreign Relations (West Germany), 1973; Grand Prize of Honor from the Argentine Writers Society, Premio Consagracion Nacional (Argentina), and Chevalier des Arts et des Lettres (France), all 1974; Prix au Meilleur Livre Etranger (Paris), 1977, for *Abaddon, el Exterminador;* Gran Cruz al Merito Civil (Spain) and Chevalier de la Legion D'Honneur (France), both 1979; Gabriela Mistral Prize from Organization of American States, 1984; Miguel de Cervantes Prize from the Spanish Ministry of Culture, 1985; Commandeur de la Legion d'Honneur (France), 1987; Jerusalem Prize, 1989.

WRITINGS:

NOVELS

El tunel, Sur, 1948, translation by Harriet de Onis published as *The Outsider,* Knopf, 1950, translation by Margaret Sayers Peden published as *The Tunnel,* Ballantine, 1988.
Sobre heroes y tumbas, Fabril, 1961, reprinted, Seix Barral, 1981, excerpt published as *Un dios desconocido: Romance de la muerte de Juan Lavalle (de "Sobre heroes y tumbas"),* A. S. Dabini, 1980, translation by Stuart M. Gross of another excerpt published as "Report on the Blind" in *TriQuarterly,* fall-winter, 1968-69, translation by Helen Lane of entire novel published as *On Heroes and Tombs,* David Godine, 1981.*
Abaddon, el Exterminador (title means "Abaddon: The Exterminator"; novel), Sudamericana, 1974.

ESSAYS

Uno y el universo (title means "One and the Universe"), Sudamericana, 1945.
Hombres y engranajes (title means "Men and Gears"), Emece, 1951, reprinted, 1985.
Heterodoxia (title means "Heterodoxy"), Emece, 1953.
El otro rostro del peronismo: Carta abierta a Mario Amadeo (title means "The Other Face of Peronism: Open Letter to Mario Amadeo"), Lopez, 1956.
El caso Sabato: Torturas y libertad de prensa—Carta abierta al Gral. Aramburu (title means "Sabato's Case: Torture and Freedom of the Press—Open Letter to General Aramburu"), privately printed, 1956.
Tango: Discusion y clave (title means "Tango: Discussion and Key"), Losada, 1963.
El escritor y sus fantasmas (title means "The Writer and His Ghosts"), Aguilar, 1963.
Tres aproximaciones a la literatura de nuestro tiempo: Robbe-Grillet, Borges, Sartre (title means "Approaches to the Literature of Our Time . . ."; essays), Universitaria (Chile), 1968.
La convulsion politica y social de nuestro tiempo (title means "The Political and Social Upheaval of Our Time"), Edicom, 1969.
Ernesto Sabato: Claves politicas (title means "Ernesto Sabato: Political Clues"), Alonso, 1971.
La cultura en la encrucijada nacional (title means "Culture in the National Crossroads"), Ediciones de Crisis, 1973.
(With Jorge Luis Borges) *Dialogos* (title means "Dialogues"), Emece, 1976.
Apologias y rechazos (title means "Apologies and Rejections"), Seix Barral, 1979.
La robotizacion del hombre y otras paginas de ficcion y reflexion (title means "The Robotization of Man and Other Pages of

Fiction and Reflection"), Centro Editorial del America Latina, 1981.

COLLECTIONS

Obras de ficcion (title means "Works of Fiction"; contains *El tunel* and *Sobre heroes y tumbas*), Losada, 1966.

Itinerario (title means "Itinerary"; selections from Sabato's novels and essays), Sur, 1969.

Obras: Ensayos (title means "Works: Essays"), Losada, 1970.

Paginas vivas (title means "Living Pages"), Kapelusz, 1974.

Antologia (title means "Anthology"), Libreria del Colegio, 1975.

Narrativa completa (title means "Complete Narrative"), Seix Barral, 1982.

Paginas de Ernesto Sabato (title means "Pages from Ernesto Sabato"), Celtia (Buenos Aires), 1983.

OTHER

(Editor) *Mitomagia: Los temas del misterio* (title means "Mitomagia: Themes of the Mysterious"), Ediciones Latinoamericanas, 1969.

(Author of introduction) *Testimonios: Chile, septiembre, 1973* (title means "Eyewitness Accounts: Chile, September, 1973"), Jus, 1973.

(With Antonio Berni) *Cuatro hombres de pueblo*, Libreria de la Ciudad, 1979.

(Editor with Anneliese von der Lipper) *Viaje a los mundos imaginarios*, Legasa, 1983.

Contributor to *Sur* and other periodicals.

SIDELIGHTS: When one considers that Argentine novelist and essayist Ernesto Sabato has published only three novels, the impact he has had on Hispanic literature is remarkable: His first novel, *The Tunnel*, was a best-seller in his native land; his second work of fiction, *On Heroes and Tombs*, according to Emir Rodriguez Monegal in the *Borzoi Anthology of Latin American Literature*, "is one of the most popular contemporary novels in Latin America." *Abaddon, the Exterminator*, his third novel, was similarly acclaimed and was granted France's highest literary award—the Prix au Meilleur Livre Etranger. Sabato's importance was officially recognized in 1985 when he received the first Miguel de Cervantes Prize (considered the equivalent of the Nobel in the Hispanic world) from Spain's King Juan Carlos. Harley Dean Oberhelman, in his study of the author titled *Ernest Sabato*, calls Sabato "Argentina's most discussed contemporary novelist." His appeal rests largely in his portrayals of Argentine society under the domination of military strongmen such as Juan Peron and others, with his recurrent themes of incest, blindness, insanity, and abnormal psychology reflecting the distress of the Argentine people.

Born into a large, prosperous family of Italian origin, at age thirteen Sabato left the rural community where he had grown up to attend school in the city of La Plata. The transition from familial life to life alone in an unfamiliar urban area was a disturbing one for the future writer, and Sabato found order in his otherwise turbulent world in the study of mathematics. His academic studies were briefly interrupted for a five year period, however, when he became involved in the Argentine communist movement. Soon, upon learning of Stalinist atrocities, he lost faith in the communist cause and decided to retreat again to his academic work.

Sabato's success as a student earned him a research fellowship for study in Paris, and, while there his interest in writing was born. Deeply impressed by the surrealist movement, he secretly began writing a novel. Although his writing started to play an

increasingly important role in his life, Sabato continued his scientific research and accepted a teaching position upon his return to Argentina. Nonetheless, his literary efforts continued and he became a regular contributor to the popular Argentine magazine, *Sur*. Teaching was to remain his livelihood until 1943 when a conflict with the Juan Peron government resulted in his dismissal from his posts.

Commenting on his departure from the scientific world, Sabato wrote in an autobiographical essay appearing in English translation in *Salmagundi*, "The open, public transition from physics to literature was not an easy one for me; on the contrary, it was painfully complicated. I wrestled with my demons a long time before I came to a decision in 1943—when I resolved to sequester myself, with wife and son, in a cabin in the sierras of Cordoba, far from the civilized world. It was not a rational decision. . . . But in crucial moments of my existence I have always trusted more in instinct than in ideas and have constantly been tempted to venture where reasonable people fear to tread."

While living in the cabin for a year Sabato wrote an award-winning book of essays, *Uno y el universo*, in which he condemned the moral neutrality of science. Two years later his first novel, *The Tunnel*, appeared. Profoundly influenced by psychological thought and existential in tone, the work evoked comparison to the writings of French authors Albert Camus and Jean-Paul Sartre. It is the story of an Argentine painter who recounts the events leading up to his murder of his mistress. As an exercise in self-analysis for the lonely painter, unable to communicate his thoughts and feelings, *The Tunnel* contains many of the themes found in Sabato's later work. "The almost total isolation of a man in a world dominated by science and reason," notes Oberhelman, "is the most important of these themes, but at the same time the reader sees the inability of man to communicate with others, an almost pathological obsession with blindness, and a great concern for Oedipal involvement as important secondary themes."

The landmark of Sabato's work stands to be his 1961 novel, *On Heroes and Tombs*, which appeared in an English edition in 1982. It tells the story of Martin del Castillo and his love for Alejandra Vidal Olmos. Alejandra's father, Fernando Vidal Olmos, apparently involved in an incestuous relationship with his daughter, is another important figure in the book along with Bruno Bassan, a childhood friend of Fernando. The work is lengthy and complex and has spawned numerous critical interpretations. "When it first appeared twenty years ago," writes *Newsweek* contributor Jim Miller, "Ernesto Sabato's Argentine epic was widely praised. This belated translation finally lets Americans see why. Bewitched, baroque, monumental, his novel is a stunning symphony of dissonant themes—a Gothic dirge, a hymn to hope, a tango in hell." Commenting on the novel's intricacy, John Butt observes in the *Times Literary Supplement*, "This monster novel . . . works on so many levels, leads down so many strange paths to worlds of madness, surrealistic self-analysis and self-repudiation, and overloads language so magnificently and outrageously, that the reader comes out of it with his critical nerve shot, tempted to judge it as 'great' without knowing why." Also noting the novel's multi-faceted contents, Ronald Christ in his *Commonweal* review referred to it as "wild, hypnotizing, and disturbing."

On Heroes and Tombs is divided into four parts, the third being a novel-within-a-novel called "Report on the Blind." *Review* contributor William Kennedy characterizes this portion of the novel—a first person exploration of Fernando's theories about a conspiracy of blind people who rule the world—as "a tour de force, a document which is brilliant in its excesses, a surreal journey into the depths of Fernando's personal, Boschian hells, which in their ultimate landscapes are the provinces of a 'terrible nocturnal divinity, a demoniacal specter that surely held supreme power over life and death.' " In his *Washington Post Book World* review Salman Rushdie calls the section "the book's magnificent high point and its metaphysical heart." In Sabato's hands Fernando's paranoidal ravings fuse with the rest of the novel making the work at once a cultural, philosophical, theological, and sociological study of man and his struggle with the dark side of his being. According to Oberhelman, *On Heroes and Tombs* "without a doubt is the most representative national novel of Argentina written in the twentieth century." Kennedy describes the impact of the work when he concludes: "We read Sabato and we shudder, we are endlessly surprised, we exult, we are bewildered, fearful, mesmerized. He is a writer of great talent and imagination."

BIOGRAPHICAL/CRITICAL SOURCES:

BOOKS

Contemporary Literary Criticism, Gale, Volume 10, 1979, Volume 23, 1983.
Oberhelman, Harley Dean, *Ernesto Sabato,* Twayne, 1970.
Rodriguez Monegal, Emir, *The Borzoi Anthology of Latin American Literature,* Knopf, 1986.

PERIODICALS

Commonweal, June 18, 1982.
Newsweek, September 21, 1981.
Review, May-August, 1981.
Salmagundi, spring-summer, 1989.
Times Literary Supplement, August 13, 1982.
Washington Post Book World, August 16, 1981.

—*Sketch by Marian Gonsior*

* * *

SABERHAGEN, Fred(erick Thomas) 1930-

PERSONAL: Born May 18, 1930, in Chicago, Ill.; son of Frederick Augustus and Julia (Moynihan) Saberhagen; married Joan Dorothy Spicci, June 29, 1968; children: Jill, Eric, Thomas. *Education:* Attended Wright Junior College, 1956-57.

ADDRESSES: Home—Albuquerque, N.M. *Agent*—Eleanor Wood, Spectrum Literary Agency, 432 Park Ave. S., Suite 1205, New York, N.Y. 10016.

CAREER: Motorola, Inc., Chicago, Ill., electronics technician, 1956-62; free-lance writer, 1962-67; *Encyclopaedia Britannica,* Chicago, assistant editor, 1967-73; free-lance writer, 1973—. *Military service:* U.S. Air Force, electrical technician, 1951-55.

MEMBER: Science Fiction Writers of America.

WRITINGS:

The Golden People, Ace Books, 1964.
The Water of Thought, Ace Books, 1965, reprinted, Pinnacle Books, 1981.
The Book of Saberhagen (short stories), DAW Books, 1975.
Specimens, Popular Library, 1975.
Love Conquers All (first published in *Galaxy* magazine, 1974-75), Ace Books, 1978.
Mask of the Sun, Ace Books, 1978.
The Veils of Azlaroc, Ace Books, 1978.
(Editor) *A Spadeful of Spacetime* (anthology), Ace Books, 1980.
(With Roger Zelazny) *Coils,* Tor Books, 1980.

Octagon, Ace Books, 1981.
Earth Descended (short stories), Tor Books, 1981.
A Century of Progress, Tor Books, 1982.
(Editor with wife, Joan Saberhagen) *Pawn to Infinity* (science fiction anthology), Ace Books, 1982.
The Frankenstein Papers, Baen Books, 1986.
Pyramids, Baen, 1987.
Saberhagen: My Best, Baen, 1987.
After the Fact, Baen, 1988.
The White Bull, Baen, 1988.

"BERSERKER" SERIES

Berserker (short stories), Ballantine, 1967.
Brother Assassin, Ballantine, 1969 (published in England as *Brother Berserker,* Macdonald & Co., 1969).
Berserker's Planet, DAW Books, 1975.
Berserker Man, Ace Books, 1979.
The Ultimate Enemy (short stories), Ace Books, 1979.
The Berserker Wars (short stories), Tor Books, 1981.
The Berserker Throne, Simon & Schuster, 1985.
(With Poul Anderson, Ed Bryant, Stephen R. Donaldson, Larry Niven, Connie Willis, and Zelazny) *Berserker Base,* Tor Books, 1985.
Berserker, Blue Death, Tor Books, 1985.

"EMPIRE OF THE EAST" SERIES

The Broken Lands, Ace Books, 1967.
The Black Mountains, Ace Books, 1970.
Changeling Earth, DAW Books, 1973.
The Empire of the East (contains *The Broken Lands, The Black Mountains,* and *Changeling Earth*), Ace Books, 1979.

"DRACULA" SERIES

The Dracula Tape, Warner Paperback, 1975.
Holmes-Dracula File, Ace Books, 1978.
An Old Friend of the Family, Ace Books, 1979.
Thorn, Ace Books, 1980.
Dominion, Tor Books, 1981.

"SWORDS" TRILOGY

The First Book of Swords, Tor Books, 1984.
The Second Book of Swords, Tor Books, 1985.
The Third Book of Swords, Tor Books, 1985.
The Complete Book of Swords: Comprising the First, Second, and Third Books, Doubleday, 1985.

"LOST SWORDS" SERIES

The First Book of Lost Swords: Woundhealer's Story, T. Doherty, 1986.
The Second Book of Lost Swords: Sightblinder's Story, Tor Books, 1987.
The Third Book of Lost Swords: Stonecutter's Story, St. Martin's, 1988.
The Lost Swords: The First Triad (book club edition; contains *Woundhealer's Story, Sightblinder's Story,* and *Stonecutter's Story*), Doubleday, c. 1988.
The Fourth Book of Lost Swords: Farslayer's Story, St. Martin's, 1989.

BIOGRAPHICAL/CRITICAL SOURCES:

BOOKS

Dictionary of Literary Biography, Volume 8: *Twentieth-Century American Science Fiction Writers,* Gale, 1981.

PERIODICALS

Extrapolation, December, 1976.

*   *   *

SACASTRU, Martin
See BIOY CASARES, Adolfo

*   *   *

SACKS, Oliver (Wolf) 1933-

PERSONAL: Born July 9, 1933, in London, England; immigrated to the United States in 1960; son of Samuel (a physician) and Elsie (a physician; maiden name, Landau) Sacks. *Education:* Queen's College, Oxford, B.A., 1954, M.A., B.M., and B.Ch., all 1958; attended University of California, Los Angeles, 1962-65.

ADDRESSES: Home and office—119 Horton St., Bronx, N.Y. 10464. *Agent*—International Creative Management, 40 West 57th St., New York, N.Y. 10019.

CAREER: Yeshiva University, Albert Einstein College of Medicine, Bronx, N.Y., 1965—, began as instructor, currently clinical professor of neurology; Beth Abraham Hospital, Bronx, staff neurologist, 1966—. Visiting professor, University of California, Santa Cruz, 1986. Consultant neurologist, Bronx State Hospital, 1966—, and at the Little Sisters of the Poor in New York City.

MEMBER: American Academy of Neurology (fellow).

AWARDS, HONORS: Hawthornden Prize, 1974, for *Awakenings;* Oskar Pfister Award, American Psychiatric Association, 1988; Guggenheim fellowship, 1989; Harold D. Vursell Memorial Award, American Academy and Institute of Arts and Letters, 1989.

WRITINGS:

Migraine: Evolution of a Common Disorder, University of California Press, 1970, revised and enlarged edition published as *Migraine: Understanding a Common Disorder,* 1985.
Awakenings, Duckworth, 1973, Doubleday, 1974, published with a new foreword by the author, Summit Books, 1987.
A Leg to Stand On, Summit Books, 1984.
The Man Who Mistook His Wife for a Hat, and Other Clinical Tales, Duckworth, 1985, Summit Books, 1986.
Seeing Voices: A Journey into the World of the Deaf, University of California Press, 1989.

Contributor to the *New York Review of Books* and to various other journals.

WORK IN PROGRESS: A study of visual memory and imagery in creative artists.

SIDELIGHTS: As a physician, professor and author of widely read books about his work in the field of neurology, Oliver Sacks has become a leading proponent of the rehumanization of the medical arts. Working day-to-day in the hospitals and nursing homes of the New York City area exploring organic disorders of the brain and their symptoms, Sacks resembles a general practitioner, "a medical man in the old-fashioned humanist tradition," in the words of *New York Times* reviewer Michiko Kakutani. "He sees medicine as part of the continuum of life." Sacks is unhurried by an overly ambitious schedule and, therefore, able to give time to patients, time for listening and discussing their conditions. He is also free of the technical bias characteristic of current medical practice, so he involves patients in developing their own treatments. "His outstanding quality is wonder,"

writes Douglas Hill in the Toronto *Globe and Mail,* "a constant amazed appreciation of how men and women afflicted with frustrating or terrifying handicaps can cope with them and even help themselves to master them."

Sacks's approach to his work is reflected in his writing. He avoids the technical language and biochemical analyses common in medical treatises. Instead, in journal articles and such books as *Migraine, Awakenings, A Leg to Stand On,* and *The Man Who Mistook His Wife for a Hat,* he uses a case history approach to write straightforward clinical biographies that go beyond medical analysis to capture the human side of illness. These human stories also chronicle Sacks's discovery of health as a complex interaction of mind, body, and lifestyle that requires a concerted effort on the part of patient and physician in order to arrive at an appropriate cure. As Walter Kendrick puts it in a *Voice Literary Supplement* article, "Sacks's aim in all his books has been to show that neuropsychologists are wrong when they confine themselves to dry tabulations of symptoms and dosages. Just as the subject ought to be the full human brain, not half of it, so the method should account for the human being—emotions, personal relationships, everything."

In his book *Migraine,* first published in 1970 and later updated and enlarged for publication in 1985, Sacks examines a condition known to mankind for thousands of years. As Sacks points out, though it is a common affliction, migraine is little understood, its cycles of agony and euphoria often different with each episode. Headache is but one of many symptoms that include convulsions, vomiting, depression, and hallucinations. Drawing upon his observation of the numerous patients he treated, Sacks focuses not on cures but on an explanation of the function migraine serves for its human sufferers. As Israel Rosenfield relates in the *New York Times Book Review,* Sacks maintains that the disorder "is part of the human repertory of passive reactions to danger. The complexity of human social activities often necessitates passivity—neuroses, psychosomatic reactions and the varieties of migraine—when the individual confronts essentially unsolvable problems."

Though useful to migraine sufferers for the answers it provides, Sacks's book has attracted a varied readership. Kakutani finds that "his commentary is so erudite, so gracefully written, that even those people fortunate enough to never have had a migraine in their lives should find it equally compelling." Rosenfield maintains that *Migraine* "should be read as much for its brilliant insights into the nature of our mental functioning as for its discussion of migraine."

Upon his arrival at Beth Abraham Hospital in the late 1960s, Sacks discovered a group of patients suffering from a range of debilitating symptoms, the worst of which was a "sleep" so deep the sufferer was beyond arousal. The patients, he learned, were survivors of a sleeping sickness epidemic that had occurred between 1916 and 1927. In his second book, *Awakenings,* Sacks tells of his attempts to help this group. Recognizing the similarities between the symptoms exhibited by his patients and those of sufferers of Parkinson's disease, Sacks decided to begin administering L-dopa, a drug proven effective in treating Parkinson's. L-dopa initially produced dramatic results; patients out of touch with the world for over four decades suddenly emerged from their sleep. However, Sacks discovered that the drug was not a miracle cure. Battling side-effects and the shock of waking a changed person in a changed world proved too much for some in the group. Some died; others withdrew into trance-like states. Others succeeded, however, but only by achieving a balance between the illness and the cure, the past and the present.

Sacks's portrayal of the complexities of this episode has earned him considerable praise from readers of *Awakenings.* "Well versed in poetry and metaphysics, [Sacks] writes from the great tradition of Sir Thomas Browne," writes *Newsweek* reviewer Peter S. Prescott. "probing through medicine and his own observations of fear, suffering and total disability toward an investigation of what it means not only to be, but to become a person." "Some would attribute this achievement to narrative skill, others to clinical insight," comments Gerald Weissman in the *Washington Post;* "I would rather call this feat of empathy a work of art."

A Leg to Stand On is a doctor's memoir of his experience as a patient. As Jerome Bruner explains in the *New York Review of Books,* Sacks's book "is about a horribly injured leg, his own, what he thought and learned while living through the terrors and raptures of recovering its function." In 1976 while mountaineering in Scandinavia, Sacks fell and twisted his left knee. Although surgery repaired the physical damage—torn ligaments and tendons—the leg remained immobile. Even worse, Sacks found he had lost its inner sense of the leg; it seemed to him detached and alien, not his own. His inability to recover disturbed him and the surgeon's dismissal of his concerns only heightened his anxiety.

"By describing his experience and its resolution," comments Vic Sussman in the *Washington Post Book World,* "Sacks shows how patients rapidly become isolated (even physician-patients) when medicine regards them as 'invalids, in-valid.'" This reflection on the doctor/patient relationship is what makes *A Leg to Stand On* more than a personal story. As Bruner notes, "It is also a book about the philosophical dilemma of neurology, about the philosophy of mind, about what it might take to create a 'neurology of the soul' while still hanging on to your scientific marbles." And, Sussman concludes, "Sacks' remarkable book raises issues of profound importance for everyone interested in health care and the humane application of science."

In his bestselling collection of case histories entitled *The Man Who Mistook His Wife for a Hat,* "Dr. Sacks tells some two dozen stories about people who are also patients, and who manifest strange and striking peculiarities of perception, emotion, language, thought, memory or action," observes John C. Marshall in the *New York Times Book Review.* "And he recounts these histories with the lucidity and power of a short-story writer." One of the case histories Sacks presents is that of an instructor of music who suffers from a visual disorder. While able to see the component parts of objects, he is unable to perceive the whole they compose. Leaving Sacks's office after a visit, this patient turns to grab his hat and instead grabs his wife's face. Another features two autistic twins unable to add or subtract but capable of determining the day of the week for any date past or present and of calculating twenty-digit prime numbers. "Blessed with deep reserves of compassion and a metaphysical turn of mind," comments Kakutani, "Dr. Sacks writes of these patients not as scientific curiosities but as individuals, whose dilemmas—moral and spiritual, as well as psychological—are made as completely real as those of characters in a novel."

Although it demonstrates the variety of abnormal conditions that can arise from damage to the brain, *The Man Who Mistook His Wife for a Hat* also touches larger themes. *Nation* contributor Brina Caplan is taken by the book's portrayal of "men and women [who] struggle individually with a common problem: how to reconcile being both a faulty mechanism and a thematic, complex and enduring self." As Walter Clemmons suggests in *Newsweek,* "Sacks's humane essays on these strange cases are deeply stirring, because each of them touches on our own fragile 'normal' identities and taken-for-granted abilities of memory, attention and concentration."

In *Seeing Voices: A Journey Into the World of the Deaf,* Sacks explores the world of the congenitally deaf—those who are born without the ability to hear or speak. The author maintains that Sign—the language in which the deaf communicate—is no less complex or effective than any spoken language, and in fact Sign is superior to spoken language in its ability to express spatial dimension. *New York Times* critic Herbert Mitgang notes that "after reading [Sacks's] latest book, it will not be possible to watch deaf people communicate without gaining new respect for their language abilities."

Commenting on his work and writing, Sacks once told an interviewer for *U.S. News and World Report,* "You get an idea of how much is given to us by nature when you see what happens if it's taken away and how the person—the human subject—survives its loss, sometimes in the most extraordinary and even creative ways." This creativity is what Sacks attempts to capture in his case histories and memoirs. *New York Times* reviewer Benedict Nightingale characterizes Sacks as "a most unusual man, as much a metaphysician as physician: passionate, inquiring, generous, imaginative and supremely literate, a sort of Isaac Bashevis Singer of the hospital ward."

Yet, Sacks's writing also serves his larger purpose. "What he's arguing for is a set of neglected values: empathetic, emotional, individual, storylike," notes Caplan. "To ignore those values, he suggests, means constructing a science of cold, rigid design." As Paul Baumann sums it up in a *Commonweal* article, "Sacks's larger ambition is to develop what he calls an 'existential neurology' or 'romantic science' that will shed the rigid computational paradigms of traditional neurology and open itself up to the dynamic 'powers' of the mind."

MEDIA ADAPTATIONS: Harold Pinter's play, "A Kind of Alaska," is based on one of the case histories from *Awakenings.* An opera, based on the title case history of *The Man Who Mistook His Wife for a Hat,* was first produced under the same title in the fall of 1986 at the London Institute of Contemporary Art.

AVOCATIONAL INTERESTS: Bicycling, swimming, mountaineering.

BIOGRAPHICAL/CRITICAL SOURCES:

BOOKS

Sacks, Oliver, *A Leg to Stand On,* Summit Books, 1984.

PERIODICALS

Chicago Tribune, November 3, 1989.
Commonweal, March 28, 1986.
Globe and Mail (Toronto), February 21, 1987, November 18, 1989.
Los Angeles Times, October 15, 1989.
Los Angeles Times Book Review, March 23, 1986, September 24, 1989.
Nation, February 22, 1986.
Newsweek, July 15, 1974, August 20, 1984, December 30, 1985.
New York Review of Books, September 27, 1984, March 2, 1986, March 13, 1986, March 27, 1986.
New York Times, May 24, 1984, June 19, 1985, January 25, 1986, September 30, 1989.
New York Times Book Review, July 7, 1985, March 2, 1986, October 8, 1989.
People, March 17, 1986.
Times (London), February 3, 1990.

Times Literary Supplement, December 14, 1973, June 22, 1984,
    February 7, 1986, January 19, 1990.
Tribune Books (Chicago), August 20, 1989.
U.S. News and World Report, July 14, 1986.
Voice Literary Supplement, February, 1986.
Washington Post, October 30, 1987.
Washington Post Book World, August 26, 1984, February 16,
    1986, September 10, 1989.

*   *   *

SACKVILLE-WEST, V(ictoria Mary) 1892-1962

PERSONAL: Born March 9, 1892, at Knole Castle, Sevenoaks,
Kent, England; died June 2, 1962, at Sissinghurst Castle, Cran-
brook, Kent, England; daughter of Lionel Edward and Victoria
Sackville-West; married Harold Nicolson (a journalist and diplo-
mat), October 1, 1913; children: Benedict, Nigel. *Education:*
Studied privately with tutors.

CAREER: Novelist and poet. Gardening correspondent for *Observer;* member of National Trust's Garden Committee. *Wartime
service:* Organizer of Kent's Women's Land Army during World
War II.

MEMBER: Royal Society (fellow).

AWARDS, HONORS: Hawthornden Prize, 1927, for *The Land;*
Heinemann Prize, 1946, for *The Garden;* Companion of Honor,
1948.

WRITINGS:

POETRY

Chatterton, privately printed, 1909.
Constantinople, privately printed, 1915.
Poems West and East, John Lane, 1918.
Orchards and Vineyards, John Lane, 1921.
The Land, Heinemann, 1927.
King's Daughter, Doubleday, 1930.
Invitation to Cast Out Care, illustrated by Graham Sutherland,
    Faber, 1931. *Sissinghurst,* Hogarth, 1931, reprinted, Na-
    tional Trust, 1972.
(Translator) Rainer Marie Rilke, *Duineser Elegien: Elegies from
    the Castle of Duino,* Hogarth, 1931.
Collected Poems: Volume I, Hogarth, 1933, Doubleday, 1934.
Some Flowers, Cobden-Sanderson, 1937.
Solitude, Hogarth, 1938, Doubleday, 1939.
Selected Poems, Hogarth, 1941.
The Garden, Doubleday, 1946.

NOVELS

Heritage, George H. Doran, 1919.
The Dragon in Shallow Waters, Putnam, 1922.
Challenge, George H. Doran, 1923, reprinted, Avon, 1976.
Grey Wethers: A Romantic Novel, George H. Doran, 1923.
The Edwardians, Doubleday, Doran, 1930, reprinted, Virago,
    1983.
All Passion Spent, Doubleday, Doran, 1931, reprinted, Hogarth,
    1965.
Family History, Doubleday, Doran, 1932.
The Dark Island, Doubleday, Doran, 1934.
Grand Canyon, Doubleday, Doran, 1942.
The Devil at Westease: The Story as Related by Roger Liddiard
    (detective story), Doubleday, 1947.
The Easter Party, Doubleday, 1953, reprinted, Greenwood
    Press, 1972.
No Sign-Posts in the Sea, Doubleday, 1961, reprinted, Penguin,
    1985.

SHORT STORIES

The Heir: A Love Story (one short story), privately printed, 1922.
The Heir: A Love Story (collection; contains "The Heir," "The
    Christmas Party," "Patience," "Her Son," and "The Par-
    rot"), George H. Doran, 1922, reprinted, Cedric Chivers,
    1973.
Seducers in Ecuador, George H. Doran, 1925.
Thirty Clocks Strike the Hour and Other Stories, Doubleday,
    Doran, 1932.
Death of Noble Godavary and Gottfried Kuenstler, Benn, 1932.

BIOGRAPHIES

(Author of introduction and notes) *The Diary of Lady Anne Clif-
    ford,* 1923, reprinted, Norwood Editions, 1979.
Aphra Ben, the Incomparable Astrea, G. Howe, 1927, Viking,
    1928, reprinted, Russell, 1970.
Andrew Marvell, Faber, 1929, reprinted, Folcroft, 1969.
St. Joan of Arc, Doubleday, 1936, reprinted, M. Joseph, 1969.
Pepita, Doubleday, 1937, reprinted, Hogarth, 1970.
*The Eagle and the Dove: A Study in Contrasts, St. Theresa of
    Avila and St. Theresa of Lisieux,* M. Joseph, 1943, Double-
    day, 1944, reprinted, M. Joseph, 1969.
*Daughter of France: The Life of Anne Marie Louise d'Orleans,
    Duchesse de Montpensier, 1627-1693, La Grande Mademoi-
    selle,* Doubleday, 1959.

BOOKS ON GARDENING

Country Notes, M. Joseph, 1939, Harper, 1940, reprinted, Books
    for Libraries, 1971.
Country Notes in Wartime, Hogarth, 1940, Doubleday, 1941, re-
    printed, Books for Libraries, 1970.
In Your Garden, M. Joseph, 1951, published as *V. Sackville-
    West's Garden Book,* edited by Philippa Nicolson, Athe-
    neum, 1968, published in England as *V. Sackville-West's
    Garden Book: A Collection Taken From In Your Garden,* M.
    Joseph, 1968, reprinted, Macmillan, 1983.
In Your Garden Again, M. Joseph, 1953.
More for Your Garden, M. Joseph, 1955.
A Joy of Gardening: A Selection for Americans, edited by Her-
    mine I. Popper, Harper, 1958.
Even More for Your Garden, M. Joseph, 1958.
The Illustrated Garden Book: A New Anthology, edited by Robin
    Lane Fox, Atheneum, 1986.

Author of gardening column for *London Observer,* 1946-61.

OTHER

Knole and the Sackvilles, Heinemann, 1923, Benn, 1950.
*Twelve Days: An Account of a Journey Across the Bakhtiari
    Mountains in Southwestern Persia,* Doubleday, 1928.
English Country Houses, Collins, 1941.
Passenger to Teheran, Penguin, 1943.
The Women's Land Army, M. Joseph, 1944.
Nursery Rhymes (a study of the history of nursery rhymes),
    Dropmore, 1947.
Faces: Profiles of Dogs, Harvill, 1961, Doubleday, 1962.
(With husband, Harold Nicolson) *Another World Than This* (an-
    thology), M. Joseph, 1945.
(Author of introduction) Alice Christiana Meynell, *Prose and
    Poetry,* J. Cape, 1947.
*Berkeley Castle: The Historic Glouchestershire Seat of the Berke-
    ley Family Since the Eleventh Century,* English Life Publica-
    tions, 1972.

Dearest Andrew: Letters From V. Sackville-West to Andrew Reiber, 1951-1952, edited by Nancy MacKnight, Scribner, 1979.

Contributor of critical essays to Royal Society of Literature of the United Kingdom, c. 1927-45.

SIDELIGHTS: Victoria Sackville-West, who was called Vita and published under the name V. Sackville-West, was a member of one of Britain's most socially prominent families. She was born in Knole Castle, which her son Nigel Nicolson described in *Portrait of a Marriage* as "the largest house in England still in private hands." Her social milieu included people of noble birth and wealth, namely, Rudyard Kipling, Auguste Rodin, Pierpont Morgan, William Waldorf Astor, and Henry Ford. She was courted by nobility, including Lord Lascelles and Lord Granby.

A solitary person, Sackville-West for many years enjoyed Knole as her only companion. "Through Knole and her preferred solitude," Nicolson revealed, "she discovered the joy of writing." Her first works, written at the age of eleven, were ballads in the Horatius manner, and the first money she ever earned was one pound for a poem published in the *Onlooker* in 1907. Commenting on her early style, her son noted: "She taught herself the techniques of narrative and dialogue by careful observation of what she read, since she had no literary mentor and was yet to go to school." A prolific young writer, she wrote eight full-length novels (one in French) and five plays between 1906 and 1910. For her plots, Sackville-West turned to the stories of Knole and of the Sackvilles. "The Sackvilles, who were on the whole a modest family given to lengthy bouts of melancholia," related Nicolson, "were transformed by Vita into troubadors who played the most dramatic roles at the most dramatic moments of English history, and behaved in every situation with the utmost gallantry."

Some of the drama in the author's life was not made public until after her death when her son discovered an autobiography that his mother wrote in 1920. Incorporated into *Portrait of a Marriage,* the autobiography described Sackville-West's relationships with two women, Rosamund Grosvenor, a relative of the Duke of Westminster, and Violet Keppel. Sackville-West's affair with Grosvenor coincided with her engagement to Harold Nicolson, and by nearly eloping with Keppel the novelist came close to destroying her marriage.

Apart from disclosing the homosexuality within Britain's upper classes, Sackville-West's autobiography is the remarkable story of the author's relationship with her husband, Harold Nicolson. Their son called his parents' marriage "the strangest and most successful union that two gifted people have ever enjoyed." Theirs "is the story of two people who married for love and whose love deepened with every passing year, although each was constantly and by mutual consent unfaithful to the other. Both loved people of their own sex, but not exclusively. Their marriage not only survived infidelity, sexual incompatibility and long absences, but it became stronger and finer as a result. . . . Marriage succeeded because each found permanent and undiluted happiness only in the company of the other," he observed.

A large part of Sackville-West's renown stems from her association with the Bloomsbury group, a clique of literary elites, and from her relationship with a member of that group, Virginia Woolf, with whom she shared a deep, lasting, and briefly sexual friendship. Some believe that Sackville-West is the central figure of *Orlando,* Woolf's experimental novel that traces a character through several centuries and identities. Based on the novelists'

friendship, the novel took on genuine importance in Sackville-West's life. Nicolson explained: "Virginia by her genius has provided Vita with a unique consolation for having been born a girl, for her exclusion from her inheritance, for her father's death earlier that year. The book, for her, was not simply a brilliant masque or pageant. It was a memorial mass."

Woolf often commented on Sackville-West's writings. In a letter dated January 26, 1926, Sackville-West summarized Woolf's reaction to *The Land.* She said: "She was disappointed, but very sweet about it. She says it is a contribution to English literature, and is a solid fact against which one can lean up without fear of its giving way. She also says it is one of the few *interesting* poems—I mean the information part." Woolf, however, did like *Seducers in Ecuador,* as she told Sackville-West in a letter written September 15, 1924. "I like its texture," Woolf wrote, "the sense of all the fine things you have dropped into it, so that it is full of beauty in itself when nothing is happening—nevertheless such interesting things do happen, so suddenly—barely, too; and I like its obscurity so that we can play about with it—interpret it different ways, and the beauty and the fantasticality of the details." Other critics also praised Sackville-West's endeavors. In *Bookman,* for example, Hugh Walpole stated: "I find among all the writers in England no one else who has achieved such distinction in so many directions. The novelists who are also poets, the poets who are also novelists, are very rare always." L. A. G. Strong made a similar observation in *Spectator:* "Every novel written by a poet is in one sense an allegory. If it moves him as a poet—and he has no business with it otherwise—its characters and scenes will bear more than their literal meaning. Like a poem, it will contain more than the poet is consciously aware of as he writes. Miss Sackville-West's work has always had this double validity. Even where she is least conscious of her intentions, the truth of her work rings on more than one level."

Among her literary works, Sackville-West's long poem *The Land,* her novel *The Edwardians,* and the biography of her grandmother *Pepita* received the most critical attention. As a writer she brought consciousness to bear on her choice of genres, and in her poetry, fiction, and biographies she stayed within traditional forms. In his critical biography, Michael Stevens put forth: "The quality most immediately apparent in VS-W's work is the beauty of her prose, an observation which applies equally to her fiction, her biographies, and her travel books. It is, however, a style that she had to discipline herself to achieve; restraint was not a trait that came naturally to her passionate nature. The tranquility and balance which are such noticeable features of *No Sign-Posts in the Sea,* her last novel, are by no means equally obvious in *Heritage,* her first."

Later in life, Sackville-West became greatly admired for her formal gardens. Her enthusiasm for this country art, about which she wrote several books, seemed at first in sharp contrast with the nonconformity of her youth. But Walpole discerned the inconsistency in Sackville-West's nature. He claimed: "She has done everything in her life, I imagine, simply because it would be a delightful thing to do. . . . I would say that she has never definitely chosen anything or anybody all her life long, but that when a place or a person or a book has appeared close to her and has seemed the sort of place or person or book natural to her, she has attached it to herself without consciously thinking about it." This makes her romantic, the reviewer continued, "because the essence of romantic living is to find pleasure in the things around one, and she has found intense pleasure in them. This intensity of approach is at the basis of all her work."

BIOGRAPHICAL/CRITICAL SOURCES:

BOOKS

Bell, Quentin, *Virginia Woolf: A Biography,* Harcourt, 1972.
Dictionary of Literary Biography, Volume 34: *British Novelists, 1890-1929, Traditionalists,* Gale, 1985.
Glendinning, Victoria, *Vita: The Life of Vita Sackville-West,* Knopf, 1983.
Nicolson, Nigel, editor, *The Diaries and Letters of Harold Nicolson,* three volumes, Atheneum, 1966-68.
Nicolson, *Portrait of a Marriage,* Atheneum, 1973.
Philippe, Juliann, and John Phillips, *The Other Woman: A Life of Violet Trefusis,* Houghton, 1976.
Rule, Jane, *Lesbian Images,* Doubleday, 1975.
Smaridge, Norah, *Famous British Women Novelists,* Dodd, 1967.
Stevens, Michael, *V. Sackville-West: A Critical Biography,* Scribner's, 1974.
Watson, Sarah Ruth, *V. Sackville-West,* Twayne, 1972.

PERIODICALS

Bookman, September, 1930.
Horticulture, July, 1977.
Newsweek, April 24, 1961, November 5, 1973.
New York Times, June 3, 1962.
PMLA, March, 1955, March, 1956.
Publishers Weekly, June 25, 1962.
Spectator, June 2, 1953.
Time, June 8, 1962, November 12, 1973.
Vogue, September 1, 1956, October 15, 1961, November, 1973.
Wilson Library Bulletin, September, 1962.

* * *

SAETONE
See CAMUS, Albert

* * *

SAGAN, Carl (Edward) 1934-

PERSONAL: Born November 9, 1934, in New York, N.Y.; son of Samuel (a cloth cutter) and Rachel (Gruber) Sagan; married Lynn Alexander, June 16, 1957 (divorced, 1963); married Linda Salzman (a painter), April 6, 1968 (divorced); married Ann Druyan (a writer); children: (first marriage) Dorian Solomon, Jeremy Ethan; (second marriage) Nicholas; (third marriage) Alexandra. *Education:* University of Chicago, A.B. (with general and special honors), 1954, B.S., 1955, M.A., 1956, Ph.D., 1960.

ADDRESSES: Office—Laboratory for Planetary Studies, Space Science Building, Cornell University, Ithaca, N.Y. 14853.

CAREER: Writer. University of California, Berkeley, Miller research fellow in astronomy, 1960-62; Harvard University, Cambridge, Mass., 1962-68, began as lecturer, became assistant professor of astronomy; Smithsonian Institution, Astrophysical Observatory, Cambridge, Mass., astrophysicist, 1962-68; Cornell University, Ithaca, N.Y., associate professor, 1968-70, professor of astronomy and space sciences, 1970—, David-Duncan Professor of Astronomy and Space Sciences, 1976—, director of Laboratory for Planetary Studies, 1968—, associate director of Center for Radiophysics and Space Research, 1972-81.

Visiting assistant professor of genetics, Stanford University Medical School, 1962-63; National Science Foundation-American Astronomical Society visiting professor at various colleges, 1963-67; Condon Lecturer, University of Oregon and Ore-

gon State University, 1967-68; National Aeronautics and Space Administration (NASA) lecturer in astronaut training program, 1969-72; Holiday Lecturer, American Association for the Advancement of Science, 1970; Vanuxem Lecturer, Princeton University, 1973; Smith Lecturer, Dartmouth University, 1974, 1977; Wagner Lecturer, University of Pennsylvania, 1975; Philips Lecturer, Haverford College, 1975; Jacob Bronowski Lecturer, University of Toronto, 1975; Anson Clark Memorial Lecturer, University of Texas at Dallas, 1976; Danz Lecturer, University of Washington, 1976; Stahl Lecturer, Bowdoin College, 1977; Christmas Lecturer, Royal Institution, London, 1977; Menninger Memorial Lecturer, American Psychiatric Association, 1978; Carver Memorial Lecturer, Tuskegee Institute, 1981; Feinstone Lecturer, United States Military Academy, 1981; Class Day lecturer, Yale University, 1981; George Pal Lecturer, Motion Picture Academy of Arts and Sciences, 1982; Phelps Dodge Lecturer, University of Arizona, 1982; H. L. Welsh Lecturer in Physics, University of Toronto, 1982. Also lecturer at numerous other colleges and universities.

President, Carl Sagan Productions, Inc. (scientific books and supplies), 1981—. Member of Committee to Review Project Blue Book (U.S. Air Force), 1956-66. Experimenter, Mariner mission to Venus, 1962, Mariner and Viking missions to Mars, 1969—, designer of Pioneer 10 and 11 and Voyager 1 and 2 interstellar messages. Member of council, Smithsonian Institution, 1975—; member, American Committee on East-West Accord, 1983—. Judge, National Book Awards, 1976—. Member of various advisory groups of National Aeronautics and Space Administration; member of advisory panel, Civil Space Station Study, Office of Technology Assessment, U.S. Congress, 1982-; consultant to National Academy of Science.

MEMBER: International Astronomical Union (member of organizing committee, Commission of Physical Study of Planets), International Council of Scientific Unions (vice chairman; member of executive council, committee on space research; co-chairman, working group on moon and planets), International Academy of Astronautics, International Society for the Study of the Origin of Life (member of council, 1980—), P.E.N. International, American Astronomical Society (councillor; chairman, division of planetary sciences, 1975-76), American Physical Society, American Geophysical Union (president, planetology section, 1980—), American Association for the Advancement of Science (fellow; chairman, astronomy section, 1975), American Institute of Aeronautics and Astronautics (associate fellow), American Astronautical Society (member of council, 1976), Federation of American Scientists (member of council, 1977), Society for the Study of Evolution, British Interplanetary Society (fellow), Astronomical Society of the Pacific, Genetics Society of America, Authors Guild, Authors League of America, Phi Beta Kappa, Sigma Xi, Explorers Club.

AWARDS, HONORS: National Science Foundation postdoctoral fellowship, 1955-60; Alfred P. Sloan Foundation research fellowship at Harvard University, 1963-67; Smith Prize, Harvard University, 1964; National Aeronautics and Space Administration, Apollo Achievement Award, 1970, medal for exceptional scientific achievement, 1972, medal for distinguished public service, 1977, 1981; Prix Galabert (international astronautics prize), 1973; Klumpke-Roberts Prize, Astronomical Society of the Pacific, 1974; John W. Campbell Memorial Award, World Science Fiction Convention, 1974; Golden Plate Award, American Academy of Achievement, 1975; Joseph Priestly Award, Dickinson College, 1975; D.Sc., from Rensselaer Polytechnic University, 1975, Denison University, 1976, and Clarkson College, 1977; D.H.L., Skidmore College, 1976;

Pulitzer Prize for Literature, 1978, for *The Dragons of Eden: Speculations on the Evolution of Human Intelligence;* Washburn Medal, 1978; Rittenhouse Medal, 1980; 75th Anniversary Award, Explorers Club, 1980; *Cosmos* named among best books for young adults, American Library Association, 1980; American Book Award nominations for *Cosmos* (hardcover) and *Broca's Brain: Reflections on the Romance of Science* (paperback), both 1981; Peabody Award, 1981, for "Cosmos"; Seaborg Prize, 1981; Roe Medal, American Society of Mechanical Engineers, 1981; Humanist of the Year Award, American Humanist Association, 1981; Ohio State University annual award for television excellence, 1982, for "Cosmos"; Stony Brook Foundation award, with Frank Press, for distinguished contributions to higher education, 1982; John F. Kennedy Astronautics Award, American Astronautical Society, 1983; Locus Award, 1986, for *Contact.*

WRITINGS:

(With W. W. Kellogg) *The Atmospheres of Mars and Venus,* National Academy of Sciences, 1961.
(With I. S. Shklovskii) *Intelligent Life in the Universe,* Holden-Day, 1963, reprinted, 1978.
(With Jonathan Leonard) *Planets,* Time-Life Science Library, 1966.
Planetary Exploration: The Condon Lectures, University of Oregon Press, 1970.
(Editor with T. Owen and H. J. Smith) *Planetary Atmospheres,* D. Reidel, 1971.
(Editor with K. Y. Kondratyev and M. Ryecroft) *Space Research XI,* two volumes, Akademie Verlag, 1971.
(With R. Littauer and others) *The Air War in Indochina,* Center for International Studies, Cornell University, 1971.
(Editor with T. Page) *UFOs: A Scientific Debate,* Cornell University Press, 1972.
(Editor) *Communication with Extraterrestrial Intelligence,* MIT Press, 1973.
(With Ray Bradbury, Arthur Clarke, Bruce Murray, and Walter Sullivan) *Mars and the Mind of Man,* Harper, 1973.
(With R. Berendzen, A. Montagu, P. Morrison, K. Stendhal, and G. Wald) *Life beyond Earth and the Mind of Man,* U.S. Government Printing Office, 1973.
(Editor) *The Cosmic Connection: An Extraterrestrial Perspective* (selection of several book clubs, including Library of Science Book Club and Natural History Book Club), Doubleday, 1973.
Other Worlds, Bantam, 1975.
The Dragons of Eden: Speculations on the Evolution of Human Intelligence (Book-of-the-Month Club selection; also selection of other book clubs, including *Psychology Today* Book Club and McGraw-Hill Book Club), Random House, 1977.
(With F. D. Drake, A. Druyan, J. Lomberg, and T. Ferris) *Murmurs of Earth: The Voyager Interstellar Record* (Book-of-the-Month Club and other book clubs selection), Random House, 1978.
Broca's Brain: Reflections on the Romance of Science (Book-of-the-Month Club and other book clubs selection), Random House, 1979.
Cosmos (also see below; Book-of-the-Month Club and Natural History Book Club main selection; also selection of other book clubs, including Library of World History Book Club and Natural Science Book Club), Random House, 1980.
(With Paul R. Ehrlich, Donald Kennedy, and Walter Orr Roberts) *The Cold and the Dark,* Norton, 1984.
Comet, Random House, 1985.
Contact, Random House, 1986.

A Path Where No Man Thought, Random House, 1989.

Also contributor to several books on science. Author of radio and television scripts, including "Cosmos," Public Broadcasting System, 1980, and scripts for Voice of America, American Chemical Society radio series, and British Broadcasting Corp. Contributor to *Encyclopedia Americana, Encyclopaedia Britannica,* and *Whole Earth Catalog,* 1971. Contributor of more than 350 papers to scientific journals, and of articles to periodicals, including *National Geographic, Saturday Review, Discovery, Washington Post, Natural History, Scientific American,* and *New York Times. Icarus: International Journal of Solar System Studies,* associate editor, 1962-68, editor-in-chief, 1968-79; member of editorial board, *Origins of Life,* 1974—, *Climatic Change,* 1976—, and *Science,* 1979—.

SIDELIGHTS: When Carl Sagan was twelve years old, his grandfather asked him what he wanted to be when he grew up. "An astronomer," answered Carl, whereupon his grandfather replied, "Yes, but how will you make your living?"

As one of the most widely known and outspoken scientists in America, Carl Sagan has made both his living and a considerable reputation in astronomy, biology, physics, and the emerging science of exobiology, the study of extraterrestrial life. In his best-selling books, such as *The Dragons of Eden: Speculations on the Evolution of Human Intelligence* and *Broca's Brain: Reflections on the Romance of Science,* and in the extremely popular television series "Cosmos" (itself adapted into book form), Sagan, according to Frederic Golden of *Time,* "sends out an exuberant message: science is not only vital for humanity's future well-being, but it is rousing good fun as well."

The Cornell University-based scientist, who published his first research article ("Radiation and the Origin of the Gene") at age twenty-two, grew up in Brooklyn, New York, the son of an American-born mother and a Russian-immigrant father. Sagan describes himself as a science-fiction addict from an early age who became hooked on astronomy after learning that each star in the evening sky represented a distant sun. He tells Golden: "This just blew my mind. Until then the universe had been my neighborhood. Now I tried to imagine how far away I'd have to move the sun to make it as faint as a star. I got my first sense of the immensity of the universe." In a *New Yorker* interview, Sagan tells Henry S.F. Cooper, Jr.: "I didn't make a decision to pursue astronomy; rather, it just grabbed me and I had no thought of escaping. But I didn't know that you could get paid for it. . . . Then, in my sophomore year in high school, my biology teacher . . . told me he was pretty sure Harvard paid [noted astronomer] Harold Shapley a salary. That was a splendid day—when I began to suspect that if I tried hard I could do astronomy full time, not just part time." At sixteen, Sagan entered the University of Chicago on a scholarship. As early as his undergraduate days, the student began earning a reputation as a maverick; according to Golden, Sagan organized a popular campus lecture series and included himself as one of the speakers. At the same time, he shunned traditional courses of study in favor of his own intellectual pursuits.

On leaving the University of Chicago with a Ph.D. in astronomy and astrophysics in 1960, Sagan began research at Harvard University where, with colleague James Pollack, he challenged standard scientific views on the periodic lightening and darkening surface of Mars. Sagan's theory—that the alternating shades of surface light were caused by wind storms—was confirmed several years later with photographs of Mars. Speculations of that type cemented Sagan's image as an iconoclast. However, writes Golden, "even Sagan's scientific friends acknowledge that he does not have the patience or persistence for the slow, painstaking experimentation that is at the heart of the scientific process. Nor has he come close to the kind of breakthrough work that wins Nobel Prizes. But he more than compensates with other significant talents. He has a penchant for asking provocative questions. Sometimes, as Sagan fully concedes, this can rile others. But such prodding can inspire students and colleagues, lead to brilliant new insights, and generally create a mood of intellectual excitement." As one of Sagan's associates tells Cooper in the *New Yorker:* "Carl sees himself as an intellectual gadfly. . . . His talent is speculating, more than data analysis or collection. He works that talent—he theorizes, he gets people to admit things they wouldn't admit earlier. He creates an expansive view of man and the universe. But the fact that he can be quite passionate in his arguments makes people mad."

It is not only his speculations, though, that have made people mad. For instance, one of Sagan's more unusual projects involves interstellar communication. For the explorer ships Pioneer 10 and 11, both slated to leave our solar system, Sagan and Cornell colleague Frank Drake designed plaques to be installed on the crafts. Using illustrations and symbolic language, the plaques depict, according to Cooper's article, "the time of the launch in relation to the history of our galaxy, . . . a sort of return address, in case they fell into the hands (or whatever) of extraterrestrial beings, . . . [and] pictures of those who had launched the craft—delineations of a nude man and woman." Cooper reports that the scientist "still gets letters from people complaining about his sending smut into space."

Sagan's writing career has evolved along with his scientific career. In 1963 he became interested in a Russian book called *Intelligent Life in the Universe* and was given permission to work on its English translation. In the process Sagan added ten new chapters (more than doubling the original length of the book), thus becoming, according to Stuart Bauer in *New York,* "more than 60 per cent responsible for the first comprehensive treatment of the entire panorama of natural evolution, covering the origin of the universe, the evolution of the stars and planets, and the beginning of life on earth." (Bauer credits Sagan's expansion of the Russian original for the fact that *Intelligent Life in the Universe* has since gone into fourteen printings.) The scientist further distinguished himself as an expert in these fields in 1971, when, according to Bauer, "the *Encyclopaedia Britannica* invited [Sagan] to write its definitive 25,000-word essay on 'Life'; in 1973, in a manner of speaking, he took out a patent on it—U.S. Patent 3,756,934 for the production of amino acids from gaseous mixtures."

The Dragons of Eden, Sagan's first popular book to delve outside the study of astronomy, was published in 1977. Essentially an exploration of human intelligence, the work has met with mixed critical reaction. Robert Manning of *Atlantic,* for instance, finds *The Dragons of Eden* "rational, elegant and witty" but warns that reading parts of it is "akin to climbing the Matterhorn without crampons or ice ax. One must pay attention to every crack and cranny." R. J. Herrnstein writes in *Commentary* that although the author is "asking his readers to change their minds about almost nothing," he does so with "grace, humor and style." John Updike finds fault with the author's subject matter. "Versatile though he is," Updike remarks in the *New Yorker,* "[Sagan] is simply not enough saturated in his subject to speculate; what he can do is summarize and, to a limited degree, correlate the results of scattered and tentative modern research on the human brain. . . . [His] speculations, where they are not cheerfully wild, seem tacked on and trivial," *Newsweek*'s Raymond Sokolov also feels that the author "tries to 'speculate' about mat-

ters beyond scientific knowledge," but he "manages to get away with such airy inquiries because he is so open about their tentative science fiction status."

On the other hand, Stephen Toulmin, in a *New York Review of Books* article, praises *The Dragons of Eden* as an "engaging and well written . . . antidote to much of the recent controversy about human evolution." Toulmin cites the author's "briskness and astringency" of style and suggests that the book shows Sagan as "a true 'natural philosopher,' . . . whose real goal is to produce a revised version of the story of human history and destiny, within the boundary conditions set by the ideas of twentieth-century science."

The inspiration for Sagan's next work, *Broca's Brain,* came during a tour of the Musee de l'Homme in Paris, where he came upon a collection of jars containing human brains. Examining one of the jars, he found he was holding the brain of Paul Broca, a distinguished nineteenth-century anatomist. The idea for a book "flashed through his mind," according to Judy Klemsrud of the *New York Times Book Review. Broca's Brain,* a compilation of essays ranging in topic from ancient astronauts to mathematically-gifted horses, became another bestseller, prompting Sagan to tell Klemsrud that he believes "the public is a lot brighter and more interested in science than they're given credit for. . . . They're not numbskulls. Thinking scientifically is as natural as breathing."

As with *The Dragons of Eden, Broca's Brain* has elicited mixed reaction from the critics. While most praise Sagan's scientific expertise, some, like Maureen Bodo in *National Review,* think "Sagan is on less firm ground when speculating on semi-philosophical topics," a view shared by *New York Times Book Review* critic Robert Jastrow. Although Jastrow writes that "the skeptical chapters on pseudoscience . . . are delightful" and that Sagan is "capable of first-class reasoning when disciplined," he adds that the scientist "soars all too often on flights of meaningless fancy." Ultimately, though, Jastrow finds *Broca's Brain* worth reading, as does *Science* magazine's Richard Berendzen. "For the nonspecialist," Berendzen writes, "the book will be frustrating reading, with uneven technical detail, loose connections, and an overabundance of polysyllabic jargon. But if the reader can make it through, this curious volume can answer old questions, raise new ones, open vistas, become unforgettable. In short, Sagan has done it again. The book's title might be *Broca's Brain,* but its subject is Sagan's."

Television has played an important part in Carl Sagan's career. In the early 1970s he appeared on "The Tonight Show" and, as *New York*'s Bauer puts it, "launched into a cosmological crash course for adults. It was one of the great reckless solos of late-night television." After the scientist finished his long monologue on the evolution of the earth, Bauer writes, "one was willing to bet that if a million teenagers had been watching, at least a hundred thousand vowed on the spot to become full-time astronomers like him." Late in 1980, Sagan's involvement with the medium led to the television series "Cosmos," an eight million-dollar Public Broadcasting System production that eventually reached a worldwide audience of 150 million viewers—or, as Sagan prefers to think of it, three per cent of the earth's population. Filmed over a period of three years on forty locations in twelve countries, "Cosmos," introduced and narrated by Sagan, and written by Sagan, Ann Druyan, and Steven Soter, uses elaborate sets and special effects to explain the wide spectrum of the universe, from the expanse of a solar black hole to the intricacies of a living cell.

"Cosmos" is "dazzling" in its theme and presentation, observes Harry F. Waters in *Newsweek;* yet the reviewer feels that "Sagan undermines the show's scientific credibility by lapsing into fanciful speculation. . . . Equally unsettling is Sagan's perpetual expression of awestruck reverence as he beholds the heavens." John S. DeMott, what likewise finds Sagan's presentation "unabashedly awestruck," writes in *Time* that "each segment [of 'Cosmos'] has flair, excellent special effects and a dash of good ethical showmanship" and calls Sagan "a man clearly in love with his subject."

As "Cosmos" became public television's most highly-rated series to date, Sagan's book adaptation, *Cosmos,* proved equally popular, topping the bestseller lists for several months. In a *Christian Science Monitor* review, R. C. Cowan labels the book "as magnificent, challenging, and idiosyncratic . . . as the TV series." James Michener, writing in the *New York Times Book Review,* also finds Cosmos "a cleverly written, imaginatively illustrated summary . . . about our universe." Sagan's style, according to Michener, is "irridescent, with lights flashing upon unexpected juxtapositions of thought." The reviewer sums up, "Cosmos is an inviting smorgasbord of nutritious ideas well worth sampling." Citing the author's "personal voice," *Washington Post* critic Eliot Marshall feels that Sagan "lends his work a resonance and coherence it would otherwise lack." Marshall concludes that *Cosmos* is "a little overbearing, but still informative and entertaining."

Jeffery Marsh, however, takes exception to the book and the television series, emphasizing in *Commentary* the one criticism that has often been leveled against Sagan's theories: "Most blameworthy of all in this avowedly serious attempt to explain the nature and essence of scientific thinking is Sagan's systematic blurring of the distinction between proof and assertion, and between fact and hypothesis." As an example Marsh points out the author's "flat assertion that 'evolution is a fact, not a theory'. . . . What Sagan should have said is that the concept of evolution is accepted by . . . modern biologists." Marsh also contends that "Sagan's unwillingness to countenance seriously any form of particularism . . . is seen also in his failure to come to grips with the significance of religion, which he basically regards as a malignant force." Yet, the critic continues, "Sagan has no qualms about expounding . . . his personal messianic belief that the receipt of a radio transmission from a superior extraterrestrial intelligence . . . will somehow transform human behavior."

In recent years, Sagan has devoted much of his time to writing and lecturing about the long-term effects of nuclear warfare. The scientist's vision of the total devastation and widespread death brought on by radiation poisoning has made him a leading spokesman in the nuclear disarmament movement. Representing this cause, Sagan appeared in a panel debate with such figures as William F. Buckley, Jr., Elie Wiesel, and Henry Kissinger, following a broadcast of the highly-publicized television film "The Day After," which dramatized the aftermath of a nuclear attack on Lawrence, Kansas.

Despite the controversies surrounding the speculative nature of his work, Carl Sagan continues to be one of modern science's most popular spokesmen. In his lectures and books, he often tries to establish man's place in relation to the universe. In *Time,* Sagan writes of the significance of man: "As long as there have been humans we have searched for our place in the cosmos. Where are we? Who are we? . . . We make our world significant by the courage of our questions and by the depth of our answers."

Several of Sagan's books, including *The Cosmic Connection, The Dragons of Eden, Broca's Brain,* and *Cosmos,* have been translated into numerous languages, including French, Portuguese, Chinese, Hebrew, Greek, Japanese, Dutch, and Serbo-Croatian.

MEDIA ADAPTATIONS: Planets has been adapted into a film.

BIOGRAPHICAL/CRITICAL SOURCES:

BOOKS

Contemporary Issues Criticism, Volume 2, Gale, 1984.
Sagan, Carl, *Cosmos,* Random House, 1980.

PERIODICALS

America, February 7, 1981.
Atlantic, August, 1977.
Chicago Tribune, May 20, 1977.
Christian Science Monitor, November 19, 1980.
Commentary, August, 1977, May, 1981.
Detroit News, May 27, 1977.
Humanist, July-August, 1981.
National Review, August 3, 1979.
New Statesman, April 4, 1980.
Newsweek, June 27, 1977, October 6, 1980, November 23, 1981.
New York, September 1, 1975.
New Yorker, June 21, 1976, June 28, 1976, August 2, 1977.
New York Review of Books, June 9, 1977.
New York Times, May 17, 1977.
New York Times Book Review, June 10, 1979, July 19, 1979, January 25, 1981.
Omni, June, 1983.
People, December 15, 1980.
Saturday Evening Post, July-August, 1982.
Saturday Review, August, 1980.
Science, July 6, 1979.
Science Digest, March, 1982.
Time, January 24, 1974, September 29, 1980, October 20, 1980, December 14, 1981.
Washington Post Book World, May 27, 1977, November 17, 1980.

*   *   *

SAGAN, Francoise
   See QUOIREZ, Francoise

*   *   *

St. CYR, Cyprian
   See BERNE, Eric (Lennard)

*   *   *

SAINT-EXUPERY, Antoine (Jean Baptiste Marie Roger) de   1900-1944

PERSONAL: Born June 29, 1900, in Lyons, France; reported missing in action, July 31, 1944; believed shot down during reconnaissance flight over southern France; son of Jean (some sources say Cesar) and Marie Boyer (de Fonscolombe) de Saint-Exupery; married Consuelo Gomez Carillo, 1931. *Education:* Attended Ecole Bossuet and Lycee Saint-Louis (naval preparatory schools), 1917-19; attended school for air cadets at Avord, France, 1922.

CAREER: Aviator and writer. Tile manufacturer, flight instructor, and truck salesperson, 1920s; Latecoere Co. (now Air

France), Toulouse, France, commercial pilot flying between France and western Africa, 1926-27, commander of airport at Cape Juby, Morocco, 1927-28, directed Argentinian subsidiary of company and established airmail route in South America from Brazil to Patagonia, 1929-31, test pilot of hydroplanes over Mediterranean Sea, Perpignan, France, 1933; publicity agent and magazine writer for Air France, 1934; foreign correspondent for newspapers, including *Paris Soir* and *Intransigeant,* covering such events as the Spanish Civil War, beginning in 1935; pilot for Air France, late 1930s; lecturer and free-lance writer in the United States, 1940-43. *Military service:* Served in French Army Air Force, 1921-26 and during World War II; became captain in Air Corps Reserve, 1939; received Croix de Guerre for courage on reconnaissance flights, 1940; instructor for flying squadron in northern Africa, 1943; reconnaissance pilot between Algeria, Italy, and southern France, 1944; began final reconnaissance mission, July 29, 1944; reported missing in action, July 31, 1944.

AWARDS, HONORS: Prix Femina (France), 1931, for *Vol de nuit;* French Legion of Honor Award, 1929, for peaceful negotiations with Spaniards and Moors in Morocco; Grand Prix from Academie Francaise, 1939, for *Terre des hommes* and previous writings; Prix des Ambassadeurs (France), 1948, for *Citadelle.*

WRITINGS:

FICTION

Courrier sud (novel), Gallimard, 1929, translation by Stuart Gilbert published as *Southern Mail,* illustrations by Lynd Ward, H. Smith & R. Haas (New York City), 1933; translation by Curtis Cate bound with *Night Flight* (also see below), Heinemann, 1971, and published separately as *Southern Mail,* Harcourt, 1972, reprinted, 1985.

Vol de nuit (novel), preface by Andre Gide, Gallimard, 1931, translation by Stuart Gilbert published as *Night Flight* (Book-of-the-Month Club choice), Century, 1932; translation by Curtis Cate bound with *Southern Mail* (also see above), Heinemann, 1971.

Le Petit Prince (for children), illustrations by the author, Reynal & Hitchcock, 1943, translation by Katherine Woods published as *The Little Prince,* Harcourt, 1943, reprinted, 1982; educational edition published as *Le Petit Prince,* edited by John Richardson Miller, Houghton, 1946, revised edition, 1970.

ESSAYS

Terre des hommes, Gallimard, 1939, translation by Lewis Galantiere published as *Wind, Sand, and Stars,* Reynal & Hitchcock, 1939, with illustrations by John O. Cosgrave II, Harcourt, 1949, revised translation, Heinemann, 1970.

Pilote de guerre, Gallimard, 1942, translation by Lewis Galantiere published as *Flight to Arras,* illustrations by Bernard Lamotte, Harcourt, 1942, reprinted, 1985; educational edition published as *Pilote de guerre,* edited by Leon Wencelius, Editions de la Maison Francaise (New York City), 1943.

Citadelle, Gallimard, 1948, translation by Stuart Gilbert published as *The Wisdom of the Sands,* Harcourt, 1950, with introduction by Wallace Fowlie, University of Chicago Press, 1979.

Carnets, Gallimard, 1953, revised edition, introduction by Pierre Chevrier, 1975.

Saint-Exupery par lui-meme, illustrations by Luc Estang, Seuil, 1956.

Un Sens a la vie, compiled and edited by Claude Reynal, Gallimard, 1956, translation by Adrienne Foulke published as *A Sense of Life,* Funk & Wagnalls, 1965.

Ecrits de guerre, 1939-1944 (includes *Lettre a un otage*), preface by Raymond Aron, Gallimard, 1982, translation by Norah Purcell published as *Wartime Writings, 1939-1944,* introduction by Anne Morrow Lindbergh, Harcourt, 1986.

LETTERS

Lettre a un otage, Brentano's, 1943 (also see below), translation by Jacqueline Gerst published as *Letter to a Hostage,* Heinemann, 1950.

Lettres de jeunesse, 1923-1931, illustrations by the author, introduction by Renee de Saussine, Gallimard, 1953 (also see below), also published as *Lettres a l'amie inventee,* Plon, 1953.

Lettres a sa mere, Gallimard, 1955, revised edition, 1984 (also see below).

Lettres de Saint-Exupery: Lettres a sa mere, Lettres de jeunesse [and] *Lettre a un otage* (also published as *Lettres*), Club du Meilleur Livre, 1960.

COLLECTIONS

Airman's Odyssey (omnibus volume; contains *Wind, Sand, and Stars; Night Flight;* and *Flight to Arras*), Reynal & Hitchcock, 1943, with introduction by Richard Bach, Harcourt, 1984.

Oeuvres completes (complete works), illustrations by the author and others, Gallimard, 1950.

Pages choisies (selected works), introduction by Michel Quesnel, Gallimard, 1962.

Oeuvres completes de Saint-Exupery (complete works), Volume 1: *Courrier sud* [and] *Terre des hommes,* Volume 2: *Vol de nuit* [and] *Pilote de guerre,* Volume 3: *Lettre a un otage* [and] *Un sens a la vie,* Volume 4: *Lettres a sa mere* [and] *Le Petit Prince,* Volumes 5 and 6: *Citadelle,* Volume 7: *Carnets,* Club de l'Honnete Homme, 1985.

OTHER

"Courrier sud" (motion picture screenplay adapted from author's novel of the same title), released in France, 1937.

Contributor to periodicals, including *Harper's, New York Times Magazine, Senior Scholastic,* and *Navire d'Argent.*

MEDIA ADAPTATIONS: Night Flight was adapted into a motion picture of the same title, Metro-Goldwyn-Mayer, 1933; *The Little Prince* was adapted into a motion picture of the same title, Paramount, 1975, with a screenplay and lyrics by Alan Jay Lerner published by Paramount, 1974. *The Little Prince* was read in English by Peter Ustinov and recorded by Argo, 1972; *Le Petit Prince* was read in French by Gerard Phillipe and Georges Poujouly and recorded by Everest, 1973.

SIDELIGHTS: "There are certain rare individuals . . . who by the mere fact of their existence put an edge on life, their ceaseless astonishment before its possibilities awakening our own latent sense of renewal and expectation. No one ever stood out more conspicuously in this respect than the French aviator and author Antoine de Saint-Exupery," extolled Nona Balakian in the *New York Times Book Review.* A pilot before and during World War II, Saint-Exupery was praised for the lyricism with which he describes the exhilaration of flight, the wonder of childhood, and his visions of both personal and global peace. Throughout his writings, which include two novels and several essays, Saint-Exupery expresses the "paradoxical truth," as noted French author Andre Gide wrote in his preface to the pilot's novel *Vol de nuit* (*Night Flight*), that an individual's contentment "lies not in freedom but in his acceptance of a duty." Even Saint-Exupery's children's tale, *Le Petit Prince* (*The Little Prince*), for which he is probably best known among English-language readers, depicts responsibility as a necessary element of love.

In both his personal and professional life, Saint-Exupery lived according to the principles he espoused in his writings. Having developed a childhood interest in flying during family vacations near the French airport at Bugey, he became a military aviator soon after failing his exams at naval school (perhaps intentionally, some biographers speculate). Saint-Exupery combined his enthusiasm for flying with a strong sense of duty to his country by serving as an air force pilot in the early 1920s and in World War II, and as a pioneering long-distance airmail pilot in Africa and South America during the interim. In 1929 he received the French Legion of Honor Award for bringing about peaceful negotiations with feuding Spaniards and Moors during his command of an airport in Morocco, and in 1940 he was awarded the Croix de Guerre for the bravery he demonstrated on reconnaissance flights during the Battle of France. He insisted on serving the air force during World War II even when told he was too old to fly, so he worked as an instructor when necessary, and as a pilot when allowed. He began his final mission—one of a series of reconnaissance flights over northern Africa, southern Italy, and southern France—on July 29, 1944. He was reported missing two days later and is believed to have been shot down over southern France.

Saint-Exupery began recording his piloting experiences during the 1920s, and he had his first book published in 1929. *Courrier sud* (*Southern Mail*), a semi-autobiographical novel about an airmail pilot's failed romance, describes the glory of flight, the potential sadness of love, and the comfort found in attending to one's responsibilities. *Night Flight*, a novel published two years later, concerns the director of a postal airline and includes descriptions of Saint-Exupery's pioneering—and often hazardous—night flights across South America. "For the most part," wrote M. Parry in *Modern Language Review*, Saint-Exupery "deals with individuals who are prepared to risk their lives for something which will endure beyond themselves."

In response to critics who accused Saint-Exupery of portraying aviators as unrealistically heroic, the author's admirers asserted that Saint-Exupery considered pilots no better than any other people. Rather, he used his often mystical airborne experiences and the ideal qualities he saw in good pilots to illustrate the spiritual contentment people sought and the ideal qualities he believed everyone could possess. "Saint-Exupery's characters are not interested in the plane as machine . . .," observed *Dictionary of Literary Biography* contributor Catharine Savage Brosman, "but in what it allows them to do." Similarly, Saint-Exupery was not interested in his characters and stories as simply pilots and events, but as metaphors to help him describe ideas he found otherwise indescribable. "The most significant passages" of *Southern Mail*, according to Parry, "deal indirectly with metaphysical ideas such as time, change and movement, and the desire to penetrate beyond the surface appearance of reality to discover an underlying essence."

In an essay in the *French Review*, Bonner Mitchell observed that Saint-Exupery "was venturing upon largely unbroken ground in choosing to write directly about 'man's fate' while remaining in the realm of belles-lettres. Like [French authors Andre] Malraux, [Jean-Paul] Sartre, and [Albert] Camus after him, he achieved his first successes in the novel, but his message fitted less and less well into that form." Saint-Exupery's writings after

Night Flight took the form of essays and vignettes, this time frankly autobiographical. *Terre des hommes* (*Wind, Sand, and Stars*) conveys the joys and perils of flight and of life itself in its many anecdotes, including one of a desert crash in which Saint-Exupery nearly perished. In 1935 he and a friend had entered a contest sponsored by the French Air Ministry to break the time record for flying from Paris to Saigon, Vietnam. More than two hundred miles into the Libyan desert they crashed and, with almost no water or food, remained for three days before being rescued by a passing Bedouin. For its combination of realistic description and philosophic discussion, *Wind, Sand, and Stars* was awarded the Grand Prix from France's Academie Francaise.

Reviewers consider Saint-Exupery's next volume of essays, *Pilote de guerre* (*Flight to Arras*), more cohesive than *Wind, Sand, and Stars*. The author based *Flight to Arras* on the 1940 reconnaissance mission over German territory for which he received the Croix de Guerre. The text begins by describing Saint-Exupery's preparations and contempt for the mission, which he considers needlessly dangerous. In the course of the flight, however, his contempt gradually transforms into an acceptance of his duty, and possible hazards concern him less as his acceptance strengthens. Brosman praised the lyricism with which Saint-Exupery camouflages potential dangers: "Literary transformations—that is, metaphors—by which he depicts the sky and earth in poetic terms disguise the treachery of the experience, in which a blue evening sky and peaceful countryside below conceal mortal danger." Saint-Exupery ultimately embraces the assignment, pointless and dangerous as the task may still be, as a selfless and patriotic act that he must perform for himself, for his countrymen, and for all of humanity, if only to demonstrate that such selflessness and loyalty are possible. "The pilot before the flight was only conscious of himself as an individual," explained Richard Rumbold and Lady Margaret Stewart in their portrait *The Winged Life*, "but [he] achieves during it a new sense of 'belonging' which is expressed in almost mystical terms."

Some commentators consider the author's conclusion in *Flight to Arras* almost unbelievably patriotic and self-sacrificing, while others admire Saint-Exupery's ideals. Rumbold and Stewart, for example, described *Flight to Arras* as "a record, sincere, passionate, heart-searching, of Saint-Exupery's own reactions to the disaster to his country which he sees, in a . . . theme fundamental to the book, as part of the deeper crisis of our times. . . . In the modern world, he believed, man has lost an essential quality, described variously as a common incentive, a sense of mutual brotherhood, and what he calls the life of the spirit as opposed to the life of the intellect." In dutifully performing his mission as a French military pilot, Rumbold and Stewart suggested, Saint-Exupery was attempting to help restore that "common incentive" among his fellow citizens. The author's success in his attempt was evidenced by the admiration and reverence with which he was regarded by his fellow pilots and compatriots.

Soon after his flight over Germany Saint-Exupery traveled to the United States, where he remained three years and wrote *The Little Prince*, his most popular work among English-language readers. Of all of Saint-Exupery's writings, *The Little Prince* is often said to provide the most accurate and personal portrait of its author. Philip A. Wadsworth, writing in *Modern Language Quarterly*, observed that Saint-Exupery frequently recalled his happy childhood in his other writings, though "he never turned to childhood as an escape; for him the past was not another world but was still alive as part of his present." The author was frequently known to doodle whimsical sketches of a small child, and at the urging of friends he drew more sketches and created a story about them. Maxwell A. Smith, writing in his *Knight of the Air: The Life and Works of Antoine de Saint-Exupery,* described the story *The Little Prince* as "a delicate and ethereal fairy tale apparently addressed to children," but he added that "its wide philosophical overtones as a parable will be understood only by adults."

The Little Prince is narrated by a pilot who has crashed in the desert—as Saint-Exupery had done in 1935—and is attempting to repair his plane before his provisions run out. Before him appears a child, the Little Prince, who has traveled to earth from his own tiny planet, and who immediately asks the pilot for a drawing of a sheep to take back home. He also requests a muzzle for the sheep, so it won't eat the beautiful rose he has cultivated and grown to love. The Little Prince tells the pilot that when he first arrived on earth he entered a garden containing hundreds of roses identical to his own, and he was filled with sadness as he suddenly realized that his rose was not unique. A fox he befriended, though, told the Little Prince that it was the time he spent loving and caring for his rose, and his responsibility for keeping the rose alive, that would make his rose special to him. The Little Prince returns to his planet—with the sheep but without the muzzle, which he has forgotten—by asking a poisonous desert snake to bite him. The pilot hopes, as he gazes toward the sky and remembers the Little Prince, that the prince has been able to prevent the sheep from eating his beloved rose.

P. L. Travers, the author of *Mary Poppins* and other children's books, believed *The Little Prince*'s interpretation of love and responsibility would "shine upon children with a sidewise gleam." Travers explained in the *New York Herald Tribune Weekly Book Review:* "It will strike them in some place that is not the mind and glow there until the time comes for them to comprehend it." Praising *The Little Prince*'s "poetic charm, . . . its freshness of imagery, its whimsical fantasy, delicate irony and warm tenderness," Maxwell A. Smith predicted in 1956 that "*The Little Prince* will join that select company of books like [Jean de] La Fontaine's *Fables,* [Jonathan] Swift's *Gulliver's Travels,* [Lewis] Carroll's *Alice in Wonderland* and [Maurice] Maeterlinck's *Blue Bird,* which have endeared themselves to children and grownups alike throughout the world." Forty years after the book's publication it had sold nearly four million copies, and it was continuing to sell two hundred thousand copies each year.

In 1943, after completing *The Little Prince,* Saint-Exupery returned to his old flying squadron as an instructor and pilot in northern Africa, southern Italy, and southern France. For several years he had been working on his lengthiest and most ambitious writing project, but had not completed it by the time of his death in 1944. The book, *Citadelle (The Wisdom of the Sands),* was published in 1948 with few editorial revisions, and it received that year's Prix des Ambassadeurs for exemplifying the spirit of France. "A huge tapestry, woven across the years in hours of solitude and leisure," according to Wadsworth, *The Wisdom of the Sands* "incorporates every thread of [Saint-Exupery's] thought and serves as a mighty backdrop for his other works." Although the book encompasses Saint-Exupery's main themes, it never mentions flying or pilots; instead, it concerns a society of desert dwellers and the reminiscences and proclamations of their leader. The French title, which means "citadel" or city fortress, noted Brosman, refers simultaneously to "the desert city which is the [book's] geographical center . . .; the city of God . . .; and the fortress within each man." Saint-Exupery's intent is to depict the "responsibility and interdependency," in Brosman's words, of the city's chief and his people—his responsibility for them, theirs for him, and theirs for each other—just as he emphasized his own country's and all of humanity's responsibility and interdependency in his earlier writings.

The Wisdom of the Sands has often been compared with the Christian Old Testament and Friedrich Nietzsche's *Thus Spake Zarathustra* because of its length and its weighty, majestic tone. Some critics, including Rumbold and Stewart, lamented the fact that Saint-Exupery could not revise *The Wisdom of the Sands* before the volume's publication, as he had done dozens of times with his other manuscripts. "It is perhaps unfair to judge a work which was never completed or revised," acknowledged Rumbold and Steward, "but, as it stands, it is little more than a series of rambling, disconnected notes, and consequently produces, particularly when taken as a whole, an impression of verbosity and even incoherence." Reviewers such as Wadsworth, however, felt that the book's "rough-draft form . . . displays the author's entire and intimate expression of thought before being revised to meet his high artistic standards. . . . If this book lacks the nervous quality, the charged meanings, to which we are accustomed in Saint Exupery," Wadsworth declared, "it has the merit of showing us the author, pen in hand, in the act of baring his soul on paper."

For Brosman, *The Wisdom of the Sands* constitutes a fitting conclusion to Saint-Exupery's *oeuvre.* "The unity of Saint-Exupery's work derives from his style, his poetic vision of the world, and his moral concern," asserted Brosman, "which begins in *Courrier sud* by focusing on the quality of the individual, seen in relation to his tasks, and ends in *Citadelle* by posing the principles for the city of man." Wadsworth likewise found the themes of morality and responsibility permeating Saint-Exupery's writings and his life. Saint-Exupery's "gift," Wadsworth declared, "was that he saw no frontier between art and life, that he identified in his personality and in all his writing the artist, the thinker, and the man of action."

BIOGRAPHICAL/CRITICAL SOURCES:

BOOKS

Children's Literature Review, Volume 10, Gale, 1986.
Dictionary of Literary Biography, Volume 72: *French Novelists, 1930-1960,* Gale, 1988.
Rumbold, Richard and Lady Margaret Stewart, *The Winged Life: A Portrait of Antoine de Saint-Exupery, Poet and Airman,* Weidenfeld & Nicolson, 1953.
Saint-Exupery, Antoine de, *Night Flight,* preface by Andre Gide, Reynal & Hitchcock, 1932.
Smith, Maxwell A., *Knight of the Air: The Life and Works of Antoine de Saint-Exupery,* Pageant Press, 1956.
Twentieth-Century Literary Criticism, Volume 2, Gale, 1979.

PERIODICALS

French Review, April, 1960.
Modern Language Quarterly, March, 1951.
Modern Language Review, April, 1974.
New York Herald Tribune Weekly Book Review, April 11, 1943.
New York Times Book Review, August 31, 1986.
Time, August 4, 1986.
Washington Post Book World, July 27, 1986.

—*Sketch by Christa Brelin*

*   *   *

St. JOHN, Philip
See del REY, Lester

SAKI
See MUNRO, H(ector) H(ugh)

*   *   *

SALINGER, J(erome) D(avid) 1919-

PERSONAL: Born January 1, 1919, in New York, NY; son of Sol (an importer) and Miriam (Jillich) Salinger; allegedly married a French physician, c. 1945, and divorced in 1947; married Claire Douglas, February 17, 1955 (divorced, October, 1967); children: (second marriage) Margaret Ann, Matthew. *Education:* Graduated from Valley Forge Military Academy, 1936; attended New York University, Ursinus College, and Columbia University (where he studied with Whit Burnett).

ADDRESSES: Home and office—Cornish, NH. *Agent*—Harold Ober Associates, Inc., 40 East 49th St., New York, NY 10017.

CAREER: Writer. Worked as an entertainer on the Swedish liner M.S. *Kungsholm* in the Caribbean, 1941. *Military service:* Army of the United States, 1942-46; served in Europe; staff sergeant; received five battle stars.

WRITINGS:

The Catcher in the Rye (novel; Book-of-the-Month Club selection), Little, 1951.
Nine Stories, Little, 1953 (published in England as *For Esme—With Love and Squalor, and Other Stories,* Hamish Hamilton, 1953).
Franny and Zooey (two stories; "Franny" first published in *New Yorker,* January 29, 1955, "Zooey," *New Yorker,* May 4, 1957), Little, 1961.
Raise High the Roof Beam, Carpenters; and, Seymour: An Introduction (two stories; "Raise High the Roof Beam, Carpenters" first published in *New Yorker,* November 19, 1955, "Seymour," *New Yorker,* June 6, 1959), Little, 1963.
Four Books by J. D. Salinger (the four preceding books in one volume), Bantam, 1967.

Also contributor to *Harper's, Story, Collier's, Saturday Evening Post, Cosmopolitan,* and *Esquire.*

MEDIA ADAPTATIONS: "Uncle Wiggily in Connecticut" (published in *Nine Stories*), was made into the motion picture "My Foolish Heart," 1950.

SIDELIGHTS: J. D. Salinger began accumulating a substantial corps of disciples, especially among young people, with the publication of his first book, the now-classic novel *Catcher in the Rye.* And, with comparatively few pages of published fiction, he became a literary phenomenon who, as Walter Allen notes, "created the dialect of a generation." Phoniness, to this college generation of the 1950s, was the cardinal sin. It was simple to distinguish the saints and pilgrims from the "phonies." Salinger continues to be widely read. But his critics became more critical and labeled him " 'cute,' 'repressed,' 'Puritanical,' or 'grossly sentimental,' " writes William Wiegand. He has been dismissed as a *New Yorker* contributor and merely "a good minor writer." Jonathan Baumbach notes that Salinger's stories became repetitive and that he takes few risks. The "Everybody's Favorite" that Alfred Kazin, with mixed feelings, wrote about himself came to be known as a bit phony. In 1965 Salinger ceased publishing.

Critical evaluations of his work have never been unanimously laudatory. He has been called both profound and immature, the inheritor of Kierkegaardian ideas as well as distrustful of ideas. But many reviewers consider his characters to be serious critics of their world. Wiegand writes that Salinger demonstrates "skepticism toward the systematic, the orderly, the explicit, the formally contrived. . . . What Salinger celebrates is the spontaneous, the passionate, the accidental. An explicit and determined universe forbids the truly spontaneous." The Glass children of his novellas mystically seek a state of *agape* instead of mundane love, and what is unbearable for them, writes Wiegand, "is not that some people are bad, but that experience is fleeting. [Therefore] everything must be retained." Donald Barr adds: "[Salinger] is preoccupied with collapses of nerve, with the cracking laugh of the outraged, with terrifying feelings of loneliness and alienation. He seems to correspond peculiarly to the psychological aura of our moment of history." He has, in short, expressed some of the values and aspirations of certain young people "in a way that nobody since Scott Fitzgerald . . . [has] done as well," writes Maxwell Geismar.

Much has been made of Salinger's preoccupations with Zen Buddhism, but Barr disagrees that such a system is dominant in Salinger's work: "Salinger's spiritual message is, I think, refracted by his eclecticism. On the one side are his acknowledged inclinations toward Zen and the evident quest, in which all the Glass children are engaged, for some ultimate experience of centrality. On the other side is Salinger's flurried oscillation between lucubration and the luscious emotions, both of which are repugnant to Zen."

The Catcher in the Rye, which took about ten years to write, continues to lead Salinger's writings in popularity, and it placed third in a *Book Week* poll of the twenty best postwar novels. It is a sensitive and humorous portrait of an adolescent and a novel of initiation. Its protagonist, the young Holden Caulfield, uses colloquial adolescent language and condemns everything that is "phony." Kay Boyle wrote: "Now that we are in the midst of the student revolution for which his book was the White Paper, I believe that his novel may now grow rather than diminish in importance in our literature." Frank Kermode, in a not altogether favorable review, called it "a book of extraordinary accomplishment." Middleton Murray wrote: "The effect of revelation is heightened by the apparently unexpressive medium: we are made to feel that the most fastidious utterance would be no more adequate to the spiritual simplicity of this generous soul than the barbarous lingo to which he is confined. To produce such an impression, of course, is a triumph of art." Geismar praised the book with reservations: "The real achievement of *The Catcher in the Rye* is that it manages so gracefully to evade just those central questions which it raises, and to preserve both its verbal brilliance and the charm of its emotions within the scope of its own dubious literary form. It is still Salinger's best work, if a highly artificial one, and the caesuras, the absences, the ambiguities at the base of this writer's work became more obvious in his subsequent books." While *Catcher* elicited artistic evaluations in the West, in Russia it was judged on moral grounds. Alexander Dymshits praised the book for reflecting "the spiritual bankruptcy of America."

Salinger began publishing stories, rather ordinary pieces about GIs, with *Collier's* during World War II. Barr believes that Salinger came to be "one of the most powerful talents . . . practising the short story" and sees his development as a story writer as organic, "if perhaps somewhat monstrous. The earlier stories, which are controlled and even conventional, seem to begin in ordinary hurts—hurts caused by social snobbery, anti-Semitism, the bitchiness of girls. . . . Then the center of anxiety shifts. How to be loved is no longer the problem, but how to love. . . . So Salinger draws in and draws in his awareness, from a general sympathy to a personal worry. These changes in Salinger's concerns are accompanied by changes in his technique. The prose thickens to a chowder of learning and expostulating; the descriptive phrases *reach* more wildly; Salinger's easy mastery of colloquial rhythms and of the insensate little violences of the metropolitan idiom is now exploited to propel longer and longer flights of abstractions." Kazin believes that it is Salinger's "intense . . . almost compulsive, need to fill in each inch of his canvas, each moment of his scene," that makes his stories exciting.

Little is known about Salinger himself; he lives in secrecy and almost total seclusion from interviewers. He began to write at fifteen and published his first story in *Story* magazine in 1940. His methods owe something to F. Scott Fitzgerald and Ring Lardner. He enjoys writing, and considers the compensations, if they come, "very beautiful."

BIOGRAPHICAL/CRITICAL SOURCES:

BOOKS

Allen, Walter, *The Modern Novel,* Dutton, 1965.
Belcher, W. F., and J. W. Lee, editors, *J. D. Salinger and the Critics,* Wadsworth, 1962.
Children's Literature Review, Volume 18, Gale, 1989.
Concise Dictionary of American Literary Biography: The New Consciousness, 1941-1968, Gale, 1987.
Contemporary Literary Criticism, Gale, Volume 1, 1973, Volume 3, 1975, Volume 8, 1978, Volume 12, 1980, Volume 56, 1989.
Dictionary of Literary Biography, Volume 2: *American Novelists since World War II,* Gale, 1978.
French, Warren, *J. D. Salinger,* Twayne, 1963.
Geismar, Maxwell, *American Moderns,* Hill & Wang, 1958.
Grunwald, Henry Anatole, editor, *Salinger: A Critical and Personal Portrait,* Harper, 1962.
Gwynn, F. L., and J. L. Blotner, *The Fiction of J. D. Salinger,* University of Pittsburgh Press, 1958.
Hamilton, Ian, *In Search of J. D. Salinger,* Random House, 1988.
Kazin, Alfred, *Contemporaries,* Atlantic Monthly Press, 1962.
Kermode, Frank, *Puzzles and Epiphanies,* Chilmark, 1962.
Laser, Marvin, and Norman Fruman, editors, *Studies in J. D. Salinger,* Odyssey, 1963.
Marsden, Malcolm M., compiler, *If You Really Want to Know: A Catcher Casebook,* Scott, 1963.
Short Story Criticism, Volume 2, Gale, 1989.

PERIODICALS

America, January 26, 1963.
Atlantic, August, 1961.
Book Week, September 26, 1965.
Catholic World, February, 1962.
Critique, spring-summer, 1965.
Harper's, October, 1962, December, 1962.
Horizon, May, 1962.
Life, November 3, 1961.
Mademoiselle, August, 1961.
Minnesota Review, May-July, 1965.
Newsweek, January 28, 1963.
Saturday Review, September 16, 1961, November 4, 1961.
Time, September 15, 1961.

*   *   *

SALISBURY, Harrison E(vans) 1908-

PERSONAL: Born November 14, 1908, in Minneapolis, Minn.; son of Percy Pritchard and Georgianna (Evans) Salisbury; married Mary Hollis, April 1, 1933 (divorced); married Charlotte Young Rand, 1964; children: (first marriage) Michael, Stephan. *Education:* University of Minnesota, A.B., 1930.

ADDRESSES: Home—Box 70, Taconic, Conn. 06079. *Agent*—Curtis Brown, 10 Astor Place, New York, N.Y. 10003.

CAREER: Minneapolis Journal, Minneapolis, Minn., reporter, 1928; United Press, reporter, London manager, Moscow manager, and foreign editor, 1930-48; *New York Times,* correspondent in Moscow, 1949-54, reporter in New York City, 1955-61, national editor, 1962-64, assistant managing editor, 1964-70, associate editor and editor of opinion-editorial page, 1971-75.

MEMBER: American Academy and Institute of Arts and Letters (president, 1975-77), Authors League of America (president, 1980-85), National Press Club (Washington, D.C.), Century Association (New York).

AWARDS, HONORS: Pulitzer Prize in international reporting, 1955, for articles on the Soviet Union.

WRITINGS:

Russia on the Way, Macmillan, 1946.
American in Russia, Harper, 1955 (published in England as *Stalin's Russia and After,* Macmillan [London], 1955).
The Shook-up Generation, Harper, 1958.
To Moscow—and Beyond: A Reporter's Narrative, Harper, 1960.
Moscow Journal: The End of Stalin, University of Chicago Press, 1961.
The Northern Palmyra Affair, Harper, 1962.
A New Russia?, Harper, 1962.
The Key to Moscow, Lippincott, 1963.
Russia, Atheneum, 1965 (published in England as *The Soviet Union,* Encyclopaedia Britannica Educational Corp., 1967).
Orbit of China, Harper, 1967.
(Editor and contributor) *The Soviet Union: The First Fifty Years,* Harcourt, 1967 (published in England as *Anatomy of the Soviet Union,* Thomas Nelson, 1967).
Behind the Lines—Hanoi, December 23, 1966-January 7, 1967, Harper, 1967.
(Editor) Andrei Sakharov, *Progress, Coexistence, and Intellectual Freedom,* Norton, 1968.
War between Russia and China, Norton, 1969 (published in England as *The Coming War between Russia and China,* Secker & Warburg, 1969).
The 900 Days: The Siege of Leningrad, Harper, 1969, reprinted with a new introduction, Da Capo Press, 1985 (published in England as *The Siege of Leningrad,* Secker & Warburg, 1969).
(Editor) Georgi K. Zhukov, *Marshal Zhukov's Greatest Battles,* Harper, 1969.
The Many Americas Shall Be One, Norton, 1971.
(Author of commentary) Emil Schulthess, *Soviet Union,* Harper, 1971.
(Editor) *The Eloquence of Protest: Voices of the 70's,* Houghton, 1972.
(Editor and contributor, with James A. Keith and Ida Prince Nelson) *Project WERC Resource Book,* Teacher Assist Center, 1972.
(Editor with David Schneiderman) *The Indignant Years: Art and Articles from the Op-Ed Page of the New York Times,* Crown/Arno Press, 1973.
To Peking—and Beyond: A Report on the New Asia, Quadrangle, 1973.
(Editor and author of foreword) Sakharov, *Sakharov Speaks,* Knopf, 1974.

The Gates of Hell, Random House, 1975.

Travels around America, Walker, 1976.

Black Night, White Snow: Russia's Revolutions, 1905-1917, Doubleday, 1978.

Russia in Revolution, Holt, 1979.

(Editor) *Russian Society since the Revolution,* Ayer Co., 1979.

Without Fear or Favor: The New York Times and Its Times, New York Times, 1980, published as *Without Fear or Favor: An Uncompromising Look at the New York Times,* Ballantine, 1981.

China: 100 Years of Revolution, Holt, 1983.

A Journey for Our Times: A Memoir, Harper, 1983.

(Editor and author of introduction) *Vietnam Reconsidered: Lessons from a War,* Harper, 1984.

The Long March: The Untold Story, Harper, 1985.

A Time of Change: A Reporter's Tale of Our Time, Harper, 1988.

The Great Black Dragon Fire: The Chinese Inferno, Little, Brown, 1989.

SIDELIGHTS: During his long career, Pulitzer Prize-winning journalist Harrison E. Salisbury has specialized in covering the Soviet Union and China. He has served as the Moscow manager for United Press and as Moscow correspondent for the *New York Times,* and he has written a number of books on recent Soviet and Chinese history. In the course of his work he has traveled to Siberia, Central Asia, Outer Mongolia, Tibet, North Vietnam and North Korea. He was the first western reporter allowed to visit Hanoi during the Vietnam War. For his book *The Long March: The Untold Story,* Salisbury retraced the arduous seven thousand mile march of the Red Chinese Army, a march that cost some eighty thousand lives. Called a "battle-scarred old reporter" by James Yuenger in *Tribune Books,* Salisbury explains in an article for *Modern Maturity:* "I am a writer. I like to write and report and have since I was in college. There is nothing I would rather do."

After leaving college in 1930, Salisbury worked for the United Press in Chicago, covering the trial of gangster Al Capone. He was soon transferred overseas to handle first the London and then the Moscow office. During the Second World War he covered the Eastern Front for United Press, reporting on the fighting between Soviet and Nazi troops. Following the war Salisbury became the Moscow correspondent for the *New York Times,* a position he held until 1954. It was during this time that Salisbury's name became "synonymous with the Soviet Union, whose politics, totalitarian leadership, and, above all, its people, preoccupied him for some 40 years," according to Robert Manning in the *New York Times.* Upon returning home in 1954 following Soviet dictator Joseph Stalin's death, Salisbury wrote a series of articles about Kremlin politics and Stalin's crimes; these articles won him the Pulitzer Prize in 1955.

Because of the extensive censorship practiced in the Soviet Union in the 1940s and 1950s, Salisbury's stories while he was a reporter there were often cut before they were allowed to be sent out of the country. It was not until he returned to the United States that he was able to speak openly about many aspects of Soviet life. His experiences in the Soviet Union were recounted in a string of books during the 1950s and 1960s, including such titles as *Stalin's Russia and After, To Moscow—and Beyond: A Reporter's Narrative,* and *Moscow Journal: The End of Stalin.*

In *A Journey for Our Times: A Memoir,* Salisbury writes about his years in the Soviet Union, a country that, Robert MacNeil notes in the *New York Times,* "has dominated much of his adult life." Salisbury explains in the book: "I've been interested in Russia as a whole, the Russianness of Russia rather than the Soviet

phase, which seems to me to be an aberration and not as interesting as the culture and tradition and the marvelous Russian literature and the nature of the people and the country." *A Journey for Our Times* covers the problems Salisbury experienced both with the Soviet censors and with his editors back home. The Soviets withheld information from him; the editors sometimes revised his stories. Salisbury also recounts his fear in 1950 that the KGB was trying to kill him with a paralyzing drug, and the possibility in 1953, just before Stalin's death, that he would be put on trial. "When [Salisbury] warms up, when he writes about what moves him," MacNeil says in his review of the book, " 'A Journey for Our Times' is superb."

Salisbury's career after his return to the United States is recounted in *A Time of Change: A Reporter's Tale of Our Time,* his second volume of memoirs. In this book he tells of covering the civil rights era and the Vietnam War, among other major stories of the 1960s. His stories about Birmingham, Alabama, during the height of civil rights turbulence, in which he warned that the city was about to explode in violence, earned him 42 charges of criminal libel and a $10 million suit against him and the *New York Times.* Salisbury and the *Times* won dismissal of the cases. During the Vietnam War, he was the first American reporter allowed to visit North Vietnam, where his stories of American bombing raids over Hanoi drew criticism from hardliners back home. He was also the first reporter allowed into Communist Albania, North Korea, and Mongolia. Aside from his travels abroad, Salisbury recounts the office politics at the *New York Times* during the 1960s and 1970s, providing what Yuenger calls "gossip of an intriguing order."

To Arnold R. Isaacs of the *Washington Post Book World, A Time of Change* is "zesty, fast-paced, a tumbling, kaleidoscopic succession of places and events and personalities and details set down vividly but not always thoughtfully or originally. . . . Most readers . . . will come away from this book with a new respect for the craft of those, like Salisbury, who undertake to observe and explain complicated, turbulent events not from a safe distance or after they have passed, but from close up and as they occur." Yuenger concludes that *A Time of Change,* along with the first volume of Salisbury's memoirs, "should be required reading for every young reporter who wants to know how it's done."

At the age of 75, Salisbury received permission to retrace the historic Long March of the Red Chinese Army, a journey of some 7,400 miles across some of the most rugged terrain in China. The Long March began in 1934 when the Red Army, chased by the much larger armies of Nationalist leader Chaing Kai-Shek, sought to escape being wiped out. When they finally reached the western Chinese province of Shaanxi after a grueling, year-long journey, only 4,000 survivors remained of the original 86,000 soldiers. The Long March has assumed legendary stature in modern Chinese history because of the important role played by Mao Zedong, later to become leader of Red China, and other prominent Chinese communists.

In *The Long March: The Untold Story,* Salisbury tells of the hardships and misery of the Long March, comparing the historic trek to his own journey over the same terrain fifty years later. Accompanied by his wife, Charlotte, and his close friend John S. Service, Salisbury followed the route of the Long March by jeep, mule, and even on foot. He also interviewed many of the original Long March participants to obtain their insights into the event, and he spoke to local historians and government officials. "Only, I felt, by traveling those 7,400 miles could I write an accurate account of the Long March," Salisbury explains in *Mod-*

ern Maturity. "Only so could I convey some small sense of the ordeal of the men and women who made the march." Salisbury's book, Judith Shapiro writes in the *New Republic,* "provides a fascinating glimpse into Maoist China's myth of its origins." Michel Oksenberg, writing in the *New York Times Book Review,* calls *The Long March* "an engrossing and revealing account . . . the best to date."

Called by Connie Lauerman in the *Chicago Tribune* "a reporter's reporter, at once tough and compassionate, worldly and naive," Salisbury is often ranked among the best known and most respected of American journalists. Peter S. Prescott in *Newsweek* describes him as "the most distinguished of postwar foreign correspondents." Yuenger finds Salisbury to be "an extraordinary piece of work—passionately romantic and coldly cynical, quick to take offense or dispense praise, relentlessly catty . . ., yet wisely tolerant of man's foibles. He wears his heart on his typewriter. And he has proven, time and time again, that he is one hell of a journalist."

BIOGRAPHICAL/CRITICAL SOURCES:

BOOKS

Salisbury, Harrison E., *A Journey for Our Times: A Memoir,* Harper, 1983.
Salisbury, Harrison E., *A Time of Change: A Reporter's Tale of Our Time,* Harper, 1988.

PERIODICALS

Chicago Tribune, August 3, 1983.
Los Angeles Times Book Review, April 3, 1988.
Modern Maturity, October-November, 1986.
Nation, May 24, 1980.
National Review, March 6, 1981.
New Republic, June 28, 1980, December 16, 1985.
Newsweek, June 6, 1983, October 14, 1985.
New York Times, June 8, 1983.
New York Times Book Review, May 18, 1980, May 15, 1983, September 29, 1985, March 20, 1988.
Publishers Weekly, October 19, 1984.
Tribune Books (Chicago), February 21, 1988.
Washington Post, June 11, 1980.
Washington Post Book World, March 6, 1988.

—Sketch by Thomas Wiloch

*   *   *

SAMIGLI, E.
See SCHMITZ, Aron Hector

*   *   *

SANCHEZ, Sonia 1934-

PERSONAL: Born September 9, 1934, in Birmingham, daughter of Wilson L. and Lena (Jones) Driver; children: Rita, Morani Neusi, Mungu Neusi. *Education:* Hunter College (now Hunter College of the City University of New York) B.A., 1955; postgraduate study, New York University. *Politics:* "Peace, freedom, and justice."

ADDRESSES: Home—407 W. Chelten Ave., Philadelphia, Pa., 19144. *Office*—Department of English/Women's Studies, Temple University, Broad and Montgomery, Philadelphia, Pa., 19122.

CAREER: Staff member, Downtown Community School, San Francisco, Calif., 1965-67, and Mission Rebels in Action,

1968-69; San Francisco State College (now University), San Francisco, instructor, 1966-68; University of Pittsburgh, Pittsburgh, Pa., assistant professor, 1969-79; Rutgers University, New Brunswick, N.J., assistant professor, 1970-71; Manhattan Community College of the City University of New York, New York City, assistant professor of literature and creative writing, 1971-73; City College of the City University of New York, teacher of creative writing, 1972; Amherst College, Amherst, Mass., associate professor, 1972-75; University of Pennsylvania, Philadelphia, Pa., 1976-77; Temple University, Philadelphia, associate professor, 1977, professor, 1979—, faculty fellow in provost's office, 1986-87, presidential fellow, 1987-88. Member, Literature Panel of the Pennsylvania Council on the Arts.

AWARDS, HONORS: PEN Writing Award, 1969; National Institute of Arts and Letters grant, 1970; Ph.D., Wilberforce University, 1972; National Endowment for the Arts Award, 1978-79; Honorary Citizen of Atlanta, 1982; Tribute to Black Women Award, Black Students of Smith College, 1982; Lucretia Mott Award, 1984; American Book Award, Before Columbus Foundation, 1985, for *homegirls & handgrenades;* Pennsylvania Governor's Award in the humanities, 1989, for bringing great distinction to herself and her discipline through remarkable accomplishment.

WRITINGS:

Homecoming (poetry), Broadside Press, 1969.
We a BaddDDD People (poetry), with foreword by Dudley Randall, Broadside Press, 1970.
It's a New Day: Poems for Young Brothas and Sistuhs (juvenile), Broadside Press, 1971.
(Editor) *Three Hundred and Sixty Degrees of Blackness Comin' at You* (poetry), 5X Publishing Co., 1971.
A Sun Lady for All Seasons Reads Her Poetry (record album), Folkways, 1971.
Ima Talken bout the Nation of Islam, TruthDel, 1972.
Love Poems, Third Press, 1973.
A Blues Book for Blue Black Magical Women (poetry), Broadside Press, 1973.
The Adventures of Fat Head, Small Head, and Square Head (juvenile), Third Press, 1973.
(Editor and contributor) *We Be Word Sorcerers: 25 Stories by Black Americans,* Bantam, 1973.
I've Been a Woman: New and Selected Poems, Black Scholar Press, 1978.
A Sound Investment and Other Stories (juvenile), Third World Press, 1979.
Crisis in Culture—Two Speeches by Sonia Sanchez, Black Liberation Press, 1983.
homegirls & handgrenades (poems), Thunder's Mouth Press, 1984.
(Contributor) Mari Evans, editor, *Black Women Writers (1950-1980): A Critical Evaluation,* introduction by Stephen Henderson, Doubleday-Anchor, 1984.
Under a Soprano Sky, Africa World, 1987.

PLAYS

"The Bronx Is Next," first produced in New York at Theatre Black, October 3, 1970 (included in *Cavalcade: Negro American Writing from 1760 to the Present,* edited by Arthur Davis and Saunders Redding, Houghton, 1971).
"Sister Son/ji," first produced with "Cop and Blow" and "Players Inn" by Neil Harris and "Gettin' It Together" by Richard Wesley as "Black Visions," Off-Broadway at New York Shakespeare Festival Public Theatre, 1972 (included in *New*

Plays from the Black Theatre, edited by Ed Bullins, Bantam, 1969).

"Uh Huh; But How Do It Free Us?", first produced in Chicago, at Northwestern University Theater, 1975 (included in *The New Lafayette Theatre Presents: Plays with Aesthetic Comments by Six Black Playwrights, Ed Bullins, J. E. Gaines, Clay Gross, Oyamo, Sonia Sanchez, Richard Wesley,* edited by Bullins, Anchor Press, 1974).

"Malcolm Man/Don't Live Here No More," first produced in Philadelphia at ASCOM Community Center, 1979.

"I'm Black When I'm Singing, I'm Blue When I Ain't," first produced in Atlanta, Georgia at OIC Theatre, April 23, 1982.

Also author of "Dirty Hearts," 1972.

CONTRIBUTOR TO ANTHOLOGIES

Robert Giammanco, editor, *Potero Negro* (title means "Black Power"), Giu. Laterza & Figli, 1968.

Le Roi Jones and Ray Neal, editors, *Black Fire: An Anthology of Afro-American Writing,* Morrow, 1968.

Dudley Randall and Margaret G. Burroughs, editors, *For Malcolm: Poems on the Life and Death of Malcolm X,* Broadside Press, 1968.

Walter Lowenfels, editor, *The Writing on the Wall: One Hundred Eight American Poems of Protest,* Doubleday, 1969.

Arnold Adoff, editor, *Black Out Loud: An Anthology of Modern Poems by Black Americans,* Macmillan, 1970.

Lowenfels, editor, *In a Time of Revolution: Poems from Our Third World,* Random House, 1970.

June M. Jordan, editor, *Soulscript,* Doubleday, 1970.

Gwendolyn Brooks, editor, *A Broadside Treasury,* Broadside Press, 1971.

Randall, editor, *Black Poets,* Bantam, 1971.

Orde Coombs, editor, *We Speak as Liberators: Young Black Poets,* Dodd, 1971.

Bernard W. Bell, editor, *Modern and Contemporary Afro-American Poetry,* Allyn & Bacon, 1972.

Adoff, editor, *The Poetry of Black America: An Anthology of the 20th Century,* Harper, 1973.

J. Chace and W. Chace, *Making It New,* Canfield Press, 1973.

Donald B. Gibson, editor, *Modern Black Poets,* Prentice-Hall, 1973.

Stephen Henderson, editor, *Understanding the New Black Poetry: Black Speech and Black Music as Poetic References,* Morrow, 1973.

J. Paul Hunter, editor, *Norton Introduction to Literature: Poetry,* Norton, 1973.

James Schevill, editor, *Breakout: In Search of New Theatrical Environments,* Swallow Press, 1973.

Lucille Iverson and Kathryn Ruby, editors, *We Become New: Poems by Contemporary Women,* Bantam, 1975.

Quincy Troupe and Rainer Schulte, editors, *Giant Talk: An Anthology of Third World Writings,* Random House, 1975.

Henry B. Chapin, editor, *Sports in Literature,* McKay, 1976.

Brooks and Warren, editors, *Understanding Poetry,* Holt, 1976.

Ann Reit, editor, *Alone amid All the Noise,* Four Winds/Scholastic, 1976.

Erlene Stetson, editor, *Black Sister: Poetry by Black American Women, 1746-1980,* Indiana University Press, 1981.

Amiri and Amina Baraka, editors, *Confirmation: An Anthology of African-American Women,* Morrow, 1983.

Burney Hollis, editor, *Swords upon this Hill,* Morgan State University Press, 1984.

Jerome Rothenberg, editor, *Technicians of the Sacred: A Range of Poetries from Africa, America, Asia, Europe and Oceania,* University of California Press, 1985.

Marge Piercy, editor, *Early Ripening: American Women's Poetry Now,* Pandora (London), 1987.

Poems also included in *Night Comes Softly, Black Arts, To Gwen With Love, New Black Voices, Blackspirits, The New Black Poetry, A Rock Against the Wind, America: A Prophecy, Nommo, Black Culture,* and *Natural Process.*

OTHER

Author of column for *American Poetry Review,* 1977-78, for *Philadelphia Daily News,* 1982-83. Contributor of poems to *Minnesota Review, Black World,* and other periodicals. Contributor of plays to *Scripts, Black Theatre, Drama Review,* and other theater journals. Contributor of articles to several journals, including *Journal of African Civilizations.*

WORK IN PROGRESS: Editing a book of critical essays on four women poets, Audre Lorde, Margaret Walker, Gwendolyn Brooks, and Sonia Sanchez; a play.

SIDELIGHTS: Sonia Sanchez is often named among the strongest voices of black nationalism, the cultural revolution of the 1960s in which many black Americans sought a new identity distinct from the values of the white establishment. C. W. E. Bigsby comments in *The Second Black Renaissance: Essays in Black Literature* that "the distinguishing characteristic of her work is a language which catches the nuance of the spoken word, the rhythms of the street, and of a music which is partly jazz and partly a lyricism which underlies ordinary conversation." Her emphasis on poetry as a spoken art, or performance, connects Sanchez to the traditions of her African ancestors, an oral tradition preserved in earlier slave narratives and forms of music indigenous to the black experience in America, as Bernard W. Bell demonstrates in *The Folk Roots of Contemporary Afro-American Poetry.* In addition to her poetry, for which she has won many prizes, Sanchez has contributed equally-well-known plays, short stories, and children's books to a body of literature called "The Second Renaissance," as Bigsby's title reflects.

Sanchez reached adulthood in Harlem, which only thirty years before had been the cradle of the first literary "renaissance" in the United States to celebrate the works of black writers. Political science and poetry were the subjects of her studies at Hunter College and New York University during the fifties. In the next decade Sanchez began to combine these interests into one activity, "the creat[ion] of social ideals," as she wrote for a section about her writings in *Black Women Writers (1950-1980: A Critical Evaluation,* edited by Mari Evans. For Sanchez, writing and performing poetry is a means of constructive political activism to the extent that it draws her people together to affirm pride in their heritage and build the confidence needed to accomplish political goals. Yet the terms of "black rhetoric," or words by themselves, are not enough, she says often in poems and interviews. Biographers cite her record of service as an educator, activist, and supporter of black institutions as proof of her commitment to this belief. Writing in the *Dictionary of Literary Biography,* Kalamu ya Salaam introduces Sanchez as "one of the few creative artists who have significantly influenced the course of black American literature and culture."

Before Sanchez became recognized as a part of the growing black arts movement of the 1960s, she worked in the Civil Rights movement as a supporter of the Congress of Racial Equality. At that time, like many educated black people who enjoyed economic stability, she held integrationist ideals. But after hearing Malcolm X say that blacks would never be fully accepted as part of mainstream America despite their professional or economic achievements, she chose to base her identity on her racial heritage. David Williams reports that the title of her first book, *Homecoming,* announces this return to a sense of self grounded in the realities of her urban neighborhood after having viewed it for a time from the outside through the lens of white cultural values. In the title poem, "Sanchez presents the act of returning home as a rejection of fantasy and an acceptance of involvement," notes Williams in *Black Women Writers (1950-1980).* For the same reasons, Sanchez did not seek a New York publisher for the book. She preferred Dudley Randall's Broadside Press, a publisher dedicated to the works of black authors, that was to see many of her books into print. Reacting to the poems in *Homecoming,* Johari Amini's review in *Black World* warns that they "hurt (but doesn't anything that cleans good) and [the] lines are blowgun dartsharp a wisdom ancient as kilimanjaro." Haki Madhubuti's essay in *Black Women Writers (1950-1980)* comments on this effect, first remarking that "Sanchez . . . is forever questioning Black people's commitment to struggle," saying again later that she is "forever disturbing the dust in our acculturated lives."

One aspect of her stand against acculturation is a poetic language that does not conform to the dictates of standard English. Madhubuti writes, "More than any other poet, [Sanchez] has been responsible for legitimizing the use of urban Black English in written form. . . . She has taken Black speech and put it in the context of world literature." Salaam elaborates, "In her work from the 1960s she restructured traditional English grammar to suit her interest in black speech patterns"—a technique most apparent, he feels, in *We a BaddDDD People.* In one poem cited by Madhubuti which he says is "concerned with Black-on-Black damage," Sanchez predicts that genuine "RE VO LU TION" might come about "if mothas programmed / sistuhs to / good feelings bout they blk / men / and I / mean if blk / fathas proved / they man / hood by fightin the enemy. . . ." These reviewers explain that by inserting extra letters in some words and extra space between lines, words, and syllables within a poem, Sanchez provides dramatic accents and other clues that indicate how the poem is to be said aloud.

The sound of the poems when read aloud has always been important to Sanchez. Her first readings established her reputation as a poet whose energetic performances had a powerful effect on her listeners. She has visited Cuba, China, the West Indies, Europe, and more than five hundred campuses in the United States to give readings, for which she is still in demand. Of her popularity, Salaam relates, "Sanchez developed techniques for reading her poetry that were unique in their use of traditional chants and near-screams drawn out to an almost earsplitting level. The sound elements, which give a musical quality to the intellectual statements in the poetry, are akin to Western African languages; Sanchez has tried to recapture a style of delivery that she felt had been muted by the experience of slavery. In her successful experimentation with such techniques, she joined . . . others in being innovative enough to bring black poetry to black people at a level that was accessible to the masses as well as enjoyable for them."

Sanchez is also known as an innovator in the field of education. During the sixties, she taught in San Francisco's Downtown Community School and became a crusader and curriculum developer for black studies programs in American colleges and universities. Materials on black literature and history were absent from the schools she had attended, and she has worked to see that other young people are not similarly disenfranchised. Opposition to this goal has often complicated her career, sometimes making it difficult for her to find or keep teaching positions; nevertheless, Sanchez has fought to remain in the academic arena to shape and encourage the next generation. She wrote two books

for her children (*The Adventures of Fat Head, Small Head, and Square Head,* and *A Sound Investment and Other Stories*) for reasons she expressed to interviewer Claudia Tate in *Black Women Writers at Work:* "I do think that it's important to leave a legacy of my books for my children to read and understand; to leave a legacy of the history of black people who have moved toward revolution and freedom; to leave a legacy of not being afraid to tell the truth. . . . We must pass this on to our children, rather than a legacy of fear and victimization."

Because she takes action against oppression wherever she sees it, she has had to contend with not only college administrators, but also the FBI, and sometimes fellow-members of political organizations. Reviewers note that while her early books speak more directly to widespread social oppression, the plays she wrote during the seventies give more attention to the poet's interpersonal battles. For example, "Uh Huh; But How Do It Free Us?" portrays a black woman involved in the movement against white oppression who also resists subjection to her abusive husband. This kind of resistance, writes Salaam, was not welcomed by the leaders of the black power movement at that time.

Sanchez resigned from the Nation of Islam after three years of membership. She had joined the Nation of Islam in 1972 because she wanted her children to see an "organization that was trying to deal with the concepts of nationhood, morality, small businesses, schools. . . . And these things were very important to me," she told Tate. As Sanchez sees it, her contribution to the Nation was her open fight against the inferior status it assigned to women in relation to men. Believing that cultural survival requires the work of women and children no less than the efforts of men, Sanchez felt compelled to speak up rather than to give up the influence she could exert through public readings of her poetry. "It especially was important for women in the Nation to see that," stated Sanchez, who also told Tate that she has had to battle the "so-called sexism" of many people outside the Nation as well.

Thus Sanchez became a voice in what Stephen E. Henderson calls "a 'revolution within the Revolution' " that grew as black women in general began to reassess their position as the vicitms not only of racial injustice but of a sexual arrogance tantamount to dual-colonialism—one from without, the other from within, the Black community," he writes in his introduction to Evans's book. This consciousness surfaces in works that treat politics in the context of personal relationships. Sanchez told Tate, "If we're not careful, the animosity between black men and women will destroy us." To avoid this fate, she believes, women must refuse to adopt the posture of victims and "move on" out of damaging relationships with men, since, in her words recorded in the interview, "If you cannot remove yourself from the oppression of a man, how in the hell are you going to remove yourself from the oppression of a country?"

Consequently, *A Blues Book for Blue Black Magical Women,* written during her membership in the Nation, examines the experience of being female in a society that "does not prepare young black women, or women period, to be women," as she told Tate. Another section tells about her political involvements before and after she committed herself to the establishment of ethnic pride. In this book, as in her plays and stories, "Sanchez uses many of the particulars of her own life as illustrations of a general condition," writes Salaam. He offers that Sanchez "remains the fiery, poetic advocate of revolutionary change, but she also gives full voice to the individual human being struggling to survive sanely and to find joy and love in life." *Love Poems* contains many of the haiku Sanchez wrote during a particularly stressful period of her life. An interview she gave to *Black Collegian* disclosed that she had been beset by the problems of relocation, illness, and poverty. Writing haiku allowed her to "compress a lot of emotion" into a few lines, which helped her to stay sane. Under the circumstances, she also felt that there was no guarantee she would have the time to finish longer works. The poems in these two books are no less political for their being more personal, say reviewers. "The haiku in her hands is the ultimate in activist poetry, as abrupt and as final as a fist," comments Williams. In Salaam's opinion, "No other poet of the 1960s and 1970s managed so masterfully to chronicle both their public and personal development with poetry of such thoroughgoing honesty and relevant and revelatory depth."

Madhubuti says of the poet, "Much of her work is autobiographical, but not in the limiting sense that it is only about Sonia Sanchez." For example, in her well-known story "After Saturday Night Comes Sunday," a woman on the verge of madness finds strength to break out of a painful liaison with a drug abuser without herself becoming trapped in self-pity or alcoholism. "It's not just a personal story," the poet, who has survived divorce, told Tate. "It might be a personal experience, but the whole world comes into it." Readers of all backgrounds can appreciate writings concerned with black identity and survival, she declares in *Black Women Writers at Work,* mentioning that her works have been translated into European languages and remarking that "you don't have to whitewash yourself to be universal." At another point in the interview, she explained why she deliberately pushes her writing beyond autobiography: "We must move past always focusing on the 'personal self' because there's a larger self. There's a 'self' of black people. And many of us will have to make a sacrifice in our lives to ensure that our bigger self continues." In her statement for *Black Women Writers (1950-1980),* she presents her own life as an example of the price that must be paid to contribute to social change: "I see myself helping to bring forth the truth about the world. I cannot tell the truth about anything unless I confess to being a student. . . . My first lesson was that one's ego always compromised how something was viewed. I had to wash my ego in the needs/ aspiration of my people. Selflessness is key for conveying the need to end greed and oppression. I try to achieve this state as write."

According to *Detroit News* contributor Carole Cook, the title of the American Book Award winner *homegirls & handgrenades* "underscores the creative tension between love and anger intrinsic to . . . young black women poets." Speaking in *Black Women Writers (1950-1980)* of the creative tension between protest and affirmation in her writing, Sanchez declared, "I still believe that the age for which we write is the age evolving out of the dregs of the twentieth century into a more humane age. Therefore I recognize that my writing must serve a dual purpose. It must be a clarion call to the values of change while it also speaks to the beauty of a nonexploitative age." Throughout her poems, Sanchez emphasizes the importance of strong family relationships, and exposes the dangers of substance abuse among people who hope to be the vital agents of change, relates Richard K. Barksdale in *Modern Black Poets: A Collection of Critical Essays.* Her message, as he notes, is that the desired revolution will not come about through "violence, anger, or rage;" rather, "political astuteness and moral power" among black people are needed to build the new world. Commenting on the content of the poems as it has broadened over the years, Madhubuti observes, "Her work has matured; she's a much better writer now than she was ten years ago. She has continued to grow, but her will has not changed," states critic Sherley Anne Williams, who told Tate that black women writers as a group have kept their

commitment to social revolution strong, while others seem to be letting it die out. In the same book, Sanchez attributes this waning, in part, to the rewards that have been given to black writers who focus on themes other than revolution. "The greatness of Sonia Sanchez," believes Salaam, "is that she is an inspiration." Madhubuti shares this view, concluding, "Sanchez has been an inspiration to a generation of young poets. . . . Her concreteness and consistency over these many years is noteworthy. She has not bought refuge from day-to-day struggles by becoming a writer in the Western tradition. . . . Somehow, one feels deep inside that in a real fight, this is the type of black woman you would want at your side."

BIOGRAPHICAL/CRITICAL SOURCES:

BOOKS

Bankier, Joanna, and Deirdre Lashgari, editors, *Women Poets of the World,* Macmillan, 1983.
Bell, Bernard W., *The Folk Roots of Contemporary Afro-American Poetry,* Broadside Press, 1974.
Bigsby, C. W. E., editor, *The Second Black Renaissance: Essays in Black Literature,* Greenwood Press, 1980.
Contemporary Literary Criticism, Volume 5, Gale, 1976.
Dictionary of Literary Biography, Volume 51: *Afro-American Poets since 1955,* Gale, 1985.
Evans, Mari, editor, *Black Women Writers (1950-1980): A Critical Evaluation,* with introduction by Stephen E. Henderson, Doubleday-Anchor, 1984.
Gibson, Donald B. editor, *Modern Black Poets: A Collection of Critical Essays,* Prentice-Hall, 1973.
Randall, Dudley, *Broadside Memories: Poets I Have Known,* Broadside Press, 1975.
Redmond, Eugene B., *Drumvoices: The Mission of Afro-American Poetry, A Critical History,* Anchor, 1976.
Sanchez, Sonia, *We a BaddDDD People,* Broadside Press, 1970.
Tate, Claudia, editor, *Black Women Writers At Work,* Continuum, 1983.

PERIODICALS

Black Creation, fall, 1973.
Black Scholar, May, 1979, January, 1980, March, 1981.
Black World, August, 1970, April, 1971, September, 1971, April, 1972, March, 1975.
Book World, January 27, 1974.
CLA Journal, September, 1971.
Ebony, March, 1974.
Essence, July, 1979.
Indian Journal of American Studies, July, 1983.
Negro Digest, December, 1969.
New Republic, February 22, 1975.
Newsweek, April 17, 1972.
Phylon, June, 1975.
Poetry, October, 1973.
Poetry Review, April, 1985.
Publishers Weekly, October 1, 1973, July 15, 1974.
Time, May 1, 1972.

*　　*　　*

SANDBURG, Carl (August) 1878-1967
(Charles Sandburg, Charles A. Sandburg; pseudonyms: Militant, Jack Phillips)

PERSONAL: Born January 6, 1878, in Galesburg, Ill.; died July 22, 1967, in Flat Rock, N.C.; buried at Remembrance Rock, Carl Sandburg Birthplace, Galesburg, Ill.; son of August (a railroad blacksmith; original surname Johnson) and Clara (Anderson) Sandburg; married Lillian ("Paula") Steichen (sister of photographer Edward Steichen), June 15, 1908; children: Margaret, Janet, Helga (originally named Mary Ellen; Mrs. George Crile). *Education:* Attended Lombard College, 1898-1902. *Politics:* Formerly Social-Democrat, later Democrat.

ADDRESSES: Home and office—Connemara Farm, Flat Rock, N.C.

CAREER: Held many odd jobs, including work as milk-delivery boy, barber shop porter, fireman, truck operator, and apprentice house painter; sold films for Underwood and Underwood; helped to organize Wisconsin Socialist Democratic Party; worked for *Milwaukee Sentinel* and *Milwaukee Daily News;* city hall reporter for *Milwaukee Journal;* secretary to Milwaukee Mayor Emil Seidel, 1910-12; worked for *Milwaukee Leader* and *Chicago World,* 1912; worked for *Day Book* (daily), Chicago, 1912-17; *System: The Magazine of Business,* Chicago, associate editor, February to early fall, 1913 (returned to *Day Book);* worked for *Chicago Evening American* for three weeks in 1917; Newspaper Enterprise Association (390 newspapers), Stockholm correspondent, 1918, ran Chicago office, 1919; *Chicago Daily News,* 1917-30, served as reporter (covered Chicago race riots), editorial writer, and motion picture editor, later continued as columnist until 1932; wrote weekly column syndicated by *Chicago Daily Times,* beginning in 1941. Presidential Medal of Freedom lecturer, University of Hawaii, 1934; Walgreen Foundation Lecturer, University of Chicago, 1940. Contributed newspaper columns to Chicago Times Syndicate and radio broadcasts such as "Cavalcade of America" and foreign broadcasts for the Office of War Information during World War II. Lectured and sang folk songs to his own guitar accompaniment. *Military service:* Sixth Illinois Volunteers, 1898; served in Puerto Rico during Spanish-American War.

MEMBER: American Academy of Arts and Letters, National Institute of Arts and Letters, Phi Beta Kappa (honorary); honorary member of Chicago's Tavern Club and Swedish Club (Chicago).

AWARDS, HONORS: Levinson Prize, *Poetry* magazine, 1914; shared Poetry Society of America prize, 1919, 1921; Friend of American Writers award; Phi Beta Kappa poet, Harvard University, 1928, William & Mary College, 1943; Friends of Literature award, 1934, for *Lincoln: The Prairie Years;* Theodore Roosevelt distinguished service medal, 1939; Pulitzer Prize in history, 1939, for *Abraham Lincoln: The War Years;* Pulitzer Prize for poetry, 1951; American Academy of Arts and Letters gold medal for history, 1952, 1953; Poetry Society of America gold medal for poetry, 1953; Taminent Institution award, 1953, for *Always the Young Strangers;* honored by Sweden's Commander Order of the North Star on his seventy-fifth birthday, January 6, 1953; New York Civil War Round Table silver medal, 1954; University of Louisville award of merit, 1955; Albert Einstein award, Yeshiva College, 1956; Roanoke-Chowan Poetry Cup, 1960, for *Harvest Poems, 1910-1960,* and 1961, for *Wind Song;* International Poet's Award, 1963; National Association for the Advancement of Colored People award, 1965, acclaiming Sandburg as "a major prophet of civil rights in our time." Litt.D., Lombard College, 1928, Knox College, 1929, Northwestern University, 1931, Harvard University, 1940, Yale University, 1940, New York University, 1940, Wesleyan University, 1940, Lafayette College, 1940, Syracuse University, 1941, Dartmouth College, 1941, University of North Carolina, 1955; LL.D., Rollins College, 1941, Augustana College, 1948, University of Illinois, 1953; Ph.D., Uppsala University, 1948.

WRITINGS:

(As Charles A. Sandburg) *In Reckless Ecstasy,* Asgard Press, 1904.

(As Charles A. Sandburg) *The Plaint of a Rose,* Asgard Press, 1905.

(As Charles A. Sandburg) *Incidentals,* Asgard Press, 1905.

(As Charles A. Sandburg) *You and Your Job,* [Chicago], ca. 1906.

(As Charles Sandburg) *Joseffy* (promotional biography; commissioned by a wandering magician), Asgard Press, 1910.

Chicago Poems, Holt, 1916.

Cornhuskers, Holt, 1918.

The Chicago Race Riots, July, 1919, Harcourt, Brace & Howe, 1919, reprinted with new introduction, 1969.

Smoke and Steel (also see below), Harcourt, Brace & Howe, 1920.

Rootabaga Stories (also see below), Harcourt, Brace, 1922.

Slabs of the Sunburnt West (also see below), Harcourt, Brace, 1922.

Rootabaga Pigeons (also see below), Harcourt, Brace, 1923.

Selected Poems of Carl Sandburg, edited by Rebecca West, Harcourt, Brace, 1926.

Songs of America, Harcourt, Brace, 1926.

(Editor) *The American Songbag,* Harcourt, Brace, 1927.

Abraham Lincoln: The Prairie Years (also see below), Harcourt, Brace, 1927.

Abe Lincoln Grows Up, Harcourt, Brace, 1928.

Good Morning, America (also see below), Harcourt, Brace, 1928.

Rootabaga Country: Selections from Rootabaga Stories and Rootabaga Pigeons, Harcourt, Brace, 1929.

Steichen, the Photographer, Harcourt, Brace, 1929.

M'Liss and Louie, J. Zeitlin (Los Angeles, Calif.), 1929.

Early Moon, Harcourt, Brace, 1930.

Potato Face, Harcourt, Brace, 1930.

(With Paul M. Angle) *Mary Lincoln, Wife and Widow,* Harcourt, Brace, 1932.

The People, Yes, Harcourt, Brace, 1936.

Smoke and Steel [and] *Slabs of the Sunburnt West,* Harcourt, Brace, 1938.

A Lincoln and Whitman Miscellany, Holiday Press, 1938.

Abraham Lincoln: The War Years (also see below), four volumes, Harcourt, Brace, 1939.

Abraham Lincoln: The Sangamon Edition, six volumes, Scribner, 1940.

Bronze Wood, Grabhorn Press, 1941.

Storm Over the Land, Harcourt, Brace, 1942.

Smoke and Steel, Slabs of the Sunburnt West [and] *Good Morning, America* (omnibus volume), Harcourt, Brace, 1942.

Home Front Memo, Harcourt, Brace, 1943.

(With Frederick Hill Meserve) *Photographs of Abraham Lincoln,* Harcourt, Brace, 1944.

Poems of the Midwest, two volumes, World Publishing, 1946.

The Lincoln Reader: An Appreciation, privately printed, 1947.

Remembrance Rock (novel), Harcourt, Brace, 1948.

Lincoln Collector: The Story of Oliver R. Barrett's Great Private Collection, Harcourt, Brace, 1949.

(Editor) *Carl Sandburg's New American Songbag,* Broadcast Music, Inc., 1950. *Complete Poems,* Harcourt, Brace, 1950, revised and enlarged edition published as *The Complete Poems of Carl Sandburg,* 1970.

Always the Young Strangers (autobiography), Harcourt, Brace, 1952.

A Lincoln Preface, Harcourt, Brace, 1953.

Abraham Lincoln: The Prairie Years and the War Years, Harcourt, 1954, reprinted, 1974.

Prairie-Town Boy, Harcourt, Brace, 1955.

The Sandburg Range, Harcourt, Brace, 1957.

Chicago Dynamic, Harcourt, Brace, 1957.

The Fiery Trial, Dell, 1959.

Address Before a Joint Session of Congress, February 12, 1959, Harcourt, Brace, 1959 (also published as *Carl Sandburg on Abraham Lincoln,* [Cedar Rapids], 1959, and as *Abraham Lincoln, 1809-1959,* J. St. Onge, 1959).

Abraham Lincoln, three volume condensation of earlier work, Dell, 1959.

Harvest Poems, 1910-1960, Harcourt, Brace, 1960.

Wind Song, Harcourt, Brace, 1960.

Six New Poems and a Parable, privately printed, 1960.

Address Upon the Occasion of Abraham Lincoln's One Hundredth Inaugural Anniversary, Black Cat Books, 1961.

Honey and Salt, Harcourt, Brace & World, 1963.

The Wedding Procession of the Rag Doll and the Broom Handle and Who Was in It (chapter of "Rootabaga" stories), Harcourt, Brace & World, 1967.

The Letters of Carl Sandburg, edited by Herbert Mitgang, Harcourt, 1968.

A Sandburg Treasury: Prose & Poetry for Young People, Harcourt, 1970.

Seven Poems, illustrated with seven original etchings by Gregory Masurovsky, Associated American Artists, 1970.

Breathing Tokens, edited by daughter Margaret Sandburg, Harcourt, 1978.

Ever the Winds of Chance, edited by daughter M. Sandburg and George Hendrick, University of Illinois Press, 1983.

Fables, Foibles and Foobles, edited by Hendrick, University of Illinois Press, 1988.

Also author of commentary for U.S. Government film "Bomber." Author of captions for "Road to Victory" mural photograph show, 1942. Collaborator on screenplay for the film "King of Kings," 1960. *The World of Carl Sandburg,* a stage presentation by Norman Corwin, was published by Harcourt in 1961. Contributor to *International Socialist Review, Tomorrow, Poetry, Saturday Evening Post, Masses, Little Review, New Leader, Nation,* and *Playboy.* (Of his experience with *Playboy* he remarked: "It was fun to be read by the most gustatory audience of readers in America, all of them definitely opposed to artificial insemination.")

SIDELIGHTS: "Trying to write briefly about Carl Sandburg," said a friend of the poet, "is like trying to picture the Grand Canyon in one black and white snapshot." His range of interests has been enumerated by his close friend, Harry Golden, who, in his study of the poet, called Sandburg "the one American writer who distinguished himself in five fields—poetry, history, biography, fiction, and music."

His poetry is basically free verse. Concerning rhyme versus nonrhyme Sandburg once said airily: "If it jells into free verse, all right. If it jells into rhyme, all right." Some critics noted that the illusion of poetry in his works was based more on the arrangement of the lines than on the lines themselves. Sandburg, aware of the criticism, wrote in the preface to *Complete Poems:* "There is a formal poetry only in form, all dressed up and nowhere to go. The number of syllables, the designated and required stresses of accent, the rhymes if wanted—they all come off with the skill of a solved crossword puzzle. . . . The fact is ironic. A proficient and sometimes exquisite performer in rhymed verse goes out of his way to register the point that the more rhyme there is in poetry the more danger of its tricking the writer into something other than the urge in the beginning." He dismissed modern poetry, however, as "a series of ear wigglings." In *Good*

Morning, America, he published thirty-eight definitions of poetry, among them: "Poetry is a pack-sack of invisible keepsakes. Poetry is a sky dark with a wild-duck migration. Poetry is the opening and closing of a door, leaving those who look through to guess about what is seen during a moment." His success as a poet has been limited to that of a follower of Whitman and of the Imagists. In *Carl Sandburg,* Karl Detzer says that in 1918 "admirers proclaimed him a latter-day Walt Whitman; objectors cried that their six-year-old daughters could write better poetry."

Admirers of his poetry, however, have included Sherwood Anderson ("among all the poets of America he is my poet"), and Amy Lowell, who called *Chicago Poems* "one of the most original books this age has produced." Miss Lowell's observations were reiterated by H. L. Mencken, who called Sandburg "a true original, his own man." No one, it is agreed, can deny the unique quality of his style. In his newspaper days, an old friend recalls, the slogan was, "Print Sandburg as is." It was Sandburg, as Golden observes, who "put America on paper," writing the American idiom, speaking to the masses, who held no terror for him. As Richard Crowder notes in *Carl Sandburg,* the poet "Had been the first poet of modern times actually to use the language of the people as his almost total means of expression. . . . Sandburg had entered into the language of the people; he was not looking at it as a scientific phenomenon or a curiosity. . . . He was at home with it." Sandburg's own Whitmanesque comment was: "I am the people—the mob—the crowd—the mass. Did you know that all the work of the world is done through me?" He has always been read by the masses, as well as by scholars. He once observed: "I'll probably die propped up in bed trying to write a poem about America."

Sandburg's account of the life of Abraham Lincoln is one of the monumental works of the century. *Abraham Lincoln: The War Years* alone exceeds the collected writings of Shakespeare by some 150,000 words. Though Sandburg did deny the story that in preparation he read everything ever published on Lincoln, he did collect and classify Lincoln material for thirty years, moving himself into a garret, storing his extra material in a barn, and for nearly fifteen years writing on a cracker-box typewriter. His intent was to separate Lincoln the man from Lincoln the myth, to avoid hero-worship, to relate with graphic detail and humanness the man both he and Whitman so admired. The historian Charles A. Beard called the finished product "a noble monument of American literature," written with "indefatigable thoroughness." Allan Nevins saw it as "homely but beautiful, learned but simple, exhaustively detailed but panoramic . . . [occupying] a niche all its own, unlike any other biography or history in the language." The Pulitzer Prize committee would apparently concur. Prohibited from awarding the biography prize for any work on Washington or Lincoln, it circumvented the rules by placing the book in the category of history. As a result of this work Sandburg was the first private citizen to deliver an address before a joint session of Congress (on February 12, 1959, the 150th anniversary of Lincoln's birth).

Perhaps Sandburg was best known to America as the singing bard—the "voice of America singing," says Golden. Sandburg was an author accepted as a personality, as was Mark Twain. Requests for his lectures began to appear as early as 1908. He was his own accompanist, and was not merely a musician of sorts; he played the guitar well enough to have been a pupil of Andres Segovia. Sandburg's songs were projected by a voice "in which you [could] hear farm hands wailing and levee Negroes moaning." It was fortunate that he was willing to travel about reciting and recording his poetry, for the interpretation his voice lent to his work is unforgettable. With its deep rich cadences, dramatic pauses, and midwestern dialect, his speech was "a kind of singing." Ben Hecht once wrote: "Whether he chatted at lunch or recited from the podium he had always the same voice. He spoke like a man slowly revealing something."

A self-styled hobo, Sandburg was the recipient of numerous honorary degrees, had six high schools and five elementary schools named for him, and held news conferences with presidents at the White House. "My father couldn't sign his name," wrote Sandburg; "[he] made his 'mark' on the CB&Q payroll sheet. My mother was able to read the Scriptures in her native language, but she could not write, and I wrote of Abraham Lincoln whose own mother could not read or write! I guess that somewhere along in this you'll find a story of America."

A Sandburg archives is maintained in the Sandburg Room at the University of Illinois. Ralph G. Newman, who is known primarily as a Lincoln scholar but who also is the possessor of what is perhaps the largest and most important collection of Sandburgiana, has said that a complete bibliography of Sandburg's works, including contributions to periodicals and anthologies, forewords, introductions, and foreign editions would number more than four hundred pages. Sandburg received 200-400 letters each week. Though, to a friend who asked how he managed to look ten years younger than he appeared on his last visit, he replied: "From NOT answering my correspondence," he reportedly filed his mail under "F" (friendly and fan letters), "No reply needed," and "Hi fi" (to be read and answered).

For all this fame, he remained unassuming. What he wanted from life was "to be out of jail, . . . to eat regular, . . . to get what I write printed, . . . a little love at home and a little nice affection hither and yon over the American landscape, . . . [and] to sing every day." He wrote with a pencil, a fountain pen, or a typewriter, "but I draw the line at dictating 'em," he said. He kept his home as it was, refusing, for example, to rearrange his vast library in some orderly fashion; he knew where everything was. Furthermore, he said, "I want Emerson in every room."

On September 17, 1967, there was a National Memorial Service at the Lincoln Memorial in Washington, D.C., at which Archibald MacLeish and Mark Van Doren read from Sandburg's poetry. A Carl Sandburg Exhibition of memorabilia was held at the Hallmark Gallery, New York City, January-February, 1968. His home is under consideration as a National Historical site.

MEDIA ADAPTATIONS: Sandburg recorded excerpts from *Always the Young Strangers,* Caedmon, 1966; he also recorded *The People, Yes, Poems for Children, A Lincoln Album, Carl Sandburg Sings His American Songbag,* and *The Poetry of Carl Sandburg,* for Caedmon.

AVOCATIONAL INTERESTS: Walking.

BIOGRAPHICAL/CRITICAL SOURCES:

BOOKS

Contemporary Literary Criticism, Gale, Volume 1, 1973, Volume 4, 1975, Volume 10, 1979, Volume 15, 1980, Volume 35, 1985.

Crane, Joan St. C., compiler, *Carl Sandburg, Philip Green Wright, and the Asgard Press, 1900-1910,* University of Virginia Press, 1975.

Crowder, Richard, *Carl Sandburg,* Twayne, 1964.

Detzer, Karl William, *Carl Sandburg,* Harcourt, 1941.

Dictionary of Literary Biography, Gale, Volume 17: *Twentieth-Century American Historians,* 1983, Volume 54: *American Poets, 1880-1945,* 1987.

Durnell, Hazel, *America of Carl Sandburg,* University Press of Washington, 1965.

Golden, Harry, *Carl Sandburg,* World Publishing, 1961.

Haas, Joseph, and Gene Lovietz, *Carl Sandburg: A Pictorial Biography,* Putnam, 1967.

Picture Book of American Authors, Sterling, 1962.

Sandburg, Carl, *Complete Poems,* Harcourt, Brace, 1950.

Sandburg, *Good Morning, America,* Harcourt, Brace, 1928.

Sandburg, *The Letters of Carl Sandburg,* edited by Herbert Mitgang, Harcourt, 1968.

Steichen, Edward, editor, *Sandburg: Photographers View Carl Sandburg,* Harcourt, 1966.

Tribute to Carl Sandburg at Seventy-Five, special edition of the Journal of the Illinois State Historical Society, Abraham Lincoln Book Shop, 1953.

Zehnpfennig, Gladys, *Carl Sandburg, Poet and Patriot,* Denison, 1963.

PERIODICALS

Books, August, 1967.

Chicago Tribune Book World, October 23, 1983.

Detroit Free Press, November 30, 1965.

Life, December 1, 1961, February 23, 1953.

Look, July 10, 1956.

Newsweek, January 12, 1953.

New York Herald Tribune Book Review, October 8, 1950.

New York Public Library Bulletin, March, 1962.

New York Times, January 10, 1968, September 25, 1968.

New York Times Book Review, June 1, 1952, January 4, 1953, January 2, 1966, September 29, 1968, January 1, 1984.

Publisher's Weekly, January 28, 1963.

Redbook, February, 1966.

Saturday Evening Post, June 6, 1964.

OBITUARIES:

PERIODICALS

New York Times, July 23, 1967.

Time, July 28, 1967, July 31, 1967.

[Sketch approved by Harry Golden]

* * *

SANDBURG, Charles
See SANDBURG, Carl (August)

* * *

SANDBURG, Charles A.
See SANDBURG, Carl (August)

* * *

SANDERS, Lawrence 1920-

PERSONAL: Born 1920 in Brooklyn, NY. *Education:* Wabash College, B.A., 1940.

ADDRESSES: Home—Pompano Beach, FL. *Agent*—c/o Putnam Publishing Group, 200 Madison Ave., New York, NY 10016.

CAREER: Macy's (department store), New York City, staff member, 1940-43; worked for various magazines as an editor and as a writer of war stories, men's adventure stories, and detective stories; feature editor for *Mechanix Illustrated,* New York City;

editor for *Science and Mechanics,* New York City; Magnum-Royal Publications, New York City, free-lance writer for men's magazines, 1967-68; novelist, 1969—. *Military service:* U.S. Marine Corps, 1943-46; became sergeant.

AWARDS, HONORS: Edgar Award for best first mystery novel, Mystery Writers of America, 1970, for *The Anderson Tapes.*

WRITINGS:

(Editor) *Thus Be Loved: A Book for Lovers,* Arco, 1966.
(With Richard Carol) *Handbook of Creative Crafts* (nonfiction), Pyramid Books, 1968.
(Under pseudonym Mark Upton) *Dark Summer,* Coward, McCann, 1979.

NOVELS

The Anderson Tapes, Putnam, 1970.
The Pleasures of Helen, Putnam, 1971.
Love Songs, Putnam, 1972.
The First Deadly Sin, Putnam, 1973.
The Tomorrow File, Putnam, 1975.
The Tangent Objective, Putnam, 1976.
The Marlow Chronicles, Putnam, 1977.
The Second Deadly Sin, Putnam, 1977.
The Tangent Factor, Putnam, 1978.
The Sixth Commandment, Putnam, 1978.
The Tenth Commandment, Putnam, 1980.
The Third Deadly Sin, Putnam, 1981.
The Case of Lucy Bending, Putnam, 1982.
The Seduction of Peter S., Putnam, 1983.
The Passion of Molly T., Putnam, 1984.
The Fourth Deadly Sin, Putnam, 1985.
The Loves of Harry Dancer, Berkley Publishing, 1986.
The Eighth Commandment, Putnam, 1986.
Tales of the Wolf, Avon, 1986.
The Dream Lover, Berkley Publishing, 1987.
The Timothy Files, Putnam, 1987.
Caper, Berkley Publishing, 1987.
Timothy's Game, Putnam, 1988.
Capital Crimes, Putnam, 1989.

Author of books under pseudonyms and of several "purse books" for Dell. Contributor of more than one hundred stories and articles to various publications.

MEDIA ADAPTATIONS: Films based on Sanders's books include "The Anderson Tapes," Columbia Pictures, 1971, and "The First Deadly Sin," Filmways, 1980.

SIDELIGHTS: "I learned my trade as a novelist," Sanders has said, "by working as an editor of pulp magazines" and writing "gag lines for cheesecake magazines." After editing various men's magazines, *Mechanix Illustrated,* and *Science and Mechanics,* he "got to the point where a lot of editors get—I said to myself that I could write the stuff better myself. And so I wrote *The Anderson Tapes*—my first novel—at age fifty."

The Anderson Tapes is the story of a Mafia-backed effort to rob an entire luxury apartment building. Foreshadowing the role electronics were to play in the political scandal known as Watergate during the early 1970s, this plot is thwarted when several governmental agencies wiretap "everything from a candy-store pay phone to Central Park itself." Christopher Lehmann-Haupt speculated that those "fashionably paranoiac and willing to believe that the whole world is plugged into a tape recorder" would "have a zippy time" with this novel. *The Anderson Tapes* was a best seller upon publication and was made into a Columbia motion picture soon thereafter.

Since becoming a full-time novelist, Sanders has settled down from the post-*Anderson Tape* days when he was "shoveling down martinis at night and waking up on Tums." "I've been working my tail off and enjoying it," he says. "I usually write about five pages a night, and it adds up." In one span Sanders produced three novels within a year, including *The Second Deadly Sin* and a story of one man's struggle to unite Africa, *The Tangent Factor.*

The Tangent Factor "depicts how one man imposes his will on whole nations, and the basic thesis is that it is not done merely through strength of character but through treachery, manipulation and carefully calculated violence," wrote Joseph McLellan. Despite objecting to its "unpleasant aftertaste," critic Thomas Lask admitted the "narrative is lean, fat free and highly readable. . . . It's hard not to admire [Sanders's] skill."

Sanders now lives in Florida and continues to share his life with his "constant and beloved" companion of thirty years, Fleurette Ballou. Though he has expressed a desire to "try to slow down to only two books a year," he readily admits: "I'm obsessed with writing. I have no hobbies. I don't fish. I'm not interested in sports. I don't even own a car. When I'm writing, my fantasies become more important than my personal life. I'm a Walter Mitty—living out my years through my characters."

BIOGRAPHICAL/CRITICAL SOURCES:

BOOKS

Bestsellers 89, Issue 4, Gale, 1989.
Contemporary Literary Criticism, Volume 41, Gale, 1987.

PERIODICALS

Chicago Tribune Book World, September 19, 1982.
Globe and Mail (Toronto), January 12, 1985.
Los Angeles Times, November 5, 1982.
Los Angeles Times Book Review, October 12, 1980, July 31, 1983, October 28, 1984.
New York Times, February 20, 1970, October 20, 1973, August 25, 1977, March 24, 1978.
New York Times Book Review, August 21, 1977, October 9, 1977, October 5, 1980, September 6, 1981, August 22, 1982.
People, November 28, 1977, September 16, 1985.
Publishers Weekly, August 2, 1976.
Time, April 27, 1970, August 29, 1977.
Tribune Books (Chicago), July 10, 1988.
Washington Post, May 4, 1978, August 6, 1981, September 2, 1984.
Washington Post Book World, August 18, 1985.

*   *   *

SANDERS, Noah
    See BLOUNT, Roy (Alton), Jr.

*   *   *

SANDERS, Winston P.
    See ANDERSON, Poul (William)

*   *   *

SANDOZ, Mari(e Susette)   1896-1966
    (Mari Macumber)

PERSONAL: Born May 11, 1896 (some sources say 1901), in Sheridan County, Neb.; died March 10, 1966, of cancer in New

York City; daughter of Jules Ami and Mary Elizabeth (Fehr) Sandoz; married Wray Macumber (a rancher), May 27, 1914 (divorced, 1919). *Education:* Attended business college for nine months and University of Nebraska, 1922-31.

ADDRESSES: Home—New York, NY.

CAREER: Held various positions, including country school teacher in Nebraska for five years, assistant in a drug laboratory, a university English reader, and proofreader and researcher on Sioux Indians for the Nebraska State Historical Society; *The School Executive,* Lincoln, Neb., associate editor, 1927-29; *Star* and *Nebraska State Journal,* Lincoln, proofreader, 1929-34; Nebraska State Historical Society, Lincoln, director of research and associate editor of Nebraska History magazine, 1934-35; writer, teacher, lecturer, Lincoln, 1935-40, Denver, Colo., 1940-43, New York City, 1943-66, summer instructor, University of Wisconsin, 1947-55. Staff leader for writers' conferences and director of short courses in writing. Cartographer.

MEMBER: Authors Guild, Authors League of America, Nebraska State Historical Society.

AWARDS, HONORS: Atlantic Monthly Press, nonfiction award, 1935, for *Old Jules;* Litt.D., University of Nebraska, 1950; award for distinguished service, Native Sons and Daughters of Nebraska, 1954; National Achievement Award of The Westerners, Chicago Corral, 1955; Headliner Award, Theta Sigma Phi, 1957; The Buffalo of the New York Posse, The Westerners, 1959, for *The Cattlemen;* Oppie Award, 1962, for *These Were the Sioux,* and 1964, for *The Beaver Men;* Western Heritage Award, 1962, for article on last frontier published in *American Heritage; The Story Catcher* was cowinner of Spur Award, 1963; Levi Straus Award for best novel on the west, 1963, for *The Story Catcher.*

WRITINGS:

These Were the Sioux (nonfiction), Hastings House, 1961, reprinted, University of Nebraska Press, 1985.
Love Song to the Plains (nonfiction), Harper, 1961.
(Author of introduction) George Bird Grinnell, *The Cheyenne Indians: Their History and Ways,* Cooper Square, 1962.
The Battle of the Little Bighorn, Lippincott, 1966.
(Author of introduction) Amos Bad Heart Bull and Helen Blish, *A Pictographic History of the Oglala Sioux,* University of Nebraska Press, 1967.

"GREAT PLAINS" SERIES; ALL NONFICTION

Old Jules (biography; Book-of-the-Month Club selection), Atlantic, 1935, revised edition, Hastings House, 1975.
Crazy Horse: The Strange Man of the Oglalas (biography), Knopf, 1942, reprinted, Hastings House, 1975.
Cheyenne Autumn, McGraw, 1953, reprinted, Avon, 1975.
The Buffalo Hunters: The Story of the Hide Men (Outdoor Life Book Club selection), Hastings House, 1954, published in England as *The Buffalo Hunters: The Slaughter of the Great Buffalo Herds,* Eyre & Spottiswoode, 1960, reprinted, University of Nebraska Press, 1978.
The Cattlemen: From the Rio Grande across the Far Marias, Hastings House, 1958, reprinted, University of Nebraska Press, 1978.
The Beaver Men: Spearheads of Empire, Hastings House, 1964.

FICTION

Slogum House (novel), Atlantic, 1937, reprinted, University of Nebraska Press, 1981.

Capital City (novel), Atlantic, 1939, reprinted, University of Nebraska Press, 1982.
The Tom-Walker (novel), Dial, 1947, reprinted, University of Nebraska Press, 1984.
Winter Thunder (novella), Westminster, 1954, reprinted, University of Nebraska Press, 1986.
Miss Morissa: Doctor of the Gold Trail (novel), McGraw, 1955, reprinted, Hastings House, 1975.
The Horsecatcher (novella), Westminster, 1957, reprinted, University of Nebraska Press, 1986.
Son of the Gamblin' Man: The Youth of an Artist (novel), C. N. Potter, 1960, reprinted, University of Nebraska Press, 1976.
The Christmas of the Phonograph Records (novel), University of Nebraska Press, 1966.
The Story Catcher (novella), Westminster, 1973.

COLLECTIONS

Hostiles and Friendlies: Selected Short Writings of Mari Sandoz, University of Nebraska Press, 1959, reprinted, 1975.
"Old Jules" Country: A Selection from "Old Jules" and Thirty Years of Writing since the Book Was Published, Hastings House, 1965.
Sandhill Sundays and Other Recollections, University of Nebraska Press, 1970.

OTHER

Contributor of more than thirty short stories and articles to anthologies and magazines, including *Scribner's, Saturday Evening Post, Blue Book,* and *Prairie Schooner.* Many of Sandoz's books have been published in Swiss and German editions. *Old Jules* was serialized and issued in half a dozen editions in Scandinavian countries. The author's correspondence and working papers are collected at the University of Nebraska Archives, along with her maps, genealogies, manuscripts, and library. The Mamie Meredith Collection of the Nebraska State Historical Society also has material by and about Mari Sandoz, her father, and the Sandoz family.

SIDELIGHTS: Mari Sandoz's writings, which explored nearly every aspect of life in the old west, were based on extensive research and personal knowledge. Born in the Sand Hills cattle country of northwest Nebraska, Sandoz was nine before she began attending school, and she knew the difficult circumstances of pioneer life from first-hand experience. When Sandoz was about fourteen, she became snowblind and later lost the use of one eye after she and her brother spent a day digging their cattle out of a blizzard snowdrift. Of her childhood responsibilities, Sandoz once told the *New York Times* that by the time she was ten she "could bake up a 49-pound-sack of flour, but would let the bread sour and the baby cry if there was anything to read."

After Sandoz completed the eighth grade, she passed the teachers examination and skipped high school to teach in the countryside. She later entered the University of Nebraska and began writing. Her first book was *Old Jules,* a biography of her father, a foul-tempered Swiss immigrant who came from the east in the 1880s to settle in the high plains of the trans-Missouri area after quarreling with his own father. In his attempts to tame the land, Sandoz's father became a leading figure in the region. Helen Stauffer explained in the *Dictionary of Literary Biography* that *Old Jules* is not only a biography of Sandoz's father, but also a chronicle of the author's home community and the surrounding area.

As *New Republic* reviewer B. E. Bettinger characterized the book upon publication, it is "a wise and memorable saga of American pioneering, recited with the expansive Western gesture, bitter and fragrant as soil and prairie growth," while K. C. Kaufman in the *Christian Science Monitor* considered *Old Jules* to be "a powerful, distinctively American history of a man, a region and an epoch." A Boston *Transcript* writer reported that "as a biography of [Sandoz's] father it has great success," commenting that the character of Jules "is clearly and warmly defined." And although a *Books* writer indicated that "the old man's virtues his toughness, perseverance and unexpected intellectual interests didn't seem to us to compensate for his insensitiveness, even brutality, toward his family and neighbors," a critic in *Forum* pointed out that "*Old Jules* is the kind of flamboyant character whom most novelists would give their eyeteeth to create." The biography is "a vigorous, devastating, and often brutal chronicle which nevertheless achieves a certain grandeur," the *Forum* reviewer concluded.

In 1935, after fourteen rejections and revisions, *Old Jules* won the *Atlantic* Nonfiction Prize of $5,000. Despite her father's disapproval of the writing profession, "Sandoz's life from then on was dedicated to writing and research," Stauffer noted. Although many of the events in *Old Jules* happened during Sandoz's lifetime, Stauffer pointed out that "she spent years researching published and private memoirs, using local and state historical society collections, listening to the old storytellers in her region, and interviewing those involved" to create the book. Sandoz then used the narrative technique of fiction to tell the story. As Stauffer observed, "This combination of meticulous historical research and narrative style became the pattern for her writing."

Throughout the rest of Sandoz's writing career, her primary goals "were to preserve history and present it accurately and to bring attention to the western frontier," said Stauffer. All of her twenty-one books, along with her articles and short stories, deal with the trans-Missouri region; Sandoz is best known for her six-book Great Plains series (also sometimes referred to as the Trans-Missouri series), a nonfiction study of man on the plains from the Stone Age to the present. Included in the series are the biographies *Old Jules* and *Crazy Horse: Strange Man of the Oglalas*, as well as *Cheyenne Autumn*, which are widely held to be Sandoz's finest works.

Both *Cheyenne Autumn* and *Crazy Horse*, the biography of the Sioux war chief and mystic, are told from the Indian point of view. Although not all reviewers found Sandoz's Indian sympathies appealing, particularly in her attempts to incorporate Indian speech patterns into the nonfictional narrative, most thought the books were well written. Discussing *Crazy Horse* in the *New Yorker*, Clifton Fadiman stated that "unquestionably, her book, the product of studious labor, will rank among the important records of the history of the American Indian," while David Lowe in the *Prairie Schooner* considered *Crazy Horse* probably Sandoz's "finest" book. In his words, "no one has written more movingly of the hopelessness of the Indian after he had seen every treaty broken, the buffalo wantonly slaughtered, the tribes decimated by the white man's disease" than Mari Sandoz in *Crazy Horse*.

Cheyenne Autumn relates the story of the 1878 fall flight of a small band of Cheyenne Indians from Indian Territory in Oklahoma, where they had been sent by the American army, to their ancestral home in Montana. Sandoz gathered some of the information for the book from the personal accounts of Indians who had participated in the journey as well as from traditional research sources. And as August Derleth commented in the *Chicago Sunday Tribune*, Sandoz did more than tell the story in *Cheyenne Autumn:* "With her customary skill, she manages to

recreate a man, a scene, an event, a page from history, so that through her prose [the tale] takes on the stature of an American epic." J. F. Dobie reported in the *New York Herald Tribune Book Review* that Sandoz's "story of the flight is as poignant in realism as her biography of her father but in the eighteen years between 'Old Jules' and 'Cheyenne Autumn' her sympathy for the tears that are in human affairs have deepened, and her art now gives the strength, vividness and unity to complexity that it began by giving to simplicity."

Sandoz also produced three novellas, *Winter Thunder, The Horsecatcher*, and *The Story Catcher*, although Stauffer remarked that "Sandoz's fiction is not as a rule as well written as her nonfiction." Sandoz was able to use fictional techniques in her historical work, but Stauffer said that she was less successful with true fiction, since her novels are often allegorical or intended to instruct and are frequently cluttered with historical digressions. "Because of her tendency toward instruction," Scott L. Greenwell indicated in *Western American Literature*, "she found much of American fiction—particularly romantic Western novels—thin, 'without anything of the push and throb of life, totally inconsequential.' " Greenwell reports that Sandoz "liked bone and muscle in literature," blaming "what she considered the poor quality of domestic fiction on the American writers' tendency to conform to the commercial market" and waging her own continuing battle to write as she felt necessary.

Sandoz expressed her political beliefs through some of her novels, particularly *Capital City*, an unflattering portrait of a state capital around election time, and *Slogum House*. In Stauffer's opinion, the publication of *Capital City* may have been a factor in Sandoz's decision to move from Lincoln to Denver in 1940, since many of the Nebraska capital's residents became hostile towards the author after the book was circulated, perhaps finding the subject matter too familiar for comfort. *Slogum House*, written directly following the publication of *Old Jules*, is generally regarded to be the better novel.

In contrast to the biography of Sandoz's father, *Slogum House* portrays the darker side of the pioneer ethic. The book's protagonist, Gulla Slogum, was described by Stauffer as a "ruthless woman whose will to power leads her to use her daughters as prostitutes in her roadhouse to extend her influence over others." Gulla, maintained Margaret Wallace in the *New York Times Book Review*, is "the rugged individualist—the very archetype of the unscrupulous builders of empire to whom the West offered, in the past century, such golden opportunity." Although, according to Greenwell the book was not overwhelmingly well-received, particularly in Nebraska where it was banned from several libraries, Wallace claimed that *Slogum House* was "a remarkably sweeping novel and ironic picture of America's last frontier during a period of half a century." Sandoz also "intended the novel as an allegorical study of a nation exerting its will to power by using force to overcome opposition," Stauffer said, indicating that Sandoz wrote the book in reaction to some of Hitler's ideas, fearing that some Americans might find them attractive.

Although Sandoz frequently used her work to convey opinion, her nonfiction, in particular, also reflects "her awareness of the power and beauty of the natural world" and man's relationship to that world, Stauffer reported. "As is true with the writings of many Western writers, Sandoz's work is closely tied to nature. She had an intimate knowledge of the land she grew up in, and all her works are based on her close association with the natural world." Some of what Stauffer called Sandoz's "finest, most lyrical" writing can be found in *Love Song to the Plains*, the Nebraska volume for Harper and Row's series on the states. "Although she sometimes uses wry humor or satire she expresses her great affection for Nebraska and the Great Plains in language at times poetic," noted Stauffer. "Some of the same information, of necessity, is repeated from earlier works, but her storytelling [in her use of anecdotal information] is never better."

One of Sandoz's final works of nonfiction, *The Battle of the Little Bighorn,* investigates the circumstances of Custer's famous last stand. In 1966, A. M. Josephy commented in the *New York Times Book Review* that the book was "probably the best account of the battle ever written." The book "is written more from the white man's point of view than was the case in 'Crazy Horse,'" Josephy pointed out, but he said that "there is enough knowledgeable interrelation of the Indian's outlook and actions to give proper understanding to all that was transpiring." According to Stauffer, *The Battle of the Little Bighorn* "drew the ire of those who objected to the author's claims that Custer's actions were based on his White House aspirations; this motive had not been suggested in many previous accounts. Other reviewers praised her ability to fit the enormous jigsaw puzzle of the day's events into recognizable order; several considered this the apogee of her works."

MEDIA ADAPTATIONS: Cheyenne Autumn was adapted into a motion picture released by Warner Brothers in December, 1964.

AVOCATIONAL INTERESTS: Young writers, human justice, justice for the American Indian, motion pictures, television, and satirical drama.

BIOGRAPHICAL/CRITICAL SOURCES:

BOOKS

Contemporary Literary Criticism, Volume 28, Gale, 1984.
Dictionary of Literary Biography, Volume 9: *American Novelists, 1910-1945,* Gale, 1981.
Pifer, Caroline Sandoz, *Making of an Author,* Gordon Journal Press, 1972.
Sandoz, Mari, *Old Jules,* Atlantic, 1935, revised edition, Hastings House, 1975.
Sandoz, *Hostiles and Friendlies: Selected Short Writings of Mari Sandoz,* University of Nebraska Press, 1959, reprinted, 1975.
Sandoz, *These Were the Sioux,* Hastings House, 1961.
Sandoz, *"Old Jules" Country: A Selection from "Old Jules" and Thirty Years of Writing since the Book Was Published,* Hastings House, 1965.
Sandoz, *Sandhill Sundays and Other Recollections,* University of Nebraska Press, 1970.
Stauffer, Helen Winter, *Story Catcher of the Plains,* University of Nebraska Press, 1982.

PERIODICALS

America, July 16, 1966.
American West, spring, 1965.
Atlantic, January, 1943.
Atlantic Bookshelf, November, 1935.
Baltimore Bulletin of Education, May-June, 1958.
Best Sellers, July 15, 1966.
Booklist, November, 1935, January 15, 1938, December 1, 1939, January 15, 1943, January 1, 1954, January 15, 1954, September 1, 1954.
Books, November 3, 1935, November 10, 1935, November 28, 1937, December 3, 1939, November 29, 1942.
Boston Transcript, November 6, 1935, November 27, 1937.

Chicago Daily Tribune, November 2, 1935.
Chicago Sunday Tribune, November 22, 1953, August 26, 1954, August 29, 1954, May 12, 1957, October 22, 1961, December 17, 1961.
Christian Science Monitor, October 30, 1935, August 26, 1954, May 9, 1957, December 13, 1961.
Nation, December 16, 1939, December 5, 1953.
New Republic, December 25, 1935, December 13, 1939.
New Yorker, December 2, 1939, December 5, 1942.
New York Herald Tribune, October 31, 1935.
New York Herald Tribune Book Review, December 13, 1953, September 5, 1954, May 12, 1957.
New York Herald Tribune Books, November 28, 1937, November 29, 1942, November 12, 1961.
New York Times, November 10, 1935, November 28, 1937, December 3, 1939, December 20, 1942, November 22 1953, August 22, 1954, June 2, 1957.
New York Times Book Review, November 28, 1937, November 22, 1953, August 22, 1954, November 20, 1955, July 3, 1966.
Prairie Schooner, spring, 1968, summer, 1971.
San Francisco Chronicle, August 29, 1954, March 4, 1962.
Saturday Review, December 12, 1953, August 21, 1954, June 28, 1958, December 16, 1961.
Saturday Review of Literature, November 2, 1935, November 27, 1937, December 2, 1939, January 2, 1943.
Springfield Republican, November 10, 1935, December 19, 1937, December 14, 1942, September 26, 1954.
Time, November 29, 1937, December 11, 1939.
Times Literary Supplement, January 9, 1987.
Western American Literature, summer, 1977.

*   *   *

SANSOM, William   1912-1976

PERSONAL: Born January 18, 1912, in London, England; died April 20, 1976; son of Ernest Brooks and Mabel (Clark) Sansom; married Ruth Grundy, 1954; children: Sean, Nicholas. *Education:* Attended Uppingham School; also studied in Europe.

CAREER: Worked in a bank, for an advertising agency, as a fireman in London during World War II, and as a script writer for motion pictures; full-time novelist and essayist since about 1943.

MEMBER: Royal Society of Literature (fellow).

AWARDS, HONORS: Society of Authors travel scholarship, 1946, literary bursary, 1947.

WRITINGS:

(With James Gordon and Stephen Spender) *Jim Braidy: The Story of Britain's Firemen,* Drummond, 1943.
Fireman Flower, and Other Stories, Hogarth, 1944, Vanguard, 1945, 3rd edition, Hogarth, 1966.
Three Stories by William Sansom, Hogarth, 1946, Reynal & Hitchcock, 1947.
(Editor) *Choice: Some New Stories and Prose,* Progress Publishing (London), 1946.
Westminster in War, Faber, 1947.
Something Terrible, Something Lovely (stories), Hogarth, 1948, Harcourt, 1954.
South: Aspects and Images from Corsica, Italy, and Southern France (travel stories), Hodder & Stoughton, 1948, Harcourt, 1950.
The Equilibriad, Hogarth, 1948.
(Editor) Edgar Allan Poe, *The Tell-Tale Heart, and Other Stories,* Lehmann, 1948.

The Body (novel), Harcourt, 1949.
The Passionate North (stories), Hogarth, 1950, Harcourt, 1953.
The Face of Innocence (novel), Harcourt, 1951.
A Touch of the Sun (stories), Hogarth, 1952, Reynal & Hitchcock, 1958.
Pleasures Strange and Simple (essays), Hogarth, 1953.
It Was Really Charlie's Castle (juvenile), Hogarth, 1953.
The Light That Went Out (juvenile), Hogarth, 1953.
A Bed of Roses (novel), Harcourt, 1954.
Lord Love Us (ballads), Hogarth, 1954.
The Loving Eye (novel), Reynal & Hitchcock, 1956.
A Contest of Ladies (stories), Reynal & Hitchcock, 1956.
Among the Dahlias, and Other Stories, Hogarth, 1957.
The Icicle and the Sun (travel), Hogarth, 1958, Reynal & Hitchcock, 1959, reprinted, Greenwood Press, 1975.
The Cautious Heart (novel), Reynal & Hitchcock, 1958.
(Translator) Astrid Bergman, *Chendru: The Boy and the Tiger,* Harcourt, 1960.
Selected Short Stories, Chosen by the Author, Penguin, in association with Hogarth, 1960.
(Editor) Kurt Otto-Wasow, *The Bay of Naples,* Viking, 1960.
The Last Hours of Sandra Lee (novel), Little, 1961, reprinted as *The Wild Affair,* Popular Library, 1964.
Blue Skies, Brown Studies (travel), Little, 1961.
(Editor) Hjalmar Soderberg, *Doctor Glas,* Chatto & Windus, 1963.
The Stories of William Sansom, introduction by Elizabeth Bowen, Little, 1963, reprinted, Ayer Co., 1986.
Away to It All (travel), Hogarth, 1964, New American Library, 1966.
The Ulcerated Milkman (stories), Hogarth, 1966.
Goodbye (novel), Hogarth, 1966, New American Library, 1967.
Grand Tour Today, Hogarth, 1968.
A Book of Christmas (Book-of-the-Month Club selection), McGraw, 1968 (published in England as *Christmas,* Weidenfeld and Nicolson, 1968).
The Verticle Ladder and Other Stories, Chatto & Windus, 1969.
Hans Feet in Love (novel), Hogarth, 1971.
The Birth of a Story, Chatto & Windus/Hogarth, 1972.
Proust and His World, Scribner, 1973, reprinted as *Proust,* Thames & Hudson, 1986.
The Marmalade Bird (short stories), Hogarth, 1973.
Skimpy (juvenile), pictures by Hilary Abrahams, Deutsch, 1974.
(Author of introduction) *Victorian Life in Photographs,* photographic research by Harold Chapman, Thames & Hudson, 1974.
A Young Wife's Tale (novel), Hogarth, 1974.

Contributor to magazines.

SIDELIGHTS: William Sansom's stories and novels were continually praised for their precision of vision, language, and craftsmanship. His works are technically flawless. On the other hand, they were often deprecated for weakness in plot and, most often, for a lack of three-dimensional characters. Walter Allen noted that Sansom was a writer "for whom the sensual surface of things seems to offer the greater part of experience. . . . His first novel, *The Body* . . . is still perhaps his best. It is, as it were, a comedy of exacerbation in which the distorted vision of the hero-narrator is expressed mainly through a minute rendering of the objects that make up the external world. They are seen in an unnatural clarity, magnified as though through an eye that is not a human eye. . . .. The result suggests the literary equivalent of paintings Rousseau might have made had he been turned loose in London immediately after the war." Richard Sullivan added: "In William Sansom's astonishingly productive career he has

written few things to which the adjective 'brilliant' does not apply. . . . [However,] even the extraordinary brilliance of the prose does not offer adequate compensation for the coolness, the aloofness, the detachment of the characterization."

"Sansom is not a writer to whom one can be indifferent," wrote James Dean Young. "The praise is, as far as one can judge, real praise; the damning almost always condescension—as if the stories needed putting down. And so they do." Young primarily objected to Sansom's explicitness and added that "Sansom's stories are written, but they are not made." Other critics contended that he was in perfect control of what he was doing. Max Cosman wrote that "Sansom's is a noticeable temperament. It is antiromantic, chance-ridden, smotheredly violent." He missed nothing that interested him. "The flesh of William Sansom's stories is their uninterrupted contour of sensory impressions," Eudora Welty wrote. "The bone is reflective contemplation. There is an odd contrast, and its pull is felt in the stories between the unhurriedness of their actual events and their racing intensity. . . . Sansom has never been anything less than a good writer. I think as time passes his writing becomes more flexible without losing its tightness of control. . . . And what is perhaps more unusual among writers so good, his work with time seems to have gained, not lost, spontaneity."

Among his novels, *The Body,* as Allen noted, is generally his most highly regarded. As a study in jealousy, according tho Harvey Breit, "it has no contemporary peer. . . . [It is] a serious, psychological novel, with sociological overtones and thriller undertones, by a man with superb control of his material and with a language and style that is simplicity itself." Herbert Barrows believed that this novel could "disappoint only those who respond to the slick." The *Times Literary Supplement* reviewer had only praise for this first novel: "The whole book is written at a high pitch of sensibility often achieved in a compressed form but seldom sustained throughout a longer work. Mr. Sansom adds to this rare power of concentration a sense of humour, acute observation, sound psychological insight and a distinguished descriptive prose style." With the publication of his second novel, *The Face of Innocence,* he was hailed as "an accomplished virtuoso." The novel's "great virtues," wrote Ernest Jones, "like the virtues of the books which preceded it, lie somewhere outside fiction, with the essay, with the best travel writing, sometimes with poetry." Breit concurred: "Sansom, I believe, writes as ably as anyone writing in English today. His language is quietly distinctive, effortless, and exact. . . . He doesn't try what he can't do. Maybe that is the reason he hasn't written a great novel. So far his works have been minor ones. But this modest phenomenon is pleasing within the current context of ego-mania."

After receiving mediocre reviews for *A Bed of Roses* he published *The Loving Eye,* of which R. C. Butz wrote: "All of Mr. Sansom's virtues are here—the freshness of vision, the sensuousness, and the melancholy gaiety similar to the acrid smell of woodsmoke." *The Cautious Heart* was also well received, though Sandra Lee, the protagonist of his *The Last Hours of Sandra Lee,* was considered by some a women's magazine heroine, and the novel was only partly saved from disaster by Sansom's virtuosity. His penultimate novel, *Hans Feet in Love,* was met with little enthusiasm from the critics, who found the main character "unattractive," to use *Books and Bookmen* contributor Diane LeClercq's word, and one *Times Literary Supplement* reviewer remarked that Hans's adventures had already been done by Sansom "with more wit, invention and care in other places." Estimations of *A Young Wife's Tale,* however, were more generous. In a *New Statesman* article, for example, Valerie Cunningham found the novel "fetchingly jokey," though *Listener* critic Neil

Hepburn did complain that the book's narration was "too elegant to believe in." Of the mixed reactions to the author's works, C. J. Rolo once offered this summary: "Sansom is a writer whose novels have at once impressed and disappointed me. He is an artist to his fingertips, and one is tempted to expect great things of him, but egregious flaws appear in his fiction." Rolo noted that a Sansom novel may hinge on an improbable situation and end with a neat resolution, but he adds that, "if these things are accepted, the rewards are large."

Although he is primarily a fiction writer, Sansom admitted that travel writing provided a respectable second income for him. David Depledge wrote: "He didn't have to seek his first commissions for travel work. 'It was about 14 years ago. An American editor saw some stories of mine which were set in Naples. I had set them there deliberately, I now realize, because I wanted to write about Naples. This American recognized something in them, and invited me to write travel pieces for him.' He has been writing for a few of the top American magazines ever since." Elizabeth Bowen praised his travel books as antiprovocative and non-egotistical. Most of these books read like collections of stories, "fresh, instant, exact, inhumanly brilliant," wrote Welty, adding that Sansom is a "wizard twice over." Elizabeth Young noted that Sansom "is not precious, meretricious, burning, or sticky." He "writes like an angel," said Jones, "and his joy in the performance communicates itself directly to the reader." Reversing the theology, J. J. Maloney added: "It is all too seldom . . . that one comes across a man who can tell a rattling good story and write like the devil."

William Sansom's manuscript collection is kept in the New York Public Library Berg Collection.

BIOGRAPHICAL/CRITICAL SOURCES:

BOOKS

Allen, Walter, *The Modern Novel,* Dutton, 1965.
Allsop, Kenneth, *The Angry Decade,* P. Owen, 1958.
Contemporary Literary Criticism, Gale, Volume 2, 1974, Volume 6, 1976.

PERIODICALS

Atlantic, September, 1949, September, 1951, February, 1957.
Books and Bookmen, September, 1968, November, 1971, December, 1973.
Chicago Sunday Tribune, January 19, 1958.
Commonweal, September 9, 1949.
Critique, spring, 1964.
Listener, September 9, 1971, February 6, 1975.
London Magazine, December, 1974/January, 1975.
Manchester Guardian, May 5, 1961.
Nation, October 14, 1950, August 18, 1951.
National Review, August 27, 1963.
New Statesman, November 3, 1961, September 3, 1971, December 13, 1974.
New Yorker, March 24, 1956, April 1, 1967.
New York Herald Tribune Book Review, April 20, 1947, October 15, 1950, August 12, 1951, October 7, 1954, January 12, 1958.
New York Review of Books, August 24, 1967.
New York Times Book Review, August 7, 1949, September 10, 1950, October 10, 1954, March 25, 1956, February 10, 1957, January 12, 1958, June 17, 1961, June 30, 1963.
Observer, June 16, 1968.
San Francisco Chronicle, August 9, 1951, February 24, 1957.
Saturday Review of Literature, August 27, 1949, September 23, 1950, April 7, 1956, September 20, 1958.

Time, September 29, 1958.
Times Literary Supplement, April 30, 1949, April 13, 1956, November 16, 1956, January 24, 1958, October 27, 1966, September 24, 1971, September 14, 1973.

OBITUARIES:

PERIODICALS

AB Bookman's Weekly, June 14, 1976.
New York Times, April 21, 1976.
Washington Post, April 24, 1976.

*   *   *

SANTMYER, Helen Hooven 1895-1986

PERSONAL: Born November 25, 1895, in Cincinnati, Ohio; died of complications brought on by chronic emphysema, February 21, 1986, in Xenia, Ohio; daughter of Joseph Wright (a former medical student, traveling salesman for a drug company, deputy county auditor for Greene County, Ohio, and manager of a rope manufacturing company), and Bertha (a Cincinnati art school graduate; maiden name, Hooven) Santmyer. *Education:* Wellesley College, B.A., 1918; Oxford University, B.Litt., 1927. *Politics:* Republican. *Religion:* Presbyterian.

ADDRESSES: Home—Hospitality Home East, 1301 Monroe Dr., Xenia, Ohio 45385.

CAREER: Charles Scribner's Sons, New York, N.Y., secretary to editor of *Scribner's* magazine, 1919-21; Xenia High School, Xenia, Ohio, teacher of English, 1921-22; Wellesley College, Wellesley, Mass., affiliated with department of English, 1922-24; Cedarville College, Cedarville, Ohio, dean of women and chairman of department of English, 1936-53; Dayton and Montgomery County Public Library, Dayton, Ohio, assistant in reference department, 1953-60.

AWARDS, HONORS: Florence Roberts Hood Memorial Award, Ohioana Library Association, 1964, for *Ohio Town;* Ohioana Book Award in Fiction, 1983, for *. . . And Ladies of the Club;* named to Women's Hall of Fame of Greene County, Ohio, and State of Ohio, 1984; honorary doctor of humanities, Wright State University, 1984; Ohio Governor's Award, 1985.

WRITINGS:

Herbs and Apples (novel), Houghton, 1925, reprinted, Harper, 1985.
The Fierce Dispute (novel), Houghton, 1929, reprinted, St. Martin's, 1987.
Ohio Town: A Portrait of Xenia (essays; selections originally published in *Antioch Review,* 1956 and 1961), Ohio State University Press, 1963, reprinted, Harper, 1984.
. . . And Ladies of the Club (novel; Book-of-the-Month Club main selection), Ohio State University Press, 1982, Putnam, 1984.
Farewell, Summer (novel), Harper, 1988.

Also author of an unpublished mystery novel, *The Hall with Eight Doors.* Contributor of essays, poetry, and stories to *Atlantic, Scribner's Magazine, Midland,* and *Antioch Review.* Helen Hooven Santmyer's papers and letters are in the collection of the Ohio State University Library.

SIDELIGHTS: Helen Hooven Santmyer is best known as the author of the 1984 bestseller *. . . And Ladies of the Club,* a mammoth novel telling the story of four generations of ordinary life in a rural Ohio town. Many of her other novels also depict the lives of people living in small-town America in the years between the end of the Civil War and the Great Depression, evoking a time when life was slower-paced and death was common among young people as well as the elderly. Celebrated for their atmosphere and historical authenticity as well as their vivid characterization, these stories are drawn largely from her own experiences, and Xenia, the Ohio town where she grew up, often provides the basis for their settings.

Helen Santmyer first came to Xenia when her father settled his family in his in-laws' home—built not long before the Civil War—in 1901. Her early years were markedly quiet and contented. "A happy childhood is valuable," she once said, "because you acquire a deep-seated habit of being happy." She felt free to climb trees, to throw seedpods around, and generally to entertain herself. Maple and tulip trees stood in the front yard; from a branch over the sidewalk, she wrote, it "was quite easy to throw down a key tied to a fine thread, or a few sycamore balls onto the Theologues heading to class at the Seminary a block away." Helen played baseball with a family of eight boys named Smith, and was skillful enough to hold her place there for several years, until the ninth Smith could swing a bat.

When Helen entered the grade school in Xenia she discovered reading, possibly the greatest joy of her life. The realization came, she later wrote, "with all the suddenness of a thunderclap when there has been no lightning." She was an omnivorous reader, taking in everything she could find, both in her family's extensive collection and in the public library, including many of her father's medical texts. Helen's parents never forbade her to read books like *Tom Sawyer* and *Huckleberry Finn,* which many parents in Xenia considered unsuitable for their children. She was especially fond of Louisa May Alcott's *Little Women* and told her mother that when she grew up she wanted to be just like Miss Alcott and write wonderful stories of her own. Her mother sympathized completely; she fixed up a room on the second floor of the house for her daughter to work in, with bookshelves all along two walls, and later added an old dining table for Helen to use as a writing desk.

Helen's determination to write dominated her high school years. She decided that in order to pursue her career she had to attend college, a thing few women did at that time. After her graduation in 1913, she applied to Wellesley, a women's college in Massachusetts, partly because some of her Xenia friends had gone there, but also because it had a very strong English department. Unfortunately, before she left for college she came down with a severe case of typhoid fever—contracted from the Xenia ice supply, which was skimmed from the surface of local ponds. The local doctor recommended a year of rest at home and Helen did not enter Wellesley until 1914. The university faculty helped nurture her gift for writing; they taught Helen how to appreciate poetry as well as prose and disciplined her ability as a novelist and essayist. To hone her skills further, Helen joined an informal group of writers called the Scribblers, who met at odd intervals to read and criticize each other's work. In 1918 she completed her bachelor's degree in English literature and composition and graduated at the top of her class.

After Helen left Wellesley, she went to New York City to work. Her first job after graduation was with suffragettes who were working to get women's votes. The work did not appeal to her: "They considered a day lost when they hadn't succeeded in getting into jail." Helen's own approach was to avoid jail at all costs, and she gave up campaigning for women's rights within a few months. Instead she tried to find work with a well established book publisher that published literary works like those of John Galsworthy and Sinclair Lewis, but settled for a position as sec-

retary to an editor of *Scribner's* magazine. The job did expose her to contemporary literary figures, including Ernest Hemingway, Sinclair Lewis, and F. Scott Fitzgerald, but she was not always impressed with them and their work. Fitzgerald, she felt, was a spoiled Princeton boy who drank too much, and the editors "should not have had to put up with his shenanigans." Lewis's *Main Street* she disliked intensely. Remembering her own happy childhood, she could not help feeling his book presented a biased picture of small-town American life.

Helen returned to Xenia in 1921 because her mother was ill and she felt that she was needed at home. Also, she wanted to enter school again—this time Oxford University in England. As her mother's health improved, her father made a bargain with her: if she would first teach in the English department at Xenia high school, he would provide the money for her study in England. Helen joined the high school staff that year, but stayed there only one year before going back to Wellesley as an assistant in the literature department until her departure for England in 1924. Although a bout of hepatitis slowed her progress, she graduated from Oxford in 1927 with a thesis on minor novels of the eighteenth century. In 1925 she published her first book—*Herbs and Apples,* a semi-autobiographical novel—the story of a young Ohio girl whose plans to go to New York and become a writer are thrown into disarray by World War I.

After graduation Helen returned to Xenia again and began work on another novel. While borrowing books from the library she made the acquaintance of Mildred Sandoe, known locally as Miss Johnny Appleseed for her vigorous campaigning on behalf of Ohio libraries, who was then developing the Xenia city library into a county-wide system. Helen knew few people there; her friends from her high school days had all either married or moved away, and, since she was invariably the last person out of the building and usually was struggling with an armload of books, Mildred offered her rides home at the end of the day. It was the beginning of a long and fruitful friendship that lasted nearly sixty years.

Helen continued her literary activities by joining the Xenia Woman's Club, a rather exclusive organization, limited to thirty-five members, which was probably the inspiration for the Waynesboro women's club featured in . . . *And Ladies of the Club.* She quickly impressed her associates with her research ability and versatility as well as her literary credentials. In 1928 she completed her second book, *The Fierce Dispute,* the story of a young girl whose mother and grandmother were feuding over her future career. The characters were entirely her own creation, but the settings were Xenian; the large house mentioned in the novel was based on an actual building on the northernmost edge of town. It was surrounded by several acres of meadow and marshland, with a small stream flowing into a pond in the yard. Three generations of women—a grandmother, her daughter and her granddaughter—lived there, with only a houseman to take care of them, the only connection between the residents and the Xenia townspeople.

Helen left Xenia again in the early 1930s to accompany her family to California, where her father had found work. She spent most of her time there writing and reading about Ohio, the Civil War, and life in America between 1860 and 1932. The writing mostly consisted of essays—which later formed the basis for *Ohio Town*—about her home town's library, courthouse, railroad station, and all the other places that, she felt sure, were common to midwestern towns. She returned to Ohio to take a post at Cedarville College, a small Presbyterian college near Xenia with a scanty budget but an excellent faculty. Helen took the position of dean of women and head of the English department, although there were times when she found herself teaching Latin and Greek as well as her own classes.

Although Helen's English class attracted many students, her activities were not limited to the school year. In the summers she organized writing clubs among her niece's ten-year-old friends, and read poetry to them. However, her projects were curtailed in the late 1930s by a severe illness. Helen suffered from the disease for more than five years. At times she was so ill that she could not walk the seven or so blocks from her apartment to the campus, and had to hold class in her living room. Eventually her doctor sent her to the Ohio State University, where her illness was diagnosed as undulant fever. She was eventually cured, but the long years of illness had damaged her digestive tract and forced her to remain on a restricted diet for the rest of her life.

Helen left Cedarville in 1953, due to disagreements with the new fundamentalist proprietors of the university. She soon obtained a position as assistant reference librarian in the library of Dayton and Montgomery County, specializing in literature, local history and biography. Helen stayed there until her retirement in 1959, when she returned to Xenia to live. Her parents had died in 1957, so Helen asked Mildred Sandoe, her old friend from her Xenia days, to live with her in the old house on West Third Street. They took their vacations together: to Canada and the Northeast for fishing; to the Southwest to visit Helen's brother Philip; and to Pennsylvania and the Midwest for Amish antiques and stories. Helen and Mildred kept up these trips for a good many years, until Helen's health made it too uncomfortable for her to travel. She had suffered a fall while working in Dayton, breaking two vertebrae and injuring her spinal cord. An arthritic knot formed at the base of her spine, and this, combined with emphysema from her constant smoking that made it hard for her to breathe, put an end to their journeys. Eventually, Helen's health deteriorated so much that she could not sit in a car for any length of time without considerable pain, making trips outside of Xenia and the surrounding area impractical.

Helen continued to write after her retirement. She set aside each afternoon, writing left-handed in longhand on lined white paper at her desk in the bedroom downstairs, or in bed when she was not feeling well. Mildred urged her to finish the essays she had begun in California, adding some new material, and to send them off to a publisher. Helen chose Weldon Kefauver of the Ohio State University Press, and mailed the manuscript of *Ohio Town* to him in 1963. She received an enthusiastic response, and the book went to press that year. *Ohio Town* received good reviews from local papers and historical journals; although it was "a book of remembrance rather than a retelling of history," as a reviewer for the *Xenia Daily Gazette* described it, the volume effectively evoked life in Xenia around the turn of the century. It remained relatively unknown, however, probably because its publication coincided with a large newspaper strike in New York. Those who heard about the book thought highly of it, and it won the Florence Roberts Head Award for excellence in literature from the Ohioana Library in 1964. Although Helen was in her mid-sixties at the time, she accepted her award personally, saying, "I am so pleased. I am so *very* pleased."

Sometime between 1964 and 1970, Helen began work on the novel she had always wanted to write, about American life in the small towns of the midwest between 1865 and 1932. She had been collecting bits and pieces of information about it since the family discussions about current events around the dining table in her childhood, but it was not until the mid-1960s that she began the actual task of composition. Helen generally set aside

two hours in the late morning and another two in the late afternoon to work on her novel; her health remained uncertain, and she did not complete the manuscript until 1975.

She sent the work to Dr. Kefauver in eleven boxes filled to the brim with typewritten manuscript. Kefauver's response was favorable; even though the Ohio State University Press did not publish much fiction, he felt that her book was a good risk, worth publishing for its historical merit as well as its literary quality. However, he added, it would have to be shortened by six or seven hundred pages. Helen's eyesight was failing her by that time, so she enlisted Mildred's assistance in cutting the novel down to two-thirds its original size. It took them nearly eighteen months to prepare a shortened version, and even then some parts of the book were never touched. They returned the manuscript to Dr. Kefauver, and, in due course, received two enormous red-bound volumes "looking more like reference books than novels." . . . *And Ladies of the Club* had arrived.

The Ohio State University Press was not sure that the novel would sell, and initially their apprehensions seemed justified; they printed 1500 copies in 1982, of which only about 200 sold, mostly to libraries. The first edition of *Ladies* proved unwieldy in several ways; the completed volume weighed over four pounds, had over 1300 pages, and cost $35.00. It made a fearsome weapon, however; one reader later wrote Helen that she had been trapped in her kitchen by a large snake, and had dropped the book on its head. "It did the work," she wrote Helen. "I read every golden word of it even though I'll admit some of the pages were pretty gory."

While some reviewers found the myriad details in . . . *And Ladies of the Club* burdensome and the prejudices and moral rigidity displayed by its characters untenable, others were enchanted by the novel's matter-of-fact, day-by-day approach. Susan Toepfer, writing in the *New York Daily News,* declares that "Santmyer's subjects are not the overblown romantics of a *Gone with the Wind,* but simple, 'decent' midwestern folk—with all the narrow-mindedness that 'decent' implies." A. C. Greene noted on the "MacNeil/Lehrer News Hour" that *Ladies* tells "the lives that most of us lead. It's not full of sudden, strange unexpected episodes, but it's well written and it relates the human experience in a pattern that, even though we're talking about 120 and some odd years ago, we can still relate to it."

Critics also commented on Helen's approach to history. Leola Floren remarked in the *Detroit News,* "Miss Santmyer clearly understands that history is more than the sterile procession of dates and events that we learned in school. . . . What she offers in this very fine story is not objectivity, or an omniscient view of the world scene, but everyday life through the eyes of people who crawled out from under the shadow of civil war, lost children to rheumatic fever and tuberculosis, watched sons march off to the Great War, and endured a series of depressions even before the Big One." Ruth Clements wrote in the Toronto *Globe and Mail* that the author "is moving us through time . . . while simultaneously asking us to step back and watch time move. It is as though time were an object that Santmyer holds the way a teacher displays a globe to a class."

Ladies did not attract much public attention until late in 1983. Mrs. Grace Sindell of Shaker Heights, a suburb of Cleveland, Ohio, overheard a library patron talking about the book; the patron said *Ladies* was the best novel she had ever read. Mrs. Sindell checked the book out, read it, and recommended it to her son Gerald, a Hollywood producer. He contacted a friend at the William Morris agency, who turned it over to the publisher G. P. Putnam's Sons, and Helen Santmyer, the small woman with the large book, shot into the public eye, an overnight phenomenon. The Putnam edition stayed on the *New York Times* bestseller list for 37 consecutive weeks and held the number-one position for seven. The Book-of-the-Month Club made *Ladies* its main selection and sold more than 162,000 copies, and a paperback edition sold more than a million copies. Helen's response was typical: "Isn't that nice. I just can't believe it." Newspeople flocked to Xenia, including reporters from all the major television news programs, from papers around the country, and from major magazines such as *Life, People, Newsweek* and *Time.*

The newspeople found, when they arrived, a lady of nearly 90 years, confined to a sheepskin-lined wheelchair. Helen was suffering from severe arthritis and emphysema, had totally lost the vision in one eye and had cataracts in the other, and weighed only 90 pounds due to her digestive trouble. Her mental condition was good, however, and her disposition was excellent; her fellow patients described her as "the little lady with the sweet smile who always waves when she goes past the door." She remained unimpressed by all the media hype about *Ladies;* "I think it's the kind of book most people are not interested in," she once said. "Part of the interest is because I'm an old lady." Trudy Krisher, writing in the Dayton *Journal Herald,* declared, "Helen taught us all something about success. That it is not measured by contracts or the number of pictures in *Life* magazine. It comes from the pleasure of doing what you love in the best way that you can." "Helen Santmyer has joined the club," Krisher concluded. "In my opinion, the company is enriched by her presence."

MEDIA ADAPTATIONS: . . . And Ladies of the Club has been optioned as a television miniseries.

AVOCATIONAL INTERESTS: Travel (especially Civil War battlefields), gardening, reading (especially mysteries), antique collecting.

BIOGRAPHICAL/CRITICAL SOURCES:

BOOKS

Contemporary Literary Criticism, Volume 33, Gale, 1985.
Dictionary of Literary Biography Yearbook: 1984, Gale, 1985.

PERIODICALS

Blade (Toledo), May 29, 1988.
Chicago Tribune, June 10, 1984.
Chicago Tribune Book World, June 10, 1984, September 9, 1984.
Christian Science Monitor, January 27, 1984.
Columbus Dispatch, August 26, 1984, December 23, 1987.
Dayton Daily News, August 4, 1963.
Detroit Free Press, January 13, 1984.
Detroit News, June 10, 1984.
Globe and Mail (Toronto), August 4, 1984.
Los Angeles Times Book Review, June 10, 1984.
Mid-Cities Daily News (Hurst, Tex.), December 5, 1984.
Newsweek, June 18, 1984.
New York Daily News, June 17, 1984.
New Yorker, July 9, 1984.
New York Times, January 12, 1984, June 1, 1984, June 4, 1984.
New York Times Book Review, June 24, 1984, September 16, 1984.
People, July 16, 1984.
Nation, July 21, 1984.
Time, July 9, 1984.
Washington Post Book World, January 22, 1984, September 2, 1984.
Wellesley Alumnae Magazine, January, 1963.

Xenia Daily Gazette, January 24, 1963, February 18, 1963, June 5, 1975.

OTHER

"MacNeil/Lehrer News Hour," Public Broadcasting Service (PBS-TV), July 5, 1984.

OBITUARIES:

PERIODICALS

AB Bookman's Weekly, March 24, 1986.
Chicago Tribune, February 23, 1986.
Circleville Herald (Circleville, Ohio), February 22, 1986.
Journal Herald (Dayton), March 1, 1986.
New York Times, February 22, 1986.
Publishers Weekly, March 7, 1986.
Sun-Times (Chicago), February 22, 1986.
Xenia Daily Gazette, February 22, 1986.

[Sketch reviewed by Mildred Sandoe, Miss Santmyer's companion, and by
Louise A. Muller, Miss Santmyer's personal secretary]

—*Sketch by Kenneth R. Shepherd*

* * *

SAROYAN, William   1908-1981
(Sirak Goryan)

PERSONAL: Born August 31, 1908, in Fresno, Calif.; died May 18, 1981, of cancer and cremated in Fresno; half of his ashes interred in Fresno, the remaining half interred near Yerevan, Armenia, U.S.S.R., May 29, 1981; son of Armenak (a Presbyterian preacher and writer) and Takoohi (Saroyan) Saroyan; married Carol Marcus, February, 1943 (divorced, November, 1949); remarried Carol Marcus, 1951 (divorced, 1952); children: Aram, Lucy. *Education:* Left high school at age fifteen.

CAREER: Short story writer, playwright, novelist. Began selling newspapers at the age of eight for the *Fresno Evening Herald;* while still in school he worked at various jobs, including that of telegraph messenger boy; after leaving school he worked in his uncle's law office, then held numerous odd jobs, including that of grocery clerk, vineyard worker, postal employee, and office manager of San Francisco Postal Telegraph Co. Co-founder of Conference Press, 1936. Organized and directed The Saroyan Theatre, August, 1942 (closed after one week). Writer in residence, Purdue University, 1961. *Military service:* U.S. Army, 1942-45.

AWARDS, HONORS: O. Henry Award, 1934, for "The Daring Young Man on the Flying Trapeze"; Drama Critics Circle Award, 1940, for "The Time of Your Life"; Pulitzer Prize, 1940, for "The Time of Your Life"—declined by the author on the principle that business should not judge the arts; Academy Award, 1943, for the screenplay "The Human Comedy"; California Literature Gold Medal, 1952, for *Tracy's Tiger;* American Book Award nomination, 1980, for *Obituaries.*

WRITINGS:

The Daring Young Man on the Flying Trapeze, and Other Stories (also see below), Random House, 1934, reprinted, Yolla Bolly, 1984.
A Christmas Psalm, Gelber, Lilienthal, 1935.
Inhale and Exhale (stories; also see below), Random House, 1936, Books for Libraries Press, 1972.
Those Who Write Them and Those Who Collect Them, Black Archer Press, 1936.

Three Times Three (stories; also see below), Conference Press, 1936.

Little Children (stories), Harcourt, 1937.

A Gay and Melancholy Flux (compiled from *Inhale and Exhale* and *Three Times Three*), Faber, 1937.

Love, Here Is My Hat, and Other Short Romances, Modern Age Books, 1938.

The Trouble with Tigers (stories), Harcourt, 1938.

A Native American, George Fields, 1938.

Peace, It's Wonderful (stories), Modern Age Books, 1939.

3 Fragments and a Story, Little Man, 1939.

The Hungerers: A Short Play, S. French, 1939.

My Heart's in the Highlands (play; produced on Broadway at Guild Theatre, April 13, 1939; first published in *One-Act Play Magazine,* December, 1937; also see below), Harcourt, 1939.

The Time of Your Life (play; produced on Broadway at Booth Theatre, October 25, 1939; produced in London, England, by Royal Shakespeare Company, 1982; also see below), Harcourt, 1939, acting edition, S. French, 1969, Methuen, 1983.

The Time of Your Life (miscellany), Harcourt, 1939.

Christmas, 1939, Quercus Press, 1939.

"A Theme in the Life of the Great American Goof " (ballet-play; also see below), produced in New York City at Center Theatre, January, 1940.

Subway Circus (play), S. French, 1940.

The Ping-Pong Game (play; produced in New York, 1945), S. French, 1940.

A Special Announcement, House of Books, 1940.

My Name Is Aram (stories; Book-of-the-Month Club selection), Harcourt, 1940, revised edition, 1966.

The Beautiful People (play; produced under the author's direction on Broadway at Lyceum Theatre, April 21, 1940), Harcourt, 1941.

Saroyan's Fables, Harcourt, 1941.

The Insurance Salesman and Other Stories, Faber (London), 1941.

Love's Old Sweet Song (play; first produced on Broadway at Plymouth Theatre, May 2, 1940; also see below), S. French, 1941.

Three Plays: My Heart's in the Highlands, The Time of Your Life, Love's Old Sweet Song, Harcourt, 1940.

Harlem as Seen by Hirschfield, Hyperion Press, 1941.

Hilltop Russians in San Francisco, James Ladd Delkin, 1941.

The People with Light Coming Out of Them (radio play; first broadcast, 1941), The Free Company (New York City), 1941.

Jim Dandy, A Play, Little Man Press (Cincinnati), 1941, reprinted as *Jim Dandy: Fat Man in a Famine,* Harcourt, 1947.

"Across the Board on Tomorrow Morning," first produced Pasadena, Calif., at Pasadena Playhouse, February, 1941, produced at Theatre Showcase, March, 1942, produced under the author's direction on Broadway at Belasco Theatre, on the same bill with "Talking to You," August, 1942.

Hello Out There (play; first produced in Santa Barbara, Calif., at Lobeto Theatre, September, 1941, produced on Broadway at Belasco Theatre, September, 1942), S. French, 1949.

Razzle-Dazzle (short plays; includes "A Theme in the Life of the Great American Goof "), Harcourt, 1942.

"Talking to You" (play), produced in New York, 1942.

"The Good Job" (screenplay based on his story "A Number of the Poor"), Loew, 1942.

48 Saroyan Stories, Avon, 1942.

The Human Comedy (novel; also see below), Harcourt, 1943, revised edition, 1966.

"The Human Comedy," (scenario based on *The Human Comedy,* Metro-Goldwyn-Mayer), 1943.

Thirty-One Selected Stories, Avon, 1943.

Fragment, Albert M. Bender, 1943.

Get Away Old Man (play; produced on Broadway at Cort Theatre, November, 1943), Harcourt, 1944.

Someday I'll Be A Millionaire Myself, Avon, 1944.

Dear Baby (stories), Harcourt, 1944.

(With Henry Miller and Hilaire Hiler) *Why Abstract?,* New Directions, 1945, Haskell House, 1974.

The Adventures of Wesley Jackson (novel; also see below), Harcourt, 1946.

The Saroyan Special: Selected Short Stories, Harcourt, 1948, Books for Libraries Press, 1970.

The Fiscal Hoboes, Press of Valenti Angelo, 1949.

Don't Go Away Mad, and Two Other Plays: Sam Ego's House; A Decent Birth, A Happy Funeral, Harcourt, 1949.

Sam Ego's House (play), S. French, 1949.

The Assyrian, And Other Stories, Harcourt, 1950.

The Twin Adventures: The Adventures of William Saroyan, A Diary; The Adventures of Wesley Jackson, A Novel, Harcourt, 1950.

"The Son" (play), produced in Los Angeles, Calif., 1950.

(Author of introduction) Khatchik Minasian, *The Simple Songs of Khatchik Minasian,* Colt Press, 1950.

Rock Wagram (novel), Doubleday, 1951.

Tracy's Tiger (fantasy), Doubleday, 1951, revised edition, Ballantine, 1967.

The Bicycle Rider in Beverly Hills (autobiography), Scribner, 1952, Ballantine, 1971.

The Laughing Matter (novel), Doubleday, 1953.

"Opera, Opera" (play), produced in New York, 1955.

Mama I Love You (novel; listed in some sources under the working title "The Bouncing Ball"), Atlantic-Little, Brown, 1956, Dell, 1986.

The Whole Voyald and Other Stories, Atlantic-Little, Brown, 1956.

Papa You're Crazy (novel), Atlantic-Little, Brown, 1957.

"Ever Been in Love with a Midget?" (play), produced in Berlin, 1957.

The Cave Dwellers (play; produced on Broadway in New York City, October 19, 1957), Putnam, 1958.

The Slaughter of the Innocents (play; produced at The Hague, Netherlands, 1957), S. French, 1958.

The William Saroyan Reader, Braziller, 1958.

Once Around the Block (play), S. French, 1959.

"The Paris Comedy; or, The Secret of Lily" (play; produced in Vienna, Austria, 1960), published as *The Paris Comedy; or, The Dogs, Chris Sick, and 21 Other Plays,* also published as *The Dogs, or The Paris Comedy, and Two Other Plays: Chris Sick, or Happy New Year Anyway, Making Money, and Nineteen Other Very Short Plays,* Phaedra, 1969.

Sam, the Highest Jumper of Them All, or The London Comedy (play; produced in London under the author's direction, 1960), Faber, 1961.

(With Henry Cecil) "Settled Out of Court" (play), produced in London, 1960.

"High Time along the Wabash" (play), produced in West Lafayette, Ind., at Purdue University, 1961.

"Ah, Man" (play), music by Peter Fricker, produced in Adelburgh, Suffolk, England, 1962.

Here Comes, There Goes, You Know Who (autobiography), Trident, 1962.

My Lousy Adventures with Money, New Strand (London), 1962.

A Note on Hilaire Hiler, Wittenborn, 1962.

Boys and Girls Together (novel), Harcourt, 1963.

Me (juvenile), Crowell-Collier, 1963.

Not Dying (autobiography), Harcourt, 1963.

One Day in the Afternoon of the World (novel), Harcourt, 1964.

After Thirty Years: The Daring Young Man on the Flying Trapeze (includes essays), Harcourt, 1964.

Best Stories of William Saroyan, Faber, 1964.

Deleted Beginning and End of a Short Story, Lowell-Adams House Printers (Cambridge, Mass.), 1965.

Short Drive, Sweet Chariot (reminiscences), Phaedra, 1966.

My Kind of Crazy and Wonderful People, Harcourt, 1966.

(Author of introduction) *The Arabian Nights,* Platt & Munk, 1966.

Look at Us; Let's See; Here We Are; Look Hard, Speak Soft; I See, You See, We All See; Stop, Look, Listen; Beholder's Eye; Don't Look Now But Isn't That You? (Us? U.S.?), Cowles, 1967.

I Used to Believe I Had Forever, Now I'm Not So Sure, Cowles, 1968.

(Author of foreword) Barbara Holden and Mary Jane Woebcke, *A Child's Guide to San Francisco,* Diablo Press, 1968.

Horsey Gorsey and the Frog (juvenile), illustrated by Grace Davidian, R. Hale, 1968.

Letters from 74 rue Taitbout, or Don't Go, But If You Must, Say Hello to Everybody, World, 1968, published as *Don't Go, But If You Must, Say Hello to Everybody,* Cassell, 1970.

Man with the Heart in the Highlands, and Other Stories, Dell, 1968.

Days of Life and Death and Escape to the Moon, Dial, 1970.

(Editor and author of introduction) *Hairenik, 1934-1939: An Anthology of Short Stories and Poems* (collection of Armenian-American literature), Books for Libraries Press, 1971.

Places Where I've Done Time, Praeger, 1972.

The Tooth and My Father, Doubleday, 1974.

"The Rebirth Celebration of the Human Race at Artie Zabala's Off-Broadway Theater" (play), first produced in New York City, July 10, 1975.

An Act or Two of Foolish Kindness, Penmaen Press & Design, 1976.

Sons Come and Go, Mothers Hang In Forever, Franklin Library, 1976.

Morris Hirschfield, Rizzoli International, 1976.

Chance Meetings, Norton, 1978.

(Compiler) *Patmuatsk'ner / Uiliem Saroyean; hayats'uts' Hovhannes Sheohmelean* (selected Armenian stories), Sewan, 1978.

Two Short Paris Summertime Plays of 1974: Assassinations and Jim, Sam and Anna, Santa Susana Press, 1979.

Obituaries, Creative Arts, 1979, second edition, 1979.

Two Short Paris Summertime Plays of 1974, California State University, Northridge Library, 1979.

Births, introduction by David Kherdian, Creative Arts, 1981.

My Name Is Saroyan (short stories; autobiographical), edited by James H. Tashjian, Coward-McCann, 1983.

The New Saroyan Reader: A Connoisseur's Anthology of the Writings of William Saroyan, edited by Brian Derwent, Creative Arts, 1984.

The Circus (juvenile), Creative Education, 1986.

The Armenian Trilogy, California State University Press, 1986.

The Pheasant Hunter: About Fathers and Sons, Redpath Press, 1986.

Madness in the Family, edited by Leo Hamalian, New Directions, 1988.

Also author of the plays "Something about a Soldier," "Hero of the World," and "Sweeney in the Trees," all produced in stock, 1940. Plays represented in anthologies, including *Famous American Plays of the 1930s,* edited by Harold Clurman, and *One Act: Eleven Short Plays of the Modern Theatre,* edited by Samuel Moon. Writer of song lyrics, including "Come On-a My House" with Ross Bagdasarian, in 1951. Contributor to *Overland Monthly, Hairenik* (Armenian-American magazine), *Story, Saturday Evening Post, Atlantic, Look, McCalls,* and other periodicals. *The Human Comedy* and *The Adventures of Wesley Jackson* have been translated into Russian.

SIDELIGHTS: William Saroyan's career began in 1934 with the publication of *The Daring Young Man on the Flying Trapeze and Other Stories.* From that time on, he wrote prolifically, producing a steady stream of short stories, plays, novels, memoirs, and essays. His career can be divided into five phases. From 1934 to 1939 he wrote short stories; from 1939 to 1943 his energies were directed toward playwriting; the years 1943-1951 saw the appearance of his first two novels (*The Human Comedy* and *The Adventures of Wesley Jackson*), as well as plays and short fiction; between 1951 and 1964 Saroyan published a series of novels dealing with marriage and the family; and finally, from 1964 until his death in 1981, Saroyan devoted himself primarily to the exploration of his past through autobiographical writings.

It is through the short story genre that Saroyan made his initial impact as a writer. During this first creative period, Saroyan published eight volumes; in the preface to *The Assyrian and Other Stories,* he estimated that during these years he wrote "five hundred short stories, or a mean average of one hundred per annum." These early collections project a wide variety of thematic concerns, yet they are united in their portrayal of America between the two world wars. Saroyan's first books reflect the painful realities of the Depression of the 1930s. The young writer without a job in his first famous story "The Daring Young Man on the Flying Trapeze" goes to be interviewed for a position and finds that "already there were two dozen young men in the place." The story "International Harvester" from the 1936 collection *Inhale and Exhale* also gives a bleak vision of complete economic collapse: "Shamefully to the depths fallen: America. In Wall Street they talk as if the end of this country is within sight."

Readers clearly saw their troubled lives vividly portrayed in Saroyan's stories; though they depicted the agony of the times, the stories also conveyed great hope and vigorously defiant good spirits. However, as Maxwell Geismar remarked in *Writers in Crisis: The American Novel, 1925-1940,* "the depression of the 1930s, apparently so destructive and so despairing," was actually a time of "regeneration" for the major writers of the period. Furthermore, "the American writer had gained moral stature, a sense of his own cultural connection, a series of new meanings and new values for his work." The crisis these writers were experiencing was, of course, more than merely economic. A deep cultural schism had rocked Europe since Friedrich Nietzsche's nineteenth-century apocalyptic prophecies and affected such American writers as Henry Miller, whose *Tropic of Cancer* appeared in the same year as Saroyan's first collection of short fiction.

Between 1939 and 1943, Saroyan published and produced his most famous plays. Works such as *My Heart's in the Highlands, The Beautiful People,* and *Across the Board on Tomorrow Morning* were well received by some critics and audiences; *The Time of Your Life* won the Pulitzer Prize as the best play of the 1939-1940 season, but Saroyan refused the award on the grounds that businessmen should not judge art. Although championed by critics like George Jean Nathan, Saroyan had a strained relationship with the theatrical world. From the time his first play appeared on Broadway, critics called his work surrealistic, sentimental, or difficult to understand. His creation of a fragile, fluid, dramatic universe full of strange, lonely, confused, and gentle people startled theatergoers accustomed to conventional plots and characterization. His instinctive and highly innovative sense of dramatic form was lost on many audiences. These plays were a wonderful amalgam of vaudeville, absurdism, sentiment, spontaneity, reverie, humor, despair, philosophical speculation, and whimsy. His plays introduced a kind of rambunctious energy into staid American drama. His "absurdity" bore a direct relationship to his sorrow at observing the waste of the true, vital impulses of life in the contemporary world. His artist figures—Joe, Jonah Webster, Ben Alexander—all feel within themselves the dying of the old order and the painful struggle to give birth to a new consciousness.

In 1941, after two active years on Broadway, Saroyan traveled to Hollywood to work on the film version of *The Human Comedy* for Metro-Goldwyn-Mayer. When the scenario was completed, it was made into a successful motion picture. From the beginning of his career, Saroyan had committed himself to celebrating the brotherhood of man, and in *The Human Comedy* he preached a familiar sermon: love one another, or you shall perish. This portrayal of love's power in small-town America offered consolation to millions ravaged by the suffering and death brought on by World War II.

Saroyan went on to publish four novels between 1951 and 1964: *Rock Wagram, The Laughing Matter, Boys and Girls Together,* and *One Day in the Afternoon of the World.* Each novel explores in fictional form the troubled years of Saroyan's own marriage to Carol Marcus and that marriage's aftermath. These thinly disguised transcriptions of Saroyan's own life might be termed the "fatherhood novels," for they are linked thematically through the author's concern with founding a family. Each Armenian-American protagonist in these novels is searching for (or has already found) a wife and children, his emblems of human community. Edward Krickel, in a 1970 *Georgia Review* article, correctly points out that sex and love in Saroyan's novels are not ends in themselves, but rather "lead to family and the honorable roles of parent and grandparent, in short the traditional view. Children are the glory of the relationship." In the novels, as in the plays and short stories, the family symbolizes the family of humanity in microcosm and localizes the desire for universal brotherhood that had always marked Saroyan's vision. The Webster family in *The Beautiful People,* the Macauleys in *The Human Comedy,* the Alexanders in *My Heart's in the Highlands,* and the Garoghlanians in *My Name Is Aram* all were his imaginary families before he sought to become a father himself and realize his dreams.

During the 1930s and 1940s, Saroyan reached the peak of his fame; by the mid-1950s his reputation had declined substantially. Many critics have dismissed Saroyan for not being what they wanted him to be, rather than considering the writer's virtues and faults on his own terms. Saroyan was aware early in his career that he was being neglected, as is apparent from his reaction in *Razzle-Dazzle* to the critical reception of the plays: "As it happened first with my short stories, my plays appeared so suddenly and continued to come so swiftly that no one was quite prepared to fully meet and appreciate them, so that so far neither the short stories nor the plays have found critical understanding worthy of them. If the critics have failed, I have not. I have both written and criticized my plays, and so far the importance I have given

them, as they have appeared, has been supported by theatrical history. If the critics have not yet agreed with me on the value of my work, it is still to be proved that I am not the writer I say I am. I shall some day startle those who now regard me as nothing more than a show-off, but I shall not startle myself." What he said of his short stories and plays proved to be true of the novels and autobiographical writings as well.

Peter Collier, in a 1972 *New York Times Book Review* essay, attributed the critical devaluation to the fact that "the generation of academic critics had now come to power who were overseeing the development of the kind of dense, cerebral literature which justified their profession." Saroyan's often flippant and antiacademic tone was not calculated to endear him to the professors. Another complaint commonly voiced by critics was Saroyan's tendency toward "escapism." Philip Rahv found Saroyan's role as lover of mankind irritating; in the September 1943 *American Mercury* Rahv wrote that in *The Human Comedy* Saroyan insisted "evil is unreal," although the world was obviously mired in pain and tragedy. Linked to this charge of escapism was Saroyan's nonpolitical stance; he supported no 'ism' and was therefore accused of lacking a social conscience. This attitude put him out of favor with the proletarian writers of the 1930s who were eager to enlist him in their cause. Although Saroyan always affirmed the brotherhood of man, he recognized no authorities, no leaders, no programs to save the world.

Among the negative comments about Saroyan's works is the charge that he was a simple-minded, sentimental romantic whose naive optimism did not reflect the terrible realities of the age. However, the angst of the twentieth century pervades his work; his brooding depression appears not only in the later books but also in an early play, *The Time of Your Life.* Saroyan's lonely and and pathetic characters sense the oncoming fury of World War II, and the knowledge that life is poised at the rim of disaster haunts their dialogue. Commentators have almost completely ignored this darker, despairing existential side of Saroyan's work.

Though the alienation and melancholy that characterize much of Saroyan's work are typical of twentieth-century literature, the feeling of rootlessness that pervades his imagination finds an important source in his Armenian heritage. In 1896, twelve years before Saroyan's birth, 200,000 Armenians were massacred by the Turks. In 1915, the Turks deported the Armenian population of 2,500,000 to Syria and Mesopotamia; more than a million and a half Armenians were killed during this process. The Armenian migration began in earnest; of those who escaped deportation, many fled to Russia and the United States. Armenak and Takoohi Saroyan were among the thousands who came to America during the first wave of the massacres. William, the only one of their four children to be born in America, was born in Fresno, California.

In California's San Joaquin Valley, Saroyan's parents found a region similar to their native land. Although Armenians would establish communities in other parts of America, California attracted the greatest number because it was the ideal region for a predominantly agricultural people. Although California seemed idyllic, the racial conflicts that had driven the Armenians to their newfound land continued. In the autobiographical *Here Comes, There Goes, You Know Who,* Saroyan remarked: "The Armenians were considered inferior, they were pushed around, they were hated, and I was an Armenian. I refused to forget it then, and I refuse to forget it now, but not because being an Armenian had, or has, any particular significance." Because the Armenians were not really absorbed into American life, isolated within their own communities, it is no accident that Saroyan's work conveys a powerful sense of not being at home in the world.

If the Armenian people were symbolically homeless in their American exile, Saroyan himself, after the age of three, was literally homeless. The death of his father in 1911 surely contributed to his lifelong obsession with death and estrangement. Saroyan's mother was forced to place him in an orphanage, and it is evident from his autobiographical writings that his childhood was often profoundly unhappy. Midway through his career, Saroyan wondered, as he says in *Here Comes, There Goes, You Know Who:* "Well, first of all, just where was my home? Was it in Fresno, where I was born? Was it in San Jose, where my father died? Was it in Oakland, where I spent four very important years? . . . Home was in myself, and I wasn't there, that's all . . . I was far from home." The poverty of his early life drove him to literature, and to the quest for meaning: "I took to writing at an early age to escape from meaninglessness, uselessness, unimportance, insignificance, poverty, enslavement, ill health, despair, madness, and all manner of other unattractive, natural, and inevitable things. I have managed to conceal my madness fairly effectively," he wrote in *Here Comes, There Goes, You Know Who.*

Saroyan returned obsessively throughout his career to the theme of "madness," to a consideration of the possible reasons for his sorrow and psychic dislocation. He revealed a kind of "race-melancholy" underlying the Armenian temperament. In the late story "The Assyrian," he explored the dark side of his sensibility under the guise of an Assyrian hero, Paul Scott: "The longer he'd lived, the more he'd become acquainted with the Assyrian side, the old side, the tired side, the impatient and wise side, the side he had never suspected existed in himself until he was thirteen and had begun to be a man." Another foreign alter ego, the Arab in *The Time of Your Life,* repeats to himself: "No foundation. All the way down the line"—at once expressing the pain of the exile and Saroyan's own sense of disorder and spiritual emptiness.

Saroyan also identified this madness with illness, which was, he declared in *The Bicycle Rider in Beverly Hills,* "an event of the soul more than of the body." He asserted in the same volume, "I have been more or less ill all my life," a statement remarkable for both its extremism and its honesty. In *Days of Life and Death and Escape to the Moon,* a late memoir, he drew together various aspects of his own self-analysis in reexamining the past: "Most of the time illnesses of one sort or another came to me regularly, all the year round. I can't believe it is all from the sorrow in my nature, in my family, in my race, but I know some of it is." Saroyan was thus aware that his psychology derived from his Armenian heritage, the effects of his family life, and some quality inherent in his own personality.

If Saroyan was not at home in the world as it was, he was very much at home in his own imaginative recreation of it in his work. There may not be "real" homes and families like the one depicted in Saroyan's play *The Beautiful People,* but that is beside the point. As Wallace Stevens pointed out, the artist must *create* nobility, must press back against the world's chaos to create a livable sphere of existence. For Saroyan, art was a way toward health, toward reconciliation, toward psychic regeneration. He observed in the preface to *Don't Go Away Mad and Two Other Plays* that he needed to write "because I hate to believe I'm sick or half-dead; because I want to get better; because writing is my therapy."

Deeply aware of the fragmentation and spiritual anarchy of life in the modern world, Saroyan exhibited a driving impulse to-

ward joy, self-realization, and psychic integration. In the introduction to *Three Plays* he remarked that "the imperative requirement of our time is to restore faith to the mass and integrity to the individual. The integration of man is still far from realized. In a single age this integration can be immeasurably improved, but it is impossible and useless to seek to imagine its full achievement. Integration will begin to occur when the individual is uninhibited, impersonal, simultaneously natural and cultured, without hate, without fear, and rich in spiritual grace." Saroyan's work, then, records the attempt to integrate the divided self.

Following the final dissolution of his marriage in 1952 Saroyan turned increasingly to the exploration of his past through a series of autobiographies, memoirs, and journals. Although he continued to publish plays and fiction, autobiography became his main form of self-expression. This impulse reflected a shift in emphasis from art to life, from "doing" to "being," from the creation of works to the creation of self. Saroyan sought in memory a key to his identity, a meaningful pattern underlying the chaos of experience. In *The Bicycle Rider in Beverly Hills,* he wrote: "I want to think about the things I may have forgotten. I want to have a go at them because I have an idea they will help make known how I became who I am." Like Whitman, Thomas Wolfe, and Henry Miller, Saroyan obsessively focused on his own responses, emotions, and experiences in search of the psychological matrices of his behavior and personality. The writings of his final phase, however, are not only an important source of biographical insights—they also represent some of his best prose.

There is in these last writings a vibrant joy, a deep pleasure taken in small details of daily living. Saroyan buys cheap second-hand books in a Paris shop, brings home basil plants to his apartment, delights in solitude and reading. He writes of casual long walks, visits to libraries, meetings with dear friends. Musing over the strange disjunctions of a long life, he remembers many people: family, writers, former teachers, childhood comrades.

Saroyan's search in these last years was the search of his youth. His continuing antipathy toward authority, repression, and the fettering of the human spirit made him an influence on writers of the Beat Generation, who responded to his innovative, hip, casual, jazzy voice. Beginning his career in San Francisco, meeting ground of the spiritual East and expansive West, Saroyan wrote of beautiful people and preached love not war; he had been a flower-child of the 1930s. It is thus no accident that he was a literary godfather to such writers as Jack Kerouac and J. D. Salinger.

In his last work published during his lifetime, *Obituaries,* he wrote: "My work is writing, but my real work is being." He was, in Rahv's conception, a literary "redskin." As Stephen Axelrod explains in *Robert Lowell: Life and Art,* Rahv believed that "American literature composes itself into a debate between 'palefaces' and 'redskins.' The 'palefaces' (Henry James, T. S. Eliot, and Allen Tate would belong to this part) produce a patrician art which is intellectual, symbolic, cosmopolitan, disciplined, cultured. The 'redskins' (Walt Whitman and William Carlos Williams would tend to belong here) produce a plebian art which is emotional, naturalistic, nativist, energetic, in some sense *uncultured.* . . . All such formulations attest to a basic bifurcation [or, rift] in American literature between writers who experience primarily with the head and those who experience primarily with the blood." Saroyan wanted to feel the world directly, intuitively—like D. H. Lawrence, "with the blood." Saroyan's work is thus a great deal more complex than many commentators have acknowledged. His writing is a blend of the affirmative, mystical, and rambunctious qualities of the American romantic sensibility and of the profound sadness that finds its source in the tragic history of the Armenian people. On the one hand, Saroyan was thoroughly American in his persistent expansiveness, verve and spontaneity. Yet he was also the Armenian grieving for his lost homeland, speaking for those lost in an alien culture.

Precisely this sense of man's essential aloneness links Saroyan's work directly to the main currents of modern philosophical thought and to the major modernist writers; he has acknowledged his deep love for the work of both Samuel Beckett and Eugene Ionesco. One of the few observers to have discerned this important aspect of Saroyan's work was Edward Hoagland, who, in a 1970 *Chicago Tribune Book World* essay, called Saroyan "brother at once to Thomas Mann and to [Beckett,] the author of *Krapp's Last Tape*." The existential strain was noted by Thelma Shinn, who remarked in *Modern Drama* that his work may be seen as the record of the search for meaning within the self. The difficulty of this quest for true meaning was also emphasized by William Fisher, who argued in his *College English* essay that in mid-career Saroyan's "novels and plays became strange battlegrounds where belief struggled with skepticism." These articles are among the few devoted to a serious consideration of Saroyan's place in modern literature.

MEDIA ADAPTATIONS: A film version of "The Human Comedy" starring Mickey Rooney was released in 1943; United Artists made film based on *The Time of Your Life* starring Jimmy Cagney in 1948; an opera version of "Hello, Out There" prepared by composer Jack Beeson was widely performed in 1953; a television adaptation of *The Time of Your Life* was produced on "Playhouse 90," October, 1958; "Ah, Sweet Mystery of Mrs. Murphy" was produced by NBC-TV, 1959; "The Unstoppable Gray Fox" was produced by CBS-TV, 1962; *My Heart's in the Highlands* was adapted for opera by Beeson and broadcast on television March 18, 1970; selections from *Making Money and 13 Other Very Short Plays* were presented on television by NET Playhouse on December 8, 1970; a musical version of "The Human Comedy" was produced on Broadway by Joseph Papp in 1986.

BIOGRAPHICAL/CRITICAL SOURCES:

BOOKS

Aaron, Daniel, *Writers on the Left,* Oxford University Press, 1977.

Agee, James, *Agee on Film,* McDowell, Obolensky, 1958.

Axelrod, Stephen Gould, *Robert Lowell: Life and Art,* Princeton University Press, 1978.

Balakian, Nona, *The Armenian-American Writer,* AGBU, 1958.

Balakian, Nona, *Critical Encounters,* Bobbs-Merrill, 1978.

Calonne, David Stephen, *William Saroyan: My Real Work Is Being,* University of North Carolina Press, 1983.

Contemporary Literary Criticism, Gale, Volume 1, 1973, Volume 8, 1978, Volume 10, 1979, Volume 29, 1984, Volume 34, 1985.

Dictionary of Literary Biography, Gale, Volume 7: *Twentieth-Century American Dramatists,* 1981, Volume 9: *American Novelists, 1910-1945,* 1981.

Dictionary of Literary Biography Yearbook: 1981, Gale, 1982.

Esslin, Martin, *The Theatre of the Absurd,* Doubleday, 1961.

Floan, Howard, *William Saroyan,* Twayne, 1966.

Geismar, Maxwell, *Writers in Crisis: The American Novel, 1925-1940,* Hill and Wang, 1966.

Gifford, Barry, and Lawrence Lee, *Saroyan: A Biography,* Harper, 1984.

Gold, Herbert, *A Walk on the West Side: California on the Brink,* Arbor House, 1981.

Kazin, Alfred, *Starting Out in the Thirties,* Vintage, 1980.

Kherdian, David, *A Bibliography of William Saroyan: 1934-1964,* Howell, 1965.

Krutch, Joseph Wood, *The American Drama since 1918,* Braziller, 1957.

Lipton, Lawrence, *The Holy Barbarians,* Messner, 1959.

Martin, Jay, *Always Merry and Bright: The Life of Henry Miller,* Penguin, 1980.

McCarthy, Mary, *Sights and Spectacles,* Farrar, 1956.

Saroyan, Aram, *William Saroyan,* Harcourt, 1983.

Saroyan, Aram, *Last Rites: The Death of William Saroyan,* Harcourt, 1983.

Saroyan, William, *The Daring Young Man on the Flying Trapeze and Other Stories,* Random House, 1934, Yolla Bolly, 1984.

Saroyan, William, *Inhale and Exhale,* Random House, 1936, Books for Libraries Press, 1972.

Saroyan, William, *The Time of Your Life,* Harcourt, 1939.

Saroyan, William, *Three Plays,* Harcourt, 1940.

Saroyan, William, *Razzle Dazzle,* Harcourt, 1942.

Saroyan, William, *Don't Go Away Mad, and Two Other Plays,* Harcourt, 1949.

Saroyan, William, *The Assyrian and Other Stories,* Harcourt, 1950.

Saroyan, William, *The Bicycle Rider in Beverly Hills* (autobiography), Scribner, 1952.

Saroyan, William, *Here Comes, There Goes, You Know Who* (autobiography), Simon & Schuster, 1962.

Saroyan, William, *Not Dying* (autobiography), Harcourt, 1963.

Saroyan, William, *Days of Life and Death and Escape to the Moon* (memoir), Dail, 1970.

Saroyan, William, *Obituaries,* Creative Arts, 1979.

Stevens, Wallace, *The Necessary Angel: Essays on Reality and the Imagination,* Knopf, 1951.

Straumann, Heinrich, *American Literature in the Twentieth Century,* Harper, 1965.

Trilling, Diana, *Reviewing the Forties,* Harcourt, 1978.

Weales, Gerald C., *American Drama since World War II,* Harcourt, 1962.

Wilson, Edmund, *The Boys in the Back Room: Notes on California Novelists,* Colt Press, 1941.

PERIODICALS

American Mercury, September, 1943.

Chicago Tribune Book World, July 5, 1970.

College English, March, 1955.

Commonweal, November 4, 1942.

Detroit Free Press, May 22, 1981.

Georgia Review, fall, 1970.

Los Angeles Times, May 19, 1981, June 7, 1981.

Modern Drama, September, 1972.

New Republic, March 1, 1943, March 9, 1953.

New York Times Book Review, April 2, 1972, August 15, 1976, May 20, 1979, August 21, 1983.

Pacific Spectator, winter, 1947.

Punch, January 31, 1973.

Quarterly Journal of Speech, February, 1944.

Saturday Review of Literature, December 28, 1940.

Theatre Arts, December, 1958.

Times Literary Supplement, June 22, 1973.

Virginia Quarterly Review, summer, 1944.

OBITUARIES:

PERIODICALS

Detroit News, May 24, 1981.

Newsweek, June 1, 1981.

New York Times, May 19, 1981.
Publishers Weekly, June 5, 1981.
Time, June 1, 1981.
Washington Post, May 19, 1981.

*   *   *

SARRAUTE, Nathalie 1900-

PERSONAL: Born July 18, 1900, in Ivanovo, Russia (now in U.S.S.R.); daughter of Ilya (a chemist) and Pauline (a writer; maiden name, Chatounovsky) Tcherniak; married Raymond Sarraute (a barrister), July 28, 1925; children: Claude, Anne, Dominique. *Education:* Sorbonne, University of Paris, licence d'anglais, 1920, licence en droit, 1925; attended Oxford University, 1921; additional study in Berlin, 1921-22.

ADDRESSES: Home—12 avenue Pierre I de Serbie, 75116 Paris, France.

CAREER: Barrister from 1926 to 1932, when she began writing her first book, *Tropismes.*

AWARDS, HONORS: Formentor Prize ($10,000) and Prix International de Litterature, both 1964, for *The Golden Fruits;* 1964; doctor honoris causa, University of Dublin Trinity College, 1976, and University of Kent at Canterbury, 1980; Grand Prix National, 1982; Prix Cavour, 1984.

WRITINGS:

FICTION

Tropismes (sketches), Denoel (Paris), 1939, revised edition, Editions de Minuit (Paris), 1957, translation by Maria Jolas published as *Tropisms* (also see below), Braziller, 1967, reprinted, Riverrun Press, 1986.
Portrait d'un inconnu (novel), preface by Jean-Paul Sartre, Robert Marin (Paris), 1948, reprinted, Gallimard (Paris), 1977, translation by Jolas published as *Portrait of a Man Unknown,* Braziller, 1958.
Martereau (novel), Gallimard, 1953, translation by Jolas, Braziller, 1959.
Le Planetarium (novel), Gallimard, 1959, 2nd edition, 1967, translation by Jolas published as *The Planetarium,* Braziller, 1960.
Les Fruits d'or (novel), Gallimard, 1963, translation by Jolas published as *The Golden Fruits,* Braziller, 1964.
Entre la vie et la mort (novel), Gallimard, 1968, translation by Jolas published as *Between Life and Death,* Braziller, 1969.
Vous les entendez? (novel), Gallimard, 1972, translation by Jolas published as *Do You Hear Them?,* Braziller, 1973.
"disent les imbeciles" (novel), Gallimard, 1976, translation by Jolas published as *"fools say,"* Braziller, 1977.
L'Usage de la parole (sketches), Gallimard, 1980, translation by Barbara Wright published as *The Use of Speech,* Braziller, 1983.
Tu ne t'aimes pas (novel), Gallimard, 1989.

CRITICISM

L'Ere du soupcon: Essais sur le roman, Gallimard, 1956, translation by Jolas published as *The Age of Suspicion: Essays on the Novel* (also see below), Braziller, 1963.
Paul Valery et l'enfant d'elephant (first published in *Les Temps modernes,* January, 1947) [and] *Flaubert le precurseur* (first published in *Preuves,* February, 1965), Gallimard, c. 1986.

PLAYS

Le Silence [and] *Le Mensonge* (also see below; both plays first broadcast on German radio, both produced in Petit Odeon at Theatre de France, January 14, 1967), Gallimard, 1967, translation by Jolas published in England as *Silence* [and] *The Lie* (also see below), Calder & Boyars, 1969.
Isma; ou, Ce qui s'appelle rien (also see below; produced at Espace Pierre-Cardin, February 5, 1973) [and] *Le Silence* [and] *Le Mensonge,* Gallimard, 1970.
Theatre (contains "C'est Beau," first performed at Theatre d'Orsay, October 24, 1975, "Elle est la," first performed at Theatre d'Orsay, January 15, 1980, "Isma," "Le Mensonge," and "Le Silence"), Gallimard, 1978, translation by Jolas and Wright published as *Collected Plays of Nathalie Sarraute* (contains "It Is There," "It's Beautiful," "Izzum," "The Lie," and "Silence"), J. Calder, 1980, Braziller, 1981.
"For No Good Reason," first produced in New York City in 1985.

CONTRIBUTOR

Visages d'aujourd'hui, Plon (Paris), 1960.
The Writer's Dilemma, introduction by Stephen Spender, Oxford University Press, 1961.
Andrew Hook, editor, *The Novel Today: Edinburgh International Festival 1962—International Writers' Conference; Programme and Notes,* R. R. Clark (Edinburgh), 1962.
Jacqueline Levi-Valensi, editor, *Les Critiques de notre temps et Camus,* Garnier (Paris), 1970.
Violoncelle qui resiste, Eric Losfeld (Paris), 1971.
Gespraeche mit . . ., Europaverlag, 1972.
Jean Ricardou and Francoise von Rossum-Guyon, editors, *Nouveau roman: Hier, aujourd'hui* (text not reviewed by Sarraute), Union Generale d'Editions (Paris), 1972.
Words and Their Masters, Doubleday, 1974.
Comment travaillent les ecrivains, Flammarion (Paris), 1978.
Frida S. Weissman, editor, *Du monologue interieur a la sous conversation,* Nizet (Paris), 1978.

OTHER

Tropisms [and] *The Age of Suspicion,* Calder & Boyars, 1964.
Enfance (autobiography), Gallimard, 1983, translation by Wright published as *Childhood,* Braziller, 1984.

Sarraute's works have been translated into twenty-five foreign languages, including German, Hebrew, Italian, Russian, and Spanish. Contributor to numerous periodicals, including the *New York Times Book Review, Washington Post Book World, Times Literary Supplement, Cahiers Renaud Barrault, Le Monde, Les Temps modernes, Nouvelle Revue francaise,* and *Preuves.*

SIDELIGHTS: As one of the outstanding writers and theoreticians of the "New Novel" in France, Nathalie Sarraute has consistently sought to create innovative forms of narrative that apprehend the psychological reality beneath the surface of daily events and conversations. Although she began writing in the 1930s, her work did not receive much critical attention until the 1950s and 1960s with the publication of her theoretical work *L'Ere du Soupcon: Essais sur le roman (The Age of Suspicion: Essays on the Novel),* and her novel *Les Fruits d'or (The Golden Fruits).* Her novels are complex studies of human interaction that question traditional elements of character and plot. While sometimes considered difficult for the uninitiated, her books challenge the reader to reassess common assumptions about literature and its relationship to life. The rewards are well worth the effort, for Sarraute's works offer a poetic, humorous, and sometimes painful vision of life.

The only child of Russian Jewish intellectuals who divorced when she was two years old, Sarraute spent much of her early childhood moving back and forth between her parents in Russia and France, soon becoming fluent in the languages of both countries. Her mother, also a novelist, remarried, with a Russian historian, and the three first settled in Paris when the child was two, and then in St. Petersburg (today called Leningrad) when the child was six. Here the young Nathalie tried writing a novel but was discouraged when a friend of her mother's told her she should learn to spell first. At age eight she returned to her father, who had remarried and started a dye factory in Paris. She remained there for the rest of her life, seeing her mother only twice.

After completing her baccalaureate degree, Sarraute easily obtained a *licence* in English at the Sorbonne and studied at Oxford for a year, working on a B.A. in history. In the winter of 1921-1922, Sarraute studied sociology in Berlin and discovered German novelist Thomas Mann's *Tonio Krueger,* which reinforced her desire to write.

Upon her return to Paris Sarraute enrolled in law school, where she met Raymond Sarraute, whom she married in 1925 and who proved to be a lifelong source of support and encouragement. Both received law degrees, and for about six years she practiced law. Between 1927 and 1933 the couple's three daughters, Claude, Anne, and Dominique, were born. In 1932 Sarraute began the first texts of her *Tropismes (Tropisms),* published in 1939 by Robert Denoel after being refused by Grasset and Gallimard. Although the book received little attention at first, Sarraute's literary career had officially begun, only to be delayed by the outbreak of World War II, when Sarraute was forced to pose as the governess of her own children in order to hide from the Germans. Since 1935, Sarraute has traveled extensively in Europe, Scandinavia, the Soviet Union, Cuba, and Israel, in addition to Egypt, the United States, South America, Japan, and India, delivering lectures on college campuses.

One of the hallmarks of Sarraute's literary work is the "tropism." Borrowing the term from the biological sciences, where it characterizes an involuntary reaction to external stimuli, as when a plant turns toward light or heat, Sarraute uses it to describe the subtle psychological responses of people to objects, words, and other human beings. In remarks published in the *Listener* in 1961, Sarraute explains tropisms as movements that "glide quickly round the border of our consciousness" and "compose the small, rapid, and sometimes very complex dramas concealed beneath our actions, our gestures, the words we speak, our avowed and clear feelings." Sarraute notes in the preface to her collection of critical essays, *The Age of Suspicion,* that she had intuited the tropistic movements during her childhood. *Tropisms* is composed of short texts that investigate what Valerie Minogue, in *Nathalie Sarraute and the War of the Words,* calls "the teeming sub-surface of life, anonymously yet intimately observed." The reader is thrust into the midst of a world of unidentified characters (nameless women gossiping in a tea salon, passersby in front of a shop window) who experience sensations that are dramatically and poetically rendered through imagery, rhythm, and repetition. Sarraute explains in the preface that "it was not possible to communicate [the tropisms] to the reader otherwise than by means of equivalent images that would make him experience analogous sensations." Character development and plot are minimal, she explains, because such novelistic traits tend to particularize experience and to "distract [the attention]

of the reader," while Sarraute is interested in portraying an underlying psychological reality common to everyone.

In *The Age of Suspicion,* the author develops many of her critical and theoretical stances regarding the novel and clarifies her own creative goals. On the paperback cover the essays are described as the "first theoretical manifestation of the 'New Novel' school," whose representatives also include French writers Alain Robbe-Grillet, Michel Butor, Marguerite Duras, Claude Simon, and Claude Ollier. Sarraute argues that both novelists and readers have become suspicious of character types, the "unforgettable figures" of tightly knit, coherent plots in nineteenth-century novels by such earlier French writers as Honore de Balzac and Gustave Flaubert. According to Sarraute, these characters and their stories if written nowadays would appear as stereotypes that no longer ring true. Aligning herself with such novelists as Fedor Dostoevski, Marcel Proust, James Joyce, and Virginia Woolf, who investigate the human psyche, Sarraute advocates a new realism. In her interview for the 1984 special issue of *Digraphe* devoted to her work, Sarraute defines the "real" as "what hasn't yet taken on the conventional forms" and holds that the writer's task is not to copy or imitate accepted reality, but to invent new forms that will help the reader perceive new realities. In her investigation of the human psyche, Sarraute makes a case for formal innovations that shape the experience of the reader. Instead of calling for controlled analyses of carefully defined feelings, she develops in *The Age of Suspicion* the notion of the "sub-conversation" which renders verbally "what is dissimulated behind the interior monologue: a countless profusion of sensations, of images, of feelings, of memories . . . which no interior language expresses." She thus portrays instinctive, instantaneous reactions before they become fully understood and named, insisting that the passage from subconversation to dialogue must be continuous: no standard formulas like "she said" or "George murmured" are to interrupt the flow of "these interior dramas made up of attacks, triumphs, defeats, caresses."

Imagery plays a major role in Sarraute's successful presentation of the unnameable sensations that make up the tropism. As Gretchen Rous Besser points out in *Nathalie Sarraute,* the novelist often utilizes the imagery of animals and insects, "whose instinctive reactions are consonant with the prerational nature of tropistic reactions." The interpersonal struggles Sarraute portrays are sometimes enacted through the use of military terminology that dramatizes seemingly minor dissensions. Olga Bernal's 1973 *Modern Language Notes* article examines the symbolic oppositions developed in Sarraute's work between images of fluids and solids. This dichotomy contrasts the external world of appearances, solid, secure, and well-defined, with the invisible movements of the tropism, fluid, hesitant, vacillating, and oozing.

In his preface to Sarraute's first novel, *Portrait d'un inconnu (Portrait of a Man Unknown),* Jean-Paul Sartre characterizes the work as an anti-novel because it contests traditional novelistic conventions. Rene Micha, in *Nathalie Sarraute,* calls her novel "a long interrogation": a first person narrator, who remains a nameless voice, "is speaking or writing or dreaming or reflecting" about a couple, father and daughter, whose relationship fascinates and perhaps obsesses him. Sarraute herself has admitted in an interview with Serge Fauchereau and Jean Ristat in *Digraphe* that the father-daughter duo is inspired by Balzac's *Eugenie Grandet,* but the narrator explores the hidden side of Balzac's solid character types. The boundaries between the narrator's imagination and his actual knowledge about the couple tend to blur because there are no linguistic markers to distinguish between fact and fiction, between objective reality and creative interpretation. *Portrait of a Man Unknown* is reminiscent of a detective story, and as Jean V. Alter remarks in an article appearing in J. H. Matthews's collection *Un Nouveau Roman?:* "The reader finds himself involved in an inquiry regarding the reality of things." But unlike a third-person omniscient narrator, whose authority would guarantee the difference between an unquestionable evaluation of the couple and a personal interpretation, the narrator of Sarraute's novel can only reveal his hesitant, anguished questions and doubts about the accuracy of his perceptions. Other New Novelists, such as Robbe-Grillet in *The Erasers,* also use the detective story format while subverting it. But while Sarraute explores the depths of psychological reality, Robbe-Grillet prefers to remain at the surface, providing a minute description of external appearances that betray the depths.

Minogue argues that *Portrait of a Man Unknown* "contains a far-reaching critique of conventional characterization," putting on trial the notion of stable, definable characters (whether one is speaking of the narrator or the couple he watches) and ultimately questioning the way the reader constructs reality and personal identity. As in Sarraute's other novels and plays, there are no heroes and little action in the sense of an adventure outside the tropisms. Descriptions of places, historical events, and characters and their surroundings are either sketchy or completely lacking. Such omissions are strategies to keep the readers from resorting to old reading habits that would distance them from the text, for Sarraute wants her readers to take an active part in her works, to share in the invisible dramas.

Sarraute's second novel, *Martereau,* increases the number of characters, including an aunt, uncle, cousin, and nephew (the first person narrator), and an outsider, Martereau, with his wife. With the social milieu expanded, the interaction becomes more complex. Although the purchase of a house is the basis for the external plot, Sarraute is again more concerned with drawing the reader into an anonymous world of relationships filtered through the vacillating perspectives of the narrating nephew. The family seems to provide Sarraute with a particularly favorable environment for depicting tropisms. Except for Martereau, characters are identified only by personal pronouns or family relationships. As in *Portrait of a Man Unknown,* the readers must make their way through this labyrinth of shifting connections by remaining attentive to certain repeated words and rhythms, which Minogue calls Sarraute's "signposts." But this radical indecision with respect to character identity is essential to Sarraute's work, because it stresses the common ground of the characters, instead of individualizing them according to an established set of reassuring categories. In all Sarraute's work, labels, proper names, and abstractions are shown to be ways of concealing the multifaceted aspects of life. Martereau, who does bear a name, is, at first, one of these stock individuals, a "traditional novel character," says Sarraute in her interview for *Digraphe,* "in the way that we see the people around us," that is, from the outside. But as the novel progresses, the external appearance disintegrates. As Minogue notes: "Martereau plays successively, in the mind of the narrator [and thus in ours], the roles of saint, adulterer, clown, and calculating crook," becoming a shadowy figure bereft of any "solidity." In her 1977 article in *PTL: A Journal for Descriptive Poetics and Theory of Literature,* Ann Jefferson explains the function of the named character: "To use a name is an index of the inauthentic in that it always goes with a deceitful venture of characterization and individuation which the novel's narrative refutes."

Regarding her novel *Le Planetarium* (*The Planetarium*), Sarraute remarked in the *Listener:* "Here I met with greater difficulties than in my previous books." In contrast to the first two, Sarraute's third novel is populated by a large cast of characters with proper names. However, as in most of Sarraute's works, the novel lacks elaborate descriptions of place and time. Sarraute may have chosen to name the characters in order to supply the reader with more recognizable markers because of the complex interaction between characters. Whatever the case, the names do not serve as a claim to uniqueness, for the novel concludes with the comment: "I think that we are all a little like that," and the characters' similarities ultimately loom larger than their differences. Although *The Planetarium* is written in the third person, there is no omniscient narrator to oversee and validate any one perspective. Instead, Sarraute uses the subconversation, which is reminiscent of Flaubert's free indirect discourse. The narrator (and reader) pass into the thoughts of a character, although the latter is referred to as a "she" or a "he," and the "thoughts" are more renderings of pre-verbal impressions than a discourse actually articulated by the character.

With the publication of her next three novels, *Les Fruits d'or* (*The Golden Fruits*), *Entre la vie et la mort* (*Between Life and Death*), and *Vous les entendez?* (*Do You Hear Them?*), Sarraute adroitly focuses her attention on artistic creation and critical reception. Even more than her previous works, these novels exemplify the self-examining character of the "New Novel," implicitly and explicitly questioning Sarraute's own literary activity through discussions about the nature of artistic value and the process of creation. Humorous, moving, self-mocking, and intricate, they reveal Nathalie Sarraute's talent at its best.

According to Leah D. Hewitt's 1983 *Modern Language Studies* article, *The Golden Fruits* "traces the rise and fall of an imaginary novel, *also* called 'Les Fruits d'or,' as it is acclaimed, criticized and almost forgotten by its readers." The imaginary novel fulfills the same role as the various objects in *The Planetarium,* serving as a pretext around which a group of anonymous voices attempt to prove the superiority of their literary judgment. As in the novels that follow, *The Golden Fruits* juxtaposes everyday colloquial language and poetic metaphors that capture the underlying emotions of the moment. Also characteristic of Sarraute's style is the continual use of elliptical sentences that trail off without finishing. These fragmentary remarks underscore the commonplace quality of the discussions and, as Sarraute explains in a letter to *CA,* imply that the reader is "supposed to know how they would finish." But they also suggest that thoughts and impressions are formed and "cross our minds very quickly. There is no time to waste for building correct, well-rounded sentences."

The Golden Fruits centers around the way one reads, experiences, and evaluates literature, calling upon Sarraute's reader to participate actively in the interrogation. The tropism is not just a phenomenon to be perceived and understood by the readers: they reenact it as they move toward and away from the speakers' comments about the imaginary novel. Although critical positions abound in the novel—ranging from the arrogant to the timid, from the "classical" which affirms that aesthetic values are established and definable, to intimate, personal experiences of reading which can only offer subjective opinions—no single stance can triumph over the others. Through the extensive use of parody and cliches, Sarraute skillfully undermines positions of authority. Consider, for example, the jargon-ridden language of a pompous critic silencing dissenting opinion: "This book, I believe, installs in literature a privileged language that succeeds in encircling a correspondence that is its very structure. It is a very new and perfect appropriation of rhythmic signs that transcend by their tension what is inessential in all semantics." The parody is comically effective and ought to make any critic wary of obscurity.

Karlis Racevskis's study of Sarraute's irony in his 1977 *French Review* article shows that the reader of *The Golden Fruits* can neither wholly espouse nor wholly reject the positions of Sarraute's fictive readers, for just as he begins to accept or to dismiss a viewpoint, another voice intervenes to indicate its weaknesses or strengths. As Hewitt notes: "Rather than providing a response to the question of value (an act which would deny the very problematic that she has dramatically set in motion), Sarraute creates a dialectical movement in which affirmations are always being undone." One voice comments near the end of the book: "Art as you say, a work of art is never a sure value. . . . One is often wrong, that's natural. How can one know? Who can say that he knows?" The open-ended questions of Sarraute's novel suggest that any work of art undergoes a continual re-evaluation according to the needs of a particular society at a given moment in history.

In *Between Life and Death,* Sarraute turns her attention to the writer's activity, pondering the act of creation from the inside, as well as the writer's interactions with his public. Minogue stresses the self-analyzing quality of the novel: "[*Between Life and Death*] recreates in its pages the writer writing about writing—writing, indeed, about the specific writing we are reading." Nevertheless, on the paperback cover of her novel, Sarraute takes care to point out that it is not autobiographical and that the reader trying to construct a hero-writer will only find "disparate parts" which cannot hold together as a character. It would indeed prove difficult to identify the writer (sometimes a "he," sometimes an "I") as one coherent being, because the "factual" elements from the past contradict each other. Racevskis aptly shows, for example, the humorous altering of details from one passage to the next. At one moment the writer maintains that he can compose only on the typewriter; at another, he uses a Bic ballpoint pen; at still another, he writes only with a pencil. Clearly, Sarraute is more concerned with problems in the perception of writers than with the portrait of a specific individual, even though there are references to particular situations and memories.

It is noteworthy that Sarraute refers to the writer as a "he" rather than a "she," a technique that distances the author Sarraute from her work, avoiding an identification between them. As in most of her works, masculine voices tend to predominate for a strategic reason. In an interview with Bettina Knapp appearing in the *Kentucky Romance Quarterly* in 1969, Sarraute maintains that the masculine is as close as one can get to a neutral voice applicable to everyone. Sarraute feels that the feminine voice tends to be automatically considered as gender-specific and particularized, a characterization she wishes to avoid.

Micha observes that Sarraute had originally thought of naming her novel "Le Cercle" ("The Circle"), and Besser explains the circular structure of *Between Life and Death:* in the beginning, the writer is already established and well known to the public; then he returns to his childhood memories, early writing attempts, and the reactions of his family and friends; at the end, he is once again a successful writer, but still grappling with the creative process. No preconceived formula can guarantee successful creation and even the writer cannot explain how he writes. The reader shares in his solitary moments of joy and anguish as he labors over his manuscript, wondering whether his writing is original, facile, or interesting, whether it is alive or dead. There is a certain magic in the way the words take shape, rising as if from a void, but the dangers of facility always lurk in the background, and the writer risks making his text too "pretty," a stylistic accomplishment devoid of any vitality or emotional charge. Once he has written something, the writer

splits himself in two to evaluate his effort. In a 1973 *Contemporary Literature* interview with Germaine Bree, Sarraute comments on this doubling: "I think each writer, each artist . . . has a kind of double, who, from time to time as he works, stands back and looks at his painting or rereads his text. He is both himself and someone else. He often becomes a completely merciless judge." Besser points out that in *Between Life and Death* "the process of autocriticism is rendered fictionally in the form of a dialogue between the artist's twin halves: his critical and creative faculties."

In the childhood scenes, the writer-as-child shows an early sensitivity to words, which are fascinating playthings as well as sources of displeasure when used in certain ways or pronounced with certain intonations. The adults around him are quick to interpret his attention to language as a sign indicating his future career and pointing to an inability to deal adequately with his physical surroundings. While contesting the predestination of the writer, Sarraute does explore the relationship between an extreme preoccupation with language and the act of writing. Do the writer's words portray an extant reality or does he create one which refers only to itself? Other New Novelists such as Robbe-Grillet have maintained that there is no reality beyond the words, that writing is a purely self-reflexive activity, but Sarraute does not share this view. In *Between Life and Death,* the writer's struggle with words is an attempt to create something that exceeds the words but cannot be communicated to others without them. In *Nouveau Roman: Hier, aujourd'hui,* Sarraute speaks of this indeterminate "something" as a vibration, a vacillation, a vague sensation at the heart of the tropistic reactions which she brings to life through metaphor and analogy.

Most of *Between Life and Death,* like *The Golden Fruits* and *Do You Hear Them?,* entails an intricate web of dialogues and subconversations. Alternately humble and proud, the writer at times seeks positive recognition from his readers while remaining fearful that they will not approve of his work. At other times, when riding the wave of success, he becomes self-satisfied, considering himself a creative genius. When interacting with his readers, he finds that roles are imposed on him despite his wishes, as they transform his most innocuous gestures (preparing tea, for example) into romanticized ceremonial rituals that confirm his unique personality. Masks presenting a stereotyped view of "The Writer" are assigned to him, but at the same time, he uses such masks to defend himself against intrusions or to bolster his own importance. Ultimately, he is the only one who can judge his work: the novel concludes with the moving image of the anxious writer holding a mirror to his work to see if a breath will cloud it, thereby attesting to the work's vitality.

Sarraute completes the trilogy of *The Golden Fruits* and *Between Life and Death* with *Do You Hear Them?,* focusing, as she says in her interview with Bree, on "the relationship between the work of art, the environment into which it falls, and its fate in general." In his home, a man and his friend contemplate a small stone figurine of primitive art while the man's children are heard laughing upstairs. The domestic drama lies in the tension between the father's love of the statue and his love for his children who rebel against what they see as his quasi-religious devotion to art, favoring free artistic creation untrammeled by rules and a weighty sense of tradition. The father interprets the children's effervescent laughter as, in turns, carefree and innocent or mocking and deceitful. Besser notes how the metaphorical descriptions of the children's gleeful voices pass from poetic cliche ("Tiny bells. Tiny drops. Fountains. Gentle water-falls. Twittering of birds.") to ominous images of persecution: "Soon the 'titters' grow 'sharp as needles,' and the water drips on its victim like a Chinese torture."

According to Besser, when asked which of the two opposing conceptions of art Sarraute would herself choose, the novelist responded that she could identify with both. Her answer is not surprising when one remembers that in *The Age of Suspicion* she had admired novelists of the past while nevertheless rebelling against certain novelistic conventions. In addition, Besser points out that, as in *Portrait of a Man Unknown,* "there is no delineation between 'real' and 'imagined' events," so that the boundaries separating the opposing positions of the father and children tend to blur. One cannot always distinguish between the father's viewpoint and the children's because the father often tries to identify with what he imagines his children are thinking. In the Bree interview, Sarraute corroborates this impression: "I wanted to show a kind of interaction between consciousnesses which are extremely close to one another to the extent that they almost fuse and communicate by a kind of osmosis. . . . What each one feels and attributes to another becomes any one of the others at any given moment."

In her next two works, *"disent les imbeciles"* (*"fools say"*) and *L'Usage de la parole* (*The Use of Speech*), Sarraute pushes the novelistic genre to the limit. In fact, *The Use of Speech* is often not considered a novel at all. In both works, there is no one story line or character to unite the fragmented episodes. Instead, the author creates a series of interpersonal exchanges in which anonymous voices react to the effects of linguistic labeling, to the power of cliches to imprison the individual in stock phrases and concrete descriptions. The unifying element lies in the relentless study of the way language intervenes in the development of ideas and of human identity. As in her other novels, the hypersensitive individuals of *"fools say"* writhe in discomfort as they find themselves condemned to play certain roles by virtue of the labels and categorizations that others ascribe to them. As Ellen W. Munley says in her 1983 *Contemporary Literature* article, "Sarraute scrutinizes the tropistic proximity and distance, the fusion and separation created by language. Words speak actions. . . . Words create a cast of characters erected at a distance: a grandmother 'sweet enough to eat,' a dual personality 'gifted but not intelligent,' 'fools.' " Minogue describes the setting of *"fools say"* as "a terrorist world, against which Nathalie Sarraute raises a voice that insists that any idea, however comforting, or however disconcerting it may be, must be treated as an idea, not as an appurtenance of a personality, group, class, nation, or race."

The Use of Speech is a collection of ten essays or sketches more reminiscent of *Tropisms* than of a conventional novel. Again, Sarraute focuses her attention on the resonances of certain verbal expressions, investigating, for example, what is contained in the word "love" or in the phrase "Don't talk to me about that." But according to Munley, *The Use of Speech* differs from Sarraute's previous works in that "it contains a self-styled narrator-doctor of words who joins all of its loosely connected vignettes by virtue of her presence." Unlike the narrators of *Portrait of a Man Unknown* or *Martereau,* this speaker does not directly participate as one of the characters in the vignettes. The new use of a first person narrator in her work perhaps anticipates Sarraute's subsequent interest in writing an account of her early years in *Childhood.*

Although Sarraute is best known for her novels, she also launched a play writing career after the publication of *The Golden Fruits* in 1963. In "Le Gant retourne" ("The Inverted Glove"), published in the *Cahiers Renaud Barrault,* Sarraute explains that she had not considered writing for the theater until

a young German, Werner Spies, asked her to write radio plays for Radio Stuttgart. After refusing several times, she finally decided to accept the challenge. Thus she composed two short plays, "Le Silence" ("Silence") and "Le Mensonge" ("The Lie"), which were first broadcast on German radio and then performed in Paris in 1967 at the Theatre de France under the direction of Jean-Louis Barrault. Sarraute was surprised at the richness of Barrault's staging, finding that the actors' work complemented her text.

Given Sarraute's enduring interest in the invisible, unspoken movements that underlie dialogue, the theater, as an oral, visual medium, presents special problems for the portrayal of tropisms. In the play format, the subconversations or pre-dialogues must be incorporated into the dialogue in order for the audience to witness and participate in them. Sarraute's dramatic dialogues are full of the hesitations, incomplete sentences, and trite expressions of everyday speech, and as in her novels, the characters are primarily anonymous, "even in the rare instances," as Besser notes, "when they are equipped with a name."

In "Silence" and "The Lie," Sarraute breaks down the social masks of commonplace dialogue with disruptive although equally banal "events." In "Silence," one character in a group of friends remains silent for most of the play. His lack of participation in the exchange begins to bother another character, who eventually communicates his discomfort to everyone else. The silence produces a series of tropistic reactions and is interpreted in every way possible: it becomes in turns a positive, negative, or indifferent sign on the part of the silent man. As was the case with the title, *The Golden Fruits,* silence is transformed into a creative generator of meaning, the whole process eventually questioning the nature of meaning and interpretations of reality. In "The Lie," a seemingly trivial white lie disturbs one character and provokes not only a discussion of the differences between truth and untruth, between play-acting and authentic action, but a dramatic enactment of the issues as well.

Unlike many of her novels, Sarraute's plays do not use physical objects as catalysts for the tropisms; instead, elements of speech trigger reactions. But the cause for irritation is so slight that the characters are constantly repeating that it's nothing even as they respond to that "nothing." For example, in "Isma" ("Izzum"), first performed in 1970, the mannered pronunciation of words ending in "ism" causes an anonymous man and woman to vent their hostility toward a family named Dubuit. In the suffocating familial atmosphere of "C'est Beau" ("It's Beautiful"), first performed in 1975, a mother and father avoid saying the simple words "it's beautiful" in their son's presence because the phrase, as Besser says, "encompasses . . . all the ideas and principles that govern the parents' lives." Like the father of *Do You Hear Them?,* they cringe at the thought that their son might scorn their aesthetic values.

Sarraute's next two plays, "Elle est la" ("It Is There"), which premiered in 1980, and "For No Good Reason," which premiered in New York in 1985, perhaps illustrate best that, in the struggles between individuals over truth or values, her characters are always seeking, as Sarraute said in her 1969 interview with Knapp, "fusion and contact with someone else." But such a desire is difficult to realize and in "For No Good Reason" an attempt at reconciliation between two old friends ends in a confirmation of their fundamental differences with respect to lifestyles and values. It is paradoxically the desire to be close to another, to find the basis for agreement, that prompts the most intense antagonisms.

It might seem surprising that Sarraute, who has steadfastly questioned the status of personal identity and unequivocal factual truth, should have written *Childhood,* a series of autobiographical texts about her early relationships with her families and her first experiences in language. But for Sarraute, autobiography is still literature, another terrain for prospecting the subterranean tropisms of her own experiences. Instead of the singular "I" usually found in autobiography, this work contains *two* narrators in dialogue: while one voice narrates episodes from the past, the other admonishes, encourages, censures, and interprets what the first has presented. Sarraute makes no attempt to connect the various episodes she relates, for identity is conceived as split or fragmented, and interpretation is acknowledged in the text as a necessary component of memory. The author's personae and her past are recognized as fictive re-creations like those in her other literary works.

John Sturrock notes in his 1983 *Times Literary Supplement* review of *Childhood* that the theme of disobedience sets the stage for many of Sarraute's memories. The pleasure of self-affirmation in rebelling against parental rule seems to foreshadow the writer's subsequent revolt against established literary conventions. But at the same time, the reader is made aware of the child's intense need to be recognized and loved by her parents: her often frustrated efforts to feel an intimacy with her mother are poignant although never self-pitying. This aspect, too, reappears in her novels and plays, as characters move toward and away from each other in the difficult act of communication. One is particularly reminded of the writer in *Between Life and Death,* although Sarraute would be the first to deny that the novel is *her* story.

With *Childhood,* Sarraute captures the humor, joys, and pain of growing up in a divided family and in different languages in an original, enthralling autobiographical account. In 1985, after its 1984 Parisian premiere, *Childhood* was performed in New York under the direction of Simone Benmussa, with Glenn Close in the starring role.

As a New Novelist, Sarraute has successfully combined an investigation of language's ability to unsettle its own stale, rigid definitions, with an intimate, relentless study of the hazardous paths human beings explore in interacting. Her exploration of the tropism has given new life to the psychological novel, and her works continue to fascinate readers who, dissatisfied with conventional narrative forms that take "reality" for granted, turn to literature in search of new ways of understanding the changing relationships between language and the world.

MEDIA ADAPTATIONS: Childhood was adapted as a play by Simone Benmussa and premiered in Paris in 1984. The American premiere, both adapted and directed by Benmussa, was produced in 1985 at the Samuel Beckett, New York City, featuring Glenn Close in the starring role.

BIOGRAPHICAL/CRITICAL SOURCES:

BOOKS

Alter, Robert, *Partial Magic: The Novel as a Self-conscious Genre,* University of California Press, 1975.

Beja, Morris, *Epiphany in the Modern Novel,* University of Washington Press, 1971.

Bell, Sheila Margaret, compiler, *Nathalie Sarraute: A Bibliography,* Grant & Cutler, 1982.

Besser, Gretchen Rous, *Nathalie Sarraute,* Twayne, 1979.

Contemporary Literary Criticism, Gale, Volume 1, 1973, Volume 2, 1974, Volume 4, 1975, Volume 8, 1978, Volume 10, 1979, Volume 31, 1985.

Cranaki, Mimica and Yvon Belaval, editors, *Nathalie Sarraute,* Gallimard, 1965.

Dictionary of Literary Biography, Gale, Volume 83: *French Novelists Since 1960,* Gale, 1989.

Edel, Leon, *The Modern Psychological Novel,* revised edition, Grosset & Dunlap-Universal Library, 1964.

Frohock, W. M., editor, *Image and Theme: Studies in Modern French Fiction,* Harvard University Press, 1969.

Hassan, Ihab, *The Dismemberment of Orpheus,* Oxford University Press, 1971.

Heath, Stephen, *The Nouveau Roman: A Study in the Practice of Writing,* Temple University Press, 1972.

Jaccard, Jean-Luc, *Nathalie Sarraute,* Juris (Zurich), 1967.

Knapp, Bettina, *Off-Stage Voices: Interviews With Modern French Dramatists,* Whitston, 1975.

Kostelanetz, Richard, *On Contemporary Literature,* Avon, 1964.

Le Sage, Laurent, *The French New Novel,* Pennsylvania State University Press, 1962.

Matthews, J. H., editor, *Un Nouveau Roman?,* La Revue des Lettres Modernes, 1964.

McCarthy, Mary, *The Writing on the Wall and Other Literary Essays,* Harcourt, 1970.

Mercier, Vivian, *The New Novel: From Queneau to Pinget,* revised edition, Farrar, Straus, 1966.

Micha, Rene, *Nathalie Sarraute,* Editions Universitaires (Paris), 1966.

Minogue, Valerie, *Nathalie Sarraute and the War of the Words: A Study of Five Novels,* Edinburgh University Press, 1981.

Moore, Harry T., *Twentieth-Century French Literature Since World War II,* Southern Illinois University Press, 1966.

Nadeau, Maurice, *The French Novel Since the War,* translation by A. M. Sheridan-Smith, Methuen, 1967.

Peyre, Henri, *The Contemporary French Novel,* Oxford University Press, 1955.

Peyre, *French Novelists of Today,* Oxford University Press, 1967.

Podhoretz, Norman, *Doings and Undoings,* Farrar, Straus, 1953, revised edition, 1964.

Rahv, Betty T., *From Sartre to the New Novel,* Kennikat Press, 1974.

Robbe-Grillet, Alain, *Pour un nouveau roman,* Gallimard, 1964.

Sarraute, Nathalie, *Portrait d'un inconnu,* preface by Jean Paul Sartre, Robert Marin, 1948, translation by Jolas published as *Portrait of a Man Unknown,* Braziller, 1958.

Sarraute, *L'Ere du soupcon: Essais sur le roman,* Gallimard, 1956, translation by Jolas published as *The Age of Suspicion: Essays on the Novel,* Braziller, 1963.

Sontag, Susan, *Against Interpretation and Other Essays,* revised edition, Farrar, Straus, 1966.

Temple, Ruth Z., *Nathalie Sarraute,* Columbia University Press, 1968.

Weightman, John, *The Concept of the Avant-Garde: Explorations in Modernism,* Alcove, 1973.

PERIODICALS

American Scholar, summer, 1963.
Arts, June 3-9, 1959.
Atlantic, June, 1960, March, 1973, May, 1977, April, 1984.
Book Week, February 9, 1964.
Books Abroad, autumn, 1972.
Bucknell Review, April, 1976.
Bulletin des jeunes romanistes, Volume 20, 1974.
Cahiers Renaud Barrault, Volume 89, 1975.
Christian Science Monitor, February 13, 1964, July 15, 1969, August 22, 1977, August 2, 1984.
Commonweal, December 18, 1959, August 22, 1969.

Contemporary Literature, spring, 1973, summer, 1983.
Critique (Paris), Volumes 86-87, 1954, Volumes 100-101, 1955, Volumes 111-112, 1956.
Critique: Studies in Modern Fiction, winter, 1963-64, Volume 14, number 1, 1972.
Digraphe, March, 1984.
Drama, autumn, 1981.
Esprit, Volume 376, 1968.
Essays in French Literature, Volume 3, 1966.
Etudes litteraires, Volume 17, number 2, 1984.
Express (Paris), April 29-May 5, 1968.
French Forum, Volume 5, 1980.
French Review, December, 1959, spring special issue, 1972, October, 1977, February, 1980, March, 1981, April, 1983.
French Studies, April, 1973, Volume 30, number 1, 1976.
Hudson Review, autumn, 1967, autumn, 1973.
International Fiction Review, January, 1974, January, 1977.
Kentucky Romance Quarterly, Volume 14, number 3, 1969.
Kenyon Review, summer, 1963.
Lettres francaises, February 4, 1960.
Lettres nouvelles, April 29, 1959.
Listener, March 9, 1961.
Los Angeles Times, April 17, 1984.
Mercure de France, Volume 336, 1959, Volume 345, 1962, Volume 348, 1963.
Modern Fiction Studies, winter, 1960-61.
Modern Language Notes, Volume 88, number 4, 1973.
Modern Language Review, July, 1978, July, 1982, January, 1986, January, 1987.
Modern Language Studies, Volume 13, number 3, 1983.
Ms., July, 1984.
Nation, March 23, 1962, March 2, 1964.
New Republic, March 21, 1964.
New Statesman, April 15, 1983.
Newsweek, February 10, 1964.
New Yorker, March 26, 1960, May 21, 1960, May 2, 1964, November 22, 1969, May 9, 1977, April 11, 1983.
New York Herald Tribune Book Review, August 3, 1958.
New York Review of Books, March 5, 1964, July 31, 1969, April 19, 1973, October 25, 1984.
New York Times, August 10, 1958, May 30, 1969, July 24, 1970, March 30, 1984.
New York Times Book Review, November 1, 1959, May 15, 1960, February 9, 1964, May 21, 1967, May 18, 1969, February 4, 1973, April 3, 1977, April 1, 1984.
Nouvelle Revue francaise, Volume 54, 1957, Volume 62, 1958, Volume 127, 1963.
Nouvelles litteraires, June 9, 1966.
Performing Arts Journal, winter, 1977.
Preuves, Volume 154, 1963.
PTL: A Journal for Descriptive Poetics and Theory of Literature, April, 1977.
Renascence, summer, 1964.
Revue de Paris, June, 1958.
Salmagundi, spring, 1970.
San Francisco Chronicle, July 10, 1960.
Saturday Review, August 2, 1958, January 2, 1960, June 11, 1960, March 16, 1963, February 15, 1964, May 6, 1967, May 24, 1969, April 2, 1977.
Symposium, winter, 1974.
Tel Quel, Volume 20, 1965.
Time, August 4, 1958, May 23, 1960, February 7, 1964.
Times Literary Supplement, January 1, 1960, January 30, 1964, July 29, 1965, July 11, 1968, January 1, 1970, February 25,

1972, July 11, 1975, April 4, 1980, July 30, 1982, June 10, 1983, April 11, 1986.
Village Voice, July 31, 1984.
Washington Post Book World, February 18, 1973, May 20, 1984.
World, July 4, 1972.
World Literature Today, summer, 1977, summer, 1979, spring, 1981, autumn, 1983, winter, 1983.
Yale French Studies, winter, 1955-56, summer, 1959, spring-summer, 1961, June, 1971.
Yale Review, winter, 1959, summer, 1960, autumn, 1973.

*   *   *

SARTON, (Eleanor) May 1912-

PERSONAL: Born May 3, 1912, in Wondelgem, Belgium; brought to United States, 1916; became naturalized U.S. citizen, 1924; daughter of George Alfred Leon (a historian of science) and Eleanor Mabel (Elwes) Sarton. *Politics:* Democrat. *Religion:* Unitarian Universalist.

ADDRESSES: Home—P.O. Box 99, York, Me. 03809. *Agent*—Russell & Volkening, Inc., 551 Fifth Ave., New York, N.Y. 10017.

CAREER: Eva Le Gallienne's Civic Repertory Theatre, New York City, apprentice, 1929-34; Associated Actors Theatre, New York City, founder, director, 1934-37; Overseas Film Unit, New York City, script writer, 1941-52; Harvard University, Cambridge, Mass., Briggs-Copeland Instructor in English Composition, 1949-52; Bread Loaf Writer's Conference, Middlebury, Vt., lecturer, 1951-53; Boulder Writers' Conference, Boulder, Colo., lecturer, 1954; Wellesley College, Wellesley, Mass., lecturer in creative writing, 1960-64; Lindenwood College, St. Charles, Mo., poet-in-residence, 1965. Danforth visiting lecturer, Arts Program, 1959; Phi Beta Kappa visiting scholar, 1960; visiting lecturer, Agnes Scott College, 1972.

MEMBER: Poetry Society of America, New England Poetry Society, American Academy of Arts and Sciences (fellow).

AWARDS, HONORS: Golden Rose Award, New England Poetry Society, 1945; Bland Memorial Prize, *Poetry,* 1945; Reynolds Lyric Award, Poetry Society of America, 1952; Lucy Martin Donnelly fellowship, Bryn Mawr College, 1953-54; Guggenheim fellow in poetry, 1954-55; Litt.D., Russell Sage College, 1958; Johns Hopkins University Poetry Festival Award, 1961; Emily Clark Balch Prize, 1966; National Endowment for the Arts grant, 1966; Litt.D., New England College, 1971; Sarah Josepha Hale Award, 1972; doctorate degrees from Clark University, 1975, Bates College, 1976, Colby College, 1976, University of New Hampshire, 1975, Thomas Starr King School of Religious Leadership, 1976, Nasson College, 1980, University of Maine, 1981, University of Bowdoin, 1983, and University of Goucher, 1985; Avon/COCOA Pioneer Woman Award, 1983; Fund for Human Dignity Award, 1985; American Book Award, Before Columbus Foundation, 1985, for *At Seventy: A Journal.*

WRITINGS:

POETRY

Encounter in April, Houghton, 1937.
Inner Landscape, Houghton, 1939.
The Lion and the Rose, Rinehart, 1948.
The Land of Silence, Rinehart, 1953.
In Time like Air, Rinehart, 1957.
Cloud, Stone, Suit, Vine, Norton, 1961.
A Private Mythology, Norton, 1966.
As Does New Hampshire, Richard R. Smith, 1967.

A Grain of Mustard Seed, Norton, 1971.
A Durable Fire, Norton, 1972.
Collected Poems: 1930-1973, Norton, 1974.
Selected Poems, Norton, 1978.
Halfway to Silence, Norton, 1980.
Letters from Maine: New Poems, Norton, 1984.
The Silence Now: New and Uncollected Earlier Poems, Norton, 1988.

FICTION

The Single Hound, Houghton, 1938.
The Bridge of Years, Doubleday, 1946.
Shadow of a Man, Rinehart, 1950.
A Shower of Summer Days, Rinehart, 1952.
Faithful Are the Wounds, Rinehart, 1955.
The Fur Person, Norton, 1956.
The Birth of a Grandfather, Rinehart, 1957.
The Small Room, Norton, 1961.
Joanna and Ulysses, Norton, 1963.
Mrs. Stevens Hears the Mermaids Singing, Norton, 1965, revised edition, 1974.
Miss Pickthorn and Mr. Hare (fable), Norton, 1966.
The Poet and the Donkey, Norton, 1969.
Kinds of Love, Norton, 1970.
As We Are Now, Norton, 1973.
Punch's Secret (juvenile), Harper, 1974.
Crucial Conversations, Norton, 1975.
A Walk through the Woods (juvenile), Harper, 1976.
A Reckoning, Norton, 1978.
Anger, Norton, 1982.
The Magnificent Spinster, Norton, 1985.
The Education of Harriet Hatfield, Norton, 1989.

NONFICTION

I Knew a Phoenix: Sketches for an Autobiography, Rinehart, 1959.
(Contributor) *The Movement of Poetry,* Johns Hopkins Press, 1962.
Plant Dreaming Deep (autobiography), Norton, 1968.
Journal of a Solitude, Norton, 1973.
A World of Light: Portraits and Celebrations, Norton, 1976.
The House by the Sea, Norton, 1977.
Writings on Writing, Puckerbrush Press, 1980.
Recovering: A Journal, Norton, 1980.
At Seventy: A Journal, Norton, 1984.
May Sarton: A Self-Portrait, edited by Marita Simpson and Martha Wheelock, Norton, 1986.

OTHER

Underground River (play), Play Club, 1947.

Also author of screenplays "Toscanini: The Hymn of Nations," 1944, and "Valley of the Tennessee," 1944. Contributor of poetry, short stories, and essays to periodicals.

SIDELIGHTS: "Examined as a whole," Lenora P. Blouin writes, "the body of May Sarton's writing is almost overwhelming. It reveals an artist who has not remained stagnant or afraid of change. 'Truth,' especially the truth within herself, has been her life-long quest." "May Sarton," Victor Howes states, "is the kind of writer whom fans and admirers write letters to, or cross the continent to consult, or just visit. Reading her poems, one comes to see why."

Sarton's poetry is calm, cultured, and urbane. A reviewer for *Poetry* describes it as "fluent, fluid, humble with a humility not entirely false, cultivated rather than worldly, tasteful, civilized, and

accomplished." James Dickey believes that Sarton "attains a delicate simplicity as quickeningly direct as it is deeply given, and does so with the courteous serenity, the clear, caring, intelligent and human calm of the queen of a small, well-ordered country." "In her most perfect poems," a reviewer for *Choice* writes, ". . . the fusion of passion and discipline is marvelously realized." Reviewing *Collected Poems,* Elizabeth Knies avows that it is "intelligently conceived and finely wrought" and calls it "the consummation of a distinguished career and a major achievement in its own right."

Other critics, however, find less to admire in Sarton's poetry. James McMichael writes that Sarton's poetry "is too self-conscious, . . . the products are dull too much of the time [and] the writing is quaint but accurate." Rosellen Brown, reviewing *Durable Fire,* comments that it contains "many brief evocations of an actual rural world, but it is, every bit of it, . . . *used* and directed."

Critical commentary about Sarton's fiction has been generally favorable. Among her harsher critics, R. L. Brown finds that Sarton's writing is "sensitive to the point of fussiness and totally without humor." Lore Dickstein criticizes Sarton's style, "which tends toward the ready cliche and occasionally teeters on the edge of sentimentality," while noting that "Sarton is best at evoking the private sensibility of one person." R. P. Corsini, however, finds that "the music of Miss Sarton's prose leaves compelling echoes in one's mind." "Sarton," Beverly Grunwald writes, "knows how to be tender and romantic, melancholy and amusing, all at once." Cade Ware notes that "Sarton is particularly adept at presenting intelligent women intelligently. . . . She is famous, too, for catching the flavor of background. . . . She is an aristocrat whose patent is clarity of mind."

"It is my hope," Sarton has written, "that all [my work] may come to be seen as a whole, the communication of a vision of life that is unsentimental, humorous, passionate, and, in the end, timeless."

BIOGRAPHICAL/CRITICAL SOURCES:

BOOKS

Blotner, Joseph, *The Modern American Political Novel: 1900-1960,* University of Texas Press, 1966.
Blouin, Lenora, *May Sarton: A Biography,* Scarecrow, 1978.
Contemporary Literary Criticism, Gale, Volume 4, 1975, Volume 14, 1980, Volume 49, 1988.
Cornillon, Susan K., *Images of Women in Fiction,* Bowling Green University Press, 1972.
Dickey, James, *Babel to Byzantium,* Farrar, Straus, 1968.
Dictionary of Literary Biography, Volume 48: *American Poets, 1880-1945, Second Series,* Gale, 1986.
Dictionary of Literary Biography Yearbook: 1981, Gale, 1982.
Henderson, Joseph, *Thresholds of Initiation,* Wesleyan University Press, 1967.
Lyons, John O., *The College Novel in America,* Southern Illinois University Press, 1962.
Rule, Jane, *Lesbian Images,* Doubleday, 1975.
Sarton, May, *I Knew a Phoenix: Sketches for an Autobiography,* Rinehart, 1959.
Sarton, *Plant Dreaming Deep,* Norton, 1968.
Sarton, *A World of Light: Portraits and Celebrations,* Norton, 1976.
Silbey, Agnes, *May Sarton,* Twayne, 1972.

PERIODICALS

Arizona Quarterly, winter, 1962.

Atlantic, January, 1953, June, 1975.
Book Week, December 29, 1963.
Boston Globe, May 14, 1950.
Chicago Tribune, May 7, 1950.
Choice, January, 1979.
Christian Science Monitor, April 8, 1939, June 10, 1950, November 13, 1978.
Chrysallis Journal, summer, 1975.
Commonweal, July 4, 1975.
Contempora, spring, 1972.
Denver Quarterly, winter, 1967.
Green River Review, summer, 1975.
Hudson Review, summer, 1967.
Los Angeles Times, March 16, 1957, December 24, 1980, October 8, 1982, April 2, 1984, April 29, 1987.
Maine Times, June 20, 1975.
Massachusetts Review, summer, 1967.
New Leader, March 28, 1955.
New Republic, June 8, 1974.
New Yorker, February 27, 1954.
New York Times, November 20, 1983.
New York Times Book Review, March 15, 1939, September 8, 1957, November 24, 1963, October 24, 1965, November 12, 1978, March 27, 1988.
Parnassus, spring/summer, 1973.
Poetry, July, 1937, April, 1968.
Publishers Weekly, June 24, 1974.
Punch, April 11, 1962.
San Francisco Chronicle, June 19, 1966.
San Francisco Examiner, November 29, 1976.
Saturday Review, March 27, 1937, October 23, 1965.
Sewanee Review, spring, 1958.
Southern Review, spring, 1967.
Time, March 21, 1938, October 1, 1965.
Village Voice, June 13, 1974.
Virginia Quarterly Review, spring, 1962.
Washington Post, October 10, 1980, December 23, 1985.
Western Humanities Review, autumn, 1971.
Yale Review, winter, 1954.

*   *   *

SARTRE, Jean-Paul 1905-1980

PERSONAL: Born June 21, 1905, in Paris, France; died April 15, 1980, of a lung ailment in Paris; son of Jean-Baptiste (a naval officer) and Anne-Marie (Schweitzer) Sartre; children: Arlette el Kaim-Sartre (adopted). *Education:* Attended Lycee Louis-le-Grand; Ecole Normale Superieure, agrege de philosophie, 1930; further study in Egypt, Italy, Greece, and in Germany under Edmund Husserl and Martin Heidegger. *Politics:* Communistic, but not Party member. *Religion:* Atheist.

ADDRESSES: Office—*Les Temps modernes,* 30 rue de l'Universite, Paris 7, France.

CAREER: Philosopher and author of novels, plays, screenplays, biographies, and literary and political criticism. Professeur of philosophy at Lycee le Havre, 1931-32 and 1934-36, Institut Francais, Berlin, 1933-34, Lycee de Laon, 1936-37, Lycee Pasteur, 1937-39, and Lycee Condorcet, 1941-44. Founded *Les Temps modernes,* 1944, editor, beginning 1945. Lecturer at various institutions in United States, including Harvard, Columbia, Yale, and Princeton universities, and in Europe, the U.S.S.R. and China. *Military service:* Meteorological Corps, 1929-31; French Army, 1939-40; prisoner of war in Germany for nine months, 1940-41. Served in Resistance Movement, 1941-44,

wrote for its underground newspapers, *Combat* and *Les Lettres Francaises.* One of the founders of the French Rally of Revolutionary Democrats.

MEMBER: American Academy of Arts and Sciences, Modern Language Association of America (honorary fellow).

AWARDS, HONORS: Roman populiste prize, 1940, for *Le Mur;* French Legion d'honneur, 1945 (refused); New York Drama Critics Award for the best foreign play of the season, 1947, for *No Exit;* French Grand Novel Prize, 1950, for *La Nausee;* Omegna Prize (Italy), 1960, for total body of work; Nobel Prize for Literature, 1964 (refused); received honorary doctorate from Hebrew University in Jerusalem, 1976.

WRITINGS:

PHILOSOPHY

L'imagination, Librairie Felix Alcan, 1936, French and European Publications, 1970, translation by Forrest Williams published as *Imagination: A Psychological Critique,* University of Michigan Press, 1962.

Esquisse d'une theorie des emotions, Hermann, 1939, translation by Bernard Frechtman published as *The Emotions: Outline of a Theory,* Philosophical Library, 1948 (translation by Philip Mairet published in England as *Sketch for a Theory of the Emotions,* Methuen, 1962).

L'imaginaire: Psychologie phenomenologique de l'imagination, Gallimard, 1940, reprinted, 1966, translation published as *The Psychology of Imagination,* Philosophical Library, 1948, reprinted, Lyle Stuart, 1980.

L'etre et le neant: Essai d'ontologie phenomenologique, Gallimard, 1943, reprinted, 1976, translation by Hazel E. Barnes published as *Being and Nothingness: An Essay on Phenomenological Ontology* (also see below), Philosophical Library, 1956, abridged edition, Citadel, 1964.

L'existentialisme est un humanisme, Nagel, 1946, reprinted, 1970, translation by Frechtman published as *Existentialism* (also see below), Philosophical Library, 1947 (translation by Mairet published in England as *Existentialism and Humanism,* Methuen, 1948, reprinted, 1973).

Existential Psychoanalysis (selections from Barnes's translation of *Being and Nothingness: An Essay on Phenomenological Ontology*), Philosophical Library, 1953.

Existentialism and Human Emotions (selections from *Existentialism* and *Being and Nothingness: An Essay on Phenomenological Ontology*), Philosophical Library, 1957.

Transcendence of the Ego: An Existentialist Theory of Consciousness, translation by Williams and Robert Kirkpatrick, Noonday, 1957, original French edition published as *La Transcendance de l'ego: Esquisse d'une description phenomenologique,* J. Vrin, 1965.

Critique de la raison dialectique: Precede de Question de methode, Gallimard, 1960, reprinted, 1986, translation by Alan Sheridan-Smith published as *Critique of Dialectical Reason: Theory of Practical Ensembles,* Humanities, 1976.

(With others) *Marxisme et Existentialisme,* Plon, 1962, translation by John Matthews published as *Between Existentialism and Marxism,* NLB, 1974.

Choix de textes, edited by J. Sebille, Nathan, 1962, 2nd edition, 1966.

Essays in Aesthetics, selected and translated by Wade Baskin, Philosophical Library, 1963.

Search for a Method, translation by Barnes, Knopf, 1963 (published in England as *The Problem of Method,* Methuen, 1964), original French edition published as *Question de methode,* Gallimard, 1967.

The Philosophy of Existentialism, edited by Baskin, Philosophical Library, 1965.

The Philosophy of Jean-Paul Sartre (translations from extracts of his work), edited by Robert Denoon Cummings, Random House, 1965.

Of Human Freedom, edited by Baskin, Philosophical Library, 1967.

Essays in Existentialism, selected and edited with a foreword by Baskin, Citadel, 1967.

The Wisdom of Jean-Paul Sartre (selections from Barnes's translation of *Being and Nothingness: An Essay on Phenomenological Ontology*), Philosophical Library, 1968.

Textes choisis, edited by Marc Beigbeder and Gerard Deledalle, Bordes, 1968.

FICTION

La Nausee, Gallimard, 1938, reprinted, Bibliotheque des chefs-d'oeuvre, 1979, translation by Lloyd Alexander published as *Nausea,* New Directions, 1949, reprinted, Robert Bentley, 1979 (published in England as *The Diary of Antoine Requentin,* J. Lehmann, 1949), new edition with illustrations by Walter Spitzer, Editions Lidis, 1964, new translation by Robert Baldick, Penguin, 1965.

Le Mur, Gallimard, 1939, reprinted, 1972, translation published as *The Wall, and Other Stories,* preface by Jean-Louis Curtis, New Directions, 1948, reprinted, 1969.

Les Chemins de la liberte, Volume 1: *L'age de raison,* Gallimard, 1945, new edition with illustrations by Spitzer, Editions Lidis, 1965, Volume 2: *Le Sursis,* Gallimard, 1945, Volume 3: *La Mort dans l'ame,* Gallimard, 1949, French and European Publications, 1972; translation published as *The Roads of Freedom,* Volume 1: *The Age of Reason,* translation by Eric Sutton, Knopf, 1947, new edition with introduction by Henri Peyre, Bantam, 1968, Volume 2: *The Reprieve,* translation by Sutton, Knopf, 1947, reprinted, Vintage Books, 1973, Volume 3: *Iron in the Soul,* translation by Gerard Hopkins, Hamish Hamilton, 1950, translation by Hopkins published as *Troubled Sleep,* Knopf, 1951, reprinted, Vintage Books, 1973.

Intimacy, and Other Stories, translation by Alexander, Berkley Publishing, 1956.

PLAYS

Les Mouches (also see below; first produced in Paris at Theatre Sarah-Bernhardt in 1942; translation by Stuart Gilbert produced as "The Flies" in New York City at President Theatre, April 17, 1947), Gallimard, 1943, new edition edited by F. C. St. Aubyn and Robert G. Marshall, Harper, 1963.

Huis-clos (also see below; first produced in Paris at Theatre du Vieux-Colombier, May 27, 1944; translation by Marjorie Gabain and Joan Swinstead produced as "The Vicious Circle" in London at Arts Theatre Club, July 17, 1946; translation by Paul Bowles produced as "No Exit" on Broadway at Biltmore Theatre, November 26, 1946), Gallimard, 1945, new edition edited by Jacques Hardre and George B. Daniel, Appleton, 1962.

The Flies (also see below) [and] *In Camera,* translation by Gilbert, Hamish Hamilton, 1946, published as *No Exit* (also see below) [and] *The Flies,* Knopf, 1947, original French edition published as *Huis-clos* [and] *Les Mouches,* Gallimard, 1964.

Morts sans sepulture (also see below; first produced with "La Putain respectueuse" in Sweden at Theatre Goeteborg, October 26, 1946; produced in Paris at Theatre Antoine, November 8, 1946; translation produced as "Men without

Shadows" on the West End at Lyric Theatre, July 17, 1947; translation produced as "The Victors" in New York City at New Stages Theatre, December 26, 1948), Marguerat, 1946, reprinted, Gallimard, 1972.

La Putain respectueuse (also see below; first produced with "Morts sans sepulture" in Sweden at Theatre Goeteberg, October 26, 1946; produced in Paris at Theatre Antoine, November 8, 1946), Nagel, 1946, translation published as *The Respectful Prostitute* (also see below; produced in New York City at New Stages Theatre, February 9, 1948; produced on Broadway at Cort Theatre, March 16, 1948), Twice a Year Press, 1948.

Theatre I (contains "Les Mouches," "Huis-clos," "Morts sans sepulture," and "La Putain respectueuse"), Gallimard, 1947.

Les jeux sont faits (screenplay; produced by Gibe-Pathe Films, 1947), Nagel, 1947, new edition edited by Mary Elizabeth Storer, Appleton, 1952, translation by Louise Varese published as *The Chips Are Down,* Lear, 1948.

Les Mains sales (also see below; first produced in Paris at Theatre Antoine, April 2, 1948; translation by Kitty Black produced as "Crime Passionnel" on the West End at Lyric Theatre, June 17, 1948, and adapted by Daniel Taradash and produced as "The Red Gloves" in New York City at Mansfield Theatre, December 4, 1948), Gallimard, 1948, published as *Les Mains sales: Piece en sept tableaux,* edited by Geoffrey Brereton, Methuen, 1963, new edition with analysis and notes by Gaston Meyer, Edition Bordas, 1971.

L'engrenage (screenplay), Nagel, 1948, translation by Mervyn Savill published as *In the Mesh,* A. Dakers, 1954.

Three Plays (contains "The Victors," "Dirty Hands" [translation of *Les Mains sales*], and "The Respectable Prostitute"), translation by Lionel Abel, Knopf, 1949.

Three Plays: Crime Passionnel, Men without Shadows, [and] *The Respectable Prostitute,* translation by Black, Hamish Hamilton, 1949.

Le Diable et le Bon Dieu (first produced in Paris at Theatre Antoine, June 7, 1951), Gallimard, 1951, reprinted, 1972, translation by Black published as *Lucifer and the Lord* (also see below), Hamish Hamilton, 1953, published as *The Devil and the Good Lord, and Two Other Plays,* Knopf, 1960.

(Adapter) Alexandre Dumas, *Kean* (also see below; first produced in Paris at Theatre Sarah-Bernhardt, November 14, 1953), Gallimard, 1954, translation by Black published as *Kean, Or Disorder and Genius,* Hamish Hamilton, 1954, Vintage Books, 1960.

No Exit, and Three Other Plays (contains "No Exit," "The Flies," "Dirty Hands," and "The Respectful Prostitute"), Random House, 1955.

Nekrassov (also see below; first produced in Paris at Theatre Antoine, June 8, 1955), Gallimard, 1956, translation by Sylvia and George Leeson published as *Nekrassov* (produced in London at Royal Court Theatre, September 17, 1957), Hamish Hamilton, 1956, French and European Publications, 1973.

Les Sequestres d'Altona (also see below; first produced in Paris at Theatre de la Renaissance, September 23, 1959), Gallimard, 1960, new edition edited and with an introduction by Philip Thody, University of London Press, 1965, translation by S. Leeson and G. Leeson published as *Loser Wins,* Hamish Hamilton, 1960, published as *The Condemned of Altona* (also see below; produced on Broadway at Vivian Beaumont Theatre, February 3, 1966), Knopf, 1961.

Crime Passionnel: A Play, translation by Black, Methuen, 1961.

Theatre (contains "Les Mouches," "Huis-clos," "Morts sans sepulture," "La Putain respecteuse," "Les Mains sales," "Le Diable et le Bon Dieu," "Kean," "Nekrassov," and "Les Sequestres d'Altona"), Gallimard, 1962.

Bariona, Anjou-Copies, 1962, 2nd edition, E. Marescot, 1967.

The Condemned of Altona, Men without Shadows, [and] *The Flies,* Penguin, 1962.

"Orphee Noir" (first published in *Anthologie de la nouvelle poesie negre et malgache de langue francaise,* Presses Universitaires de France, 1948), translation by S. W. Allen published as *Black Orpheus,* University Place Book Shop, c. 1963.

La Putain respecteuse, piece en un acte et deux tableaux: Suivi de Morts sans sepulture, piece en deux actes et quatre tableax, Gallimard, 1963.

The Respectable Prostitute [and] *Lucifer and the Lord,* translation by Black, Penguin, 1965.

(Adapter) Euripides, *Les troyennes* (first produced in Paris at Theatre National Populaire, March 10, 1965), Gallimard, 1966, translation by Ronald Duncan published as *The Trojan Women* (also see below), Knopf, 1967.

Three Plays (contains "Kean, Or Disorder and Genius," "Nekrassov," and "The Trojan Women"), Penguin, 1969.

Five Plays (contains "No Exit," "The Flies," "Dirty Hands," "The Respectful Prostitute," and "The Condemned of Altona"), Franklin Library, 1978.

Also author of screenplay "Typhus," 1944, of an unpublished play "All the Treasures of the Earth," and of screenplay "Les Sorcieres de Salem" adapted from Arthur Miller's *The Crucible.*

LITERARY CRITICISM AND POLITICAL WRITINGS

Reflexions sur la question juive, P. Morihien, 1946, translation by George J. Becker published as *Anti-Semite and Jew,* Schocken, 1948 (translation by Erik de Mauney published in England as *Portrait of the Anti-Semite,* Secker & Warburg, 1948).

Baudelaire, Gallimard, 1947, translation by Martin Turnell published as *Baudelaire,* Horizon (London), 1949, New Directions, 1950.

Situations I, Gallimard, 1947, reprint published as *Critiques litteraires,* 1975.

Situations II, Gallimard, 1948.

Qu'est-ce que le litterature? (first published in *Situations II*), Gallimard, 1949, translation by Frechtman published as *What Is Literature?,* Philosophical Library, 1949, published as *Literature and Existentialism,* Citadel, 1962.

Situations III, Gallimard, 1949.

(With David Rousset and Gerard Rosenthal) *Entretiens sur la politique,* Gallimard, 1949.

Saint Genet, comedien et martyr, Gallimard, 1952, translation by Frechtman published as *Saint Genet: Actor and Martyr,* Braziller, 1963.

Literary and Philosophical Essays (excerpts from *Situations I* and *III*), translation by Annette Michelson, Criterion, 1955.

Literary Essays (excerpts from *Situations I* and *III*), translation by Michelson, Philosophical Library, 1957, reprinted, Citadel, 1978.

Sartre on Cuba, Ballantine, 1961.

Situations IV: Portraits, Gallimard, 1964, translation by Benita Eisler published as *Situations,* Braziller, 1965.

Situations V: Colonialisme et neo-colonialisme, Gallimard, 1964.

Situations VI: Problemes du Marxisme, Part I, Gallimard, 1966.

(Contributor) Aime Cesaire, *Das politische Denken Lumumbas,* Verlag Klaus Wagenbach, 1966.

Situations VII: Problemes du Marxisme, Part II, Gallimard, 1967.

On Genocide, with a summary of the evidence and the judgments of the International War Crimes Tribunal by Sartre's adopted daughter, Arlette el Kaim-Sartre, Beacon, 1968.

The Ghost of Stalin, translation by Martha H. Fletcher and John R. Kleinschmidt, Braziller, 1968 (translation by Irene Clephane published in England as *The Spectre of Stalin,* Hamish Hamilton, 1969).

Les Communistes et la paix (first published in *Situations VI*), Gallimard, 1964, translation by Fletcher and Kleinschmidt (bound with "A Reply to Claude Lefort" translated by Philip R. Berk) published as *The Communists and Peace,* Braziller, 1968.

El Intelectual frente a la revolucion, Ediciones Hombre Nuevo, 1969.

Les Communistes ont peur de la revolution, J. Didier, 1969.

(With Vladimir Dedijer) *War Crimes in Vietnam,* Bertrand Russell Peace Foundation, 1971.

L'idiot de la famille, Gallimard, 1971, translation by Carol Cosman published as *The Family Idiot,* three volumes, University of Chicago Press, 1981-89.

Situations VIII: Autour de 1968, French and European Publications, 1972.

Situations IX: Melanges, French and European Publications, 1972.

Situations X: Politique et Autobiographie, French and European Publications, 1976, translation by Paul Auster and Lydia Davis published as *Life/Situations: Essays Written and Spoken,* Pantheon, 1977.

OTHER

(Contributor) *L'Affaire Henri Martin* (title means "The Henry Martin Affair"), Gallimard, 1953.

Sartre par lui-meme, edited by Francis Jeanson, Editions du Seuil, 1959, translation by Richard Seaver published as *Sartre by Himself,* Outback Press, 1978.

(Author of text) Andre Masson, *Vingt-Deux Dessins sur le Theme du Desir,* F. Mourtot, 1961.

Les Mots (autobiography), Gallimard, 1963, translation by Frechtman published as *The Words,* Braziller, 1964 (translation by Clephane published in England as *Words,* Hamish Hamilton, 1964).

Sartre por Sartre, edited by Juan Jose Sebreli, Jorge Alvarez, 1968.

(Editor with Bertrand Russell) *Das Vietnam Tribunal,* Rowohlt Verlag, 1970.

Gott ohne Gott (contains *Bariona* and a dialogue with Sartre), edited by Gotthold Hasenhuttl, Graz Verlag (Austria), 1972.

Un theatre de situations, compiled and edited by Michel Contat and Michel Rybalka, Gallimard, 1973, translation by Frank Jellinck published as *Sartre on Theater,* Pantheon, 1976.

Oeuvres romanesques, edited by Contat and Rybalka, Gallimard, 1981.

Cahiers pour une morale, Gallimard, 1983.

Carnets de la drole de guerre, Gallimard, 1983.

(With Simone de Beauvoir) *Lettres au Castor et a quelques autres,* Volume 1: *1926-1939,* Volume 2: *1940-1963,* Gallimard, 1984.

Le scenario Freud, Gallimard, 1984, translation by Quintin Hoare published as *The Freud Scenario,* University of Chicago Press, 1985.

The War Diaries of Jean-Paul Sartre, Random House, 1985.

Contributor to numerous books, anthologies, and periodicals. Editor of *La Cause du peuple,* beginning 1970, *Tout!,* beginning 1970, and *Revolution!,* beginning 1971.

SIDELIGHTS: Jean-Paul Sartre was one of the major intellectual figures of the twentieth century, doubtless the greatest of his immediate generation in France. In the words of Sartrean scholars Michel Contat and Michel Rybalka in *The Writings of Jean-Paul Sartre,* he was "uncontestably the most outstanding philosopher and writer of our time." The eminent scholar Henri Peyre, in his preface to *The Condemned of Altona,* called Sartre "the most powerful intellect at work . . . in the literature of Western Europe," the "Picasso of literature." Since his death in 1980, Sartre's reputation has not waned, and with perspective it has become clear that he represented his age much as, in different ways, Voltaire (1694-1778), Victor Hugo (1802-1885), and Andre Gide (1869-1951) represented theirs. "To understand Jean-Paul Sartre," wrote the novelist Iris Murdoch in *Sartre: Romantic Rationalist,* "is to understand something important about the present time."

Sartre was the chief proponent of French existentialism, a philosophic school—influenced by Soeren Kierkegaard and German philosophy—that developed around the close of the World War II. Existentialism stressed the primacy of the thinking person and of concrete individual experience as the source of knowledge; this philosophy also emphasized the anguish and solitude inherent in the making of choices.

Sartre's worldwide fame was based substantially on his existentialism, but it would be a mistake to consider him significant only for a philosophy that represented his thinking at a relatively early stage of his career. It would be a still greater mistake to reduce his existentialism to very simplistic elements, such as crude nihilism, as often has been done.

Sartre's literary and philosophic careers were inextricably bound together and are best understood in relation to one another and to their biographic context. An only child, Sartre decided at an early age to be a writer. According to *The Words,* the autobiography of his youth, this decision was made in conscious opposition to the wishes of his grandfather, Charles Schweitzer (who, after the death of Sartre's father, raised the boy with the help of Sartre's grandmother). Schweitzer, a domineering old Protestant who was nevertheless very fond of his grandson and extremely indulgent with him, appeared to young Sartre as insincere, a consummate charlatan. Charles Schweitzer preached the serious values of the bourgeoisie and tried to denigrate a career in letters as precarious, unsuitable for stable middle-class people. As a reaction, Sartre proposed to make writing *serious,* to adopt it as the center of his life and values. He also chose it as a kind of self-justification in a world where a child was not taken seriously. "By writing I was existing. I was escaping from the grown-ups," he wrote in *The Words.*

When his mother remarried, Sartre moved from Paris to La Rochelle with her and his stepfather, a solemn professional man with whom he felt little in common. All the same, young Sartre followed the path of a professional, finishing his lycee studies in Paris and completing university work at the Ecole Normale Superieure. There he met Simone de Beauvoir, who was to be a lifelong companion, though by no means his only love interest.

As a student, Sartre became interested in philosophy, pursuing it through the *agregation* (the highest French degree preparing for a teaching career). Sartre was steeped in the Cartesian rationalist tradition (whereby the subject's existence is proven by his thought), although eventually he largely departed from this phi-

losophy. The topic of his thesis, the imagination, shows how his philosophic concerns supported his early interest in creative writing. Other of his treatises of the 1930s concern the emotions and what Sartre called the transcendence of the ego—or the nature of the self—which, he argued, is created by the individual instead of being a given. At the same time that he was pursuing these investigations on the imagination, Sartre became acquainted with phenomenology, a branch of philosophy associated with such German scholars as Edmund Husserl, with whom Sartre studied for a year in Berlin.

Throughout the 1930s, Sartre's philosophic and literary pursuits supported each other and developed along parallel lines. At the beginning of the decade Sartre began work on a fictional piece first called "A Pamphlet on Contingency" (contingency being lack of foundation), which developed into his first novel, *Nausea.* It illustrates what Simone de Beauvoir called his "opposition aesthetics"—his desire to use literature as a critical tool. The novel's title indicates the hero's reaction toward existence: when he discovers that life is absurd, he feels repulsed. Nothing, it would seem, can save him, except the discovery that he might be able to write a novel that would have internal necessity and be a rival to life; he proposes to save himself through an act of aesthetic creation. Sartre said in *The Words:* "At the age of thirty, I executed the masterstroke of writing in *Nausea*—quite sincerely, believe me—about the bitter unjustified existence of my fellow men and of exonerating my own."

Nausea was received with praise and had considerable success. In his 1938 *Esprit* review, for instance, Armand Robin wrote that *Nausea* "is undoubtedly one of the distinctive works of our time." Later, in *Sartre: A Philosophic Study,* Anthony Richards Manser called it "that rare thing: a genuinely philosophic novel."

Sartre revealed himself to be a master psychologist in his next fictional work, the short story collection *The Wall.* These works are superb examples of the storyteller's craft. Particularly impressive is the title story, which recounts an episode from the Spanish Civil War, and the final one, "The Childhood of a Leader," which, while autobiographical to a considerable degree, has as its main plot thread the making of a Fascist. All the stories reveal the author's command of dialogue and metaphor and illustrate exceptionally interesting ideas about human relationships, sexuality, insanity, childhood development, and the meaning of action.

By the end of the 1930s, Sartre was known as a promising writer but he was not yet considered an important philosopher. This assessment changed in 1943 when Sartre produced *Being and Nothingness: An Essay on Phenomenological Ontology,* the major philosophical work of the first half of his career. While closely related to his treatises on imagination and to the views of experience he had expressed in his fiction, *Being and Nothingness* is not confined to these subjects. Rather, in defining being, or what *is,* as what *appears,* it explores all phenomena. The essay examines man, the being who questions being, and concludes that he is both his body occupying a place in the world—that is, an object among objects—and a subject or a consciousness reflecting on objects. Sartre contends that all consciousness is consciousness of *something.* Since it is basically a negating—or distinguishing—function (saying that this chair, for instance, is *not* this table), consciousness produces the concept of nothingness; man is the being by whom negation is introduced into an otherwise complete world. Though its influence penetrated slowly, *Being and Nothingness* helped assure its authors fame after 1945.

In *Being and Nothingness*, Sartre wrote that one of the most important characteristics of consciousness is its freedom. He soon drew explicitly the corollary that ontological freedom, in which man is "condemned to be free," as he wrote in *Being and Nothingness*, must entail political freedom also. That is, freedom is a goal as well as a given and must be embodied in praxis (practical action). The very popular *The Flies*, which retells the Greek story of the murder of Clytemnestra by her children Orestes and Electra, emphasizes man's fundamental freedom, against which even the gods are powerless. *No Exit*, often anthologized and perhaps the best known of all of Sartre's works, deals with the absence of freedom when one allows oneself to exist through and for others, rather than living authentically. Sartre stated in *L'Express* that its famous conclusion, "Hell is other people," did not describe what *had to be* true concerning human relationships, but what *was* true when relationships with others became corrupt or twisted.

The theme of freedom may be even more elaborately treated in less famous Sartre plays of the 1940s. *Morts sans sepulture* (usually translated as *The Victors*), which shocked the sensibilities of many theatergoers because it dealt with torture during the Occupation, indicates how extreme the Sartrean view of freedom could be. The play offers the view that even under torture and threat of death, one is free to choose; that this choice cannot be evaded, nor can it be made other than in utter loneliness; and that one is responsible for all its consequences. *Les Mains sales* (sometimes translated as "Dirty Hands"), treats the difficulty of political choice, the necessity of political compromise, and the refusal to let one's freedom be alienated or appropriated by others.

Between 1945 and 1950 Sartre also published three more novels—*The Age of Reason, The Reprieve,* and *Troubled Sleep*—collectively called *Roads to Freedom*. These works deal with an ineffectual hero in a morally and politically indifferent France before World War II. The series illustrates what Sartre described in "What Is Literature" as a literature of praxis: "action in history and on history . . . a synthesis of historical relativity and moral and metaphysical absolute." In *The Reprieve,* the second volume of this trilogy, Sartre carries further than any other French writer of his period the techniques of jumping from one plot thread to another, without transition, and of pursuing simultaneous plots. While making for very difficult reading, these techniques suggest collective action and thus support his portrait of what it was like to be in Europe at the time of the Munich Crisis (1938).

After the war Sartre also published many articles on literature and politics, notably the important essay "What Is Literature?" in *Situations II*. Here he stated that all prose literature is necessarily committed to making a political and social statement and is directed to one's own contemporaries; the practice of literature, he insisted, is built on freedom (the writer's, the reader's). As he put it in *Situations II,* literature is "the subjectivity of a society in permanent revolution."

After the war, though considerably lionized and taken by many youthful readers to be the preeminent spokesman for their generation, Sartre continued to develop intellectually and undergo changes that were to have far-reaching effects on his work. In the prewar years, he had been generally uninterested in politics. While despising Fascist parties and the bourgeoisie from which they—and he—came, Sartre had not participated in political action, nor even bothered to vote. He considered then that his fiction and philosophic texts were sufficient expressions of his unfavorable views of society. But he eventually became thoroughly politicized, speaking out on such issues as the French presence in Indochina, which he opposed, and even participating in a leftist, but non-Communist, postwar political movement.

By the close of the decade, with the advent of the Cold War, Sartre accepted that a non-Communist leftist party was a contradiction. He returned to Karl Marx's writings, with which he had previously been only roughly familiar, and began steeping himself in Marxism to rework his positions and think *against* what he had previously held. Throughout the rest of his career Sartre denounced many of his previous attitudes and practiced systematic self-debate. Although he became a resolute neo-Marxist, he was never a member of the French Communist Party but was instead often its critic and that of the Soviet Union (as when it invaded Hungary in 1956 and Czechoslovakia in 1968). However, he was always staunchly opposed to Western capitalism, NATO, and the United States.

The radicalization of his thinking seemed essential to Sartre because the fame that had overtaken him during the 1940s had the effect, or so he thought, of making him a public being; he felt that he was being appropriated by others. This threat increased his sense of alienation. He also resented what he felt would be his inevitable acceptance by the bourgeoisie; he was becoming respectable, read by the middle classes. This attitude explains why, in 1964, he refused the Nobel Prize for Literature; to him, it was a middle-class recognition that would have the effect of making him appear inoffensive.

In a 1964 *Le Monde* interview with Jacqueline Piatier, Sartre summarized his political changes: "I discovered abruptly that alienation, exploitation of man by man, undernourishment, relegated to the background metaphysical evil, which is a luxury." This discovery led to profound transformations in Sartre as a writer. Although he continued to regard his earlier works as well written, he also now viewed them as inauthentic because they had resulted from a bourgeois decision to write, a decision based on personal rebellion and on the idolatry of words. Moreover, he came to believe that fiction could no longer serve his purpose. He even abandoned drama, although he had argued earlier that theatre is an ideal means of showing characters in situations where they must commit themselves wholly to their actions and thereby create values.

In short, Sartre's career as a semipopular writer came to a close in 1950. Yet several works published after that date are among his greatest. The *Critique of Dialectical Reason,* his second major philosophic work, is essential to the understanding of all he wrote after his radicalization and is so closely connected to certain of his other texts that whole sections were transferred from one to another. It is far from a popular work; even more than in *Being and Nothingness,* the vocabulary and concepts of its 750-plus pages are difficult, and the analysis is so abstruse and sometimes meandering that even professional philosophers have found some of it incomprehensible.

Intended as a synthesis of existentialist philosophy and Marxism, the *Critique* calls on and belongs to disciplines as various as anthropology, history, psychology, economics, and philosophy. Its aim is to give a philosophical basis to Marxism and, on that basis, to investigate further the dialectic of history and its intelligibility. Dialectical reasoning, which is opposed to the analytic method, involves the Hegelian synthesis of contraries. Sartre's thesis is that, whereas analytical reason has been the tool of the oppressive classes, dialectical reason, which offers a different understanding of history and its possibilities, is "the objective spirit of the working class," as he put it in the *Critique*. While still insisting on the possibility of human freedom, the treatise shows how this freedom is conditioned, alienated, made powerless by historical and social developments.

In the field of biography, Sartre published in 1947 a short volume on the poet Charles Baudelaire. Using what in *Being and Nothingness* he called existential psychoanalysis, Sartre explains Baudelaire's character and career as an original conscious choice—the choice to remain infantile, narcissistic, dependent on his mother, a failure. In opposition to Freud, Sartre shows that the poet's choice reveals psychological freedom, not psychological determinism. The next biography, *Saint Genet: Actor and Martyr,* is a masterly analysis of the writer Jean Genet, a convicted thief and multiple offender known as the author of shocking plays and novels concerned with homosexuality, anarchy, and rebellion against authority. The biography ascribes Genet's career as a thief to a conscious decision made in childhood to be what others accused him of being. To Sartre, Genet is a splendid example of a man who *made himself* as he wanted to be by inverting other people's values.

Some twelve years later, Sartre published his autobiography, a self-accusatory work. The title, *The Words,* refers to the idolatry of literature he had practiced up to about 1950. The autobiography was judged by Francis Jeanson in *Sartre dans sa vie* as "the most accessible, and doubtless the most successful, of all the non-philosophical works of Sartre." It demolishes "the myth of a Messiah-writer of a dechristianized bourgeoisie," according to *Revue des Sciences Humaines* contributor Marc Bensimon. As a study in characters (his mother, his grandfather, the Alsatian bourgeoisie from which they sprang, his father's family), it is superb. As self-analysis, it is even more outstanding. Few writers have portrayed so searchingly their early childhood and their choice of a vocation or have judged so severely the adult who grew from the child. The book was, Sartre says within its pages, the fruit of an awakening from "a long, bitter, and sweet delusion." *The Words* reads almost like fiction; it is brief and its style is witty, aphoristic, penetrating—classical, in a word, although its method is dialectical.

At the opposite extreme is Sartre's final biographic work, *The Family Idiot,* a 2,800-page analysis of Gustave Flaubert. Flaubert had long interested Sartre, both attracting him and repulsing him. Sartre wanted to explore chiefly the particular circumstances and the dialectical relationships that made Flaubert into a bourgeois who hated the bourgeoisie, a passive man incapable of pursuing an ordinary career, and, generally, a misfit and a neurotic, as well as a great writer. The investigation ranges far afield, from Flaubert's antecedents and family, to his infancy (reconstructed with the help of Sartre's dialectical method, here called progressive-regressive) and youth, to all aspects of the social and economic situation in which he matured. Sartre wished to show, he said in an interview given to *Le Monde,* that "everything can be communicated . . . that every human being is perfectly capable of being understood if the appropriate methods are used."

After 1950 Sartre published and saw into production two theatrical adaptations and three original plays, two of which are surely among his greatest. *The Devil and the Good Lord,* his personal favorite, is, like the volume on Genet, concerned with values, absolutely and pragmatically. An uncompromising statement of atheism, the play explores in a historical context (sixteenth-century Reformation Germany) the interdependency of good and evil and illustrates the necessity of adopting means that suit the ends. A second major play of the 1950s is the lengthy *The Condemned of Altona,* which concerns a German World War II veteran who has barricaded himself in his room for years.

Tended only by his sister, the veteran has persuaded himself that Germany won the war. Although concerned explicitly with that conflict and its aftermath, the play was intended to refer also to the Algerian War, then in progress. The play impugns Nazi Germany and the type of men it produced—not just SS soldiers but also members of the upper bourgeoisie who found Nazism useful because it served their economic interests. More generally, it condemns capitalist Europe, whose conflicts over markets and expansion had caused two world wars.

Declaring to John Gerassi—in a 1971 *New York Times Magazine* interview—that "commitment is an *act,* not a word," Sartre expressed his political beliefs by participating in demonstrations, marches, and campaigns, although he was not well (he suffered from failing eyesight and circulatory troubles, among other ailments). Sartre took stands on literally dozens of political and social issues around the world. Such topics as decent housing in France, conscientious objection in Israel, the Vietnamese War, repression in the Congo, Basque separatism, the troubles in Northern Ireland, torture in Argentina, and the Russian invasion of Afghanistan show the range of his concerns. Denouncing as ossified the French Communist Party and all other parties intellectually dependent upon the Soviet Union, Sartre supported Maoist attempts at a new radicalization of Marxist theory and action. This political activity both increased interest in his writings and made him notorious throughout Europe.

From the beginning of his career, Sartre wanted to make people think, feel, see, and ultimately act differently. Like his earlier views, summarized in *Existentialism Is a Humanism,* Sartre's later morality is both a difficult and a hopeful one. People *can* change, he proclaimed, but they would prefer to remain in their errors (to practice injustice, for instance) or to cling to what he had called bad faith. Because of the acceleration of violence and international competition, they *must* change, he insisted. Since the oppressive and privileged classes will not willingly give up their privileges, these must be wrested from them by violence and revolution; then new relationships between human beings, based on reciprocity and openness instead of rivalry and secrecy, will be possible, Sartre declared.

As his health deteriorated, Sartre wrote less but gave lengthy interviews that are a sort of intellectual autobiography. He remained fascinated with himself and his career, perhaps more so than other great writers, but more surprisingly so, since he had wished to move away from the cult of the individual to the idea of the *general* man, "anyone at all," as he put it in *The Words.* He was, as Josette Pacaly declared in *Sartre au miroir,* "a Narcissus who does not like himself."

Seen as a whole, Sartre's career reveals numerous contradictions. A bourgeois, he hated the middle classes and wanted to chastise them; "I became a traitor and remained one," he wrote in *The Words.* Yet he was not a true proletarian writer. An individualist in many ways and completely opposed to regimentation, he nevertheless attacked the individualistic tradition and insisted on the importance of the collectivity; he moved from the extremely solitary position of an existentialist to concern for society above all. A writer possessed of an outstanding ear for language and other literary skills, he came to suspect literature as inauthentic and wrote a superb autobiography to denounce writing. An atheist, he often spoke with the fervor of an evangelist and repeated that man was responsible for his own errors and must mend his ways. A reformer and moralist, he led an existence that would seem to many decidedly immoral. Of such contradictions, he was of course, aware.

MEDIA ADAPTATIONS: "The Chips Are Down," a film based on Sartre's screenplay *Le jeux sont faits,* was produced by Lopert in 1949; "Les Mains sales," a film based on Sartre's play of the same title, was produced by Rivers Films in 1951 and later released in the United States as "Dirty Hands"; "La Putain respectueuse," a film based on Sartre's play of the same title, was produced by Agiman Films and Artes Films in 1952; "The Respectable Prostitute," a film based on Sartre's play *La Putain respectueuse,* was produced by Gala in 1955; "Les orgueilleux," a film based on Sartre's original screenplay "Typhus," was produced by Jean Productions in 1953 and was released in the United States as "The Proud and the Beautiful" by Kingsley in 1956; "Huis-clos," a film based on Sartre's play of the same title, was produced by Jacqueline Audry in 1954; "Kean, Genio e Sregolatezza," a film based on an Alexandre Dumas play adapted by Sartre, was produced by Lux Films in 1957; "Les sequestres d'Altona," a film based on Sartre's play of the same title, was produced by Titanus Films in 1963 and released in the United States as "The Condemned of Altona" by Twentieth Century-Fox Film Corp. in 1963; a television production based on *Huis-clos* was broadcast on O.R.T.F. (French Radio-Television) in October, 1965; "Le Mur," a film based on Sartre's short story of the same title, was produced by Niepce Films in 1967; "The Roads to Freedom," a thirteen-week television serial based on Sartre's novels, *The Age of Reason, The Reprieve,* and *Troubled Sleep* was produced by the British Broadcasting Corp. in 1970.

BIOGRAPHICAL/CRITICAL SOURCES:

BOOKS

Aron, Raymond, *History and the Dialectic of Violence: Analysis of Sartre's "Critique de la raison dialectique,"* Harper, 1975.

Aronson, Ronald, *Jean-Paul Sartre,* Schocken, 1980.

Astruc, Alexandre and Michel Contat, *Sartre by Himself,* Urizen Books, 1978.

Barnes, Hazel, *Sartre,* Lippincott, 1973.

Bauer, George H., *Sartre and the Artist,* University of Chicago Press, 1969.

Beauvoir, Simone de, *Memoirs of a Dutiful Daughter,* World Publishing, 1959.

Beauvoir, Simone de, *The Prime of Life,* World Publishing, 1962.

Beauvoir, Simone de, *The Force of Circumstance,* Putnam, 1965.

Beauvoir, Simone de, *All Said and Done,* Putnam, 1974.

Beauvoir, Simone de, *Adieux: A Farewell to Sartre,* Pantheon, 1984.

Bree, Germaine, *Camus and Sartre: Crisis and Commitment,* Delacorte, 1972.

Catalano, Joseph S., *A Commentary on Jean-Paul Sartre's "Being and Nothingness,"* Harper, 1974.

Caws, Peter, *Sartre,* Routledge & Kegan Paul, 1979.

Champigny, Robert, *Stages on Sartre's Way,* Indiana University Press, 1959.

Champigny, Robert, *Humanism and Human Racism: A Critical Study of Essays by Sartre and Camus,* Mouton and Co., 1972.

Champigny, Robert, *Sartre and Drama,* French Literature Publications, 1982.

Chiodi, Pietro, *Sartre and Marxism,* Harvester, 1976.

Collins, Douglas, *Sartre as Biographer,* Harvard University Press, 1980.

Contat, Michel and Michel Rybalka, compilers, *The Writings of Jean-Paul Sartre,* Northwestern University Press, 1974.

Contemporary Literary Criticism, Gale, Volume 1, 1973, Volume 4, 1975, Volume 7, 1977, Volume 9, 1978, Volume 13, 1980, Volume 18, 1981, Volume 24, 1983, Volume 44, 1987, Volume 50, 1988, Volume 52, 1989.

Cranston, Maurice, *Sartre,* Oliver & Boyd, 1962.

Cranston, Maurice, *The Quintessence of Sartrism,* Harper, 1971.

Cumming, Robert D., *The Philosophy of Jean-Paul Sartre,* Random House, 1965.

Danto, Arthur, *Jean-Paul Sartre,* Viking, 1975.

Dempsey, Peter J. R., *The Psychology of Sartre,* Cork University Press, 1950.

Dictionary of Literary Biography, Volume 72: *French Novelists, 1930-1960,* Gale, 1988.

Fell, Joseph P. III, *Emotion in the Thought of Sartre,* Columbia University Press, 1965.

Grene, Marjorie, *Sartre,* New Viewpoints, 1973.

Halpern, Joseph, *Critical Fictions: The Literary Criticism of Jean-Paul Sartre,* Yale University Press, 1976.

Hayim, Gila J., *The Existential Sociology of Jean-Paul Sartre,* University of Massachusetts Press, 1980.

Howells, Christina, *Sartre's Theory of Literature,* Modern Humanities Research Association, 1979.

Jeanson, Francis, *Sartre and the Problem of Morality,* Indiana University Press, 1950.

Jeanson, Francis, *Sartre dans sa vie,* Editions du Seuil, 1974.

Kaelin, Eugene Francis, *An Existentialist Ethic: The Theories of Sartre and Merleau-Ponty,* University of Wisconsin Press, 1962.

King, Thomas M., *Sartre and the Sacred,* University of Chicago Press, 1974.

Kirsher, Douglas, *The Schizoid World of Jean-Paul Sartre and R. D. Laing,* Humanities, 1976.

La Capra, Dominick, *A Preface to Sartre,* Cornell University Press, 1978.

Laing, R. D. and D. G. Cooper, *Reason and Violence: A Decade of Sartre's Philosophy, 1950-1960,* Tavistock, 1964.

Lapointe, Francois and Claire Lapointe, *Jean-Paul Sartre and His Critics,* Philosophy Documentation Center, Bowling Green State University, 1980.

Manser, Anthony Richards, *Sartre: A Philosophic Study,* Athlone Press, 1966.

McCall, Dorothy, *The Theatre of Jean-Paul Sartre,* Columbia University Press, 1969.

McMahon, Joseph H., *Human Being: The World of Jean-Paul Sartre,* University of Chicago Press, 1971.

Molnar, Thomas S., *Sartre: Ideologue of Our Time,* Funk, 1968.

Morris, Phyllis S., *Sartre's Concept of a Person: An Analytic Approach,* University of Massachusetts Press, 1976.

Murdoch, Iris, *Sartre: Romantic Rationalist,* Yale University Press, 1953.

Peyre, Henri, *Jean-Paul Sartre,* Columbia University Press, 1968.

Plank, William, *Sartre and Surrealism,* UMI Research Press, 1981.

Ranwez, Alain D., *Jean-Paul Sartre's "Les Temps Modernes": A Literary History, 1945-1952,* Whitson, 1981.

Salvan, Jacques, *To Be or Not to Be: An Analysis of Jean-Paul Sartre's Ontology,* Wayne State University Press, 1962.

Salvan, Jacques, *The Scandalous Ghost: Sartre's Existentialism,* Wayne State University Press, 1967.

Sartre, Jean-Paul, *Situations II,* Gallimard, 1948.

Sartre, Jean-Paul, *Sartre par lui-meme,* edited by Francis Jeanson, Editions du Seuil, 1959, translation by Richard Seaver published as *Sartre by Himself,* Outback Press, 1978.

Sartre, Jean-Paul, *Les Mots,* Gallimard, 1963, translation by Bernard Frechtman published as *The Words,* Braziller, 1964.

Schilpp, Paul, editor, *The Philosophy of Jean-Paul Sartre,* Open Court, 1981.

Scriven, Michael, *Sartre's Existential Biographies,* Macmillan, 1984.
Sheridan, James F., *Sartre: The Radical Conversion,* Ohio University Press, 1969.
Stack, George, *Sartre's Philosophy of Social Existence,* Warren Green, 1977.
Stern, Alfred, *Sartre: His Philosophy on an Existential Psychoanalysis,* Liberal Arts Press, 1953, revised edition, Delacorte, 1967.
Streller, Justus, *Jean-Paul Sartre: To Freedom Condemned,* Philosophical Library, 1960.
Thody, Philip, *Jean-Paul Sartre: A Literary and Political Study,* Hamish Hamilton, 1960.
Warnock, Mary, *The Philosophy of Sartre,* Hutchinson Library Service, 1965.
Warnock, Mary, *Sartre: A Collection of Critical Essays,* Doubleday, 1971.
Wilcocks, Robert, *Jean-Paul Sartre: A Bibliography of International Criticism,* University of Alberta Press, 1975.
Wilson, Colin, *Anti-Sartre,* Borgo, 1981.

PERIODICALS

Esprit, Number 38, 1938.
Le Figaro, June 26, 1951.
Le Monde, April 18, 1964.
L'Express, October 11, 1965.
New Republic, June 1, 1968, August 30, 1975.
Newsweek, October 5, 1964.
New York Review of Books, August 7, 1975.
New York Times, October 23, 1964, September 1, 1971.
New York Times Book Review, October 11, 1964, December 27, 1981.
New York Times Magazine, October 17, 1971.
Revue des Sciences Humaines, July/September, 1965.
Times (London), November 22, 1984, November 28, 1985, July 11, 1986.
Times Literary Supplement, April 2, 1964, June 25, 1976, January 29, 1982, May 11, 1984, July 11, 1986.

OBITUARIES:

PERIODICALS

AB Bookmans Weekly, May 5, 1980.
Chicago Tribune, April 16, 1980.
Los Angeles Times, April 16, 1980.
New York Times, April 16, 1980, April 20, 1980.
Publishers Weekly, May 9, 1980.
Times (London), April 16, 1980, April 17, 1980.
Washington Post, April 16, 1980, April 17, 1980.

* * *

SASSOON, Siegfried (Lorraine) 1886-1967
(Saul Kain, Pinchbeck Lyre, S. S.)

PERSONAL: Born September 8, 1886, in Brenchley, Kent, England; died September 1, 1967, in Wiltshire, England; buried in Mells, Somerset, England; son of Alfred and Theresa (Thornycroft) Sassoon; married Hester Gatty, December 18, 1933; children: George Thornycroft. *Education:* Attended Clare College, Cambridge. *Politics:* Labour. *Religion:* Catholic.

CAREER: Poet and author. Literary editor of the *Daily Herald,* 1919. *Military service:* British Army, 1914-18; served with Royal Welch Fusiliers; became captain; received Military Cross.

MEMBER: Reform Club (London).

AWARDS, HONORS: Hawthornden Prize and James Tait Black Memorial Prize, both 1928, both for *Memoirs of a Fox-Hunting Man;* D.Litt. from University of Liverpool, 1932, and Oxford University, 1965; Commander of the Order of the British Empire, 1951; Queen's Medal for Poetry, 1957.

WRITINGS:

POETRY; PUBLISHED ANONYMOUSLY

Poems, privately printed, 1906.
Orpheus in Diloeryium, J. E. Francis, 1908.
Sonnets, privately printed, 1909.
Sonnets and Verses, privately printed, 1909.
Melodies, privately printed, 1912.
Morning Glory, privately printed, 1916.

POETRY

Twelve Sonnets, privately printed, 1911.
Poems, privately printed, 1911.
An Ode for Music, privately printed, 1912.
Hyacinth: An Idyll, privately printed, 1912.
Amyntas, privately printed, 1913.
(Under pseudonym Saul Kain) *The Daffodil Murderer, Being the Chantrey Prize Poem,* John Richmond, 1913.
Discoveries, privately printed, 1915.
The Redeemer, W. Heffer, 1916.
To Any Dead Officer, Severs, 1917.
The Old Huntsman and Other Poems, Heinemann, 1917, Dutton, 1918.
Counter-Attack and Other Poems, introduction by Robert Nichols, Dutton, 1918.
Four Poems, Severs, 1918.
The War Poems of Siegfried Sassoon, Heinemann, 1919, reprinted, Faber, 1983.
Picture Show, privately printed, 1919, enlarged edition, Dutton, 1920.
Recreations, privately printed, 1923.
Lingual Exercises for Advanced Vocabularians, privately printed, 1925.
Selected Poems, Heinemann, 1925.
Satirical Poems, Viking, 1926, enlarged edition, Heinemann, 1933.
Siegfried Sassoon, Benn, 1926.
Nativity, designs by Paul Nash, Rudge, 1927.
The Heart's Journey, Crosby Gaige, 1927.
To My Mother, illustrations by Stephen Tennant, Faber & Gwyer, 1928.
On Chatterton: A Sonnet, privately printed, 1930.
In Sicily, illustrations by Tennant, Faber, 1930.
(Under pseudonym Pinchbeck Lyre) *Poems,* Duckworth, 1931.
To the Red Rose, illustrations by Tennant, Faber, 1931.
Prehistoric Burials, illustrations by Witold Gordon, Knopf, 1932.
The Road to Ruin, Faber, 1933.
Vigils, Douglas Cleverdon, 1934, enlarged edition, Heinemann, 1935, Viking, 1936.
Rhymed Ruminations, Chiswick Press, 1939, enlarged edition, Faber, 1940, Viking, 1941.
Poems Newly Selected, 1916-1935, Faber, 1940.
Early Morning Long Ago, Chiswick Press, 1941.
Selected Poems, Eyre & Spottiswoode, 1943.
Collected Poems, Faber, 1947, Viking, 1949.
Common Chords, Mill House Press, 1950.
Emblems of Experience, Rampant Lions Press, 1951.
The Tasking, Cambridge University Press, 1954.
Faith Unfaithful, Stanbrook Abbey, c. 1954.

Renewals, Stanbrook Abbey, 1954.

(Under pseudonym S. S.) *An Adjustment,* foreword by Philip Gosse, Golden Head Press, 1955.

Sequences, Faber, 1956, Viking, 1957.

Poems, selected by Dennis Silk, Marlborough College Press, 1958.

Lenten Illuminations and Sight Sufficient, privately printed, 1958, Downside Review, 1959.

The Path to Peace: Selected Poems, Stanbrook Abbey Press, 1960.

Arbor Vitae and Unfoldment, Stanbrook Abbey Press, 1960.

Awaitment, Stanbrook Abbey Press, 1960.

A Prayer at Pentecost, Stanbrook Abbey Press, 1960.

Collected Poems, 1908-1956, Faber, 1961, reprinted, 1986.

Something about Myself, illustrations by Margaret Adams, Stanbrook Abbey Press, 1966.

An Octave: 8 September 1966, Arts Council of Great Britain, 1966.

Selected Poems, Faber, 1968.

A Poet's Pilgrimage, edited by Felicitas Corrigan, Gollancz, 1973.

PROSE

(Published anonymously) *Memoirs of a Fox-Hunting Man* (novel), Faber & Gwyer, 1928, Coward, 1929, new edition, Faber, 1954.

(Published anonymously) *Memoirs of an Infantry Officer* (novel), Faber, 1930, (published under name Seigfried Sassoon) Coward-McCann, 1930, reprinted with illustrations by Barnett Freedman, Faber, 1966, Collier, 1969.

Sherston's Progress (novel), Doubleday, Doran, 1936.

The Memoirs of George Sherston (contains *Memoirs of a Fox-Hunting Man, Memoirs of an Infantry Officer,* and *Sherston's Progress*), Doubleday, Doran, 1937, reprinted, Stackpole Books, 1967 (published in England as *The Complete Memoirs of George Sherston,* Faber, 1937, reprinted, 1964).

The Old Century and Seven More Years (autobiography), Faber, 1938, Viking, 1939, reprinted with introduction by Michael Thorpe, Faber, 1968.

On Poetry: Arthur Skemp Memorial Lecture, University of Bristol, 1939.

The Flower Show Match and Other Pieces, Faber, 1941.

The Weald of Youth (autobiography), Viking, 1942.

Siegfried's Journey, 1916-1920 (autobiography), Faber, 1945, Viking, 1946, reprinted, White Lion, 1973.

Meredith, A Biography, Viking, 1948.

(Author of introduction) Isaac Rosenberg, *The Collected Poems,* Chatto & Windus, 1962.

Letters to a Critic, introduction and notes by Michael Thorpe, Kent Editions, 1976.

Siegfried Sassoon Diaries, 1915-1918, edited by Rupert Hart-Davis, Faber, 1981.

Siegfried Sassoon Diaries, 1920-1922, edited by Hart-Davis, Faber, 1983.

SIDELIGHTS: Siegfried Sassoon is best known for his angry and compassionate poems of the First World War, which brought him public and critical acclaim. Avoiding the sentimentality and jingoism of many war poets, Sassoon wrote of the horror and brutality of trench warfare and contemptuously satirized generals, politicians, and churchmen for their incompetence and their blind support of the war. His later poems, often concerned with religious themes, were less appreciated, but the autobiographical trilogy *The Complete Memoirs of George Sherston* won him two major awards.

Born into a wealthy Jewish family, sometimes called the "Rothschilds of the East" because the family fortune was made in India, Sassoon lived the leisurely life of a cultivated country gentleman before the First World War, pursuing his two major interests, poetry and fox hunting. His early work, which was privately printed in several slim volumes between 1906 and 1916, is considered minor and imitative, heavily influenced by John Masefield (of whose work *The Daffodil Murderer* is a parody).

Following the outbreak of the First World War, Sassoon served with the Royal Welch Fusiliers, seeing action in France in late 1915. He received a Military Cross for bringing back a wounded soldier during heavy fire. After being wounded in action, Sassoon wrote an open letter of protest to the war department, refusing to fight any more. "I believe that this War is being deliberately prolonged by those who have the power to end it," he wrote in the letter. At the urging of Bertrand Russell, the letter was read in the House of Commons. Sassoon expected to be court-martialed for his protest, but poet Robert Graves intervened on his behalf, arguing that Sassoon was suffering from shell-shock and needed medical treatment. In 1917, Sassoon was hospitalized.

Counter-Attack and Other Poems collects some of Sassoon's best war poems, all of which are "harshly realistic laments or satires," according to Margaret B. McDowell in the *Dictionary of Literary Biography.* The later collection *The War Poems of Siegfried Sassoon* included 64 poems of the war, most written while Sassoon was in hospital recovering from his injuries. Public reaction to Sassoon's poetry was fierce. Some readers complained that the poet displayed little patriotism, while others found his shockingly realistic depiction of war to be too extreme. Even pacifist friends complained about the violence and graphic detail in his work. But the British public bought the books because, in his best poems, Sassoon captured the feeling of trench warfare and the weariness of British soldiers for a war that seemed never to end. "The dynamic quality of his war poems," according to a critic for the *Times Literary Supplement,* "was due to the intensity of feeling which underlay their cynicism." "In the history of British poetry," McDowell wrote, "[Sassoon] will be remembered primarily for some one hundred poems . . . in which he protested the continuation of World War I."

After the war, Sassoon became involved in Labour Party politics, lectured on pacifism, and continued to write. His most successful works of this period were his trilogy of autobiographical novels, *The Memoirs of George Sherston.* In these, he gave a thinly-fictionalized account, with little changed except names, of his wartime experiences, contrasting them with his nostalgic memories of country life before the war and recounting the growth of his pacifist feelings. Some have maintained that Sassoon's best work is his prose, particularly the first two Sherston novels. *Memoirs of a Fox Hunting Man* was described by a critic for the *Springfield Republican* as "a novel of wholly fresh and delightful content," and Robert Littrell of *Bookman* called it "a singular and a strangely beautiful book."

That book's sequel was also well received. The *New Statesman* critic called *Memoirs of an Infantry Officer* "a document of intense and sensitive humanity." In a review for the *Times Literary Supplement,* after Sassoon's death, one critic wrote: "His one real masterpiece, *Memoirs of an Infantry Officer* . . . is consistently fresh. His self scrutiny is candid, critical, and humourous. . . . If Sassoon had written as well as this consistently, he would have been a figure of real stature. As it is, English literature has one great work from him almost by accident."

Sassoon's critical biography of Victorian novelist and poet George Meredith was also well received. In this volume, he recounted numerous anecdotes about Meredith, portraying him vividly as a person as well as an author: "The reader lays the book down with the feeling that a great author has become one of his close neighbors," wrote G. F. Whicher in the *New York Herald Tribune Weekly Book Review.* The critical portions of the book were also praised, though some found the writing careless. But the *New Yorker* critic noted Sassoon's "fresh and lively literary criticism," and the reviewer for the *Times Literary Supplement* declared that "Mr. Sassoon gives us a poet's estimate, considered with intensity of insight, skilfully shaped as biography, and written with certainty of style."

In 1957 Sassoon became a convert to Catholicism. For some time before, his spiritual concerns had been the predominant subject of his writing. Though his later poems are usually considered markedly inferior to those written between 1917 and 1920, *Sequences* (published shortly before his conversion) has been praised by some critics. Derek Stanford, in *Books and Bookmen,* claimed that "the poems in *Sequences* constitute some of the most impressive religious poetry of this century."

Speaking of Sassoon's war poetry in a 1981 issue of the *Spectator,* P. J. Kavanagh claimed that "today they ring as true as they ever did; it is difficult to see how they could be better." Looking back over Sassoon's long literary career, Peter Levi wrote in *Poetry Review:* "One can experience in his poetry the slow, restless ripening of a very great talent; its magnitude has not yet been recognised. . . . He is one of the few poets of his generation we are really unable to do without."

BIOGRAPHICAL/CRITICAL SOURCES:

BOOKS

Contemporary Literary Criticism, Volume 36, Gale, 1986.
Corrigan, Felicitas, *Siegfried Sassoon: A Poet's Pilgrimage,* Gollancz, 1973.
Dictionary of Literary Biography, Volume 20: *British Poets, 1914-1945,* Gale, 1983.
Fussell, Paul, *The Great War and Modern Memory,* Oxford University Press, 1975.
Keynes, Geoffrey, *A Bibliography of Siegfried Sassoon,* Hart-Davis, 1962.
Sassoon, Siegfried, *The Memoirs of George Sherston,* Doubleday, Doran, 1937.
Sassoon, *The Old Century and Seven More Years,* Viking, 1939.
Sassoon, *The Weald of Youth,* Viking, 1942.
Sassoon, *Siegfried's Journey, 1916-1920,* Viking, 1946.
Sassoon, *Siegfried Sassoon Diaries, 1915-1918,* edited by Rupert Hart-Davis, Faber, 1981.
Sassoon, *Siegfried Sassoon Diaries, 1920-1922,* edited by Hart-Davis, Faber, 1983.
Thorpe, Michael, *Siegfried Sassoon: A Critical Study,* Oxford University Press, 1966.

PERIODICALS

Bookman, March, 1929.
Books and Bookmen, November, 1973.
New Statesman, September 20, 1930.
New Yorker, October 9, 1948.
New York Herald Tribune Weekly Book Review, October 24, 1948.
New York Times, January 27, 1918, February 3, 1929, October 12, 1930, January 2, 1949.
Poetry, August, 1936.
Poetry Review, autumn, 1966.

Saturday Review of Literature, February 23, 1929, January 29, 1949.
Spectator, October, 17, 1981.
Springfield Republican, March 3, 1929.
Times Literary Supplement, July 11, 1918, June 3, 1926, November 1, 1947, September 18, 1948, January 4, 1957, December 7, 1973.

OBITUARIES:

PERIODICALS

Newsweek, September 18, 1967.
New York Times, September 3, 1967.
Publishers Weekly, September 18, 1967.
Time, September 15, 1967.
Times (London), September 4, 1967.

* * *

SATTERFIELD, Charles
See del REY, Lester and POHL, Frederik

* * *

SAUNDERS, Caleb
See HEINLEIN, Robert A(nson)

* * *

SAUSER-HALL, Frederic 1887-1961
(Blaise Cendrars)

PERSONAL: Born September 1, 1887, in Paris, France; died January 21, 1961, in Paris; married second wife (an actress); children: two sons. *Education:* University of Paris, B.A., 1907.

CAREER: Writer. Worked variously in business, horticulture, journalism, and motion pictures. *Military service:* Served with French Foreign Legion during World War I.

WRITINGS:

UNDER PSEUDONYM BLAISE CENDRARS; IN ENGLISH

Le Panama; ou, Les Aventures de mes sept oncles, [Paris], 1918, translation by John Dos Passos published as *Panama; or, The Adventures of My Seven Uncles,* Harper, 1931.
(Compiler) *L'Anthologie negre,* Editions de la Sirene, 1921, revised edition, Correa, 1947, reprinted, Le Livre de Poche, 1972, translation by Margery Bianco published as *The African Saga,* Payson & Clarke, 1927, reprinted, Negro University Press, 1969.
Kodak, Stock, 1924, translation by Ron Padgett published under same title, *Adventures in Poetry,* 1976.
L'Or: La Merveilleuse Histoire du general Johann August Suter (novel), B. Grasset, 1925, reprinted, 1964, translation by Henry Longan Stuart published as *Sutter's Gold,* Harper, 1926, published as *Gold: Being the Marvelous History of General John Augustus Sutter,* translation by Nina Rootes, Michael Kesend, 1984.
Moravagine (novel), B. Grasset, 1926, reprinted, 1956, translation by Alan Brown published under same title, P. Owen, 1968, Projection Books, 1970.
Dan Yack, Volume 1: *Le Plan de l'aiguille,* Au Sans Pariel, 1927, translation by Rootes published as *Dan Yack,* Michael Kesend, 1987, Volume 2: *Les Confessions de Dan Yack,* [Paris], 1929, translation by Rootes published as *Confessions of Dan Yack,* P. Owen, 1990, published together in

one-volume edition, [Paris], 1946, translation published as *Antarctic Fugue,* Pushkin Press, 1948.

Petite contes negres pour les enfants des blancs, [Paris], 1928, translation by Bianco published as *Little Black Stories for Little White Children,* Payson & Clarke, 1929.

Une nuit dans la foret, [France], 1929, translation by Margaret K. Ewing published as *Night in the Forest,* University of Missouri Press, 1985.

(Editor) Hans Bringolf, *I Have No Regrets: Being the Memoirs of Lieutenant Bringolf,* translated from the original French by Warre B. Wells, Jarrolds, 1931.

L'Homme foudroye (autobiographical novel), Denoel, 1945, reprinted, Gallimard, 1973, translation by Rootes published as *The Astonished Man,* Owen, 1970.

La Main Coupee (title means "The Cut-off Hand"), Denoel, 1946, reprinted, Gallimard, 1973, translation by Rootes published as *Lice,* Owen, 1973.

Bourlinguer (title means "Reminiscences"), Denoel, 1948, abridged translation by Rootes published as *Planus,* Owen, 1972.

Emmene-moi au bout du monde!, Denoel, 1956, translation by Brown published as *To the End of the World,* P. Owen, 1967.

Selected Writings, translated from the original French, edited by Walter Albert, New Directions, 1966, reprinted as *Selected Writings of Blaise Cendrars,* Greenwood Press, 1978.

Complete Postcards From the Americas: Poems of Road and Sea, translated from the original French, University of California Press, 1976.

Pathe Baby, translated from the original French, City Lights, 1980.

Knockabout, Scarborough House, 1982.

Shadow (juvenile), translation and with illustrations by Marcia Brown, Scribner's, 1982.

UNDER PSEUDONYM BLAISE CENDRARS; IN FRENCH

La Legende de novgorode, [France], 1909.

Sequences, [France], 1912.

Les Paques a New York, [France], 1912.

La Prose du trans-siberien et la petite Jehanne de France (title means "The Prose of the Trans-Siberian and of Little Jehanne of France"), [France], 1913, reprinted as *Le Trans-siberien,* P. Seghers, 1957.

Profound aujourd'hui, LaBelle, 1917.

J'ai tue, [France], 1918.

Du Monde entier au coeur du monde (poems; title means "From the Entire World"), Editions de la Nouvelle revue francaise, 1919, reprinted, Denoel, 1957.

(With Abel Gance) *J'accuse,* [France], 1919.

Dix neuf poemes elastiques (title means "Nineteen Elastic Poems"), [France], 1919.

La Fin du monde, Editions de la Sirene, 1919, reprinted, P. Seghers, 1949.

J'ai saigne, [France], 1920.

(With Gance) *La Roue,* [France], 1922.

Feuilles de route, Au Sans Pareil, 1924.

ABC de cinema, [France], 1926.

L'Eloge de la vie dangereuse, [France], 1926.

Rhum: L'Aventure de Jean Galmot, B. Grasset, 1930, reprinted, 1960.

Aujourd'hui, B. Grasset, 1931.

Vol a voiles (autobiographical), Payot, 1932.

Hollywood: La Mecque de cinema, B. Grasset, 1936.

(Translator) O. Henry, *Hors la Loi!: La Vie d'outlaw american racontee par lui-meme,* [France], 1936.

Histoires vraies, B. Grasset, 1938.

La Vie dangereuse (title means "The Dangerous Life"), B. Grasset, 1938.

D'Oultremer a indigo, B. Grasset, 1940.

Poesies completes, Denoel, 1944.

Blaise Cendrars, Nouvelle Revue critique, 1947.

Oeuvres choisies, [France], 1948.

La Banlieue de Paris, La Builde du livre, 1949.

Le Lotissement du ciel (title means "Heaven in Lots"), Denoel, 1949.

Blaise Cendrars vous parle, Denoel, 1952.

Le Bresil: Des Hommes sont venus, Documents d'art, 1952.

Trop c'est trop (title means "Too Much"), Denoel, 1957.

A L'Aventure, Denoel, 1958.

Films sans images, Denoel, 1959.

Saint Joseph de Cupertino, Club de livre chretien, 1960.

Amours (poems), P. Seghers, 1961.

Blaise Cendrars, 1887-1961, Mercure de France, 1962.

Serajevo, Theatre universitaire, 1963.

Oeuvres completes, eight volumes, Club francais du livre, 1968-71.

Dites-nous, Monsieur Blaise Cendrars, edited by Hughes Richard, Editions Recontre, 1969.

Ineduts secrets, Club francais du livre, 1969.

SIDELIGHTS: When Blaise Cendrars ran away from home at age fifteen, he embarked on the first of many journeys that would span his lifetime and take him to such places as Siberia, Panama, China, Persia, Mongolia, North America, and the greater part of Europe. His novels and poems, celebrated for their rich images and striking effects, are largely autobiographical, evolved from his own experiences and travels.

BIOGRAPHICAL/CRITICAL SOURCES:

BOOKS

Blaise Cendrars: Discovery and Re-Creation, University of Toronto Press, 1978.

Contemporary Literary Criticism, Volume 18, Gale, 1981.

PERIODICALS

Chicago Tribune Book World, August 1, 1982.

Los Angeles Times, November 24, 1987.

Newsweek, April 9, 1984.

New York Times Book Review, August 4, 1968, October 3, 1982, March 18, 1984, March 13, 1988.

Paris Review, April, 1966.

Times Literary Supplement, February 16, 1967, February 4, 1983, May 29, 1987, January 26, 1990.

OBITUARIES:

PERIODICALS

New York Times, January 22, 1961.

Publishers Weekly, February 13, 1961.

*   *   *

SAYERS, Dorothy L(eigh) 1893-1957
(H. P. Rallentando)

PERSONAL: Born June 13, 1893, in Oxford, England; died of a thrombosis, December 17, 1957, in Witham, Essex, England; daughter of Henry (a clergyman and schoolmaster) and Helen Mary (one source says Helen May; maiden name, Leigh) Sayers; married Oswald Atherton (one source says Oswald Arthur) "Mac" Fleming (a journalist) in 1926 (died, 1950); children: one son. *Education:* Somerville College, Oxford, earned first class honors, 1915, B.A., M.A., B.C.L., all in 1920. *Religion:* Anglican.

ADDRESSES: Home—24 Newland St., Witham, Essex, England; and 24 Great James St., London W.C.1., England.

CAREER: Hull High School for Girls, Yorkshire, England, teacher, 1915-17; Blackwell's (publishers), Oxford, England, editor, 1917-19; Ecole des Roches (boys' school), Normandy, France, teacher, 1919-20; Benson's (advertising agency), London, England, copywriter, 1922-31; full-time writer, 1931-57.

MEMBER: Modern Language Association (president, 1939-45), Detection Club (president, 1949-57, and co-founder).

AWARDS, HONORS: D.Litt. from University of Durham, 1950.

WRITINGS:

POETRY

Op. I, Longmans, Green, 1916.
Catholic Tales and Christian Songs, McBride, 1918.
(Contributor and editor with Wilfred R. Childe and Earp) *Oxford Poetry, 1917,* Blackwell, 1918.
(Contributor and editor with Earp and E. F. A. Geach) *Oxford Poetry, 1918,* Blackwell, 1919.
(Contributor and editor with Earp and Siegfried Sassoon) *Oxford Poetry, 1919,* Blackwell, 1920.
Lord, I Thank Thee, Overbrook, 1943.

EDITED WORKS

Great Short Stories of Detection, Mystery, and Horror, Gollancz, 1928, published as *The Omnibus of Crime,* Payson & Clarke, 1929, abridged edition published as *Human and Inhuman Stories,* Macfadden-Bartell, 1963.
Great Short Stories of Detection, Mystery, and Horror—Second Series, Gollancz, 1931, published as *The Second Omnibus of Crime,* Coward-McCann, 1932, published as *The World's Greatest Crime Stories,* Blue Ribbon, 1932.
Great Short Stories of Detection, Mystery, and Horror-Third Series, Gollancz, 1934, published as *The Third Omnibus of Crime,* Coward-McCann, 1935.
Tales of Detection, Dent, 1936, published as *Great Tales of Detection: Nineteen Stories,* 1976.
(With Muriel St. Clare Byrne) *Bridgeheads,* Methuen, 1941-46.

CRIME NOVELS

Whose Body?, Boni & Liveright, 1923, reprinted, Harper, 1987.
Clouds of Witness, Unwin, 1925, Dial, 1927, reprinted, Harper, 1987.
Unnatural Death, Benn, 1927, reprinted, Harper, 1987, published as *The Dawson Pedigree,* Dial, 1928, illustrated edition published under original title, Gollancz, 1972.
The Unpleasantness at the Bellona Club, Payson & Clarke, 1928, reprinted as *The Unpleasantness at the Bellona Club: A Lord Peter Wimsey Mystery with Harriet Vane,* Harper, 1986.
(With Robert Eustace) *The Documents in the Case,* Brewer & Warren, 1930, reprinted, Harper, 1987.
Strong Poison, Brewer & Warren, 1930, reprinted as *Strong Poison: A Lord Peter Wimsey Mystery with Harriet Vane,* Harper, 1987.
Suspicious Characters, Brewer, Warren & Putnam, 1931 (published in England as *The Five Red Herrings,* Gollancz, 1931, crime series edition, New English Library, 1972).
(With members of the Detection Club) *The Floating Admiral,* Hodder & Stoughton, 1931, Doubleday, Doran, 1932.

Have His Carcase, Warren & Putnam, 1932, reprinted, New English Library, 1974, reprinted as *Have His Carcase: A Lord Peter Wimsey Mystery with Harriet Vane,* Harper, 1987.
Murder Must Advertise: A Detective Story, Harcourt, 1933, reprinted, Harper, 1986.
(With members of the Detection Club) *Ask a Policeman,* Mortow, 1933, reprinted, Berkely Publishing, 1987.
The Nine Tailors: Changes Rung on an Old Theme in Two Short Touches and Two Full Peals, Harcourt, 1934, modern classics edition, Harcourt, Brace, 1962, reprinted, New English Library, 1972.
Gaudy Night, Gollancz, 1935, Harcourt, 1936, reprinted as *Gaudy Night: A Lord Wimsey Mystery with Harriet Vane,* Harper, 1988.
Busman's Honeymoon: A Love Story With Detective Interruptions (adapted from the play "Busman's Honeymoon,"), Harcourt, 1937, reprinted, Harper, 1987.
(With members of the Detection Club) *Double Death: A Murder Story,* edited by John Chancellor, Gollancz, 1939.
(With others) *Crime on the Coast and No Flowers by Request,* Berkley Publishing, 1987.

SHORT STORY COLLECTIONS

Lord Peter Views the Body, Gollancz, 1928, Payson & Charles, 1929, reprinted, Harper, 1986.
Hangman's Holiday, Harcourt, 1933, abridged edition (omits "Sleuths on the Scent" and "Murder in the Morning"), Bestseller Mysteries, c. 1942, reprinted, Harper, 1987.
(With others) *Six Against Scotland Yard,* Doubleday, 1936 (published in England as *Six Against the Yard: In Which Margery Allingham, Anthony Berkeley, Freeman Wills Crofts, Dorothy L. Sayers, and Russell Thorndike Commit the Crime of Murder, Which Ex-Superintendent Cornish, C.I.D., Is Called Upon to Solve,* Selwyn & Blount, 1936.
In the Teeth of the Evidence, and Other Stories, Gollancz, 1939, Harcourt, 1940, reprinted, Harper, 1987.
Even the Parrot: Exemplary Conversations for Enlightened Children, illustrations by Sillince, Methuen, 1944.
A Treasury of Sayers Stories (contains the texts of *Lord Peter Views the Body* and *Hangman's Holiday*), Gollancz, 1958.
Lord Peter: A Collection of All the Lord Peter Wimsey Stories, edited by James Sandoe, coda by Carolyn Heilbrun, and codetta by E. C. Bentley, Harper, 1972, 2nd edition (includes three final Lord Peter Wimsey stories), Harper, 1972, reprinted, 1987.
Striding Folly: Including the Three Final Lord Peter Wimsey Stories, introduction by Janet Hitchman, New English Library, 1972.

Also contributed stories to numerous anthologies.

ESSAYS

The Greatest Drama Ever Staged (contains "The Greatest Drama Ever Staged" and "The Triumph of Easter"; both originally published in the *Sunday Times,* April, 1938), Hodder & Stoughton, 1939.
Strong Meat, Hodder & Stoughton, 1939.
Begin Here: A War-Time Essay, Gollancz, 1940, published as *Begin Here: A Statement of Faith,* Harcourt, 1941.
The Mind of the Maker, Harcourt, 1941, reprinted, Greenwood Press, 1971.
Unpopular Opinions, Gollancz, 1946, Harcourt, 1947.
Creed or Chaos? and Other Essays in Popular Theology, Methuen, 1946, Harcourt, 1949.
(With others) *The Great Mystery of Life Hereafter,* Hodder Stoughton, 1957.

The Poetry of Search and the Poetry of Statement, and Other Post-humous Essays on Literature, Religion, and Language, Gollancz, 1963.

Christian Letters to a Post-Christian World: A Selection of Essays, selected and introduced by Roderick Jellema, Eerdmans, 1969, published as *The Whimsical Christian: Eighteen Essays,* Macmillan [New York], 1978.

Are Women Human?, introduction by Mary McDermott Shideler, Eerdmans, 1971.

A Matter of Eternity: Selections From the Writings of Dorothy L. Sayers, edited by Rosamond Kent Sprague, Eerdmans, 1973.

PLAYS

(With Muriel St. Clare Byrne) *Busman's Honeymoon: A Detective Comedy in Three Acts* (first produced in the West End at Comedy Theatre, December 16, 1936; produced in Mt. Kiscoe, N.Y., at the Westchester Playhouse, July 12, 1937), Gollancz, 1937, Dramatists Play Service, 1939.

The Zeal of Thy House (four scenes; first produced at the Canterbury Festival in England, June 12, 1937; produced in the West End at Westminster Theatre, March 29, 1938), Harcourt, Brace, 1937, reprinted with preface and notes by C. H. Rieu, Methuen, 1961.

He That Should Come: A Nativity Play in One Act (radio play; first broadcast by the British Broadcasting Corp., December 25, 1938), Gollancz, 1939.

The Devil to Pay: Being the Famous History of John Faustus, the Conjurer of Wittenberg in Germany: How He Sold His Immortal Soul to the Enemy of Mankind, and Was Served Twenty-four Years by Mephistopheles, and Obtained Helen of Troy to His Paramour, With Many Other Marvels; and How God Dealt With Him at the Last (four scenes; first produced at the Canterbury Festival, June 10, 1939, produced in the West End at His Majesty's Theatre, July 20, 1939), Harcourt, 1939.

Love All (first produced in London at Torch Theatre, April 10, 1940), Kent State University Press, 1984.

"The Golden Cockerel" (radio play; adapted from the story of the same title by Aleksander Pushkin), first broadcast by British Broadcasting Corp., December 27, 1941.

The Man Born to Be King: A Play-Cycle on the Life of Our Lord and Saviour Jesus Christ (twelve-episode radio series; first broadcast by the British Broadcasting Corp., December, 1941, to October, 1942), Gollancz, 1943, Harper, 1949.

The Just Vengeance (first produced in Lichfield, England, June 15, 1946), Gollancz, 1946.

(With members of the Detection Club) "Where Do We Go From Here?" (radio play), first broadcast for the "Mystery Playhouse" series by British Broadcasting Corp., 1948.

The Emperor Constantine: A Chronicle (first produced at the Colchester Festival in England, at the Playhouse Theatre, July 3, 1951; abridged version produced in London as "Christ's Emperor," February 5, 1952), Harper, 1951.

Also author of episodes for British Broadcasting Corp. radio series "Behind the Screen" (episode of June 28, 1930) and "The Scoop" (episodes of January 10, 1931, and April 4, 1931).

CRITICISM

Introductory Papers on Dante, Methuen, 1954, Harper, 1955.

Further Papers on Dante, Harper, 1957, reprinted, Greenwood Press, 1980.

Wilkie Collins: A Critical and Biographical Study, edited by E. R. Gregory, Friends of the Toledo Public Libraries, 1977.

OTHER

Papers Relating to the Family of Wimsey, privately printed, 1936.

An Account of Lord Mortimer Wimsey, the Hermit of the Wash, privately printed, 1937.

The Wimsey Papers, published serially in *Spectator,* November 24, 1939-January 26, 1940.

The Days of Christ's Coming (juvenile), illustrations by Fritz Wegner, Harper, 1960.

The Wimsey Family: A Fragmentary History Compiled from Correspondence With Dorothy L. Sayers, compiled by C. W. Scott-Giles, Harper, 1977.

Also translator of several books. Contributor of essays to and author of introduction for several books. Contributed poems, essays, and stories to periodicals, including *Time and Tide, Times Literary Supplement, Atlantic Monthly, London Mercury, Ellery Queen's Mystery Magazine, London Mercury, Sewanee Review, National Review, Punch, Saturday Review of Literature, Spectator,* and *Times Literary Supplement.* Also author of a poem for the Westminster *Gazette* under the pseudonym H. P. Rallentando and of numerous book reviews for the *London Sunday Times.*

WORK IN PROGRESS: Cat O'Mary, an unfinished novel.

SIDELIGHTS: Dorothy L. Sayers achieved her greatest recognition for her eleven novels and twenty-one short stories featuring the aristocratic, Oxford-educated amateur sleuth Lord Peter Wimsey. The Wimsey mysteries and Sayers's essays on the history and aesthetics of detective fiction, which with the exception of one short story were published in the two decades between the World Wars, established the author as one of the foremost practitioners and defenders of detective fiction during the golden age of the British mystery.

In her works about Wimsey, Sayers constantly experimented with and expanded the mystery formula. She invented innovative methods for murder, such as injecting an air bubble into an artery or copper-plating a victim. She broke the rules she herself helped establish as a member of the group of writers that called themselves the Detection Club—the principle, for example, that love should not take a dominant role in a detective story: in breaking these rules, she moved detective fiction in the direction of the novel of manners. She worked toward a high standard of artistic craftsmanship, achieved most notably in her novels *The Nine Tailors* and *Gaudy Night,* both of which present complex characters and intertwine the solving of a crime with moral and social themes.

Sayers's clever plots, appealing characters, witty dialogue, social satire, and well-drawn settings have brought the Wimsey novels popular success and critical accolades, both before and since her death in 1957. Scholar and mystery writer Carolyn Heilburn remarked in an essay for *American Scholar* that "many a detective story reader . . . would, if they could, offer her resurrection on condition that she produce more Lord Peter novels." Between 1972 and 1975, the British Broadcasting Corporation (BBC-TV) televised versions of five of the Wimsey novels, thereby introducing Wimsey to a new generation of readers who responded as enthusiastically to Sayers's mysteries as had earlier generations; as a result, her mysteries—both the novels and the short stories—were reissued in paperback editions. In addition, the revival of interest in Wimsey directed attention to previously unpublished Sayers manuscripts: the short story "Talboys" (written in 1942), which features Wimsey, his wife Harriet, and their three sons, was printed in the second edition of the *Lord Peter* short story collection; a final unfinished Wimsey novel entitled *Thrones,*

Dominations is archived in the Marion E. Wade Collection at Wheaton College in Illinois; and papers, speeches, and newspaper clippings detailing the history of the Wimsey family back to the time of William the Conqueror have been compiled by C. W. Scott-Giles in *The Wimsey Family.*

Sayers's writings also include critical discussions of the detective story that have long been acknowledged as first-rate introductions to the genre. Even critic Julian Symons, who discussed Sayers "from a point of view a long way short of idolatry" in his book *Mortal Consequences,* stated that Sayers's introductions to the three-volume collection *Great Short Stories of Detection, Mystery, and Horror* show "an acute intelligence at work." In her history and criticism of the mystery genre, especially the introductions mentioned by Symons and her 1935 essay "Aristotle on Detective Fiction," Sayers analyzed the works of Edgar Allan Poe, Arthur Conan Doyle, Wilkie Collins, and E. C. Bentley, the masters and shapers of the genre and writers who strongly influenced her own mystery writing. Conceding that detective fiction did not begin to flower until the mid-nineteenth century when societies came to see their constabularies as more heroic than their criminals, Sayers identified a fascination with detection in such early works of literature as the *Aeneid,* Aesop's *Fables,* and the apocryphal books of the Bible. In addition to these writings about detective fiction, Sayers collected materials throughout her life for a proposed biography of nineteenth-century mystery novelist Wilkie Collins. E. R. Gregory edited Sayers's manuscripts on Collins and completed the biography in 1977.

Critics have noted several major themes that reappear in Sayers's writings. "The sacramental value of work," argued Margaret P. Hannay in the introduction to *As Her Whimsey Took Her: Critical Essays on the Work of Dorothy L. Sayers,* "is the theme which unifies Dorothy L. Sayers's writings in many genres." Elsewhere in *As Her Whimsey Took Her,* critic Alzina Stone Dale identified as common to Sayers's works the author's whimsical sense of humor, her Christian convictions, and her ability to translate ideas from one generation to another. In the *Sayers Review,* Joe R. Christopher presented Carole Sperous's definition of the unifying links in Sayers's writings: "The dramatic character of the incarnation and the absolute necessity and relevancy of doctrine; . . . the significance of creativity and work; . . . beliefs about education and the process of thinking; and . . . views about women." Leroy Lad Panek, contradicting any view that separates Sayers's mysteries from her religious writings, contended in *Watteau's Shepherds,* that the writer's detective novels may be her "best pieces of theology."

Although readers can detect biographical elements in the Wimsey canon, most critics, including Tischler, stress Wimsey's literary parentage. Trevor H. Hall argued in *Dorothy L. Sayers: Nine Literary Studies* that Sherlock Holmes influenced the characterization of Wimsey, a plausible theory, given Sayers's series of essays on Holmes and Watson. Hall notes references to Holmes and Watson in the Wimsey canon, Wimsey's scientific knowledge, his interests in books and music, and his address: 10 A, almost half of Holmes's 221 B. Panek noted that Wimsey, who examines crime scenes using his monocle, his cane, his matchbox, and his servant Bunter—as photographer—resembles R. Austin Freeman's scientific detective Dr. Thorndyke. Panek suggested further that Sayers may well have intended to parody the "strong, silent, quietly intelligent, stern-faced Englishmen" who were popular as literary detectives in the decade before she began to write. Certainly, her Wimsey is the antithesis of this stereotype: he is short, pampered, garrulous, and not particularly attractive.

Among critics, Wimsey has always been a controversial character. In *The Dyer's Hand and Other Essays,* W. H. Auden referred to Wimsey as a "priggish superman"; in *Mortal Consequences,* Julian Symons called Sayers's mysteries "ludicrously snobbish." Wimsey is seen as a prig and a snob, no doubt, because of his aristocratic tastes, habits, behavior, and possessions. In Sayers's short stories "The Entertaining Episode of the Article in Question" and "The Fascinating Problem of Uncle Meleager's Will," collected in *Lord Peter Views the Body,* an overrefined Wimsey wears mauve silk pajamas, sings French songs in his bath, refers to himself as "Tory, if anything," lives in an apartment filled with daffodils, and dresses to perfection, thanks to Bunter's ministrations. E. C. Bentley's delightful parody "Greedy Night" emphasized other signs of Wimsey's upper-class life-style: his collection of incunabula—books printed during the fifteenth century—his Oxford education, his love of vintage wines and gourmet food, his expensive cars, and his membership in several exclusive clubs. In *The Puritan Pleasures of the Detective Story,* Eric Routley denied that Sayers's creation was an act of snobbery: "Once you have accepted his background and met his relatives as rarely as is decent," Routley wrote, "you have heard the last of English high life. Not one of the stories is placed in a country house, and there are fewer aristocratic titles per story than there are in the Holmes or the Poirot adventures."

In several of Sayers's short stories, such as "The Abominable History of the Man With Copper Fingers" and "The Incredible Elopement of Lord Peter Wimsey," Wimsey acts, god-like, to bring about justice. In *The Nine Tailors,* however, Sayers blends the detective formula and theological concerns to create a rich, complex novel, and Peter Wimsey is shown as a spiritual man, not a sanctimonious one. Many critics, such as John Cawelti, Lionel Basney, and Eric Routley, praised the novel as Sayers's finest. In *As Her Whimsey Took Her* Basney lauded the book's ambiguities and ironies as it presents guilt and innocence. John Cawelti declared, in *Adventure, Mystery, and Romance,* "Miss Sayers's powers of invention, organization, mystification, and style seem to have reached their peak in *The Nine Tailors,* perhaps because this story deeply embodied her own deepest social and religious feelings . . . and her sense of what was most basic about the detective story." In this novel, Wimsey, stranded in Fenchurch St. Paul when his car runs off the road, agrees to aid the innocent, good-hearted Reverend Venables by replacing an ill bellringer at the New Year's Eve nine-hour change-ringing. Much later Wimsey himself is nearly killed by the bells while trapped in the belfry as a flood-warning peal is sounded, and he realizes that he and the other ringers unknowingly killed a man as they rang the bells at the New Year. Wimsey comes to recognize that life is a mystery no detective can resolve, that sin inevitably brings its own punishment, and that all humans are both murderers and victims.

Critics have lauded Sayers's development of Peter Wimsey's character from the frivolous "Oh, Damn!" that begins *Whose Body?* to the heartrending "Oh, Damn!" that closes *Busman's Honeymoon.* As the stories move from conventional detective fiction toward the novel of manners, Wimsey becomes more human; he grows older and more concerned with his mortality. A relatively carefree bachelor in the early novels, Wimsey changes when he falls in love with Harriet Vane in *Strong Poison.* A man who has always had what he wanted when he wanted it, Wimsey learns, in the course of several novels, to be patient as Harriet works to balance the claims of head and heart. They both have to work, in *Busman's Honeymoon,* to create a marriage, a partnership, that is "polyphonic." As the series progresses, Wimsey becomes increasingly disillusioned and depressed as he contemplates modern society: the fantasies promised by advertising and drugs, the emptiness of avant-garde movements in art and politics, the atrophying aristocracy, and the endless international tensions that always threaten to erupt into war. As he matures, Wimsey turns more and more to traditional English and Christian values.

Enriching Sayers's mysteries and raising them above a conventional puzzle mystery like Christie's *The Murder of Roger Ackroyd* is the social criticism that pervades all her writings. In Sayers's mysteries, as in her essays and speeches, she argued that human beings need meaningful work and that women need to be treated as human beings. In the essay "Living to Work," she contended that society must concern itself not just with hours, wages, and working conditions but with changing the nature of work so that people might find happiness through employment not through escaping it. In the essays "Are Women Human?" and "The Human-Not-Quite-Human," Sayers criticized society, and specifically the Church, for treating the sexes as opposites, as almost separate species, rather than as individual people sharing needs for respect, love, and meaningful work. These two ideas come together in the novel *Unnatural Death.* In this book Wimsey explains to Charles Parker why he has established "The Cattery," an investigative agency managed by Miss Climpson and staffed by "superfluous" single women: "Miss Climpson . . . is a manifestation of the wasteful way in which this country is run. Look at electricity. Look at water-power. Look at the tides. Look at the sun. Millions of power units being given off into space every minute. Thousands of old maids, simply bursting with useful energy, forced by our stupid social system into hydros and hotels and communities and hostels and posts as companions, where their magnificent gossip-powers and units of inquisitiveness are allowed to dissipate themselves or even become harmful to the community, while the ratepayers' money is spent on getting work, for which these women are providentially fitted, inefficiently carried out by ill-equipped policemen like you. My god! it's enough to make a man write to John Bull. And then bright young men write nasty little patronising books called 'Elderly Women,' and 'On the Edge of the Explosion'— and the drunkards make songs upon 'em, poor things."

After *Busman's Honeymoon,* a novelization of the popular play, Sayers virtually stopped writing detective fiction and began to produce dramas and essays, speeches and reviews, mostly on political and theological topics. Much critical attention has centered around Sayers's reasons for abandoning the mystery form. In *As Her Whimsey Took Her* Hannay contended, "Lord Peter Wimsey had become so nearly real that he wandered out of the detective novel altogether." Elaine Bander in *The Armchair Detective* observed that "The Wimsey Papers," serialized in the *Spectator* from November 1939 to January 1940, features characters from the Wimsey novels acting as spokesmen for Sayers, expressing opinions on World War II and other subjects. Perhaps, Bander suggested, Sayers decided to speak more directly to the public through speeches and essays and theatrical and scholarly writing. Panek pointed out that Sayers, in *The Mind of the Maker,* contrasted the "finite, solvable, mathematical nature of the detective story with the insolvable, protean, and transcendental problems of the world, the flesh, and the devil." To deal with the problems of world, flesh, and devil, especially on the eve of World War II, Panek suggested, "Sayers felt that she had to move to more practical and honest ways of coping with the world than the detective story offered." Perhaps a more plausible explanation is that, with the success of the play *Busman's Honeymoon,* Sayers found her interest in drama revived; therefore, in 1937 and 1938, instead of writing mysteries, she accepted

offers to write plays for the Friends of Canterbury Cathedral, including *The Zeal of Thy House,* and for the BBC, including the nativity play *He That Should Come.* The plays, essays, and speeches allowed Sayers open expression of her political, social, and theological views, which had been creeping more and more into her detective fiction, stretching the form to—or even beyond—its limits.

During the war years, Sayers, freed from the confines of the mystery formula, wrote prolifically in many forms and on many subjects. Yet, in the plays and various prose writings, certain ideas recur: the importance of recognizing and understanding evil, the nature and significance of Christ, and the weaknesses of modern "progressive" thinking. In all the works of this period, she seemed driven to show the relevance of Christian dogma to an age of world crisis.

In the last section of *Even the Parrot* and in the essays "Creed or Chaos?" and "They Tried to Be Good" Sayers pointed out that Britain's failure to understand the nature and inevitability of evil led to the devastation of World War II. She chided the British, specifically, for making a weak peace treaty after World War I, for perceiving the Nazis as "naughty" rather than evil, and for refusing to prepare for war, believing naively that not preparing would prevent warfare. In *The Just Vengeance,* a miracle play written in 1946 to celebrate the 750th anniversary of the Lichfield Cathedral, an airman is trying to sort out his life, to come to terms with the killing he has perpetrated during the war. The aviator wants to believe that the future will bring justice, progress, and happiness. Instead he learns, from the biblical figures of Adam and Eve, Cain and Abel, Christ and Judas, that life always has been and always will be filled with suffering, death, injustice, and bewilderment and that humankind's hope is to believe, not in earthly utopia, but in divine mercy and grace.

Sayers's master work of theology and aesthetic theory is *The Mind of the Maker* which tests Christian creed and speculates about the nature of the creative process by examining the metaphor of God as creative artist. In Sayers's metaphor, God becomes Idea, Christ becomes Energy, and the Holy Spirit becomes Power. As she applied this trinity to both Christian dogma and the process of creating art, she explained much, including, for example, the existence of both evil and bad art. In an essay for *As Her Whimsey Took Her,* Richard T. Webster commented that he had "never read such a trenchant and convincing metaphysical exposition on the problem of evil" as he found in *The Mind of the Maker.* Yet the book is not unreadably theoretical. As always, Sayers reaches out for the common reader. Webster concluded his essay by noting that the subject matter of this work could lead a writer to Dante, which is precisely what happened to Sayers.

On December 17, 1957, Dorothy L. Sayers died in her home at Witham. She left to the world writings spanning the genres— from popular fiction to verse translations of medieval classics, from poetry to radio speeches, from newspaper articles to theological plays and essays. Her works were as varied as her interests, but throughout them all a certain voice and certain themes resound. In *The Mind of the Maker,* Sayers acknowledged the central unifying motif in all her writings: "I know it is no accident that *Gaudy Night,* coming towards the end of a long development in detective fiction, should be a manifestation of precisely the same theme as the play *The Zeal of Thy House,* which followed it and was the first in a series of creatures embodying a Christian theology. They are variations upon a hymn to a Master Maker: and now, after nearly twenty years, I can hear in *Whose Body?* the notes of that tune sounding unmistakably under the tripping melody of a very different descant: and further back still, hear it again, in a youthful set of stanzas in *Catholic Tales.* . . . The end is clearly there in the beginning."

Always Sayers was aware of a "Master Maker"; her Christian beliefs were implicit in all she wrote. Additionally, she consistently displayed a sense of humor and a love of learning in her writings, common sense, clear-sightedness, meticulous scholarship, and concern for the fate of her own society. Sayers also stressed the importance of education, creativity, and rational thinking and the need, in modern society, for economic responsibility, political realism, honesty in language, and justice in dealing with all human beings. Finally, she chose to translate her ideas to a mass audience through her clear, direct, lively style and through her use of popular media such as radio, newspapers, detective fiction, and the stage. That Sayers achieved the popularity she sought without sacrificing her intellectual rigor or compromising her often unpopular opinions is perhaps her greatest achievement.

MEDIA ADAPTATIONS: The film "The Silent Passenger" was adapted from Sayers' unpublished short story of the same title and released by Phoenix Films in 1935. *Busman's Honeymoon* was filmed by Metro-Goldwyn-Mayer [British Studios,] 1940, (released in the U.S. as "The Haunted Honeymoon," 1940), was filmed for television by the British Broadcasting Corp. (BBC-TV), October 2, 1947, and adapted for radio by the British Broadcasting Corp. (BBC-Radio) series "Curtain's Up!," August 3, 1949. *Whose Body?* was adapted for radio by the BBC-Radio's "Mystery Playhouse," from December 2, 1947, to January 6, 1948. *Murder Must Advertise* was adapted for radio by BBC-Radio, April 22, 1957, and filmed for television by the BBC-TV's "Masterpiece Theatre," in June, 1973. *Strong Poison* was adapted for radio by the BBC-Radio's "Saturday Night Theatre," May 25, 1963. *Unnatural Death* was adapted for radio by the BBC-Radio's "Saturday Night Theatre," March 18, 1972. *Clouds of Witness* was filmed for television by the BBC-TV's "Masterpiece Theatre," April 15, 1972, and was televised in the United States by the Public Broadcasting Service. *The Unpleasantness at the Bellona Club* was filmed for television by the BBC-TV's "Masterpiece Theatre," June 2, 1974. *The Five Red Herrings* was filmed for television by the BBC-TV's "Masterpiece Theatre," July 23, 1975 (one source says in March, 1975). "Lord Peter Wimsey Stories," a weekly radio series based on seven stories from the collection *Lord Peter Views the Body* and the short story "In the Teeth of the Evidence," was broadcast by BBC-Radio from April 6, 1970, to June 1, 1970.

BIOGRAPHICAL/CRITICAL SOURCES:

BOOKS

Auden, W. H., *The Dyer's Hand, and Other Essays,* Random House, 1962.
Cawelti, John, *Adventure, Mystery, and Romance: Formula Stories as Art and Popular Culture,* University of Chicago Press, 1976.
Dale, Alzina Stone, *Maker and Craftsman: The Story of Dorothy L. Sayers,* Eerdmans, 1978.
Dictionary of Literary Biography, Gale, Volume 10: *British Dramatists, 1940-1945,* 1982, Volume 36: *British Novelists, 1890-1929: Modernists,* 1985, Volume 77: *British Mystery Writers, 1920-1939,* 1989.
Hall, Trevor H., *Dorothy L. Sayers: Nine Literary Studies,* Duckworth, 1980.
Hannay, Margaret P., editor, *As Her Whimsey Took Her,* Kent State University Press, 1979.

Panek, Leroy Lad, *Watteau's Shepherds: The Detective Novel in Britain, 1914-1940,* Popular Press, 1979.
Routley, Eric, *The Puritan Pleasures of the Detective Story: From Sherlock Holmes to Van de Valk,* Gollancz, 1972.
Sayers, Dorothy L., *Lord Peter,* compiled by James Sandoe, Avon, 1972.
Sayers and others, editors, *Oxford Poetry, 1918,* Blackwell, 1919.
Sayers, *Unnatural Death,* Benn, 1927, reprinted, Harper, 1987.
Sayers, *Lord Peter Views the Body,* Gollancz, 1929, reprinted, Harper, 1986.
Sayers, *The Mind of the Maker,* Harcourt, 1941, reprinted, Greenwood Press, 1971.
Symons, Julian, *The Detective Story in Britain,* revised edition, Longmans, Green, 1969.
Symons, *Mortal Consequences: A History From the Detective Story to the Crime Novel,* Schocken, 1973.
Tischler, Nancy, *Dorothy L. Sayers: A Pilgrim Soul,* John Knox, 1980.
Twentieth-Century Literary Criticism, Gale, Volume 2, 1979, Volume 15, 1985.

PERIODICALS

American Scholar, spring, 1968.
Armchair Detective, October, 1977, spring, 1981.
New York Times Book Review, February 21, 1937, May 18, 1941, November 9, 1975.
Sayers Review, June, 1978, January, 1980, January, 1981.
Time, May 30, 1949, December 30, 1957.
Times Literary Supplement, June 12, 1937, January 27, 1940, June 23, 1961, April 22, 1977.

*   *   *

SCHAEFFER, Susan Fromberg 1941-

PERSONAL: Born March 25, 1941, in Brooklyn, N.Y.; daughter of Irving (a clothing manufacturer) and Edith (Levine) Fromberg; married Neil Jerome Schaeffer (a college English professor), October 11, 1970; children: Benjamin Adam, May Anna. *Education:* Attended Simmons College; University of Chicago, B.A., 1961, M.A. (with honors), 1963, Ph.D. (with honors), 1966. *Religion:* Jewish.

ADDRESSES: Office—Department of English, Brooklyn College of the City University of New York, Brooklyn, N.Y. 11210. *Agent*—Timothy Seldes, Russell & Volkening, Inc., 50 West 29th St., New York, N.Y. 10001.

CAREER: Novelist and poet. Wright Junior College, Chicago, Ill., instructor in English, 1963-64; Illinois Institute of Technology, Chicago, assistant professor of English, 1964-67; Brooklyn College of the City University of New York, Brooklyn, N.Y., assistant professor, 1967-73, associate professor, 1973-75, professor of English, 1975—, Broeklundian Professor of English, 1985—. Guest lecturer at University of Chicago, Cornell University, University of Arizona, and University of Maine. Has given readings of work at Yale University, University of Massachusetts, University of Texas, University of Houston, and other universities.

MEMBER: Modern Language Association of America, PEN, Authors Guild, Authors League of America, Poetry Society of America.

AWARDS, HONORS: Edward Lewis Wallant Award, 1974, and Friends of Literature Award, both for *Anya;* National Book Award nomination, 1974, for *Granite Lady;* O. Henry Award, 1977, for "The Exact Nature of the Plot"; Lawrence Award,

Prairie Schooner, 1984; Guggenheim fellowship, 1984-85; *Centennial Review*'s award for poetry, 1985.

WRITINGS:

The Witch and the Weather Report (poetry), Seven Woods Press, 1972.
Falling (novel), Macmillan, 1973.
Anya (novel), Macmillan, 1974.
Granite Lady (poetry), Macmillan, 1974.
The Rhymes and Runes of the Toad (poetry), Macmillan, 1975.
Alphabet for the Lost Years (poetry), Gallimaufry, 1976.
The Red, White and Blue Poem, Ally Press, 1977.
Time in Its Flight (novel), Doubleday, 1978.
The Bible of the Beasts of the Little Field (poetry), Dutton, 1980.
The Queen of Egypt (short fiction), Dutton, 1980.
Love (novel), Dutton, 1980.
The Madness of a Seduced Woman (novel), Dutton, 1983.
Mainland (novel), Linden Press, 1985.
The Dragons of North Chittendon (children's novel), Simon & Schuster, 1986.
The Injured Party (novel), St. Martin's, 1986.
Buffalo Afternoon (novel), Knopf, 1989.

Contributor of critical articles to numerous periodicals, including *Centennial Review, Modern Fiction Studies, Great Ideas Today, London Review of Books,* and *New York Times.*

WORK IN PROGRESS: The Day in Its Parts, poetry; *The Death of the Dog and Other Short Fiction,* a novel.

SIDELIGHTS: Although highly respected for both her poetry and shorter pieces of fiction, Susan Fromberg Schaeffer is perhaps more widely known for her novels. As Elizabeth Ward observes in the *Washington Post Book World,* Schaeffer is "a born storyteller, with a rare ability to transport the reader bodily into her various fictional worlds, all criticism suspended. [She has a] genuinely original voice, at once light, versatile, stylish and informed by a sharp eye and ear for the life-giving detail."

Sybil S. Steinberg writes in *Publishers Weekly* that reading Schaeffer's novels "is rather like falling into a time warp and experiencing events through total immersion in the mind of the protagonist. So carefully does she build character, so meticulously does she convey details of time and place and social mores that one wonders with each new novel if the author is writing autobiography in the guise of fiction."

Schaeffer's first novel, *Falling,* was very well received by critics, and its author was hailed as a novelist with much promise. In *Falling* the reader watches a young Jewish graduate student, Elizabeth Kamen, as she slowly rises from a near-suicidal existence to a hopeful future; a *Time* reviewer calls *Falling* "the blunt but quietly humorous story of a New York girl who lifts herself out of depression by her own pantyhose." Wayne C. Booth states in the *New York Times Book Review:* "I love this novel—first reading, second reading, browsing. . . . [Elizabeth's] journey is not only convincing, it is for the most part very funny. I can't think of any other treatment of 'the way those young people live now' that has made me laugh so much." And Pearl K. Bell writes in the *New Leader* that Schaeffer "is a writer of uncommon talent and honesty blessed with a natural command of humor and perception, and she has crafted one of the most engaging and genuinely funny books I've read in years. . . . *Falling* is at once poignant, hilarious and luminous."

In *Falling,* as in many of her subsequent works, Schaeffer effectively and dramatically uses the narrative voice to draw the reader deeper into the plot. Cynthia MacDonald explains in the

Washington Post Book World: "Fromberg is a fine storyteller. You care about her characters and want to know what is going to happen next. . . . Description functions as a part of character so it is never extraneous, never like those paste wedding cake decorations, something to remove before eating." In his review of *Falling* Booth remarks that the reader is "engaged with remarkable intensity in this young woman's fight for a life of her own; somehow, as in the best of Bellow, the very possibility of life in such a world seems at stake. As we catch through her eyes occasional images of beauty and mystery, images that transform the intellectual deciphering into promises of meaning, we come to care very much about whether this sharp-eyed lost woman can find a way to live without self-deception, as acceptance of all that has been done against her and all that she has done to destroy herself."

Schaeffer's second novel, *Anya,* explores the plight of a Jewish woman trying to survive in a turbulent era. The book begins in the 1930s and takes Anya through the Nazi massacre of Jews in Poland up to the present day in America. As such, maintains Judith Thurman of *Ms.,* "*Anya* is one of the few 'Holocaust' novels to begin long enough before the war to give us a full, material sense of what was lost." D. A. Parente similarly believes *Anya* is unique because it transforms the "reader into a totally involved participant." In a *Best Sellers* review Parente writes: "Anya, the narrator, becomes of course our most intimate acquaintance and those to whom she is the closest . . . are portrayed in depth. . . . This novel is a thoroughly worthwhile experience on all levels—moral, psychological, social, historical, and artistic. . . . It is perhaps, however, the final tribute to Mrs. Schaeffer's artistry that she has created a life experience so realistic and convincing that we can only believe at the end that it is a reproduction of a historical life."

In the *Washington Post Book World,* Mary Richie similarly comments that in *Anya,* "out of blown-away dust Susan Fromberg Schaeffer has created a world. A writer of remarkable power, . . . she has taken on the biggest moral questions, made us see the holocaust anew as if we had never heard of it." Continues the critic: "*Anya* unfolds before us like a superb film, so detailed it seems many minds and hands must have gone into decorating the set, clothing the performers, and detailing the dialogue. It is like a *makimono,* those narrative scrolls to be unrolled slowly from one ivory cylinder to another so that the panoramic story is experienced image by image, as it was envisioned. It is a vision, set down by a fearless, patient poet, a fabulist who knows that whatever is created never dies, that it is truly good to see and tell."

Just as with *Falling,* many reviewers credit powerful characterization aided by the use of a convincing narrative voice for making *Anya* especially moving. Thurman believes "the compelling horror of the [Holocaust] does not distract us from the real business of the book—of any fiction—to create an awareness of character which grows, changes, and deepens. *Anya*'s power as a novel is its extraordinary specificity. Its focus is the woman herself—who she was, what happened to her, and because of that, what she became." Thurman comments further: "I have read few books that are more tangible. The reality is solid—it bears the full weight of one's trust. The story is told in the first person, with a depth of vision that seems to be memory, that imitates memory, but is really something much less passive and more interesting: an author in possession of someone she has fully imagined."

Another of Schaeffer's historical novels, *Time in Its Flight,* is a family saga set in nineteenth-century New England that covers several generations over more than a hundred years. Clifton Fadiman writes in the *Book-of-the-Month Club News* magazine that in *Time in Its Flight* "Schaeffer contrives to turn time backward in its flight, to give us the feeling, the shape of a whole stubborn Yankee rural culture. This she manages not merely through vivid details of manners and dress, but by an extraordinary photographic genius. These are real voices, dozens of them, using the idiom of their time and place, but always colored by a precise notation of individuality. In a way we do not read this book. We hear it, or overhear it."

Webster Schott, however, remarks in the *New York Times Book Review* that *Time in Its Flight* "will satisfy if you need to kill time or want to know how the rural rich once lived in America. But it's a poor intellectual companion. It's capriciously organized and confusing without purpose." "Schaeffer has a teeming imagination, and scatters ideas, anecdotes, and descriptions with a prodigal hand," Lynne Sharon Schwartz comments in *Saturday Review*. "Unfortunately, only a portion of these contribute to any formal design or movement. Similarly, Schaeffer's attempt to render a photographic reality of affectionate family life yields tedium." In contrast, a reviewer for the *New Yorker* writes that "the abundant dialogue and reminiscences are entertaining and informative. Articulate women abound . . . and Mrs. Schaeffer manages to keep her characters and readers curious about what the future has in store for them."

As Cynthia MacDonald observes, however, Schaeffer's saga is perhaps too all-encompassing to be entirely successful. Explains MacDonald in the *Washington Post Book World:* "The ambition [in *Time in Its Flight*] is to incorporate a whole world, take it into the body of the novel and into each character. Much of the ambition is realized, much in the novel is wonderful, but there is too much. More shaping, more order, more discarding were needed. Yet I would say read this book; Susan Fromberg Schaeffer is a good enough writer to make even a flawed book worth reading."

Schaeffer's fourth novel, *Love,* is the story of two generations of Jewish families, the Lurias and the Romanoffs, beginning with events in Russia and ending with a new life in America. Susanne Freeman writes in the *Washington Post* of *Love:* "In her fourth novel, Susan Fromberg Schaeffer takes us trudging through Russian snows, dancing through Jewish weddings, noshing in Brooklyn kitchens. She gives us childbirth, divorce and nightmares that come true. She serves up murder, pogroms and talking dogs. This can all be pretty steamy stuff—the thick soup of family life in a story that spans a hundred years—but Schaeffer is too clever for that. Family sagas are her specialty, and she knows just how to spoon them out—in short dream passages as thin as broth, followed by meatier scenes, just dense and sweet enough to make us wish for more."

Love also met with mixed reviews similar to those of *Time in Its Flight.* Dorothy Wickenden, for instance, remarks in *Saturday Review* that "Schaeffer knows what ingredients insure a novel's commercial success. *Love* captures Jewish family tradition, celebrates the lives of the hardworking and the obscure, and is punctuated with wry anecdotes about daily domestic crises. Still, Schaeffer's glimmers of wit aren't enough to sustain one throughout this overwritten and carelessly edited novel." Nevertheless, critics once again praised Schaeffer's skillful use of the narrative voice. For example, Lore Dickstein remarks in the *New York Times Book Review* that "Schaeffer has constructed this novel in large sections of flashback interspersed with narratives written in the voices of the characters, a device she has used in previous novels. Although many of these first-person accounts sound very much like verbatim transcripts of tape-recorded in-

terviews, they are quite wonderful in the way they foretell and retell the story and they save the novel from mediocrity. Only in these sections can one hear distinctly individual voices, a quiet chuckle, and ironic comment."

The idea behind Schaeffer's next book, *The Madness of a Seduced Woman,* germinated for almost twenty years before Schaeffer wrote a novel concerning, as Schaeffer explained to *CA,* "the spectacle of a body gone to war with the mind." While doing research for *Time in Its Flight,* Schaeffer came across five newspaper articles describing the murder trial of a woman accused of killing another woman after discovering they were both engaged to the same man. Following the shooting, the young woman attempted suicide, but failed and was put on trial for her crime. Schaeffer told *Publishers Weekly:* "I thought then: what an awful fate, that no matter what she did to herself she was destined to go on living. And that led me to speculate about any usual person finding happiness in life, especially one with an obsessive determination to change the nature of reality. And the seductive possibility of being able to visualize a better world than the one you were given by birth or inheritance."

Julie Greenstein writes in *Ms.* that *The Madness of a Seduced Woman,* "set at the turn of the century in New England, possesses the subtle allure of an Andrew Wyeth painting. Beautifully constructed and intelligently written, *Madness* is a gothic tale of romance, passion, and oddly enough, feminism." Mary Kathleen Benet comments in the *Times Literary Supplement* that Schaeffer "has written not so much a novel as an example of the sort of novel women really ought to be reading." And Edmund White remarks in *Nation* that "at the heart of the novel beats the fibrillating pulse of an obsession. . . . Many books (trashy ones) blandly accept the genre of romantic fiction without a pause—they repeat every cliche. But serious books, such as this honest, intelligent novel, re-examine the cliches by observing even the most hackneyed situations with a deeper, more powerful vision."

"[*The Madness of a Seduced Woman*] is much more complex and satisfying than its romantic plot suggests," Rosellen Brown likewise states in the *New York Times Book Review.* She continues: "Schaeffer's earnest exploration of questions of mind versus body, family history versus personal freedom, does distance her novel from the common run of good reads about the travails of beautiful wantons. But in the end, the story of Agnes, who 'would love the world if she didn't have to live in it,' is an absorbing, wonderfully inventive psychological tale of a woman imagined as we would never dare, or want, to be."

Schaeffer's next novel, *Mainland,* tells the story of Eleanor, a forty-six-year-old college professor who, after undergoing cataract surgery, takes a look at her seemingly happy marriage and family and decides she is no longer content with her life. After embarking on an affair with her Chinese chauffeur, Eleanor begins to undergo a slow transformation and finds real happiness at last. Susan Allen Toth asks in the *New York Times Book Review:* "Who wants to read another novel about an upper-middle-class New York City wife, unhappy despite (or because of) her prosperous husband and bright, healthy children? . . . In bare outline, Susan Fromberg Schaeffer's *Mainland* sounds tediously familiar. But this short, lilting novel offers many delightful surprises, not only in its underlying optimism but in its fresh, funny and often poetic prose." While Alice Kavounas reports in the *Times Literary Supplement* that "it's debatable whether the author intended *Mainland* to be more than the enjoyable read it is," she also points out that Schaeffer "keeps the pace of the narrative lively" and "endows her central character with [a] special brand of self-deprecating wit."

Because of her insightful and sensitive treatment of much of her subject matter and the background of many of her main characters, many critics have described Schaeffer as a "Jewish-American writer." As William Novack explains in the *New York Times Book Review:* "[Recently] there have been signs of a new trend that reflects a growth in the Jewish-American consciousness. Writers like Cynthia Ozick and Arthur A. Cohen, together with some of their younger colleagues, have begun to produce a literature about Jews which is more identifiably Jewish than anything we have seen until now in the work of American-born authors. This new writing is more concerned with Jewish history, culture and even theology than with questions of how Jews live in American society." According to Novack, Schaeffer's *Anya* in particular is "a perhaps unintentional part of this phenomenon" that "represents a new stride toward maturity in Jewish-American writing. The novel looks history straight in the eye, engaging it with a stubborn fierceness. It is a triumph of realism in art."

Although many of her characters are Jewish, Schaeffer takes issue with reviewers labeling her as a "Jewish-American writer." As she explains to interviewer Harold U. Ribalow in *The Tie That Binds: Conversations with Jewish Writers,* "Partly the reason I wouldn't call myself a Jewish writer is because I'm not trying deliberately to write on Jewish themes." According to Susan Kress in *Dictionary of Literary Biography,* "Schaeffer says she is not an observant Jew and never has been, but she regards her sensibility as profoundly Jewish. Her primary concerns are not Jewish themes and Jewish identity. . . . Nevertheless, her Jewish identity is important to Susan Fromberg Schaeffer; in her own words, she regards her Jewishness as 'like the wallpaper in every room [she has] ever been in.'"

MEDIA ADAPTATIONS: The film rights to *The Madness of a Seduced Woman* have been purchased.

BIOGRAPHICAL/CRITICAL SOURCES:

BOOKS

Contemporary Literary Criticism, Gale, Volume 6, 1976, Volume 11, 1979, Volume 22, 1982.
Dictionary of Literary Biography, Volume 28: *Twentieth-Century American-Jewish Fiction Writers,* Gale, 1984.
Ribalow, Harold U., editor, *The Tie That Binds: Conversations with Jewish Writers,* A. S. Barnes, 1980.

PERIODICALS

American Book Review, January-February, 1981.
Antioch Review, fall, 1981.
Best Sellers, October 1, 1974.
Book-of-the-Month Club News, July, 1978.
Chicago Tribune Book World, January 27, 1980, May 3, 1981, April 17, 1983.
Library Journal, September 15, 1974, June 15, 1978.
Los Angeles Times, July 24, 1983, August 20, 1985.
Los Angeles Times Book Review, March 15, 1981.
Ms., March, 1975, November, 1975, February, 1980, July, 1983.
Nation, July 9-16, 1983.
New Leader, August 6, 1973.
New Yorker, July 31, 1978.
New York Times Book Review, May 20, 1973, July 14, 1974, October 20, 1974, March 20, 1975, May 18, 1975, August 13, 1978, February 24, 1980, January 11, 1981, May 22, 1983, July 8, 1984, July 7, 1985.

Open Places, fall/winter, 1975-76.
Partisan Review, fall, 1973.
Poetry, July, 1975.
Prairie Schooner, fall, 1977.
Publishers Weekly, April 8, 1983.
Saturday Review, June 24, 1978, January, 1981.
Time, July 18, 1973, December 31, 1973, October 14, 1974.
Times Literary Supplement, March 23, 1984, January 17, 1986.
Washington Post, January 26, 1981, October 17, 1986.
Washington Post Book World, August 11, 1974, November 17, 1974, June 18, 1978, February 3, 1980, June 12, 1983.

* * *

SCHLAFLY, Phyllis 1924-

PERSONAL: Born August 15, 1924, in St. Louis, Mo.; daughter of John Bruce (an engineer) and Odille (Dodge) Stewart; married John Fred Schlafly (a lawyer), October 20, 1949; children: John F., Bruce S., Roger S., P. Liza Forshaw, Andrew L., Anne V. *Education:* Attended Maryville College of the Sacred Heart for two years; Washington University, St. Louis, Mo., A.B., 1944, J.D., 1978; Radcliffe College, M.A., 1945.

ADDRESSES: Home—68 Fairmount, Alton, Ill. 62002. *Office*—Eagle Forum, Box 618, Alton, Ill. 62002.

CAREER: Lawyer, 1979—. First National Bank and St. Louis Union Trust Company, St. Louis, Mo., librarian and researcher, 1946-49; homemaker, 1949—. Delegate to Republican national conventions; candidate for Congress, 1952, 1970; president, Illinois Federation of Republican Women, 1960-64; first vice-president, National Federation of Republican Women, 1965-67; national chairman, Stop ERA, 1972—; member, Illinois Commission on the Status of Women, 1975-85; founder and president, Eagle Forum, 1975—. Member, Administrative Conference of the United States, 1983—, and Commission on the Bicentennial of the United States Constitution, 1985—. Commentator on "Matters of Opinion," WBBM Radio, Chicago, Ill., 1973-75, on "Spectrum," CBS Radio Network 1973-78, and on CNN Cable Television Network, 1980-83.

MEMBER: Authors Guild, Authors League of America, American Conservative Union, Daughters of the American Revolution (national chairman of American history committee, 1965-68; member of bicentennial committee, 1967-70, and of national defense committee, 1977-80 and 1983—), Junior League of St. Louis, Phi Beta Kappa, Pi Sigma Alpha.

AWARDS, HONORS: Named woman of achievement in public affairs by *St. Louis Globe-Democrat,* 1963; named Woman of the Year by Illinois Federation of Republican Women, 1969; awarded ten George Washington Honor Medals by Freedoms Foundation; Brotherhood Award, National Conference of Christians and Jews, 1975; LL.D., Niagara University, 1976; named one of the ten "most admired women in the world" by *Good Housekeeping* magazine, 1977—.

WRITINGS:

A Choice Not an Echo, Pere Marquette, 1964.
(With Chester C. Ward) *The Gravediggers,* Pere Marquette, 1964.
(With Ward) *Strike from Space,* Pere Marquette, 1965.
Safe—Not Sorry, Pere Marquette, 1967.
(With Ward) *The Betrayers,* Pere Marquette, 1968.
Mindszenty the Man, Cardinal Mindszenty Foundation, 1972.
(With Ward) *Kissinger on the Couch,* Arlington House, 1975.
Ambush at Vladivostok, Pere Marquette, 1976.
The Power of the Positive Woman, Arlington House, 1977.

The Power of the Christian Woman, Standard Publishing, 1981.
(Editor) *Equal Pay for Unequal Work,* Eagle Forum Education
   and Legal Defense Fund, 1984.
Child Abuse in the Classroom, Pere Marquette, 1984.
Pornography's Victims, Pere Marquette, 1987.

Also author of *The Phyllis Schlafly Report* (monthly national
newsletter), 1967—. Contributor of syndicated column to newspapers through Copley News Service.

SIDELIGHTS: Phyllis Schlafly, a housewife turned political activist, is a leading spokeswoman for the conservative, pro-family
viewpoint on issues such as women's rights, national defense, education, the law, and politics. Schlafly's organizational techniques and outspoken personal leadership are widely cited as the
forces that defeated the Equal Rights Amendment in 1982 after
a ten-year battle; her nationwide Eagle Forum continues to represent the concerns of families and political conservatives. A tireless worker known for her unflappable demeanor, Schlafly is
"one of the best loved and the most loathed women in the country," according to *New York Review of Books* contributor Frances FitzGerald. Opinion is indeed sharply divided on Schlafly
and her goals. In the *Washington Post,* Sally Quinn notes that on
the podium Schlafly "comes on like a female George Wallace.
She is tough and aggressive, totally unlike the role she espouses
for most women." Conversely, a *National Review* correspondent
calls her "one of the most remarkable women in American history," a dynamo who "has triumphed over the major media, the
bureaucrats (and bureaucrettes), and the 'women's movement,'
almost singlehandedly." Supporters and detractors alike concede, however, that Schlafly is enormously successful at galva-
nizing support and influencing public policy. In the *New York
Times Magazine,* Joseph Lelyveld observes that she "has become
one of the most relentless and accomplished platform debaters
of any gender to be found on any side of any issue."

Schlafly was born Phyllis Stewart in St. Louis, Missouri on August 15, 1924. Her conservatism was nurtured from earliest
childhood by her parents. Even when her father lost his job in
the Depression, forcing the family into dire financial straits, he
continued to champion the free enterprise system and traditional
values. Family circumstances forced Phyllis's mother to work
outside the home, and she was the head librarian at the St. Louis
Art Museum for 25 years. The young Miss Stewart rewarded her
mother's diligence by graduating first in her Catholic school
class and earning a college scholarship. She began her undergraduate education at Maryville College of the Sacred Heart, but
transferred to Washington University, graduating Phi Beta
Kappa in three years. While attending Washington University
during World War II, she worked the night shift at a federal factory where she tested both rifles and machine guns for ammunition accuracy from midnight until eight in the morning, and then
attended her classes during the day. "It was a strictly budgeted,
time-managed life," Schlafly told the *New York Times.* In 1944
she won yet another scholarship, for graduate work at Radcliffe
College. A year later she had earned her master's degree in political science. Deciding against a career in academia she served
briefly as a researcher for several Washington congressmen, then
helped to run the successful campaign of Republican Congressman Claude I. Bakewell of St. Louis. In 1946 she took a job as
a researcher and librarian in a St. Louis bank and continued her
Republican political activities in her spare time.

The newsletter that Phyllis Stewart helped to write for the bank
brought her to the attention of Fred Schlafly, a successful lawyer
from Alton, Illinois, who had similar conservative views. Fred
and Phyllis Schlafly were married on October 20, 1949, and the

bride quit her job to become a homemaker and a mother. Although she soon had six children, Schlafly continued to take an
interest in politics and community volunteer work. She ran for
Congress unsuccessfully in 1952 and has served as a delegate to
Republican national conventions since the 1950s.

A new avenue of expression opened to Schlafly in 1964 when she
published her first book, *A Choice Not an Echo.* The paperback,
published by a company she and her husband created, championed Senator Barry M. Goldwater for the Republican presidential nomination. Over three million copies of *A Choice Not an
Echo* were sold; political analysts contend that the work helped
Goldwater to secure his party's nomination. Thereafter Schlafly
teamed with a retired military man, Admiral Chester Ward, to
coauthor more titles on the subjects of national defense policy
and nuclear strategy. In works such as *The Gravediggers, Strike
from Space, The Betrayers,* and *Kissinger on the Couch,* Schlafly
and Ward find fault with a series of presidential advisors who,
in their view, weakened the United States' defenses and paved
the way for Soviet nuclear superiority. FitzGerald explains:
"The central thesis of these books was that certain powerful government officials were plotting the unilateral disarmament of the
United States." In 1980, Schlafly served on the Defense Policy
Advisory Group; her work brought praise from President Ronald Reagan.

In 1965 Schlafly was elected first vice-president of the National
Federation of Republican Women. She ran for president of the
organization in 1967 but was narrowly defeated by a more liberal
candidate. That same year she began the Eagles Trust Fund to
support conservative political candidates and founded her
monthly newsletter, *The Phyllis Schlafly Report,* in which she
outlined the concerns of the Republican right. In 1970 she ran
for Congress again in Illinois's twenty-third district, but she lost
to a Democratic incumbent. Ironically, her campaign slogan, "A
woman's place is in the House," was used the same year by another candidate, feminist Bella Abzug. Having lost her bid for
Congress, Schlafly returned to her writing, concentrating on exposing the communist menace and calling for more vigilant national defense. Indeed, *Newsweek* quotes Schlafly as calling the
atomic bomb "a marvelous gift that was given to our country by
a wise God."

Schlafly's first blast against the Equal Rights Amendment was
printed in the February, 1972 issue of *The Phyllis Schlafly Report.* She told *Newsweek* that she "didn't set out to confront the
whole women's lib movement. These tasks were thrust upon
me." Once convinced that the ERA would undermine family
life, take away the legal rights of wives, and thrust women into
military combat, however, Schlafly turned her full attention to
a crusade to quash the amendment. She founded Stop ERA in
1972 and the Eagle Forum in 1975, both of which became sophisticated grass-roots lobby organizations with the goal of defeating ERA. She also testified against the amendment in 30 state
legislatures. *New Republic* contributor Morton Kondracke observes that when state-by-state ratification of the amendment
began to slow down, "it was caught up to and walloped by antifeminist firebrand Phyllis Schlafly, one of the most gifted practitioners of political diatribe in the country today. Most of Schlafly's major arguments against ERA [were] outrageous fabrica-
tions, but they [were] so artful and so brazenly repeated that
Schlafly . . . put ERA proponents on the defensive in state after
state." Although polls showed that a majority of Americans favored ERA, Schlafly and her corps of trained volunteers "made
the ERA so controversial that legislators preferred to avoid it—
thus turning the weight of inertia against the amendment," according to FitzGerald. Schlafly's pro-family movement pooled

forces with the burgeoning American Conservative Union, the Moral Majority, and the Catholic, Baptist, Orthodox Jewish, and Mormon churches to reach state legislators individually. She made speeches against ERA repeatedly, often driving hostile audiences to hysteria with her calmly-expressed and unshakable convictions. *Newsweek* quotes Chicago feminist Diann Smith, who said, "The only way to debate Phyllis Schlafly is to jump up and down and shout 'Liar, liar, liar!' "

The Power of the Positive Woman, Schlafly's 1977 book, outlines her views on the status of American women. The Positive Woman, she writes, "rejoices in the creative capability within her body and the power potential of her mind and spirit. She understands that men and women are different, and that those very differences provide the key to her success as a person and fulfillment as a woman." The Women's Liberation Movement, she contends, is peopled by "a bunch of bitter women seeking a constitutional cure for their personal problems" and "Typhoid Marys carrying a germ called lost identity." In the *New York Times*, Gail Sheehy reacts to Schlafly's thesis: "Phyllis Schlafly's formula for the better life, then, is based on marrying a rich professional, climbing the pedestal to lady of leisure, and pulling up the rope behind her, thereby breaking any painful identifications with women who are still powerless, women who didn't have the wits to find a high-status male or the initiative to bind him legally into taking 'beautiful' care of them." FitzGerald also finds *The Power of the Positive Woman* a "guerrilla attack" on the feminist movement, "where the enemy has a fixed position but the attacker does not. . . . Schlafly must know better, but she consistently assumes that all American women are rich enough so that they don't have to go to work." Kondracke comments that Schlafly "has clearly tapped elemental currents of resentment, fear and anger running beneath the surface of American society. . . . Though she is hardly one of them, Schlafly represents the stay-at-homes who look at women's liberation and the working lifestyle as a threat and a rebuke. The old rules decreed that women got married and had babies, and millions of women dutifully followed the pattern. Now the rules are suddenly being changed, and these women are being told they have wasted their lives. They won't sit for it . . . and Schlafly is leading the way." Such comments about her views, Schlafly tells *CA*, "are ridiculous and have no relation to my life or writings."

Despite Congressional extension of the ratification deadline, ERA was defeated in 1982. Since then, Schlafly and her Eagle Forum have been actively involved in other political issues including aid to Nicaragua's *contra* rebels, support for the Strategic Defense Initiative and for parental rights in public schools, lobbies to revise public school curricula, and aid to conservative political candidates. Schlafly still conducts most of her business from her home in Alton, Illinois, where she lives with her husband. Sheehy characterizes the well-groomed activist as a "moral boss" who is "unencumbered by empathy on a personal level or by the democratic process on a political level." Other observers are not as critical; at a 1982 post-ERA dinner, Schlafly was lauded by John Lofton, editor of *Conservative Digest*, the Reverend Jerry Falwell, Morton Blackwell, a special assistant to President Reagan, and others, who praised her work on a wide variety of national concerns. She has also received ten George Washington Honor Medals from the Freedoms Foundation and citations from *Good Housekeeping* magazine. When asked about her own accomplishments, Schlafly usually speaks with pride of her six grown children, and thanks her husband for allowing her to pursue her causes. In *People* magazine, former National Organization of Women chief Karen DeCrow put Schlafly's achieve-

ments in perspective. "If I had a daughter," DeCrow commented, "I'd like her to be a housewife just like Phyllis Schlafly."

BIOGRAPHICAL/CRITICAL SOURCES:

BOOKS

Authors in the News, Volume I, Gale, 1976.
Contemporary Issues Criticism, Volume I, Gale, 1982.
Felsenthal, Carol, *The Sweetheart of the Silent Majority: The Biography of Phyllis Schlafly*, Doubleday, 1981.
Schlafly, Phyllis, *The Power of the Positive Woman*, Arlington House, 1977.

PERIODICALS

Christian Century, April 24, 1985.
Modern Age, winter, 1977.
Ms., March, 1974, May, 1981, January, 1982, September, 1982.
National NOW Times, December, 1977.
National Review, June 6, 1975, February 3, 1978, May 15, 1981, August 6, 1982.
New Republic, April 30, 1977.
Newsweek, July 25, 1977, February 28, 1983, December 23, 1985.
New York Daily News, November 22, 1977.
New York Review of Books, November 19, 1981.
New York Times, December 15, 1975, October 14, 1977, January 24, 1980.
New York Times Book Review, October 30, 1977.
New York Times Magazine, April 17, 1977.
People, March 30, 1981.
Rolling Stone, November 26, 1981.
Time, July 3, 1978, May 4, 1981, July 12, 1982.
Washington Post, July 11, 1974.

*   *   *

SCHLESINGER, Arthur M(eier), Jr. 1917-

PERSONAL: Name originally Arthur Bancroft Schlesinger; born October 15, 1917, in Columbus, Ohio; son of Arthur Meier (a professor of history and author) and Elizabeth (Bancroft) Schlesinger; married Marian Cannon (an author and artist), August 10, 1940 (divorced, 1970); married Alexandra Emmet, July 19, 1971; children: (first marriage) Stephen Cannon and Katharine Bancroft Kinderman (twins), Christina, Andrew Bancroft; (second marriage) Robert Emmet Kennedy. *Education:* Harvard University, A.B. (summa cum laude), 1938. *Politics:* Democrat. *Religion:* Unitarian.

ADDRESSES: Office—Graduate School and University Center, City University of New York, 33 West 42nd St., New York, N.Y. 10036-8099.

CAREER: Affiliated with Office of War Information, Washington, D.C., 1942-43, and with Office of Strategic Services, Washington, D.C., London, England, and Paris, France, 1943-45; free-lance writer, Washington, D.C., 1945-46; Harvard University, Cambridge, Mass., associate professor, 1946-54, professor of history, 1954-62; special assistant to President John F. Kennedy, 1961-63, and to President Lyndon B. Johnson, 1963-64; City University of New York, New York City, Albert Schweitzer Professor in the Humanities, beginning in 1966. Chairman, Franklin Delano Roosevelt Four Freedoms Foundation, beginning in 1983. Trustee of Robert F. Kennedy Memorial, Recorded Anthology of American Music, and Twentieth Century Fund. Adviser, Arthur and Elizabeth Schlesinger Library on the History of Women in America, and Library of America. Member, boards of Harry S. Truman Library Institute, John Fitzgerald Kennedy Library, Ralph Bunche Institute, and Harriman Institute of Russian Studies. Member, Adlai Stevenson presidential campaign staff, 1952 and 1956. Consultant, Economic Cooperation Administration, 1948, and Mutual Security Administration, 1951-52. *Military service:* U.S. Army, 1945; served in Europe.

MEMBER: American Historical Association, American Academy and Institute of Arts and Letters (president, 1981-84, chancellor of the Academy, 1985-88), Library of Congress Council of Scholars, Association for the Study of Afro-American Life and History, Organization of American Historians, Society for Historians of American Foreign Relations, Center for Inter-American Relations, Council on Foreign Relations, Americans for Democratic Action (national chairman, 1953-54), American Civil Liberties Union (member of national council), Massachusetts Historical Society, Colonial Society of Massachusetts, Phi Beta Kappa.

AWARDS, HONORS: Henry Fellow, Cambridge University, 1938-39; Harvard Fellow, 1939-42; Pulitzer Prize for history, 1946, for *The Age of Jackson,* and for biography, 1966, for *A Thousand Days: John F. Kennedy in the White House;* Guggenheim fellow, 1946; American Academy of Arts and Letters grant, 1946; Francis Parkman Prize, Society of American Historians, 1957, and Frederic Bancroft Prize, Columbia University, 1958, both for *The Age of Roosevelt,* Volume 1: *The Crisis of the Old Order;* National Book Award, 1966, for *A Thousand Days: John F. Kennedy in the White House,* and 1979, for *Robert Kennedy and His Times;* gold medal in history and biography, National Institute and American Academy of Arts and Letters, 1967; Ohio Governor's Award for history, 1973; Sidney Hillman Foundation Award, 1973, for *The Imperial Presidency;* Eugene V. Debs Award in education, 1974; Fregene Prize for literature, Italy, 1983. Honorary degrees from many schools and universities, including New School for Social Research, 1966, Utah State University, 1978, University of Louisville, 1978, Rutgers University, 1982, State University of New York at Albany, 1984, University of New Hampshire, 1985, University of Oxford (England), 1987, and Brandeis University, 1988.

WRITINGS:

Orestes A. Brownson: A Pilgrim's Progress (Catholic Book Club selection), Little, Brown, 1939, published as *A Pilgrim's Progress: Orestes A. Brownson,* 1966.

The Age of Jackson, Little, Brown, 1945, reprinted, 1968, abridged edition, New American Library, 1962.

The Vital Center: The Politics of Freedom, Houghton, 1949 (published in England as *The Politics of Freedom,* Heinemann, 1950).

(With Richard H. Rovere) *The General and the President and the Future of American Foreign Policy,* Farrar, Straus, 1951, revised edition published as *The MacArthur Controversy and American Foreign Policy,* 1965.

The Age of Roosevelt, Volume 1: *The Crisis of the Old Order, 1919-1933* (Book-of-the-Month Club selection), Houghton, 1957, reprinted, 1988, Volume 2: *The Coming of the New Deal* (Book-of-the-Month Club selection), Houghton, 1959, reprinted, 1988, Volume 3: *The Politics of Upheaval* (Book-of-the-Month Club selection), Houghton, 1960, reprinted, 1988.

Kennedy or Nixon: Does It Make Any Difference?, Macmillan, 1960.

The Politics of Hope (essays), Houghton, 1963.

(With John M. Blum and others) *The National Experience,* Harcourt, 1963, 7th edition, 1989.

A Thousand Days: John F. Kennedy in the White House, Houghton, 1965, reprinted, Greenwich House, 1983.

The Bitter Heritage: Vietnam and American Democracy, 1941-1966, Houghton, 1967.

The Crisis of Confidence: Ideas, Power, and Violence in America, Houghton, 1969.

(With Lloyd C. Gardner and Hans J. Morgenthau) *The Origins of the Cold War,* Ginn-Blaisdell, 1970.

The Imperial Presidency (Book-of-the-Month Club selection), Houghton, 1973.

Robert Kennedy and His Times, Houghton, 1978.

The Cycles of American History, Houghton, 1986.

EDITOR

(With others) *Harvard Guide to American History,* Harvard University Press, 1954.

(With Quincy Howe) *Guide to Politics, 1954,* Dial, 1954.

(With Morton White) *Paths of American Thought,* Houghton, 1963.

Herbert Croly, *The Promise of American Life,* Belknap, 1967.

Edwin O'Connor, *The Best and the Last of Edwin O'Connor,* Little, Brown, 1970.

(With Fred L. Israel and William P. Hansen) *History of American Presidential Elections, 1789-1972,* four volumes, Chelsea House, 1971, supplemental volume, *1972-1984,* 1986.

The Coming to Power: Critical Presidential Elections in American History, Chelsea House, 1972.

The Dynamics of World Power: A Documentary History of United States Foreign Policy, 1945-1973, Chelsea House, 1973, Volume 1: *Western Europe,* Volume 2: *Eastern Europe and the Soviet Union,* Volume 3: *Latin America,* Volume 4: *Far East,* Volume 5: *United Nations, Middle East, Subsaharan Africa.*

History of U.S. Political Parties, Chelsea House, 1973, Volume 1: *1789-1860: From Factions to Parties,* Volume 2: *1860-1910: The Gilded Age of Politics,* Volume 3: *1910-1945: From Square Deal to New Deal,* Volume 4: *1945-1972: The Politics of Change.*

(With Roger Bruns) *Congress Investigates: A Documented History, 1792-1974,* five volumes, Chelsea House, 1975.

The American Statesmen, forty-five volumes, Chelsea House, 1982.

(With John S. Bowman) *The Almanac of American History,* Putnam, 1983.

OTHER

(Contributor) *Four Portraits and One Subject: Bernard De Voto,* Houghton, 1963.

(Author of foreword) Arthur M. Schlesinger, Sr., *Paths to the Present,* revised and enlarged edition, Houghton, 1964.

(Author of preface) Schlesinger, *The American as Reformer,* Harvard University Press, 1968.

(Author of introduction) Schlesinger, *The Birth of a Nation: A Portrait of the American People on the Eve of Independence,* Knopf, 1968.

(Author of introduction) Schlesinger, *Nothing Stands Still: Essays,* Belknap Press, 1969.

(Author of foreword) *Robert Kennedy in His Own Words: The Unpublished Recollections of the Kennedy Years,* Bantam, 1989.

Also author of television screenplay, "The Journey of Robert F. Kennedy." Author of pamphlets on political subjects. Author of introductions for "World Leaders Past & Present" series, more than fifty volumes, and "Know Your Government" series, for Chelsea House. Movie reviewer for *Show,* 1962-64, *Vogue,* 1966-72, and *Saturday Review,* 1977-80; member of jury, Cannes Film Festival, 1964. Contributor to magazines and to newspapers, including *Wall Street Journal.* Schlesinger's White House staff papers are collected in the John F. Kennedy Library in Boston, Mass.

SIDELIGHTS: "Since World War II," reports Edwin A. Miles in the *Dictionary of Literary Biography,* "Arthur Meier Schlesinger, Jr., has been perhaps the nation's most widely known and controversial historian." Twice awarded the Pulitzer Prize and the National Book Award, Schlesinger's oeuvre has gained widespread popularity as well as serious critical attention. He has also attracted attention through his political activism, especially his outspoken advocacy of a liberal position in the Democratic party. "There is perhaps no single name more closely associated with the history, the biography, the political experience and the intellectual positions of liberalism's 'vital center,' " declares Benjamin R. Barber in *The New York Times Book Review,* "than that of Mr. Schlesinger."

Schlesinger seemed destined for a remarkable career from an early age. His father, the senior Arthur M. Schlesinger, was a distinguished American historian who helped guide his son's career. The younger Schlesinger majored in history and literature at Harvard University, where he won the LeBaron Russell Briggs Prize for a freshman essay. His senior honors thesis, on the nineteenth-century American Catholic intellectual Orestes A. Brownson, was later published as *Orestes A. Brownson: A Pilgrim's Progress* and was acclaimed by many prominent authorities. The famous American historian Henry Steele Commager, for instance, declares in the *New York Times Book Review* that Schlesinger's study "not only rescues from undeserved oblivion a striking and authentic figure in our history, but announces a new and distinguished talent in the field of historical portraiture."

The impact of the Brownson biography brought Schlesinger material awards as well. He received fellowships to both Cambridge and Harvard universities and was invited to lecture on the period of President Andrew Jackson's administration by the Lowell Institute in Boston. The lectures Schlesinger delivered there in the fall of 1941 provided the groundwork for *The Age of Jackson,* a reevaluation of Andrew Jackson's presidency that "stands as a significant landmark in the writing of the nation's history," according to Miles. The volume captured the Pulitzer Prize for history in 1946 and provoked a controversy among historians that continues today.

In *The Age of Jackson* Schlesinger challenges the accepted interpretation of Jacksonian democracy as essentially a frontier phenomenon. Historians relying on Frederick Jackson Turner's "frontier thesis" see the political battles of Jackson's era as a sectional struggle between a firmly democratic West and the established powers of the East. Schlesinger argues that in fact Jacksonian democracy received much of its support from laborers living in Eastern states and suggests that it represented a clash of classes rather than of sections. He also maintains that Jackson's concept of democracy represented a significant change from Thomas Jefferson's ideal because of its willingness to use strong government to protect individuals from corporate interests, and draws parallels between Jacksonian politics and the philosophy of Franklin Roosevelt's New Deal programs.

In addition to the Pulitzer Prize, *The Age of Jackson* won Schlesinger a Guggenheim fellowship, sold more than 90,000 copies, and got its author an associate professorship in Harvard's history

department—this for a twenty-eight-year-old who held only a bachelor's degree and had little teaching experience. Yet although many reviewers acclaim *The Age of Jackson* for its readability and thought-provoking analysis, others find Schlesinger's approach too partisan in its advocacy of Jacksonian principles. Allan Nevins, writing in the *New York Times,* calls the book "excessively hostile to Whig leaders and Whig ideas, the caustic treatment of Daniel Webster and Horace Greeley seeming especially unfair. It sometimes rides its thesis a bit too hard." "But," he adds "it is a remarkable piece of analytical history, full of vitality, rich in insights and new facts, and casting a broad shaft of illumination over one of the most interesting periods of our national life."

In the mid 1950s, Schlesinger began what many historians feel is his greatest contribution to the field: his multivolume *The Age of Roosevelt,* still in progress more than thirty years after its beginning. The three volumes that appeared between 1957 and 1960 were all Book-of-the-Month Club selections, and all "attest to his superb style, felicity of phrase, keen sense of drama, and successful blending of narrative and analytical history," says Miles. Yet although the first volume, *The Crisis of the Old Order, 1919-1933,* won prestigious awards from historical and scholastic institutions, it was not universally acclaimed. Norman MacKenzie, writing in the *New Statesman,* declares that it "lacked a cutting edge," and adds, "Mr. Schlesinger's appraisal is not only smooth; it is curiously isolated from the outside world." Many prominent reviewers and historians feel otherwise. "Probably no more thoughtful or surgical or compassionate study of the period in the United States has been written," asserts the *New Yorker;* and C. Vann Woodward maintains in the *Saturday Review* that the book "is a permanent enrichment of our historical literature."

Schlesinger sustained a presence in politics as well as in academics. Many of his works championed Democratic and liberal policies; *The Vital Center: The Politics of Freedom* reflects Schlesinger's anti-Communism, for instance, while *Nixon or Kennedy: Does It Make Any Difference?* urged voters to select the Democratic ticket in the 1960 election, and *The Politics of Hope* expressed his liberal philosophy and hopes for the Kennedy administration. In 1952 and 1956 he took leaves of absence from Harvard to support Adlai Stevenson's presidential campaigns as an adviser and speech writer. After John F. Kennedy won his presidential bid in 1960, Schlesinger joined the administration as a special assistant to the President. Working with President Kennedy, Schlesinger helped formulate the "New Frontier" and, in foreign policy, the "Alliance for Progress." He also provided innovations, stimulated new ideas, and linked the scholastic, intellectual, and cultural communities with Kennedy's government.

The historian recalls his role in the Kennedy Administration in his book *A Thousand Days: John F. Kennedy in the White House,* which won Schlesinger his first National Book Award and his second Pulitzer Prize. "I felt I owed it," he says, "both to the memory of the President and to the historical profession to put it all down." The volume draws on notes Schlesinger had kept at Kennedy's request for the president's own memoirs, and caused much contention through its revelations about Kennedy's political circle, especially his frustration with Secretary of State Dean Rusk. John Roger Fredland, writing in *Saturday Review,* was one who found Schlesinger "unduly hard on Dean Rusk," calling his depiction of Kennedy's Secretary of State, the State Department as a whole, and the Foreign Service "both mischievous and unjust." But the book is not so much a history of the Kennedy administration as it is a description of its deliberations and decisions as Schlesinger remembers them. Some reviewers who expected a more scholarly treatment have been disappointed, but many others agree with Fredland in saying that "as a primary source . . . for future historians *A Thousand Days* deserves success and acclaim." James MacGregor Burns declares in the *New York Times Book Review* that "this is Arthur Schlesinger's best book. A great President has found—perhaps he deliberately chose—a great historian."

The late 1960s and 1970s proved disappointing politically for Schlesinger. He left the government soon after President Kennedy's assassination, disillusioned with Lyndon Johnson's administration. The historian criticized Johnson's Vietnam policy in *The Bitter Heritage: Vietnam and American Democracy, 1941-1966,* and backed Robert Kennedy's bid for the Democratic nomination in the 1968 election. Senator Robert Kennedy's murder in June of 1968 profoundly affected Schlesinger's ideology, according to Miles. In 1969 he produced *The Crisis of Confidence: Ideas, Power, and Violence in America,* a book that rejected the optimism of *The Politics of Hope* published just six years earlier, and in 1973 he censured several presidents, including Johnson and Richard Nixon, for their misuse of presidential powers in *The Imperial Presidency.* Even the election of Democrat Jimmy Carter in 1976 did not lighten Schlesinger's gloom; he "called him the most conservative Democratic president since Grover Cleveland, and pronounced his administration the most incompetent since that of Warren G. Harding," declares Miles.

In 1978, perhaps as a reaction to the Carter presidency, Schlesinger published *Robert Kennedy and His Times,* an enormous project that won him his second National Book Award. The book reexamines the idealism of the Kennedy years in what Henry Fairlie, writing in the *New Republic,* calls "really a page-by-page revision of [*A Thousand Days*]." Yet there are marked differences between the two volumes: while *A Thousand Days* is a personal memoir, *Robert Kennedy* is a formal biography, and many reviewers found the later book more controversial than its predecessor. While succumbing to the fascination of the work, some commentators were disappointed in its uncritical portrait of Bobby Kennedy and believed that Schlesinger had created "something like a 916-page promotional pamphlet of exculpation and eulogy," as *New York Review of Books* contributor Marshall Frady puts it. "Schlesinger is, of course, scrupulously candid about the nature of the book in this regard," reports Eliot Fremont-Smith in the *Village Voice,* "but candor does not excuse everything. There's no question that he puts the most favorable light . . . on Kennedy's mistakes and flaws." However, he concludes, after "all this [is] said, I think *Robert Kennedy and His Times* is pretty good."

The election of Republican Ronald Reagan in 1980 further delayed Schlesinger's anticipation of a resurgent liberalism. *The Cycles of American History,* a collection of essays on the history of American government published in 1986, "may be taken as the testament of a confirmed liberal forced to endure the age of Reagan," reports Barry Gewen in the *New Leader.* Yet the book is not a tirade against the Republican government, but rather a historical analysis of mechanisms that, Schlesinger believes, shape American history. He also suggests how these mechanisms may be used to shape tomorrow's America. In fourteen essays on subjects ranging from "The Future of the Vice Presidency" to "Affirmative Government and the American Economy," Schlesinger attempts "to measure America's behavior against America's aspirations," according to *Time* contributor Melvin Maddocks. John Kenneth Galbraith, writing for *Tribune Books,* calls the collection "a brilliant evocation of his view of the uses of history."

Misgivings about his political activism aside, professional historians value the contributions Schlesinger has made to their craft. Alan Brinkley, writing in the *New Republic,* states that, "despite the countless ways in which he has violated the conventions of his profession, he remains one of [the historical occupation's] most important voices." "It is not simply because he possesses a literary grace that few American scholars can match," he continues, "and not simply because the range of his interests and knowledge far exceeds that of most historians in this age of narrow specialization. It is because he possesses a rare ability to make history seem important, because he is willing to argue that the search for an understanding of the past is not simply an aesthetic exercise but a path to the understanding of our own time." "He is a reminder to professional historians," Brinkley concludes, "of the possibilities of reaching beyond their own ranks to the larger world in which they live."

BIOGRAPHICAL/CRITICAL SOURCES:

BOOKS

Authors in the News, Volume 1, Gale, 1976.
Brandon, Henry, *Conversations with Henry Brandon,* Deutsch, 1966.
Cunliffe, Marcus and Robin W. Winks, editors, *Pastmasters: Some Essays on American Historians,* Harper, 1969.
Dictionary of Literary Biography, Volume 17: *Twentieth-Century American Historians,* Gale, 1983.
Fitzgerald, Carol B., editor, *American History: A Bibliographic Review,* Volume 1, Meckler, 1985.
Garraty, John A., *Interpreting American History: Conversations with American Historians,* Macmillan, 1970.
Heller, Deane and David Heller, *Kennedy Cabinet,* Monarch, 1961.
Ross, Mitchell S., *The Literary Politicians,* Doubleday, 1978.
Schlesinger, Arthur Meier, Sr., *In Retrospect: The History of a Historian,* Harcourt, 1963.

PERIODICALS

Akron Beacon Journal, December 30, 1973.
American Heritage, October, 1978.
American Historical Review, January, 1940, April, 1946, October, 1957, October, 1959, April, 1961.
Esquire, September 26, 1978.
Globe and Mail (Toronto), March 7, 1987.
Harper's, September, 1978.
Life, July 16, 1965.
Los Angeles Times, March 22, 1979.
Los Angeles Times Book Review, October 26, 1986.
Nation, July 22, 1939, October 20, 1945, March 23, 1957, January 31, 1959, November 12, 1960, August 6, 1977, August 20, 1977, September 30, 1978.
National Review, October 27, 1978.
New Leader, May 8, 1967, November 17, 1986.
New Republic, June 7, 1939, October 22, 1945, March 4, 1957, October 27, 1958, November 10, 1958, January 12, 1959, September 26, 1960, December 4, 1965, February 11, 1967, September 9, 1978, December 1, 1986.
New Statesman, August 17, 1957, May 26, 1961, November 10, 1978.
Newsweek, November 19, 1973, September 4, 1978, October 27, 1986.
New Yorker, September 15, 1945, March 16, 1957, September 10, 1960, December 11, 1965, December 10, 1973, November 17, 1986.
New York Herald Tribune Book Review, September 11, 1960.

New York Review of Books, January 6, 1966, February 23, 1967, December 13, 1973, October 12, 1978, November 6, 1986.

New York Times, April 23, 1939, September 16, 1945, March 3, 1957, January 4, 1959, November 24, 1965, January 16, 1967, October 31, 1985, November 13, 1986, April 14, 1988.

New York Times Book Review, January 4, 1959, April 7, 1963, November 28, 1965, April 9, 1967, June 4, 1967, June 22, 1969, November 18, 1973, January 7, 1979, November 16, 1986.

Playboy, May, 1966.

Saturday Review, March 2, 1957, December 4, 1965, February 4, 1967, September 18, 1971.

Time, March 11, 1957, January 19, 1959, December 17, 1965, November 26, 1973, September 4, 1978, December 1, 1986.

Times Literary Supplement, November 25, 1965, January 26, 1967, November 30, 1973, November 10, 1978, March 13, 1987.

Tribune Books (Chicago), November 2, 1986.

Village Voice, December 20, 1973, September 11, 1978.

Wall Street Journal, September 8, 1978.

Washington Post, February 18, 1970.

Washington Post Book World, December 14, 1986.

OTHER

Schlesinger, Arthur M., Jr., "A Conversation with Arthur M. Schlesinger, Jr." (recording), Center for Cassette Studies, 1975.

*   *   *

SCHMITZ, Aron Hector   1861-1928
(E. Samigli, Italo Svevo)

PERSONAL: Birth-given name Italianized as Ettore Schmitz; best known as Italo Svevo; born December 19, 1861, in Trieste (part of the Austro-Hungarian Empire; now in Italy); died September 13, 1928, in Motta di Livenza, Treviso, Italy; son of Francesco and Allegra (Moravia) Schmitz; married Livia Veneziani, July 30, 1896 (civil ceremony), and August 25, 1897 (Catholic rite); children: Letizia Fonda Savio. *Education:* Attended Brussel'sche Handels-und Erzichungsinstitut (Segnitz-am-Main, Germany), 1874-78; attended Istituto Superiore Commerciale Revoltella (now University of Trieste), 1874-80.

CAREER: Novelist, short story writer, playwright, essayist, and journalist. Correspondence clerk at Trieste branch of Viennese Unionbank, 1880-99; instructor in French and German commercial correspondence at Istituto Superiore Commerciale Revoltella, 1893-1900; industrialist with Ditta Veneziani (manufacturer of marine paints), 1899-1928. Director of Lega Nazionale, Societa Triestina di Ginnastica, and Societa Patria.

MEMBER: P.E.N. (Paris, France), Il Convegno (Milan, Italy), Gabinetto di Minerva, Circolo Musicale, Circolo Artistico, Schopenhauergesellschaft.

WRITINGS:

FICTION, UNDER PSEUDONYM ITALO SVEVO

Una vita (novel), [Italy], c. 1892, Edizioni Studi Tesi, 1985, translation by Archibald Colquhoun published as *A Life,* Knopf, 1963, reprinted, Penguin, 1982.

Senilita (novel), [Italy], 1898, Dall'Oglio, 1967, translation by Beryl De Zoete published as *As a Man Grows Older,* with introduction by Stanislaus Joyce, Putnam, 1932, reprinted, with essay by Edouard Roditi, Greenwood Press, 1977.

La coscienza di Zeno (novel), [Bologna, Italy], 1923, revised edition, with preface by Eugenio Montale, Dall'Oglio, 1976,

translation by De Zoete published as *Confessions of Zeno,* Putnam, 1930, reprinted, Greenwood Press, 1973, published with essay by Renato Poggioli, New Directions, 1947, published with note on Svevo by Roditi, Secker & Warburg, 1962, Random House, 1989.

Una burla riuscita (first published as a short story), translation by De Zoete published as *The Hoax,* Leonard & Virginia Woolf, 1929, Harcourt, 1930, reprinted, Arden Library, 1978.

La novella del buon vecchio e della bella fanciulla e altri scritti (novella), [Italy], 1929, Dall'Oglio, 1966, translation by L. Collison-Morley published as *The Nice Old Man and the Pretty Girl and Other Stories,* with introductory note by Montale, Leonard & Virginia Woolf, 1930.

Corto viaggio sentimentale e altri racconti inediti (short stories; title means "Short Sentimental Journey and Other Unpublished Stories"), edited with preface by Umbro Apollonio, Mondadori, 1949, reprinted, 1966, published as *Corto viaggio sentimentale: Racconto,* Dall'Oglio, 1978.

Due racconti: La tribu, Lo specifico del dottor Menghi (two short stories), All'insegna del pesce d'oro, 1967.

Further Confessions of Zeno (contains fragments and drafts of Svevo's unpublished sequel to *Confessions of Zeno* [also see above], the play "Regeneration," and the stories "The Old, Old Man," "An Old Man's Confessions," "Umbertino," "A Contract," and "This Indolence of Mine"), translation from the Italian by Ben Johnson and P. N. Furbank, University of California Press, 1969.

NONFICTION, UNDER PSEUDONYM ITALO SVEVO

James Joyce (transcript of lecture delivered by Svevo in Milan, Italy, in 1926), translation by Stanislaus Joyce, New Directions, 1950, reprinted, City Lights Books, 1969.

Saggi e pagine sparse (essays, articles, and diary entries), edited with preface by Apollonio, Mondadori, 1954.

"Profilo autobiografico" (autobiographical sketch), published in *Vita di mio marito con altri inedite di Italo Svevo,* by Livia Veneziani Svevo and Lina Galli, Edizioni dello Zibaldone, 1958.

Commedie (plays), edited with preface by Apollonio, Mondadori, 1960.

Diario per la fidanzata, 1896 (title means "Diary for My Fiancee, 1896"), edited by Bruno Maier and Anita Pittoni, with introduction by Maier, Edizioni dello Zibaldone, 1962.

Critical Edition of the Works of Italo Svevo, edited by Maier, Edizioni Studio Tesi, 1985.

LETTERS, UNDER PSEUDONYM ITALO SVEVO

Corrispondenza con Valery Larbaud, Benjamin Cremieux e Marie Anne Comnene, [Italy], 1953.

Lettere alla moglie (title means "Letters to My Wife"), edited by Pittoni with introduction by Maier, Edizioni dello Zibaldone, 1963.

Lettere, con gli scritti di Montale su Svevo (correspondence and Montale's writings on Svevo), De Donato, 1966.

Saba, Svevo, Comisso: Lettere inedite (correspondence between Svevo and poets Umberto Saba and Giovanni Comisso), edited by Mario Sutor with introduction by George Pullini, Gruppo di lettere moderne, 1968.

Carteggio con gli scritti di Montale su Svevo (correspondence and Montale's writings on Svevo), edited by Giorgio Zampa, Mondadori, 1976.

Carteggio con James Joyce, Valery Larbaud, Benjamin Cremieux, Marie Anne Comnene, Eugenio Montale, Valerio Jahier, edited by Maier, Dall'Oglio, 1978.

COLLECTED WORKS, UNDER PSEUDONYM ITALO SVEVO

Opere di Italo Svevo (title means "The Works of Italo Svevo"; includes *Una vita, Senilita, La coscienza di Zeno,* and *La novella del buon vecchio e della bella fanciulla*), edited with introduction and bibliography by Maier, Dall'Oglio, 1954, reprinted, 1964.

Opera Omnia, edited by Maier, Dall'Oglio, Volume 1: *Epistolario,* 1966; Volume 2: *Romanzi: Una Vita, Senilita, La coscienza di Zeno,* 1969; Volume 3: *Racconti, saggi, pagine sparse,* 1968; Volume 4: *Commedie,* introduction and note by Apollonio, 1969.

The Works of Italo Svevo, University of California Press, 1967-80, Volume 1: *Confessions of Zeno,* translated from the Italian by De Zoete, with note by Roditi; Volume 2: *As a Man Grows Older,* translated from the Italian by De Zoete; Volume 3: *A Life,* translated from the Italian by Colquhoun; Volume 4: *Short Sentimental Journal and Other Stories,* translated from the Italian by De Zoete, Collison-Morley, and Johnson; Volume 5: *Further Confessions of Zeno,* translated from the Italian by Johnson and Furbank.

OTHER

Contributor of newspaper articles and short stories to periodicals, including *L'Indipendente,* under pseudonym E. Samigli.

SIDELIGHTS: Writing about Italo Svevo for *Modern Fiction Studies,* Beno Weiss declared: "When we speak of modern European literature, we think of [James] Joyce, [Luigi] Pirandello, [Franz] Kafka, [Robert] Musil, [Marcel] Proust, [D. H.] Lawrence, [Andre] Gide, and [Thomas] Mann as seminal forces. Certainly Italo Svevo, for his distinct originality, for his sensitivity to the new European currents which dominated his time, for his wealth of interests and his intuitive capacity in the inner probings of man, has been fully accepted and rightfully belongs among the ranks of these great writers. If we wish to study this period of Italian letters, we must, therefore, start with Svevo." Indeed, he was the first Italian—if not European—author to make use of Austrian neurologist Sigmund Freud's new and, in Svevo's time, revolutionary ideas of psychoanalysis. Yet in spite of his vast critical acclaim Svevo remained something of a problematic figure for Italian readers—particularly those obsessed with and nurtured under the influence of the aesthetic ideals of Benedetto Croce and Gabriele D'Annunzio—who found it difficult to classify Svevo's experimentation in style, language, themes, and narrative techniques.

Born Aron Hector Schmitz, Svevo was a son of a patriarchal Jewish family that had migrated to Trieste from Hungary and had Italianized itself in the port city of the Austro-Hungarian empire. Though it was by no means fanatical in its religious observances, the Schmitz family respected certain Jewish customs. Called Ettore, the Italian form of Hector, the child was sent at the age of twelve to study in Germany, where he attended a commercial school frequented predominantly by Jewish boys. His father believed that in order to be a successful businessman in Trieste one had to have a good knowledge of the German language and that a traditional German education, with its formality and discipline, would be useful for his son's eventual career in business. This paternal choice was to have a great influence on Svevo's formation as a writer. At school in Segnitz-am-Main he began to read widely—from William Shakespeare to Ivan Turgenev—and quench his great thirst for knowledge. He was particularly fond of the German classics: Friedrich Schiller, Johann Wolfgang von Goethe, and Arthur Schopenhauer; in the wry humor of Friedrich Richter he found a special attraction. Indeed, Svevo's experiences at Segnitz-am-Main inspired him to

become a writer. At seventeen he returned to Trieste where he attended for two years—but without much interest—the Istituto Superiore Commerciale Revoltella. His father, totally absorbed by his business ventures, failed to appreciate Svevo's literary longings. Only his younger brother Elio fully understood Svevo's nature and encouraged his literary aspirations. Grasping the value of the older boy's excitement and still disorganized ideas, Elio kept abreast of all Svevo's attempts at writing, including his failures and partial successes.

Financial difficulties compelled Svevo to leave school in 1880. He then found a job as a correspondence clerk at the Unionbank, where he endured nineteen long years of unsatisfying work. His experiences as a petty-bourgeois bank employee are well described in several of his writings, particularly in *A Life (Una vita)* in which he takes to task the mediocrity and hypocrisy of the Triestine middle class. With Elio's prodding and counsel, he realized that in order to succeed as an Italian writer he had to study Italian authors; he thus devoted much of his free time to this task at the public library of Trieste. He read Niccolo Machiavelli, Francesco Guicciardini, Giovanni Boccaccio, and Giosue Carducci, using literary historian Francesco De Sanctis as a guide. But soon he was attracted to the novel and to the French naturalists, reading Gustave Flaubert, Honore de Balzac, Alphonse Daudet, and finally Emile Zola, who immediately became his idol. Nonetheless, Svevo revealed years later in his autobiographical sketch "Profilo autobiografico" (published in wife Livia Veneziani Svevo's memoirs, *Vita di mio marito con altri inedite di Italo Svevo*) that Schopenhauer soon became his favorite author. Alfonso, the protagonist of Svevo's first novel, *A Life,* "was supposed to be the very personification of the Schopenhauerian affirmation of life so near its negation," Svevo wrote. "Hence, perhaps, the harsh and abrupt conclusion of the novel, like a part of a syllogism."

In 1880 Svevo began his long association with *L'Indipendente,* a Triestine newspaper that advocated the city's independence from Austria. In *L'Indipendente* he published his first article, "Shylock," under the pseudonym E. Samigli. He continued to use this pseudonym until 1892, when he published *A Life* as Italo Svevo, a name chosen to underline the dual aspects of the author's cultural roots: Italian and Swabian (German). Joking about the use of the pseudonym, Svevo repeatedly claimed that he had chosen it because he felt sorry for that lonely vowel surrounded by so many consonants in his surname Schmitz.

Trieste, due to its geographical and political position, was a meeting place of heterogeneous peoples and cultures, as well as a clearing house of new cultural movements and ideas. In this international city where the arts flourish many theatres and concert halls featured the most popular Italian and European plays and artists. Svevo, who was very much drawn to the cultural life of the city, felt that he had been born for the stage and dreamed of becoming an actor and a playwright. Indeed, Svevo wrote plays throughout his life, for he was convinced that through the theatre more than through his novels he could communicate directly the themes that interested him. Regarding the theatre as "the form of forms," he wrote his novels and short stories only after he had experienced continuous setbacks with his plays, which are neither scarce, secondary, nor marginal to his novels. They are, in fact, the genesis of his fiction.

In 1886 Svevo's brother Elio died after a long illness. His death was a terrible blow for Svevo, who then felt utterly alone, discouraged, and bewildered. Other deaths and family misfortunes implanted an abiding bitterness in the aspiring writer. Only literature could offer him solace and purpose. In 1889, when he was working on his first novel, Svevo made the following entry in his diary: "Today I am 28 years old. My dissatisfaction with myself and with others could not be worse. I record these feelings so that if in a few years I should look back, I'll be able to call myself a fool anew and perhaps even get some comfort in finding that my situation hasn't improved. My financial position is growing worse; I'm not happy with either my health, my work, or the people around me. It's only fitting that since I myself am not satisfied with my work, I can't expect others to be. Regardless of all the exaggerated ambitions I once had, it is terrible not to have found anyone, no one at all, who would take an interest in what I was thinking or doing; I find myself instead forced always to take an interest in other people's doings, since that's the only way of getting their attention. Exactly two years ago I began that novel which was supposed to be God knows what. Instead it's mere rubbish that will eventually sicken me. Hope has always been my strength, but alas even that is diminishing." Notwithstanding this dejection, Svevo persevered and gradually began to make a name for himself in Trieste, where he wrote plays and published articles and short stories. In 1890 he met the Triestine painter Umberto Veruda, who introduced him to impressionism and who appears as the sculptor Balli in Svevo's second novel, *As a Man Grows Older* (*Senilita*). This friendship filled the void of Elio's death and decreased Svevo's loneliness and pessimism, for Veruda's understanding of Svevo was complete, and both shared their thoughts and creations.

In 1892 Svevo's father died, and the same year he published *A Life* at his own expense. The novel, except for a few positive reviews in the local press and a brief but encouraging mention in the prestigious newspaper *Il Corriere Della Sera,* was otherwise greeted with complete silence. Svevo wrote in "Profilio autobiografico" that if *A Life* had been better received, he would have left his ill-paying job and improved his "neglected literary preparation." This silence on the part of the Italian critics marked the beginning of the now notorious "Svevo case," which was to plague Svevo's reputation until the post-Fascist era. The term is used to describe his inability to gain recognition from the Italian critics due in part to his being a Jew, his not being completely Italian (he retained his Austrian passport until 1918), and his living in an international city, as well as to his particular style, language, and choice of subject matter and characters. Even after his "discovery" and as late as 1928 he could not find a publisher willing to print the second edition of *As a Man Grows Older* unless he paid for it himself.

In 1893, Svevo began part-time teaching of German and French correspondence at the Istituto Commerciale Superiore Revoltella, which after World War I became the University of Trieste and where, with Svevo's help, writer James Joyce was appointed professor of English, teaching from 1911 to 1920. In 1896 Svevo's mother died. That same year he married his cousin Livia Veneziani in a civil ceremony. Livia and her parents exerted extreme pressure on Svevo to convert to Catholicism; his wife, who was suffering from a difficult pregnancy, feared that she would die in mortal sin if she was not married in church. Svevo reluctantly converted and married Livia in a religious ceremony in 1897. The conversion was a mere formality for Svevo, who was an agnostic, yet for years he felt guilty about his apostasy. In several letters, he expressed his uneasiness and incompatibility with Christianity, particularly when his daughter's education was to be decided.

Svevo published *As a Man Grows Older* in 1898, again at his own expense. This novel prompted even less response than his first one, a fact that caused him great bitterness and frustration. Once again, as he had done on previous occasions, he took stock of his

literary efforts, and as Livia reported in *Vita di mio marito,* he concluded bitterly: "I can't understand this incomprehension. It shows that people just do not understand. It's useless for me to write and publish." He withdrew within himself, giving up his literary ambitions and no longer speaking to his friends about his writings; nevertheless, during his free time, he continued to read incessantly and to write. According to Livia, he frequently declared, "In this world one is compelled to write, but not necessarily to publish."

In 1899, after nineteen years at the Unionbank, Svevo went to work for his wife's family, thus greatly improving his financial position. The Veneziani family owned a very successful factory that produced protective underwater paints for ships' hulls. The new job allowed Svevo to travel on the continent and also often to England, where he set up a branch of the factory. He eventually became a very prosperous businessman, but this new way of life did not fulfill his inner needs. Only writing, it seemed, could do that. He thus began to make notes and collect scraps of paper on which he analyzed everything he saw or thought, hoping to gain a better understanding of himself and to improve his writing: "I believe, I sincerely believe, that there is no better way of becoming a serious writer than to scribble every day. One must try to bring out from the depths of one's innermost being a sound, an accent, a fossil or a vegetable residue of something that may or may not be a feeling, or rather a whim, a regret, a sorrow, something sincere, dissected and that's all. . . . In other words there is no salvation except in the pen," he recorded in a diary entry for October 2, 1899.

Svevo's work at the Veneziani enterprise demanded more and more of him, leaving little time or energy for his hidden passion. Again and again he tried with little success to give up writing, finding at times some compensation by playing his violin. Svevo's perennial seesaw of renouncing and then resuming his literary yearning was similar to his lifelong resolutions to give up tobacco. Like Zeno, the protagonist of his last novel, Svevo, too, used to write himself resolutions vowing to give up his addiction, without ever managing to fulfill the promise of the "last cigarette."

Svevo's friend Veruda died in 1904. The next year Svevo met writer James Joyce, who had come to Trieste to teach English at the Berlitz School. Svevo, who often traveled to England and wished to improve his knowledge of English, eventually became the Irish writer's pupil. However, instead of concerning themselves with English grammar—Svevo used to call Joyce *il mercante di gerundi* (gerund-dealer)—they discussed at length literature and their own writings. According to Stanislaus Joyce's recollections in his introduction to *As a Man Grows Older,* when his brother James read his story "The Dead" to Svevo, Livia Svevo, "who took lessons with her husband, gathered a bunch of flowers and presented it to my brother. It was the first genuine and spontaneous sign of pleasure in the literary work of that outcast artist that I can recollect."

The most important aspect of this new friendship was that Svevo again had someone to talk to about his writings, someone who gave him the necessary encouragement and made him aware that his writings were far better than he had realized. According to Stanislaus Joyce, his brother James, who never praised or disparaged half-heartedly, "told Svevo impulsively that there were pages of *Senilita* that could not have been written better by the greatest French master. He already knew parts of it by heart, and quoted them with huge satisfaction. He expressed his opinion roundly, as is his wont, of the obtuseness of critics. Svevo was amazed at hearing his almost forgotten novels commended in such unambiguous terms."

When Svevo read parts of Joyce's novel *A Portrait of the Artist as a Young Man,* his warm response stimulated Joyce to go on writing and to send off once again his story collection *Dubliners,* for which he had been unable to find a publisher. When Joyce was planning to write his masterpiece novel *Ulysses,* he discussed it at great length with Svevo, whose knowledge of Jewish customs proved invaluable for the creation of one of the novel's central characters, Leopold Bloom. According to Stanislaus, Joyce scholar Richard Ellmann, and others, Bloom is modeled to a large extent on Svevo. Stanislaus wrote that once, when he substituted for his brother at a lesson, "Svevo asked me to tell him something about Ireland and the Irish. My brother had been talking so much about Jews that Svevo wished to get even with him by holding forth on Ireland."

This long-lasting friendship with the great Irish writer instilled in Svevo a new sense of purpose that inspired him to undertake his third novel after almost twenty years of silence. When he wrote *Confessions of Zeno (La coscienza di Zeno)* in 1919, he was no longer haunted by uncertainties and feelings of insecurity. He had read Freud and translated some of his writings into Italian; he had written many plays, short stories, and articles, as well as a treatise on universal peace; Italy had taken part in World War I, and Svevo had participated in the political struggle for the Italianization of Trieste. He no longer had doubts about literature, nor did he feel his earlier hesitance to write. Livia wrote that these were days full of excitement for Svevo, that he "fully embraced literature."

Confessions of Zeno was published in 1923, once again at the author's expense. The novel was greeted by what Svevo, according to Stanislaus Joyce, called perfect unanimity: "There is no unanimity so perfect as the unanimity of silence." Only Silvio Benco and a few other local writers paid any attention to the novel. As an act of rebellion against this blatant hostility on the part of the Italian press, Svevo sent the novel to Joyce, who was then in Paris. Joyce showed *Confessions of Zeno* and Svevo's other novels to critics Benjamin Cremieux and Valery Larbaud, key figures on the Parisian literary scene. Both were fascinated by Svevo's works and promised to bring their author to the attention of the French public. Recognition instead came when the poet Eugenio Montale devoted a profound and ample study to Svevo's works in his periodical *Esame,* thus bringing him to the attention of Italian readers. Finally, in 1926, after many delays, Cremieux and Larbaud's efforts came to fruition: an entire issue of the newly founded Parisian periodical *Le Navire d'Argent* was devoted to Svevo, thereby making him known to France and the world. Many critiques and articles were published about him, hailing him erroneously as the "Italian Proust." He gave lectures and interviews and participated in various functions as a celebrity. He prepared new editions of his novels and supervised various translations of his works; he also began to write a long sequel to *Confessions of Zeno.*

Just when Svevo was beginning to enjoy his delayed but much deserved success, he suffered a broken femur in a car accident and died unexpectedly a few days later in September of 1928. Since he had been ailing for many years with a heart condition, aggravated by his excessive smoking, the cause of Svevo's death is thought to be shock from the accident. According to his daughter's account in *Iconografia Sveviana,* when Svevo knew that he was about to die, he asked for a cigarette. When it was refused, he said, "This one would definitely have been the last cigarette." Umberto Saba recalled in *Prose* that when Svevo be-

came aware that he had already smoked his very last cigarette, he stopped being afraid of death. "Dying," he said to his family, "is far easier than writing a novel." Shortly thereafter, his heart stopped. He was buried in a shroud, according to Jewish tradition.

A Life, Svevo's first novel, introduces subjects explored in Svevo's later works: ineptitude, the frustrated artist, antiheroic characters, autobiography, craving for self-fulfillment and love, old age, disease, death, introspection and propensity for dreams, the bourgeoisie and its decadence, and crises of modern man. It also presents Svevo's characteristic antitheses: old age/youth; health/disease; real illness/imaginary illness; heroism/antiheroism; life/art; life/death. The novel tells the story of a young man who has come to Trieste to work at a bank but finds difficulty in adjusting to city life and to the demeaning, tedious work of a low-paid business correspondent. Alfonso Nitti, the protagonist, lives as a boarder with the Lanuccis, a wretched family that has fallen on hard times. His incompetence at the bank results in harsh reprimands from his superiors. He partly overcomes his uneasiness and frustration by going to the library where he is free to indulge in his true vocation: that of a writer. Eventually, in spite of his timidity, he befriends Annetta Maller, his boss's spoiled but beautiful daughter. Though she is vain, arrogant, and treats him as an inferior, he is intrigued by her and by the new respect he receives at the bank because of this relationship. Ultimately he seduces the girl—one might say she seduces him—but instead of improving his condition in life by marrying Annetta, he uses his mother's illness as a pretext to run away from her. At home in his village he finds out that his mother truly is dying. His return to the city marks his end: He is demoted at the bank, loses Annetta, and ultimately must choose between certain death at the hands of Annetta's brother or suicide.

As attested by Svevo himself, the novel can be regarded as a spiritual autobiography inasmuch as the protagonist experiences the same problems of identity, frustration, anxiety, and timidity encountered by the author while working at the bank. By and large, the dark mood of *A Life* and its depiction of the social and economic problems in the life of the Triestine middle class—particularly the careful description of the Lanuccis—are naturalistic. However, Svevo went beyond the canons of French naturalism by presenting a new social situation that reflected the changes occurring in the bourgeoisie of central Europe. Georgio Luti declared in *Italo Svevo e altri studi sulla letteratura italiana del primo Novecento* that *A Life* presents "the vivid documentation of the bourgeois anguish of those years and the novel, precisely because of this new dimension, leaves behind the naturalistic heritage. In Svevo's work we find the development of the grand picture of the early 20th Century, the authentic portrait of contemporary man."

Svevo's protagonist Nitti is typical of his other antiheroic characters. In "Note on Svevo," which prefaces the 1930 translation of *Confessions of Zeno,* Edouard Roditi stated that these figures "all seem to be tormented by an intense lust for self-improvement, spiritual or social, for education, wisdom or learning to better them or their positions; however old, they still think themselves unprepared for the serious business of living. . . . Nitti is reduced, by the insincerity of his love and by the very real misery of such unreal happiness, to a passive listlessness which ends in suicide. This is not, however, [a] romantic escape. . . . [Nitti's] despair goes even farther than the confused decadentism of the decadent; weaker and even more completely defeated by reality and his surroundings, Nitti is led to suicide without any will to resist or defy fate, or to affirm himself even self-destructively. Life and reality are his enemies; he remains innocent of his own death." The original title "Un inetto" ("An Inept"), later changed at the insistence of the publisher, captures Nitti's incapacity for action and his inability to make bold decisions because he finds himself in an environment where decisive actions are only possible on blind impulse. He, like Shakespeare's character Hamlet, is a man undone by his doubts. His brooding intellect and introspective intellectuality lead him to meditation and inaction. Though intrigued with Annetta, he does not really love her. In "Svevo: News From the Past," a 1963 review essay that appeared in *New Republic,* Richard Gilman pointed out that Annetta represents merely "the daughter of a bank president, a powerful, remote man whom [Nitti] is in awe of as the embodiment of the force and unassailable being which he lacks. . . . It is the father Nitti wants, not the daughter, yet not even the father but his aura of strength."

Sergio Pacifici wrote in *The Modern Italian Novel: From Manzoni to Svevo* that *A Life* "creates a climate not of a city but of a way of life whose dominating traits are futility, boredom, and senselessness of purpose—the unmistakable flaws of the twentieth-century bourgeoisie. . . . No matter how desperately Alfonso strives to learn the ways of the world, the strange art of living in a society whose rules he does not comprehend, he fails miserably [, for] he lacks the stuff that makes for the kind of individual he would like to be." Indeed, it is only in his dreams that he can perform heroic action.

As a Man Grows Older, which first appeared in serialized form in *L'Indipendente,* is based on Svevo's own infelicitous experiences with a seductive woman from the lower classes who, after a stormy affair, left Trieste and became a circus equestrienne. The novel tells of an unhappy love affair between Emilio Brentani, an inexperienced thirty-five-year-old bachelor, and Angiolina Zarri, a much younger and more knowledgeable working-class girl of doubtful respectability. Emilio leads an uneventful and unfulfilled life together with his comely spinster sister, Amalia. The only bright lights in his desolate existence are his fading reputation as the author of a novel written in his youth and his friendship with Balli, a sculptor and notorious ladies' man of whom, however, he is extremely envious. In spite of Angiolina's vulgarity and infidelities, Emilio becomes inexorably entrapped by her and by his newly awakened passion. His turbulent liaison arouses in Amalia a craving for love, and she falls desperately in love with Balli, who is totally unaware of her sentiments. Finally, due to Balli's advice and then Amalia's illness and death, Emilio is compelled to break with Angiolina. At the end, his life resumes its monotonous course and in his fantasy the unhappy sister and the beautiful mistress—who has run off with a thief—blend together in one feminine image that he will always cherish. He looks back at that experience as "the most important and the most luminous in his life. He lived on it like an old man on the memories of his youth. Angiolina underwent a strange metamorphosis in the writer's idle imagination. She preserved all her own beauty, but acquired as well all the qualities of Amalia, who died a second time in her." (These are some of the lines of the novel that James Joyce recited by heart.)

The title captures the sad, negative qualities of Emilio, who does not suffer yet from the degenerative processes of old age but rather from an affliction of the mind and will. Emilio is a kindred soul to Alfonso, only somewhat older and more experienced, though lacking Alfonso's ambition for love and success. Emilio's condition—which Bruno Maier, writing in *Italo Svevo,* labeled "metaphysical" old age—is characterized by inertia, introspection, gloom, defeat, resignation, and inability to survive. In a 1961 *Modern Language Notes* article, Russell Pfohl called it "a

disease rooted in a propensity to create images illuminating, rather than disguising, the bitterness of reality. . . . Like a grey miasma, 'senility' may permeate the universe inhabited by the other characters and smother any state of real youth or health." In 1927, trying to explain the selection of his title, Svevo wrote in the preface to the second edition of *As a Man Grows Older:* "Now that I know what real senility is all about, I, too, at times smile when I think that I regarded it with such an overabundance of love. . . . For me it would appear to be mutilating the book by depriving it of its title; for me it seems to explain and justify something. I was guided by that title and I actually lived it."

The literary tradition to which *As a Man Grows Older* belongs is that of the nineteenth-century European social novel. Still, it is far more than a social document in view of its modernity and psychological inquiry into the irrational motivations of the characters. "By the time of *Senilita,*" wrote P. N. Furbank in his *Italo Svevo: The Man and the Writer,* "Svevo had found the focus he wanted, a 'single thing' which he went on exploring throughout the rest of his writing. This 'single thing' was the Unconscious, in its aspect of unconscious motivation. . . . What Svevo did was to isolate unconscious motivation as an everyday phenomenon, not as a special case but as a general one." Like Joyce, Montale showed in his 1925 *Esame* article on Svevo a marked preference for *As a Man Grows Older.* He considered it original and "not only perhaps Svevo's masterpiece, but also a book of rare power [in which Svevo] no longer reminds us of any other author, he reminds us only of himself."

Confessions of Zeno, generally considered Svevo's best book, is the first truly psychoanalytic Italian novel. When written it was an original experiment in form, technique, and theme. The simple linear plots of the other novels are replaced by a collection of incidents in the life of Zeno Cosini, which are recorded retrospectively in the form of a diary. The novel presents two levels of action. The first is a loosely knit sequence of overlapping events in which the narrated facts are not always in chronological order but arranged thematically into six episodes in the life of Zeno: The Last Cigarette, The Death of My Father, The Story of My Marriage, Wife and Mistress, A Business Partnership, and Psychoanalysis. The second level of action is found in the unconscious. As Zeno tries to come to terms with life and his neuroses, he probes deeply into the human mind and explores the recesses of his unconscious. As Sandro Maxia pointed out in *Svevo e la prosa del Novecento,* the novel contains "two distinct temporal planes: one of actuality, of the present (Zeno's 'now as I am writing') in which the writing of the recollections and the psychoanalytic cure occur contemporaneously. . . . The other level concerns the recollected events that go back twenty-five years."

Zeno Cosini, a fifty-six-year-old businessman from Trieste, suffers from various complexes and psychoneurotic disorders characterized by an obsessive preoccupation with real and imagined physical illnesses. Above all, he is concerned with his addiction to tobacco. He decides to subject himself to a new and revolutionary treatment: psychoanalysis. The analyst suggests that the patient keep a diary that will be part of the therapy. For six months Zeno uses the technique of free association and thereby succeeds in producing material from his unconscious. He records everything: dreams, memories, feelings. When Zeno is told by the doctor that he is cured, he at first believes the man, even though psychosomatic pains continue to torment him. But when he is told that "the diagnosis is exactly the same as the one that Sophocles drew up long ago for poor Oedipus: I was in love with my mother and wanted to murder my father," he laughs, realizing that "the surest proof that I never had the disease is that I have not been cured of it." When Zeno stops the therapy, the analyst publishes the diary as a means of punishing his patient for having withdrawn from his care and robbed him of the fruits of his labor. Because the therapy and diary have been interrupted, the sources of Zeno's illness remain a mystery to the reader. Perhaps a psychic trauma is responsible for the protagonist's neuroses, the causes of which lie buried in his unconscious. He realizes that there are no cures for life, which is viewed by him as being "neither ugly nor beautiful, only original," and that death is the only remedy for human misery. Therefore, he declares himself cured.

Although Zeno has many similarities to Alfonso and Emilio—his younger alter egos—and shares many neuroses with them, he is able to function because, unlike them, he does understand life. He knows its limitations as well as its rewards, and he recognizes above all that his suffering is not caused by his own failings but rather is simply the condition of man. Zeno is a figure who, though beset by psychoneuroses, nevertheless manages to come to terms with them. In *Italo Svevo, the Writer From Trieste: Reflections on His Background and His Work,* Charles C. Russell paraphrased the novel's theme: "Life is difficult, amoral, absurd, meaningless and paradoxical, but if you can accept it as such, expect nothing [bear in mind Zeno the Stoic] and ask nothing, accept it simply as original, then, in a way, you are free; and when you are free, you can laugh. Zeno laughs, and perhaps the most wonderful thing in this novel is the sound of his laughter which echoes through the pages of his confession." Gilman wrote that "what Svevo promised to cure us of was precisely our desire to be cured. We were, as it turned out, without being able to formulate it or speak in its behalf, sick of health as the world defined it, tired of striving for strength, psychological heroism and muscular self-determination, and *Confessions of Zeno,* as no other book we had known, showed us the possibility of the imagination for taking us out of the hopeless business. [Svevo] had taken illness as the conditions of existence itself, making uprootedness, alienation, moral uncertainty and social weakness—as opposed to unseeing robustness and coerced integrity—into agencies of wily enduring and liberating instruments of self-knowledge." When Svevo wrote *Confessions of Zeno* he had already been afflicted by what Giacomo Debenedetti, writing in *Il romanzo del Novecento,* considered Svevo's strength: "the analytical corrosion of narrative texture," which paved the way in Italy for the advent of a new prose, a new style, and a new approach to life and art. In his last novel, Svevo no longer lingers near the surface of his characters but searches deeper as he gnaws away at their psyches.

In 1925 Montale regarded *Confessions of Zeno* as Svevo's attempt to "give us a poem of our complicated contemporary madness. Having broken through the barriers of the [old style] novel, . . . that nevertheless had spurred his inspiration, Svevo projects into his world the ambiguous and subterranean current of psychoanalysis. The writer who was quite conscious of rigorous choice, now records, jots down and doesn't eschew any risk. The book must issue from the subconscious, it must shape and define itself on its own. . . . There is an emotional mass, a concrete center, but it is outwardly projected, made to flow outward, at times one might say, illusory and gratuitous. It is here that Svevo touches one of the most painful experiences of contemporary art: for this reason he is additionally very much alive, if anyone is today."

When *Confessions of Zeno* was published, Svevo, confident that he had made a contribution to psychoanalysis, asked Dr. Edoardo Weiss, a prominent Triestine psychiatrist, Freud's friend and disciple, and perhaps the model for Dr. S. in the novel, to give him his professional opinion of the novel. Weiss promised to review it in a Viennese journal. Shortly thereafter, however, he told Svevo that he couldn't do it because the novel had nothing to do with psychoanalysis. Svevo's correspondence in 1927 and 1928 with Valerio Jahier, a young admirer who was considering undergoing analysis and years later killed himself, shows that eventually Svevo doubted Freud's ideas. In one letter he wrote: "Our Freud is a great man, far more for novelists than the sick." In another letter he pointed out that Freud himself had doubts, and that "in literature Freud is certainly more interesting. I only wish I had undergone a cure with him. My novel would have been more complete." Carlo Fonda, in *Svevo e Freud: Proposta di interpretazione della "Coscienza di Zeno,"* noted that notwithstanding Svevo's reservations, *Confessions of Zeno* shows psychoanalysis to be both a failure and a success: "A success because it explains the causes of our illness, but a failure because it cannot cure us."

In *The Spirit of the Letter: Essays in European Literature,* Renato Poggioli wrote of Svevo: "The man born old always grew younger with time: and the same is already happening to his work, through the wonders of glory and the miracle of death. In the annals of contemporary literature very few books will remain so youthfully fresh as the pages of a writer like Svevo, who spent all his life drawing a 'portrait of the artist as an old man.'"

BIOGRAPHICAL/CRITICAL SOURCES:

BOOKS

Biasin, Gian-Paolo, *Literary Diseases: Theme and Metaphor in the Italian Novel,* University of Texas Press, 1975.

Debenedetti, Giacomo, *Il romanzo del Novecento,* Garzanti, 1971.

De Castris, A. Leone, *Italo Svevo,* Nistri-Lischi, 1959.

Ellmann, Richard, *James Joyce,* New York & Oxford University Press, 1965.

Fonda, Carlo, *Svevo e Freud: Proposta di interpretazione della "Coscienza di Zeno,"* Longo Editore, 1978.

Fonda Savio, Letizia and Bruno Maier, *Iconografia sveviana: Scritti parole e immagini della vita privata di Italo Svevo,* Edizioni Studio Tesi, 1981.

Furbank, P. N., *Italo Svevo: The Man and the Writer,* Secker & Warburg, 1966.

Hays, Peter L., *The Limping Hero: Grotesques in Literature,* New York University Press, 1971.

Lebowitz, Naomi, *Italo Svevo,* Rutgers University Press, 1978.

Luti, Giorgio, *Italo Svevo e altri studi sulla letteratura italiana del primo Novecento,* Lerici, 1961.

Luti, Giorgio, *Svevo,* Il Castoro, 1967, 2nd edition, La Nuova Italia, 1972.

Maier, Bruno, *Italo Svevo,* Mursia, 1968, 4th revised edition, 1975.

Maxia, Sandro, *Svevo e la prosa del Novecento,* Laterza, 1977.

Moloney, Brian, *Italo Svevo: A Critical Introduction,* Edinburgh University Press, 1974.

Pacifici, Sergio, *The Modern Italian Novel: From Manzoni to Svevo,* Southern Illinois University Press, 1967.

Pacifici, Sergio, *From Verismo to Experimentalism: Essays on the Modern Italian Novel,* Indiana University Press, 1969.

Poggioli, Renato, *The Spirit of the Letter: Essays in European Literature,* Harvard University Press, 1965.

Russell, Charles C., *Italo Svevo, the Writer From Trieste: Reflections on His Background and His Work,* Longo Editore, 1978.

Saba, Umberto, *Prose,* Mondadori, 1964.

Sutor, Mario, editor, *Saba, Svevo, Comisso: Lettere inedite,* Gruppo di Lettere Moderne dell'Universita di Padova, 1967-68.

Twentieth-Century Literary Criticism, Volume 2, Gale, 1979.

Veneziani Svevo, Livia with Lina Galli, *Vita di mio marito con altri inedite di Italo Svevo,* Edizioni dello Zibaldone, 1958.

Weiss, Beno, *An Annotated Bibliography on the Theatre of Italo Svevo,* Pennsylvania State University Libraries, 1974.

Wisse, Ruth R., *The Schlemiel as Modern Hero,* University of Chicago Press, 1971.

PERIODICALS

Belfagor, July, 1959, March, 1974.
Esame, November-December, 1925.
Il Convegno, January 25, 1929, February 25, 1929.
Il Corriere Della Sera, December 11, 1892.
Italian Quarterly, summer, 1959.
Italian Studies, Volume 31, 1976.
Italica, summer, 1963, summer, 1971, winter, 1971, summer, 1978, winter, 1978, winter, 1979, winter, 1981.
James Joyce Quarterly, summer, 1964.
La Fiera Letteraria, September 23, 1928.
Language and Style, Number 3, 1971.
Le Navire d'Argent, February, 1926.
Literature and Psychology, Volume 20, 1970.
Modern Fiction Studies, spring, 1972.
Modern Language Notes, February, 1953, January, 1962, January, 1969, January, 1975.
Monograph Series (University of Tulsa Department of English), Number 6, 1969.
New Republic, November 2, 1963.
New York Times Book Review, January 21, 1968.
Nuovi Argomenti, Numbers 63-64, 1979.
Otto/Novecento, November-December, 1978.
Psychoanalytic Review, Volume 18, 1931.
Revue des Etudes Italiennes, Numbers 3-4, 1966, Number 1, 1967, Number 1, 1970.
Rivista di Letterature Moderne e Comparati, September-December, 1963.
Sin Nombre, October-December, 1980.
Solaria, March-April, 1929.
Studies in Short Fiction, summer, 1973.
Times Literary Supplement, March 30, 1962.

* * *

SCHWARTZ, Delmore (David) 1913-1966

PERSONAL: Born December 8, 1913, in Brooklyn, N.Y.; died of a heart attack, July 11, 1966, in New York, N.Y.; son of Harry and Rose (Nathanson) Schwartz; married Gertrude Buckman; married second wife, Elizabeth Pollet, 1949. *Education:* Attended University of Wisconsin, 1931; New York University, B.A. in philosophy, 1935; attended Harvard University, 1935-37. *Religion:* Jewish.

CAREER: Editor of *Mosaic* (a small magazine) while still a student; Harvard University, Cambridge, Mass., Briggs-Copeland Instructor in English Composition, 1940, assistant professor of English composition, 1946-47; *Partisan Review,* New Brunswick, N.J., editor, 1943-47, associate editor, 1947-55; associated with *Perspectives,* a Ford Foundation publication, 1952-53; poetry editor of *New Republic,* 1955-57. Visiting lecturer at New York University, Kenyon School of English, Indiana School of Letters, Princeton University, and University of Chicago; visiting

professor, Syracuse University. Literary consultant to New Directions (publishers).

AWARDS, HONORS: Guggenheim fellow, 1940 and 1941; National Institute of Arts and Letters grant in literature, 1953; *Kenyon Review* fellow, 1957; Levinson Prize, *Poetry* magazine, 1959; Bollingen Prize in poetry, and Shelley Memorial Award, both 1960, both for *Summer Knowledge.*

WRITINGS:

In Dreams Begin Responsibilities (story, poem, lyrics, and a play), New Directions, 1938.
(Translator) Jean Rimbaud, *A Season in Hell,* New Directions, 1939, 2nd edition, 1940.
Shenandoah (one-act verse play; produced Off-Off-Broadway, 1969), New Directions, 1941.
Genesis, Book One (prose and poetry), J. Laughlin (New York), 1943.
The World is a Wedding (stories), New Directions, 1948.
Vaudeville for a Princess, and Other Poems, New Directions, 1950.
(With John Crowe Ransom and John Hall Wheelock) *American Poetry at Mid-Century,* Gertrude Whittall Poetry and Literature Fund, 1958.
Summer Knowledge: New and Selected Poems, 1938-1958, Doubleday, 1959, published as *Selected Poems: Summer Knowledge, 1938-1958,* New Directions, 1967.
Successful Love, and Other Stories, Corinth, 1961.
(Compiler and author of foreword) *Syracuse Poems, 1964,* Department of English, Syracuse University, 1965.
Selected Essays of Delmore Schwartz, edited by Donald A. Dike and David H. Zucker, University of Chicago Press, 1970.
In Dreams Begin Responsibilities and Other Stories, edited by James Atlas, New Directions, 1978.
I Am Cherry Alive, the Little Girl Sang, Harper, 1979.
Last and Lost Poems of Delmore Schwartz, edited by Robert Phillips, Vanguard, 1979, revised edition, New Direction, 1989.
Letters of Delmore Schwartz, edited by Phillips, Ontario Review Press, 1985.
Portrait of Delmore: Journals and Notes of Delmore Schwartz, 1939-1959, Farrar, Straus, 1986.
The Ego Is Always at the Wheel: Bagatelles, introduction by Phillips, New Directions, 1986.

Author of an unpublished manuscript, "The Imitation of Life, and Other Problems of Literary Criticism." Contributor to *New York Times Book Review, Commentary, New Yorker, Poetry, Southern Review,* and other publications.

SIDELIGHTS: Delmore Schwartz had, writes Alfred Kazin, "a feeling for literary honor, for the highest standards, that one can only call *noble*—he loved the nobility of example presented by the greatest writers of our century, and he wanted in this sense to be noble himself, a light unto the less talented. . . . So he suffered, unceasingly, because he had often to disappoint himself—because the world turned steadily more irrational and incomprehensible—because the effort of his intellectual will, of his superb intellectual culture, was not always enough to sustain him. . . . He was the prisoner of his superb intellectual training, a victim of the logic he respected beyond anything else. He was of the generation that does not come easily to concepts of the absurd."

Mental illness haunted Schwartz for approximately twenty years. Marlene Nadle reported that it sent him "in and out of sanatoriums and into and out of the isolation of hotel rooms. It was an illness he accepted almost fatalistically." "Lost he was," said Kazin, "but he was not enough 'lost' in the demonic poet's tradition of losing himself to this world and finding himself in a richer world of private vision. . . . He was not a seer, not a visionary of 'the lost traveller's dream under the hill,' of the 'holy madness' that Yeats claimed to find in Ireland itself—the madness that Christopher Smart knew, and Hoelderlin, and Blake."

Schwartz nevertheless possessed a dazzling intellect, one equally fascinated by the ideas of Marx and Freud and by popular culture. He spoke quickly and emotionally, his words often running together, and was once clocked talking for eight hours straight. After the death of Dylan Thomas he inherited the role of house poet at the White Horse Tavern in New York. He was known to amuse his friends with a dialogue in which he played both himself and T. S. Eliot. He could turn his humor on himself; Nadle recalls how "he couldn't quite see Delmore as a name for a nice Jewish boy. To explain this exotic happening he embroidered elaborate tales about his being named after a Tammany politician. Other times the story would be that he was named after a pullman car, or a building on Riverside Drive."

Kazin remembers the author as one who "believed in nothing so much as the virtue and reason of poetry. . . . In Delmore's world of writer-heroes, none was greater than Joyce," the critic continued, noting that Schwartz was known to carry with him a heavily-annotated copy of *Finnegans Wake*. "Joyce, after all, had proved that naturalist art could attain to the condition of poetry. But beyond this intense loyalty to the great modern tradition—this was Delmore's religion and his faith—it was his need to be intellectually *serious,* in his favorite form of irony, that explains the extraordinary style of *The World is a Wedding.*"

The author's view of life was a tragic one. Morton Seiff called him a "desperate counterpart of Rimbaud. . . . Both [were] aware that the supports of their respective cultures [were] tottering and new beliefs must be found to nourish the religious impulse of man." Schwartz wrote of the city, about which he had no illusions. He was "concerned with fundamentals, with the problem of identity, of knowledge and belief, haunted by the noise time makes, able to write wittily and movingly," according to Babette Deutsch. He chose as his theme "the wound of consciousness," he once said, and he wanted to show the miraculous character of daily existence. M. L. Rosenthal said that Schwartz "has many moments of pure music to offer, and some moments in which he speaks in the accents of greatness, and he holds us even in his failures with the honesty and contemporaneity of his voice."

He died, ostensibly of a heart attack, outside a stranger's door with no one to come to his aid. For three days no one came to claim his body. His friends, who reported that Schwartz had dropped out of sight for a year prior to his death, learned of his death by reading the obituaries. He died at the Columbia Hotel in New York, in the city whose artifacts were contributing to "our anguished diminution until we die."

In 1975, when Saul Bellow's novel, *Humboldt's Gift,* was published by Viking, Karyl Roosevelt stated that the protagonist Humboldt was "a thinly disguised portrait of the late poet Delmore Schwartz, with whom Bellow had a complex friendship in real life." Walter Clemons and Jack Kroll wrote of that same character as "a loving portrait of Delmore Schwartz, whose precocious early poems prefigured the flowering of the powerful generation of poets who came to the fore in the '40s—Robert Lowell, Randall Jarrell, John Berryman." As Craig Tapping summarized the writer's life and work in a *Dictionary of Literary Biography* essay: "The clashes which Schwartz believed his name embodied—between social aspirations and cultural values, old world civility and new world philistinism, and generational dif-

ferences between immigrants and their American-born offspring—are the subject of much of his prose fiction and poetry. All of Schwartz's writing attempt[ed] to evoke, analyze, and at times transcend what he saw as the inevitable disappointments and profound disillusionment which life forces on people."

BIOGRAPHICAL/CRITICAL SOURCES:

BOOKS

Contemporary Literary Criticism, Gale, Volume 2, 1974, Volume 4, 1975, Volume 10, 1979, Volume 45, 1987.
Dictionary of Literary Biography, Gale, Volume 28: *Twentieth-Century Jewish-American Fiction Writers,* 1984, Volume 48: *American Poets, 1880-1945, Second Series,* 1986.

PERIODICALS

Book Week, October 9, 1966.
Books Abroad, spring, 1967.
Commentary, December, 1950.
Jewish Social Studies, October, 1951.
Nation, June 11, 1960.
New Republic, November 9, 1959.
New York Times Book Review, November 5, 1950.
New York Herald Tribune Books, March 5, 1939.
Poetry, May, 1939, February, 1960, December, 1966.
Saturday Review, April 29, 1939.
Village Voice, July 21, 1966.

OBITUARIES:

PERIODICALS

Newsweek, July 25, 1966.
Publishers Weekly, July 25, 1966.

*   *   *

SCHWARTZ, Muriel A.
See ELIOT, T(homas) S(tearns)

*   *   *

SCIASCIA, Leonardo   1921-1989

PERSONAL: Born January 8, 1921, in Racalmuto, Sicily; son of a sulphur miner; came to Italy.

ADDRESSES: Home—Via Redentore 131, Caltanissetta, Italy.

CAREER: Functionary in a Fascist agency concerned with requisitioning produce from farms; elementary school teacher in Calatanissetta, 1949-57, and in Palermo, 1957-68; writer, 1968—.

AWARDS, HONORS: Premio Crotone; Premio Libera Stampa Lugano; Premio Prato.

WRITINGS:

IN ENGLISH

Le parrocchie di Regalpetra (essays; title means "The Parishes of Regalpetra"; also see below), Laterza, 1956, translation published as *Salt in the Wound* (includes *Death of the Inquisitor*), Orion Press, 1969.
Gli zii di Sicilia (four novelettes), Einaudi, 1958, translation by N. S. Thomson published as *Sicilian Uncles,* Carcanet, 1986.
Il giorno della civetta (novel), Einaudi, 1961, translation by Archibald Colquhoun and Arthur Oliver published as *Mafia*

Vendetta, J. Cape, 1963, Knopf, 1964, later published as *The Day of the Owl* (also see below).

Il consiglio d'Egitte, Einaudi, 1963, translation by Adrienne Foulke published as *The Council of Egypt,* Knopf, 1966.

A ciasuno il suo, Einaudi, 1966, translation by Foulke published as *A Man's Blessing,* Harper, 1968, reprinted as *To Each His Own,* Carcanet, 1989.

Il contesto (title means "The Contest"; also see below), Einaudi, 1971, first American edition in Italian edited by Iole Fiorillo Magri, Houghton, 1976, translation by Foulke published as *Equal Danger* (also see below), Harper, 1973.

Il mare colore del vino (short stories), Einaudi, 1973, translation by Avril Bardoni published as *The Wine-Dark Sea,* Carcanet, 1985.

Todo modo (title means "In Every Way"; also see below), Einaudi, 1974, translation by Foulke published as *One Way or Another,* Harper, 1977.

Todo Modo; Il contesto, Club degli editore, 1975.

La scomparsa di Majorana, Einaudi, 1975, translation by Sacha Rabinovitch published as *The Moro Affair and The Mystery of Majorana,* Carcanet, 1987.

Candido: ovvero, Un sogno fatto in Sicilia, Einaudi, 1977, translation by Foulke published as *Candido; or, A Dream Dreamed in Sicily,* Harcourt, 1979.

L'Affare Moro, Sellerio, 1978, translation by Rabinovitch published as *The Moro Affair and The Mystery of Majorana,* Carcanet, 1987.

The Day of the Owl and Equal Danger, Godine, 1983.

1912 1, translation by Rabinovitch and Ian Thomson, Adelphi, 1987.

OTHER

Favole della dittatura (title means "Fables of the Dictatorship"), Bardi (Rome, Italy), 1950.

Pirandello e il pirandellismo, privately printed, 1953.

Pirandello e la Silicia, privately printed, 1961.

Morte dell'inquisitore (biography; title means "Death of the Inquisitor"; also see below), Laterza, 1964.

Feste religiose in Sicilia, Leonardo da Vinci editrice, 1965.

L'onorevole, dramma in tre atti (title means "The Honorable One: A Play in Three Acts"), Einaudi, 1965.

La corda pazza. Scrittori e cose della Sicilia, Einaudi, 1970.

Le parrocchie di Regalpetra; Morte dell'inquisitore, Laterza, 1973.

(With Rosario La Duca) *Palermo felicissima,* Il punto, 1973.

(With others) *Mostra retrospettiva della opere di Christian Hess: Palermo Palazzo del turismo, 26 novembre-10 dicembre 1974,* Cassa centrale di risparmio Vittorio Emanuele per le province siciliane, 1974.

Il fuoco nel mare, Emme Edizioni, 1975.

L'onorevole; Recitazione della controversia liparitana; I mafiosi (collected works), Einaudi, 1976.

I pugnalatori (also see below), Einaudi, 1976.

I pugnalatori; La scomparsa di Majorana, Club degli editori, 1977.

Atti relativi alla morte di Raymond Roussel, Sellerio, 1977.

Nero du nero, Einaudi, 1979.

Dalle parti degli infideli, Sellerio, 1979.

La Sicilia come metafora: Intervista di Marcelle Padovani, Mondadori, 1979.

Conversazione in una stanza chiusa, Sperling & Kupfer, 1981.

Il teatro della memoria, Einaudi, 1981.

Kermesse, Sellerio, 1982.

La palma va a nord, Gammalibri, 1982.

Cruciverba, Einaudi, 1983.

Il cavaliere e la morte, Adelphi (Milan), 1989.

Author of *La Sicilia, il suo cuore* (title means "Sicily, Its Heart"), 1952; *La Morte di Stalin,* 1960; *Santo Marino,* 1963; *Racconti Siciliani,* 1966. Also author of the play *Recitazione della controversia liparitana dedicata ad A. D. [Alexander Dubcek],* 1969. Contributor to periodicals, including *New York Times.*

SIDELIGHTS: In Italy, Leonardi Sciascia is considered one of the finest novelists writing today. Herbert Mitgang reported in the *New York Times Book Review,* however, that Sciascia "was puzzled and saddened when I told him that in the United States his books sometimes fall into the mystery bin." But Sciascia replied, "At least I hope they will be regarded as metaphysical mysteries." The author has reason not to be satisfied with the mystery fiction label. Stefano Tani places Sciascia among novelists who have gone beyond the usual limits of detective fiction to create a new form he called "literary" detective fiction. In *The Doomed Detective: The Contribution of the Detective Novel to Postmodern American and Italian Fiction,* Tani explains that, like master novelists Umberto Eco and Italo Calvino, Sciascia writes "a postmodern form or variety of forms that reshape the seeming dead-end rationality of the British mystery into an original 'something else.' This something else is what I will describe as the anti-detective novel, a high-parodic form that stimulates and tantalizes its readers by disappointing common detective-novel expectations." Sciascia, whose works have also been translated into French, Spanish, and German, has succeeded in winning over many American critics. As Mitgang observed, "Sciascia is a careful and slow writer who has turned out a unified body of work in the last 20 years." He also described Sciascia as "a novelist respected by his peers and readers for grappling with old themes that reach down to the condition of life and justice."

Sciascia's main subject is the people of Sicily and the relevance of the problems of their culture to the rest of the world. A former school teacher on the island, he has kept a close eye on local politics and has expressed his views on his findings in nonfiction as well as in novels. *La parrocchie di Regalpetra* (*Salt in the Wound*) is a collection of partly fictional essays referred to by a *Book World* critic as the "social biography of an imaginary Sicilian town." The book chronicles the suffering of peasants through "centuries under the combined forces of the rich and the Church, later to be joined by the Fascist and Christian Democratic parties and the Mafia." Though not strictly documentary, these essays on fictional Regalpetra communicate the tenor of life in Sciascia's birthplace, Racalmuto. Some reviewers called the book a delightful read, but the reviewer for *Book World* was less impressed. "What finally disappoints about the work," noted the *Book World* critic, "is the author's sense of hopelessness about the conditions he describes. For all its concern, *Salt in the Wound* is a cry of protest against seemingly immovable forces rather than an angry demand that they be removed."

Sciascia's bending of the essay form in *Salt in the Wound* presaged his bending of conventional forms of fiction. The pieces in *Gli zii di Sicilia* (*Sicilian Uncles*), are in the form of short stories, but the uncles described include Uncle Sam and Uncle Stalin. Though Sciascia's technique varies from novel to novel, his alterations are not experimental. They are deliberate designs best suited to his materials and his purpose. *Mafia Vendetta* relies on long sequences of dialogue to tell the story of a policeman's efforts to solve a murder. Sciascia supplies very little narrative so that the reader's experience of discovering clues more closely replicates the experience of the investigator.

For *Il consiglio d'Egitto* (*The Council of Egypt*), a novel in which the author raises questions about the reliability of written history, Sciascia chose the form of the historical novel. Set during the late eighteenth-century on the eve of the Enlightenment, it shows the conflict between Paolo Di Blasi, a man of reason, and Guiseppe Vella, an opportunistic forger. Economic power granted to the aristocracy erodes when Vella "finds" an Arabic manuscript which awards priority to the crown in the event of inheritance disputes. The manuscript which causes this economic revolution is a fake. "The story of the forged historical manuscripts allows Sciascia to delve further into the relationship between writing and reality," Verina Jones writes in *Writing and Society in Contemporary Italy: A Collection of Essays.* The questions it raises, she says, include "What status does Vella's historical fraud have in relation to historical truth? Is it any more fraudulent than the skilful weaving of the feudal legal tradition which Vella's manuscript is now attempting to subvert? Is it not in fact simply the reversed mirror image of the fraud of history? Does history contain any truth at all when it has been the history of 'i re, i vicere, i papi, i capitani' '(kings, viceroys, popes, generals'), when it has ignored the lives of those who have been unable to write their own history?" Again, Sciascia raises questions and offers no solutions. *New Yorker* critic Anthony West called the novel "a very cooly ironic and detached piece of storytelling concerned mainly with social hypocrisy in the manner of Voltaire or Anatole France."

In comparison to *The Council of Egypt,* West remarked that *A Man's Blessing* was a "homage of imitation to Graham Greene." Similar to Greene's *The Man Within, A Man's Blessing* concerns a professor's attempt to solve the murder of a friend. However, as his search takes him into the criminal world, he is less willing to go to the police with his dangerous information; he cares more about finding out who killed his friend than in seeing the killers brought to justice. He has not yet discovered the role of the Church in the murders, yet the questions he has asked have already marked him as a person who knows too much. When his friend's widow talks the professor into speaking to the police, it is to set him up to be murdered. After his death, the townspeople reveal, ironically, that throughout the story they knew the solution to the murder, but were bound by the code of silence that protected them from retribution for their own crimes, and preserved their lives. Of *A Man's Blessing,* West wrote: "This graceful piece of storytelling is in fact a savagely expressed cry of despair. Sciascia has moved on from the belief that life is a comedy, which would be much more enjoyable for the actors if they would only be a little more reasonable and a little less emotional, to discover its tragic essence. This account of his discovery, in the form of a novel, is at once moving and horrifying, and may well in time win itself recognition as one of the minor classics of extreme pessimism."

Tani relates this pessimism to Sciascia's larger purpose, which he says "is to paint a critical portrait of the sad state of Sicilian (and generally, Italian) affairs, a portrait of the social and political condition of his island ruled by a secret power (the Mafia) which has corrupted the official power (the state) so deeply that by now the two are nearly identical. In an island that has been dominated and exploited by all the civilizations in the Mediterranean basin . . . a sort of conspiracy, a network of secret solidarity among the inhabitants, was first a necessity in order to survive and to resist the rulers, but it became a means of local power used by Sicilians themselves against each other when, after the Italian unification, Sicily was no longer a conquered land but, at least on paper, part of Italy, with equal rights and equal duties." In novels and essays, and short satires, Sciascia consistently exposes the problems of Sicily as a warning to the rest of the world. He delared in an interview cited in the introduction to *A ciascuno*

il suo, "The problems of the Sicilian microcosm are the ones which can kill the world." Therefore, his works take on importance beyond their regional historical value.

Though a mystery novel normally satisfies the reader by providing answers, Sciascia's novels reward in other ways. Datchery noted, "The crimes in his stories do not demand solutions; they serve, rather, as vehicles for social comment: to show how justice can be removed to a plateau where it is concerned only with its forms." Phoebe Adams agreed with Datchery. She observed that the chase in the novel "turns into a fable about power exercised for its own sake regardless of the purposes for which it was conferred and therefore spreading universal criminality." The serious nature of Sciascia's message is balanced by his sense of irony, humor, and mastery of technique. Writing in *Critic,* Dick Datchery called *Equal Danger* "an intellectual suspense novel." Datchery found the story of Inspector Rogas and his search for the murderer of several judges to be "a serious parody, complex and sometimes vague, but always rewarding."

Critics also applaud the author's ability to create memorable characters. Sciascia's *One Way or Another* is the story of a curious driver who decides to investigate a mysterious sign on the road. He discovers a secret religious order run by Don Gaetano who wears spectacles similar to those of Satan in a painting. John Ahern called Don Gaetano "one of the strongest, most intriguing characters that Sciascia has ever created. A brilliant intellect, a widely read, cynical master of paradox, a scornful, ruthless manipulator of the rich and powerful for his own ends." *Newsweek* reviewer Peter S. Prescott, however, was not as impressed. He claimed that *One Way or Another* "lacks the wit, the aphorisms and the scathing cynicism that distinguished the author's earlier books." Prescott also found the characters "familiar" and added that "their arguments are tiresome."

Prescott enjoyed the 1979 novel *Candido: ovvero, Un sogno fatto in Sicilia* more. Candido, the main character, is convinced that everything is simple. He is so innocent of self-interest that he is regarded as "a monster" by his neighbors. The young Sicilian inherits an estate, and is rejected first for trying to work the land himself, then for trying to give it away. Not even the Communists will accept it because of their aversion to private ownership and to cooperative farming. Like the mysteries in which the killers remain unnamed, "this story, too, has a quicksilver quality—no one in it ever does or says quite what the occasion requires." However, Prescott adds, Sciascia's "wintry pessimism seems warmer here." Victor Carrabino comments in *World Literature Today,* "Once again Sciascia offers the reader a work of art which is truly entertaining and yet invites him to reflect on the true meaning of life." In addition to "the lightness and the humor with which these pages have been written, the seriousness and commitment of Sciascia's thought," says Carrabino, ask the reader to identify with the youth who sees that everything "is simple."

Though individual novels by Sciascia sometimes are reviewed unfavorably, his work as a whole commands international attention for its contribution to the development of new forms of fiction that reflect a new understanding of man in the late twentieth century. Tani concludes that anti-detective fiction such as Sciascia's is "a crossroad of multifold preoccupations: tradition and postmodernism, mass culture and high culture, Italy and United States, Italy-United States and Western societies. The sense of an ending or of a new beginning, the twilight zone between the nuclear age and what comes after it, between rationality and mystery, can be clarified through a study of anti-detective fiction, the crossroad where unsolvable mysteries and doomed detectives meet with a less optimistic but clearly more mature sense of man and his limits."

MEDIA ADAPTATIONS: Equal Danger was made into the film *Illustrious Corpses* by Francesco Rosi.

BIOGRAPHICAL/CRITICAL SOURCES:

BOOKS

Contemporary Literary Criticism, Gale, Volume 8, 1978, Volume 9, 1978, Volume 41, 1987.
Jones, Verina, *Writing and Society in Contemporary Italy: A Collection of Essays,* Berg Publishers, 1984.
Sciascia, Leonardo, *A ciascuno il suo,* 5th edition, Einaudi, 1977.
Tani, Stefano, *The Doomed Detective: The Contribution of the Detective Novel to Postmodern American and Italian Fiction,* Southern Illinois University Press, 1984.
Vidal, Gore, *The Second American Revolution and Other Essays (1976-1982),* Random House, 1982.

PERIODICALS

Best Sellers, April 15, 1968, June 1, 1969.
Books and Bookmen, number 350, November, 1984.
Book World, September 7, 1969.
Critic, November/December, 1973.
Italian Quarterly, summer-fall, 1965.
Kirkus Reviews, March 15, 1977.
Listener, October 25, 1984.
Los Angeles Times Book Review, June 12, 1988.
Modern Fiction Studies, autumn, 1983.
New Republic, September 17, 1977.
Newsweek, June 16, 1973, May 9, 1977, September 24, 1979, December 23, 1985.
New Yorker, May 3, 1969, July 4, 1977.
New York Times, October 7, 1979, November 20, 1985.
New York Times Book Review, September 16, 1973, October 7, 1979, November 24, 1985, August 24, 1986, April 5, 1987.
Partisan Review, fall, 1972.
Times (London), August 21, 1986.
Times Literary Supplement, October 5, 1973, January 30, 1976, March 25, 1977, May 2, 1980, March 30, 1984, October 26, 1984, December 20, 1985, February 6, 1987, March 20, 1987, March 3, 1989, July 21, 1989.
World Literature Today, winter, 1979.

*   *   *

SCOTLAND, Jay
See JAKES, John (William)

*   *   *

SCOTT, Paul (Mark)   1920-1978

PERSONAL: Born March 25, 1920, in Palmers Green, England; died March 1, 1978, in London, England; married Nancy Edith Avery, 1941; children: Carol, Sally. *Education:* Attended public schools in England.

ADDRESSES: Agent—David Higham Associates, 5-8 Lower John St., Golden Sq., London W1R 4HA, England.

CAREER: Novelist. Company secretary, Falcon Press and Grey Walls Press, both London, England, 1946-50; director of Pearn Pollinger and Higham, now David Higham Associates (literary agents), London, 1950-60; free-lance writer, 1960-78. British Council lecturer, India, 1972; visiting lecturer, University of

Tulsa, Oklahoma, 1976-77. *Military service:* British Army, served in India, 1940-43; served in Indian Army, Malaya, 1943-46.

MEMBER: Royal Society of Literature (fellow).

AWARDS, HONORS: Eyre & Spottiswoode literary fellowship, 1951; Arts Council grant, 1969; Yorkshire Post book of the year award for finest fiction, 1971, for *The Towers of Silence;* Booker Prize, 1977.

WRITINGS:

NOVELS

Johnnie Sahib, Eyre & Spottiswoode, 1952.
Six Days in Marapore, Morrow, 1953 (published in England as *The Alien Sky,* Eyre & Spottiswoode, 1953, reprinted, Panther, 1974).
A Male Child, Eyre & Spottiswoode, 1956, Dutton, 1957, reprinted, Carroll & Graf, 1987.
The Mark of the Warrior, Morrow, 1958.
The Love Pavilion, Morrow, 1960, reprinted, Carroll & Graf, 1985 (published in England as *The Chinese Love Pavilion,* Eyre & Spottiswoode, 1960).
The Birds of Paradise, Morrow, 1962, reprinted, Carroll & Graf, 1986.
The Bender, Morrow, 1963, reprinted, Carroll & Graf, 1986 (published in England as *The Bender: Pictures From an Exhibition of Middle Class Portraits,* Secker & Warburg, Morrow, 1966).
The Corrida of San Feliu, Morrow, 1964.
The Jewel in the Crown (first novel in tetralogy; also see below), Heinemann, 1966.
The Day of the Scorpion (second novel in tetralogy; also see below), Morrow, 1968.
The Towers of Silence (third novel in tetralogy; also see below), Heinemann, 1971, Morrow, 1972.
A Division of the Spoils (fourth novel in tetralogy; also see below), Morrow, 1975.
The Raj Quartet (tetralogy; includes *The Jewel in the Crown, The Day of the Scorpion, The Towers of Silence,* and *A Division of Spoils*), Morrow, 1976. *Staying On,* Morrow, 1977.

OTHER

I Gerontius (verse), Favil Press, 1941.
(Contributor) H. F. Rubinstein, *Four Jewish Plays* (includes his play "Pillars of Salt"), Gollancz, 1948.
Contributor) *Essays by Divers Hands,* Oxford University Press, 1970.
After the Funeral (short story), Whittington Press, 1979.
The Making of "The Jewel in the Crown," St. Martin's Press, 1983.
My Appointment With the Muse, edited by Shelley C. Reece, Heinemann, 1986.
On Writing and the Novel, edited by Reece, Morrow, 1987.

Author of the radio plays "Lines of Communication," 1951, "The Alien Sky" (adapted from his novel), 1954, and "Sahibs and Memsahibs," 1958. Author of the televion play "The Mark of the Warrior" (adapted from his novel), 1959. Also contributor of articles to British newspapers and periodicals, including *Country Life* and the London *Times.*

SIDELIGHTS: Paul Scott was perhaps best known as the chronicler of the decline of the British occupation of India. His most famous works are those of *The Raj Quartet.* They center on a single dramatic event, the rape of an English woman by several Indians, but proceed to describe life for both the British and the

Indian under the British raj, or rule. This seemed to be characteristic of Scott's novels; or "as more than one reviewer pointed out he dealt less with events than with the situation created by these events."

Scott's novels have consistently drawn positive reviews. A *Punch* reviewer once described Scott as "a professional novelist of the expansive, humane, nineteenth-century type, though with mid-twentieth-century sensibilities. . . . Mr. Scott has two great qualities that are rarely found together, excitement with material and control. His work is packed, not crammed."

A *Times Literary Supplement* critic reviewing *The Day of the Scorpion* wrote: "The characters, while they successfully represent aspirations and conflicts which are bigger than themselves, never cease to be individuals. The conversations have subtlety and a quality of plenteousness which is none the less welcome for being out of fashion. Above all, the reader is impressed, and given confidence, by the feeling which Mr. Scott can generate of a writer who has thoroughly mastered his material, and who can, because of this, work through a maze of fascinating detail without for a moment losing sight of distant, and considerable objectives." A *Listener* critic agreed: "Paul Scott's is one of those rare books that express not only themselves but something of the essence of their genre. Prose fiction does many things, but nothing more characteristic than the intricate relating of private lives to public issues. When this is done with the subtlety, wisdom and grace of *The Day of the Scorpion,* the triumph is more than a personal one for the author. It vindicates a whole tradition of literary endeavour."

John Leonard of the *New York Times Book Review* commented that the strength of Scott's last novel, *Staying On,* lay in "its portrayal of hitherto unsuspected dignity, of depths of feeling hiding in the ordinary." In contrast, Malcolm Muggeridge noted that he had difficulty in trying "to work up sympathy with any of the characters to care about what happened to them."

The last novel in *The Raj Quartet* led Webster Schott to write: "Sometimes [Scott] seemed to be writing mostly history. Other times a study of racist psychology. And now and then an outrageously long love letter to a land and people unable to decide whether they liked or loathed what fate had dealt them."

Scott once said that he preferred "to write about people in relation to their work, which strikes me as a subject no less important than their private lives." Although during his years in the army he wrote poetry and plays, nearly all of his published works are novels; he viewed the novel as the ultimate form of literature. "He was no miniaturist. He required a broad canvas, he never wrote a short story, for example," commented Thomas Lask. In addition, Jean G. Zorn observed: "The world of Scott's Indian novels is so extraordinarily vivid in part because it is constructed out of such accuracies of detail as the proper name or the precise sum that a retired colonel's widow could expect to receive as a pension. Scott's vision is both precise and painterly."

Summing up Scott's career as a novelist, Margaret B. Lewis concluded in *Contemporary Novelists:* "Critical acclaim came late to Paul Scott and only in the last years of his life did a wide readership develop for his work. Although the slow pace of his novels with their gradual accumulation of detail may be very much against the modern trend to short, elliptical novels, the reader finds in the very complexities of his later works an invitation to share in the complexities of life itself, and to emerge with an extended vision as a result." Scott's novels have been translated into Dutch, German, Polish, Swedish, Spanish, French, and Finnish.

MEDIA ADAPTATIONS: J. Mitchell adapted *Staying On* for television in 1981.

BIOGRAPHICAL/CRITICAL SOURCES:

BOOKS

Bhaskara Rao, K., *Paul Scott,* Twayne, 1980.
Contemporary Literary Criticism, Volume 9, Gale, 1978.
Contemporary Novelists, St. Martin's Press, 1986.
Dictionary of Literary Biography, Volume 14, *British Novelists since 1960,* Gale, 1983.
Swinden, Patrick, *Paul Scott: Images of India,* Macmillan, 1980.

PERIODICALS

Best Sellers, March 1, 1969.
Books and Bookmen, November, 1968.
Listener, September 5, 1968.
Newsweek, February 11, 1985.
New York Times Book Review, November 10, 1968, July 26, 1977, August 21, 1977, March 15, 1987.
Observer Review, September 1, 1968.
Punch, September 4, 1968.
Times Literary Supplement, September 12, 1968, February 27, 1987.
Washington Post Book World, January 11, 1987.

OBITUARIES:

PERIODICALS

New York Times, March 3, 1978.

*   *   *

SEBASTIAN, Lee
  See SILVERBERG, Robert

*   *   *

SEDGES, John
  See BUCK, Pearl S(ydenstricker)

*   *   *

SEFERIADES, Giorgos Stylianou   1900-1971
  (George Seferis, Georgios Sepheriades)

PERSONAL: Born February 29, 1900, in Smyrna (now Izmir), Turkey; died September 20, 1971, in Athens, Greece; emigrated to Athens, Greece, in 1914; son of Stelios P. (a lawyer) and Dhespo (Tenekidhis) Seferiades; married Marie Zannou, 1941. *Education:* Attended University of Athens and Sorbonne, University of Paris.

ADDRESSES: Home—Agzas 20, Athens 501, Greece.

CAREER: Held various diplomatic posts with Royal Greek Ministry of Foreign Affairs, 1926-62, including vice-consul in London, England, 1931-34, and in Athens, Greece, 1934-36, consul in Albania, 1936-38, and in Athens, 1938-41, served with Free Greek Government in South Africa, Egypt, Palestine, England, and Italy, 1941-44, returned to regular diplomatic service in Ankara, Turkey, 1948-50, and in London, 1951-53, ambassador to Lebanon and minister to Syria, Iraq, and Jordan, 1953-56, ambassador to the United Nations, 1956-57, and to Great Britain, 1957-62; full-time writer and translator, 1962-71.

MEMBER: American Academy of Arts and Sciences (honorary foreign member), St. James' Club and Travellers' Club (both London).

AWARDS, HONORS: William Foyle Poetry Prize (England), 1961; Nobel Prize for Literature, 1963; Kostis Palamys prize for poetry, for *The Thrush;* Order of Holy Sepulchre; Grand Cross of the Cedar; Grand Cross of Order of Merit (Syria); Knight Commander of Order of George I (Greece); Grand Cross of Order of Phoenix (Greece). Litt.D., Cambridge University, 1960; D.Phil., University of Thessaloniki, 1964; D.Litt., Oxford University, 1964, and Princeton University, 1965.

WRITINGS:

UNDER PSEUDONYM GEORGE SEFERIS

Strophe (title means "The Turning Point"), [Athens], 1931.
I Sterna (title means "The Cistern"), [Athens], 1932.
Gymnopedia, [Athens], 1936.
A Dialogue on Poetry, [Athens], 1939.
Log Book I (also see below), [Athens], 1940.
Exercise Book, 1928-1937, [Athens], 1940.
Poems I, [Athens], 1940.
Dokimes (literary criticism), [Cairo], 1944, 4th edition, Icarus (Athens), 1981.
Log Book II (also see below), [Alexandria], 1944.
Erotokritos (essay), [Athens], 1946.
Kichli (title means "The Thrush"), Icarus, 1947.
The King of Asine and Other Poems, translated by Bernard Spencer, Nanos Valaoritis, and Lawrence Durrell, Lehmann, 1948.
Collected Poems, 1924-1946, Icarus, 1950, 5th edition, 1964.
Three Days at the Monasteries of Cappadocia, French Institute (Athens), 1953.
To Cyprus, Icarus, 1955.
Log Book III (also see below), Icarus, 1955.
Poems (includes *Mythistorema* [also see below], *Log Book I, Log Book II,* and *Log Book III*), translated by Rex Warner, Little, Brown, 1960, reprinted, David R. Godine, 1979.
(Contributor) Philip Sherrard and Edmund Keeley, editors and translators, *Six Poets of Modern Greece,* Knopf, 1961.
Delphoi, [Athens], 1963, translation by Sherrard published as *Delphi,* William Heinman, 1963.
On the Greek Style: Selected Essays in Poetry and Hellenism, translated by Warner and T. Frangopoulos, Atlantic/Little, Brown, 1966.
Collected Poems, 1924-1955, edited and translated by Sherrard and Keeley, Princeton University Press, 1967, 3rd and expanded edition published as *George Seferis: Collected Poems, 1924-1955,* 1981.
Tria Krifka Poema, Icarus, 1967, translation by Walter Kaiser published as *Three Secret Poems,* Harvard University Press, 1969.
(Contributor) *Modern Poetry in Translation,* Grossman, 1968.
(Contributor) *Giorgos Seferis, Mikhail Snolokhov, Henryk Sienkiewicz [and] Carl Spitteler,* A. Gregory, 1971.
Days of 1945-1951: A Poet's Journal, translated by Athan Anagnostopoulos, Belknap Press, 1974.
Mythistorima and Gymnopaidia, translation by Mary Cooper Walton, Lycabettus (Athens), 1977.
Metagraphes, Lesche (Athens), 1980.
(With Adamantios Diamantes) *Allelographia 1953-1971* (correspondences), Stigme (Athens), 1985.
Meres 20 Aprili 1951-4 Avgoustou 1956 (journal), Icarus, 1986.

Also author of *Mythistorema,* 1935, and *Cyprus,* 1953. Translator of numerous works into Greek, including T. S. Eliot's *The Waste Land and Other Poems,* 1936, reprinted, Icarus, 1967, and *Murder in the Cathedral,* Icarus, 1963, Sidney Keyes's *The Wilderness,* 1954, *Antigraphes,* Icarus, 1965, *Song of Solomon,* Ica-

rus, 1966, and *The Apocalypse of John,* Icarus, 1967. Contributor to *Nea Grammata, Nea Hestia, New Directions, Poetry, Folder, Atlantic, Western Humanities Review, Harvard Advocate, Prairie Schooner, Perspective, Quarterly Review of Literature, Wake, Accent, Partisan Review,* and other journals.

SIDELIGHTS: Giorgos Seferiades, better known to his readers as George Seferis (a pseudonym he derived not only from his own name but from the Arabic word *sefer* "journey" as well), was Greece's only Nobel Prize winner. A poet who received his award from the Swedish Academy "for his eminent lyrical writings inspired by a deep feeling for the Hellenic world of culture," Seferis spent most of his life traveling and living in countries far from his beloved homeland. Yet it was this very distance, many critics maintained, that enabled him to comment on the tragic state of twentieth-century Greece with such a touching blend of Hellenic tradition and modern sensibility.

Born in Smyrna (now Izmir) on the Aegean coast of Turkey, Seferis passed his childhood in the area's large Greek community until the coming of World War I forced his family to flee to Athens and later Paris, where the young man completed his education. The subsequent destruction of Smyrna (and its Greek community) in the Greek-Turkish war of 1922 left Seferis with a deep sense of personal loss and rootlessness that eventually manifested itself both in the themes and in the somber, resigned tone of his poetry. His choice of career, too, reinforced his view of himself as a perpetual wanderer; a diplomat with the Greek government, Seferis held posts in more than a dozen locations during a thirty-six-year period.

Though it was not of the confessional type, Seferis's poetry nevertheless reflected many of his innermost feelings. Drawing on Greek history and classical mythology (especially the works of Homer) for inspiration, the poet most often chose to speak via the character of Odysseus, a heroic figure Seferis regarded as representative of every wanderer in search of a spiritual fulfillment he cannot seem to find. Yet Seferis did not dwell exclusively on the past, on the glory that was Greece; instead he bridged what Anthony N. Zahareas of *Books Abroad* termed "the abyss between a great past and a dismal present."

Often compared to other poets—most notably T. S. Eliot, W. B. Yeats, Paul Valery, and Ezra Pound—who turned to myths and ancient ruins to illustrate contemporary waste and disintegration, Seferis developed a poetry in which "the legends of Mycenae or of Hercules, or the reverberations of a phrase from Aeschylus are set side by side with the spiritual impoverishment, the sense of imprisonment of modern life," as a *Times Literary Supplement* critic once observed. Explained Edmund Keeley in the *Kenyon Review:* "[Seferis's] poetry fully exploits the survival of mythic gods and heroes in the landscape of modern Greece, and it does so as naturally, as unpretentiously as one would expect in a poet of genius. . . . Seferis' secret (in addition to his advantage) is that he always offers an appropriate setting—a poetically realistic setting—before he allows any ghosts to appear on his stage; before he attempts to carry the reader to the level of myth, the level of timeless universalities, he wins his sympathy and belief by convincingly representing the present reality sustaining his myth."

Mythistorema, a sequence of twenty-four related poems based for the most part on lines, characters, and scenes in Homer's *Odyssey,* was widely regarded as Seferis's masterpiece as well as a turning point in the history of Greek poetry as a whole, for in this "mythistory" the poet reconciled Classical and nonclassical elements by means of a then-new, austere, free-verse style that betrayed an underlying passion and denseness of meaning. As the *Times Literary Supplement* critic pointed out, Seferis sought to demonstrate in his epic "the contrast between a past which, however tragic, was responsive to the eternal needs of the human spirit, and a present in which man feels estranged because he cannot find substitutes for the old values of life, and has become the victim of sterile and constricting routines."

With the exception of Odysseus and a few other more "glamorous" figures, most of the characters who tell their stories in *Mythistorema* are ordinary sailors and soldiers, those referred to only in passing in the various legends about Odysseus and Jason. Zahareas noted that the narrator, speaking as "we" or "I," created a "compound voice of multiple identities [that] moves back and forth in time until the borderline between past and present is completely blurred." As a result, the critic continued, Seferis's imaginary Mediterranean voyage becomes "an act of self-examination and a meditation upon the human condition [that straddles], as it were, the diverse times of civilization, by wandering among the various mirrors of myth and reality. . . . The 'mythistorical' voyager is the common man found anywhere in all times of Greek history, who endures through time and survives the changes in political, social, and religious philosophies because he lives, necessarily, by a basic philosophy which is a law of life—one lives as one can." Concluded Zahareas: "The combination of regionalism and universality makes [Seferis's] poems engrossing, utterly faithful to their own terms. [He] invents a mythical Aegean world complete and living in all its details and his journeys into the Aegean Sea stand as a parable or legend of Greek history and man's history. . . . The recollection of past splendor is a reminder that, in the face of death and annihilation, all pretensions of glory are puny and futile."

Despite the fact that he explored man's plight specifically in terms of the suffering of the modern Greek people, Seferis avoided commenting directly on politics in his poetry. Keeley once remarked in *Encounter* that his poetry was political "only in the broadest sense of the term" in that he lamented mankind's tendency to engage in senseless wars (exemplified, the poet felt, by the legendary one waged in Troy many centuries ago). According to Victor Lange of the *New Republic*, Seferis viewed himself not as a social critic but as the "heir and recorder of an incomparable tradition that is present in worn and fragmentary monuments, not as promise or challenge, but as a fractured reminder of greatness." Nevertheless, commented James Goodman, another *New Republic* critic, Seferis's tragic vision was undeniably linked to events in modern Greece. Wrote Goodman: "No poet has expressed Greece's pain better than George Seferis. With a visceral understanding of the plight of his native land . . ., Seferis' poetry never loses sight of Greece. . . . Bold in style, utilizing a minimum of words . . ., his poetry draws from a reservoir of history and mythology. . . . [His] genius rested in his ability to capture in simple but moving images a suffering Greece. . . . For Seferis, his sense of the tragic is harnessed to the hope that his poetry will somehow awaken his people to a 'Greekness' shattered by present politics."

That his appeal was universal, however, was never in dispute. As the *Times Literary Supplement* critic once declared: "More than any other of his contemporaries or successors Seferis has extended the frontiers of Greek literature and created for it a poetry which is attuned to the poetic idiom of the contemporary western world. He has introduced new harmonies and discords into poetic diction and subtilized the use of figurative language, and in doing all this he has employed the 'demotic' tongue and vindicated his lifelong conviction that the poetry of his country can and must be written in the language of everyday speech. Other Greek poets may have surpassed him as word-musicians

or as masters of a wider range of poetic forms. [But] Seferis is uniquely gifted in finding expression for the complexity, the paradoxical and evanescent characters of the modern sensibility."

BIOGRAPHICAL/CRITICAL SOURCES:

Contemporary Literary Criticism, Gale, Volume 5, 1976, Volume 11, 1979.

PERIODICALS

Books Abroad, winter, 1967, spring, 1968, autumn, 1969.
Book Week, December 15, 1963.
Encounter, March, 1972.
Hudson Review, autumn, 1968.
Kenyon Review, June, 1966.
L'Express, October 31, 1963.
London Magazine, June, 1967.
Nation, September 16, 1968, February 7, 1972.
New Republic, February 17, 1968, September 7, 1974.
Newsweek, November 4, 1963.
New Yorker, August 5, 1974.
New York Times Book Review, November 17, 1963, March 17, 1968, July 7, 1974.
Poetry, May, 1969.
Publishers Weekly, November 4, 1963.
Saturday Review, November 30, 1963.
Texas Quarterly, spring, 1964.
Time, November 1, 1963, November 3, 1967.
Times Literary Supplement, September 12, 1968, December 12, 1986.
Virginia Quarterly Review, summer, 1968, summer, 1969, spring, 1975.
Washington Post Book World, March 3, 1968, May 30, 1982.

OBITUARIES:

PERIODICALS

Commonweal, October 29, 1971.
Time, October 4, 1971.
Washington Post, September 21, 1971.

*　　*　　*

SEFERIS, George
　　See SEFERIADES, Giorgos Stylianou

*　　*　　*

SEGAL, Erich (Wolf) 1937-

PERSONAL: Born June 16, 1937, in Brooklyn, N.Y.; son of Samuel Michael (a rabbi) and Cynthia (Shapiro) Segal; married Karen Llona Marianne James (an editor), June 10, 1975; children: Francesca. *Education:* Harvard University, A.B., 1958, A.M., 1959, Ph.D., 1965. *Religion:* Jewish.

ADDRESSES: Home—London, England; Essex, Conn. *Office*—c/o Lazarow, Rm. 1106, 119 West 57th St., New York, N.Y. 10019. *Agent*—Ed Victor Ltd., 162 Wardour St., London W1V 4AB, England.

CAREER: Yale University, New Haven, Conn., visiting lecturer, 1964-65, assistant professor, 1965-68, associate professor of classics and comparative literature, 1968-72, adjunct professor of classics, 1981—; author and adapter of stage plays and screenplays, novelist and lyricist. Visiting professor at University of Munich, 1973, Princeton University, 1974-75, Tel Aviv University, spring, 1976, and Dartmouth College, fall, 1976, and 1977;

visiting fellow, Wolfson College, Oxford University, 1978, 1979, 1981, and 1986; honorary research fellow, University College, University of London, 1983—. Member of National Advisory Council of Peace Corps, 1970; jury member, Cannes Film Festival, 1971, and National Book Award for Arts and Letters, 1971. Sports commentator at Olympic Games, for American Broadcasting Companies, Inc. (ABC-TV), 1972, and 1976, and during pre-Olympic coverage, for National Broadcasting Company, Inc. (NBC-TV), 1980; French-language radio commentator at Olympic Games for RT-Radio (Paris, France), 1972, and 1976; occasional commentator on NBC-TV's "Sports World" and ABC-TV's "Wide World of Sports"; host of Public Broadcasting Service (PBS-TV)'s "Masterpiece Theater" presentation of "Morning Becomes Electra."

MEMBER: American Philological Association, American Comparative Literature Association, Dramatists Guild, Writers Guild of America, West, American Society of Composers, Authors and Publishers (ASCAP), Academy for Literary Studies.

AWARDS, HONORS: Guggenheim fellowship, 1968; Golden Globe Award from Hollywood Foreign Press Association, 1971, for screenplay "Love Story"; nominated for Academy Award ("Oscar") for best screenplay, 1971, for "Love Story"; Presidential commendation, 1972, for service to the Peace Corps; Humboldt Stiftung award (West Germany), 1973; Premio Bancarella (Italy) and Prix Deauville (France), both 1986, for *The Class.*

WRITINGS:

NOVELS

Love Story (Literary Guild alternate selection; based on Segal's screenplay of the same title; also see below), Harper, 1970.
Fairy Tale (juvenile), Harper, 1973.
Oliver's Story (also see below), Harper, 1977.
Man, Woman and Child (also see below), Harper, 1980.
The Class (Literary Guild main selection), Bantam, 1985.
Doctors, Bantam, 1987.

MUSIC

"Sing Muse," produced Off-Broadway, 1960.
"Odyssey," produced at Kennedy Center, Washington, D.C., December, 1974.

Also author of revue, "Voulez-Voux?," produced in Boston, Mass., songs for a one-man show of Dutch star Toon Hermans, and several adaptations from the French, including "Madame Mousse."

SCREENPLAYS

(With others) "Yellow Submarine," United Artists, 1968.
"Love Story," Paramount, 1970.
"The Games," Twentieth Century-Fox, 1970.
"R.P.M.," Columbia, 1970.
"Jennifer on My Mind," United Artists, 1971.
(With John Korty) "Oliver's Story" (based on Segal's novel of the same title), Paramount, 1978.
"A Change of Seasons," Twentieth Century-Fox, 1981.
(With David Z. Goodman) "Man, Woman and Child" (based on Segal's novel of the same title), Paramount, 1983.

EDITOR OR CO-EDITOR

Euripides: A Collection of Critical Essays, Prentice-Hall, 1968.
(And translator) *Plautus: Three Comedies* (contains "The Braggart Soldier," "The Brothers Menaechmus," and "The Haunted House"), Harper, 1969, revised edition, Bantam, 1985.

Scholarship on Plautus, 1965-1976, Classical World Surveys, 1981.
(With Fergus Millar) *Caesar Augustus: Seven Essays,* Clarendon Press, 1984.
Greek Tragedy: Modern Essays in Criticism, Harper, 1983 (published in England as *Oxford Readings in Greek Tragedy,* Oxford University Press, 1983).
Plato's Dialogues, Bantam, 1986.

OTHER

Roman Laughter: The Comedy of Plautus, Harvard University Press, 1968, revised and expanded edition, Oxford University Press, 1987.

Also author of two television specials, "The Ancient Games," 1972, and "Olympathon '80," 1980. Contributor of reviews and articles to numerous periodicals, including *New York Times Book Review, New Republic,* and *Times Literary Supplement.* Member of editorial board, *Diacritics,* 1971—.

WORK IN PROGRESS: Editing *Scholarship on Plautus, 1976-1985;* writing a screenplay based on his novel *The Class.*

SIDELIGHTS: Judging by the list of Erich Segal's accomplishments, compiled by Robert Thomas, Jr., for the *New York Times Book Review,* Segal has led a very successful life. He graduated from Harvard as the first student in the school's history to be both Latin Salutatorian and Class Poet. He taught at Yale where, according to Thomas, his classes "drew overflow attendance and were branded 'star performances' " by his students. His first screenplay was the highly successful "Yellow Submarine." His first novel, *Love Story,* went through twenty-one hardcover printings in a little more than a year, and its first paperback run, Thomas notes, "produced the largest initial print order in the history of publishing [up until that time], 4,350,000" copies. Not only was Segal's novel the best-selling book on the *New York Times Book Review*'s list for a year, but it was also translated into twenty-three languages and eventually sold eleven million copies in the United States alone.

Since Thomas's article was published, more success has come Segal's way, including several more best-selling novels and well-received scholarly publications on his specialty, classical Greco-Roman comedy. But along with these successes have also come disappointments. For example, *Love Story* was informally nominated for the 1971 National Book Award, but the five-judge panel threatened to resign if the book was not dropped from consideration. That same year, Segal was denied tenure at Yale, something he wanted badly. And, despite the immense popularity of his books, especially in Europe, reviews have been almost always no better than mixed.

For instance, while in *Publishers Weekly* Barbara A. Bannon called *Love Story*'s characterizations "memorable," in *Newsweek* S. K. Oberbeck wrote that the novel's "banality . . . skips from cliche to cliche with an abandon that would chill the blood of a *True Romance* editor." Segal's longest novel, *The Class,* fared no better. In *People,* for example, Andrea Chambers called the book a "slick yet perceptive saga," while in the *New York Times Book Review* Susan Isaacs noted: "Segal is able to . . . keep the plot moving. He is a good enough storyteller that despite the dead language, the reader still wants to find out what happens to his characters."

Despite lukewarm reviews and other setbacks, including nearly dying from a blood disorder in 1982, Segal has managed to persevere. "I'll never be the critics' darling," Segal told Wendy Smith in a *Chicago Tribune* interview, "[But] I would like to be a better writer. . . . It's the opposite of running, where you get slower every year. In writing, you sometimes get better every year. I'd like to keep on improving."

Segal's next novel, *Doctors,* shows the desired improvement, say the critics. The book chronicles the challenges faced by a class of students at Harvard Medical School in the early 1960s. Characters from a wide assortment of socioeconomic backgrounds allow the author to explore topics such as professional ethics, racial prejudice, and mercy-killing. "There is enough action here to keep several emergency rooms busy round the clock. . . . [Segal] seems to have done impressive research, in that the situations ring true," Grace Lichtenstein comments in a *Washington Post Book World* review. Lichtenstein also commends Segal's descriptions of the pressures these students must endure—and their realistic responses to stress, which are not always admirable. *Doctors,* she relates, "is also quite pointed in dealing with professional backstabbing, whether it involves blowing the whistle on a negligent colleague . . . or the sexist treatment of female doctors." *Chicago Tribune* contributor Carol Kleiman suggests that *Doctors* succeeds because of Segal's focus on the relationship between psychiatrist Barney Livingston and neonatologist Laura Castellano, the riddle of love that remains Segal's "personal territory."

MEDIA ADAPTATIONS: Author, with Martin Ransohoff, of story "Frost on the Apples," from which the movie "Consenting Adults" (1979) was adapted. Film rights to *The Class* have been purchased for a television miniseries.

AVOCATIONAL INTERESTS: Running, playing the piano.

BIOGRAPHICAL/CRITICAL SOURCES:

BOOKS

Bestsellers 89, Number 1, Gale, 1989.
Contemporary Literary Criticism, Gale, Volume 3, 1975, Volume 10, 1979.
Dictionary of Literary Biography Yearbook: 1986, Gale, 1987.

PERIODICALS

Atlantic, June, 1970.
Chicago Tribune, May 5, 1985, August 19, 1988.
Christian Science Monitor, April 30, 1970.
Classical World, December, 1968.
Detroit News, May 5, 1985, June 5, 1985.
Houston Post, April 27, 1975.
Los Angeles Times Book Review, May 19, 1985.
Newsweek, March 9, 1970, April 9, 1973, May 5, 1980, May 13, 1985.
New York Times, February 13, 1970, February 25, 1977, March 21, 1977, May 23, 1980.
New York Times Book Review, March 8, 1970, December 20, 1970, March 25, 1973, March 6, 1977, June 8, 1980, April 21, 1985.
New York Times Magazine, June 13, 1971.
People, May 13, 1985.
Publishers Weekly, December 1, 1969, February 2, 1970, July 15, 1988.
Saturday Review, February 14, 1970, December 26, 1970.
Time, March 15, 1971, March 21, 1977, May 26, 1980, May 13, 1985.
Times (London), May 13, 1977, May 13, 1980.
Times Literary Supplement, April 17, 1969, September 4, 1970, May 13, 1977.
Washington Post, March 24, 1987.

Washington Post Book World, March 20, 1977, May 18, 1980, April 28, 1985, August 7, 1988.
West Coast Review of Books, May, 1977.
Yale Review, December, 1968.

* * *

SEIFERT, Jaroslav 1901-1986

PERSONAL: Born September 23, 1901, in Prague, Czechoslovakia; died following an apparent heart attack, January 10, 1986, in Prague, Czechoslovakia; son of Antonin (a blacksmith) and Marie Seifert; married Marie Ulrichova, 1928; children: Jana, Jaroslav. *Education:* Attended secondary school in Prague, Czechoslovakia. *Religion:* Roman Catholic.

ADDRESSES: Home—Brevnov U Ladronky 23/1338, Prague 6, Czechoslovakia.

CAREER: Journalist and editor of periodicals in Czechoslovakia, 1920-49, including *Rovnost,* Brno, 1922, *Srsatec, Rude pravo,* 1922-25, *Nova scena* (theatre monthly), 1930, *Pestre kvety* (weekly), 1931-33, *Ranni noviny* (daily), 1933-39, *Narodni prace,* 1939-45, *Prace* (daily), 1945-49, and *Kytice* (literary monthly), 1946-48; full-time writer, 1949-86. Co-founder of Devetsil Art Association, 1920.

MEMBER: Union of Czechoslovak Writers (acting chairman, 1968-69; chairman, 1969-70).

AWARDS, HONORS: Czechoslovakian State Prize for Literature, 1936, for *Ruce Venusiny,* 1954, for *Maminka,* and 1968; named National Artist of Czechoslovakia, 1966; Nobel Prize for literature, 1984.

WRITINGS:

Mesto v slzach (poems; title means "The City in Tears"), [Czechoslovakia], 1921, Ceskoslovensky spisovatel, 1979.
Sama laska (poems; title means "Nothing But Love"), Vecernice, 1923.
Na vlnach T.S.F. (poems; title means "On Radio Waves"), [Czechoslovakia], 1925.
Slavik zpiva spatne (poems; title means "The Nightingale Sings Badly"), [Czechoslovakia], 1926.
Svatebni cesta, [Czechoslovakia], 1928, Ceskoslovensky spisovatel, 1982.
Hvezdy nad Rajskou zahradou (essays; title means "Stars Over Paradise Garden"), [Czechoslovakia], 1929.
Postovni holub (poems; title means "The Carrier Pigeon"), Skerik, 1929.
Jablko z klina (poems; title means "An Apple From the Lap"), [Czechoslovakia], 1933, Borovy, 1947.
Ruce Venusiny (poems; title means "The Hands of Venus"), [Czechoslovakia], 1936, Melantrich, 1967, Sixty-eight Publishers (Toronto), 1984.
Zpivano do rotacky, [Czechoslovakia], 1936.
Jaro sbohem, [Czechoslovakia], 1937, Ceskoslovensky spisovatel, 1980.
Osm dni (poems), Melantrich, 1937, Ceskoslovensky spisovatel/Vimperk, 1968, translation by Paul Jagasich and Tom O'Grady published as *Eight Days: An Elegy for Thomas Masaryk,* Spirit That Moves Us (Iowa City, Iowa), 1985.
Podzim v cechach, [Czechoslovakia], 1937.
Zhasnete svetla (poems; title means "Put Out the Lights"), Melantrich, 1938.
Pantoumy o lasce, [Czechoslovakia], 1939.
Vejir Bozeny Nemcove, [Czechoslovakia], 1940, Ceskoslovensky spisovatel, 1976.

Svetlem odena (poems; title means "Dressed in Light"; also see below), [Czechoslovakia], 1940, Ceskoslovensky spisovatel, 1962.

Jablon se strunami pavucin, [Czechoslovakia], 1943.

Ruka a plamen, [Czechoslovakia], 1943, Borovy, 1948.

Kamenny most (poems; title means "The Stone Bridge"; also see below), [Czechoslovakia], 1944, Borovy, 1947.

Devet rondeaux, [Czechoslovakia], 1945.

Prilba hliny (poems; title means "The Helmet of Clay"), Prace, 1945.

Suknice andelu, [Czechoslovakia], 1946.

Dokud nam neprsi na rakev, [Czechoslovakia], 1947.

Sel malir chude do sveta, [Czechoslovakia], 1949, Ceskoslovensky spisovatel, 1956.

Pozdrav Frantisku Halasovi, [Czechoslovakia], 1949.

Pisen o Viktorce (poems), Ceskoslovensky spisovatel, 1950.

Mozart v Praze: Trinact rondeaux, [Czechoslovakia], 1951, Ceskoslovensky spisovatel, 1956, bilingual edition published as *Mozart v Praze/Mozart in Prague,* Spirit That Moves Us, 1985.

Petrin, [Czechoslovakia], 1951.

Maminka (juvenile poems; title means "Mother"), [Czechoslovakia], 1954, Statni nakl. detske knihy, 1960, Ceskoslovensky spisovatel, 1966, 1975.

Prsten Trebonski Madone, [Czechoslovakia], 1954, Ceske Budejovice, 1966.

Dilo, Ceskoslovensky spisovatel, 1956.

Chlapec a hvezdy, Ceskoslovensky spisovatel, 1956.

Praha a venec sonetu, [Czechoslovakia], 1956.

Vytrzene stranky. Frenstatske koledy, romance a pisne, [Czechoslovakia], 1957.

Pisen domova: Vybor z dila, Statni nakl. detske knihy, 1958.

Praha: Vybox versu z let 1929-1947, Nakl. ceskoslovenskych vytvarnych umelcu, 1958.

Mesto v slzach, Ceskoslovensky spisovatel, 1960.

Jeste jednou jaro, Klub pratel poezie, 1961.

Verse o Praze, Ceskoslovensky spisovatel, 1962.

Polibek na cestu: vybor milostne lyriky, Ceskoslovensky spisovatel, 1965.

Koncert na ostrove (poems), Ceskoslovensky spisovatel, 1965.

Halleyova kometa (poems), Statni nakl. detske knihy, 1967.

Odlevani zvonu (poems), Ceskoslovensky spisovatel, 1967, translation by Paul Jagasich and Tom O'Grady published as *The Casting of Bells,* Spirit That Moves Us, 1983.

Zpevy o Praze, Ceskoslovensky spisovatel, 1968.

Vidim zemi sirou, Sirena, 1968.

Nejkrasnejsi byva silena, Mlada fronta, 1968.

Milostna rondeaux, Vimperk, 1969.

Morovy Sloup (poem), Index (Cologne, West Germany), 1977, Ceskoslovensky spisovatel, 1981, translation by Ewald Osers published as *The Plague Column,* Terra Nova Editions, 1979, translation by Lyn Coffin published as *The Plague Monument,* [Silver Spring, Md.], 1980.

Svetlem odena [and] *Kamenny most,* Ceskoslovensky spisovatel, 1978.

Destnik z Piccadilly (poems), Ceskoslovensky spisovatel, 1979, translation by Ewald Osers published as *An Umbrella from Piccadilly,* London Magazine Editions, 1983.

Dve basny, Charta 77 Foundation (Stockholm, Sweden), 1981.

Zapas s andelem, Ceskoslovensky spisovatel, 1981.

Vsecky krasy sveta (memoirs; title means "All the Beauties of the World"), Sixty-eight Publishers, 1981, Ceskoslovensky spisovatel, 1982.

Byti basnikem (poems; title means "To Be a Poet"), Ceskoslovensky spisovatel, 1983.

The Selected Poetry of Jaroslav Seifert, translation by Ewald Osers and George Gibian, Macmillan, 1986.

Also translator of poetry and contributor to periodicals.

SIDELIGHTS: When Czech writer Jaroslav Seifert won the 1984 Nobel Prize for literature, his achievement merely capped a career that had already earned him the respect and love of his countrymen. He was admired both for his courage and integrity in the face of political repression and for his artistry, as revealed in more than thirty volumes of lyric poetry published over a span of sixty years. He had survived a Nazi dictatorship, Stalinist purges, and Communist power struggles to become the best-loved poet in a nation of poetry-lovers.

Seifert, son of a working-class family, published his first volume of poems in 1921 and, together with other young intellectuals, joined the newly-formed Communist party. In 1929, when that party's leadership changed its course, seven foremost writers among its members, including Seifert, protested publicly and were expelled. After his break with the Communists, Seifert worked as a literary editor, mostly on social democratic periodicals, and published one collection of poems after another. In the Munich crisis of 1938 and the subsequent catastrophes that eventually shattered Czechoslovakia, leaving its people dominated by German leader Adolf Hitler, Seifert became a highly visible spokesman and penned many poems urging resistance.

During the post-World War II period Seifert directed an eclectic review, *The Bouquet,* but this was shut down in 1948 when the Communists seized power. A regime unfriendly toward writers of independent views, the Communists silenced Seifert and many other writers for failing to promote the slogans of social realism. A series of poems by Seifert in 1950 honoring his native village and rural novelist Bozena Nemcova, a greatly admired Czech novelist and female rebel of the classic period of Czech literature, earned him the denunciation of official critics as disloyal, bourgeois, escapist, and a traitor to his class. Seifert then turned to writing children's literature, a genre to which his direct, simple style well suited him. One of these efforts, *Maminka,* has become a classic of Czech literature, epitomizing, according to Alfred French in *Czech Writers and Politics, 1945-1969,* "a whole trend of literature away from the monumental to the humble; from public themes to private; from the pseudoreality of political slogans to the known reality of Czech home life which was the product of its past."

In 1956, when the Soviet regime in Czechoslovakia tightened controls on artistic freedom, Seifert spoke out in protest at a writers' association meeting on behalf of imprisoned and silenced writers. His speech had little immediate effect beyond infuriating the establishment sufficiently to suspend publication of his new works, but the poet was from that time on generally regarded as the dean of Czech letters, a man from the old days whose contemporaries were almost all dead, who could always be counted on to speak the truth.

Seifert re-emerged in the mid-1960s at the forefront of the drive among Czech writers to support the liberalization and de-Sovietization of the communist regime, a national movement that led to the catastrophic Warsaw Pact invasion of Czechoslovakia in August, 1968. The following October the National Writers Union elected Seifert president to replace the exiled Eduard Goldstucker, but the country's leaders dissolved the union in 1970. Seifert refused to join a new government-backed writers union and was one of the first to sign the Charter 77 human rights manifesto. Consequently, the poet was again out of favor, and for a decade the Czech authorities published no new work of his. However, Seifert never became active in Prague's dissident scene, preferring instead to live and write in relative seclusion, expressing himself in poems about love and nature.

His new writings were published mainly privately or abroad, the best known of which was *Morovy Sloup,* published in Czech in 1977 by the emigre publishing house Index in Cologne, West Germany, and later translated into English. A single, long poem described by *World Literature Today* contributor William E. Harkins as "probably Seifert's masterpiece," it celebrates the monument erected by the people of Prague soon after the end of the Thirty Years War in thanksgiving for deliverance from the plague. According to Harkins, the monument "seems to represent a great and terrifying image of the unity of Czech fate and Czech history, bringing together past and present, and symbolizing a destiny for the land . . . of a small people eternally invaded, occupied, and encroached upon."

In view of Seifert's great popularity and the passing of his eightieth birthday, Czech officials relented and published an edition of *Morovy Sloup* in 1981. A year later they also issued Seifert's memoirs, *Vsecky Krasy sveta,* a recollection of his childhood and youth. In fact, during the last years of his life, noted Harkins, Seifert enjoyed a unique position among his fellow writers: he had been a dissident and published abroad, yet he was, at the end of his long career, acceptable to the Prague regime. "He is not liked by the state, but they cannot silence him because he is so famous," exiled Czech poet Pavel Kohout told United Press International on the day of the Swedish Academy's announcement of the 1984 Nobel Prize winner, adding, "He's really a voice of the people."

Seifert spent his final years in a villa in a quiet district of Prague, surrounded by his vast collection of cactus plants—and still writing. He once said, "I'm being laughed at for being old and still writing love poems, but I shall write them until the end."

Seifert's career as a poet ranged from an intensely lyrical period when he began writing in the 1920s, to a surrealistic phase in the 1930s, to vehement patriotism during the Nazi occupation, and finally to a meditative, philosophical stage toward the end of his life. But throughout, his themes remained constant: celebration of his homeland and his native Prague, a deep concern for the suffering of others, and a sensuous delight in the beauty of the physical world and the love of women. Critics credit his appeal as a poet to certain qualities that make his work outstanding, notably that it is utterly simple and unpretentious, haunting and lyrical.

As a young man Seifert passed through the then-dominant phase of "proletarian" poetry, as revealed in his first two collections, *Mesto v slzach* and *Sama laska,* celebrations of the common person and the bright future of socialism. He also embraced the succeeding "pure poetry" phase, with its emphasis on exotic and playful imagery, as evidenced by *Na vlnach T.S.F.* and *Slavik zpiva spatne.* Seifert's poetic maturity reputedly began with the cycle of poems *Postovni holub* and peaked with *Jablko z klina,* a collection in which the clever manner and fireworks of earlier works had been abandoned for a new style, one notable for its sincerity and directness and for its cultivation of natural, unaffected images rendered in fresh, at times almost colloquial, language. Love, including its sensual aspects, a frequent theme in Seifert's earlier collections, is his main subject in *Jablko z klina* and continues to dominate his next collection, *Ruce Venusiny.*

The national catastrophe at Munich in 1938 and the Nazi occupation that followed brought out Seifert's deep patriotism, reflected in some of his most acclaimed collections. These include

Zhasnete svetla, which expresses the poet's anxiety after the betrayal of Czechoslovakia at Munich, *Svetlem odena,* a poetic tribute to Prague written by Seifert during the Nazi occupation of Czechoslovakia, and *Prilba hliny,* several cycles of patriotic verses published after the war, celebrating in particular the Prague uprising against the remnants of the occupying Nazi army in May of 1945. In *Prilba hliny,* a tremendously popular collection that is generally credited with establishing Seifert as a national poet, he pits the brief violence and the eerie excitement of improvised barricades against the startling beauty of the lilacs, the acacias, and the chestnuts in bloom. With his patriotic poems, wrote Josef Skvorecky in *New Republic,* "full of both linguistic beauty and encoded messages—clear to the Czechs, impenetrable to the Nazi censor, the poet boosted the morale of the nation." They were poems that, in the words of *Listener* contributor Karel Janovicky, "plucked the secret strings of the nation's soul while the Nazi censor looked on bewildered."

When the Swedish Academy awarded Seifert the Nobel Prize for literature in 1984, his work was relatively unknown in the United States except among scholars and Americans of Czechoslovak origin. Only three of his nearly thirty volumes of poetry were available in English, *Odlevani zvonu,* translated by Tom O'Grady and Paul Jagasich as *The Casting of Bells* in 1983, *Destnik z Piccadilly,* translated by Ewald Osers as *An Umbrella from Piccadilly,* also in 1983, and *Morovy Sloup,* translated by Osers as *The Plague Column* in 1979 and by Lyn Coffin as *The Plague Monument* in 1980.

Following Seifert's reception of the Nobel Prize, however, more of his poetry and prose appeared in English translation. Noteworthy among these publications is *The Selected Poetry of Jaroslav Seifert,* a collection of some sixty-two of Seifert's poems, ranging from his first published work, *Mesto v slzach,* to his last, *Byti basnikem,* along with ten prose excerpts from his memoirs, *Vsecky krasy sveta.*

Several commentators have noted the difficulty experienced by English-speaking critics in assessing the value of Seifert's work. They cite as problems the dearth of translations, the difficulty of translating what Seifert called his poems' "inner rhythms," the lack of previous criticism and commentary, and the presence in Seifert's writing of many allusions that escape the non-Czech reader. Yet critics have always acknowledged Seifert's respected position in Central European literature and praised his poetry for its sensuality and humor, its accessible, conversational style, and its celebration of Czechoslovakia's cultural heritage. Perhaps the most memorable accolade given Seifert is contained in his Nobel Prize citation, which honors him for work "which, endowed with freshness, sensuality, and rich inventiveness, provides a liberating image of the indomitable spirit and versatility of man."

BIOGRAPHICAL/CRITICAL SOURCES:

BOOKS

Contemporary Literary Criticism, Volume 34, 1985, Volume 44, Gale, 1987.
French, Alfred, *Czech Writers and Politics, 1945-1969,* Columbia University Press, 1982.
French, Alfred, *The Poets of Prague,* Oxford University Press, 1969.

PERIODICALS

Best Sellers, November, 1986.
Hudson Review, spring, 1987.
Listener, October 18, 1984.

London Magazine, April, 1986, May, 1986.
New Republic, February 18, 1985.
New Yorker, November 5, 1984.
New York Review of Books, November 22, 1984.
New York Times, October 12, 1984, October 15, 1984, December 20, 1984.
New York Times Book Review, June 30, 1985.
People, January 7, 1985.
Spectator, January 12, 1985.
Time, October 22, 1984, December 17, 1984.
Times Literary Supplement, February 24, 1984, October 26, 1984, October 31, 1986.
Washington Post, October 12, 1984, November 28, 1984.
World Literature Today, autumn, 1984, winter, 1985, spring, 1985, winter, 1986, spring, 1986, winter, 1987.

OBITUARIES:

PERIODICALS

Chicago Tribune, January 11, 1986.
Detroit Free Press, January 11, 1986, January 22, 1986.
Globe and Mail (Toronto), January 11, 1986.
Los Angeles Times, January 11, 1986.
Newsweek, January 20, 1986.
New York Daily News, January 11, 1986.
New York Times, January 11, 1986.
Publishers Weekly, January 31, 1986.
Time, January 20, 1986.
Times (London), January 11, 1986.
Washington Post, January 11, 1986.

*   *   *

SELVON, Sam
    See SELVON, Samuel (Dickson)

*   *   *

SELVON, Samuel (Dickson)   1923-
    (Sam Selvon)

PERSONAL: Born May 20, 1923, in Trinidad, West Indies; son of an Indian father and a half-Scottish mother; immigrated to England, 1950; married Draupadi Persaud, 1947 (divorced); married Althea Nesta Daroux, 1963; children: (first marriage) Shelley Sarojini; (second marriage) Michael, Leslie, Debra Jane. *Education:* Attended Naparima College.

CAREER: Writer, c. 1940—. *Trinidad Guardian* (newspaper and weekly magazine), Trinidad, West Indies, journalist, 1946-50; British Broadcasting Corp. (BBC), London, England, journalist, c. 1950; Indian Embassy, London, civil servant, 1950-53; free-lance writer during early 1950s. *Military service:* Royal Navy Reserve, 1940-45; wireless operator patrolling Caribbean Sea on minesweepers and torpedo boats.

AWARDS, HONORS: Fellow of the John Simon Guggenheim Memorial Foundation, 1954 and 1968; traveling scholarship from the Society of Authors, 1958; grants from the Arts Council of Great Britain, 1967 and 1968; Hummingbird Medal of the Order of the Trinity from the Prime Minister's Office of the Trinidad and Tobago Government, 1969; D.Litt., University of West Indies, 1985, and University of Warwick, 1989.

WRITINGS:

A Brighter Sun (novel), Wingate, 1952, Viking, 1953, reprinted, Longman Caribbean, 1985.
An Island Is a World (novel), Wingate, 1955.

The Lonely Londoners (novel), St. Martin's, 1956, published as *The Lonely Ones,* Brown, Watson, 1959, reprinted, Longman, 1978.
Ways of Sunlight (short stories), St. Martin's, 1957, reprinted, Three Continents Press, 1979.
Turn Again Tiger (novel), MacGibbon & Kee, 1958, St. Martin's, 1959.
I Hear Thunder (novel), Wingate, 1962, St. Martin's, 1963.
The Housing Lark (novel), MacGibbon & Kee, 1965.
The Plains of Caroni (novel), MacGibbon & Kee, 1970.
Those Who Eat the Cascadura (novel), Davis-Poynter, 1972.
(Under name Sam Selvon) *Moses Ascending* (novel), Davis-Poynter, 1975.
(Under name Sam Selvon) *Moses Migrating* (novel), Longman, 1983.
(Under name Sam Selvon) *Highway in the Sun and Other Plays,* Peepal Tree, 1988 (also see below).
(Under name Sam Selvon) *Foreday Morning* (short stories), Longman, 1989.

Also author of radio plays, including "Lost Property," 1965; "A House for Teena," 1965; "Highway in the Sun," 1967; "Rain Stop Play," 1967; "You Right in the Smoke," 1968; "Worse Than Their Bite," 1968; "Bringing in the Sheaves," 1969; "Perchance to Dream," 1969; "Eldorado West One," 1969; "Home Sweet India," 1970; "Mary Mary Shut Your Gate," 1971; "Voyage to Trinidad," 1971; "Those Who Eat the Cascadura," 1971; "Water for Veronica," 1972; "Cry Baby Brackley," 1972; "The Harvest in Wilderness," 1972; "Milk in the Coffee," 1975; and "Zeppi's Machine," 1977. Adapted "The Magic Stick" for radio, from a work by Ismith Khan, 1971.

Contributor to periodicals, including *London Magazine, New Statesman, Nation,* and London *Sunday Times.*

SIDELIGHTS: Award-winning West Indian writer Samuel Selvon captures the spirit of a changing culture in his short stories and novels. The author is a native of Trinidad, an island in the Atlantic located off the northeastern coast of Venezuela, bordering the southern portion of the Caribbean Sea. Acquired by England in 1802, the island did not become part of an independent state until 1962. Selvon's evocations of Caribbean life explore the ramifications of the British influence on Trinidad as well as the racial tensions existing between black Africans and Indians living in the West Indies. Judged by critics to be impassioned, charming, and sometimes ribald works of fiction, the author's writings are noted for their vibrant local color, faithfulness to the Trinidadian dialect, and conversational tone. In an interview with Kenneth Ramshand for *Canadian Literature,* Selvon asserted, "If I have anything significant to say on an issue it is to be found inside my novels and short stories."

Selvon was a popular short story writer in Trinidad before moving to England in 1950. His first novel, *A Brighter Sun,* garnered considerable acclaim in both England and the United States upon its publication in the early 1950s. The story revolves around Urmilla and Tiger, a rural East Indian couple who, following an arranged marriage, live and grow through the turbulence that World War II brings to their native land. Despite some criticism that Selvon dealt too lightly with the problems of illiteracy, racial conflict, poverty, and psychological depression among the villagers, Anthony West, writing in the *New Yorker,* dubbed the book "a delightful first novel." West further contended, "Selvon is a writer with a sharp eye; his characters and the world they inhabit have a substantial reality." In an article for the *New York Times Book Review,* Edith Efron explained, "Tiger's drama lies in his superiority of mind and imagination which drives him constantly to transcend the restricted economic and spiritual horizons of his native neighbors."

Selvon's 1956 book, *The Lonely Londoners,* was greeted enthusiastically. Generally regarded as a more mature work than *A Brighter Sun, The Lonely Londoners* is an exploration of clashing cultures. The novel takes place during the years following World War II and focuses on black West Indians living in London. Selvon illuminates the poor living conditions and racial discrimination that the immigrants faced, creating what Whitney Baillett hailed "a nearly perfect work of its kind." The critic proclaimed, "This is the blessedly balanced realism that skirts completely the depressing passion of the naturalist novelist—the romance of total misery."

The Housing Lark picks up on the issue of white prejudice, depicting the efforts of freewheeling Trinidadians to save enough money to purchase a home and thereby liberate themselves from exploitation by crooked white landlords. Portraits of both expatriate West Indians living in London and the people of Trinidad in their native milieu, the short stories in the 1957 collection *Ways of Sunlight* also contain Selvon's signature characters, leading "precarious lives . . . with difficulty but also with gusto," according to Rye Vervaet in the *New York Times Book Review.* K. W. Purdy noted in *Saturday Review* that while the tales in the volume "are not notable for dramatic tension," Selvon's character studies—such as that of the wrinkle-faced, space-toothed black farm woman, Ma Procop, "who gripped a dirty clay pipe firmly with her gums . . . and smoked cheap black tobacco"—convey "a warming, balanced conviction of the indestructibility of the human spirit."

Selvon broke new ground with his 1962 novel *I Hear Thunder,* centering on the educated native bourgeoisie living in the West Indies. In the story, a black Trinidadian returns to the island from London with a medical degree and a white wife. Selvon portrays Trinidad in *I Hear Thunder* as an island where white skin "was more desired than food." Yet color in no way impedes a series of partner-swapping seductions that occur throughout the course of the novel. Some critics complained that Selvon failed to address the complex social consequences of intermarriage—especially during the 1960s. Dion Reilly, writing in the *New York Times Book Review,* ventured that the development of the narrative might be somewhat misleading in its implication that "money and education, more than race or color" are the "important keys to the apparently somewhat skittish social conditions of Trinidad." Still, Reilly conceded, "Selvon writes with great charm and a fresh, earthy naivete."

The author's later novels, including *The Plains of Caroni* and *Moses Ascending,* were generally faulted for their thin plots but praised for their beautifully evocative scenes and authentic language. Selvon explained in the *Canadian Literature* interview that he is more concerned with "the translation of emotions, feelings, and situations" in his works than in the creation of "an epic or saga" documenting West Indian history. "There is more than enough history and drama here for others to do more comprehensive and detailed studies," the author reasoned. Selvon's humorous and optimistic brand of realism—if not entirely representative of the difficulties faced by the natives of Trinidad—brings what West called a "vigor" to the "new literature of the West Indies." Commenting on the value of Selvon's works, Vervaet concluded that the spirited writer "finds both humor and pathos in the human condition," and "he also believes a little in obeah (magic)."

BIOGRAPHICAL/CRITICAL SOURCES:

BOOKS

Selvon, Samuel, *Ways of Sunlight,* St. Martin's, 1957.
Selvon, Samuel, *I Hear Thunder,* St. Martin's, 1963.

PERIODICALS

Atlantic Monthly, March, 1953.
Canadian Literature, winter, 1982.
New Statesman, August 29, 1975.
New Yorker, February 14, 1953, January 18, 1958.
New York Times Book Review, January 18, 1953, November 2, 1958, August 18, 1963.
Saturday Review, November 15, 1958.
Times Literary Supplement, January 31, 1958, April 1, 1965.

*   *   *

SENDAK, Maurice (Bernard)   1928-

PERSONAL: Born June 10, 1928, in Brooklyn, N.Y.; son of Philip and Sarah (Schindler) Sendak. *Education:* Attended Art Students' League, New York, N.Y., 1949-51.

ADDRESSES: Home—200 Chestnut Hill Rd., Ridgefield, Conn. 06877.

CAREER: Writer and illustrator of children's books, 1951—. Worked for comic book syndicate All American Comics part time during high school, adapting the "Mutt and Jeff" newspaper strip for comic books; Timely Service (window display house), New York City, window display artist, 1946; F.A.O. Schwartz, New York City, display artist, 1948-51. Illustrations have been displayed in one-man shows at School of Visual Arts, New York City, 1964, Rosenbach Foundation, Philadelphia, Pa., 1970 and 1975, Galerie Daniel Keel, Zurich, Switzerland, 1974, Ashmolean Museum, Oxford University, 1975, American Cultural Center, Paris, France, 1978, and Pierpont Morgan Library, New York City, 1981. Set and costume designer for a number of opera productions in the United States and Great Britain, including Wolfgang Amadeus Mozart's "The Magic Flute," for Houston Grand Opera, 1980, Leos Janacek's "The Cunning Little Vixen," for New York City Opera, 1981, Serge Prokofiev's "Love for Three Oranges," for Glyndebourne Opera, 1982, "The Abduction from the Seraglio," for New York City Opera, 1984, and two one-act operas by Ravel, for Glyndebourne Opera, 1986.

MEMBER: Authors' Guild, Authors' League of America.

AWARDS, HONORS: Recipient of eighteen *New York* Times awards for illustrations, 1952-76; Caldecott Medal, American Library Association, 1964, for *Where the Wild Things Are,* runner-up for his illustrations in *A Very Special House, Little Bear's Visit, The Moon Jumpers, Mr. Rabbit and The Lovely Present,* and *What Do You Say, Dear?;* Hans Christian Andersen International Medal (first American to receive this award), 1970, for the entire body of his work; L.H.D., Boston University, 1977; American Book Award nomination, 1980, for *Higglety Pigglety Pop!; or, There Must Be More to Life;* American Book Award, *New York Times* Best Illustrated Children's Book Award, and *Boston Globe-Horn Book* Awards, all 1982, all for *Outside Over There;* Laura Ingalls Wilder Award, Association for Library Service to Children, 1983, for "a substantial and lasting contribution to childrens' literature;" Best Young Picture Books Paperback Award, *Redbook,* 1984, for *Where the Wild Things Are; New York Times* Best Illustrated Children's Book Award, 1985, for Ralph Manheim's translation of E. T. A. Hoffman's *Nutcracker.*

WRITINGS:

CHILDREN'S BOOKS; ALL SELF ILLUSTRATED, EXCEPT AS INDICATED

Kenny's Window, Harper, 1956.
Very Far Away, Harper, 1957.
The Sign on Rosie's Door, Harper, 1960.
Chicken Soup with Rice (also see below), Harper, 1962, reprinted (cassette included), Scholastic, Inc., 1986.
One Was Johnny (also see below), Harper, 1962.
Alligators All Around (also see below), Harper, 1962.
Pierre (also see below), Harper, 1962.
Nutshell Library (contains *Chicken Soup with Rice, One Was Johnny, Alligators All Around,* and *Pierre*), Harper, 1962.
Where the Wild Things Are, 1963, reprinted, Penguin, 1979, 25th anniversary edition, Harper, 1988.
Hector Protector [and] *As I Went Over the Water,* Harper, 1965.
Higglety Pigglety Pop!; or, There Must Be More to Life, Harper, 1967.
In the Night Kitchen, Harper, 1970.
Ten Little Rabbits: A Counting Book with Mino the Magician, Philip H. Rosenbach, 1970.
Fantasy Sketches (published in conjunction with one-man show at Rosenbach Foundation), Philip H. Rosenbach, 1970.
Pictures by Maurice Sendak, Harper, 1971.
(Author of introduction) *Maxfield Parrish Poster Book,* Crown, 1974.
Maurice Sendak's Really Rosie (based on the television program of the same title; also see below), Harper, 1975.
(Author of appreciation) *The Publishing Archive of Lothar Meggendoifer,* Schiller, 1975.
(With Matthew Margolis) *Some Swell Pup; or, Are You Sure You Want a Dog?,* Farrar, Straus, 1976.
(Editor) *The Disney Poster Book,* illustrated by Walt Disney Studios, Harper, 1977.
Seven Little Monsters, Harper, 1977.
Outside Over There, Harper, 1981.
(Author of introduction) Jonathan Cott, *Victorian Color Picture Books,* Stonehill Publishing Co./Chelsea House, 1985.
Posters, Harmony Books, 1986.
Caldecott & Co.: Notes on Books & Pictures, Michael Di Capua Books/Farrar, Straus, 1988.

ILLUSTRATOR; CHILDREN'S BOOKS, EXCEPT AS INDICATED

M. L. Eidinoff and H. Ruchlis, *Atomics for the Millions* (adult book), McGraw, 1947.
Robert Garvey, *Good Shabbos, Everybody!,* United Synagogue Commission on Jewish Education, 1951.
Marcel Ayme, *The Wonderful Farm,* Harper, 1951.
Ruth Krauss, *A Hole Is to Dig,* Harper, 1952.
Ruth Sawyer, *Maggie Rose: Her Birthday Christmas,* Harper, 1952.
Beatrice S. de Regniers, *The Giant Story,* Harper, 1953.
Meindert De Jong, *Hurry Home,* Candy, 1953.
De Jong, *Shadrach,* Harper, 1953.
Krauss, *A Very Special House,* Harper, 1953.
Hyman Chanover, *Happy Hanukkah, Everybody,* United Synagogue Commission on Jewish Education, 1954.
Krauss, *I'll Be You and You Be Me,* Harper, 1954.
Edward Tripp, *The Tin Fiddle,* Oxford University Press, 1954.
Ayme, *Magic Pictures,* Harper, 1954.
Betty MacDonald, *Mrs. Piggle-Wiggle's Farm,* Lippincott, 1954.
De Jong, *The Wheel on the School,* Harper, 1954.
Krauss, *Charlotte and the White Horse,* Harper, 1955.
De Jong, *The Little Cow and the Turtle,* Harper, 1955.

Jean Ritchiq, *Singing Family of the Cumberlands,* Oxford University Press, 1955.
de Regniers, *What Can You Do with a Shoe?,* Harper, 1955.
Jack Sendak (brother), *Happy Rain,* Harper, 1956.
De Jong, *The House of Sixty Fathers,* Harper, 1956.
Krauss, *I Want to Paint My Bathroom Blue,* Harper, 1956.
Krauss, *Birthday Party,* Harper, 1957.
J. Sendak, *Circus Girl,* Harper, 1957.
Ogden Nash, *You Can't Get There from Here,* Little, Brown, 1957.
Else Minarik, *Little Bear,* Harper, 1957.
De Jong, *Along Came a Dog,* Harper, 1958.
Minarik, *No Fighting, No Biting!,* Harper, 1958.
Krauss, *Somebody Else's Nut Tree,* Harper, 1958.
Sesyle Joslyn, *What Do You Say, Dear?,* W. R. Scott, 1958.
Minarik, *Father Bear Comes Home,* Harper, 1959.
Janice Udry, *The Moon Jumpers,* Harper, 1959.
Hans Christian Andersen, *Seven Tales,* Harper, 1959.
Wilhelm Hauff, *Dwarf Long-Nose,* Random House, 1960.
Minarik, *Little Bear's Friend,* Harper, 1960.
Krauss, *Open House for Butterflies,* Harper, 1960.
Udrey, *Let's Be Enemies,* Harper, 1961.
Clemens Brentano, *The Tale of Gockel, Hinkel & Gackeliah,* Random House, 1961.
Minarik, *Little Bear's Visit,* Harper, 1961.
Joslyn, *What Do You Do, Dear?,* Young Scott Books, 1961.
Brentano, *Schoolmaster Whackwell's Wonderful Sons,* Random House, 1962.
Charlotte Zolotow, *Mr. Rabbit and the Lovely Present,* Harper, 1962.
De Jong, *The Singing Hill,* Harper, 1962.
Leo Tolstoy, *Nikolenka's Childhood,* Harper, 1963.
Robert Keeshan, *She Loves Me, She Loves Me Not,* Harper, 1963.
Randall Janell, *The Bat-Poet,* Collier, 1964.
Amos Vogel, *How Little Lori Visited Times Square,* Harper, 1964.
Jan Wahl, *Pleasant Fieldmouse,* Harper, 1964.
William Engvick, editor, *Lullabies and Night Songs,* Pantheon, 1965.
Janell, *The Animal Family,* Pantheon, 1965.
Isaac Bashevis Singer, *Zlateh the Goat and Other Stories,* Harper, 1966.
George MacDonald, *The Golden Key,* Harper, 1967.
Robert Graves, *The Big Green Book,* Crowell, 1968.
Frank Stockton, *Griffin and the Minor Canon,* Collins, 1968.
Minarik, *A Kiss for Little Bear,* Harper, 1968.
MacDonald, *The Light Princess,* Bodley Head, 1969.
Stockton, *The Bee-Man of Orn,* Holt, 1971.
Doris Orgel, *Sarah's Room,* Bodley Head, 1971.
Jakob Grimm and Wilhelm Grimm, *The Juniper Tree, and Other Tales from Grimm,* Farrar, Straus, 1973.
Marie Catherine Jumelle de Berneville Aulnoy, *Fortunia: A Tale by Mme. D'Aulnoy,* translation by Richard Schaubeck, Frank Hallman, Harper, 1974.
Janell, *Fly by Night,* Farrar, Straus, 1976.
J. Grimm and W. Grimm, *King Grisley Beard,* Harper, 1978.
E. T. A. Hoffman, *Nutcracker* (also see below), translation by Ralph Manheim, Crown, 1984.
Frank Corsaro, *The Love for Three Oranges,* Farrar, Straus, 1984.
Philip Sendak, *In Grandpa's House,* translated and adapted by Seymour Barofsky, Harper, 1985.
Dear Mili: An Old Tale by Wilhelm Grimm, based on a letter by Wilhelm Grimm translated by Manheim, Michael Di Capua Books/Farrar, Straus, 1988.

OTHER

(Author, director, and lyricist) *Really Rosie* (thirty-minute animated television special; based on characters from *The Nutshell Library* and *Sign on Rosie's Door* [also see below]; produced on Columbia Broadcasting System, 1975), music composed and performed by Carol King, Harper, 1975.

(Lyricist and set designer) "Really Rosie" (musical play; based on television special of the same title), music by King, first produced Off-Broadway, October, 1980.

(Lyricist, set designer, and costume-designer) "Where the Wild Things Are" (opera; based on his book of the same title), music by Oliver Knussen, first produced in Belgium by Brussels Opera, November, 1980, produced at New York City Opera, 1984.

(Designer) *Nutcracker* (film; based on E. T. A. Hoffman's book of the same name), 1986.

Many of Sendak's book have been translated into foreign languages. Contributor of illustrations to *McCall's* and *Ladies' Home Journal,* 1964.

SIDELIGHTS: In the fall of 1963, Maurice Sendak published a picture book that would prove to be as popular as it is controversial, *Where the Wild Things Are.* Not only did the book (a 1964 Caldecott Medal winner) launch Sendak's international reputation as an author-illustrator, it also launched a philosophical argument about the nature of children's literature that has yet to be resolved. Because the graphically illustrated text depicts a small child's rage at his mother, some psychologists and librarians consider it unsuitable for children. These critics advocate a prescriptive form of children's literature that depicts what a child ought to be, not what he is. "To this tradition," reports Saul Braun in the *New York Times Magazine,* "Maurice Sendak appears as a virtual one-man revolution or counterculture. Sendak shouts a resounding 'No!' to the idea that there is something inherently good about a tidy, obedient child." According to *Newsweek's* Walter Clemons, "Sendak belongs, not with sensible, sociologically oriented concocters of edifying kiddie books, with audience age ('5 to 8') coded on the jacket, but with the great eccentric visionaries like Lewis Carroll and George MacDonald who simply wrote books they had to write."

Sendak, the only American ever to be awarded the Hans Christian Andersen International Medal for the body of his illustration, shares this view of his work: "I don't write for children specifically," he told Virginia Haviland in a conversation reprinted in the *Quarterly Journal of the Library of Congress.* "I certainly am not conscious of sitting down and writing a book for children. I think it would be fatal if one did. So I write books, and I hope that they are books anybody can read."

Enjoyed by readers of all ages, Sendak's books are nonetheless inspired by elements of childhood—elements, Sendak told Selma Lanes, that come from his deepest self. Later in that *New York Times Book Review* article, Sendak explains how the artist "draws on a peculiar vein of childhood that is always open and alive. That is his particular gift. The artist understands that children know a lot more than people give them credit for. Children are willing to deal with many dubious subjects that grownups think they shouldn't know about. But children are small courageous people who have to deal every day with a multitude of problems, just as we adults do." The majority of critics applaud his insight. Writing in the *Washington Post Book World,* for example, Jonathan Cott commends Sendak's "uncanny ability to make us, as adults, reexperience the way a child experiences his or her earliest emotions." And Saul Braun expresses a similar view: "To Sendak, the truth of childhood lies in his recollected

emotions, and truth is what he wants most of all in his books. The passionate involvement of his boys and girls is Sendak's own."

In his quest for truth and excellence, Sendak may well have opened new doors in the world of children's literature. Lanes credits him with elevating the "American children's picture book to a high art form," while Farrar, Straus & Giroux editor Michael di Capua told Braun that Sendak has "turned the entire tide of what is acceptable to put in a children's book illustration. There is nobody to compare with Maurice."

The youngest of three children born to Jewish immigrants, Maurice was a sickly baby who spent most of his early years indoors. "I was miserable as a kid, I couldn't make friends. I couldn't play stoopball terrific, I couldn't skate great. I stayed home and drew pictures," he told an interviewer from *Rolling Stone.* "You know what they all thought of me: sissy Maurice Sendak. When I wanted to go out and do something, my father would say: 'You'll catch a cold.' And I did. . . . I did whatever he told me."

To pass the time, young Sendak spent many hours gazing out his apartment window or listening with his brother and sister to the tales his father would often tell. In *The Art of Maurice Sendak,* Lanes suggests that these elaborate stories—spun of fantasy and Jewish folklore—"constituted the first important source from which his work developed. One tale that he remembers vividly was about a child taking a walk with his parents. 'Somehow he becomes separated from them, and snow begins to fall. The child shivers in the cold and huddles under a tree, sobbing in terror. Then, an enormous, angelic figure hovers over him and says, as he draws the boy up, "I am Abraham, your father." His fear gone, the child looks up and also sees Sarah. When his mother and father find him, he is dead.' "

Such melancholy tales coupled with his own frail health to color Sendak's vision. So, too, did the succession of lower-middle-class Brooklyn neighborhoods in which he lived. "My mother, for some reason, could not bear the smell of paint," he told *Washington Post* reporter Paul Richard. "So every three years, rather than repaint the walls, we would change apartments. She liked to move. I hated it." Occasionally, Maurice would take trips with his family into Manhattan. His memories of the city, with its bright lights and tall buildings, its elegant theatres and fashionable restaurants, would later figure in his work.

Another significant childhood recollection concerns the day his sister brought him *The Prince and the Pauper,* which he describes as "my first book. . . . A ritual began with that book which I recall very clearly," he told Haviland. "The first thing was to set it up on the table and stare at it for a long time. Not because I was impressed with Mark Twain; it was just such a beautiful object. Then came the smelling of it. I think the smelling of books began with *The Prince and the Pauper,* because it was printed on particularly fine paper, unlike the Disney books I had gotten previous to that, which were printed on very poor paper and smelled poor. *The Prince and the Pauper*—smelled good and it had a shiny cover. I flipped over that. And it was very solid. I mean, it was bound very tightly. I remember trying to bite into it, which I don't imagine is what my sister intended when she bought the book for me. But the last thing I did was to read it. It was all right. But I think it started then, a passion for books and book-making."

Throughout his youth and adolescence, Sendak was an apathetic student, but his enthusiasm and talent got him an illustrating job when he was still in high school. Working for All American Comics, Sendak adapted the popular "Mutt and Jeff" newspaper strip for comic books. After graduation, he took a job at a window-display house in lower Manhattan, where he helped create life-size storybook characters from papier-mache. He left the job in 1948 when a promotion took him away from the work he enjoyed.

That summer he and his brother Jack set up a home workshop and built elaborate mechanical toys based on eighteenth-century German models. Jack engineered the moveable parts and Maurice did the carving and painting. When they took their collection to F.A.O. Schwarz, they were told that their beautifully crafted pieces were much too expensive to mass produce. But the window-dresser was so impressed with the craftsmanship that he offered Maurice a job.

The store featured an excellent children's book department, which served both to educate and to inspire the young artist. One day, when some of his sketches were on display throughout the building, his co-workers arranged to have children's editor Ursula Nordstrom drop by. "He was very young when I met him," Nordstrom recalled in a conversation with Braun. "Very shy. . . . He didn't project his personality." Nonetheless, she was sufficiently impressed with his drawings to invite him to illustrate *The Wonderful Farm.*

Some time later, Nordstrom asked to review Sendak's personal sketchbook, and what she saw convinced her that Maurice was the right choice for an exciting project. "We had already turned down a number of illustrators for the new Ruth Krauss book, *A Hole Is to Dig.* We needed something very special, and Maurice's sketchbook made me think he would be perfect for it," she told Braun.

A series of definitions made up by children, the book is now considered a modern classic. Its publication in 1952 not only established Sendak's career as an illustrator, it also prompted a rash of imitations. But, of these competitors, Nordstrom observed: "None of them have Maurice's vision. He has a tremendous number of imitators, but nobody has his emotional equipment."

With book-illustration offers pouring in, Sendak was able to quit his F.A.O. Schwarz job and become a free-lance illustrator. In just a few years, he was writing books of his own, the first of which, *Kenny's Window,* he completed in 1955. "Looked at today," Lanes writes in *The Art of Maurice Sendak,* "*Kenny's Window* is a dreamlike and tentative evocation of the new kind of hero and heroine Sendak would introduce to young children's books. Though the story is overlong and overwritten, it is a treasure trove of the themes, situations, and psychological excursions that would become the core of Sendak's mature work."

Sendak considers not only *Kenny's Window,* but all his early works to be illustrated books, i.e., books in which the pictures are secondary to the text. But in the early 1960s Sendak was ready to attempt a project in which the illustrations would carry as much weight as the story; in other words, a picture book. As it turned out, his first endeavor would be his most successful, for the picture book he created was *Where the Wild Things Are.*

The brief 338-word text tells the story of a little boy named Max who dresses up in a wolf suit and behaves mischievously. When his mother calls him a "Wild Thing" and sends him to bed without supper, he says, "I'll eat you up." Once in his room, Max watches as trees grow from his bedposts and a magical forest springs up all around, carrying him to a land where the wild things are. After taming them, Max becomes their king and he leads them on an uninhibited romp through the wild. Soon, however, Max tires of the game and, growing lonely, longs to be "where someone loves him best of all." Retracing his steps, Max

finds himself back in his own bedroom, where his supper is waiting—"and it was still hot."

Though Max's adventure is a fantasy, his journey is motivated by actual events. "In *Where the Wild Things Are,*" notes Lanes, "the hero's adventure among the wild things is preceded by the real-life fact of his rage against his mother—which is precipitated by another fact: he has been sent to bed without any supper." Lanes believes that these factors lend the book its underlying strength. Complimenting Sendak's understanding of young children, Constantine Georgiou writes in *Children and Their Literature,* that the book "offers the momentary escape that most children need. It vicariously provides wild adventure and a refreshed return to a relatively calmer reality. This need for release or escape is common to humankind and to children particularly, on whom so many social limits for conformity are imposed."

But child psychologist Bruno Bettelheim attacks the book, stating in the *Ladies' Home Journal* that "the author was obviously captivated by an adult psychological understanding of how to deal with destructive fantasies in the child. What he failed to understand is the incredible fear it evokes in the child to be sent to bed without supper, and this by the first and foremost giver of food and security—his mother." Bettelheim also notes that his objections were based strictly on principle—he had not actually read the book. *Saturday Review* contributing critic Alice Dalgliesh argues that the "book has disturbing possibilities for the child who does not need this catharsis," and concludes that "how children feel about the whole book remains to be seen."

If sales figures are any indication, children feel very good about the book indeed. *Where the Wild Things Are* has sold over 700,000 hardback copies and been translated into thirteen foreign languages. An additional 1,800,000 paperback copies of the book have been sold in the school market alone. "Those adults who were apprehensive about the possibility of the wild things . . . frightening children seem to have been mistaken," conclude May Hill Arbuthnot and Zena Sutherland in *Children and Books.* "The pictures amuse and delight small children, and many Sendak fans have sent him their own pictures of wild things. And children see the reassurance in Max's return home from his fantasy land when he wanted to be where someone loved him best of all."

Sendak has said that the book marked an important stage in his development. "I feel that I am at the end of a long apprenticeship," he remarked on accepting the Caldecott Medal. "By that I mean all my previous work now seems to have been an elaborate preparation for it. I believe [*Where the Wild Things Are*] is an immense step forward for me, a critical stage in my work."

Despite his professional success, Sendak experienced personal hardships during the next few years. His mother was afflicted with cancer, he suffered a heart attack, and the dog he had cherished for fourteen years, a Sealyham named Jennie, had to be put to sleep. The turmoil of this period is reflected in a book he dedicated to Jennie in 1967—*Higglety, Pigglety, Pop!; or, There Must Be More to Life.* ("Somehow it was easier to work up an anxiety about the dog's dying than about my mother," Sendak explained to Lanes in *The Art of Maurice Sendak,* "because that was just too much to go for.")

In the story, Jennie, a pampered pet with "two pillows, two bowls, a red wool sweater, eyedrops, eardrops, two different bottles of pills" and a master who loves her, decides "there must be more to life than having everything" and runs away from home. "What she wants, of course," says Eliot Fremont-Smith in the

New York Times, "is an identifying experience; she is Everyman in the guise of Everydog, and will risk even death to have her day." Jennie's search takes her to a house where she is welcomed as a new nurse for Baby. Only Baby, apparently abandoned by her parents, has already had six nurses, all of whom have been fed to the downstairs lion when they couldn't get Baby to eat. Jennie fares no better, gobbling up the baby's food herself. But, the dog redeems herself by putting her head into the lion's mouth to protect Baby and is herself saved by a piece of luck. Her reward for this experience is a leading role in the World Mother Goose Theatre production of "Higglety, Pigglety, Pop."

The book has been widely reviewed by critics, many of whom feel that it is equally appealing to children and adults. "A triumph," proclaims Fremont-Smith, "and outside of genre. A children's book, of course, but one could just as well call it a mind-expanding novel, an anthropomorphic Pilgrim's Progress, a psychoanalytic revision of Mother Goose or anything else. Names don't matter; it's a delight, which should be exciting enough."

Other critics focus on the skillful intermingling of real and fantastic elements that characterizes not only this, but so much of Sendak's work. "For those who have followed Sendak's development from the dark night when the Wild Things danced, it becomes increasingly clear that his sensibility is engaged in a continuing dialogue between the real and the fantastic," writes Barbara Novak O'Doherty in the *New York Times Book Review.* And the *National Observer* critic suggests that what the author makes of Mother Goose's simple rhyme is "unmistakably Sendak, a surreal excursion worthy of Lewis Carroll."

Although it features a different style of illustration, *In the Night Kitchen* also recounts a fantastic voyage. A little boy named Mickey (in honor of Mickey Mouse, one of Sendak's childhood heroes) is awakened from slumber, falls through the dark, out of his pajamas (much to the dismay of conservative librarians), and into the night kitchen where buildings are shaped like bottles, salt shakers, and jelly jars. Here three bakers, each the image of Oliver Hardy, mistake him for the milk they need and bake him into a cake. Mickey escapes by fashioning an airplane from the dough and flies up to the Milky Way to fetch the real ingredient from a giant milk bottle. Mission accomplished, he slides back down, returning home "cakefree and dried."

Unlike the somber undercurrents which run through *Higglety Pigglety Pop!,* the fantasy in the night kitchen is a happy one which "poses few problems for its hero and asks nothing of its audience beyond the willingness to surrender to its own inexpressible dream logic," Lanes says. Here, according to Margot Hentoff in the *New York Review of Books,* "the elevated trains still run, and the dark starry sky is the one which, in the imagination of a Thirties child, appeared nightly over Radio City Music Hall." Sendak himself has acknowledged to Haviland that the book "is a kind of homage to New York City, the city I loved so much and still love. . . . It also is homage to the things that really affected me esthetically. I did not get to museums, I did not see art books. I was really quite rough in the sense of what was going on artistically. 'Fantasia' was perhaps the most esthetic experience of my childhood, and that's a very dubious experience. But mainly there were the comic books and there was Walt Disney."

With its full-color illustrations and balloons of conversation, the book is indeed reminiscent of certain comics, but according to George A. Woods in the *New York Times Book Review,* it also possesses "a newness as if Sendak were picking up where comic books went wrong and pointing a new direction. Where other il-

lustrators remain static in development as colorists, collagists, cartoonists, his talent grows."

One reason for his continued growth is Sendak's experimentation with various techniques of illustration. "To get trapped in a style," he told Haviland, "is to lose all flexibility. And I have worked very hard not to get trapped that way. . . . I worked up a very elaborate pen and ink style in *Higglety,* which is very finely cross-hatched. But I can abandon that for a magic marker as I did in *Night Kitchen* and just go back to very simple, outlined, broad drawings with flat, or flatter, colors. Each book obviously demands an individual stylistic approach. If you have one style, then you're going to do the same book over and over, which is, of course, pretty dull."

In 1981, Sendak completed *Outside Over There,* a book that is stylistically as different from *In the Night Kitchen* as *In the Night Kitchen* is different from his first picture book *Where the Wild Things Are.* And yet, as Sendak explains to Lanes, the three "are all variations on the same theme: how children master various feelings—anger, boredom, fear, frustration, jealousy—and manage to come to grips with the realities of their lives." For this reason, Sendak views the books as a trilogy.

In *Outside Over There*—as in all his storybooks—Sendak completed the text before he conceived the pictures. "Not many of the artist's admirers are aware of how seriously he takes the texts of his own tales," says Lanes. "*Outside Over There,* a story with only 359 words, took almost a year and a half—and more than one hundred drafts—to complete. 'I have a hostility towards books which are not well written,' Sendak says."

Set in a rural eighteenth-century landscape that was sketched while Sendak listened to Mozart, *Outside Over There* dramatizes what *Newsweek* reviewer Clemons calls "fears, rages, and appetites that adults would prefer to believe children don't experience. But *Outside Over There* . . . deals with the more complex feelings of an older child." As the story opens, nine-year-old Ida, whose father is away at sea and whose mother is in the arbor, sits absentmindedly watching her baby sister and playing her Magic Horn. When goblins come and steal the baby away, replacing it with a figure of ice, Ida doesn't even notice. But once the ice melts and she realizes what has happened, she dons an enormous yellow rain cloak and sets off to rescue the babe. "Unlike Max and Mickey, who rampage unhindered in fantasy worlds of their own," notes Clemons, "Ida is discovered in a difficult relation with others—a ruminative, preoccupied mother, an absent father whose approval Ida wants . . . and a heavy baby she dutifully tends but never directly looks at until the story's climactic moment."

John Gardner calls it, "a book for children that treats the childreader as a serious, intelligent, troubled and vulnerable human being. Another writer might have softened the tale's effect by humor," he continues in the *New York Times Book Review,* "Mr. Sendak does something better: By the lyricism and gentle irony of his words and pictures, he transmutes guilt and insecurity—the dual bane of every child's existence—the things one can muse on without undue fear and escape triumphant. More specifically, he examines, with great accuracy and tenderness, the archetypal older girl-child's longing-filled love for her father and her jealousy toward her mother and younger sibling, and he shows how the father's love and respect are won."

"Like most great fairy tales," notes *Washington Post Book World* contributing reviewer Jonathan Cott, *Outside Over There* "has the simplicity of an elemental story and at the same time the mysteriousness, the depth, and the multiplicity of meanings of a dream . . . as we, like Ida, enter the underworld of the goblins' cave, where what is outer becomes inner, and where what is lost is found."

The complexity of its theme has led several reviewers to conclude that *Outside Over There* may not be a "children's book" at all. Clemons expresses this opinion, and so does Christopher Lehmann-Haupt when he writes in the *New York Times* that the child within him is "bewildered" by much of the book. "There is a grandeur and complexity about the pictures that intimidate. . . . They have a quality of nightmare. That is not necessarily a bad thing in a book such as this. In fact, it may be a very good thing. But, so far, my child isn't absolutely certain."

Sendak told *Publishers Weekly* that "the book is a release of something that has long pressured my internal self. It sounds hyperbolic but it's true; it's like profound salvation. If for only once in my life, I have touched the place where I wanted to go and, when Ida goes home, I go home. No other work of art has given me this inner peace and happiness. I have caught the thing that has eluded me for so long, so critical to living; and knowing that means everything, regardless of what anyone else says about the book. I'm not a happy man. I'm notorious for that. *Outside Over There* made me happy."

MEDIA ADAPTATIONS: Where the Wild Things Are was made into a filmstrip by Western Woods in 1968; *Really Rosie* was filmed as "Really Rosie Starring the Nutshell Kids," by Western Woods in 1976; *Pierre, Chicken Soup with Rice, Alligators All Around,* and *One Was Johnny* were made into filmstrips with cassettes, all by Western Woods, all 1976; an opera version of *Higglety, Pigglety, Pop!,* with a libretto written by Sendak, was performed by the Glyndebourne Opera in England, October, 1984.

BIOGRAPHICAL/CRITICAL SOURCES:

BOOKS

Arbuthnot, May Hill and Zena Sutherland, *Children and Books,* 4th edition, Scott, Foresman, 1972.
Children's Literature Review, Volume 1, Gale, 1976.
Dictionary of Literary Biography, Volume 61: *American Writers for Children since 1960: Poets, Illustrators, and Nonfiction Authors,* Gale, 1987.
Georgiou, Constantine, *Children and Their Literature,* Prentice-Hall, 1969.
Hopkins, Lee Bennett, *Books Are by People,* Citation Press, 1969.
Lanes, Selma G., *The Art of Maurice Sendak,* Abrams, 1980.
Sendak, Maurice, *Where the Wild Things Are,* Harper, 1963.
Sendak, *Higglety, Pigglety, Pop!; or, There Must Be More to Life,* Harper, 1967.
Sendak, *In the Night Kitchen,* Harper, 1970.
Smith, Jeffrey Jon, *A Conversation with Maurice Sendak,* Smith (Illinois), 1974.

PERIODICALS

Books and Bookmen, June, 1969.
Chicago Tribune, July 17, 1980.
Chicago Tribune Book World, May 3, 1981.
Ladies' Home Journal, March, 1969.
Los Angeles Times, February 6, 1981, December 10, 1982.
National Observer, November 27, 1967.
Newsweek, May 18, 1981.
New Yorker, January 22, 1966.
New York Review of Books, December 17, 1970.

New York Times, November 1, 1967 December 9, 1970, October 15, 1980, April 11, 1981, June 1, 1981, November 30, 1981, November 8, 1987.
New York Times Book Review, October 22, 1967, November 1, 1970, April 29, 1979, April 26, 1981.
New York Times Magazine, June 7, 1970.
Publishers Weekly, April 10, 1981.
Quarterly Journal of the Library of Congress, Volume 28, number 4, 1971.
Rolling Stone, December 30, 1976.
Saturday Review, December 14, 1963.
School Library Journal, December, 1970.
Time, July 6, 1981.
Times Literary Supplement, July 2, 1971.
Washington Post, November 1, 1978, November 20, 1981.
Washington Post Book World, May 10, 1981.

* * *

SENDER, Ramon (Jose) 1902-1982

PERSONAL: Born February 3, 1902, in Chalamera de Cinca, Spain; immigrated to United States, 1942, naturalized citizen, 1946; died of emphysema, January 15, 1982, in San Diego, Calif.; son of Jose (a farmer) and Andrea (Garces) Sender; married Amparo Barayon, January 7, 1934 (died October 11, 1936); married Elizabeth de Altube, 1937 (divorced); married Florence Hall, August 12, 1943 (divorced September 3, 1963); children: (first marriage) Ramon, Andrea; (second marriage) Emmanuel. *Education:* Instituto de Segunda Ensenanza de Teruel, Bachillerato, 1917; University of Madrid, Licenciado en filosofia y letras, 1924.

ADDRESSES: Home—San Diego, Calif. *Agent*—American Literary Agency, 11 Riverside Dr., New York, N.Y. 10023.

CAREER: El Sol, Madrid, Spain, editor and literary critic, 1924-30; free-lance writer in Madrid, 1930-36, and in Mexico, 1939-41; Amherst College, Amherst, Mass., professor of Spanish literature, 1943; Metro-Goldwyn-Mayer, Inc., New York, N.Y., translator and adapter, 1943-45; University of Denver, Denver, Colo., professor of Spanish literature, 1946; University of New Mexico, Albuquerque, professor of Spanish literature, 1947-63; University of Southern California, Los Angeles, professor of Spanish literature, until 1973. Visiting professor of Spanish at Ohio State University, 1950, University of California, Los Angeles, 1962, and University of Southern California, 1965. *Military service:* Served as reserve officer on Spanish infantry mission to Morocco, 1923-24; received Medal of Morocco and Military Cross of Merit. Spanish Republican Army, 1936-39; became major on general staff.

MEMBER: Hispanic Society of America, Spanish Confederated Societies (New York; honorary member), Ateneo (Spain; member of governing board and secretary of Ibero-American section), National Council on Culture (Spain), Alliance of Intellectuals for the Defense of Democracy (Spain), Phi Sigma Iota, Alpha Mu Gamma.

AWARDS, HONORS: National Prize for Literature (Spain), 1935, for *Mister Witt en el canton;* Guggenheim fellow, 1942-43; Premio de la Literatura, 1966; D.Litt., University of New Mexico, 1968, and University of Southern California; Planeta Prize (Spain), 1969, for *En la vida de Ignacio Morel;* nominated for Nobel Prize for Literature, 1979.

WRITINGS:

El problema religioso en Mejico (nonfiction), preface by Ramon del Valle-Inclan, Imprenta Argis (Madrid), 1928.

Iman (novel), Editorial Cenit (Madrid), 1930, reprinted, Ediciones Destino (Barcelona), 1976, translation by James Cleugh published as *Earmarked for Hell,* Wishart, 1934, published as *Pro Patria,* Houghton, 1935.

Teresa de Jesus, Editorial Zeus (Madrid), 1931.

El verbo se hizo sexo (nonfiction), Sociedad Anonima Editorial (Madrid), 1931.

Siete domingos rojos (novel), Coleccion Balague (Barcelona), 1932, revised edition, Editorial Proyeccion (Barcelona), 1973, translation by Sir Peter Chalmers Mitchell published as *Seven Red Sundays,* Liveright, 1936, reprinted, Collier, 1961.

La noche de las cien cabezas (novel), Imprenta de J. Pueyo (Madrid), 1934.

Viaje a la aldea del crimen (nonfiction), Imprenta de J. Pueyo, 1934.

Mister Witt en el canton (novel), Espasa-Calpe (Madrid), 1936, reprinted, Alianza Editorial (Madrid), 1976, translation by Mitchell published as *Mr. Witt Among the Rebels,* Faber, 1937, Houghton, 1938.

Counter-attack in Spain (nonfiction), translated from the original Spanish manuscript by Mitchell, Houghton, 1937 (published in England as *The War in Spain: A Personal Narrative,* Faber, 1937).

Proverbio de la muerte (novel), Ediciones Quetzal (Mexico), 1939, revised edition published as *La esfera,* Aguilar (Madrid), 1969, translation by F. Giovanelli published as *The Sphere,* Hellman, Williams (New York), 1949.

El lugar del hombre (novel), Ediciones Quetzal, 1939, reprinted, Ediciones Destino, 1960, translation by Oliver La Farge published as *A Man's Place,* Duell, 1940, revised Spanish edition published as *El lugar de un hombre,* Ediciones CNT (Mexico), 1958, reprinted, Ediciones Destino, 1976.

Hernan Cortes (nonfiction), Ediciones Quetzal, 1940.

Mexicayotl (nonfiction), Ediciones Quetzal, 1940.

O. P.: Orden publico (novel), Publicaciones Panamericanas (Mexico), 1941.

Epitalamio del prieto Trinidad (novel), Ediciones Quetzal, 1942, reprinted, Ediciones Destino, 1973, translation by Eleanor Clark published as *Dark Wedding,* Doubleday, 1943.

Cronica del alba, Editorial Nuevo Mundo (Mexico), 1942, translation by Willard R. Trask published as *Chronicle of Dawn* (also see below), Doubleday, 1944, annotated Spanish edition, edited and introduced by Florence Hall, Crofts, 1946.

El rey y la reina (novel), Editorial Jackson, 1949, reprinted, Ediciones Destino, 1972, translation by Mary Low published as *The King and the Queen,* Vanguard, 1948.

El verdugo afable (novel), Nascimento (Santiago, Chile), 1952, translation by Hall published as *The Affable Hangman,* J. Cape, 1954, Las Americas Publishing Co., 1963.

Mosen Millan (novel), [Mexico], 1953, Heath, 1964, published as *Requiem por un campesino espanol/Requiem for a Spanish Peasant* (parallel English and Spanish texts), translated by Elinor Randall, Las Americas Publishing Co., 1960, Spanish text reprinted, Ediciones Destino, 1976.

Hipogrifo violento (novel), [Mexico], 1954, translation by F. W. Sender published as *Violent Griffin* in *Before Noon: A Novel in Three Parts* (also see below), University of New Mexico Press, 1957.

Ariadna (novel), [Mexico], 1955, published as *Los cinco libros de Ariadna,* Ediciones Iberica (New York), 1957, reprinted, Ediciones Destino, 1977.

Unamuno, Valle-Inclan, Baroja y Santayana (critical essays), Ediciones de Andrea (Mexico), 1955.

Before Noon: A Novel in Three Parts (contains *Chronicle of Dawn, Violent Griffin,* and *The Villa Julieta* [translation by F. W. Sender from original Spanish manuscript of *La Quinta Julieta*]), University of New Mexico Press, 1957.

El diantre: Tragicomedia para el cine segun un cuento de Andreiev, Ediciones de Andrea, 1958.

Los laureles de Anselmo (novel), Ediciones Atenea (Mexico), 1958.

Emen hetan (novel), Libro Mex (Mexico), 1958.

El mancebo y los heroes (novel), Ediciones Atenea, 1960.

Las imagenes migratorias (poems), Ediciones Atenea, 1960.

La llave (novel; also see below), Editorial Alfa (Montevideo, Uruguay), 1960.

(With Valle-Inclan) *Memorias del marques de Bradomin,* Las Americas Publishing Co., 1961.

Examen de ingenios: Los noventayochos (critical essays), Las Americas Publishing Co., 1961.

Novelas ejemplares de Cibola, Las Americas Publishing Co., 1961, translation by Hall and others published as *Tales of Cibola,* 1964.

La tesis de Nancy (novel), Ediciones Atenea, 1962.

La luna de los perros, Las Americas Publishing Co., 1962.

Los tontos de la concepcion (nonfiction), Editorial Coronado (Sandoval, New Mexico), 1963.

Carolus Rex (historical novel), Editores Mexicanos Unidos (Mexico), 1963.

Jubileo en el zocalo: Retablo commemorativo, edited by Hall, Appleton, 1964.

La aventura equinoccial de Lope de Aguirre, antiepopeya (novel), Las Americas Publishing Co., 1964.

Cabrerizas altas, Editores Mexicanos Unidos, 1965.

El bandido adolescente, Ediciones Destino (Barcelona), 1965.

Valle-Inclan y la dificultad de la tragedia (nonfiction), Editorial Gredos (Madrid), 1965.

El sosia y los delegados (nonfiction), B. Costa-Amic (Mexico), 1965.

Tres novelas teresianas (fiction), Ediciones Destino, 1967.

Las Gallinas de Cervantes y otras narraciones parabolicas (nonfiction), Editores Mexicanos Unidos, 1967.

Ensayos sobre el infringimiento cristiano, Editores Mexicanos Unidos, 1967.

La llave y otras narraciones (fiction), Editorial Magisterio Espanol (Madrid), 1967.

Las criaturas saturnianas, Ediciones Destino, 1968.

Don Juan en la mancebia: Drama liturgico en cuatro actos, Editores Mexicanos Unidos, 1968.

El extrano Senor Photynos y otras novelas (fiction), Ayma (Barcelona), 1968.

Novelas de otro jueves, Aguilar, 1969.

Comedia del Diantre y otras dos, Ediciones Destino, 1969.

En la vida de Ignacio Morel (novel), Editorial Planeta (Barcelona), 1969.

Nocturno de los 14 (novel), Iberama Publishing Co. (New York), 1969.

Tres ejemplos de amor y una teoria (nonfiction), Alianza Editorial, 1969.

Ensayos del otro mundo, Ediciones Destino, 1970.

Relatos fronterizos, Editores Mexicanos Unidos, 1970.

Tanit (novel), Editorial Planeta, 1970.

Zu, el angel anfibio (novel), Editorial Planeta, 1970.

La antesala, Ediciones Destino, 1971.

El fugitivo, Editorial Planeta, 1972.

Paginas escogidas, edited and introduced by Marcelino C. Penuelas, Editorial Gredos (Madrid), 1972.

Donde crece la marihuana: Drama en cuatro actos, Escelicer (Madrid), 1973.

Tupac Amaru, Ediciones Destino, 1973.

Una virgen llama a tu puerta, Ediciones Destino, 1973.

Libro armilar de poesia y memorias bisiestas, Aguilar, 1974.

La mesa de las tres moiras (novel), Editorial Planeta, 1974.

Nancy, doctora en gitaneria, Editorial Magisterio Espanol, 1974.

Nancy y el bato loco, Editorial Magisterio Espanol, 1974.

Las tres sorores, Ediciones Destino, 1974.

Cronus y la senora con rabo, AKAL (Madrid), 1974.

El futuro comenzo ayer: Lecturas mosaicas, CVS Ediciones (Madrid), 1975.

La efemerides (novel), Sedmay Ediciones (Madrid), 1976.

Arlene y la gaya ciencia, Ediciones Destino, 1976.

El pez de oro, Ediciones Destino, 1976.

Obra completa, Ediciones Destino, 1976.

El Alarido de Yauri, Ediciones Destino, 1977.

Gloria y vejamen de Nancy, Editorial Magisterio Espanol, 1977.

El Mechudo y la Llorona, Ediciones Destino, 1977.

Adela y yo, Ediciones Destino, 1978.

El superviviente, Ediciones Destino, 1978.

(Editor) *Cinco poetas disidentes escrito en Cuba,* Transaction, 1978.

Solanar y lucernario aragones, Heraldo de Aragon (Saragossa, Spain), 1978.

La mirada inmovil, Editorial Argos Vergara, 1979.

Also author of novel *La Quinta Julieta* (also see above), B. Costa-Amic, and of one-act plays "The House of Lot," "The Secret," and "The Photograph"; author of introduction to *Reflejos de Espana* by A. Monros, Federacion Social de Montreal. Contributor to magazines and literary periodicals.

WORK IN PROGRESS: Poetry; works in philosophy and history.

SIDELIGHTS: Though Ramon Sender was forced to spend more than half his life in countries other than his native Spain, he was nevertheless regarded as one of that nation's most distinguished novelists. Sender's path to exile began during his years at the University of Madrid, where his political activities on behalf of various reformist causes angered school authorities and ultimately led to his expulsion and even to a brief period of imprisonment. Sender did, however, manage to earn a degree, and in 1924 he went to work as an editor and literary critic for the liberal publication *El Sol.* Six years later he severed his official ties with *El Sol* and became a free-lance writer contributing to many different newspapers and journals and publishing novels, essays, and plays.

When civil war broke out in Spain in the summer of 1936 Sender was among the first to join the army of the Republic in its fight against the forces of Generalissimo Francisco Franco. But the young writer's military career was brief; Sender left Spain in 1937, not long after learning that his wife and brother had been executed by the Fascists for sympathizing with the republican cause. In an attempt to garner support for the beleaguered government, Sender then set out on a speaking tour of Europe and the United States as a representative of the Republic. The victory of Franco's troops in 1939, however, meant that Sender faced the prospect of permanent exile. After traveling and writing in Mexico for several years, he settled in the United States, spending most of the remaining forty years of his life in the Southwest and writing (in Spanish) about the world he had left behind in 1937.

Critics have tended to divide Sender's best-known works of fiction into two categories that correspond to these two major periods in his life. In the first category are novels Sender wrote *before*

leaving Spain, such as *Iman* and *Siete domingos rojos;* in the second category are novels he wrote *after* leaving Spain, including *La esfera* and *Cronica del alba* and its sequels, a series many believe is his greatest achievement. For the most part, noted John Devlin in his book *Spanish Anticlericalism: A Study in Modern Alienation,* "the earlier group evokes the fights, illusions and hardships of [Sender's] fellow Spaniards before and during the Republic. [The] latter works reveal a continual philosophic evolution and search for values in the twentieth century world of turmoil."

Iman, Sender's first novel, is one of those works concerned with the political and social atmosphere of pre-civil war Spain. A fictionalized account of events the author witnessed during the Spanish military's attempt to suppress a revolt among the Moors in Morocco in the early 1920s, *Iman* reflects on the uselessness of the campaign and the brutal sacrifices expected of the lower classes in the name of patriotism and economic gain. Commenting on the English translation of *Iman* which was published in the United States as *Pro Patria,* Charles C. King remarks in his critical study, *Ramon J. Sender,* that this particular novel is significant not only because it is Sender's first, "but also because in style and human content it accurately foreshadows [his] prolific . . . novelistic production of the next four decades." Viance, the army private who serves as the principal narrator of the story, is, according to King, "both an individual soldier and a symbol of the Spanish underprivileged masses. . . . There is a parallel between the treatment meted out to Viance by his officers and the treatment of the Spanish lower classes by the upper classes through the centuries. . . . In the end Viance breaks national boundaries, becoming a universal symbol of the common man as victim of injustice and man's inhumanity to man." In addition, wrote the critic, *Pro Patria* resembles subsequent Sender novels in that it displays "a direct, sober, verbal style, an impersonal distancing of the author from the work, the same grim—sometimes gruesome—humor . . . , the same interweaving of objective and subjective realities to create the novel's own private world, the harshest of visual detail alongside lyrical and metaphysical fantasy, the flight into delirium and dreams which sometimes cast a surrealistic spell over the action, and the ever-present probing of ultimate reality, mystery."

In a review written at the time of the book's publication in 1935, a *Times Literary Supplement* critic remarked that it is appropriate to regard *Pro Patria* "less as a work of fiction than as an impressive piece of journalism contributing an unpublished page to the detailed history of the present." But as Paul Allen observed in *Books,* Sender was not entirely successful at blending the two genres. Observed the critic: "All this is not for the squeamish certainly. Nor for the strong. For it seems hardly possible that any one can have stomach or nerves strong enough to read it unmoved. Nor can one take refuge in doubt. Senor Sender was on the scene. . . . But so intense was his desire to cram into the book all the searing things he had felt and seen he forgot he was writing a novel."

The *Christian Century*'s Raymond Kresensky also noted that *Pro Patria* lacks many of the qualities of a good novel. "There is no romance, no sentiment, and very little humaneness [in this book]," he began. "Not once is it lightened by even a glimmer of humor. Those with weak stomachs will not be able to read through the three hundred pages of ghastly experiences."

Though Otis Ferguson of the *New Republic* agreed that "as a novel [*Pro Patria*] is confusing and incomplete, half this, half that," he went on to state that it is nevertheless "more valuable, in what it has to tell us of things we could not imagine, than any five-foot shelf of Life and Death in Recent Leading Fiction." V. S. Pritchett expressed a similar view, declaring in the *New Statesman and Nation* that "*Pro Patria* has dignity but no great distinction, and the attempt to create a symbolical Spanish soldier type is not very successful. . . . [Yet] it would be a pity if, after our glut of war books, this intelligent and sensitive Spanish document were put aside."

A few reviewers were somewhat more generous in their praise of Sender's first novel. Commented a *Saturday Review of Literature* critic: "[*Pro Patria*] is as full of humanity as it is of terror. It is like so many current war stories, a narrative of futility. . . . If it makes the reader shudder, [it] also inevitably makes him think." William Plomer of the *Spectator* noted that "only a man of rare imaginative power and literary skill, a man both honest and brilliant, could have produced this record of a prolonged and complicated nightmare. Senor Sender makes it clear that he had no need to invent anything. . . . Private Viance has as great a significance as any character in recent fiction."

Unlike those reviewers who did not like the author's documentary approach, the *Nation*'s Florence Codman was pleased to see that Sender disclaimed all "literary and aesthetic prejudices" before beginning *Pro Patria.* "The agreeable thing about this book," Codman stated, "is its total lack of pretenses—sentimental, egotistic, social, or artistic. In fact, I recall no recent examples of war fiction in which there is so little attitude and so generous a permission to let bare incidents, within their context, speak for themselves. It is Sender's compliment to his subject to have realized that no inflation could make it more ghastly or render his hero more pitiable or more dignified."

Sender's second novel, *Siete domingos rojos,* continued the examination of politics and society in pre-civil war Spain, this time from the point of view of a group of communists, anarchists, and trade unionists who stage an unsuccessful general strike in Madrid. Though this book also struck many critics at the time of its publication as more documentary than literary in style, it nevertheless demonstrated the author's growing preoccupation with experimental philosophies and different ways of perceiving reality. Discussing the English translation, *Seven Red Sundays,* Sherman H. Eoff suggested in *The Modern Spanish Novel* that Sender's interest in "the mysterious 'presence' that lurks behind commonplace existence" and in "the notion that the heart of human reality is concealed in a nonrational and phantomlike quality" foreshadowed the French existentialists in some ways. Explained Eoff: "Bolder—and less organized—than the French in his expression of ideas, and less dedicated to novelistic technique as a goal in itself, [Sender] evinces a lusty primitivism whose existentialist affinity is an aspect rather than a systematic trend of thought." King observed in his book that "Sender uses external or ordinary reality in *Seven Red Sundays* as a solid base of operations, as a kind of trampoline from which to launch his leaps to 'higher' realities. The chapter in which the moon becomes a character is an example of unrestrained imagination which clearly violates the usual norms for a 'realistic' work. . . . [Thus,] the 'realism' of *Seven Red Sundays* is a strange fusion of ordinary reality with other 'realities,' imaginative 'realities' that sometimes add an intellectual dimension, at others a lyrical or metaphysical overtone."

Perhaps the most philosophical of Sender's many works is *La esfera,* the first novel he wrote after leaving Spain. The English translation, *The Sphere,* is described by King as "an ambitious attempt to fuse into an artistic unity the realistic, the lyrical-metaphysical, the fantastic, and the symbolic." *The Sphere* follows a Spanish refugee on a transatlantic voyage that is marred by several murders, a mutiny, and a shipwreck. In this complex story, Sender explored a variety of universal opposites—life and death, love and hate—and tried to synthesize them into higher unities or "spheres" that incorporated elements of the purely rational and conventional "everyday" world as well as the chaotic and fragmented world of the subconscious and the unconscious. According to King, "The dramatic tension of *The Sphere,* as it is in all of Sender's fiction, is . . . between [these] two worlds. . . . Sender seeks ever to write in the twilight zone where [they] merge."

One of the more unusual, yet significant, "opposites" the author discussed in *The Sphere* was "man" and "person." As Sender himself explained in a passage from the novel, a man is (in a somewhat mystical sense) "the source of all truth, of each universal and innate truth," and "an integral part of *the infinite intellect of God.*" A "person," on the other hand, is the individualized "mask" that begins to develop soon after birth and continues to grow and change throughout life—in essence, the sum of those qualities that makes one man different from another. In Sender's view, this process of individualization isolates a man from his fellow man and gradually takes him farther and farther away from his instinctive nature.

In his essay on *The Sphere,* King pointed to this man-person antithesis as the source of Sender's major philosophical convictions. It was, for instance, the basis for his belief in the "natural unity of all created objects" and his "deep faith in the value of man *simply because he is man*"; it also led him ultimately to deny the existence of death. (According to Sender, man, the "eternal substance," is immortal; what "dies" is the person, "that growing individualization of the human being.")

Sender demonstrated his preoccupation with these and other thought-provoking concepts in many of his subsequent works of fiction, including *El lugar del hombre, Epitalamio del prieto Trinidad, El rey y la reina,* and *El verdugo afable.* For the most part, critics found these books bewildering yet fascinating in their symbolic complexity and blend of reality and fantasy. One particular group of post-exile novels, however, did not exhibit quite the same abstruseness. Known by the general title of the first work in this particular series, *Chronicle of Dawn,* these novels depict early twentieth-century Spain in a tenderly nostalgic light, primarily through the eyes of a republican refugee, Pepe Garces, as he lies dying in a French prison camp during the final months of the civil war. Though Sender's series is, as Bertram Wolfe observed in *New York Herald Tribune Books,* first and foremost "a remarkably beautiful tale of romantic and heroic childhood which will take its place alongside the very best in its genre," it is also, declared the *New York Times*'s Marjorie Farber, a war story unlike any other in its portrayal of "what happens to the good men, and to all men, in the course of the fight."

Nearly all the critics who were familiar with the English translations of three novels in the series—*Chronicle of Dawn, Violent Griffin,* and *The Villa Julieta*—were charmed as well as saddened by the author's simple narrative of youth. In his *Nation* review, for example, Paul Blackburn called *Before Noon* "one of the sweetest-tempered books I have read in a long time. In fact, I can recall no book of prose at all with which to set it. I thought that only poetry could be this warm. This does not seem to be so much a result of Mr. Sender's style (an enviable clarity in itself), as of his attitude toward his character, Pepe Garces. I don't think Pepe can avoid being mostly Ramon Sender, ages ten to twelve. I do not know what Mr. Sender thinks of himself as man, but he adores that boy! I am grateful; you will be too. . . . The fabric of the book will catch you up, both in its gross take and in its delicacies, so that you will read, impatient for the next development."

Isaac Rosenfeld of the *New Republic* found that the technique of beginning the story in the present and then returning to the past creates "an idyllic effect. . . . But it is the tone in which remembered experience is set down and the purpose these scenes serve which give *Chronicle of Dawn* its quality of delight." The critic was also impressed by "the renewed ease" with which the author handled symbolism in the book. Remarked Rosenfeld: "[In previous novels Sender's] symbolism appeared to be getting out of hand, even at times symbolizing nothing so much as itself in an iconography run riot, religious in its overtones but wary of the reality to which it owed some final commitment. *Chronicle of Dawn* is to my mind a very welcome reconstruction of the symbol."

Farber applauded Sender for at last writing "an astonishingly true and moving" book which examines "the total truth of our tragedy"—in short, "the whole monstrous discrepancy between human potential and the inhuman, mechanized result: the love perverted or corrupted, the courage exploited, the nobility thrown away." She was also pleased to note Sender's "tone of respect" and "unusual honesty and clarity" in recording "the physical details and the passionate emotions of childhood," explaining that "Sender's humor contains none of the underlying contempt of [novelist Booth] Tarkington's attitude toward Penrod; nor does he ever allow nostalgia to falsify his memories into the pastel prettiness of [William] Saroyan. Pepe may be young, but he is a human being—a young man in the most dignified literal sense."

Unlike Farber, however, *Nation* critic Diana Trilling did not find Sender's portrait of Pepe particularly dignified. "For all Mr. Sender's good prose," she stated, "[*Chronicle of Dawn*] was marred for me by the fatal coyness with which Mr. Sender reproduces the mind of a ten-year-old." Others, too, had some less-than-flattering observations to make about the book. As Edwin Honig commented in the *Saturday Review:* "Despite the delicacy and charm of its details, the novel is somber and bare, and at times appears too far removed from the sources of feeling it exploits. . . . After the first true heat and *vraisemblance* are struck in *Chronicle of Dawn,* the novel seems to jerk along without developing characters or situations beyond the passing events themselves." In his *Commonweal* review, Paule Berault described *Chronicle of Dawn* as a childhood memory "with all the weaknesses and the charm of this form" and expressed his disappointment with Sender's all-too-brief mention of that "drama [the Spanish civil war] which was the forerunner of that which spread all over the world." As far as Berault was concerned, Sender's sober yet powerful explanation of how and why the dying Pepe came to tell his story "far surpasses the rest of the book."

At least two critics believed that Sender did not err in downplaying the political and social realities of the 1930s in his novel. *Saturday Review*'s Ralph Bates, for example, speculated that the author, "driven out of his own land with memories too horrible for contemplation," probably felt "compelled to reorder his thinking [and thus] deliberately returned to that [time when] the spirit was whole and hard and pure." Continued the critic: "Sender must go back, as [Pepe] must do, not in order to comfort the heart with dreams of a Golden Epoch, but in order to collect and concentrate himself, to pare off the impurities, particularly the uncleanness of the political world of compromise and ungodly tolerance . . . This return to childhood is a kind of voluntary seclusion, a monasticism of the spirit that is far more rigorous than

the imprisonments which have been made to serve the same purpose by other writers. . . . That is the significance of this simple, astonishing book. That is why it is so singularly pure, for against its one banal memory there are set within it scores of startling and altogether beautiful things."

Rosenfeld agreed that Sender's "reconstruction of [Pepe's] childhood is . . . not an escape from political responsibility, nor even a simple flight from hopelessness. It is, rather, a justification of the hopeless. . . . Only through the reconstruction of the times and experiences in which the ideal had meaning—the childhood of hope—can one examine, with the most unsparing honesty, the significance of the ideal, and know, without delusion, precisely what was lost when 'all was lost.' "

Sender's lifelong desire to determine "precisely what was lost when 'all was lost' " did not, however, leave him bitter or pessimistic. It is true, noted critic John Devlin, that as "a novelist with philosophical inclinations" Sender did continually seek out the "explanations behind reality—not only the reality of Spain of his day, but of human existence, as well." Nevertheless, concluded Devlin, "an examination of [his] first novel reveals, under literary symbols, that he discovered in the worst of situations and people a small light shining in the midst of the surrounding darkness of chaos and cruelty. This note is [Sender's] saving grace; it pervades and becomes the touchstone of all his major works."

BIOGRAPHICAL/CRITICAL SOURCES:

BOOKS

Contemporary Literary Criticism, Volume 8, Gale, 1978.
Devlin, John, *Spanish Anticlericalism: A Study in Modern Alienation,* Las Americas Publishing Co., 1966.
Eoff, Sherman H., *The Modern Spanish Novel,* New York University Press, 1961.
King, Charles C., *Ramon J. Sender,* Twayne, 1974.
Sender, Ramon, *Chronicle of Dawn,* annotated Spanish edition, edited and introduced by Florence Hall, Crofts, 1946.

PERIODICALS

Books, October 6, 1935, October 11, 1936.
Christian Century, November 6, 1935.
Christian Science Monitor, May 12, 1937, May 24, 1949.
Commonweal, May 26, 1944.
Manchester Guardian, May 1, 1936, April 23, 1937.
Nation, October 2, 1935, October 24, 1936, November 2, 1940, April 24, 1943, March 18, 1944, April 19, 1958.
New Republic, October 16, 1935, October 14, 1936, February 3, 1941, April 5, 1943, April 24, 1944, May 31, 1948, November 30, 1963.
New Statesman and Nation, September 8, 1934, January 16, 1937, April 10, 1937.
New Yorker, April 19, 1958.
New York Herald Tribune Weekly Book Review, March 28, 1943, March 12, 1944, May 16, 1948.
New York Times, September 22, 1935, October 18, 1936, January 30, 1938, November 3, 1940, March 28, 1943, February 20, 1944, June 27, 1948, May 1, 1949, January 19, 1958.
San Francisco Chronicle, June 19, 1949, February 16, 1958.
Saturday Review of Literature, October 19, 1935, September 26, 1936, January 29, 1938, December 21, 1940, May 15, 1943, April 15, 1944, June 4, 1949, April 12, 1958, September 7, 1963.
Spectator, September 14, 1935, April 16, 1937.
Times Literary Supplement, October 25, 1934, May 2, 1936, April 17, 1937.
Washington Post Book World, September 29, 1963.

OBITUARIES:

PERIODICALS

AB Bookman's Weekly, February 22, 1982.
Chicago Tribune, January 19, 1982.
Times (London), January 19, 1982.

*   *   *

SENGHOR, Leopold Sedar   1906-
(Silmang Diamano, Patrice Maguilene Kaymor)

PERSONAL: Born October 9, 1906, in Joal, Senegal (part of French West Africa; now Republic of Senegal); son of Basile Digoye (a cattle breeder and groundnut planter and exporter) and Nyilane (Bakoume) Senghor; married Ginette Eboue, September, 1946 (divorced, 1956); married Collette Hubert, October 18, 1957; children: (first marriage) Francis-Aphang, Guy-Waly (deceased); (second marriage) Philippe-Maguilen (deceased). *Education:* Baccalaureate degree from Lycee of Dakar, 1928; Sorbonne, University of Paris, agregation de grammaire, 1933, studied African languages at Ecole des Hautes Etudes, Paris, 1929-32.

ADDRESSES: Home—Corniche Ouest, Dakar, Senegal Republic; 1 square de Tocqueville, 75017 Paris, France. *Office*—c/o Presidence de la Republique, Dakar, Senegal Republic.

CAREER: Lycee Descartes, Tours, France, instructor in Greek and Latin classics, 1935-38; Lycee Marcelin Berthelot, St. Maur-des-Fosses, France, instructor in literature and African culture, 1938-40 and 1943-44; Ecole Nationale de la France d'Outre Mer, professor, 1945; French National Assembly, Paris, France, and General Council of Senegal, Dakar, Senegal, elected representative, beginning in 1946; Bloc Democratique Senegalais, Dakar, founder, 1948; French Government, Paris, delegate to United Nations General Assembly in New York City, 1950-51, Secretary of State for scientific research, and representative to UNESCO conferences, 1955-56, member of consultative assembly, 1958, minister-counsellor to Ministry of Cultural Affairs, Education, and Justice, 1959-60, advisory minister, beginning in 1960; City of Thies, Senegal, mayor, beginning in 1956; Senegalese Territorial Assembly, elected representative, beginning in 1957; founder and head of Union Progressiste Senegalaise, beginning in 1958; Mali Federation of Senegal and Sudan, president of Federal Assembly, 1959-60; Republic of Senegal, President of the Republic, 1960-80, Minister of Defense, 1968-69; Socialist Inter-African, chairman of executive bureau, 1981—; Haut Conseil de la Francophonie, vice-president, 1985—. Co-founder, with Lamine Gueye, of Bloc Africain, 1945; representative for Senegal to French Constituent Assemblies, 1945 and 1946; official grammarian for writing of French Fourth Republic's new constitution, 1946; sponsor of First World Festival of Negro Arts, Dakar, 1966; chairman of Organisation Commune Africaine et Malgache, 1972-74; established West African Economic Community, 1974; chairman of ECONAS, 1978-79. *Military service:* French Army, infantry, 1934-35; served in infantry battalion of colonial troops, 1939; prisoner of war, 1940-42; participated in French Resistance, 1942-45; received serviceman's cross, 1939-45.

MEMBER: Comite National des Ecrivains, Societe des Gens de Lettres, Societe Linguistique de France.

AWARDS, HONORS: Numerous awards, including corresponding membership in Bavarian Academy, 1961; International French Friendship Prize, 1961; French Language Prize (gold medal), 1963; International Grand Prize for Poetry, 1963; Dag Hammarskjoeld International Prize Gold Medal for Poetic Merit, 1963; Marie Noel Poetry Prize, 1965; Red and Green International Literature Grand Prix, 1966, German Book Trade's Peace Prize, 1968; associate membership in French Academy of Moral and Political Sciences, 1969; Knokke Biennial International Poetry Grand Prix, 1970; membership in Academy of Overseas Sciences, 1971; membership in Black Academy of Arts and Sciences, 1971; Grenoble Gold Medal, 1972; Haile Selassie African Research Prize, 1973; Cravat of Commander of Order of French Arts and Letters, 1973; Apollinaire Prize for Poetry, 1974; Prince Pierre of Monaco's Literature Prize, 1977; Prix Eurafrique, 1978; Alfred de Vigny Prize, 1981; Aasan World Prize, 1981; election to Academie Francaise, 1983; Jawaharlal Nehru Award, 1984; Athinai Prize, 1985; also Grand Cross of French Legion of Honor, Commander of Academic Palms, Franco-Allied Medal of Recognition, membership in Agegres de Grammaire and American Academy of Arts and Letters. Numerous honorary doctorates, including those from Fordham University, 1961; University of Paris, 1962; Catholic University of Louvain (Belgium), 1965; Lebanese University of Beirut, 1966; Howard University, 1966; Laval University (Quebec), 1966; Harvard University, 1971; Oxford University, 1973; and from the universities of Ibadan (Nigeria), 1964; Bahia (Brazil), 1965; Strasbourg (France), 1965; Al-Azan (Cairo, Egypt), 1967; Algiers (Algeria), 1967; Bordeaux-Talence (France), 1967; Vermont, 1971; California at Los Angeles, 1971; Ethiopia Haile Selassie I, 1971; Abidjan (Ivory Coast), 1971; and Lagos (Nigeria), 1972.

WRITINGS:

POETRY

Chants d'ombre (title means "Songs of Shadow"; includes "Femme noire" and "Joal"; also see below), Seuil, 1945.
Hosties noires (title means "Black Sacrifices"; includes "Au Gouverneur Eboue," "Mediterranee," "Aux Soldats Negro-Americains," "Tyaroye," and "Priere de paix"; also see below), Seuil, 1948.
Chants pour Naeett (title means "Songs for Naeett"; also see below), Seghers, 1949.
Chants d'ombre [suivi de] *Hosties noires* (title means "Songs of Shadow" [followed by] "Black Sacrifices"), Seuil, 1956.
Ethiopiques (includes "Chaka," poetic adaptation of Thomas Mofolo's historical novel *Chaka;* "A New York"; and "Congo"), Seuil, 1956, critical edition with commentary by Papa Gueye N'Diaye published as *Ethiopiques: Poemes,* Nouvelles Editions Africaines, 1974.
Nocturnes (includes *Chants pour Naeett,* "Elegie de minuit," and "Elegie a Aynina Fall: Poeme dramatique a plusieurs voix" [title means "Elegy for Aynina Fall: Dramatic Poem for Many Voices"]), Seuil, 1961, translation by John Reed and Clive Wake published as *Nocturnes,* Heinemann Educational, 1969, with introduction by Paulette J. Trout, Third Press, 1971.
Elegie des Alizes, original lithographs by Marc Chagall, Seuil, 1969.
Lettres d'hivernage, illustrations by Marc Chagall, Seuil, 1973.
Paroles, Nouvelles Editions Africaines, 1975.

Poems published in periodicals such as *Chantiers, Les Cahiers du Sud, Les Lettres Francaises, Les Temps Modernes, Le Temp de la Poesie, La Revue Socialiste, Presence Africaine,* and *Prevue.*

CRITICAL AND POLITICAL PROSE

(With Robert Lemaignen and Prince Sisowath Youteyong) *La Communaute imperiale francaise* (includes "Views on Africa; or, Assimilate, Don't Be Assimilated"), Editions Alsatia, 1945.

(With Gaston Monnerville and Aime Cesaire) *Commemoration du centenaire de l'abolition de l'esclavage,* introduction by Edouard Depreux, Presses Universitaires de France, 1948.

(Contributor) *La Nation en construction,* [Dakar], 1959.

Rapport sur la doctrine et le programme du parti, Presence Africaine, 1959, translation published as *Report on the Principles and Programme of the Party,* Presence Africaine, 1959, abridged edition edited and translated by Mercer Cook published as *African Socialism: A Report to the Constitutive Congress of the Party of African Federation,* American Society of African Culture, 1959.

Rapport sur la politique generale, [Senegal], 1960.

Nation et voie africaine du socialisme, Presence Africaine 1961, new edition published as *Liberte 2: Nation et voie africaine du socialisme,* Seuil, 1971, translation by Mercer Cook published as *Nationhood and the African Road to Socialism,* Presence Africaine, 1962, abridged as *On African Socialism,* translation and introduction by Cook, Praeger, 1964.

(Contributor) *Cultures de l'Afrique noire et de l'Occident,* Societe Europeenne de Culture, 1961.

Rapport sur la doctrine et la politique generale; ou, Socialisme, unite africaine, construction nationale, [Dakar], 1962.

(With Pierre Teilhard de Chardin) *Pierre Teilhard de Chardin et la politique africaine* [and] *Sauvons l'humanite* [and] *L'Art dans la ligne de l'energie humaine* (the first by Senghor, the latter two by Teilhard de Chardin), Seuil, 1962.

(With others) *Le Racisme dans le monde,* Julliard, 1964.

Theorie et pratique du socialisme senegalais, [Dakar], 1964.

Liberte 1: Negritude et humanisme, Seuil, 1964, selections translated and introduced by Wendell A. Jeanpierre published as *Freedom 1: Negritude and Humanism,* [Providence, R.I.], 1974.

(In Portuguese, French, and Spanish) *Latinite et negritude,* Centre de Hautes Etudes Afro-Ibero-Americaines de l'Universite de Dakar, 1966.

Negritude, arabisme, et francite: Reflexions sur le probleme de la culture (title means "Negritude, Arabism, and Frenchness: Reflections on the Problem of Culture"), preface by Jean Rous, Editions Dar al-Kitab Allubmani (Beirut), 1967, republished as *Les Fondements de l'Africanite; ou, Negritude et arabite,* Presence Africaine, 1967, translation by M. Cook published as *The Foundations of "Africanite"; or, "Negritude" and "Arabite,"* Presence Africaine, 1971.

Politique, nation, et developpement moderne: Rapport de politique generale, Imprimerie Nationale (Rufisque), 1968.

Le Plan du decollage economique; ou, La Participation responsable comme moteur de developpement, Grande Imprimerie Africaine (Dakar), 1970.

Pourquoi une ideologie negro-africaine? (lecture), Universite d'Abidjan, 1971.

La Parole chez Paul Claudel et chez les Negro-Africains, Nouvelles Editions Africaines, 1973.

(With others) *Litteratures ultramarines de langue francaise, genese et jeunesse: Actes du colloque de l'Universite du Vermont,* compiled by Thomas H. Geno and Roy Julow, Naaman (Quebec), 1974.

Paroles (addresses), Nouvelles Editions Africaines, 1975.

(Contributor) *La Senegal au Colloque sur le liberalisme planifie et les voies africaines vers le socialisme, Tunis, 1-6 juillet 1975* (includes *Pour une relecture africaine de Marx et d'Engels;* also see below), Grand Imprimerie Africaine (Dakar), 1975.

Pour une relecture africaine de Marx et d'Engels (includes "Le socialisme africain et la voie senegalaise"), Nouvelles Editions Africaines, 1976.

Pour une societe senegalaise socialiste et democratique: Rapport sur la politique generale, Nouvelles Editions Africaines, 1976.

Liberte 3: Negritude et civilisation de l'universel (title means "Freedom 3: Negritude and the Civilization of the Universal"), Seuil, 1977.

(With Mohamed Aziza) *La Poesie de l'action : Conversations avec Mohamed Aziza* (interviews), Stock (Paris), 1980.

Ce que je crois: Negritude, francite, et la civilisation de l'universel, Grosset, 1988.

Also author of *L'Apport de la poesie negre,* 1953; *Langage et poesie negro-africaine,* 1954; *Esthetique negro-africain,* 1956; and *Liberte 4: Socialisme et planification,* 1983. Author of four technical works on Wolof grammar. Author of lectures and addresses published in pamphlet or booklet form, including *The Mission of the Poet,* 1966; *Negritude et germanisme,* 1968; *Problemes de developpement dans les pays sous-developpes,* 1975; *Negritude et civilisations mediterraneennes,* 1976; and *Pour une lecture negro-africaine de Mallarme,* 1981. Contributor, sometimes under the pseudonyms Silmang Diamano or Patrice Maguilene Kaymor, of critical, linguistic, sociological, and political writings to periodicals and journals, including *Journal de la Societe des Africanists, Presence Africaine,* and *L'Esprit.*

OTHER

(Editor) *Anthologie de la nouvelle poesie negre et malgache de langue francaise* [precede de] *Orphee noir, par Jean Paul Sartre* (poetry anthology; title means "Anthology of the New Negro and Malagasy Poetry in French [preceded by] Black Orpheus, by Jean-Paul Sartre"), introduction by Sartre, Presses Universitaires de France, 1948, 4th edition, 1977.

(With Abdoulaye Sadji) *La Belle Histoire de Leuk-le-Lievre* (elementary school text; title means "The Clever Story of Leuk-the-Hare"), Hachette, 1953, reprinted as *La Belle Histoire de Leuk-le-Lievre: Cours elementaire des ecoles d'Afrique noir,* illustrations by Marcel Jeanjean, Hachette, 1961, British edition (in French) edited by J. M. Winch, illustrations by Jeanjean, Harrap, 1965, adaptation published as *Les Aventures de Leuk-le-Lievre,* illustrations by G. Lorofi, Nouvelles Editions Africaines, 1975.

(Author of introductory essay) *Anthologie des poetes du seizieme siecle* (anthology), Editions de la Bibliotheque Mondiale, 1956.

(Contributor of selected texts) *Afrique Africaine* (photography), photographs by Michel Huet, Clairfontaine, 1963.

(Contributor) *Terre promise d'Afrique: Symphonie en noir et or* (poetry anthology), lithographs by Hans Erni, Andre et Pierre Gonin (Lausanne), 1966.

(Contributor of selected texts) *African Sojourn* (photography), photographs by Uwe Ommer, Arpel Graphics, 1987.

Author of prose tale "Mandabi" (title means "The Money Order"). Translator of poetry by Mariane N'Diaye. Founder of journals, including *Condition Humaine;* with Aime Cesaire and Leon Gontran Damas, *L'Etudiant Noir;* and, with Alioune Diop, *Presence Africaine.*

OMNIBUS VOLUMES

Leopold Sedar Senghor (collection of prose and poems; with biographical-critical introduction and bibliography), edited by Armand Guibert, Seghers, 1961, reprinted as *Leopold Sedar*

*Senghor: Une Etude d'Armand Guibert, avec un choix de po-
emes [et] une chronologie bibliographique,* "Leopold Sedar
Senghor et son temps," Seghers, 1969.
(In English translation) John Reed and Clive Wake, editors and
translators, *Selected Poems,* introduction by Reed and
Wake, Atheneum, 1964.
Poemes (includes *Chants d'ombre, Hosties noires, Ethiopiques,
Nocturnes,* and "poemes divers"), Seuil, 1964, 4th edition,
1969, reprinted 1974, new edition, 1984.
L. S. Senghor: Poete senegalais, commentary by Roger Mercier,
Monique Battestini, and Simon Battestini, F. Nathan, 1965,
reprinted, 1978.
(In English translation) *Prose and Poetry,* selected and translated
by Reed and Wake, Oxford University Press, 1965, Heine-
mann Educational, 1976.
(In French with English translations) *Selected Poems/Poesies
choisies,* English-language introduction by Craig William-
son, Collings, 1976.
(In French) *Selected Poems of Leopold Sedar Senghor,* edited,
with English-language preface and notes, by Abiola Irele,
Cambridge University Press, 1977.
Elegies majeures [suivi de] *Dialogue sur la poesie francophone,*
Seuil, 1979.
(In English translation) *Poems of a Black Orpheus,* translated by
William Oxley, Menard, 1981.

SIDELIGHTS: President of the Republic of Senegal from the
proclamation of that country's independence in 1960 until he
stepped down in 1980, Leopold Sedar Senghor is considered, according to *Time,* "one of Africa's most respected elder statesmen." Yet until 1960 Senghor's political career was conducted
primarily in France rather than in Africa. He is a product of the
nineteenth-century French educational system, a scholar of
Greek and Latin, and a member of the elite Academie Francaise,
but he is best known for developing "negritude," a wide-ranging
movement that influenced black culture worldwide. As the chief
proponent of negritude, Senghor is credited with contributing to
Africa's progress toward independence from colonial rule and,
according to Jacques Louis Hymans in his *Leopold Sedar Senghor: An Intellectual Biography,* with "setting in motion a whole
series of African ideological movements." Senghor first gained
widespread recognition, however, when his first collection of poetry was published in 1945; he followed that volume with a
highly esteemed body of verse that has accumulated numerous
prestigious honors, most notably consideration for the Nobel
Prize in Literature. Senghor, thus, seems to be, as Hymans suggests, "the living symbol of the possible synthesis of what appears irreconcilable: he is as African as he is European, as much
a poet as a politician, . . . as much a revolutionary as a traditionalist."

From the outset, disparate elements comprised Senghor's life.
He was born in 1906 in Joal, a predominantly Moslem community established by Portuguese settlers on the Atlantic coast
south of Dakar, a major Senegalese port and capital of what was
then known as French West Africa. Senghor's mother was a
Roman Catholic, and through maternal or paternal lines Senghor was related to the Fulani ethnic group, the Mandingo tribe,
and the Serer ethnic group—said to provide a connection between Senghor and Serer royalty. His early childhood afforded
contact with traditional customs and beliefs, with indigenous poetry, and with the surrounding natural setting. These contacts,
critics note, strongly influenced Senghor's later life. As Sebastian
Okechukwu Mezu explained in his 1973 study, *The Poetry of Leopold Sedar Senghor:* "This early childhood gave Senghor the
material for his lyric poems. . . . Despite the splendours of po-

litical life, perhaps because of the excess of its paraphernalia,
[Senghor] comes back to these memories of childhood . . . in his
poems, events evoked several times in his public speeches and
television interviews, images that have become a kind of obsession, romanticized during the years of his absence from Senegal,
and because of this process of nostalgic remembrance, taken to
be reality itself. Poetic life for Senghor as a result of this becomes
a continual quest for the kingdom of childhood, a recovery, a recapture of this idyllic situation."

As a child Senghor demonstrated a lively intelligence and an
early ambition to become a priest or a teacher, and was accordingly enrolled in a Catholic elementary school in 1913. The following year he began living in a boarding house four miles from
Joal at N'Gasobil, where he attended the Catholic mission
school operated by the Fathers of the Holy Spirit. There Senghor
was encouraged to disparage his ancestral culture while he
learned Latin and studied European civilization as part of a typical nineteenth-century French teaching program. In 1922 he entered Libermann Junior Seminary in Dakar. In his four years
there Senghor acquired a sound knowledge of Greek and Latin
classics. Obliged to leave the seminary when he was deemed ill-
suited to the priesthood, Senghor, disappointed, entered public
secondary school at a French-style lycee in Dakar. There he
earned numerous scholastic prizes and distinction for having
bested white pupils in academic performance. Senghor obtained
his secondary school degree with honors in 1928 and was
awarded a half scholarship for continued study in France.

In Paris Senghor boarded at the Lycee Louis-le-Grand, where
top-ranking French students study for entrance exams to
France's elite higher education programs. One of Senghor's
classmates was Georges Pompidou, later prime minister and,
eventually, president of France. Pompidou exposed Senghor to
the works of French literary masters Marcel Proust, Andre
Gide, and Charles Baudelaire. During this time Senghor was also
influenced by the writings of Paul Claudel, Arthur Rimbaud,
and Maurice Barres. Senghor's lycee education in Paris emphasized methodology for rigorous thought and instilled habits of
intellectual discipline, skills that Senghor embraced. He meanwhile continued to observe Roman Catholicism and expressed
support for a restoration of the French government to monarchy. According to Hymans, Senghor in his student days was considered fully assimilated into Paris's intellectual milieu, which
began including political and social liberation movements such
as socialism, rationalism, humanism, and Marxism.

Europe was also reassessing African cultural traditions. European writers, artists, and musicians were exploring Africa's cultural wealth and incorporating what they discovered into their
own creations. Paris of the late 1920s was permeated with Europe's new cultural appreciation of Africa, and in this atmosphere an exciting period of discovery began for Senghor. He
began meeting with black students from the United States, Africa, and the Caribbean, and soon a friendship grew between
Senghor and Aime Cesaire, a writer from the French West Indian territory of Martinique. Another of Senghor's acquaintances was Paulette Nardal, a West Indian and the editor of a
journal, *La Revue du Monde Noir.* Published in French and English, the journal was intended to provide a forum for black intellectuals writing literary and scientific works, to celebrate black
civilization, and to increase unity among blacks worldwide.
Through its editor Nardal, Senghor met West Indian writers
Etienne Lero and Rene Maran and read the poetry of black
Americans.

In *The New Negro,* an anthology published in 1925, Senghor encountered the works of prominent writers such as Paul Laurence Dunbar, W. E. B. Du Bois, Countee Cullen, Langston Hughes, Claude McKay, Zora Neale Hurston, James Weldon Johnson, and Jean Toomer. The anthology's editor, Alain Locke, was a professor of philosophy at Harvard University and a contributor to *La Revue du Monde Noir;* Senghor met him through Nardal as well. When Senghor, Cesaire, and Leon Gontran Damas, a student from French Guiana, sought a name for the growing francophone interest in African culture, they borrowed from the title of Locke's anthology and dubbed the movement "neonegre" or "negre-nouveau." These labels were later replaced by "negritude," a term coined by Cesaire. Senghor credits Jamaican poet and novelist Claude McKay with having supplied the values espoused by the new movement: to seek out the roots of black culture and build on its foundations, to draw upon the wealth of African history and anthropology, and to rehabilitate black culture in the eyes of the world. With Cesaire and Darnas, Senghor launched *L'Etudiant Noir,* a cultural journal.

In exalting black culture and values, Senghor emphasized what he perceived as differences between the races. He portrayed blacks as artistic geniuses less gifted in the areas of scientific thought, attributing emotion to blacks and reason to whites. Europe was seen as alien, dehumanized, and dying, while Africa was considered vital, nourishing, and thriving. As racism and fascism swept through Europe in the 1930s, Senghor's attitudes were affected. For a brief period he became disillusioned with Europe in general and abandoned his religious faith. "By Senghor's own admission," Hymans revealed, "the same Romantic anti-rationalism that fathered racism among the Fascists of the 1930s underlay his early reaction against the West." But Senghor observed the increasing turmoil in Europe caused by Fascist regimes in Italy and Germany and understood the dangers of racism. Accordingly he modified his position.

Senghor nevertheless continued to cite what he considered to be differences between the races, such as an intuitive African way of understanding reality. But more importantly, as negritude evolved, he emphasized racial pride as a way of valuing black culture's role in a universal civilization. In this vein, he published an essay in 1939 titled "What the Negro Contributes." Themes that Senghor introduced to negritude at this time included a humanism based on the solidarity of all races, a moderate position that gave primacy to culture and maintained respect for other values. As Senghor told an audience he addressed in Dakar in 1937: "Assimilate, don't be assimilated." He later developed negritude further, however, by working to insure not only that African cultural identity became accessible to blacks worldwide, but that the unique aspects of African life were accorded status in the cultural community of society as a whole. Once African modes of thought and artistic expression are restored to their proper place among the world's cultures, Senghor proposed, then a sort of cultural cross-breeding can occur. This mixing of the races, according to Mezu, was conceived as "a symbiotic union where blacks will bring to the rendezvous of the races their special . . . talents." Hymans examined this development of negritude since its inception in the 1930s and quoted Senghor's retrospective assessment of the movement: "Like life, the concept of negritude has become historical and dialectical. It has evolved."

Much of what later informed negritude had yet to be developed when in 1933 Senghor became the first African to obtain the coveted agregation degree. This distinction led to his first teaching position, at the Lycee Descartes in Tours, France. Senghor's new appreciation for Africa, coupled with his estrangement from his homeland, created an internal conflict that found resolution when he began writing poetry. Influenced by the works of Andre Breton and other surrealist writers, Senghor drew on surrealist techniques for his poetic style. Surrealism, with its emphasis on the irrational, depended on a creative process that tapped latent energies and subconscious sources of imagination without drawing a distinction between the fantastic and the real. Senghor found this process similar to traditional African modes of thought and employed it in his poetry. "By adopting the surrealist techniques," Mezu explained, "he was at the same time modern and African: educated and modernist from the white European viewpoint, traditional and faithful to the motherland from the African viewpoint. This dualism, or rather ambivalence, is ever present in Senghor's theories, poetry and actions." Nevertheless, Mezu noted, "there is a difference between the surrealist norm and the Senghorian philosophy. The difference is basically one of degree. For the surrealists, their effort, and an effort only, was to discover the point where reality and dream merge into one. For Senghor . . . this principle is already possessed, already a part of the ancestral culture."

The poems Senghor wrote in the late 1930s were later published in the collection *Chants d'ombre.* For the most part, these poems express Senghor's nostalgia for Africa, his sense of exile, estrangement, and cultural alienation, and his attempt to recover an idealized past. In a style based on musical rhythms, the poet evokes the beauty of the African landscape and peoples, the richness of Africa's past and the protecting presence of the dead, and the innocence and dignity inherent in his native culture. These poems, critics note, celebrate an Africa Senghor knew as a child, one transformed by nostalgia into a paradise-like simplicity. In some of the volume's other poems Senghor laments the destruction of the continent's culture and the suffering of its people under colonial rule. One of the collection's frequently cited pieces, "Femme noir," employs sensual yet worshipful language intended to glorify all black women. In "Joal" Senghor returns to his native village, revisiting places and inhabitants he had once known very well; it is, according to Mezu, "easily one of the most beautiful poems created by Senghor." When *Chants d'ombre* was published in 1945 it was well received in Paris and brought Senghor to public attention as a voice of black Africa. "In recreating the distant continent by verse," Hymans observed, "Senghor helped blaze the trail that led to the phenomenon of negritude."

World War II intervened between the writing of the poems collected in *Chants d'ombre* and their eventual publication. Germany invaded Poland in September, 1939, and Senghor was immediately called to active duty to protect France at the German border. While the holder of a high academic degree is usually made a commissioned officer, Senghor as a black man was made a second-class soldier in the Colonial Infantry. France fell to the German assault in June, 1940, the same month Senghor was captured and interned in a German prison camp. At the time of his capture he was almost shot along with some other Senegalese prisoners, but a French officer interceded on his behalf. While in prison Senghor met African peasants who had been recruited into the French Army, and began to identify with their plight. He wrote a number of poems that he sent by letter to his old classmate and friend Georges Pompidou; they were hand-delivered by a German guard who had been a professor of Chinese at the University of Vienna before the war. These poems later formed the core of Senghor's second published collection, *Hosties noires,* which appeared in 1948.

Hosties noires documents Senghor's realization that he was not alone in his exile from Africa, explores his increasing sense of unity with blacks as an exploited race, and elucidates the positive meaning Senghor finds in the sacrifices blacks have made. In poems such as "Au Gouveneur Eboue," which treats a black man's willingness to die for the salvation of the white world, Senghor memorializes blacks fighting for Europe. Elsewhere in *Hosties noires,* Senghor protests the exploitation of black soldiers and attacks western sources of power and violence. In other poems, such as "Mediterranee" and "Aux Soldats Negro-Americains," he rejoices in the common bonds formed with fellow soldiers and with American blacks. And with "Priere de paix" and "Tyaroye" Senghor hopes for unity and peace; while denouncing colonialism, he calls for an end to hatred and welcomes the new life that succeeds death. The collection, according to Mezu, is "the most homogeneous volume of Senghor's poetry, from the point of view not only of theme but also of language and sentiment."

Through the influence of West Indian colleagues Senghor was released from prison in June, 1942, and resumed teaching at the lycee in suburban Paris where he had earlier served as instructor of literature and African culture. He joined a Resistance group and also participated in activities involving colonial students. During the war, negritude had gained momentum, and when *Chants d'ombre* appeared in 1945, a new group of black intellectuals eagerly embraced Senghor's poetry and cultural theories. That year he published the influential essay "Views on Africa; or, Assimilate, Don't Be Assimilated." While in the 1930s Senghor concentrated on cultural rather than political issues, after the war he was encouraged by colonial reforms extended to French West Africans. He decided to run for election as one of Senegal's representatives in the French National Assembly. With Lamine Gueye, Senghor formed the Bloc Africain to involve Senegalese in their political fate. France was forming a new constitution, and in recognition of his linguistic expertise, France's provisional government appointed Senghor the document's official grammarian. Senghor founded the Bloc Democratique Senegalais (BDS) in 1948; throughout the 1950s the BDS dominated Senegalese politics.

Senghor's literary activities also continued. In 1947 he founded, with Alioune Diop, the cultural journal *Presence Africaine.* Along with a publishing house of the same name, *Presence Africaine* under Diop's direction became a powerful vehicle for black writing worldwide. As editor of *Anthologie de la nouvelle poesie noire et malgache de langue francaise,* published in 1948, Senghor brought together contemporary poetry written by francophone blacks. An essay titled "Orphee noir" ("Black Orpheus"), by French philosopher and writer Jean Paul Sartre, introduced the anthology. Sartre's essay outlined the cultural aims of black peoples striving to recapture their heritage. In the process Sartre defined and gained notoriety for the philosophy of negritude, portraying negritude as a step toward a united society without racial distinction. Many consider "Black Orpheus" to be the most important document of the negritude movement.

After 1948 Senghor became increasingly active politically, serving as France's delegate to the 1949 Council of Europe and as a French delegate to the United Nations General Assembly in 1950 and 1951; he won resounding reelection to the French National Assembly in 1951 as well. In 1955 and 1956 Senghor served in the cabinet of French president Edgar Faure as secretary of state for scientific research and attended UNESCO conferences as a representative of France. While some French-held territories sought independence from colonial rule, often with accompanying violence, Senghor pushed for an arrangement giving French overseas territories equal status in a federation relationship facilitating economic development. He constantly modified his stance while avoiding violence and making small gains. In

Dakar in 1953, according to Hymans, Senghor defined politics as "the art of using a method which, by approximations that are constantly corrected, would permit the greatest number to lead a more complete and happy life."

A collection of poems Senghor had been working on since 1948 was published as *Ethiopiques* in 1956. These poems reflect Senghor's growing political involvement and his struggle to reconcile European and African allegiances through crossbreeding, both figurative and literal. The year *Ethiopiques* was published Senghor divorced his African wife to marry one of her friends, a white Frenchwoman; critics have suggested that Senghor's views on cross-breeding represent an attempt to resolve his personal conflict by eliminating the divisive social elements that divided his loyalties. One of *Ethiopiques*'s poems, "Chaka," is a dramatic adaptation of Thomas Mofolo's novel about a Zulu hero who forged and ruled a vast domain in the early nineteenth century. Mezu called "Chaka" Senghor's "most ambitious piece." Others have drawn parallels between Senghor's life and the poem's attempt to combine in the character of Chaka both the poet and politician. In "Chaka" Senghor applied his theories about the combination of music, dance, and poetry found in native African art forms. As Mezu noted, "Senghor aimed to illustrate what he considered an indigenous form of art where music, painting, theatre, poetry, religion, faith, love, and politics are all intertwined." In addition to musical and rhythmic elements, native plants and animals also figure prominently in *Ethiopiques,* whose other poems include "A New York," and "Congo."

When France's Fourth Republic collapsed in 1958 and France began to form a new constitution—along with new African policies—Senghor joined the advocates of independence for African territories. The French government, under Charles de Gaulle, appointed Senghor to the consultative assembly that would formulate the new constitution and policies. De Gaulle's proposed constitution, which was adopted in late 1958, accorded French West African territories autonomy within the French Community. At the same time De Gaulle warned Senghor that complete independence for West Africa would mean a cessation of technical and financial aid. In 1959 Senghor countered with the Mali Federation, linking Senegal and the Sudan (now Mali). The Mali Federation proclaimed its independence in June, 1960, but two months later Senegal withdrew and reproclaimed its independence. A Senegalese constitution was drawn up in August, 1960, and the following month Senghor was elected to a seven-year term as president of the new Republic of Senegal. Almost twenty-five years later Senghor told *Time,* "The colonizing powers did not prepare us for independence."

Poems Senghor wrote during the tumultuous years leading up to his election as president of Senegal were published in the 1961 collection *Nocturnes,* which featured a group of love poems previously published as *Chants pour Naeett* in 1949. In *Nocturnes* Senghor ponders the nature of poetry and examines the poetic process. Critics have noted that in this volume, particularly in poems such as "Elegie de minuit," Senghor reveals his regret for time spent in the empty pomp of political power, his nostalgia for his youth, and his reconciliation with death. Mezu called "Elegie de minuit" the poet's " 'last' poem."

After 1960, Senghor wrote mainly political and critical prose, tied closely to the goals, activities, and demands of his political life. During this time he survived an attempted coup d'etat staged in 1962 by Senegal's prime minister, Mamadou Dia. The following year Senghor authorized the Senegalese National Assembly to draw up a new constitution that gave more power to the president, elected to five-year terms. Known for his ability to hold factions together, he remained in power, reelected in 1968 and 1973, despite more coup attempts, an assassination plot in 1967, and civil unrest in the late 1960s. Much of Senghor's writing from this era outlines the course he feels Africa must hold to, despite upheavals. Commenting on the instability suffered after African nations achieved independence, Senghor told *Time:* "The frequency of coups in Africa is the result of the backwardness in civilization that colonization represented. . . . What we should all be fighting for is democratic socialism. And the first task of socialism is not to create social justice. It is to establish working democracies."

According to Hymans, Senghor's brand of socialism, often called the African Road to Socialism, maps out a middle position between individualism and collectivism, between capitalism and communism. Senghor sees socialism as a way of eliminating the exploitation of individuals that prevents universal humanism. Some of Senghor's writings on this topic were translated by Mercer Cook and published in 1964 as *On African Socialism.* Appraising *On African Socialism* for *Saturday Review,* Charles Miller called its selections "exquisitely intellectual tours de force." Senghor's important political writings include *Liberte 1: Negritude et humanisme,* of which portions are available in translation; a work translated by Cook as *The Foundations of "Africanite": or, "Negritude" and "Arabite"; Politique, nation, et developpement moderne; Liberte 3: Negritude et civilization de l'universel;* and *Liberte 4: Socialisme et planification.* In a collection of interviews with Mohamed Aziza published in 1980, Senghor discussed poetry and both his politics and his life. Senghor "comes across in these interviews as a brilliant, sincere, and steadfast leader who has yet managed to retain a sense of humility," wrote Eric Sellin, reviewing the collection for *World Literature Today.* Sellin continued: "His unswerving fidelity to personal and national programs is more readily understandable in light of his autobiographical introspections about his youth and education." Published as *La Poesie de l'action,* the volume, Sellin concluded, is "an important and interesting book." Later in 1980, Senghor stepped down from Senegal's presidency when his protege, Prime Minister Abdou Diouf, took office.

Senghor is revered throughout the world for his political and literary accomplishments and a life of achievement that spans nearly six decades. He was widely thought to have been under consideration in 1962 for the Nobel Prize in Literature in recognition of his poetic output. When a major English-translation volume devoted to Senghor's body of poetry appeared in 1964, *Saturday Review* likened Senghor to American poet Walt Whitman and determined that the poems represented were "written by a gifted, civilized man of good will celebrating the ordinary hopes and feelings of mankind." The *Times Literary Supplement* called Senghor "one of the best poets now writing in [French]" and marveled at his "astonishing achievement to have combined so creative a life with his vigorous and successful political activities." Senghor was elected to one of the world's most prestigious and elite intellectual groups, the Academie Francaise, in 1983.

When a new collected edition of Senghor's poetry appeared in 1984, Robert P. Smith, Jr., writing in *World Literature Today* identified Senghor as a "great poet of Africa and the universe." Praising the masterly imagery, symbolism, and versification of the poetry, Smith expressed particular admiration for Senghor's "constant creation of a poetry which builds up, makes inquiries, and expands into universal dimensions," and cited an elegy Senghor wrote for his deceased son as "one of the most beautiful in modern poetry." Critics characterize Senghor's poetic style as serenely and resonantly rhetorical. While some readers detect a lack of tension in his poetry, most admire its lush sensuality and

uplifting attitude. Offered as a means of uniting African peoples in an appreciation of their cultural worth, Senghor's poetry, most agree, extends across the chasm that negritude, at least in its early form, seemed to have created in emphasizing the differences between races. "It is difficult to predict whether Senghor's poetry will excite the same approbation when the prestige of the President and that of the idealist no longer colour people's view of the man," Mezu acknowledged. "The Senegalese poet will certainly survive in the history of the Black Renaissance as the ideologist and theoretician of negritude."

Senghor's negritude in its more evolved form refuses to choose between Africa and Europe in its quest for worldwide national, cultural, and religious integration. Himself a synthesis of disparate elements, Senghor, in his role as reconciler of differences, holds to negritude as a median between nationalism and cultural assimilation. "Politically, philosophically, Senghor has been a middle-of-the-roader, a man of conciliation and mediation," Mezu declared, adding: "Negritude should . . . be seen as a stage in the evolution of the literature of the black man. . . . The contemporary trend in African poetry seems to be away from the negritude movement as the racism and colonialism that inspired this literature dies out or becomes less barefaced." Senghor's life, according to Hymans, "might be summarized as an effort to restore to Africa an equilibrium destroyed by the clash with Europe." For those who see contradictions in Senghor's effort over more than five decades, Hymans observed that "one constant in his thought appears to surmount the contradictions it contains: universal reconciliation is his only goal and Africa's only salvation."

MEDIA ADAPTATIONS: Senghor's prose tale "Mandabi" was adapted for film by Ousmane Sembene.

BIOGRAPHICAL/CRITICAL SOURCES:

BOOKS

Blair, Dorothy S., *African Literature in French,* Cambridge University Press, 1976.

Bureau de Documentation de la Presidence de la Republique, *Leopold Sedar Senghor: Bibliographie,* 2nd edition, Fondation Leopold Sedar Senghor, 1982.

Contemporary Literary Criticism, Volume 54, Gale, 1989.

Crowder, Michael, *Senegal: A Study in French Assimilation Policy,* Oxford University Press, 1962.

Guibert, Armand, *Leopold Sedar Senghor: L'Homme et l'oeuvre,* Presence Africaine, 1962.

Hymans, Jacques Louis, *Leopold Sedar Senghor: An Intellectual Biography,* University Press, Edinburgh, 1971.

Markovitz, Irving Leonard, *Leopold Sedar Senghor and the Politics of Negritude,* Atheneum, 1969.

Mezu, Sebastian Okechuwu, *The Poetry of Leopold Sedar Senghor,* Fairleigh Dickinson University Press, 1973.

Moore, Gerald, *Seven African Writers,* Oxford University Press, 1962.

Neikirk, Barend van Dyk Van, *The African Image (Negritude) in the Work of Leopold Sedar Senghor,* A. A. Balkema 1970.

Rous, Jean, *Leopold Sedar Senghor,* J. Didier, 1968.

PERIODICALS

Black World, August 14, 1978.
Ebony, August, 1972.
Essence, September, 1987.
French Review, May, 1982.
Saturday Review, January 2, 1965.
Time, June 9, 1978, January 16, 1984.
Times Literary Supplement, June 11, 1964.

World Literature Today, spring, 1965, autumn, 1978, summer, 1981, winter, 1985.

* * *

SEPHERIADES, Georgios
   See SEFERIADES, Giorgos Stylianou

* * *

SETIEN, Miguel Delibes
   See DELIBES SETIEN, Miguel

* * *

SEUSS, Dr.
   See GEISEL, Theodor Seuss

* * *

SEXTON, Anne (Harvey)   1928-1974

PERSONAL: Born November 9, 1928, in Newton, Mass.; died October 4, 1974, by her own hand, in Weston, Mass.; daughter of Ralph Churchill (a salesman) and Mary Grab (Staples) Harvey; married Alfred M. Sexton II (a salesman), August 16, 1948 (divorced, 1974); children: Linda Gray, Joyce Ladd. *Education:* Attended Garland Junior College, 1947-48.

ADDRESSES: Home—14 Black Oak Rd., Weston, Mass. 02193. *Agent*—Sterling Lord, 75 East 55th St., New York, N.Y. 10022.

CAREER: Fashion model in Boston, Mass., 1950-51; Wayland High School, Wayland, Mass., teacher, 1967-68; Boston University, Boston, lecturer in creative writing, 1970-71, professor of creative writing, 1972-74; writer. Scholar, Radcliffe Institute for Independent Study, 1961-63; Crawshaw Professor of Literature, Colgate University, 1972. Gave numerous poetry readings at colleges and universities.

MEMBER: Poetry Society of America, Royal Society of Literature (fellow), New England Poetry Club, Phi Beta Kappa (honorary member).

AWARDS, HONORS: Audience Poetry Prize, 1958-59; Robert Frost fellowship at Bread Loaf Writers Conference, 1959; Levinson Prize, *Poetry,* 1962; American Academy of Arts and Letters traveling fellowship, 1963-64; Ford Foundation grant for year's residence with professional theater, 1964-65; first literary magazine travel grant, Congress for Cultural Freedom, 1965-66; Shelley Memorial Award, 1967; Pulitzer Prize, 1967, for *Live or Die;* Guggenheim fellowship, 1969; Litt.D. from Tufts University, 1970, Regis College, 1971, and Fairfield University, 1971.

WRITINGS:

POETRY

To Bedlam and Part Way Back, Houghton, 1960.
All My Pretty Ones (also see below), Houghton, 1962.
Selected Poems, Oxford University Press, 1964.
Live or Die (also see below), Houghton, 1966.
(With Thomas Kinsella and Douglas Livingstone) *Poems,* Oxford University Press, 1968.
Love Poems (also see below), Houghton, 1969.
Transformations, Houghton, 1971.
The Book of Folly, Houghton, 1972.
O Ye Tongues, Rainbow Press, 1973.
The Death Notebooks, Houghton, 1974.
The Awful Rowing toward God, Houghton, 1975.

45 Mercy Street, edited by daughter, Linda Gray Sexton, Houghton, 1976.
The Heart of Anne Sexton's Poetry (contains *All My Pretty Ones, Live or Die,* and *Love Poems*), three volumes, Houghton, 1977.
Words for Dr. Y: Uncollected Poems with Three Stories, edited by L. G. Sexton, Houghton, 1978.
The Complete Poems, Houghton, 1981.
Selected Poems of Anne Sexton, edited by Diane W. Middlebrook and Diana H. George, Houghton, 1988.
Love Poems of Anne Sexton, Houghton, 1989.

OTHER

(With Maxine W. Kumin) *Eggs of Things* (juvenile), Putnam, 1963.
(With Kumin) *More Eggs of Things* (juvenile), Putnam, 1964.
45 Mercy Street (play; first produced Off-Broadway at American Place Theatre, October 11, 1969), edited by L. G. Sexton, Houghton, 1976.
(With Kumin) *Joey and the Birthday Present* (juvenile), McGraw, 1971.
(With Kumin) *The Wizard's Tears* (juvenile), McGraw, 1975.
Anne Sexton: A Self Portrait in Letters (correspondence), edited by L. G. Sexton and Lois Ames, Houghton, 1977.
No Evil Star: Selected Essays, Interviews, and Prose, edited by Steven E. Colburn, University of Michigan Press, 1985.

Poems represented in numerous anthologies. Contributor to many magazines, including *Harper's, New Yorker, Partisan Review, Saturday Review,* and *Nation.*

SIDELIGHTS: Much of Anne Sexton's poetry is autobiographical and concentrates on her deeply personal feelings, especially anguish. In particular, many of her poems record her battles with mental illness. She spent many years in psychoanalysis, including several long stays in mental hospitals. As she told Beatrice Berg, her writing began, in fact, as therapy: "My analyst told me to write between our sessions about what I was feeling and thinking and dreaming." Her analyst, impressed by her work, encouraged her to keep writing, and then, she told Berg, she saw (on television) "I. A. Richards [a poet and literary critic] describing the form of a sonnet and I thought maybe I could do that. Oh, I was turned on. I wrote two or three a day for about a year." Eventually, Sexton's poems about her psychiatric struggles were gathered in *To Bedlam and Part Way Back* which recounts, as James Dickey wrote, the experiences "of madness and near-madness, of the pathetic, well-meaning, necessarily tentative and perilous attempts at cure, and of the patient's slow coming back into the human associations and responsibilities which the old, previous self still demands."

This kind of poetry, which unveils the poet's innermost feelings, is usually termed confessional poetry, and it is the subject of much critical controversy. A *Times Literary Supplement* reviewer, for example, said of *Live or Die* that "many of Mrs. Sexton's new poems are arresting, but such naked psyche-baring makes demands which cannot always be met. Confession may be good for the soul, but absolution is not the poet's job, nor the reader's either." A *Punch* critic added, "When her artistic control falters the recital of grief and misery becomes embarrassing, the repetitive material starts to grow tedious, the poetic gives way to the clinical and the confessional." Many reviewers raised at least two questions. First, should her poetry be classified as confessional? Second, does her work consistently demonstrate the artistic control which many critics feel is an essential quality of good poetry?

Concerning the first question, Erica Jong objects to the classification: "Whenever Anne Sexton's poems are mentioned, the term 'confessional poetry' is not far behind. It has always seemed a silly and unilluminating term to me; one of those pigeonholing categories critics invent so as not to talk about poetry as poetry. . . . The mind of the creator is all-important, and the term 'confessional' seems to undercut this, implying that anyone who spilled her guts would be a poet." Sexton also often denigrated the term, but at times she applied it to herself. She told Berg that "for years I railed against being put in this category. Then . . . I decided I was the only confessional poet." Moreover, in an interview with Patricia Marx, Sexton discussed the effect on her work of another poet often called confessional, W. D. Snodgrass, and acknowledged the confessional quality of her writing: "If anything influenced me it was W. D. Snodgrass' *Heart's Trouble*. . . . It so changed me, and undoubtedly it must have influenced my poetry. At the same time everyone said, 'You can't write this way. It's too personal; it's confessional; you can't write this, Anne,' and everyone was discouraging me. But then I saw Snodgrass doing what I was doing, and it kind of gave me permission."

The second question is perhaps best answered in critics' specific responses to several of her individual books. Like many of Sexton's volumes, *To Bedlam and Part Way Back* received a mixed response. Dickey praised the subject of the work, but found that "the poems fail to do their subject the kind of justice which I should like to see done. . . . As they are they lack concentration, and above all the profound, individual linguistic suggestibility and accuracy that poems must have to be good." On the other hand, Melvin Maddocks believed that "Mrs. Sexton's remarkable first book of poems has the personal urgency of a first novel. It is full of the exact flavors of places and peoples remembered, familiar patterns of life recalled and painstakingly puzzled over. . . . A reader finally judges Mrs. Sexton's success by the extraordinary sense of first-hand experience he too has been enabled to feel." Barbara Howes thinks that many of the poems are flawed, but overall she judged *Bedlam* "an honest and impressive achievement."

All My Pretty Ones also garnered mixed reviews. Peter Davison found one poem, "The Operation," "absolutely superb," but he felt that none of the others are nearly as good. Dickey's critique was even stronger: "Miss Sexton's work seems to me very little more than a kind of terribly serious and determinedly outspoken soap-opera." Yet in an essay on both *Bedlam* and *Pretty Ones*, Beverly Fields argued that Sexton's poetry is mostly misread. She contended that the poems are not as autobiographical as they seem, that they are poems, not memoirs, and she went on to analyze many of them in depth in order to show the recurrent symbolic themes and poetic techniques that she felt make Sexton's work impressive.

Dissent among the reviewers continued with the appearance of *Live or Die,* Sexton's best known book. A *Virginia Quarterly Review* critic believed that Sexton was "a very talented poet" who was perhaps too honest: "Confession, while good for the soul, may become tiresome for the reader if not accompanied by the suggestion that something is being held back. . . . In [*Live or Die*] Miss Sexton's toughness approaches affectation. Like a drunk at a party who corners us with the story of his life, . . . the performance is less interesting the third time, despite the poet's high level of technical competence." Joel O. Conarroe, however, had a more positive view of Sexton's candor. "Miss Sexton is an interior voyager," commented Conarroe, "describing in sharp images the difficult discovered landmarks of her own inner landscape. . . . Poem after poem focuses on the

nightmare obsessions of the damned: suicide, crucifixion, the death of others . . ., fear, the humiliations of childhood, the boy-child she never had. . . . It is, though, through facing up to the reality (and implications) of these things that the poet, with her tough honesty, is able to gain a series of victories over them. . . . All in all, this is a fierce, terrible, beautiful book, well deserving its Pulitzer award."

Transformations, a retelling of Grimm's fairy tales, marked a shift away from the confessional manner of her earlier work, which several commentators found to be a fruitful change. Gail Pool, for example, contended that the tales provided Sexton with "a rich medium for her colorful imagery," a distance from her characters which allowed wit, an eerie realm "where she had always been her sharpest," and "the structure she needed and so often had difficulty imposing on her own work. At last she had found material to which she could bring her intelligence, her wit, all that she knew, and she created, in Stanley Kunitz's words, 'a wild, blood-curdling, astonishing book.' " Christopher Lehmann-Haupt echoed Pool's analysis, arguing that Sexton's earlier work tended to lack control, that perhaps she worked too closely with firsthand experience. Lehmann-Haupt continued, "by using the artificial as the raw material of *Transformations* and working her way backwards to the immediacy of her personal vision, she draws her readers in more willingly, and thereby makes them more vulnerable to her sudden plunges into personal nightmare." Similarly, Louis Coxe discovers a new objectivity and distance in *Transformations,* which he considers "a growth of the poet's mind and strength."

In *The Death Notebooks, The Awful Rowing toward God,* and *45 Mercy Street,* the last two published posthumously, Sexton returned to the confessional method. While these books have been praised, they have also been more severely criticized than her early writings, many readers detecting a deterioration in quality. William Heyen remarked that Sexton's "poems went almost 'steadily downhill, became less intense, less dramatic, less interesting as one book followed another. . . . There were moments, occasional lines or even poems that wept or raged with her old power," but overall her voice became often "maudlin or patently melodramatic or simply silly." Heyen added that *Awful Rowing* continues the downward trend; it is touching, "but it's not very good." Robert Mazzocco seconded Heyen, commenting that while the early poems "depict intensely introverted states in highly extroverted style" and are well constructed, the later poems "seem to me less commanding, strike dissonant strains, chromatize the keyboard, or become programmatic." In like manner, Patricia Meyer Spacks argued that Sexton's poems become more and more sentimental in that they overindulge in emotion and fail to evaluate that emotion. The sentimentalism becomes "painfully marked" in *Awful Rowing,* "with its embarrassments of religious pretension. . . . The problem of internal division, the perception of divinity, the will to rebuild the soul: all alike register unconvincingly. The poetry through which these vast themes are rendered is simply not good enough."

On the other hand, not all critics disparaged the later books. In a response to Spacks's critique, Jong commented: "Let's be fair about Sexton's poetry. She was uneven and excessive, but that was because she dared to be a fool and dared to explore the dark side of the unconscious." Moreover, Sandra M. Gilbert believed that *The Death Notebooks* "goes far beyond [the earlier volumes] in making luminous art out of the night thoughts that have haunted this poet for so long." Finally, Jong, in a review of *Notebooks,* assessed Sexton's poetic significance and contended that her artistry is often overlooked: "She is an important poet not only because of her courage in dealing with previously forbidden subjects, but because she can make the language sing. Of what does [her] artistry consist? Not just of her skill in writing traditional poems. . . . But by artistry, I mean something more subtle than the ability to write formal poems. I mean the artist's sense of where her inspiration lies. . . . There are many poets of great talent who never take that talent anywhere. . . . They write poems which any number of people might have written. When Anne Sexton is at the top of her form, she writes a poem which no one else could have written."

MEDIA ADAPTATIONS: A stage production entitled ". . . about Anne" and based on a compilation of Sexton's poems was produced in Los Angeles in 1986.

BIOGRAPHICAL/CRITICAL SOURCES:

BOOKS

Concise Dictionary of American Literary Biography: The New Consciousness, 1941-1968, Gale, 1987.
Contemporary Authors Bibliographical Series, Gale, Volume 2, 1986.
Contemporary Literary Criticism, Gale, Volume 2, 1974, Volume 4, 1975, Volume 6, 1976, Volume 8, 1978, Volume 10, 1979, Volume 15, 1980, Volume 53, 1989.
Dictionary of Literary Biography, Volume 5: *American Poets since World War II,* Gale, 1980.
George, Diana Hume, *Oedipus Anne: The Poetry of Anne Sexton,* University of Illinois Press, 1987.
Hungerford, Edward, editor, *Poets in Progress,* Northwestern University, 1967.
McClatchy, J. D., editor, *Anne Sexton: The Artist and Her Critics,* Indiana University Press, 1978.
Northouse, Cameron and Thomas P. Walsh, *Sylvia Plath and Anne Sexton: A Reference Guide,* G. K. Hall, 1974.
Phillips, Robert, *The Confessional Poets,* Southern Illinois University Press, 1973.

PERIODICALS

Atlantic, November, 1962.
Centennial Review, spring, 1975.
Christian Science Monitor, September 1, 1960.
Concerning Poetry, spring, 1974.
Epoch, fall, 1960.
Harper's, September, 1963.
Hollins Critic, June, 1984.
Hudson Review, winter, 1965-66.
Los Angeles Times, May 3, 1986.
Moons and Lion Tailes, Volume 2, number 2, 1976.
Ms., March, 1974.
Nation, February 23, 1963, September 14, 1974, November 21, 1981.
New Boston Review, spring, 1978.
New Republic, November 22, 1969, October 16, 1971, November 11, 1981.
Newsday, March 23, 1975.
New Statesman, June 16, 1967.
New Yorker, April 27, 1963.
New York Review of Books, June 6, 1968.
New York Times, March 8, 1969, October 28, 1969, November 2, 1969, November 9, 1969, September 27, 1971, May 18, 1988.
New York Times Book Review, April 28, 1963, May 30, 1976, July 25, 1976, November 26, 1978, October 18, 1981.
Observer Review, May 14, 1967.
Paris Review, spring, 1971.
Parnassus: Poetry in Review, Volumes 12-13, numbers 1-2, 1985.

Poetry, February, 1961, May, 1967.
Punch, July 5, 1967.
Reporter, January 3, 1963.
Saturday Review, December 31, 1966.
Shenandoah, summer, 1967.
Times Literary Supplement, May 18, 1967.
Village Voice, November 6, 1969.
Virginia Quarterly Review, winter, 1967.
Washington Post Book World, November 22, 1981.

OBITUARIES:

PERIODICALS

AB Bookman's Weekly, December 2, 1974.
New York Times, October 6, 1974.
Publishers Weekly, October 28, 1974.
Time, October 14, 1974.
Washington Post, October 6, 1974.

*   *   *

SHACKLETON, C. C.
See ALDISS, Brian W(ilson)

*   *   *

SHAFFER, Peter (Levin) 1926-
(Peter Anthony, a joint pseudonym)

PERSONAL: Born May 15, 1926, in Liverpool, England; son of Jack (a realtor) and Reka (Fredman) Shaffer. *Education:* Trinity College, Cambridge, B.A., 1950. *Politics:* Conservative anarchist. *Religion:* Humanist.

ADDRESSES: Home—173 Riverside Dr., New York, N.Y. 10024.

CAREER: Playwright and critic. Worked in the New York Public Library, New York, N.Y., 1951-54, and for Bosey & Hawkes (music publishers), London, England, 1954-55; literary critic for *Truth,* 1956-57; music critic for *Time and Tide,* 1961-62. *Wartime service:* Served as a conscript in coal mines in England, 1944-47.

MEMBER: Dramatists Guild, Garrick Club (London).

AWARDS, HONORS: Evening Standard Drama Award, 1958, and New York Drama Critics Circle Award, 1960, both for *Five Finger Exercise;* Antoinette Perry Award (Tony), Outer Critics Circle Award, and New York Drama Critics Circle Award, all 1975, all for *Equus;* Tony Award, 1980, and best play of the year award from *Plays and Players,* both for *Amadeus;* New York Film Critics Circle Award, 1984, Los Angeles Film Critics Association Award, 1984, and Academy Award of Merit (Oscar) from the Academy of Motion Picture Arts and Sciences, 1985, all for screenplay adaptation of *Amadeus;* named Commander of the British Empire, 1987.

WRITINGS:

PLAYS

Five Finger Exercise (also see below; first produced on the West End at the Comedy Theatre, July 16, 1958; produced on Broadway at the Music Box Theater, December 2, 1959), Hamish Hamilton, 1958, Harcourt, 1959.
The Private Ear [and] *The Public Eye* (also see below; two one-acts; first produced on the West End at the Globe Theatre, May 10, 1962; produced on Broadway at the Morosco The-

atre, October 9, 1963), Hamish Hamilton, 1962, Stein & Day, 1964.

"The Merry Rooster's Panto," first produced on the West End at Wyndham's Theatre, December, 1963.

The Royal Hunt of the Sun: A Play Concerning the Conquest of Peru (first produced by the National Theatre Co. at the Chichester Festival, July 7, 1964; produced on Broadway at the ANTA Theatre, October 26, 1965), Samuel French (London), 1964, Stein & Day, 1965.

"A Warning Game," first produced in New York, 1967.

Black Comedy (also see below; one-act; first produced by the National Theatre Co. at the Chichester Festival, July 27, 1965; produced on Broadway at the Ethel Barrymore Theatre with "White Lies" [also see below], February 12, 1967; produced on the West End at the Lyric Theatre as "Black Comedy and The White Liars" [also see below], 1968), Samuel French, 1967.

The White Liars, Samuel French, 1967.

Black Comedy [and] *White Lies,* Stein & Day, 1967 (published in England as *The White Liars* [and] *Black Comedy,* Hamish Hamilton, 1968).

"It's about Cinderella," first produced in London, 1969.

Equus (also see below; first produced by the National Theatre Co. on the West End at the Old Vic Theatre, July 26, 1973; produced on Broadway at the Plymouth Theater, October 24, 1974), Deutsch, 1973, Samuel French, 1974.

Shrivings (also see below; three-act; first produced on the West End at the Lyric Theatre as "The Battle of Shrivings," February 5, 1970), Deutsch, 1974.

Equus [and] *Shrivings,* Atheneum, 1974.

Three Plays (contains *Five Finger Exercise, Shrivings,* and *Equus*), Penguin, 1976.

Four Plays, Penguin, 1981.

Amadeus (also see below; first produced on the West End by the National Theatre Co. at the Olivier Theatre, November 2, 1979; produced on Broadway at the Broadhurst Theater, December 17, 1980), Deutsch, 1980, Harper, 1981.

Collected Plays of Peter Shaffer, Crown, 1982.

"Yonadab: The Watcher," first produced on the West End by the National Theatre Co. at the Olivier Theatre, December 4, 1985, published as *Yonadab: A Play,* Harper, 1988.

"Lettice and Lovage," first produced on the West End at the Globe Theatre, 1987; produced on Broadway at the Ethel Barrymore Theater, March 25, 1990.

NOVELS; WITH BROTHER, ANTHONY SHAFFER

(Under joint pseudonym Peter Anthony) *Woman in the Wardrobe,* Evans Brothers, 1951.

(Under joint pseudonym Peter Anthony) *How Doth the Little Crocodile?,* Evans Brothers, 1952, published under names Peter Shaffer and Anthony Shaffer, Macmillan, 1957.

Withered Murder, Gollancz, 1955, Macmillan, 1956.

SCREENPLAYS

(With Peter Brook) "Lord of the Flies," Walter Reade, 1963.

"The Pad (and How to Use It)" (adaptation of *The Private Ear*), Universal, 1966.

"Follow Me!," Universal, 1971.

"The Public Eye" (based on Shaffer's play of the same title), Universal, 1972.

"Equus," United Artists, 1977.

"Amadeus," Orion Pictures, 1984.

TELEVISION PLAYS

"The Salt Land," Independent Television Network, 1955.

"Balance of Terror," British Broadcasting Corp., 1957.

RADIO PLAYS

"The Prodigal Father," British Broadcasting Corp., 1955.

OTHER

Contributor of articles to periodicals, including *Theatre Arts, Atlantic, Encore,* and *Sunday Times.*

SIDELIGHTS: "Whatever else Peter Shaffer may lack, it isn't courage, it isn't derring-do. His plays traverse the centuries and the globe, raising questions that have perplexed minds from Job to Samuel Beckett," Benedict Nightingale writes in the *New York Times.* Shaffer examines the conflict between atheism and religion in "The Royal Hunt of the Sun," the nature of sanity and insanity in modern society in "Equus," the role of genius in "Amadeus," and Old Testament ethics in "Yonadab: The Watcher." These epic plays are always a visual spectacle, but some critics feel that Shaffer's spectacles mask superficial stories. *Newsweek* contributor Jack Kroll characterizes the typical Shaffer play as "a large-scale, large-voiced treatment of large themes, whose essential superficiality is masked by a skillful theatricality reinforced by . . . extraordinary acting." Despite such criticism, Shaffer's plays are enormously popular—both "Equus" and "Amadeus" had Broadway runs of more than one thousand performances each.

Shaffer's first major success was "The Royal Hunt of the Sun," based on Francisco Pizarro's sixteenth-century expedition to the Incan Empire of Peru. To force the Incan people to give him the gold he desired, Pizarro took their leader, Atahuallpa, prisoner. But Atahuallpa refused to concede defeat and the resulting battle between Pizarro's forces and the Incan Indians proved disastrous for his people. In the ensuing battle, Atahuallpa is killed. But Pizarro had befriended the Incan leader. When Atahuallpa dies, Pizarro renounces Catholicism to adopt the Incan religion.

"The Royal Hunt of the Sun" is considered unique because of its historical subject and its stylized theatrical techniques, including mime and adaptations of Japanese Kabuki theater. To enhance the visual spectacle of the play, Shaffer specified that the Indians wear dramatic Incan funeral masks during Atahuallpa's death scene; many in the audience later claimed to have seen the masks change expression during the production. "They hadn't, of course," Shaffer told Richard Schickel in *Time.* "But the audience invested so much emotion in play that it looked as if they had."

Despite this positive emotional response from audiences, critics feel the play's language and theatrical devices are not effective. *Drama* critic Ronald Hayman thinks that Shaffer borrows from so many different traditions and uses so many theatrical devices that "instead of unifying to contribute to the same effect, the various elements make their effects separately and some of them are superfluous and distracting." Warren Sylvester Smith in the *Dictionary of Literary Biography* indicates that the language "sometimes fail[s] to achieve the magnitude of the characters or to match the scope of the events." And Hayman faults the dialogue for being "lustreless, tumbling into cliches and even pleonasms like 'trapped in time's cage' when nothing less than poetry would take the strain Shaffer is putting on it."

But other critics, and many playgoers, had a more generous response to "The Royal Hunt of the Sun." These reviewers mention that the elaborate sets and costumes, the epic story, and the innovative rendition of history were exciting additions to the contemporary dramatic scene. John Russell Taylor writes in *Peter Shaffer* that as a "piece of sheer theatrical machinery the play is impeccable." He concludes that "The Royal Hunt of the Sun" is "at once a spectacular drama and a thinkpiece."

In Shaffer's 1973 play, "Equus," he confronts the question of sanity in the modern world. Despite its morbid focus, "Equus" was so well-liked that the opening-night Broadway audience gave it a five-minute standing ovation. "It's never happened to me before," Shaffer told Schickel. "I cry every time I think about it." "Equus" is based on a newspaper report of a boy who blinded several horses in a north England stable. The play revolves around psychiatrist Martin Dysart's treatment of the boy, Alan Strang, for the offense he committed.

During his examination of the boy, Dysart discovers that Strang is a pagan who believes that horses are gods. Therefore, when a stable girl attempts to seduce him in front of the horses, Strang is impotent. In frustrated rage that they have seen his failure, Strang blinds the horses. Dysart tries to treat him in a conventional manner, but eventually finds that he prefers Strang's primitive passion to his own rational, controlled personality. Brendan Gill notes in the *New Yorker* that Dysart "poses questions that go beyond the sufficiently puzzling matter of the boy's conduct to the infinitely puzzling matter of why, in a world charged with insanity, we should seek to 'cure' anyone in the name of sanity."

"Equus" brought complaints from some reviewers who argue that it superficially portrays insanity and psychoanalysis. "Equus," John Simon suggests in *New York*, "falls into that category of worn-out whimsy wherein we are told that insanity is more desirable, admirable, or just saner than sanity." *Commentary* contributor Jack Richardson states that "Equus" seems to be a "perfect case-study in the mediocrity of insight necessary nowadays for a play to enjoy a popular reputation for profundity." Simon concludes that no "amount of external embellishment can overcome the hollowness within."

Other reviewers feel that because of the enthusiastic audience response to the play, "Equus" may be depicting a significant trend in modern society. Gerald Weals reports in *Commonweal* that "Equus" "clearly touches a nerve in the New York audience, as it did earlier in London, which means that it is something more serious . . . than the effectively theatrical play it so obviously is. . . . *Equus,* it seems, is more than a highclass melodrama. It is a cry for the power of irrationality. Or an echo."

Shaffer's next play, "Amadeus," is based on the life of eighteenth-century composer Wolfgang Amadeus Mozart. Richard Christiansen of the *Chicago Tribune* believes that the characters in "Amadeus" and "Equus" are similar, remarking that "here again, as in 'Equus,' an older, learned man of the world is struck and amazed by the wild inspiration of a much younger man who seemingly is possessed with divine madness." The older man in "Amadeus" is Antonio Salieri, a second-rate composer who is consumed by jealousy because of young Mozart's greater talent.

Shaffer became interested in the rivalry between Mozart and Salieri upon reading material about Mozart's mysterious death. Shaffer at first suspected that Salieri may have murdered the composer, but further research proved this to be wrong. "But by then the cold eyes of Salieri were staring at me . . . ," Shaffer tells Roland Gelatt in the *Saturday Review.* "The conflict between virtuous mediocrity and feckless genius took hold of my imagination, and it would not leave me alone."

In "Amadeus," Salieri has made a bargain with God. He is to remain pious in return for being made the most popular composer of his time. As court composer in Vienna, Salieri is satisfied that his bargain with God has been kept. But then Mozart arrives at the court, playing music Salieri considers to be the finest he

has ever heard. And in contrast to Salieri's piety, Mozart is a moral abomination—a bastard, a womanizer, and an abrasive man with a scatological sense of humor. Salieri feels cheated and angry, and begins to sabotage Mozart's budding career by spreading rumors about him. These rumors, along with Mozart's contentious personality, serve to ostracize him from polite society and cause him to lose his pupils. Eventually Mozart becomes ill and dies, and the play asks whether he was killed by Salieri or died from natural causes.

"*Amadeus* . . . is about the ravaging of genius by mediocrity," Robert Brustein writes in the *New Republic.* Some critics believe Shaffer handled his material in much the same manner, charging him with a superficial portrayal of Mozart's life. Brustein argues that "at the same time that the central character—a second-rate kapellmeister named Antonio Salieri—is plotting against the life and reputation of a superior composer named Wolfgang Amadeus Mozart, a secondary playwright named Peter Shaffer is reducing this genius, one of the greatest artists of all time, to the level of a simpering, braying ninny."

Despite complaints from reviewers, audiences received "Amadeus" enthusiastically, and it played in many European cities. Bernard Levin, writing in the London *Times,* sums up the feelings of many theatergoers by writing that "those who go to ["Amadeus"] prepared to understand what it is about will have an experience that far transcends even its considerable value as drama." Impressed with the play's serious intentions, Gelatt writes that "*Amadeus* gives heartening evidence that there is still room for the play of ideas."

Perhaps Shaffer's most famous work is the screenplay adaptation of "Amadeus," written in collaboration with director Milos Forman and producer Saul Zaentz. This 1984 film won several coveted Academy Awards, including best screenplay adaptation and best picture of the year.

For the movie, Shaffer and his collaborators kept the basic story of the play, but changed several key points. For example, Shaffer tells Kakutani that in the play, Salieri had been "too much the observer of the calamities he should have been causing." In the movie, Salieri takes a more active role in Mozart's death. Vincent Canby comments in the *New York Times* that this new version of Salieri's character "may not be history, but it's the high point of this drama."

Another difference between the play and film is the way music is used. Shaffer and Forman thought music was very important to the film. Shaffer remarks to Kakutani: "In a way, Milos and I, as it were, met on that middle ground—he from film, I from the stage; he from the visual, I from the verbal. We met on ground that is neither visual nor verbal, but acoustic and abstract—we met there in music." The movie incorporated staged sequences from some of Mozart's operas and used Mozart's music in the entire soundtrack—things that were impossible to do in the play. The result, writes David Denby in *New York,* is "perhaps the juiciest dramatization in movie history of the emotional power of classical music."

"Amadeus" was filmed with Shaffer's characteristic visual spectacle in the centuries-old cathedrals and churches of Prague, Czechoslovakia. Geoff Brown comments in the London *Times* on the ambience of the production, writing that "so many films lie on the screen today looking shrivelled or inert; *Amadeus* sits there resplendent, both stately and supple, a compelling, darkly comic story of human glory and human infamy."

Critics voiced many of the same complaints with the movie that they had with the play, particularly attacking the supposed pretentiousness of the story. Jascha Kessler, for example, says in a radio broadcast for KUSC-FM, Los Angeles, that "Amadeus" offers us "a heavy dose of pseudoprofundities, in a formulation composed of nothing but worn-out truisms. . . . I think everyone who had anything to do with making ["Amadeus"], an example of cultural pretentiousness at its intellectual best today, ought to be ashamed."

Critic Richard A. Blake, however, writes in *America* that "Amadeus" was "the most powerful film I have seen in a long time" and praises the characters, setting, and music. In contrast to Kessler's finding, Blake believes that in the conflict between Salieri and Mozart "rests the plight of the human condition, that furious tension between what might be and what really is. For believers, there remains the question: Why is the Incarnation so capricious? Why does the spark of divinity glow in such unlikely crevices: dissolute artists, unbearable saints? . . . Salieri could not answer those questions, and they drove him to murder and insanity. Neither could Shaffer, and they drove him to drama."

In December of 1985, Shaffer's play "Yonadab: The Watcher" opened to mixed reviews. Based on the Old Testament account of King David's reign in ancient Jerusalem, the play focuses on court hanger-on Yonadab, who believes an ancient superstition that incest committed between members of the royal family promotes wisdom in government. He convinces Amnon, King David's son, to rape his own sister, Tamar. Commenting on the strikingly different subject matter of this play, Shaffer tells Higgins: "I never want to repeat myself, so it is essential to come up in a different place every time."

Although some critics express many of the same complaints about "Yonadab: The Watcher" that they have about previous Shaffer plays—historical inaccuracies, superficial treatment of theme, lack of character development—Shaffer remains undaunted. Dan Sullivan reports in the *Los Angeles Times* that Shaffer told Associated Press's Matt Wolf: "Audiences are very excited by the play; that's the main thing."

Audience reaction to 1987's "Lettice and Lovage" was also positive. Wolf writes in the *Chicago Tribune* that the play, "an overtly commercial, out-and-out comedy," was winning "nightly bravos and may even get an award or two." Shaffer wrote the play as a gift for actress Maggie Smith, who starred in his earlier work "Black Comedy" and plays the lead role of Lettice.

The fact that audiences are excited by Shaffer's plays is a testament to his popularity and staying power. Smith concludes that though Shaffer is sometimes slighted by critics, "none of [his] imputed failings has inhibited the lines at the box office or deterred serious theatergoers from expressing gratitude for the revitalization [he] has brought to contemporary drama."

MEDIA ADAPTATIONS: "The Royal Hunt of the Sun" was filmed by CBS's Cinema Center Films; "Five Finger Exercise" was filmed by Columbia in 1962.

BIOGRAPHICAL/CRITICAL SOURCES:

BOOKS

Brustein, Robert, *The Third Theatre,* Knopf, 1969.
Contemporary Literary Criticism, Gale, Volume V, 1976, Volume XIV, 1980, Volume XVIII, 1981, Volume XXXVII, 1986.
Dictionary of Literary Biography, Volume XIII: *British Dramatists since World War II,* Gale, 1982.
Lumley, Frederick, *New Trends in 20th Century Drama,* Oxford University Press, 1967.
McCrindle, J. F., editor, *Behind the Scenes,* Holt, 1971.

Taylor, John Russell, *Anger and After,* Methuen, 1962.
Taylor, John Russell, *Peter Shaffer,* Longman, 1974.

PERIODICALS

America, October 13, 1984.
American Imago, fall, 1974.
Chicago Tribune, March 7, 1983, September 19, 1984, November 15, 1987.
Commentary, February, 1975.
Commonweal, April 25, 1975.
Drama, autumn, 1970, January, 1980.
Encounter, January, 1975.
Film Comment, September/October, 1984, January/February, 1985.
Globe and Mail (Toronto), June 13, 1987.
Guardian, August 6, 1973.
Harper's, July, 1981.
Hudson Review, summer, 1967.
Listener, February 12, 1970, December 12, 1985.
Los Angeles Times, December 10, 1982.
Modern Drama, September, 1978, March, 1985.
Monthly Film Bulletin, January, 1985.
Nation, February 27, 1967, January 17, 1981.
National Review, October 19, 1984.
New Leader, February 27, 1967.
New Republic, January 17, 1981, October 22, 1984.
New Statesman, February 13, 1970.
Newsweek, February 20, 1967, November 4, 1974, December 29, 1980.
New York, November 11, 1974, September 24, 1984.
New Yorker, February 25, 1967, November 4, 1974, March 10, 1980, December 29, 1980.
New York Times, September 29, 1968, December 23, 1979, December 18, 1980, September 16, 1984, September 19, 1984, December 22, 1985, February 13, 1987, March 26, 1990.
New York Times Magazine, August 17, 1973, October 25, 1974, October 27, 1974, April 13, 1975.
Observer, February 25, 1968, December 8, 1985.
Partisan Review, spring, 1966.
Plays and Players, November, 1979, February, 1980.
Punch, February 28, 1968.
Reporter, March 9, 1967.
Saturday Review, February 25, 1967, February, 1981.
South Atlantic Quarterly, autumn, 1980.
Spectator, March 1, 1968.
Time, November 11, 1974, December 29, 1980.
Times (London), January 9, 1985, January 18, 1985, November 28, 1985, December 6, 1985, November 17, 1988.
Vogue, March 15, 1967.
Washington Post, July 5, 1979, November 9, 1980, November 13, 1980, November 23, 1980, March 26, 1990.

OTHER

Kessler, Jascha, "Peter Shaffer: 'Amadeus,'" broadcast on KUSC-FM, Los Angeles, Calif., October 12, 1984.

*   *   *

SHANGE, Ntozake 1948-

PERSONAL: Original name Paulette Williams; name changed in 1971; name pronounced "En-to-zaki Shong-gay"; born October 18, 1948, in Trenton, N.J.; daughter of Paul T. (a surgeon) and Eloise (a psychiatric social worker and educator) Williams; married second husband, David Murray (a musician), July, 1977 (divorced). *Education:* Barnard College, B.A. (with honors),

1970; University of Southern California, Los Angeles, M.A., 1973; graduate study, University of Southern California.

ADDRESSES: Office—Department of Drama, University of Houston—University Park, 4800 Calhoun Rd., Houston, Tex. 77004.

CAREER: Writer and performer. Faculty member in women's studies, California State College, Sonoma Mills College, and the University of California Extension, 1972-75; artist in residence, New Jersey State Council on the Arts; creative writing instructor, City College of New York; associate professor of drama, University of Houston, beginning in 1983. Lecturer at Douglass College, 1978, and at many other institutions, such as Yale University, Howard University, Detroit Art Institute, and New York University. Dancer with Third World Collective, Raymond Sawyer's Afro-American Dance Company, Sounds in Motion, West Coast Dance Works, and For Colored Girls Who Have Considered Suicide (Shange's own dance company); has appeared in Broadway and Off-Broadway productions of her own plays, including "For Colored Girls Who Have Considered Suicide/When the Rainbow Is Enuf," and "Where the Mississippi Meets the Amazon." Director of several productions including "The Mighty Gents," produced by the New York Shakespeare Festival's Mobile Theatre, 1979, "A Photograph: A Study in Cruelty," produced in Houston's Equinox Theatre, 1979, and June Jordan's "The Issue" and "The Spirit of Sojourner Truth," 1979. Has given poetry readings.

MEMBER: Actors Equity, National Academy of Television Arts and Sciences, Dramatists Guild, PEN American Center, Academy of American Poets, Poets and Writers, Inc., Women's Institute for Freedom of the Press, New York Feminist Arts Guild.

AWARDS, HONORS: Obie Award, Outer Critics Circle Award, Audelco Award, Mademoiselle Award, and Tony, Grammy, and Emmy award nominations, all 1977, all for "For Color Girls Who Have Considered Suicide/When the Rainbow Is Enuf"; Frank Silvera Writers' Workshop Award, 1978; *Los Angeles Times* Book Prize for Poetry, 1981, for *Three Pieces;* Guggenheim fellowship, 1981; Medal of Excellence, Columbia University, 1981; Obie Award, 1981, for "Mother Courage and Her Children"; Pushcart Prize.

WRITINGS:

For Colored Girls Who Have Considered Suicide/When the Rainbow Is Enuf: A Choreopoem (first produced in New York City at Studio Rivbea, July 7, 1975; produced Off-Broadway at Anspacher Public Theatre, 1976; produced on Broadway at Booth Theatre, September 15, 1976), Shameless Hussy Press (San Lorenzo, Calif.), 1975, revised version, Macmillan, 1976.
Sassafrass (novella), Shameless Hussy Press, 1976.
Melissa & Smith, Bookslinger Editions, 1976.
"A Photograph: A Study of Cruelty" (poem-play), first produced Off-Broadway at Public Theatre, December 21, 1977, revised version, "A Photograph: Lovers in Motion" (also see below), produced in Houston, Texas, at the Equinox Theatre, November, 1979.
(With Thulani Nkabinde and Jessica Hagedorn) "Where the Mississippi Meets the Amazon," first produced in New York City at Public Theatre Cabaret, December 18, 1977.
Natural Disasters and Other Festive Occasions (prose poems), Heirs, 1977.
Nappy Edges (poems), St. Martin's, 1978.

Boogie Woogie Landscapes (play; also see below; first produced in New York City at Frank Silvera Writers' Workshop, June, 1979, produced on Broadway at the Symphony Space Theatre, produced in Washington, D.C., at the Kennedy Center), St. Martin's, 1978.
"Spell #7: A Geechee Quick Magic Trance Manual" (play; also see below), produced on Broadway at Joseph Papp's New York Shakespeare Festival Public Theater, July 15, 1979.
"Black and White Two Dimensional Planes" (play), first produced in New York City at Sounds in Motion Studio Works, February, 1979.
"Mother Courage and Her Children" (an adapted version of Bertolt Brecht's play), first produced Off-Broadway at the Public Theatre, April, 1980.
Three Pieces: Spell #7; A Photograph: Lovers in Motion; Boogie Woogie Landscapes (plays), St. Martin's, 1981.
A Photograph: Lovers in Motion, Samuel French, 1981.
Spell #7: A Theatre Piece in Two Acts, Samuel French, 1981.
Sassafrass, Cypress & Indigo: A Novel, St. Martin's, 1982.
"Three for a Full Moon" and "Bocas," first produced in Los Angeles, Calif., at the Mark Taper Forum Lab, Center Theatre, April 28, 1982.
(Adapter) Willy Russell, "Educating Rita" (play), first produced in Atlanta, Ga., by Alliance Theatre Company, 1982.
A Daughter's Geography (poems), St. Martin's, 1983.
See No Evil: Prefaces, Essays and Accounts, 1976-1983, Momo's Press, 1984.
From Okra to Greens: Poems, Coffee House Press, 1984.
From Okra to Greens: A Different Kinda Love Story; A Play with Music and Dance (first produced in New York City at Barnard College, November, 1978), Samuel French, 1985.
Betsey Brown: A Novel, St. Martin's, 1985.
"Three Views of Mt. Fuji" (play), first produced at the Lorraine Hansberry Theatre, June, 1987, produced in New York City at the New Dramatists, October, 1987.
Ridin' the Moon in Texas: Word Paintings (responses to art in prose and poetry), St. Martin's, 1987.

Also author of *Some Men* (poems in a pamphlet that resembles a dance card), 1981. Author of the play "Mouths" and the operetta "Carrie," both produced in 1981. Has written for a television special starring Diana Ross, and appears in a documentary about her own work for WGBH-TV. Contributor to periodicals, including *Black Scholar, Third World Women, Ms.,* and *Yardbird Reader.*

WORK IN PROGRESS: "In the Middle of a Flower," a play; a film adaptation of her novella *Sassafrass;* a novel.

SIDELIGHTS: Born to a surgeon and an educator, Ntozake Shange—originally named Paulette Williams—was raised with the advantages available to the black middle class. But one by one, the roles she chose for herself—including war correspondent and jazz musician—were dismissed as "no good for a woman," she told Stella Dong in a *Publishers Weekly* interview. She chose to become a writer because "there was nothing left." Frustrated and hurt after separating from her first husband, Shange attempted suicide several times before focusing her rage against the limitations society imposes on black women. While earning a master's degree in American Studies from the University of Southern California, she reaffirmed her personal strength based on a self-determined identity and took her African name, which means "she who comes with her own things" and she "who walks like a lion." Since then she has sustained a triple career as an educator, a performer/director in New York and Houston, and a writer whose works draw heavily on her experiences and the frustrations of being a black female in America.

"I am a war correspondent after all," she told Dong, "because I'm involved in a war of cultural and esthetic aggression. The front lines aren't always what you think they are."

Though she is an accomplished poet and an acclaimed novelist, Shange became famous for her play, "For Colored Girls Who Have Considered Suicide/When the Rainbow Is Enuf." A unique blend of poetry, music, dance and drama called a "choreopoem," it is still being produced around the country more than ten years after it "took the theater world by storm" in 1975. Before it won international acclaim, "For Colored Girls," notes Jacqueline Trescott in the *Washington Post,* "became an electrifying Broadway hit and provoked heated exchanges about the relationships between black men and women. When [it] debuted, [it] became the talk of literary circles. Its form—seven women on the stage dramatizing poetry—was a refreshing slap at the traditional, one-two-three-act structures." Whereas plays combining poetry and dance had already been staged by Adrienne Kennedy, Mel Gussow of the *New York Times* states that "Miss Shange was a pioneer in terms of her subject matter: the fury of black women at their double subjugation in white male America."

Shange's anger was not always so evident. "I was always what you call a nice child," she told *Time* magazine contributor Jean Vallely. "I did everything nice. I was the nicest and most correct. I did my homework. I was always on time. I never got into fights. People now ask me, 'Where did all this rage come from?' And I just smile and say it's been there all the time, but was just trying to be nice."

Shange's childhood was filled with music, literature, and art. Dizzy Gillespie, Miles Davis, Chuck Berry, and W. E. B. Du Bois were among the frequent guests at her parents' house. On Sunday afternoons Shange's family held variety shows. She recalled them in a self-interview published in *Ms.:* "my mama wd read from dunbar, shakespeare, countee cullen, t. s. eliot. my dad wd play congas & do magic tricks. my two sisters & my brother & i wd do a soft-shoe & then pick up the instruments for a quartet of some sort: a violin, a cello, flute & saxophone. we all read constantly. anything. anywhere. we also tore the prints outta art books to carry around with us. sounds/images, any explorations of personal visions waz the focus of my world."

However privileged her childhood might have seemed, Shange felt that she was "living a lie." As she explained to *Newsday* reviewer Allan Wallach: "[I was] living in a world that defied reality as most black people, or most white people, understood it—in other words, feeling that there was something that I could do, and then realizing that nobody was expecting me to do anything because I was colored and I was also female, which was not very easy to deal with."

Writing dramatic poetry became a means of expressing her dissatisfaction with the role of black women in society. She and a group of friends, including various musicians and the choreographer-dancer Paula Moss, would create improvisational works comprised of poetry, music, and dance, and they would frequently perform them in bars in San Francisco and New York. When Moss and Shange moved to New York City, they presented "For Colored Girls" at a Soho jazz loft, the Studio Rivbea. Director Oz Scott saw the show and helped develop the production as it was performed in bars on the Lower East Side. Impressed by one of these, black producer Woodie King, Jr., joined Scott to stage the choreopoem Off-Broadway at the New Federal Theatre, where it ran successfully from November, 1975, to the following June. Then Joseph Papp became the show's producer at the New York Shakespeare Festival's Anspacher Public The-

atre. From there, it moved to the Booth Theatre uptown. "The final production at the Booth is as close to distilled as any of us in all our art forms can make it," Shange says of that production in the introduction to *For Colored Girls,* published in 1976. "The cast is enveloping almost 6,000 people a week in the words of a young black girl's growing up, her triumphs and errors, [her] struggle to be all that is forbidden by our environment, all that is forfeited by our gender, all that we have forgotten."

In "For Colored Girls," poems dramatized by the women dancers recall encounters with their classmates, lovers, rapists, abortionists, and latent killers. The women survive the abuses and disappointments put upon them by the men in their lives and come to recognize in each other, dressed in the colors of Shange's personal rainbow, the promise of a better future. As one voice, at the end, they declare, "i found god in myself / and i loved her / . . . fiercely." To say this, remarks Carol P. Christ in *Diving Deep and Surfacing: Women Writers on Spiritual Quest,* is "to say . . . that it is all right to be a woman, that the Black woman does not have to imitate whiteness or depend on men for her power of being." "The poetry," says Marilyn Stasio in *Cue,* "touches some very tender nerve endings. Although roughly structured and stylistically unrefined, this fierce and passionate poetry has the power to move a body to tears, to rage, and to an ultimate rush of love."

While some reviewers are enthusiastic in their praise for the play, others are emphatically negative. "Some Black people, notably men, said that . . . Shange broke a taboo when her 'For Colored Girls . . .' took the theater world by storm," Connie Lauerman reports in the *Chicago Tribune.* "[Shange] was accused of racism, of 'lynching' the black male." But the playwright does not feel that she was bringing any black family secrets to light. She told Lauerman, "Half of what we discussed in 'For Colored Girls' about the dissipation of the family, rape, wife-battering and all that sort of thing, the U.S. Census Bureau already had. . . . We could have gone to the Library of Congress and read the Census reports and the crime statistics every month and we would know that more black women are raped than anyone else. We would know at this point that they think 48 per cent of our households are headed by single females. . . . My job as an artist is to say what I see."

If these conditions are unknown to some, Shange feels it is all the more important to talk about them openly. Defending her portrayal of the acquaintance who turned out to be a rapist, she told interviewer Claudia Tate that men who deal with the issues by saying they have never raped anyone trouble her: "Maybe we should have a Congressional hearing to find out if it's the UFOs who are raping women. . . . After all, that is a denial of reality. It does *not* matter if you did or did not do something. . . . When is someone going to take responsibility for what goes on where we live?" In the same interview, printed in *Black Women Writers at Work,* Shange explained that she wrote about Beau Willie Brown, a war veteran who is on drugs when he drops two small children off a high-rise balcony, because she "refuse[s] to be a part of this conspiracy of silence" regarding crimes that hurt black women.

Some feminist responses to the play were negative, reports *Village Voice* critic Michele Wallace, who suspects "that some black women are angry because 'For Colored Girls' exposes their fear of rejection as well as their anger at being rejected. They don't want to deal with that so they talk about how Shange is persecuting the black man." Sandra Hollin Flowers, author of the *Black American Literature Forum* article " 'Colored Girls': Textbook for the Eighties," finds most inappropriate the charges that

Shange portrays black men as stupidly crude and brutal. "Quite the contrary, Shange demonstrates a compassionate vision of black men—compassionate because though the work is not without anger, it has a certain integrity which could not exist if the author lacked a perceptive understanding of the crisis between black men and women. And there is definitely a crisis. . . . This, then is what makes *Colored Girls* an important work which ranks with [Ralph] Ellison's *Invisible Man,* [Richard] Wright's *Native Son,* and the handful of other black classics—it is an artistically successful female perspective on a long-standing issue among black people."

"Shange's poems aren't war cries," Jack Kroll writes *Newsweek* review of the Public Theatre production of "For Colored Girls." "They're outcries filled with a controlled passion against the brutality that blasts the lives of 'colored girls'—a phrase that in her hands vibrates with social irony and poetic beauty. These poems are political in the deepest sense, but there's no dogma, no sentimentality, no grinding of false mythic axes." Critic Edith Oliver of the *New Yorker* remarks: "The evening grows in dramatic power, encompassing, it seems, every feeling and experience a woman has ever had; strong and funny, it is entirely free of the rasping earnestness of projects of this sort. The verses and monologues that constitute the program have been very well chosen—contrasting in mood yet always subtly building."

While Wallace was not completely satisfied with "For Colored Girls" and complained of the occasional "worn-out feminist cliches," she was still able to commend Shange. She wrote: "There is so much about black women that needs retelling; one has to start somewhere, and Shange's exploration of this aspect of our experience, admittedly the most primitive (but we were all there at some time and, if the truth be told, most of us still are) is as good a place as any. All I'm saying is that Shange's 'For Colored Girls' should not be viewed as the definitive statement on black women, but as a very good beginning." She continued: "Very few have written with such clarity and honesty about the black woman's vulnerability and no one has ever brought Shange's brand of tough humor and realism to it."

Reviews of Shange's next production, "A Photograph: A Study of Cruelty," are less positive, although critics are generally impressed with the poetic quality of her writing. "Miss Shange is something besides a poet but she is not—at least not at this stage—a dramatist," Richard Eder declares in a *New York Times* review. "More than anything else, she is a troubadour. She declares her fertile vision of the love and pain between black women and black men in outbursts full of old malice and young cheerfulness. They are short outbursts, song-length; her characters are perceived in flashes, in illuminating vignettes."

Shange's next play, "Spell #7: A Geechee Quick Magic Trance Manual," more like "For Colored Girls" in structure, elicits a higher recommendation from Eder. Its nine characters in a New York bar discuss the racism black artists contend with in the entertainment world. At one point, the all-black cast appears in overalls and minstrel-show blackface to address the pressure placed on the black artist to fit a stereotype in order to succeed. "That's what happens to black people in the arts no matter how famous we become. . . . Black Theater is not moving forward the way people like to think it is. We're not free of our paint yet," Shange told Tate. "On another level, Spell #7 deals with the image of the black woman as a neutered workhorse, who is unwanted, unloved, and unattended by anyone," notes Elizabeth Brown in the *Dictionary Literary Biography.* "The emphasis is still on the experiences of the black woman but it is broadened and deepened, and it ventures more boldly across the sexual di-

vide," Eder writes in the *New York Times.* Don Nelson, writing in the *New York Daily News,* deems the show "black magic. . . . The word that best describes Shange's works, which are not plays in the traditional sense, is power."

To critics and producers who have complained that Shange's theater pieces do not present an easily marketable issue or point, Shange responds that a work's emotional impact should be enough. As she told Tate, "Our society allows people to be absolutely neurotic and totally out of touch with their feelings and everyone else's feelings, and yet be very respectable. This, to me, is a travesty. So I write to get at the part of people's emotional lives that they don't have control over, the part that can and will respond. . . . *For Colored Girls* for me is not an issue play. . . . There are just some people who are interesting. There's something there to make you feel intensely. Black writers have a right to do this," she said, although such works are not often rewarded with financial success. She names a number of successful plays that don't have a point except to celebrate being alive, and claims, "Black and Latin writers have to start demanding that the fact we're alive is point enough!" Furthermore, works which rely on emotional appeal reach a larger audience, she maintains in the same interview: "The kind of esteem that's given to brightness/smartness obliterates average people or slow learners from participating fully in human life. But you cannot exclude any human being from emotional participation."

Shange writes to fulfill a number of deeply felt responsibilities. Describing the genesis of *For Colored Girls,* for instance, Shange told Tate that she wrote its poems because she wanted young black women "to have information that I did not have. I wanted them to know what it was truthfully like to be a grown woman. . . . I don't want them to grow up in a void of misogynist lies." It is her commitment to break the silence of mothers who know, but don't tell their daughters, that "it's a dreadful proposition to lose oneself in the process of tending and caring for others," she said. The play "calls attention to how male-oriented black women . . . [and] women in general are," and how their self-esteem erodes when they allow themselves to be exploited, writes Tate. Says Shange, "When I die, I will not be guilty of having left a generation of girls behind thinking that anyone can tend to their emotional health other than themselves."

Speaking of her works in general, she said, "I think it was Adrienne Rich or Susan Griffin who said that one of our responsibilities as women writers is to discover the causes for our pain and to respect them. I think that much of the suffering that women and black people endure is not respected. I was also trained not to respect it. For instance, we're taught not to respect women who can't get their lives together by themselves. They have three children and a salary check for $200. The house is a mess; they're sort of hair-brained. We're taught not to respect their suffering. So I write about things that I know have never been given their full due. . . . I want people to at least understand or have the chance to see that *this* is a person whose life is not only valid but whose life is valiant. My responsibility is to be as honest as I can and to use whatever technical skills I may possess to make these experiences even clearer, or sharper, or more devastating or more beautiful." Women writers should also demand more respect for writing love poems, for seeing "the world in a way that allows us to care more about people than about military power. The power we see is the power to feed, the power to nourish and to educate. . . . It's part of our responsibility as writers to make these things important," Shange said.

Shange's poetry books, like her theater pieces, are distinctively original. *Nappy Edges,* containing fifty poems, is too long, says Harriet Gilbert in the *Washington Post Book World;* however, she claims, "nothing that Shange writes is ever entirely unreadable, springing, as it does, from such an intense honesty, from so fresh an awareness of the beauty of sound and of vision, from such mastery of words, from such compassion, humor and intelligence." Alice H. G. Phillips relates in the *Times Literary Supplement,* "Comparing herself to a jazzman 'takin a solo', she lets go with verbal runs and trills, mixes in syncopations, spins out evocative hanging phrases, variations on themes and refrains. Rarely does she come to a full stop, relying instead on line breaks, extra space breaking up a line, and/or oblique strokes. . . . She constantly tries to push things to their limit, and consequently risks seeming overenthusiastic, oversimplistic or merely undisciplined. . . . But at its best, her method can achieve both serious humour and deep seriousness."

In her poetry, Shange takes many liberties with the conventions of written English, using nonstandard spellings and punctuation. Some reviewers feel that these innovations present unnecessary obstacles to the interested readers of *Nappy Edges, A Daughter's Geography,* and *From Okra to Greens: Poems.* Explaining her "lower-case letters, slashes, and spelling" to Tate, she said that "poems where all the first letters are capitalized" bore her; "also, I like the idea that letters dance. . . . I need some visual stimulation, so that reading becomes not just a passive act and more than an intellectual activity, but demands rigorous participation." Her idiosyncratic punctuation assures her "that the reader is not in control of the process." She wants her words in print to engage the reader in a kind of struggle, and not be "whatever you can just ignore." The spellings, she said, "reflect language as I hear it. . . . The structure is connected to the music I hear beneath the words."

Shange's rejection of standard English serves deeper emotional and political purposes as well. In a *Los Angeles Times Book Review* article on Shange's *See No Evil: Prefaces, Essays and Accounts, 1976-1983,* Karl Keller relates, "[Shange] feels that as a black female performer/playwright/poet, she has wanted 'to attack deform n maim the language that i was taught to hate myself in. I have to take it apart to the bone.'" Speaking to Tate, she declared, "We do not have to refer continually to European art as the standard. That's absolutely absurd and racist, and I won't participate in that utter lie. My work is one of the few ways I can preserve the elements of our culture that need to be remembered and absolutely revered."

Shange takes liberties with the conventions of fiction writing with her first full-length novel, *Sassafrass, Cypress & Indigo.* "The novel is unusual in its form—a tapestry of narrative, poetry, magic spells, recipes and letters. Lyrical yet real, it also celebrates female stuff weaving, cooking, birthing babies," relates Lauerman. Its title characters are sisters who find different ways to cope with their love relationships Sassafrass attaches herself to Mitch, a musician who uses hard drugs and beats her; she leaves him twice, but goes back to him for another try. To male readers who called Mitch a "weak" male character, Shange replied to Lauerman, "[He] had some faults, but there's no way in the world you can say [he wasn't] strong. . . . I think you should love people with their faults That's what love's about." Cypress, a dancer in feminist productions, at first refuses to become romantically involved with any of her male friends. Indigo, the youngest sister, retreats into her imagination, befriending her childhood dolls, seeing only the poetry and magic of the world. The music she plays on her violin becomes a rejuvenating source for her mother and sisters. "Probably there is a little bit of all three sisters in Shange," Lauerman suggests, "though she says that her novel is not autobiographical but historical, culled from the experiences of blacks and from the 'information of my feelings.'"

Critics agree that Shange's poetry is more masterfully wrought than her fiction, yet they find much in the novel to applaud. Writes Doris Grumbach in the *Washington Post Book World,* "Shange is primarily a poet, with a blood-red sympathy for and love of her people, their folk as well as their sophisticated ways, their innocent, loving goodness as much as their lack of immunity to powerful evil. . . . But her voice in this novel is entirely her own, an original, spare and primary-colored sound that will remind readers of Jean Toomer's *Cane.*" In Grumbach's opinion, "Whatever Shange turns her hand to she does well, even to potions and recipes. A white reader feels the exhilarating shock of discovery at being permitted entry into this world she couldn't have known " apart from the novel.

"There is poetry in . . . *Sassafrass, Cypress & Indigo:* the poetry of rich lyrical language, of women you want to know because they're so original even their names conjure up visions," comments Joyce Howe in the *Village Voice. Betsey Brown: A Novel,* "lacks those fantastical qualities, yet perhaps because this semi-autobiographical second novel is not as easy to love, it is the truer book." Betsey is thirteen, growing into young womanhood in St. Louis during the 1950s. "An awakening sense of racial responsibility is as important to Betsey as her first kiss," relates Patchy Wheatley, a *Times Literary Supplement* reviewer. As one of the first students to be bused to a hostile white school, Betsey learns about racism and how to overcome it with a sense of personal pride. Says the reviewer, "By interweaving Betsey's story with those of the various generations of her family and community, Shange has also produced something of wider significance: a skillful exploration of the Southern black community at a decisive moment in its history."

"Black life has always been more various than the literature has been at liberty to show," comments Sherley Anne Williams in a *Ms.* review. Though she is not impressed with *Betsey Brown* "as a literary achievement," she welcomes this important-because-rare look at the black middle class. In a *Washington Post* review, Tate concurs and notes the differences between *Betsey Brown* and Shange's previous works: "Shange's style is distinctively lyrical; her monologues and dialogues provide a panorama of Afro-American diversity. Most of Shange's characteristic elliptical spelling, innovative syntax and punctuation is absent from 'Betsey Brown.' Missing also is the caustic social criticism about racial and sexual victimization. . . . 'Betsey Brown' seems also to mark Shange's movement from explicit to subtle expressions of rage, from repudiating her girlhood past to embracing it, and from flip candor to more serious commentary." Shange told Dong that she is as angry and subversive as ever, but does not feel as powerless, she said, "because I *know where to put my anger,* and I don't feel alone in it anymore."

MEDIA ADAPTATIONS: A musical-operetta version of Shange's novel *Betsey Brown* was produced by Joseph Papp's Public Theater in 1986.

AVOCATIONAL INTERESTS: Playing the violin.

BIOGRAPHICAL/CRITICAL SOURCES:

BOOKS

Betsko, Kathleen and Rachel Koenig, editors, *Interviews with Contemporary Women Playwrights,* Beech Tree Books, 1987.

Christ, Carol P., *Diving Deep and Surfacing: Women Writers on Spiritual Quest,* Beacon Press, 1980.
Contemporary Literary Criticism, Gale, Volume 8, 1978, Volume 25, 1983, Volume 38, 1986.
Dictionary of Literary Biography, Volume 38: *Afro-American Writers after 1955: Dramatists and Prose Writers,* Gale, 1985.
Shange, Ntozake, *For Colored Girls Who Have Considered Suicide/When the Rainbow Is Enuf,* Shameless Hussy Press, 1975, Macmillan, 1976.
Shange, Ntozake, *See No Evil: Prefaces, Essays and Accounts, 1976-1983,* Momo's Press, 1984.
Squier, Susan Merrill, editor, *Women Writers and the City: Essays in Feminist Literary Criticism,* University of Tennessee Press, 1984.
Tate, Claudia, editor, *Black Women Writers at Work,* Continuum, 1983.

PERIODICALS

American Book Review, September, 1983, March, 1986.
Black American Literature Forum, summer, 1981.
Black Scholar, March, 1979, March, 1981, December, 1982, July, 1985.
Chicago Tribune, October 21, 1982.
Chicago Tribune Book World, July 1, 1979, September 8, 1985.
Christian Science Monitor, September 9, 1976, October 8, 1982, May 2, 1986.
Cue, June 26, 1976.
Daily News, July 16, 1979.
Detroit Free Press, October 30, 1978.
Ebony, August, 1977.
Essence, November, 1976, May, 1985, June, 1985.
Freedomways, Third Quarter, 1976.
Horizon, September, 1977.
Los Angeles Times, October 20, 1982, June 11, 1985, July 28, 1987.
Los Angeles Times Book Review, August 22, 1982, October 20, 1982, January 8, 1984, July 29, 1984, June 11, 1985, July 19, 1987.
Mademoiselle, September, 1976.
Ms., September, 1976, December, 1977, June, 1985, June, 1987.
New Leader, July 5, 1976.
Newsday, August 22, 1976.
New Statesman, October 4, 1985.
Newsweek, June 14, 1976, July 30, 1979.
New York Amsterdam News, October 9, 1976.
New Yorker, June 14, 1976, August 2, 1976, January 2, 1978.
New York Post, June 12, 1976, September 16, 1976, July 16, 1979.
New York Theatre Critics' Reviews, Volume XXXVII, number 16, September 13, 1976.
New York Times, June 16, 1976, December 22, 1977, June 4, 1979, June 8, 1979, July 16, 1979, July 22, 1979, May 14, 1980, June 15, 1980.
New York Times Book Review, June 25, 1979, July 16, 1979, October 21, 1979, September 12, 1982, May 12, 1985, April 6, 1986.
New York Times Magazine, May 1, 1983.
Plays & Players, Volume 27, number 3, December, 1979.
Publishers Weekly, May 3, 1985.
Saturday Review, February 18, 1978, May/June, 1985.
Time, June 14, 1976, July 19, 1976, November 1, 1976.
Times (London), April 21, 1983.
Times Literary Supplement, December 6, 1985, April 15, 1988.

Washington Post, June 12, 1976, June 29, 1976, February 23, 1982, June 17, 1985.
Washington Post Book World, October 15, 1978, July 19, 1981, August 22, 1982, August 5, 1984.
Variety, July 25, 1979.
Village Voice, August 16, 1976, July 23, 1979, June 18, 1985.

*   *   *

SHAPIRO, Karl (Jay)   1913-

PERSONAL: Born November 10, 1913, in Baltimore, Md.; son of Joseph and Sarah (Omansky) Shapiro; married Evalyn Katz (a literary agent), March 25, 1945 (divorced, January, 1967); married Teri Kovach, July 31, 1967; children: (first marriage) Katharine, John Jacob, Elizabeth. *Education:* Attended University of Virginia, 1932-33, Johns Hopkins University, 1937-39, and Enoch Pratt Library School, 1940. *Politics:* None. *Religion:* None.

ADDRESSES: Home—2223 Amador Ave., Davis, Calif. 95616. *Office*—Sproul Hall, University of California, Davis, Calif. 95616.

CAREER: Library of Congress, Washington, D.C., consultant in poetry, 1947-48; Johns Hopkins University, Baltimore, Md., associate professor of writing, 1948-50; *Poetry,* Chicago, Ill., editor, 1950-56; University of Nebraska, Lincoln, professor of English, 1956-66; University of Illinois at Chicago Circle, professor of English, 1966-68; University of California, Davis, professor of English, 1968—. Lecturer in India, summer of 1955, for U.S. Department of State. Visiting professor or lecturer at University of Wisconsin, 1948, Loyola University, 1951-52, Salzburg Seminar in American Studies, 1952, University of California, 1955-56, and University of Indiana, 1956-57. Member, Bollingen Prize Committee, 1949. *Military service:* U.S. Army, 1941-45.

MEMBER: National Institute of Arts and Letters, Phi Beta Kappa.

AWARDS, HONORS: Fellow in American Letters, Library of Congress; Jeanette S. Davis Prize and Levinson prize, both from *Poetry* in 1942; *Contemporary Poetry* prize, 1943; American Academy of Arts and Letters grant, 1944; Pulitzer Prize in poetry, 1945, for *V-Letter and Other Poems;* Shelley Memorial Prize, 1946; Guggenheim Foundation fellowships, 1944, 1953; Kenyon School of Letters fellowship, 1956-57; Eunice Tietjens Memorial Prize, 1961; Oscar Blumenthal Prize, *Poetry,* 1963; Bollingen Prize, 1968.

WRITINGS:

English Prosody and Modern Poetry, Johns Hopkins Press, 1947, reprinted, Folcroft Library Editions, 1975.
A Bibliography of Modern Prosody, Johns Hopkins Press, 1948, reprinted, Folcroft Library Editions, 1976.
(Editor with Louis Untermeyer and Richard Wilbur) *Modern American and Modern British Poetry,* Harcourt, 1955.
(Author of libretto) *The Tenor* (opera; music by Hugo Weisgall), Merion Music, 1956.
(Editor) *American Poetry* (anthology), Crowell, 1960.
(Editor) *Prose Keys to Modern Poetry,* Harper, 1962.
(With Robert Beum) *Prosody Handbook,* Harper, 1965.
Edsel (novel), Geis, 1970.
(Editor with Robert Phillips) *Letters of Delmore Schwartz,* Ontario Review Press/Persea Books, 1984.
The Younger Son: Poet; An Autobiography in Three Parts, Volume 1: *The Youth and War Years of a Distinguished American Poet,* Algonquin Books, 1988.

POETRY

Poems, Waverly, 1935.
(Contributor) *Five Young American Poets,* New Directions, 1941.
Person, Place, and Thing, Reynal, 1942.
The Place of Love, Comment Press, 1942.
V-Letter and Other Poems, Reynal, 1944.
Essay on Rime, Secker & Warburg, 1945.
Trial of a Poet and Other Poems, Reynal, 1947.
(Contributor) *Poets at Work,* Harcourt, 1948.
Poems: 1940-1953, Random House, 1953.
The House, privately printed, 1957.
Poems of a Jew, Random House, 1958.
The Bourgeois Poet, Random House, 1964.
Selected Poems, Random House, 1968.
White-Haired Lover, Random House, 1968.
Adult Book Store, Random House, 1976.
Collected Poems: 1948-1978, Random House, 1978.
Love and War, Art and God, Stuart Wright, 1984.
Adam and Eve, edited by John Wheatcroft, Press Alley, 1986.
New and Selected Poems, 1940-1986, University of Chicago Press, 1987.

LITERARY CRITICISM

Beyond Criticism, University of Nebraska Press, 1953, published as *A Primer for Poets,* 1965.
In Defense of Ignorance, Random House, 1960.
(With James E. Miller, Jr. and Beatrice Slote) *Start it with the Sun: Studies in Cosmic Poetry,* University of Nebraska Press, 1960.
(With Ralph Ellison) *The Writer's Experience,* Library of Congress, 1964.
Randall Jarrell, Library of Congress, 1967.
To Abolish Children and Other Essays, Quadrangle Books, 1968.
The Poetry Wreck: Selected Essays, 1950-1970, Random House, 1975.

AUTHOR OF INTRODUCTION

Pawel Majewski, editor, *Czas Niepokoju* (anthology; title means "Time of Unrest"), Criterion, 1958.
Jack Hirschman, *A Correspondence of Americans,* Indiana University Press, 1960.
Bruce Cutler, *The Year of the Green Wave,* University of Nebraska Press, 1960.

OTHER

Also author of screenplay "Karl Shapiro's America," 1976. Work appears in anthologies. Contributor of articles, poetry, and reviews to *Partisan Review, Poetry, Nation, Saturday Review,* and other periodicals. Editor, *Newberry Library Bulletin,* 1953-55, and *Prairie Schooner,* 1956-63.

SIDELIGHTS: Karl Shapiro's poetry received early recognition, winning a number of major poetry awards during the 1940s. Strongly influenced by the traditionalist poetry of W. H. Auden, Shapiro's early work is "striking for its concrete but detached insights," Alfred Kazin writes in *Contemporaries.* "It is witty and exact in the way it catches the poet's subtle and guarded impressions, and it is a poetry full of clever and unexpected verbal conceits. It is a very professional poetry—supple [and] adaptable." Stephen Stepanchev notes in *American Poetry since 1945: A Critical Survey* that Shapiro's poems "found impetus and subject matter in the public crises of the 1940's [and all] have their social meaning."

Although his early traditionalist poetry was successful, Shapiro doubted the value and honesty of that kind of poetry. In many of his critical essays, he attacked the assumptions of traditionalist poetry as stifling to the poet's creativity. "What he wants," Paul Fussell, Jr. maintains in *Partisan Review,* "is a turning from received and thus discredited English and European techniques of focus in favor of honest encounters with the stuff of local experience."

In the poetry of both Walt Whitman and the Beat poets, Shapiro found a confirmation of his own idea of feeling over form. In his collection *The Bourgeois Poet,* Shapiro broke with his traditional poetic forms in favor of the free verse of Whitman and the Beats. Hayden Carruth sees these poems as bearing "little resemblance to [Shapiro's] previous work. Blocky, free, prose-like, iconoclastic, touched with apocalyptic insight, they seemed, coming from Shapiro, actually shocking. Today their shock is gone; yet they remain fresh, shrewd poems." Writing in *American Poets from the Puritans to the Present,* Hyatt H. Waggoner finds *The Bourgeois Poet* "a work of greater poetic integrity than any of Shapiro's earlier volumes."

Examining Shapiro's career as a whole, Laurence Leiberman sees him as one of "a generation of poets who . . . wrote a disproportionate number of superbly good poems in early career, became decorated overnight with honors . . . and spent the next twenty-odd years trying to outpace a growing critical notice of decline." Leiberman judges *The Bourgeois Poet* to be Shapiro's attempt to "recast the poetic instrument to embody formerly intractable large sectors of [his life]" and to win "a precious freedom to extend the limits of [his art]." Leiberman sees the two styles in Shapiro's poetry, the traditionalist and free verse, enhancing each other. He believes that Shapiro's "future work stands an excellent chance of merging the superior qualities of two opposite modes: the expressiveness of candid personal confession and the durability of significant form."

BIOGRAPHICAL/CRITICAL SOURCES:

BOOKS

Bartlett, Lee, *Karl Shapiro: A Descriptive Bibliography,* Garland Publishing, 1979.
Contemporary Authors Autobiography Series, Volume 6, Gale, 1987.
Contemporary Literary Criticism, Gale, Volume 4, 1975, Volume 8, 1978, Volume 15, 1980, Volume 53, 1989.
Dictionary of Literary Biography, Volume 48: *American Poets, 1880-1945, Second Series,* Gale, 1986.
Jarrell, Randall, *The Third Book of Criticism,* Farrar, Straus, 1969.
Kazin, Alfred, *Contemporaries,* Little, Brown, 1962.
Nemerov, Howard, *Poetry and Fiction,* Rutgers University Press, 1963.
Rosenthal, M. L., *The Modern Poets: A Critical Introduction,* Oxford University Press, 1960.
Scannell, Vernon, *Not without Glory,* Woburn Press, 1976.
Spears, Monroe K., *Dionysus and the City,* Oxford University Press, 1970.
Stepanchev, Stephen, *American Poetry since 1945: A Critical Survey,* Harper, 1965.
Waggoner, Hyatt H., *American Poets from the Puritans to the Present,* Houghton, 1968.
White, William, *Karl Shapiro: A Bibliography,* Wayne State University Press, 1960.

PERIODICALS

Antioch Review, Volume 31, Number 3, 1971.

Books, March, 1964.
Book Week, August 2, 1964.
Book World, July 28, 1968.
Carleton Miscellany, spring, 1965.
Christian Science Monitor, July 3, 1968.
College English, February, 1946.
Commonweal, September 19, 1958, January 20, 1960, October 4, 1968.
Esquire, April, 1968.
Harper's, August, 1964.
Hollins Critic, December, 1964.
Hudson Review, autumn, 1975, summer, 1988.
Kenyon Review, winter, 1946.
Literary Times, June, 1967.
Los Angeles Times, July 7, 1968.
Nation, July 5, 1958, September 24, 1960, August 24, 1964, November 11, 1978.
New Republic, November 24, 1958.
New Yorker, November 7, 1964.
New York Herald Tribune Book Review, May 8, 1960.
New York Times, July 29, 1968, January 6, 1969, October 4, 1971.
New York Times Book Review, September 7, 1958, May 8, 1960, July 14, 1968, August 18, 1968, July 25, 1976, March 31, 1985.
Paris Review, spring, 1986.
Partisan Review, winter, 1969.
Poetry, June, 1965, April, 1969, July, 1969, February, 1970, June, 1985.
Prairie Schooner, winter, 1965.
Saturday Review, September 27, 1958, April 15, 1978.
Sewanee Review, winter, 1965.
Southern Review, winter, 1973.
Time, August 2, 1968.
Tribune Books (Chicago), October 30, 1988.
Village Voice, March 29, 1976.
Virginia Quarterly Review, winter, 1969.
Wall Street Journal, July 7, 1976.
Washington Post, January 4, 1980, December 9, 1988.
Western Review, spring, 1954.
Yale Review, winter, 1954, June, 1975.

* * *

SHARON, Rose
See MERRIL, Judith

* * *

SHAW, Bernard
See SHAW, George Bernard

* * *

SHAW, G. Bernard
See SHAW, George Bernard

* * *

SHAW, George Bernard 1856-1950
(G. B. S., Bernard Shaw, G. Bernard Shaw; Corno di Bassetto, a pseudonym)

PERSONAL: Born July 26, 1856, in Dublin, Ireland (now Republic of Ireland); died November 2, 1950; son of George Carr (an agricultural merchant) and Lucinda Elizabeth (a singer, musician, and music teacher; maiden name, Gurly) Shaw; married Charlotte Francis Payne-Townshend, 1898 (died, September, 1943). *Education:* Attended Wesleyan Connexional School (now Wesleyan College).

CAREER: Playwright, novelist, essayist, critic, and lecturer. Cashier for a land agent in Dublin, Ireland, c. 1872-73; writer and commercial laborer, c. 1876-85; co-founder of Fabian Society, 1884. Vestryman and borough councilor in London, c. late 1880s.

MEMBER: Society of Authors, Playwrights, and Composers, Fabian Society, Royal Automobile Club, Burlington Fine Arts Club.

AWARDS, HONORS: Nobel Prize for literature from the Swedish Academy, 1925.

WRITINGS:

PLAYS—INDIVIDUAL WORKS; UNDER NAME BERNARD SHAW, EXCEPT AS NOTED

Widowers' Houses (first produced in London at the Royalty Theatre, December 9, 1892), Henry, 1893, Brentano's, 1913.
"The Man of Destiny," first produced in Croydon at the Grand Theatre, July 1, 1897, produced in London at the Royal Court Theatre, June 4, 1907.
"The Gadfly; or, The Son of the Cardinal," first produced in Bayswater at the Bijou Theatre, March, 1898.
Man and Superman (first produced in London at the Royal Court Theatre, May 21, 1905; revised version, including "Don Juan in Hell," first produced in Edinburgh at the Lyceum Theatre, June 11, 1915 [also see below]; revised version produced in London at the Regent Theatre, October 23, 1925), University Press, 1903, reprinted with introduction and notes by A. C. Ward, Longman, 1947, reprinted with introduction by Lewis Casson, illustrated by Charles Mozley, Heritage Press, 1962.
"How He Lied to Her Husband," first produced in New York at the Berkeley Lyceum Theatre, September 26, 1904, produced in London at the Royal Court Theatre, February 28, 1905.
Passion, Poison, and Petrifaction; or, The Fatal Gazogene (first produced in London at the Theatrical Garden Party, Regent's Park, July 14, 1905), H. B. Clafin, 1905.
The Devil's Disciple (first produced in Albany, N.Y., at Hermanus Bleecker Hall, October 1, 1897, produced in London at the Savoy Theatre, October 14, 1907), Constable, 1906, Brentano's, 1913, reprinted with an introduction and notes by Ward, Longman, 1958, reprinted with illustrations by Leonard Everett Fisher, F. Watts, 1967.
You Never Can Tell (first produced in London at the Royalty Theatre, November 26, 1899), Constable, 1906, Brentano's, 1913, reprinted with introduction by Margery M. Morgan, Hicks Smith, 1967.
Captain Brassbound's Conversion (first produced in London at the Strand Theatre, December 16, 1900), Constable, 1906, Brentano's, 1913.
"The Interlude at the Playhouse," first produced in London at the Playhouse Theatre, January 28, 1907.
"Don Juan in Hell," first produced in London at the Royal Court Theatre, June 4, 1907 (also see above).
The Doctor's Dilemma (first produced in London at the Royal Court Theatre, November 20, 1906), Constable, 1908, Brentano's, 1911, revised with preface, 1913, Dodd, 1941, re-

printed with an introduction and notes by Ward, Longman, 1957.

(Under name George Bernard Shaw) *The Admirable Bashville; or, Constancy Unrewarded* (based on Shaw's novel *Cashel Byron's Profession;* first produced in London at the Imperial Theatre, June 7, 1903), Brentano's, 1909.

The Shewing-up of Blanco Posnet (first produced in Dublin at the Abbey Theatre, August 25, 1909, produced in London at the Everyman Theatre, March 14, 1921), Brentano's, 1909.

Press Cuttings (first produced in Manchester at the Gaiety Theatre, September 27, 1909), Brentano's, 1909.

"Misalliance," first produced in London at the Duke of York's Theatre, February 23, 1910.

"The Dark Lady of the Sonnets," first produced in London at the Haymarket Theatre, November 24, 1910.

"Fanny's First Play," first produced in London at the Little Theatre, April 19, 1911.

Arms and the Man (first produced in London at the Avenue Theatre, April 21, 1894), Brentano's, 1913, reprinted with introduction by Ward, Longman, 1956, reprinted with introduction by Louis Kronenberger, Bantam, 1960, authoritative edition with critical material and introduction by Henry Popkin, Avon, 1967, revised edition with introduction and notes by Louis Crompton, Bobbs-Merrill, 1969, definitive text edition, Penguin, 1977.

Mrs. Warren's Profession (first produced in London at the New Lyric Club, January 5, 1902), Brentano's, 1913 (also see below).

Candida (first produced in Aberdeen at Her Majesty's Theatre, July 30, 1897, produced in London at the Royal Court Theatre, April 26, 1904), Brentano's, 1913, reprinted with an introduction and notes by Ward, Longman, 1956.

John Bull's Other Island (first produced in London at the Royal Court Theatre, November 1, 1904), Brentano's, 1913.

The Philanderer (first produced in London at the New Stage Club, Applegate Institute, February 20, 1905, produced in London at the Royal Court Theatre, February 5, 1907), Brentano's, 1913.

Major Barbara (first produced in London at the Royal Court Theatre, November 28, 1905), Brentano's, 1913, Dodd, 1941, reprinted with introduction and notes by Ward, Longman, 1958, revised edition edited by Elizabeth T. Forter, Appleton-Century-Crofts, 1971.

Caesar and Cleopatra (first produced in Berlin at the Neues Theatre, March 31, 1906, produced in New York at the New Amsterdam Theatre, October 30, 1906, produced in London at the Savoy Theatre, November 25, 1907), Brentano's, 1913, reprinted, Penguin, 1964, revised edition edited by Forter, Appleton-Century-Crofts, 1965.

Getting Married (first produced in London at the Haymarket Theatre, May 12, 1908), Brentano's, 1913.

Pygmalion (first produced in Siegfried Trebitsch's German translation in Vienna at the Hofburg Theatre, October 16, 1913; first produced in English in London at His Majesty's Theatre, April 11, 1914), German translation by Trebitsch, S. Fischer, 1913, English-language edition first published in 1920, reprinted with an introduction by Ward, Longman, 1957, reprinted with reader's supplement, Washington Square Press, 1968, definitive text edition, illustrated by Feliks Topolski, Penguin, 1982.

"Great Catherine," first produced in London at Vaudeville Theatres, November 18, 1913.

"The Music-Cure," first produced in London at the Little Theatre, January 28, 1914.

Overruled (first produced in London at the Duke of York's Theatre, October 14, 1912), Constable, 1915.

"The Inca of Perusalem," first produced in Birmingham at the Repertory Theatre, October 7, 1916, produced in London at the Criterion Theatre, December 16, 1917.

"Augustus Does His Bit," first produced in London at the Royal Court Theatre, January 21, 1917.

"Annajanska, the Wild Grand Duchess," first produced in London at the London Coliseum, January 21, 1918.

"O'Flaherty, V. C.," first produced in New York at the 39th Street Theatre, June 21, 1920, produced in London at the Lyric Theatre, Hammersmith, December 19, 1920.

Back to Methuselah (first produced in New York at the Garrick Theatre, February 27, 1922, produced in London at the Royal Court Theatre, February 18, 1924), Brentano's, 1921, revised edition with a postscript, Oxford University Press, 1946, definitive text edition, Penguin, 1977, reprinted as *Back to Methuselah: A Metabiological Pentateuch,* Penguin, 1988.

"Jitta's Atonement" (adapted from Siegfried Trebitsch's *Frau Gittas Suehne*), first produced in Washington, D.C., at the Shubert Theatre, January 8, 1923, produced in New York at the Comedy Theatre, January 17, 1923, produced in London at the Arts Theatre, April 30, 1930.

Saint Joan (first produced in New York at the Garrick Theatre, December 28, 1923, produced in London at the New Theatre, March 26, 1924), Brentano's, 1923, revised edition edited and with an introduction and notes by Stanley Weintraub, Bobbs-Merrill, 1971.

"The Glimpse of Reality," first produced in London at the Arts Theatre Club, November 20, 1927.

"The Fascinating Foundling," first produced in London at the Arts Theatre Club, January 28, 1928.

The Apple Cart (first produced in Warsaw at the Teatr Polski, June 14, 1929, produced in Malvern at the Malvern Theatre Festival, August 19, 1929, produced in London at the Queen's Theatre, September 17, 1929), Constable, 1930, Brentano's, 1931, reprinted, Penguin, 1956.

"Too True to Be Good," first produced in Boston at the National Theatre, February 29, 1932, produced in New York at the Guild Theatre, April 4, 1932.

"On the Rocks," first produced in London at the Winter Garden Theatre, November 25, 1933.

"Village Wooing," first produced in Dallas at the Little Theatre, April 16, 1934, produced in Tunbridge Wells at the Pump Room, May 1, 1934.

(With Jean Froissart and Auguste Rodin) *The Six of Calais* (first produced in London at the Open Air Theatre, Regent's Park, July 17, 1934), privately printed, 1934.

"The Simpleton of the Unexpected Isles," first produced in New York at the Guild Theatre, February 18, 1935.

"The Millionairess," first produced in Vienna at the Akademie Theatre, January 4, 1936, produced in Melbourne at the King's Theatre, March 7, 1936.

Cymbeline Refinished (first produced in London at the Embassy Theatre, Swiss Cottage, November 16, 1937), privately printed, 1937.

Geneva (first produced in Malvern at the Festival Theatre, August 1, 1938, produced in London at the Saville Theatre, November 22, 1938), Constable, 1939.

"In Good King Charles's Golden Days" (first produced in Malvern at the Festival Theatre, August 12, 1939, produced in London at the Streatham Hill Theatre, April 15, 1940), illustrated by Topolski, Constable, 1939.

Buoyant Billions (first produced in Zurich at the Schauspielhaus, October 21, 1948, produced in Malvern at the Festival Theatre, August 13, 1949), Constable, 1949.

"Shakes Versus Shav" (puppet play), first produced in Malvern at the Waldo Lanchester Marionette Theatre, Lyttleton Hall, August 9, 1949, produced in Battersea Park at the Riverside Theatre, June 10, 1951.

"Farfetched Fables," first produced in London at the Watergate Theatre, September 6, 1950.

Androcles and the Lion (first produced in Berlin at Kleines Theatre, November 25, 1912, produced in London at St. James's Theatre, September 1, 1913), Penguin, 1951, reprinted with an introduction and notes by Ward, Longman, 1957.

"Why She Would Not," first produced in New York by the Shaw Society of America at the Grolier Club, January 21, 1957.

Heartbreak House (first produced in New York at the Garrick Theatre, November 10, 1920, produced in London at the Royal Court Theatre, October 18, 1921), Penguin, 1964.

LETTERS, CONVERSATIONS, AND DIARIES; UNDER NAME BERNARD SHAW, EXCEPT AS NOTED

(Under name George Bernard Shaw) *Table-Talk of G. B. S.: Conversations on Things in General Between George Bernard Shaw and His Biographer,* compiled and edited by Archibald Henderson, Harper, 1925.

Ellen Terry and Bernard Shaw: A Correspondence, edited by Christopher St. John, Putnam, 1931, reprinted with illustrations, Theatre Arts Books, 1969.

(Under name George Bernard Shaw) *Some Unpublished Letters of George Bernard Shaw,* edited by Julian Park, [Buffalo], 1939.

Florence Farr, Bernard Shaw, and W. B. Yeats, edited by Clifford Bax, Cuala Press, 1941, Dodd, 1942.

Bernard Shaw and Mrs. Patrick Campbell: A Correspondence, edited by Alan Dent, Knopf, 1952.

Advice to a Young Critic, and Other Letters, notes and introduction by E. J. West, Crown, 1955.

Bernard Shaw's Letters to Harley Granville Barker, edited by C. B. Purdom, Phoenix, 1956, Crown, 1957.

My Dear Dorothea: A Practical System of Moral Education for Females, Embodied in a Letter to a Young Person of That Sex, illustrated by Clare Winsten, with a note by Stephen Winsten, Phoenix, 1956, Vanguard Press, 1957.

To a Young Actress: The Letters of Bernard Shaw to Molly Tompkins, edited with an introduction by Peter Tompkins, Potter, 1960.

Collected Letters, four volumes, edited by Dan H. Laurence, Volume 1: *1874-1897,* Dodd, 1965, Volume 2: *1898-1910,* Dodd, 1965, Volume 3: *1911-1925,* Viking, 1985, Volume 4: *1926-1950,* Viking, 1988.

Bernard Shaw and Alfred Douglas: A Correspondence, edited by Mary Hyde, Ticknor & Fields, 1982.

The Playwright and the Pirate: Bernard Shaw and Frank Harris, a Correspondence, edited with an introduction by Weintraub, Pennsylvania State University Press, 1982.

Agitations: Letters to the Press, 1875-1950, edited by James Rambeau and Laurence, Ungar, 1985.

Bernard Shaw's Letters to Siegfried Trebitsch, edited by Samuel A. Weiss, Stanford University Press, 1986.

Bernard Shaw: The Diaries, 1885-1897, edited and annotated by Weintraub, transliterated from shorthand notation by Stanley Rypins, additional transliterations and transcriptions by Blanche Patch, Pennsylvania State University Press, 1986.

Monologues From George Bernard Shaw, edited by Ian Michaels, Dramaline Publications, 1988.

Dear Mr. Shaw: Selections From Bernard Shaw's Postbag, edited by Vivian Elliot, Bloomsbury, 1988.

COLLECTIONS; UNDER NAME BERNARD SHAW

Plays: Pleasant and Unpleasant, two volumes, Stone, 1898, reprinted, Constable, 1957.

Three Plays for Puritans, Stone, 1901, abridged edition published as *Two Plays for Puritans,* illustrated by George Him, Heritage Press, 1966).

The Wisdom of Bernard Shaw (passages from Shaw's works), selected by Charlotte F. Shaw, Brentano's, 1913.

The Socialism of Shaw, edited with an introduction by James Fuchs, Vanguard Press, 1926.

The Works of Bernard Shaw, Collected Edition, thirty volumes, Constable, 1930-1932, revised edition published as *The Works of Bernard Shaw, Ayot St. Lawrence Edition,* Wise, 1931-1932, enlarged edition published as *Standard Edition of the Works of Bernard Shaw,* thirty-six volumes, Constable, 1947-1952.

The Complete Plays of Bernard Shaw, Constable, 1931, reprinted, Hamlyn Publishing, 1965.

Major Critical Essays, Constable, 1932, reprinted as *Major Critical Essays: The Quintessence of Ibsenism, the Perfect Wagnerite, the Sanity of Art,* Penguin, 1986, reprint of 1932 edition, Reprint Services, 1988.

Short Stories, Scraps and Shavings, illustrated by John Farleigh, Dodd, 1934, published as *The Black Girl in Search of God, and Some Lesser Tales,* Penguin, 1964.

Three Plays: Too True to Be Good, Village Wooing, and On the Rocks, Dodd, 1934, reprinted, Constable, 1963.

Prefaces, Constable, 1934, reprinted, Scholarly Press, 1971, reprinted as *Prefaces by Bernard Shaw,* Reprint Services, 1988.

Nine Plays, Dodd, 1935.

Six Plays (a companion to *Nine Plays*), Dodd, 1941.

Selected Novels, introduction by Arthur Zeiger, Caxton House, 1946.

Selected Plays (includes prefaces), Dodd, 1948-1957.

Plays and Players: Essays on the Theatre, selected with an introduction by Ward, Oxford University Press, 1952.

Selected Prose, selected by Diarmuid Russell, Dodd, 1952.

Selected Plays and Other Writings, introduction by William Irvine, Rinehart, 1956.

The Illusions of Socialism, Together With Socialism: Principles and Outlook, Shaw Society, 1956.

Shaw's Dramatic Criticism: 1895-1898 (selections from the author's contributions to *Saturday Review*), edited by John F. Matthews, Hill & Wang, 1959.

A Prose Anthology, selected with introduction and notes by H. M. Burton, preface by Ward, Fawcett, 1959.

Selected Nondramatic Writings of Bernard Shaw, edited by Laurence, Houghton, 1965.

Bernard Shaw: Selections of His Wit and Wisdom, compiled by Caroline Thomas Harnsberger, Follett, 1965.

The Complete Prefaces of Bernard Shaw, Hamlyn Publishing, 1965.

Bernard Shaw's Ready-Reckoner, edited with an introduction by N. H. Leigh-Taylor, Random House, 1965.

Four Plays, foreword and introduction by Paul Kozelka, Washington Square Press, 1965.

Selected One-Act Plays, Penguin, 1965.

Seven Plays With Prefaces and Notes, Dodd, 1966.

Three Shorter Plays, Heinemann Educational, 1968.

Bernard Shaw's Plays, edited by Warren Sylvester Smith, Norton, 1970.

The Bodley Head Bernard Shaw, seven volumes, Bodley Head, 1970, Reinhardt, 1970-1974, published as *Collected Plays With Their Prefaces,* Dodd, 1975. *The Road to Equality: Ten Unpublished Lectures and Essays, 1884-1918,* introduction by Crompton, edited by Crompton and Hilayne Cavanaugh, Beacon Press, 1971.

Collected Music Criticism, Vienna House, 1973.

The Portable Bernard Shaw, edited with an introduction by Weintraub, Penguin, 1977.

The Collected Screenplays of Bernard Shaw, edited by Bernard F. Dukore, University of Georgia Press, 1980.

Selected Plays, preface by Rex Harrison, introductory essay by David Bearinger, Dodd, 1981.

Facsimile editions of plays published as *Early Texts: Play Manuscripts in Facsimile,* twelve volumes, edited by Laurence, Garland, 1981.

OTHER; UNDER NAME BERNARD SHAW, EXCEPT AS NOTED

Cashel Byron's Profession (novel), Harper, 1886, revised edition, Stone, 1901, reprinted alone with preface by Harry T. Moore, edited with an introduction by Weintraub, Southern Illinois University Press, 1968, definitive text edition edited by Laurence, Penguin, 1979.

An Unsocial Socialist (novel), Lowry, 1887, Brentano's, 1900, reprinted, Scholarly Press, 1970.

(Editor) *Fabian Essays in Socialism,* Fabian Society, 1889, reprinted, Peter Smith, 1967.

The Quintessence of Ibsenism, Tucker, 1891, enlarged edition, Brentano's, 1913, 3rd edition, Constable, 1922, revised enlarged edition published as *Shaw and Ibsen: Bernard Shaw's The Quintessence of Ibsenism and Related Writings,* edited by J. L. Wisenthal, University of Toronto Press, 1979.

The Perfect Wagnerite, G. Richards, 1898, Stone, 1899, reprinted, Dover, 1967.

(Editor) *Fabianism and the Empire: A Manifesto by the Fabian Society,* G. Richards, 1900.

Love Among the Artists (novel), Stone, 1900, reprinted, Viking, 1962.

The Common Sense of Municipal Trading, Constable, 1904, revised edition with preface, A. C. Fifield, 1908, John Lane, 1911.

The Author's Apology From Mrs. Warren's Profession: The Tyranny of Police and Press, introduction by John Corbin, Brentano's, 1905 (also see above).

The Irrational Knot (novel), Brentano's, 1905, reprinted, Constable, 1950.

(Under name G. Bernard Shaw) *An Essay on Going to Church,* J. W. Luce, 1905.

(Under name G. Bernard Shaw) *Dramatic Opinions and Essays,* with a word by James Huneker, Brentano's 1906, reprinted (under name Bernard Shaw) with an apology by Shaw, 1907.

The Sanity of Art, Tucker, 1908.

Socialism and Superior Brains, John Lane, 1910.

Peace Conference Hints, Constable, 1919.

Imprisonment Brentano's, 1925, published as *The Crime of Imprisonment,* illustrated by William Gropper, Greenwood Press, 1946, reprinted, 1969.

Translations and Tomfooleries, Brentano's, 1926.

The Intelligent Woman's Guide to Capitalism and Socialism, Brentano's, 1928, reprinted with an introduction by Susan Moller Okin, Transaction Books, 1984, published as *The Intelligent Woman's Guide to Socialism, Capitalism, Sovietism, and Fascism,* Penguin, 1965.

Bernard Shaw and Karl Marx: A Symposium, 1884-1889, Georgian Press, 1930, Norwood, 1978.

Immaturity, Constable, 1931.

What I Really Wrote About the War, Constable, 1931, Brentano's, 1932.

Doctor's Delusions, Crude Criminology, and Sham Education, Constable, limited edition, 1931, revised standard edition, 1932.

Pen Portraits and Reviews, Constable, 1932, reprinted, 1963.

Essays in Fabian Socialism, Constable, 1932, reprinted, 1961.

Our Theatres in the Nineties, Constable, 1932.

The Adventures of the Black Girl in Her Search for God, Constable, 1932, Dodd, 1933.

Music in London, 1890-1894 (criticisms originally published in *World*), Constable, 1932, reprinted, Scholarly Press, 1977.

(Under name George Bernard Shaw) *American Boobs,* E. O. Jones, 1933, published as *The Future of Political Science in America,* Dodd, 1933 (published in England as *The Political Madhouse in America and Nearer Home,* Constable, 1933).

William Morris As I Knew Him, Dodd, 1936, reprinted, Folcroft, 1969.

London Music in 1888-1889 as Heard by Corno di Bassetto, Dodd, 1937, reprinted, Vienna House, 1973.

Shaw Gives Himself Away: An Autobiographical Miscellany, Gregynog Press, 1939.

Everybody's Political What's What, Dodd, 1944.

Sixteen Self Sketches, Dodd, 1949.

Shaw on Vivisection, compiled and edited by G. H. Bowker, Allen & Unwin, 1949, published as *Are Doctors Really Inhuman?,* Fridtjof-Karla, 1957.

Shaw on Music, selected by Eric Bentley, Doubleday, 1955.

Shaw on Theatre, edited by E. J. West, Hill & Wang, 1958.

An Unfinished Novel, edited by Weintraub, Dodd, 1958.

How to Become a Musical Critic, edited by Laurence, Hart-Davis, 1960, Hill & Wang, 1961.

Platform and Pulpit, edited by Laurence, Hill & Wang, 1961.

Shaw on Shakespeare, Dutton, 1961, edited with an introduction by Edwin Wilson, Books for Libraries Press, 1971.

G. B. S. on Music, foreword by Alec Robertson, Penguin, 1962.

The Matter With Ireland, edited with an introduction by David H. Greene and Laurence, Hill & Wang, 1962.

(Under name George Bernard Shaw) *On Language,* edited with an introduction and notes by Abraham Tauber, foreword by James Pitman, Philosophical Library, 1963.

Religious Speeches, edited by Smith, foreword by Arthur N. Nethercot, Pennsylvania State University Press, 1963.

(Under name George Bernard Shaw) *The Rationalization of Russia,* edited with an introduction by Harry M. Geduld, Indiana University Press, 1964.

Shaw on Religion, edited with an introduction and notes by Smith, Dodd, 1967.

Shaw: An Autobiography, 1856-1898, compiled and edited by Weintraub, Weybright & Talley, 1969.

Shaw: An Autobiography; The Playwright Years, 1898-1950, compiled and edited by Weintraub, Weybright & Talley, 1970.

Practical Politics: Twentieth-Century Views on Politics and Economics, edited by Lloyd J. Hubenka, University of Nebraska Press, 1976.

The Great Composers: Reviews and Bombardments, edited with an introduction by Crompton, University of California Press, 1978.

(Presumed author) *Lady, Wilt Thou Love Me?* (eighteen love poems to Ellen Terry attributed to Bernard Shaw), edited with introduction and notes by Jack Werner, Stein & Day, 1980.

Shaw's Music, three volumes, edited by Laurence, Dodd, 1981.

Shaw on Dickens, edited with introduction by Laurence and Martin Quinn, Ungar, 1985.

Music critic for such periodicals as London *Star, World,* and *Saturday Review* in 1880s. Drama critic for *Saturday Review* in 1880s. Contributor to newspapers and periodicals, including *Pall Mall Gazette, Daily Telegraph, Daily Sketch, World* (under name G. B. S.), and *Star* (under pseudonym Corno di Bassetto).

SIDELIGHTS: George Bernard Shaw has earned almost universal recognition as the chief English-speaking dramatist of the modern age, second only to William Shakespeare in his contribution to the British theatrical tradition. "One after another," H. W. Nevinson wrote in a 1929 *New Leader,* "his plays and the prefaces to his plays have laid bare the falsities and hypocrisies and boastful pretensions of our . . . time. I can think of no modern prophet who has swept away so much accepted rubbish and cleared the air of so much cant." A great innovator, Shaw invented the theater of ideas, turned the stage into a forum for moral instruction, altered outmoded and unrealistic theatrical conventions, and paved the way for later symbolist drama and the theater of the absurd. As such, he is credited with returning intellect to the theater. As Joseph Knight wrote in *Athenaeum* in 1907, before Shaw had even written his masterpieces: "Mr. Shaw is the playwright who has put new brains into the theatre, and ruthlessly taxed the brains of his audiences. He it is who has shown that it is possible to have an intellectual drama even in England, and an intellectual drama that shall be amusing." According to Archibald Henderson in *European Dramatists,* "Back of all surface manifestations lies the supreme conviction of Shaw that the theatre of today, properly utilized, is an instrumentality for the molding of character and the shaping of conduct no whit inferior to the Church and the School."

Recognition as a major force in the theater came slowly for Shaw, partly because he was already a celebrity when his first performed play, "Widowers' Houses," reached the stage in 1892. By that time Shaw had developed a public personality as the impudent, iconoclastic, paradoxical, and witty "G. B. S." who combined elements of the clown and the crank in his strident platform utterances and devastating published criticism of art, literature, music, and drama. J. I. M. Stewart later wrote in *Eight Modern Writers* that Shaw "consistently employed arts of showmanship that are not commonly held becoming in a writer unquestionably eminent."

Shaw's own career in the theater developed in four phases. In the initial period—from 1892 to 1902—his plays appeared in suburban and matinee performances in England and won wider audiences only through publication. During the second period, running from 1903 to the eve of World War I, Shaw secured a place in the London theater, scoring successes at the Royal Court Theatre and in the commercial West End. The third phase began in 1914 with intense public disapproval of his "Common Sense About the War" but took a turn in 1923 with public adulation for "Saint Joan" and peaked in 1925 with Shaw receiving the Nobel Prize for literature. In the final stage, which extended from 1929 to his death, Shaw became preoccupied with political issues, and he alienated many people with his often controversial views on European dictators.

In retrospect, the first period of Shaw's dramatic career suggested surprising reluctance on the part of critics to recognize his genius. His plays had short runs in small cities; only a few were staged in London. "Widower's Houses," Shaw's first staged play, was performed only twice in London, in 1892. Shaw's next several plays were staged only after difficulties. "The Philanderer," a satire, found no producer until 1905, and "Mrs. Warren's Profession," addressing the social issues implicit in prostitution, was banned by the Lord Chamberlain, thus limiting it to club performances until the ban was removed late in 1924. In 1897 Shaw's first study in greatness, his playlet on Napoleon called "The Man of Destiny," had one performance in the London suburb of Croydon. "Candida," which presented a memorable woman choosing her conventional husband over an admiring young poet for unconventional reasons, also had one 1897 performance in Aberdeen, Scotland, and "The Devil's Disciple," an inverted melodrama set in America during the war for independence, had one 1897 performance in Albany, New York.

Although Shaw's plays also had a few London performances at the turn of the century—"You Never Can Tell" in 1899 and "Captain Brassbound's Conversion" in 1900—his impact on the stage was almost nonexistent. His importance came when his works appeared in print. When he published *Plays: Pleasant and Unpleasant* he provided elaborate prefaces raising the significant issues of his plays. He also wrote his stage directions in a narrative form more congenial than the terse notations common to dramatic scripts. As T. F. Evans commented in *Shaw: The Critical Heritage,* Shaw took great pains with every detail of publication: "[He] had much to say to Grant Richards on the physical appearance of the books, the type, the binding, the advertisements, the sales policy and the author's royalties."

Shaw's plays were criticized on several counts. One common charge was that his plays were not really plays at all. Arnold Bennett, writing for *Academy,* felt that Shaw's works were "decidedly not drama" even if they included "amusing and edifying dialogue." Another charge that critics frequently leveled at Shaw concerned the supposed heartlessness of his approach to life and the ostensibly inhuman nature of his characters. Responding to "Arms and the Man," Archer commented in *World,* "To look at nothing but the seamy side may be to see life steadily, but is not to see it whole. As an artist, Mr. Shaw suffers from this limitation; and to this negative fault, if I may call it so, he superadds a positive vice of style." Further, Archer criticized Shaw for his "peculiar habit of straining all the red corpuscles out of the blood of his personages. They have nothing of human nature except its pettinesses; they are devoid alike of its spiritual and its sensual instincts."

During this second phase, some critics expressed greater understanding of Shaw's methods. In 1900, reviewing *Captain Brassbound's Conversion* in *World,* Archer ridiculed theater managers' failures to realize that Shaw's plays could be commercially successful in West End theaters. Archer contended that audiences enjoyed Shaw's plays thoroughly despite the disapproval of drama critics. Max Beerbohm, reviewing the published volume *Man and Superman* for *Saturday Review* in 1903, also blamed theater managers for the commercial failure of Shaw's plays. "It is only the theatrical managers," he wrote, "who stand between him and the off-chance of a real popular success."

"Man and Superman" was an important turning point in Shavian drama, presenting for the first time a coherent statement—in the "Don Juan in Hell" interlude—of Shaw's ideal of the "Life Force." To the consternation of Shaw's socialist friends, the play treats Fabianism comically, satirizing socialist movements among the brigands and commenting—specifically in the *Revolutionist's Handbook* appended to the public version of the play—that Fabianism is one of socialism's failed experiments. In *The Bishop of Everywhere,* Warren Sylvester Smith declared that the play's "subject is simply: *The Life Force, acting through the will of woman, subdues man to its purpose, and thereby moves the race to its next higher level.* That is the subject that gives unity to the play, even though it proves somewhat limiting to its philosophical development." Smith agreed with Alfred Turco, Jr., who in *Shaw's Moral Vision* noted that "Man and Superman" is the culmination of Shaw's career, "the first play in which Shaw's belief in the possibility of an *effective* idealism is presented with real conviction."

More important to Shaw's popular success were the 1904-1907 seasons of the Royal Court Theatre, which began its association with Shaw with six matinee performances of "Candida" in April and May of 1904. Following the popularity of the matinees, the Royal Court performed "John Bull's Other Island" in November of 1904, launching Shaw's stage career in England. The play drew large audiences and favorable responses, and it was given a command performance for King Edward VII. Subsequent performances of Shaw's plays at the Royal Court included "Man and Superman," "Major Barbara," "The Doctor's Dilemma," "Captain Brassbound's Conversion," "The Philanderer," "The Man of Destiny," and "Don Juan in Hell." Of 988 performances during the years 1904 to 1907 at the Royal Court, 701 were of plays by Shaw. These productions clearly established the viability of Shaw's work in performance and attracted a larger theatergoing audience to his plays.

After staging several plays of limited appeal, Shaw produced three works that sealed his reputation as a playwright. "Fanny's First Play," which began a record run of 622 performances at London's Little Theatre on April 19, 1911, and "Androcles and the Lion," which premiered in 1913, and "Pygmalion," which premiered the next year, completed Shaw's triumph in West End theater. By this time, Shaw had gained recognition as both a new force in drama and as a commercially successful playwright. He also began to find defenders of his drama, and many agreed with the assessment of Dixon Scott in *Bookman* that when "the limitations of the plays are realized they cease to possess any; once you see that Shaw has done the best he could for us under the circumstances, then his effort is seen in relation to those circumstances and its errors instinctively allowed for. Recognize that a passion for purity, gentleness, truth, justice, and beauty is the force at the base of all his teaching, and you will find his message one of the most tonic of our time."

The third phase of Shaw's dramatic career—the years 1914 to 1925—saw him fall to the lowest point of his popularity only to rise again to the height of international fame. When World War I broke out in August of 1914, Shaw turned down several remunerative offers and withdrew to write "Common Sense About the War," collected in the 1931 publication *What I Really Wrote About the War.* When "Common Sense" first appeared in November, 1914, it sold more than seventy-five thousand copies and managed to alienate practically everyone with its contention that England must bear its share of responsibility for a war that would be ruinous for all parties. Shaw's stance was so disturbing to superpatriots that he found himself unwanted even at the Dramatists' Club, where he was the most eminent member. The essay proved extremely damaging to Shaw's reputation, destroying a popularity that his best efforts had taken more than two decades to establish.

Eventually the British government realized the accuracy of Shaw's farsightedness, and by 1917 he was invited to Flanders to report from the front for the *Daily Sketch.* As T. S. Eliot commented in *Dial,* "It might have been predicted that what he said then would not seem so subversive or blasphemous now. The public has accepted Mr. Shaw not by recognizing the intelligence of what he said then, but by forgetting it." By the close of World War I in 1918, Shaw had emerged as virtually the only public figure who had seen the folly of the war from its inception, and from his wartime experiences grew his greatest plays.

During the war Shaw wrote only a few light pieces, and it became fashionable to represent him as on the wane. John Leslie Palmer actually entitled a 1915 *Fortnightly Review* article "Mr. Bernard Shaw: An Epitaph." Shaw's plays from this period, infrequently staged, lampooned aspects of World War I. "The Inca of Perusalem," produced in 1916, spoofed Kaiser Wilhelm; "Augustus Does His Bit," staged one year later, satirized well-meaning but self-important, befuddled bureaucrats whose incompetence undermined the war effort; and "O'Flaherty, V. C.," which was not performed in London until after the armistice, satirized the ambiguous role of the Irish in the war by showing that O'Flaherty, winner of the Victoria Cross, dreaded meeting his mother because she thought he was fighting against the English.

Still, Shaw drew what some critics consider his three greatest plays—"Heartbreak House," "Back to Methuselah," and "Saint Joan"—from the crucible of his 1914-1918 experiences. In *Shakes Versus Shav,* Shaw explicitly identified "Heartbreak House" as his "King Lear." Begun during the war and performed in 1920, "Heartbreak House" examines the prewar spiritual impoverishment that made World War I inevitable. Shaw's most ambitious work, "Back to Methuselah," is a five-part cycle that dramatizes the workings of Creative Evolution as a solution to man's propensity for self-slaughter.

Neither "Heartbreak House" nor "Back to Methuselah" received enthusiastic responses. But "Saint Joan," which concerns the religious martyr Joan of Arc, restored Shaw to the highest place in public esteem. As Alexander Woolcott commented in the New York *Herald,* "for most of those who see *Saint Joan* this will be their image of her." For Stewart, Joan "at last" revealed Shaw's capability to create a real human being. Instead of ending the play with Joan's execution, which would impress upon an audience the inevitability of tragedy, Shaw provided an epilogue that presents Joan ultimately triumphant over the religious and secular forces that combined to oppose her. Despite her canonization, however, Joan is once again vilified, revealing the paradox that humanity fears and even kills its saints and heroes for the very qualities that ennoble them. Such rejection, Shaw suggests, will continue until saintly and heroic qualities become universal among humankind.

When Shaw won the Nobel Prize in 1925, he reportedly joked that it was in recognition of his not having written a play for that year. He then refused the prize money, suggesting that it fund an Anglo-Swedish literary foundation, which it ultimately did. After "Saint Joan," Shaw wrote no plays for six years. From 1923 to 1928 he worked on *The Intelligent Woman's Guide to Capitalism and Socialism,* and when he returned to writing plays, he gave most of them a political bent. His 1929 work "The Apple Cart," drawing its ideas from *The Intelligent Woman's Guide,* contrasts the ineptitude of popular leaders with the superiority of a competent aristocrat, thus alienating those who regarded Shaw's elevation of King Magnus as a direct attack on parliamentary government.

In "Too True to Be Good," written in 1932, Shaw takes an absurdist stance toward several aspects of the British military presence in other lands, while "On the Rocks" predicts the collapse of parliamentary democracy in the face of overwhelming economic problems. In "Geneva," Shaw presents a ridiculously futile League of Nations trying to control thinly disguised caricatures of Benito Mussolini, Adolf Hitler, and Francisco Franco, suggesting that his sympathy for "benevolent" despots lingered until the eve of World War II.

These apparent rejections of democracy alienated many theatergoers almost as thoroughly as Shaw's misunderstood stance in "Common Sense" had alienated the English during World War I. Coupled with the unpopularity of Shaw's political position during this period was the recognition of his waning dramatic powers, although a waning Shaw remained more vital in the theater than many of the younger generations that owed so much to his pioneering efforts. Still, critics who had come to accept and to respect Shaw over the years were disappointed with "The Simpleton of the Unexpected Isles," written in 1934 and first performed the following year, which applies a "day of judgment" solution to the ills of the world by having angels eliminate all those who are worthless. Critics speculate that Shaw was running short of inspiration at this point, as he had after completing "Saint Joan." Written in 1938 and 1939, his " 'In Good King Charles's Golden Days' "—a fanciful discussion among Charles II, Sir Isaac Newton, George Fox, Nell Gwynn, and others—returns to the aristocratic motifs of "The Apple Cart."

Between the end of World War II and his death in 1950, Shaw seemed to write in the spirit of his comment "as long as I live I must write" (from his preface to the published edition of "Buoyant Billions"), returning to earlier concerns in his grappling for something to convey. "Buoyant Billions" reworks the themes of the 1936 play "The Millionairess," "Farfetched Fables" takes a post-atomic view of the future, "Shakes Versus Shav" provides a discussion between Shakespearean and Shavian puppets on their relative merits, and "Why She Would Not" employs the "born boss" and duel-of-sex themes that Shaw had used earlier. These last plays failed to match the success of Shaw's greater works, but at his death he was still considered a premier dramatist.

Although some critics contend that Shaw's acceptance as a major playwright was much more gradual than it should have been, his many contributions to the theater are undeniable. By insisting that the theater provide moral instruction, for instance, he invented the theater of ideas, which ranks as one of his greatest achievements. He also created his own genre—serious farce—by inverting melodramatic conventions and using the techniques of comedy to advance serious views on human conduct, social institutions, and political systems. Ronald Peacock described this in *The Poet in the Theatre* as a "remarkable feat." Maxwell Anderson expressed equally great praise for Shaw in *Off Broadway* when he wrote, "The worth of his work lies in this—that in expounding, defending, attacking, and laying bare all the conceivable aspects of belief and all the possible motives for action he has irradiated almost the whole of a century with the unquenchable wildfire of an extraordinary brain."

MEDIA ADAPTATIONS: Among the films adapted from Shaw's plays are "Arms and the Man," 1932 and 1962; "Pygmalion," 1938; "Major Barbara," 1941; "Caesar and Cleopatra," 1946; "Androcles and the Lion," 1952; "Saint Joan," 1957; "The Doctor's Dilemma," 1958; "The Devil's Disciple," 1959; "The Millionairess," 1960; "Mrs. Warren's Profession," 1960; and "Great Catherine," 1968. "Pygmalion" was also adapted as the stage musical "My Fair Lady," which was adapted for film in 1964.

BIOGRAPHICAL/CRITICAL SOURCES:

BOOKS

Anderson, Maxwell, *Off Broadway: Essays About the Theater,* William Sloane, 1947.
Dictionary of Literary Biography, Volume 10: *Modern British Dramatists, 1940-1945,* Gale, 1982.
Evans, T. F., *Shaw: The Critical Heritage,* Routledge & Kegan Paul, 1976.
Henderson, Archibald, *European Dramatists,* Appleton, 1926.
Henderson, Archibald, *George Bernard Shaw: Man of the Century,* Appleton-Century, 1956.
Huneker, J. G., *Iconoclasts: A Book of Dramatists,* Scribner, 1905.
Peacock, Ronald, *The Poet in the Theatre,* Harcourt, 1946, revised edition, Hill & Wang, 1960.
Shaw, Bernard, *Plays: Pleasant and Unpleasant,* two volumes, Stone, 1898.
Shaw, Bernard, *Plays,* foreword by Eric Bentley, New American Library, 1960.
Shaw, Bernard, *Collected Plays With Their Prefaces,* eight volumes, Dodd, 1975.
Smith, Warren Sylvester, *The Bishop of Everywhere,* Pennsylvania State University Press, 1982.
Stewart, J. I. M., *Eight Modern Writers,* Clarendon Press, 1963.
Turco, Alfred, Jr., *Shaw's Moral Vision: The Self and Salvation,* Cornell University Press, 1976.
Twentieth-Century Literary Criticism, Gale, Volume 3, 1980, Volume 9, 1983, Volume 21, 1986.

PERIODICALS

Academy, February 9, 1901.
Athenaeum, July 27, 1907.
Bookman, September, 1913, December, 1924.
Dial, October, 1921.
English Review, September, 1931.
Fortnightly Review, March 1, 1915, April/May, 1926.
New Leader, August 23, 1929.
New Statesman, July 9, 1921.
New York Herald, December 29, 1923.
Saturday Review, February 1, 1902, September 12, 1903.
Times Literary Supplement, June 24, 1988.
World, April 25, 1894.

*   *   *

SHAW, Irwin 1913-1984

PERSONAL: Born February 27, 1913, in New York, N.Y.; died May 16, 1984, in Davos, Switzerland; son of William and Rose (Tompkins) Shaw; married Marian Edwards, October 13, 1939 (divorced); children: Adam. *Education:* Brooklyn College (now of the City University of New York), B.A., 1934.

CAREER: Novelist and playwright. Script writer for the "Andy Gump" and "Dick Tracy" radio shows, 1934-36; *New Republic,* Washington, D.C., drama critic, 1947-48; New York University, New York City, instructor in creative writing, 1947-48. *Military service:* U.S. Army, 1942-45; became warrant officer.

AWARDS, HONORS: O. Henry Award, 1944, for "Walking Wounded," and second prize, 1945; National Institute of Arts and Letters grant, 1946; *Playboy* Awards, 1964, 1970, and 1979; Brooklyn College, honorary doctorate.

WRITINGS:

NOVELS

The Young Lions, Random House, 1948, reprinted, Dell, 1984.
The Troubled Air, Random House, 1950, reprinted, Dell, 1987.
Lucy Crown, Random House, 1956, reprinted, Dell, 1971.
Two Weeks in Another Town, Random House, 1960, reprinted, Dell, 1971.
Voices of a Summer Day, Delacorte, 1965, reprinted, Dell, 1978.
Rich Man, Poor Man, Delacorte, 1970.
Evening in Byzantium, Delacorte, 1973.
Nightwork, Delacorte, 1975.
Beggarman, Thief, Delacorte, 1977.
The Top of the Hill (also see below), Delacorte, 1979.
Bread upon the Waters, Delacorte, 1981.
Acceptable Losses, Arbor House, 1982.

PLAYS

Bury the Dead (one-act; first produced on Broadway at the Ethel Barrymore Theatre, April, 1936), Random House, 1936.
"Siege," first produced on Broadway at the Longacre Theatre, December, 1937.
The Gentle People: A Brooklyn Fable (first produced on Broadway at the Belasco Theatre, January, 1939), Random House, 1939.
"Quiet City," first produced on Broadway at the Belasco Theatre, March, 1939.
"Retreat to Pleasure," first produced on Broadway at the Belasco Theatre, 1940.
Sons and Soldiers (first produced on Broadway at the Morosco Theatre, May, 1943), Random House, 1944.
The Assassin (first produced on Broadway at the American National Theatre and Academy, October, 1945), Random House, 1946.
(With Peter Viertel) *The Survivors* (first produced on Broadway at the Playhouse Theatre, January, 1948), Dramatists Play Service, 1948.
(Adaptor) Marcel Achard, "Patate," first produced in New York City, 1958.
Children from Their Games (first produced on Broadway at the Morosco Theatre, April, 1963), Samuel French, 1962.
"A Choice of Wars," first produced in Salt Lake City, Utah, 1967.
"The Shy and Lonely" (one-act), first produced in Los Angeles; produced with "Sailor Off the Bremen" (based on Shaw's story; also see below) by William Kramer under joint title "I, Shaw," in New York City at the Jewish Repertory Theatre, February 19, 1986.

STORY COLLECTIONS

Sailor Off the Bremen and Other Stories, Random House, 1939.
Welcome to the City and Other Stories, Random House, 1942.
Act of Faith and Other Stories, Random House, 1946.
Mixed Company: Collected Short Stories, Random House, 1950.
Tip on a Dead Jockey and Other Stories, Random House, 1957.
Selected Short Stories, Modern Library, 1961.
In the French Style (screenplay and stories; also see below), MacFadden, 1963.
Love on a Dark Street and Other Stories, Delacorte, 1965.
Short Stories, Random House, 1966.
Retreat and Other Stories, New English Library, 1970.
Whispers in Bedlam: Three Novellas, Weidenfeld & Nicolson, 1972.
God Was Here, But He Left Early, Arbor House, 1973.
Short Stories: Five Decades, Delacorte, 1978.

SCREENPLAYS

"The Big Game," RKO, 1936.
"Commandos Strike at Dawn," Columbia, 1942.
(With Daniel Fuchs and Jerry Wald) "The Hard Way," Warner Bros., 1942.
(With Sidney Buchman) "Talk of the Town," RKO, 1942.
(With Chester Erskine and David Shaw) "Take One False Step," Universal, 1949.
"I Want You," RKO, 1951.
"Act of Love," United Artists, 1953.
"Fire Down Below," Columbia, 1957.
"Desire under the Elms," Paramount, 1958.
(With Rene Clement) "This Angry Age," Columbia, 1958.
"The Big Gamble," Twentieth Century-Fox, 1961.
"In the French Style," Columbia, 1963.
"Survival 1967," United Film, 1968.

Also author, with Charles Schnee, of "Easy Living," 1949, and, with others, of "Ulysses," 1955.

OTHER

(Contributor) *Famous Plays of 1936,* Gollancz, 1936.
(Contributor) Zozlenko, editor, *American Scenes,* Day, 1941.
Report on Israel, Simon & Schuster, 1950.
In the Company of Dolphins (travel book), Geis, 1964.
Paris! Paris!, Harcourt, 1977.
"The Top of the Hill" (television script; based on the novel of the same title), WPIX-TV (New York City), February 6-7, 1980.
(Author of text) *Paris/Magnum: Photographs, 1935-1981,* Harper, 1981.

Contributor to *New Yorker, Esquire, Yale Review,* and other publications.

SIDELIGHTS: During a writing career spanning four decades, the late Irwin Shaw practiced his natural storytelling talent in a host of genres. When he was twenty-three his play *Bury the Dead* was a Broadway hit. His short stories are ranked among the very best produced by writers of his generation; *Newsweek* called him "a master of the short story." *The Young Lions* established him as one of the major novelists of the 1950s while his later novels, although critically snubbed, sold in the millions of copies.

Shaw was once described by William Brashler in the *Chicago Tribune Book World* as "an old pro, a craftsman and a storyteller." Michael M. Thomas, writing in the *Washington Post,* called Shaw "a fine and serious writer. . . . He hasn't shirked the challenge of the novelist's task, which is to take a view . . . of the world and its workings, and to particularize that view through characterization and plot. To enlighten and entertain, the latter shyly drawing aside the curtain to reveal the former." Ross Wetzsteon of *Saturday Review* found Shaw's writing strengths to be popular with the reading audience but generally out of favor with the critical establishment. "Shaw's strengths as a novelist," Wetzsteon maintained, "are those of another century—relentlessly fluid narrative, dramatically focused set pieces, and sharp, incisive dialogue—which help account for both his critical disfavor . . . and his commercial success. . . . In short, Shaw is that most contemptible of contemporary writers—a believer in *stories.*"

Shaw began his career at the age of twenty-one as a radio script writer on the "Andy Gump" and "Dick Tracy" shows, two popular radio programs of the 1930s. For three years he wrote nine serial episodes a week. This led to a stint as a film writer in Hollywood, but Shaw soon grew dissatisfied with the film industry and returned to New York City. In 1935 a play writing contest sponsored by the New Theatre League caught his attention, and Shaw wrote a one-act play for the competition. Though his entry did not win, it was produced on Broadway at the Ethel Barrymore Theatre in 1936.

A searing antiwar play, *Bury the Dead* is set during "the second year of the war that is to begin tomorrow night," as Shaw explained in the text. It concerns a group of dead soldiers who refuse to be buried. They argue that they never had a chance to finish their lives. The play ends with the soldiers walking off the stage, ignoring the pleas of their family and commanding officers to stay and be buried. Stark Young of the *New Republic* thought *Bury the Dead* "presents the finest image that has appeared in our theatre this year. . . . When these six dead men arise from their graves and refuse to be buried, the imagination is shocked and caught by the sheer sight of them. . . . As theatre image this motif ranks with the entrance of Oedipus with his blinded eyes, in Sophocles' play, with the sleep-walking scene in 'Macbeth,' with Lear in the storm, with, that is, such consummations of action, the visual and the idea as are rare even in first-rank drama."

Bury the Dead was an immediate success. Because it reflected the antiwar rhetoric of the Popular Front of the time it also became, a writer for the London *Times* recounted, "one of the radically chic events of the 1930s." Joseph Wood Krutch, reviewing the play for the *Nation,* called it "incomparably the best of the left-wing dramas seen this year." But Shaw was later to disavow the work's pacifism. Jack Jones and William Tuohy of the *Los Angeles Times* quoted him explaining: "I'm not a pacifist. I don't believe you can be. Lie down and let people walk over you? Some wars have to be fought." Although Shaw devoted the next few years to writing plays, and had new works produced until the 1960s, he never again enjoyed such a popular success as *Bury the Dead.*

But in another field of writing he gained lasting critical acceptance. During the late 1930s Shaw began to contribute short stories to such magazines as the *New Yorker* and *Esquire.* His first collection, *Sailor Off the Bremen and Other Stories,* appeared in 1939 and established his reputation as a short story writer. Shaw's stories, Walter W. Ross explained in the *Dictionary of Literary Biography Yearbook: 1984,* are what "many critics regard as his best work." As Hubert Saal maintained in the *Saturday Review,* "Shaw's high place among contemporary writers rests largely on his short stories."

William Goldman, writing in the *New York Times Book Review,* cited Shaw's storytelling talent as the key to his successful short stories. "What he is," Goldman wrote, "is this: a tale teller. There is narrative interest in everything the man puts down. . . . Coupled with the narrative gift is the ability to write with an ease and a clarity that only Fitzgerald had." A reviewer for the *Washington Post Book World* also found this quality in Shaw's work: "He knows, with wonderful exactitude, how to tell a story. Not just some of the story, not merely the parts of the story that please him, not more of the story than we need to know, but the very tale itself; and when it's over, it stops."

Shaw's ability to create believable characters was cited by several critics as another strength of his short stories. Robert Cromie, writing in the *Saturday Review,* thought that Shaw "has the gift of all great storytellers: when he's really swinging, he creates characters as genuine as that odd couple across the street, the curious patrons of the corner bar, the tragic figures from the headlines. They are individuals who walk into the living room of your

mind, ensconce themselves, and refuse to be dislodged." Also writing in *Saturday Review,* William Peden believed that "Shaw's power lies in his ability to capture the essence of a character by the revealing statement, gesture, or thought. . . . Shaw's people seem wonderfully alive, even when the author descends to caricature and burlesque. Like Dickens, Mr. Shaw has created, prodigally, a crowded gallery of memorable people."

Jonathan Yardley of the *Washington Post Book World* commented on Shaw's recreation of the texture and tone of the world around him. "Shaw is less a creative artist," Yardley argued, "than a reporter—but . . . like O'Hara, he is a very good one. He sees clearly, he understands what he sees, and he describes it pointedly." Cromie, too, saw this ability: "Shaw is a fine observer with a well-trained ear; his conversations, whether real or invented, give the impression of inevitability."

Shaw's stories underwent several changes in the course of his long career. As Stefan Kanfer of *Time* reported: "In the '30s Shaw sang a chant of social significance; the tales are filled with laborers and struggling families. . . . But by the '40s he had found his own voice, a Shavian mix of irony and poignance. [After that] the supple prose [was], like Cheever's, dominated by sexual themes and by the attempt to lend common experiences and ordinary people a secular grace." Despite the changes in his stories, his work "consistently remained on a high level of craftsmanship," as Herbert Ruhm wrote in *National Review.*

A continuing theme of Shaw's short fiction was war and violence. Peden believed that Shaw's "best-known and most memorable stories are those directly or indirectly connected with war and the effect of war, violence, and intolerance." Willie Morris, in an article for the *Washington Post,* agreed with this assessment: "The war molded [Shaw] irrevocably and inspired many of his most enduring stories." One such story is "Sailor Off the Bremen," in which an American athlete fights a Nazi sailor who has attacked his communist brother. Their fight becomes "a graphic dramatization on a small scale of the clash between the forces of Teutonic fascism and communism," Ross wrote in the *Dictionary of Literary Biography.*

War and violence also provided the impetus for Shaw's first novel, *The Young Lions,* published in 1948. Following the lives of three young soldiers—two Americans, Michael Whitacre and Noah Ackerman, and a German, Christian Diestl—during World War II, the novel brings the three men together at a concentration camp at the close of the war. There Whitacre "finds meaning beyond all the bloodshed which has consumed his life for the last four years. He realizes if struggle and sacrifice will bring about the survival of a few men of decency, then all their hardships have been worth the cost," Ross explained in the *Dictionary of Literary Biography.* John Lardner of the *New Yorker* found the novel's climax to be "particularly well and movingly written," and called Shaw "one of the most skillful storytellers extant." In the *Saturday Review of Literature,* Lee Rogow called *The Young Lions* "a fine, full, intelligent book, packed with wonderful talk and crackling writing."

Publication of *The Young Lions* marked a turning point in Shaw's career. The book was praised by the critics of the time and is still held in high esteem today. Bart Barnes of the *Washington Post* explained that it was "hailed as one of the most important novels to come out of the war." Writing in the *Times Literary Supplement,* William Boyd described *The Young Lions* as "one of the few genuinely praiseworthy 'big' novels to come out of the Second World War," while Morris called it "the finest novel of the European theater." But perhaps more important to Shaw's later career was the book's financial success. *The Young*

Lions made the best-seller lists and was adapted as a movie. "It enabled Shaw," Ross reported in the *Dictionary of Literary Biography Yearbook: 1984,* "to rise above a hand-to-mouth existence as a struggling author." Because of the lucrative rewards available in the genre, Shaw devoted most of his remaining years to writing novels. As Richard Haver Costa stated in the *Dictionary of Literary Biography Yearbook: 1984,* the success of *The Young Lions* "convinced him that only in the novel could he find the passport to economic self-sufficiency."

The Troubled Air, Shaw's second novel, concerns a radio station director who must investigate press charges that five of his employees are communist agents. He is caught between the right-wing attackers who demand dismissal of the employees because of their political beliefs and the left-wingers who defend the accused regardless of their actual activities. The novel demonstrated, Stephen Stepanchev wrote in the *Nation,* that "radicalism is no longer fashionable on the air waves and can, as a matter of fact, spin careers downward to economic ruin and suicide." A London *Times* writer reported that *The Troubled Air* "was disliked by some because Shaw did not find Communism perfect, but it remains his most psychologically convincing" novel. Writing in the *New York Herald Tribune Book Review,* Milton Rugoff found *The Troubled Air* to be "Shaw at his characteristic best, seizing passionately on a vital social issue and presenting it with a firm grasp not only of the intellectual and moral values but of the many kinds of human beings it involves."

Soon after publishing *The Troubled Air* in 1950 Shaw left the United States to live in Europe. As Ross quoted Shaw explaining in the *Dictionary of Literary Biography Yearbook: 1984,* "America was not a good place to live in then." Shaw continued to write about Americans, however, and in the years to follow he produced a string of popular best-sellers. Speaking to the *Paris Review* about his decision to live in Europe, Shaw stated: "The charge that I've become less American is ridiculous. . . . I think I gained a whole lot of insight by living in Europe."

Although Shaw's later novels made him a popular and wealthy writer, they damaged his early critical reputation. During the 1950s and 1960s he was widely believed to have squandered his potential in order to make money with unambitious commercial fiction. This evaluation of his work riled Shaw. He once told the *New York Times:* "I cringe when critics say I'm a master of the popular novel. . . . What's an unpopular novel? Can you beat the ending of the 'Odyssey' or the Gospels? They're enormously entertaining. Now I'm sometimes regarded as just a popular writer, but so were Tolstoy, Dickens and Balzac and the ghost looking over all our shoulders, Shakespeare." Goldman explained Shaw's differences with the critics in this way: "He was not skillful enough to surmount the ultimate obstacle: popularity. Before the war, when no one was reading him, he was a critic's darling. They never forgave him for [the success of] 'The Young Lions.' "

Shaw's novels after *The Troubled Air* often concern a large cast of characters in a host of exotic locales and occupy what R. V. Cassill described in the *Chicago Tribune Book World* as "the borderland where serious art and commercial sentimentalities blur comfortably." Few of these novels received kind reviews from the critics. Speaking of *The Top of the Hill,* for example, Curt Suplee of the *Washington Post* complained that "nearly 1,000 trees have already fallen to provide the paper for Irwin Shaw's new novel. By any literary standard, those trees have died in vain." Stanley Kauffmann of the *Chicago Tribune Book World* called "writers like Shaw . . . retailers of the serious" who offer "pasteurized social-historical insight [and] tragedy 'worked' for

easy pathos." But other critics praised Shaw's continued ability to create worthwhile, entertaining stories. Among these reviewers, Charles Champlin of the *Los Angeles Times* believed Shaw to be "a strong storyteller first and always. . . . Shaw's writing, whether unabashedly commercial or more intensely personal, reveals his knowledge of time, place, character and history, and the artist's sure control of his materials." Mark Goodman of *Time* commented that Shaw had the "ability to create a bestseller with moral resonance."

Undoubtedly Shaw's most successful novel was the 1970 bestseller *Rich Man, Poor Man,* which has sold well over six million copies and was made into the first television miniseries. As Barnes recounted, "it is generally credited with inspiring the television craze for mini-series based on novels that continues today." The novel tells the saga of the Jordache family, descended from a New York baker, and ranges over the whole of American society. As W. G. Rogers maintained in the *New York Times Book Review,* "this is the dawn-to-dusk, 1940's-to-1970's, success-to-failure, poor-to-rich spectrum."

Though the novel was extremely popular, its critical reception was as cold as that given to previous Shaw efforts. Christopher Lehmann-Haupt of the *New York Times* simply called *Rich Man, Poor Man* "bad, bad." John Leggett of the *Saturday Review* allowed that "along with nearly everyone else, I was, and am, in awe of Irwin Shaw. . . . He is the kind of craftsman—sincere, knowledgeable, unassuming—that I am drawn to and want to see confirmed as one of our great writers. It is my agonizing duty to report that *Rich Man, Poor Man* does not redeem his long-standing promise." Rogers stated that "few of our younger technicians can beat Irwin Shaw's expertise. . . . His pace doesn't slacken for chapter after chapter. Incidents lead to incidents—and they are uncommonly appealing. . . . 'Rich Man, Poor Man' is exciting reading. It's a book you can't put down. Once you do, it wouldn't occur to you to pick it up again."

Upon Shaw's death in 1984, Barnes described him as "one of the most prolific of contemporary American authors [and one] whose novels, short stories and plays portrayed a kaleidoscope of the human experience." Shaw's books have sold over fourteen million copies and have been translated into twenty-eight languages. Several of his novels have been adapted as popular movies and television programs. But despite his commercial success, Shaw's critical reputation is still mixed. His early short stories are highly regarded but many critics, Ross explained in the *Dictionary of Literary Biography Yearbook: 1984,* believe that Shaw "decided he could earn big money writing bestsellers and traded his integrity as a writer for slick novels."

But this judgment is contested by Gay Talese. Writing in the *Washington Post,* Talese stated that Shaw "deserved kinder treatment than he got from the book critics, but their resentment of him had less to do with his work than with the way he lived. Irwin Shaw enjoyed living—in a way so few writers do. He was an outdoor man in an indoor sport, and his international fame served to inspire envy and some cruelty in critics. Irwin accepted this, and he left behind a body of work any good writer should envy." Also writing in the *Washington Post,* Jonathan Yardley described Shaw as "a professional writer with standards. His short stories (at which he was best) and novels were intended, without embarrassment, to entertain, and this they often did very well. . . . He seems always to have believed that he was writing for intelligent people; his prose was clean, literate and polished, and he usually had something interesting to say. He was certainly a 'popular' writer, but he could hold his head high in polite company and indeed was revered, as a personal and professional example, by many writers with larger literary reputations than his own." Morris believed Shaw to be "the author of . . . many of the finest short stories in the English language" and a "worldly and profoundly sensitive American writer, one of our great ones." Speaking to the *Miami Herald,* Shaw once explained his goal as a writer: "Starting with the first minute I got my first paycheck, my object was to be an absolute pro. What does that mean? A man who does hard things and makes them look easy. Who doesn't get rattled, who knows what to do, when to do it, who takes his time."

BIOGRAPHICAL/CRITICAL SOURCES:

BOOKS

Aldridge, John W., *After the Lost Generation,* Noonday, 1951.
Authors in the News, Volume 1, Gale, 1976.
Concise Dictionary of American Literary Biography: The New Consciousness, 1941-1968, Gale, 1987.
Contemporary Literary Criticism, Gale, Volume 7, 1977, Volume 23, 1983, Volume 34, 1985.
Dictionary of Literary Biography, Volume 6: *American Novelists since World War II,* second series, Gale, 1980.
Dictionary of Literary Biography Yearbook: 1984, Gale, 1985.
Eisinger, Chester E., *Fiction of the Forties,* University of Chicago Press, 1963.
Lewis, Allan, *American Plays and Playwrights of the Contemporary Theatre,* Crown, 1965.
Newquist, Roy, *Counterpoint,* Rand McNally, 1964.

PERIODICALS

Atlantic, November, 1948, February, 1960, February, 1973.
Chicago Tribune Book World, March 7, 1965, September 27, 1970, November 4, 1979, August 30, 1981, November 7, 1982, December 26, 1982.
Commentary, July, 1956.
Commonweal, March 18, 1960, April 23, 1965.
Detroit News, September 6, 1981, September 12, 1982.
English Journal, November, 1951.
Esquire, October, 1975.
Los Angeles Times, August 28, 1981.
Los Angeles Times Book Review, September 26, 1982, January 9, 1983.
Miami Herald, December 15, 1974.
Midwest Quarterly, Number 2, 1961.
Nation, May 6, 1936, October 9, 1948, June 23, 1951.
National Review, February 16, 1979.
New Republic, May 13, 1936, February 2, 1942.
New Statesman, August 7, 1981.
Newsweek, November 5, 1962, November 3, 1975.
New Yorker, October 2, 1948, October 20, 1975, November 14, 1977, December 24, 1979.
New York Herald Tribune, January 25, 1942, October 22, 1945.
New York Herald Tribune Book Review, June 10, 1951.
New York Times, October 22, 1945, January 26, 1948, March 9, 1965, September 27, 1970, January 15, 1973, March 28, 1973, September 18, 1975, March 15, 1977, October 17, 1977, October 30, 1979, June 1, 1981, August 29, 1981, September 28, 1982, February 17, 1983.
New York Times Book Review, August 25, 1946, February 28, 1965, October 4, 1970, February 4, 1973, April 1, 1973, June 9, 1974, September 7, 1975, October 23, 1977, November 12, 1978, February 10, 1980, July 13, 1980, August 23, 1981, October 3, 1982.
Paris Review, Number 1, 1953, spring, 1979.

Saturday Review, November 18, 1950, June 9, 1951, March 31, 1956, August 3, 1957, March 6, 1965, October 2, 1965, October 17, 1970, August, 1981.
Saturday Review of Literature, September 2, 1939, October 2, 1948, February 12, 1949.
Time, December 29, 1975, November 6, 1978.
Times Literary Supplement, October 28, 1965, December 8, 1972, April 22, 1977, November 25, 1977, July 31, 1981.
Washington Post, December 11, 1979, August 27, 1981, November 19, 1982, May 18, 1984, May 21, 1984.
Washington Post Book World, April 22, 1973, November 5, 1978, December 3, 1978.

OBITUARIES:

PERIODICALS

Chicago Tribune, May 18, 1984.
Detroit News, May 17, 1984.
Los Angeles Times, May 17, 1984.
Newsweek, May 28, 1984.
New York Times, May 17, 1984.
Publishers Weekly, June 1, 1984.
Time, May 28, 1984.
Times (London), May 18, 1984.
Washington Post, May 17, 1984.

*   *   *

SHEED, Wilfrid (John Joseph) 1930-

PERSONAL: Born December 27, 1930, in London, England; came to the United States in 1940; son of Francis Joseph (an author and publisher) and Maisie (an author and publisher; maiden name Ward) Sheed; married Miriam Ungerer; children: Elizabeth Carol, Francis, Marion. *Education:* Lincoln College, Oxford, B.A. 1954, M.A., 1957. *Religion:* Roman Catholic.

ADDRESSES: Home—Sag Harbor, N.Y. 11963. *Agent*—Lantz-Donadio, 111 West 57th St., New York, N.Y. 10019.

CAREER: Jubilee, New York, N.Y., movie reviewer, 1959-61, associate editor, 1959-66; *Commonweal,* New York City, drama critic and book editor, 1964-71; *Esquire,* New York City, movie critic, 1967-69; *New York Times,* New York City, columnist, 1971—. Visiting lecturer in creative arts, Princeton University, 1970-71; Book of the Month Club judge, 1972—; reviewer for numerous publications.

MEMBER: PEN.

AWARDS, HONORS: National Book Award nomination, 1966, for *Office Politics,* and 1971, for *Max Jamison;* "best fiction book of 1970" citation from *Time* magazine, 1971, for *Max Jamison;* Guggenheim fellowship and National Institute and American Academy award in literature, both 1971.

WRITINGS:

FICTION

Joseph (juvenile), Sheed, 1958.
A Middle Class Education: A Novel, Houghton, 1960.
The Hack (novel), Macmillan, 1963, reprinted, Vintage Books, 1980.
Square's Progress: A Novel, Farrar, Straus, 1965.
Office Politics: A Novel, Farrar, Straus, 1966.
The Blacking Factory & Pennsylvania Gothic: A Short Novel and a Long Story, Farrar, Straus, 1968.
Max Jamison: A Novel, Farrar, Straus, 1970 (published in England as *The Critic: A Novel,* Weidenfeld & Nicolson, 1970).
People Will Always Be Kind (novel), Farrar, Straus, 1973.

Transatlantic Blues (novel), Dutton, 1978.
The Boys of Winter (novel), Knopf, 1987.

NONFICTION

(Editor) G. K. Chesterton, *Essays and Poems,* Penguin, 1958.
The Morning After: Selected Essays and Reviews, Farrar, Straus, 1971.
Three Mobs: Labor, Church, and Mafia, Sheed, 1974.
Muhammad Ali: A Portrait in Words and Photographs, New American Library, 1975.
(Author of introduction) James Thurber, *Men, Women and Dogs,* Dodd, 1975.
The Good Word & Other Words, Dutton, 1978.
Clare Boothe Luce, Thorndike Press, 1982.
Frank & Maisie: A Memoir with Parents, Simon & Schuster, 1985.
(Editor) *Sixteen Short Novels,* Dutton, 1986.
(Author of text) *The Kennedy Legacy: A Generation Later,* Viking, 1988.

OTHER

Also author of *Vanishing Species of America,* 1974. Contributor to numerous periodicals, including *New York Times Book Review, Esquire, Sports Illustrated,* and *Commonweal.*

SIDELIGHTS: Novelist and critic Wilfrid Sheed has been a prominent man of letters in America for nearly thirty years. *Time* correspondent John Skow calls Sheed "almost certainly the best American reviewer of books," an elegant writer who is also "a novelist of wit and intelligence." Sheed, who was raised both in England and the United States, is often cited as an essayist who is penetrating but not pompous—"an acute and twinkling observer, adept at both irony and slapstick farce, compassionate to a fault and a most clever and accomplished stylist," to quote Eliot Fremont-Smith in the *New York Times.* The author may be slightly better known for his reviews, but he has also penned almost a dozen works of fiction, many of which draw upon his personal experiences from childhood to maturity. *Washington Post Book World* columnist Jonathan Yardley finds Sheed "a novelist of depth, complexity and compassion. . . . Sheed gets better with each new novel, and there are few writers of whom that can be said." All of Sheed's works share two essential components, according to his critics: they display finely-wrought prose and subtle, ironic humor. In *Newsweek,* Peter S. Prescott contends that Sheed "is a very funny man, but (especially in recent years) his wit has been used in the service of humaneness, a kind of domestic service to the family of man."

Sheed may have seemed destined for a literary life from his birth. Four years before he was born his parents, Frank Sheed and Maisie Ward Sheed, established the prestigious publishing firm of Sheed & Ward, "one of the most respected religious publishers in the world," according to Walter W. Ross III in the *Dictionary of Literary Biography.* Thus Sheed and his sister grew up surrounded by the important Catholic writers and thinkers of their day; both children were encouraged to excel in their studies and to enjoy vigorous exercise. When Sheed was nine the Second World War erupted, and the family moved to America, settling in Torresdale, Pennsylvania. Sheed spent his early teen years there, fascinated by American sports, especially baseball. His own budding athletic talent was squelched abruptly at fourteen when he contracted the dreaded polio, an event that shadowed the rest of his youth. Having recovered after a long convalescence, Sheed returned to England to attend preparatory school and Oxford University. Where he had been considered British in Pennsylvania, he was now looked on as an American in his native land. This too contributed to his conception of himself, both in his actions and in his philosophy.

Sheed told the *New York Times Book Review* that he "picked up . . . writing on the very day" his father died, as a meager consolation for the loss. Soon he was supporting himself by doing book and movie reviews for magazines and writing fiction in his spare time. "I guess I just sort of backed into writing," he told *Publishers Weekly.* "Probably I do not understand the craft at all, and how difficult it is. Theoretically, I may not even approve of the kind of writing I do and such a markedly personal style, but I didn't seem to have a heck of a lot of choice in the matter. I have taken off from family experiences sometimes as if they were daydreams." Indeed, much of Sheed's fiction contains autobiographical elements, although the author admits that he alters incidents immensely. "I use settings I know," he said. "I wait until things have distilled, fomented. The boyhood episodes in my novels are less and less based on anything that really happened." Still, many of Sheed's early novels deal with themes that mirror his youth. *A Middle Class Education,* his first novel, is a satire on school life in England and America. *The Blacking Factory* and *Pennsylvania Gothic* explore childhood isolation in rural Pennsylvania, and *People Will Always Be Kind* concerns a teenager stricken with polio. One theme remains more or less constant throughout all of Sheed's fiction: his protagonists, regardless of age, are prone to self-analysis of the most intense sort. As *New York Times* contributor Christopher Lehmann-Haupt puts it, Sheed's works are studies "in agonized self-consciousness."

Several of Sheed's best known novels, including *Office Politics, The Hack, Max Jamison,* and *The Boys of Winter,* deal with the wry and sometimes sordid worlds of journalism and publishing. According to John Blades in a Chicago *Tribune Books* review, Sheed "comes from a publishing family, and few writers cover the territory so confidently, or write about it with so much vim and vitriol, such malicious afore- and afterthought." For instance, *Office Politics,* which was nominated for the National Book Award in 1966, analyzes a vicious power struggle that ensues among members of a magazine staff after the editor-in-chief becomes ill. In an essay for *Wisconsin Studies in Contemporary Literature,* Richard Lehan writes that *Office Politics* "uses the drab world of New York City to intensify the drab, sordid, meaningless routine that turns young men into cynics and romantic expectation into despair." *New York Times* commentator Charles Poore suggests that Sheed "has a splendid gift for dramatizing the search-and-destroy diabolism of outrageous fortune. His characters are multidimensional without hazing off into the pretentiously symbolic."

Not every reviewer finds Sheed's characters so multidimensional. In a *New York Review of Books* essay, Robert Towers contends that Sheed's novels "read more like demonstrations than imaginative works of fiction. . . . His novels seem stronger in documentation than in invention and regularly give the *appearance* of autobiography only slightly transmuted—even when the characters and their circumstances are obviously 'made up.' They have trouble progressing beyond their initial premise or situation into a freely moving story, with the result that their denouements are often unconvincing . . . or melodramatic." *Village Voice* contributor James Wolcott likewise sees Sheed's fiction as working in a "self-created void: the characters are storewindow mannequins, the scenery consists of painted back-drops. Nothing is at stake, no giddy risks are taken, so the jokes become only curlicues in his elegant doodling." Other critics have responded warmly to Sheed's work. A *Time* reviewer writes: "Sheed constructs a bright, cutting prose from the dross of everyday slang. He wields that prose with a subtle ear for speech rhythms and a sardonic eye for the tell-tale gesture. . . . His protagonists are ordinary guys desperately trying to fend off the world's idiocies and evils long enough to define themselves and do the decent thing. They rarely succeed completely." In the *New Republic,* Yardley maintains that Sheed has moved "toward a fiction which, while the dazzle remains, has gained measurably in depth and subtlety. . . . Even at his darkest, he is a joy to read. His wit and perceptiveness are marvelous. . . . It is a measure of his achievement that we only rarely feel that the glitter is for its own sake."

Max Jamison, published in 1970, is one of Sheed's most successful novels. In another case of thinly-veiled autobiography, the book spotlights a Broadway theatre critic whose life is consumed by his work. *Saturday Review* correspondent Robert Cromie calls it "a darkly engaging book, which may be read purely as entertainment, or, as I am sure Sheed intended it should, as a sympathetic, occasionally ribald, always engrossing portrait of a tragi-comic man, mired in a profession he no longer respects or truly enjoys, a man doomed to boredom and despair, with only an occasional slight flash of pleasure in prospect to keep him alive until the fall of the final curtain." *Max Jamison* also received a nomination for the National Book Award and has been generally well-received by critics. *Commonweal* essayist David Lodge finds in the work "impressive evidence of the mature poise and skill Wilfrid Sheed has achieved as a novelist," and a *National Observer* contributor calls the book "one of the most unhappily accurate accounts of a critic's day-to-day life ever committed to paper." In a *New Republic* review, Yardley finds the unhappy Max "nonetheless a curiously admirable character for whom, in the end, one grieves. His pomposity is maddening, but in his insistence upon 'standards' there is an old-fashioned deference to tradition which one must honor; he is a man of genuine if dubiously exercised integrity. For all his stiffness, his infuriating withdrawal from the turmoil and pain of life, he inspires sadness and sympathy."

Transatlantic Blues, Sheed's 1978 novel, concerns the travails of a continent-hopping television personality with roots in England and America. *New York Times Book Review* correspondent Julian Moynahan finds the work "fictional autobiography structured as a general confession in the old Catholic sense of the term. . . . It turns out to be a tale of growing up between two countries and is one we have been waiting for from Wilfrid Sheed. . . . That isn't, of course, to pretend that the book is Sheed's own confession." According to Walter Clemons in *Newsweek, Transatlantic Blues* "is a rich mess of a novel, the funniest and freest Sheed has written. The miserable [protagonist] Chatworth is endowed with a ripped-open version of a transatlantic style Sheed has made his own, in which Oxonian clarity joins with American lowdown colloquial. . . . Chatworth's confessional prose is rawer and speedier, edgier and more combative than anything we have heard from Sheed before. At full throttle it is exciting and explosively funny." Many observers have found Sheed's use of first person narration in the book more conducive to his humor and prose style. *Critic* essayist Laurence P. Smith calls the book "clearly Sheed's finest novel to date. . . . His voice seems less coldly detached, revealing an emotional concern for his characters that his sardonic, cutting style has often obscured. *Transatlantic Blues* is a novel filled with so much humor that the temptation is to speak of nothing else. It is rich in the irony, parody, satire and witty verbal gymnastics that have earned Sheed his reputation as a leading novelist of manners. Yet his vision is the entire sad human predicament. . . . It is humor with a serious purpose." Smith elaborates: "Between the laughs are the leads, the themes and insights which help to explain the

chaos within every man. Tear-washed eyes, from laughter or grief, may offer the clearest view of the truth, or at least of one's own soul."

Nine years separate the publication dates of *Transatlantic Blues* and *The Boys of Winter,* a tragi-comic novel about struggling authors and their editors set in the rural reaches of Long Island. As Herbert Gold notes in the *New York Times Book Review,* the subject of the tale "is not so much the life of literature as careerism—also sex and softball—in an exurban Long Island colony." Sheed makes forays into the jealousies between competing fiction writers, the vagaries of the book business, and the macho antics of grown men let loose on a softball diamond. Gold writes that *The Boys of Winter* "brings Grub Street to contemporary times and the exurbs—and it's funny. Finally it does the satirist's good work of demolition, but it also, alas, tells much of the truth about literary politicking. . . . The gloomy conditions of publishing are not rubbed in our faces, and the implications are among the subtexts adroitly not emphasized. There is a nostalgia for times when the Word really did seem haunted and holy." *Los Angeles Times Book Review* contributor Art Seidenbaum concludes: "Anyone unfortunate enough to earn or learn a living in the book business will relish the back-biting behind the back-slapping in this artful novel about the wiles of writers, editors, publishers and hangers-on. Every character, as a matter of fiction, is a hanger-on here, trying to survive over somebody else's live body."

Sheed began his career as a critic writing reviews for popular periodicals, and even now he prefers a more colloquial and less academic style for his criticism—and a popular rather than academic forum. "The ideal critic, after all, is not an Aristotle or Solon or Lionel Trilling, stuffing laws down the artists' and readers' throats;" writes Mitchell S. Ross in the *Chicago Tribune Book World,* "he is a stimulator, even an agitator, whose first responsibility is to rouse his readers and irritate the cogitative cells, a task at which Sheed succeeds brilliantly. . . . His is the sort of critic who makes the ordinary labels of reviewers seem trivial—which is to say, the only kind of critic who really counts. . . . If this is not criticism, then nothing being written today is worthy of that great classification." Sheed's essays and reviews have appeared in such disparate places as *Sports Illustrated, Life, Esquire,* and the *New York Times Book Review.* The best of them are collected in two works, *The Morning After: Selected Essays and Reviews* and *The Good Word and Other Words.* Morris Freedman describes Sheed's criticism in the *New Republic:* "Mr. Sheed writes to order, mostly pithy essays on movies, plays or books, in the pages of [magazines]. The formal demands of this occasional writing, like those of the heroic couplet itself, force a concentration on the epigram, the compact summation, the striking generalization. . . . To this highly professional skill Sheed fortunately brings the restraint of common sense, balance and, most importantly, a sense of responsibility." George Stade puts it another way in the *New York Times Book Review.* "The bright, quick sentences flash through the reader's head, depositing pictures and patterns that only fade behind the rush of new ones, the sequence and sum by no means altogether without subtlety," Stade comments. ". . .Sheed is not the kind of bullying guide who in a fit of naive vanity wants to put the skeptical tourist in his place. There are no significant pauses before dark solemnities or pointed gestures toward an ineffable murk."

Sheed's fiction is widely respected, but his criticism has made his national name. According to Thomas Edwards in the *New York Times Book Review,* Sheed's work "is much in demand at the quality and slick publications alike, and one sees how his shameless lack of sham would tickle the 'inside' world of writers, editors, publishers and professional reviewers, where the pretense that the game of literature is deadly serious, somehow less political, commercial and self-advancing than the other games in town, must get positively suffocating." *Time* commentator John Skow claims that Sheed is not a critic but a reviewer, "and in his weight class, one of the best in America. He has the good taste to know that glibness is slightly shabby. . . . Sheed's opinions seem right most of the time, but not so invariably right as to be insufferable. Too much rightness shuts off debate and stifles the thought process. Sheed provides a good mixture of wisdom and nonsense." In a *New Republic* assessment, Ross concludes that Sheed's works of criticism "stand beside the works of the academics like . . . fresh and crusty loaves beside stacks of Wonder Bread."

In recent years Sheed has added full-length biographies to his list of publications. Both *Clare Boothe Luce* and *Frank and Maisie: A Memoir with Parents* are intimate accounts of their subjects, less scholarly than personal. In a *Chicago Tribune Book World* review of *Clare Boothe Luce,* Ronald Steel finds the work "a brilliantly written pastiche," adding: "Sheed is a masterly prose stylist, as addictive as chocolates, and as biting at one-liners as the lady herself. . . . Although he doesn't unveil what makes Clare tick, he does make her human. And in doing so he shows one way that an intelligent and ambitious woman made it in America in the days before affirmative action." Likewise, *New York Times* contributor John Gross notes that in *Frank and Maisie* Sheed "has not attempted to provide a full-scale portrait of his parents. Instead, he has written an account of what it was like to grow up as one of their two children. . . . But the book is Frank and Maisie's, beyond a doubt, and a very eloquent memorial to them it is—both entertaining and deeply felt, full of wry insights into the contradictions of human nature, a demonstration (if one is needed) that love and what in the end can only be called filial piety are no barrier to the incisiveness that readers of Mr. Sheed's novels and journalism have come to expect of him."

Transatlantic novelist, respected critic, and gentle biographer, Sheed has enjoyed a lengthy stay in the literary sphere. *Nation* essayist Vivian Mercier contends that Sheed has "made it," not with a bestseller, "but as a critic and novelist and something more than either—a man of letters." In his *Chicago Tribune Book World* piece, Ross writes: "The man is a natural critic who happens to write novels. A natural critic? Yes, and much more; indeed, a naturalness beautifully embellished. This is a critic with a thousand phrases on his sleeve, a playful adventurer among books. This is a man who does not need the framework of a story in order to impose his imagination upon us; Sheed is the rare critic who can stamp his personality on every page he writes. Why does the man bother with novel-writing when his talent for criticism is so great? . . . He can do the job with some skill . . . and so he continues doing it." Stade comments that in Sheed's various works, "the prose, the pace, the humor are pleasures neither old-fashioned nor new-fangled, but simply unique. . . . So is a certain quality of moral intelligence, one graced by an unflappable and chastened sanity, a charity precise and unsentimental." In the *Washington Post Book World,* Webster Schott concludes of Sheed: "He is one of our brightest reflectors. Let's urge him on in our mutual education."

Sheed is quoted on his occupation in the *Dictionary of Literary Biography.* "Circumstances have obliged me to do a good deal of reviewing (the last refuge of the light essayist): books, plays, etc.," he said. "I find this work painful, but it serves a couple of selfish purposes. It enables me to work out various aesthetic ideas, while unloading my little burden of didacticism in a safe place; and it gives me a certain thin-lipped benignity towards my own critics, when they turn the cannon round and aim it in my direction." Sheed told the *New York Times Book Review* that, as an experience, "fiction is more rewarding, even if it dumps you out of a flying door into a mudbath. But, whatever the word on that, one's nonfiction gains tremendously from having known the pressure, just as a political commentator would gain from running for office. Whatever you can still do when you can't be fastidious is your essence."

AVOCATIONAL INTERESTS: Baseball, softball, boxing.

BIOGRAPHICAL/CRITICAL SOURCES:

BOOKS

Contemporary Literary Criticism, Gale, Volume 2, 1973, Volume 4, 1975, Volume 10, 1979.
Dictionary of Literary Biography, Volume 6: *American Novelists since World War II, Second Series,* Gale, 1980.
Sheed, Wilfrid, *Frank and Maisie: A Memoir with Parents,* Simon & Schuster, 1985.

PERIODICALS

America, November 9, 1963.
Atlantic, May, 1973, March, 1978.
Chicago Tribune Book World, December 17, 1978, February 7, 1982.
Commonweal, January 24, 1969, May 8, 1970, June 24, 1977, April 14, 1978.
Critic, summer, 1978, December, 1978.
Horizon, Autumn, 1971.
International Fiction Review, January, 1974.
Kenyon Review, Volume XXXI, number 2, 1969.
Life, April 18, 1969.
Los Angeles Times, October 30, 1985.
Los Angeles Times Book Review, July 19, 1987, August 28, 1988.
Nation, December 20, 1971, February 20, 1982.
National Observer, October 28, 1968, May 11, 1970.
National Review, February 9, 1971.
New Leader, November 4, 1968.
New Republic, May 23, 1970, October 2, 1971, May 5, 1973, January 21, 1978.
New Statesman, January 18, 1974.
Newsweek, October 4, 1971, January 16, 1978, February 22, 1982, August 24, 1987.
New Yorker, November 30, 1968, March 13, 1978, December 9, 1985.
New York Review of Books, May 17, 1973, October 30, 1975, January 26, 1978, November 8, 1979, April 1, 1982, May 8, 1986.
New York Times, August 23, 1965, September 19, 1968, May 7, 1970, April 11, 1973, September 15, 1975, January 13, 1978, December 21, 1978, February 10, 1982, October 15, 1985, July 30, 1987.
New York Times Book Review, August 22, 1965, September 8, 1968, May 3, 1970, October 10, 1971, April 8, 1973, September 21, 1975, January 15, 1978, January 21, 1979, February 21, 1982, November 10, 1985, August 2, 1987.
People, August 31, 1987.
Publishers Weekly, February 6, 1978.
Saturday Review, September 4, 1965, September 14, 1968, June 6, 1970, January 20, 1979, July, 1982.
Spectator, January 26, 1974.
Sports Illustrated, November 11, 1968.
Time, September 20, 1968, January 6, 1975, September 8, 1975, January 27, 1978, December 25, 1978, February 22, 1982, November 18, 1985, August 3, 1987.

Times (London), August 5, 1982.
Times Literary Supplement, November 4, 1965, February 9, 1967, August 14, 1969, July 31, 1970, January 18, 1974, November 23, 1979, October 1, 1982, May 30, 1986.
Tribune Books (Chicago), July 19, 1987.
Village Voice, August 26, 1971, January 23, 1978.
Washington Post Book World, January 7, 1968, September 22, 1968, April 29, 1973, February 5, 1978, December 24, 1978, February 14, 1982, January 5, 1986, August 19, 1987, October 16, 1988.
Wisconsin Studies in Contemporary Literature, summer, 1967.

—*Sketch by Anne Janette Johnson*

*   *   *

SHEEHY, Gail 1936(?)-

PERSONAL: Born November 25, 1936 (one source says November 27, 1937), in Mamaroneck, N.Y.; daughter of Harold Merritt (an advertising executive) and Lillian (a singer; maiden name, Rainey) Henion; married Albert Sheehy (an internist), August 20, 1960 (divorced, 1968); children: Maura; Mohm (foster daughter). *Education:* University of Vermont, B.S., 1958; Columbia University, graduate study, 1970.

ADDRESSES: Home—New York, N.Y. *Office*—c/o William Morrow & Co., 105 Madison Ave., New York, N.Y. 10016. *Agent*—Paul R. Reynolds Inc., 12 East 41st St., New York, N.Y. 10017.

CAREER: Democrat and Chronicle, Rochester, N.Y., fashion editor, 1961-63; *New York Herald Tribune,* New York City, feature writer, 1963-66; *New York* (magazine), New York City, contributing editor, 1968-77; free-lance writer. Has worked as a traveling home economist.

MEMBER: Authors Guild, Authors League of America, P.E.N. American Center (member of national advisory board), Common Cause, National Organization for Women, Cambodian Crisis Committee, Girls Clubs of America, Newswomen's Club of New York.

AWARDS, HONORS: Front Page Award from Newswomen's Club of New York, 1964, for most distinguished feature of interest to women, and 1973, for best magazine feature; National Magazine Award, 1972, for reporting excellence; Alicia Patterson Foundation fellowship, 1974.

WRITINGS:

Lovesounds, Random House, 1970.
Panthermania: The Clash of Black against Black in One American City, Harper, 1971.
Speed Is of the Essence, Pocket Books, 1971.
Hustling: Prostitution in Our Wide Open Society, Delacorte, 1973.
Passages: Predictable Crises of Adult Life, Dutton, 1976.
Pathfinders, Morrow, 1981.
Spirit of Survival, Morrow, 1986.
Character: America's Search for Leadership, Morrow, 1988.
Gorbachev: The Man Who Changed the World, Harper, 1990.

Contributor to *Cosmopolitan, McCall's, Glamour, Good Housekeeping, London Sunday Telegraph, Paris Match,* and *New York Times Magazine.*

SIDELIGHTS: Gail Sheehy's first book, *Lovesounds,* deals with the breakup of a marriage. But, as Judith Martin of the *Washington Post* points out, it may be a disappointment to "devotees of the genre, who know how to enjoy first her side, then his side, and then the counselor's view showing that they both had faults but could learn to correct them and have another baby." In this book there are no major faults in the characters. Sheehy has created a good wife and a good husband, both of whom love their child and have rewarding careers, but who are nonetheless getting a divorce. Martin says that "it would seem to be a step backwards in novel writing because we have all been brought up to believe that everything in books, if not in life, happens for a reason." Here, this is clearly not the case, but "once you accept the fact that the marriage was a good one, and that its dissolution is something that neither husband nor wife wished and for which neither was deliberately responsible, you find a good study of the pure emotions involved."

Israel Horovitz states that with *Lovesounds* "Gail Sheehy has written the most brutal indictment of hypocrisy in marriage, the most incisive analysis of the daily experience, the most hearty yet subtle feminist line since that Friday morning in July when Anton Chekhov died in Olga Knipper's arms. She has written a truly pop novel: a book that reads as easily as any of R. Art Crumb's comix, yet stays as firmly lodged in your stomach as Grandma's kreplach. *Lovesounds* is a fine, fine piece of writing that should be read by anyone who is married, was married, or will be married." But Paul D. Zimmerman, in a *Newsweek* review, insists that the book is a failure. His explanation: "Imprisoned in nearly every journalist lives a captive novelist struggling to get out. . . . But the rules of the novel are different. The subject stands inside the characters, not across the table taking notes, and the language that serves so well to capture the surface tensions of a tow-away depot or the anxieties of a student revolutionary cannot necessarily handle the swollen emotions of inner life bursting apart." Zimmerman concludes that "Gail Sheehy has broken out as a novelist all right. But this book at least makes it doubtful that it was worth the struggle."

Sheehy's best-known work is probably *Passages: Predictable Crises of Adult Life.* The theme of the book, as Jill Tweedie puts it in a *Saturday Review* article, is that "not only are there crises in every life, not only do they occur with reasonable predictability, but they are (cheeringly) entirely natural—comparable, say, to the seasons of the year or to the germination of a seed." Sheehy contends that there are four main "passages" in life; she terms them "Pulling up Roots," "The Trying Twenties," "Passage to the Thirties," and "The Deadline Decade: Setting off on the Midlife Passage." She feels that everyone must confront each of these milestones and must pass through each in order to advance to the next.

Reviewing the book for *Ms.,* Patricia O'Brien writes: "I barely made it past the Introduction to *Passages* before I found myself underlining passages—not because I was learning startling new facts, but because finally somebody was putting universal human fears and uncertainties about change and growing old into a manageable perspective. On the whole, *Passages* succeeds most when it is defining these fears, and not when Sheehy is presenting her numerous case histories." O'Brien calls it "a book that gives us the chance to track ourselves. Sheehy particularly makes it easier for us to understand the lonely polarization that may occur between men and women by pointing out that the sexes are rarely in the same identity and career questions at the same time."

Maurice Hart of *Best Sellers* says that the writing in *Passages* "is basically journalistic in style, and the arguments are not as clearly and precisely stated as they should be in a scholarly presentation. Consequently, for a definitive work on the stages of adult life one will have to look elsewhere—possibly to one of Ms. Sheehy's sources." Around those sources centers a noteworthy controversy. In researching this subject Sheehy talked with such experts as Yale psychologist Daniel Levinson, Harvard psychiatrist George Vaillant, and U.C.L.A. psychiatrist Roger Gould. She also attributes some of her information to Erik Erikson, Else Frenkel-Brunswick, Margaret Hennig, and Margaret Mead. When the book first appeared, *Time* noted that Levinson "outlined the 'mentor phenomenon'—that in middle age a man feels the need to promote the fortunes of a younger worker," and that Hennig "reported on the importance of mentors to women in corporate life" in 1970.

Levinson was somewhat perturbed at Sheehy's allegedly unauthorized use of his research, saying "she is incomplete, to put it mildly, in acknowledging her use of my published and unpublished material." But Hennig, according to *Time,* had no complaints. "She used my stuff," she said, "but this is real life and I'm not upset about it. She gave me credit." Roger Gould, however, was furious. A *Time* writer said that he "filed a plagiarism suit against Sheehy and Dutton [her publisher]. The case was settled out of court: Gould received $10,000 and 10% of the book's royalties." Gould contended that he was under the impression that he was to be a collaborator on the book, but after he had discussed his research with Sheehy, found that she considered him a paid consultant. She claimed that it was made clear from the beginning that Gould was not to be a co-author.

In defense of Sheehy, Roderick MacLeish of the *Washington Post* emphasizes that "by her own assertion, Gail Sheehy is not the central theorist of her work. . . . What Sheehy has done is to gather together the materials of the relatively new social science of adult development, codify it into skillfully popularized form, invest it with the classy, vernacular prose style for which she is justifiably admired and arrive at a generalist's conclusions—there's more hope in the aging process than you've been led to believe." And, as MacLeish goes on to conclude, "I'm sure that specialists will quarrel with what she has done. That's what specialists are for. But the hope, wit and de-mythification of adulthood that permeates Sheehy's book make *Passages* a work of revelation for the layman as he tries to understand the inevitable movement of his life. It is a stunning accomplishment."

BIOGRAPHICAL/CRITICAL SOURCES:

BOOKS

Contemporary Issues Criticism, Volume 2, Gale, 1984.

PERIODICALS

Best Sellers, August 1, 1971, September, 1976.
Chicago Tribune, May 13, 1988, May 29, 1988.
Los Angeles Times, May 25, 1988, June 10, 1988.
McCall's, August, 1970.
Ms., August, 1976.
Newsweek, August 10, 1970, August 30, 1973.
New York, July 21, 1969, August 3, 1970.
New York Review of Books, October 28, 1976.
New York Times, August 16, 1976.
New York Times Book Review, September 5, 1971, May 25, 1986, May 29, 1988.
Saturday Review, July 24, 1971, May 15, 1976.
Time, May 10, 1976.
Village Voice, August 20, 1970.
Washington Post, August 29, 1970, August 5, 1988.
Washington Post Book World, March 23, 1976.

SHEEN, Fulton J(ohn)　1895-1979

PERSONAL: Original given name Peter, took the name John at confirmation and later adopted mother's maiden name; born May 8, 1895, in El Paso, Ill.; died December 9, 1979, in New York, N.Y.; buried in St. Patrick's Cathedral, New York, N.Y.; son of Newton Morris (a farmer) and Delia (Fulton) Sheen. *Education:* St. Viator College, B.A., 1917, M.A., 1919; St. Paul Seminary, St. Paul, Minn., seminarian, 1919; Catholic University of America, S.T.B. and J.C.B., 1920; University of Louvain, Ph.D., 1923, agrege en philosophie, 1925; University of Rome, S.T.D., 1924; also attended Sorbonne (University of Paris) and Collegio Angelico.

CAREER: Ordained Roman Catholic priest, 1919, appointed papal chamberlain with title Very Reverend Monsignor, 1934, raised to domestic prelate with title Right Reverend Monsignor, 1935, consecrated as Titular Bishop of Cesariana and Auxiliary to the Archbishop of New York, 1951, consecrated as Titular Archbishop of Newport, 1969; St. Edmund's College, Ware, England, professor of dogmatic theology, 1925; St. Patrick's Church, Peoria, Ill., curate, 1925-26; Catholic University of America, Washington, D.C., 1926-50, began as instructor in philosophy of religion, became professor of philosophy; Society for the Propagation of the Faith, New York City, national director, 1950-66; auxiliary bishop of New York City, 1951-66; Bishop of Rochester, Rochester, N.Y., 1966-69. Host of weekly radio program "Catholic Hour," National Broadcasting Co., 1930-52, weekly television program "Life Is Worth Living," 1951-57, and television series "Life of Christ" and "Quo Vadis? America"; narrator, "The Story of the Vatican" (part of "March of Time" series). Preacher at summer conferences, Westminster Cathedral, London, England, 1925 and 1928-31; lecturer, Catholic Summer School, Cambridge University, 1930 and 1931; visiting preacher, Santa Suzanna, Rome, summer, 1933. Annual Lenten orator at St. Patrick's Cathedral, New York, beginning 1931.

MEMBER: American Catholic Philosophical Association, Mediaeval Academy of America, American Geographical Association, Catholic Literary Guild.

AWARDS, HONORS: LL.D., St. Viator College and Loyola University (Chicago), 1929, University of Notre Dame, 1934, and St. Bonaventure College (New York), 1939; Litt.D., Marquette University, 1934; Cardinal Mazalla Philosophy Medal, Georgetown University, 1936; L.H.D., St. John's University (Brooklyn), 1941; Academy of Television Arts and Sciences Emmy Award, 1952, for "Life Is Worth Living" program.

WRITINGS:

God and Intelligence in Modern Philosophy, introduction by G. K. Chesterton, Longmans, Green, 1925, Image Books, 1958.
Religion Without God, Longmans, Green, 1928, Garden City Books, 1954.
The Life of All Living, Century, 1929, reprinted, Doubleday, 1979.
The Divine Romance, revised edition, Century, 1930.
Old Errors and New Labels, Century, 1931, reprinted, Kennikat, 1970.
Moods and Truths, Century, 1932, reprinted, Kennikat, 1970.
Way of the Cross, Appleton, 1932, reprinted, Garden City Books, 1956.
The Seven Last Words, Century, 1933, reprinted, Alba, 1982.
Hymn of the Conquered, Kenedy, 1933.
The Eternal Galilean, Appleton, 1934, reprinted, Garden City Publishing, 1950.

Philosophy of Science, Bruce, 1934.

The Mystical Body of Christ, Sheed & Ward, 1935.

Calvary and the Mass, Kenedy, 1936, reprinted, Garden City Books, 1953.

The Moral Universe, Bruce, 1936, reprinted, Books for Libraries, 1967.

The Cross and the Beatitudes, Kenedy, 1937.

Communism: The Opium of the People, St. Anthony Guild, 1937.

The Cross and the Crisis, Kenedy, 1938, reprinted, Books for Libraries, 1969.

Liberty, Equality and Fraternity, Macmillan, 1938.

The Rainbow of Sorrow, Kenedy, 1938, reprinted, Garden City Books, 1953.

Victory Over Vice, Kenedy, 1939, reprinted, Garden City Books, 1953.

Whence Come Wars, Sheed & Ward, 1940.

The Seven Virtues, Kenedy, 1940.

Freedom Under God, Bruce, 1940.

War and Guilt (collection of nineteen radio broadcasts), National Council of Catholic Men, 1941.

For God and Country, Kenedy, 1941.

A Declaration of Dependence, Bruce, 1941.

Peace (collection of seventeen radio broadcasts), National Council of Catholic Men, 1942.

God and War, Kenedy, 1942.

The Divine Verdict, Kenedy, 1943.

The Armour of God: Reflections and Prayers for Wartime, Kenedy, 1943.

Philosophies at War, Scribner, 1943.

Crisis in Christendom (collection of eighteen radio broadcasts), National Council of Catholic Men, 1943.

Love One Another, Kenedy, 1944.

Seven Words to the Cross, Kenedy, 1944.

Seven Pillars of Peace, Scribner, 1944.

Seven Words of Jesus and Mary, Kenedy, 1945.

You (collection of eighteen radio broadcasts), National Council of Catholic Men, 1945.

One Lord, One World, National Council of Catholic Men, c. 1945.

Preface to Religion, Kenedy, 1946.

Characters of the Passion, Kenedy, 1947.

Jesus, Son of Mary (for children), McMullen, 1947, reprinted, Seabury, 1980.

Light Your Lamps (collection of eleven radio broadcasts), National Council of Catholic Men, 1947.

Love on Pilgrimage (collection of twelve radio broadcasts), National Council of Catholic Men, 1947.

Communism and the Conscience of the West, Bobbs-Merrill, 1948.

The Modern Soul in Search of God (collection of thirteen radio broadcasts), National Council of Catholic Men, 1948.

Philosophy of Religion, Appleton, 1948.

Peace of Soul, McGraw, 1949.

The Love That Waits for You, National Council of Catholic Men, 1949.

Lift up Your Heart, McGraw, 1950, reprinted, Image Books, 1975.

Three to Get Married, Appleton, 1951.

The World's First Love, McGraw, 1952, reprinted, Doubleday, 1976, abridged edition published as *The World's Great Love,* Seabury, 1978.

Life Is Worth Living (collection of television broadcasts), McGraw, Volume I, 1953, Volume II, 1954, Volume III, 1955, Volume IV, 1956, Volume V, 1957, selections from

Volumes I and II published in one volume, Doubleday, 1978.

The Life of Christ, Maco Magazine Corp., 1954.

The Way to Happiness, Maco Magazine Corp., 1954.

The Way to Inner Peace, Maco Magazine Corp., 1954.

The Way to Happy Living, Maco Magazine Corp., 1955.

God Love You, Garden City Books, 1955, reprinted, Doubleday, 1981.

Thinking Life Through, McGraw, 1955.

The True Meaning of Christmas, McGraw, 1955.

Thoughts for Daily Living, Garden City Books, 1956.

(Contributor) Henry Babcock Adams, editor, *Selected Sermons of Fulton J. Sheen and Harry Emerson Fosdick,* Department of Speech and Drama, Stanford University, 1956.

(With S. Andhil Fineberg and Daniel A. Poling) *The Ideological Fallacies of Communism,* U.S. Government Printing Office, 1957.

(With Henri Daniel-Rops) *This Is the Mass,* Hawthorn, 1958.

Life of Christ, McGraw, 1958, reprinted, Image Books, 1977.

(With Henry Canova Vollam Morton) *This Is Rome,* Hawthorn, 1960.

Go to Heaven, McGraw, 1960.

(With Morton) *This Is the Holy Land,* Hawthorn, 1961.

These Are the Sacraments, Hawthorn, 1962.

Science, Psychiatry and Religion, Dell, 1962.

Love, Marriage and Children, Dell, 1963.

The Priest Is Not His Own, McGraw, 1963.

Missions and the World Crisis, Bruce, 1963.

The Church, Communism and Democracy, Dell, 1964.

The Power of Love, Maco Magazine Corp., 1964.

Walk With God, Maco Magazine Corp., 1965.

Christmas Inspirations, Maco Publishing Co., 1966.

(Compiler) *That Tremendous Love,* Harper, 1967.

Guide to Contentment, Simon & Schuster, 1967.

Footprints in a Darkened Forest, Meredith, 1967.

The Quotable Fulton J. Sheen, edited by F. Gushurst and others, Droke, 1967.

The Fulton J. Sheen Treasury, Popular Library, 1967.

Lenten and Easter Inspirations, Maco Publishing Co., 1967.

The Wit and Wisdom of Bishop Fulton J. Sheen, edited by Bill Adler, Prentice-Hall, 1968.

Children and Parents, Simon & Schuster, 1970.

Those Mysterious Priests, Doubleday, 1974.

The Electronic Christian (readings), Macmillan, 1979.

A Fulton Sheen Reader, Carillon Books, 1979.

Treasure in Clay: The Autobiography of Fulton J. Sheen, Doubleday, 1980.

Also author of *God of Peace,* 1942; author of booklets, including a series of five on communism, 1937. Author of columns "God Love You," Catholic Press, and "Bishop Sheen Speaks," syndicated in secular publications. Contributor to *Commonweal, America, New Scholasticism,* and other periodicals. Editor, *Mission* and *World-Mission.*

SIDELIGHTS: For nearly forty of his eighty-four years, Fulton J. Sheen was one of the American Catholic church's most prominent spokesmen. At its peak in 1950, his "Catholic Hour" radio program reached an audience of some four million people in the United States alone; his television series, "Life Is Worth Living," attracted up to thirty million viewers per week, beating such competition as Frank Sinatra and Milton Berle. (There was, in fact, a lighthearted rivalry between "Uncle Miltie" and "Uncle Fultie," with Berle once going so far as to remark that Sheen "had better writers." Sheen was careful to thank all four of them—"Matthew, Mark, Luke and John"—when he won an

Emmy in 1952.) In short, the *New York Times* noted, he was "one of the most effective evangelists that the broadcasting era has produced."

According to this same *New York Times* reporter, Sheen first distinguished himself as a young priest "by his furious dedication and passion. He neither smoked nor drank; he took no holidays; he was indifferent to food and amusements; he gave away nearly all his earnings." An almost lifelong conservative, he often took stands that generated controversy. He was, for example, a fiery opponent of communism, siding with Francisco Franco in the Spanish Civil War and once criticizing a visiting group of Russian Orthodox clergymen so severely that they complained to the Vatican. He also scorned the concept of Freudian psychoanalysis (which he felt was based on nothing but "materialism, hedonism, infantilism and eroticism") to such an extent that Catholic therapists feared he would dissuade people from seeking psychiatric treatment. He advocated an active role for both religion and corporal punishment in the schools, commenting that "it is about time that politics ceased setting a limit to religion and that religion begin setting a limit to politics." His 1967 break with the church over the presence of American troops in Vietnam—Sheen favored immediate withdrawal, while the church supported the president—at first glance might have seemed uncharacteristic for a conservative, but it did manage to land him squarely in the middle of a very characteristic imbroglio. He later changed his mind, however, and chose to back President Richard Nixon's plan of gradual withdrawal.

Sheen's tenure as bishop of Rochester, New York (his first pastoral post in forty years) was also marked by controversy. As the *New York Times* recalled, "he named a young priest who had been active among blacks as his vicar for urban affairs, gave his priests permission to say mass in private homes, moved the favored age of confirmation up from the traditional 7 to 12 years to the late teens, proposed that the church give 5 percent of its revenues to the poor and said no new church should be built at a cost of more than $1 million." He also offered to donate a church in his diocese for use as low-income housing, an offer his parishioners felt he did not have the right to make. Some attribute his early "retirement" from the bishopric to the widespread complaints this last proposal sparked. At any rate, Rochester proved to be Sheen's final forum; increasingly poor health forced him to spend most the 1970s confined to his New York City apartment.

In a review of *Treasure in Clay,* Sheen's autobiography, *America*'s John Jay Hughes traced the bishop's tendency to stir up controversy back to his childhood. After quoting Sheen's comment that "I struggled to be a leader in the class, and I would come home with holy pictures and medals, but I would never receive one word of praise from my parents," Hughes wrote: "In their commendable attempt to avoid spoiling their brilliant son, [Sheen's] well-meaning parents instilled in him, probably without ever knowing it, the insatiable hunger for praise which constituted his single serious vice: vanity. Against this besetting sin Bishop Sheen waged a lifelong battle." Robert Nordberg of *Best Sellers* also noticed what he called "a strange duality about the man. . . . There was the Fulton Sheen who taught philosophy at the Catholic University of America and produced such distinguished works as *God and Intelligence in Modern Philosophy.* Then there was Fulton Sheen the popularizer, the winner of converts, the radio and television curator. . . . The world being what it is, it was the popularizer who received tremendous adulation. The professor was all but forgotten."

Concluded Hughes: "Bishop Sheen was a curious blend of intellectual brilliance, uncontrolled romanticism and total naivete about practical affairs. It is difficult to imagine a man less suited to be chief pastor of a diocese. . . . [But] if Bishop Sheen failed as an administrator, he towered above others in the bishop's primary task of preaching and teaching. . . . [In the pages of his autobiography,] that memorable voice continues to speak, reminding us of truths too often forgotten today."

BIOGRAPHICAL/CRITICAL SOURCES:

BOOKS

Baker, Gladys, *I Had to Know,* Appleton, 1951.
Nizer, Louis, *Between You and Me,* Beechurst, 1948.
Sheen, Fulton J., *Treasure in Clay: The Autobiography of Fulton J. Sheen,* Doubleday, 1980.

PERIODICALS

America, November 8, 1980.
Best Sellers, January, 1981.
Christian Century, August 14, 1963, May 27, 1964.
Collier's, January 4, 1953.
Life, March 24, 1952, April 6, 1953.
Newsweek, June 4, 1951, February 16, 1959, October 27, 1969.
New York Times, October 29, 1969.
Ramparts, November, 1967.
Reader's Digest, June, 1947, July, 1952, January, 1966.
Saturday Review, March 6, 1954.
Theatre Arts, December, 1952.
Time, May 6, 1946, April 14, 1952, October 31, 1960.

OBITUARIES:

PERIODICALS

New York Times, December 10, 1979.
Chicago Tribune, December 11, 1979, December 12, 1979.
Newsweek, December 24, 1979.

*   *   *

SHELDON, Alice Hastings Bradley   1915-1987
(Raccoona Sheldon, James Tiptree, Jr.)

PERSONAL: Born August 24, 1915, in Chicago, Ill.; died after shooting her husband and herself, May 19, 1987, in McLean, Va.; daughter of Herbert Edwin (an attorney, explorer, big-game collector, and naturalist) and Mary Wilhelmina (a writer, explorer, and linguist; maiden name, Hastings) Bradley; married William Davey (a poet and polo-player), 1934 (divorced, 1938); married Huntington Denton Sheldon (in business and U.S. Government), September 22, 1945. *Education:* Attended Sarah Lawrence College, University of California, Berkeley, Rutgers Agricultural College, and Johns Hopkins University; American University, B.A. (summa cum laude), 1959; George Washington University, Ph.D. (magna cum laude), 1967. *Religion:* "Atheist; ethical imperatives consonant with Christian New Testament, rationalized on basic principle of striving against entropy. (e.g., greed is more entropic than altruism; truth is less entropic than lies.)"

ADDRESSES: Home and office—6037 Ramshorn Pl., McLean, Va. 22101. *Agent*—Robert P. Mills Ltd., 333 Fifth Ave., New York, N.Y. 10016.

CAREER: Graphic artist and painter, work exhibited in Corcoran Gallery, Washington, D.C., and Chicago Art Institute, 1925-41; *Chicago Sun,* Chicago, Ill., art critic, 1941-42; partner with husband, Huntington Sheldon, of custom hatching business in New Jersey, 1946-52; Central Intelligence Agency, Washington, D.C., in photo-intelligence, 1952-55; taught experimental psychology and statistics at American University and George Washington University, Washington, D.C., 1955-68. *Military service:* U.S. Army Air Force, 1942-46; became major; was first female American photo-intelligence officer.

MEMBER: American Civil Liberties Union, American Psychological Association, Science Fiction Writers of America, National Organization for Women, American Association for the Advancement of Science, American Museum of Natural History, Smithsonian Associates, Audubon Society, Friends Service Committee, Friends of Democracy, Esperanto Society of Washington, Psi Chi, Sigma Xi.

AWARDS, HONORS: Nebula Award from Science Fiction Writers of America, for best short story, 1973, for "Love Is the Plan, the Plan Is Death," for best novella, 1976, for "Houston, Houston, Do You Read?," and for best novelette, 1977, for "The Screwfly Solution"; Hugo Award from World Science Fiction Convention, for best novella, 1973, for "The Girl Who Was Plugged In," and 1976, for "Houston, Houston, Do You Read?"; Jupiter Award for best novella, 1976, for "Houston, Houston, Do You Read?"; Locus Award for best short story, 1985, for "Beyond the Dead Reef."

WRITINGS:

SCIENCE FICTION; UNDER PSEUDONYM JAMES TIPTREE, JR.

Ten Thousand Light-Years from Home (short stories), Ace, 1973.
Warm Worlds and Otherwise (short stories), Ballantine, 1975.
(Contributor) Robert Silverberg, editor, *The New Atlantis and Other Novellas of Science Fiction* (includes "A Momentary Taste of Being"), Hawthorn, 1975.
Star-Songs of an Old Primate (short stories), Ballantine, 1978.
Up the Walls of the World (novel), Berkley, 1978.
Out of the Everywhere and Other Extraordinary Visions (short stories), Ballantine, 1981.
Brightness Falls from the Air (novel), Tor, 1985.
The Starry Rift, Tor, 1986.
Tales of the Quintana Roo (short stories), Arkham House, 1986.
Crown of Stars (short stories), Tor, 1988.

Contributor of short stories, sometimes under pseudonym Raccoona Sheldon, to many science fiction magazines and anthologies.

WORK IN PROGRESS: A novel, working title, *Planetary Passions, Astral Angst;* a novella, tentatively entitled *Right-to-Life Adoption Center Number Seven;* a short story.

SIDELIGHTS: Alice H. B. Sheldon, best known under her pseudonym James Tiptree Jr., wrote "some of the finest s.f. short stories of the last decade," according to Gerald Jonas in a 1978 *New York Times Book Review* critique. Virginia Bemis, writing in the *Dictionary of Literary Biography,* declared that "Tiptree is considered one of the most important new writers of the 1970s." Her stories have appeared in numerous magazines and anthologies, in addition to several collections of her own works. One such collection, *Warm Worlds and Otherwise,* inspired Jonas to say, "If it made any sense to talk about a successor to Cordwainer Smith among contemporary S.F. writers, the most likely candidate would be James Tiptree, Jr."

Perhaps Sheldon's vivid imagination, evident in her science fiction stories and novels, developed during her adventurous child-

hood spent largely in Africa and India on expeditions with her parents, Herbert and Mary Bradley. Often sponsored by organizations such as the American Museum of Natural History, the Field Museum, and the National and Royal Geographic Societies, the Bradleys made their first trip to Africa in 1919, where they sought the Central African mountain gorilla. From 1924 until 1925 Herbert Bradley led his family on foot across the Mountains of the Moon (Mount Ruwenzori) and over two hundred miles of unknown territory west of former Lake Edward, making the first European contact with the cannibals there. The Bradleys left Africa in 1925 to travel through India, several Southeast Asian countries, and to the interior of then Indo-China, hunting tiger and gaur, which Sheldon describes as "a whopping great buffalo-thing with armor-plated brains (if any)."

During 1929 and 1930 the Bradleys made the first crossing of the African continent by automobile, witnessing, according to Sheldon, "the speed of Colonial despoilment of Africa's peoples, land, and wildlife." The group of explorers also nearly encountered death when a short side-trip on foot led them into an area devastated by drought. What seemed a friendly native told them to continue ahead; that "fine water" flowed in a place only two days away. They took his advice until Herbert, on a hunch, ordered the group to turn back. They were left with only four ounces of water daily per person in 110 degree heat, and later learned there had been no water ahead; the land was long known to be dry, and the messenger had been sent to send the intruders to their deaths. "Such was the ambience of the last trip to Africa," Sheldon wrote. "No one desired to return."

By the time she was fourteen, Alice had experienced more of the world than many do in a lifetime, and, although her travels were undoubtedly educational, Alice felt displaced. Writing about her early travels, Sheldon told *CA:* "This future writer was plunged into half a world of alien environments all before she was old enough to be allowed to enter an American movie house, and as with places, so with people. She found herself interacting with adults of every color, size, shape, and condition—lepers, black royalty in lionskins, white royalty in tweeds, Arab slavers, functional saints and madmen in power; poets, killers, and collared eunuchs, world-famous actors with headcolds, blacks who ate their enemies and a white who had eaten his friends; and above all, women; chattel-women deliberately starved, deformed, blinded and enslaved; women in nuns' habits saving the world; women in high heels committing suicide, and women in low heels shooting little birds; an English-woman in bloomers riding out from her castle at the head of her personal Moslem army; women, from the routinely tortured, obscenely-mutilated slave-wives of the 'advanced' Kibuyu, to the free, propertied, Sumatran matriarchs who ran the economy and brought six hundred years of peaceful prosperity to the Menang-Kabau; all these were known before she had a friend or playmate of her own age. And finally, she was exposed to dozens of cultures and sub-cultures whose values, taboos, imperatives, religions, languages, and mores conflicted with each other as well as with her parents. And the writer, child as she was, had continuously to learn this passing kaleidoscope of Do and Don't lest she give offense, or even bring herself or the party into danger. But most seriously, this heavy jumble descended on her head before her own personality or cultural identity was formed. The result was a profound alienation from any nominal peers, and an enduring cultural relativism. Her world, too, was suffused with sadness; everywhere it was said, or seen, that great change was coming fast and much would be forever gone."

Sheldon was exposed to writing through her mother, who wrote prolifically about their travels, and on other issues as well, including women's rights. She often expressed a competitive spirit that she developed as the daughter of a woman who could do, and had done, "everything." Mary Bradley also served as a World War II correspondent on the European fronts, being the first American woman to survey and report on some of the gruesome German deathcamps. She issued more than thirty-five books during her lifetime, and her influence on her daughter can be seen in Sheldon's first published story, a fiction/fact piece for the *New Yorker* in 1946. Entitled "The Lucky Ones," the story was a plea to Americans for more humane treatment of "displaced persons," survivors of Nazi labor camps who had been taken into American custody after the war. Sheldon began writing science fiction years later as a way of relaxing after completing her doctoral dissertation and because it was a genre that her mother had not tried.

Sheldon soon demonstrated a mastery of the genre, drawing on her own expertise in the social sciences. Bemis explained, "Her work is primarily social science fiction, drawing on her extensive knowledge of psychology, anthropology, and related areas." *Up the Walls of the World,* her first novel, presents a sophisticated, three-fold plot involving humans working on a government ESP project, squid-like inhabitants of the planet Tyree, and a lonely planet-eating organism that floats freely in space. "The level of excellence on all three channels is Master Class, and when they all come together they heterodyne," remarked Spider Robinson in *Analog.* "It's probably the best thing Tiptree has published so far." Carl Macek of the *West Coast Review of Books* commented: "*Up the Walls of the World* is unrelenting. It is [an] excellent example of the sophistication achieved by contemporary science fiction writers."

The Tiptree pseudonym was chosen at random to use for Sheldon's early stories, which she did not really expect to sell. "The plan was to use a new name for each new batch of stories, so as to avoid permanent identification with the slush-pile," Sheldon said. The first stories did sell, however, so Tiptree stuck and was used on all correspondence and in all business deals for eleven years. But Sheldon kept her involvement in Tiptree's work a secret; not even Tiptree's agent knew the author's true identity. "This had to be kept secret," Sheldon wrote. "The news that I was writing science fiction would have wakened prejudice enough to imperil my grant, and destroy my credibility with the psychology departments of George Washington and American universities, and for any possible future employment with the CIA." When answering letters from fans, Tiptree told the truth about his background; that is, Alice Sheldon imparted the details of her life, including the facts of her parents' lives. She had detailed Mary Bradley's life so well, in fact, that when Mary died in 1977, Tiptree's followers correctly identified Tiptree and Sheldon as one by the facts in Mary's obituary. "James Tiptree, Jr., was blown for good, leaving an elderly lady in McLean, Virginia, as his only—astral—contact," Sheldon wrote. Suddenly critics viewed Tiptree in a new light. "Only the feminist world remained excited, but on a different basis having nothing to do with the stories," Sheldon continued. "Tiptree by merely existing unchallenged for eleven years, had shot the stuffing out of male stereotypes of women writers. Even non-feminist women were secretly gleeful. The more vulnerable males discovered simultaneously that Tiptree had been much overrated, and sullenly retired to practice patronizing smiles."

After her pseudonym was disclosed, Sheldon wrote less science fiction. "Frankly, I came unglued," she told Jean Ross in a *Contemporary Authors* interview. "A woman writing of the joy and terror of furious combat, or of the lust to torture and kill, or of the violent forms of evil—isn't taken quite seriously. . . . I

think that for all of us the sense of being in contact with something that has the potential to do—or maybe (wow!) has done—real evil, gives a little thrill to reading. Some people seem to have projected that onto Tiptree. Maybe I did a little too. So to write on as a toothless tiger was shaming." In a fit of depression, Alice Sheldon took her own life in the spring of 1987.

For an interview with this author, see *Contemporary Authors,* Volume 108, Gale, 1983.

AVOCATIONAL INTERESTS: Nishikigoi (ornamental Koi), hydrogen as an energy source, bright young people, learning to speak, read and write English.

BIOGRAPHICAL/CRITICAL SOURCES:

BOOKS

Contemporary Literary Criticism, Gale, Volume 48, 1988, Volume 50, 1988.
Dictionary of Literary Biography, Volume 8: *Twentieth-Century American Science Fiction Writers,* Gale, 1981.
Dozois, Gardner, *The Fiction of James Tiptree, Jr.,* Algol Press, 1977.
Staicar, Tom, editor, *The Feminine Eye: Science Fiction and the Women Who Write It,* Ungar, 1982.

PERIODICALS

New York Times Book Review, March 23, 1975, February 26, 1978.
Times Literary Supplement, August 8, 1975.
Analog Science Fiction/Science Fact, June, 1978.
Fantasy and Science Fiction, September, 1978.
West Coast Review of Books, July, 1979.

OBITUARIES:

PERIODICALS

International Herald Tribune, May 21, 1987.
Los Angeles Times, May 22, 1987.
New York Times, May 21, 1987.
Pittsburgh Post-Gazette, May 21, 1987.
Washington Post, May 20, 1987.

*   *   *

SHELDON, Raccoona
See SHELDON, Alice Hastings Bradley

*   *   *

SHELDON, Sidney 1917-

PERSONAL: Born February 11, 1917, in Chicago, Ill.; son of Otto (a salesman) and Natalie (Marcus) Sheldon; married Jorja Curtright (an actress), March 28, 1951 (died, 1985); children: Mary Sheldon Dastin. *Education:* Attended Northwestern University, 1935-36. *Religion:* Church of Religious Science.

ADDRESSES: Home—Bel Air, California. *Office*—c/o William Morrow & Co., 105 Madison Ave., New York, N.Y. 10016.

CAREER: Writer. Former script reader for Universal and Twentieth Century-Fox Studios; creator, producer, and writer of television shows, Los Angeles, Calif., 1963—, including "The Patty Duke Show," "I Dream of Jeannie," "Nancy," and "Hart to Hart." *Military service:* U.S. Army Air Forces, 1941.

MEMBER: Freedom to Read Foundation.

AWARDS, HONORS: Academy Award ("Oscar") for best original screenplay, Academy of Motion Picture Arts and Sciences,

1948, for "The Bachelor and the Bobby-Soxer"; Screen Writers' Guild Award for best musical of the year, 1948, for "Easter Parade," and 1950, for "Annie Get Your Gun"; Antoinette Perry Award ("Tony"), 1959, for book of "Redhead"; Emmy Awards for "I Dream of Jeannie"; Edgar Award for best first mystery novel, Mystery Writers of America, and *New York Times* citation for best first mystery novel, both 1970, both for *The Naked Face;* recipient of a star on the Hollywood Walk of Fame.

WRITINGS:

NOVELS

The Naked Face, Morrow, 1970.
The Other Side of Midnight, Morrow, 1974.
A Stranger in the Mirror, Morrow, 1976.
Bloodline, Morrow, 1977.
Rage of Angels, Morrow, 1980.
Master of the Game, Morrow, 1982.
If Tomorrow Comes, Morrow, 1985.
Windmills of the Gods, Morrow, 1987.
The Sands of Time, Morrow, 1988.
Sheldon Boxed Set: Bloodline, A Stranger in the Mirror, Rage of Angels, Warner Books, 1988.
Memories of Midnight, Morrow, 1990.

PLAYS

(Adaptor with Ben Roberts) "The Merry Widow" (operetta), first produced on Broadway, August 4, 1943.
"Jackpot," first produced on Broadway, January 13, 1944.
(With Roberts and Dorothy Kilgallen) "Dream with Music," first produced on Broadway, May 18, 1944.
(With Ladislaus Bush-Fekete and Mary Helen Fay) "Alice in Arms," first produced on Broadway, January 31, 1945.
(With Dorothy and Herbert Fields, and David Shaw) "Redhead" (musical), first produced on Broadway, February 5, 1959.
"Roman Candle," first produced on Broadway, February 3, 1960.

Also author of "Gomes," produced in London.

SCREENPLAYS

(Author of story with Roberts) "Borrowed Hero," Monogram, 1941.
(With Jack Natteford) "Dangerous Lady," Producers Releasing Corp., 1941.
(Author of story with Roberts) "Gambling Daughters," Producers Releasing Corp., 1941.
(With Roberts) "South of Panama," Producers Releasing Corp., 1941.
(Author of story with Roberts) "Fly by Night," Paramount, 1942.
"She's in the Army," Monogram, 1942.
(With Roberts) "The Carter Case," Republic, 1947.
"The Bachelor and the Bobby-Soxer," RKO, 1947.
(With Albert Hackett and Frances Goodrich) "Easter Parade" (musical), Metro-Goldwyn-Mayer, 1948.
"Annie Get Your Gun" (adapted from the musical by Irving Berlin), Metro-Goldwyn-Mayer, 1950.
"Nancy Goes to Rio," Metro-Goldwyn-Mayer, 1950.
(With Dorothy Cooper) "Rich, Young, and Pretty" (musical), Metro-Goldwyn-Mayer, 1951.
"No Questions Asked," Metro-Goldwyn-Mayer, 1951.
"Three Guys Named Mike," Metro-Goldwyn-Mayer, 1951.
"Just This Once," Metro-Goldwyn-Mayer, 1952.

(With Herbert Baker and Alfred L. Levitt, and director) "Dream Wife," Metro-Goldwyn-Mayer, 1953.
"Remains to Be Seen," Metro-Goldwyn-Mayer, 1953.
"You're Never Too Young," Paramount, 1955.
"Anything Goes" (adapted from the musical by Cole Porter), Paramount, 1956.
"Pardners," Paramount, 1956.
(And director and producer with Robert Smith) "The Buster Keaton Story," Paramount, 1957.
"All in a Night's Work," Paramount, 1961.
"Billy Rose's Jumbo" (also titled "Jumbo"), Metro-Goldwyn-Mayer, 1962.
(With Preston Sturges) "The Birds and the Bees," Paramount, 1965.

OTHER

Also author of a children's book, published in Japan. Author of more than 250 scripts, occasionally under a pseudonym, for "The Patty Duke Show," 1963-66, and "I Dream of Jeannie," 1965-70.

SIDELIGHTS: At age fifty, at the top of his profession as a film and television producer of hits like "I Dream of Jeannie," Sidney Sheldon had no hint of another, even more successful career ahead of him. "[Novels] never occurred to me," Sheldon told *Detroit News* reporter Ruth Pollack Coughlin. "I wasn't a novelist. I was writing for motion pictures and television and Broadway. For me, writing novels was an unnatural next step." Why then, would the winner of Oscar, Tony, and Emmy Awards turn to fiction? The author explained his decision to Sarah Booth Conroy of the *Washington Post:* "I got an idea that was so introspective I could see no way to do it as a television series, movie or Broadway play, because you had to get inside the character's mind. With much trepidation, I decided I'd try a novel." The result was *The Naked Face,* which despite winning awards as the best first mystery novel of the year, initially sold only 17,000 copies. "I was horrified," Sheldon told Conroy, "because 20 million people watched ['I Dream of] Jeannie.' " Nevertheless, Sheldon persisted in his efforts, and his next work, *The Other Side of Midnight,* sold over three million copies in paperback. Since then, Sheldon has published seven more million-selling novels, and is now considered the best-selling writer in the world, with books in print in thirty-nine countries.

The typical Sheldon potboiler features a beautiful and determined heroine enacting revenge on her enemies; as Conroy describes, in Sheldon's novels "the beautiful but often poor and pure heroines are raped, sodomized and defrauded, and go on to avenge themselves by questionable, often illegal, but ingenious methods." These works, with their rapid momentum and mass appeal, "evidently satisfy . . . everyone except most literary critics, who regard popularity and quality as incompatible," *Los Angeles Times* arts editor Charles Champlin comments. Indeed, Sheldon's work has not fared well with critics, who often fault his plots and characters as unbelievable, and his prose as "staccato [and] lackluster," as *New York Times Book Review* contributor Mel Watkins states.

Some reviewers, however, find some merit in Sheldon's work; as Carol E. Rinzler notes in the *Washington Post,* "there aren't a whole lot of writers around who can be depended on to produce good junk reading time after time; Sheldon is one of the few." *Washington Post* reviewer Joseph McLellan similarly observes that in *Rage of Angels* "craftsmanship is the keynote, as a matter of fact, in this novel that ticks along like an intricate, beautifully designed piece of clockwork, full of characters and incidents that are usually interesting even if they are slightly unreal." "Although this may be literary junk food," *New York Times Book Review* contributor Robert Lekachman comments, "it is hard to put down once you get started. . . . Sheldon's smooth, serviceable, if unmemorable, prose carries one along, much like the movie serials of the Great Depression."

Because of their brisk pace, Sheldon's novels are often characterized as being "less like a book than like a movie," according to *New York Times* writer Janet Maslin, a description their author refutes: "I am accused constantly of writing books as movies," Sheldon told Paul Rosenfield of the *Los Angeles Times*. "But it just isn't true. What's true is that I write *visually*. It's my training from movies and TV." Sheldon does, however, strive for a captivating effect in his books: "I have this goal," the author remarked to Rosenfield. "And it's for a reader to not be able to go to sleep at night. I want him to keep reading another four pages, then one more page. The following morning, or night, he's anxious to get back to the book."

MEDIA ADAPTATIONS: The Other Side of Midnight was made into a film by Twentieth Century-Fox in 1977; *Bloodline* was filmed by Paramount in 1979, and was re-edited by Sheldon and shown as an ABC miniseries in 1982; *Rage of Angels,* for which Sheldon served as executive producer, became an NBC miniseries in 1983, and inspired a 1986 sequel which Sheldon also produced; CBS broadcast miniseries adaptations of *Master of the Game* in 1984, *If Tomorrow Comes* in 1986, and *Windmills of the Gods* in 1988; *The Naked Face* was filmed by Cannon in 1985; *The Sands of Time* has been optioned.

BIOGRAPHICAL/CRITICAL SOURCES:

BOOKS

Authors in the News, Volume 1, Gale, 1976.
Bestsellers 89, Issue 1, Gale, 1989.

PERIODICALS

Detroit News, February 8, 1987.
Los Angeles Times, October 3, 1982, March 12, 1987.
Newsweek, June 13, 1977.
New Yorker, July 11, 1977.
New York Times, July 24, 1947, July 1, 1948, July 22, 1979.
New York Times Book Review, January 27, 1974, May 2, 1976, February 19, 1978, August 29, 1982, March 10, 1985.
Publishers Weekly, November 25, 1988.
Time, June 20, 1977.
Washington Post, July 12, 1982, February 19, 1985, December 6, 1988.
Washington Post Book World, February 18, 1979.

*   *   *

SHEPARD, Sam   1943-

PERSONAL: Given name Samuel Shepard Rogers VII; born November 5, 1943, in Fort Sheridan, Ill.; son of Samuel Shepard (a teacher and farmer) and Elaine (Schook) Rogers; married O-Lan Johnson (an actress), November 9, 1969 (divorced); currently living with Jessica Lange (an actress and film producer); children: (first marriage) Jesse Mojo; (with Lange) Hannah Jane, Samuel Walker. *Education:* Attended Mount Antonio Junior College, 1960-61.

ADDRESSES: Office—Lois Berman, Little Theatre Building, 240 West 44th St., New York, N.Y. 10036. *Agent*—Toby Cole, 234 West 44th St., New York, N.Y. 10036.

CAREER: Writer, 1964—. Conley Arabian Horse Ranch, Chino, Calif., stable hand, 1958-60; Bishop's Company Repertory Players (touring theatre group), actor, 1962-63; Village Gate, New York City, busboy, 1963-64. Rock musician (drums and guitar) with Holy Modal Rounders, 1968-71; playwright in residence at Magic Theatre, San Francisco, Calif., 1974-84; actor in feature films, including "Days of Heaven," 1978, "Resurrection," 1980, "Raggedy Man," 1981, "Frances," 1982, "The Right Stuff," 1983, "Country," 1984, "Fool for Love," 1985, and "Crimes of the Heart," 1986.

MEMBER: American Academy and Institute of Arts and Letters.

AWARDS, HONORS: Obie Awards from *Village Voice* for best plays of the Off-Broadway season, 1966, for "Chicago," "Icarus's Mother," and "Red Cross," 1967, for "La Turista," 1968, for "Forensic and the Navigators" and "Melodrama Play," 1973, for "The Tooth of Crime," 1975, for "Action," 1977, for "Curse of the Starving Class," 1979, for "Buried Child," and 1984, for "Fool for Love"; grant from University of Minnesota, 1966; Rockefeller Foundation grant and Yale University fellowship, 1967; Guggenheim Foundation memorial fellowships, 1968 and 1971; National Institute and American Academy award for literature, 1974; Brandeis University creative arts award, 1975-76; Pulitzer Prize for drama, 1979, for "Buried Child"; Academy Award nomination for best supporting actor from Academy of Motion Picture Arts and Sciences, 1984, for "The Right Stuff "; Golden Palm Award from Cannes Film Festival, 1984, for "Paris, Texas"; New York Drama Critics' Circle Award, 1986, for "A Lie of the Mind."

WRITINGS:

PLAYS

"Cowboys" (one-act), first produced Off-Off-Broadway at St. Mark Church in-the-Bowery, October 16, 1964.
"The Rock Garden" (one-act; also see below), first produced Off-Off-Broadway at St. Mark Church in-the-Bowery, October 16, 1964.
"4-H Club" (one act; also see below), first produced Off-Broadway at Cherry Lane Theatre, 1965.
"Up to Thursday" (one-act), first produced Off-Broadway at Cherry Lane Theatre, February 10, 1965.
"Dog" (one-act), first produced Off-Broadway at La Mama Experimental Theatre Club, February 10, 1965.
"Chicago" (one-act; also see below), first produced Off-Off-Broadway at St. Mark Church in-the-Bowery, April 16, 1965.
"Icarus's Mother" (one-act; also see below), first produced Off-Off-Broadway at Caffe Cino, November 16, 1965.
"Fourteen Hundred Thousand" (one-act; also see below), first produced at Firehouse Theater, Minneapolis, Minn., 1966.
"Red Cross" (one-act; also see below), first produced Off-Broadway at Martinique Theatre, April 12, 1966.
La Turista (two-act; first produced Off-Broadway at American Place Theatre, March 4, 1967; also see below), Bobbs-Merrill, 1968.
"Cowboys #2" (one-act; also see below), first produced Off-Broadway at Old Reliable, August 12, 1967.
"Forensic and the Navigators" (one-act; also see below), first produced Off-Off-Broadway at St. Mark Church in-the-Bowery, December 29, 1967.
(Contributor) "Oh! Calcutta!," first produced on Broadway at Eden Theatre, 1969.
"The Unseen Hand" (one-act; also see below), first produced Off-Broadway at La Mama Experimental Theatre Club, December 26, 1969.

"Holy Ghostly" (one-act; also see below), first produced in New York, N.Y., 1970.

Operation Sidewinder (two-act; first produced Off-Broadway at Vivian Beaumont Theatre, March 12, 1970; also see below), Bobbs-Merrill, 1970.

"Shaved Splits" (also see below), first produced Off-Broadway at La Mama Experimental Theatre Club, July 29, 1970.

"Mad Dog Blues" (one-act; also see below), first produced Off-Off-Broadway at St. Mark Church in-the-Bowery, March 4, 1971.

(With Patti Smith) "Cowboy Mouth" (also see below), first produced at Transverse Theatre, Edinburgh, Scotland, April 2, 1971, produced Off-Broadway at American Place Theatre, April 29, 1971.

"Back Bog Beast Bait" (one-act; also see below), first produced Off-Broadway at American Place Theatre, April 29, 1971.

"The Tooth of Crime" (two-act; also see below), first produced at McCarter Theatre, Princeton, N.J., 1972, produced Off-Off-Broadway at Performing Garage, March 7, 1973.

"Blue Bitch" (also see below), first produced Off-Off-Broadway at Theatre Genesis, February, 1973.

(With Megan Terry and Jean-Claude van Itallie) "Nightwalk" (also see below), first produced Off-Off-Broadway at St. Clement's Church, September 8, 1973.

"Geography of a Horse Dreamer" (two-act; also see below), first produced at Theatre Upstairs, London, England, February 2, 1974.

"Little Ocean," first produced at Hampstead Theatre Club, London, England, March 25, 1974.

"Action" (one-act; also see below), first produced Off-Broadway at American Place Theatre, April 4, 1975.

"Killer's Head" (one-act; also see below), first produced Off-Broadway at American Place Theatre, April 4, 1975.

"Angel City" (also see below), first produced at Magic Theatre, San Francisco, Calif., 1976.

"Curse of the Starving Class" (two-act; also see below), first produced Off-Broadway at Newman/Public Theatre, March, 1978.

"Buried Child" (two-act; also see below), first produced Off-Broadway at Theatre of the New City, November, 1978.

"Seduced" (also see below), first produced Off-Broadway at American Place Theatre, February 1, 1979.

"Suicide in B-flat" (also see below), first produced Off-Off-Broadway at Impossible Ragtime Theatre, March 14, 1979.

"Tongues," first produced at Eureka Theatre Festival, Calif., 1979, produced Off-Off-Broadway at The Other Stage, November 6, 1979.

"Savage/Love," first produced at Eureka Theater Festival, Calif., 1979, produced Off-Off-Broadway at The Other Stage, November 6, 1979.

True West (two-act; first produced Off-Broadway at Public Theatre, December 23, 1980), Doubleday, 1981.

(Also director of original production) "Fool for Love" (one-act; also see below), first produced at Magic Theatre, San Francisco, 1983, produced Off-Broadway by Circle Repertory Company, May 27, 1983.

"The Sad Lament of Pecos Bill on the Eve of Killing His Wife" (one-act; also see below), first produced Off-Broadway at La Mama Experimental Theatre Club, September 25, 1983.

"Superstitions" (one-act), first produced Off-Broadway at La Mama Experimental Theatre Club, September 25, 1983.

(Also director of original production) *A Lie of the Mind* (three-act; first produced Off-Broadway at Promenade Theatre, December, 1985), published with *The War in Heaven* (also see below), New American Library, 1987.

"Hawk Moon" (adapted from his collection of the same title), produced at the Gate, London, 1989.

PLAY COLLECTIONS

Five Plays by Sam Shepard (contains "Icarus's Mother," "Chicago," "Melodrama Play," "Red Cross," and "Fourteen Hundred Thousand"), Bobbs-Merrill, 1967.

"The Unseen Hand" and Other Plays (contains "The Unseen Hand," "4-H Club," "Shaved Splits," "Forensic and the Navigators," "Holy Ghostly," and "Back Bog Beast Bait"), Bobbs-Merrill, 1971.

"Mad Dog Blues" and Other Plays (includes "Mad Dog Blues," "The Rock Garden," "Cowboys #2," "Cowboy Mouth," "Blue Bitch," and "Nightwalk"), Winter House, 1972.

The Tooth of Crime [and] *Geography of a Horse Dreamer*, Grove, 1974.

"Angel City," "Curse of the Starving Class" and Other Plays (includes "Angel City," "Curse of the Starving Class," "Killer's Head," and "Action"), Urizen Books, 1976.

Buried Child, Seduced, Suicide in B-flat, Urizen Books, 1979.

Four Two-Act Plays by Sam Shepard (contains "La Turista," "The Tooth of Crime," "Geography of a Horse Dreamer," and "Operation Sidewinder"), Urizen Books, 1980.

"Chicago" and Other Plays, Urizen Books, 1981.

"The Unseen Hand" and Other Plays, Urizen Books, 1981.

Seven Plays by Sam Shepard, Bantam, 1981.

Fool for Love [and] *The Sad Lament of Pecos Bill on the Eve of Killing His Wife*, City Lights Books, 1983.

"Fool for Love" and Other Plays, Bantam, 1984.

SCREENPLAYS

(With Michelangelo Antonioni, Tonino Guerra, Fred Graham, and Clare Peploe) *Zabriskie Point* (produced by Metro-Goldwyn-Mayer, 1970), Cappelli (Bologna, Italy), 1970, published with Antonioni's *Red Desert,* Simon & Schuster, 1972.

(With L. M. Kit Carson) "Paris, Texas," Twentieth Century-Fox, 1984.

"Fool for Love" (based on Shepard's play of the same title), Golan Globus, 1985.

(And director) "Far North," Alive Enterprises, 1988.

Also author, with Robert Frank, of "Me and My Brother" and, with Murray Mednick, of "Ringaleerio."

OTHER

Hawk Moon: A Book of Short Stories, Poems, and Monologues, Black Sparrow Press, 1973.

Rolling Thunder Logbook, Viking, 1977.

Motel Chronicles, City Lights Books, 1982.

(With Joseph Chaikin) *The War in Heaven* (radio drama; first broadcast over WBAI in January, 1985; produced on stage at Theatre Upstairs, London, 1987), published with *A Lie of the Mind,* New American Library, 1987.

SIDELIGHTS: Sam Shepard has devoted more than two decades of his life to a highly eclectic—and critically acclaimed—career in the performing arts. Considered the preeminent literary playwright of his generation, he is an author whose prolific output and imaginative intensity consistently outpace his contemporaries. Throughout his career Shepard has never confined himself merely to pen and paper; he has also directed plays of his authorship, played drums and guitar in rock bands and jazz ensembles, and acted in major feature films. He is perhaps best known to the American public for his movie appearances, including leading roles in "The Right Stuff " and "Country," but acting is a sideline for the man *Newsweek*'s Jack Kroll calls "the poet laureate of America's emotional Badlands." Despite his success in Hollywood, Shepard is first and foremost a playwright whose dramas explore mythic images of modern America in the nation's own eccentric vernacular.

Shepard established himself by writing numerous one-act plays and vignettes for the Off-Off-Broadway experimental theatre. Although his audiences have grown, and his plays have been widely produced in America and abroad, he has not yet staged a production on Broadway. *New Republic* contributor Robert Brustein, who finds Shepard "one of our most celebrated writers," contends that the lack of attention from Broadway "has not limited Shepard's powers." Indeed, continues Brustein, "unlike those predecessors who wilted under such conditions, Shepard has flourished in a state of marginality. . . . Shepard's work has been a model of growth and variety." From his early surreal one-acts to his more realistic two- and three-act plays, Shepard has placed stress on artistic integrity rather than on theatrical marketability. As a result, contends Kroll, Shepard plays have "overturned theatrical conventions and created a new kind of drama filled with violence, lyricism and an intensely American compound of comic and tragic power." The numerous awards Shepard has received for his work stand as evidence of his plays' extraordinary originality; Shepard has won more than ten Obie Awards for best Off-Broadway plays, a Pulitzer Prize for "Buried Child," and a prestigious New York Drama Critics' Circle Award in 1986 for "A Lie of the Mind." *Plays and Players* magazine contributor Richard A. Davis comments that Shepard has both "a tremendous ability to make bring the imagination of an audience to life" and "a talent for creating with words alone extremely believable emotional experiences."

According to *Village Voice* correspondent Michael Feingold, Shepard "has the real playwright's gift of habitually transposing his feelings and visions into drama as a mere matter of praxis. He speaks through the theatre as naturally as most of us speak through the telephone." The analogy is apt; Shepard's plays make use of modern idiomatic language as well as the prevailing legends of American popular culture, particularly those of the American West and the glittering worlds of Hollywood and the rock and roll industry. "No one knows better than Sam Shepard that the true American West is gone forever," writes Frank Rich in the *New York Times,* "but there may be no writer alive more gifted at reinventing it out of pure literary air." Shepard's inventions based on the pioneer ethos have an ironic twist, however. His modern cowboys, drifters, farmers, and other offspring of the frontier era experience nostalgia for a purer past that may never have existed as they jostle for power and quarrel with family members in the neurotic present. *Journal of Popular Culture* contributor George Stambolian maintains that like many of his fellow playwrights, Shepard "knows that the old frontier myths of America's youth are no longer a valid expression of our modern anxieties, even though they continue to influence our thoughts." From this point of origin, claims Stambolian, Shepard seeks "a new mythology that will encompass all the diverse figures of our cultural history together with the psychological and social conditions they represent. . . . Shepard's greatest contribution to a new American mythology may well be his elaboration of a new myth of the modern artist."

The theatre of Sam Shepard is marked by "a spirit of comedy that tosses and turns in a bed of revulsion," in the words of *New York Times* correspondent Richard Eder. Malicious mischief and comic mayhem heighten the intensity of Shepard's tragic vision; in many of his plays the action is vigorous and the dialogue is peppered with language of the playwright's invention. As

David Richards explains in the *Washington Post,* actors and directors "respond to the slam-bang potential in [Shepard's] scripts, which allows them to go for broke, trash the furniture, and generally shred the scenery. Whatever else you've got, you've got a wild and woolly fight on your hands." The theatrical fisticuffs are played out sometimes with physical violence and sometimes with verbal badinage based on the overriding rhythms of American music. *New York Times* theatre critic Clive Barnes remarks: "Mr. Shepard writes mythic plays in American jazz-poetry. . . . He is trying to express truths wrapped up in legends and with the kind of symbolism you often find nowadays in pop music. His command of language is daring and inventive—some of the words sound new, and quite a few of them actually are." Richard L. Homan makes a similar point in *Critical Quarterly:* "Shepard's vivid use of language and flair for fantasy have suggested something less like drama and more like poetry in some unfamiliar oral tradition." Also in the *New York Times,* Barnes suggests that Shepard's expressive dialogue "follows along the lines of the Mad Hatter's tea party." The critic adds: "I find myself wondering whether this is altogether bad. At least he leaves a taste in the soul, disenchanted and disturbing."

While Shepard's subjects—nostalgia, power struggles, family tensions—may seem simple and quintessentially American at a cursory glance, his plays remain "extraordinarily resistant to thematic exegesis," according to Richard Gilman in his introduction to *Seven Plays by Sam Shepard.* Gilman finds the standard critical vocabulary inadequate for the assessment of Shepard's work because the dramatist "slips out of all the categories" and seems to have come "out of no literary or theatrical tradition at all but precisely for the breakdown or absence—on the level of art if not of commerce—of all such traditions in America." Gilman further comments that a number of the plays "seem like fragments, chunks of various sizes thrown out from some mother lode of urgent and heterogeneous imagination in which [Shepard] has scrabbled with pick, shovel, gun-butt and hands. The reason so many of them seem incomplete is that they lack the clear boundaries as artifact, the internal order, the progress toward a denouement . . . and the consistency of tone and procedure that ordinarily characterize good drama. . . . Another difficulty is that we tend to look at all plays for their single 'meanings' or ruling ideas but find this elusive in Shepard and find, moreover, his plays coalescing, merging into one another in our minds."

In *American Dreams: The Imagination of Sam Shepard,* Michael Earley also remarks that Shepard "seems to have forged a whole new kind of American play that has yet to receive adequate reckoning." Earley calls the playwright "a true American primitive, a literary naif coursing the stage of American drama as if for the first time" who brings to his work "a liberating interplay of word, theme and image that has always been the hallmark of the romantic impulse. His plays don't work like plays in the traditional sense but more like romances, where the imaginary landscape (his version of America) is so remote and open that it allows for the depiction of legend, adventure, and even the supernatural. . . . Even though Shepard is one of our most modernist playwrights . . . what he more keenly resembles is a transcendentalist or new romantic whose 'innocent eye' wonders at all it surveys and records experience without censure." *Partisan Review* contributor Ross Wetzsteon contends that viewers respond to Shepard's plays "not by interpreting their plots or analyzing their characters or dissecting their themes, but simply by experiencing their resonance. . . . Shepard's arias seek to soar into a disembodied freedom, to create emotions beyond rational structure, to induce in both player and audience a trancelike state of grace."

Shepard was born in Fort Sheridan, Illinois, on November 5, 1943, and was given the name his forebears had used for six generations—Samuel Shepard Rogers. His father was a career army officer, so as a youngster Shepard moved from base to base in the United States and even spent some time in Guam. When Shepard's father retired from the service, the family settled on a ranch in Duarte, California, where they grew avocados and raised sheep. Although the livelihood was precarious, Shepard enjoyed the atmosphere on the ranch and liked working with horses and other animals. Influenced by his father's interest in Dixieland jazz, Shepard gravitated to music; he began to play the drums and started what *Dictionary of Literary Biography* contributor David W. Engel calls "his lifelong involvement with rock and roll music and its subculture." He graduated from Duarte High School in 1960 and spent one year studying agricultural science at the local junior college, but his family situation deteriorated as his father began drinking excessively. Shepard fled the "hysterical" family scene by joining a touring theatrical group called the Bishop's Company Repertory Players. At the age of nineteen, he found himself in New York City, determined to seek his fortune with only a few months' acting experience to his credit.

By chance Shepard encountered a high school friend in New York, Charles Mingus, Jr., son of the renowned jazz musician. Mingus found Shepard a job at the Village Gate, a jazz club, and the two young men became roommates. While working at the Village Gate, Shepard met Ralph Cook, founder of the Off-Off-Broadway company Theatre Genesis. Cook encouraged Shepard to write plays, and Shepard obliged him by producing "Cowboys" and "The Rock Garden," two one-acts that became part of the first Theatre Genesis show at St. Mark Church in-the-Bowery. Though Engel notes that most of the critics regarded Shepard's first two works as "bad imitations of [Samuel] Beckett," the *Village Voice* columnist "gave the plays a rave review." Shepard began to turn out one-act pieces in rapid fashion; many of them were performed Off-Off-Broadway, and they attracted a cult following within that theatrical circuit. Shepard also continued his association with jazz and rock music, incorporating the rhythms into his dialogue and including musical riffs in the scripts. He reminisced about his early career in *New York* magazine: "When I arrived in New York there was this environment of *art* going on. I mean, it was really tangible. And you were right *in* the thing, especially on the Lower East Side. La Mama, Theatre Genesis, . . . all those theaters were just starting. So that was a great coincidence. I had a place to go and put something on without having to go through a producer or go through the commercial network. All of that was in response to the tightness of Broadway and Off-Broadway, where you couldn't get a play done."

Shepard told *New York* that his early work was done very hastily. "There wasn't much rewriting done," he said. "I had this whole attitude toward that work that it was somehow violating it to go back and rework it. . . . Why spend the time rewriting when there was another one to do?" Jack Kroll comments on the personal stream-of-consciousness nature of Shepard's first one-act plays: "The true artist starts with his obsessions, then makes them ours as well. The very young Sam Shepard exploded his obsessions like firecrackers; in his crazy, brilliant early plays he was escaping his demons, not speaking to ours." *New York Times* correspondent Mel Gussow, who has followed Shepard's career closely, characterizes the playwright's early works as "a series of mystical epics (on both a large and small scale) mixing figures

from folklore with visitors from the outer space of fantasy fiction." The Shepard one-acts, still frequently performed at theatre festivals and universities, utilize dramatic collage to juxtapose visual and verbal images, often in unexpected combinations. Stambolian contends that the technique "forces the spectator to view the surface, so to speak, from behind, from within the imagination that conceived it."

Modern Drama critic Charles R. Bachman describes the cultural wellspring from which the young Shepard nourished his imagination: "Shepard draws much of his material from popular culture sources such as B-grade westerns, sci-fi and horror films, popular folklore, country and rock music and murder-mysteries. In his best work he transforms the original stereotyped characters and situations into an imaginative, linguistically brilliant, quasi-surrealistic chemistry of text and stage presentation which is original and authentically his own." According to Stanley Kauffmann in the *New Republic,* the deliberate use of movie types "is part of Shepard's general method: the language and music of rock, spaceman fantasies, Wild West fantasies, gangster fantasies—pop-culture forms that he uses as building blocks, rituals of contemporary religion to heighten communion." Engel observes that Shepard's purpose in his early plays is "to capture the energetic diversity of American culture in an off-beat and poetic form. . . . The fantasy of his plays tears down and ridicules the middle-class world. Paradoxically, however, his plays often mourn the loss of traditional values."

Some critics have dismissed Shepard's early work as undisciplined, obscure, and lacking in sufficient self-awareness. For instance, *Massachusetts Review* essayist David Madden finds the plays "mired in swampy attitudes toward Mom and Dad. Their main line of reasoning seems to be that if Mom and Dad's middle class values are false, that if they and the institutions they uphold are complacent and indifferent, the only alternative is some form of outlaw behavior or ideology." Other national drama critics have evaluated the one-act plays quite differently. In the *New York Review of Books,* Robert Mazzocco writes: "If one is content to follow this hard-nosed, drug-induced, pop-flavored style, this perpetual retuning of old genres and old myths, one encounters, finally, a profuse and unique panorama of where we are now and where we have been." Stambolian declares that Shepard "is in fact showing to what extent the mind, and particularly the modern American mind, can become and has become entrapped by its own verbal and imaginative creations." And according to Barnes, Shepard "is so sweetly unserious about his plays, and so desperately serious about what he is saying. . . . There is more in them than meets the mind. They are very easy to be funny about, yet they linger oddly in the imagination." In his own assessment of his first plays, Shepard told *New York* he thinks of them as "survival kits, in a way. They were explosions that were coming out of some kind of inner turmoil in me that I didn't understand at all. There are areas in some of them that are still mysterious to me."

Shepard's first major production, "Operation Sidewinder," premiered at the Vivian Beaumont Theatre on March 12, 1970. Engel describes the two-act play as "an excellent example of how [Shepard] combines the roles of poet, musician, and playwright." Set in the Hopi Indian country of the American Southwest, "Operation Sidewinder" follows the attempts of many different factions of American society to control a huge mechanical rattlesnake originally designed to trace unidentified flying objects. Air force commandos, Hopi snake-worshippers, black power activists, and even a beautiful but foolish blonde named Honey try to use the computerized sidewinder for their own ends. Engel notes that the "playful and satiric action is amplified by Shepard's production techniques. He assaults the senses of the audience by the use of intense sound and lights, and by various chants and songs." Shepard himself helped to provide the music in the play by performing with a rock band, the Holy Modal Rounders. Although Engel claims that "the psychological resonance of stylized production, and not its sociological satire, is Shepard's aim," critics have found the work overly moralistic and stylistically confusing. "The difficulty of the play is in the writing," Barnes states in his *New York Times* review. "The symbolic progression, while clearly charting the progress to atomic holocaust, is altogether too symbolic." Kroll maintains that the play's energy "has congealed in a half-slick pop machine with the feel of celluloid and the clackey sound of doctrinaire contemporaneity." Martin Gottfried offers a different assessment of the play in *Women's Wear Daily.* "Everything about Sam Shepard's 'Operation Sidewinder' is important to our theatre," writes Gottfried. "More than any recent major production, it is built upon exactly the style and the mentality energizing the youth movement in America today."

In 1971 Shepard took his wife and infant son and moved to England. Having long experimented with drugs, the playwright sought escape from the abusive patterns he saw destroying fellow artists in New York. He also hoped to become more involved with rock music, still a central obsession in his life. He did not accomplish that goal, but as Engel notes, he did "write and produce some of his finest works" while living in London. Shepard discovered that by distancing himself from America he was made more aware of the pull of his nation's culture and the stresses placed on an artist in that national milieu. Gussow writes of this period: "As the author became recognized as an artist and found himself courted by such unearthly powers as Hollywood, he went through a Faustian phase. The result was a series of plays about art and the seduction of the artist." Plays such as "Angel City," "Geography of a Horse Dreamer," and "The Tooth of Crime" explore various aspects of the artist/visionary's dilemma when faced with public tastes or corporate profit-taking. Mazzocco feels that at this stage in his career Shepard chose to examine "not so much in political or economic parallels as in those of domination and submission, the nature of power in America. Or, more precisely, the duplicitous nature of 'success' and 'failure,' where it's implied that a failure of nerve and not that of a 'life' is at the basis of both." The playwright also discovered, in the words of Richard A. Davis, that "it is only within the individual mind that one finds his 'shelter' from the world; and even this shelter is not permanent, for the mind and body are tied together. To a great extent, Shepard's dramas have all been caught in this continual exploration of the same human problem."

"The Tooth of Crime," first produced in 1972, further strengthened Shepard's literary reputation. A two-act study of rock and roll stars who fight to gain status and "turf," the play "depicts a society which worships raw power," in Engel's words. London *Times* reviewer Irving Wardle writes of the work: "Its central battle to the death between an aging superstar and a young pretender to his throne is as timeless as a myth . . . and . . . has proved a durably amazing reflection of the West Coast scene. If any classic has emerged from the last 20 years of the American experimental theatre, this is it." "Moving freely from gangster movies of the 40's to punk rock of the 70's, Mr. Shepard speaks in a language that is vividly idiomatic," Gussow claims in the *New York Times.* "The imagery is visceral and sexual, a necromantic view of a rapacious society where, for an achiever, there is no acceptable alternative to being on top of the charts." Mazzocco calls "The Tooth of Crime" "undoubtedly the quintessen-

tial Shepard play" and "a dazzlingly corrosive work . . . one of the most original achievements in contemporary theater. It is also the play that best illustrates the various facets—at once highly eclectic and highly singular—of [Shepard's] genius."

"The Tooth of Crime" also proved to be a stylistic departure from previous Shepard plays. Bachman contends that the work "utilizes . . . the traditional dramatic values of taut, disciplined structure, vivid and consistent characterization, and crescendo of suspense." More recently these criteria have come to play more prominent roles in Shepard's work, although the transition from modernist to traditional style has hardly been either abrupt or thorough. According to Richard L. Homan in *Critical Quarterly,* Shepard has learned "to express the outrage, which gave rise to the experimental theatre, in plays which work through realistic conventions to challenge our everyday sense of reality." Shepard told *New York* that he sees a growing emphasis on character in his plays since 1972. "When I started writing," he said, "I wasn't interested in character at all. In fact, I thought it was useless, old-fashioned, stuck in a certain way. . . . I preferred a character that was constantly unidentifiable, shifting through the actor, so that the actor could almost play anything, and the audience was never expected to identify with the character. . . . But I had broken away from the idea of character without understanding it." Shepard's more recent plays explore characters—especially idiosyncratic and eccentric ones—for dramatic effect.

Mel Gussow believes that Shepard's writing has entered a new phase, one which reflects the changes in his own life as he ages. The playwright increasingly seeks to expose "the erosion and the conflagration of the ill-American family," according to Gussow. Mazzocco also claims that Shepard has "turned from the game to the trap, from the trail back to the hearth, from warfare in a 'buddy culture' to warfare among kith and kin." Four of Shepard's plays, "Buried Child," "Curse of the Starving Class," "True West," and "A Lie of the Mind," document in scenes of black humor the peculiar savagery of modern American family life. *New York Times* contributor Benedict Nightingale finds these plays peopled by a "legion of the lost," whose "essential tragedy . . . seems . . . to be that they are simultaneously searching for things that are incompatible and possibly not attainable anyway: excitement and security, the exhilaration of self-fulfillment and a sense of belonging, freedom and roots." In *Time,* T. E. Kalem notes that the works "display no traces of cozy domesticity. There is only the baleful sense of wary enemies endlessly circling and stalking each other, waiting to deliver, or receive, an invisible dagger thrust."

"Buried Child" and "A Lie of the Mind"—separated by seven years of the playwright's career—both traverse the psychological topography of disturbed families. In "Buried Child," notes *Washington Post* contributor David Richards, Shepard "delivers a requiem for America, land of the surreal and home of the crazed. . . . Beyond the white frame farmhouse that contains the evening's action, the amber waves of grain mask a dark secret. The fruited plain is rotting and the purple mountain's majesty is like a bad bruise on the landscape." The action in "Buried Child" unfolds when son Vince arrives at his midwestern farm home after a long absence. He is confronted with a dangerously unbalanced cast of relatives who harbor secrets of incest and murder. As Richard Christiansen points out in the *Chicago Tribune,* the Pulitzer Prize-winning play is "a Norman Rockwell portrait created for Mad Magazine, a scene from America's heartland that reeks with 'the stench of sin.' " Similarly, the 1985 play "A Lie of the Mind" presents a tale of "interior domestic violence, the damage that one does to filial, fraternal and marital bonds—and the love that lingers in the air after the havoc has run its natural course," according to Gussow. In that work, two families are galvanized into violence by the near-fatal beating a jealous husband administers to his wife. Gussow calls the drama "a play of penetrating originality" while noting that it "follows a clear naturalistic plotline, with characters who behave like normal, irrational human beings." "A Lie of the Mind" won the New York Drama Critics' Circle Award for best new Off-Broadway play of 1985, and Shepard himself directed the original production.

Shepard also directed his 1983 play "Fool for Love"—probably his best-known work. The one-act piece has been produced for stage and has also been made into a feature film in which Shepard performed the starring role. "Fool for Love" charts a course of alternating submission and rejection between two lovers who may also be half-brother and half-sister. New York *Daily News* critic Douglas Watt maintains that the ninety-minute nonstop drama "is Sam Shepard's purest and most beautiful play. An aching love story of classical symmetry, it is . . . like watching the division of an amoeba in reverse, ending with a perfect whole." "Fool for Love," writes *New York Times* reviewer Frank Rich, "is a western for our time. We watch a pair of figurative gunslingers fight to the finish—not with bullets, but with piercing words that give ballast to the weight of a nation's buried dreams. . . . As Shepard's people race verbally through the debris of the West, they search for the identities and familial roots that have disappeared with the landscape of legend." In the *New Republic,* Brustein finds "nothing very thick or complicated about either the characters or the plot" and a lack of resolution to the play's ending. The critic concludes nevertheless that "Fool for Love" is "not so much a text as a legend, not so much a play as a scenario for stage choreography, and under the miraculous direction of the playwright, each moment is rich with balletic nuances." Clive Barnes concludes in the *New York Post* that the drama "moves with a deathless effortlessness through planes of meaning. Everything . . . is always what it seems but then a little bit more."

Shepard's film work has not been confined to his 1985 appearance in "Fool for Love." Since 1978 he has taken a major movie role each year and has, despite his discomfort with the image, assumed a certain matinee idol status. "Shepard did not become famous by writing plays," declares Stephen Fay in *Vogue.* "Like it or not, acting [has] made him a celebrity." Shepard does *not* like to be considered a screen celebrity; his attitude toward film work is ambivalent, and public scrutiny has driven him into near-seclusion. He told *New York:* "There's a definite fear about being diminished through film. It's very easy to do too much of it, to a point where you're lost. Image-making is really what film acting is about. It's image-making, as opposed to character-making, and in some cases it's not true." *Film Comment* essayist David Thomson contends, however, that Shepard's long-standing fascination with movies lures him into that sort of work. "His sternness wants to be tested against their decadence," writes Thomson. "His restraint struggles to reconcile a simultaneous contempt and need for movies. The uneasiness hovers between passion and foolishness, between the lack of skill and a monolith of intractability." Some critics, including *Washington Post* correspondent Harry Haun, maintain that Shepard's disdain for Hollywood publicity is a calculated device to strengthen his personal mystique. "He chooses to hide out from the world on the silver screen," notes Haun. "That fine irony is the stuff that animates many a Shepard work. He is The Recluse as Superstar, the man who has arrived on his own terms, carefully sculpting a special myth for himself."

Many of the roles Shepard has taken tend to contradict the contention that he is devising his own heroic persona. In "Country," for instance, he portrays a farmer who wilts under pressure when threatened with foreclosure, and in "Fool for Love" he appears as a womanizing, luckless rodeo rider. According to Thomson, Shepard brings the same sort of integrity to his movie roles that he brings to his writing. "For five years or so," Thomson states, "he has been prowling around the house of cinema, coming in a little way, armored with disdain, slipping out, but coming back, as if it intrigued and tempted his large talent. And movies need him, for his talent and because of the change that would be necessary in them for him to be a star or a writer . . . or a director. But as with all prowlers, there remains a doubt as to whether this roaming, wolfen, mongrel lurcher wants to live in the house or tear it to pieces with his jaws and then howl at the desert moon, queen of dead worlds." Shepard phrased his reaction to film work less poetically in *New York:* "I'm a writer. The more I act, the more resistance I have to it. Now it seems to me that being an actor in films is like being sentenced to a trailer for twelve weeks."

In 1983, German director Wim Wenders commissioned Shepard to write a screenplay based loosely on the playwright's book *Motel Chronicles.* The resulting work, "Paris, Texas," was a unanimous winner of the Golden Palm Award at the 1984 Cannes Film Festival. The film recasts many of Shepard's central concerns—broken families, the myth of the loner, and the elegy for the old West—in a story of reunion between a father and a son. In *People* magazine, Peter Travers calls "Paris, Texas" the "most disturbing film ever about the roots of family relationships. Shepard's words and Wenders' images blend in a magical poetry." *New York* reviewer David Denby finds the film "a lifeless art-world hallucination—a movie composed entirely of self-conscious flourishes," but most other critics praise the work. In the *Los Angeles Times,* Sheila Benson, for one, writes: "This is a deeply affecting film about family, separation, loss and a man's last act of repentance. . . . Its beautiful parable about rootlessness has gone deep into our unconscious."

For all his work in other media, Shepard is still most highly regarded for the plays he writes. "He is indeed an original," writes Edith Oliver in the *New Yorker,* "but it might be pointed out that the qualities that make him so valuable are the enduring ones—good writing, wit, dramatic invention, and the ability to create characters." George Stambolian comments that whatever judgment is finally made on Shepard's work, "it is certain that in a society drifting rapidly into the escapism of a permanent, and often instant, nostalgia, Shepard's plays are a sign of artistic health and awareness, and are, therefore, worthy of our attention." John Lahr elaborates on this idea in *Plays and Players:* "Shepard, who has put himself outside the killing commercial climate of American life and theatre for the last few years, seems to be saying . . . that the only real geography is internal." And, as *New York Times* correspondent Walter Kerr concludes, "everyone's got to admire [Shepard's] steadfast insistence on pursuing the vision in his head."

Shepard himself sees room for growth in his writing. "I guess I'm always hoping for one play that will end my need to write plays," he told *Vogue.* "Sort of the definitive piece, but it never happens. There's always disappointment, something missing, some level that hasn't been touched, and the more you write the more you struggle, even if you are riding a wave of inspiration. And if the piece does touch something, you always know you haven't got to the depths of certain emotional territory. So you go out and try another one." According to *New Statesman* reviewer Benedict Nightingale, "we can rely on [Shepard] to continue bringing a distinctively American eye, ear and intelligence to the diagnosis of what are, if you think about it, universal anxieties." The playwright told the *New York Times* that he plans to continue the multifaceted career that has made him as recognizable to the American public as he has always been to discriminating theatregoers. Quite simply, he concluded, "I want to do the work that fascinates me."

MEDIA ADAPTATIONS: "Fourteen Hundred Thousand" was filmed for "NET Playhouse," 1969; "Blue Bitch" was filmed by the British Broadcasting Corporation (BBC), 1973; "True West" was filmed for the Public Broadcasting Service (PBS) series "American Playhouse."

AVOCATIONAL INTERESTS: Polo, rodeo.

BIOGRAPHICAL/CRITICAL SOURCES:

BOOKS

Contemporary Literary Criticism, Gale, Volume 4, 1975, Volume 6, 1976, Volume 17, 1981, Volume 34, 1985, Volume 41, 1987, Volume 44, 1987.
Dictionary of Literary Biography, Volume 7: *Twentieth-Century American Dramatists,* Gale, 1981.
Marranca, Bonnie, editor, *American Dramas: The Imagination of Sam Shepard,* Performing Arts Journal Publications, 1981.
The New York Times Theatre Reviews, New York Times Company, 1971.
Shepard, Sam, *Five Plays by Sam Shepard,* Bobbs-Merrill, 1967.
Shepard, Sam, *"Mad Dog Blues" and Other Plays,* Winter House, 1972.
Shepard, Sam, *Seven Plays by Sam Shepard,* Bantam, 1981.
Shewey, Don, *Sam Shepard,* Dell, 1985.
Weales, Gerald, *The Jumping-Off Place: American Drama in the 1960's,* Macmillan, 1969.

PERIODICALS

After Dark, June, 1975.
America, November 5, 1983.
American Film, October, 1984.
Canadian Forum, March, 1985.
Chicago Tribune, December 15, 1978, December 7, 1979, July 2, 1980, April 23, 1982, December 16, 1985, December 18, 1985, November 23, 1988.
Christian Century, November 21, 1984.
Christian Science Monitor, June 9, 1983.
Commonweal, June 14, 1968, May 8, 1970, November 30, 1984.
Cosmopolitan, January, 1985.
Critical Quarterly, spring, 1982.
Cue, April 11, 1970, July 18, 1970, February 17, 1973, March 31, 1973, March 18, 1978.
Drama, winter, 1965, spring, 1969, autumn, 1973, summer, 1976.
Educational Theatre Journal, October, 1977.
Esquire, February, 1980.
Film Comment, November-December, 1983, June, 1984.
Globe and Mail (Toronto), December 21, 1985.
Guardian, February 20, 1974.
Harper's Bazaar, September, 1985.
Hudson Review, spring, 1979, spring, 1984.
Journal of Popular Culture, spring, 1974.
Listener, September 26, 1974.
London Magazine, December, 1968.
Los Angeles Times, May 12, 1982, February 12, 1983, October 1, 1983, December 12, 1983, March 14, 1984, November 16, 1984, September 25, 1985, December 6, 1985, January 25, 1986, April 11, 1986, August 11, 1986, November 9, 1988.
Maclean's, October 29, 1984, December 24, 1984, January 13, 1986.
Mademoiselle, March, 1985.
Massachusetts Review, autumn, 1967.
Modern Drama, December, 1976, March, 1979, March, 1981.
Ms., November, 1984.
Nation, February 21, 1966, April 4, 1966, March 30, 1970, March 26, 1973, May 3, 1975, January 10, 1976, February 24, 1979, January 31, 1981, October 27, 1984, December 29, 1984-January 5, 1985, January 11, 1986, February 22, 1986.
New Leader, April 10, 1967.
New Republic, April 21, 1973, April 8, 1978, January 31, 1981, June 27, 1983, October 29, 1984, December 3, 1984, December 23, 1985, September 29, 1986, February 2, 1987.
New Statesman, August 24, 1984, October 12, 1984, March 1, 1985, July 4, 1986.
Newsweek, March 23, 1970, January 5, 1981, June 6, 1983, October 1, 1984, November 19, 1984, November 11, 1985, December 16, 1985.
New York, November 27, 1978, February 19, 1979, June 13, 1983, December 5, 1983, October 15, 1984, November 19, 1984, December 9, 1985.
New York Daily News, May 27, 1983.
New Yorker, May 11, 1968, March 21, 1970, March 17, 1973, May 5, 1975, December 22, 1975, November 29, 1982, October 1, 1984, September 2, 1985, January 27, 1986, December 15, 1986.
New York Post, May 27, 1983.
New York Review of Books, April 6, 1967, May 9, 1985.
New York Times, February 11, 1965, April 13, 1966, May 28, 1968, April 13, 1969, March 15, 1970, April 2, 1970, March 8, 1971, June 28, 1971, March 7, 1973, September 17, 1977, March 3, 1978, April 28, 1978, November 7, 1978, December 10, 1978, February 2, 1979, March 4, 1979, March 14, 1979, April 17, 1979, June 3, 1979, February 7, 1980, March 12, 1980, December 24, 1980, November 9, 1981, January 6, 1982, October 18, 1982, March 2, 1983, May 27, 1983, June 5, 1983, September 20, 1983, September 25, 1983, May 27, 1983, January 29, 1984, September 28, 1984, September 30, 1984, November 9, 1984, November 14, 1984, November 18, 1984, November 22, 1984, November 29, 1984, November 30, 1984, December 16, 1984, August 15, 1985, October 1, 1985, October 4, 1985, November 14, 1985, December 1, 1985, December 6, 1985, December 15, 1985, January 12, 1986, January 21, 1986, April 13, 1986.
Partisan Review, Volume 41, number 2, 1974, Volume 49, number 2, 1982.
People, December 26, 1983, January 2, 1984, October 15, 1984, November 5, 1984, December 9, 1985, January 6, 1986.
Plays and Players, June, 1970, October-November, 1971, April, 1974, May, 1974, November, 1974, April, 1979.
Quill and Quire, February, 1980.
Rolling Stone, August 11, 1977, December 18, 1986-January 1, 1987.
Saturday Review, December, 1984.
Theatre Journal, March, 1984.
Theatre Quarterly, August, 1974.
Time, November 27, 1972, June 6, 1983, October 8, 1984, August 12, 1985, December 2, 1985, December 16, 1985.
Times (London), September 24, 1983, September 26, 1983, October 6, 1984, January 7, 1986, October 10, 1987, April 25, 1989.
Times Literary Supplement, November 24, 1978, March 1, 1985.

Village Voice, April 4, 1977, August 15, 1977, February 12, 1979.
Vogue, February, 1984, February, 1985.
Washington Post, January 14, 1979, June 2, 1979, March 5, 1983, April 22, 1983, October 23, 1983, April 12, 1985, October 15, 1985, May 1, 1986, September 12, 1986, November 8, 1988, November 23, 1988, December 12, 1988.
Women's Wear Daily, March 13, 1970, May 27, 1983.

*   *   *

SHEPHERD, Michael
See LUDLUM, Robert

*   *   *

SHIRER, William L(awrence) 1904-

PERSONAL: Surname is pronounced *"Shy-*rer"; born February 23, 1904, in Chicago, Ill.; son of Seward Smith (a lawyer) and Josephine (Tanner) Shirer; married Theresa Stiberitz (an artist), January 30, 1931 (divorced, 1970); remarried in the 1970s and divorced; married Irina Lugovskaya (a Russian instructor), December 25, 1987; children: (first marriage) Eileen Inga, Linda Elizabeth. *Education:* Coe College, B.A., 1925; College de France, Paris, courses in European history, 1925-27. *Politics:* Independent. *Religion:* Presbyterian.

ADDRESSES: Box 487, 34 Sunset Ave., Lenox, Mass. 01240. *Agent*—Don Congdon, Harold Matson Co., Inc., 276 Fifth Ave., New York, N.Y. 10001.

CAREER: Chicago Tribune, Paris edition, reporter in Paris, France, 1925-27, foreign correspondent in Paris, London, England, Geneva, Switzerland, Rome, Italy, Dublin, Ireland, Vienna, Austria, and Prague, Czechoslovakia, 1927-29, chief of Central European bureau in Vienna, 1929-32; European correspondent for Paris edition of *New York Herald,* 1934; Universal News Service, foreign correspondent in Berlin, Germany, 1935-37; Columbia Broadcasting System (CBS), continental representative in Vienna, 1937-38, and in Prague and Berlin, 1938-40, war correspondent, 1939-45, radio commentator in the United States, 1941-47; radio commentator for Mutual Broadcasting System, 1947-49; full-time writer, 1950—. Columnist for *New York Herald Tribune* and its syndicate, 1942-48.

MEMBER: Authors Guild (president, 1953-57), PEN, Council on Foreign Relations, Foreign Policy Association, Phi Beta Kappa, Tau Kappa Epsilon, Century Club.

AWARDS, HONORS: Headliners Club Award, 1938, for coverage of the Austrian Anschluss, and 1941, for general excellence in radio reporting; Litt.D., Coe College, 1941; Chevalier, Legion d'Honneur; George Foster Peabody Award, 1947; Wendell Willkie One World Award, 1948; National Book Award and Sidney Hillman Foundation Award, both 1961, for *The Rise and Fall of the Third Reich;* Emmy Award from National Academy of Television Arts and Sciences for cultural documentary, 1967-68, for "The Rise and Fall of the Third Reich"; *Los Angeles Times* Book Prize nomination in biography, 1984, and nonfiction award from Society of Midland Authors, c. 1985, for *Twentieth-Century Journal,* Volume II: *The Nightmare Years: 1930-1940.*

WRITINGS:

Berlin Diary: The Journal of a Foreign Correspondent, 1934-1941 (Book-of-the-Month Club selection), Knopf, 1941, reprinted, Little, Brown, 1988.
End of a Berlin Diary, Knopf, 1947.

The Traitor (novel), Farrar, Straus, 1950, reprinted, Pocket Books, 1971.
Midcentury Journey: The Western World Through Its Years of Conflict (Literary Guild selection), Farrar, Straus, 1952.
Stranger Come Home (novel), Little, Brown, 1954.
The Challenge of Scandinavia: Norway, Sweden, Denmark, and Finland in Our Time, Little, Brown, 1955, reprinted, Greenwood Press, 1977.
The Consul's Wife (novel), Little, Brown, 1956.
The Rise and Fall of the Third Reich: A History of Nazi Germany (Book-of-the-Month Club selection), Simon & Schuster, 1960, reprinted, 1981.
The Rise and Fall of Adolf Hitler (for children), Random House, 1961 (published in England as *All About the Rise and Fall of Adolf Hitler,* W. H. Allen, 1962).
The Sinking of the Bismarck (for children), Random House, 1962 (published in England as *All About the Sinking the Bismarck,* W. H. Allen, 1963).
The Collapse of the Third Republic: An Inquiry Into the Fall of France in 1940 (Book-of-the-Month Club selection), Simon & Schuster, 1969.
Twentieth-Century Journey: A Memoir of a Life and the Times, Volume I: *The Start, 1904-1930,* Simon & Schuster, 1976, Volume II: *The Nightmare Years, 1930-1940,* Little, Brown, 1984, Volume III: *A Native's Return, 1945-1988,* Little, Brown, 1990.
Gandhi: A Memoir, Simon & Schuster, 1980.

Contributor to *Harper's, Atlantic, Reader's Digest, Look,* and other publications.

WORK IN PROGRESS: A book tentatively titled *The Road to Yasnaya Polyana: The Last Days of Leo Tolstoy,* for Bantam.

SIDELIGHTS: In the summer of 1925, twenty-one-year-old William L. Shirer left his home in Cedar Rapids, Iowa, and set out for Paris on what was intended to be one last youthful fling before settling into a stateside job in the fall. Having borrowed two hundred dollars (enough money, he figured, to last him about two months) from his uncle and the president of his alma mater, Coe College, the young man proceeded to work his way across the Atlantic on a cattle boat, arriving in the French capital with dreams of becoming a writer of fiction and poetry. Shirer found his new life to be far more "intellectually stimulating and less personally restrictive" than his life had been in the United States, reports Alice Henderson in the *Dictionary of Literary Biography,* and he soon decided to try his luck at obtaining a newspaper job in Paris. (Shirer had served as editor of his college paper and as sports editor of the *Cedar Rapids Republican.*) But editors of two major American newspapers with Paris editions, the *New York Herald* and the *Chicago Tribune,* could offer him little encouragement; hundreds of other job-seeking men and women had been there before him, all with similar stories and requests.

Resigned to the prospect of having to return to what he called the land of "Prohibition, fundamentalism, puritanism, Coolidgeism, [and] Babbitry" when his money ran out, Shirer vowed to make the most of his remaining time in Paris. But on the morning of his last day in the city, after a particularly lively farewell night on the town, he awoke to discover a note from the editor of the *Chicago Tribune* asking him to report to the newspaper office that very evening for a possible job. Thus, at 9 o'clock, Shirer found himself at the *Tribune* copy desk sitting next to a fellow expatriate-turned-copywriter, James Thurber.

Shirer spent the next two years in Paris working for the *Tribune,* specializing in sports, human interest stories, and international political news. Though still very interested in literature, Shirer was also, says Henderson, becoming increasingly "concerned that Americans were unaware of the threat of war in Europe and unwilling to read serious articles by overseas correspondents." As Shirer himself recalls in the first volume of his autobiography: "After a year in Paris I was beginning to know myself well enough to see that, as Jim [Thurber] said of himself, I was not going to be a Fitzgerald or a Hemingway or a Dos Passos or even a lesser creator of fiction and poetry. I had another disposition. Whereas they, as all good novelists must do, had turned inward to find the sources of their creativity . . . I was beginning to turn outward—after a year of trying to write poetry and short stories—to what was going on in the world. History now seemed more interesting to me, especially contemporary history. . . . Vaguely the idea began to take root that there might be a great deal of history to write about from here for a daily newspaper back home." Shirer's superiors at the *Tribune* evidently thought so, too; impressed by his talent for reporting and aware of his preoccupation with current events, they soon made him a foreign correspondent for the home paper.

Until December, 1940, Shirer roamed from one European capital to another, first for the *Tribune* and subsequently for the Paris edition of the *New York Herald,* the Universal News Service, and the Columbia Broadcasting System. He spent much of this time in Vienna, Berlin, and Prague, reporting on Adolf Hitler and the Nazis during crucial phases of their rise to power. His observations of these tumultuous years formed the basis of two voluminous best-sellers, each one a blend of journalism and history: *Berlin Diary* and *The Rise and Fall of the Third Reich.*

Berlin Diary was Shirer's first book. It opens on January 11, 1934, when the author was vacationing in Spain, and ends on December 13, 1940, as he was on board a ship heading back to America. Published in mid-1941, the book met with virtually unqualified praise, as in this *Saturday Review of Literature* article by W. L. White: "[*Berlin Diary*] is the best book on Germany in many years, and it will be many more before a better one can be written. . . . [The author] is gifted with an eye for significant detail. . . . I have yet to find anyone who picked the book up who was able to put it down unfinished." Joseph Barnes of *Books* agrees that *Berlin Diary* is "the most important and exciting book written out of Germany since long before the war began. This is, first of all, an absorbing book. Most of it reads like the scenario of a partly forgotten but important nightmare, written down with footnotes."

"I shall be surprised if *Berlin Diary* does not outdo every other war-book in popularity," declares the *Spectator*'s Wilson Harris. "As you read, your confidence in Mr. Shirer's eye for the essential, soundness of judgment, and fairness even to characters he dislikes most increases. The result is a book of engrossing interest and solid value." Clifton Fadiman of the *New Yorker* also applauds *Berlin Diary* as "a book of unusual interest and timeliness. We have had reports from Germany by the score, but none, I think, covering so long a period, none so fresh, so realistic, so (in the best sense) reportorial. No matter how carefully you have followed the news, no matter how large a proportion of Shirer's notes appears merely recapitulative, you will find *Berlin Diary* compelling reading."

Only a few reviewers disagree with these assessments of *Berlin Diary.* The *Catholic World* critic, for instance, despite calling the book "a vivid picture deftly drawn," feels that "judicious readers will be wary about accepting [Shirer's] implications and deductions." The lack of material on subjects "not in the headlines" prompts *Commonweal*'s Max Fischer to "seriously question [the

book's] quality." Continues the reviewer: "Mr. Shirer is just the typical newspaperman, whose interests are restricted to his profession. I admit he is an excellent reporter, but his book seems to me rather sterile."

Edward Weeks takes issue with Fischer's remarks. "[The author] makes mistakes and admits them," the critic states in his *Atlantic* review. "But if you identify yourself unhesitatingly with Shirer, it is because he is conscientious and right-minded. Finally—and this, I think, will make the *Diary* live—he is a man of letters: he writes with the power and beauty, with the anger and pity, that come straight from the incandescent movements he lived through. He doesn't deal in venom. He lets the evidence speak."

After the publication of *Berlin Diary,* Shirer continued his career in radio and newspaper reporting until being blacklisted during the McCarthy era for supporting the Hollywood Ten. "I became unemployable," he told the *New York Times Book Review*'s John L. Hess. "I was broke, with two kids in school. Some of my friends were editors and would pay me for a piece, but nothing was ever published. I then decided I would speak my piece on the lecture trail. I spent almost five years when my sole income was from these one-night stands at universities. They were almost the only place in the country that still had some sort of respect for freedom of speech."

Being blacklisted did, however, give Shirer the time he needed to research and write the book many regard as his best, the massive (1,245 pages) *Rise and Fall of the Third Reich.* "The work of a newspaperman, not a university scholar," as the author describes it, *The Rise and Fall of the Third Reich* took Shirer ten years to complete; among his major sources were his own reports on events of the era, transcripts of the Nuremberg Trial, diaries, and captured German documents. The result, says G. A. Craig of the *New York Herald Tribune Book Review,* is "a book that will please [Shirer's] admirers, make him many new ones, and perhaps, by the force of its narrative, help restore the perspective of a generation which, in its preoccupation with present world dangers, has forgotten how desperate our situation seemed when Hitler's monstrous tyranny was at the height of its power. . . . Mr. Shirer's own intense interest in his subject has been reflected in his writing: and this and his excellent taste in anecdotes and striking details make this an immensely readable book."

Many critics marvel at the author's ability to organize and present a wealth of basically familiar material in such an attention-riveting fashion. As Bernard Levin reports in the *Spectator,* Shirer took the available information "and sifted and kneaded it until it takes on a new, clear, polished aspect." Though the *New York Times Book Review*'s H. R. Trevor-Roper would like to have seen Shirer cover certain topics in greater detail or with more skill, he decides that such criticism is "trivial" when one considers "the greatness of his achievement" in bringing together the memories of living witnesses and "historical truth." "This is a splendid work of scholarship," Trevor-Roper adds, "objective in method, sound in judgment, inescapable in its conclusions." In short, declares Alan Bullock in his *Guardian* review, "neither Mr. Shirer nor the reader has any reason to regret the five years' hard work he put into writing [*The Rise and Fall of the Third Reich*]. . . . There are half a dozen books on Nazi Germany which I should rate higher as historical studies of particular aspects, but I can think of none which I would rather put in the hands of anyone who wanted to find out what happened In Germany between 1930 and 1945, and why the history of those years should never be forgotten."

Both Naomi Bliven of the *New Yorker* and Telford Taylor of *Saturday Review* are pleased to note that despite Shirer's obvious hatred of Hitler and Nazism, he does not try to moralize. Bliven, for example, points out that "Shirer knew a great deal about the Nazis before he began his researches; he was, in fact, an expert—a man who knows so much that he knows how much more there is to know. His book is a judicious blend of several kinds of knowledge. . . . [The result is] a literary scale model of an era. And while it is impossible to write a book about Nazi Germany without writing a book against Nazi Germany, Mr. Shirer neither moralizes nor argues but simply presents." Taylor agrees with this assessment, stating: "Some history is Olympian and objective; this is personal and passionate. . . . Passionately written as it is, [*The Rise and Fall of the Third Reich*] is rarely marred by prejudice. For the most part, the diction is restrained and poised, and the judgments tempered and well-supported. The level of factual accuracy is high. . . . Mr. Shirer is a journalist, and his book carries the marks of his profession at its best."

A few critics express some reservations about what they feel is Shirer's tendency to dwell on the more lurid and well-publicized excesses of the Nazi era. The *New Statesman*'s R. H. S. Crossman, who regards *The Rise and Fall of the Third Reich* as "not a history of Nazi Germany but a biography of Hitler," finds the presentation "perilously lopsided" and "overblown," while the *New York Herald Tribune Book Review*'s Craig notes that Shirer "cloys the appetite [he] feeds. There is such a thing as too much of a good thing. . . . The book is also to my way of thinking out of balance. . . . [Shirer] has concentrated on those aspects of Nazi history that have been most written about and skipped over the periods about which it is time historians had something new and fresh to say."

Geoffrey Barraclough, commenting in the *Nation,* worries that those readers who did not live through the Nazi era "may be more impressed by the melodrama than by the lessons. We all see what we want to in a book; and I fear that, as things are, what most readers will see is Hitler in cinerama. . . . It is a terrifying thought that Mr. Shirer may unwittingly have popularized what he set out to condemn. Of course, the Third Reich *was* lurid, melodramatic, sensational. But that is only part of the picture and not the most important."

As the *Time* reviewer observes, however, it is this very element of sensationalism that makes *The Rise and Fall of the Third Reich* so readable. Explains the critic: "To his huge task Shirer brings only modest writing gifts, but he has an advantage that swamps all shortcomings: his material is horribly fascinating. He has done thorough research. . . . The result is a panoramic exposure of Naziism in practice that may lack literary stature and new insights, but seizes the reader's interest and holds it to the end."

This ability to "seize the reader's interest and hold it to the end" has been a hallmark of Shirer's work since his days as a news correspondent. As a *Best Sellers* reviewer once noted, Shirer always "had the good fortune to be in the important places when things began to happen, and the ability to relate these events in a graphic manner." And according to the *Dictionary of Literary Biography*'s Henderson, it was those first few years the young reporter spent in Paris that made the difference. Concludes the critic: "Although Shirer did not publish any poetry or fiction during the years he lived in Paris, as he had originally hoped to do, his Paris experience was pivotal in his life. It changed him from a relatively inexperienced, although well-read, youth to a journalist with wide interests and a concern for careful research.

These traits, combined with a clear and vigorous writing style gave him unprecedented success as a journalist-historian."

MEDIA ADAPTATIONS: The Rise and Fall of the Third Reich was adapted as a three-part documentary miniseries for American Broadcasting Companies (ABC-TV), March 6, 1968; Shirer's second volume of memoirs, *The Nightmare Years: 1930-1940,* was adapted as a four-part miniseries for TNT cable television, September 17, 1989.

AVOCATIONAL INTERESTS: Walking, sailing, attending the theater and ballet, listening to symphonic and chamber music.

BIOGRAPHICAL/CRITICAL SOURCES:

BOOKS

Dictionary of Literary Biography, Volume 4: *American Writers in Paris, 1920-1939,* Gale, 1980.
Shirer, William L., *Berlin Diary: The Journal of a Foreign Correspondent, 1934-1941,* Knopf, 1941.
Shirer, William L., *Twentieth-Century Journey: A Memoir of a Life and the Times,* Volume I: *The Start, 1904-1930,* Simon & Schuster, 1976, Volume II: *The Nightmare Years, 1930-1940,* Little, Brown, 1984, Volume III: *A Native's Return, 1945-1988,* Little, Brown, 1990.

PERIODICALS

Atlantic, September, 1941, December, 1960, December, 1969.
Best Sellers, December, 1976.
Books, June 22, 1941.
Catholic World, October, 1941.
Chicago Sunday Tribune, October 16, 1960.
Chicago Tribune, February 24, 1985.
Chicago Tribune Book World, May 20, 1984.
Christian Science Monitor, June 30, 1941, October 20, 1960.
Commonweal, August 1, 1941.
Detroit News, June 3, 1984.
Guardian, November 11, 1960.
Living Age, August, 1941.
Los Angeles Times, February 3, 1980, July 11, 1984, December 26, 1984, January 17, 1990, February 4, 1990.
Los Angeles Times Book Review, July 1, 1984.
Nation, July 19, 1941, October 29, 1960.
National Review, November 26, 1976.
New Republic, June 30, 1941, November 14, 1960, February 12, 1977.
New Statesman, November 5, 1960.
Newsweek, January 28, 1980.
New Yorker, June 21, 1941, October 29, 1960, September 27, 1976.
New York Herald Tribune Book Review, October 16, 1960.
New York Times, June 22, 1941, September 11, 1976, January 7, 1980, May 25, 1984, January 12, 1986, January 12, 1990, February 3, 1990.
New York Times Book Review, October 16, 1960, November 9, 1969, October 10, 1976, July 24, 1977, January 20, 1980, May 27, 1984, April 7, 1985, January 21, 1990.
Saturday Review, October 15, 1960, August 21, 1976, January 19, 1980.
Saturday Review of Literature, June 28, 1941.
Spectator, October 3, 1941, November 18, 1960.
Time, October 27, 1941, October 17, 1960, November 21, 1969, June 25, 1984.
Times Literary Supplement, December 2, 1960.
Tribune Books, February 4, 1990.
Washington Post Book World, November 9, 1969.

Washington Post, January 29, 1980, August 10, 1989, February 9, 1990.

Washington Post Book World, May 20, 1984.

* * *

SHOLOKHOV, Mikhail (Aleksandrovich) 1905-1984

PERSONAL: Surname is pronounced *Shaw*-loh-khoff; born May 24, 1905, in Kruzhlino, Russia (now U.S.S.R.); died February 21 (some sources say February 20), 1984, in Veshenskaya, Rostov-on-Don, U.S.S.R., after a long illness; buried in Veshenskaya; son of Aleksander Mikhailovich (a farmer, cattle buyer, clerk, and owner of a power mill) and Anastasiya Danilovna (Chernikova) Sholokhov; married Maria Petrovna Gromoslavskaya (a teacher), 1923; children: four. *Education:* Attended public schools in Voronezh; studied under Ossip Brik and Viktor Shklovsky. *Politics:* Communist.

ADDRESSES: Home—Stanitsa Veshenskaya, Rostov Region, U.S.S.R. *Office*—Union of Soviet Writers, Ulitsa Vorovskogo 52, Moscow, U.S.S.R.

CAREER: Writer. Held a variety of jobs, including teacher, laborer, musician, playwright, actor, and journalist; worked as a war correspondent during World War II. Elected Deputy to the Supreme Soviet, 1937; member of Communist Party of Soviet Union Central Committee and of Committee for Defense of Peace. *Military service:* Red Army, c. 1920-22, served in various capacities, including journalist, freight handler, food inspector, mason, and machine gunner.

MEMBER: Academy of Sciences of the U.S.S.R., Union of Soviet Writers.

AWARDS, HONORS: Stalin Prize, 1941, for *Tikhii Don;* Nobel Prize for literature, 1965; named Hero of Socialist Labor, 1967; received Order of Lenin eight times.

WRITINGS:

IN ENGLISH TRANSLATION

Donskie rasskazy (short stories), [Moscow], 1925, reprinted, 1975, translation by H. C. Stevens published as *Tales From the Don,* Putnam, 1961, published as *Tales of the Don,* Knopf, 1962.

Tikhii Don (novel; title means "The Quiet Don"), Volumes 1-3 serialized in *Oktiabr,* 1928-32, Volume 4 serialized in *Novyi Mir,* 1937-40, revised Russian edition of Volumes 1-4 published in 1953, translation of Volumes 1-2 by Stephen Garry published as *And Quiet Flows the Don,* Putnam, 1934, reprinted, Knopf, 1973, translation of Volumes 3-4 by Garry published as *The Don Flows Home to the Sea,* Putnam, 1940, Knopf, 1941, reprinted, Random House, 1989, translation of Volumes 1-4 published as *The Silent Don,* Knopf, 1941.

Podniataia tselina (novel), Volume 1 published serially in *Novyi Mir,* 1932, revised Russian edition, 1953, Volume 2 published serially in *Pravda, Ogonyok,* and *Oktiabr,* 1955-60, translation of Volume 1 by Garry published as *Seeds of Tomorrow,* Knopf, 1935, reprinted, 1959 (published in England as *Virgin Soil Upturned,* Putnam, 1935), translation of Volume 2 by Stevens published as *Harvest on the Don,* Putnam, 1960, Knopf, 1961.

Nauka nenavisti, [Moscow], 1942, translation published as *Hate,* Foreign Languages Publishing House, 1942.

Oni srazhalis' za rodinu (novel), Volume 1, [Moscow], 1943, translation published as *They Fought for Their Country* in

Soviet Literature, July and August, 1959, excerpts from Volume 2 published in *Pravda,* 1969.

Sobranie sochinenii (collected works), eight volumes, Goslitzdat (Moscow), 1956-60, translation published as *Collected Works in Eight Volumes,* State Mutual Book, 1985.

Sud'ba cheloveka, [Moscow], 1957, reprinted, 1975, translation by Robert Daglish published as *The Fate of a Man,* Foreign Languages Publishing House, 1957, published as *The Fate of Man,* Von Nostrand, 1960, translation by Stevens contained in *One Man's Destiny, and Other Stories, Articles, and Sketches* (also see below), Knopf, 1967.

Slovo o rodine (title means "A Word on Our Country"), [Moscow], 1965, translation by Stevens contained in *One Man's Destiny, and Other Stories, Articles, and Sketches,* Knopf, 1967.

Early Stories (contains "The Birthmark," "The Herdsman," "The Bastard," "The Azure Steppe," "The Foal," "Alien Blood"), translation by Daglish and Yelena Oltshuler, Progress Publishers, 1966.

Fierce and Gentle Warriors (short stories; contains "The Colt," "The Rascal," "The Fate of a Man"), translation by Miriam Morton, Doubleday, 1967.

Selected Tales From the Don (biography in English; stories in Russian), introduction and notes by C. G. Bearne, Pergamon Press, 1967.

Po veleniiu dushi, [Moscow], 1970, translation by Olga Shartse published as *At the Bidding of the Heart,* Progress Publishers, 1973.

Stories (includes "The Fate of a Man"), Progress Publishers, 1975.

OTHER

Nakhalenok, 1925, reprinted, [Moscow], 1967.

Lazorevaya Steppe (short stories; title means "The Azure Steppe"), [Moscow], 1925.

Sbornik statei, Izdvo Leningradskogo Universiteta, 1956.

Rannie rasskazy, Sovetskaia Rossia, 1961.

Plesums, romans, [Riga], 1961.

Put'dorozhen'ka, Molodaia Gvardiia, 1962.

Izbrannoe, Molodaia Gvardiia, 1968.

Rossiia v serdtse, [Moscow], 1975.

(With others) *Slovo k molodym* (addresses, essays, and lectures), [Moscow], 1975.

SIDELIGHTS: Few writers have been more revered by Soviet officials than Mikhail Sholokhov. *The Quiet Don,* his epic about life in a Cossack village from 1912 to 1922, and *Virgin Soil Upturned,* his story of the collectivization of agriculture, are part of the curriculum in all Soviet schools. Sholokhov has been showered with honors by the Communist regime, including the Stalin Prize and the Order of Lenin. In 1955 his fiftieth birthday was declared a national celebration. But Sholokhov's fame extended far beyond the borders of the Soviet Union. His works have been translated into more than forty languages and have sold millions of copies. In recognition of "the artistic power and integrity with which, in his epic of the Don, Sholokhov has given expression to the history of the Russian people," the Swedish Academy awarded him the Nobel Prize for literature in 1965.

Despite these laurels, in the 1960s Sholokhov came under increasing attack by liberal Russian intellectuals and Western observers. Some critics accused him of being nothing more than an apologist for Communism. Others suggested that *The Quiet Don* was plagiarized. Although there has been a tendency to portray Sholokhov in black-and-white terms, he was, as Alexander Werth pointed out, "an extremely puzzling man." Sholokhov ardently defended the concept of socialist realism, which holds that the purpose of art is to glorify socialism, even though his own work was not always acceptable to government censors. He repeatedly declared his loyalty to the Soviet regime, but on occasion criticized authorities.

If this "extremely puzzling man" is ever to be understood, an examination of his background is essential. He was born on a farm not far from the river Don. This region was dominated by the Cossacks, a privileged group of people who were required to serve in the Russian Army and who were often used by the czar to suppress revolutionary movements. Sholokhov's father, Alexander Mikhailovich Sholokhov, was an "outlander" whose family had moved to Veshenskaya from the Ryazan region near Moscow. His mother, Anastasiya Danilovna Chernikova, was half-Turkish and half-Cossack. While working as a maid in the Sholokhov household, she met and fell in love with the young Alexander Mikhailovich. When she discovered she was pregnant, the older Sholokhovs were so dismayed by the prospect of their son wedding a peasant that they quickly married the servant girl off to an elderly Cossack officer. Not one to be thwarted by his parents, Alexander Mikhailovich collected his inheritance, purchased his own house, and hired Anastasiya Danilovna as his servant.

Since her legal husband was a Cossack, when she gave birth to Mikhail in 1905 he inherited all the rights and privileges of the Cossacks. When the old man died in 1912, however, Anastasiya Danilovna and Alexander Mikhailovich were officially married. This act meant that Mikhail lost his Cossack status. "What problems this may have caused a seven-year-old boy we do not know," D. H. Stewart noted in *Mikhail Sholokhov: A Critical Introduction,* "though echoes of traumatic discomfiture can be detected in Sholokhov's early stories about children. The crucial fact is that Sholokhov lacked full Cossack status."

Although Sholokhov's father had received little schooling, he was a well-read man. In contrast, his mother was illiterate. It was only after her son was sent away to school that she learned to read and write, for she wanted to keep in contact with him. Sholokhov attended public school in Boguchar, Voronezh Province, but was forced to leave school because of the German invasion. Upon his return home, he devoted much of his time to reading. Despite the fact that the area he was living in was dominated by the Whites, he began to develop a sympathy for the revolutionary movement. At the age of fifteen he went to work for the Revolutionary Committee. He performed a variety of tasks, including writing and acting in plays and establishing a collective youth theatre at Veshenskaya. For a time he served as a machine gunner with a Red Army supply detachment, hunting down kulaks (anti-Bolshevik farmers) and White Guards.

In 1922 Sholokhov went to Moscow to resume his education. While he was in that city he came under the tutelage of writers Ossip Brik and Viktor Shklovsky, and his essays and short stories began to appear in print. He returned to Veshenskaya in 1923 to marry Maria Gromoslavskaya, the daughter of a clerk in a Cossack regiment. After living for a short time in Moscow, Sholokhov and his wife settled down in the Don Region, where he lived until his death in 1984. Sholokhov found living on his native turf to be much more conducive to his writing than big-city life. He distrusted the urban intellectuals whom he had met in Moscow; besides, he had already determined that his literary creations would deal with the people of the Don Region. "I wanted," he later recalled, "to write about the people among whom I was born and whom I knew."

This regional interest is reflected in his first two books, *Tales of the Don* and *The Azure Steppe,* both of which were published in 1925. In retrospect, some critics discerned in these short story collections the same qualities that distinguish Sholokhov's subsequent work. For instance, Marc Slonim remarked in *Modern Russian Literature: From Chekhov to the Present,* " 'Tales of the Don' contains all the elements that later made Sholokhov a master of representational narrative; tense dramatic plots, fresh landscape, catching humor and a racy, uninhibited popular idiom. It is true that they are lacking in depth and character portrayal, but these primitive stories about primitive men are interesting as a document of an unsettled time, and they offer revealing material about the origins of an important Soviet writer." Commenting on the stories in *The Azure Steppe,* Ernest J. Simmons declared in *Russian Fiction and Soviet Ideology: Introduction to Fedin, Leonov, and Sholokhov,* that "we see in embryo in these early tales the future powerful psychological realist as he creates characters and bold, dramatic situations."

In October of 1925, when he was only twenty-one, Sholokhov began writing his masterpiece, *The Quiet Don,* a work that took him nearly fourteen years to complete. From 1925 to 1930 he worked on *The Quiet Don* almost constantly. In order to collect material for his book, he examined documents in the archives in Moscow and Rostov, listened to the tales of his Don Cossack neighbors, and read newspapers from the czarist era. The first two segments of *The Quiet Don* were published serially in *Oktiabr* in 1928 and 1929. Because of objections by Communist officials that the book was not sufficiently proletarian in outlook, publication ceased in April of 1929. It did not resume until 1932, when Sholokhov gained full membership into the Communist party. At this time the novelist became increasingly involved with public affairs. This new demand on his time, coupled with further censorship problems, delayed the publication of the final installment of *The Quiet Don* until 1940. *The Quiet Don* was published in English in two parts: *And Quiet Flows the Don* and *The Don Flows Home to the Sea.*

Sholokhov's epic portrays the life of the Don Cossacks during World War I and the Bolshevik Revolution. Because of the book's huge cast of characters and panoramic sweep, some critics have termed it "Tolstoyan." The central figure in the story is Gregor Melekhov, a young Cossack so beset by conflicting loyalties that he comes to believe that all is meaningless. Most Western critics feel that *The Quiet Don* demonstrates the principle of historical inevitability, in which people must either adapt to or be destroyed by historical forces. Rufus W. Mathewson, for instance, commented in *The Positive Hero in Russian Literature* that the theme of *The Quiet Don* is that "private moral judgment is sometimes irrelevant to the higher struggles of historical forces, and . . . in this fact there is genuine human tragedy."

Sholokhov's deep feeling for the land and for the people of the Don Region is evident throughout *The Quiet Don.* The book is filled with lyrical descriptions of nature. "Of the Russian authors I have read, Sholokhov is almost the only one with a highly developed sense of locality," Malcolm Cowley asserted in an article for the *New Republic.* He went on: "But besides his sense of locality, he also has a sense of people that is somewhat commoner in Russian fiction, though rare enough in the literature of any country. He writes about them as if he had always known and loved them and wanted the outside world to understand just why they acted as they did." Numerous critics describe Sholokhov's characters as primitive, and many feel that he excels at describing the instinctual urges of people rather than in capturing psychological depth. Helen Muchnic, for example, commented in *Russian Writers: Notes and Essays* that "the primitive, the naive, the elemental are [Sholokhov's] province: palpable matter, physical actions, simple feelings; the impact of a blow, the reflex of anger, the surging of lust; and also sentiment, gentleness."

One of the most striking characteristics of *The Quiet Don* is its dispassionate objectivity. Sholokhov's allegiance to the Communist party, Slonim pointed out, "did not affect his artistic integrity and his objectivity in description. . . . *The Quiet Don* told a story of nation-wide significance. . . . Sholokhov never subordinated these stories to his political ideas, never used his plot to drive a point home." Writing in *Introduction to Russian Realism*, Simmons also remarked upon the lack of political posturing in *The Quiet Don*: "*The Quiet Don* . . . represents with near perfection that fusion of traditional Russian realism with Soviet socialist realism, and was written by a Communist who, because of his artistic integrity, all but refused to sacrifice either the logic of his design or—in the Tolstoyan sense—the truth of his hero to extraneous demands of Party doctrine. If there is any point in the old cliche that all literature is propaganda, but not all propaganda is literature, then it may be said that propaganda is brilliantly sublimated in *The Quiet Don.*"

Between the publication of the third and fourth volumes of *The Quiet Don*, Sholokhov began work on *Virgin Soil Upturned*. This novel tells the story of the efforts to organize collective farming in the Cossack village of Gremyachy Log. Sholokhov had witnessed both the virtues and the drawbacks of this system in his own village of Veshenskaya. In 1933 he became so incensed at some of the injustices perpetrated against the Cossack farmers that he wrote a letter of complaint to Stalin. Later, in 1937 and 1938, he displayed a similar courage when he helped reinstate some local Communist officials who had been wrongfully convicted.

In Volume I of *Virgin Soil Upturned*, as in his personal life, Sholokhov had the courage to point out both the pros and cons of collective farming. A critic for the *Saturday Review* wrote that in this book, "the artist in Sholokhov triumphs over the propagandist, for not only are we presented with the wonderfully sympathetic picture of the Cossacks' love for their land and their fierce determination to acquire it for themselves, but the absurdities of the whole Soviet mechanising system and the stupidities of its officials are relentlessly exposed with an audacity that is almost incredible." The explanation for Sholokhov's audacity, Mihajlo Mihajlov observed in *Russian Themes*, "lies in the fact that Sholokhov had been dedicated to the Party heart and soul all his life and was a true believer in Communism, just like the people who crucified Russia, and he could therefore allow himself to depict reality much more truthfully than those who did not share his belief. He described reality honestly because he believed that in spite of all sacrifices the imposed collectivization would benefit Russia in the long run."

In Volume II of *Virgin Soil Upturned* (published in the United States as *Harvest on the Don*), the propaganda is much more overt. More than twenty-five years elapsed between the publication of the first and second volumes, and rumors circulated that the reason for the long delay in publication was that Sholokhov had been fighting with Communist censors about the conclusion of the novel. When the final installment of *Virgin Soil Upturned* appeared in *Pravda* in February of 1960, Sholokhov denied that he had changed the ending to conform with the party line. Many American critics, however, complained about the book's rigid adherence to Communist dogma, and several felt that he had let ideological considerations take precedence over artistic integrity. Anthony West asserted in the *New Yorker* that "it is all too clear in 'Harvest on the Don' that Sholokhov's gifts have been eroded

by a lifetime in a literary world ruled by the inevitably second-rate utilitarian aesthetics that fosters this kind of thing. His intuitive grasp of what writing can and should be . . . has deserted him, and he now alternates uneasily between broad vulgarities and parodies of the official style."

Despite *Harvest on the Don*'s bias, commentators did find much of merit in the book. Its warmth, humor, and powerful evocation of the Russian landscape were widely praised. Many critics valued it as a realistic portrayal of an important period in Soviet history. "To Americans its slant may seem rather obvious and its view of good men and bad men ingenuous, but it should still be recognized as the most intimate and vivid record of Russian rural life during the most momentous social change of our time," Milton Rugoff contended. Similarly, George Reavey maintained that "I know of no better account in fiction of this period of 'enforced civil war.' "

In *They Fought for Their Country,* Sholokhov set out to give a fictional account of the Soviet people's valiant struggles during the German invasion of World War II. Sholokhov had ample opportunity to observe the war effort, for he served as a correspondent on the front lines. Volume I of *They Fought for Their Country,* published in 1943, describes the Russian retreat in the Don area. Further installments of the novel were not published until 1969, when excerpts began to appear in *Pravda*. At that time it was announced that Volume II would be published shortly, but it has never appeared. The excerpts in *Pravda* contained an unfavorable depiction of Stalin's capacity as a wartime leader, and some observers believe that the complete book was never published because of this negative portrait.

In his well-known short story, "The Fate of a Man," Sholokhov again dramatizes the heroism of the Russian people during World War II. The protagonist of the story, Andrei Sokolov, is a Soviet soldier who escapes from a Nazi prison camp. He returns home only to discover that his entire family has been killed in the fighting. His sole consolation is the war orphan whom he adopts. Muchnic described "The Fate of a Man" as "a story of physical endurance and spiritual fortitude, and so long as memory lasts, no one is likely to question that Andrei Sokolov is a typical example, not an exception, of that stoic Russian heroism which roused the world's admiration in the great sieges and defenses of World War II." Although some critics complained about the Communist dogma contained in the story, most readers found the tale sentimental but moving. E. J. Czerwinski noted that the story "adheres to all the strictures of Socialist Realism and yet somehow manages to overcome the handicaps that such a narrow artistic policy forces upon a work of art."

Aside from "The Fate of a Man" and Volume II of *Virgin Soil Upturned*, Sholokhov published very little since the war. Indeed, he never again matched his years of great creativity between 1925 and 1930. One reason for his scanty output was the active role he played in the Communist party. "I am first and foremost a Communist; only thereafter am I a writer," Sholokhov once declared. Sholokhov was elected to the Supreme Soviet in 1937 and in 1939 became a member of the Academy of Sciences. Over the years he was frequently called upon to make public appearances and to write propaganda pieces for the government; as a result, the time that he devoted to literary pursuits was limited.

Another reason for Sholokhov's relative silence in the past four decades was censorship problems. Despite his avowal that he was "first and foremost a Communist," Sholokhov often quarreled with censors when they attempted to inject political messages into his literary work. In the 1930s he was compelled by censors to make many revisions in the original text of *The Quiet*

Don. In an edition that was published in 1953, the novel was revised extensively to adhere more closely to the Communist party line. It is not clear whether this bowdlerized version was prepared with the approval of Sholokhov, however. In 1956, after Stalin's death, a new edition of *The Quiet Don* came out, similar in nearly every way to the original. As mentioned previously, there are also reports that Sholokhov had difficulties getting *Harvest on the Don* and *They Fought for Their Country* past government censors.

Whatever difficulties Sholokhov may have had with censors in private, publicly he stoutly denied allegations that he had to alter his work. In 1965, when asked about literary freedom in the Soviet Union, he asserted: "No one is being prevented from writing anything he wants to. The only problem is how to write it and for what purpose. There is a way of writing everything honestly. I stand for those writers who look honestly into the face of Soviet power and publish their works here and not abroad." Although there is evidence that Sholokhov often chafed under the bonds of socialist realism, he publicly averred that he was a supporter of that doctrine. In his Nobel Prize acceptance speech, he extolled socialist realism because "it expresses a philosophy of life that accepts neither a turning away from the world nor a flight from reality, a philosophy that enables one to comprehend goals that are dear to the hearts of millions of people and to light up their path in the struggle."

Those writers who have refused to deal with Soviet authorities or who have eschewed the doctrine of socialist realism earned Sholokhov's scorn. He vilified Boris Pasternak as "a poet for old maids" and a "hermit crab." In 1966, after a celebrated trial in which Andrei Sinyavsky and Yuri Daniel were convicted of publishing anti-Soviet propaganda abroad, he delivered an address before the twenty-third congress of the Communist party in which he insinuated that the two writers should have been summarily shot rather than sentenced to prison terms. Later, he described Aleksandr Solzhenitsyn as a "Colorado beetle" who should be exterminated. He also castigated Andrei Voznesensky and Yevgeny Yevtushenko for criticizing Soviet society in their poetry and for taking trips to the United States to recite their works.

Sholokhov's criticism of his fellow writers aroused the anger of many literary figures on both sides of the Iron Curtain. After his attack on Sinyavsky and Daniel, Soviet writer Lydia Chukovskaya wrote a scathing open letter to him in which she accused him of literary sterility. In an even more vociferous attack, Solzhenitsyn denounced Sholokhov as a plagiarist. Specifically, he charged that *The Quiet Don* was actually written by Fyodor Kryukov, a Cossack who had served with the Whites during the Civil War. After Kryukov died in 1920, Solzhenitsyn maintained, Sholokhov got his hands on the manuscript, added some sections sympathetic to the Communist cause, and then passed it off as his own.

Solzhenitsyn's charges are nothing new. Rumors began circulating that Sholokhov plagiarized *The Quiet Don* as early as 1928. In 1977 Roy Medvedev wrote a study of the case, *Problems in the Literary Biography of Mikhail Sholokhov.* Among the arguments that Medvedev cites as evidence that Sholokhov was not the sole author of *The Quiet Don* are his young age when he began writing the novel, the low level of his succeeding work, and the humanism displayed in *The Quiet Don* (which Medvedev thinks Sholokhov has never personally demonstrated). Other commentators have suggested that Sholokhov may have used Kryukov's manuscript as source material, but that he reworked it into his own novel. It is unlikely that the issue will ever be re-

solved. The original manuscript of the book was destroyed during a German bombing raid in World War II, so it can provide no clues for investigators. Sholokhov always dismissed charges of plagiarism as nonsense.

Assaults on Sholokhov's character tended to depict him as a man who once had the courage to fight for his art, but who in old age became little more than a bloody-minded party hack. But to dismiss Sholokhov as a toady is too simplistic. Striving to explain the many contradictions in this bewildering man, Stewart pointed out: "Sholokhov's relationship with Communism was symbiotic—if not altogether healthy for his art. They share the same impulse to glorify 'mankind' just as they share a purely aesthetic disinterestedness about the fate of individuals. This is perhaps why they can be sentimentally humanitarian one moment but adamantly cruel the next. During the time when Sholokhov achieved equilibrium between the two, his artistic impulse balanced his Communist allegiance and he composed his one masterpiece, *The Quiet Don.* . . . The difficulties he overcame no less than the form his art took made Sholokhov the best example of the virtues and limitations of Soviet literature as a whole during its first fifty years—from epic heroism to drudgery."

MEDIA ADAPTATIONS: The Quiet Don, Virgin Soil Upturned, and "The Fate of a Man" have all been produced as motion pictures. Ivan Dzerzhinsky has written operas based on *The Quiet Don* and *Virgin Soil Upturned. Virgin Soil Upturned* has also been dramatized as a four-act play.

AVOCATIONAL INTERESTS: Fishing, hunting, breeding cattle.

BIOGRAPHICAL/CRITICAL SOURCES:

BOOKS

Alexandrova, Vera, *A History of Soviet Literature,* translated by Mina Ginsburg, Doubleday, 1963.

Carlisle, Olga, *Voices in the Snow,* Random, 1962.

Contemporary Literary Criticism, Gale, Volume 7, 1977, Volume 15, 1980.

Ermolaev, Herman, *Mikhail Sholokhov and His Art,* Princeton University Press, 1983.

Hayward, Max and Edward L. Crowley, editors, *Soviet Literature in the Sixties,* Praeger, 1964.

Klimenko, Michael, *World of Young Sholokhov: Vision of Violence,* Christopher Publishing House, 1972.

Mathewson, Rufus W., Jr., *The Positive Hero in Russian Literature,* Columbia University Press, 1958, 2nd edition, Stanford University Press, 1975.

Medvedev, Roy A., *Problems in the Literary Biography of Mikhail Sholokhov,* Cambridge University Press, 1977.

Mihajlov, Mihajlo, *Russian Themes,* Farrar, Straus, 1968.

Muchnic, Helen, *From Gorky to Pasternak,* Random, 1961.

Muchnic, *Russian Writers: Notes and Essays,* Random House, 1971.

Simmons, Ernest J., *Russian Fiction and Soviet Ideology: Introduction to Fedin, Leonov, and Sholokhov,* Columbia University Press, 1958.

Simmons, *Introduction to Russian Realism,* Indiana University Press, 1965.

Slonim, Marc, editor, *Modern Russian Literature: From Chekhov to the Present,* Oxford University Press, 1953.

Stewart, D. H., *Mikhail Sholokhov: A Critical Introduction,* University of Michigan Press, 1967.

PERIODICALS

Atlantic Monthly, March, 1961.

Books, July 1, 1934, August 3, 1941.
Books Abroad, autumn, 1933, winter, 1967, spring, 1971.
Books and Bookmen, November, 1977.
Book Week, May 7, 1967.
Christian Science Monitor, November 20, 1935, February 23, 1961.
Columbia University Forum, winter, 1961.
Commonweal, May 11, 1962, October 20, 1967.
London Magazine, April, 1967.
Nation, July 11, 1934, August 16, 1941.
New Republic, August 15, 1934, December 25, 1935, August 18, 1941, May 8, 1961.
New Statesman, October 29, 1960, May 6, 1977.
New Yorker, August 9, 1941, April 29, 1961.
New York Herald Tribune, July 3, 1934.
New York Review of Books, June 15, 1967.
New York Times, November 10, 1935, August 3, 1941, March 4, 1962, October 16, 1965, December 1, 1965, December 10, 1965, December 11, 1965, April 2, 1966, May 27, 1969, June 25, 1970.
New York Times Book Review, February 19, 1961, March 4, 1962, March 5, 1967, August 20, 1967.
Observer Review, February, 1967.
Russian Review, April, 1957.
Saturday Review, October 26, 1935, February 18, 1961, February 24, 1962, June 17, 1967.
Saturday Review of Literature, July 7, 1934, August 9, 1941.
Slavic Review, September, 1964.
Soviet Literature, August, 1948, September, 1963.
Spectator, April 6, 1934, October 11, 1935, October 18, 1940.
Survey, April-June, 1961.
Thought, spring, 1951.
Time, February 24, 1961, September 16, 1974.
Times Literary Supplement, April 5, 1934, October 5, 1940, November 4, 1960, December 1, 1961, February 16, 1967.
World Literature Today, Winter, 1978.
Yale Review, autumn, 1941.

OBITUARIES:

PERIODICALS

Chicago Tribune, February 23, 1984.
Newsweek, March 5, 1984.
New York Times, February 22, 1984.
Time, March 5, 1984.
Times (London), February 22, 1984.
Washington Post, February 22, 1984.

* * *

SHONE, Patric
See HANLEY, James

* * *

SIDDONS, (Sybil) Anne Rivers 1936-

PERSONAL: Born January 9, 1936, in Atlanta, GA; daughter of Marvin (an attorney) and Katherine (a secretary; maiden name, Kitchens) Rivers; married Heyward L. Siddons (a business partner and creative director), in 1966; children: (stepsons) Lee, Kemble, Rick, David. *Education:* Auburn University, B.A.A., 1958; attended Atlanta School of Art, c. 1958. *Avocational interests:* Sailing, swimming, cooking, reading, cats.

ADDRESSES: Home—3767 Vermont Rd. N.E., Atlanta, GA 30319; (summer) Haven Colony, Brooklin, ME 04616.

CAREER: Worked in advertising with Retail Credit Co., c. 1959, Citizens & Southern National Bank, 1961-63, Burke-Dowling Adams, 1967-69, and Burton Campbell Advertising, 1969-74; full-time writer, 1974—. Woodward Academy, member of governing board; Auburn University, member of publications board and arts and sciences honorary council, 1978-83.

MEMBER: Chevy Chase Club (Chevy Chase, MD), Every Saturday Club and Ansley Golf Club (both Atlanta, GA).

AWARDS, HONORS: Alumna achievement award in arts and humanities, Auburn University, 1985.

WRITINGS:

John Chancellor Makes Me Cry (essays), Doubleday, 1975.
Heartbreak Hotel (novel), Simon & Schuster, 1976.
The House Next Door (horror novel), Simon & Schuster, 1978.
Go Straight on Peachtree, Dolphin Books, 1978.
Fox's Earth (novel), Simon & Schuster, 1980.
Homeplace (novel), Harper, 1987.
Peachtree Road (novel), Harper, 1988.
King's Oak (novel), Harper, 1990.

Contributor to *Gentleman's Quarterly, Georgia, House Beautiful, Lear's, Reader's Digest, Redbook,* and *Southern Living.* Senior editor, *Atlanta* magazine, 1964-67.

MEDIA ADAPTATIONS: Heartbreak Hotel was adapted as the film "Heart of Dixie," Orion Pictures, 1989.

WORK IN PROGRESS: Hot Water, for Harper.

SIDELIGHTS: Siddon's first book, *John Chancellor Makes Me Cry,* chronicles one year of her life in Atlanta, Georgia, humorously reflecting on the frustrations and joys of life—serving jury duty, hosting parties, and taking care of a husband suffering with the flu. The author's style in *John Chancellor Makes Me Cry* has been favorably compared to that of Erma Bombeck, whose own review of the book praised Siddons: "She is unique. She's an original in her essays that combine humor, intimacy and insight into a marriage." Bombeck found the most "poignant and very real" chapter to be the one describing "the month [Siddons's] husband lost his job, her Grandmother died, a Siamese cat they were keeping for a friend was hit by a car, their house was burgled and their Persian cat contracted a $50-a-week disease."

Heartbreak Hotel is a novel about a young Southern woman who must choose between her two suitors and the very different lifestyles they represent. Katha Pollitt asserted: "The author dissects the 1950's, Southern style, with a precision that is anything but nostalgic; and yet somehow the very wealth of detail she provides makes 'Heartbreak Hotel' a good-natured rather than an angry look backward. . . . This is a marvelously detailed record of a South as gone with the wind as Scarlett O'Hara's."

Jane Larkin Crain was disappointed with the lack of drama in Siddons's third novel, *The House Next Door.* This tale of an affluent young couple whose lives are changed by the mysterious evils occurring in a neighboring house, according to Crain, "is suffused with tacit New Class moralism and snobbery and populated with characters of such smugness and self-satisfaction that it is hard to work up much sympathy or distress when they are forced into the author's idea of extremity. . . . With lives as bland and complacent as those in this novel, one would think that all concerned might welcome a little murder and mayhem in the neighborhood, just to liven things up a bit." Siddons, in an interview in *Publishers Weekly,* called the book "something of a lark. It's different from anything I've ever written, or probably ever will. But I like to read occult, supernatural stories. Some of the world's great writers have written them, and I guess I wanted to see what I could do with the genre."

Later novels, such as *Homeplace* and *Peachtree Road*, won greater favor with critics and became best-sellers. Noted Bob Summers in *Publishers Weekly*, *Homeplace* "struck a national chord" with its account of an independent Southern-born woman returning home after more than twenty years. *Peachtree Road* is Siddons's "love letter to Atlanta," according to *Chicago Tribune* contributor Joyce Slater. "Siddons does an admirable job of tracing the city's rebirth after World War II without idealizing it." Concluded the reviewer, it is Siddons's "most ambitious [book] to date."

BIOGRAPHICAL/CRITICAL SOURCES:

BOOKS

Siddons, Anne Rivers, *John Chancellor Makes Me Cry*, Doubleday, 1975.
Bestsellers 89, Issue 2, Gale, 1989.

PERIODICALS

Chicago Tribune, June 14, 1987, November 11, 1988.
Chicago Tribune Book World, June 28, 1981.
Journal and Constitution (Atlanta), October 9, 1988.
Library Journal, June 15, 1975.
New York Times, September 16, 1989.
New York Times Book Review, April 13, 1975, September 12, 1976, October 23, 1977, December 10, 1978.
Publishers Weekly, November 18, 1988.
Tribune Books (Chicago), June 14, 1987.
Washington Post, August 3, 1987.

* * *

SILLANPAA, Frans Eemil 1888-1964

PERSONAL: Born September 16, 1888, in Hameenkyro, Finland; died June 3, 1964, in Helsinki, Finland; son of Frans Henrik (a farmer) and Loviisa Vilhelmiina (a farmer; maiden name Makela) Sillanpaa; married Sigrid Maria Salomaki, September 11, 1916; children: Saara, Esko, Helmi, Paula, Eero, Juhani, Heikki, Kristiina. *Education:* Attended Helsingin Yliopisto/ Helsingfors Universitet, 1908-13.

CAREER: Free-lance writer, 1916-20; full-time writer, 1920-57; editor of literary publication *Panu*, 1921-27.

MEMBER: Finnish P.E.N. (chairman, 1924-26), Society of Finnish Authors.

AWARDS, HONORS: Finnish state pension for authors, 1920; honorary doctorate, State University of Finland, 1936; Aleksis Kivi Prize, 1937; Kordelin Prize from the Kordelin Foundation, 1938; honorary prize from the Frenckell Foundation, 1938; Nobel Prize for literature from the Swedish Academy, 1939.

WRITINGS:

Elama ja aurinko (novel; title means "Life and Sun"), [Helsinki], 1916, reprinted, Otava, 1962.
Ihmislapsia elaman saatossa (short stories; title means "The Procession of Life"), [Helsinki], 1917.
Hurskas kurjuus (novel), [Helsinki], 1919, reprinted, Otava, 1971, translation by Alexander Matson published as *Meek Heritage*, Knopf, 1938, translation revised by John R. Pitkin, Otava, 1971, reprinted, Paul Eriksson, 1973.
Rakas isanmaani (short stories; title means "My Dear Fatherland"), [Helsinki], 1920.

Hiltu ja Ragnar (novel; title means "Hilda and Ragner"), [Helsinki], 1923, reprinted, Otava, 1981.
Enkelten soujatit, [Helsinki], 1923.
Maan tasalta (title means "From the Level of the Earth"), Soderstrom, 1924.
Tollinmaki (short stories), [Helsinki], 1925.
Rippi, [Helsinki], 1928.
Kiitos hetkistaa, Herra . . . , [Helsinki], 1929.
Nuorena nukkunut (novel), [Helsinki], 1931, reprinted, Otava, 1958, translation by Matson published as *The Maid Silja: The History of the Last Offshoot of an Old Family Tree*, Macmillan, 1933, reprinted, Norman S. Berg, 1974 (translation by Matson published in England as *Fallen Asleep While Young: The History of the Last Offshoot of an Old Family Tree*, Putnam, 1933).
Miehen tie (title means "A Man's Road"), [Helsinki], 1932.
Virran pohjalta, [Helsinki], 1933.
Ihmiset suviyossa (vignettes), [Helsinki], 1934, reprinted, Otava, 1976, translation by Alan Blair published as *People in the Summer Night*, introduction by Thomas Warburton, University of Wisconsin Press, 1966.
Viidestoista, [Helsinki], 1936.
Elokuu (novel; title means "Harvest Month"), Otava, 1941, reprinted, 1963.
Ihmiselon ihanuus ja kurjuus (title means "The Joy and Misery of the Human Life"), Otava, 1945, reprinted, 1962.
Eraan elaman satoa (short stories; title means "The Harvest of a Life"), selected by Rafael Koskimies, Otava, 1947.
Poika eli elamaansa (memoir), [Helsinki], 1953.
Paivia korkeimmillaan (memoir), Otava, 1957.
Ajatelmia ja luonnehdintoja, edited by Aarne Laurila, Otava, 1960.
Kuvia ja tarinoita, Otava, 1960.
Novellit (collection), edited by Laurila, Otava, 1961.
Piika ja muita kertomuksia, edited by Hannu Makela, Otava, 1978.

Works represented in numerous anthologies. Contributor of articles and short stories to magazines and newspapers.

OMNIBUS VOLUMES

Kootut teokset (title means "Complete Works"), 12 volumes, [Helsinki], 1932-48.
Valitut teokset (title means "Selected Works"), Otava, 1956.

SIDELIGHTS: Nobel laureate Frans Eemil Sillanpaa is generally regarded as the finest Finnish writer of the twentieth century. Set against the landscape of his native countryside, the author's lyrical prose works focus on unsophisticated human beings struggling to exist in a changing and confounding world. Most critics maintain that Sillanpaa achieves a balance between reality and idealism in his novels and short stories, suffusing his treatment of Finland's military struggles with a sense of mystery and compassion and a belief in the inexplicable natural forces guiding human destiny. In *A History of Finnish Literature*, Jaakko Ahokas theorized that "Sillanpaa received the Nobel Prize [for literature in 1939] because he reflected the spirit of his time."

Born into a family of peasant farmers, the author financed his study of natural science at the University of Helsinki with a loan from friends. But his ensuing association with members of southern Finland's intelligentsia, especially composer Jean Sibelius, together with an exposure to the works of Norwegian writer Knut Hamsun and Belgian symbolist Maurice Maeterlinck, sparked Sillanpaa's interest in the arts. Consequently, he decided to pursue writing as a career and left the university in 1913 without receiving a degree.

Sillanpaa gained notoriety as a free-lance writer before completing his first novel, *Elama ja aurinko* (title means "Life and Sun"), in 1916. The story of a young man's simultaneous affairs with two women of vastly different social stature, *Elama ja aurinko* took the author more than two years to compose. He finally finished the manuscript under great duress, having been incarcerated in a Helsinki hotel room by his publishers until its completion.

With the publication of *Hurskas kurjuus* in 1919, Sillanpaa's reputation as an esteemed writer spread throughout Europe. Translated as *Meek Heritage,* this stark depiction of peasant life appeared in the wake of Finland's bitter civil war, which saw the defeat of the leftist Red Army by the German-backed conservative White Army. The plot revolves around impoverished farmhand Juha Toivola, a simpleminded human being caught up in the Finnish struggle for independence. Beginning with the sixty-year-old Juha's execution by members of the White Army, the novel goes on to chronicle the peasant's entire existence, recalling his birth into poverty and maturation within an unjust social system. Having lived through the famine of the 1860s, the death of his wife, impending bankruptcy, and his daughter's suicide, the naive Juha becomes embroiled in a Red Army plot for Finland's liberation, the ramifications of which are beyond his comprehension. Accused of a murder he could not have committed, Juha suffers as much degradation in death as he did in life.

In *Meek Heritage,* Sillanpaa mourns the legacy of oppression that enshrouded Finland through the end of World War II, writing, "In every phase of every stratum of the Finnish people, everything turns mostly to tragedy, a strange thin tragedy. Fate, instead of exterminating the nation, has subjected it to slow torture." In an article for the *New York Times Book Review,* John Cournos pointed to an unusual lack of sentimentality in Sillanpaa's compelling narrative and suggested that "the inevitable climax of violence [in *Meek Heritage*] resolves a situation which has evolved naturally." The critic further noted that Juha's "senile deprivations [and] brief triumphs . . . are a natural result of social evils of which he has been an innocent victim."

Sillanpaa's 1931 novel *Nuorena nukkunut,* translated as *The Maid Silja,* brought the author international success. Similar in several ways to *Meek Heritage,* the work is an evocation of peasant life in the midst of the Finnish civil war. Following the loss of the family farm and the death of her mother, young Silja and her father become the icons of a dying generation. Lauri Viljanen, writing in *American Scandinavian Review,* described the changing times against which the story is told as a period in Finland's history when "old standards [were] beginning to disintegrate under the impact of new ideas." Silja's father soon dies; shortly thereafter, so, too, does Silja, the young maid who had symbolized humanity in its unspoiled state. Deeming *The Maid Silja* Sillanpaa's "supreme achievement," Agnes Rothery asserted in the *Virginia Quarterly Review* that a "sense of spiritual awareness, of spiritual intensity and suspense, and above all, of immense and eternal spiritual significance, infuses [the author's] novels with an almost intolerable poignancy."

Two of Sillanpaa's subsequent works, *Miehen tie* (title means "A Man's Road") and *Ihmiset suviyossa* (translated as *People in the Summer Night*), earned the author comparisons to renowned British writer D. H. Lawrence. In *Miehen tie,* published in 1932, young farmer Paavo Ahrola abandons his childhood love to marry a wealthy older woman who is in ill health. The marriage is an unhappy one, and, following his wife's death, Paavo de-

spairs until he is reunited with his former lover. While several critics complained that the author spent an inordinate amount of time describing the farmer's mistakes, Ahokas considered the story to be "on the level of [Sillanpaa's] best compositions." The critic also noted the author's use of natural symbolism, especially evident in "the connection between the rhythm of nature expressed in the seasons and the changes in the lives of his characters."

Although not his most popular work, *People in the Summer Night,* originally published in 1934, is generally regarded as Sillanpaa's most exquisitely constructed composition. More a series of poetic sketches than a true novel, the work documents the events of a summer night—cyclical events of birth and death, hope and frustration—and the effects of those events on a variety of characters, creating a microcosm of reality. John H. Wuorinen, writing in *Saturday Review,* suggested that the story "has an elusive quality not easy to capture." Viljanen called *People in the Summer Night* a "little masterpiece" in which action is fueled by a power "flowing from unknown cosmic depths."

A reflection of both his peasant background and the political and social history of his native country, Sillanpaa's poetic fiction earned him international acclaim in his lifetime. Deeming the author "the first great modernist in Finnish literature," Viljanen further ventured that "in all European fiction it is difficult to find anything to equal his peculiar psychological method of seeing."

MEDIA ADAPTATIONS: A Man's Road was adapted for a film titled "One Man's Way," [Helsinki], 1940.

BIOGRAPHICAL/CRITICAL SOURCES:

BOOKS

Ahokas, Jaakko, *A History of Finnish Literature,* Indiana University Publications, 1973.
Contemporary Literary Criticism, Volume 19, Gale, 1981.
Koskimies, K. R., *Frans Eemil Sillanpaa,* [Helsinki], 1948.
Laurila, Aarne, *Frans Eemil Sillanpaa vousina 1888-1958,* [Helsinki], 1958.

PERIODICALS

American Scandinavian Review, March, 1940.
Nation, September 24, 1938.
New York Times Book Review, November 19, 1933, September 18, 1938.
Poet Lore, winter, 1940.
Saturday Review, November 11, 1933, June 11, 1966.
Times Literary Supplement, May 28, 1938.
Virginia Quarterly Review, spring, 1940.

*   *   *

SILLITOE, Alan 1928-

PERSONAL: Born March 4, 1928, in Nottingham, England; son of Christopher Archibald (a tannery laborer) and Sylvina (Burton) Sillitoe; married Ruth Esther Fainlight (a poet, writer, and translator), November 19, 1959; children: David Nimrod, Susan (adopted). *Education:* Left school at the age of fourteen.

ADDRESSES: Home—c/o Savage Club, 9 Fitzmaurice Pl., London S.W. 1, England. *Agent*—Tessa Sayle, 11 Jubilee Pl., London SW3 3TE, England.

CAREER: Worked in a bicycle plant, in a plywood mill, and as a capstan-lathe operator; air traffic control assistant, 1945-46;

free-lance writer, beginning in 1948. *Military service:* Royal Air Force, radio operator in Malaya, 1946-49.

MEMBER: Society of Authors, Royal Geographical Society (fellow), Writers Action Group, Savage Club.

AWARDS, HONORS: Author's Club prize, 1958, for *Saturday Night and Sunday Morning;* Hawthornden Prize for Literature, 1960, for *The Loneliness of the Long-Distance Runner;* honorary fellow, Manchester Polytechnic, 1977.

WRITINGS:

POEMS

Without Beer or Bread, Outpost Publications (London), 1957.
The Rats and Other Poems, W. H. Allen, 1960.
A Falling Out of Love and Other Poems, W. H. Allen, 1964.
Shaman and Other Poems, Turret Books, 1968.
Love in the Environs of Voronezh and Other Poems, Macmillan (London), 1968, Doubleday, 1969.
(Contributor) *Poems* [by] *Ruth Fainlight, Ted Hughes, Alan Sillitoe,* Rainbow Press, 1971.
Storm and Other Poems, W. H. Allen, 1974.
Barbarians and Other Poems, Turret Books, 1974.
Snow on the North Side of Lucifer, W. H. Allen, 1979.
Sun before Departure, Grafton & Co., 1984.
Tides and Stone Walls, Grafton & Co., 1986.

NOVELS

Saturday Night and Sunday Morning (also see below), W. H. Allen, 1958, Knopf, 1959, revised edition, with an introduction by the author and commentary and notes by David Craig, Longmans, Green, 1968.
The General (also see below), W. H. Allen, 1960, Knopf, 1961.
Key to the Door, W. H. Allen, 1961, Knopf, 1962.
The Death of William Posters (first volume of trilogy), Knopf, 1965.
A Tree on Fire (second volume of trilogy), Macmillan (London), 1967, Doubleday, 1968.
A Start in Life, W. H. Allen, 1970, Scribner, 1971.
Travel in Nihilon, W. H. Allen, 1971, Scribner, 1972.
The Flame of Life (third volume of trilogy), W. H. Allen, 1974.
The Widower's Son, W. H. Allen, 1976, Harper, 1977.
The Storyteller, W. H. Allen, 1979, Simon & Schuster, 1980.
Her Victory, F. Watts, 1982.
The Lost Flying Boat, Little, Brown, 1983.
Down from the Hill, Granada, 1984.
Life Goes On (sequel to *A Start in Life*), Grafton & Co., 1985.
Out of the Whirlpool, Hutchinson, 1987, Harper, 1988.
The Open Door, Grafton & Co., 1989.
Last Loves, Grafton & Co., 1990.

SHORT STORIES

The Loneliness of the Long-Distance Runner (also see below), W. H. Allen, 1959, Knopf, 1960, bound with *Sanctuary,* by Theodore Dreiser, and related poems, edited by Roy Bentley, Book Society of Canada, 1967.
The Ragman's Daughter and Other Stories, W. H. Allen, 1961, Knopf, 1964.
Guzman Go Home and Other Stories, Macmillan (London), 1968, Doubleday, 1969.
A Sillitoe Selection, Longmans, Green, 1968.
Men, Women and Children, W. H. Allen, 1973, Scribner, 1974.
The Second Chance and Other Stories, Simon & Schuster, 1981.

PLAYS

"Saturday Night and Sunday Morning" (screenplay; based on novel of same title), Continental, 1960.
"The Loneliness of the Long-Distance Runner" (screenplay; based on short story of same title), Continental, 1961.
"Counterpoint" (screenplay; based on novel *The General*), Universal, 1968.
(Translator and adapter with Ruth Fainlight) Lope de Vega, *All Citizens Are Soldiers* (two acts; first produced at Theatre Royal, Stratford, London, 1967), Macmillan (London), 1969, Dufour, 1970.
Three Plays: The Slot Machine, The Interview, Pit Strike ("The Slot Machine," first produced as "This Foreign Field" in London at Round House, 1970; "Pit Strike," produced by British Broadcasting Corporation, 1977; "The Interview," produced at the Almost Free Theatre, 1978), W. H. Allen, 1978.

OTHER

Road to Volgograd (travel), Knopf, 1964.
(Author of introduction) Arnold Bennett, *Riceyman Steps,* Pan Books, 1964.
(Author of introduction) Bennett, *The Old Wives' Tale,* Pan Books, 1964.
The City Adventures of Marmalade Jim (juvenile), Macmillan, 1967.
Raw Material (memoir), W. H. Allen, 1972, Scribner, 1973.
Mountains and Caverns: Selected Essays, W. H. Allen, 1975.
Big John and the Stars (juvenile), Robson Books, 1977.
The Incredible Fencing Fleas (juvenile), Robson Books, 1978.
Marmalade Jim on the Farm (juvenile), Robson Books, 1979.
The Saxon Shore Way (travel), Hutchinson, 1983.
Marmalade Jim and the Fox (juvenile), Robson Books, 1985.
Nottinghamshire (travel; photography by David Sillitoe), Grafton, 1987.

Also author of film script "Che Guevara," 1968, and *Every Day of the Week,* 1987.

WORK IN PROGRESS: A novel; a collection of poems.

SIDELIGHTS: "I was twenty years old when I first tried to write, and it took ten years before I learned how to do it," remarked Alan Sillitoe in reference to *Saturday Night and Sunday Morning,* the novel that catapulted the thirty-year-old self-educated Briton into the literary limelight. Described by the *New Yorker's* Anthony West as a "brilliant first book," *Saturday Night and Sunday Morning* broke new ground with its portrayal of "the true robust and earthy quality characteristic of English working-class life." Only one year later, Sillitoe was again the center of critical attention, this time for "The Loneliness of the Long-Distance Runner," the title novella in a collection of short stories which also contained some frank representations of working-class life in Britain. Although he has since written numerous novels and short stories, as well as several poems and plays, Sillitoe has almost always been evaluated in terms of these first two works. Both, in fact, are the focus of a debate that has yet to be resolved: is Alan Sillitoe a traditionalist, a sentimental throwback to writers of an earlier age, or is he a genuine "revolutionary," an Angry Young Man of the modern age?

On a thematic level, Sillitoe seems to draw inspiration from both the old and the new. As is true of many contemporary writers, he often centers his stories around an individual isolated from society, studying what the *Guardian's* Roy Perrot calls "the spirit of the outsider, the dissenter, the man apart." But instead of limiting himself strictly to the psychological confines of this one person and allowing the rest of the world to remain somewhat shadowy, Sillitoe places his rebellious outsider in a gritty, distinctive milieu—Nottingham, an English industrial town (and the author's birthplace) where, as Charles Champlin explains in the *Los Angeles Times*, "the lower-middle and working classes rub, where breaking even looks like victory, and London is a long way South." This strong regionalism, reminiscent of the regionalism common in nineteenth-century British fiction, is one of the most striking features of Sillitoe's writing.

Sillitoe populates his rather grim world with factory workers, shop girls, and other types not often depicted from the inside in English literature. Whether they are at home, at work, or relaxing in the pubs, these characters reveal themselves to be "unfamiliar with the great world of London or country houses or what is called high culture," says the *Chicago Tribune Book World*'s Kendall Mitchell. "And they don't care—they have their lives to live, their marriages to make and wreck, their passions to pursue." "The cumulative impression of Sillitoe's people," notes Champlin, "is of their strength and will to survive, however forces beyond their control blunt their prospects."

These "forces beyond their control" play a major role in the author's fiction; Sillitoe's conception of fate, however, differs from the classical one in that economic and social factors, not the whim of the gods, determine one's destiny. As James Gindin writes in *Postwar British Fiction: New Accents and Attitudes:* "Nothing really changes Sillitoe's jungle world. A man may win or lose, depending on the wheel of chance, but he cannot control the wheel or change his position. Often, too, the wheel is rigged, for the same numbers keep coming up as privilege and power keep reinforcing themselves." In short, comments Saul Maloff in *Contemporary British Novelists*, "for Sillitoe, class is fate."

John W. Aldridge expands on this idea in the book *Time to Murder and Create: The Contemporary Novel in Crisis*, but suggests that Sillitoe's belief in the power of fate hinders rather than helps the reader to understand his characters and their motivations. States the critic: "To the extent that his people are the victims of their economic situation, they are people without the power of moral freedom. And to the extent that they are unfree, and lack even the opportunity to be enticed to choose freedom and to be damned by it, they are grossly oversimplified as fictional characters, pawns in a chess game in which every move is necessary and therefore none is possible." Aldridge continues, "Hence, nothing they think is interesting, nothing they do is finally worth doing, and nothing they want will in the end be of any value whatever to them. There can be no doubt that one may be impressed by this and frequently moved to compassion. But one is emphatically not moved to understanding."

Yet as even Aldridge admits, Sillitoe is a master at presenting his material in such a way that compassion, and not disgust, is what most readers feel for his rough-edged characters. Several critics, including the *Washington Post*'s Daniel O'Neill, credit the author with an "ability to blend cold-blooded rendering of the exterior world with insightful and sensitive representation of the inner workings of the characters' minds." According to Max Cosman of *Commonweal*, "such is Mr. Sillitoe's interest in his fellow man and such his skill in compelling attention, that ignoble, or subnormal as his Nottinghamites are, they can [bring] forth compassion even in the midst of disapproval."

Others, however, feel that this emphasis on compassion makes Sillitoe less an Angry Young Man with a special talent for describing the plight of the proletariat than a sentimentalist who idealizes the lives of his working-class heroes. Though the *New Republic*'s Irving Howe is pleased by the lack of romanticization,

"moral nagging [and] political exhortation" in *Saturday Night and Sunday Morning*, for instance, he nevertheless concludes that "in its hard-headed and undeluded way it is not quite free from sentimentality." *New York Review of Books* contributor Stanley Kauffmann is especially critical of what he feels is Sillitoe's mishandling of pathos, pointing out that "often he appeals for sympathy with music-hall blatancy." David Boroff of the *Saturday Review* agrees that Sillitoe is "sometimes betrayed by his own sentimentality," as does a *Times Literary Supplement* critic, who suggests that such lapses may stem not from the author's attitude toward his subject but from "the difficulties presented by the use of a fictitious narrator who is not supposed to be as articulate or as sophisticated as the writer himself."

Sillitoe's practice of speaking through a narrator who is less articulate and sophisticated than himself has resulted in a style many critics have trouble classifying. As Champlin notes, "at times the essayist, social historian and social reporter in Sillitoe seems simply to have chosen fiction as the best carrier of impressions he wants to leave and points he wants to make." Consequently, remarks Kauffmann, his writing "fluctuates from straight hard prose to Nottingham slang to the most literary effusions, often all on the same page." In most other respects, comment a number of reviewers, including the *Times Literary Supplement*'s John Lucas, Sillitoe's style is "peculiarly artless" in that "even the best of [the stories] work in a manner that is unusual or unorthodox." There is, for example, no particularly strong emphasis on plot in a Sillitoe story, no "half hidden thread that can be traced," no sudden flash or insight that makes everything clear; as Lucas states, "nothing happens: there is no revelation, the story hardly seems to be a story at all." West also notices that Sillitoe's stories are "so firmly rooted in experience, and so ably handled, that they do not seem to have been written at all; they seem to be occurrences of a most engrossing and absorbing kind." Gene Baro agrees with this assessment of the author, writing in the *New York Herald Tribune Book Review* that "Sillitoe exhibits . . . lucid design, pace, a gift for salty vernacular, an unerring eye for the telling gesture, a robust and yet a restrained sense of the comic. . . . All is achieved simply, matter-of-factly, without apparent striving for effect."

A *Times Literary Supplement* critic is especially impressed by Sillitoe's "integrity of style that never falsifies the writer's role—which is why, for instance, he refuses to go on 'like a penny-a-liner to force an ending' if inspiration stops before he knows what to do with the character he has created. There may not even *be* an ending to a Sillitoe story." John Updike notices this same feature in Sillitoe's writing, pointing out in a *New Republic* article that his stories "have a wonderful way of going on, of not stopping short . . . that lifts us twice, and shows enviable assurance and abundance in the writer."

P. H. Johnson of the *New Statesman* also regards Sillitoe as "highly gifted technically: he is an excellent story-teller, and his style is perfectly adapted to his subject-matter; he has literary tact and a sense of design." *The Saturday Review*'s James Yaffe reports that among Sillitoe's "many wonderful qualities" are "a fluent, often brilliant command of language, an acute ear for dialect, [and] a virtuoso ability to describe the sight, sound, and smell of things."

What reviewers cannot agree upon in their evaluations of Sillitoe's work is whether he writes in the tradition of an earlier age (notably the American proletarian novelists of the 1930s) or in the tradition of certain British authors of the 1950s and 1960s whose bitter attacks on the political and social establishment earned them the name "Angry Young Men." Kauffmann, for one, feels Sillitoe is a victim of the cultural "time-lag" that exists between the United States and England and is therefore merely rediscovering the themes that once preoccupied American writers such as John Steinbeck, Erskine Caldwell, Theodore Dreiser, and John Dos Passos. Maloff shares this view, commenting: "Sillitoe is a throwback, an old-fashioned realist—in fact, a regionalist. He has attempted to make viable as art what was called, without embarrassment or sneering, the 'proletarian novel' in the 1930's. His protagonists are profoundly rooted in their class, and draw such strengths as they possess—or come finally to possess—from that identification." This, he adds, makes Sillitoe very different from other post-war writers. "[He] is a historical surprise. In the utterly changed circumstances of the fifties and sixties, he has partially validated as art the 'proletarian novel' of the thirties; and standing eccentrically against the current driven by his defter contemporaries, he has made possible a working-class novel."

Aldridge suggests that part of Sillitoe's inspiration may date back even earlier than the 1930s. States the critic: "Sillitoe stands as a comforting reminder to the English that the grand old roistering 'low life' tradition of Fielding and Dickens may have lost its sting, but is not yet dead. . . . Although [the author] does have his grievances, he seems basically content to keep the working man in his place, and as a writer he evidently wants to remain a working man." Aldridge indicates, however, that other writers "did all that he has done first and better than he. It might be objected that working-class life is, after all, Sillitoe's material, and that he ought to have a perfect right to use it if he so chooses. But there is little virtue in repeating the discoveries or the mistakes of one's predecessors, or in trying to make literature out of a cultural lag that merely social reform and the payment of some money can rectify."

Allen R. Penner of *Contemporary Literature* also sees traces of an old-fashioned literary tradition in Sillitoe's works—but with a modern twist. Explains Penner: " 'The Loneliness of the Long-Distance Runner' . . . is written in a tradition in English fiction which dates at least from Elizabethan times, in . . . the rogue's tale, or thief's autobiography." In his opinion Sillitoe "has reversed the formula of the popular crime tale of fiction, wherein the reader enjoys vicariously witnessing the exploits of the outlaw and then has the morally reassuring pleasure of seeing the doors of the prison close upon him in the conclusion. Sillitoe begins his tale in prison, and he ends it before the doors have opened again, leaving us with the unsettling realization that the doors will indeed open and that the criminal will be released unreformed." This emphasis on unrepentant rebellion, says Penner, proves that "Sillitoe was never, really, simply an 'angry young man.' His hostility was not a transitory emotion of youth, but a permanent rancor well grounded in class hatred. 'The Loneliness of the Long-Distance Runner' contains the seeds of the revolutionary philosophy which would eventually attain full growth in his works."

On the other hand, some critics see nothing but youthful anger in Sillitoe's writings. Commenting in the *New York Times Book Review,* Malcolm Bradbury notes that "if the heroes of some . . . English novels are angry young men, Mr. Sillitoe is raging; and though he doesn't know it, he is raging for much the same reasons." Champlin remarks that Sillitoe's emergence was "a sharp signaling of an end to quiet acceptance of the way things are. It was a protest, fueled by the war, against the stratified status quo. . . . Unlike some of Britain's angry young men who have matured and prospered into more conservative postures, Sillitoe remains the poet of the anonymous millions in the council flats and the cold-water attached houses, noting the ignored, remembering the half-forgotten."

Though John R. Clark of the *Saturday Review* also sees Sillitoe as an Angry Young Man, he feels that "his anger and fictions have altered with time. In [his] early work there was something single-minded and intense in the actions and scenes, particularly in the shorter novels." On the other hand, "Later novels reveal a broader social and political horizon. Sillitoe's characters not only privately rebel but become dedicated to larger 'movements.' "

Prairie Schooner's Robert S. Haller rejects the notion that Sillitoe is an Angry Young Man. "If this title is justified for any writers," he begins, "it would be so for [those] men with university training who wanted room at the top but who resented the moral and aesthetic cost of getting there. But it hardly applies to Sillitoe [and others] who are authentically of the working class, self-educated, and uninterested in the matter of rising to the upper classes. . . . Anger is the resentment of frustrated ambition; neither Sillitoe nor his early heroes see in established values and styles anything to aspire to."

Nor is Sillitoe's style based on that of any grand literary tradition, Haller goes on to state. In fact, declares the critic, the author's "commitment to his [Nottinghamite] people has been an expression of a refusal to mimic the educated literary man." Consequently, books like *Saturday Night and Sunday Morning* and *The Loneliness of the Long-Distance Runner* "have been continuous best sellers because they provide a mirror for working-class readers and a window for others into a culture with its own richness of circumstance and its own integrity."

Sillitoe himself sees little merit in arguing about whether he is traditional or modern, sentimental or angry. As he told Igor Hajek in a *Nation* interview: "I cannot understand why people are always looking for trends and movements. Writers work just as all others: miners, engineers, psychologists. From their point [of view] trends do not exist. Why should they exist in writing? Although I admit that looking from a distance some similarities may appear, the writer himself usually does not realize it."

In this same interview, Sillitoe reveals that he is not at all dismayed by the fact that he is best known for his earliest works, especially "The Loneliness of the Long-Distance Runner." "I think those people [who remember me primarily as the author of 'The Loneliness of the Long-Distance Runner'] are absolutely right," he says. "This story of a working-class youth is at the same time the statement of my artistic integrity. I shall never write anything to uphold this Establishment and this society. And I'm ready to stick to my principles even to a self-damaging extent."

Continues the author: "Whatever I have against [English society] I say through my characters: every character in my books has an opinion, and they are all mine. On the other hand, it is very difficult to write about something you hate, you have to try to understand and even show some sympathies. That is why people, who consider writers from a political rather than artistic viewpoint, accuse them of being treacherous: they take this for sympathizing with enemy. . . . If they ask me what I am, a Communist or Socialist, etc., I can only answer that I'm on the Left, beyond that I can't say much." In his opinion, "A writer never stands still. When you are young, everything is simple, but I am not young any more, [which] means that I am leaving a lot of simplicities behind. Basic beliefs stay, but things now look more complex."

In short, concludes Sillitoe, "Each individual has to make a choice: either to accept this society or stand up against It. In this country, as in any other, a writer is liked if he is loyal to the system. But it is the writer's duty in a sense to be disloyal. In the modern world, he is one of the few people who are listened to, and his primary loyalty should be to his integrity and to his talent. He can speak up in many ways; the best way is to write a book."

BIOGRAPHICAL/CRITICAL SOURCES:

BOOKS

Aldridge, John W., *Time to Murder and Create: The Contemporary Novel in Crisis,* McKay, 1966.
Authors in the News, Volume I, Gale, 1976.
Contemporary Authors Autobiography Series, Volume II, Gale, 1985.
Contemporary Literary Criticism, Gale, Volume I, 1973, Volume III, 1975, Volume VI, 1976, Volume X, 1979, Volume XIX, 1981.
Dictionary of Literary Biography, Volume XIV: *British Novelists since 1960,* Gale, 1983.
Gindin, James, *Postwar British Fiction: New Accents and Attitudes,* University of California Press, 1962.
Shapiro, Charles, editor, *Contemporary British Novelists,* Southern Illinois University Press, 1965.

PERIODICALS

Chicago Tribune Book World, October 26, 1980, August 31, 1981.
Commonweal, September 4, 1959, April 29, 1960, March 27, 1964.
Contemporary Literature, Volume X, number 2, 1969.
Globe and Mail (Toronto), September 7, 1985.
Guardian, September 25, 1959.
Los Angeles Times, October 1, 1980, April 21, 1981.
Los Angeles Times Book Review, November 21, 1982, March 20, 1988.
Milwaukee Journal, November 10, 1974.
Nation, January 27, 1969.
New Republic, August 24, 1959, May 9, 1960.
New Statesman, October 3, 1959.
New Yorker, September 5, 1959, June 11, 1960.
New York Herald Tribune Book Review, August 16, 1959, May 29, 1960.
New York Review of Books, March 5, 1964.
New York Times Book Review, August 16, 1959, April 10, 1960, September 28, 1980, April 19, 1981, December 12, 1982.
Prairie Schooner, winter, 1974/75.
San Francisco Chronicle, November 29, 1959, May 1, 1960.
Saturday Review, September 5, 1959, April 16, 1960, January 25, 1964, October 16, 1971.
Sewanee Review, summer, 1975.
Spectator, September 25, 1959.
Time, April 18, 1960.
Times (London), November 10, 1983, November 15, 1984, October 10, 1985, February 23, 1989.
Times Literary Supplement, October 2, 1959, October 19, 1973, January 15, 1981, January 23, 1981, October 15, 1982, November 11, 1983, June 7, 1985, April 7, 1989, May 18, 1990.
Washington Post, June 2, 1981, December 10, 1982.
Washington Post Book World, October 26, 1980.
Yale Review, September, 1959.

SILONE, Ignazio   1900-1978
(Pasquini)

PERSONAL: Name originally Secundo Tranquilli; surname pronounced See-*low*-nay; born May 1, 1900, in Pescina, Italy; died August 23, 1978, in Geneva, Switzerland; son of Paolo (a small landowner) and Annamaria (a weaver; maiden name, Delli Quadri) Tranquilli; orphaned at age 14; married Darina Laracy (an Irish writer), 1944. *Education:* Attended Jesuit and other Catholic schools in the Abruzzi and in Rome. *Politics:* Independent Socialist.

CAREER: Secretary of the Federation of Land Workers of the Abruzzi, 1917; member of the Italian Socialist Youth Movement, 1917-21; editor of *Avanguardia,* a leftist weekly paper published in Rome, and *Il Lavoratore,* a Trieste daily leftist paper, 1921-22; became a communist and helped establish the Italian Communist Party which in 1921 sent him to Russia and in 1923 to Spain; twice imprisoned in Spain for political reasons, first in Madrid and then in Barcelona; in 1925, returned to Rome and engaged in work against the Fascist Regime as a militant communist; contributed to various newspapers and magazines in Italy and abroad, many of them printed clandestinely, 1921-29; broke away from the Communist Party, 1930, then was smuggled across the border to Switzerland in 1941; Political Secretary in Zurich of the Foreign Center of the Italian Socialists, and involved with the Resistance movements in Germany, Austria, France, and the Balkans; broadcasted an appeal for civil resistance in Italy in 1942 and was consequently briefly imprisoned by the Swiss; after the Liberation he returned to Rome and joined the Socialist Party in 1945, becoming editor of *Avanti!,* the Socialist daily newspaper; founder of Teatro del Popolo, 1945, and president; member of the Italian Constituent Assembly, 1946-48, and active participant in the political life of the country; secretary of the Unitary Socialist Party in 1950; retired from politics to devote himself to literature, 1950.

MEMBER: National Institute of Arts and Letters (corresponding member), PEN, Italian Pen Club (president, 1945-59), Association for the Freedom of Italian Culture (chairman).

AWARDS, HONORS: Marzotto Prize, 1965; honorary doctorates from Yale University, 1965, and University of Toulouse, 1969; Campiello award, 1968; Jerusalem Prize, 1969.

WRITINGS:

FICTION

Fontamara, first published in German, translation by Nettie Sutro, Oprecht & Helbling, 1930, first Italian edition, Nuove Edizione Italiani (Zurich and Paris), 1933, English translation by Eric Mosbacher and Gwenda David, Methuen, 1934, translation by Michael Wharf, Smith & Haas, 1934, revised Italian edition, Mondadori (Milan), 1958, revision translated by Harvey Fergusson II, with a preface by Malcolm Cowley, Atheneum, 1960.
Mr. Aristotle (short stories), translation by Samuel Putnam, R. M. McBride (New York), 1935.
Pane e vino, first published in translation by Mosbacher and David as *Bread and Wine,* Methuen, 1936, Harper, 1937, first Italian edition, Nuove Edizione di Capolago (Lugano), 1937, revised Italian edition published as *Vino e pane,* Mondadori, 1955, revision translated by Fergusson, with a new preface by the author, Atheneum, 1962.
Il seme sotto la neve, first published in German translation as *Der Sam en unterm Schnee,* [Zurich], 1941, first Italian edition, Faro (Rome), 1945, translation by Frances Frenaye pub-

lished as *The Seed Beneath the Snow,* Harper, 1942, translation by Fergusson, Atheneum, 1965.

Una manciata di more, Mondadori, 1952, translation by wife, Darina Silone, published as *A Handful of Blackberries,* Harper, 1953.

Il segreto di Luca, Mondadori, 1956, translation by D. Silone published as *The Secret of Luca,* Harper, 1958.

La volpe e le camelie, Mondadori, 1960, translation by Mosbacher published as *The Fox and the Camelias,* Harper, 1961.

OTHER

Der Fascismus: Seine Entstehung und seine Entwicklung, Europa-Verlag (Zurich), 1934.

Un viaggio a Parigi, [Zurich], 1934.

La scuola dei dittatori, [Zurich], 1938, translation by Mosbacher and David published as *The School for Dictators,* Harper, 1938, translation by William Weaver, published with a preface by Silone, Atheneum, 1963.

(Editor) *Mazzini,* 1939, translation published as *The Living Thoughts of Mazzini,* Longmans, Green, 1939.

Ed egli si nascose (4-act play), first published in German translation, Buechergilde Gutenberg (Zurich), 1944, first Italian edition, [Rome], 1945, English translation by D. Silone published as *And He Hid Himself,* Harper, 1946, (published in England as *And He Did Hide Himself,* J. Cape, 1946), revised Italian version, Edizioni Mondiali, 1966.

Uscita di sicurezza (essay), first published in *The God That Failed: Six Studies in Communism,* edited by Richard Crossman, Harper, 1949, Italian edition, [Florence], 1951, Associazione Italiana per la Liberta della Cultura (Rome), 1955, new edition, Vallecchi (Florence), 1965, translation published as *Emergency Exit: Autobiographical Fragments that Combine The Chronicle of a Life with a Spiritual Self-portrait,* Harper, 1968.

(With Ivan Anissimov) *Un dialogo difficile: Sono liberi gli scrittori russi?* (dialogue), [Rome], 1950, published as *An Impossible Dialogue Between Ivan Anissimov and Ignazio Silone,* Institute of Political and Social Studies, 1957.

La scelta dei compagni, Associazione Italiana per la Liberta della Cultura, 1954.

(Editor) *A trent'anni dal Concordata,* Parenti (Florence), 1959.

Mi paso por el comunismo, Asociacion Argentina por la Libertad de la Cultura (Buenos Aires), 1959.

(With others) *Per una legge sull'obiezione di coscienza,* Associazione Italiana per la Liberta della Cultura, 1962.

L'Avventura d'un povero cristiano (play), Mondadori, 1968, translation by Weaver published as *The Story of a Humble Christian,* Harper, 1971.

Paese dell'anima, edited by Maria Letizia Cassata, U. Mursia (Milan), 1968.

Severina, edited by D. Silone, Mondadori, 1982.

Contributor to anthologies, including *Modern Italian Short Stories,* 1954, and *Italian Short Stories,* 1965. Contributor to numerous Italian journals, magazines, and newspapers, sometimes under pseudonym Pasquini. Editor, with Nicola Chiaromonte, *Tempo Presente* (magazine), until 1970.

SIDELIGHTS: Ignazio Silone wrote his first novel *Fontamara* in 1930 when he was a political exile in Davos, Switzerland. "Since I was alone there," he wrote in the preface to the revised edition which appeared several years later, "—a stranger with an alias to evade the efforts of the Fascist police to find me— writing became my only means of defense against despair." At that time Silone believed he had not long to live and he wrote hurriedly, "with unspeakable affliction and anxiety, to set up as

best I could that village into which I put the quintessence of myself and my native heath so that I could at least die among my own people." The village which he created, *Fontamara* (the name means "bitter fountain"), is not unlike Pescina, the village of his own youth, with the same endless cycle of life, work, poverty, and death. "A village, in short, like many others," Silone has said, "but for those who are born and die there, the world." The story concerns the life of the peasants and their hopeless struggles against the tyrannies of the landowners and petty officials. But, underlying this theme is an affirmation of the dignity of man even among the indignities of life and, above all, a profound compassion for suffering humanity. Sergio Pacifici, author of *A Guide to Contemporary Italian Literature,* has called *Fontamara* "a kind of classic, a book that illuminates its own time and man's condition." Silone's vision in *Fontamara* was of a world where ultimately the peasants would unite with their fellow sufferers and would triumph over officialdom and fascism. In his review of the book, Anthony West wrote: "It is one of those rare novels that really deserves to be called important." Another reviewer commented: "It is written with passion and also with wonderful realism of language and economy of means. Its vitality transcends the circumstances of its creation."

A storm of controversy attended the publication of *Fontamara.* "Nobody not rabidly anti-fascist can be conceived either as believing it or as liking it," said Mark Van Doren. Nevertheless, *Fontamara* was translated into seventeen languages and became a best seller in fourteen European countries. Few today would deny the propagandist character of the book, even in the revised edition which omitted many of the unrelieved political passages, but would now agree with H. E. Bates who wrote: "It is lifted right out of the ordinary propagandist class by Silone's art. His simple, bitterly humorous, savagely satirical style is without a flaw." Silone himself made no secret of the fact that his fiction has a message, social, political, and human. Brotherhood and freedom were the ideals he strove for and the themes he wove into his writing and, as Pacifici has observed, his stories dramatize the need for action.

During his years as a communist, Silone entirely identified with the Party which became his "family, school, church, and barracks." The day he broke away was, he admits, "a very sad day for me, a day of deep mourning, of mourning for my youth." He has described his involvement and eventual disillusionment with communism in a lengthy essay which was published along with testimonies from other former communists under the title *The God That Failed.* Iris Origo feels that Silone was possibly never meant, by temperament, to be a Party man. "Nevertheless," she continues, "it is not possible to separate his positions as a political rebel and as a writer: both spring from the same patient, persistent preoccupation with the condition and destiny of man."

Later novels by Silone repeat in essence the themes implicit in *Fontamara,* although some were less successful. Reviewing *The Fox and the Camelias,* Marc Slonim observed in the *New York Times Book Review* that Silone "appears again as a moralist deeply concerned with ethical problems and the political reality of our times," but, comparing this with the earlier novel, Slonim considered this effort "more limited in scope and less comprehensive in its vision of life." *Bread and Wine,* however, which first appeared in English, and *School for Dictators,* a political discussion rather after the style of Plato's *Republic,* both met with praise from reviewers.

Of one of Silone's last works, a six-act play entitled *The Story of a Humble Christian,* Emile Capouya wrote in *Saturday Review:* "In his earlier books the polity that might incarnate our values had come more and more to appear incompatible with government. In this play, his conclusion is more explicitly anarchist: men cannot find God or the good while their institutions separate them from their fellows. It is our privilege that so sound a moralist is also a great artist."

Silone is best known as the author of *Bread and Wine*, a document against Italian Fascism. "To readers of any political faith *Bread and Wine* must needs be a compelling novel," wrote Fanny Butcher. "The peasants live in these pages as naturally as a trillium grows on the banks of the Des Plaines river. They are neither sentimentalized nor looked at through a microscope." H. S. Canby believed that, "in spite of the tragedy depicted, it is also a humorous book, and often tender and very touching." A *Forum* reviewer called the novel "a grand, resounding parable. . . . Here is the voice of Italy's Sinclair Lewis, repeating more subtlely, more poetically—'It *has* happened here.'" Silone wrote "this compassionate, sunny, wonderfully sensitive book," said Alfred Kazin, "in a spirit that is as rare in modern letters as it is in modern consciousness. It is not easy to name that spirit, with its supple, tragic sense of good feeling that pervades everything he writes. Part of it is the serenity and the gaiety of the folk writer, the joyous tenderness of a man who is fond of his own people, his hosts in time of danger. It is the tenderness of a man who has an immense faith in the masses, who is democratic by instinct." With this novel Philip Rahv believes that Silone became recognized "as one of the most truly contemporary and significant writers of our time."

To a great extent the extraordinary power of Silone's writing lies in the incredible simplicity of his style. The language is often rich in imagery and vividly colloquial, but it is always immediate and direct. At times, it reveals a sad and melancholy poetry. Silone avoids complex grammatical structure and self-conscious symbolism, allowing the natural, vigorous dialect of the peasants to lend strength and vibrancy to the narration. The stark and somber background against which their lives are led is depicted with bitter irony, occasionally illuminated by flashes of humor or heightened by descriptive passages of rare and haunting beauty.

The mistrust with which Silone was once regarded in Italy has now been replaced by a very genuine admiration. Iris Origo noted wryly: "To admire Silone has now become not only the fashion, but almost a certificate of integrity," but for too long, she said, he was "undervalued both as a thinker and a writer." Until his death, Silone continued to survey the political and social scene and to write "in order to understand."

MEDIA ADAPTATIONS: "Le Grain sous la neige," a play by Daniel Guerin (Del Duca, 1961), was based on *Il seme sotto la neve.*

AVOCATIONAL INTERESTS: Football.

BIOGRAPHICAL/CRITICAL SOURCES:

BOOKS

Contemporary Literary Criticism, Volume 4, Gale, 1975.
Pacifici, Sergio, *A Guide to Contemporary Italian Literature,* Meridian, 1962.
Scott, Nathan A., *Rehearsals of Discomposure: Alienation and Reconciliation in Modern Literature: Franz Kafka, Ignazio Silone, D. H. Lawrence, and T. S. Eliot,* John Lehmann (London), 1952.
Silone, Ignazio, *Fontamara,* revised Italian edition, Mondadori (Milan), 1958.

PERIODICALS

Atlantic, March, 1967.
Best Sellers, May 5, 1971.
Book World, December 5, 1968.
Books and Bookmen, July, 1969, February, 1971.
Books, April 11, 1937, October, 1969.
Chicago Daily Tribune, April 3, 1937.
Forum, June, 1937.
London Magazine, June, 1969.
Nation, October 3, 1934, April 10, 1937.
New York Times, December 26, 1968, March 22, 1972.
New Statesman and Nation, November 10, 1934.
New York Times Book Review, May 28, 1961, December 29, 1968.
Observer Review, August 3, 1969.
Partisan Review, fall, 1939.
Personalist, Volume 36, 1953.
Saturday Review, April 3, 1937, November 9, 1968, April 24, 1971.
Times Literary Supplement, January 7, 1965.
Variety, April 2, 1969.

OBITUARIES:

PERIODICALS

New York Times, August 23, 1978.
Time, September 4, 1978.

*   *   *

SILVERBERG, Robert 1935-

(T. D. Bethlen, Walker Chapman, Dirk Clinton, Roy Cook, Walter Drummond, Dan Eliot, Don Elliott, Franklin Hamilton, Paul Hollander, Ivar Jorgenson, Calvin M. Knox, Dan Malcolm, Webber Martin, Alex Merriman, David Osborne, George Osborne, Lloyd Robinson, Eric Rodman, Lee Sebastian, Hall Thornton, Richard F. Watson; Gordon Aghill, Ralph Burke, Robert Randall, Ellis Robertson, joint pseudonyms; Robert Arnette, Alexander Blade, Richard Greer, E. K. Jarvis, Warren Kastel, Clyde Mitchell, Leonard G. Spencer, S. M. Tenneshaw, Gerald Vance, house pseudonyms)

PERSONAL: Born January 15, 1935, in New York, N.Y.; son of Michael (an accountant) and Helen (Baim) Silverberg; married Barbara H. Brown (an engineer), August 26, 1956 (separated, 1976; divorced, 1986). *Education:* Columbia University, B.A., 1956.

ADDRESSES: P.O. Box 13160, Station E, Oakland, Calif. 94661. *Agent*—Kirby McCauley, Ltd., 432 Park Ave. S., Suite 1509, New York, N.Y. 10016.

CAREER: Writer, 1956—; president, Agberg Ltd., 1981—.

MEMBER: Science Fiction Writers of America (president, 1967-68), Hydra Club (chairman, 1958-61).

AWARDS, HONORS: Hugo Award, World Science Fiction Convention, 1956, for best new author, and 1969, for novella "Nightwings"; *Lost Race of Mars* was chosen by the *New York Times* as one of the best hundred children's books of 1960; Spring Book Festival Award, *New York Herald Tribune,* 1962, for *Lost Cities and Vanished Civilizations,* and 1967, for *The Auk, the Dodo, and the Oryx: Vanished and Vanishing Creatures;* National Association of Independent Schools award, 1966, for *The Old Ones: Indians of the American Southwest;* Guest of Honor, World Science Fiction Convention, 1970; Nebula Award, Science Fiction Writers of America, 1970, for story "Passengers," 1972, for story "Good News from the Vatican," 1972, for novel *A Time of Changes,* 1975, for novella "Born with the Dead," and 1986, for novella *Sailing to Byzantium;* John W. Campbell Memorial Award, 1973, for excellence in writing; Jupiter Award, 1973, for novella "The Feast of St. Dionysus"; Prix Apollo, 1976, for novel *Nightwings;* Milford Award, 1981, for editing; Locus Award, 1982, for fantasy novel *Lord Valentine's Castle.*

WRITINGS:

SCIENCE FICTION

Master of Life and Death (also see below), Ace Books, 1957, reprinted, Tor Books, 1986.

The Thirteenth Immortal (bound with *This Fortress World* by J. E. Gunn), Ace Books, 1957.

Invaders from Earth (also see below; bound with *Across Time* by D. Grinnell), Ace Books, 1958, published separately, Avon, 1968, published as *We, the Marauders* (bound with *Giants in the Earth* by James Blish) under joint title *A Pair in Space,* Belmont, 1965.

Stepsons of Terra (bound with *A Man Called Destiny* by L. Wright), Ace Books, 1958, published separately, 1977.

The Planet Killers (bound with *We Claim These Stars!* by Poul Anderson), Ace Books, 1959.

Collision Course, Avalon, 1961, reprinted, Ace Books, 1982.

Next Stop the Stars (story collection; bound with *The Seed of Earth* [novel] by Silverberg), Ace Books, 1962, each published separately, 1977.

Recalled to Life, Lancer Books, 1962, reprinted, Ace Books, 1977.

The Silent Invaders (bound with *Battle on Venus* by William F. Temple), Ace Books, 1963, published separately, 1973.

Godling, Go Home! (story collection), Belmont, 1964.

Conquerors from the Darkness, Holt, 1965, reprinted, Tor Books, 1986.

To Worlds Beyond: Stories of Science Fiction, Chilton, 1965.

Needle in a Timestack (story collection), Ballantine, 1966, revised edition, Ace Books, 1985.

Planet of Death, Holt, 1967.

Thorns, Ballantine, 1967.

Those Who Watch, New American Library, 1967.

The Time-Hoppers (also see below), Doubleday, 1967.

To Open the Sky (story collection), Ballantine, 1967.

Hawksbill Station, Doubleday, 1968 (published in England as *The Anvil of Time,* Sidgwick & Jackson, 1968).

The Masks of Time (also see below), Ballantine, 1968 (published in England as *Vornan-19,* Sidgwick & Jackson, 1970).

Dimension Thirteen (story collection), Ballantine, 1969.

The Man in the Maze (also see below), Avon, 1969.

Nightwings (also see below), Avon, 1969.

(Contributor) *Three for Tomorrow: Three Original Novellas of Science Fiction,* Meredith Press, 1969.

Three Survived, Holt, 1969.

To Live Again, Doubleday, 1969.

Up the Line, Ballantine, 1969, revised edition, 1978.

The Cube Root of Uncertainty (story collection), Macmillan, 1970.

Downward to the Earth (also see below), Doubleday, 1970.

Parsecs and Parables: Ten Science Fiction Stories, Doubleday, 1970.

A Robert Silverberg Omnibus (contains *Master of Life and Death, Invaders from Earth,* and *The Time-Hoppers*), Sidgwick & Jackson, 1970.

Tower of Glass, Scribner, 1970.

Moonferns and Starsongs (story collection), Ballantine, 1971.

Son of Man, Ballantine, 1971.

A Time of Changes, New American Library, 1971.

The World Inside, Doubleday, 1971.

The Book of Skulls, Scribner, 1972.

Dying Inside (also see below), Scribner, 1972.

The Reality Trip and Other Implausibilities (story collection), Ballantine, 1972.

The Second Trip, Doubleday, 1972.

(Contributor) *The Day the Sun Stood Still,* Thomas Nelson, 1972.

Earth's Other Shadow: Nine Science Fiction Stories, New American Library, 1973.

(Contributor) *An Exaltation of Stars: Transcendental Adventures in Science Fiction,* Simon & Schuster, 1973.

(Contributor) *No Mind of Man: Three Original Novellas of Science Fiction,* Hawthorn, 1973.

Unfamiliar Territory (story collection), Scribner, 1973.

Valley beyond Time (story collection), Dell, 1973.

Born with the Dead: Three Novellas about the Spirit of Man (also see below), Random House, 1974.

Sundance and Other Science Fiction Stories, Thomas Nelson, 1974.

The Feast of St. Dionysus: Five Science Fiction Stories, Scribner, 1975.

The Stochastic Man, Harper, 1975.

The Best of Robert Silverberg, Volume 1, Pocket Books, 1976, Volume 2, Gregg, 1978.

Capricorn Games (story collection), Random House, 1976.

Shadrach in the Furnace, Bobbs-Merrill, 1976.

The Shores of Tomorrow (story collection), Thomas Nelson, 1976.

The Songs of Summer and Other Stories, Gollancz, 1979.

Lord Valentine's Castle, Harper, 1980.

The Desert of Stolen Dreams, Underwood-Miller, 1981.

A Robert Silverberg Omnibus (contains *Downward to the Earth, The Man in the Maze,* and *Nightwings*), Harper, 1981.

Majipoor Chronicles, Arbor House, 1982.

World of a Thousand Colors (story collection), Arbor House, 1982.

Valentine Pontifex, Arbor House, 1983.

The Conglomeroid Cocktail Party (story collection), Arbor House, 1984.

Sailing to Byzantium, Underwood-Miller, 1985.

Tom O'Bedlam, Donald I. Fine, 1985.

Beyond the Safe Zone: Collected Short Stories of Robert Silverberg, Donald I. Fine, 1986.

Star of Gypsies, Donald I. Fine, 1986.

Robert Silverberg's Worlds of Wonder, Warner, 1987.

At Winter's End, Warner, 1988.

Born with the Dead (bound with *The Saliva Tree* by Brian W. Aldiss), Tor Books, 1988.

The Masks of Time, Born with the Dead, Dying Inside, Bantam, 1988.

The Time of the Great Freeze, Tor Books, 1988.

To the Land of the Living, Gollancz, 1989.

(With Karen Haber) *The Mutant Season,* Foundation/Doubleday, 1989.

Worlds Imagined: Fifteen Short Stories, Crown, 1989.

JUVENILE FICTION

Revolt on Alpha C, Crowell, 1955.
Starman's Quest, Gnome Press, 1959.
Lost Race of Mars, Winston, 1960.
Regan's Planet, Pyramid Books, 1964, revised edition published as *World's Fair, 1992,* Follett, 1970.
Time of the Great Freeze, Holt, 1964.
The Mask of Akhnaten, Macmillan, 1965.
The Gate of Worlds, Holt, 1967, reprinted, Tor Books, 1984.
The Calibrated Alligator and Other Science Fiction Stories, Holt, 1969.
Across a Billion Years, Dial, 1969.
Sunrise on Mercury and Other Science Fiction Stories, Thomas Nelson, 1975.
(Editor with Charles G. Waugh and Martin H. Greenberg) *The Science Fictional Dinosaur,* Avon, 1982.

NONFICTION

First American into Space, Monarch Books, 1961.
Lost Cities and Vanished Civilizations, Chilton, 1962.
Empires in the Dust: Ancient Civilizations Brought to Light, Chilton, 1963.
The Fabulous Rockefellers: A Compelling, Personalized Account of One of America's First Families, Monarch Books, 1963.
Akhnaten: The Rebel Pharaoh, Chilton, 1964.
(Editor) *Great Adventures in Archaeology,* Dial, 1964.
Man before Adam: The Story of Man in Search of His Origins, Macrae Smith, 1964.
The Great Wall of China, Chilton, 1965, published as *The Long Rampart: The Story of the Great Wall of China,* 1966.
Scientists and Scoundrels: A Book of Hoaxes, Crowell, 1965.
Bridges, Macrae Smith, 1966.
Frontiers in Archaeology, Chilton, 1966.
The Auk, the Dodo, and the Oryx: Vanished and Vanishing Creatures, Crowell, 1967.
Light for the World: Edison and the Power Industry, Van Nostrand, 1967.
Men against Time: Salvage Archaeology in the United States, Macmillan, 1967.
Mound Builders of Ancient America: The Archaeology of a Myth, New York Graphic Society, 1968.
The Challenge of Climate: Man and His Environment, Meredith Press, 1969.
The World of Space, Meredith Press, 1969.
If I Forget Thee, O Jerusalem: American Jews and the State of Israel, Morrow, 1970.
The Pueblo Revolt, Weybright & Talley, 1970.
Before the Sphinx: Early Egypt, Thomas Nelson, 1971.
Clocks for the Ages: How Scientists Date the Past, Macmillan, 1971.
To the Western Shore: Growth of the United States, 1776-1853, Doubleday, 1971.
The Longest Voyage: Circumnavigators in the Age of Discovery, Bobbs-Merrill, 1972.
The Realm of Prester John, Doubleday, 1972.
(Contributor) *Those Who Can,* New American Library, 1973.
Drug Themes in Science Fiction, National Institute on Drug Abuse, 1974.
(Contributor) *Hell's Cartographers: Some Personal Histories of Science Fiction Writers,* Harper, 1975.

JUVENILE NONFICTION

Treasures beneath the Sea, Whitman Publishing, 1960.
Fifteen Battles That Changed the World, Putnam, 1963.

Home of the Red Man: Indian North America before Columbus, New York Graphic Society, 1963.
Sunken History: The Story of Underwater Archaeology, Chilton, 1963.
The Great Doctors, Putnam, 1964.
The Man Who Found Nineveh: The Story of Austen Henry Layard, Holt, 1964.
Men Who Mastered the Atom, Putnam, 1965.
Niels Bohr: The Man Who Mapped the Atom, Macrae Smith, 1965.
The Old Ones: Indians of the American Southwest, New York Graphic Society, 1965.
Socrates, Putnam, 1965.
The World of Coral, Duell, 1965.
Forgotten by Time: A Book of Living Fossils, Crowell, 1966.
To the Rock of Darius: The Story of Henry Rawlinson, Holt, 1966.
The Adventures of Nat Palmer: Antarctic Explorer and Clipper Ship Pioneer, McGraw, 1967.
The Dawn of Medicine, Putnam, 1967.
The Morning of Mankind: Prehistoric Man in Europe, New York Graphic Society, 1967.
The World of the Rain Forest, Meredith Press, 1967.
Four Men Who Changed the Universe, Putnam, 1968.
Ghost Towns of the American West, Crowell, 1968.
Stormy Voyager: The Story of Charles Wilkes, Lippincott, 1968.
The World of the Ocean Depths, Meredith Press, 1968.
Bruce of the Blue Nile, Holt, 1969.
Vanishing Giants: The Story of the Sequoias, Simon & Schuster, 1969.
Wonders of Ancient Chinese Science, Hawthorn, 1969.
Mammoths, Mastodons, and Man, McGraw, 1970.
The Seven Wonders of the Ancient World, Crowell-Collier, 1970.
(With Arthur C. Clarke) *Into Space: A Young Person's Guide to Space,* Harper, revised edition (Silverberg not associated with earlier edition), 1971.
John Muir: Prophet among the Glaciers, Putnam, 1972.
The World within the Ocean Wave, Weybright & Talley, 1972.
The World within the Tide Pool, Weybright & Talley, 1972.
Project Pendulum, Walker & Co., 1987.

EDITOR

Earthmen and Strangers: Nine Stories of Science Fiction, Duell, 1966.
Voyagers in Time: Twelve Stories of Science Fiction, Meredith Press, 1967.
Men and Machines: Ten Stories of Science Fiction, Meredith Press, 1968.
Dark Stars, Ballantine, 1969.
Tomorrow's Worlds: Ten Stories of Science Fiction, Meredith Press, 1969.
The Ends of Time: Eight Stories of Science Fiction, Hawthorn, 1970.
Great Short Novels of Science Fiction, Ballantine, 1970.
The Mirror of Infinity: A Critics' Anthology of Science Fiction, Harper, 1970.
The Science Fiction Hall of Fame, Doubleday, Volume 1, 1970 (published in England as *Science Fiction Hall of Fame,* Volumes 1 and 2, Sphere, 1972).
Worlds of Maybe: Seven Stories of Science Fiction, Thomas Nelson, 1970.
Four Futures, Hawthorn, 1971.
Mind to Mind: Nine Stories of Science Fiction, Thomas Nelson, 1971.

The Science Fiction Bestiary: Nine Stories of Science Fiction, Thomas Nelson, 1971.

To the Stars: Eight Stories of Science Fiction, Hawthorn, 1971.

Beyond Control: Seven Stories of Science Fiction, Thomas Nelson, 1972.

Invaders from Space: Ten Stories of Science Fiction, Hawthorn, 1972.

Chains of the Sea: Three Original Novellas of Science Fiction, Thomas Nelson, 1973.

Deep Space: Eight Stories of Science Fiction, Thomas Nelson, 1973.

Other Dimensions: Ten Stories of Science Fiction, Hawthorn, 1973.

Three Trips in Time and Space, Hawthorn, 1973.

Infinite Jests: The Lighter Side of Science Fiction, Chilton, 1974.

Mutants: Eleven Stories of Science Fiction, Thomas Nelson, 1974.

Threads of Time: Three Original Novellas of Science Fiction, Thomas Nelson, 1974.

Windows into Tomorrow: Nine Stories of Science Fiction, Hawthorn, 1974.

(With Roger Elwood) *Epoch,* Berkley Publishing, 1975.

Explorers of Space: Eight Stories of Science Fiction, Thomas Nelson, 1975.

The New Atlantis and Other Novellas of Science Fiction, Warner Books, 1975.

Strange Gifts: Eight Stories of Science Fiction, Thomas Nelson, 1975.

The Aliens: Seven Stories of Science Fiction, Thomas Nelson, 1976.

The Crystal Ship: Three Original Novellas of Science Fiction, Thomas Nelson, 1976.

Earth Is the Strangest Planet: Ten Stories of Science Fiction, Thomas Nelson, 1977.

Galactic Dreamers: Science Fiction as Visionary Literature, Random House, 1977.

The Infinite Web: Eight Stories of Science Fiction, Dial, 1977.

Triax: Three Original Novellas, Pinnacle Books, 1977.

Trips in Time: Nine Stories of Science Fiction, Thomas Nelson, 1977.

Lost Worlds, Unknown Horizons: Nine Stories of Science Fiction, Thomas Nelson, 1978.

The Androids Are Coming: Seven Stories of Science Fiction, Elsevier-Nelson, 1979.

(With Greenberg and Joseph D. Olander) *Car Sinister,* Avon, 1979.

(With Greenberg and Olander) *Dawn of Time: Prehistory through Science Fiction,* Elsevier-Nelson, 1979.

The Edge of Space: Three Original Novellas of Science Fiction, Elsevier-Nelson, 1979.

(With Greenberg) *The Arbor House Treasury of Great Science Fiction Short Novels,* Arbor House, 1980.

(With Greenberg) *The Arbor House Treasury of Modern Science Fiction,* Arbor House, 1980.

The Best of Randall Garrett, Pocket Books, 1982.

The Nebula Awards, Arbor House, 1983.

(With Greenberg) *The Arbor House Treasury of Science Fiction Masterpieces,* Arbor House, 1983.

(With Greenberg) *The Fantasy Hall of Fame,* Arbor House, 1983.

(With Greenberg) *The Time Travelers: A Science Fiction Quartet,* Donald I. Fine, 1985.

(With Greenberg) *Neanderthals,* New American Library, 1987.

(With Greenberg) *The Mammoth Book of Fantasy All-Time Greats,* Robinson, 1988.

(With Karen Haber) *Universe 1,* Foundation/Doubleday, 1990.

EDITOR; "ALPHA" SERIES

Alpha, Volumes 1-6, Ballantine, 1970-76.

Alpha, Volumes 7-9, Berkley Publishing, 1977-78.

EDITOR; "NEW DIMENSIONS" SERIES

New Dimensions, Volumes 1-5, Doubleday, 1971-75.

New Dimensions, Volumes 6-10, Harper, 1976-80.

The Best of New Dimensions, Pocket Books, 1979.

(With Marta Randall) *New Dimensions,* Volumes 11-12, Pocket Books, 1980-81.

UNDER PSEUDONYM WALKER CHAPMAN

The Loneliest Continent: The Story of Antarctic Discovery, New York Graphic Society, 1964.

(Editor) *Antarctic Conquest: The Great Explorers in Their Own Words,* Bobbs-Merrill, 1966.

Kublai Khan: Lord of Xanadu, Bobbs-Merrill, 1966.

The Golden Dream: Seekers of El Dorado, Bobbs-Merrill 1967, published as *The Search for El Dorado,* 1967.

UNDER PSEUDONYM DON ELLIOTT

Flesh Peddlers, Nightstand, 1960.

Passion Trap, Nightstand, 1960.

Backstage Sinner, Nightstand, 1961.

Lust Goddess, Nightstand, 1961.

Sin Cruise, Nightstand, 1961.

Kept Man, Midnight, 1962.

Shame House, Midnight, 1962.

Sin Hellion, Ember, 1963.

Sin Servant, Nightstand, 1963.

Beatnik Wanton, Evening, 1964.

Flesh Bride, Evening, 1964.

Flesh Prize, Leisure, 1964.

Flesh Taker, Ember, 1964.

Sin Warped, Leisure, 1964.

Switch Trap, Evening, 1964.

Nudie Packet, Idle Hour, 1965.

The Young Wanton, Sundown, 1965.

Depravity Town, Reed, 1973.

Jungle Street, Reed, 1973.

Summertime Affair, Reed, 1973.

Also author of eighty other novels, 1959-65, under pseudonyms Dan Eliot and Don Elliott.

OTHER

(With Randall Garrett, under joint pseudonym Robert Randall) *The Shrouded Planet,* Gnome Press, 1957, published under names Robert Silverberg and Randall Garrett, Donning, 1980.

(Under pseudonym Calvin M. Knox) *Lest We Forget Thee, Earth,* Ace Books, 1958.

(Under pseudonym David Osborne) *Aliens from Space,* Avalon, 1958.

(Under pseudonym Ivar Jorgenson) *Starhaven,* Avalon, 1958.

(Under pseudonym David Osborne) *Invisible Barriers,* Avalon, 1958.

(With Randall Garrett, under joint pseudonym Robert Randall) *The Dawning Light,* Gnome Press, 1959, published under names Robert Silverberg and Randall Garrett, Donning, 1981.

(Under pseudonym Calvin M. Knox) *The Plot against Earth,* Ace Books, 1959.

(Under pseudonym Walter Drummond) *Philosopher of Evil,* Regency Books, 1962.

(Under pseudonym Walter Drummond) *How to Spend Money,* Regency Books, 1963.

(Under pseudonym Franklin Hamilton) *1066,* Dial, 1963.

(Under pseudonym Calvin M. Knox) *One of Our Asteroids Is Missing,* Ace Books, 1964.

(Under pseudonym Paul Hollander) *The Labors of Hercules,* Putnam, 1965.

(Under pseudonym Franklin Hamilton) *The Crusades,* Dial, 1965.

(Under pseudonym Lloyd Robinson) *The Hopefuls: Ten Presidential Candidates,* Doubleday, 1966.

(Under pseudonym Roy Cook) *Leaders of Labor,* Lippincott, 1966.

(Under pseudonym Lee Sebastian) *Rivers,* Holt, 1966.

(Under pseudonym Franklin Hamilton) *Challenge for a Throne: The Wars of the Roses,* Dial, 1967.

(Under pseudonym Lloyd Robinson) *The Stolen Election: Hayes versus Tilden,* Doubleday, 1968.

(Under pseudonym Ivar Jorgenson) *Whom the Gods Would Slay,* Belmont, 1968.

(Under pseudonym Paul Hollander) *Sam Houston,* Putnam, 1968.

(Under pseudonym Lee Sebastian) *The South Pole,* Holt, 1968.

(Under pseudonym Ivar Jorgenson) *The Deadly Sky,* Pinnacle Books, 1971.

"Dying Inside" (recording), Caedmon, 1979.

"Robert Silverberg Reads 'To See the Invisible Man' and 'Passengers' " (recording), Pelican Records, 1979.

Lord of Darkness (fiction), Arbor House, 1983.

Gilgamesh the King (fiction), Arbor House, 1984.

Contributor, sometimes under pseudonyms, to *Omni, Playboy, Amazing Stories Science Fiction, Fantastic Stories Science Fiction, Magazine of Fantasy and Science Fiction,* and other publications.

SIDELIGHTS: Robert Silverberg is one of the best known of contemporary science fiction writers. He has won the field's Nebula and Hugo Awards and has received more award nominations for his work than any other science fiction writer. He is also, according to Brian M. Stableford in *Masters of Science Fiction,* "the most prolific science fiction writer of the past two decades." But despite his prominence in the field, Silverberg's science fiction work makes up, "at the most, fifteen percent of his output," Barry M. Malzberg writes in the *Magazine of Fantasy and Science Fiction.* Indeed, Silverberg has even left the field entirely on two separate occasions. Most of his work has been nonfiction on such varied topics as archaeology, conservation, history, and the natural sciences. He has received awards for several of these nonfiction books, while his *Mound Builders of Ancient America: The Archaeology of a Myth* is considered one of the standard works on the subject. Still, this considerable success in the nonfiction field is overshadowed by his continuing popularity in science fiction. As George R. R. Martin, writing in the *Washington Post Book World,* admits, Silverberg "is best known and best regarded for his work within science fiction."

Silverberg began his writing career while still a student at Columbia University in the 1950s. He had decided to become a science fiction writer because of his own reaction to the genre as a boy. As he tells Jeffrey M. Elliot in *Science Fiction Voices #2:* "When I was a boy, I read science fiction and it did wonderful things for me. It opened the universe to me. I feel a sense of obligation to science fiction to replace what I had taken from it, to add to the shelf, to put something there for someone else that would do for them what other writers had done for me." Silverberg's first sales were to the science fiction magazines of the 1950s, and his first book was a juvenile science fiction novel.

Upon graduation from Columbia in 1956, he became a full-time free-lance writer. His work was already so popular that the World Science Fiction Convention, a gathering of the genre's devotees, voted him the Hugo Award as the best new writer of the year.

During the 1950s Silverberg produced hundreds of stories for the science fiction magazines. His production was so high that he was obliged to publish much of this work under a host of pseudonyms. Silverberg recalls that time to Charles Platt in *Dream Makers: The Uncommon People Who Write Science Fiction,* "I was courted by editors considerably back then, because I was so dependable; if they said, 'Give me a story by next Thursday,' I would." These early stories, George W. Tuma writes in the *Dictionary of Literary Biography,* "conform closely to the conventions of science fiction: alien beings, technological gadgetry, standard plot devices, confrontations between [Earthlings] and extraterrestrial beings, and so forth." In 1959 a downturn in sales forced many science fiction magazines out of business. Silverberg was no longer able to support himself by writing for the genre. He turned to writing articles for the popular magazines instead, maintaining his high level of production by turning out two pieces every working day.

In the early 1960s Silverberg moved from writing magazine articles to writing nonfiction books, a change he remembers with some relief in his *Contemporary Authors Autobiography Series* article. "I severed my connections with my sleazy magazine outlets and ascended into this new, astoundingly respectable and rewarding career," he recalls. In a few years he had established himself as one of the most successful nonfiction writers in the country, publishing books about Antarctica, ancient Egypt, the American space program, medical history, and a host of other topics. "I was considered one of the most skilled popularizers of the sciences in the United States," Silverberg remembers.

During these early years Silverberg maintained a prolific writing pace, publishing nearly two million words per year. He tells Elliot that he managed to write so much due to intense concentration. "I concentrated on a point source and the words just came out right," Silverberg recalls. Malzberg allows that "the man is prolific. Indeed, the man may be, in terms of accumulation of work per working year, the most prolific writer who ever lived."

But the years of prolific writing finally ended in the middle 1960s. Silverberg has cited two factors for the slowdown in his production at that time. The first was a hyperactive thyroid gland, brought on by prolonged overwork, which forced him in 1966 to slow his working pace considerably. The second factor was a fire in early 1968 at Silverberg's New York City home. This fire, he writes in the *CA Autobiography Series,* "drained from me, evidently forever, much of the bizarre energy that had allowed me to write a dozen or more significant books in a single year."

It was also in the middle 1960s that Silverberg returned to the science fiction field after an absence of several years. It is the work from this period that most observers credit as the beginning of Silverberg's serious fiction in the genre. Thomas D. Clareson, although noting in his book *Robert Silverberg* that "from the beginning, he was a skilled storyteller," nonetheless marks 1969 to 1976 as the period when Silverberg "conducted his most deliberate experiments and attained the most consistent command of his material." Malzberg claims that "in or around 1965 Silverberg put his toys away and began to write literature."

The change in Silverberg's science fiction of the 1960s can be explained in part by changes in the field as a whole. The New

Wave, a movement of younger writers trying break out of the pulp formulas of science fiction and utilize the techniques of modernist literature, had a powerful influence on many writers in the field, including Silverberg. New subjects and approaches were suddenly suitable for commercial science fiction. Silverberg began to experiment with technique and style, producing the award-winning novels *A Time of Changes* and *Nightwings,* several award-winning stories and novellas, and other novels nominated for major awards. Speaking of several books from this period in an article for the *New York Times Book Review,* Theodore Sturgeon finds that Silverberg "changed into something quite new and different—his own man, saying his own things his own way, and doing it with richness and diversity." Tuma also sees a transformation in Silverberg's work, stating that he "found his unique approach to science fiction, in terms of both content and writing style."

This new seriousness is evident, too, in the concerns of Silverberg's 1960s fiction. Russell Letson, writing in *Extrapolation,* finds that Silverberg's fiction "pursued the modernist themes of anxiety and alienation" while Silverberg "shaped science fiction materials to deal with themes that were not previously part of the American sf mainstream." Speaking of the novels *Thorns* and *Hawksbill Station,* and of the story "To See the Invisible Man," all works of the 1960s, Stableford sees Silverberg as using "science fictional ideas to dramatize situations of extreme alienation."

Through his experiments with style and narrative structure Silverberg sought to extend the range of science fiction. "Having already proved that he could write every kind of s.f. story at least as well as anyone else," Gerald Jones comments in the *New York Times Book Review,* "Silverberg set out . . . to stretch both the genre and himself." In *Son of Man,* for example, called by Stableford a "surreal novel," the story is told as a series of bizarre adventure sequences set on "not the physical planet Earth but the Earth of human perception—the model world of the mind," as Stableford relates. Sandra Miesel, writing in *Extrapolation,* calls *Son of Man* a "sensuous, didactic, and witty novel" in which "the dream fantasy is stretched to the breaking point."

This new approach in his work put Silverberg in the forefront of the science fiction field. "By the 1970s Silverberg was writing science fiction much as such of his contemporaries as Barth, Reed, Bartheleme, and Coover were presenting their renditions of everyday American life," Clareson writes in *Voices for the Future: Essays on Major Science Fiction Writers.* But Silverberg was dissatisfied with the response to his work. His books won awards, but their sales were poor and they often met with uninformed critical comments from science fiction purists. "I was at first bewildered by the response I was getting from the audience," Silverberg tells Platt. "There are passages in *Dying Inside* or in *Nightwings* which I think are sheer ecstatic song, but people would come up to me and say, Why do you write such depressing books? Something was wrong." By 1975 all of Silverberg's more serious books, upon which he had placed such importance, were out of print. At that point he announced his retirement from science fiction.

For the next four years Silverberg wrote no new science fiction. He devoted his time to the garden of his California home. "I had had my career," Silverberg writes in his *CA Autobiography Series* article. "Now I had my garden." But in 1978, he was pushed back into the field. Silverberg needed to buy a house for his wife, from whom he was separated. To raise the necessary money, he decided to write one last book. The result was *Lord Valentine's Castle,* a massive novel that set a record when it was offered to

publishers at auction. Harper & Row paid the largest sum ever given for a science fiction novel—$127,500—and Silverberg was a writer again.

In *Lord Valentine's Castle* Silverberg mixes elements from science fiction and heroic fantasy. The science fiction elements include a far future setting, the imaginary planet of Majipoor, and a host of exotic alien life forms. But the plot, a quest by a disinherited prince to regain his throne, is common to the fantasy genre. The clever combination of genre elements was praised by Jack Sullivan in the *New York Times Book Review.* Sullivan calls *Lord Valentine's Castle* "an imaginative fusion of action, sorcery and science fiction, with visionary adventure scenes undergirded by scientific explanations." In his book *Robert Silverberg,* Clareson states that "whatever else it does, *Lord Valentine's Castle* demands that its readers re-examine the relationship between science fiction and fantasy, for in this narrative Silverberg has fused the two together."

The rich diversity of the planet Majipoor was remarked upon by several reviewers, including Patrick Parrinder of the *Times Literary Supplement.* "Silverberg's invention," Parrinder writes, "is prodigious throughout. The early sections . . . are a near-encyclopaedia of unnatural wonders and weird ecosystems. I suspect this book breaks all records in the coinage of new species." John Charnay of the *Los Angeles Times Book Review,* although believing the book "lacks depth of dialogue and emotion to match the grandeur of scenery and plot," still finds that "Silverberg's inventiveness is intriguing."

The success of *Lord Valentine's Castle* drew Silverberg back into the writing life again. He began to write stories for *Omni* magazine, where several old friends were working, and in 1982 he published *Majipoor Chronicles,* a novel fashioned from several short stories set on the planet introduced in *Lord Valentine's Castle.* Each story is an episode from Majipoor's history which has been stored on an experience-record. By using a futuristic reading-machine, a young boy is able to "relive" these historical events. "As a result," Michael Bishop writes in the *Washington Post Book World,* "the stories become something more than stories—vivid initiation experiences in the boy's struggle to manhood. A neat trick, this." Sturgeon, in his review of the book for the *Los Angeles Times Book Review,* expresses his "absolute awe at Silverberg's capacity for creating images—wonder upon wonder, marvel upon marvel, all with verisimilitude. . . . This is a beautiful book."

With *Valentine Pontifex,* Silverberg did what he had once vowed he would never do: write a sequel to *Lord Valentine's Castle.* Colin Greenland of the *Times Literary Supplement,* who believes *Lord Valentine's Castle* a weak novel because it "satisfied readers' wishes for a great big safe world where nice things flourish and evil succumbs to forgiveness," sees *Valentine Pontifex* as "Silverberg's act of conscience for *Lord Valentine's Castle.*" In the sequel, Lord Valentine, now restored to his position as ruler of Majipoor, faces opposition from the Piurivars, an aboriginal race dispossessed years before by Earthling colonists. The Piurivars release plagues and deadly bio-engineered creatures upon the humans. The reviewer for the *Voice Literary Supplement* finds that "the lazy pace through time and space" found in *Lord Valentine's Castle* gives way in this novel "to a dance of conflicting emotions and political intrigue." Greenland is disappointed with the book's hopeful ending, explaining that the characters "all live happily ever after." But the *Voice Literary Supplement* reviewer, seeing *Lord Valentine's Castle, Majipoor Chronicles,* and *Valentine Pontifex* as related works forming a loose trilogy, believes that "the trilogy becomes a whole in a way that the form rarely achieves."

Over a professional writing career spanning three decades, Silverberg has produced an immense body of work in several genres. Commenting on this diversity, Martin writes that "few writers, past or present, have had careers quite as varied, dramatic, and contradictory as that of Robert Silverberg." As a writer of nonfiction, Silverberg has enjoyed particular success. But as a writer of science fiction, he is among a handful of writers who have helped to shape the field into what it is today. He is, Elliot declares, "a titan in the science fiction field." "Few science fiction readers," Elliot goes on, "have not been enriched and inspired by his contributions to the genre, contributions which reflect his love of the field and his deep respect for its readers." Silverberg's contributions to the field, Clareson writes in the *Magazine of Fantasy and Science Fiction,* are of predictably high quality: "He will tell a good story, he will fuse together content and form, and he will add to our perception of the human condition." In his introduction to *Galactic Dreamers: Science Fiction as Visionary Literature,* Silverberg explains what he has been striving to attain in his work: "To show the reader something he has never been able to see with his own eyes, something strange and unique, beautiful and troubling, which draws him for a moment out of himself, places him in contact with the vastness of the universe, gives him for a sizzling moment a communion with the fabric of space and time, and leaves him forever transformed, forever enlarged."

MEDIA ADAPTATIONS: Film rights for *The Book of Skulls* have been sold.

BIOGRAPHICAL/CRITICAL SOURCES:

BOOKS

Aldiss, Brian and Harry Harrison, editors, *Hell's Cartographers: Some Personal Histories of Science Fiction Writers,* Harper, 1975.
Clareson, Thomas D., editor, *Voices for the Future: Essays on Major Science Fiction Writers,* Volume 2, Bowling Green State University Popular Press, 1979.
Clareson, Thomas D., *Robert Silverberg,* Starmont House, 1983.
Clareson, Thomas D., *Robert Silverberg: A Primary and Secondary Bibliography,* G. K. Hall, 1983.
Contemporary Authors Autobiography Series, Volume 3, Gale, 1986.
Contemporary Literary Criticism, Volume 7, Gale, 1977.
Dictionary of Literary Biography, Volume 8: *Twentieth-Century American Science-Fiction Writers,* Gale, 1981.
Elliot, Jeffrey M., *Science Fiction Voices #2,* Borgo Press, 1979.
Magill, Frank N., editor, *Survey of Science Fiction,* Salem Press, 1979.
Platt, Charles, *Dream Makers: The Uncommon People Who Write Science Fiction,* Berkley Publishing, 1980.
Rabkin, Eric S. and others, editors, *No Place Else,* Southern Illinois University Press, 1983.
Schweitzer, Darrell, editor, *Exploring Fantasy Worlds: Essays on Fantastic Literature,* Borgo Press, 1985.
Silverberg, Robert, editor, *Galactic Dreamers: Science Fiction as Visionary Literature,* Random House, 1977.
Stableford, Brian M., *Masters of Science Fiction,* Borgo Press, 1981.
Staircar, Tom, editor, *Critical Encounters II,* Ungar, 1982.
Walker, Paul, *Speaking of Science Fiction: The Paul Walker Interviews,* Luna Press, 1978.

PERIODICALS

Analog, November, 1979.
Atlantic, April, 1972.
Essays in Arts and Sciences, August, 1980.
Extrapolation, summer, 1979, winter, 1980, winter, 1982.
Fantasy Newsletter, June-July, 1983.
Los Angeles Times Book Review, May 18, 1980, April 18, 1986.
Magazine of Fantasy and Science Fiction, April, 1971, April, 1974.
Megavore, March, 1981.
National Review, November 3, 1970.
New Statesman, June 18, 1976.
New York Times Book Review, May 9, 1965, November 3, 1968, March 5, 1972, August 24, 1975, August 3, 1980, August 4, 1985, November 23, 1986.
Science Fiction: A Review of Speculative Literature, September, 1983.
Science Fiction Chronicle, January, 1985, May, 1985.
Starship, November, 1982.
Times Literary Supplement, June 12, 1969, March 15, 1974, November 7, 1980, August 3, 1984.
Voice Literary Supplement, December, 1983.
Washington Post Book World, February 28, 1982, May 8, 1983.
Writer, November, 1977.

*   *   *

SIM, Georges
See SIMENON, Georges (Jacques Christian)

*   *   *

SIMAK, Clifford D(onald)   1904-1988

PERSONAL: Born August 3, 1904, in Millville, Wis.; died April 25, 1988, in Minneapolis, Minn.; son of John Lewis and Margaret (Wiseman) Simak; married Agnes Kuchenberg, April 13, 1929; children: Scott, Shelley. *Education:* Attended University of Wisconsin.

ADDRESSES: Home—Minnetonka, Minn. *Agent*—Blassingame, McCauley & Wood, 60 East 42nd St., New York, N.Y. 10017.

CAREER: Worked with various newspapers in Midwest during 1930s; *Minneapolis Star and Tribune,* Minneapolis, Minn., 1939-76, news editor of *Minneapolis Star,* beginning 1949, coordinator of *Minneapolis Tribune*'s Science Reading Series, beginning 1961.

MEMBER: Sigma Delta Chi.

AWARDS, HONORS: International Fantasy Award for best science fiction novel, 1953, for *City;* Hugo Award for best science fiction novelette, 1958, for "The Big Front Yard," for best science fiction novel, 1963, for *Way Station,* and for short story, 1982, for "Grotto of the Dancing Deer"; Minnesota Academy of Science Award, 1967, for distinguished service to science; First Fandom Hall of Fame Award, 1973; Juniper Award for best novel, Instructors of Science Fiction in Higher Education, 1977, for *A Heritage of Stars;* Grand Master Award, Science Fiction Writers of America, 1977, for lifetime achievement; Jupiter Award, 1979, for *A Heritage of Stars;* Nebula Award from Science Fiction Writers of America, and Locus Award, both 1982, both for "Grotto of the Dancing Deer."

WRITINGS:

SCIENCE FICTION AND FANTASY

The Creator (novelette), Crawford, 1946, recent edition, Locus Press, 1981.

Cosmic Engineers, Gnome Press, 1950, reprinted, Paperback Library, 1970.

Empire, Galaxy, 1951.

Time and Again, Simon & Schuster, 1951, reprinted, Ace, 1976, published as *First He Died,* Dell, 1952.

City, Gnome Press, 1952, recent edition, Ace, 1981.

Ring around the Sun, Simon & Schuster, 1953.

Time Is the Simplest Thing, Ace, 1961, reprinted, Nordon Publications, 1977.

The Trouble Trouble with Tycho, Ace, 1961, reprinted, 1983.

They Walked Like Men, Doubleday, 1962, reprinted, Avon, 1979.

Way Station, Doubleday, 1963, recent edition, Ballantine, 1986.

All Flesh Is Grass, Doubleday, 1965.

Why Call Them Back from Heaven?, Doubleday, 1967.

The Werewolf Principle, Putnam, 1967.

The Goblin Reservation, Putnam, 1968.

Out of Their Minds, Putnam, 1970.

Destiny Doll, Putnam, 1971.

A Choice of Gods, Putnam, 1972.

Cemetery World, Putnam, 1973.

Our Children's Children, Putnam, 1974.

Enchanted Pilgrimage, Berkley, 1975.

Shakespeare's Planet, Berkley, 1976.

A Heritage of Stars, Berkley, 1977.

The Fellowship of the Talisman, Ballantine, 1978.

Mastodonia, Ballantine, 1978.

The Visitors, Ballantine, 1980.

Project Pope, Ballantine, 1981.

Where the Evil Dwells, Ballantine, 1982.

Special Deliverance, Ballantine, 1982.

Highway of Eternity, Ballantine, 1986.

SHORT STORY COLLECTIONS

Strangers in the Universe, Simon & Schuster, 1956.

The Worlds of Clifford Simak, Simon & Schuster, 1960 (published in England as *Aliens for Neighbours,* Faber, 1961).

All the Traps of Earth and Other Stories, Doubleday, 1962, reprinted, Avon, 1979, published as *The Night of the Puudly,* Four Square, 1964.

Other Worlds of Clifford Simak, Doubleday, 1962.

Worlds without End, Belmont Books, 1964.

Best Science Fiction Stories of Clifford Simak, Faber 1967, Doubleday, 1971.

So Bright the Vision, Ace, 1968.

(Editor) *Nebula Award Stories #6,* Doubleday, 1971.

The Best of Clifford D. Simak, Sidgwick & Jackson, 1975.

Skirmish: The Great Short Fiction of Clifford D. Simak, Berkley, 1977.

Also author of *The Marathan Photographer and Other Stories,* 1986, and *Brother and Other Stories,* 1987. Work represented in anthologies. Contributor of more than two hundred short stories to science fiction magazines.

NONFICTION

The Solar System: Our New Front Yard, St. Martin's, 1962.

Trilobite, Dinosaur, and Man: The Earth's Story, St. Martin's, 1965.

(Editor) *From Atoms to Infinity: Readings in Modern Science,* Harper, 1965.

Wonder and Glory: The Story of the Universe, St. Martin's, 1969.

Prehistoric Man: The Story of Man's Rise to Civilization, St. Martin's, 1971.

(Editor) *The March of Science,* Harper, 1971.

Author of columns "Science in the News," *Minneapolis Star,* and "Medical News," *Minneapolis Tribune.*

SIDELIGHTS: Clifford D. Simak's best-known work is *City,* a future history of mankind and its eventual destruction through the misuse of technology. "Once Simak had written *City . . . ,*" Thomas D. Clareson believes, "American science fiction could never again be what it had been. . . . [No] one, so thoroughly as Simak, had condemned man's surrender to that technology which led him to Hiroshima and the Moon." Clareson concludes that Simak "did more, perhaps, than any of his contemporaries to free science fiction from its established patterns and to create credible, imaginary worlds better able to sustain metaphors of the condition of man. As few other writers before him, he gave the genre a moral stature."

Simak's own view of *City* differed from that of the critics. He told *CA* that although the book "is used in the classroom, . . . perhaps is my best-known work, [and] did have some impact on the field, . . . that doesn't make it my major work." He hoped that one of his later works would prove still better.

Simak's story "How-2" has been adapted as a musical. His books have been translated into numerous languages including French, Russian, Italian, and Hebrew.

BIOGRAPHICAL/CRITICAL SOURCES:

BOOKS

Amis, Kingsley, *New Maps of Hell,* Harcourt, 1960.

Clareson, Thomas D., editor, *Voices for the Future,* Volume I, Bowling Green University Press, 1976.

Contemporary Literary Criticism, Gale, Volume 1, 1973, Volume 55, 1989.

De Camp, L. Sprague, *Science Fiction Handbook,* Hermitage, 1953.

Dictionary of Literary Biography, Volume 8: *Twentieth-Century American Science-Fiction Writers,* 1981.

Moskowitz, Samuel, *Seekers of Tomorrow,* World Publishing, 1966.

Wollheim, Donald A., *The Universe Makers,* Harper, 1971.

PERIODICALS

Amazing Stories, December, 1961, June, 1965, June, 1973.

Analog, April, 1954, July, 1969, December, 1971, January, 1977.

Books and Bookmen, June, 1968.

Books West, October, 1977.

Detroit News, June 21, 1981.

Galaxy, October, 1952, June, 1967, July, 1971.

Magazine of Fantasy and Science Fiction, October, 1960, March, 1966, February, 1969.

Natural History, November, 1966.

New Statesman, February 3, 1967.

New York Times Book Review, June 26, 1977, June 8, 1986.

Observer, April 14, 1968.

Punch, April 3, 1968.

Saturday Review, May 15, 1971.

Science Books, March, 1966.

Sky and Telescope, October, 1970.

Spectator, July 30, 1977.

Times Literary Supplement, March 24, 1966, August 8, 1975.

Washington Post Book World, April 26, 1981, June 22, 1986.

OBITUARIES:

PERIODICALS

Los Angeles Times, April 29, 1988.
New York Times, April 28, 1988.
Times (London), April 29, 1988.
Washington Post, April 30, 1988.

*   *   *

**SIMENON, Georges (Jacques Christian)   1903-1989
(Bobette, Christian Brulls, Germain d'Antibes,
Jacques Dersonnes, Georges d'Isly, Luc Dorsan,
Jean Dorsange, Jean Dossage, Jean du Perry,
Georges Martin Georges, Gom Gut, Kim, Plick et
Plock, Georges Sim, Gaston Vialis, G. Violis)**

PERSONAL: Born February 13, 1903, in Liege, Belgium; died
September 4, 1989, in Lausanne, Switzerland; son of Desire (an
insurance clerk) and Henriette (Brull) Simenon; married Regine
Renchon, March 24, 1923 (divorced, June 21, 1950); married
Denyse Ouimet, June 22, 1950 (separated c. 1970); children:
(first marriage) Marc; (second marriage) Jean, Marie-Georges
(deceased), Pierre. *Education:* Educated in Liege, Belgium.

ADDRESSES: Home—12 Avenue des Figuiers, 1007, Lausanne,
Switzerland.

CAREER: Writer, beginning 1922. Worked as a baker's apprentice and bookstore clerk in Liege, Belgium; *Liege Gazette,* Liege,
began as police reporter, became comic columnist. *Wartime service:* Worked with refugees in Vichy, France, during World War
II.

MEMBER: Acadame Royale de Langue et Litterature Francaise
(Brussels), American Academy of Arts and Letters, Mystery
Writers of America (former president).

AWARDS, HONORS: Received Grand Masters Award from
Mystery Writers of America.

WRITINGS:

"MAIGRET" SERIES

Pietr-le-Letton, Fayard, 1931, translation published as *The
Strange Case of Peter the Lett,* Covici-Friede, 1933, transla-
tion by Anthony Abbott published as "The Case of Peter
the Lett" in *Inspector Maigret Investigates,* Hurst & Black-
ett, 1934, translation by Daphne Woodward published as
Maigret and the Enigmatic Lett, Penguin, 1963.
Au rendez-vous des terre-neuvas, Fayard, 1931, translation by
Margaret Ludwig published as "The Sailors Rendezvous"
in *Maigret Keeps a Rendezvous,* George Routledge, 1940,
Harcourt, 1941.
Le Charretier de la "Providence," Fayard, 1931, translation published as *The Crime at Lock 14* [with] *The Shadow on the
Courtyard,* Covici-Friede, 1934, translation by Robert Bald-
ick published as *Maigret Meets a Milord,* Penguin, 1963.
Le Chien jaune, Fayard, 1931, translation by Geoffrey Sainsbury
published as "A Face for a Clue" in *The Patience of Mai-
gret,* George Routledge, 1939, Harcourt, 1940, published as
A Face for a Clue [with] *A Crime in Holland,* Penguin, 1952,
translation by Linda Asher published as *Maigret and the
Yellow Dog,* Harcourt, 1987.
La Danseuse du Gai-Moulin, Fayard, 1931, translation by Sains-
bury published as "At the Gai-Moulin" in *Maigret Abroad,*
Harcourt, 1940, published as *At The Gai-Moulin* [with] *A
Battle of Nerves,* Penguin, 1951.

M. Gallet decede, Fayard, 1931, translation published as *The
Death of Monsieur Gallet,* Covici-Friede, 1932, translation
by Abbott published as "The Death of M. Gallet" in *Intro-
ducing Inspector Maigret,* Hurst & Blackett, 1933, transla-
tion by Margaret Marshall published as *Maigret Stone-
walled,* Penguin, 1963.
La Nuit du carrefour, Fayard, 1931, translation published as *The
Crossroad Murders,* Covici-Friede, 1933, translation by
Abbot published as "The Crossroad Murders" in *Inspector
Maigret Investigates,* Hurst & Blackett, 1933, published as
La Nuit de carrefour, edited and adapted by P. W. Packer,
Oxford University Press, 1935, translation by Baldick published as *Maigret at the Crossroads,* Penguin, 1963, reprinted, 1984.
Le Pendu de Saint-Phiolien, Fayard, 1931, translation by Abbot
published as *The Crime of Inspector Maigret,* Covici-Friede,
1933, published as "The Crime of Inspector Maigret" in *In-
troducing Inspector Maigret,* Hurst & Blackett, translation
by Tony White published as *Maigret and the Hundred Gib-
bets,* Penguin, 1963, published as *Maigret et le Pendu de
Saint-Pholien,* edited by Geoffrey Goodall, St. Martin's,
1965.
Un Crime en Hollande, Fayard, 1931, translation by Sainsbury
published as "A Crime in Holland" in *Maigret Abroad,*
Harcourt, 1940, published as *A Crime in Holland* [with] *A
Face for a Clue,* Penguin, 1952.
La Tete d'un homme (L'Homme de la Tour Eiffel), Fayard,
1931, translation by Sainsbury published as "A Battle of
Nerves" in *The Patience of Maigret,* George Routledge,
1939, Harcourt, 1940, published as *A Battle of Nerves* [with]
At the Gai-Moulin, Penguin, 1950, published as *Maigret's
War of Nerves,* Harcourt, 1986.
L'Affaire Saint Fiacre, Fayard, 1932, translation by Ludwig pub-
lished as "The Saint-Fiacre Affair" in *Maigret Keeps a Ren-
dezvous,* George Routledge, 1940, Harcourt, 1941, translation by Baldick published as *Maigret Goes Home,* Penguin,
1967.
Chez les Flamands, Fayard, 1932, translation by Sainsbury pub-
lished as "The Flemish Shop" in *Maigret to the Rescue,*
George Routledge, 1940, Harcourt, 1941.
Le Fou de Bergerac, Fayard, 1932, translation by Sainsbury pub-
lished as "The Madman of Bergerac" in *Maigret Travels
South,* Harcourt, 1940.
La Guinguette a deux sous, Fayard, 1932, translation by Sains-
bury published as "Guinguette by the Seine" in *Maigret to
the Rescue,* George Routledge, 1940, Harcourt, 1941.
Liberty Bar, Fayard, 1932, translation by Sainsbury published as
"Liberty Bar" in *Maigret Travels South,* Harcourt, 1940.
L'Ombre Chinoise, Fayard, 1932, translation published as *The
Shadow in the Courtyard* [with] *The Crime at Lock 14,*
Covici-Friede, 1934, published in England as "The Shadow
in the Courtyard" in *The Triumph of Inspector Maigret,*
Hurst & Blackett, 1934, translation by Jean Stewart pub-
lished as *Maigret Mystified,* Penguin, 1965.
Le Port des brumes, Fayard, 1932, translation by Stuart Gilbert
published as "Death of a Harbormaster" in *Maigret and M.
L'Abbe,* George Routledge, 1941, Harcourt, 1942.
L'Ecluse no. 1, Fayard, 1933, translation by Ludwig published
as "The Lock at Charenton" in *Maigret Sits It Out,* Har-
court, 1941.
Maigret, Fayard, 1934, translation by Ludwig published as
"Maigret Returns" in *Maigret Sits It Out,* Harcourt, 1941.
Cecile est morte (also see below), Gallimard, 1942, translation by
Eileen Ellenbogen published as *Maigret and the Spinster,*
Harcourt, 1977.

Maigret et les Caves du Majestic (also see below), [France], 1942, translation by Caroline Hiller published as *Maigret and the Hotel Majestic,* Hamish Hamilton, 1977, Harcourt, 1978.

La Maison du juge (also see below), [France], c. 1942, translation by Ellenbogen published as *Maigret in Exile,* Hamish Hamilton, 1978, Harcourt, 1979.

Maigret a New York, Presses de la Cite, 1947, translation by Adrienne Foulke published as *Maigret in New York's Underworld,* Doubleday, 1955, published as *Inspector Maigret in New York's Underworld,* New American Library, 1956.

Maigret se fache, Presses de la Cite, 1947.

La Pipe de Maigret, Presses de la Cite, 1947, translation by Stewart published as *Maigret's Pipe,* Harcourt, 1985.

Maigret et son morte, Presses de la Cite, 1948, translation by Stewart published as *Maigret's Dead Man,* Doubleday, 1964 published as *Maigret's Special Murder,* Hamish Hamilton, 1964.

Les Vacances de Maigret, Presses de la Cite, 1948, translation by Sainsbury published as *Maigret on Holiday,* Routledge & Kegan Paul, 1950, published as *No Vacation for Maigret,* Doubleday, 1953.

Maigret chez le coroner, Presses de la Cite, 1949, translation by Francis Keene published as *Maigret at the Coroner's,* Harcourt, 1980 (published in England as *Maigret and the Coroner,* Hamish Hamilton, 1980).

Maigret et la vieille dame, Presses de la Cite, 1949, translation by Robert Brain published as *Maigret and the Old Lady,* Hamish Hamilton, 1958.

Mon ami Maigret, Presses de la Cite, 1949, translation by Nigel Ryan published as *My Friend Maigret,* Hamish Hamilton, published as *The Methods of Maigret,* Doubleday, 1957.

La Premier Enquette de Maigret, 1913, Presses de la Cite, 1949, translation by Robert Brain published as *Maigret's First Case,* Hamish Hamilton, 1965.

L'Amie de Mine Maigret, Presses de la Cite, 1950, translation by Helen Sebba published as *Madame Maigret's Own Case,* Doubleday, 1959, published as *Madame Maigret's Friend* (also see below), Hamish Hamilton, 1960.

Les Petits Cochons sans queues, Presses de la Cite, 1950, published as *Maigret et les petits cochons sans queues,* 1957.

Les Memoires de Maigret, Presses de la Cite, 1951, translation by Stewart published as *Maigret's Memoires,* Hamish Hamilton, 1963, Harcourt, 1985.

Maigret en mueble, Presses de la Cite, 1951, translation by Robert Brain published as *Maigret Takes a Room,* Hamish Hamilton, 1960, published as *Maigret Rents a Room,* Doubleday, 1961.

Maigret et la grande perche, Presses de la Cite, 1951, translation by J. Maclaren-Ross published as *Maigret and the Burglar's Wife,* Hamish Hamilton, 1955, published as *Inspector Maigret and the Burglar's Wife,* Doubleday, 1956.

Les Memories de Maigret, Presses de la Cite, 1951, translation by Stewart published as *Maigret's Memories,* Hamish Hamilton, 1963.

Maigret, Longnon et les gangsters, Presses de la Cite, 1952, translation by Louise Varese published as *Maigret and the Killers,* Doubleday, 1954, published as *Maigret and the Gangsters,* Hamish Hamilton, 1974.

Le Revolver de Maigret, Presses de la Cite, 1952, translation by Ryan published as *Maigret's Revolver,* Doubleday, 1956, reprinted, Harcourt, 1984.

Maigret et l'homme du banc, Presses de la Cite, 1953, translation by Ellenbogen published as *Maigret and the Man on the Bench,* Harcourt, 1975 (published in England as *Maigret and the Man on the Boulevard,* Hamish Hamilton, 1975).

Maigret a peur, Presses de la Cite, 1953, translation by Margaret Duff published as *Maigret Afraid,* Hamish Hamilton, 1961, Harcourt, 1983, published as *Maigret se trompe,* Presses de la Cite, 1953, translation by Alan Hodge published as "Maigret's Mistake" in *Maigret Right and Wrong,* Hamish Hamilton, 1957, published as *Maigret's Mistake,* Harcourt, 1988.

Maigret a l'ecole, Presses de la Cite, 1954, translation by Woodward published as *Maigret Goes to School,* Hamish Hamilton, 1957, Harcourt, 1988.

Maigret chez le ministre, privately printed, 1954, translation by Moura Budberg published as *Maigret and the Calame Report,* Harcourt, 1969, reprinted, 1987 (published in England as *Maigret and the Minister,* Hamish Hamilton, 1969).

Maigret et la jeune morte, Presses de la Cite, 1954, translation by Woodward published as *Inspector Maigret and the Dead Girl,* Doubleday, 1955 (published in England as *Maigret and the Young Girl,* Hamish Hamilton, 1955).

Maigret et le corps sans tete, privately printed, 1955, translation by Ellenbogen published as *Maigret and the Headless Corpse,* Hamish Hamilton, 1967, Harcourt, 1968, reprinted, 1985.

Maigret tend un piege, Presses de la Cite, 1955, translation by Woodward published as *Maigret Sets a Trap,* Hamish Hamilton, 1965, Harcourt, 1972.

Un Echec de Maigret, Presses de la Cite, 1956, translation by Woodward published as *Maigret's Failure,* Hamish Hamilton, 1962.

Maigret s'amuse, Presses de la Cite, 1957, translation by Richard Brain published as *Maigret's Little Joke,* Hamish Hamilton, 1957, published as *None of Maigret's Business,* Doubleday, 1958.

Maigret voyage, Presses de la Cite, 1958, translation by Stewart published as *Maigret and the Millionaires,* Harcourt, 1974.

Les Scrupules de Maigret, Presses de la Cite, 1959, translation by Robert Eglesfield published as *Maigret Has Scruples,* Hamish Hamilton, 1959, Harcourt, 1988, published as "Maigret Has Scruples" in *Versus Inspector Maigret,* Doubleday, 1960, published as *Maigret Has Scruples* [with] *Maigret and the Reluctant Witness,* Ace Books, 1962.

Une Confidence de Maigret, Presses de la Cite, 1959, translation by Lyn Moir published as *Maigret Has Doubts,* Hamish Hamilton, 1968, Harcourt, 1982.

Maigret et les temoins recalcitrants, Presses de la Cite, 1959, translation by Woodward published as "Maigret and the Reluctant Witness" in *Versus Inspector Maigret,* Doubleday, 1960.

Maigret aux assises, Presses de la Cite, 1960, translation by Robert Brain published as *Maigret in Court,* Hamish Hamilton, 1961, Avon, 1988.

Maigret et les vieillards, Presses de la Cite, 1960, translation by Eglesfield published as *Maigret in Society,* Hamish Hamilton, 1962.

Maigret et le voleur paresseux, Presses de la Cite, 1961, translation by Woodward published as *Maigret and the Lazy Burglar,* Hamish Hamilton, 1963.

Maigret et les braves gens, Presses de la Cite, 1962, translation by Helen Thomson published as *Maigret and the Black Sheep,* Harcourt, 1976.

Maigret et le client du samedi, Presses de la Cite, 1962, translation by White published as *Maigret and the Saturday Caller,* Hamish Hamilton, 1964.

Maigret et l'inspecteur malgracieux, Presses de la Cite, 1962.

La Colere de Maigret, Presses de la Cite, 1963, translation by Eglesfield published as *Maigret Loses His Temper,* Hamish Hamilton, 1965, Harcourt, 1974.

Maigret et le clochard, Presses de la Cite, 1963, translation by Stewart published as *Maigret and the Bum,* Harcourt, 1973 (published in England as *Maigret and the Dosser,* Hamish Hamilton, 1973).

Maigret et le fantome, Presses de la Cite, 1964, translation by Ellenbogen published as *Maigret and the Apparition,* Harcourt, 1976 (published in England as *Maigret and the Ghost,* Hamish Hamilton, 1976).

Maigret se defend, Presses de la Cite, 1964, translation by Alistair Hamilton published as *Maigret on the Defensive* (also see below), Hamish Hamilton, 1966, Avon, 1987.

La Patience de Maigret, Presses de la Cite, 1965, translation by Hamilton published as *The Patience of Maigret* (also see below), Hamish Hamilton, 1966, published as *Maigret Bides His Time,* Harcourt, 1985.

Maigret et l'affair Nahour, Presses de la Cite, 1966, translation by Hamilton published as *Maigret and the Nahour Case,* Hamish Hamilton, 1967, Harcourt, 1986.

Le Voleur de Maigret, Presses de la Cite, 1967, translation by Ryan published as *Maigret's Pickpocket* (also see below), Harcourt, 1968, reprinted, 1985.

L'Ami d'enfance de Maigret, Presses de la Cite, 1968, translation by Ellenbogen published as *Maigret's Boyhood Friend,* Harcourt, 1970.

Maigret a Vichy, Presses de la Cite, 1968, translation by Ellenbogen published as *Maigret in Vichy,* Harcourt, 1969, reprinted, 1984 (published in England as *Maigret Takes the Waters* [also see below], Hamish Hamilton, 1969).

Maigret hesite, Presses de la Cite, 1968, translation by Moir published as *Maigret Hesitates* (also see below), Harcourt, 1970, reprinted, 1986.

Maigret et le tueur, Presses de la Cite, 1969, translation by Moir published as *Maigret and the Killer* (also see below), Harcourt, 1971, published as *Le Meurtre d'un etudiant,* edited by Frederick Ernst, Holt, 1971.

La Folle de Maigret, Presses de la Cite, 1970, translation by Ellenbogen published as *Maigret and the Madwoman,* Harcourt, 1972.

Maigret et le marchand de vin, Presses de la Cite, 1970, translation by Ellenbogen published as *Maigret and the Wine Merchant,* Harcourt, 1971.

Maigret et l'homme tout seul, Presses de la Cite, 1971, translation by Ellenbogen published as *Maigret and the Loner,* Harcourt, 1975.

Maigret et l'indicateur, Presses de la Cite, 1971, translation by Moir published as *Maigret and the Informer,* Harcourt, 1972 (published in England as *Maigret and the Flea,* Hamish Hamilton, 1972).

Maigret et Monsieur Charles, Presses de la Cite, 1972, translation by Marianne A. Sinclair published as *Maigret and Monsieur Charles,* Hamish Hamilton, 1973.

Maigret on the Riviera (originally published in France, 1940), translation by Sainsbury, Harcourt, 1988.

Maigret and the Fortuneteller (originally published in France, 1944), translation by Sainsbury, Harcourt, 1989.

Also author of *Maigret au "Picratts,"* Presses de la Cite, translation by Cornelia Schaffer published as *Inspector Maigret and the Strangled Stripper,* Doubleday, 1956, translation by Woodward published as "Maigret in Montmartre" in *Maigret Right and Wrong,* Hamish Hamilton, 1954.

NOVELS

Le Relais d'Alsace, Fayard, 1931, translation by Gilbert published as "The Man From Everywhere" in *Maigret and M. Labbe,* George Routledge, 1941, Harcourt, 1942, published

as *The Man from Everywhere* [with] *Newhaven-Dieppe,* Penguin, 1952.

Le Passageur du "Polarlys," Fayard, 1932, translation by Gilbert published as "The Mystery of the 'Polarlys' " in *Two Latitudes,* George Routledge, 1942, Harcourt, 1943, translation by Victor Kosta published as "Danger at Sea" in *On Land and Sea,* Hanover House, 1954.

Les Treize Coupables, Fayard, 1932.

Les Treize Enigmes, Fayard, 1932.

Les Treize Mysteries, Fayard, 1932.

L'Ane rouge, Fayard, 1933, translated by Stewart published as *The Nightclub,* Harcourt, 1979.

Le Coup de lune, Fayard, 1933, translation by Gilbert published as "Tropic Moon" in *Two Latitudes,* George Routledge, 1942, Harcourt, 1943, published as *Tropic Moon,* Berkeley, 1958.

Les Fiancailles de M. Hire, Fayard, 1933, translation by Woodward published as "Mr. Hire's Engagement" in *The Sacrifice,* Hamish Hamilton, 1958.

Les Gens d'en face, Fayard, 1933, translation by Sainsbury published as *The Window Over the Way* [with] *The Gendarme's Report,* Routledge & Kegan Paul, 1951, translation by Kosta published as "Danger Ashore" in *On Land and Sea,* Hanover House, 1954, translation by Baldick published as *The Window Over the Way,* Penguin, 1966.

Le Haut-mal, Fayard, 1933, translation by Gilbert published as "The Woman in the Grey House" in *Affairs of Destiny,* George Routledge, 1942, Harcourt, 1944.

La Maison du Canal, Fayard, 1933, translation by Sainsbury published as *The House by the Canal* [with] *The Ostenders,* Routledge & Kegan Paul, 1952.

Les Suicides, Nouvelle Revue Francaise, 1934, translation by Gilbert published as "One Way Out" in *Escape in Vain,* George Routledge, 1943, Harcourt, 1944.

L'Homme de Londres, Fayard, 1934, translation by Gilbert published as "Newhaven-Dieppe" in *Affairs of Destiny,* George Routledge, 1942, Harcourt, 1944, published as *Newhaven-Dieppe* [with] *The Man From Everywhere,* Penguin, 1952.

La Locataire, Nouvelle Revue Francaise, 1934, translation by Gilbert published as "The Lodger" in *Escape in Vain,* George Routledge, 1943, Harcourt, 1944, published as *The Lodger,* Harcourt, 1983.

Les Clients d'Avrenos, Nouvelle Revue Francaise, 1935.

Les Pitard, Nouvelle Revue Francaise, 1935, translation by Sainsbury published as *A Wife at Sea* [with] *The Murderer,* Routledge & Kegan Paul, 1949.

Quartier Negre, Nouvelle Revue Francaise, 1935.

Les Demoiselles de Concarneau, Nouvelle Revue Francaise, 1936, translation by Gilbert published as "The Breton Sisters" in *Havoc by Accident,* Harcourt, 1943.

L'Evade, Nouvelle Revue Francaise, 1936, translation by Sainsbury published as *The Disintegration of J.P.G.,* George Routledge, 1937.

Long cours, Nouvelle Revue Francaise, 1936, translation by Ellenbogen as *The Long Exile,* Harcourt, 1983.

45 a l'hombre, Nouvelle Revue Francaise, 1936.

L'Assassin, Nouvelle Revue Francaise, 1937, translation by Sainsbury published as *The Murderer* [with] *A Wife at Sea,* Routledge & Kegan Paul, 1947, published as *The Murderer,* Harcourt, 1986.

Le Blanc a lunettes, Nouvelle Revue Francaise, 1937, translation by Gilbert published as "Tatala" in *Havoc by Accident,* Harcourt, 1943.

Faubourg, Nouvelle Revue Francaise, 1937, translation by Gilbert published as "Home Town" in *On the Danger Line,* Harcourt, 1944.

Le Testament Donadieu, Nouvelle Revue Francaise, 1937, translation by Gilbert published as *The Shadow Falls,* Harcourt, 1945.

Ceux de la soif, Nouvelle Revue Francaise, 1938.

Chemin sans issue, Nouvelle Revue Francaise, 1938, translation by Gilbert published as *Blind Alley,* Reynal & Hitchcock, 1946, published as "Blind Alley" in *Lost Moorings,* George Routledge, 1946.

Le Cheval blanc, Nouvelle Revue Francaise, 1938, translated by Norman Denny as *The White Horse Inn,* Harcourt, 1980.

L'Homme qui regardait passer les trains, Nouvelle Revue Francaise, 1938, translation by Gilbert published as *The Man Who Watched the Trains Go By,* Musson, 1942, Reynal & Hitchcock, 1946.

La Marie du port, Nouvelle Revue Francaise, 1938, translation by Sainsbury published as *A Chit of a Girl* [with] *Justice,* Routledge & Kegan Paul, 1949, published as *The Girl in Waiting* [with] *Justice,* Pan Books, 1957.

La Mauvaise Etoile, Nouvelle Revue Francaise, 1938.

Monsieur La Souris, Nouvelle Revue Francaise, 1938, translation by Sainsbury published as *Monsieur La Souris* [with] *Poisoned Relations,* Routledge & Kegan Paul, 1950, translation by Baldick published as *The Mouse,* Penguin, 1966.

Les Rescapes du "Telmaque," Nouvelle Revue Francaise, 1938, translation by Gilbert published as *The Survivors* [with] *Black Rain,* Routledge & Kegan Paul, 1949, published as *The Survivors,* Harcourt, 1985.

Les Soeurs Lacroix, Nouvelle Revue Francaise, 1938, translation by Sainsbury published as *Poisoned Relations* [with] *Monsieur La Sours,* Routledge & Kegan Paul, 1950.

Le Suspect, Nouvelle Revue Francaise, 1938, translation by Gilbert published as "The Green Thermos" in *On the Danger Line,* Harcourt, 1944.

Touriste de bananes (ou, Les Dimanches de Tahiti), Nouvelle Revue Francaise, 1938, translation by Gilbert published as "Banana Tourist" in *Lost Moorings,* George Routledge, 1946.

Les Trois Crimes de mes amis, Nouvelle Revue Francaise, 1938.

Le Bourgmestre de Furnes, Nouvelle Revue Francaise, 1939, translation by Sainsbury published as *The Bourgomaster of Furnes,* Routledge & Kegan Paul, 1952.

Chez Krull, Nouvelle Revue Francaise, 1939, translation by Woodward published as "Chez Krull" in *A Sense of Guilt,* Hamish Hamilton, 1955, published as *Chez Krull,* New English Library, 1966.

Le Coup de vague, Nouvelle Revue Francaise, 1939.

Les Inconnus dans la maison, Nouvelle Revue Francaise, 1940, translation by Sainsbury published as *Strangers in the House,* Routledge & Kegan Paul, 1951, Doubleday, 1954.

Malempin, Nouvelle Revue Francaise, 1940, translation by Isabel Quigly published as *The Family Lie,* Hamish Hamilton, 1978.

Bergelon, Nouvelle Revue Francaise, 1941, translation by Ellenbogen published as *The Delivery,* Harcourt, 1981.

Cour d'Assises, Nouvelle Revue Francaise, 1941, translation by Sainsbury published as *Justice* [with] *A Chit of a Girl,* Routledge & Kegan Paul, 1949, published as *Justice,* Harcourt, 1983.

Il pleut bergere, Nouvelle Revue Francaise, 1941, translation by Sainsbury published as *Black Rain,* Reynal & Hitchcock, 1947, published as *Black Rain* [with] *The Survivors,* Routledge & Kegan Paul, 1949.

La Maison des sept jeunes filles, Gallimard, 1941.

L'Outlaw, Gallimard, 1941, translation by Howard Curtis published as *The Outlaw,* Harcourt, 1986.

Le Voyageur de la Toussaint, Nouvelle Revue Francaise, 1941, translation by Sainsbury published as *Strange Inheritance,* Routledge & Kegan Paul, 1970.

Les Fantomes du chapelier, Presses de la Cite, 1941, translation by Ryan published as "The Hatter's Ghost" in *The Judge and the Hatter,* Hamish Hamilton, 1956, translation by Willard Trask published as *The Hatter's Phantoms,* Harcourt, 1976.

Le Fils Cardinaud, 1942, translation by Richard Brain published as "Young Cardinaud" in *The Sacrifice,* Hamish Hamilton, 1956, published as *Young Cardinaud,* New English Library, 1966.

Oncle Charles s'est enferme, Nouvelle Revue Francaise, 1942, translation published as *Uncle Charles Has Locked Himself In,* Harcourt, 1987.

La Verite sur Bebe Donge, Nouvelle Revue Francaise, 1942, translation by Sainsbury published as *The Trial of Bebe Donge,* Routledge & Kegan Paul, 1952, translation by Varese published as "I Take This Woman" in *Satan's Children,* Prentice-Hall, 1953.

La Veuve couderc, Nouvelle Revue Francaise, 1942, translation by Robert J. P. Hewitton (under pseudonym John Petrie) published as *Ticket of Leave,* Routledge & Kegan Paul, 1954, published as *The Widow* [with] *Magician,* Doubleday, 1955.

La Rapport du gendarme, Nouvelle Revue Francaise, 1944, translation by Sainsbury published as *The Gendarme's Report* [with] *Window Over the Way,* Routledge & Kegan Paul, 1951.

L'Aine des ferchaux, Gallimard, 1945, translation by Sainsbury published as *Magnet of Doom,* George Routledge, 1948, published as *The First Born,* Reynal & Hitchcock, 1949.

Le Fenetre des Rouet, Editions de la Jeune Parque, 1945, translation by Hewitton (under pseudonym John Petrie) published as *Across the Street,* Routledge & Kegan Paul, 1954.

La Fuite de Monsieur Monde, Editions de la Jeune Parque, 1945, translation by Stewart published as *Monsieur Monde Vanishes,* Hamish Hamilton, 1967, Harcourt, 1977.

Je me souviens, Presses de la Cite, 1945.

Trois Chambres a Manhattan, Presses de la Cite, 1945, translation by Lawrence G. Blochman published as *Three Beds in Manhattan,* Doubleday, 1964.

Le Cercle des Mahe, Gallimard, 1946.

Les Noces de Poitiers, Gallimard, 1946, translation by Ellenbogen published as *The Couple from Poitiers,* Harcourt, 1985.

Au Bout du rouleau, Presses de la Cite, 1947.

Le Clan des Ostendais, Gallimard, 1947, translation by Sainsbury published as *The Ostenders* [with] *The House by the Canal,* Routledge & Kegan Paul, 1952.

Lettre a mon juge, Presses de la Cite, 1947, translation by Varese published as *Act of Passion,* Prentice-Hall, 1952.

Le Passager clandestin, Editions de la Jeune Parque, 1947, translation by Ryan published as *The Stowaway,* Hamish Hamilton, 1957.

Le Bilan maletras, Gallimard, 1948, translation by Emily Read published as *The Reckoning,* Harcourt, 1984.

Le Destin des Malou, Presses de la Cite, 1948, translation by Dennis George published as *The Fate of the Malous,* Hamish Hamilton, 1962.

La Jument perdu, Presses de la Cite, 1948.

La Neige etait sale, Presses de la Cite, 1948, translation by Varese published as *The Snow Was Black,* Prentice-Hall, 1950, translation by Hewitton (under pseudonym John Petrie) published as *The Stain on the Snow*, Routledge & Kegan Paul, 1953.

Pedigree, Presses de la Cite, 1948, translation by Baldick published as *Pedigree*, Hamish Hamilton, 1962.

Le Fond de la bouteille, Presses de la Cite, 1949, translation by Schaffer published as "The Bottom of the Bottle" in *Tidal Wave*, Doubleday, 1954 (published in England as *The Bottom of the Bottle*, Hamish Hamilton, 1977).

Les Quatre Jours du pauvre homme, Presses de la Cite, 1949, translation by Varese published as "Four Days in a Lifetime" in *Satan's Children*, Prentice-Hall, 1953, published as *Four Days in a Lifetime*, Hamish Hamilton, 1977.

L'Enterrement de Monsieur Bouvet, Presses de la Cite, 1950, translation by Eugene MacCowan published as "The Burial of Monsieur Bouvet" in *Destinations*, Doubleday, 1955, published as *Inquest on Bouvet*, Hamish Hamilton, 1958.

Un Nouveau dans la ville, Presses de la Cite, 1950.

Tante Jeanne, Presses de la Cite, 1950, translation by Sainsbury published as *Aunt Jeanne*, Routledge & Kegan Paul, 1953.

Les Volets verts, Presses de la Cite, 1950, translation by Varese published as *The Heart of a Man*, Prentice-Hall, 1951 (published in England as "The Heart of a Man" in *A Sense of Guilt*, Hamish Hamilton 1955).

Marie qui louche, Presses de la Cite, 1951, translation by Varese published as *The Girl with a Squint*, Harcourt, 1978.

Le Temps d'Anais, Presses de la Cite, 1951, translation by Varese published as *The Girl in His Past*, Prentice-Hall, 1952.

Une Vie comme neuve, Presses de la Cite, 1951, translation by Joanne Richardson published as *A New Lease on Life*, Doubleday, 1963.

Les Freres Rico, Presses de la Cite, 1952, translation by Ernst Pawel published as "The Brothers Rico" in *Tidal Wave*, Doubleday, 1954 (published in England as "The Brothers Rico" in *Violent Ends*, Hamish Hamilton, 1964).

La Morte de Belle, Presses de la Cite, 1952, translation by Varese published as "Belle" in *Tidal Wave*, Doubleday, 1954 (published in England as "Belle" in *Violent Ends*, Hamish Hamilton, 1954).

Antoine et Julie, Presses de la Cite, 1953, translation by Sebba published as *Magician* [with] *The Widow*, Doubleday, 1955, published as *Magician*, Berkeley, 1956 (published in England as *The Magician*, Hamish Hamilton, 1974).

L'Escalier de fer, Presses de la Cite, 1953, translation by Ellenbogen published as *The Iron Staircase*, Hamish Hamilton, 1963, Harcourt, 1977.

Feux Rouges, Presses de la Cite, 1953, translation by Denny published as "The Hitchhiker" in *Destinations*, Doubleday, 1955, published as "Red Lights" in *Danger Ahead*, Hamish Hamilton, 1955, published as *The Hitchhiker*, Signet, 1957.

Crime impuni, Presses de la Cite, 1954, translation by Varese published as *Fugitive*, Doubleday, 1955, translation by White published as *Account Unsettled*, Hamish Hamilton, 1962.

Le Grand Bob, Presses de la Cite, 1954, translation by Eileen Lowe published as *Big Bob*, Hamish Hamilton, 1969.

L'Horloger d'Everton, Presses de la Cite, 1954, translation by Denny published as "The Watchmaker of Everton" in *Danger Ahead*, Hamish Hamilton, 1955, published as *The Watchmaker of Everton* [with] *Witnesses*, Doubleday, 1956.

Les Temoins, privately printed, 1954, translation by Budberg published as *Witnesses* [with] *The Watchmaker of Everton*, Doubleday, 1956 (published in England as "The Witnesses" in *The Judge and the Hatter*, Hamish Hamilton, 1956).

La Boule noire, Presses de la Cite, 1955.

Les Complices, Presses de la Cite, 1955, translation by Bernard Frechtman published as *The Accomplices* [with] *The Blue Room*, Harcourt, 1964, published as *The Accomplices*, Hamish Hamilton, 1966, Harcourt, 1977.

En Case de malheur, Presses de la Cite, 1956, translation by Sebba published as *In Case of Emergency*, Doubleday, 1958.

Le Fils, Presses de la Cite, 1957, translation by Woodward published as *The Son*, Hamish Hamilton, 1958.

Le Negre, Presses de la Cite, 1957, translation by Sebba published as *The Negro*, Hamish Hamilton, 1959.

Le Petit Homme d'Arkhangelsk, Presses de le Cite, 1957, translation by Ryan published as *The Little Man From Arkangel*, Hamish Hamilton, 1957, published as *The Little Man From Arkangel* [with] *Sunday*, Harcourt, 1966.

Le Passage de la Ligne, Presses de la Cite, 1958.

Le President, Presses de la Cite, 1958, translation by Woodward published as *The Premier*, Hamish Hamilton, 1961, published as *The Premier* [with] *The Train*, Harcourt, 1966.

Strip-Tease, Presses de la Cite, 1958, translation by Robert Brain published as *Striptease*, Hamish Hamilton, 1959.

Dimanche, Presses de la Cite, 1959, translation by Ryan published as *Sunday*, Hamish Hamilton, 1960, published as *Sunday* [with] *The Little Man From Arkangel*, Harcourt, 1966.

La Vieille, Presses de la Cite, 1959.

L'Ours en pluche, Presses de la Cite, 1960, translation by John Clay published as *Teddy Bear*, Hamish Hamilton, 1971, Harcourt, 1972.

Le Veuf, 1960, translation by Baldick published as *The Widower*, Hamish Hamilton, 1961.

Betty, Presses de la Cite, 1961, translation by Hamilton published as *Betty*, Harcourt, 1975.

Le Train, Presses de la Cite, 1961, translation by Baldick published as *The Train*, Hamish Hamilton, 1964, published as *The Train* [with] *The Premier*, Harcourt, 1966.

Les Autres, Presses de la Cite, 1962, translation by Hamilton published as *The House on Quai Notre Dame*, Harcourt, 1975 (published in England as *The Others*, Hamish Hamilton, 1975).

La Porte, Presses de la Cite, 1962, translation by Woodward published as *The Door*, Hamish Hamilton, 1964.

Les Anneaux de Bicetre, Presses de la Cite, 1963, translation by Stewart published as *The Patient*, Hamish Hamilton, 1963, published as *The Bells of Bicetre*, Harcourt, 1964.

La Chambre bleue, Presses de la Cite, 1964, translation by Ellenbogen published as *The Blue Room* [with] *The Accomplices*, Harcourt, 1964, published as *The Blue Room*, Hamish Hamilton, 1965.

L'Homme au petit chien, Presses de la Cite, 1964, translation by Stewart published as *The Man With the Little Dog*, Hamish Hamilton, 1965, Harcourt, 1989.

Le Petit Saint, Presses de la Cite, 1965, translation by Frechtman published as *The Little Saint*, Harcourt, 1965.

Le Train de Venise, Presses de la Cite, 1965, translation by Hamilton published as *The Venice Train*, Harcourt, 1974.

Le Confessional, Presses de la Cite, 1966, translation by Stewart published as *The Confessional*, Hamish Hamilton, 1967, Harcourt, 1968.

La Mort d'Auguste, Presses de la Cite, 1966, translation by Frechtman published as *The Old Man Dies*, Harcourt, 1967.

Le Chat, Presses de la Cite, 1967, translation by Frechtman published as *The Cat*, Harcourt, 1967.

Le Demenagement, Presses de la Cite, 1967, translation by Christopher Sinclair-Stevenson published as *The Move*,

Harcourt, 1968 (published in England as *The Neighbors,* Hamish Hamilton, 1968).

La Main, Presses de la Cite, 1968, translation by Budberg published as *The Man on the Bench in the Barn,* Harcourt, 1970.

La Prison, Presses de la Cite, 1968, translation by Moir published as *The Prison,* Harcourt, 1969.

Il y a encore des noisetiers, Presses de la Cite, 1969.

Novembre, Presses de la Cite, 1969, translation by Stewart published as *November,* Harcourt, 1970.

Le Riche Homme, Presses de la Cite, 1970, translation by Stewart published as *The Rich Man,* Harcourt, 1971.

Le Cage de verre, Presses de la Cite, 1971, translation by Antonia White published as *The Glass Cage,* Harcourt, 1973.

La Disparition d'Odile, Presses de la Cite, 1971, translation by Moir published as *The Disappearance of Odile,* Harcourt, 1972.

Les Innocents, Presses de la Cite, 1972, translation by Ellenbogen published as *The Innocents,* Hamish Hamilton, 1973, Harcourt, 1974.

The Rules of the Game, translation by Curtis, Harcourt, 1988.

UNDER PSEUDONYM GEORGES SIM

Au pont des arches, Benard (Liege), 1921.
Les Ridicules, Benard, 1921.
Les Larmes avant le bonheur, Ferenczi, 1925.
Le Feu s'eteint, Fayard, 1927, reprinted, 1954.
Les Voleurs de bavires (adventure), Tallindier, c. 1927, reprinted, 1954.
Defense d'aimer, Ferenczi, 1927.
Le Cercle de la soif (adventure), Ferenczi, 1927, published as *Le Cercle de la mort,* 1933.
Paris-Leste, Editions Paris-Plaisirs, 1927.
Un Monsieur libidineux, Editions Prima, 1927.
Les Coeurs perdus, Tallandier, 1928.
Le Secret des Lamas (adventure), Tallandier, 1928, reprinted, 1954.
Les Maudits du Pacifique (adventure), Tallandier, 1928, reprinted, 1954.
Le Monstre blanc de la terre de feu, Ferenczi, 1928, published (under pseudonym Christian Brulls) as *L'Ile de la desolation,* 1933.
Miss Baby, Fayard, 1928.
Le Semeur de larmes, Ferenczi, 1928.
Le Roi des glaces (adventure), Tallandier, 1928, reprinted, 1954.
Le Sousmarin dans la foret, Tallandier, 1928, reprinted, 1954.
La Maison sans soleil, Fayard, 1928, reprinted, 1954.
Aimer d'amour, Ferenczi, 1928.
Songes d'ete, Ferenczi, 1928.
Le Lac d'angoisse (adventure), Ferenczi, 1928, published (under pseudonym Christian Brulls) as *Le Lac des esclaves,* 1933.
Le Sang des gitanes, Ferenczi, 1928.
Chair de beaute, Fayard, 1928.
Les Memoires d'un prostitute, Editions Prima, 1929.
En Robe de mariee, Tallandier, 1929.
La Panthere borgne (adventure), "Panther"), Tallandier, 1929.
La Fiancee aux mains de glace, Fayard, 1929.
Les Bandits de Chicago (adventure), Fayard, 1929.
L'Ile des hommes roux (adventure), Tallandier, 1929.
Le Roi du Pacifique (adventure), Ferenczi, 1929, abridged edition published as *Le Bateau d'or,* Ferenczi, 1955.
Le Gorille-Roi, Tallandier, 1929.
Les Contrabaniers de l'alcool (adventure), Fayard, 1929.
La Femme qui tue, Fayard, 1929.
Destinees, Fayard, 1929, reprinted, 1954.

L'Ile des maudits (adventure), Ferenczi, c. 1929, abridged edition published as *Naufrage du "Pelican,"* 1933.
La Femme en deuil, Tallandier, 1929.
L'Oeil de l'Utah (adventure), Tallandier, 1930.
L'Homme qui tremble (adventure), Fayard, 1930.
Nez d'argent (adventure), Ferenczi, 1930, abridged edition published as *Le Paria des bois sauvages,* 1933.
Mademoiselle Million, Fayard, 1930, published as *Les Ruses de l'amour* 1954.
Le Pecheur de bouees (adventure), Tallandier, 1930.
Le Chinois de San-Francisco, Tallandier, 1930.
La Femme 47, Fayard, 1930.
Katia, Acrobate, Fayard, 1931.
L'Homme a la cigarette, Tallandier, 1931.
L'Homme de poire, Fayard, 1931, reprinted, 1952.
Les Errants, Fayard, 1931, reprinted, 1954.
La Maison de l'inquietude (crime novel), Tallandier, 1932.
L'Epave, Fayard, 1932, reprinted, 1952.
Matricule 12 (crime novel), Tallandier, 1932.
La Fiance du diable, Fayard, 1932.
La Femme rousse (crime novel), Tallandier, 1933.
Le Chateau des sables rouges, Tallandier, 1933.
Le Yacht fantome (adventure), originally published (under pseudonym Christian Brulls) as *Le Desert du froid qui tue,* Ferenczi, 1928), Ferenczi, 1933.
Deuxieme Bureau (crime novel), Tallandier, 1933.
Les Nains des cataractes (adventure), Tallandier, 1954.

NOVELS UNDER PSEUDONYM JEAN du PERRY

Le Roman d'une dactylo, Ferenczi, 1924.
Amour d'exile, Ferenczi, c. 1924.
L'Oiseau blesse, Ferenczi, 1925.
L'Heureuse fin, Ferenczi, 1925.
Pour la sauver, Ferenczi, 1925.
Ceux qu'on avait oubles . . ., [France], 1925.
Pour qu'il soit heureux, [France], 1925.
Amour Afrique, [France], 1925.
A l'assaut d'un coeur, [France], 1925.
L'Orgueil d'aimer, [France], 1926.
Celle qui est aimee, [France], 1926.
Les Yeux qui ordonnent, [France], 1926.
Que ma mere l'ignore, [France], 1926.
De la rue au bonheur, [France], 1926.
Un Peche de jeunesse, [France], 1926.
Lili Tristesse, [France], 1927.
Un Tout petit coeur, Editions du Livre National, 1927.
Le Fou d'amour, [France], 1928.
Coeur Exalte, [France], 1928.
Trois Coeurs dans la tempete, [France], 1928.
Les Amants de la mansarde, [France], 1928.
Un Jour de soleil, [France], 1928.
La Fille de l'autre, [France], 1929.
L'Amour et l'argent, [France], 1929.
Coeur de poupee, [France], 1929.
Une Femme a tue, [France], 1929.
Deux Coeurs de femme, [France], 1929.
L'Epave d'amour, [France], 1929.
Le Mirage de Paris, [France], 1929.
Celle qui passe, [France], 1930.
Petite Exile, [France], 1930.
Les Amants de malheur, [France], 1930.
La Femme ardente, [France], 1930.
La Porte close, [France], 1930.
Le Poupee brisee, [France], 1930.
Pauvre Amante, [France], 1931.

Le Reve qui meurt, F. Rouff, 1931.
Marie-Mystere, Fayard, 1931.

NOVELS UNDER PSEUDONYM GEORGES-MARTIN GEORGES

L'Orgueil qui meurt, Editions du Livre National, 1925.
Un Soir de veritage, Ferenczi, 1928.
Brin d'amour, Ferenczi, 1928.
Les Coeurs vides, Ferenczi, 1928.
Cabotine . . ., Ferenczi, 1928.
Amier, Mourir, Ferenczi, 1928.
Voleuse d'amour, Ferenczi, 1929.
Une Ombre dans la nuit, Ferenczi, 1929.
Nuit de Paris, Ferenczi, 1929.
La Victime, Ferenczi, 1929.
Un Nid d'amour, Ferenczi, 1930.
Bobette, mannequin, Ferenczi, 1930.
La Puissance du souvenir, Ferenczi, 1930.
Le Bonheur de Lili, Ferenczi, 1930.
Le Double Vie, Ferenczi, 1931.

NOVEL UNDER PSEUDONYM GEORGES d'ISLY

Etoile de cinema, F. Rouff, 1925.

NOVELS UNDER PSEUDONYM CHRISTIAN BRULLS

La Pretresse des vaudoux (adventure), Tallandier, 1925.
Nox l'insaissable (crime novel), Ferenczi, 1926.
Se Ma Tsien, le sacrificateur (adventure), Tallandier, 1926.
Le Desert du froid qui tue (adventure), Ferenczi, 1928, published (under pseudonym Georges Sim) as *Le Yacht fantome* 1933.
Mademoiselle X . . ., Fayard, 1928.
Annie, danseuse, Ferenczi, 1928.
Dolorosa, Fayard, 1928.
Les Adolescents passionnes, Fayard, 1929.
L'Amant sans nom, Fayard, 1929.
Un Drame au Pole Sud, (adventure), Fayard, 1929.
Les Pirates du Texas (adventure), Ferenczi, 1929, published as *La Chasse au whiskey,* 1934.
Capitan S.O.S. (adventure), Fayard, 1929.
Jacques d'Antifer, roi des Iles du Vent (adventure), [France], 1930, published as *L'Heritier du Corsaire,* 1934.
L'Inconnue, Fayard, 1930.
Train de nuit, Fayard, 1930.
Pour venger son pere, Ferenczi, 1931.
La Maison de la haine, Fayard, 1931.
La Maison des disparus, Fayard, 1931.
Les Forcats de Paris, Fayard, 1932.
La Figurante, Fayard, 1932.
Fievre, Fayard, 1932.
L'Ile de la desolation (adventure; originally published [under pseudonym Georges Sim] as *Le Monstre blanc de la terre de feu,* 1928) Ferenczi, 1933.
Le Lac des esclaves, (originally published [under pseudonym Georges Sim] as *Le Lac d'angoisse,* 1928), Ferenczi, 1933.
L'Evasion, Fayard, 1934.
L'Ils empoisonne (adventure), Ferenczi, 1937.
Seul parmi les gorilles (adventure), Ferenczi, 1937.

NOVELS UNDER PSEUDONYM GOM GUT

Un Viol aux q'uat'z arts, Prima, 1925.
Perversites frivotes, Prima, 1925.
Au grand 13, Prima, 1925.
Plaisirs charnes, Prima, 1925.
Aux vingt-huit negresses, Prima, 1925.
La Noche a Montmartre, Prima, 1925.
Liquettes au vent, Prima, 1926.

Une Petite tres sensuelle, Prima, 1926.
Orgies bourgoise, Prima, 1926.
L'Homme aux douze etreintes, Prima, 1927.
Entreintes passionnees, Prima, 1927.
Une Mome dessalee, Prima, 1927.
L'Amant fantome, Prima, 1928.
L'Amour a Montparnasse, Prima, 1928.
Les Distractions d'Helene, Prima, 1928.

NOVELS UNDER PSEUDONYM PLICK ET PLOCK

Voluptueues Etreintes, Prima, 1925.
Le Cheri de Tantine, Prima, 1925.

NOVELS UNDER PSEUDONYM LUC DORSAN

Histoire d'un pantalon, Prima, 1926.
Nini violce, Prima, 1926.
Nichonnette, Prima, 1926.
Memoires d'un vieux suiveur, Prima, 1926.
Nuit de noces, doubles noces, les noces ardents, Prima, 1926.
Le Pucelle de Benouville, Prima, Ferenczi, 1928.

UNDER PSEUDONYM BOBETTE

Bobette et ses satyres, Ferenczi, 1928.

UNDER PSEUDONYM KIM

Un Petit Poison, Ferenczi, 1928.

NOVELS UNDER PSEUDONYM JACQUES DERSONNES

Un Seul Basier, Ferenczi, 1928.
La Merveilleuse Adventure, Ferenczi, 1929.
Les Etapes du Mensonge, Ferenczi, 1930.
Baisers mortels, Ferenczi, 1930.
Victime de son fils, Ferenczi, 1931.

NOVELS UNDER PSEUDONYM JEAN DORSANGE

L'Amour meconnu, Ferenczi, 1928.
Celle qui revient, Ferenczi, 1929.
Coeur de jeune fille, Ferenczi, 1930.
Soeurette, Ferenczi, 1930.
Les Chercheurs de bonheur, Ferenczi, 1930.

NOVELS UNDER PSEUDONYM GASTON VIALIS

Un Petit Corps blesse, Ferenczi, 1928.
Hair a force d'amier, Ferenczi, 1928.
Le Parfum du passe, Ferenczi, 1929.
Lili-sourire, Ferenczi, 1930.
Folie d'un soir, Ferenczi, 1930.
Ame de jeune fille, Ferenczi, 1931.

NOVEL UNDER PSEUDONYM GERMAIN d'ANTIBES

Helas!, Ferenczi, 1929.

NOVEL UNDER PSEUDONYM JEAN DOSSAGE

Les Deux Maitresses, Ferenczi, 1929.

NOVEL UNDER PSEUDONYM G. VIOLIS

Trop belle pour elle!, Ferenczi, 1929.

SHORT STORIES

Les Sept Minutes, Nouvelle Revue Francaise, 1938.
Maigret revient, Nouvelle Revue Francaise, 1942.
Le Petit Docteur, Nouvelle Revue Francaise, 1943, translation by Stewart published as *The Little Doctor,* Harcourt, 1978.
Les Nouvelles Enquetes de Maigret, Nouvelle Revue Francaise, 1944.

Signe Picpus, Nouvelle Revue Francaise, 1944, translation by Sainsbury published as *To Any Lengths,* Penguin.

Les Dossiers de l'agence O, Nouvelle Revue Francaise, 1945.

Le Commissaire Maigret et L'Inspecteur Malchanceaux (four novellas), Presses de la Cite, 1947.

Un Noel de Maigret, Presses de la Cite, 1951, translation by Stewart published as *Maigret's Christmas: Nine Stories,* Hamish Hamilton, 1976, Harcourt, 1977.

Les Tournants dangereux (four novellas), Appleton, 1953.

Le Bateau d'Emile, Gallimard, 1954.

The Short Cases of Inspector Maigret, Doubleday, 1959.

La Rue aux trois poussins, Presses de la Cite, 1963.

A Maigret Quartet, Hamish Hamilton, 1964.

Les Enquetes du Commissaire Maigret, Presses de la Cite, Volume 1, 1966, Volume 2, 1967.

Maigret Triumphant, Hamish Hamilton, 1969.

Choix de Simenon Appleton, 1972.

La Piste du Hollandais, Presses de la Cite, 1973.

Maigret Victorious, Hamish Hamilton, 1975.

Complete Maigret Short Stories, two volumes, Hamish Hamilton, 1976, Harcourt, 1977.

Maigret and the Mad Killers, Doubleday, 1980.

OTHER

Je me souviens, Presses de la Cite, 1945, reprinted, 1970.

Lone Cours dur les rivieres et canaux (illustrated nonfiction), Editions Dynamo (Liege), 1952.

Le Roman de l'homme (lectures and essays), Presses de la Cite, 1959, translation by Frechtman published as *The Novel of Man,* Harcourt, 1964.

La Femme en France (illustrated nonfiction), Presses de la Cite, 1960.

Entretien avec Roger Stephanie (interview), Radio Television Francaise, 1963.

Ma Conviction profonde (unedited writings), Callier, 1963.

Le Paris de Simenon (illustrated nonfiction), Tehou, 1969, translation published as *Simenon's Paris,* Dial, 1970.

Quand j'etais vieux (autobiography), translation by Helen Eustis published as *When I Was Old,* Harcourt, 1971.

Lettre a ma mere (autobiography), Presses de la Cite, 1974, translation by Ralph Manheim published as *Letter to My Mother,* Harcourt, 1976.

Un Homme comme un autre (biography), Presses de la Cite, 1975.

(With Francis Lacassin and Sigaux) *A la decouverte de la France,* Union General d'Editions, 1976.

(With Lacassin and Sigaux) *A la recherche de l'homme nu,* Union General d'Editions, 1976.

DIARIES

Des Traces de pas, Presses de la Cite, 1975.

Vent du nord, vent du sud, Presses de la Cite, 1976.

Les Petits Hommes, Presses de la Cite, 1976.

De la cave au grenier, Presses de la Cite, 1977.

A l'abri de notre arbre, Presses de la Cite, 1977.

Un Banc au soleil, Presses de la Cite, 1977.

Tant que je suis vivant, Presses de la Cite, 1978.

Vacances obligatoires, Presses de la Cite, 1978.

A quoi bon jurer?, Presses de la Cite, 1979.

Au-dela de ma port-fenetre, Presses de la Cite, 1979.

Je suis reste un enfant de choeur, Presses de la Cite, 1979.

Point-virgule, Presses de la Cite, 1979.

Les Libertes qu'il nous reste, Presses de la Cite, 1980.

On dit que j'ai soixante-quinze ans, Presses de la Cite, 1980.

Le Prix d'un homme, Presses de la Cite, 1980.

Quand vient le froid, Presses de la Cite, 1980.

Le Femme endormie, Presses de la Cite, 1981.

Jour et Nuit, Presses de la Cite, 1981.

Memoires intimes, Presses de la Cite, 1981, translation by Harold J. Salemson published as *Intimate Memoires,* Harcourt, 1984.

WORK IN PROGRESS: Publication of diaries and miscellaneous writings.

SIDELIGHTS: Georges Simenon was one of the world's most prolific writers, having produced hundreds of novels, stories, and other works over a span of five decades. Although he wrote exclusively in French, his work is available world-wide in more than forty languages. It has been said that at the peak of his writing career, when he was regularly producing four or more books per year, a new Simenon translation was appearing somewhere in the world on the average of once every three days. But of all his writing, he was best known as the creator and chronicler of the cases of his detective-Inspector Jules Maigret.

In 1922 Simenon left Belgium for Paris to concentrate on a career as a full-time writer of fiction. His early attempts met with rejection and led him to consult Sidonie-Gabrielle Colette, the renowned novelist, who was at that time the editor of *Le Matin.* Colette, too, rejected Simenon's material for publication and suggested that his writing was "too literary" for the mass market. She advised him to simplify and clarify his writing. Simenon's efforts in this direction resulted in the development of his skills as a storyteller of the first rank. He began writing pulp fiction at the rate of eighty pages per day. Simenon published hundreds of books and stories under various pseudonyms during the next several years and soon found that he was able to afford such luxuries as a chauffeur-driven car and, finally, a yacht, the *Ostrogot.*

In 1929, while traveling throughout Europe aboard his yacht, Simenon wrote *The Strange Case of Peter the Lett,* which was the first novel to feature Inspector Maigret. Simenon's detective represented a departure from the conventional portrayal of a supersleuth. When his editors at Fayard first saw the Maigret manuscript, they were doubtful of the novel's chances for success with the reading public. Trudee Young wrote: "They [the Maigrets] were not like other detective novels. The main character, Inspector Maigret—a heavy-set, pipe-smoking detective—did not use scientific means to solve his cases, only his intuition; there were no love affairs; there were no truly good guys and bad guys; and, finally, the story ended neither bad nor good." Inspector Maigret also differs from most famous fictional crime fighters (particularly his American counterparts) in that he rarely carries a gun, rarely throws a punch or takes one, and hardly ever is involved in a chase either on foot or in a car. In fact, Maigret does not know how to drive. Although in the later novels he owns a car, his wife, Madame Maigret, drives him to Meung-sur-Loire for quiet weekends at their country house.

If to all outward appearances Maigret is an ordinary man, of ordinary habits and tastes (although while on a case, he can and does consume inordinate amounts of alcohol), the opposite is true of his abilities and methods as a policeman. Maigret's outstanding traits are his unerring intuition, his compassion for both victim and murderer, and his extraordinary patience. While investigating a murder, Maigret spends hours, and more often days, in watchful waiting—seeking insights into the lives and minds of both the victim and his assassin. Only when he finally and thoroughly understands the reasons why the crime came to be committed does he arrest his suspect. About Maigret and his methods of investigation, Otto Penzler stated in his *The Private Lives of Private Eyes, Spies, Crime Fighters and Other Good Guys,* "unlike most of the great detectives of literature, Maigret does not have immense powers of deduction. He cannot obtain a few clues, consider their ramifications, then swoop down like an avenging hawk of justice and triumphantly carry away a killer to stand trial. "Maigret's powers are intuitive. . . . He attempts to slip into the skin of his quarry and think like him, act like him—indeed become him as nearly as possible. When he has practically assumed his suspect's identity, he is sure of his man and is able to arrest him."

In the same way that Inspector Maigret is unlike most famous fictional sleuths, Simenon's crafting of the stories themselves differs from the traditional form of the mystery and detection genre. Anthony Boucher observed that Simenon's work in this area departed "from the well-shaped plot and the devious gimmick (though he could be very good at these when he chose) to lay stress on the ambience and milieu of the crime and on the ambivalent duel . . . between the murderer and Maigret." Similarly, Edward Galligan made a distinction between traditional mystery fiction and Simenon's Maigret stories. According to Galligan, the Maigrets "are, in a sense, fables demonstrating the ways of the creative, or intuitive intelligence. They most definitely are not mere mystery stories. They are free of the gimmicks and cliches that make most mystery stories tedious to all but the addicts of the genre. Much more concerned with the why's of murder than with the who's, the Maigrets are perceptive about the realities of human behavior. And like all of his work, they are written in a beautifully spare, unpretentious style that Simenon developed in his twenties, when he trained himself as a writer by grinding out an incredible number of commercial fictions."

As much as Maigret is admired and enjoyed by readers of crime fiction, Simenon himself has not always been one of the Inspector's fans. After completing nineteen Maigret novels, Simenon gave up the series for a number of years to concentrate on writing more serious novels, which he termed *romans-crise,* or novels of crisis. These books focus on the psychological motivations of characters as they approach and experience a crisis in their lives. But although Simenon "attempted to persuade critics and publishers that he should be taken seriously as an author of *romans serieux* [serious novels]," observed *Dictionary of Literary Biography* contributor Catharine Savage Brosman, "sales figures suggest that the Maigret series and a few other books in the same vein have the most appeal, and his fame continues to rest principally on them." As Brosman later explained, "His serious novels do not offer wisdom or illumination, and, despite the strong characterization, the reader does not enter into their world. . . . In the detective mode, however, his work sets the standard, rather than following it."

But Andre Gide, an admirer and long-time critical correspondent of Simenon, asserted that there is a "profound psychological and ethical interest" in all Simenon's books. Gide stated: "This is what attracts and holds me in him. He writes for 'the vast public,' to be sure, but delicate and refined readers find something for them too as soon as they begin to take him seriously. He makes one reflect; and this is close to being the height of art; how superior he is in this to those heavy novelists who do not spare us a single commentary! Simenon sets forth a particular fact, perhaps of general interest; but he is careful not to generalize; that is up to the reader." Claude Mauriac felt that although "the reader may be easily disappointed by a given book of Simenon's . . . surprise and admiration often come with the last pages, which renew, renovate and clarify the preceding chapters retrospectively. . . . The very last lines of Georges Simenon's novels most always have the greatest value: it is there that in a

few very simple words, insignificant in appearance, he reveals what he knows about *the secrets of men.*"

In an article entitled "Simenon on Simenon" for the *Times Literary Supplement,* Simenon revealed to his readers some of his thoughts about himself, not as a writer, but as a man. "Simenon," he wrote, "is truly a modest man. He knows his own limitations and does not make for himself the claims that have sometimes been made for him by some of his more florid admirers. He describes himself as a craftsman, has a healthy distrust of intellectuals, of *belle-lettriens,* of literary occasions and intellectual conversations, feels ill at ease at social functions, and is quite unambitious in conventional terms: recognition, decorations, and so on. He can, it is true, well afford to be."

After producing over five hundred novels and novellas, Simenon retired from writing fiction in 1974, devoting himself to nonfiction and the taping of his diaries, which were then transcribed and published. In 1978, the author suffered the greatest tragedy in his life when his daughter, Marie-Georges, whom he called Marie-Jo, committed suicide in her apartment. Devastated by his loss, Simenon felt the need to write about it; the result was his lengthy *Intimate Memoirs,* which begins with the discovery of Marie-Jo's body and is reminiscent of the openings of one of the author's Maigret novels. "Simenon," described Leslie Garis in a *New York Times Magazine* interview with Simenon, "using the insightful probing into human character and clear-eyed equilibrium that have always distinguished his best work, applied his skills to unravelling the causes of her death."

Intimate Memoirs was an exhausting book for the writer to compose and was his last published work. It also "continues to be the best seller of Simenon's career," according to Garis. In this last published interview with Simenon, Garis asked him whether all his numerous books cover all he had wanted to say. "There's always something more to say," replied Simenon, "but we don't have time. Life is short, short, it's so short. I've lived 80 years now and I have the impression that it was yesterday that I was a child."

MEDIA ADAPTATIONS: Approximately two dozen films and television shows have been produced based on Simenon's books, including the 1983 film "L'Etoile du Nord," written by Jean Aurenche and directed by Pierre Granier-Deferre, which is based on the novel, *La Locataire.*

BIOGRAPHICAL/CRITICAL SOURCES:

BOOKS

Barzun, Jacques and W. H. Taylor, *Catalogue of Crime,* 1971.
Contemporary Literary Criticism, Gale, Volume 1, 1973, Volume 2, 1974, Volume 3, 1975, Volume 8, 1978, Volume 18, 1981, Volume 47, 1988.
Dictionary of Literary Biography, Volume 72: *French Novelists, 1930-1960,* Gale, 1988.
Gide, Andre, *The Journals of Andre Gide,* Volume 4: *1938-1949,* translated by Justin O'Brien, Knopf, 1951.
Mauriac, Claude, *The New Literature,* translated by Samuel I. Stone, Braziller, 1959.
Penzler, Otto, *The Private Lives of Private Eyes, Spies, Crime Fighters and Other Good Guys,* Grosset, 1977.
Simenon, Georges, *Pedigree,* translated by Robert Baldick, Hamish Hamilton, 1962.
Simenon, Georges, *When I Was Old,* translated by Helen Eustis, Harcourt, 1971.
Simenon, Georges, *Letter to My Mother,* translated by Ralph Manheim, Harcourt, 1976.

Symons, Julian, *Mortal Consequences: A History—From the Detective Story to the Crime Novel,* Harper, 1972.

Young, Trudee, *Georges Simenon,* Scarecrow, 1976.

PERIODICALS

Adam International Review, autumn, 1969.
Armchair Detective, January, 1971, October, 1977, winter, 1980.
Chicago Tribune Book World, December 25, 1983, July 1, 1984.
Critic, January/February, 1972, January/February, 1974.
Globe and Mail (Toronto), November 23, 1985.
Journal of Popular Culture, summer, 1978.
Life, May 9, 1969.
Listener, February 17, 1983.
Los Angeles Times, February 27, 1981.
Los Angeles Times Book Review, May 24, 1981, July 2, 1983, June 24, 1984, August 5, 1984, November 18, 1984, April 10, 1988.
National Review, June 23, 1972, April 30, 1976, December 10, 1976.
New Republic, March 4, 1940, March 10, 1941.
New Statesman, March 5, 1965, October 17, 1969, June 27, 1980, October 21, 1983.
New Statesman and Nation, February 10, 1940, May 25, 1940, August 13, 1955.
Newsweek, April 27, 1970, February 19, 1973, January 9, 1984, June 25, 1984.
New Yorker, January 17, 1970, April 7, 1975, April 24, 1978, April 2, 1979, June 28, 1982, January 17, 1983, December 23, 1985.
New York Herald Tribune Book Review, May 11, 1958, July 19, 1959.
New York Review of Books, October 12, 1978.
New York Times, December 12, 1980, June 27, 1984, September 4, 1989.
New York Times Book Review, September 4, 1932, February 5, 1933, March 4, 1934, October 11, 1953, July 11, 1954, November 28, 1954, January 27, 1957, August 25, 1957, June 20, 1965, August 18, 1968, March 16, 1969, August 8, 1971, February 25, 1973, November 4, 1973, November 24, 1974, August 4, 1975, November 21, 1976, May 22, 1977, July 1, 1979, May 30, 1982, October 10, 1983, July 1, 1984.
New York Times Magazine, April 22, 1984.
Publishers Weekly, November 13, 1978, January 24, 1986.
Reporter, January 14, 1965.
Saturday Review, February 21, 1953.
South Atlantic Quarterly, autumn, 1967.
Spectator, June 13, 1941, October 3, 1941, March 23, 1951.
Time, March 14, 1969, June 18, 1984.
Times (London), August 21, 1984, August 22, 1984.
Times Literary Supplement, December 14, 1940, November 25, 1960, July 29, 1983, August 12, 1988.
Tribune Books (Chicago), April 24, 1988, July 2, 1989, September 3, 1989.
Washington Post, September 17, 1972.
Washington Post Book World, September 27, 1970, May 18, 1980, January 18, 1981.
World, May, 1973.

OBITUARIES:

PERIODICALS

Globe and Mail (Toronto), September 9, 1989.
Washington Post, September 7, 1989.

SIMON, Claude 1913-

PERSONAL: Surname is pronounced See-moan; born October 10, 1913, in Tananarive, Madagascar; French citizen by birth; son of Louis (a career officer) and Suzanne (Denamiel) Simon; married Yvonne Ducing, 1951 (marriage ended); married Rhea Karavas, May 29, 1978. *Education:* Educated in France.

ADDRESSES: Home—3 Place Monge, 75005 Paris, France. *Office*—Editions de Minuit, 7 rue Bernard-Palissy, 75006 Paris, France.

CAREER: Writer. *Military service:* French Cavalry, 1939-40; became brigadier.

AWARDS, HONORS: Prix de l'Express, 1960, for *La Route des Flandres;* Prix Medicis, 1967, for *Histoire;* Nobel Prize for literature, 1985.

WRITINGS:

NOVELS

Le Tricheur (title means "The Cheat"), Sagittaire, 1945.
La Corde raide (title means "The Taut Rope"), Editions de Minuit, 1947.
Gulliver, Calmann-Levy, 1952.
Le Sacre du printemps (title means "The Crowning of Spring"), Calmann-Levy, 1954.
(Author of text) *Femmes,* paintings by John Miro, Maeght (Paris), 1966, Simon's text reprinted as *La Chevelure de Berenice,* Editions de Minuit, 1983.
Orion aveugle (title means "Blind Orion"), Skira, 1970.
Discours de Stockholm, Editions de Minuit, 1986.
L'Invitation, Editions de Minuit, 1987.

NOVELS WITH ENGLISH TRANSLATIONS

Le Vent: Tentative de restitution d'un retable baroque, Editions de Minuit, 1957, translation by Richard Howard published as *The Wind,* Braziller, 1959, reprinted, 1986.
L'Herbe, Editions de Minuit, 1958, translation by Howard published as *The Grass,* Braziller, 1960, reprinted, Riverrun, 1986.
La Route des Flandres, Editions de Minuit, 1960, translation by Howard published as *The Flanders Road,* Braziller, 1961, reprinted, Riverrun, 1986.
La Palace, Editions de Minuit, 1962, translation by Howard published as *The Palace,* Braziller, 1963.
Histoire, Editions de Minuit, 1967, translation by Howard published under same title, Braziller, 1968.
La Bataille de Pharsale, Editions de Minuit, 1969, translation by Howard published as *The Battle of Pharsalus,* Braziller, 1971.
Les Corps conducteurs, Editions de Minuit, 1971, translation by Helen Lane published as *Conducting Bodies,* Viking, 1974.
Triptyque, Editions de Minuit, 1973, translation by Lane published as *Triptych,* Viking, 1976, revised edition, Riverrun, 1986.
Lecon de choses, Editions de Minuit, 1975, translation by Daniel Weissbort published as *The World about Us,* Ontario Review Press, 1983.
Les Georgiques, Editions de Minuit, 1981, translation by Beryl Fletcher and John Fletcher published as *The Georgics,* Riverrun Press, 1989.

WORK IN PROGRESS: A novel.

SIDELIGHTS: Though considered one of the most important New Novelists in France, Claude Simon has been slow to gain recognition in the United States. Because at first glance Simon's writing "seems incoherent, merely a series of disconnected fragments, a lyrical but meaningless collection of images," observed Morton P. Levitt, "even a reasonably conscientious reader is apt to be confused by what appears to be, in the worst modern tradition, a narrative experiment without meaning or substance. These impressions are misleading, however, for Simon is one of the finest living novelists."

Four of Simon's novels, *The Grass, The Flanders Road, The Palace,* and *Histoire,* form part of a single work connected by various recurring characters and incidents. The best known of the four is *Histoire,* which won the Prix Medicis in 1967.

Superficially, *Histoire* is "the history of the narrator's story of his family as it is captured on the page by reminiscences of intimately evocative material possessions: the ancestral home, bits of furniture, family portraits, faded album photos and postal cards," stated the *Virginia Quarterly Review.* But Georges Schlocker noted that "the essence of the book lies in the confrontation of its characters with passing time and in the states of mind resulting therefrom." The book attempts to recall and recreate reality, which to Simon is "made up of occurrences scattered in time and space, yet belonging to the same emotional or spiritual experience." As a result, all the characters and events are jumbled together. "The past often invades the present without the usual typographical warnings of a new sentence or paragraph," Leo Bersani observed, "and the mixture is made even more confusing by the fact that the whole novel is written in past tenses. The 'he' referred to in one line may not be the same person as the 'he' mentioned in the next line."

Some critics were put off by the vagaries of the text. For example, the book jacket explains that one of the central occurrences in *Histoire* is the "suicide of a cousin adored but somehow betrayed by the narrator." Hugh Kenner complained: "At the publishing house they will have given 'Histoire' more than one reading, and 'somehow' was still the best they could do. ('Hey, George, how the heck shall I say he betrayed her?' 'Somehow.')" But Levitt defended the novel: "If it is incomplete, it is only because the narrator refuses to fill in all the gaps; if it seems disordered, it is because it is the product of a disordered point of view. The narrator fails in his effort to know himself, and, because form and function are here indistinguishable, we can know him only if we can understand the method of his narrative." A *Time* reviewer explained it this way: "Simon is at ease with uncertainties and loose ends. In fact, loose ends are his antennae. How he uses them to convey his own private perceptions is his mystery and his art."

In the tradition of other New Novelists such as Sarraute, Robbe-Grillet, and Butor, Simon attempts to create an awesome awareness of reality through experimentation with different points of view. But Simon transcends the New Novel by exploring the possibilities of language and by sympathetically presenting each of his characters as "a kind of every-man who suffers for all men," noted Levitt. The *Virginia Quarterly Review* contended that "what distinguished 'Histoire' from so many dreary and boring nouveau roman attempts at capturing the truths of reality is that Claude Simon structures his remembrances around crucial centripetal happenings that manage to sustain the reader's interest."

Numerous critics have pointed out the influence of Faulkner and Proust on Simon's writing. The *Tri-Quarterly* noted that "a Simon novel translated by an American reads so like a Faulkner novel" because of the long, convoluted sentences, lack of punctuation, abrupt transitions, and confused chronology. Simon himself once commented that *The Sound and the Fury* "truly revealed to me what writing could be. But what I prefer in Faulkner is his Joycean and Proustian side." In a similar vein, Hugh Kenner remarked that "Simon is investing his Proustian material with Faulknerian mechanisms and mannerisms." In 1985, Simon finally won wide recognition when he was awarded the Nobel Prize for literature. Writing in the *Dictionary of Literary Biography,* Doris Y. Kadish reported that "the Nobel Academy praised Simon for having combined the creativity of the poet and the painter and expressed a profound sense of time and the human condition."

BIOGRAPHICAL/CRITICAL SOURCES:

BOOKS

Contemporary Literary Criticism, Gale, Volume 4, 1975, Volume 9, 1978, Volume 15, 1980, Volume 39, 1986.
Dictionary of Literary Biography, Volume 83: *French Novelists since 1960,* Gale, 1989.

PERIODICALS

Best Sellers, April 15, 1971.
Books Abroad, spring, 1968.
Chicago Tribune, October 18, 1985.
Critique, Volume 12, number 1, 1970.
Globe and Mail (Toronto), October 19, 1985, December 14, 1985.
Kenyon Review, Issue 1, 1967.
Los Angeles Times Book Review, July 26, 1987.
New Republic, June 8, 1968.
New York Times, November 28, 1967, October 18, 1985, October 20, 1985, October 30, 1985, November 4, 1985.
New York Times Book Review, January 21, 1968, July 14, 1968, September 15, 1974, April 1, 1984, October 1, 1989.
Saturday Review, April 17, 1971.
Spectator, April 18, 1969, July 19, 1969.
Time, March 29, 1968.
Times (London), October 26, 1985, June 8, 1989.
Times Literary Supplement, June 8, 1967, December 24, 1971, July 11, 1975, December 4, 1981, November 17, 1989.
Tribune Books (Chicago), September 17, 1989.
Tri-Quarterly, winter, 1967.
Virginia Quarterly Review, autumn, 1968, summer, 1971.
Washington Post Book World, August 15, 1976.

*   *   *

SIMON, Kate (Grobsmith) 1912-1990

PERSONAL: Given name originally Kaila; born December 5, 1912, in Warsaw, Poland; immigrated to United States, 1917, naturalized citizen; died February 4, 1990, in New York, N.Y., of cancer; daughter of Jacob (in the shoe design business) and Lina (a corsetiere; maiden name, Babicz) Grobsmith; married Stanley Goldman (a doctor; died, 1942); married Robert Simon, 1947 (a publisher; divorced, 1960); children: (first marriage) Alexandra (died, 1954). *Education:* Hunter College of the City University of New York, B.A., 1935.

ADDRESSES: Home and office—160 East 27th St., New York, N.Y. 10016. *Agent*—Kristine Dahl Agency, 264 Fifth Ave., New York, N.Y. 10001.

CAREER: Writer. Worked for Book-of-the-Month Club, for a printing firm, and for *Publishers Weekly;* book reviewer for *New Republic* and *Nation;* free-lance writer for Alfred A. Knopf, Inc., 1952-55.

MEMBER: PEN, Authors League.

AWARDS, HONORS: Awards of honor from Hunter College and English Speaking Union; National Book Critics Circle named *Bronx Primitive: Portraits in a Childhood* among the most distinguished books published in 1982.

WRITINGS:

New York Places and Pleasures: An Uncommon Guidebook, illustrations by Bob Gill, Meridian Books, 1959, 4th revised edition, Harper, 1971.
New York, photographs by Andrea Feininger, Viking, 1964.
Mexico: Places and Pleasures, Doubleday, 1965, 4th edition, Harper, 1988.
Paris Places and Pleasures: An Uncommon Guidebook, Putnam, 1967.
London Places and Pleasures: An Uncommon Guidebook, Putnam, 1968.
Italy: The Places In Between, Harper, 1970, revised and expanded edition, Harper, 1984.
Rome: Places and Pleasures, Knopf, 1972.
England's Green and Pleasant Land, Knopf, 1974.
Fifth Avenue: A Very Social Story, Harcourt, 1978.
Bronx Primitive: Portraits in a Childhood (autobiography), Viking, 1982.
A Wider World: Portraits in an Adolescence (autobiography), Harper, 1986.
A Renaissance Tapestry: The Gonzaga of Mantua (nonfiction), Harper, 1988.

Contributor of articles to periodicals, including the *New York Times, Vogue, Harper's, National Geographic, Harper's Bazaar, Saturday Review, Holiday,* and *Travel and Leisure.*

WORK IN PROGRESS: A third volume of her autobiography, tentatively entitled *Etchings on an Hour Glass,* for Harper.

SIDELIGHTS: According to *Time* magazine reviewer R. Z. Sheppard, Kate Simon was "one of those rare writers who is preternaturally incapable of composing a dull sentence." Widely praised for her colorful, richly detailed prose, Simon first established her literary reputation as an author of travel guides, which Sybil S. Steinberg described in a *Publishers Weekly* article as being "in a class by themselves, distinctly personal guides of rare good taste and discernment, expressed in an urbane and witty style." Simon captivated her readers—globetrotters and armchair travelers alike—since the 1959 publication of her first book, *New York Places and Pleasures.* "There is no more wonderful guidebook than this," J. H. Plumb announced in the *New York Times Book Review,* proclaiming the eventual bestseller a work "written with a real love for a city and sparkling with gaiety, wit, and recondite knowledge."

Simon went on to write similar guides for such cities as Mexico, Paris, London, and Italy, eliciting accolades for "her saunterings in areas which only the most enterprising tourists would find for themselves," as a *Times Literary Supplement* reviewer commented; for giving "the distinct impression [she] did all this research on her own two feet and not in a library," according to *Washington Post Book World's* John Crosby; and for writing "for travelers who want to possess [a place], not for vacationers seeking a brief flirtation," as Stanley Carr stated in the *New York Times Book Review.* Plumb remarked that Simon "has made of the guidebook, one of the dullest forms of literature, a brilliant work of art. And to do that requires genius."

Simon also demonstrated her descriptive powers in *Fifth Avenue: A Very Social Story,* her 1978 book that delves into the glamorous past of New York City's Fifth Avenue and the mansions once lining it. The work also explores the lives of the great homes' occupants, including such famous and wealthy families as the Vanderbilts, the Astors, the Stuyvesants, the Guggenheims, and the Rockefellers. "Ambling up Fifth Avenue in a leisurely, neo-Proustian fashion," remarked *Saturday Review* critic Robert F. Moss, Simon "mixes elaborate architectural commentary with an unauthorized biography of nineteenth-century American nobility." Bruce Bliven, Jr., writing for the *New York Times Book Review,* judged *Fifth Avenue* "a generous book—large and handsome—filled with a multitude of treasures and pleasures," adding that "we owe a debt to the author for capturing as much of [the mansions] as she has in words, which is preservation of a kind."

Until the publication of her autobiographical *Bronx Primitive: Portraits in a Childhood,* few of Simon's readers would have guessed that she began life in a Warsaw, Poland, ghetto. She was not, as *Los Angeles Times* writer Elaine Kendall pointed out, "wheeled through the Borghese Gardens in her pram; shepherded through the city museums on rainy afternoons; [and] rewarded for good behavior with petits fours at Rumplemeyer's." Rather, at age four she immigrated to America as a steerage passenger aboard the *Susquehanna* with her mother and younger brother, her father having made the journey three years earlier. Simon then spent the remainder of her childhood in a poor immigrant neighborhood in the northernmost borough of New York City, where "her Borghese garden was Crotona Park, her cultural mecca the neighborhood library, [and] her Museum of Natural History the tenement hallways," noted Kendall.

In *Bronx Primitive* Simon recounts this childhood, casting her father as an overbearing and selfish shoemaker who decided that young Kate would become a famous concert pianist and make him rich, a husband and father who was more concerned for his newly-arrived immigrant cousins than for his own wife and children. Simon reserves higher regard for her mother, a proud woman who later confessed to her daughter that she'd had thirteen abortions—which, as *Time's* Sheppard related, "was not a neighborhood record." Simon's younger sister was born only after Dr. James—brother of novelist Henry and compassionate gynecologist to the poor—refused to give Simon's mother her fourteenth abortion. With the arrival of the new baby, eldest Kate, who had been expected to also care for her younger brother, took charge of another sibling, while her brother was allowed to amuse himself as he pleased. "While he," Simon reflected, "the grasshopper, sang and danced, I, the ant, sat demurely rocking the carriage. He was in the full sun, I in the shade; he was young, I was old."

Within this familial framework, however, life for the author was not undiluted dissatisfaction, squalor, and pain; Simon invokes fond memories in *Bronx Primitive* as well. She tells, for instance, of the two weeks her family spent at a small rented beach house on Coney Island, and describes an outing with her mother and brother: "When my mother walked into the street in her new brown suit and beaver hat on the first day of Passover, she was so beautiful that I couldn't see her; her radiance blinded me. My brother, in spite of our steady urge to mayhem, appeared all gold and dazzling as he played stickball in the street." In this scene Simon herself feels "complete and smooth as a fresh pea pod."

Critics greeted *Bronx Primitive* enthusiastically, praising Simon's aptitude for description and applauding the lucid, unidealized tone of the work. "She approaches [her experiences] with a clear eye in two senses," observed *Washington Post* critic Linda Barrett Osborne. "She is both strongly visual and vivid in re-creating scenes and people, and uncompromisingly straightforward in assessing them. She makes the era attractive because her style is lively, humorous, tough, and not sentimental or nostalgic." Echoing Osborne, Helen Yglesias wrote in the *New York Times Book Review* that "the reader is in safe hands, delivered from the dangers of shallow nostalgia or a generalizing sentimentality." As Kendall concluded, Simon "recalls the 1920s with piercing clarity, and while the ingredients are familiar, the results are often unexpected. There are unfiltered memories of the immigrant experience, with the grounds still settling and a slight sharp aftertaste."

Simon followed *Bronx Primitive* with a second volume of memoirs titled *A Wider World: Portraits in an Adolescence.* In this book Kate Simon has become a rebellious, quick-witted, and artistically gifted Depression-era teenager who embraces literature-induced fantasies of worldliness, fame, and romantic passion, seeing herself as "the girl who was to be immortal, the bright fantasist and loony wanderer." Informed by her father upon graduation from primary school that she may only attend high school for one year of secretarial training, she responds with what Sheppard termed "pluck and clarity of intent [that] are completely captivating." Her determination lands her in the academically challenging James Monroe High School, where she shines as a sharp English student and essayist. At fifteen she breaks free of her father's tyrannical grip and leaves home to become a live-in babysitter for the eccentric and politically radical Bergson family, who introduce her to a potent world of culture. She adopts an avant-garde bohemian lifestyle, the trappings of which include a long gray raincoat, gold borsalino hat, gypsy earrings, beads, and black stockings. To further prove her independence she also shares a flat for a time with the shy and sensitive Davy, earning a reputation among her high school classmates as an "utterly uninhibited sexpot and total free spirit"—despite the fact that the couple's awkwardness prevents them from consummating their relationship for several years.

Simon's treatment of sexuality in *A Wider World* is forthright and even humorous at times, as when she describes an arrangement wherein Jones, a free-love friend-of-a-friend, eagerly agrees to initiate the virginal young Kate. His lesson is unsuccessful, however; during his preamble on the wonders of nature's fecundity, she falls asleep. But the author acknowledges the darker side of sexuality, too, when recounting her two abortions, the first of which was "the result of drinking deeply of synthetic gin and romping with an anonymous beauty over house roofs and down some stairs or other, to roll on the grass in a nearby park." Simon's frank but gruesome recollection of the actual abortion procedure prompted *Washington Post Book World* contributor Robert Lekachman to comment that "right-to-lifers could read with profit what it was like to get a cheap abortion without anesthesia."

Such straightforward, vivid writing earned Simon critical applause similar to that which greeted *Bronx Primitive.* Comparing *A Wider World* with such celebrated American works as Willa Cather's *My Antonia,* F. Scott Fitzgerald's *The Great Gatsby,* and Mario Puzo's *The Godfather, New York Times Book Review* writer Robert Pinskey decided that Simon's "modest, distinctive and feminist account may be all the more essentially American precisely because the transitional climb is a matter not of heroic determination or overwhelming genius, but of shining intelligence, good luck, and a tough, likable vitality." The critic also deemed Simon "unsentimental, judgmental, passionate in dislike and in loyalty, [and] coolly meticulous of eye," and praised "her clean and unpretentious prose style, her aristocratic disdain for cant, her frank worldliness and the unforced breadth of reference." *New York Times* critic Michiko Kakutani echoed Pinskey, finding in *A Wider World* "memories [that] move us not

with the faded, antique charm of dog-eared photos in an album, but with the hard, bright passions of life." Sheppard concluded that "together, *Bronx Primitive* and *A Wider World* qualify as a minor American classic."

Simon turned to the concerns of another country in another era for her next book, *A Renaissance Tapestry: The Gonzaga of Mantua.* *New Yorker*'s Naomi Bliven likened the work to Simon's earlier travel series, calling *A Renaissance Tapestry* "an all-inclusive tour of four extraordinary centuries conducted at an easy tempo by an unpretentious, friendly, knowledgeable guide." The Gonzaga family ruled Mantua, a province of the Lombardy region of northern Italy, from the early fourteenth century until the early 1700s. Focusing primarily on the lives of Francesco Gonzaga, Marquis of Mantua from the late fifteenth century to the early sixteenth century, and his wife, Isabella d'Este, Simon presents a history of politics, war, and culture, in which the lords of Mantua served as soldiers of fortune for wealthier rulers of other Italian city-states, prospered from sound farming practices in the region's fertile land, founded Italy's first tapestry industry, and became known as excellent horse breeders. The author also describes the Gonzaga penchant for ostentation ("their clothes were gaudy, their jewels flashy, their dwarfs the smallest they could find," notes Bliven) and fratricide, while portraying them as earnest patrons of the arts whose payroll included artists Leonardo da Vinci, Titian, Andrea Mantegna, and Peter Paul Rubens, as well as composer Claudio Monteverdi and builder and architect Filippo Brunelleschi. Remarking on *A Renaissance Tapestry* in the *New York Times Book Review,* Mark Phillips wrote that "a colorful, troubled, egotistical age is alive in Miss Simon's readable narrative." Bliven commended Simon on her characteristically forthright, unaffected style: "Her narrative poise . . . eschews the 'gee whizz' wonderment that often addles writers about the Renaissance. Her book is simply accurate, and its unargumentative precision demonstrates—at this moment in history, anyhow—the Italian Renaissance has lost some of its appeal."

At the time of her death in 1990, Simon had finished the manuscript for a third volume of her autobiography. Tentatively entitled *Etchings on an Hour Glass,* Simon's last book contained recollections of her college years, marriages, career, and included accounts of her most recent travels.

BIOGRAPHICAL/CRITICAL SOURCES:

BOOKS

Simon, Kate, *Bronx Primitive: Portraits in a Childhood,* Viking, 1982.
Simon, Kate, *A Wider World: Portraits in an Adolescence,* Harper, 1986.

PERIODICALS

Los Angeles Times, May 4, 1982.
Ms., June, 1982, July, 1986.
Newsweek, May 12, 1986.
New Yorker, July 28, 1962, May 10, 1982, April 11, 1988.
New York Times, March 24, 1970, March 3, 1978, May 24, 1982, February 15, 1986, April 5, 1988.
New York Times Book Review, June 16, 1968, September 8, 1968, June 7, 1970, April 16, 1978, May 23, 1982, February 23, 1986, April 10, 1988.
Observer, February 14, 1971.
Publishers Weekly, May 14, 1982.
Saturday Review, June 26, 1965, April 29, 1978.
Time, July 14, 1967, April 19, 1982, February 24, 1986.
Times Literary Supplement, August 1, 1968, February 19, 1970.

Washington Post, May 11, 1982.
Washington Post Book World, September 1, 1968, April 10, 1988.

OBITUARIES:

PERIODICALS

New York Times, February 5, 1990.

* * *

SIMON, (Marvin) Neil 1927-

PERSONAL: Born July 4, 1927, in Bronx, N.Y.; son of Irving (a garment salesman) and Mamie Simon; married Joan Baim (a dancer), September 30, 1953 (died, 1973); married Marsha Mason (an actress), 1973 (separated, 1983); married Diana Lander, 1986; children (first marriage) Ellen, Nancy. *Education:* Attended New York University, 1946, and University of Denver.

ADDRESSES: Office—c/o Albert Da Silva, Esq., Da Silva & Da Silva, 502 Park Ave., New York, N.Y. 10022.

CAREER: Playwright. Owner of the Eugene O'Neill Theatre, New York City. Warner Brothers, Inc. (CBS), New York City, mailroom clerk, 1946; Columbia Broadcasting System, New York City, comedy writer for Goodman Ace, late 1940s; comedy writer for "The Phil Silvers Arrow Show," National Broadcasting Co. (NBC-TV), 1948, "The Tallulah Bankhead Show," NBC-TV, 1951, "The Sid Caesar Show," NBC-TV, 1956-57, "The Phil Silvers Show," CBS-TV, 1958-59, "The Garry Moore Show," CBS-TV, 1959-60, for "The Jackie Gleason Show" and "The Red Buttons Show," both CBS-TV, and for NBC-TV specials. *Military service:* U.S. Army Air Force Reserve; sports editor of *Rev-Meter,* the Lowry Field (Colorado) base newspaper, 1946.

MEMBER: Dramatists Guild, Writers Guild of America.

AWARDS, HONORS: Academy of Television Arts and Sciences Award (Emmy), 1957, for "The Sid Caesar Show," and 1959, for "The Phil Silvers Show"; Antoinette Perry Award (Tony) nomination, 1963, for "Little Me" and "Barefoot in the Park," 1968, for "Plaza Suite," 1969, for "Promises, Promises," 1970, for "Last of the Red Hot Lovers," 1972, for "The Prisoner of Second Avenue," and 1987, for "Broadway Bound"; Tony Award, 1965, for best playwright, and 1985, for "Biloxi Blues"; Writers Guild Award nomination, 1967, for "Barefoot in the Park"; *Evening Standard* Drama Award, 1967, for "Sweet Charity"; Sam S. Shubert Foundation Award, 1968; Academy of Motion Picture Arts and Sciences Award (Oscar) nomination, 1968, for "The Odd Couple"; Writers Guild Award, 1969, for "The Odd Couple," 1970, for "Last of the Red Hot Lovers," 1971, for "The Out-of-Towners," and 1972, for "The Trouble with People"; named Entertainer of the Year, *Cue* magazine, 1972; L.H.D., Hofstra University, 1981; New York Drama Critics Circle Award, 1983, for "Brighton Beach Memoirs"; elected to the Theater Hall of Fame, Uris Theater, 1983; a Neil Simon tribute show was held at the Shubert Theater, March 1, 1987; the Neil Simon Endowment for the Dramatic Arts has been established at Duke University.

WRITINGS:

PUBLISHED PLAYS

(With William Friedberg) *Adventures of Marco Polo: A Musical Fantasy* (music by Clay Warnick and Mel Pahl), Samuel French, 1959.
(Adaptor with Friedberg) *Heidi* (based on the novel by Johanna Spyri; music by Warnick), Samuel French, 1959.

(With brother, Danny Simon) *Come Blow Your Horn* (also see below; first produced in New Hope, Pa., at the Bucks County Playhouse, August, 1960; produced on Broadway at the Brooks Atkinson Theatre, February 22, 1961; produced on the West End at the Prince of Wales Theatre, February 17, 1962), Doubleday, 1963.
Barefoot in the Park (also see below; first produced, under title "Nobody Loves Me," in New Hope, Pa., at the Bucks County Playhouse, 1962; produced on Broadway at the Biltmore Theatre, October 23, 1963; produced on the West End, 1965), Random House, 1964.
The Odd Couple (also see below; first produced on Broadway at the Plymouth Theatre, March 10, 1965; produced on the West End at the Queen's Theatre, October 12, 1966; revised version first produced in Los Angeles at the Ahmanson Theatre, April 6, 1985; produced on Broadway at the Broadhurst Theatre, June, 1985), Random House, 1966.
Sweet Charity (musical; based on the screenplay "The Nights of Cabiria" by Federico Fellini; music and lyrics by Cy Coleman and Dorothy Fields; first produced on Broadway at the Palace Theatre, January 29, 1966; produced on the West End at the Prince of Wales Theatre, October 11, 1967), Random House, 1966.
The Star-Spangled Girl (also see below; first produced on Broadway at the Plymouth Theatre, December 21, 1966), Random House, 1967.
Plaza Suite (also see below; three one-acts entitled "Visitor from Hollywood," "Visitor from Mamaroneck," and "Visitor from Forest Hills"; first produced on Broadway at the Plymouth Theatre, February 14, 1968; produced on the West End at the Lyric Theatre, February 18, 1969), Random House, 1969.
Promises, Promises (also see below; musical; based on the screenplay "The Apartment" by Billy Wilder and I. A. L. Diamond; music by Burt Bacharach; lyrics by Hal David; first produced on Broadway at the Shubert Theatre, December 1, 1968; produced on the West End at the Prince of Wales Theatre, October 2, 1969), Random House, 1969.
Last of the Red Hot Lovers (also see below; three-act; first produced in New Haven at the Shubert Theatre, November 26, 1969; produced on Broadway at the Eugene O'Neill Theatre, December 28, 1969; produced in London, 1979), Random House, 1970.
The Gingerbread Lady (also see below; first produced in New Haven at the Shubert Theatre, November 4, 1970; produced on Broadway at the Plymouth Theatre, December 13, 1970; produced in London, 1974), Random House, 1971.
The Prisoner of Second Avenue (also see below; first produced in New Haven at the Shubert Theatre, October 12, 1971; produced on Broadway at the Eugene O'Neill Theatre, November 11, 1971), Random House, 1972.
The Sunshine Boys (also see below; first produced in New Haven at the Shubert Theatre, November 21, 1972; produced on Broadway at the Broadhurst Theatre, December 20, 1972; produced in London, 1975), Random House, 1973.
The Good Doctor (also see below; musical; adapted from stories by Anton Chekhov; music by Peter Link; lyrics by Simon; first produced on Broadway at the Eugene O'Neill Theatre, November 27, 1973), Random House, 1974.
God's Favorite (also see below; first produced on Broadway at the Eugene O'Neill Theatre, December 11, 1974), Random House, 1975.
California Suite (also see below; first produced in Los Angeles, April, 1976; produced on Broadway at the Eugene O'Neill

Theatre, June 30, 1976; produced in London, 1976), Random House, 1977.

Chapter Two (also see below; first produced in Los Angeles, 1977; produced on Broadway at the Imperial Theatre, December 4, 1977; produced in London, 1981), Random House, 1979.

They're Playing Our Song (musical; music by Marvin Hamlisch; lyrics by Carol Bayer Sager; first produced in Los Angeles, 1978; produced on Broadway at the Imperial Theatre, February 11, 1979; produced in London, 1980), Random House, 1980.

I Ought to Be in Pictures (also see below; first produced in Los Angeles, 1980; produced on Broadway at the Eugene O'Neill Theatre, April 3, 1980; produced in London at the Offstage Downstairs, December, 1986), Random House, 1981.

Fools (first produced on Broadway at the Eugene O'Neill Theatre, April, 1981), Random House, 1982.

Brighton Beach Memoirs (also see below; first produced in Los Angeles at the Ahmanson Theatre, December, 1982; produced on Broadway at the Alvin Theatre, March 27, 1983), Random House, 1984.

Biloxi Blues (also see below; first produced in Los Angeles at the Ahmanson Theatre, December, 1984; produced on Broadway at the Neil Simon Theatre, March, 1985), Random House, 1986.

Broadway Bound (first produced at Duke University, October, 1986; produced on Broadway at the Broadhurst Theatre, December, 1986), Random House, 1987.

OMNIBUS COLLECTIONS

The Comedy of Neil Simon (contains *Come Blow Your Horn, Barefoot in the Park, The Odd Couple, The Star-Spangled Girl, Promises, Promises, Plaza Suite,* and *Last of the Red Hot Lovers*), Random House, 1971, published as *The Collected Plays of Neil Simon,* Volume 1, New American Library, 1986.

The Collected Plays of Neil Simon, Volume 2 (contains *The Sunshine Boys, Little Me* [also see below], *The Gingerbread Lady, The Prisoner of Second Avenue, The Good Doctor, God's Favorite, California Suite,* and *Chapter Two*), Random House, 1979.

UNPUBLISHED PLAYS

(Contributor of sketches) "Tamiment Revue," first produced in Tamiment, Pa., 1952-53.

(Contributor of sketches, with D. Simon) "Catch a Star!" (musical revue), first produced on Broadway at the Plymouth Theatre, November 6, 1955.

(Contributor of sketches, with D. Simon) "New Faces of 1956," first produced on Broadway at the Ethel Barrymore Theatre, June 14, 1956.

(Adaptor) "Little Me" (musical; based on the novel by Patrick Dennis), music by Coleman, first produced on Broadway at the Lunt-Fontanne Theatre, November 17, 1962, produced on the West End at the Cambridge Theatre, November 18, 1964.

(Contributor of sketch) "Broadway Revue" (satirical musical revue), first produced in New York City at the Karruit Bloomgarden Theatre, November, 1968.

(Editor of book for musical) "Seesaw" (based on "Two for the Seesaw" by William Gibson), first produced on Broadway, March 18, 1973.

"Rumors," first produced in San Diego at the Old Globe Theater, 1988, produced on Broadway at the Broadhurst Theater, November, 1988.

"Jake's Women," first produced in San Diego at the Old Globe Theater, March 8, 1990.

SCREENPLAYS

(With Cesare Zavattini) "After the Fox," United Artists, 1966.

"Barefoot in the Park" (based on Simon's play of the same title), Paramount, 1967.

"The Odd Couple" (based on Simon's play of the same title), Paramount, 1968.

"The Out-of-Towners," Paramount, 1970.

"Plaza Suite" (based on Simon's play of the same title), Paramount, 1971.

"Last of the Red Hot Lovers" (based on Simon's play of the same title), Paramount, 1972.

"The Heartbreak Kid" (based on short story by Bruce Jay Friedman), Twentieth Century-Fox, 1972.

"The Sunshine Boys" (based on Simon's play of the same title), Metro-Goldwyn-Mayer, 1974.

"The Prisoner of Second Avenue" (based on Simon's play of the same title), Warner Bros., 1975.

"Murder by Death," Columbia, 1976.

"The Goodbye Girl," Warner Bros., 1977.

"The Cheap Detective," Columbia, 1978.

"California Suite" (based on Simon's play of the same title), Columbia, 1978.

"Chapter Two" (based on Simon's play of the same title), Columbia, 1979.

"Seems Like Old Times," Columbia, 1980.

"Only When I Laugh," Columbia, 1981.

"I Ought to Be in Pictures" (based on Simon's play of the same title), Twentieth Century-Fox, 1982.

"Max Dugan Returns," Twentieth Century-Fox, 1983.

(With Ed Weinberger and Stan Daniels) "The Lonely Guy," Universal, 1984.

"The Slugger's Wife," Columbia, 1985.

"Brighton Beach Memoirs" (based on Simon's play of the same title), Universal, 1986.

"Biloxi Blues" (based on Simon's play of the same title), Universal, 1988.

TELEVISION SCRIPTS

"The Trouble with People," National Broadcasting Co., 1972.

Also coauthor of "Happy Endings," 1975.

WORK IN PROGRESS: "A Foggy Day," a musical incorporating music and lyrics written by the late Ira and George Gershwin.

SIDELIGHTS: "When I was a kid," playwright Neil Simon tells Tom Prideaux of *Life,* "I climbed up on a stone ledge to watch an outdoor movie of Charlie Chaplin. I laughed so hard I fell off, cut my head open and was taken to the doctor, bleeding and laughing. . . . My idea of the ultimate achievement in a comedy is to make a whole audience fall onto the floor, writhing and laughing so hard that some of them pass out." In his own comedies Simon has often come close to realizing this ideal. "At *The Odd Couple,*" Prideaux notes, "at least two people a week do—literally—fall out of their seats laughing."

For some thirty years Simon's comedies have dominated the Broadway stage and have been adapted as popular Hollywood films as well. As David Richards explains in the *Washington Post,* Simon's comedies have always run "forever on Broadway and made him pots of money, after which they were turned into movies that made him pots more." Such plays as "Barefoot in the Park," "The Odd Couple," "Plaza Suite," "The Prisoner of Second Avenue," "The Sunshine Boys," and the autobiographical trilogy of "Brighton Beach Memoirs," "Biloxi Blues," and "Broadway Bound," have ensured Simon a position as "one of America's most popular and prolific playwrights" and "the most formidable comedy writer in American theatre," as Sheila Ennis Geitner reports in the *Dictionary of Literary Biography.*

Even though Simon's plays are often "detonatingly funny," as a critic for *Time* claims, in recent years they have grown more serious too, confronting issues of importance, the humor developing naturally from the characters and their interactions. With these plays, Simon has gained a new respect for his work. "Simon's mature theatre work," Robert K. Johnson writes in his *Neil Simon,* "combines comedy with moments of poignance and insight." Speaking of the Tony Award-winning "Biloxi Blues," Frank Rich of the *New York Times* argues that in this play Simon "at last begins to examine himself honestly, without compromises, and the result is his most persuasively serious effort to date." In his review of the same play, Clive Barnes of the *New York Post* calls it "a realistic comedy of the heart" and allows that it "is funny, often heartrendingly funny, but, nowadays Simon will not compromise character for a laugh."

Simon began his career as a radio writer in the 1940s. He and his brother Danny Simon worked as a team, writing comedy sketches for radio personality Goodman Ace. In the 1950s the pair graduated to television, working with such popular entertainers as Sid Caesar, Phil Silvers, and Jackie Gleason, and with such other writers as Mel Brooks and Woody Allen. But after some ten years in the business, Simon wanted out. "I hated the idea of working in television and having conferences with network executives and advertising executives who told you what audiences wanted and in what region they wanted it," Simon tells the *New York Times Magazine.* With the success of his play "Come Blow Your Horn," written with Danny, Simon was finally able to leave television and devote his efforts to the stage. He has never regretted the move. As he tells Richards, "I would rather spend my nights writing for an audience of 1,000, than an audience of 14 million."

Since the initial success of "Come Blow Your Horn," which ran for eighty-four weeks on Broadway, Simon has seldom had a disappointing reception to his work. His second play, "Barefoot in the Park," ran for more than 1,500 performances on Broadway; "The Odd Couple" for more than 900 performances; "Plaza Suite" for more than 1,000 performances; and "Last of the Red Hot Lovers" and "The Prisoner of Second Avenue" ran for more than 700 performances each. Richards notes that "all but a handful of Simon's plays" have made a profit, while Simon is reputedly "the richest playwright alive and arguably the richest ever in the history of the theater." "Most of Simon's plays," Richard Christiansen remarks in the *Chicago Tribune,* "have been good box office. [And] he still holds the record for having the most plays running simultaneously on Broadway (four)." Speaking of Simon's phenomenal career Christine Arnold of the *Chicago Tribune* calls him "America's most successful playwright, more prolific and far less troubled than Tennessee Williams, more popular than Eugene O'Neill or Lanford Wilson or Sam Shepard. Critics may dismiss or embrace his work, but they cannot dispute his genius for creating plays that resonate for vast audiences."

Although Simon's plays have dealt with a wide range of situations and characters, certain elements recur in all of them. The setting is usually Simon's hometown of New York, the characters are often native New Yorkers, and their problems are similar to those experienced by Simon himself. "Come Blow Your Horn," for instance, is a thinly-disguised version of Simon and brother Danny coming of age and leaving home. "The Odd Couple" stems from Danny's experience of sharing an apartment with a divorced friend. And "Chapter Two" concerns Simon's recovery following the death of his first wife in 1973. Simon tells Leslie Bennetts of the *New York Times* about how he has incorporated events from his own life into his plays: "The theme is me, my outlook on life. If you spread [my career] out like a map, you can chart my emotional life: some of the growth, some of the changes, some of the side trips."

Critics often point out that Simon has an admirable ability to accurately depict American domestic life. "Simon has a gift for sketching America in small-scale situations," states Joe Brown of the *Washington Post.* Writing in the *Humanist,* Julius Novick claims that Simon immerses "himself in the minutiae of modern American upper-middle-class existence, which no one conveys with more authority—or, anyhow, more assiduity—than he."

Simon's plays usually focus on the members of one family or on a small group of friends, and often concern the more disruptive problems of modern life: divorce, urban crime and congestion, conflicts between children and parents, infidelity. These conflicts occur in a closed environment: an apartment or the family home. "Many of my plays [deal] with people being dumped together in a confined space, physically and emotionally," Bennetts quotes Simon as explaining. He uses this confined space with expert skill. David Kehr of the *Chicago Tribune* claims that Simon has "a kind of genius—a genius for stagecraft, the art of getting characters on and off a stage as unobtrusively as possible and of finding plausible, natural excuses for restricting a whole range of dramatic action to the confines of a single set. As a master of logistics, Simon is without peer."

Although Simon's plays are often concerned with domestic troubles, they nonetheless find humor in these painful situations. In his critique of "The Odd Couple" for the *Saturday Review,* Henry Hewes explains that Simon "makes comic cadenzas out of our bleats of agony." Simon's characters, Hewes maintains, "are blissfully unhappy but the pain of what they do to each other and to themselves is exploded into fierce humor." In his analysis of what makes Simon's plays funny, T. E. Kalem of *Time* finds that "the central aspect of his plays is that the central characters are not funny at all. They never laugh, and they are frequently utterly miserable. . . . Why does the audience laugh? Two reasons suggest themselves. The first is the catharsis of relief—thank God, this hasn't happened to me. The second is to ward off and suppress anxiety—by God, this might happen to me." Speaking to Paul D. Zimmerman of *Newsweek,* Simon explains: "My view is 'how sad and funny life is.' I can't think of a humorous situation that does not involve some pain. I used to ask, 'What is a funny situation?' Now I ask, 'What is a sad situation and how can I tell it humorously?'"

This fusion of the sad and funny in Simon's work is noted by several critics who see it as a central reason for his theatrical success. Marilyn Stasio writes in her review of "Last of the Red Hot Lovers": "There is nothing at all funny about the painfully neurotic and really quite profoundly unhappy characters in this play, which is actually about the disintegration of our moral codes and the chaos which such a breakdown has made of our emotional lives. What makes the play so wildly funny is not its author's vision, for Simon's is close to tragedy, but his conceptualization of that vision as high comedy-of-manners. It is neither the personae of the characters nor the situations of their drama which Simon treats humorously, but only the superficial foibles which they have erected as elaborate defenses against their own anxieties." Prideaux argues that Simon's comic characters—who, like his audience, are usually from the middle class—offer something more than simple entertainment. "By making a modern audience feel that its foibles and vices are not too serious because he makes them seem so funny," Prideaux writes, "Simon is also selling a sort of forgiveness: absolution by laughter."

In her *Neil Simon: A Critical Study,* Edythe M. McGovern argues that in his early plays Simon also advocates compromise and moderation. In "Barefoot in the Park," for instance, a newly-married couple are opposites: she is spontaneous; he is overly-careful. Their different outlooks on life threaten to pull them apart. But by play's end, they have moderated their behavior so that they can live comfortably together. "Simon," McGovern writes, "has made a point here regarding the desirability of following a middle course in order to live pleasurably without boredom, but with a sensible regard for responsibility."

The same theme is returned to in "The Odd Couple," in which two divorced male friends share an apartment, only to find that the disagreeable personality traits which led them to get divorces also make their living together impossible. They are "two rather nice human beings who will never be able to communicate with one another simply because each man has a completely different way of viewing the world and is committed to what amounts to an extreme position with no intention of compromise," as McGovern explains. Their unyielding attitudes lead to an angry confrontation and eventual break. In showing the consequences of their inability to compromise, Simon again argues for "a middle course rather than an extremely polarized position," McGovern writes. Speaking of Simon's handling of such important themes in his comedies, McGovern claims that "to Neil Simon, . . . the comic form provides a means to present serious subjects so that audiences may laugh to avoid weeping."

But not all critics have been kind to Simon. Some believe his long string of hit comedies to be filled with funny one-liners and little else. Jack Kroll of *Newsweek* refers to Simon's image as "Gagman Laureate." Writing in his *Uneasy Stages: A Chronicle of the New York Theater, 1963-73,* John Simon claims that "the basic unit of [Simon's] playmaking is the joke. Not the word, the idea, the character, or even the situation, but the gag. It kills him if here and there a monosyllable resists funnying up, if now and then someone has to make a move that won't fracture the audience." According to Gerald M. Berkowitz, writing in *Players,* "Simon is a critical embarrassment. . . . A Neil Simon comedy makes the audience laugh. . . . [But] the secret of his special comic talent is a matter of pure technique; . . . it is not the content of his plays, but the manner in which the content is presented that generates most of the laughter."

For many years, Simon was taken less than seriously even by critics who enjoyed his work. A *Time* reviewer, for example, once claimed that "Santa Claus is just an alias for Neil Simon. Every year just before Christmas, he loads up packets of goodies and tosses two unbridled hours of laughter to Broadway audiences." Johnson notes that many people saw Simon as "a sausage grinder turning out the same pleasing 'product' over and over again. The 'product' is a play or movie realistic in style and featuring New Yorkers who spout a lot of funny lines." Geitner remarks that Simon's reputation as "the most formidable comedy writer in American theatre . . . prevented his being considered a serious dramatist by many critics."

With the production of the trilogy "Brighton Beach Memoirs," "Biloxi Blues," and "Broadway Bound" in the 1980s, however, critical opinion about Simon's work has improved enormously. Speaking of the critical reception of "Brighton Beach Memoirs," Richards explains that "the critics, who have sometimes begrudged the playwright his ability to coin more funny lines per minute than seems humanly possible, have now decided that he has a very warm heart." And "Biloxi Blues," his twenty-first Broadway play, won Simon in 1985 his first Tony Award for best drama. (He had twenty years earlier won the Tony for best playwright.)

The trilogy is based on Simon's own childhood and youth in the 1930s and 1940s, although he tells Charles Champlin of the *Los Angeles Times:* "I hate to call it autobiographical, because things didn't necessarily happen, or happen to me. It's an Impressionist painting of that era and that place. But there are bits and pieces of me in several of the characters." "Broadway Bound" is close enough to the truth, however, for William A. Henry III of *Time* to report that both Simon "and his brother Danny have wept openly while watching it in performance."

"Brighton Beach Memoirs" is set in the Brooklyn of 1937 and tells of a Jewish family, the Jeromes, and their financial troubles during the Depression. When an aunt loses her job, she and her son move in with the Jeromes, and the family, now seven people in a cramped house, must survive their financial crisis and the aggravatingly close proximity to each other. Rich explains that "Simon uses the family's miseries to raise such enduring issues as sibling resentments, guilt-ridden parent-child relationships and the hunger for dignity in a poverty-stricken world." Simon's alter ego is the family's teenage son, Eugene, who comments on his family's problems in asides to the audience. Eugene, Richards explains, "serves as the play's narrator and [his] cockeyed slant on the family's tribulations keeps the play in comic perspective."

The play has earned Simon some of the best reviews of his career. Brown writes that "Brighton Beach Memoirs" has "plenty of laughs," but "Simon avoids the glib, tenderly probing the often-awkward moments where confused emotions cause unconscious hurts. . . . Simon's at his best, finding the natural wit, wisecracking and hyperbole in the words and wisdom of everyday people." Barnes finds "Brighton Beach Memoirs" to be "a very lovely play." He continues: "I am certain—if the kids of our academic establishment can get off their pinnacles and start taking Simon as seriously as he deserves—*Brighton Beach Memoirs* will become a standard part of American dramatic literature."

Eugene Jerome joins the Army in "Biloxi Blues," the second play of the trilogy. The story follows Eugene through his ten weeks of basic training in Biloxi, Mississippi. During this training, one recruit is jailed for his homosexuality; one comes into constant conflict with his superior officers; and Eugene faces anti-Semitic insults from another soldier. Eugene, an aspiring writer, records these events faithfully in his diary, learning to examine his life and the lives of his friends honestly, and developing personal values in the process. Eugene's dream of becoming a writer is greatly furthered when he is assigned to work on an Army newspaper instead of being sent to the front, a fortunate turn of events that nonetheless makes him feel guilty.

Eugene's Army career is virtually identical to Simon's own stint in the military. Simon explains to Michiko Kakutani of the *New York Times* that writing the play was an act of self-discovery: "I wanted to know how this extremely shy, not enormously well-educated boy came to do what I consider a very hard thing to do—write plays. I wanted to see how I became the person I am.

I seem to be, in my own mind, a very unlikely candidate for success."

This self-examination has been well received by the critics, who find that Simon realistically presents life in the Army. "For all the familiarity of its set pieces," Dan Sullivan of the *Los Angeles Times* says of "Biloxi Blues," "it feels like life, not 'Gomer Pyle.'" Critics have also been impressed with how Simon subordinates the play's humor to its more serious concerns. As Howard Kissel writes in *Women's Wear Daily*, "Biloxi Blues" "is certainly Simon's best play, to my mind the first in which he has had the courage to suggest there are things that matter more to him than the reassuring sound of the audience's laughter. My admiration for the play is deep and unqualified." Richards claims that "Biloxi Blues" "may be the most touching play ever written about the rigors of basic training."

The story of Eugene Jerome continues in "Broadway Bound," in which Eugene and his older brother, Simon, become comedy writers, leave home, and take jobs with a major network radio show. The breakup of their parents' marriage, the family's resistance to their new profession, and Eugene's realization that life does not enjoy the happy endings found in art form the basis of the plot. Danny Simon tells Nina Darnton of the *New York Times* that "Broadway Bound" "is the closest in accuracy" of the three autobiographical plays.

Eugene's mother is the primary character in "Broadway Bound." "Through much of the comedy," Christiansen notes, "she has been the needling, nagging Jewish mother who gets the old, familiar laughs. But by the end of the play, with her personal life a shambles, she has turned into a creature of great sorrow and weariness, as well." After recounting to Eugene the story of how she once danced with actor George Raft—an exhilarating and romantic moment she still recalls fondly—Eugene asks his mother to dance with him. "In this," Kroll observes, "perhaps the most delicate and highly charged moment in any Simon play, we feel the waste of a woman's unlived life and the shock of a young man who feels in his arms the repressed rhythm of that life." Eugene "sees that behind his mother's depressed exterior," Mel Gussow comments in the *New York Times*, "is the heart of a once vibrant and hopeful young woman; she is someone who has been defeated by the limits she has imposed on her life."

According to Sylvie Drake of the *Los Angeles Times*, "Broadway Bound" "is the third and best and final segment of Simon's semi-autobiographical trilogy. . . . There is plenty of comedy left, but of a different order. The one-liners are gone, replaced by a well-timed visceral humor that is coated in melancholy." Drake concludes that "Broadway Bound" is Simon "not only at his finest, but at his most personal and complex." Similarly, although he sees some flaws in "Broadway Bound," Rich admits that it "contains some of its author's most accomplished writing to date—passages that dramatize the timeless, unresolvable bloodlettings of familial existence as well as the humorous conflicts one expects." And Holly Hill, writing for the London *Times*, believes that Eugene's mother "is the most masterful portrait Neil Simon has ever drawn."

Although primarily known for his plays, Simon also has written a score of popular films. These include the screen adaptations of many of his own hit plays including "Barefoot in the Park," "The Odd Couple," and "The Sunshine Boys"—as well as such original screenplays as "The Cheap Detective," "Murder by Death," and "The Goodbye Girl." Simon's best screen work is found in films where he creates a desperate situation, Vincent Canby argues in the *New York Times*. Simon's "wisecracks define a world of mighty desperation," Canby writes, "in which

every confrontation, be it with a lover, a child, a husband, a friend or a taxi driver, becomes a last chance for survival. When he writes a work in which the desperation is built into the situations, Mr. Simon can be both immensely funny and surprisingly moving."

But not all critics appreciate Simon's film work. Gene Siskel of the *Chicago Tribune,* for one, declares: "I dread going to see a movie of Neil Simon's. In fact, I would see anything but a Disney live-action film rather than a Neil Simon movie. Anything. Even a mad-slasher movie." Simon's adaptations of his own plays, while often successful at the box office, have sometimes been criticized for being too stagey, like "photographed plays," as Johnson puts it. Yet, most of Simon's films, especially "The Heartbreak Kid" and "Only When I Laugh," have been extremely popular with audiences and critics alike.

"The Heartbreak Kid" concerns a young couple who get divorced during their honeymoon in Florida after the husband meets another woman. Simon creates humor in this film, as Johnson allows, "out of situations which are not basically surefire comedy material." It is this blend of the humorous and the essentially tragic—with the humor emerging naturally from the actions and speech of the characters—which makes "The Heartbreak Kid" "the best film created thus far from a Neil Simon script," Johnson believes.

"Only When I Laugh" was also a critical success for Simon. It tells the story of Georgia Hines, an alcoholic Broadway actress who, despite rehabilitation, cannot beat her dependence. Georgia "is one of the most interesting, complicated characters that Mr. Simon, the master of the sometimes self-defeating one-liner, has ever written," according to Canby. Johnson finds "Only When I Laugh" "one of the most absorbing pieces of work that Simon has written."

"Writing is an escape from a world that crowds me," Simon tells John Corry of the *New York Times*. "I like being alone in a room. It's almost a form of meditation an investigation of my own life." He explains to Henry how he begins a play: "There's no blueprint per se. You just go through the tunnels of your mind, and you come out someplace." Simon admits to Zimmerman that the writing process still frightens him. "Every time I start a play," he explains, "I panic because I feel I don't know how to do it. . . . I keep wishing I had a grownup in the room who would tell me how to begin." Accepting his success as a writer has also been difficult. "I was depressed for a number of years," Simon tells Corry. The opening of a new play always filled him with guilt. It took psychoanalysis, and a consultation with his second wife's swami, before Simon learned to enjoy his accomplishments.

Simon writes on a daily basis, although much of his work is never completed. Richards reports that "Simon's desk overflows with the plays he's begun over the years. On an average, for every one he finishes, there are 10 he abandons after 15 or 20 pages." Generally, if Simon gets past page thirty-five he will finish the play, a process that takes four months for a first draft, longer for the final draft. "Come Blow Your Horn," for example, was rewritten twenty times before Simon was satisfied with it. In "Broadway Bound," Simon has his alter ego, Eugene, say: "I love being a writer. It's the writing that's hard."

Despite the difficulty involved in writing, Simon has managed to produce an impressive body of work. A new Simon comedy every theatrical season has been a Broadway staple for three decades. Henry calls him "America's foremost stage comedist" and places Simon "in the top rank of American playwrights." Rich calls him "not just a show business success but an institution." After surveying Simon's many achievements during his long career as a writer for the stage and screen, Johnson concludes by calling him "one of the finest writers of comedy in American literary history."

MEDIA ADAPTATIONS: "Come Blow Your Horn" was filmed by Paramount in 1963; "Sweet Charity" was filmed by Universal in 1969; "The Star-Spangled Girl" was filmed by Paramount in 1971; "Barefoot in the Park" was adapted as a television series by American Broadcasting Co. (ABC) in 1970; "The Odd Couple" was adapted as a television series by ABC in 1970-75, and as "The New Odd Couple," ABC, in 1982-83; "Neil Simon: Not Just for Laughs," a biographical portrait of Simon aired on the Public Broadcasting Corporation (PBS) "American Masters" series in 1989.

BIOGRAPHICAL/CRITICAL SOURCES:

BOOKS

Authors in the News, Volume 1, Gale, 1976.
Contemporary Literary Criticism, Gale, Volume 6, 1976, Volume 9, 1979, Volume 31, 1985, Volume 39, 1986.
Dictionary of Literary Biography, Volume 7: *Twentieth-Century American Dramatists,* Gale, 1981.
Johnson, Robert K., *Neil Simon,* Twayne, 1983.
Kerr, Walter, *Thirty Plays Hath November,* Simon & Schuster, 1969.
McGovern, Edythe M., *Neil Simon: A Critical Study,* Ungar, 1979.
Monaco, James, *American Film Now,* Oxford University Press, 1979.
Simon, John, *Uneasy Stages: A Chronicle of the New York Theater, 1963-73,* Random House, 1975.
Simon, Neil, *Broadway Bound,* Random House, 1987.

PERIODICALS

America, May 20, 1961, May 29, 1965.
American Film, March, 1978.
Chicago Tribune, March 26, 1982, April 7, 1986, November 2, 1986, December 31, 1986, August 23, 1989.
Christian Science Monitor, January 17, 1970, November 11, 1970.
Commonweal, November 15, 1963, April 2, 1965.
Critic's Choice, December, 1969.
Cue, January 3, 1970, January 15, 1972.
Daily News (New York), April 4, 1980, April 7, 1981, March 29, 1985.
Horizon, January, 1978.
Hudson Review, spring, 1978.
Humanist, September/October, 1976.
Life, April 9, 1965, March 6, 1970, May 7, 1971.
Los Angeles Times, December 5 1982, December 11, 1982, August 24, 1984, December 15, 1984, April 6, 1985, April 8, 1985, December 6, 1986, December 25, 1986, March 25, 1988, November 19, 1988, November 23, 1988, August 19, 1989, September 8, 1989, March 10, 1990, April 7, 1990.
Nation, March 4, 1968, July 3, 1976.
National Observer, November 20, 1971.
New Republic, January 16, 1971.
New Statesman, November 1, 1974.
Newsweek, January 9, 1967, February 26, 1968, February 2, 1970, November 23, 1970, December 10, 1973, April 26, 1976, February 26, 1979, April 14, 1980, April 20, 1981, December 15, 1986.
New York, January 13, 1975, April 11, 1983.

New Yorker, January 10, 1970, December 23, 1974.
New York Post, December 22, 1966, November 12, 1971, April 7, 1981, March 28, 1983, March 29, 1985.
New York Times, August 4, 1968, December 2, 1968, December 31, 1969, November 17, 1971, December 9, 1973, December 12, 1974, December 22, 1974, December 1, 1977, June 23, 1978, December 22, 1978, December 19 1980, March 23, 1981, April 5, 1981, April 7, 1981, April 12, 1981, September 23, 1981, March 25, 1983, March 27, 1983, March 28, 1983, April 3, 1983, March 29, 1985, April 1, 1985, April 7, 1985, April 16, 1985, June 9, 1985, August 29, 1986, November 30, 1986, December 5, 1986, December 14, 1986, December 25, 1986, December 26, 1986, January 8, 1987, January 25, 1987, August 17, 1987, December 9, 1987, March 25, 1988, April 15, 1988, November 13, 1988, November 18, 1988.
New York Times Magazine, March 7, 1965, March 22, 1970, May 26, 1985.
Philadelphia Inquirer, March 27, 1988.
Playbill, January, 1969.
Playboy, February, 1979.
Players, February/March, 1972, September, 1977.
Plays and Players, February, 1975, July, 1975, September, 1977.
Saturday Review, March 27, 1965.
Seventeen, November, 1979.
Show Business, January 10, 1970.
Spectator, November 2, 1974.
Time, November 1, 1963, January 12, 1970, January 15, 1973, December 23, 1974, April 8, 1985, December 15, 1986.
Times (London), April 20, 1983, April 10, 1985, December 4, 1986, January 3, 1987, June 4, 1987.
TV Guide, November 4, 1972.
Variety, December 24, 1969, February 25, 1970, November 4, 1970, September 8, 1971, December 27, 1972, December 5, 1973.
Village Voice, January 8, 1970.
Vogue, April 1, 1968, October 1, 1968, January 1, 1970.
Washington Post, January 13, 1970, February 9, 1971, April 10, 1983, December 14, 1984, April 6, 1985, July 16, 1985, June 12, 1986, September 12, 1986, October 19, 1986, December 25, 1986, December 26, 1986, March 25, 1988, December 20, 1988.
Women's Wear Daily, November 15, 1971, April 4, 1980, March 29, 1985.
World Journal Tribune, December 22, 1966.

*   *   *

SIMPSON, Dorothy 1933-

PERSONAL: Born June 20, 1933, in Blaenavon, Monmouthshire, Wales; daughter of Robert Wilfrid (a civil servant) and Gladys (a teacher of elocution; maiden name, Jones) Preece; married Keith Taylor Simpson (a barrister), July 22, 1961; children: Mark Taylor, Ian Robert, Emma Morag. *Education:* University of Bristol, B.A. (with honors), 1954, teaching diploma, 1955. *Religion:* Christian.

ADDRESSES: Home—Leeds, England. *Agent*— Anne McDermid, Curtis Brown Ltd., 162-168 Regent St., London W1R 5TA, England.

CAREER: Teacher of English and French at Dartford Grammar School for Girls, Dartford, England, 1955-59, and Erith Grammar School, Erith, England, 1959-61; Senacre School, Maidstone, Kent, England teacher of English, 1961-62; marriage guidance counsellor, 1969-82; writer, 1975—.

MEMBER: Crime Writers Association, Society of Authors, Mystery Writers of America.

AWARDS, HONORS: Silver Dagger Award from Crime Writers Association of Great Britain, 1985, for *Last Seen Alive.*

WRITINGS:

MYSTERY NOVELS

Harbingers of Fear (suspense novel), Macdonald & Janes, 1977.

"INSPECTOR THANET" SERIES; PUBLISHED BY SCRIBNER

The Night She Died, 1981.
Six Feet Under, 1982.
Puppet for a Corpse, 1983.
Close Her Eyes, 1984.
Last Seen Alive, 1985.
Dead on Arrival, 1986.
Element of Doubt, 1987.
Suspicious Death, 1988.
Dead by Morning, 1989.

OTHER

Contributor to *Ellery Queen's Mystery Magazine* and *Alfred Hitchcock's Mystery Magazine.*

WORK IN PROGRESS: More books in the "Inspector Thanet" series; additional crime stories.

SIDELIGHTS: It was mid-life for Dorothy Simpson before she wrote her first book, *Harbingers of Fear.* Accepted by the first publisher it was submitted to, this suspense novel was generally well-received by British readers. Although her husband sensed her literary ability and for years urged her to try her hand at writing, Simpson felt uninspired to toil away on a book. However, as she explained to *CA:* "I began to write after a long illness in 1975, which gave me plenty of time for reflection and reassessment. I was fortunate in that my first book found an agent immediately, and a publisher and serialization in a major women's magazine."

Following this initial success, Simpson wrote three books that were all rejected by various publishers. As a result, Simpson took a serious look at her talents, assessed her strengths, and decided to devote her next efforts to creating an intriguing murder mystery staged around an engaging sleuth. After months of molding and planning, Inspector Luke Thanet and his loyal assistant, Sergeant Lineham were created to solve the murder in *The Night She Died.*

Described as "an absolutely first rate mystery" by *Publishers Weekly, The Night She Died* was greeted enthusiastically by reviewers and readers not only in Simpson's homeland of England but in the United States as well. In a *Washington Post Book World* review of *The Night She Died* Jean M. White states that "Simpson neatly interweaves past and present with deft double-plotting. Her characters take on real-life dimension, notably Inspector Thanet, a policeman with a bad back, an interesting wife, and a compassionate curiosity about human beings. This is a first-rate job from a writer with subtlety and an unobtrusive literate style." Since *The Night She Died,* Simpson has added eight more books to her "Inspector Thanet" series and has built a following of loyal readers who eagerly await each new book.

Much of the reason for her success can be attributed to the popularity of Inspector Thanet himself. Simpson portrays Thanet as an average British policeman. Although he seems blessed with great detective skills, he still is very human—besieged with the problems of everyday life, such as experiencing and coping with

a chronic bad back, the joys and tribulations of fatherhood, and the efforts needed to maintain a good marriage.

"Detective Inspector Luke Thanet [is] a man of gentle mien, he is inclined to use psychology and tact, rather than showboat heroics, when pursuing his murder inquiries," comments a critic for the *New York Times Book Review.* And Douglas Hill remarks in Toronto's *Globe and Mail:* "Thanet comes across as gentle, human, civilized; his approach to [a] particular crime [and] specific people, leads to a rewarding psychological synthesis. Just don't read Simpson after a dose of the neo-Hammett, shoot-'em-up, down-and-dirty school of detective writing. Then you may be disappointed with Luke Thanet and his quiet ways. That would be a pity."

Reviewers have frequently compared Simpson's mystery novels with those of fellow countrywomen Agatha Christie and Margery Allingham. Like these two detective novelists, Simpson presents a meticulously designed mystery with a cast of characters and vividly detailed local settings as developed and integral as her plot. Charles Champlin writes in the *Los Angeles Times Book Review:* "The country village murder cases as Christie and Allingham used to write them, complete with manor house, eccentric vicar and a map for a frontispiece, are an endangered species. But Dorothy Simpson writes them fondly and well."

BIOGRAPHICAL/CRITICAL SOURCES:

PERIODICALS

Booklist, December 1, 1986.
Los Angeles Times Book Review, January 1, 1989.
Listener, July 2, 1987.
Library Journal, January, 1987.
New York Times Book Review, January 1, 1989.
Publishers Weekly, May 1, 1981, August 2, 1985, January 29, 1988.
Times, April 25, 1986.
Times Literary Supplement, May 28, 1982, April 5, 1985.
Washington Post Book World, June 21, 1981, November 17, 1985.

*　　*　　*

SIMPSON, George Gaylord 1902-1984

PERSONAL: Born June 16, 1902, in Chicago, Ill.; died of pneumonia, October 6, 1984, in Tucson, Ariz.; son of Joseph Alexander (a lawyer) and Helen Julia (Kinney) Simpson; married Lydia Pedroja, February 2, 1923 (divorced April, 1938); married Anne Roe (a psychologist and writer), May 27, 1938; children: (first marriage) Helen (Mrs. Wolf Vishniac), Gaylord (Mrs. Frank Bush; deceased), Joan (Mrs. James Bums), Elizabeth (Mrs. John Wuri). *Education:* University of Colorado, student, 1918-19, 1920-22; Yale University, Ph.B., 1923, Ph.D., 1926. *Politics:* Democrat. *Religion:* "Nondogmatic."

ADDRESSES: Office—Simroe Foundation, 5151 East Holmes St., Tucson, Ariz. 85711.

CAREER: American Museum of Natural History, New York, N.Y., field assistant, 1924, assistant curator, 1927, associate curator of vertebrate paleontology, 1928-42, curator of fossil mammals, 1942-59; chairman of department of geology and paleontology, 1944-58; Columbia University, New York City, professor of vertebrate paleontology, 1945-59; Harvard University, Museum of Comparative Zoology, Cambridge, Mass., Alexander Agassiz Professor of Vertebrate Paleontology, 1959-70; University of Arizona, Tucson, professor of geoscience, 1967-82; Simroe Foundation, Tucson, president and trustee, 1968-84. National Research Council fellow in biological science, British Museum of Natural History, 1926-27. Special lectureships at Princeton University, Harvard University, Yale University, University of California, Columbia University, and other universities, 1946-83. Member of American Museum of Natural History expeditions to western United States, 1924, 1929, 1932, 1935, 1936, 1946-50, and 1952-54, southeastern United States, 1929-30, Patagonia region of Argentina and Chile, 1930-31, 1933-34, Venezuela, 1938-39, Brazil, 1954-55, 1956, Spain, 1960, East Africa, 1961, and others. *Military service:* U.S. Army, 1942-44; became major.

MEMBER: Paleontological Society, American Society of Mammalogists, American Society of Zoologists (president, 1964), Geological Society of America (fellow), Society for the Study of Evolution (president, 1946), Society of Systematic Zoology (president, 1962-63), Society of Vertebrate Paleontology (president, 1942-43), American Academy of Arts and Sciences (fellow; councillor, 1960-63), American Philosophical Society (fellow; councillor, 1946-49), National Academy of Sciences, Academia de Ciencias (Venezuela, Brazil, Argentina), Sociedad Cientifica Argentina (corresponding member), Sociedad Argentina de Estudios Geographia Gaea (honorary correspondent), Asociacion Paleontologica Argentina (honorary member), Deutsche Gesellschaft fur Saugetier Kunde, Senkenbergische Naturforschende Gesellschaft, Accademia Nazionale dei Lincei (Italy), Academia Nazionale dei XL (Italy), Phi Beta Kappa, Sigma Xi; foreign member of Royal Society, Linnean Society, and Zoological Society (all London); also member of numerous other societies in the United States, South America, Europe, Australia, and New Zealand.

AWARDS, HONORS: Lewis Prize, American Philosophical Society, 1942; National Academy of Sciences, Thompson Medal, 1943, and Elliott Medal, 1944, 1961; Gaudry Medal, Societe Geologique de France, 1947; Hayden Medal, Philadelphia Academy of Sciences, 1950; Penrose Medal, Geological Society of America, 1952; Andre H. Dumont Medal, Geological Society of Belgium, 1953; Darwin-Wallace Medal, Linnean Society of London, 1958; Darwin Plakette, Deutsche Akademie Naturforscher Leopoldina, 1959; Darwin Medal, Royal Society of London, 1962; Linnean Gold Medal, 1962; National Medal of Science, 1965; Verrill Medal, Yale University, 1966; distinguished achievement medal, American Museum of Natural History, 1969; Wilbur Cross Medal, Yale Graduate Association, 1969; Paleontological Society Medal, 1973; International Award for distinguished contributions to natural history, Smithsonian Institution, 1976; distinguished service award, American Institute of Biological Science, 1978. Sc.D. from Yale University, 1946, Princeton University, 1947, University of Durham, 1951, Oxford University, 1951, University of New Mexico, 1954, University of Chicago, 1959, Cambridge University, 1965, York University, 1966, Kenyon College, 1968, University of Colorado, 1968; LL.D., University of Glasgow, 1951; Dr.h.c., University of Paris, 1965, Universidad de La Plata, 1978.

WRITINGS:

A Catalogue of the Mesozoic Mammalia in the Geological Department of the British Museum, British Museum, 1928, reprinted, Ayer Co., 1980.
American Mesozoic Mammalia, Elliot's Books, 1929.
(Contributor) *Memoirs of the Peabody Museum of Yale University,* Volume III, Yale University Press, 1929, reprinted, Ayer Co., 1980.

Attending Marvels: A Patagonian Journal, Macmillan, 1934, reprinted, University of Chicago Press, 1982.
The Fort Union of the Crazy Mountain Field, Montana, and Its Mammalian Faunas, U.S. National Museum, 1937, reprinted with *Paleocene Primates of the Fort Union, with Discussion of Relationships of Eocene Primates* by James W. Gidley, AMS Press, 1978.
(With wife, Anne Roe) *Quantitative Zoology,* McGraw, 1939, revised edition (with Anne Roe and Richard Lewontin), Harcourt, 1960.
Los Indios Kamarakotos, Revista de Fomento (Caracas), 1940.
Tempo and Mode in Evolution, Columbia University Press, 1944, reprinted, 1984.
The Principles of Classification and a Classification of Mammals, American Museum of Natural History, 1945.
The Beginning of the Age of Mammals in South America, American Museum of Natural History, Part I, 1948, Part II, 1967.
The Meaning of Evolution: A Study of the History of Life and Its Significance for Man, Yale University Press, 1949, revised and abridged edition, New American Library, 1951, revised edition, Yale University Press, 1967.
Horses: The Story of the Horse Family in the Modern World and Through Sixty Million Years of History, Oxford University Press, 1951, published with new preface, Anchor Books, 1961.
Life of the Past (an introduction to paleontology), Yale University Press, 1953.
The Major Features of Evolution, Columbia University Press, 1953.
Evolution and Geography (Condon Lectures), Oregon State System of Higher Education, 1953.
(With Carlos de Paula Cauto) *The Mastodonts of Brazil,* American Museum of Natural History, 1957.
(With C. S. Pittendrigh and L. H. Tiffany) *Life: An Introduction to Biology,* Harcourt, 1957, revised edition (with William S. Beck), with instructor's manual, 1965, abridged edition, with student guide, 1970.
(Editor with Anne Roe) *Behavior and Evolution,* Yale University Press, 1958.
Principles of Animal Taxonomy, Columbia University Press, 1961.
This View of Life: The World of an Evolutionist, Harcourt, 1964.
The Geography of Evolution (collected essays), Chilton, 1965.
Biology and Man, Harcourt, 1969.
Mammals Around the Pacific, University of Washington Press, 1966.
Penguins: Past and Present, Here and There, Yale University Press, 1976.
Concession to the Improbable: An Unconventional Autobiography, Yale University Press, 1979.
Splendid Isolation: The Curious History of South American Mammals, Yale University Press, 1980.
Why and How: Some Problems and Methods in Historical Biology, Pergamon, 1980.
(Author of introduction) Charles Darwin, *Book of Darwin,* WSP, 1983.
Fossils and the History of Life, W. H. Freeman, 1984.
Discoverers of the Lost World: An Account of Some of Those Who Brought Back to Life South American Mammals Long Buried in the Abyss of Time, Yale University Press, 1984.
Simple Curiosity: Letters From George Gaylord Simpson to His Family, 1921-1927, edited by Leo F. Laporte, University of California Press, 1987.

Contributor of numerous articles, reports, essays, and reviews, to journals.

WORK IN PROGRESS: Essays and reviews for journals.

SIDELIGHTS: George Gaylord Simpson told *CA:* "I am primarily an earth scientist but have written not only technical studies but also textbooks and popular books covering broad fields in a number of different sciences. Outside of the sciences I read detective stories and study languages and linguistics from ancient Egyptian to modern Arabic, Hawaii, and other languages."

Simpson's book *Splendid Isolation: The Curious History of South American Mammals* presented its topic "successfully and readably, though the subject matter is highly specialized and somewhat technical," wrote David Snow in the *Time Literary Supplement.* Excavating South America's past, Simpson pieced together evidence which shows the relationship between its geologic history and the evolution of its mammals. Mammals distinctly South American, he found, developed where the continent was separated from North America during the late Cretaceous and the Tertiary periods. When continental drift united the two land masses, South America's peculiar mammals began their struggle to survive the invasion by North America's more advanced species. "This book shows Simpson's characteristic thoroughness, carefully measured thought, and admirable clear prose style," commented a *Washington Post Book World* reviewer. "Although aimed at anyone with a general interest in natural history," Snow added, *Splendid Isolation* "will . . . be referred to as much by working biologists as by the general reader and will be enjoyed by both."

AVOCATIONAL INTERESTS: Travel.

BIOGRAPHICAL/CRITICAL SOURCES:

BOOKS

Simpson, George, *Concession to the Improbable: An Unconventional Autobiography,* Yale University Press, 1979.

PERIODICALS

Nature, April 26, 1984.
New York Times Book Review, March 23, 1980.
Science, May 16, 1980, November 16, 1984.
Times Literary Supplement, August 1, 1980, November 2, 1984.
Washington Post Book World, September 4, 1983.

OBITUARIES:

PERIODICALS

Chicago Tribune, October 9, 1984.
Los Angeles Times, October 10, 1984.
New York Times, October 8, 1984.
Washington Post, October 13, 1984.

*   *   *

SIMPSON, Harriette
      See ARNOW, Harriette (Louisa) Simpson

*   *   *

SIMPSON, Louis (Aston Marantz) 1923-

PERSONAL: Born March 27, 1923, in Kingston, Jamaica, British West Indies; son of Aston and Rosalind (Marantz) Simpson; married Jeanne Rogers, 1949 (divorced, 1953); married Dorothy Roochvarg, 1955 (divorced, 1979); children: (first marriage) Matthew; (second marriage) Anne, Anthony. *Education:* Columbia University, B.S., 1948, M.A., 1950, Ph.D., 1959.

ADDRESSES: Home—P.O. Box 91, Port Jefferson, New York 11777. *Office*—Department of English, State University of New York, Stony Brook, N.Y. 11794.

CAREER: Bobbs-Merrill Publishing Co., New York City, editor, 1950-55; Columbia University, New York City, instructor in English, 1955-59; University of California, Berkeley, 1959-67, began as assistant professor, became professor of English; State University of New York at Stony Brook, professor of English and comparative literature, 1967—. Has given poetry readings at colleges and poetry centers throughout the United States and Europe and on television and radio programs in New York, San Francisco, and London. *Military service:* U.S. Army, 1943-46; became sergeant; awarded Bronze Star with oak leaf cluster, Purple Heart (twice), Presidential Unit Citation.

AWARDS, HONORS: Fellowship in literature (Prix de Rome) at American Academy in Rome, 1957; *Hudson Review* fellowship, 1957; Columbia University, distinguished alumni award, 1960, Medal for Excellence, 1965; Edna St. Vincent Millay Award, 1960; Guggenheim fellowships, 1962, 1970; American Council of Learned Societies grant, 1963; Pulitzer Prize for poetry, 1964, for *At the End of the Open Road;* American Academy of Arts and Letters award in literature, 1976; D.H.L., Eastern Michigan University, 1977; Institute of Jamaica Centenary Award, 1980; National Jewish Book Award, 1981.

WRITINGS:

POEMS

The Arrivistes: Poems, 1940-1949, Fine Editions, 1949.
Good News of Death and Other Poems, Scribner, 1955.
A Dream of Governors, Wesleyan University Press, 1959.
Louis Simpson Reads from His Own Works (sound recording), Carillon Books, 1961.
At the End of the Open Road, Wesleyan University Press, 1963, reprinted, 1982.
(Contributor) Thom Gunn and Ted Hughes, editors, *Five American Poets,* Faber, 1963.
Selected Poems, Harcourt, 1965.
(With others) *Today's Poets 1* (sound recording), Folkways, 1967.
Tondelayo, Slow Loris Press, 1971.
Adventures of the Letter I, Harper, 1972.
The Mexican Woman, Pomegranate Press, 1973.
Searching for the Ox: New Poems and a Preface, Morrow, 1976.
The Invasion of Italy, Main Street (Northampton, Mass.), 1976.
Armidale: Poems and a Prose Memoir, Boa Editions, 1979.
Out of Season, Deerfield Press (Deerfield, Mass.), 1979.
Caviare at the Funeral, Watts, 1980.
The Best Hour of the Night, Ticknor & Fields, 1983.
People Live Here: Selected Poems 1949-1983, Boa Editions, 1983.
Collected Poems, Paragon House, 1988.
(With Nicolo D'Alessandro) *Poems-Drawings,* translation by Nat Scammacca, Cross-Cultural Communications, 1989.

Another recording of Simpson reading his poetry is available in "Spoken Arts Treasury of 100 Modern American Poets Reading Their Poems," Volume 15, Spoken Arts.

OTHER

(Editor with Donald Hall and Robert Pack) *New Poets of England and America,* Meridian, 1957, reprinted, New English Library, 1974.
Riverside Drive (novel), Atheneum, 1962.
James Hogg: A Critical Study, St. Martin's, 1962, reprinted, Arden Library, 1977.

(Contributor) Michael Benedikt and George E. Wellwarth, editors, *Modern French Theatre* (contains Simpson's "The Breasts of Tiresias," an adaptation of Apollinaire's play), Dutton, 1964 (published in England as *Modern French Plays,* Faber, 1965).

(Editor) *An Introduction to Poetry,* St. Martin's, 1967, 3rd edition, 1986.

North of Jamaica (autobiography), Harper, 1972 (published in England as *Air with Armed Men,* London Magazine Editions, 1972).

Three on the Tower: The Lives and Works of Ezra Pound, T. S. Eliot and William Carlos Williams, Morrow, 1975.

A Revolution in Taste: Studies of Dylan Thomas, Allen Ginsberg, Sylvia Plath and Robert Lowell, Macmillan, 1978.

A Company of Poets, University of Michigan Press, 1981.

The Character of the Poet, University of Michigan Press, 1986.

Selected Prose, Paragon House, 1989.

Also author of plays *The Father Out of the Machine: A Masque* (published in *Chicago Review,* winter, 1950), *Good News of Death* (published in *Hudson Review,* summer, 1952), and *Andromeda* (published in *Hudson Review,* winter, 1956). Contributor of poems, plays, and articles to literary periodicals, including *American Poetry Review, Listener, Hudson Review, Paris Review,* and *Critical Quarterly.*

SIDELIGHTS: In a discussion of Louis Simpson's early poetry, Yohma Gray comments that he "never departs from traditional form and structure and yet he never departs from contemporary themes and concerns." Gray describes one poem, for example, in which Simpson "handles a modern psychological situation in the delicate cadence of seventeenth century verse." Ronald Moran makes a similar comment in regard to *The Arrivistes,* Simpson's first book. Moran finds that Simpson often sounds "like an Elizabethan song-maker or like a Cavalier poet." Gray argues that this juxtaposition of traditional form (ordered meter and rhyme) and modern subjects emphasizes, particularly in the poems about the world wars, the chaotic quality and the tensions of contemporary life. Gray finds that Simpson neither complains nor moralizes about modern problems; rather he clarifies difficulties and presents rational insights.

Gray also praises Simpson for his ability to make his readers heed that which usually passes undiscerned. As Gray remarks: "Even in the most mundane experience there is a vast area of unperceived reality and it is Louis Simpson's kind of poetry which brings it to our notice. It enables us to see things which are ordinarily all about us but which we do not ordinarily see; it adds a new dimension to our sensational perception, making us hear with our eyes and see with our ears." In addition, Gray contends that Simpson's art "imposes order from within on chaos without, gives meaning to the apparently meaningless, suggests fresh vantage points from which to probe experience." Gray comments in conclusion that poetry seeks the same goal as religious belief, "to formulate a coherent and significant meaning for life. The poetry of Louis Simpson offers us that meaning."

After 1959, the publication date of *A Dream of Governors,* Simpson's work changed, and Stephen Stepanchev contends that it changed for the better. Notes Stepanchev: "The prosaism of his early work—which required metrics and rhyme in order to give it character as verse—now gave way to rich, fresh, haunting imagery. His philosophical and political speculations achieved a distinction and brilliance that they had lacked before." A *Chicago Review* critic also remarks on the shift in Simpson's poetry, "*A Dream of Governors* has wit, sophistication, perceptiveness, intelligence, variety, and knowingness, but it comes perilously

close to being a poetry of chic." The reviewer goes on to say that this early work lacks a depth of feeling. However, he continues, "*At the End of the Open Road* (1963) . . . is a different story entirely. Simpson has found the secret of releasing the meaning and power of his themes. . . . It is not that his stanzas . . . are becoming more flexible and experimental: this in itself does not mean very much. . . . What is more fundamental, it seems to me, is that greater stylistic flexibility should be the sign of growth in the character and thought of the speaker. Simpson is becoming more able to be a part of what he writes about, and to make what he writes about more a part of him."

Not all critics appreciate the change in Simpson's verse. In a review of *Selected Poems,* which contains twelve new poems in addition to selections of earlier work, Harry Morris states that "Mr. Simpson's first three volumes are better" than his new poetry. Morris believes that Simpson's "new freedoms" have not helped him convey his themes more effectively. T. O'Hara, in a critique of *Adventures of the Letter I,* also questions Simpson's new manner: "What has happened to Louis Simpson's energy? . . . It almost appears that success has mellowed the tough poetic instinct that once propelled him, for this present collection barely flexes a muscle." Yet Marie Borroff, speaking of the same book, avows that "when the remaining decades of the twentieth century have passed ignominiously into history along with the 1960's, these stanzas and other gifts will remain to us." And Christopher Hope deems *Adventures* "a work of pure, brilliant invention."

Critical dissent continues in reviews of *Searching for the Ox.* Derwent May finds the quiet, reflective mood of the poems attractive. Nikki Stiller, on the other hand, feels that "Louis Simpson's work now suggest too much comfort: emotional, physical, intellectual. He has stopped struggling, it seems, for words, for rhythms, for his own deepest self." Yet in contrast to this, Peter Stitt remarks that *Searching for the Ox* "is a tremendously refreshing book. . . . The style in which [the poems] are written presents us with no barriers—it is plain, direct and relaxed. Moreover, the poems tell a story, or stories, in which we can take a real interest."

Simpson's poetry throughout the 1970s and 1980s is marked by this more pedestrian form as the poet began to feel more empathy with his adopted country. Among his more recent books which are concerned with the everyday lives of modern Americans, *Caviare at the Funeral* is often considered to be one of the poet's most accomplished collections. "The astonishing thing about *Caviare at the Funeral,*" emphasized Stitt in a *Georgia Review* article, "is its radical presentation of American life. . . . Somehow the fact that [Simpson] was born and raised in Jamaica and came to this country only in his eighteenth year has enabled him to see us, our land and our ways, with unusually clear vision. His earlier work," Stitt continues, "especially in *At the End of the Open Road,* shows an understanding of America rarely seen. . . . In *Caviare at the Funeral* Simpson carries his insights several steps further in the creation of a poetry of everyday American life." G. E. Murray similarly observes in *Hudson Review* that "just when it seems that Simpson has reached the comfortable heights of his powers, as evidenced by six formidable earlier collections, including the Pulitzer Prize-winning *At the End of the Open Road,* he penetrates forward with *Caviare at the Funeral.*"

The poet's next book, *The Best Hour of the Night,* "reflects Simpson's increasing focus on life in the suburbs," according to *Nation* critic Richard Tillinghast. Although some would not consider suburban life a lofty subject for a poet, Tillinghast believes that the subject is a valid and even important one, and applauds Simpson's willingness to write about the ordinary middle-class American. "Someone who knew nothing of present-day America would get little idea of our life from most contemporary poetry," writes Tillinghast, who later adds: "If you cling to the impression that poetry is by nature obscure, forbidding and otherworldly, buy one of these books by Louis Simpson. You may be the only passenger on the 5:51 reading it, but you will feel a shock of recognition at poems that dare to come to terms with this country we live in."

Simpson has also ventured into other genres: novel, autobiography, and literary critical study. Robert Massie writes in the *New York Times Book Review*: "Into fragments of dialogue, [Simpson] packs more meaning and drama than many novelists can bring off in a chapter. . . . As novels go, *Riverside Drive* is not a tragedy to shake the Gods—but it should stir most of its readers. From the first chapter to the last, it has the ring of truth." William Cole calls Simpson's autobiography, *North of Jamaica,* "magnificent." Concerning *A Revolution in Taste,* a literary critical study, Paul Zweig comments: "[Simpson] has provided a series of engaging portraits of poets whom he presents less as cultural exemplars than as individuals struggling, as Baudelaire wrote, to absolve the pain of their lives with the grace of an enduring poem. It is the life narrowing intensely and heatedly into the act of writing that interests Simpson, the life pared to the poem. And this has enabled him to write a series of compact literary biographies that have the pithiness of a 17th-century 'character' and a literary good sense that reminds me of [Samuel] Johnson's 'Lives of the Poets.' "

The most recent Simpson books have been collected works, including *People Live Here: Selected Poems 1949-1983, Collected Poems,* and *Selected Prose.* Critics have found the author's books of collected poetry to be especially rewarding, for works like *People Live Here* exhibit "drastic, unpredictable, and yet characteristic change" in the poet's writing, according to *Kenyon Review* contributor T. R. Hummer. "*People Live Here* makes it clear not that Simpson's work is divisible into phases (though from one angle of view, of course, it is); this book makes it clear that Simpson wants us to see a different truth about his and any good poet's way of working: that there are never absolute divisions, and that no poet can ever afford to turn his back on any possibility, because just when he does, that which he has rejected or neglected will turn out to be precisely what is called for."

Simpson's manuscript collection is kept at the Library of Congress, Washington, D.C. The Poetry Center of San Francisco State University and the State University of New York at Stony Brook have videotapes of his readings.

BIOGRAPHICAL/CRITICAL SOURCES:

BOOKS

Contemporary Authors Autobiography Series, Volume 4, Gale, 1986.
Contemporary Literary Criticism, Gale, Volume 4, 1975, Volume 7, 1977, Volume 9, 1978, Volume 32, 1985.
Dictionary of Literary Biography, Volume 5: *American Poets since World War II,* Gale, 1980.
Hungerford, Edward, editor, *Poets in Progress: Critical Prefaces to Thirteen Modern American Poets,* Northwestern University Press, 1967.
Lensing, George S., and Ronald Moran, *Four Poets and the Emotive Imagination,* Louisiana State University Press, 1976.
Moran, Ronald, *Louis Simpson,* Twayne, 1972.
Stepanchev, Stephen, *American Poetry since 1945,* Harper, 1965.

PERIODICALS

American Poetry Review, January-February, 1979.
Best Sellers, June 15, 1972.
Chicago Review, Volume 19, number 1, 1966.
Chicago Tribune Book World, February 22, 1981, June 10, 1984.
Georgia Review, spring, 1981, fall, 1983.
Harper's, October, 1965.
Hudson Review, spring, 1981, spring, 1984.
Kenyon Review, summer, 1984.
Listener, November 25, 1976.
London Magazine, February-March, 1977, February, 1982.
Los Angeles Times Book Review, October 5, 1980.
Midstream, December, 1976.
Nation, February 11, 1984.
New Statesman, January 31, 1964.
New York Herald Tribune Books Review, November 15, 1959, May 13, 1962.
New York Times Book Review, September 27, 1959, May 13, 1962, May 9, 1976, December 17, 1978, November 2, 1980, March 14, 1982, January 29, 1984, November 13, 1988, May 7, 1989.
New York Times Magazine, May 2, 1965.
Poetry, April, 1960, December, 1981.
Saturday Review, May 21, 1960.
Saturday Review/World, April 3, 1976.
Sewanee Review, spring, 1969.
Time, May 18, 1962.
Times Literary Supplement, June 9, 1966, January 4, 1980, June 5, 1981, September 11, 1981, July 4, 1986, May 5, 1989.
Tribune Books (Chicago), March 5, 1989.
Washington Post Book World, May 3, 1981.
Yale Review, March, 1964, October, 1972.

*   *   *

SINCLAIR, Andrew (Annandale) 1935-

PERSONAL: Born January 21, 1935, in Oxford, England; son of Stanley Charles (in the British Colonial Service) and Hilary (a writer; maiden name, Nash-Webber) Sinclair; married Marianne Alexandre, 1960 (divorced); married Miranda Seymour, October 18, 1972 (divorced June 6, 1984); married Sonia Melchett (a writer), July 25, 1984; children: (first marriage) Timon Alexandre; (second marriage) Merlin George. *Education:* Cambridge University, B.A. (double first honors in history), Trinity College, 1958, Ph.D., Churchill College, 1963.

ADDRESSES: Home—16 Tite St., London SW3 4HZ, England. *Agent*—Gillon Aitkens, 17 South Eaton Pl., London SW1W 9ER, England.

CAREER: Cambridge University, Churchill College, Cambridge, England, founding fellow and director of historical studies, 1961-63; University of London, London, England, lecturer in American history, 1965-67; managing director, Lorrimer Publishing, London, 1967-84, and Timon Films, 1969-84; Raleigh Promotions Ltd., London, chairman of operations, 1984-88. Writer and filmmaker. *Military service:* British Army, Coldstream Guards, 1953-55; became lieutenant.

MEMBER: Association of Cinematograph and Television Technicians, Royal Society of Literature (fellow), Society of American Historians (fellow).

AWARDS, HONORS: Commonwealth fellow, Harvard University, 1959-61; American Council of Learned Societies fellow, 1963-65; Somerset Maugham Literary Prize, 1967, for *The*

Emancipation of the American Woman; Venice Film Festival award, 1971, and Cannes Film Festival prize, 1972, both for "Under Milk Wood."

WRITINGS:

NOVELS

The Breaking of Bumbo (also see below), Simon & Schuster, 1959.

My Friend Judas (also see below), Faber, 1959, Simon & Schuster, 1961.

The Project, Simon & Schuster, 1960.

The Paradise Bum, Atheneum, 1963 (published in England as *The Hallelujah Bum,* Faber, 1963).

The Raker, Atheneum, 1964.

Gog, Macmillan, 1967.

Magog, Harper, 1972.

The Surrey Cat, M. Joseph, 1976, published as *Cat,* Sphere, 1977.

A Patriot for Hire, M. Joseph, 1978, published as *Sea of the Dead,* Sphere, 1981.

The Facts in the Case of E. A. Poe, Holt, 1980.

Beau Bumbo, Weidenfeld & Nicolson, 1985.

NONFICTION

The Era of Excess, introduction by Richard Hofstadter, Atlantic-Little, Brown, 1962, published as *The Era of Excess: A Social History of the Prohibition Movement,* Harper, 1964.

The Available Man: The Life behind the Masks of Warren Gamaliel Harding, Macmillan, 1965.

The Better Half: The Emancipation of the American Woman, Harper, 1965, published as *The Emancipation of the American Woman,* 1966, reprinted under original title, Greenwood Press, 1981.

A Concise History of the United States, Viking, 1967.

The Last of the Best: The Aristocracy of Europe in the Twentieth Century, Macmillan, 1969.

Che Guevara, Viking, 1970 (published in England as *Guevara,* Fontana, 1970).

Dylan Thomas: No Man More Magical, Holt, 1975 (published in England as *Thomas: Poet of His People,* M. Joseph, 1975).

The Savage: A History of Misunderstanding, Weidenfeld & Nicolson, 1977.

Jack: A Biography of Jack London, Harper, 1977.

John Ford: A Biography, Dial, 1979.

Corsair: The Life of J. Pierpont Morgan, Little, Brown, 1981.

The Other Victoria: The Princess Royal and the Great Game of Europe, Weidenfeld & Nicolson, 1981.

(With Ladislas Farago) *Royal Web,* McGraw, 1982.

Sir Walter Raleigh and the Age of Discovery, Penguin, 1984.

S. P. Eagle: A Biography of Sam Spiegel, Little, Brown, 1988.

PLAYS

"My Friend Judas" (adapted from author's novel of same title), first produced in London at Arts Theatre, October 21, 1959.

(Adapter) Dylan Thomas, *Adventures in the Skin Trade* (first produced at Hampstead Theatre Club, March 7, 1965; produced in Washington, D.C., at Washington Theatre Club, February 25, 1970), Dent, 1967, New Directions, 1968.

"The Blue Angel" (adapted from screenplay of Josef von Sternberg's film of same title), first produced in Liverpool, England, at Liverpool Playhouse, October 1, 1983.

SCRIPTS

"Before Winter Comes" (based on Frederick L. Keefe's short story "The Interpreter"), Columbia, 1969.

"The Breaking of Bumbo" (based on author's novel of same title), directed by Sinclair, Associated British Pictures Corp., 1970.

"The Voyage of the Beagle" (television script), CBS Films, 1970.

Under Milk Wood (based on Dylan Thomas's play of same title; directed by Sinclair; produced by Timon Films, 1971), Simon & Schuster, 1972.

"Malachi's Cove," Timon Films, 1973.

"Martin Eden" (television script; based on novel by Jack London), RAI, 1981.

Also author of television scripts "The Chocolate Tree," 1963, and "Old Soldiers," 1964.

TRANSLATOR

Selections from the Greek Anthology, Weidenfeld & Nicolson, 1967, Macmillan, 1968.

(With Carlos P. Hanserv) *Bolivian Diary: Ernesto Che Guevara,* Lorrimer, 1968.

(With former wife, Marianne Alexandre) Jean Renoir, *La Grande Illusion* Lorrimer, 1968.

Masterworks of the French Cinema, Lorrimer, 1974.

OTHER

(Author of introduction) Homer, *The Iliad,* translated by W. H. D. Rouse, Heron Books, 1969.

Inkydoo, the Wild Boy (children's story), Abelard (London), 1976, published as *Carina and the Wild Boy,* Beaver/Hamlyn, 1977.

(Editor) *GWTW: The Screenplay* (script for "Gone with the Wind"), Macmillan, 1979.

(Editor) Jack London, *The Call of the Wild, White Fang, and Other Stories,* introduction by James Dickey, Penguin, 1981.

(Editor and author of introduction) Jack London, *The Sea Wolf and Other Stories,* Penguin, 1989.

Contributor to *Atlantic, Harper's, Observer, Guardian, Spectator, New Statesman,* and other periodicals and newspapers.

SIDELIGHTS: Among Andrew Sinclair's most imaginative works are the allegorical novel *Gog* and its sequel, *Magog.* A blend of fiction, history, and myth, the books examine Great Britain's past and present through the eyes of half-brothers Gog and Magog, names that evoke the twin giants of British legend whose statues stood guard over London's Guildhall until they were destroyed by German bombs in 1940. As Richard Freedman explains in the *Saturday Review,* Sinclair's modern versions of these age-old figures "symbolize the best and worst people and events from ancient Albion to Labourite Britain."

In the first novel, which begins just after the end of World War II, a seven-foot-tall man is washed ashore on the coast of Scotland, naked and suffering from amnesia. After a brief convalescence, the man—who remembers only that his name is Gog—sets out for London, hoping to learn more about his identity and, therefore, his past. The rest of the novel chronicles his many adventures as he journeys south. In the picaresque tradition, Gog meets a variety of fictional, historical, and mythological characters along the way. Some display concern and offer him assistance and advice; others (including his own wife and half-brother) regard him as "the perfect victim" and derive much pleasure from making him suffer. By the end of the novel, the one-time innocent has developed a less idealistic, more pragmatic attitude toward life, one that acknowledges the existence of evil and corruption and the need for each person to fight his or her own battles.

In their evaluations of *Gog,* critics have tended to rate it in one of two ways: as an unsuccessful attempt at sophisticated satire or as a highly ambitious and imaginative product of genius. An adherent of the former view is *New Statesman* reviewer Kenith Trodd, who characterizes *Gog* as "a series of funny production numbers: droll, but the laughs are hollow where they need to be edgy; the wrong sort of punch." Frank McGuinness also believes *Gog* lacks the proper sort of "punch." Writing in *London Magazine,* McGuinness declares that the book exhibits "perhaps more satirical pretensions than the author's talent for ribald and extravagant inventiveness can finally support. . . . The truth is that if the novel is not without distinction as a study of a mind hovering between sanity and madness, its satirical aims are lost in a welter of scholarly clowning, crude farce and the sort of glib cynicism that is so often mistaken for cold, hard-headed intellectualism."

A similar opinion is expressed by J. D. Scott in the *New York Times Book Review.* "Mr. Sinclair has too much talent to fail to make an impression," the critic begins. "But the impression is confused by too much frenetic action, and softened by long lapses into flat, sometimes merely clever, sometimes merely banal, prose. *Gog* is a monument of myth and slapstick, violence and parody, drama-of-evil and custard-pie comedy. Like some great Gothic folly seen through the mist, it fails to communicate its meaning."

On the other side of the discussion are those reviewers who regard *Gog* as excitingly original and entertaining. Though he thinks the novel is "much too long," Roger Sale comments in the *Hudson Review* that "the end is rich and satisfying, a book the likes of which I have not seen in a long time." In his study *The Situation of the Novel,* Bernard Bergonzi praises Sinclair's "extraordinary imaginative exuberance" and terms *Gog* "an intensely personal book, whose approach could not be followed by writers who do not share Sinclair's preoccupations, knowledge and temperament." Even more enthusiastic is critic Philip Callow, who asserts in *Books and Bookmen:* "[*Gog*] sears and scalds, it's the vision of a cold, planetary eye, and somehow it all founders in the end, goes mad like a cancer and finally smashes in a blind fury of destruction. I'm still reeling. I think there's genius in it."

Rachel Trickett more or less agrees with this assessment of *Gog,* stating in the *Yale Review* that it is "most extraordinary and ambitious. . . . A mixture of traditional genres, the allegory, the romance, and the picaresque tale, it is at once realistic and a fantasy, didactic and mythical, precise and comprehensive. Sinclair complains that most reviewers have misunderstood it, but he can hardly be surprised; it attempts so much. . . . The love of life and a compulsive literary energy are what make *Gog* so impressive a book. . . . Confusion and carelessness are its worst faults, but its inclusiveness is also its strength. Self-indulgent and undisciplined, it nevertheless shows a clumsy but powerful genius which can only leave one astonished, occasionally repelled, but consistently grateful for so much imaginative vigor and breadth."

Magog, the sequel to *Gog,* examines many of the same social, political, and moral issues from the point of view of Gog's half-brother and spiritual opposite—Magog, the "symbol of power, authority, centralization, the tyranny of material success and fashion," as Trickett describes him. Like *Gog, Magog* begins in 1945, just after the end of the war. Sinclair portrays his title character as a young civil servant whose promising career with the government comes to an abrupt end when an investigation reveals the extent of his dishonest dealings. Despite this apparent setback, Magog moves on to successively more powerful positions as head of a film production company, an urban developer, and, finally, master of a new college at Cambridge. The focus of the book is on these various stages in Magog's career and on what *Dictionary of Literary Biography* writer Judith Vincent refers to as his ultimate realization "that his material success is hollow and that an inevitably changing order must deprive him of power."

Reviewers have greeted *Magog* with somewhat less enthusiasm than *Gog.* "Gobbling great hunks of time, a vast *dramatis personae;* tossing off puns, inside jokes, bits of mythology; insisting that the life of a man and of an empire have much in common, *Magog* trivializes all it touches," declares Patricia Meyer Spacks in the *Hudson Review.* "It's funny sometimes, sometimes even sad, but the lack of sharp authorial perspective makes it seem purposeless."

Commenting in the *New York Times Book Review,* Anthony Thwaite remarks that *Magog* "suffers, as sequels are apt to do, from the disabilities of its predecessor: lumbering in its episodic movement, spotty in its characterization, arbitrary in its action, and megalomaniac in its overview. . . . This book is not an epic, whatever its author's purpose may have been. Nor, despite its blurb, is it a 'wonderfully sardonic morality tale.' Sinclair's juggled universe bears little resemblance to any known world, no matter how hard he tries to reinforce everything with documentary and travelogue. *Magog* is a febrile, self-indulgent, opinionated and finally rather squalidly boring fling at the picaresque."

Unlike their colleagues, reviewers from the *Times Literary Supplement* and *Books and Bookmen* temper their criticism with praise. The *Times Literary Supplement* critic, for example, believes that "too many events" make *Magog* read like "a first-draft synopsis of a twelve-volume novel series, full of bright ideas, sharp comments and ambitions not yet realized." Nevertheless, the critic adds, "Sinclair is always interesting and convincing about [the] details of high life, which he treats with disdain." Oswell Blakeston also has some positive observations, particularly regarding the author's "ear for civil service dialogue." In general, says Blakeston in *Books and Bookmen,* this makes for "a splendid beginning" to the novel. "But then, alas, [Sinclair] plunges into farce," the critic continues. "[And] after one has laughed at a well-aimed poisoned dart of brilliant criticism, it's hard to accept the old custard pie as a devastating weapon."

Kenn Stitt and Lee T. Lemon are among those whose praise for *Magog* is almost without qualification. In a *New Statesman* article, Stitt describes the novel as "a rich and complex book, mirroring the complexities of the world it is set in, its strands intricately and carefully interwoven." Though he finds the theme somewhat trite, Lemon observes in *Prairie Schooner* that the author "does a fine job of showing the reader the peculiar anguish of the successful but hollow man [and] the intricacies of power." Like several other critics, he also finds that Sinclair "has a talent for the memorable turn of phrase." In short, concludes the reviewer, *Magog* "just might be one of the best novels of the past few years"—even better than *Gog.* "The earlier book was a stumbling romp through the history and mythology of the British Isles," says Lemon. "But *Magog* is a different book. Magog . . . is not hindered by his brother [Gog's] ponderous memories. He is a kind of gadfly of meaningless change. . . . By the end of the novel, Magog the manipulator has learned that time brings new and shrewder manipulators, and that one does not have to manipulate for the things which give satisfaction."

In a letter to *CA,* Sinclair comments on the ideas that inspired *Gog* and *Magog* and explains how *King Ludd* will complete the trilogy. "*Gog* is based on Eliot's principle that time past and present and future are all the same. It also attempts to bring alive the legendary and mystical history of Britain as seen in the struggle of the people against the power of the government, of London, of King Ludd's town. There is no resolution to the fight of Gog against Magog, of the land against the city, of the ruled against the ruler, but in that fight lies the spirit and the glory of Albion, whatever it may be. *Magog*'s world is the machinations of power, and how its misuse drove Britain down after the end of the Second World War. *King Ludd* will deal with England from the time of the Luddites opposing the industrial revolution through the neurosis of the 1930s to the odd conflicts of today, where the descendants of the Tolpuddle martyrs now have their unions and use the workers' power to oppress the rest. When brother fights brother, Magog and King Ludd will always rule."

BIOGRAPHICAL/CRITICAL SOURCES:

BOOKS

Bergonzi, Bernard, *The Situation of the Novel,* University of Pittsburgh Press, 1970.
Contemporary Authors Autobiography Series, Volume 5, Gale, 1987.
Contemporary Literary Criticism, Gale, Volume 2, 1974, Volume 14, 1980.
Dictionary of Literary Biography, Volume 14: *British Novelists since 1960,* Gale, 1982.
Morris, Robert K., editor, *Old Lines, New Forces: Essays on the Contemporary British Novel, 1960-1970,* Fairleigh Dickinson University Press, 1976.

PERIODICALS

Best Sellers, October 1, 1967.
Books and Bookmen, May, 1967, June, 1967, June, 1972.
Book World, September 24, 1967.
Chicago Tribune Book World, April 1, 1979, October 5, 1981.
Drama, summer, 1967.
Hudson Review, winter, 1967, autumn, 1972.
Listener, April 4, 1968.
London Magazine, June, 1967.
Los Angeles Times, April 7, 1981.
New Statesman, June 9, 1967, May 5, 1972.
New York Times, April 21, 1981.
New York Times Book Review, January 22, 1967, September 10, 1967, October 8, 1967, July 2, 1972, October 12, 1980.
Observer Review, June 1, 1967, January 1, 1970.
Prairie Schooner, spring, 1974.
Punch, January 20, 1970.
Saturday Review, September 16, 1967.
Spectator, April 25, 1969.
Time, September 1, 1967.
Times (London), January 21, 1982.
Times Literary Supplement, June 8, 1967, July 13, 1967, May 5, 1970, June 26, 1981.
Variety, January 15, 1969.
Washington Post, April 30, 1981.
Yale Review, spring, 1968.

*   *   *

SINCLAIR, Emil
See HESSE, Hermann

SINCLAIR, Upton (Beall) 1878-1968
(Clarke Fitch, Frederick Garrison, Arthur Stirling)

PERSONAL: Born September 20, 1878, in Baltimore, Md.; died November 25, 1968, in Bound Brook, N.J.; son of Upton Beall (a traveling salesman) and Priscilla (Harden) Sinclair; married Meta H. Fuller, 1900 (divorced, 1913); married Mary Craig Kimbrough (a poet), April 21, 1913 (died April 26, 1961); married Mary Elizabeth Willis, October 14, 1961 (died December 18, 1967); children: (first marriage) David. *Education:* City College (now City College of the City University of New York), A.B., 1897; graduate studies at Columbia University, 1897-1901. *Politics:* Formerly Socialist, then left-wing Democrat.

ADDRESSES: Home—Bound Brook, N.J. *Agent*—Bertha Klausner International Literary Agency, Inc., 71 Park Ave., New York, N.Y. 10016.

CAREER: Supported himself while an undergraduate by writing jokes, light verse, short stories, and other commissioned works for comic papers and adventure magazines; wrote nearly one hundred pseudonymous "dime novels" while attending graduate school; full-time writer, 1898-1962. Founder, Intercollegiate Socialist Society (now League for Industrial Democracy), Helicon Home Colony, Englewood, N.J., 1906, and EPIC (End Poverty in California) League, 1934; assisted U.S. Government in investigation of Chicago stock yards, 1906; established theater company for performance of socialist plays, 1908. Socialist candidate for U.S. House of Representatives from New Jersey, 1906, and from California, 1920, for U.S. Senate from California, 1922, and for governor of California, 1926 and 1930; Democratic candidate for governor of California, 1934. Occasional lecturer.

MEMBER: Authors League of America (founder), American Institute of Arts and Letters, American Civil Liberties Union (founder of Southern California chapter).

AWARDS, HONORS: Nobel Prize for literature nomination, 1932; Pulitzer Prize, 1943, for *Dragon's Teeth;* New York Newspaper Guild Page One Award, 1962; United Auto Workers Social Justice Award, 1962.

WRITINGS:

NOVELS

Springtime and Harvest: A Romance, Sinclair Press, 1901, published as *King Midas,* Funk, 1901, 2nd edition, Heinemann, 1906.
The Journal of Arthur Stirling, revised and condensed edition, Appleton, 1903, new edition, Heinemann, 1907.
Prince Hagen: A Phantasy, L. C. Page and Co., 1903, reprinted, Arno, 1978.
Manassas: A Novel of the War, Macmillan, 1904, reprinted, Scholarly Press, 1969, revised edition published as *Theirs Be the Guilt: A Novel of the War between the States,* Twayne, 1959.
The Jungle, Doubleday, 1906, reprinted, Penguin, 1980, unabridged edition, Doubleday, 1988.
A Captain of Industry, Being the Story of a Civilized Man, The Appeal to Reason, 1906, reprinted, Haldeman-Julius Publications, 1924.
The Overman, Doubleday, Page and Co., 1907.
The Moneychangers, B. W. Dodge and Co., 1908, reprinted, Gregg, 1968.
The Metropolis, Moffat, Yard and Co., 1908.
Samuel the Seeker, B. W. Dodge and Co., 1910.
Love's Pilgrimage, M. Kennerley, 1911, reprinted, Laurie, 1933.

The Millennium: A Comedy of the Year 2000, Laurie, 1912, reprinted, 1929.

Damaged Goods (novelization of play "Les Avaries" by Eugene Brieux), Winston, 1913, reprinted, Laurie, 1931, published as *Damaged Goods: A Novel about the Victims of Syphilis,* Haldeman-Julius Publications, 1948.

Sylvia, Winston, 1913, reprinted, Scholarly Press, 1970.

Sylvia's Marriage, Winston, 1914.

King Coal, Macmillan, 1917, reprinted, AMS Press, 1980.

Jimmie Higgins, Boni & Liveright, 1919, reprinted, University Press of Kentucky, 1970.

100%: The Story of a Patriot (also see below), privately printed, 1920 (published in England as *The Spy,* Laurie, 1920).

They Call Me Carpenter: A Tale of the Second Coming, Boni & Liveright, 1922, reprinted, Chivers, 1971.

Oil!, A. & C. Boni, 1927, reprinted, Robert Bentley, 1980, four-act play adaptation, privately printed, 1929.

Boston: A Documentary Novel of the Sacco-Vanzetti Case, A. & C. Boni, 1928 (published in England as *Boston: A Novel,* Laurie, 1929), reprinted, Robert Bentley, 1978, condensed edition published as *August 22,* Award Books, 1965 (published in England as *Boston: August 22,* Heinemann, 1978).

Mountain City, A. & C. Boni, 1930.

Peter Gudge Becomes a Secret Agent (excerpted from *100%*), State Publishing House, 1930.

Roman Holiday, Farrar & Rinehart, 1931.

The Wet Parade, Farrar & Rinehart, 1931.

Co-op: A Novel of Living Together, Farrar & Rinehart, 1936.

The Gnomobile: A Gnice Gnew Gnarrative with Gnonsense, but Gnothing Gnaughty (juvenile), Farrar & Rinehart, 1936, reprinted, Bobbs-Merrill, 1962.

No Pasaran! (They Shall Not Pass): A Story of the Battle of Madrid, Laurie, 1937.

Little Steel, Farrar & Rinehart, 1938, reprinted, AMS Press, 1976.

Our Lady, Rodale Press, 1938.

Limbo on the Loose: A Midsummer Night's Dream, Haldeman-Julius Publications, 1948.

Marie and Her Lover, Haldeman-Julius Publications, 1948.

Another Pamela; or, Virtue Still Rewarded, Viking, 1950.

What Didymus Did, Wingate, 1954, published as *It Happened to Didymus,* Sagamore Press, 1958.

Cicero: A Tragedy of Ancient Rome, privately printed, 1960.

Affectionately Eve, Twayne, 1961.

The Coal War: A Sequel to King Coal, edited by John Graham, Colorado Associated University Press, 1976.

POLITICAL, SOCIAL, AND ECONOMIC STUDIES

The Industrial Republic: A Study of the America of Ten Years Hence, Doubleday, Page and Co., 1907, reprinted, Hyperion Press, 1976.

(With Michael Williams) *Good Health and How We Won It, with an Account of the New Hygiene,* F. A. Stokes, 1909.

The Fasting Cure, M. Kennerley, 1911.

The Profits of Religion: An Essay in Economic Interpretation, privately printed, 1918, Vanguard, 1927, reprinted, AMS Press, 1970.

The Brass Check: A Study of American Journalism, privately printed, 1919, 11th edition, 1936, reprinted, Arden Library, 1979.

The Book of Life, Mind and Body, Macmillan, 1921, 4th edition, privately printed, 1926.

The Goose-step: A Study of American Education, privately printed, 1923, revised edition, Haldeman-Julius Publications, 1923, reprinted, AMS Press, 1970.

The Goslings: A Study of the American Schools, privately printed, 1924, reprinted, AMS Press, 1970.

Mammonart: An Essay in Economic Interpretation, privately printed, 1925, reprinted, Hyperion Press, 1975.

Letters to Judd, An American Workingman, privately printed, 1926, revised edition published as *This World of 1949 and What to Do about It: Revised Letters to a Workingman on the Economic and Political Situation,* Haldeman-Julius Publications, 1949.

The Spokesman's Secretary, Being the Letters of Mame to Mom, privately printed, 1926.

Money Writes!, A. & C. Boni, 1927, reprinted, Scholarly Press, 1970.

Upton Sinclair Presents William Fox, privately printed, 1933, reprinted, Arno, 1970.

The Way Out: What Lies Ahead for America, Farrar & Rinehart, 1933.

I, Governor of California, and How I Ended Poverty: A True Story of the Future, Farrar & Rinehart, 1933.

The Lie Factory Starts, End Poverty League, 1934.

The EPIC Plan for California, Farrar & Rinehart, 1934.

EPIC Answers: How to End Poverty in California, End Poverty League, 1934, 2nd edition, 1935.

I, Candidate for Governor, and How I Got Licked, Farrar & Rinehart, 1935 (published in England as *How I Got Licked and Why,* Laurie, 1935).

We, People of America, and How We Ended Poverty: A True Story of the Future, National EPIC League, 1935.

The Flivver King: A Story of Ford-America, Haldeman-Julius Publications, 1937 (published in England as *The Flivver King: A Novel of Ford-America,* Laurie, 1938), reprinted, Chivers, 1971.

(With Eugene Lyons) *Terror in Russia?: Two Views,* Richard R. Smith, 1938.

Your Million Dollars, privately printed, 1939 (published in England as *Letters to a Millionaire,* Laurie, 1939).

Expect No Peace!, Haldeman-Julius Publications, 1939.

What Can Be Done about America's Economic Troubles, privately printed, 1939.

Telling the World, Laurie, 1940.

The Cup of Fury, Channel Press, 1956.

PLAYS

Plays of Protest (includes "The Naturewoman," "The Machine," "The Second-story Man," and "Prince Hagen"), M. Kennerley, 1912, reprinted, Scholarly Press, 1970.

Hell: A Verse Drama and Photo-play, privately printed, 1923.

Singing Jailbirds: A Drama in Four Acts, privately printed, 1924.

Bill Porter: A Drama of O. Henry in Prison, privately printed, 1925.

Depression Island, Laurie, 1935.

Wally for Queen!: The Private Life of Royalty, privately printed, 1936.

Marie Antoinette, Vanguard, 1939.

A Giant's Strength, Laurie, 1948.

The Enemy Had It Too (three-act), Viking, 1950.

OTHER

(Under pseudonym Frederick Garrison) *Off for West Point; or, Mark Mallory's Struggle,* Street & Smith, 1903.

(Under Garrison pseudonym) *On Guard; or, Mark Mallory's Celebration,* Street & Smith, 1903.

(Editor) *The Cry for Justice: An Anthology of the Literature of Social Protest,* Winston, 1915, revised edition, Lyle Stuart, 1963.

Mental Radio, A. & C. Boni, 1930 (published in England as *Mental Radio: Does It Work, and How?,* Laurie, 1930), reprinted, Macmillan, 1971, revised edition, C. C Thomas, 1962.

American Outpost: A Book of Reminiscences, Farrar & Rinehart, 1932 (published in England as *Candid Reminiscences: My First Thirty Years,* Laurie, 1932), reprinted, Kennikat, 1969.

The Book of Love, Laurie, 1934.

An Upton Sinclair Anthology, compiled by I. O. Evans, Farrar & Rinehart, 1934, revised edition, Murray & Gee, 1947.

What God Means to Me: An Attempt at a Working Religion, privately printed, 1935, Farrar & Rinehart, 1936.

A Personal Jesus: Portrait and Interpretation, Evans Publishing Co., 1952, 2nd edition published as *The Secret Life of Jesus,* Mercury Books, 1962.

My Lifetime in Letters, University of Missouri Press, 1960.

Autobiography, Harcourt, 1962.

(Author of foreword) Morton T. Kelsey, *Tongue Speaking,* Doubleday, 1964.

"LANNY BUDD" SERIES; NOVELS

World's End, Viking, 1940, reprinted, Curtis Books, 1968.

Between Two Worlds, Viking, 1941, reprinted, Curtis Books, 1968.

Dragon's Teeth, Viking, 1942, reprinted, New American Library, 1968.

Wide Is the Gate, Viking, 1943.

Presidential Agent, Viking, 1944.

Dragon Harvest, Viking, 1945.

A World to Win, 1940-1942, Viking, 1946.

Presidential Mission, Viking, 1947.

One Clear Call, Viking, 1948.

O Shepherd, Speak, Viking, 1949.

The Return of Lanny Budd, Viking, 1953.

JUVENILE NOVELS; UNDER PSEUDONYM CLARKE FITCH

Courtmartialed, Street & Smith, 1898.

Saved by the Enemy, Street & Smith, 1898.

Wolves of the Navy; or, Clif Faraday's Search for a Traitor, Street & Smith, 1899.

A Soldier Monk, Street & Smith, 1899.

A Soldier's Pledge, Street & Smith, 1899.

Clif, the Naval Cadet; or, Exciting Days at Annapolis, Street & Smith, 1903.

From Port to Port; or, Clif Faraday in Many Waters, Street & Smith, 1903.

The Cruise of the Training Ship; or, Clif Faraday's Pluck, Street & Smith, 1903.

A Strange Cruise; or, Clif Faraday's Yacht Chase, Street & Smith, 1903.

SIDELIGHTS: "He was a man with a cause, and his weapon was an impassioned pen." With these words, a *National Observer* reporter summed up the life of Upton Sinclair, one of the twentieth century's foremost novelists, journalists, and pamphleteers. A "muckraker" whose motto was the same as that of American reformer Wendell Phillips (1811-1884)—"If anything can't stand the truth, let it crack"—Sinclair spent most of his ninety years engaged in what William A. Bloodworth, Jr., in the *Dictionary of Literary Biography* calls "idealistic opposition to an unjust society." Time and time again, in books like the international bestseller *The Jungle* (a graphic portrayal of the wretched lives of workers in Chicago's meat-packing plants), the socialist crusader set out to reveal what he described as "the breaking of human hearts by a system which exploits the labor of men and women for profits."

According to Bloodworth, Sinclair pursued his theme of social justice for all with "single-minded intensity." He regarded all art as propaganda, continues the critic, using the novel not only to denounce wealth, corruption, and "loose morals" (alcohol and promiscuity were favorite targets) with puritanical fierceness, but also "to publicize and interpret contemporary events that he felt had not been adequately covered by the news media." And because Sinclair believed that the primary purpose of his books was to bring about improvement in the human condition, he placed more emphasis on content than on form, a major factor in the development of his reputation as a writer who displayed more zeal than style.

In addition to zeal, Sinclair was noted for his morally simple view of history, a view that is especially evident in the "Lanny Budd" novels. This eleven-volume series, begun in 1940 and completed in 1953, traces the political history of the Western world from 1913 to 1950. It describes historical change in terms of international conspiracy and conflict, primarily between the forces of progress (socialism and communism) and the forces of oppression (fascism). As the series moves forward in time, however, America of the 1930s and 1940s takes up the cause of progress to do battle with both fascism and Soviet-style communism. (Sinclair enthusiastically supported Franklin Roosevelt and abhorred Stalinism.)

The author had an equally simple view of human nature, evident in his characterization. Virtually all of his figures are two-dimensional, more symbolic than real. His typical hero, for instance, is a young and noble paragon of socialism; his typical villain, on the other hand, is usually the personification of a specific trait such as greediness or corruption. Explains V. F. Calverton in the *Nation:* "[Sinclair's] characters are rational—or cerebral if you will—rather than emotive creations. One can see them but not experience them. This is partly due to the fact that, in the main, they are types instead of individuals, types that you know. . . . Sinclair tends to portray his characters in terms of straight lines instead of in terms of all those zigzags of personality, those intricate and irrational contradictions of self, which create individuality in life as well as in fiction."

In his book *Sketches in Criticism,* Van Wyck Brooks presents a more pointed assessment of Sinclair's characters. It is hardly surprising, he says, that "Sinclair should be popular with the dispossessed: they who are so seldom flattered find in his pages a land of milk and honey. Here all the workers wear haloes of pure golden sunlight and all the capitalists have horns and tails; socialists with fashionable English wives invariably turn yellow at the appropriate moment, and rich men's sons are humbled in the dust, winsome lasses are always true unless their fathers have money in the bank, and wives never understand their husbands, and all those who are good are also martyrs, and all those who are patriots are also base. Mr. Sinclair says that the incidents in his books are based on fact and that his characters are studied from life. . . . But Mr. Sinclair, like the rest of us, has seen what he wanted to see and studied what he wanted to study; and his special simplification of the social scene is one that almost inevitably makes glad the heart of the victim of our system."

Granville Hicks, commenting in *College English,* believes this flatness of characterization is not a deliberate effort on Sinclair's part to idealize and stereotype, but it is "an inherent defect of the genre in which [he] is writing. In the historical novel, whether its subject is in the remote or the recent past, if the emphasis is on history, attention is directed outward rather than inward. . . . One cannot say that Sinclair has a meager imagination, for there are magnificent passages [in his books] to prove the contrary; but one can say that the very nature of both his practical and his literary interests will not allow him to exploit his insight."

On the subject of Sinclair's writing style, however, Hicks is less willing to blame genre limitations for any deficiencies. Like many of his colleagues, the critic notes that "the writing, if seldom downright bad, . . . is not distinguished. Years ago Sinclair perfected a fluent, lucid style, easy to read and probably not very hard to write. . . . No experimentalist of these recent years, in fact no writer of the twentieth century, has influenced his style. He editorializes as readily as any Victorian, is not afraid of cliches, uses and sometimes misuses the colloquialisms of the day. It is a style rather painful to those who crave either artifice or art, but it is clear and it does move." Sinclair (who took pleasure in responding to his critics) had a simple explanation for his commonplace style and tendency toward oversimplification. "Somebody has to write for the masses and not just the Harvard professors," he once remarked. "I have tried to make my meaning plain so that the humblest can understand me."

Sinclair's strong identification with "the masses" is most often attributed to the circumstances of his youth. He was born into an aristocratic but impoverished Southern family whose financial difficulties dated back to the Civil War era. His father, Upton Beall, a traveling salesman who turned to alcohol to cope with the unaccustomed pressures of having to work for a living, rarely made enough money to provide Upton and his mother with some measure of comfort. This life of genteel hardship contrasted sharply with that of Priscilla Sinclair's wealthy Baltimore relatives; it was a difference that disturbed young Sinclair, who could not understand why some people were rich and others poor. (Many years later, at the age of eighty-five, he remarked at a gathering held in his honor that he still did not understand.)

A sickly but precocious child, Sinclair entered New York's City College at the age of fourteen. Determined to become financially independent from his unreliable father, he immediately began submitting jokes, riddles, poems, and short stories to popular magazines; by the time he graduated, Sinclair was selling full-length adventure novels (which appeared under various pseudonyms) to Street & Smith, one of the day's foremost publishers of pulp fiction. During this period, the teenager learned to write quickly, prolifically, and with a minimum of effort, turning out an average of six to eight thousand words per day, seven days per week.

After receiving his degree from City College, Sinclair went on to graduate school at Columbia University, where he was attracted to the romantic poets and their belief in the power of literature to make an appreciable difference in the world. The thought of being able to influence the course of human events was so appealing to the young student that he decided to give up hack writing and concentrate on "real" writing instead.

The next few years were filled with nothing but misery for Sinclair, his wife, and their infant son as the writer watched his first three highly idealistic, semi-autobiographical novels fade into oblivion soon after being published. Increasingly bitter, depressed, and even physically ill from his life of deprivation, Sinclair decided to make one last attempt to write a popular romantic work. His dream of a Civil War trilogy never went beyond the first volume, *Manassas,* but this single novel proved to be the turning point in his career. With its theme of a rich young Southerner who rejects plantation life to join the abolitionist movement, *Manassas* demonstrated the author's growing interest in

radical politics and eventually brought him to the attention of the American Socialists.

Once in contact with members of the socialist movement, Sinclair began studying philosophy and theoretics in earnest and was soon invited to contribute articles to major socialist publications. In late 1904, Fred D. Warren, editor of the magazine *Appeal to Reason,* approached Sinclair and challenged him to write about the "wage slaves" of industry in the same way he had written about the "chattel slaves" on the Southern plantations of *Manassas.* Encouraged by his editor at Macmillan, Sinclair accepted Warren's challenge and took as his starting point an article he had worked on that very summer dealing with an unsuccessful strike in the Chicago meat-packing industry. Thus in November, 1904, having moved his wife and son to a small New Jersey farm he had bought with the five-hundred dollar advance he received for his novel-to-be, *The Jungle,* Sinclair set out for Chicago, promising to "shake the popular heart and blow the roof off of the industrial tea-kettle." It was, notes Bloodworth in his study *Upton Sinclair,* a trip that "made a traumatic, life-long impression on him." Explains the critic: "What World War I meant to Ernest Hemingway, what the experiences of poverty and crime meant to Jack London, the combination of visible oppression and underlying corruption in Chicago in 1904 meant to Upton Sinclair. *This* kind of evidence, *this* kind of commitment to social justice became the primal experience of his fiction. For at least the next four decades, . . . Sinclair would continually retell the story of what happened to him in Chicago."

Sinclair's investigative work for *The Jungle* took seven weeks, during which time the young man talked with workers and visited packing plants, both on an official basis and in disguise. "I sat at night in the homes of the workers, foreign-born and native, and they told me their stories, one after one, and I made notes of everything," he once recalled. "In the daytime I would wander about the yards, and their friends would risk their jobs to show me what I wanted to see."

Returning to New Jersey in December, 1904, Sinclair began writing with his customary compulsiveness. "For three months," he said, "I worked incessantly. I wrote with tears and anguish, pouring into the pages all that pain which life had meant to me. Externally, the story had to do with a family of stockyards workers, but internally it was the story of my own family. Did I wish to know how the poor suffered in winter time in Chicago? I had only to recall the previous winter in the cabin, where we had only cotton blankets, and had to put rugs on top of us, and cowered shivering in our separate beds. It was the same with hunger, with illness, with fear."

Sinclair fashioned his story around the experiences of Jurgis Rudkus, a fictional Lithuanian immigrant who arrives in Chicago with his family "expecting to achieve the American dream," Bloodworth writes. "Instead," the critic continues, "their life becomes a nightmare of toil, poverty, and death. . . . [Rudkus] not only sees his father, wife, and son die, but he is also brutalized by working conditions in the Chicago packing houses and exploited by corrupt politics." To dramatize his story of pain and oppression, Sinclair included some unpleasant passages on the meat-packing process itself, focusing on the diseased and chemically-tainted condition of the products manufacturers were offering to the American public.

Having spent most of his novel chronicling the tragedy of life in Packingtown, Sinclair was left with the problem of ending *The Jungle* on a note of socialist hope. It was not enough to show that capitalism crushed the lives of workers, he decided; he had to prove that socialism was the best way to overcome capitalist exploitation. Though Sinclair wanted to avoid sermonizing, he saw no alternative: his hero, devastated by his brutal experiences, was in no condition to lead a revolution. Thus, the author has the despondent Rudkus stumble into a political meeting where he undergoes what most critics call a "religious conversion" to socialism as he listens to the words of various orators. Explains Bloodworth: "Sinclair finally presents Socialistic concepts in the closing chapters of [*The Jungle*] as part of a radical morality play in which the hero comes to accept as sinful the way in which he has worked unresistingly and individualistically within the capitalist system."

Sinclair completed *The Jungle* in late 1905. Though a serialized version in *Appeal to Reason* had begun to attract attention as early as the summer of that year, the book version caused officials at Macmillan and four other companies the author approached to balk at the idea of publishing potentially libelous material. Eventually, however, after sending investigators to Chicago to check out Sinclair's facts, the firm of Doubleday, Page and Company agreed to bring out *The Jungle.*

The book appeared early in 1906 and, in an ironic twist of fate, was promoted not as a socialist novel, but as an expose of "the flagrant violations of all hygienic laws in the slaughter of diseased cattle . . . and in the whole machinery of feeding a nation." Published at a time of growing public outcry against contaminated food, *The Jungle* shocked and infuriated Americans; it was, in fact, this widespread revulsion that made the book a best seller and its author a world-famous writer. (Well aware of the real reason for *The Jungle*'s success, Sinclair once remarked, "I aimed at the public's heart, and by accident I hit it in the stomach.") Observes Alfred Kazin in his book *On Native Grounds:* "*The Jungle* attracted attention because it was obviously the most authentic and most powerful of the muckraking novels. The romantic indignation of the book gave it its fierce honesty, but the facts in it gave Sinclair his reputation, for he had suddenly given an unprecedented social importance to muckraking. The sales of meat dropped, the Germans cited the book as an argument for higher import duties on American meat, Sinclair became a leading exponent of the muckraking spirit to thousands in America and Europe, and met with the President. No one could doubt it, the evidence was overwhelming: here in *The Jungle* was the great news story of a decade written out in letters of fire."

While few reviewers dispute the remarkable emotional impact of *The Jungle,* many believe its "letters of fire" do not constitute great literature. Its plot and characterization have come under particularly heavy fire in the years since 1906. *Bookman*'s Edward Clark Marsh, for instance, finds it "impossible to withhold admiration of Mr. Sinclair's enthusiasm" as he describes the "intolerable" conditions in Packingtown. But "when [the author] betakes himself to other scenes, and attempts to let his characters breathe the air of a more familiar life," continues the critic, "it is impossible not to recognize his ignorance." Furthermore, declares Marsh, "we do not need to be told that thievery, and prostitution, and political jobbery, and economic slavery exist in Chicago. So long as these truths are before us only as abstractions they are meaningless."

Another "meaningless abstraction," Marsh goes on to note, is Sinclair's main character, Jurgis Rudkus, whom the reviewer calls "a mere puppet." Explains Marsh: "He is too obviously manipulated, his experiences are too palpably made to order, to signify anything one way or the other. Jurgis Rudkus is neither individual or type. He is a mere jumble of impossible qualities labelled a man, and put through certain jerky motions at the hands

of an author with a theory to prove." In short, Marsh concludes, Sinclair's "reasoning [in *The Jungle*] is so false, his disregard of human nature so naive, his statement of facts so biased, his conclusions so perverted, that the effect can be only to disgust many honest, sensible folk with the very terms he uses so glibly."

Walter Rideout, commenting in *The Radical Novel in the United States,* takes issue with Marsh's opinion on characterization in *The Jungle.* Remarks the critic: "Jurgis is admittedly a composite figure who was given a heaping share of the troubles of some twenty or thirty packing workers with whom Sinclair had talked, and the author's psychology of character is indeed a simple one. . . . [It is also true that during the course of the book Jurgis and the other characters] gradually lose their individuality, becoming instead any group of immigrants. . . . Yet paradoxically, the force and passion of the book are such that this group of lay figures with Jurgis at their head, these mere capacities for infinite suffering, finally do come to stand for the masses themselves."

Several reviewers are disappointed with the book's ending, especially the abrupt switch from fiction to political rhetoric that occurs when Jurgis is "converted" to socialism. Writing in *The Strenuous Age in American Literature,* Grant C. Knight observes that the final section "is uplifting but it is also artificial, an arbitrary re-channelling of the narrative flow, a piece of rhetoric instead of a logical continuation of story." Rideout accepts the notion of a religious-like conversion to socialism as being "probable enough," but declares that from that point onward *The Jungle* becomes "intellectualized" as political philosophy supplants Jurgis as the novel's focus. In short, notes Bloodworth, Sinclair failed to "carry out his intentions of a heart-breaking story with imminent Socialism. Instead, he settled for an uneven story dealing mainly with proletarian experience until the last four chapters, which switch disturbingly to the Socialist movement, its leaders, and its ideas."

Some critics regard this ending not so much as a demonstration of Sinclair's lack of literary skill as a confirmation of his elitism and essentially nineteenth-century liberal (rather than socialist) bent. Like several of his colleagues, Rideout finds that Sinclair had more in common with someone like Charles Dickens than with most other socialist writers, observing that the two men championed not "blood and barricades, but . . . humanitarianism and brotherly love." Hicks, commenting in his book *The Great Tradition,* maintains Sinclair's socialism "has always been of the emotional sort, a direct response to his own environment, and, as a result of his failure to undergo an intense intellectual discipline, he has never eradicated the effects of his bourgeois upbringing. Though his aim has been socialistic, his psychology has remained that of the liberal. Therefore, whether he realizes it or not, he is always writing for the middle class, trying to persuade his fellows to take their share of the burden of humanity's future, to pity the poor worker and strive for his betterment." Bloodworth also believes that Sinclair's socialism "had an obvious middle-class bias to it. Although he spoke *for* the lowest working classes, he spoke *to* a much wider audience in *The Jungle.* . . . [In the last few chapters of the novel] Sinclair's attitudes towards his protagonist and the lower social class he represents seem to take on qualities of paternalism and condescension. . . . The overcoming of capitalism that the orator speaks of does not really seem to be the task of the working class. The responsibilities fall mainly on the shoulders of men like himself—articulate, educated, even wealthy spokesmen." Brooks, noting that Sinclair fosters "the emotion of self-pity" among members of the working class because he chooses to depict "the helplessness, the benightedness, [and] the naivete of the American workers' movement," wonders how the author expects such an inept group to master their own fate and advance the cause of socialism.

To most critics, however, questions regarding the amount of literary skill or philosophical consistency in *The Jungle* are beside the point; what does count, they say, is the book's undeniably strong emotional impact. Writes Bloodworth: "As a work of modern fiction measured against the aesthetic achievements of a Henry James or a William Faulkner or a James Joyce, *The Jungle* hardly merits any discussion at all. Psychological complexity is alien to Sinclair's characterization, style is a matter of piling up details and modifiers, and structure is confused after the first twenty-one chapters." Nevertheless, the reviewer continues, "while such criticisms are common as well as obvious, they seem out of place, almost completely unrelated to the features of *The Jungle* that contribute to or detract from its significance and power. . . . In [simple] terms, *The Jungle* is a muckraking novel directed at documenting conditions and striving for an emotional response on the part of readers. In his novel Sinclair attacks traditional distinctions between literature and life. With *The Jungle* literature is less a way of ordering and interpreting experience—less the imposition of a particular artistic vision—than a way of simply presenting life and, in the subjective way that Sinclair does this, responding to it with regret, shame, and anger."

Robert Herrick of the *New Republic* is even more emphatic in his defense of Sinclair. "Sophisticated readers, professors and critics, hold that Mr. Sinclair's novels are not 'literature'—whatever that may mean," he begins. "If a passionate interest in the substance of all great literature—life, if a wide acquaintance with its special manifestations of the writer's own day, if a deep conviction about the values underlying its varied phenomena and the ability to set them forth, count in the making of enduring literature, all these Mr. Sinclair has demonstrated again and again that he possesses."

"I am willing to grant that Sinclair's aim . . . automatically bars him from the highest range of literary achievement," writes Hicks, commenting on this occasion in *College English.* "Yet what he has done, he has done well. . . . If Tolstoys came by the dozen, we could afford to smile at Upton Sinclair, but the actual state of contemporary literature scarcely warrants condescension. . . . It may be true, as some critics say, that in the future only social historians will be interested in his work; but even that is a larger claim on posterity than most of his contemporaries will be able to make."

Never again did Sinclair write a novel with quite the impact of *The Jungle.* In fact, Bloodworth contends, the success of this one book "virtually guaranteed that the rest of [Sinclair's] career would be anticlimactic." In the book *Sixteen to One,* David Karsner expands on this idea, stating: "I cannot help but feel that *The Jungle* gave Sinclair a bad start by making him famous before he had reached his maturity as an artist. It chained him to propaganda and placed him in the literary pulpit where [he continued to preside] over our social morals and economic manners. . . . The true artist does not address his readers from a rostrum."

Because of his many highly publicized failures and eccentricities, as well as his tendency to polarize readers and critics, Sinclair has proven to be somewhat of a problem for those attempting to determine his place in American literature. As Bloodworth points out in his study of the author: "Sympathetic critics have generally seen him as a passionate crusader who selflessly attacked injustice whenever it reared its ugly head in American life and who shied away from few subjects, however unpopular they

were at the time. . . . On the other hand, detractors have always found Sinclair an easy target. Politically, he is not only open to attacks from conservative critics, but his liberal ideas are often inconsistent, his radicalism often naive. His support of such quackish causes as fasting and psychic healing has often been an embarrassment to readers who might agree with him politically. Recent radical critics, those with a New Left orientation, have found little inspiration in Sinclair. Above all, he has been scorned by literary critics and scholars who find him simple-minded and shallow beside the great twentieth-century writers who were, after all, his competitors in the race for reputation and recognition."

Noting that Sinclair was "never a great writer in the terms of style and structure, never a symbolist or a modernist, interested in the external affairs of society and politics rather than in the internal affairs of human consciousness, journalistic and populistic rather than poetic and eloquent," Bloodworth goes on to characterize the author as "a nineteenth century moral idealist somewhat ill at ease in the twentieth century but almost totally committed to the exploration and, where possible, reform of the world around him. . . . No writer ever made [this subject] so exclusively his or her *raison d' etre* as Sinclair did. Even within a larger realization of his literary weaknesses and intellectual ambivalences, and taking into account even his blindness to racial oppression, Sinclair's commitment to social justice commands respect. . . . [His works have] survived to be read and to produce often striking effects." In short, concludes the critic, "no picture of twentieth century American life could pretend to be complete without him."

"Sinclair originated *none* of the ideas for which he propagandized, nor did he claim to have," observes Leon Harris in his book *Upton Sinclair: American Rebel.* "But he convinced millions of people all over the world of them. Other of his contemporary muckrakers played a greater role than he in effecting particular social change. But not one of them approached his total influence in regard to all the ideas he advocated. In the variety of his work and in his incomparable success in having it widely reprinted, discussed, attacked, and kept in print, Sinclair outweighed all other individual muckrakers."

These sentiments were echoed by Arthur Koestler in this eightieth birthday tribute to Sinclair: "Perhaps a writer is judged by posterity not so much by the actual text of his work as by the size of the hole that would be left in the fabric of history had he never lived. Other authors in our age outshone Sinclair in artistic quality, subtlety of characterization, and so on, but I can think of no contemporary writers whose non-existence would leave such a gaping hole in the face of the twentieth century than Upton Sinclair's."

Sinclair's personal papers, books, manuscripts, and other materials are in the Lilly Library at Indiana University.

MEDIA ADAPTATIONS: Several films have been based on books by Sinclair, including "The Adventurer," U.S. Amusement Corp., 1917, "The Money Changers," Pathe Exchange, 1920, "Marriage Forbidden," Criterion, 1938, and "The Gnome-Mobile," Walt Disney Productions, 1967.

BIOGRAPHICAL/CRITICAL SOURCES:

BOOKS

Blinderman, Abraham, editor, *Critics on Upton Sinclair,* University of Miami Press, 1975.
Bloodworth, William A., Jr., *Upton Sinclair,* Twayne, 1977.
Brooks, Van Wyck, *Sketches in Criticism,* Dutton, 1932.

Brooks, *The Confident Years,* Dutton, 1952.

Contemporary Literary Criticism, Gale, Volume 1, 1973, Volume 9, 1979, Volume 15, 1980.

Cowley, Malcolm, editor, *After the Genteel Tradition: American Writers since 1910,* Norton, 1937, published as *After the Genteel Tradition: American Writers 1910-1930,* Southern Illinois University Press, 1964.

Dekle, Bernard, *Profiles of Modern American Authors,* Tuttle, 1969.

Dell, Floyd, *Upton Sinclair: A Study in Social Protest,* Doubleday, 1927, reprinted, AMS Press, 1970.

Dictionary of Literary Biography, Volume 9: *American Novelists, 1910-1945,* Gale, 1981.

Evans, I. O., compiler, *An Upton Sinclair Anthology,* Farrar & Rinehart, 1934.

Harris, Leon, *Upton Sinclair: American Rebel,* Crowell, 1975.

Harte, James Lambert, *This Is Upton Sinclair,* Rodale Press, 1938.

Hicks, Granville, *The Great Tradition,* revised edition, Biblo & Tannen, 1967.

Karsner, David, *Sixteen Authors to One,* Books for Libraries, 1968.

Kazin, Alfred, *On Native Grounds: An Interpretation of Modern American Prose Literature,* Harcourt, 1942.

Knight, Grant C., *The Strenuous Age in American Literature,* University of North Carolina Press, 1954.

Loggins, Vernon, *I Hear America . . .,* Crowell, 1937.

Millgate, Michael, *American Social Fiction,* Oliver & Boyd, 1964, Barnes & Noble, 1967.

Rideout, Walter, *The Radical Novel in the United States 1900-1954: Some Interrelations of Literature and Society,* Harvard University Press, 1956.

Schreiber, Georges, editor, *Portraits and Self-Portraits,* Houghton, 1936.

Sinclair, Upton, *American Outpost* (autobiography), Farrar & Rinehart, 1934.

Sinclair, *The Autobiography of Upton Sinclair,* Harcourt, 1962.

Yoder, John A., *Upton Sinclair,* Ungar, 1975.

PERIODICALS

Atlantic, August, 1946.
Bookman, April, 1906.
Chicago Tribune, April 16, 1932.
Christian Century, October 19, 1932.
College English, January, 1943, December, 1959.
Critic, December, 1962-January, 1963.
Harper's, March, 1961.
Nation, February 4, 1931, April 13, 1932.
New Republic, October 7, 1931, June 22, 1932, February 24, 1937, June 24, 1940, January 11, 1943, September 29, 1958, December 1, 1962.
New York Herald Tribune, February 11, 1960.
New York Herald Tribune Books, December 9, 1962.
New York Times, March 3, 1906, June 16, 1906, August 22, 1988.
New York Times Book Review, May 13, 1962.
Saturday Review, March 3, 1928, August 28, 1948.
Saturday Review of Literature, May 7, 1932.
Spectator, July 9, 1932.
Time, December 14, 1962.

OBITUARIES:

PERIODICALS

Detroit Free Press, November 26, 1968.
Nation, December 9, 1968.

National Observer, December 2, 1968.
New York Times, November 27, 1968.
Publishers Weekly, December 9, 1968.
Time, December 6, 1968.
Times (London), November 27, 1968.
Washington Post, November 27, 1968.

*   *   *

SINGER, Isaac
See SINGER, Isaac Bashevis

*   *   *

SINGER, Isaac Bashevis   1904-
(Isaac Bashevis, Isaac Singer; pseudonym: Isaac Warshofsky)

PERSONAL: Born July 14, 1904, in Radzymin, Poland; came to United States in 1935, naturalized in 1943; son of Pinchos Menachem (a rabbi and author) and Bathsheba (Zylberman) Singer; married first wife, Rachel (divorced); married Alma Haimann, February 14, 1940; children: (first marriage) Israel. *Education:* Attended Tachkemoni Rabbinical Seminary, 1920-27. *Religion:* Jewish.

ADDRESSES: Home—209 West 86th St., New York, N.Y. 10024.

CAREER: Novelist, short story writer, children's author, and translator. Worked in Poland for the Yiddish and Hebrew press, 1923-35; *Literarishe Bletter,* Warsaw, Poland, proofreader and translator, 1923-33; *Globus,* Warsaw, co-editor, 1932; *Jewish Daily Forward,* New York, N.Y., member of staff, 1935—.

MEMBER: Jewish Academy of Arts and Sciences (fellow), National Institute of Arts and Letters (fellow), Polish Institute of Arts and Sciences in America (fellow), American Academy of Arts and Sciences, PEN.

AWARDS, HONORS: Louis Lamed Prize, 1950, for *The Family Moskat,* 1956, for *Satan in Goray;* National Institute of Arts and Letters and American Academy award in literature, 1959; Harry and Ethel Daroff Memorial Fiction Award, Jewish Book Council of America, 1963, for *The Slave;* D.H.L., Hebrew Union College, Los Angeles, Calif., 1963; National Council on the Arts grant, 1966; National Endowment for the Arts grant, 1967; *Playboy* magazine award for best fiction, 1967; Newbery Honor Book Award, 1967, for *Zlateh the Goat and Other Stories,* 1968, for *The Fearsome Inn;* Bancarella Prize, 1968, for Italian translation of *The Family Moskat;* Brandeis University Creative Arts Medal for Poetry-Fiction, 1970; National Book Award for children's literature, 1970, for *A Day of Pleasure,* for fiction, 1974, for *A Crown of Feathers and Other Stories;* D.Litt. from Texas Christian University, 1972, and Colgate University, 1972; Ph.D., Hebrew University, Jerusalem, 1973; Litt.D., Bard College, 1974; Agnon Gold Medal, 1975; Nobel Prize for Literature, 1978; Gold Medal for Fiction, American Academy and Institute of Arts and Letters, 1989.

WRITINGS:

NOVELS; ORIGINALLY IN YIDDISH

Der Satan in Gorey, [Warsaw], 1935, translation by Jacob Sloan published as *Satan in Goray,* Noonday, 1955, reprinted, Fawcett, 1980.

(Under name Isaac Bashevis) *Di Familie Mushkat,* two volumes, [New York], 1950, translation by A. H. Gross published under name Isaac Bashevis Singer as *The Family Moskat,* Knopf, 1950, reprinted, Farrar, Straus, 1988.

The Magician of Lublin, translation by Elaine Gottlieb and Joseph Singer, Noonday, 1960, reprinted, Fawcett, 1985.

The Slave, translation by author and Cecil Hemley, Farrar, Straus, 1962, reprinted, Fawcett, 1984.

The Manor, translation by Gottlieb and J. Singer, Farrar, Straus, 1967, reprinted, 1987.

The Estate, translation by Gottlieb, J. Singer, and Elizabeth Shub, Farrar, Straus, 1969.

Enemies: A Love Story (first published in *Jewish Daily Forward* under title "Sonim, di Geshichte fun a Liebe," 1966), translation by Aliza Shevrin and Shub, Farrar, Straus, 1972, reprinted, 1987.

Shosha, Farrar, Straus, 1978.

Reaches of Heaven: A Story of the Baal Shem Tov, Farrar, Straus, 1981.

The Penitent, Farrar, Straus, 1983.

King of the Fields, limited edition, Farrar, Straus, 1988.

SHORT STORY COLLECTIONS; ORIGINALLY IN YIDDISH

Gimpel the Fool and Other Stories, translation by Saul Bellow and others, Noonday, 1957, reprinted, Fawcett, 1985.

The Spinoza of Market Street and Other Stories, translation by Gottlieb and others, Farrar, Straus, 1961, reprinted, Fawcett, 1980.

Short Friday and Other Stories, translation by Ruth Whitman and others, Farrar, Straus, 1964, reprinted, Fawcett, 1985.

Selected Short Stories, edited by Irving Howe, Modern Library, 1966.

The Seance and Other Stories, translation by Whitman, Roger H. Klein, and others, Farrar, Straus, 1968.

A Friend of Kafka and Other Stories, Farrar, Straus, 1970.

An Isaac Bashevis Singer Reader, Farrar, Straus, 1971.

A Crown of Feathers and Other Stories, Farrar, Straus, 1973.

Passions and Other Stories, Farrar, Straus, 1975.

Old Love: And Other Stories, Farrar, Straus, 1979.

The Collected Stories of Isaac Bashevis Singer, Farrar, Straus, 1982.

Gifts, Jewish Publication Society of America, 1985.

The Image and Other Stories, Farrar, Straus, 1985.

The Death of Methuselah: And Other Stories, Farrar, Straus, 1988.

JUVENILE; ORIGINALLY IN YIDDISH; TRANSLATION BY SINGER AND ELIZABETH SHUB

Mazel and Schlimazel; or, The Milk of a Lioness, Harper, 1966.

Zlateh the Goat and Other Stories, Harper, 1966, reprinted, 1984.

The Fearsome Inn, Scribner, 1967.

When Schlemiel Went to Warsaw and Other Stories, Farrar, Straus, 1968, reprinted, 1986.

Elijah the Slave: A Hebrew Legend Retold (nonfiction), Farrar, Straus, 1970, reprinted, 1988.

Joseph and Koza; or, The Sacrifice to the Vistula, Farrar, Straus, 1970.

Alone in the Wild Forest, Farrar, Straus, 1971.

The Topsy-Turvy Emperor of China, Harper, 1971.

The Wicked City (nonfiction), Farrar, Straus, 1972.

The Fools of Chelm and Their History, Farrar, Straus, 1973, reprinted, 1988.

Why Noah Chose the Dove (nonfiction), Farrar, Straus, 1974.

A Tale of Three Wishes, Farrar, Straus, 1975.

Naftali the Storyteller and His Horse, Sus, and Other Stories, Farrar, Straus, 1976.

The Power of Light: Eight Stories for Hanukkah, Farrar, Straus, 1980.

The Golem, limited edition, Farrar, Straus, 1982.

Stories for Children, Farrar, Straus, 1984.

AUTOBIOGRAPHY; ORIGINALLY IN YIDDISH; UNDER PSEUDONYM ISAAC WARSHOFSKY

Mayn Tatn's Bes-din Shtub, [New York], 1956, translation by Channah Kleinerman-Goldstein published under name Isaac Bashevis Singer as *In My Father's Court,* Farrar, Straus, 1966.

A Day of Pleasure: Stories of a Boy Growing Up in Warsaw (juvenile), translation by author and Shub, Farrar, Straus, 1969.

A Little Boy in Search of God: Mysticism in a Personal Light (also see below), Doubleday, 1976.

A Young Man in Search of Love (also see below), Doubleday, 1978.

Lost in America (also see below), Doubleday, 1981.

Love and Exile: A Memoir (includes *A Little Boy in Search of God: Mysticism in a Personal Light, A Young Man in Search of Love,* and *Lost in America*), Doubleday, 1984.

PLAYS; ORIGINALLY IN YIDDISH

"The Mirror" (also see below), produced in New Haven, Conn., 1973.

(With Leah Napolin) *Yentle, the Yeshiva Boy* (produced on Broadway at Atkinson Theatre, 1974), Samuel French, 1978.

"Schlemiel the First," produced in New Haven, Conn., 1974.

(With Eve Friedman) *Teibele and Her Demon* (first produced in Minneapolis at Guthrie Theatre, 1978, produced on Broadway at Atkinson Theatre, December 16, 1979), Samuel French, 1984.

TRANSLATOR INTO YIDDISH

Knut Hamsen, *Pan,* Wilno (Warsaw), 1928.

Erich Maria Remarque, *All Quiet on the Western Front,* Wilno, 1930.

Thomas Mann, *The Magic Mountain,* four volumes, Wilno, 1930.

Remarque, *The Road Back,* Wilno, 1930.

Leon S. Glaser, *From Moscow to Jerusalem,* privately printed, 1938.

OTHER

(Editor with Elaine Gottlieb) *Prism 2,* Twayne, 1965.

(Contributor) Anatol Filmus, *Tully Filmus,* Jewish Publication Society of America, 1971.

(With Ira Moscowitz) *The Hasidim: Paintings, Drawings, and Etchings,* Crown, 1973.

Nobel Lecture, Farrar, Straus, 1979.

The Gentleman from Cracow; The Mirror, illustrated with water colors by Raphael Soyer, introduction by Harry I. Moore, Limited Editions Club, 1979.

Isaac Bashevis Singer on Literature and Life, University of Arizona Press, 1979.

Also author under name Isaac Singer. Contributor of stories and articles to periodicals in the United States and Poland, including *Die Yiddische Welt, Commentary, Esquire, New Yorker, Globus, Literarishe Bletter, Harper's,* and *Partisan Review.*

SIDELIGHTS: Widely proclaimed to be the foremost living writer of Yiddish literature, Isaac Bashevis Singer stands clearly outside the mainstream and basic traditions of both Yiddish and American literature. Singer's writing has proven difficult to cate-

gorize, with critics attaching to him various and sometimes contradictory labels in an attempt to elucidate his work. He has been
called a modernist, although he personally dislikes most contemporary fiction, and he has also been accused of being captivated
by the past, of writing in a dying language despite his English
fluency, of setting his fiction in a world that no longer exists, the
shtetls (Jewish ghettos) of Eastern Europe which were obliter-
ated by Hitler's campaign against the Jews. Despite the attention
called to the mysticism, the prolific presence of the supernatural,
and the profoundly religious nature of his writing, he has been
called both a realist and a pessimist. Undeniably a difficult author to place in critical perspective, Singer addresses himself to
the problems of labeling his work in an interview with Cyrena
N. Pondrom: "People always need a name for things, so whatever you will write or whatever you will do, they like to put you
into a certain category. Even if you would be new, they would
like to feel that a name is already prepared for you in advance. . . . I hope that one day somebody will find a new name
for me, not use the old ones."

Commenting on the paradoxical nature of Singer and his work,
Irving Howe states: "Singer writes in Yiddish, a language that
no amount of energy or affection seems likely to save from extinction. He writes about a world that is gone, destroyed with a
brutality beyond historical comparison. He writes within a culture, the remnant of Yiddish in the Western world, that is more
than a little dubious about his purpose and stress. . . . And he
does all this without a sigh or apology, without so much as a Jewish groan. It strikes one as a kind of inspired madness: here is
a man living in New York City, a sophisticated and clever writer,
who composes stories about places like Frampol, Bilgoray,
Kreshev, *as if they were still there.*"

More than with most writers, the key to Singer's work lies in his
background, in his roots in the Polish Yiddish-speaking Jewish
ghettos. "I was born with the feeling that I am part of an unlikely
adventure, something that couldn't have happened, but happened just the same," Singer once remarked to a *Book Week* interviewer. Born in a small Polish town, his father was a Hassidic
rabbi and both his grandfathers were also rabbis. Visiting his maternal grandfather in Bilgoray as a young boy, Singer learned of
life in the *shtetl*, which would become the setting of much of his
later work. The young Singer received a basic Jewish education
preparing him to follow his father and grandfathers' steps into
the rabbinical vocation; he studied the Torah, the Talmud, the
Cabala, and other sacred Jewish books. An even stronger influence than his education and his parents' orthodoxy was his older
brother, the novelist I. J. Singer, who broke with the family's orthodoxy and began to write secular stories. Attempting to overcome the influence of his brother's rationalism and to strengthen
the cause of religion, his parents told him stories of *dybbuks*
(wandering souls in Jewish folklore believed to enter a human
body and control its actions), possessions, and other spiritual
mysteries. Singer has commented that he was equally fascinated
by his parents' mysticism and his brother's rationalism. Although he was eventually to break from both traditions, this dualism characterizes his writing.

His desire to become a secular writer caused a painful conflict
within Singer and with his family; it represented a break from
traditional ways. Aaron, the writer-protagonist of *Shosha*,
"senses that the literary vocation cannot provide a substitute for
the life-giving bread of the Jewish religion from which he has
separated himself," according to Edward Alexander. Both
Shosha and *A Young Man in Search of Love*, Alexander further
elaborates, "dwell on the special difficulties of the Yiddish
writer, who felt isolated and frustrated not only because his

choice of such a vocation made him a *meshumad* (apostate) in
the eyes of the religious, but, also, because he was 'stuck with a
language and culture no one recognized outside a small circle of
Yiddishists and radicals.' Here was a sort of double exile." Reviewing the autobiographical *In My Father's Court*, Herbert Leibowitz comments: "What Singer writes of his brother becomes
true of himself later: 'he had deserted the old, but there was nothing in the new that he could call his own.' The two brothers became that familiar figure in the modern landscape (and in Singer's fiction): the spiritual outlander, the man whose soul is the
battleground for a war between the sacred and the profane, the
erotic and the ascetic."

Eventually, Singer rejected his parents' orthodoxy, although not
their faith in God. He joined his brother in Warsaw and began
working for the Hebrew and Yiddish press and also began to
publish stories. At first he wrote in Hebrew but switched to Yiddish because he felt that Hebrew was a dead language (this was
before its revival as the national language of Israel). Feeling that
the Nazis would certainly invade Poland, Singer followed his
brother to the United States where he began to write for the *Jewish Daily Forward*. Here he wrote fiction under the name Isaac
Bashevis and nonfiction under the pseudonym Isaac Warshofsky. Most of Singer's stories appeared first in the *Jewish Daily
Forward* in their original Yiddish; the novels appeared in serialized form.

Singer still does all of his writing in Yiddish, and much of his
large body of writing remains untranslated. Before he felt sufficiently fluent in English, Singer had to rely on other people to
do the translations; his nephew Joseph Singer was responsible for
much of it. Now, Singer usually does a rough translation into English himself and has someone help him polish the English version and work on the idioms. The English translations are often
a "second original," according to Singer, differing structurally
from the Yiddish. "I used to play with the idea [of writing in En-
glish]," Singer has admitted, "but never seriously. Never. I always knew that a writer has to write in his own language or not
at all." Inevitably, much of Singer's fine style is lost in translation. Although some Yiddish critics have accused him of stylistic
ineptitude in Yiddish, Irving Howe believes that "no translation
. . . could possibly suggest the full idiomatic richness and syntactical verve of Singer's Yiddish. Singer has left behind the ora-
torical sententiousness to which Yiddish literature is prone, he
has abandoned its leisurely meandering pace, which might be
called the *shtetl* rhythm, and has developed a style that is both
swift and dense, nervous and thick. His sentences are short and
abrupt; his rhythms coiled, intense, short-breathed."

Lance Morrow defines Yiddish as "that subtle, rich, vital, and
probably doomed tongue. . . . Yiddish, based originally on a
Middle High German dialect, developed in the tenth century and
eventually became a wonderfully supple international language
with borrowings from almost every Indo-European language.
Among Jews, Hebrew was the language of piety: Yiddish, quivering with life and idiom, was the medium of the street. Before
World War II it was the principal language of some eleven million people; now it is spoken by four million and fading yearly."
More optimistic than Morrow about the fate of the Yiddish language, Singer calls Yiddish in his Nobel lecture "a language of
exile, without a land, without frontiers, not supported by any
government, a language which possesses no words for weapons,
ammunition, military exercises, war tactics; a language that was
despised by both gentiles and emancipated Jews. . . . Yiddish
has not yet said its last word. It contains treasures that have not
been revealed to the eyes of the world. It was the tongue of martyrs and saints, of dreamers and cabalists—rich in humor and

in memories that mankind may never forget. In a figurative way, Yiddish is the wise and humble language of us all, the idiom of the frightened and hopeful humanity."

Yet Singer is realistic about the fate of Yiddish. Morrow quotes him as saying that the language "is a tragedy and a responsibility." Singer has commented on the dwindling Yiddish-reading audience: "You don't feel very happy about writing in a language when you know it dies from day to day. . . . The only thing is, I don't have this feeling while I write; I don't choose to remember it. . . . When I sit down to write I have a feeling that I'm talking maybe to millions or maybe to nobody." In a lighter vein, Singer told Morrow that one of the reasons he writes in Yiddish is that "I like to write ghost stories and nothing fits a ghost better than a dying language. The deader the language, the more alive is the ghost. Ghosts love Yiddish, and as far as I know, they all speak it."

Awarding him the Nobel Prize for Literature in 1978, the Swedish Academy cited Singer for "his impassioned narrative art which, with roots in a Polish-Jewish cultural tradition, brings universal human conditions to life." In his acceptance speech, Singer said that "the high honor bestowed upon me by the Swedish Academy is also a recognition of the Yiddish language." Yet Singer's sternest detractors are other Yiddish writers and American Yiddishists. Besides the charge of stylistic ineptitude, Yiddish critics, according to Lothar Kahn, have accused Singer of "deliberately misrepresenting life in the *shtetls* and city ghettos of Poland. . . . He has been faulted for a morbid fascination with animal slaughter, blood, demons . . . and with the dominant presence of sex and fantasy. . . . His critics have also been visibly disturbed by the fact that Singer has not sentimentalized Jewish life in a world that is no more, and whose inhabitants were ruthlessly slain."

Singer has deliberately disassociated himself from the American Yiddishists. He said in the interview with Pondrom: "Yiddish culture and I are two different things. Though I love Yiddish, I'm not a Yiddishist, because these people really want to create a movement. They always talk about a movement—the Jewish literature, the Jewish theater, or the Yiddish theater. I'm not a man of movements at all. . . . I know that movements and mediocrity always go together. Whatever becomes a mass movement . . . would be bad. . . . Also, these people were all on the socialistic side. They always thought about creating a better world. And, because of this, they were sentimental, which is not my way; I would also like to see a better world, but I don't think, really, that men can create it." Kahn points out that Singer believes "what human contentment is attainable can be found on the individual, not the social level, in the moral and spiritual and not the sociopolitical sphere, in man's quest for self-improvement more than in dicta and programs from above and for all. . . . Singer thus cannot be expected to please progressives, socialists, utopians or those preaching a politically committed literature. He might faintly suggest that the artist more than the statesman can achieve progress and human satisfaction." According to Howe, Singer is not caught up in the Enlightenment as most Yiddish writers are. He "shares very little in the collective sensibility . . . of the Yiddish masters; he does not unambiguously celebrate in the common man as a paragon of goodness; he is impatient with the sensual deprivation implicit in the value of *edelkeit* (refinement, nobility); and above all he moves away from a central assumption of both Yiddish literature in particular and the 19th century in general, the assumption of an immanent fate or end in human existence."

The criticism of the Yiddishists that Singer's work is saturated with sex has some validity. Stefan Kanfer believes Singer to be "one of the least explicit but most sexually charged of modern writers." Singer himself told Kenneth Turan: "I like to write about sex and love, which is not kosher to the orthodox people. I believe in God, but I don't believe that God wants man to run away completely from pleasure. If he has created men and women with a great desire to love and be loved, there must be something in it; it can't be all bad. Love and sex are the things that give life some value, some zest. Miserable as flesh and blood is, it is still the best you can get."

Although his preoccupation with sex links him to much of twentieth-century literature, Singer dislikes modern fiction which focuses on the writer revealing his inner self and complaining about his problems and complexes. Singer commented to Edith Gold, "There is more art, more challenge in writing a real story than in just sitting there and complaining." He also denigrates the tendency for the writer to take on a cause, to be not motivated by art for its own sake but by political, sociological, or psychological postures. Singer told Harold Flender that one of the things he learned from his brother was that "while facts never become obsolete or stale, commentaries *always* do. . . . Imagine Homer explaining the deeds of his heroes according to the old Greek philosophy, or the psychology of his time. Why nobody would read Homer! Fortunately, Homer just gives us the images and the facts; and because of this the *Iliad* and the *Odyssey* are fresh in our time."

Singer believes that the only role of fiction is entertainment. As he comments to Sanford Pinsker: "I never thought that my fiction—my kind of writing—had any other purpose than to be read and enjoyed by the reader. I never sit down to write a novel to make a better world or to create good feelings towards the Jews or for any other purpose. I knew this from the very beginning, that writing fiction has no other purpose than to give enjoyment to a reader. . . . I consider myself an entertainer. . . . I mean an entertainer of good people, of intellectual people who cannot be entertained by cheap stuff. And I think this is true about fiction in all times. . . . Whatever other good things come out from fiction are to say sheer profit." He reiterated this theory of the function of literature to Pondrom: "Literature is a force without direction. . . . Literature stirs the mind; it makes you think about a million things, but it does not lead you." He told Alexandra Johnson, "Whenever a writer tries to be more than a storyteller, he becomes less."

Singer is the ultimate storyteller; according to Gold, "for Singer . . . literature means storytelling." Considered to be a master of the short story, it is his most effective and favorite genre because, as he has explained, it is more possible to be perfect in the short story than in a longer work. Also Singer doesn't think that the supernatural, which is his element, lends itself well to longer, novelistic writing. Singer's style in the short story is simple, spare, in the tradition of the spoken tale. Paddy Chayefsky writes: "There is none of the cumbersome complexity of modern writing, no obsession with the externals of relationships, no fumbling about for profundity beneath the civilized sigh." In a *Commentary* interview, Singer remarked: "When I tell a story, I tell a story. I don't try to discuss, criticize, or analyze my characters." Irving Howe calls him "above and beyond everything else . . . a great performer in ways that remind one of Twain, Dickens, Sholom Aleichem," and in another writing states that Singer "simply as a literary performer has few peers among living writers." Maureen Howard says that in his short stories Singer "writes as if words themselves were not questioned in high literary circles, as if we had been lectured and analyzed quite enough, as if, given the possibility of thorough destruction, stories still matter." Singer borrows from everyday life in order to produce his stories; he told Gold, "every encounter with a human being is for me a potential story." Moreover, Singer feels that it is the writer's responsibility to find the stories which best fit him. "Every human being—not only every writer—has stories which only he can tell," he commented in an interview with Alexandra Johnson. "These are his stories. The important thing for a writer is to find and trust these stories."

For Singer, his special stories, the ones that belong to him, are placed for the most part in the nineteenth- and early twentieth-century *shtetl.* He has been criticized for his overuse of this setting, with some critics suggesting that he is not effective in any other surrounding. Singer told Morrow: "I prefer to write about the world which I knew, which I know, best. This is Bilgoray, Lublin, the Jews of Kreshev. This is enough for me. I can get from these people art. I don't need to go to the North Pole and write a novel about the Eskimos who live in that neighborhood. I write about the things where I grew up, and where I feel completely at home." Ruth R. Wisse believes that the *shtetl* stories "vivify a world whose beatific fictional existence is set into fiercely tragic perspective by its historical extinction. Most of Singer's stories inspire a fresh awareness of human malignancy and remorseless fate." Morrow calls Singer's world "a pure act of devotional memory, protected and elaborated, made to move, brought alive by a tender and sinister imagination. . . . By writing about a lost world, he achieves an eerie distancing effect, an undertone something like what Hawthorne accomplished in his demon-ridden tales of earliest Puritan New England."

Jacob Sonntag notes that even in those stories which take place in a modern setting, such as *Enemies: A Love Story* which has modern-day New York City as its background, "the people we encounter are the same we have met before in Warsaw or Tzvikev and other *shtetls* and villages in pre-war Poland. It is as if Singer was looking for them among the new arrivals, those who have survived the ghettos, concentration camps, and the deportations to Siberia and, after the war, had found their way to the New World; and having found them, had made them once again the vehicle of his imagery and morbid philosophy." Singer's new settings follow the classical pattern of the European Jewish emigre—from East European ghetto to New York or Miami. A *Virginia Quarterly Review* writer believes that "Singer, like Nabokov, is a great spanner of widely different cultures—and this makes him very modern and very American." Michael Wood points out that more than half the stories in *A Crown of Feathers and Other Stories* deal with immigrants to the New World. "Singer is thus forced to find in isolated individuals what he formerly found in the re-created memories of small East European communities: an image of the ongoing Jewish enterprise, a mark of the indefatigable persistence of the past."

Wisse makes another connection to the *shtetl* setting and the use of Old World characters, linking them to Singer's use of Yiddish. According to Wisse, Singer wrote an essay in 1943 which complained that Yiddish in America was in a serious decline. There were no new expressions to match the modern experience of Jews in America. "This explains," wrote Singer, "why the best Yiddish prose writers consciously or unconsciously avoid writing about American life. They don't want to fake the dialogue, and they are fed up with describing yet again the narrow circle of coarse aging immigrants. . . . The prose writer, who must develop a broad cast of characters, has to yield to linguistic pressure, recognizing that he is a slave to the past, where Yiddish was thoroughly at home." According to Wisse, Singer "plucks Yiddish prose out of the 20th century to move it back to its roots,

to a culture ruled by the impulses of evil and good rather than by the id and superego, or fascism and democracy. . . . His analysis serves as a kind of justification for returning artistically to a world he had abandoned in fact. . . . Others have justified Singer's method, noting that in these traditional Jewish settings, the demonic still retains the power to anger and shock . . . [and the *shtetl*] provided him with the only convincing medium for the representation of sin on a still-human scale."

Singer is preoccupied with the problem of sin, with man's capacity to know God, but because he does not insert philosophy or commentary directly into his work, the characters must speak for him. William Peden calls his characters "prodigious, insatiable, indomitable talkers; one has the feeling that if the hydrogen bomb is finally dropped, the last sound on earth will be that of one of Singer's wonderful people, relating a tale of love, lust, betrayal, passion, demonic possession, madness, success, frustration, suicide, life." Maureen Howard also finds the Singerian characters delightful and links them to the folktale-like quality of his work. "These inspired characters, rabbis, charlatans, whores, so good, so evil, are out of a world that can never be parochial, a world out of our childhood legends, out of medieval romance, out of episodic sagas," Howard writes. "These are the stories that were once told to sustain life and community of an evening in any house, any town. But being at least partially literary in origin, Singer's tales are also more sophisticated than we first imagine. . . . In Singer's balance of innocence and sophistication is really where his magic lies."

The word magic is not misplaced, for Singer uses the irrational—the world of ghosts, possessions, *dybbuks,* magicians, seances, religious fanaticism, sexual perversion, pacts with the devil—prolifically in his stories. A *Virginia Quarterly Review* writer comments that one of Singer's aims is "to present the irrational in the clearest and most disciplined of styles." A *Times Literary Supplement* reviewer writes: "What gives his stories their undoubted strength is a quality common to all folk literature: an exact literalness about the visible combined with an unquestioned acceptance of the invisible." In his tales, replete with mysticism, imps, and ghosts, it is not unusual to see the dead move and dance among the living. Reviewing *The Slave,* David Boroff writes: "Few writers since Shakespeare have been able to evoke so harrowingly the nightmare world of savage animals . . . and of man's kinship with them." Singer believes in the possibility that the supernatural entities of which he writes are real. As he told Gold, "there are many things we do not yet understand. We are surrounded by secrets and entities of which we have no inkling. These things may all exist, just as electricity existed before Franklin discovered it." Singer uses the electricity analogy often, commenting that a pre-Franklin man probably thought that the sparks which emanated from his wool sweater on a dark night were of supernatural origin. "We also see sparks," notes Singer, "but we ignore them." He told Pinsker that he writes about *dybbuks* and devils "because these facts express the subconscious better than any other events a writer can write about. The story of the *dybbuk* is always the story of a suppressed human spirit. . . . I think all my heroes are possessed people—possessed by a mania, by a fixed idea, by a strange level of fear or passion." Yet Singer makes clear that his demonic possessions are not merely Freudian appellations. "I believe that there may be such a thing as possession, I actually believe that there are powers in this world of which we have no inkling, but which have an influence on our lives and on our way of thinking. . . . I personally believe in God and in spirits and in many things about which other men think are only superstition and folklore."

Singer's personal belief in God permeates his work, making him, as Donald Phelps says, "a pre-eminently religious writer." He commented to Pinsker that "by losing religion we have lost a lot of our spirit, a lot of what sustained us and kept us alive. It is true that I am a Jewish writer, but I am also, in a way, a philosophic writer. My philosophy is expressed not in philosophical terms but in events, in stories. But the eternal questions bother me all my life. . . . What is expressed in my stories is the doubt about realities, the question of the problem of human suffering and so on and so on. But even though it is Jewish, it is also universal because these are the questions which all men ask in all times and in all places." Indeed, Linda G. Zatlin believes that Singer's obsession with "the individual's struggle to find a viable faith in an age possessed by this very problem" places him in some perspective as far as being a twentieth-century writer. According to Zatlin, although most of his stories are placed in nineteenth-century Eastern Europe and appear on the surface to be simple folk tales, they portray the dilemma of modern man. "Specifically Singer predicates his fiction on the idea that the presence or absence of human faith in God is an eternal, omnipresent dilemma which the individual must resolve for himself, and he consistently shows that man's fate . . . is directly correlated to his degree of faith in God." Zatlin views Singer's characters as allegorical representations of three postures of individual belief. She outlines these categories of Singerian characters as the "God-chooser; he directs his energy toward living consistently within His laws; . . . the God-denier; he has already submitted to the forces of evil by embracing Satan; the doubter; he ruminates at length about God's existence but utilizes his drives in resolving his conflict and arrives ultimately at complete faith in or denial of Him. This last group illustrates most clearly the dilemma of modern man."

Yet Singer allows himself a healthy skepticism; he has been called, despite his deep faith in God, a profoundly pessimistic writer. Phelps comments that "by the token of Singer's faith, skepticism is not a self-protective distrust of any certainty, but a recognition of reality's rich elusiveness." Kahn also calls attention to Singer's skeptical and doubting nature, calling him "both a skeptic and a pessimist. He is dubious about human nature which can so quickly succumb to lusts and savagery. He is even more dubious about men's ability to know God or the ultimate secrets of the universe. . . . He is attracted to a past world which never doubted the moral importance of life, but he knows the clock cannot be turned back." Compared by an interviewer to other Yiddish masters, Singer commented: "I consider myself—in spite of all my beliefs—a modern man, more free to think, more free to doubt." That he doubts about man's future is clear in his comments to Harold Flender. "Nothing will save us," says Singer. "We will make a lot of progress, but we will keep on suffering, and there will never be an end to it. We will always invent new sources of pain. Being a pessimist to me means to be a realist."

Ted Hughes summarizes Singer's extraordinary talent: "No psychological terminology or current literary method has succeeded in rendering such a profound, unified and fully apprehended account of the Divine, the Infernal, and the suffering space of self-determination between, all so convincingly interconnected, and fascinatingly peopled. . . . [To] isolate his decisive virtue: whatever region his writing inhabits, it is blazing with life and actuality. His powerful, wise, deep, full-face paragraphs make almost every other modern fiction seem by comparison labored, shallow, overloaded with alien and undigested junk, too fancy, fuddled, not quite squared up to life."

MEDIA ADAPTATIONS: The movie, *Yentl,* Metro-Goldwyn-Mayer/United Artists, 1983, starring Barbara Streisand, was based on *Yentle, the Yeshiva Boy; Enemies: A Love Story* was adapted as a film directed and produced by Paul Mazursky and with a screenplay by Mazursky and Roger L. Simon, Twentieth Century-Fox, 1989.

BIOGRAPHICAL/CRITICAL SOURCES:

BOOKS

Allentuck, Marcia, editor, *The Achievement of Isaac Bashevis Singer,* Southern Illinois University Press, 1967.
Authors in the News, Gale, Volume 1, 1976, Volume 2, 1976.
Buchen, Irving H., *Isaac Bashevis Singer and the Eternal Past,* New York University Press, 1968.
Burgin, Richard, *Conversations with Isaac Bashevis Singer,* Farrar, Straus, 1986.
Children's Literature Review, Volume 1, Gale, 1976.
Cohen, Sarah Blacher, editor, *From Hester Street to Hollywood: The Jewish-American Stage and Screen,* Indiana University Press, 1983.
Concise Dictionary of American Literary Biography: The New Consciousness, 1941-1968, Gale, 1987.
Contemporary Literary Criticism, Gale, Volume 1, 1973, Volume 3, 1975, Volume 6, 1976, Volume 9, 1978, Volume 11, 1979, Volume 15, 1980, Volume 23, 1983, Volume 38, 1986.
Dictionary of Literary Biography, Gale, Volume 6: *American Novelists since World War II,* 1980, Volume 28: *Twentieth-Century American-Jewish Fiction Writers,* 1984, Volume 52: *American Writers for Children since 1960: Fiction,* 1986.
Gass, William H., *Fiction and the Figures of Life,* Knopf, 1970.
Hyman, Edgar, *Standards: A Chronicle of Books for Our Time,* Horizon Press, 1966.
Kazin, Alfred, *Contemporaries,* Atlantic Monthly Press, 1962.
Kazin, Alfred, *Bright Book of Life: American Novelists and Storytellers from Hemingway to Mailer,* Atlantic Monthly Press, 1973.
Kostelanetz, Richard, editor, *On Contemporary Literature,* Avon, 1964.
Kresh, Paul, *Isaac Bashevis Singer: The Magician of West 86th Street,* Dial, 1979.
Madison, Charles A., *Yiddish Literature: Its Scope and Major Writers,* Ungar, 1968.
Malin, Irving, editor, *Critical Views of Isaac Bashevis Singer,* New York University Press, 1969.
Malin, Irving, *Isaac Bashevis Singer,* Ungar, 1972.
Phelps, Donald, *Covering Ground,* Ascot Press, 1969.
Pinsker, Sanford, *The Schlemiel as Metaphor: Studies in the Yiddish and American Jewish Novel,* Southern Illinois University Press, 1971.
Singer, Isaac Beshevis, *Selected Short Stories,* introduction by Irving Howe, Modern Library, 1966.
Singer, Isaac Beshevis, *In My Father's Court,* Farrar, Straus, 1966.
Singer, Isaac Beshevis, *A Day of Pleasure: Stories of a Boy Growing Up in Warsaw,* Farrar, Straus, 1969.
Singer, Isaac Bashevis, *A Little Boy in Search of God: Mysticism in a Personal Light,* Doubleday, 1976.
Singer, Isaac Bashevis, *A Young Man in Search of Love,* Doubleday, 1978.
Singer, Isaac Bashevis, *Lost in America,* Doubleday, 1981.

PERIODICALS

Atlantic, August, 1962, January, 1965, July, 1970, January, 1979.
Best Sellers, October 1, 1970.

Books and Bookmen, October, 1973, December, 1974.
Book Week, July 4, 1965.
Book World, October 29, 1967, March 3, 1968, September 1, 1968, November 25, 1979.
Chicago Review, spring, 1980.
Chicago Tribune, October 25, 1980, June 23, 1987.
Chicago Tribune Book World, July 12, 1981, March 21, 1982, November 6, 1983, July 21, 1985.
Christian Century, May 16, 1979.
Christian Science Monitor, October 28, 1967, September 5, 1978, September 18, 1978.
Commentary, November, 1958, October, 1960, November, 1963, February, 1965, February, 1979.
Contemporary Literature, winter, 1969.
Critical Quarterly, spring, 1976.
Criticism, fall, 1963.
Critique, Volume 11, number 2, 1969, Volume 14, number 2, 1972.
Detroit Free Press, October 6, 1978, October 24, 1979.
Detroit News, December 29, 1985, May 17, 1987.
Encounter, March, 1966.
Globe & Mail (Toronto), May 3, 1980, November 23, 1985, June 13, 1988.
Harper's, October, 1965, September, 1978.
Hudson Review, winter, 1966-67, spring, 1974.
Illustrated London News, March 9, 1967.
Jewish Currents, November, 1962.
Jewish Quarterly, winter, 1966-67, autumn, 1972.
Judaism, fall, 1962, winter, 1974, spring, 1977, winter, 1979.
Kenyon Review, spring, 1964.
London Magazine, December, 1982-January, 1983.
London Review of Books, September 2, 1982.
Los Angeles Times, November 8, 1978, December 28, 1981, November 18, 1983, March, 18, 1984, December 4, 1986, December 12, 1989.
Los Angeles Times Book Review, November 16, 1980, August 16, 1981, May 2, 1982, February 6, 1983, December 9, 1984, August 25, 1985, May 1, 1988.
Midstream, March, 1967.
Minnesota Review, Volume 7, number 3, 1967.
Nation, November 19, 1983.
New Leader, August 14, 1978.
New Republic, November 24, 1958, January 2, 1961, November 13, 1961, June 18, 1962, November 3, 1973, October 25, 1975, September 16, 1978, October 21, 1978.
New Review, June, 1976.
Newsweek, June 26, 1972, November 12, 1973, April 12, 1982, September 26, 1983.
New Yorker, August 17, 1981.
New York Magazine, December 31, 1979.
New York Review of Books, April 22, 1965, February 7, 1974, December 7, 1978.
New York Times, October 30, 1966, January 29, 1967, July 10, 1978, July 22, 1978, December 9, 1978, October 17, 1979, December 5, 1979, December 16, 1979, December 17, 1979, April 19, 1980, June 15, 1982, November 30, 1982, September 22, 1983, October 7, 1984, November 7, 1984, October 30, 1985, November 17, 1985, June 24, 1986, September 28, 1986, November 8, 1986, July 6, 1987, April 12, 1988, May 18, 1989, July 30, 1989, December 10, 1989, December 13, 1989.
New York Times Book Review, December 29, 1957, June 26, 1960, October 22, 1961, June 17, 1962, November 15, 1964, October 8, 1967, June 25, 1972, November 4, 1973, November 2, 1975, April 30, 1978, July 23, 1978, October 28, 1979,

January 18, 1981, June 21, 1981, January 31, 1982, March 21, 1982, November 14, 1982, September 25, 1983, November 11, 1984, June 30, 1985, October 27, 1985, October 16, 1988.
Paris Review, fall, 1968.
People, December 11, 1978.
Publishers Weekly, February 18, 1983 (interview).
Punch, April 5, 1967.
Reporter, April 22, 1965.
Saturday Review, January 25, 1958, November 25, 1961, June 16, 1962, November 21, 1964, September 19, 1970, July 22, 1972, July 8, 1978.
Sewanee Review, fall, 1974.
Southern Review, spring, 1972, spring, 1973.
Spectator, October 17, 1958, September 15, 1961, May 11, 1962, June 10, 1966.
Studies in Short Fiction, summer, 1974, fall, 1976.
Time, October 20, 1967, September 21, 1970, October 27, 1975, November 3, 1975, June 15, 1981, April 5, 1982, October 17, 1983, October 28, 1984, July 15, 1985.
Times (London), April 10, 1980, March 8, 1984.
Times Literary Supplement, January 2, 1959, May 4, 1962, April 11, 1980, July 16, 1982, July 22, 1983, March 23, 1984, October 19, 1984, May 3, 1985, April 4, 1986, May 1, 1987, October 21, 1988, September 1, 1989.
Tribune Books (Chicago), April 10, 1988, November 6, 1988.
Village Voice, February 2, 1976.
Virginia Quarterly Review, spring, 1976.
Vogue, April, 1979.
Washington Post, October 6, 1978, October 16, 1979, October 26, 1979, November 4, 1981, September 17, 1984.
Washington Post Book World, November 30, 1980, June 28, 1981, March 28, 1982 (interview), November 7, 1982, July 7, 1985, September 21, 1986, October 23, 1988.
Wilson Library Bulletin, December, 1962.
World Literature Today, spring, 1979.

*   *   *

SIRIN, V.
   See NABOKOV, Vladimir (Vladimirovich)

*   *   *

SITWELL, Dame Edith   1887-1964

PERSONAL: Born September 7, 1887, in Scarborough, England; died December 9, 1964; daughter of Sir George Reresby and Lady Ida Emily Augusta (Denison) Sitwell. *Education:* Privately educated. *Religion:* Roman Catholic convert, 1955.

CAREER: Writer. Visiting professor, Institute of Contemporary Arts, 1957.

MEMBER: Royal Society of Literature (fellow; vice-president, 1958), American Institute of Arts and Letters (honorary associate).

AWARDS, HONORS: Benson Medal, Royal Society of Literature, 1934; created Dame, Commander Order of the British Empire, 1954 (the first poet to be so honored); William Foyle Poetry Prize, 1958, for *Collected Poems;* with Robert Lowell and W. H. Auden, shared Guiness Poetry Award, 1959; Litt.D., University of Leeds, 1948; D.Litt., University of Durham, 1948, Oxford University, 1951, University of Sheffield, 1955, University of Hull, 1963.

WRITINGS:

The Mother and Other Poems, Basil Blackwell, 1915.

(With brother, Osbert Sitwell) *Twentieth Century Harlequinade and Other Poems,* Basil Blackwell, 1916.

Clown's Houses (poems), Longmans, Green, 1918.

The Wooden Pegasus (poems), Basil Blackwell, 1920.

Facade (poems), Favil Press, 1922, new edition with introduction by Jack Lindsay, Duckworth, 1950.

Bucolic Comedies (poems), Duckworth, 1923.

The Sleeping Beauty (poems), Duckworth, 1924.

(With brothers Osbert and Sacheverell Sitwell) *Poor Young People* (poems), Fleuron, 1925.

(Author of introduction) Ann Taylor, *Meddlesome Matty and Other Poems for Infant Minds,* John Lane, 1925.

Poetry and Criticism, L. and V. Woolf, 1925, Holt, 1926, Folcroft Press, 1969.

Troy Park (poems), Duckworth, 1925.

Elegy on Dead Fashion, Duckworth, 1926, reprinted, Folcroft, 1977.

Twelve Poems, E. Benn, 1926.

Rustic Elegies, Knopf, 1927.

Popular Song (poems), Faber and Gwyer, 1928.

Five Poems, Duckworth, 1928.

Gold Coast Customs (poems), Duckworth, 1929.

Alexander Pope, Cosmopolitan Book Corp., 1930, reprinted, Ayer Co., 1972.

The Collected Poems of Edith Sitwell, Duckworth, 1930, Vanguard, 1968.

(Editor) *The Pleasures of Poetry: A Critical Anthology,* Duckworth, Volume 1: *First Series, Milton and the Augustan Age,* 1930, Volume 2: *Second Series, The Romantic Revival,* 1931, Volume 3: *Third Series, The Victorian Age,* 1932, Norton, 1934.

Children's Tales from the Russian Ballet, [London], 1930.

Epithalamium, Duckworth, 1931.

Jane Barston, 1719-1746, Faber, 1931.

In Spring (poems), privately printed, 1931.

Bath, Faber, 1932, new edition, 1948, 1932 edition reprinted, Hyperion Press, 1980.

(Author of introductory essay to translation by Helen Rootham) Rimbaud, *Prose Poems from Les Illuminations,* Faber, 1932.

Five Variations on a Theme, Duckworth, 1933.

The English Eccentrics, Houghton, 1933, revised and enlarged edition, Vanguard, 1957, abridged edition, Arrow Books, 1960.

Aspects of Modern Poetry, Duckworth, 1934, Scholarly Press, 1972.

Selected Poems, Duckworth, 1936.

Some Recent Developments in English Literature, University of Sydney, 1936.

Victoria of England, Houghton, 1936, revised edition, Faber, 1949.

(Author of introductory essay) Sacheverell Sitwell, *Collected Poems,* Duckworth, 1936.

I Live Under a Black Sun (novel), Gollancz, 1937, Doubleday, Doran, 1938, reprinted, Greenwood Press, 1973, new edition, Lehmann, 1948.

(With Osbert and Sacheverell Sitwell) *Trio: Dissertations on Some Aspects of National Genius,* Macmillan, 1938, published as *Triad of Genius,* British Book Centre, 1953, reprinted, Rebecca West, 1979.

(Editor) *Edith Sitwell's Anthology,* Gollancz, 1940.

Poems New and Old, Faber, 1940.

(Editor) *Look! The Sun,* Gollancz, 1941.

English Women, Collins, 1942.

Street Songs, Macmillan, 1942.

A Poet's Notebook, Macmillan, 1943, Little, Brown, 1950, reprinted, Greenwood Press, 1972.

Green Song and Other Poems, Macmillan, 1944, Vanguard, 1946.

(Compiler) *Planet and Glow-Worm: A Book for the Sleepless,* Macmillan, 1944.

The Song of the Cold (poems), Macmillan, 1945, Vanguard, 1948.

Fanfare for Elizabeth, Macmillan, 1946, Dufour, 1989.

The Shadow of Cain (blank verse), Lehmann, 1947, reprinted, Folcroft, 1977.

A Notebook of William Sheakespeare, Macmillan, 1948, Beacon, 1961.

The Canticle of the Rose: Selected Poems, 1920-1947, Macmillan, 1949, Vanguard, 1949.

(Author of foreword) Charles Henri Ford, *Sleep in a Nest of Flames,* New Directions, 1949.

(Compiler) *A Book of the Winter* (poems and prose), Macmillan, 1950, Vanguard, 1951.

Poor Men's Music, Fore Publications, 1950.

(Editor) *The American Genius,* Lehmann, 1951.

Facade: An Entertainment with Poems by Edith Sitwell, with music by William Turner Walton (performed in 1922), Oxford University Press, 1951. (Compiler) *A Book of Flowers,* Macmillan, 1952.

Gardeners and Astronomers: New Poems, Vanguard, 1953.

Collected Poems, Vanguard, 1954.

(Editor) *The Atlantic Book of British and American Poetry,* Little, Brown, 1958.

(Author of introduction) Jose Garcia Villa, *Selected Poems and New,* McDowell, Oblensky, 1958.

(Editor) Algernon Charles Swinburne, *Swinburne: A Selection,* Harcourt, 1960.

Edith Sitwell (poems), Vista Books, 1960.

The Queens and the Hive, Little, Brown, 1962.

The Outcasts (poems), Macmillan, 1962.

Music and Ceremonies (poems), Vanguard, 1963.

Taken Care Of (autobiography), Atheneum, 1965.

Selected Poems, compiled with an introduction by John Lehmann, Macmillan, 1965.

Selected Letters, 1919-1964, edited by Lehmann and Derek Parker, Macmillan, 1970, Vanguard, 1971.

Facade and Other Poems, 1920-1935, Duckworth, 1971.

Edith Sitwell: A Fire of the Mind, An Anthology, compiled by Elizabeth Salter and Allanah Harper, Joseph, 1976.

Editor of *Wheels,* an annual anthology of modern verse, 1916-21.

SIDELIGHTS: In the introduction to *The Canticle of the Rose* British poet Dame Edith Sitwell wrote: "At the time I began to write, a change in the direction, imagery and rhythms in poetry had become necessary, owing to the rhythmical flaccidity, the verbal deadness, the dead and expected patterns, of some of the poetry immediately preceding us." Her early work was often experimental, creating melody, using striking conceits, new rhythms, and confusing private allusions. Her efforts at change were resisted, but, as the *New Statesman* observed, "losing every battle, she won the campaign," and emerged the high priestess of twentieth-century poetry.

The *Times* (London) stated in 1955 that "she writes for the sake of sound, of color, and from an awareness of God and regard for man." She believed that "Poetry is the deification of reality, and one of its purposes is to show that the dimensions of man are, as Sir Arthur Eddington said, 'half way between those of an atom and a star.'" An admiring critic, John Lehmann, admitted that "her tendency has always been rather to overwork her symbolism; by a certain overfluid quality in her imagination to make the use of the symbols sometimes appear confused and indiscriminate." This Baroque quality has its admirers, however. Babette Deutsch in *Poetry in Our Time* wrote: "like the medieval hangings that kept the cold away from secular kings and princes of the Church, the finest of [Dame Edith's] poems have a luxurious beauty that serves to grace the bareness, to diminish the chill of this bare, cold age." Writing in the London *Times,* Geoffrey Elborn commented that Sitwell's best work was written in the 1920s, collected in the volumes *Bucolic Comedies, The Sleeping Beauty,* and *Troy Park.* "These . . . [were] written with a highly indvidual use of language still unsurpassed for its peculiar, inimitable artifice. Far from being trivial, these early poems by one 'a little outside life' should now find a greater acceptance in an era more concerned with Sitwell's concepts than her own age, earning her the deserved and secure reputation for which she herself so earnestly but recklessly fought."

The *New Statesman* has said that Sitwell's place in poetry is "roughly commensurate with that of Christina Rossetti in the previous century," and insists on the primacy of her personality. The sister of Osbert and Sacheverell was indeed not to be trifled with. Says Sacheverell: "She was always determined to be remarkable and she has succeeded." The *New Statesman* described her thus: "great rings load the fingers, the hands are fastidiously displayed, the eye-sockets have been thumbed by a master, the eyes themselves haunt, disdain, trouble indifference, and the fashions are century-old with a telling simplification." At times, and perhaps not unintentionally, she looked like a Tudor monarch. The author of a study of Elizabeth I, she once remarked: "I've always had a great affinity for Queen Elizabeth. We were born on the same day of the month and about the same hour of the day and I was extremely like her when I was young." Dame Edith always insisted that she was no eccentric: "It's just that I am more alive than most people."

Her outspoken manner and rebellion against accepted modes of behavior led to encounters with such as Wyndham Lewis and Geoffrey Grigson. When *Facade* was first performed in London in 1922, the response of the audience and of critics was derisive and indignant. Dame Edith recalled: "I had to hide behind the curtain. An old lady was waiting to beat me with an umbrella." (In 1949 the work was enthusiastically received in New York.) She remained wonderfully candid. On a visit to America she revealed that her most serious objection to certain Beat poets was that they smelled bad, and found she liked the late Marilyn Monroe, "largely because she was ill treated. She was like a sad ghost."

Robert K. Martin summed up Sitwell's literary career in *Dictionary of Literary Biography:* "Sitwell's reputation has suffered from the exceptional success of *Facade,* which was often treated as if it were the only work she had ever written. Inadequate attention has been paid to her development as a social poet, as a religious poet, and as a visionary. Her career traces the development of English poetry from the immediate post-World War I period of brightness and jazzy rhythms through the political involvements of the 1930s and the return to spiritual values after World War II. Her technique evolved, and, although she always remained a poet committed to the exploration of sound, she came to use sound patterns as an element in the construction of deep philosophic poems that reflect on her time and on man's condition. Edith Sitwell needs to be remembered not only as the bright young parodist of *Facade,* but as the angry chronicler of social injustice, as a poet who has found forms adequate to the atomic age and its horrors, and as a foremost poet of love. Her work displays enormous range of subject and of form. With her contemporary [T. S.] Eliot she remains one of the most important voices of twentieth-century English poetry."

AVOCATIONAL INTERESTS: Music, silence, reading.

BIOGRAPHICAL/CRITICAL SOURCES:

BOOKS

A Marrianne Moore Reader, Viking, 1961.
Bogan, Louise, *Selected Criticism,* Noonday, 1955.
Brophy, I. D., *Edith Sitwell,* Southern Illinois University Press, 1968.
Contemporary Literary Criticism, Gale, Volume 2, 1974, Volume 9, 1978.
Dictionary of Literary Biography, Volume 20: *British Poets, 1914-1945,* Gale, 1983.
Deutsch, Babette, *Poetry in Our Time,* Columbia University Press, 1956.
Fifoot, Richard, *A Bibliography of Edith, Osbert, and Sacheverell Sitwell,* Hart/Davis, 1963.
Lehmann, John, *Edith Sitwell,* Longmans, Green, 1952.
Lehmann, *A Nest of Tigers: The Sitwells in Their Times,* Little, Brown, 1968.
Megroz, R. L., *The Three Sitwells,* Doran, 1927, reprinted, Kennikat, 1969.
Mills, Ralph J., Jr., *Edith Sitwell: A Critical Essay,* Eerdmans, 1966.
Salter, Elizabeth, *The Last Years of a Rebel: A Memoir of Edith Sitwell,* Houghton, 1967.
Sitwell, Edith, and Osbert Sitwell, *Triad of Genius,* Part 1, British Book Centre, 1954.
Villa, J. G., *Celebrations for Edith Sitwell,* New Directions, 1948.

PERIODICALS

Criticism, winter, 1967.
Encounter, May, 1966.
Life, January 4, 1963.
London Magazine, September, 1970.
Nation, June 7, 1965.
New Republic, April 24, 1965.
New Statesman and Nation, January 23, 1954.
New York Times, December 10, 1964.
Observer, April 4, 1965.
Time, December 18, 1964.
Times (London), September 7, 1987.
Vogue, July, 1960.

*   *   *

SKINNER, B(urrhus) F(rederic) 1904-1990

PERSONAL: Born March 20, 1904, in Susquehanna, Pa.; son of William Arthur (an attorney) and Grace (Burrhus) Skinner; married Yvonne Blue, November 1, 1936; children: Julie (Mrs. Ernest Vargas), Deborah (Mrs. Barry Buzan). *Education:* Hamilton College, A.B., 1929; Harvard University, M.A., 1930, Ph.D., 1931.

ADDRESSES: Home—11 Old Dee Rd., Cambridge, Mass. 02138. *Office*—William James Hall, Harvard University, Cambridge, Mass. 02138.

CAREER: Harvard University, Cambridge, Mass., research fellow with National Research Council, 1931-32, junior fellow in Harvard Society of Fellows, 1933-36; University of Minnesota, Minneapolis, instructor, 1936-37, assistant professor, 1937-39, associate professor of psychology, 1939-45; Indiana University—Bloomington, professor of psychology and department chairman, 1945-48; Harvard University, Cambridge, William James Lecturer, 1947, professor of psychology, 1948-57, Edgar Pierce Professor of Psychology, 1958-74, professor emeritus, 1974—. Lecturer. Conducted war research for the Office of Scientific Research and Development, 1942-43.

MEMBER: American Psychological Association, American Association for the Advancement of Science, Society of Experimental Psychologists, National Academy of Sciences, American Philosophical Society, American Academy of Arts and Sciences, Royal Society of Arts (fellow), Swedish Psychological Society, Phi Beta Kappa, Sigma Xi.

AWARDS, HONORS: Howard Crosby Warren Medal, 1942; Guggenheim fellow, 1944-45; National Institute of Mental Health career grant; American Psychological Association award, 1958; National Medal of Science, 1968; American Psychological Association gold medal, 1971; Joseph P. Kennedy, Jr., Foundation award, 1971; Humanist of the Year Award, American Humanist Society, 1972; Creative Leadership in Education Award, New York University, 1972; American Educational Research Association award, 1978; National Association for Retarded Citizens first annual award, 1978. Honorary degrees from twenty-five universities and colleges, including: Sc.D., University of Chicago, 1967, University of Exeter, 1969, and McGill University, 1970; Litt.D., Ripon College, 1961; LH.D., Rockford College, 1971; L.L.D., Ohio Wesleyan University, 1971.

WRITINGS:

(Editor with father, William A. Skinner) *A Digest of Decisions of the Anthracite Board of Conciliation,* [Scranton, Pa.], 1928.

Behavior of Organisms: An Experimental Analysis, Appleton-Century-Croft, 1938, reprinted, Prentice-Hall, 1966.

(With others) *Current Trends in Psychology* (lectures), University of Pittsburgh Press, 1947, reprinted, Arden Library, 1982.

Walden Two (novel), Macmillan, 1948, revised edition, Macmillan (London), 1969, published with introduction by Skinner, Macmillan, 1976.

Science and Human Behavior, Macmillan, 1953, reprinted, Irvington, 1979. (Editor with Peter B. Dews) *Techniques for the Study of Behavioral Effects of Drugs,* Annals of the New York Academy of Sciences, 1956.

(With C. B. Ferster) *Schedules of Reinforcement,* Prentice Hall, 1957. *Verbal Behavior,* Prentice-Hall, 1957.

(Editor) *Cumulative Record: A Selection of Papers,* Prentice Hall, 1959, 3rd edition, 1972.

(With James G. Holland) *The Analysis of Behavior: A Program for Self-Instruction,* McGraw, 1961.

Teaching Machines, Freeman, 1961.

(With others) *Understanding Maps: A Programmed Text,* Allyn, 1964.

(With Sue-Ann Krakower) *Handwriting with Write and See* (patented method of teaching writing), Lyons & Carnahan, 1968.

The Technology of Teaching, Prentice-Hall, 1968.

Earth Resources (textbook), Prentice-Hall, 1969, 2nd edition, 1976.

Contingencies of Reinforcement: A Theoretical Analysis, Prentice-Hall, 1969.

(With Arnold J. Toynbee and others) *On the Future of Art* (lectures), Viking, 1970.

Beyond Freedom and Dignity, Knopf, 1971.

About Behaviorism, Knopf, 1974.

Particulars of My Life (also see below; autobiography), Knopf, 1976.

Reflections on Behaviorism and Society, Prentice-Hall, 1978.

The Shaping of a Behaviorist: Part Two of an Autobiography (also see below), Knopf, 1979.

Notebooks, Prentice-Hall, 1981.

Skinner for the Classroom: Selected Papers, edited by Robert Epstein, Research Press (Champaign, Ill.), 1982.

A Matter of Consequences: Part Three of an Autobiography (also see below), Knopf, 1983.

(With M. E. Vaughan) *Enjoy Old Age: A Program of Self Management,* Norton, 1983 (published in England as *How to Enjoy Your Old Age,* Sheldon Press, 1985).

Particulars of My Life [and] *The Shaping of a Behaviorist* [and] *A Matter of Consequences* (three-book set), New York University Press, 1984.

Upon Further Reflection, Prentice-Hall, 1987.

Recent Issues in the Analysis of Behavior, Merrill, 1989.

RECORDINGS

(With Carl Rogers) "A Dialogue on Education and the Control of Human Behavior," Jeffrey Norton, 1976.

(With Rogers) "Sound Seminars," Jeffrey Norton, 1976.

Also recorded on three albums from the Center for the Study of Democratic Institutions.

SIDELIGHTS: An influential and controversial figure in modern psychology, B. F. Skinner is "the most famous of behaviorist psychologists," Harold Kaplan states in *Commentary.* Writing in *Behavioral and Brain Sciences,* Joseph M. Scandura calls Skinner "contemporary behaviorism personified." His belief that man is controlled solely by external factors in his environment—specifically, that rewarded behavior is encouraged and unrewarded behavior is extinguished—and his rejection of man as an autonomous being capable of independent, self-willed action have made Skinner notorious among many of his colleagues. His supporters believe, however, that Skinner has made an important contribution to behaviorism and that his insights can be used to radically improve society.

Behaviorism is a "scientific theory that takes as its domain the behavior of living organisms and tries to explain how they learn this behavior and how it changes," Peter Caws explains in the *New Republic.* This emphasis on behavior grows out of a belief that human consciousness is beyond scientific analysis. The ideas and findings of behaviorist psychologists have had a tremendous impact on such areas as drug and alcohol rehabilitation where the chief concern is behavior modification. Skinner stands out from most other behaviorists in that he not only dismisses the scientific analysis of human consciousness but also believes that "feelings and mental processes are just the meaningless byproducts of [the] endless cycle of stimulus and response," John Leo writes in *Time.* As Skinner explains in *A Matter of Consequences,* the third volume of his autobiography, "I . . . do not think feelings are important. Freud is probably responsible for the current extent to which they are taken seriously." Skinner also advocates the use of "behavioral technology" to restructure society. He suggests that the same techniques that successfully train laboratory animals can be used to control man's negative behavior and thereby eliminate such social ills as crime, poverty, and war. Because his critics see a totalitarian danger in his suggestions for social change, they have called Skinner "politely, a social engineer; less politely, a neo-fascist," Elizabeth Mehren writes in the *Los Angeles Times.* Despite such criticism, "Skinner has influenced everything from crib toys for babies to inventory management systems in industry," Webster Schott writes in the *Washington Post Book World.*

Skinner's behaviorist beliefs were derived from a series of laboratory experiments he conducted during the 1930s and 1940s. At that time Skinner experimented with rats and pigeons. By rewarding his test animals whenever they performed desired behavior—a process he calls positive reinforcement—Skinner succeeded in training them to do a number of difficult tasks. His pigeons could play Ping Pong, dance, walk in figure eights, and distinguish between colors. He taught rats to push buttons, pull strings, and press levers to receive food and drink. These experiments convinced Skinner that behavior control could be achieved through the control of environmental stimuli. The special environment in which Skinner's animals were trained, an enclosed, soundproof box equipped with buttons, levers, and other training devices, was "a marvelous tool for conditioning animals," John Langone admits in *Discover.* Widely used by other researchers, this training environment became known as the Skinner Box.

Convinced that the techniques used on his pigeons and rats could work on human beings as well, Skinner built a training box for children in 1943. Called the Air-Crib by Skinner, but popularly dubbed the "baby box" by the media, the device was "nothing more than an elaborate, insulated, glassed-in crib with the temperature carefully controlled," Langone re-ports. It was designed to provide a child with "a very comfortable, stimulating environment," Skinner tells Lawrence Meyer in the *Washington Post.* Skinner raised his daughter Deborah in the box for two and a half years. When his account of the child rearing experiment was published in the *Ladies' Home Journal,* it sparked a national controversy. Skinner was accused of monstrous experiments with his own children. Newspaper editorials attacked him; he was featured on radio shows and in newsreels. His daughter suffered no ill effects from the experiment, grew up normally, and is still on good terms with her father. Nonetheless, Skinner's attempt to market the "baby box" under the name "Heir Conditioner" was a failure.

In 1948, Skinner speculated on how the findings from his laboratory work and his experiment with his daughter's upbringing could be applied to the structuring of society. In his novel *Walden Two,* he portrays a behaviorist society in which positive and negative reinforcements are built into the social structure. The novel's plot revolves around a tour of the community taken by two college professors. As T. Morris Longstreth writes in the *Christian Science Monitor,* the community "is a sort of managed democracy." Children, raised in communal nurseries, are taught to think and learn instead of called upon to memorize specific facts. Theology and history are suppressed. All members of the society encourage social harmony by practicing positive reinforcement for approved behavior. "One can admire much of this and only marvel that such large adjustments in human nature are to be bought at such cheap price," Longstreth writes. Tabitha M. Powledge points out in *Nation* that in *Walden Two* "ideal social behavior is shaped by gentle means for good ends; the fascist dystopia which is equally possible from such techniques seems not to trouble [Skinner]." In his review of the novel for the *New York Times Book Review,* Charles Poore wonders "why anyone should want to spend his days in this antiseptic elysium," but allows that the book is "a brisk and thoughtful foray in search of peace of mind, security, and a certain amount of balm for burnt-fingered moderns." Mehren describes *Walden Two* as "a kind of behavioristic book of the Bible: a road map to a future in which free will would recede to the positive and negative reinforcements of culture and the environment." Speaking to *Psychology*

Today, Skinner expresses some reservations about the book. "If were to rewrite *Walden Two,*" he explains, "I would have more in it about the nitty-gritty conditions of incentive systems. I was counting on everybody being willing to give four hours a day in exchange for the privilege of living in the community. That's Marx, and I don't think it really works. I would change *Walden Two*'s education. . . . I dealt too timidly with sex. . . . Also, *Walden Two* has no criminals, no psychotics, no retardates—I would do something about them now."

Where Skinner spoke fictionally about a new society in *Walden Two,* in *Beyond Freedom and Dignity,* described by Kaplan as "the culminating book of [Skinner's] career," he openly argues for radical social change based on behaviorist findings. "Almost all our major problems involve human behavior, and they cannot be solved by physical and biological technology alone. What is needed is a technology of behavior," Skinner asserts in the book. This proposed technology of behavior would utilize our knowledge about "the interaction between organism and environment" to design a society capable of altering man's destructive behavior through a system of positive and negative reinforcements. But before this can come about, Skinner maintains, the belief in autonomous, self-directed man and the relating concepts of freedom and dignity must he discarded. Freedom and dignity, Skinner writes, "are the possessions of the autonomous man of traditional theory, and they are essential to practices in which a person is held responsible for his conduct and given credit for his achievements. A scientific analysis shifts both the responsibility and the achievement to the environment."

Reaction to *Beyond Freedom and Dignity* was divided. Those critics opposed to Skinner's ideas thought his denial of man's autonomy and his plans for social manipulation were incorrect and possibly dangerous. Writing in the *National Review,* Michael S. Gazzaniga states: "No one denies reinforcement is an important controlling influence on our behavior. Skinner is correct to say we could order our society a little more logically than we do. But to extend the limited benefits of the obvious to a new world-view that eliminates concepts such as free will is both pretentious and incredibly naive." Kaplan calls Skinner's proposals "nothing less than a bid for power by a new leader class, called, in [Skinner's] words, the 'technologists of behavior.'" Robert Claiborne, in a review of the book for *Book World,* insists that Skinner "knows almost nothing about human beings," an opinion echoed by Richard Sennett in the *New York Times Book Review,* who claims that Skinner "appears to understand so little, indeed to care so little, about society itself that the reader comes totally to distrust him."

But those who found value in *Beyond Freedom and Dignity* point to its basic insight that man's behavior is shaped by his environment, although some critics disagreed with Skinner's conclusions based on that insight. As Michael Novak writes in *Beyond the Punitive Society: Operant Conditioning, Social and Political Aspects,* "few question the technical validity of his laboratory work, or even the technically expressed theory interpreting it. Many do question Professor Skinner's extrapolation therefrom." In another article for *Beyond the Punitive Society,* Karl H. Pribram argues that because of information omitted from the book, such as evidence that the human brain is modified by experience, Skinner's conclusions are not entirely correct. "Designs of cultures, therefore, cannot, in and of themselves, completely specify behavior," Pribram writes. But there is "much good in the book," Pribram maintains, including "a good case for . . . behavioral technology." Pribram also admires "Skinner's contributions to our knowledge of the environmental contingencies that lead to reinforcement." W. F. Day, writing in *Contemporary Psy-*

chology, states that Skinner's "frontal attack on what he calls the concept of autonomous man" is essentially correct. We do "incalculable damage . . . to ourselves, to those we love, and to those others for whom we want to assume some responsibility when we base our social decisions on the model of autonomous man," Day declares. Gerald Marwell counters critics who see Skinner's suggestions as totalitarian. In a *Contemporary Sociology* article, Marwell contends that what Skinner proposes is a society in which those who are controlled have power over society's control mechanisms. Skinner "asserts that social control over populations will be exercised by someone. The choice which remains is only *who* shall control and by what means," Marwell explains.

The questions raised in *Beyond Freedom and Dignity* continue to be addressed in Skinner's three volumes of autobiography—*Particulars of My Life, The Shaping of a Behaviorist,* and *A Matter of Consequences.* Each of these books covers a particular time span in the course of Skinner's career: *Particulars of My Life* traces Skinner's childhood and education; *The Shaping of a Behaviorist* addresses his years of research during the 1930s and 1940s; and *A Matter of Consequences* chronicles his later life as one of the leading psychologists in the country. Skinner's writing style reflects his beliefs about behavior and motivation. As he explains in *A Matter of Consequences:* "I have tried to report my life *as it was lived.* . . . I have seldom mentioned later significances. When I first bent a wire in the shape of a lever to be pressed by a rat, I was making the prototype of many thousands of levers, but did not know it then, and mentioning it would have been a mistake." This approach leads Christopher Lehmann-Haupt in the *New York Times* to complain that "instead of reflecting on or trying to pick out and organize whatever shaped him as a behaviorist, Mr. Skinner simply slogs his way chronologically through the years." But Eugene Kennedy writes in the *Chicago Tribune Book World* that *The Shaping of a Behaviorist* "opens to us the life of a genius."

The publication of the autobiographies gave critics the opportunity to appraise Skinner's contributions to his field. Schott finds that "Skinner has been working at what scientists everywhere work at: meaning. Except he has devoted his life to the refinement of what precedes meaning—observation and description." In the Toronto *Globe and Mail,* Andrew Nikiforuk holds that Skinner "has long argued that a scientific analysis of human behavior need not slight the dignity of mankind. Behaviorism, he says, examines what people do and why they do it, points to conditions that can be changed and shows the inadequacies of other views."

Although "the vast majority of psychologists disagree strongly with his basic theories," as Langone writes, Skinner is "the undisputed leader of modern behaviorism" and "may be the most influential American psychologist who ever lived," Harvey Mindess states in the *Los Angeles Times Book Review.* Kennedy admits that Skinner "has been the favorite villain of a wide range of supposedly intellectual Americans." But he is also, Kennedy believes, "a model for scientists of all kinds, since his hypotheses flowed from the work he was doing, rather than from the fashion of the day." Skinner "has made enormous contributions to [psychology] and demonstrated the awesome control the experimenter can have over the behavior of an animal under specified conditions," George W. Barlow writes in *Behavioral and Brain Sciences.* Gazzaniga believes that Skinner "is a man of many talents. He is a superb writer, a brilliant polemicist, a clever inventor and a trained scientist. He is also a philosopher manque and an incredible egotist."

The controversy Skinner's life and writings have caused continues unabated, and the focus of this controversy still rests on the validity of applying Skinner's laboratory findings about animal behavior and control to the structuring of modern society. Rosemary Dinnage states her objections to Skinner's ideas in the *New York Times Book Review:* "The control it is possible to exercise over the behavior of small caged animals . . . has led Professor Skinner into the almost appealingly naive view that there is a science of behavior that can be used to control wars and all the other social problems that beset us. He has still to give practical proof of how this could be done." But within the field of psychology Skinner has many supporters for his theories. H. J. Eysenck writes in *Behavioral and Brain Sciences* that Skinner "resembles [Sigmund] Freud, and it is no wonder that both men have formed a tightly knit group of supporters, founded their own journals, and have, in their attempt to inaugurate a new psychology, separated themselves from the broad basis of general psychology." Outside criticism has not diminished the intensity of Skinner's belief that behaviorist research can be used to alter man's behavior. "Despite decades of controversy," Leo reports, "Skinner remains convinced that his principles of fifty years are correct." As Skinner writes in *A Matter of Consequences:* "I am sometimes asked, 'Do you think of yourself as you think of the organisms you study?' The answer is yes."

BIOGRAPHICAL/CRITICAL SOURCES:

BOOKS

Chomsky, Noam, *For Reasons of State,* Pantheon, 1973.
Contemporary Issues Criticism, Volume 2, Gale, 1984.
Koestler, Arthur, *The Ghost in the Machine,* Hutchinson, 1967.
Skinner, B. F., *Beyond Freedom and Dignity,* Knopf, 1971.
Skinner, B. F., *Particulars of My Life,* Knopf, 1976.
Skinner, B. F., *The Shaping of a Behaviorist: Part Two of an Autobiography,* Knopf, 1979.
Skinner, B. F., *A Matter of Consequences: Part Three of an Autobiography,* Knopf, 1983.
Wheeler, Harvey, editor, *Beyond the Punitive Society: Operant Conditioning, Social and Political Aspects,* W. H. Freeman, 1973.

PERIODICALS

American Journal of Sociology, September, 1980.
Behavioral and Brain Sciences, December, 1984.
Book World, October 10, 1971.
Chicago Tribune Book World, May 20, 1979.
Christian Science Monitor, June 24, 1948.
Commentary, February, 1972.
Contemporary Psychology, September, 1972, September, 1979.
Contemporary Sociology, January, 1972.
Discover, September, 1983.
Globe and Mail (Toronto), March 10, 1984.
Journal of Individual Psychology, Volume 26, 1970.
Journal of the Experimental Analysis of Behavior, May, 1969, March, 1971.
Los Angeles Times, September 22, 1982.
Los Angeles Times Book Review, October 9, 1983.
Nation, July 28-August 4, 1979.
National Review, November 5, 1971, November 22, 1974.
New Republic, October 16, 1971, June 1, 1974, August 4, 1979.
New Yorker, October 9, 1971.
New York Review of Books, December 30, 1971.
New York Times, June 6, 1979, August 25, 1987, September 13, 1987.
New York Times Book Review, June 13, 1948, October 24, 1971, July 14, 1974, May 20, 1979, January 1, 1984.

Psychology Today, September, 1983.
Saturday Review, October 9, 1971.
Science, June 8, 1979.
Time, October 10, 1983.
Times Literary Supplement, February 29, 1975, December 4, 1981.
Washington Post, August 24, 1982.
Washington Post Book World, July 8, 1979.

*   *   *

SKVORECKY, Josef (Vaclav) 1924-

PERSONAL: Surname pronounced *Shquor*-et-skee; born September 27, 1924, in Nachod, Czechoslovakia; immigrated to Canada, 1969; son of Josef Karel (a bank clerk) and Anna Marie (Kurazova) Skvorecky; married Zdena Salivarova (a writer and publisher), March 31, 1958. *Education:* Charles University, Prague, Ph.D., 1951. *Politics:* Christian socialist. *Religion:* Roman Catholic.

ADDRESSES: Home—487 Sackville St., Toronto, Ontario, Canada M4X 1T6. *Office*—Erindale College, University of Toronto, 3599 Mississagua Rd., Clarkson, Ontario, Canada; and 68 Publishers, 164 Davenport Rd., Toronto, Ontario, Canada M5R 1J2.

CAREER: Odeon Publishers, Prague, Czechoslovakia, editor of Anglo-American department, 1953-56; *World Literature Magazine,* Prague, assistant editor-in-chief, 1956-59; free-lance writer in Prague, 1963-69; University of Toronto, Erindale College, Clarkson, Ontario, special lecturer in English and Slavic drama, 1969-71, writer-in-residence, 1970-71, associate professor, 1971-75, professor of English, 1975—. Founder and editor-in-chief, 68 Publishers, 1972—. *Military service:* Czechoslovak Army, 1951-53.

MEMBER: International PEN, International Association of Crime Writers, Authors Guild, Authors League of America, Mystery Writers of America, Royal Society of Canada (fellow), Crime Writers of Canada, Canadian Writers Union, Czechoslovak Society of Arts and Letters (honorary member).

AWARDS, HONORS: Literary Award of Czechoslovakian Writers Union, 1968; Neustadt International Prize for Literature, 1980; Guggenheim fellowship, 1980; Silver Award for Best Fiction Publication in Canadian Magazines of 1980, 1981; nominated for the Nobel Prize in literature, 1982; Governor General's Award for Best Fiction, 1984; recipient, 1985 City of Toronto Book Award; D.H.L., State University of New York, 1986.

WRITINGS:

Zbabelci (novel), Ceskoslovensky spisovatel (Prague), 1958, 4th edition, Nase vojsko (Prague), 1968, translation by Jeanne Nemcova published as *The Cowards,* Grove, 1970.
Legenda Emoke (novel; title means "The Legend of Emoke"), Ceskoslovensky spisovatel, 1963, 2nd edition, 1965.
Sedmiramenny svicen (stories; title means "The Menorah"), Nase vojsko, 1964, 2nd edition, 1965.
Napady ctenare detektivek (essays; title means "Reading Detective Stories"), Ceskoslovensky spisovatel, 1965.
Ze zivota lepsi spolecnosti (stories; title means "The Life of Better Society"), Mlada fronta (Prague), 1965.
Babylonsky pribeh (stories; title means "A Babylonian Story"), Svobodne Slovo (Prague), 1965.
Smutek porucika Boruvka (stories), Mlada fronta, 1966, translation published as *The Mournful Demeanor of Lieutenant Boruvka,* Gollancz, 1974.
Konec nylonoveho veku (novel; title means "The End of the Nylon Age"), Ceskoslovensky spisovatel, 1967.

O nich—o nas (essays; title means "About Them—Which Is about Us"), Kruh (Hradec Kralove), 1968.
(With Evald Schorm) *Fararuv Konec* (novelization of Skvorecky's filmscript "Konec farare"; title means "End of a Priest"; also see below), Kruh, 1969.
Lvice (novel), Ceskoslovensky spisovatel, 1969, translation published as *Miss Silver's Past,* Grove, 1973.
Horkejsvet: Povidky z let, 1946-1967 (title means "The Bitter World: Selected Stories, 1947-1967"), Odeon (Prague), 1969.
Tankovy prapor (novel; title means "The Tank Corps"), 68 Publishers (Toronto), 1971.
All the Bright Young Men and Women: A Personal History of the Czech Cinema, translation from the original Czech by Michael Schonberg, Peter Martin Associates, 1971.
Mirakl (novel; title means "The Miracle Play"), 68 Publishers, 1972.
Hrichy pro patera Knoxe (novel), 68 Publishers, 1973, translation by Kaca Polackova-Henley published as *Sins for Father Knox,* Norton, 1989.
Prima Sezona (novel), 68 Publishers, 1974, translation published as *The Swell Season,* Lester & Orpen Dennys, 1982.
Konec porucika Boruvka (novel; title means "The End of Lieutenant Boruvka"), 68 Publishers, 1975.
Pribeh inzenyra lidskych dusi (novel), 68 Publishers, 1977, translation published as *The Engineer of Human Souls: An Entertainment of the Old Themes of Life, Women, Fate, Dreams, the Working Class, Secret Agents, Love, and Death,* Knopf, 1984.
The Bass Saxophone, translation from the original Czech by Polackova-Henley, Knopf, 1979.
Navrat porucika Boruvka (novel; title means "The Return of Lieutenant Boruvka"), 68 Publishers, 1980.
Jiri Menzel and the History of the "Closely Watched Trains" (comparative study), University of Colorado Press, 1982.
Scherzo capriccioso (novel), 68 Publishers, 1984, translation published as *Dvorak in Love,* Knopf, 1986.
Talkin' Moscow Blues (essays), Lester & Orpen Dennys, 1988.

EDITOR

Selected Writings of Sinclair Lewis, Odeon, 1964-69.
(With P. L. Doruzka) *Tvar jazzu* (anthology; title means "The Face of Jazz"), Statni hudebni vydavatelstvi (Prague), Part 1, 1964, Part 2, 1966.
Collected Writings of Ernest Hemingway, Odeon, 1965-69.
Three Times Hercule Poirot, Odeon, 1965.
(With Doruzka) *Jazzova inspirace* (poetry anthology; title means "The Jazz Inspiration"), Odeon, 1966.
Nachrichten aus der CSSR (title means "News from Czechoslovakia"), translation from the original Czech by Vera Cerna and others, Suhrkamp Verlag (Frankfurt), 1968.

OTHER

Also author of movie screenplays, including "Zlocin v divci skole" (title means "Crime in a Girl's School"), 1966; "Zlocin v santanu" (title means "Crime in a Night Club"), 1968; "Konec farare" (title means "End of a Priest"), 1969; "Flirt se slecnou Stribrnou" (title means "Flirtations with Miss Silver"), 1969; and "Sest cernych divek" (title means "Six Brunettes"), 1969. Author of scripts for television programs. Author of prefaces and introductions to Czech and Slovak editions of the works of Saul Bellow, Bernard Malamud, Stephen Crane, Rex Stout, Dorothy Sayers, Charles Dickens, Sinclair Lewis, and others. Translator of numerous books from English to Czech, including the works of Ray Bradbury, Henry James, Ernest Hemingway, William Faulkner, Raymond Chandler, and others.

WORK IN PROGRESS: The Bride from Texas, a novel about the Czechs in General Sherman's army.

SIDELIGHTS: "In his native country, Josef Skvorecky is a household word," fellow Czech author Arnost Lustig tells the *Washington Post.* Skvorecky wrote his first novel, *The Cowards,* in 1948 when he was twenty-four. Not published until 1958, the book caused a flurry of excitement that led to "firings in the publishing house, ragings in the official press, and a general purge that extended eventually throughout the arts," according to Neal Ascherson in the *New York Review of Books.* The book was banned by Czech officials one month after publication, marking "the start of an incredible campaign of vilification against the author," a *Times Literary Supplement* reviewer reports. Skvorecky subsequently included a "cheeky and impenitent Introduction," Ascherson notes, in the novel's 1963 second edition. "In spite of all the suppression," the *Times Literary Supplement* critic explains, "*The Cowards* became a milestone in Czech literature and Joseph Skvorecky one of the country's most popular writers." Formerly a member of the central committees of the Czechoslovak Writers' Union and the Czechoslovak Film and Television Artists, Skvorecky chose exile and immigrated to Canada in 1969 following the Soviet invasion of his country.

Ascherson explains why *The Cowards* caused so much controversy: "It is not at all the sort of mirror official Czechoslovakia would wish to glance in. A recurring theme is . . . pity for the Germans, defeated and bewildered. . . . The Russians strike [the main character] as alluring primitives (his use of the word 'Mongolian' about them caused much of the scandal in 1958)." The *Times Literary Supplement* writer adds, "The novel turned out to be anti-Party and anti-God at the same time; everybody felt himself a victim of the author's satire." Set in a provincial Bohemian town, the story's events unfold in May, 1945, as the Nazis retreat and the Russian army takes control of an area populated with "released prisoners of war, British, Italian, French and Russian (Mongolians, these, whom the locals do not find very clean), and Jewish women survivors from a concentration camp," writes Stuart Hood in the *Listener.* The narrator, twenty-year-old Danny Smiricky, and his friends—members of a jazz band—observe the flux of power, human nature, and death around them while devoting their thoughts and energies to women and music. "These are, by definition, no heroes," states Hood. "They find themselves caught up in a farce which turns into horror from one minute to the next." The group may dream of making a bold move for their country, but, as Charles Dollen notes in *Best Sellers,* "they never make anything but music."

Labeled "judeonegroid" (Jewish-Negro) and suppressed by the Nazis, their jazz is, nonetheless, political. To play blues or sing scat is to stand up for "individual freedom and spontaneity," states Terry Winch in *Washington Post Book World.* "In other words, [jazz] stood for everything the Nazis hated and wanted to crush." Skvorecky, like his narrator, was a jazz musician during the Nazi "protectorate." The author wields this music as a "goad, the 'sharp thorn in the sides of the power-hungry men, from Hitler to Brezhnev,' " Saul Maloff declares in the *New York Times Book Review.* Described as a "highly metaphorical writer" by Winch, Skvorecky often employs jazz "in its familiar historical and international role as a symbol (and a breeding-ground) of anti-authoritarian attitudes," according to Russell Davies, writing in the *Times Literary Supplement.*

Skvorecky follows the life of Danny Smiricky in his *Tankovy prapor, Mirakl, The Bass Saxophone,* and *The Engineer of Human*

Souls: An Entertainment of the Old Themes of Life, Women, Fate, Dreams, the Working Class, Secret Agents, Love, and Death. The Bass Saxophone contains a memoir and two novellas first published individually in Czechoslovakia during the 1960s. Like *The Cowards,* the memoir "Red Music," observes Maloff, "evokes the atmosphere of that bleak time [during World War II], the strange career of indigenous American music transplanted abroad to the unlikeliest soil." Although it is only a "brief preface to the stories," Winch maintains that the memoir "in some ways is the more interesting section" of the book. Davies believes that the "short and passionate essay" shows how, "since [the jazz enthusiast in an Iron Curtain country] has sorrows other than his own to contend with, the music must carry for him not just a sense of isolation and longing but a bitterly practical political resentment."

"Emoke," the novella that follows, is "fragile, lyrical, 'romantic' and, like its title character, "fabulous: precisely the materials of fable," comments Maloff. Davies adds that "in its poetic evocation of Emoke, a hurt and delicate creature with an array of spiritual cravings, . . . the story has a . . . depth of soul and concern." Winch, however, feels the woman "is not a vivid or forceful enough character to bear the burden of all she is asked to represent." The three critics believe that the title story, "The Bass Saxophone," is more successful, "perhaps because music, Skvorecky's real passion, is central to the narrative," Winch explains. Here, writes Davies, "music . . . emerges as a full symbolic and ideological force," whereas in "Emoke" it was "a mere undercurrent." The story of a boy playing music while under Nazi rule, claims Maloff, is "sheer magic, a parable, a fable about art, about politics, about the zone where the two intersect." Writing in the *Atlantic,* Benjamin De Mott calls *The Bass Saxophone* "an exceptionally haunting and restorative volume of fiction, a book in which literally nothing enters except the fully imagined, hence the fully exciting."

Following Danny's travels to Canada as an immigrant, Skvorecky's writing continues to parallel his own life when the main character of *The Engineer of Human Souls* accepts a position at a small University of Toronto college. The main theme, brought out by the author's use of humor in the book, concerns the dangers of dogmatic thinking, the political naivete of Westerners, and the injustices of totalitarianism. *Quill and Quire* critic Mark Czarnecki asserts that as "an exhaustive, insightful document of modern society in both East and West, [*The Engineer of Human Souls*] has no equal." In a *Canadian Forum* review, Sam Solecki notes that *The Engineer of Human Souls* is also a "transitional novel for Skvorecky, in which we see him extending his imagination beyond his Czechoslovak past while still including it." Solecki also writes that this novel, which portrays Smiricky in his sixties, will probably bring "the Smiricky cycle to a close."

However, the theme of music which Skvorecky maintains throughout the Smiricky books is continued in the author's next novel, *Dvorak in Love.* The book is a fictionalized account of Skvorecky's compatriot, composer Antonin Dvorak, and his visit to New York City. The life of Dvorak, whose music was influenced by black folk music and jazz, provided the author with the perfect subject for discussing the synthesis "of the two dominant musical cultures of our time—the classical European tradition . . . and the jazzy American tradition," as William French put it in a *Globe and Mail* review. Although some reviewers like Barbara Black have found the narrative structure of the opening chapters of *Dvorak in Love* too complicated to enjoy, the author's characteristic humor later enlivens the story. "Best of all" in this book, remarks Black, "Skvorecky celebrates Dvorak and the musical trail he blazed."

Summarizing the writer's accomplishments in all his works, Hood comments that "Skvorecky is a novelist of real stature, who writes without sentimentality about adolescence, war and death." Yet it is not plot that impresses Winch. He points out that Skvorecky "is a poetic writer whose work depends more on the interplay of words and images than on story-line." Concludes Maloff: "We have had to wait a very long time for the . . . English translation and . . . American publication of [Skvorecky's] superlative, greatly moving works of art. . . . Fortunately, [his] work has lost none of its immediacy or luster, nor is it likely to for a long time to come."

AVOCATIONAL INTERESTS: Film, jazz (Skvorecky plays the saxophone), American folklore.

BIOGRAPHICAL/CRITICAL SOURCES:

BOOKS

Contemporary Authors Autobiography Series, Volume 1, Gale, 1984.
Contemporary Literary Criticism, Gale, Volume 15, 1980, Volume 39, 1986.
Contemporary Literary Criticism Yearbook: 1985, Gale, 1986.

PERIODICALS

Atlantic, March, 1979.
Best Sellers, November 1, 1970.
Canadian Forum, August-September, 1984.
Chicago Tribune, June 9, 1987.
Chicago Tribune Book World, August 12, 1984, March 1, 1987.
Encounter, July-August, 1985.
Globe and Mail (Toronto), November 25, 1986, November 29, 1986, June 25, 1988.
Library Journal, July, 1970.
Listener, October 8, 1970, March 11, 1976, August 17, 1978.
Los Angeles Times Book Review, July 1, 1984, February 15, 1987, August 23, 1987, June 12, 1988, February 26, 1989.
Nation, August 4, 1984.
New Republic, August 27, 1984.
Newsweek, August 13, 1984.
New York Review of Books, November 19, 1970, September 27, 1984.
New York Times, July 23, 1984, August 9, 1984.
New York Times Book Review, September 21, 1975, January 14, 1979, August 19, 1984, January 12, 1986, February 22, 1987, September 6, 1987.
Observer, March 3, 1985.
Publishers Weekly, June 22, 1984.
Quill and Quire, May, 1984.
Time, July 30, 1984.
Times Literary Supplement, October 16, 1970, June 23, 1978, August 12, 1983, March 8, 1985, January 23, 1987.
Washington Post, December 4, 1987.
Washington Post Book World, July 29, 1984, March 29, 1987.
World Literature Today, autumn, 1978.

*   *   *

SMITH, Florence Margaret   1902-1971
(Stevie Smith)

PERSONAL: Born September 20, 1902, in Hull, Yorkshire, England; died of a brain tumor, March 7, 1971; daughter of Charles Ward (a shipping agent) and Ethel Rahel (Spear) Smith. *Education:* Attended high school in Palmers Green, London, and North London Collegiate School.

CAREER: Newnes Publishing Co., London, England, secretary, 1923-53; writer and broadcaster. Gave poetry readings for British Broadcasting Corp. radio and television; read and sang poems set to music (based on plainsong and folk music) at festivals in London, Edinburgh, Stratford on Avon, and elsewhere in England. Member of literature panel of Arts Council.

AWARDS, HONORS: Cholmondeley Poetry Award, 1966; Queen's Gold Medal for Poetry, 1969.

WRITINGS:

POETRY; UNDER NAME STEVIE SMITH; SELF-ILLUSTRATED

A Good Time Was Had by All, J. Cape, 1937.
Tender Only to One, J. Cape, 1938.
Mother, What is Man?, J. Cape, 1942.
Harold's Leap, Chapman & Hall, 1950.
Not Waving but Drowning, Deutsch, 1957.
Selected Poems (also see below), Longmans, Green, 1962, New Directions, 1964.
The Frog Prince and Other Poems (also see below), Longmans, Green, 1966.
(With Edwin Brock and Geoffrey Hill) *Penguin Modern Poets 8,* Penguin, 1966.
The Best Beast, Knopf, 1969.
Two in One (includes *Selected Poems* and *The Frog Prince and Other Poems*), Longman, 1971.
Scorpion and Other Poems, Longman, 1972.
Collected Poems, A. Lane, 1975, Oxford University Press, 1976.

Contributor of poetry to numerous anthologies, including *Faber Book of Twentieth-Century Verse,* 2nd edition, 1965, and *Poetry 1900 to 1965,* 1967.

OTHER; UNDER NAME STEVIE SMITH

Novel on Yellow Paper; or, Work It out for Yourself, J. Cape, 1936, Morrow, 1937.
Over the Frontier (novel), J. Cape, 1938.
The Holiday (novel), Chapman & Hall, 1949.
Some Are More Human than Others (drawings and captions), Gaberbocchus, 1958.
(Editor) *T. S. Eliot: A Symposium for His 70th Birthday,* Hart-Davis, 1958.
(Editor) *The Poet's Garden,* Viking, 1970 (published in England as *The Batsford Book of Children's Verse,* Batsford, 1970).
Me Again: Uncollected Writings of Stevie Smith, edited by Jack Barbera and William McBrien, Virago, 1981, Farrar, Straus, 1982.

Contributor of poems and reviews to *Observer, Times Literary Supplement, Listener, New Yorker, Nation,* and other periodicals.

SIDELIGHTS: Calling Stevie Smith's *Not Waving but Drowning* "the best collection of new poems to appear in 1957," *Poetry* contributor David Wright observed that "as one of the most original women poets now writing [Stevie Smith] seems to have missed most of the public accolades bestowed by critics and anthologists. One reason may be that not only does she belong to no 'school'—whether real or invented as they usually are—but her work is so completely different from anyone else's that it is all but impossible to discuss her poems in relation to those of her contemporaries." "Without identifying itself with any particular school of modern poetics," Linda Rahm Hallett similarly noted in the *Dictionary of Literary Biography,* "[Smith's] voice is nevertheless very much that of what she once called the 'age of unrest' through which she lived." Combining a deceptively simple form and mannered language with serious themes, Smith was able "both to compass the pity and terror of her themes and to respond to them with rueful courage and humour," a *Times Literary Supplement* reviewer remarked.

Smith's "seemingly light verse," stated Hallett, contains a "sometimes disconcerting mixture of wit and seriousness . . ., making her at once one of the most consistent and most elusive of poets." "We say that her poetry is childlike, everyone is charmed, delighted," Jerome McGann explained in *Poetry*. "She goes self-consciously to Blake, to nursery rhymes, to naive ballad forms, and offers us afterwards imaginary gardens with real toads in them." Smith's writings, however, frequently demonstrated a fascination with death and also explored "the mysterious, rather sinister reality which lurks behind appealing or innocent appearances," Hallett described. As a result, Wright commented, "the apparent geniality of many of her poems is in fact more frightening than the solemn keening and sentimental despair of other poets, for it is based on a clear-sighted acceptance, by a mind neither obtuse nor unimaginative, but sharp and serious, innocent but far from naive, and because feminine having a bias towards life and survival, of the facts as they are and the world as it is."

Contributing to the deceptive quality of the poet's work was her language, which the *Times Literary Supplement* reviewer termed "Smith's most distinctive achievement." The critic elaborated: "The cliches, the excesses, the crabbed formalities of this speech are given weight by the chillingly amusing or disquieting elements; by the sense of a refined, ironic unhappiness underlying the poems; and by the variety of topics embraced by the poet's three or four basic and serious themes." Although the writer found some of Smith's work "indulgent, even trivial . . . it ought at last to be recognized that Miss Smith's is a purposeful and substantial talent. From below the surface oddness, her personal voice comes out to us as something questing, discomfiting, compassionate." Smith's "highly individualistic poetic style [was] vulnerable to shifts in critical taste and to the charges of eccentricity, a charge which Smith risked, and in a sense even flirted with, throughout her career," Hallett concluded. "However, the integrity with which she adhered to her own style earned Stevie Smith a considerable amount of respect, and, more than ten years after her death, her reputation with both readers and fellow poets is deservedly high."

MEDIA ADAPTATIONS: Smith recorded, with three other poets, a reading of her own poems, "The Poet Speaks," Arco, 1965; a recorded poetry reading was released by Marwell Press, 1966, and she recorded her poems for Listener Records, 1967.

BIOGRAPHICAL/CRITICAL SOURCES:

BOOKS

Barbera, Jack, and William McBrien, *Stevie: A Biography of Stevie Smith,* Oxford University Press, 1986.
Contemporary Literary Criticism, Gale, Volume 3, 1975, Volume 8, 1980, Volume 25, 1983, Volume 44, 1987.
Dictionary of Literary Biography, Volume 20: *British Poets, 1914-1945,* Gale, 1983.

PERIODICALS

Poetry, August, 1958, March, 1965, December, 1970.
Spectator, August 30, 1969.
Times (London), November 19, 1981.
Times Literary Supplement, January 19, 1967.

SMITH, Rosamond
See OATES, Joyce Carol

*　　*　　*

SMITH, Stevie
See SMITH, Florence Margaret

*　　*　　*

SMITH, Wilbur (Addison) 1933-

PERSONAL: Born January 9, 1933, in Broken Hill, Northern Rhodesia (now Zambia); son of Herbert James and Elfreda (Lawrence) Smith; married Jewell Slabbert, August 28, 1964; married second wife, Danielle Thomas, February, 1971; children: two sons. *Education:* Rhodes University, Bachelor of Commerce, 1954.

ADDRESSES: Home—Sunbird Hill, 34 Klassens Rd., Constantia 7800, South Africa. *Agent*—Charles Pick Consultancy, Flat 3, 3 Bryanston, London W1H 7FN, England.

CAREER: Affiliated with Goodyear Tire & Rubber Co., Port Elizabeth, South Africa, 1954-58, and H. J. Smith & Son Ltd., Salisbury, Rhodesia (now Zambia), 1958-63; writer, 1964—.

MEMBER: Chartered Institute of Secretaries, Rhodesian Wildlife Conservation Association, British Sub Aqua Club.

WRITINGS:

NOVELS

When the Lion Feeds, Viking, 1964.
The Train From Katanga, Viking, 1965 (published in England as *The Dark of the Sun,* Heinemann, 1965).
Shout at the Devil, Coward, 1968.
Gold Mine, Doubleday, 1970.
The Diamond Hunters, Heinemann, 1971, Doubleday, 1972.
The Sunbird, Heinemann, 1972, Doubleday, 1973.
Eagle in the Sky, Doubleday, 1974.
Eye of the Tiger, Doubleday, 1974.
Cry Wolf, Doubleday, 1975.
A Sparrow Falls, Doubleday, 1976.
Hungry as the Sea, Doubleday, 1977.
Wild Justice, Doubleday, 1978.
A Falcon Flies, Doubleday, 1979.
Men of Men, Doubleday, 1980.
The Delta Decision, Doubleday, 1981.
Flight of the Falcon, Doubleday, 1982.
The Angels Weep, Doubleday, 1983.
The Leopard Hunts in Darkness, Doubleday, 1984.
The Burning Shore, Doubleday, 1985.
Power of the Sword, Little, Brown, 1986.
Rage, Little, Brown, 1987.
The Courtneys, Little, Brown, 1988.

Writer for British Broadcasting Corp. programs.

WORK IN PROGRESS: A Time to Die.

SIDELIGHTS: Wilbur Smith is known for his colorful adventures set in the African jungles. He told *CA:* "I am essentially a writer of entertainment fiction. So far most of my work is against the background of southern Africa. My interests are the history of this land, its wildlife, and its people. However, none of my work deals with present day politics or racial problems. I speak Afrikaans and some African dialects, including Zulu."

AVOCATIONAL INTERESTS: Fishing and wildlife conservation.

MEDIA ADAPTATIONS: The Dark of the Sun was filmed by MGM and released in 1968; *Gold Mine* was filmed by Hemdale and released in 1974.

BIOGRAPHICAL/CRITICAL SOURCES:

BOOKS

Contemporary Literary Criticism, Volume 33, Gale, 1985.

PERIODICALS

New Statesman, October 20, 1972.
New York Times Book Review, October 25, 1970, April 23, 1972, July 29, 1973, May 30, 1976, September 4, 1977, February 24, 1980, April 26, 1981.
Times (London), April 30, 1981.
Washington Post, October 7, 1985, September 20, 1986.

*   *   *

SNODGRASS, William D(e Witt) 1926-
(S. S. Gardons)

PERSONAL: Born January 5, 1926, in Wilkinsburg, Pa.; son of Bruce DeWitt (an accountant) and Jesse Helen (Murchie) Snodgrass; married Lila Jean Hank, June 6, 1946 (divorced, December, 1953); married Janice Marie Ferguson Wilson, March 19, 1954 (divorced August, 1966); married Camille Rykowski, September 13, 1967 (divorced, 1978); married Kathleen Ann Brown, June 20, 1985; children: (first marriage) Cynthia Jean; (second marriage) Kathy Ann Wilson (stepdaughter), Russell Bruce. *Education:* Attended Geneva College, 1943-44, 1946-47; University of Iowa, B.A., 1949, M.A., 1951, M.F.A., 1953.

ADDRESSES: Home—308 Delaware Circle, Newark, Del. 19711.

CAREER: Worked as hotel clerk and hospital aide in Iowa; Cornell University, Ithaca, N.Y., instructor in English, 1955-57; University of Rochester, Rochester, N.Y., instructor, 1957-58; Wayne State University, Detroit, Mich., assistant professor of English, 1959-67; Syracuse University, Syracuse, N.Y., professor of English and speech, 1968-77; Old Dominion University, Norfolk, Va., visiting professor, 1978-79; University of Delaware, Newark, Del., distinguished professor, 1979-80, distinguished professor of creative writing and contemporary poetry, 1980—. Leader of poetry workshop, Morehead Writers' Conference, 1955, Antioch Writers' Conference, 1958, 1959, and Narrative Poetry Workshop, State University of New York at Binghamton, 1977. Lectures and gives poetry readings. *Military service:* U.S. Navy, 1944-46.

MEMBER: National Institute of Arts and Letters, Academy of American Poets (fellow).

AWARDS, HONORS: Ingram Merrill Foundation Award, 1958; *Hudson Review* fellowship in poetry, 1958-59; Longview Foundation Literary Award, 1959; Poetry Society of America citation, 1960; National Institute of Arts and Letters grant, 1960; Pulitzer Prize for poetry, 1960, British Guinness Award, 1961, both for *Heart's Needle;* Yaddo resident award, 1960, 1961, 1965; Ford Foundation grant, 1963-64; Miles Poetry Award, 1966; National Endowment for the Arts grant, 1966-67; Guggenheim fellowship, 1972; Bicentennial medal from College of William and Mary, 1976; centennial medal from government of Romania, 1977.

WRITINGS:

Heart's Needle (poetry), Knopf, 1959, reprinted, 1983.

(Translator with Lore Segal) Christian Morgenstern, *Gallows Songs,* University of Michigan, 1967.
After Experience (poetry), Harper, 1967.
(Under pseudonym S. S. Gardons) *Remains,* Perishable Press, 1970, revised edition, BOA Editions, 1985.
In Radical Pursuit (critical essays), Harper, 1975.
(Translator) *Six Troubadour Songs,* Burning Deck Press, 1977.
The Fuehrer Bunker: A Cycle of Poems in Progress (poetry; also see below), BOA Editions, 1977.
(Translator) *Traditional Hungarian Songs,* Seluzicki Fine Books, 1978.
If Birds Build with Your Hair (poetry), Nadja Press, 1979.
"The Fuehrer Bunker" (play; adaptation of book of poetry of the same title), first produced Off-Broadway at American Place Theatre, May 26, 1981.
Six Minesinger Songs, Burning Deck, 1983.
Heinrich Himmler: Platoons and Flies, Pterodactyl Press, 1985.
Selected Poems, 1957-1987, Soho Press, 1987.
The Death of Cock Robin: Poems by W. D. Snodgrass, Paintings by Deloss McGraw, University of Delaware Press, 1987.
(With Deloss McGraw) *W. D.'s Midnight Carnival,* Artra, 1988.

AUTHOR OF INTRODUCTION

Tom Marotta, *For They Are My Friends,* Art Reflections, 1976.
Barton Suffer, *Cedarhome* (poetry), BOA Editions, 1977.
Rainer Maria Rilke, *The Roses and the Windows,* translated by A. Poulin, Graywolf, 1979.
Michael Jennings, *The Hardeman Country Poems* (based on photographs by Dorothea Lange), Heliographics, 1980.

CONTRIBUTOR

From the Iowa Poetry Workshop, Prairie Press, 1951.
Reading Modern Poetry, Scott, 1955.
New Poets of England and America, Meridian, 1957.
New World Writing, New American Library, 1957.
Theodore Roethke: Essays on the Poetry, University of Washington Press, 1965.

OTHER

Also translator, with Rosmarie Waldrop, of *Biedermann and the Firebugs,* by Max Frisch. Contributor, to the *Syracuse Scholar,* of translation of the four sonnets which are the basis of Vivaldi's "The Four Seasons." Contributor of poems, poetry translations (from the German and the Romanian), literary criticism, essays, and reviews to magazines, journals, and newspapers.

WORK IN PROGRESS: A second volume in *The Fuehrer Bunker* cycle; two collections of song translations, one of songs by troubadours and Renaissance composers, the other of folk ballads; translations of the epitaphs from the Sapintza graveyard in Transylvania, Romania.

SIDELIGHTS: W. D. Snodgrass is often credited with being one of the founding members of the "confessional" school of poetry, even though he dislikes the term confessional and does not regard his work as such. Nevertheless, his Pulitzer Prize-winning first collection, *Heart's Needle,* has had a tremendous impact on that particular facet of contemporary poetry. The style was imitated and, in some cases, surpassed by other poets. This fact leads *Yale Review*'s Laurence Lieberman to comment that a later book, *After Experience,* reveals "an artist trapped in a style which . . . has reached a dead end," because the group style had taken a different direction than Snodgrass's own.

The combination of the traditional and the confessional in Snodgrass's writing prompts Thomas Lask of the *New York Times* to write, "In *Heart's Needle,* . . . Snodgrass spoke in a distinctive voice. It was one that was jaunty and assertive on the surface but somber and hurt beneath. . . . It is one of the few books that successfully bridged the directness of contemporary free verse with the demands of the academy." Peter Porter echoes this opinion when he writes in *London Magazine:* "Snodgrass is a virtuoso, not just of versification but of his feelings. He sends them round the loops of self analysis with the same skill he uses to corset them into his poetry." The impact of Snodgrass' self-analytical approach is clearly felt in Stanley Moss's statement in the *New Republic* that the poet "has found a place for emotions felt, but previously left without words and out of consciousness. He has identified himself with exquisite suffering and guilt and with all those who barely manage to exist on the edge of life."

Regarding Snodgrass's translation (with Lore Segal) of Christian Morgenstern's *Gallows Songs,* Louise Bogan writes in *New Yorker:* "German . . . here takes on a demonic life of its own. . . . To translate Morgenstern is a very nearly impossible task, to which the present translators have faced up bravely and well." Even though some critics may not agree with Bogan— Hayden Carruth of *Poetry* calls the translation "dreadful"— *Books Abroad*'s Sidney Rosenfeld finds that in spite of its possible shortcomings, *Gallows Songs* opens "a door onto the world of Christian Morgenstern and impart[s] to the English reader some sense of the playfully profound genius that enlivens it."

Paul Gaston points out that Snodgrass's critical essays and translations help develop his talents and prevent him from reaching the complete dead end of Lieberman's prediction. "These endeavors," writes Gaston in his book *W. D Snodgrass,* "reveal a poet intent on carefully establishing his creative priorities and perfecting his language." He continues, "Snodgrass's criticism gives the impressions of a mind reaching beyond the pleasures of cleverness to the hard-won satisfactions of wisdom." And finally, "[His] work with translations . . . has encouraged the increasing linguistic, metrical, and structural diversity of his own work."

This diversity is apparent in Snodgrass's third volume of original poetry, *The Fuehrer Bunker,* which uses dramatic monologues to recreate what was said by the men and women who shared Hitler's bunker from April 1 to May 1, 1945. "In these poems," writes Gertrude M. White in *Odyssey: A Journal of the Humanities,* "we are overhearing people talking to themselves, each character speaking in a verse form expressive of his or her personality, revealing who and what they are with a dramatic power that carries conviction almost against our will." Robert Peters, writing in the *American Book Review,* believes that the volume is "a rare example of ambitious, on-going verse sculpture. . . . It will be around for a long time to inspire writers who've come to realize the sad limitations of the locked-in, private, first lesson, obsessional poem."

Snodgrass told *CA* that "These Trees Stand . . .," a poem which originally appeared in *Heart's Needle,* has been made into a volume "bound in exquisite leather in an edition of ten copies and two artist's proofs." The volume is illustrated with photographs by Robert Mahon. Several of Snodgrass's song translations have been performed by early music groups, including the Waverley Consort, Columbia Colleguim (New York), Persis Ensor (Boston), and the Antiqua Players (Pittsburgh).

AVOCATIONAL INTERESTS: Tennis, singing, playing guitar, lute, psaltery, and sax.

BIOGRAPHICAL/CRITICAL SOURCES:

BOOKS

Carroll, Paul, *The Poem in Its Skin,* Follett, 1968.
Contemporary Literary Criticism, Gale, Volume 2, 1974, Volume 6, 1976, Volume 10, 1979, Volume 18, 1981.
Gaston, Paul, *W. D. Snodgrass,* Twayne, 1978.
Howard, Richard, *Alone with America,* Atheneum, 1969.
Hungerford, Edward, editor, *Poets in Progress,* revised edition, Northwestern University Press, 1967.
Mazzaro, Jerome, editor, *Modern American Poetry: Essays in Criticism,* McKay, 1970.
Phillips, Robert, *The Confessional Poets,* Southern Illinois University Press, 1973.
Rosenthal, M. L., *The New Poets,* Oxford University Press, 1967.
Spiller, Robert E., editor, *A Time of Harvest,* Hill & Wang, 1962.
White, William, compiler, *W. D. Snodgrass, A Bibliography,* Wayne State University Press, 1960.

PERIODICALS

American Book Review, December, 1977.
Book World, April 14, 1968.
Detroit Free Press, Sunday supplement, June 6, 1965.
Kenyon Review, summer, 1959.
Literary Times, April, 1965.
London Magazine, March, 1969.
Los Angeles Times Book Review, August 2, 1987, November 1, 1987, January 3, 1988.
Massachusetts Review, spring, 1975.
Nation, September 16, 1968.
New Republic, June 15, 1968, February 15, 1975.
New Yorker, October 24, 1959.
New York Times, March 30, 1968, June 3, 1981.
New York Times Book Review, April 28, 1968, September 13, 1987.
Observer Review, December 15, 1968.
Odyssey: A Journal of the Humanities, April, 1979.
Papers on Language and Literature, summer, 1977, fall, 1977.
Poetry, November, 1959, September, 1968.
Salmagundi, spring, 1972, spring, 1973, summer, 1973.
Shenandoah, summer, 1968.
Southwest Review, summer, 1975.
Tri-Quarterly, spring, 1960.
Western Humanities Review, winter, 1970.
Yale Review, autumn, 1968.

*   *   *

SNOW, C(harles) P(ercy) 1905-1980

PERSONAL: Born October 15, 1905, in Leicester, England; died of a perforated ulcer, July 1, 1980, in London, England; son of William Edward (an organist and shoe factory clerk) and Ada Sophia (Robinson) Snow; married Pamela Hansford Johnson (a novelist and critic), July 14, 1950 (died June 18, 1981); children: Philip Charles Hansford. *Education:* University College, Leicester, B.Sc. (London; first class honours in chemistry), 1927, M.Sc. (London; physics), 1928; Christ's College, Cambridge, Ph.D. (physics), 1930.

ADDRESSES: Home—85 Eaton Ter., London S.W. 1, England. *Agent*—Curtis Brown Ltd., 575 Madison Ave., New York, N.Y. 10022.

CAREER: Cambridge University, Christ's College, Cambridge, England, fellow, 1930-50, tutor, 1935-45; British Civil Service, London, England, commissioner, 1945-60; English Electric Co.

Ltd., London, physicist and director of scientific personnel, 1944-47, director, 1947-64; British Ministry of Technology, London, parliamentary under-secretary, 1964-66. Writer, 1932-80. Director, Educational Film Centre Ltd., 1961-64; member of board of directors, London bureau, University of Chicago Press; member, Arts Council, 1971-80. Rede Lecturer, Cambridge University, 1959; Godkin Lecturer, Harvard University, 1960; Regent's Professor of English, University of California, Berkeley, 1960. Rector, St. Andrews University, 1962-64; fellow, Morse College, Yale University, 1962. Member of Royal College of Malta Commission, 1956-60. *Wartime service:* British Ministry of Labour, director of technical personnel, 1942-45.

MEMBER: Royal Society of Literature (fellow), American Academy of Arts and Sciences—National Institute of Arts and Letters (honorary member), Society for European Culture, British Migraine Association (president, 1965), Library Association (president, 1961), H. G. Wells Society (vice-president, 1964); Savile Club, Athenaeum Club, and Marylebone Cricket Club (all London); Century Club (New York).

AWARDS, HONORS: Commander, Order of the British Empire, 1943, for services to the Ministry of Labour; British Annual of Literature medal, 1949, for *Time of Hope;* James Tait Black Memorial Prize, Edinburgh University, 1955, for *The Masters* and *The New Men;* knighted, 1957; created life peer Baron Snow of Leicester, 1964; Diamond Jubilee medal, Catholic University of America, 1964; Centennial Corporation award, Albert Einstein Medical Center, 1965; resolution of esteem, Congressional Committee on Science and Aeronautics, 1966; Centennial Engineering medal, Pennsylvania Military College, 1966; Cambridge University, extraordinary fellow of Churchill College and honorary fellow of Christ's College, both 1966; honorary fellow, Hatfield Polytechnic College, and York University, Toronto, both 1967; award for creative leadership in education, School of Education, New York University, 1969; International Dimitrov Prize, Bulgaria, 1980. Recipient of honorary doctorates and other academic awards from American, Canadian, English, Scottish, and Soviet universities, colleges, and academies, including LL.D. from University of Leicester, 1959, University of Liverpool, 1960, St. Andrews University, 1962, Brooklyn Polytechnic Institute, 1962, University of Bridgeport, 1966, York University, Toronto, 1967, Loyola University, 1970, Newfoundland University, 1973, and Hull University, 1980, D.Litt. from Dartmouth College, 1960, Bard College, 1962, Temple University, 1963, Syracuse University, 1963, University of Pittsburgh, 1964, Ithaca College, 1967, Westminster College, 1968, Western Ontario University, 1971, University of Cincinnati, 1976, New York University, 1976, Widener University, 1978, and Union College, 1979, D.H.L. from Kenyon College, 1961, Washington University, 1963, University of Michigan, 1963, Hebrew Union College, 1968, Alfred University, 1969, University of Akron, 1969, University of Louisville, 1976, and Pace University, 1977, Doctor of Philological Sciences from Rostov State University, 1963, and D.Sc. from Pennsylvania Military College, 1966.

WRITINGS:

NOVELS

Death under Sail (mystery), Doubleday, 1932, reprinted, Scribner, 1981, revised edition, Heinemann, 1959.
New Lives for Old (science fiction; published anonymously), Gollancz, 1933.
The Search, Gollancz, 1934, Bobbs-Merrill, 1935, reprinted, Penguin, 1965, revised edition, Macmillan (London), 1959.
The Malcontents, Scribner, 1972.
In Their Wisdom, Scribner, 1974.

A Coat of Varnish (mystery), Scribner, 1979.

Also author of unpublished novels, *Youth Searching,* and *The Devoted.*

"STRANGERS AND BROTHERS" CYCLE; NOVELS

Strangers and Brothers, Faber, 1940, Scribner, 1960, reprinted, Scribner, 1985, published as *George Passant* (also see below), Penguin, 1973.
The Light and the Dark (also see below), Faber, 1947, Macmillan, 1948, reprinted, Penguin, 1979.
Time of Hope (also see below), Faber, 1949, Macmillan, 1950, reprinted, Penguin, 1978.
The Masters (British Book Society selection; also see below), Macmillan, 1951, reprinted, Scribner, 1979.
The New Men (also see below), Macmillan (London), 1954, Scribner, 1955.
Homecoming, Scribner, 1956 (published in England as *Homecomings* (also see below), Macmillan, 1956, reprinted, Penguin, 1979).
The Conscience of the Rich (also see below), Scribner, 1958, reprinted, Penguin, 1979.
The Affair (British Book Society and Book-of-the-Month Club selection; also see below), Scribner, 1960, reprinted, Penguin, 1979.
Corridors of Power (also see below), Scribner, 1964.
The Sleep of Reason (Book-of-the-Month Club selection; also see below), Macmillan (London), 1968, Scribner, 1969.
Last Things (Book-of-the-Month Club selection; also see below), Scribner, 1970.
Strangers and Brothers: Omnibus Edition, Volume 1: *Time of Hope, George Passant, The Conscience of the Rich, The Light and the Dark,* Volume 2: *The Masters, The New Men, Homecomings, The Affair,* Volume 3: *Corridors of Power, The Sleep of Reason, Last Things,* Scribner, 1972.

ESSAYS, ADDRESSES, AND LECTURES

The Two Cultures and the Scientific Revolution (Rede Lecture), Cambridge University Press, 1959, expanded edition published as *The Two Cultures: And a Second Look* (also see below), 1963, New American Library, 1964.
The Moral Un-Neutrality of Science (also see below), [Philadelphia], 1961.
Science and Government (Godkin Lectures; also see below), Harvard University Press, 1961.
Recent Thoughts on the Two Cultures, Birkbeck College, University of London, 1961.
A Postscript to "Science and Government," Harvard University Press, 1962.
On Magnanimity (Rector's Address), St. Andrews University, 1962.
The State of Siege (John Findlay Greene Foundation Lectures; also see below), Scribner, 1969.
Kinds of Excellence (Kenneth Aldred Spencer Lecture), University of Kansas Libraries, 1970.
Public Affairs (lectures; includes "The Two Cultures: And a Second Look," "The Moral Un-Neutrality of Science," "Science and Government," "The State of Siege," and "The Case of Leavis and the Serious Case"), Scribner, 1971.

Also contributor to *Essays and Studies,* English Association, 1961.

CRITICISM

Richard Aldington: An Appreciation, Heinemann, 1938.

The English Realistic Novel, Modern Language Teachers' Association of Sweden, 1957.

Variety of Men (biographies and reminiscences), Scribner, 1967.

Trollope: His Life and Art, Scribner, 1975 (published in England as *Trollope,* Macmillan, 1975).

The Realists: Eight Portraits, Scribner, 1978 (published in England as *The Realists: Portraits of Eight Novelists—Stendhal, Balzac, Dickens, Dostoevsky, Tolstoy, Galdos, Henry James, Proust,* Macmillan, 1978).

The Physicists: A Generation That Changed the World (history), Little, Brown, 1981.

PLAYS

"The Ends of the Earth," televised by British Broadcasting Corp., 1949, produced on stage as "Views over the Park," in Hammersmith at Lyric Theatre, 1950.

(With wife, Pamela Hansford Johnson) *The Supper Dance,* Evans Brothers, 1951.

(With P. Johnson) *Family Party,* Evans Brothers, 1951.

(With P. Johnson) *Spare the Rod,* Evans Brothers, 1951.

(With P. Johnson) *To Murder Mrs. Mortimer,* Evans Brothers, 1951.

(With P. Johnson) *Her Best Foot Forward,* Evans Brothers, 1951.

(With P. Johnson) *The Pigeon with the Silver Foot: A Legend of Venice* (one-act), Evans Brothers, 1951.

"The Young and Antient Men: A Chronicle of the Pilgrim Fathers," BBC-TV, 1952.

(Adapter with P. Johnson, and author of introduction) Georgi Dzhagarov, *The Public Prosecutor* (produced in London at Hampstead Theatre Club, 1967), translated from the Bulgarian by Marguerite Alexieva, University of Washington, 1969.

Also author of unproduced play, "Nights Ahead," and, with William Gerhardi, of play "The Fool of the Family."

CONTRIBUTOR

Arthur Bryant, editor, *Imaginary Biographies,* Allen & Unwin, 1936.

Alister Kershaw and Frederic-Jacques Temple, *Richard Aldington: An Intimate Portrait,* Southern Illinois University Press, 1966.

Maurice Goldsmith, *The Science of Society,* Penguin, 1966.

B. S. Benedikz, editor, *On the Novel: A Present for Walter Allen on His 60th Birthday from His Friends and Colleagues,* Dent, 1971.

Dora B. Weiner and William R. Keylor, editors, *From Parnassus: Essays in Honor of Jacques Barzun,* Harper, 1976.

OTHER

(Editor with Johnson) *Winter's Tales 7: Stories from Modern Russia,* St. Martin's, 1961, published as *Stories from Modern Russia,* 1962.

(Author of introduction) Arnold A. Rogow, *The Jew in a Gentile World,* Macmillan, 1961.

(Author of preface) Jessica Brett Young, *Francis Brett Young: A Biography,* Heinemann, 1962.

C. P. Snow: A Spectrum—Science, Criticism, Fiction (selections from novels, speeches, and articles), edited by Stanley Weintraub, Scribner, 1963.

(Author of introduction) Charles Reznikoff, *By the Waters of Manhattan: Selected Verse,* New Directions, 1962.

(Author of preface) Ronald Millar, *The Affair, The New Men and The Masters* (three plays based on Snow's novels of the same titles), Macmillan (London), 1964.

(Author of introduction) John Holloway, *A London Childhood,* Routledge & Kegan Paul, 1966, Scribner, 1967.

(Author of foreword) G. H. Hardy, *A Mathematician's Apology,* Cambridge University Press, 1967.

(Author of introduction) Sir Arthur Conan Doyle, *The Case-Book of Sherlock Holmes,* Murray & Cape, 1974.

"The Role of Personality in Science" (sound recording; read by the author), J. Norton Publishers, 1974.

"The Two Cultures of C. P. Snow: A Contemporary English Intellectual Discusses Science and the State of Man" (sound recording), Center for Cassette Studies, 1975.

Also contributor of many scientific papers, primarily on infrared investigation of molecular structures, to *Proceedings of the Royal Society,* 1928-29, 1930-32, and 1935. Contributor of weekly articles on Cambridge cricket to *The Cricketer,* summers, 1937-39. Editor, "Cambridge Library of Modern Science" series, beginning 1931. Contributor to periodicals, including *New Statesman, Nation, Look, Sunday Times, Financial Times,* and *Science.* Editor, *Discovery,* 1938-40.

WORK IN PROGRESS: A second series of *Variety of Men* (biographies and reminiscences).

SIDELIGHTS: C. P. Snow was "an attentive observer of life in three disparate worlds—the world of science, the world of literature, and the world of government and administration—and to some extent a participant in all of them," according to Arthur C. Turner in the *New York Times Book Review.* Alan Gardner in *Saturday Review* further characterized him as possessing "the intellect of a professor; the confidence of a soothsayer; the erudition of a top-flight statesman; the devil-may-care approach of a warm-blooded novelist; and the hardsell technique of a successful businessman." "In truth," Gardner concluded, he was "all these things." Trained as a scientist, Snow achieved success as an administrator and novelist, and his name became "a household word in many places and [had] a celebrity achieved by few writers after Shaw and Hemingway," stated *New Yorker* contributor George Steiner. "All of his life," announced a reporter for the *National Observer,* "[was] spent combining and understanding the interactions of science, art, and government, and he [became] an accepted master in all three disciplines."

Snow began his career as a scientist through necessity rather than by choice. The second of four sons born to parents of low income, Snow's education was limited to what he could afford. In order to attend college at all he required financial aid, and at that time the only assistance available to students from his background was in the sciences. So, in 1925, he enrolled in the newly created department of physics and chemistry at Leicester University College. As his brother Philip Snow stated in his *Stranger and Brother: A Portrait of C. P. Snow,* "It would not have been possible to do this from the school's Arts side to which, he told me, he would have otherwise transferred as early as he could."

Although Snow proved to be a first-rate student of theory, professors soon realized that in handling laboratory equipment he was less than adept. Nonetheless, he won another scholarship to Cambridge University, based on his performance at Leicester. Soon after he received his Ph.D. he was elected a fellow of Christ's College, "which meant that he might hope to find a permanent place at the University: among scientists he was beginning to be spoken of . . . as a bright young man," wrote William Cooper in his study *C. P. Snow.* In 1933, however, "a piece of research that went wrong through oversight" helped convince Snow that his true vocation lay elsewhere, stated Cooper. Philip Snow further suggested that his brother's awkwardness in the laboratory "was the real reason for his abandoning scientific research, especially as some of his technical predictions turned out to be false."

Instead, Snow turned his energies to writing and there, as Turner declared, the "young Cambridge scientist of the 1930's found his true metier." In 1932, Snow published a murder mystery, *Death under Sail,* which met with some popular success. He then produced an anonymous science-fiction story and a mainstream novel, *The Search.* Of the latter Philip Snow remarked, "It reflected some of his agony over his scientific failure, the main character abandoning science to write a book on the political state of Europe." Snow's work met with enough critical success to convince him fully that his future lay in literature. "From then on," stated Cooper, "he did no more research. However, he continued to teach science in the university, and was appointed to a college Tutorship in 1934."

Snow's horizons expanded during the 1940s. At the onset of the Second World War, he left Cambridge for government service. He was approached by a branch of the Royal Society to assist in recruiting other scientists for Britain's war effort, a function later assumed by the Ministry of Labour. During the war, Cooper stated, Snow's "chief role was to exercise personal judgement on how individual scientists might best be employed, in research, in government research establishments or industry, or as technical officers in the Armed Forces; and to plan how the number of scientists and engineers in the country might be increased." Snow continued in this line of work as a commissioner for scientific appointments in the civil service after the war. From 1945 until 1960, said Cooper, he "participated in all the major appointments of scientists to the government service; and he acted as an essential point of reference in questions of official policy relating to scientific manpower and technological education." For his services in these areas, a knighthood was conferred upon him in 1957. In 1964 he was awarded a life peerage to enable him to serve the government in the House of Lords as parliamentary secretary to the newly formed Ministry of Technology. "The route [Snow's] career took was not especially devious," stated Russell Davies in the *New York Review of Books,* "but on the other hand it was longer and steeper than such ascents are likely to be again, now that society is no longer surprised to discover brains among the poor."

The circumstances of Snow's education and his unique career as an administrator, a scientist and a writer gave him an original perspective on the relationship of science and literature. He saw that people interested in literature and people engaged in scientific pursuits were unable to talk to one another. The disparity between the two groups was so great that he began referring to them as "The Two Cultures." Philip Snow indicated that this phrase, coined by his brother, and "likely to be used for a good many years yet, was a product of his upbringing; it was partly the result of the range of his early reading, partly of the lack of educational opportunity at a crucial stage which forced him towards science." Snow articulated his views on these subjects in the Cambridge University Rede lecture of 1959, which he called *The Two Cultures and the Scientific Revolution.*

In *The Two Cultures and the Scientific Revolution* Snow highlighted two weaknesses in modern thought which he saw as ultimately disastrous for Western civilization. Snow's first thesis suggested that scientists and other educated people can no longer communicate effectively with each other; scientists tend to regard literature as unproductive, while literary thinkers see science as incomprehensible. According to Cooper, Snow felt that this condition "is in any case intellectually and socially undesirable," and "in the case of a country in the particular situation

that [Great Britain] is in, it could in a short time be catastrophic." Why? Because what Snow labelled the "scientific revolution"—the industrial application of electronics, the peaceful use of atomic energy, and the expansion of robotics and automation—will change the world to an even greater extent than did the industrial revolution of the nineteenth century. Snow argued, said Cooper, that this lack of communication between scientists and non-scientists would lead to disaster; he stated that "the splintering of a culture into an increasing number of fragments, between which communication becomes less and less possible, inevitably leads to attrition and decay." A way to change this situation, Snow suggested, is through educational reforms which stress sciences and mathematics in the elementary levels and the humanities in the higher grades.

Snow's second thesis, according to Cooper, was that this lack of communication between scientists and others "obscures the existence of the major gap in the world today, namely that between the countries which are technologically advanced and the rest—major because it is a more deep-seated cause of possible world conflict than any other." Snow saw the contrast between the poverty of the undeveloped Third World nations and the wealth of the Western powers as a threat to world peace. He believed that "the prime social task of the advanced countries, for the sake of their own continued peaceful existence if no one else's, is to reduce the gap. This can only be done by helping the less advanced countries to industrialize as rapidly as possible," declared Cooper. In order for Western civilization to survive, Snow suggested, the entire world must be advanced to their level. "It is technically possible to carry out the scientific revolution in India, Africa, South-east Asia, Latin America, the Middle East, within fifty years," Snow stated in his lecture. "There is no excuse for western man not to know this. And not to know that this is the one way out through the three menaces which stand in our way—H-bomb war, over-population, the gap between the rich and the poor. This is one of the situations where the worst crime is innocence." Snow concluded, "We have very little time. So little that I dare not guess at it."

Snow's theses were recognized as important by many critics and inspired a variety of interpretations. For instance, John Wren-Lewis pointed out in the *New Statesman* that although Snow's message was "assumed to have been a warning about the danger of lack of communication between 'humanities' and 'sciences,' " Snow was really more concerned "with a much larger issue than this: indeed, the whole point of his lecture was to argue that the failures of communication that beset our academic life are merely symptoms of a much more fundamental division in western society which extends back through the Victorian era and beyond." Wren-Lewis declared that Snow's "message was that our civilisation has to come to terms not only with the actual discoveries and applications of science, but, much more important, with the cultural revolution that made the advances of science and technology over the past three centuries possible." "In other words," he concluded, "we have to come to terms with the experimental spirit, which is not at all the same thing as 'doing more science' or even 'knowing more science.' "

Snow's own career demonstrated that the two cultures need not be mutually exclusive. Robert Gorham Davis asserted in his study *C. P. Snow,* "A scientist by training, a writer by vocation, Snow offers himself as a unique living bridge between the two cultures. But his capacities and experience extend further than this." Davis pointed out that Snow was an executive as well as a scientist and author, and that a knowledge of science was at least as necessary to people in that occupation as to people with a literary background. "If we are to speak of 'cultures' in the plural," he said, "there is no need to be limited to two. Administrators in the universities, in business, and government belong neither to science nor the arts, and may be considered a culture of their own. 'One of the most bizarre features of any industrial society in our time,' Snow wrote in *Science and Government,* 'is that the cardinal choices have to be made by a handful of men . . . who cannot have a first-hand knowledge of what these choices depend upon or what their results may be.' Nonscientific administrators now decide how science is to be organized and used." Snow's unique position enabled him to act as a sort of arbiter; Davis declared, "By bringing together two kinds of imagination which he had himself experienced, [Snow] could enable scientists and literary men to appreciate each other, and the lay public to appreciate both."

Reaction to Snow's theses varied. It impressed a variety of people ranging from then-Senator John F. Kennedy to Bertrand Russell to the Russian ambassador to Britain. What Charles Snow had to say, Philip Snow declared, "had long been obvious to thinking people but nothing was being done about it. . . . [H]is honest account of the lack of communication between scientists and non-scientists on everyday and more critically important levels aroused the deepest feelings of anxiety. Many found the truth unpalatable, and books and articles—from the highly commendatory to unwarrantably vituperative—came pouring out." Philip Snow quotes Kennedy as calling *The Two Cultures and the Scientific Revolution* "one of the most provocative discussions that I have ever read of this intellectual dilemma which at the same time is of profound consequence to our public policy." The greatest assault came from F. R. Leavis, whose vitriolic attack was published in the *Spectator* in 1962. Leavis's onslaught, which included personal slights on Snow's character, "seemed to do Snow little professional harm at first, but it has had some destructive effects in later years," said Davies. "For one thing, Leavis was abominably rude to Snow, who accepted this with a kind of stolid disgust," Davies continued, "and the result has been that ever since, many British critics and less-than-critics have been able to disparage Snow freely, happy in the knowledge that he has suffered worse." Snow finally responded to Leavis's criticisms in an article in the *Times Literary Supplement* in 1970.

Critics recognized that the theses stated in *The Two Cultures and the Scientific Revolution* reintroduced themes found in Snow's novels and reflected his career as an administrator as well. As Davis put it, "Not since Disraeli has a popular, political-minded novelist been so intimately involved with the actual exercise of power. Not since H. G. Wells has a popular, social-minded novelist known so much at first hand about science. For nearly twenty years before 1958, Snow had been in an ideal position to carry out in his fiction the program defined in 'The Two Cultures.'" Davis concluded that Snow "could dramatize for his readers the struggle toward those social goods which he condemned the major writers of his century for betraying," especially in works such as *The Sleep of Reason, The Masters,* and *Corridors of Power.*

Snow addressed this struggle, along with other questions, in what is generally regarded as his greatest work, the eleven books that make up the cycle called *Strangers and Brothers.* In these novels, declared Douglas Hill of the Toronto *Globe and Mail,* the author examined "the world of public affairs, the academic, scientific and political arenas judged as moral testing grounds." Snow first conceived of a sequence of interrelated novels early in 1935. Philip Snow remarked, "It was to take him five years to plan the sequence in general and to produce, as his next book after *The Search* in 1934, the first of the *Strangers and Brothers* series, initially entitled *Strangers and Brothers* [published in

1940] and later changed to *George Passant.* This was to be followed by *The Conscience of the Rich, The Masters,* and *Time of Hope.*"

Snow's program was interrupted by the war, and later volumes in the sequence were delayed because of his work for the government. However, he kept the idea alive, and by the war's end had a firm idea of what the sequence should be. Philip Snow quoted from a note written by his brother in 1945: "Each of the novels [in the *Strangers and Brothers* sequence] will be intelligible if read separately, but the series is planned as one integral work of art and I should like it so considered and so judged. The work has two explicit intentions—first to carry out an investigation into human nature . . . through a wide variety of characters, major and minor, second, to depict a number of social backgrounds in England in the period 1920-50 from the dispossessed to Cabinet Ministers. For each major character, the narrator is occupied with the questions: How much of his fate is due to the accident of his class and time? and how much to the essence of his nature which is unaffected by class and time?" "All the social backgrounds are authentic," Snow concluded. "I have lived in most of them myself; and the one or two I have not lived in I know at very close second-hand."

Readers familiar with Snow's life and career detected many elements from the author's experiences in his novels. Philip Snow pointed out that Snow based many of his characters on people he had known. Many readers identified Lewis Eliot, the narrator of the entire sequence, with Snow himself; one reason for this was because Eliot was born in 1905, the same year as Snow. *Dictionary of Literary Biography* contributor David Shusterman commented, "Though dissimilarities exist between the author and his narrator—the main one being that Lewis Eliot is a lawyer—there are some striking similarities. The chief of these is that the narrator becomes a member of the Labour party and lives securely, for the most part, within the establishment." In one case, at least, fiction anticipated life. In the novel *Corridors of Power* Eliot was chosen by defense minister Roger Quaife as his closest political associate; the year the book was published, Snow himself joined Harold Wilson's government. However, some critics have questioned how closely Snow and Eliot should be identified. "Though it may be unwise to assert that Eliot's reactions throughout the sequence are Snow's, nevertheless many readers of the sequence have made this assertion," declared Shusterman. "Certainly there is not much evidence, except of the most superficial kind, that the two are very different."

The character of Lewis Eliot is one of the factors that ties these novels together. According to Cooper, the structure of the sequence is basically simple; the accounts trace "the life-story of the narrator, Lewis Eliot, in terms of alternation between what Snow himself [called] 'direct experience' and 'observed experience.'" In some of the novels, the actions of the narrator Lewis Eliot himself were emphasized; this was what Snow called "direct experience." In other books, Eliot functioned as an interested third party, observing the actions of the featured characters and commenting on them. This was what Snow called "observed experience." Cooper continued, "The design of the sequence is continuously cyclical. With *Time of Hope* Lewis Eliot first of all tells his own story over a certain period of time and then, in the next five novels, the stories of some of his friends during more or less the same period. . . . With *Homecomings* Lewis begins a second similar cycle over a later period. And *Last Things,* again a novel of 'direct experience,' draws the whole work together."

Alfred Kazin in his book *Contemporaries* characterized the novels in this sequence as "remarkably intelligent," and called them the product of long and hard thought. "The action," said Davis, "consists largely of talk among small groups of people. This talk is directed toward practical or emotional ends; rarely are literary, scientific, or political ideas developed for their own sake. In Snow's novels people seldom write letters, and they telephone chiefly to arrange face-to-face meetings. At these meetings something unexpected is usually revealed—often reluctantly, hesitantly, as a result of close questioning—which makes it necessary to plan at once a meeting with somebody else." He explained, "The novels consist of a series of short dramatic chapters, each marking a stage in the careful step-by-step development of some issue or affair."

One of the components which made Snow's novels effective, claimed Cooper, was his prose style. He stated that "the major point about Snow's style is that it has been developed firstly to give *absolute conviction on the plane of immediate fact,* though it has been developed so flexibly that it can also be used for both narrative and analytical purposes." "It has a compelling tone which arises not only, or even mainly, from knowledge, but from the author's total involvement in what he is doing," concluded Cooper. "To read it is to believe it." G. S. Fraser, a contributor to *The Politics of Twentieth-Century Novelists,* defined Snow's efforts as "a sort of puritan prose; he does not convey the oddly self-enjoying quality of human life half as much in his novels as he does in some of his prose memoirs. He writes, I think, good puritan, or perhaps good early Royal Society, prose: a naked, plain, and natural style." "In effect," concluded Rubin Rabinovitz in *The Reaction against Experiment in the English Novel, 1950-1960,* "this means that Snow has eschewed all devices such as allusion, symbolism, the stream of consciousness, complex uses of time (there are rarely even any flashbacks in his books); little attention is given to the sounds of words or the rhythm of sentences; rarely are there any vivid passages or striking metaphors; and there is no conscious use of allegory or myth. Instead the prose is straightforward and never difficult to understand—'readable,' as Snow puts it."

Other reviewers felt differently; Bernard Bergonzi, writing in *The Situation of the Novel,* declared that "Snow's linguistic resources are still inadequate to meet his emotional demands." Julian Symons in his *Critical Occasions* found an "alkaline flatness" in Snow's writing, but asserted, "The style is that of a lucid and uncommonly honest recorder, rather than of an artist." Stanley Weintraub, writing in *MOSAIC,* declared, "The administrative, often scientific, prose, precise, flat and unemotional, with its figures of speech more often from chemistry or anthropology or medicine than from aesthetics, seems Snow's personal bridging of the 'Two Cultures.'"

Some critics viewed Snow's style as old-fashioned, but recognized that this was not necessarily a defect in his work. Symons commented that Snow "ignores half a century of experimental writing." He continued, "Mr. Snow is not imperceptive of the revolution in the novel's technique connected with the names of James Joyce, Wyndham Lewis, Joyce Cary and many others; he ignores them deliberately in pursuit of an aesthetic which has never been openly formulated, but is perhaps his own version of realism—a realism that looks back to Trollope rather than to the symbolic naturalism of Zola." Davis also compared Snow's work to that of Anthony Trollope. "Trollope's Barsetshire novels," he concluded, "[have] many of the same ingredients as the 'Strangers and Brothers' series, dramatized in the same way. Complex institutions—governmental and clerical—are staffed by the worldly, the selfish, the conscientious, the refractory, battling for principles, place, and power." Davies saw similarities between Snow's work and that of seventeenth-century French novelist

Jean-Louis Balzac. "It was Balzac's mock-modest claim that society was doing the storytelling, and that his own function was merely 'secretarial,'" the critic explained.

Part of the reason Snow's novels differ from most modern literary works is that they are intended to be didactic rather than artistic. Kazin suggested that Snow was reactionary in the form his novels took because his interest was not in the book itself, but in the questions and ideas raised by it: "Snow, in opposing his work to the formal esthetic of [Virginia] Woolf and Joyce, has also saved himself from artistic risks and demands in which he is not interested." Peter Fison, writing in *Twentieth Century,* declared, "[To] blame Snow's style for lacking virtues which are not only irrelevant but would be completely out of place in the character of his work is . . . inadequate." Frederick R. Karl stated in *The Politics of Conscience: The Novels of C. P. Snow,* "In short, Snow is that phenomenon among twentieth-century novelists: a serious moralist concerned with integrity, duty, principles, and ideals. . . . His novelistic world is not distorted or exaggerated; his work rests not on artistic re-creation but on faithful reproduction, careful arrangement, and commonsensical development of character and situation." In short, Karl maintained, "Snow has attempted in his modest way to bring fiction back to a concern with commonplace human matters without making the novel either journalistic, naturalistic, or prophetic."

On one level, Snow's novels concern people faced with old questions in the new world of the twentieth century. *Strangers and Brothers* is, as Robert K. Morris described it in *Continuance and Change: The British Novel Sequence,* the "most sustained attempt at codifying fictionally the dilemmas and directions of our age." "Specifically, Snow asks," stated Karl, "what is man like in the twentieth century? how does a good man live in a world of temptations? how can ambition be reconciled with conscience? what is daily life like in an age in which all things are uncertain except one's feelings?" But Snow also used the sequence to describe the placement and use or abuse of power in twentieth-century society. His depiction of the workings of power politics, stated Fraser, deal "with centrally important questions of 'pure' politics, in the sense that I have defined that: the relationships between knowledge and power (or knowledge and charisma), between expedience and justice, between one's affection for a certain person, say, and one's perception that another person, for whom one has little affection, is the better man for a certain job." Snow's novels, he declared, "are at least unique in modern fiction in giving us a dry but accurate notion of how we are ruled and some quite deep insights into the consciences of our rulers."

On another level, *Strangers and Brothers* is about relations between people. Cooper declared, "In content [the cycle] is essentially a personal story—the story of a man's life, through which is revealed his psychological and his moral structure—yet by extension and implication it is an enquiry into the psychological and moral structure of a large fraction of the society of our times." Philip Snow cited a letter C. P. Snow wrote to Mrs. Maryke Lanius in 1961, reading in part: "The phrase Strangers and Brothers is supposed to represent the fact that in part of our lives each person is alone (each of us lives in isolation and in such parts of the individual life we are all strangers) and in part of our lives, including social activities, we can and should feel for each other like brothers." Snow continued, "Socially I am optimistic and I believe that men are able to grapple with their social history. That is, the brothers side of the overall theme contains a completely definite hope. But some aspects of the individual life do not carry the same feeling. Have you ever seen anyone you love die of disseminated sclerosis? This is the strangers part of the thing. I don't believe we subtract from our social optimism if we see the individual tragedies with clear eyes. On the contrary, I believe we strengthen ourselves for those tasks which are within our power."

Snow's tasks were for the most part finished by 1970. He left government service in 1966 and returned to writing full-time, completing the *Strangers and Brothers* sequence with *Last Things*. Between lectures and addresses he continued to attend debates in the House of Lords, and completed three novels and several works of nonfiction. As the sixties and seventies progressed, however, his optimism began to fade. "The Vietnam war, antagonism between Russia and America, the unsettled state of the Third World were all causes for concern," declared Philip Snow, and attacks of what, at the time, was believed to be migratory arthritis also contributed to his depression. Snow's health worsened and he died in 1980 of a massive hemorrhage precipitated by a perforated gastric ulcer. His last book, *The Physicists*, a series of biographical sketches, was published posthumously.

In spite of Snow's tendency toward pessimism in his later years, stated Karl, "It is possible to see Snow's entire career as a way of bringing people closer together, not of course through the vulgar way of the evangelist or the popular humanitarian, but through demonstrating man's common aims." This is evident in Snow's novels and in his lectures, Kazin claimed; the author, he said, "is simply pursuing the same theme: that the similarities among men are sufficiently great to warrant their rapprochement." In this reconciliation of brother with brother, Cooper declared, one can still see a strain of optimism. "The split in the culture [alarmed] him; and the gap between the rich advanced nations and the poverty-stricken backward ones [troubled] him both practically and morally," Cooper asserted. "But both gaps can be reduced by men of goodwill if they set themselves out to do it. There is no reason why the human *social* condition should be tragic. It can be affected by human action. There *is* hope for the future."

MEDIA ADAPTATIONS: Sir Ronald Millar adapted several of Snow's novels as plays, including *The Affair,* a three-act play produced in London at the Strand Theatre in 1961-62, and published by Scribner in 1962; it also opened in Boston at the Henry Miller Theater on September 6, 1982. "The New Men" was first produced in Brighton at the Theatre Royal in 1962, but later that year it moved to London, where it was produced at the Strand Theatre. *The Masters: A Play* was first produced in London at the Savoy Theatre on May 29, 1963, and published by Samuel French in 1964. These three were also published by Macmillan of London in one volume under the title *The Affair, The New Men and The Masters* in 1964. Other Millar versions include *The Case in Question: A Play,* an adaptation of *In Their Wisdom,* produced at the Theatre Royal in Haymarket in 1975, and published by Samuel French in the same year, and *A Coat of Varnish: A Play in Two Acts,* produced at the Theatre Royal in Haymarket in 1982, and published by Samuel French in 1983. Arthur and Violet Ketels adapted "Time of Hope" to the stage; it was produced in Philadelphia in 1963.

BIOGRAPHICAL/CRITICAL SOURCES:

BOOKS

Allen, Walter, *The Modern Novel,* Dutton, 1965.
Allsop, Kenneth, *The Angry Decade,* P. Owen, 1958.
Atkins, John, *Six Novelists Look at Society,* Calder, 1977.
Bergonzi, Bernard, *The Situation of the Novel,* University of Pittsburgh Press, 1970.

Boytinck, Paul, *C. P. Snow: A Reference Guide,* G. K. Hall, 1980.
Bradbury, Malcolm, *Possibilities: Essays on the State of the Novel,* Oxford University Press, 1973.
Burgess, Anthony, *The Novel Now: A Guide to Contemporary Fiction,* Norton, 1967.
Contemporary Literary Criticism, Gale, Volume 1, 1973, Volume 4, 1975, Volume 6, 1976, Volume 9, 1978, Volume 13, 1980, Volume 19, 1981.
Cooper, William (pseudonym of Harry Summerfield Hoff), *C. P. Snow,* Longmans, Green, 1959.
Davis, Robert Gorham, *C. P. Snow,* Columbia University Press, 1965.
Dictionary of Literary Biography, Volume 15: *British Novelists, 1930-1959,* Gale, 1983, Volume 77: *British Mystery Writers, 1920-1939,* Gale, 1989.
Enright, D. J., *Conspirators and Poets,* Dufour, 1966.
Fuller, Edmund, *Books with Men behind Them,* Random House, 1959.
Greacen, Robert, *The World of C. P. Snow,* London House & Maxwell, 1963.
Halperin, John, *C. P. Snow: An Oral Biography; Together with a Conversation with Lady Snow (Pamela Hansford Johnson),* St. Martin's, 1983.
Johnson, Pamela Hansford, *Important to Me: Personalia,* Macmillan, 1974, Scribner, 1975.
Karl, Frederick R., *A Reader's Guide to the Contemporary English Novel,* Farrar, Straus, 1962.
Karl, *C. P. Snow: The Politics of Conscience,* Southern Illinois University Press, 1963.
Kazin, Alfred, *Contemporaries,* Little, 1962.
Leavis, F. R., *The Two Cultures: The Significance of C. P. Snow,* Random House, 1963.
Morris, Robert K., *Continuance and Change: The Contemporary British Novel Sequence,* Southern Illinois University Press, 1972.
Newquist, Roy, *Counterpoint,* Simon & Schuster, 1964.
Panichas, George, editor, *The Politics of Twentieth-Century Novelists,* Hawthorne, 1971.
Rabinovitz, Robin, *The Reaction against Experiment in the English Novel, 1958-1960,* Columbia University Press, 1967.
Ramanthan, Suguna, *The Novels of C. P. Snow,* Macmillan (London), 1978.
Raymond, John, editor, *The Baldwin Age,* Eyre & Spottiswoode, 1960.
Schusterman, David, *C. P. Snow,* Twayne, 1975.
Snow, C. P., *The Two Cultures and the Scientific Revolution,* Cambridge University Press, 1959.
Snow, Philip, *Stranger and Brother: A Portrait of C. P. Snow,* Macmillan, 1982, Scribner, 1983.
Symons, Julian, *Critical Occasions,* Hamish Hamilton, 1966.
Thale, Jerome, *C. P. Snow,* Oliver & Boyd, 1964.
Wain, John, *Essays on Literature and Ideas,* St. Martin's 1963.
Weintraub, Stanley, editor, *C. P. Snow: A Spectrum—Science, Criticism, Fiction,* Scribner, 1963.

PERIODICALS

American Scholar, summer, 1965.
Atlantic, February, 1955, April, 1958, June, 1960, November, 1964, February, 1969, September, 1970, June, 1972, December, 1974, January, 1980.
Best Sellers, September 15, 1964, May 1, 1967, January 15, 1969, June 15, 1969, September 15, 1970.
Books and Bookmen, March, 1965, January, 1969, February, 1969, December, 1970, November, 1971, December, 1971,

August, 1972, January, 1973, May, 1973, March, 1975, April, 1979, November, 1979.

Chicago Tribune Book World, November 11, 1979, September 20, 1981.

Choice, April, 1970, February, 1985.

Christian Science Monitor, January 13, 1955, October 11, 1956, February 27, 1958, May 12, 1960, September 29, 1960, September 17, 1964, May 4, 1967, January 16, 1969, August 27, 1970.

Commonweal, December 21, 1951, February 4, 1955, June 27, 1958, February 12, 1960, May 13, 1960, October 2, 1964.

Critical Quarterly, winter, 1973.

Detroit News, May 30, 1972.

Economist, November 21, 1970.

Encounter, January, 1965.

Esquire, March, 1969.

Globe and Mail (Toronto), March 31, 1984.

Guardian, April 14, 1960.

Harper's Magazine, February, 1969.

Library Journal, May 15, 1969, July, 1970.

Life, April 7, 1961, May 5, 1967, January 17, 1969.

Listener, October 31, 1968, October 10, 1974, September 13, 1979.

London Magazine, January, 1969.

Los Angeles Times, October 18, 1981.

Los Angeles Times Book Review, June 28, 1987.

MOSAIC, spring, 1971.

Nation, December 8, 1956, March 15, 1958, June 25, 1960, July 17, 1967, December 9, 1968, April 28, 1969, May 29, 1972.

National Observer, November 18, 1968, January 13, 1969.

National Review, October 6, 1964, May 22, 1967, February 25, 1969, June 8, 1979, June 13, 1980.

New Leader, August 28, 1967.

New Republic, February 23, 1948, October 8, 1956, June 2, 1958, April 11, 1960, May 30, 1960, April 13, 1963, November 28, 1964, May 27, 1967, February 1, 1969, November 27, 1971, October 25, 1975, December 16, 1978.

New Statesman, October 6, 1956, March 29, 1958, June 6, 1959, April 16, 1960, March 6, 1964, November 6, 1964, May 26, 1967, November 1, 1968, September 19, 1969, October 30, 1970, October 29, 1971, July 7, 1972, October 18, 1974, November 3, 1978, September 14, 1979, October 10, 1980.

New Statesman and Nation, December 6, 1947, August 4, 1951, May 1, 1954, September 6, 1956, September 22, 1956.

Newsweek, September 14, 1964, April 24, 1967, August 17, 1970.

New Yorker, November 3, 1956, May 10, 1958, May 28, 1960, December 16, 1961, November 7, 1964, May 27, 1967, July 12, 1969, May 13, 1972, January 13, 1975, November 20, 1978, November 26, 1979.

New York Herald Tribune Book Review, February 22, 1948, July 16, 1950, October 28, 1951, January 9, 1955, October 7, 1956, February 23, 1958, March 2, 1958, May 8, 1960, October 2, 1960.

New York Review of Books, November 5, 1964, August 3, 1967, March 11, 1971, September 21, 1972, August 3, 1967, February 21, 1980, December 17, 1981.

New York Times, February 29, 1948, July 16, 1950, December 16, 1951, January 9, 1955, October 7, 1956, February 23, 1958, February 11, 1969, April 26, 1972, May 7, 1972, October 30, 1972, October 17, 1979.

New York Times Book Review, January 3, 1960, May 8, 1960, September 25, 1960, September 13, 1964, April 23, 1967, January 19, 1969, August 23, 1970, December 6, 1970, December 26, 1971, May 7, 1972, October 27, 1974, December 2, 1979, March 22, 1981, July 12, 1981, December 27, 1981.

Partisan Review, volume 30, 1963.

Prairie Schooner, fall, 1972.

Publishers Weekly, November 30, 1959, April 14, 1969.

Punch, May 24, 1967, October 11, 1967, October 30, 1968.

Reporter, October 8, 1964.

San Francisco Chronicle, February 22, 1948, May 9, 1960, October 13, 1960.

Saturday Review, November 3, 1951, January 8, 1955, October 13, 1956, February 22, 1958, May 7, 1960, October 1, 1960, March 4, 1961, March 4, 1964, September 12, 1964, October 23, 1965, November 26, 1966, December 17, 1966, April 1, 1967, May 27, 1967, January 11, 1969, August 22, 1970, December 25, 1971, May 27, 1972, June 17, 1972, January 11, 1975, January 6, 1979.

Saturday Review and World, April 6, 1974.

Saturday Review of Literature, March 27, 1948, July 15, 1950.

Saturday Review of the Arts, June 17, 1972.

Scientific American, June, 1964.

South Atlantic Quarterly, summer, 1965, autumn, 1973.

Southern Review, spring, 1973.

Spectator, May 14, 1954, September 14, 1956, April 11, 1958, August 7, 1959, April 15, 1960, March 9, 1962, June 16, 1967, November 15, 1968, November 7, 1970, July 8, 1972, December 5, 1981.

Time, October 8, 1956, May 16, 1960, April 20, 1962, September 18, 1964, January 3, 1969, January 10, 1969, August 24, 1970, June 12, 1972, November 25, 1974, October 12, 1981.

Times Educational Supplement, August 22, 1980, March 26, 1982.

Times Literary Supplement, November 8, 1947, July 20, 1951, May 7, 1954, September 7, 1956, March 28, 1958, August 15, 1958, April 15, 1960, November 5, 1964, May 18, 1967, October 31, 1968, July 3, 1969, July 9, 1970, October 23, 1970, November 19, 1971, June 30, 1972, December 25, 1972, October 11, 1974.

Twentieth Century, March, 1960, June, 1960.

Village Voice Literary Supplement, March, 1982.

Vogue, March 1, 1961.

Washington Post, November 24, 1971, December 6, 1978.

Washington Post Book World, January 5, 1969, August 23, 1970, May 7, 1972, September 17, 1972, November 19, 1978, November 18, 1979, March 15, 1981, October 4, 1981, September 26, 1982, July 12, 1987.

Wilson Library Bulletin, January, 1954, January, 1961.

Yale Review, spring, 1955, June, 1960, spring, 1969.

OBITUARIES:

PERIODICALS

AB Bookman's Weekly, August 11, 1980.

Bookseller, July 17, 1980.

Chicago Tribune, July 3, 1980.

Daily Telegraph (London), July 2, 1980, July 3, 1980, July 7, 1980, July 12, 1980, July 31, 1980, September 15, 1980, September 26, 1980.

Financial Times (London), July 12, 1980.

Guardian, July 2, 1980.

Newsweek, July 14, 1980.

New York Times, July 2, 1980.

Observer, July 6, 1980, September 15, 1980.

Publishers Weekly, July 25, 1980.

Saturday Review, August, 1980.

Sunday Times (London), July 6, 1980.

Time, July 14, 1980.

Times (London), July 2, 1980, July 11, 1980, September 15, 1980, September 26, 1980.

Times Educational Supplement, July 11, 1980.
Washington Post, July 3, 1980.

*   *   *

SOFTLY, Edgar
    See LOVECRAFT, H(oward) P(hillips)

*   *   *

SOFTLY, Edward
    See LOVECRAFT, H(oward) P(hillips)

*   *   *

SOLO, Jay
    See ELLISON, Harlan

*   *   *

SOLWOSKA, Mara
    See FRENCH, Marilyn

*   *   *

SOLZHENITSYN, Aleksandr I(sayevich) 1918-

PERSONAL: Surname is pronounced "sohl-zhe-*neet*-sin"; born December 11, 1918, in Kislovodsk, Russia (now U.S.S.R.); immigrated to United States, 1976; father was an artillery officer in World War I; mother was a typist and stenographer; married Natalya Reshetovskaya (a professor and research chemist), April 27, 1940 (divorced); remarried Natalya Reshetovskaya, 1956 (divorced, 1972); married Natalya Svetlova (a mathematics teacher), April, 1973; children: (from marriage to Svetlova) Yermoli, Ignat, Stepan (sons); one stepson. *Education:* Moscow Institute of History, Philosophy, and Literature, correspondence course in philology, 1939-41; University of Rostov, degree in mathematics and physics, 1941.

ADDRESSES: Home—Cavendish, Vermont.

CAREER: Writer. First Secondary School, Morozovka, Rostov, U.S.S.R., physics teacher, 1941; arrested 1945, while serving as commander in Soviet Army; sent to Greater Lubyanka Prison, Moscow, 1945; convicted of anti-Soviet actions and sentenced to eight years in prison; sent to Butyrki Prison, Moscow, and worked in construction, 1946; transferred to Marfino Prison and worked as mathematician in radio and telephone communications research, 1947-50; sent to Ekibastuz labor camp in Kazakhstan in Asian U.S.S.R., and worked as bricklayer and carpenter, 1950-53; released from prison, 1953; exiled to Kok-Terek in Kazakhstan and worked as mathematics teacher; released from exile, 1956; teacher of mathematics and physics in Riazan, U.S.S.R., until early 1960s; banned from teaching and exiled from Moscow; arrested, 1974; sent to Lefortovo Prison and charged with treason, 1974; exiled from U.S.S.R., 1974. Lecturer. *Military service:* Soviet Army, 1941-45; became captain of artillery unit; decorated twice; stripped of rank and decorations when arrested (see above).

MEMBER: American Academy of Arts and Sciences, Hoover Institute on War, Revolution, and Peace (honorary).

AWARDS, HONORS: Nominated for Lenin Prize, 1964; Prix du Meilleur Livre Etranger (France), 1969, for *The First Circle* and *Cancer Ward;* Nobel Prize for Literature, 1970; Freedoms Foundation Award from Stanford University, 1976; prize for "progress in religion" from Templeton Foundation; honorary degrees from various institutions, including Harvard University, 1978, and Holy Cross, 1984.

WRITINGS:

Odin den'Ivana Denisovicha (novella), first published in *Novy Mir,* 1962, Flegon Press (London), 1962, translation by Ralph Parker published as *One Day in the Life of Ivan Denisovich,* Dutton, 1963.

Dlya polzy'dela (novella), first published in *Novy Mir,* 1963, Russian Language Specialties, 1963, translation by David Floyd and Max Hayward published as *For the Good of the Cause,* Praeger, 1964.

Sluchay na stantsii Krechetovka [i] Matrenin dvor (two short novels; titles mean "An Incident at Krechetovka Station" and "Matryona's House"), first published in *Novy Mir,* 1963, Flegon Press, 1963, translation by Paul W. Blackstock published as *We Never Make Mistakes,* University of South Carolina Press, 1963.

"Ztiudy i Krokhotnye Rasskazy" (short story), first published in *Grani* (Frankfurt), 1964, published as *Krokhotnye Rasskazy,* Librarie des Cinq Continents (Paris), 1970.

Sochininiia (selected works), [Frankfurt], 1966.

V kruge pervom (novel), Harper, 1968, translation by Thomas P. Whitney published as *The First Circle,* Harper, 1968.

Rakovyl korpus (novel), Bodley Head, 1968, translation by Nicholas Bethell and David Burg published as *Cancer Ward* (two volumes), Bodley Head, 1968-69, published as *The Cancer Ward,* Farrar, Straus, 1969.

Olen'i shalashovka (play), Flegon Press (London), 1968, translation by Bethell and Burg published as *The Love Girl and the Innocent,* Farrar, Straus, 1969.

Svecha na vetru (play), Flegon Press, 1968, published in *Grani,* 1969, translation by Keith Armes and Arthur Hudgins published as *Candle in the Wind,* University of Minnesota Press, 1973.

Les Droits de l'ecrivain (title means "The Rights of the Writer"), Editions du Seuil, 1969.

Krasnoe koleso (multi-volume novel), translation published as *The Red Wheel;* Volume 1: *Avgust chetyrnadtsatogo,* Flegon Press (London), 1971, English translation by Michael Glenny published as *August 1914,* Farrar, Straus, 1972, revised edition, YMCA Press (Paris), 1983, translation by Harry Willetts, Farrar, Straus, 1989; Volume 2: *Oktyabr' shestnadtsatogo,* YMCA Press, 1984, translation by Harry Willetts published as *October 1916,* Farrar, Straus, in press.

Stories and Prose Poems by Aleksandr Solzhenitsyn, translated by Glenny, Farrar, Straus, 1971.

Six Etudes by Aleksandr Solzhenitsyn, translated by James G. Walker, College City Press, 1971.

Nobelevskara lektsira po literature, YMCA Press, 1972, English translation by F. D. Reeve published as *Nobel Lecture by Aleksandr Solzhenitsyn,* Farrar, Straus, 1972.

A Lenten Letter to Pimen, Patriarch of All Russia, translated by Theofanis G. Staurou, Burgess, 1972.

Arkhipelag Gulag, 1918-1956: Op 'bit khudozhestvennopo issledovaniia, YMCA Press, 1973, translation published as *The Gulag Archipelago, 1918-1956: An Experiment in Literary Investigation,* Harper, Volume 1, translated by Thomas P. Whitney, 1974, Volume 2, translated by Whitney, 1976, Volume 3, translated by Willetts, 1979.

Mir i nasilie (title means "Peace and Violence"), [Frankfurt], 1974.

Prusskie nochi: pozma napisappaja v lagere v 1950 (title means "Prussian Nights: Epic Poems Written at the Forced Labor Camp, 1950"), YMCA Press, 1974.

Pis'mo vozhdram Sovetskogo Soruza, YMCA Press, 1974, translation by Hilary Sternberg published as *Letter to the Soviet Leaders,* Harper, 1974.

Solzhenitsyn: A Pictorial Autobiography (photographs by Solzhenitsyn and others), Farrar, Straus, 1974.

Bodalsra telenok s dubom, YMCA Press, 1975, translation published as *The Oak and the Calf,* Association Press, 1975, translation by Willetts published as *The Oak and the Calf: Sketches of Literary Life in the Soviet Union,* Harper, 1980.

Lenin v Tsiurikhe, YMCA Press, 1975, translation by Willetts published as *Lenin in Zurich,* Farrar, Straus, 1976.

Amerikanskie rechi (title means "American Speeches"), YMCA Press, 1975.

(With others) *From under the Rubble,* English translation by Michael Scammell, Little, Brown, 1975, published as *From under the Ruins,* Association Press, 1975.

(With others) *Detente: Prospects for Democracy and Dictatorship,* Transaction Books, 1975.

Warning to the West, Farrar, Straus, 1976.

A World Split Apart (commencement address), Harper, 1979.

The Mortal Danger, Harper, 1981.

Victory Celebrations: A Comedy in Four Acts [and] Prisoners: A Tragedy (plays), translated by Helen Rapp and Nancy Thomas, Bodley Head, 1983.

Also author of unpublished works, including "The Right Hand" (story); "The Light That Is in You" (play); "The Tanks Know the Truth" (screenplay); "Feast of the Victors" (play). Contributor to periodicals, including *New Leader.*

MEDIA ADAPTATIONS: The Love Girl and the Innocent was adapted for the stage by Paul Avila Mayer as "A Play by Aleksandr Solzhenitsyn," 1970.

WORK IN PROGRESS: The Red Wheel's final volumes, to be published in translation as *March 1917* and *April 1917.*

SIDELIGHTS: Very rarely does an author burst so dramatically upon the world as Aleksandr Solzhenitsyn, who became famous seemingly overnight with the publication of his novella *One Day in the Life of Ivan Denisovich.* The first published Soviet work of its kind, the novella centers on the concentration camps in which millions died under dictator Joseph Stalin. *Ivan Denisovich,* which initially seemed to signal the beginning of relaxed Soviet censorship, instead contributed to the political demise of Premier Nikita Khrushchev, who supported de-Stalinization before being deposed in 1964. There followed a decade of creativity and conflict for Solzhenitsyn. Ultimately, this was to the chagrin of Soviet authorities, who deported him in 1974.

An appraisal of Solzhenitsyn's life and work must address irresolvable paradoxes—he has acquired fame as a protest writer, but at heart he is an aesthete. His moral and spiritual authority come from the way he has borne witness to twentieth-century totalitarianism, but his dislike of publicity and his reclusiveness makes him an anachronism. Solzhenitsyn's work needs to be discussed in relation to the tradition from which it comes, for he responds to Socialist Realism, which was proclaimed in 1932 as the only acceptable form of art in the Soviet Union. Socialist Realism literature resembles many Western best-sellers in its accessible style, positive heroes, and happy endings, and thus it cut off Russian literature from its rich heritage of the nineteenth and early twentieth centuries.

In his own way, Solzhenitsyn is engaged in an ongoing attempt to restore wholeness to Russian society by reconnecting the pre- and post-revolutionary periods. He writes to make sense of the evolution of twentieth-century Russia in terms of the lives and works of the nineteenth-century Russian classics. Accordingly, he knows intimately the works of Russian masters such as Aleksandr Pushkin, Nikolay Gogol, Yury Lermontov, Ivan Turgenev, Leo Tolstoy, Fyodor Dostoyevsky, and Anton Chekhov.

The paradoxes of Solzhenitsyn's life began very early. He never knew his father, who died in a hunting accident before Solzhenitsyn was born, and his mother, daughter of a wealthy landowner, was denied sufficient employment by the Soviet government, thus mother and son lived in relative squalor from 1924 to 1936. Young Solzhenitsyn was a child of his era: the parades and speeches of the Pioneers, the Soviet equivalent of the Boy Scouts, had an effect on him, and he later joined the Communist Youth League. In *Solzhenitsyn: A Biography,* Michael Scammell quotes him as saying of this period: "Inside me I bore this social tension—on one hand, they used to tell me everything at home, and on the other, they used to work on our minds at school. And so this collision between two worlds gave birth to such social tensions within me that it somehow defined the path I was to follow for the rest of my life."

Perhaps it was such conflict that prompted Solzhenitsyn to begin writing in his youth. He had some sense of his literary ambition by the age of nine, and before he was eighteen he resolved to write a major novel about the Revolution. But he regrets that his literary education was haphazard and that he read little Western literature. Yet his aestheticism breaks out even in the most adverse conditions. After he was arrested in 1945 and sent to Moscow's notorious Lubyanka prison, which had a relatively good library, he read otherwise unobtainable works by such authors as Yevgeny Zamyatin, the great Soviet prose writer of the 1920s, and American novelist John Dos Passos, whose expressionist style later influenced Solzhenitsyn's own writing.

Solzhenitsyn turned to poetry in the years 1946 to 1950, when he was interred just outside of Moscow at a *sharashka,* or special prison. This was a unique creation of Stalinism—a high-level research institute in which all the scientists and technicians were prisoners. Because everything he wrote was subject to constant inspection, Solzhenitsyn composed poetry in his head and kept his memory precise by repeating certain portions of his verse each day. He continued to compose what was essentially oral poetry during the years 1950-1953, which he spent in a Central Asian concentration camp in Ekibastuz, Kazakhstan.

In March of 1953 Solzhenitsyn was released from the concentration camp and sent into exile in Kok-Terek in Central Asia, where he taught mathematics and physics in a secondary school. In Kok-Terek, he had pen and paper and wrote down both a long poem and some plays. He also began making notes for a novel. Freed from exile in April of 1956, he returned to central Russia, and, in September of 1957, he took a position as a teacher of physics and astronomy in the city of Ryazan.

During this time Solzhenitsyn had been reading aloud carefully selected excerpts from his works to acquaintances in Ryazan and Moscow. Encouraged by the progress of de-Stalinization, they urged him to submit something to poet and editor Aleksandr Tvardovsky's *Novy Mir.* Solzhenitsyn initially resisted, believing that nothing of his would be published while he was alive. Nevertheless, he allowed himself to be persuaded that "Shch-854," a short prose work which he wrote in 1959, might pass censorship. Though skeptical, he eventually sent the story—which became *Ivan Denisovich*—to *Novy Mir,* where it made its way from sub-editors to Tvardovsky and then to Khrushchev himself.

Ivan Denisovich presents a day in the life of a simple prisoner who wants only to serve out his sentence with a certain integrity. Solzhenitsyn's strategy was to reverse the usual procedure of Socialist Realism, which imposed thoughts and feelings on its readers, and thus he rendered his tale in an ironic, understated, elliptical manner. His purpose with this sparse style was to elicit feelings, rather than impose them, as the official propaganda had done for so long.

With *Ivan Denisovich* Solzhenitsyn realized considerable success. The issue of *Novy Mir* in which the story appeared sold out immediately, and editor Tvardovsky kept asking Solzhenitsyn for new works. In 1963, Solzhenitsyn published three more stories in *Novy Mir:* "Matryona's House," a story about the quiet dignity of an elderly woman who had been his landlady; "Incident at Kochetovka Station," about an over-zealous young officer who turns an innocent man over to the secret police; and "For the Good of the Cause," which involves the abuse of power by local party officials.

Solzhenitsyn's principal fiction achievements of the 1960s, however, were his novels *The First Circle* and *Cancer Ward.* In *The First Circle* he drew on his experiences in the *sharashka,* or special prison, in the late 1940s, and in *Cancer Ward,* he drew on his stay in a Tashkent hospital where he was treated for cancer in the 1950s. Both works are set in institutions cut off from society, and both feature characters with diverse backgrounds and philosophies debating the issues of the day.

The First Circle begins outside the prison with Innokenty Volodin, an idealistic young diplomat who makes a telephone call to the American embassy, a call that eventually results in his arrest and imprisonment in a *sharashka.* The principal prisoners are Lev Rubin, a Jew and a dedicated Communist; Dmitry Sologdin, an engineer and idiosyncratic spiritual teacher; and Gleb Nerzhin, a scientist and aspiring writer. At the end of the novel, Nerzhin is taken away to a far more difficult camp, Sologdin is about to gain a pardon, and Rubin is kept behind. With *The First Circle* Solzhenitsyn countered stifling Socialist Realism by relating his work to both Russian classics and Western culture. The three principal prisoners, for example, each correspond to the siblings of Dostoyevsky's *Brothers Karamazov,* while the *sharashka*—and the title itself—recall the first circle of hell in Dante's *Inferno.*

Like *The First Circle, Cancer Ward* presents an isolated environment. The latter work, drawing a parallel between the hospital and Soviet society, thus constitutes another meditation on the human condition. The work's principal protagonists present two extremes, yet their illness makes them draw back into themselves instead of widening their sympathies and understanding. Pavel Rusanov, a bureaucrat with connections to the secret police, expects special treatment and deference, while Oleg Kostoglotov, a former camp inmate, tolerates no elitism. Both benefit from their treatment, but each leaves the hospital with unchanged attitudes.

Solzhenitsyn's most important work of nonfiction is unquestionably *The Gulag Archipelago,* a detailed account of Stalinist repression. *Gulag* is predicated on the fact that arrest and torture were everyday practices in the Soviet Union. Solzhenitsyn proceeds as a scientist might, creating a taxonomy of arrests and tortures. In one unforgettable passage, he even invites readers to participate with him in deciding which forms of torture belong in which categories. Solzhenitsyn makes his narrative vivid and direct. Again and again, he speaks of his own experiences, such as his arrest and confinement in different prisons and concentration camps. He also includes many personal narratives, replete with horrifying detail from other victims of arbitrary violence.

In *Gulag* Solzhenitsyn finds all Russians—including himself—accountable for the horrors of Stalinism. "We didn't love free-

dom enough," he writes. "We purely and simply deserved everything that happened afterward." He also observes that the line dividing good and evil cuts through the heart of every human being. A lesson of *Gulag,* then, is that to divide the world into good and evil is itself a fallacy and evil.

Solzhenitsyn wrote *Gulag* between 1964 and 1968. Through intermediaries, he sent the manuscript to Paris, where it was published on December 28, 1973. A few months later he was expelled from the Soviet Union.

In 1970 Solzhenitsyn received the Nobel Prize for literature, but he had only just begun what he thought of as his life's work—a multi-volume novel to be known as *The Red Wheel.* Much of *August 1914,* the first volume in the series, centers on the battle of Tannenberg, which is filtered through the eyes of two important characters in the entire *Red Wheel:* Colonel Georgy Vorotyntsev, a graduate of the Russian equivalent of West Point, and Arseny Blagodaryov, an enlisted man whom Vorotyntsev befriends. Vorotyntsev and Blagodaryov see various kinds of action, ultimately serving with a group of Russian soldiers who are surrounded by advancing German troops and who succeed in breaking through enemy lines.

Like Solzhenitsyn's other major works, *August 1914* is polyphonic in its technique. This remarkably diverse novel consists of fifty-eight fictional chapters, two newspaper sections, five film segments (passages written in a cryptic style designed to have a cinematic quality), four historical surveys of troop movements, one interpretive historical essay, and six collections of contemporary documents. Both the film segments and the selections of newspaper clippings from the time show the continuing influence of Dos Passos.

The second *Red Wheel* volume, *October 1916,* is approximately twice as long as *August 1914* and contains proportionately more characters, thereby creating a society in all its intriguing variety. If *August 1914* is a war novel, then *October 1916* is a peace novel. It presents very little military action but emphasizes the effect of the war on the home front. Among the various storylines is one involving Vorotyntsev, who is married but nonetheless falls in love with a woman professor at Petrograd University.

The Russian-language publication of *March 1917* in 1986 and 1987 marked another major change in the emphasis of *The Red Wheel.* In this extraordinarily long volume—it occupies four books and runs to well over two thousand pages—the fictional characters all but disappear. There are a few isolated chapters on Vorotyntsev in Moscow, but virtually all the action takes place in revolutionary Petrograd, and virtually all the characters are historical ones. Politicians such as Pavel Milyukov and Vasily Maklakov connive and deal; generals consult each other; and members of the imperial family convey their uncertainty and anxiety. There are scenes of public confusion and domestic tranquility. Solzhenitsyn minutely details various episodes, describing weather and clothing as well as actions and emotions. He therefore allows his readers to experience what happens when a society slowly but inexorably falls apart.

Throughout his canon, from *One Day in the Life of Ivan Denisovich* through *The Red Wheel,* Solzhenitsyn's great theme is not the effect of the revolution—for no revolution or reformation in the Marxist-Leninist sense actually occurred in Russia—but both the dissolution of an anachronistic, deeply divided society under the stress of great events and the response of individuals to that dissolution. His achievement, like his ambition, is admirable.

AVOCATIONAL INTERESTS: Photography, bicycling, hiking, gardening.

BIOGRAPHICAL/CRITICAL SOURCES:

BOOKS

Allaback, Steven, *Alexander Solzhenitsyn,* Taplinger, 1978.
Barker, Francis, *Solzhenitsyn: Politics and Form,* Barnes & Noble, 1977.
Carter, Stephen, *The Politics of Solzhenitsyn,* Macmillan, 1977.
Contemporary Literary Criticism, Gale, Volume 1, 1973, Volume 2, 1974, Volume 4, 1975, Volume 7, 1977, Volume 9, 1978, Volume 10, 1979, Volume 18, 1981, Volume 26, 1983, Volume 34, 1985.
Curtis, James M., *Solzhenitsyn's Traditional Imagination,* University of Georgia Press, 1984.
Dunlop, John B., and others, editors, *Solzhenitsyn in Exile: Critical Essays and Documentary Materials,* Hoover Institution Press, 1985.
Dunlop, John B., Richard Haugh, and Alexis Klimoff, editors, *Aleksandr Solzhenitsyn: Critical Essays and Documentary Materials,* Nordland, 1973.
Feuer, Kathryn, editor, *Solzhenitsyn: A Collection of Critical Essays,* Prentice-Hall, 1976.
Labedz, Leopold, *Solzhenitsyn: A Documentary Record,* Indiana University Press, 1973.
Medvedev, Zhores, *Ten Years After "Ivan Denisovich,"* Knopf, 1973.
Rothberg, Abraham, *Alexander Solzhenitsyn: The Major Novels,* Cornell University Press, 1971.
Scammell, Michael, *Solzhenitsyn: A Biography,* Norton, 1984.
Solzhenitsyn, Aleksandr I., *The Gulag Archipelago, 1918-1956: An Experiment in Literary Investigation,* Harper, 1974-1979.

PERIODICALS

Nation, October 7, 1968.
National Review, October 15, 1976.
New Republic, May 11, 1963.
New Yorker, August 14, 1971.
New York Review of Books, December 19, 1968.
The New York Times Book Review, September 15, 1968, September 10, 1972, March 3, 1974.
Saturday Review, August 23, 1975.

*   *   *

SOMERS, Jane
    See LESSING, Doris (May)

*   *   *

SONTAG, Susan   1933-

PERSONAL: Born January 16, 1933, in New York, N.Y.; married Philip Rieff (a professor of sociology), 1950 (divorced, 1958); children: David. *Education:* Attended University of California, Berkeley, 1948-49; University of Chicago, B.A., 1951; Harvard University, M.A. (English), 1954, M.A. (philosophy), 1955, Ph.D. candidate, 1955-57; St. Anne's College, Oxford, graduate study, 1957.

ADDRESSES: Office—Farrar, Straus & Giroux, 19 Union Sq. W., New York, N.Y. 10003.

CAREER: University of Connecticut, Storrs, instructor in English, 1953-54; *Commentary,* New York City, editor, 1959; lecturer in philosophy, City College (now City College of the City University of New York), New York City, and Sarah Lawrence College, Bronxville, N.Y., 1959-60; Columbia University, New York City, instructor in department of religion, 1960-64; Rutgers University, New Brunswick, N.J., writer-in-residence, 1964-65. Novelist, short-story writer, critic, and essayist. Director of motion pictures "Duet for Cannibals," 1969, "Brother Carl," 1971, "Promised Lands," 1974.

MEMBER: PEN American Center (president, 1987).

AWARDS, HONORS: Fellowships from American Association of University Women, 1957, Rockefeller Foundation, 1966, 1974, Guggenheim Memorial Foundation, 1966, 1975; George Polk Memorial Award, 1966, for contributions toward better appreciation of theatre, motion pictures, and literature; National Book Award nomination, 1966, for *Against Interpretation, and Other Essays;* Brandeis University Creative Arts Award, 1975; National Institute and American Academy award for literature, 1976; National Book Critics Circle prize for criticism, 1978, for *On Photography.*

WRITINGS:

NONFICTION

Against Interpretation, and Other Essays, Farrar, Straus, 1966.
Styles of Radical Will, Farrar, Straus, 1969.
Trip to Hanoi, Farrar, Straus, 1969.
(Contributor) Douglas A. Hughes, editor, *Perspectives on Pornography,* St. Martin's, 1970.
(Author of introduction) Dugald Stermer, compiler, *The Art of Revolution,* McGraw, 1970.
(Author of introduction) E. M. Cioran, *The Temptation to Exist,* translated by Richard Howard, Quadrangle, 1970.
(Editor and author of introduction) *Antonin Artaud: Selected Writings,* Farrar, Straus, 1976.
On Photography, Farrar, Straus, 1977.
Illness as Metaphor, Farrar, Straus, 1978.
Under the Sign of Saturn, Farrar, Straus, 1980.
(Editor and author of introduction) *A Roland Barthes Reader,* Farrar, Straus, 1982.
A Susan Sontag Reader, introduction by Elizabeth Hardwick, Farrar, Straus, 1982.
AIDS and Its Metaphors, Farrar, Straus, 1989.

FICTION

The Benefactor (novel), Farrar, Straus, 1963.
Death Kit (novel), Farrar, Straus, 1967.
I, etcetera (short stories), Farrar, Straus, 1978.

SCREENPLAYS

(And director) *Duet for Cannibals* (produced by Sandrew Film & Teater AB [Sweden], 1969), Farrar, Straus, 1970.
(And director) *Brother Carl: A Filmscript* (produced by Sandrew Film & Teater AB and Svenska Filminstitutet [Sweden], 1971), Farrar, Straus, 1974.

Also writer and director of films of films "Promised Lands," 1974, and "Unguided Tour," 1983.

OTHER

Author of *Literature* (monograph), 1966. Contributor to *Great Ideas Today,* 1966; also contributor of short stories, reviews, essays, and articles to numerous periodicals, including *Atlantic Monthly, American Review, Playboy, Partisan Review, Nation, Commentary, Harper's,* and *New York Review of Books.*

SIDELIGHTS: Susan Sontag is an American intellectual whose works on modernist writing and Western culture form an important modern critical canon. Considered "one of the few bold and original minds to be found among the younger critics," to quote *Partisan Review* contributor William Phillips, Sontag has penned controversial essays on topics ranging from "camp" to cancer, encompassing her views on literature, plays, film, photography, and politics. Though best known for her nonfiction, the author has also written novels and short stories and has written and directed several films; in an introduction to *A Susan Sontag Reader,* Elizabeth Hardwick calls Sontag a "foraging pluralist" who is attracted to "waywardness," "outrageousness," and "the unpredictable, along with extremity." *New York Times Book Review* correspondent David Bromwich notes that her "subjects bear witness to Miss Sontag's range as well as her diligence. She keeps up—appears, at times, to do the keeping-up for a whole generation. . . . From ground to summit, from oblivion to oblivion, she covers the big movements and ideas and then sends out her report, not without qualms. For the art she most admires, an inward and recalcitrant art, exists in tension with her own role as its advocate." According to Susan Walker in the *Dictionary of Literary Biography,* Sontag's career as a writer "has been marked by a seriousness of pursuit and a relentless intelligence that analyzes modern culture on almost every possible level: artistic, philosophical, literary, political, and moral. . . . Sontag has produced a stimulating and varied body of work which entertains the issues of art while satisfying the rigors of her own intellect."

In an essay for *World Literature Today,* Leon S. Roudiez contends that, from the start, "Sontag's interests have been very catholic—that is, she did not enter the stage as a literary critic pure and simple. Her prose covers a broad spectrum, ranging from articles dealing with individual writers, to general considerations on literature, playwrights and the theatre, films and directors, to various aspects of our culture." *Chicago Tribune Book World* contributor Bernard Rodgers calls Sontag "an enthusiast and an explorer, a partisan and a provocatrice. She is also a constant challenge and disconcerting anomaly to those who want their writers easy to pigeonhole, tag and file. A film critic and experimental fictionist, social critic and political activist, historian of ideas and cultural journalist, Sontag has more in common with such thinkers as Roland Barthes and Walter Benjamin, of whom she has written with such sympathy and understanding, than with the New York intellectuals with whom she is usually linked. For although she carries an American passport, her most profound allegiance has always been to the tradition of the cosmopolitan European intellectual which has been both her model and her most congenial subject." In a *New Republic* review, Leo Braudy finds a theme that links Sontag's disparate works—that of "the critic/artist in search of an audience that by its understanding will bring him into being." Braudy elaborates: "Since her first essays began appearing in the mid-1960s, all of Sontag's critical writing has focused on the question of intellectual connection: what is the central tradition of Western thought in the 20th century and which writers have contributed most to its creation?" The answer, in Sontag's view, is the modernist sensibility, in its preoccupations with "alienation, deracination, powerlessness, blockage of perception and communication, death of relationship, rage for transformation, search for new consciousness and (no skipping this) the bourgeois West as . . . moral collapse," in the words of *Atlantic* correspondent Benjamin DeMott.

Sontag has been a shaper of contemporary criticism through her call for a new formal aestheticism. Michiko Kakutani observes

in the *New York Times* that Sontag argues "that art and morality have no common ground, that it is style, not content, that matters most of all." Likewise, *Saturday Review* contributor Edward Grossman suggests that Sontag takes "distinctions between art and science, between high and low, to be largely, though not entirely, false and irrelevant," and she also dismisses the "old, mainly literary notion that art is the criticism of life." According to Stanley Aronowitz in the *Voice Literary Supplement,* Sontag's reactions "against the dessication of literature by sociology," seen especially in her works *Against Interpretation, and Other Essays* and *Styles of Radical Will,* have offered "a liberating vision." Although her ideas have evolved over the more than twenty years she has been writing, Sontag is still deeply involved in aesthetic awareness and is an advocate of sensuous perception of the arts. *Commentary* essayist Alicia Ostriker notes, however, that as an author, Sontag "is distinguished less by a decided or passionate point of view . . . than by an eagerness to explore anything new." Ostriker concludes: "Sensitive people are a dime a dozen. The rarer gift Miss Sontag has to offer is brains."

From a very early age Sontag nurtured a fascination for literature and philosophy. Born in New York City, she was raised in Tucson, Arizona, and Los Angeles. She graduated from high school in 1948, at the age of fifteen, and enrolled at the University of California, Berkeley the same year. Reminiscing on her youthful ambitions in *Publishers Weekly,* she said she wanted to study medicine and write in her spare time until she realized, in her mid-teens, that writing should be her only career. "In high school," she said, "I used to buy *Partisan Review* at a newsstand at Hollywood and Vine and read Lionel Trilling and Harold Rosenberg and Hannah Arendt. My greatest dream was to grow up and come to New York and write for *Partisan Review* and be read by 5,000 people." Eventually she fulfilled that dream, after having studied English and philosophy at the University of Chicago, Harvard, and St. Anne's College, Oxford. Sontag began writing essays and book reviews in the early 1960s, and her first novel, *The Benefactor,* was published in 1963. By 1966, when she released *Against Interpretation, and Other Essays,* she was able to quit teaching on the college level in order to write full time; her readership had far exceeded the "5,000 people" she once hoped would see her work.

As a young critic writing for *Partisan Review, Harper's, Nation* and the *New York Review of Books,* Sontag became known as a champion of European artists and thinkers. *Chicago Tribune Book World* contributor Seymour Krim writes: "Although she was reared in Arizona and California, . . . Sontag has been much more at home with modern Europe than with this country. She made this plain . . . when she gave us fresh studies of such people as Simone Weil, Camus, Marxist critic Georg Lukacs, Nathalie Sarraute, Eugene Ionesco, etc. In Sontag's hands the distant and blurred became sharp and immediate, and [she] . . . is a trail-blazer of what might be called America's new cultural internationalism." Braudy states that Sontag's particular polemic has been "to celebrate the leopards in the temple of literature, not those cool and calm consciousnesses . . . who abided all questions and saw life whole, but those whose own derangement allowed them to explode the lies of order so that better forms might be discovered. In her criticism she labors to turn even the most self-isolating, uncompromising, and personally outrageous of such figures . . . into humane teachers, whose flame, all the brighter for being trimmed, she will pass on to future generations." With a tone of "eminent rationality," to quote Wendy Lesser in *Threepenny Review,* Sontag has acquainted readers with "the artist as exemplary sufferer" and with "the fragmentation, exaggeration, morbidity, and lunacy with which art has responded to the modern world."

Walter Kendrick suggests in the *Nation* that as an American explorer of European artistic trends, Sontag "stands midway between the two continents, in what one might call the Sargasso Sea of thought." Belonging wholeheartedly to neither culture, the critic has taken a position "from which she can see both cultures whole." She therefore seeks to illuminate crucial European modernist sensibilities reacting to the peculiar rigors of twentieth-century life. According to Roudiez, her literary essays "almost invariably raise issues that transcend the topic at hand—and that is one reason they are worth preserving. . . . She has tended to write about European (mostly French) authors rather than about American ones; this . . . is what has led her to allow general or even theoretical considerations to intrude and it has made her essays more interesting. It has also permitted her to act as go-between for European and American traditions." Phillips sees Sontag as a critic who has made "a break with the kind of adaptation to popular taste in the last few decades that made literature so conventional in form and in subject. The effect is to rescue the experimental tradition from its loss of power and the exhaustion of its subject, from its unbearable isolation as it struggled to remain both pure and advanced."

From case studies of neglected artists, Sontag moved to theoretical essays on the aims of modern art and the relationship between art and criticism. Her works "encourage, in art and criticism, . . . respect for sensuous surfaces, for feeling, for form, for style," according to Ostriker. A *Times Literary Supplement* reviewer observes that in *Against Interpretation, and Other Essays,* Sontag "is tired of interpretive criticism and mimetic art. . . . She proposes instead an art which is joyously itself and a criticism which enthusiastically dwells on the fact." John S. Peterson elaborates in the *Los Angeles Times:* "Sontag has argued that critical interpretation tends to be stifling and reactionary, and that the job of the critic is not to assign 'meanings' but to show how a work of art is what it is. Her own writings [are] not to be regarded as criticism, strictly speaking, but as case studies for an aesthetic, a theory of her own sensibility." *Nation* essayist Robert Sklar suggests that Sontag makes this aesthetic criticism a form of philosophical inquiry: "Art, particularly the language arts, are themselves caught in the trap of consciousness. When consciousness as we know it is destroyed, art as we know it will also come to an end—art as expression or representation, art as truth and beauty. The 'minimal art' of our own time, in painting, sculpture, the new novel, already aims, in this sense, at the abolition of art." Sklar concludes that Sontag's "form of prophecy and critical insight, this mode of radical will, can be extremely clarifying and stimulating for the willing reader."

Against Interpretation, and Other Essays and *Styles of Radical Will,* both published in the 1960s, assured Sontag a wide and controversial reputation. In *Atlantic,* Hilton Kramer describes how the American intellectual community reacted to her works: "Sontag seemed to have an unfailing faculty for dividing intellectual opinion and inspiring a sense of outrage, consternation, and betrayal among the many readers—especially older readers—who disagreed with her. And it was just this faculty for offending respectable opinion that, from the outset, was an important part of her appeal for those who welcomed her pronouncements. She was admired not only for what she said but for the pain, shock, and disarray she caused in saying it. Sontag thus succeeded in doing something that it is given to very few critics to achieve. She made criticism a medium of intellectual scandal, and this won her instant celebrity in the world where ideas are absorbed into fashions and fashions combine to create a new cultural atmo-

sphere." Phillips contends that since Sontag was taken as a spokesperson for "The New," she was perceived "as someone to take a stand for or against. Hence, as with so many of the younger writers, the reactions to her have fallen into the stereotypes of polarization. But because she is so articulate and takes all questions as her theoretical province, because her writing has political as well as literary implications, the polarization is both sharper and more distorting. Susan Sontag is both an exponent and a victim of the new polarization; an exponent in that she doesn't go in for modulation and adjustment, a victim because her concern with speculative and literary problems often falls outside the prevailing left-right fashions."

A near-fatal case of cancer interrupted Sontag's career in the early 1970s, but as she recovered she wrote two of her best-known works, *On Photography* and *Illness as Metaphor.* In the *Washington Post Book World,* William McPherson describes *On Photography* as "a brilliant analysis of the profound changes photographic images have made in our way of looking at the world, and at ourselves over the last 140 years. . . . *On Photography* merely describes a phenomenon we take as much for granted as water from the tap, and how that phenomenon has changed us—a remarkable enough achievement, when you think about it." William H. Gass offers even stronger praise for the National Book Critics Circle prize-winning work in the *New York Times Book Review.* Every page of *On Photography,* writes Gass, "raises important and exciting questions about its subject and raises them in the best way. In a context of clarity, skepticism and passionate concern, with an energy that never weakens but never blusters, and with an admirable pungency of thought and directness of expression that sacrifices nothing of subtlety or refinement, Sontag encourages the reader's cooperation in her enterprise. . . . The book understands exactly the locale and the level of its argument." *Time* columnist Robert Hughes expresses a similar opinion. "It is hard to imagine any photographer's agreeing point for point with Sontag's polemic," Hughes concludes. "But it is a brilliant, irritating performance, and it opens window after window on one of the great *faits accomplis* of our culture. Not many photographers are worth a thousand of her words."

Illness as Metaphor is not an autobiographical account of Sontag's own experience with cancer, but rather an examination of the cultural myths that have developed around certain diseases, investing them with meaning beyond mere human debilitation. *New Republic* contributor Edwin J. Kenney, Jr. calls the book "a critical analysis of our habitual, unconscious, and even pathological ways of conceptualizing illness and of using the vocabulary of illness to articulate our feelings about other crises, economic, political, and military. Sontag is seeking to go behind the language of the mind to expose and clarify the assumptions and fears the language masks; she wants to liberate us from the terrors that issue not from disease itself, but from our ways of imagining it." Braudy writes: "In *Illness as Metaphor* [Sontag] condemns the way we have used metaphoric language to obscure and mystify the physical and material world, turning diseases into imagery, metamorphosing the final reality of bodily decay and death into the shrouded fantasies of moral pollution and staining sin." DeMott claims that the work "isn't conceived as an act of conversion. It presents itself as an attack on some corrupt uses of language. In a series of ten meditations on the human failure to grasp that sickness is not a metaphor, not a sign standing in for something else, not a symbol of a moral or cultural condition, Miss Sontag develops the thesis that it is therefore wrong to use sickness as a means of interpreting the character of either individuals or nations."

Discussing Sontag's fiction, a *Times Literary Supplement* reviewer writes: "Miss Sontag has had the misfortune (as a novelist) to become well-known for her high, serious, and argumentative mind (as a critic). Much is therefore expected, indeed searched for, in any novel she may write—much, particularly, to do with technical experiment, learned and subtle allusion, comment on the predicament of the American intellectual today." Technical experiment indeed characterizes much of the author's fiction; in his *Bright Book of Life: American Novelists and Storytellers from Hemingway to Mailer,* Alfred Kazin notes that in Sontag's novels as in her essays, "she is concerned with producing a startling esthetic which her words prolong." Kazin continues: "She is interested in advancing new positions to the point of making her clever, surprisingly sustained novels experiments in the trying-out of an idea. One respects these books, even their total intellectual solemnity, because they are entirely manifestations of Sontag's personal will over esthetic situations defined as those in which originality functions by asserting itself." *Washington Post Book World* correspondent John B. Breslin finds Sontag's fiction highly commendable. Breslin states: "At her best, . . . Sontag illuminates our contemporary situation with the peculiar radiance that comes from the fusion of wide learning, precise thinking and deep feeling. Suddenly we see our own face in the mirror and hear our own voice with a shock of recognition all the greater for the restraint with which the revelation is made." In *Partisan Review,* Tony Tanner contends that Sontag's novels are about a particularly modern theme: "how the head gets rid of the world. . . . The energies of disburdenment—or the fatigues of relinquishment—are very evident." Roudiez concludes: "Consciously or not, we are all creators of fictions, what is known as reality being but one of them; some of us have the ability to translate those vague creations into an architecture of words and in so doing strike a responsive chord among those less gifted than they—and Susan Sontag is surely one of them."

Sontag's novels, *The Benefactor* and *Death Kit,* have received mixed reviews. Both works "emphasize fiction as a construct of words rather than as a mimesis," to quote Roudiez. In a *New Republic* piece, Stanley Kauffmann calls *The Benefactor* "a skillful amalgam of a number of continental sources in fiction and thought" and adds that it contains "a good deal of well fashioned writing." Kauffmann maintains, however, that the book "remains a neat knowledgeable construct, reclining on the laboratory table." Conversely, Kazin feels that the novel "works because its author really sees the world as a series of propositions about the world. Her theoreticalness consists of a loyalty not to certain ideas but to life as the improvisation of ideas. She is positive only about moving on from those ideas, and this makes her an interesting fantasist about a world conceived as nothing but someone thinking up new angles to it." *New York Review of Books* essayist Denis Donoghue finds *Death Kit* "an extremely ambitious book," but notes that it is "undermined by the fact that its ideas never become its experience: the ideas remain external, like the enforced correlation of dream and act in *The Benefactor.*" Maureen Howard, on the other hand, praises *Death Kit* in a *Saturday Review* column. "The writing is vigorous, the plot highly imaginative," Howard claims. "*Death Kit . . .* is about the endless and insane demands put upon us to choose coherence and life over chaos and death."

In 1978 Sontag released *I, etcetera,* a collection of eight short stories previously published in periodicals. *New York Times Book Review* correspondent Robert Towers notes that the stories "are not quite the autonomous and self-sufficient verbal constructs that [Sontag's] esthetic position would seem to advocate. They

are chock-full of reference to the exhausted world we inhabit; they abound in 'meaning'—meaning that calls not for interpretation but for small, repeated sighs of recognition. All of them bear the impress of an active, questing intelligence that can apply language with neurosurgical skill to isolate and cut away the necrotic tissues of our collective modern consciousness." *Ms.* magazine reviewer Laurie Stone also observes that in *I, etcetera,* Sontag "is not so much interested in abstract ideas and experimental styles as she is in revealing human character. . . . Sontag is focused simply (artfully) on the dear, idiosyncratic, alienating behavior of human beings." According to Howard, the stories show a "surrender to imaginative language, a release of [Sontag's] amazing articulateness into a taut, richly associative prose style." The reviewer concludes that *I, etcetera* "is a pleasure to read—inventive, witty, intelligent, of course—but a pleasure."

Some critics express reservations about Sontag's work, most notably about her critical stance and her highly erudite presentations. For instance, Kendrick claims that the author's "eminence in American letters is disproportionate to the quality of her thought" because "she perpetuates a tradition of philosophical naivete that has always kept America subservient to Europe and that surely should have run its course by now." *Saturday Review* correspondent James Sloan Allen calls Sontag "a virtuoso of the essay, the Paganini of criticism," who "has often overwhelmed her subjects and intimidated her readers with intellectual pyrotechniques, pretentious erudition, and cliquish hauteur. Lacking has been the quality of mind that deals in modern but sure understanding rather than bravura." Donoghue offers a similar opinion in the *New York Times Book Review:* "Her mind is powerful rather than subtle; it is impatient with nuances that ask to be heard, with minute discriminations that, if entertained, would impede the march of her argument." In his book *The Confusion of Realms,* Richard Gilman states that while Sontag's essays are "true extensions of our awareness," they nevertheless reveal that beneath the "clean-functioning, superbly armed processes of her thought exists a confused, importunate, scarcely acknowledged desire that culture, the culture she knows so much about, be other than it is in order for her to be other than she is."

Phillips believes that Sontag has suffered from over-publicity and from a process of symbolization by "her culture-hungry interpreters." He writes: "A popular conception of [Sontag] has been rigged before a natural one could develop." If this is true, the conception is hardly universally negative; many critics praise her works as original and thought-provoking. "There are perhaps half a dozen critics in America whose silence would be a loss to writing itself," Robert Hughes claims in *Time,* "and Sontag is one of them." A *Times Literary Supplement* contributor contends that the author has "a widely informed, tirelessly argumentative, thoroughly contemporary mind of a high order." In the *New York Times Book Review,* Lawrence M. Bensky notes that the techniques Sontag employs "have something for everyone in the mind game: vast fields of reference, an easy use of traditional philosophical and literary analysis, ruthless self-criticism, a shifting focus of investigation. But since she uses such techniques better than almost any other writer today, Susan Sontag cannot be called fashionable, any more than a statue can be called statuesque. She's simply there, thoroughly herself." Both Phillips and Gilman suggest that Sontag's essays have more relevance to modern literary theory than does traditional criticism. Despite his reservations about her work, Gilman concludes that Sontag is "one of the most interesting and valuable critics we possess, a writer from whom it's continually possible to learn, even when you're most dissatisfied with what she's saying, or perhaps especially at those times." "To read Sontag," observes

Rodgers, "is to spend time with a writer for whom ideas are as real as things, as exciting as a pennant race, as vital as the day's reports from Lebanon. And there are far too few critics like that around."

"Thinking about Susan Sontag in the middle of her career is to feel the happiness of more, more, nothing ended," writes Hardwick. Indeed, although a compendium of her work was published in 1982 as *A Susan Sontag Reader,* the author continues to write, especially fiction. In the *Village Voice,* Kendrick suggests that Sontag is engaged in the lifetime project of "making a multifaceted creative and critical presence of herself." She undertakes this task with very exacting standards, as she told the *New York Times Book Review:* "Of course, I want readers, and I want my work to matter. Above all I don't just want the work to be good enough to last, I want it to deserve survival. That's a very great ambition because one knows that 99.9 percent of everything that's written at any given time is not going to last." Still in her fifties, Sontag remains a prominent figure in the American literary community; her presence in the intellectual world is felt through speeches as well as writings. Reflecting on her accomplishments in the *Threepenny Review,* Sontag once said, "What readers do with it, whether I am (as I hope) making work which will last—my part ends with my doing the best I can."

BIOGRAPHICAL/CRITICAL SOURCES:

BOOKS

Bellamy, Joe David, editor, *The New Fiction: Interviews with Innovative American Writers,* University of Illinois Press, 1974.
Contemporary Literary Criticism, Gale, Volume 1, 1973, Volume 2, 1974, Volume 10, 1979, Volume 13, 1980, Volume 31, 1985.
Dictionary of Literary Biography, Gale, Volume 2: *American Novelists Since World War II,* 1978, Volume 67: *Modern American Critics since 1955,* 1988.
Gilman, Richard, *The Confusion of Realms,* Random House, 1970.
Kazin, Alfred, *Bright Book of Life: American Novelists and Storytellers from Hemingway to Mailer,* Little, Brown, 1973.
Smith, Sharon, *Women Who Make Movies,* Hopkinson & Blake, 1975.
Solotaroff, Theodore, *The Red Hot Vacuum,* Atheneum, 1970.
Sontag, Susan, *A Susan Sontag Reader,* introduction by Elizabeth Hardwick, Farrar, Straus, 1982.
Vidal, Gore, *Reflections upon a Sinking Ship,* Little, Brown, 1969.

PERIODICALS

Antioch Review, spring, 1978.
Atlantic, September, 1966, November, 1978, September, 1982.
Best Sellers, April, 1979.
Books, November, 1966.
Book Week, September 22, 1963.
Boston Review, Volume 1, number 1, 1975.
Chicago Tribune, December 11, 1988.
Chicago Tribune Book World, December 10, 1978, October 9, 1980 January 9, 1983.
College English, February, 1986.
Columbia Magazine, November, 1981.
Commentary, June, 1966.
Commonweal, February 3, 1978.
Detroit News, January 15, 1967.
Encounter, November, 1978.
Esquire, July, 1968, February, 1978.

Harper's, January, 1979, February, 1983.
Hudson Review, autumn, 1969, summer, 1983.
Listener, February 22, 1979.
Los Angeles Times, December 22, 1980.
Los Angeles Times Book Review, November 19, 1978, December 12, 1982.
Ms., March, 1979.
Nation, October 2, 1967, March 24, 1969, June 2, 1969, October 23, 1982.
New Boston Review, spring, 1978.
New Leader, August 28, 1967.
New Republic, September 21, 1963, February 19, 1966, September 2, 1967, May 3, 1969, January 21, 1978, July 8, 1978, November 25, 1978, November 29, 1980.
New Statesman, March 24, 1967.
Newsweek, December 5, 1977, June 12, 1978, October 11, 1982.
New York Arts Journal, Number 13, 1979.
New York Review of Books, June 9, 1966, September 28, 1967, March 13, 1969, July 20, 1978, January 25, 1979, November 6, 1980.
New York Times, August 18, 1967, February 4, 1969, May 2, 1969, October 3, 1969, November 14, 1977, January 30, 1978, June 1, 1978, November 11, 1978, October 13, 1980, November 11, 1980, January 26, 1989, February 23, 1989.
New York Times Book Review, September 8, 1963, January 23, 1966, August 27, 1967, July 13, 1969, February 13, 1972, December 18, 1977, July 16, 1978, November 26, 1978, November 23, 1980, September 12, 1982, October 24, 1982.
Out, April, 1974.
Partisan Review, summer, 1968, Volume 36, number 3, 1969.
Psychology Today, July, 1978.
Publishers Weekly, October 22, 1982.
Salmagundi, fall, 1975.
Saturday Review, February 12, 1966, August 26, 1967, May 3, 1969, December 10, 1977, October 28, 1978, October, 1980.
Sewanee Review, summer, 1974.
Spectator, March 17, 1979.
Threepenny Review, fall, 1981.
Time, August 18, 1967, December 26, 1977, January 27, 1986.
Times (London), March 13, 1989.
Times Literary Supplement, March 16, 1967, April 25, 1967, January 8, 1970, March 17, 1978, November 23, 1979, December 10, 1982.
Tri-Quarterly, fall, 1966.
Village Voice, August 31, 1967, October 15-21, 1980.
Vogue, August 1, 1971.
Voice Literary Supplement, November, 1982.
Washington Post, March 16, 1982, March 25, 1989.
Washington Post Book World, February 5, 1978, June 25, 1978, December 17, 1978, October 26, 1980.
World Literature Today, spring, 1983.

*   *   *

SOYINKA, Wole 1934-

PERSONAL: Name is pronounced "*Woh*-leh Shaw-*yin*-ka"; given name, Akinwande Oluwole; born July 13, 1934, in Isara, Nigeria; son of Ayo (a headmaster) and Eniola Soyinka. *Education:* Attended University of Ibadan; University of Leeds, B.A. (with honors), 1959. *Religion:* "Human liberty."

ADDRESSES: Office—Department of Dramatic Arts, University of Ife, Ife-Ife, Oyo, Nigeria. *Agent*—Greenbaum, Wolff & Ernst, 437 Madison Ave., New York, N.Y. 10022.

CAREER: Playwright, poet, and novelist. University of Ibadan, Nigeria, research fellow in drama, 1960-61, chairman of department of theatre arts, 1967-71; University of Ife, professor of drama, 1972; Cambridge University, Cambridge, England, fellow of Churchill College, 1973-74; University of Ife, chairman of department of dramatic arts, 1975. Director of own theatre groups, Orisun Players and 1960 Masks, in Lagos and Ibadan, Nigeria. Visiting professor at University of Sheffield, 1974, University of Ghana, 1975, and Cornell University, 1986.

MEMBER: International Theatre Institute (president), Union of Writers of the African Peoples (secretary-general).

AWARDS, HONORS: Rockefeller Foundation grant, 1960; John Whiting Drama Prize, 1966; Dakar Negro Arts Festival award, 1966; *New Statesman* Jock Campbell Award, 1968, for *The Interpreters;* Nobel Prize in Literature, 1986; named Commander of the Federal Republic of Nigeria by General Ibrahim Babangida, 1986; D.Litt., Yale University and University of Leeds; Prisoner of Conscience Prize, Amnesty International.

WRITINGS:

POETRY

Idanre and Other Poems, Methuen, 1967, Hill & Wang, 1969.
Poems from Prison, Rex Collings, 1969, expanded edition published as *A Shuttle in the Crypt,* Hill & Wang, 1972.
(Editor and author of introduction) *Poems of Black Africa,* Hill & Wang, 1975.
Ogun Abibiman, Rex Collings, 1976.
Mandela's Earth and Other Poems, Methuen, 1990.

PLAYS

"The Invention," first produced in London at Royal Court Theatre, 1955.
A Dance of the Forests (also see below; first produced in London, 1960), Oxford University Press, 1962.
The Lion and the Jewel (also see below; first produced at Royal Court Theatre, 1966), Oxford University Press, 1962.
Three Plays (includes "The Trials of Brother Jero" [also see below], one-act, produced Off-Broadway at Greenwich Mews Playhouse, November 9, 1967; "The Strong Breed" [also see below], one-act, produced at Greenwich Mews Playhouse, November 9, 1967; and "The Swamp Dwellers" [also see below]), Mbari Publications, 1962, Northwestern University Press, 1963.
Five Plays (includes "The Lion and the Jewel," "The Swamp Dwellers," "The Trials of Brother Jero," "The Strong Breed," and "A Dance of the Forests"), Oxford University Press, 1964.
The Road (produced in Stratford, England, at Theatre Royal, 1965), Oxford University Press, 1965.
Kongi's Harvest (also see below; produced Off-Broadway at St. Mark's Playhouse, April 14, 1968), Oxford University Press, 1966.
Three Short Plays, Oxford University Press, 1969.
The Trials of Brother Jero, Oxford University Press, 1969, published with "The Strong Breed" as *The Trials of Brother Jero and The Strong Breed: Two Plays,* Dramatists Play Service, 1969.
"Kongi's Harvest" (screenplay), produced by Calpenny-Nigerian Films, 1970.
Madmen and Specialists (two-act; produced in Waterford, Conn., at Eugene O'Neill Memorial Theatre, August 1, 1970), Methuen, 1971, Hill & Wang, 1972.
(Contributor) *Palaver: Three Dramatic Discussion Starters* (includes "The Lion and the Jewel"), Friendship Press, 1971.
Before the Blackout (revue sketches; also see below), Orisun Acting Editions, 1971.

(Editor) *Plays from the Third World: An Anthology,* Doubleday, 1971.
The Jero Plays (includes "The Trials of Brother Jero" and "Jero's Metamorphosis"), Methuen, 1973.
(Contributor) *African Theatre: Eight Prize Winning Plays for Radio,* Heinemann, 1973.
Camwood on the Leaves, Methuen, 1973, published with "Before the Blackout" as *Camwood on the Leaves and Before the Blackout,* Third Press, 1974.
(Adapter) *The Bacchae of Euripides: A Communion Rite* (first produced in London at Old Vic Theatre, August 2, 1973), Methuen, 1973, Norton, 1974.
Collected Plays, Oxford University Press, Volume 1, 1973, Volume 2, 1974.
Death and the King's Horseman (produced at University of Ife, 1976; produced in Chicago at Goodman Theatre, 1979; produced in New York at Vivian Beaumont Theatre, March, 1987), Norton, 1975.
Opera Wonyosi (light opera), Indiana University Press, 1981.
A Play of Giants, Methuen, 1984.
Six Plays, Methuen, 1984.
Requiem for a Futurologist, Rex Collings, 1985.

Also author of television script, "Culture in Transition."

OTHER

The Interpreters (novel), Deutsch, 1965.
(Translator) D. O. Fagunwa, *The Forest of a Thousand Daemons: A Hunter's Saga* (novel), Nelson, 1967, Humanities, 1969.
(Contributor) D. W. Jefferson, editor, *The Morality of Art,* Routledge & Kegan Paul, 1969.
(Contributor) O. R. Dathorne and Wilfried Feuser, editors, *Africa in Prose,* Penguin, 1969.
The Man Died: Prison Notes of Wole Soyinka, Harper, 1972, 2nd edition, Rex Collings, 1973.
Season of Anomy (novel), Rex Collings, 1973.
Myth, Literature and the African World (essays), Cambridge University Press, 1976.
Ake: The Years of Childhood (autobiography), Random House, 1981.
Art, Dialogue, and Outrage (essays), New Horn, 1988.
Isara: A Voyage around "Essay," (biography of the author's father), Random House, 1989.

Co-editor, *Black Orpheus,* 1961-64; editor, *Transition* (now *Ch'Indaba*), 1974-76.

SIDELIGHTS: Many critics consider Wole Soyinka Africa's finest writer. The Nigerian playwright's unique style blends traditional Yoruban folk-drama with European dramatic form to provide both spectacle and penetrating satire. Soyinka told *New York Times Magazine* writer Jason Berry that in the African cultural tradition, the artist "has always functioned as the record of the mores and experience of his society." His plays, novels, and poetry all reflect that philosophy, serving as a record of twentieth-century Africa's political turmoil and its struggle to reconcile tradition with modernization. Eldred Jones states in his book *Wole Soyinka* that the author's work touches on universal themes as well as addressing specifically African concerns: "The essential ideas which emerge from a reading of Soyinka's work are not specially African ideas, although his characters and their mannerisms are African. His concern is with man on earth. Man is dressed for the nonce in African dress and lives in the sun and tropical forest, but he represents the whole race."

As a young child, Soyinka was comfortable with the conflicting cultures in his world, but as he grew older he became increasingly aware of the pull between African tradition and Western modernization. Ake, his village, was mainly populated wth people from the Yoruba tribe, and was presided over by the *ogboni*, or tribal elders. Soyinka's grandfather introduced him to the pantheon of Yoruba gods and to other tribal folklore. His parents were key representatives of colonial influences, however: his mother was a devout Christian convert and his father acted as headmaster for the village school established by the British. When Soyinka's father began urging Wole to leave Ake to attend the government school in Ibadan, the boy was spirited away by his grandfather, who administered a scarification rite of manhood. Soyinka was also consecrated to the god Ogun, ruler of metal, roads, and both the creative and destructive essence. Ogun is a recurring figure in Soyinka's work and has been named by the author as his muse.

Ake: The Years of Childhood, Soyinka's account of his first ten years, stands as "a classic of childhood memoirs wherever and whenever produced," states *New York Times Book Review* contributor James Olney. Numerous critics have singled out Soyinka's ability to recapture the changing perspective of a child as the book's outstanding feature; it begins in a light tone but grows increasingly serious as the boy matures and becomes aware of the problems faced by the adults around him. The book concludes with an account of a tax revolt organized by Soyinka's mother and the beginnings of Nigerian independence. "Most of 'Ake' charms; that was Mr. Soyinka's intention," writes John Leonard of the *New York Times*. "The last 5O pages, however, inspire and confound; they are transcendent." Olney agrees that "the lyricism, grace, humor and charm of 'Ake' . . . are in the service of a profoundly serious viewpoint that attempts to show us how things should be in the community of men and how they should not be. Mr. Soyinka, however, does this dramatically, not discursively. Through recollection, restoration and re-creation, he conveys a personal vision that was formed by the childhood world that he now returns to evoke and exalt in his autobiography. This is the ideal circle of autobiography at its best. It is what makes 'Ake,' in addition to its other great virtues, the best introduction available to the work of one of the liveliest, most exciting writers in the world today."

Soyinka published some poems and short stories in *Black Orpheus,* a highly regarded Nigerian literary magazine, before leaving Africa to attend the University of Leeds in England. There his first play was produced. "The Invention" is a comic satire based on a sudden loss of pigment by South Africa's black population. Unable to distinguish blacks from whites and thus enforce its apartheid policies, the government is thrown into chaos. "The play is Soyinka's sole direct treatment of the political situation in Africa," notes Thomas Hayes in the *Dictionary of Literary Biography Yearbook: 1986.* Soyinka returned to Nigeria in 1960, shortly after independence from colonial rule had been declared. He began to research Yoruba folklore and drama in depth and incorporated elements of both into his play "A Dance of the Forests."

"A Dance of the Forests" was commissioned as part of Nigeria's independence celebrations. In his play, Soyinka warned the newly independent Nigerians that the end of colonial rule did not mean an end to their country's problems. It shows a bickering group of mortals who summon up the *egungun* (spirits of the dead, revered by the Yoruba people) for a festival. They have presumed the *egungun* to be noble and wise, but they discover that their ancestors are as petty and spiteful as any living people. "The whole concept ridicules the African viewpoint that glorifies the past at the expense of the present," suggests John F. Povey in *Tri-Quarterly.* "The sentimentalized glamor of the past is exposed so that the same absurdities may not be reenacted in the future. This constitutes a bold assertion to an audience awaiting an easy appeal to racial heroics." Povey also praises Soyinka's skill in using dancing, drumming, and singing to reinforce his theme: "The dramatic power of the surging forest dance [in the play] carries its own visual conviction. It is this that shows Soyinka to be a man of the theatre, not simply a writer."

After warning against living in nostalgia for Africa's past in "A Dance of the Forests," Soyinka lampooned the indiscriminate embrace of Western modernization in "The Lion and the Jewel." A *Times Literary Supplement* reviewer calls this play a "richly ribald comedy," which combines poetry and prose "with a marvellous lightness in the treatment of both." The plot revolves around Sidi, the village beauty, and the rivalry between her two suitors. Baroka is the village chief, an old man with many wives; Lakunle is the enthusiastically Westernized schoolteacher who dreams of molding Sidi into a "civilized" woman. In *Introduction to Nigerian Literature,* Eldred Jones comments that "The Lion and the Jewel" is "a play which is so easily (and erroneously) interpreted as a clash between progress and reaction, with the play coming down surprisingly in favour of reaction. The real clash is not between old and new or between real progress and reaction. It is a clash between the genuine and the false; between the well-done and the half-baked. Lakunle the school teacher would have been a poor symbol of any desirable kind of progress. . . . He is a man of totally confused values. [Baroka's worth lies in] the traditional values of which he is so confident and in which he so completely outmaneouvres Lakunle who really has no values at all." Bruce King, editor of *Introduction to Nigerian Literature,* names "The Lion and the Jewel" "the best literary work to come out of Africa."

Soyinka was well established as Nigeria's premier playwright when in 1965 he published his first novel, *The Interpreters.* The novel allowed him to expand on themes already expressed in his stage dramas and to present a sweeping view of Nigerian life in the years immediately following independence. Essentially plotless, *The Interpreters* is loosely structured around the informal discussions among five young Nigerian intellectuals. Each has been educated in a foreign country and returned hoping to shape Nigeria's destiny. They are hampered by their own confused values, however, as well as the corruption they encounter everywhere. Some reviewers liken Soyinka's writing style in *The Interpreters* to that of James Joyce and William Faulkner. Others take exception to the formless quality of the novel, but Eustace Palmer asserts in *The Growth of the African Novel:* "If there are reservations about the novel's structure, there can be none about the thoroughness of the satire at society's expense. Soyinka's wide-ranging wit takes in all sections of a corrupt society—the brutal masses, the aimless intellectuals, the affected and hypocritical university dons, the vulgar and corrupt businessmen, the mediocre civil servants, the illiterate politicians and the incompetent journalists. [The five main characters are all] talented intellectuals who have retained their African consciousness although they were largely educated in the western world. Yet their western education enables them to look at their changing society with a certain amount of detachment. They are therefore uniquely qualified to be interpreters of this society. The reader is impressed by their honesty, sincerity, moral idealism, concern for truth and justice and aversion to corruption, snobbery and hypocrisy; but anyone who assumes that Soyinka presents all the interpreters as models of behaviour will be completely misreading the novel. He is careful to expose their selfishness, egoism, cynicism and aimlessness. Indeed the conduct of the intellectuals both in and out of the university is a major preoccupation of Soyinka's in this novel. The aimlessness and superficiality of the lives of most of the interpreters is patent."

Neil McEwan points out in *Africa and the Novel* that for all its seriousness, *The Interpreters* is also "among the liveliest of recent novels in English. It is bright satire full of good sense and good humour which are African and contemporary: the highest spirits of its author's early work. . . . Behind the jokes of his novel is a theme that he has developed angrily elsewhere: that whatever progress may mean for Africa it is not a lesson to be learned from outside, however much of 'modernity' Africans may share with others." McEwan further observes that although *The Interpreters* does not have a rigidly structured plot, "there is unity in the warmth and sharpness of its comic vision. There are moments which sadden or anger; but they do not diminish the fun." Palmer notes that *The Interpreters* notably influenced the African fiction that followed it, shifting the focus "from historical, cultural and sociological analysis to penetrating social comment and social satire."

The year *The Interpreters* was published, 1965, also marked Soyinka's first arrest by the Nigerian police. He was accused of using a gun to force a radio announcer to broadcast incorrect election results. No evidence was ever produced, however, and the PEN writers' organization launched a protest campaign, headed by William Styron and Norman Mailer. Soyinka was released after three months. He was next arrested two years later, during Nigeria's civil war. Soyinka was completely opposed to the conflict, and especially to the Nigerian Government's brutal policies toward the Ibo people who were attempting to form their own country, Biafra. He traveled to Biafra to establish a peace commission composed of leading intellectuals from both sides; when he returned, the Nigerian police accused him of helping the Biafrans to buy jet fighters. Once again he was imprisoned. This time Soyinka was held for more than two years, although he was never formally charged with any crime. Most of that time he was kept in solitary confinement. When all of his fellow prisoners were vaccinated against meningitis, Soyinka was passed by; when he developed serious vision problems, they were ignored by his jailers. He was denied reading and writing materials, but he manufactured his own ink and began to keep a prison diary, written on toilet paper, cigarette packages and in between the lines of the few books he secretly obtained. Each poem or fragment of journal he managed to smuggle to the outside world became a literary event and a reassurance to his supporters that Soyinka still lived, despite rumors to the contrary. He was released in 1969 and left Nigeria soon after, not returning until a change of power took place in 1975.

Published as *The Man Died: Prison Notes of Wole Soyinka,* the author's diary constitutes "the most important work that has been written about the Biafran war," believes Charles R. Larson, contributor to *Nation.* " 'The Man Died' is not so much the story of Wole Soyinka's own temporary death during the Nigerian Civil War but a personified account of Nigeria's fall from sanity, documented by one of the country's leading intellectuals." Gerald Weales's *New York Times Book Review* article suggests that the political content of *The Man Died* is less fascinating than "the notes that deal with prison life, the observation of everything from a warder's catarrh to the predatory life of insects after a rain. Of course, these are not simply reportorial. They are vehicles to carry the author's shifting states of mind, to convey the real subject matter of the book; the author's attempt to survive as a man, and as a mind. The notes are both a means to that survival and a record to it." Larson underlines the book's political

impact, however, noting that ironically, "while other Nigerian writers were emotionally castrated by the war, Soyinka, who was placed in solitary confinement so that he wouldn't embarrass the government, was writing work after work, books that will no doubt embarrass the Nigerian Government more than anything the Ibo writers may ever publish." A *Times Literary Supplement* reviewer concurs, characterizing *The Man Died* as "a damning indictment of what Mr. Soyinka sees as the iniquities of wartime Nigeria and the criminal tyranny of its administration in peacetime."

Many literary commentators feel that Soyinka's work changed profoundly after his prison term, darkening in tone and focusing on the war and its aftermath. In the *Dictionary of Literary Biography Yearbook: 1986,* Hayes quotes Soyinka on his concerns after the war: "I have one abiding religion—human liberty. . . . conditioned to the truth that life is meaningless, insulting, without this fullest liberty, and in spite of the despairing knowledge that words alone seem unable to guarantee its possession, my writing grows more and more preoccupied with the theme of the oppressive boot, the irrelevance of the color of the foot that wears it and the struggle for individuality."

In spite of its satire, most critics had found *The Interpreters* to be ultimately an optimistic book. In contrast, Soyinka's second novel expresses almost no hope for Africa's future, says John Mellors in *London Magazine:* "Wole Soyinka appears to have written much of *Season of Anomy* in a blazing fury, angry beyond complete control of words at the abuses of power and the outbreaks of both considered and spontaneous violence. . . . The plot charges along, dragging the reader (not because he doesn't want to go, but because he finds it hard to keep up) through forest, mortuary and prison camp in nightmare visions of tyranny, torture, slaughter and putrefaction. The book reeks of pain. . . . Soyinka hammers at the point that the liberal has to deal with violence in the world however much he would wish he could ignore it; the scenes of murder and mutilation, while sickeningly explicit, are justifed by . . . the author's anger and compassion and insistence that bad will not become better by our refusal to examine it."

Like *Season of Anomy,* Soyinka's postwar plays are considered more brooding than his earlier work. "Madmen and Specialists" is called "grim" by Martin Banham and Clive Wake in *African Theatre Today.* In the play, a doctor returns from the war trained as a specialist in torture and uses his new skills on his father. The play's major themes are "the loss of faith and rituals" and "the break-up of the family unit which traditionally in Africa has been the foundation of society," according to Charles Larson in the *New York Times Book Review.* Names and events in the play are fictionalized to avoid censorship, but Soyinka has clearly "leveled a wholesale criticism of life in Nigeria since the Civil War: a police state in which only madmen and spies can survive, in which the losers are mad and the winners are paranoid about the possibility of another rebellion. The prewar corruption and crime have returned, supported by the more sophisticated acts of terrorism and espionage introduced during the war." Larson summarizes: "In large part 'Madmen and Specialists' is a product of those months Soyinka spent in prison, in solitary confinement, as a political prisoner. It is, not surprisingly, the most brutal piece of social criticism he has published." In a similar tone, "A Play of Giants" presents four African leaders—thinly disguised versions of Jean Bedel Bokassa, Sese Seko Mobutu, Macias Ngeuma, and Idi Amin—meeting at the United Nations building, where "their conversation reflects the corruption and cruelty of their regimes and the casual, brutal flavor of their rule," discloses Hayes. In Hayes's opinion, "A Play of Giants" demonstrates that "as Soyinka has matured he has hardened his criticism of all that restricts the individual's ability to choose, think, and act free from external oppression. . . . [It is] his harshest attack against modern Africa, a blunt, venomous assault on . . . African leaders and the powers who support them."

In *Isara: A Voyage around "Essay,"* Soyinka provides a portrait of his father, Akinyode Soditan, as well as "vivid sketches of characters and culturally intriguing events that cover a period of 15 years," Charles Johnson relates in the *Washington Post.* The narrative follows S. A., or "Essay," and his classmates through his years at St. Simeon's Teacher Training Seminary in Ilesa. Aided by documents left to him in a tin box, Soyinka dramatizes the changes that profoundly affected his father's life. The Great Depression that brought the Western world to its knees during the early 1930s was a time of economic opportunity for Africans. The quest for financial gain transformed African culture, as did Mussolini's invasion of Ethiopia and the onset of World War II. More threatening was the violent civil war for the throne following the death of their king. An aged peacemaker named Agunrin resolved the conflict by an appeal to the people's common past. "As each side presents its case, Agunrin, half listening, sinks into memories that unfold his people's collective history, and finally he speaks, finding his voice in a scene so masterfully rendered it alone is worth the price of the book," Johnson claims. The book is neither a strict biography nor a straight historical account. However, "in his effort to expose Western readers to a unique, African perspective on the war years, Soyinka succeeds brilliantly," Johnson comments. *New York Times* reviewer Michiko Kakutani writes that, in addition, "Essay emerges as a high-minded teacher, a mentor and companion, blessed with dignity and strong ideals, a father who inspired his son to achievement."

Soyinka's work is frequently described as demanding but rewarding reading. Although his plays are widely praised, they are seldom performed, especially outside of Africa. The dancing and choric speech often found in them are unfamiliar and difficult for non-African actors to master, a problem Holly Hill notes in her London *Times* review of the Lincoln Center Theatre production of "Death and the King's Horseman." She awards high praise to the play, however, saying it "has the stateliness and mystery of Greek tragedy." When the Swedish Academy awarded Soyinka the Nobel Prize in Literature in 1986, its members singled out "Death and the King's Horseman" and "A Dance of the Forests" as "evidence that Soyinka is 'one of the finest poetical playwrights that have written in English,'" reports Stanley Meisler of the *Los Angeles Times.* Hayes summarizes Wole Soyinka's importance: "His drama and fiction have challenged the West to broaden its aesthetic and accept African standards of art and literature. His personal and political life have challenged Africa to embrace the truly democratic values of the African tribe and reject the tyranny of power practiced on the continent by its colonizers and by many of its modern rulers."

BIOGRAPHICAL/CRITICAL SOURCES:

BOOKS

Banham, Martin and Clive Wake, *African Theatre Today,* Pitman Publishing, 1976.

Banham, *Wole Soyinka's "The Lion and the Jewel,"* Rex Collings, 1981.

Contemporary Literary Criticism, Gale, Volume 3, 1975, Volume 5, 1976, Volume 14, 1980, Volume 36, 1986, Volume 44, 1987.

Dictionary of Literary Biography Yearbook: 1986, Gale, 1987.

Dunton, C. P., *Notes on "Three Short Plays,"* Longman, 1982.

Gakwandi, Shatto Arthur, *The Novel and Contemporary Experience in America,* Heinemann, 1977.

Gibbs, James, editor, *Study Aid to "Kongi's Harvest,"* Rex Collings, 1973.

Gibbs, editor, *Critical Perspectives on Wole Soyinka,* Three Continents, 1980.

Gibbs, editor, *Notes on "The Lion and the Jewel,"* Longman, 1982.

Gibbs, *Wole Soyinka,* Macmillan, 1986.

Gibbs, Ketu Katrak and Henry Gates, Jr., editors, *Wole Soyinka: A Bibliography of Primary and Secondary Sources,* Greenwood Press, 1986.

Goodwin, K. L., *Understanding African Poetry,* Heinemann, 1979.

Jones, Eldred, editor, *African Literature Today, Number 5: The Novel in Africa,* Heinemann, 1971.

Jones, editor, *African Literature Today, Number 6: Poetry in Africa,* Heinemann, 1973.

Jones, *Wole Soyinka,* Twayne, 1973 (published in England as *The Writings of Wole Soyinka,* Heinemann, 1973).

Katrak, Ketu, *Wole Soyinka and Modern Tragedy: A Study of Dramatic Theory and Practice,* Greenwood Press, 1986.

King, Bruce, editor, *Introduction to Nigerian Literature,* Africana Publishing, 1972.

Larson, Charles R., *The Emergence of African Fiction,* revised edition, Indiana University Press, 1972.

Laurence, Margaret, *Long Drums and Cannons: Nigerian Dramatists and Novelists,* Praeger, 1968.

McEwan, Neil, *Africa and the Novel,* Humanities Press, 1983.

Moore, Gerald, *Wole Soyinka,* Africana Publishing, 1971.

Morell, Karen L., editor, *In Person—Achebe, Awoonor, and Soyinka at the University of Washington,* African Studies Program, Institute for Comparative and Foreign Area Studies, University of Washington, 1975.

Ogunba, Oyin, *The Movement of Transition: A Study of the Plays of Wole Soyinka,* Ibadan University Press, 1975.

Ogunba and others, editors, *Theatre in Africa,* Ibadan University Press, 1978.

Palmer, Eustace, *The Growth of the African Novel,* Heinemann, 1979.

Parsons, E. M., editor, *Notes on Wole Soyinka's "The Jero Plays,"* Methuen, 1982.

Pieterse, Cosmo, and Dennis Duerden, editors, *African Writers Talking: A Collection of Radio Interviews,* Africana Publishing, 1972.

Probyn, editor, *Notes on "The Road,"* Longman, 1981.

Ricard, Alain, *Theatre et Nationalisme: Wole Soyinka et LeRoi Jones,* Presence Africaine, 1972.

Roscoe, Adrian A., *Mother Is Gold: A Study in West African Literature,* Cambridge University Press, 1971.

Soyinka, Wole, *The Man Died: Prison Notes of Wole Soyinka,* Harper, 1972.

Soyinka, *Myth, Literature and the African World,* Cambridge University Press, 1976.

Soyinka, *Ake: The Years of Childhood,* Random House, 1981.

Tucker, Martin, *Africa in Modern Literature: A Survey of Contemporary Writing in English,* Ungar, 1967.

PERIODICALS

America, February 12, 1983.

Ariel, July, 1981.

Black Orpheus, March, 1966.

Book Forum, Volume 3, number 1, 1977.

Books Abroad, summer, 1972, spring, 1973.
British Book News, December, 1984, April, 1986.
Chicago Tribune Book World, October 7, 1979.
Christian Science Monitor, July 31, 1970, August 15, 1970.
Commonweal, February 8, 1985.
Detroit Free Press, March 20, 1983, October 17, 1986.
Detroit News, November 21, 1982.
Globe and Mail (Toronto), June 7, 1986, January 6, 1990.
London Magazine, April/May, 1974.
Los Angeles Times, October 17, 1986.
Los Angeles Times Book Review, October 15, 1989.
Nation, October 11, 1965, April 29, 1968, September 15, 1969, November 10, 1969, October 2, 1972, November 5, 1973.
New Republic, October 12, 1974, May 9, 1983.
New Statesman, December 20, 1968.
Newsweek, November 1, 1982.
New Yorker, May 16, 1977.
New York Review of Books, July 31, 1969, October 21, 1982.
New York Times, November 11, 1965, April 19, 1970, August 11, 1972, September 23, 1982, May 29, 1986, May 31, 1986, June 15, 1986, October 17, 1986, November 9, 1986, March 1, 1987, March 2, 1987, November 3, 1989.
New York Times Book Review, July 29, 1973, December 24, 1973, October 10, 1982, January 15, 1984, November 12, 1989.
New York Times Magazine, September 18, 1983.
Research in African Literatures, spring, 1983.
Saturday Review/World, October 19, 1974.
Spectator, November 6, 1959, December 15, 1973, November 24, 1981.
Time, October 27, 1986.
Times (London), October 17, 1986, April 6, 1987, March 15, 1990.
Times Literary Supplement, April 1, 1965, June 10, 1965, January 18, 1968, December 31, 1971, March 2, 1973, December 14, 1973, February 8, 1974, March 1, 1974, October 17, 1975, August 5, 1977, February 26, 1982, September 23, 1988, March 22-29, 1990.
Tribune Books (Chicago), November 19, 1989.
Tri-Quarterly, fall, 1966.
Village Voice, August 31, 1982.
Washington Post, October 30, 1979, October 17, 1986, November 10, 1989.
World, February 13, 1973.
World Literature Today, winter, 1977, autumn, 1981, summer, 1982.

*   *   *

SPARK, Muriel (Sarah) 1918-
(Evelyn Cavallo)

PERSONAL: Born February 1, 1918, in Edinburgh, Scotland; daughter of Bernard (an engineer) and Sarah Elizabeth (Uezzell) Camberg; married S. O. Spark, 1937 (divorced); children: Robin (son). *Education:* Attended schools in Edinburgh, Scotland. *Religion:* Roman Catholic.

ADDRESSES: Home—Italy. *Agent*—Harold Ober Associates, Inc., 40 East 49th St., New York, N.Y. 10017.

CAREER: Writer. Wrote news items for political intelligence department of British government, 1944-45; affiliated with *Argentor* (jewelry trade magazine); press agent for businessmen; founder, *Forum* (literary magazine), 1949; part-time editor, Peter Owen Ltd. (publishing company).

MEMBER: Royal Society of Literature (fellow), Poetry Society (general secretary, 1947-49), PEN, American Academy and Institute of Arts and Letters (honorary member).

AWARDS, HONORS: Observer short story prize, 1951, for "The Seraph and the Zambesi"; Prix Italia, 1962, for radio play adaptation of *The Ballad of Peckham Rye;* Yorkshire Post Book of the Year Award, 1965, and James Tait Black Memorial Prize, 1966, both for *The Mandelbaum Gate;* commander, Order of the British Empire, 1967; LL.D., University of Strathclyde, 1971; Booker McConnell Prize nomination, 1981, for *Loitering with Intent;* short stories in translation prize, 1988, for the Editions Fayard translation of *The Stories of Muriel Spark.*

WRITINGS:

FICTION

The Comforters (also see below), Lippincott, 1957, reprinted, Perigee Books, 1984.
Robinson, Lippincott, 1958, Avon, 1978.
Memento Mori (also see below), Macmillan (London), 1958, Lippincott, 1959, reprinted, Perigee Books, 1982.
The Go-Away Bird and Other Stories (short stories), Macmillan (London), 1958, Lippincott, 1960.
The Ballad of Peckham Rye (also see below), Lippincott, 1960, reprinted, Perigee Books, 1982.
The Bachelors, Macmillan (London), 1960, Lippincott, 1961, reprinted, Perigee Books, 1984.
Voices at Play (short stories and radio plays), Macmillan (London), 1961, Lippincott, 1962.
The Prime of Miss Jean Brodie, Macmillan (London), 1961, Lippincott, 1962, New American Library, 1984.
A Muriel Spark Trio (contains *The Comforters, Memento Mori,* and *The Ballad of Peckham Rye*), Lippincott, 1962.
The Girls of Slender Means, Knopf, 1963, reprinted, Perigee Books, 1982.
Doctors of Philosophy (play; first produced in London, 1962), Macmillan (London), 1963, Knopf, 1966.
The Mandelbaum Gate, Knopf, 1965.
Collected Stories I (short stories), Macmillan (London), 1967, Knopf, 1968.
The Public Image, Knopf, 1968.
The Very Fine Clock (juvenile), Knopf, 1968.
The Driver's Seat, Knopf, 1970.
Not to Disturb, Macmillan (London), 1971, Knopf, 1972.
The Hothouse by the East River, Viking, 1973.
The Abbess of Crewe, Viking, 1973.
The Takeover (also see below), Viking, 1976.
Territorial Rights, Coward, 1979.
Loitering with Intent, Coward, 1981.
Bang-Bang You're Dead and Other Stories, Panther Books, 1983.
The Only Problem, Coward, 1984, Perigree Books, 1985.
A Far Cry from Kensington, Houghton, 1988, Thorndike Press, 1989.
The Stories of Muriel Spark, New American Library, 1986.
Symposium, Houghton, 1990.

POETRY

The Fanfarlo and Other Verse, Hand and Flower Press, 1952.
Collected Poems I, Macmillan (London), 1967, Knopf, 1968, published as *Going Up to Sotheby's and Other Poems,* Panther Books, 1982.

NONFICTION

Child of Light: A Reassessment of Mary Wollstonecraft Shelley, Tower Bridge Publications, 1951, reprinted, Richard West, 1978.

(With Derek Stanford) *Emily Bronte: Her Life and Work,* P. Owen, 1953, London House and Maxwell, 1960, reprinted, Merrimack Book Service, 1982.

John Masefield, Nevill, 1953, Norwood, 1978.

Mary Shelley, New American Library, 1988.

Mary Shelley: A Biography, Dutton, 1989.

EDITOR

(And author of introductions with Stanford) *Tribute to Wordsworth,* T. Brun, 1950, reprinted, Kennikat, 1970.

(And author of introduction) *A Selection of Poems by Emily Bronte,* Grey Walls Press, 1952.

(With Stanford) *My Best Mary: The Letters of Mary Shelley,* Wingate, 1953.

The Letters of the Brontes: A Selection, University of Oklahoma Press, 1954 (published in England as *The Bronte Letters,* Nevill, 1954).

(With Stanford) *Letters of John Henry Newman,* P. Owen, 1957.

OTHER

Also author of a film adaptation of *The Takeover.* Contributor of short stories to the *New Yorker* and of poems, articles, and reviews to magazines and newspapers, occasionally under the pseudonym Evelyn Cavallo. Editor, *Poetry Review,* 1947-49; review editor, *European Affairs,* 1949-50.

SIDELIGHTS: Often described as one of the best, yet one of the most unappreciated, of today's novelists, Muriel Spark puzzles those readers and critics who have an affinity for labels and categories. Explains Richard Sullivan in *Book World:* "For those who take comfort in instant classification Muriel Spark keeps posing a mischievous problem. She's elusive. There is no question about her quality: her work to date has demonstrated it. . . . Yet she doesn't fit neatly into any pigeonhole. . . . She is—and probably without bothering in the least about it, prefers to be—an original."

Spark had already achieved some recognition as a critic and poet when she entered what was virtually her first attempt at fiction, the short story "The Seraph and the Zambesi," in a 1951 Christmas writing contest sponsored by the *Observer.* The fanciful tale of a troublesome angel who bursts in on an acting troupe staging a holiday pageant on the banks of Africa's Zambesi River, "The Seraph and the Zambesi" won top honors in the competition and attracted a great deal of attention for its unconventional treatment of the Christmas theme. Several other stories set in Africa and England followed; soon Sparks's successes in fiction began to overshadow those in criticism and poetry.

In 1954 Spark's publisher, Macmillan, urged her to try writing a novel. Spark reluctantly agreed. "I thought it was an inferior way of writing," she told Frank Kermode in a *Partisan Review* interview. "So I wrote a novel to work out the technique first, to sort of make it all right with myself to write a novel at all." At the same time she was working out the technique for writing a novel, Spark was "working out" something else far more important in her life—her conversion to Roman Catholicism. The daughter of a Jewish father and a Presbyterian mother, Spark had for many years practiced the Anglican faith. During the early 1950s, however, the inadequacy of her old beliefs became more and more unsettling; soon she found herself searching for new and better answers in the works of English theologian John Cardinal Newman, an early nineteenth-century Anglican convert to Catholicism. Reading Newman, explains Spark in *Twentieth Century,* "helped me find a definite location," and her eventual conversion, though marked by tremendous spiritual and physical turmoil, "provided my norm . . . something to measure from."

With financial and moral support from both Macmillan and author Graham Greene, Spark struggled for nearly three years to sort out the aesthetic, psychological, and religious questions raised by her conversion and her attempt at writing longer fiction. Drawing on the tenets of her new faith, which she believes is especially "conducive to individuality, to finding one's own individual point of view," the young writer formulated her own theory of the novel. According to Kermode in his book *Continuities,* this theory suggests that "a genuine relation exists between the forms of fiction and the forms of the world, between the novelist's creation and God's." In essence, Spark sees the novelist as very God-like—omniscient and omnipotent, able to manipulate plot, character, and dialogue at will. Viewed in this light, Kermode and others contend, Spark's first novel, *The Comforters,* is obviously "an experiment designed to discover whether . . . the novelist, pushing people and things around and giving 'disjointed happenings a shape,' is in any way like Providence."

Because Spark's Catholicism figures so prominently in *The Comforters* and subsequent works, it is "much more than an item of biographical interest," in the opinion of Victor Kelleher. Comments Kelleher in *Critical Review:* "Spark does not stop short at simply bringing the question of Catholicism into her work; she has chosen to place the traditionally Christian outlook at the very heart of everything she writes. . . . [Her tales proclaim] the most basic of Christian truths: that all man's blessings emanate from God; that, in the absence of God, man is nothing more than a savage." Catharine Hughes makes a similar assessment of Spark's religious sentiment in an article in *Catholic World.* Observes the critic: "[Spark satirizes] humanity's foibles and incongruities from a decidedly Catholic orientation. One is conscious that she is a writer working within the framework of some of Christianity's greatest truths; that her perspective, which takes full cognizance of eternal values, is never burdened by a painful attempt to inflict them upon others."

Despite their acknowledgment of Spark's unmistakably Catholic outlook, most critics hasten to point out that she is not at all what is usually thought of as a "Catholic writer." "[There] is a difference between a Catholic who writes novels and a Catholic Novelist," declares D. J. Enright in his book *Man Is an Onion.* "This latter term evokes, even if it shouldn't, an unholy mixture of the Claudelic, the Mauriacesque and the Greenean, a browbeating either direct or indirect, a stifling odour of incense or of fallen sweat or of both. Mrs. Spark's writing seems to me altogether dissimilar: even a lapsed Wesleyan can approach her without too painful a sense of intimidation or exclusion. . . . Granville Hicks has faintly deplored her as 'a gloomy Catholic, like Graham Greene and Flannery O'Connor, more concerned with the evil of man than with the goodness of God.' Far from gloomy, I would even have thought [Spark] positively funny, and . . . concerned with the evil of man no more than is to be expected in a fair-minded though shrewd observer of humanity. . . . Spark neither despises nor hates her fellow humans nor dotes simple-mindedly on her Catholicism. . . . What emerges [in her work] is a chastened Christianity not so far removed in matters of this world from the chastened humanism which is the only sort of humanism our age can allow."

Ann Dobie also takes issue with those who label Spark a "Catholic novelist." In *Critique: Studies in Modern Fiction,* Dobie insists that "it is doubtful that a reader who is not aware of [the author's] religious affiliation would know that she is a Roman Catholic. Muriel Spark is never didactic about her religion. Her purpose is to intrigue, not teach. She awakens the reader's imagination and curiosity instead of making firm the ideas which she brings to the novel. . . . Spark's novels are therefore written to express a moral or spiritual truth. Though they entertain by their wit and originality, their basic purpose lies in their endeavor to make a statement about the nature of the universe and man's place in it."

At first glance, however, Spark's novels do not seem to reflect her strong religious and moral preoccupations. In terms of setting, for example, the author usually chooses to locate her modern morality tales in upper-class urban areas of England or Italy. Her "fun-house plots, full of trapdoors, abrupt apparitions, and smartly clicking secret panels," as John Updike describes them in a *New Yorker* article, focus on the often bizarre behavior of people belonging to a small, select group: elderly men and women linked by long-standing personal relationships in *Memento Mori;* unmarried male and female residents of the same London district in *The Bachelors;* students and teachers at a Scottish girls' school in *The Prime of Miss Jean Brodie;* servants on a Swiss estate in *Not to Disturb;* guests at a pair of neighboring Venetian hotels in *Territorial Rights.* The "action" in these stories springs from the elaborate ties Spark concocts between the members of each group—ties of blood, marriage, friendship, and other kinds of relationships. Commenting in her study of the author, critic Patricia Stubbs observes that the use of such a technique reflects Spark's fascination with "the way in which the individual varies in different settings, or different company." "By taking this restricted group of protagonists," explains Stubbs, "[Spark] is able to create multiple ironies, arising from their connecting and conflicting destinies: by her selection of such a restricted canvas, she can display the many facets of her creatures' personalities, and the different roles which they, or society, decree they should play."

Like her settings and plots, Spark's characters belie her strong Catholic convictions. In fact, as many reviewers have noticed, she has few qualms about depicting her coreligionists (who figure prominently in her fiction) in a manner that creates a decidedly objectionable image for their faith. For instance, Robert Maurer, writing in the *Saturday Review,* describes Spark's cast of characters as a "strange collection of eccentrics, self-deceivers, misfits, and purveyors of reprehensible madness." Because of their interrelatedness, all are equally important to the story line, though one or two usually stand out somewhat from the rest. These protagonists, most often female Catholic converts, "are frequently intelligent and talented women who, because they demand much of life, insist on a broad view of its possibilities," reports Dobie. "At the same time they desire the security of certain ultimate laws which limit man's actions." Spark generally portrays them in the midst of a struggle to understand themselves and their chaotic environments within the context of their religion. Though their struggle may be a noble one, they are not necessarily heroic or even very likable people. According to Gail Kessler Kmetz in *Ms.,* the typical Spark heroine "believes herself to be above ordinary standards of right and wrong. . . . She is an autocrat, an elitist, a tyrant convinced that God's standards are identical to her own." In short, remarks Derek Stanford in his study of the author, Spark's protagonists, "encased in the self-love of their own rightness or superiority, . . . do not attract us to identify ourselves with them or their self-willed fates."

Secondary characters fare little better in most of Spark's novels; as Dobie notes, they are among those "despicable people" who "misuse religious faith to achieve their own gain: money, social position, personal pride." Mean-spirited liars, meddlers, and bores, they are Catholic only in that they have "the articles of an ancient creed built into their grid of reflexes, predispositions, and quirks," writes Updike. Yet as Samuel Hynes points out in *Commonweal,* they are not truly evil: "[Spark] is not, like that other distinguished convert, Graham Greene, devil-ridden; the diabolic creatures who turn up in her books are more grotesque than terrifying, and their deeds are rather annoying than destroying. They are . . . the kind of people who bring out the pettiness and uncharitableness in us, not the kind who lead us to damnation."

Spark often emphasizes the diabolicism of a particular person or event by introducing supernatural forces into a setting that is otherwise quite ordinary. The appearance of these inscrutable forces is always unpredictable, and they may take a variety of forms: an enigmatic stranger with unusual powers, disembodied voices, untraceable telephone calls. Whatever their form, they exert considerable influence over human activities; according to Dobie, however, their purpose is neither to harm nor to help, but to disrupt routine, provoke thought, and inspire spiritual growth. As such, the supernatural is as important an element in Spark's world as the natural.

Both Hynes and Dobie view this intrusion of the supernatural as "a more pervasive, less specific" manifestation of Spark's religious feeling, to use Hynes's words. Explains Dobie: "Those characters [in Spark's fiction] who recognize [supernatural forces] for what they are acquire 'vision'. . . . That is, such characters are given the opportunity to comprehend more fully the nature of themselves and the world. If the characters accept the opportunity, their new concept of reality is a liberating one, for the limitations which they had previously accepted are destroyed by a new grasp of the enormity of the real world which reaches far beyond what the human being can observe by his senses and prove by his reason." In short, as Dobie and many others have concluded, Spark makes us take a second look at the world and the people we think we know; she transfigures the commonplace, blending the ordinary and the supernatural ("complementary parts of a whole and rich reality") in such a way that "a new concept of reality emerges, one which is closer to truth."

In contrast to the complexities of plot, characterization, and theme in her fiction, Spark is noted for what Stubbs refers to as a "frugality of method." Precise, economical, and matter-of-fact, her prose leaves most readers "wondering why other writers must babble on and on to twice that length," declares a reviewer for *Time.* States Edmund White in the *New York Times Book Review:* "Details, no matter how prosaic, are presented with the utmost clarity, even severity, and this classic exactitude holds our interest, for it is the tone of the professor during the opening lectures of a course that we know is quickly going to get bewilderingly out of hand. . . . Dozens of scenes are compressed into a single slim volume, but each is displayed in the dry, unemphatic, seemingly leisurely style for which the author is renowned." Malcolm Bradbury makes a similar observation in *Critical Quarterly,* remarking that Spark's books "possess a high tactical authority and a singular clarity so that every compositional decision, every rhetorical device, every perspective in every sentence has the high economy of, for example, one of Hemingway's better stories, the same air of exchanging language at the very best possible rate." As White asserts, "this efficiency and orderliness . . . are [Spark's] real artistic achievements."

In the tradition of the intellectual novelist, Spark avoids florid descriptions of the physical world, preferring instead to concentrate on dialogue, on "the play of ideas and experiences upon the mind, and the interplay of minds upon each other," in Hynes's words. Her characterizations are quick, sharp, and concise; in a *New Statesman* article, for instance, Walter Allen writes that the author "pins [her types] to the page quivering in their essential absurdity." As a result, says *Newsweek* reviewer Raymond A. Sokolov, "a [typical Spark] character is born, with a deft flick of the author's wrist, in an effortless few pages."

Spark teams her technical virtuosity with an elegant, acerbic wit and condescending attitude that most readers find highly entertaining. As Melvin Maddocks declares in *Life:* "Reading a Muriel Spark novel remains one of the minor pleasures of life. Like a perfect hostess, she caters to our small needs. In the manner available to only the best British novelists, she ordains a civilized atmosphere—two parts what Evelyn Waugh called creamy English charm, one part acid wit. She peoples her scene discriminatingly, showing a taste for interesting but not overpowering guests. . . . As the evening moves along, she has the good sense to lower the drawing-room lights and introduce a pleasantly chilling bit of tension—even violence—just to save us all, bless her, from the overexquisite sensibilities of the lady novelist."

Charles Alva Hoyt traces the source of Spark's humor to her conception of the novelist as a God-like figure. Noting in the book *Contemporary British Novelists* that Spark is "a thoroughly mischievous writer," Hoyt goes on to explain: "By that I do not mean only that she plays tricks upon her characters—although she does—or upon the reader—she treats him even worse—but that she also views the universe itself as mischievous. The cosmos is neither void of all sense, nor is it sentient but preoccupied: it is both aware of individuals and fond of meddling with them for its own amusement. . . . [Spark's universe] reveals its playfulness in an almost continuous flow of irony, but it is quite as fond of comedy as it is of tragedy. There is furthermore in her work an almost irresponsible impertinence towards everyday reality. . . . What we have here is . . . not the scientist's or the theologian's attempt to reason the demons out of the thunderstorm, but the magician's effort to make the demons do his bidding."

Yet, as Barbara Grizzuti Harrison reminds readers in a *New York Times Book Review* article, Spark is at heart "a profoundly serious comic writer whose wit advances, never undermines or diminishes, her ideas." This sentiment is shared by Harrison's fellow *New York Times Book Review* critic Leonard Graver, who writes: "Sinister metaphysical farce has always been one of Muriel Spark's specialties. . . . [But] lurid entertainment is only part of [her] intention. She has always been a novelist who wishes to tease readers into serious thought. . . . [Her work] has the cleverness to entertain and the intelligence to provoke thought."

The effects of Spark's malevolent wit are intensified by the air of authorial omniscience and condescension that permeates her fiction. Reflecting what David Pryce-Jones describes in the *London Magazine* as a desire "to observe man disposing what God has proposed," Spark deliberately sets up a distance between herself and her characters (and, to a somewhat lesser extent, between herself and her readers) that clearly gives the impression she knows much more than she cares to reveal. One is always well aware, says Hoyt, of "the cool, clever female mind in control. This level scrutiny from the distance plays continuously though mildly upon every frenzied human action like the soft, semi-contemptuous gaze of the household cat. Muriel Spark is ever the reasonable recorder of unreason: she is the Jane Austen

of the surrealists." As such, maintains a *Times Literary Supplement* critic, Spark "makes it refreshingly clear that modern satire can be more than anger or tittle-tattle."

Not all reviewers, however, are quite as charmed by Spark's biting humor and cool detachment. To some, these trademarks of her writing are a source of uneasiness. States Thomas R. Brooks in the *New Leader:* "On the surface, [a typical Spark novel] might pass for a decaying comedy of manners. . . . Yet underneath the deftly paced plot and the gleaming prose there lurks a disconcerting darkness that goes beyond black humor. The trouble, I think, is that the characters are dislikable to a degree that is fatal." *Los Angeles Times* critic Jascha Kessler asserts that this is because "the narrator [Spark] usually employs is too often the stereotypical convert, joyless and sexless; sometimes it's a disembodied voice, literally a spook; or it's intellectualist, bored by the drab English, or English (African) colonial, life; or it's neuter, hysterical, grim, as though suffering from menopause from the onset of puberty, and wishing only to find refuge or surcease from the life of the whole person. And that refuge is too easily found in an attitude that is self-consciously catty and complacent, spiritualistic rather than spiritual, smug about rosaries, icons, rituals, embarrassed by faith and not exalted or empowered by it, as though faith demands a show of warmth that is in poor taste."

Gillian Tindall, on the other hand, believes that it is the author's omniscient tone that makes her characters so unattractive. Says Tindall in the *New Statesman:* "[Spark's] insistence that for all her characters the future *is already there,* and that she can reveal it if she has a mind to, tends to belittle them and, by depriving them of self-determination, turns them into demented automata." Christopher Ricks views Spark's tendency to create unsympathetic characters in more negative terms. In a *New York Review of Books* article, Ricks declares: "[Spark's works] exemplify more than any other writing known to me, a body of work guilty of all that which it finds most hateful and which it most eagerly exposes. . . . 'Merciless,' the reviewers have always said. Leave aside the question of why something which is a vice in life becomes a virtue in literature; but why fabricate characters at whose expense you can then exercise your mercilessness?"

According to a few critics, Spark's omniscient tone also gives her work an overall air of inconsequentiality. Margaret Drabble, for instance, notes in the *New York Times Book Review* that Spark is "an enigmatic novelist, and her forte is to imply that she knows much more than . . . she chooses to say. . . . She writes of the rich, the clever, the sophisticated, the experienced; the innocent and the unknowing receive hardly more than a derisory nod or an astonished salute in her collected works. . . . [Her characters] are the jet set of fiction. . . . But, as ever, Muriel Spark raises the question: what lies beneath this dazzling game? Anything? Nothing? And, as ever, she leaves us on our own . . . to try to answer it. At times one suspects she may not know the answer herself. It is easy to appear knowing if one says little, or if one works . . . on the level of tediously protracted fantasy." Commenting in *The Modern English Novel,* Bernard Harrison also characterizes Spark's novels as "too spun-out. They seem all surface, and a rather dry, sparsely furnished, though elegant and mannered surface at that. . . . [They] seem, while one is reading them, to be profoundly, if obscurely, preoccupied with morality, not to say moral theology. Indeed they seem to be about nothing else. But there is no denying the obscurity. . . . Nothing is ever fully explained or given depth."

Even Maurer, who believes that requesting Spark to "alter these characteristics in her work would be [asking] her to surrender her uniqueness—and, one hastens to add, much of her delight and pleasure," has reservations about her "self-controlled poise, the intellectuality of her pessimism, her crisp sort of kindness, her impatience with moral obliquity." In short, observes the critic, "one wonders how vast a reserve of sympathy lies beneath the iceberg of her consciousness, and how far beyond trickery her work would go if she let it show through."

John Updike suspects that differences between American and English sensibilities account for much of the negative criticism reviewers have expressed regarding Spark's coolly distant attitude. Though he himself finds that "her hard, unflecked prose seems laid on from a calculated distance that this admirer, sometimes, would be relieved to see reduced," he nevertheless maintains that "detachment is the genius of her fiction. We are lifted above her characters, and though they are reduced in size and cryptically foreshortened, they are all seen at once, and their busy interactions are as plain and pleasing as a solved puzzle. The use by a serious author of [such techniques] may strike American readers as incongruous. We are accustomed to honest autobiographical shapelessness. . . . Our novels tend to be about education rather than products of it; they are soul-searching rather than worldly-wise. English fiction, for all the social and philosophical earthquakes since Chaucer, continues to aspire, with the serenity of a treatise, to a certain dispassionate elevation above the human scene. Hence its greater gaiety and ease of contrivance, its (on the whole) superior finish, and its flattering air of speaking to the reader who, himself presumably educated, may be spared the obvious."

Others also find Spark's attitude appropriate and not at all callous. "There is certainly a remoteness, a lack of ordinary compassion, in [Spark's] dealing with characters," admits Kermode in the *New Statesman.* "But this is part of the premise of her fiction; if we feel sorry in the wrong way, it's because our emotions are as messy and imprecise as life, part of the muddle she is sorting out." Hynes makes a similar observation, stating: "Compassion is there, but Mrs. Spark's religion protects her from that too-easy compassion which we call sentimentality. She is neither cold nor soft-hearted; on the whole she is amiably disposed toward her characters, finds material for comedy in them, and records their nastier qualities without rancor. . . . If she is detached in her attitude toward her characters, this is understandable in a novelist who sees people in terms of the designs into which they fit."

Despite all that has been written about her and her fiction, Muriel Spark remains an enigma to most critics, concerning herself as she does "with matters beyond reality, with forces that do not lend themselves to facile explanations," according to Florence Rome in the *Chicago Tribune Book World.* Described by Sybille Bedford in the *Saturday Review* as "an artist, a serious—and most accomplished—writer, a moralist engaged with the human predicament, wildly entertaining, and a joy to read," Spark has nevertheless, in Stubbs's opinion, "succeeded triumphantly in evading classification." Updike, too, contends that Spark possesses a truly exceptional talent—a talent that without a doubt makes her an unclassifiable "original." In fact, he declares in the *New Yorker,* Spark "is one of the few writers of the language on either side of the Atlantic with enough resources, daring, and stamina to be altering, as well as feeding, the fiction machine."

Shirley Hazzard also counts herself among those who believe Muriel Spark is indeed "a remarkable writer." Elaborating on the subject in a lengthy *New York Times Book Review* article, Hazzard states: "At this moment when, in all the arts, novelty is frequently confused with quality, Mrs. Spark's writings dem-

onstrate how secondary—in fact, how incidental—are innovations of style and form to the work of the truly gifted. . . . When the word 'humorous' has little currency in literature or in life, her wit is employed to produce effects and insights only matched in contemporary fiction, in this reviewer's opinion, by the glittering jests of Vladimir Nabokov. At a time when our 'tolerance' tends to take the form of general agreement that we are all capable of the worst crimes had we but the conditions for committing them, Mrs. Spark interests herself instead in our capacities for choice and in the use we make of them; and in those forces of good and evil that she picks out unerringly, often gleefully, beneath their worldly camouflage." Noting that the author "does not posture instructively, nor does she shade her work to appease reviewers and gladden the hearts of publishing companies," Hazzard concludes that Muriel Spark writes for the best possible reason: "She writes to entertain, in the highest sense of that word—to allow us the exercise of our intellect and imagination, to extend our self-curiosity and enrich our view."

MEDIA ADAPTATIONS: Several of Muriel Spark's novels have been adapted for the stage, film, and television. A dramatization of *Memento Mori* was produced on stage in 1964. Jay Presson Allen's dramatization of *The Prime of Miss Jean Brodie,* published by Samuel French in 1969, was first produced in Torquay, England, at the Princess Theatre beginning April 5, 1966, then in Boston at the Colonial Theatre from December 26, 1967, to January 6, 1968, and finally on Broadway at the Helen Hayes Theatre beginning January 9, 1968. Allen also wrote the screenplay for the 1969 film version of the same novel, a Twentieth Century-Fox production starring Maggie Smith. John Wood's dramatization of *The Prime of Miss Jean Brodie* was produced in London at Wyndham's Theatre in 1967. A six-part adaptation appeared on public television in England in 1978 and in the United States in 1979. *The Driver's Seat* was filmed in 1972, and in 1974 *The Girls of Slender Means* was adapted for television. *The Abbess of Crewe* was filmed and released in 1976 under the title "Nasty Habits."

BIOGRAPHICAL/CRITICAL SOURCES:

BOOKS

Contemporary Literary Criticism, Gale, Volume 2, 1974, Volume 3, 1975, Volume 5, 1976, Volume 8, 1978, Volume 13, 1980, Volume 18, 1981, Volume 40, 1987.
Dictionary of Literary Biography, Volume 15: *British Novelists, 1930-1959,* Gale, 1983.
Enright, D. J., *Man Is an Onion: Reviews and Essays,* Chatto & Windus, 1972.
Josipovici, Gabriel, editor, *The Modern English Novel: The Reader, the Writer and the Work,* Open Books, 1976.
Kemp, Peter, *Muriel Spark,* Elek, 1974, Barnes & Noble, 1975.
Kermode, Frank, *Continuities,* Random House, 1968.
Malkoff, Karl, *Muriel Spark,* Columbia University Press, 1968.
Shapiro, Charles, editor, *Contemporary British Novelists,* Southern Illinois University Press, 1965.
Stanford, Derek, *Muriel Spark: A Biographical and Critical Study,* Centaur Press, 1963.
Stanford, Donald E., editor, *Nine Essays in Modern Literature,* Louisiana State University Press, 1965.
Stubbs, Patricia, *Muriel Spark,* Longman, 1973.
Whittaker, Ruth, *The Faith and Fiction of Muriel Spark,* Macmillan (London), 1978.

PERIODICALS

Atlantic, August, 1959, October, 1968.
Best Sellers, November 1, 1968, November 1, 1970.

Book Week, September 15, 1963.
Book World, September 29, 1968, November 23, 1969.
Books and Bookmen, July, 1968, April, 1973.
Catholic World, August, 1961.
Chicago Sunday Tribune, January 1, 1961.
Chicago Tribune Book World, April 29, 1973, May 24, 1981, November 3, 1985.
Christian Science Monitor, November 14, 1968.
Commonweal, August 23, 1957, September 18, 1959, February 23, 1962, December 3, 1965, January 14, 1966.
Critical Quarterly, autumn, 1972.
Critical Review, Number 18, 1976.
Critique: Studies in Modern Fiction, Volume 5, no. 2, 1962, Volume 12, no. 1, 1970, Volume 15, no. 1, 1973.
Detroit News, June 21, 1981, July 8, 1984.
Harper, November, 1963.
Hudson Review, autumn, 1972.
Insight, July 6, 1987.
Kenyon Review, Volume 31, no. 2, 1969.
Life, October 11, 1968.
Listener, December 7, 1967, September 24, 1970.
London Magazine, July, 1968.
Los Angeles Times, July 14, 1968, July 26, 1984, July 29, 1987, July 14, 1988.
Manchester Guardian, February 12, 1957.
Ms., May, 1976.
Nation, October 5, 1970.
New Leader, November 30, 1970, July 30, 1979.
New Republic, January 29, 1962.
New Statesman, July 5, 1958, March 28, 1959, March 5, 1960, October 15, 1960, November 3, 1961, September 27, 1963, September 25, 1970, March 2, 1973, April 27, 1979.
New Statesman and Nation, February 23, 1957.
Newsweek, October 21, 1968, November 30, 1970, May 18, 1981, July 2, 1984, September 16, 1985.
New Yorker, June 13, 1959, August 27, 1960, September 30, 1961, September 14, 1963, January 27, 1968, June 8, 1981.
New York Review of Books, October 28, 1965, December 19, 1968, November 28, 1974, November 11, 1976.
New York Times, September 1, 1957, October 19, 1958, March 29, 1972, November 26, 1974, October 7, 1976, May 19, 1979, May 28, 1981, June 26, 1984, September 18, 1985, July 20, 1987.
New York Times Book Review, May 17, 1959, August 28, 1960, September 29, 1968, March 26, 1972, October 3, 1976, May 20, 1979, May 31, 1981, July 15, 1984, October 20, 1985, September 6, 1987, July 31, 1988.
Partisan Review, spring, 1963.
Saturday Review, November 19, 1960, April 8, 1961, January 20, 1962, September 14, 1963, October 16, 1965, October 5, 1968, September 18, 1976.
Spectator, February 22, 1957, November 3, 1961, December 22, 1967, June 7, 1968.
Time, August 15, 1960, January 19, 1962, January 13, 1967, November 1, 1968, October 26, 1970, June 11, 1979, July 6, 1981, July 16, 1984.
Times (London), September 6, 1984, April 16, 1987.
Times Literary Supplement, June 27, 1958, March 4, 1960, October 11, 1960, November 3, 1961, October 25, 1963, October 14, 1965, September 25, 1970, May 22, 1981.
Twentieth Century, autumn, 1961.
Washington Post, May 4, 1979.
Washington Post Book World, October 3, 1976, June 24, 1979, May 24, 1981, September 29, 1985, August 23, 1987, .

Yale Review, autumn, 1957, December, 1958, January, 1959, June, 1959, June, 1961.

*   *   *

SPAULDING, Douglas
See BRADBURY, Ray (Douglas)

*   *   *

SPAULDING, Leonard
See BRADBURY, Ray (Douglas)

*   *   *

SPENCE, J. A. D.
See ELIOT, T(homas) S(tearns)

*   *   *

SPENCER, Elizabeth   1921-

PERSONAL: Born July 19, 1921, in Carrollton, Miss.; daughter of James L. (a farmer) and Mary J. (McCain) Spencer; married John Rusher (an educator), September 29, 1956. *Education:* Belhaven College, B.A., 1942, Vanderbilt University, M.A., 1943. *Politics:* Democrat. *Religion:* Episcopalian.

ADDRESSES: Home—402 Longleaf Dr., Chapel Hill, N.C. 27514.

CAREER: Writer, 1948—. Concordia University, Montreal, Canada, professor of creative writing, 1976-86; University of North Carolina—Chapel Hill, professor of creative writing, 1986—.

MEMBER: National Institute of Arts and Letters.

AWARDS, HONORS: Women's Democratic Committee Award, 1949; National Institute of Arts and Letters award, 1952; Guggenheim fellowship, 1953; Rosenthal Foundation award from American Academy of Arts and Letters, 1956; Kenyon College fellow in fiction, 1957; McGraw-Hill fiction award, 1960; Bryn Mawr College Donnelly fellow, 1962; Henry Bellamann Award for creative writing and LL.D., Southwestern University, both 1968; Award of Merit Medal for the Short Story from American Academy and Institute of Arts and Letters, 1983; National Endowment for the Arts, creative award grant, 1983, senior award grant in literature, 1988; D.L., Concordia University, 1988.

WRITINGS:

Fire in the Morning, Dodd, 1948, reprinted, McGraw, 1968.
This Crooked Way, Dodd, 1952, reprinted, McGraw, 1968.
The Voice at the Back Door, McGraw, 1956, reprinted with an introduction by the author, Time-Life, 1982.
The Light in the Piazza, McGraw, 1960, reprinted, Penguin Books, 1986.
Knights and Dragons, McGraw, 1965.
No Place for an Angel, McGraw, 1967.
Ship Island and Other Stories, McGraw, 1968.
The Snare, McGraw, 1972.
(Contributor) *76: New Canadian Stories,* Oberon, 1976.
The Stories of Elizabeth Spencer, Doubleday, 1981.
Marilee, University Press of Mississippi, 1981.
The Salt Line, Doubleday, 1984.
Jack of Diamonds and Other Stories, Viking, 1988.
"For Lease or Sale" (play), first produced by Playmakers Repertory Company, Chapel Hill, N.C., 1989.

Contributor of stories to *Redbook, New Yorker, Southern Review, Texas Quarterly,* and *Atlantic.*

WORK IN PROGRESS: A novel.

SIDELIGHTS: Elizabeth Spencer's many works of fiction draw upon her experiences as a Southerner, a world traveller, and a college-trained educator. Over a period of more than forty years, Spencer "has produced a number of distinguished works marked for their range in subject and style," to quote *Dictionary of Literary Biography* contributor Peggy Whitman Prenshaw. Spencer was born and raised in Mississippi, but she has spent much of her life in Canada and Italy; *Washington Post Book World* reviewer Garrett Epps finds her "a Southern writer . . . whose art has been shaped by exile."

Indeed, though her settings range from Montreal to New Orleans to Italy, Spencer exhibits a recognizably Southern sensibility. She has drawn critical praise for those qualities that distinguish what *Publishers Weekly* correspondent Amanda Smith calls "the grand tradition of Southern writers"—evocative dialogue, spirited narrative, and a well-defined sense of place. Other critics see her work as broader-based, however. In the *Los Angeles Times,* for instance, Elaine Kendall cites Spencer for "a special attention to idiosyncratic idiom, an intense awareness of social distinctions, and a passionate concern with family ties—a literary attitude that can exist without a shred of Spanish moss or a single black-eyed pea." *Saturday Review* essayist Robert Tallant notes that Spencer "writes with clarity and honesty, often with beauty." The critic adds: "Her people live, and her ear for dialogue is fine. She has a magnificent sense of narrative and the gift of sympathy."

Spencer's parents were prosperous farmers, and she grew up in an environment rich in traditional literature. "We were very family and land oriented," she told *Publishers Weekly.* "Both sides of my family had been in [Mississippi] since the Indians. . . . I was fragile when I was a child, and my mother used to pass the time reading to me, mostly fairy stories and myths." Spencer attended Belhaven College and then went to graduate school at Vanderbilt University, the seat of a resurgence of Southern literature. There, as she began her own creative writing about Mississippi, she confronted the powerful legacy of other living Southern writers, including William Faulkner and Eudora Welty. Spencer told *Mississippi Quarterly* that the mid-1940s "was both a very good and a very bad time to be writing, . . . because the giants in literature were people who were dealing with the same people I wanted to deal with. So these were tremendously strong influences for a young writer to shake off. The problem was both to use the same environment and to search your own identity as a writer. This was extremely difficult." At the same time, she told *Publishers Weekly,* the public's revived interest in works by Southerners helped her to find an audience. "Southern literature was in the ascendancy, and people were looking for new Southern writers as a matter of course," she said, "so I seemed to fill that need."

According to Charles Champlin in the *Los Angeles Times,* Spencer quickly "made her reputation as an uncommonly accurate, sensitive and lyrical writer about her Mississippi origins." The author's first three novels, *Fire in the Morning, This Crooked Way,* and *The Voice at the Back Door,* are all set in her native state. *South Atlantic Quarterly* contributor Nash K. Burger suggests that Spencer "ranges widely in time and society within this milieu; and her narratives, in the Southern and nineteenth-century tradition, are rich with happenings and complicating incidents." In the *New Yorker,* Brendan Gill claims that these early works "give off the characteristic ghostly phosphorescence of

something (slavery? the plantation system? the War between the States?) that went bad down there a long time ago and that threatens to go on flickering through the swamps and bayous till Kingdom come."

Spencer's early novels cover recognizable terrain—"the rural South during the first half of the twentieth century," to quote Prenshaw—but they also exhibit an independence in both substance and style. *New York* magazine reviewer Anthony West maintains that Spencer's "limpid and attractive prose, accurate and sharp about tastes, smells, appearances, and emotions . . . pleasingly enlarges one's picture of the South." In the *New York Times Book Review,* Reynolds Price praises Spencer for her "distinctive timbre in which to sing familiar scores," adding that the dangers of monotony "are combated by the serene rhythm and salty compassion with which the voice examines its findings." Other critics cite Spencer for her realistic depictions of race relations, especially in her 1956 work *The Voice at the Back Door.* "No other voice so clearly reminded me of a way of life obscured by outrage and oversimplified by headlines," writes John Malcolm Brinnin in the *Washington Post Book World.* ". . . Like other realists before her, Elizabeth Spencer had written of the life she knew with the kind of bare documentary exactitude which time lifts into metaphor—as though, from the mythological murk of Faulkner territory, she had emerged holding up a crisp photograph negative on which black is visible only in relation to white, and vice versa." Tallant puts it more succinctly. Spencer, he concludes, "knows her South, her country, and she draws it with justice."

In 1953 Spencer left the South for what turned out to be a long sojourn abroad. She lived in Italy for five years, and then married a British businessman and settled in Quebec Province, Canada. Spencer told *Publishers Weekly:* "Italy had a lot to do with changing the focus of my work over the years. Before I went to Italy I thought I would always be encased in the Southern social patterns and lineage and tradition, and if the South changed, then I wanted to be part of that change. I didn't see myself as separated from it. Then, especially after I married, I had to come to terms with a life that was going to be quite separate from that. I got to thinking that the Southerner has a certain mentality, especially Southern women—you can no more change a Southern woman than you can a French woman; they're always going to be French no matter what you do. So I thought that really nothing was going to happen to me as far as my essential personality was concerned, that it could broaden and include more scope and maybe get richer. I looked at that from the standpoint of my characters, that the Southern approach was going to be valued no matter where they found themselves. It seemed to me that there wasn't any need in sitting at home in the cottonfield just to be Southern, that you could be Southern elsewhere, in Florence, or Paris, or anywhere you found yourself."

Spencer has written several books set in Italy, including her well-known work *The Light in the Piazza.* She has also crafted a number of short stories set in Europe or Canada, many of which center upon displaced American women who must meet and deal with quiet crises. Champlin notes that the Spencer stories reveal "those moments when the young girls, the young women, the wives and careerists of the stories come to realize the concealed truth of a situation . . . or the inescapable truths about themselves and their lives—where they were, and have arrived at." Critics praise Spencer's sensitivity to the expatriate condition as well as her ability to create compelling characters. Prenshaw observes that the author "shows keen psychological insight into the irrepressible motive for the nonrational, the human need for mystery and awe, the longing for faith." *Saturday Review* contributor John Fludas calls Spencer's male characters "detailed, vivid, and convincing," concluding however that it is "the women of Elizabeth Spencer, in longing childhood and youth, through marriage and divorce, in Canada or Alabama or her beloved Italy, who have inspired her finely hued perceptions."

According to George Core in the *Washington Post,* Spencer "has worked in the shadow of William Faulkner, Eudora Welty and other leading Southern authors. Now, by dint of long persistence and considerable accomplishment, she may be coming into her own so far as critical recognition is concerned." A number of Spencer's early works have been reprinted, and her 1984 novel, *The Salt Line,* received wide review. In 1986 she was invited to a part-time professorship of creative writing at the University of North Carolina—Chapel Hill; after decades of living elsewhere, she has returned to the South. Kendall, for one, feels that Spencer has always retained her ties to the country of her youth. "For her less ambitious and intrepid people," writes the critic, "geography, like biology, will often be destiny. In all cases, it's the enduring power of place to shape lives that supplies these stories with their internal momentum; Spencer's uncanny understanding of the relationship between place and personality that lends them distinction." In the *Washington Post,* Garrett Epps suggests that the author's voice "is deeply feminine; but at a time when many 'women's books' have taken on a kind of hectoring insecurity, she is at her best rendering the ways in which self-confident women stake out a corner of the world—larger or smaller as luck and talent dictate—and claim it for their own." Kendall concludes: "Just off the monotonous freeways and beyond the tacky strip shopping centers, individuality still thrives, revealed and celebrated by a writer whose vision penetrates the blanket of homogeneity that blurs the American landscape."

BIOGRAPHICAL/CRITICAL SOURCES:

BOOKS

Contemporary Literary Criticism, Volume 22, Gale, 1982.
Dictionary of Literary Biography, Volume 6: *American Novelists since World War II,* Gale, 1980.
French, Warren, editor, *The Fifties: Fiction, Poetry, Drama,* Everett/Edwards, 1970.
Prenshaw, Peggy Whitman, *Elizabeth Spencer,* Twayne, 1985.

PERIODICALS

Books in Canada, March, 1981.
Chicago Tribune, August 24, 1988.
Delta Review, autumn, 1964.
Georgia Review, winter, 1974.
Globe & Mail (Toronto), February 11, 1984, March 23, 1985, January 25, 1986.
Los Angeles Times, February 20, 1981, January 12, 1984, September 16, 1988.
Mississippi Quarterly, fall, 1975, fall, 1976.
Nation, September 25, 1948.
National Review, March 30, 1973.
New Republic, June 26, 1965.
New York, March 22, 1952.
New Yorker, December 15, 1956.
New York Times, January 7, 1984.
New York Times Book Review, November 20, 1960, October 26, 1967, March 1, 1981, January 29, 1984, September 4, 1988.
Notes on Mississippi Writers, fall, 1968, fall, 1970, winter, 1974.
Publishers Weekly, September 9, 1988.
Saturday Review, November 6, 1948, October 20, 1956, February, 1981.
South Atlantic Quarterly, summer, 1964, Volume 63, 1964.

Time, February 13, 1984, August 15, 1988.
Times Literary Supplement, July 17, 1969.
Village Voice, September 20, 1988.
Washington Post, August 9, 1988.
Washington Post Book World, March 8, 1981, May 15, 1983.
Weekend Magazine, August 12, 1978.

—*Sketch by Anne Janette Johnson*

*   *   *

SPENCER, Leonard G.
   See SILVERBERG, Robert

*   *   *

SPENDER, Stephen (Harold)   1909-

PERSONAL: Born February 28, 1909, in London, England; son of Edward Harold (a journalist and lecturer) and Violet Hilda (Schuster) Spender; married Agnes Marie Pearn, 1936 (divorced); married Natasha Litvin (a pianist), 1941; children: (second marriage) Matthew Francis, Elizabeth. *Education:* Attended University College, Oxford, 1928-30.

ADDRESSES: Home—15 Loudoun Rd., London NW8, England (winters); Maussane-Les-Alpieles, Provence, France (summers).

CAREER: Writer. University of London, University College, London, England, professor of English, 1970-77, professor emeritus, 1977—. Counselor in Section of Letters, UNESCO, 1947. Holder of Elliston Chair of Poetry, University of Cincinnati, 1953; Beckman Professor, University of California, 1959; visiting lecturer, Northwestern University, 1963; Clark lecturer, Cambridge University, 1966; Northcliffe lecturer, University of London, 1969; visiting professor at University of Connecticut, 1969, Vanderbilt University, 1979, and University of South Carolina, 1981. Fellow of Institute of Advanced Studies, Wesleyan University, 1967. Consultant in poetry in English, Library of Congress, Washington, D.C., 1965. *Wartime service:* National Fire Service, fireman, 1941-44.

MEMBER: PEN International (president, English Centre, 1975—); American Academy of Arts and Letters and National Institute for Arts and Letters (honorary), Phi Beta Kappa (Harvard University; honorary member), Beefsteak Club.

AWARDS, HONORS: Commander of the British Empire, 1962; Queen's Gold Medal for Poetry, 1971; named Companion of Literature, 1977; knighted by Queen Elizabeth II, 1983; nominated for 1986 *Los Angeles Times* Book Award in poetry for *Collected Poems, 1928-1985;* honorary fellow, University College, Oxford; D.Litt. from University of Montpelier, Cornell University, and Loyola University.

WRITINGS:

POETRY

Nine Experiments: Being Poems Written at the Age of Eighteen, privately printed, 1928.
Twenty Poems, Basil Blackwell, 1930.
Poems, Faber, 1933, Random House, 1934, revised edition, Faber, 1934.
Perhaps (limited edition), privately printed, 1933.
Poem (limited edition), privately printed, 1934.
Vienna, Faber, 1934, Random House, 1935.
At Night, privately printed, 1935.
The Still Centre, Faber, 1939.
Selected Poems, Random House, 1940.

I Sit by the Window, Linden Press, c. 1940.
Ruins and Visions: Poems, 1934-1942, Random House, 1942.
Poems of Dedication, Random House, 1947.
Returning to Vienna, 1947: Nine Sketches, Banyan Press, 1947.
The Edge of Being, Random House, 1949.
Sirmione Peninsula, Faber, 1954.
Collected Poems, 1928-1953, Random House, 1955, reprinted, 1975, revised edition published as *Collected Poems, 1928-1985,* Faber, 1985.
Inscriptions, Poetry Book Society (London), 1958.
Selected Poems, Random House, 1964.
The Generous Days: Ten Poems, David Godine, 1969, enlarged edition published as *The Generous Days,* Faber, 1971.
Descartes, Steam Press (London), 1970.
Art Student, Poem-of-the-Month Club (London), 1970.
Recent Poems, Anvil Press Poetry (London), 1978.

PLAYS

Trial of a Judge: A Tragedy in Five Acts (first produced in London at Rupert Doone's Group Theatre on March 18, 1938), Random House, 1938.
(Translator and adapter with Goronwy Rees) *Danton's Death* (first produced in London, 1939; adaptation of a play by Georg Buechner), Faber, 1939.
"To the Island," first produced at Oxford University, 1951.
(Adapter) "Lulu" (adaptation from plays by Frank Wedekind; also see below), produced in New York, 1958.
(Translator and adapter) *Mary Stuart* (adaptation of a play by Johann Christoph Friedrich von Schiller; produced on the West End at Old Vic, 1961; produced on Broadway at Vivian Beaumont Theatre, November 11, 1971), Faber, 1959, reprinted, Ticknor & Fields, 1980.
(Translator and adapter) *The Oedipus Trilogy—King Oedipus, Oedipus at Colonos, Antigone: A Version by Stephen Spender* (three-act play; revision of play produced at Oxford Playhouse, 1983), Faber, 1985.

ESSAYS

The Destructive Element: A Study of Modern Writers and Beliefs, J. Cape, 1935, Houghton, 1936, reprinted, Folcroft, 1970.
Forward from Liberalism, Random House, 1937.
The New Realism: A Discussion, Hogarth, 1939, Folcroft, 1977.
Life and the Poet, Secker & Warburg, 1942, Folcroft, 1974.
European Witness, Reynal, 1946.
(Contributor) Richard H. Crossman, editor, *The God that Failed: Six Studies in Communism,* Harper, 1950.
Learning Laughter, Weidenfeld & Nicolson, 1952, Harcourt, 1953.
The Creative Element: A Study of Vision, Despair, and Orthodoxy among Some Modern Writers, Hamish Hamilton, 1953, Folcroft, 1973.
The Making of a Poem, Hamish Hamilton, 1955, Norton, 1962.
The Imagination in the Modern World: Three Lectures, Library of Congress, 1962.
The Struggle of the Modern, University of California Press, 1963.
Chaos and Control in Poetry, Library of Congress, 1966.
The Year of the Young Rebels, Random House, 1969.
Love-Hate Relations: A Study of Anglo-American Sensibilities, Random House, 1974.
Eliot, Fontana, 1975, published as *T. S. Eliot,* Viking, 1976.
Henry Moore: Sculptures in Landscape, Studio Vista (London), 1978, C. N. Potter, 1979.
The Thirties and After: Poetry, Politics, People, 1933-1970, Random House, 1978.
(Contributor) *America Observed,* C. N. Potter, 1979.

(With David Hockney) *China Diary,* with illustrations by Hockney, Thames & Hudson, 1982.
In Irina's Garden with Henry Moore's Sculpture, Thames and Hudson, 1986.

EDITOR

W. H. Auden, *Poems,* privately printed, 1928.
(With Louis MacNeice) *Oxford Poetry 1929,* Basil Blackwell, 1929.
(With Bernard Spencer) *Oxford Poetry 1930,* Basil Blackwell, 1930.
(With John Lehmann and Christopher Isherwood) *New Writing, New Series I,* Hogarth, 1938.
(With Lehmann and Isherwood) *New Writing, New Series II,* Hogarth, 1939.
(With Lehmann and author of introduction) *Poems for Spain,* Hogarth, 1939.
Spiritual Exercises: To Cecil Day Lewis (poems), privately printed, 1943.
(And author of introduction) *A Choice of English Romantic Poetry,* Dial, 1947, reprinted, Books for Libraries Press, 1969.
(And author of introduction) Walt Whitman, *Selected Poems,* Grey Walls Press (London), 1950.
Martin Huerlimann, *Europe in Photographs,* Thames & Hudson, 1951.
(With Elizabeth Jennings and Dannie Abbse) *New Poems 1956: An Anthology,* M. Joseph, 1956.
(And author of introduction) *Great Writings of Goethe,* New American Library, 1958.
(And author of introduction) *Great German Short Stories,* Dell, 1960.
(And author of introduction) *The Writer's Dilemma,* Oxford University Press, 1961.
(With Irving Kristol and Melvin J. Lasky) *Encounters: An Anthology from the First Ten Years of "Encounter" Magazine,* Basic Books, 1963.
(With Donald Hall) *The Concise Encyclopedia of English and American Poets and Poetry,* Hawthorn, 1963, revised edition, Hutchinson, 1970.
(And author of introduction) *A Choice of Shelley's Verse,* Faber, 1971.
(And author of introduction) *Selected Poems of Abba Kovne* [and] *Selected Poems of Nelly Sachs,* Penguin, 1971.
The Poems of Percy Bysshe Shelley, Limited Editions Club (Cambridge), 1971.
D. H. Lawrence: Novelist, Poet, Prophet, Harper, 1973.
W. H. Auden: A Tribute, Macmillan (New York), 1975.

TRANSLATOR

(And author of introduction and, with J. B. Leishman, commentary) Rainer Maria Rilke, *Duino Elegies* (bilingual edition), Norton, 1939, 4th edition, revised, Hogarth, 1963.
(With Hugh Hunt) Ernst Toller, *Pastor Hall* (three-act play; also see below), John Lane, 1939.
(With Hunt) Toller, *Pastor Hall* (bound with *Blind Man's Buff* by Toller and Denis Johnson), Random House, 1939.
(With J. L. Gili) Federico Garcia Lorca, *Poems,* Oxford University Press (New York), 1939.
(With Gili) *Selected Poems of Federico Garcia Lorca,* Hogarth, 1943.
(With Frances Cornford) Paul Eluard, *Le Dur desir de Durer,* Grey Falcon Press, 1950.
(And author of introduction) Rilke, *The Life of the Virgin Mary (Das Marien-Leben)* (bilingual edition), Philosophical Library, 1951.

(With Frances Fawcett) Wedekind, *Five Tragedies of Sex,* Theatre Arts, 1952.

(With Nikos Stangos) C. P. Cavafy, *Fourteen Poems,* Editions Electo, 1977.

Wedekind, *Lulu Plays and Other Sex Tragedies,* Riverrun, 1979.

OTHER

The Burning Cactus (short stories), Random House, 1936, reprinted, Books for Libraries Press, 1971.

The Backward Son (novel), Hogarth, 1940.

(With William Sansom and James Gordon) *Jim Braidy: The Story of Britain's Firemen,* Lindsay Drummond, 1943.

(Author of introduction and notes) *Botticelli,* Faber, 1945, Pitman, 1948.

(Author of introduction) Patrice de la Tour du Pin, *The Dedicated Life in Poetry* [and] *The Correspondence of Laurent de Cayeux,* Harvill Press, 1948.

World Within World: The Autobiography of Stephen Spender, Harcourt, 1951.

Engaged in Writing, and The Fool and the Princess (short stories), Farrar, Straus, 1958.

(With Nicholas Nabokov) *Rasputin's End* (opera), Ricordi (Milan), 1963.

(Contributor with Patrick Leigh Fermor) *Ghika: Paintings, Drawings, Sculpture,* Lund, Humphries, 1964, Boston Book and Art Shop, 1965.

(Reteller) *The Magic Flute: Retold* (juvenile; based on the opera by Mozart), Putnam, 1966.

(Author of introduction) *Venice,* Vendome, 1979.

Letters to Christopher: Stephen Spender's Letters to Christopher Isherwood, 1929-1939, with "The Line of the Branch"—Two Thirties Journals, Black Sparrow, 1980.

(Author of introduction) *Herbert List: Photographs, 1930-1970,* Thames & Hudson, 1981.

(Contributor) Martin Friedman, *Hockney Paints the Stage,* Abbeville Press, 1983.

The Journals of Stephen Spender, 1939-1983, Random House, 1986.

The Temple (novel), Grove, 1988.

Contributor to numerous anthologies. Editor, with Cyril Connolly, of *Horizon,* 1939-41; co-editor, with Melvin J. Lasky, 1953-66, and corresponding editor, 1966-67, *Encounter;* co-founder of *Index on Censorship* (bimonthly magazine).

SIDELIGHTS: Stephen Spender is the last surviving member of the generation of British poets who came to prominence in the 1930s, a group that included W. H. Auden, Christopher Isherwood, D. Day Lewis, and Louis MacNeice. In *World within World: The Autobiography of Stephen Spender* the author speculates that the names of the members of the group became irreversibly linked in the minds of critics for no other reason other than having their poems included in the same important poetic anthologies of the early thirties. However, in *The Angry Young Men of the Thirties* Elton Edward Smith finds that the poets had much more in common and states that they shared a "similarity of theme, image, and diction." According to Smith, the poets also all rejected the writing of the immediately preceding generation. Gerald Nicosia reaches the same conclusion in his *Chicago Tribune Book World* essay on Spender's work. "While preserving a reverence for traditional values and a high standard of craftsmanship," Nicosia writes, "they turned away from the esotericism of T. S. Eliot, insisting that the writer stay in touch with the urgent political issues of the day and that he speak in a voice whose clarity can be understood by all." Comparing the older and younger generations of writers, Smith notes that while

the poets of the 1920s focused on themes removed from reality, "the poets of the 1930s represented a return to the objective world outside and the recognition of the importance of the things men do together in groups: political action, social structure, cultural development."

Spender's name is most frequently associated with that of W. H. Auden, perhaps the most famous poet of the thirties; yet some critics, including Alfred Kazin and Helen Vendler, find the two poets dissimilar in many areas. In the *New Yorker,* for example, Vendler observes that "at first [Spender] imitated Auden's self-possessed ironies, his determined use of technological objects. . . . But no two poets can have been more different. Auden's rigid, brilliant, peremptory, categorizing, allegorical mind demanded forms altogether different from Spender's dreamy, liquid, guilty, hovering sensibility. Auden is a poet of firmly historical time, Spender of timeless nostalgic space." In the *New York Times Book Review* Kazin similarly concludes that Spender "was mistakenly identified with Auden. Although they were virtual opposites in personality and in the direction of their talents, they became famous at the same time as 'pylon poets'— among the first to put England's gritty industrial landscape of the 1930's into poetry."

The term "pylon poets" refers to "The Pylons," a poem by Spender which many critics describe as typical of the Auden generation. The much-anthologized work, included in one of Spender's earliest collections, *Poems,* as well as in his compilation of a lifetime's accomplishments, *Collected Poems, 1928-1985,* is characteristic of the group's imagery and also reflects the political and social concerns of its members. Smith recognizes that in such a poem "the poet, instead of closing his eyes to the hideous steel towers of a rural electrification system and concentrating on the soft green fields, glorifies the pylons and grants to them the future. And the nonhuman structure proves to be of the very highest social value, for rural electrification programs help create a new world of human equality."

The decade of the thirties was marked by turbulent events that would shape the course of history: the world-wide economic depression, the Spanish Civil War, and the beginnings of the Second World War. Seeing the established world crumbling around them, the writers of the period sought to create a new reality to replace the old which in their minds had become obsolete. According to D. E. S. Maxwell, commenting in his *Poets of the Thirties,* "the imaginative writing of the thirties created an unusual *milieu* of urban squalor and political intrigue. This kind of statement—a suggestion of decay producing violence and leading to change—as much as any absolute and unanimous political partisanship gave this poetry its marxist reputation. Communism and 'the communist' (a poster-type stock figure) were frequently invoked." For a time Spender, like many young intellectuals of the era, was a member of the Communist party. "Spender believed," Smith notes, "that communism offered the only workable analysis and solution of complex world problems, that it was sure eventually to win, and that for significance and relevance the artist must somehow link his art to the Communist diagnosis." Smith describes Spender's poem, "The Funeral" (included in *Collected Poems: 1928-1953* but omitted from the 1985 revision of the same work), as "a Communist elegy" and observes that much of Spender's other works from the same early period as "The Funeral," including his play, "Trial of a Judge," his poems from *Vienna,* and his essays in *The Destructive Element: A Study of Modern Writers and Beliefs* and *Forward from Liberalism* deal with the Communist question.

Washington Post Book World contributor Monroe K. Spears finds "The Funeral," one of Spender's least successful poems, but, nevertheless acknowledges that it reveals some of the same characteristics of the poet as his better work: "an ardent idealism, an earnest dedication that leaves him vulnerable in his sympathy for the deprived and exploited, his hopes for a better world, [and] his reverence for greatness and heroism, especially in art." Critics note that Spender's attitudes, developed in the thirties, have continued to influence the poet throughout his life. As Peter Stansky points out in the *New Republic:* "The 1930s were a shaping time for Spender, casting a long shadow over all that came after. . . . It would seem that the rest of his life, even more than he may realize, has been a matter of coming to terms with the 1930s, and the conflicting claims of literature and politics as he knew them in that decade of achievement, fame, and disillusion." Stansky also observes, as do other reviewers, that Spender is at his best when he is writing autobiography. The poet himself seems to point out the truth in this statement when he writes in the postscript to *Thirties and After: Poetry, Politics, People, 1933-1970:* "I myself am, it is only too clear, an autobiographer. Autobiography provides the line of continuity in my work. I am not someone who can shed or disclaim his past."

The past has often become the subject of Spender's recent writing. His books of the eighties—particularly *The Journals of Stephen Spender, 1939-1983, Collected Poems, 1928-1985,* and *Letters to Christopher: Stephen Spender's Letters to Christopher Isherwood, 1929-1939, with "The Line of the Branch"—Two Thirties Journals*—place a special emphasis on autobiographical material that reviewers find reveal Spender as both an admirable personality and a notable writer. In a *New York Times Book Review* commentary by Samuel Hynes on the collection of Spender's letters, for instance, the critic expresses his belief that "the person who emerges from these letters is neither a madman nor a fool, but an honest, intelligent, troubled young man, groping toward maturity in a troubled time. And the author of the journals is something more; he is a writer of sensitivity and power." Discussing the same volume in the *Times Literary Supplement* Philip Gardener notes, "If, since the war, Spender's creative engine has run at less than full power, one remains grateful for his best work, the context of which is fascinatingly provided by these letters and journals." "Some of Spender's poems, criticism, memoirs, translations have contributed to the formation of a period, which to some extent, they now represent . . . ," Robert Craft observes in his *New York Review of Books* critique of *The Journals of Stephen Spender, 1939-1983.* "Yet Spender himself stands taller than his work. The least insular writer of his generation and the most generous, he is a kinder man—*hypocrite lecteur!*—than most of us deserve."

Collections of Spender's papers can be found at Northwestern University in Evanston, Illinois, and in the Bancroft Library at the University of California at Berkeley.

BIOGRAPHICAL/CRITICAL SOURCES:

BOOKS

Contemporary Literary Criticism, Gale, Volume 1, 1973, Volume 2, 1974, Volume 5, 1976, Volume 10, 1979, Volume 41, 1987.
Dictionary of Literary Biography, Volume 20: *British Poets, 1914-1945,* Gale, 1983.
Maxwell, D. E. S., *Poets of the Thirties,* Barnes & Noble, 1969.
Smith, Elton Edmund, *The Angry Young Men of the Thirties,* Southern Illinois University Press, 1975.
Spender, Stephen, *World Within World: The Autobiography of Stephen Spender,* Harcourt, 1951.

Spender, Stephen, *The Thirties and After: Poetry, Politics, People, 1933-1970,* Random House, 1978.

PERIODICALS

Chicago Tribune Book World, January 12, 1986.
New Republic, September 23, 1978.
New Yorker, November 10, 1986.
New York Review of Books, January 25, 1979, April 24, 1986.
New York Times Book Review, February 1, 1981, January 26, 1986.
Times Literary Supplement, April 17, 1981.
Washington Post Book World, January 12, 1986.

—*Sidelights by Marian Gonsior*

*   *   *

SPILLANE, Frank Morrison 1918-
(Mickey Spillane)

PERSONAL: Born March 9, 1918, in Brooklyn, N.Y.; son of John Joseph (a bartender) and Catherine Anne Spillane; married Mary Ann Pearce, 1945 (divorced); married Sherri Malinou, November, 1965 (divorced); married Jane Rodgers Johnson, October, 1983; children: (first marriage) Kathy, Mark, Mike, Carolyn; (third marriage; stepdaughters) Britt, Lisa. *Education:* Attended Kansas State College (now University). *Religion:* Converted to Jehovah's Witnesses in 1952.

ADDRESSES: Home—Murrells Inlet, Myrtle Beach, S.C.; and 225 East 57th St., New York, N.Y. 10022.

CAREER: Writer of mystery and detective novels, short stories, books for children, comic books, and scripts for television and films. Spillane, with producer Robert Fellows, formed an independent film company in Nashville, Tenn., called Spillane-Fellows Productions, which filmed features and television productions, 1969. Creator of television series "Mike Hammer," 1984-87. Actor; has appeared in over 110 commercials for Miller Lite Beer. *Military service:* U.S. Army Air Forces; taught cadets and flew fighter missions during World War II; became captain.

AWARDS, HONORS: Junior Literary Guild Award, 1979, for *The Day the Sea Rolled Back.*

WRITINGS:

UNDER NAME MICKEY SPILLANE; MYSTERY NOVELS

I, the Jury (also see below), Dutton, 1947, reprinted, New American Library, 1973.
Vengeance Is Mine! (also see below), Dutton, 1950.
My Gun Is Quick (also see below), Dutton, 1950, reprinted, Signet, 1988.
The Big Kill (also see below), Dutton, 1951, reprinted, New English Library, 1984.
One Lonely Night, Dutton, 1951, reprinted, New English Library, 1987.
The Long Wait, Dutton, 1951, reprinted, New American Library, 1972.
Kiss Me, Deadly (also see below), Dutton, 1952.
The Deep, Dutton, 1961.
The Girl Hunters (also see below), Dutton, 1962.
Day of the Guns, Dutton, 1964, reprinted, New American Library, 1981.
The Snake, Dutton, 1964.
Bloody Sunrise, Dutton, 1965.
The Death Dealers, Dutton, 1965, reprinted, New American Library, 1981.

The Twisted Thing, Dutton, 1966, published as *For Whom the Gods Would Destroy,* New American Library, 1971.
The By-Pass Control, Dutton, 1967.
The Delta Factor, Dutton, 1967.
Body Lovers, New American Library, 1967.
Killer Mine, New American Library, 1968.
Me, Hood!, New American Library, 1969.
Survival: Zero, Dutton, 1970.
Tough Guys, New American Library, 1970.
The Erection Set, Dutton, 1972.
The Last Cop Out, New American Library, 1973.
The Flier, Corgi, 1973.
Mickey Spillane: Five Complete Mike Hammer Novels (contains *I, the Jury, Vengeance Is Mine!, My Gun Is Quick, The Big Kill,* and *Kiss Me, Deadly*), Avenel Books, 1987.
The Killing Man, Dutton, 1989.

Also author of *Return of the Hood.*

OTHER

"The Girl Hunters" (screenplay; based on Spillane's novel of the same title and starring Spillane in role of Mike Hammer), Colorama Features, 1963.
The Day the Sea Rolled Back (children's book), Windmill Books, 1979.
The Ship That Never Was (children's book), Bantam, 1982.
Tomorrow I Die (short stories), Mysterious Press, 1984.

Also author of *The Shrinking Island.* Creator and writer of comic books. Author of several television and movie screenplays. Contributor of short stories to magazines.

SIDELIGHTS: Mickey Spillane started his writing career in the early 1940s scripting comic books for Funnies, Inc. Spillane made the switch from comic books to novels in 1946 when, needing one thousand dollars to buy a parcel of land, he decided the easiest and quickest way to earn the money was to write a novel. Three weeks later, he sent the finished manuscript of *I, the Jury* to Dutton. Although the editorial committee questioned its good taste and literary merit, they felt the book would sell. *I, the Jury* did indeed sell—well over twelve million copies have been sold to date. In addition to buying the property, Spillane was able to construct a house on the site as well. This book would be the start of a long and prolific career that would make Spillane famous, wealthy, and a personality in his own right.

Spillane described himself to Margaret Kirk in the *Chicago Tribune* in this manner: "I'm a money writer, I write when I need money. And I'm not writing for the critics. I'm writing for the public. An author would never do that. They write one book, they think they're set. I'll tell you when you're a good writer. When you're successful. I'd write like Thomas Wolfe if I thought it would sell."

Not only did *I, the Jury* introduce Spillane to the book buying public, but it also gave birth to the character Mike Hammer, a 6-foot, 190-pound, rough and tough private investigator. Spillane's next several novels recorded the action-packed adventures of Hammer as he drank, fought, and killed his way through solving mystery after mystery. While Hammer is not featured in all of Spillane's mysteries, he is undoubtedly the most popular of Spillane's leading men. Art Harris describes Hammer in the *Washington Post:* "There was no one like Hammer. Sam Spade was tame. Never before had a private eye spilled blood on such a vast scale. He shot quick, punched hard, fought off beautiful women and always got the bad guys. Mobsters got it. Commies got it. And if a woman deserved it, well, she got it, too."

Spillane's audience has been very loyal to his Hammer character and his other mystery novels. During his more than forty year career, over 180 million copies of his books have been sold in over sixteen languages. Seven of his books are still listed among the top fifteen all-time fiction best sellers published in the last fifty years. "I'm the most translated writer in the world, behind Lenin, Tolstoy, Gorki, and Jules Verne," Spillane said to Harris. "And they're all dead." Spillane went on to declare: "I have no fans. You know what I got? Customers. And customers are your friends."

Although his first eight novels sold very well most reviewers dismissed his work, calling it mindless as well as much too violent and too sexual. For example, a critic for the *Saturday Review* describes *I, the Jury* as the prototype for future Spillane novels with its "lurid action, lurid characters, lurid plot, lurid finish." And Newgate Callendar explains in the *New York Times Book Review* that "the usual Spillane mix [is a mix of] sex, sadism, assorted fun and games with gun and fist."

"Spillane is like eating takeout fried chicken: so much fun to consume, but you can feel those lowlife grease-induced zits rising before you've finished the first drumstick," notes Sally Eckhoff in the *Voice Literary Supplement.* "*My Gun Is Quick* is just the book to have with you on a Hamptons weekend or a stint at an exclusive art colony where everybody else is reading Huysmans. Guaranteed they leave you alone. But don't try to slide into *Me, Hood* unless you want to permanently transform yourself into a snarling closet crimebuster. Any more of those seamed stockings, pawnshops, and stereotypical Irish gumshoes, and you'll be screaming for a Bergman movie to break your trance." In his 1951 review of *The Big Kill, New York Times* writer Anthony Boucher comments: "As rife with sexuality and sadism as any of his novels, based on a complete misunderstanding of law and on the wildest coincidence in detective fiction, it still can boast the absence of the hypocritical 'crusading' sentiments of Mike Hammer. For that reason, and for some slight ingenuity in its denouement, it may rank as the best Spillane—which is the faintest praise this department has ever bestowed."

In 1952, Spillane began a nine year break from writing mystery novels. Some people have attributed this hiatus to his religious conversion to the sect of Jehovah's Witnesses, while others feel that Spillane earned enough money from his writings and by selling the film rights to several of his books to live comfortably, enjoying life in his new beach home on Murrells Inlet located in Myrtle Beach, South Carolina. Although he stopped writing mysteries, Spillane wrote short stories for magazines and scripts for television and films. He also appeared on a number of television programs often performing in parodies of his tough detective characters.

Spillane reappeared on the publishing scene in 1961 with his murder mystery *The Deep* and in the following year Mike Hammer returned to fight crime in *The Girl Hunter.* The public was ecstatic—buying copies of the novel as soon as they were placed on the shelf. Reviewers seemed to soften their criticism somewhat at Hammer's return. For example, Boucher writes in his review of *The Girl Hunter* that "Spillane's rough tough Mike Hammer has been away for so long . . . that it's possible for even an old enemy of his, like me, to view him afresh and recognize that he does possess a certain genuine vigor and conviction lacking in his imitators."

Many of Spillane's later books also were somewhat praised by critics. For example, a reviewer for the *Times Literary Supplement* remarks: "Nasty as much of it is, [*The Deep*] has a genuine narrative grip; and there is a certain sociological conscience at work in the presentation of the street which has bred so much crime and an unusual perception in the portrait of an old Irish patrol officer." And Callendar comments in the *New York Times Book Review* that "editorials were written condemning [Spillane's novels], and preachers took to the pulpit. But things have changed, and one reads Spillane's . . . *The Erection Set* with almost a feeling of sentimental *deja vu.* The sex, sadism and assorted violence remain. Basically, what the Spillane books are about is the all-conquering hero myth. We all like to escape into a fantasy world to identify with the figure who is all-knowing, all-powerful, infinitely virile, sending off auras of threat in solar pulsations."

In 1979 Spillane's publisher dared him to write a children's book. A number of editors at the company felt he could never change his style of writing in order to appeal or be acceptable to a much younger, more impressionable audience. Not one to back down from a challenge, Spillane produced *The Day the Sea Rolled Back* and three years later, *The Ship that Never Was.* In general, reviewers have praised the books for their suspense and clean-cut high adventure. For example, a critic for the *Washington Post Book World* notes: "Yes, Mickey Spillane has written a kids' book, and quite an entertaining one too. As you might expect there's plenty of suspense, but violence is held in the wings; Spillane has trimmed his sails a bit for the young set."

In 1984 Spillane shared these thoughts with the *Washington Post:* "I'm 66. . . . If you're a singer, you lose your voice. A baseball player loses his arm. A writer gets more knowledge, and if he's good, the older he gets, the better he writes. They can't kill me. I still got potential."

MEDIA ADAPTATIONS: I, the Jury was filmed in 1953, *The Long Wait* in 1954, *Kiss Me, Deadly* in 1955, and *My Gun Is Quick* in 1957, all by United Artists; *The Delta Factor* was filmed in 1970 by Colorama Features; a remake of "I, the Jury" was filmed in 1981 by Twentieth Century-Fox. "Mickey Spillane's Mike Hammer," a television series based on Spillane's mystery novels and his character, Mike Hammer, was produced by Revue Productions, distributed by MCA-TV Ltd., and premiered in 1958; another television series based on Spillane's writings, "Mike Hammer," starring Stacey Keach, was produced and broadcasted from 1984-87.

BIOGRAPHICAL/CRITICAL SOURCES:

BOOKS

Contemporary Literary Criticism, Gale, Volume 3, 1975, Volume 13, 1980.

PERIODICALS

Books and Bookmen, September, 1967, June, 1969.
Chicago Tribune, April 18, 1986.
Chicago Tribune Magazine, April 8, 1984.
Christian Century, January 29, 1969.
Detroit Free Press, June 11, 1967, March 23, 1969.
Detroit News, September 14, 1967.
Globe and Mail (Toronto), December 23, 1989.
Los Angeles Times, March 26, 1989.
Los Angeles Times Book Review, January 14, 1990.
New York Times, November 11, 1951, October 26, 1952, June 14, 1989.
New York Times Book Review, October 14, 1962, February 27, 1966, August 13, 1967, February 27, 1972, May 20, 1973, October 15, 1989.
People, July 28, 1986.
Publishers Weekly, May 15, 1967.

Saturday Review, May 29, 1965, September 27, 1970, March 25, 1972, April 7, 1973.
Times Literary Supplement, November 10, 1961, September 19, 1980.
Tribune Books, November 26, 1989.
Voice Literary Supplement, July, 1988.
Washington Post, October 24, 1984.
Washington Post Book World, May 10, 1981.
Writer's Digest, September, 1976.

*   *   *

SPILLANE, Mickey
   See SPILLANE, Frank Morrison

*   *   *

SPOCK, Benjamin (McLane)   1903-

PERSONAL: Born May 2, 1903, in New Haven, Conn.; son of Benjamin Ives and Mildred Louise (Stoughton) Spock; married Jane Davenport Cheney, June 25, 1927 (marriage dissolved, 1975); married Mary Morgan, 1976; children: (first marriage) Michael, John Cheney; (second marriage) one stepdaughter. *Education:* Yale University, B.A., 1925; Yale Medical School, student, 1925-27; Columbia University, College of Physicians and Surgeons, 10022. M.D., 1929.

ADDRESSES: Office—Box N, Rogers, AR 72756.

CAREER: Presbyterian Hospital, New York City, intern in medicine, 1929-31; New York Nursery and Child's Hospital, service in pediatrics, 1931-32; New York Hospital, service in psychiatry, 1932-33, assistant attending pediatrician, 1933-47; practice in pediatrics, New York City, 1933-44 and 1946-47; Cornell University, Medical College, New York City, instructor in pediatrics, 1933-47; New York City Health Department, consultant in pediatric psychiatry, 1942-47; Mayo Clinic, Rochester, Minn., consultant in psychiatry, 1947-51; Mayo Foundation for Medical Education and Research, Rochester, associate professor of psychiatry, 1947-51; University of Pittsburgh, Pittsburgh, Pa., professor of child development, 1951-55; Western Reserve University (now Case Western Reserve University), Cleveland, Ohio, professor of child development, 1955-67. Lecturer and writer "for peace and justice." *Military service:* United States Naval Reserve, lieutenant commander, Medical Corps, 1944-46.

MEMBER: National Committee for a Sane Nuclear Policy (SANE), National Conference for a New Politics (NCNP; member of executive board, 1967—).

AWARDS, HONORS: Family Life Book Award, 1963, for *Problems of Parents;* Thomas Paine Award, National Emergency Civil Liberties Committee, 1968. Honorary degrees from University of Durham, Yale University, and University of Hartford.

WRITINGS:

The Common Sense Book of Baby and Child Care, Duell, Sloan & Pearce, 1946, published as *The Pocket Book of Baby and Child Care,* Pocket Books, 1949, 2nd edition published as *Baby and Child Care,* 1957, revised edition with Michael B. Rothenberg published as *Dr. Spock's Baby and Child Care: Fortieth Anniversary Edition,* Dutton, 1985.
(With John Reinhart) *A Baby's First Year,* Duell, Sloan, Pearce, 1955.
(With Miriam F. Lowenberg) *Feeding Your Baby and Child,* Duell, Sloan, Pearce, 1955.
Dr. Spock Talks with Mothers: Growth and Guidance, Houghton, 1961, reprinted, Greenwood Press, 1982.

On Being a Parent. . . of a Handicapped Child, National Society for Crippled Children and Adults (Chicago), 1961.

Problems of Parents, Houghton, 1962, reprinted, Greenwood Press, 1978.

Prejudice in Children: A Conversation with Dr. Spock, Anti-Defamation League of B'nai B'rith (New York), 1963.

(With M. O. Lerrigo) *Caring for Your Disabled Child,* Macmillan, 1965.

(With J. Darnell Barnard and Celia Stendler) *Macmillan Science Series* (science textbooks, grades 1-9; nine volumes), Books 1-6: *Science for Tomorrow's World,* Book 7: *Science: A Search for Evidence,* Book 8: *Science A Way to Solve Problems,* Book 9: *Science: A Key to the Future,* Macmillan, 1966—.

(With Mitchell Zimmerman) *Dr. Spock of Vietnam,* Dell, 1968.

Decent and Indecent: Our Personal and Political Behavior, McCalls Publishing, 1970, revised edition, Fawcett World Library, 1971.

A Teenager's Guide to Life and Love, Simon & Schuster, 1970 (published in England as *A Young Person's Guide to Life and Love,* Bodley Head, 1971).

Raising Children in a Difficult Time, Norton, 1974 (published in England as *Bringing Up Children in a Difficult Time,* Bodley Head).

Dr. Spock on Parenting: Sensible Advice from America's Most Trusted Child-Care Expert, Simon & Schuster, 1988.

Spock on Spock: A Memoir of Growing Up with the Century, edited by wife, Mary Morgan, Pantheon, 1989.

SOUND RECORDINGS

Women's Lib, Politics and Children (cassette) Encyclopedia Americana/CBS News Audio Resource Library, 1973.

(With Claude Steiner) *Children, Parents and Education,* Big Sur Recordings, 1975.

(With Steiner) *Power: Abuses and Uses,* Big Sur Recordings, 1975.

(With Steiner) *T.A. Demonstrations* (cassette), Big Sur Recordings, 1975.

(With Steiner) *Views on Political Movements* (cassette), Big Sur Recordings, 1975.

SIDELIGHTS: Twenty-eight million copies of *Dr. Spock's Baby and Child Care* have been sold since its first printing in 1946. It has been published in some thirty languages, including Catalan, Russian, and Urdu. *Baby and Child Care* has changed with the times. According to a *Parade* reviewer, the latest edition ". . . contains a section on working mothers, pays more attention to male participation in child-rearing, avoids sexual stereo-typing, even updates baby formulas." A *Washington Post* columnist agrees: "Spock has changed—somewhat. . . . He plans to keep recommending that infants receive constant parental care, but will no longer specify which parent should curtail his career to supply it. . . . He'll continue to state that sexual identity is necessary to mental health, but no longer suggest that it be reinforced through the selection of toys and clothes." Spock is, however, angered and appalled at the growing attitude that childraising is burdensome and unfullilling work. He told a *New York Times* reporter, "If our society can get it through its noodle that rearing children is exciting and creative work, we'll have accomplished something useful."

With regard to childrearing, many people blame Spock for the restlessness and rebellion in today's youth. *Newsweek* states: "It has been commonplace during the past couple of decades to speak of our children as the Spock Generation. . . . what we really seem to say when we speak of the Spock Generation is that

America's children have been nurtured indulgently and permissively." A three-year study of 1,000 students at the University of California, Berkeley and San Francisco State University was conducted by psychologists M. Brewster Smith, Norma Haan and Jeanne H. Block to test the relationship of parental guidance to social involvement and unrest. Many of the students involved in the study had been jailed for participation in demonstrations. According to *Newsweek* the psychologists found that those students actively involved in demonstrations "described their parents as being more permissive and less authoritarian than did the other, uninvolved students. These parents had a close relationship with their children and avoided imposing flat prohibitions and arbitrary punishments on them." Then the psychologists ". . . concluded—quite approvingly—'that the emergence of a dedicated spontaneous generation concerned with humanitarian values and personal authenticity is a triumph of Spockian philosophy.'"

Spock himself was involved in demonstrations against the Vietnam War and was indicted by a Federal Grand Jury on January 5, 1968, for conspiring to counsel American youths to avoid the draft. He was later acquitted on appeal of his case. When questioned about his involvement, Spock said, "What is the use of physicians like myself trying to help parents to bring up children, healthy and happy, to have them killed in such numbers for a cause that is ignoble?"

Reviewing *Decent and Indecent,* a *Time* reporter wrote: "Spock's most useful perception, perhaps, is his understanding that man in the 20th century has indulged in such an orgy of self-depreciation that he grows violent in self-revulsion. There is, mourns Spock, 'an unprecedented loss of belief in man's worthiness.' Art becomes grotesquerie, music a concert where the players splinter their instruments in a convulsion that suggests strychnine poisoning. 'This represents emotional regression all the way back to the one-to-two-year-old level,' Spock writes briskly, 'when the child in a spell of anger wants to antagonize and mess and destroy on a titanic scale.' What troubles the doctor is that such impulses escape the nursery; fathers and mothers, artists, politicians, scientists and generals—all of them go around breaking things. Medicine cannot cope with civilization as tantrum."

BIOGRAPHICAL/CRITICAL SOURCES:

BOOKS

Bloom, Lynn Z., *Dr. Spock: Biography of a Conservative Radical,* Bobbs-Merrill, 1972.

Mitford, Jessica, *The Trial of Dr. Spock,* Knopf, 1969.

PERIODICALS

Best Sellers, January 15, 1971.
Christian Century, October 22, 1969.
Detroit News, October 3, 1971, January 31, 1990.
Esquire, February, 1969, May, 1970, December, 1983.
Harper's, May, 1968.
L'Express, September, 1970.
Life, May 17, 1968, September 12, 1969.
Los Angeles Times, November 3, 1989, November 22, 1989.
Nation, March 11, 1968, October 13, 1969.
National Observer, June 17, 1968, July 2, 1968.
New Republic, February 7, 1970.
Newsweek, September 23, 1968, September 15, 1969, February 2, 1970, May 3, 1976, July 3, 1978, March 4, 1985.
New York Times, December 14, 1968, August 6, 1969, January 28, 1970, November 3, 1970, March 1, 1985, December 30, 1989.

New York Times Book Review, February 16, 1969, March 15, 1970, November 5, 1989.
Parade, March 14, 1976.
People, May 13, 1985.
Publishers Weekly, November 2, 1984.
Time, February 16, 1970, November 16, 1970, April 8, 1985.
Times (London), May 2, 1988.
Village Voice, April 25, 1968.
Washington Post, September 24, 1971, December 4, 1971, October 22, 1989, November 27, 1989.

*   *   *

STACY, Donald
See POHL, Frederik

*   *   *

STAFFORD, Jean   1915-1979

PERSONAL: Born July 1, 1915, in Covina, Calif.; died March 26, 1979, in White Plains, N.Y.; buried in Greenriver Cemetery, East Hampton, N.Y.; daughter of John Richard (a writer of westerns under pseudonym Jack Wonder) and Mary (McKillop) Stafford; married Robert Lowell (a Pulitzer Prize winning poet), April 2, 1940 (divorced, 1948); married Oliver Jensen (a writer), January 28, 1950 (divorced, 1953); married A. J. Liebling (a columnist for the *New Yorker*), April, 1959 (died, 1963). *Education:* University of Colorado, B.A. and M.A., 1936; Heidelberg University, additional study, 1936-37. *Politics:* Democrat.

ADDRESSES: Agent—James Oliver Brown Associates, Inc., 25 West 43rd St., New York, N.Y. 10031.

CAREER: Novelist and short story writer. Instructor, Stephens College, Columbia, Mo., 1937-38; lecturer, Queens College (now Queens College of the City University of New York), 1945; adjunct professor, Columbia University, 1967-69. Secretary, *Southern Review,* 1940-41. Fellow, Center for Advanced Studies, Wesleyan University, 1964-65.

MEMBER: Cosmopolitan Club (New York).

AWARDS, HONORS: Mademoiselle's merit award, 1944; National Institute of Arts and Letters grant in literature, 1945; Guggenheim fellowships in Fiction, 1945, 1948; National Press Club Award, 1948; O. Henry Memorial Award, 1955, for best short story of the year; Ingram-Merrill grant, 1969; Chapelbrook grant, 1969; Pulitzer Prize, 1970, for *The Collected Stories of Jean Stafford.*

WRITINGS:

Boston Adventure (novel), Harcourt, 1944, reprinted, 1967.
The Mountain Lion (novel), Harcourt, 1947, reprinted, University of New Mexico Press, 1977.
The Catherine Wheel (novel), Harcourt, 1952, reprinted, Ecco Press, 1981.
Children Are Bored on Sunday (short stories), Harcourt, 1953.
(With others) *New Short Novels,* Ballantine, 1954.
(With others) *Stories,* Farrar, Straus, 1956.
Elphi: The Cat with the High I.Q. (juvenile), Farrar, Straus, 1962.
(Editor and author of introduction) *The Lion and the Carpenter* (juvenile), Macmillan, 1962.
Bad Characters (short stories), Farrar, Straus, 1966.
A Mother in History (based on interviews with the mother of Lee Harvey Oswald), Farrar, Straus, 1966.
The Collected Stories of Jean Stafford, Farrar, Straus, 1969.

Also author of an unfinished novel. Contributor of articles and stories to *New Yorker, Vogue, Harper's, Mademoiselle, Holiday, Horizon, Reporter, New Republic,* and other magazines.

SIDELIGHTS: Jean Stafford was a writer of traditionally structured and painstakingly crafted novels and short stories. H. M. Jones wrote in the *Saturday Review* that "there is no sentence in [*Children Are Bored on Sunday*] which does not have its clean, precise line. Difficult ideas are stated with effortless ease, the difficulty of the idea not being a metaphysical difficulty but a difficulty of conveying to the reader the impression made upon some problematical personality by a particular human situation."

Jones also appreciated Stafford's neat, crisp style, and he once wrote in a review that "Stafford writes with brilliance. Scene after scene is told with unforgettable care and tenuous entanglements are treated with wise subtlety. She creates a splendid sense of time, of the unending afternoons of youth, and of the actual color of noon and of night." And Thomas Lask wrote in an article in the *New York Times* that he felt "Jean Stafford can teach almost anything one could want to know about swiftly and deftly developing characters balancing them in delicate counterpoint or wrenching conflict, and probing their thoughts and emotions." Once acknowledging that each novel and short story was a much deliberated literary project, Stafford told an interviewer: "I am a rather slow person, in that experience has to sink in for years before I can use it. . . . I have to let impressions and experience age within me."

Although her first three books were novels and were generally well received, critics seemed much more impressed and enthusiastic with Stafford's short stories. As *Dictionary of Literary Biography* contributor Jeanette Mann pointed out: "Stafford works within the traditional forms of Chekhov and James in her short fiction. Some critics believe that this form is more compatible to her than is that of the novel. In each story she creates a moment of experience, through the use of realistic settings, characters, and dialogues, so as to present, often through the device of dramatic irony, the sudden illumination of understanding, the symbolic crisis, or the unresolved glimpse into the heart of the situation. She relies heavily upon the use of the symbolic object and often uses it to reflect changes and development within the characters." It might be this effective use of the short story genre that won Stafford the reputation of being an extremely gifted and sensitive author, reflecting what many readers feel was "a sympathetic yet ultimately bleak vision of alienation and innocence."

However, Eleanor Perry does not agree that Stafford's reputation for sensitivity is well deserved. Illustrating that Stafford's characterization shows a possible lack of sensitivity, and definitely a lack of depth, Perry wrote: "No fault can be found with Miss Stafford's talents, but what happens as one reads one story after another is that a nagging, sometimes boring, similarity surrounds her 'good' characters. They are all weak, defenseless, long-suffering. They rarely act upon or even interact much with their enemies. They suffer from a paralysis of will, they are vitiated by guilt."

Many critics feel that her reputation of sensitivity also encompasses her reflection of the "feminine mind." One such critic, Pete Axthelm, felt that "Stafford is one of a group of modern female writers who share an intensely introspective, feminine, sensibility. . . . She has explored obscure and intriguing corners of the feminine mind within the fairly conventional framework of the modern short story."

Several critics have written that this special sensitivity is reflected especially in her book *A Mother in History,* which was the result of a three-day interview with Marguerite Oswald, the mother of Lee Harvey Oswald. Lask wrote that "the character and psychology of that woman, who sought the spotlight and who felt that not enough had been made of her, were as vividly captured as anything in Miss Stafford's fiction." Marya Mannes wrote in *Book Week* that Stafford let Mrs. Oswald speak for herself. "There Jean Stafford's great skill is manifest in the brief interpolations, between Mrs. Oswald's copious stream, in which [Stafford] manages to convey the trauma of her own involvement with this woman without ever raising her voice. . . . Certainly, *A Mother in History* could be nothing less than a shocking account; an aversion to Marguerite Oswald on the basis of her past behaviour and continuing greediness for attention is understandable. What is disturbing is that so many readers should have construed this report as a tasteless 'expose.'. . . This small book is a triumph of control not only over material but over the writer's emotions."

BIOGRAPHICAL/CRITICAL SOURCES:

BOOKS

Breit, Harvey, editor, *The Writer Observed,* World Publishing, 1956.
Contemporary Literary Criticism, Gale, Volume 4, 1975, Volume 7, 1977, Volume 19, 1981.
Dictionary of Literary Biography, Volume 2: *American Novelists since World War II,* Gale, 1978.

PERIODICALS

Book Week, October 11, 1964.
Critique, spring, 1962.
New Republic, October 31, 1964.
Newsweek, April 9,1979.
New York Times, March 28, 1979.
New York Times Book Review, October 11, 1964, February 16, 1969.
Saturday Review, May 9, 1953.
Saturday Review of Literature, March 1, 1947.
Time, April 9, 1979.
Washington Post, March 29, 1979.
Western Review, spring, 1955.

*   *   *

STAINES, Trevor
See BRUNNER, John (Kilian Houston)

*   *   *

STAUNTON, Schuyler
See BAUM, L(yman) Frank

*   *   *

STEAD, Christina (Ellen)   1902-1983

PERSONAL: Born July 17, 1902, in Rockdale, Sydney, New South Wales, Australia; died March 31, 1983, in Sydney, Australia; daughter of David George (a naturalist) and Ellen (Butters) Stead; married William James Blake, 1952 (an author; surname originally Blech; died, 1968). *Education:* Attended Teachers' College, Sydney University, received teacher's certification.

ADDRESSES: Home—Sydney, Australia. *Agent*—Joan Daves, 59 East 54th St., New York, NY 10022.

CAREER: Novelist, short story writer, editor, and translator. Worked as a public school teacher, a teacher of abnormal chil-

dren, and a demonstrator in the psychology laboratory of Sydney University, all in Australia; grain company clerk, London, England, 1928-29; bank clerk in Paris, France, 1930-35; lived in the United States during the late 1930s and 1940s; senior writer for Metro-Goldwyn-Mayer, 1943; instructor in Workshop in the Novel, New York University, 1943-44; lived in Surbiton, England, from 1953 to 1968; permanently returned to Australia, 1974.

AWARDS, HONORS: Aga Khan Prize, *Paris Review,* 1966; Arts Council of Great Britain grant, 1967; fellow in creative arts, 1969, emeritus fellow, 1981-82, both from Australian National University at Canberra; first recipient of Patrick White Award, 1974; honorary member, American Academy and Institute of Arts and Letters, 1982; Victorian Fellowship, Australian Writers Awards, 1986, for *Ocean of Story;* Premiere's Award for Literature, Premiere of New South Wales, Australia; several times nominated for the Nobel Prize.

WRITINGS:

NOVELS

Seven Poor Men of Sydney, Appleton, 1935.
The Beauties and Furies, Appleton, 1936.
House of All Nations, Simon & Schuster, 1938.
The Man Who Loved Children, Simon & Schuster, 1940, reprinted with introduction by Randall Jarrell, Holt, 1965.
For Love Alone, Harcourt, 1944.
Letty Fox: Her Luck, Harcourt, 1946.
A Little Tea, a Little Chat, Harcourt, 1948.
The People with the Dogs, Little, Brown, 1952.
Dark Places of the Heart, Holt, 1966 (published in England as *Cotters' England,* Secker & Warburg, 1966).
The Little Hotel, Angus & Robertson, 1973, Holt, 1975.
Miss Herbert (the Suburban Wife), Random House, 1976.
I'm Dying Laughing: The Humorist, Holt, 1987.

STORIES

The Salzburg Tales, Appleton, 1934.
The Puzzleheaded Girl (four novellas), Holt, 1967.
Ocean of Story (uncollected stories), edited by R. G. Geering, Viking, 1986.

OTHER

(Contributor) *The Fairies Return,* P. Davies, 1934.
(Editor with husband, William J. Blake) *Modern Women in Love,* Dryden Press, 1946.
(Editor) *South Sea Stories,* Muller, 1955.
(Translator) Fernand Gigon, *Colour of Asia,* Muller, 1955.
(Translator) Jean Giltene, *The Candid Killer,* Muller, 1956.
(Translator) August Piccard, *In Balloon and Bathyscape,* Cassell, 1956.
A Christina Stead Reader, selected by Jean B. Read, Random House, 1978.

Contributor of short stories to *Southerly, Kenyon Review,* and *Saturday Evening Post,* and of reviews to various papers. Stead's novels have been translated into foreign languages.

WORK IN PROGRESS: Short stories.

SIDELIGHTS: Australian-born novelist and short story author Christina Stead—whose work went unregarded for a large part of her life—is considered by many critics to be one of the most gifted writers of the twentieth century. Her novel *The Man Who Loved Children,* which depicts a boisterous, often cruel family led by an idealist father, is generally regarded as her masterpiece—although when first published in 1940 it was both a critical and popular failure. For years, it led an underground existence, read and admired by the cognoscenti. In a 1965 reprint edition, Randall Jarrell proclaimed: "If I were asked to name a good book that we don't read but that people of the future will read, I'd answer, almost with confidence, *The Man Who Loved Children*." He goes on: "It seems to me as plainly good as *Crime and Punishment* and *Remembrance of Things Past* and *War and Peace* are plainly great. I call it a good book, but it is a better book, I think, than most of the novels people call great; perhaps it would be fairer to call it great. It has one quality that, ordinarily, only a great book has: it makes you a part of one family's immediate existence as no other book quite does. One reads the book, with an almost ecstatic pleasure of recognition. You get used to saying, 'Yes, that's the way it is'; and you say many times, but can never get used to saying, 'I didn't know *anybody* knew that. Henny, Sam, Louie, and the children are entirely real to the reader, and reality is rare in novels."

Critics praised Stead for her masterful and original depictions of characters, emotions, and atmosphere, yet she was also placed among writers of the nineteenth century. Christopher Ricks wrote: "In its sense of growth and of generations, in its generality and specificity, above all in the central place which it accords to feelings of indignation and embarrassment, *The Man Who Loved Children* is in the best tradition of the nineteenth-century novel. . . . Like George Meredith at his best, [Stead] is fascinated by the way we speak to ourselves in the privacy of our skulls, and she is able to remind us of what we would rather forget—that we are all continually employing, to ourselves and to others, a false rhetoric, overblown, indiscriminately theatrical, and yet indisputably ours." Ricks continued: "Everything in the book deserves notice. Its narrative skill; its sense of how much it matters to have money; its creation of locality (Washington, Baltimore); its pained insistence on the rights of women and children; its political acuteness, especially in its feeling for what underlies those people and those moments which protest that they are non-political; its presentation of a religious soft-soaping secularism: these are not extraneous but the fiber of the book." Eleanor Perry similarly remarked that the novel is "not a slice of life. It is life." Jose Yglesias proclaimed *The Man Who Loved Children* "a funny, painful, absorbing masterpiece, obviously the work of a major writer."

Jarrell wrote: "There is a bewitching rapidity and lack of self-consciousness about Christina Stead's writing; she has much knowledge, extraordinary abilities, but is too engrossed in what she is doing ever to seem conscious of them, so that they do not cut her off from the world but join her to it." Although best known for her achievements in *The Man Who Loved Children*, "in all her work, Stead displays a similar originality of concept, a brilliant, almost obsessive hold on subject and character and a headlong rush of language, more like a force of nature than a literary process, which is her unique signature," Helen Yglesias commented in the *Los Angeles Times Book Review*. The obituary writer for the London *Times* wrote that "in the end [Stead] did achieve a fame almost commensurate with her towering and always human achievement. She was one of the great originals, by whom it was almost impossible to be influenced." Yglesias called her "a master novelist of our time, for whom a resting place in the literature of the English language is assured."

BIOGRAPHICAL/CRITICAL SOURCES:

BOOKS

Contemporary Literary Criticism, Gale, Volume 4, 1975, Volume 5, 1976, Volume 8, 1978, Volume 32, 1985.
Geering, R. G., *Christina Stead*, Twayne, 1969.

PERIODICALS

Atlantic, March, 1965, June, 1965.
Book Week, April 18, 1965.
Chicago Tribune Book World, December 24, 1978.
Los Angeles Times, May 19, 1986.
Los Angeles Times Book Review, October 4, 1987, November 8, 1987.
Nation, April 5, 1965.
New York Review of Books, June 17, 1965.
New York Times Book Review, March 15, 1981, May 25, 1986.
Saturday Review, April 10, 1965.
Southerly (Sydney), 1962.
Times (London), January 12, 1985.
Times Literary Supplement, September 25, 1981, May 16, 1986, April 24, 1987.
Tribune Books (Chicago), October 4, 1987.
Washington Post Book World, May 25, 1986, December 20, 1987.

OBITUARIES:

PERIODICALS

New York Times, April 13, 1983.
Times (London), April 7, 1983.

*   *   *

STEEL, Danielle (Fernande) 1947-

PERSONAL: Born August 14, 1947, in New York, N.Y.; daughter of John and Norma (Stone) Schuelein-Steel; married third husband, John Traina; children: nine. *Education:* Educated in France; attended Parsons School of Design, 1963, and New York University, 1963-67.

ADDRESSES: Home—New York, N.Y. *Agent*—Morton L. Janklow Associates, Inc., 598 Madison Ave., New York, N.Y. 10022.

CAREER: Has worked as copywriter, Grey Advertising, San Francisco, 1973-74, and other positions in public relations and advertising; writer.

WRITINGS:

NOVELS

Going Home, Pocket Books, 1973.
Passion's Promise, Dell, 1977.
The Promise (based on a screenplay by Garry Michael White), Dell, 1978.
Now and Forever, Dell, 1978.
Season of Passion, Dell, 1979.
Summer's End, Dell, 1980.
The Ring, Delacorte, 1980.
Remembrance, Delacorte, 1981.
Palomino, Dell, 1981.
To Love Again, Dell, 1981.
Crossings, Delacorte, 1982.
Once in a Lifetime, Dell, 1982.
A Perfect Stranger, Dell, 1982.
Changes, Delacorte, 1983.
Thurston House, Dell, 1983.
Full Circle, Delacorte, 1984.
Secrets, Delacorte, 1985.
Family Album, Delacorte, 1985.
Wanderlust, Delacorte, 1986.
Fine Things, Delacorte, 1987.
Kaleidoscope, Delacorte, 1987.

Zoya, Delacorte, 1988.
Star, Delacorte, 1989.
Daddy, Delacorte, 1989.

JUVENILE

Loving (young adult novel), Dell, 1981.
Martha's Best Friend, Doubleday, 1989.
Martha's New Daddy, Doubleday, 1989.
Martha's New School, Doubleday, 1989.
Max and the Baby-Sitter, Doubleday, 1989.
Max's Daddy Goes to the Hospital, Doubleday, 1989.
Max's New Baby, Doubleday, 1989.

OTHER

Love Poems: Danielle Steel (poetry), Dell, 1981, abridged edition, Delacorte, 1984.
(Co-author) *Having a Baby* (nonfiction), Dell, 1984.

Contributor of articles and poetry to numerous periodicals, including *Viva, California Living, San Francisco, Good Housekeeping, McCall's, Ladies' Home Journal,* and *Cosmopolitan.*

WORK IN PROGRESS: More novels.

SIDELIGHTS: Introducing a review of Danielle Steel's *Family Album, Washington Post Book World* writer Susan Dooley states: "From *Pamela* to *Peyton Place,* there have been books that everyone reads. Sometimes they titillate while professing to teach, and sometimes they make no sense at all. They do not win literary prizes, serious readers ignore them, and they are as popular as potato chips." After producing a score of romance novels, which are generally dismissed by critics but almost always embraced by readers, Steel has distinguished herself as nothing less than "a publishing phenomenon," Jacqueline Briskin reports, adding in her *Los Angeles Times Book Review* article that according to industry figures, the author sold more than 13 million mass-market paperbacks in a two-year period.

Steel's fiction is peopled by women in powerful or glamorous positions; often they are forced to choose the priorities in their lives. Thus in *Changes* a New York anchorwoman who weds a Beverly Hills surgeon must decide whether her career means more to her than her long-distance marriage does. And while reviewers seldom express admiration for the style of romance novelists in general—*Chicago Tribune Book World* critic L. J. Davis claims that *Changes* is written in "the sort of basilisk prose that makes it impossible to tear your eyes from the page even as your brain is slowly [turning] to stone"—some reviewers, such as a *Detroit News* writer, find that the author's "flair for spinning colorful and textured plots out of raw material . . . is fun reading. The topic [of *Changes*] is timely and socially relevant." Toronto *Globe & Mail* contributor Peggy Hill similarly concludes about 1988's *Zoya:* "Steel has the ability to give such formula writing enough strength to not collapse into an exhausted state of cliche. *Zoya* is a fine example of that achievement."

MEDIA ADAPTATIONS: Now and Forever was adapted into a movie and released by Inter Planetary Pictures in 1983; *Crossings* was made into an ABC-TV miniseries in 1986; several of Steel's other novels have been optioned for television miniseries.

BIOGRAPHICAL/CRITICAL SOURCES:

BOOKS

Bestsellers '89, Issue 1, Gale, 1989.

PERIODICALS

Chicago Tribune Book World, August 28, 1983.

Detroit News, September 11, 1983.
Globe & Mail (Toronto), July 9, 1988.
Los Angeles Times, January 6, 1988.
Los Angeles Times Book Review, April 14, 1985.
New York Times Book Review, September 11, 1983, August 19, 1984, March 3, 1985.
Time, November 25, 1985.
Washington Post Book World, July 3, 1983, March 3, 1985.

*   *   *

STEGNER, Wallace (Earle)   1909-

PERSONAL: Born February 18, 1909, in Lake Mills, Iowa; son of George H. and Hilda (Paulson) Stegner; married Mary Stuart Page, September 1, 1934; children: Stuart Page. *Education:* University of Utah, B.A., 1930; additional study at University of California, 1932-33; State University of Iowa, M.A., 1932, Ph.D., 1935.

ADDRESSES: Home—13456 South Fork Lane, Los Altos Hills, Calif. 94022. *Agent*—Brandt & Brandt, 1501 Broadway, New York, N.Y. 10036.

CAREER: Augustana College, Rock Island, Ill., instructor, 1933-34; University of Utah, Salt Lake City, instructor, 1934-37; University of Wisconsin—Madison, instructor, 1937-39; Harvard University, Cambridge, Mass., Briggs-Copeland Instructor of Composition, 1939-45; Stanford University, Stanford, Calif., professor of English, 1945-69, Jackson Eli Reynolds Professor of Humanities, 1969-71, director of creative writing program, 1946-71; University of Toronto, Toronto, Ont., Bissell Professor of Canadian-U.S. Relations, 1975.

Writer in residence, American Academy in Rome, 1960; Phi Beta Kappa visiting scholar, 1960-61; Tanner Lecturer, University of Utah, 1980. Assistant to the Secretary of the Interior, 1961; National Parks Advisory Board, member, 1962-66, and chairman, 1965-66.

MEMBER: American Academy of Arts and Sciences, American Institute and Academy of Arts and Letters, American Antiquarian Society, Phi Beta Kappa.

AWARDS, HONORS: Little, Brown Prize, 1937, for *Remembering Laughter;* O. Henry Awards, 1942, 1950, and 1954; Houghton-Mifflin Life-in-America Award and Anisfield-Wolfe Award, both 1945, both for *One Nation;* Guggenheim fellow, 1949-51 and 1959; Rockefeller fellowship, 1950-51, to conduct seminars with writers throughout the Far East; Wenner-Gren Foundation grant, 1953; Center for Advanced Studies in the Behavioral Sciences fellow, 1955-56; D.Litt., University of Utah, 1968; D.F.A., University of California, 1969, and Utah State University, 1972; National Endowment for the Humanities senior fellow, 1972; Pulitzer Prize, 1972, for *Angle of Repose;* D.L., University of Saskatchewan, 1973; Western Literature Association Award, 1974; National Book Award for fiction, 1977, for *The Spectator Bird;* D.H.L., University of Santa Clara, 1979; Robert Kirsch Award for body of work, *Los Angeles Times,* 1980; Montgomery fellow, Dartmouth College, 1980; National Book Critics Circle Award nomination, 1987, for *Crossing to Safety;* has also received five Commonwealth Club medals.

WRITINGS:

NOVELS

Remembering Laughter, Little, Brown, 1937.
The Potter's House, Prairie Press, 1938.
On a Darkling Plain, Harcourt, 1940.
Fire and Ice, Duell, 1941.

The Big Rock Candy Mountain, Duell, 1943, reprinted, University of Nebraska Press, 1983.

Second Growth, Houghton, 1947, reprinted, University of Nebraska Press, 1985.

The Preacher and the Slave, Houghton, 1950, published as *Joe Hill: A Biographical Novel,* Doubleday, 1969.

A Shooting Star, Viking, 1961.

All the Little Live Things, Viking, 1967.

Angle of Repose, Doubleday, 1971.

The Spectator Bird, Doubleday, 1976.

Recapitulation, Doubleday, 1979.

Crossing to Safety, Random House, 1987.

COLLECTIONS

The Women on the Wall (stories), Houghton, 1948, reprinted, University of Nebraska Press, 1980.

The City of the Living and Other Stories, Houghton, 1956.

The Sound of Mountain Water: The Changing American West (essays), Doubleday, 1969, reprinted, University of Nebraska Press, 1985.

One Way to Spell Man (essays), Doubleday, 1982.

Collected Stories of Wallace Stegner, Random House, 1990.

EDITOR

(With others) *An Exposition Workshop: Readings in Modern Controversy,* Little, Brown, 1939.

(With others) *Readings for Citizens at War,* Harper, 1941.

(With Richard Scowcroft and Boris Ilyin) *The Writer's Art: A Collection of Short Stories,* Heath, 1950, reprinted, Greenwood Press, 1972.

This Is Dinosaur: Echo Park and Its Magic Rivers, Knopf, 1955, reprinted, Roberts, Rinehart, 1985.

J. W. Powell, *The Exploration of the Colorado River of the West,* University of Chicago Press, 1957.

(With wife, Mary Stegner) *Great American Short Stories,* Dell, 1957, reprinted, 1985.

Selected American Prose, 1841-1900: The Realistic Movement, Rinehart, 1958.

Samuel Clemens, *The Adventures of Huckleberry Finn,* Dell, 1960.

Bret Harte, *The Outcasts of Poker Flat,* New American Library, 1961.

Powell, *Report on the Lands of the Arid Region of the United States,* Harvard University Press, 1962.

(With others) *Modern Composition,* four volumes, Holt, 1964.

The American Novel: From James Fenimore Cooper to William Faulkner, Basic Books, 1965.

A. B. Guthrie, Jr., *The Big Sky,* Houghton, 1965.

(With Scowcroft) *Twenty Years of Stanford Short Stories,* Stanford University Press, 1966.

Nathaniel Hawthorne, *Twice-Told Tales,* Heritage Press, 1967.

The Letters of Bernard DeVoto, Doubleday, 1975.

Editor, with Scowcroft, of *Stanford Short Stories* (annual), Stanford University Press, 1946-68. West Coast editor, Houghton-Mifflin Co., 1945-53; editor in chief, *American West Magazine,* 1966-68.

OTHER

Mormon Country, Duell, 1941, reprinted, University of Nebraska Press, 1981.

(With the editors of *Look* magazine) *One Nation,* Houghton, 1945.

The Writer in America (lectures), Hokuseido Press (Tokyo), 1951, Folcroft Press, 1969.

Beyond the Hundredth Meridian: John Wesley Powell and the Second Opening of the West, Houghton, 1954, reprinted, University of Nebraska Press, 1982.

Wolf Willow: A History, a Story, and a Memory of the Last Plains Frontier, Viking, 1962, reprinted, University of Nebraska Press, 1980.

The Gathering of Zion: The Story of the Mormon Trail, McGraw, 1964, reprinted, Howe Brothers, 1982.

Teaching the Short Story, Department of English, University of California, Davis, 1965.

Discovery!: The Search for Arabian Oil, Middle East Export Press, 1971.

Variations on a Theme of Discontent, Utah State University Press, 1972.

Robert Frost and Bernard DeVoto, Association of the Stanford University Libraries, 1974.

The Uneasy Chair: A Biography of Bernard DeVoto, Doubleday, 1974.

(Author of foreword) Ansel Adams, *Images, 1923-1974,* New York Graphic Society, 1974.

(With son, Page Stegner, and Eliot Porter) *American Places,* Dutton, 1981.

(With Richard Etulain) *Conversations with Wallace Stegner on Western History and Literature,* University of Utah Press, 1983.

The American West As Living Space, University of Michigan Press, 1987.

On the Teaching of Creative Writing, edited by Edward C. Lathem, University Press of New England, 1989.

A Sense of Place (audio cassette), Tioga, 1989.

CONTRIBUTOR

Look at America: The Central Northwest, Houghton, 1947.

Edward R. Murrow, compiler, *This I Believe,* Simon & Schuster, 1952.

H. Mosley, editor, *The Romance of North America,* Houghton, 1958.

Alvin V. Josephy, editor, *American Heritage Book of Great Natural Wonders,* American Heritage Publishing, 1963.

Four Portraits and One Subject: Bernard DeVoto, Houghton, 1963.

R. E. Spiller and others, editors, *Literary History of the United States,* 3rd edition, Macmillan, 1963.

C. R. Anderson and others, editors, *American Literary Masters,* Holt, 1965.

Maurice Sheehy, editor, *Michael/Frank: Studies on Frank O'Connor,* Knopf, 1969.

Harold Hayes, editor, *The Best of California: Some People, Places, and Institutions of the Most Exciting State in the Nation, as Featured in California Magazine, 1976-86,* Borgo, 1988.

Contributor of short stories, essays, and articles to *Esquire, Vogue, Atlantic, Harper's, Saturday Review, Mademoiselle, New York Times Book Review, Virginia Quarterly Review, New Republic,* and other publications.

SIDELIGHTS: The American West has figured prominently in the writings of Wallace Stegner for five decades. He has written two major works on the history of the Mormons, a biography of Western explorer John Wesley Powell, and a remembrance of the plains of Saskatchewan where he spent his boyhood. His novel *The Big Rock Candy Mountain* ranges over North Dakota, Washington, Minnesota, and Saskatchewan and concerns "that place of impossible loveliness that pulled the whole nation westward," as Stegner writes in the book. The Pulitzer Prize-winning

Angle of Repose follows a professor in California who writes a book about his grandmother, an illustrator and writer of the old West.

"Stegner is a regional writer in the richest sense of that word," James D. Houston maintains in the *Los Angeles Times Book Review*, "one who manages to dig through the surface and plumb a region's deepest implications, tapping into profound matters of how a place or a piece of territory can shape life, character, actions, dreams. Something elemental about the West emerges, comes pushing through his prose." Although admitting that Stegner's fiction is "almost invariably set in the western United States," Richard H. Simpson of the *Dictionary of Literary Biography* believes that the author's "main region is the human spirit. . . . Each [novel] explores a question central in Stegner's life and in American culture: How does one achieve a sense of identity, permanence, and civilization—a sense of home—in a place where rootlessness and discontinuity dominate?" In their study *Wallace Stegner*, Merrill and Lorene Lewis agree with Simpson: "The central theme of all his work is the quest for identity, personal and regional, artistic and cultural."

Stegner was born in Iowa and raised in Utah, North Dakota, Washington, Montana, Wyoming, and Saskatchewan. After graduating from the University of Utah in 1930, he went to the State University of Iowa for his graduate degrees. He taught at the University of Utah, the University of Wisconsin—Madison, and Harvard University before moving to Stanford University in California, where Stegner was a professor of English for 26 years. During his years at Stanford, Stegner "founded and orchestrated one of the country's most prestigious writing programs," as Houston states. The Lewises maintain that Stegner's "success as a teacher of creative writing, as well as his success as a writer, has given him opportunities and honors that not many regional writers have obtained. He has had access to major libraries for research; he has had the opportunity to travel and the leisure to write."

A book contest sponsored by the publishing house of Little, Brown in 1936 first prompted Stegner to try his hand at writing a novel. *Remembering Laughter,* his entry in the contest, won the top prize of $2,500 and was published in 1937. Over the next five years Stegner was to publish three more novels—*The Potter's House, On a Darkling Plain,* and *Fire and Ice.* All of these early novels are short, novella-length works and explore the relationships between individuals and their communities. *Remembering Laughter,* for instance, concerns a love triangle between a farmer, his wife, and his wife's sister. When the sister becomes pregnant, the truth about the child's parentage is kept secret for fear of the puritanical reaction of the community. *On a Darkling Plain* tells the story of Edwin Vickers, a disabled soldier who becomes a farmer on the Saskatchewan prairie. Though seeking self-sufficient isolation from others, Vickers is drawn back into the community when an outbreak of influenza threatens the local town and he must go to the aid of his neighbors. *Fire and Ice* follows a college student who works untiringly for the campus branch of the Young Communist League. His devotion to party discipline is undone, however, when an outburst of drunken violence forces him to leave town. The Lewises see this novel as a sign of Stegner's "rejection of closed systems" and indicative of his "early conservatism regarding any ready-made radical political or utopian economic solutions to human inequities. . . . The portrayal of the self-destructiveness of Calvinism in *Remembering Laughter,* the failure of isolationist Thoreauvian individualism in *On a Darkling Plain* both indicate, too, that Stegner expects the human lot to be a complex one, without formulas for success."

With the publication of *The Big Rock Candy Mountain* in 1942 Stegner achieved his first popular and critical success. A much longer and more fully developed novel than its predecessors, *The Big Rock Candy Mountain* "confirmed Stegner's place as an important American writer," as Simpson states. It chronicles the lives of Bo Mason, his wife Elsa, and their two sons from 1906 to 1942. The family history is one of continuous travel across the American and Canadian West as Bo, convinced that there is a place where opportunity awaits him, seeks to make his fortune. The Lewises explain that *The Big Rock Candy Mountain* is "more than the dream of the bitch goddess Success. It is the 'dream of taking from life exactly what you wanted,' and the quest for the Promised Land."

Critics particularly praise Stegner's handling of character and his evocation of the hardships of Western life. Milton Rugoff of the *Weekly Book Review* believes that "who Bo Mason was and what he did and how he lived Wallace Stegner conveys to us with a vividness and a fullness hardly less than that with which we know our own fathers." Edward Weeks of *Atlantic* speaks of "the ever deepening sympathy which [he feels] for the man and wife" of the story. Commenting on Stegner's ability to recreate Western life, J. W. Beach of the *New York Times* writes that "Stegner has felt the spell of mountain and prairie, of drought, flood and blizzard; he can write of moving accidents and hair-breadth escapes which give us the feel of frontier life better than phrases about the stars and seasons." Orville Prescott, writing in the *Yale Review,* concludes that *The Big Rock Candy Mountain* "is a sound, solid, intelligent, interesting novel, a good story and an excellent interpretation of an important phase of American life." Robert Canzoneri of the *Southern Review* calls *The Big Rock Candy Mountain* "a once-in-a-lifetime book."

Stegner was not to enjoy another such success until *A Shooting Star* in 1961, a book that was a Literary Guild selection and sold over 150,000 copies. Sabrina Castro, the novel's troubled protagonist, "is Stegner's first strong and rebellious woman," Kerry Ahearns writes in the *Western Humanities Review*. Sabrina's infidelity and the resultant breakup of her marriage, her mother's strength and compassion during her trials, and the efforts of the two women to insure that the development of the family's land will include a city park, are what the Lewises call Stegner's "old themes of familial and community concern." Simpson finds Sabrina's mother to be "portrayed with skill," and believes that Stegner's "skillful portrait of this woman may serve as an example of one of his important achievements as a writer: throughout his career, Stegner has intelligently explored the experience of women." Writing in *Commonweal,* Martin Tucker maintains that "the ever-radiant undercurrent of compassion, of the idea that everyone needs love-and-understanding, and that the only way to get it is to start giving it, streaks through the book and cannot fail to make it a moving experience."

In 1972 Stegner won the Pulitzer Prize for his novel *Angle of Repose,* a work Houston explains is now "recognized as a masterpiece." The story is set in California and concerns a retired history professor, Lyman Ward, who is editing the papers of his grandmother, a writer and illustrator of the nineteenth century. Ward has taken on this project so that he can forget his health and marital problems. Because he has lost a leg to a degenerative disease, Ward's wife has left him. As he imagines the lives of his grandparents through his grandmother's letters, Ward reflects upon his own life, and so Stegner "manages to bring past and present together in a brilliant fabric of memory interwoven with intuition," as Fred Rotondaro writes in *Best Sellers.*

Ward's grandparents embody the tensions of America itself. His grandmother is Eastern, cultured, and genteel; his grandfather is a western mining engineer and a rugged pioneer. "The relationship that emerges is one of complex unease," Janet Burroway remarks in the *New Statesman*. "Neither East nor West is the true region of [Stegner's] novel," Glendy Culligan explains in the *Saturday Review*, "but rather the human soul and the tension between its poles."

Through his investigation of his grandparents' lives, Ward finally comes to an understanding of his own life. "From them," Culligan writes, "he learns that 'wisdom is knowing what you have to accept.'" This sense of tranquillity is reflected in the novel's title, Burroway explains: "Peace-seeking in the poisoned American West is a recurrent theme of Wallace Stegner's novels. He seems now to have found its ideal image in *Angle of Repose*, the geological term for the slope at which rocks cease to roll." William Abrahams of the *Atlantic* sees Stegner as using family history to create an ultimately personal statement. *Angle of Repose*, he writes, "is neither the predictable historical-regional Western epic, nor the equally predictable four-decker family saga. . . . For all the breadth and sweep of the novel, it achieves an effect of intimacy, hence of immediacy, and, though much of the material is 'historical,' an effect of discovery also, of experience newly minted rather than a pageantlike re-creation."

Ahearns believes that *Angle of Repose* represents a culmination for Stegner. "That this novel," she writes, "is his most ambitiously and perfectly crafted only hints at how fully it grew from the thinking and experience most moving to him over the years. The story of the Ward family has the scope of an epic and the control of a lyric because it draws together all the threads of Stegner's thinking about the West and about that final man-woman judgment." Similarly, Simpson finds that *Angle of Repose* "brings some of the most important elements of Stegner's work into sharp relief," including "his enduring concern with the family, especially the subtle shadings of emotional relations between parents and children, husbands and wives."

The Spectator Bird concerns another search of the past. Joe Allston is a seventy-year-old literary agent who lives in California. A chance postcard from an old friend moves him to read over his journal of a trip he made to Denmark some twenty years earlier, looking for his family's roots. The journal is a gothic tale that even includes Danish writer Isak Dinesen as a character. While reading the journal, Allston seeks some answers to his life. He wants to know "how to live and grow old inside a head I'm contemptuous of, in a culture I despise." David Dillon of *Southwest Review* describes Allston as "a sardonic commentator on his own professional failures and geriatric disorders, hostile critic of contemporary fiction, sexual liberation, and anything connected with youth culture, [and] thinks of himself as a spokesman for traditional ethical and social values but acts like someone on the lam from life."

Several critics find Allston to be a cantankerous, unpleasant character. A *New Yorker* reviewer, for example, notes that "Stegner's writing is smooth and clear, and Allston is a believable and frequently sympathetic character, but so much of the book consists of dyspeptic diatribes . . . that one often finds oneself reading the book as if it were a letter from an intelligent but rather petulant elderly relative." But other reviewers appreciate Allston as a charming creation. "For some time [Stegner's] narrators have been older people . . . ," a *Time* critic notes. "They mount the crow's-nest of age to look back (and down) on current civilization. The resulting author's voice is full of a distinctive sardonic ruefulness that produces a style of its own."

Although a *Saturday Review* critic finds *The Spectator Bird* "a disappointment" because Stegner "simply refused to exploit the dramatic tension to be found in the life his protagonist looks back on," P. L. Adams of the *Atlantic* disagrees. "The tale," Adams writes, "can be interpreted in several ways, but regardless of interpretation, it is consistently elegant and entertaining reading, with every scene adroitly staged and each effect precisely accomplished." *The Spectator Bird* received a National Book Award for fiction in 1977.

Stegner's concern with the influence of the past on the present and with a personal and societal sense of identity is most obvious in his nonfiction books, many of which deal with Western history and historical figures. In his essay "On the Writing of History," included in *The Sound of Mountain Water: The Changing American West*, Stegner defines the best history writing as a branch of literature, combining historical fact with the narrative prose of fiction. The proper blending of history and fiction "should help to unveil those continuities between past and present which have remained obscure," as Forrest G. Robinson and Margaret G. Robinson explain in their study, *Wallace Stegner*. Speaking to Dillon in the *Southwest Review*, Stegner explains his attraction to the writing of history: "I think to become aware of your life, to examine your life in the best Socratic way, is to become aware of history and of how little history is written, formed, and shaped. I also think that writers in a new tradition, in a new country, invariably, by a kind of reverse twist of irony, become hooked on the past, which in effect doesn't exist and therefore has to be created even more than the present needs to be created."

Having lived in Salt Lake City and attended the University of Utah, Stegner was naturally drawn to write about the region and the people who live there. His first nonfiction hook was *Mormon Country*, an account of the geography of Utah and a short history of the Mormons who settled it. Stegner's "process of fusing personal experience with historical fact . . . took its first important nonfictional expression in *Mormon Country*," the Robinsons maintain. Combining fiction, straight historical narrative, and personal anecdotes, the book examines a central feature of Mormon life and one of Stegner's primary concerns—the sense of community. The Mormon community, achieved by strict discipline imposed by a theocratic religion, was in stark contrast to the rugged individualism of non-Mormon pioneers. But the stability of Mormon society earned Stegner's admiration. The Robinsons find that his account of Mormon life is therefore biased, ignoring the drawbacks of Mormon culture and exaggerating the faults of other ways of life.

In his second book on the Mormons, *The Gathering of Zion: The Story of the Mormon Trail*, Stegner achieves an impartiality about his subject, according to the Robinsons. As he states in the book, Stegner is writing "as a non-Mormon but not a Mormon-hater." The book tells the story of the Mormon Trail, the long and arduous journey the Mormons underwent from Illinois to Utah from 1846 to 1869. Based on journals kept by the participants, Stegner's account achieves an "understanding of the eminently human pioneers," D. L. Morgan writes in the *Saturday Review*. G. M. Greesley of *Library Journal* believes that Stegner's account is so vivid that "the reader can almost hear the wail of the undernourished infant and the creak of wagons." It is, R. A. Billington writes in *Book Week*, "the best single volume to appear on the Mormon migration. . . . [Stegner's] sensitivity to human beings and his ability to understand the spirit motivating the oft-persecuted Latter Day Saints allow him insights missed by earlier writers."

The nineteenth-century Western explorer and naturalist John Wesley Powell is the subject of Stegner's biography *Beyond the Hundredth Meridian: John Wesley Powell and the Second Opening of the West.* Powell led the first expeditions on the Green and Colorado rivers and conducted some of the earliest geological surveys of the West. "Ethnology and Indian policies, public land policy and the structure of government science stem back to his trail blazing efforts," a *Kirkus* reviewer explains. Stegner sees Powell, he writes in the book, as "the personification of an ideal of public service that seems peculiarly a product of the American experience."

Critical reaction to *Beyond the Hundredth Meridian* was favorable. The *New Yorker* reviewer calls it "an important book and, what is more, an exciting one." Mari Sandoz of *Saturday Review* finds it "a complex story, but no man is better fitted by understanding and artistry to tell it than Wallace Stegner." J. H. Jackson of the *San Francisco Chronicle* believed the book to have "a fine chance to qualify either as biography or history when the 1954 Pulitzer awards are made next spring." The Robinsons, looking back on the book in 1977, find it to be "the longest, the most scholarly, perhaps the best written, and certainly the most valuable of Stegner's contributions to historical nonfiction."

Stegner successfully combines history and fiction in his *Wolf Willow: A History, a Story, and a Memory of the Last Plains Frontier.* Returning to the small town in Saskatchewan where he lived for a time as a boy, Stegner searches the past for his own identity much as his fictional characters do in his novels. "I may not know who I am," Stegner writes in the book, "but I know where I came from." Stegner's return to his boyhood town is contrasted with a history of the region, a short story set in Saskatchewan, and studies of prairie and small town life. "By combining history, fiction and his own memories," Hal Borland writes in the *New York Times Book Review,* "Wallace Stegner . . . has summarized the frontier story and interpreted it as only one who was a part of it could do. The result is a memorable and rewarding book." Although finding a few faults with *Wolf Willow,* a *Times Literary Supplement* reviewer still judges it to be "an honest, modest, sensitive and memorable book." Speaking of *Wolf Willow* and *Beyond the Hundredth Meridian,* R. L. Perkins of *Saturday Review* states that "Stegner . . . has written two of the most important Western books of the decade. . . . Both are, so to speak, geo-history, intensified, sharpened, made viable and useful by poetic insights and a keen intelligence."

In his essay collections *The Sound of Mountain Water* and *One Way to Spell Man,* Stegner writes of the history and geography of the West, reflects on being a Western writer, and examines the culture and literature of the region. Though the essays collected in these two books were written over a period of several decades, Stegner's concerns remain remarkably consistent. One such concern is his fervent environmentalism. "We need," he writes in *The Sound of Mountain Water,* "wilderness preserved—as much as is still left, and as many kinds—because it was the challenge against which our character as a people was formed." Another of Stegner's continuing interests is the need for a moral reference in American society. He "speaks of the survival of a lifelong essential code of conduct and esthetics, the belief in conscience and in American pride," Karl Shapiro explains in the *Chicago Tribune Book World.* Speaking of *One Way to Spell Man,* Vance Bourjaily writes in the *New York Times Book Review* that the book contains "the attitudes and beliefs of a humane and civilized man who is both an artist and a Westerner."

As "one of our finest Western novelists," as Shapiro describes him, as well as a writer of award-winning nonfiction, Stegner "has made an extensive, permanently valuable contribution to American letters," Simpson maintains. Richard G. Lillard, writing in the *Los Angeles Times Book Review,* speaks of Stegner's nonfiction in the highest of terms. Stegner, Lillard believes, "writes in the great tradition of narrative history, that of Francis Parkman, Henry Adams, or Bernard DeVoto. His style and substance are enriched by a wide knowledge of literature and natural science and by the skills he has developed during a career of writing." Referring to Stegner's work as a fiction writer, David C. Taylor of *Library Journal* calls him "one of America's most important living novelists."

Speaking to Dillon, Stegner sees the course of his life as having been characteristically American: "I've made a kind of American hegira from essential poverty through the academic world, from real ignorance (my parents never finished the sixth grade) to living in a world where my natural companions are people of real brilliance. As Americans, it seems to me, we are expected to make the whole pilgrimage of civilization in a single lifetime. That's a hell of a thing to ask of anybody. It seems to me an extra hardship. It may also he an extra challenge, and it may be good for us."

MEDIA ADAPTATIONS: Angle of Repose was adapted as an opera by Andrew Imbrie and Oakley Hall and produced by the San Francisco Opera Company in 1976.

BIOGRAPHICAL/CRITICAL SOURCES:

BOOKS

Authors in the News, Volume 1, Gale, 1976.
Contemporary Authors Autobiography Series, Gale, 1989.
Contemporary Literary Criticism, Gale, Volume 9, 1978, Volume 49, 1988.
Dictionary of Literary Biography, Volume 9: *American Novelists, 1910-1945,* Gale, 1981.
Eisinger, Chester E., *Fiction of the Forties,* University of Chicago Press, 1963.
Lewis, Merrill and Lorene Lewis, *Wallace Stegner,* Boise State College, 1972.
Robinson, Forrest G. and Margaret G. Robinson, *Wallace Stegner,* Twayne, 1977.

PERIODICALS

Atlantic, November, 1943, April, 1971, June, 1976.
Best Sellers, April 1, 1971.
Book Week, October 3, 1943, January 10, 1965.
Brigham Young University Studies, winter, 1974.
Chicago Tribune Book World, April 4, 1982.
Christian Science Monitor, November 16, 1967, February 12, 1979.
College English, December, 1958.
Commonweal, July 14, 1961.
Courier-Journal & Times (Louisville), July 28, 1974.
Dialogue: A Journal of Mormon Thought, winter, 1966.
Library Journal, October 1, 1964, April 1, 1971.
Los Angeles Times Book Review, March 25, 1979, November 23, 1980, November 1981, September 6, 1987.
New Statesman, May 26, 1961, September 17, 1971.
New Yorker, October 2, 1943, September 25, 1954, June 5, 1971, June 21, 1976.
New York Times, September 26, 1943, July 27, 1967, March 24, 1971, February 24, 1979.
New York Times Book Review, October 28, 1962, February 10, 1974, May 30, 1982, September 20, 1987, March 18, 1990.
Notes on Contemporary Literature, March, 1973.
Per Se, fall, 1968.

Publishers Weekly, September 25, 1987.
Quarry, Number 4, 1975.
San Francisco Chronicle, September 12, 1954.
Saturday Review, September 1954, May 20, 1961, December 1962, January 16, 1965, March 20, 1971, May 15, 1976.
Saturday Review of Literature, October 2, 1943.
Sewanee Review, winter, 1962.
South Dakota Review, spring, 1971.
Southern Review, autumn, 1973.
Southwestern Review, summer, 1976, spring, 1977.
Time, July 12, 1976.
Times Literary Supplement, April 26, 1963.
Tribune Books (Chicago), September 20, 1987.
Washington Post, December 28, 1987.
Washington Post Book World, May 2, 1982, September 13, 1987, October 4, 1987.
Weekly Book Review, October 3, 1943.
Western American Literature, summer, 1970, summer, 1975.
Western Humanities Review, spring, 1977.
Western Review, autumn, 1955.
Yale Review, winter, 1944, spring, 1968.

* * *

STEIN, Gertrude 1874-1946

PERSONAL: Born February 3, 1874, in Allegheny, PA; died of cancer, July 27, 1946, in the American Hospital at Neuilly-sur-Seine, France; daughter of Daniel and Amelia (Keyser) Stein. *Education:* Radcliffe College, Harvard University, B.A., 1897; attended Johns Hopkins Medical School, 1897-1901. *Avocational interests:* Collecting postimpressionist art.

CAREER: Poet, short story writer, novelist, literary experimentalist.

AWARDS, HONORS: Medal of French Recognition from the French government, for services during the Second World War.

WRITINGS:

Three Lives: Stories of the Good Anna, Melanctha, and the Gentle Lena, Grafton Press, 1909.
Tender Buttons: Objects, Food, Rooms, Claire Marie, 1914.
Geography and Plays, Four Seas, 1922.
The Making of Americans: Being a History of a Family's Progress, Contact Editions (Paris), 1925, published as *The Making of Americans: The Hersland Family,* Harcourt, 1934.
Composition as Explanation, Hogarth, 1926.
Useful Knowledge, Payson & Clarke, 1928.
An Acquaintance with Description, Seizin Press, 1929.
Lucy Church, Amiably, Imprimerie "Union," 1930.
How to Write, Plain Edition, 1931.
Operas and Plays, Plain Edition, 1932.
The Autobiography of Alice B. Toklas, Harcourt, 1933.
Matisse, Picasso and Gertrude Stein, Plain Edition, 1933.
Portraits and Prayers, Random House, 1934.
Lectures in America, Random House, 1935.
Narration, University of Chicago Press, 1935.
The Geographical History of America; or, The Relation of Human Nature to the Human Mind, Random House, 1936.
Everybody's Autobiography, Random House, 1937.
Picasso, Floury, 1938, English translation by Alice B. Toklas, Scribner, 1939.
The World . . . Is Round, W. R. Scott, 1939.
Paris France, Scribner, 1940.
What Are Masterpieces, Conference Press, 1940.
Ida, a Novel, Random House, 1941.
Wars I Have Seen, Random House, 1945.

Brewsie and Willie, Random House, 1946.
In Savoy; or, Yes Is for a Very Young Man, a Play of the Resistance in France, Pushkin Press, 1946.
Selected Writings of Gertrude Stein, edited by Carl Van Vechten, Random House, 1946.
Four in America, Yale University Press, 1947.
The Gertrude Stein First Reader & Three Plays, M. Fridberg (London), Houghton, 1948.
Blood on the Dining-Room Floor, Banyan Press, 1948.
Last Operas and Plays, edited by Van Vechten, Rinehart, 1949.
Things As They Are, A Novel in Three Parts, Banyan Press, 1950.
The Yale Edition of the Unpublished Writings of Gertrude Stein, edited by Van Vechten, Yale University Press, Volume 1: *Two: Gertrude Stein and Her Brother, and Other Early Portraits, 1906-12,* 1951, Volume 2: *Mrs. Reynolds and Five Earlier Novelettes,* 1952, Volume 3: *Bee Time Wine, and Other Pieces, 1913-1927,* 1953, Volume 4: *As Fine as Melanctha, 1914-1930,* 1954, Volume 5: *Painted Lace, and Other Pieces, 1914-1937,* 1955, Volume 6: *Stanzas in Meditation, and Other Poems, 1929-1933,* 1956, Volume 7: *Alphabets and Birthdays,* 1957, Volume 8: *A Novel of Thank You,* 1958.
Selected Writings, edited by Van Vechten, Modern Library, 1962.
Gertrude Stein's America, edited by Gilbert A. Harrison, R.B. Luce, 1965.
Writings and Lectures 1911-1945, edited by Patricia Meyerowitz, Owen, 1967.
Gertrude Stein on Picasso, edited by Edward Burns, Liveright (in cooperation with the Museum of Modern Art), 1970.
Selected Operas and Plays of Gertrude Stein, edited by John Malcolm Brinnin, University of Pittsburg Press, 1970.
Fernhurst, Q.E.D., and Other Early Writings, Liveright, 1971.
Look at Me Now and Here I Am; Writings and Lectures 1909-45, edited by Meyerowitz, Penguin, 1971.
Matisse, Picasso, and Gertrude Stein, with Two Shorter Stories, Something Else Press, 1972.
The Previously Uncollected Writings of Gertrude Stein, edited by Robert Bartlett Haas, Black Sparrow Press, Volume 1: *Reflection on the Atomic Bomb,* 1973, Volume 2: *How Writing Is Written,* 1974.
Dear Sammy: Letters from Gertrude Stein and Alice B. Toklas, edited by Samuel M. Steward, Houghton, 1977.

LIBRETTOS; MUSIC BY VIRGIL THOMSON

Four Saints in Three Acts; An Opera to Be Sung (first produced at the Wadsworth Atheneum in Hartford, Connecticut, February, 1934), Random House, 1934.
Capital, Capitals; For Four Men and a Piano, [New York], 1947.
The Mother of Us All (first produced at Columbia University in 1947), Music Press, 1947.
Preciosilla; For Voice and Piano, G. Schirmer, 1948.

OTHER

(Contributor) *The Collectors: Dr. Claribel and Miss Etta Cone; with a Portrait by Gertrude Stein,* by Barbara Pollack, Bobbs-Merrill, 1962.

Also contributor of two articles to the Harvard *Psychological Review,* 1896 and 1898.

SIDELIGHTS: From the time she moved to France in 1903 until her death in Neuilly-sur-Seine in 1946, American writer Gertrude Stein was a central figure in the Parisian art world. An advocate of the avant garde, Stein helped shape an artistic movement that demanded a novel form of expression and a conscious break with the past. The salon she shared with Alice B. Toklas, her lifelong companion and secretary, at 27, rue de Fleurus became a gathering place for the "new moderns," as the talented young artists supporting this movement came to be called. Among those whose careers she helped launch were painters Henri Matisse, Juan Gris, and Pablo Picasso. What these creators achieved in the visual arts, Stein attempted in her writing. A bold experimenter and self-proclaimed genius, she rejected the linear, time-oriented writing characteristic of the nineteenth century for a spatial, process-oriented, specifically twentieth-century literature. The results were dense poems and fictions, often devoid of plot or dialogue, which yielded memorable phrases ("Rose is a rose is a rose") but not commercially successful books. In fact, her only bestseller, *The Autobiography of Alice B. Toklas,* a memoir of Stein's life written in the person of Alice B. Toklas, was a standard narrative, conventionally composed.

Though commercial publishers slighted her experimental writings and critics dismissed them as incomprehensible, Stein's theories did interest some of the most talented writers of the day. During the years between World War I and World War II, a steady stream of expatriate American and English writers, whom Stein dubbed "the Lost Generation," found their way to her soirees. Ernest Hemingway, F. Scott Fitzgerald, and Sherwood Anderson were among those exposed to her literary quest for what she called an "exact description of inner and outer reality." Whether or not Stein influenced these and other major modern writers—including James Joyce, whose masterpiece of modernist writing, *Ulysses,* was composed after his exposure to Stein—remains an issue of some contention. Critics do agree, however, that whatever her influence, her own work, and particularly her experimental writing, is largely neglected. As Edmund Wilson noted in *Axel's Castle,* "Most of us balk at her soporific rigmaroles, her echolaliac incantations, her half-witted-sounding catalogues of numbers; most of us read her less and less. Yet, remembering especially her early work, we are still always aware of her presence in the background of contemporary literature."

If Stein's importance as a literary figure has largely been relegated to a secondary role, her influence as a personality should not be underestimated. She was an imposing figure, possessed of a remarkable self-confidence and a commanding manner. When couples came to visit her salon, Stein typically entertained the men, while shuttling the wives off to sit with Toklas. Writing in the *Dictionary of Literary Biography,* Volume 4: *American Writers in Paris, 1920-1939,* James R. Mellow suggests that Stein's unconventional lifestyle and "her openness to vanguard trends may have been encouraged by her erratic family life."

Born in Allegheny, Pennsylvania, in 1874, Stein moved frequently and was exposed to three different languages before mastering one. When she was six months old, her parents took her and her two older brothers, Michael and Leo, abroad for a five-year European sojourn. Upon their return, they settled in Oakland, California, where Stein grew up. At eighteen, she followed her brother Leo to Baltimore; while he attended Harvard, she enrolled in the Harvard Annex (renamed Radcliffe College before she graduated). At this time Stein's primary interest was the study of psychology under noted psychologist William James. With his encouragement, she published two research papers for the Harvard *Psychological Review* ("Normal Motor Automatism," 1896, and "Cultivated Motor Automatism," 1898) and enrolled in the Johns Hopkins Medical School. After failing several courses, Stein quit the program without taking a degree. Instead she followed Leo first to London, and then to Paris, where he had settled early in 1903 to pursue a career as an artist. "Paris was the place," Stein is quoted in Gilbert A. Harrison's *Gertrude*

Stein's America, "that suited us who were to create the twentieth century art and literature."

As soon as she arrived, Stein submerged herself in the bohemian community of the avant-garde, described by her brother Leo as an "atmosphere of propaganda." With guidance from her eldest brother Michael—an art collector who lived just a few blocks away—Stein began to amass a modern art collection of her own. She also, at age twenty-nine, dedicated herself in earnest to her writing.

Stein published her first—and some say her best—book in 1909. *Three Lives* is comprised of three short tales, each of which investigates the essential nature of its main character. Of these, "Melanctha," the portrait of a young mulatto girl who suffers an unhappy affair with a black doctor, has been particularly singled out for praise. A reworking of an autobiographical story Stein wrote about an unhappy lesbian affair, the story "attempts to trace the curve of a passion, its rise, its climax, its collapse, with all the shifts and modulations between dissension and reconciliation along the way," Mark Schorer wrote in *The World We Imagine.* Mellow commended it as "one of the earliest and most sensitive treatments of Negro experience," attributing much of its success to "the racy, almost vernacular style of the dialogue."

Not just the dialogue, but other facets of the story reflect the influence of Stein's psychological training under James. "The identity of her characters as it is revealed in unconscious habits and rhythms of speech, the classification of all possible character types, and the problem of laying out as a continuous present knowledge that had accumulated over a period of time"—all are Jamesian questions that surface in the tale, according to Meredith Yearsley in the *Dictionary of Literary Biography,* Volume 54: *American Poets, 1880-1945.* Since few—if any—writers had ever isolated these themes in this particular manner, the work remains significant. "Both for historical reasons and for intrinsic merit, 'Melanctha' must be ranked as one of the three of four thoroughly original short stories which have been produced in this century," Oscar Cargill concluded in his *Intellectual America.*

As she developed her craft, Stein became more experimental in her writing. Since her works were not published in the order in which they were composed, it is difficult to chart the progression of her experiments, but critics mark *The Making of Americans: Being a History of a Family's Progress* (written between 1906-1908 and published in 1925) as a milestone. A 900-page novel without dialogue or action, the book held no commercial interest and went unpublished for seventeen years. It began as a chronicle of a representative family and evolved into a history of the entire human race, reflecting both her interest in psychology and her obsession with the process of experience. Not trusting narration to convey the complexity of human behavior, Stein employed description to achieve what she called "a continuous present." She compared the technique to a motion picture camera, which freezes action into separate frames. Though no two frames are exactly alike, when viewed in sequence they present a flowing continuity.

In a critique of *The Making of Americans,* Katherine Anne Porter compared the experience of reading the book to walking into "a great spiral, a slow, ever-widening, unmeasured spiral unrolling itself horizontally. The people in this world appear to be motionless at every stage of their progress, each one is simultaneously being born, arriving at all ages and dying. You perceive that it is a world without mobility, everything takes place, has taken place, will take place; therefore nothing takes place, all at once," she wrote in *The Collected Essays and Occasional Writ-*

ings of Katherine Anne Porter. Porter maintained that such writing was not based upon moral or intellectual judgments but simply upon Stein's observations of "acts, words, appearances giving her view; limited, personal in the extreme, prejudiced without qualification, based on assumptions founded in the void of pure unreason." In his *I Hear America,* Vernon Loggins described Stein's language as "thought in the nude—not thought dressed up in the clothes of time-worn rhetoric." Mark Schorer also noted her process-oriented approach: "Her model now is Picasso in his cubist phase and her ambition a literary plasticity divorced from narrative sequence and consequence and hence from literary meaning. She was trying to transform literature from a temporal into a purely spatial art, to use words for their own sake alone."

Stein carried this technique even further in *Tender Buttons: Objects, Food, Rooms,* which appeared in 1914. Published at her own expense, the book contains passages of automatic writing and is configured as a series of paragraphs about objects. Devoid of logic, narration, and conventional grammar, it resembles a verbal collage. "*Tender Buttons* is to writing . . ., exactly, what cubism is to art," wrote W. G. Rogers in his *When This You See Remember Me: Gertrude Stein in Person.* "Both book and picture appeared in, belong to, can't be removed from our time. That particular quality in them which is usually ridiculed, the disparate, the dispersed, the getting onto a horse and riding off in all directions, the atomization of their respective materials, the distorted vision, all that was not imagined but rather drawn out of their unique age. If the twentieth century makes sense, so do Stein and Picasso." Despite its inaccessibility, W. G. Rogers called *Tender Buttons* "essential, for here is the kind of Stein that launched a thousand jibes; this represents the big break with the sort of books to which we had been accustomed, and once you have succumbed to it, you can take anything, you have become a Stein reader."

Stein explained the theory behind her techniques in *Composition as Explanation,* published in 1926. But even those critics who understood her approach were largely skeptical of her ability to reduce language to abstraction and still use it in a way that had meaning to anyone beyond herself. As Alfred Kazin noted in the *Reporter,* "she let the stream of her thoughts flow as if a book were only a receptacle for her mind. . . . But the trouble with these pure thinkers in art, criticism, and psychology is that the mind is always an instrument, not its own clear-cut subject matter." When Stein did embrace conventional subjects, as she did in her memoir, *The Autobiography of Alice B. Toklas,* she was a resounding success.

Published in 1933, *The Autobiography of Alice B. Toklas* recounts Stein's experiences in the colorful art world of Paris between the world wars. It was written by Stein from Toklas's point of view, a technique that "enables Miss Stein to write about herself while pretending she is someone dearly devoted to herself," in the words of *New Outlook* contributor Robert Cantwell. Notwithstanding the enormous egotism behind the endeavor, readers flocked to the publication (which was to be Stein's only bestseller), fascinated by the vivid portrait of a genuinely creative world. As Ralph Thompson noted in *Current History,* "The style is artful, consciously naive, at times pompous, but it is never boring or obscure, and is often highly amusing. *The Autobiography of Alice B. Toklas* should convince even the most skeptical that Miss Stein is gifted and has something to say."

In addition to writing books, Stein also contributed librettos to several operas by Virgil Thompson, notably *Four Saints in Three Acts* and *The Mother of Us All.* The year after her autobiography

appeared, Stein returned to the United States to celebrate the successful staging of *Four Saints* at the Wadsworth Atheneum in Hartford, Connecticut, and conduct a lecture tour. Though she had been absent for thirty years, Stein was treated royally and her return was front page news in the major daily papers. She described her six-month visit in a second memoir, *Everybody's Autobiography,* published in 1937. Her tour completed, Stein returned to France where she remained for the rest of her life, though she moved from Paris to an unoccupied village near the Swiss border during the Second World War. Many of her later writings took the war as a subject, notably the 1946 publication *Brewsie and Willie,* which sought to capture the life of common American soldiers through their speech.

Remembered today largely as an interesting personality, whose works are seldom read, Gertrude Stein nonetheless has left her stamp upon modern literature. As John Ashbery concluded in *ARTnews,* "Her structures may be demolished; what remains is a sense of someone's having built."

BIOGRAPHICAL/CRITICAL SOURCES:

BOOKS

Cargill, Oscar, *Intellectual America: Ideas on the March,* Macmillan, 1941.
Concise Dictionary of Literary Biography, 1917-1929, Gale, 1989.
Dictionary of Literary Biography, Gale, Volume 4: *American Writers in Paris, 1920-1939,* 1980, Volume 54: *American Poets, 1880-1945, Third Series,* 1987.
Loggins, Vernon, *I Hear America . . . Literature in the United States since 1900,* Crowell, 1937.
Porter, Katherine Anne, *The Collected Essays and Occasional Writings of Katherine Anne Porter,* Delacorte Press, 1970.
Rogers, W. G., *When This You See Remember Me: Gertrude Stein in Person,* Rinehart & Co., 1948.
Schorer, Mark, *The World We Imagine: Selected Essays,* Farrar, Straus, 1968.
Stein, Gertrude, *The Autobiography of Alice B. Toklas,* Harcourt, 1933.
Stein, Gertrude, *Everybody's Autobiography,* Random House, 1937.
Stein, Gertrude, *Gertrude Stein's America,* edited by Gilbert A. Harrison, R. B. Luce, 1965.
Twentieth-Century Literary Criticism, Gale, Volume 1, 1978, Volume 6, 1982, Volume 28, 1988.
Wilson, Edmund, *Axel's Castle: A Study in the Imaginative Literature of 1870-1930,* Scribner, 1931.

PERIODICALS

ARTnews February, 1971.
Current History, January, 1934.
New Outlook, October, 1933.
Reporter, February 18, 1960.

—*Sketch by Donna Olendorf*

*   *   *

STEINBECK, John (Ernst) 1902-1968
(Amnesia Glasscock)

PERSONAL: Born February 27, 1902, in Salinas, Calif.; died December 20, 1968, of heart disease, in New York, N.Y.; buried in Salinas, Calif.; son of John Ernst (a county treasurer) and Olive (a schoolteacher; maiden name, Hamilton) Steinbeck; married Carol Henning, 1930 (divorced, 1943); married Gwyn Conger (a writer, singer, and composer), March 29, 1943 (divorced,

1948); married Elaine Scott, December 29, 1950; children: (second marriage) Tom, John. *Education:* Stanford University, special student, 1919-25.

ADDRESSES: Home—New York, N.Y. *Agent*—McIntosh & Otis, Inc., 475 Fifth Ave., New York, N.Y. 10017.

CAREER: Variously employed as hod-carrier, fruit-picker, apprentice painter, laboratory assistant, caretaker, surveyor, and reporter; writer. Foreign correspondent in North Africa and Italy for *New York Herald Tribune,* 1943; correspondent in Vietnam for *Newsday,* 1966-67. Special writer for U.S. Army Air Forces, during World War II.

AWARDS, HONORS: General Literature Gold Medal, Commonwealth Club of California, 1936, for *Tortilla Flat,* 1937, for *Of Mice and Men,* and 1940, for *The Grapes of Wrath;* New York Drama Critics Circle Award, 1938, for play, "Of Mice and Men"; Pulitzer Prize in novel, 1940, for *The Grapes of Wrath;* Academy Award (Oscar) nomination for best original story, Academy of Motion Picture Arts and Sciences, 1944, for "Lifeboat," and 1945, for "A Medal for Benny"; Nobel Prize for literature, 1962; Paperback of the Year Award, Best Sellers, 1964, for *Travels with Charley: In Search of America.*

WRITINGS:

NOVELS

Cup of Gold: A Life of Henry Morgan, Buccaneer, Robert McBride, 1929, reprinted, Penguin, 1976.
The Pastures of Heaven, Viking, 1932, new edition, 1963, reprinted, Penguin, 1982.
To a God Unknown, Viking, 1933, reprinted, Penguin, 1976.
Tortilla Flat, Viking, 1935, illustrated edition, 1947, reprinted, Penguin, 1977.
In Dubious Battle, Viking, 1936, new edition, 1971.
Of Mice and Men (also see below; Book-of-the-Month Club selection), Viking, 1937, reprinted, Bantam, 1970.
The Red Pony (also see below), Covici, Friede, 1937, reprinted, Penguin, 1989.
The Grapes of Wrath, Viking, 1939, published with introduction by Carl Van Doren, World Publishing, 1947, revised edition, edited by Peter Lisca, 1972, reprinted, Penguin, 1989.
The Forgotten Village (also see below), Viking, 1941.
The Moon Is Down (also see below), Viking, 1942, reprinted, Penguin, 1982.
Cannery Row, Viking, 1945, new edition, 1963, published with manuscript, corrected typescript, corrected galleys, and first edition, Stanford Publications Service, 1975.
The Wayward Bus (Book-of-the-Month Club selection), Viking, 1947, reprinted, Penguin, 1979.
The Pearl (also see below), Viking, 1947, reprinted, Bantam, 1986.
Burning Bright: A Play in Story Form (also see below), Viking, 1950, reprinted, Penguin, 1979.
East of Eden, Viking, 1952, reprinted, Penguin, 1979.
Sweet Thursday, Viking, 1954, reprinted, Penguin, 1979.
The Short Reign of Pippin IV: A Fabrication (Book-of-the-Month Club selection), Viking, 1957, reprinted, Penguin, 1977.
The Winter of Our Discontent, Viking, 1961, reprinted, Penguin, 1982.

SHORT STORIES

Saint Katy the Virgin (also see below), Covici, Friede, 1936.
Nothing So Monstrous, Pynson Printers, 1936, reprinted, Porter, 1979.

The Long Valley (contains fourteen short stories, including "The Red Pony," "Saint Katy the Virgin," "Johnny Bear," and "The Harness"), Viking, 1938, reprinted, Penguin, 1986, published as *Thirteen Great Short Stories from the Long Valley,* Avon, 1943, published as *Fourteen Great Short Stories from the Long Valley,* Avon, 1947.
How Edith McGillicuddy Met R. L. S., Rowfant Club (Cleveland), 1943.
The Crapshooter, Mercury Publications (New York), 1957.

PLAYS

(With George S. Kaufman) *Of Mice and Men: A Play in Three Acts* (based on novel of same title; first produced on Broadway at The Music Box Theatre, November 23, 1937), Viking, 1937, reprinted, Dramatist's Play Service, 1964, published in *Famous American Plays of the Nineteen Thirties,* edited by Harold Clurman, Dell, 1980.
The Moon Is Down: Play in Two Parts (based on novel of same title; first produced on Broadway at Martin Beck Theatre, April 7, 1942), Dramatist's Play Service, 1942.
Burning Bright: Play in Three Acts (based on novel of same title; first produced on Broadway at Broadhurst Theatre, October 18, 1950), acting edition, Dramatist's Play Service, 1951, reprinted, Penguin, 1979.

SCREENPLAYS

"Forgotten Village" (based on novel of same title), independently produced, 1939.
"Lifeboat," Twentieth Century-Fox, 1944.
"A Medal for Benny," Paramount, 1945 (published in *Best Film Plays—1945,* edited by John Gassner and Dudley Nichols, Crown, 1946).
"The Pearl" (based on novel of same title), RKO, 1948.
"The Red Pony" (based on novel of same title), Republic, 1949.
Viva Zapata! (produced by Twentieth Century-Fox, 1952), edited by Robert E. Morsberger, Viking, 1975.

OMNIBUS VOLUMES

Steinbeck, edited by Pascal Covici, Viking, 1943, enlarged edition published as *The Portable Steinbeck,* 1946, revised edition, 1971, reprinted, Crown, 1986 (published in Australia as *Steinbeck Omnibus,* Oxford University Press, 1946).
Short Novels: Tortilla Flat, The Red Pony, Of Mice and Men, The Moon Is Down, Cannery Row, The Pearl, Viking, 1953, new edition, 1963.
East of Eden [and] *The Wayward Bus,* Viking, 1962.
The Red Pony, Part I: The Gift [and] *The Pearl,* Macmillan (Toronto), 1963.
The Pearl [and] *The Red Pony,* Viking, 1967.
Cannery Row [and] *Sweet Thursday,* Heron Books, 1971.
To a God Unknown [and] *The Pearl,* Heron Books, 1971.
Of Mice and Men [and] *Cannery Row,* Penguin (Harmondsworth, England), 1973, Penguin (New York), 1978.
The Grapes of Wrath [and] *The Moon Is Down* [and] *Cannery Row* [and] *East of Eden* [and] *Of Mice and Men,* Heinemann, 1976.
John Steinbeck, 1902-1968 (contains *Tortilla Flat, Of Mice and Men,* and *Cannery Row*), limited edition, Franklin Library, 1977.
The Short Novels of John Steinbeck (contains *Tortilla Flat, The Red Pony, Of Mice and Men, The Moon Is Down, Cannery Row,* and *The Pearl*), introduction by Joseph Henry Jackson, Viking, 1981.

OTHER

"Their Blood Is Strong" (factual story of migratory workers), Simon J. Lubin Society of California, 1938.

A Letter to the Friends of Democracy, Overbrook Press, 1940.

(With Edward F. Ricketts) *Sea of Cortez* (description of expedition to Gulf of California), Viking, 1941, published as *Sea of Cortez: A Leisurely Journal of Travel,* Appel, 1971, revised edition published as *The Log from the "Sea of Cortez": The Narrative Portion of the Book, "Sea of Cortez,"* Viking, 1951, reprinted, Penguin, 1977.

Bombs Away: The Story of a Bomber Team (account of life and training in U.S. Army Air Forces), Viking, 1942.

A Russian Journal (description of tour to Russia), photographs by Robert Capa, Viking, 1948.

Once There Was a War (collection of dispatches and anecdotes from World War II), Viking, 1958, reprinted, Penguin, 1977.

Travels with Charley: In Search of America, Viking, 1962, reprinted, Penguin, 1980.

Letters to Alicia (collection of newspaper columns written as a correspondent in Vietnam), [Garden City, N.J.], 1965.

America and Americans (description of travels in United States), Viking, 1966.

Journal of a Novel: The "East of Eden" Letters, Viking, 1969.

Steinbeck: A Life in Letters (collection of correspondence), edited by wife, Elaine Steinbeck, and Robert Wallsten, Viking, 1975.

The Acts of King Arthur and His Noble Knights: From the Winchester Manuscripts of Thomas Malory and Other Sources, edited by Chase Horton, Farrar, Straus, 1976.

The Collected Poems of Amnesia Glasscock (poems published by Steinbeck under pseudonym Amnesia Glasscock in *Monterey Beacon,* January-February, 1935), Manroot Books (San Francisco), 1976.

Letters to Elizabeth: A Selection of Letters from John Steinbeck to Elizabeth Otis, edited by Florian J. Shasky and Susan F. Kiggs, Book Club of California (San Francisco), 1978.

The Harvest Gypsies: On the Road to the Grapes of Wrath, Heyday, 1988.

Working Days: The Journals of the Grapes of Wrath, edited by Robert DeMott, Penguin, 1989.

Short stories and short novels have appeared in numerous anthologies. Author of syndicated column written during tour of Vietnam, 1966-67. Contributor of numerous short stories, essays, and articles to popular magazines and periodicals.

SIDELIGHTS: Throughout his long and controversial career, John Steinbeck extolled the virtues of the American dream while he warned against what he believed to be the evils of an increasingly materialistic American society. Although his subject and style varied with each book, the themes of human dignity and compassion, and the sense of what a *Time* critic called "Steinbeck's vision of America," remained constant. Steinbeck was a uniquely American novelist, the critics contended, whose distrust and anger at society was offset by his faith and love for the land and its people. Of his seventeen novels, *The Grapes of Wrath* is perhaps the best example of Steinbeck's philosophy, perception, and impact. It is Steinbeck's "strongest and most durable novel," the *Time* reviewer commented, "a concentration of Steinbeck's artistic and moral vision."

Published in 1939, *The Grapes of Wrath* is a novel of social protest that caused a furor of both praise and denunciation. Although many protest novels appeared during the 1930s, none was as widely read nor as effective as Steinbeck's. According to Daniel Aaron, Steinbeck possessed a "special combination of marketable literary talent, sense of historical timing, eye for the significant subject, and power of identification," that made the book "the first of the Thirties protest novels to be read on a comparable scale with . . . best-selling novels." Peter Lisca recalled the impact of this combination: "*The Grapes of Wrath* was a phenomenon on the scale of a national event. It was publicly banned and burned by citizens; it was debated on national radio hookups; but above all it was read."

Written during the Depression, *The Grapes of Wrath* concerns the Joad family and their forced migration from the Dust Bowl of Oklahoma to what they had been told was "the land of promise," California. What they find, however, is a land of waste, corruption, and poverty. Expecting to find work, decent wages, and a chance to someday acquire their own land, they are instead introduced to a system of degrading migrant labor camps, menial wages, and near starvation. F. W. Watt commented: "The Paradise in front of them is a fallen world, . . . the place they have reached is as filled with suffering as the place from which they have fled. The subtle but relentless stages by which the realisation comes makes the irony all the more intense—to hear and gradually understand the term 'Okies' and to know that they are Okies; to realise that 'Hooverville'—any and every rough camp on a town's outskirts or garbage dump, named as an ironical tribute to the President who saw prosperity just around the corner—Hooverville was their home; to discover that the rich lands all around them are owned and controlled by large impersonal companies; to be hired for daily wages that barely cover the day's food, then to have those wages cut, and finally to be beaten and driven off at a sign of protest."

The Grapes of Wrath was Steinbeck's second attempt at gaining support and sympathy for the migrants' condition. The first, *L'Affaire Lettuceberg,* had been a satire that Steinbeck destroyed because he felt that it failed to promote understanding and came dangerously close to ridiculing the very people he wanted to help. In 1937, shortly after the publication of his first major success, *Of Mice and Men,* Steinbeck left for Oklahoma. There he joined a group of farmers embarking for California. For two years Steinbeck lived and worked with the migrants, seeking to lend authenticity to his account and to deepen his understanding of their plight. "To make their story convincing, he had to report their lives with fidelity," Aaron explained, and Watt noted that Steinbeck's "personal involvement was intimate and his sympathies were strongly aroused by the suffering and injustice he saw at first hand." Critics contended that this combination of concern, first-hand knowledge, and commitment produced what a reviewer for the London *Times* termed "one of the most arresting [novels] of its time."

One of the most prevalent themes in *The Grapes of Wrath* is the misuse and waste of lives and land. "The real power of *The Grapes of Wrath* is the savage anger at the impersonal process that uproots men from the land and rapes it, substituting rattletraps and highways for place and kindred," Nancy L. McWilliams and Wilson C. McWilliams wrote. Steinbeck was appalled at an economic system that, having collapsed, bankrupted and forced thousands of farmers from work on their own land to work on massive and impersonal farms concerned only with profit. On these highly productive "agricultural 'factories,'" Aaron contended, the migrants "slaved and starved." Watt elaborated: "Here the land is not sick, but the system that is supposed to distribute the land's fruitfulness has broken down, and so in the midst of plenty men are starving: produce is being destroyed because it will not fetch the price of marketing, while the starving watch."

Steinbeck saw this "large-scale commercial and industrial exploitation of the land" as the end of "pioneer ideals," Watt commented. He opposed the continued growth of powerful private interest groups, such as "the growers and their . . . financial allies," Aaron explained, at the expense of individual rights and dignity. "The Okies have had their ramshackle but cherished homes snatched away from them by the insatiable behemoth of big-scale agriculture," John S. Kennedy wrote. "What is wrong with this, it is suggested, is not the pooling of hundreds of family-farms, but the fact of the alien ownership of the amalgam." Steinbeck advocated what Aaron described as a "cooperative commonwealth" attitude, a return to "neighborly interdependence."

Certain groups, however, misinterpreted this message and charged Steinbeck with writing a Communist tract. "Publicists for the big California growers and the right-wing press denounced [*The Grapes of Wrath*] as a pack of lies," Aaron reported. "Spokesmen for the Association Farmers, incorporated in 1934 to combat unionism and other 'subversive activities,' accused Steinbeck of writing a brief for Communism."

In reality, Steinbeck "was a conservative, a man who valued and even clung to the old America," McWilliams and McWilliams noted. What he wrote, Aaron remarked, was "the insider's plea to the popular conscience, not a call for revolution." While Steinbeck criticized what he believed were evil and immoral institutions, he offered what critics contended was an optimistic picture of the American ideal. He presented the migrants as the "preservers of the old American verities, innocent of bourgeois proprieties, perhaps, but courteous, trusting, friendly, and generous," Aaron commented. "What preserved them in the end, and what would preserve all America, was a recovery of a neighborly interdependence that an acquisitive society had almost destroyed." Although Steinbeck recorded "the symptoms of his sick society," Aaron continued, "[he] did not regard himself as one of its gravediggers."

In *The Grapes of Wrath*, as well as in his other novels, Steinbeck took a "biological view" towards man. He did not look for the causes or motives behind a given situation. Instead, he sought to objectively observe the actuality of a situation rather than what that situation could or should have been. Frederick Bracher described this as "a way of looking at things characteristic of a biologist."

Because he held a biological view of man, Steinbeck believed that the evolutionary concepts of adaption and "survival of the fittest" applied to men as well as animals. "The ability to adapt to new conditions is one of man's most valuable biological attributes, and the loss of it might well lead to man's extinction," is an important concept in Steinbeck's work, according to Bracher. Although Steinbeck is sympathetic toward the migrants in *The Grapes of Wrath*, "he is not blind to [their] defects," Warren French noted. "He shows clearly that he writes about a group of thoughtless, impetuous, suspicious, ignorant people." As such, French suggested, they too are bound by the laws of nature and "must also change if they are to survive." Thus, French described the book as "a dynamic novel about people who learn that survival depends upon their adaptability to new conditions." Jackson L. Benson noticed an example of this evolutionary concept in *Of Mice and Men*, a short novel concerning two itinerant farm hands, George and Lennie. George, the "fittest" of the two, is compelled to shoot the strong but feeble-minded Lennie after the latter inadvertently kills their employer's daughter-in-law: "Lennie kills without malice—animals and people die simply because of his strength. Lennie himself must die simply because within the society of man he is an anomaly and weak."

The concept of "group-man" was another aspect of Steinbeck's biological view. This idea was later outlined in *Sea of Cortez*, Steinbeck's and marine biologist Ed Ricketts' account of their expedition to the Gulf of California. According to Peter Shaw: "The book took each day's observations of sea life as an occasion for the drawing of biological parallels with human society. The most striking parallel for Steinbeck was the seeming existence of a group instinct in man similar to that found in schools of fish and colonies of marine fauna. Man, Steinbeck suggested, . . . could be regarded as a group phenomenon as well as an individual one. Accordingly, it might be possible to discover more about an individual by studying his behavior as it related to the group than by studying him in isolation." Steinbeck took this premise one step further by suggesting that man as an individual has no identity and that mankind as a whole is the only reality. This idea is expressed by Doc Burton in Steinbeck's novel about a fruit picker's strike, *In Dubious Battle*: "I want to watch these group men, for they seem to me to be a new individual, not at all like single men. A man in a group isn't himself at all; he's a cell in an organism that isn't like him any more than the cells in your body are like you." Kennedy found the concept of group-man to be "the central point in Steinbeck's concept of life." He added: "Permeating his works is this idea, which is the very heart of his philosophy of life: that the concrete person is in himself virtually nothing, whereas the abstraction 'humanity' is all."

Throughout his work, Steinbeck maintains what R. W. B. Lewis called "a celebrational sense of *life*." This quality, critics have remarked, set him apart from his contemporaries and accounted for much of his popular appeal. "He has a generous indignation at the spectacle of human suffering," Walter Allen noted. "But apart from this, he is the celebrant of life, any kind of life, just because it is life." Alfred Kazin claimed that while other Depression era authors "saw life as one vast Chicago slaughterhouse, a guerrilla war, a perpetual bomb raid," Steinbeck displayed "a refreshing belief in human fellowship and courage; he had learned to accept the rhythm of life." This is not to suggest, however, that Steinbeck held any unrealistically optimistic illusions. Kennedy noted: "He depicts human existence as conflict, unremitting and often savage battle. But he suggests that life is worth living, flagellant and baffling though it may be. . . . In a time when the prevalent note in creative literature is that of despondency and abandonment to malign fate, . . . Steinbeck's assertion of the resiliency and tough durability of life has set him off from the generality."

Although Steinbeck possessed a "moving approach to human life," as Kazin described it, he was generally unsuccessful at bringing his characters to life. Reviewers frequently criticized his people for appearing to be manipulated, stage-like creations. "Nothing in his books is so dim, significantly enough, as the human beings who live in them," Kazin wrote, "and few of them are intensely imagined as human beings at all." Edmund Wilson found that the characters in *The Grapes of Wrath* "are animated and put through their paces rather than brought to life." He added: "They are like excellent character actors giving very conscientious performances in a fairly well-written play. Their dialect is well managed, but they always sound a little stagy."

Steinbeck's descriptive ability, on the other hand, has been widely praised. The *Time* critic contended that Steinbeck wrote with "cinematic clarity." Aaron compared the effects of the images and descriptions in *The Grapes of Wrath* to those rendered by a "camera eye." He found that the novel "unfolds cinematically almost as if Steinbeck had conceived of it as a documentary film."

Critics have suggested that Steinbeck's best novels are those set in his birthplace, northern California's Salinas Valley. "He was a Californian," McWilliams and McWilliams remarked, "and his writings never succeeded very well when he tried to walk alien soil." They defined his California as "a very special one, . . . sleepy California that time passed by." Bruce Cook noted that while Steinbeck was "a writer of international reputation, he was almost a regionalist in his close concentration on the 50 miles or so of California that surrounded his birthplace. The farming towns up and down the Salinas Valley," Cook continued, "and the commercial fishing port of Monterey just a few miles across the mountains provided the settings for most of his best books."

Steinbeck often used this setting to stress his theme of the importance of the "relationship between man and his environment," Shaw claimed. "The features of the valley at once determined the physical fate of his characters and made symbolic comment on them." Moreover, while Steinbeck dwelled on the beauty and "fruitfulness" of the valley, he "did not make it a fanciful Eden," Shaw commented. "The river brought destructive floods as well as fertility, and the summer wind could blow hot for months without let-up." Thus, "Man struggled within a closed system that both formed and limited him; there he was responsible for his acts and yet unable to control the larger forces."

After *The Grapes of Wrath;* Steinbeck's reputation as a novelist began to decline. Although his later works, such as *The Moon Is Dawn, East of Eden,* and *The Winter of Our Discontent,* have been public favorites and best sellers, they have also been considered critical disappointments. Too often, the reviewers contended, Steinbeck's later work is flawed by sentimentality, obvious symbolism, and the inability to achieve the power and statement of *The Grapes of Wrath.*

The first such novel to have provoked critical attack is *The Moon Is Down.* Published in 1942, it deals with a mythical European town and its invasion by what Watt described as a "totalitarian and inhumane power which arouses, instead of crushing, the desire of the conquered for freedom." The novel, most critics have agreed, is a thinly disguised account of Germany's occupation of Norway. It was written, according to Watt, "in the interest of the Office of Strategic Services in helping resistance movements in Occupied Europe." Steinbeck wrote the novel with the same sense of objectivity that had characterized his earlier work. He tried to present the Nazi-like characters as fully as possible; they are good as well as evil, strong as well as weak. In this instance, however, Steinbeck's objectivity worked against him. Kennedy explained: "His Nazi characters emerged as something like human beings, by no means admirable, but by no means demoniac either. For not making them intrinsically and uniformly monstrous, at a time when some of our most celebrated writers were trying to whip Americans up to a frenzy of indiscriminate hatred, Steinbeck was pilloried." Although at the novel's end the Europeans triumph over their enemy, Steinbeck was nevertheless accused, as French recalled, of being "soft toward the Nazis." Later critics, however, detached from the immediate tensions aroused by the war, found more serious fault with what French regarded as the novel's "artificiality."

East of Eden and *The Winter of Our Discontent* similarly fell short of critical expectations. The former, a biblical allegory of the Cain and Abel story, is considered Steinbeck's most ambitious novel. Yet the *Time* critic claimed that "the Biblical parallels of Cain and Abel are so relentlessly stenciled upon the plot that symbolized meaning threatens to overwhelm the narrative surface." *The Winter of Our Discontent,* Steinbeck's last novel,

"is spoilt by sentimentality and the consequent evasion of the moral issues raised," the reviewer for the London *Times* remarked. "Steinbeck was unable in any of his later work to master the problems he seems to have set himself, and though several of his books were widely popular, they appeared too small an achievement to be worthy of the author of *The Grapes of Wrath.*" Max Westbrook echoed this claim when he wrote: "The general feeling is that novels like *East of Eden . . .* and *The Winter of Our Discontent . . .* ought to be like *The Grapes of Wrath* but are not. . . . Neither novel comes to grips with the problems handled so courageously in *The Grapes of Wrath.*"

French blamed these later failures on the popular and critical reaction to *Cannery Row.* Written after the war, the novel is a satire "on contemporary American life with its commercialised values, its ruthless creed of property and status, and its relentlessly accelerating pace," according to Watt. For the most part, however, the novel has been misread as lighthearted, escapist fare. French commented: "Another letter of advice to an erring world; but, as had happened before, the advice went not only unheeded but unperceived. After this, Steinbeck was to strain to make his points clear to the reader; and as he belabored his points, the quality of his fiction suffered."

In 1962, Steinbeck was awarded the Nobel Prize, an honor that many believed "had been earned by his early work," noted the London *Times* critic, rather than for his later efforts. Several reviewers, however, thought this attitude was unjust. Watt, for example, offered this assessment: "Like America itself, his work is a vast, fascinating, paradoxical universe: a brash experiment in democracy; a naive quest for understanding at the level of the common man; a celebration of goodness and innocence; a display of chaos, violence, corruption and decadence. It is no neatly-shaped and carefully-cultivated garden of artistic perfections, but a sprawling continent of discordant extremes." Shaw was seemingly in agreement when he wrote: "When one begins to talk about the shape of a career rather than about single books, one is talking about a major writer. Steinbeck used to complain that reviewers said each new book of his showed a falling-off from his previous one, yet they never specified the height from which his apparently steady decline had begun. What he was noticing was the special kind of concern for a grand design that readers feel when they pick up the book of a writer whose career seems in itself to be a comment on the times."

Steinbeck's books have appeared in translations around the world.

MEDIA ADAPTATIONS: Several of Steinbeck's works have been adapted for films, the stage, and television. *The Grapes of Wrath,* with Henry Fonda, was filmed by Twentieth Century-Fox in 1940. *Of Mice and Men,* starring Burgess Meredith and Lon Chaney, was produced by United Artists in 1939, in 1970 it premiered as an opera, adapted by Carlisle Floyd, at the Seattle Opera House, and was also adapted as a teleplay by E. Nick Alexander. *Tortilla Flat,* featuring Spencer Tracy, was filmed by Metro-Goldwyn-Mayer in 1942. *The Moon Is Down,* produced by Twentieth Century-Fox in 1943, starred Sir Cedric Hardwicke and Lee J. Cobb. *East of Eden,* with James Dean and Jo Van Fleet, who won an Oscar for her performance, was filmed by Warner Bros. in 1954, and was later made into a television mini-series; it was also adapted into a musical, "Here's Where I Belong," which opened at the Billy Rose Theatre, in 1968. "Pipe Dream," a 1955 musical adapted by Oscar Hammerstein II, with music by Richard Rogers, was based on Steinbeck's *Sweet Thursday.* Twentieth Century-Fox produced *The Wayward Bus* in 1957. The National Broadcasting Co. has produced the following works for television: *America and Americans,* 1967, and *Travels with Charley,* 1968, both narrated by Henry Fonda; "The Harness," a story from *The Pastures of Heaven,* was televised in 1971 and featured Lorne Greene; *The Red Pony,* starring Henry Fonda and Maureen O'Hara, was shown in 1973. *Cannery Row* was adapted as a film starring Nick Nolte and Debra Winger by Metro-Goldwyn-Mayer, 1982.

BIOGRAPHICAL/CRITICAL SOURCES:

BOOKS

Allen, Walter, *The Modern Novel,* Dutton, 1965.

Beach, Joseph Warren, *American Fiction: 1920-1940,* Russell & Russell, 1960.

Bode, Carl, editor, *The Young Rebel in American Literature,* Heinemann, 1959.

Concise Dictionary of American Literary Biography: The Age of Maturity, 1929-1941, Gale, 1989.

Contemporary Literary Criticism, Gale, Volume 1, 1973, Volume 5, 1976, Volume 9, 1978, Volume 13, 1980, Volume 21, 1982, Volume 34, *Yearbook, 1984,* 1985, Volume 45, 1987.

Davis, Robert Murray, editor, *Steinbeck: A Collection of Critical Essays,* Prentice-Hall, 1972.

Dictionary of Literary Biography, Gale, Volume 7: *Twentieth-Century American Dramatists,* 1981, Volume 9: *American Novelists, 1910-1945,* 1981.

Dictionary of Literary Biography Documentary Series, Volume 2, Gale, 1982.

Fontenrose, Joseph, *John Steinbeck: An Introduction and Interpretation,* Barnes & Noble, 1963.

French, Warren, *John Steinbeck,* Twayne, 1961.

Frohock, W. M., *The Novel of Violence in America,* University Press in Dallas, 1950, revised edition, Southern Methodist University Press, 1957.

Gardiner, Harold C., editor, *Fifty Years of the American Novel,* Scribner, 1951.

Geismar, Maxwell, *Writers in Crisis,* Houghton, 1942.

Hayashi, Tetsumaro, editor, *John Steinbeck: A Dictionary of His Fictional Characters,* Scarecrow, 1976.

Hedgpeth, Joel W., editor, *The Outer Shores,* Mad River Press, 1978.

Kazin, Alfred, *On Native Grounds: An Interpretation of Modern American Prose Literature,* Harcourt, 1942.

Levant, Howard, *The Novels of John Steinbeck: A Critical Study,* University of Missouri Press, 1974.

Lisca, Peter, *The Wide World of John Steinbeck,* Rutgers University Press, 1958.

Lisca, Peter, *Steinbeck: The Man and His Work,* Oregon State University Press, 1971.

McCarthy, Paul, *John Steinbeck,* Ungar, 1980.

Moore, Harry Thornton, *The Novels of John Steinbeck: A First Critical Study,* Normandie House, 1939.

Snell, George, *The Shapers of American Fiction: 1798-1947,* Dutton, 1947.

Steinbeck, John, *In Dubious Battle,* Viking, 1936, new edition, 1971.

Tedlock, E. W., Jr., and C. V. Wicker, editors, *Steinbeck and His Critics: A Record of Twenty-Five Years,* University of New Mexico Press, 1957.

Timmerman, John H., *John Steinbeck's Fiction: The Aesthetics of the Road Taken,* University of Oklahoma Press, 1986.

Watt, F. W., *John Steinbeck,* Grove, 1962.

Westbrook, Max, editor, *The Modern American Novel: Essays in Criticism,* Random House, 1966.

William Faulkner, Eugene O'Neill, John Steinbeck (Nobel Prize presentation addresses and acceptance speeches), Gregory, 1971.

Wilson, Edmund, *The Boys in the Back Room,* Colt Press, 1941.

Wilson, Edmund, *Classics and Commercials: A Literary Chronicle of the Forties,* Noonday Press, 1950.

PERIODICALS

Antioch Review, spring, 1967.
Chicago Tribune, April 21, 1989.
Christian Science Monitor, September 25, 1952.
Commonweal, May 9, 1969.
Detroit Free Press, January 9, 1967.
Esquire, November, 1969.
Globe and Mail (Toronto), December 20, 1986, April 22, 1989.
Life, November 2, 1962.
Los Angeles Times, December 6, 1987, May 1, 1989.
Modern Fiction Studies, summer, 1974.
National Observer, December 23, 1968.
New Republic, October 6, 1952, August 21, 1961.
New Statesman, June 30, 1961.
Newsweek, November 5, 1962, January 30, 1967.
New York Herald Tribune Books, February 28, 1937.
New York Times, June 2, 1969, August 11, 1989.
New York Times Book Review, February 16, 1947, September 21, 1952, April 14, 1957, November 16, 1958, June 25, 1961, July 29, 1962, October 24, 1976, April 9, 1989.
Novel: A Forum on Fiction, spring, 1977.
Observer, December 22, 1968.
Pacific Spectator, winter, 1948.
Ramparts, July, 1967.
Saturday Review, September 20, 1952, November 1, 1958, September 28, 1968, February 8, 1969.
Steinbeck Quarterly, winter and spring, 1981.
Studies in Short Fiction, summer, 1971, winter, 1977.
Time, December 27, 1968.
Times Literary Supplement, July 7, 1961.
Washington Post, December 21, 1968, December 23, 1969.
Washington Post Book World, April 16, 1989.
Western American Literature, summer, 1971.
Yale Review, December, 1961.

OBITUARIES:

PERIODICALS

Antiquarian Bookman, January 6-8, 1969.
Books Abroad, spring, 1969.
Current Biography, February, 1969.
Newsweek, December 30, 1968.
New York Times, December 21, 1968.
Publishers Weekly, December 30, 1968.
Time, December 27, 1968.
Times (London), December 21, 1968.

*   *   *

STEINEM, Gloria 1934-

PERSONAL: Born March 25, 1934, in Toledo, Ohio; daughter of Leo and Ruth (Nuneviller) Steinem. *Education:* Smith College, B.A. (magna cum laude), 1956; University of Delhi and University of Calcutta, India, graduate study, 1957-58.

ADDRESSES: Office—Ms. Foundation for Education and Communication, Inc., One Times Square, 10th Floor, New York, N.Y. 10036.

CAREER: Editor, writer, lecturer. Independent Research Service, Cambridge, Mass., and New York City, director, 1959-60; *Glamour* magazine, New York City, contributing editor, 1962-69; *New York* magazine, New York City, co-founder and contributing editor, 1968-72; *Ms.* magazine, New York City, co-founder and editor, 1972-87, columnist, 1980-87, consulting editor, 1987. Contributing correspondent to NBC's "Today" show. Active in civil rights and peace campaigns, including those of United Farm Workers, Vietnam War Tax Protest, and Committee for the Legal Defense of Angela Davis; active in political campaigns of Adlai Stevenson, Robert Kennedy, Eugene McCarthy, Shirley Chisholm, and George McGovern. Editorial consultant to Conde Nast Publications, 1962-69, Curtis Publishing, 1964-65, Random House Publishing, 1988—, and McCall Publishing.

MEMBER: PEN, National Press Club, Society of Magazine Writers, Authors Guild, Authors League of America, American Federation of Television and Radio Artists, National Organization for Women, Women's Action Alliance (co-founder; chairperson, 1970—), National Women's Political Caucus (founding member; member of national advisory committee, 1971—), Ms. Foundation for Women (co-founder; member of board, 1972—), Coalition of Labor Union Women (founding member, 1974), Voters for Choice (co-founder), Phi Beta Kappa.

AWARDS, HONORS: Chester Bowles Asian fellow in India, 1957-58; Penney-Missouri journalism award, 1970, for *New York* article "After Black Power, Women's Liberation"; Ohio Governor's journalism award, 1972; named Woman of the Year, *McCall's* magazine, 1972; Doctorate of Human Justice from Simmons College, 1973; Bill of Rights award, American Civil Liberties Union of Southern California, 1975; Woodrow Wilson International Center for Scholars fellow, 1977; Ceres Medal from United Nations; Front Page Award; Clarion Award; nine citations from *World Almanac* as one of the twenty-five most influential women in America.

WRITINGS:

The Thousand Indias, Government of India, 1957.
The Beach Book, Viking, 1963.
(Contributor) Peter Manso, editor, *Running against the Machine,* Doubleday, 1969.
(With G. Chester) *Wonder Woman,* Holt, 1972.
(Author of introductory note) Marlo Thomas and others, *Free to Be . . . You and Me,* McGraw, 1974.
Outrageous Acts and Everyday Rebellions, Holt, 1983.
Marilyn: Norma Jeane, Holt, 1986.
Bedside Book of Self-Esteem, Little, Brown, 1989.

Writer for television, including series "That Was the Week That Was," NBC, 1964-65. Author of films and political campaign material. Former author of column, "The City Politic," in *New York.* Contributor to periodicals, including *Esquire, Ms., Show, Vogue, Life,* and *Cosmopolitan.* Editorial consultant, *Seventeen,* 1969-70, and *Show.*

WORK IN PROGRESS: A book about the women in America's most rich and powerful families, for Simon & Schuster.

SIDELIGHTS: Gloria Steinem is recognized as one of the foremost organizers of the modern women's movement. Her grandmother, Pauline Steinem, was the president of a turn-of-the-century women's suffrage group and was a representative to the 1908 International Council of Women, but Gloria was not substantially influenced by her while growing up in Toledo, Ohio. Her parents divorced when she was young, and at the age of ten Gloria was left alone to care for herself and her mentally ill

mother. She left home when she was seventeen to attend Smith College on a scholarship. Like most women in that era, she was engaged by her senior year; however, Steinem broke her engagement to continue her political science studies in India. She adjusted quickly to life there, adopting native dress and ways. Because English served as the common language, she was "able to really talk, and tell jokes, and understand political arguments," she told Miriam Berkley in *Publishers Weekly.* Steinem was also able to free-lance for Indian newspapers. She supplemented her university studies by seeking out the company of the activists who were then working for an independent India. As a member of a group called the Radical Humanists, she traveled to southern India at the time of the terrible caste riots there, working as a member of a peacemaking team. Her experiences in India gave her a deep sympathy for the underclasses, as well as an enduring love of that country.

When the time came for her to return to the United States, Steinem did so filled with an "enormous sense of urgency about the contrast between wealth and poverty," she stated in her interview with Berkley. But because she "rarely met people who had shared this experience," it became "like a dream. It had no relation to my real, everyday life. . . . I couldn't write about it." Instead, she established a successful free-lance career writing articles about celebrities, fashions, and tropical vacations, while devoting her spare time to work for the civil rights movement. Berkley describes Steinem's life in the early 1960s as "schizophrenically split between career and conscience." "I was . . . divided up into pieces as a person," the author told Elisabeth Bumiller in the *Washington Post.* "I was working on one thing, and caring about another, which I think is the way a lot of us have to live our lives. I'm lucky it came together."

Steinem's best-known article from her early career is "I Was a Playboy Bunny." Assigned to cover the 1963 opening of the New York City Playboy Club for *Show* magazine, she went undercover to work as a "Bunny," or waitress, for two weeks. The resulting article is an "excellent, ironic, illuminating bit of reporting," says Angela Carter in the *Washington Post Book Review.* Steinem was instructed by the "Bunny Mother" in techniques for stuffing her bodice and bending over to serve drinks; she was cautioned against sneezing, which would split the seams of a Bunny costume; she was presented with a copy of the "Bunny Bible," the lengthy code of conduct for Playboy waitresses; and she was informed that all new Bunnies were required to have a pelvic examination performed by the club's specially appointed doctor. "I Was a Playboy Bunny" is "hysterically funny," according to Ann Marie Lapinski in the *Chicago Tribune,* but it is also "full of feminist consciousness as some of [Steinem's] later reportage," believes Carter, who comments, "If it is implicit rather than explicit, it is no less powerful for that." Of her experiences in the club, Steinem remarked to *Los Angeles Times* interviewer Elenita Ravicz, "Being a Bunny was more humiliating than I thought it would be. True, it was never the kind of job I would have considered under ordinary circumstances, but I expected it to be more glamorous and better paid than it was. . . . Customers there seemed to be there because they could be treated as superiors. . . . There is a real power difference when one group is semi-nude and the other is fully-clothed."

By the mid-sixties, Steinem was getting more substantial writing assignments and earning respect for her pieces on political figures. In 1968 she and Clay Felker founded *New York* magazine; Steinem supplied the monthly column "The City Politic" and articles such as "Ho Chi Minh in New York." She was still seen as something of a trendy celebrity by many in the male-dominated world of journalism, however. Bumiller quotes a 1969

Time article describing Steinem as "one of the best dates to take to a New York party these days. . . . Writers, politicians, editors, publishers and tuned-in businessmen are all intensely curious about her. Gloria is not only a successful free-lance writer and contributing editor of *New York* magazine; she is also a trim, undeniably female, blonde-streaked brunette. . . . She does something for her soft suits and clinging dresses, has legs worthy of her miniskirts, and a brain that keeps conversation lively without getting tricky." But her popularity was about to wane because of her interest in controversial women's issues.

Her colleagues' reactions to a 1969 article she wrote about a New York abortion hearing shocked Steinem. She told Ravicz, "I went to that hearing and listened to women stand up and talk about how dangerous and difficult it was for them to get an illegal abortion. . . . They had tears running down their faces as they talked, many of them for the first time, about how they'd had to risk permanent injury and even give sexual favors to their abortionists. I wrote an article about the hearing and my male colleagues, really nice men I got along well with, took me aside one by one and said, 'don't get involved with these crazy women. You've taken so much trouble to establish your reputation as a serious journalist, don't throw it all away.' That was when I realized men valued me only to the extent I imitated them."

Instead of abandoning the subject, Steinem followed up her coverage of the abortion hearing with an extensively researched article on reproductive and other feminist issues. Her article "After Black Power, Women's Liberation" won her the Penney-Missouri journalism award, but it also "unleashed a storm of negative reactions . . . from male colleagues. The response from the publishing establishment, and its reluctance to publish other work on the subject, opened her eyes. She began to pursue not only writing but also speaking engagements and became an active part of the women's movement she had once only observed," relates Berkley. Steinem came to believe that a magazine controlled by women was necessary if a truly open forum on women's issues was to exist. Accordingly, she and others began working toward that goal. Clay Felker offered to subsidize a sample issue and to include a thirty-page excerpt of the new publication in *New York* magazine; Steinem and the rest of the staff worked without pay and produced the first issue of *Ms.* in January of 1972. "We called it the spring issue," Steinem recalled to Berkley. "We were really afraid that if it didn't sell it would embarrass the women's movement. So we called it Spring so that it could lie there on the newsstands for a long time." Such worries were unfounded, for the entire 300,000-copy run of *Ms.* sold out in eight days.

Steinem was suddenly the editor of a very successful monthly magazine. She was somewhat ambivalent about the position: "I backed into [starting *Ms.*]," she admitted to Beth Austin in an interview for the *Chicago Tribune*. "I felt very strongly there should be a feminist magazine. But I didn't want to start it myself. I wanted to be a free-lance writer. I'd never had a job, never worked in an office, never worked with a group before. It just happened, through a series of events that included my having worked for *New York* magazine." Steinem believed that she would turn the editorship of *Ms.* over to someone else as soon as the magazine was squarely on its feet. "I said, 'I'm going to do this two years, that's it.' I kept on saying that until . . . I'd already been doing it for almost seven years. Then I took a fellowship at the Woodrow Wilson Center, which is part of the Smithsonian Institution in Washington. So I was away from the office for the first time for substantial periods of time. . . . I just missed it terribly. And I suddenly realized that, where I thought I'd been delaying life, there *was* life."

As a spokesperson for the women's movement, Steinem has been criticized as subversive and strident by some and as overly tolerant and conservative by others. An overview of her opinions and her development as a feminist is provided by her 1983 publication *Outrageous Acts and Everyday Rebellions*. It is a collection representing twenty years of her writing on a variety of subjects, including politics, pornography, her mother, and Marilyn Monroe. Carter criticizes the book, complaining that Steinem presents only "the acceptable face of feminism" and that she is "straightjacketed by her own ideology." But Diane Johnson offers a more favorable appraisal in the *New York Times Book Review*: "Reading Miss Steinem's essays . . . one is struck by their intelligence, restraint and common sense, as well as by the energetic and involved life they reflect. . . . This is a consciousness-raising book. . . . Her views, like her writing itself, are characterized by engaging qualities of unpretentious clarity and forceful expression." Douglas Hill concurs in the Toronto *Globe and Mail*: "Honesty, fairness and consistency gleam in these pages. And Steinem writes superbly. . . . It's her special strength to write as cleanly and affectingly about her mother's mental illness as about the practice of genital mutilation endured by 75 million women worldwide or the inadequacies of William Styron's fiction." *Detroit News* reviewer Fiona Lowther concludes, "Make no mistake: Whether you disagree with or espouse wholly or in part what Steinem stands for—or what you think she stands for—she is a worthy observer and reporter of the contemporary scene."

Steinem's next book grew from the essay in *Outrageous Acts* concerning Marilyn Monroe, the actress who became internationally famous for her "sex goddess" image in the 1950s and died by her own hand in 1962. When photojournalist George Barris decided to publish a series of photographs taken of Monroe shortly before her death, Steinem was asked to contribute the text. While researching *Marilyn: Norma Jeane,* she became aware that although over forty books had already been published about the late film star, only a few were written by women. Most of the biographies focused on the scandalous aspects of Monroe's death and personal relationships, or reinforced her image as the ultimate pin-up. Steinem explained to *Washington Post* interviewer Chip Brown, "I tried to take away the fantasy of Marilyn and replace it with reality. . . . The book doesn't have a thesis so much as an emphasis—an emphasis on Norma Jeane, on the private, real, internal person. I hadn't read a book about Marilyn that made me feel I knew her. My purpose was to try to get to know or to portray the real person inside the public image." Commenting on the ironic fact that Monroe derived little pleasure from her physical relationships, Steinem suggested to Brown, "It's hard for men to admit that a sex goddess didn't enjoy sex. . . . It's part of the desire to believe she was murdered—the same cultural impulse that says if she's a sex goddess she had to have enjoyed sex doesn't want to believe she killed herself, doesn't want to accept her unhappiness. . . . This country is media-sick. People who are seen in the media are considered to be more real, or different, or special or magic. . . . I tried to make Marilyn real."

"Steinem's 'Marilyn' is a sort of feminist rebuttal to Norman Mailer's conquer-and-transcend biography of the same name," offers Brown. "His book is an extravagant concerto for the 'Stradivarius of sex.' Monroe is the supreme object. . . . Steinem's approach is not so mystical. . . . And while at times her writing is wheat germ to Mailer's caviar, she makes some sensible arguments. . . . She draws Monroe as a prisoner of childhood, compulsively using sex to get 'childlike warmth and nurturing'. . . . [She] stresses the limited choices women had then—and underscores Monroe's struggle for independence, her desire to be taken seriously." London *Times* reviewer Fiona MacCarthy finds fault with Steinem's "passionate involvement with the helpless child in Marilyn," believing that it is an example of "the new phenomenon of women letting women off too lightly. . . . Her sentimental vision of the real Marilyn entrapped in the sex-goddess body sometimes makes one wonder where is now the Gloria Steinem who worked on the campaign trail in the 1960s both as a reporter and an aide to George McGovern. Has she lost all astuteness?" But Diana Trilling argues that *Marilyn: Norma Jeane* is "thoughtful and absorbing." Her *New York Times Book Review* evaluation calls the biography "a quiet book; it has none of the sensationalism that has colored other purportedly serious books about the film star, Norman Mailer's in particular. . . . In writing about Marilyn Monroe, Gloria Steinem for the most part admirably avoids the ideological excess that we have come to associate with the women's movement—Monroe emerges from her book a far more dimensional figure than she would have been if she had been presented as simply the victim of a male-dominated society."

"One aspect of writing about a woman like Marilyn is that you feel you're exploiting her all over again," Steinem disclosed to George James in the *New York Times Book Review*. That feeling led her to donate all her earnings from *Marilyn: Norma Jeane* to the establishment of the Marilyn Monroe Children's Fund. Under the auspices of Ms. Foundation for Women, which sponsors feminist causes, the Marilyn Monroe Children's Fund finances a variety of children's welfare projects. Steinem continues to work energetically for social change through her writing, fund-raising, and speaking engagements. Bumiller asked the feminist leader about the state of the women's movement today: "She says it's not dead or even sick, but has instead spread out from the middle class to be integrated into issues like unemployment and the gender gap. Feminism, she says, has brought America closer to the democracy it ought to be, and has found words like sexual harrassment for events that '10 years ago were called life.' She sees four enormous goals ahead: 'reproductive freedom, democratic families, a depoliticized culture and work redefined. . . . Remember. We are talking about overthrowing, or humanizing—pick your verb, depending on how patient you feel—the sex and race caste systems. Now that is a big job."

MEDIA ADAPTATIONS: "I Was a Playboy Bunny" was produced by Joan Marks as an ABC television movie, "A Bunny's Tale," starring Kirstie Alley, first broadcast February 25, 1985.

BIOGRAPHICAL/CRITICAL SOURCES:

PERIODICALS

Chicago Tribune, October 2, 1983, January 11, 1987.
Detroit News, August 28, 1983.
Esquire, June, 1984.
Globe and Mail (Toronto), February 8, 1986.
Los Angeles Times, December 11, 1984, December 10, 1986, May 6, 1987.
New York Times, April 4, 1987, May 10, 1988.
New York Times Book Review, September 4, 1983, December 21, 1986.
People, June 11, 1984, February 25, 1985.
Publishers Weekly, August 12, 1983.
Times (London), February 19, 1987.
Washington Post, October 12, 1983, December 7, 1986.
Washington Post Book World, October 9, 1983.

STEINER, George 1929-

PERSONAL: Born April 23, 1929, in Paris, France; came to the United States in 1940, naturalized citizen, 1944; son of Frederick George (a banker) and Elsie (Franzos) Steiner; married Zara Alice Shakow (a university professor), July 7, 1955; children: David Milton, Deborah Tarn. *Education:* University of Chicago, B.A., 1948; Harvard University, M.A., 1950; Oxford University, Ph.D., 1955.

ADDRESSES: Home—32 Barrow Rd., Cambridge, England.

CAREER: Economist, London, England, member of editorial staff, 1952-56; Princeton University, Princeton, N.J., fellow of Institute for Advanced Study, 1956-58, Gauss Lecturer, 1959-60; Cambridge University, Cambridge, England, fellow of Churchill College, 1961-69, Extraordinary Fellow, 1969—; University of Geneva, Geneva, Switzerland, professor of English and comparative literature, 1974—. Visiting professor at New York University, 1966-67, University of California, 1973-74, and at Harvard University, Yale University, Princeton University, and Stanford University.

MEMBER: English Association (president, 1975), Royal Society of Literature (fellow), German Academy of Literature (corresponding member), Athenaeum Club (London), Savile Club (London), Harvard Club (New York).

AWARDS, HONORS: Bell Prize, 1950; Rhodes scholar, 1955; Fullbright professorship, 1958-59; O. Henry Short Story Prize, 1959; Morton Dauwen Zabel Award from National Institute of Arts and Letters, 1970; Guggenheim fellowship, 1971-72; Cortina Ulisse Prize, 1972; Remembrance Award, 1974, for *The Language of Silence;* PEN-Faulkner Award nomination, 1983, for *The Portage to San Cristobal of A. H.;* named Chevalier de la Legion d'Honneur, 1984. Numerous honorary degrees, including University of East Anglia and Mount Holyoke College.

WRITINGS:

Tolstoy or Dostoevsky: An Essay in the Old Criticism, Knopf, 1959, reprinted, University of Chicago Press, 1985.
The Death of Tragedy, Knopf, 1961, reprinted, Oxford University Press, 1980.
(Editor with Robert Fagles) *Homer: A Collection of Critical Essays,* Prentice-Hall, 1962.
Anno Domini: Three Stories, Atheneum, 1964.
(Editor and author of introduction) *The Penguin Book of Modern Verse Translation,* Penguin Books, 1966, reprinted as *Poem into Poem: World Poetry in Modern Verse Translation,* 1970.
Language and Silence: Essays on Language, Literature, and the Inhuman, Atheneum, 1967.
Extraterritorial: Papers on Literature and the Language Revolution, Atheneum, 1971.
In Bluebeard's Castle: Some Notes towards the Redefinition of Culture, Yale University Press, 1971.
Fields of Force: Fischer and Spassky in Reykjavik, Viking, 1973 (published in England as *The Sporting Scene: White Knights in Reykjavik,* Faber, 1973).
After Babel: Aspects of Language and Translation, Oxford University Press, 1975.
On Difficulty and Other Essays, Oxford University Press, 1978.
Martin Heidegger, Viking, 1978 (published in England as *Heidegger,* Fontana, 1978).
The Portage to San Cristobal of A. H. (novel), Simon & Schuster, 1981.
George Steiner: A Reader, Oxford University Press, 1984.

Antigones: How the Antigone Legend Has Endured in Western Literature, Art, and Thought, Oxford University Press, 1984.
Real Presences, University of Chicago Press, 1989.

Columnist and book reviewer for the *New Yorker;* contributor of essays, reviews, and articles to numerous periodicals, including *Commentary, Harper's,* and *Nation.*

SIDELIGHTS: "George Steiner is the most brilliant cultural journalist at present writing in English, or perhaps in any language," a *Times Literary Supplement* reviewer writes. Steiner, who teaches at Cambridge University and the University of Geneva, is known on two continents for his literary criticism and far-ranging essays on linguistics, ethics, translation, the fine arts, and science. According to Pearl K. Bell in the *New Leader,* few present-day literary critics "can match George Steiner in erudition and sweep. Actually, he resists confinement within the fields of literature, preferring more venturesome forays into the history of ideas. . . . Steiner has proceeded on the confident assumption that no activity of the human mind is in any way alien or inaccessible to his own." Steiner writes for the educated general reader rather than for the academic specialist; London *Times* contributor Philip Howard calls the author "an intellectual who bestrides the boundaries of cultures and disciplines." In addition to his numerous books, including *Language and Silence: Essays on Language, Literature, and the Inhuman* and *After Babel: Aspects of Language and Translation,* Steiner produces regular columns for the *New Yorker* magazine, where he serves primarily as a book reviewer. Almost always controversial for his bold assertions and assessments of highly specialized theories, Steiner "has been called both a mellifluous genius and an oversimplifying intellectual exhibitionist," to quote Curt Suplee in the *Washington Post. National Review* correspondent Scott Lahti claims, however, that most readers find Steiner's "provocative manner of expression . . . by turns richly allusive, metaphoric, intensely concerned, prophetic, apocalyptic—and almost always captivating."

Much of Steiner's criticism reflects his own sensitivity to the shaping events of modern history. "One way or another," writes a *Times Literary Supplement* reviewer, "in his view, the word has been pushed into a corner; non-verbal forms of discourse have taken over so many fields where writing once reigned supreme. . . . There is also the terrible cloud that has been cast over language and literature by the actions of a thoroughly literate and cultured people between 1933 and 1945. This bears doubly on the critic: first there is the need to expose all such dehumanization of the word . . . and secondly the changed sense of proportion and perspective that it must give to any concern with literature, however ancient or academic." In the *New Republic,* Theodore Solotaroff proposes that Steiner, himself a Jew who escaped France just before the Nazi atrocities descended, regards himself as heir to a European intellectual community that was annihilated by the Holocaust. Solotaroff suggests that Steiner stands "in a deep sense for the whole generation of his peers—these children who did not survive, who left this great tradition bereft of its natural proteges, who make such a haunting absence today in the life of the European mind. . . . There is a driving, obsessive quality to Steiner's acquisitiveness, a fever in his point of view which goes beyond curiosity and self-assertion." Indeed, one of Steiner's central preoccupations, discussed in both his fiction and his nonfiction, is the relation between high culture and barbarism—how, for instance, a concentration camp guard could enjoy a novel or a symphony after sending people to the gas chambers. *Punch* contributor Melvyn Bragg writes: "The drive, the necessity, the fate which kept Sisyphus going has been, with Steiner, the Holocaust. In that blaze, he has written, not

only did a people burn, but words turned to ashes, meaning and value were powdered to be ground into dirt by the heels of vacant inheritors." Steiner himself told the *New York Times Book Review* that central to everything he is and believes and has written "is my astonishment, naive as it seems to people, that you can use human speech both to bless, to love, to build, to forgive and also to torture, to hate, to destroy and to annihilate."

Rootlessness—or, as he puts it, extraterritoriality, also serves as a foundation for Steiner's essays on language and literature. *Dictionary of Literary Biography* contributor Bruce Robbins sees in Steiner "the willed trace of a radical homelessness that he has made a personal motif for almost thirty years." Steiner was born in Paris to Viennese parents; he was only eleven when his family fled to the United States in 1940. Thus he grew up with a full command of three languages—English, French, and German—and his adult life has included extensive work on the nature and limitations of human communication. "The recent preoccupation of all thoughtful practitioners of the humanities with language is [Steiner's] preoccupation," writes David H. Stewart in the *Western Humanities Review.* "Semantics, semiotics, psycholinguistics, structuralist literary criticism: these are his concerns. These he orchestrates into his continuing effort to explain how human beings communicate and what their *manner* of communication does to the content and style of their minds." In *Book World,* Richard Freedman contends that Steiner's interests have led him to investigate "the very roots of communication: . . . how the special patterns of the some 4,000 languages now spoken in the world determine not only the course of the literature, but of the psychology, philosophy, and even the physiology of the people who speak and write them." As Malcolm Bradbury puts it in the London *Times,* part of Steiner's appeal is that he "celebrates, and *is,* the great scholar-reader for whom endless reinterpretation of major ideas and myths is fundamental to existence. He becomes himself the case in point: native in three languages, read in many more, learned over a massive range, requiring of those who study or debate with him an unremitting dedication. All this is expressed with a charismatic power which makes even difficulty seem easy, and invites rebellion against low educational standards, intellectual simplifications, and false prophesy."

Steiner was educated on two continents, having studied at the University of Chicago, Harvard, and Oxford University on a Rhodes scholarship. His first book, published the year he turned thirty, concerns not English literature but the works of two great Russian writers, Tolstoy and Dostoevsky. Entitled *Tolstoy or Dostoevsky: An Essay in the Old Criticism,* the book "announces the particular place Steiner has assigned himself," writes Robbins. "Neither Europe nor America, his Russia is a no-man's-land that permits him to remain, to use his term, unhoused." In addition to offering an analysis of the two writers' lives, thoughts, and historical milieus, the work challenges the *au courant* "New Criticism" by assigning moral, philosophical, and historical worth to the texts. A *Times Literary Supplement* correspondent observes that Steiner "is concerned not with a catalogue of casual, incidental parallels between life and fiction but with the overmastering ideas which so preoccupied the two men that they could not help finding parallel expression in their lives and their works." Another *Times Literary Supplement* reviewer likewise declares that Steiner "feels he is addressing not professional scholars merely, safely shut in the confines of one particular discipline, but all thinking men who are aware of the larger world of social and political realities about them. Dr. Steiner's style derives part of its force from his seeing intellectual questions against the background of historical crises and catastrophes."

In 1967 Steiner published *Language and Silence,* a collection of essays that establish the author's "philosophy of language." The book explores in depth the vision of the humanely educated Nazi and the diminution of the word's vitality in an audio-visual era. Solotaroff maintains that *Language and Silence* "casts a bright and searching light into the murky disarray of current letters and literacy: it looks back to a darkness and disruption of Western culture that continues to plague and challenge the moral purpose of literature, among other fields, and it looks forward to possibilities of art and thought that may carry us beyond our broken heritage. It provides an articulate and comprehensive discussion of the impact of science and mass communications on the ability of language to describe the realities of the earth and the world." Steiner's conclusion—that silence and the refusal to write is the last-resort moral act in the face of bestiality—has aroused conflicting opinions among his reviewers. In the *New York Times Book Review,* Robert Gorham Davis suggests that the author "displaces onto language many of his feelings about history and religion. He makes it an independent living organism which can be poisoned or killed." The critic adds, however, that throughout the volume, "thoughts are expressed with such a fine and knowledgeable specificity that when we are forced to disagree with Steiner, we always know exactly upon what grounds. He teaches and enlightens even where he does not convince." *New York Times* contributor Eliot Fremont-Smith concludes that *Language and Silence* "will confirm, if confirmation is necessary, [Steiner's] reputation as one of the most erudite, resourceful and unrelentingly serious critics working today."

Most observers agree that *After Babel* is Steiner's monumental work, a "deeply ambivalent hymn to language," as Geoffrey H. Hartman puts it in the *New York Times Book Review.* The book offers a wide-ranging inquiry into the fields of linguistics and translation, with commentary on the vagaries of communication both inside and between languages. *Washington Post Book World* reviewer Peter Brunette explains that in *After Babel* Steiner proposes "the radical notion that the world's many diverse languages (4000 plus, at last count) were created to disguise and hide things from outsiders, rather than to assist communication, as we often assume. A corollary is that the vast majority of our day-to-day language production is internal, and is not meant to communicate at all." In *Listener,* Hyam Maccoby contends that Steiner's predilection is for a view "that a language is the soul of a particular culture, and affects by its very syntax what can be said or thought in that culture; and that the differences between languages are more important than their similarities (which he calls 'deep but trivial')." The book has brought Steiner into a debate with linguists such as Noam Chomsky who are searching for the key to a "universal grammar" that all human beings share. Many critics feel that in *After Babel* Steiner presents a forceful challenge to the notion of innate, universal grammar. According to Raymond Oliver in the *Southern Review,* the book "is dense but lucid and often graceful; its erudition is balanced by sharpness of insights, its theoretical intelligence by critical finesse; and it pleads the cause of poetry, language, and translation with impassioned eloquence. . . . We are ready to be sustained and delighted by the sumptuous literary feast [Steiner] has prepared us." *New Yorker* columnist Naomi Bliven likewise points out that Steiner's subject "is extravagantly rich, and he ponders it on the most generous scale, discussing how we use and misuse, understand and misunderstand words, and so, without always being aware of what we are doing, create art, history, nationality, and our sense of belonging to a civiliza-

tion. . . . He is frequently ironic and witty, but for the most part his language and his ideas display even-handedness, seriousness without heaviness, learning without pedantry, and sober charm."

"Steiner's performance is mindful of a larger public," writes Robbins. Not surprisingly, therefore, the author does not shy from forceful communication or controversial conclusions. For instance, in his novel *The Portage to San Cristobal of A. H.,* Steiner gives readers an opportunity to ponder world history from Adolf Hitler's eloquent point of view. Some critics have found the novel morally outrageous, while others cite it for its stimulating—if not necessarily laudable—ideas. Steiner's essays also have their detractors. Bradbury suggests that his nonfiction has "a quality of onward-driving personal history, and it is not surprising that they have left many arguments in their wake." Bradbury adds that Steiner's impact "in provoking British scholars to a much more internationalist and comparative viewpoint has been great, but not always gratefully received." Lahti, for one, finds Steiner's conclusions "often fragmentary, and his frequent resort to extravagant assertions and perverse generalizations lessens the force of his arguments." Similarly, *New York Review of Books* essayist D. J. Enright faults Steiner for "a histrionic habit, an overheated tone, a melodramatization of what (God knows) is often dramatic enough, a proclivity to fly to extreme positions. The effect is to antagonize the reader on the brink of assent."

Other reviewers suggest that Steiner intends to challenge his audience, deliberately provoking strong opinions. In the *New Republic,* Robert Boyers writes: "Readers will sense, on every page, an invitation to respond, to argue, to resist. But so nimble and alert to possibility is the critic's articulating voice that one will rather pay careful attention than resist. Ultimately, no doubt, 'collaborative disagreement' may seem possible, but few will feel dismissive or ungrateful. . . . No reader will fail to feel Steiner's encouragement as he moves out on his own." According to Edward W. Said in *Nation,* Steiner "is that rare thing, a critic propelled by diverse enthusiasms, a man able to understand the implications of trends in different fields, an autodidact for whom no subject is too arcane. Yet Steiner is to be read for his quirks, rather than in spite of them. He does not peddle a system nor a set of norms by which all things can be managed, every text decoded. He writes to be understood by nonspecialists, and his terms of reference come from his experience—which is trilingual, eccentric and highly urbane—not from something as stable as doctrine or authority. This is the other side of his egotism: that he, George Steiner, conscientiously tries to register every response accurately, work through every difficulty, test every feeling, authenticate each experience of the best that is known and thought. As such, then, the critic functions as a real if very unusual person, not an academic abstraction." Bradbury states that what can always be said of Steiner "is that what he questions and quarrels with, he reads and knows. And, whatever the quarrels, Steiner is a major figure, who has sustained a profoundly enquiring philosophy of literature." Fremont-Smith expresses a similar opinion. "Whether or not one agrees with Mr. Steiner's analyses," the reviewer concludes, "he does set one thinking, and thinking, moreover, about issues that are paramount."

MEDIA ADAPTATIONS: The Portage to San Cristobal of A. H. was adapted for the stage under the same title by Christopher Hampton, first produced in America at Hartford Stage, Hartford, Connecticut, January 7, 1983.

AVOCATIONAL INTERESTS: Music, chess, hiking.

BIOGRAPHICAL/CRITICAL SOURCES:

BOOKS

Contemporary Literary Criticism, Volume 24, Gale, 1983.
Dictionary of Literary Biography, Volume 67: *American Critics since 1955,* Gale, 1988.

PERIODICALS

Book World, January 2, 1972.
Christian Science Monitor, May 25, 1975.
Commentary, October, 1968, November, 1975.
Commonweal, May 12, 1961, October 27, 1967.
Detroit News, April 25, 1982.
Listener, April 27, 1972, January 30, 1975, March 22, 1979, July 3, 1980.
London Magazine, December, 1967.
Los Angeles Times, October 23, 1980.
Los Angeles Times Book Review, April 11, 1982, November 18, 1984.
Nation, March 2, 1985.
National Review, December 31, 1971, August 31, 1979, June 11, 1982, July 26, 1985.
New Leader, June 23, 1975.
New Republic, May 13, 1967, January 27, 1979, May 12, 1979, April 21, 1982, November 19, 1984.
New Statesman, November 17, 1961, October 20, 1967, October 22, 1971, January 31, 1975, December 1, 1978, June 27, 1980.
Newsweek, April 26, 1982.
New Yorker, January 30, 1965, May 5, 1975.
New York Review of Books, October 12, 1967, November 18, 1971, October 30, 1975, April 19, 1979, August 12, 1982, December 6, 1984.
New York Times, March 20, 1967, June 22, 1971, July 1, 1974, May 7, 1975, April 16, 1982, January 7, 1983.
New York Times Book Review, May 28, 1967, August 1, 1971, October 13, 1974, June 8, 1975, January 21, 1979, May 2, 1982, December 16, 1984.
Observer, December 17, 1978.
Punch, June 17, 1981.
Southern Review, winter, 1978.
Spectator, April, 1960, December 2, 1978, July 19, 1980.
Time, July 26, 1971, March 29, 1982.
Times (London), March 20, 1982, June 23, 1984, June 28, 1984.
Times Literary Supplement, March 11, 1960, September 28, 1967, December 17, 1971, May 19, 1972, May 18, 1973, January 31, 1975, November 17, 1978, June 12, 1981.
Voice Literary Supplement, April, 1982, December, 1984.
Washington Post, May 13, 1982.
Washington Post Book World, January 14, 1979, May 2, 1982, December 30, 1984, January 19, 1986.
Western Humanities Review, autumn, 1979.
Yale Review, autumn, 1967.

—*Sketch by Anne Janette Johnson*

*   *   *

STEPHEN, Virginia
  See WOOLF, (Adeline) Virginia

*   *   *

STEPTOE, Lydia
  See BARNES, Djuna

STEVENS, Wallace   1879-1955
(Peter Parasol)

PERSONAL: Born October 2, 1879, in Reading, Pa.; died of cancer, August 2, 1955, in Hartford, Conn.; buried in Cedar Hills Cemetery, Hartford, Conn.; son of Garrett Barcalow (a lawyer) and Margaretha Catharine (a schoolteacher; maiden name, Zeller) Stevens; married Elsie Viola Kachel, September 21, 1909; children: Holly Bright. *Education:* Attended Harvard University, 1897-1900; New York Law School, LL.B., 1903.

ADDRESSES: Home—118 Westerly Terrace, Hartford, CT 06112.

CAREER: Poet and insurance lawyer. *New York Tribune,* New York City, reporter, 1900-01; law clerk for W. G. Peckham in New York City, 1903-04; admitted to the Bar in New York State, 1904; law partner with Lyman Ward, c. 1904; worked in various law firms in New York City, 1904-08; American Bonding Co. (became Fidelity and Deposit Co.), New York City, lawyer, 1908-13; Equitable Surety Co. (became New England Equitable Insurance Co.), New York City, resident vice-president, 1914-16; Hartford Accident and Indemnity Co., Hartford, Conn., 1916-55, became vice-president, 1934. Lecturer.

MEMBER: National Institute of Arts and Letters.

AWARDS, HONORS: Prize from Players Producing Co., c. 1916, for "Three Travelers Watch a Sunrise"; Levinson Prize from *Poetry,* 1920; poetry prize from *Nation,* 1936; Harriet Monroe Poetry Award, 1946; Bollingen Prize in Poetry, 1950; gold medal from Poetry Society of America, 1951; National Book Award for best poetry, 1951, for *The Auroras of Autumn;* National Book Award for best poetry and Pulitzer Prize for poetry, both 1955, both for *The Collected Poems of Wallace Stevens;* L.H.D., from Hartt College of Music, 1955; Litt.D., from Bard College, 1951, Harvard University, 1951, Mount Holyoke College, 1952, Columbia University, 1952; and Yale University, 1955.

WRITINGS:

Harmonium (poetry; includes "Le Monocle de Mon Oncle," "The Comedian as the Letter C," "The Emperor of Ice Cream," "Thirteen Ways of Looking at a Blackbird," "Peter Quince at the Clavier," "Sunday Morning," "Sea Surface Full of Clouds," and "In the Clear Season of Grapes"), Knopf, 1923, revised edition, 1931.
Ideas of Order (poetry; includes "Farewell to Florida," "The Idea of Order at Key West," "Academic Discourse at Havana," "Like Decorations in a Nigger Cemetery," and "A Postcard From the Volcano"), Alcestis Press, 1935, enlarged edition, Knopf, 1936.
Owl's Clover (poetry; also see below), Alcestis Press, 1936.
The Man With the Blue Guitar, and Other Poems (poetry; includes "The Man With the Blue Guitar," "A Thought Revolved," and "The Men That Are Falling"), Knopf, 1937.
Parts of a World (poetry; includes "The Poems of Our Climate," "The Well Dressed Man With a Beard," and "Examination of the Hero in a Time of War"), Knopf, 1942.
Notes Toward a Supreme Fiction (poetry; also see below), Cummington Press, 1942.
Esthetique du Mal (poetry; also see below), Cummington Press, 1945.
Transport to Summer (poetry; includes "The Pure Good of Theory," "A Word With Jose Rodriguez-Feo," "Description Without Place," "The House Was Quiet and the World

Was Calm," *Notes Toward a Supreme Fiction,* and *Esthetique du Mal*), Knopf, 1947.

Three Academic Pieces: The Realm of Resemblance, Someone Puts a Pineapple Together, Of Ideal Time and Choice (essays; also see below), Cummington Press, 1947.

A Primitive Like an Orb (poetry; also see below), Gotham Book Mart, 1948.

The Auroras of Autumn (poetry; includes "The Auroras of Autumn," "Large Red Man Reading," "In a Bad Time," "The Ultimate Poem Is Abstract," "Bouquet of Roses in Sunlight," "An Ordinary Evening in New Haven," and *A Primitive Like an Orb*), Knopf, 1950.

The Relations Between Poetry and Painting (lecture), Museum of Modern Art, 1951.

The Necessary Angel: Essays on Reality and the Imagination (essays; includes "The Noble Rider and the Sound of Words," "The Figure of the Youth as Virile Poet," "Effects of Analogy," "The Realm of Resemblance," "Someone Puts a Pineapple Together," and "Of Ideal Time and Choice" from *Three Academic Pieces*), Faber, 1960.

Selected Poems, Fortune Press, 1952.

Selected Poems, Faber, 1953.

Raoul Duly: A Note (nonfiction), Pierre Beres, 1953.

The Collected Poems of Wallace Stevens (includes *The Rock,* previously unpublished section featuring "The Poem That Took the Place of a Mountain," "A Quiet Normal Life," "Final Soliloquy of the Interior Paramour," "The Rock," "The Planet on the Table," and "Not Ideas About the Thing but the Thing Itself"), Knopf, 1954, reprinted, Random House, 1982.

Opus Posthumous (includes *Owl's Clover* and essays "The Irrational Element in Poetry," "The Whole Man: Perspectives, Horizons," "Preface to Time of Year," "John Crowe Ransom: Tennessean," and "Adagia"), edited by Samuel French Morse, Knopf, 1957, reprinted, Random House, 1982.

Poems by Wallace Stevens, edited by Morse, Vintage Books, 1959.

Letters of Wallace Stevens, edited by daughter, Holly Stevens, Knopf, 1966.

The Palm at the End of the Mind: Selected Poems and a Play by Wallace Stevens, edited by Holly Stevens, Knopf, 1971.

Also author of preface to *William Carlos Williams's Collected Poems, 1921-1931,* Objectivist Press, 1934. Author of plays "Three Travelers Watch a Sunrise," 1916, "Carlos Among the Candles," 1917, and "Bowl, Cat, and Broomstick," c. 1917. Work represented in numerous anthologies, including *Modern American Poetry, The New Pocket Anthology of American Verse,* and *The Norton Anthology of Modern Poetry.* Contributor to periodicals, including *Accent, American Letters, Botteghe Oscure, Broom, Contact, Dial, Halcyon, Horizon, Hound and Horn, Kenyon Review, Life and Letters Today, Little Review, Measure, Modern School, Nation, New Republic, Others, Poetry* (some works published under pseudonym Peter Parasol, c. 1914), *Poetry London, Quarterly Review of Literature, Rogue, Secession, Soil, Southern Review, Voices,* and *Wake.*

SIDELIGHTS: Wallace Stevens is one of America's most respected poets. He was a master stylist, employing an extraordinary vocabulary and a rigorous precision in crafting his poems. But he was also a philosopher of aesthetics, vigorously exploring the notion of poetry as the supreme fusion of the creative imagination and objective reality. Because of the extreme technical and thematic complexity of his work, Stevens was sometimes considered a willfully difficult poet. But he was also acknowl-

edged as an eminent abstractionist and a provocative thinker, and that reputation has been sustained throughout the more than thirty years that have passed since his death. In 1975, for instance, noted literary critic Harold Bloom, whose writings on Stevens include the imposing *Wallace Stevens: The Poems of Our Climate,* called him "the best and most representative American poet of our time."

Stevens was born in 1879 in Reading, Pennsylvania. His family belonged to the Dutch Reformed Church, and when Stevens became eligible he enrolled in parochial schools. Stevens's father contributed substantially to the son's early education by providing their home with an extensive library and by encouraging reading. At age twelve Stevens entered public school for boys and began studying classics in Greek and Latin. In high school he became a prominent student, scoring high marks and distinguishing himself as a skillful orator. He also showed early promise as a writer by reporting for the school's newspaper, and after completing his studies in Reading he decided to continue his literary pursuits at Harvard University.

Encouraged by his father, Stevens devoted himself to the literary aspects of Harvard life. By his sophomore year he wrote regularly for the Harvard *Advocate,* and by the end of his third year, as biographer Samuel French Morse noted in *Wallace Stevens: Poetry as Life,* he had received all of the school's honors for writing. In 1899 Stevens joined the editorial board of the *Advocate*'s rival publication, the Harvard Monthly, and the following year he assumed the board's presidency and became editor. By that time Stevens had already published poems in both the *Advocate* and the *Monthly,* and as editor he additionally produced stories and literary sketches. Because there was a frequent shortage of manuscript during his tenure as editor, Stevens often published several of his own works in each issue of the *Monthly.* He thus gained further recognition on campus as a prolific and multi-talented writer. Unfortunately, his campus literary endeavors ended in 1900 when a shortage of family funds necessitated his withdrawal from the university.

Leaving Harvard was hardly a setback, though, for Stevens was not working towards a college degree and was not particularly invigorated by the school's literary environment. Once out of Harvard, Stevens decided to work as a journalist, and shortly thereafter he began reporting for the *New York Evening Post.* He published regularly in the newspaper, but he found the work dull and inconsequential. The job proved most worthwhile as a means for Stevens to acquaint himself with New York City. Each day he explored various areas and then recorded his observations in a journal. In the evenings he either attended theatrical and musical productions or remained in his room writing poems or drafting a play.

Stevens soon tired of this life, however, and questioned his father on the possibility of abandoning the newspaper position to entirely devote himself to literature. But his father, while a lover of literature, was also prudent, and he counseled his son to cease writing and commence law studies. Stevens heeded the advice, and in October, 1901, he enrolled at the New York School of Law. Two years later Stevens graduated, and in 1904 he was admitted to the New York Bar. He then worked briefly in a law partnership with former Harvard classmate Lyman Ward. After parting from Ward, Stevens worked for various law firms in New York City. In 1908 he accepted a post with the American Bonding Company, an insurance firm, and he stayed with the company when it was purchased by the Fidelity and Deposit Company.

Stevens's early years with the insurance firm brought great personal change. Financially secure, he proposed marriage to Elsie Viola Kachel, who accepted and became his wife in September, 1909. Two years later Stevens's father died, and in 1912 his mother also died. During this period Stevens apparently wrote no poetry, but he involved himself in New York City's artistic community through his association with several writers, including poets Marianne Moore and William Carlos Williams. Of keen interest to Stevens at this time were the art exhibitions at the many museums and galleries in the city. He developed a fondness for modern painting eventually becoming a connoisseur and collector and for Asian art, including painting, pottery, and jewelry. He particularly admired Asian works for their vivid colors and their precision and clarity, qualities that he later imparted to his own art.

By 1913 Stevens was enjoying great success in the field of insurance law. Unlike many aspiring artists, however, he was hardly stifled by steady employment. He soon resumed writing poetry, though in a letter to his wife he confided that writing was "absurd" as well as fulfilling. In 1914 he nonetheless published two poems in the modest periodical Trend, and later that year he produced four more verses-portions from an ultimately uncompleted work, "Phases for Harriet Monroe's publication *Poetry*. None of these poems were included in Stevens's later volumes, but they are often considered his first mature writings.

After he began publishing his poems Stevens changed jobs again, becoming resident vice-president, in New York City, of the Equitable Surety Company (which, in turn, became the New England Equitable Company). He left that position in 1916 to work for the Hartford Accident and Indemnity Company, where he remained employed for the rest of his life, becoming vice-president in 1934.

This period of job changes was also one of impressive literary achievements for Stevens. In 1915 he produced his first important poems, "Peter Quince at the Clavier" and "Sunday Morning," and in 1916 he published his prize-winning play, "Three Travelers Watch a Sunrise." Another play, "Carlos Among the Candles," followed in 1917, and the comic poem "Le Monocle de Mon Oncle" appeared in 1918. During the next few years Stevens began organizing his poems for publication in a single volume. For inclusion in that prospective volume he also produced several longer poems, including the masterful "Comedian as the Letter C." This poem, together with the early "Sunday Morning" and "Le Monocle de Mon Oncle," proved key to Stevens's volume *Harmonium* when it was published in 1923.

Harmonium bears ample evidence of Stevens's wide-ranging talents: an extraordinary vocabulary, a flair for memorable phrasing, an accomplished sense of imagery, and the ability to both lampoon and philosophize. "Peter Quince at the Clavier," among the earliest poems in Harmonium, contains aspects of all these skills. In this poem, a beautiful woman's humiliating encounter with lustful elders becomes a meditation on the nature of beauty (and the beauty of nature). Stevens vividly captures the woman's plight by dramatically contrasting the tranquility of her bath with a jarring interruption by several old folk. Consistent with the narrator's contention that "music is feeling," the woman's plight is emphasized by descriptions of sounds from nature and musical instruments. The poem culminates in a reflection on the permanence of the woman's physical beauty, which, it is declared, exists forever memory and through death in the union of body and nature: "The body dies; the body's beauty lives. / So evenings die, in their green going, / A wave, interminably flowing."

"Peter Quince at the Clavier," with its notion of immortality as a natural cycle, serves as a prelude to the more ambitious "Sunday Morning," in which cyclical nature is proposed as the sole alternative to Christianity in the theologically bankrupt twentieth century. Here Stevens echoes the theme of "Peter Quince at the Clavier" by writing that "death is the mother of beauty," thus confirming that physical beauty is immortal through death and the consequent consummation with nature. Essentially an analysis of one woman's ennui, "Sunday Morning" ends by stripping the New Testament's Jesus Christ of transcendence and consigning him, too, to immortality void of an afterlife but part of "the heavenly fellowship / of men that perish." In this manner "Sunday Morning" shatters the tenets, or illusion, of Christianity essentially, the spiritual alterlife—and substantiates nature— the joining of corpse to earth as the only channel to immortality. In her volume *Wallace Stevens: An Introduction to the Poetry,* Susan B. Weston perceived the replacement of Christianity with nature as the essence of the poem, and she called "Sunday Morning" the "revelation of a secular religion."

Less profound, perhaps, but no less impressive are *Harmonium*'s comedic highlights, "Le Monocle de Mon Oncle" and "The Comedian as the Letter C." In "Le Monocle de Mon Oncle" the narrator, a middle-aged poet, delivers an extended, rather flamboyantly embellished, monologue to love in all its embodiments and evocations. He reflects on his own loves and ambitions in such carefree detail that the work seems an amusing alternative to T. S. Eliot's pessimistic poem "The Love Song of J. Alfred Prufrock." Like "Sunday Morning," "Le Monocle de Mon Oncle" celebrates change, and it further suggests that even in fluctuation there is definition—"that fluttering things have so distinct a shade."

In the mock epic "Comedian as the Letter C" Stevens presents a similarly introspective protagonist, Crispin, who is, or has been, a poet, handyman, musician, and rogue. The poem recounts Crispin's adventures from France to the jungle to a lush, Eden-like land where he establishes his own colony and devotes himself to contemplating his purpose in life. During the course of his adventures Crispin evolves from romantic to realist and from poet to parent, the latter two roles being, according to the poem, mutually antagonistic. The poem ends with Crispin dourly viewing his six daughters as poems and questioning the validity of creating anything that must, eventually, become separate from him.

"The Comedian as the Letter C" is a fairly complex work, evincing Stevens's impressive, and occasionally intimidating, vocabulary and his penchant for often obscure humor. Stevens later declared that his own motivations in writing the poem derived from his enthusiasm for "words and sounds." He stated: "I suppose that I ought to confess that by the letter C I meant the sound of the letter C; what was in my mind was to play on that sound throughout the poem. While the sound of that letter has more or less variety . . . all its shades maybe said to have a comic aspect. Consequently, the letter C is a comedian."

Although the aforementioned poems are perhaps the most substantial in *Harmonium,* they are hardly the volume's only noteworthy ones. Also among the more than fifty poems that comprise Stevens's first book are "Thirteen Ways of Looking at a Blackbird," an imagistic poem highly reminiscent of the Japanese poetry form haiku, and "The Emperor of Ice Cream," an eloquent exhortation that death is an inevitable aspect of living. These and the other entries in *Harmonium* reveal Stevens as a poet of delicate, but determined, sensibility, one whose perspective is precise without being precious, and whose wit is subtle but not subdued. As Harriet Monroe, founder and first editor of *Poetry,* wrote in reviewing *Harmonium* for her own periodical, "The delight which one breathes like a perfume from the poetry of Wallace Stevens is the natural effluence of his own clear and untroubled and humorously philosophical delight in the beauty of things as they are."

Few critics, however, shared Monroe's enthusiasm, or even her familiarity, concerning *Harmonium* following its publication in 1923. The book was ignored in most critical quarters, and was dismissed as a product of mere dilettantism by some of the few reviewers that acknowledged Stevens's art. Although apparently undaunted by the poor reception accorded *Harmonium,* Stevens produced only a few poems during the next several years. Part of this unproductiveness was attributed by Stevens to the birth of his daughter, Holly, in 1924. Like his autobiographical character Crispin, Stevens found that parenting thwarted writing. In a letter to Harriet Monroe he noted that the responsibilities of parenthood were a "terrible blow to poor literature."

In 1933, nine years after his daughter's birth, Stevens finally resumed writing steadily. The following year he published his second poetry collection, *Ideas of Order,* and in 1935 he produced an expanded edition of that same work. The poems of *Ideas of Order* are, generally, sparer and gloomier than those of *Harmonium.* Prominent among these bleak works is "Like Decorations in a Nigger Cemetery," comprised of fifty verses on subjects such as aging and dying. Perhaps in reference to these fifty short verses, the racist title refers to the litter that, in Stevens's opinion, accumulated in blacks' cemeteries. He ends this poem by noting the futility of attempts to thwart nature and by commending those individuals who adapt to change: "Union of the weakest develops strength / Not wisdom. Can all men, together, avenge / One of the leaves that have fallen in autumn? / But the wise avenges by building his city in snow."

Stevens more clearly explicated his notion of creative imagination in "The Idea of Order in Key West," among the few invigorating poems in *Ideas of Order* and one of the most important works in his entire canon. In this poem Stevens wrote of strolling along the beach with a friend and discovering a girl singing to the ocean. Stevens declares that the girl has created order out of chaos by fashioning a sensible song from her observations of the swirling sea. The concluding stanza extolls the virtues of the singer's endeavor ("The maker's rage to order words of the sea") and declares that the resulting song is an actual aspect of the singer. In his book *Wallace Stevens: The Making of the Poem,* Frank Doggett called the concluding stanza Stevens's "hymn to the ardor of the poet to give order to the world by his command of language."

Following the publication of *Ideas of Order* Stevens began receiving increasing recognition as an important and unique poet. Not all of that recognition, however, was entirely positive. Some critics charged that the obscurity, abstraction, and self-contained, art-for-art's-sake tenor of his work were inappropriate and ineffective during a time of international strife that included widespread economic depression and increasing fascism in Europe. Stevens, comfortably ensconced in his half-acre home in Hartford, responded that the world was improving, not degenerating further. He held himself relatively detached from politics and world affairs, although he briefly championed leading Italian fascist Benito Mussolini, and contended that his art actually constituted the most substantial reality. "Life is not people and scene," he argued, "but thought and feeling. The world is myself. Life is myself."

Stevens contended that the poet's purpose was to interpret the external world of thought and feeling through the imagination. Like his alter-ego Crispin, Stevens became preoccupied with articulating his perception of the poet's purpose, and he sought to explore that theme in his 1936 book, *Owl's Clover.* But that book comprised of five explications of various individuals' relations to art proved verbose and thus uncharacteristically excessive. Immensely displeased, Stevens immediately dismantled the volume and reshaped portions of the work for inclusion in a forthcoming collection.

That volume, *The Man With the Blue Guitar,* succeeded where *Owl's Clover* failed, presenting a varied, eloquently articulated contention of the same theme the poet, and therefore the imagination, as the explicator of thought and feeling that had undone him earlier. In the title poem Stevens defends the poet's responsibility to shape and define perceived reality: "They said, 'You have a blue guitar, / You do not play things as they are.' / The man replied, 'Things as they are / Are changed upon the blue guitar.' " For Stevens, the blue guitar was the power of imagination, and the power of imagination, in turn, was "the power of the mind over the possibility of things" and "the power that enables us to perceive the normal in the abnormal."

The Man With the Blue Guitar, particularly the thirty-three-part title poem, constituted a breakthrough for Stevens by indicating a new direction: an inexhaustive articulation of the imagination as the supreme perception and of poetry as the supreme fiction. Harold Bloom, in acknowledging Stevens's debacle *Owl's Clover,* described *The Man With the Blue Guitar* as the poet's "triumph over . . . literary anxieties" and added that with its completion Stevens renewed his poetic aspirations and vision. "The poet who had written *The Man With the Blue Guitar* had weathered his long crisis," Bloom wrote, "and at fifty-eight was ready to begin again."

In subsequent volumes Stevens singlemindedly concentrated on his idea of poetry as the perfect synthesis of reality and the imagination. Consequently, much of his poetry is about poetry. In his next collection, *Parts of a World,* his writing frequently adopts a solipsistic perspective in exemplifying and explicating his definition of poetry. Such poems as "Prelude to Objects," "Add This to Rhetoric," and "Of Modern Poetry" all address, to some extent, the self-referential nature of poetry. In "Of Modern Poetry" Stevens defined the genre as "the finding of a satisfaction, and may / Be of a man skating, a woman dancing, a woman / Combing. The poem of the act of the mind." In *Wallace Stevens: An Introduction to the Poetry,* Susan B. Weston wrote that in "Of Modern Poetry," as with many poems in *Parts of a World,* "Stevens cannot say what the mind wants to hear; he must be content to write about a poetry that would express what the mind wants to hear, and to render the satisfaction that might ensue." She added, "Stevens's is a conditional world indeed."

Stevens followed *Parts of a World* with *Notes Toward a Supreme Fiction,* which is usually considered his greatest poem on the nature of poetry. This long poem, more an exploration of a definition than it is an actual definition, exemplifies the tenets of supreme fiction even as it articulates them. The poem is comprised of a prologue, three substantial sections, and a coda. The first main section, entitled "It Must Be Abstract," recalls *Harmonium*'s themes by hailing art as the new deity in a theologically deficient age. Abstraction is necessary, Stevens declares, because it fosters the sense of mystery necessary to provoke interest and worship from humanity. The second long portion, "It Must Change," recalls "Sunday Morning" in citing change as that which ever renews and sustains life: "Winter and spring, cold

copulars, embrace / And for the particulars of rapture come."
And in "It Must Give Pleasure," Stevens expresses his conviction that poetry must always be "a thing final in itself and, therefore, good: / One of the vast repetitions final in themselves and,
therefore, good, the going round / And round and round, the
merely going round, / Until merely going round is a final good,
/ The way wine comes at a table in a wood." *Notes Toward a Supreme Fiction* concludes with verses describing the poet's pursuit
of supreme fiction as "a war that never ends." Stevens, directing
these verses to an imaginary warrior, wrote: "Soldier, there is a
war between the mind / And sky, between thought and day and
night. It is / For that the poet is always in the sun, / Patches the
moon together in his room / to his Virgilian cadences, up down,
/ Up down. It is a war that never ends." This is perhaps Stevens's
most impressive description of his own sense of self, and in it he
provides his most succinct appraisal of the poet's duty.

Although *Notes Toward a Supreme Fiction* elucidates Stevens's
notions of poetry and poet, it was not intended by him to serve
as a definitive testament. Rather, he considered the poem as a
collection of ideas about the idea of supreme fiction. Writing to
Henry Church, to whom the poem is dedicated, Stevens warned
that it was not a systematized philosophy but mere notes—"the
nucleus of the matter is contained in the title." He also reaffirmed his contention that poetry was the supreme fiction, explaining that poetry was supreme because "the essence of poetry
is change and the essence of change is that it gives pleasure."

Notes Toward a Supreme Fiction was published as a small volume in 1942 and was subsequently included in the 1947 collection, *Transport to Summer*. Also featured in the collection is *Esthetique du Mal*, another long poem first published separately.
In this poem Stevens explored the poetic imagination's response
to specific provocations: pain and evil. Seconding philosopher
Friedrich Nietzsche, Stevens asserted that evil was a necessary
aspect of life, and he further declared that it was both inspirational and profitable to the imagination. This notion is most
clearly articulated in the poem's eighth section, which begins:
"The death of Satan was a tragedy / For the imagination. A capital / Negation destroyed him in his tenement / And, with him,
many blue phenomena." In a later stanza, one in which Bloom
found the poem's "central polemic," Stevens emphasizes the positive aspect of evil: "The tragedy, however, may have begun, /
Again, in the imagination's new beginning, / In the yes of the
realist spoken because he must / Say yes, spoken because under
every no / Lay a passion for yes that had never been broken."
In *Wallace Stevens: The Poems of Our Climate*, Bloom called *Esthetique du Mal* Stevens's "major humanistic polemic" of the
mid-1940s.

In 1950 Stevens published his last new poetry collection, *The Auroras of Autumn*. The poems in this volume show Stevens further
refining and ordering his ideas about the imagination and poetry.
Among the most prominent works in this volume is "An Ordinary Evening in New Haven," which constitutes still another set
of notes toward a supreme fiction. Here Stevens finds the sublime
in the seemingly mundane by recording his contemplations of a
given evening. The style here is spare and abstract, resulting in
a poem that revels in ambiguity and the elusiveness of definitions: "It is not the premise that reality / Is solid. It may be a
shade that traverses / A dust, a force that traverses a shade." In
this poem Stevens once again explicates as the supreme synthesis
of perception and the imagination and produces a poem about
poetry: "This endlessly elaborating poem / Displays the theory
of poetry, / As the life of poetry." Other poems in *The Auroras
of Autumn* are equally self-reflexive, but they are ultimately less
ambitious and less provocative, concerned more with rendering

the mundane through abstraction and thus prompting a sense of
mystery and, simultaneously, order. As fellow poet Louise
Bogan noted in a *New Yorker* review of the collection, only Stevens "can describe the simplicities of the natural world with
more direct skill," though she added that his "is a natural world
strangely empty of human beings."

Stevens followed *The Auroras of Autumn* with a prose volume,
The Necessary Angel, in which he articulated his poetic notions
without resorting to abstraction and obfuscation. In the essay
"The Noble Ride and the Sound of Words" he addressed the
imagination's response to adversity, and in "The Figure of the
Youth as Virile Poet" he once again championed the imagination
as the medium toward a reality transcending mere action and rationalization. Consistent in the volume is Stevens's willingness
to render his ideas in a precise, accessible manner. Thus *The Necessary Angel* considerably illuminates his poetry.

By the early 1950s Stevens was regarded as one of America's
greatest contemporary poets, an artist whose precise abstractions
exerted substantial influence on other writers. Despite this widespread recognition, Stevens kept his position at the Hartford
company, perhaps fearing that he would become isolated if he
left his lucrative post. In his later years with the firm, Stevens
amassed many writing awards, including the Bollingen Prize for
Poetry, the National Book Award for *The Auroras of Autumn*,
and several honorary doctorates. His greatest accolades, however, came with the 1955 publication of *The Collected Poems of
Wallace Stevens*, which earned him the Pulitzer Prize for poetry
and another National Book Award. In this volume Stevens gathered nearly all of his previously published verse, save *Owl's Clover*, and added another twenty-five poems under the title "The
Rock." Included in this section are some of Stevens's finest and
most characteristically abstract poems. Appropriately, the final
poem in "The Rock" is entitled "Not Ideas About the Thing But
the Thing Itself," in which reality and the imagination are depicted as fusing at the instant of perception: "That scrawny
cry—it was / A chorister whose *c* preceded the choir. / It was
part of the colossal sun, / Surrounded by its choral rings, / Still
far away. It was like / A new knowledge of reality."

After publishing his collected verse Stevens succumbed increasingly to cancer and was repeatedly hospitalized. He died in August, 1955. In the years since his death Stevens's reputation has
remained formidable. The obscurity and abstraction of his poetry has proven particularly appealing among students and academicians and has consequently generated extensive criticism.
Among the most respected interpreters of Stevens's work are
Helen Hennessy Vendler, who has demonstrated particular expertise on the longer poems, and Harold Bloom, whose *Wallace
Stevens: The Poems of Our Climate* is probably the most provocative and substantial, if also dense and verbose, of the many volumes attending to Stevens's entire canon. For Bloom, Stevens is
"a vital part of the American mythology."

MEDIA ADAPTATIONS: Poems from Harmonium were set to
music by Vincent Persichetti to form a song cycle; "Thirteen
Ways of Looking at a Blackbird" was set to music by John
Gruen to form a song cycle and by J. Wisse to form a secular
cantata.

AVOCATIONAL INTERESTS: Collecting paintings, walking.

BIOGRAPHICAL/CRITICAL SOURCES:

BOOKS

Alvarez, A., *Stewards of Excellence: Studies in Modern English
and American Poets*, Scribner, 1958.

Baird, James, *The Dome and the Rock: Structure in the Poetry of Wallace Stevens,* Johns Hopkins University Press, 1968.

Bates, Milton J., *Wallace Stevens: A Mythology of Self,* University of California Press, 1985.

Beckett, Lucy, *Wallace Stevens,* Cambridge University Press, 1974.

Benarnou, Michel, *Wallace Stevens and the Symbolist Imagination,* Princeton University Press, 1972.

Blackmur, R. P., *The Double Agent: Essays in Craft and Elucidation,* Peter Smith, 1962.

Blessing, Richard Allen, *Wallace Stevens' "Whole Harmonium,"* Syracuse University Press, 1970.

Bloom, Harold, *Figures of Capable Imagination,* Seabury, 1976.

Bloom, *Wallace Stevens: The Poems of Our Climate,* Cornell University Press, 1976.

Bornstein, George, *Transformations of Romanticism in Yeats, Eliot, and Stevens,* University of Chicago Press, 1976.

Boroff, Marie, *Language and the Poet: Verbal Artistry in Frost, Stevens, and Moore,* University of Chicago Press, 1979.

Boroff, editor, *Wallace Stevens: A Collection of Critical Essays,* Prentice-Hall, 1963.

Brazeau, Peter, *Parts of a World: Wallace Stevens Remembered,* Random House, 1983.

Brown, Ashley, and Robert S. Haller, editors, *The Achievement of Wallace Stevens,* Lippincott, 1962.

Brown, Merle E., *Wallace Stevens: The Poem as Act,* Wayne State University Press, 1970.

Burney, William, *Wallace Stevens,* Twayne, 1968.

Buttel, Robert, *Wallace Stevens: The Making of "Harmonium,"* Princeton University Press, 1967.

Buttel and Frank Doggett, editors, *Wallace Stevens: A Celebration,* Princeton University Press, 1980.

Doggett, *Stevens' Poetry of Thought,* Johns Hopkins University Press, 1966.

Doggett, *Wallace Stevens: The Making of the Poem,* Johns Hopkins University Press, 1980.

Donaghue, Denis, *Connoisseurs of Chaos: Ideas of Order in Modern American Poetry,* Faber, 1965.

Donaghue, *The Ordinary Universe: Soundings in Modern Literature,* Faber, 1968.

Ehrenpreis, Irvin, editor, *Wallace Stevens: A Critical Anthology,* Penguin, 1973.

Enck, John J., *Wallace Stevens: Images and Judgments,* Southern Illinois University Press, 1964.

Hines, Thomas J., *The Later Poetry of Wallace Stevens: Phenomenological Parallels With Husserl and Heidegger,* Bucknell University Press, 1976.

Kenner, Hugh, *A Homemade World: The American Modernist Writers,* Knopf, 1975.

Kermode, Frank, *Wallace Stevens,* Oliver & Boyd, 1960.

Kessler, Edward, *Images of Wallace Stevens,* Rutgers University Press, 1972.

LaGuardia, David M., *Advance on Chaos: The Sanctifying Imagination of Wallace Stevens,* University Press of New England, 1983.

Lentricchia, Frank, *The Gaiety of Language: An Essay on the Radical Poetics of W. B. Yeats and Wallace Stevens,* University of California Press, 1968.

Litz, A. Walton, *Introspective Voyager: The Poetic Development of Wallace Stevens,* Oxford University Press, 1972.

McNamara, Peter L., editor, *Critics on Wallace Stevens,* University of Miami Press, 1972.

Morris, Adalaide Kirby, *Wallace Stevens: Imagination and Faith,* Princeton University Press, 1974.

Morse, Samuel French, *Wallace Stevens: Poetry as Life,* Pegasus, 1970.

Nasser, Eugene Paul, *Wallace Stevens: An Anatomy of Figuration,* University of Pennsylvania Press, 1965.

O'Connor, William Van, *The Shaping Spirit: A Study of Wallace Stevens,* Regnery, 1950.

Pack, Robert, *Wallace Stevens: An Approach to His Poetry and Thought,* Rutgers University Press, 1958.

Perlis, Alan, *Wallace Stevens: A World of Transforming Shapes,* Bucknell University Press, 1976.

Richardson, Joan, *Wallace Stevens: The Early Years,* Morrow, 1986.

Riddel, Joseph N., *The Clairvoyant Eye: The Poetry and Poetics of Wallace Stevens,* Louisiana State University Press, 1965.

Sexson, Michael, *The Quest of Self in the Collected Poems of Wallace Stevens,* Edwin Mellen, 1981.

Stern, Herbert J., *Wallace Stevens: Art of Uncertainty,* University of Michigan Press, 1966.

Stevens, Holly, *Souvenirs and Prophecies: The Young Wallace Stevens,* Knopf, 1977.

Sukenick, Ronald, *Wallace Stevens: Musing the Obscure,* New York University Press, 1967.

Tindall, William York, *Wallace Stevens,* University of Minnesota Press, 1961.

Twentieth-Century Literary Criticism, Gale, Volume 3, 1980, Volume 12, 1984.

Vendler, Helen Hennessy, *On Extended Wings: Wallace Stevens' Longer Poems,* Harvard University Press, 1969.

Vendler, *Wallace Stevens,* Harvard University Press, 1986.

Wells, Henry W., *Introduction to Wallace Stevens,* Indiana University Press, 1964.

Weston, Susan B., *Wallace Stevens: An Introduction to the Poetry,* Columbia University Press, 1977.

Woodman, Leonora, *Stanza My Stone: Wallace Stevens and the Hermetic Tradition,* Purdue University Press, 1983.

Woodward, Kathleen, *At Last, the Real Distinguished Thing: The Later Poems of Eliot, Pound, Stevens, and Williams,* Ohio State University Press, 1980.

PERIODICALS

American Poetry Review, September-October, 1978.

Arizona Quarterly, autumn, 1955.

Colorado Quarterly, summer, 1960.

Commonweal, September 23, 1955.

Comparative Literature, winter, 1959.

Contemporary Literature, autumn, 1975.

Critical Quarterly, autumn, 11960.

Criticism, winter, 1960, summer, 1965.

Encounter, November, 1979.

English Journal, October, 1959.

Georgia Review, spring, 1976, summer, 1976.

Hudson Review, autumn, 1957.

Journal of Modern Literature, May, 1982.

Kenyon Review, winter, 1957, winter, 1964.

Literary Review, autumn, 1963.

Modern Language Quarterly, September, 1969.

Nation, April 5, 1947.

New England Quarterly, December, 1971.

New Yorker, October 28, 1950.

Poetry, March, 1924, December, 1931, February, 1937, January, 1956.

Sewanee Review, autumn, 1945, spring, 1952, winter, 1957.

Southern Review, July, 1971, July, 1976, October, 1979, January, 1982.

Studies in Romanticism, spring, 1982.

Western Review, autumn, 1955.
Yale Review, spring, 1955, spring, 1967, winter, 1982.

*   *   *

STEVENSON, Anne (Katharine) 1933-

PERSONAL: Born January 3, 1933, in Cambridge, England; American citizen born abroad; daughter of Charles Leslie (a philosopher) and Louise (Destler) Stevenson; previously married and divorced; married Peter Lucas, September 3, 1987; children: Caroline Margaret Hitchcock, John Gawain Elvin, Charles Lionel Elvin. *Education:* University of Michigan, B.A., 1954, M.A., 1962. *Politics:* Democrat.

ADDRESSES: Home—30 Logan St., Langley Park, Durham DH7 9YN, England.

CAREER: Poet and critic. Fellow in writing at University of Dundee, Scotland, 1973-75, Lady Margaret Hall, Oxford, 1975-77, and Bulmershe College, Reading, 1977-78; The Poetry Bookshop, Hay-on-Wye, Wales, co-proprietor, 1978-81; Northern Arts Literary Fellow at University of Newcastle-upon-Tyne and University of Durham, 1981-82; writer in residence at University of Edinburgh, beginning in mid-1980s. Member of advisory panel of Arts Council of Great Britain, 1983-85. Part-time teacher of cello in Cambridge, England; cellist in string orchestra connected with Cambridge University.

MEMBER: Royal Society of Literature (fellow), Phi Beta Kappa.

AWARDS, HONORS: Avery and Jules Hopwood Award, University of Michigan, 1950, 1952, 1954; Scottish Arts Council Award, 1974; Welsh Arts Council Award, 1980.

WRITINGS:

POETRY, EXCEPT AS INDICATED

Living in America, Generation, 1965.
Elizabeth Bishop (criticism), Twayne, 1966.
Reversals, Wesleyan University Press, 1969.
Correspondences: A Family History in Letters, Wesleyan University Press, 1974.
Travelling behind Glass, Oxford University Press, 1974.
"Correspondences" (radio play), broadcast by British Broadcasting Corp. (BBC), 1975.
"Child of Adam" (radio play), broadcast by BBC, 1976.
Enough of Green, Oxford University Press, 1977.
A Morden Tower Reading 3, Morden Tower (Newcastle upon Tyne, England), 1977.
Cliff Walk: A Poem, Keepsake Press (Richmond, England), 1977.
Sonnets for Five Seasons, Five Seasons Press (Hereford, England), 1979.
Green Mountain, Black Mountain, Rowan Tree Press (Boston), 1982.
Minute by Glass Minute, Oxford University Press, 1982.
New Poems, Other Branch Readings (Leamington Spa, England), 1982.
Making Poetry, Pisces Press (Oxford, England), 1983.
A Legacy, Taxus Press (Durham, England), 1983.
Black Grate Poems, Inky Parrot Press (Oxford), 1984.
The Fiction-Makers, Oxford University Press, 1985.
Winter Time, Mid-Northumberland Arts Group (Ashington, England), 1986.
(Editor) Frances Bellerby, *Selected Poems,* Enitharmon (London, England), 1986.

(Editor with Amy Clampitt and Craig Raine) *1985 Anthology: The Observer and Ronald Duncan Foundation International Poetry Competition on Behalf of the Arvon Foundation,* Arvon Foundation (Beaworthy, England), 1987.
Selected Poems, 1956-1986, Oxford University Press, 1987.
Bitter Fame: A Life of Sylvia Plath (biography), Houghton, 1989.

Contributor to *Times Literary Supplement* and other periodicals in Great Britain and the United States. Former poetry critic for *Listener.* Co-editor, *Other Poetry Magazine.*

SIDELIGHTS: Anne Stevenson "has what Henry James call[ed] 'sensibility to the scenery of life,' " comments Dorothy Donnelly in *Michigan Quarterly Review.* "Her poems have added considerably to the scenery of our own landscapes." Stevenson's poetry, a *Times Literary Supplement* critic writes, is "remarkable for a fresh, authentic brand of realist observation and an impressive capacity to reflect intelligently on what it sees." Ralph J. Mills, Jr. in *Poetry* calls Stevenson "one of the most promising young women poets."

The landscape that Stevenson creates is a shifting one, built upon the ambiguous borders between England and America, family and self, dependence and independence, tradition and nonconformity. "The landscape created by Anne Stevenson's poems . . . shimmers with the tenuous colors and outlines of reflections in water," Donnelly says of *Reversals.* "The poet hesitates, caught between reality and illusion, moving through a flickering, borderless region, a land behind the land. . . . Stevenson's poems evoke with delicacy the misty, the insubstantial, the indefinite, 'the line between land and water,' the view from which 'there is no end to illusion.' " Nicholas Brooke in *New Review* observes that the poems in *Travelling behind Glass* "characterize America and Europe from no fixed base."

Stevenson herself comments upon the feeling of movement and duality her poetry elicits. "Although I am an American . . . I have lived almost constantly in Great Britain since 1962," she writes. "This has meant a measure of flexibility and a constant sense of flux . . . [as well as] the sense I have constantly of a divided life between the Old World and the New."

Stevenson has developed this theme of "flux" in much of her work. In many of her poems it takes the form of the narrator questioning her own actions or the direction her life has taken. Stevenson is "given to querying life," states Donnelly, "and the frequent questions asked in these poems [in *Reversals*] indicate their prevailingly tentative tone. Answers are usually avoided, sometimes suggested, often simply not to be had." Kaye Boyd, a principal character in *Correspondences: A Family History in Letters,* questions her decision to become an author—a decision which also entails leaving her family home: "Dear Father, I love you but can't know you./ I've given you all that I can./ Can these pages make amends for what was not said?/ Do justice to the living, to the dead?" In "Victory," included in *Reversals,* the narrator is compelled to ask her infant son, "Why do I have to love you?"

Although the "landscape" in which Stevenson moves is "tentative," "flickering," and "borderless," her responses to it are not. *Times Literary Supplement*'s Andrew Motion observes, "The characteristic method of *Enough of Green* is to confront the harsh realities of life, acknowledge the temptation to evade them, and then discover rewards in them as well as disappointments."

Correspondences: A Family History in Letters is Stevenson's most ambitious accomplishment. The book traces the Chandler family from its pre-Revolution, New England roots to the present. "*Correspondences* . . . is an ambitious book," asserts Richard

Caram in *Open Places*. "[It] just burns to be an American epic, to combine the insights of history with the characterizations of fiction and the fine aesthetic harmonies of poetry. And it works, in the end, far better than it has a right to—particularly as a very readable form of history, a mythopoetic look backward." Notes Stewart Conn in *Listener:* "With penetrating insight, Anne Stevenson depicts successive generations blighted by drink and estrangement, woe within marriage and a wonderment that man has deserved propagation at all in this wicked world."

Stevenson's characteristic sense of ambiguity is also present in *Correspondences*. Caram concludes that the final section of the book "does most deftly what poetry can do better than history: hold the ambiguities of the lives of the surviving members of the family in lifelike suspension, unwilling to resolve them into finalities, swirling them round and round in a mixture rhetorically rich enough to seem almost a resolution."

Other critics, however, feel that *Correspondences* tries to accomplish too great a task. Douglas Dunn in *Encounter* notes that the work "has been worked hard at, not only as a poem, but as something to hold the reader's attention; unfortunately, the impression is that the clever writer was conjuring with too many gimmicks, for all the weightiness of her critique of America." *New Review*'s Brooke comments that since the poems in *Correspondences* "are not long, it follows they are overloaded, and the story is reduced to familiar types. . . . A novelist would do more than this; a poet should not do less." Concurs Robert Garfitt in *London Magazine:* "Moving as some of [*Correspondences*] is . . . one is left wondering what it has achieved that a novel couldn't have achieved and, more important, whether a more intimate and telling exploration, accessible only to poetry, hasn't been missed."

Despite these criticisms, Stevenson's reputation remains secure. "Her formal dexterity, her determination to include alternative responses to any given situation, and her ability to write with a detachment which is both objective and engaging prove her a poet of exceptional distinction," states Motion.

AVOCATIONAL INTERESTS: Music, traveling, and reading.

BIOGRAPHICAL/CRITICAL SOURCES:

BOOKS

Contemporary Authors Autobiography Series, Volume 9, Gale, 1989.
Contemporary Literary Criticism, Gale, Volume 7, 1977, Volume 33, 1985.
Dictionary of Literary Biography, Volume 40: *Poets of Great Britain and Ireland Since 1960,* Gale, 1985.

PERIODICALS

Encounter, December, 1974, April, 1978.
Globe and Mail (Toronto), October 28, 1989.
Lines Review 50, September, 1974.
Listener, November 28, 1974.
London Magazine, November, 1974.
Los Angeles Times Book Review, August 20, 1989.
Michigan Quarterly Review, fall, 1966, spring, 1971.
New Review, October, 1974.
New Statesman, November 28, 1974, February 10, 1978.
New York Times, August 9, 1989.
New York Times Book Review, November 15, 1987, August 27, 1989.
Open Places, spring/summer, 1976.
Ploughshares, autumn, 1978.
Poetry, February, 1971, November, 1975.

Times Literary Supplement, July 19, 1974, November 25, 1977, May 6, 1983, January 10, 1986, July 17, 1987, May 20, 1988, October 27, 1989.
Tribune Books (Chicago), August 13, 1989.
Washington Post Book World, August 20, 1989.

*   *   *

STEWART, J(ohn) I(nnes) M(ackintosh) 1906- (Michael Innes)

PERSONAL: Born September 30, 1906, in Edinburgh, Scotland; son of John (in education) and Eliza Jane (Clark) Stewart; married Margaret Hardwick (a physician), 1932; children: three sons, two daughters. *Education:* Oriel College, Oxford, M.A., 1928.

ADDRESSES: Home—Fawler Copse, Fawler, Wantage, Oxon OX12 9QJ, England.

CAREER: Writer. University of Leeds, Yorkshire, England, lecturer in English, 1930-35; University of Adelaide, Adelaide, South Australia, jury professor of English, 1935-45; Queen's University, Belfast, Ireland, lecturer, 1946-48; Oxford University, Oxford, England, reader in English literature, 1969-73. Student of Christ Church, Oxford, 1949-73; Walker Ames Professor at University of Washington, 1961.

AWARDS, HONORS: Matthew Arnold Memorial Prize, 1929; D.Litt., University of New Brunswick, 1962, University of Leicester, 1979, St. Andrews University, 1980.

WRITINGS:

NOVELS

Mark Lambert's Supper, Gollancz, 1954.
The Guardians, Gollancz, 1955, Norton, 1957.
A Use of Riches, Norton, 1957, reprinted, University of Chicago Press, 1983.
The Man Who Won the Pools, Norton, 1961.
The Last Tresilians, Norton, 1963.
An Acre of Grass, Norton, 1965.
The Aylwins, Norton, 1966.
Vanderlyn's Kingdom, Norton, 1967.
Avery's Mission, Norton, 1971.
A Palace of Art, Norton, 1972.
Mungo's Dream, Norton, 1973.
The Gaudy (first book in "A Staircase in Surrey" quintet), Gollancz, 1974, Norton, 1975.
Young Pattullo (second book in "A Staircase in Surrey" quintet), Gollancz, 1975, Norton, 1976.
A Memorial Service (third book in "A Staircase in Surrey" quintet), Norton, 1976.
The Madonna of the Astrolabe (fourth book in "A Staircase in Surrey" quintet), Norton, 1977.
Full Term (fifth book in "A Staircase in Surrey" quintet), Norton, 1978.
Andrew and Tobias, Norton, 1980.
A Villa in France, Norton, 1982.
An Open Prison, Norton, 1984.
The Naylors, Norton, 1985.

NOVELS UNDER PSEUDONYM MICHAEL INNES

Death at the President's Lodging, Gollancz, 1936, reprinted, Penguin, 1964, published as *Seven Suspects,* Dodd, 1937, reprinted, Doubleday, 1962.
Hamlet, Revenge!, Dodd, 1937, reprinted, Penguin, 1976.

Lament for a Maker, Dodd, 1938, reprinted, New English Library, 1964.

The Spider Strikes Back, Dodd, 1939 (published in England as *Stop Press,* Gollancz, 1939).

The Secret Vanguard (also see below), Gollancz, 1940, Dodd, 1941.

A Comedy of Terrors (also see below), Dodd, 1940 (published in England as *There Came Both Mist and Snow,* Gollancz, 1940, reprinted, 1972).

Appleby on Ararat, Dodd, 1941, reprinted, Greenwood Press, 1971.

The Daffodil Affair, Dodd, 1942, reprinted, Garland Publishing, 1976.

The Weight of the Evidence, Gollancz, 1943, Dodd, 1944.

Appleby's End, Dodd, 1945, reprinted, Greenwood Press, 1970.

What Happened at Hazelwood, Gollancz, 1944, Dodd, 1947, reprinted, Gollancz, 1973.

Unsuspected Chasm, Dodd, 1946 (published in England as *From London Far,* Gollancz, 1946).

Night of Errors, Gollancz, 1947, Dodd, 1948, reprinted, Gollancz, 1974.

The Case of the Journeying Boy, Dodd, 1949 (published in England as *The Journeying Boy,* Gollancz, 1949).

Paper Thunderbolt, Dodd, 1951 (published in England as *Operation Pax,* Gollancz, 1951).

One Man Show (also see below), Dodd, 1952 (published in England as *A Private View,* Gollancz, 1952).

Christmas at Candleshoe, Dodd, 1953.

The Man from the Sea, Dodd, 1955.

A Question of Queens, Dodd, 1956 (published in England as *Old Hall, New Hall,* Gollancz, 1956).

Death on a Quiet Day, Dodd, 1957 (published in England as *Appleby Plays Chicken,* Gollancz, 1957).

The Long Farewell, Dodd, 1958.

Hare Sitting Up, Dodd, 1959.

The Case of Sonia Wayward, Dodd, 1960 (published in England as *The New Sonia Wayward,* Gollancz, 1960).

Silence Observed, Dodd, 1961.

The Crabtree Affair, Dodd, 1962 (published in England as *A Connoisseur's Case,* Gollancz, 1962).

Money From Holme, Gollancz, 1964, Dodd, 1965.

The Bloody Wood, Dodd, 1966.

A Change of Heir, Dodd, 1966.

Death by Water, Dodd, 1968.

Appleby at Allington, Dodd, 1968.

Picture of Guilt, Dodd, 1969 (published in England as *A Family Affair,* Gollancz, 1969).

Death at the Chase, Dodd, 1970.

An Awkward Lie, Dodd, 1971.

The Open House, Dodd, 1972.

Appleby's Answer, Dodd, 1973.

Appleby's Other Story, Gollancz, 1973, Dodd, 1974.

The Mysterious Commission, Gollancz, 1974, Dodd, 1975.

The Gay Phoenix, Gollancz, 1976, Dodd, 1977.

Honeybath's Haven, Gollancz, 1977, Dodd, 1978.

The Ampersand Papers, Dodd, 1978.

Going It Alone, Dodd, 1980.

Lord Mullion's Secret, Dodd, 1981.

Sheiks and Adders, Dodd, 1982.

Appleby and Honeybath, Dodd, 1983.

Carson's Conspiracy, Dodd, 1984.

Appleby and the Ospreys, Dodd, 1986.

OTHER

(Editor) Michel Eyquem de Montaigne, *Montaigne's Essays: John Florio's Translation,* Random House, 1931.

Educating the Emotions, [Adelaide], 1944.

(Contributor) Raynor Heppenstall, editor, *Imaginary Conversations: Eight Radio Scripts,* Secker & Warburg, 1948.

Character and Motive in Shakespeare: Some Recent Appraisals Examined, Longman, 1949.

The Man Who Wrote Detective Stories and Other Stories, Norton, 1959.

Eight Modern Writers, Oxford University Press, 1963.

Rudyard Kipling, Dodd, 1966.

(Author of introduction) J. B. Priestley, *Thomas Love Peacock,* Penguin, 1966.

(Editor) Wilkie Collins, *Moonstone,* Penguin, 1966.

(Editor and author of introduction) William Makepeace Thackeray, *Vanity Fair,* Penguin, 1968.

Joseph Conrad, Dodd, 1968.

Cucumber Sandwiches and Other Stories, Norton, 1969.

Thomas Hardy: A Critical Biography, Dodd, 1971.

Shakespeare's Lofty Scene, Oxford University Press for the British Academy, 1971.

Our England Is a Garden (short stories), Norton, 1979.

The Bridge at Arta (short stories), Norton, 1981.

My Aunt Christina: And Other Stories, Norton, 1983.

Myself and Michael Innes: A Memoir, Gollancz, 1987, Norton, 1988.

OTHER; UNDER PSEUDONYM MICHAEL INNES

(With Heppenstall) *Three Tales of Hamlet,* Gollancz, 1950.

Dead Man's Shoes, Dodd, 1954 (published in England as *Appleby Talking: Twenty-Three Detective Stories,* Gollancz, 1954).

Appleby Talks Again: Eighteen Detective Stories, Gollancz, 1956, Dodd, 1957.

Appleby Intervenes: Three Tales From Scotland Yard (contains *One Man Show, A Comedy of Terrors,* and *The Secret Vanguard*), Dodd, 1965.

The Appleby File: Detective Stories, Gollancz, 1975, Dodd, 1976.

Parlour 4 and Other Stories, Gollancz, 1986.

SIDELIGHTS: J. I. M. Stewart has distinguished himself as both a novelist and literary scholar. His mysteries, written under the pseudonym Michael Innes, have been acknowledged by critics for their intellectual tone and erudite quality; and critics, notably Rayner Heppenstall, have compared some of his other novels to those of Henry James. His scholarly work, *Thomas Hardy,* is considered by many reviewers to be a valuable source of information on that particular author.

Stewart's first two biographies, *Rudyard Kipling* and *Joseph Conrad,* were not as successful as the later *Thomas Hardy.* Rudyard Kipling* was viewed by one writer for *Times Literary Supplement* as a "useful introduction" to the British author. However, the same writer also complained about the lack of fresh information in Stewart's book. The critic warned that "for those for whom introductions are no longer needed its pleasures are rather those of reading about the familiar than of deeper exploration or critical enlightenment."

Stephen Miller held *Joseph Conrad* in a more favorable light. Citing Bertrand Russell's lament that "Conrad, I suppose, is in process of being forgotten . . .," Miller claimed that Stewart's book would renew appreciation for the novelist. But Heppenstall was less enthusiastic. Although he conceeded that *Joseph Conrad* "will meet, I feel sure, a need," he also remarked that the book "somehow has the effect of putting him back into the nonsense world" where too much theorizing is done on certain novelists. Heppenstall voiced his disappointment by writing, "Now, I thought, people would just have to stop talking and writing nonsense about Hardy, James, Shaw, Conrad, Kipling, Yeats, Joyce, and Lawrence."

Stewart's third biography, *Thomas Hardy,* received many enthusiastic reviews. A critic for *Economist* wrote, "Anyone who enjoys reading Hardy's fiction will get a great deal of pleasure and stimulation from reading the commentaries on the novels." The same critic declared that Stewart's "familiarity with the whole file of Hardy studies is abundantly evident, but his contribution differs from most of the worthy discourses in its relaxed and often humorous tone." John Bayley called *Thomas Hardy* "concise, elegant, and witty." James Gindin was similarly impressed, calling it "a highly praiseworthy and provocative book." Gindin also admired Stewart's approach to Hardy, deeming it "biographical, but biographical in an intelligent and flexible way that avoids the dogma implicit in the set of consistent philosophy or structural criticism."

Stewart's novel, *Vanderlyn's Kingdom,* also received a great deal of critical attention, although not always of a positive nature. R. G. G. Price compared Stewart to "a great journalist," and commented that "he can fill a paragraph with things never noticed before; but people and places lose substantiality as events roll." A critic for the *Times Literary Supplement* described the novel as "basically about the dangers of trying to organize and direct the creative life of an artist when one has no intrinsic feeling for the end product," but noted that "it falls short of complete achievement." Alan Pryce-Jones blamed the novel's failure on a lack of significant characters. He wrote that Stewart "has omitted to populate his places with people." Guy Davenport was ambivalent about *Vanderlyn's Kingdom.* "The result is not bad," he observed, "but is less than convincing."

Critics were in disagreement concerning Stewart's *Mungo's Dream.* His story of a friendship shrouded in impending doom was called "a stilted demonstration of what a novel should not be" by Jeanne Kinney. In a difference of opinion, a reviewer for the *Times Literary Supplement* wrote, "Mr. Stewart, in true detective style, keeps everyone guessing to the final chapter. And he spins out his illusion with a good deal of light-hearted literary cavorting." Martin Amis noted both the flaws and fine points of *Mungo's Dream* in his review. "It appears that Mr. Stewart has . . . fallen victim to the diversity of his own talents," he wrote. After observing that there is some of both the mystery-writer and academic imposed in the work, Amis did assert that "there is a lot going on in *Mungo's Dream;* the interest never flags and Mr. Stewart's sharp eye makes up for his cauliflower ear."

The Gaudy concerns Duncan Pattullo, an alumnus of Oxford University who has returned after twenty years to attend a reunion. Melody Hardy wrote that Stewart "captures the romance of an Oxford education and its impact on the men who experience it." She further remarked, "In telling this tale, reminiscent of C. P. Snow, Stewart has captured an environment." A reviewer for the *Times Literary Supplement,* taking into account that *The Gaudy* is the first of five novels featuring Pattullo, was less impressed. "The present reviewer . . .," it was noted, "hopes to be spared the next four installments." The writer added, "One feels that Mr. Stewart would have written better if he had known Christ Church, Oxford, less well."

Young Pattullo is the second of five novels featuring Duncan Pattullo. Victoria Glendinning wrote, "There is nostalgia on every page, expressed in elegant, well-made sentences." She called the novel "an educated, subtle discourse for readers whom the writer

is courteous enough to suppose as educated and subtle as himself." Lalage Pulvertaft agreed with Glendinning that *Young Pattullo* contains "wonderful accounts of undergraduate life." However, like the critic who wrote on *The Gaudy* for the *Times Literary Supplement,* Pulvertaft felt that Stewart was too close to his subject. "The trouble," she wrote, "is that Mr. Stewart's highly wrought, tense tangential style mirrors this society all too closely."

Stewart's third novel in the Duncan Pattullo series, referred to collectively as "A Staircase in Surrey," is *A Memorial Service.* While both Julian Barnes and Susan Kennedy found the novel enjoyable, they both also pointed out Stewart's use of a serial-convention. "One of the drawbacks of the serial novel is the need to remind the reader . . . of people and events introduced in earlier volumes," wrote Kennedy. "Mr. Stewart's way of handling this is to take up old threads in after-dinner conversations or on leisurely, companionable walks." And Barnes wrote that *A Memorial Service* "has pleasures analogous to those of the hightable dinners [Stewart] so regularly describes."

Aside from his scholarly works and novels, Stewart also penned a collection of short stories, *Cucumber Sandwiches.* The tales, often reminiscent of Henry James's shorter works, were deemed "perfect" by a critic for the *New York Times Book Review.* Neil Millar noted that *Cucumber Sandwiches* "exhales the drama of every battle between flesh and spirit. Its flesh never undresses in public, and nearly always dresses for dinner. Its spirit rarely raises—and never lowers—its kindly, cultured, understanding voice." The writer for the *New York Times Book Review* also noted that Stewart "shapes and polishes each sentence with respectful craftsmanship." The same writer added, "Little enough is left us these days. Let us give deep thanks to J. I. M. Stewart for his intellect, his respect for undecayed English, and his preservative humor."

Stewart has also written numerous mysteries under the pseudonym of Michael Innes. Many of the novels feature Sir John Appleby, a resourceful crime-solver who rose in rank to become chief police commissioner before retiring. Even in retirement, though, he has been present in Stewart's recent mysteries such as *The Gay Phoenix, Appleby and Honeybath,* and *Appleby and the Ospreys.* The novels have been praised for their Victorian style although some critics have found them exceedingly erudite and, according to one critic, "boring." However, the character of Appleby is a popular one with both British and American readers. *Washington Post Book World* contributor George L. Scheper calls the Appleby mysteries "highly literate, witty and, as they say, 'donnish.' " Scheper concludes: "Other literate mystery writers since Dorothy L. Sayers have put their oar in, and have come and gone, but Innes has stayed the course for 50 years."

BIOGRAPHICAL/CRITICAL SOURCES:

BOOKS

Contemporary Authors Autobiography Series, Volume 3, Gale, 1986.
Contemporary Literary Criticism, Gale, Volume 7, 1977, Volume 14, 1980, Volume 32, 1985.
Penzler, Otto, *The Great Detectives,* Little, Brown, 1978.
Symons, Julian, *Mortal Consequences: A History—From the Detective Story to the Crime Novel,* Harper, 1972.

PERIODICALS

Best Sellers, June, 1975.
Books and Bookmen, June, 1983.

Book World, November 28, 1971.
British Book News, May, 1982.
Chicago Tribune Book World, June 8, 1980, March 28, 1982.
Christian Science Monitor, June 13, 1970.
Economist, January 15, 1972.
Listener, July 29, 1982.
London Review of Books, December 30, 1982.
Los Angeles Times Book Review, April 3, 1983.
National Review, April 9, 1968.
New Leader, September 9, 1968.
New Statesman, December 20, 1968, September 24, 1971, February 9, 1973, June 13, 1975, April 30, 1976, July 7, 1978, August 10, 1979, November 12, 1982, May 20, 1983.
New York Times, December 11, 1982, December 2, 1983, June 19, 1987.
New York Times Book Review, April 7, 1968, June 19, 1970, May 29, 1977, June 11, 1978, April 29, 1979, February 14, 1982, February 13, 1983, January 1, 1984, July 29, 1984, September 15, 1985.
Observer, August 19, 1979.
Southwest Review, autumn, 1977.
Spectator, September 22, 1967, October 31, 1981.
Times (London), April 18, 1987.
Times Literary Supplement, January 19, 1967, September 21, 1967, December 25, 1969, February 2, 1973, October 25, 1974, June 6, 1975, May 7, 1976, July 7, 1978, January 16, 1981, June 19, 1981, July 2, 1982, November 26, 1982, January 25, 1985, January 31, 1986, September 25, 1987.
Virginia Quarterly Review, winter, 1972.
Washington Post Book World, November 9, 1979, July 18, 1982, October 30, 1988.

*   *   *

STIRLING, Arthur
See SINCLAIR, Upton (Beall)

*   *   *

STONE, Irving 1903-1989

PERSONAL: Surname originally Tannenbaum, name legally changed, 1911; born July 14, 1903, in San Francisco, Calif.; died of heart failure, August 26, 1989, in Los Angeles, Calif.; son of Charles Tannenbaum and Pauline (Rosenberg) Tannenbaum Stone; married Jean Factor (his editor since 1933), February 11, 1934; children: Paula Hubbell, Kenneth. *Education:* University of California, Berkeley, B.A., 1923, graduate study, 1924-26; University of Southern California, M.A., 1924. *Politics:* Independent. *Religion:* Jewish.

ADDRESSES: Home—Beverly Hills, Calif. *Office*—c/o Doubleday & Co., 666 Fifth Ave., New York, N.Y. 10103.

CAREER: University of Southern California, Los Angeles, instructor in economics, 1923-24; University of California, Berkeley, instructor in economics, 1924-26; writer, 1926—. Visiting professor of creative writing, University of Indiana, 1948, University of Washington, 1961, and Gustavus Adolphus College, 1982; lecturer, University of Southern California and California State Colleges, 1966, New York University and Johns Hopkins University, 1985. Specialist on cultural exchange for U.S. State Department to Soviet Union, Poland, and Yugoslavia, 1962; contributing member, American School of Classical Studies, Athens, Greece, 1965—. Member of advisory board, University of California Institute for Creative Arts, 1963—; founder, Cali-

fornia State Colleges Committee for the Arts, 1967; member, Center for the Study of Evolution and the Origin of Life, University of California, Los Angeles, 1985. Member, U.S. delegation to Writers Conference, Kiev, Soviet Union, 1982; panelist, Nobel Conference on "Darwin's Legacy"; member, Soviet-American Writers Conference, Pepperdine University, 1984; Regents' professor, University of California, Los Angeles, 1984—.

Member of California Civil War Centennial Commission, 1961-65, California Citizens' Committee for Higher Education, 1964, and California State Committee on Public Education, 1966-67. Member of Eleanor Roosevelt Memorial Foundation, 1963; vice-president, Eugene V. Debs Foundation, 1963—; trustee, Douglass House Foundation, 1967-74; chairman, Allan Nevins Memorial Fund, Huntington Library, 1972—. Member of American Assembly, Columbia University, 1963-67; president, Beverly Hills Improvement Association, 1964-65. Founder with wife, Jean Stone, of two annual $1000 awards for the best biographical and historical novels published; founder, Jean and Irving Stone Honors Commons, University of California, Los Angeles, 1985.

MEMBER: Authors League of America, PEN, Society of American Historians, National Society of Arts and Letters (member of advisory council, 1976—), Academy of American Motion Picture Arts and Sciences, Academy of Political Science, Academy of American Poets (founder), Western Writers of America, Renaissance Society of America, California Writers Guild (president, 1960-61), California Writers Club (honorary life member), Historical Society of Southern California, Fellows for Schweitzer (founder and president, 1955—), Berkeley Fellows (charter member), Los Angeles Dante Alighieri Society (president, 1968-69).

AWARDS, HONORS: Christopher Award and Silver Spur Award from Western Writers of America, both 1957, for *Men to Match My Mountains;* Golden Lily of Florence, Rupert Hughes Award from Author's Club, Gold Medal from Council of American Artist Societies, and Gold Medal from Commonwealth Club of California, all for *The Agony and the Ecstasy;* named commendatore of Republic of Italy; American Revolution Round Table Award and Literary Father of the Year Award, both 1966, for *Those Who Love;* Gold Trophy from American Women in Radio and Television, 1968; Herbert Adams Memorial Medal from National Sculpture Society, 1970; Golden Plate Award from American Academy of Achievement, 1971; Alumnus of the Year from University of California, Berkeley, 1971; honorary citizen of Athens, Greece, 1972; Corpus Litterarum Award from Friends of the Libraries, University of California, Irvine, 1975; Distinguished Alumni Award from Los Angeles Unified School District, 1976; Author of the Year Award from Book Bank USA, 1976.

Distinguished body of work annual award, Los Angeles PEN Center, 1980; Rupert Hughes Award for excellence in writing from Author's Club, 1980; Call Achievement Award from University of Southern California, 1980; named Grand Ufficiale of the Italian Republic, 1982; Neil H. Jacoby Award from International Student Center, University of California, Los Angeles, 1983; honorary citation from Union of Soviet Writers, 1983; Commandeur dans l'Ordre des Arts et des Lettres from French Ministry of Culture, 1984. D.L. from University of Southern California, 1965; D.Litt. from Coe College, 1967, and California State Colleges, 1971; LL.D. from University of California, Berkeley, 1968; H.H.D. from Hebrew Union College, 1978.

WRITINGS:

Pageant of Youth, A. H. King, 1933.

Lust for Life (biographical novel about Vincent van Gogh; also see below), Longmans, Green, 1934, published with foreword by the author, Modern Library, 1939, reprinted, 1962, published with reader's supplement, Washington Square Press, 1967, published as limited edition with portfolio of drawings by van Gogh, Franklin Library, 1980.

(Editor with wife, Jean Stone) *Dear Theo: The Autobiography of Vincent van Gogh,* Doubleday, 1937, reprinted, New American Library, 1969.

Sailor on Horseback (biographical novel about Jack London), Houghton, 1938, published as *Jack London, Sailor on Horseback,* Doubleday, 1947, reprinted, New American Library of Canada, 1969, published with twenty-eight stories by London as *Irving Stone's Jack London, His Life, Sailor on Horseback,* Doubleday, 1977.

False Witness (novel), Doubleday, 1940.

Clarence Darrow for the Defense (biography), Doubleday, 1941, abridged edition, Bantam, 1958, reprinted, New American Library, 1971.

Immortal Wife (biographical novel about Jessie Benton Fremont; also see below), Doubleday, 1944, condensed edition, 1954, reprinted, New American Library, 1972.

They Also Ran: The Story of the Men Who Were Defeated for the Presidency, Doubleday, 1945, reprinted, New American Library, 1966.

Adversary in the House (biographical novel about Eugene V. Debs), Doubleday, 1947, reprinted, New American Library, 1969.

Earl Warren: A Great American Story (biography), Prentice-Hall, 1948.

The Passionate Journey (biographical novel about John Noble), Doubleday, 1949.

We Speak for Ourselves: A Self-Portrait of America, Doubleday, 1950.

The President's Lady (biographical novel about Rachel and Andrew Jackson; also see below), Doubleday, 1951, reprinted, New American Library, 1968.

Love Is Eternal (biographical novel about Mary Todd and Abraham Lincoln), Doubleday, 1954, reprinted, New American Library, 1969, condensed large type edition, Ulverscroft, 1976.

Men to Match My Mountains: The Opening of the Far West, 1840-1900, Doubleday, 1956, reprinted, Berkley Publishing, 1982.

The Agony and the Ecstasy (biographical novel about Michelangelo Buonarroti; also see below), Doubleday, 1961, illustrated edition, 1963, published with illustrations by Bruce Waldman, Franklin Library, 1977, abridged juvenile edition with illustrations by Joseph Cellini published as *The Great Adventures of Michelangelo,* Doubleday, 1965.

(Editor with J. Stone) *I, Michelangelo, Sculptor: An Autobiography Through Letters,* translated by Charles Speroni, Doubleday, 1962.

(Editor with Allan Nevins) *Lincoln: A Contemporary Portrait,* Doubleday, 1962.

Two Faces of Love: Lust for Life [and] Immortal Wife, Doubleday, 1962.

The Irving Stone Reader, Doubleday, 1963.

The Story of Michelangelo's Pieta, Doubleday, 1964.

Those Who Love (biographical novel about Abigail and John Adams), Doubleday, 1965.

(Editor and author of introduction) *There Was Light: Autobiography of a University; Berkeley,* Doubleday, 1970.

The Passions of the Mind (biographical novel about Sigmund Freud; Collectors Edition Club choice), Doubleday, 1971.

The Greek Treasure (biographical novel about Henry and Sophia Schliemann), Doubleday, 1975.

The Origin (biographical novel about Charles Darwin), Doubleday, 1980.

Irving Stone: Three Complete Novels (includes *Lust for Life, The Agony and the Ecstasy,* and *The President's Lady*), Avenel Books, 1981.

Depths of Glory (biographical novel about Camille Pissarro and the French impressionists), Doubleday, 1985.

The Science, and the Art, of Biography (Naumburg Memorial lecture; monograph), Division of Honors, University of California, Los Angeles, 1986.

CONTRIBUTOR

The People's Reader, Consolidated, 1949.

Isabel Leighton, editor, *The Aspirin Age,* Simon & Schuster, 1949.

Rudolf Flesch, editor, *Best Articles, 1953,* Hermitage House, 1953.

Three Views of the Novel: Lectures by Irving Stone, John O'Hara, and MacKinlay Kantor, Library of Congress, 1957.

American Panorama: West of the Mississippi, Doubleday, 1960.

The Good Housekeeping Treasury, Simon & Schuster, 1960.

(Author of introduction) *The Drawings of Michelangelo,* Borden Publishing, 1961.

Bucklin Moon, editor, *A Doubleday Anthology,* Doubleday, 1962.

Donald C. Rehkoff, editor, *Portraits in Words,* Odyssey, 1962.

Roy Newquist, editor, *Counterpoint,* Rand McNally, 1964.

My Most Inspiring Moment, Doubleday, 1965.

Bromberg and Greene, editors, *Biography for Youth,* Globe, 1965.

Tanner and Vittetoe, editors, *A Guide for Objective Writing,* Ginn, 1968.

Charles L. Hamrum, editor, *Nobel Conference XVII: Darwin's Legacy,* Harper, 1983.

OTHER

"Magnificent Doll" (screenplay), Universal, 1946.

Also author of *The Biographical Novel: A Lecture Presented at the Library of Congress,* 1957, *Evolution of an Idea,* 1965, and *Mary Todd Lincoln: A Final Judgment?,* 1973. Author of plays "The Dark Mirror," 1928, "The White Life" (about Baruch Spinoza), 1929, and "Truly Valiant," 1936, all produced in New York. Also contributor to *Fourteen Radio Plays,* edited by Arch Oboler, Random House. Art critic for the *Los Angeles Times Mirror,* 1959-60. Contributor to popular magazines, including *American Weekly, California Monthly, Catholic Digest, Coronet, Family Weekly, Good Housekeeping, Holiday, Horizon, Life, Saturday Evening Post, Saturday Review,* and *Suburbia Today.*

SIDELIGHTS: "Irving Stone is far and away the most magisterial of all the popular novelists working today," writes Peter Andrews in the *New York Times Book Review.* Although he has written both fiction and biography, Stone is considered the "undisputed king of the literary genre he terms 'biographical novel' " by critics such as Edwin McDowell of the *New York Times Book Review.* Ever since the publication of *Lust for Life,* his popular and enduring fictionalized biography of Vincent van Gogh, Stone has written best-selling biographical novels about such influential figures as Michelangelo in *The Agony and the Ecstasy,* Sigmund Freud in *The Passions of the Mind,* Charles Darwin in *The Origin,* and more recently, Camille Pissarro and the French impressionists in *The Depths of Glory*. While critics have been somewhat reluctant to appreciate the genre itself—considering it a mongrelized form that ultimately fails as biography as well as fiction—and have faulted Stone for what they perceive to be tedious, fact-laden tomes, they nonetheless commend his perseverance and meticulous research. "Searching relentlessly for evidence—letters, documents, records, scraps of paper—Stone has written a series of widely acclaimed books," says Marshall Berges in the *Los Angeles Times*, "each time focusing on a long-departed giant and vividly restoring not only the era and the scene but most of all the person."

"I have always loved human stories, both the reading and the writing of them," relates Stone in a *Contemporary Authors Autobiography Series* essay. "I decided early on that I would read all the great tales that had been written, and those which had not yet been set down I would create myself." Although Stone studied economics and political science in college, the desire to become a writer ultimately proved to be more powerful than the inclination to complete his doctorate and eventually led him to Paris in the 1920s. "During my fifteen months in Paris, Antibes and Florence, I wrote seventeen full-length plays, thirty-one one-act plays, several essays and random chapters of novels that never got any further," continues Stone. "The work literally poured out of my fountain pen; yet in some dim way I knew that this was an act of regurgitation rather than creativity." The plays were unsuccessful, but Berges notes that Stone, having been "dazzled" by detective stories as a child, "supported himself by writing penny-a-word detective stories. Later, he adopted detective-like methods to become one of the world's best-selling authors."

In the introduction to *The Irving Stone Reader,* Joseph Henry Jackson observes that working on these early detective stories taught Stone "the necessity of careful plotting, the trick of keeping a narrative on the move, the techniques of construction." Jackson suggests, however, that "the kind of spark that would fire his imagination . . . was character-ready-made, the story of someone who had lived, whose acts could be found in the record and whose motives might be traced by patient, careful, sympathetic investigation." What motivates Stone to bring a given character to life is "any suspicion that such a character had been misunderstood, perhaps even misrepresented through historical accident or through an early biographer's prejudice." While critical response to Stone's work has not paralleled his popularity, Peter Gorner maintains in the *Chicago Tribune* that most people are probably indebted to Stone for what they know about van Gogh, Freud, and Michelangelo, and that "Stone also has written about lesser-known folks he felt people should learn about. . . . And he has been quick to portray great lives he believes were unfairly wounded by cheap shots."

In *The Science, and the Art, of Biography* (his Naumburg Memorial Lecture at the University of California, Los Angeles), Stone presents his thoughts on the genre he has fostered and on the author's responsibility toward it: "The biographical novel is a true and documented story of one human being's journey across the face of the years, transmuted from the raw material of life into the delight and purity of an authentic art form. It is based on the conviction that the best of all plots lie in human character; and that human character is endlessly colorful and revealing. The biographical novel sets out to document this truth, for character is plot; character development is action; and character fulfillment is resolution." Stone also explains that while biography involves three persons—the subject, the reader, and the author as a mediator between them—the biographical novel involves but two, since the author merges with his subject: "The author becomes the main character by years of intense study of his diaries, journals, correspondence, recorded dialogues, writings about him, his finished work, his character, personality, his manner of speaking, acting; geographic place in the world. The author slips slowly and authentically into his bloodstream, the millions of cells in his brain, the feelings in his gut and nervous system. A total portrait of this one human being's values, his beatings and failures, accomplishments and fulfillments."

Stone indicates to Grace Glueck in the *New York Times* that his preference for the biographical novel over nonfictionalized biography is partially due to the opportunity it affords him to use the "novelistic skills" he acquired during his early attempts at writing plays. But he also says: "I know from experience that biographies have a limited audience. We have thousands of readers who love [the biographical novel] and are thrilled by it, who'd never get near a conventional biography." In *The Science, and the Art, of Biography,* Stone asserts that "the research, dedication and techniques of the biographical novelist are identical to those of the biographer. The major difference is one of dramatization." Perhaps because of his efforts to champion the underdog or to set the historical record straight, Stone is aware of his responsibility for accurate representation in his work and has produced monumentally impressive research for each book. Moreover, Stone's patient and careful research has brought much previously unpublished and important information into print. In addition to the letters of Michelangelo, Stone has had access to van Gogh's letters and Freud's papers, as well as access to the friends and relatives of his more contemporary subjects.

The persistent effort to uncover remnants of an individual's existence calls for ingenuity and tenacity as well as stamina; but to revivify such an existence also requires creative imagination. Stone suggests in Roy Newquist's *Counterpoints* that "even if there is endless documentation it would be impossible to know what a man thought inside his own mind." A vital question is thereby raised, says Stone: "Do you push your character around, and distort history, or do you study [him] so carefully, identify him so totally and with such honesty, that when you come to the point where documentation leaves off, and you must put yourself inside the heart and mind of this man or woman, can you think and feel as he (or she) would have, in the given circumstances? This is the creative part of the book, and if you are honest, if you are sincere, if you have worked hard, if you are determined to be true and to achieve exact identity and to plumb the depths of a man's feelings, I think you have a good chance of doing the job proudly."

Stone's research for *Lust for Life* included a stay not only in van Gogh's asylum cell but also, on the fortieth anniversary of his death, in the very room in which van Gogh died. As Stone recalls in *The Science, and the Art, of Biography:* "On the very night that Vincent died I went to bed about midnight, surrounded by colored reproductions of his canvases. I pored over them until one o'clock when I began to feel faint. I could not understand why until I realized that Vincent had died in that very bed at 1:20 in the morning. I grew fainter, until finally at 1:19 I threw off the covers, dashed to the back window, stuck my head out and took in deep lungsful of the night air."

Stone's intense identification with his subjects has prompted several critics to question the extent of his objectivity. In a review of *Lust for Life* in the *Nation,* for instance, Robert Morse suggests that "from a novelist one might have hoped for a dispassionate and honest attempt to clarify and explain the behavior of an extremely interesting human being. . . . I began to suspect that . . . Stone had fallen into the old attitude of unquestioning sentimental identification with his hero." However, a reviewer for the *Boston Transcript* notes in his defense of the novel: "Stone did not need to call this fiction. Many biographers have taken more liberties with less results. There is reality here, pathos, humor, a knowledge of art and artists, and a delightful, nonchalant style which keeps us fascinated . . . to the end."

Decrying Stone's method of interpreting the life and motivation of his subject by "becoming" that character, some critics suggest that Stone tends toward idealization. R. J. Clements, for example, finds *The Agony and the Ecstasy* "an important and thoroughly enjoyable novel," but says in the *Saturday Review* that "Stone's Michelangelo is an idealized version, purged not only of ambisexuality, but of the egotism, fault-finding, harsh irony, and ill temper that we know were characteristic of Michelangelo." And although a *Kirkus Reviews* contributor calls *The Agony and the Ecstasy* "an enormous book, in scope, in historical background, in depth perception and characterization," others feel it is simply not a very good novel. Moreover, despite the enormous sales of his novels, many critics seem to agree that Stone is better suited to historical and biographical nonfiction. In the *New York Herald Tribune Lively Arts,* for example, Richard Winston distinguishes between Stone's weaknesses and his obvious talent: "How elegant and convincing some of . . . Stone's shrewd guesses and fictional insights might have been in a straight biography—whereas here they are so often embarrassing and give rise to uneasiness and dissatisfaction."

The critics' obvious admiration for Stone's impressive research does not prevent them from questioning his manipulation of the collected data. In the *Atlantic,* Steven Marcus praises Stone's fictionalized biography of Freud, *The Passions of the Mind,* for its bibliography, calling it "daunting in its compendiousness, impressive evidence of the earnestness with which [Stone] has taken this work to himself." However, he also believes that "the novel constitutes itself by an incessant, indiscriminate, and incontinent regurgitation of second-hand information." Similarly, Richard Locke refers to the book in the *New York Times* as "a 'massively researched' erector set of a novel crammed with biographical, architectural, gastronomical, geographical, medical, historical details." And while Edwin Fadiman, Jr., observes in *Saturday Review* that "the author's integrity is revealed in every line," he adds that "it is precisely this glacial earnestness, this obsession with detail that make *The Passions of the Mind* praiseworthy yet dull." In *Time,* Brad Darrach calls Stone "the taxidermist of biography" and suggests that he "seems more interested in the facts than he is in Freud." Several critics think that the accumulation of detail inhibits the reader's awareness of any inner evolution on the part of the subject. Marcus, for instance, writes: "There is suggested none of the pathological involvement without which a genius of Freud's magnitude is almost unthinkable. It is Freud without the warts." Yet Rosalind Wade calls the book "a magnificent memorial to Freud's achievement" in *Contemporary Review.* "Apart from being an excellent narrative in its own right the book affords an illuminating blue-print of the means by which psychotherapy was belatedly accepted during the 'twenties and 'thirties in the London teaching hospitals."

Stone's techniques may have an undesired effect, suggests Redmond O'Hanlon in the *Times Literary Supplement:* "The making of lists, the fussy accumulation of historical detail, far from bringing a period to life, may actually museum it away, stiff and distant." And some reviewers even wonder whether a profusion of facts, no matter how comprehensive, can disclose accurately a sense of the individual. Calling Stone's *Origin* "743 pages of catalogues," Anthony Astrachan writes in the *Washington Post Book World* that the novel "conveys nothing of Darwin's emo-

tions, and little of his intellect beyond what can be gleaned from documents." Further, Astrachan finds that "nowhere . . . is there any of the one thing that would justify a novel about Darwin: a re-creation of the feelings and the mental processes of one of the great figures of the nineteenth century." Webster Schott acknowledges in the *New York Times Book Review* that the book is "a work of vast research, much pleasure and modest insights," yet he also senses that it "seldom seems to reach the essence of the man who went through physical anguish . . . as he wrestled with conflicts created by his extraordinary ideas and their public reception." Perhaps Stone has "encountered a character he can observe in almost limitless detail, but not fully reveal," suggests Schott.

Noting, however, that Darwin poses a "severe challenge for a biographical novelist," S. J. Gould adds in *Science* that "Stone's success with such a recalcitrant subject is a testimony to the power of an art that he has promoted assiduously for many years." While Christopher Lehmann-Haupt of the *New York Times* admits that *The Origin* "does sound a few major chords amid its endless stream of notes," he thinks that "such chords could have just as well been sounded by a conventional biography." And despite the shared belief that "there is little sense of the man . . . and no large attempt to follow the intricacies of his work," O'Hanlon maintains that "this is far and away . . . Stone's best researched and best written book to date."

Some critics feel that because Stone's research is so thorough he may be overwhelmed by its sheer mass. Susan Isaacs, for example, finds that Stone's book about Camille Pissarro and the French impressionists, *The Depths of Glory,* "lacks the verve, narrative device and structure that made his earlier work so enjoyable." She adds in the *New York Times Book Review* that "this book is little more than mere data." Believing the purpose of detail should be "to flesh out character or add texture to the setting," Isaacs thinks "Stone seems overwhelmed by the piles of information he's gathered, and manages only the weakest narrative thread." However, Daniel Fuchs notes in the *Los Angeles Times Book Review* that Stone "willingly forgoes the useful devices of fiction—the suspense that comes from organized plot and drama, the winning, fictional characters, the manufactured pleasures and excitement and surprise of the actual event." Stone expressed to Glueck that he would like to see Camille Pissarro become as well-known as Vincent van Gogh, and Glueck remarks that "though as a subject, Pissarro lacks the glamour of Van Gogh and Michelangelo . . . Stone has spared no detail that might pique the reader's interest. He gives a full picture of Pissarro's travails as a painter and a family man . . . and conjures up a Paris art world where the schmaltz runs deep."

Stone admits that as a writer he may be verbose. His wife edits all his work and routinely cuts about ten percent of it before a finished product is achieved—a finished product which some reviewers may claim is still too long. Stone and his work, though, have prevailed over the critics, whom he refers to in *The Science, and the Art, of Biography* as "my sometimes critics—and how barren an author's life would be without critics!" The popularity of his work is certainly confirmed by the many languages into which it has been translated: French, German, Spanish, Italian, Greek, Swedish, Turkish, Arabic, Japanese, Russian, Finnish, Norwegian, Danish, Dutch, Portuguese, Polish, Hungarian, Rumanian, Czech, Slovene, Hebrew, Assamese, Hindu, Tamil, Gujarati, Kannada, Marathi, Kanarese, Bengali, Malayan, Latvian, Serbo-Croatian, Persian, Bratislavian, and Icelandic. Surmising that "the secret of the popularity of . . . Stone's novels may very well lie in their unreadability," Peter Andrews remarks in the *New York Times Book Review* that getting through one of his books "gives one a sense of accomplishment." Perhaps, however, the secret rests in the formula Stone uses for his books. "The recurring theme," notes Gorner, "is one man (or woman) against the world, succeeding no matter what." Stone elaborated on this theme to Berges: "My goal always is to tell a universal story, meaning it's about a person who has an idea, a vision, a dream, an ambition to make the world somewhat less chaotic. He or she suffers hardships, defeats, miseries, illnesses, poverty, crushing blows. But ultimately that person accomplishes a big, beautiful, gorgeous job of work, leaving behind a testimonial that the human mind can grow and accomplish fantastic ends."

MEDIA ADAPTATIONS: Stone's novel *False Witness* was filmed by Republic in 1941 as "Arkansas Judge" and was released in Great Britain under its original title; *Immortal Wife* became a film by Twentieth Century-Fox in 1953 under the title "The President's Lady," starring Charlton Heston and Susan Hayward; *Lust for Life* was filmed by Metro-Goldwyn-Mayer in 1956 and starred Kirk Douglas and Anthony Quinn in an Academy Award-winning performance; *The Agony and the Ecstasy* was filmed by Twentieth Century-Fox in 1963 and starred Charlton Heston and Rex Harrison.

AVOCATIONAL INTERESTS: Collecting art.

BIOGRAPHICAL/CRITICAL SOURCES:

BOOKS

Authors in the News, Volume 1, Gale, 1976.
Contemporary Authors Autobiography Series, Volume 3, Gale, 1986.
Contemporary Literary Criticism, Volume 7, Gale, 1977.
Newquist, Roy, *Counterpoint,* Rand McNally, 1964.
Stone, Irving, *The Irving Stone Reader,* introduction by Joseph Henry Jackson, Doubleday, 1963.
Stone, *The Science, and the Art, of Biography* (Naumberg Memorial Lecture), Division of Honors, University of California, Los Angeles, 1986.

PERIODICALS

Atlantic, May, 1961, April, 1971.
Books, September 30, 1934, October 19, 1941.
Boston Transcript, September 26, 1934.
Catholic World, August, 1961.
Chicago Sunday Tribune, March 26, 1961.
Chicago Tribune, August 26, 1980.
Christian Science Monitor, October 17, 1934, September 27, 1951, October 14, 1954, August 30, 1962.
Contemporary Review, July, 1971.
Fort Lauderdale News, January 10, 1975.
Forum, October, 1938.
Kirkus Reviews, July 15, 1956, January 15, 1961.
Los Angeles Times Book Review, November 18, 1984, October 20, 1985.
Nation, November 7, 1934.
New Republic, September 21, 1938, June 5, 1971.
Newsweek, November 1, 1965.
New York Herald Tribune, September 26, 1934.
New York Herald Tribune Book Review, September 28, 1947, August 22, 1954, September 30, 1956.
New York Herald Tribune Lively Arts, March 19, 1961.
New York Times, September 30, 1934, September 18, 1938, April 14, 1940, November 9, 1941, October 1, 1944, March 27, 1971, August 7, 1980, October 16, 1985.
New York Times Book Review, March 19, 1961, August 26, 1962, March 14, 1965, November 7, 1965, March 14, 1971, Octo-

ber 12, 1975, September 14, 1980, August 9, 1981, September 16, 1984, October 20, 1985.
San Francisco Chronicle, October 7, 1951, September 23, 1956, March 17, 1961.
Saturday Review, August 21, 1954, March 18, 1961, May 15, 1965, November 20, 1965, April 10, 1971, May 27, 1972, August, 1980.
Saturday Review of Literature, September 30, 1944, September 29, 1951.
Science, January 16, 1981.
Springfield Republican, September 30, 1956, August 19, 1962.
Time, September 19, 1938, November 5, 1965, April 5, 1971, September 15, 1975, October 10, 1977, November 11, 1985.
Times Literary Supplement, July 13, 1967, April 6, 1971, January 2, 1976, June 19, 1981.
Washington Post, April 2, 1971.
Washington Post Book World, August 22, 1980.
World Literature Today, winter, 1980.

OBITUARIES:

PERIODICALS

Chicago Tribune, August 28, 1989.
Los Angeles Times, August 28, 1989.
New York Times, August 28, 1989.
Times (London), August 29, 1989.
Washington Post, August 28, 1989.

*   *   *

STONE, Robert (Anthony) 1937-

PERSONAL: Born August 21, 1937, in New York, N.Y.; son of C. Homer and Gladys Catherine (a teacher; maiden name, Grant) Stone; married Janice G. Burr, December 11, 1959; children: Deidre M., Ian A. *Education:* Attended New York University, 1958-60, and Stanford University, 1962-64.

ADDRESSES: Agent—Candida Donadio & Associates, 231 West 22nd St., New York, N.Y. 10011.

CAREER: Novelist and screenwriter. *New York Daily News,* New York City, copyboy and caption writer, 1958-60; worked at various jobs, 1960-62, in a coffee factory and as an actor in New Orleans, La., and as an advertising copywriter in New York City; *National Mirror,* New York City, writer, 1965-67; freelance writer in London, England, Hollywood, Calif., and Saigon, South Vietnam (now Ho Chi Minh City, Vietnam), 1967-71; Princeton University, Princeton, N.J., writer in residence, 1971-72, faculty member, 1985 and 1986; Amherst College, Amherst, Mass., associate professor of English, 1972-75, writer in residence, 1977-78; writer in residence at Stanford University, 1979, University of Hawaii at Manoa, 1979-80, and Harvard University, 1981; faculty member at University of California, Irvine, 1982, New York University, 1983-84, and University of California, San Diego, 1985. *Military service:* U.S. Navy, 1955-58; served in amphibious force of the Atlantic Fleet and as senior enlisted journalist on Operation Deep Freeze Three in Antarctica; became petty officer third class.

MEMBER: PEN (member of executive board), Authors League of America, Authors Guild, Writers Guild of America, West.

AWARDS, HONORS: Wallace Stegner fellowship, Stanford University, 1962-64; Houghton-Mifflin literary fellowship, 1967, and William Faulkner Foundation Award for notable first novel, 1968, both for *A Hall of Mirrors;* Guggenheim fellowship, 1971; National Book Award, 1975, for *Dog Soldiers;* nomination for best script adapted from another medium, Writers Guild of America, 1979, for "Who'll Stop the Rain"; *Los Angeles Times Book Prize,* 1982, for *A Flag for Sunrise;* nominations for American Book Award, National Book Critics Circle Award, and PEN/Faulkner Award, all 1982, all for *A Flag for Sunrise;* runner-up for Pulitzer Prize in fiction, 1982, for *A Flag for Sunrise;* American Academy and Institute of Arts and Letters Award, 1982; John Dos Passos Prize for literature, 1982; National Endowment for the Arts fellowship, 1983; co-recipient of Harold and Mildred Strauss Livings award, 1988; grant from National Institute of Arts and Letters.

WRITINGS:

NOVELS

A Hall of Mirrors, Houghton, 1967.
Dog Soldiers, Houghton, 1974.
A Flag for Sunrise, Knopf, 1981.
Children of Light, Knopf, 1986.
Outerbridge Reach, Weidenfeld & Nicolson, 1989.

SCREENPLAYS

"WUSA" (based on his novel *A Hall of Mirrors*), Paramount, 1970.
(With Judith Roscoe) "Who'll Stop the Rain" (based on his novel *Dog Soldiers*), United Artists, 1978.

CONTRIBUTOR

Richard Scowcroft and Wallace Stegner, editors, *Twenty Years of Stanford Short Stories,* Stanford University Press, 1966.
New American Review 6, New American Library, 1969.
David Burnett and Martha Foley, editors, *Best American Short Stories, 1970,* Houghton, 1970.
James B. Hall and Elizabeth Hall, editors, *The Realm of Fiction: Seventy-four Short Stories,* McGraw, 1977.
Theodore Solotaroff, editor, *American Review 26,* Bantam, 1977.
William O'Rourke, editor, *On the Job: Fiction about Work by Contemporary American Writers,* Vintage, 1977.
Rust Hills and Tom Jenks, editors, *Esquire Fiction Reader,* Volume I, Wampeter, 1985.
Images of War (nonfiction), Boston Publishing, 1986.

Also contributor to *Who We Are,* a collection of articles on aspects of the war in Vietnam.

OTHER

Contributor of articles and reviews to periodicals, including *Atlantic, Harper's, Life, New York Times Book Review, Manchester Guardian,* and *TriQuarterly.*

WORK IN PROGRESS: A novel set in New England.

SIDELIGHTS: In just four novels, Robert Stone has established himself as one of America's most stringent political voices and an artist of considerable caliber. His books, many critics acknowledge, are not for everyone. A typical Stone protagonist is a down-and-out, cynical drifter engrossed in the drug culture or otherwise at odds with the law. Stone's stories have taken readers to the bowels of society, from the underbelly of New Orleans to the jungles of Vietnam, from the brutality of war-torn Central America to the artificial glamour of Hollywood. In this way the author is often compared to Graham Greene, Joseph Conrad, John Dos Passos, and Nathanael West, but Stone's individuality ultimately distinguishes him as "the apostle of strung out," as *New York Times Book Review* critic Jean Strouse sees him.

Stone has earned that epithet. A native of Brooklyn, New York, a product of Catholic school upbringing, the young man started his career in the 1950s as a newspaper copyboy, but soon Stone and his wife dropped their conventional life to see America. "They got as far as New Orleans, where they both worked at a variety of menial jobs that never lifted them above the poverty level," reports Sybil Steinberg in *Publishers Weekly.* Finally, the Stones, joined by a daughter born in a charity hospital, returned to New York City. There the author joined the emerging bohemian scene, counting Jack Kerouac among his confederates, and the group's dedication to discovery took them to northern California and to Ken Kesey.

Stone's days in Louisiana undoubtedly provided him with the background material for his first novel, *A Hall of Mirrors.* While this story of a young man's encounter with class politics is set in New Orleans, the book is really about all of America, as several reviewers suggest. "The unspoken theme of *A Hall of Mirrors* is the relation between the prosperous official society and its necessary underworld of drop-outs and cast-offs," notes *Commonweal* critic Emile Capouya. "These parallel systems meet in the persons of two characters. One is the millionaire demagogue, who wants to get more power than he already has by exploiting the fears of the poor white trash. The other is Rheinhardt, the pattern of the available 'intellectual,' the disabused journeyman liar of the communications industries." The communications industry in question is WUSA, a rightwing propagandist radio station that Rheinhardt infiltrates. The author's "breadth of mind and . . . seriousness [set] him apart from any number of merely talented writers, for he instinctively makes the connection between the accidents of his fable and the world of his readers' experience," says Capouya, adding that Rheinhardt is "[Albert] Camus' Stranger in a less abstract, less absolute form."

"Stone's language is a joy," declares Ivan Gold in his *New York Times Book Review* piece on *A Hall of Mirrors.* "Rich yet unobtrusive, self-effacing but in complete control—here is a growing sense of awe, once one has finished the book, at what the effort must have cost him. When so accomplished a style is joined to an ear which encompasses the dictions of hippies, and senators, and a good portion of the worlds in between; which seems incapable of producing or reproducing a line of dialogue which does not ring true, it takes an act of willfulness on the part of the reader not to be drawn in, and moved, and altered."

The serious scholarly attention accorded Stone's first novel is summed up in the words of L. Hugh Moore, who says in *Critique: Studies in Modern Fiction:* "Stone's vision of the modern world and society is a profoundly pessimistic one. The implications of his main, related metaphors—the undersea world and evolution—are, indeed, disturbing. To see the world as an environment, an ecological system, that is as cold, hostile, and brutal as the sea floor is hardly new. Nor is his view of his characters as denizens of the deep profoundly original. What disturbs and what makes the novel contemporarily relevant is the fact that Stone offers no melioristic possibility. To survive in the new ice age is immoral; neither work, bitter humor, nor withdrawal is humanly possible. 'Despair and die' is the final message of the novel."

Suspenseful, convincing, cruel, funny and frightening are just some of the words critics use to describe Stone's next novel, *Dog Soldiers.* Like *A Hall of Mirrors,* this book exposes corruption and greed, this time in settings ranging from Saigon to California. During the waning days of the Vietnam war, journalist John Converse, stationed in Saigon, gets an offer he cannot refuse: If he smuggles three kilograms of pure heroin back to the States, he will earn $40,000. Engaging an accomplice, Ray Hicks, into the scheme, Converse manages to get the package to California and to leave it in possession of his wife, Marge. "The stark evil in this plan quickly flows into nightmare," *Time*'s Paul Gray writes, as Converse and his cohorts are pursued by agents for a corrupt federal officer.

Dog Soldiers "is more than a white-knuckled plot; it is a harrowing allegory," continues Gray. "The novice smugglers evade a sense of their own villainy through sophistry or indifference. Converse rationalizes that in a world capable of producing the horrors of war, 'people are just naturally going to want to get high.'" *New York Review of Books* critic Roger Sale takes a different view. "The more seriously Stone takes his characters, the more carefully he brings their aimlessness to a decision, the more he eventually either jettisons the aimlessness or falsifies the decisiveness and its importance. I'm not sure how he could better have pondered his materials and his wonderful first half, but the remainder is good writing that seems divorced from a wider purpose than its own existence, and so seems just like writing."

Despite his reservations, however, Sale concludes that *Dog Soldiers* ultimately shows the author's "clear eye for detail and clear-eyed determination to see these lives through to some end without sentimentalizing them. Throughout, thus, his integrity gives us a sense of learning at first hand what most of us have known only as hearsay or freakout. He brings the news, as novelists are supposed to do; he makes one think we have only begun to understand our immediate past." And a *Washington Post Book World* reviewer, labeling *Dog Soldiers* the most important novel of the year, adds that "Stone writes like a Graham Greene whose God is utterly dead, and he favors the same sort of setting, the same juxtaposition of the exotic and the banal."

Stone's third novel, *A Flag for Sunrise*, "is about Catholics—a nun, a priest, an anthropologist, a drifter—caught up among spies, gun runners, murderers, maniacs, and revolutionaries in a poor Central American country ruled by American business interests and the CIA through a local military regime," summarizes Leonard Michaels in the *Saturday Review*. "The plot is complicated and built upon short scenes, some of them so intensely dramatic they could be published independently. What holds them together is suspenseful action, an atmosphere of neurasthenic menace, and Stone's prose style. Lean, tough, quick, and smart, it is perfect for violent action, yet lyrical enough for Stone's nun as she contemplates her own mind, her 'inward place.'"

To *Los Angeles Times Book Review* writer Carolyn See, Stone "does American imperialism so well it is possible to read his third novel as a purely aesthetic experience. The decay is so attractive, so muted, so 'literary,' that reading it is . . . like curling up with Graham Greene in Africa or Joseph Conrad in the deep Pacific." William Logan finds distinct ties between the author's first and third books. *A Flag for Sunrise*, he notes in the *Chicago Tribune Book World*, "so carefully duplicates the structure of 'A Hall of Mirrors,' even to the rhythm of its title. In each, the narration emanated from three characters whose careless intertwinnings led to a cataclysm only one escaped alive."

Jonathan Yardley has criticism for the author's style. While Stone "writes very well, [creating] plausible characters [with] a deft hand for dramatic incident," the critic says in the *Washington Post Book World*, the author "is a preacher masquerading in novelist's clothing, indulging himself in rhetoric right out of SDS or the IWW. It is the politics of his novels rather than the craft of them that seems ultimately to interest him the most; the problem is that there is nothing interesting about his politics." Elaborating, Yardley points out that the nun character, Sister Justin, "is clearly intended to be the novel's moral center, but she is sim-

ply too good to be true." Also, Stone "trivializes what he hopes to glorify. The stock roles that his characters play and the stock rhetoric that they utter are nothing more than safe, comfortable responses to a situation that is considerably more complex and ambiguous than Stone appears to realize." However, Yardley remarks, when the author "gets off his soapbox and pays attention to the craft of fiction, he is very good."

On the other hand, *Commonweal* critic Frank McConnell calls *A Flag for Sunrise* "an important political novel precisely because it is such a perceptive religious novel." Further, Stone offers "an indication of a new trend in the American sensibility. For Conrad, Greene, and [John] LeCarre can be considered the elegists of Britain's dreams of empire and the explorers of that vaster, richer territory of the spirit that lies beyond the hope of triumph over history. Robert Stone is the first American writer I know of who shares that melancholy, that maturity, and that bitter sanity. And if his novel is fierce in its despair, it is even fiercer in its unvoiced suggestion of a sensibility that renders despair itself mute before the absurd, unending possibility of love." "*Flag* is a disturbing book in many ways, some of them not intended," in Richard Poirier's opinion. Poirier, in the *New York Review of Books*, adds that he is "not referring to Stone's politics as such but to the degree to which they may reveal more about his opportunism as a novelist than about his anxieties as a citizen."

Stone's first two novels were made into feature films. While he contributed to both screenplays, "WUSA," based on *A Hall of Mirrors*, and "Who'll Stop the Rain," based on *Dog Soldiers*, are remarkable for the unfavorable responses both received from film critics and audiences. Many factors go into the fate of a film, however—the work of the director, cast, crew and production company included—and Stone has stated in interviews that the finished products were never even close to the screen treatments he had originally conceived. Still, his experiences in film provided the author with the impetus for his fourth novel, *Children of Light*. Set on the location of a film, it chronicles the wasted days of a washed-up screenwriter and a schizophrenic actress; the novel offers "a fine, complex, often funny tale, full of lights and shadows, with great dialogue and a sharp sense of character and place," according to Jean Strouse in the *New York Times Book Review*.

The book "is jampacked with people pretending to be other than they are, people with masks, people who have become their lies. Even the film location, Mexico pretending to be Louisiana, is schizoid. The only sane person is the mad one, [the actress] Lee Verger, notes *Washington Post Book World* critic Stephen Dobyns. The author "has taken some spectacular risks, particularly with his climax," says Christopher Lehmann-Haupt. "His drama plays, and one's sense of dread builds up like a bank of storm clouds."

Lehmann-Haupt, commenting in a *New York Times* article, continues that while *Children of Light* is Stone's "most dramatically coherent performance to date," nevertheless "there is a mechanical quality about the way [he] manipulates his characters that keeps the reader's mind divided. Part of one's reaction is to be amazed at the effects he is pulling off, but another part is to wonder why his characters are so remorselessly condemned to their respective fates. Why is [main character] Gordon Walker a drunk and a coke addict? Why is Lee Verger schizophrenic? Why are all the film types so wiseacre, heartless and nasty? What do all the drugs and alcohol mean? Are they no more than God's way of telling Hollywood that it has too much money? Not that this reader was able to figure out."

Again, Stone's dialogue wins wide praise. Not only does the author's language "snap like a bullwhip," feels *Globe and Mail* reviewer Norman Snider, but the author, "having paid hard dues in Hollywood, has an acute sense of how the patois of the film biz equally encompasses relationships as well as professional arrangements. [A character's] husband, for instance, 'takes a walk' out of the marriage in exactly the same way performers or directors would walk off a film they suspect will damage their career."

Children of Light "seems far more slanted than anything Stone has written before," in A. Alvarez's opinion. "He has always kept apart from the current fashion that confuses fiction with the art of the self and is suspicious of anyone with a strong gift for narrative. Stone, who has a strong imaginative grip on the contemporary American scene and writes like an angel—a fallen, hard-driving angel—is also a marvelous storyteller. He does not take sides and is as much at one with Pablo, the murderous speed freak, as he is with Holliwell, the liberal intellectual," writes Alvarez in the *New York Review of Books.* The critic sums up that in order for the author to reach his own level of truth, "he has sacrificed the intricate, gallows-humor detachment that has made him, in his previous books, one of the most impressive novelists of his generation."

In a 1981 *Washington Post* interview, Stone explained his reasons for telling the stories he does: He believes that by exposing readers to the darker side of society, he is abetting "the awareness of ironies and continuities, showing people that being decent is really hard and that we carry within ourselves our own worst enemy."

Stone told *CA* that the combination of teaching college English courses at various universities and writing books "works rather well. It tends to give the week a certain kind of shape, and it doesn't hurt to talk about writing, because it helps me find out what I believe about writing. The great thing about writing courses is that even if you can't teach anybody to write—which you certainly can't—you get to talk about everything. Writing courses are really more the philosophy of composition than they are anything else. You can't teach people how to write, but you can talk about life, about how it is, how people are. That's not a bad way to pass a couple of hours."

AVOCATIONAL INTERESTS: Scuba diving, acting.

BIOGRAPHICAL/CRITICAL SOURCES:

BOOKS

Contemporary Literary Criticism, Gale, Volume V, 1976, Volume XXIII, 1983, Volume XLII, 1987.

PERIODICALS

Atlantic, November, 1981.
Chicago Tribune Book World, October 25, 1981, March 9, 1986.
Commentary, March, 1982.
Commonweal, April 5, 1968, March 12, 1982, May 23, 1986.
Critique: Studies in Modern Fiction, Volume XL, number 3, 1969.
Encounter, September, 1975.
Esquire, August, 1985.
Globe and Mail (Toronto), April 26, 1986.
Harper's, April 28, 1975.
Los Angeles Times Book Review, November 8, 1981, March 23, 1986.
Modern Fiction Studies, spring, 1984.
New Boston Review, February, 1982.
New Republic, January 4, 1975, November 18, 1981, April 28, 1986.

Newsweek, November 11, 1974, October 26, 1981, March 17, 1986.
New York Review of Books, April 3, 1975, December 3, 1981, April 10, 1986.
New York Times, October 31, 1974, October 16, 1981, March 13, 1986.
New York Times Book Review, September 24, 1967, November 3, 1974, October 18, 1981, April 15, 1984, March 16, 1986.
Publishers Weekly, March 21, 1986.
Saturday Review, November, 1981.
Time, November 11, 1974, October 26, 1981, March 10, 1986.
Times Literary Supplement, May 30, 1975, December 4, 1981, March 21, 1986.
TriQuarterly, winter, 1982.
Washington Post, November 15, 1981.
Washington Post Book World, December 8, 1974, November 1, 1981, March 23, 1986.

*   *   *

STONE, Rosetta
See GEISEL, Theodor Seuss

*   *   *

STONE, Zachary
See FOLLETT, Ken(neth Martin)

*   *   *

STOPPARD, Tom   1937-

PERSONAL: Original name, Tom Straussler; born July 3, 1937, in Zlin, Czechoslovakia; son of Eugene Straussler (a physician) and Martha Stoppard; married Jose Ingle, 1965 (divorced, 1972); married Miriam Moore-Robinson (a physician), 1972; children: (first marriage) two sons; (second marriage) two children. *Education:* Educated in Europe and England.

ADDRESSES: Home—Iver Grove, Iver, Bucks, England. *Agent*—Peter Fraser Dunlop, The Chambers, 5th Floor, Chelsea Harbor, London SW10 OXF, England.

CAREER: Playwright, novelist, radio and television script writer. *Western Daily Press,* Bristol, England, reporter and critic, 1954-58; *Evening World,* Bristol, reporter, 1958-60; free-lance reporter, 1960-63. Director of play, "Born Yesterday," in London, England, at Greenwich Theatre, 1973.

AWARDS, HONORS: Ford Foundation grant to Berlin, 1964; John Whiting Award, 1967; *Evening Standard* drama award for most promising playwright, 1967, for best play of the year for "Jumpers," 1972, and for best comedy of the year for "Travesties," 1974; Prix Italia, 1968; Antoinette Perry (Tony) Award for best play for "Rosencrantz and Guildenstern Are Dead," 1968, and for "Travesties," 1976; New York Drama Critics Circle Award for best play for "Rosencrantz and Guildenstern Are Dead," 1968, and for best play for "Travesties," 1976; London *Evening Standard* awards, 1978, for *Night and Day* and 1982, for *The Real Thing;* Antoinette Perry (Tony) Award for best play, 1984, for *The Real Thing;* Academy Award (Oscar) nomination for best original screenplay, 1985, for "Brazil."

WRITINGS:

Lord Malquist and Mr. Moon (novel), Anthony Blond, 1966, Knopf, 1968.

PLAYS

"The Gamblers," produced in Bristol, England, 1965.

Rosencrantz and Guildenstern Are Dead (three-act; first produced at Edinburgh Festival at Cranston Street Hall, August 24, 1966; produced on the West End at Old Vic Theatre, April 12, 1967; produced on Broadway at Alvin Theatre, October 16, 1967), Samuel French, 1967.

Enter a Free Man (broadcast as "A Walk on the Water" in England for BBC-TV, 1963; broadcast as "A Walk on the Water" in Hamburg, 1964; broadcast as "The Preservation of George Riley," 1964; first produced in London, 1968; produced in Olney, Maryland, at Olney Theatre, August 4, 1970; produced Off-Broadway at St. Clements Theatre, December 17, 1974), Faber, 1968, Grove, 1972.

Tango (based on the play by Slawomir Mrozek; produced in London, 1966; produced on the West End at Aldwych Theatre, May 25, 1968), J. Cape, 1968.

The Real Inspector Hound (one-act; first produced on the West End at Criterion Theatre, June 17, 1968; produced in Providence at Brown University Summer Theatre, August 2, 1970), Samuel French, 1968.

After Magritte (one-act; first produced in London at Green Banana Restaurant, April 9, 1970; produced Off-Broadway at Theatre Four, April 23, 1972), Faber, 1971, Grove, 1972.

Jumpers (first produced on the West End at Old Vic Theatre, February 2, 1972; produced in Washington, D.C., at Kennedy Center, February 18, 1974; produced on Broadway at Billy Rose Theatre, April 22, 1974), Grove, 1972, revised edition, Faber, 1986.

"The House of Bernarda" (based on the play by Garcia Lorca), produced in London at Greenwich Theatre, March, 1973.

Travesties (produced on the West End at Aldwych Theatre, June 10, 1974; produced on Broadway at Ethel Barrymore Theatre, October 30, 1974), Grove, 1975.

Dogg's Our Pet (produced in London, 1971), published in *Six of the Best,* Inter-Action Imprint, 1976.

Dirty Linen and New-Found-Land (produced in London, 1976; produced on Broadway at John Golden Theatre, January 11, 1977), Grove, 1976.

Albert's Bridge, and Other Plays, Grove, 1977 (also see below).

Every Good Boy Deserves Favor [and] *The Professional Foul* (the former was produced; the latter produced as a screenplay for Public Broadcasting Service, April 26, 1978), Grove, 1978.

Night and Day, Grove, 1979, revised edition, Samuel French, 1980.

Undiscovered Country (adapted from Arthur Schnitzler's "Das Weite Land"; produced at the Hartford Stage Company, Conn., 1981), Samuel French, 1984 (also see below).

On the Razzle (adapted from Johann Nestroy's "Einen Jux Will Er Sich Machen"; produced in London, 1982; produced by the West Coast Ensemble in Los Angeles, Calif., 1985), Faber, 1981.

The Real Thing (produced on Broadway, 1982), Faber, 1982, revised edition, 1983.

The Dog It Was That Died, and Other Plays, Faber, 1983 (also see below).

Squaring the Circle: Poland, 1980-81, Faber, 1985 (also see below).

Rough Crossing (adaptation of Ferenc Molnar's "The Play's the Thing"; produced in London, 1984; produced in New York, N.Y. at the New Theater of Brooklyn, 1990), Faber, 1985.

"Dalliance" (adapted from a play by Arthur Schnitzler; produced in London, 1986) published in *Dalliance; and, Undiscovered Country,* Faber, 1986 (also see below).

Dalliance; and, Undiscovered Country, Faber, 1986.

(Translator) Vaclav Havel, *Largo Desolato,* Faber, 1987.

Hapgood (produced in London and New York, N.Y., 1988), Faber, 1988.

Also author of "Home and Dry," and "Riley."

SCREENPLAYS

(Co-author) "The Romantic Englishwoman," New World Pictures, 1975.

"The Human Factor" (adapted from a novel by Graham Greene), Metro-Goldwyn-Mayer, 1980.

(With Terry Gilliam and Charles McKeown) "Brazil," Universal, 1985.

"Empire of the Sun" (adapted from J. G. Ballard's autobiographical novel), Warner Bros., 1987.

Also author of screenplays "Despair," adapted from the novel by Vladimir Nabokov, 1978, and "The Russia House," adapted from the novel by John Le Carre, 1989.

TELEVISION PLAYS

(Adaptor) "A Separate Peace," British Broadcasting Corporation (BBC-TV), 1966, published in *Playbill 2,* edited by Alan Durband, Hutchinson, 1969.

"Teeth," BBC-TV, 1967.

"Another Moon Called Earth," BBC-TV, 1967.

"Neutral Ground," BBC-TV, 1968.

"The Engagement," National Broadcasting Company, (NBC-TV), for "Experiment in Television," 1970.

"One Pair of Eyes," BBC-TV, 1972.

(With Clive Exton) "Eleventh House," BBC-TV, 1975.

(With Exton) "Boundaries," BBC-TV, 1975.

"Three Men in a Boat" (based on the novel by Jerome K. Jerome), 1975.

"Squaring the Circle," BBC-TV, 1985.

RADIO PLAYS; ALL BROADCAST BY BRITISH BROADCASTING CORPORATION (BBC)

"The Dissolution of Dominic Boot," 1964.

"M Is for Moon Among Other Things," 1964.

Albert's Bridge and If You're Glad I'll Be Frank: Two Plays for Radio (the former produced, 1965; the latter produced, 1967, produced as one-act play in Washington, D.C., at Saint Albans Repertory Theatre, June 24, 1969), Faber, 1969.

Artist Descending a Staircase and Where Are They Now?: Two Plays for Radio ("Where Are They Now?" 1970; "Artist Descending a Staircase," 1972), Faber, 1973.

Four Plays for Radio, Faber, 1984.

Also author of "The Dog It Was That Died," 1982. Contributor of short stories to *Introduction 2,* edited by Francis Hope, Faber, 1964. Reviewer for *Scene* magazine, 1962.

SIDELIGHTS: "Basically, I like them as people. Shakespeare suggests they're black conspirators in alliance with the King. But to me they seem like just men thrust into a situation they know little about, then killed for reasons they know nothing about, not having sinned against God or anyone." This was Tom Stoppard's assessment of his title characters in his phenomenally successful "Rosencrantz and Guildenstern Are Dead" as he revealed it to *Newsweek* writer Irwin Goodwin. "I feel like three cherries have come up on my slot machine," Stoppard said of the unexpected critical and financial rewards his play had amassed.

Stoppard's delight at his play's debut was justified, for his writing now commands the sort of attention which led Clive Barnes to place Stoppard "among the finest English-speaking writers of our stage." "Rosencrantz and Guildenstern LIVE!" reported Barnes. "I'm beginning to feel like a popular Argentinian corned-beef millionaire," Stoppard told a *Look* critic, who pointed out that this treatment of "*Hamlet*'s two most forgettable figures" included "an original play-within-a-play, complete with metaphysics, existential absurdity and snappy vaudeville-style patter."

Interwoven with Shakespeare's blank verse, "Rosencrantz and Guildenstern" is nevertheless an original and imaginative attempt to explain the *raison d'etre* of the title characters within an existential framework. In the tradition of Pirandello, Beckett, and Pinter, Stoppard deals thematically with the question of "free will versus predestination," noted John Simon, and with the question of whether life's meaning is actually to be answered in death rather than in life. It was Jeremy Kingston's feeling that Rosencrantz and Guildenstern "define themselves by choosing to die" rather than by existing as "the littlest wheels in the machinery of other people's lives." Charles Marowitz called the play "a blinding metaphor about the absurdity of life," and a *Time* reviewer compared Rosencrantz and Guildenstern with "the two tramps who wait for Godot."

The bulk of Stoppard criticism has pointed to the syntactic brilliance of his dialogue as the unique characteristic of his work. Through the use of stichomythia, puns, and other rhetorical devices, "Stoppard's lines pant with inner panic" in "Rosencrantz and Guildenstern," noted *Time*. Like Beckett, Stoppard often juxtaposes stichomythia with "periodic bursts of busy activity across the calmer, reflective passages" while his dialogue provides a realistic mirror of Shakespeare's language, observed Kingston. Tom Prideaux echoed this assessment and added that Stoppard's achievement in "Rosencrantz and Guildenstern" lay in his recreation of Shakespeare's "comic word play" rather than in any futile attempt to recreate his poetry in this "elaborate club sandwich of Shakespeare and Stoppard." *Newsweek* called attention to the "Wonderlandish language games" played by these "Elizabethan Ritz Brothers" who, noted *Village Voice*'s Michael Smith, ultimately "talk themselves out of existence." About his style, Stoppard told Giles Gordon: "It's taken me a long time to shake the illusion that everything I write is self-evident, that it's self-evident in the way it is intended to be performed, spoken, moved and so on. Not at all! I write with a very dominant sense of rhythm in the dialogue, and to me the orchestration of that dialogue has a kind of inevitability. . . . I'm hooked on style." It was Bruce Cook's feeling that Stoppard's international upbringing resulted in a "version of English [that] seems always to have something of a foreign language—that sense of freshness and verbal discovery, of sport with words."

Other critics have discussed Stoppard's displays of verbal genius as they appear in his very successful "Travesties," a play based on a 1917 meeting in Zurich of three reactionaries: Lenin, James Joyce, and Tristan Tzara. In a manner similar to that in "Rosencrantz and Guildenstern," Stoppard uses plot line and characterization from Oscar Wilde's "The Importance of Being Earnest" to parallel and emphasize his own plot structure. John Beaufort called the play "a dazzling skyrocket . . . a breathtaking word flight into the Wilde blue yonder of Tom Stoppard's imagination." Jack Kroll discussed the play in terms of Stoppard's stylistic debts to other writers, such as his use of stream of consciousness in the manner of James Joyce and his comedic play with limericks in the manner of Oscar Wilde. "I fall into comedy like a man falling into bed," Stoppard told Kroll, to which Kroll added that "underneath the mattress is a hard board—

Stoppard's lust for ideas." Again, Stoppard's characters operate within an existential framework of despair and absurdity.

Various reviewers have attempted to analyze and define Stoppard's philosophical position as he presents and develops it within his plays. Most often his ideas are considered from an existentialist perspective and encompass such concepts as man's alienation and consequent anguish. According to T. E. Kalem, Stoppard "chain-smokes ideas like cigarettes and emits the smoke with puffs of mirth" in his treatment of "the abyss of non-belief" in which "man [is] devoid of metaphysical absolutes" and so cannot act effectively. David J. Gordon observed that, with Stoppard, nothing is sacred, for he takes standard situations and turns them to his own literary advantage: "Old-fashioned melodrama, drawing-room comedy, ladies' magazine fiction, westerns, vaudeville, cinema, but especially absurdist literature . . . are grist to his parodic mill." Kroll stated that "Stoppard's special trick is finding the sweet, sad craziness hidden in real behavior," and Jack Richardson declared him to be "the best playwright around today, the only writer . . . capable of making the theater a truly formidable and civilized experience again."

BIOGRAPHICAL/CRITICAL SOURCES:

BOOKS

Bigsby, Christopher William Edgar, editor, *Writers and Their Work,* Longman, 1976.
Brustein, Robert, *The Third Theatre,* Knopf, 1969.
Contemporary Literary Criticism, Gale, Volume 1, 1973, Volume 3, 1975, Volume 4, 1975, Volume 5, 1976, Volume 8, 1978, Volume 15, 1980, Volume 29, 1984, Volume 34, 1985.
Dictionary of Literary Biography, Volume 13: *British Dramatists since World War II,* Gale, 1982.
Dictionary of Literary Biography Yearbook, 1985, Gale, 1985.
Taylor, John Russell, *The Second Wave: British Drama for the Seventies,* Hill & Wang, 1971.

PERIODICALS

Atlantic, May, 1968.
Christian Science Monitor, April 25, 1974, November 6, 1975.
Commentary, December, 1967, June, 1974.
Commonweal, November 10, 1967.
Drama, summer, 1968, fall, 1969, summer, 1972, winter, 1973, autumn, 1974.
Encounter, September, 1974.
Hudson Review, Volume 10, number 4, winter, 1967-68, Volume 21, number 2, summer, 1968.
Illustrated London News, April 22, 1967.
Life, February 9, 1968.
Listener, April 11, 1968, April 18, 1968, June 20, 1974.
London Magazine, August, 1968.
Look, December 26, 1967.
Nation, November 6, 1967, May 11, 1974, May 18, 1974.
National Observer, October 23, 1967.
National Review, December 12, 1967.
New Republic, June 15, 1968, May 18, 1974, November 22, 1975.
New Statesman, June 14, 1974.
Newsweek, August 7, 1967, August 31, 1970, March 4, 1974, January 8, 1975, November 10, 1975.
New Yorker, May 6, 1967, October 28, 1967, May 4, 1968, May 6, 1972, March 4, 1974, May 6, 1974, January 6, 1975, January 24, 1977.
New York Magazine, March 11, 1974, May 13, 1974, August 26, 1974.
New York Post, April 23, 1974.

New York Times, October 18, 1967, October 29, 1967, March 24, 1968, May 8, 1968, June 19, 1968, July 8, 1968, October 15, 1968, April 23, 1974, July 29, 1979, November 25, 1979.
New York Times Book Review, August 25, 1968.
Observer Review, April 16, 1967, December 17, 1967, June 23, 1968.
Playboy, May, 1968.
Plays and Players, July, 1970.
Punch, April 19, 1967.
Reporter, November 16, 1967.
Saturday Review, January 8, 1977.
Saturday Review of the Society, August 26, 1972.
Show Business, April 25, 1974.
Spectator, June 22, 1974.
Stage, February 10, 1972.
Time, October 27, 1967, August 9, 1968, March 11, 1974, May 6, 1974.
Times Literary Supplement, March 21, 1968.
Transatlantic Review, summer, 1968.
Village Voice, May 4, 1967, October 26, 1967, May 2, 1974.
Vogue, November 15, 1967, April 15, 1968.
Wall Street Journal, March 11, 1974, November 3, 1975.
Washington Post, May 11, 1969, June 25, 1969, July 9, 1969.
Women's Wear Daily, April 24, 1974.

*   *   *

STOREY, David (Malcolm) 1933-

PERSONAL: Born July 13, 1933, in Wakefield, Yorkshire, England; son of Frank Richmond (a coal miner) and Lily (Cartwright) Storey; married Barbara Rudd Hamilton, 1956; children: two sons, two daughters. *Education:* Slade School of Art, diploma, 1956.

ADDRESSES: Home—2 Lyndhurst Gardens, London NW3, England. *Agent*—c/o Jonathan Cape Ltd., 32 Bedford Square, London WC1B 3EL, England.

CAREER: Novelist and playwright. Worked as art teacher, farm worker, postman, tent erector, and bus conductor; player for Leeds Rugby League Club, 1952-56; director of television productions "Portrait of Margaret Evans" and "Death of My Mother," 1963; associate artistic director of Royal Court Theatre, London, England, 1972-74; currently fellow at University College, London.

AWARDS, HONORS: Macmillan Award, 1959, for *This Sporting Life;* John Llewelyn Rhys Memorial Prize, 1961, and Somerset Maugham Award, 1963, both for *Flight into Camden;* drama award, *Evening Standard,* 1967, for most promising playwright; award from London Theatre Critics, 1970, Writer of the Year award from Variety Club of Great Britain, 1971, and award from New York Drama Critics Circle, 1974, all for "The Contractor"; drama award from *Evening Standard,* 1970, award from New York Drama Critics Circle, 1971, and nomination for Antoinette Perry (Tony) Award from League of New York Theatres and Producers, 1971, all for "Home"; award from New York Drama Critics Circle and nomination for Tony Award, both 1973, both for "The Changing Room"; Geoffrey Faber Memorial Award, 1973, for *Pasmore;* Obie drama award, *Village Voice,* 1974; Booker Prize for Fiction, 1976, for *Saville.*

WRITINGS:

NOVELS

This Sporting Life, Macmillan, 1960.
Flight into Camden, Longmans, Green, 1960, Macmillan, 1961, J. Cape, 1982.

Radcliffe, Longmans, Green, 1963, Coward, 1964, J. Cape, 1982.
Pasmore, Longmans, 1972, Dutton, 1974.
A Temporary Life, Allen Lane, 1973, Dutton, 1974.
Saville, J. Cape, 1976, Harper, 1977.
A Prodigal Child, Dutton, 1983.
Present Times, J. Cape, 1984.

PLAYS

The Restoration of Arnold Middleton (three-act; first produced in Edinburgh, Scotland, at Traverse Theatre, November, 1966; produced on West End at Criterion Theatre, 1967), J. Cape, 1967, Samuel French, 1968.
In Celebration (two-act; first produced in London at Royal Court Theatre, April 22, 1969; produced in New York City at Sutton East Theatre, 1977), J. Cape, 1969, Grove, 1975.
The Contractor (three-act; first produced in London at Royal Court Theatre, October 20, 1969; produced on West End at Fortune Theatre, April 6, 1970; produced in New York City, October, 1973), J. Cape, 1970, Random House, 1970.
Home (two-act; also see below; first produced in London at Royal Court Theatre, June 17, 1970; produced on Broadway at Morosco Theatre, November 17, 1970), J. Cape, 1970, Random House, 1971.
The Changing Room (three-act; also see below; first produced in London at Royal Court Theatre, November 9, 1971; produced on Broadway at Morosco Theatre, March 6, 1973), J. Cape, 1972, Random House, 1972.
Cromwell (first produced in London at Royal Court Theatre, 1973), J. Cape, 1973.
The Farm (produced in London, 1973), J. Cape, 1973.
Life Class (also see below; first produced in London, 1974), J. Cape, 1975.
"Sisters" (also see below), first produced in Manchester, England, 1978, produced in London, 1989.
"Early Days" (also see below), first produced in London at National Theatre, 1980, produced in Washington, D.C. at the Eisenhower Theater, John F. Kennedy Center for the Performing Arts, May, 1981.
Home with Changing Room and Mother's Day, Penguin, 1979.
Early Days with Sisters and Life Class, Penguin, 1980.

Also author of "Night," 1976.

OTHER

"This Sporting Life" (screenplay; based on the novel), Continental, 1963.
(Contributor) *Writers on Themselves,* BBC Publications, 1964.
"Home" (teleplay; based on the play), Public Broadcasting Service, 1971.
"Grace" (teleplay), for television series "Play for Today," British Broadcasting Corporation, 1974.
Edward (juvenile), Allen Lane, 1973.
"In Celebration" (screenplay; based on the novel), American Film Theatre, 1975.

SIDELIGHTS: British writer David Storey is well known for his novels and his plays. His play "In Celebration" has been translated into thirty languages and applauded by audiences around the world, Benedict Nightingale reports in the *New York Times. This Sporting Life,* Storey's first novel, won the Macmillan Award in 1959, and his second, *Flight into Camden,* won several awards in the early 1960s. His most highly acclaimed novel is *Saville,* a "detailed and perceptive portrait of a South Yorkshire miner's son who gradually finds himself alienated from his family and his village by a grammar-school education. Not the least of the book's virtues is the way in which the predicaments of its characters illuminate entire movements of economic and social change in post-World War II England," Elizabeth Ward comments in the *Washington Post Book World*. *Saville* was awarded the Booker Prize in 1976.

Though his novels have won the nation's highest prizes for literature, critics and Storey himself have noted his preference for the dramatic form as opposed to the novel. John Russell Taylor commented in *The Second Wave: British Drama for the Seventies* that Storey's adaptation of *The Sporting Life* revealed an understanding of "the advantages of the dramatic media for directing an audience's responses through angling and selection, in a way which is much more difficult in the more expansive medium of the novel." In the same article, Storey compared writing a novel with "launching an unmanned ship" and added that "a play is like a properly crewed ship: you can modify from moment to moment, take account of the climate of feeling at any particular performance, test out ideas and if they don't work as you want them to, change them." In an interview with Ronald Hayman printed in *Playback*, Storey observed that with a novel it is unnecessary to maintain focus on every character, while the dramatic form demands that visible characters be justifiably engaged "even if they are passive—they've got to be engaged in a way that's just as important, as informative, as the people who are talking."

Basic to an understanding of Storey's themes and characters is a consideration of his pre-literary experiences. His four years as a professional rugby player provided the background for *This Sporting Life*, *The Changing Room*, and *Present Times;* a stint as a tent erector inspired the stage action of *The Contractor; Flight into Camden* is based on his years in art school.

In a *Listener* article, Storey described the weekly four-hour train journey from his London art endeavors to the Leeds rugby field as a "life . . . neatly divided into half," thereby recalling the tension vital to his writings. "I seemed, through these two activities," wrote Storey, "to be trying to resolve two sides of my temperament which were irreconcilable—the courtship of a self-absorbed, intuitive kind of creature with a hard, physical, extroverted character: the one the very antithesis of the other." He related the despair he felt at being "continually torn between the two extremes of my experience, the physical and the spiritual, with the demand to be effective in both." The physical demands of life are a major motif in *The Sporting Life,* and the urgencies of the artistic soul are represented in *Flight into Camden.* Storey told an interviewer that he combined the two extremes in *Radcliffe* with two major characters reflecting both sides of his own personality.

The 1982 novel *Present Times* "contains specific as well as general autobiographical elements," notes Peter Stothard in the London *Times*. A personal battle against the education authorities in which he challenged them to set higher standards for student achievement gave him background for this novel. The battle accounts for "a new tone in David Storey's writing," Stothard notes. "A much harder and more individualist view of the world emerged." Enraged during most of the writing, Storey felt that he had also written "a funny book. . . . Nearly every character is an idiot, trapped into living by some horrendous orthodoxy which they think is some glorious freedom," he told Stothard. Critics contend there is more irony in the book than humour. Storey agreed, telling Stothard, "Well, perhaps it is irony more than humour. In *This Sporting Life* the orthodoxies were all masculine and the women were broken on them. In *Present Times* the orthodoxies are feminist and the women are broken on them. From where I stand now, that is a comic irony." In this "political

novel," says the reviewer, Storey is "poking lethal fun at the fads of change and progress, putting up a gentle preference for the world's known ways."

AVOCATIONAL INTERESTS: Painting.

BIOGRAPHICAL/CRITICAL SOURCES:

BOOKS

Contemporary Literary Criticism, Gale, Volume 2, 1974, Volume 4, 1975, Volume 5, 1976, Volume 8, 1978.
Gindin, James, *Postwar British Fiction: New Accents and Attitudes,* University of California Press, 1962.
Hayman, Ronald, *Playback,* Davis-Poynter Ltd., 1973.
Taylor, John Russell, *The Second Wave: British Drama for the Seventies,* Hill & Wang, 1971.
Taylor, *David Storey,* Longman, 1974.

PERIODICALS

Books and Bookmen, March, 1972.
Cambridge Quarterly, summer, 1966, autumn, 1970.
Listener, August 1, 1963.
New York Times, November 11, 1984.
New York Times Book Review, April 10, 1983.
Times (London), May 3, 1984.
Times Literary Supplement, July 2, 1982.
Washington Post Book World, April 19, 1983.

*   *   *

STOW, (Julian) Randolph 1935-

PERSONAL: Born November 28, 1935, in Geraldton, Western Australia; son of Cedric Ernest (a barrister and solicitor) and Mary (Sewell) Stow. *Education:* University of Western Australia, B.A., 1956. *Religion:* Church of England.

ADDRESSES: c/o Richard Scott Simon Ltd., 32 College Cross, London N1 1PR, England.

CAREER: Novelist and poet. Worked at various times on a mission for aborigines in northwest Australia, and as assistant to the government anthropologist in New Guinea; has lived in East Anglia, Scotland, and Malta, teaching English betweentimes in Australia at the University of Adelaide, 1957, and University of Western Australia, 1963-64, and in England at the University of Leeds, 1962, 1968-69. Harkness fellow, 1964-66.

AWARDS, HONORS: Miles Franklin Award, 1958; Britannica Australia Award, 1966; Patrick White Award, 1979, for *The Girl Green as Elderflower.*

WRITINGS:

A Haunted Land (novel), Macdonald & Co., 1956, Macmillan, 1957.
The Bystander (novel), Macdonald & Co., 1957.
Act One (poems), Macdonald & Co., 1957.
To the Islands (novel), Macdonald & Co., 1958, Little, Brown, 1959, revised edition, Taplinger, 1982.
Outrider (poems), Macdonald & Co., 1962.
Tourmaline (novel), Macdonald & Co., 1963.
(Editor) *Australian Poetry 1964,* Angus & Robertson, 1964.
The Merry-Go-Round in the Sea (novel), Macdonald & Co., 1965, Morrow, 1966.
Midnite: The Story of a Wild Colonial Boy (novel for children), Macdonald & Co., 1967, Prentice-Hall, 1968.
A Counterfeit Silence: Selected Poems, Angus & Robertson, 1969.
Visitants (novel), Secker & Warburg, 1979, Taplinger, 1981.

The Girl Green as Elderflower (novel), Viking, 1980.
The Suburbs of Hell (novel), Taplinger, 1984.

Also author, with Peter Maxwell Davies, of "Eight Songs for a Mad King," 1969, and "Miss Donnithorne's Maggot," 1974, both music theater.

SIDELIGHTS: Randolph Stow is a novelist and poet known for his chilling examinations of contemporary problems in works that capture the dialect and character of his native Australia. His early novels include *A Haunted Land,* about an Australian family's attempt to achieve emotional stability after experiencing a death; *To the Islands,* about an aged missionary's struggle to find his identity and lost spirituality; and *The Merry-Go-Round,* about an Australian boy growing up during World War II. Often exploring the same themes of childhood, love, and death as his fiction, Stow's poetry has appeared in the volumes *Act One, Outrider,* and *A Counterfeit Silence.* Stow also wrote a novel for children, *Midnite,* as well as more recent novels, including his award-winning 1980 effort, *The Girl Green as Elderflower,* and his 1984 crime novel, *The Suburbs of Hell.*

BIOGRAPHICAL/CRITICAL SOURCES:

BOOKS

Contemporary Literary Criticism, Volume 48, Gale, 1988.
Hassall, Anthony J., *Strange Country: A Study of Randolph Stow,* University of Queensland Press, 1986.

PERIODICALS

Globe and Mail (Toronto), May 19, 1984.
London Review of Books, April 19-May 2, 1984.
Los Angeles Times Book Review, August 10, 1980.
National Review, May 31, 1985.
Sewanee Review, winter, 1984.
Spectator, February 27, 1982, April 7, 1984.
Times (London), April 5, 1984.
Times Literary Supplement, May 16, 1980, March 12, 1982.

*   *   *

STRAUB, Peter (Francis) 1943-

PERSONAL: Born March 2, 1943, in Milwaukee, Wis.; son of Gordon Anthony and Elvena (Nilsestuen) Straub; married Susan Bitker (a counselor), August 22, 1966; children: Benjamin Bitker, Emma Sydney Valli. *Education:* University of Wisconsin—Madison, B.A., 1965; Columbia University, M.A., 1966; attended University College, Dublin, 1969-72. *Politics:* "Mainstream undecided."

ADDRESSES: Home—P.O. Box 395, Greens Farms, Conn. 06436.

CAREER: University School, Milwaukee, Wis., English teacher, 1966-69; writer, 1969—.

MEMBER: International PEN, Authors Guild, Authors League of America, Writers Action Group.

AWARDS, HONORS: "Best Novel" nomination, World Fantasy Awards, 1981, for *Shadowland;* British Fantasy Award and August Derleth Award, both 1983, for *Floating Dragon;* World Fantasy Award, 1989, for *Koko.*

WRITINGS:

Ishmael (poetry), Turret Books, 1972, Underwood/Miller, 1973.
Open Air (poetry), Irish University Press, 1972.
Marriages (novel), Coward, 1973.

Julia (also see below; novel), Coward, 1975, reprinted in England as *Full Circle,* Corgi, 1977.
If You Could See Me Now (also see below; novel), Coward, 1977.
Ghost Story (novel), Coward, 1979.
Shadowland (novel), Coward, 1980.
The General's Wife (story), D. M. Grant, 1982.
Floating Dragon (novel), Putnam, 1983.
Leeson Park and Belsize Square: Poems 1970-1975, Underwood/ Miller, 1983.
(With Stephen King) *The Talisman* (novel), Viking, 1984.
Wild Animals: Three Novels (contains *Julia, If You Could See Me Now,* and *Under Venus;* also see below), Putnam, 1984.
Blue Rose (novella), Underwood/Miller, 1985.
Under Venus, Berkley, 1985.
Koko (novel), Dutton, 1988.

Straub's novels appear in a number of foreign languages.

SIDELIGHTS: One of the most popular practitioners of horror and suspense fiction—more than ten million copies of his novels have been sold—American writer Peter Straub is the author of such well-known titles as *Ghost Story, Shadowland, Floating Dragon, The Talisman* (with Stephen King), and *Koko.* Straub employs an array of ghastly elements—hauntings, vengeful agents of murder, gruesome deaths, fantastical happenings—and is especially good at, as *Maclean's* Barbara Matthews notes, "stark cold horror—the kind worshippers of the genre love to spirit away and read quickly, inhaling fright and holding it in their lungs until it becomes brittle enough to shatter if so much as a telephone rings." More than spine-tingling thrillers, however, Straub's novels are also imaginative explorations into the realistic, often personal, roots of the unreal. Patricia L. Skarda writes in *Dictionary of Literary Biography Yearbook* that Straub's "best work . . . focuses on private experiences on the margin where nature and supernature meet, where reality converges with dream, where writing leaves off and the imagination takes over." Straub commented to Joseph Barbato in *Publishers Weekly* on the effects he wishes to elicit: "I want readers to feel as if they've left the real world behind just a little bit, but are still buoyed up and confident, as if dreaming. I want them left standing in midair with a lot of peculiar visions in their heads."

Straub decided to become a novelist—though not a horror novelist—in the early 1970s, after abandoning an academic career in English. A former high school teacher who left the United States for Dublin's University College, Straub was at work on a doctorate when he became disenchanted. "The plan was to get a Ph.D. and come back to get a better job," he told Joseph McLellan in the *Washington Post.* "Then, in Ireland, I suddenly realized what the trouble really was: I had always thought of myself as a novelist although I had not written a novel. I could feel fiction growing inside me, characters and situations forming themselves in my mind as I walked down the street." Already a published poet, Straub began work in 1972 on his first novel, *Marriages,* about the extramarital affair of an American businessman in Europe. Published a year later, *Marriages* received favorable reviews. Ronald Bryden in the *Listener* called it "the other side of the Jamesian tradition: an American chronicle of the quest for European richness, complexity and depth," while a *Times Literary Supplement* critic characterized Straub as a "poetic novelist," adding, "it may be this skill which enables him to place so securely the sense of gesture, and the texture of atmosphere, which characterizes *Marriages.*"

Straub was at work on a second novel, *Under Venus,* when financial reasons prompted a change to his writing efforts. " 'Marriages' had not done very well," he told Barbato, ". . . just about the time that publishers were beginning to cut back on midlist— and bottom-list—authors. And I was one of those guys coming along with more of the same. It unnerved me. I knew I could never hold a real job—that I'd be an impossible employee anywhere. I had to save my life by writing a book that could get published." Furthermore, despite numerous revisions, *Under Venus* failed to attract a publisher (later it appeared in the three-novel collection *Wild Animals*). Straub's agent stepped in and suggested he try writing a Gothic. "I found that I had a natural bent toward this kind of thing," he told Barbato. "Later, I had to deal with that, because I had never seen myself as that type of writer. I dealt with it by trying to see just how much I could do with that peculiar stock of imagery and leaden conventions that you're given as a horror novelist."

Straub's horror debut occurred in 1975 with *Julia*, the harrowing tale of an American woman in England haunted by the torturous ghost of a murdered child, and the emerging knowledge of responsibility in the death of her own daughter (the victim of an emergency tracheotomy). While some reviewers noted inconsistent plotting and characterization, many acknowledged Straub's flair for the gothic. "In the last resort, *Julia* . . . succeeds in the brutal business of delivering supernatural thrills," wrote Michael Mason in the *Times Literary Supplement;* Straub "has thought of a nasty kind of haunting, and he presses it upon the reader to a satisfying point of discomfort." Valentine Cunningham in *New Statesman* called the book "an extraordinarily gripping and tantalising read. . . . Every dubious solution and ambivalent pattern is possible, for almost anything becomes believable under the novelist's stunningly gothic manipulations."

After *Julia*, Straub wrote *If You Could See Me Now*, a tale set in the midwestern United States about the vengeful spirit of a murdered girl who returns to inflict horrors upon the community where she died. Critics particularly praised the novel's narrative timing, structure, and the authenticity of local settings. "Straub is good at slick manipulation of pace," wrote Jonathan Keates in *New Statesman*, "punctuating the story with chunks of police statement . . ., and he has an equally nifty way with rustic grotesques." Keates called the book "crisp, classy buggaboo . . . full of neatly managed understatements and chillingly calculated surprises." Peter Ackroyd in *Spectator* singled out the book's "filmic" qualities: "*If You Could See Me Now* makes great play, for example, with contrasts of speech and silence, of crowd scenes and empty landscapes, and of the ways in which a written 'close-up' can be employed to suggest deep 'emotion.' Some of the book's scenes, in fact, can only be understood in visual terms."

Following these ventures, Straub embarked upon the novel that would become his breakthrough, the 1979 bestselling *Ghost Story*. Drawing upon various horror story motifs and conventions, *Ghost Story* is the tale of a rural New England community terrorized when a young woman, killed years earlier, returns to exact retribution from four elderly townsmen (The Chowder Society) responsible for her death. The Chowder Society's members, who regularly meet to exchange ghost stories, become involved in a frantic race to save themselves and the town from the gruesome revenge of the "shapeshifter" Eva Galli. "What's interesting about 'Ghost Story' is that Mr. Straub . . . seems to have decided to write a summarizing American tale of the supernatural, and to throw into it every scrap of horror-cliche and campfire trash that he can muster," commented Christopher Lehmann-Haupt in the *New York Times*. "Still, because Mr. Straub is so good at writing eerie set-pieces and because the very complexity of his story keeps it baffling to the end, I look back

on the time spent reading 'Ghost Story' as on an interval distorted by fever."

Straub's aim in *Ghost Story*, as Jennifer Dunning quotes the author in the *New York Times*, was to "take the genre and pull it upstairs a little bit. . . . Not exactly transcend the genre, but make a little more of the material than has been made of it in the recent past." *Ghost Story* draws from early masters in the field, including Nathaniel Hawthorne, Henry James, Edgar Allen Poe, and Sheridan Le Fanu. Some reviewers objected to the novel's overt deference to these influences. "Although Straub's 'affection' for the proven devices of his betters is estimable, many of these allusions seem rather pedantic and pointless," wrote Jack Sullivan in the *Washington Post Book World*. Douglas Hill commented in *Maclean's* that "at times the book stumbles over its structure: all the epigraphs and cute chapter titles are merely pretentious." "There was a certain amount of audacity in the overt references to the great writers," Straub admitted to Thomas Lask in the *New York Times*, "but today the form is debased, and it is a messianic thing to me to elevate it and make it honorable." A number of reviewers were, however, impressed with Straub's creation. Gene Lyons in the *New York Times Book Review* called *Ghost Story* "a quite sophisticated literary entertainment," while Valerie Lloyd remarked in *Newsweek* that "with considerable technical skill, Peter Straub has constructed an extravagant entertainment which, though flawed, achieves in its second half some awesome effects." She concluded: "It is, I think, the best thing of its kind since Shirley Jackson's 'The Haunting of Hill House.' "

Straub moved back to the United States after the success of *Ghost Story* and embarked upon a period which produced some of his best known and bestselling titles. His next novel *Shadowland*, however, received mixed reviews and, according to Skarda, "confused an audience expecting ghoulish ghosts." The story of two boys who become involved in a world of magic where anything happens, *Shadowland*'s "prophecy and telepathy, use and misuse of sleights of hand and mind convert a strange Arizona prep school and a Vermont home into a platonic inversion where every shadow seems substance." Lehmann-Haupt noted that in *Shadowland* Straub "appears to be taking the classic elements of the Grimms' fairy tale as far as they can go." Some critics remarked that the fantastical events in the novel appeared too much at random, thereby diminishing the suspense. "*Shadowland* ultimately has neither the gnomic simplicity of the fairy-tale nor the eery sense of a grossly interrupted reality, which [Straub] caught more successfully in *Ghost Story*," commented Thomas Sutcliffe in the *Times Literary Supplement*.

Straub's 1983 bestselling novel, *Floating Dragon*, seemed to meet the expectations generated by *Ghost Story*. In a sweeping story of a malevolent spirit which periodically visits an affluent Connecticut suburb with death and destruction, Straub creates "a compendium of horrors designed to punish the shallow housewives, adulterers, corporate tycoons, and even the children in a commuter community," notes Skarda. "*Floating Dragon*, beneath its remarkable repertoire of horrific details, is a simple moral tale of the confrontation between good and evil," wrote Alan Bold in the *Times Literary Supplement*. "Nevertheless, it represents a new level of sophistication in the Gothic novel. Straub plays games with the structure, rapidly switching from third-person to first-person narrative, and teases the reader with biblical symbols and red herrings. The novel is sustained with great skill as the battle between good and evil is impressively, if agonizingly, stretched over the disturbingly supernatural plot." Alan Ryan commented in the *Washington Post Book World:* "If *Floating Dragon* is sometimes baffling, flawed in some structural elements, and perhaps a little too long for its own good, it is at the same time both ruthlessly contemporary and steeped in tradition, gruesomely chilling, and told with a narrative strength and a lively colloquial style that readers should welcome."

In his next novel, Straub teamed up with friend and fellow horror writer Stephen King—via word processors connected by telephone—to produce the 1984-85 blockbuster *The Talisman*. Drawing upon both writers' immense popularity, the book was an instant bestseller; critics, however, felt that it was a bit overstocked with mad capers and special effects. The fantasy/adventure story of a boy who goes in search of a magic object to cure his dying mother, *The Talisman* outlines a power struggle between good and evil in a strange world. "There's a dizzying amount of flipping in this book," noted Peter Gorner in the *Chicago Tribune*, "and often the point is elusive." Lehmann-Haupt wrote that *The Talisman* "suffers from a surfeit of monstrosity. It takes forever to develop its smallest plot complications. It telegraphs its clues with the subtlety of falling telephone poles. It stoops to outrageous sentimentality over its boy hero. . . . It repeats and repeats unto silliness." These elements, however, are also part of the book's appeal, according to Frank Herbert in the *Washington Post Book World*: "*The Talisman* is exactly what it sets out to be—a fine variation on suspense and horror filled with many surprises, a ground King and Straub have plowed before with great success, together and individually. Together, they demonstrate once more that they are the Minnesota Fats of the novel-into-film. When they say six ball in the side pocket, that's where the six ball goes."

Straub's 1988 bestseller, *Koko*, is a notable departure from his past supernatural novels. A psychological suspense thriller, *Koko* is the story of four Vietnam War veterans who travel to the Far East to track down a former platoon member they believe has become a deranged killer. Straub remarked to *Bestsellers 89* on his change of direction: "By the time I began *Koko*, I had pretty much done everything I could think to do with supernatural fiction. . . . Whether I knew it or not, I was saying goodbye to imagery and situations involving hallucination versus reality with which I had been involved for years. . . . What I wanted to do next was to work with the set of feelings that lay behind horror—to move in closer to the world, to work more strictly within the realistic tradition." Straub's venture has been well-received. A reviewer for *Publishers Weekly* called *Koko* "a dizzying spin through those eerie psychic badlands where nightmare and insanity seem to fuse with reality." Emily Tennyson added in the *Detroit Free Press*: "Like the war that Straub seeks to analyze and explain, 'Koko' wrenches the spirits of those who took part and were taken apart by Vietnam. Much more than a tale of escape and murder, 'Koko' is an examination of fear in the human soul." While *Koko* affirms Straub's ability to create terror, it is also a positive sign of a new scope to his fiction. Lucius Shepard remarks in the *Washington Post Book World*: "Judged as a thriller, *Koko* deserves to be compared with the best of the genre, to novels such as *Gorky Park* and *The Honorable Schoolboy*. . . . *Koko* is vastly entertaining, often brilliantly written, full of finely realized moments and miniatures of characterization. . . . What all this most hearteningly signals is that Peter Straub is aspiring toward a writerly range which may cause his future novels to face more discriminating judgments yet."

MEDIA ADAPTATIONS: Julia was adapted for the 1981 Peter Fetterman film, "The Haunting of Julia" (entitled "Full Circle" in England); *Ghost Story* was adapted for the 1981 Universal Pictures film of the same title. *Floating Dragon* was adapted for cassette by Listen for Pleasure Cassettes in 1987; *Koko* was adapted for cassette by Simon & Schuster Audioworks in 1989.

AVOCATIONAL INTERESTS: Jazz, opera.

BIOGRAPHICAL/CRITICAL SOURCES:

BOOKS

Bestsellers 89, Issue 1, Gale, 1989.
Contemporary Literary Criticism, Volume 28, Gale, 1984.
Dictionary of Literary Biography Yearbook: 1984, Gale, 1985.

PERIODICALS

Chicago Tribune, May 16, 1979, December 16, 1981, November 8, 1984, January 23, 1990.
Detroit Free Press, November 13, 1988.
Globe and Mail (Toronto), January 27, 1990.
Listener, March 15, 1973.
Maclean's, May 21, 1979, January 12, 1981, March 14, 1983.
New Statesman, February 27, 1976, June 24, 1977.
Newsweek, March 26, 1979, December 24, 1984.
New York Times, April 3, 1979, April 27, 1979, May 20, 1979, October 24, 1980, December 16, 1981, January 26, 1983, November 8, 1984.
New York Times Book Review, April 8, 1979, March 6, 1983.
People, January 28, 1985.
Publishers Weekly, January 28, 1983, May 11, 1984, August 12, 1988.
Spectator, July 9, 1977.
Times (London), February 24, 1990.
Times Literary Supplement, March 23, 1973, February 27, 1976, April 17, 1981, March 11, 1983.
Washington Post, October 31, 1980, February 6, 1981, February 16, 1981, November 27, 1984.
Washington Post Book World, April 8, 1979, October 14, 1984, August 21, 1988, February 11, 1990.

*　　*　　*

STUART, Don A.
  See CAMPBELL, John W(ood, Jr.)

*　　*　　*

STUART, Ian
  See MacLEAN, Alistair (Stuart)

*　　*　　*

STURGEON, Theodore (Hamilton) 1918-1985
(Frederick R. Ewing, E. Waldo Hunter, Ellery Queen, E. Hunter Waldo)

PERSONAL: Original name, Edward Hamilton Waldo; name legally changed upon adoption by stepfather; born February 26, 1918, in St. George, Staten Island, N.Y.; died May 8, 1985, of pneumonia, in Eugene, Ore.; son of Edward (a retail paint businessman) and Christine (a teacher and writer; maiden name, Dicker) Waldo; married Dorothy Fillingame, 1940 (divorced, 1945); married Mary Mair (a singer), 1949 (divorced, 1951); married third wife, Marion, 1951; married Wina Bonnie Golden (a television personality), April 16, 1969 (divorced); married Jayne Enelhart; children: Colin, Patricia, Cynthia, Robin, Tandy, Noel, Timothy, Andros. *Education:* Attended Pennsylvania State Nautical School. *Religion:* Episcopal.

CAREER: Science fiction writer, 1938-85. Worked as an engine room wiper in the Merchant Marine, 1935-38; manager of a resort hotel in the West Indies, 1940-41; manager of a tractor lubrication center for the U.S. Army in Puerto Rico, 1941; bulldozer operator in Puerto Rico, 1942-43; copy editor for an advertising agency, 1944; literary agent in New York City, 1946-47; *Fortune* (magazine), New York City, circulation staff member, 1948-49; story editor for *Tales of Tomorrow* (magazine), 1950; *If* (magazine), New York City, feature editor, 1961-64, contributing editor, 1972-74. Teacher at workshops and writing conferences.

MEMBER: Writers Guild of America.

AWARDS, HONORS: Argosy magazine story award, 1947, for "Bianca's Hands"; International Fantasy Award, 1954, for *More Than Human;* guest of honor at Twentieth World Science Fiction Convention, 1962; Nebula Award, 1970, and Hugo Award, 1971, both for "Slow Sculpture"; World Fantasy Award for life achievement, World Fantasy Convention, 1986.

WRITINGS:

NOVELS

The Dreaming Jewels, Greenberg, 1950, published as *The Synthetic Man,* Pyramid, 1961, reprinted, Bluejay, 1984.
More Than Human, Farrar, Straus, 1953, reprinted, Ballantine, 1981.
The King and Four Queens (Western novel; based on a story by Margaret Fitts), Dell, 1956.
(Under pseudonym Frederick R. Ewing) *I, Libertine* (historical novel), Ballantine, 1956.
The Cosmic Rape, Dell, 1958.
Venus Plus X, Pyramid, 1960, reprinted, Carroll & Graf, 1988.
Some of Your Blood (also see below), Ballantine, 1961.
Voyage to the Bottom of the Sea (based on the screenplay by Irwin Allen and Charles Bennet), Pyramid, 1961.
(Under pseudonym Ellery Queen) *The Player on the Other Side,* Random House, 1963.
Two Complete Novels (contains "And My Fear Is Great" and "Baby Is Three"), Galaxy, 1965.
The Rare Breed, Fawcett, 1966.
Amok Time (based on one of his "Star Trek" television scripts), Bantam, 1978.
Godbody, limited edition, Donald I. Fine, 1986, New American Library, 1987.

STORY COLLECTIONS

"It" (single story), Prime Press, 1948.
Without Sorcery, with introduction by Ray Bradbury, Prime Press, 1948, revised edition published as *Not without Sorcery,* Ballantine, 1961.
E Pluribus Unicorn, Abelard, 1953.
Caviar, Ballantine, 1955.
A Way Home, Funk, 1955 (published in England as *Thunder and Roses,* M. Joseph, 1957).
A Touch of Strange, Doubleday, 1958.
Aliens 4, Avon, 1959.
Beyond, Avon, 1960.
The Unexpected, compiled by Leo Margulies, Pyramid, 1961.
Sturgeon in Orbit, Pyramid, 1964.
The Joyous Invasions, Gollancz, 1965.
Starshine, Pyramid, 1966.
(With Ray Bradbury and Oliver Chadwick Symmes) *One Foot and the Grave,* Avon, 1968.
Sturgeon Is Alive and Well, Putnam, 1971.
The Worlds of Theodore Sturgeon, Ace Books, 1972.
To Here and the Easel, Gollancz, 1973.
(With Don Ward) *Sturgeon's West,* Doubleday, 1973.
Case and the Dreamer, New American Library, 1974.
Visions and Venturers, Dell, 1978.

Maturity, Science Fiction Society (Minneapolis), 1979.
The Golden Helix, Doubleday, 1979.
The Stars Are the Styx, Dell, 1979.
Slow Sculpture, Pocket Books, 1982.
Alien Cargo, Bluejay, 1984.
To Marry Medusa, Baen Books, 1987.
A Touch of Sturgeon, Simon & Schuster, 1988.

RADIO AND TELEVISION SCRIPTS

Author of radio scripts, including "Incident at Switchpath," 1950; "The Stars Are the Styx," 1953; "Mr. Costello Here," 1956; "Saucer of Loneliness," 1957; "More Than Human," 1967; "The Girl Had Guts," "The Skills of Xanadu," and "Affair with a Green Monkey." Also author of television scripts for "Beyond Tomorrow," "Star Trek," "Playhouse 90," "CBS Stage 14," "Schlitz Playhouse," "Land of the Lost," "Wild, Wild West," "The Invaders," and other television series. Also author, with Ed MacKillop, of television script "Killdozer!" (based on his short story), 1974.

OTHER

(Contributor) Leo Margulies and O. J. Friend, editors, *My Best Science Fiction Story,* Merlin Press, 1949.
"It Should Be Beautiful" (play), first produced in Woodstock, N.Y., c.1963.
(Contributor) Reginald Bretnor, editor, *Science Fiction: Today and Tomorrow,* Harper, 1974.
(Contributor) Bretnor, editor, *The Craft of Science Fiction,* Harper, 1976.
"Psychosis: Unclassified" (play; based on his novel *Some of Your Blood*), first produced in 1977.
(Editor) *New Soviet Science Fiction,* Macmillan (London), 1980.

Work included in many anthologies. Also author of comic book scripts. Author of column, *National Review,* 1961-73. Contributor of short stories, sometimes under pseudonyms, to *Unknown, Astounding Science Fiction, Omni, Galaxy,* and other magazines. Book reviewer, *Venture,* 1957-58, *Galaxy,* 1972-74, *New York Times,* 1974-75, and *Hustler,* 1983.

SIDELIGHTS: The late Theodore Sturgeon was one of a handful of science fiction writers whose work revolutionized the genre. Beginning as a pulp writer in the late 1930s, Sturgeon became one of science fiction's Golden Age writers of the 1940s, a period when many of the genre's most popular writers came to prominence. Sturgeon published his stories in such influential magazines as *Astounding Science Fiction* and *Unknown.* His stream-of-consciousness technique, concern for humane values, and ability to create unlikely characters and situations, endeared him to readers and influenced a score of other writers. Kurt Vonnegut, Jr., is believed to have modeled his character Kilgore Trout, a prolific and inventive science fiction writer, on Sturgeon.

After dropping out of high school as a teenager, Sturgeon joined the Merchant Marine, worked in the West Indies and Puerto Rico, and finally found himself in the middle 1940s in New York City, working as a writer of science fiction and, for a time, as a literary agent for other writers in the field. His first widely acclaimed book, *More Than Human,* appeared in 1953; it won the International Fantasy Award. Later books, usually collections of short stories, established Sturgeon as one of science fiction's most accomplished and popular writers.

Donald L. Lawler, writing in the *Dictionary of Literary Biography,* credited Sturgeon for his role in "extending the boundaries of the [science fiction] genre into the soft sciences." Sturgeon's stories, Lawler believed, "emphasized the personal and psychological dimensions of human experience with science," while "loneliness and alienation are two persistent themes in his writing." "More than any other figure in Science Fiction's 'Golden Age,'" wrote Bob Collins in *Fantasy Review*, "[Sturgeon] consistently attempted profound themes." Speaking to Charles Platt in *Dream Makers, Volume II: The Uncommon Men and Women Who Write Science Fiction*, Sturgeon explained: "I have my own definition of science, which derives from *scientia*, which is the Latin word that means knowledge. To me, science fiction is *knowledge* fiction, and it's knowledge not only of physical and chemical laws but also the quasi- and soft sciences, and also matters of the human heart and mind. This is all knowledge, and so to me it's all legitimate science fiction."

Among the subjects that Sturgeon made into legitimate science fiction was sex, particularly sex of an unusual or even abberant nature. He was the first writer in science fiction to include homosexual characters in his work, and to portray them as being worthy of tolerance. His story "The World Well Lost" concerns a pair of homosexual lovers from another planet who are aided in their escape from outraged spacemen by an Earthman who empathizes with them. Sturgeon's early story "Bianca's Hands," first written in 1939 but considered too erotically daring by science fiction magazines of the 1940s, was finally published in the British adventure magazine *Argosy* in 1947. It won a $1,000 fiction prize, beating out entries by such writers as Graham Greene. The story tells of the deformed idiot Bianca, who possesses hands which "have a life and will of their own," as Lawler explained. Bianca's friend Ran becomes obsessed with the hands, desiring nothing else but to be strangled by them. Sturgeon's novel *Venus Plus X* features a utopian society of the future whose citizens undergo surgery at birth to render themselves hermaphroditic. This sexual change allows them to transcend the normal conflicts between men and women. In many of Sturgeon's stories, love was seen as the surest method of overcoming the adversities of life. Sturgeon "never abandoned belief in the therapeutic power of love," Collins noted.

An eccentric and outspoken man whose daring ideas made his fiction continually popular, Sturgeon was an iconoclast in his thinking. A long-time columnist for the conservative *National Review*, Sturgeon also wrote book reviews for the explicit men's magazine *Hustler*. He was a nudist, a vegetarian, and a believer in herbal medicines and vitamin cures. "I have a right to my own life-style," he explained to Platt, "and I don't like yahoos coming along to correct me. . . . I like to protect my own way of thinking." Speaking of his political persuasion, Sturgeon told Platt: "Libertarian, at the moment, feels more like home to me than anything else." In private life Sturgeon was also known for his unorthodox attitude toward finances. As Sam Moskowitz observed, "If ever an author epitomized the skittishness and sensitivity attributed to the 'artist,' it is Theodore Sturgeon. While he appreciated the need for money, his primary motivation was not the dollar. Despite the knowledge that he could sell *anything* of a fantastic nature he cared to write . . ., it was typical of him to take a couple of months off to write a three-act play *free* for a small-town theater, with the review in a local weekly his sole reward."

Sturgeon is credited with two observations that have become known not only in science fiction circles but among a wider audience as well. "Sturgeon's Law," so called because he claimed that it applied in every field of endeavor, is stated in polite terms as: "90% of everything is trash." His other abiding observation was the "concept of the 'Prime Directive'" created for the "Star Trek" television program, as Lawler noted. Sturgeon wrote two episodes for the popular series ("Amok Time" and "Shore Leave"). The "Prime Directive," or overriding law of the United Federation of Planets, "prohibits Federation interference with the normal development of alien life and societies," according to Bjo Trimble in *A Star Trek Concordance*.

In his fiction Sturgeon displayed a wide variety of styles, adapting his approach to the story he wanted to tell. Moskowitz, writing in *Seekers of Tomorrow: Masters of Modern Science Fiction*, stated that Sturgeon "strives in *every* story to be as differently and bizarrely off-trail as he is able" and claimed that Sturgeon possessed an "adroitness at altering the rhythm of his writing to conform to the subject [which] gives him as many styles as stories." Lawler agreed. Sturgeon, he wrote, "uses a remarkable variety of styles, points of view, and narrative devices." Lawler also credited the author with having "pointed the way for new developments in the genre by combining the subject matter, themes, and formulas of science fiction with the ideas, modes of treatment, and stylistic features of mainstream literature."

Sturgeon's influence on other science fiction writers, and on the parameters of the genre as a whole, was impressive. Lawler explained that Sturgeon's influence was "great because it is so diffuse. It is not so much an acknowledged influence as it is pervasive, and it tends to be strongest in matters of tone, style, attitudes, and values." Among those writers influenced by Sturgeon were Ray Bradbury, Samuel R. Delaney, Philip K. Dick, Ursula K. LeGuin, and Kurt Vonnegut, Jr.

Vonnegut modeled his character Kilgore Trout on Sturgeon. Trout is a science fiction writer who has authored hundreds of books filled with wildly inventive concepts. But Trout lives in poverty and obscurity because the ridiculous titles he gives his books, and the pornographic magazines in which his stories appear, severely limit his audience. Trout is both homage to Sturgeon for his inventiveness and his ability to confront major themes and a satire of Sturgeon's eccentricity.

At the time of Sturgeon's death in 1985, commentators noted that he had a tremendous reputation both as an individual and as a writer. Reginald Bretnor emphasized in the *Dictionary of Literary Biography Yearbook: 1985* that "*I have never heard anyone—fellow writer or editor or fan—say a bad word about him. I found him to be warm and open, tremendously interested in people and what they did and what made them tick. I felt immediately that he genuinely liked people.*" James Gunn agreed. "Ted loved life, loved people, and loved writing," Gunn recalled in *Fantasy Review*.

Poul Anderson found Sturgeon's work to be among the best in science fiction. Writing in *National Review*, Anderson stated: "One can raise quibbles about Sturgeon, his touches of doctrinaire liberalism (though never, never collectivism), his ungrammatical treatment of 'thou,' his sometimes overly neat plots, nits like that. So what? It's as easy to pick them off Rembrandt and Beethoven, easier off Shakespeare, and none of these are lessened thereby, nor is Sturgeon. He is reliably a joy." In his tribute to Sturgeon for the *Washington Post Book World*, Stephen King noted that as a writer Sturgeon had "entertained, provoked thought, terrified, and occasionally ennobled. He fulfilled, in short, all the qualifications we use to measure artistry in prose."

MEDIA ADAPTATIONS: The film rights to many of Sturgeon's novels and short stories have been sold.

BIOGRAPHICAL/CRITICAL SOURCES:

BOOKS

Contemporary Literary Criticism, Gale, Volume 22, 1982, Volume 39, 1986.
Dictionary of Literary Biography, Volume 8: *Twentieth Century American Science Fiction Writers,* Gale, 1981.
Dictionary of Literary Biography Yearbook: 1985, Gale, 1986.
Ketterer, David, *New Worlds for Old: The Apocalyptic Imagination, Science Fiction, and American Literature,* Anchor Press, 1974.
Moskowitz, Sam, *Explorers of the Infinite,* World Publishing, 1963.
Moskowitz, Sam, *Seekers of Tomorrow: Masters of Modern Science Fiction,* World Publishing, 1965.
Platt, Charles, *Dream Makers, Volume II: The Uncommon Men and Women Who Write Science Fiction,* Berkley, 1983.
Trimble, Bjo, *A Star Trek Concordance,* Ballantine, 1976.

PERIODICALS

Bloomsbury Review, February, 1986.
Books and Bookmen, January, 1969.
Extrapolation, summer, 1979, fall, 1985.
Magazine of Fantasy and Science Fiction, December, 1971.
National Review, May 4, 1971.
Washington Post Book World, May 26, 1985.

OBITUARIES:

PERIODICALS

AB Bookman's Weekly, June 24, 1985.
Fantasy Review, May, 1985.
Los Angeles Times, May 11, 1985.
New York Times, May 11, 1985.
Pittsburgh Post-Gazette, May 10, 1985.
Publishers Weekly, May 31, 1985.
Science Fiction Chronicle, July, 1985.
Washington Post, May 13, 1985.

—*Sketch by Thomas Wiloch*

*   *   *

STYRON, William 1925-

PERSONAL: Born June 11, 1925, in Newport News, Va.; son of William Clark (a shipyard engineer) and Pauline (Abraham) Styron; married Rose Burgunder, May 4, 1953; children: Susanna, Paola, Thomas, Alexandra. *Education:* Attended Christchurch School, Middlesex County, Va., and Davidson College; Duke University, A.B., 1947; studied writing at New School for Social Research. *Politics:* Democrat.

ADDRESSES: Home and office—Roxbury, Conn.; and Vineyard Haven, Mass. (summer).

CAREER: Writer. McGraw-Hill Book Co. (publishers), New York, N.Y., associate editor, 1947. Honorary consultant in American Letters to the Library of Congress; fellow of Silliman College, Yale University. *Military service:* U.S. Marine Corps, World War II; became first lieutenant; recalled briefly in 1951.

MEMBER: National Institute of Arts and Letters, American Academy of Arts and Sciences, American Academy of Arts and Letters (inducted, 1988), Signet Society of Harvard (honorary), Phi Beta Kappa.

AWARDS, HONORS: American Academy of Arts and Letters Prix de Rome, 1952, for *Lie Down in Darkness;* Pulitzer Prize,

1968, and Howells Medal of the American Academy of Arts and Letters, 1970, both for *The Confessions of Nat Turner;* American Book Award, National Book Critics Circle Award nominee, both 1980, both for *Sophie's Choice;* Connecticut Arts Award, 1984; Commandeur, Ordre des Arts et des Lettres (France), 1987; Edward MacDowell Medal, 1988.

WRITINGS:

Lie Down in Darkness, Bobbs-Merrill, 1951.
The Long March, Vintage, 1957.
Set This House on Fire, Random House, 1960.
The Confessions of Nat Turner, Random House, 1967.
In the Clap Shack (three-act play; first produced in New Haven at Yale Repertory Theatre, December 15, 1972), Random House, 1973.
Sophie's Choice, Random House, 1979.
This Quiet Dust (essays), Random House, 1982.
(Author of introduction) Robert Satter, *Doing Justice: A Trial Judge at Work,* American Lawyer Books/Simon & Schuster, 1990.
Darkness Visible, Random House, 1990.

Editor of *Paris Review: Best Short Stories,* published by Dutton. Contributor to *Esquire, New York Review of Books,* and other publications. Manuscript collections of Styron's work are held by the Library of Congress, Washington, D.C., and Duke University, Durham, North Carolina.

WORK IN PROGRESS: A semi-autobiographical novel about the Marine Corps.

SIDELIGHTS: William Styron's novels have brought him major literary awards, broad critical notice, and a reputation for raising controversial issues. In *The Confessions of Nat Turner* and *Sophie's Choice,* Styron writes about two victims of oppression: a slave and a concentration camp survivor. Although some critics question his approach, most praise Styron for probing into difficult subjects. Reviewers consider Styron's timing a positive factor in the success of these two books; *Sophie's Choice,* published during renewed concern about the Holocaust, and *The Confessions of Nat Turner,* published during the racially explosive late Sixties, both found large audiences. George Steiner comments in the *New Yorker:* "The crisis of civil rights, the new relationships to each other and to their own individual sensibilities that this crisis has forced on both whites and Negroes . . . give Mr. Styron's fable [*The Confessions of Nat Turner*] a special relevance."

Styron based *The Confessions of Nat Turner* on the transcript of testimony given by a slave, Nat Turner, who had led a brief revolt against slave owners in Virginia's Tidewater district. Styron considers his book a "meditation on history" rather than a strict retelling of events. He explains in a letter to the Nation that "in writing *The Confessions of Nat Turner* I at no time pretended that my narrative was an exact transcription of historical events; had perfect accuracy been my aim I would have written a work of history rather than a novel." Philip Rahv asserts that Styron's viewpoint is more valuable than a historical perspective. He writes in the *New York Review of Books:* "This narrative is something more than a novelistic counterpart of scholarly studies of slavery in America; it incarnates its theme, bringing home to us the monstrous reality of slavery in a psychodynamic manner that at the same time does not in the least neglect social or economic aspects."

Styron's subjective approach draws ire from critics who feel that his portrait of Nat is based on white stereotypes. A *Negro Digest* critic takes particular issue with Styron's depiction of Nat's sexuality: "In the name of fiction, Mr. Styron can do whatever he likes with History. When his interpretation, however, duplicates what is white America's favorite fantasy (i.e., every black male—especially the leader—is motivated by a latent(?) desire to sleep with the Great White Woman), he is obligated to explain (in the structure of the novel, of course) this coincidental duplication—or to be criticized accordingly. Since there is no such explanation in the technique of the novel and since it offers no vision or new perspective, but rather reaffirms an old stale, shameful fantasy (which is still quite salable) it is at best a good commercial novel." Albert Murray concurs in the *New Leader:* "Alas, what Negroes will find in Styron's 'confessions' is much the same old failure of sensibility that plagues most other fiction about black people. That is to say, they will all find a Nat Turner whom many white people may accept at a safe distance, but hardly one with whom Negroes will easily identify."

Other critics argue that Styron is entitled to give a personal interpretation of the story, whatever his views. Steiner asserts that Styron "has every artistic right to make of his Nat Turner less an anatomy of the Negro mind than a fiction of complex relationships, of the relationship between a present-day white man of deep Southern roots and the Negro in today's whirlwind." Stylistically, Styron is often compared with William Faulkner, who shares his Southern white background and his interest in depicting Black characters. According to Philip Rahv, "Styron has gained greatly from his ability to empathize with his Negro figures—with the protagonist, Nat, as well as with some of his followers—to live in them, as it were, in a way inconceivable even for Faulkner, Styron's prose-master. Whereas Faulkner's Negroes are still to some extent the white man's Negroes, Styron's are starkly themselves."

Styron writes about human suffering in a more contemporary setting—post-World War II Brooklyn—in *Sophie's Choice.* Sophie is a beautiful Polish gentile who survived Auschwitz but lost two of her children and much of her self-esteem there. Her lover, Nathan (mad, brilliant, and Jewish) is haunted by the atrocities of the Holocaust, although he personally escaped them, and he torments Sophie with reminders. Stingo, a young writer who lives downstairs from Sophie and Nathan, narrates. According to Geoffrey Wolff of *Esquire,* "Stingo is in the tradition of *The Great Gatsby*'s Nick Carraway. Like Nick, he bears witness to the passion of characters he chances upon and tries modestly to judge and pardon. Like Nick, he is a refugee from settled values—Virginia's Tidewater country—back from a great war to make his way in the great world."

David Caute of the *New Statesman* hears additional voices. For him, the "neo-Biblical cadences of Southern prose, of Wolfe and Faulkner, jostle with the cosmopolitan sensibility of an F. Scott Fitzgerald." Other critics agree that the influence of other writers sometimes muffles Styron's own voice. Jack Beatty writes in the *New Republic* that *Sophie's Choice* "is written in an unvaryingly mannered style—High Southern—that draws constant spell-destroying attention to itself." The "Southern style" associated with Faulkner and Thomas Wolfe is characterized by elaborate, even Gothic descriptions, and although Styron is "a novelist hard to categorise," he shows his allegiance to that style here and "in all of [his] writing," according to Caute, with "a tendency towards post-Wolfian inflation, a reluctance to leave any noun uncaressed by an adjective." Paul Gray of *Time* agrees, noting that Styron "often lets Stingo pile up adjectives in the manner of Thomas Wolfe: 'Brooklyn's greenly beautiful, homely, teeming, begrimed and incomprehensible vastness'. . . . True, Stingo is pictured as a beginning writer, heavily in debt to Faulkner, Wolfe and the Southern literary tradition,

but Styron may preserve more redundant oratory than the effect of Stingo's youth strictly requires."

Robert Towers, writing in the *New York Review of Books,* also faults Styron for verbosity. " 'All my life, I have retained a strain of uncontrolled didacticism,' says Stingo at one point," Towers notes, "and *Sophie's Choice* bears him out. The novel is made to drag along an enormous burden of commentary, ranging all the way from the meaning of the Holocaust, the ineluctable nature of evil, the corrosive effects of guilt, the horrors of slavery, and the frailty of goodness and hope to such topics as the misunderstanding of the South by Northern liberals, Southern manners as opposed to those of New York taxi drivers, and the existence of prejudice and cruelty in even the best of us." But Wolff defends Styron, observing that "the book's narrative flow is suspenseful if languid, if sometimes even glacial," and that "*Sophie's Choice* achieves an almost palpable evocation of its place and time—Poland before and during the war, Brooklyn and Coney Island immediately after." And Caute, despite his criticisms, contends that Styron's prose is "marked also by clarity, honesty and accessibility."

As evidence of Styron's narrative power, Gray asserts that he gives Sophie "a core of individuality that elevates her role beyond that of a symbolic victim." Styron explains that his sympathy toward Sophie's character stems from personal experience. He modelled her after a woman he met when—like Stingo—he was an aspiring writer living in a Brooklyn rooming house. Inspiration for the story came, he tells Tony Schwartz in *Newsweek,* when one day "I woke up with the remembrance of a girl I'd once known, Sophie. It was a very vivid half-dream, half-revelation, and all of a sudden I realized that hers was a story I had to tell." As in *Confessions,* Styron expanded on the original historical data when he wrote his story. "The fact is," he relates, "I didn't get to know [Sophie's prototype] very well and the story as it evolves in the book is made up. But what I realized is that it was necessary for me to write about Auschwitz. . . . It was the same sort of territory, modernized, that I explored in *The Confessions of Nat Turner.*"

In response to critics who question the validity of *Confessions* and *Sophie's Choice* on the grounds of Styron's personal background, Towers argues that "it should not be necessary to defend the right of Styron—a non-Jew, a Southern Protestant in background—to this subject matter—any more than his right to assume, in the first person, the 'identity' of the leader of a slave rebellion in Virginia in 1831." Gray agrees. "The question," he writes, "is not whether Styron has a right to use alien experiences but whether his novel proves that he knows what he is writing about. In this instance, the overriding answer is yes."

MEDIA ADAPTATIONS: Sophie's Choice was filmed for Universal Pictures in 1982; it featured Meryl Streep in the title role.

BIOGRAPHICAL/CRITICAL SOURCES:

BOOKS

Allen, Walter, *The Modern Novel,* Dutton, 1965.

Baumbach, Jonathan, *The Landscape of Nightmare,* New York University Press, 1965.

Concise Dictionary of American Literary Biography: Broadening Views, 1968-1988, Gale, 1989.

Contemporary Literary Criticism, Gale, Volume 1, 1973, Volume 3, 1975, Volume 5, 1976, Volume 11, 1979, Volume 15, 1980.

Cowley, Malcolm, *Writers at Work: The "Paris Review" Interviews,* First Series, Viking, 1958.

Crane, John K., *The Root of All Evil: The Fiction of William Styron,* University of South Carolina Press, 1985.

Dictionary of Literary Biography, Volume 2: *American American Novelists since World War II,* Gale, 1978.

Dictionary of Literary Biography Yearbook: 1980, Gale, 1981.

Fossum, Robert H., *William Styron,* Eerdmans, 1968.

Friedman, Melvin J., *William Styron,* Bowling Green University, 1974.

Geismar, Maxwell, *American Moderns,* Hill & Wang, 1958.

Gossett, Louise Y., *Violence in Recent Southern Fiction,* Duke University Press, 1965.

Kostelanetz, Richard, editor, *On Contemporary Literature,* Avon, 1964.

Mackin, Cooper R., *William Styron,* Steck Vaughn, 1969.

Moore, Harry T., editor, *Contemporary American Novelists,* Southern Illinois University Press, 1964.

Pearce, Richard, *William Styron* (Pamphlets on American Writers Series, No. 98), University of Minnesota Press, 1971.

Waldmeir, Joseph J., editor, *Recent American Fiction,* Michigan State University Press, 1963.

West, James L., *William Styron: A Descriptive Bibliography,* G. K. Hall, 1977.

PERIODICALS

American Dialog, spring, 1968.

Book World, October 1, 1967, October 8, 1967.

Boston Globe Sunday Magazine, July 7, 1985.

Chicago Tribune, July 3, 1989.

Chicago Tribune Book World, May 27, 1979, January 16, 1983.

Commonweal, December 22, 1967.

Detroit News, June 24, 1979.

Esquire, July 3, 1979, December 1, 1985.

Harper's, July, 1967.

Kenyon Review, Volume 30, number 1, 1968.

Los Angeles Times, December 14, 1983.

Los Angeles Times Book Review, January 16, 1983.

Nation, October 16, 1967, April 22, 1968, July 7, 1979.

Negro Digest, February, 1968.

New Leader, December 4, 1967.

New Republic, June 30, 1979.

New Statesman, May 7, 1979.

Newsweek, October 16, 1967, May 28, 1979.

New Yorker, November 25, 1967, June 18, 1979.

New York Review of Books, October 26, 1967, September 12, 1968, July 19, 1979.

New York Times, August 5, 1967, October 3, 1967, May 29, 1979, November 27, 1982.

New York Times Book Review, October 8, 1967, August 11, 1968, May 27, 1979, June 6, 1982, November 21, 1982, December 12, 1982.

Observer Review, May 5, 1968.

Partisan Review, winter, 1968, summer, 1968.

Spectator, October 13, 1979.

Time, October 13, 1967, June 11, 1979.

Times Literary Supplement, May 19, 1968, November 30, 1979, June 10, 1983.

Village Voice, December 14, 1967.

Washington Post, May 18, 1979, January 4, 1983.

Washington Post Book World, May 20, 1979, December 5, 1982.

Yale Review, winter, 1968.

SUAREZ LYNCH, B.
See BIOY CASARES, Adolfo and BORGES, Jorge Luis

*   *   *

SUSANN, Jacqueline   1921-1974

PERSONAL: Born August 20, 1921, in Philadelphia, Penn.; died of cancer, September 21, 1974, in New York, N.Y.; daughter of Robert (a portrait artist) and Rose (a teacher; maiden name, Jans) Susann; married Irving Mansfield (a television and film producer); children: Guy. *Education:* Studied ballet and drama in New York, N.Y.

ADDRESSES: Home—112 Central Park S., New York, N.Y. 10019.

CAREER: Began as model, and later actress, appearing in more than twenty Broadway plays and road company productions, including "The Women," 1937, "She Gave Him All She Had" and "When We Are Married," 1939, "My Fair Ladies" and "Banjo Eyes," 1941, "Jackpot" and "The Lady Says Yes," 1944, and Off-Broadway in "The Madwoman of Chaillot," 1970; author and novelist, 1962-74. Made frequent appearances on television dramas, panels, and commercials.

AWARDS, HONORS: Valley of the Dolls has been cited in the *Guinness Book of World Records* as the best-selling novel of all time.

WRITINGS:

(With Beatrice Cole) "Lovely Me" (play), produced on Broadway, 1946.

Every Night, Josephine! (nonfiction), Geis, 1963.

Valley of the Dolls: A Novel, Geis, 1966.

The Love Machine (novel), Simon & Schuster, 1969.

Once Is Not Enough (novel), Morrow, 1973.

Dolores (novel), Morrow, 1976.

Yargo, Bantam, 1978.

Contributor to magazines.

WORK IN PROGRESS: At the time of her death, Susann was working on *Good Night, Sweet Princess,* and a sequel to *Every Night, Josephine!*

SIDELIGHTS: Jacqueline Susann was the first author to publish two number-one best-sellers back to back, and simultaneously to face the nearly unanimous outrage of critics. When asked if she read the reviews of her novels *Valley of the Dolls* and *The Love Machine,* the actress-turned-writer responded: "I'd like to have the critics like me, I'd like to have everybody like what I write. But when my book sells, I know people like the book. That's the most important thing, because writing is communication." Moreover Susann contended, "The day is over when the point of writing is just to turn a phrase that critics will quote, like Henry James. *I'm* not interested in turning a phrase; what matters to *me* is telling a *story* that *involves* people. The hell with what critics say. I've made characters live, so that people talk about them at cocktail parties, and that, to me, is what counts. You have to have a divine conceit in your judgment. I have it."

When the author of *Valley of the Dolls* was criticized as being a writer of pornography, she explained such was not her motivation: "I don't think it is a dirty book," she told Roy Newquist. "I do believe, however, that you cannot define characters without identifying them with the sexual acts they would commit and the language they would use. For example, it is one sort of person who would say, 'Oh, for goodness' sake!' when a rehearsal went wrong. You would know that woman has restraint, a basic dignity, and is likely to be in command of a given situation. But when a performer blows sky-high, loses control of herself and her tongue, and lashes out at everyone in sight, then you are aware of the deficiencies in personality and character that will play themselves out in later events in the novel. . . . If I didn't sometimes show these characters at their more bestial, weaker moments, I'd have written a dishonest book. Frankly, I'd rather risk being called the author of a dirty book than the author of a weak or inaccurate one."

As Nora Ephron noted, "If Jacqueline Susann is no literary figure, she is nevertheless an extraordinary publishing phenomenon. . . . With the possible exception of *Cosmopolitan* magazine, no one writes about sadism in modern man and masochism in modern woman quite as horribly and accurately as Jacqueline Susann." In addition, Ephron was able to identify the reason behind the incredible success of Susann's first best-seller: "*Valley* had a message that had a magnetic appeal for women readers: it described the standard female fantasy—of going to the big city, striking it rich, meeting fabulous men—and went on to show every reader that she was far better off than the heroines in the book—who took pills, killed themselves, and made general messes of their lives. It was, essentially, a morality tale. And despite its reputation, it was not really a dirty book. Most women, I think, do not want to read hard-core pornography. They do not even want to read anything terribly technical about the sex act. What they want to read about is lust. And Jacqueline Susann gave it to them."

Susann's second best-seller, *The Love Machine,* evoked another storm of criticism. Setting up the criterion for passing judgment on it, Christopher Lehmann-Haupt remarked that since it was going to "be devoured like popcorn at a Saturday matinee, . . . it's irrelevant to judge it by any standard other than popcorn." He found it "salty (lots of four-letter words sprinkled into a morally square container). It dissolves in your mouth (the characters are so flat and interchangeable that at times I even forgot who Robin Stone was). It doesn't fill you up (I doubt if I've ever read a novel that made less of an impression). It goes down quickly and easily. It is the kernel of an idea, the seed of an inspiration, exploded into bite-sized nothingness."

To Jonathan Baumbach, "reading *The Love Machine* is a numbingly mindless experience. Its effect is narcotic. Miss Susann asks her readers not to think, not to feel, and, before all, not to see—nothing is asked and all is given. In a sense, the book is a collaboration—a shared inhuman cultural fantasy between author and readers, a reinforcement of culture-induced fantasies. Where real literature disturbs, books like *The Love Machine* comfort. It is only child's play to read but offers gratifyingly easy solutions. . . . The subliminal message of the novel is *stay as stupid as you are.*" He continued, "The main thrust of the novel is hedonistic—characters hop in and out of bed with one another in various combinations—but the novel opts finally for the middle-class puritan verities. . . . On the face of it, *The Love Machine* deplores the amoral world it describes. . . . Integrity and love triumph over hedonism and ambition. *The Love Machine* subscribes to cultural convention so successfully because it believes in it. There is no discernible vision in the novel outside popular culture's vision of itself, no higher intelligence, no other context." Baumbach concluded that "the novel is written in the very language of its world—a language wholly incapable of accounting for human experience, a language geared to genocide."

MEDIA ADAPTATIONS: Among Susann's best-sellers adapted as screenplays are "Valley of the Dolls," released by Twentieth Century-Fox in 1967, "The Love Machine," released by Columbia in 1971, and "Once Is Not Enough," released by Paramount in 1975.

BIOGRAPHICAL/CRITICAL SOURCES:

BOOKS

Authors in the News, Volume 1, Gale, 1976.
Contemporary Literary Criticism, Volume 3, Gale, 1975.

PERIODICALS

Chicago Tribune, February 17, 1983.
Cosmopolitan, January, 1967.
Harper's, October, 1969.
Life, May 30, 1969.
Nation, September 1, 1969.
New Statesman, March 8, 1968.
New York Times Book Review, May 11, 1969.
Punch, January 31, 1968.
Saturday Evening Post, February 24, 1968.
Village Voice, January 25, 1968.

*   *   *

SUZUKI, D. T.
   See SUZUKI, Daisetz Teitaro

*   *   *

SUZUKI, Daisetz T.
   See SUZUKI, Daisetz Teitaro

*   *   *

SUZUKI, Daisetz Teitaro   1870-1966
   (D. T. Suzuki, Daisetz T. Suzuki, Teitaro Suzuki)

PERSONAL: Name originally Teitaro Suzuki; born October 18, 1870, in Kanazawa, Japan; died July 12, 1966, in Tokyo, Japan; son of Ryojun (a physician) and Masu (Kojima) Suzuki; married Beatrice Erskine Lane (a teacher and writer), 1911 (died, 1938). *Education:* Attended Imperial University. *Avocational interests:* Walking.

CAREER: Zen scholar. Worked as English teacher in Japan, 1888; novice Zen monk in Kamakura, Japan, in 1890s; Open Court Publishing Co., La Salle, IL, proofreader, editor, and translator, 1897-1908; Imperial University, Tokyo, Japan, professor of English, 1909-14; professor of English at Gakushuin in early 1920s; Otani University, Kyoto, Japan, professor of English and of Buddhist philosophy, 1921-40; writer. Visiting professor at Columbia University, 1955-57; lecturer at numerous institutions, including Cornell University, Yale University, Harvard University, Cambridge University, and Oxford University. Participant at various conferences, including World Congress of Faith, 1936, East-West Philosophers' Conference, 1949, and World Congress of Buddhists, 1952. Founder and director of Matsuga-oka Bunko (library), 1946; president of Tibetan Tripitak Research Institute.

AWARDS, HONORS: D.Litt. from Otani University; named to Academy of Japan; medals from Japanese emperor, 1949, and from *Asahi,* 1955.

WRITINGS:

(Translator under name Teitaro Suzuki) *Acvaghosha's Discourse on the Awakening of Faith in the Mahayana,* Open Court, 1900, reprinted, Chinese Material Center, 1976.

(Translator under name Teitaro Suzuki, with Dr. Paul Carus) Lao Tze, *T'ai-shang kan-yang p'ien: Treatise of the Exalted One on Response and Retribution,* Open Court, 1906, later edition published as *Treatise on Response and Retribution,* with translators' names listed as D. T. Suzuki and Paul Carus, 1973.

Outlines of Mahayana Buddhism, Luzac, 1907, reprinted with preface by Alan Watts, Schocken, 1963.

A Brief History of Early Chinese Philosophy, Probsthain, 1914.

Essays in Zen Buddhism, Luzac, 1st series, 1927, 2nd series, 1933, 3rd series, 1934, reprinted, Grove, 1989.

Studies in the Lankavatara Sutra, One of the Most Important Texts of Mahayana Buddhism, in Which Almost All Its Principal Tenets Are Presented, Including the Teachings of Zen, Routledge, 1932, reprinted, Prajna Press, 1981.

An Introduction to Zen Buddhism (also see below), Eastern Buddhist Society, 1934, edited by Christmas Humphreys, foreword by C. G. Jung, Philosophical Library, 1949, reprinted, Grove, 1987.

The Training of the Zen Buddhist Monk, illustrations by Zenchu Sato, Eastern Buddhist Society, 1934, published as *The Zen Monk's Life,* Olympia Press, 1972, published under original title, Wingbow Press, 1974.

A Manual of Zen Buddhism, Eastern Buddhist Society, 1935, reprinted, Grove, 1987.

Buddhist Philosophy and Its Effect on the Life and Thought of the Japanese People, Society for International Cultural Relations, 1936, published as *Buddhism in the Life and Thought of Japan,* Buddhist Lodge, 1937, published as *Zen Buddhism and Its Influence on Japanese Culture,* Eastern Buddhist Society, 1938, revised edition published as *Zen and Japanese Buddhism,* C. E. Tuttle, 1958, 2nd revised edition published as *Zen and Japanese Culture,* Pantheon Books, 1959, 3rd edition, Japan Travel Bureau, 1965.

Japanese Buddhism, Board of Tourist Industry, Japanese Government Railways, 1938.

The Essence of Buddhism (also see below), Buddhist Society, 1946, reprinted in *What Is Zen?,* 2nd edition, 1947.

The Zen Doctrine of No-Mind: The Significance of the Sutra of Hui-neng, Rider, 1949, reprinted, Weiser, 1981.

Living by Zen, Rider, 1950, reprinted, Weiser, 1982.

Studies in Zen, edited by Humphreys, Philosophical Library, 1955.

(Under name D. T. Suzuki) *Zen Buddhism: Selected Writings of D. T. Suzuki,* edited by William Barrett, Doubleday, 1956.

(Translator) *The Lankavatara Sutra: A Mahayana Text,* Routledge & Kegan Paul, 1956, reprinted, Routledge Chapman & Hall, 1972.

Mysticism: Christian and Buddhist, the Eastern and Western Way, Harper, 1957, reprinted, Greenwood Press, 1975.

(Contributor) Erich Fromm, editor, *Zen Buddhism and Psychoanalysis,* Harper, 1960.

(Under name Daisetz T. Suzuki) *The Essentials of Zen Buddhism: Selected From the Writings of Daisetz T. Suzuki,* edited by Bernard Philips, Dutton, 1962, published as *The Essentials of Zen Buddhism: An Anthology of the Writings of Daisetz T. Suzuki,* Rider, 1963.

On Indian Mahayana Buddhism, edited by Edward Conze, Harper, 1968.

The Field of Zen: Contributions to "The Middle Way," the Journal of the Buddhist Society, edited by Humphreys, Buddhist Society, 1969, Harper, 1970.

Shin Buddhism, Harper, 1970.

What Is Zen? (includes *The Essence of Buddhism*), Buddhist Society, 1971, Harper, 1972.

(Translator) Soyen Shaku, *Sermons of a Buddhist Abbot: Addresses on Religious Subjects, Including the Sutra of Forty-two Chapters,* Weiser, 1971, published as *Zen for Americans: Including the Sutra of Forty-two Chapters,* Open Court, 1974.

(Under name Daisetz T. Suzuki) *Sengai, the Zen Master,* preface by Eva von Hoboken, New York Graphic Society, 1971.

Japanese Spirituality, ten volumes, Japan Society for the Promotion of Science, 1972, reprinted, Greenwood Press, 1988.

Collected Writings on Shin Buddhism, edited by Eastern Buddhist Society, Shinashu Otaniha, 1973.

(Translator) Shinran, *The Kyogyoshin-sho,* Shinshu Otaniha, 1973.

An Introduction to Zen Buddhism (includes *An Introduction to Zen Buddhism* and *A Manual of Zen Buddhism*), introduction by Charles San, Causeway Books, 1974.

(Translator under name D. T. Suzuki, with Paul Carus) Laotze, *The Canon of Reason and Virtue,* Open Court, 1974.

The Awakening of Zen, edited by Humphreys, Prajna Press, 1980.

Also author and editor of works in Japanese; translator of works into Japanese, including *Self-Reliance of Noble Wisdom,* edited by Dwight Goddard, 1932. Contributor to periodicals.

SIDELIGHTS: During a career that spanned more than half of the twentieth century, Daisetz Teitaro Suzuki was probably the Western world's foremost authority on Zen Buddhism. His many writings influenced several leading thinkers—including writer Aldous Huxley, psychiatrist Carl Jung, and fellow Buddhists Christmas Humphreys and Alan Watts—and established Suzuki as an unrivaled exponent and interpreter of the Zen method and perspective. In a 1957 profile for *New Yorker,* Winthrop Sargeant asserted, "Dr. Suzuki is, in fact, merely the most celebrated and most eloquent international commentator on a branch of Buddhist thought that is followed, in a popular form, by millions of laymen in Japan . . . , and, in a more advanced form, is practiced with rigorous austerity by thousands of monks and acolytes in various secluded Japanese monasteries."

Zen is an elusive subject to define. Although it derived from Buddhism, it is not a religion. Neither is it a philosophy as that subject is perceived in the Western world, for its method explicitly refutes rational thought and analysis. Perhaps Zen is most accurately perceived as a method of perspective, one that dwells on the contemplation of specific questions, called *koans,* which are, in turn, designed to inspire enlightenment, or *satori.* Typical of this method is the contemplation of a koan that poses a question such as, "What is the sound of one hand clapping?" In considering this seemingly irrational problem, the student eventually achieves a higher level of insight, one that exposes the futility of rationality and thus prompts *satori.* The time devoted to study of a specific koan is, understandably, varied. Some Zen aspirants devote years to a single koan, while more accomplished followers master thousands of the seemingly obscure exercises and enjoy countless moments of enlightenment.

Suzuki's own acquaintance with Zen practices began after he had already worked as an English teacher in a small fishing village during the late 1880s. After leaving the village to study in Tokyo at the Imperial University, he became increasingly active in the Zen monastery in nearby Kamakura. Perhaps sensing his student's penchant for explication, Zen master Soyen Shaku eventually found a job for Suzuki as a translator for Open Court publishers in Illinois. Suzuki assumed the position in 1897, and for the next eleven years he worked at Open Court—primarily as a translator, but also as a proofreader and even an editor.

At Open Court, Suzuki translated Acvaghosha's *Discourse on the Awakening of Faith in the Mahayana,* a Chinese classic, and collaborated with Paul Carus on a translation of Lao Tze's *Treatise on Response and Retribution,* a noted volume in Chinese mysticism. In addition, Suzuki wrote *Outlines of Mahayana Buddhism,* in which he related the rituals and myths of the particularly mystical—and thus non-Zen—Mahayana faith.

After leaving Open Court in 1908, Suzuki worked in Europe translating works—including those of the Swedish mystic philosopher Emanuel Swedenborg—into Japanese. In 1909 Suzuki returned to Japan, and for the next thirty-one years he worked as a teacher of English and Buddhism. During this period he wrote his first important works on Zen, including the three-volume *Essays in Zen Buddhism* and *An Introduction to Zen Buddhism.* Many scholars consider these works most valuable to readers already familiar with Zen. Alan Watts, for instance, wrote in the introduction to his book *The Way of Zen* that Suzuki's Essays in Zen Buddhism were "an unsystematic collection of scholarly papers on various aspects of the subject, enormously useful for the advanced student but quite baffling to the general reader with an understanding of the general principles." Similarly, Watts referred to Suzuki's *Introduction to Zen* as a "delightful" but "narrow and specialized" volume.

During World War II Suzuki drew the ire of his countrymen for criticizing Japan's militaristic policies, and he even came under surveillance by Japanese police. After the war Suzuki moved back to the United States, where he lived in New York City and lectured at various institutions, including Columbia University in the mid-1950s. It was at this time that Suzuki gained prominence as an authority on Zen. His *Essays in Zen Buddhism* were reprinted to great acclaim, with Gerald, Heard countering Alan Watts in a *New York Times* article by contending that the volumes provide "a clear introduction to the subject."

As Suzuki's reputation grew in the West, so did the popularity of Zen. Its influence was evident in music, particularly jazz, and in literature, notably the fiction of J. D. Salinger. Watts, too, contributed to public interest in Zen through works such as *The Way of Liberation in Zen Buddhism* and *The Way of Zen.* But he acknowledged his debt to Suzuki, whose works Watts found especially important to his own *Spirit of Zen,* written in 1936 but reprinted in the mid-1950s. Watts also noted Suzuki's influence in the works of British Buddhist Humphreys, particularly his *Zen Buddhism.*

In the 1950s Suzuki enjoyed particular success with his volume *Mysticism: Christian and Buddhist,* in which he traced similarities between the two religions and supplemented his findings with translations of Japanese mystics. J. M. Kitigawa, reviewing the book in *Christian Century,* described it as "very rewarding" and cited Suzuki as "the most prominent authority on Zen Buddhism." Suzuki also reached readers through anthologies compiled from his previous works. His *Zen Buddhism,* edited by William Barrett, was even accessible to the general public, for Barrett had organized the volume into chapters exploring specific aspects of Zen. Noteworthy in the book are sections such as "The Meaning of Zen Buddhism" and "The Historical Background of Zen Buddhism," both of which feature provocative accounts of early Zen masters illustrating the elusive simplicity of the actual subject.

Suzuki devoted himself to more specialized subjects in other works. *Zen and Japanese Culture,* for instance, is concerned with detailing and analyzing the presence of Zen in Japan's art and social customs. This work earned more praise for Suzuki upon publication in the late 1950s. Christopher Logue called it "a good book" in *New Statesman* and added that it was "an amiable, intelligent account." N. W. Ross, writing in the *New York Times Book Review,* also complimented Suzuki, declaring that the scholar had produced "a rewarding volume." Ross added, "As one turns the pages of this delightful book one seems to catch intimations of how and why certain aspects of the 'spirit of Zen' are making themselves felt in America today."

Suzuki died in 1966 at age ninety-five. Since his death, however, several more of his writings have appeared, including translations of Buddhist texts. More anthologies have also been published, and his lectures have been collected in volumes such as *Shin Buddhism.* In addition, his earlier works are often reprinted, thus assuring his continued stature as Zen's most accomplished and articulate interpreter for Western readers.

BIOGRAPHICAL/CRITICAL SOURCES:

BOOKS

Watts, Alan Wilson, *The Way of Zen,* Pantheon, 1957.

PERIODICALS

Christian Century, December 28, 1949, June 8, 1955, April 10, 1957, March 18, 1970.
Crozer Quarterly, October, 1949, October, 1950.
Guardian, November 4, 1960.
Journal of Religion, April, 1960.
Nation, August 15, 1959.
New Statesman, August 29, 1959.
New Yorker, August 31, 1957.
New York Times, June 4, 1950.
New York Times Book Review, July 12, 1959, October 16, 1960.
Saturday Review, November 16, 1957.
Times Literary Supplement, May 13, 1955, April 15, 1960, February 17, 1961, July 7, 1972.

OBITUARIES:

PERIODICALS

Current Biography, November, 1966.
New York Times, July 12, 1966.

* * *

SUZUKI, Teitaro
  See SUZUKI, Daisetz Teitaro

* * *

SVEVO, Italo
  See SCHMITZ, Aron Hector

* * *

SWENSON, May 1919-1989

PERSONAL: Born May 28, 1919, in Logan, Utah; daughter of Dan Arthur (a teacher) and Anna M. (Helberg) Swenson. *Education:* Utah State University, B.A., 1939.

ADDRESSES: Home—73 The Boulevard, Sea Cliff, Long Island, N.Y. 11579. *Office*—c/o Little, Brown and Co., 34 Beacon St., Boston, Mass. 02114.

CAREER: Poet, living in New York City, 1949—. Formerly worked as an editor for New Directions, New York City; writer in residence at Purdue University, Lafayette, Ind., 1966-67, University of North Carolina, 1968-69 and 1974, Lothbridge University, Alberta, Canada, 1970, and University of California, Riverside, 1976. Has lectured and given readings at more than fifty American universities and colleges, as well as at the New York YM-YWHA Poetry Center, and San Francisco Poetry Center. Conductor of workshops at University of Indiana Writers' Conference and Breadloaf, Vermont. Participant at the Yaddo and MacDowell colonies for writers.

AWARDS, HONORS: Poetry Introductions Prize, 1955; Robert Frost Poetry Fellowship for Bread Loaf Writers' Conference, 1957; Guggenheim fellowship, 1959; William Rose Benet Prize of the Poetry Society of America, 1959; Longview Foundation award, 1959; National Institute of Arts and Letters award, 1960; Amy Lowell Travelling Scholarship, 1960; Ford Foundation grant, 1964; Brandeis University Creative Arts Award, 1967; Rockefeller Writing fellowship, 1967; Distinguished Service Medal of Utah State University, 1967; Lucy Martin Donnelly Award of Bryn Mawr College, 1968; Shelley Poetry Award, 1968; National Endowment for the Arts Grant, 1977; National Book Award nomination, 1978, for *New and Selected Things Taking Place;* Academy of American Poets fellowship, 1979; Bollingen Poetry Award, 1981; MacArthur Award, 1987; National Book Critics Circle award nomination (poetry), 1987, for *In Other Words.*

WRITINGS:

POETRY

Another Animal, Scribner, 1954.
A Cage of Spines, Rinehart, 1958.
To Mix With Time: New and Selected Poems, Scribner, 1963.
Poems to Solve (for children "14-up"), Scribner, 1966.
Half Sun Half Sleep (new poems and her translations of six Swedish poets), Scribner, 1967.
Iconographs, Scribner, 1970.
More Poems to Solve, Scribner, 1971.
(Translator with Leif Sjoberg) *Windows and Stones, Selected Poems of Tomas Transtromer* (translated from Swedish), University of Pittsburgh Press, 1972.
New and Selected Things Taking Place, Little, Brown, 1978.
In Other Words, Knopf, 1988.

PLAYS

"The Floor" (one-act), first produced under the program title "Doubles and Opposites" in New York at American Place Theater, May 11, 1966, on a triple bill with "23 Pat O'Brien Movies," by Bruce Jay Friedman, and "Miss Pete," by Andrew Glaze.

CONTRIBUTOR

A Treasury of Great Poems, edited by Louis Untermeyer, Simon & Schuster, 1955.
New Poets 2, Ballentine, 1957.
New Poets of England & America, edited by Donald Hall, Robert Pack, and Louis Simpson, Meridian, 1957.
A Country in the Mind, edited by Ray B. West, Angel Island Publications, 1962.
Twentieth-Century American Poetry, edited by Conrad Aiken, Modern Library, 1963.
100 American Poems of the Twentieth Century, Harcourt, 1963.
The Modern Poets, edited by John Malcolm Brinnin and Bill Read, McGraw, 1963.
The New Modern Poetry, edited by M. L. Rosenthal, Macmillan, 1967.

OTHER

Works represented in other anthologies. Poems also included in translation in anthologies published in Italy and Germany. Contributor of poetry, stories, and criticism to *Poetry, Nation, Saturday Review, Atlantic, Harper's, New Yorker, Southern Review, Hudson Review,* and other periodicals. Swenson's work is included in the sound recording *Today's Poets: Their Poems, Their Voices,* Volume 2, Scholastic Records, 1968, and recordings for the Library of Congress, Spoken Arts Records, Folkways Records, and others. Her poems have been set to music by Otto Leuning, Howard Swanson, Emerson Meyers, Joyce McKeel, Claudio Spies, Lester Trimble, and Warren Benson.

SIDELIGHTS: May Swenson's poetry has been praised for its imagery, which is alternately precise and beguiling, and for the quality of her personal and imaginative observations. In addition, her poetry "exhibits . . . her continuing alertness to the liveliness of nature. Correspondences among all life forms pour from her work, confirming that nothing is meaningless. The universe's basic beauty and balance is the stuff and soul of her poems," Eloise Klein Healy observes in the *Los Angeles Times.*

Richard Howard emphasizes in a *Tri-Quarterly* review that Swenson's enterprise is "to get out of herself and into those larger, warmer energies of earth, and to do so by liturgical means." Howard writes: "When May Swenson, speaking in her thaumaturgical fashion of poetry, says that 'attention to the silence in between is the amulet that makes it work,' we are reminded, while on other occasions in her work we are reassured, that there is a kind of poetry, as there used to be a kind of love, which dares not speak its name." Thus Swenson's "orphic cadences," her "siren-songs, with their obsessive reliance on the devices of incantation," are the means by which she seeks to "discover runes, the conjurations by which she can not only apostrophize the hand, the cat and the cloud in their innominate otherness, but by which she can, in some essential and relieving way, become them, leave her own impinging selfhood in the paralyzed region where names are assigned, and assume instead the energies of natural process."

In *Book Week,* Chad Walsh notes: "In most of Miss Swenson's poems the sheer thingness of things is joyfully celebrated." Walsh calls her "the poet par excellence of sights and colors." Stephen Stepanchev, author of *American Poetry since 1945,* agrees that Swenson's "distinction is that she is able to make . . . her reader see clearly what he has merely looked at before." Stepanchev, however, is one of the few critics to find her poems less than completely effective. "Miss Swenson," he writes, "works in a free verse that is supple but rather prosaic, despite her picture-making efforts."

Howard, writing of Swenson's development as a poet, states that "from the first . . . Swenson has practiced, in riddles, chants, hex-signs and a whole panoply of invented sortilege unwonted in Western poetry since the Witch of Endor brought up Samuel, the ways not only of summoning Being into her grasp, but of getting herself out of that grasp and into alien shapes, into those emblems of power most often identified with the sexual." Of the more recent poems, Howard writes: "They are the witty, resigned poems of a woman . . . eager still to manipulate the phenomenal world by magic, but so possessed, now, of the means of her identity that the ritual, spellbinding, litaneutical elements of her art, have grown consistent with her temporal, conditioned, suffering experience and seem—to pay her the highest compliment she could care to receive—no more than natural."

Other critics were also enthusiastic about Swenson's recent collection, *Half Sun Half Sleep. New York Times Book Review* contributor Karl Shapiro writes: "[Swenson's] concentration on the verbal equivalent of experience is so true, so often brilliant, that one watches her with hope and pleasure, praying for victory all the way." In a *Poetry* review of *Half Sun Half Sleep,* William Stafford says of this collection: "No one today is more deft and lucky in discovering a poem than May Swenson. Her work often appears to be proceding calmly, just descriptive and accurate; but then suddenly it opens into something that looms beyond the material, something that impends and implies. . . . So graceful is the progression in her poems that they launch confidently into any form, carrying through it to easy, apt variations. Often her way is to define things, but the definitions have a stealthy trend; what she chooses and the way she progresses heap upon the reader a consistent, incremental effect." And Shapiro offers this analysis of Swenson's achievement in this book: "The whole volume is an album of experiments . . . that pay off. It is strange to see the once-radical *carmen figuratum,* the calligraphic poem, spatial forms, imagist and surreal forms—all the heritage of the early years of the century—being used with such ease and unself-consciousness." Swenson's poetry, however, is by no means random experiment. Not only has she carefully analyzed the material with which she works, she has also examined the "experience of poetry" and, as a result, has derived effective methods of presenting her material in the terms of poetry, a means which, according to Howard, can be called the "Higher Fabrication, that *poesis* which is the true baptism."

Swenson herself writes that the experience of poetry is "based in a craving to get through the curtains of things as they *appear,* to things as they are, and then into the larger, wilder space of things as they *are becoming.* This ambition involves a paradox: an instinctive belief in the senses as exquisite tools for this investigation and, at the same time, a suspicion about their crudeness." Although the senses may deceive and distort, the poet is nevertheless aware that deception is taking place and that there exists a reality whose nature must be apprehended other than sensually. This awareness leads Swenson to state: "Sometimes one gets the inkling that there are extrasenses as yet nameless, within the apperceptive system, if only one could differentiate them and identify their organs." The poet's task then, becomes an incessant quest for a means of interpreting "the vastness of the unknown beyond his consciousness." Swenson continues: "The poet, tracing the edge of a great shadow whose outline shifts and varies, proving there is an invisible moving source of light behind, hopes (naively, in view of his ephemerality) to reach and touch the foot of that solid whatever-it-is that casts the shadow. If sometimes it seems he does touch it, it is only to be faced with a more distant, even less accessible mystery. Because all is movement—all is breathing change."

Among the "strategies and devices, the shamanism and sorcery this poet deploys," as Howard admiringly describes them, is Swenson's use of the riddle in *Poems to Solve.* The book may be enjoyed by both children and adults; the poems here are neither frivolous nor cute but another serious attempt to accommodate "the mystery that only when a thing is apprehended as something else can it be known as itself." Swenson writes of these poems: "It is essential, of course, with a device such as this to make not a riddle-pretending-to-be-a-poem but a poem that is also, and as if incidentally, a riddle—a solvable one. The aim is not to mystify or mislead but to clarify and make recognizable through the reader's own uncontaminated perceptions. By bringing into play the sensual apparatus of the reader, the poem causes him to realize the content eye-wise, ear-wise, taste, touch, and

musclewise *before* beginning to cerebralize. The analyzing intellect ought not to be the first but the last tool that is applied to a poem, for applied alone, as it sometimes is, it can inhibit organic associative responses, can bypass initial curiosity and individual exploration, resulting in little more than a mechanistic contact with the poem."

Coming to Swenson's poems for the first time, the reader cannot fail to recognize that he is experiencing the work of a poet who loves her medium and her task. Shapiro writes: "She draws everything into her ken, into a sharp focus which is inescapable. And the reader laughs with joy that she has done it. . . . May Swenson is a true artist, giving the object its due and trying to flirt it down."

BIOGRAPHICAL/CRITICAL SOURCES:

BOOKS

Brinnin, John Malcolm, and Bill Read, editors, *The Modern Poets,* McGraw, 1963.
Contemporary Literary Criticism, Gale, Volume 4, 1975, Volume 14, 1980.
Contemporary Poets, St. Martin's Press, 1980.
Deutsch, Babette, editor, *Poetry in Our Time,* 2nd edition, Doubleday, 1963.
Dictionary of Literary Biography, Volume 5: *American Poets since World War II,* Gale, 1980.
Hoffman, Daniel, editor, *The Harvard Guide to American Writing,* Belknap Press, 1977.
Nemerov, Howard, editor, *Poets on Poetry,* Basic Books, 1966.
Poems for Young Readers: Selections from Their Own Writing by Poets Attending the Houston Festival of Contemporary Poetry, National Council of Teachers of English, 1966.
Stepanchev, Stephen, *American Poetry Since 1945,* Harper, 1965.
Untermeyer, Louis, editor, *A Treasury of Great Poems, English and American,* Simon & Schuster, 1955.

PERIODICALS

Atlantic, February, 1968.
Book Week, June 4, 1967; Volume 4, number 30.
Christian Science Monitor, February 12, 1979.
Los Angeles Times, March 22, 1979.
New York Times, March 19, 1979, June 16, 1987.
New York Times Book Review, September 1, 1963, May 7, 1967, February 11, 1979.
Poetry, December, 1967, February, 1979.
Prairie Schooner, spring, 1968.
Tri-Quarterly, fall, 1966.

*   *   *

SWIFT, Augustus
  See LOVECRAFT, H(oward) P(hillips)

*   *   *

SWITHEN, John
  See KING, Stephen (Edwin)

*   *   *

SYLVIA
  See ASHTON-WARNER, Sylvia (Constance)

SYMMES, Robert Edward
See DUNCAN, Robert (Edward)

*   *   *

SYMONS, Julian (Gustave) 1912-

PERSONAL: Born May 30, 1912, in London, England; son of Morris Albert (an auctioneer) and Minnie Louise (Bull) Symons; married Kathleen Clark, October 25, 1941; children: Marcus Richard Julian. *Education:* Educated in state schools in England. *Politics:* "Left wing, with no specific party allegiance."

ADDRESSES: Home—Groton House, 330 Dover Rd., Walmer, Deal, Kent, England. *Agent*—Curtis Brown, Ltd., 1 Craven Hill, London W2 3EP, England.

CAREER: Shorthand typist and secretary in London, England, 1929-41; advertising copywriter in London, 1944-47; full-time writer, 1947—. Founder and editor, *Twentieth Century Verse,* 1937-39; reviewer, *London Sunday Times,* London, 1958-68. Member of council, Westfield College, University of London, 1972—. *Military service:* British Army, Royal Armoured Corps, 1942-44.

MEMBER: Crime Writers Association (chairman, 1958-59), Society of Authors (chairman of committee of management, 1970-71), Mystery Writers of America, PEN, Detective's Club (president, 1976-85), Royal Society of Literature (fellow).

AWARDS, HONORS: Crime Writers Association, Crossed Red Herrings Award for best crime story of the year, 1957, for *The Color of Murder,* special award, 1966, for *Crime and Detection;* Mystery Writers of America, Edgar Allan Poe Award for best crime story of the year, 1961, for *The Progress of a Crime,* special award, 1973, for *Bloody Murder;* Grand Master of Swedish Academy of Detection, 1977, Danish Poe-Kluhben, 1979, and Mystery Writers of America, 1982.

WRITINGS:

NOVELS

The Immaterial Murder Case, Gollancz, 1945, Macmillan, 1957.
A Man Called Jones, Gollancz, 1947, reprinted, Collins, 1963.
Bland Beginning, Harper, 1949, reprinted, Carroll & Graf, 1987 (published in England as *Bland Beginning: A Detective Story,* Gollancz, 1949).
The 31st of February (also see below), Harper, 1950, reprinted, Carroll & Graf, 1987 (published in England as *The Thirty-First of February: A Mystery Novel,* Gollancz, 1950).
The Broken Penny, Gollancz, 1952, Harper, 1953, reprinted, Carroll & Graf, 1988.
The Narrowing Circle, Harper, 1954, reprinted, Garland Publishing, 1983 (published in England as *The Narrowing Circle: A Crime Novel,* Gollancz, 1954).
The Paper Chase, Collins, 1956, published as *Bogue's Fortune,* Harper, 1957, reprinted, Carroll & Graf, 1988.
The Color of Murder, Harper, 1957.
The Gigantic Shadow, Collins, 1958, published as *The Pipe Dream,* Harper, 1959, reprinted, Prescott Press, 1988.
The Progress of a Crime (also see below), Harper, 1960.
The Plain Man, Harper, 1962 (published in England as *The Killing of Francie Lake,* Collins, 1962).
The End of Solomon Grundy (also see below), Harper, 1964.
The Belting Inheritance, Harper, 1965.
The Julian Symons Omnibus (contains *The 31st of February, The Progress of a Crime,* and *The End of Solomon Grundy*), Collins, 1966, reprinted, Penguin, 1984.
The Man Who Killed Himself, Harper, 1967.

The Man Whose Dreams Came True, Harper, 1968.
The Man Who Lost His Wife, Harper, 1970.
The Players and the Game, Harper, 1972.
The Plot against Roger Rider, Harper, 1973.
A Three-Pipe Problem, Harper, 1975.
The Blackheath Poisonings: A Victorian Murder Mystery, Harper, 1978.
Sweet Adelaide: A Victorian Puzzle Solved, Harper, 1980.
The Detling Secret, Viking, 1982 (published in England as *The Detling Murders,* Macmillan, 1982).
The Name of Annabel Lee, Viking, 1983.
A Criminal Comedy, Viking, 1985 (published in England as *The Criminal Comedy of the Contented Couple,* Macmillan, 1985).
The Kentish Manor Murders, Viking, 1988.

POETRY

Confusions about X, Fortune Press, 1939.
The Second Man, Routledge & Kegan Paul, 1943.
A Reflection on Auden, Poem-of-the-Month Club, 1973.
The Object of an Affair, and Other Poems Tragara Press, 1974.
Seven Poems for Sarah, Tragara Press, 1979.

OTHER

(Editor) *An Anthology of War Poetry,* Penguin, 1942.
(Editor and author of introduction) Samuel Johnson, *Selected Writings of Samuel Johnson,* Grey Walls Press, 1949, British Book Centre (New York), 1950.
A. J. A. Symons: His Life and Speculations (biography), Eyre & Spottiswoode, 1950.
Charles Dickens (biography), Roy, 1951, 2nd edition, Arthur Barker, 1969.
Thomas Carlyle: The Life and Ideas of a Prophet, Oxford University Press (New York), 1952, reprinted, Books for Libraries, 1970.
Horatio Bottomley: A Biography, Cresset Press, 1955.
(Editor) Thomas Carlyle, *Selected Works, Reminiscences and Letters,* Clarke, Irwin & Co., 1956, Harvard University Press, 1957.
The General Strike: A Historical Portrait, Cresset Press, 1957, Dufour, 1963.
A Reasonable Doubt: Some Criminal Cases Re-examined, Cresset Press, 1960.
The Thirties: A Dream Resolved, Cresset Press, 1960, Greenwood Press, 1973, revised edition, Faber, 1975.
Murder, Murder (short story collection) Fontana Books, 1961.
The Detective Story in Britain, Longmans, Green, 1962.
Buller's Campaign, Cresset Press, 1963.
Francis Quarles Investigates (short story collection), Panther Books, 1965.
England's Pride: The Story of the Gordon Relief Expedition, Hamish Hamilton, 1965.
Critical Occasions, Hamish Hamilton, 1966.
A Pictorial History of Crime, Crown, 1966 (published in England, as *Crime and Detection: An Illustrated History from 1840,* Studio Vista, 1966).
(Editor) *A. J. A. Symons, Essays and Biographies,* Cassell, 1969.
Mortal Consequences: A History—from the Detective Story to the Crime Novel, Harper, 1972, revised edition published as *Bloody Murder,* Viking, 1985 (published in England as *Bloody Murder: From the Detective Story to the Crime Novel: A History,* Faber, 1972).
(Editor and author of introduction) *Between the Wars: Britain in Photo,* Batsford, 1972.
Notes from Another Country, Alan Ross, 1972.

(Editor and author of introduction) Wilkie Collins, *The Woman Who Wore White,* Penguin, 1974, reprinted as *The Woman in White,* 1982.

(Editor) *The Angry Thirties,* Eyre & Spottiswoode, 1976.

The Tell-Tale Heart: The Life and Works of Edgar Allan Poe, Harper, 1978.

(Editor) *Verdict of Thirteen: A Detection Club Anthology,* Harper, 1979.

Portrait of an Artist: Conan Doyle (biography), Whizzard/Deutsch, 1980.

(Editor) Edgar Allan Poe, *Selected Tales,* Oxford University Press, 1980.

(Editor and author of introduction) Agatha Christie, *The ABC Murders,* Collins, 1980.

(Editor and author of introduction) Freeman Wills Crofts, *The Loss of the Jane Vosper,* Collins, 1980.

(Author of commentary) Tom Adams, *Agatha Christie, the Art of Her Crimes: The Paintings of Tom Adams,* Everest House, 1981 (published in England as *Tom Adams' Agatha Christie Cover Story,* introduction by John Fowles, Paper Tiger, 1981).

(Author of preface) Arthur Conan Doyle, *The Complete Sherlock Holmes,* Secker & Warburg, 1981.

Great Detectives: Seven Original Detectives, illustrated by Adams, Abrams, 1981.

Critical Observations, Ticknor & Fields, 1981.

The Tigers of Subtopia, and Other Stories (also see below), Viking, 1982.

Crime and Detection Quiz, Weidenfeld & Nicolson, 1983.

(Editor) *The Penguin Classic Crime Omnibus,* Penguin, 1984.

Dashiell Hammett (biography), Harcourt, 1985.

(Editor) Anton Chekov, *The Shooting Party,* translated by A. E. Chamot, Deutsch, 1986.

Makers of the News: The Revolution of Literature, Random House, 1987.

(Editor) Wyndham Lewis, *The Essential Wyndham Lewis: An Introduction to His Work,* Deutsch, 1989.

Also author of radio plays "Affection Unlimited," 1968, and "Night Rider to Dover," 1969, and of television plays "Miranda and a Salesman," 1963, "The Witnesses," 1964, "The Finishing Touch," 1965, "Curtains for Sheila," 1965, "Tigers of Subtopia," based on the author's short story collection of the same title, 1968, "The Pretenders," 1970, and "Whatever's Peter Playing At?," 1974; editor, *New Poetry 9,* 1983. Editor, "Penguin Mystery" series, 1974-79. Contributor to *Times Literary Supplement, New York Times,* and other newspapers and magazines. Reviewer, *Manchester Evening News,* 1947-56, and *Sunday Times,* 1958—. Part of Symons' manuscript collection is housed at the University of Texas at Austin.

SIDELIGHTS: A staunch believer in the literary value of crime and detective novels, Julian Symons is best known as a novelist and critic of these genres, though he is also a respected historian, biographer, and poet. Many of the English novelist's ideas about the crime fiction genre are expressed in his book, *Bloody Murder,* which traces the history of detective and crime novels over the past two centuries. Symons' "most important contribution to the study of the genre," attests Larry E. Grimes in the *Dictionary of Literary Biography,* "is his assertion that much of the focus in crime writing in the twentieth century has changed" from the "classical detective story" to the "crime novel." The detective story, explains Grimes, "is built around a great detective and upon a plot deception," while a crime novel "is based on the psychology of its characters, uses the lines of those characters (not methods, clues, and puzzles) as the basis of the story."

Symons has written novels that fall under both categories, but most of these works have one commonality: the author's interest in the surprising capability for violence that any person may release under the right circumstances. "The thing that absorbs me most in our age," remarks Symons in his introduction to *The Julian Symons Omnibus,* "is the violence behind respectable faces, the civil servant planning how to kill Jews most efficiently, the judge speaking with passion about the need for capital punishment, the quiet obedient boy who kills for fun. These are extreme cases, but if you want to show the violence that lives behind the bland faces most of us present to the world, what better vehicle can you have than the crime novel?"

In his initial attempts to write mysteries, Symons feels his results were unsatisfactory. "My first three crime stories, including the unfortunate [*The Immaterial Murder Case*]" he reveals in his *Contemporary Authors Autobiography Series* entry, "I look back on without pleasure. They were set in one orthodox pattern of the British crime story at that time, consciously light, bright, and determinedly 'civilized.' The fourth, *The Thirty-First of February* . . . , is another matter. I must at this time have had some nascent ideas about doing all the things in the form of the crime story that one can do in a 'straight' novel, in the way of character development, and saying something about the form and shape of society." As with many of Symons' crime stories, *The Thirty-First of February* is not so much a murder mystery as it is a study in human psychology and sociology. The novel involves "Andy" Anderson, an advertising businessman who, after the apparently accidental death of his wife, is accused of her murder. His employers are completely unsympathetic to Anderson's situation and force him to return to work without a period for mourning, while also burdening him with an important account. At the same time, the police, who are certain Anderson is guilty, continually harass him. Though he is never convicted, the unrelenting pressures on him eventually lead to Anderson's insanity.

Similarly, the protagonist in *The Narrowing Circle,* David Nelson, is never convicted of the murder charges brought against him; but the events he experiences nevertheless effectively rob him of his sense of humanity. However, it is not so much the accusation of homicide that brings about Nelson's downfall; rather, as Grimes explains, it is his continued desire to climb up the social and financial ladder that "choke[s] off his ability to be human and know love." "A large part of the horror at the end of *The Narrowing Circle,*" writes Steven R. Carter in *Armchair Detective,* "comes from the reader's awareness that David Nelson is killing an essential part of himself by his decision to accept the sleazy material success which an ulcer-ridden entrepreneur offers him."

About the same time *The Color of Murder* was published, Symons was becoming an influential figure among crime writers. From 1958 to 1959 he was a chairman of the Crime Writer's Association, and in 1958 he began work as a reviewer of mystery fiction for the *London Sunday Times. The Color of Murder* won the Crime Writer's Association Red Herrings Award in 1957, and in 1961 *The Progress of a Crime* won the Edgar Allan Poe Award. These books continue the pattern Symons previously established of using crime fiction as an instrument for social commentary. Like *The Thirty-First of February, The Color of Murder* ends with the insanity of an innocent man accused of a homicide. But in *The Progress of a Crime,* Symons reverses this plot so that the a guilty man is found innocent. Criticizing the misuse of force by the police, the desire of newspapers to capitalize on people's misfortunes in order to sell more papers, and lawyers who care only about winning their cases, *The Progress of a Crime* "is one of the truest and most sensible . . . English crime novels" of its time, opines *Spectator* critic Christopher Pym.

Some of Symons' most complex novels are also among his best, according to a number of reviewers. *The Man Who Killed Himself,* for example, features a protagonist who creates a double identity to commit the perfect crime. One of his identities, Alan Brownjohn, murders his wife and then is, in turn, "murdered" by Major Easonby Mellon, Brownjohn's alter ego. William R. Evans, a *Best Sellers* critic, praises this novel as being "a brilliant portrait of a fascinating murderer along with an extremely ingenious and suspenseful plot." But, as Grimes reveals, *The Man Who Killed Himself* is not a simple murder mystery, "for Easonby/Brownjohn has plotted a perfect murder, not for murder's sake, but for the sake of freedom from an imperfect world." Grimes explains this in more detail in his comments about *The End of Solomon Grundy,* where he notes that in Symons' books the author portrays the world as a place where "one must either become a criminal or remain a hypocrite." Symons' characters are never all good or all evil; indeed, in some of his books it is difficult to find a character with whom the reader can sympathize completely.

The Players and the Game, another example of one of Symons' more intricate plots, is one such book that lacks sympathetic characters. As Leo Harris notes in *Books and Bookmen,* none of the people portrayed in this novel are "very nice." Symons' mysteries, Harris adds, "have always the rebarbative surface of warts-and-all truthfulness, and he has a cold, perceptive, but not entirely unforgiving eye for human frailty." *The Players of the Game* tells two stories: one describes a business executive's journey toward self-destruction as he strives for success; the other is narrated by a character who calls himself "Dracula," and portrays a world in which criminal behavior is considered normal. "One of the most intriguing and unusual aspects of Symons' writing" that is illustrated in *The Players and the Game,* remarks Carter, "is his stress on games." Carter elucidates that "Symons has implied often that anyone might become a criminal by being subjected to too much pressure, by having insufficient outlets for release from pressure, or by surrendering to his fantasies."

Not long after *The Players of the Game,* Symons indulged his interest in the Victorian era by writing three novels set in late nineteenth-century England. These books include *The Blackheath Poisonings: A Victorian Murder Mystery, Sweet Adelaide: A Victorian Puzzle Solved,* and *The Detling Secret.* According to Symons in the *Contemporary Authors Autobiography Series,* he was "pleased" with the first book, while the other two "seemed to me less good." William McPhearson echoes the author's assessment of *The Blackheath Poisonings,* praising the mystery as a "skillfully written, thoroughly researched and deftly plotted novel." As to Symons' other Victorian mysteries, critics have generally been more positive in their evaluations than the novelist himself.

One of these books, *Sweet Adelaide,* is based on an actual murder case in England. Still interested in studying how innocent-looking people can commit murder, Symons investigates the reasons why Adelaide Bartlett, a woman as infamous in England as Lizzie Borden is in the United States, could be driven into pouring liquid chloroform down her husband's throat. Bartlett was found not guilty, relates Michael Malone in the *New York Times Book Review,* "by a jury that could not believe this demure little lady had either the will or the expertise" to kill her husband. Symons proposes, however, that she did possess these qualities, and proceeds to describe in his novel what could push a woman like Bartlett over the edge. *Los Angeles Times Book* critic Alan Cheuse lauds the writer's portrayal of Bartlett, saying that "Sy-

mons' masterly construction of Adelaide's mind—and journal—as she lives through years of suffering her husband's patronage of prostitutes . . . keep[s] us fascinated with each moment of this woman's inevitable slide toward murder." In *The Detling Secret,* Symons explores the more sinister impulses that lurk behind even civilized, upper-class members of society. A more traditional English mystery, critics have praised *The Detling Secret* for its authentic recreation of Edwardian England and the novelist's expert handling of plot. *New York Times Book Review* contributor Mary Cantwell praises the author's research, reporting that "Mr. Symons' use of period detail is both scrupulous and economical." And *Los Angeles Times* critic Carolyn See avers that as a murder mystery *The Detling Secret* "is simply perfect of its kind."

With *The Name of Annabel Lee,* Symons returned to contemporary settings for his novels, "having proved my ability to write such a story—at least to my own satisfaction," he says in *Contemporary Authors Autobiography Series.* Some critics have given this work a chilly reception, however. *Los Angeles Times* reviewer Art Seidenbaum, for one, feels that "the resolution of the mystery . . . leaves substance to be desired." But although Derrick Murdoch similarly believes that Symons' plot appears weak in this case, the reviewer notes in *Globe and Mail* that the novel succeeds in other ways. *The Name of Annabel Lee,* Murdoch writes, "uses the form of the mystery novel to provide a sardonic study of the extent of modern decadence as scathing as his Victorian murder mysteries were of nineteenth-century injustice and hypocrisy." In a more light-hearted fashion, Symons' *A Criminal Comedy* also gibes capitalist society by painting "a savagely comic picture of Headfield [England] and its colour supplement *bourgeoisie,*" according to T. J. Binyon's *Times Literary Supplement* review.

A Criminal Comedy has generally been well received by critics; but, more than this, to one *Time* contributor it also proves that Symons has not allowed his story-telling powers to diminish over the years as has happened with some other mystery writers. "At 73," the reviewer declares, "Julian Symons has . . . published perhaps his best mystery ever." By this time, too, the author had long been a respected biographer and critic. Among other subjects, Symons' interest in mystery authors led him to write biographies of Edgar Allan Poe, Dashiell Hammett, and Sir Arthur Conan Doyle, whose famous creation, Sherlock Holmes, Symons honors with modern versions of the great detective in *A Three-Pipe Problem* and *The Kentish Manor Murders.* The author's biographies have received mixed reviews from critics, the most negative reactions being awarded to *The Tell Tale Heart: The Life and Works of Edgar Allan Poe.* For example, in a *New Republic* article Megan Marshall calls Symons' biography of Poe "steadfastly superficial" and observes that the writer "fails to cover the full dimension of his subject." *Spectator* contributor Benny Green similarly comments that "what we get [in *The Tell Tale Heart*] is not so much a reassessment as a rearrangement" of Poe's life and work.

However, Symons' *Dashiell Hammett* and *Conan Doyle: Portrait of an Artist* have been better received, although *Los Angeles Times* critic Carolyn See feels that Symons' English background puts him at a "cultural disadvantage" in interpreting Hammett's distinctly American works. One *Washington Post* contributor, on the other hand, states that the author writes "with zestful, sometimes revisionist appreciation of the [Hammett] novels." Symons is more in his element when he talks about the much-admired Doyle; and though "this isn't a definitive work," according to Margaret Cannon in *Globe and Mail,* ". . . it's a carefully written, delightfully illustrated introduction" to Doyle.

But more than for his common interest in these giants of the crime fiction genre, Symons is unique in his fascination for lesser-known literary figures; and much of his critical writing focuses on such writers as Wyndham Lewis, Frances Newman, James Branch Cabell, and Peggy Hopkins Joyce. Indeed, in his *Makers of the New: The Revolution in Literature, 1912-1939,* Symons ranks Lewis with the likes of Ezra Pound, James Joyce, and T. S. Eliot. Some critics, like *Washington Post* contributor Charles Trueheart, feel that including Lewis among these authors is an "injustice." Even though some reviewers are puzzled by Symons' emphasis on these relatively minor writers, others see his attention to such details as being a virtue. In a review of the author's *Critical Observations,* Valentine Cunningham writes in the *Times Literary Supplement:* "Symons' greatest distinction as a critic . . . is [his] ungrudging affection for literary merit wherever it crops up. It's a critical versatility that rebuts the fixity of canons, without ever sinking into the flaccidities of a too liberal tastelessness."

Just as Symons tries to bring more obscure literary figures to public attention, he has attempted throughout his career to elevated the status of crime fiction. "The crime story is a wonderfully literary form," he writes in *Contemporary Authors Autobiography Series.* "In the hands of a good writer it can be used for anything from Kafkan ambiguity to raw slices of Zolaesque realism. A criminal theme is the sturdiest of backbones for a plot, and there is nothing intrinsically sensational or trivial about it— the sensationalism and triviality come, if they do, in the treatment." As for Symons himself, his work in the crime genre— especially as a device for social commentary—has made a distinct impression. As Carter attests, Symons "has proven how flexible a vehicle [the mystery genre] is for presenting a personal vision of the stresses of modern western civilization."

AVOCATIONAL INTERESTS: Cricket, football.

BIOGRAPHICAL/CRITICAL SOURCES:

BOOKS

Contemporary Authors Autobiography Series, Volume 3, Gale, 1986.
Contemporary Literary Criticism, Gale, Volume 2, 1974, Volume 14, 1980, Volume 32, 1985.
Dictionary of Literary Biography, Volume 87: *British Mystery and Thriller Writers since 1940,* Gale, 1989.
Scarte, Francis, *Auden and After: The Liberation of Poetry, 1930-1941,* Routledge & Kegan Paul, 1942.
Symons, Julian, *The Julian Symons Omnibus,* Collins, 1966.

PERIODICALS

Armchair Detective, January, 1979.

Best Sellers, April 15, 1972.
Books and Bookmen, October, 1972.
Book World, May 28, 1972.
Detroit News, November 8, 1981.
Georgia Review, fall, 1972.
Globe and Mail (Toronto), January 28, 1984, January 16, 1988, April 9, 1988.
Los Angeles Times, February 14, 1983, November 2, 1983, April 8, 1985.
Los Angeles Times Book Review, October 19, 1980, September 14, 1986, January 24, 1988, July 10, 1988.
National Observer, January 5, 1970.
New Republic, August 26, 1978, September 2, 1978.
New Statesman, December 23, 1966, October 20, 1978.
Newsweek, February 14, 1983.
New Yorker, April 1, 1972.
New York Herald Tribune Book Review, June 22, 1958, November 4, 1962.
New York Times, October 23, 1949, November 9, 1952, April 24, 1955, June 29, 1958, July 3, 1978, January 10, 1986, November 6, 1987.
New York Times Book Review, July 21, 1965, January 8, 1967, May 14, 1967, December 9, 1973, July 9, 1978, February 4, 1979, November 16, 1980, December 13, 1981, March 20, 1983, January 29, 1984, May 5, 1985, January 10, 1988, August 14, 1988.
Observer, July 23, 1978.
Publishers Weekly, July 2, 1982, October 25, 1985.
Spectator, October 26, 1951, July 29, 1960, August 11, 1973, June 29, 1974, March 22, 1975, November 11, 1978, January 19, 1980.
Time, February 14, 1983, February 24, 1986.
Times (London), November 19, 1981, May 13, 1982, September 22, 1983.
Times Literary Supplement, April 8, 1965, February 1, 1975, August 11, 1978, May 9, 1980, January 22, 1982, June 25, 1982, September 17, 1982, November 18, 1983, March 28, 1986, April 25, 1986, November 4, 1988, March 17, 1989.
Washington Post, December 26, 1978.
Washington Post Book World, July 9, 1978, November 2, 1980, March 17, 1985, March 16, 1986, January 3, 1988, August 21, 1988.

—*Sketch by Kevin S. Hile*

*   *   *

SYRUC, J.
See MILOSZ, Czeslaw

T

TAGORE, Rabindranath 1861-1941

PERSONAL: Some sources transliterate name as Ravindranatha Thakura; born May 7 (some sources say May 6), 1861, in Calcutta, Bengal, British India (now Calcutta, West Bengal, India); died August 7, 1941, in Calcutta, West Bengal, India; cremated; son of Debendranath (a philosopher, scholar, religious reformer, and writer) and Sarada Devi Tagore; married Mrinalini Devi Raichaudhuri, December 9, 1883; children: Madhurilata (daughter; also known as Bela), Rathindranath (son), Renuka (daughter), Mira (daughter), Samindranath (son). *Education:* Attended University College, London, 1879-1880.

CAREER: Poet, playwright, novelist, essayist, short story writer, musician, painter, actor, producer, director, political and social activist, and educator. Co-founder of Sarasvat Samaj (a literary organization), 1882; secretary of Adi Brahmo Samaj (a religious society), beginning in 1884; manager of Tagore family estates, beginning in 1890; vice-president of Academy of Bengali Letters, beginning in 1894; co-founder of businesses in Calcutta and Kushtia, 1895-1902; founder of and educator at school at Santiniketan (became Visva-Bharati University in 1918), 1901; founder of weaving school at Kushtia, 1905; founder of agricultural cooperative bank at Patisar, 1905; founder of Sriniketan (a rural reconstruction institute); founder of literary journals, including *Sadhana,* 1891, and *Santiniketan Patra,* 1919.

AWARDS, HONORS: Nobel Prize for Literature, 1913, for *Gitanjali;* D.Litt. from University of Calcutta, 1913, University of Dacca, 1936, Osmania University, 1938, and Oxford University, 1940.

WRITINGS:

PUBLISHED IN INDIA IN BENGALI

Kavi-Kahini (poetry), 1878.
Bana-Phul (poetry), 1880.
Valmiki Pratibha (play), 1881.
Bhagnahriday (play), 1881.
Rudrachanda (play), 1881.
Europe-Pravasir Patra (letters), 1881.
Kal-Mrigaya (play), 1882.
Sandhya Sangit (poetry; title means "Evening Songs"), 1882.
Prabhat Sangit (poetry; title means "Morning Songs"), 1883.
Bau-Thakuranir Hat (novel), 1883.
Vividha Prasanga (essays), 1883.

Chhabi O Gan (poetry; title means "Pictures and Songs"), 1884.
Nalini (play), 1884.
Saisav Sangit (poetry), 1884.
Bhanusimha Thakurer Padavali (songs), 1884.
Alochana (essays), 1885.
Rabichchhaya (songs), 1885.
Kari O Kamal (poetry; title means "Sharps and Flats"), 1886.
Rajarshi (novel), 1887.
Chithipatra (essays), 1887.
Samalochana (essays), 1888.
Mayar Khela (play), 1888.
Manasi (poetry; title means "The Mind's Creation"), 1890.
Europe Yatrir Diary (travel), Part 1, 1891, Part 2, 1893.
Goday Galad (play), 1892, new edition published as *Sesh Raksha,* 1928.
Sonar Tari (poetry; title means "The Golden Boat"), 1894.
Chhota Galpa (short stories), 1894.
Vichitra Galpa (short stories), Parts 1 and 2, 1894.
Katha-Chatushtay (short stories), 1894.
Galpa-Dasak (short stories), 1895.
Nadi (poetry), 1896.
Chitra (poetry), 1896.
Chaitali (poetry), first published in *Kavya Granthavali,* 1896.
Vaikunther Khata (play), 1897.
Panchabhut (essays), 1897.
Kanika (poetry), 1899.
Katha (poetry), 1900.
Kalpana (poetry), 1900.
Kshanika (poetry), 1900.
Kahini (poetry and verse drama), 1900.
Naivedya (poetry; title means "Offerings"), 1901.
Smaran (poetry), first published in *Kavya-Grantha,* 1903.
Sisu (poetry), first published in *Kavya-Grantha,* 1903.
Karmaphal (story), 1903.
Atmasakti (essays), 1905.
Baul (songs), 1905.
Bharatvarsha (essays), 1906.
Kheya (poetry; title means "Ferrying Across"), 1906.
Vichitra Prabandha (essays), 1907.
Charitrapuja (essays), 1907.
Prachin Sahitya (essays), 1907.
Lokasahitya (essays), 1907.
Sahitya (essays), 1907.
Adhunik Sahitya (essays), 1907.

Hasya-Kautuk (plays), 1907.
Vyangakautuk (essays and plays), 1907.
Prajapatir Nirbandha (novel), 1908.
Raja Praja (essays), 1908.
Samuha (essays), 1908.
Svades (essays), 1908.
Samaj (essays), 1908.
Siksha (essays), 1908.
Mukut (play), 1908.
Sabdatattva (essays), 1909.
Dharma (sermons), 1909.
Santiniketan, Parts 1-8, 1909, Parts 9-11, 1910, Parts 12-13, 1911, Parts 14-15, 1915, Parts 15-16, 1916.
Prayaschitta (play; title means "Atonement"), 1909, new edition published as *Paritran,* 1929.
Vidyasagar-Charit (essays), c. 1909.
Galpa Chariti (short stories), 1912.
Achalayatan (play), 1912, new edition published as *Guru,* 1918.
Utsarga (poetry), 1914.
Gitali (songs), 1914.
Atati Galpa (short stories), c. 1915.
Sanchay (essays), 1916.
Parichay (essays), 1916.
Galpasaptak (short stories), 1916.
Palataka (poetry), 1918.
Payla Nambar (short stories), 1920.
Sisu Bholanath (poetry), 1922.
Vasanta (play), 1923.
Puravi (poetry), 1925.
Grihapraves (play), 1925.
Pravahini (songs), 1925.
Chirakumar Sabha (play), 1926.
Sodhbodh (play), 1926.
Lekhan (epigrams), 1927.
Rituranga (plays), 1927.
Yatri (diary), 1929.
Yogayog (novel), 1929.
Tapati (play), 1929.
Bhanusimher Patravali (letters), 1930.
Navin (play), 1931.
Vanavani (poems and songs), 1931.
Sapmochan (play), 1931.
Punascha (poetry; title means "Postscript"), 1932.
Parisesh (poetry), 1932.
Kaler Yatra (play), 1932.
Manusher Dharma (lectures), 1933.
Vichitrita (poetry), 1933.
Taser Des (play), 1933.
Bharatpathik Rammohan Roy (essays and addresses), 1933.
Sravan-Gatha (play), 1934.
Shesh Saptak (poetry; title means "Last Octave"), 1935.
Sur O Sangati (letters), 1935.
Vithika (poetry), 1935.
Chhanda (essays), 1936.
Nrityanatya Chitrangada (play), 1936.
Japane-Parasye (travel), 1936.
Sahityer Pathe (essays), 1936.
Praktani (addresses), 1936.
Khapchhada (rhymes), 1937.
Kalantar (essays), 1937.
Sey (stories), 1937.
Chhadar Chhabi (poetry), 1937.
Visva-Parichay (essays), 1937.
Pathe O Pather Prante (letters), 1938.
Banglabhasha Parichay (essays), 1938.

Semjuti (poetry; title means "Evening Lamp"), 1938.
Prahasini (poetry), 1939.
Akas-Pradip (poetry), 1939.
Pather Sanchay (essays and letters), 1939.
Nabajatak (poetry; title means "Newly Born"), 1940.
Sanai (poetry), 1940.
Tin Sangi (short stories), 1940.
Galpasalpa (stories and poetry), 1941.
Janmadine (poetry), 1941.
Asramer Rup O Vikas (essays), 1941.
Chhada (poetry), 1941.
Smriti (letters), 1941.
Chithipatra I (letters), 1942.
Chithipatra II (letters), 1942.
Chithipatra III (letters), 1942.
Atmaparichay (essays), 1943.
Sahiryer Svarup (essays), 1943.
Chithipatra IV (letters), 1943.
Sphulinga (poetry), 1945.
Chithipatra V (letters), 1945.
Muktir Upay (comedy), 1948.
Mahatma Gandhi (essays and addresses), 1948.
Visvabharati (addresses), 1951.
Baikali (songs and poetry), 1951.
Samavayaniti (essays), 1954.
Chitravichitra (poetry), 1954.
Itihas (essays), 1955.
Buddhadeva (essays and poetry), 1956.
Khrishta (essays and poems), 1959.
Chithipatra VI (letters), 1960.
Chithipatra VII (letters), 1960.
Chhinnapatravali (letters), 1960.

POETRY IN ENGLISH TRANSLATION

Gitanjali (title means "Song Offerings"), [India], 1910, translation by the author, introduction by W. B. Yeats, India Society (London), 1912, Macmillan (New York), 1913, Branden Press, 1978, translation by Brother James, University Press (Khaka, Bangladesh), 1983.
The Gardener, translation by the author, Macmillan (New York), 1913, reprinted, Macmillan (London), 1931.
The Crescent Moon, translation by the author, Macmillan (London), 1913, reprinted, 1957, Macmillan (New York), 1916.
Balaka, [India], 1916, translation by Aurobindo Bose published as *A Flight of Swans: Poems from Balaka,* foreword by S. Radhakrishnan, J. Murray, 1955, reprinted, 1962.
Fruit-Gathering, Macmillan (New York), 1916, reprinted, Macmillan (London), 1943.
Stray Birds, Macmillan (New York), 1916, reprinted, Macmillan (London), 1967.
Lover's Gift and Crossing, Macmillan (New York), 1918, reprinted, Macmillan (London), 1943.
The Fugitive and Other Poems, Santiniketan Press, 1919.
The Fugitive (poetry, songs, and plays), Macmillan (New York), 1921.
Lipika (poetry, allegories, and stories), [India], 1922, translation by A. Bose, Jaico Publishing House (Bombay), 1969.
Poems from Tagore, introduction by C. F. Andrews, Macmillan (Calcutta), 1923.
Rabindranath Tagore: Twenty-two Poems, translation by Edward J. Thompson, E. Benn, 1925.
Fireflies, Macmillan (New York), 1928, Collier Books, 1975.
Sheaves, Poems, and Songs by Rabindranath Tagore, compiled and translated by Nagendranath Gupta, Indian Press (Allahabad), 1929, 2nd edition, Greenwood Press, 1971.

The Child (originally published in English), Allen & Unwin, 1931.

Patraput (title means "Cupful of Leaves"), [India], 1935, translation by Sisir Chattopadhyaya, foreword by Kalidas Bhattacharya, Patrhikrit Prakashani (Calcutta), 1969.

Syamali, [India], 1936, translation by Sheila Chatterjee and the author, Visva-Bharati, 1955.

Prantik (title means "The Borderland"), [India], 1938 [and *Rogashajyaya* (title means "From the Sickbed"), [India], 1940 [and] *Arogya* (title means "Recovery"), [India], 1940 [and] *Sesh Lekha* (title means "Last Writings"), [India], 1941, translated together by A. Bose as *Wings of Death: The Last Poems of Rabindranath Tagore,* foreword by Gilbert Murray, J. Murray, 1960.

The Herald of Spring: Poems from Mohua, translation by A. Bose, J. Murray, 1957.

Ode to a Parted Love, Jaico Publishing House (Bombay), 1959.

Shesh Lekha: The Last Poems of Rabindranath Tagore, translation by Pritish Nandy, Dialogue Publications (Calcutta), 1973.

PLAYS IN ENGLISH TRANSLATION

Prakritir Pratisodh (verse drama), [India], 1884, translation by Edwin Lo-tien Fang published as *Sanyasi,* Commercial Press (Shanghai), 1936; also published as *Sanyasi; or, The Ascetic* in *Sacrifice and Other Plays,* Macmillan (New York), 1917.

Raja O Rani (verse drama), [India], 1889, translation published as *The King and Queen* in *Sacrifice and Other Plays,* Macmillan (New York), 1917; translation by Shakuntala Rao Sastri published as *Devouring Love,* East West Institute (New York), 1961.

Visarjan (verse drama), [India], 1890, translation published in *Sacrifice and Other Plays,* Macmillan (New York), 1917; new version edited and translated by R. K. Bamsal, published as *Sacrifice,* Uniteck Publications (Agra), 1971.

Chitrangada (verse drama), [India], 1892, translation by Birenda Nath Roy, Sribhumi Publishing Co., 1957; translation by the author published as *Chitra, the India Society* (London), 1913, Macmillan (New York), 1926.

Viday-Abhisap (verse drama), [India], 1894, translation by Thompson published as *The Curse at Farewell,* Harrap, 1924; also published as "Kach and Debjani" in *The Fugitive,* Macmillan (New York), 1921.

Malini, first published in *Kavya Granthavali,* Satyaprasad Gangopadhyaya, 1896, translation published in *Sacrifice and Other Plays,* Macmillan (New York), 1917.

Saradotsav (one-act), [India], 1908 (new edition published as *Rinsodh,* 1921), translation published as *Autumn Festival,* Brahmo Mission Press (Calcutta), 1919.

Raja, [India], 1910 (new edition published as *Arup Ratan,* 1920), translation by the author published as *The King of the Dark Chamber,* Macmillan (New York), 1914, reprinted, Macmillan (London), 1961.

Dak-Ghar, [India], 1912, translation by Devabrata Mukerjea published as *The Post Office,* preface by W. B. Yeats, Cuala Press (Ireland), 1914, T. M. MacGlinchey, 1971, new translation published as *The Post Office,* Macmillan (New York), 1914, Verry, 1978.

Phalguni, [India], 1916, translation by Andrews and Nishi-Kanta Sen with revision by the author published as *The Cycle of Spring,* Macmillan (New York), 1917.

Sacrifice and Other Plays, Macmillan (New York), 1917, Macmillan (London), 1963.

Mukta-dhara, [India], 1922, translation published as *The Waterfall* in *Modern Review,* 1922; translation by Marjorie Sykes published in *Three Plays,* Oxford University Press (Bombay), 1950.

Rakta-karavi, [India], 1924, translation published as *Red Oleanders,* illustrations by Gagendranath Tagore, in *Visva-Bharati Quarterly,* September, 1924, translation published as *Red Oleanders,* Macmillan (London), 1925, Macmillan (New York), 1926.

Natir Puja, [India], 1926 (first produced at Santiniketan, May 7, 1926), translation by Sykes published serially in *Visva-Bharati Quarterly,* February-October, 1945, published as "Dancing Girl's Worship" in *Three Plays,* Oxford University Press (Bombay), 1950.

Chandalika, [India], 1933 (first produced in Calcutta at Madan Theatre, September 12, 1933), translation and introduction by Kripalani published in *Visva-Bharati Quarterly,* February, 1938, translation by Sykes published in *Three Plays,* Oxford University Press (Bombay), 1950.

Chandalika Nrityanatya (dance drama), [India], 1938, translation by Shyamaree Devi published in *Orient Review,* January-February, 1956.

Syama, [India], 1939 (first produced in Calcutta, October 10, 1936), translation by Bharatendu Chakravarti published in *Eastern Post,* winter, 1955-56, translation by P. K. Saha published in *Thought,* July 31, 1971.

Bansari, Visva-Bharati, 1943, reprinted, 1948.

Three Plays (contains *Mukta-dhara, Natir Puja,* and *Chandalika*), translation by Sykes, Oxford University Press (Bombay), 1950, Oxford University Press (New York), 1970.

Three Riddle Plays (contains *The Test, The Reception,* and *The Patron*), translation by Prithvindra Chakravarti, Ind-US, 1983.

NOVELS IN ENGLISH TRANSLATION

Nashtanir, [India], 1901, translation by Mary M. Lago and Supriya Sen published as *The Broken Nest,* introduction by Lago, University of Missouri Press, 1971.

Chokher Bali (first published serially in *Bangadarsan,* 1901), [India], 1903, translation by Surendranath Tagore published as *Eyesore* in *Modern Review,* January-December, 1914, translation by Kripalani published as *Binodini,* W. S. Heinman (New York), 1959, revised edition, Sahitya Akademi (New Delhi), 1968.

Nauka Dubi (first published serially in *Bangadarsan,* 1903), [India], 1906, translation by J. G. Drummond published as *The Wreck,* Macmillan (New York), 1921, reprinted, Macmillan (London), 1963.

Gora (first published serially in *Pravasi,* 1907-10), [India], 1910, translation by W. W. Pearson published serially in *Modern Review,* January-December, 1923, translation by the author with revision by Surendranath Tagore, Macmillan (London), 1924, Macmillan (New York), 1925; abridged and simplified edition by E. F. Dodd, Macmillan (London), 1963.

Chaturanga, [India], 1916, translation published serially as *A Story in Four Chapters* in *Modern Review,* February-May, 1922, translation published as *Broken Ties,* Macmillan (London), 1925, translation by Asok Mitra published as *Chaturanga,* Sahitya Academi (New Delhi), 1963, Interculture Associates, 1974.

Ghare-Baire, [India], 1916, translation by Surendranath Tagore published serially as *At Home and Outside* in *Modern Review,* January-December, 1918, translation with revision by the author published as *The Home and the World,* Macmillan (New York), 1919, Verry, 1978.

Sesher Kavita, [India], 1929, translation by Kripalani published as *Farewell My Friend,* New India Publishing Co. (London), 1946.

Dui Bon, [India], 1933, translation by Kripalani published as *Two Sisters,* Visva-Bharati, 1945, reprinted, 1964.

Malancha, [India], 1934, translation by Kripalani published with *Sesher Kavita* as *Farewell My Friend* [and] *The Garden,* Jaico Publishing House (Bombay), 1956, reprinted, 1966.

Char Adhyay, [India], 1934, translation published as *Novelette of Young India: Four Chapters in Asia,* December, 1936-April, 1937, translation by Surendranath Tagore published as *Four Chapters,* Visva-Bharati, c. 1950.

SHORT FICTION IN ENGLISH TRANSLATION

Glimpses of Bengal Life, translation and introduction by Rajani Ranjan Sen, G. A. Nateson & Co. (Madras), 1913.

The Hungry Stones and Other Stories, translation by the author, Andrews, Thompson, Panna Lal Basu, Prabhat Kumar Mukerji, and Sister Nivedita, Macmillan (New York), 1916, AMS Press, 1970.

Mashi and Other Stories, Macmillan (New York), 1918, Arno Press, 1978.

"Tota-Kahini," translation published as *The Parrot's Training,* Thacker, Spink & Co., 1918, published in Bengali in *Lipika,* 1922.

The Trial of the Horse, Brahmo Mission Press (Calcutta), 1919, published in *The Parrot's Training and Other Stories.*

Broken Ties and Other Stories, Macmillan (London), 1925, Arno Press, 1978.

The Runaway and Other Stories, edited by Somnath Maitra, Visva-Bharati, 1958.

NONFICTION IN ENGLISH TRANSLATION

Jivansmriti (autobiography; first published serially in *Pravasi,* 1911), [India], 1912, translation by Surendranath Tagore published serially in *Modern Review* as *My Reminiscences,* January-December, 1916, Macmillan (New York), 1917, Gordon Press, 1978, published as *Reminiscences,* Macmillan (London), 1946, reprinted, 1971.

Sadhana: The Realisation of Life, Macmillan (New York), 1913, Omen Press (Tuscon, Ariz.), 1972.

Personality, Macmillan (New York), 1917, Macmillan (Madras), 1970.

Nationalism (lectures), Macmillan (New York), 1917, Greenwood Press, 1973.

Japan Yatri, [India], 1919, translation by Shakuntala Rao Sastri published as *A Visit to Japan,* edited by Walter Donald Kring, East West Institute, 1961.

Greater India, S. Ganesan (Madras), 1921.

Thought Relics, translation by the author, Macmillan (New York), 1921, enlarged edition published as *Thoughts from Rabindranath Tagore,* edited by Andrews, 1929.

Creative Unity, Macmillan (New York), 1922, Gordon Press, 1978.

Ethics of Destruction, Ganesh & Co. (Madras), 1923.

Talks in China: Lectures Delivered in April and May, 1924, Visva-Bharati, 1925.

The Religion of Man (lectures), Macmillan (New York), 1931, AMS Press, 1981.

India and the Pacific, Allen & Unwin, 1937.

The True India: A Plea for Understanding, Allen & Unwin, 1939.

Chhelebela, [India], 1940, translation by Sykes published as *My Boyhood Days,* Visva-Bharati (Santiniketan), 1940, 2nd edition, Visva-Bharati (Calcutta), 1941, reprinted, 1968.

Man (lectures), Kitabistan (Allahabad), 1946, Andhra University Press (Waltair), 1965.

My Early Life, edited by Rajendra Verma, Macmillan (Madras), 1952, Macmillan (Bombay), 1955.

Visva-Bharati and Its Institutions, Pulinbihari Sen (Santiniketan), 1956.

Our Universe (first published as *Visva-Parichaya*), translation by Indu Dutt, foreword by Malcolm MacDonald, Meridian Books (London), 1958, Interculture Associates, 1969.

Towards Universal Man (essays), edited by Bhabani Bhattacharya, introduction by Humayan Kabir, Asia Publishing House (New York), 1961, reprinted, 1962.

Pioneer in Education: Essays and Exchanges Between R. Tagore and L. K. Elmhirst, J. Murray, 1961.

Rabindranath Tagore on Rural Reconstruction, Publications Division, Ministry of Information and Broadcasting (New Delhi), 1962.

The Cooperative Principle (essays and addresses), edited by Pulinhihari Sen, translation by Surendranath Tagore, Apurvakumar Chanda, Somnath Maitra, and Jitendranarayan Sen, Visva-Bharati, 1963.

Mahatma Gandhi, compiled by Pulinbihari Sen, Visva-Bharati, 1963.

Gagendranath Tagore (art criticism), edited by Pulinbihari Sen, Indian Society of Oriental Art (Calcutta), 1972.

LETTERS IN ENGLISH TRANSLATION

Chhinnapatra, [India], 1912, translation by Surendranath Tagore published as *Glimpses of Bengal,* Macmillan (London), 1911, Macmillan (New York), 1921.

Letters, Macmillan (New York), 1917.

Letters from Abroad (first published serially in *Modern Review,* October, 1921-December, 1922), S. Ganesan (Madras), 1924, enlarged edition published as *Letters to a Friend,* edited by Andrews, Allen & Unwin, 1928.

Paschim Yatrir Diary, [India], 1924, translation by Dutt published as *The Diary of a Westward Voyage,* Asia Publishing House (New York), 1962, Greenwood Press, 1975.

Russiar Chithi, [India], 1931, translation by Sasadhar Sinha published as *Letters from Russia,* Visva-Bharati, 1960.

(With Mahatma Gandhi) *Mahatmaji and the Depressed Humanity,* Visva-Bharati Book Shop (Calcutta), 1932.

(With Gilbert Murray) *East and West,* Allen & Unwin, 1935.

(With Yone Noguchi) *Poet to Poet,* Visva-Bharati, 1939.

Rolland and Tagore: Letters and Transcripts of Conversations, 1919-1930, translation by Indira Chaudhurani and Alex Aronson, edited by Aronson and Kripalani, Visva-Bharati, 1945.

Imperfect Encounter: Letters of William Rothenstein and Rabindranath Tagore, 1911-1941, edited with introduction and notes by Mary M. Lago, Harvard University Press, 1972.

OTHER

Author of numerous songs. Translator of numerous works, and contributor of works in a variety of genres to books and periodicals.

MEDIA ADAPTATIONS: Tagore's "Samapti" was filmed by Satyajit Ray as "Teen Kanya" (title means "Three Daughters"), 1961; another version was released in the United States as "Two Daughters," 1963. The film "Charulata" (title means "The Lonely Wife") was adapted by Ray from a story by Tagore, R. D. Bansal, 1961. The novel *Ghare-Baire* (title means *The Home and the World*) was adapted by Ray for film and released by European Classics, 1985.

SIDELIGHTS: On his seventieth birthday, in an address delivered at the university he founded in 1918, Rabindranath Tagore said: "I have, it is true, engaged myself in a series of activities. But the innermost me is not to be found in any of these. At the end of the journey I am able to see, a little more clearly, the orb of my life. Looking back, the only thing of which I feel certain is that I am a poet (*ami kavi*)."

Though Tagore thought of himself essentially as a poet, he also made notable contributions to literature as a dramatist, novelist, short story writer, and writer of nonfictional prose, especially essays, criticism, philosophical treatises, journals, memoirs, and letters. In addition, he expressed himself as musician, painter, actor-producer-director, educator, patriot, and social reformer. Referring to the variety and abundance of Tagore's creative output, Buddhadeva Bose declared in *An Acre of Green Grass:* "It would be trite to call him versatile; to call him prolific very nearly funny." Bose added, "The point is not that his writings run into a hundred thousand pages of print, covering every form and aspect of literature, though this matters: he is a source, a waterfall, flowing out in a hundred streams, a hundred rhythms, incessantly."

A man of prodigious literary and artistic accomplishments, Tagore played a leading role in the Indian cultural renaissance and came to be recognized, along with Mahatma Gandhi, as one of the architects of modern India. India's first Prime Minister, Jawaharlal Nehru, wrote in *Discovery of India:* "Tagore and Gandhi have undoubtedly been the two outstanding and dominating figures in the first half of the twentieth century. . . . [Tagore's] influence over the mind of India, and especially of successive rising generations has been tremendous. Not Bengali only, the language in which he himself wrote, but all the modern languages of India have been molded partly by his writings. More than any other Indian, he has helped to bring into harmony the ideals of the East and the West, and broadened the bases of Indian nationalism."

Tagore's career, extending over a period of more than sixty years, reflected the artistic, cultural, and political vicissitudes of India in the late nineteenth and the first half of the twentieth century. Tagore wrote in "My Life," an essay collected in *Lectures and Addresses,* that he "was born and brought up in an atmosphere of the confluence of three movements, all of which were revolutionary": the religious reform movement started by Raja Rammohan Roy, the founder of the Bramo Samaj (Society of Worshipers of the One Supreme Being); the literary revolution pioneered by the Bengali novelist Bankim Chandra Chatterjee, who "lifted the dead weight of ponderous forms from our language and with a touch of his magic aroused our literature from her age-long sleep"; and the Indian National Movement, protesting the political and cultural dominance of the West. Members of the Tagore family had actively participated in all the three movements, and Tagore's own work, in a broad sense, represented the culmination of this three-pronged revolution.

Tagore began writing poetry at a very early age, and during his lifetime he published nearly sixty volumes of verse, in which he experimented with many poetic forms and techniques—lyric, sonnet, ode, dramatic monologue, dialogue poems, long narrative and descriptive works, and prose poems. Many of Tagore's poems are expressions of a mystical experience he had while looking at the sunrise one day: "As I continued to gaze, all of a sudden a covering seemed to fall away from my eyes, and I found the world bathed in a wonderful radiance, with waves of beauty and joy swelling on every side. This radiance pierced in a moment through the folds of sadness and despondency which had accumulated over my heart, and flooded it with this universal light," he recalled in *Reminiscences.* He recounted this experience in greater detail in *The Religion of Man:* "I felt sure that some Being who comprehended me and my world was seeking his best expression in all my experiences, uniting them into an ever-widening individuality which is a spiritual work of art. To this Being I was responsible; for the creation in me is His as well as mine." He called this Being his *Jivan devata* ("The Lord of His Life"), a new conception of God as man's intimate friend, lover, and beloved that was to play an important role in his subsequent work.

This sense of all-pervading joy in the universe expressed itself in *Chhabi O Gan* (1884; *Pictures and Songs*) and *Kari O Kamal* (1886; *Sharps and Flats*), in which he boldly celebrated the human body. He described *Kari O Komal* as "the Song of Humanity standing on the road in front of the gateway of the Palace of Life" and believed it to be an important landmark in the evolution of his poetic outlook. It was, however, his later contemplative, mystical, religious, and metaphysical tone dominating that gave his lyrical poetry depth, maturity, and serenity and that eventually brought him world renown with the publication of the English translations of *Gitanjali* in 1912.

The publication of *Gitanjali* was the most significant event in Tagore's writing career, for, following the volume's appearance, he won the Nobel Prize in Literature in 1913—the first such recognition of an Eastern writer. This slender volume of poems was "hailed by the literary public of England as the greatest literary event of the day" and which created "the literary sensation of the day" in America, according to the editors of the *Literary History of the United States.*

Gitanjali was written shortly after the deaths of Tagore's wife, his two daughters, his youngest son, and his father. But as his son, Rathindranath, testified in *On the Edges of Time,* "he remained calm and his inward peace was not disturbed by any calamity however painful. Some superhuman *sakti* [force] gave him the power to resist and rise above misfortunes of the most painful nature." *Gitanjali* was his inner search for peace and a reaffirmation of his faith in his *Jivan devata.* Its central theme was the realization of the divine through self-purification and service to humanity. When presenting Tagore the Nobel Prize, Harold Hjarne noted: "The *Gitanjali* is Mysticism, but not a mysticism that, relinquishing personality, seeks to become absorbed in the All to a point of Nothingness, but one that, with all the faculties of soul at highest pitch, eagerly sets forth to meet the Living Father of all Creation." Sarvepalli Radhakrishnan said in *The Philosophy of Rabindranath Tagore,* "The poems of *Gitanjali* are the offerings of the finite to the infinite." In his introduction to *Gitanjali,* Yeats called it "the work of supreme culture" and confessed, "I have carried the manuscript of these translations about me for days, reading it in railway trains, or on top of omnibuses and in restaurants, and I have often had to close it lest some stranger would see how it moved me." Ezra Pound, in his *Fortnightly Review* essay, described *Gitanjali* as a "series of spiritual lyrics" and compared it to "the *Paradiso* of Dante." Yeats and Pound set the tone of Tagore criticism in the West, and *Gitanjali* came to be looked upon as his most characteristic work.

The publication of *Gitanjali* was followed by five major poetical works in English translation: *The Gardener* (1913), *The Crescent Moon* (1913), *Fruit-Gathering* (1916), *Lover's Gift and Crossing* (1918), and *The Fugitive and Other Poems* (1919). *The Gardener* was a feast of love lyrics, though it also included mystical and religious poems, nature poems, and even a few poems with political overtones. *The Crescent Moon,* a book of songs about children, celebrated their beauty, innocence, charity, divinity, and primordial wisdom. Thompson called these poems a "revelation of a child's mind, comparable to the best that any language had seen." The combined *Lover's Gift and Crossing* contained some of Tagore's best lyrics, and *The Fugitive and Other Poems* included "Urvashi," Tagore's rapturous incantation of the Eternal Female, suggesting affinities with Shelley's "Hymn to Intellectual Beauty." In "Urvashi," observed Thompson, there was "a meeting of East and West indeed, a glorious tangle of Indian mythology, modern science, and legends of European romance."

J. C. Ghosh noted in *Bengali Literature* that "the more substantial and virile side of [Tagore's] work, such as his social, political, descriptive, and narrative poetry and his poetry of abstract thought, was either never presented at all or was presented in a terribly mutilated and emasculated form." Reviewing Tagore's literary reception in the West, Nabaneeta Sen in a *Mahfil* essay came to the conclusion that "Rabindranath only became a temporary craze, but never a serious literary figure in the Western scene. He was intrinsically an outsider to the contemporary literary tradition of the West, and after a short, misunderstood visit to the heart of the West, he again became an outsider."

In 1916 appeared *Balaka* (*A Flight of Swans*), which pointed to the new direction Tagore's poetry was to take. "The poems of *Balaka,*" wrote Lago in *Rabindranath Tagore,* "reflect a time of account-taking and of Tagore's reactions to the turbulence of the past four years: the excitement surrounding the Nobel award and the knighthood that followed in 1915, the premonitions of political disaster, and the anxieties of the World War." The flying swans symbolized, for the poet, movement, restlessness, a longing for faraway sites, an eternal quest for the unknown.

In the last decade of his life, as he became conscious of his approaching death, Tagore turned to radical experimentation in poetic techniques and to purely humanistic concepts dealing with the problems of life and death. His poems "became increasingly terse, luminous and precise in the use of imagery," wrote Amiya Chakravarty in *A Tagore Reader.* In *The Later Poems of Tagore,* Sisir Kumar Ghose said: "Full of dramatic discords, through alternate rhythms of intensity and exhaustion, the[se] poems unfold the history of a conflict, long and carefully concealed, at the heart of the Rabindrean imagination." He concluded, "To accept the best among the later poems is to alter our total conception of Tagore's poetry." "But," he added, "its hour is not yet. In order to do this as it should be done the ideal critic of Tagore needs to be as, if not more, sensitive than the poet himself. . . . Such a critic we do not have, unless he is in hiding."

Tagore also published more than forty plays, most of which were written for production in the open air for his students at Santiniketan. He himself took part in their performance as actor, producer, director, composer, and choreographer. He "mocked the commercial Bengali theater, burdened with heavy sets and realistic decor, and created a lyrical theater of the imagination," wrote Balwant Gargi in his *Folk Theater of India.* Though Tagore was influenced by Western dramatic techniques and his plays, as Mohan Lal Sharma pointed out in a *Modern Drama* essay, "have close affinity with the poetic or symbolist European drama of the present century typified in the works of such writers as Maurice Maeterlinck," he upheld the classical Indian tradition of drama as the depiction of emotion or *rasa* rather than of action. He blended this classical element with the folk tradition of Bengali *Jatra* performance—a combination of group singing, dancing,

and acting induced by a trance-like state—to achieve a synthesis of music, poetry, dance, drama, and costume. Consequently, most of Tagore's plays are interspersed with songs and are either lyrical or symbolic with subtle emotional and metaphysical overtones. The main principle of his plays, as he said himself, was "the play of feeling and not of action." Judged by the standards of Western drama, therefore, they seem static, ill-constructed, and unsuitable for commercial production.

Perhaps the most popular and the most frequently performed among Tagore's plays is *Dak-Ghar* (*The Post Office*), which dramatizes the story of a lonely boy, Amal, confined to his sickroom, longing to be free. Day after day, he sits at the window, watching the colorful spectacle of life passing him by, until death brings him deliverance from earthly pain and confinement. The play was produced in 1913 by the Abbey Theatre Company in Dublin and in London. Kripalani reported that after attending a performance of the play in London, William Butler Yeats testified: "On the stage the little play shows that it is very perfectly constructed, and conveys to the right audience an emotion of gentleness and peace." "Judged by a London standard," wrote Ernest Rhys in *Rabindranath Tagore: A Biographical Study,* "it may seem that all [Tagore's] dramatic work is lacking in ordinary stage effect, but to this criticism one can only reply that his plays were written to attain a naturalness of style and a simplicity of mode which only Irish players have so far realised for us." A London *Times* reviewer called the play "dreamy, symbolical, spiritual . . . a curious play, leaving to a certain extent a sense of incompleteness, since it ends before the climax, rich in poetical thought and imagery, as well as a kind of symbolism that must not be pressed too closely." Since *The Post Office* can be read on two levels, the naturalistic and the symbolic, it has remained a special favorite with Tagore readers. In his book *Rabindranath Tagore,* Thompson paid the play a high compliment: "*The Post Office* does what both Shakespeare and Kalidas failed to do. It succeeds in bringing on the stage a child who neither shows off nor is silly."

Following the public controversy that broke out between Mahatma Gandhi and Tagore in 1921 over the poet's opposition to Gandhi's noncooperation movement and his cult of the *charkha* (spinning wheel), Tagore's popularity suffered a steep decline and he found himself more and more publicly isolated. Gandhi, failing to enlist the poet's support, remarked: "Well, if you can do nothing else for me you can at least . . . lead the nation and spin." Tagore immediately replied: "Poems I can spin, songs I can spin, but what a mess I would make, Gandhiji, of your precious cotton!" There the controversy stopped. But the churnings in the poet's mind over the political situation in the country produced *Mukta-dhara* in January, 1922, a symbolic play with political overtones. A distant echo of *Prayaschitta* (1909; *Atonement*), the play has been regarded by several critics as a noble tribute to Mahatma Gandhi and his campaign of nonviolence. Tagore was making preparations to stage the play, but when he heard the news of Gandhi's arrest in March, 1922, he abandoned the preparations and *Mukta-dhara* was never produced.

Like Gandhi, Tagore preached against and fought the Indian caste system that fostered the concept of untouchability. The first number of Gandhi's weekly *Harijan,* issued in Poona on February 11, 1933, carried a poem by Tagore, "The Cleanser," on its front page. The same year, Tagore wrote *Chandalika* (*The Untouchable Girl*), a drama based on the Buddhist legend of *Sardulakarnavadana.* This is the story of a young untouchable girl, Prakriti, who falls in love with a handsome Buddhist monk, Ananda, when the latter asks her to give him some water to drink. As Ananda drinks water from her hands, she feels redeemed, spiritually reborn, newly aware of herself as a woman, and emancipated from the bondage of her birth and caste. No one could have paid a better tribute to Gandhi's cause of Harijan uplift than Tagore did in this poetic play. It remains a personal testament of Tagore the humanist, exemplifying his faith in the dignity of humanity.

With *Binodini,* titled in the original Bengali *Chokher Bali*—literally, "Eyesore"—Tagore "paved the way for the truly modern novel in India, whether realistic or psychological or concerned with social problems," wrote its English translator Krishna R. Kripalani in his foreword to the 1959 edition. The novel gives an intimate picture of domestic relations in an upper middle-class Bengali Hindu family at the turn of the century and portrays the plight of a young widow, Binodini, who "asserts her right to love and happiness." In Kripalani's view, "Of all women characters created by Tagore in his many novels, Binodini is the most real, convincing, and full-blooded. In her frustrations and suffering is summed up the author's ironic acceptance of the orthodox Hindu society of the day."

In *Gora* Tagore created a socio-political novel voicing the aspirations of the resurgent India. Published in 1910, the year of the *Gitanjali* series of poems, it represented the peak of his fictional career. "This work," wrote Naravane in *An Introduction to Rabindranath Tagore,* "has everything that one might expect from a masterpiece: brilliant delineation of characters; a story which offers surprises till the very end; a fluent, powerful style interspersed with bursts of poetic imagery, and absolute serenity." Though heavily filled with polemics reflecting the social, religious, and political issues of the time, the novel projected Tagore's concept of liberal nationalism based on the ideal of *vishwabandhutva* or international brotherhood. In a March 13, 1921, letter to Andrews, Tagore declared: "All humanity's greatest is mine. The infinite personality of man has come from the magnificent harmony of all races. My prayer is that India may represent the cooperation of all the people of the earth." In the extraordinary character and personality of the protagonist Gourmohan or Gora, Tagore tried to bring about the fusion of the East and the West to exemplify his ideal of the Universal Man. In *Rabindranath Tagore,* Lago declared *Gora* "a study of the relation between Hindu orthodoxy and Indian nationalism." Gora's sudden discovery that he has no parents, no home, no country, no religion, brings him freedom from all barriers: "But today I am free—yes, am standing freely in the center of a vast truth. Only now do I have the right to serve India. Today I have truly become an Indian. For me there is no conflict between Hindu, Muslim and Christian."

The subject of *The Home and the World* is the political agitation resulting from the partition of Bengal in 1905. Tagore was at the time deeply involved in the Indian National Movement. But when militant Hindu nationalism began to turn to violence and terrorist methods, he took a public stand against this development and openly condemned the excesses of the Swadeshi (*swa,* self; *deshi,* national) movement, which advocated the use of goods made in India. This position made him so unpopular with the nationalist Hindu intelligentsia that, in utter disillusionment, he withdrew from active politics and retreated into what he called the "poet's corner." But to answer his critics who had accused him of desertion and to reaffirm his own faith in the principles of truth and nonviolence, he wrote *The Home and the World,* which, as Bhabani Bhattacharya noted in an article that appeared in *Rabindranath Tagore: A Centenary Volume,* "roused a storm of controversy when it first appeared in serial form in the literary magazine *Subui Patra* and harsh pens assailed it not only as 'unpatriotic' but 'immoral.' "

E. M. Forster, in a review that first appeared in *Athenaeum* and was later reprinted in *Abinger Harvest,* admired the novel's theme but was repelled by its persistent "strain of vulgarity." He wrote, "throughout the book one is puzzled by bad tastes that verge upon bad taste." He thought the novel contained much of "a boarding-house flirtation that masks itself in mystic or patriotic talk." "Yet the plain fact is," as Bhattacharya pointed out, "that in matters of sex Tagore always retained in him a conservative core that was near-prudery, and his moments of realism in the context of such relationships were a whole epoch apart from the trends which our modern literary idiom calls 'naturalistic.' "

Though Tagore was the first modern Indian writer to introduce psychological realism in his fiction, his novels were generally looked upon as old-fashioned in form. From the artistic point of view, however, Tagore excelled in the art of short story writing. He was not only a pioneer in Bengali literature, but he also paved the way for modern writers like Premchand and such contemporary writers as Mulk Raj Anand, Raja Rao, and R. K. Narain. Bose acknowledged in *An Acre of Green Grass* that Rabindranath "brought us the short story when it was hardly known in England." Naravane wrote in *An Introduction to Rabindranath Tagore,* "The modern short story is Rabindranath Tagore's gift to Indian literature."

Tagore dictated his last poem a few hours before his death on August 7, 1941. The leading newspapers of the world published editorials paying tribute to him as "India's greatest man of letters," "the soul of Bengal," and "ambassador of friendship between East and West." But the *Washington Post* provided perhaps the most telling of assessments: "Tagore believed that East and West do not represent antagonistic and irreconcilable attitudes of the human mind, but that they are complementary, and since Tagore's own work and thought represented a fusion of East and West, the fate of his poems and dramas at the hands of later generations . . . may be the test of whether the age-old gulf between Asia and Europe can ever be bridged."

BIOGRAPHICAL/CRITICAL SOURCES:

BOOKS

Aronson, Alexander, *Rabindranath through Western Eyes,* Kitabistan (Allahabad), 1943.

Aronson, Alexander and Krishna R. Kripalani, editors, *Rolland and Tagore,* Visva-Bharati (Calcutta), 1945.

Bose, Abinash Chandra, *Three Mystic Poets: A Study of W. B. Yeats, A. E., and Rabindranath Tagore,* Folcroft, 1970.

Bose, Buddhadeva, *An Acre of Green Grass: A Review of Modern Bengali Literature,* Orient Longmans (Calcutta), 1948.

Bose, Buddhadeva, *Tagore: Portrait of a Poet,* University of Bombay, 1962.

Chatterjee, Ramananda, editor, *The Golden Book of Tagore,* Golden Book Committee (Calcutta), 1931.

Forster, E. M., *Abinger Harvest,* Harcourt, 1964.

Gargi, Balwant, *Folk Theater of India,* University of Washington Press, 1966.

Ghose, Sisir Kumar, *The Later Poems of Tagore,* Asia Publishing House (London), 1961.

Ghosh, Jyotis Chandra, *Bengali Literature,* Oxford University Press (London), 1948.

Kripalani, Krishna R., *Rabindranath Tagore: A Biography,* Oxford University Press (London), 1962.

Lago, Mary M., *Imperfect Encounter: Letters of William Rothenstein and Rabindranath Tagore, 1911-1941,* Harvard University Press, 1972.

Lago, Mary M., *Rabindranath Tagore,* Twayne, 1976.

Leny, V., *Rabindranath Tagore: His Personality and World,* translation by Guy McKeever, Phillips, Allen & Unwin, 1939.

Naravane, Vishwanath S., *An Introduction to Rabindranath Tagore,* Macmillan (Madras), 1977.

Nehru, Jawaharlal, *Discovery of India,* John Day, 1946.

Ray, Nihar-Ranjan, *An Artist in Life: A Commentary on the Life and Works of Rabindranath Tagore,* University of Kerala (Trivandrum), 1967.

Rhys, Ernest, *Rabindranath Tagore: A Biographical Study,* Macmillan (London), 1915.

Spiller, Robert E. and others, editors, *Literary History of the United States,* Macmillan (New York), 1962, 4th edition, 1974.

Tagore, Rabindranath, *Sonar Tari,* [India], 1894.

Tagore, Rabindranath, *Gitanjali,* Macmillan (New York), 1913.

Tagore, Rabindranath, *My Reminiscences,* Macmillan (New York), 1917.

Tagore, Rabindranath, *Letters to a Friend,* edited by C. F. Andrews, Allen & Unwin, 1928.

Tagore, Rabindranath, *My Boyhood Days,* translation by Marjorie Sykes, Visva-Bharati (Santiniketan), 1940.

Tagore, Rabindranath, *Binodini,* translated by Krishna R. Kripalani, Sahitya Akademi (New Delhi), 1959.

Tagore, Rabindranath, *A Tagore Reader,* edited by Amiya Chakravarty, Macmillan (New York), 1961.

Tagore, Rabindranath, *A Tagore Testament,* translation by Indu Dutt, Jaico Publishing House (Bombay), 1969.

Tagore, Rabindranath, *Lectures and Addresses,* Macmillan (New Delhi), 1970.

Tagore, Rabindranath, *Sadhana: The Realisation of Life,* Macmillan (New York), Omen Press (Tuscon, Ariz.), 1972.

Tagore, Rathindranath, *On the Edges of Time,* Orient Longmans (Calcutta), 1958.

Thompson, Edward J., *Rabindranath Tagore: Poet and Dramatist,* 2nd edition, revised, Oxford University Press (London), 1948.

Thompson, Edward J. and Arthur Mariman Spencer, *Rabindranath Tagore: His Life and Work,* YMCA Publishing House (Calcutta), 1921.

Twentieth Century Literary Criticism, Volume 3, Gale, 1980.

PERIODICALS

American Quarterly, fall, 1962.

Fortnightly Review, March, 1913.

Indian Literature, Volume 9, number 5, 1976; September-October, 1980.

Mahfil: A Quarterly of South Asian Literature, Volume 3, 1966.

Modern Drama, May, 1970.

Times (London), July 11, 1913.

Washington Post, August 8, 1941.

*   *   *

TALESE, Gay 1932-

PERSONAL: Given name originally Gaetano; born February 7, 1932, in Ocean City, N.J.; son of Joseph Francis and Catherine (DePaulo) Talese; married Nan Ahearn (a vice president and executive editor at a publishing company), June 10, 1959; children: Pamela, Catherine. *Education:* University of Alabama, B.A., 1953.

ADDRESSES: Home—109 East 61st St., New York, N.Y. 10021; and 154 East Atlantic Blvd., Ocean City, N.J. 08226 (summer).

CAREER: New York Times, New York, N.Y., 1953-65, began as copy boy, became reporter; full-time writer, 1965—. *Military service:* U.S. Army, 1953-55; became first lieutenant.

MEMBER: Authors League of America, Sigma Delta Chi, Phi Sigma Kappa.

AWARDS, HONORS: Best Sports Stories Award-Magazine Story, E. P. Dutton & Co., 1967, for "The Silent Season of a Hero"; Christopher Book Award, 1970, for *The Kingdom and the Power.*

WRITINGS:

NONFICTION

New York: A Serendipiter's Journey, Harper, 1961.

The Bridge, Harper, 1964.

The Overreachers, Harper, 1965.

The Kingdom and the Power (Book-of-the-Month Club alternate selection), World Publishing, 1969.

Fame and Obscurity, World Publishing, 1970.

Honor Thy Father (Literary Guild selection), World Publishing, 1971.

Thy Neighbor's Wife (Literary Guild special selection), Doubleday, 1980.

(Editor with Robert Atwan) *The Best American Essays 1987,* Ticknor & Fields, 1987.

Contributor of articles to magazines, including *Reader's Digest, New York Times Magazine,* and *Saturday Evening Post.* Contributing editor, *Esquire,* beginning in 1966.

WORK IN PROGRESS: A book on the Italian migration to America at the turn of the century, for Doubleday.

SIDELIGHTS: As a pioneer of the new journalism, Gay Talese was one of the first writers to apply the techniques of fiction to nonfiction. In a *Writer's Digest* interview with Leonard Wallace Robinson, Talese described how and why he began writing in this style while reporting for the *New York Times:* "I found I was leaving the assignment each day, unable with the techniques available to me or permissible to the *New York Times,* to really tell, to report, all that I saw, to communicate through the techniques that were permitted by the archaic copy desk. . . . [So] I started . . . to use the techniques of the short story writer in some of the *Esquire* pieces I did in the early Sixties. . . . It may read like fiction, it may give the impression that it was made up, over-dramatizing incidents for the effect those incidents may cause in the writing, but without question . . . there is reporting. There is reporting that fortifies the whole structure. Fact reporting, leg work."

Now considered classics of the genre, Talese's *Esquire* articles probed the private lives of celebrities such as Frank Sinatra, Joe DiMaggio, and Floyd Patterson. The success of these stories prompted Talese to apply this new technique to larger subjects, and, in 1969, he produced his first best-seller, *The Kingdom and the Power,* a nonfiction work about the *New York Times* written in novelistic style. Since then Talese has explored such controversial topics as the Mafia, in *Honor Thy Father* (1971), and sexuality in America, in *Thy Neighbor's Wife* (1980). Widely respected as a master of his craft, Talese has thought of writing fiction, but, as he explained to the *Los Angeles Times*'s Wayne Warga, nonfiction challenges him more: "I suggest there is art in journalism. I don't want to resort to changing names, to fictionalizing. The reality is more fascinating. My mission is to get deep into the heart and soul of the people in this country."

Talese grew up in Ocean City, a resort town in New Jersey that he describes as "festive and bright in the summertime" and "depressing" the rest of the year. As the son of an Italian immigrant, young Talese was "actually a minority within a minority" according to *Time* magazine's R. Z. Sheppard. He was Catholic in a Protestant community and Italian in a predominately Irish parish. A repressed, unhappy child, Talese remembers himself as a loner who failed most of the classes at his conservative parochial school. Then, when he was thirteen, he made a discovery. "I became involved with the school newspaper," he told Francis Coppola in an *Esquire Film Quarterly* interview, and realized that "you can be shy, as I was, but you can still approach strangers and ask them questions." Throughout high school and college, Talese continued his writing, majoring in journalism at the University of Alabama, contributing sports columns to the campus newspaper, and hoping to work someday for the *New York Herald Tribune,* where his literary idol, Red Smith, had a column of his own. After graduation Talese made the rounds of the major New York newspapers, applying for a job and finally being offered one by the paper where he thought his chances were least promising—the *New York Times.* Hired as a copy boy, he was promoted to reporter in just two years.

In 1961 Talese published his first book, *New York: A Serendipiter's Journey.* Composed largely of material from his *New York Times* articles, the book was a critical success and sold about 12,000 copies, mostly in New York. His next venture was *The Bridge,* a book in which, according to *Playboy* magazine, "he took the plunge into the book-length nonfiction novel style." To prepare for this story, Talese spent over a year observing the workers who built the Verrazano-Narrows Bridge connecting Brooklyn and Staten Island. In the *New York Times Book Review* Herbert Mitgang calls the book "a vivid document," noting that Talese "imparts drama and romance to this bridge-building story by concentrating on the boomers, the iron workers who stitch steel and live high in more ways than one." While the publication was not a best-seller, it was critically well received, and *Playboy* reports that "it was a minor classic in demonstrating how deeply—and subjectively—a reporter could involve himself in the lives of his subjects and bring the flesh and blood of real people to paper in a way that was usually expected only in novels." Furthermore, critics believe it set the scene for the three larger works which would follow in the next sixteen years.

The first of these was *The Kingdom and the Power,* an intimate portrait of the *New York Times* where Talese worked as a reporter for ten years. Published four years after he left the paper, the book is "rich in intimate detail, personal insights and characterizations," according to Ben H. Bagdikian in the *New York Times Book Review.* "In this book," Bagdikian continues, "the men of The Times emerge not as godlike models of intrepid journalism, but as unique individuals who, in addition to other human traits, have trouble with ambitions, alcohol, wives and analysts." In his author's note, Talese describes the book as "a human history of an institution in transition." Specifically, Talese relates the infighting between James ("Scotty") Reston, respected columnist and head of the *New York Times* Washington bureau, and E. Clifton Daniel, managing editor of the paper, for control of the Washington bureau, which had maintained independent status for years. In the end, Reston wins and is appointed executive editor. But "that outcome, of great moment inside the *Times,* is of less than secondary interest to the rest of the world," according to a *Time* critic who adds that "to curry reader excitement, Talese has had to transform the newsroom on the third floor of the *Times* building into a fortress of Machiavel-

lian maneuver. (One wonders, sometimes, how the paper ever got put out at all.)"

Talese's decision to dramatize the story, to relate the process of change at an American institution from the human perspective has been more praised than criticized. Detractors feel that the *New York Times* owners and employees are ultimately unworthy of such elaborate attention, that their petty squabbling diminishes the institution they represent. Supporters argue that Talese's approach is the best way to reveal the inside story and is an example of new journalism at its best.

Among the critics of this approach is John Leo, who writes in *Commonweal:* "The new journalist in Talese is forever trying to capture the real *Times* by a telling scene of explaining what everyone felt at a critical moment. But the effort doesn't amount to much. . . . It is often spectacularly effective in delineating a person, a small group of people or a social event. But for an institution, and a ponderous non-dramatic one at that, well, maybe only the boring old journalism will do." Because his focus is on personality rather than issues, some critics believe the perspective is skewed. Among them is Harold E. Fey who writes in the *Christian Century* that Talese "seems unable to understand or to formulate adequately the *Times*'s high purpose, its worthy conceptions of public responsibility, its firm identification of personal with journalistic integrity. These also have something to do with power. And they have much to do with the *New York Times.* They help to explain, as Talese does not, why the *Times,* in his own words, 'influences the world.' " Fred Powledge in the *Nation,* however, found merit in Talese's approach: "Talese does not attempt to resolve questions [about journalistic procedure and social responsibility,] and some may consider this a fault. I do not think so. If he had entered this vast and relatively unexplored territory the book would have lost some of its timeless, surgically clean quality." And, writing in *Life,* Murray Kempton notes that "by talking about their lives [Talese] has done something for his subjects which they could not do for themselves with their product, and done it superlatively well." Another supporter is David Bernstein. "There are surely criticisms to be made [of the great power the *New York Times* wields over public opinion]," he writes in *New Leader,* "but they are meaningless without an understanding of the private worlds of individual reporters, editors, and publishers and of how these worlds interact. Gay Talese is quite right to place his emphasis upon all this when he describes the kingdom that is the *Times.* What might appear at first glance to be a frivolous book is in fact a serious and important account of one of the few genuinely powerful institutions in our society." Powledge agrees: "The inner conflicts and passions of these men are beautifully documented in *The Kingdom and the Power.* It is no less than a landmark in the field of writing about journalism."

In 1971, Talese produced what many consider to be another landmark—*Honor Thy Father,* an inside look at the life of mafioso Bill Bonanno and a book so popular that it sold more than 300,000 copies within four months of its publication. Like all of Talese's efforts, the story was extensively researched and written in the intimate style of the new journalism. Almost six years elapsed between the day in 1965 when Talese first met Bill Bonanno outside a New York courtroom and the publication of the book. During that time Talese actually lived with the Bonanno family and persuaded them to talk about their business and personal lives, becoming, to use his words, "a source of communication within a family that had long been repressed by a tradition of silence."

While the tone of the book is nonjudgmental, Talese's compassionate portrayal of underworld figures—including Bill and his father, New York boss Joseph Bonanno—incited charges that Talese was giving gangsters moral sanction. Writing in the *New York Times Book Review,* Colin McInnes says that "Gay Talese has become so seduced by his subject and its 'hero,' that he conveys the impression that being a mobster is much the same as being a sportsman, film star or any other kind of public personality." But others, such as the *Times Literary Supplement* critic, defend Talese's treatment, noting that "Mr. Talese's insight will do more to help us understand the criminal than any amount of moral recrimination." And writing in the *New York Review of Books,* Wilfrid Sheed expresses a similar view: "Gay Talese has been criticized for writing what amounts to promotional material for the Bonanno family, but his book is an invaluable document and I don't know how such books can be obtained without some compromise. It is a lot to ask of an author that he betray the confidence of a Mafia family. As with a tapped phone call, one must interpret the message. . . . Talese signals occasionally to his educated audience—dull, aren't they? Almost pathetic. But that's all he can do."

Furthermore, Sheed argues, the technique of new journalism, "an unfortunate strategy for most subjects, is weirdly right" here: "The prose matches the stiff watchful facade of the Mafia. One is reminded of a touched-up country wedding photo, with the cheeks identically rouged and the eyes glazed, of the kind the Bonanno family might have ordered for themselves back in Sicily."

After the success of *Honor Thy Father,* Doubleday offered Talese a $1.2 million contract for two books. "I was interested in sexual changes and how . . . morality was being defined," Talese told a *Media People* interviewer. To gather material for a chronicle of the American sexual revolution, Talese submerged himself in the subculture of massage parlors, pornographic publishing, blue movies, and, ultimately, Sandstone, the California sexual retreat. He also studied First Amendment decisions in the Supreme Court and law libraries, tracing the effect of Puritanism on American's free rights. As his research stretched from months into years, however, Talese realized that what began as a professional exploration had become a personal odyssey. And because he was asking others to reveal their most intimate sexual proclivities, he felt it would be hypocritical not to reveal his own. Thus, before he had written a word of his book, Talese became the subject of two revealing profiles in *Esquire* and *New York* magazines, the latter entitled "An Evening in the Nude with Gay Talese." The public was titillated, and the resulting publicity virtually guaranteed the book's financial success (and "the critics' wrath," according to Nan Talese in a letter to *CA*). In October, 1979, months before the publication reached bookstores, United Artists bid a record-breaking $2.5 million for film rights to the book Talese entitled *Thy Neighbor's Wife.* Published in 1980, the book became a best-seller and was number one on the *New York Times* best-seller list for three consecutive months.

Despite its popularity, *Thy Neighbor's Wife* received negative reviews from many literary critics. But Nan Talese believes the reasons have less to do with the quality of the book than with its subject matter and the circumstances under which it was written. In her letter to *CA*, she explains: "Because [the] book took so long and was about sex, surely a most intimate and volatile subject, because of the early publicity, the enormous movie sale and the fact that it would be published in fourteen countries abroad, the success was too much and the critics pounced. . . . Writers had a heyday with our marriage, and the book, which is a sociological study as well as a contemporary re-creation, was misrep-

resented except by serious-minded sociologists and psychologists (who I suppose are less shocked by the human condition)."

Virginia Johnson-Masters, the respected sex researcher, foresaw the ensuing controversy when she wrote an early *Vogue* review saying that Talese "shows us many things about ourselves and the social environment in which we live. Some of them we may not appreciate or want any part of. However, Talese, the author, is fair. Read carefully and perceive that he really does not proselytize, he informs." Johnson-Masters goes on to say: "*Thy Neighbor's Wife* is a scholarly, readable and thoroughly entertaining book. . . . It is a meticulously researched context of people, events, and circumstances through which a reader can identify the process of breakdown in repressive sexual myths dominating our society until quite recently."

Writing in the *New York Times Book Review,* psychiatrist Robert Coles notes that Talese "has a serious interest in watching his fellow human beings, in listening to them, and in presenting honestly what he has seen and heard. He writes clear unpretentious prose. He has a gift, through phrase here, a sentence there, of making important narrative and historical connections. We are given, really, a number of well-told stories, their social message cumulative: A drastically transformed American sexuality has emerged during this past couple of decades." Despite such praise from sociologists and psychologists, many reviewers criticize the book. Objections range from Ernest van den Haag's charge in the *National Review* that *Thy Neighbor's Wife* is "remarkably shallow" to Robert Sherrill's allegation in the *Washington Post* that it is "constructed mostly of the sort of intellectual plywood you find in most neighborhood bars: part voyeurism, part amateur psychoanalysis, part sixpack philosophy." The most common objections include Talese's apparent lack of analysis, his omission of homosexuality, and his supposed anti-female attitude.

In his *Playboy* review of the book, critic John Leonard articulates each of these objections: "Since Talese parajournalizes so promiscuously—reaching into [his subjects'] minds, reading their thoughts, scratching their itches—one would expect at the very least to emerge from his book, as if from a novel, with some improved comprehension of what they stand for and a different angle on the culture that produced them. One emerges instead, as if from a soft-porn movie in the middle of the afternoon, reproached by sunlight and feeling peripheral to the main business of the universe. If Talese expects us to take his revolutionaries as seriously as he himself takes them, he has to put them in a social context and make them sound interesting. He doesn't." Furthermore, Leonard continues, "Talese almost totally ignores feminism. Gay liberation doesn't interest him. Children, conveniently, do not exist; if they did exist, they would make group sex—Tinkertoys! Erector Sets!—an unseemly hassle. . . . Missing from *Thy Neighbor's Wife* are history and stamina and celebration and mystery, along with birth, blood, death and beauty, not to mention earth, fire, water, politics, and everything else that isn't our urgent plumbing, that refuses to swim in our libidinal pool." The book, responds Nan Talese, "is a sociological study of where we have been in regards to sex and how the sexual revolution changed us. It is fair to say that homosexuality is not represented and the women's movement not annotated, although there are many women in the book and quite a few of them are feminists. But one book cannot do everything and I think now it was a mistake for Doubleday to delete the subtitle *Lust and Longing in America* from the book. Gay had meant it to indicate, along with the title, that it was written very much about men from a man's point of view."

When asked by *Playboy* interviewer Larry DuBois if he were vulnerable to charges that he wrote "only as a reporter telling a series of dramatic stories without understanding and conveying the deeper philosophical meaning of those stories," Talese said he was not. "The characters are described, are understood, are understood in their historical time, and the historical time of the twentieth century is reflected against the background of the nineteenth century. If the book were what you described, I could have done it in six months." It was not, however, only the depth of his research, but also the fact that he refused to change names or use composite characters that made the book eight years in the making. "The book reports fantasy," he told *Washington Post* interviewer Tom Zito. "It reports intimacy. Getting releases from people to use their real names is what took me eight years. I had to develop relationships with these people. I had to convince them that they were typical of their time. And what the book may be able to do is convince other people that what they're doing in private isn't bad, isn't abnormal." Talese considers it the most important story of his life. The negative reviews, he believes, will not matter in the long run. "Ten years from now this will read as a historical book," he told Clarence Petersen in the *Chicago Tribune.* "The gossip will be forgotten." In the meantime, Talese maintains his composure. "In my personal life certainly there is much that I am willing to apologize for," he told DuBois. "But not in my work. I never apologize for the work I do. That is deliberate, very carefully crafted, done with love and care. I have never been ashamed of anything I have written. Success is marvelous, but all I'm really committed to is writing well."

MEDIA ADAPTATIONS: Honor Thy Father was filmed as a made-for-television movie by Columbia Broadcasting System in 1973.

BIOGRAPHICAL/CRITICAL SOURCES:

BOOKS

Authors in the News, Volume 1, Gale, 1976.
Contemporary Issues Criticism, Volume 1, Gale, 1982.
Contemporary Literary Criticism, Volume 37, Gale, 1986.

PERIODICALS

Chicago Tribune, June 8, 1980, October 2, 1987.
Christian Century, October 8, 1969.
Commonweal, October 17, 1969.
Esquire Film Quarterly, July, 1981.
Life, June 27, 1969.
Los Angeles Times, May 23, 1980.
Los Angeles Times Book Review, April 27, 1980.
Media People, May 1980.
Nation, September 15, 1969.
National Review, August 12, 1969, March 6, 1981.
New Leader, May 26, 1969.
Newsweek, July 21, 1969, April 28, 1980.
New York Review of Books, July 20, 1972.
New York Times, May 21, 1969, October 5, 1971, April 30, 1980.
New York Times Book Review, January 17, 1965, June 8, 1969, August 2, 1970, October 31, 1971, May 4, 1980.
New York Times Magazine, April 20, 1980.
People, April 14, 1980.
Playboy, May, 1980.
Publishers Weekly, January 7, 1983.
Time, July 4, 1969, October 4, 1971.
Times Literary Supplement, May 14, 1971, April 4, 1972, July 4, 1980.
Vogue, June, 1980.

Washington Post, October 18, 1979, April 27, 1980, May 7, 1980, May 15, 1980.
Washington Post Book World, November 15, 1987.
Writer's Digest, January, 1970.

* * *

TANNER, William
See AMIS, Kingsley (William)

* * *

TARASSOFF, Lev
See TROYAT, Henri

* * *

TATE, (John Orley) Allen 1899-1979

PERSONAL: Born November 19, 1899, in Winchester, Ky.; died February 9, 1979, in Nashville, Tenn.; son of John Orley and Eleanor (Varnell) Tate; married Caroline Gordon (a novelist), November 3, 1924 (divorced, 1959); married Isabella Stewart Gardner, August 27, 1959 (divorced, 1966); married Helen Heinz, July 30, 1966; children: (first marriage) Nancy Meriwether, (third marriage) John Allen, Michael Paul (deceased), Benjamin Lewis Bogan. *Education:* Vanderbilt University, B.A. (magna cum laude), 1922. *Politics:* Democrat. *Religion:* Roman Catholic convert, 1950.

ADDRESSES: Home—113 Groome Dr., Nashville, Tenn. 37205. *Office*—Department of English, 127 Vincent Hall, University of Minnesota, Minneapolis, Minn. *Agent*—Laurence Pollinger Ltd., 18 Maddox St., London W1, England.

CAREER: Writer, 1922-79. *Telling Tales,* New York, N.Y., assistant editor, 1924-25; Southwestern College, Memphis, Tenn., lecturer in English, 1934-36; University of North Carolina, Women's College, Greensboro, professor of English, 1938-39; Princeton University, Princeton, N.J., poet in residence, 1939-42; Library of Congress, Washington, D.C., chair of poetry, 1943-44, fellow in American letters, 1944-50; *Sewanee Review,* Sewanee, Tenn., editor, 1944-46; New York University, New York, N.Y., lecturer, 1947-51; University of Chicago, Chicago, Ill., visiting professor of humanities, 1949; University of Minnesota, Minneapolis, professor of English, 1951-66, Regents' Professor of English, 1966-68. Member of Columbia Broadcasting System (CBS) radio program "Invitation to Learning," 1940-41. Fulbright professor, University of Rome, 1953-54, Oxford University, 1958-59. Member of American delegation to UNESCO Conference on the Arts, and American representative to the International Exposition of the Arts (Congress for Cultural Freedom), both 1952. Lecturer for Department of State in England, France, Italy, and India, 1956. Senior fellow, Indiana School of Letters. Visiting lecturer and poet at numerous universities and public readings.

MEMBER: National Institute of Arts and Letters (president, 1968-69), American Academy of Arts and Letters, American Academy of Arts and Sciences, Society of American Historians, Southern Historical Association, Phi Beta Kappa (senate, 1952-53), Century Association, Princeton Club, Authors Club (London).

AWARDS, HONORS: Guggenheim fellowships, 1928 and 1929; National Institute of Arts and Letters award, 1948; Bollingen Prize for poetry, 1956; Brandeis University Medal for poetry,

1961; gold medal from Dante Society, Florence, Italy, 1962; Academy of American Poets award, 1963; Oscar Williams award, Mark Rothko award, Ingram Merrill award, and National Medal for Literature, all 1976. Numerous honorary degrees, including University of Louisville, 1948, Coe College, 1955, Colgate University, 1956, University of Kentucky, 1960, and Carleton College, 1963.

WRITINGS:

POETRY

(With Ridley Wills) *The Golden Mean, and Other Poems,* privately printed, 1923.
Mr. Pope, and Other Poems, Minton, 1928.
(Contributor) *Fugitives: An Anthology of Verse,* Harcourt, 1928.
Three Poems: Ode to the Confederate Dead, Message from Abroad, [and] The Cross, Minton, 1930.
Poems: 1928-1931, Scribner, 1932.
The Mediterranean and Other Poems, Alcestis, 1936.
Selected Poems, Scribner, 1937.
Sonnets at Christmas, Cummington, 1941.
(Translator) Pervigilium Veneris, *Vigil of Venus,* Cummington, 1943.
The Winter Sea, Cummington, 1944.
Fragment of a Meditation/MCMXXVIII, Cummington, 1947.
Poems, 1920-1945, Eyre, 1948.
Poems: 1922-1947, Scribner, 1948, enlarged edition, 1960.
Two Conceits for the Eye To Sing, If Possible, Cummington, 1950.
Poems, Scribner, 1960.
Christ and the Unicorn, Cummington, 1966.
The Swimmers and Other Selected Poems, Oxford University Press, 1970, Scribner, 1971.
Collected Poems, 1919-1976, Farrar, Straus, 1977.

PROSE

Stonewall Jackson: The Good Soldier, Minton, 1928.
Jefferson Davis: His Rise and Fall, Minton, 1929.
(Contributor) *I'll Take My Stand: The South and the Agrarian Tradition by Twelve Southerners,* Harper, 1930.
(With others) *The Critique of Humanism,* 1930.
(Contributor) *The Best Short Stories, 1934,* Houghton, 1934.
(Editor and contributor) *Who Owns America?: A New Declaration of Independence,* Houghton, 1936.
Reactionary Essays on Poetry and Ideas, Scribner, 1936.
(Contributor) *A Southern Harvest,* Houghton, 1937.
(With A. Theodore Johnson) *America through the Essay,* Oxford University Press, 1938.
The Fathers (novel; also see below), Putnam, 1938, revised edition, A.Swallow, 1960.
Reason in Madness: Critical Essays, Putnam, 1941.
(With Huntington Cairns and Mark Van Doren) *Invitation to Learning,* Random House, 1941.
On the Limits of Poetry: Selected Essays, 1928-1948, A. Swallow, 1948.
The Hovering Fly and Other Essays, Cummington, 1948.
The Forlorn Demon: Didactic and Critical Essays, Regnery, 1953.
The Man of Letters in the Modern World: Selected Essays, 1928-1955, Meridian, 1955.
Collected Essays, A. Swallow, 1959, revised and enlarged edition published as *Essays of Four Decades,* 1968.
Mere Literature and the Lost Traveller, George Peabody College for Teachers, 1969.
The Translation of Poetry, Gertrude Clark Whittall Poetry and Literature Fund, 1972.

John Tyree Fain and Thomas Daniel Young, editors, *The Literary Correspondence of Donald Davidson and Allen Tate,* University of Georgia Press, 1974.
Memoirs and Opinions, 1926-1974, Swallow, 1975 (published in England as *Memoirs & Essays Old and New, 1926-1974,* Carcanet, 1976).
The Fathers and Other Fiction, Louisiana State University Press, 1977.
Thomas Daniel Young and John J. Hindle, editors, *The Republic of Letters in America: The Correspondence of John Peale Bishop and Allen Tate,* University Press of Kentucky, 1981.
Ashley Brown and Frances Neel Cheney, editors, *The Poetry Reviews of Allen Tate,* Louisiana State University Press, 1983.

EDITOR

White Buildings: Poems by Hart Crane, Horace Liveright, 1926.
The Language of Poetry, Princeton University Press, 1942.
Princeton Verse between Two Wars: An Anthology, Princeton University Press, 1942.
(With John Peale Bishop) *American Harvest: Twenty Years of Creative Writing in the United States,* L. B. Fischer, 1942.
Recent American Poetry and Poetic Criticism: A Selected List of References, Library of Congress, 1943.
Sixty American Poets, 1896-1944, Library of Congress, 1945, revised edition, 1954.
A Southern Vanguard: The John Peale Bishop Memorial Volume, Prentice-Hall, 1947.
The Collected Poems of John Peale Bishop, Scribner, 1948.
(With wife, Caroline Gordon) *The House of Fiction: An Anthology of the Short Story, with Commentary,* Scribner, 1950, revised edition, 1960.
(With David Cecil) *Modern Verse in English,* Macmillan, 1958.
(With Ralph Ross and John Berryman) *The Arts of Reading,* Crowell, 1960.
(With Robert Penn Warren) *Selected Poems by Denis Devlin,* Delacorte, 1966.
T. S. Eliot, the Man and His Work: A Critical Evaluation by Twenty-six Distinguished Writers, Delacorte, 1967.
Complete Poetry and Selected Criticism of Edgar Allan Poe, New American Library, 1968.
Six American Poets from Emily Dickinson to the Present: An Introduction, University of Minnesota Press, 1971.

OTHER

Editor, *Kenyon Review,* 1938-42. Contributor of essays and poetry to numerous periodicals, including *Double-Dealer, Hound and Horn, The Fugitive, Literary Review, Nation, New Republic, Minnesota Review, Shenandoah, Kenyon Review, Partisan Review, Yale Review, Criterion, Le Figaro Litteraire,* and *Sewanee Review.* Tate's papers are collected at the Princeton University Library, the Columbia University Library, and the University of Victoria Library, British Columbia.

SIDELIGHTS: The late Allen Tate was a well-known man of letters from the American South, a central figure in the fields of poetry, criticism, and ideas. In the course of a career spanning the middle decades of the twentieth century, Tate authored poems, essays, translations, and fiction; *Dictionary of Literary Biography* contributor James T. Jones claimed that his "influence was prodigious, his circle of acquaintances immense." Tate relished his "man of letters" reputation—he consistently held for the highest standards of literature, feeling that the best creative writing offers the most cogent expressions of human experience. *Sewanee Review* correspondent J. A. Bryant, Jr. called Tate a "sage" who "kept bright the instrument of language in our time and . . . made it illuminate as well as shine."

Tate was born and raised in Kentucky, the youngest of three sons of John Orley and Eleanor Varnell Tate. His family moved frequently when he was young, so his elementary education was erratic. Influenced by his mother's love of literature, however, he did extensive reading on his own; he was admitted to Vanderbilt University in 1918. There Tate proved an excellent student, earning top honors and membership in Phi Beta Kappa. More importantly, while an undergraduate he became aware of the special circumstances of Southern culture and sensibility. *Dictionary of Literary Biography* essayist James A. Hart wrote: "With a Border background [Tate] had to face the question of whether he was a Southerner or an American. Affirming the first, he had to confront the dominant positivist and materialistic Yankee values which were supplanting the older values of the South." Under the influence of his teachers Walter Clyde Curry, Donald Davidson, and John Crowe Ransom, Tate began to analyze his inheritance from a critical, but respectful, perspective.

Tate was the only undergraduate to be admitted to membership in the Fugitives, an informal group of Southern intellectuals that included Ransom, Davidson, Merrill Moore, and Robert Penn Warren. The Fugitives met once a week to discuss poetry—their own and others'—and to mount a defense against the notion that the South did not possess a significant literature of its own. In the periodical *The Fugitive,* and later in an important anthology called *I'll Take My Stand,* Tate argued that the Southern agrarian way of life reflected the artistic beauty, intelligence, and wit of the ancient classic age. Hart explained that Tate and his fellow Fugitives "believed that industrialism had demeaned man and that there was a need to return to the humanism of the Old South." The Agrarian movement, Hart added, "would create or restore something in 'the moral and religious outlook of Western Man.' " Whatever its beliefs, the Fugitive group exerted an enormous influence on American letters in the 1920s and on into the Depression era. A number of its members, including Tate, became the literary spokesmen for their generations.

Although Tate spent several years between 1928 and 1932 in France, he continued to write almost exclusively about the South. While he socialized with Ernest Hemingway, Gertrude Stein, and the other expatriate American writers in Paris, Tate still explored his own personal philosophical and moral ties to his homeland. He wrote two biographies of Southern Civil War heroes, *Stonewall Jackson: The Good Soldier* and *Jefferson Davis: His Rise and Fall,* he began his most important poem, "Ode to the Confederate Dead," and he worked on his only novel, *The Fathers. Southern Literary Journal* contributor George Core maintained that Tate was aware of the failings of the Old South, but it still remained "his chief model for his whole life. . . . Hence Tate's connections with the South—by inheritance, kinship, custom, and manner—have furnished him with . . . a central allegiance. Out of the tension between Tate's personal allegiance and his awareness of what he has called 'a deep illness of the modern mind' has come the enkindling subject of his work as a whole."

Not surprisingly, Tate's poetry has seemed to come from "a direct sensuous apprehension . . . of the Southern experience—the Southern people, animals, terrain, and climate," to quote Donald E. Stanford in the *Southern Review.* In many of his poems, Tate confronted the relation between an idealized past and a present deficient in both faith and tradition. *New York Times Book Review* correspondent Hilton Kramer found the author "deeply immersed in the materials of history, and there could never be any question of separating *his* literary achievements from their attachment to the historical imagination." Kramer added that the particular history upon which Tate drew

was "the history of a lost world carried in the mind of a Southerner, a classicist and an artist exiled to a Northern culture in which the imperatives of industrialism, philistinism and bourgeois capitalism reinforce a sense of irretrievable defeat." Likewise, *Southern Review* essayist Alan Williamson wrote that the stance in Tate's poetry "is that the individual is deeply unworthy, and should desire only to bring himself closer . . . to the destiny and the standards of the ancestors." Williamson concluded, however, that in some of Tate's later work "there is an undercurrent of contrary feeling: a bitter suspicion that the domination of the past, rather than the deficiencies of modern thought, is responsible for the sense of suffocation and unreality in present experience."

The Old South was semifeudal, agrarian, backward-looking, and religious, much like the European communities of the Middle Ages. Some critics have detected in Tate's work a return to somewhat medieval patterns of thought. In *Renascence,* Sister Mary Bernetta wrote: "In the Middle Ages there was one drama which took precedence over all other conflict . . . the Struggle of Everyman to win beatitude and to escape eternal reprobation. Tate recognizes the issue as a subject most significant for literature." Furthermore, like Dante, a poet he admired, Tate employed the most demanding poetic forms, which became "a compelling ritual to which the reader must submit in order to approach this poet's meaning," according to Robert B. Shaw in *Poetry.* As Louise Cowan noted in her book *The Southern Critics,* Tate's "quest throughout all his writing was for the sacramental vision such as Dante's Christianity embodied; for the unity of being, achieved in the philosophy of Thomism; for the classical-Christian synthesis of thought and feeling, formed in the Middle Ages and still underlying, albeit fragmentarily, the Southern sensibility."

One of Tate's preoccupations was indeed "man suffering from unbelief." His modern Everyman, however, faced a more complex situation than the simple medieval morality tale hero. *Michigan Quarterly Review* contributor Cleanth Brooks explained: "In the old Christian synthesis, nature and history were related in a special way. With the break-up of that synthesis, man finds himself caught between a meaningless cycle on the one hand, and on the other, the more extravagant notions of progress—between a nature that is oblivious of man and a man-made 'unnatural' utopia." Even though he had periods of skepticism himself, Tate felt that art could not survive without religion. To quote Pier Francesco Listri in *Allen Tate and His Work: Critical Evaluations,* "In a rather leaden society governed by a myth of science, [Tate's] poetry conducts a fearless campaign against science, producing from that irony a measure both musical and fabulous. In an apathetic, agnostic period he [was] not ashamed to recommend a Christianity to be lived as intellectual anguish."

Tate expounded upon many of the same themes in his criticism. Because he believed in the autonomy of art and the aesthetic formalist basis of critical analysis, he was classified among the "New Critics" of the mid-twentieth century. In *On Native Grounds: An Interpretation of Modern American Prose Literature,* Alfred Kazin observed that, in order to save criticism from the "scientists," Tate "disengaged literature itself from society and men, and held up the inviolate literary experience as the only measure of human knowledge. Literature in this view was not only the supreme end; it was also the only end worthy of man's ambition." Ferman Bishop claimed in his book *Allen Tate* that for the author, "the distinctively literary quality of a poem, play, or novel is the manner of its presentation." *Accent* correspondent Richard Foster contended that Tate was "less a technical literary critic than an essayist using literature as the frame of reference within which he criticizes the mind and life of his time in the light of his convictions about the proper ends of man. He speaks as a twentieth-century humanist intellectual, isolated and virtually unheard in the barbaric society whose larger deformities it is his concern to examine and minister to." *Sewanee Review* essayist Eliseo Vivas concluded: "At the heart of [Tate's] criticism, informing it throughout and giving it remarkable consistency and force, is his protest against the meaning of the present and of the probable future."

Having had a classical education himself, Tate employed numerous classical allusions in his work; he also often wrote intensely personal poetry that would not reveal itself instantly to a reader. In the *Sewanee Review*, Cowan called Tate "the most difficult poet of the twentieth century," and other critics have offered similar assessments. Brooks, for one, noted: "Tate puts a great burden upon his reader. He insists that the reader himself, by an effort of his own imagination, cooperate with the poet to bring the violent metaphors and jarring rhythms into unity." *Georgia Review* contributor M. E. Bradford also contended that Tate, with "his preference for the lyric and for the agonized *persona* in that genre—along with the admiration which his ingenuities in the employment of all manner of strategies have together inspired—have confirmed his reputation for obscurity, allusive privacy, and consequent difficulty. Were it not for his politics, his poetics, and his honesty about them both, he could have become the object of coterie enthusiasms."

Monroe K. Spears offered some reasons why Tate never became merely the "object of coterie enthusiasms." In the *Sewanee Review*, Spears praised Tate for his "independence and common sense and avoidance of cant" as well as for "his stubborn honesty and candor; his ideal of poise, integrity, and intelligence." *New Republic* contributor James Dickey also found Tate to be more than a "Southern writer." Dickey wrote: "[Tate's] situation has certain perhaps profound implications for every man in every place and every time. And they are more than implications; they are the basic questions, the possible solutions to the question of existence. How does each of us wish to live his only life?" Bishop concluded that Tate's place in American letters "is secure," adding: "He is one of a very small number of American writers who have had the ability to present the intellectual as well as the emotional side of the American experience. In a culture which has seemed so often to encourage and even depend on the anti-intellectual, he has emphasized the opposite. Ultimately, . . . he will be proved to have dealt with the truly significant elements in our experience."

BIOGRAPHICAL/CRITICAL SOURCES:

BOOKS

Allen, Walter, *The Modern Novel: In Britain and the United States,* Dutton, 1965.
Arnold, W. B., *Social Ideas of Allen Tate,* Humphries, 1955.
Bishop, Ferman, *Allen Tate,* Twayne, 1967.
Bradbury, John M., *The Fugitives: A Critical Account,* University of North Carolina Press, 1958.
Contemporary Literary Criticism, Gale, Volume 2, 1974, Volume 4, 1975, Volume 6, 1976, Volume 9, 1978, Volume 11, 1979, Volume 14, 1980, Volume 24, 1983.
Cowan, Louise, *The Fugitive Group: A Literary History,* Louisiana State University Press, 1959.
Deutsch, Babette, *Poetry in Our Time,* Holt, 1952.
Dictionary of Literary Biography, Gale, Volume 4: *American Writers in Paris, 1920-1939,* 1980, Volume 45: *American Poets, 1880-1945, Third Series,* 1986, Volume 63: *Modern American Critics, 1920-1955,* 1988.

Dupree, Robert S., *Allen Tate and the Augustinian Imagination: A Study of the Poetry,* Louisiana State University Press, 1983.
Fallwell, Marshall, Jr., *Allen Tate: A Bibliography,* Lewis, 1969.
Foster, Richard, *The New Romantics: A Reappraisal of the New Criticism,* Indiana University Press, 1962.
Frye, Northrop, *Northrop Frye on Culture and Literature: A Collection of Review Essays,* University of Chicago Press, 1978.
Hemphill, George, *Allen Tate,* University of Minnesota Press, 1964.
Kazin, Alfred, *On Native Grounds: An Interpretation of Modern American Prose Literature,* Reynal & Hitchcock, 1942.
Meiners, R. K., *The Last Alternatives: A Study of the Works of Allen Tate,* Swallow, 1963.
Pratt, William, editor, *The Fugitive Poets: Modern Southern Poetry in Perspective,* Dutton, 1965.
Pritchard, John Paul, *Criticism in America,* University of Oklahoma Press, 1956.
Purdy, Rob Roy, editor, *Fugitives Reunion: Conversations at Vanderbilt,* Vanderbilt University Press, 1959.
Ransom, John Crowe, editor, *The Kenyon Critics,* World, 1951.
Rizzardi, Alfredo, *Ode ai Caduti Confederati e Altre Poesie,* Arnoldo Mondadori, 1970.
Rubin, Louis and R. D. Jacobs, editors, *South: Modern Southern Literature in Its Cultural Setting,* Doubleday, 1961.
Spears, Monroe K., *Dionysus and the City: Modernism in Twentieth-Century Poetry,* Oxford University Press, 1970.
Squires, Radcliffe, *Allen Tate: A Literary Biography,* Bobbs-Merrill, 1971.
Squires, Radcliffe, editor, *Allen Tate and His Work: Critical Evaluations,* University of Minnesota Press, 1972.
Stewart, John L., *The Burden of Time: The Fugitives and the Agrarians,* Princeton University Press, 1965.
Stineback, David C., *Shifting World: Social Change and Nostalgia in the American Novel,* Associated University Presses, 1976.
West, Thomas R., *Nature, Community, & Will: A Study in Literary and Social Thought,* University of Missouri Press, 1976.

PERIODICALS

American Scholar, autumn, 1976.
Book World, March 2, 1969.
Commonweal, May 29, 1953.
Critique, spring, 1964.
Georgia Review, spring, 1968, spring, 1971.
Intercollegiate Review, winter, 1973-74.
Michigan Quarterly Review, fall, 1971.
New Republic, April 29, 1936, July 24, 1965, October 1, 1975.
New York Times Book Review, May 4, 1969, December 11, 1977, January 8, 1978, April 8, 1979.
Partisan Review, February, 1949, summer, 1968.
Poetry, May, 1968, April, 1970, January, 1972.
Renascence, spring, 1971.
Sewanee Review, January, 1954, autumn, 1959, summer, 1968, spring, 1972, summer, 1974, spring, 1978, spring, 1979.
Shenandoah, spring, 1961, winter, 1968.
South Atlantic Quarterly, autumn, 1967.
Southern Literary Journal, autumn, 1969.
Southern Review, winter, 1936, winter, 1940, summer, 1971, autumn, 1972, autumn, 1976, April, 1978.
Virginia Quarterly Review, summer, 1969.
Washington Post, May 7, 1969.

OBITUARIES:

PERIODICALS

Chicago Tribune, February 10, 1979.
New York Times, February 10, 1979.
Publishers Weekly, February 26, 1979.
Washington Post, February 10, 1979.

—*Sketch by Anne Janette Johnson*

*   *   *

TAYLOR, A(lan) J(ohn) P(ercivale) 1906-

PERSONAL: Born March 25, 1906, in Southport, Birkdale, Lancashire, England; son of Percy Lees and Constance (Thompson) Taylor; married third wife, Eva (a historian), 1976; children: Giles, Sebastian, Amelia, Sophia, Crispin, Daniel. *Education:* Bootham School, student, 1919-24; Oriel College, Oxford, B.A., 1927, M.A., 1932. *Politics:* Labour Party.

ADDRESSES: Home—32 Twisden Rd., London NW5 1DN, England.

CAREER: Rockefeller Fellow in social sciences, 1929-30; Manchester University, Manchester, England, lecturer in history, 1930-38; Oxford University, Oxford, England, fellow of Magdalen College, 1938-76, honorary fellow, 1976—, tutor in modern history, 1938-63, university lecturer in international history, 1953-63, Ford's Lecturer in English History, 1955-56, honorary fellow of Oriel College, 1980—. Leslie Stephen Lecturer, Cambridge University, 1961-62; Creighton Lecturer, London University, 1973; Benjamin Meaker Visiting Professor of History, University of Bristol, 1976-78. In charge of Beaverbrook Library.

MEMBER: British Academy (fellow), American Academy of Arts and Sciences (honorary member), Yugoslav Academy of Sciences (honorary member), Hungarian Academy of Sciences (honorary member), National Union of Journalists, City Music Society (London; president).

AWARDS, HONORS: Honorary degrees include D.C.L. from New Brunswick College, Oxford, 1961, D.Litt. from University of Bristol, 1978, University of Warwick, 1981, and University of Manchester, 1982.

WRITINGS:

The Italian Problem in European Diplomacy, 1847-1849, Manchester University Press, 1934, Barnes & Noble, 1970.
Germany's First Bid for Colonies, 1884-1885: A Move in Bismarck's European Policy, Macmillan, 1938, Archon, 1967.
The Habsburg Monarchy, 1815-1918, Macmillan, 1941, revised edition published as *The Habsburg Monarchy, 1809-1918: A History of the Austrian Empire and Austria-Hungary,* 1949, University of Chicago Press, 1976.
The Course of German History: A Survey of the Development of German History since 1815, Hamish Hamilton, 1945, revised edition, Coward-McCann, 1946, reprinted, Methuen, 1961.
From Napoleon to Stalin: Comments on European History, Hamish Hamilton, 1950.
Rumours of Wars, Hamish Hamilton, 1952.
The Struggle for Mastery in Europe, 1848-1918, Clarendon Press, 1954.
Bismarck: The Man and the Statesman, Knopf, 1955.
Englishmen and Others, Hamish Hamilton, 1956.
The Trouble Makers: Dissent over Foreign Policy, 1792-1939, Hamish Hamilton, 1957, Indiana University Press, 1958.

"The Russian Revolution" (television script), Associated Television, 1959.
Politics in the First World War, [London], 1959.
Lloyd George: Rise and Fall, Cambridge University Press, 1961.
The Origins of the Second World War, Hamish Hamilton, 1961, Atheneum, 1962, 2nd edition, Fawcett, 1966.
The First World War: An Illustrated History, Hamish Hamilton, 1963, published as *An Illustrated History of the First World War,* Putnam, 1964, published as *A History of the First World War,* Berkeley, 1966.
Politics in Wartime and Other Essays, Hamish Hamilton, 1964, Atheneum, 1965.
English History, 1914-1945 (Oxford History of England), Clarendon Press, 1965, reprinted, 1985.
From Sarajevo to Potsdam, Thames & Hudson, 1966, Harcourt, 1967.
From Napoleon to Lenin: Historical Essays, Harper, 1966.
Europe: Grandeur and Decline, Penguin, 1967.
(With Robert Rhodes James, J. H. Plumb, Basil Liddell Hart, and Anthony Storr) *Churchill Revised: A Critical Assessment,* Dial, 1969.
War by Timetable: How the First World War Began, American Heritage Press, 1969.
Beaverbrook, Simon & Schuster, 1972.
(With others) *Churchill: Four Faces and the Man,* Penguin, 1973.
Essays in English History, Hamish Hamilton, 1976.
The Last of Old Europe: A Grand Tour with A. J. P. Taylor, Sidgwick & Jackson, 1976.
The War Lords, Hamish Hamilton, 1977, Atheneum, 1978.
The Russian War, 1941-1945, edited by Daniela Mrazkova and Vladimir Remes, J. Cape, 1978.
How Wars Begin, Atheneum, 1979.
Revolutions and Revolutionaries, Hamish Hamilton, 1980.
Politicians, Socialism and Historians, Hamish Hamilton, 1980, Stein & Day, 1982.
A Personal History (autobiography), Atheneum, 1983.
In Search of C. S. Lewis, Bridge Publications, 1983.
An Old Man's Diary, Hamish Hamilton, 1984.
How Wars End, Hamish Hamilton, 1985.

EDITOR

(And co-translator) Heinrich Friedjung, *The Struggle for Supremacy in Germany, 1859-1866,* Macmillan, 1935.
(With R. Reynolds) *British Pamphleteers,* Volume 2, Wingate, 1948-51.
(With Alan Louis Charles Bullock) *A Select List of Books on European History, 1815-1914,* Clarendon Press, 1949, 2nd edition, 1957.
(With Richard Pares) *Essays Presented to Sir Lewis Namier,* St. Martin's, 1956, reprinted, Books for Libraries Press, 1971.
William Maxwell Aitken and Baron Beaverbrook, *The Abdication of King Edward VIII,* Atheneum, 1966.
(And author of introduction) K. Marx and F. Engels, *The Communist Manifesto,* Penguin, 1967.
(With Mortimer Wheeler and Hugh Trevor-Roper) Winston S. Churchill, *History of English-Speaking Peoples: Based on the Text of "A History of the English-Speaking Peoples,"* twelve volumes, New Caxton Library Service, 1969-74.
Lloyd George: Twelve Essays, Hamish Hamilton, 1971.
Frances Stevenson, *Lloyd George: A Diary,* Hutchinson, 1971.
W. P. Crozier, *Off the Record: Political Interviews, 1933-1943,* Hutchinson, 1973.
The Second World War: An Illustrated History, Putnam, 1975.

My Darling Pussy: The Letters of Lloyd George and Frances Stevenson, 1913-41, Weidenfeld & Nicolson, 1975.
The Illustrated History of the World Wars, Octopus, 1978.

OTHER

(Author of introduction) F. Fertig, editor, *1848: The Opening of an Era,* Howard Fertig, 1967.
(Author of foreword) Arthur Schnitzler, *My Youth in Vienna,* Weidenfeld & Nicolson, 1971.

Also author of *The Russian Revolution of 1917,* 1958. Contributor to *Sunday Express, Observer, New Statesman,* and other publications. Editor in chief, "History of the Twentieth Century," for B.P.C. Publishing. A bibliography of Taylor's writings, articles, and TV lectures has been compiled by A. Wrigley.

SIDELIGHTS: A. J. P. Taylor "must be the most widely read English historian since G. M. Trevelyan, quite possibly since Lord Macaulay, and with good reason," states John Gross in the *New York Times Book Review.* Taylor is familiar to many Britons through his long career as a television commentator, his columns in popular papers such as the *Sunday Express,* and through his television series. Woodrow Wyatt, writing in the London *Times,* calls his television work "the best possible history lesson, combining entertainment with instruction," and adds that "A. J. P. Taylor is the most gifted teacher on television." "My guess," Goss declares, "is that he is relatively better known in Britain than, say, John Kenneth Galbraith or Arthur Schlesinger Jr. is in America."

Taylor's books are also widely acclaimed by critics. London *Times* contributor David Marquand declares that the historian is "capable of a sinewy, apparently effortless prose of bewitching grace." John Kenneth Galbraith, writing in the *Washington Post Book World,* asserts that "when [Taylor] turns to his historical writing, he has been as careful, even meticulous, as the better scholars in his areas of competence, and, in addition, he has shown a phenomenally greater capacity for continuous, committed labor." "He writes," Goss notes, "with a verve which will insure that books like his study of dissent in foreign policy, 'The Trouble Makers,' or 'English History 1914-1945' (in my opinion, his masterpiece) will survive on their literary merits even when they have been overtaken by subsequent research." "Where he excels most of all is in his ability to master a great mass of material, and to weave it into a continuous narrative, of which he is always in control," Marquand maintains. "In . . . *English History 1914-1945,* he did this better than anyone since Macaulay. It is hard to believe that anyone will do it as well again."

BIOGRAPHICAL/CRITICAL SOURCES:

BOOKS

Gilbert, Martin, editor, *A Century of Conflict, 1850-1950: Essays in Honour of A. J. P. Taylor,* Hamish Hamilton, 1966, Atheneum, 1967.
Sked, Alan, and Chris Cook, editors, *Crisis and Controversy: Essays in Honour of A. J. P. Taylor,* Macmillan, 1976.
Taylor, A. J. P., *A Personal History* (autobiography), Hamish Hamilton, 1983.
Taylor, A. J. P., *An Old Man's Diary,* Hamish Hamilton, 1984.
Wrigley, Chris, editor, *Warfare, Diplomacy and Politics: Essays in Honour of A. J. P. Taylor,* Hamish Hamilton, 1986.

PERIODICALS

Los Angeles Times Book Review, February 10, 1985.
New York Times Book Review, September 25, 1983, June 30, 1985.

Times (London), April 11, 1983, June 2, 1983, April 19, 1984, April 4, 1985.
Times Literary Supplement, May 27, 1983, June 15, 1984, July 19, 1985.
Washington Post Book World, September 4, 1983.

[Sketch reviewed by wife, Eva Taylor]

*   *   *

TAYLOR, Elizabeth 1912-1975

PERSONAL: Born July 3, 1912, in Reading, Berkshire, England; died November 19, 1975; daughter of Oliver and Elsie (Fewtrell) Coles; married John William Kendall Taylor (in business), March 11, 1936; children: Renny, Joanna (Mrs. David Routledge). *Education:* Attended the Abbey School, Reading. *Politics:* Labour. *Religion:* None.

ADDRESSES: Home—Grove's Barn, Penn, Buckinghamshire, England. *Agent*—Brandt & Brandt, 101 Park Ave., New York, N.Y. 10017.

CAREER: Writer. Worked as a governess and in a library.

MEMBER: P.E.N., Society of Authors.

WRITINGS:

At Mrs. Lippincote's, P. Davies, 1945, Knopf, 1946.
Palladian, P. Davies, 1946, Knopf, 1947, reprinted, Virago, 1985.
A View of the Harbour, Knopf, 1949, reprinted, Penguin, 1987.
A Wreath of Roses, Knopf, 1949, reprinted, Penguin, 1987.
A Game of Hide-and-Seek, Knopf, 1951, reprinted, Virago, 1986.
The Sleeping Beauty, Viking, 1953, reprinted, Popular Library, 1976.
Hester Lilly: Twelve Short Stories, Viking, 1954 (published in England as *Hester Lilly and Other Stories,* P. Davies, 1954).
Angel, Viking, 1957.
The Blush and Other Stories, P. Davies, 1958, Viking, 1959, reprinted, Virago, 1987.
In a Summer Season, Viking, 1961.
The Soul of Kindness, Viking, 1964.
A Dedicated Man and Other Stories, Viking, 1965.
Mossy Trotter (for children), Harcourt, 1967.
The Wedding Group, Viking, 1968.
(Contributor) J. Burnley, editor, *Penguin Modern Stories 6,* Penguin, 1970.
Mrs. Palfrey at the Claremont, Viking, 1971.
The Devastating Boys and Other Stories, Viking, 1972.
Blaming, Viking, 1976.

Contributor of short stories to *Harper's, New Yorker,* and *Vogue.*

SIDELIGHTS: Shortly before Elizabeth Taylor's death, a *Times Literary Supplement* critic called her one of "the four or five most distinguished living practitioners of the art of the short story in the English-speaking world." Other reviewers wrote similarly of Taylor's talents as a short story writer and a novelist. In the *New York Times Book Review* Martin Levin referred to the author as "a pastel stylist," and a *Harper's* reviewer noted, "Taylor couldn't write an inelegant sentence if she tried and her prose is a delight." In *Library Journal,* Elizabeth Thalman once listed the "literary qualities that have won . . . Taylor a devoted following." According to Thalman these were "irony, humor, artful structuring and stylistic grace."

Some critics, however, found Taylor's characters insufficiently developed. A *Times Literary Supplement* reviewer, for example, wrote that in *The Wedding Group* "Taylor . . . left too much unsaid, too many superb opportunities to expand a scene or a character only half explored." And Joyce Carol Oates, writing in the *Washington Post Book World,* remarked: "The people [Taylor] deals with in her fiction are not people, but characters. They are imagined as interior creations, existing within the confines of their particular stories."

Despite such negative criticism, Guy Davenport noted in *National Review* that Taylor's readers "realize that [they] are in the hands of a real novelist, the kind of analytical and unfoolable mind that invented the novel in the first place." Summing up Taylor's work, Alice McCahill wrote in *Best Sellers,* "Elizabeth Taylor . . . has to her credit a list of several novels, . . . all showing the same keen understanding of people, the ability to share that understanding with her readers, a sense of humor, and a gift and feeling for words."

MEDIA ADAPTATIONS: "A Dedicated Man" and *Mrs. Palfrey at the Claremont* were both adapted for television.

AVOCATIONAL INTERESTS: Travel in Greece.

BIOGRAPHICAL/CRITICAL SOURCES:

BOOKS

Contemporary Literary Criticism, Gale, Volume 2, 1974, Volume 4, 1975, Volume 29, 1984.

PERIODICALS

Best Sellers, April 1, 1968.
Encounter, September, 1972.
Harper's, August, 1964.
Isis, January 28, 1959.
Library Journal, February 1, 1968.
National Review, April 23, 1968.
New Republic, August 22, 1964.
New Statesman, August 27, 1971.
New York Times Book Review, March 31, 1968, April 23, 1972, March 29, 1987.
Review of English Literature (London), April, 1960.
Times Literary Supplement, September 24, 1964, May 9, 1968, August 27, 1971, June 9, 1972, July 1, 1983, November 29, 1985, December 19, 1986, September 18-24, 1987.
Washington Post Book World, April 30, 1972, August 21, 1983.

OBITUARIES:

PERIODICALS

London Times, November 21, 1975.

*   *   *

TAYLOR, Peter (Hillsman) 1917-

PERSONAL: Born January 8, 1917, in Trenton, Tenn.; son of Matthew Hillsman (an attorney) and Katherine (Taylor) Taylor; married Eleanor Lilly Ross (a poet), June 4, 1943; children: Katherine Baird, Peter Ross. *Education:* Attended Vanderbilt University, 1936-37, and Southwestern at Memphis, 1937-38; Kenyon College, A.B., 1940.

ADDRESSES: Home—1841 Wayside Pl., Charlottesville, Va. 22903. *Office*—Department of English, Wilson Hall, University of Virginia, Charlottesville, Va. 22901.

CAREER: Writer. University of North Carolina at Greensboro, 1946-67, became professor of English; University of Virginia, Charlottesville, professor of English, beginning in 1967, director of creative writing program, 1967-87. Visiting lecturer at Indiana University, 1949, University of Chicago, 1951, Kenyon College, 1952-57, Oxford University, 1955, Ohio State University, 1957-63, and Harvard University, 1964 and 1972-73. *Military service:* U.S. Army, 1941-45; became sergeant.

MEMBER: National Academy and Institute of Arts and Letters, American Academy of Arts and Sciences.

AWARDS, HONORS: Guggenheim fellowship in fiction, 1950; National Institute of Arts and Letters grant in literature, 1952; Fulbright fellowship to France, 1955; first prize, O. Henry Memorial Awards, 1959, for short story "Venus, Cupid, Folly and Time"; Ohioana Book Award, 1960, for *Happy Families Are All Alike;* Ford Foundation fellowship, to England, 1961; Rockefeller Foundation grant, 1964; second prize, *Partisan Review-Dial,* for short story "The Scoutmaster"; National Academy and Institute of Arts and Letters gold medal for literature, 1979; fellowship from National Endowment for the Arts, 1984; Faulkner Award for fiction, PEN American Center, 1986, for *The Old Forest and Other Stories;* American Book Award nomination, 1986, Ritz-Hemingway Prize, 1987, and Pulitzer Prize for fiction, 1987, all for *A Summons to Memphis.*

WRITINGS:

A Long Fourth and Other Stories, introduction by Robert Penn Warren, Harcourt, 1948.
A Woman of Means (novel), Harcourt, 1950.
The Widows of Thornton (short stories and a play), Harcourt, 1954.
Tennessee Day in St. Louis (play), Random House, 1959.
Happy Families Are All Alike: A Collection of Stories, Astor Honor, 1959.
Miss Leonora When Last Seen and Fifteen Other Stories, Astor Honor, 1963.
(Editor with Robert Lowell and Robert Penn Warren) *Randall Jarrell, 1914-1965,* Farrar, Straus, 1967.
The Collected Stories of Peter Taylor, Farrar, Straus, 1969.
A Stand in the Mountains (play; first produced in Abingdon, Va., at Barter Theatre, 1971), first published in *Kenyon Review,* 1965, Pantheon, 1984.
Presences: Seven Dramatic Pieces (contains "Two Images," "A Father and a Son," "Missing Person," "The Whistler," "Arson," "A Voice through the Door," and "The Sweethearts"), Houghton, 1973.
In the Miro District and Other Stories, Knopf, 1977.
(Editor) *The Road and Other Modern Stories,* Cambridge University Press, 1979.
The Old Forest and Other Stories, Doubleday, 1985.
A Summons to Memphis (novel), Knopf, 1986.

Contributor of stories to numerous anthologies, including: *The Best American Short Stories,* edited by Martha Foley, Houghton, 1945-46, 1950, 1959, and 1965, edited by Foley and David Burnett, 1960 and 1961; *Prize Stories of 1950: The O. Henry Awards,* edited by Herschell Bricknell, Doubleday, 1950; *The Literature of the South,* edited by R. C. Beatty and others, Scott, Foresman, 1952; *Stories from the Southern Review,* edited by Cleanth Brooks and Robert Penn Warren, Louisiana State University Press, 1953; *Prize Stories 1959: The O. Henry Awards,* edited by Paul Engle, Doubleday, 1959; *Prize Stories 1961: The O. Henry Awards,* edited by Richard Poirier, Doubleday, 1961; *Prize Stories 1965: The O. Henry Awards,* edited by Poirier and William Abrahams, Doubleday, 1965; and *The Sense of Fiction,* edited by Robert L. Welker and Herschel Gover, Prentice-Hall, 1966.

Contributor of short stories to *Sewanee Review, Virginia Quarterly Review, Kenyon Review, New Yorker,* and numerous other journals.

WORK IN PROGRESS: A novel; short stories; a play titled "The Girl from Forked Deer."

SIDELIGHTS: Although Peter Taylor has received critical acclaim for his novel *A Woman of Means* and for his plays, he is best known for his work in short fiction. Gene Baro, in a *New York Herald Tribune Book Review* article, calls Taylor "one of the most accomplished short-story writers of our time." And John Leonard of the *New York Times* says that "Peter Taylor makes stories the way Mercedes-Benz makes automobiles: to last."

Born in Tennessee and now living in Virginia, Taylor is considered by many critics to be a Southern writer in the tradition of William Faulkner and Flannery O'Connor. A *Village Voice* reviewer notes that Taylor "often writes about the decay of the gentrified South (something he has observed firsthand)." In the *Times Literary Supplement,* Zachary Leader says that Taylor's "roots in the Southern literary tradition are deep . . . [and an understanding of his] complex relation to the tradition this background fostered is helpful to an appreciation of his stories."

Leader cites Allen Tate (literary critic and poet) and Andrew Lytle (novelist and editor of *Sewanee Review*) as two of Taylor's early influences. As an undergraduate at Vanderbilt University, the author met and became friends with several members of the Southern Agrarian movement, including Randall Jarrell and Robert Penn Warren. Later, Taylor, Jarrell, and another friend, Robert Lowell, studied under well-known poet and critic John Crowe Ransom. Ransom was the acknowledged leader of the Agrarians, who advocated, among other things, a return to a non-industrialized South, one free of Northern influence and exploitation. Out of this philosophy, writes Leader, "grew the dream of the 'Old South,' or what Taylor calls 'the old times.'. . . These writings look past the South's supposedly aristocratic origins to the pre-settlement wilderness, an Eden whose native inhabitants were as unspoilt and unspoiling as the surroundings from which they drew their character."

Yet, despite this foundation in Southern literature, Taylor is as often praised for the universality of his stories as for their superior quality. When his first collection, *A Long Fourth and Other Stories,* appeared in 1948, a *New Yorker* critic said that these stories were "particularly notable for a vein of unobtrusive humor and for a complete lack of the regional chauvinism that Southern authors so frequently exhibit when writing about their own." Coleman Rosenberger, in the *New York Herald Tribune Weekly Book Review,* wrote: "These seven short stories by Peter Taylor are a little island of excellence in the flood of books from the South. They have the qualities of permanence: a fine craftsmanship, integrity, and the imprint of a subtle and original intelligence."

Critical response to Taylor's next collection, *The Widows of Thornton,* solidified his reputation as a master in his field. Mack Morriss, in a *Saturday Review* article, called the book "as free of ugliness as the lingering nutmeg and as unpretentious as cold-water cornbread. . . . [Taylor] has created a wistful, clinging, but utterly non-depraved image of the Deep South that some of us, his regional contemporaries, have been trying to recall from our childhood." F. H. Lyell of the *New York Times* commented: "The stories in [this book] are outwardly simple but psychologically complex and powerful, and under the surface of events in the regions he knows best the author discloses the universal long-

ings of the human heart." In the *New York Herald Tribune Book Review,* Dan Wickenden declared, "It seems improbable that any American work of fiction more distinguished and enduring than *The Widows of Thornton* will appear this year."

Through the years, praise for Taylor's work in short fiction has continued, with emphasis on his natural ear for dialogue, his smooth, finely paced style, and especially his sensitive character portrayal. A *Times Literary Supplement* critic calls him "a cautious writer with an intellectual respect for his characters. Every change of mood and feeling is something he considers worth recording." And, in *Saturday Review,* William Peden writes: "[Taylor's] stories succeed because his characters and their words are real, moving, and convincing. In each story there is always at least one character who becomes 'finely aware' (the phrase is Henry James's) of the situations in which they find themselves. It is this fine awareness that gives the 'maximum of sense' to what befalls them, which makes these quietly effective stories so meaningful to the reader." In *Sewanee Review,* well-respected novelist, editor, and short-story writer George Garrett states: "There are few American writers, living or dead, who have for so long a time received so much praise—and this from the most honored quarters—for artistic achievement. For thirty years now . . . [Taylor's] stories have been admired, analyzed, anthologized, preserved as major models of excellence for all other writers." Finally, in a *Saturday Review* article, Linda Kuehl concludes, "I am tempted to say that Peter Taylor is the greatest living short-story writer, but I shall be prudent and suggest he is the greatest one writing in English today."

Despite his acclaim among scholars and critics, Taylor remained unrecognized and relatively unknown to the general reading public until the mid-1980s, when his collection *The Old Forest and Other Stories* won the 1986 Faulkner Award. His novel *A Summons to Memphis* was nominated for an American Book Award the same year, but Taylor declined the award in advance to protest the naming of three candidates before the announcement of a winner, a practice he felt made "losers" of the two talented artists who did not receive the prize. Taylor received more notice in 1987, when *A Summons to Memphis* garnered him both the Ritz-Hemingway Prize and the Pulitzer Prize for fiction.

A Summons to Memphis centers on the Carvers, a Tennessee family that moves from Nashville to Memphis after domineering father George Carver is betrayed by a longtime business partner. The novel is narrated by Carver's grown son Philip, who, while reminiscing about his father's interference in his children's romantic involvements, also relates how the now-resentful Carver siblings try to thwart George's impending second marriage. Reviewers praised *A Summons to Memphis* for its evocation of place and its compelling characterizations, and placed the novel among Taylor's most memorable works. "As in his short stories, Taylor has in his novel produced a masterful piece of writing. . . . Descriptions are sharp, dialogue is clear and unburdened, situations are believable," commended David Shiflett in *Insight.* Also impressed was *New York Times*'s Michiko Kakutani, who wrote, "Taylor's sympathy for the chiaroscuro of familial emotion, combined with his command of naturalistic detail, remains so assured, so persuasive, that we finish the novel feeling we've not only come to know his characters, but also come to share their inner truth." "Though one can argue about which of his stories will survive the longest," Jonathan Yardley of the *Washington Post* declared, "there can be no question that this novel . . . will be among them."

BIOGRAPHICAL/CRITICAL SOURCES:

BOOKS

Contemporary Literary Criticism, Gale, Volume 1, 1973, Volume 4, 1975, Volume 18, 1981, Volume 37, 1986, Volume 44, 1987, Volume 50, 1988.
Dictionary of Literary Biography Yearbook, 1981, Gale, 1982.
Eisinger, Charles E., *Fiction of the Forties,* University of Chicago Press, 1963.
Griffith, Albert, *Peter Taylor,* Twayne, 1970.
Rubin, Louis D., Jr., and Robert D. Jacobs, *South: Modern Southern Literature in Its Cultural Setting,* Doubleday, 1961.

PERIODICALS

Book Week, March 8, 1964.
Chicago Sunday Tribune, May 14, 1950, December 6, 1959.
Chicago Tribune, May 9, 1988.
Critique, Volume IX, number 3, 1967.
Georgia Review, winter, 1970.
Globe and Mail (Toronto), December 6, 1986.
Insight, November 10, 1986.
Los Angeles Times Book Review, February 3, 1985, October 5, 1986.
New Republic, March 8, 1948, June 26, 1950, October 18, 1969, May 7, 1977.
New Statesman, August 6, 1960.
Newsweek, October 20, 1969, September 29, 1986.
New Yorker, March 13, 1948.
New York Herald Tribune Book Review, May 2, 1950, May 2, 1954, December 6, 1959.
New York Herald Tribune Weekly Book Review, March 14, 1948.
New York Review of Books, June 11, 1964.
New York Times, March 21, 1948, June 11, 1950, May 2, 1954, October 11, 1969, April 7, 1977, May 7, 1986, September 24, 1986.
New York Times Book Review, November 22, 1959, March 29, 1964, October 19, 1969, February 12, 1970, April 3, 1977, February 17, 1984, October 19, 1986.
Publishers Weekly, January 18, 1985.
San Francisco Chronicle, May 13, 1954.
Saturday Review, May 8, 1954, November 28, 1959, October 18, 1969, May 14, 1977, March 15, 1980.
Saturday Review of Literature, March 27, 1948.
Sewanee Review, autumn, 1962.
Shenandoah, winter, 1973, winter, 1977, summer, 1978.
Southern Review, Volume VII, number 1, 1971, winter, 1979.
Time, May 15, 1950, September 29, 1986.
Times (London), August 15, 1985.
Times Literary Supplement, August 19, 1960, September 30, 1977, January 22, 1982.
Tribune Books (Chicago), October 26, 1986.
Village Voice, April 28, 1980.
Virginia Quarterly Review, spring, 1978.
Washington Post, March 15, 1980, April 20, 1987.
Washington Post Book World, October 7, 1984, September 14, 1986.

*   *   *

TAYLOR, Telford 1908-

PERSONAL: Born February 24, 1908, in Schenectady, N.Y.; son of John Bellamy (an electrical engineer) and Marcia Estabrook (Jones) Taylor; married Mary Eleanor Walker (an attorney), July 2, 1937 (divorced); married Toby Barbara Golick (an attorney), August 9, 1974; children: (first marriage) Joan Penderwell, Ellen Estabrook, John Bellamy II; (second marriage) Benjamin Waite, Samuel Bourne. *Education:* Williams College, A.B., 1928, M.A., 1932; Harvard University, LL.B., 1932. *Politics:* Democratic. *Religion:* Protestant.

ADDRESSES: Office—School of Law, Columbia University, 435 West 116th St., New York, N.Y. 10027.

CAREER: Williams College, Williamstown, Mass., instructor in history and political science, 1928-29; law clerk to U.S. Circuit Court judge, New York City, 1932-33; U.S. Government, Washington, D.C., assistant solicitor, Department of the Interior, 1933-34, senior attorney, Agricultural Adjustment Administration, 1934-35, associate counsel, U.S. Senate Committee on Interstate Commerce, 1935-39, special assistant to U.S. Attorney General, 1939-40, general counsel, Federal Communications Commission, 1940-42; U.S. Army, 1942-49, went on active duty as major in Military Intelligence, 1942, promoted to brigadier general, 1946, member of staff of chief of counsel and U.S. representative for prosecution of war criminals, 1945-46, chief of counsel for war crimes, U.S. Office of Military Government, 1946-49; Taylor, Ferencz & Simon (law firm), New York City, partner, 1951—; Yale University, School of Law, New Haven, Conn., visiting lecturer, 1957-76; Columbia University, School of Law, New York City, visiting lecturer, 1958-63, professor of law, 1963—. Counsel, Joint Council for Educational Television, 1951-61; New York City Advisory Board of Public Welfare, member, 1960-65, chairman, 1960-63.

MEMBER: American Law Institute, American Academy of Arts and Sciences (fellow), American Military Institute, Authors Guild, Authors League of America, American Society of Composers, Authors and Publishers, Association of the Bar of the City of New York.

AWARDS, HONORS: Military—Distinguished Service Medal, 1946; Order of Orange-Nassau (Netherlands), 1950; Order of the British Empire; Legion of Honor (France); Polonia Restituta (Poland); Lateran Cross, third class (Vatican). Civilian—LL.D. from Williams College, 1949; overseas fellow, Churchill College, Cambridge University, 1969; National Book Critics Circle award, 1979, for *Munich: The Price of Peace.*

WRITINGS:

Sword and Swastika: Generals and Nazis in the Third Reich, Simon & Schuster, 1952.
Grand Inquest: The Story of Congressional Investigations, Simon & Schuster, 1955, reprinted, Da Capo Press, 1974.
The March of Conquest, Simon & Schuster, 1958.
The Breaking Wave: The German Defeat in the Summer of 1940, Simon & Schuster, 1967.
Two Studies in Constitutional Interpretation, Ohio State University Press, 1969.
Nuremberg and Vietnam: An American Tragedy, Random House, 1970.
Guilt, Responsibility, and the Third Reich (lectures), Heffer, 1970.
(With others) *Perspectives on Justice,* Northwestern University Press, 1975.
(With Alan Dershowitz, George Fletcher, Leon Lipson, and Melvin Stein) *Courts of Terror: Soviet Criminal Justice and Jewish Emigration,* Knopf, 1976.
Munich: The Price of Peace, Doubleday, 1979.

Contributor of articles to periodicals.

WORK IN PROGRESS: Nuremberg: A Personal Memoir.

SIDELIGHTS: Attorney Telford Taylor writes of the role of law and justice in the policies of modern states. Because Taylor served as chief of counsel for the Nuremberg trials of Nazi war criminals, he is uniquely qualified to investigate and comment upon the legal aspects of governmental actions. *Nuremberg and Vietnam: An American Tragedy* compares the war crimes of the Nazis during the Second World War with the conduct of American soldiers during the Vietnam War. *Courts of Terror: Soviet Criminal Justice and Jewish Emigration* recounts the efforts of a group of American lawyers to free wrongfully imprisoned Jews in the Soviet Union. *Munich: The Price of Peace* examines the events surrounding British Prime Minister Neville Chamberlain's meeting with Adolf Hitler in 1938, with particular emphasis on the willingness of Chamberlain and other Western leaders to ignore the treaties and international laws broken by the Nazis.

At the height of the Vietnam War, Taylor wrote *Nuremberg and Vietnam,* a study of the relationship between Nazi war crimes and American actions and an attempt to determine if American conduct of the Vietnam War had violated international law. "Although Taylor writes about the applicability of Nuremberg to Vietnam," Richard Wasserstrom states in the *New York Review of Books,* "the application is an extremely restrictive and guarded one." Taylor's cautious study is, according to Richard A. Falk in the *New York Times Book Review,* "the minimum conclusion that an honest, conservative, and well-informed man can make about the criminal status of American war policies in Vietnam." This careful approach makes Taylor's conclusions all the more powerful. He finds that the documented crimes of American soldiers in Vietnam are comparable to some of those committed by the Nazis during World War II. Further, Taylor believes the responsibility for these crimes reaches to the highest levels of civilian and military command. Although Wasserstrom sees Taylor as too narrow in his definition of war crimes and would like to see American officials charged with "crimes against peace and humanity," he still judges the book to be "valuable and important just because it has made discussions of the applicability of Nuremberg to Vietnam legitimate."

Another example of governmental policies violating law is related in *Courts of Terror.* The book grew out of an effort by Taylor and other American lawyers to free Jews in Soviet prison camps. Because of their desire to emigrate from the Soviet Union to Israel, these Jews had been arrested and imprisoned on trumped-up charges. One man was accused of knocking a cake from a woman's hands and using obscene language. He was sentenced to three years in a labor camp. Another man, accused of overcharging for his services as a carpenter, received a five-year sentence. Taylor and the other lawyers hoped to prove that, under Soviet law, some nineteen Jews had been wrongfully imprisoned and should be released. Although the American group had no legal standing in the Soviet Union, they hoped that by well-reasoned arguments based on the appropriate Soviet legal statutes they could persuade the authorities to reevaluate the cases. After their carefully prepared legal briefs were rejected by Soviet officials, who claimed there was nothing wrong with the trials, Taylor "concluded that the miscarriages of justice were not accidental," Harrison E. Salisbury writes in the *New York Times Book Review,* "but directed by the highest officials."

Unable to secure the release of the prisoners, the group decided to publish their findings in the hope that a wider awareness of Soviet anti-semitism might bring international pressure to bear. *Courts of Terror* "contains excerpts from the briefs and the full text of four legal memoranda that Taylor's group submitted," Joshua Rubenstein explains in *Commentary.* "In a subdued, logical manner, these documents confirm what Soviet dissidents

have said all along—that Soviet justice remains subordinate to ideological priorities." Rubenstein lists such flagrant judicial abuses as denying the defendants' right to choose their own counsel, refusing the chance for defense witnesses to speak, and even forcibly removing one prosecution witness from the courtroom when his testimony became favorable to the accused. "One of the fascinations of *Courts of Terror,*" Richard Bernstein states in *Time,* "is its depiction of a government in the tortuous process of subverting its own laws for reasons of propaganda and political expediency." Salisbury reveals that the author of the Soviet constitution, Nikolai Bukharin, was himself arrested by Josef Stalin and "shot in the basement of Lubyanka prison" in violation of Soviet law. "There is only slightly more concordance today between the word and the deed of Soviet justice," Salisbury concludes, "than there was in Stalin's day."

In *Munich: The Price of Peace,* Taylor looks at the 1938 Munich meeting between Adolf Hitler and British Prime Minister Neville Chamberlain at which the German occupation of parts of Czechoslovakia was approved. This meeting followed a string of provocative moves by Hitler in defiance of treaties and international agreements. In 1933, Germany withdrew from the Disarmament Conference and the League of Nations. In 1935, Hitler repudiated the arms provisions of the Versailles Treaty, provisions which limited the size and strength of the German military, and began publicly to rebuild the German war machine. In 1936, German troops reoccupied the Rhineland, a territory along the Rhine River rich in coal and iron which, under the Versailles Treaty, was to remain demilitarized. All of these acts were met with virtual indifference by the Western powers. Expressions of outrage and disapproval were made, but no concrete steps were taken to stop Hitler.

The meeting in Munich went much the same way. Hitler asked that German-speaking areas of Czechoslovakia be incorporated into Germany and Chamberlain agreed, hoping that this concession would satisfy Hitler and prevent war. Chamberlain's willingness to appease Hitler was long believed by historians to be a sign of his personal weakness and naivete. But Taylor shows that Chamberlain had the overwhelming support of the British public and of prominent business and political leaders as well. France also approved of the agreement. As Gordon A. Craig reports in the *New Republic,* the Western powers "were the victims of a persistent unwillingness to face up to unpleasant realities and to make the hard decisions these called for." Because of the failure of this meeting to prevent war, Munich has become a symbol for diplomatic weakness and shortsightedness.

"Taylor," Stanley Hoffmann writes in the *Washington Post Book World,* "is far from the first to tell this sinister story. And yet his book is both a masterful synthesis and an original contribution." Comparing *Munich* to other works dealing with the same period, James Joll of the *New York Times Book Review* finds it "the biggest and fullest of them all." Joll further believes that Taylor's "own experience as a member of the prosecuting team at Nuremberg, his continuing preoccupation with problems of recent history and his lawyer's ski at marshaling, examining, and presenting evidence will all insure that [*Munich*] will command respect."

BIOGRAPHICAL/CRITICAL SOURCES:

PERIODICALS

Best Sellers, January 15, 1971.
Chicago Tribune Book World, March 25, 1979.
Christian Science Monitor, September 8, 1980.
Commentary, May, 1976.

National Review, July 23, 1976, March 16, 1979.
New Republic, April 24, 1971, April 14, 1976.
New Statesman, September 15, 1967.
New Yorker, April 19, 1969.
New York Review of Books, June 3, 1971, March 22, 1979.
New York Times, November 18, 1970.
New York Times Book Review, December 27, 1970, April 18, 1976, April 1, 1979.
Observer, June 11, 1967.
Punch, June 14, 1967.
Saturday Review, June 28, 1969.
Time, November 23, 1970, June 14, 1976.
Times Literary Supplement, June 15, 1967.
Washington Post Book World, July 8, 1976, April 29, 1979.

*   *   *

TELLER, Edward 1908-

PERSONAL: Born January 15, 1908, in Budapest, Hungary; came to the United States in 1935, naturalized March 4, 1941; son of Max (a lawyer) and Ilona (Deutch) Teller; married Augusta Harkanyi, February 26, 1934; children: Paul, Susan Wendy. *Education:* Studied at Karlsruhe Technical Institute, Karlsruhe, Germany, 1926-28, and University of Munich, 1928-29; University of Leipzig, Ph.D., 1930.

ADDRESSES: Home—1573 Hawthorne Ter., Berkeley, Calif. 94708. *Office*—Hoover Institution, Stanford, Calif. 94305.

CAREER: Research associate at University of Leipzig, Leipzig, Germany, 1929-31, and University of Gottingen, Gottingen, Germany, 1931-33; Rockefeller Foundation fellow at University of Coppenhagen, Copenhagen, Denmark, 1934; University of London, London, England, lecturer in physics, 1934-35; George Washington University, Washington, D.C., professor of physics, 1935-41; Columbia University, New York, N.Y., professor of physics, 1941-42; physicist for Manhattan Project at University of Chicago, Chicago, Ill., 1942-43, and Los Alamos Scientific Laboratory, Los Alamos, N.M., 1943-46; University of Chicago, professor of physics, 1946-52, on leave as assistant director of Los Alamos Scientific Laboratory, 1949-52; University of California, professor of physics at Berkeley, 1953-60, professor of physics-at-large, 1960-70, university professor, 1970-75, university professor emeritus, 1975—, chairman of department of applied science, Davis-Livermore, 1963-66, consultant to Livermore branch, University of California Radiation Laboratory, 1952-53, associate director of Lawrence Radiation Laboratory, Livermore, 1954-75, associate director emeritus, 1975—, director of Lawrence Radiation Laboratory, 1958-60; Hoover Institution, Stanford, Calif., senior research fellow, 1975—. Visiting professor, Arthur Spitzer Chair of Energy Management, Pepperdine University, 1976-77.

Early researcher in thermonuclear reactions; helped develop atomic bomb, and worked on development and function of other nuclear weapons after Hiroshima (including the hydrogen bomb); currently concerned with peaceful applications of nuclear energy. Director, Thermo Electron Corp.; member of president's Foreign Intelligence Advisory Board; member of scientific advisory board, U.S. Air Force; member of general advisory committee, U.S. Atomic Energy Commission, 1956-58; member of board of directors, Defense Intelligence School and Naval War College; member of other committees, councils, and advisory boards.

MEMBER: National Academy of Sciences, American Nuclear Society (fellow), American Physical Society (fellow), American Academy of Arts and Sciences, American Ordnance Association, American Geophysical Union, Society of Engineering Science, International Platform Association, American Association for the Advancement of Science, American Defense Preparedness Association, Americans for More Power Sources (member of advisory board), Atlantic Union, Center for the Survival of the Western Democracies, Hungarian Unity Association (member of advisory board), Western Goals Foundation (member of advisory board).

AWARDS, HONORS: Joseph Priestley Memorial Award, Dickinson College, 1957; Albert Einstein Award, 1959; General Donovan Memorial Award, 1959; Midwest Research Institute Award, 1960; Living History Award from Research Institute of America, 1960; Thomas E. White Award, 1962; Enrico Fermi Award, 1962; Robins Award of America, 1963; Leslie R. Groves gold medal, 1974; Harvey Prize, 1975; Semmelweiss Medal, 1977; Albert Einstein Award, Technion Institute of Israel, 1977; Henry T. Heald Award, Illinois Institute of Technology, 1978; American College of Nuclear Medicine gold medal, 1980; Man of the Year, Achievement Rewards for College Scientists, 1980; Paul Harris Award, Rotary Club, 1980; A. C. Eringen Award, Society of Engineering Science, 1980; named distinguished scientist by National Science Development Board, 1981, and by Phil-American Academy of Science and Engineering, 1981; National Medal of Science, 1983. Honorary degrees: D.Sc., Yale University, 1954, University of Alaska, 1959, Fordham University, 1960, George Washington University, 1960, University of Southern California, 1960, St. Louis University, 1960, Rochester Institute of Technology, 1962, University of Detroit, 1964, Clemson University, 1966, Clarkson College, 1969; LL.D., Boston College, 1961, Seattle University, 1962, University of Cincinnati, 1962, University of Pittsburgh, 1963, Pepperdine University, 1974, and University of Maryland, 1977; L.H.D., Mount Mary College, 1964; Ph.D., Tel Aviv University, 1972; Doctor of Natural Science, De La Salle University, Manila, 1981.

WRITINGS:

(With J. H. Hibben) *Raman Effect and Its Chemical Applications,* Reinhold, 1939.
(With F. O. Rice) *The Structure of Matter,* Wiley, 1949.
(With A. L. Latter) *Our Nuclear Future,* Criterion, 1958.
(With others) *Education of the Scientist in a Free Society,* Marquette, 1959.
Basic Concepts of Physics, Part 1, California Book Co., 1960.
(With Allen Brown) *The Legacy of Hiroshima,* Doubleday, 1962, reprinted, Greenwood Press, 1975.
The Reluctant Revolutionary, University of Missouri Press, 1964.
(With G. W. Johnson, W. K. Talley, and G. H. Higgins) *The Constructive Uses of Nuclear Explosives,* McGraw, 1968.
(With Paul V. Yoder) *Great Issues '72: Important Questions Facing the American Public,* Troy State University, 1973.
Power and Security, Lexington Books, 1976.
Energy from Heaven and Earth, W. H. Freeman, 1979, revised edition, 1981.
The Pursuit of Simplicity, Pepperdine University Press, 1980.
Fusion: Magnetic Confinement, Academy Press, 1981.
(With others) *Great Issues '83: A Forum on Important Questions Facing the American Public,* Troy State University, 1983.
Better a Shield Than a Sword: Perspectives on Defense and Technology, Free Press, 1987.

Also author of *Great Men of Physics,* 1969, *The Miracle of Freedom,* 1972, *Energy: A Plan for Action,* 1975, *Nuclear Energy in the Developing World,* 1977, and *In Search of Solutions for Defense and for Energy,* Hoover Institution.

SIDELIGHTS: Edward Teller's work with the Manhattan Project during the Second World War, and later with the Los Alamos Scientific Laboratory, was instrumental in developing atomic weapons for the United States. Teller, in fact, is credited with being the father of the hydrogen bomb. Since the 1950s he has been at work developing peaceful uses for atomic energy, pioneering in methods to safely harness atomic power with magnetic confinement and laser techniques.

Speaking soon after the first hydrogen bomb was tested in 1952, Teller told *Newsweek:* "I would rather work on defense than on aggressive weapons." This desire was realized during the Reagan administration when Teller's proposal for a Strategic Defense Initiative, a system of satellites to shoot down and destroy incoming missiles, was met with enthusiasm. Although criticized at the time by some scientists, and by the Soviet Union, the SDI system is under development. Teller's book *Better a Shield Than a Sword: Perspectives on Defense and Technology* presents his argument for the proposal.

BIOGRAPHICAL/CRITICAL SOURCES:

BOOKS

Blumberg, Stalney A. and Gwinn Ownes, *Energy and Conflict: The Life and Times of Edward Teller,* Putnam, 1976.
Shepley, James and Clay Blair, Jr., *The Hydrogen Bomb,* David McKay, 1954.
Teller, Edward, *Better a Shield Than a Sword: Perspectives on Defense and Technology,* Free Press, 1987.

PERIODICALS

Life, September 6, 1954.
Los Angeles Times Book Review, March 22, 1981.
New Scientist, September 2, 1982.
Newsweek, August 2, 1954, October 18, 1954.
New York Review of Books, March 31, 1988.
New York Times, January 31, 1954, June 3, 1954, June 16, 1954, June 17, 1954, July 4, 1954.
Science, November 19, 1982.
Tribune Books (Chicago), July 12, 1987.
Washington Post, January 19, 1980, November 18, 1988.

*   *   *

TENNANT, Kylie
   See RODD, Kylie Tennant

*   *   *

TENNESHAW, S. M.
   See SILVERBERG, Robert

*   *   *

TERKEL, Louis   1912-
   (Studs Terkel)

PERSONAL: Born May 16, 1912, in New York, N.Y.; son of Samuel and Anna (Finkel) Terkel; married Ida Goldberg, July 2, 1939; children: Paul. *Education:* University of Chicago, Ph.B., 1932, J.D., 1934.

ADDRESSES: Home—85O West Castlewood Terr., Chicago, Ill. 60640. *Office*—WFMT, Inc., 5OO North Michigan Ave., Chicago, Ill. 6O611.

CAREER: Worked as a civil service employee in Washington, D.C., and as a stage actor and movie house manager, during the 1930 and 1940s; host of interview show "Wax Museum" on radio station WFMT, Chicago, Ill., 1945—. Moderator of television program "Studs' Place," Chicago, Ill., 1950-53. Actor in stage plays, including "Detective Story," 1950, "A View from the Bridge," 1958, "Light Up the Sky," 1959, and "The Cave Dwellers," 1960. Master of ceremonies at Newport Folk Festival, 1959 and 196O, Ravinia (Ill.) Music Festival, 1959, University of Chicago Folk Festival, 1961, and others.

AWARDS, HONORS: Ohio State University award, 1959, and UNESCO Prix Italia award, 1962, both for "Wax Museum"; University of Chicago Alumni Association Communicator of the Year award, 1969; National Book Award nominee, 1975; Pulitzer Prize in nonfiction, 1985, for *"The Good War": An Oral History of World War II;* Society of Midland Authors Award, 1982, for *American Dreams: Lost and Found,* and 1983, for best writer.

WRITINGS:

UNDER NAME STUDS TERKEL

Giants of Jazz, Crowell, 1957, revised edition, Harper, 1975.
Division Street, America, Pantheon, 1967.
Hard Times: An Oral History of the Great Depression, Pantheon, 1970.
Working: People Talk about What They Do All Day and How They Feel about What They Do, Pantheon, 1974.
Talking to Myself: A Memoir of My Times, Pantheon, 1977.
American Dreams: Lost and Found, Pantheon, 1980.
"The Good War": An Oral History of World War II, Pantheon, 1984.
(Author of foreword) Hollinger F. Barnard, editor, *Outside the Magic Circle: Autobiography of Virginia Foster Durr,* University of Alabama Press, 1985.
(With Nelson Algren) *The Neon Wilderness,* Writers and Readers, 1986.
Chicago, Pantheon, 1986.
The Great Divide: Second Thoughts on the American Dream, Pantheon, 1988.

Also author of play, "Amazing Grace," first produced in Ann Arbor, Mich., by the University of Michigan's Professional Theater Program, 1967. Featured on sound recordings, including "Television: The First Fifty Years," Center for Cassette Studies, 1975.

SIDELIGHTS: "Next to Richard Nixon, the person whose life has been most dramatically affected by the tape recorder is Studs Terkel," according to Paul Gray in *Time.* For some two decades, Terkel has been the sympathetic ear to the American people, devoting several of his books to their intimate, revealing, first-person narratives. Armed with his tape machine, Terkel travels cross-country to get his interviews. His subjects speak out on topics as distinct as the Great Depression, World War II, and their jobs and as nebulous as their definition of the American Dream. Some of Terkel's interviews are with celebrities, but his most remembered—and some say his best—are with "real people." "I celebrate the non-celebrated," the author once told *Philadelphia Bulletin* contributor Lewis Beale. "I've found that average people want to talk about themselves, their hopes, dreams, aspirations, provided they sense that you're interested in what they're saying." And, as Terkel explained in a 1985 talk to the Friends of Libraries U.S.A., he has also discovered that "the average American has an indigenous intelligence, a native wit. It's only a question of piquing that intelligence."

Born Louis Terkel in New York City, the writer is closely associated with his years living and working in Chicago; he adopted the name Studs from another colorful Chicago character, the fictional Studs Lonigan. Trained in law, Terkel became a successful actor and broadcaster. He was also an enthusiastic liberal whose fall from favor with the House Un-American Activities Committee during the 1950s led to the early cancellation of his television talk show, "Studs' Place." As Terkel explains to Lee Michael Katz in a *Washington Post* interview, he was never a Communist, but he "belonged to a left-wing theatre group. Basically my name appeared on many petitions. Rent control. Ending Jim Crow. Abolishing the poll tax. You know, as subversive issues as that. Coming out in favor of Social Security prematurely. You think I'm kidding? These were very controversial issues, considered commie issues." But the writer also feels that the blacklisting helped his career: "If it weren't for the blacklist I might have been emceeing [today] on these network TV shows and have been literally dead because . . . I'd have said something that would have knocked me off [the air], obviously. But I would never have done these books, I would never have gone on to the little FM station playing classical music. So, long live the blacklist!"

Perhaps Terkel's best-known book of interviews is *Working: People Talk about What They Do All Day and How They Feel about What They Do.* A compendium of several dozen interviews from Americans in all walks of life, *Working* is described by *Washington Post Book World* reviewer Bernard Weisberger as "good talk—earthy, passionate, honest, sometimes tender, sometimes crisp, juicy as reality, seasoned with experience." Peter S. Prescott of *Newsweek* calls *Working* "an impressive achievement. . . . This is, I think, a very valuable document, a book that would be of use to writers and sociologists if only for the vast amount of technical information it contains." Terkel's *American Dreams: Lost and Found* and *The Great Divide: Second Thoughts on the American Dream* continue the same approach, each book containing some one hundred interviews with a diverse range of Americans.

In *"The Good War": An Oral History of World War II,* Terkel confines his interviews to those who experienced the war firsthand, providing a kind of informal history of that time. "As in Terkel's previous oral histories," Jonathan Yardley notes in the *Washington Post Book World,* "'The Good War' is a clangorous but carefully orchestrated jumble of voices." Louden Wainwright in the *New York Times Book Review* finds that the book "gives the American experience in World War II great immediacy. Reading it, I felt a renewed connection with that slice of my own past and a surprisingly powerful kinship with the voices from it. . . . [The book] certainly offers the sharp and unlaundered glimpses of a generation and a conflict they've grown up seeing romanticized in late night television movies."

MEDIA ADAPTATIONS: Working was adapted as a musical by Stephen Schwartz and first produced on Broadway, May 14, 1978, and later taped for a television broadcast; *Talking to Myself* was adapted as a play by Paul Sills and first produced in Evanston, Ill., at the Northlight Theater in 1988.

BIOGRAPHICAL/CRITICAL SOURCES:

BOOKS

Authors in the News, Volume 1, Gale, 1976.
Terkel, Studs, *Talking to Myself: A Memoir of My Times,* Pantheon, 1977.

PERIODICALS

Atlantic, July 1977, November, 1980.
Newsweek, April 1, 1974, April 18, 1977, October 13, 1980, October 15, 1984.
New York Times Book Review, April 19, 1970, March 21, 1974, March 22, 1974, April 11, 1977, May 14, 1978, September 24, 1980, September 26, 1984.
Philadelphia Bulletin, April 17, 1974.
Time, May 13, 1974, April 18, 1977, September 29, 1980, October 8, 1984.
Washington Post, May 5, 1974, April 24, 1977, October 5, 1980, September 30, 1984.
Washington Post Book World, May 5, 1974, April 24, 1977, October 5, 1980, September 30, 1984, December 22, 1985.

*   *   *

TERKEL, Studs
See TERKEL, Louis

*   *   *

THEOBALD, Lewis, Jr.
See LOVECRAFT, H(oward) P(hillips)

*   *   *

THEROUX, Paul (Edward) 1941-

PERSONAL: Surname rhymes with "skiddoo"; born April 10, 1941, in Medford, Mass.; son of Albert Eugene (in sales) and Anne (Dittami) Theroux; married Anne Castle (a broadcaster), December 4, 1967; children: Marcel Raymond, Louis Sebastian. *Education:* Attended University of Maine, 1959-60; University of Massachusetts, B.A., 1963; Syracuse University, further study, 1963.

ADDRESSES: Home—35 Elsynge Rd., London SW18 2HR, England.

CAREER: Soche Hill College, Limbe, Malawi, lecturer in English, 1963-65; Makerere University, Kampala, Uganda, lecturer in English, 1965-68; University of Singapore, Singapore, lecturer in English, 1968-71; professional writer, 1971—. Visiting lecturer, University of Virginia, 1972-73. Has given numerous lectures on literature in the United States and abroad.

MEMBER: American Academy and Institute of Arts and Letters.

AWARDS, HONORS: Robert Hamlet one-act play award, 1960; *Playboy* Editorial Award, 1971 and 1976; *New York Times Book Review* "Editors' Choice" citation, 1975, for *The Great Railway Bazaar: By Train Through Asia;* American Academy and Institute of Arts and Letters award for literature, 1977; American Book Award nominations, 1981, for *The Old Patagonian Express: By Train Through the Americas,* and 1983, for *The Mosquito Coast.*

WRITINGS:

FICTION

Waldo (novel), Houghton, 1967.
Fong and the Indians (novel), Houghton, 1968.
Girls at Play (novel), Houghton, 1969.
Murder in Mount Holly (novel), Alan Ross, 1969.
Jungle Lovers (novel), Houghton, 1971.
Sinning With Annie and Other Stories (short stories), Houghton, 1972.

Saint Jack (novel; also see below), Houghton, 1973.

The Black House (novel), Houghton, 1974.

The Family Arsenal (novel; Book-of-the-Month Club selection), Houghton, 1976.

The Consul's File (short stories), Houghton, 1977.

Picture Palace (novel), Houghton, 1978.

World's End and Other Stories (short stories), Houghton, 1980.

The Mosquito Coast (novel; Book-of-the-Month Club selection), with woodcuts by David Frampton, Houghton, 1982.

The London Embassy (short stories), Houghton, 1982.

Doctor Slaughter (novel; also see below), Hamish Hamilton, 1984.

Half Moon Street: Two Short Novels (contains *Doctor Slaughter* and *Doctor DeMarr*), Houghton, 1984.

O-Zone (novel; Book-of-the-Month Club alternate selection), Putnam, 1986.

My Secret History (autobiographical novel; Book-of-the-Month Club and Quality Paperback Book Club featured selection), Putnam, 1989.

NONFICTION

V. S. Naipaul: An Introduction to His Works, Africana Publishing, 1972.

The Great Railway Bazaar: By Train Through Asia, Houghton, 1975.

The Old Patagonian Express: By Train Through the Americas, Houghton, 1979.

Sailing Through China, illustrated by Patrick Procktor, Houghton, 1984.

The Kingdom by the Sea: A Journey Around Great Britain, Houghton, 1985.

(With Steve McCurry) *The Imperial Way: By Rail From Peshawar to Chittagong,* Houghton, 1985.

Sunrise With Seamonsters: Travels and Discoveries 1964-1984, Houghton, 1985.

(With Bruce Chatwin) *Patagonia Revisited,* Houghton, 1986.

Riding the Iron Rooster: By Train Through China, Putnam, 1988.

FOR CHILDREN

A Christmas Card, illustrated by John Lawrence, Houghton, 1978.

London Snow: A Christmas Story, illustrated by Lawrence, Houghton, 1979.

OTHER

(With Peter Bogdanovich and Howard Sackler) "Saint Jack" (screenplay), produced by New World/Shoals Creek/ Playboy/Copa de Oro, 1979.

"The Autumn Dog" (play), produced in New York, 1981.

(Translator) Abdelrahman Munif, *Cities of Salt,* Random, 1988.

Contributor of fiction to *Encounter, Atlantic, Commentary, Playboy, Harper's Bazaar,* and other periodicals; contributor of numerous reviews and essays to *New York Times, New York Times Book Review, New Statesman,* London *Times,* and other periodicals in the United States and England.

SIDELIGHTS: In a career spanning two decades, author Paul Theroux has established a reputation as one of modern literature's most respected chroniclers of the expatriate experience. His novels find themes in the anomalies of postimperial life in such exotic locales as Malawi, Singapore, and Honduras, as well as in the economic and social decay besetting Great Britain. As Samuel Coale notes in *Critique:* "Drastic change indeed stalks the world of [Theroux's] fiction, that precisely rendered realm where cultures clash and characters encounter each other as society's pawns in a larger pattern." An American citizen who lives in London most of the year, Theroux has gained equal renown for his nonfiction travel books, some of which feature continent-crossing railway journeys of months' duration. By traveling, suggests *New Yorker* contributor Susan Lardner, "Theroux has tested a belief in the continuing strangeness of the world, and discovered openings for melodrama and romantic gestures that other writers have given up for lost." Helen Dudar writes in the *Chicago Tribune Book World* that Theroux has become "our foremost fictional specialist in the outsized outsider, the ravenous wanderer who sees or knows or wants more than most of us allow ourselves to hope for."

Critics tend to place Theroux's work on a thematic continuum with that of some of the twentieth century's most notable fiction writers. James Fenton of the London *Times* suggests: "There is a line of writing to be travelled, if you get on at Joseph Conrad: Graham Greene is the next stop, then V. S. Naipaul, and after that most of the trains call at . . . Paul Theroux." Other reviewers liken Theroux to Henry James, Somerset Maugham, and Evelyn Waugh, noting as does Robert Towers in the *New York Times Book Review* that Theroux has "staked out for himself a fictional terrain that is generally thought of as British." A concurrent opinion is offered by William McPherson in the *Washington Post Book World.* McPherson finds that Theroux's affinities "are very English: the acerbic wit of Evelyn Waugh, Graham Greene's rich pessimism reduced here to arid scorn; Joseph Conrad's menacing atmosphere, and the exile's eye of Henry James." *Times Literary Supplement* contributor Valentine Cunningham gives reasons for the comparison: "Like Greene, Theroux keeps animating the lust for frontier excitements and their attendant anxieties. . . . In their way, all Theroux's frontier-crossers are smugglers—smuggling displaced selves into alien places, perpetually a risky business."

Timothy J. Evans suggests in the *Dictionary of Literary Biography* that Theroux's writing "contains little technical innovation, an attribute often associated with contemporary novelists." Evans nevertheless adds: "What Theroux does seem to share with other contemporary writers is a vision of a meaningless, chaotic world enveloping his characters. They are unable to draw meaning from their lives or surroundings, and therefore they attempt to impose some kind of order, generally either through violence, or through writing, or both." Coale offers a similar assessment: "Theroux's fictional techniques are precisely those of the literary realist. His remarkable lucid and emblematic style is based on careful and precise observation, the seizing of sharp and clear images, and the documentary urge to record what happens during the conflicts that ensue." Coale also writes: "The encounters between East and West, between different cultures, and between the temperaments of different characters provide the formal antitheses of Theroux's fiction. . . . Theroux's is a world palpably at war with itself, split down the middle, trapped in a continuing dialectic of power and impotence, chaos and order, personal appetite and socio-cultural conventions, that reveals no signs of healing or mending." Coale concludes that Theroux's "searingly accurate perception of decay, the contemporary wasteland of much of the Third World and the American's ambiguous place in it," reveals the efforts of "a dedicated and thorough artist."

Theroux's family background and upbringing in the "prim suburbs of Boston" hardly seem adequate preparation for his adult role as an award-winning novelist, essayist, and world traveler. He was born in Medford, Massachusetts, in 1941, to working-class parents who had, he claims in the *New York Times,* "no place, no influence, no money nor power." They did, however, have numerous children. In his essay collection *Sunrise With Seamonsters: Travels and Discoveries 1964-1984,* Theroux writes: "It was part of my luck to have been born in a populous family of nine unexampled wits." Included in this roster of six siblings are two elder brothers—Eugene, a Washington, D.C.-based lawyer and expert in Sino-American trade, and Alexander, a novelist whose critical reception has rivaled Paul's. *New York Times* contributor James Atlas characterizes the three oldest Theroux brothers as "collective tutors in the acquisition of culture" who "shared their various talents among themselves and passed them down to their younger brothers." Theroux remembers his family fondly but is unsparing in his condemnation of the public education he received at Medford High School. In *Sunrise With Seamonsters* he describes the "willfully uninspiring" teachers and the "mediocre—non-intellectual rather than anti-intellectual" curriculum that left him decidedly unmotivated. "For twenty years," he comments, "I tried to account for my choice of this [writing] profession. I mentioned books I had read in high school. But the books I read . . . had not made me a writer. . . . I . . . pored much more seriously over the L. L. Bean catalog which advertised tents, hand-warmers and snow-shoes. So: what intellectual upbringing? Television, radio, comic books, camping manuals and *The American Rifleman?* I didn't play baseball and wasn't interested in electronics. That ought to have left me with plenty of time for the library, but in fact I chose guns, bombs and fires."

The fascination with guns and bombs did not persist into Theroux's college years. As a sophomore at the University of Massachusetts, he declared himself to be a pacifist and insisted on receiving an exemption from the mandatory R.O.T.C. program. Though "neither a brilliant nor inspired student," according to Atlas, Theroux called further attention to himself in 1962 by being arrested for leading an antiwar demonstration—"when demonstrations were rare and actually bothered people"—he notes in *Sunrise With Seamonsters.* Upon graduation from the University of Massachusetts in 1963, Theroux joined the Peace Corps, an organization he describes in *Sunrise With Seamonsters* as "a sort of Howard Johnson's on the main drag to maturity." He was sent to Limbe, Malawi, in south central Africa to teach English.

For a time Theroux supplemented his Peace Corps stipend by writing articles for the *Christian Science Monitor* and several African periodicals. In the course of his stay in Malawi, he found himself on friendly terms with a group of political leaders who eventually fell from favor with the unstable Hastings Banda regime. This association, as well as a duplicitous use of some of Theroux's articles by the German equivalent of the C.I.A., led to Theroux's deportation from Malawi in 1965 under the charge of spying. Several years later, Theroux described the incident in an essay that has been reprinted in *Sunrise With Seamonsters.* "My readiness to say yes to favors may suggest a simplicity of mind, a fatal gullibility," he wrote, "but I was bored, and the daily annoyance of living in a dictatorship, which is like suffering an unhappy family in a locked house, had softened my temper to the point where anything different, lunch with a stranger, the request for an article, the challenge of a difficult task, changed that day and revived my mind. The risk was usually obvious, but it always seemed worth it—better that than the tyranny of the ordinary." Theroux was expelled from the Peace Corps and fined for "six months' unsatisfactory service," but no further government action ensued based on the events in Malawi.

Immediately following his expulsion from the Peace Corps, Theroux returned to Africa, where he became a lecturer in En-

glish at Makerere University in Kampala, Uganda. He remained in Uganda until 1968, when he and his wife, Anne Castle, were attacked during a political demonstration against the policies of white-controlled Rhodesia. The violent end to his stay in Uganda notwithstanding, Theroux found much-needed intellectual stimulation at the university, as well as the time to work on his writing. In 1966 author V. S. Naipaul visited Makerere University and struck up an amiable but exacting working relationship with the young writer. Theroux remembers the period in *Sunrise With Seamonsters:* "It was like private tuition—as if, at this crucial time in my life, . . . he had come all the way to Africa to remind me of what writing really was and to make me aware of what a difficult path I was setting out on. . . . With me he was a generous, rational teacher." It was Naipaul, Theroux claims, who suggested that he write fiction about Africa, with attention to the comic and the tragic aspects of life there. Theroux, in turn, published a critical appraisal of Naipaul's work, entitled *V. S. Naipaul: An Introduction to His Works,* in 1972.

Waldo, Theroux's first novel, was published in 1967, while the author was still living in Uganda. Timothy J. Evans notes that the work "deals with the theme of a man trying to find or create order in his life" and that the book is the first expression of themes that Theroux continues to use. "Order is not discovered by the characters" in *Waldo,* states Evans, "and it is not imposed by the writer on the novel." Evans claims that critical reaction to *Waldo* falls in extremes of praise and disparagement but that the book's quality falls rather midway between the two poles. "The novel does have a point," Evans concludes, "and it has some humorous, satiric passages which make it worth reading, but it is very episodic, with vignettes of uneven quality." A *Times Literary Supplement* reviewer offers a concurrent assessment: "Most of the time, *Waldo* seems to wander along, quite amiably and quite readably, but without much sense of direction."

In 1968 Theroux left Uganda and took a teaching position at the University of Singapore. While there he published three novels set in Africa, *Fong and the Indians, Girls at Play,* and *Jungle Lovers.* As a group, the works explore the frustrating and potentially tragic difficulties of social interaction in postcolonial Africa. Robert Towers writes of Theroux: "Unafraid of ethnic generalizations, he spares no one—African, Englishman, Chinaman, Indian, American—in his wildly absurd confrontations between the old and the new exploiters and the poor bastards caught in the middle; recklessly he juxtaposes the crumbling institutions of colonialism with some of the more bizarre outgrowths of the Third World." In *Fong and the Indians,* for instance, Theroux describes the misadventures of a Chinese Catholic grocer in an imaginary African state. According to *Saturday Review* contributor Constance Wagner, the novel depicts "Africans, Asians, whites, cheating, despising, mistrusting one another. . . . With a smile Theroux lays bare the myopic self-serving not of Africa but of man. . . . Laugh as you will, you realize in the end that this short novel contains more of sanity and truth than a dozen fat morality plays on ugly Americanism."

Critics find elements of satire and hopelessness in Theroux's novels about Africa. In a *Times Literary Supplement* review of *Jungle Lovers,* a writer states: "Increasingly a more wryly observed Africa emerges from the condescension or primitivism of expatriate fiction. . . . [Theroux's] fable, with roots in satiric caricature and documentary terror, uses the linguistic complexity to underscore the wavering relationships between lingering British, Africans, and the two American protagonists." *Spectator* contributor Auberon Waugh calls *Jungle Lovers* "the most vivid account of the sheer hopelessness of independent Black Africa" and "a serious and excellent novel, welcome above all for its refreshing pessimism." Evans suggests that a "repeated assertion of empathy for the blacks does not convincingly cover an attitude of paternalism" on the author's part in *Jungle Lovers.* Evans nevertheless adds that in the book, "the British and American settlers are also viewed with ridicule, and Theroux seems content to leave the Americans' plans for change open to question." The destructive implications of one particularly naive American's plans for change form the violent climax of *Girls at Play,* a work one *Times Literary Supplement* critic characterizes as "unremittingly depressing." Susan Lardner feels that Theroux's novels set in Africa reveal him to be "a connoisseur of the conflict of ideals and illusions with things as they turn out to be." Irony, she concludes, "is his natural style."

Theroux had published five novels by the time he turned thirty in 1971. Three of these received considerable critical acclaim, especially in Great Britain. On the strength of this success, and on the conviction that writing and teaching were not necessarily compatible forms of employment, Theroux quit his position at the University of Singapore. He moved to a suburb of London with his wife and children and continued to work on fiction, essays, and book reviews. With the exception of a brief visiting lectureship at the University of Virginia, he has depended upon his professional writing for a livelihood since that time.

While teaching in Singapore, Theroux was made to promise that he would not write any fiction about that island. The informal constraint was removed when he relocated in London, and he published *Saint Jack,* a novel set in Singapore. *Atlantic* reviewer Edward Weeks calls the work "a highly professional, often amusing, withering account of prostitution in the once glamorous East." A low-key first person narrative by a middle-aged, expatriate American pimp, *Saint Jack* has received generous praise from critics. "There has never been any question about the quality of Theroux's prose or the bite of his satire," writes Jonathan Yardley in the *Washington Post Book World.* "In *Saint Jack,* more than in any of his previous fiction, the sardonic is balanced with compassion, and in Jack Flowers we are given a character whose yearnings touch upon our own." Evans feels that the protagonist "could never change, because he represents life in Singapore. . . . Jack may dream of an ideal existence and wish that he could write the novel which would depict it, but he cannot. . . . Life will be a treadmill for him." Though Weeks suggests that under the surface humor "one is aware of the author's scorn for this disheveled, corrupt memento of colonialism," other reviewers cite Theroux for a sympathetic portrayal of a quixotic hero. "Jack Flowers is funny, endearing, outrageous, poignant, noble—and utterly believable," contends Yardley. "He is Paul Theroux's finest accomplishment." In 1979, Peter Bogdanovich directed the movie version of *Saint Jack,* based on a screenplay that Theroux helped to write.

Theroux's commercial and critical success was still to a certain extent dependent upon his British readership when he published *The Black House* in 1974. The novel, a gothic tale with psychological dimensions set in a rural part of England, has garnered mixed reviews. *New York Times Book Review* contributor Michael Mewshaw feels that while "it is a tribute to [Theroux's] integrity and ambition that he is not content to keep repeating himself," the work in question, "an abrupt departure from the comic vision of his earlier work, does a serious disservice to his talent." Claire Tomalin offers a different viewpoint in the *New Statesman.* "The book is about a man panicked by doubts about just where he and other creatures do belong," Tomalin writes. "The degree of skill with which Theroux handles these various themes, and the level of mastery of his writing, have produced a novel of unusual scope and promise still more for the future."

The Black House has gained added notoriety for being the manuscript Theroux dropped at the publishing house on his way to the train station for his now-famous transcontinental rail trip. In *Sunrise With Seamonsters* he writes: "Travel is a creative act— not simply loafing and inviting your soul, but feeding the imagination, accounting for each fresh wonder, memorizing and moving on. The discoveries the traveler makes in broad daylight— the curious problems of the eye he solves—resemble those that thrill and sustain a novelist in his solitude." Boarding a train at Victoria Station in London, Theroux set off on a four-month odyssey through Asia, the Far East, and the Soviet Union, eventually returning to his point of departure with "four thick notebooks" on his lap. The edited notebooks became *The Great Railway Bazaar: By Train Through Asia.*

Though travel accounts are not generally known for their commercial appeal, *The Great Railway Bazaar* was an enormous success. Writing for *Publishers Weekly,* John F. Baker calls Theroux's accomplishment an "amazing first." Baker notes: "He had made his way onto the best seller list . . . with nothing more than a travel book, . . . thereby becoming probably the first writer since Mark Twain whose travels made a more than fleeting impression in booksellers' accounts." Critics have lavished praise on the work. *Washington Post Book World* contributor David Roberts claims that the account "represents travel writing at its very best—almost the best, one is tempted to say, that it can attain. Paul Theroux . . . here transforms what was clearly a long, ultimately tedious journey by train . . . into a singularly entertaining book." "Though it is a travel book and not a novel," Robert Towers comments, "it incorporates many of the qualities of Theroux's fiction: it is funny, sardonic, wonderfully sensuous and evocative in its descriptions, casually horrifying in its impact." Arthur Cooper makes a similar observation in *Newsweek:* "Rarely have subject and sensibility been so splendidly conjoined: aside from his love for the rails, Theroux demonstrates . . . that he embarks on every project with all of his senses fully engaged." British reviewers have been equally enthusiastic about *The Great Railway Bazaar.* In a *New Statesman* piece, V. S. Pritchett suggests that Theroux "has Dickens's gift for getting the character of a man or woman in a flash. . . . The whole book is more than a rich and original entertainment. His people, places and asides will stay a long time jostling in the mind of the reader." Hunter Davies likewise writes in the *Spectator:* "The main fascination of the book is watching Mr. Theroux as he keeps his narrative flowing, avoiding, if only just, the temptation to improve on reality. . . . I suppose that all fans of Mr. Theroux will be delighted by this journey around himself."

The success of *The Great Railway Bazaar,* combined with an admitted wanderlust, have led Theroux to pen several subsequent travel memoirs. Best known among these are *The Old Patagonian Express: By Train Through the Americas* and *The Kingdom by the Sea: A Journey Around Great Britain.* Employing the same techniques of rail travel, walking excursion, and personal rumination, these works explore Central and South America and the coastline regions of the British Isles, respectively. Neither volume has enjoyed the critical reception that attended publication of *The Great Railway Bazaar;* some reviewers find the works scornful and repetitive. As Patrick Breslin notes of *The Old Patagonian Express* in the *Washington Post Book World:* "Theroux so loses himself in the mechanics of how he got to Patagonia, and the people who irritated him along the way, that there is little room in the book for anything else. And since not very much out of the ordinary happened to him, one's interest flags." In the *New York Times,* John Leonard comments that Theroux's traveling style "tends to be contentious; at the drop of an offhand remark in a bar or a dining car, he will opinionize." Leonard adds, however: "One forgives him because one tends to agree with his opinions." *Chicago Tribune Book World* editor John Blades, reviewing *The Kingdom by the Sea,* finds Theroux's tone refreshing: "Through all the rigors of his travel, . . . Theroux never lost his wit; as much as anything else, his journals are notable for their malign humor, which he turns on himself as well as almost everyone and everything he encounters. . . . With undisguised contempt for the people and customs of the countries he visits, with no synthetic bonhomie, Theroux has a certain arrogant charm, a cruel honesty that becomes infectious and disarming."

Concurrent with his travel books, Theroux has continued to write fiction, some of which reveals a London rife with economic problems and emotional malaise. *The Family Arsenal,* published in 1976, follows the exploits of a band of political terrorists awaiting orders in the London slums. "The sense of urban rot edging toward ruin is palpable on every page," claims Lawrence Graver in the *New York Times Book Review.* "London has rarely looked dingier or more sinister." *Newsweek* critic Peter S. Prescott calls the novel "the work of a self-assured artist" and asserts that Theroux writes "about spiritual despair, a London from which moral and political sanity have fled, a world waiting, possibly deserving, to blow up. . . . When the violence comes, it is not even remotely in aid of a social idea." The absence of moral and political sanity also serves as a theme in *Dr. Slaughter,* published as the first part of *Half Moon Street: Two Short Novels.* In that work, a young American scholar visiting London begins moonlighting as a highly-paid prostitute, and she ultimately falls into a ring of international blackmailers and assassins. According to Webster Schott in a *Washington Post Book World* review of *Half Moon Street,* Theroux "combines unlikely elements—mystery, character study, the Gothic nightmares of industrialized society—in fiction that shimmers with implications, possibilities, and warnings."

The Mosquito Coast, a novel published in 1982, is among Theroux's best-known works of fiction. Told from the point of view of a thirteen-year-old narrator, the story explores a family's exodus from Massachusetts to the jungles of Honduras under the domination of a manic and eccentric father, Allie Fox. *Times Literary Supplement* contributor Valentine Cunningham comments on Theroux's characterization: "Allie Fox . . . [is] a truly amazing and unforgettable figure, an American titan whose actions unlock the essences of oppressive Americanism, revealing evils we're to take as intrinsic to the rationality and mechanization that helped make his country what it is." Robert Towers likewise cites the theme of "Yankee-ingenuity-gone-berserk" in the *New York Review of Books,* adding that Theroux handles the concept "with commendable skill." "Though Allie Fox is an archetypal character whose career follows an emblematic line," Towers writes, "Theroux has avoided the sterility of much quasi-allegorical writing by endowing his main character with a lively and dense specificity." "In Allie Fox, Theroux has created his first epic hero," claims Jonathan Raban in the *Saturday Review.* "If one can imagine an American tradition that takes in Benjamin Franklin, Captain Ahab, Huey Long, and the Reverend Jim Jones, then Allie Fox is its latest, most complete incarnation."

The Mosquito Coast garnered an American Book Award nomination and numerous highly favorable reviews. Raban, for instance, terms the work "not just [Theroux's] finest novel so far. It is—in a characteristically hooded way—a novelist's act of self-definition, a midterm appraisal of his own resources. It is a wonderful book, with so many levels to it that it feels bottomless." The novel does not, however, meet with universal approval. *Los Angeles Times Book Review* contributor Edward M. White writes

that *The Mosquito Coast* is "an abstract and witty book, embodying Theroux's usual themes about the conflict of cultures. The abstraction is particularly damaging, here, however, where it becomes authorial manipulation of characters and plotting in the interests of theoretical design." William Logan complains in the *Chicago Tribune Book World* that because Theroux "cannot create a human referent for his characters, the narrative is labored and overlong, the irony clumsy, and the end congested with symbolism." In his *New York Times Book Review* article, Thomas R. Edwards offers an opposite view. "Theroux's book . . . is, characteristically, a fine entertainment, a gripping adventure story, a remarkable comic portrait of minds and cultures at cross-purposes. But under its unintimidating surface, . . . 'The Mosquito Coast' shows a cosmopolitan expatriate novelist pondering his imaginative sources as an American writer, and the relation of those sources to the world as it now seems to be. This excellent story . . . is also an impressively serious act of imagination."

In addition to his novels and nonfiction, Theroux has produced four collections of short stories. W. M. Spackman, in a *New Republic* review of *The London Embassy,* suggests that the short story "looks so natural" to Theroux "that it may turn out to be the form he prefers." The author's stories bear a thematic resemblance to his longer works; many of the characters are, in the words of *New York Times Book Review* contributor Benjamin DeMott, "travelers, truants and transplants." "The notion of the undoing of innocents abroad, of outsiders and castaways struggling to cope with alien ways," serves to unite the tales in *World's End and Other Stories,* according to *Washington Post Book World* reviewer Allen Wier. Critics find Theroux's style conducive to success in the shorter medium. "His natural gift for place is a means of capitalising on his passion for travel," writes Alan Hollinghurst in *New Statesman,* "and the short story with its emphasis on plot and its need for quick and shapely resolution is an ideal form for him." Frank Tuohy, reviewing for the *Times Literary Supplement,* concludes that Theroux's writing techniques "distinguish him from his American contemporaries: he is an experimental writer who uses a studied archaism" that includes a range of short story styles that had seemed obsolete. Bruce Cook likewise points out in the *Washington Post Book World* that Theroux "is a rather austere stylist who works with the economy of a real short story writer, concentrating not on lush passages of description but rather on bits and pieces of incident." Cook feels that this more English method of creation is the correct choice for Theroux. "It suits his temper well," the critic concludes.

Theroux has long labored outside of the realm of academia, and he has occasionally expressed mild contempt for university creative writing programs and patronage in the form of fellowships, endowments, and grants. Succinctly stating his position in *Sunrise With Seamonsters,* he comments: "The writer doesn't want a patron half so badly as he wants a paying public." The takeover of creative writing by the universities in the United States has, he contends, "changed the profession out of all recognition. It has made it narrower, more rarified, more neurotic; it has altered the way literature is taught and it has diminished our pleasure in reading." Theroux's own writing, highly successful commercially, has not gained a great deal of attention within the academic community. As Theroux tells *Publishers Weekly,* however, "No serious writer writes for money alone, but it's equally a mistake to think that if your writing makes money you're not serious." He is more greatly concerned, he admits in a *Chicago Tribune Book World* interview, that his writing should continue to entertain readers. "My fear is that I'll be boring," he states.

"You never actually run out of ideas, but you might run out of ideas that are intelligent, amusing, original. I don't want to be a bore. I would rather open a beauty parlor—I swear."

A prolific and eclectic author, Theroux seems determined to maintain a writing pace that seems almost contrary to the working habits of his particular group of contemporaries. "One needs energy to keep up with the extraordinary, productive restlessness of Paul Theroux," notes Jonathan Raban. Raban claims that Theroux, still in his forties, is "the most gifted, most prodigal writer of his generation. . . . He has moved in skips and bounds, never staying long enough in one place for the moss of a mannered style to grow on his writing." According to Jonathan Yardley, Theroux is to be read "for his unsparingly witty eviscerations of human vanity and pretense. At his best he is a merciless chronicler of the deceptions that people practice on themselves as well as others, of the nuances of affectation and self-display, of the implacable barriers that separate alien cultures." In the *Hudson Review*, William H. Pritchard concludes of Theroux: "As a steadily producing writer of long and short fiction, travel books, essays and reviews—of 'letters' generally—no American writer matters more than this gifted and possessed word-man."

MEDIA ADAPTATIONS: Saint Jack was adapted, with Theroux's assistance, for a film directed by Peter Bogdanovich in 1979; *The Mosquito Coast* was filmed in 1986; *Doctor Slaughter* was adapted as the film "Half Moon Street" in 1986.

BIOGRAPHICAL/CRITICAL SOURCES:

BOOKS

Contemporary Literary Criticism, Gale, Volume 5, 1976, Volume 8, 1978, Volume 11, 1979, Volume 15, 1980, Volume 28, 1984, Volume 46, 1988.
Dictionary of Literary Biography, Volume 2: *American Novelists since World War II,* Gale, 1978.
Theroux, Paul, *Sunrise With Seamonsters: Travels and Discoveries 1964-1984,* Houghton, 1985.

PERIODICALS

Antioch Review, winter, 1977.
Atlantic, October, 1973, April, 1976, October, 1983.
Books Abroad, summer, 1969, winter, 1971.
Chicago Tribune, January 7, 1987.
Chicago Tribune Book World, September 16, 1979, February 21, 1982, August 15, 1982, March 27, 1983, November 13, 1983, June 30, 1985, February 9, 1986, September 7, 1986.
Choice, July, 1973.
Christian Science Monitor, September 5, 1968.
Commentary, June, 1967.
Critique, March, 1981.
Detroit News, June 4, 1978, September 9, 1979, November 13, 1983, February 16, 1986, July 23, 1989.
Encounter, July, 1973.
Esquire, December, 1971, April, 1983.
Express, June, 1982.
GEO, November, 1983.
Globe and Mail (Toronto), October 19, 1985, October 11, 1986, June 17, 1989.
Harper's, May, 1967, March, 1976, September, 1977, April, 1982.
Hudson Review, winter, 1974-75, autumn, 1978.
Kenyon Review, September, 1967.
Life, May 21, 1971.
London Magazine, January, 1970.
Los Angeles Times, November 13, 1983, October 25, 1984, September 26, 1986, November 26, 1986, December 16, 1986.
Los Angeles Times Book Review, October 7, 1979, September 21, 1980, April 18, 1982, March 13, 1983, September 21, 1986, May 8, 1988, May 29, 1988, June 11, 1989.
Manchester Guardian Weekly, July 9, 1989.
National Observer, October 6, 1969.
National Review, June 29, 1971, November 10, 1972.
New Republic, November 29, 1969, September 25, 1976, November 27, 1976, September 22, 1979, February 24, 1982, April 11, 1983.
New Statesman, June 11, 1971, October 4, 1974, October 17, 1975, March 26, 1976, September 1, 1978, October 24, 1980.
Newsweek, September 24, 1973, November 11, 1974, September 8, 1975, June 19, 1976, August 15, 1977, September 10, 1979, March 1, 1982, April 25, 1983, October 24, 1983, October 22, 1984, August 12, 1985, September 15, 1986.
New Yorker, November 11, 1967, November 8, 1969, December 29, 1975, January 7, 1985.
New York Review of Books, September 23, 1971, September 30, 1976, November 10, 1977, August 17, 1978, April 15, 1982, June 2, 1983.
New York Times, May 29, 1971, July 22, 1976, August 23, 1977, April 30, 1978, May 31, 1978, April 27, 1979, August 28, 1979, February 11, 1982, February 28, 1983, October 13, 1983, October 1, 1984, June 5, 1985, August 30, 1986, November 21, 1986, November 26, 1986, December 7, 1986, May 30, 1989.
New York Times Book Review, November 3, 1968, September 28, 1969, August 8, 1971, November 5, 1972, September 9, 1973, September 8, 1974, August 24, 1975, December 28, 1975, July 11, 1976, August 21, 1977, June 18, 1978, July 22, 1979, August 26, 1979, August 24, 1980, February 14, 1982, March 20, 1983, October 23, 1983, April 22, 1984, October 28, 1984, June 2, 1985, November 10, 1985, September 14, 1986, June 19, 1988, June 4, 1989.
North American Review, winter, 1972.
Observer (London), February 8, 1987.
Ontario Review, fall, 1974, fall-winter, 1976-77.
Playboy, January, 1973.
Publishers Weekly, July 26, 1976.
Punch, December 10, 1969, October 13, 1982.
Saturday Review, September 28, 1968, July 24, 1976, September 3, 1977, July 8, 1978, October 27, 1979, February, 1982, November-December, 1983.
Spectator, June 12, 1971, October 12, 1974, March 15, 1975, October 18, 1975, March 27, 1976, June 4, 1977, September 16, 1978, October 17, 1981, June 30, 1984, June 29, 1985, August 7, 1989.
Time, August 23, 1968, August 25, 1975, August 2, 1976, September 5, 1977, June 5, 1978, February 22, 1982, October 31, 1983, July 1, 1985, May 22, 1989.
Times (London), October 6, 1983, June 6, 1985, September 1, 1986, October 11, 1986, October 16, 1986, February 6, 1987, September 15, 1988, June 29, 1989.
Times Literary Supplement, April 11, 1968, June 12, 1969, June 25, 1971, November 17, 1972, April 27, 1973, October 4, 1974, March 14, 1975, March 26, 1976, June 3, 1977, October 31, 1980, November 21, 1980, October 16, 1981, October 8, 1982, October 28, 1983, June 8, 1984, August 2, 1985, October 31, 1986, September 9-15, 1988, July 7-13, 1989.
Tribune (London), October 5, 1979.
Tribune Books, May 22, 1988, June 4, 1989.
U.S. News and World Report, December 17, 1979.
Village Voice, November 15, 1983, July 30, 1985.

Virginia Quarterly Review, winter, 1969, winter, 1970, winter, 1974.

Voice Literary Supplement, March, 1982.

Washington Post, September 20, 1979, November 23, 1985, December 19, 1986.

Washington Post Book World, February 8, 1970, August 8, 1971, September 14, 1973, September 15, 1974, September 7, 1975, May 30, 1976, July 11, 1976, August 21, 1977, June 25, 1978, September 2, 1979, August 17, 1980, March 6, 1983, October 16, 1983, December 9, 1984, July 7, 1985, June 5, 1988, June 11, 1989.

Yale Review, spring, 1979.

*   *   *

THEVENIN, Denis
See DUHAMEL, Georges

*   *   *

THIBAULT, Jacques Anatole Francois   1844-1924
(Anatole France; Gerome, a house pseudonym)

PERSONAL: Born April 16, 1844, in Paris, France; died October 12, 1924, in Saint-Cyr-sur-Loire, Indre-et-Loire, France; buried in Neuilly, France; son of Francois-Noel (a bookseller) and Antoinette (Gallas) Thibault; married Marie-Valerie Guerin de Sauville, April 28, 1877 (divorced, August 12, 1893); married Emma Laprevotte (a housekeeper), 1920; children: (first marriage) Suzanne.

CAREER: Writer. Assistant at Librairie de France (father's bookstore), Paris, France, during 1860s; editorial assistant at Bachelin-Deflorenne publishing house, Paris, during mid-1860s; schoolteacher in Ivry-sur-Seine, France, 1869; Lemerre publishing house, Paris, reader and editor, c. 1869-75; Senate Library, Paris, assistant librarian, 1876-c. 1889.

MEMBER: French Academy, League of the Rights of Man.

AWARDS, HONORS: Award from French Academy, 1881, for *Le Crime de Sylvestre Bonnard;* French Legion of Honor, chevalier, 1884, officer, 1895; honorary doctorate from University of Athens, 1919; Nobel Prize in literature, 1921.

WRITINGS:

NOVELS; UNDER NAME ANATOLE FRANCE

Jocaste [and] *Le Chat maigre,* Calmann-Levy, 1879; translation by Agnes Farley published as *Jocasta* [and] *The Famished Cat,* John Lane, 1912.

Le Crime de Sylvestre Bonnard, membre de l'Institut, Calmann-Levy, 1881, revised, 1902; translation by Lafcadio Hearn published as *The Crime of Sylvestre Bonnard, Member of the Institute,* Harper, 1890.

Les Desirs de Jean Servien, Lemerre, 1882; translation by Alfred Allinson published as *The Aspirations of Jean Servien,* John Lane, 1912.

Thais, Calmann-Levy, 1890; translation by A. D. Hall published as *Thais,* N. C. Smith (Chicago), 1891; translation by Ernest De Lancey Pierson published as *Thais; or, The Vengeance of Venus,* Minerva (New York), 1892.

La Rotisserie de la Reine Pedauque, Calmann-Levy, 1893; translation by Joseph A. V. Stritzko published as *The Queen Pedauque,* Gibbings, 1910, Boni & Liveright, 1923; translation by Mrs. Wilfrid Jackson published as *At the Sign of the Reine Pedauque,* John Lane, 1912; translation published as

The Romance of the Queen Pedauque, Halcyon House, 1950.

Le Lys rouge, Calmann-Levy, 1894; translation published as *The Red Lily,* Brentano's (New York), 1898.

L'Orme du mail (first in "Histoire contemporaine" series), Calmann-Levy, 1897; translation by M. P. Willcocks published as *The Elm-Tree on the Mall: A Chronicle of Our Own Times,* John Lane, 1910.

Le Mannequin d'osier (second in "Histoire contemporaine" series), Calmann-Levy, 1897; translation by M. P. Willcocks published as *The Wicker Work Woman: A Chronicle of Our Own Times,* John Lane, 1910.

L'Anneau d'amethyste (third in "Histoire contemporaine" series), Calmann-Levy, 1899; translation by B. Drillien published as *The Amethyst Ring,* John Lane, 1919.

Monsieur Bergeret a Paris (fourth in "Histoire contemporaine" series), Calmann-Levy, 1901; translation by B. Drillien published as *Monsieur Bergeret in Paris,* John Lane, 1921.

Histoire comique, Calmann-Levy, 1903; translation by Charles E. Roche published as *A Mummer's Tale,* John Lane, 1921.

L'Ile des pingouins, Calmann-Levy, 1908; translation by A. W. Evans published as *Penguin Island,* John Lane, 1909.

Les Dieux ont soif, Calmann-Levy, 1912; translation by Alfred Allinson published as *The Gods Are Athirst,* John Lane, 1913; translation by Frederick Davies published as *The Gods Will Have Blood,* Penguin Books, 1979.

Les Anges, Editions de Gil Blas, 1913, revised edition published as *La Revolte des anges,* Calmann-Levy, 1914; translation by Mrs. Wilfrid Jackson published as *The Revolt of the Angels,* John Lane, 1914.

Les Autels de la peur (title means "The Altars of Fear"; first published serially in *Le Journal des debats,* March 2, 1884, to March 16, 1884), Joseph Place, 1926, Nizet, 1971.

Also author of the unfinished novel "Victor Mainvielle."

SHORT STORIES; UNDER NAME ANATOLE FRANCE

Abeille, Charavay freres, 1883, Bias, 1973; translation by Mrs. John Lane published as *Honey-bee,* John Lane, 1911; translation by Peter Wright published as *Bee, Princess of the Dwarfs,* Dutton, 1912.

Nos Enfants: Scenes de la ville et des champs, Hachette, 1887; translation by Alfred Allinson published as *Child Life in Town and Country* [bound with] *The Merrie Tales of Jacques Tournebroche,* John Lane, 1910; translation by A. G. Wippern published as *In All France: Children in Town and Country,* A. Whitman (Chicago), 1930; published in two volumes as *Nos Enfants: Scenes de la ville et des champs* and *Filles et Garcons: Scenes de la ville et des champs,* Hachette, 1900; translation published in two volumes as *Our Children: Scenes From the Country and the Town,* Duffield, 1917, and *Girls and Boys: Scenes From the Country and the Town,* Duffield, 1913.

Balthasar (includes *Abeille*), Calmann-Levy, 1889, published as *Balthasar et la reine Balkis,* Carteret, 1900; translation by Mrs. John Lane published as *Balthasar,* John Lane, 1909.

L'Etui de nacre (includes "Le Procurateur de Judee" and "Le Jongleur de Notre-Dame"), Calmann-Levy, 1892; translation by Henri Pene Du Bois published as *Tales From a Mother-of-Pearl Casket,* G. H. Richmond (New York), 1896; translation by Frederic Chapman published as *Mother of Pearl,* John Lane, 1908.

Le Puits de Sainte Claire, Calmann-Levy, 1895; translation by Alfred Allinson published as *The Well of Saint Claire,* John Lane, 1909.

Clio, Calmann-Levy, 1900; translation by Winifred Stephens, Dodd, 1922.

L'Affaire Crainquebille (includes "L'Affaire Crainquebille"), Pelletan, 1901, revised, Cahiers de la Quinzaine, 1902, revised edition published as *Crainquebille, Putois, Riquet, et plusieurs autres recits profitables,* Calmann-Levy, 1904; translation by Winifred Stephens published as *Crainquebille, Putois, Riquet, and Other Profitable Tales,* John Lane, 1915; translation by Jacques Le Clerq published as *Crainquebille,* Heritage Press (New York), 1949.

Les Contes de Jacques Tournebroche, Calmann-Levy, 1908, enlarged edition (includes *Clio*), 1921; translation by Alfred Allinson published as *The Merrie Tales of Jacques Tournebroche* [bound with] *Child Life in Town and Country,* John Lane, 1910.

Les Sept Femmes de la Barbe-Bleue et autres contes merveilleux, Calmann-Levy, 1909; translation by D. B. Stewart published as *The Seven Wives of Bluebeard and Other Marvellous Tales,* John Lane, 1920.

Marguerite (first published in *Les Lettres et les arts,* December 1, 1886), Coq, 1920; translation by J. Lewis May, John Lane, 1921.

Le Comte Morin, depute (first published in *La Revue Independante,* December, 1886), Mornay, 1921; translation by J. Lewis May published as *Count Morin, Deputy,* John Lane, 1921.

"PIERRE NOZIERE" SERIES OF AUTOBIOGRAPHICAL STORIES; UNDER NAME ANATOLE FRANCE

Le Livre de mon ami, Calmann-Levy, 1885; translation by J. Lewis May published as *My Friend's Book,* John Lane, 1913.

Pierre Noziere, Lemerre, 1899; translation by J. Lewis May, John Lane, 1916.

Le Petit Pierre, Calmann-Levy, 1918; translation by J. Lewis May published as *Little Pierre,* John Lane, 1920.

La Vie en fleur, Calmann-Levy, 1922; translation by J. Lewis May published as *The Bloom of Life,* Dodd, 1923.

PLAYS; UNDER NAME ANATOLE FRANCE

Au petit bonheur (one-act; first performed in Paris, France, June 1, 1898), Pour Pierre Dauze, 1898.

(With Gaston de Caillavet) "Le Lys rouge" (adapted from his novel of the same title), first performed at Vaudeville Theatre, February 25, 1899.

Crainquebille (three-act; adapted from his short story "L'Affaire Crainquebille"; first performed at Theatre de la Renaissance, March 28, 1903), Calmann-Levy, 1903; translation by Barrett H. Clark published as *Crainquebille: A Comedy,* Samuel French, 1915.

"Le Mannequin d'osier" (adapted from his novel of the same title), first performed at Theatre de la Renaissance, 1904.

La Comedie de celui qui epousa une femme muette (two-act; first published in *L'Illustration,* Christmas, 1908; first performed at Porte-Saint-Martin, May 30, 1912), Calmann-Levy, 1913; translation by Curtis Hidden Page published as *The Man Who Married a Dumb Wife,* John Lane, 1915.

POEMS; UNDER NAME ANATOLE FRANCE

Les Poemes dores (title means "Golden Poems"; includes groups of poems titled "Les Poemes dores" and "Idylles et legendes"), Lemerre, 1873.

Les Noces corinthiennes (dramatic poem), Lemerre, 1876, revised, Pelletan, 1902, revised, Lemerre, 1923; translation by Wilfrid Jackson and Emilie Jackson published as *The Bride* of Corinth in *The Bride of Corinth, and Other Poems and Plays,* John Lane, 1920.

Poesies (includes *Les Poemes Dores* and *Les Noces Corinthiennes*), Lemerre, 1896.

COLLECTED ARTICLES AND SPEECHES; UNDER NAME ANATOLE FRANCE

La Vie litteraire (first published in *Le Temps*), four volumes, Calmann-Levy, 1888-92; published as *On Life and Letters,* Volume I: translation by A. W. Evans, John Lane, 1911, Volume II: translation by A. W. Evans, John Lane, 1914, Volume III: translation by D. B. Stewart, John Lane, 1922, Volume IV: translation by Bernard Miall, Dodd, 1924.

Les Opinions de Monsieur Jerome Coignard (first published in *L'Echo de Paris*), Calmann-Levy, 1893; translation by Mrs. Wilfrid Jackson published as *The Opinions of Jerome Coignard,* John Lane, 1913.

Le Jardin d'Epicure (first published in *Le Temps*), Calmann-Levy, 1895; translation by Alfred Allinson published as *The Garden of Epicurus,* John Lane, 1908.

Opinions sociales (title means "Social Opinions"), two volumes, Bellais, 1902.

Vers les temps meilleurs, Pelletan, 1906; translation by J. Lewis May published as *The Unrisen Dawn: Speeches and Addresses,* Dodd, 1928.

Le Genie latin (prefaces), Lemerre, 1913; translation by Wilfrid S. Jackson published as *The Latin Genius,* Dodd, 1924.

Sur la Voie Glorieuse, Champion, 1915; translation by Alfred Allinson published as *The Path of Glory,* John Lane, 1916.

Prefaces, Introductions, and Other Uncollected Papers, translation by J. Lewis May, John Lane, 1927, Dodd, 1928.

LETTERS; UNDER NAME ANATOLE FRANCE

Lettres inedites d'Anatole France a Jacques Lion, edited by Marie-Claire Bancquart, Societe Anatole France, 1965.

Lettres inedites d'Anatole France a Paul-Louis Couchoud et sa femme, edited by Gerald Bloch, Societe Anatole France, 1968.

Lettres inedites d'Anatole France a Paul Grunebaum-Ballin, edited by Jean Diedisheim, Societe Anatole France, 1971.

Quelques lettres inedites d'Anatole France et de Madame Arman de Caillavet a Charles Maurras, edited by Max Philippe Delatte, Societe Anatole France, 1972.

Anatole France a l'Academie Francaise: lettres inedites, Societe Anatole France, 1975.

Le Secret du 'Lys rouge': Anatole France et Madame de Caillavet; Lettres intimes, 1888-1889, edited by Jacques Suffel, Nizet, 1984.

OTHER; UNDER NAME ANATOLE FRANCE, EXCEPT AS NOTED

Alfred de Vigny (biographical study), Bachelin-Deflorenne, 1868.

(Editor and author of introduction) *Oeuvres de Jean Racine* (anthology), Lemerre, five volumes, 1874-75.

Le Livre du bibliophile, Lemerre, 1874.

(Editor and author of introduction) *Lucile de Chateaubriand* (anthology), Charavay freres, 1879.

Le Chateau de Vaux-le-Vicomte (study), Lemercier, 1888, Calmann-Levy, 1933.

L'Elvire de Lamartine: Notes sur Monsieur et Madame Charles, Champion, 1893.

(With Octave Greard) *Discours prononces dans la seance publique tenue par l'Academie Francaise, pour la reception de Monsieur Anatole France, le 24 decembre 1896,* Firmin-

Didot, 1896, published as *Seance de l'Academie Francaise du 24 decembre 1896: Discours de reception de Anatole France,* Calmann-Levy, 1897.

La Liberte par l'etude, Editions des Cahiers, 1902.

Discours prononce a l'inauguration de la statue d'Ernest Renan, Calmann-Levy, 1903.

L'Eglise et la Republique (essay; title means "The Church and the Republic"), Pelletan, 1904, Pauvert (Utrecht), 1964.

Sur la pierre blanche (philosophical dialogue), Calmann-Levy, 1905; translation by Charles E. Roche published as *The White Stone,* John Lane, 1910.

Vie de Jeanne d'Arc (biography), two volumes, Calmann-Levy, 1908; translation by Winifred Stephens published as *The Life of Joan of Arc,* John Lane, 1909.

(With others) *Aux etudiants,* Pelletan, 1910.

Les Poemes du Souvenir, Pelletan, 1910.

Dernieres pages inedites d'Anatole France, issued by Michel Corday, Calmann-Levy, 1925.

Under the Rose (philosophical dialogues), translation by J. Lewis May, Dodd, 1926.

Les Dieux asiatiques aux premiers siecles de l'ere chretienne, Imprimerie Ducros et Cloas, 1928.

Rabelais (biography), first published in *Oeuvres completes illustres,* 1928 (see below); translation by Ernest Boyd, Holt, 1929.

Associated with *Histoire de France* (title means "History of France"), 1881. Author of introductions to numerous works, including Marquis de Sade, *Dorci; ou, La Bizarrerie du sort,* Charavay, 1881; Marcel Proust, *Les Plaisirs et les jours,* Calmann-Levy, 1896; Paul Grunebaum-Ballin, *La Separation des Eglises et de l'Etat,* Bellais, 1905; Michel Eyquem de Montaigne, *Essais,* J. Povolowsky, 1920; Jack London, *Le Talon de fer,* Cres, 1925.

Contributor to numerous periodicals, including *Le Bibliophile francais illustre, L'Echo de Paris, Le Figaro, L'Humanite, Revue de Paris, Le Temps, L'Univers illustre* (sometimes under house pseudonym Gerome), *La Vogue parisienne.* Member of editorial board of *Le Bibliophile francais illustre* and *Parnasse contemporain;* literary adviser of *L'Humanite.*

COLLECTED WORKS; UNDER NAME ANATOLE FRANCE

Oeuvres completes illustrees, twenty-five volumes, edited by Leon Carias and Gerard Le Prat, Calmann-Levy, 1925-35.

Oeuvres completes, Cercle du Bibliophile, 1968-70.

Oeuvres, four volumes, edited by Marie-Claire Bancquart, Gallimard, 1984-89.

The Works of Anatole France, forty volumes, Gordon Press, 1975.

SIDELIGHTS: Anatole France was principally a lover of the written word whose childhood environment and education had conditioned him to critique others' writings as well as to create his own pieces. His depth of knowledge and critical sense gave him a decided advantage over other French intellectuals of his time. Until the age of forty he was a detached spectator, a humanist, a dilettante using several literary alter egos as his mouthpieces and leading an epicurean life. By the mid-1890s he had built a solid reputation as a novelist and short story writer, a literary critic, and a journalist. At fifty-three, having won literary fame, he suddenly became politically and socially active by opting for the Dreyfusard position in the controversy surrounding the alleged spying by French Army Captain Alfred Dreyfus. Beginning in 1897, he produced his best prose works, which reflected in large part his new commitment to socialism and various left-wing causes. Fleetingly he shared the idealism of leftist

philosophies, but generally his writings bore the stamp of skepticism that often became pessimism expressed with irony, scoring every French institution perceived as oppressive, especially the church. France was an inveterately subjective writer whose work was a sounding board for his ideas. In remarkably clear and elegant language, this turn-of-the-century Voltaire conveyed the message that humans should be free of all fetters; but he held out little hope for the future of mankind. As Jacques Suffel records in *Anatole France par lui-meme,* France once declared, "It is difficult for me to conceive that serious-minded and sensible men entertain the hope of one day making bearable the sojourn on this little sphere which, awkwardly circling the yellow and already half-obscured sun, supports us like a vermin on its decaying surface."

France spent his childhood among the bookstalls lining the quays of Paris and in the quiet setting of the Librairie de France, his father's bookshop, which became a depository for the most important collection of material on the French Revolution then in existence. A host of famous writers, noted historians, assorted book-lovers, and other distinguished clients made the shop a haven and filled young France's ears with stimulating conversations. Although France enjoyed average success during two years at preparatory school in St. Mary's Institute, his seven years at the senior school, the famous College Stanislas secondary school, were painful. His hatred of his stern teachers not only caused him to earn mediocre grades and to fail the *baccalaureat* several times, finally passing it at the embarrassingly advanced age of twenty, but also fostered his lifelong antiauthoritarianism and anticlericalism. Perhaps the only clear benefit of the Stanislas experience was exposure to the classics, which he memorized and adored; but he undoubtedly learned more from observing his fellow Parisians in the streets, from his father's customers, and from the books he voraciously read than he did from his mentors.

France's early occupations included a post as editorial assistant for the publisher Bachelin-Deflorenne and editor and manuscript reader for Alphonse Lemerre. The latter position brought France into contact with the Parnasse poets, who comprised an anti-Romantic, art-for-art's-sake literary movement during the mid-nineteenth century. Since most of the famous Parnasse poets contributed to Lemerre's new journal, *Parnasse contemporain,* France found his way into an important segment of the literary world. Editing meant drudgery and boredom, but reviewing manuscripts was an invaluable experience for an aspiring writer. Even so, he was already looking beyond Lemerre's. France revived an almost defunct periodical, *Le Chasseur bibliographe,* and contributed to others. Determined to earn a reputation as a poet, he used *Le Chasseur* to publish his first lengthy poem of any consequence, "La Legende de Sainte-Thais" ("The Legend of Saint Thais," 1867).

As a member of the Parnasse circle, France entered the social whirl of the Paris salons, especially that of Nina de Villard (Anne-Marie Gaillard, Countess Hector de Callias). France edited her contribution to the second *Parnasse contemporain* collection, which included two of his own poems, thinly-veiled jabs at Emperor Napoleon III; the young writer also engaged in a brief love affair with Nina, which ended when he was physically attacked in a Left Bank cafe by Charles Cros, another Parnassian and a competitor for Nina's affections. In 1869 France's position as a part-time reader at Lemerre's became permanent, and he began to display his talent as a journalist and literary critic by starting his first regular column in the newspaper *Le Rappel.*

France's first collection, *Les Poemes dores* ("Golden Poems"), was published by Lemerre in 1873. Although these poems are generally undistinguished, many of them featured a theme which would recur in France's writings, that of a woman who chooses religion over sexual love. He next completed a five-volume edition of the works of Jean Racine, and his literary judgment was now so trusted that he was promoted from contributor to member of the editorial committee of the third *Parnasse contemporain.* Asserting his newfound authority, he rejected pieces for the new collection by Charles Cros (petty revenge for the Nina de Villard confrontation), by Verlaine, and by Stephane Mallarme (whose famous *Apres-midi d'un faune* [*Afternoon of a Faun*] was cast aside), decisions that would haunt France for the rest of his life. A place in the issue was found for the first part of France's own impressive but not great dramatic poem, *Les Noces corinthiennes* (*The Bride of Corinth*). Published in its entirety by Lemerre the same year (1876), it was admired for its style but impugned for its undisguised sources in Johann Wolfgang von Goethe's *Die Braut von Korinth* (*Bride of Corinth*) and Rene de Chateaubriand's *Atala.* According to Reino Virtanen in *Anatole France,* "France's poem can be read as a neo-pagan reply to Chateaubriand's combination of exotic Romanticism and religiosity," and, in *Anatole France, un sceptique passionne,* Marie-Claire Bancquart terms it "an absolute and passionate rejection of christian morality as one opposed to all natural growth and development."

Eighteen seventy-six marked France's logical transition from objective Parnasse poetry to subjective prose writing. It also saw substantial changes in his professional and personal life. In August of that year he became assistant librarian at the Senate Library for an annual salary of 2,200 francs. His newfound prestige no doubt helped facilitate France's spring, 1877, marriage to Marie-Valerie Guerin de Sauville, who brought with her a dowry of 50,000 francs.

For several years France served as editor and book reviewer for small magazines; after 1875, he had acquired sufficient repute to be welcomed as a contributor and literary critic by the more respected and widely circulated periodicals. In 1878 France decided to move from Lemerre to the more prestigious publishing house of Calmann-Levy, yet he incredibly signed conflicting contracts with both, sparking a lawsuit with Lemerre that was finally resolved, in France's favor, in 1911. Calmann-Levy became his primary publisher and from 1888 to 1892 published a four-volume collection of critical essays from one of France's columns, *La Vie litteraire* ("Literary Life"), which had appeared originally in *Le Temps.* Although the 300-odd articles revealed the writer's erudition, their style and tone were casual, even nonchalant. Despite inconsistencies, prejudices, and deliberate subjectivity, these essays were generally viewed as authoritative. France wrote in the preface to *La Vie litteraire:* "The good critic is the one who tells about the adventures of his soul among the masterpieces." Suffel declares in *Anatole France par lui-meme* that France "truly knew how to judge most of the great writers of the century, by recognizing the strong and the weak points, by showing their influence." Lemerre published his critical prefaces in 1913 as *Le Genie latin* ("The Latin Genius").

France's career as a storyteller really began in 1878. From that time on much of his prose fiction appeared first in the pages of leading periodicals before being expanded and published as books. He was as much a subjective writer of prose fiction as he was a subjective critic, contended Suffel, who wrote that France "romanticizes the story of his life and of his feelings, constantly mixing fiction with reality." Short stories, novellas, and novels were the major thrust of his writing career.

In 1881 Calmann-Levy published *Le Crime de Sylvestre Bonnard* (*The Crime of Sylvestre Bonnard*). It was a revision of two short stories that had already been serialized in Paris journals. He made them share a principal character, a type whose personal qualities were those of the old scholarly gentlemen who had been his father's customers, and thus created his first really successful novel. A lyrical hymn to Paris, the book conveys a message of moderation in living, of a Montaigne-like concept of human happiness, epicurean but reasonable. Although *Bonnard* was popular, it could not successfully challenge naturalism or survive the test of time. Yet it brought France recognition from colleagues such as Maurice Barres, Jules Lemaitre, Renan, and Taine; and it earned him an Academy prize.

Lemerre, with legal support, confiscated *Histoire de France* ("History of France") as part of the 1878 contract and, once the rights were confirmed, postponed its publication. Because it was necessary to appease Lemerre, smarting from the success of *Bonnard,* France paid his debt by reworking *Les Desirs de Jean Servien* (*The Aspirations of Jean Servien*), a tale of the Franco-Prussian war and the Paris Commune, which he had drafted and cast aside a decade earlier. Lemerre published the short novel in 1882, but its moment had clearly passed. Although this and other early post-*Bonnard* works commanded little attention, France's impact on French literary life during the early 1880s was enough that in 1884 he was named a chevalier in the French Legion of Honor.

Success had a profound effect on France's personal and professional life, giving him full access to French cultural circles. Paris boasted several prominent literary salons at the time, one of the most influential being that of Madame Albert Arman de Caillavet (Leontine Lippmann) at 12 avenue Hoche. From the time he first visited her home in 1883, France was strongly attracted to the witty, charming Madame Arman, who had agreed with her husband, in the early 1870s, to live independent lives under the same roof. By 1888 France had become the central figure not only in Leontine's salon but also in her private life. His relationship with his pretentious and overbearing wife, Valerie, had been foundering in spite of his closeness to his frail and affectionate little daughter Suzanne. France finally left his wife in 1892, and when his 1893 divorce freed him of his domestic concerns, it also liberated his muse. His relationship with Leontine signaled the beginning of the most intense and creative years of his life. At the age of forty-eight, France moved first to an apartment on the rue de Sontay and then in 1894 to a mansion he purchased at 5 villa Said, which would remain his official home for twenty years. However, he spent most of his time at Leontine's residence, where he took all his meals despite the presence of his mistress's husband and son and where Madame Arman even provided a private study and library next to her bedroom. Being able to work in a quiet atmosphere and to help her entertain the country's most prominent writers at Sunday soirees was, for France, the ultimate in convenience and opportunity. Except for one brief fling with an actress in 1909, France was loyal to Leontine until her death.

France's next real success following *The Crime of Sylvestre Bonnard* was the first of four autobiographical stories. *Le Livre de mon ami* (*My Friend's Book*) painted scenes of childhood domestic bliss in Second Empire Paris. The publication in 1889 of *Balthasar,* a collection of strange tales, closed out France's fiction-writing activities in the 1880s.

The 1890s were years of intense literary production for France; most of his truly significant short story collections and novels appeared during that decade. As early as 1888, installments of an exotic tale of an Egyptian monk's passion for an actress—her progressive sanctification and his moral degradation—had appeared in *La Revue des deux mondes;* France had needed the influence of his mistress to convince the editor, who mercilessly cut the text, to accept it. This descendant of Flaubert's *Tentation de Saint Antoine (The Temptation of Saint Anthony,* 1874), replete with sensualism and religious skepticism, originally bore the monk's name, *Paphnuce,* but Calmann-Levy gave it the more phonetically appealing heroine's name, *Thais,* when it was produced in book form in 1890. Inspired by one of France's early poems and other background writings, the poignant love story was a colossal success in its time, made even more so when it became the basis for composer Jules Massenet's opera and played at the Paris Opera House beginning in March, 1894. In *Anatole France, un sceptique passionne,* Bancquart calls *Thais* "the novel of sensual coming-of-age, and the release from a great haunting fear of sexual failure." Two significant short story collections also reached the French public during the 1890s. The first, *L'Etui de nacre (Mother of Pearl,* 1892), included sixteen stories, several of them tales of the Revolution. Although as a whole the book was less than impressive, two historical legends steeped in irony are recognized as masterpieces of the genre: "Le Procurateur de Judee" ("The Procurator of Judea"), depicting the Crucifixion, and "Le Jongleur de Notre Dame" ("The Juggler of Notre Dame"), a charming Christmas fable. The second collection, *Le Puits de Sainte Claire (The Well of Saint Claire),* published in 1895, contained eleven stories. The background of these tales was drawn from France's 1893 Italian "honeymoon" with Leontine; the inspiration of these stories came from historical events and legends of Italy, and their tone was satirical and anticlerical.

For Anatole France, the 1890s were most significant because they were years of transition from a passive creative writer and literary critic to an active, committed, politically oriented author and social critic. French politics in the 1890s witnessed a rise in leftist activity, and France's political and social opinions found their expression in several very successful books. In October of 1892 he contributed to *L'Echo de Paris* the first of fifty-four installments of *La Rotisserie de la Reine Pedauque (At the Sign of the Queen Pedauque),* which draws its title from the name of a small restaurant where the action takes place. Published in book form in March, 1893, this widely acclaimed novel introduced the character of epicurean and scholar Jerome Coignard, a lecherous, drunken abbe reminiscent of the sixteenth-century French novelist Francois Rabelais. The cleric's bizarre eighteenth-century adventures, which combine comedy, mystery, philosophy, and the occult, provided a context for France's opinions on contemporary problems. A varied cast of supporting characters, an assortment of historical figures including Voltaire and Denis Diderot, and a rich style result in a masterpiece of wit and irony exposing France's humanistic and liberal attitudes. Like Sylvestre Bonnard and later Monsieur Bergeret, Coignard is his author's alter ego, whose adventures are told by the grill owner's son, protagonist Jacques Tournebroche. Suffel says in *Anatole France par lui-meme:* "Here finally is a broad narrative, rich in colors, full of variety and cheer, cast in magnificent language. And this book is something else: a sort of crucible into which all of the eighteenth-century . . . seems to have been melted and poured, to compose a porcelain of incomparable brilliance."

While he was composing *At the Sign of the Queen Pedauque,* France was rapidly writing a series of columns bearing the title *Les Opinions de Monsieur Jerome Coignard (The Opinions of Jerome Coignard)* for publication in *L'Echo de Paris* every two weeks. These essays attacked social and political policies of the

Third Republic, especially the ascendancy of capitalism, by deploring the excesses of the Bourbon kings and of the French Revolution. Since the author blamed religious, political, military, and judicial authorities for his country's social ills, the essays revealed his increasing compassion for the common man and his struggle for freedom. *The Opinions,* collected in one volume and published by Calmann-Levy in the fall of 1893 as a sequel to *At the Sign of the Queen Pedauque,* fully established France's reputation as a social critic.

During a visit to Florence in 1893, Madame Arman decided that France should write a novel treating their relationship. From the idea came the writer's first novel of contemporary society, a work originally titled "La Terre des morts" ("The Land of the Dead") but later retitled *Le Lys rouge (The Red Lily),* for the scarlet lily on Florence's coat of arms. Leontine believed that Paris was the only logical setting for most of the book's intrigue but that Florence and its romantic memories also should be represented in what she termed "their" novel. There is obviously much autobiographical material in the sensual love story of Jacques Dechartre and Therese Martin-Belleme. Though it seemed atypical of its author and was marred by some pretentious dialogue, the book, published in July, 1894, was received with enthusiasm by the critics and the reading public. *The Red Lily* proved to be the most successful of France's books to date because of the sincerity of its love story and its only incidental political and social commentary.

Conditions in 1897 intensified France's interest in social issues. A writer who had long condemned political fanatics from either end of the spectrum, he particularly hated discrimination, especially that practiced by the Catholic church, and many of his writings had already included anticlerical barbs. To express his views in that area, he began publishing in 1897 a series of scenes of provincial intrigue focusing on a power struggle to name the bishop of a diocese. Many of the slice-of-life anecdotes were not structured for dramatic impact, and some even had no denouement. Instead of drawing on ideas derived from books or from his imagination, the author, for the first time, created intensely realistic situations based on observation. Collected under the general title "Histoire contemporaine" ("Contemporary History"), which Suffel terms "a broad fresco, powerfully realistic," the scenes offer a panoramic view of French social life. The collection's four volumes—*L'Orme du mail (The Elm-Tree on the Mall,* 1897), *Le Mannequin d'osier (The Wicker Work Woman,* 1897; adapted as a stage play in 1904), *L'Anneau d'amethyste (The Amethyst Ring,* 1899), and *Monsieur Bergeret a Paris (Monsieur Bergeret in Paris,* 1901)—really constitute a new type of novel. Presenting a microcosm of French society of the late 1890s, the works create a series of well-defined characters that are mostly unsympathetic prototypes. The erudite but self-effacing professor and philosopher, Lucien Bergeret, who is the sole exception to this rule, has become a classic literary character.

The first two volumes, published in 1897, contain a large dose of political statement as well as autobiographical content. The political, social, and military circles described are precisely those forming the backdrop for the Dreyfus affair. The case had been reopened several months earlier when suspicion of having divulged military secrets to the Prussians shifted from Captain Dreyfus, who had been condemned to Devil's Island in 1894, to another French Army officer, Major Ferdinand Walsin Esterhazy. During the fall of 1897 the polarization of the French nation over the issue was at its most acute. As he began to compose *The Amethyst Ring,* Anatole France had not publicly sided with the right or the left, but suddenly his social and political conscience was awakened. Possibly conditioned by his association with members of Paris's Jewish community, notably Madame Arman and Marcel Proust, France abruptly committed to the left, to socialism, and to the fight against anti-Semitism when he heard Zola explain the position he assumed in his famous letter "J'Accuse." France was compelled publicly to endorse Zola's Dreyfusard position and later to testify on his behalf at Zola's trial for libel, though such other prominent writers as Alphonse Daudet and Francois Coppee and most of the French academicians took the nationalist view. The affair led him to scorn the Legion of Honor, in which he was then an officer, and boycott the *Institut.*

From a passive cynic, Anatole France had become an active liberal who would henceforth speak out publicly for a variety of socialist causes even though his stance cost him many friendships. The Dreyfus case and France's newly adopted militant attitude also affected his work. The ecclesiastical intrigue of *The Amethyst Ring,* the third volume of "Contemporary History," reflects the Dreyfus affair as Bergeret defends the cause with surprising vigor, and the fourth volume, *Monsieur Bergeret in Paris,* can be regarded as a pure socialist outcry. The stepped-up irony and political satire of the second half of "Contemporary History" overshadowed the novels' charm and subtle wit. France's sustained support was to be rewarded when in the summer of 1906 Alfred Dreyfus, reinstated as an officer of the French Army, was admitted to the Legion of Honor.

In 1904 Jean Jaures founded *L'Humanite,* which soon became socialism's leading newspaper and which, by 1921, had turned to communism. France, who was immediately appointed literary adviser, contributed to *L'Humanite* until just before his death. His first column was a long political and philosophical dialogue that became *Sur la pierre blanche* (*The White Stone,* 1905), a utopian fantasy attempting unsuccessfully to recapture the eloquence of *The Opinions of Jerome Coignard. The White Stone* presents dialogues from the past, present, and future, in which speakers confront the futures of their own particular eras. The conversations—from Roman antiquity, the twentieth century, and the twenty-third century—preach political, religious, economic, and social messages that reflect France's optimistic albeit uncertain positions at the time. Though in 1907 he began work on a socialist novel, "Victor Mainvielle" (later abandoned), his hopes for a better socialist world had already been shattered by Czar Nicholas II's repression of Russian revolutionaries in 1905.

France's writings for the remainder of the decade attempted to escape contemporary reality, to divorce his creative efforts from his political activism, often through a return to medieval subjects. His first project of this sort was a venture into historical writing, his *Vie de Jeanne d'Arc* (*The Life of Joan of Arc,* 1908). He had for twenty-five years been preparing the story, but the effort was doomed to failure. A critic proud of his subjective approach and a scholar who, despite his erudition, was always hard-pressed to organize his content could hardly be expected to produce an objective historical work. After four years and more than a thousand pages in two volumes, France's obvious anticlerical effort to remove the legendary halo and the supernatural aura from Joan of Arc foundered for many reasons. His attempt to humanize her displeased both the Catholics who considered her a saint and the free-thinkers who looked on her as a patriot; historians rejected it as valid biographical history because, though entertaining, it lacked focus, drew few logical conclusions, and contained many errors.

The failure of his try at serious history was a disappointment for France, but he took refuge in *L'Ile des pingouins* (*Penguin Island,* 1908), a burlesque epic saga of a civilization of penguins that satirically ranged from the beginning of time to the future, cleverly held up history itself to ridicule, and made everybody forget *The Life of Joan of Arc.* Though *Penguin Island* reduced the past to absurdity and offered an extremely pessimistic view of the future, it was a great success.

During the first decade of the twentieth century France's personal life was marked by difficulties. In 1899, to fulfill the still unresolved contract with Lemerre, he hurriedly collected scenes from his childhood that had appeared in magazines since 1890 and allowed Lemerre to publish them as *Pierre Noziere,* the second of his purely autobiographical works. The next year his daughter Suzanne made the first of two troubled marriages, the complications of which caused a schism between her and France that remained unresolved when Suzanne died in 1917. Moreover, by 1904 Madame Arman's health was declining; France's dependency on her had been reduced by his association with Jaures, and he had transferred most of his professional activity, writing, and entertaining to the Villa Said from the avenue Hoche mansion where he now just took his meals. As time wore on, Madame Arman became increasingly suspicious and with good reason, for her lover was, in fact, beginning to stray. To escape the temper tantrums and violent arguments, he accepted an invitation to make an all-expenses-paid lecture tour in South America. From May to August, 1909, enthusiastic but small audiences in Brazil, Argentina, and Uruguay heard his lectures on Rabelais and Auguste Comte, but the major excitement came from France's scandalous affair with a middle-aged actress, Jeanne Brindeau, a member of the touring Comedie Francaise troupe. The Brindeau affair ended as soon as the party returned home, and France spent weeks trying to rekindle his relationship with Madame Arman. When she died in January, 1910, France's grief was deep and sincere; by December of that year, however, he felt free enough to invite Emma Laprevotte, one of Madame Arman's maids, to live with him.

The years with Emma were extremely productive ones as France composed the most masterful works of his career. Though several chapters of two books, *Les Dieux ont soif* (*The Gods Are Athirst,* 1912) and *La Revolte des anges* (*The Revolt of the Angels,* 1913-14), had already been drafted before Leontine's death, they were essentially composed after 1910. *The Gods Are Athirst,* which borrowed its title from Camille Desmoulins, a famous journalist of the Revolution, was the best structured and most impressive of all France's fictional works. Its success derived in part from the youthful hours France had spent absorbing details of the French Revolution as he worked the card file of his father's bookstore. Bancquart declares the novel "a work which is scrupulously accurate even in its chronology and its locales . . . attempting to balance the fictitious subject matter with the cultural elements with which it is fraught." France also set aside his usual ironic tone and, combining clearly delineated characters with well-conducted intrigue, effectively told the tragic story of Evariste Gamelin. Where he had failed with legitimate history, he succeeded with the historical novel. Suffel announces that "the work is warm, sensitive, pulsating with life," calling it "a painting produced with incomparable vigor and richness of color." Critics and the reading public have justifiably acclaimed *The Gods Are Athirst* as France's best effort and one of the greatest French novels.

The Revolt of the Angels was to *The Gods Are Athirst* what *Penguin Island* had been to *The Life of Joan of Arc;* the recreation of a historical reality coincided with the invention of a fantasy tale of epic proportions. *The Revolt of the Angels* portrayed angels reduced to the human condition and plotting a second revolt where modern military methods would insure victory and avenge Lucifer's original defeat. French society and its institutions were again fair game for the writer's satirical barbs, especially the church and its belief in the intervention of angels in human existence. This new parody, an even greater commercial success than *The Gods Are Athirst,* showed once more that one of France's greatest strengths was his ability to spin an excellent, Voltaire-like philosophical tale, steeped in wit and irony. His books reflected a pervading pessimism that did not square with the idealism of his socialist colleagues; he found it hard to believe in the socialist recipe for a better world because of his conviction that man was essentially evil.

France compensated for his nondoctrinaire attitude by militantly supporting socialism as the clouds of war gathered over Europe. Proclaiming in a speech in London in 1913, "I am a socialist because socialism is justice, I am a socialist because socialism is truth," he served the cause by defending individuals, traveling to Russia, Germany, and Austria, attending socialist functions, participating in demonstrations, and continuing to write for *L'Humanite.* Sure that socialism would produce restraint, he vigorously promoted peace and preached tolerance. In that effort, he added his prestige and voice to that of Jaures, who was tirelessly pleading with his fellow citizens to avoid war. Unfortunately, many French nationalists considered proponents of peace unpatriotic. When a fanatic assassinated Jaures in the summer of 1914 and the initial battles of World War I were in progress, France was overwhelmed with grief but still found it impossible to abandon his dream of a peaceful world.

After the bombardment of the cathedral at Reims France answered a request to bolster the people's spirits with an encouraging message in the periodical *La Guerre sociale,* concluding, "when we have conquered the last army and reduced the last fortress to ashes, we shall proclaim that the French people accept as friends the vanquished enemy." Such a declaration, which seemed at best weakness and at worst treason, generated a hail of insults, even threats, and nearly destroyed the man who had been the country's leading author. A pathetic, futile effort to explain his stance, followed by thoughts of suicide and a ludicrous attempt to enlist in the army at the age of seventy, left him exhausted, emotionally drained, physically ill, and truly a broken man.

During the following months, France gradually regained his health and control of his life. He composed a series of articles, collected under the title *Sur la Voie Glorieuse (The Path of Glory)* in 1915, intended to illustrate his patriotism; proceeds from the book's sale were designated for wounded French soldiers. As the war raged in the north, France spent more than two years renovating his newly purchased home at Saint-Cyr-sur-Loire near Tours, acquiring surrounding buildings, settling down with his possessions, and caring for Emma's precarious health. Life was peaceful enough for him to work on the third book in his autobiographical series, *Le Petit Pierre (Little Pierre),* published in 1918 and warmly received by his war-weary fellow citizens. He was keenly aware of the happenings in the capital and even saw fit in 1916 to attend an Academy meeting for the first time in fifteen years. He regained his position in the mainstream of French cultural life, and by 1918 his Sunday afternoon receptions attracted prominent people from throughout France.

After the armistice Anatole France was again plunged into politics. Jaures's assassin, who had committed the crime five years earlier and whose guilt the evidence overwhelmingly supported,

was not tried until 1919. When the murderer was incredibly acquitted, France was incensed and again became active in the League of the Rights of Man, renewing his ties with the party and with *L'Humanite.* Without being fully aware of the implications of the action, he found himself linked to the new Communist party in 1920 but, by 1922, though he still embraced the leftist philosophy, he balked at dictatorial demands that French intellectuals submit to party discipline. His last significant political act was to contribute the essay "Salut aux Soviets" ("Greetings to the Soviets") to the front page of *L'Humanite* in 1922 to celebrate the fifth anniversary of the Russian Revolution. In 1924, just before he died, he decided that the socialists and communists over the years had exploited his prestige, and he disavowed his political ties.

France's nonpolitical literary activities during his final years amounted to an essay on Stendhal in the *Revue de Paris* in 1920 and the fourth and last volume of the autobiographical Pierre Noziere series on his youth, *La Vie en fleur (The Bloom of Life),* published in 1922. Honors continued to come to him, notably the prestigious Nobel Prize for literature in 1921. Although the Catholic church placed all his works on the Index of Forbidden Books in 1922, his personal life at last conformed to accepted social standards. He returned to the rebuilt Villa Said in 1920 and later in the year married Emma. His books were immensely popular; royalties and translation income and play and film rights insured a comfortable existence. His old age was made more tolerable by the presence of Suzanne's son, his only grandchild, Lucien Psichari, then in his teens. From 1922 on France's health steadily declined. His eightieth birthday brought wishes from all over the world, but in August, 1924, he became bedridden until his death on October 12. A national funeral in Paris was followed by burial at Neuilly. A suitable epitaph might be Suffel's comment in *Anatole France par lui-meme:* "Never was a Frenchman more French than this left-bank Parisian."

MEDIA ADAPTATIONS: Le Crime de Sylvestre Bonnard was adapted as a play by Pierre Frondaie, published in 1918, as a film, [France], 1929, and as the film "Chasing Yesterday," RKO, 1935; *Thais* was adapted as an opera with music by Jules Massenet and libretto by Louis Gallet, Calmann-Levy, 1894, translated by Charles Alfred Byrne, Burden (New York), 1907, and as films, [France], 1911, Goldwyn, 1917; *La Rotisserie de la Reine Pedauque* was adapted as a play by Georges Ducqois, Calmann-Levy, 1920; "L'Affaire Crainquebille" was adapted as films, [France], 1922 and 1934, and as the film "Mort aux vaches," [France], 1953.

BIOGRAPHICAL/CRITICAL SOURCES:

BOOKS

Axelrad, Jacob, *Anatole France: A Life Without Illusions, 1844-1924,* Harper, 1944.

Bancquart, Marie-Claire, *Anatole France, un sceptique passionne,* Calmann-Levy, 1984.

Bresky, Duskan, *The Art of Anatole France,* Mouton (The Hague), 1969.

Carias, Leon, *Anatole France,* Rieder, 1931.

Cerf, Barry, *Anatole France: The Degeneration of a Great Artist,* Dial Press, 1926.

Chevalier, Haakon M., *The Ironic Temper: Anatole France and His Time,* Oxford University Press, 1932.

Dargan, Edwin Preston, *Anatole France: 1844-1896,* Oxford University Press, 1937.

Jefferson, Carter, *Anatole France: The Politics of Skepticism,* Rutgers University Press, 1965.

May, James Lewis, *Anatole France, the Man and His Work,* Lane, 1924.

McEwen, Marjorie Richards, *Anatole France in the United States,* Edwards Brothers (Ann Arbor), 1945.

Sachs, Murray, *Anatole France: The Short Stories,* Edward Arnold, 1974.

Shanks, Lewis Piaget, *Anatole France: The Mind and the Man,* Harper, 1932.

Smith, Helen B., *The Skepticism of Anatole France,* Presses Universitaires de France, 1927.

Stewart, Herbert L., *Anatole France the Parisian,* Dodd, 1927.

Suffel, Jacques, *Anatole France,* Editions du Myrte, 1946.

Suffel, Jacques, editor, *Anatole France par lui-meme,* Seuil, 1954.

Twentieth-Century Literary Criticism, Gale, Volume 9, 1983.

Tylden-Wright, David, *Anatole France,* Walker, 1967.

Virtanen, Reino, *Anatole France,* Twayne, 1968.

Walton, Loring Baker, *Anatole France and the Greek World,* Duke University Press, 1950.

PERIODICALS

Conradiana, summer, 1983.
History Today, November, 1975.
Journal of the History of Ideas, January, 1972.
Nation, November 5, 1924, April 22, 1944.
New Republic, September 7, 1932, December 7, 1932, October 24, 1934.
New York Times, April 23, 1944.
Nineteenth-Century French Studies, fall-winter, 1976-77.
PMLA, March, 1932.
Revue de Paris, December 1, 1924.
Romanic Review, October, 1942, December, 1970.
Le Soir (Brussels), September 2, 1950.
Times Literary Supplement, September 29, 1966.

*   *   *

THOMAS, Audrey (Callahan) 1935-

PERSONAL: Born November 17, 1935, in Binghamton, NY; daughter of Donald Earle (a teacher) and Frances (Corbett) Callahan; married Ian Thomas (a sculptor and art teacher), December 6, 1958 (divorced, 1978); children: Sarah, Victoria, Claire. *Education:* Smith College, B.A., 1957; University of British Columbia, M.A., 1963, currently doctoral candidate in English.

ADDRESSES: Home—R.R. #2, Galiano Island, British Columbia V0N 1P0, Canada.

CAREER: Writer. Visiting assistant professor of creative writing, Concordia University, 1978; visiting professor of creative writing, University of Victoria, 1978-79; writer in residence, Simon Fraser University, 1981-82, University of Ottawa, 1987.

MEMBER: PEN, Writers Union of Canada, Federation of British Columbia Writers.

AWARDS, HONORS: CBC Literary Competition, second prize for fiction, 1980, second prize for memoirs, 1981; second prize for fiction, National Magazine Awards, 1980; second prize, Chatelaine Fiction Competition, 1981; senior Canadian-Scotland literary fellowship, Edinburgh University.

WRITINGS:

NOVELS

Mrs. Blood (also see below), Bobbs-Merrill, 1970.
Munchmeyer and Prospero on the Island, Bobbs-Merrill, 1972.
Songs My Mother Taught Me, Bobbs-Merrill, 1973.
Blown Figures, Talonbooks (Vancouver), 1974, Knopf, 1975.

Latakia, Talonbooks, 1979.
Intertidal Life, Beaufort Books, 1984.

RADIO PLAYS

(With Linda Sorenson and Keith Pepper) *Once Your Submarine Cable Is Gone, What Have You Got?,* first broadcast on Canadian Broadcasting Corp. (CBC-Radio), October 27, 1973.

Mrs. Blood, first broadcast on CBC-Radio, August 16, 1975.
Untouchables, first broadcast on CBC-Radio, December 5, 1981.
The Milky Way, first broadcast on CBC-Radio, November 26, 1983.
The Axe of God, first broadcast as part of *Disasters! Act of God or Acts of Man?,* CBC-Radio, February 24, 1985.
The Woman in Black Velvet, first broadcast on CBC-Radio, May 17, 1985.
In the Groove, first broadcast on CBC-Radio, November 4, 1985.
On the Immediate Level of Events Occurring in Meadows, first broadcast as part of *Sextet,* CBC-Radio, January 26, 1986.

Also author of five other radio plays.

SHORT STORY COLLECTIONS

Ten Green Battles, Bobbs-Merrill, 1967.
Ladies & Escorts, Oberon (Ottawa), 1977.
Real Mothers, Talonbooks, 1981.
Goodbye Harold, Good Luck, Viking/Penguin, 1986.

OTHER

Contributor of short stories to periodicals, including *Atlantic, Maclean's, Saturday Night, Toronto Life, Capilano Review, Fiddlehead, Canadian Literature,* and *Interface.*

SIDELIGHTS: An American-born Canadian author of novels, short stories, and radio plays, Audrey Thomas has won a number of literary prizes, yet, as Urjo Kareda observes in *Saturday Night,* "somehow she has never achieved her rightful place in the hierarchy of Canada's best writers. Her writing tends to be racier, ruder, more raw than that of her contemporaries in the Ontario-centered, female-dominated literary establishment." Thomas's work, as a number of critics have noted, is autobiographical in nature, and displays an interest in feminism and a love of experimentation, both with language and literary devices. Employing these techniques in a number of different ways to shed light on her common theme of personal isolation and loneliness, the author has said that her stories are about "the terrible gap between men and women," quotes Margaret Atwood in her *Second Words: Selected Critical Prose.* But she also sometimes expands this theme of separation to involve children, who are often the casualties in broken marriages. *Saturday Night* contributor Eleanor Wachtel maintains that as a writer who reveals these "politics of the family, . . . Audrey Thomas [is] one of [our] most astute commentators."

A divorced mother of three children, Thomas is well acquainted with the problems of family life about which she writes. Having once resided in Ghana during the 1960s, she also "likes to tell her stories of Americans or Canadians set down in an alien culture so that their problems will appear more starkly," writes *Open Letter* critic George Bowering. The author's first novel, *Mrs. Blood,* is about one such character who suffers a miscarriage while living in Africa. It is a stream-of-consciousness novel in which the protagonist, Isobel Cleary, while lying in the hospital, contemplates the problems of her marriage and her painful affair with another man. Critics like Joan Caldwell, a *Canadian Literature* reviewer, have been particularly impressed by the writing skills demonstrated in this first effort. "*Mrs. Blood* is accomplished writing," praised Caldwell; "it does not bear the marks of a first novel and it must surely not be Audrey Thomas's last."

Thomas has written two sequels to *Mrs. Blood, Songs My Mother Taught Me* and *Blown Figures.* The first of these takes Isobel back to her childhood, an unhappy time in her life during which she is caught between her parents—an "inadequate man and [a] compulsive angry woman," describes *Saturday Night* contributor Anne Montagnes. Longing for love, Isobel does not find happiness until she gets a job at an asylum, where, as Constance Rooke relates in the *Dictionary of Literary Biography,* "she learns something of compassion and something of the madness which has been concealed in her family. Finally, she chooses to be vulnerable." The subject of madness is also a part of *Blown Figures,* which takes up the story of Isobel with her return to Africa to find the body of her miscarried baby. "She is now clearly schizophrenic and addresses many of her remarks to a Miss Miller—an imaginary confidante," remarks Rooke. "Blatantly experimental, *Blown Figures* has numerous nearly blank pages which serve to isolate the fragments (cartoons, one-liners, and so forth) which appear here. The novel depends heavily on Africa as a metaphor for the unconscious." "In hands less skillful than Miss Thomas's," praises Atwood in a *New York Times Book Review* article, "such devices could spell tedious experimentation for its own sake, self-indulgence, or chaos. But she is enormously skillful, and instead of being a defeating pile of confusions 'Blown Figures' is amazingly easy to read."

The other three novels that Thomas has written, *Munchmeyer and Prospero on the Island, Latakia,* and *Intertidal Life,* all concern male-female relationships and also share in common protagonists who are women writers. These characters, reports Wayne Grady in *Books in Canada,* are all "trying to come to terms in their books with the fact that they have been rejected by men who have loved them." Of these books, critics have generally found *Intertidal Life,* the story of a woman named Alice whose husband leaves her after fourteen years of marriage, to be the most significant effort. Grady calls *Intertidal Life* "undoubtedly Thomas's best novel to date." And although Kareda feels that this novel "doesn't rank with Audrey Thomas's finest writing," he asserts that ". . . its desire to reach us, to tell so much, to keep questioning, are the strengths of an exceptional, expressive will."

Thomas, according to Alberto Manguel's *Village Voice* review, also seems to resolve an issue that was raised in her earlier work. *Intertidal Life,* he says, "appears as the culmination of the search for a character that was never quite defined before. Perhaps in the much-neglected *Blown Figures* or in *Songs My Mother Taught Me,* there are sketchier versions of Alice circling the primary question: Who am I? In *Intertidal Life* the question is answered." Rooke explains further that, in being separated from her husband, Alice is able to assert her independence while overcoming her feelings of isolation by becoming "inextricably involved with others and most particularly with [her] female friends and children."

The themes that Thomas explores in her novels are also echoed in her short story writing, which, along with the work she has done for radio, has amounted to a large ouevre since the 1970s. But, laments Atwood in her book, despite this concerted effort and "its ambition, range and quality, she has not yet received the kind of recognition such a body of work merits, perhaps because she is that cultural hybrid, an early-transplanted American. Of course her work has flaws; everyone's does. She can be sentimen-

tal, repetitious, and sometimes merely gossipy. But page for page, she is one of [Canada's] best writers."

BIOGRAPHICAL/CRITICAL SOURCES:

BOOKS

Atwood, Margaret, *Second Words: Selected Critical Prose,* House of Anansi, 1982.
Authors in the News, Volume 2, Gale, 1976.
Contemporary Literary Criticism, Gale, Volume 7, 1977, Volume 13, 1980, Volume 37, 1986.
Dictionary of Literary Biography, Volume 60: *Canadian Writers since 1960, Second Series,* Gale, 1987.

PERIODICALS

Books in Canada, December, 1979; February, 1982; May, 1985.
Canadian Forum, May-June, 1974; June-July, 1980.
Canadian Literature, autumn, 1971; summer, 1975.
Fiddlehead, January, 1983.
Globe and Mail (Toronto), April 16, 1977; April 18, 1987.
Los Angeles Times Book Review, February 10, 1985.
New York Times Book Review, February 1, 1976.
Open Letter, summer, 1976.
Saturday Night, July, 1972; May, 1974; April, 1982; January, 1985.
Village Voice, August 6, 1985.
Wascana Review, fall, 1976.

—*Sketch by Kevin S. Hile*

*   *   *

THOMAS, D(onald) M(ichael) 1935-

PERSONAL: Born January 27, 1935, in Redruth, Cornwall, England; son of Harold Redvers (a builder) and Amy (a housewife; maiden name, Moyle) Thomas; children: Caitlin, Sean, Ross. *Education:* New College, Oxford, B.A. (with first class honors), 1958, M.A., 1961.

ADDRESSES: Home—10 Greyfriars Ave., Hereford, England. *Agent*—John Johnson, Clerkenwell Green, London ECR 0HT, England.

CAREER: Grammar school English teacher in Teignmouth, Devonshire, England, 1960-64; Hereford College of Education, Hereford, England, lecturer, 1964-66, senior lecturer in English, 1966-79, head of department, 1977-79; writer, 1979—. Visiting lecturer in English, Hamline University, 1967; visiting professor of literature, American University, spring, 1982 (resigned). *Military service:* British Army, two years.

MEMBER: Bard of the Cornish Gorseth.

AWARDS, HONORS: Richard Hilary Award, 1960; Translators award from British Arts Council, 1975, for translations of works by Anna Akhmatova; Chomondeley Award, 1978, for poetry; *Guardian*-Gollancz Fantasy Novel Award, 1979, for *The Flute-Player;* Cheltenham Prize, *Los Angeles Times* Book Award, and Booker McConnell Prize nomination, all 1981, all for *The White Hotel.*

WRITINGS:

POETRY

Personal and Possessive, Outposts, 1964.
(With Peter Redgrove and D. M. Black) *Modern Poets 11,* Penguin, 1968.
Two Voices, Grossman, 1968.
Lover's Horoscope: Kinetic Poem, Purple Sage, 1970.

Logan Stone, Grossman, 1971.
The Shaft, Arc, 1973.
Symphony in Moscow, Keepsake Press, 1974.
Lilith-Prints, Second Aeon Publications, 1974.
Love and Other Deaths, Merrimack Book Service, 1975.
The Honeymoon Voyage, Secker & Warburg, 1978.
Protest: A Poem after a Medieval Armenian Poem by Frik, privately printed, 1980.
Dreaming in Bronze, Secker & Warburg, 1981.
Selected Poems, Viking, 1983.
(With Sylvia Kantaris) *News from the Front,* Arc, 1983.

FICTION

The Devil and the Floral Dance (juvenile), Robson, 1978.
The Flute-Player (novel), Dutton, 1979.
Birthstone (novel), Gollancz, 1980.
The White Hotel (novel; also see below), Gollancz, 1980, Viking, 1981.
Ararat (first novel in "The Russian Quartet"), Viking, 1983.
Swallow (second novel in "The Russian Quartet"), Viking, 1984.
Sphinx (third novel in "The Russian Quartet"), Gollancz, 1986, Viking, 1987.
Summit (fourth novel in "The Russian Quartet"), Gollancz, 1987, Viking, 1988.

EDITOR

The Granite Kingdom: Poems of Cornwall, Barton, 1970.
Poetry in Crosslight (textbook), Longman, 1975.
Songs from the Earth: Selected Poems of John Harris, Cornish Miner 1820-84, Lodenek Press, 1977.

TRANSLATOR

Anna Akhmatova, *Requiem, and Poem without a Hero,* Ohio University Press, 1976.
Akhmatova, *Way of All the Earth,* Ohio University Press, 1979.
Yevgeny Yevtushenko, *Invisible Threads,* Macmillan, 1981.
Alexander Pushkin, *The Bronze Horseman,* Viking, 1982.
Yevtushenko, *A Dove in Santiago,* Viking, 1983.
Akhmatova, *You Will Hear Thunder: Poems,* Ohio University Press, 1985.
Akhmatova, *Selected Poems,* Penguin Books, 1989.

OTHER

Memories and Hallucinations: A Memoir, Viking, 1988.

Contributor to anthologies, including *Best SF: 1969,* edited by Harry Harrison and Brian W. Aldiss, Putnam, 1970; *Inside Outer Space,* edited by Robert Vas Dias, Anchor Books, 1970; and *Twenty-Three Modern British Poets,* edited by John Matthias, Swallow Press, 1971. Contributor to literary journals in England and the United States.

SIDELIGHTS: In 1980, after spending nearly a year closeted in a small study at Oxford University, D. M. Thomas emerged with the manuscript for his third novel. Known until that time primarily as a poet and translator of Russian verse, Thomas had first branched out into adult fiction with the 1979 book *The Flute-Player,* a fantasy-like meditation on art and its struggle to endure and even flourish in a totalitarian regime. A second fantasy novel, *Birthstone,* followed soon after; it tells the story of a woman trying to create a single, stable identity out of the fragmented parts of her personality. Both works—especially *The Flute-Player,* which won a contest for best fantasy novel—received praise for their imaginative, poetic treatments of familiar themes. But neither work sold more than a few hundred copies.

Upon its publication in late 1980, Thomas's new novel, *The White Hotel,* seemed destined for the same fate. A complex blend of the real and the surreal and of the apparent dichotomy between the Freudian concepts of the pleasure instinct and the death instinct, the work generated relatively little interest among British critics and readers; what reaction there was, the author later recalled in a *New York Times Magazine* article, could best be summed up as "restrained approval." Within just a few months, however, it became clear that on the other side of the Atlantic, at least, that would not be the case. Appearing in the United States in the spring of 1981, *The White Hotel* met with what William Borders referred to in the *New York Times* as a "thunderclap of critical praise" that sparked sales and made Thomas an instant celebrity. Already into its second printing before the official publication date, *The White Hotel* eventually sold more than 95,000 copies in its hardcover edition and almost 1.5 million copies in the paperback reprint—making it without a doubt "the sleeper novel of the season," to quote a *Publishers Weekly* writer.

Less than two years before, Thomas had been at a crucial turning point in his life and career. When government budget cuts led to the closing of the Hereford College of Education, the forty-four-year-old head of the English department found himself suddenly jobless (but with a full year's severance pay to live on while he searched for a new position). Thomas's first thought was to return to Oxford University and pursue another degree, a move his former tutor advised against—unless he had some other compelling reason to be there. As it turned out, he did. "I was becoming dissatisfied at writing my ideas as poems," Thomas told *Publishers Weekly* interviewer Ion Trewin. "I wanted a larger form, and in our age I think you can only do that as a novel. But with the college closing down I wanted to be more involved in human lives, which I found I could be with a novel. And again, I think that by middle age you find you've gathered a lot of material that's waiting to be used, material that was no good for a poem."

Some of this material "waiting to be used" included parts of a poem that Thomas had been working on for quite some time. Based on an image of two young lovers on a train journey in 1912 (with Karl Jung and Sigmund Freud as fellow passengers), the verses he had composed never seemed quite finished to Thomas, and the image continued to haunt him. Then, while searching for a long book to read on a flight to the United States, he came across Anatoli Kuznetsov's *Babi Yar,* a description of the wartime massacre of Jews at Kiev in the Soviet Union. As Thomas explained to Trewin: "The account of the Holocaust suddenly connected to my poems. Everything fell into place. And I didn't go to the United States after all—I started to write the novel instead." He spent the next nine months at Oxford, expanding on the image of the train journey, Freud, and the Holocaust, weaving a tale that is part epistolary, part poetic, and part straight narrative.

Divided into seven distinct sections, *The White Hotel* begins with a prologue that consists of a series of letters to, from, or about Freud and several of his colleagues in which the doctor discusses the case of one of his female patients, "Frau Anna G.," who is suffering from a severe hysterical illness. Her psychic distress manifests itself physically as asthma, anorexia, pains in the left breast and ovary, and a general feeling of anxiety that conventional treatments have not alleviated. In his letters, Freud speculates that the case of "Frau Anna G." will substantiate his theory of a death instinct that coexists with the erotic one.

Following the prologue are two sections devoted to writings by the mysterious "Frau Anna G." herself. The first sample is a long poem in which "Anna" describes an erotic fantasy she has concerning an affair with Freud's son. The affair begins in a train compartment and continues at a lakeside "white hotel," where a series of explicit and unusual love scenes are played out against a backdrop of horrible death and destruction involving other guests at the hotel; none of the violence, however, interferes with or diminishes the lovers' passion and self-absorbed pursuit of physical pleasure. The second writing sample, ostensibly written at Freud's request, is an expanded prose version of "Anna's" fantasy, "a wild, lyrical, irrational embroidery upon her original," remarked Thomas Flanagan in the *Nation*. According to *Village Voice* critic Laurie Stone, it is this prose version that serves as "a key to [Anna's] fears, imaginative transformations, and clairvoyant projections."

The fourth section of *The White Hotel* is comprised of Freud's long analysis of the case of "Frau Anna G.," now revealed to be Lisa Erdman, an opera singer of Russian-Jewish descent. A pastiche of actual case histories written by Freud, the section connects Lisa's fantasies to events in her real life and concludes with the doctor's observation that "she was cured of everything but life, so to speak. . . . She took away with her a reasonable prospect of survival, in an existence that would doubtless never be less than difficult."

The fifth and sixth sections of the novel chronicle in detached prose the course of Lisa's life after she is treated and "cured" by Dr. Freud. The conventional narrative ends with a chilling account of her execution in 1941 at Babi Yar along with thousands of other Russian Jews; the reader then discovers what Lisa's fantasies have always meant in terms of her life and death and, in a broader sense, all of European history in the twentieth century.

The White Hotel's seventh and final section is a surreal epilogue in which Lisa, now in a purgatory-like land that is unmistakably Palestine, is reunited with people who had figured prominently in her life, including her mother and Freud. There, too, in this strange place are thousands of other souls awaiting forgiveness, love, and understanding; Lisa is last seen agreeing to help the latest wave of "immigrants" settle in: "No one could, or would, be turned away; for they had nowhere else to go."

The initial reaction to *The White Hotel* among British critics was "bafflingly contradictory," as Thomas himself reported in the *New York Times Magazine*. Among the few major periodicals that published reviews, the discussions often highlighted the novel's "pornographic" content, especially the two chapters containing Lisa's poetic and prose versions of her fantasy. *Punch* reviewers Mary Anne Bonney and Susan Jeffreys, for example, dismissed the entire book as "humourlessly insubstantial" and singled out Lisa's poem in particular as "a sexual fantasy of some crudity and little literary worth." This view was shared by Brian Martin, who added in a *New Statesman* article that "no amount of fumbling with artistic devices and excuses makes it any different." Commenting in the *Times Literary Supplement*, Anne Duchene agreed that the early sections of the book "are not for the squeamish," but conceded that "they have to be undergone, by committed readers, as part of the raw material for the later, much more interesting sections."

Though *London Review of Books* critic Robert Taubman also found the sexual scenes "not real or erotic," with an "unconvincing look of pornography," he nevertheless went on to declare: "The analysis that follows sounds an authentic note. . . . At the same time, it provides the reader with an absorbing Chinese box narrative of hidden memories, reversals of meaning and deceptions uncovered." A reviewer for *Encounter* compared reading *The White Hotel* to watching an Ingmar Bergman film: "You are battered with symbolism, in perpetual pursuit of images, of references, of bizarre surrealist objects. . . . I'm not sure that I enjoyed it, but I am certainly respectful; this is a powerful piece of writing, highly complex, carefully structured. Its meanings and intention fall gradually into place; I suspect that it would improve still further on subsequent readings. . . . The novel either has to be accepted on its own terms or not at all. Either the reader enters into [the author's] psychological construction . . . or he doesn't."

In the months immediately following *The White Hotel*'s publication in Britain, it seemed that few people were willing to accept the novel on *any* terms. As Thomas put it in the *New York Times Magazine*, "Any serious novel needs a miracle to bring it to the public's attention, and that miracle did not happen in Britain. It happened, instead, in the United States." By and large, American critics lauded *The White Hotel* as an ambitious, brilliant, and gripping *tour de force*. According to Thomas, their reviews were "individual, lengthy, well-considered, and concentrated within a short period of time; in Britain [*The White Hotel*] generally appeared among a miscellaneous bundle of three or four novels. . . . The British reviews stressed the book's complexity; the American reviews stressed its readability. The Americans seemed more open to largeness of theme and inventiveness of form. Their lips weren't so pursed."

The Americans, for example, were far less inclined than the British to make an issue out of *The White Hotel*'s "pornographic" content. The few who even raised the possibility described Thomas's poem and its prose rendition as highly erotic rather than pornographic; several reviewers mentioned that the decision to use such a technique was an unusual and very effective way of revealing the soul of Lisa Erdman.

Though George Levine commented in the *New York Review of Books* that the author's language is occasionally "merely vulgar, or banal," he went on to note that it often achieves "a lush, romantic intensity, with a remarkable precision of imagery. [The] writing is full of dislocation and surprise; it is seductive, frightening, and beautifully alive. . . . Such language immediately establishes the mysterious 'Anna G.' as a powerful presence." Leslie Epstein expressed a similar opinion, declaring in the *New York Times Book Review* that "the poem seems to speak directly from the unconscious." In short, declared *Time*'s Paul Gray, *The White Hotel* "easily transcends titillation. Those who come to [Thomas's] novel with prurient interests alone will quickly grow baffled and bored."

While British reviewers by no means focused exclusively on the subject of eroticism in *The White Hotel*, they did devote less space than their American counterparts to discussions of the novel's other major features. Its structure in particular impressed a number of critics on this side of the Atlantic, most of whom praised it as an innovative mixture of traditional forms that results in "what feels like entirely new fictional terrain," to use Stone's words.

Because she felt *The White Hotel* is much more than a novel, Elaine Kendall hesitated referring to it as such. Instead, she maintained in her *Los Angeles Times* review, it is "a *belles lettres* revival in itself, encompassing not only the three traditional disciplines [of fiction, poetry and drama] but also history, myth, biography and science. D. M. Thomas has written a book that enlarges the usual notion of the novel, so radically that to classify it with a single noun diminishes the author's intent and achievement."

Newsweek's Peter S. Prescott found the book "in its conception and design a daring enterprise, brought off with dazzling virtuosity. . . . [Thomas] has made of his story a full-dress tragedy incorporating a variety of moods and narrative styles which reinforce each other to an astonishing degree. Each segment succeeds in its own way . . . yet they are bound together by a repetition of symbol and event whose significance shifts slightly from one segment to the next, always adding to our understanding of the whole. By the end . . . Thomas has achieved the kind of serenity we associate with Sophocles and Shakespeare."

Writing in the *Nation,* Thomas Flanagan described *The White Hotel* as "a book of extraordinary beauty, power and audacity—powerful and beautiful in its conception, audacious in its manner of execution. It is as stunning a work of fiction as has appeared in a long while. . . . [Thomas] is not one of those writers who, having been informed by the hum of the general culture that 'narrative' has fallen from favor, has looked about for more modish equivalents. His form issues directly from his vision, is compelled by his vision. . . . It becomes literally impossible to respond to the novel . . . without disentangling the submerged narrative from the manner of its telling, the shifting viewpoints and chronologies, the rich and shifting imagery."

Partisan Review critic Frank Conroy suggested that these contrasting modes and shifting viewpoints serve to link *The White Hotel*'s structure with Freudian methods and theories of psychotherapy, especially the idea of a life instinct-death instinct, a major thematic component of the novel. As Conroy explained, *The White Hotel*'s seven separate sections "come at the story from different angles, creating the effect of the author circling in on his subject in a spiral," a method that "echoes the process of psychoanalysis" developed by Freud. The eminent doctor is, in fact, a major character in the novel, and Thomas's realistic portrayal garnered many compliments from American as well as British reviewers.

Freud and his life instinct-death instinct theory are first introduced via the letters that form *The White Hotel*'s prologue. In one of these letters, the doctor mentions to a colleague that the writings of a young female patient of his "seem to lend support to my theory: an extreme of libidinous phantasy combined with an extreme of morbidity." Several sections later, following the poetry and prose versions of Lisa's fantasy, Freud appears again as the author of the case history of "Frau Anna G." According to *New Republic* reviewer Michele Slung, "the Freud Thomas gives us, viewed through the lens of fiction, does not seem to be different from the Freud of contemporary witnesses: he is kind, diplomatic, tolerant, insightful, self-assured." Thomas's imitation of a case history, said Gray, "is uncannily accurate and convincing. It has the same whodunit intensity of the originals, the same bristling of symbols, the same gentle prodding to make the patient reveal more than she wants to know." The *Spectator*'s Paul Ableman remarked that "the document is so finely-attuned to the style of the founder of psychoanalysis that it seems merely fortuitous that 'Anna G.' never occupied the famous couch in the Berggasse." Thus, it is within this "model of affectionate impersonation," to use Flanagan's words, that Lisa's fantasy "is artfully joined to her painfully remembered past."

As Thomas makes clear, however, the fictional Freud is aware that there remain images in Lisa's fantasies that cannot be readily explained in terms of her childhood and early life. During the course of the case history, it is revealed that Lisa has "telepathic powers"—an ability to foresee the future without actually understanding it—a talent that Freud dismisses at first but eventually comes to accept. The reader's acceptance of Lisa's gift (or

"curse," to use her words) is crucial, for the entire second half of the novel builds on the premise that her physical pains and violent fantasies are related to *future* events, not past ones, and that her personal suffering prefigures and eventually becomes part of the horror of the Holocaust. In short, observed Flanagan, Thomas proposes that "far more has been at stake [in *The White Hotel*] than Lisa Erdman's damaged psyche. The fate of our culture has been implied."

Whether a reviewer was able to make the "imaginative leap" necessary at this point in the story usually determined how he or she ultimately felt about *The White Hotel*. For some, the leap was impossible, often because they believed that neither Lisa Erdman's character nor Freud's life instinct-death instinct theory was developed enough to sustain such a metaphor. For others, like the *New York Times*'s Christopher Lehmann-Haupt, the poetic transformation of Lisa's tragic personal history into a collective one was nothing less than "heart-stunning."

Susan Fromberg Schaeffer, for instance, stated in the *Chicago Tribune Book World* that "the bones of a wonderful story are here [in *The White Hotel*], but Lisa Erdman and her world do not come alive. . . . [Thomas] clearly means to pay tribute to Freud's vision, and [he] does. In the process, however, [he] loses sight of the real Freud, who always refused easy comfort, either in religion or in mysticism. Worse still, Thomas loses sight of his own characters, his own obligation to breathe life and power into his fictional world." Epstein agreed, pointing out that Lisa "seems to float through the various crises that afflict her," and she has "no intellectual life" despite the complex political, social, and cultural forces that swirl around her. She is, in essence, no more than a "casualty at first of her psyche and then of history," in Taubman's opinion. In addition, Epstein contended, "the notion of the death instinct is shaky enough in Freud's own theory, and the application of a 'struggle between the life instinct and the death instinct' to this poor patient strikes me as nothing more than a bald assertion, unsupported by the evidence."

Though he described Thomas's "expansion of imagery and structure from the fate of an individual to the fate of the culture itself " as "a dazzling accomplishment," Flanagan nonetheless concluded that the author's decision to authenticate his case by making Lisa clairvoyant "has exacted a price. . . . The device remains a device, a willed literary artifice that demands, but cannot fully claim, our assent. And at the end we are left with a 'solution' more esthetically satisfying, perhaps, than that of the rational psychologist, but just as arbitrary. Thomas is no less imprisoned by the conditions of his art than was Freud by his. His deepest theme, the joined threads of desolation and joy, is communicable only through images that are mute save in their power and their beauty, [and] his 'explanation' [of them] imperils both of these qualities."

Among those who were of a different opinion was Daphne Merkin, who affirmed in the *New Leader* that "despite intricate schema of interlocking myths and recurring symbols, the novel manages to sustain a clear, pure intention, always presenting Lisa in terms of her own story. Her desires and the impediments to their fulfillment are never less than unique, yet within the remarkable context of their telling they acquire the weight of allegory."

New York magazine critic Edith Milton made a similar observation, declaring that Thomas's "interweaving of psychological symbols and cultural myth, of prophetic intuition and the dismal truths of twentieth-century history, did not seem to me merely the fabric of a convincing fiction, but the brilliant representation and clarification of some troubled and important mystery at the heart of my own world. . . . Lisa's dream of love and death is more than an exercise in clairvoyance. It is an apocalyptic vision of the eternal destruction and resurrection of the human spirit. And Freud's interpretation of it is the rational man's battle to make some sense of the senseless equilibrium between chaos and survival."

The White Hotel's epilogue requires readers to make yet another imaginative leap, one that most reviewers, including several of those who had criticized Lisa's clairvoyance as an implausible device, found possible and even somewhat exhilarating in light of what Levine called "Thomas's refusal to end his novel with the shocking finality of Babi Yar." Set in a dreamlike world beyond death that is almost, but not quite, paradise, the epilogue weaves together all the novel's symbols and images "into a somehow reassuring unity, reassuring even in the aftermath of the agony," observed Slung. More important, it underscores the author's belief that the forces on the side of life and love are more powerful than those on the side of death and hatred, transforming what has appeared to be a vision of despair into a vision of hope.

To Richard A. Blake of *America,* the ending of *The White Hotel* tells us that Lisa "can never really die, because she is the race itself, a victim of its own deep mysterious evil, yet resilient, responsive to love and ever hopeful. Lisa can, it seems, return one day to her 'white hotel,' the womb where she rests secure from her nightmares and her memory." Even Epstein, who was critical of Thomas's decision to propel the story forward by giving Lisa telepathic powers and a death instinct, felt that the ending overcame the weaknesses in the earlier section. "It is a remarkable and perhaps even necessary conclusion," the reviewer wrote. "It made me realize that I had, after all, read the story of a particular life, that it was one I could respect and for which I had come to feel real fondness."

"Thomas's conclusion is audacious, yet it seems exactly right for all that has gone before," declared Gray. "Given the many mysteries in Lisa's life, the last one is almost commonplace. . . . [*The White Hotel*] is a reminder that fiction can amaze as well as inform." As *Esquire*'s James Wolcott put it, "*The White Hotel* is so cleanly propelled by its obsessions that it slices through platitude and serves as a tribute to the silenced millions—to all those whose blood crimsoned the bayonet's edge. [It] is one of the rare novels written for grown-ups that aren't afraid to leap over the railing into passionate, lyrical excess."

For others, including a few who found the rest of *The White Hotel* moving, the ending was anticlimactic, a disappointment—somewhat of a "technicolour sunset with angelic choir," as Duchene remarked. Her British colleague Taubman voiced a similar opinion, maintaining that "it's more of a sentimental fantasy than that of the white hotel at the beginning, and too insubstantial for Lisa's final conviction—'we were made to be happy and to enjoy life'—to carry much weight." At least one of the American critics, Conroy, supported this contention that the ending is too weak to sustain the rest of the story. "The various sections of [*The White Hotel*] are like elaborate, highly decorated checks for vast amounts," he wrote, "and the end is like a trip to the bank, where one discovers, sadly, that they can't be cashed."

Levine, too, was not entirely satisfied with the ending, especially its pervasive sense of hope, which he believed was not entirely justified. Nevertheless, he defended *The White Hotel* as "a novel of immense ambition and virtuosity" based on a fictional world of "unmanageable, inexpressible reality." Continued the critic: "It is inevitable that a book taking so many risks, in a manner distinctly less English than continental, or even American,

should be marked by some unevenness. Whatever one's doubts its strengths remain. The image of the 'white hotel' is an image of the womb, an image of peace, but the novel that takes this image for its title suggests that life can be seen neither as a matter of peace or of violence. . . . In his emotionally precise and inventive prose, Thomas suggests a reality at once vital and deadly, and more accessible than we—protected behind our documents and books—might care to know."

Ableman, one of the few British reviewers who praised Thomas's novel virtually without qualification, agreed that "*The White Hotel* is a work of vast ambition and impressive achievement. It aspires to being little less than a comprehensive synthesis of the forces of life and death operating on this planet in the context of a civilisation that apparently obeys quite different laws but in which their influence is always present. If that sounds forbidding it should immediately be added that it is also a gripping human story." Echoing Levin's observation, Ableman concluded, "*The White Hotel* transcends the parochialism of most contemporary English novels and shows that fiction, when it escapes the dead conventions of the nineteenth century and, of course, when written by a major talent, is still full of vitality."

Since the success of *The White Hotel,* which made its author a very reluctant celebrity, Thomas has published two additional novels (part of a proposed trilogy), two poetry collections, and three translations. Despite the variety of his output, he considers himself primarily a poet who also happens to write novels. "It's a problem," he told *Publishers Weekly* interviewer Trewin. "Trying to be a juggler and keep two balls in the air is difficult enough, but to be a translator too. . . ." What is most important for him to keep in mind regarding his work, Thomas believes, is to keep his distance from the critical and commercial hype and continue writing. "I can enjoy the bursts of travel, and the small vanities of success," he remarked in the *New York Times Magazine.* "Yet [I] know that the reality is where the blank sheet rests in the typewriter, where the new novel or poem is as great a struggle as ever. . . . I know [too that with each new book] the critics will be breathing down my neck . . . , but that doesn't worry me. I simply carry on writing the best way I know how, and enjoy it." As he further explained to Borders in a *New York Times* interview: "Serious work can come only from your psyche. You go along for years and then all of a sudden there comes a divine spark and it all works. All I can do now, as I write, is hope and pray that it will strike again."

AVOCATIONAL INTERESTS: "Besides sex and death, I am interested in Russian literature, music, most sport, and my Celtic homeland, Cornwall."

BIOGRAPHICAL/CRITICAL SOURCES:

BOOKS

Contemporary Literary Criticism, Gale, Volume 13, 1980, Volume 22, 1982, Volume 31, 1985.
Dictionary of Literary Biography, Volume 40: *Poets of Great Britain and Ireland since 1960,* Gale, 1985.
Dictionary of Literary Yearbook: 1982, Gale, 1983.
Thomas, D. M., *The White Hotel,* Gollancz, 1980, Viking, 1981.
Thomas, D. M., *Memories and Hallucinations: A Memoir,* Viking, 1988.

PERIODICALS

America, October 17, 1981, April 16, 1983.
Atlantic, April, 1983.
Best Sellers, May, 1981.
Books and Bookmen, July, 1980, March, 1983.

Chicago Tribune Book World, March 22, 1981, June 12, 1983.
Commentary, August, 1981.
Commonweal, October 7, 1983.
Detroit News, March 22, 1981, June 12, 1983.
Encounter, August 1981, July-August, 1983.
Esquire, April, 1981, November, 1982.
Globe and Mail (Toronto), March 10, 1984, July 21, 1984.
Hudson Review, autumn, 1983.
Listener, July 19, 1979, January 22, 1981, March 3, 1983.
London Review of Books, February 5, 1981, April 1, 1983.
Lone Star Review, April, 1981.
Los Angeles Times, March 17, 1981.
Los Angeles Times Book Review, October 31, 1982, April 3, 1983, November 18, 1984.
Maclean's, April 11, 1983, June 25, 1984.
Nation, May 2, 1981, April 23, 1983.
New Leader, April 20, 1981, May 30, 1983.
New Republic, March 28, 1981, April 4, 1983.
New Statesman, June 22, 1979, March 21, 1980, January 16, 1981, March 4, 1983, June 29, 1984.
Newsweek, March 16, 1981, March 15, 1982, April 4, 1983.
New York, March 16, 1981.
New Yorker, March 30, 1981.
New York Review of Books, May 28, 1981, June 16, 1983, November 22, 1984.
New York Times, March 13, 1981, March 24, 1981, September 21, 1982, March 29, 1983, October 31, 1984.
New York Times Book Review, March 15, 1981, June 28, 1981, September 26, 1982, March 27, 1983.
New York Times Magazine, June 13, 1982.
Observer, June 24, 1979, February 27, 1983, July 1, 1984.
Partisan Review, January, 1982.
People, June 29, 1981.
Poetry, May, 1971.
Publishers Weekly, March 27, 1981, April 17, 1981, January 8, 1982.
Punch, October 14, 1981, March 2, 1983.
Saturday Review, March, 1981, July, 1981.
Spectator, July 7, 1979, January 17, 1981, March 19, 1983, June 30, 1984.
Time, March 16, 1981, April 25, 1983.
Times (London), January 15, 1981, June 9, 1983, March 10, 1984, June 28, 1984.
Times Literary Supplement, November 30, 1979, March 14, 1980, January 16, 1981, January 22, 1982, June 29, 1983, June 29, 1984.
Village Voice, March 18, 1981, April 26, 1983.
Virginia Quarterly Review, summer, 1981.
Voice Literary Supplement, October, 1982.
Washington Post, December 15, 1979, January 27, 1982.
Washington Post Book World, March 15, 1981, May 16, 1982, March 27, 1983, September 9, 1984.
West Coast Review of Books, May-June, 1983.

OTHER

Kessler, Jascha, "D. M. Thomas: *Selected Poems,*" (radio broadcast), KUSC-FM, Los Angeles, Calif., May 18, 1983.

* * *

THOMAS, Dylan (Marlais) 1914-1953

PERSONAL: Born October 27, 1914, in Swansea, Carmarthenshire (now Glamorganshire), Wales; died of pneumonia caused by acute alcoholism (some sources list cause of death as a cerebral ailment), November 9, 1953, in New York, N.Y.; buried at St. Martin's Churchyard, Laugharne, Wales; son of D. J. (a grammar school master) and Florence (Williams) Thomas; married Caitlin Macnamara, July 11, 1937; children: Llewellyn (son), Colm (son), Aeron (daughter). *Education:* Completed grammar school in Swansea, Wales.

CAREER: Poet and prose writer. Reporter for the *South Wales Daily Post,* a reviewer for the *Herald of Wales,* and an actor; British Ministry of Information, scriptwriter during the mid-1930s; British Broadcasting Corporation (BBC), documentary scriptwriter and radio commentator on poetry during the 1940s; gave public poetry readings, including extensive lecture tours in the United States, 1950-53.

WRITINGS:

POEMS

Eighteen Poems, Sunday Referee and Parton Bookshop, 1934.
Twenty-five Poems, Dent, 1936.
New Poems, New Directions, 1943.
Deaths and Entrances, Dent, 1946, revised edition edited with notes by Walford Davies, illustrated by John Piper, Gwasg Gregynog, 1984.
Selected Writings of Dylan Thomas, New Directions, 1946.
Twenty-six Poems, Dent, 1950.
In Country Sleep and Other Poems, Dent, 1952.
Collected Poems, 1934-1952, Dent, 1952, published as *The Collected Poems of Dylan Thomas,* New Directions, 1953, reprinted, 1971, reprinted as *Collected Poems, 1934-1952,* Dent, 1984.
The Colour of Saying: An Anthology of Verse Spoken by Dylan Thomas, edited by Ralph Maud and Aneirin Talfan Davies, Dent, 1963, published as *Dylan Thomas's Choice,* New Directions, 1964.
Collected Poems, Dutton, 1966.
Poem in October, Coach House Press, 1970.
The Poems of Dylan Thomas, New Directions, 1971, revised edition, Dent, 1978.
Poems, edited by Daniel Jones, Dent, 1974.
Selected Poems of Dylan Thomas, Dent, 1975.

Poems represented in anthologies; contributor of poems to such periodicals as *Living Age, Poetry, New English Weekly,* and *New Verse.*

SHORT STORIES AND ESSAYS

Portrait of the Artist as a Young Dog (autobiographical short stories; includes "Peaches" and "One Warm Saturday"), New Directions, 1940, reprinted, 1956.
Quite Early One Morning, preface and notes by Aneirin Talfan Davies, Dent, 1954, enlarged edition, New Directions, 1954.
A Child's Christmas in Wales, New Directions, 1955, new edition illustrated with woodcuts, 1959, Godine, 1984.
A Prospect of the Sea, and Other Stories and Prose Writings, edited by Daniel Jones, Dent, 1955.
Adventures in the Skin Trade and Other Stories, New Directions, 1955 (published in England as *Adventures in the Skin Trade,* with a foreword by Vernon Watkins, Putnam [London], 1955, new edition with drawings by Ceri Richards, 1982).
The Collected Prose of Dylan Thomas, New Directions, 1969.
Early Prose Writings of Dylan Thomas, edited by Walford Davies, Dent, 1971, reprinted, 1983, New Directions, 1972.
The Collected Stories, Dent, 1983, New Directions, 1984.

Short stories represented in anthologies, including *Welsh Short Stories,* Faber, 1937, and *Short Story Study: A Critical Anthology,* edited by A. Smith and W. H. Mason, Edward Arnold, 1961. Contributor of short stories and essays to periodicals, including *New English Weekly, New World Writing, Life and Letters Today, Janus, Contemporary Poetry and Prose, Delta,* and *Mademoiselle.*

POETRY AND PROSE COLLECTIONS

The World I Breathe, New Directions, 1939.
The Map of Love, Dent, 1939.
Selected Writings of Dylan Thomas, New Directions, 1946, revised edition edited by J. P. Harries, Heinemann, 1970.
Miscellany: Poems, Stories, Broadcasts, Dent 1963, reprinted as *Miscellany One: Poems, Stories, Broadcasts,* 1974.
Miscellany Two: A Visit to Grandpa's, and Other Stories and Poems, Dent, 1966.
Miscellany Three: Poems and Stories, Dent, 1978.

LETTERS AND NOTEBOOKS

Letters to Vernon Watkins, edited with introduction by Vernon Watkins, New Directions, 1957.
Selected Letters of Dylan Thomas, edited by Constantine Fitz-Gibbon, Dent, 1956, published as *Selected Letters,* New Directions, 1967.
The Notebooks of Dylan Thomas, edited by Ralph Maud, New Directions, 1967 (published in England as *Poet in the Making: The Notebooks of Dylan Thomas,* Dent, 1968).
Twelve More Letters, Daedalus Press, 1969.
Collected Letters of Dylan Thomas, edited by Paul Ferris, Macmillan, 1985.

FILM SCRIPTS

The Doctor and the Devils (based on a short story by Donald Taylor), New Directions, 1953, published with an introduction by John Ormond, Time, 1964.
The Beach of Falesa (based on a short story by Robert Louis Stevenson), Stein & Day, 1963, 2nd edition, 1983.
Twenty Years A-Growing (based on a short story by Maurice O'Sullivan), Dent, 1964.
The Doctor and the Devils and Other Scripts, New Directions, 1966.
Me and My Bike (unfinished screenplay; introduction by Sydney Box, illustrations by Leonora Box), McGraw, 1965.

Also author or co-author of numerous educational film scripts for the British Ministry of Information.

SOUND RECORDINGS

Selections From the Writings of Dylan Thomas (five records), Caedmon, 1952-60.
Under Milk Wood: A Play for Voices (two records), Argo, 1954.
An Evening With Dylan Thomas Reading His Own And Other Poems, Caedmon, 1963.
Dylan Thomas Reading His Complete Recorded Poetry (two records), Caedmon, 1963.
Dylan Thomas Reading From His Own Work, Caedmon, 1971.
In Country Heaven: The Evolution of a Poem, Caedmon, 1971.
The Complete Recorded Stories and Humorous Essays, Caedmon, 1972.
Return Journey to Swansea (radio play; performed by Thomas and a supporting cast), Caedmon, 1972.
Dylan Thomas Reads From His Adventures in the Skin Trade and Two Poems, Caedmon, 1975.

OTHER

Under Milk Wood: A Play for Voices (first produced in New York City at the Young Men's/Young Women's Hebrew Association, May 14, 1953), New Directions, 1954, new edition, with preface and musical settings by Daniel Jones, published as *Under Milk Wood: A Play in Two Acts,* 1958, new edition, Dent, 1962.
Conversation About Christmas, privately printed, 1954.
Quite Early One Morning: Broadcasts by Dylan Thomas, with preface and notes by Ichiro Nishizaki and Nobutko Suto, Hokuseido Press (Tokyo), 1956.
Rebecca's Daughters, Little, Brown, 1965.
(With John Davenport) *The Death of the King's Canary* (novel), introduction by Constantine FitzGibbon, Hutchinson, 1977.
Two Tales: Me and My Bike [and] *Rebecca's Daughters,* illustrated by Leonora Box, Sphere, 1968

SIDELIGHTS: The work of Dylan Thomas has occasioned much critical commentary, although critics share no consensus on how bright his star shines in the galaxy of modern poetry. In fact, it is a curious phenomenon that so many critics seem obsessed with deciding once and for all whether Thomas's poems belong side by side with those of T. S. Eliot and W. H. Auden, or whether they are—in the words of a reputable critic quoted by Henry Treece in *Dylan Thomas: "Dog Among the Fairies"*— "intellectual fakes of the highest class." The latter is definitely a minority opinion; yet even Treece, an acquaintance of Thomas's, had to admit that the poet's work is "extremely ill-balanced."

The estimation of the work has often been colored by an estimation of the man. Until Constantine FitzGibbon's *The Life of Dylan Thomas* in 1965, Thomas's biography was dominated by numerous unflattering published reminiscences, among them the graphically detailed account of John Malcolm Brinnin's *Dylan Thomas in America,* concerning, in part, the poet's drinking and philandering during his last years in America. Though FitzGibbon sympathetically glossed over Thomas's drinking habits, the facts reported by Brinnin and others and corroborated in Paul Ferris's *Dylan Thomas* support the idea that Thomas frequently drank to excess, and that such drinking adversely affected his social behavior. Personal details such as these tended to render objective evaluations of the poetry difficult. Indeed, the legend of Dylan Thomas grew: the hard-drinking bard, the erratic chanter of his own songs, the romantic artist at odds with the modern world.

Thomas began writing poetry as a child, publishing his work in school magazines. By 1930 he had taken to writing poems in penny notebooks; a number of his poems were published in the "Poet's Corner" of the *Sunday Referee* and in the influential *New Verse.* After Thomas's death Ralph Maud, in *Entrances to Dylan Thomas's Poetry,* declared that the writer's first published poem was the subsequently popular "And death shall have no dominion," which appeared on May 8, 1933, in the *New English Weekly.*

The notebooks in which Thomas composed between 1930 and 1934, when he was sixteen to twenty years old, reveal the young poet's struggle with a number of personal crises, the origins of which are rather obscure. In his 1965 *Dylan Thomas,* Jacob Korg described them as "related to love affairs, to industrial civilization, and to the youthful problems of finding one's identity." Revised versions of some of the notebooks' poems became in 1934 his first published volume of poetry, *Eighteen Poems.*

Eighteen Poems was published in December, 1934, a short time after Thomas moved to London. The volume received little notice at first, but by the following spring some influential newspapers and journals had reviewed it favorably. Ferris quoted from an anonymous review in the *Morning Post* that called the poems "individual but not private" and went on to strike a note that later became a frequent criticism: "a psychologist would observe Mr. Thomas's constant use of images and epithets which are secretory or glandular." Ferris also quoted a critic for *Time and Tide,* who wrote: "This is not merely a book of unusual promise; it is more probably the sort of bomb that bursts not more than once in three years." The book was also reviewed favorably by *Spectator, New Verse,* and the *Times Literary Supplement.*

Like James Joyce before him, Dylan Thomas was obsessed with words—with their sound and rhythm and especially with their possibilities for multiple meanings. This richness of meaning, an often illogical and revolutionary syntax, and catalogues of cosmic and sexual imagery render Thomas's early poetry original and difficult. In a letter to Richard Church, included by FitzGibbon in *Selected Letters,* Thomas commented on what he considered some of his own excesses: "Immature violence, rhythmic monotony, frequent muddle-headedness, and a very much overweighted imagery that leads often to incoherence." Similarly, in a letter to Glyn Jones, he wrote: "My own obscurity is quite an unfashionable one, based, as it is, on a preconceived symbolism derived (I'm afraid all this sounds wooly and pretentious) from the cosmic significance of the human anatomy."

This discussion of the difficulty of *Eighteen Poems* does not discount the fact that most of the poems have yielded their meanings to persistent readers—and books like William York Tindall's *A Reader's Guide to Dylan Thomas* and Clark Emery's *The World of Dylan Thomas* aid the reader's comprehension. Such poems as "I see the boys of summer," "A process in the weather of the heart," and the popular "The force that through the green fuse drives the flower" merit repeated readings, both for the artistic pleasure they give through their highly structured forms and for their embodiment of some of the key themes that run throughout the volume and, indeed, throughout much of Thomas's work. Among these themes are the unity of time, the similarity between creative and destructive forces in the universe, and the correspondence of all living things. This last theme was identified by Elder Olson in *The Poetry of Dylan Thomas* as part of the tradition of the microcosm-macrocosm: "He analogizes the anatomy of man to the structure of the universe . . . and sees the human microcosm as an image of the macrocosm, and conversely."

During the almost two years between the publication of *Eighteen Poems* in 1934 and *Twenty-five Poems* in 1936, Thomas moved back and forth between London and Wales a great deal. In London he began to meet influential people in the literary world: Herbert Read, Geoffrey Grigson, Norman Cameron, and Vernon Watkins, among others. He became particularly close to Watkins, an older man whose sedate lifestyle contrasted markedly with Thomas's. Watkins and Thomas would criticize each other's poetry, and Watkins became a frequent source of money for the continually destitute Thomas. At this time Thomas was carrying on a mostly long-distance relationship with the poet and novelist Pamela Hansford Johnson, later the wife of novelist C. P. Snow. While the affair lasted—it was finally torn asunder by Thomas's drinking—Thomas shared with her in letters his personal insecurities and his misgivings about his work. Paul Ferris cited this letter written from Laugharne, Wales, circa May 21, 1934: "I am tortured today by every doubt and misgiving that an hereditarily twisted imagination, an hereditary thirst and a commercial quenching, a craving for a body not my own, a chequered education and too much egocentric poetry, and a wild, wet day in a tided town, are capable of conjuring up out of their helly deeps." During this period Thomas's drinking became a se-

rious problem, and his friends would sometimes take him off to out-of-the-way places in Cornwall and Ireland to remove him from temptation with the hope that he would do more writing.

Thomas's second volume of poetry, *Twenty-five Poems,* was published in September, 1936. Most of the poems were revised from the notebooks; FitzGibbon reported in *The Life of Dylan Thomas* that "only six entirely new poems, that is to say poems written in the year and a half between the publication of [*Eighteen Poems*] and the despatch of the second volume to the printers, are to be found in that volume." Ferris noted that "the reviews were generally favourable, but with one exception they were not as enthusiastic as they were for [*Eighteen Poems*]." This exception, however, almost assured the volume's commercial success; it was a laudatory review by Dame Edith Sitwell in the *Sunday Times.* As cited by Ferris, the review proclaimed: "The work of this very young man (he is twenty-two years of age) is on a huge scale, both in theme and structurally. . . . I could not name one poet of this, the youngest generation, who shows so great a promise, and even so great an achievement."

Though most of the works in *Twenty-five Poems* were mined from older material, the volume includes a significant sonnet sequence of ten poems, "Altarwise by owl-light," written in Ireland the year before publication. In these sonnets Thomas moved from the pre-Christian primitivism of most of the *Eighteen Poems* to a Christian mythology based upon love. G. S. Fraser commented in *Vision and Rhetoric* that "the sonnets, a failure as a whole, splendid in parts . . . are important because they announce the current of orthodox Christian feeling—feeling rather than thought—which was henceforth increasingly to dominate Thomas's work in poetry." Olson saw these sonnets as a break with the past, in method as well as philosophic-religious outlook: "It is notable that after the 'Altarwise by owl-light' sonnets, he discards nearly all of this particular body of symbols, transforms the remainder and gradually develops new symbols and new diction to correspond with his changing view of life." Olson, who worked out an elaborate schema of interpretation involving Hercules in the zodiac, also called these sonnets "surely among the greatest poems of the century." Tindall remarked in *A Reader's Guide to Dylan Thomas* that the theme of these sonnets is really Thomas himself. Tindall commented, "Although cheerfully allowing the presence of Jesus, Hercules, the stars, the zodiac, and a generally neglected voyage, I think them analogies, not to be confused with the theme." Korg, commenting on the obscurity of the sequence, said that "all that is reasonably clear is that it concerns the crucifixion and the resurrection as foci of spiritual conflict."

While much of the attention given to *Twenty-five Poems* has been focused on the religious sonnets, the volume as a whole contains indications of a shift in emphasis in Thomas's writing. Richard Morton noted in *An Outline of the Works of Dylan Thomas* that the poems of this volume are "concerned with the relationship between the poet and his environment," particularly the natural environment. "In *Twenty-five Poems,* we can see the beginnings of the pastoral mode which reaches its fulfillment in the great lyrics of Thomas's last poems." And, as Korg said, "at least three of the poems in the second volume are about the poet's reactions to other people, themes of an entirely different class from those of [*Eighteen Poems*]; and these three anticipate [Thomas's] turning outward in his later poems toward such subjects as his aunt's funeral, the landscape, and his relations with his wife and children."

Some of the best poems in the book are rather straightforward pieces—"This bread break," "The hand that signed the paper,"

"And death shall have no dominion"—but others, such as "I, in my intricate image," are as involved and abstruse as the poems of the earlier volume. Derek Stanford noted that still "there are traces of doubt, questioning, and despair in many of these pieces." Thomas, however, chose to place the optimistic "And death shall have no dominion" at the end of the volume. This poem has always been one of Thomas's most popular works, perhaps because, as Clark Emery noted, it was "published in a time when notes of affirmation—philosophical, political, or otherwise—did not resound among intelligent liberal humanists, [and thus] it answered an emotional need. . . . It affirmed without sentimentalizing; it expressed a faith without theologizing."

The "Altarwise by owl-light" poems as well as "And death shall have no dominion" inevitably raise questions concerning the extent to which Dylan Thomas can be called a religious writer. In an essay for *A Casebook on Dylan Thomas* W. S. Merwin was one of the first to deal with this issue; he found Thomas to be a religious writer because he was a "celebrator in the ritual sense: a maker and performer of a rite. . . . That which he celebrates is creation, and more particularly the human condition." However, the positions on this issue can be—and have been—as various as the definitions of what constitutes a religious outlook. At one end of the scale, critics do not dispute that Thomas used religious imagery in his poetry; at the other end, critics generally agree that, at least during certain periods of his creative life, Thomas's vision was not that of any orthodox religious system. The range of interpretations was summarized by R. B. Kershner, Jr., in *Dylan Thomas: The Poet and His Critics:* "He has been called a pagan, a mystic, and a humanistic agnostic; his God has been identified with Nature, Sex, Love, Process, the Life Force, and with Thomas himself."

On July 11, 1937, Thomas married Caitlin Macnamara; they were penniless and lacked the blessings of their parents. After spending some time with each of their reluctant families, they moved to a borrowed house in Laugharne, Wales. This fishing village became their permanent address, though they lived in many temporary dwellings in England and Wales through the war years and after, until Thomas's death in 1953. The borrowing of houses and money became recurring events in their married life together. Korg associated these external circumstances in the poet's life with his artistic development: "Thomas's time of settling in Laugharne coincides roughly with the period when his poetry began to turn outward; his love for Caitlin, the birth of his first child, Llewellyn, responses to the Welsh countryside and its people, and ultimately events of the war began to enter his poetry as visible subjects."

Thomas's third book, *The Map of Love,* appeared in August, 1939, the year war broke out in Europe. It comprised a strange union of sixteen poems and seven stories, the stories having been previously published in periodicals. The volume was a commercial failure, perhaps because of the war. Ferris reported that "the book was respectfully and sometimes warmly reviewed, with a few dissenters"; yet these works of Thomas's middle period are his least successful. The short stories are inferior to those that appeared the next year in *Portrait of the Artist as a Young Dog.* They are mannered, misty, cumbersome—dealing often with dreams and vague imaginings. Some of these stories have been called surrealistic, opening up a vein of controversy, since Thomas often disavowed his use of surrealism. Annis Pratt, in *Dylan Thomas's Early Prose,* suggested that although surrealistic features exist in the stories, Thomas exercised careful control over his material. She quoted Thomas on this point: "I do not mind from where the images of a poem are dragged up; drag them up, if you like, from the nethermost sea of the hidden self;

but, before they reach paper, they must go through all the rational processes of the intellect."

While the poems of *The Map of Love,* with one or two exceptions, are not among the best Thomas wrote, they are interesting for the light they shed on his development of a more outward-looking and less cosmic aesthetic. At least one of the poems, "I make this in a warring absence," treats an early marital conflict with Caitlin. "If my head hurt a hair's foot" appears to be a celebration of the birth of the poet's son. Two very interesting poems have to do with the uncertainties of the poet. Clark Emery has associated "On no word of words" with Coleridge's "Dejection" and Milton's Sonnet XVI in its lament over lost powers and the passage of time. "After the funeral," considered the best poem of the volume, is an elegy for his rural aunt, Ann Jones. John Fuller concluded in an essay from *Dylan Thomas: New Critical Essays* that "the poem rehearses for Thomas the idea that out of the practice of grief can come real grief and love."

In sharp contrast to the stories in *The Map of Love* are those published the following year, 1940, in *Portrait of the Artist as a Young Dog.* Thomas claimed in a letter to Vernon Watkins that he "kept the flippant title for—as the publishers advise—money-making reasons." He also said that the title was not a parody of James Joyce's *A Portrait of the Artist as a Young Man*—a dubious proposition—though he did acknowledge the general influence of Joyce's *Dubliners.* These Thomas stories are different from the earlier ones in their particularity of character and place, their straightforward plot lines, and their relevance to Thomas's childhood in Wales. Thomas wrote to Watkins in August, 1939: "I've been busy over stories, pot-boiling stories for a book, semi-autobiographical, to be finished by Christmas."

Reviews of the book were mixed, and it didn't sell well at the time, though it later became enormously popular. According to Ferris, a reviewer for the *Times Literary Supplement* found that "the atmosphere of schoolboy smut and practical jokes and poetry is evoked with lingering accuracy but with nothing more." Subsequent critics have detected more in the stories, though most agree that Thomas is primarily a poet and only secondarily a writer of fiction. Korg commented that "taken as a group, [the stories] seem to trace the child's emergence from his domain of imagination and secret pleasures into an adult world where he observes suffering, pathos, and dignity." Two of the more successful stories in the collection are "The Peaches"—the first story—and "One Warm Saturday"—the last.

"The Peaches" features a youthful main character named Dylan who goes to his aunt's farm for a holiday; this is quite clearly the farm of Ann Jones of "After the funeral" and the farm celebrated in "Fern Hill." Harold F. Mosher, Jr., in his *Studies in Short Fiction* essay, summed up the conflict of the story and the means by which it is dramatized: "Through the juxtaposition of characters, the opposition of images, and the variation of pace and tempo, Thomas unifies his story and clarifies the conflict between imaginative life and dull existence." "One Warm Saturday" contains disillusionment comparable to that found in Joyce's story "Araby." After falling in love with a girl in a park and drinking with her and her friends in a bar, the hero of the story goes with the group to the girl's apartment, but loses his way in the hall after going to the bathroom and never finds the apartment again. Once more, this story depicts the conflict between the imaginative dreams of love and the real world of pain and confusion. In his *Studies in Short Fiction* essay Richard Kelly contrasted this story with Joyce's *Portrait of the Artist as a Young Man:* "Whereas Joyce's wading girl provides [the main character] with aesthetic and emotional autonomy, the girl in the antiromantic 'One Warm Saturday' fills the young man with anguish and frustration and returns him to an ugly, hostile world."

Constantine FitzGibbon reported that Thomas considered World War II a "personal affront." For a while he contemplated filing for conscientious objector status, but in the end he seems to have avoided service because of medical problems. Ferris quoted Thomas's mother, who claimed "punctured lungs" were the reason he didn't serve. Ferris suggested that the disability may have been a psychological one. Whatever his particular unfitness, Thomas was able to secure employment during the war years writing documentary scripts for the British Broadcasting Corporation (BBC). While he considered it hack work, it provided the first regular income since his newspaper days and also allowed him to spend a good deal of time in London pubs. This pragmatic writing was the beginning of a career that Thomas pursued until his death; it did not, however, replace what he considered his more important work, the writing of poems. In addition to the documentaries, he wrote radio scripts and eventually screenplays for feature films. Though his income from these activities was moderate, it did not allow him and Caitlin relief from debt or their friends relief from the frequent begging letters.

In 1940 Thomas began writing *Adventures in the Skin Trade,* a novel that he never completed, though its first section was subsequently published. It is essentially the time-honored story of a country boy in the big city. Annis Pratt commented that Thomas intended the story to be "a series of 'adventures' in which the hero's 'skins' would be stripped off one by one like a snake's until he was left in a kind of quintessential nakedness to face the world."

Thomas's work next saw publication in a 1946 poetry collection, *Deaths and Entrances,* containing many of his most famous poems. This volume included such works as "A Refusal to Mourn the Death, by Fire, of a Child in London," "Poem in October," "The Hunchback in the Park," and "Fern Hill." *Deaths and Entrances* was an instant success. Ferris noted that three thousand copies sold in the first month after its publication and that the publisher, Dent, ordered a reprint of the same number. In *Vision and Rhetoric* G. S. Fraser said of the volume that "it increases the impression of variety and of steady development, which the earlier volumes, read in the order of their appearance, give." T. H. Jones, in his *Dylan Thomas,* declared the volume to be the core of Thomas's achievement. The poems of *Deaths and Entrances,* while still provoking arguments about interpretation, are less compressed and less obscure than the earlier works. Some, like "Fern Hill," illustrate an almost Wordsworthian harmony with nature and other human beings but not without the sense of the inexorability of time. As Jacob Korg said of these poems, "the figures and landscapes have a new solidity, a new self-sufficiency, and the dialectic vision no longer penetrates them as though they were no more than windows opening on a timeless universe."

"A Refusal to Mourn the Death, by Fire, of a Child in London," one of Thomas's more accessible poems, illustrates well the almost sacramental view of nature that characterizes this later poetry. At the same time it is topical in its reference to the firebombing of London during the war. The child, like the poet, enters the "synagogue of corn," the holiness of nature, at her death. Yet the poem is richly ambiguous in its final line, "After the first death, there is no other." As Tindall observed, this statement can be taken either as a pledge of eternal life or as a realization that death is death, that one is dead forever—or both. "Fern Hill" presents a similar sacramental imagery—"And the sabbath rang slowly / In the pebbles of the holy streams"—and a pervasive sense of unity between the speaker and nature. But over the whole poem broods "Time," which at the end is triumphant: "Time held me green and dying / Though I sang in my chains like the sea." In an essay for *English Journal* Jack L. Jenkins summarized: "The predominate tone of the poem is still green, touched by the bittersweet knowledge of the last lines but green nonetheless. There is nothing harsh or bitter or dark about the poem, only an inevitable acceptance of the irony."

Mention has already been made of Thomas's obsession with words, and while these later poems in *Deaths and Entrances* are less compressed than the earlier ones, they reveal no less verbal facility or less concern for what is generally called poetic style. Thomas was always a highly individual stylist. Sound was as important as sense in his poems—some would even say more important. He made ample use of alliteration, assonance, internal rhyme, and approximate rhyme. In *The Craft and Art of Dylan Thomas,* William T. Moynihan describes his rhythm as "accentual syllabic": "its stress pattern generally sounds as though it is iambic, but this very justifiable assumption cannot always be borne out by traditional scansion. Thomas may, in fact, have depended upon an iambic expectancy, as he varied his rhythms beyond any customary iambic formulation and then—by completely unprecedented innovations—created his own rhythm, which is very close to iambic."

By the time of the publication of *Deaths and Entrances* Thomas had become a living legend. Through his very popular readings and recordings of his own work, this writer of sometimes obscure poetry gained mass appeal. For many, he came to represent the figure of the bard, the singer of songs to his people. Kershner asserted that Thomas "became the wild man from the West, the Celtic bard with the magical rant, a folk figure with racial access to roots of experience which more civilized Londoners lacked." His drinking, his democratic tendencies, and the frank sexual imagery of his poetry made him the focal point of an ill-defined artistic rebellion.

In 1949 Thomas and his family moved to the Boat House of Laugharne, Wales, a house provided for them by one of Thomas's benefactors, Mrs. Margaret Taylor. For the last four years of his life he moved between this dwelling and the United States, where he went on four separate tours to read his poetry and receive the adulation of the American public. The often sordid accounts of these tours are provided in John Malcolm Brinnin's *Dylan Thomas in America.* Thomas's last separate volume of poetry before the *Collected Poems, 1934-1952* (1952) was *Country Sleep,* published by New Directions in the United States in 1952. As originally published, this book contained six of the poet's most accomplished works: "Over Sir John's hill," "Poem on his Birthday," "Do not go gentle into that good night," "Lament," "In the white giant's thigh," and "In country sleep." Concerning this volume, Rushworth M. Kidder commented in *Dylan Thomas: The Country of the Spirit* that "the fact of physical death seems to present itself to the poet as something more than distant event. . . . These poems come to terms with death through a form of worship: not propitiatory worship of Death as deity, but worship of a higher Deity by whose power all things, including death, are controlled." Tindall called these poems "Thomas at his mellowest." In "Do not go gentle into that good night," a poem written during his father's illness and in anticipation of his death, the son exhorts the father to affirm life in his dying. Similarly, though the women of "In the white giant's thigh" have died childless, the poet, as Korg pointed out, "memorializes their vitality by means of the paradox that their fertility survives through the memory of their many loves."

It has already been mentioned that Thomas began writing scripts during the war. Several of his film scripts have been published, including *The Doctor and the Devils* and *The Beach at Falesa.* Neither of these was produced, but they gave Thomas the opportunity to develop his dramatic skills. These skills culminated in his radio play, *Under Milk Wood,* written over a long period of time and frantically revised in America during the last months of his life. The play grew out of the story "Quite Early One Morning," which was broadcast by the BBC in 1945. *Under Milk Wood* is set in a small Welsh town called Llareggub and covers one day in the lives of its provincial characters. These characters are disembodied voices who reveal their nighttime dreams and their daily monotonous lives. Richard Morton commented that "the trivialities of small-town life are more than evocative, however; they are presented to us in ceremonial order, as though they have a kind of esoteric significance." The characters in the play are satisfied with their lives, and Thomas himself seems to accept and affirm their rural simplicity. Raymond Williams, in an essay for *Dylan Thomas: A Collection of Critical Essays,* said that *Under Milk Wood* is "not a mature work, but the retained extravagance of an adolescent's imaginings. Yet it moves, at its best, into a genuine involvement, an actual sharing of experience, which is not the least of its dramatic virtues." Thomas read the play as a solo performance in Cambridge, Massachusetts, on May 3, 1953; the first group reading was on May 14. In the following November Dylan Thomas died in New York of ailments complicated by alcohol and drug abuse.

The originality that is the hallmark of Thomas's work makes categorization very difficult. As Kershner commented, "The fact remains that Thomas throughout his career stayed generally aloof from literary cliques, groups, and movements." Unlike other prominent writers of the 1930s—W. H. Auden and Stephen Spender, for example—Thomas had little use for socialistic ideas in his art. He seems to have admired much of T. S. Eliot's earlier poetry but became disenchanted with what Kershner called Eliot's "unsensual and religious poetry." It is safe to say that Thomas was influenced by such modern movements as symbolism and surrealism, but he borrowed without adhering to any creed. He was particularly concerned with disassociating himself from the surrealist movement because he felt his conscious craftsmanship was contrary to the methods of that group. In the late 1930s and the 1940s a movement called the Apocalypse, which heralded myth and decried the machine and politics, claimed Thomas for its own; but though he did say he mostly believed in its principles, he refused to sign the group's manifesto. Clearly, Thomas can be seen as an extension into the twentieth century of the general movement called romanticism, particularly in its emphasis on imagination, emotion, intuition, spontaneity, and organic form; but attempts to identify him with a particular "neo-romantic" school have failed. As Kershner said, "The historical perspective, while valuable, is self-limiting; poetry either crosses temporal boundaries or else it has no essential purpose." That Dylan Thomas wrote poems that cross temporal boundaries guarantees their essential purpose.

MEDIA ADAPTATIONS: The Doctor and the Devils was adapted for stage and performed at the Vanbrugh Theatre, Royal Academy of Dramatic Arts, 1961, and filmed by Ronald Harwood in 1985; the poem "The force that through the green fuse drives the flower" was adapted for soprano voice and orchestra by David Harden and released as a sound recording by University Microfilms, 1968; "Under Milk Wood" was performed and broadcast in Britain and the United States by the British Broadcasting Corporation (BBC), and filmed in 1971; several of Thomas's works were adapted into a play, "Dylan Thomas: Return Journey," directed by Anthony Hopkins and produced at the Hudson Guild, New York City, 1990.

BIOGRAPHICAL/CRITICAL SOURCES:

BOOKS

Brinnin, John Malcolm, *Dylan Thomas in America,* Atlantic/ Little, Brown, 1955.

Brinnin, John Malcolm, editor, *A Casebook on Dylan Thomas,* Crowell, 1960.

Cox, C. B., editor, *Dylan Thomas: A Collection of Critical Essays,* Prentice-Hall, 1966.

Davies, Walford, editor, *Dylan Thomas: New Critical Essays,* Dent, 1972.

Dictionary of Literary Biography, Gale, Volume 13: *British Dramatists Since World War II,* 1982, Volume 20: *British Poets, 1914-1945,* 1983.

Emery, Clark, *The World of Dylan Thomas,* University of Miami Press, 1962.

Ferris, Paul, *Dylan Thomas,* Dial, 1977.

FitzGibbon, Constantine, *The Life of Dylan Thomas,* Little, Brown, 1965.

FitzGibbon, Constantine, editor, *Selected Letters of Dylan Thomas,* New Directions, 1967.

Fraser, G. S., *Dylan Thomas,* Longman, revised edition, 1972.

Fraser, G. S., *Vision and Rhetoric,* Faber, 1959.

Jones, Daniel, editor, *Dylan Thomas: The Poems,* New Directions, 1971.

Jones, T. H., *Dylan Thomas,* Barnes & Noble, 1963.

Kershner, R. B., Jr., *Dylan Thomas: The Poet and His Critics,* American Library Association, 1976.

Kidder, Rushworth M., *Dylan Thomas: The Country of the Spirit,* Princeton University Press, 1973.

Korg, Jacob, *Dylan Thomas,* Twayne, 1965.

Maud, Ralph, *Entrances to Dylan Thomas's Poetry,* University of Pittsburgh Press, 1963.

Maud, Ralph, editor, *Poet in the Making: The Notebooks of Dylan Thomas,* New Directions, 1967.

Maud, Ralph and Albert Glover, *Dylan Thomas in Print: A Bibliographical History,* University of Pittsburgh Press, 1970.

Morton, Richard, *An Outline of the Works of Dylan Thomas,* Forum House, 1970.

Moynihan, William T., *The Craft and Art of Dylan Thomas,* Cornell University Press, 1966.

Olson, Elder, *The Poetry of Dylan Thomas,* University of Chicago Press, 1954.

Pratt, Annis, *Dylan Thomas's Early Prose: A Study in Creative Mythology,* University of Pittsburgh Press, 1970.

Stanford, Derek, *Dylan Thomas,* Neville Spearman, revised edition, 1964.

Tedlock, E. W., editor, *Dylan Thomas: The Legend and the Poet; A Collection of Biographical and Critical Essays,* Heinemann, 1960.

Thomas, Caitlin, *Leftover Life to Kill,* Atlantic/Little, Brown, 1957.

Tindall, William York, *A Reader's Guide to Dylan Thomas,* Farrar, Straus, 1962.

Treece, Henry, *How I See Apocalypse,* Lindsay Drummond, 1946.

Treece, Henry, *Dylan Thomas: "Dog Among the Fairies,"* Benn, 1956.

Twentieth-Century Literary Criticism, Gale, Volume 1, 1978, Volume 8, 1982.

West, Paul, *Doubt and Dylan Thomas,* University of Toronto Press, 1970.

Williams, Robert Coleman, editor, *A Concordance to the Collected Poems of Dylan Thomas,* University of Nebraska Press, 1967.

PERIODICALS

Atlantic Monthly, February, 1954, December, 1954, June, 1957, October, 1965, November, 1965.
Bucknell Review, March, 1966.
Critical Quarterly, spring, 1962.
English Journal, January, 1966, December, 1966.
English Language Notes, March, 1969.
Los Angeles Times, May 21, 1989.
National Library of Wales Journal, summer, 1968.
New Republic, June 10, 1967.
New York Times, March 1, 1989, February 23, 1990.
PMLA, September, 1963, December, 1964.
Queen's Quarterly, autumn, 1964.
Southern Review, October, 1967.
Studies in Short Fiction, fall, 1969, winter, 1969.
Texas Quarterly, summer, 1966.
Wall Street Journal, June 8, 1967.

OBITUARIES:

PERIODICALS

New York Times, November 10, 1963.
Observer (London), November 15, 1953.
Poetry, January, 1954.
Spectator (London), November 13, 1953.
Time, November 16, 1953.
Times (London), November 10, 1953.
Wilson Library Bulletin, January, 1954.

*   *   *

THOMAS, Joyce Carol   1938-

PERSONAL: Born May 25, 1938, in Ponca City, Okla.; daughter of Floyd Dave (a bricklayer) and Leona (a housekeeper; maiden name, Thompson) Haynes; married Gettis L. Withers (a chemist), May 31, 1959 (divorced, 1968); married Roy T. Thomas, Jr. (a professor), September 7, 1968 (divorced, 1979); children: Monica Pecot, Gregory Withers, Michael Withers, Roy T. Thomas III. *Education:* Attended San Francisco City College, 1957-58, and University of San Francisco, 1957-58; College of San Mateo, A.A., 1964; San Jose State College (now University), B.A., 1966; Stanford University, M.A., 1967.

ADDRESSES: Home—Berkeley, Calif. *Agent*—Mitch Douglas, International Creative Management, 40 West 57th St., New York, N.Y. 10019.

CAREER: Worked as a telephone operator in San Francisco, Calif., 1957-58; Ravenwood School District, East Palo Alto, Calif., teacher of French and Spanish, 1968-70; San Jose State College (now University), San Jose, Calif., assistant professor of black studies, 1969-72; Contra Costa College, San Pablo, Calif., teacher of drama and English, 1973-75; St. Mary's College, Moranga, Calif., professor of English, 1975-77; San Jose State University, San Jose, reading program director, 1979-82, professor of English, 1982-83; full-time writer, 1982—. Visiting associate professor of English at Purdue University, spring, 1983; member of Berkeley Civic Arts Commission.

MEMBER: International Reading Association, Authors Guild, Western Reading Association, Sigma Delta Pi, Spanish Honors Society.

AWARDS, HONORS: Danforth Graduate Fellow at University of California at Berkeley, 1973-75; Stanford University scholar, 1979-80, and Djerassi Fellow, 1982 and 1983; *Marked by Fire* was named outstanding book of the year by *New York Times* and a best book by American Library Association, both in 1982; Before Columbus American Book Award from Before Columbus Foundation (Berkeley, Calif.), 1982, and the National Book Award for Children's fiction from the Association of American Publishers, 1983, both for *Marked by Fire;* Coretta Scott King Award from American Library Association, 1984, for *Bright Shadow.*

WRITINGS:

NOVELS

Marked by Fire (young adult), Avon, 1982.
Bright Shadow (young adult), Avon, 1983.
Water Girl, Avon, 1986.
The Golden Pasture (young adult), Scholastic, Inc., 1986.
Journey, Scholastic, Inc., 1988.
Amber, Scholastic, Inc., in press.

POETRY

Bittersweet, Firesign Press, 1973.
Crystal Breezes, Firesign Press, 1974.
Blessing, Jocato Press, 1975.
Black Child, Zamani Productions, 1981.
Inside the Rainbow, Zikawana Press, 1982.

PLAYS

(And producer) "A Song in the Sky" (two-act), first produced in San Francisco at Montgomery Theatre, 1976.
"Look! What a Wonder!" (two-act), first produced in Berkeley at Berkeley Community Theatre, 1976.
(And producer) "Magnolia" (two-act), first produced in San Francisco at Old San Francisco Opera House, 1977.
(And producer) "Ambrosia" (two-act), first produced in San Francisco at Little Fox Theatre, 1978.
"Gospel Roots" (two-act), first produced in Carson, Calif., at California State University, 1981.

OTHER

Contributor to periodicals, including *American Poetry Review, Black Scholar, Calafia, Drum Voices, Giant Talk,* and *Yardbird Reader.* Editor of *Ambrosia* (women's newsletter), 1980.

WORK IN PROGRESS: An Act of God, a novel, for Scholastic, Inc.; *House of Light,* a novel.

SIDELIGHTS: Often favorably compared to such prominent black female writers as Maya Angelou, Alice Walker, and Toni Morrison, Joyce Carol Thomas first established her literary reputation as a poet and playwright in the San Francisco Bay area of California. Raised in Oklahoma during the 1940s as the fifth child in a family of nine, Thomas developed an early fascination for storytelling when, during harvest time, sharing anecdotes and exchanging bits of family lore were popular sources of entertainment. Her works reflect this ingrained talent for telling stories; her first book, the 1982 award-winning young adult novel, *Marked by Fire,* earned the author critical acclaim for what *San Francisco Chronicle Book World* reviewer Patricia Holt called Thomas's "ear for language and dialect, her gift for simplicity in description and the absolute authenticity of her setting and characters."

Marked by Fire chronicles twenty years in the life of Abyssinia Jackson, beginning with her birth in a cotton field, where she is scarred by a spark from a brush fire. As such, she is "marked for unbearable pain and unspeakable joy," according to Mother Barker, the character who serves as the local healer, spiritual adviser, and, eventually, Abyssinia's mentor. Set in Ponca City, Oklahoma—Thomas's birthplace—the story depicts Abyssinia as an especially bright, happy child who is gifted with an extraordinarily beautiful singing voice. At age ten, however, she loses this gift when an elder member of her church brutally rapes her. The incident brings the prophesied "unbearable pain" and a bitter questioning of her faith in God, but with time—and the support of the women in the close-knit community—Abyssinia gradually recovers from the ordeal. The remainder of *Marked by Fire* traces the heroine's passage into young womanhood and concludes with her decision to follow in Mother Barker's footsteps, attending to the needs of the town's troubled and sick.

The novel met with enthusiastic reviews and became required reading in many high school and university classrooms throughout the United States. "Thomas writes with admirable simplicity and finds a marvelous fairy tale quality in everyday happenings," wrote *New York Times Book Review* critic Alice Childress. Holt declared the book a "hauntingly and beautifully written novel" that "reads with the rhythm and beauty of poetry" and deemed *Marked by Fire* "the kind of novel that *no one* should miss." California's *Peninsula Times Review* writer Charles Beardsley praised Thomas's portrayal of the main character, describing Abyssinia as "drawn full scale, shining forth as an unforgettable individual who welcomes life and thereby experiences as much joy as sorrow, life's ignomiy and the grandeur of its heritage." Beardsley added that *Marked by Fire* "is no 'made up' story, but the sensitive distillation of the black experience as seen through the eyes of a remarkable writer."

In *Bright Shadow,* the 1983 sequel to *Marked by Fire,* Abyssinia enters college to prepare for a medical career. She meets and falls in love with Carl Lee Jefferson and, despite initial disapproval from Abyssinia's father, their relationship thrives. Together they endure the painful aftermath of the gruesome murder of Abyssinia's favorite aunt as well as the death of Carl Lee's abusive father, an event that reveals the truth of Carl Lee's ancestry.

Critical reception of *Bright Shadow* did not match that of its predecessor, but was nevertheless recommended in library and publishing journals and won the Coretta Scott King Award offered by the American Library Association in 1984. Thomas plans additional novels for the "Abyssinia" series.

MEDIA ADAPTATIONS: Marked by Fire was adapted by James Racheff and Ted Kociolek for the stage musical "Abyssinia," first produced in New York City at the CSC Repertory Theater in 1987.

BIOGRAPHICAL/CRITICAL SOURCES:

BOOKS

Contemporary Literary Criticism, Volume 35, Gale, 1985.
Dictionary of Literary Biography, Volume 33: *Afro-American Fiction Writers after 1955,* Gale, 1984.
Something about the Author Autobiography Series, Volume 7, Gale, 1989.
Yalom, Marilyn, editor, *Women Writers of the West Coast,* Capra Press, 1983.

PERIODICALS

New York Times, November 30, 1982.
New York Times Book Review, April 18, 1982, December 5, 1982, March 18, 1984.
Peninsula Times Tribune (California), March 20, 1982.

San Francisco Chronicle Book World, April 12, 1982.

*   *   *

THOMAS, Lewis 1913-

PERSONAL: Born November 25, 1913, in Flushing, N.Y.; son of Joseph S. (a surgeon) and Grace Emma (Peck) Thomas; married Beryl Dawson, January 1, 1941; children: Abigail, Judith, Eliza. *Education:* Princeton University, B.S., 1933; Harvard University, M.D., 1937.

ADDRESSES: Home—333 East 68th St., New York, N.Y. 10021. *Office*—Memorial Sloan-Kettering Cancer Center, 1275 York Ave., New York, N.Y. 10021.

CAREER: Boston City Hospital, Boston, Mass., intern, 1937-39; Neurological Institute, New York City, resident in neurology, 1939-41; Boston City Hospital, Tilney Memorial Fellow at Thorndike Laboratory, 1941-42; Rockefeller Institute for Medical Research, New York City, visiting investigator, 1942-46; Johns Hopkins University, Baltimore, Md., assistant professor of pediatrics, 1946-48; Tulane University, New Orleans, La., associate professor, 1948-50, professor of medicine, 1950, director of Division of Infectious Disease, 1948-50; University of Minnesota, Minneapolis, professor of pediatrics and medicine and director of pediatric research laboratories at Heart Hospital, 1950-54; New York University, New York City, professor of pathology, 1954-69, head of department, 1954-58, director of University Hospital, 1959-66, dean of School of Medicine, 1966-69; Yale University, New Haven, Conn., professor of pathology and head of department, 1969-72, dean of School of Medicine, 1971-73; Memorial Sloan-Kettering Cancer Center, New York City, president and chief executive officer, 1973-80, chancellor, 1980-83, emeritus president and member of Sloan-Kettering Institute, 1983—.

Professor at Cornell University; adjunct professor at Rockefeller University (also member of board of trustees); member of board of overseers of Harvard University, 1976—; member of scientific advisory board of C. V. Whitney Laboratory for Experimental Marine Biology and Medicine, at University of Florida, 1976—; member of council of visitors of Bank Street College of Education, 1975—; associate fellow of Ezra Stiles College, Yale University. Pediatrician at Harriet Lane Home for Invalid Children, of Johns Hopkins University, 1946-48; director of medical divisions at Bellevine Hospital, 1958-66, president of Medical Board, 1963-66; chief of pathology at Yale-New Haven Hospital, 1969-73; attending physician at Memorial Hospital; member of scientific advisory committee of Massachusetts General Hospital, 1969-72; member of scientific advisory board of Scripps Clinic and Research Foundation, 1973-78. Member of board of directors of New York City Public Health Research Institute, 1960-69; member of board of trustees of C. S. Draper Laboratory, 1974—, Cold Spring Harbor Laboratory, 1974—, and Hellenic Anticancer Institute (Athens), 1977—; member of scientific advisory committee of Fox Chase Institute for Cancer Research, 1976—; member of scientific council of International Institute of Cellular and Molecular Pathology (Brussels), 1977—. Member of Commission on Streptococcal and Staphylococcal Diseases, of U.S. Department of Defense's Armed Forces Epidemiological Board, 1950-62; member of New York City Board of Health, 1955-60, and Health Research Council, 1974-75 (head of narcotics advisory committee, 1961-63); member of National Advisory Health Council, 1958-62, and National Advisory Child Health and Human Development Council, 1963-67; member of President's Science Advisory Committee,

1967-70; head of National Academy of Sciences committee to review national cancer plan, 1972; member of special medical advisory group to U.S. Veterans Administration. Member of board of trustees of Guggenheim Foundation, 1975—, and board of directors of Squibb Corp., 1969—, and Josiah Macy, Jr. Foundation, 1975—. *Military service:* U.S. Naval Reserve, Medical Corps, active duty, 1941-46; became lieutenant commander.

MEMBER: International Academy of Pathology, Association of American Physicians, American Academy and Institute of Arts and Letters (inducted, 1984), American Pediatric Society, American Association of Immunologists, Society for Experimental Biology and Medicine, American Academy of Microbiology (charter member), American Rheumatism Association, American Society for Clinical Investigation, National Academy of Sciences Institute of Medicine (member of council, 1973-76), American Philosophical Society, American Academy of Arts and Sciences, American Association of University Professors, Peripatetic Clinical Society, Practitioners Society, Harvey Society, Interurban Clinical Club, Phi Beta Kappa, Alpha Omega Alpha, Century Association, Harvard Club.

AWARDS, HONORS: Honorary degrees include M.A. from Yale University, 1969, Sc.D. from University of Rochester, 1974, Princeton University, 1976, Medical College of Ohio, 1976, and Columbia University, 1978, LL.D. from Johns Hopkins University, 1976, L.H.D. from Duke University, 1976, and Reed College, 1977; National Book Award in Arts and Letters, 1974, for *The Lives of a Cell;* distinguished achievement award from *Modern Medicine,* 1975; visiting scholar of Phi Beta Kappa, 1977-78; American Academy and Institute of Arts and Letters award, 1980; American Book Award for science, 1981, for *The Medusa and the Snail.*

WRITINGS:

The Lives of a Cell: Notes of a Biology Watcher, Viking, 1974.

The Medusa and the Snail: More Notes of a Biology Watcher, Viking, 1979.

The Youngest Science: Notes of a Medicine-Watcher, Viking, 1983.

Late Night Thoughts on Listening to Mahler's Ninth Symphony, Viking, 1984.

CONTRIBUTOR

Rheumatic Fever: A Symposium, University of Minnesota Press, 1952.

Gregory Schwartzman, editor, *The Effects of ACTH and Cortisone Upon Infection and Resistance,* Columbia University Press, 1953.

Russell Cecil and R. F. Loeb, editors, *A Textbook of Medicine,* Saunders, 1953.

H. S. Lawrence, editor, *Cellular and Humoral Aspects of the Hypersensitive States,* Paul B. Hoeber, 1959.

Biological Problems of Grafting, Les Congres et Colloques de L'Universite de Liege, 1959.

Streptococcus, Rheumatic Fever, and Glomerulonephritis, Williams & Wilkins, 1964.

W. Braun and M. Landy, editors, *Bacterial Endotoxins,* Rutgers University, Institute of Microbiology, 1964.

The Inflammatory Process, Academic Press, 1965.

The Modern Hospital, McGraw, 1967.

P. A. Miescher, C. Henze, and R. Schett, editors, *The Modern University: Structure, Functions, and Its Role in the New Industrial State,* Georg Thieme Verlag, 1969.

Microbial Toxins, Volume 3, Academic Press, 1970.

G. I. Gallagher, editor, *Immunological Disorders of the Nervous System,* Williams & Wilkins, 1971.

I. Z. Bowers and E. F. Purcell, editors, *Advances in American Medicine: Essays at the Bicentennial,* Josiah Macy, Jr. Foundation, 1976.

Contributor of a poem to *New Yorker.* Contributor of about two hundred articles to medical and scientific journals, including *Science, Nature, Daedalus,* and *Saturday Review of Science.* Author of column, "Notes of a Biology Watcher," in *New England Journal of Medicine,* 1971—. Member of editorial board of *Human Pathology, Journal of Immunology, American Journal of Pathology, Cellular Immunology, Journal of Medicine and Philosophy, Inflammation, Perspectives in Biology and Medicine, Human Nature, Journal of Developmental and Comparative Immunology,* and *Daedalus.*

SIDELIGHTS: The observation of the natural world has long been Lewis Thomas's vocation and avocation. Although his medical specialty is pathology, Thomas's interest has been captured by the range of natural phenomena from the unit of the cell to human social patterns. In 1971 he began contributing a popular column, "Notes of a Biology Watcher," to the prestigious *New England Journal of Medicine.* Some of these essays were collected and published in 1974 as *The Lives of a Cell: Notes of a Biology Watcher.* The book, which according to a *Time* reviewer combined wit and "imagination" with a "bold, encouraging vision of both man and nature," received a National Book Award the same year. Critics were dazzled with Thomas's accomplishment, but he was somewhat embarrassed by his newfound status as a book author. "I mean it's not really fair to have a book with a cover and everything when you never wrote a book, except in such little tiny bits," he told Barbara Yuncker. "I love having it, but it doesn't seem as though I'd earned it."

Symbiosis—the mutually beneficial relationship between organisms—is the main theme of *The Lives of a Cell.* "There is a tendency for living things to join up," explains Thomas, "establish linkages, live inside each other, return to earlier arrangements, get along whenever possible. This is the way of the world." He decries man's attempt to remove himself from nature, and concludes that "the whole dear notion of one's own self-marvelous old free-willed, free-enterprising, autonomous, independent, isolated island of a Self—is a myth."

New Yorker reviewer John Updike noted that Thomas's "absorption in the marvels of symbiotic interconnection intoxicates this scientist, and leads him into flights of what must be fantasy." Some of his ideas, Updike commented, seem "more mystical than demonstrable." He continued: "Dr. Thomas has the mystic's urge toward total unity. He views the earth as a single cell in its membrane of atmosphere. . . . Not that he professes any use for old-fashioned supernaturalist religion. Yet his doctrine of universal symbiosis soars with an evangelical exultation, and it is interesting that even his careful prose lapses into the grammar of teleology."

In the *New York Times Book Review,* Joyce Carol Oates pondered what tack to take in praising Thomas's work. She remarked: "A reviewer who concentrates upon Dr. Thomas's effortless, beautifully-toned style, even to the point of claiming that many of the twenty-nine essays in this book are masterpieces of the 'art of the essay,' would direct attention away from the sheer amount of scientific information these slender essays contain. A reviewer who deals with the book as 'science' would be forced, by Dr. Thomas's marvelous use of paradox, to admit that the book might not yield its wisdom at a single reading." She continued: "One might as well rise to the higher speculation that [this book] anticipates the kind of writing that will appear more and more frequently, as scientists take on the language of poetry in order to communicate human truths too mysterious for old-fashioned common sense."

Since the publication of *The Lives of a Cell,* more of Thomas's essays have been collected in *The Medusa and the Snail: More Notes of a Biology Watcher, The Youngest Science: Notes of a Medicine-Watcher,* and *Late Night Thoughts on Listening to Mahler's Ninth Symphony.* Barbara Brotman writes in the *Chicago Tribune* of *The Medusa and the Snail,* "Despite all his intense concentration through powerful microscopes at minute particles of life, Thomas never has stopped marveling at the Big Picture, how well everything on this Earth works: the civility of the symbiotic relationship between the sea slug and the jellyfish or medusa, the subject of the title essay, the mysterious way warts can actually be *thought* away, the almost always accurate pinpointing and destruction by our antibodies of foreign cells."

Many of Thomas's essays end on an upbeat note. The title essay of *The Lives of a Cell* succinctly expresses Thomas's perception of man's place in the universe and his belief in the continued existence of that universe. He wrote: "We are told that the trouble with Modern Man is that he has been trying to detach himself from nature. He sits on the topmost tiers of polymer, glass, and steel, dangling his pulsing legs, surveying at a distance the writhing life of the planet. In this scenario, Man comes on as a stupendous lethal force, and the earth is pictured as something delicate, like rising bubbles at the surface of a country pond, or flights of fragile birds. But it is an illusion to think that there is anything fragile about the life of the earth; surely this is the toughest membrane imaginable in the universe, opaque to probability, impermeable to death. We are the delicate part, transient and vulnerable as cilia."

BIOGRAPHICAL/CRITICAL SOURCES:

BOOKS

Contemporary Literary Criticism, Volume 35, Gale, 1985.
Thomas, Lewis, *The Lives of a Cell: Notes of a Biology Watcher,* Viking, 1974.

PERIODICALS

Chicago Tribune, July 11, 1979.
Detroit News, May 27, 1979.
Newsweek, June 24, 1974.
New Yorker, July 15, 1974.
New York Post, June 29, 1974.
New York Review of Books, November 28, 1974.
New York Times, April 27, 1979, February 9, 1983, November 5, 1983.
New York Times Book Review, May 26, 1974.
Time, July 22, 1974, May 14, 1979.
Village Voice, June 27, 1974.
Washington Post, August 28, 1979, September 1, 1979.

*   *   *

THOMAS, Paul
See MANN, (Paul) Thomas

*   *   *

THOMAS, R(onald) S(tuart) 1913-

PERSONAL: Born March 29, 1913 in Cardiff, Wales; son of T. H. (a sailor); married Mildred E. Eldridge (a painter), 1940; chil-

dren: Gwydion (son). *Education:* University College of North Wales, B. A., 1935; attended St. Michael's College, Llandaff, 1935-36.

ADDRESSES: Home—Sarn-y-Plas, Y Rhiw, Pwllheli, Gwynedd, Wales.

CAREER: Ordained a deacon of the Anglican Church, 1936, priest, 1937; curate of Chirk, Denbighshire, 1936-40; curate in charge of Tallarn Green, Hanmer, Flintshire, 1940-42; rector of Manafon, Montgomeryshire, 1942-54; vicar of St. Michael's, Eglwysfach, Cardiganshire, 1954-67; vicar of St. Hywyn, Aberdaron, Gwynedd, with St. Mary, Bodferin, 1967-78; rector of Rhiw with Llanfaelrhys, 1972-78.

MEMBER: Campaign for Nuclear Disarmament (committee member and representative of county branch).

AWARDS, HONORS: Heinemann Award, Royal Society of Literature, 1955, for *Song at the Year's Turning: Poems, 1942-1954;* Queen's Gold Medal for Poetry, 1964; Welsh Arts Council award, 1968 and 1976; Cholmondeley Award, 1978.

WRITINGS:

POEMS

The Stones of the Field, Druid Press, 1946.
An Acre of Land, Montgomeryshire Printing Company, 1952.
The Minister (verse play; first produced on Welsh BBC Radio, 1953), Montgomeryshire Printing Company, 1953.
Song at the Year's Turning: Poems, 1942-1954, with introduction by John Betjeman, Hart-Davis, 1955.
Poetry for Supper, Hart-Davis, 1958, Dufour, 1961.
Judgment Day, Poetry Book Society, 1960.
Tares, Dufour, 1961.
(With Lawrence Durrell and Elizabeth Jennings) *Penguin Modern Poets 1,* Penguin (London), 1962.
The Bread of Truth, Dufour, 1963.
Pieta, Hart-Davis, 1966.
Not That He Brought Flowers, Hart-Davis, 1968.
(With Roy Fuller) *Pergamon Poets 1,* edited by Evan Owen, Pergamon, 1968.
Postcard: Song, Fishpaste Postcard Series, 1968.
The Mountains, illustrations by John Piper, Chilmark Press, 1963.
H'm: Poems, St. Martin's, 1972.
Young and Old (children's poems), Chatto & Windus, 1972.
Selected Poems, 1946-1968, Hart-Davis MacGibbon, 1973, St. Martin's, 1974.
What Is a Welshman?, Christopher Davies, 1974.
Laboratories of the Spirit, Macmillan (London), 1975, Godine, 1976.
The Way of It, illustrations by Barry Hirst, Ceolfrith Press, 1977.
Frequencies, Macmillan (London), 1978.
Between Here and Now, Macmillan (London), 1981.
Later Poems, 1972-1982, Macmillan (London), 1983.
A Selection of Poetry, edited by D. J. Hignett, Hignett School Services, 1983.
Poet's Meeting, Celandine, 1984.
Ingrowing Thoughts, Poetry Wales Press, 1985.
Destinations, Celandine, 1985.
Poems of R. S. Thomas, University of Arkansas Press, 1985.
Experimenting with an Amen, Macmillan (London), 1986.
Welsh Airs, Poetry Wales Press, 1987.

EDITOR

The Batsford Book of Country Verse, Batsford, 1961.
The Penguin Book of Religious Verse, Penguin, 1963.

Edward Thomas, *Selected Poems,* Faber, 1964.
A Choice of George Herbert's Verse, Faber, 1967.
A Choice of Wordsworth's Verse, Faber, 1971.

OTHER

Words and the Poet (W. D. Thomas Memorial Lecture), University of Wales Press, 1964.
Selected Prose, edited by Sandra Anstey, Poetry Wales Press, 1983, Dufour, 1984.
Neb: Golygwyd gan Gwenno Hywyn (autobiography in Welsh), Gwasg Gwynedd, 1987.

SIDELIGHTS: Recognized as one of the leading poets of modern Wales, R. S. Thomas writes about the people of his country in a style that some critics have compared to that nation's harsh and rugged terrain. Using few of the common poetic devices, Thomas's work exhibits what Alan Brownjohn of the *New Statesman* calls a "cold, telling purity of language." James F. Knapp of *Twentieth Century Literature* explains that "the poetic world which emerges from the verse of R. S. Thomas is a world of lonely Welsh farms and of the farmers who endure the harshness of their hill country. The vision is realistic and merciless." Despite the often grim nature of his subject matter, Thomas's poems are ultimately life-affirming. "What I'm after," John Mole of *Phoenix* quotes Thomas explaining, "is to demonstrate that man is spiritual." As Louis Sasso remarks in *Library Journal,* "Thomas's poems are sturdy, worldly creations filled with compassion, love, doubt, and irony. They make one feel joy in being part of the human race."

The son of a sailor, Thomas spent much of his childhood in British port towns where he and his mother would live while his father was away at sea. His early education began late and was only sporadically pursued until his father found steady work with a ferry boat company operating between Wales and Ireland, and the family was able to settle in the Welsh town of Caergybi. After graduating from school Thomas studied for the Anglican priesthood, a career first suggested to him by his mother. As he recounts in his article for the *Contemporary Authors Autobiography Series,* "Shy as I was, I offered no resistance."

In 1936, Thomas was ordained a deacon in the Anglican Church and was assigned to work as a curate in the Welsh mining village of Chirk. In 1937 he became an Anglican priest. The post in Chirk was the first of a series of positions he was to hold in the rural communities of Wales. Between 1936 and 1978, Thomas served in churches located in six different Welsh towns. These appointments gave him a firsthand knowledge of Welsh farming life and provided him with a host of characters and settings for his poetry.

Although he had written poetry in school, it was only after meeting Mildred E. Eldridge, the woman who was to become his wife, that Thomas began to write seriously. At the time they met she had already earned a reputation as a painter, and, as Thomas remarks in his article for the *Contemporary Authors Autobiography Series,* "this made me wish to become recognised as a poet." He began to compose poetry about the Welsh countryside and its people, influenced by the writings of Edward Thomas, Fiona Macleod, and William Butler Yeats.

Perhaps Thomas's best known character is Iago Prytherch, a farm laborer who appears in many of his poems. Thomas describes him in the poem "A Peasant" as "an ordinary man of the bald Welsh hills." Writing in *British Poetry since 1970: A Critical Survey,* Colin Meir explains that Prytherch epitomizes Welsh hill-farming life and "is seen as embodying man's fortitude." A. E. Dyson, in an article for *Critical Quarterly,* finds that Pry-

therch, being a farmer, is "cut off from culture and poetry, and cut off too . . . from religion. . . . Yet [he] has an elemental reality and power in his life which is in part to be envied."

Prytherch is a kind of archetypal rural Welshman, standing as a symbol for his people. As Knapp remarks, Prytherch "represents the Welsh peasants in all their aspects throughout [Thomas's] poetry." According to Dyson, Prytherch is also used by Thomas as a symbol for humanity itself. His hard labor in an unyielding landscape, though representative of Welsh farmers, also exemplifies the hardships common to all men. "It seems then," Dyson states, "that in finding in the Welsh peasants a 'prototype' of man, Thomas is making a universal statement. . . . This pared-down existence, in a land of ruined beauty belonging to the past, is more human than any educated sophistication. Or perhaps one should say, it is more truly symbolic of the human predicament."

Many of Thomas's poems set his farming characters against the bleak and forbidding landscape of Wales, focusing on the difficulties of rural existence. "Many of his poems offer an unsparingly bleak view of man," Knapp admits, "and . . . even in those cases where hope seems clearly offered, the elements of the drama are still exceedingly grim. . . . The basic postulate is a kind of minimal man, struggling to endure in his little universe. . . . Mostly the visual aspect of the poetry concerns lone figures, working the stony fields, walking along the roads." Comparing Thomas's work with that of Robert Frost, who also wrote of rural life, C. A. Runcie of *Poetry Australia* notes that Thomas's "farmers and labourers and hillmen, unlike Frost's, are not philosophers. Thought has been worked out of them year after year. Only life and a little, obtuse, silent feeling remain."

As a clergyman, Thomas imbues his poetry with a consistently religious theme, often speaking of "the lonely and often barren predicament of the priest, who is as isolated in his parish as Prytherch is on the bare hillside," as Meir writes. "In Christian terms," Dyson explains, "Thomas is not a poet of the transfiguration, of the resurrection, of human holiness. . . . He is a poet of the Cross, the unanswered prayer, the bleak trek through darkness, and his theology of Jesus, in particular, seems strange against any known traditional norm." Anne Stevenson of the *Listener* describes Thomas as "a religious poet" who "sees tragedy, not pathos, in the human condition. . . . He is one of the rare poets writing today who never asks for pity."

Writing in the *Contemporary Authors Autobiography Series,* Thomas asserts that "as long as I was a priest of the Church, I felt an obligation to try to present the Bible message in a more or less orthodox way. I never felt that I was employed by the Church to preach my own beliefs and doubts and questionings. Some people were curious to know whether I did not feel some conflict between my two vocations. But I always replied that Christ was a poet, that the New Testament was poetry, and that I had no difficulty preaching the New Testament in its poetic context."

Although he had already published three books of poetry, Thomas did not gain widespread recognition as a poet until the appearance of *Song at the Year's Turning: Poems, 1942-1954.* This volume, brought out by a major publisher and with an introduction by poet John Betjeman, introduced Thomas to a national audience and "caused quite a stir," according to W. J. Keith in the *Dictionary of Literary Biography.* The collection's poems, marked by a spare and controlled language, earned Thomas widespread critical praise. With each subsequent volume his reputation has increased.

Like the Welsh countryside he writes about, Thomas's poetry is often harsh and austere, written in plain, somber language, with a meditative quality. Runcie describes Thomas's style as consisting of "simple words and short nouns, nouns of such authentic meaning that they rarely need modifiers, moving as beats at a controlled pace in stress accent metre—a constant technique to effect a constant tone, his own inexhaustibly haunting tone that lingers like sounds in a darkness." Writing in *Eight Contemporary Poets,* Calvin Bedient also notes this spare style, claiming that "Thomas puts little between himself and his subject. . . . His poems are ascetic. . . . To seem at once lean and sensuous, transparent and deeply crimsoned, is part of his distinction." Thomas reveals his stylistic intentions in *Words and the Poet:* "A recurring ideal, I find, is that of simplicity. At times there comes the desire to write with great precision and clarity, words so simple and moving that they bring tears to the eyes."

Thomas's interest in such things as his Welsh homeland, his religion, the natural world, and a spare and simple poetic style reflect his disenchantment with the modern world. In *Neb: Golygwyd gan Gwenno Hywyn,* an autobiography, Thomas speaks of his tendency to "look back and see the past as better," according to Gwyneth Lewis in *London Magazine.* On several occasions he has expressed his dismay at this century's industrialization of Wales, arguing that the country's natural beauty has been ruined. In his article for the *Contemporary Authors Autobiography Series,* Thomas lists among his recent concerns "the assault of contemporary lifestyles on the beauty and peace of the natural world." Thomas notes too that religious faith has declined with the emergence of our technological civilization. "We are told with increasing vehemence," he writes in the *Times Literary Supplement,* "that this is a scientific age, that science is transforming the world, but is it not also a mechanized and impersonal age, an analytic and clinical one; an age in which under the hard gloss of affluence there can be detected the murmuring of the starved heart and the uneasy spirit?"

Runcie believes that with Thomas, the poet and the poetry are one. He describes Thomas as "a Welshman and a parson, a tidy, boney man with a thin face rutted by severity. And the poems are the man. Austere and simple and of repressed power." Similarly, William Cole in the *Saturday Review/World* comments that "Thomas is austere, tough-minded, but can bring tears." Looking back on his long career, Thomas writes in the *Contemporary Authors Autobiography Series* that he "moved in unimportant circles, avoiding, or being excluded from the busier and more imposing walks of life." He claims that the critical praise he has received is due to "a small talent for turning my limited thoughts and experience and meditation upon them into verse."

Despite what he sees as a "small talent," Thomas is often ranked among the most important Welsh poets of this century. Writing in the *Anglo-Welsh Review,* R. George Thomas finds him to be "the finest living Welsh poet writing in English." Keith reports that Thomas is "now recognized as a prominent voice in British poetry of the second half of the twentieth century" and "has strong claims to be considered the most important contemporary Anglo-Welsh poet." Meir concludes that Thomas's work expresses a religious conviction uncommon in modern poetry. Thomas, according to Meir, believes that "one of the important functions of poetry is to embody religious truth, and since for him as poet that truth is not easily won, his poems record the struggle with marked honesty and integrity, thereby providing the context for the necessarily infrequent moments of faith and vision which are expressed with a clarity and gravity rarely matched by any of his contemporaries."

BIOGRAPHICAL/CRITICAL SOURCES:

BOOKS

Anstey, Sandra, *Critical Writings on R. S. Thomas,* Poetry Wales Press, 1982.
Bedient, Calvin, *Eight Contemporary Poets,* Oxford University Press, 1974.
Contemporary Authors Autobiography Series, Volume 4, Gale, 1986.
Contemporary Literary Criticism, Gale, Volume 6, 1976, Volume 13, 1980, Volume 48, 1988.
Dictionary of Literary Biography, Volume 27: *Poets of Great Britain and Ireland, 1945-1960,* Gale, 1984.
Dyson, A. E., *Yeats, Eliot, and R. S. Thomas: Riding the Echo,* Macmillan (London), 1981.
Jones, Peter and Michael Schmidt, editors, *British Poetry since 1970: A Critical Survey,* Carcanet Press, 1980.
Keith, W. J., *The Poetry of Nature,* University of Toronto Press, 1980.
Merchant, William Moelwyn, *R. S. Thomas,* Verry, 1979.
New Pelican Guide to English Literature, Pelican, 1983.
Phillips, Dewi, *R. S. Thomas: Poet of the Hidden God,* Macmillan (London), 1986.
Thomas, R. George, *R. S. Thomas,* Longman, 1964.
Thomas, R. S., *Words and the Poet,* University of Wales Press, 1964.
Ward, J. P., *The Poetry of R. S. Thomas,* Poetry Wales Press, 1987.

PERIODICALS

Anglo-Welsh Review, February, 1970, autumn, 1971.
Books and Bookmen, September, 1974.
Critical Quarterly, winter, 1960, summer, 1978, autumn, 1985.
Daily Telegraph Magazine, November 7, 1975.
Hudson Review, spring, 1987.
Library Journal, September 1, 1976.
Listener, April 15, 1976.
London Magazine, December, 1986-January, 1987.
Midwest Quarterly, summer, 1974.
New Statesman, September 29, 1972.
Phoenix, winter, 1972.
Poetry, April, 1974.
Poetry Australia, 1972.
Poetry Wales, spring, 1972.
Review of English Literature, October, 1962.
Saturday Review/World, April 20, 1974.
Spectator, November 8, 1975, April 1, 1978.
Times Literary Supplement, March 3, 1966, June 2, 1978.
Twentieth Century Literature, January, 1971.

*   *   *

THOMPSON, Francis Clegg
See MENCKEN, H(enry) L(ouis)

*   *   *

THOMPSON, Hunter S(tockton) 1939-

PERSONAL: Born July 18, 1939, in Louisville, Ky.; son of Jack R. (an insurance agent) and Virginia (Ray) Thompson; married Sandra Dawn, May 19, 1963; children: Juan. *Education:* Attended public schools in Louisville, Ky. *Politics:* Anarchist. *Religion:* None.

ADDRESSES: Home—Owl Farm, Woody Creek, Colo. 81656.

CAREER: New York Herald Tribune, New York, N.Y., Caribbean correspondent, 1959-60; *National Observer,* New York, N.Y., South American correspondent, 1961-63; writer, 1963—. *Rolling Stone* (magazine), national affairs editor, 1970-76, affiliated with the magazine until 1981; global affairs correspondent, *High Times,* 1977—; media critic, *San Francisco Examiner,* 1985—. *Military service:* U.S. Air Force, 1956-58.

MEMBER: Overseas Press Club, American Civil Liberties Union, National Rifle Association.

WRITINGS:

Hell's Angels: A Strange and Terrible Saga, Random House, 1966.
Fear and Loathing in Las Vegas: A Savage Journey to the Heart of the American Dream, illustrated by Ralph Steadman, Random House, 1972.
Fear and Loathing on the Campaign Trail '72, illustrated by Steadman, Straight Arrow Books, 1973.
The Great Shark Hunt: Strange Tales from a Strange Time, Summit Books, 1979.
The Curse of Lono, illustrated by Steadman, Bantam, 1983.
Generation of Swine: Gonzo Papers, Volume Two; Tales of Shame and Degradation in the '80s, Summit Books, 1988.

Contributor to *Esquire, New York Times Magazine, Nation, Reporter, Harper's,* and other publications.

WORK IN PROGRESS: The Silk Road, a novel set in the Florida Keys during "The Great Cuban Freedom Flotilla."

SIDELIGHTS: Hunter S. Thompson ranks among the first and foremost practitioners of New Journalism, a genre that evolved in the 1960s to reflect the particular mood of those times. Thompson, who has called his contributions "Gonzo Journalism," was among the most visible—and vituperative—of New Journalism correspondents; as national affairs editor for *Rolling Stone* and author of such widely read books as *Hell's Angels: A Strange and Terrible Saga, Fear and Loathing in Las Vegas: A Savage Journey to the Heart of the American Dream,* and *Fear and Loathing on the Campaign Trail '72,* he caught both the disillusionment and the delirium of a volatile era. According to Morris Dickstein in *Gates of Eden: American Culture in the Sixties,* Thompson "paraded one of the few original prose styles of recent years," a style that indulged in insult and stream-of-invective to an unparalleled degree. He pioneered a new approach to reporting, allowing the story of covering an event to become the central story itself, while never disguising the fact that he was "a half-cranked geek journalist caught in the center of the action," to quote Jerome Klinkowitz in *The Life of Fiction.*

Critics have responded enthusiastically to Thompson's mad, drug-ridden forays into the heart of a corpulent and complacent America. *Saturday Review* contributor Joseph Kanon notes that Thompson has brought a great originality to his work. "There is no one quite like him," Kanon writes, "and we turn to [him] not for 'objective' reporting . . . but to watch an interesting sensibility engaged in high drama. . . . His eccentricity works for him—he seems a rare individual voice in a world of homogenized telecasts. His raving excess is what we read him *for,* and, as with all good writers, his style—a wild mishmash of put-on, fantasy, and cultivated lunacy—seems an extension of personality. He is the kind of writer who talks to you right on the page." Klinkowitz, among others, praises Thompson for employing the technique "of simultaneously leading the parade and heckling oneself from the curb, to capture the spirit of the age in himself." By this means, Klinkowitz contends, Thompson "turns himself into a laboratory for the study of what's going on in contempo-

rary America." *New York Times Book Review* correspondent Leo E. Litwak observes that Thompson's "language is brilliant, his eye is remarkable, and his point of view is reminiscent of Huck Finn's. He'll look at anything; he won't compromise his integrity. Somehow his exuberance and innocence are unaffected by what he sees." In his book *Wampeters Foma & Granfalloons,* Kurt Vonnegut, Jr., concludes that Thompson "is that rare sort of American author who must be read. He makes exciting, moving collages out of carefully selected junk."

Thompson was considered a seasoned journalist while still in his twenties. Between 1959 and 1965 he served as a Caribbean correspondent for the *New York Herald Tribune* and South American correspondent for the *National Observer* and also contributed to magazines such as the *Nation, Harper's, Reporter* and *Scanlan's.* His early works were conventional, but as his own experiments with drugs increased, and the tenor of the nation began to change, he embraced the nascent New Journalism style. *New York Times Book Review* contributor Crawford Woods explains that New Journalism's roots lay in "the particular sense of the nineteen-sixties that a new voice was demanded by the way people's public and private lives were coming together in a sensual panic stew, with murder its meat and potatoes, grass and acid its spice. How to tell the story of a time when all fiction was science fiction, all facts lies? The New Journalism was born." Dickstein notes that the genre "developed parallel to the chief organs of information, influencing them only subtly and gradually, in tandem with the influence of the age. . . . This work included a broad spectrum of underground writing—political, countercultural, feminist, pornographic, and so on—that dealt with cultural developments ignored, distorted, or merely exploited by the media." Riding and drinking with the Hell's Angels motorcycle gang, taking massive quantities of hallucinogenic drugs, and careening to assignments on little food and less sleep, Thompson became the "professional wildman" of the New Journalists, to quote *Village Voice* contributor Vivian Gornick. He also became a nationally known figure whose work "in particular caused currents of envy in the world of the straight journalists, who coveted his freedom from restraint," according to an *Atlantic* essayist.

In *Critique: Studies in Modern Fiction,* John Hellmann writes: "By conceiving his journalism as a form of fiction, Thompson has been able to shape actual events into meaningful works of literary art." Thompson's "Gonzo Journalism" narratives are first-person accounts in which the author appears as a persona, sometimes Raoul Duke, but more commonly Dr. Hunter S. Thompson, a specialist variously in divinity, pharmaceuticals, or reporting. Hellmann describes this self-caricature in his book *Fables of Fact: The New Journalism as New Fiction.* It is "a paradox of compulsive violence and outraged innocence, an emblem of the author's schizophrenic view of America. . . . But the persona also has a determined belief in the power of good intentions and right methods which runs counter to his violent impulses. Despite the psychotic threatening, his artistic aims include the corrective impulse of satire." Hellmann elaborates: "The created persona is essentially defined by the title phrase 'fear and loathing,' for it embodies both the paranoia with which the persona perceives the ominous forces pervading actuality, and the aggression with which he seeks to survive it. This latter trait is particularly crucial, for despite the comic buffoonery and paranoia delusions, Thompson's persona is hardly a passive anti-hero. A descendant of the trickster character of folklore, the Vice of medieval drama, the picaro of early prose narratives, he is a self-portrait of the journalist as rogue. . . . But as a journalist and a human being attempting to report contemporary events, the dangers he meets are psychological and spiritual. Defining himself through opposition, he counters them with violence and laughter."

With talent and a significant measure of recklessness, Thompson has created "fantasies which record the spirit—if not the misleading 'actual' facts—of the life they've experienced," according to Klinkowitz. The critic suggests that Thompson "multiplies himself" in his works through several methods: by "making as much of the conditions under which he's writing as he does of the subject matter itself," by "including references to his own mythology as a writer," by "dividing his own personality into mutually exclusive personae," and by "constantly downgrading his own paranoid fantasies in proportion to the raving madness of the so-called straight world." Gornick sees Thompson's work in a simpler light. "He poses variously as a maverick journalist, a nonstop drug user, an enemy of Main Street America and the Corporate State," she writes, "but being wild is really what his profession is. . . . Savaging everything in sight is his real target." Whatever his aims and methods might be, however, Hellmann notes in *Fables of Fact* that Thompson "has developed a journalism which communicates, both formally and thematically, his black humorist vision. The pervasive theme of Thompson's work is one of 'doomed alienation on your own turf.' In his 'fear and loathing' works he has expressed this malaise through an innovative application of the same parodic devices found in black-humor fictions. The result is journalism which reads as savage cartoon."

Hell's Angels, Thompson's 1966 account of the infamous California motorcycle gang, is the most conventional of his book-length works. The young author rode with the Angels for almost a year, recording their road rallies, their home lives, and their sexual adventures. The book strives to present the gang objectively while exposing the fact that its brutal reputation was primarily the creation of the scandal-mongering media. *New Republic* contributor Richard M. Elman observes that in *Hell's Angels* Thompson has "managed to correct many popular misconceptions about [the Angels], and in the process, provided his readers with a tendentious but informative participant-observer study of those who are doomed to lose." In the *Nation,* Elmer Bendiner likewise notes that throughout the book "Thompson's point of view remains eminently sane and honest. He does not weep for the Angels or romanticize them or glorify them. Neither does he despise them. Instead, he views them as creatures of an irresponsible society, given their image by an irresponsible press, embodying the nation's puerile fantasy life. He sees the menace not so much in the Hell's Angels themselves, as in the poverty of spirit and perennial adolescence that spawned them." *Hell's Angels* has garnered a mixture of critical reactions. *Atlantic* correspondent Oscar Handlin contends that Thompson's "lurid narrative, despite its sympathy for his subjects, reveals the threat they pose." Conversely, William Hogan in *Saturday Review* calls the work "a jarring piece of contemporary Californiana, as well as an examination of a weird branch of present-day show business." According to Elman, Thompson's "fascinating invocation to, evocation of, and reportage about the Hell's Angels . . . is certainly the most informative, thorough, and vividly written account of this phenomenon yet to appear."

In 1972 Thompson published *Fear and Loathing in Las Vegas,* perhaps his best known work. Hellmann describes the book in *Fables of Fact:* "*Fear and Loathing in Las Vegas* is, in barest outline, the author's purported autobiographical confession of his failure to fulfill the magazine's assignment to 'cover' two events in Las Vegas, the Fourth Annual 'Mint 400' motorcycle desert race and the National Conference of District Attorneys Seminar on Narcotics and Dangerous Drugs. It is more exactly the au-

thor's (or 'Raoul Duke's') tale of his hallucinations and adventures while with a 300-pound Samoan attorney called Dr. Gonzo, actually a Chicano lawyer named Oscar Zeta Acosta, . . . who serves as a parody of noble savage 'sidekicks' from Chingachgook to Tonto. The book is, then, even in its most general subject and presentation, either a report of an actual experience which was largely fantasy or an actual fantasy which is disguised as report." The author poses as Raoul Duke in the first-person narrative, and he relates a series of episodic adventures revolving around drug use and carte blanche access to Las Vegas's finest hotels. *National Observer* contributor Michael Putney calls the book "a trip, literally and figuratively, all the way to bad craziness and back again. It is also the most brilliant piece of writing about the dope subculture since Tom Wolfe's *Electric Kool-Aid Acid Test* and, at the same time, an acid, wrenchingly funny portrait of straight America's most celebrated and mean-spirited pleasure-dome, Las Vegas."

Critics have argued about how much of *Fear and Loathing in Las Vegas* is fact or "journalism," and how much of it is fiction, but most have praised the work for its originality and humor. *New York Times* columnist Christopher Lehmann-Haupt finds favor with the book's "mad, corrosive prose poetry," and in *Fables of Fact* Hellmann calls it "an important report on the American unreality of the late 1960's." Woods writes that *Fear and Loathing in Las Vegas* is "a custom-crafted study of paranoia, a spew from the 1960's and—in all its hysteria, insolence, insult, and rot—a desperate and important book, a wired nightmare. . . . The book's highest art is to be the drug it is about, whether chemical or political. To read it is to swim through the highs and lows of the smokes and fluids that shatter the mind, to survive again the terror of the politics of unreason."

Thompson continues to explore "the politics of unreason" in his 1973 book, *Fear and Loathing on the Campaign Trail '72,* a collection of articles that first appeared in *Rolling Stone* magazine. *Nation* correspondent Steven d'Arazien calls the work "a New Journalism account of the [1972 presidential] campaign from before New Hampshire to Miami and beyond. . . . It will be regarded as a classic in the genre." As national affairs editor for *Rolling Stone,* Thompson travelled with the press corps who followed George McGovern; Dickstein notes that the author "recorded the nuts and bolts of a presidential campaign with all the contempt and incredulity that other reporters must feel but censor out." According to Jules Witcover in *Progressive* magazine, the book's "heavily personalized writing-on-the-run, riddled here and there by the clear eye of hindsight, does convey an honest picture of a political writer picking his way through all the hoopla, propaganda, tedium, and exhaustion of a campaign." Critics' opinions on the book depend on their assessment of Thompson's reporting style. *Columbia Journalism Review* essayist Wayne C. Booth characterizes the work as "an inflated footnote on how [Thompson] used the campaign to achieve a 'very special kind of High.'" The critic concludes: "Cleverness, energy and brashness cannot, finally, make up for ignorance and lack of critical training." On the other hand, Kanon finds *Fear and Loathing on the Campaign Trail '72* "the best political reporting in some time—it manages to give politics, after years of televised lobotomy, some flesh." In the *New York Times,* Lehmann-Haupt concludes that while Thompson "doesn't exactly see America as Grandma Moses depicted it, or the way they painted it for us in civics class, he does in his own mad way betray a profound democratic concern for the polity. And in its own mad way, it's damned refreshing."

Thompson's two subsequent books, *The Great Shark Hunt: Strange Tales from a Strange Time* and *The Curse of Lono,* continue to mine his vein of personal, high-energy reporting. *Los Angeles Times Book Review* correspondent Peter S. Greenburg notes that *The Great Shark Hunt* "is not so much an attack on America as it is a frightfully perceptive autopsy of our culture. . . . In each story—or rather adventure—he leads us on a scattered but very personal journey of experience. The bottom line is that he's really a Charles Kuralt for crazy people, but Thompson's version of 'On the Road' is filled with so many detours that ultimately there isn't just one fork in the road but a complete service for eight. Nevertheless, there seems to be method in his madness. He is the master of the cosmic metaphor and combines this talent with all the subtlety of a run at someone's jugular with a red-hot rail spike." In *The Curse of Lono* Thompson recounts his antics during a visit to Hawaii with his longtime illustrator, Ralph Steadman. Once again the author demonstrates his "very nearly unrelieved distemper," an attribute William F. Buckley describes as "the Sign of Thompson" in the *New York Times Book Review. Washington Post Book World* reviewer Michael Dirda claims of the work: "No one writes like Hunter Thompson, though many have tried, and *The Curse of Lono* dispenses pages rabid with his hilarious, frenzied rantings, gusts of '60s madness for the stuffy '80s."

A media critic for the *San Francisco Examiner* beginning in 1985, Thompson published a collection of his columns in 1988 as *Generation of Swine: Gonzo Papers, Volume Two; Tales of Shame and Degradation in the '80s*. The book contains Thompson's opinions on a variety of people who figure prominently in the media. Much of the volume is devoted to lambasting those associated with the conservatism of the 1980s, including Ronald Reagan, George Bush, and members of their respective cabinets. Thompson also attacks the televangelists, calling Oral Roberts—as quoted by Steve Johnson in the *Chicago Tribune*—"a greed-crazed white-trash lunatic who should have been hung upside down from a telephone pole on the outskirts of Tulsa 44 years ago before he somehow transmogrified into the money-sucking animal that he became when he discovered television." A number of critics were disappointed with *Generation of Swine*, including Michael Edens in the *Washington Post*. Edens claimed, "Hardly a trace of that talent [displayed in Thompson's earlier works] remains in 'Generation of Swine.' The columns collected here . . . are shallow, sloppy and redundant beyond belief." Herbert Mitgang of the *New York Times* partially agreed: "He's a little more strident this time out, but if you happen to share his public enemies, Mr. Thompson's your man."

Needless to say, Thompson's paeans to hallucinogenic drugs and his bouts of colorful invective have not found universal favor. In the *Washington Monthly*, Joseph Nocera calls the author "a manifestation of an old and ignoble strain in American journalism. We have always had our share of writers more interested in being fashionable, or snide, or above the fray than in understanding or enlightening." Nocera concludes his essay with the remark that Thompson "has given New Journalism a bad name, and the damage he did may take a long time to undo." Likewise, *London Magazine* contributor Jonathan Raban finds Thompson "a professionally unreliable witness; you feel you are listening to an impossible skein of truth mixed up with falsehood, and he implores you to quit bothering about which is which." According to a *New Republic* reviewer, Thompson is either unwilling or unable to get beneath what he sees, and therefore is "yet another carrier of journalism's current typhus: he transmits surface description as analysis."

More critics praise Thompson than disparage him, however. Klinkowitz writes: "For all of the charges against him, Hunter S. Thompson is an amazingly insightful writer. His 'journalism' is not in the least irresponsible. On the contrary, in each of his books he's pointed out the lies and gross distortions of conventional journalism. . . . Moreover, his books are richly intelligent." According to Gornick, Thompson's talent "lies in his ability to describe his own manic plunge into drink, drugs, and madness through a use of controlled exaggeration that is truly marvelous. There are many moments in his stories—all having to do with paranoia finally induced after hours and days of swallowing, snorting, slugging down amounts of pills, powders, and alcohol that would long ago have killed an army of Berbers— that are so wonderfully funny you are left shaking with laughter and the happiness of literary creation." John Leonard expresses a similar opinion in the *New York Times*. Thompson, Leonard writes, "became, in the late 1960's, our point guard, our official crazy, patrolling the edge. He reported back that the paranoids were right, and they were. The cool inwardness, . . . the hugging of the self to keep from cracking up, is not for him. He inhabits his nerve endings; they are on the outside, like the skin of a baby; he seeks thumbprints. . . . He is also, as if this needs to be said, hilarious."

The dust jacket of *Fear and Loathing in Las Vegas* describes Thompson as an author who "continues to work his own strange tangents, seemingly oblivious [to] public outrage, acclaim, or criticism of any sort. He is known, to his handful of friends, as a compulsive hermit with an atavistic fondness for the .44 Magnum and extremely amplified music." Thompson's own self-parody has served to inspire another parodist of modern culture. Garry Trudeau, author of the "Doonesbury" cartoon strip, has modeled his "Uncle Duke" character on Thompson and his manic exploits. A denizen of Woody Creek, Colorado—where he once ran for sheriff on the "Freak Power" ticket—Thompson works, he says, only when he needs money to "crank up" his lifestyle. He told the *New York Times Book Review:* "I never liked to write very much. For me, journalism was just a way to have someone pay you to get out there and see what was happening."

MEDIA ADAPTATIONS: "Where the Buffalo Roam," a 1980 Universal Studios film starring Bill Murray, was based on a Thompson character.

BIOGRAPHICAL/CRITICAL SOURCES:

BOOKS

Contemporary Literary Criticism, Gale, Volume 9, 1978, Volume 17, 1981, Volume 40, 1986.

Dickstein, Morris, *Gates of Eden: American Culture in the Sixties*, Basic Books, 1977.

Hellmann, John, *Fables of Fact: The New Journalism as New Fiction*, University of Illinois Press, 1981.

Klinkowitz, Jerome, *The Life of Fiction*, University of Illinois Press, 1977.

Thompson, Hunter S., *Fear and Loathing in Las Vegas: A Savage Journey to the Heart of the American Dream*, illustrated by Ralph Steadman, Random House, 1972.

Thompson, Hunter S., *The Great Shark Hunt: Strange Tales from a Strange Time*, Summit Books, 1979.

Vonnegut, Kurt, Jr., *Wampeters Foma & Granfalloons*, Delacorte, 1974.

PERIODICALS

Atlantic, February, 1967, July, 1973.

Chicago Tribune, December 7, 1989.

Columbia Journalism Review, November-December, 1973, September-October, 1979.

Commonweal, April 7, 1967.

Critique: Studies in Modern Fiction, Volume 21, number 1, 1979.

Detroit News, August 26, 1979, November 27, 1983.
Harper's, July, 1973.
London Magazine, June-July, 1973.
Los Angeles Times Book Review, August 12, 1979.
Nation, April 3, 1967, August 13, 1973, October 13, 1979.
National Observer, August 5, 1972.
New Republic, February 25, 1967, October 14, 1972, October 13, 1973, August 25, 1979.
Newsweek, March 6, 1967.
New Yorker, March 4, 1967.
New York Review of Books, October 4, 1973.
New York Times, February 23, 1967, June 22, 1972, May 18, 1973, August 10, 1979, August 11, 1988.
New York Times Book Review, January 29, 1967, March 5, 1967, July 23, 1972, July 15, 1973, December 2, 1973, August 5, 1979, October 14, 1979, January 15, 1984.
Progressive, July, 1973.
Saturday Review, February 18, 1967, April 21, 1973.
Times (London), May 12, 1982.
Times Literary Supplement, January 11, 1968, November 3, 1972.
Village Voice, November 19, 1979.
Washington Monthly, April, 1981.
Washington Post, August 2, 1988, December 16, 1989.
Washington Post Book World, August 19, 1979, December 18, 1983.

*   *   *

THORNTON, Hall
See SILVERBERG, Robert

*   *   *

THORSTEIN, Eric
See MERRIL, Judith

*   *   *

THURBER, James (Grover) 1894-1961

PERSONAL: Born December 8, 1894, in Columbus, Ohio; died November 2, 1961, in New York, N.Y., of pneumonia following a stroke; son of Charles Leander (name later changed to Lincoln; a politician) and Mary Agnes (Fisher) Thurber; married Althea Adams, May 20, 1922 (divorced, May 24, 1935); married Helen Wismer, June 25, 1935; children: (first marriage) Rosemary. *Education:* Attended Ohio State University, 1913-1918.

CAREER: Columbus Dispatch, Columbus, Ohio, reporter, 1921-24; *Chicago Tribune,* Chicago, Ill., reporter for Paris edition, 1925-26; *New York Evening Post,* New York City, reporter, 1926; *New Yorker,* New York City, managing editor, 1927, staff writer, chiefly for "Talk of the Town" column, 1927-33, regular contributor, 1933-61. Artwork was exhibited in several one-man shows, including shows at the Valentine Gallery, New York City, 1933, and the Storran Gallery, London, England, 1937. *Wartime service:* Code clerk at the Department of State, Washington, D.C., and at the American Embassy, Paris, France, 1918-20.

MEMBER: Authors League of America, Dramatists Guild, Phi Kappa Psi, Sigma Delta Chi.

AWARDS, HONORS: Ohioana Book Award, Martha Kinney Cooper Ohioana Library Association, 1946, for *The White Deer;* Laughing Lions of Columbia University Award, 1949; Litt.D.,

Kenyon College, 1950, and Yale University, 1953; L.H.D., Williams College, 1951; Sesquicentennial Career Medal, Martha Kinney Cooper Ohioana Library Association, 1953; T-Square Award, American Cartoonists Society, 1956; Library and Justice Award, American Library Association, 1957, for *Further Fables for Our Time;* Antoinette Perry ("Tony") Special Award, 1960, for *A Thurber Carnival;* Certificate of Award from Ohio State University Class of 1916 for "Meritorious Service to Humanity and to Our Alma Mater," 1961.

WRITINGS:

(With E. B. White) *Is Sex Necessary?; or, Why You Feel the Way You Do,* Harper, 1929, reprinted, 1984.
The Owl in the Attic and Other Perplexities, Harper, 1931, reprinted, 1965.
The Seal in the Bedroom and Other Predicaments, Harper, 1932, reprinted, 1950.
My Life and Hard Times, Harper, 1933, reprinted, 1973.
The Middle-Aged Man on the Flying Trapeze: A Collection of Short Pieces, Harper, 1935, reprinted, Queens House, 1977.
Let Your Mind Alone!, and Other More or Less Inspirational Pieces, Harper, 1937, reprinted, Queens House, 1977.
The Last Flower: A Parable in Pictures, Harper, 1939, reprinted, Queens House, 1977.
Cream of Thurber, Hamish Hamilton, 1939.
Fables for Our Time and Famous Poems Illustrated, Harper, 1940, reprinted, 1983.
My World and Welcome to It, Harcourt, 1942, reprinted, 1983.
Thurber's Men, Women, and Dogs, Harcourt, 1943, reprinted, Dodd, 1975.
The Thurber Carnival, Harper, 1945, reprinted, 1975, abridged edition published as *Selected Humorous Stories from "The Thurber Carnival,"* edited by Karl Botzenmayer, F. Shoeningh, 1958.
The Beast in Me and Other Animals, Harcourt, 1948, reprinted, 1973.
The Thurber Album: A New Collection of Pieces about People, Simon & Schuster, 1952, reprinted, 1965.
Thurber Country: A New Collection of Pieces about Males and Females, Simon & Schuster, 1953, reprinted, 1982.
Thurber's Dogs: A Collection of the Master's Dogs, Simon & Schuster, 1955.
A Thurber Garland, Hamish Hamilton, 1955.
Further Fables for Our Time, Simon & Schuster, 1956, reprinted, Penguin, 1962.
Alarms and Diversions, Harper, 1957, reprinted, 1981.
The Years with Ross (Book-of-the-Month Club selection), Little, Brown, 1959, reprinted, Penguin, 1984.
Lanterns and Lances, Harper, 1961.
Credos and Curios, Harper, 1962, reprinted, 1983.
Vintage Thurber, two volumes, Hamish Hamilton, 1963.
Thurber & Company, Harper, 1966.
Snapshot of a Dog, Associated Educational Services, 1966.
The Secret Life of Walter Mitty, Associated Educational Services, 1967, reprinted, Creative Education, Inc., 1983.
The Catbird Seat, Associated Educational Services, 1967.
Selected Letters of James Thurber, edited by his wife, Helen Thurber, and Edward Weeks, Little, Brown, 1981.
The Night the Ghosts Got In, Creative Education, Inc., 1983.
Collecting Himself, edited by Michael Rosen, Hamish Hamilton, 1989.

PLAYS

(With Elliott Nugent) *The Male Animal* (three-act; first pro-
    duced on Broadway at the Cort Theatre, January 9, 1940),
    Random House, 1940.
"Many Moons" (also see below), produced in New York, 1947.
A Thurber Carnival (produced in Columbus, Ohio, at the Hart-
    man Theatre, January 7, 1960; first produced on Broadway
    at the ANTA Theatre, February 26, 1960), Samuel French,
    1962.

Also author of librettos for "Oh My, Omar" and other musicals
produced by the Scarlet Mask Club, Columbus, and of the play
"Nightingale" (two-act musical).

JUVENILES

Many Moons, illustrations by Louis Slobodkin, Harcourt, 1943,
    reprinted, 1973.
The Great Quillow, illustrations by Doris Lee, Harcourt, 1944,
    reprinted, Peter Smith, 1984.
The White Deer, illustrations by Thurber and Don Freeman,
    Harcourt, 1945, reprinted, 1968.
The 13 Clocks (also see below), illustrations by Marc Simont,
    Simon & Schuster, 1950, reprinted, 1977.
The Wonderful O (also see below), illustrations by Simont,
    Simon & Schuster, 1957, reprinted, 1976.
The 13 Clocks [and] The Wonderful O, illustrations by Ronald
    Searle, Penguin, 1962.

ILLUSTRATOR

Margaret Samuels Ernst, *The Executive's in a Word Book,*
    Knopf, 1939, reprinted, Belmont Books, 1963.
Elizabeth Howes, *Men Can Take It,* Random House, 1939.
James R. Kinney, *How to Raise a Dog,* Simon & Schuster, 1953
    (published in England as *The Town Dog,* Harvill, 1954, re-
    printed, 1966).

SIDELIGHTS: Called "one of the world's greatest humorists"
by Alistair Cooke in the *Atlantic,* James Thurber was one of the
mainstays of the *New Yorker* magazine, where his short stories,
essays, and numerous cartoons were published for over thirty
years. "Comedy is his chosen field," Malcolm Cowley wrote in
Thurber: A Collection of Critical Essays, "and his range of effects
is deliberately limited, but within that range there is nobody who
writes better than Thurber, that is, more clearly and flexibly,
with a deeper feeling for the genius of the language and the value
of words." After losing an eye in a childhood accident—playing
William Tell with his brother—Thurber later developed a condition that robbed him of sight in his remaining eye. Despite his
handicap, Thurber continued to work as a popular cartoonist
and illustrator and to write some of the best humor of his time.
Alan Coren of the *Times Literary Supplement* emphasized "the
magnitude of the tragedy which Thurber overcame in order to
produce the dazzling magnitude of his comedy."

"I'm always astounded when my humor is described as gentle,"
Thurber is quoted as saying in Burton Bernstein's *Thurber.* "It's
anything but that." An underlying tension, a desperation, is
present in Thurber's work. Richard C. Tobias, writing in his *The
Art of James Thurber,* pointed out that he made "laughter possible for us by deliberately choosing subjects that will create nervous, unsettling and unbearable tensions." Charles S. Holmes,
in his *Thurber: A Collection of Critical Essays,* also noted "the
pessimism and the sense of disaster which give Thurber's world
its special atmosphere." Speaking of himself and other "writers
of light pieces" in his foreword to *My Life and Hard Times,*
Thurber wrote: "The notion that such persons are gay of heart

and carefree is curiously untrue. . . . To call such persons 'humorists,' a loose-fitting and ugly word, is to miss the nature of
their dilemma and the dilemma of their nature. The little wheels
of their invention are set in motion by the damp hand of melancholy." "Thurber's genius," John Updike wrote in *Thurber: A
Collection of Critical Essays,* "was to make of our despair a humorous fable."

Although Thurber's writings cover a wide range of genres, including essays, short stories, fables, and children's books, it is his
stories concerned with middle-class domestic situations, often
based on actual events in Thurber's own life, that made his reputation. In these stories, timid and befuddled men are overwhelmed by capable and resourceful women or by the mechanical contraptions of modern life. The conflict between the sexes—
inspired in part by Thurber's troubled first marriage—and the
dangerously precarious nature of everyday life are the recurring
subjects in all of Thurber's work.

Thurber's career began after a stint as a code clerk in Paris during World War I. Unable to join the Army because of his bad
eyesight, Thurber instead worked for the Department of State.
When the war ended, Thurber returned to his native Columbus,
Ohio, where he worked as a newspaper reporter for the *Columbus Dispatch.* For a time he wrote a weekly column for the paper
entitled "Credos and Curios" in which he covered current books,
films, and plays. After marrying in 1922, Thurber and his wife
left for Paris. Thurber was attracted to Paris by the budding literary scene of American exiles there. He found work with the
Paris edition of the *Chicago Tribune.* Although, as Judith S.
Baughman wrote in the *Dictionary of Literary Biography,*
"France does not figure prominently as a subject in James Thurber's works," the country was a favorite of Thurber's; he lived
there for three extended periods during the 1920s and 1930s.
These European visits, Baughman related, "provided Thurber
with norms against which to measure the American attitudes
and manners examined in his best essays, stories, and drawings."

It was not until 1927, when he joined the staff of the *New Yorker*
magazine, that Thurber's career blossomed. Thurber had met E.
B. White at a Greenwich Village party in February of that year.
White, already working for the *New Yorker,* thought Thurber
might make a fine addition to the staff. He introduced him to
Harold Ross, editor of the magazine, and Thurber was hired as
managing editor. "I found out that I was managing editor three
weeks later," Thurber wrote in *The Years with Ross,* "when I
asked my secretary why I had to sign the payroll each week, approve the items in Goings On [the *New Yorker* calendar of
events], and confer with other editors on technical matters."
Thurber did not last long as managing editor. "An editor and organizer Thurber was not," Peter A. Scholl admitted in the *Dictionary of Literary Biography,* "but he could not convince Ross
that he would be happier and more effective as a staff writer.
Ross was finally convinced when Thurber returned two days late
from a visit to Columbus, having overstayed his leave to look for
his lost dog." In *The Years with Ross,* Thurber remembered
Ross's reaction to this incident: "I thought you were an editor,
goddam it," Ross said, "but I guess you're a writer, so write."

Thurber wrote for the *New Yorker* full time until 1933 and was
a regular contributor to the magazine until his death in 1961.
"Between 1927 and 1935," Baughman wrote, "Thurber became
one of the most prolific and best known of the *New Yorker* writers." He always credited White with having helped him fine tune
his writing style for the magazine. "I came to the *New Yorker,*"
Scholl quoted Thurber explaining, "a writer of journalese and it
was my study of White's writing, I think, that helped me to

straighten out my prose so that people could see what I meant." This style, described by Thurber as "played-down," was economical, lean, and conversational. Because many of his humorous subjects bordered on the bizarre, Thurber deliberately chose a writing style that was calm and precise. Thurber understood, Scholl argues, "that the comedy is heightened by the contrast between the unexcitable delivery and the frenetic events described." Michael Burnett, in his contribution to *Thurber: A Collection of Critical Essays,* also noted the unobtrusive nature of Thurber's style. "It is a style," Burnett wrote, "which does its best not to call attention to itself through any deviations from the norm." Louis Hasley, writing in the *South Atlantic Quarterly,* found that Thurber "was, it must be conceded, a fastidious stylist with psychological depth, subtlety and complexity; with a keen sense of pace, tone, ease, and climax; and with imagination that often wandered into surrealism."

White was also instrumental in bringing Thurber's drawings to public attention. Thurber often doodled cartoons while working at the office, absently filling pads of notepaper with pencil drawings. As Brendan Gill recounted in his *Here at the New Yorker,* he even drew upon the walls of the *New Yorker* offices: "There were Thurber drawings of men marching up endless flights of stairs, of dogs romping or fighting . . ., and of men and women engaged in contests wholly mysterious to us, thanks to Thurber's having failed to provide any captions for the drawings." White urged Thurber to submit his drawings to the magazine's art department, but he refused. One day White, who shared an office with Thurber, retrieved some of the discarded drawings from Thurber's wastebasket, inked them in, and took them to the *New Yorker* art editor. To everyone's surprise, the drawings were accepted.

Because he had no formal art training, Thurber's cartoons were simple and rudimentary. Dorothy Parker, in her foreword to *The Seal in the Bedroom and Other Predicaments,* fondly remarked that all of Thurber's characters "have the outer semblance of unbaked cookies." Thurber told Cooke that "somebody once asked Marc Connelly how you could tell a Thurber man from a Thurber woman. He said, 'The Thurber women have what appears to be hair on their heads.' " Thurber noted in his preface to *The Thurber Carnival* that his drawings "sometimes seemed to have reached completion by some other route than the common one of intent." One famous Thurber cartoon was indeed unintentional. Attempting to draw a crouching woman at the top of a staircase, Thurber got the perspective wrong and the woman was instead perched on the top of a bookcase. Unperturbed, Thurber drew in three other characters, two men and a woman, standing on the floor. One of the men is speaking: "That's my first wife up there, and this is the present Mrs. Harris." "My husband," Helen Thurber wrote in her introduction to *Thurber & Company,* "never cared much for the label of cartoonist, but he was equally reluctant about being called an artist. He had so much fun drawing pictures that he never really took them seriously."

Thurber's writing career, Tobias noted, falls into three loosely defined periods. The first, from 1929 until about 1937, "develops the comedy of the little man menaced by civilization." The second period is a time of exploration for Thurber, when he published fables like *The Last Flower: A Parable in Pictures* and *Fables for Our Time and Famous Poems Illustrated,* had his play *The Male Animal* successfully produced, and wrote the first of his children's books. The last period, the 1950s, saw Thurber return to the subject matter of his early work but with a deeper understanding. The books of Thurber's first period, collections of short pieces and drawings first published in the *New Yorker,* are generally considered to contain most of his best work. Many later titles reprint pieces from these books, sometimes including other Thurber material not previously reprinted from the *New Yorker.*

In 1929 Thurber teamed with White to produce a spoof of the sex manual genre. Their effort, entitled *Is Sex Necessary?; or, Why You Feel the Way You Do,* covered such topics as "Osculatory Justification," "Schmalhausen Trouble" (when couples live in small apartments), and "The Nature of the American Male: A Study of Pedestalism." As Edward C. Simpson of the *Dictionary of Literary Biography* reported, the two authors "parody the serious writers on the subject, making light of complexities, taking a mock-serious attitude toward the obvious, delighting in reducing the case-history technique to an absurdity, and making fun of those writers who proceeded by definition." The two men wrote alternate chapters of the manual, while Thurber provided the illustrations. The artwork—some forty drawings—took Thurber only one night to produce. "The next morning," Thurber told Cooke, "we took them down to the publishers, and when we got there, we put them down on the floor. Three bewildered and frightened publishers looked at them, and one man, the head publisher, said, 'These I suppose are rough sketches for the guidance of some professional artist who is going to do the illustrations?' and Andy [E. B. White] said, 'Those are the actual drawings that go in the book.' " The drawings were included. In his foreword to the manual, White found in Thurber's artwork "a strong undercurrent of grief " and described Thurber's men as "frustrated, fugitive beings." White went on to speak of "the fierce sweep, the economy, and the magnificent obscurity of Thurber's work. . . . All I, all anybody, can do is to hint at the uncanny faithfulness with which he has caught—caught and thrown to the floor—the daily, indeed the almost momently, severity of life's mystery, as well as the charming doubtfulness of its purpose." *Is Sex Necessary?* has gone through over twenty-five printings since its initial publication.

The Owl in the Attic and Other Perplexities, Thurber's second book and first collection of *New Yorker* pieces, includes eight stories, a section of drawings and short writings about pets, and the "Ladies' and Gentlemen's Guide to Modern English." Most of the stories are taken from Thurber's own life and feature the character John Monroe in domestic battles with his wife and with uncooperative household products. Some of the marital battles are based on Thurber's stormy first marriage. The Monroe stories, Tobias believed, combine the comic with the tragic. John Monroe "has more potential for pathos than comedy," Tobias wrote, "but his frightening and agonizing situations are more extreme than that and thus comic. Further, the situations also suggest that behind the comic mask is a raw human experience which the writer, by his craft, has subdued for our pleasure. What is painful in life is transformed into a finer tone by the comic vision." Scholl reported that with the publication of *The Owl in the Attic* "Thurber's reputation as a writer and an artist was firmly established." Tobias found *Is Sex Necessary?* and *The Owl in the Attic* to be "astonishing performances for the beginning of a career."

The Seal in the Bedroom and Other Predicaments, a collection of Thurber's drawings, takes its title from one of his most famous cartoons. Like other of his works, this cartoon evolved by accident. The original cartoon—drawn in pencil while doodling at the office—showed a seal on a rock in the arctic waste. In the distance are two specks. "Hmmm, explorers," says the seal. The published version of the cartoon is quite different. After drawing the seal on the rock, this time in ink, Thurber decided that his rock looked less like a rock and more like a headboard for a bed.

So he added a couple lying in the bed. The wife is saying, "All right, have it your way—you heard a seal bark!"

Perhaps the most important of Thurber's early books is the story collection *My Life and Hard Times,* which recounts some outlandish events and disastrous misunderstandings from Thurber's childhood. Included here are "The Night the Bed Fell," "The Night the Ghost Got In," and "The Day the Dam Broke." Charles S. Holmes, writing in *The Clocks of Columbus: The Literary Career of James Thurber,* called *My Life and Hard Times* "the peak achievement of Thurber's early career. . . . For many readers it is his one unquestioned masterpiece." One of the chief virtues of the collection is the distance that Thurber maintained between himself and his past experiences, allowing him to use his own life to comic effect. As he wrote in "A Note at the End," the afterword to the collection, "the confusions and the panics of last year and the year before are too close for contentment. Until a man can quit talking loudly to himself in order to shout down the memories of blunderings and gropings, he is in no shape for the painstaking examination of distress and the careful ordering of event so necessary to a calm and balanced exposition of what, exactly, was the matter."

My Life and Hard Times, Scholl stated, "is Thurber's best single collection of integrated stories, a series that can be read as a well-wrought and unified work of art." Hasley wrote that, "despite its autobiographical basis, [*My Life and Hard Times*] is the most consistently creative and humorous of all his books." Hasley found, too, that it displayed "Thurber's eminence in the portrayal of actual people." Holmes analyzed the stories in this collection and believed that throughout the book Thurber had celebrated "what might be called the Principle of Confusion. . . . Nearly every episode shows the disruption of the orderly pattern of everyday life by the idiosyncratic, the bizarre, the irrational." With *My Life and Hard Times,* Holmes concluded, Thurber "arrived at full artistic maturity."

In *The Middle-Aged Man on the Flying Trapeze,* a book described by Baughman as a "generally darker-toned miscellany," there is one curiously unfunny piece that sheds light on Thurber's personal life. The story "One Is a Wanderer" portrays a lonely middle-aged man in New York City who lives alone, drinks too much, and has alienated most of his friends. Taken from Thurber's situation during his first marriage, when he lived alone in New York while his wife and daughter lived in the country, the story ends with the revelation that "Two is company, four is a party, three is a quarrel. One is a wanderer." In the humorous stories, too, there are depictions of Thurber's troubled life. "The quarrels, the fights, the infidelities, and the loneliness of these years are animated in the humorous pieces," Scholl commented. In "Mr. Preble Gets Rid of His Wife," for example, Thurber successfully blends the absurdly comic with the tragic. Mr. Preble wants his wife to go in the cellar with him. She knows he wants to kill her there. But, because she is tired of arguing about it and because she is as dissatisfied with their marriage as he is, Mrs. Preble accompanies him. Another argument develops in the cellar over Mr. Preble's choice of murder weapon. Mrs. Preble does not wish to be hit on the head with a shovel. The story ends with the husband leaving for the store to buy a more suitable weapon. His wife waits patiently in the cellar for his return.

In *Let Your Mind Alone!* Thurber returned to the satirical mode of *Is Sex Necessary?,* this time writing a self-help psychology book. It is, Kenneth Burke remarked in *The Critic as Artist: Essays on Books, 1920-1970,* "a very amusing burlesque of psychoanalysis." Thurber proposed in the book that "the undisciplined mind . . . is far better adapted to the confused world in which we live today than the streamlined mind." He then gives examples of real-life cases where this idea is proven to be true. E. L. Tinker of the *New York Times* judged it to be "intelligent humor of a particularly refreshing brand which is very rare today. It appeals to the adult and sophisticated mind." The *Canadian Forum* reviewer thought popular psychology had been handled in "a brilliantly amusing fashion."

In his second period Thurber explored new types of writing, although he also continued to write the essays and short stories that had made his reputation. During the 1940s he wrote fables, a play, and children's books in addition to several collections of *New Yorker* pieces. In *The Last Flower,* published in 1940, Thurber created a picture book fable for adults that tells the story of World War XII and what survived: a man, a woman, and a single flower. From these three items, love emerges in the waste land. But love leads to family, to tribe, to civilization, and, inevitably and sadly, to another war. The book was inspired by the Spanish Civil War of the 1930s and the joint Soviet and Nazi invasion of Poland in 1939. It was published shortly before America's entry into World War II. The book "is not funny," the *Boston Transcript* reviewer wrote. "It isn't meant to be funny. 'The Last Flower' is magnificent satire." "The message of the work," E. Charles Vousden stated in the *Dictionary of Literary Biography,* ". . . is . . . one of despair—humanity will never learn to avoid war."

Thurber returned to the allegorical fable in his *Fables for Our Time,* a collection of Aesop parodies that Fred Schwed, Jr., of the *Saturday Review of Literature* thought showed "rather conclusively, I'm afraid, that at its worst the human race is viciously silly, while at its best it is just silly." Containing what Vousden called "astute observations on the human condition," *Fables for Our Time* commented on such contemporary figures as Adolf Hitler and had fun with some of the more familiar fairy tale situations. Thurber's version of "Little Red Riding Hood," for instance, ended with Little Red shooting the wolf with a pistol. "You can read as much or as little as you please into these light and perfectly written little tales," G. W. Stonier wrote in the *New Statesman and Nation.*

The Male Animal, Thurber's first produced play, was written with his old friend Elliott Nugent and staged in 1940. It is set at a midwestern college where an English professor finds himself at odds with a university trustee who is more interested in football and alumni support than with academic values. "For the first time," Tobias remarked, "the tart, astringent Thurber dialogue gets a larger framework." Thurber learned some important things concerning the differences between writing a play and having it produced. He told *New Yorker* colleague Wolcott Gibbs: "During rehearsal you discover that your prettiest lines do not cross the footlights, because they are too pretty, or an actor can't say them, or an actress doesn't know what they mean. . . . On the thirteenth day of rehearsal, the play suddenly makes no sense to you and does not seem to be written in English." *The Male Animal* was a huge success for Thurber, running for 243 performances in New York and being adapted as a film starring Henry Fonda.

"The Secret Life of Walter Mitty," one of Thurber's most famous short stories, is included in the collection *My World and Welcome to It.* The story concerns a man who daydreams heroic adventures to escape from a domineering wife and a boring job. "The story is a masterpiece of associational psychology," Hasley wrote, "in its shuttling between the petty, humiliating details of his outer life and the flaming heroism of his self-glorifying reveries." In this story, Carl M. Lindner stated in the *Georgia Review,* Thurber "touched upon one of the major themes in American literature—the conflict between individual and society."

It was during this second period, too, that Thurber began to write books for children, publishing *Many Moons, The Great Quillow,* and *The White Deer.* All of these books are fairy tales subtly modernized by Thurber's perspective. *The White Deer,* the story of an enchanted princess and the three princes who must do an impossible labor to free her, was called "a serene and beautiful fantasy" by Isabelle Mallet of the *New York Times.* Edmund Wilson, in his review for the *New Yorker,* compared Thurber's children's books to the works of Frank Stockton. Like Stockton, Wilson maintained, Thurber took traditional fairy tale situations and made "them produce unexpected results."

Thurber's later children's books, *The 13 Clocks* and *The Wonderful O,* are also fairy tales. The evil duke of *The 13 Clocks* is so bad that time itself has stopped because of him. When he holds his niece captive in a castle, the hero of the story must save her and in so doing restore time to the kingdom. Irwin Edman of the *New York Herald Tribune Book Review* called the book "a fairy tale, a comment on human cruelty and human sweetness or a spell, an incantation, compounded of poetry and logic and wit." While noting that Thurber had employed traditional fairy tale elements in *The 13 Clocks,* the *New Yorker* critic thought the story to be essentially an "ingenius satire on that form, written in a many-tiered, poetic prose style."

Perhaps Thurber's most important book of the 1950s is *The Years with Ross.* An informal biography of Harold Ross, founder and editor of the *New Yorker,* the book is also a history of the magazine and a recounting of Thurber's friendship with Ross. Told in a rambling and anecdotal style, the book is divided into sections dealing with various aspects of Ross's life and career, treating each one "as an entity in itself," as Thurber explained in the book's foreword. "The unity I have striven for," Thurber wrote, "is one of effect." Thurber relied on his own memories of Ross, the memories of other *New Yorker* staff members, and on letters and published articles to trace Ross's career. The book fared well with the critics, although several reviews found Thurber's portrait of Ross a bit unclear. Gerald Weales of *Commonweal,* for example, said that he "came out with the feeling that Thurber must still know something that he has failed to tell me." But Peter Salmon of the *New Republic* called *The Years with Ross* "a great book," while Weales concluded that it is "often fascinating." "This is a book to savor," Mark Schorer wrote in the *San Francisco Chronicle,* "and to treasure. It has two heroes: The first, obviously, is Harold Ross himself, a flashing and fascinating man; the second is James Thurber, a retiring and a great one." The criticism that especially hurt Thurber came from his friends. E. B. White and his wife Katharine, friends of both Thurber and Ross for many years, did not like the book. Scholl noted, however, that *The Years with Ross* "has a lasting power to entertain and move the reader."

Thurber's last major work, "A Thurber Carnival," is a series of skits, some of which are adapted from earlier stories and some of which are new material. In one skit a woman reads from *The Last Flower* and displays the book's illustrations on an easel. Some of Thurber's cartoons were enlarged and used as backdrops for the New York production of the play. "A Thurber Carnival," Kenneth Hurren wrote in *Spectator,* "managed to turn a lot of the stories and observations of the minutiae of American living into engaging sketches." After premiering in Thurber's hometown of Columbus, the play opened on Broadway on February 26, 1960. There was also a national road tour. When ticket

sales for the Broadway production slowed, Thurber himself joined the cast, playing himself in one of the skits for some 88 performances. Ticket sales increased. A critical and popular success, "A Thurber Carnival" won a special Tony Award in 1960.

On October 3, 1961, Thurber suffered a stroke at his home in New York City. While in the hospital he developed pneumonia and on November 2, 1961, Thurber passed away. Towards the end of his life it seemed to many observers that Thurber's work had become pessimistic. "During the last ten years of his life," Hasley noted, "Thurber turned more and more to serious treatments of literary subjects and people. . . . While he never yielded wholly to despair, the note of gloom is unmistakable." Holmes, too, found this bleak outlook. "The theme of all of Thurber's late work is decline—of form, style, good sense, 'human stature, hope, humor,'" he wrote. This outlook is reflected in his personal life, too. Scholl quoted Thurber as saying to Elliott Nugent shortly before his death, "I can't hide anymore behind the mask of comedy. . . . People are not funny; they are vicious and horrible and so is life!"

But much of this pessimism has been attributed to Thurber's developing illness. "In his old age, racked by disease and incapacitated by blindness," John Seelye wrote in *Thurber: A Collection of Critical Essays,* "Thurber became a sort of resident western curmudgeon, snarling at a changing world he could not comprehend." Jesse Bier argued in *The Rise and Fall of American Humor* that "Thurber's last stage represents a retreat from humor. And his irritabilities, his explicitness, his animus, his borderline perversities and grotesqueries, his final hopelessness, and his ingrownness are indices to the whole contemporary epoch, not only to his own career."

Holmes defines two ways of approaching Thurber's body of work: "The humanistic view sees Thurber as the defender of the individual in an age of mass culture, the champion of imagination over the logic-and-formula-ridden mind, the enemy of political fanaticism. . . . The darker view focuses on Thurber as a man writing to exorcise a deep inner uncertainty, to come to terms with fears and resentments which threatened his psychic balance." In *Thurber: A Collection of Critical Essays,* Robert H. Elias examined Thurber's place in American literature and found that many Thurber stories are "as well shaped as the most finely wrought pieces of Henry James, James Joyce and Ernest Hemingway, as sensitively worded as the most discriminatingly written prose of H. L. Mencken, Westbrook Pegler and J. D. Salinger, and as penetrating . . . as the most pointed insights of those two large poets of our century, E. A. Robinson and Robert Frost." Jonathan Yardley, writing in the *Washington Post Book World,* judged Thurber's contribution to letters to be of lasting value. "Thurber's humor" Yardley wrote, "has a timeless quality that should guarantee him a readership far into the future."

MEDIA ADAPTATIONS: My Life and Hard Times was filmed as "Rise and Shine," Twentieth Century-Fox, 1941; *The Male Animal* was filmed by Warner Bros., 1942, and as "She's Working Her Way Through College," Warner Bros., 1952; "The Secret Life of Walter Mitty" was filmed by RKO, 1949; "A Unicorn in the Garden" was adapted as an animated film by Leaming Corp. of America, 1952; *The 13 Clocks* was adapted as an opera and as a television special in 1954; several of Thurber's stories were adapted as the play "Three by Thurber," written by Paul Ellwood and St. John Terrell, first produced in New York at the Theatre de Lys, 1955; some of Thurber's work was adapted for the film "Fireside Book of Dog Stories," State University of Iowa, 1957; *The Last Flower* was adapted as a dance by a French ballet company, 1959; "The Catbird Seat" was filmed as "The Battle of the Sexes," Continental Distributing, 1960; *Many Moons* was filmed by Rembrandt Films, c. 1960, was adapted as a filmstrip by H. M. Stone Productions, 1972, and adapted as an animated film by Contemporary Films/McGraw, 1975; *My World and Welcome to It* was adapted as a television series in 1969; several of Thurber's stories were adapted as "The War between Men and Women," National General Pictures Corp., 1972. Many of his works have also been recorded.

BIOGRAPHICAL/CRITICAL SOURCES:

BOOKS

Atteberry, Brian, *The Fantasy Tradition in American Literature,* Indiana University Press, 1980.
Bernstein, Burton, *Thurber,* Dodd, 1975, published as *Thurber: A Biography,* Ballantine, 1976.
Bier, Jesse, *The Rise and Fall of American Humor,* Holt, 1968.
Black, Stephen Ames, *James Thurber: His Masquerades,* Mouton, 1970.
Blair, Walter and Hamlin Hill, *America's Humor: From Poor Richard to Doonesbury,* Oxford University Press, 1978.
Bowden, Edwin T., *James Thurber: A Bibliography,* Ohio State University Press, 1968.
Concise Dictionary of Literary Biography: The Age of Maturity, 1929-1941, Gale, 1989.
Contemporary Literary Criticism, Gale, Volume 5, 1976, Volume 11, 1979, Volume 25, 1983.
Cowley, Malcolm, *Writers at Work: The Paris Review Interviews,* Viking, 1959.
Dictionary of Literary Biography, Gale, Volume 4: *American Writers in Paris, 1920-1939,* 1980, Volume 11: *American Humorists, 1800-1950,* 1982, Volume 22: *American Writers for Children, 1900-1960,* 1983.
Eastman, Max, *The Enjoyment of Laughter,* Simon & Schuster, 1936.
Gill, Brendan, *Here at the New Yorker,* Random House, 1975.
Holmes, Charles S., *The Clocks of Columbus: The Literary Career of James Thurber,* Atheneum, 1972.
Holmes, Charles S., editor, *Thurber: A Collection of Critical Essays,* Prentice-Hall, 1974.
Kramer, Dale, *Ross and the "New Yorker,"* Doubleday, 1951.
Morseberger, Robert E., *James Thurber,* Twayne, 1964.
Sheed, Wilfrid, *The Good Word and Other Words,* Dutton, 1978.
Shirer, William L., *Twentieth Century Journey, a Memoir of a Life and the Times: The Start, 1904-1930,* Simon & Schuster, 1976.
Thurber, James and E. B. White, *Is Sex Necessary?, or, Why You Feel the Way You Do,* Harper, 1929, reprinted, 1984.
Thurber, James, *The Seal in the Bedroom and Other Predicaments,* Harper, 1932, reprinted, 1950.
Thurber, James, *My Life and Hard Times,* Harper, 1933, reprinted, 1973.
Thurber, James, *The Middle-Aged Man on the Flying Trapeze: A Collection of Short Pieces,* Harper, 1935, reprinted, Queens House, 1977.
Thurber, James, *Let Your Mind Alone!, and Other More or Less Inspirational Pieces,* Harper, 1937, reprinted, Queens House, 1977.
Thurber, James, *The Thurber Carnival,* Harper, 1945, reprinted, 1975.
Thurber, James, *The Years with Ross,* Little, Brown, 1959, reprinted, Penguin, 1984.
Thurber, James, *Thurber & Company,* Harper, 1966.
Tobias, Richard C., *The Art of James Thurber,* Ohio State University Press, 1969.
Yates, Norris W., *The American Humorist: Conscience of the Twentieth Century,* Iowa State University Press, 1964.

PERIODICALS

Atlantic, August, 1956.
Books, November 24, 1935, November 1, 1942.
Boston Transcript, December 9, 1939.
Christian Science Monitor, May 28, 1959, December 14, 1981.
Commonweal, July 17, 1959.
Economist, February 13,1982.
Esquire, August, 1975.
Georgia Review, summer, 1974.
Listener, January 28, 1982.
Lost Generation Journal, winter, 1975.
Maclean's, January 18, 1982.
Nation, June 13, 1959, November 21, 1981.
National Review, April 2, 1982.
New Republic, September 20, 1940, June 29, 1959.
New Statesman, December 14, 1962.
New Statesman and Nation, December 23, 1939, December 14, 1940, December 19, 1942.
Newsweek, March 24, 1975.
New Yorker, October 27, 1945, December 9, 1950, November 11, 1961, June 23, 1975.
New York Herald Tribune Book Review, December 3, 1950.
New York Times, February 22, 1931, September 12, 1937, February 4, 1945, September 30, 1945, May 31, 1959.
New York Times Book Review, March 25, 1973, November 8 1981.
New York Times Magazine, December 4, 1949.
Reader's Digest, September, 1972.
Saturday Review, November 17, 1956, March 22, 1975.
Saturday Review of Literature, December 2, 1939, November 23, 1940, February 3, 1945.
Smithsonian, January, 1977.
South Atlantic Quarterly, autumn, 1974.
Spectator, July 5, 1975.
Time, July 9, 1951, March 31, 1975.
Times Literary Supplement, January 29, 1982.
Washington Post Book World, November 8, 1981.
Yale Review, autumn, 1965.

OBITUARIES:

PERIODICALS

Illustrated London News, November 11, 1961.
Newsweek, November 13, 1961.
New York Times, November 9, 1961.
Publishers Weekly, November 13, 1961.
Time, November 10, 1961.

*   *   *

TIGER, Derry
See ELLISON, Harlan

*   *   *

TILLICH, Paul (Johannes) 1886-1965

PERSONAL: Surname pronounced *Till*-ik; born August 20, 1886, in Starzeddel, Kreis Guben, Prussia; died October 22, 1965, in the United States; came to America in 1933, naturalized in 1940; son of Johannes (a Lutheran pastor) and Mathilde (Durselen) Tillich; married Hannah Werner, 1924; children: Erdmuthe Tillich Farris, Rene Descartes. *Education:* Studied at University of Berlin, 1904-05, 1908, University of Tuebingen, 1905, University of Halle, 1905-07; University of Breslau, Ph.D., 1911; University of Halle, Licentiat of Theology, 1912.

ADDRESSES: Home—84 Woodlane, Easthampton, Long Island, N.Y. *Office*—Divinity School, University of Chicago, 5801 South Ellis, Chicago, Ill.

CAREER: Ordained minister of Evangelical Lutheran Church, 1912. University of Berlin, Berlin, Germany, privat-dozent, 1919-24; University of Marburg, Marburg, Germany, professor of theology, 1924-25; University of Dresden, Dresden, Germany, professor of theology, 1925-29; University of Leipzig, Leipzig, Germany, professor of theology, 1928-29; University of Frankfurt-am-Main, Frankfurt, Germany, professor of philosophy, 1929-33; Union Theological Seminary, New York, N.Y., professor of theology and philosophy, 1933-54; Harvard University, Cambridge, Mass., University Professor, 1955-62; University of Chicago, Divinity School, Chicago, Ill., John Nuven Professor of Theology, 1962-65. Visiting lecturer at numerous universities in the United States, Europe, and Japan, including Tailor Lecturer, Yale University, 1935, Terry Lecturer, Yale, 1950, and Gifford Lecturer, University of Edinburgh, 1953. Co-founder of Self-Help for Emigres from Central Europe, Inc.; member of executive committee of American Committee for Christian Refugees; vice-chairman of Center for German and Austrian Art and Handicraft; provisional chairman of Council for a Democratic Germany. *Military service:* German Army, chaplain, 1914-18; awarded Iron Cross, First Class.

MEMBER: American Philosophical Association, American Theological Association, American Academy of Arts and Sciences, Philosophy Club, Academy of Religion and Mental Health.

AWARDS, HONORS: Grosse Verdienstkreuz from West German Republic, 1956; Goethe Medal from City of Frankfurt, 1956; Hanseatic Goethe Prize from City of Hamburg, 1958; Stern zum Grossen Verdienstkreuz from West German Republic, 1961; Academy of Religion and Mental Health Award, 1962; Paul Tillich Chair created at Union Theological Seminary, 1971. Numerous honorary degrees, including University of Halle, 1926, Yale University, 1940, University of Glasgow, 1951, Princeton University, 1953, Harvard University, 1954, University of Chicago, 1955, New School for Social Research, 1955, Brandeis University, 1955, Free University of Berlin, 1956, Franklin and Marshall College, 1960, and Bucknell College, 1960.

WRITINGS:

Die religiose Lage der Gegenwart, Ullstein, 1926, translation by H. Richard Niebuhr published in America as *The Religious Situation,* Henry Holt, 1932.
Religiose Verwirklichung, Furche, 1929.
Die sozialistische Entscheidung, A. Protte, 1933, 2nd edition, Bollwerk, 1948.
The Interpretation of History, Scribner, 1936.
Christian Answers by Paul J. Tillich and Others, Scribner, 1945.
The Shaking of the Foundations (sermons), Scribner, 1948.
The Protestant Era, University of Chicago Press, 1948, abridged edition, 1957.
Systematic Theology, University of Chicago Press, Volume 1, 1951, Volume 2, 1959, Volume 3, 1963.
Christianity and the Problem of Existence, Henderson, 1951.
Politische Bedeutung der Utopie im Leben der Voelker, Gebr. Weiss, 1951.
The Courage to Be (Terry Lectures), Yale University Press, 1952.

Die Judenfrage: Ein christliches und ein deutsches Problem, Gebr. Weiss, 1953.
Love, Power, and Justice, Oxford University Press, 1954.
The New Being (sermons), Scribner, 1955.
Biblical Religion and the Search for Ultimate Reality, University of Chicago Press, 1955, 2nd edition, 1964.
Dynamics of Faith, Harper, 1956.
Die Philosophie der Macht, Colloquium, 1956.
(Contributor) *Religion and Health: A Symposium,* Association Press, 1958.
Theology of Culture, Oxford University Press, 1959.
Gesammelte Werke, Evangelisches Verlagswerk, 1959.
Fruhe Hauptwerke, Evangelisches Verlagswerk, 1959.
Wesen und Wandel des Glaubens, Ullstein, 1961.
Philosophie und Schicksal, Evangelisches Verlagswerk, 1961.
Auf der Grenze: Aus dem Lebenswerk Paul Tillichs, Evangelisches Verlagswerk, 1962.
Der Protestantismus als Kritik und Gestaltung, Evangelisches Verlagswerk, 1962.
(Contributor) Reinhold Niebuhr, *A Prophetic Voice in Our Time: Essays in Tribute,* Seabury, 1962.
Christianity and the Encounter of the World Religions, Columbia University Press, 1963.
Morality and Beyond, Harper, 1963.
The Eternal Now, Scribner, 1963.
Das religiose Fundament des moralischen Handelns, Verlagswerk, 1965.
The World Situation, Fortress Press, 1965 (first published as a chapter in the symposium *The Christian Answer*).
Ultimate Concern: Tillich in Dialogue, Harper, 1965.
The Future of Religions, Harper, 1966.
On the Boundary (revision and new translation of part one of *The Interpretation of History*), Scribner, 1966.
My Search for Absolutes, with illustrations by Saul Steinberg, Simon & Schuster, 1967.
Perspectives on 19th and 20th Century Protestant Theology, Harper, 1967.
A History of Christian Thought, Harper, 1968.
My Travel Diary, 1936: Between Two Worlds, with illustrations by Alfonso Ossorio, Harper, 1970.
Political Expectation, Harper, 1971.
Begegnungen (collected works), Evangelisches Verlagswerk, 1972.
E. J. Tinsley, editor, *Paul Tillich 1886-1965* (collected works), Epworth, 1973.
Mysticism and Guilt-Consciousness in Schelling's Philosophical Development, English translation by Victor Nuovo, Bucknell University Press, 1974.
The Construction of the History of Religion in Schelling's Positive Philosophy: Its Presuppositions and Principles, English translation by Nuovo, Bucknell University Press, 1975.
Philosophical Development, English translation by Nuovo, Bucknell University Press, 1975.
Perry LeFevre, editor, *The Meaning of Health: The Relation of Religion and Health,* North Atlantic, 1981.
James L. Adams, editor, *Political Expectation,* Mercer University Press, 1981.
Das System der Wissenschaften nach Gegenstanden und Methoden, published in America as *The System of the Sciences According to Objects and Methods,* Bucknell University Press, 1981.
The Socialist Decision, English translation by Franklin Sherman, University Press of America, 1983.
John Dillenberger and Jane Dillenberger, editors, *Paul Tillich on Art and Architecture,* Crossroad, 1987.

F. Forrester Church, editor, *The Essential Tillich: An Anthology of the Writings of Paul Tillich,* Macmillan, 1987.

Religiose Reden, De Gruyter, 1987.

J. Mark Thomas, editor, *The Spiritual Situation in Our Technical Society,* Mercer University Press, 1988.

Contributor to journals, including *Christian Century, History of Ideas,* and *Social Research.* Member of editorial board, *Daedalus, Pastoral Psychology, Aufbau,* and *Journal of Religion and Mental Health.*

SIDELIGHTS: Paul Tillich was perhaps the best known Protestant theologian in America from 1933 until his death in 1965. One of the first non-Jewish academicians to be expelled from Nazi Germany for his opposition to Hitler, Tillich spent the most productive years of his life at the Union Theological Seminary in New York City. From his base there he wrote numerous works in both English and German and delivered innumerable sermons and lectures on the meaning of the Christian faith for twentieth-century man. "Paul Tillich was a giant among us," wrote colleague Reinhold Niebuhr in the *New York Times Book Review.* "His influence extended beyond theological students and circles to include many from other disciplines. . . . He combined theological with philosophical and psychological learning, and also, he combined religious insights with an understanding and appreciation of the arts. Thus he displayed to the American communities of learning and culture, the wholeness of religious philosophy and of the political and social dimensions of human existence."

From his earliest years Tillich was passionate about both Christianity and scholarship. He was born in Prussia in 1886, the son of a Lutheran pastor of high standing. Tillich attended school in Brandenburg and later in Berlin, earning sufficient grades to qualify for university training. This he took at colleges in Halle, Breslau, Tuebingen, and Berlin, eventually earning a Ph.D. and a Licentiate of Theology. He was ordained as a minister of Germany's Evangelical Lutheran Church in 1912. During World War I, Tillich served as a chaplain to the German ground forces, earning decoration for his work among the troops. At the war's conclusion he accepted the post of *privat-dozent* of theology at the University of Berlin, the first of several prestigious universities on whose faculties he would serve.

Tillich quickly established a reputation as one of Germany's most important philosopher/theologians, whose "influence on . . . religious life was maximal," to quote Niebuhr. Throughout the 1920s he authored a number of important works, including *Die religiose Lage der Gegenwart,* translated into English as *The Religious Situation.* In this and other books, Tillich proposed his central theme, namely that religion is the ultimate concern overriding all human activities, and that only by discerning God could modern man discover the courage to be. Tillich expanded on these notions in his English-language books after the Nazi regime dismissed him from his post and more or less forced him to emigrate.

It was Reinhold Niebuhr, in fact, who helped Tillich secure a position at Union Theological Seminary in 1933. Tillich stayed at the seminary for more than twenty years, during which he wrote a number of books, lectures, and sermons aimed primarily at the lonely and alienated "contemporary" man. The author often said that he considered himself an explorer "on the boundary" between religion, philosophy, and psychology. In books such as *The Shaking of the Foundation* and *The Courage to Be* he was able to integrate existential philosophy with the religious basis of human life, suggesting that religion could be a "unifying center" for existence. Tillich's scholarly yet humanistic works pro-

vided a welcome alternative for American Protestants who were not comfortable with fundamentalist interpretations of the Bible. To quote Niebuhr, he "emancipated the intellectually questioning in the churches from literalistic dogma."

By the time of his death in 1965 Tillich had written more than forty full-length works, some in German and some in English. During the 1950s and the 1960s he was given prizes and honorary doctorates in America and in his native land for his memorable contributions to Protestant theology. In the *New Republic,* Roger Hazelton contended that Tillich's greatness as a thinker lay "in the fact that he [knew] what man is made of, what he suffers from, and what he can hope for." A *Times Literary Supplement* reviewer likewise found Tillich "a great constructive thinker" who "was a very human and humane personality." The reviewer added: "His remarkable ability to identify himself with others in their happiness and in their anguish is reflected again and again."

Not surprisingly, Tillich's influence has survived his passing, especially in academic circles. No less than fifteen works have been published posthumously, including collections in both German and English, and Union Theological Seminary has honored the professor by creating a chair in his name. As John K. Roth put it in the *Los Angeles Times Book Review,* Tillich's philosophical theology "decisively influenced mainline American Protestantism during its heyday in the middle third of this century. . . . Tillich explored the uncertainties of human existence and, in spite of those conditions, helped people to discern the God who provides the courage to be."

BIOGRAPHICAL/CRITICAL SOURCES:

BOOKS

Freeman, David Hugh, *Tillich,* Presbyterian & Reformed, 1962.

Half Century of Union Theological Seminary, 1896-1945, Scribner, 1954.

Harcourt, Melvin, editor, *Thirteen for Christ,* Sheed, 1963.

Kegley, C., *The Theology of Paul Tillich,* Macmillan, 1952.

Kilsey, D. H., *The Fabric of Paul Tillich's Theology,* Yale University Press, 1967.

Leibrecht, Walter, editor, *Religion and Culture: Essays in Honor of Paul Tillich,* Harper, 1959.

Nelson, James, editor, *Wisdom,* Norton, 1958.

O'Meara, T. A., and C. D. Weisser, editors, *Paul Tillich in Catholic Thought,* Priory Press, 1964.

Tavard, G. H., *Paul Tillich and the Christian Message,* Scribner, 1962.

Thomas, J. Heyward, *Paul Tillich: An Appraisal,* Westminster, 1963.

Thomas, *Paul Tillich,* John Knox, 1966.

Tillich, Paul, *The Interpretation of History,* Scribner, 1936.

Tillich, Paul, *On the Boundary,* Scribner, 1966.

Tillich, Paul, *My Search for Absolutes,* with illustrations by Saul Steinberg, Simon & Schuster, 1967.

PERIODICALS

Book Week, February 23, 1964.

Churchman, February 1, 1937.

Commentary, April, 1967.

Encounter, winter, 1967, summer, 1967.

Los Angeles Times Book Review, November 22, 1987.

New Republic, January 6, 1968.

Newsweek, May 17, 1954.

New York Herald Tribune Book Review, March 8, 1953.

New York Post, May 1, 1940.

New York Times, June 4, 1950.

New York Times Book Review, June 27, 1948, October 24, 1965, October 15, 1967, May 10, 1970.

Time, October 20, 1952, March 16, 1959.

Times Literary Supplement, December 4, 1970, January 28, 1972.

*   *   *

TIPTREE, James, Jr.
See SHELDON, Alice Hastings Bradley

*   *   *

TOFFLER, Alvin 1928-

PERSONAL: Born October 28, 1928, in New York, N.Y.; married Adelaide Farrell, April 29, 1950; children: Karen. *Education:* New York University, B.A., 1949.

CAREER: Washington correspondent for various newspapers and magazines, 1957-59; *Fortune* magazine, New York, N.Y., associate editor, 1959-61; free-lance writer, 1961—. Member of faculty, New School for Social Research, 1965-67; visiting professor, Cornell University, 1969; visiting scholar, Russell Sage Foundation, 1969-70. Member of board of trustees, Antioch University. Consultant to organizations, including Rockefeller Brothers Fund, American Telephone & Telegraph Co., Institute for the Future, and Educational Facilities Laboratories, Inc.

MEMBER: American Society of Journalists and Authors, Society for the History of Technology (member of advisory council).

AWARDS, HONORS: Award from National Council for the Advancement of Educational Writing, 1969, for *The Schoolhouse in the City;* McKinsey Foundation Book Award, 1970, and Prix du Meilleur Livre Etranger (France), 1972, both for *Future Shock; Playboy* magazine best article award, 1970; Doctor of Laws from University of Western Ontario, D.Litt. from University of Cincinnati and Miami University, and D.Sc. from Rensselaer Polytechnic Institute, all 1972; Doctor of Letters, Ripon College, 1975; Author of the Year Award, American Society of Journalists and Authors, 1983; American Association for the Advancement of Science fellow, 1984; Centennial Award, Institute of Electrical and Electronics Engineers, 1984; Officier de l'Ordre des Arts et des Lettres, 1984; Doctor of Laws, Manhattan College, 1984.

WRITINGS:

The Culture Consumers: A Study of Art and Affluence in America (Literary Guild selection), St. Martin's, 1964.

(Editor) *The Schoolhouse in the City,* Praeger, 1968.

Future Shock, Random House, 1970.

(Editor) *The Futurists,* Random House, 1972.

(Editor) *Learning for Tomorrow: The Role of the Future in Education,* Random House, 1974.

The Eco-Spasm Report, Bantam, 1975.

The Third Wave, Morrow, 1980.

Previews and Premises, Morrow, 1983.

The Adaptive Corporation, McGraw, 1984.

Powershift: Knowledge, Wealth and Violence in the 21st Century, Bantam, 1990.

CONTRIBUTOR

Bricks and Mortarboards, Educational Facilities Laboratories, Inc., 1966.

B. M. Gross, editor, *A Great Society?,* Basic Books, 1968.

K. Baier and N. Rescher, editors, *Values and the Future,* Free Press, 1969.

Gross, editor, *Social Intelligence for America's Future,* Allyn & Bacon, 1969.

Cultures beyond the Earth, Vintage, 1975.

Anticipatory Democracy, Vintage, 1975.

Science Fiction at Large, Gollancz, 1976.

Order out of Chaos, Bantam, 1984.

Work appears in anthologies, including *Politics, U.S.A.,* edited by A. M. Scott and E. Wallace, 2nd edition, Macmillan, 1965; *Essays Today,* edited by William Moynihan, Harcourt, 1968; *The Sociology of Art and Literature,* edited by M. C. Albrecht and others, Praeger, 1970.

Contributor to *Fortune, Life, Reader's Digest, Horizon, New York Times Magazine, Saturday Review, Playboy, New Republic, Nation,* and other publications.

SIDELIGHTS: In *Future Shock* and *The Third Wave,* Alvin Toffler presents his speculations about future developments in our society and his recommendations for adapting to the problems and opportunities these changes will create. "I'm no prophet," Toffler tells Edwin McDowell of the *New York Times Book Review.* "I don't believe anybody knows the future. . . . What I do is throw out large-scale hypotheses, new ideas, in hopes of stimulating fresh thinking."

In the best-selling *Future Shock,* Toffler indeed stimulated some fresh thinking. He argues in this book that the rate of change in contemporary society is now so fast that many people are being overwhelmed by it. The term "future shock," explains Arnold A. Rogow in the *Saturday Review,* refers to "a condition of confusion and dislocation" brought on by sudden, massive societal change. Toffler bases his concept on the anthropological idea of "culture shock," the inability of some primitive cultures to adapt when first coming into contact with a highly advanced culture. Applying this idea to our own constantly changing society, Toffler argues that members of our society are experiencing a clash between the culture they grew up in and the emerging technological culture around them, which is replacing and destroying their familiar world. "Future shock is a time phenomenon," Toffler writes in his book, "a product of the greatly accelerated rate of change in society. It arises from the superimposition of a new culture on an old one. It is culture shock in one's own society."

Toffler believes there is a limit to the amount of change that human beings can readily accept, and that we may be reaching that limit. "We have," Elting E. Morison states in the *New York Times Book Review,* ". . . discoverable limits, physiological and emotional, to the numbers of signals we can take in from the world to come." The rising rates for divorce, drug use, and crime all point, Toffler states, to the disastrous effects that future shock is having on Western Society. But, writes John Greenway in the *American Journal of Sociology,* the "limits of change the human organism can absorb are discoverable and are therefore controllable." Toffler suggests several ways to control the ill effects of future shock. Children should read more science fiction, he believes, contemporary rituals should be developed to celebrate technological progress, and the study of the future should be given a more prominent place in our society.

Although he finds *Future Shock* "monstrous, mind-coshing, premeditatedly inexact, over-and-overstated and, above all, over-long," P. M. Grady of *Book World* nonetheless believes the book "might assist us not only in preparing for a softer landing into the future, but also in diagnosing more keenly some of today's social puzzles." Calling *Future Shock* "the most prophetic, disturbing, and stimulating social study of this year," Edward Weeks of the *Atlantic Monthly* goes on to agree with Toffler's argument that "we have it in our power to shape change; we may choose one future over another." Neil Millar of the *Christian Science Monitor* also sees an optimism in *Future Shock*. "It oversimplifies some issues . . . ," he writes, "[but] it also opens bright vistas of hope."

This hope is also found in *The Third Wave,* a book which extends and develops the ideas first presented in *Future Shock.* The great changes Toffler warns about in *Future Shock* are presented in *Third Wave* as the harbingers of a new and potentially liberating form of civilization. "This new civilization," Toffler writes, "brings with it new family styles; changed ways of working, loving, and living; a new economy; new political conflicts; and beyond all this an altered consciousness as well."

The first two "waves" of history, Toffler explains, were the invention of agriculture ten thousand years ago and the industrial revolution of a few centuries ago. The "third wave" involves the restructuring of industrial civilization along more humane lines. Decentralization, renewable energy sources, high technology, and new forms of participatory democracy are all features of this coming civilization.

Several critics disparage Toffler's writing style in *Third Wave* but believe he does raise some important questions for further discussion. "Toffler's style suffers from evangelism: sonorous, incremental cascades, prose panoramas," Anatole Broyard writes in the *New York Times.* "While he is often right, he has the hortatory tone we associate with being wrong. . . . Even so, 'The Third Wave' has many virtues. In his hectic way, Mr. Toffler raises all sorts of good questions." Similarly, Langdon Winner of the *New York Times Book Review* believes Toffler "offers many provocative observations about contemporary social trends, especially on patterns evolving in work and family life. But he's in such a hurry to package his ideas in flashy conceptual wrappers that he seldom completes a thought."

Rosalind H. Williams, reviewing *Third Wave* for *Technology Review,* disagrees with some of Toffler's interpretations of present-day trends. Toffler sees, for example, current high technology industries as harbingers of his "third wave" civilization. Williams, however, believes "these developments would prolong the present order, not alter it radically. New markets do not make a new civilization. . . . Toffler's problem is not that he dares to predict, but that his prophecies overlook possible extensions of the community- and energy-intensive civilization of today." But Williams still finds much value in *Third Wave* as "a manual of survival strategies" and as a "stimulus to the imagination." Reviewing the book for *American Anthropologist,* Magorah Maruyama writes that "overall, the shortcomings of the book are very minor compared to its contribution in encouraging readers to revise many of their assumptions and patterns of thinking about cultural processes."

Toffler stresses to Charles Platt in *Dream Makers,* Volume II: *The Uncommon Men and Women Who Write Science Fiction* that in all his work he has promoted the idea of citizen participation in the decisions regarding future technological developments. "These decisions," he explains, "can no longer be left to scientific, business, or political elites. . . . If you do not give people that voice, you are not giving them a voice in the selection of their own future." He believes his own role is "to open up the reader's mind to other ways of conceptualizing our political and social structures. I think that that helps people adapt; and to have a repertoire of alternatives is necessary."

BIOGRAPHICAL/CRITICAL SOURCES:

BOOKS

Platt, Charles, *Dream Makers,* Volume II: *The Uncommon Men and Women Who Write Science Fiction,* Berkley Publishing, 1983.
Toffler, Alvin, *Future Shock,* Random House, 1970.
Toffler, *The Third Wave,* Morrow, 1980.

PERIODICALS

American Anthropologist, Volume LXXXIII, Number 2, 1981.
American Journal of Sociology, July, 1971.
Atlantic Monthly, August, 1970.
Book World, September 6, 1970.
Chicago Tribune Book World, March 23, 1980.
Christian Science Monitor, August 6, 1970.
Commentary, October, 1971.
Contemporary Issues Criticism, Volume I, Gale, 1982.
Economist, June 21, 1980.
Fortune, November, 1970.
Los Angeles Times, April 4, 1980, February 20, 1989.
Los Angeles Times Book Review, March 23, 1980.
Maclean's, April 14, 1980.
Nation, January 25, 1971.
New Society, October 1, 1970.
New Statesman, October 2, 1970.
Newsweek, August 24, 1970.
New York Times, March 22, 1980, July 3, 1980.
New York Times Book Review, July 26, 1970, March 30, 1980, July 17, 1983.
Psychology Today, April, 1980.
Saturday Review, December 12, 1970, March 29, 1980.
Social Science, summer, 1976.
Technology Review, October, 1980.
Time, March 24, 1980.
Times Literary Supplement, August 8, 1975, October 31, 1980.
Washington Post Book World, May 4, 1980, June 12, 1983.

* * *

TOLAND, John (Willard) 1912-

PERSONAL: Born June 29, 1912, in La Crosse, Wis.; son of Ralph (a concert singer) and Helen (Snow) Toland; married present wife, Toshiko Matsumura, March 12, 1960; children: (previous marriage) Diana, Marcia; (present marriage) Tamiko (daughter). *Education:* Williams College, B.A., 1936; attended Yale University, 1937.

ADDRESSES: Home—1 Long Ridge Rd., Danbury, Conn. 06810. *Agent*—Carl D. Brandt, Brandt & Brandt Literary Agents Inc., 1501 Broadway, New York, N.Y. 10036.

CAREER: Writer. Advisor to the National Archives. *Military service:* U.S. Air Force, six years; became captain.

MEMBER: Overseas Press Club, Writers Guild, PEN.

AWARDS, HONORS: Overseas Press Club award, 1961, for *But Not in Shame,* 1967, for *The Last 100 Days,* 1970, for *The Rising Sun: The Decline and Fall of the Japanese Empire, 1936-1945,* and 1976, for *Adolf Hitler;* L.H.D., Williams College, 1968; Van Wyck Brooks Award for nonfiction, 1970, and Pulitzer Prize for nonfiction, 1970, both for *The Rising Sun;* L.H.D., University of Alaska, 1977; National Society of Arts and Letters gold medal, 1977, for *Adolf Hitler;* Accademia del Mediterrano, 1978; L.H.D., University of Connecticut, 1986.

WRITINGS:

Ships in the Sky, Holt, 1957.
Battle: The Story of the Bulge, Random House, 1959.
But Not in Shame, Random House, 1961.
The Dillinger Days, Random House, 1963.
The Flying Tigers (juvenile), Random House, 1963.
The Last 100 Days, Random House, 1966.
The Battle of the Bulge (juvenile), Random House, 1966.
*The Rising Sun: The Decline and Fall of the Japanese Empire,
    1936-1945,* Random House, 1970.
Adolf Hitler, Doubleday, 1976.
Hitler: The Pictorial Documentary of His Life, Doubleday, 1978.
No Man's Land: 1918, The Last Year of the Great War, Double-
    day, 1980.
Infamy: Pearl Harbor and Its Aftermath, Doubleday, 1982.
Gods of War (novel), Doubleday, 1985.
Occupation (novel), Doubleday, 1987.

Contributor of articles to *Look, Life, Reader's Digest, Saturday
Evening Post,* and other magazines.

SIDELIGHTS: John Toland's "approach to history," Diana
Loercher writes in the *Christian Science Monitor,* "is that of an
investigative reporter." For each of his books Toland interviews
the participants in a historic event, sometimes several hundred
of them, in order to get all sides of a story from those people who
know it best. He then presents these interviews as objectively as
is possible. "I believe it's my duty," Toland explains, "to tell you
everything and let you draw your own conclusions. I keep my
opinions to a minimum."

Among Toland's more popular books are the Pulitzer Prize-
winning *The Rising Sun: The Decline and Fall of the Japanese
Empire, 1936-1945;* his *Adolf Hitler,* a biography; *No Man's
Land: 1918, The Last Year of the Great War; Infamy: Pearl Harbor and Its Aftermath;* and the novel *Gods of War.* Many of these
titles have been best-sellers and have helped to establish Toland
as "a superb popular historian of World War II," as Jack Lessenberry states in the *Detroit News.*

Toland's most successful book is *The Rising Sun,* which traces
the collapse of the Japanese Empire after its fatal decision to
wage war during the 1930s. It is a "big, absorbing and finally
very moving history of the Pacific war, told primarily from the
Japanese viewpoint," as Walter Clemons explains in the *New
York Times.* William Craig of the *Washington Post Book World*
believes that "nowhere in American literature has the Japanese
side of the war in the jungles been so well told."

To uncover the Japanese version of the Second World War, Toland interviewed hundreds of participants, "ranging from former
generals and admirals to former first-class privates of the Imperial Army and housewives who somehow lived through Hiroshima," the *Times Literary Supplement* critic states. He interweaves this material with relevant written documents to produce
a narrative history of Imperial Japan. "Although in the main a
narrative account," the *Times Literary Supplement* critic writes,
"[*The Rising Sun*] is not devoid of passages of shrewd analytical
insight." Craig believes that "*The Rising Sun* makes a significant
contribution to our knowledge of the recent past. . . . Toland
has fashioned a compelling portrait of Japan at the brink of national suicide."

The extensive research for *The Rising Sun* resulted in the clearing up of historical inaccuracies and the unearthing of new information. Toland found, for example, that a simple misunderstanding during Japanese-American negotiations prior to World
War II was one of the reasons Japan went to war. During these

negotiations, the United States had demanded that the Japanese
remove their troops from China. Although agreeable to a withdrawal from China, the Japanese assumed that this demand included Manchuria, an area of China they wished to keep, and
so refused to withdraw. In fact, the United States had not meant
to include Manchuria in its demand. If this point had been clarified, Japanese-American relations may have been normalized
and the subsequent war averted. "In showing how just about all
of the Japanese leaders in 1941 sincerely hoped to avoid war,"
notes F. X. J. Homer in *Best Sellers,* "Toland makes it possible
for us to recognize that Pearl Harbor was the result of failings
on the part of American diplomacy as well as of Japanese aggression. . . . Toland adds a new dimension to orthodox military
history in going beyond grand strategy to portray the human side
of the conflict."

In *Adolf Hitler,* a study of the National Socialist leader of World
War II Germany, Toland's research again uncovered new facts
and dispelled some widely believed misinformation. As with Toland's previous books, *Adolf Hitler* relies on extensive interviews.
Toland spoke to almost two hundred people who knew or
worked with Hitler. Piecing together their accounts, he constructs a multi-faceted portrait of one of the pivotal figures of the
war. Because this portrait presents observations from "generals
and diplomats [and] some of Hitler's closest friends and atten-
dants," as W. Warren Wagar notes in the *Saturday Review, Adolf
Hitler* contains "hundreds of chatty anecdotes and odd glimpses
into Hitler's life that help to give him a human, if often unpleas-
ing, face."

Toland's book reveals that until the Second World War began,
Hitler was overwhelmingly popular in Germany. He had
brought his country out of a depression, instituted a series of
massive building programs that provided much-needed jobs, established sweeping social reforms, and given the German people
a sense of common purpose. Internationally, Hitler enjoyed an
equally favorable reputation. Gertrude Stein believed he deserved a Nobel Peace Prize. George Bernard Shaw praised him
in newspaper articles. The Vatican cooperated with him. Toland
states that "if Hitler had died in 1937 . . . he would undoubtedly
have gone down as one of the greatest figures in German history."

Critical reaction to *Adolf Hitler* particularly praised the sheer
mass of information that Toland gathers into one book. "Put
simply," Peter S. Prescott comments in *Newsweek,* "Toland tells
us more about Hitler than anyone knew before." And because
of the vast amount of information provided in the book, *Adolf
Hitler* is one of the most comprehensive studies of its subject
available. "Not only is 'Adolf Hitler' marvelously absorbing
popular history," Christopher Lehmann-Haupt writes in the
New York Times, "it also must be ranked as one of the most complete pictures of Hitler we have yet had." "Toland's book," Eliot
Freemont-Smith claims in the *Village Voice,* "is very good, in
most ways the best Hitler biography so far. . . . What makes it
'best' is Toland's superb command of an enormous amount of
detail, of where to place emphasis in order to increase our understanding and of tone."

In *No Man's Land: 1918, The Last Year of the Great War,* Toland turned from his studies of World War II to look at how
World War I had ended. The last year of that conflict saw stunning military reversals and massive casualties. It began with a
stalemate on the Western Front, where soldiers on both sides endured a stagnant and bloody trench warfare. But in the spring
of 1918 the Kaiser completed a peace treaty with Russia and was
able to move troops from the Russian front to the Western

Front. With some 600,000 men, far more than the French and British armies could muster, the Germans launched "the greatest military assault in history," as Timothy Foote writes in *Time*. It appeared as if the Germans would soon capture Paris.

But in July the Allies counterattacked, driving the German army back some twenty miles. The French and British armies then captured around 50,000 German soldiers in one battle near Amiens and put an end to the Kaiser's hopes of victory. When American troops began to arrive shortly thereafter, at the rate of 250,000 a month, the German high command realized that the war was lost. Toland's account of the dramatic finish of World War I is "scrupulously accurate while at the same time absorbing and dramatic," according to Richard M. Watt of the *New York Times Book Review*.

Some reviewers were critical of Toland's approach. Brian Bond of the *Times Literary Supplement* calls *No Man's Land* "essentially a story without any real attempt to analyse issues, reappraise evidence or reach conclusions." In the *Detroit News*, Bernard A. Weisberger complains that Toland "seems to have relied on first-hand accounts by soldiers who still had some notion of the war as an adventure." But the London *Times*'s Laurence Cotterell praises Toland's objectivity. "While describing in exhaustive detail the direction and course of battle," writes Cotterell, "Toland displays remarkably little partisanship [and] yet evokes all the intrinsic colour and passion of the situation, enabling the reader to form his or her own conclusions."

With *Infamy: Pearl Harbor and Its Aftermath*, Toland examined the tragic attack which brought the United States into the Second World War. Some 2,400 American servicemen died when the Japanese fleet staged a surprise attack on the naval base at Pearl Harbor, Hawaii, on December 7, 1941. Toland had written about this event in his *The Rising Sun* in 1970. But, he tells Andrew R. McGill of the *Detroit News*, "I made a mistake in *The Rising Sun* by saying the attack was a total surprise. . . . Subsequently, enough people came to me with contrary information that I learned I had fallen into a trap."

Toland argues in *Infamy* that President Franklin D. Roosevelt and a handful of top government officials wanted to provoke a war with Japan but were held back by the isolationism of the American people. Their provocations finally drove the Japanese to plan an attack on Pearl Harbor, America's largest naval base in the Pacific. When Roosevelt learned of the upcoming attack, he and his aides deliberately kept the information from the Naval commanders at Pearl Harbor. Roosevelt's purpose was to make the Japanese fire the first shot and "make Americans so mad they'd abandon their isolationism and plunge into the confrontation with fascism," as Jeff Lyon explains in the *Chicago Tribune Book World*.

Reaction to Toland's assertion that Roosevelt knew of the coming Pearl Harbor attack and did nothing to stop it drew some harsh criticism. "I'm getting the greatest hatred on this," Toland told Lyon. And yet, his conclusions are based on what D. J. R. Bruckner of the *New York Times Book Review* calls "tons of documents unsealed by the Freedom of Information Act." Among the evidence are reports that radio messages from the Japanese naval force were intercepted days before the attack; that a Dutch diplomat who visited the navy's Washington command center in early December of 1941 watched as intelligence officers tracked the Japanese fleet on its way to Hawaii; and that a British double agent alerted the United States that a Pearl Harbor attack was planned. "The evidence [Toland] has gathered . . .," Lyon writes, "is fresh and compelling." Bill Stout of the *Los Angeles Times Book Review* finds that *Infamy*'s evidence amounts to "a

strong indictment of Franklin D. Roosevelt and most of his wartime inner circle."

After writing for more than twenty years about recent history, particularly about the Second World War, Toland decided in 1985 to transform historical fact into fiction. *Gods of War*, his first novel, traces the experiences of two families during World War II: the McGlynns are an American family; the Todas, a Japanese family. Together, their stories provide a panoramic look at the entire war in the Pacific. "Toland makes a majestic sweep of conditions, events and personalities," Webster Schott explains in the *New York Times Book Review*.

Although Lessenberry believes that *Gods of War* "is a ponderous, 598-page pedestrian work in which the substance of characters range from cardboard to knotty pine," other critics find much to praise. While admitting that "Toland is an analyst of history, not personality," and that "his characters act rather than struggle," Schott concludes that *Gods of War* "is compelling as information and impressive as performance. It's history dressed as fiction. Very well dressed." Noel Barber of the *Washington Post Book World* maintains that, "small faults aside, this is a massive novel, broad in its scope and fascinating in its detail. Like all good sagas based on recent war history, it cannot fail."

BIOGRAPHICAL/CRITICAL SOURCES:

PERIODICALS

American Historical Review, February, 1972.
Ann Arbor News, June 6, 1982.
Best Sellers, February 1, 1971.
Books and Bookmen, July, 1977.
Book World, January 3, 1971.
Chicago Tribune Book World, September 28, 1980, May 15, 1982, April 14, 1985.
Christian Science Monitor, March 3, 1966, October 27, 1976.
Detroit News, October 19, 1980, June 13, 1982, March 10, 1985.
Los Angeles Times, December 28, 1980.
Los Angeles Times Book Review, May 9, 1982, March 3, 1985.
Modern Age, fall, 1966.
Nation, January 22, 1977.
National Review, April 29, 1977.
New Republic, November 20, 1976, June 16, 1979.
Newsweek, March 7, 1966, December 28, 1970, September 20, 1976.
New York Herald Tribune Book Review, February 18, 1966.
New York Review of Books, May 26, 1977, December 18, 1980, May 27, 1982.
New York Times, December 7, 1970, October 12, 1976.
New York Times Book Review, November 29, 1970, September 26, 1976, November 12, 1980, August 22, 1982, April 21, 1985.
North American Review, summer, 1977.
Progressive, February, 1977.
Saturday Review, March 12, 1966, January 2, 1971, September 18, 1976, September, 1980.
Time, December 7, 1970, December 6, 1976, September 22, 1980.
Times (London), December 11, 1980.
Times Literary Supplement, September 1, 1972, February 6, 1981.
Village Voice, November 15, 1976.
Virginia Quarterly Review, summer, 1977.
Wall Street Journal, February 28, 1966.
Washington Post, October 27, 1980, May 3, 1982, October 29, 1987.

Washington Post Book World, January 3, 1971, September 5, 1976, April 23, 1985.
Yale Review, June, 1971.

*   *   *

TOLKIEN, J(ohn) R(onald) R(euel) 1892-1973

PERSONAL: Surname is pronounced *"Tohl-keen";* born January 3, 1892, in Bloemfontein, South Africa; brought to England in April, 1895; died of complications resulting from a bleeding gastric ulcer and a chest infection, September 2, 1973, in Bournemouth, England; buried in Wolvercote Cemetary, Oxford; son of Arthur Reuel (a bank manager) and Mabel (Suffield) Tolkien; married Edith Mary Bratt (a pianist), March 22, 1916 (died November 29, 1971); children: John, Michael, Christopher, Priscilla. *Education:* Exeter College, Oxford, B.A., 1915, M.A., 1919. *Religion:* Roman Catholic.

CAREER: Author and scholar. Assistant on *Oxford English Dictionary,* 1918-20; University of Leeds, Leeds, England, reader in English, 1920-24, professor of English language, 1924-25: Oxford University, Oxford, England, Rawlinson and Bosworth Professor of Anglo-Saxon, 1925-45, Merton Professor of English Language and Literature, 1945-59, fellow of Pembroke College, 1926-45, honorary resident fellow of Merton College, 1972-73. Free-lance tutor, 1919; Leverhulme research fellow, 1934-36; Sir Israel Gollancz Memorial Lecturer, British Academy, 1936; Andrew Lang Lecturer, St. Andrews University, 1939; W. P. Ker Lecturer, University of Glasgow, 1953; O'Donnell Lecturer, Oxford University, 1955. *Military service:* Lancashire Fusiliers, 1915-18.

MEMBER: Royal Society of Literature (fellow), Philological Society (vice-president), Science Fiction Writers of America (honorary), Hid Islenzka Bokmenntafelag (honorary).

AWARDS, HONORS: New York Herald Tribune Children's Spring Book Festival award, 1938, for *The Hobbit;* Dr. en Phil. et Lettres, Liege, 1954; D.Litt., University College, Dublin, 1954, and Oxford University, 1972; International Fantasy Award, 1957, for *The Lord of the Rings;* Benson Medal, 1966; Commander, Order of the British Empire, 1972; *Locus* Award for best fantasy novel, 1978, for *The Silmarillion.*

WRITINGS:

(Editor with C. L. Wiseman, and author of introductory note) Geoffrey Bache Smith, *A Spring Harvest* (poems), Erskine Macdonald, 1918.
A Middle English Vocabulary, Clarendon Press, 1922.
(Editor with Eric V. Gordon) *Sir Gawain and the Green Knight,* Clarendon Press, 1925, 2nd edition, revised by Norman Davis, 1967.
(With Gordon and others) *Songs for the Philologists* (verse), Department of English, University College, Oxford, 1936.
Beowulf: The Monsters and the Critics (originally published in *Proceedings of the British Academy,* 1936; also see below), Oxford University Press, 1937, reprinted, 1958.
Chaucer as a Philologist, Oxford University Press, 1943.
(Self-illustrated) *The Hobbit; or, There and Back Again,* Allen & Unwin, 1937, Houghton, 1938, 2nd edition, 1951, 3rd edition, 1966, 4th edition, 1978.
Farmer Giles of Ham (also see below), Allen & Unwin, 1949, Houghton, 1950, 2nd edition, Allen & Unwin, 1975, Houghton, 1978.
The Lord of the Rings, Houghton, Volume 1: *The Fellowship of the Ring,* 1954, Volume 2: *The Two Towers,* 1954, Volume

3: *The Return of the King,* 1955, with new foreword by the author, Ballantine, 1966, 2nd edition, Allen & Unwin, 1966, Houghton, 1967.
The Adventures of Tom Bombadil and Other Verses from the Red Book (also see below), Allen & Unwin, 1962, Houghton, 1963, 2nd edition, Houghton, 1978.
(Editor) *Ancrene Wisse: The English Text of the Ancrene Riwle,* Oxford University Press, 1962.
Tree and Leaf (includes "On Fairy-Stories" and "Leaf By Niggle" [originally published in *Dublin Review,* 1945]; also see below), Allen & Unwin, 1964, Houghton, 1965, reprinted, 1989, 2nd edition, Allen & Unwin, 1975.
The Tolkien Reader (includes "The Homecoming of Beorhtnoth" [originally published in *Essays and Studies,* English Association, 1953; also see below], *Tree and Leaf, Farmer Giles of Ham,* and *The Adventures of Tom Bombadil*), introduction by Peter S. Beagle, Ballantine, 1966.
The Road Goes Ever On: A Song Cycle, music by Donald Swann, Houghton, 1967.
Smith of Wootton Major (also see below), Houghton, 1967, 2nd edition, Allen & Unwin, 1975, Houghton, 1978.
Smith of Wootton Major [and] *Farmer Giles of Ham,* Ballantine, 1969.
(Translator) *Sir Gawain and the Green Knight, Pearl,* [and] *Sir Orfeo,* edited by Christopher Tolkien, Houghton, 1975.
Tree and Leaf, Smith of Wootton Major, The Homecoming of Beorhtnoth, Unwin Books, 1975.
Farmer Giles of Ham, The Adventures of Tom Bombadil, Unwin Books, 1975.
The Father Christmas Letters, edited by Baillie Tolkien, Houghton, 1976.
The Silmarillion, edited by Christopher Tolkien, Houghton, 1977.
Pictures by J. R. R. Tolkien, foreword and notes by Christopher Tolkien, Houghton, 1979.
Unfinished Tales of Numenor and Middle-Earth, edited by Christopher Tolkien, Houghton, 1980.
Poems and Stories, Allen & Unwin, 1980.
The Letters of J. R. R. Tolkien, selected and edited by Humphrey Carpenter and Christopher Tolkien, Houghton, 1981.
(Author of text and commentary, and translator) *The Old English Exodus,* edited by Joan Turville-Petre, Oxford University Press, 1981.
Mr. Bliss (reproduced from Tolkien's illustrated manuscript), Allen & Unwin, 1982, Houghton, 1983.
Finn and Hengest: The Fragment and the Episode, edited by Alan Bliss, Allen & Unwin, 1982, Houghton, 1983.
The Monsters and the Critics and Other Essays, edited by Christopher Tolkien, Allen & Unwin, 1983, Houghton, 1984.
Oliphaunt (verse), Contemporary Books, 1989.

"HISTORY OF MIDDLE EARTH" SERIES; EDITED BY CHRISTOPHER TOLKIEN

The Book of Lost Tales, Part 1, Allen & Unwin, 1983, Houghton, 1984.
The Book of Lost Tales, Part 2, Houghton, 1984.
The Lays of Beleriand, Houghton, 1985.
The Shaping of Middle-Earth: The Quenta, the Ambarkanta, and the Annals, Houghton, 1986.
The Lost Road and Other Writings: Language and Legend before The Lord of the Rings, Houghton, 1987.
The Return of the Shadow: The History of The Lord of the Rings, Part 1, Houghton, 1988.
The Treason of Isengard: The History of The Lord of the Rings, Part 2, Houghton, 1989.

OTHER

(Contributor) G. D. H. Cole and T. W. Earp, editors, *Oxford Poetry, 1915,* B. H. Blackwell, 1915.

(Contributor) *A Northern Venture: Verses by Members of the Leeds University English School Association,* Swan Press, 1923.

(Contributor) G. S. Tancred, editor, *Realities: An Anthology of Verse,* Gay & Hancock, 1927.

(Contributor) *Report on the Excavation of the Prehistoric, Roman, and Post-Roman Sites in Lydney Park,* Gloucestershire, Reports of the Research Committee of the Society of Antiquaries of London, Oxford University Press, 1932.

(Author of foreword) Walter E. Haigh, *A New Glossary of the Dialect of the Huddersfield District,* Oxford University Press, 1928.

(Author of preface) John R. Clark Hall, *Beowulf and the Finnesburg Fragment: A Translation into Modern English Prose,* edited by C. L. Wrenn, Allen & Unwin, 1940.

(Contributor) *Essays Presented to Charles Williams,* Oxford University Press, 1947.

(Author of preface) *The Ancrene Riwle,* translated by M. Salu, Burns & Oates, 1955.

(Contributor) *Angles and Britons: O'Donnell Lectures,* University of Wales Press, 1963.

(Contributor) Caroline Hillier, editor, *Winter's Tales for Children: 1,* St. Martin's, 1965.

(Contributor) William Luther White, *The Image of Man in C. S. Lewis,* Abingdon Press, 1969.

(Contributor) Roger Lancelyn Green, *The Hamish Hamilton Book of Dragons,* Hamish Hamilton, 1970.

(Contributor) Jared Lobdell, editor, *A Tolkien Compass,* Open Court, 1975.

(Contributor) Mary Salu and Robert T. Farrell, *J. R. R. Tolkien: Scholar and Storyteller,* Cornell University Press, 1979.

Contributor of translations to *The Jerusalem Bible,* Doubleday, 1966. Contributor to *The Year's Work in English Studies,* 1924 and 1925, *Transactions of the Philological Society,* 1934, *English Studies,* 1947, *Studia Neophilologica,* 1948, and *Essais de philologie moderne,* 1951. Contributor to periodicals, including *The King Edward's School Chronicle, Oxford Magazine, Medium Aevum, Dublin Review, Welsh Review,* and *Shenandoah: The Washington and Lee University Review.*

SIDELIGHTS: J. R. R. Tolkien is best known to most readers as the author of *The Hobbit* and *The Lord of the Rings,* regarded by Charles Moorman in *Tolkien and the Critics* as "unique in modern fiction," and by Augustus M. Kolich in the *Dictionary of Literary Biography* as "the most important fantasy stories of the modern period." From 1914 until his death in 1973, Tolkien drew on his familiarity with Northern and other ancient literatures and his own invented languages to create not just his own story, but his own world: Middle-earth, complete with its own history, myths, legends, epics and heroes. "His life's work," Kolich continues, ". . . encompasses a reality that rivals Western man's own attempt at recording the composite, knowable history of his species. Not since Milton has any Englishman worked so successfully at creating a secondary world, derived from our own, yet complete in its own terms with encyclopedic mythology; an imagined world that includes a vast gallery of strange beings: hobbits, elves, dwarfs, orcs, and, finally, the men of Westernesse." His works—especially *The Lord of the Rings*—have pleased countless readers and fascinated critics who recognize their literary depth.

Tolkien began to create his secondary world while still in school, shortly before enlisting to fight in World War I. In 1914, Humphrey Carpenter states in *Tolkien: A Biography,* Tolkien wrote a poem based on a line from the works of an Old English religious poet. Entitled "The Voyage of Earendel, the Evening Star," the poem marked the first appearance in his work of the mariner who sails across the heavens through the night, and was "the beginning of Tolkien's own mythology"—the stories that, edited by Christopher Tolkien, appeared after the author's death in "The History of Middle Earth" and *The Silmarillion.* Nearly all of Tolkien's fiction drew on these stories for their background. *The Hobbit* had at first no connection with Tolkien's legendary histories; he wrote it to please his own children and later remarked that "Mr. Baggins got dragged against my original will" into his imagined mythos. *The Lord of the Rings* also moved into the realm of legend until it became the chronicle of the last days of the Third Age of Middle-earth. After *The Lord of the Rings,* Tolkien published a sequence of related poems, *The Adventures of Tom Bombadil,* but the other fiction he published during his lifetime, including the satirical *Farmer Giles of Ham,* the allegorical *Leaf by Niggle,* and *Smith of Wooten Major,* one of his last works, drew on other sources.

However, Tolkien held another reputation not as well known to readers of his fantasies: he "was in fact one of the leading philologists of his day," Kolich reports. His essay "Beowulf: The Monsters and the Critics"—a plea to study the Old English poem "Beowulf" as a poem, and not just as a historical curiosity—is regarded as a classic critical statement on the subject, and his renditions of the Middle English poems "Sir Orfeo," "Sir Gawain and the Green Knight," and "Pearl" into Modern English are used as texts in some literature classes. His academic work, teaching English language and literature at Leeds and later at Oxford, heavily influenced his fiction; Tolkien himself wrote that "a primary 'fact' about my work [is] that it is all of a piece, and *fundamentally linguistic* in inspiration." " 'Philology,' " says T. A. Shippey in *The Road to Middle Earth,* quoting Tolkien, "is indeed the only proper guide to a view of Middle-earth 'of the sort which its author may be supposed to have desired.' " Carpenter declares, "There were not two Tolkiens, one an academic and the other a writer. They were the same man, and the two sides of him overlapped so that they were indistinguishable—or rather they were not two sides at all, but different expressions of the same mind, the same imagination."

What is philology? The concise edition of the *Oxford English Dictionary*—a book that focuses on the meaning of words through time, rather than just their present definition, and on which Tolkien himself worked—derives the word "philology" from two Greek stems: *philo,* meaning "love of," and *logos,* meaning "words" or "language," and defines it as "the study of literature in a wide sense, including grammar, literary criticism and interpretation, the relation of literature and written records to history, etc." Tolkien was a philologist in the literal sense of the word: a lover of language. It was a passion he developed early and kept throughout his life, exploring tongues that were no longer spoken and creating languages of his own. Carpenter explains, "It was a deep *love* for the look and sound of words [that motivated him], springing from the days when his mother had given him his first Latin lesson." After learning Latin and Greek, Tolkien taught himself some Welsh, Old and Middle English, Old Norse, and Gothic, a language with no modern descendant—he wrote the only poem known to exist in that speech. Later he added Finnish to his list of beloved tongues; the Finnish epic *The Kalevala* had a great impact on his *Silmarillion,* and the language itself, says Carpenter, formed the basis for "Quenya," the High-elven tongue of his stories.

But philology also refers to a discipline: linguistics, the science of language, the application of observed, consistent change of tongues through time to reconstruct languages no longer spoken. After recognizing the common ancestry of certain tongues, philologists devised laws—such as Grimm's Law of Consonants, devised by the great philologist Jacob Grimm, of *Grimm's Fairy Tales* fame—to describe the changes these languages underwent in their development to modern form. Because the changes were regular, these laws make it possible to reconstruct words that do not exist in written records. Reconstructed words are marked with an asterisk (*) to show that the word in question is inferred and does not appear in any known document. Modern philologists have used the principles of linguistics to recover and interpret ancient languages and their literatures ranging from Mycenaean Linear B script—the language contemporary with *The Iliad's* heroes—to the Hittite language of Old Testament times.

Throughout his fiction, from the early tales of *The Silmarillion* to *The Hobbit* and *The Lord of the Rings,* Tolkien exercised his philological talents and training to create an "asterisk-epic"—an inferred history—that revealed elements of the Northern (and especially the English) literature he loved, and of which so little remains. "The dwarf-names of 'Thorin and Company,' as well as Gandalf's," declares Shippey, "come from a section of the Eddic poem *Voluspa,* often known as the *Dvergatal* or 'Dwarves' Roster.'" "In the case of the 'ents,'" states A. N. Wilson in the *Spectator,* quoting Tolkien, ". . . 'as usual with me they grew rather out of their name than the other way about. I always felt that something ought to be done about the peculiar Anglo-Saxon word *ent* for a "giant" or a mighty person of long ago—to whom all old works are ascribed.' He was not content to leave the ents as they appear on the page of *Beowulf,* shadowy, unknown figures of an almost forgotten past." "That is lovely," writes Ursula Le Guin in *The Language of the Night: Essays on Fantasy and Science Fiction;* "that is the Creator Spirit working absolutely unhindered—making the word flesh."

The value of linguistics, or comparative philology, lies in its applicability. Knowing the history of the words forgotten people used can reveal something about the way those people thought and about the modern languages descended from their tongues. Once philologists recognized the relationship between English and Gothic (the oldest recorded Germanic language), for instance, they proved able to explain why certain English words are pronounced and spelled the way they are: "a whole series of things which people said, and still *say,* without in the least knowing why, turn out to have one very old but clear, 100 per cent predictable reason. It's almost like genetics," declares Shippey. Historians frequently use linguistic principles to trace patterns of settlement through place names. In England, for example, towns whose names end in the element *-caster* or *-chester* (from the Latin *castrum,* a fort) mark sites where Roman legions built fortifications, according to the *Oxford English Dictionary.* Towns whose names end in *-ham* or *-wich* were once inhabited by speakers of Old English; in that language, *wic* is an encampment or village, while *hamme* can mean a meadow or a manorhouse. Towns whose names end in *-by,* however, were settled by invading Vikings; *byr* is an Old Norse term for a dwelling-place. Tolkien, Shippey points out, uses place names in a "Celtic 'style,' to make subliminally the point that hobbits were immigrants too, that their land had a history before them." The Carrock, the rocky island in the middle of the river of Wilderland in *The Hobbit,* is derived from the Welsh *carrecc,* a rock, while the town of

Bree in *The Lord of the Rings* comes from a Welsh word for a hill.

One of the reasons that philologists have to rely on terms like place names is that so few manuscript sources have survived from ancient times. "The philologist," writes E. Christian Kopff in *Chronicles of Culture,* "lives in the tragic world of the partially lost or broken. He knows the 18th-century fire that ate away just that page of *Beowulf* that explains why the dragon attacks after so many years." Of the sixteen epic poems that originally told the entire history of the Trojan War and its aftermath, only Homer's *Iliad* and *Odyssey* remain intact; the others survive only in fragments or summaries. But careful examination of the fragments of ancient literature that do survive can often reveal facets of the writer's culture, and can contain echoes of still older tales. In *Finn and Hengest: The Fragment and the Episode,* writes Kopff, "Tolkien takes a brief and fragmentary tale sung by a bard in *Beowulf* and a fragment of a separate version of the same story that survives on a single manuscript page and tries to reconstruct the history that lies behind the two sources."

This sense of loss helps explain why Tolkien came to write the history of Middle-earth. "Like Walter Scott or William Morris before him," Shippey declares, "he felt the perilous charm of the archaic world of the North, recovered from bits and scraps by generations of inquiry. He wanted to tell a story about it simply, one feels, because there were hardly any complete ones left." "J. R. R. Tolkien," says Jessica Yates in *British Book News,* "began to write *The Book of Lost Tales* in 1916-17, as his first attempt on 'a mythology for England.' He felt that the English people, as opposed to the Greeks or the Celts for example, had no 'body of . . . connected legend' of their own. All we had was *Beowulf* (imported from Denmark) and our native fairy stories. So partly with the sense of mission and partly as an escape from the horrors of the First World War, he wrote a series of tales about the creation of the world and the coming of the Elves, of evil Melko and the wars of Elves and Men against him."

Tolkien used the evocative power of language to create his English legend. Names in Tolkien's fiction are not merely identifying sounds, Shippey points out; they are also descriptions of the people, places and creatures that bear them. The name Gandalf, for instance, is made up of two Norse words: *gandr,* a magical implement (probably a staff), and *alfr,* an elf. Tolkien's Gandalf, therefore, is an elf with a staff, or a wizard. Shippey explains, "Accordingly when Gandalf first appears [in *The Hobbit*], 'All that the unsuspecting Bilbo saw that morning *was an old man with a staff.'.* . . He turns out not to be an elf, but by the end of *The Lord of the Rings* it is clear he comes from Elvenhome." The character Gollum continually refers to himself and to the Ring throughout *The Hobbit* and *The Lord of the Ring* as "my precious"; Douglas A. Anderson, in his notes to *The Annotated Hobbit,* cites Constance B. Hieatt, who declares that "Old Norse gull/goll, of which one inflected form would be *gollum,* means 'gold, treasure, something precious' and can also mean 'ring,' a point which may have occurred to Tolkien." In the last appendix to *The Lord of the Rings,* Shippey points out, Tolkien derives the word *hobbit* itself from an Old English asterisk-word—**holbytla,* meaning "hole-dweller" or "-builder"—although he worked out the meaning long after he first used the word.

Tolkien also drew on ancient words for inspiration. Shippey traces the origins of the Balrog—the evil creature Gandalf faces on the bridge in Moria—to an article Tolkien published in two parts in the journal *Medium Aevum* on the Anglo-Saxon word *Sigelhearwan,* used to translate Latin biblical references to natives of Ethiopia. Tolkien suggested that the element *sigel* meant both 'sun' and 'jewel,' and that the element *hearwa* was related to the Latin *carbo,* meaning soot. He further conjectured that when an Anglo-Saxon used the word, he did not picture a dark-skinned man but a creature like the fire-giants of Northern myth. "What was the point of the speculation," asks Shippey, "admittedly 'guess-work,' admittedly 'inconclusive'? It offers some glimpses of a lost mythology, suggested Tolkien with academic caution, something 'which has coloured the verse-treatment of Scripture and determined the diction of poems.' A good deal less boringly, one might say, it had helped to naturalise the 'Balrog' in the traditions of the North, and it had helped to create (or corroborate) the image of the *silmaril,* that fusion of 'sun' and 'jewel' in physical form." "Tolkien's attitude to language," writes Janet Adam Smith in the *New York Review of Books,* "is part of his attitude to history . . . to recapture and reanimate the words of the past is to recapture something of ourselves; for we carry the past in us, and our existence, like Frodo's quest, is only an episode in an age-long and continuing drama."

Tolkien's ability to use ancient tongues—"tending," according to Shippey, "to focus on names and words and the things and realities which lie behind them"—helps create a sense of history within Middle-earth, a feeling many reviewers have noticed. Joseph McLellan writes in the *Washington Post Book World,* "Tolkien's stories take place against a background of measureless depth. . . . That background is ever-present in the creator's mind and it gives Frodo and company a three-dimensional reality that is seldom found in this kind of writing." Shippey explains that Tolkien's use of language "gave *The Lord of the Rings* a dinosaur-like vitality which cannot be conveyed in any synopsis, but reveals itself in so many thousands of details that only the most biased critical mind could miss them all." "In the Tolkinian world," states C. S. Lewis in *Time and Tide,* "you can hardly put your foot down anywhere from Esgaroth to Forlindon or between Ered Mithrin and Khand without stirring the dust of history."

Although many readers have viewed *The Lord of the Rings* as an allegory of modern history (especially of the Second World War), Tolkien explicitly rejected such an interpretation; in the foreword to the Ballantine edition of *The Lord of the Rings,* he stated, "As for any inner meaning or 'message,' it has in the intention of the author none. It is neither allegorical nor topical." "I cordially dislike allegory in all its manifestations," he continued, "and have always done so since I grew old and wary enough to detect its presence. I much prefer history, true or feigned, with its varied applicability to the thought and experience of readers. I think that many confuse 'applicability' with 'allegory'; but the one resides in the freedom of the reader, and the other in the purposed dominations of the author." He expanded on these comments in a letter to his publisher Stanley Unwin: "There is a 'moral,' I suppose, in any tale worth telling. But that is not the same thing. Even the struggle between light and darkness (as [Rayner Unwin] calls it, not me) is for me just a particular phase of history, one example of its pattern, perhaps, but not The Pattern; and the actors are individuals—they each, of course, contain universals or they would not live at all, but they never represent them as such." "You can make the Ring into an allegory of our own time, if you like," he concluded: "an allegory of the inevitable fate that waits for all attempts to defeat evil power by power. But that is only because all power magical or mechanical does always so work. You cannot write a story about an apparently simple magic ring without that bursting in, if you really take the ring seriously, and make things happen that would happen, if such a thing existed."

Tolkien did, however, suggest that his work had an underlying theme. "*The Lord of the Rings,*" he wrote in a letter to the Jesuit Father Robert Murray, "is of course a fundamentally religious and Catholic work; unconsciously so at first, but consciously in the revision." Shippey points out that the rejoicing of the forces of the West after the downfall of Sauron in *The Return of the King* is an example of what Tolkien called a "eucatastrophe." Tolkien wrote to his son Christopher that in his essay "On Fairy Stories" "I coined the word 'eucatastrophe': the sudden happy turn in a story which pierces you with a joy that brings tears (which I argued it is the highest function of fairy-stories to produce). And I was there led to the view that it produces its peculiar effects because it is a sudden glimpse of Truth." "It perceives," he explained, ". . . that this is indeed how things really do work in the Great World for which our nature is made. And I concluded by saying that the Resurrection was the greatest 'eucatastrophe' possible in the greatest Fairy Story—and produces that essential emotion: Christian joy which produces tears because it is qualitatively so like sorrow, because it comes from those places where Joy and Sorrow are at one." "Of course," he added, "I do not mean that the Gospels tell what is *only* a fairy-story; but I do mean very strongly that they do tell a fairy-story: the greatest. Man the story-teller would have to be redeemed in a manner consonant with his nature: by a moving story."

"A good way to understand *The Lord of the Rings* in its full complexity," says Shippey, "is to see it as an attempt to reconcile two views of evil, both old, both authoritative, each seemingly contradicted by the other." To the orthodox Christian Evil does not exist by itself, but springs from an attempt to separate one's self from God—an opinion expressed most clearly in *The Consolation of Philosophy,* a work by the early medieval thinker Boethius, a Roman senator imprisoned and later executed for his views. Tolkien was probably most familiar with it through King Alfred's Old English translation, made in the 9th century A.D. An alternate view—labelled Manichaean, and considered heretical by the church—is that Good and Evil are separate forces, equal and opposite, and the world is their battleground. King Alfred's own career, campaigning against marauding Norsemen, writes Shippey, emphasizes the "strong point of a 'heroic' view of evil, the weak point of a Boethian one: if you regard evil as something internal, to be pitied, more harmful to the malefactor than the victim, you may be philosophically consistent but you may also be exposing others to sacrifices to which they have not consented (like being murdered by Viking ravagers or, as *The Lord of the Rings* was being written, being herded into gas-chambers)." In *The Lord of the Rings,* Shippey states, Tolkien strikes a balance between these two views of evil, using the symbol of the shadow: "Shadows are the absence of light and so don't exist in themselves, but they are still visible and palpable just as if they did." Tolkien's attitude "implies the dual nature of wickedness," which can also be found in the Lord's Prayer: " 'And lead us not into temptation; but deliver us from evil.' Succumbing to temptation is our business, one might paraphrase, but delivering us from evil is God's." "At any rate," Shippey concludes, "on the level of narrative one can say that *The Lord of the Rings* is neither a saint's life, all about temptation, nor a complicated wargame, all about tactics. It would be a much lesser work if it had swerved towards either extreme."

Nonetheless, Tolkien implies, to take *The Lord of the Rings* too seriously might be a mistake. "I think that fairy story has its own mode of reflecting 'truth,' different from allegory or (sustained) satire, or 'realism,' and in some ways more powerful," he stated. "But first of all it must succeed just as a tale, excite, please, and even on occasion move, and within its own imagined world be accorded literary belief. To succeed in that was my primary object." "The tale is after all in the ultimate analysis a tale," Tolkien wrote, "a piece of literature, intended to have literary effect, and not real history. That the device adopted, that of giving its setting an historical air or feeling, and (an illusion of ?) three dimensions, is successful, seems shown by the fact that several correspondents have treated it in the same way . . . as if it were a report of 'real' times and places, which my ignorance or carelessness had misrepresented in places or failed to describe properly in others." "Having set myself a task," he concluded, "the arrogance of which I fully recognized and trembled at: being precisely to restore to the English an epic tradition and present them with a mythology of their own: it is a wonderful thing to be told that I have succeeded, at least with those who have still the undarkened heart and mind."

MEDIA ADAPTATIONS: Recordings of J. R. R. Tolkien reading from his own works include "Poems and Songs of Middle-earth," "The Hobbit and The Fellowship of the Ring" and "The Lord of the Ring," have all been released by Caedmon. Christopher Tolkien reads "The Silmarillion: Of Beren and Luthien," also for Caedmon. Tolkien's illustrations from *Pictures by J. R. R. Tolkien* have been published in various editions of his books, and have appeared on calendars, posters, and postcards. Rankin-Bass animated a version of "The Hobbit" for television, which aired in 1977. Ralph Bakshi directed a theater film based on *The Fellowship of the Ring* and bits and pieces of *The Two Towers,* which was released as "The Lord of the Rings" in 1978. A Bunraku-style puppet version of "The Hobbit" was produced in Los Angeles in 1984 by Theatre Sans Fil of Montreal.

BIOGRAPHICAL/CRITICAL SOURCES:

BOOKS

Anderson, Douglas A., author of introduction and notes, *The Annotated Hobbit,* Houghton, 1988.

Authors in the News, Volume 1, Gale, 1976.

Carpenter, Humphrey, *J. R. R. Tolkien: A Biography,* Allen & Unwin, 1977, published as *Tolkien: A Biography,* Houghton, 1978.

Carpenter, Humphrey, *The Inklings: C. S. Lewis, J. R. R. Tolkien, Charles Williams and Their Friends,* Allen & Unwin, 1978, Houghton, 1979.

Carter, Lin, *Tolkien: A Look behind The Lord of the Rings,* Houghton, 1969.

Compact Edition of the Oxford English Dictionary, Oxford University Press, 1971.

Contemporary Literary Criticism, Gale, Volume 1, 1973, Volume 2, 1974, Volume 3, 1975, Volume 8, 1978, Volume 12, 1980, Volume 38, 1986.

Day, David, *A Tolkien Bestiary,* Ballantine, 1979.

Dictionary of Literary Biography, Volume 15: *British Novelists, 1930-1959,* Gale, 1983.

Ellwood, Gracia F., *Good News from Tolkien's Middle Earth: Two Essays on the Applicability of The Lord of Rings,* Eerdmans, 1970.

Fonstad, Karen Wynn, *The Atlas of Middle-Earth,* Houghton, 1981.

Foster, Robert, *A Guide to Middle-Earth,* Mirage Press, 1971, revised edition published as *The Complete Guide to Middle-Earth,* Del Rey, 1981.

Fuller, Edmund, and others, *Myth, Allegory and Gospel: An Interpretation; J. R. R. Tolkien, C. S. Lewis, G. K. Chesterton, Charles Williams,* Bethany Fellowship, 1974.

Isaacs, Neil D., and Rose A. Zimbardo, editors, *Tolkien and the Critics,* University of Notre Dame Press, 1968.

Johnson, Judith A., *J. R. R. Tolkien: Six Decades of Criticism,* Greenwood Press, 1986.

Kocher, Paul H., *Master of Middle-Earth: The Fiction of J. R. R. Tolkien,* Houghton, 1972.

Le Guin, Ursula K., *The Language of the Night: Essays on Fantasy and Science Fiction,* edited and with an introduction by Susan Wood, Putnam, 1979.

Lobdell, Jared, editor, *A Tolkien Compass,* Open Court, 1975.

Purtill, Richard L., *Lord of the Elves and Eldils: Fantasy and Philosophy in C. S. Lewis and J. R. R. Tolkien,* Zondervan, 1974.

Ready, William B., *The Tolkien Relation: A Personal Inquiry,* Regnery, 1968.

Shippey, T. A., *The Road to Middle-Earth,* Allen & Unwin, 1982, Houghton, 1983.

Stimpson, Catherine R., *J. R. R. Tolkien,* Columbia University Press, 1969.

Strachey, Barbara, *Journeys of Frodo: An Atlas of J. R. R. Tolkien's The Lord of the Rings,* Ballantine, 1981.

Tolkien, J. R. R., *The Letters of J. R. R. Tolkien,* selected and edited by Humphrey Carpenter and Christopher Tolkien, Houghton, 1981.

West, Richard C., compiler, *Tolkien Criticism: An Annotated Checklist,* Kent State University Press, 1970, revised edition, 1981.

PERIODICALS

Atlantic, March, 1965.
Book Week, February 26, 1967.
British Book News, December, 1984.
Chicago Tribune Book World, March 22, 1981.
Chronicles of Culture, April, 1985.
Commentary, February, 1967.
Commonweal, December 3, 1965.
Criticism, winter, 1971.
Critique, spring-fall, 1959.
Encounter, November, 1954.
Esquire, September, 1966.
Hudson Review, number 9, 1956-57.
Kenyon Review, summer, 1965.
Los Angeles Times Book Review, January 4, 1981, February 10, 1985.
Nation, April 14, 1956.
New Republic, January 16, 1956.
New York Review of Books, December 14, 1972.
New York Times Book Review, March 14, 1965, October 31, 1965, November 16, 1980, May 27, 1984, June 17, 1984.
New York Times Magazine, January 15, 1967.
Saturday Evening Post, July 2, 1966.
Sewanee Review, fall, 1961.
South Atlantic Quarterly, summer, 1959, spring, 1970.
Spectator, November, 1954.
Sunday Times (London), September 19, 1982.
Thought, spring, 1963.
Time and Tide, August 14, 1954, October 22, 1955.
Times Literary Supplement, July 8, 1983, July 19, 1985, December 23, 1988.
Washington Post Book World, September 4, 1977, December 9, 1980, February 13, 1983.

OBITUARIES:

PERIODICALS

Newsweek, September 17, 1973.
New York Times, September 3, 1973.
Publishers Weekly, September 17, 1973.

Time, September 17, 1973.
Washington Post, September 3, 1973.

—*Sketch by Kenneth R. Shepherd*

* * *

TOOMER, Jean 1894-1967

PERSONAL: Born December 26, 1894, in Washington, D.C.; died March 30, 1967, in Doylestown, Pa.; son of Nathan and Nina (Pinchback) Toomer; married Margery Latimer, October 20, 1931 (deceased); married Marjorie Content, September 1, 1934; children: Margery. *Education:* Attended University of Wisconsin—Madison, 1914, Massachusetts College of Agriculture, 1915, American College of Physical Training, 1916, University of Chicago, 1916, New York University, 1917, and City College of New York (now of the City University of New York), 1917; also attended Gurdjieff Institute (France). *Religion:* Quaker.

ADDRESSES: Home—Bucks County, Pa.

CAREER: Writer. Worked as teacher in Georgia, 1920-21; associated with Gurdjieff Institute in Harlem, N.Y., 1925, and Chicago, Ill., 1926-33.

WRITINGS:

Cane (novel comprised of poems and short stories), Boni & Liveright, 1923, reprinted, Norton, 1987.
(Contributor) Alain Locke and Montgomery Gregory, editors, *Plays of Negro Life: A Source-Book of Native American Drama,* Harper, 1927, Negro University Press, 1970.
(Contributor) *The New American Caravan,* Macaulay, 1929.
Essentials (aphorisms and apothegms), Lakeside Press, 1931, reprinted, Xerox University Microfilms (Ann Arbor, Mich.), 1975.
An Interpretation of Friends Worship, Committee on Religious Education of Friends General Conference, 1947.
The Flavor of Man (lecture), Young Friends Movement of the Philadelphia Yearly Meetings, 1949, reprinted, 1974.
Darwin Turner, editor, *The Wayward and the Seeking: A Miscellany of Writings,* Howard University Press, 1978.

Author of plays, including "Portage Potential," 1931, "Eight-Day World," 1932, and an autobiography, "Outline of Autobiography," 1934. Short stories and poetry included in numerous anthologies. Contributor of short stories, poetry, and criticism to periodicals, including *Broom, Crisis, Dial, Liberator, Little Review, Modern Review, Nomad, Prairie,* and *Adelphi.*

SIDELIGHTS: Toomer's major contribution to literature is *Cane,* a novel comprised of poetry and prose which Robert Bone in *The Negro Novel in America* hailed as the product of a "universal vision." Upon the publication of *Cane* in 1923, Toomer was ranked with Ralph Ellison and Richard Wright as a leading figure in the Harlem Renaissance. In his introduction to *Cane,* Waldo Frank wrote that "a poet has arisen among our American youth who has known how to turn the essences and material of his Southland into the essences and materials of literature."

Cane's structure is of three parts. The first third of the book is devoted to the black experience in the Southern farmland. As Bernard W. Bell noted in *Black World,* "Part One, with its focus on the Southern past and the libido, presents the rural thesis." In his book *Black Literature in America,* Houston A. Baker, Jr., called Toomer's style "Southern psychological realism." The characters inhabiting this portion of the book are faced with an inability to succeed. Citing the story "Fern" as an example,

Baker wrote: "The temptations and promises presented by Fern's body are symbolic of the temptations and promises held out by the road of life . . . which stretches before the rural black American, and the frustration experienced by men in their affairs with Fern is symbolic of the frustration of the life journey. Men are willing to give their all, but the result is simply frustration, haunting memory, and hysteria." Toomer infused much of the first part with poetry. "In the sketches, the poet is uppermost," wrote *New Republic* contributor Robert Littell. "Many of them begin with three of four lines of verse, and end with the same lines, slightly changed. The construction here is musical."

The second part of *Cane* is more urban oriented and concerned with Northern life. The writing style throughout is much the same as the initial section with poetry interspersed with stories. Charles W. Scruggs noted in *American Literature* that Toomer revealed the importance of the second section in a letter to the author's brother shortly before the publication of *Cane.* "From three angles, Cane's design is a circle," Scruggs quoted Toomer as writing. "Aesthetically, from simple forms to complex ones, and back to simple forms. Regionally, from the South up into the North, and back into the South again." But Toomer, in the same letter, also cited the completion of the "circle" as the story "Harvest Song," which is contained in the second section. As Scruggs explained, "Toomer is describing *Cane* in organic terms, and therefore it never really ends." Scruggs noticed the acceleration of the narrative as the novel's focus moved from South to North. "The spiritual quest which gains momentum in the agrarian South 'swings upward' in the electric beehive of Washington," he declared. "The 'cane-fluted' world does not die in the North. It continues to haunt the dreams and lives of those who have strayed far from their roots to dwell in the cities."

The concluding third of the novel is a prose piece entitled "Kabnis." Bell called this final part "a synthesis of the earlier sections." The character of Kabnis, Bell claimed, represented "the Black writer whose difficulty in reconciling himself to the dilemma of being an Afro-American prevents him from tapping the creative reservoir of his soul." Littell, as opposed to seeing "Kabnis" as a "synthesis" of the earlier portions, called it a "strange contrast to the lyric expressionism of the shorter pieces." Of the three sections, he wrote, "Kabnis" was by "far the most direct and most living, perhaps because it seems to have grown so much more than been consciously made. There is no pattern in it, and very little effort at poetry."

Many critics have offered interpretations of the title *Cane.* "Toomer uses Cain as a symbol of the African in a hostile land," wrote Scruggs, "tilling the soil of the earth, a slave, without enjoying her fruits. Yet strangely enough, this Cain receives another kind of nourishment from the soil, spiritual nourishment, which the owners of it are denied." Bell owned a slightly different perspective regarding the title. He wrote: "Equally important as a symbol of the rural life is sugar cane itself. Purple in color, pungently sweet in odor, mysteriously musical in sound, and deep-rooted in growth, cane represents the beauty and pain of living close to nature. It also represents the Gothic qualities of the Black American's African and southern past, especially his ambivalent attitude toward this heritage." Baker acknowledged the validity of the *Cane* image in the Northern portion of the novel. He contended that "even when Toomer deals with the life of the urban black American . . . he still presents the rhythms and psychological factors that condition life in the land of sugar cane, a land populated by the 'sons of Cane.'"

Praise for Toomer's writing is extensive. Baker cited his "mysterious brand of Southern psychological realism that has been matched only in the best work of William Faulkner." Kenneth Rexroth, in his book *American Poetry in the Twentieth Century,* was no less impressed. "Toomer is the first poet to unite folk culture and the elite culture of the white avant-garde," he contended, "and he accomplishes this difficult task with considerable success. He is without doubt the most important Black poet." Critics such as Bell and Gorham Munson preferred to dwell on Toomer's use of language. "There can be no question of Jean Toomer's skill as a literary craftsman," asserted Munson. "Toomer has found his own speech, now swift and clipped for violent narrative action, now languorous and dragging for specific characterizing purposes, and now lean and sinuous for the exposition of ideas, but always cadenced to accord with an unusually sensitive ear." Bell attributed *Cane*'s "haunting, illusive beauty" to "Toomer's fascinating way with words." He wrote, "The meaning of the book is implicit in the arabesque pattern of imagery, the subtle movement of symbolic actions and objects, the shifting rhythm of syntax and diction, and the infrastructure of a cosmic consciousness."

After the publication of *Cane,* Toomer continued writing prodigiously. However, most of his work was rejected by publishers. He became increasingly interested in the teachings of George I. Gurdjieff, a Greek spiritual philosopher, and turned to teaching Gurdjieff's beliefs in America. Finally, Toomer embraced the Quaker religion and lived his last decade as a recluse. In an article for *Phylon,* S. P. Fullwinder summed up Toomer's life as "a story of tragedy." He wrote: "As long as he was searching he was a fine creative artist; when the search ended, so did his creative powers. So long as he was searching his work was the cry of one caught in the modern human condition; it expressed modern man's lostness, his isolation. Once Toomer found an identity-giving absolute, his voice ceased to be the cry of modern man and became the voice of the schoolmaster complacently pointing out the way—his way."

BIOGRAPHICAL/CRITICAL SOURCES:

BOOKS

Baker, Houston A., Jr., *Black Literature in America,* McGraw, 1971.
Benson, Bryan Joseph, and Mabel Mayle Dillard, *Jean Toomer,* Twayne, 1980.
Bone, Robert A., *The Negro Novel in America,* Yale University Press, 1965.
Bontemps, Arna, editor, *The Harlem Renaissance Remembered,* Dodd, 1972.
Concise Dictionary of American Literary Biography, Volume 3: *The Twenties,* Gale, 1989.
Contemporary Literary Criticism, Gale, Volume 1, 1973, Volume 4, 1975, Volume 13, 1980, Volume 22, 1982.
Dictionary of Literary Biography, Gale, Volume 45: *American Poets, 1880-1945, First Series,* 1986, Volume 51: *Afro-American Writers From the Harlem Renaissance to 1940,* 1987.
McKay, Nellie Y., *Jean Toomer, Artist,* University of North Carolina Press, 1984.
Rexroth, Kenneth, *American Poetry in the Twentieth Century,* Herder, 1971.
Short Story Criticism, Volume 1, Gale, 1988.
Toomer, Jean, *Cane,* introduction by Waldo Frank, Boni & Liveright, 1923, University Place Press, 1967.
Turner, Darwin T., *In a Minor Chord: Three Afro-American Writers and Their Search for Identity,* Southern Illinois University Press, 1971.

PERIODICALS

American Literature, May, 1972.
Black World, September, 1974.
Crisis, February, 1924.
New Republic, December 26, 1923.
Opportunity, September, 1925.
Phylon, winter, 1966.

*   *   *

TORLEY, Luke
    See BLISH, James (Benjamin)

*   *   *

TORRE, Raoul della
    See MENCKEN, H(enry) L(ouis)

*   *   *

TORRES BODET, Jaime   1902-1974

PERSONAL: Born April 17, 1902, in Mexico City, Mexico; committed suicide by gunshot, May 13, 1974, at his home in Mexico City; son of Alejandro Torres Girbent (a theatrical producer and businessman) and Emilia Bodet de Torres; married Josefina Juarez, March, 1929. *Education:* Studied law at University of Mexico, 1918-1920.

ADDRESSES: Home—Mexico City, Mexico.

CAREER: Diplomat, statesman, writer, orator, and educator. National Preparatory School, Mexico City, Mexico, secretary and teacher of literature, 1921-22; Mexican Ministry of Education, Mexico City, head of libraries department, 1922-24; University of Mexico, Mexico City, professor of French literature, 1924-28; Mexican legation, Madrid, Spain, third secretary, 1929-31; Mexican embassy, Paris, France, second secretary, 1931-32; Mexican embassy, The Hague, Netherlands, acting charge d'affaires, 1932-34; Mexican embassy, Buenos Aires, Argentina, acting charge d'affaires, 1934-35; Mexican embassy, Paris, first secretary, 1935-36; Ministry of Foreign Affairs, Mexico, head of diplomatic department, 1936-37; Mexican embassy, Brussels, Belgium, charge d'affaires, 1937-40; Mexican Under-Secretary for Foreign Affairs, 1940-43; Mexican Minister of Education, 1943-46; Mexican Minister of Foreign Affairs, 1946-48; United Nations Educational, Scientific, and Cultural Organization (UNESCO), Paris, director-general, 1948-52; Mexican ambassador to France, 1954-58; second term as Mexican Minister of Education, 1958-64. Head of Mexican delegation to Ninth International Conference of American States (Bogota), 1948, which drafted the Charter of the Organization of American States; represented Mexico at Conference of Education and Economic and Social Development in Latin America, 1962.

MEMBER: International PEN.

AWARDS, HONORS: Gold medal, Pan American League; gold medal, French Legion of Honor; National Prize for Literature (Mexico), 1966; doctor honoris causa, University of New Mexico and University of Southern California; decorations from Order of the Glittering Stars (China), Order of the Cedar (Lebanon), Order of Polonia Restituta (Poland), Order of the Polar Star (Sweden), Order of Leopold and Order of the Crown (both Belgium), Order of Merit Carlos Manuel de Cespedes (Cuba), Order of Juan Pablo Duarte and Order of Christophe Colomb (both Dominican Republic), Order of Vasco Nunez de Balboa (Panama), Order of Morazan (Honduras), Knight Commander of Order of Quetzal (Guatemala), Order of the Liberator (Venezuela), Order of the Sun (Peru), Great Officer of Order of the Andean Condor (Bolivia), Order of "Al Merito" (Ecuador), Order of Boyaca (Colombia), Order of Merit (Chile), Great Cross of the Order of San Martin the Liberator (Argentina).

WRITINGS:

POEMS

Fervor (title means "Fervor"), introduction by E. Gonzalez Martinez, Ballesca (Mexico), 1918, reprinted, [Mexico], 1968.

Canciones (title means "Songs"), Cultura (Mexico), 1922.

El corazon delirante (title means "The Impassioned Heart"), introduction by Arturo Torres Rioseco, Porrua (Mexico), 1922.

La casa (title means "The House"), Herrero (Mexico), 1923.

Los dias (title means "The Days"), Herrero, 1923.

Nuevas canciones (title means "New Songs"), Calleja (Madrid), 1923.

Poemas (title means "Poems"), Herrero, 1924.

Biombo (title means "Folding Screen"), Herrero, 1925.

Poesias (anthology), Espasa-Calpe (Madrid), 1926.

Destierro (title means "Exile"), Espasa-Calpe (Madrid), 1930.

Cripta (title means "Crypt"), R. Loera y Chavez (Mexico), 1937.

Sonetos (title means "Sonnets"), Grafica Panamericana (Mexico), 1949.

Seleccion de poemas, selected by Xavier Villaurrutia, Nueva Voz (Mexico), 1950.

Fronteras (title means "Frontiers"), Fondo de Cultura Economica (Mexico), 1954.

Poesias escogidas (selections from previous works), Espasa-Calpe (Buenos Aires), 1954.

Sin tregua (title means "No Truce"), Fondo de Cultura Economica, 1957.

Trebol de cuatro hojas (title means "Four-Leaf Clover"), privately printed (Paris), 1958, Universidad Veracruzana, 1960.

Poemes (French translations of Torres Bodet's poems), Gallimard (Paris), 1960.

Selected Poems of Jaime Torres Bodet (text in English and Spanish), edited and translated by Sonja Karsen, Indiana University Press, 1964.

Poesia de Jaime Torres Bodet, Finisterre (Mexico), 1965.

Versos y prosas, introduction by Karsen, Ediciones Iberoamericanas (Madrid), 1966.

Obra poetica (collected poems, 1916-66), introduction by Rafael Solona, two volumes, Porrua, 1967.

Viente poemas, Ediciones Sierra Madre (Monterrey, Mexico), 1971.

FICTION

Margarita de niebla (novel; title means "Margaret's Fog"), Cultura, 1927.

La educacion sentimental (novel; title means "The Sentimental Education"), Espasa-Calpe (Madrid), 1929.

Proserpina rescatada (novel; title means "Proserpina Rescued"), Espasa-Calpe (Madrid), 1931.

Estrella de dia (novel; title means "Movie Star"), Espasa-Calpe (Madrid), 1933.

Primero de enero (novel; title means "First of January"), Ediciones Literatura (Madrid), 1935.

Sombras (novel; title means "Shades"), Cultura, 1937.

Nacimiento de Venus y otros relatos (stories; title means "Birth of Venus and Other Stories"), Nueva Cultura (Mexico), 1941.

CRITICISM

Perspectiva de la literatura mexicana actual 1915-1928 (title means "View of Present-Day Literature 1915-1928"), Contemporaneos, 1928.

Contemporaneos: Notas de critica (essays; title means "Contemporaries: Notes on Literary Criticism"), Herrero, 1928.

Tres inventores de realidad: Stendhal, Dostoyevski, Perez Galdos (essays; title means "Three Inventors of Reality: Stendhal, Dostoyevski, Perez Galdos"), Imprenta Universitaria (Mexico), 1955.

Balzac, Fondo de Cultura Economica, 1959.

Maestros venecianos (essays on painters; title means "Venetian Masters"), Porrua, 1961.

Leon Tolstoi: Su vida y su obra (title means "Leo Tolstoy: His Life and Work"), Porrua, 1965.

Ruben Dario: Abismo y cima (title means "Ruben Dario: Fame and Tragedy"), Universidad Nacional Autonoma de Mexico/Fondo de Cultura Economica, 1966.

Tiempo y memoria en la obra de Proust (title means "Time and Memory in Proust's Work"), Porrua, 1967.

SPEECHES

Educacion mexicana: Discursos, entrevistas, mensajes (main title means "Mexican Education"), Secretaria de Educacion Publica (Mexico), 1944.

La escuela mexicana: Exposicion de la doctrina educativa, Secretaria de Educacion Publica, 1944.

Educacion y concordia internacional: Discursos y mensajes (1941-1947) (main title means "Education and International Concord"), El Colegio de Mexico, 1948.

Teachers Hold the Key to UNESCO's Objectives, Naldrett Press, 1949.

Doce mensajes educativos (title means "12 Educational Messages"), Secretaria de Educacion Publica, 1960.

Doce mensajes civicos (title means "Twelve Civic Messages"), Secretaria de Educacion Publica, 1961.

La voz de Mexico en Bogota y Los Angeles (title means "The Voice of Mexico in Bogota and Los Angeles"), Secretaria de Educacion Publica, 1963.

Patria y cultura, Secretaria de Educacion Publica, 1964.

Discursos (1941-1964), Porrua, 1964.

A number of speeches by Torres Bodet have been published individually.

OTHER

(Translator from the French and author of introductory essay) Andre Gide, *Los limites del arte y algunas reflexiones de moral y de literatura,* Cultura, 1920.

(Editor and author of prologue) Jose Marti, *Nuestra America,* Secretaria de Educacion Publica, 1945.

Tiempo de arena (also see below; autobiography; title means "Time of Sand"), Fondo de Cultura Economica, 1955.

Obras escogidas (selected works; contains poems, essays, speeches, and reprint of *Tiempo de arena*), Fondo de Cultura Economica, 1961.

Liberar el alsa de America con la luz de la educacion, [Mexico], 1962.

(Editor and author of introduction) Ruben Dario, *Antologia de Ruben Dario* (anthology), Universidad Nacional Autonoma de Mexico/Fondo de Cultura Economica, 1967.

Memorias (memoirs), Porrua, Volume 1: *Anos contra el tiempo,* 1969, Volume 2: *La victoria sin alas,* 1970, Volume 3: *El desierto internacional,* 1971, Volume 4: *La tierra prometida,* 1972.

Equinoccio, Porrua, 1974.

Founder of literary reviews, including *La Falange,* with Ortiz de Montellano, 1922, and *Contemporaneos,* 1928.

WORK IN PROGRESS: Another volume of his autobiography, left unfinished at the time of his death.

SIDELIGHTS: "Quintessentially the intellectual-in-politics," according to *Time,* Mexico's Jaime Torres Bodet was both an accomplished statesman and writer. According to Sonja Karsen in her book *Jaime Torres Bodet,* he "achieved the unusual distinction of successfully combining the qualities of the man of action with the sensitivity of the man of letters." During his long career in government, Torres Bodet was famous as an advocate of literacy and education. As Mexico's Minister of Education in the 1940s, he developed a campaign entitled "Each One Teach One," which in two years increased the literate population in Mexico by more than one million people. Later, as director-general of the United Nations Educational, Scientific, and Cultural Organization (UNESCO), he advocated that world peace and liberty hinged upon people being educated, especially upon their being able to read. From his post at UNESCO, he led the development of specialized educational materials for individual countries, until he resigned in 1952 when his budget was cut by over $2.5 million. Torres Bodet also worked many years in the Mexican diplomatic service and in the late 1940s was Mexican Minister of Foreign Affairs. He represented his country at numerous international conferences, and in 1948 led the Mexican delegation which helped formulate the Charter of the Organization of American States.

As a writer, Torres Bodet authored over twenty books of poetry, six novels, a volume of short stories, and numerous critical studies, ranging from studies of Balzac, Tolstoy, and Ruben Dario, to European painting. He was a leading member of the group called "The Contemporaneos," which sparked a revival of Mexican lyric poetry in the 1920s and 1930s. He was also known for his novels and essays; some scholars, such as Antonio Castro Leal, have ranked his prose among the finest of Mexican writers. Karsen states that his novels, like those of other "Contemporaneos" writers who produced fiction, were influenced by innovations of European writers of the period such as Kafka, Joyce, and Proust. Like Proust, Torres Bodet especially held the importance of memory to the writer. According to Karsen, poetry and prose represented to him "different ways of approximation and expression of the same poetic substance, from which he trie[d] to lift the opaque veil which hides the secret of life." The main themes of his poetry, also at work in his fiction, include "the haunting . . . search for his own identity and the attempt to establish an identity with his fellow men, . . . one of utter loneliness, of nothingness, of being and not being, . . . [and] a constant preoccupation with the evanescence of time which finally leads us to the theme of death." In his prose, Torres Bodet was "less interested in the nature of the activities to be observed, than in observing all activities in a special way," creating thereby, according to Karsen, "a sensibility hitherto unknown in Mexical letters."

Torres Bodet's contributions as a writer were officially recognized in 1966 when President Diaz Ordaz bestowed him with the Mexican National Prize for Literature. From 1969 to 1972, Torres Bodet published four volumes of an autobiography, *Memorias,* which recounted his years as a statesman within Mexican and world politics. In 1974, he committed suicide at his home in Mexico City. The *New York Times* reported that Torres Bodet, suffering from prostate cancer, wrote in a final note: "I prefer to call on death myself at the right time."

BIOGRAPHICAL/CRITICAL SOURCES:

BOOKS

Carballo, Emmanuel, *Jaime Torres Bodet,* Empresas Editoriales (Mexico), 1968.
Cowart, Billy F., *La obra educativa de Torres Bodet en lo nacional y lo internacional,* El Colegio de Mexico, 1966.
Forster, Merlin H., *Los Contemporaneos 1920-1932,* Ediciones De Andrea, 1964.
Jaime Torres Bodet en quince semblanzas, Ediciones Oasis (Mexico), 1965.
Jarnes, Benjamin, *Ariel disperso,* Stylo (Mexico), 1946.
Karsen, Sonja, *A Poet in a Changing World,* Skidmore College, 1963.
Karsen, Sonja, *Jaime Torres Bodet,* Twayne, 1971.
Kneller, George F., *The Education of the Mexican Nation,* Columbia University Press, 1951.
Laves, Walter L. C., and Charles A. Thomson, *UNESCO: Purpose, Progress, Prospects,* Indiana University Press, 1957.

PERIODICALS

Americas, March, 1949, August, 1969.
Antioch Review, winter, 1968-69.
Books Abroad, spring, 1967, autumn, 1970.
Christian Science Monitor, September 14, 1946.
Nature, December 4, 1948.

OBITUARIES:

PERIODICALS

New York Times, May 14, 1974.
Time, May 27, 1974.

*   *   *

TORSVAN, Ben Traven
  See TRAVEN, B.

*   *   *

TORSVAN, Benno Traven
  See TRAVEN, B.

*   *   *

TORSVAN, Berick Traven
  See TRAVEN, B.

*   *   *

TORSVAN, Berwick Traven
  See TRAVEN, B.

*   *   *

TORSVAN, Bruno Traven
  See TRAVEN, B.

*   *   *

TORSVAN, Traven
  See TRAVEN, B.

TOURNIER, Michel (Edouard) 1924-

PERSONAL: Born December 19, 1924, in Paris, France; son of Alphonse and Marie-Madeleine (Fournier) Tournier. *Education:* Attended University of Paris and University of Tuebingen.

ADDRESSES: Home—Le Presbytere, Choisel, 78460 Chevreuse, France. *Office*—Editions Plon, 8 rue Garanciere, Paris 6, France.

CAREER: Producer and director, R.T.F., 1949-54; newspaper work, 1955-58; Editions Plon, Paris, France, director of literary services, 1958-68; writer.

MEMBER: Academie Goncourt.

AWARDS, HONORS: Grand Prix du Roman from Academie Francaise, 1967, for *Vendredi; ou, Les Limbes du Pacifique;* Prix Goncourt, 1970, for *Le Roi des aulnes;* Officier de la Legion d'Honneur.

WRITINGS:

Vendredi; ou, Les Limbes du Pacifique (novel), Gallimard, 1967, revised edition, 1978, translation by Norman Denny published as *Friday,* Doubleday, 1969 (published in England as *Friday; or, The Other Island,* Collins, 1969), juvenile edition published as *Vendredi; ou, La Vie sauvage,* Flammarion, 1971, translation by Ralph Manheim published as *Friday and Robinson: Life on Esperanza Island,* Knopf, 1972.

Le Roi des aulnes (novel), Gallimard, 1970, translation by Barbara Bray published as *The Ogre,* Doubleday, 1972 (published in England as *The Erl King,* Collins, 1972).

Les Meteores (novel), Gallimard, 1975, translation by Anne Carter published as *Gemini,* Doubleday, 1981.

Le Vent paraclet (essays), Gallimard, 1977.

Canada: Journal de voyage (nonfiction), La Press, 1977.

Le Coq de bruyere (short stories), Gallimard, 1978, translation by Barbara Wright published as *The Fetishist,* Doubleday, 1984.

Des clefs et des serrures (essays), Editions du Chene, 1979.

Gaspard, Melchior et Balthazar (novel), Gallimard, 1980, translation by Manheim published as *The Four Wise Men,* Doubleday, 1982.

Vus de dos, Gallimard, 1981.

Le Vol du Vampire, Mercure de France, 1981.

Gilles et Jeanne (novel), Gallimard, 1983, translation by Alan Sheridan published as *Gilles and Jeanne,* Methuen, 1987.

(With Konrad R. Mueller) *Francois Mitterand,* Flammarion, 1984.

(With Jean-Max Toubeau) *Le Vagabond immobile,* Gallimard, 1984.

(Author of introduction) Marianne Fulton, *Lucien Clergue,* New York Graphic Society/Little, Brown, 1985.

A Garden at Hammamet, translation by Wright of *Un Jardin a Hammamet,* Lord John, 1985.

La Goutte d'or, Gallimard, 1986, translation by Wright published as *The Golden Droplet,* Doubleday, 1987.

The Wind Spirit: An Autobiography, translation by Arthur Goldhammer, Beacon Press, 1988.

Le Medianoche Amoureux, Gallimard, 1989.

Le Tabor et le Sinai, Belfond, 1989.

SIDELIGHTS: Winner of two prestigious French literary prizes, Michel Tournier, as a *Times Literary Supplement* critic once observed, "writes slowly but successfully." After completing three novels he declined to submit to publishers because he judged them unworthy of publication, Tournier wrote two more novels, *Friday* and *The Ogre,* which quickly established him as one of the most remarkable writers to appear on the postwar French literary scene. The products of a highly imaginative mind, his novels—consisting primarily of philosophical speculation—are not for the casual reader. Like the works of Thomas Pynchon, John Barth, and Vladimir Nabokov, Tournier's tales are densely packed with a complex network of symbols and allusions. They have been criticized for their pretentiousness and, on occasion, for their somewhat disturbing and even frightening themes. Narrators of his tales include a pederast and a fetishist who is obsessed with lingerie. "Tournier's stories," says Richard Eder in the *Los Angeles Times Book Review,* "are . . . aimed at turning some aspect of the received world inside out." The controversial nature of his subjects has brought him much critical attention. Furthermore, says *Times Literary Supplement* reviewer John Sturrock, Tournier "has no rival among French novelists of his generation for writing books that are at once vivid and intellectually provocative."

Friday, described by the *New Statesman*'s Gillian Tindall as "an idiosyncratic Frenchman's reconstruction of our petrified classic [*Robinson Crusoe*], with 20th century insights," was the first of Tournier's novels to appear in print. Beginning with the traditional Robinson Crusoe formula (which views man as a rational, tool-using creature who seeks to control his world through the imposition of physical and social order), Tournier deviates from the Daniel Defoe version somewhat to stress the existence of other alternatives—mainly non-rational and non-technical ones—that man has at his disposal to deal with the environment. While both Defoe and Tournier's castaways at first strive to "civilize" life on their little island, Tournier, unlike Defoe, has his Crusoe gradually become less and less interested in imposing his will on nature as he grows mystically closer to his surroundings. By the time his would-be savior Friday arrives, Crusoe is ready to go completely "native"; with Friday as his teacher, he learns to abandon the old European conventions as he sheds his clothes, worships the sun, and eats, sleeps, and works only when he feels like it. In a particularly ironic twist, Tournier has Friday, not Crusoe, join the crew of a rescue ship upon its departure for Europe; Crusoe chooses instead to remain on the island. Thus, as opposed to the rationalism espoused by the eighteenth-century Defoe, Tournier, using the same basic material, suggests another, more "modern" approach to determining one's place in the natural world—an approach that is more sensual and spontaneous.

At first glance, the *New Yorker* critic found all of this philosophizing to be "not a particularly attractive prospect" for a novel. Yet, he concludes, "Tournier is a cultivated and disciplined writer, and his Robinson . . . is most likable." The *New Statesman*'s Tindall also admits that the story of Crusoe "as a microcosm of Man everywhere is not a symbolism with immediate appeal to me," yet, she insists, "do try the book. There is much more in it. . . . A French critic apparently described the work as 'Crusoe seen through the eyes of Freud, Jung and Claude Levi-Strauss'; while this encapsulation sounds glib, it does sum up usefully the author's overall approach."

T. J. Fleming of the *New York Times Book Review* reports that there is "a remarkable heady French wine in the old English bottle. . . . [Tournier] has attempted nothing less than an exploration of the soul of modern man [in *Friday*]. . . . Again and again, he finds fresh and original ways of viewing primary experiences such as time and work and religious faith, the relationship of men to animals and trees and their own shadowy selves, to civilization and the essential earth. The telling is intensely French. The focus is on thinking, and thinking about feeling. . . . [*Friday*] works, because the framework of the classic makes this abracadabra of believability convincing."

With the publication of his second novel, a fable-like tale called *The Ogre,* Tournier received world-wide attention. Based in part on Goethe's poem "The Erl King" and often compared to Guenter Grass's *The Tin Drum, The Ogre* is set in Germany between 1938 and 1945, where an imprisoned giant of a Frenchman, Abel Tiffauges, serves his Nazi captors as a procurer of young boys for an elite Hitler youth camp. Haunted by the symbolic nature of his own actions and of the destructive actions of mankind in general, the brooding Tiffauges views his role in life as that of a "beast of burden," a man who will save himself by saving others. Readers, however, find his role difficult to determine, for while Tiffauges seems to be a somewhat shadowy symbol of resistance (he dies after marching into a bog while carrying a Jewish child he rescued from a concentration camp), he can also—as the author suggests when someone attempts to assassinate him on July 20, 1944—be regarded as an embodiment of Hitler as well. As the *Times Literary Supplement* reviewer explains: "The book as a whole is a journey from a contrived surrealism to, as it were, the real thing. The novel is so charged with symbols that it is hard to tell whether it is intended to have one meaning or many, or just how menacing an ogre Tiffauges is. . . . He is no simple monster."

Other critics, too, have been baffled by the multiplicity of ideas and interpretations present in the story, yet they still regard it as a worthwhile literary experience. *Newsweek*'s Peter Prescott calls it a "fine novel" that is "more likely to be praised than read. A good demanding fable, a meditative story of unaccustomed viscosity that rewards a second reading, it also seems curiously old-fashioned. . . . *The Ogre* is built in the way Bach built his fugues; themes and statements are introduced, inverted, tangled and marched past each other, all to be resolved in loud, majestic chords. . . . And yet the symbols and correspondences of this story, which are far more complex than I have been able to indicate, would be insufficient to sustain it as fiction. Tournier's achievement rests in his remarkable blend of myth with realism. . . . He offers a succession of scenes . . . which, as Abel says, not only decipher the essence of existence, but exalt it."

On the other hand, the *New York Review of Books*'s Karl Miller writes: "*The Ogre* is a very clever book in its belletristic way. . . . It may not be a likely story, but it is an absorbing one. Tiffauges' obsessions . . . are conveyed in an alliterative rhetoric of rare words and allusions. . . . There is clearly some renewal here of the profundities and affirmations of [*Friday*], and I imagine that it wouldn't be easy to say why one should be dazzled by the first book and repelled by its successor." Miller claims that his main objection to *The Ogre* lies in "the weakness of the distinction it draws between the malignity of the Nazis and the comparative benignity of this creature who achieves an apotheosis in the Nazi heartland. And its picture of the malignity of the Nazis is very dubious anyway. . . . Tournier documents [their] behavior . . . with reference to the evidence obtained for the Nuremburg Trials. . . . But it would appear that he has misrepresented that history while using it as a setting for an account of a fairly exotic psychological state." Miller concludes, *The Ogre* "is all too mysterious and magical for me. . . . Tournier's imaginings come no closer to the condition of life in Nazi Germany than his Academician's prose does to the delusions of a supposedly ignorant obsessional."

"Like a good Hegelian, Tournier presents his thesis and antithesis," admits R. Z. Sheppard of *Time.* "But he is also a good Jungian. Signs, symbols and archetypes are pried from every inci-

dent and lofted chaotically into the mythological vacuum of the modern world. The presumption is that these fragments are awaiting a supersign that will unify them into some sort of new mythic order. When this in fact occurs in Tournier' book, the effect is one not of artistic revelation but of melodramatic kitsch." Commenting on his technique, Tournier told *Publisher's Weekly* interviewer Herbert R. Lottman, "A fable has its moral spelled out in black and white; the short story a la Maupassant or Chekhov contains a message that there isn't any message—the world is meaningless. I prefer *tales,* which include elements both of fable and of short story—say, the Bible stories, the Hassidic legends, Grimm, Perrault, Kipling. But in a tale the precise meaning is hidden; it's like dipping into muddy water looking for fish. The reader has to do half the work."

Marian Engel's reaction to *The Ogre* is more appreciative of the novel's complexity. As she notes in her *New York Times Book Review* article: "There are passages of great descriptive beauty [in *The Ogre*], and Tournier does not artistically shy away from them. . . . [His book] can be taken as an explication of the German role in World War II and as a hundred other things as well. The book's French title was that of Goethe's poem 'The Erl King'—and, though I have also tied it to the Childe Harold legend, it is capable of other interpretations. In its richness and strangeness it encompasses also that other French anarchic misfit, Big Meaulnes, incorporating his loneliness in the Wagnerian web of *Goetterdaemmerung.* As you read the book, you, too, are drawn into that web, an experience that is dangerous and purging. . . . Abel Tiffauges is as complex and dangerous in English as in French; his themes are eternal and disturbing. To follow his dark path is a magnificent experience."

Tournier believes that any writer is necessarily at odds with convention. He told Lottman: "[A writer is] . . . always the enemy of power. When I received the Legion of Honor decoration, I was accused of having sold out to government. I reminded my critics of what Erik Satie said about Maurice Ravel when Ravel refused the Legion of Honor: 'He rejects the Legion of Honor, but all his work accepts it.' I can say that I accepted the medal although all my work refuses it. I'll continue to write books that could send me to prison." Theodore Zeldin comments in an *Observer* review that the resulting novels "are like fireworks, packed with amazingly intelligent observations on every kind of subject, dazzling in their gyrations, even when the explosion is frightening. He is particularly ingenious at discovering the unexpected in what seems banal."

As he reveals in the essay collection *Le Vent paraclet,* Tournier makes a conscious effort to include "eternal and disturbing" elements in novels that are otherwise conventional (as opposed to experimental) in form. In the novel *The Four Wise Men,* for example, a fourth seeker of the Christ Child misses the Nativity, spends the next thirty-three years in prison, misses the crucifixion, eats the leftovers from the last supper, and is welcomed into heaven. And *Gemini* explores the experiences of identical twins, including questions of identity and homosexual incest.

According to a *Times Literary Supplement* reviewer, Tournier confesses to adhering to an orthodox structure "partly as bait, in order to get people to read what they might otherwise refuse. Deception is needed because he is a metaphysical novelist, more likely to find charm and inspiration in Leibniz or Spinoza than in the work of other novelists. . . . He adapts the supposedly safe conventions of realism to fantastic, transcendent ends." This strategy makes Tournier's novels more accessible than the works of other fabulists. Roger Shattuck explains in the *New York Review of Books,* "Insofar as they adapt existing legends and celebrate earlier forms of wisdom, his works leave behind the preoccupation with originality that has propelled the arts for the last two centuries. . . . By sparing himself the need to innovate in form, he has been able to direct his inventive powers simultaneously toward elaborating a story line and toward marshalling a powerful style."

Though a *French Review* critic has said that Tournier's novels are too playful to be "taken very seriously," a *World Literature Today* reviewer insists that they are worthy of serious attention. "Tournier's tales in their symbolic significance are more convincing than realistic fiction," she declares. "They represent a poetic rendering of his relationship to the world. Concretizing arcane reality through delusion or enchantment, Tournier is a magician who gives us the reassurance that there is a secret garden next to our backyard, that there is another world behind the mirror and that there is a small island in the Pacific Ocean where we lived happily once upon a time." Tournier's skill at combining elements of fiction and philosophy with the unorthodox and unexpected has led critics to recognize him as France's most exciting novelist, a writer on par with winners of the Nobel Prize.

MEDIA ADAPTATIONS: A dramatisation of *The Fetishist* was presented Off Broadway at the Perry Theatre in 1984.

BIOGRAPHICAL/CRITICAL SOURCES:

BOOKS

Contemporary Literary Criticism, Gale, Volume 6, 1976, Volume 23, 1983, Volume 36, 1986.
Dictionary of Literary Biography, Volume 83: *French Novelists since 1960,* Gale, 1989.

PERIODICALS

Antioch Review, June, 1973.
Books and Bookmen, January, 1973.
Chicago Tribune Book World, September 6, 1981, October 25, 1987.
French Review, May, 1978, April, 1979.
Journal of Popular Culture, summer, 1974.
Los Angeles Times Book Review, September 16, 1984, May 19, 1985, December 27, 1987.
New Republic, February 21, 1985.
New Statesman, February 7, 1969.
Newsweek, October 4, 1972.
New Yorker, June 14, 1969.
New York Review of Books, November 30, 1972, December 14, 1972, April 28, 1983.
New York Times Book Review, April 13, 1969, October 3, 1972, October 4, 1981, October 24, 1982, September 9, 1984, November 1, 1987.
Observer, January 30, 1983.
Publishers Weekly, September 14, 1984 (interview).
Time, August 21, 1972, November 18, 1982.
Times Literary Supplement, October 23, 1970, October 7, 1977, October 13, 1978, February 13, 1981, October 16, 1981, November 5, 1987, August 11, 1989.
Washington Post Book World, November 21, 1982, October 28, 1984, December 27, 1987, December 11, 1988.
World Literature Today, spring, 1979.

*   *   *

TOURNIMPARTE, Alessandra
  See GINZBURG, Natalia

TOWNSEND, Sue 1946-

PERSONAL: Born April 2, 1946, in Leicester, Leicestershire, England. *Education:* Attended English secondary school. *Politics:* Socialist. *Religion:* Atheist.

ADDRESSES: Home—Leicester, Leicestershire, England. *Agent*—Giles Gordon, 43 Doughty Street, London, England.

CAREER: Worked in various capacities, including garage attendant, hot dog saleswoman, dress shop worker, factory worker, and trained community worker; full-time writer, 1982—.

AWARDS, HONORS: Thames Television Bursary, 1979, for "Womberang."

WRITINGS:

"Womberang" (one-act play), first produced in Leicester, England, at the Leicester Haymarket Theatre, 1979; produced on the West End at the Soho Poly (also see below).
"Bazaar and Rummage" (teleplay), British Broadcasting Corporation, 1983 (also see below).
"Groping for Words" (two-act play), first produced in London at the Croydon Warehouse, 1983 (also see below).
"The Great Celestial Cow," first produced In Leicester, at the Leicester Haymarket Theatre, October, 1984; produced on the West End at the Royal Court Theatre.
"Secret Diary of A. Mole" (radio series), British Broadcasting Corporation Radio 4, first broadcast in January, 1982 (also see below).
The Secret Diary of Adrian Mole, Aged 13 3/4, Methuen, 1982 (also see below).
Bazaar and Rummage, Groping for Words [and] *Womberang* (play collection), Methuen, 1984 (also see above).
The Growing Pains of Adrian Mole, Methuen, 1984.
The Secret Diary of Adrian Mole, Aged 13 3/4 (two-act play; first produced in Leicester at the Phoenix Theatre, September, 1984; produced on the West End at Wyndham's Theatre, December 12, 1984), with songs by Ken Howard and Alan Blaikley, Methuen, 1985 (also see above).
"Secret Diary of A. Mole" (television series), Thames TV, first broadcast September, 1986 (also see above).
The Adrian Mole Diaries (contains *The Secret Diary of Adrian Mole, Aged 13 3/4* and *The Growing Pains of Adrian Mole*), Methuen, 1985, Grove Press, 1986 (also see above).
Rebuilding Coventry: A Tale of Two Cities (novel), Methuen, 1988.
"Ear, Nose and Throat" (play), first produced in Cambridge, England, 1989.

Contributor to periodicals, including the London *Times, New Statesman, Airport, Guardian, Observer,* and *Marxism Today.*

SIDELIGHTS: Though British author Sue Townsend has had many of her plays produced on London's West End, she is best known as the creator of Adrian Mole, a character whose teen-aged musings have been the subject of two books, radio and stage plays, a television series, and a column in *Woman's Realm* magazine. The books, *The Secret Diaries of Adrian Mole, Aged 13 3/4* and *The Growing Pains of Adrian Mole,* have been a huge success in England, together selling more than five million copies. Most critics account for the popularity of Townsend's character with the theory that Adrian Mole has struck a national and generational chord; Richard Eder of the *Los Angeles Times* quoted the *Listener* as predicting, "When the social history of the 1980s comes to be written, the Mole books . . . will probably be considered as key texts."

In *The Secret Diaries of Adrian Mole,* Townsend's protagonist is a boy approaching fourteen years old and beginning a diary in the English Midlands. Adrian records his trials, which include his parents' extramarital affairs, the acne on his chin, the octogenarian he is assigned to visit as a member of the Good Samaritans organization, suffocating school rules, and his relationship with his girlfriend, Pandora, who belongs to a higher social class. Added to these problems of an ordinary adolescent is the fact that Adrian is attempting to become an intellectual. In one of his diary entries, Adrian writes: "I am very unhappy and have once again turned to great literature for solace. It's no surprise to me that intellectuals commit suicide, go mad or die from drink. We feel things more than other people. We know that the world is rotten and that chins are ruined by spots. I am reading 'Progress, Coexistence and Intellectual Freedom' by [Soviet dissident] Andrei D. Sakharov." Though Adrian records that "It is an 'inestimably important document' according to the cover," his next entry reveals that " 'Progress, Coexistence and Intellectual Freedom' is inestimably boring, according to me, Adrian Mole." His pursuit of intellectualism also includes sending poetry to the British Broadcasting Corporation (BBC) in hopes that it might be read on the air, but his literary efforts are kindly rejected in personal letters from BBC producer John Tydeman.

If intellectual, Adrian is also somewhat naive. He doesn't understand why his mother's lover asks for a blood test when his mother has a baby, nor why his father becomes alarmed when his former illicit lover—whom Adrian labels "Stick Insect"—arrives on their doorstep looking as though she has gained weight. Upon bursting into his parents' bedroom after their reconciliation, Adrian concludes: "I think the central heating must need turning down because my parents were both very red in the face."

The second book, *The Growing Pains of Adrian Mole,* follows its hero past his sixteenth birthday. In it Adrian recounts his attempts at rebellion, which include joining a gang of punks and running away from home. Spending his birthday at the Sheffield rail station, he reflects on turning sixteen—he now has the legal right in England to have sex, purchase cigarettes, operate a moped, and live on his own. "Strangely," he confesses, "I don't want to do any of them." Adrian's relationships with his parents and Pandora continue to be problematic, and his adventures in this volume also include a blind date, looking for *Guardian* editorials in the dog's basket, and a family vacation in Skegness. By the end of the book Adrian, realizing that he has been blind to many of his parents' foibles, has lost his naivete. Noting that his diary entries for the period of his parents' respective infidelities are filled only with his "childish fourteen-year-old thoughts and preoccupations," Adrian wonders if the wife of Victorian-era British murderer Jack the Ripper had similarly obtuse diary observations, such as: "10:30 pm Jack late home. Perhaps he is kept late at the office," and "12:10 am Jack home covered in blood; an offal cart knocked him down."

Many reviewers have cited the universal appeal of Adrian's adolescent struggles. Jessica Saraga in the *Times Educational Supplement* invited Townsend's character to "join the roll-call of the world's great teenagers," including the literary creations "Huck Finn and Tom Sawyer, Romeo and Juliet, [and] Holden Caulfield." Also comparing Adrian Mole to author J. D. Salinger's mutinous character Holden Caulfield, Thomas M. Disch noted in the *Washington Post* that Adrian was the more realistic creation. "Like Adrian," he explained, "we might have had to restrain our rebellion against school authorities, not having Holden's golden parachute, but even as we did our homework we seethed inside, and we knew ourselves to be, intellectually, the

equals of anyone." Disch concluded that the combined *Adrian Mole Diaries* would meet with as much success in the United States as they have in England. Other critics disagreed, though, complaining that despite a glossary of British terms the books were too grounded in British society to appeal to Americans. Eder remarked that "the comedy in 'Adrian Mole' has become waterlogged somewhere in mid-Atlantic."

If the distinctly British flavor of Townsend's Mole books lessens their universality, however, it helps provide an interesting reflection of what Eder termed "Margaret Thatcher's Britain." Adrian fails a geography test when he states that the Falkland Islands are a part of Argentina, and he accounts for the elimination of hot school lunches by musing, "Perhaps Mrs Thatcher wants us to be too weak to demonstrate in the years to come."

Townsend also wrote the successful television and stage versions of Adrian's first diary. Three of her other plays have been collected in one volume that contains *Bazaar and Rummage,* about agoraphobics, *Groping for Words,* concerning adult literacy, and *Womberang,* which centers on a gynecological clinic. According to Diana Devlin, critiquing the collection in *Drama,* Townsend's "characters are affectionately drawn" and "her situations capture the bizarre aspects of what passes for 'normal' life." Devlin also lauded the works' movements "towards the triumph of a kind of collective life force."

AVOCATIONAL INTERESTS: "Reading, Canadian canoeing, gardening, traveling on trains, listening to the radio, buying shoes, domestic architecture, drinking, listening to opera, but not attending the opera."

BIOGRAPHICAL/CRITICAL SOURCES:

BOOKS

Townsend, Sue, *The Secret Diaries of Adrian Mole, Aged 13 3/4,* Methuen, 1982.
Townsend, Sue, *The Growing Pains of Adrian Mole,* Methuen, 1984.

PERIODICALS

Drama, winter, 1984.
Los Angeles Times, May 28, 1986.
New Statesman, November 26, 1982, August 24, 1984.
New York Times Book Review, April 22, 1990.
Publishers Weekly, August 23, 1985, March 21, 1986.
Times (London), November 28, 1984, September 30, 1988, November 16, 1988.
Times Educational Supplement, December 23, 1983.
Times Literary Supplement, November 30, 1984.
Washington Post, May 24, 1986, May 3, 1990.

*   *   *

TRAVEN, B. ?-1969
(Ret Marut)

PERSONAL: "B. Traven" is a pseudonym for a writer whose identity has only been conjectured. Alternatively identified as Hermann Albert Otto Maximilian Feige, born February 28, 1882, in Swiebodzin, Poland, son of a brickworker, adopting names Ret Marut in 1907 and Traven Torsvan in 1926; or as born May 3, 1882, in Germany, perhaps the son of Burton and Dorothy (Ottarent) Marut; or as Traven Torsvan, born March 5, 1890, in Chicago, Ill., perhaps the son of Burton and Dorothy Torsvan; also identified with names Hal Croves and Ben, Benno, Berick, Berwick, and Bruno Traven Torsvan. Married Rosa

Elena Lujan, May 16, 1957; died March 26, 1969, in Mexico City, Mexico. *Politics:* Left wing.

CAREER: Writer. One version lists career as going to sea as cabinboy, around 1900 or 1912; later became a seaman; spent some time in London and Berlin, before settling in Mexico, about 1920-22. Also identified as being an apprentice locksmith for four years; worked as actor under name Ret Marut in Germany, 1907-15; became political activist and published journal *Der Ziegelbrenner,* 1917-22; worked as press minister in brief leftist government in Munich, 1919; arrested and jailed, escaping to England, 1923; jailed as illegal alien, 1923-24; moved to Mexico, assuming name Traven Torsvan; government photographer on expedition to Chiapas, Mexico, 1926.

WRITINGS:

FICTION

Das Totenschiff: Die Geschichte eines amerikanischen Seemans, Buechergilde Gutenberg (Berlin), 1926, 2nd edition, W. Krueger (Hamburg), 1951, U.S. edition, prepared by author, published as *The Death Ship: The Story of an American Sailor,* Knopf, 1934, translation from the German by Eric Sutton published under same title, Chatto & Windus, 1934.

Der Wobbly, Buchmeister Verlag (Berlin), 1926, published as *Die Baumwollpfluecker,* 1929, translation by Eleanor Brockett published as *The Cotton-Pickers,* R. Hale, 1956, U.S. edition, prepared by author, published under same title, Hill & Wang, 1969.

Der Schatz der Sierra Madre, Buechergilde Gutenberg, 1927, U.S. edition, prepared by author, published as *The Treasure of Sierra Madre,* Knopf, 1935, translation by Basil Creighton published under same title, Chatto & Windus, 1935.

Land des Fruehlings, Buechergilde Gutenberg, 1928.

Die Bruecke im Dschungel, Buechergilde Gutenberg, 1929, English language edition, prepared by author, published as *The Bridge in the Jungle,* Knopf, 1938.

Die weisse Rose, Buechergilde Gutenberg, 1929, H. Fel Kraus, 1946, English language edition, prepared by author, published as *The White Rose,* R. Hale, 1965.

Der Busch (short stories), Buechergilde Gutenberg, 1930.

Der Karren, Buechergilde Gutenberg, 1931, translation by Basil Creighton published as *The Carreta,* Chatto & Windus, 1935, U.S. edition, prepared by author, published under same title, Hill & Wang, 1970.

Regierung, Buechergilde Gutenberg, 1931, translation by Creighton published as *Government,* Chatto & Windus, Hill & Wang, 1971.

Der Marsch ins Reich der Caoba: Ein Kriegsmarsch, Buechergilde Gutenberg, 1933, translation published as *March to Caobaland,* R. Hale, 1960, published as *March to the Monteria,* 1963.

Die Troza, Buechergilde Gutenberg, 1936.

Die Rebellion der Gehenkten, Buechergilde Gutenberg, 1936, translation from the German by Charles Duff published as *The Rebellion of the Hanged,* R. Hale, 1952, translation from the Spanish edition published under same title, Knopf, 1952.

Djungelgeneralen, translated from the German manuscript by Arne Holmstrom, Axel Holmstrom (Stockholm), 1939, published in original German as *Ein General kommt aus dem Dschungel,* 1940, translation by Desmond Vesey published as *General from the Jungle,* R. Hale, 1954, Hill & Wang, 1972.

Macario, Buechergilde Gutenberg, 1950, translation by wife, Rosa Elena Lujan, published under same title, Houghton, 1971.

Aslan Norval, Desch (Munich), 1960.

Stories by the Man Nobody Knows: Nine Tales, Regency Books, 1961.

Khundar: Das erste Buch Begegnungen, Clou Verlag (Egnach, Switzerland), 1963.

The Night Visitor and Other Stories, Hill & Wang, 1966.

Erzaehlungen, Limmat-Verlag, 1968.

The Kidnapped Saint and Other Stories, Lawrence Hill, 1975.

(Under pseudonym Ret Marut) *To the Honorable Miss S., and Other Stories,* translated by Peter Silcock, Chicago Review Press, 1981.

OTHER

O Cloveku Ktery Stvoril Slunce (South American Indian legends), translated from the English manuscript by Vincenc Svoboda, F. J. Mueller (Prague), 1934, English language edition published as *The Creation of the Sun and the Moon,* Hill & Wang, 1968.

Der Banditendoktor: Mexikanische Erzaehlungen, Limmat-Verlag (Zurich), 1957.

(Editor) Fritz Thurn, *Die Weisheiten der Aspasia,* Inter-Verlag (Luxembourg), 1966.

Also author, under pseudonym Ret Marut, of *Das Fruewerk,* 1977. Work included in *Vagabunden: Three Modern German Stories,* edited by Wolfgang Paulsen, Holt, 1950.

SIDELIGHTS: B. Traven's work has been published in 36 languages and over 500 editions since April, 1926. He is "probably the most mysterious and baffling of all modern writers," E. R. Hagemann once commented, "a man who has seemingly courted obscurity as another might court fame and notoriety, courted oblivion with an almost pathological intensity. Occasionally, this mysteriousness has been lessened by a letter or communication from him (irritating in its vagueness), or by an article either by one who puts forth claims of personal acquaintanceship or second-hand familiarity, or by one who seems deliberately to confuse the picture even more with wild and totally imaginative writing. The result, for one interested in Traven as a man and as a writer, is more than another 'quest for Corvo.' At best," the critic continued, "one can only patch together a chaotic *melange* of what appear to be facts, guesses, legends, myths, and downright unadorned lies; and after completing his patchwork, can but suggest that his *may* be Traven's biography, but nothing more."

At different times, Traven has been identified as various individuals: Jack London, who, some believe, only pretended to die; ex-President Lopez Mateos of Mexico (who was only five years old when Traven's first book was published, although his sister, Esperanza Lopez Mateos, assisted the writer in translations); writer Ambrose Bierce, who disappeared in Mexico and was presumed dead; Ret Marut, a Bavarian socialist; a black man fleeing from American injustice; an expatriate of the old Industrial Workers of the World (a Wobbly); a leper; a fugitive Austrian archduke; an American capitalist who wrote proletarian novels to salve his conscience; the illegitimate son of Kaiser Wilhelm II of Germany; and even as the collaboration of two men. At one time the *Times Literary Supplement* added facetiously that "two highly promising lines of speculation that have so far not been explored are that Traven is T. E. Lawrence and that Traven is the Empress Anastasia."

When *The Death Ship* went to press, Traven's German publishers wrote the author in Mexico asking him for photographs and biographical material. Traven replied: "My personal history would not be disappointing to readers, but it is my own affair which I want to keep to myself. . . . I am in fact in no way more important than is the typesetter for my books, the man who works the mill; . . . no more important than the man who binds my books and the woman who wraps them and the scrubwoman who cleans up the office." Another reason for his reluctance to identify himself might have been attributed to his opinion of American publicity methods which, he claimed, reduced "authors to the status of tight rope walkers, sword swallowers, and trained animals." "Such resolute shunning of the limelight," the *Times Literary Supplement* continued, "has, of course, made the limelight search for him all the more avidly. And in the forty years since the publication of *The Death Ship,* Traven has had a steady following of detective readers. *Life* magazine even offered a large prize to anyone who could identify him."

Although Traven was thought to be a German, he always claimed to be a native-born American. He insisted that he always wrote in English and that he tried to interest an American publisher in *The Death Ship* before a German-Swiss translator encouraged a German firm to publish it. "This being the case," wrote William Weber Johnson, "it is strange that British editions of his books appeared as translations from German by different translators—Eric Sutton, Basil Creighton, Charles Duff, Eleanor Brockett. Why it was necessary to translate from the German when the originals, according to Traven, were written in English, has never been explained—though it led to one of the more fanciful theories about Traven: that he is really Jack London, . . . the linguistic migration from English to German and back to English again occurring in order to disguise his readily identifiable style."

The critic further explained that "Traven's writing did not appear in the United States until the early 1930's, when Alfred A. Knopf, hearing in Europe of Traven's popularity, began publishing some of the mysterious author's novels. The Knopf texts differed from the British translations and may have been taken from Traven's original manuscripts. In *The Night Visitor and Other Stories* . . . it is curious to find that one of the stories appears to be taken from the British translation of a German translation. . . . There are enough Traven textual mysteries to occupy a generation of Ph.D. candidates." Harlan Ellison once said, while speaking of *Stories by the Man Nobody Knows:* "I let Scott Meredith, Traven's agent in New York, know that I wanted to publish some new material in the collection as well as those they had recently gotten published in magazines. These three stories came then, and they simply amazed me. They were so crudely written. I had heard that Traven took editing, but nothing that Knopf got from him could have looked like these. I had to do everything to them, short of rewriting them myself." Ellison suspected that someone else was writing from Traven's notes.

Warner Brothers purchased the rights to *The Treasure of Sierra Madre* for $5,000 and, in 1947, John Huston, scenarist and director, began filming. By correspondence, Traven expressed admiration for Huston's script and thus was invited to serve as consultant on the film. In Mexico City, Huston was confronted by a man who claimed to be Traven's representative and whose card read "Hal Croves, Translator, Acapulco." It was suspected that Croves was Traven and upon completion of the film, Huston wrote an article to this effect. Following this lead and knowing that Croves traveled on an American passport, a Mexican novelist, Luis Spota, checked Mexican immigration records and found

that a Mexican "Form-14" passport gave his full name as Traven Torsvan, born in Chicago on March 5, 1890. His parents were listed as Burton and Dorothy Torsvan and described as Norwegian-Swedish immigrants. Spota found that he also used the name Berick Traven Torsvan at times. Traven had denied that his name was B. Traven (or Ben or Benno or Bruno).

Years ago, William Weber Johnson received an unsigned letter that he assumed was written by Traven or Esperanza Lopez Mateos. "On reading Traven, it read, one will find it some times not very easy. His style, his way to express himself, is now and then clumsy, cumbersome, twisted, mangled, and his English will frequently shock men and women of culture, although the ideas he wished to drive home are always clear. . . . Yet one must not forget that he has been a sailor for many years, that he has had to earn his own living and stand on his own two feet since he was seven. . . . Until he was thirty-five [he] had no more than twenty-six days of education in grammar school. He came to Mexico for the first time when he was twelve, then being cabin boy on a Dutch freighter. He jumped ship on the West Coast of Mexico, stayed for a good time in Mexico, working as an electrician's assistant before returning to his home country. Since then, with occasional interruptions to sail ships again, he has lived in Latin America the greater half of his life, most of the time in Mexico."

The Traven myths evolve around the untraceable years from 1910 to 1920. The German theory was that Traven's true identity was to be found under the name Ret Marut. As reported by Gerd Heidemann in *Stern,* Richard Maurhut, Robert Marut, or Ret Marut was an actor and writer of obscure origins. Before World War I he was improperly registered with the German police as English, born in San Francisco in 1882. With the outbreak of the war, Marut changed his passport to read "American" and thus was a neutral. He then started his own paper, *Der Ziegelbrenner* (*The Brickmaker*) which attacked Hindenberg, the war, and the Pope. Because of his post-war Bavarian revolutionary career he was forced to flee the country and escaped to Mexico in 1923. Here, according to the Heidemann theory, he took the name of Traven Torsvan. Heidemann claimed that there was a good reason for Traven to hide his identity. Traven's wife, Rosa Elena Lujan, told Heidemann that in "a weak hour in Berlin" Traven had told her that his father's name was William—Kaiser Wilhelm II. Heidemann also claimed that the birthdate on Spota's discovered passport was false and that Traven was born May 3, 1882. A two-part *Ramparts* article claimed that Judy Stone "was given an unprecedented series of interviews with the mysterious novelist." The man she interviewed, however, was Hal Croves—who still insisted that he was only a close friend of Traven's. His wife's name was Rosa Elena Lujan.

Reporting Traven's death in 1969, many newspapers and magazines identified him as Traven Torsvan (one account reported Rosa Elena had given out the information). Even that did not end the mystery. Donald D. Chankin, author of *Anonymity and Death: The Fiction of B. Traven,* told *CA:* "Senora Lujan also admitted that he was in fact Ret Marut; thus he was most likely born in 1882. She does not seem to have noticed the contradiction—in 1907 Ret Marut was already appearing as actor and director in Essen. Throughout his life Traven always maintained that he was born in Chicago, but there is no birth certificate or other documentary proof (for the probable reasons for lack of documents, see *The Death Ship*). I think he should be accepted as American, not because he was born here, but because his main protagonists are American—Gales, Dobbs, Howard."

In Russia, Traven is regarded as an important American proletarian writer. His books have sold well and have been enthusiastically received in Germany and elsewhere, though not in the United States. Many critics believe a possible explanation for this is that Americans are unaccustomed to discovering an author's excellence without some knowledge of his personal life. Anthony West offered another theory: "The Traven mystery, insofar as there is one, resides in the question of how Mr. Traven has been able to make himself a reputation with writing of this order. . . . In the twenties, when [Traven] . . . was settling himself into his newly adopted Mexican habitat, his work, unpublished in the United States, was being lapped up in Germany. An immense vogue for adventure stories in general, and for Westerns in particular, swept over Germany in the postwar decade. Dreamstuff about a free zone beyond the advancing frontiers of civilization, a place outside the urbanized world of rules and restraints where there was elbowroom and where action was all important, had an enormous appeal for disillusioned and frustrated people in Europe. Mr. Traven's stories," the critic elaborated, "are about men who leave their law- and custom-bound selves behind and prove their virility with guns and knives while regaining contact, through the Indians, with an ancient wisdom of the instincts whose secrets Europeans have forgotten in the process of becoming civilized. [At that time,] this particular brand of baloney could not be sold in a Southwest whose distances were only just beginning to surrender to the Model T Ford. . . . Mr. Traven's West is a region of the mind, wholly unrelated to the West of reality—an un-place that might best be described as its creator's anti-Chicago."

As the unsigned letter to Johnson maintained, Traven's style was often clumsy. The opening sentence of *The Treasure of Sierra Madre*, for example, reads: "The bench on which Dobbs was sitting was not so good." Bruce Cook explained that Traven's " 'untranslated' English versions read as though they had been worked out laboriously by someone who was fairly fluent in English yet not entirely at home with it. There is a good deal of self-conscious use of dated slang. . . . This sort of thing, intended to make the text idiomatically up-to-date and very American, actually stamps it indelibly as foreign and quite old-fashioned. On the other hand, B. Traven writes a good standard literary German, free from slang and replete with those long dependent clauses with which Mark Twain had so much fun in his essay, 'The Awful German Language.' " But the author's "gift for spinning a yarn," wrote Johnson, "outweighs the occasional awkwardness of language."

Traven's books have recurrent themes: sickness, death, cruelty, hard work for low wages, loneliness, fear, and superstition. He passionately defended the underdog. "It is an anarchist message," noted the *Times Literary Supplement,* "the anarchism of the Wobblies, of Thoreau and of Tolstoy (though without Tolstoy's Christianity). It is totally committed to the proletariat, the oppressed, committed to life and to enjoyment of physical reality: it is equally committed to opposing capitalism, authority, bureaucracy, the state, the oppressor. *The Treasure of Sierra Madre,* for example, is a polemic against the concept of gold as a commercial substance. Gold is a pretty metal, useful for making ornaments but not much more; the ignorant Mestizo murderers of Dobbs are right in their valuation when they mistake gold dust for sand and scatter it to the winds. Similarly Traven's references to capitalism are frequent, and never complimentary: 'Sing Sing is the residence of all New Yorkers who get caught. The rest have offices in Wall Street.' " Desmond MacNamara was similarly impressed with the author's work, concluding: "Of all the proletarian writers [Traven] alone shares honors with Jack London. Indeed, for me he is far better. As a storyteller he is superb and his feeling for Latin American politics on a backyard or jun-

gle-clearing level is the best available. He can make the sun-sodden realities of the cactus lands as logical as an eviction in Kentish Town."

MEDIA ADAPTATIONS: The Treasure of Sierra Madre was made into an award-winning motion picture by Warner Brothers in 1948, directed by John Huston and starring Humphrey Bogart; *Rebellion of the Hanged* was filmed in 1954; *Das Totenschiff* was filmed by a German company in 1959; *Macario* was made into an award-winning Mexican film. *The White Rose,* filmed in Mexico under the title "Rosa Blanca" in 1962, was purchased by the Mexican government and not released until 1972, allegedly for political reasons; after government censorship problems, a version of *Bridge in the Jungle* written by director Pancho Kohner was filmed and finally released by United Artists in 1970. The same Mexican bureau confiscated ten rolls of a German production of *The Cotton-Pickers* in 1969 for presenting a false impression of modern Mexico.

BIOGRAPHICAL/CRITICAL SOURCES:

BOOKS

Baumann, Michael L., *B. Traven: An Introduction,* University of New Mexico Press, 1976.
Chankin, Donald D., *Anonymity and Death: The Fiction of B. Traven,* Pennsylvania State University Press, 1975.
Contemporary Literary Criticism, Gale, Volume 8, 1978, Volume 11, 1979.
Dictionary of Literary Biography, Gale, Volume 9: *American Novelists, 1910-1945,* 1981, Volume 56: *German Fiction Writers, 1914-1945,* 1987.
Stone, Judy, *The Mystery of B. Traven,* William Kaufmann, 1977.

PERIODICALS

Bibliographical Society of America, January, 1959.
Listener, January 4, 1979, January 11, 1979.
Los Angeles Times, July 19, 1970.
National Observer, November 27, 1967.
New Statesman, June 23, 1967.
New Yorker, July 22, 1967.
New York Post, April 3, 1969.
New York Times, May 7, 1967.
New York Times Book Review, April 17, 1966, June 1967.
Ramparts, September, October, 1967.
Time, April 1977.
Times Literary Supplement, June 22, 1967.

OBITUARIES:

PERIODICALS

Newsweek, April 7, 1969.
New York Times, March 27, 1969.
Publishers Weekly, April 21, 1969.
Time, April 4, 1969.
Times (London), March 28, 1969.
Washington Post, March 29, 1969.

*   *   *

TREMBLAY, Michel   1942-

PERSONAL: Born June 25, 1942 (some sources say 1943 or 1944), in Montreal, Quebec, Canada; son of Armand (a linotype operator) and Rheauna Tremblay. *Education:* Attended Institut des Arts Graphiques.

ADDRESSES: Home—571 rue Davaar, Outremont, Montreal, Quebec H2V 1G2, Canada.

CAREER: Writer. Worked as a linotype operator, 1963-66.

MEMBER: Union of Quebec Writers.

AWARDS, HONORS: First prize in Radio Canada's Young Author's Competition, 1964, for unpublished play "Le Train"; Canada Council Award, 1971; Prix Victor-Morin from Societe Saint-Jean-Baptiste de Montreal, 1974; Canadian Film Festival Award for best scenario, 1975, for "Francoise Durocher, Waitress"; Ontario Lieutenant-Governor's Medal, 1976 and 1977; Prix France-Quebec from Quebec Ministere des Relations Internationales, 1981, for novel *Therese et Pierrette a l'ecole des Saints-Anges;* named Chevalier de l'ordre des arts et des lettres in France, 1984; Prix France-Quebec, 1985, for novel *La Duchesse et le Roturier; Albertine, en cinq temps* was named best play at Le Festival du theatre des Ameriques, 1985; Montreal's Prix de la Critique, 1986, for *Albertine, en cinq temps;* Floyd S. Chalmers Canadian Play Award from Ontario Arts Council, 1986.

WRITINGS:

PLAYS

"Le Train" (originally broadcast by Radio Canada, 1964), first produced at Theatre de la Place Ville-Main, 1965.

"Cinq" (one-act plays; includes "Berthe," "Johnny Mangano and His Astonishing Dogs," and "Gloria Star"), first produced in Montreal, 1966, revised version published as *En pieces detachees* (first produced in Montreal, 1969), Lemeac, 1972, translation by Allan Van Meer published as *Like Death Warmed Over,* (produced in Winnipeg, 1973), Playwrights Co-op (Toronto), 1973, translation published as *Montreal Smoked Meat* (produced in Toronto, 1974), Talon Books, 1975, translation also produced as "Broken Pieces," Vancouver, 1974.

Les Belles-Soeurs (title means "The Sisters-In-Law"; two-act; first produced in Montreal, 1968), Holt (Montreal), 1968, translation by John Van Burek and Bill Glassco published as *Les Belles-Soeurs,* Talon Books, 1974.

"La Duchesse de Langeais" (two-act; also see below), first produced in Montreal, 1970.

En pieces detachees [and] *La Duchesse de Langeais,* Lemeac, 1970.

"Les Paons" (one-act fantasy), first produced in 1971.

Trois Petit Tours (television adaptations of "Berthe," "Johnny Mangano and His Astonishing Dogs," and "Gloria Star"; also see below), Lemeac, 1971.

A toi, pour toujours, ta Marie-Lou (one-act; first produced in Montreal, 1971), introduction by Michel Belair, Lemeac, 1971, translation by Van Burek and Glassco published as *Forever Yours, Marie-Lou,* Talon Books, 1975.

Demain matin, Montreal m'attend (title means "Tomorrow Morning, Montreal Wait for Me"; first produced in Montreal, 1972), Lemeac, 1972.

"Hosanna" (two-act; also see below), first produced in Montreal, 1973, produced on Broadway, translation by Van Burek and Glassco published as *Hosanna,* Talon Books, 1974.

Hosanna [and] *La Duchesse de Langeais,* Lemeac, 1973.

Bonjour, la, bonjour (title means "Hello, There, Hello"; first produced in Ottawa, 1974), Lemeac, 1974, translation by Van Burek and Glassco published as *Bonjour, la, bonjour,* Talon Books, 1975.

Sainte-Carmen de la Main (two-act; first produced in Montreal, 1976), Lemeac, 1976, translation by Van Burek published at *Sainte-Carmen of the Main,* Talon Books, 1981.

Les Heros de mon enfance (title means "My Childhood Heroes"; musical comedy; first produced in Eastman, Quebec, 1975), Lemeac, 1976.

"Surprise! Surprise!" (one-act; also see below), first produced in Montreal, 1975.

La Duchesse de Langeais and Other Plays (includes "La Duchesse de Langeais," "Trois Petit Tours," and "Surprise! Surprise!"), translations by Van Burek, Talon Books, 1976.

"Damnee Manon, sacree Sandra" (one-act; also see below), first produced in Montreal, 1977, translation by Van Burek published as *Damnee Manon, sacree Sandra,* Talon Books, 1981.

Damnee Manon, sacree Sandra [and] *Surprise! Surprise!,* Lemeac, 1977.

L'Impromptu d'Outremont (two-act; first produced in Montreal, 1980), Lemeac, 1980, translation by Van Burek published as *The Impromptu of Outremont,* Talon Books, 1981.

Les Anciennes Odeurs (first produced in Montreal, 1981), Lemeac, 1981, translation by John Stowe published as *Remember Me,* Talon Books, 1984.

Albertine, en cinq temps (first produced in Ottawa, 1984), Lemeac, 1984, translation by Van Burek and Glassco published as *Albertine in Five Times,* Talon Books, 1987.

Le Vrai Monde? (first produced concurrently in Ottawa and in Montreal, 1987), Lemeac, 1987, translation produced as "The Real World?," London, 1990.

FICTION

Contes pour buveurs attardes (stories; also see below), Editions du Jour, 1966, translation by Michael Bullock published as *Stories for Late Night Drinkers,* Intermedia Press, 1977.

La Cite dans l'oeuf (fantasy novel; title means "The City Inside the Egg"), Editions du Jour, 1969.

C't a ton tour, Laura Cadieux (title means "It's Your Turn, Laura Cadieux"), Editions du Jour, 1973.

La Grosse Femme d'a cote est enciente (first novel in "Chroniques du plateau Mont-Royal" tetralogy), Lemeac, 1978, translation by Sheila Fischman published as *The Fat Woman Next Door Is Pregnant,* Talon Books, 1981.

Therese et Pierrette a l'ecole des Saints-Anges (second in tetralogy), Lemeac, 1980, translation by Fischman published as *Therese and Pierrette and the Little Hanging Angel,* McClelland & Stewart, 1984.

La Duchesse et le Roturier (third in tetralogy), Lemeac, 1982.

Des nouvelles d'Edouard (fourth in tetralogy), Lemeac, 1984.

Le Coeur decouvert: Roman d'amours, Lemeac, 1986, translation by Fischman published as *The Heart Laid Bare,* McClelland & Stewart, 1989.

FILMS

(Author of screenplay and dialogue, with Andre Brassard) "Francoise Durocher, Waitress," National Film Board of Canada, 1972.

(Author of scenario and dialogue, with Brassard) "Il etait une fois dans l'est" (title means "Once Upon a Time in the East"), Cine Art, 1974.

(Author of scenario and dialogue) "Parlez-vous d'amour" (title means "Speak to Us of Love"), Films 16, c. 1976.

(Author of scenario and dialogue) "Le Soleil se leve en retard," Films 16, c. 1977.

DRAMATIC ADAPTATIONS

"Messe noir" (adapted from selected stories in *Contes pour buveurs attardes*), first produced in Montreal, 1965.

(With Andre Brassard) *Lysistrata* (translated and adapted from Aristophanes's *Lysistrata;* first produced in Ottawa, 1969), Lemeac, 1969.

L'Effet des rayons gamma sur les vieux-garcons (translated and adapted from Paul Zindel's *The Effect of Gamma Rays on Man-in-the-Moon Marigolds;* first produced in Montreal, 1970), Lemeac, 1970.

". . . Et Mademoiselle Roberge boit un peu . . ." (three-act; translated and adapted from Zindel's *And Miss Reardon Drinks a Little;* first produced in Montreal, 1972), Lemeac, 1971.

"Le Pays du Dragon" (translated and adapted from four of Tennessee Williams's one-act plays), first produced in Montreal, 1971.

"Mistero buffo" (translated and adapted from Dario Fo's play of the same name), first produced in Montreal, 1973.

Mademoiselle Marguerite (translated and adapted from Roberto Athayde's *Aparaceu a Margarida;* first produced in Ottawa, 1976), Lemeac, 1975.

(With Kim Yaroshevskaya) *Oncle Vania* (translated and adapted from Anton Chekhov's play of the same name), Lemeac, 1983.

Le Gars de Quebec (adapted from Nikolay Gogol's *Le Revizov;* first produced in Montreal, 1985), Lemeac, 1985.

OTHER

Six heures au plus tard, Lemeac, 1986.

Contributor to periodicals, including *La Barre de Jour.*

SIDELIGHTS: Michel Tremblay is "the most important Quebecois artist of his generation," declared Salem Alaton in a 1986 Toronto *Globe and Mail* review. Beginning his career in the mid-1960s, the French-Canadian playwright, fiction writer, and screenwriter has become best known for dramatic works that challenge traditional myths of French-Canadian life. Indeed, for years critics contended that Tremblay's concentration on the social and cultural problems of Quebec earned him local acclaim at the expense of more universal recognition. In the 1980s, however, Tremblay began to command an international audience. Alaton theorized that it is the "edgy, Quebecois specificity" of Tremblay's work, once considered a liability, that is responsible for the playwright's success. With his work widely translated and produced, Tremblay is now regarded as a world-class dramatist who, in the words of *Quill and Quire* reviewer Mark Czarnecki, provides a persuasive example "of the much-debated cultural proposition that the more local the reference, the more universal the truth."

Tremblay grew up in the east end of Montreal, in the working-class neighborhood of the rue Fabre. The oppressive conditions of life in this impoverished area, along with the glitzy nightlife of the Main district, later provided the backdrop for much of Tremblay's work. Despite the inauspicious environment of his youth, Tremblay began writing when quite young and was a promising student who at thirteen received a scholarship to a classical college. Unable to endure the elitist attitudes fostered at the school, however, Tremblay left after several months to study graphic arts and become a linotype operator. He nevertheless continued to write during those years and by the time he was eighteen had completed his first play, "Le Train." Several years later, in 1964, it won first prize in Radio Canada's Young Author Competition.

Shortly thereafter, Tremblay made Quebec theater history. Eschewing the classical French typically used in works for the stage, Tremblay wrote a play, *Les Belles-Soeurs,* in *joual,* the language of the people. Though Tremblay had not intended to create a political work, his use of *joual*—regarded by many as a debased form of the French language—signaled to his detrac-

tors and supporters alike the desire to supplant the province's traditional French culture with an independent Quebec culture. His critics decried the play while his admirers lauded it as a contribution to what is known in Quebec as the "theatre of liberation."

Written in 1965 but denied production until 1968, *Les Belles-Soeurs* catapulted the young dramatist to fame. But the play was not radical for its language alone. *Les Belles-Soeurs* was also controversial for its naturalistic view of French-Canadian life. Its plot is straightforward: after winning one million trading stamps, Gabriel Lauzon, an average east-end Montreal housewife, invites her women friends to a stamp-pasting gathering; by play's end, the women have turned on one another in a battle for the stamps. *Les Belles-Soeurs,* averred John Ripley in a critique for *Canadian Literature,* "explodes two centuries of popular belief, ecclesiastical teaching, and literary myth about Quebecois women. Far from being the traditional guardians of religious and moral values, happy progenitors of large families, and good-humored housekeepers, they stand revealed as malevolent misfits, consumed with hatred of life and of themselves."

Les Belles-Soeurs is the first in what became an eleven-play cycle, a cycle which in its entirety many critics regarded as Tremblay's finest achievement. Ripley suggested that Quebec's "recent past, characterized by a desperate struggle to replace authoritarianism, negative identity, and destructiveness with self-respect, love, and transcendence, is nowhere better encapsulated than in the *Les Belles-Soeurs* cycle." Ripley's sentiments were echoed by critic Renate Usmiani, who in a *Contemporary Literary Criticism* extract stated: "The most general underlying theme of all [Tremblay's] works is the universal desire of the human being to transcend his finite condition." More specifically, Usmiani proposed that the typical Tremblay character is either trying to escape from family life as represented by the rue Fabre, from the false world of the Main, or from the limitations of self into a transcendent ecstasy.

One picture of life along the rue Fabre is offered by *A toi, pour toujours, ta Marie-Lou.* Deemed "a devastating psycho-social analysis of the traditional working-class Quebecois family" by Ripley, the play presents four characters juxtaposed in two different time periods. Marie-Louise is a housewife whose problems manifest themselves as sexual frigidity and religious fanaticism; Leopold, her husband, is a factory worker who becomes an alcoholic. Their marriage, according to Ripley, "is a sado-masochistic battle with no prospect of victory for either side," and thus Leopold ends their lives in a suicidal car crash. The drama progresses as, ten years later, their daughters discuss the tragedy and its impact on their lives. Manon, still living in the family home, has remained loyal to her mother and taken refuge in a similar fanaticism, seemingly unable to save herself. For Carmen, who has managed to make a life for herself as a singer in the Main district, there appears to be some hope. Both characters return in subsequent plays.

Although Leopold and Marie-Louise die to escape the rue Fabre, Tremblay's pen finds others searching for alternatives in the world of the Main. For them, "the Main stands for glamour, freedom, life itself," asserted Usmiani. Typified by prostitutes and transvestites, however, the Main, in Usmiani's opinion, "turns out to be ultimately as inbred, frustrating and limiting, in its own kinky way, as the petty household world around rue Fabre." *La Duchesse de Langeais* and *Hosanna,* whose title characters seek escape from reality in homosexuality, provide two examples. The former is a dramatic monologue delivered by the Duchess, an aging transvestite prostitute who has been rejected by a younger lover. Ripley theorized that the Duchess has chosen to "escape from male impotence" by "the adoption of a role precisely the opposite of the one normally expected." Cast aside by his young partner, however, the Duchess fails to find satisfaction and remains an essentially pathetic character. More optimistically, *Hosanna* finds lovers Hosanna (Claude), who is forever role-playing, and Cuirette (Raymond) beginning to communicate after a particularly humiliating crisis. They are eventually able to discard their female personas and accept themselves as male homosexuals, freely admitting their love for one another. In so doing, according to Ripley, the two realize that although they are deviants, they still have a place in the world.

In *Damnee Manon, sacree Sandra,* the final play of the cycle, Tremblay moves away from the nightmare of family life and illusions of the Main to explore the possibility of fulfillment through mysticism. The drama unfolds through the monologues of two characters. Manon, from the earlier *A toi, pour toujours, ta Marie-Lou,* represents an attempt at transcendence through religious mysticism. Sandra, who also appeared previously in Tremblay's work, is a transvestite who seeks transcendence through sex. Both now live on the rue Fabre, as they did in childhood, and during the course of the play each comes to appreciate that the other has chosen a different path toward the same goal. Usmiani described the two characters as "physical incarnations, exteriorizations, of the two paths toward ecstasy conceived by the author," adding that on one level their world "is not a physical reality on the rue Fabre, but the psychological reality of the poet's own mind." The critic concluded that in Tremblay's work "there is no transcendence beyond that which the self can provide."

By the time Tremblay finished the *Belles-Soeurs* cycle in 1977, the political climate in Quebec had improved, and he gave permission, previously withheld, for his plays to be produced in English in Quebec. At this juncture he also switched genres, beginning work on a series of semi-autobiographical novels. The playwright's venture into fiction has been successful, and thus far, at least two of the volumes in his "Chroniques du plateau Mont-Royal" tetralogy have been translated into English. The first volume in the series, *La Grosse Femme d'a cote est enciente,* was translated as *The Fat Woman Next Door is Pregnant.* Not only are the characters of this novel residents of the rue Fabre, as in so many of Tremblay's dramas, but the fat woman of the title is Tremblay's mother, and the story is based on the author's recollections of life in the apartment of his birth. *Quill and Quire* reviewer Czarnecki contended that *The Fat Woman*'s one-day time frame achieves "a similar effect" to that of James Joyce's famed *Ulysses.* Reviewing for the same publication, Philip Stratford called *The Fat Woman* "a generous, good-natured fresco teeming with life and invention." Regarded as both funny and sentimental, the book became a best-seller in Quebec.

Its sequel, *Therese et Pierrette a l'ecole des Saints-Anges,* translated as *Therese and Pierrette and the Little Hanging Angel,* also fared well, winning the prestigious Prix France-Quebec in 1981. Set during a four-day time period, the volume concentrates on three eleven-year-old students at the Ecole des Saints-Anges, a Roman Catholic girls' school. In this novel censuring the religious education system, Tremblay exhibits "epic gifts," in Czarnecki's opinion, that "extend to capturing life in its smallest details, creating an imaginative world complete in itself, ready to immerse and rebaptize the reader."

Tremblay concluded his tetralogy with *La Duchesse et le Roturier* in 1982 and *Des nouvelles d'Edouard* in 1984. During the 1980s, however, Tremblay also returned to writing plays. Although some critics regard his dramas of the eighties as unequal to his earlier work, many of them appraise the 1987 *Le Vrai Monde?* as his best.

In this play Tremblay looks back to 1965, to his own beginning as an artist, and questions what right he had to use the lives of family and friends in service to his art. Calling it both "an expression of guilt" and "an eloquent statement about the relationship between art and life," *Globe and Mail* critic Matthew Fraser found *Le Vrai Monde?* "a masterful piece of drama." Another reviewer for the *Globe and Mail,* Ray Conlogue, contended that it is "a formidable play" in which Tremblay tries "to defend his art." In his interview for the Toronto paper with Alaton, Tremblay offered a slightly different perspective, telling the critic: "It is almost a condemnation of what an artist does to real life." And when Alaton asked him why he wrote, the dramatist responded: "Maybe I am an artist because artists give purpose to a thing which has not purpose, which is life. . . . You put [a play] before 500 people every night and you say, 'Sometimes, this is what life might mean.' And people who live the same nonsense life as you understand this."

BIOGRAPHICAL/CRITICAL SOURCES:

BOOKS

Anthony, Geraldine, *Stage Voices: Twelve Canadian Playwrights Talk About Their Lives and Work,* Doubleday, 1978.
Contemporary Literary Criticism, Volume 29, Gale, 1984.
Dictionary of Literary Biography, Volume 60: *Canadian Writers Since 1960, Second Series,* Gale, 1987.
Usmiani, Renate, *Michel Tremblay: A Critical Study,* Douglas & McIntyre, 1981.

PERIODICALS

Books in Canada, January/February, 1986.
Canadian Drama, Number 2, 1976.
Canadian Literature, summer, 1980.
Canadian Theatre Review, fall, 1979.
Chicago Tribune, March 8, 1980.
Globe and Mail (Toronto), November 16, 1986, April 25, 1987, October 3, 1987.
Maclean's, April 30, 1984, April 22, 1985.
New York Times, December 11, 1983.
Quill and Quire, February, 1982, April, 1982, June, 1984.
Washington Post, June 22, 1978.

*   *   *

TREVOR, William
See COX, William Trevor

*   *   *

TRIFONOV, Yuri (Valentinovich) 1925-1981

PERSONAL: Given name sometimes transliterated as Yury, Iurii, or Uri; born August 28, 1925, in Moscow, U.S.S.R.; died after surgery, March 28, 1981, in Moscow, U.S.S.R.; son of Valentin A. Trifonov; children: Valentin. *Education:* Graduated from Gorky Institute of Literature, 1949.

CAREER: Writer, 1947-81.

AWARDS, HONORS: Received Stalin Prize, 1951, for *Students.*

WRITINGS:

NOVELS IN ENGLISH TRANSLATION

Students, translation from the Russian by Ivy Litvinova and Margaret Wettlin, Foreign Languages Publishing House (Moscow), 1953.

The Impatient Ones, translation from the Russian by Robert Daglish, Progress Publishers (Moscow), 1978.

The Long Goodbye: Three Novellas (contains *The Exchange, Taking Stock,* and *The Long Goodbye*), translation from the Russian by Helen P. Burlingame and Ellendea Proffer, Harper, 1978.

Another Life [and] *The House on the Embankment,* translation from the Russian by Michael Glenny, Simon & Schuster, 1983.

The Old Man, translation from the Russian by Jacqueline Edwards and Mitchell Schneider, Simon & Schuster, 1984.

OTHER

"Exchange" (play), first produced in London, England, at the Vaudeville Theatre, February, 1990.

Also author of a posthumously published novel, *Vremia i mesto* (title means "Place and Time").

SIDELIGHTS: Often called "the Soviet Anton Chekhov," Yuri Trifonov chronicled the everyday lives and aspirations of the new Russian middle class in a series of novellas that earned him acclaim in the Soviet Union and abroad. The son of a Bolshevik revolutionary who was executed during Communist dictator Joseph Stalin's political purges of the 1930s, Trifonov used his work to subtly explore the ways in which the fear and betrayals of the Stalinist past had helped shape the values and morality of contemporary Soviet society. In so doing, he rejected broad political and ideological themes to focus on personal moral conflicts that reflect both Soviet history and the universal human dilemma. Trifonov, who died in 1981 at the age of fifty-five, was highly regarded for his stylistic artistry as well as his thematic originality.

Trifonov enjoyed success and official recognition early in his career, winning the prestigious Stalin Prize in 1951 at age twenty-six for his first book, *Students,* a novel of university life in the post-World War II years. When the Stalinist era drew to a close not long afterward, he began writing novellas that dealt candidly with the often petty, materialist ambitions and careerist rivalries common among the intelligentsia in a supposedly socialist society. Never a political dissident, Trifonov did not criticize the Soviet system as such but rather the obstinate human reality that gave the lie to official propaganda declaring the end of class divisions and egotistical behavior. Indeed, the novelist depicted unscrupulous self-seeking as usually the best way to "get ahead" in the official bureaucracy and secure scarce living space and consumer luxuries. Trifonov's moralistic rather than political approach allowed him to accommodate the Soviet censor and publish freely in his own country. His low political profile, however, contributed to his relative obscurity in the West during his lifetime.

The three novellas published in the United States under the title *The Long Goodbye* typify Trifonov's themes of moral choice, family conflicts, and career dilemmas among Moscow's petty bourgeoisie and his Chekhovian attention to the emotional nuances of everyday life. *The Exchange* describes a couple who attempt to secure a roomier apartment for themselves by having the husband's dying mother move in with them, thus appearing to deserve more living space. *Taking Stock* compares the petty

passions of a quarreling family with the exhausted vigor of old religious icons, now collected by the middle class as decorative objects. The title work, finally, recounts the loves, triumphs, and disappointments of a Moscow actress. In a later novella, *Another Life,* Trifonov offered perhaps his most artfully realized portrait of a couple's failed marriage and frustrated careers, showing their personal and professional fates joined by character and history. *New York Times Book Review* critic Richard Lourie judged the work "nearly flawless," remarking that the author moves "from the errands and arguments of daily existence to memory and then back again with perfect ease. . . . By placing his story far in the background and by allowing himself to be absorbed in minutiae, Trifonov seems to say that our lives are made of small enduring traces, and all the rest, no matter how much harm it does us, really doesn't matter in the end."

In *The House on the Embankment,* published in the Soviet Union in 1976, Trifonov adds a more direct historical and autobiographical context to his familiar themes of professional rivalry and personal opportunism. Glebov, the novella's anti-hero, is an ambitious young literature student whose tenuous moral sense fails him when his favorite professor and prospective father-in-law is falsely accused of disseminating counterrevolutionary ideology during the Stalinist era. Returning later in life to the large riverside apartment house where the professor and other prominent thinkers and revolutionaries had once lived, Glebov finds the building shabby and dilapidated, a mirror of the talent and ideals lost to the bureaucratic purges to which he owed his own career. Trifonov modeled the novella's apartment house on the Moscow building in which he lived as a boy with his grandmother after his parents were imprisoned in the 1930s. The building housed high government officials and the families of revolutionary heroes, and Trifonov later recalled witnessing numerous midnight arrests as Stalin consolidated his regime during that decade of terror.

Appearing during the conservative years of Soviet leader Leonid Brezhnev's administration, *The House on the Embankment* caused a stir with its clear evocation of the suppressed Stalinist past. But the novella, Trifonov's most popular work in the Soviet Union, also owed its success to its many literary merits. Trifonov tempered his somber historical narrative with subtly satirical jabs at the intelligentsia and the new managerial class, and his study of human values and motivations transcended the Soviet setting. "The tortuous and dismal light in which Trifonov observes Russian character has changed very little, ironically, since the time of [writer Fedor] Dostoevski," Martin Lebowitz observed in a review for the *Chicago Tribune Book World.* "Indeed he is a critic not of Russia but of human nature. His unusual talent may be unique among current Russian writers."

Trifonov brought the Soviet Union's tumultuous early history more fully into focus in *The Old Man,* one of the last works he completed before his death. In fact, as *New York Times Book Review* critic Harlow Robinson remarked, the terrible years of civil war following the 1917 revolution are "the protean and elusive protagonist" of this work, which is considered unique to the author's *oeuvre.* The old man of the title is Pavel Evgrafovich Letunov, a civil war veteran driven by the need to make moral sense of his past and the chaotic events in which he played a part. His particular preoccupation is his conduct toward the cossack Migulin, a Bolshevik military commander and later a suspected counterrevolutionary who had married Letunov's youthful love, Asya. After lengthy research through the historical archives, Letunov writes an article urging that Migulin be politically "rehabilitated," i.e., restored his status as a member of the Communist party. Letunov receives a letter in response from Asya that he hopes will shed light on his personal role in Migulin's tragedy. Throughout the novella Trifonov contrasts Letunov's ethical and historical concerns with his children's petty bickering over the use of a summerhouse, suggesting ironically that the moral failure of the earlier generation may have sown the barrenness and frivolity of the latter.

Stylistically, the author underscores his theme of moral ambiguity and shifting history with a fragmented and disjointed narrative that makes use of flashbacks, interior monologues, and passages from real and fictitious war documents. Dubbing *The Old Man* Trifonov's most ambitious effort, *New York Times* critic Walter Goodman noted that the novella also refers autobiographically to Trifonov's years of effort to rehabilitate his father's name. "In its evocation of the intoxicating civil war years," the reviewer surmised, "this novel is a considerable feat of imagination, bringing alive the unremitting threats and improvised responses, the daily bursts of panic, the chronic power struggles and the rough-and-ready justice." Trifonov died shortly after completing his final novel, *Place and Time,* a semi-autobiographical account of the life of a Soviet novelist.

BIOGRAPHICAL/CRITICAL SOURCES:

BOOKS

Contemporary Literary Criticism, Volume 45, Gale, 1987.

PERIODICALS

Chicago Tribune Book World, February 19, 1984.
Los Angeles Times, December 22, 1983.
Nation, September 9, 1978.
New Leader, September 10, 1979.
New York Times, October 2, 1984.
New York Times Book Review, March 18, 1984, February 3, 1985.
Times (London), February 24, 1990.
Washington Post Book World, November 11, 1978.

OBITUARIES:

PERIODICALS

New York Times, March 29, 1981.
Washington Post, March 29, 1981.

*   *   *

TRILLIN, Calvin   1935-

PERSONAL: Born December 5, 1935, in Kansas City, Mo.; son of Abe and Edyth (Weitzman) Trillin; married Alice Stewart, August 13, 1965; children: Abigail, Sarah. *Education:* Yale University, B.A., 1957.

ADDRESSES: Office—*New Yorker,* 25 West 43rd St., New York, NY 10036.

CAREER: Time magazine, New York City, 1960-63, began as reporter in Atlanta and New York City, became writer in New York City; *New Yorker,* New York City, staff writer, 1963—.

AWARDS, HONORS: National Book Award nomination (paperback), 1980, for *Alice, Let's Eat: Further Adventures of a Happy Eater.*

WRITINGS:

An Education in Georgia (nonfiction), Viking, 1964.
Barnett Frummer Is an Unbloomed Flower, and Other Adventures of Barnett Frummer, Rosalie Mondle, Roland Magruder, and Their Friends (short stories), Viking, 1969.
U.S. Journal (nonfiction), Dutton, 1971.

American Fried: Adventures of a Happy Eater (nonfiction), Doubleday, 1974.
Runestruck (novel), Little, Brown, 1977.
Alice, Let's Eat: Further Adventures of a Happy Eater (nonfiction), Random House, 1978.
Floater (novel), Ticknor & Fields, 1980.
Uncivil Liberties (collected columns) Ticknor & Fields, 1982.
Third Helpings (nonfiction), Ticknor & Fields, 1983.
Killings (nonfiction), Ticknor & Fields, 1984.
With All Disrespect: More Uncivil Liberties (collected columns), Ticknor & Fields, 1985.
If You Can't Say Something Nice, Ticknor & Fields, 1987.
If You Don't Have Anything Nice to Say, Ticknor & Fields, 1987.
Travels With Alice, Ticknor & Fields, 1989.

OTHER

Author of the column "Uncivil Liberties," *Nation,* 1978-85, King Features Syndicate, 1986—. Contributor to periodicals, including *Atlantic, Harper's, Life, Esquire,* and *New York Times Magazine.*

SIDELIGHTS: Calvin Trillin is a journalist, critic and novelist who has won acclaim "partly because of his wayward scrambles across [America] in search of unusual regional food . . . and partly because he has mastered a television manner that communicates his understated, tongue-in-cheek humor," according to Barry Siegel in a *Los Angeles Times* article. But in some ways, continues Siegel, "it is regrettable that Trillin is so funny, because this quality tends to obscure the fact that in his *U.S. Journal* [a continuing series in the *New Yorker*] he may be offering some of the most valuable and unique reporting in the country today."

Trillin's early career saw him working at *Time,* where as a journalistic "floater" he migrated from one department to the next. As the author told *Publishers Weekly* interviewer John F. Baker, he spent some time in the "Medicine" section: "I didn't care for that—it seemed to tend toward the intestinal whenever I was there, with weekly breakthroughs in spleen research" and also had a stint in the "Religion" section, which ill-suited Trillin. "I finally got out of that by prefixing everything with 'alleged'; I'd write about 'the alleged parting of the Red Sea,' even 'the alleged Crucifixion,' and eventually they let me go."

Apparently, Trillin gained enough insight from his career at *Time* to produce, years later, a comic novel titled *Floater.* The fictional newsweekly through which protagonist Fred Becker floats is populated with trend-obsessed editors, egomaniacal writers, and eccentrics of every description. Becker enjoys his unfettered career until a rumor provided to him by a remarkably unreliable source threatens his future. The rumor—that the President's wife is pregnant—could cause Becker to be promoted to an odious bureau chief position if he is the first to report it truthfully. While Becker ponders what to do with his scoop, he accidentally leaks the rumor, only to find that the scoop is phony, "part of an elaborate, internecine power struggle at the magazine that is as unlikely as it is hilarious," according to Dan Wakefield in *Nation.*

Some critics find the novel too thin. In *Los Angeles Times Book Review* contributor Stuart Schoffman's opinion, "the chief flaw . . . is that the characters are so bloodless and inactive, pounded into two-dimensionality like paperthin slices of veal." John D. Callaway shares this view, noting in the *Chicago Tribune Book World* that, while *Floater's* humor often appealed to him, the characters "are less memorably drawn than the actors who star in 30-second commercials."

Wakefield, on the other hand, finds Trillin's satire "sure and sharp but never mean-spirited. A kind of affection for the magazine comes through, and when Becker considers leaving it, he thinks how much he would miss the camaraderie, the gossip and stories and daily routines." Wakefield concludes that "Trillin is one of those rare writers who possess grace as well as wit."

Trillin's nonfiction, gleaned from his magazine pieces, covers a wide range. There are the humor collections *Uncivil Liberties* and *With All Disrespect: More Uncivil Liberties,* the essay collection *U.S. Journal,* and a study of homicide, *Killings.* With *U.S. Journal* the author recalls his travels across America, finding stories in everyday events in which there may be no apparent "news value." These subjects befit Trillin, who grew up in Kansas City, Missouri, and has always considered himself a Midwesterner, despite his years of living in New York City. He sees his subjects as worthy of examination, even if they are not famous or important. "Upwardly mobile reporters tend to gauge themselves by the importance of the people they interview," Trillin told Siegel. "I don't think like that. Most of the people I talk to have never spoken to a reporter before. I began the U.S. Journal series partly because I wanted to stay in touch with the country. I like regional stories. The fact is, government and politics are important, but they aren't the country."

Writing about *U.S. Journal* in the *New York Times Book Review,* Evan S. Connell states: "Trillin's scales usually are balanced; he is a judicious journalist and has presented an agreeable collection. More important, several passages show compelling depth. As cautious as he is, he can create a wave of emotion in the reader—usually a wave of rage at the bigots, paralytic bureaucrats and myopic hucksters who infest [the book]. His account of desperate people in South Carolina is guaranteed to spoil your lunch."

In 1978, Trillin began to write "Uncivil Liberties," a humor column for the *Nation.* More recently published in syndication throughout the country, the column has been both a popular and critical success. *Uncivil Liberties* and *With All Disrespect: More Uncivil Liberties,* which present that work in collected form, are likewise praised for the author's slightly skewed views of today's culture. "At the outset, Trillin defined the column as 'a thousand words every three weeks for saying whatever's on my mind, particularly if what's on my mind is marginally ignoble,' " as Jonathan Yardley reports in a *Washington Post* review. "Even in his less-inspired efforts," says Yardley, "he is perceptive, funny and iconoclastic." Trillin is "consistently sharp and imaginative" in *Uncivil Liberties,* according to a *Detroit News* critic, "but don't expect a banquet of belly laughs from these 50 easy pieces. They're more likely to elicit appreciative smiles at the author's capacity for setting up and delivering clever dissections of his chosen prey."

Equally well received was Trillin's 1984 collection, *Killings.* Based on several *New Yorker* articles, the book examines the kinds of murder that don't ordinarily make national headlines—those occurring in small towns, their victims uncelebrated individuals. "Trillin's interest—and ours—lies not in how some of us die but in how we live," notes *Nation* reviewer Ann Jones. The author, continues Jones, finds that the motivation for some of the murders should be viewed within the context of the social tensions in the cities and towns where the killings took place. "He describes what sociologists would call a conflict of cultures," says Jones. "A hillbilly guns down a trespassing filmmaker. A frustrated Navajo abducts a New Mexico mayor. . . . Sometimes the conflict is more intimate [as in the case of] Lawrence Hartman, an exemplary Iowa farmer who in middle age, bedaz-

zled by the big city and a young cocktail waitress, beat his wife to death." "In several cases the killing seems inadvertent, as if the killer didn't actually want to do it, but couldn't think of any other way to pass through the situation. Lack of imagination may be a motive," Anatole Broyard points out in a *New York Times* piece.

In *Killings,* Trillin "fashions suspense by starting with ordinary, day-to-day details; the violence grows imperceptibly," as Richard Eder explains. "He roots his pieces in some particular community and set of circumstances and makes them so real that the death becomes not an extraordinary event but a natural process that has failed. Some of the most vivid reflections are those of neighbors who ask themselves what went wrong," Eder writes in the *Los Angeles Times.* To *Washington Post* critic Jonathan Yardley, the author "is a practitioner of hit-and-run journalism in the sense that he pounces on a locality, tells its story, and then moves on to the next. But he rises well above the genre for two reasons: His unusually deep interest in people . . . and his desire to find meaning in what at first seems meaningless. 'Killings' is more than just another collection of magazine pieces; its internal coherence, unusual in such volumes, derives from the empathy and intelligence of its author."

If empathy and intelligence characterize Trillin's attitude toward people, most critics agree that passion and poignancy describe his attitude toward food. The author has made his true love known in three volumes, each celebrating the variety of American cuisine. Indeed, Trillin's eloquence on such matters as fried chicken and Chicago-style pizza has caused him to be labeled "the Walt Whitman of American eats" by Craig Claiborne in the *New York Times Book Review* and a "food pornographer" by Nelson W. Polsby in *Harper's. American Fried: Adventures of a Happy Eater* is the first in Trillin's trilogy, and is "composed of a blend of waspish sociology and a sensuality so explicit as to border on the prurient," warns a *Saturday Review* critic. In his review, Polsby appreciates the author's dilemma as a roving gourmand. When Trillin arrives in town, explains Polsby, the gentry "refuse to tell him where [the good] restaurants are. Instead, they are forever touting him onto high-priced fake 'Continental' eateries, places with lots of decor, long-winded menus, revolving views of the surrounding wasteland, and terrible food. When hunger strikes in a strange town, he despairs of interviewing local informants, and he has taken to rummaging through the restaurant section of the Yellow Pages, looking for restaurants having no display ads or those called by only the first name of the proprietor."

"Some will say [that, in *American Fried,* Trillin] has written a nasty satire on gourmets, but they err who think so," claims *Washington Post Book World* writer Henry Mitchell. "Trillin genuinely loves all the stuff he writes about, no doubt of that. Love transforms all. As Proust took the simple madeline and with genius made it a glory of his book, so Trillin takes the hamburger, takes the chili-dog, takes the pizza, and does as much or more."

An entreaty to his wife comprises the title of Trillin's second food-appreciation book, *Alice, Let's Eat: Further Adventures of a Happy Eater.* Alice, it seems, does not quite share her husband's enthusiasm for barbecue and burgers, and the couple's conflicts figure as a dramatic element in the volume. While Trillin has some fun at his wife's expense in *Alice, Let's Eat,* Alice told her side of the story in a *Nation* review of her husband's book. "I am not against quests for the perfect ham hock or the perfect barbecue or even, for that matter, for the perfect roast polecat haunch," Alice Trillin explained. "But I think that anyone starting out on such a quest should be aware that his guide is someone who will travel all the way to a place called Horse Cave, Ky. because he likes the way the name Horse Cave, Ky. sounds when he drops it to me over the phone. . . . This is offered as a warning by someone who has been assigned the role of heavy in her husband's book just because she likes to say fettuccine with white truffles and cream occasionally—a dish considered by some to represent the elitist Eastern Establishment."

New Republic reviewer Ben Yagoda regrets that there is some "bad news" about *Alice, Let's Eat:* the book "is not quite as consistently delightful as *American Fried.* I blame this in part on the fact that in the new book Trillin is disappointed a number of times—by the Kentucky mutton, by a Vermont wildgame supper where he can't tell the beaver from the buffalo. . . . Also, he ventures away from the US too often: there's a trip to Martinique, one to France, and two to England." Outside of America, claims Yagoda, "Trillin seems somehow out of place, like a hamburger stand on the Champs Elysees. But read *Alice, Let's Eat,*" concludes the critic, who calls Trillin "a worthy celebrant of one of the few authentic triumphs of American culture. His book will bring a smile to your lips and a growl to your stomach."

Third Helpings is perhaps the most radical of Trillin's food books: it contains a campaign "to have the national Thanksgiving dish changed from turkey to spaghetti carbonara." The author defends his stance with a retelling of the First Thanksgiving legend. In Trillin's version the Indians joined the Pilgrims for a Thanksgiving feast, taking the precaution "of [bringing] along one dish of their own. They brought a dish their ancestors had been taught earlier by Christopher Columbus, discoverer of the New World. The dish was spaghetti carbonara."

As in the other two works, American patriotism figures into *Third Helpings.* After sampling the food at a Mediterranean resort, Trillin declares that the fancy fare is no better "than the Italian sausage sandwiches he dotes upon on Mulberry Street in lower Manhattan," as *Newsweek's* Gene Lyons relates. "Neither, for that matter, does the Italian cuisine surpass the roast duck and dirty rice at Didee's in Baton Rouge or Opelousas, La."

In pieces such as the account of the Crawford County, Kansas, fried chicken war between Chicken Annie and Chicken Mary, Trillin proves to Beryl Lieff Benderly that "under cover of a mania for dim sum, spaghetti carbonara, and pit barbecue, [the author] is actually a superlative prose stylist, an inimitable humorist, and an absolutely first-rate people writer." In a *Washington Post Book World* article, Benderly adds that Trillin's articles "concern not only comestibles but characters; they concentrate on talented devotees who take what they eat and serve every bit as seriously as Trillin does."

BIOGRAPHICAL/CRITICAL SOURCES:

BOOKS

Authors in the News, Volume I, Gale, 1976.
Trillin, Calvin, *Third Helpings,* Ticknor & Fields, 1983.

PERIODICALS

Chicago Tribune, February 26, 1984.
Chicago Tribune Book World, November 30, 1980, March 18, 1984.
Commentary, August, 1971.
Detroit News, May 30, 1982.
Harper's, August, 1974.
Kansas City Magazine, November, 1974.
Los Angeles Times, November 18, 1980, March 11, 1984, March 23, 1984.

Los Angeles Times Book Review, December 7, 1980, April 24, 1984.
Life, November 7, 1969.
Nation, October 21, 1978, October 11, 1980, March 3, 1984, December 22, 1984.
New Republic, April 17, 1971, October 7, 1978.
Newsweek, October 27, 1980, April 4, 1983, February 13, 1984.
New York Times, November 7, 1969, July 2, 1971, May 12, 1977, October 14, 1980, May 26, 1982, April 14, 1983, January 28, 1984.
New York Times Book Review, January 25, 1970, May 16, 1971, March 6, 1977, November 23, 1980, April 17, 1983, February 19, 1984, April 14, 1985, October 22, 1989.
Publishers Weekly, November 21, 1980.
Saturday Review, May 8, 1971, May 18, 1974.
Time, March 22, 1971, December 22, 1980, July 5, 1982, March 5, 1984.
Village Voice, September 25, 1978.
Voice Literary Supplement, October, 1989.
Washington Post, October 23, 1980, December 4, 1980, May 19, 1982, February 8, 1984, April 16, 1985.
Washington Post Book World, October 26, 1969, June 2, 1974, April 10, 1983.

* * *

TRILLING, Diana (Rubin) 1905-

PERSONAL: Born July 21, 1905, in New York, N.Y.; daughter of Joseph (a businessman) and Sadie (Forbert) Rubin; married Lionel Trilling (a critic and professor of English), June 12, 1929 (died November 5, 1975); children: James Lionel. *Education:* Radcliffe College, A.B., 1925.

ADDRESSES: Home—35 Claremont Ave., New York, N.Y. 10027.

CAREER: Nation, New York, N.Y., fiction critic, 1942-49; freelance writer and critic, beginning in 1949. Chairman of American Committee for Cultural Freedom, 1955-57.

MEMBER: American Academy of Arts and Sciences (fellow), Phi Beta Kappa, Radcliffe Club (New York chapter).

AWARDS, HONORS: Guggenheim fellowship, 1950-51; grants from National Endowment for the Humanities and Rockefeller Foundation, 1977-79; Pulitzer Prize nomination, 1982, for *Mrs. Harris: The Death of the Scarsdale Diet Doctor.*

WRITINGS:

Claremont Essays, Harcourt, 1964.
We Must March My Darlings: A Critical Decade (essays), Harcourt, 1977.
Reviewing the Forties (fiction criticism), introduction by Paul Fussell, Harcourt, 1978.
Mrs. Harris: The Death of the Scarsdale Diet Doctor, Harcourt, 1981.

Also author of column "Here and Now," for *New Leader,* 1957-59. Contributor to volume on D. H. Lawrence published by Weidenfeld & Nicolson. Also contributor of essays and reviews on literary, sociological, and political subjects to *Partisan Review, New York Times, New York Herald Tribune, Harper's, Harper's Bazaar, Vogue, Esquire, Reporter, American Scholar, Encounter, Commentary, Times Literary Supplement,* and other periodicals.

EDITOR

(And author of introduction) *The Portable D. H. Lawrence,* Viking, 1947, reprinted, Penguin, 1977.

(And author of introduction) *Selected Letters of D. H. Lawrence,* Farrar, Straus, 1958.

(And author of introduction) Mark Twain, *Tom Sawyer,* Crowell-Collier, 1962.

Lionel Trilling, *The Last Decade: Essays and Reviews, 1965-1975,* Harcourt, 1979.

L. Trilling, *Prefaces to the Experience of Literature,* Harcourt, 1979.

L. Trilling, *Of This Time, of That Place, and Other Stories,* Harcourt, 1979.

L. Trilling, *Speaking of Literature and Society,* Harcourt, 1980.

Also editor of *Uniform Edition of the Works of Lionel Trilling,* 1978-80. Member of editorial board of *American Scholar.*

WORK IN PROGRESS: "A childhood memoir."

SIDELIGHTS: Although Diana Trilling was trained and prepared for an operatic singing career, her aspirations were thwarted by a serious thyroid condition that left her unable to pursue her chosen occupation and unsure about any future plans. In 1941, the literary editor of *Nation* asked the well-respected educator and literary critic Lionel Trilling to suggest someone to fill a book reviewer position that was open at the magazine. After some discussion, Trilling recommended his wife, Diana, and in 1942 Diana Trilling began her career as a literary and social critic by writing very short, unsigned book reviews. Within one year, she was composing full-length literary criticism for the magazine as its fiction critic. According to Nathan A. Scott, Jr. in *Commonweal,* Trilling soon earned the respect of her peers "by virtue of the wit and intelligence and courtesy with which she scrutinized and evaluated the current fiction that came across her desk week after week."

A selection of reviews Trilling wrote during her years as fiction critic was published in 1978 under the title *Reviewing the Forties.* Of this collection, a reviewer for *Publishers Weekly* remarks: "Reading her reviews is a stimulating experience. Even when the books are now forgotten, her pungent comments are still provocative. And her literary judgments are always clear-cut and candid." Writing in *Nation,* Emile Capouya offers this opinion of Trilling's reviews: "What appears to be characteristic and characterological is her delight in the real thing, which, when she comes upon it in a writer, lifts her own writing to an intensity of praise which is ravishing in its music, its clarity and its subtle discriminations. . . . At such moments she is herself wonderfully moving and infects the reader with a sympathy that seems less an emotion than a form of knowledge. That is a great gift. It transforms good literary journalism into art."

Scott points out that many of the reviews included in *Reviewing the Forties* are brief critiques, "hardly more than a page," and "thus she had no chance for the spacious, leisurely estimate. Yet it was just her way of reckoning with this restriction that revealed her talent for the swift, central judgement of the essential drift of a career or of a particular book. And it is a brilliance of this kind which is most noticeable, as one moves through the ninety-some pieces that are here assembled." In his introduction to *Reviewing the Forties,* Paul Fussell states that in her literary criticism Trilling writes as if she "is not satisfied to leave literature sitting there uninterpreted in its fullest psychological, social, and political meaning, for she perceived that 'literature is no mere decoration of life but an index of the health or sickness of society.'" And Michiko Kakutani explains in the *Chicago Tri-*

bune that "in all her work, Diana Trilling has been interested in the relationship among esthetics, morality, and society."

"To the extent that America has an intellectual conscience," Elizabeth Janeway writes in the *Los Angeles Times Book Review,* "Diana Trilling is part of it, a literary critic who knows that literature can't be understood apart from its context in social, cultural, and political life. She has been disagreed with, but no one has ever thought her opinions shabby, easily come by or uninteresting." And in his *New York Times Book Review* critique of Trilling's first book, *Claremont Essays,* Frank Kermode labels Trilling as "Arnoldian" and places her in the group of "intellectuals who labor to understand the current of ideas, and to examine not only the art but also the main public issues of their times."

Trilling has long been recognized as a liberal, a rationalist and a moralist with strong beliefs and convictions. Political at an early age, Trilling helped a black student government candidate organize a third party to challenge the existing two-party system while a student at Brooklyn's Erasmus Hall High School. Years later, in a 1968 letter to the editor of *Commentary* magazine, American poet Robert Lowell questioned (many readers felt somewhat unfairly) Trilling's real contribution to liberalism: "On the great day, when she meets her Maker, John Stuart Mill on his right hand and Diderot on his left, they will say, 'Liberalism gave you a standard; what have you done for liberalism?'" To this query Trilling answered: "Well, rationalist that I am, this particular confrontation has not been much of a concern to me. [Nevertheless,] to Mill I shall say that I did my best to see the truth, and to Diderot I shall say that I did my best to look beneath the appearance of things, especially the things which announce themselves as virtues. And surely it is not impossible that I'll get by."

In 1971 Trilling returned to Radcliffe College, her alma mater, to interview some of its current students and to see, in her words, "what similarities and differences I might find between the present-day undergraduate and my own college generation." Trilling and her husband, Lionel, spent nearly nine weeks on the campus, living in the same dormitory that she lived in during her senior year at Radcliffe. This experience resulted in Trilling's book of essays *We Must March My Darlings.*

One difference she discovered during these interviews, as she reported to *Harper's* in 1977, was that "I and my college contemporaries wanted to 'do' something or at most to 'be' something, by which we meant that we wanted to find an activity, no matter what, which justified our feeling of having moved beyond the women who hadn't our educational advantage. Now apparently a Radcliffe graduate is enough satisfied that she *is* something to wish to turn her energies to influencing and changing the lives of others."

"Trilling's essays are an incisive commentary on the cultural and political upheavals of the last decade," states a reviewer for *Publishers Weekly.* "She fears that we are losing our commitment to the liberal ideal of human interdependence." *New York Times* reviewer John Leonard remarks that "in a way, *We Must March My Darlings* is written in the spirit of the superego—stern, unforgiving, shape up, get a grip on yourself, defer those gratifications, tote that bale. I find this bracing because I'm tired of being told that we're all wonderful and innocent or would be if we took a course or a pill."

We Must March My Darlings stirred up a controversy in the literary world before it was published. Consistent with the book's main theme of examining past and present social issues and concerns, Trilling composed a section entitled "Liberal Anti-Communism Revisited." Michiko Kakutani explains in the *Chicago Tribune* that Trilling "raised questions about *Scoundrel Time,* Lillian Hellman's account of the McCarthy years, and re-examined the rift that has existed for decades between intellectuals who remained vaguely sympathetic with communism and those who broke openly with the party." Little, Brown & Co. originally wanted to publish Trilling's work but refused to do so unless the references to Hellman were deleted. (Little, Brown considered Hellman one of its more popular authors and was also the publisher of *Scoundrel Time.*) Trilling refused to change the paragraphs in question, so the publisher decided to void the contract. Trilling then took the manuscript to Harcourt Brace Jovanovich Inc., which published it in 1977.

A writer for *Newsweek* remarks that "when one of the passages was made public, it seemed so esoteric and ideological that it was hard to imagine anyone being upset. Indeed, the big surprise was that there was a brouhaha at all. Trilling had said that disagreements originating at an anti-Communist symposium in 1967 still divided the intellectual community, but with 'always diminishing intellectual force.' She used Hellman's . . . best seller, *Scoundrel Time,* as an example of the division." And in *Esquire* Alfred Kazin writes, "the imbroglio is funny enough in its way," and comments that after examining *We Must March My Darlings* he found "no hysterical personal attack on Lillian Hellman. There is a stiffly courteous, reasoned and documented critique of Hellman's longstanding inability to understand the nature of Soviet society."

Although author of numerous volumes of literary and social criticism, Trilling has achieved her greatest recognition with her portrayal of Jean Harris, the former girls' school headmistress convicted of murdering the famous diet doctor, Herman Tarnower. "What makes *Mrs. Harris: The Death of the Scarsdale Diet Doctor* different from Trilling's previous work is its promise to reach a popular audience and become a financial success," states Michiko Kakutani in the *New York Times.* Bruce Cook explains in *Saturday Review:* "Although her work has appeared over a period of four decades, Diana Trilling is hardly a writer with a large public. To a certain readership, so loyal and intense one is almost tempted to call it a constituency, she is very well known indeed. These readers are the survivors and enthusiasts of the late great literary wars of New York."

According to a reporter for the *New York Times,* Trilling decided to write about the Harris case just two days after the slaying. "Six months later, before the trial, I had completed a first draft, and thought I had only to add a summary of the trial and the verdict," Trilling told the reporter. "I couldn't have been more wrong. Things were not as cut and dried as they seemed, and I wound up tossing the whole thing out and starting over again."

Questioned many times during the trial as to her motivation for writing this book, Trilling remarked to Anthony Holden of the *Times Literary Supplement:* "I'd been asked, not too unkindly, whether it wasn't ghoulish, an exploitation, to make a book out of so terrible a personal tragedy." She explains by expressing her fascination with "the kind of world that Dr. Tarnower and Mrs. Harris inhabited together and what happened between them for their relationship to ensue in such tragedy." Referring to this statement by Trilling, Elizabeth Janeway writes in the *Los Angeles Times Book Review:* "In the past, such moral dilemmas were the material for serious fiction; not now. But their significance remains; it deserves study—and reporting. A little uneasy about

the moral position of an investigative reporter, Trilling still feels the job necessary and valuable. I agree."

Kakutani suggests that Trilling's book concerning the Harris/Tarnower relationship is somewhat similar to the books she herself reviewed early in her career. "In fact," Kakutani writes in the *New York Times,* "for Mrs. Trilling the story of Harris is a kind of literary text, containing 'love and sexual passion, honor, money, envy, jealousy, greed, death, greatness and meanness of spirit, the anguishing anatomy of class differences'—all the themes that were once the province of the nineteenth-century novel." Josephine Henden comments in *New Republic* that *Mrs. Harris* is "a riveting narrative, progressing by a sifting of fact and emotion toward the judgment of one woman by another. . . . *Mrs. Harris* is the work of a seasoned writer with large resources of knowledge and intelligence."

And in a review of this book published in *Nation,* Elizabeth Pochoda writes that *Mrs. Harris* demonstrates that Trilling "is a good reporter—vivid and witty, with a gift for extracting narrative flow from the pokiest trial in recent history."

Writing in *Library Journal,* G. A. Preston remarks that while "the trial coverage is good, . . . what is most interesting is Trilling's analysis of the cultural and psychological motivations of its principals." And a reviewer for the *Washington Post* believes that Trilling "is best when she is employing her powers of observation and commentary. Especially when she is writing about money and/or class, she is perceptive and interesting. Her comments on the social situation of the Jews of Westchester County are thoughtful; her description of the students and parents of Madeira is clinical and unsparing. Her most useful remarks about Jean Harris have to do with that woman's position 'on the outside looking in'—a person employed by the wealthy in order to oversee the education of their daughters, but not allowed full admission into their world." Bette Howland points out in the *Chicago Tribune Book World* that "Trilling is good on Harris' character. She catches the aggression 'masquerading as moral superiority'; the moments when Harris reveals her feeling toward others: anger; and toward herself: pity."

Extremely prolific in recent years, Trilling, in addition to writing about Jean Harris, has taken on the editing duties of several collections of her late husband's work. As she told John Firth of the *Saturday Review,* "There's such an enormous amount to do after Lionel's death—putting his papers in order, looking at the unpublished material." In a review of *Speaking of Literature and Society,* Robert Alter writes in the *New York Times Book Review* that "the appearance of this selection of previously uncollected critical writings . . . is a rare homage to pay to a recent American writer, especially to a literary critic, and it obviously reflects a confidence that [Lionel] Trilling now deserves a place both on the library shelves and in the minds of the literate public as a major American author. . . . Mrs. Trilling's selection of these miscellaneous publications, most of them reviews, is both generous and intelligent."

In a summation of Trilling and her writings, Thomas R. Edwards states in the *New York Times Book Review:* "Trilling brings to the peculiar confusions of our time a moral and intellectual disposition that is strong and clear. Like what she says or not, one always knows who and where she is, what standards of judgement she applies to the case at hand."

MEDIA ADAPTATIONS: The movie rights to *Mrs. Harris: The Death of the Scarsdale Diet Doctor* have been sold.

BIOGRAPHICAL/CRITICAL SOURCES:

BOOKS

Diana Trilling, *We Must March My Darlings,* Harcourt, 1977.
Diana Trilling, *Reviewing the Forties,* Harcourt, 1978.

PERIODICALS

Chicago Tribune, November 29, 1981.
Chicago Tribune Book World, November 1, 1981, November 14, 1982.
Christian Science Monitor, August 5, 1977.
Commentary, July, 1977, January, 1979, March, 1979.
Commonweal, September 28, 1979.
Detroit News, November 24, 1981.
Esquire, August, 1977.
Harper's, April, 1977.
Library Journal, November 15, 1981.
Los Angeles Times Book Review, November 1, 1981.
Nation, October 21, 1978, November 21, 1981.
New Republic, October 28, 1978, November 4, 1981.
New York, October 26, 1981.
New York Times, May 19, 1977, October 10, 1981, October 13, 1981, November 16, 1981.
New York Times Book Review, May 28, 1977, May 29, 1977, May 14, 1978, June 3, 1979, May 25, 1980, October 12, 1980, October 25, 1981, November 14, 1982.
Newsweek, October 11, 1976, October 19, 1981.
Publishers Weekly, April 25, 1977, July 31, 1978, July 30, 1979, August 13, 1982.
Saturday Review, May 28, 1977, November, 1981.
Time, June 13, 1977, October 19, 1981, January 4, 1982.
Times Literary Supplement, May 14, 1982.
Washington Post Book World, October 25, 1981.

*   *   *

TRILLING, Lionel   1905-1975

PERSONAL: Born July 4, 1905, in New York, N.Y.; died November 5, 1975; son of David W. (a businessman) and Fannie (Cohen) Trilling; married Diana Rubin (a writer and critic), June 12, 1929; children: James Lionel. *Education:* Columbia University, B.A., 1925, M.A., 1926, Ph.D., 1938.

ADDRESSES: Home—35 Claremont Ave., New York, N.Y. 10027. *Office*—Hamilton Hall, Columbia University, New York, N.Y. 10027.

CAREER: Literary and social critic, educator, editor, essayist, and author. University of Wisconsin, Madison (now University of Wisconsin—Madison), instructor in English, 1926-27; Hunter College (now Hunter College of the City University of New York), New York City, instructor in English, 1927-30; Columbia University, New York City instructor, 1931-39, assistant professor, 1939-45, associate professor, 1945-48, professor of English, 1948-65, George Edward Woodberry Professor of Literature and Criticism, 1965-70, university professor, 1970-74, professor emeritus and special lecturer, 1974-75. George Eastman Visiting Professor, Oxford University, 1964-65; Charles Eliot Norton Professor of Poetry, Harvard University, 1969-70. Visiting fellow, All Souls College, Oxford University, 1972-73. Organizer with John Crowe Ransom and F. O. Mattheissen and senior fellow, Kenyon School of Letters, Kenyon College.

MEMBER: American Academy of Arts and Sciences, National Institute of Arts and Letters, Phi Beta Kappa, Athenaeum Club (London), Century Club (New York).

AWARDS, HONORS: D.Litt. from Trinity College (Hartford, Conn.), 1955, Harvard University, 1962, Case Western Reserve University, 1968, University of Durham, 1973, and University of Leicester, 1973; L.H.D. from Northwestern University, 1964, Brandeis University, 1974, and Yale University, 1974; Mark Van Doren Award from the student body of Columbia College, 1966; Brandeis University Creative Arts Award, 1967-68; Thomas Jefferson Award from National Endowment for the Humanities, 1972.

WRITINGS:

Matthew Arnold, Norton, 1939, 2nd edition, Columbia University Press, 1949, reprinted, Harcourt, 1979.
E. M. Forster, New Directions, 1943, revised edition, 1965, reprinted, Harcourt, 1980 (published in England as *E. M. Forster: A Study,* Hogarth, 1944).
The Middle of the Journey (novel), Viking, 1947, reprinted with new introduction by Trilling, Scribner, 1975.
The Liberal Imagination: Essays on Literature and Society, Viking, 1950, reprinted, Harcourt, 1979.
(Author of introduction) Leo Tolstoy, *Anna Karenina,* Cambridge University Press, 1951.
The Opposing Self: Nine Essays in Criticism, Viking, 1955, reprinted, Harcourt, 1979.
Freud and the Crisis of Our Culture, Beacon Press, 1955.
A Gathering of Fugitives (essays), Beacon Press, 1956, reprinted, Harcourt, 1978.
(Author of introduction) Isaak Babel, *The Collected Stories,* Criterion, 1957.
(Author of introduction) Saul Bellow, *The Adventures of Augie March,* Modern Library, 1965.
Beyond Culture: Essays on Literature and Learning, Viking, 1965, reprinted, Harcourt, 1980.
Sincerity and Authenticity (lectures), Harvard University Press, 1972.
Mind in the Modern World (Thomas Jefferson Lectures in the Humanities), Viking, 1973.
The Last Decade: Essays and Reviews, 1965-1975, edited by Diana Trilling, Harcourt, 1979.
Prefaces to the Experience of Literature, edited by D. Trilling, Harcourt, 1979.
Of This Time, Of That Place, and Other Stories, edited by D. Trilling, Harcourt, 1979.
Speaking of Literature and Society, edited by D. Trilling, Harcourt, 1980.

EDITOR

(And author of introduction) Mark Twain, *Adventures of Huckleberry Finn,* Holt, 1948.
(And author of introduction) *The Portable Matthew Arnold,* Viking, 1949, reprinted, Penguin, 1980 (published in England as *The Essential Matthew Arnold,* Chatto & Windus, 1969).
(And author of introduction) John Keats, *Selected Letters of John Keats,* Farrar, Straus, 1951.
(And author of introduction) John O'Hara, *Selected Short Stories of John O'Hara,* Modern Library, 1956.
(And author of introduction) Jane Austen, *Emma,* Houghton, 1957.
(With Steven Marcus) Ernest Jones, *The Life and Work of Sigmund Freud,* Basic Books, 1961.
(With Charles Kaplan and author of critical commentary) *The Experience of Literature: A Reader with Commentaries,* Holt, 1967, revised edition, 1969.
(And author of introduction) *Literary Criticism: An Introductory Reader,* Holt, 1970.

(Co-editor) *The Oxford Anthology of English Literature,* Oxford University Press, 1972.

(With Harold Bloom) *Victorian Prose and Poetry,* Oxford University Press, 1973.

CONTRIBUTOR

Malcolm Cowley, editor, *After the Genteel Tradition: American Writers, 1910-1930,* Norton, 1937, revised edition, Southern Illinois University Press, 1964.

Morton Dauwen Zabel, editor, *Literary Opinion in America,* Harper, 1937, 3rd revised edition, 1962.

Margaret Denny and William H. Gilman, editors, *The American Writer and the European Tradition,* University of Minnesota Press, 1950.

Chandler Brossard, editor, *The Scene Before You: A New Approach to American Culture,* Rinehart, 1955.

Irving Howe, editor, *Modern Literary Criticism,* Beacon Press, 1958.

Harold Beaver, editor, *American Critical Essays: Twentieth Century,* Oxford University Press, 1959.

Meyer Howard Abrams, editor, *English Romantic Poets: Modern Essays in Criticism,* Oxford University Press, 1960.

Sylvan Barnet, Morton Berman, and William Burto, editors, *The Study of Literature: A Handbook of Critical Essays and Terms,* Little, Brown, 1960.

Alfred Kazin, editor, *The Open Form: Essays for Our Time,* Harcourt, 1961.

Frederick J. Hoffman, editor, *The Great Gatsby: A Study,* Scribner, 1962.

Northrup Frye, editor, *Romanticism Reconsidered: Selected Papers from the English Institute,* Columbia University Press, 1963.

Carroll Camden, editor, *Literary Views: Critical and Historical Essays,* University of Chicago Press, 1964.

Norman Podhoretz, editor, *The Commentary Reader: Two Decades of Articles and Stories,* Atheneum, 1966.

Work represented in many anthologies, including *The Stature of Theodore Dreiser: A Critical Survey of His Life and His Work,* edited by Alfred Kazin and Charles Shapiro, Indiana University Press, 1955, *Literature in America,* edited by Philip Rahv, Meridian Books, 1957, *The Art of the Essay,* edited by Leslie Fiedler, Crowell, 1958, 2nd edition, 1969, *Hemingway and His Critics: An International Anthology,* edited by Carlos Baker, Hill & Wang, 1961, and *Modern British Fiction: Essays in Criticism,* edited by Mark Schorer, Oxford University Press, 1961. Contributor to *Menorah Journal, Partisan Review, New York Evening Post, Nation, New Republic, New York Times Book Review, New Yorker, Commentary, Poetry,* and numerous other periodicals. Member of editorial board of *Partisan Review* and *Kenyon Review.*

SIDELIGHTS: "In the hands of Lionel Trilling, criticism became not merely a consideration of a work of literature but also of the ideas it embodied and what these ideas said of the society that gave them birth," Thomas Lask stated in the *New York Times.* "Criticism was a moral function, a search for those qualities by which every age in its turn measured the virtuous man and the virtuous society."

Generally considered to be a major force in the world of literary criticism, Trilling was also a well-respected educator (his students included Allen Ginsberg, John Hollander, and Norman Podhoretz) and author of a novel and several short stories. He was once described by Steven Marcus in the *New York Times Book Review* as being the rather unlikely combination of "an American academic who was also a genuine intellectual in the non-academic sense [and] a professor of English who could really think, whose writing—elegant and elaborate as it often was—moved to the movement of ideas. And these ideas, one felt, were important."

"For perhaps a decade and a half, Trilling was a kind of cultural hero to a limited number of young men and women in America," Bruce Cook remarked in the *Detroit News.* "And for them, Lionel Trilling provided not just a model but an inspiration as well. No other critic seemed as brilliant, as much in command of the whole vast range of Western culture as he did. To read an essay by Trilling was not just to learn something, but also to find out what there remained yet to learn. He had a remarkable way of opening the mind to the whole vast range of English and continental intellectual influences that have shaped Western thought in the 20th century." And Lewis Leaty pointed out in *Sewanee Review* that "the death of Lionel Trilling brings an inevitable pause to literary discourse. For twenty-five years his voice has been compellingly persuasive, inviting people of liberal imagination to join with him in explorations of the life of the mind. It can be said of him what he once said of Edmund Wilson, that 'he seemed to represent the life of letters in an especially cogent way, by reason of the orderliness of his mind and the bold lucidity of his prose.' "

With the publication of *Matthew Arnold,* Trilling's criticism was almost immediately recognized for its unique contribution to the literary world. Because of his incomparable method of examining his subjects, Trilling revealed to his readers fresh insights into the work of the nineteenth-century English poet and critic. He not only studied Arnold's writing but also examined his thoughts as they related to his role in society. As Trilling explained in the preface: "I have undertaken in this book to show the thought of Matthew Arnold in its complex unity and to relate it to the historical and intellectual events of his time. . . . However, because I have treated Arnold's ideas in their development, this study may be thought of as a biography of Arnold's mind." James Orrick commented in the *Saturday Review of Literature* that "the importance of the book is that it is a comprehensive study of the whole man. For Matthew Arnold was not primarily a literary critic; the clue to his enigma is that he was really a social critic. . . . With learning, penetration, and common sense Mr. Trilling analyzes Arnold's career from lyric poetry, through literary and political criticism, to the religious writings which his contemporaries found so baffling." H. F. Lowry remarked in the *New York Times:* "Because he is concerned with Arnold's organic unity and not merely with a catalogue of his manoeuvres, Mr. Trilling has given us a valuable book. With intelligence and artistry and a sincerity that ennobles every chapter, he well advances his appointed task. . . . The most interesting part of the book is its psychological criticism, its account of the organic unity behind Arnold's multifold activity." And Edward Sackville-West wrote of *Matthew Arnold* in *Spectator:* "[This is] a book of which it would, I think, be hard to overestimate the value. I personally have no hesitation in acclaiming it as the most brilliant piece of biographical criticism issued in English during the last ten years."

A number of critics have written at length of the similarities between Trilling and Matthew Arnold. John Henry Raleigh compared the two in his book *Matthew Arnold and American Culture* and pointed out that some readers believed Arnold was an unconscious model for Trilling. Raleigh explained that Trilling's "particular blend of literary sensibility, learning, historical orientation and a civilized, urbane and ironical prose style is all too rare, and getting rarer. What he has tried to do in his career as a whole, as I understand it, is to perform in twentieth-century

America the two roles that Matthew Arnold performed in nineteenth-century England: the conservor of what was valuable from the past and the proponent of the free play of the critical intelligence on the present." And John Wain comments in *Spectator* that in his criticism Trilling's "tone is not conversational or intimate, but rather Arnoldian, without sharing Arnold's tendency to nag or preach. And, far more than Arnold, he had the true critic's gift of describing exactly the thing he is talking about. His criticism is not technical, nor aesthetic, but moral. What makes a great book great, for him, is the spiritual and moral health it embodies."

Edward Joseph Shoben also commented on the influence of Arnold on Trilling. Shoben wrote in his book *Lionel Trilling:* "What Trilling brought to his encounter with Arnold and what, as a result of it, established Arnold as his lifelong mentor go far toward accounting for one of the major themes in his work. If Arnold's conception of criticism provided the bases for Trilling's own ideas of the proper task of the critic, and if Arnold's frequent preoccupation with extraliterary issues and problems legitimized Trilling's primary focus on moral and cultural matters, Arnold's most crucial legacy to Trilling was an approach to the question of how society changes and of how it *ought* to change." As a result of this focus, Malcolm Bradbury suggested in *New Statesman,* "a key part of Trilling's [literary] effort was to recreate the public, political meaning of the novel form, the form, he said in 'Art and Fortune,' 'that provides the perfect criticism of ideas by attaching them to their appropriate actuality.' It was also an effort to reach into the roots of the modern mind, as it evolved through romanticism into modernism."

Several notable reviewers have proposed that Trilling wrote with a desire to view literature as an integral element of cultural society. Trilling strived to maintain a philosophical framework which was at the same time the core and purpose of his literary criticism. Irving Howe explained in *New Republic* Trilling's purpose in writing: "Trilling, while often performing superbly as an interpreter of texts, was not read primarily for literary guidance. His influence has to do with that shaded area between literature and social opinion, literature and morality; he kept returning to 'our' cultural values, 'our' premises of conduct for he was intent upon a subtle campaign to transform the dominant liberalism of the American cultivated classes into something richer, more quizzical and troubled than it had become during the years after World War II. One way of saying this may be that he sought to melt ideological posture into personal sensibility." And Denis Donoghue stated in the *New York Times Book Review* that he felt Trilling's "constant preoccupation was the question of literature and society. He thought literature important because it examined, under conditions of formal lucidity, the tension between self and society. Society was Trilling's cardinal term. His criticism fostered the social sentiment as the best form in which people at large can be presented to one another. As he used the word, it meant the attitudes and aspirations we hold in common, so far as they may be embodied in the convention, rituals and institutions we meet in daily life." In short, explained Jacques Barzun in *Encounter,* in Trilling's work "the maxim that literature is a criticism of life is given its continuation and counterpart: life is and ought to be a criticism of literature."

His views on the battle between society and the individual led many of Trilling's evaluators to describe him as a moralist. "To lead 'the moral life,' in his view," James Atlas explained in the *New York Times,* "was to challenge those assumptions implicit in our culture's values not for any revolutionary purpose, but in order to salvage what was valuable in them and to establish their 'authenticity'—another charged word in Trilling's vocabulary—

through criticism. Whether the subject was Hawthorne or Jane Austen, Freud or a college English curriculum, Trilling sought to challenge from within the liberal orthodoxies that had come to be so influential in his time: that society was capable of regulating itself, that human nature could be altered and that people were essentially good."

Trilling's philosophy of looking at each person as an individual separate from society carried over to his method of reviewing literature. He ignored the established rules of criticism and chose to regard each piece of writing apart from its larger context or place in literature as a whole. A writer for *Time* explained that in *Beyond Culture,* Trilling argued that "the primary function of art and thought is to liberate the individual from the tyranny of his culture in the environmental sense and to permit him to stand beyond it in an autonomy of perception and judgment." As G. F. Whicher noted in the *New York Herald Tribune,* this approach manifested itself in Trilling's reluctance "to commit himself to any single critical attitude. He cherished a freedom to experiment, to use a combination of methods and a diversity of standards as tools at his disposal."

Trilling's contemporaries were generally impressed with this distinctive method of viewing the subjects or issues in his works of literary and social criticism. "Each of Trilling's books represents a determination to redeem and enforce the values consecrated in such words as reason, mind, sincerity, pleasure, society, self, and criticism," remarked Denis Donoghue in *Sewanee Review.* "Witness the attempt to speak up for mind in *Beyond Culture,* self in *The Opposing Self,* idea in *The Liberal Imagination,* virtue in *The Middle of the Journey.* A classic occasion was Trilling's defense of reason, maintained in *Sincerity and Authenticity.*"

A number of critics agreed that it was just this defense of a particular way of thinking that was revealed in Trilling's second published critical study. Whicher stated in a review of *E. M. Forster* published in the *New York Herald Tribune Weekly Book Review* that "this mature and vibrant book is more important than its status in a series of critical studies might seem to imply. It is far from being a merely perfunctory contribution: it is a manifesto. . . . Those who are reluctant to accept the sad spiritual fascism of T. S. Eliot as the characteristic voice of our epoch will do well to ponder Mr. Trilling's pages. They will find there a notable study of a culture in disintegration, along with exciting premonitions of a new faith about to rise from the ashes of the old." And Clifton Fadiman explained in the *New Yorker* that *E. M. Forster* "is a model of the kind of criticism not too easily discoverable among us today—restrained, balanced, unashamed of its roots in a long intellectual tradition, academic in the finest sense. It is an admirable introduction to and summation of a novelist whose work, still largely unappreciated in America, quietly refuses to die."

However, George Mayberry wrote in the *New Republic:* "On the whole I think that Professor Trilling has taken Forster too seriously. I say this with the instruction and delight that Forster so frequently offers fully in mind, but it must be said of the writer who justifies the claim of England's most important living novelist, or we put too high a value upon him and upon the modern English novel."

E. M. Forster was followed five years later by Trilling's first and only novel, *The Middle of the Journey.* As is true of Trilling's other books, *The Middle of the Journey* requires the reader to look within himself for the answers to the questions subtly proposed by Trilling. As Lloyd Morris observed in the *New York Herald Tribune Weekly Book Review:* "*The Middle of the Journey* is both moving and intellectually provocative, but readers, like this reviewer, may find that its strongest effects lie in what is implied and suggested rather than in what is directly represented. It is a book so sensitively written, so deliberately loaded with implications of a larger significance than that actually expressed that its excellences may in part be revealed only by means of what readers bring to it."

"This mature and intelligent novel will be welcomed by those readers of the best contemporary American fiction who are growing weary of historical tales, group narratives in the Grand Hotel pattern, and the wistful, nostalgic family sagas of a lost generation," stated R. A. Cordell in *Saturday Review of Literature.* "*The Middle of the Journey* is a novel of ideas, objective, subtle, teasing in a sort of incompleteness as though the fastidious novelist would avoid the banality of telling too much. There are paragraphs that require rereading before they yield full meaning, not because they are vague or ambiguous, for the writing is of such a consistent excellence that one is tempted to fall back on some such cliche as 'classic style' to describe it, but because the thought is subtle."

Although Mark Shechner wrote in *Salmagundi* that to his mind *The Middle of the Journey* "is more a document than a realized piece of fiction," he concluded that "its values lie in its grasp of an historical moment and of a generation's disillusionment and conversion, out of which came not only a revised and subdued politics but a reconstituted aesthetics as well." Finally Morton Dauwen Zabel stated in *Nation* that Trilling's novel is "a brilliant example of a new mode of fiction, one whose function in the moral dilemmas of our age his acute critical sense has seen, and whose claims on the imaginative resources of his generation the finely controlled, humanly faithful art of this novel demonstrates. It is a book that brings the best critical intelligence now discernible in America into play with an absolutely honest creative talent."

In 1950 Trilling's first collection of critical essays was published. A number of critics agreed with E. J. Shoben's statement in his book *Lionel Trilling* that *The Liberal Imagination: Essays on Literature and Society* brought Trilling "immediate and widespread recognition. Established as a literary critic of the first rank and of distinctive range in the kinds of topics to which he addressed himself, and in the nature of his insights into human condition, he found his career assured. For the next twenty-five years with grace and an unassuming confidence, he walked the critic's path of his own choosing, a deeply respected and frequently honored figure in the intellectual world." Steven Marcus agreed that it was after the publication of this book that "Trilling began to acquire the wide recognition he would subsequently enjoy." Marcus went on to remark in the *New York Times* that "*The Liberal Imagination* was much more than a book of essays with an intermittently overt political interest. To those of us who read it at the time, it was unmistakable that a major figure in modern literary criticism had put in his appearance. Trilling at once took his place beside F. R. Leavis and Edmund Wilson as one of the three or four dominating and decisive presences in 20th century critical discourse—that discourse in which literature, culture, history, ideas and values freely and richly mingle."

In his review of *The Liberal Imagination,* Philip Toynbee noted in the *New York Times* that "this is a brilliant, apposite and eloquent book." And Milton Wilson remarked in *Canadian Forum* that "Lionel Trilling is a critic who has a great deal to say, and he can write. Unlike most critics, he perpetually stimulates the reader to revise or reorganize his own values, he shows us (to use his own terms) the work of art functioning as subject as well as

object, with an existence of its own beyond our partial comprehensions."

The Opposing Self: Nine Essays in Criticism was released five years after *The Liberal Imagination.* "Only Trilling, in *The Opposing Self,* could have caught so eloquently the modern self's 'intense and adverse imagination of the culture in which it has its being,' an imagination 'characterized by certain powers of indignant perception,'" stated Anatole Broyard in the *New York Times.* A critic for *Kirkus Reviews* commented that "this is as distinguished and richly rewarding a book of criticism as has appeared in America in many years." However, David Daiches commented in the *Manchester Guardian* that "Mr. Trilling has led us to expect so much more from him than from other critics that we are disappointed in not finding in this collection of essays—perceptive and illuminating though they often are—both the larger illumination and the careful assessment of the individual work."

In 1955 Trilling's *Freud and the Crisis of Our Culture* was published. Since his student days Trilling had spent much time reading and writing about the man he once described as "one of the few great Plutarchian characters of our time." In fact, many reviewers feel that Sigmund Freud was as great an influence on Trilling as Matthew Arnold had been. Shoben remarked in his critical study that "no set of ideas so consistently, so dominantly, preoccupied Lionel Trilling throughout his career as those formulated by Sigmund Freud in *Civilization and Its Discontents.* . . . In a number of ways, his familiarity with Freud increasingly shaped and gave a language to some of Trilling's most intimate experiences and lent a distinctive color to some of his central values."

"Trilling's deep absorption with Freud must have had its source in . . . the sense that Freud recognized, as almost no one else in our time has, the power of imagination to go beyond the routines of mimesis, to startle and terrify us with all that it might bring up," commented Irving Howe in *New Republic.* "Just as Freud saw the role of the analyst as that of a mediator in the battle between what we have made of ourselves and what we have made it from, so Trilling would turn toward a work of literature, attentive to its modes of order and strategies of control but also on the lookout for the unexpected. Freud was probably the single greatest influence on Trilling's work." However, Shechner wrote in *Salmagundi* that in "view of Trilling's ardent declarations of admiration and intellectual indebtedness, perhaps nothing is so remarkable about him as the discrepancy between his zeal for Freud and his use of him. While many of Trilling's essays on literature and culture over the years may be read as applied Freud, they are largely applications of his character and his outlook rather than his ideas about the constitution of the mind. Indeed, the reader who has been struck by the discrepancy might feel justified in wondering whether such lionizing of Freud was not done at the expense of psychoanalysis as such, for it is plain that the figure of the man in Trilling's thought greatly overshadowed the method."

Two additional collections of critical essays, *A Gathering of Fugitives* and *Beyond Culture: Essays on Literature and Learning,* followed Trilling's book on Freud. After reading *A Gathering of Fugitives,* Leon Edel remarked in the *New Republic* that Trilling "is perhaps at his best in his literary essays. . . . There are . . . a number of evocative autobiographical passages in the essays, a conscious effort at measurement of the Trilling self." And R. G. Davis wrote in the *New York Times* that "few contemporary critics demonstrate so consistently as Lionel Trilling the art of right thinking."

In 1972 the text from six lectures Trilling gave at Harvard University was published under the title *Sincerity and Authenticity.* Laurence Lerner suggested in a review of this book published in *New Statesman* that "like all good critics, Trilling is both predictable and unpredictable. All his criticism bears the stamp of contemporary concern and of a gifted, individual mind." Writing in the *National Review* D. K. Mano commented that *Sincerity and Authenticity* "flashes brilliance—better than brilliance, wisdom." Anatole Broyard agreed, writing in the *New York Times* that "it would be difficult to imagine anyone else writing Trilling's *Sincerity and Authenticity,* a brilliant study of our 'moral life in process of revising itself.' "

In *Mind in the Modern World,* the last book Trilling published before his death, the general theme of the place of the "mind" in culture still was present. Trilling urged the adoption of objectivity and the separation of an individual's intellect from common functional matters. In a review of *Mind in the Modern World,* a critic for *Virginia Quarterly Review* stated that "Trilling is a great critic in the tradition of Matthew Arnold. Like Arnold, Professor Trilling instructs and persuades through the example of his style, learning, and insight. He upholds the ideals of dispassionate objectivity, order, and urbanity."

Since Trilling's death several collections of his writings (containing some previously unpublished work) have been compiled, edited, and published. Trilling's wife, the highly-respected literary and social critic Diana Trilling, has taken on the editing duties for several of these collections, including *Prefaces to the Experience of Literature, The Last Decade, Of This Time, Of That Place, and Other Stories,* and *Speaking of Literature and Society.*

"Trilling has become, since his death in 1975, a modern classic," remarked James Atlas in the *New York Times.* "Such canonization is not entirely undeserved. Few would dispute his originality as a literary critic, or his ingenious critique of our culture from a vantage achieved by his unique command of its history and literature." Broyard stated in a *New York Times* review of *The Last Decade* and *Prefaces to the Experience of Literature* that "everyone who cares about contemporary literature, or contemporary life, ought to be grateful to Trilling's publisher for reissuing his collected works. To have them on one's shelf is a secure feeling. When it sometimes seems as it must, that 'the ceremony of innocence is drowned,' we can always go to that shelf for conciliation." And Mark Shechner concludes in *Nation:* "When Lionel Trilling died in 1975 it was generally agreed that literature had lost the most influential critic of the postwar era and that, if in effect, an office of literary studies had fallen vacant. Trilling had long since become something more than just a critic; he was a *figure,* and almost that rarest of creatures, an academic celebrity. Even when he spoke for no one but himself he was looked upon as a spokesman and came, in time, to be something of a standard source."

BIOGRAPHICAL/CRITICAL SOURCES:

BOOKS

Anderson, Quentin, Stephen Donadio, and Steven Marcus, editors, *Art, Politics, and Will: Essays in Honor of Lionel Trilling,* Basic Books, 1977.
Bishop, John Peale, *Collected Essays,* edited by Edmund Wilson, Scribner, 1948.
Blackmur, R. P., *The Lion and the Honeycomb: Essays in Solicitude and Critique,* Harcourt, 1955.
Chace, W. M., editor, *Lionel Trilling: Criticism and Politics,* Stanford University Press, 1980.

Contemporary Literary Criticism, Gale, Volume 9, 1978, Volume 11, 1979, Volume 24, 1983.
Dictionary of Literary Biography, Gale, Volume 28: *Twentieth-Century American-Jewish Fiction Writers,* 1984, Volume 63: *Modern American Critics, 1920-1955,* 1988.
Eisinger, Chester E., *Fiction of the Forties,* University of Chicago Press, 1963.
Feidelson, Charles, Jr., and Paul Brodtkorb, Jr., editors, *Interpretations of American Literature,* Oxford University Press, 1959.
Fraiberg, Louis Benjamin, *Psychoanalysis and American Literary Criticism,* Wayne State University Press, 1960.
Frank, Joseph, *The Widening Gyre: Crisis and Mastery in Modern Literature,* Rutgers University Press, 1963.
Green, Martin, *Science and the Shabby Curate of Poetry,* Longmans, 1964, Norton, 1965.
Milne, Gordon, *The American Political Novel,* University of Oklahoma Press, 1966.
Raleigh, John Henry, *Matthew Arnold and American Culture,* University of California Press, 1957.
Scott, Nathan A., Jr., *Three American Moralists: Mailer,* Bellow, Trilling, University of Notre Dame Press, 1973.
Shoben, Edward Joseph, *Lionel Trilling,* Ungar, 1981.
Trilling, Lionel, *Matthew Arnold,* Norton, 1939, 2nd edition, Columbia University Press, 1949.
Trilling, *Beyond Culture: Essays on Literature and Learning,* Viking, 1965, reprinted, Harcourt, 1980.
Warfel, Harry Redcay, *American Novelists of Today,* American Book Co., 1951.
Warshow, Robert, *The Immediate Experience: Movies, Comics, Theatre and Other Aspects of Popular Culture,* Doubleday, 1962.
Zabel, Morton Dauwen, *Craft and Character: Texts, Method and Vocation in Modern Fiction,* Viking, 1957.

PERIODICALS

American Scholar, winter, 1978.
Atlantic, June, 1950.
Best Sellers, September 1, 1967.
Book World, September 24, 1964.
Canadian Forum, October 5, 1950.
Christian Science Monitor, May 20, 1939.
Commentary, April, 1968, March, 1979.
Commonweal, September 24, 1943, November 14, 1947, March 9, 1956.
Detroit News, November 25, 1977.
Encounter, August, 1966.
Library Journal, February 1, 1955.
Manchester Guardian, March 21, 1939, August 23, 1955.
Nation, March 11, 1939, August 7, 1943, October 18, 1947, March 5, 1955, August 13, 1955, October 19, 1970, September 17, 1977.
New Republic, March 22, 1939, September 6, 1943, November 19, 1956, March 13, 1976, March 13, 1979.
New Review, April, 1975.
New Statesman, March 11, 1939, August 13, 1955, April 11, 1975.
Newsweek, July 27, 1959.
New Yorker, August 14, 1943, October 12, 1947, January 21, 1956.
New York Herald Tribune, April 9, 1950, April 3, 1955.
New York Herald Tribune Weekly Book Review, September 5, 1943, October 12, 1947.
New York Review of Books, December 9, 1965.

New York Times, January 29, 1939, August 15, 1943, October 12, 1947, April 9, 1950, February 13, 1955, November 4, 1956, October 26, 1965, April 11, 1968, July 9, 1979, October 26, 1979.

New York Times Book Review, February 13, 1955, November 14, 1965, December 31, 1967, January 20, 1980, October 12, 1980.

Partisan Review, summer, 1966.

Poetry, December, 1968.

Salmagundi, spring, 1978.

Saturday Review, February 12, 1955, February 14, 1958, November 6, 1965.

Saturday Review of Literature, January 28, 1939, August 28, 1943, October 11, 1947, February 14, 1948, April 15, 1950.

Sewanee Review, spring, 1976, spring, 1978.

Spectator, April 28, 1939, July 29, 1955.

Studies in Short Fiction, winter, 1976.

Time, October 20, 1947.

Times Literary Supplement, March 11, 1939, August 26, 1955, August 21, 1981.

OBITUARIES:

PERIODICALS

AB Bookman's Weekly, December 8, 1975.

New Statesman, November 14, 1975.

New York Times, November 7, 1975.

New York Times Book Review, February 8, 1976.

Newsweek, November 17, 1975.

Publishers Weekly, November 17, 1975.

Time, November 17, 1975.

Washington Post, November 7, 1975.

*   *   *

TRIMBALL, W. H.
See MENCKEN, H(enry) L(ouis)

*   *   *

TRISTRAM
See HOUSMAN, A(lfred) E(dward)

*   *   *

TROYAT, Henri 1911-
(Lev Tarassoff)

PERSONAL: Born November 1, 1911, in Moscow, Russia; left Russia with family during 1917 Revolution, settling in Paris three years later; son of Aslan (a merchant) and Lydie (Abessolomoff) Tarassoff; name legally changed to Henri Troyat; married Marguerite Saintagne, September 23, 1948; stepchildren: Jean-Daniel, Michele (Mrs. J. Donoghue McKeown). *Education:* Lycee Pasteur, Neuilly-sur-Seine, licencie en droit. *Religion:* Orthodox.

ADDRESSES: Home—5 rue Bonaparte, Paris 6e, France. *Office*—Academie Francaise, 23 quai de Conti, Paris 6e, France.

CAREER: Editorial staff member, Prefecture de la Seine, 1935-41; novelist and writer, 1941—.

MEMBER: Academie Francaise.

AWARDS, HONORS: Prix Populiste, 1935, for *Faux Jour;* Prix Goncourt, 1938, for *L'Araigne;* Prix Louis Barthou de l'Academie Francaise, 1938, for body of work; Grand Prix Litteraire de Monaco, 1952, for *La Neige en deuil;* Commandeur, Legion d'Honneur; Notable Book citation, American Library Association, 1981, for *Catherine the Great.*

WRITINGS:

NOVELS

Faux Jour, Plon, 1935.

Le Vivier, Plon, 1935, new edition, 1967.

Grandeur Nature, Plon, 1936, translation by James Whitall published as *One Minus Two,* I. Washburn, 1938.

L'Araigne, Plon, 1938, translation by Anthea Bell published as *The Web,* A. Ellis, 1984.

Judith Madrier, Plon, 1940, translation by Whitall published under same title, I. Washburn, 1941.

Le Mort saisit le vif, Plon, 1942.

Le Signe du taureau, Plon, 1945.

Tant que la terre durera, Table Ronde, Volume 1: *Tant que la terre durera,* 1947, translation by David Hapgood published as *My Father's House,* Sloan & Pearce, 1951, Volume 2: *Le Sac et la cendre,* 1948, translation by Anthony Hinton published as *The Red and the White,* Crowell, 1956 (published in England as *Sackcloth and Ashes,* Arco, 1956), Volume 3: *Etrangers sur la terre,* 1950, translation by Hinton published as *Strangers on Earth,* Crowell, 1958.

La Tete sur les epaules, Plon, 1951.

La Neige en deuil, Flammarion, 1952, translation by Constantine Fitz Gibbon published as *The Mountain,* Simon & Schuster, 1953.

Les Semailles et les moissons, Plon, translations published as *The Seed and the Fruit,* Simon & Schuster, Volume 1: *Les Semailles et les moissons,* 1953, translation by Lily Duplaix published as *Amelie in Love,* 1956, Pocket Books, 1974, Volume 2: *Amelie,* 1955, translation by M. V. Dodge published as *Amelie and Pierre,* 1957, Pocket Books, 1974, Volume 3: *La Grive,* 1956, translation by Nicolas Monjo published as *Elizabeth,* 1959, Pocket Books, 1974, Volume 4: *Tendre et violente Elizabeth,* 1957, translation by Mildred Marmur published as *Tender and Violent Elizabeth,* 1960, Pocket Books, 1974, Volume V: *La Rencontre,* 1958, translation by Gerard Hopkins published as *The Encounter,* 1962, Pocket Books, 1974.

La Lumiere des justes, Flammarion, translations published as *The Light of the Just,* Simon & Schuster, Volume 1: *Les Compagnons du coquelicot,* 1959, translation by Elisabeth Abbott published as *The Brotherhood of the Red Poppy,* 1961, Volume 2: *La Barynia,* 1960, translation by Frances Frenaye published as *The Baroness,* 1961, Volume 3: *La Gloire des vaincus,* 1961, Volume 4: *Les Dames de Siberie,* 1962, Volume 5: *Sophie, ou lafin des combats,* 1963.

Une Extreme Amitie, Table Ronde, 1963, translation by Joyce Emerson published as *An Intimate Friendship,* Redman, 1967, translation by Eugene Paul published as *An Extreme Friendship,* Phaedra, 1968.

Les Eygletiere, Flammarion, Volume 1: *Les Eygletiere,* 1965, Volume 2: *La Faim des lionceaux,* 1966, Volume 3: *La Malandre,* 1967.

Les Heritiers de l'avenir, Flammarion, Volume 1: *Le Cahier,* 1968, Volume 2: *Cent un coups de canon,* 1969, Volume 3: *L'Elephant blanc,* 1970.

La Tete sur les epaules, Plon, 1970.

La Pierre, lafeuille et les ciseaux, Flammarion, 1972.

Anne Predaille, Flammarion, 1973.

Le Moscovite, Flammarion, Volume 1: *Le Moscovite,* 1974, Volume 2: *Le Front dans les nuages,* 1976, Volume 3: *Le Prisonnier numero 1,* 1978.

Viou, Flammarion, 1980, translation by published as *Sylvie,* A. Ellis, 1982.

Grimbosq, Flammarion, 1976.

Le Pain de l'Etranger, Flammarion, 1982, translation published as *The Children,* A. Ellis, 1983.
La Derision, Flammarion, 1983.
Marie Karpovna, Flammarion, 1984.
Le Bruit solitaire du coeur, Flammarion, 1985.
A demain, Sylvie, Flammarion, 1986, translation published as *Sylvie, Her Teen-Age Years,* A. Ellis, 1988.
Le troisieme bonheur, Flammarion, 1987.
Toute ma vie sera mensonge, Flammarion, 1988.
Sylvie-Happiness, translation by Bell, A. Ellis, 1989.
An Act of Treachery, translation by Bell, A. Ellis, 1990.

BIOGRAPHY

Dostoievsky, Fayard, 1940, translation by Norbert Guterman published as *Firebrand: The Life of Dostoevsky,* Roy, 1946.
Pouchkine, A. Michel, 1946, translation by Randolph T. Weaver published as *Pushkin,* Pantheon, 1950, translation by Nancy Amphoux published as *Pushkin,* Doubleday, 1970.
L'Etrange Destin de Lermontov, Plon, 1952.
Tolstoi, Fayard, 1965, new edition, 1967, translation by Amphoux published as *Tolstoy,* Doubleday, 1967.
Gogol, Flammarion, 1971, translation by Amphoux published as *Divided Soul: The Life of Gogol,* Doubleday, 1973.
Catherine la Grande, Flammarion, 1977, translation published as *Catherine the Great,* Dutton, 1980.
Pierre le Grand, Flammarion, 1979, translation by Joan Pinkham published as *Peter the Great,* Dutton, 1987.
Alexander Ier, Flammarion, 1980, translation published as *Alexander of Russia: Napoleon's Conqueror,* Fromm International, 1983.
Kisling, 1891-1953, J. Kisling, 1982, printed in two volumes, Abner Schram (New Jersey).
Ivan le Terrible, Flammarion, 1984, translation published as *Ivan the Terrible,* Dutton, 1984.
Tourgueniev, Flammarion, 1985, translation by Amphoux published as *Turgenev,* Dutton, 1980.
Tchekov, translation by Michael Henry Heim published as *Chekhov,* Dutton, 1986.
Gorki, Flammarion, 1986, translation by Lowell Bair published as *Gorky: A Biography,* Crown, 1989.
Flaubert, Flammarion, 1988.

SHORT FICTION

La Clef de voute [and] *Monsieur Citrine,* Plon, 1937.
La Fosse commune (contains "Les Cobayes," "La Dame noire," "Le Tandem," "Erratum," "L'Assasin," "L'Etrange Histoire de Mr. Breadborough," "Le Vertige," "Le Ratuset," and "Le Ressac"), Plon, 1937.
Le Jugement de Dieu [and] *Le Puy Saint-Clair* [and] *Le Merveilleux Voyage de Jacques Mazeyrat,* Plon, 1941, reprinted, Plon, 1976.
Du Philanthrope a la rouquine (collected stories), Flammarion, 1945.
La Maison des betes heureuses (juvenile story), Bias, 1956.
Le Geste d'Eve (collected stories), Flammarion, 1964.
Les Ailes du Diable (collected stories), Flammarion, 1966.

NONFICTION

Les Ponts de Paris, Flammarion, 1946.
La Case de l'Oncle Sam (travelogue), Table Ronde, 1948.
De Gratteciel en cocotier, a travers l'Amerique latine (travelogue), Plon, 1955.
Sainte Russie: Souvenirs et reflexions, Grasset, 1956.
La Vie quotidienne en Russie au temps du dernier Tsar, Hachette, 1959, translation by Malcolm Barnes published as *Daily*

Life in Russia under the Last Tsar, Allen & Unwin, 1961, Macmillan, 1962.
Naissance d'une Dauphine: Reportage, Gallimard, 1960.
Un si long chemin, Stock, 1976.

OTHER

Also author of plays, "Les Vivants," 1946, "Sebastien," 1949, and "Madame d'Arches a dit peut-etre," 1952.

SIDELIGHTS: Works by Henri Troyat have been translated into English, Spanish, Hebrew, and Chinese.

MEDIA ADAPTATIONS: La Neige en deuil was adapted for film as "The Mountain" by Paramount, 1956.

BIOGRAPHICAL/CRITICAL SOURCES:

BOOKS

Contemporary Literary Criticism, Volume 23, Gale, 1983.
Discours de reception a l'Academie francaise, et reponse de M. le marechal Juin, Plon, 1960.

PERIODICALS

Chicago Tribune Book World, November 9, 1980, September 2, 1984.
Christian Science Monitor, December 3, 1970.
Los Angeles Times, December 3, 1980.
Los Angeles Times Book Review, March 13, 1983, September 2, 1984, November 16, 1986, August 2, 1987, March 6, 1988.
Nation, August 20, 1971.
New York Times, November 30, 1980, October 28, 1986, November 13, 1986, August 31, 1987, June 16, 1989.
New York Times Book Review, December 28, 1980, December 28, 1986, September 13, 1987.
Observer Review, March 10, 1968.
Time, June 18, 1984, November 10, 1986.
Times (London), March 3, 1988, April 23, 1989.
Times Literary Supplement, October 14, 1983, March 2, 1984, July 6, 1984, January 11, 1985, May 8, 1987, March 11, 1988, May 20, 1988, October 13, 1989.
Tribune Books (Chicago), October 12, 1986.
Washington Post Book World, August 30, 1987.

*   *   *

TRUMAN, (Mary) Margaret 1924-

PERSONAL: Born February 17, 1924, in Independence, Mo.; daughter of Harry S. (the U. S. president) and Elizabeth Virginia (Wallace) Truman; married E. Clifton Daniel, Jr. (a newspaper editor), April 21, 1956; children: Clifton, William, Harrison, Thomas. *Education:* George Washington University, A. B., 1946. *Politics:* Democrat. *Religion:* Episcopalian.

ADDRESSES: Home—New York, N. Y. *Agent*—Scott Meredith, Scott Meredith Literary Agency, Inc., 845 Third Ave., New York, N. Y. 10022.

CAREER: Writer. Opera coloratura, touring nationwide and appearing on radio and television, 1947-54; host of radio program "Authors in the News," 1954-61; co-host, with Mike Wallace, of radio program "Weekday," 1955-56; host of television program "CBS International Hour," 1965; summer stock actress. Director of Riggs National Bank, Washington, D.C.; trustee of Harry S. Truman Institute at Georgetown University; secretary of Harry S. Truman Scholarship Fund.

AWARDS, HONORS: L.H.D., Wake Forest University, 1972; Litt.D., George Washington University, 1975; H.H.D., Rockhurst College, 1976.

WRITINGS:

(With Margaret Cousins) *Souvenir: Margaret Truman's Own Story,* McGraw, 1956.
White House Pets, McKay, 1969.
Harry S. Truman (Book-of-the-Month Club selection), Morrow, 1972.
Women of Courage, Morrow, 1976.
(Editor) *Letters from Father: The Truman Family's Personal Correspondence,* Arbor House, 1981.
Bess W. Truman, Macmillan, 1986.

MYSTERY NOVELS

Murder in the White House, (Book-of-the-Month Club alternate selection), Arbor House, 1980.
Murder on Capitol Hill, Arbor House, 1981.
Murder in the Supreme Court (Book-of-the-Month Club alternate selection), Arbor House, 1982.
Murder in the Smithsonian, Arbor House, 1983.
Murder on Embassy Row, Arbor House, 1984.
Murder at the FBI, Arbor House, 1985.
Murder in Georgetown, Arbor House, 1986.
Murder in the CIA, Random House, 1987.
Murder at the Kennedy Center, Random House, 1989.

SIDELIGHTS: When Margaret Truman published her first mystery novel in 1980, *Murder in the White House,* some observers scoffed at her. As the daughter of U.S. President Harry S. Truman, she had long been a familiar figure to the nation's news media, and had garnered a reputation as a concert singer, radio and television personality, and nonfiction writer. But her move to fiction writing was unexpected, even by her. Although she had long been a reader of mystery novels, trying her hand at writing one was accidental. Speaking to Carol Lawson of the *New York Times Book Review,* Truman explains: "I had been working on a nonfiction book—a history of White House children—but lost interest in it. I was with my agent one day . . ., and I told him I had an idea for a mystery: 'Murder in the White House.' I don't know where those words came from." Because she had unique credentials to write a mystery set in the White House, having lived there for seven years during her father's administration, her agent encouraged her to do the book. "It's a combination of the setting and my name. . . .," Lawson quotes Truman as saying about the book's appeal. "Seeing my name with this setting startles people, don't you think?"

Murder in the White House centers on the murder of Lansard Blaine, the corrupt Secretary of State, who is found strangled to death in the family quarters of the White House. Because Blaine had been a shady businessman, a powerful politican, and a womanizer, there are numerous suspects in the case. "Blaine may have been put out of business by one of these females," Chris Chase of the *Chicago Tribune* explains, "or he may have been killed by the agent of a foreign power . . ., or he may have been killed by 'someone fairly highly placed in the White House.' " The ensuing investigation of the murder exposes personal and political scandals among the First Family and their staff.

Critics were divided as to the merits of *Murder in the White House,* pointing out that Truman handled some elements of the novel better than others. William French of the Toronto *Globe and Mail* notes that "Miss Truman seems to have studied Agatha Christie on how to introduce false leads, point to the wrong suspect and generally confuse the issue. She does this with a certain amount of technical dexterity, but it's too mechanical and juiceless." Edwin J. Miller of *Best Sellers* maintains that the idea for the novel "could have made a first-rate book," but that Tru-

man's story was only an "excellent outline." Peter Andrews of the *New York Times Book Review* claims that "a bit more thought and some rudimentary editing might have turned the book into a really interesting story. . . . All the evidence indicates that Margaret Truman is capable of doing much more interesting work than this." Reactions from the reading public were far more positive. *Murder in the White House* made the bestseller lists, was optioned for a television movie, and earned Truman over $200,000 for the paperback rights alone.

After her initial success as a mystery writer Truman settled into a one-novel-a-year writing schedule, and these subsequent mysteries have proven to be popular with readers and critics alike. In each one, she draws on her intimate knowledge of Washington and its environs, setting her mysteries in such famous locations as the CIA headquarters, the Supreme Court, the Smithsonian Institution, the U.S. Congress, and the offices of the FBI. "From reading Margaret Truman," writes Dan McCoubrey in the *Washington Post,* "one would gather that the cleaning people in Washington spend much of their time washing blood from the floors of our most noted public buildings."

Charles Champlin notes in the *Los Angeles Times Book Review* that Truman also "draws on her close knowledge of government as seen from the White House" to write her novels. And, Champlin admits, "she is very good." Her characters are bureaucrats, diplomats, and the other influential men and women who are found in Washington society, and she views them with a cynical eye. Her plots are complicated and fast-moving, while the Washington milieu is painted with precision. Jean M. White of the *Washington Post Book World* reports that Truman "writes a lively Washington scene with the sure hand of one who knows her way around the streets, institutions, restaurants, watering holes, people and politics." McCoubrey concludes: "I suspect Truman's novels of Washington will continue to entertain both mystery and Washington buffs. Even now, Give-'em-Hell Harry's daughter likely is zooming in on her next historical site."

Despite the success of her mystery novels, Truman has admitted on several occasions that she does not find writing to be a pleasant activity. "Writing," she told *CA,* "is the hardest and most exacting career I've ever had." And Truman has had several careers. For many years before she began to write, Truman was a concert singer. She debuted in 1947 on a national radio program with the Detroit Symphony Orchestra and was soon touring the nation, performing a program of operatic arias and light classics. Live concerts soon led to regular appearances on radio and television, and in 1949 she signed a recording contract with RCA-Victor Records. In 1956, while hosting the radio program "Weekday" with Mike Wallace, Truman married Clifton Daniel, an editor at the *New York Times.* Except for acting in summer stock, Truman quit her performing work at this time.

She was prompted to write her first book, *Souvenir: Margaret Truman's Own Story,* only because an unauthorized biography was in the planning stages and she wanted to head it off. *Souvenir* recounts incidents from her girlhood in Missouri, her years living in the White House as the president's only child, and her successful career as a concert singer. N. L. Browning of the *Chicago Sunday Tribune* calls the book "a fascinating chronicle. . . . It projects the simple dignity, warmth, and genuine modesty of a plain, unaffected midwest girl." Ishbel Ross of the *New York Herald Tribune Book Review* finds *Souvenir* to be "a gracefully written tale of an average American girl drawn by chance into the White House."

After the success of *Souvenir* in 1956, Truman did not write another book until 1969, when her *White House Pets,* a far less ambitious work, enjoyed some popularity with readers. But in 1972 Truman completed a project she had long wanted to do, a biography of her father. Her biography, published as *Harry S. Truman*, provides a behind-the-scenes look at Harry Truman as president and family man, revealing his personal side in a way no other biography could do. In her review for the *Christian Science Monitor,* Pamela Marsh explains that in this book, the former president is "shown through the eyes of a deeply loving, loyal daughter" who "can give what no one else can, a closeup of an undramatic man dramatically thrust into awesome power—and coping with it." Vera Glaser of the *Akron Beacon Journal* calls the book "a warm memoir based on her father's personal papers and [Margaret Truman's] own recollections." While disagreeing with some of the book's partisan judgments about Truman and his administration, Wilson C. McWilliams of the *New York Times Book Review* sees value in the portrait it gives of Truman. He finds that "it is the personal, familial side of [Truman's] biography that makes it valuable. . . . Every anecdote adds human dimension to the Trumans as a family and to Harry as a man." The book has sold well over one million copies and was a selection of a major book club.

In 1986 Truman followed up her success by publishing a biography of her mother, entitled *Bess W. Truman,* a book considered by several critics to be of special interest for its intimate portrait of the president's wife. Because her mother preferred to burn her correspondence rather than let historians read it, little is known of Bess Truman's private thoughts and emotions. Her daughter's biography is one of the few personal accounts available. It is, according to Helen Thomas of the *New York Times Book Review,* "a refreshing, real and touching biography." Similarly, the critic for *Time* calls the book "a gentle, warmhearted biography." A. L. Yarnell of *Choice* calls *Bess W. Truman* "the most revealing view of the personal side of the Truman relationship now available."

Although White maintains that Truman "has proved herself to be a competent professional writer of mysteries" and both her mystery novels and biographies have been bestsellers, Truman is nonetheless still uneasy about the writing life. "I am always glad," she told *CA,* "when a book or a magazine article is finished. I promise myself never to write another one, but I shall probably do one."

MEDIA ADAPTATIONS: Film rights to *Murder in the White House* have been sold to Dick Clark Cinema Productions.

BIOGRAPHICAL/CRITICAL SOURCES:

BOOKS: Truman, Margaret, *Souvenir: Margaret Truman's Own Story,* McGraw, 1956.

PERIODICALS

Akron Beacon Journal, March 3, 1974.
Armchair Detective, spring, 1986.
Best Sellers, July, 1980.
Biography News, April, 1974.
Chicago Sunday Tribune, May 27, 1956.
Chicago Tribune, July 6, 1980.
Chicago Tribune Book World, June 21, 1981.
Choice, September, 1986.
Christian Science Monitor, January 3, 1973.
Globe and Mail (Toronto), June 26, 1980.
Los Angeles Times Book Review, November 1, 1987.
New York Herald Tribune Book Review, May 20, 1956.
New York Times, April 24, 1980, June 24, 1983.
New York Times Book Review, December 24, 1972, July 20, 1980, August 17, 1980, April 13, 1986, September 17, 1989.

People, June 16, 1980.
Time, May 19, 1986.
Washington Post, June 27, 1983.
Washington Post Book World, July 19, 1981, August 18, 1985, November 15, 1987, July 16, 1989.

* * *

TRUNDLETT, Helen B.
See ELIOT, T(homas) S(tearns)

* * *

TRYON, Thomas 1926-
(Tom Tryon)

PERSONAL: Born January 14, 1926, in Hartford, Conn.; son of Arthur Lane (a clothier) and Elizabeth (Lester) Tryon; married Anne Lilienthal, June, 1955 (divorced). *Education:* Yale University, B.A. (with honors), 1949; further study at Art Students League and Neighborhood Playhouse (New York). *Politics:* Democrat.

ADDRESSES: c/o Alfred A. Knopf, Inc., 201 East 50th Street, New York, N.Y. 10022.

CAREER: Actor under name Tom Tryon, 1952-71, writer and producer, 1971—. Set painter and assistant stage manager, Cape Playhouse, Dennis, Cape Cod, Mass., 1950. Production assistant, Columbia Broadcasting System, Inc. (CBS-TV); worked occasionally as an extra on television shows. Appeared in Broadway production of "Wish You Were Here," 1952; joined Jose Ferrer Repertory Co. at New York City Center, 1953, performed in "Cyrano de Bergerac" and "Richard III." Went to California in 1955, appeared in films "The Scarlet Hour," 1956, "Screaming Eagles," 1956, "Three Violent People," 1958, "The Unholy Wife," 1958, "I Married a Monster from Outer Space," 1958, "Texas John Slaughter" for television, 1958, "The Story of Ruth," 1960, "Marines, Let's Go!," 1961, "Moon Pilot," 1962, "The Longest Day," 1962, "Something's Got to Give," 1962, "The Cardinal," 1963, "In Harm's Way," 1965, "The Glory Guys," 1965, "Momento Mori," 1968, "Color Me Dead," 1969, and "The Narco Men," 1971. Also appeared in title role of Walt Disney's television series "Texas John Slaughter," 1958, in television movie "Winchester '73," 1967, and in popular television western series, "The Virginian," "Big Valley," and "Men from Shiloh." *Military service:* U.S. Navy, 1943-46.

AWARDS, HONORS: Prix Femina de Belgique for outstanding male performance, and Laurel Award, Motion Picture Exhibitors, both 1964, both for "The Cardinal"; Ann Radcliffe Award, Count Dracula Society, 1974.

WRITINGS:

The Other (novel; also see below), Knopf, 1971, reprinted, Fawcett, 1987.
(And executive producer) "The Other" (screenplay based upon his novel of same title), Twentieth Century-Fox, 1972.
Harvest Home (novel; Literary Guild selection; also see below), Knopf, 1973.
Lady, Knopf, 1974.
Crowned Heads (novellas; contains "Fedora" [also see below], "Lorna," "Bobbitt," and "Willie"), Knopf, 1976.
All That Glitters: Five Novellas (Literary Guild main selection), Knopf, 1986.
The Night of the Moonbow (novel), Knopf, 1988.
Opal and Cupid (juvenile), Viking, 1990.
The Wings of the Morning, Knopf, 1990.

Also author of unpublished work, "What Is the Answer, What Was the Question?." Contributor to *Ladies Home Journal* and *Reader's Digest,* 1976.

WORK IN PROGRESS: Kingdom Come, a historical novel.

SIDELIGHTS: Introduced to the theatre after initially preparing for a career in art, Thomas Tryon journeyed to Hollywood in the mid-1950s, appearing in several films before his big career break occurred in 1963 with a memorable performance in the title role of Otto Preminger's "The Cardinal." Described by Larry Swindell in the *Akron Beacon Journal* as an actor with "a reputation for intensity," Tryon remembers the entire filming of "The Cardinal" as an "anguishing" experience, however, adding to John Blades in a Chicago *Tribune Books* interview, "I got to the point where I didn't want to be in front of the camera any more. I lost my actor's nerve." Recalling how he assuaged offscreen anxieties with alcohol and cocaine, he relates in Dennis Wholey's *The Courage to Change: Personal Conversations about Alcoholism,* "If anyone ever picked the wrong profession, I did when I became an actor." Spurning a successfully established acting career in the late 1960s to pursue writing instead, Tryon achieved bestseller status as well as critical plaudits with his first literary attempt.

Tryon's chilling first novel, *The Other,* which remained on the bestseller list for seven months, concerns "the boyhood of a deranged and demonic schizophrenic," notes an *English Journal* contributor. In the *Saturday Review,* I. P. Heldman likens the work to "a Jamesian nightmare of psychological tension in a brooding atmosphere of insidious terror and madness." Calling it "one of the most compelling terror fictions written in this century," Leonard Wolf adds in *Horror: A Connoisseur's Guide to Literature and Film* that the novel is "lucid, luminous and rare, and it gives lovers of terror fiction several fine opportunities to be scared to death." Hailing Tryon for his storytelling mastery in this psychological thriller, several critics perceived in him great promise as a writer of American Gothic. Tryon remained in the genre for his second novel, *Harvest Home,* about a couple who exchange urban tribulations for rural ones when the community they adopt becomes increasingly mysterious and sinister in its practices. Yet, despite acknowledging Tryon's skills as a storyteller, some critics found the story itself implausible and the novel generally disappointing. But even though Pamela March, for instance in the *Christian Science Monitor,* remarks that the novel "reads like a parody," she deems Tryon "a practiced spellbinder." And as Stephen King remarks in the *New York Times Book Review,* "Sentence by sentence, paragraph by paragraph, it is a true book; it says exactly what Tryon wanted it to say."

In *Lady,* however, Tryon moved away from the thriller genre with a novel that explores a young boy's lifelong fascination with a woman. As he once indicated in an interview with Frank Gagnard for the New Orleans *Times-Picayune,* "I wanted to try something different without going totally out of my territory, my proven ground, so to speak. I wanted to try to make strides in another direction." Praising especially the novel's "excellent character sketches," Barton Wimble, in a *Library Journal* review, deems it Tryon's best thus far. Despite the estimation of some critics, such as Martin Levin in the *New York Times Book Review,* that the novel was somewhat overwritten, the general response to it was favorable. As Bruce Cook describes it in the *National Observer*—"evocative and elegiac, full of remembered warmth for times past."

In *Crowned Heads,* the first of what Tryon foresees as a quartet of companion pieces, he draws upon his own film experience and focuses upon the familiar world of Hollywood and its luminaries.

Comprised of four novellas in which Tryon depicts the golden days of stardom of four leading actresses. In the opinion of Webster Schott, "Tryon seems to have been born with a silver story in his mouth." Pointing out that "Tryon plays to the senses," and that the book holds something for each reader, Schott adds in the *New York Times Book Review:* "He watches manners, introduces details, covers settings with a Peeping Tom passion. His stories ripple with plots and subplots." A *Virginia Quarterly Review* contributor contends that it "may be the best 'Hollywood novel' you will find" and that "Tryon convincingly depicts what becoming a film star can do to a person." And although *Time*'s Paul Gray suggests that "weaving fiction around such a monstrously self-mythologizing place as Hollywood is like gilding a plastic lily," he calls the book a "loving reconstruction of a fading era."

In a Chicago *Tribune Books* review of Tryon's fifth work, *All That Glitters: Five Novellas,* in which the author returns to the subject of Hollywood and the entertainment industry from the perspective of five actresses whose careers have ebbed, Daniel Fuchs echoes the sentiment that Tryon is "a true fan." Calling it "a study of archetypical Hollywood figures," a *West Coast Review of Books* contributor adds that it is "a ragout of drama and showbiz extravaganza that should more than satisfy the appetites of those who dote on Tinseltown's travails. Most of it is fiction. Guess which parts aren't." Fuchs maintains, though, that "these are amusing stories, nothing to alarm, no malice in them . . . and you can read all day." And although Carolyn See describes the novel in the *Los Angeles Times* as "old news," Bruce VanWyngarden suggests in the *Washington Post* that "Tryon, a former actor, knows his subject, and he knows it for what it is—delicious cotton candy." According to Tom Nolan in the *New York Times Book Review* the novel "is like a great B-movie—irresistible, a little vulgar and once in a while surprisingly moving."

"It is very difficult for people to allow me to be a writer because they have slotted me as an actor," observed Tryon in the New Orleans *Times-Picayune* interview. In the nearly two decades since his decision to abandon acting as a profession, writing has become an obsession with Tryon, who sometimes averages ten to fourteen hour days. Despite the occasional assessment of some critics that his subsequent work fails to fulfill the extraordinary potential they found exhibited in his initial effort, Tryon continues to attract a large and loyal readership with his bestselling work, much of which has been translated into several other languages. And while critical validation of his work might gratify the author, it does not govern his pursuit of a literary career. As he summarizes in *The Courage to Change:* "There is no place for fear as a writer or as an actor. You can't be afraid. . . . I'm not afraid anymore. I'm just not afraid. I was . . . so eager to please, to make the best impression, to be liked. Now I don't care if they don't like me. I like me. I'm a nice guy. I really am."

MEDIA ADAPTATIONS: A television movie based upon Tryon's novel *Harvest Home* was produced in 1973; "Fedora," based upon one of the novellas comprising *Crowned Heads,* was filmed by Gevial Rialto/United Artists in 1978, featuring William Holden, Marthe Keller, and Jose Ferrer.

AVOCATIONAL INTERESTS: Collecting films, painting, antiques.

BIOGRAPHICAL/CRITICAL SOURCES:

BOOKS

Authors in the News, Volume 1, Gale, 1976.

Contemporary Literary Criticism, Gale, Volume 3, 1975, Volume 11, 1979.

Wholey, Dennis, *The Courage to Change: Personal Conversations about Alcoholism,* Houghton, 1984.

Wolf, Leonard, *Horror: A Connoisseur's Guide to Literature and Film,* Facts on File, 1989.

PERIODICALS

Akron Beacon Journal, July 1, 1973.
Christian Science Monitor, June 27, 1973.
English Journal, October, 1973.
Library Journal, October 15, 1974.
Life, May 14, 1971.
Los Angeles Times, November 3, 1986.
National Observer, January 18, 1975.
New York Times Book Review, July 1, 1973, July 11, 1976, October 24, 1976, November 9, 1986.
Philadelphia Inquirer, November 17, 1974.
Saturday Review, June 5, 1971.
Time, June 28, 1976.
Times-Picayune, November 23, 1974.
Tribune Books (Chicago), January 25, 1987.
Virginia Quarterly Review, Volume 53, number 1, 1977.
Washington Post, December 6, 1986.
West Coast Review of Books, April, 1986.

—*Sketch by Sharon Malinowski*

* * *

TRYON, Tom
See TRYON, Thomas

* * *

TSVETAEVA (EFRON), Marina (Ivanovna) 1892-1941

PERSONAL: Given name also transliterated as Maryna and Mariny; surname also transliterated as Tsvetayeva, Cvetaeva, Zwetajewa, Zvetaieva, Cvetajevova, Tzvetaeva, Tzvetayeva, Cwietajewa, and Tsvetaevoi; born in 1892 in Moscow, Russia (now U.S.S.R.); committed suicide, August 31, 1941, in Elabuga, Tatar Republic (now U.S.S.R.); daughter of an art history professor and a homemaker; married Sergej Efron (a soldier); children: Ariadna, another daughter (deceased), Georgij. *Education:* Attended University of Paris (Sorbonne).

CAREER: Poet, essayist, critic, translator.

WRITINGS:

Vechernii al'bom: Stikhi (poetry; title means "Evening Album"), A. N. Mamonmova, 1910.

Volshebnyi fonar': Vtoraia kniga stikhov (poetry; title means "The Magic Lantern"), Ole-Lukoie, 1912, YMCA-Press (Paris), 1979.

Iz dvukh knig (poetry; title means "From Two Books"), Ole-Lukoie, 1913.

Versty II (poetry; title means "Mileposts II"), Kostry, 1921.

Versty I (poetry; title means "Mileposts I"; includes "Poema gory"), Gosudarstevnnoe Izdatel'stvo, 1922, facsimile edition, Ardis, 1972, Prideaux Press (Letchworth, England), 1979.

Stikhi k Bloku (poetry; title means "Poems to Blok"), Ogon'ki (Berlin), 1922, Prideaux Press, 1978.

Tsar'-Devitsa (epic poem; title means "The King-Maiden"), Epokha, 1922, published as *Tsar'-Devitsa: The King Maiden,* Prideaux Press, 1971.

Razluka (poetry; title means "Parting"; includes "Na krasnom kone"), Gelikon, 1922.

Psikheia (poetry; title means "Psyche"), Z. I. Grzhebina, 1923,

Remeslo (poetry; title means "Craft"), Gelikon, 1923, reprinted with introduction and notes by Efim Etkind, W. A. Meeuws, 1981.

Molodets (poems; title means "The Swain"), Plamia, 1924, published as *Molodets: Poems,* Prideaux Press, 1971.

Posle Rossii, 1922-1925 (poetry; title means "After Russia"), Parizh, 1928, reprinted, YMCA-Press, 1976.

Proza (essays; title means "Prose"), Chekhov Publishing House, 1953, published with introduction by Valentina S. Coe as *Proza: Prose [of] Marina Tsvetaeva,* Bradda, 1969.

Izbrannoe (title means "Selected Works"), Goslitizdat, 1961.

Izbrannye proizvedeniia (title means "Selected Works"), Sovetskii Pisatel', 1965, reprinted, 'Mastatskaia Literatura, 1984.

Moi Pushkin (title means "My Pushkin"), Sovetskii Pisatel', 1967, published as *Moi Pushkin: My Pushkin,* Prideaux Press, 1977.

(Translator) *Prosto serdtse: Stikhi zarubezhnykh poetov v perevode Mariny Tsvetaevoi* (title means "Simply the Heart: Poems of Foreign Poets in Marina Tsvetaeva's Translations"), Progress, 1967.

Pis'ma k A. Teskovoi (title means "Letters to Teskova"), Academia, 1969, reprinted with introductory articles by Zdenek Mathauser and Vadim Morkovin as *Pis'ma k Anne Teskovoi,* Versty, 1982.

Stikhotvoreniia (poetry), reprint of original edition, introduction by J. Norbury, Bradda, 1969.

Nesobrannye proizvedeniia (title means "Uncollected Works"), W. Fink, 1971.

Neizdannye pis'ma (title means "Unpublished Letters"; includes April 1925 letter to Ariadna Kolbasina), edited by Gleb Struve and Nikita Struve, YMCA-Press, 1972.

Neizdannoe: Stikhi, teatr, proza (title means "Unpublished Works: Poetry, Drama, Prose"), YMCA-Press, 1976.

Metel' (verse play; title means "The Snowstorm") [and] *Prikliuchenie* (verse play; title means "An Adventure") [and] *Ariadna,* Prideaux Press, 1978.

Izbrannaia v dvukh tomakh: 1917-1937 (title means "Selected Prose in Two Volumes"; includes essays "Geroj truda," "Zhivoe o zhivom," "Mat' i muzyka," "Poet o kritike," "Natalia Goncharova," "Zemnye primety," "Epos i lirika sovremennoj Rossii," and "Iskusstvo pri svete Sovesti"), two volumes, Russica (New York), 1979.

Stikhotvoreniia i poemy (title means "Lyric Poems and Longer Poems"; includes collection *Junosheskie stikhi*), Sovetskii Pisatel', 1979, Russica, 1980.

Sochinenia v dvukh tomakh (title means "Selected Prose in Two Volumes"), two volumes, Russica, 1979, Khudozhestvennaya Literatura, 1980.

Stikhotvoreniia i poemy v piati tomakh (selected poems; title means "Lyric Poems and Longer Poems in Five Volumes"), five volumes, Russica, 1980—.

Stikhi i poemy (selected poems), Vaga, 1988.

Also author of unpublished manuscript titled "Tvoia smert' "; author of unproduced verse plays "Chervonnij valet" (title means "Jack of Hearts"), 1918, "Kamennyj angel" (title means "The Stone Angel"), 1919, *Fortuna* (title means "Fortuna"), 1919, and *Konets Kazanovy* (title means "Casanova's End"), 1919, revised and expanded version published as *Feniks* (title means "Phoenix"), 1924.

Contributor of "Krysolov" (title means "The Rat Catcher"), "Poema kontsa" (title means "Poem of the End"), "Poema gory" (title means "Poem of the Hill"), and other poems to Russian journals, including *Sovremennye zapiski, Volja Rossii, Novyj mir,* and *Novyj zhurnal;* correspondence published in Russian journals. Editor of *Kovcheg,* 1926.

IN ENGLISH TRANSLATION

Lebedinyi stan (poetry; includes "Oh, My Little Mushroom"), originally published in 1957, reprinted, YMCA-Press, 1971, bilingual English and Russian edition with translation, introduction, notes, and commentaries by Robin Kemball published as *The Demesne of the Swans,* Ardis, 1980.

Selected Poems of Marina Tsvetayeva, translated by Elaine Feinstein, foreword by Max Hayward, Oxford University Press, 1971, revised and enlarged edition with literal versions by Angela Livingstone and others, 1981, Dutton, 1987.

A Captive Spirit: Selected Prose, edited and translated by J. Marin King, Ardis, 1980, reprinted with introduction by Susan Sontag, Virago, 1983.

Three Russian Women Poets: Anna Akhmatova, Marina Tsvetayeva, Bella Akhmadulina (poetry), translated by Mary Maddock, introduction by Edward J. Brown, Crossing Press, 1983.

Letters, Summer 1926: Boris Pasternak, Marina Tsvetayeva, Rainer Maria Rilke, edited by Yevgeny Pasternak, Yelena Pasternak, and Konstantin M. Azadovsky, translated by Margaret Wettlin and Walter Arndt, Harcourt, 1985, reprinted, Oxford University Press, 1988.

Selected Poems, translated by David McDuff, Bloodaxe Books, 1987.

Contributor to *The Diary of Valery Bryusov (1893-1905),* edited and translated with an introduction by Joan Delaney Grossman, University of California Press.

SIDELIGHTS: Marina Tsvetaeva is an important Soviet poet. Although the auspicious beginning of her literary career was borne out artistically in numerous volumes of poetry and essays, her early success belied the immense hardships that she would face during the rest of her life. Many of these hardships were occasioned by historical events; revolution and civil war led to emigration, political troubles, and ill-advised repatriation leading to personal deprivation and poverty. Yet the major difficulties Tsvetaeva encountered were in the realm of her art, where they were voluntarily assumed, dictated by the integrity and strong sense of responsibility with which she carried out her poetic task. Despite the personal and professional adversity out of which they arose, Tsvetaeva's poetry and essays now enjoy widespread critical respect and receive increasing Western attention and admiration.

In October, 1910, Tsvetaeva began her literary career with a book of verse titled *Vechernii al'bom* ("Evening Album"), which appeared in Moscow in a private printing of five hundred copies. An unknown eighteen-year-old schoolgirl at the time, Tsvetaeva had the volume published at her own expense "for reasons," as she declared in her 1925 essay "Geroj truda," ("A Hero of Labor"), "extraneous to literature, but related to poetry—in place of a letter to a person with whom I was deprived of the possibility of communicating in any other way." No announcements or advertisements heralded the appearance of the book; even the young poet's family remained unaware of its existence for some time.

Given *Vechernii al'bom*'s highly personal nature and its modest publication, critical response was astonishing. No fewer than four prominent writers took notice of the book and published highly laudatory reviews praising the poet's talent, originality, and artistic independence. They noted the remarkable intimacy achieved in the verse, responded with interest to the poetic themes that appeared in it, and spoke highly of the intuitive grasp of the laws of poetry evident in the collection.

It was at least in part thanks to the success of *Vechernii al'bom* that Tsvetaeva became acquainted with the poet Maksimilian Voloshin, who became her personal friend and literary mentor. Voloshin, whose spirit Tsvetaeva later captured in her 1933 essay "Zhivoe o zhivom" ("A Living Word About a Living Man"), broadened the young poet's literary tastes by supplying her with reading material and by introducing her at Musaget, the editorial office of a prominent publishing house and a site of literary gatherings. Here Tsvetaeva had the opportunity to meet with some of the principal writers of her time and to be accepted as a fellow poet. In an anthology of contemporary Russian verse Musaget published in 1911, two of her poems appeared beside works by the major poets of the time.

In 1912 Tsvetaeva published her second book of verse, *Volshebnyi fonar'* ("The Magic Lantern"), and in 1913 her third, *Iz dvukh knig* ("From Two Books"), a selection of poems from the first two collections. The thematically naive poems of *Volshebnyi fonar',* like those of *Vechernii al'bom,* revealed a remarkably mature mastery of poetic idiom, but the concerns they expressed were still adolescent ones. A prevalent theme, for example, was the writer's reluctance to leave the magical realm of childhood to enter the mundane adult world. Tsvetaeva's second and third books did not meet with the same enthusiasm that *Vechernii Al'bom* had generated, since they were essentially a continuation of the first collection and thus a part of the initial manifestation of Tsvetaeva's artistic potential but not the further development that the critics expected and that was, in fact, to come.

Already in these early works Tsvetaeva's vision of the world was inextricably linked with her artistic philosophy. In his book *Marina Tsvetaeva: The Woman, Her World and Her Poetry,* Simon Karlinsky remarked on a central feature that Tsvetaeva's early collections share with her more mature works: "Like all of her lyric poetry those first two books are a diary of her life, encounters, interests and current reading, all of it transfigured by the alchemy of poetry into higher reality." Indeed, for Tsvetaeva poetry itself became that higher reality and the only genuine source of perception. She herself later explained in the philosophical autobiographical essay "Mat' i muzyka" ("Mother and Music"): "Thus throughout my entire life, in order to understand the simplest thing, I have had to immerse it in poetry, to see it *from there.*" Each of Tsvetaeva's poems represents just such an examination of existence from the larger perspective of her art.

The widening scope of Tsvetaeva's personal experiences and literary schooling is reflected in each of her subsequent collections. The title *Junosheskie stikhi* ("Juvenilia"), for a fourth volume of poems—written between 1913 and 1915 but not published during Tsvetaeva's lifetime—would have been more appropriate for the earlier collections, since the poems appearing in this book show a distinct transition from the romantic youthfulness of Tsvetaeva's first three volumes to the more fully developed outlook found in the subsequent collection, *Versty I* (title means "Mileposts I"). Written in 1916, the poems of *Versty I* must be counted among Tsvetaeva's mature works and demonstrate the rapid development of her talent. "Stylistically and technically," Karlinsky wrote, *Versty I* "was the most daringly experimental of Tsvetaeva's collections and it constituted a watershed in her poetic evolution. In it, she not only learned whatever the great age of Russian poetry in which she lived had to teach her, but she also became a major innovator in her own right."

In some of the poems of *Versty I* Tsvetaeva cultivated a carefully crafted simplicity of language, while in others she displayed a broad range of poetic diction that encompassed elevated Church Slavonic, colloquial expressions, regional dialects, and folk speech. Her command of varied linguistic levels paralleled her ability to assume widely different personae in the poems. Metrically, too, she went beyond the technical mastery she had exhibited from the onset of her career and created new rhythmic forms. At the center of the collection is a theme that draws the diverse elements together: Moscow, Tsvetaeva's native city, whose history, architecture, and traditional Russian spirit she extolled. By stressing her personal identification with Moscow, Tsvetaeva intentionally set herself apart from the well-established Petersburg poets, including Aleksandr Blok, Anna Akhmatova, and Osip Mandelstam. Tsvetaeva's interest in and respect for history and tradition, coupled with a fiercely independent, highly individualistic spirit, were evident in *Versty I.*

The next stage in Tsvetaeva's artistic development coincided with the period of Russian history that included the February and October revolutions of 1917 and the civil war that followed them. During this time, generally known as the War Communism period, Tsvetaeva experienced extreme hardships. Her husband, Sergej Efron, traveled to southern Russia, where he joined the anti-Bolshevik White Army. Tsvetaeva, as helpless in daily life as she was masterful in her poetry, was stranded in Moscow for the next five years with her two daughters, the younger of whom died of malnutrition. In *Marina Tsvetaeva,* Karlinsky vividly described Tsvetaeva's ordeal: "At the most difficult time imaginable, she was trapped in Moscow with two small children, with no income and entirely on her own for the first time in her life. She was twenty-five years old, very near-sighted and utterly impractical. She was terrified of automobiles and elevators and she easily lost her way in the streets and even inside buildings. She survived the harrowing five years of cold, starvation and terror because of her tremendous human vitality and with the help of kindly friends and neighbors." To this list must be added yet another far more important source of Tsvetaeva's survival—the intense artistic vitality that enabled her to transcend the horrors of the daily life of that period and to find a higher purpose for existence. Early on, Tsvetaeva distinguished sharply between mundane reality, designated in Russian by the word *byt,* and true existence, designated by *bytie;* she dedicated herself entirely to *bytie.*

As was to happen again later, after Tsvetaeva left the Soviet Union, the years of greatest physical deprivation became the most fruitful artistically. Tsvetaeva recorded the period 1917 to 1922 in poems that were included in the collections *Lebedinyi stan (The Demesne of the Swans),* which was not published in its entirety until 1957, *Versty II* ("Mileposts II"), comprised of poems dating from 1917 to 1921, and *Remeslo* ("Craft"), a volume of poems from the years 1921 and 1922.

In *The Demesne of the Swans* Tsvetaeva identified with a legendary medieval Russian chronicler who had recorded troubled times in the history of his country. In this collection, as always in her art and life, Tsvetaeva's sympathy was with the underdog—the White Army that her husband had joined and that was then fighting a losing battle against the Bolsheviks. The stance Tsvetaeva adopted was politically untenable and contributed to the steadily increasing hardships she endured during this time. Her adamant refusal to compromise her views in the face of public, political, and social pressures was characteristic of her insistence on a larger, truer perspective untrammeled by temporary animosities and prejudices. In 1914, when war had broken out with Germany and anti-German sentiment raged in Russia, Tsvetaeva had recited verse in which she praised German culture. Similarly, in Bolshevik-controlled Moscow she recited verses praising the White resistance before an audience comprised largely of Red soldiers. This gesture was not political—Tsvetaeva abhorred politics—but human. With it she protested the narrow designations, whether religious, national, or political, that are applied to people or movements and that limit perception and understanding. Tsvetaeva insisted that in the context of a higher reality such divisions are meaningless. In the poem "Oh, My Little Mushroom," for example, she wrote of the dead on a battlefield: "One was White but turned red: Blood made him crimson. / Another was Red but turned white: Death whitened him."

Both the quantity and the quality of the verse Tsvetaeva wrote during this difficult time attest to her artistic victory, against all odds, over *byt,* day-to-day life. In these years Tsvetaeva honed her lyrics and developed further the range of their diction and highly original rhythmic structures. At the same time she also turned to other artistic forms—epic poetry, drama, and prose. Between 1920 and 1922 she wrote the epic poem *Tsar'-Devitsa* ("The Tsar-Maiden"), "Na krasnom kone" ("On a Red Steed"), and *Molodets* ("The Swain"), all of which reflect in subject and in manner her study of Russian folklore. In 1918 and 1919 Tsvetaeva also wrote five plays in verse: *Metel'* ("The Snowstorm"), "Chervonnyj valet" ("Jack of Hearts"), *Prikliuchenie* ("An Adventure"), "Kamennyj angel" ("The Stone Angel"), *Konets Kazanovy* ("Casanova's End", published in expanded version under the title *Feniks* ["Phoenix"] in 1924), and *Fortuna* ("Fortuna"). None of the plays were performed, and only three of them—"An Adventure," "Casanova's End" (and its expanded version "Phoenix"), and "Fortuna"—were published in Tsvetaeva's lifetime. Although the majority of the plays in verse were set in the eighteenth century, Tsvetaeva's prose works of these years took the form of memoirs or diary entries and depicted the times in which they were written.

Although not all of Tsvetaeva's works found immediate publication, her reputation as a writer gradually grew. Fortunately, these productive years in the late 1910s and early 1920s coincided with a period when Soviet cultural policy did not yet place the severe restrictions on artistic method that were soon to follow. These restrictions were imposed, however, just as Tsvetaeva received word that her husband, from whom she had not heard since he had entered the White Army in 1917, was in Prague, Czechoslovakia, and left Russia to join him. In May of 1922 she was granted an exit visa and traveled to Berlin with her surviving daughter, Ariadna. There she was greeted by a thriving, appreciative Russian emigre literary community and had the opportunity to meet a number of fellow writers. After a brief stay during which she continued to write lyric poetry, Tsvetaeva traveled on to Czechoslovakia, where she remained for the next three years.

During her Czech years Tsvetaeva assembled the collection *Psikheia* ("Psyche"), which consists of both new poems and some that had already appeared elsewhere. She also wrote the poems that, along with the twenty-one she had written in Berlin, comprise *Posle Rossii* (title means "After Russia"). *Posle Rossii* holds a special place among Tsvetaeva's works, for it represents both the pinnacle of her development as a lyric poet and her final collection of lyric verse. This collection provides a synthesis of the diction, metrical forms, and themes with which Tsvetaeva had experimented in her earlier works. In *Posle Rossii* Tsvetaeva retained her dynamic and often passionate tone, and at the same time achieved a detached, philosophical outlook. Shakespeare's *Hamlet,* Racine's *Phedre,* the myths of Ariadne, of Orpheus and Eurydice, and of the Cumaean Sibyl, all, in Tsvetaeva's interpretation, became a means of conveying the increasingly focused poetic philosophy that she continued to develop in her prose. The indivisibility of form and content on which Tsvetaeva insisted is demonstrated in the verse of *Posle Rossii,* in which she united exquisite use of language with profoundly innovative rhythmic structures. Like all of Tsvetaeva's verse, the poems in this collection are based on her personal experience of life and of literature, experience that played a vital role in her maturity as an artist. Tsvetaeva directed many of the poems to Boris Pasternak, whose work she had discovered in the early 1920s and whom she had come to regard as a kindred spirit in the realm of poetry.

Tsvetaeva also continued to develop the larger poetic form. The long poems "Poema gory" ("Poem of the Hill"), "Poema kontsa" ("Poem of the End"), the folklore-based "The Swain," and part of "Krysolov" ("The Rat-Catcher"), published serially in 1925 and 1926, all date from Tsvetaeva's Czech period. Whether her subject was intensely personal, as in "Poema gory" and "Poema kontsa," which describes the termination of a passionate love affair, or more broadly social and ethical, as in "Krysolov," which attacks philistine obtuseness and complacency, Tsvetaeva succeeded in preserving specific personal detail even as she extrapolated universal significance from it. In these longer works, as in her lyric poetry, her verbal, metrical, and thematic structures are highly original, dynamic, and varied. Even the most impassioned lyrics are perfectly controlled.

In November of 1925 Tsvetaeva, her daughter Ariadna, and her son Georgij, who had been born in Czechoslovakia, moved to Paris, where Efron later joined them. The large Russian emigre community in Paris greeted Tsvetaeva as a celebrity. She found at once a sizeable reading public, received considerable praise, and was published in a variety of Russian literary journals. The public reading she gave in February 1926 in Paris was hailed as a major literary event. Tsvetaeva was pleased by this reception, but it did not weaken her deep mistrust of fame, which, she believed, almost inevitably resulted from the wrong (that is, extraliterary) reasons and had the dangerous potential of diverting the artist from the solitary path of his art. Her reply to the community that had welcomed her was the 1926 essay "Poet o kritike" ("A Poet on Criticism"). Written in a highly innovative prose style that incorporated many of Tsvetaeva's poetic traits, the piece defined her view of the poet and the poet's art and discussed the role of the critic. The lucid formulation of highly complex artistic concerns in "Poet o kritike" revealed the extent to which Tsvetaeva had thought through her views on the creation and perception of art in general and specifically her own. It offered an account of how Tsvetaeva worked and of the demands she placed on herself and on her reader. Tsvetaeva's profound regard for language can be seen in the scathing condemnation of vague or careless use of language. Furthermore, the essay was a devastating attack on critics who passed judgment on writers and works without having arrived at a genuine understanding of them. The critical opinions Tsvetaeva expressed in "Poet o kritike" were just as valid as her artistic observations, yet the essay enraged the Russian literary community in Paris and earned Tsvetaeva many lifelong enemies. The reason for their outrage lay in the negative and highly unflattering way Tsvetaeva described some of the most respected critics of the day. The poet who had been welcomed with praise was now showered with invective. Tsvetaeva's gesture was seen as one of intentional alienation, and the isolation to which it led can be regarded to a large extent as self-imposed.

At the same time, Tsvetaeva's poetry was becoming more difficult, placing considerable demands on her readers. Tsvetaeva was conscious of the difficulty of her works, but this difficulty was not, as some hostile critics suggested, the poet's intentional posturing. It was rather the inevitable result of her poetic evolution. Tsvetaeva answered not to the demands of her reader but to the higher demands of her art. As she declared in "Poet o kritike": "To please the reader with beautifully plashing words is not the goal of creation. My goal, when I sit down to work is not to make anyone happy, neither myself nor anyone else, but to give a work as perfect as possible." From her reader Tsvetaeva expected active participation in the creative process, as she also made clear in "Poet o kritike": "And what is reading but deciphering, interpretation, the extraction of the secrets that remain beyond the lines, beyond the limits of words. . . . Reading is—above all—co-creation. If a reader is lacking in imagination no book will survive." The reader, in Tsvetaeva's view, bore considerable responsibility toward the work of art, and in "A Poet on Criticism" Tsvetaeva recognized the extent of her demand without mitigating it: "The reader's exhaustion is not devastating but creative. Co-creative. It does honor both to the reader and to me."

The ideal reader that Tsvetaeva described here was not easy to find. Although she still had a number of devotees who appreciated her work, her publications—and thus her income—decreased, even as she remained the sole breadwinner for her family. Daily life again became difficult, marked by extreme poverty. Tsvetaeva continued to write poetry but turned increasingly to prose, which, while highly idiosyncratic, was more readily comprehensible and therefore more publishable than her verse. The last ten years of Tsvetaeva's sojourn abroad, 1928 to 1939, were years dominated by prose. Tsvetaeva described her transition to prose in a letter to Anna Teskova, dated November 24, 1933, and collected in *Pis'ma k A. Teskovoi* (title means "Letters to Teskova"): "I write almost no poetry and this is why: I cannot limit myself to a single poem—they emerge in families, in cycles, like a vortex or even a maelstrom that *draws me in,* consequently it is also a matter of time. . . . And, forgetting that I am a poet, no one accepts my poems anywhere—not one line. . . . Being an emigre is turning me into a writer of prose. Of course the prose is also *mine,* and the best thing in the world after poetry *is* lyrical prose, but still, only *after* poetry!"

Tsvetaeva's allegiance to poetry is reflected stylistically in her prose works. Valentina S. Coe observed in her introduction to *Proza: Selected Prose of Marina Tsvetaeva,* a 1969 collection of four of Tsvetaeva's essays: "Even when she is writing prose, Tsvetaeva is first of all a poet. This is to say two things: firstly that she is as much concerned with words themselves (their beauty, their novelty, their ability to suggest new meanings, the way new verbal forms can be made from old ones) as with the things she has to say through them; and secondly that it is with a special kind of joy and assertive fierceness that she constantly seizes on a telling detail and magnifies, concentrates, deepens it, often exaggerating it, giving it significance through her own unique emotional awareness of it."

During her final years outside Russia Tsvetaeva commenced her third prose period. From 1917 to 1920 she had produced memoirs and diary entries, and from 1922 to 1931 she had written essays in criticism, tributes inspired by the deaths of poets Tsvetaeva admired, and a piece about the painter Natalia Goncharova. The third and final period of Tsvetaeva's prose was dominated by her interest in her past in relation to far broader artistic concerns. As J. Marin King observed—in an essay published in *A Handbook of Russian Literature,* edited by Victor Terras—"In

1933 Tsvetaeva's prose began to draw heavily on her past, although few of the some twenty prose pieces of this period can be called 'autobiographical' in the usual sense of that word. Rather, the prose begins from Tsvetaeva's strongly-sensed duty to preserve a vanished past and then plunges beyond autobiography into a mythic recreation of her childhood that serves, in turn, as a metaphor for the genesis and destiny of the poet." To a significant extent all of Tsvetaeva's writing—poetry, prose, and the several volumes of personal letters that exist—are about poetry and the poet, and nearly everything Tsvetaeva wrote can be regarded as a "mythic recreation" of the world.

In the late 1930s it became known that Tsvetaeva's husband had become an agent for the Soviet secret police and had participated in a political murder—a fact Tsvetaeva refused to believe. She was shunned by most of the Russian emigre community, which could not find her professed ignorance of her husband's activities credible. In mid-1939 Tsvetaeva made the difficult and dangerous decision to return to the Soviet Union, prompted not so much by the awkwardness of her situation in France as by the demands of her family, especially her son, whom she adored. The full extent of the Stalinist terror was not known at this time in the West, and Efron and Ariadna, who had become increasingly pro-Soviet during their years in France, were the first of her family to decide to repatriate. Georgij insisted that he had no future in France and wanted to do the same. Tsvetaeva, whose works had been harshly criticized in the Soviet Union for both subject matter and style, spent approximately a year copying and editing her manuscripts and organizing her archives. She then acquiesced to her son's demands, leaving a significant portion of her works and letters in the West for safekeeping. This last gesture indicates that she was at least partially aware that in Stalinist Russia there was little place for a writer of her breadth, originality, and individuality. She did not, however, fully grasp the severity of the repressions until after she had returned to the Soviet Union.

On June 18, 1939, shortly after Tsvetaeva and Georgij arrived in Moscow, Ariadna and Efron (who was later shot) were arrested. Tsvetaeva's sister, Anastasija Tsvetaeva, she learned, had been imprisoned two years earlier. Most of Tsvetaeva's former friends, including several prominent writers, were afraid to associate with her. Politically, Tsvetaeva's situation was precarious; artistically, it was impossible. The proclamation in the 1930s of Socialist Realism as the only acceptable form for Soviet arts precluded publication of any of Tsvetaeva's highly original works in the Soviet Union.

Shortly after Germany invaded Russia in the summer of 1941, Tsvetaeva became concerned for her son's safety and joined a group of writers being evacuated from Moscow to the Tatar Republic. More privileged authors in the politically determined hierarchy were given accommodation in the town of Chistopol, but Tsvetaeva and Georgij found themselves in Elabuga, a small, provincial village where there was neither a literary community nor the prospect of work. They rented a room in the hut of a local couple; here Tsvetaeva hanged herself on August 31, 1941. No one attended her funeral, and she was buried in an unmarked common grave.

"The age for my poems—as for precious wines—will come," Tsvetaeva wrote in a 1913 poem that was included in the collection "Juvenilia." This orientation towards the future was characteristic of Tsvetaeva, as in much of her poetry and prose she insisted on the timelessness of her art. Her youthful prophecy reveals both the profundity of her faith in her poetry and her artistic clairvoyance, for the prophecy is in fact being fulfilled.

In the 1950s the publication of Tsvetaeva's poetry, prose, and letters began growing steadily, as did her readership. Although a sizeable part of her canon has not, for political reasons, been published in the Soviet Union, selected works have appeared there in increasing number, thanks largely to the efforts of Ariadna, who survived imprisonment and exile and devoted the remainder of her life to getting her mother's poetry into print. There have also appeared in the Soviet Union memoirs and biographies of Tsvetaeva, including one by Anastasija, that alter what are considered the politically unacceptable details of her life. More accurate accounts of Tsvetaeva's life and work and the most complete collections of her poetry, prose, and letters have appeared in the West, and, together with a rapidly expanding body of Soviet and Western scholarship, they have increased readers' understanding and appreciation of this remarkable poet.

Despite the impressive volume and generally high quality of studies treating Tsvetaeva, however, the best source for a genuine understanding of her verse lies in her own writings. In the course of her career Tsvetaeva developed a highly consistent artistic credo, which she exemplified in her verse and formulated in her prose. Her personal letters, too, provide rich material, revealing, like her artistic works, her search for poetic truth.

Tsvetaeva perceived the universe as split into a temporally and spatially bounded physical world and an unbounded nonphysical world. A sworn enemy of the mundane and physical, she regarded daily life as inimical to art. In a *Slavic Review* essay, Ieva Vitins wrote: "Her aversion to this world stemmed in part from an active dislike and discomfort with its physicality. . . . For her this physicality was the main obstacle which prevented direct contact with the essence of beings and things." Life, according to Tsvetaeva, gained significance only through art. In a letter to Teskova dated December 30, 1925, she insisted: "I do not like life as such; for me it begins to carry meaning, i.e., to obtain significance and weight, only if it is transformed, i.e., in art." The demand for this artistic transformation of life arose from a need to overcome the limitations of the physical world in order to realize the greater potential of the human spirit in the creative process.

Tsvetaeva's frequent expressions of hostility toward the mundane and of longing to become entirely part of the nonphysical are balanced by her insistence that the poet must unite these two worlds, that art is a means to a larger end. In the fragments of her uncompleted book of prose that was to have been titled "Zemnye primety" ("Earthly Signs") she insisted: "Art is not an end in itself. It is a bridge, not a goal." By means of this bridge the poet could "create the other world in these worlds," as Tsvetaeva declared in her essay "A Hero of Labor."

Tsvetaeva's artistic concerns dominated her life and to a significant extent dictated her death. The difficulty of her life was emblematic of the enormity of the artistic demands she placed on herself. At odds with the world surrounding her, she felt at home only within the infinite realm she embodied in her work. Much of Tsvetaeva's writing and artistic philosophy was based on contrast, oxymoron, and paradox, yet these devices, were used to provide fresh perspectives that ultimately contributed to a wholeness of vision. Although Tsvetaeva was a rebellious, independent, innovative, demanding, solitary, and highly idiosyncratic poet, she considered herself, above all, part of the indivisible and eternal force of poetry that she served: "Because," as she wrote in "Epos i lirika sovremennoj Rossii," "poetry is not divided into or among poets. In all its manifestations poetry is one, the same, complete in each—just as there are in essence not poets but only *the* poet, one and the same, world beginning to world end."

BIOGRAPHICAL/CRITICAL SOURCES:

BOOKS

Efron, Ariadna, *Straniitsy vospominanii* (title means "Pages of Reminiscences"), Lev, 1979.

Feinstein, Elaine, *A Captive Lion: The Life of Marina Tsvetayeva,* Dutton, 1987.

Gladkova, Tatiana L., and Lev A. Mnukhin, *Marina Tsvetaeva: Bibliografija: Bibliographie des oeuvres de Marina Tsvetaeva* (title means "A Marina Tsvetaeva Bibliography"), Bibliotheque de l'Institut d'Etudes Slaves, 1982.

Karlinsky, Simon, *Marina Cvetaeva: Her Life and Art,* University of California Press, 1966.

Karlinsky, Simon, *Marina Tsvetaeva: The Woman, Her World and Her Poetry,* Cambridge University Press, 1985.

Proffer, Ellendea, editor, *Tsvetaeva: A Pictorial Biography,* translation by J. Marin King, Ardis, 1980.

Razumovsky, Maria, *Marina Zwetajewa, 1892-1941: Mythos und Wahrheit* (title means "Marina Tsvetaeva: Myth and Reality"), Age d'Homme-Karolinger, 1981.

Struve, Gleb, and Nikita Struve, editors, *Neizdannye pis'ma,* YMCA-Press, 1972.

Terras, Victor, editor, *A Handbook of Russian Literature,* Yale University Press, 1985.

Tsvetaeva, Anastasija, *Vospominanija* (title means "Memoirs"), Sovetskii Pisatel', 2nd edition, 1974.

Tsvetaeva, Marina, *Izbrannaia proza v dvukh tomakh,* Russica, 1979.

Tsvetaeva, Marina, *Stikhotvoreniia i poemy,* Sovetskii Pisatel', 1979.

Tsvetaeva, Marina, *The Demesne of the Swans,* translation with introduction, notes, and commentaries by Robin Kemball, Ardis, 1980.

Tsvetaeva, Marina, *Pis'ma k A. Teskovoi,* Academia, 1969.

Tsvetaeva, Marina, *Proza: Selected Prose of Marina Tsvetaeva,* introduction by Valentina S. Coe, Bradda, 1969.

Twentieth Century Literary Criticism, Volume 7, Gale, 1982.

PERIODICALS

Iowa Review, Volume 9, number 4, 1978.
Los Angeles Times Book Review, January 4, 1981.
New York Times Book Review, October 12, 1980.
Times Literary Supplement, March 6, 1981, January 8, 1982.
Weiner Slawistischer Alamanach, Sonderband 3, 1981.

*   *   *

TUCHMAN, Barbara W(ertheim) 1912-1989

PERSONAL: Born January 30, 1912, in New York, N.Y.; died following a stroke, February 6, 1989; daughter of Maurice (a banker) and Alma (Morgenthau) Wertheim; married Lester R. Tuchman (a physician), 1940; children: Lucy, Jessica, Alma. *Education:* Radcliffe College, B.A., 1933.

ADDRESSES: Agent—Timothy Seldes, Russell & Volkening, Inc., 50 West 29th St., New York, N.Y. 10001.

CAREER: Institute of Pacific Relations, New York City, research and editorial assistant, 1933-35; *Nation,* New York City, staff writer and foreign correspondent, 1935-37, correspondent in Madrid, 1937, correspondent in the United States, 1939; Office of War Information, New York City, editor, 1943-45. Trustee, Radcliffe College, 1960-72. Appointed Jefferson Lec-

turer for the National Endowment for the Humanities, 1980. Lecturer at Harvard University, University of California, U.S. Naval War College, and other institutions.

MEMBER: Society of American Historians (president, 1970-73), Authors Guild (treasurer), Authors League of America (member of council), American Academy of Arts and Letters (president, 1979), American Academy of Arts and Sciences, Cosmopolitan Club.

AWARDS, HONORS: Pulitzer Prize, 1963, for *The Guns of August,* and 1972, for *Stilwell and the American Experience in China, 1911-1945;* gold medal for history, American Academy of Arts and Sciences, 1978; Regent Medal of Excellence, State University of New York, 1984; Sarah Josepha Hale Award, 1985; Abraham Lincoln Literary Award, Union League Club, 1985; received Order of Leopold from the Kingdom of Belgium; D.Litt. from Yale University, Columbia University, New York University, Williams College, University of Massachusetts, Smith College, Hamilton College, Mount Holyoke College, Boston University, Harvard University, and other schools.

WRITINGS:

The Lost British Policy: Britain and Spain since 1700, United Editorial, 1938.

Bible and Sword: England and Palestine from the Bronze Age to Balfour, New York University Press, 1956.

The Zimmermann Telegram, Viking, 1958, new edition, Macmillan, 1966.

The Guns of August (Book-of-the-Month Club selection), Macmillan, 1962 (published in England as *August, 1914,* Constable, 1962).

The Proud Tower: A Portrait of the World before the War, 1890-1914 (Book-of-the-Month Club selection), Macmillan, 1966.

Stilwell and the American Experience in China, 1911-1945 (Book-of-the-Month Club selection), Macmillan, 1971 (published in England as *Sand against the Wind: Stilwell and the American Experience in China, 1911-1945,* Macmillan [London], 1971).

Notes from China, Collier Books, 1972.

A Distant Mirror: The Calamitous Fourteenth Century, Knopf, 1978.

Practicing History: Selected Essays, Knopf, 1981.

The March of Folly: From Troy to Vietnam, Knopf, 1984.

The First Salute: A View of the American Revolution, Random House, 1989.

Contributor to *Harper's, Atlantic, New York Times, American Scholar, Foreign Affairs,* and other publications.

SIDELIGHTS: Barbara Tuchman writes narrative histories that are strongly literary in nature, believing that the work of most historians is often too obscure for the average reader. "Historians who stuff in every item of research they have found, every shoe-lace and telephone call of a biographical subject, are not doing the hard work of selecting and shaping a readable story," she tells *CA.* "And besides, they seem not to have an ear for clear lucid prose, are not thinking of their readers." Tuchman favors the literary approach. "There should be a beginning, a middle, and an end," she states, "plus an element of suspense to keep a reader turning the pages." Her approach to history has won her two Pulitzer Prizes. Tuchman is also "a bestselling author and America's foremost popular historian," as Wendy Smith writes in *Publishers Weekly.*

Although not trained as a historian, Tuchman does not see that as a disadvantage. "I never took a Ph.D.," she admits. "It's what saved me, I think. If I had taken a doctoral degree, it would have stifled any writing capacity." To prepare for her books, Tuchman first researches the available information and then visits the appropriate historical sites. For *The Guns of August,* she walked the battlefields of World War I; for *A Distant Mirror: The Calamitous Fourteenth Century,* she crossed the same mountains the Crusaders of the fourteenth century crossed.

Tuchman explains to Jim Miller of *Newsweek* that it was difficult for her to become a writer of history. "It was a struggle," she states. "I had three small children and no status whatever." Tuchman's ambitions seemed out of place in a family prominent in politics and banking. Her grandfather had been U.S. ambassador to Turkey and Mexico under President Woodrow Wilson. Her father was a banker and an owner of the *Nation* magazine. An uncle served as the secretary of the treasury under President Franklin D. Roosevelt. "To come home, close a door and feel that it was your place to work," Tuchman tells Miller, "that was very difficult, particularly when you were—well, just a Park Avenue matron."

It wasn't until her third book, *The Zimmermann Telegram,* that Tuchman achieved success as a writer. A best-seller, the book concerns the infamous German telegram to Mexico during World War I which promised the Mexican government portions of the American Southwest if it would enter the war on Germany's behalf. The exposure of the telegram was instrumental in bringing the United States into the war against Germany. As Ferdinand Kuhn explains in *Saturday Review,* "The blundering telegram was important in history, and for this reason the story is worth telling." Tuchman's account of the pivotal affair is singled out for its remarkable detail. "There can only be praise," writes a *Times Literary Supplement* critic, "for the writer's mastery of a mass of documents treating all sides of this amazing affair." Ernest S. Pisko of the *Christian Science Monitor* notes Tuchman's "stupendous knowledge of all the facts and all the persona even remotely involved in the dramatic story."

The Guns of August, a look at the opening days of World War I, was Tuchman's next best-seller and winner of her first Pulitzer Prize. It is, Bruce Blivenn, Jr. writes in the *New Yorker,* a "neatly perfect literary triumph." Focusing on the opening strategies and battles of the war, Tuchman argues that errors on all sides in the conflict led to the stalemate of trench warfare—a four-year period of enormous and largely pointless casualties. "There is much of battle orders, of tactical, strategic, and logistical problems in the pages of 'The Guns of August,' " Pisko writes. "But such is the skill of the author that these technical issues become organic parts of an epic never flagging in suspense." Although Cyril Falls of the *New York Times Book Review* finds that "the errors and omissions of 'The Guns of August' mount to a formidable total," he judges the book to be "a lucid, fair, critical and witty account." Blivenn claims that "Tuchman leans toward seeing issues as black and white, but her control of her material is so certain and her opinions are so passionate that it would be risky to argue with her."

With *The Proud Tower: A Portrait of the World before the War, 1890-1914,* Tuchman turned to an examination of society before the First World War and of the events and forces which led to the war. World War I, she writes in the book, "lies like a band of scorched earth dividing that time from ours. In wiping out so many lives which would have been operative on the years that followed, in destroying beliefs, changing ideas, and leaving incurable wounds of disillusion, it created a physical as well as psychological gulf between two epochs." In eight chapters, each covering a different topic, Tuchman provides varied glimpses of

pre-war society. "*The Proud Tower,*" Oscar Handlin comments in the *Atlantic,* "is consistently interesting. [Tuchman] is a skillful and imaginative writer. She has the storyteller's knack for getting the maximum dramatic effect out of the events which crowd her pages."

Tuchman won her second Pulitzer Prize for the 1971 book *Stilwell and the American Experience in China, 1911-1945.* It follows the career of Joseph Warren Stilwell, an American military officer who served in China in various capacities from 1911 to 1944. Stilwell's years in China saw that country's transformation from a feudal society to a communist state. The book is, Anthony Grey writes in the *Washington Post Book World,* "an extremely creditable compendium of the mightiness, the miseries, the personalities, the perversities, the facts and frustrations of China in the past half-century seen through unhappy American eyes." O. Edmund Clubb, writing in the *Saturday Review,* finds *Stilwell and the American Experience in China* to be "an admirably structured work that is excellent as narrative and fascinating as history," while Allen S. Whiting, in a review for the *Nation,* calls it "the most interesting and informative book on U.S.-China relations to appear since World War II."

Although Tuchman's most popular books had dealt with twentieth-century history, in 1978 she published a book about the Middle Ages, *A Distant Mirror: The Calamitous Fourteenth Century.* Her interest in the period stemmed from what she saw as similarities between the fourteenth century and our own time; the book's title refers to this similarity. David Benson, writing in the *Spectator,* lists the "resemblances between that period and our own" as "almost continual warfare, both civil and international, widespread political instability and popular uprisings, a crisis of confidence in almost all institutions, especially the Church, and a rise of individualism combined with a general decline in authority." The central event of the fourteenth century was the bubonic plague, which swept across Europe and Asia, killing nearly a third of the population. Tuchman compares the plague to the possible devastation a nuclear war might cause in our own century.

Following the career of Enguerrand de Coucy VII, a French knight and nobleman, *A Distant Mirror* becomes an "ambitious, absorbing historical panorama," as Naomi Bliven writes in the *New Yorker.* De Coucy was related to both the French and English royal families and owned land near the troublesome Flemish border, so his life touched upon many key events and personalities of the time. Tuchman's narrative brings these events and personalities to vivid life. Despite the book's several drawbacks, Laurence Stone of the *New York Review of Books* finds it "beautifully written, careful and thorough in its scholarship, extensive in the range of topics peripherally touched upon, and enlivened by consistently intelligent comment. What Mrs. Tuchman does superbly is to tell how it was, to convey a sense of time and place." This ability to recreate the texture of fourteenth-century life is also noted by Brian Tierney of the *Washington Post Book World.* Tuchman's "special gift," Tierney writes, "is to bring a past age to life by the accumulation of countless concrete details, lovingly collected and deftly presented. . . . The result is a kind of brilliant, dazzling, impressionistic picture of the surface of medieval life."

In *The March of Folly: From Troy to Vietnam,* Tuchman ranges over Western history from the mythical Trojan horse of ancient Greece to the Vietnam War, examining in depth four episodes in which governmental "folly" is most evident: the Trojans' decision to bring the wooden horse into their city; the corruption of the Renaissance popes, which helped to provoke the Protestant

Reformation; the English policy towards the rebellious American colonies; and the American involvement in the Vietnam War. These episodes were similar, Michael Howard explains in the *Washington Post Book World,* in that "the actors involved pursued a course of action which was not only foolish but seen at the time to be foolish; which was the responsibility of an entire group or class rather than a single misguided individual, and to which a sensible and feasible alternative was quite obviously available." *The March of Folly* is a change in approach for Tuchman. "I've done what I always said I would never do," she told Smith, "and that is to take a theory before I wrote a book. My other books were narrative, and I tried not to adopt a thesis except what emerged from the material. It's what I don't believe in when writing history, actually."

Some critics took exception to the thesis of *The March of Folly.* Jack Lessenberry of the *Detroit News,* speaking of the four historic events that Tuchman discusses, asks: "What common thread links these events? I can't tell, and I read the book." Christopher Lehmann-Haupt of the *New York Times* believes that much of what Tuchman discusses in the book has been better handled by other writers: "Any way one approaches 'The March of Folly,' it is unsatisfying. . . . Better books have been written about Vietnam, the American Revolution, the Renaissance Popes and the Trojan Horse. Better things have been said about human folly."

But, as H. J. Kirchhoff of the Toronto *Globe and Mail* maintains, "there are many good reasons to recommend" *The March of Folly.* Kirchhoff believes that "Tuchman writes well about the major players in turbulent times. She researches her subjects with exemplary thoroughness, and discusses them with imagination and clear good sense. And her analysis of political folly . . . offers valuable (and sobering) insights into the political process." Writing in the *New York Times Book Review,* John Keegan states that Tuchman identifies political folly "with precision, dissects it with delicacy and dismisses it with contempt." Theodore Draper of the *New Republic* finds that "one admires Tuchman's ability to assimilate, organize, and dramatize enormous gobs of disparate material. She never ceases to be vivid and vigorous. Most readers will be carried along by her storytelling art."

In her collection *Practicing History: Selected Essays,* Tuchman presents her own ideas on how history should best be written. Divided into three parts—"The Craft," "The Practice," and "Learning from History"—the book reveals many of the assumptions and concerns which have made Tuchman one of the most popular historians in the country. She particularly emphasizes the importance of narrative writing. "The historian's basic mode," Marcus Cunliffe explains in his review of the book for the *Washington Post Book World,* "is that of narration: movement through time, so as to disclose to the reader in a clear, compelling sequence a set of significant events."

Tuchman's emphasis on narrative has helped to make her books best-sellers, though it is in sharp contrast to the approach taken by many academic historians. "Most academics," Miller writes, "lack the talent or inclination to write for a general audience. Into this vacuum has stepped Tuchman. . . . Her imaginative choice of topics and flair for words have enabled her to satisfy the popular hunger for real history spiced with drama, color and a dash of uplifting seriousness." Writing in the *New Republic,* Jack Beatty maintains that "Tuchman's books provide [her readers] with examples that lift the level of their lives. Before the academic deluge this was what history was supposed to do—to teach philosophy by example—and few writers have performed this office more inspiritingly than Barbara Tuchman."

Despite some criticism of her work by the academic world—Walter Kendrick of the *Village Voice* reports that "academic historians disdain her work now and always will"—few observers doubt the sheer power of Tuchman's writing. "Tuchman may not be a historian's historian," Laurence Freedman admits in the *Times Literary Supplement,* "but she is a pleasure for the layman to read." "Whatever her subject," Smith writes, "Tuchman brings to it a flair for the dramatic, a striking ability to combine narrative sweep with individual character analysis, and a vividly entertaining prose style." Because of her ability to turn "complex historical muddles into narrative that preserves an air of complexity but can be simply read," Kendrick argues, Tuchman will be remembered "as an entertainer, one who made the past palatable to millions of readers."

MEDIA ADAPTATIONS: The Guns of August was filmed in 1964.

BIOGRAPHICAL/CRITICAL SOURCES:

BOOKS

Bestsellers 89, Issue 1, Gale, 1989.
Bowman, Kathleen, *New Women in Social Sciences,* Creative Education Press, 1976.
Contemporary Issues Criticism, Volume I, Gale, 1982.
Tuchman, Barbara, *The Proud Tower: A Portrait of the World before the War, 1890-1914,* Macmillan, 1966.
Tuchman, Barbara, *Practicing History: Selected Essays,* Knopf, 1981.

PERIODICALS

America, February 5, 1966.
American Historical Review, July, 1966.
American Political Science Review, June, 1972.
Atlantic, February, 1966, October, 1978, April, 1984.
Books and Bookmen, May, 1979.
Book Week, January 9, 1966.
Book World, February 28, 1971.
Boston Globe, March 4, 1984.
Business Week, September 25, 1978.
Chicago Tribune Book World, March 4, 1984.
Christian Century, May 14, 1975.
Christian Science Monitor, October 2, 1958, February 1, 1962, March 24, 1971, September 18, 1978, October 7, 1986.
Chronicle Review, October 2, 1978.
Commentary, December, 1978.
Contemporary Review, April, 1982.
Cosmopolitan, January, 1967.
Critic, April-May, 1966.
Current History, May, 1966.
Detroit News, March 25, 1984.
Economist, February 26, 1966.
Esquire, June, 1971.
Globe and Mail (Toronto), April 21, 1984.
Harper's, February, 1966.
Journal of American History, September, 1966, December, 1971.
Life, February 19, 1971.
Listener, January 6, 1972, March 29, 1979.
Los Angeles Times, February 11, 1989.
Los Angeles Times Book Review, March 18, 1984, October 2, 1988.
Ms., July, 1979.
Nation, February 14, 1966, April 26, 1971.
National Review, February 8, 1966, December 8, 1978.
New Leader, October 9, 1978.

New Republic, March 27, 1971, October 28, 1978, October 21, 1981, March 26, 1984.

New Statesman, June 22, 1962.

Newsweek, February 15, 1971, September 25, 1978, March 12, 1984.

New Yorker, April 14, 1962, February 5, 1966, November 13, 1978, April 21, 1986.

New York Review of Books, February 3, 1966, July 22, 1971, August 9, 1973, September 28, 1978, March 29, 1984.

New York Times, February 15, 1971, February 27, 1979, September 29, 1981, September 7, 1982, March 7, 1984, September 20, 1987.

New York Times Book Review, January 28, 1962, January 9, 1966, February 7, 1971, April 22, 1973, November 12, 1978, September 27, 1981, March 11, 1984, March 24, 1985, October 16, 1988.

Observer, July 15, 1979.

Progressive, June, 1971.

Publishers Weekly, March 2, 1984.

Punch, March 9, 1966.

Saturday Review, October 18, 1958, January 27, 1962, January 15, 1966, February 20, 1971, October 28, 1978.

Spectator, March 31, 1979, July 21, 1984.

Time, February 9, 1962, January 14, 1966, February 15, 1971, March 26, 1984.

Times (London), May 17, 1984, March 4, 1989.

Times Literary Supplement, March 20, 1959, June 8, 1962, December 10, 1971, June 22, 1984.

Village Voice, June 19, 1978, September 30, 1981.

Virginia Quarterly Review, summer, 1966.

Wall Street Journal, January 14, 1966.

Washington Post, October 5, 1978.

Washington Post Book World, February 13, 1972, October 8, 1978, September 27, 1981, February 2, 1984, October 2, 1988.

* * *

TUTUOLA, Amos 1920-

PERSONAL: Born 1920, in Abeokuta, Nigeria; son of Charles (a cocoa farmer) and Esther (Aina) Tutuola; married Alake Victoria, 1947; children: Olubunmi, Oluyinka, Erinola. *Education:* Attended schools in Nigeria. *Religion:* Christian.

ADDRESSES: P.O. Box 2251, Ibadan, Nigeria. *Home*—Ago-Odo, West Nigeria. *Office*—Nigerian Broadcasting Corp., Ibadan, Nigeria, West Africa.

CAREER: Worked on father's farm; trained as a coppersmith; employed by Nigerian Government Labor Department, Lagos, and by Nigerian Broadcasting Corp., Ibadan, Nigeria. Freelance writer. Visiting research fellow, University of Ife, 1979; associate, international writing program at University of Iowa, 1983. *Military service:* Royal Air Force, 1943-45; served as metal worker in Nigeria.

MEMBER: Mbari Club (Nigerian authors; founder).

AWARDS, HONORS: Named honorary citizen of New Orleans, 1983; *The Palm-Wine Drinkard and His Dead Palm-Wine Tapster in the Dead's Town* and *My Life in the Bush of Ghosts* received second place awards in a contest held in Turin, Italy, 1985.

WRITINGS:

The Palm-Wine Drinkard and His Dead Palm-Wine Tapster in the Dead's Town, Faber, 1952, Grove, 1953.

My Life in the Bush of Ghosts, Grove, 1954, reprinted, Faber, 1978.

Simbi and the Satyr of the Dark Jungle, Faber, 1955.

The Brave African Huntress, illustrated by Ben Enwonwu, Grove, 1958.

The Feather Woman of the Jungle, Faber, 1962.

Ajaiyi and His Inherited Poverty, Faber, 1967.

(Contributor) *Winds of Change: Modern Short Stories from Black Africa,* Longman, 1977.

The Witch-Herbalist of the Remote Town, Faber, 1981.

The Wild Hunter in the Bush of the Ghosts (facsimile of manuscript), edited with an introduction and a postscript by Bernth Lindfors, Three Continents Press, 1982, 2nd edition, 1989.

Pauper, Brawler, and Slanderer, Faber, 1987.

WORK REPRESENTED IN ANTHOLOGIES

Rutherford, Peggy, editor, *Darkness and Light: An Anthology of African Writing,* Drum Publications, 1958.

Hughes, Langston, editor, *An African Treasury: Articles, Essays, Stories, Poems by Black Africans,* Crown, 1960.

Hughes, Langston, and Christiane Reynault, editors, *Anthologie africaine et malgache,* Seghers, 1962.

Ademola, Frances, editor, *Reflections,* African Universities Press, 1962, new edition, 1965.

Sainville, Leonard, editor, *Anthologie de la litterature negroafricaine: Romanciers et conteurs negro africains,* two volumes, Presence Africaine, 1963.

Whiteley, W. H., compiler, *A Selection of African Prose,* two volumes, Oxford University Press, 1964.

Rive, Richard, editor, *Modern African Prose,* Heinemann Educational, 1964.

Komey, Ellis Ayitey and Ezekiel Mphahlele, editors, *Modern African Stories,* Faber, 1964.

Tibble, Anne, editor, *African-English Literature: A Survey and Anthology,* Peter Owen, 1965.

Edwards, Paul, compiler, *Through African Eyes,* two volumes, Cambridge University Press, 1966.

Mphahlele, Ezekiel, editor, *African Writing Today,* Penguin, 1967.

Beier, Ulli, editor, *Political Spider: An Anthology of Stories from "Black Orpheus,"* Heinemann Educational, 1969.

Larson, Charles, editor, *African Short Stories: A Collection of Contemporary African Writing,* Macmillan, 1970.

MEDIA ADAPTATIONS: Kola Ogunmola has written a play in Yoruba entitled *Omuti,* based on *The Palm-Wine Drinkard,* published by West African Book Publishers.

SIDELIGHTS: With the publication of his novel *The Palm-Wine Drinkard and His Dead Palm-Wine Tapster in the Dead's Town* in 1952, Amos Tutuola became the first internationally recognized Nigerian writer. Since that time, Tutuola's works, in particular *The Palm-Wine Drinkard,* have been the subject of much critical debate. *The Palm-Wine Drinkard* was praised by critics outside of Nigeria for its unconventional use of the English language, its adherence to the oral tradition, and its unique, fantastical characters and plot. Nigerian critics, on the other hand, described the work as ungrammatical and unoriginal. Discussing the first criticism in his book *The Growth of the African Novel,* Eustace Palmer writes: "Tutuola's English is demonstrably poor; this is due partly to his ignorance of the more complicated rules of English syntax and partly to interference from Yoruba." The second criticism, concerning Tutuola's lack of originality, is based on similarities between Tutuola's works and those of his predecessor, O. B. Fagunwa, who writes in the Yoruba language.

The influence of Fagunwa's writings on Tutuola's work has been noted by several critics, including Abiola Irele, who writes in *The African Experience in Literature and Ideology:* "It is clear that much of the praise and acclaim that have been lavished upon Tutuola belong more properly to Fagunwa who provided not only the original inspiration but indeed a good measure of material for Tutuola's novels. The echoes of Fagunwa in Tutuola's works are numerous enough to indicate that the latter was consciously creating from a model provided by the former." Irele adds, however, "that despite its derivation from the work of Fagunwa, Tutuola's work achieves an independent status that it owes essentially to the force of his individual genius."

Tutuola's genius is described by reviewers as an ability to refashion the traditional Yoruba myths and folktales that are the foundation of his work. Eustace Palmer notes, for instance, in *The Growth of the African Novel:* "Taking his stories direct from his people's traditional lore, he uses his inexhaustible imagination and inventive power to embellish them, to add to them or alter them, and generally transform them into his own stories conveying his own message." O. R. Dathorne comments in an essay published in *Introduction to Nigerian Literature:* "Tutuola is a literary paradox; he is completely part of the folklore traditions of the Yorubas and yet he is able to modernize these traditions in an imaginative way. It is on this level that his books can best be approached. . . . Tutuola deserves to be considered seriously because his work represents an intentional attempt to fuse folklore with modern life."

In *The Palm-Wine Drinkard,* for example, the Drinkard's quest for his tapster leads him into many perilous situations, including an encounter with the Red Fish, a monster Tutuola describes as having thirty horns "spread out as an umbrella," and numerous eyes that "were closing and opening at the same time as if a man was pressing a switch on and off." Tutuola also amends a traditional tale concerning a Skull who borrows appendages belonging to other persons in order to look like a "complete gentleman" to include references to modern warfare. Tutuola writes: "If this gentleman went to the battle field, surely, enemy would not kill him or capture him and if bombers saw him in a town which was to be bombed, they would not throw bombs on his presence, and if they did throw it, the bomb itself would not explode until this gentleman would leave that town, because of his beauty." Gerald Moore observes in *Seven African Writers* that these descriptions are evidence "of Tutuola's easy use of the paraphernalia of modern life to give sharpness and immediacy to his imagery."

The Palm-Wine Drinkard was hailed by critics such as V. S. Pritchett and Dylan Thomas, the latter of whom describes the work in the *Observer* as a "brief, thronged, grisly and bewitching story." Thomas concludes: "The writing is nearly always terse and direct, strong, wry, flat and savoury. . . . Nothing is too prodigious or too trivial put down in this tall, devilish story." The work also has been favorably compared to such classics as *The Odyssey, Pilgrim's Progress,* and *Gulliver's Travels.* Some critics, however, expressed reservations about Tutuola's ability to repeat his success. According to Charles R. Larson's *The Emergence of African Fiction,* critic Anthony West stated, *"The Palm-Wine Drinkard* must be valued for its own freakish sake, and as an unrepeatable happy hit."

Despite the reservations of critics like West, Tutuola went on to publish seven additional works, and while critics are, as Larson observes in *The Emergence of African Fiction,* "a little less awed now than they were in the early 1950's," Tutuola's works continue to merit critical attention. Among the more widely reviewed of these books is *The Witch-Herbalist of the Remote Town.* Published thirty years after *The Palm-Wine Drinkard,* this book involves a quest initiated by the protagonist, a hunter, to find a cure for his wife's barrenness. The journey to the Remote Town takes six years; along the way the hunter encounters bizarre and sometimes frightening places and people, including the Town of the Born-and-Die Baby and the Abnormal Squatting Man of the Jungle, who can paralyze opponents with a gust of frigid air by piercing his abdomen. The hunter eventually reaches the Remote Town, and the witch-herbalist gives him a broth guaranteed to make his wife fertile. The plot is complicated though, when the hunter, weak from hunger, sips some of the broth.

As with *The Palm-Wine Drinkard,* critical commentary of *The Witch-Herbalist of the Remote Town* focuses in particular on Tutuola's use of the English language. Edward Blishen, for instance, comments in the *Times Educational Supplement:* "The language is wonderfully stirring and odd: a mixture of straight translation from Yoruba, and everyday modern Nigerian idiom, and grand epical English. The imagination at work is always astonishing. . . . And this, not the bargain, is folklore not resurrected, but being created fresh and true in the white heat of a tradition still undestroyed." *Voice Literary Supplement* critic Jon Parales writes: "His direct, apparently simple language creates an anything-can-happen universe, more whacky and amoral than the most determinedly modern lit." *Washington Post Book World* contributor Judith Chettle offers this view: "Tutuola writes with an appealing vigor and his idiosyncratic use of the English idiom gives the story a fresh and African perspective, though at times the clumsiness of some phrasing does detract from the thrust of the narrative. No eye-dabbing sentimentalist, Tutuola's commentary is clear-eyed if not acerbic, but underlying the tale is a quiet and persistent lament for the simpler, unsophisticated and happier past of his people."

An *Africa Today* contributor, Nancy J. Schmidt, observes that Tutuola's language has become increasingly more like that of standard English over the years. She cites other differences between this work and earlier ones as well. "Tutuola's presence is very evident in *Witch-Herbalist,* but the strength of his presence and his imagination are not as strong as they once were," writes Schmidt, who adds that "neither Tutuola nor his hero seem to be able to take a consistent moral stand, a characteristic that is distinctly different from Tutuola's other narratives." Commenting on the reasons for these differences, Schmidt writes: "They may reflect contemporary Yoruba culture, Tutuola's changing attitude toward Yoruba and Nigerian cultures as well as his changing position in Yoruba and Nigerian cultures, the difficulties of writing an oral narrative for an audience to whom oral narratives are becoming less familiar and less related to daily behavior, and the editorial policies for publishing African fictional narratives in the 1980s."

In the *New York Times Book Review* Charles Larson likewise notes Tutuola's use of standard English, but maintains that "the outstanding quality of Mr. Tutuola's work—the brilliance of the oral tradition—still remains." Larson concludes: " 'The Witch-Herbalist of the Remote Town' is Mr. Tutuola at his imaginative best. Every incident in the narrative breathes with the life of the oral tradition; every episode in the journey startles with a kind of indigenous surrealism. Amos Tutuola is still his continent's most fantastic storyteller."

BIOGRAPHICAL/CRITICAL SOURCES:

BOOKS

Collins, Harold R., *Amos Tutuola,* Twayne, 1969.
Contemporary Literary Criticism, Gale, Volume 5, 1976, Volume 14, 1980, Volume 29, 1984.
Herskovits, Melville J. and Francis S. Herskovits, *Dahomean Narrative: A Cross-Cultural Analysis,* Northwestern University Press, 1958.
Irele, Abiola, *The African Experience in Literature and Ideology,* Heinemann, 1981.
King, Bruce, editor, *Introduction to Nigerian Literature,* Evans Brothers, 1971.
Larson, Charles R., *The Emergence of African Fiction,* revised edition, Indiana University Press, 1972.
Laurence, Margaret, *Long Drums and Cannons: Nigerian Dramatists,* Praeger, 1969.
Lindfors, Bernth, editor, *Critical Perspectives on Amos Tutuola,* Three Continents Press, 1975.
Lindfors, Bernth, *Early Nigerian Literature,* Africana Publishing, 1982.
Moore, Gerald, *Seven African Writers,* Oxford University Press, 1962.
Palmer, Eustace, *The Growth of the African Novel,* Heinemann, 1979.
Tucker, Martin, *Africa in Modern Literature: A Survey of Contemporary Writing in English,* Ungar, 1967.
Tutuola, Amos, *The Palm-Wine Drinkard and His Dead Palm-Wine Tapster in the Dead's Town,* Faber, 1952, Grove, 1953.

PERIODICALS

Africa Today, Volume 29, number 3, 1982.
Ariel, April, 1977.
Books Abroad, summer, 1968.
Critique, fall/winter, 1960-61, fall/winter, 1967-68.
Journal of Canadian Fiction, Volume 3, number 4, 1975.
Journal of Commonwealth Literature, August, 1974, August, 1981, Volume 17, number 1, 1982.
Listener, December 14, 1967.
London Review of Books, April 2, 1987.
Los Angeles Times Book Review, August 15, 1982.
Nation, September 25, 1954.
New Statesman, December 8, 1967.
New Yorker, April 23, 1984.
New York Times Book Review, July 4, 1982.
Observer, July 6, 1952, November 22, 1981.
Okikie, September, 1978.
Presence Africaine, 3rd trimestre, 1967.
Spectator, October 24, 1981.
Times Educational Supplement, February 26, 1982.
Times Literary Supplement, January 18, 1968, February 26, 1982, August 28, 1987, May 18, 1990.
Voice Literary Supplement, June, 1982.
Washington Post, July 13, 1987.
Washington Post Book World, August 15, 1982.

*   *   *

TYLER, Anne 1941-

PERSONAL: Born October 25, 1941, in Minneapolis, Minn.; daughter of Lloyd Parry (a chemist) and Phyllis (Mahon) Tyler; married Taghi Modarressi (a psychiatrist and writer), May 3, 1963; children: Tezh, Mitra. *Education:* Duke University, B.A., 1961; graduate study at Columbia University, 1961-62. *Religion:* Quaker.

ADDRESSES: Home—222 Tunbridge Rd., Baltimore, Md. 21212. *Agent*—Russell & Volkening, 50 West 29th St., New York, N.Y. 10001.

CAREER: Writer. Duke University Library, Durham, N.C., Russian bibliographer, 1962-63; McGill University Law Library, Montreal, Quebec, Canada, assistant to the librarian, 1964-65.

MEMBER: P.E.N., American Academy and Institute of Arts and Letters, Authors Guild, Phi Beta Kappa.

AWARDS, HONORS: Mademoiselle award for writing, 1966; Award for Literature, American Academy and Institute of Arts and Letters, 1977; National Book Critics Circle fiction award nomination, 1980, Janet Heidinger Kafka prize, 1981, and American Book Award nomination in paperback fiction, 1982, all for *Morgan's Passing;* National Book Critics Circle fiction award nomination, 1982, and American Book Award nomination in fiction, P.E.N./Faulkner Award for fiction, and Pulitzer Prize nomination for fiction, all 1983, all for *Dinner at the Homesick Restaurant;* National Book Critics Circle fiction award and Pulitzer Prize nomination for fiction, both 1985, both for *The Accidental Tourist.*

WRITINGS:

NOVELS; PUBLISHED BY KNOPF

If Morning Ever Comes, 1964.
The Tin Can Tree, 1965.
A Slipping-Down Life, 1970.
The Clock Winder, 1972.
Celestial Navigation, 1974.
Searching for Caleb, 1976.
Earthly Possessions, 1977.
Morgan's Passing, 1980.
Dinner at the Homesick Restaurant, 1982.
The Accidental Tourist, 1985.
Breathing Lessons, 1988.

OTHER

(Editor with Shannon Ravenel, and author of introduction) *Best American Short Stories 1983,* Houghton, 1983.

Contributor of short stories to *Saturday Evening Post, New Yorker, Seventeen, Critic, Antioch Review,* and *Southern Review.*

SIDELIGHTS: Despite her status as a best-selling novelist, Anne Tyler remains a private person who rarely lets public demands interfere with family life. She shuns most interviewers, avoids talk show appearances, and prefers Baltimore, Maryland—where she lives with her husband and two daughters—to New York City. Nonetheless she is a well-established writer, having earned what former *Detroit News* reporter Bruce Cook calls "a solid *literary* reputation . . . that is based solely on the quality of her books."

Tyler's work has always been critically well received, but reviews of her early novels were generally relegated to the back pages of the book sections. Not until the publication of *Celestial Navigation* (1974), when she captured the attention of novelist Gail Godwin, and *Searching for Caleb* (1976), when John Updike recommended her to readers, did she gain widespread acclaim. "Now," says Cook, "her books are reviewed in the front of the literary journals and that means she is somebody to reckon with. No longer one of America's best unknown writers, she is now recognized as one of America's best writers. Period."

Born in Minnesota, Tyler lived in various Quaker communes throughout the Midwest and South before settling in the mountains of North Carolina for five years. She attended high school in Raleigh and at sixteen entered Duke University, where she fell under the influence of Reynolds Price, then a promising young novelist who had attended her high school. It was Price who encouraged the young Russian major to pursue her writing, and she did—but it remained a secondary pursuit until 1967, the year she and her husband settled in Baltimore.

In an interview with Bruce Cook, published in the *Saturday Review,* Tyler describes the city as "wonderful territory for a writer—so many different things to poke around in." And the longer she stays there, the more prominently Baltimore figures in her books, lending them an ambience both citified and southern and leading Reynolds Price to proclaim her "the nearest thing we have to an urban Southern novelist." Writing in the *New Yorker,* John Updike compares her to Flannery O'Connor, Carson McCullers, and Eudora Welty, noting: "Anne Tyler, in her gifts both of dreaming and of realizing, evokes comparison with these writers, and in her tone and subject matter seems deliberately to seek association with the Southern ambience that, in less cosmopolitan times, they naturally and inevitably breathed. Even their aura of regional isolation is imitated by Miss Tyler as she holds fast, in her imagination and in her person, to a Baltimore with only Southern exits; her characters when they flee, never flee north. Yet she is a citizen of the world, born in Minneapolis, a graduate student of Russian at Columbia, and now married to a psychiatrist from Iran. The brand names, the fads, the bastardized vistas of our great homogenized nation glint out at us from her fiction with a cheerful authority."

Other reviewers, such as Katha Pollitt, find Tyler's novels more difficult to classify. "They are Southern in their sure sense of family and place," she writes in the *New York Times Book Review,* "but lack the taste for violence and the Gothic that often characterizes self-consciously Southern literature. They are modern in their fictional techniques, yet utterly unconcerned with the contemporary moment as a subject, so that, with only minor dislocations, her stories could just as well have taken place in the twenties or thirties. The current school of feminist-influenced novels seems to have passed her by completely: her women are strong, often stronger than the men in their lives, but solidly grounded in traditional roles."

The key to Tyler's writing may well lie in the homage she pays to Eudora Welty, her favorite writer and one to whom she is repeatedly compared. "Reading her taught me there were stories to be written about the mundane life around me," she told Cook. Or as Tyler phrased it to Marguerite Michaels in the *New York Times Book Review,* "Reading Eudora Welty when I was growing up showed me that very small things are often really larger than the large things." Thomas M. Disch is one of several critics who believes that Tyler's insight into the lives of ordinary people is her special gift. Writing in the *Washington Post Book World,* he calls it an "uncommon accomplishment that she can make such characters interesting and amusing without violating their limitations." Despite their resemblances to people we meet in real life, Tyler's characters are totally fictitious. "None of the people I write about are people I know," she told Marguerite Michaels. "That would be no fun. And it would be very boring to write about me. Even if I led an exciting life, why live it again on paper? I want to live other lives. I've never quite believed that one chance is all I get. Writing is my way of making other chances." She perceives the "real heroes" of her books as "first the ones who manage to endure and second the ones who are somehow able to grant other people the privacy of the space around them and yet still produce some warmth."

Her major theme, according to Mary Ellen Brooks in the *Dictionary of Literary Biography,* "is the obstinate endurance of the human spirit, reflected in every character's acceptance or rejection of his fate and in how that attitude affects his day to day life. She uses the family unit as a vehicle for portraying 'how people manage to endure together—how they grate against each other, adjust, intrude and protect themselves from intrusions, give up, and start all over again in the morning.' " Frequently her characters respond to stress by running away, but their flight, Brook continues, "proves to be only a temporary and ineffectual means of dealing with reality."

Because the action of her novels is so often circular—ending exactly where it begins—Tyler's fiction has been criticized for lack of development. This is especially true of her early novels where the narratives are straightforward and the pacing slow. In fact, what impressed reviewers most about Tyler's first book, *If Morning Ever Comes,* was not the story itself but the promise it seemed to hold for future fictions. "The trouble with this competently put-together book is that the hero is hardly better defined at the end than he is at the beginning," observes Julian Gloag in the *Saturday Review.* "Writing about a dull and totally humorless character, Miss Tyler has inevitably produced a totally humorless and mainly dull novel. Anne Tyler is only twenty-two, and in the light of this her refusal to take risks is a bit puzzling. I'd like to see what she could do if she stopped narrowing her own eyes and let herself go. It might be very good." The *Times Literary Supplement* reviewer echoes these sentiments: "It will be surprising if a writer so young does not outgrow her hesitant efforts to produce big answers to emotional muddles and her sometimes over-literary sentences, and let her considerable gift for dialogue and comedy produce a very good novel indeed."

For her part, Tyler reportedly now hates her first book—and also her second, which received similar criticism. Written largely to pass the time while she was looking for a job, *The Tin Can Tree* concerns the inhabitants of a three-family house on the edge of a North Carolina tobacco field and their reactions to the accidental death of the six-year-old girl who lives there. Though the family is initially devastated by the tragedy, their emotional balance is restored in the end, and, for this reason, some critics find the novel static. Millicent Bell, for example, writes in the *New York Times Book Review:* "Life, this young writer seems to be saying, achieves its once-and-for-all shape and then the camera clicks. This view, which brings her characters back on the last page to where they started, does not make for that sense of development which is the true novel's motive force. Because of it, I think, her book remains a sketch, a description, a snapshot. But as such, it still has a certain dry clarity. And the hand that has clicked its shutter has selected a moment of truth."

Perhaps the most salient feature of Tyler's next novel, *A Slipping-Down Life* (which was misclassified as young adult literature and thus not widely reviewed), is its genesis. In discussing her craft with Marguerite Michaels, Tyler said: "Sometimes a book will start with a picture that pops into my mind and I ask myself questions about it and if I put all the answers together, I've got a novel. A real picture would be the old newspaper clipping about the Texas girl who slashed 'Elvis' in her forehead." In the novel, this incident is transformed into an episode in the life of Evie Decker, a fictive teenager grappling for her identity. "I believe this is the best thing I've ever done," Evie says of her self-mutilation. "Something out of character. Definite." In the *Dictionary of Literary Biography,* Mary Ellen Brooks describes the novel as "an accurate description of loneliness, failure to communicate, and regrets over decisions that are irreversible—problems with which any age group can identify. Tyler, who describes *A Slipping-Down Life* as one of her most bizarre works, believes that the novel 'is flawed, but represents, for me, a certain brave stepping forth.' "

So, too, does Tyler's fifth novel, *Celestial Navigation,* a book that the author wrote while "fighting the urge to remain in retreat even though the children had started school." In the character of Jeremy Paulding, an agoraphobic artist who is afraid to leave his Baltimore block, Tyler sees much of herself. While her characters are not usually autobiographical, Tyler told Brooks that creating Jeremy was a way of investigating her own "tendency to turn more and more inward."

The story opens with the death of Jeremy's mother and moves quickly to an exploration of the relationship he establishes with the woman who will take her place—a self-sufficient boarder named Mary Tell. Attracted by her sunny self-confidence, Jeremy proposes marriage and soon Mary has stepped in as Jeremy's intermediary to the outside world. As years pass, he comes to feel dwarfed by Mary's competence—she does not even alert him when she leaves for the hospital to have his fifth child because she knows he dreads the trip. Suffocated by her over-protectiveness, the disoriented artist withdraws even further into the private world of his studio where he fashions collages from scraps of other people's lives. Eventually Mary and the children abandon him, and Jeremy does venture out to find them. But the price he pays for conquering his fear is that he loses them for good. At the novel's end, Mary and Jeremy each remain in a separate existence, each still dominated by what Brooks calls "his innate driving characteristic. Jeremy returns to his life as a reclusive artist in a crumbling dark house while Mary prepares for winter in a rundown shack, knowing that another man will eventually provide for her."

Told from the viewpoints of six different characters, *Celestial Navigation* is far more intricate than Tyler's earlier novels, and most critics consider it a breakthrough. Katha Pollitt finds the work "extraordinarily moving and beautiful," while Doris Grumbach proclaims Tyler's "ability to enmesh the reader in what is a simple, uneventful story a notable achievement." In her *New York Times Book Review* article, Gail Godwin explains how "Tyler is especially gifted at the art of freeing her characters and then keeping track of them as they move in their unique and often solitary orbits. Her fiction is filled with displaced persons who persist stubbornly in their own destinies. They are 'oddballs,' visionaries, lonely souls, but she has a way of transcribing their peculiarities with such loving wholeness that when we examine them we keep finding more and more pieces of ourselves."

In her eighth novel, *Morgan's Passing,* Tyler turns from an exploration of the "oddball" as introvert to the "oddball" as extrovert in the creation of Morgan Gower—a 42-year-old hardware store manager with a knack for assuming other roles. Simply put, Morgan is an imposter, a man who changes identities every time he changes clothes. "You're walking down the street with him and this total stranger asks him when the International Brotherhood of Magicians is meeting next," his wife Bonny explains. "You're listening to a politician's speech and suddenly you notice Morgan on the platform, sitting beside a senator's wife with a carnation in his buttonhole. You're waiting for your crabs at Lexington Market and who's behind the counter but Morgan in a rubber apron, telling the other customers where he caught such fine oysters." These fantasies contrast sharply with the dullness of Morgan's actual life. At home, in the brick colonial house ac-

quired with his wife's money, he feels overwhelmed by the clutter of his wife, their seven daughters, his adult sister, and his feeble-minded mother.

The novel opens with one of Morgan's escapades. During the performance of a puppet show, the puppeteer, Leon Meredith, emerges from behind the curtains to request a doctor's assistance: his wife Emily has gone into labor. Morgan steps forward and, posing as a doctor, delivers the baby in the back seat of his car. In the process he becomes fascinated by what he perceives to be the simple existence of the Merediths. Emily, in particular, becomes "an emblem for Morgan of that spartan order he longs to bring to his over-furnished life," says Thomas M. Disch in the *Washington Post Book World.* But neither Emily nor Leon are as blithe as they seem, and by juxtaposing the reality of these characters with Morgan's fantasies of them, Tyler creates her drama, critics say.

Though *Morgan's Passing* was nominated for a National Book Critics Circle Award in hardback and an American Book Award in paperback fiction, critics are sharply divided in their assessment of the work. Those who like it praise Tyler's handling of character and her artful mingling of comedy and seriousness. "Though she allows her tale to veer toward farce, Tyler always checks it in time with the tug of an emotion, a twitch of regret," writes *Time*'s Paul Gray. He concludes: "*Morgan's Passing* is not another novel about a mid-life crisis, it is a buoyant story about a struggle unto death." Tyler acknowledged in her *Detroit News* interview with Bruce Cook that her "big worry in doing the book was that people would be morally offended by [Morgan]." But critic Marilyn Murray Willison sings his praises. "In spite of his inability to restore order to his life, his nicotine-stained hands and teeth, his silly wardrobe, his refusal to accept reality, Morgan emerges from Tyler's book a true hero," she writes in the *Los Angeles Times Book Review.*

Other critics, however, dislike the character and consider the book a disappointment. "For all its many felicities of observation and incident, *Morgan's Passing* does not come up to the high standard of Anne Tyler's other recent work. There is a self-indulgence in the portraiture of Morgan himself, whose numerous identity assumptions became for me merely tiresome," Paul Binding writes in the *New Statesman.* And *New York Review of Books* contributing critic James Wolcott dismisses *Morgan's Passing* as "a book of small compass, pent-up energy. Long before Morgan and Emily link arms, the reader has connected the dots separating them, so there's no suspense, no surprise. Instead, the book is stuffed with accounts of weddings, crowded dinners, cute squabbles, and symbolic-as-all-get-out puppet shows. Sentence by sentence, the book is engaging, but there's nothing beneath the jokes and tussles to propel the reader through these cluttered lives. It's a book with an idle motor." Writing in the *New Yorker,* John Updike explains his disappointment: "Anne Tyler continues to look close, and to fabricate, out of the cardboard and Magic Markers available to the festive imagination, images of the illusory lives we lead. More than that it would be unkind to ask, did we not imagine, for the scope of the gift displayed, that something of that gift is still being withheld."

With *Dinner at the Homesick Restaurant,* her ninth and, some say, finest novel, Tyler redeems herself in many critics' eyes. Updike, for instance, maintains that this book achieves "a new level of power and gives us a lucid and delightful yet complex and sombre improvisation on her favorite theme, family life." Writing in the *Chicago Tribune Book World,* Larry McMurtry echoes these sentiments: "She recognizes and conveys beautifully the alternations of tragedy and farce in family life, and never more beautifully than in *Dinner at the Homesick Restaurant.*" Benjamin Demott is even more impressed. "Funny, heart-hammering, wise, [the novel] edges deep into truth that's simultaneously (and interdependently) psychological, moral and formal—deeper than many living novelists of serious reputation have penetrated, deeper than Miss Tyler herself has gone before. It is a border crossing," he writes in the *New York Times Book Review.*

The story's plot is a simple one—"deceptively simple," Sarah English notes in the *Dictionary of Literary Biography Yearbook.* Eighty-five-year-old Pearl Tull—who married late in life and bore three children before being deserted by her traveling salesman husband—is lying on her deathbed recollecting the past. She reconstructs the moment, thirty-five years before, when Beck Tull announced he was leaving, the years of struggle that ensued as she singlehandedly (and sometimes heartlessly) raised her children, and the scars which Cody, Jenny, and Ezra still bear. "Something," Pearl thought, "was wrong with all her children. They were so frustrating—attractive, likeable people, the three of them, but closed off from her in some perverse way. She wondered if her children blamed her for something. Sitting close at family gatherings they tended to recall only poverty and loneliness. [They] referred continually to Pearl's short temper, displaying it against a background of stunned, childish faces so sad and bewildered that Pearl herself hardly recognized them. Honestly, she thought, wasn't there some statute of limitations here?"

In this darkest of Tyler's novels, the answer is no. "None of the three Tull children manages to cut loose from the family past," explains Demott. "Each is, to a degree, stunted; each turns for help to Pearl Tull in an hour of desperate adult need; and Pearl's conviction that something is wrong with each of them never recedes from the reader's consciousness."

The novel unfolds in a series of self-contained chapters, each, in Updike's words, "rounded like a short story," and each reflecting a different family member's point of view. This narrative technique, as Sarah English notes, "allows [Tyler] to juxtapose past and present and thus to convey the vision—that she has always had—of the past not as a continuum but as layer of still, vivid memories. The wealth of points of view also allows Tyler to show more fully than ever the essential subjectivity of the past. Cody and Jenny remember Pearl as a witch; Ezra remembers her as a source of strength and security. Every character's vision of the past is different."

Larry McMurtry believes that the book "amply demonstrates the tenacity of familial involvement," while *Los Angeles Times* reporter Carolyn See says Tyler shows how a family "is alive with needs of its own; it never relaxes its hold. Even when you are far away (especially when you're far away), it immobilizes you in its grip, which can—in another way—be looked at as a caress."

This portrait of family entanglements is too somber for some critics' tastes, including Cynthia Propper Seton's. "What may be the trouble with *Dinner at the Homesick Restaurant,*" she writes in the *Washington Post Book World,* "is that the Tull family is not marginal enough, its members are too grave a proposition for a mind so full of mischief as Anne Tyler's. They depressed her." In her *Detroit News* review, however, Cynthia King maintains that "despite the joyless atmosphere, the author's humor bubbles through in Pearl's tackiness, in Jenny's self-protective flippancy. And more than a few times—awful as Pearl is, warped and doomed as her children are—what keeps us turning pages is the suspicion that there may be a bit of each of them in each of us."

Concludes Benjamin Demott: "What one wants to do on finishing such a work as *Dinner at the Homesick Restaurant* is maintain balance, keep things intact for a stretch, stay under the spell as long as possible. The before and after are immaterial; nothing counts except the knowledge, solid and serene, that's all at once breathing in the room. We're speaking obviously, about an extremely beautiful book."

The Accidental Tourist, Tyler's tenth novel, again combines the author's subtle, understated probing into human nature and her eye for comic detail. The title serves both as a reference to the protagonist's occupation and as a metaphor for his life. Macon Leary writes travel guides for people who dislike traveling and who would prefer to stay in the comfort and familiarity of their own homes. The guide books—the series is titled *The Accidental Tourist*—advise reluctant travelers on how to visit foreign places without experiencing the annoyances and jarring peculiarities that each new city offers. Thus, Macon counsels his readers on where they can find American-style hamburgers in Amsterdam, for instance, or on the type of reading material to carry on the plane so as to ward off chatty neighbors.

Macon's suggestions are indicative of his own nature. Insular and wary of anything foreign or unexpected, Macon surrounds himself with rituals in an attempt to make his life ordered and safe. When his twelve-year-old son is murdered in a restaurant, he retreats even further into his cocoon, driving off his wife in the process. His son's dog, Edward, though, does not respond well to the changes in his environment. As Macon fills his life with more elaborate rituals, Edward develops a mean streak and begins to terrorize Macon's friends and relatives. Eventually, Edward requires a trainer, and it is this trainer that shocks Macon into reassessing his life. Muriel Pritchett is everything that Macon is not: impetuous, carefree, and disordered. Macon becomes attracted to Muriel and her odd life-style, seeing in it all the vitality and passion that his life lacks. When his wife changes her mind and asks Macon to resume their marriage, Macon is forced to choose between the two women. He opts for Muriel, recognizing the exuberance for life that she has awakened in him.

As with her previous novels, reviewers praised the gently ironic humor and sympathetic, likable characters that Tyler creates in *The Accidental Tourist.* Richard Eder of the *Los Angeles Times Book Review* notes that the character of Macon Leary "is an oddity of the first water, and yet we grow so close to him that there is not the slightest warp in the lucid, touching and very funny story of an inhibited man moving out into life." Other critics observes that in this book Tyler fuses the mix of tragedy and comedy that appears in most of her previous books. Larry McMurtry, writing in the *New York Times Book Review* about "the mingling of misery and contentment in the daily lives of her families" that Tyler constructs, comments that "these themes, some of which she has been sifting for more that twenty years, cohere with high definition in the muted . . . personality of Macon Leary." Some reviewers criticize Tyler for her tendency to draw sympathetic characters and to infuse humor into so many of her scenes. *Chicago Tribune Book World* critic John Blades wonders whether "Tyler, with her sedative resolutions to life's most grievous and perplexing problems, can be taken seriously as a writer." Most reviewers, though, only praise the book and its author. As Eder notes, "I don't know if there is a better American writer going."

In her eleventh novel, *Breathing Lessons,* Tyler examines the themes of marriage, love, and regret. The story concerns Maggie and Ira Moran, married for twenty-eight years, and a journey they make to the funeral of an old friend. During the trip they both reflect on their years together—some happy, some sad. Maggie is gregarious and curious, while Ira is practical and withdrawn. Both at times regret their decision to marry, but they also recognize the strength of the bond between them. Critics still remark on Tyler's ability to evoke sympathy for her characters and her talent for constructing humorous scenes. Eder, again writing in the *Los Angeles Times Book Review,* sums up critical reaction by noting that "there are moments when the struggle among Maggie, Ira, and the melancholy of time passing forms a fiery triangle more powerful and moving . . . than anything she has done."

MEDIA ADAPTATIONS: The Accidental Tourist was adapted into a film and released by Warner Brothers in 1988.

BIOGRAPHICAL/CRITICAL SOURCES:

BOOKS

Bestsellers 89, Issue 1, Gale, 1989.
Contemporary Literary Criticism, Gale, Volume 7, 1977, Volume 11, 1979, Volume 18, 1981, Volume 28, 1984, Volume 44, 1987.
Dictionary of Literary Biography, Gale, Volume VI: *American Novelists since World War II, Second Series,* 1980, *Yearbook: 1982,* 1983.

PERIODICALS

Atlantic Monthly, March, 1976.
Chicago Tribune Book World, March 23, 1980, March 21, 1982, July 20, 1986.
Detroit News, April 6, 1980, April 18, 1982.
Globe and Mail (Toronto), September 21, 1985, October 8, 1988.
Los Angeles Times, March 30, 1982, September 14, 1983.
Los Angeles Times Book Review, March 30, 1980, September 15, 1985, September 11, 1988.
Ms., August, 1977.
National Observer, May 30, 1977.
New Republic, May 13, 1972, May 28, 1977, March 22, 1980.
New Statesman, April 4, 1975, December 5, 1980.
Newsweek, April 5, 1982, September 9, 1985.
New Yorker, March 29, 1976, June 6, 1977, June 23, 1980, April 5, 1982.
New York Review of Books, April 3, 1980.
New York Times, May 3, 1977, March 17, 1980, March 22, 1982, September 30, 1983, September 3, 1988.
New York Times Book Review, November 22, 1964, November 21, 1965, March 15, 1970, May 21, 1972, April 28, 1974, January 18, 1976, May 8, 1977, March 14, 1982, September 8, 1985.
Saturday Review, December 26, 1964, November 20, 1965, June 17, 1972, March 6, 1976, September 4, 1976, March 15, 1980.
Time, May 9, 1977, March 17, 1980, April 5, 1982, September 16, 1985.
Times (London), January 12, 1989.
Times Literary Supplement, July 15, 1965, May 23, 1975, December 9, 1977, October 31, 1980, October 29, 1982, October 4, 1985, January 20, 1989.
Tribune Books (Chicago), August 28, 1988.
Washington Post Book World, March 16, 1980, April 4, 1982, September 4, 1988.

* * *

TYNAN, Kenneth (Peacock) 1927-1980

PERSONAL: Born April 2, 1927, in Birmingham, England; died of emphysema, July 26, 1980, in Santa Monica, Calif.; buried in England; son of Sir Peter Peacock and Letitia Rose Tynan; married Elaine Bundy (an American writer), January 25, 1951 (divorced, 1964); married Kathleen Halton (a writer), June, 1967; children: (first marriage) Tracy; (second marriage) Roxanna Nell, Matthew. *Education:* Magdalen College, Oxford, B.A., 1948. *Politics:* Socialist. *Religion:* None.

ADDRESSES: Agent—Curtis Brown Ltd., 10 Astor Pl., New York, N.Y. 10003.

CAREER: Drama critic and writer. Director of weekly repertory company, Lichfield, Staffordshire, England, 1949; director of "Man of the World," Lyric Theatre, London, England, 1950, and "Othello," for the Arts Council Tour, 1950; drama critic, *Spectator,* London, 1950-51, *Evening Standard,* London, 1952-53, and *Daily Sketch,* London, 1953-54; *Observer,* London, drama critic, 1954-58 and 1960-63, film critic, 1964-66, arts columnist, 1968-69; *New Yorker,* New York, N.Y., drama critic, 1958-60; British National Theatre, literary manager, 1963-69, literary consultant, 1969-73; *New Yorker,* feature writer, 1976-80. Actor in Alec Guinness's "Hamlet," New Theatre, London, 1951; co-producer of Rolf Hochhuth's "Soldiers," New Theatre, 1968. Head of script department, Ealing Films, 1954-56; creator of British television feature "We Dissent," 1960; editor of British television program "Tempo," 1961; television producer, 1961-62. Former member of British Council drama panel.

MEMBER: Royal Society of Literature (fellow).

WRITINGS:

He That Plays the King, Longmans, Green, 1950.
Persona Grata, photographs by Cecil Beaton, Wingate, 1953, Putnam, 1954.
Alec Guinness: An Illustrated Study of His Work for Stage and Screen, with a List of His Appearances, Rockliff, 1953, Macmillan, 1955, 3rd edition, Macmillan, 1961.
Bull Fever, Harper, 1955, enlarged edition, Atheneum, 1966.
"Nowhere to Go" (screenplay), Metro-Goldwyn-Mayer, 1958.
(Contributor) Torn Maschler, editor, *Declaration,* MacGibbon & Kee, 1959.
(With Harold Lang) *The Quest for Corbett* (radio play; first produced by British Broadcasting Corp.-Radio, 1956), Gabberbocchus, 1960.
Curtains, Atheneum, 1961.
Tynan on Theatre, Penguin, 1964.
(Editor) George Farquhar, *The Recruiting Officer* (National Theatre production), Hart-Davis, 1965.
(Editor) William Shakespeare, *Othello* (National Theatre production), Hart-Davis, 1966, Stein & Day, 1967.
(Author of introduction) Lenny Bruce, *How to Talk Dirty and Influence People,* P. Owen, 1966.
Tynan Right and Left: Plays, Films, People, Places and Events, Atheneum, 1967.
"The Actors" (television documentary script), Independent Television (ITV), 1968.
(Deviser and contributor) *Oh! Calcutta! An Entertainment with Music* (first produced Off-Broadway at Eden Theatre, June 17, 1969; produced in London at The Roundhouse, July 27, 1970), Grove, 1969, reprinted, Applause Theatre Book Publications, 1986.
(Contributor) Douglas A. Hughes, editor, *Perspectives on Pornography,* St. Martin's, 1970.
(With Roman Polanski) "Macbeth" (screenplay; based on Shakespeare's play of the same title), Columbia, 1971.
The Sound of Two Hands Clapping, Holt, 1975.
A View of the English Stage, 1944-1963, Methuen, 1975.

Show People: Profiles in Entertainment, Simon & Schuster, 1980.

Also author of *Carte Blanche,* 1976. Contributor to periodicals in England and the United States.

WORK IN PROGRESS: Profiles of Laurence Olivier and Maggie Smith.

SIDELIGHTS: "A critic," as Kenneth Tynan was once quoted by Richard West in the *Los Angeles Times,* "is a man who knows the way but can't drive the car." For three decades this critic expressed his views in books and in such periodicals as the *Spectator,* the *Observer,* and the *New Yorker.* "Regarded by many in England as 'the greatest theater critic since Shaw,' " notes Michiko Kakutani in the *New York Times,* "Mr. Tynan exerted a lasting influence on the stage." Harold Clurman, reviewing Tynan's 1961 book *Curtains,* drew this profile of the author/critic: "What makes Tynan that rare phenomenon, a genuine theatre critic, is that he is disposed toward the theatre in the sense that we speak of certain people being naturally musical." Clurman added, "[He] experiences the theatre with his nerves, body, mind and spirit. He possesses in regard to the theatre something like absolute pitch." Tynan was also a noted writer of celebrity profiles and the creator of "Oh! Calcutta!," a theatre piece which, because of its countercultural tone and its onstage nudity, became one of the most notorious successes of the 1960s.

Tynan's contributions to the lively arts were remembered by *New York Times* contributor Robert Cushman, who on the occasion of Tynan's death recalled the critic's emergence onto the 1950s theatre scene: "He was dissatisfied with the state of contemporary English drama; . . . he was uncertain what should be put in its place. All he knew is that he wanted a break from plays set in Mayfair flats or swank country houses." Cushman explained that John Osborne's play " 'Look Back in Anger,' with its articulate, poverty-stricken and discontented hero struck a chord; *this,* [Tynan] proclaimed, was what he'd waited for. He became the critical spokesman for what soon proved to be a new generation of socially aware left-wing playwrights."

Show People: Profiles in Entertainment, published just months before its author's death, is a compendium of several *New Yorker* sketches that Tynan wrote during the 1970s. As Jack Richardson noted in a *New York Times Book Review* article, "Mr. Tynan concedes in his foreword there is no theme or overview connecting these portraits except the admiration he feels for his subjects and the wish to include them all in an ideal dinner party." The five subjects are British actor Sir Ralph Richardson, playwright Tom Stoppard, writer/comic Mel Brooks, silent-screen star Louise Brooks, and television personality Johnny Carson. About these subjects, Tynan revealed, in the words of *Saturday Review* contributor Stephen Harvey, "minute biographical trivia, painstakingly analyzing the themes and techniques that have marked these figures' professional achievements, watching and describing them at work when possible, interviewing his subjects and their friends and colleagues at length."

"Tynan's elegant, lean essays cruise along smoothly at top speed," commented Jean Strouse in *Newsweek,* "and he uses the English language with all the grace and precision of a well-muscled athlete exercising his body." And according to Richardson, "As any good host should, Mr. Tynan tries to treat all his guests with equal interest and courtesy. However, being human, he does betray a greater affection for certain members of the gathering and, as an unregenerate critic, he is from time to time compelled to lecture them on their shortcomings." Strouse characterized Tynan's collection as a blend of "companionable chat with delightful anecdote and shrewd surmise." Concluded Michael Dirda in a *Washington Post Book Review* article, "Kenneth Tynan once described himself as 'a student of craftsmanship, with a special passion for imaginative craftsmen.' These pieces allow one to share his passion, and to admire—as people have for 30 years—the gifts of a splendid writer, still our finest connoisseur of the performing arts."

BIOGRAPHICAL/CRITICAL SOURCES:

PERIODICALS

Detroit News, August 10, 1980.
New Republic, August 23, 1980.
Newsweek, February 11, 1980.
New York Review of Books, March 6, 1980.
New York Times, January 22, 1980, August 17, 1980.
New York Times Book Review, March 19, 1961, January 20, 1980.
Saturday Review, February 2, 1980.
Spectator, January 31, 1981.
Time, January 21, 1980.
Times Literary Supplement, January 2, 1981.
Washington Post Book World, February 17, 1980.

OBITUARIES:

PERIODICALS

Chicago Tribune, July 30, 1980.
Los Angeles Times, July 29, 1980.
Newsweek, August 11, 1980.
New York Times, July 29, 1980.
Time, August 11, 1980.
Times (London), July 29, 1980.

U

UCHIDA, Yoshiko 1921-

PERSONAL: Surname is pronounced "Oo-*chee*-dah"; born November 24, 1921, in Alameda, Calif.; daughter of Dwight Takashi (a businessman) and Iku (Umegaki) Uchida. *Education:* University of California, Berkeley, A.B. (cum laude), 1942; Smith College, M.Ed., 1944. *Politics:* Democrat. *Religion:* Protestant.

ADDRESSES: Home—1685 Solano Ave., Apt. 102, Berkeley, Calif. 94707.

CAREER: Elementary school teacher in Japanese relocation center in Utah, beginning 1942; Frankford Friends' School, Philadelphia, Pa., teacher, 1944-45; membership secretary, Institute of Pacific Relations, 1946-47; secretary, United Student Christian Council, 1947-52; full-time writer, 1952-57; University of California, Berkeley, secretary, 1957-62; full-time writer, 1962—.

AWARDS, HONORS: Ford Foundation research fellow in Japan, 1952; Children's Spring Book Festival honor award, *New York Herald Tribune*, 1955, for *The Magic Listening Cap;* Notable Book citation, American Library Association, 1972, for *Journey to Topaz;* medal for best juvenile book by a California author, Commonwealth Club of California, 1972, for *Samurai of Gold Hill;* Award of Merit, California Association of Teachers of English, 1973; citation, Contra Costa chapter of Japanese American Citizens League, 1976, for outstanding contribution to the cultural development of society; Morris S. Rosenblatt Award, Utah State Historical Society, 1981, for article, "Topaz, City of Dust"; Distinguished Service Award, University of Oregon, 1981; Commonwealth Club of California medal, 1982, for *A Jar of Dreams;* award from Berkeley Chapter of Japanese American Citizens League, 1983; Best Book of 1985 citation, Bay Area Book Reviewers, 1985, for *The Happiest Ending.*

WRITINGS:

FOR CHILDREN

The Dancing Kettle and Other Japanese Folk Tales, illustrations by Richard C. Jones, Harcourt, 1949, reprinted, Creative Arts Book Co., 1986.

New Friends for Susan, illustrations by Henry Sugimoto, Scribner, 1951.

(Self-illustrated) *The Magic Listening Cap—More Folk Tales from Japan,* Harcourt, 1955, reprinted, Creative Arts Book Co., 1987.

(Self-illustrated) *The Full Circle* (junior high school study book), Friendship, 1957.

Takao and Grandfather's Sword, illustrations by William M. Hutchinson, Harcourt, 1958.

The Promised Year, illustrations by Hutchinson, Harcourt, 1959.

Mik and the Prowler, illustrations by Hutchinson, Harcourt, 1960.

Rokubei and the Thousand Rice Bowls, illustrations by Kazue Mizumura, Scribner, 1962.

The Forever Christmas Tree, illustrations by Mizumura, Scribner, 1963.

Sumi's Prize, illustrations by Mizumura, Scribner, 1964.

The Sea of Gold, and Other Tales from Japan, illustrations by Marianne Yamaguchi, Scribner, 1965.

Sumi's Special Happening, illustrations by Mizumura, Scribner, 1966.

In-Between Miya, illustrations by Susan Bennett, Scribner, 1967.

Hisako's Mysteries, illustrations by Bennett, Scribner, 1969.

Sumi and the Goat and the Tokyo Express, illustrations by Mizumura, Scribner, 1969.

Makoto, the Smallest Boy: A Story of Japan, illustrations by Akihito Shirawaka, Crowell, 1970.

Journey to Topaz: A Story of the Japanese-American Evacuation, illustrations by Donald Carrick, Scribner, 1971, revised edition, Creative Arts Book Co., 1985.

Samurai of Gold Hill, illustrations by Ati Forberg, Scribner, 1972, revised edition, Creative Arts Book Co., 1985.

The Birthday Visitor, illustrations by Charles Robinson, Scribner, 1975.

The Rooster Who Understood Japanese, illustrations by Robinson, Scribner, 1976.

Journey Home (sequel to *Journey to Topaz*), illustrations by Robinson, McElderry Books, 1978.

A Jar of Dreams, McElderry Books, 1981.

The Best Bad Thing (sequel to *A Jar of Dreams*), McElderry Books, 1983.

Tabi: Journey through Time, Stories of the Japanese in America, United Methodist Publishing House, 1984.

The Happiest Ending (sequel to *The Best Bad Thing*), McElderry Books, 1985.

The Two Foolish Cats, illustrations by Margot Zemach, McElderry Books, 1987.

FOR ADULTS

We Do Not Work Alone: The Thoughts of Kanjiro Kawai, Folk Art Society (Japan), 1953.
(Translator of English portions) Soetsu Yanagi, editor, *Shoji Hamada,* Asahi Shimbun Publishing, 1961.
The History of Sycamore Church, Sycamore Congregational Church, 1974.
Desert Exile: The Uprooting of a Japanese-American Family, University of Washington Press, 1982.
Picture Bride (novel), Northland Press, 1987.

CONTRIBUTOR OF SHORT STORIES FOR CHILDREN

Scribner Anthology for Young People, Scribner, 1976.
Sense, Scott, Foresman, 1977.
Image, Scott, Foresman, 1977.
Question and Form in Literature, Scott, Foresman, 1979.
The Abracadabras, Addison-Wesley, 1981.

OTHER

Author of regular column, "Letter from San Francisco," in Craft Horizons, 1958-61. Contributor to exhibit catalogue of Oakland Museum, 1976. Contributor of adult stories and articles to newspapers and periodicals, including *Woman's Day, Gourmet, Utah Historical Quarterly, Far East,* and *California Monthly.*

SIDELIGHTS: Yoshiko Uchida's appreciation for her heritage has made her the author of more than twenty books on Japanese culture for readers of all ages. "In fiction, the graceful and lively books of Yoshiko Uchida have drawn upon the author's own childhood to document the Japanese-American experience for middle-grade readers," Patty Campbell comments in the *New York Times Book Review.* And among her non-fiction works for adults are studies of Japanese folk artists such as *We Do Not Work Alone: The Thoughts of Kanjiro Kawai,* as well as a memoir of wartime imprisonment, *Desert Exile: The Uprooting of a Japanese-American Family.*

After the bombing of Pearl Harbor, Americans of Japanese descent were incarcerated by order of the government. Uchida was a senior at the University of California, Berkeley, when her family was sent to Tanforan Racetrack, where thousands of Japanese Americans lived in stables and barracks. After five months at Tanforan, they were moved to Topaz, a guarded camp in the Utah desert. Uchida taught in the elementary schools there until the spring of 1943 when she was released to accept a fellowship for graduate study at Smith College. Her parents were also released that year.

Uchida earned a master's degree in education; but because teaching limited her time for writing, she found a secretarial job that allowed her to write in the evenings. As she explains in her contribution to *Something about the Author Autobiography Series,* "I was writing short stories at the time, sending them to the *New Yorker, Atlantic Monthly* and *Harper's*—and routinely receiving printed rejection slips. After a time, however, the slips contained encouraging penciled notes and a *New Yorker* editor even met with me to suggest that I write about my concentration camp experiences. . . . And many of the short stories I wrote during those days were published eventually in literature anthologies for young people."

By the time *Women's Day* accepted one of her stories, Uchida found that writing for children promised more success. Her first book, *The Dancing Kettle and Other Japanese Folk Tales,* was well received, and when a Ford Foundation grant enabled Uchida to visit Japan, she collected more traditional tales. In addition, she became fascinated with Japanese arts and crafts, and she learned more about them from philosopher Soetsu Yanagi and other founders of the Folk Art Movement in Japan. But her most important gain from the visit, she writes, was the awareness "of a new dimension of myself as a Japanese American and [a] deepened . . . respect and admiration for the culture that had made my parents what they were."

The death of the author's mother in 1966 prompted Uchida to write a book for her parents "and the other first-generation Japanese (the Issei), who had endured so much." The result was the book *Journey to Topaz: A Story of the Japanese-American Evacuation.* Based on her own experiences in the camps during the war, it marked a shift in emphasis from Japanese culture to the Japanese-American experience in the United States. Every book Uchida has written since *Journey to Topaz* responds to the growing need for identity among third generation Japanese Americans. Uchida once explained to *CA:* "Through my books I hope to give young Asian Americans a sense of their past and to reinforce their self-esteem and self-knowledge. At the same time, I want to dispel the stereotypic image still held by many non-Asians about the Japanese and write about them as real people. I hope to convey the strength of spirit and the sense of hope and purpose I have observed in many first-generation Japanese. Beyond that, I write to celebrate our common humanity, for the basic elements of humanity are present in all our strivings."

Uchida speaks Japanese and French, and her books have been translated into German, Dutch, Afrikaans, and Japanese.

AVOCATIONAL INTERESTS: Fine arts, folk crafts.

BIOGRAPHICAL/CRITICAL SOURCES:

BOOKS

Children's Literature Review, Volume VI, Gale, 1984.
Something about the Author Autobiography Series, Volume I, Gale, 1986.

PERIODICALS

Children's Book World, November 5, 1967.
Los Angeles Times Book Review, August 9, 1987.
New York Times Book Review, February 9, 1986.
Young Readers' Review, January, 1967.

*   *   *

UNAMUNO (y JUGO), Miguel de   1864-1936

PERSONAL: Born September 29, 1864, in Bilbao, Spain; died December 31, 1936, in Salamanca, Spain; married Concepcion Lizarraga Ecenarro, 1891; children: ten. *Education:* Attended Colegio de San Nicolas and Instituto Vizacaino, Bilbao, Spain; University of Madrid, Ph.D., 1884.

CAREER: Educator, poet, novelist, and playwright. University of Salamanca, Salamanca, Spain, professor of Greek, 1891-1924, 1930-34, and rector, 1901-1914, 1934-36; exiled to Canary Islands, 1924, and lived and wrote in France, 1924-30; placed under house arrest for criticism of Franco government, 1936. Cortes (Spanish parliament) deputy from Salamanca; president, Council for Public Education. Taylor lecturer, Oxford University.

AWARDS, HONORS: Cross of the Order of Alfonso XII, 1905; honorary doctorate, University of Grenoble, 1934.

WRITINGS:

FICTION

Paz en la guerra, F. Fe, 1897, translation by Allen Lacy and Martin Nozick with Anthony Kerrigan published as *Peace in War* (Volume 1 of "Selected Works"), edited by Kerrigan, Princeton University Press, 1983.

Amor y pedogogia, 1902, Espasa-Calpe, 1934.

El espejo de la muerte (also see below), 1913, Compania Iberoamericana de Publicaciones, 1930.

Niebla, 1914, Renacimiento, 1928, translation by Warner Fite published as *Mist,* Knopf, 1928.

Abel Sanchez: Una historia de pasion, Renacimiento, 1917, translation published as *Abel Sanchez,* edited by Angel del Rio and Amelia de del Rio, Holt, 1947.

Tres novelas ejemplares y un prologo, Espasa-Calpe, 1920, translation by Angel Flores published as *Three Exemplary Novels and a Prologue,* A. & C. Boni, 1930.

La tia Tula (also see below), Renacimiento, 1921.

San Manuel Bueno, martir, y tres historias mas (also see below), Espasa-Calpe, 1933, translation by Francisco de Segovia and Jean Perez published in bilingual edition as *San Manuel Bueno, martir,* Harrap, 1957.

Cuentos (stories), edited by Eleanor Krane Paucker, Minotauro, 1961.

Ver con los ojos y otros relatos novelescos (stories), Espasa-Calpe, 1973.

San Manuel Bueno, martir [and] *La novela de don Sandalio, jugador de ajedrez* (title means "The Novel of Don Sandalio, Chessplayer"; also see below), edited with introduction and notes by C. A. Longhurst, Manchester University Press, 1984.

Also author of *Tulio Montalban y Julio Macedo,* 1920.

PLAYS

El otro, misterio en tres jornadas y un epilogo (title means "The Other"; also see below), Espasa-Calpe, 1932.

El hermano Juan; o, El mundo es teatro, Espasa-Calpe, 1934.

La esfinge (also see below), 1934, Alfil, 1960.

Soledad (also see below), Espasa-Calpe, 1957.

El pasado que vuelve, edited by Manuel Garcia Blanco, Alfil, 1960.

Also author of *La venda* (also see below), *La princesa,* [and] *Dona Lambra,* 1913, *Fedra* (also see below), 1924, *Sombras de sueno,* 1931, *Raquel encadenada* (also see below), 1933, *La difunta,* 1959, and *Medea* (also see below).

POETRY

Poesias, J. Rojas, 1907.

Rosario de sonetos liricos, Imprenta Espanola, 1911.

El Cristo de Velazquez, Calpe, 1920, translation by Eleanor L. Turnbull published as *The Christ of Velazquez,* Johns Hopkins Press, 1951.

Teresa, Renacimiento, 1923.

De Fuerteventura a Paris (verse and prose), Excelsior, 1925.

Poems, translation by Turnbull, Johns Hopkins Press, 1952.

Cancionero: Diario poetico, edited by Federico de Onis, Losada, 1953.

Cincuenta poesias ineditas (previously unpublished work), edited by Garcia Blanco, Papeles de Son Armadans, 1958.

Poemas de los pueblos de Espana, selected by Garcia Blanco, Anaya, 1961.

Poesias escogidas, selected by Guillermo de Torre, Losada, 1965.

The Last Poems of Miguel de Unamuno, translation by Edita Mas-Lopez, Fairleigh Dickinson University Press, 1974.

Also author of *Rimas de dentro,* 1923.

ESSAYS

En torno al casticismo, F. Fe, 1902.

Vida de Don Quijote y Sancho, F. Fe, 1905, translation by Homer P. Earle published as *The Life of Don Quixote and Sancho,* Knopf, 1927.

Mi religion y otros ensayos breves, 1910, Espasa-Calpe, 1942, translation by Stuart Gross published as *Perplexities and Paradoxes,* Philosophical Library, 1945.

Soliloquios y conversaciones, 1911, Espasa-Calpe, 1942.

Del sentimiento tragico de la vida en los hombres y en los pueblos, 1913, Renacimiento, 1928, translation by J. E. Crawford Flitch published as *The Tragic Sense of Life in Men and in Peoples,* Macmillan, 1926.

La agonia del cristianismo, 1925, Renacimiento, 1931, translation by Pierre Loving published as *The Agony of Christianity,* Payson & Clark, 1928, translation by Kurt F. Reinhardt published as *The Agony of Christianity,* Ungar, 1960.

Essays and Soliloquies, translation and introduction by Flitch, Knopf, 1925.

Como se hace una novela (title means "How to Make a Novel"; also see below), Alba, 1927.

Dos articulos y dos discursos, Historia Nueva, 1930.

Algunas consideraciones sobre la literatura hispano-americana, Espasa-Calpe, 1947.

Visiones y comentarios, Espasa-Calpe, 1949.

Espana y los espanoles (also see below), edited with notes by Garcia Blanco, Aguado, 1955.

Inquietudes y meditaciones, prologue and notes by Garcia Blanco, Aguado, 1957.

La vida literaria, Espasa-Calpe, 1967.

El gaucho Martin Fierro, Americalee, 1967.

Also author of *Tres ensayos,* 1900, and *El porvenir de Espana,* with Angel Ganivet, 1912 (also see below).

JOURNALISTIC PIECES

Pensamiento politico, edited by Elias Diaz, Tecnos, 1965.

Desde el mirador de la guerra, edited by Louis Urrutia, Centre de Recherches Hispaniques (Paris), 1970.

Discursos y articulos, Escelicer, 1971.

En torno a las artes: Del teatro, el cine, las bellas artes, la politica y las letras, Espasa-Calpe, 1976.

Escritos socialistas: Articulos ineditos sobre el socialismo, 1894-1922, edited by Pedro Ribas, Ayuso, 1976.

Articulos olvidados sobre Espana y la primera guerra mundial, edited by Christopher Cobb, Tamesis, 1976.

Cronica politica espanola (1915-1923), edited by Vicente Gonzalez Martin, Almar, 1977.

Republica espanola y Espana republicana, edited by Gonzalez Martin, Almar, 1979.

Unamuno: Articulos y discursos sobre Canarias, edited by Francisco Navarro Artiles, Cabildo Insular de Fuerteventura, 1980.

Ensueno de una patria: Periodismo republicano, 1931-36 (political), Pre-Textos, 1984.

LETTERS

(With Juan Maragall) *Epistolario,* Edimar, 1951, revised edition, Distribuidora Catalonia, 1976.

(With Juan Zorrilla de San Martin) *Correspondencia,* [Montevideo], 1955.

Trece cartas ineditas de Miguel de Unamuno a Alberto Nin Frias, La Mandragora, 1962.
Cartas ineditas, compiled by Sergio Fernandez Larrain, Zig-Zag, 1965.
(With Alonso Quesada) *Epistolario,* edited by Lazaro Santana, Museo Canario, 1970.
Cartas 1903-1933, compiled by Carmen de Zulueta, Aguilar, 1972.
Unamuno "agitador de espiritus" y Giner: Correspondencia inedita, edited by D. Gomez Molleda, 1976.
(With Leopoldo Gutierrez Abascal and Juan de la Encina) *Cartas intimas: Epistolario entre Miguel de Unamuno y los hermanos Gutierrez Abascal,* edited with notes by Javier Gonzalez de Durana, Equzki, 1986.
(With Jose Ortega y Gasset) *Epistolario completo Ortega-Unamuno,* edited by Laureano Robles Carcedo with Antonio Ramos Gascon, El Arquero, 1987.

AUTOBIOGRAPHY

Recuerdos de ninez y de mocedad, V. Suarez, 1908, selected and edited by William Atkinson, Longmans, Green, 1929.
En el destierro (recuerdos y esperanzas), selected and annotated by Garcia Blanco, Pegaso, 1957.
Mi vida y otros recuerdos personales, complied by Garcia Blanco, Losada, 1959.
Diario intimo (also see below), edited by P. Felix Garcia, Escelicer, 1970.
De mi vida, Espasa-Calpe, 1979.

OMNIBUS VOLUMES IN ENGLISH

Abel Sanchez and Other Stories, translated by Kerrigan, Regnery, 1956.
Our Lord Don Quixote and Sancho with Related Essays (Volume 3 of "Selected Works"), translated and edited by Kerrigan, Princeton University Press, 1967.
The Tragic Sense of Life in Men and Nations (Volume 4 of "Selected Works"), translated and edited by Kerrigan, Princeton University Press, 1972.
The Agony of Christianity and Essays on Faith (Volume 5 of "Selected Works"), translated and edited by Kerrigan, Princeton University Press, 1974.
Novela/Nivola (Volume 6 of "Selected Works"; includes *How to Make a Novel*), translated and edited by Kerrigan, Princeton University Press, 1976.
Ficciones: Four Stories and a Play (Volume 7 of "Selected Works"; includes *The Other, Tia Tula,* and *The Novel of Don Sandalio, Chessplayer*), translated and edited by Kerrigan, Princeton University Press, 1976.
The Private World: Selections from the Diario Intimo and Selected Letters (Volume 2 of "Selected Works"), translated by Kerrigan, Lacy, and Nozick, edited by Kerrigan, Princeton University Press, 1984.

ANTHOLOGIES AND OMNIBUS VOLUMES IN SPANISH

Ensayos (essays), seven volumes, Fortanet, 1916-18, revised edition, two volumes, Aguilar, 1942.
Ensayos y sentencias de Unamuno, edited with introduction and notes by Wilfred A. Beardsley, Macmillan, 1932.
Prosa diversa, selected by J. L. Gili, Oxford University Press, 1939.
Antologia poetica (poetry), edited by Luis Felipe Vivanco, Escorial, 1942.
Antologia poetica (poetry), edited by Jose Maria de Cossio, Espasa-Calpe, 1946.
Obras selectas (selected works), Pleyade, 1946.

De esto y de aquello, edited by Garcia Blanco, Sudamericana, 1950.
Obras completas (collected works), Aguado, 1950-51.
Teatro: Fedra. Soledad. Raquel encadenada. Medea. (plays), edited by Garcia Blanco, Juventud, 1954.
Obras completas (complete works), ten volumes, edited by Garcia Blanco, Aguado, 1958-61.
Teatro completo, edited by Garcia Blanco, Aguilar, 1959.
Antologia, edited by Luis Gonzalez Seara, Doncel, 1960.
Antologia, Fondo de Cultura Economica, 1964.
El espejo de la muerte, y otros relatos novelescos, Juventud, 1965.
Cancionero: Antologia (poetry), selected by Ramos Gascon, Taurus, 1966.
Unamuno: Sus mejores paginas, edited by Philip Metzidakis, Prentice-Hall, 1966.
Obras completas, Las Americas, Volume 1: *Paisajes y ensayos,* Volume 2: *Novelas,* Volume 3: *Nuevos ensayos,* Volume 4: *La raza y la lengua,* Volume 5: *Teatro completo y monodialogos,* Volume 6: *Poesia,* Volume 7: *Meditaciones y ensayos espirituales,* 1966-69.
La agonia del cristianismo, Mi religion, y otros ensayos (collected essays), Las Americas, 1967.
Tres nivolas de Unamuno (novels), edited by Demetrios Basdekis, Prentice-Hall, 1971.
El porvenir de Espana y los espanoles (contains *El porvenir de Espana* and *Espana y los espanoles*), Espasa-Calpe, 1972.
Novela (novels), edited by Eugenio de Bustos Tovar, Noguer, 1976.
Antologia poetica (poetry), edited by Jose Maria Valverde, Alianza, 1977.
Antologia poetica (poetry), edited by Mercedes Santos Moray, Editorial Arte y Literatura, 1979.
Jubilacion de don Miguel de Unamuno: Cuaderno de la Magdalena y otros papeles (papers), Libreria Estudio, 1980.
Unamuno multiple: Antologia, edited by Amelia de del Rio, University of Puerto Rico, 1981.
La esfinge; La venda; Fedra (plays), edited by Jose Paulino, Castalia, 1987.
Poesia completa, Alianza, 1987—.

Works also published in multiple editions.

OTHER

Paisajes (travel), 1902, Aguado, 1950.
De mi pais (travel), F. Fe, 1903.
Por tierras de Portugal y de Espana (travel), V. Prieto, 1911.
Contra esto y aquello, Renacimiento, 1912.
(Editor) *Simon Bolivar, libertador de la America del Sur, por los mas grandes escritores americanos,* Renacimiento, 1914, reprinted with prologue by Manuel Trujillo as *Bolivar,* Biblioteca Ayacucho, 1983.
Andanzas y visiones espanolas (travel), Renacimiento, 1922.
Romancero del destierro, Alba, 1928.
La ciudad de Henoc: Comentario 1933, Seneca, 1941.
Cuenca iberica (lenguaje y paisaje), Seneca, 1943.
El caballero de la triste figura, Espasa-Calpe, 1944.
Almas de jovenes, Espasa-Calpe, 1944.
La dignidad humana, Espasa-Calpe, 1944.
Paisajes del alma, Revista de Occidente, 1944.
La enormidad de Espana, Seneca, 1945.
Madrid, Aguado, 1950.
Mi Salamanca, selected by Mario Grande Ramos, Escuelas Graficas de la Santa Casa de Misericordia, 1950.
(With Ruben Dario) *Don Jose Lazaro, 1862-1947,* edited by Antonio R. Rodriguez Monino, Castalia, 1951.
Viejos y jovenes, Espasa-Calpe, 1956.

Autodialogos, Aguilar, 1959.

Escritos de toros, Union de Bibliofilos Taurinos, 1964.

Mi bochito, selected by Garcia Blanco, Libreria Arturo, 1965.

La raza vasca y el vascuence: En torno a la lengua espanola, Espasa-Calpe, 1968.

(Translator) Arthur Schopenhauer, *Sobre la voluntad en la naturaleza,* Alianza, 1970.

Solitana (bilingual edition), edited by Pablo Bilbao and Emilia Doyaga, Washington Irving, 1970.

Libros y autores espanoles contemporaneos, Espasa-Calpe, 1972.

Monodialogos, Espasa-Calpe, 1972.

Gramatica y glosario del Poema del Cid, edited by Barbara D. Huntley and Pilar Liria, Espasa-Calpe, 1977.

La muerte de Ramirez y las olvidadas memorias del general Anacleto Medina, A. Pena Lillo, 1980.

Also translator of *Etica de las prisiones, Exceso de legislacion, De las leyes en general,* by Herbert Spencer, three volumes, 1895, *Historia de la economia politica,* by J. K. Ingram, c. 1895, and *Historia de las literaturas castellana y portuguesa,* by Ferdinand J. Wolf, two volumes, 1895-96.

SIDELIGHTS: "At his death in 1936," Arthur A. Cohen claimed in the *New York Times Book Review,* "Miguel de Unamuno was the most influential thinker in Spain, more renowned than his younger contemporary [Jose] Ortega y Gasset and regarded by his own aficionados as the greatest stylist in the Spanish language since Cervantes." Author of fiction, drama, poetry, philosophical essays, and a variety of nonfiction, Unamuno "dug deeper into the national spirit than any of his contemporaries, a generation whose collective project was the exploration of Spanishness," Enrique Fernandez proposed in the *Voice Literary Supplement.* "Quixote incarnate, he lived out his nationality to its logical philosophical conclusions. . . . The soul-searching of the first Spanish moderns, who would be called the generation of 1898, found its fullest expression in Unamuno. In poems, plays, novels, and essays," the critic continued, Unamuno questioned "Spanishness, modernity, science, politics, philosophy, faith, God, everything."

The foremost questions for Unamuno were often existential, exploring issues of death, mortality, and faith. "Written all over [Unamuno] are the passions and yearnings of a sincere religious searcher," Paul Ilie commented in *Unamuno: An Existential View of Self and Society.* "[He] is, at the same time, clouded by the doubts and anguish of a rational mind too sophisticated for the simple faith of ordinary men." These religious doubts led to several turbulent spiritual crises, from which Unamuno "developed the dominant convictions of his later life," as Howard T. Young described in *The Victorious Expression: A Study of Four Contemporary Spanish Poets:* "to struggle for the sake of struggle, to believe in the need to believe, even if he himself could not believe. His paradoxes symbolize a lasting insecurity." Indeed, as Frances Wyers noted in *Miguel de Unamuno: The Contrary Self,* Unamuno's work was marked by paradox, "a persistent contrariness, an almost desperate need to set up oppositions and then collapse them into a single entity, to take sides and then switch, to deny and then deny the denial or to assert that what was denied was really affirmed. . . . Unamuno's paradoxes are the result of an unexamined, almost frantic, effort to tie together opposing aspirations."

In searching for resolutions to his doubts, Unamuno brought a profound passion to his writing, an intensity which informs all his work. "On whatever page we open one of his writings we find an identical atmosphere, a permanent and invariable note, forced into use with equal passion . . . throughout all of his volumes

and all of his life," Julian Marias stated in his study *Miguel de Unamuno.* This repetition of atmosphere and theme reflected the author's foremost concern: "Man in his entirety, man who goes from his birth to his death, with his flesh, his life, his personality, and above all his desire never to die completely," as Marias defined it. "It is living, suffering man who interests Unamuno, not the abstraction humanity," A. Dobson said in a *Modern Languages* essay. "What makes man authentically human is his fear of death, and for Unamuno, the preservation of the individual's personality is his supreme task."

"The evolution of [Unamuno's] thought was marked by three books or great essays, more professions of faith than philosophical treatises:" *The Life of Don Quixote and Sancho, The Tragic Sense of Life in Men and Peoples,* and *The Agony of Christianity,* as Arturo and Ilsa Barea catalogued in their book *Unamuno.* In these works, Unamuno fought what *Nation* contributor Mark Van Doren referred to as "the windmills of despair," an emotion inspired by his knowledge of his own mortality. Nevertheless, the critic added, "Unamuno fights because he knows there is not a chance in the world to win. He has tasted the glory of absurdity. He has decided to hope what he cannot believe. He has discovered grounds for faith in the very fact that there are no grounds." Thus it was this "continuous struggle with death," according to Cohen, that for Unamuno "makes [life] worth living. . . . Any means by which a man subverts the kingdom of death is a triumph for life and, in Unamuno's clever logic, for eternity."

This conflict between faith and reason, between "the truth thought and the truth felt," Salvador de Madariaga remarked in *The Genius of Spain,* became the primary focus of Unamuno's meditations. "It is because *The Tragic Sense of Life* is the most direct expression of [Unamuno's conflict] that this book is his masterpiece." In this essay, Angel and Amelia A. de del Rio recounted in the introduction to *Abel Sanchez,* "Unamuno analyzes what he calls the tragic essence of modern civilization, resulting from the longing for knowledge which, guided by reason, has destroyed man's faith in God and in immortality, a faith necessary for his emotional life. Hence, modern humanity, incapable of solving the problem, is forced to struggle in uncertainty, and at the same time to strive after truth, a struggle and agony inherently tragic." In a style that would characterize all Unamuno's essays, the Bareas asserted, *The Tragic Sense of Life* "was not meant as an orderly philosophical treatise on the human condition, but as one man's record of his thoughts on life and death, confessed before his fellow-mortals with all the passionate sincerity of which that man was capable." The work "is the greatest of the many monologues Unamuno wrote," the critics continued. "Every bit of reasoning in it springs from his intimate spiritual needs; nothing is 'objective.' This is as he meant it to be, and he argues at the very beginning of the book that this subjectivity is the only truthful approach possible." The result, as Van Doren described it, was "modern Catholicism's richest, most passionate, most brilliant statement of the grounds that exist for faith in immortality, now that reason and science have done their worst".

In *The Life of Don Quixote and Sancho* Unamuno brought a new approach to the literary essay. As Demetrios Basdekis summarized in his *Miguel de Unamuno,* "it is literary criticism which is not quite a critical essay; it is a novelizing of a particular novel and a theory of the novel in general; it is creative prose which is not quite prose fiction, although it sometimes borders on this." In arguing that the character of Don Quixote surpassed his creator—that Cervantes was unaware of his own work's implications—Unamuno "set forth the essential premise of all his intellectual criticism: madness is reality, and historical objectivity is madness," Cohen stated. Thus, "the chivalric vocation and undertakings of Don Quixote, continuously pragmatized by his sympathetic squire [Sancho Panza], are treated by Unamuno as the ultimate pilgrimage." "Don Quixote became in the eyes of Unamuno a prophet, a divinely inspired figure preaching the doctrine of quixotism, which is the doctrine of immortality through mundane glory, salvation through high-minded battle against the mean reality of the world," Young postulated. "Turning Cervantine irony into the tragic irony of life, Unamuno exalted Don Quixote as a stirring figure struggling against human fate." "Unamuno's *The Life of Don Quixote and Sancho,*" concluded Basdekis, "is a major theoretical doctrine; in turn it is a huge step toward his 'novel of extreme situations' entitled *Mist.*"

"As a novelist, Unamuno was often ahead of his time, especially in his denial of the usual boundaries between life and art," Allen Lacy maintained in a *Nation* article. Novels such as *Mist, Abel Sanchez,* and *San Manuel Bueno, martir,* are "very fresh even in the 1960s," said Lacy, "especially for [their] improvisatory technique. His sense of the novel as a vehicle of serious play, as a comic metaphysic, has strong affinities to the best work of Jorge Luis Borges and John Barth." Proposing a new form which he called a "nivola," Unamuno attempted a spontaneous creation that would give its characters their own existence. "With the guiding principle of the nonreality of the material world in view, the *nivolas* eliminate all externals, particularly settings and character descriptions," in order to focus on the individual characters, L. Livingstone noted in *Hispania.* "The destruction of form in the *nivola . . .* gives it an other-worldliness, a timelessness and freedom from spatial dimensions, that reproduce the author's hunger for immortality."

As Jose Ferrater Mora explained in *Unamuno: A Philosophy of Tragedy,* the author "emphasized that the characters he depicted—or more exactly, in whose innards he poked about—were truly intimate because of what they revealed of themselves. With the 'soul of their soul' laid bare, Unamuno held, they were indistinguishable from truly existing beings." This theory is exemplified in several works, especially the last chapter of *Mist,* in which, Carlos Blanco Aguinaga related in *Modern Language Notes,* "the conventions of Fiction, and therefore of existence, are broken." Wanting to discuss the possibility of suicide, the protagonist Augusto Perez travels to Salamanca to speak to Unamuno, whom he knows as a learned philosopher—only to learn that he is a fictional character subject to the whims of his creator and thus unable to commit suicide. Augusto returns to his home and soon dies after a strangely compulsive bout of over-eating, leaving the reader to wonder whether Unamuno or Augusto willed the death. *Mist* "abounds in ingenious conceptions and paradoxes," the del Rios observed, resting "on an idea that is eminently paradoxical, as Unamuno's ideas regularly are."

Despite his success as an essayist and novelist, Unamuno "maintained that he would be best remembered by his poetry," the Bareas reported. "His rough-tongued poems with their blend of fervour and contemplation brought indeed a new note into Spanish lyrical poetry at the turn of the century, but their poetic form was never strong enough to absorb the sentiments and thoughts that inspired them." As Young outlined, Unamuno believed that "ideas—and, consequently, feelings, for in Unamuno the two could never be separated—take precedence over all other considerations. What the poet says is more important than how he says it; meter, rhyme, and pattern are secondary to content and emotion."

As a result, much of Unamuno's poetry tended to be prosaic and "inelegant," as Young termed it; thus, it is a "pleasant surprise" to discover "the Miltonic flow of *The Christ of Velazquez,* and the subdued sadness of his later sonnets." The former work, a book-length poem, "is Unamuno's major accomplishment in poetry," Basdekis remarked, a "blank verse hymn . . . liberally sprinkled with paraphrase and quotations from the Old and New Testaments." Inspired by seventeenth-century Spanish painter Diego Velazquez's masterpiece depicting Christ's crucifixion, Unamuno's poem reflects his usual focus by "sing[ing] in resounding tones of the Incarnation, Death, and Resurrection of Jesus, and derives from these beliefs his hope of escaping total death," Martin Nozick suggested in his study *Miguel de Unamuno.* "Free of the mesh of doctrine and philosophy, he is carried away by pure love, by a fundamental devotion to Gospel whose meanings he deepens, embroiders, and personalizes." Despite the length of the poem, Madariaga stated, it "easily maintains [a] lofty level throughout, and if he had written nothing else Unamuno would still remain as having given to Spanish letters the noblest and most sustained lyrical flight in the language. It abounds in passages of ample beauty, and often strikes a note of primitive strength in the true Old Testament style." *The Christ of Velazquez,* concluded Nozick, is "a major work of unflagging vitality and resonances, a Cantata to the Son of God on the Cross, made up of wave upon wave of Whitmanesque rhythms, or what Unamuno himself called 'a sort of rhythmoid, dense prose.' "

The intense emotions Unamuno brought to *The Christ of Velazquez* and his other works have led critics to observe a poetic sense in all his writing. "For Unamuno, a poem or novel (and he holds that a novel is but a poem) is the outpouring of a man's passion, the overflow of the heart which cannot help itself and lets go," Madariaga proposed. The Bareas similarly commented that "Unamuno's true poetic creation was the personality he projected into all his work; his 'agony,' his ceaseless struggle with himself and the universe, was the core of every one of his novels and stories, poems and essays." "His style, rather than the clear, orderly style of a philosopher, is always that of a poet, impassioned, full of images, sometimes difficult because of the abundance of allusions, paradoxes, digressions, parentheses, exclamations, and ingenious plays upon words and ideas," the del Rios wrote. Ferrater Mora similarly declared that in analyzing Unamuno's work, "it must always be kept in mind that a poetic *elan* breathes within it, that the written word is meant to be only a shadow of the creative voice. . . . Unamuno wanted to dissolve all 'genres,' all classifications, to fuse all 'genres' together in the deathless fountain of poetry. For Unamuno the only 'literary form' was the poem, and the numerous, perhaps infinite, forms that the poem adopts."

The author's poetic emphasis and concern with human mortality have led many critics to characterize his work as distinctively Spanish. Calling Unamuno "the greatest literary figure of Spain [of his time]," Madariaga asserted that the author "is head and shoulders above [his contemporaries] in the highness of his purpose and in the earnestness and loyalty with which, Quixote-like, he has served all through his life. . . . Unamuno, by the cross which he has chosen to bear, incarnates the spirit of modern Spain," the critic continued. "His eternal conflict between faith and reason, between life and thought, between spirit and intellect, between heaven and civilization, is the conflict of Spain herself." Cohen likewise noted a unique Spanish temperament in the author's work; "the principal debate, the argument that undergirds all of Unamuno's life and thought and gives to it a power most peculiarly Spanish and most thoroughly universal . . . is

Unamuno's contest with death." The critic elaborated, stating that "Spain, a culture which has stylized violence, is overwhelmed with death and committed to resurrection."

"In the last analysis, it is useless to attempt to define the subject matter, the ideas, and the substance of Unamuno's writing," the del Rios suggested, "because his combined work, his life, and his personality, have for root and impulse a dynamic or dialectical contraction whose import Unamuno formulated again and again." The critics added that Unamuno's "metaphysical concepts of desperation, anguish, and agony . . . are, for him, the essence of the Spanish spirit, composed of dissonances, with its perpetual conflict between the ideal and reality, between heaven and earth, between its Sancho Panza-like sense of the immediate and its quixotic yearning for immortality." "[It was] for Unamuno, a figure who transcends the notion of generations and who speaks, at one and the same time, as both modern and universal man, to synthesize and spell out in his poetry, essays and, especially, in his 'nivolas' the dilemma of the individual 'of flesh and bones,' as he was found of saying, alienated both psychologically and metaphysically in the twentieth century," J. F. Tull contended in the *Humanities Association Bulletin.* "Though he ravaged all genres," Fernandez remarked, "Unamuno is hard to classify as a writer—if he even *is* a writer." His fiction and poetry, "though powerful, is more philosophical than lyrical," the critic continued, and his philosophical writings "are emotional and personal" rather than logical or theoretical. "Too writerly to be a philosopher, too philosophical to be an artist," Fernandez concluded, "Unamuno is, as he deserves to be, a category unto himself."

MEDIA ADAPTATIONS: Julio de Hoyos adapted one of the novellas from *Tres novelas ejemplares, Nada menos que todo un hombre,* into a drama titled "Todo un hombre."

BIOGRAPHICAL/CRITICAL SOURCES:

BOOKS

Barea, Arturo and Ilsa Barea, *Unamuno,* translated by I. Barea, Bowes & Bowes, 1952.
Basdekis, Demetrios, *Unamuno and Spanish Literature,* University of California Press, 1967.
Basdekis, Demetrios, *Miguel de Unamuno,* Columbia University Press, 1969.
Bleiberg, Herman and E. Inman Fox, editors, *Spanish Thought and Letters in the Twentieth Century: Miguel de Unamuno: 1864-1964,* Vanderbilt University Press, 1966.
Ferrater Mora, Jose, *Unamuno: A Philosophy of Tragedy,* translated by Philip Silver, University of California Press, 1962.
Ilie, Paul, *Unamuno: An Existential View of Self and Society,* University of Wisconsin Press, 1967.
Lacy, Allen, *Miguel de Unamuno: The Rhetoric of Existence,* Mouton & Co., 1967.
Lopez, Julio, *Unamuno,* Jucar, 1985.
Madariaga, Salvador de, *The Genius of Spain, and Other Essays on Spanish Contemporary Literature,* Oxford University Press, 1923.
Marias, Julian, *Miguel de Unamuno,* translated by Frances M. Lopez-Morillas, Harvard University Press, 1966.
Nozick, Martin, *Miguel de Unamuno,* Twayne, 1971.
Rubia Barcia, Jose, and M. A. Zeitlin, editors, *Unamuno: Creator and Creation,* University of California Press, 1967.
Rudd, Margaret Thomas, *The Lone Heretic: A Biography of Miguel de Unamuno y Jugo,* University of Texas Press, 1963.
Twentieth-Century Literary Criticism, Gale, Volume 2, 1979, Volume 9, 1983.

Unamuno, Miguel de, *Abel Sanchez,* edited by Angel del Rio and Amelia de del Rio, Holt, 1947.
Wyers, Frances, *Miguel de Unamuno: The Contrary Self,* Tamesis, 1976.
Young, Howard T., *The Victorious Expression: A Study of Four Contemporary Spanish Poets,* University of Wisconsin Press, 1964.

PERIODICALS

Hispania, December, 1941.
Humanities Association Bulletin, winter, 1970.
Modern Language Notes, Volume 79, number 2, 1964.
Modern Languages, June, 1973.
Nation, May 17, 1922, June 24, 1968.
New York Times Book Review, December 16, 1973.
Voice Literary Supplement, May, 1987.

—*Sketch by Diane Telgen*

* * *

UNDSET, Sigrid   1882-1949

PERSONAL: Born May 20, 1882, in Kalundborg, Denmark; died after a stroke, June 10, 1949, in Lillehammer, Norway; daughter of Ingvald Martin (an archeologist) and Anna Charlotte Undset; married Anders C. Svarstad (an artist), 1912 (marriage annulled, 1924); children: Anders, Maren Charlotte, Hans. *Education:* Received secretarial certificate from Christiania Commercial College, c. 1898. *Religion:* Roman Catholic.

CAREER: German Electric Company, Christiania (now Oslo), Norway, secretary, c. 1898-1908. Full-time writer, 1908-49.

AWARDS, HONORS: Nobel Prize for literature from the Swedish Academy, 1928; Grand Cross of the Order of Saint Olav from King Haakon VII, 1947.

WRITINGS:

CONTEMPORARY NOVELS

Fru Marta Oulie (title means "Mrs. Marta Oulie"), Aschehoug, 1907, reprinted, 1977.
Jenny, Aschehoug, 1911, reprinted, 1967, translation by W. Emme published under the same title, Knopf, 1921, reprinted, Fertig, 1975.
Vaaren (title means "Spring"), Aschehoug, 1914.
Gymnadenia, Aschehoug, 1929, reprinted, 1973, translation by Arthur G. Chater published as *The Wild Orchid,* Knopf, 1931.
Den brennende busk, Aschehoug, 1930, reprinted, 1974, translation by Chater published as *The Burning Bush,* Knopf, 1932.
Ida Elisabeth, Aschehoug, 1932, translation by Chater published under the same title, Knopf, 1933.
Den trofaste hustru, Aschehoug, 1936, translation by Chater published as *The Faithful Wife,* Knopf, 1937.

HISTORICAL NOVELS

Fortellingen om Viga-Ljot og Vigdis [and] *Sankt Halvards liv, dod og jaertgen,* Aschehoug, 1909, translation of the former by Chater published as *Gunnar's Daughter,* Knopf, 1936.
Kristin Lavransdatter, three volumes, Aschehoug, Volume I: *Kransen,* 1920, translation by Charles Archer and J. S. Scott published as *The Bridal Wreath,* Knopf, 1923 (published in England as *The Garland,* Knopf, 1930), reprinted, Bantam, 1978; Volume II: *Husfrue,* 1921, translation by Archer published as *The Mistress of Husaby,* Knopf, 1925, reprinted,

Bantam, 1978; Volume III: *Korset,* 1922, translation by Archer published as *The Cross,* Knopf, 1927, reprinted, Bantam, 1978; single volume Nobel Prize edition translated by Archer and Scott published as *Kristin Lavransdatter,* Knopf, 1929.

Olav Audunsson i Hestviken, two volumes, Aschehoug, 1925, two-volume translation by Chater published as *The Axe,* Knopf, 1928, and *The Snake Pit,* Knopf, 1929 (both volumes included in *The Master of Hestviken;* also see below).

Olav Audunsson og hans born, two volumes, Aschehoug, 1927, two-volume translation by Chater published as *In the Wilderness,* Knopf, 1929, and *The Son Avenger,* Knopf, 1930 (both volumes included in *The Master of Hestviken;* also see below).

The Master of Hestviken (contains novels *The Axe, The Snake Pit, In the Wilderness,* and *The Son Avenger*), translated by Chater, Nobel Prize edition, Knopf, 1934, reprinted, New American Library, 1978.

Madame Dorthea, Aschehoug, 1939, reprinted, 1968, translation by Chater published under the same title, Knopf, 1940.

OTHER

Den lykkelige alder (stories; title means "The Happy Age"), Aschehoug, 1908.

Fattige skjebner (stories; title means "Poor Fortunes"; contains "Forste mote," "Simonsen," "Selma Broter," "Omkring sedelighetaballet," "Froken Smith Tellefsen," and "Nikkedukken"), Aschehoug, 1912, translations of "Simonsen," "Selma Broter," and "Froken Smith Tellefsen" by Naomi Walford published in *Four Stories,* Knopf, 1959 (also see below).

Fortellinger om Kong Artur og ridderne av det Runde bord (adapted from Thomas Mallory's tales of King Arthur), Aschehoug, 1915.

Splinten av troldspeilet (contains *Fra Hjeld* and *Fra Waage*), Aschehoug, 1917, translation of *Fra Hjeld* by Chater published as *Images in a Mirror,* Knopf, 1938.

De kloge jomfruer (stories; title means "The Wise Virgins"; contains "Smaspiker," "Thjodolf," and "Gunvald og Emma"), Aschehoug, 1918, reprinted, 1968, translation of "Thjodolf" by Walford published in *Four Stories,* Knopf, 1959 (also see below).

Et kvindesynspunkt (essays), Aschehoug, 1919, reprinted, 1982.

Die saga von Vilmund Vidutan und seinen Gefaehrten (children's story), Hausen Verlagagesellschaft, 1931, translation published as *Sigurd and His Brave Companions: A Tale of Medieval Norway,* illustrations by Gunvor Bull Teilman, Knopf, 1943.

Etapper: Ny rakke (essays), Aschehoug, 1933, translation by Chater published as *Stages on the Road,* Knopf, 1934, reprinted, Books for Libraries Press, 1969.

Elleve aar (autobiography), Aschehoug, 1934, reprinted, 1966, translation by Chater published as *The Longest Years,* Knopf, 1935, reprinted, 1971.

Norske helgener (essays), Aschehoug, 1937, translation by E. C. Ramsden published as *Saga of Saints,* Longmans, Green, 1934, reprinted, Books for Libraries Press, 1968.

Selvportretter og landskapsbilleder (essays), Aschehoug, 1938, translation by Chater published as *Men, Women, and Places,* Knopf, 1939, reprinted, Books for Libraries Press, 1969.

Return to the Future (autobiography), translated by Henrietta C. K. Naeseth, Knopf, 1942.

(Editor) *True and Untrue, and Other Norse Tales* (based on original stories from Asbjoernsen and Moe's *Folkeeventyr*), illustrations by Frederick T. Chapman, Knopf, 1945.

Lykkelige dager (reminiscences), [Oslo], 1947, reprinted, Aschehoug, 1971, translation by Joran Birkeland published as *Happy Times in Norway,* Knopf, 1948, reprinted, Greenwood Press, 1979.

Caterina av Siena (biography), Aschehoug, 1951, translation by Kate Austin-Lund published as *Catherine of Siena,* Sheed & Ward (New York), 1954.

Artikler og taler fra krigstiden, edited by A. H. Winsnes, Aschehoug, 1952.

Four Stories (contains "Thjodolf," "Selma Broter," "Simonsen," "Miss Smith-Tellefsen"), translated by Naomi Walford, Knopf, 1959, reprinted, 1978.

Kirke og klosterliv: Tre essays fro norsk middelalder, Cappelen, 1963.

Djaere dea (letters), edited with foreword by Christianne Undset Svarstad, Cappelen, 1979.

Kritikk og tro: Tekster (essays), edited by Liv Bliksrud, St. Olav, 1982.

Sigrid Undset skriver hjem: En vandring gjennom enigrantarene i Amerika (letters), edited by Arne Skouen, Aschehoug, 1982.

Also author of a play titled "In the Gray Light of Dawn" and a verse collection; translator of various Icelandic tales. Work represented in anthologies, including *A Woman's Point of View,* 1919. Contributor to periodicals.

COLLECTED WORKS

Middelalder-romaner (medieval novels), ten volumes, Aschehoug, 1949.

Romaner og fortellinger fra nutiden (contemporary works), ten volumes, Aschehoug, 1964-65, reprinted as *Natidsverker,* twelve volumes, 1983.

Middelalder-verker (medieval works), eight volumes, Aschehoug, 1982.

Works also published in other collections.

SIDELIGHTS: Sigrid Undset won a secure place in literary history as one of the foremost authors of historical novels and as the most prominent Catholic author Scandinavia has produced. Carl F. Bayerschmidt, in his critical study *Sigrid Undset,* labeled the Norwegian novelist "one of the greatest realistic writers of the first half of the twentieth century." A. H. Winsnes, in *Sigrid Undset: A Study in Christian Realism,* called the author "the Christian realist *par excellence.*" Undset's works are powerful not only because of their moral message but also because of her mastery of technique: few other novelists have so accurately painted background and setting or so completely banned romanticism from their works. As Winsnes pointed out, Undset has been called "the [Emile] Zola of the Middle Ages." Very few other writers have understood so fully the past and its connection with the present. Winsnes noted that "history is Sigrid Undset's muse. No one since [thirteenth-century poet and historian] Snorri Sturluson has presented medieval Norway with such power."

Although Undset's fame was secured by her novels of medieval Norway, she also wrote realistic novels of contemporary life, a play, a collection of poems, many volumes of short stories and essays, and works of literary criticism. She followed the events of her day with attention and made significant contributions in fiction and nonfiction to the awakening movement for women's rights. She protested against the "new paganism" of materialism and was an untiring champion of democracy.

The story of Unset's life is one of self-sacrifice and responsibility. Born in Kalundborg, Denmark, she was the eldest of three daughters of Anna Charlotte Undset and the renowned Norwegian archeologist Ingvald Undset. Ingvald Undset had come from Trondelag, an area of Norway accurately described in his daughter's masterpiece, *Kristin Lavransdatter* (1920-22). Anna Charlotte Undset, who was a reserved and proud woman, inspired respect in her daughter but not the deep affection that the child felt for her father—in the portrayal of Kristin's father Lavrans in *Kristin Lavransdatter,* Undset paid tribute to her own father. At the age of two, she moved with her family to the city of Christiania (now Oslo), where her father was associated with the archeological section of the University Museum. As Ingvald Undset's health declined (he had caught malaria on an expedition to the Mediterranean), the family moved frequently, and Undset became intimately acquainted with many areas of the city of Oslo. As the daughter of an archeologist, she acquired an acute sense of history; the Undset home was filled with books, and the child was encouraged by her father to read extensively, especially works of history and Old Norse sagas. When Undset was eleven years old, her father died, and the family experienced genuine poverty. Her autobiographical memoir, *Elleve aar* (*The Longest Years,* 1934), records memories of the first eleven years of her life. That she gave herself the name "Ingvild" in these memoirs suggests the strength of her attachment to and identification with her father.

Although Undset attended the liberal school of Ragna Nielsen and had the opportunity to enroll in the university, she chose at the age of fifteen to prepare for a secretarial career at the Christiania Commercial College. Her certificate from this school a year later helped her to obtain a position in the local office of the German Electric Company, where she worked for ten years. Undset's intimate acquaintance with young working girls provided the material for many of her earliest works. In her free time from her secretarial job, Undset turned her hand to writing. She submitted a historical novel to the Gyldendal publishing house in Copenhagen only to be told that she should turn to modern themes that seemed more suited to her talents. Undset followed this advice, and her first contemporary social novel, *Fru Marta Oulie* (title means "Mrs. Marta Oulie"), appeared in the fall of 1907. After the publication of three additional works of moderate success, Undset felt secure enough to quit her job for a full-time career as a writer. In 1909 she received a travel grant from the Norwegian government and went to Rome, where she met her future husband, the painter Anders Svarstad. Married in 1912, the couple lived first in London and later in Norway, where Undset continued to produce fiction, nonfiction, and translations. After the births of three children—Anders, Maren Charlotte, and Hans—Svarstad and Undset eventually became estranged, and their marriage was annulled when she accepted the Catholic faith on All Saints' Day, November 24, 1924.

Remaining in Lillehammer, Norway, until 1940, Undset devoted herself both to her work, for which she received the Nobel Prize for literature in 1928, and to her children. Maren Charlotte, who was born retarded, lived only to the age of twenty-three; Anders, Undset's eldest son, was killed in 1940 when German armies invaded Norway. With Hans, her only surviving child, Undset then made the long journey through Sweden to Russia, from there to Japan, and from there to San Francisco. During the war, she channeled her considerable energies into the war effort, giving lectures, writing propaganda, and calling attention to the plight of occupied Norway. In August, 1945, she returned to her

homeland, and in 1947 King Haakon VII conferred upon her the Grand Cross of the Order of Saint Olav for service to her country. On June 10, 1949, Undset died in Lillehammer. Her life provided the impetus for her works: her religious faith, her pride in the past of her people, and her assessment of motherhood as woman's most important calling are all mirrored in her imaginative works and clearly stated in her nonfiction.

Although there is no clear chronological division between Undset's novels of contemporary life and her works set in earlier historical periods (in 1909 she published a pastiche of the Icelandic saga, and contemporary social novels reoccur in the 1930s), most of her early writing was inspired by her knowledge of the working class of Oslo. *Fru Marta Oulie* treats infidelity in marriage. The novel, which is written in diary form, begins with the confession, "I have been unfaithful to my husband." Undset's only play, "In the Gray Light of Dawn," is likewise concerned with adultery, and this theme is prominent in Undset's novels of the Middle Ages as well. Two collections of short stories, *Den lykkelige alder* (title means "The Happy Age," 1908) and *Fattige skjebner* (title means "Poor Fortunes," 1912), address themselves to problems of adolescence, motherhood, and spinsterhood in the lower economic classes of Norwegian urban society.

The novel *Jenny* (1912), which caused a sensation in Scandinavian feminist circles, is the story of a promising young artist who commits suicide. Jenny has, along the way, had an affair with her fiance's father, borne a child out of wedlock, suffered through the death of that child, and experienced frustration as a creative artist. Whether Jenny's suicide is caused by her failure as an artist or by her failure in erotic and maternal relationships is open to interpretation. In any case, the work is the most successful of all of Undset's social novels with contemporary settings.

Several later works also treat realistically problems of sexual fidelity and parenthood, stressing the importance of forgiveness and presenting the child as the element that can weld the most disparate parents together. *Vaaren* (title means "Spring," 1914) describes the marriage of a young couple; *Splinten av troldspeilet* (half of which was later translated as *Images in a Mirror,* 1917) contains two short stories that deal with infidelity and a young wife's conflict between family and career; *De kloge jomfruer* (title means "The Wise Virgins," 1918) emphasizes the importance of motherhood. Written towards the end of Undset's career, *Ida Elisabeth* (1932) presents a wife who sacrifices her personal happiness to remain faithful to her marriage vows, and *Den trofaste hustru* (*The Faithful Wife,* 1936) records the disintegration of a childless marriage, though in the latter work a religious element new to the social novels is introduced. Through these novels Undset was placed squarely at the head of the women's movement in Scandinavia, whether she wished to be in that position or not. An intelligent, creative working woman who also experienced marriage and motherhood, she could write eloquently of the problems that beset such women.

As controversial as some of her novels of contemporary life may have been, none of them could compare with Undset's masterpieces of medieval life. Critics agree that it is the multi-volume *Kristin Lavransdatter* and the *Olav Audunsson* series (*The Master of Hestviken,* 1925-27), that have secured her place in literary history. Showing a mastery of style lacking in the novels of contemporary life, these works also reveal the understanding of vanished cultures and love of the past instilled in the writer by her father. Her intimate knowledge of the laws, culture, and history of earlier ages had given her a sense of the continuity of life. Despite the copious and meticulously accurate historical details that embellish these novels, there is nothing strange about the people who inhabit that distant world.

Kristin Lavransdatter consists of three volumes: *Kransen (The Bridal Wreath,* 1920), *Husfrue (The Mistress of Husaby,* 1921), and *Korset (The Cross,* 1922). In the first volume, the affectionate relationship between the upright Lavrans Bjrgulfsson and his beloved daughter Kristin is vividly portrayed; however, when Kristin defies her father to marry the man whom she loves and her father deems unworthy, the relationship is strained. The novel ends with a pregnant Kristin finally joined in wedlock with Erlend Nikulausson, the man of her choice. She has forced her father to acquiesce to her will, but she has used deception and is unaffected by the worst sin: she and Erlend have forced the suicide of Eline Ormsdatter, Erlend's former mistress and mother of his two illegitimate children. The Norwegian title *Kransen* is significant in more than one way. As a child Kristin had been frightened in the woods by an elf-maiden, who beckoned to her with a garland of flowers; according to Bayerschmidt, the elf-maiden "is a symbol of the beautiful but dangerous world of the senses which makes use of all its snares and temptations to entice people who would put their own desires and gratifications above the higher order of a supernatural will." Furthermore, in the second novel, Kristin must make a pilgrimage to the shrine of St. Olav and offer her golden "krans," symbol of her virginity, to the priests. The meaning in the garland and virginal golden ornament is thus twofold.

The second and third volumes of *Kristin Lavransdatter* detail further hardships. *The Mistress of Husaby* documents the unhappy marriage of Erlend and Kristin, whose selfish passion has brought unhappiness to many. Kristin must suffer the infidelity of her husband, his seeming indifference to their seven sons, and the loss of his estate because of his attempted coup against King Magnus. Kristin herself has been petty and vindictive; the thoughtless Erlend is never allowed to forget all the wrongs he has done her, and finally he leaves her to retire to a shack in the mountains—the last bit of property he owns. The third volume, *The Cross,* relates Kristin's disappointment in her sons after the violent death of Erlend—the oldest two join a monastery (the second of the youths has been afflicted with blindness), the youngest dies of illness, her twins move away to serve Knights in other parts of the country, another of the young men travels to Iceland, and the son who takes over the estate of Kristin's father is revealed as a weakling. In despair, Kristin joins a convent, where she is stricken with the Black Death and dies. In the course of the trilogy Kristin Lavransdatter has to learn to accept whatever destiny God inflicts on her; she has to learn to subjugate her own will to the supernatural will, embodied in the figure of a holy monk, Brother Edvin. Here the work stresses the Medieval belief that the spiritual world has primacy over the material one, a belief with which Undset herself concurred but found lacking in most of her twentieth-century contemporaries.

Undset thoroughly researched the period of Norwegian history treated in her novel, although she deliberately chose for the setting an epoch for which sources are few. While some figures mentioned in the novel are historical (King Magnus, Erling Vidkunsson, Queen Ingibjrg), most of the characters are created; critics maintain that all are credible, and the unfolding of Undset's vast panorama is natural and effortless. The reader senses the religious nature of the fourteenth century but also the newness of Christianity. Superstition is rife: witches, ghosts, and elf-maidens seem to exist, and some of the people revert to heathen sacrifice in desperation when the Black Death devastates the population. *Kristin Lavransdatter* contains realistic, graphic depiction of childbirth and death, of marriage and inheritance laws

and customs, of religious practices, and of military and chivalrous codes of conduct. What is most striking in the work, however, is that the individual does not perceive himself as an individual but as a member of a family and a clan. It is in his relationships that he is important; as an individual he does not exist. This mentality seems very foreign to the self-absorbed twentieth century.

The Master of Hestviken, which stretches from the second half of the thirteenth century to the early part of the fourteenth century, also pivots around guilt and unconfessed sin. In this work, as in *Kristin Lavransdatter,* two young people who love each other are separated by circumstances. When the young woman Ingunn becomes pregnant by the Icelander Teit, the protagonist Olav kills his rival and disposes of the body. He marries Ingunn and claims the child as his own. Throughout his life he bears the burden of his secret guilt. The book presents a gloomy picture: Olav, who has been moved by love for Ingunn and who cared for her tenderly throughout an extended illness, is unable to win the affection of Ingunn's child and of the daughter they have together. Eventually Olav is wounded and deformed in battle and at the end of the novel is prevented from confessing his crime by a stroke which deprives him of the power of speech. While Winsnes saw the novel's conclusion as pessimistic, Margaret Mary Dunn, in her two *Scandinavian Studies* articles, disagreed, contending that Olav eventually comes to realize that the greatest sin "is to despair of God's mercy." Chosen by God to bear much, the Job-like Olav thus becomes the man who "does full penance." "Throughout a lifetime of purgation," Dunn asserted, "Olav's spirit has been purified like gold in a furnace, and it is thus exultant at the end of the novel."

Undset's descriptions of nature in *Kristin Lavransdatter* and *The Master of Hestviken* reveal her appreciation of the land. Moreover, nature is used to suggest the medieval consciousness of the continuity of life. Characters feel themselves links in a chain tied to a single location: ancestors and coming generations thus take precedence over individuals. The emphasis on genealogy, on the extended family, and on topography is reminiscent of the old Icelandic family sagas, by which Undset was heavily influenced. In *The Longest Years,* for instance, she recorded the thematic and stylistic importance of Norse sagas—especially *Nal's Saga*—on her own work.

Undset's last historical novel is *Madame Dorthea,* published in incomplete form in 1939. The writer abandoned the work when she fled Norway at the onset of World War II, and after 1939 she turned her energies to the war effort and to nonfiction. Set in the eighteenth century, the Age of Enlightenment, *Madame Dorthea* charts the title figure's efforts to solve the mystery of her husband's unexplained disappearance. An intelligent and rational woman, she seeks logical explanations to an enigma. Much of the almost plotless novel concerns the contrast between Madame Dorthea's intellectualism and the fervent belief of the Catholic, Scharlach.

Madame Dorthea, the medieval historical novels, and some of the social novels of contemporary times clearly contain religious themes. At least two of the later novels with modern settings may be regarded primarily as Catholic propaganda. *Gymnadenia (The Wild Orchid,* 1929) and its sequel, *Den Brennende busk (The Burning Bush,* 1930), chart the conversion to Catholicism of Paul Selmer. Bayerschmidt stated that Paul's long struggle for truth "reflects Sigrid Undset's own development from an agnostic or freethinker to a believing Christian, so that the novel [cycle] may be considered the most autobiographical of all her works." Once again in these works the theme of the renunciation of selfish passion in favor of familial responsibility is explored.

In addition to her fictional works, Undset wrote countless essays on issues of the day. Many of these essays deal with the role of the mother in contemporary society and with the question of women's rights. "Some Observations on the Emancipation of Women," published in the journal *Samtiden* and collected in *A Woman's Point of View,* expressed Undset's views on the importance of home and family to women. Other essays were literary criticism, often on the Icelandic sagas but also on other subjects: "On the Ballad" pointed out the relationship between popular didactic literature and religious elements in the ballad form. Many of her articles explained and defended her religious views, criticized Martin Luther and the Reformation, and praised the saints (Undset's biography of St. Catherine of Siena was published posthumously in 1951). And during the war years Undset tirelessly defended democracy.

Whether they are set in modern times or in the Middle Ages, Undset's works explore both the importance of the family and the dangers inherent in selfish physical passion. Undset had an understanding of sensuality and a dislike of prudishness, but she also realized the risks to the psyche passion poses. As Bayerschmidt explained, "Physical love has no rights of its own when it comes into conflict with moral and ethical laws. This is a thought which finds a constant echo in [Undset's] entire literary production." Although an emancipated woman herself, the novelist considered the natural desire of women to be for home and children and felt that a career should not be pursued instead of motherhood but only in addition to it. In "Some Observations on the Emancipation of Women," the writer claimed that "the loneliest and most worn-out worker at a typewriter, in office, shop or factory, or at a sewing machine has the right to hope and wait and dream of a happiness as a lover and wife and mother." The heroine of the early novel *Jenny* longs for family and despairs over the death of her child; art cannot fill the void for her. She realizes, according to Bayerschmidt, that "women can never reach the point where their work means everything to them." Motherhood is, in Undset's view, woman's inescapable destiny.

The question of whether Undset was a feminist or an antifeminist is a thorny one; selective quoting can produce arguments for either side. Bayerschmidt maintained that "Sigrid Undset was not a militant feminist, but neither was she an antifeminist. She believed that every woman should be free to practice an art or a profession or occupy herself in any form of work without losing the right to love and to establish a family." It was after the children were in bed that the author worked on her novels. In her portrait of Kristin Lavransdatter, Undset presents in a negative light Kristin's defiance of her father. On the other hand, Undset shows us a Kristen who lives for her seven sons and who, as mistress of Husaby, efficiently manages an estate and a family. Thus, if Undset's message is conservative in essence, it is also liberal in the respect that it confirms a woman's right to excel in whatever field she might choose.

Undset was apparently a careful and constant seeker. As a child she rejected organized religion and became an agnostic, then a free thinker. She was alert to the problems of her society, and from her extensive reading and her familiarity with vanished cultures, she weighed the civilizations of the past against those of the present. She ultimately chose the attitude of medieval man that the individual is nothing more than a cog in a great wheel, a contributing member of clan, society, and human brotherhood. Once Undset embraced this position, it followed naturally that she should become an articulate apologist for the Catholic Church. She lived according to her beliefs and became the greatest moralist that the northern countries have ever produced. In accurately and forcefully evoking the world of medieval man, Undset sought to teach contemporary man.

BIOGRAPHICAL/CRITICAL SOURCES:

BOOKS

Bayerschmidt, Carl F., *Sigrid Undset,* Twayne, 1970.
Beach, Joseph Warren, *The Twentieth Century Novel: Studies in Technique,* Appleton-Century-Crofts, 1932.
Gustafson, Alrik, *Six Scandinavian Novelists,* Princeton University Press, 1940.
McFarlane, James Walter, *Ibsen and the Temper of Norwegian Literature,* Oxford University Press, 1960.
Monroe, N. Elizabeth, *The Novel and Society: A Critical Study of the Modern Novel,* University of North Carolina Press, 1941.
Slochower, Harry, *Three Ways of Modern Man,* International, 1937.
Twentieth-Century Literary Criticism, Volume 3, Gale, 1980.
Vinde, Victor, *Sigrid Undset: A Nordic Moralist,* translated by Babette Hughes and Glenn Hughes, University of Washington Book Store, 1930.
Winsnes, A. H., *Sigrid Undset: A Study in Christian Realism,* translated by P. G. Foote, Sheed & Ward, 1953.

PERIODICALS

American-Scandinavian Review, June, 1929, July, 1929.
Books Abroad, winter, 1950.
Critic, January-February, 1974.
Literary Review, April, 1923.
Ms., January, 1981.
New Republic, October 5, 1921.
Saturday Review of Literature, June 2, 1928.
Scandinavian Studies, November, 1966, August, 1968.
Thought, spring, 1965.

*   *   *

UPDIKE, John (Hoyer) 1932-

PERSONAL: Born March 18, 1932, in Shillington, Pa.; son of Wesley Russell (a teacher) and Linda Grace (an author; maiden name, Hoyer) Updike; married Mary Entwistle Pennington, June 26, 1953 (divorced, 1977); married Martha Ruggles Bernhard, September 30, 1977; children: (first marriage) Elizabeth Pennington, David Hoyer, Michael John, Miranda; (second marriage) three stepchildren. *Education:* Harvard University, A.B. (summa cum laude), 1954; attended Ruskin School of Drawing and Fine Art, Oxford, 1954-55. *Politics:* Democrat. *Religion:* Christian.

ADDRESSES: Home—58 West Main St., Georgetown, Mass. 01833.

CAREER: Novelist, critic, short story writer, poet, essayist, and dramatist. Visited the U.S.S.R. as part of a cultural exchange program of U.S. Department of State, 1964.

MEMBER: American Academy and Institute of Arts and Letters (chancellor).

AWARDS, HONORS: Guggenheim fellowship in poetry, 1959; American Academy and National Institute of Arts and Letters Richard and Hinda Rosenthal Foundation Award, 1960, for *The Poorhouse Fair;* National Book Award in fiction, 1963, for *The Centaur;* Prix Medicis Etranger, 1966, for *The Centaur;* O.

Henry Award for fiction, 1966, for short story, "The Bulgarian Poetess"; Fulbright fellow in Africa, 1972; American Book Award nomination, 1980, for *Too Far to Go;* Edward MacDowell Medal for Literature, MacDowell Colony, 1981; Pulitzer Prize for fiction, American Book Award, and National Book Critics Circle award for fiction, all 1982, all for *Rabbit Is Rich;* National Book Critics Circle award for criticism, 1984, for *Hugging the Shore: Essays in Criticism;* Medal of Honor for Literature, National Arts Club (New York City), 1984; National Book Critics Circle award in fiction nomination, 1986, for *Roger's Version;* PEN/Malamud Memorial Prize, PEN/Faulkner Award Foundation, 1988, for "excellence in short story writing."

WRITINGS:

NOVELS

The Poorhouse Fair (also see below), Knopf, 1959, reprinted, Fawcett, 1988.
Rabbit, Run (also see below), Knopf, 1960.
The Centaur, Knopf, 1963.
Of the Farm, Knopf, 1965, reprinted, 1987.
The Poorhouse Fair [and] *Rabbit, Run,* Modern Library, 1965.
Couples, Knopf, 1968.
Rabbit Redux (also see below), Knopf, 1971.
A Month of Sundays, Knopf, 1975.
Marry Me: A Romance, Knopf, 1976.
The Coup, Knopf, 1978.
Rabbit Is Rich (also see below), Knopf, 1981.
Rabbit Is Rich/Rabbit Redux/Rabbit, Run, Quality Paperback Book Club, 1981.
The Witches of Eastwick, Knopf, 1984.
Roger's Version, Knopf, 1986.
S., Knopf, 1988.
Rabbit at Rest, Knopf, 1990.

POETRY

The Carpentered Hen and Other Tame Creatures (also see below), Harper, 1958, reprinted, Knopf, 1982, published as *Hoping for a Hoopoe,* Gollancz, 1959.
Telephone Poles and Other Poems (also see below), Knopf, 1963.
Verse: The Carpentered Hen and Other Tame Creatures/ Telephone Poles and Other Poems, Fawcett, 1965.
The Angels (poem; limited edition), King and Queen Press (Pensacola, Fla.), 1968.
Bath after Sailing (poem; limited edition), Pendulum Press (Monroe, Conn.), 1968.
Midpoint and Other Poems, Knopf, 1969.
Seventy Poems, Penguin, 1972.
Six Poems (limited edition), Oliphant Press, 1973.
Cunts (poem; limited edition), Frank Hallman, 1974.
Tossing and Turning, Knopf, 1977.
Sixteen Sonnets (limited edition), Halty Ferguson (Cambridge, Mass.), 1979.
Five Poems (limited edition), Bits Press, 1980.
Spring Trio (limited edition), Palaemon Press (Winston-Salem, N.C.), 1982.
Jester's Dozen (limited edition), Lord John (Northridge, Cal.), 1984.
Facing Nature: Poems, Knopf, 1985.

SHORT STORIES

The Same Door, Knopf, 1959, reprinted, Vintage, 1981.
Pigeon Feathers and Other Stories, Knopf, 1962.
Olinger Stories: A Selection, Vintage, 1964.
The Music School, Knopf, 1966.
Bech: A Book, Knopf, 1970.

Museums and Women and Other Stories, Knopf, 1972.
Warm Wine: An Idyll (short story; limited edition) Albondocani Press (New York), 1973.
Couples: A Short Story (limited edition), Halty Ferguson, 1976.
From the Journal of a Leper (short story; limited edition), Lord John, 1978.
Too Far to Go: The Maples Stories, Fawcett, 1979.
Three Illuminations in the Life of an American Author (short story; limited edition), Targ (New York), 1979.
Problems and Other Stories, Knopf, 1979.
Your Lover Just Called: Stories of Joan and Richard Maple, Penguin Books, 1980.
The Chaste Planet (short story; limited edition), Metacom (Worcester, Mass.), 1980.
People One Knows: Interviews with Insufficiently Famous Americans (limited edition), Lord John, 1980.
Invasion of the Book Envelopes (short story; limited edition), Ewert (Concord, Mass.), 1981.
Bech Is Back, Knopf, 1982.
The Beloved (short story; limited edition), Lord John, 1982.
Confessions of a Wild Bore (short story; limited edition), Tamazunchale Press, 1984.
More Stately Mansions: A Story (short story; limited edition), Nouveau Press (Jackson, Miss.), 1987.
Trust Me: Short Stories, Knopf, 1987.

ESSAYS

Assorted Prose, Knopf, 1965.
On Meeting Authors (essay; limited edition), Wickford (Newburyport, Mass.), 1968.
A Good Place (essay; limited edition), Aloe, 1973.
Picked-Up Pieces, Knopf, 1975.
Hub Fans Bid Kid Adieu (essay; limited edition), Lord John, 1977.
Talk from the Fifties (limited edition), Lord John, 1979.
Ego and Art in Walt Whitman (essay; limited edition), Targ, 1980.
Hawthorne's Creed (essay; limited edition), Targ, 1981.
Hugging the Shore: Essays and Criticism, Knopf, 1983.
Emersonianism (essay; limited edition), Bits Press, 1984.
Just Looking: Essays on Art, Knopf, 1989.

OTHER

(Contributor of short story) Martin Levin, editor, *Five Boyhoods,* Doubleday, 1962.
(Adapter with Warren Chappell of libretto of Mozart's opera) *The Magic Flute* (juvenile fiction), Knopf, 1962.
(Adapter with Chappell of libretto of Wagner's opera) *The Ring* (juvenile fiction), Knopf, 1964.
A Child's Calendar (juvenile poetry), Knopf, 1965.
Three Texts from Early Ipswich (historical pageant; produced in Ipswich, Mass., 1968), 17th Century Day Committee of the Town of Ipswich, 1968.
(Adapter) *Bottom's Dream* (from William Shakespeare's *A Midsummer Night's Dream;* juvenile fiction), Knopf, 1969.
(Editor) David Levine, *Pens and Needles: Literary Caricatures,* Gambit, 1970.
(Contributor of translations) Norman Thomas di Giovanni, editor, Jorge Luis Borges, *Selected Poems: 1923-1967,* Delacorte, 1972.
A Good Place: Being a Personal Account of Ipswich, Massachusetts, Aloe Editions (New York), 1973.
Buchanan Dying (play; produced in Lancaster, Mass., 1976), Knopf, 1974.

(Author of introduction) Henry Green, *Loving, Living, Party Going,* Penguin Books, 1978.
(Author of introduction) Bruno Schulz, *Sanatorium under the Sign of the Hourglass,* Penguin Books, 1979.
(Author of afterword) Edmund Wilson, *Memoirs of Hecate County,* Nonpareil, 1980.
(Editor with Shannon Ravenel and author of introduction) *The Best American Short Stories: 1984,* Houghton, 1984.
Self-Consciousness: Memoirs, Knopf, 1989.

Also author with Gunther Schuller of words and music for "The Fisherman and His Wife," performed at Savoy Theatre in Boston, Mass., by the Opera Company of Boston, May, 1970. "Talk of the Town" reporter, *New Yorker,* 1955-57. Contributor of short stories, book reviews, and poems to the *New Yorker.* Contributor of reviews and short stories to numerous periodicals.

SIDELIGHTS: John "Updike has earned an . . . imposing stance on the literary landscape," writes *Los Angeles Times* contributor Katherine Stephen, "earning virtually every American literary award, repeated best-sellerdom and the near-royal status of the American author-celebrity." However hailed by critics and readers as one of America's great novelists, John Updike has also acquired his share of detractors. As Joseph Kanon explains in *Saturday Review:* "The debate over John Updike's work has long since divided itself into two pretty firmly entrenched camps: those who admire the work consider him one of the keepers of the language; those who don't say he writes beautifully about nothing very much."

Updike acknowledges this charge but believes the complaint lacks validity. "There is a great deal to be said about almost anything," Updike explained to Jane Howard in a *Life* magazine interview. "Everything can be as interesting as every other thing. An old milk carton is worth a rose. . . . The idea of a hero is aristocratic. Now either nobody is a hero or everyone is. I vote for everyone. My subject is the American Protestant small town middle class. I like middles. It is in middles that extremes clash, where ambiguity restlessly rules. . . . There's a 'yes-but' quality about my writing that evades entirely pleasing anybody. It seems to me that critics get increasingly querulous and impatient for madder music and stronger wine, when what we need is a greater respect for reality, its secrecy, its music."

Debate about the effectiveness of Updike's writing began in 1957 with publication of *The Poorhouse Fair,* his first novel. As Curt Suplee notes in his *Washington Post* profile of the author: "Updike's fiction is not overburdened by action, and his spare story lines are embellished with a lush and elegantly wrought style that some readers find majestic (John Barth calls him the Andrew Wyeth of American writers) and others intolerable. Norman Podhoretz described his prose in 'The Poorhouse Fair' as 'overly lyrical, bloated like a child who has eaten too much candy.' " Other critics saw the novel differentlt than Podhoretz; in the *New York Times,* for example, Donald Barr called the book "a work of art." And, in the *Chicago Sunday Tribune* Fanny Butcher referred to "the author's brilliant use of words and . . . his subtle observations."

"There is one point on which his critics all agree," observes Rachael C. Burchard in *John Updike: Yea Sayings.* "His style is superb. His work is worth reading if for no reason other than to enjoy the piquant phrase, the lyric vision, the fluent rhetoric." In a cover story on the author *Time* magazine's Paul Gray claimed: "No one else using the English language over the past two and a half decades has written so well in so many ways as he." And, a reviewer for *Books Abroad* noted, "Critics continually comment on the technical virtuosity of Updike," while in

John Updike Suzanne Henning Uphaus declared, "In the midst of diversity there are certain elements common to all of Updike's writing. Most important, there is Updike's remarkable mastery of language."

However, in direct contrast to the glowing evaluations of Burchard, Gray, and others that might agree with them, are the opinions of still other commentators who fail to see Updike's work in such a favorable light. For example, in her *Partisan Review* commentary on *Couples* Elizabeth Dalton asserts, "In its delicacy and fullness Updike's style seems to register a flow of fragments almost perfectly toned. And yet, after pages and pages of his minutely detailed impressions, the accumulated effect is one of waste." John W. Aldridge writes in *Time to Murder and Create: The Contemporary Novel in Crisis* that the novelist "has none of the attributes we conventionally associate with major literary talent. He does not have an interesting mind. He does not possess remarkable narrative gifts or a distinguished style. He does not create dynamic or colorful or deeply meaningful characters. . . . In fact, one of the problems he poses for the critic is that he engages the imagination so little that one has real difficulty remembering his work long enough to think clearly about it." "Updike has difficulty in reining in his superfluous facility with words," Edward Hoagland complains in the *New York Times Book Review.* "He is too fluent."

"Much criticism of John Updike's fiction derives from the same middle-class repressions he writes about," Robert Detweiler notes in *Twentieth Century Literature.* Thus, many of the most disparaging reviews of Updike's work have come from critics that object not only to his writing style, but also to the author's subject matter. Commenting on the frenzy of criticism from reviewers that met the 1968 publication of *Couples,* Updike's explicit look at sexual freedom in a small New England town, Detweiler notes in *John Updike,* "As frequently happens, the furor accompanying the depiction of sexual amorality increased the difficulty of judging the novel's artistic quality. Most of the reviews appeared to be impulsive reactions to the subject matter rather than measured assessments." In the case of this novel, negative critical response did nothing to tone down public enthusiasm for the work: it appeared on the *Publishers Weekly* bestseller list for thirty-six weeks.

Couples wasn't the first Updike novel to deal with the sexual habits of middle-class America or to receive disapproving reviews from commentators upset by the author's frank language. "Looking back," writes Eliot Fremont-Smith in the *Village Voice,* "it must have been the sexuality that so upset the respectable critics of *Rabbit, Run* in 1960. Their consternation had to do with what seemed a great divide between John Updike's exquisite command of prose . . . and the apparent no-good vulgar nothing he expended it on." *Rabbit, Run* was the first installment in Updike's continuing saga of Harry "Rabbit" Angstrom which would later include *Rabbit Redux* and, the highly celebrated *Rabbit Is Rich.* Published at ten-year intervals, the novels follow the life of "Rabbit" as he first tries to leave his marriage, later, as he discovers his wife has been unfaithful and finds himself laid off from his blue-collar job, and, later yet, as he confronts middle-age.

Although the third volume in Updike's series of Rabbit novels received the Pulitzer Prize, the National Book Critics Circle award, and the American Book Award, some critics found its sexual focus offensive. While claiming the book "reeks of vulgarity," in his *Washington Post* review of *Rabbit Is Rich,* for example, Jonathan Yardley wrote, "Updike fancies himself the chronicler of the common man, and he fills page after page with the most clinical evidence of that fellow's gaucherie." Others viewed the sexual content of the book (and the other two volumes in the planned tetralogy) as merely a part of what they considered to be Updike's accurate depictions of U. S. society. Anthony Quinton's London *Times* review seems to summarize the feeling of many critics when he observes, "The Rabbit novels are John Updike's best since they give the fullest scope to his remarkable gifts as observer and describer. What they amount to is a social and, so to speak, emotional history of the United States over the last twenty years or more, the period of Rabbit's and his creator's conscious life."

America's sexual mores have continued to be a dominant subject in Updike's fiction along with the additional theme of religion. In his *John Updike and the Three Great Secret Things* George Hunt suggests that sex and religion along with art "characterize the predominant subject matter, thematic concerns, and central questions found throughout [Updike's] adult fiction." According to *Contemporary Authors Bibliographical Series* contributor Donald J. Greiner, Updike criticism has in fact shifted since the 1960s from a consideration of the novelist's style to a focus on his themes and how they interrelate. "Later commentators," Greiner asserts, "are concerned with his intellectually rigorous union of theology and fiction and with his suggestion that sex is a kind of emerging religion in the suburban enclaves of the middle class."

Exploring the interrelatedness of sex and religion in Updike's fiction, Jean Strouse observes in a *Newsweek* review of Updike's *Bech Is Back,* "Readers and critics have accused Updike of being obsessed with sex. Maybe—but I think he is using Harry Angstrom [from his "Rabbit" novels], and Piet Hanema in "Couples," and Richard Maple in "Too Far to Go," to explore that modern search for 'something behind all this . . . that wants me to find it.' Melville—and many others—may have announced the demise of God, but nobody has managed to excise the desire for something beyond death and daily life, a desire that has in the 20th century shifted its focus from God to sex." The *New York Times*'s Machiko Kakutani offers a similar explanation of the development of what he calls Updike's "favorite preoccupations" in his review of *Roger's Version.* "His heroes, over the years, have all suffered from 'the tension and guilt of being human.' Torn between vestigial spiritual yearnings and the new imperatives of self-fulfillment, they hunger for salvation even as they submit to the importunate demands of the flesh."

Updike's skill in portraying the anxieties and frustrations of middle-America seems to be the feature most mentioned by approving critics. "He is our unchallenged master at evoking the heroic void of ordinary life," Suplee maintains, "where small braveries contend in vain against the nagging entropy of things, where the fear of death drips from a faulty faucet and supermarket daydreams turn to God. With heart-clutching clarity, he transmutes the stubborn banality of middle-class existence into tableaux that shiver with the hint of spiritual meaning." "His work has not only lyrically defined the joys and sorrows of the American middle class," Kakutani concludes, "but also gives—as he once wrote of another author—'the happy impression of an oeuvre, of a continuous task carried forward variously, of a solid personality, of a plenitude of gifts explored, knowingly.' "

A collection of Updike's papers are found in the Houghton Library, Harvard University.

MEDIA ADAPTATIONS: Couples was purchased by United Artists in 1969; *Rabbit, Run* was filmed by Warner Bros. in 1970; *Bech: A Book* was adapted for a play entitled, "Bech Takes Pot Luck," produced in New York at Theatre Guild, 1970; *The*

Music School was networked by Public Broadcasting System, 1976; *Two Far to Go* was made into a television movie by National Broadcasting Co. in March, 1979, later revised and released for theater distribution by Sea Cliff Productions, 1982; director George Miller's movie "The Witches of Eastwick," 1987, was loosely based on Updike's novel of the same title; "The Christian Roommates," a short story, was made into a ninety-minute movie for television.

BIOGRAPHICAL/CRITICAL SOURCES:

BOOKS

Aldridge, John W., *Time to Murder and Create: The Contemporary Novel in Crisis,* McKay, 1966.
Burchard, Rachael C., *John Updike: Yea Sayings,* Southern Illinois University Press, 1971.
Concise Dictionary of American Literary Biography, 1968-1987, Gale, 1989.
Contemporary Authors Bibliographical Series, Volume 1, Gale, 1986.
Contemporary Literary Criticism, Gale, Volume 1, 1973, Volume 2, 1974, Volume 3, 1975, Volume 5, 1976, Volume 7, 1977, VOlume 9, 78, Volume 13, 1980, Volume 15, 1980, Volume 23, 1983, Volume 34, 1985, Volume 43, 1987.
Detweiler, Robert, *John Updike,* Twayne, 1972, revised edition, 1984.
Dictionary of Literary Biography, Gale, Volume 2: *American Novelists since World War II,* 1978, Volume 5: *American Poets since World War II,* 1980.
Dictionary of Literary Biography Documentary Series, Volume 3, 1983.
Dictionary of Literary Biography Yearbook, Gale, *1980,* 1981, *1982,* 1983.
Greiner, Donald J., *John Updike's Novels,* Ohio University Press, 1984.
Greiner, Donald J., *Adultery in the American Novel: Updike, James, Hawthorne,* University of South Carolina Press, 1985.
Hunt, George, *John Updike and the Three Great Secret Things,* Eerdmans, 1980.
Tallent, Elizabeth, *Married Men and Magic Tricks: John Updike's Erotic Heroes,* Creative Arts, 1981.
Thorburn, David, and Howard Eiland, editors, *John Updike: A Collection of Critical Essays,* G. K. Hall, 1982.
Updike, John, *Self-Consciousness: Memoirs,* Knopf, 1989.
Uphaus, Suzanne Henning, *John Updike,* Ungar, 1980.

PERIODICALS

Books Abroad, winter, 1967.
Chicago Sunday Tribune, January 11, 1959.
Life, November 4, 1966.
Los Angeles Times, January 4, 1987.
Modern Fiction Studies, spring, 1974, autumn, 1975.
Newsweek, November 15, 1971, September 28, 1981, October 18, 1982.
New York Review of Books, April 11, 1968, August 8, 1974, April 3, 1975, November 19, 1981, November 18, 1982, November 24, 1983, June 14, 1984, December 4, 1986.
New York Times, January 11, 1959, October 7, 1982, August 27, 1986.
New York Times Book Review, March 18, 1962, April 7, 1963, April 7, 1968, June 21, 1970, November 14, 1971, September 27, 1981, October 17, 1982, September 18, 1983, May 13, 1984, August 31, 1986, April 26, 1987.
New York Times Sunday Magazine, December 10, 1978.
Partisan Review, winter, 1969.

Saturday Review, March 17, 1962, September 30, 1972.
Time, April 26, 1968, October 18, 1982, August 25, 1986.
Times (London), January 14, 1982.
Times Literary Supplement, January 15, 1982, January 20, 1984, September 28, 1984, October 24, 1986.
Twentieth Century Literature, April, 1966, July, 1967, October, 1971, winter, 1978.
Village Voice, September 30, 1981.
Washington Post, September 27, 1981, April 26, 1982.

—*Sketch by Marian Gonsior*

* * *

UPSHAW, Margaret Mitchell
See MITCHELL, Margaret (Munnerlyn)

* * *

URIS, Leon (Marcus) 1924-

PERSONAL: Born August 3, 1924, in Baltimore, Md.; son of Wolf William and Anna (Blumberg) Uris; married Betty Katherine Beck, 1945 (divorced January, 1968); married Margery Edwards, September 8, 1968 (died February 20, 1969); married Jill Peabody (a photographer), February 15, 1970; children: (first marriage) Karen Lynn, Mark Jay, Michael Cady; (third marriage) Rachael, one other child. *Education:* Attended public schools in Baltimore, Md.

ADDRESSES: Home—Aspen, Colo. *Office*—c/o Doubleday Publishing Co., Inc., 245 Park Ave., New York, N.Y. 11530.

CAREER: Former newspaper driver, *San Francisco Call-Bulletin,* San Francisco, Calif. Full-time writer, 1950—. *Military service:* U.S. Marine Corps, 1942-45.

MEMBER: Writers League, Screenwriters Guild.

AWARDS, HONORS: Daroff Memorial Award, 1959; National Institute of Arts and Letters grant, 1959; California Literature Medal Award, silver medal, 1962, for *Mila 18,* and gold medal, 1965, for *Armageddon;* honorary doctorates, University of Colorado, 1976, Santa Clara University, 1977, Wittenberg University, 1980, and Lincoln College, 1985; John F. Kennedy Medal, Irish/American Society of New York, 1977; gold medal, Eire Society of Boston, 1978; Jobotinsky Medal, State of Israel, 1980; (with wife, Jill Uris) Hall Fellowship, Concord Academy, 1980; Scopus Award, Hebrew University of Jerusalem, 1981; *Exodus* selected as one of the "Books for the Teen Age," New York Public Library, 1980, 1981, and 1982.

WRITINGS:

NOVELS

Battle Cry (also see below), Putnam, 1953, reprinted, Bantam, 1982.
The Angry Hills, Random House, 1955, reprinted, Bantam, 1972.
Exodus (also see below) Doubleday, 1957, reprinted, Bantam, 1983.
Mila 18, Doubleday, 1960, reprinted, Bantam, 1983.
Armageddon, Doubleday, 1964, reprinted, Dell, 1985.
Topaz, McGraw, 1967.
QB VII, Doubleday, 1970.
Trinity, Doubleday, 1976.
The Haj, Doubleday, 1984.
Mitla Pass (Literary Guild main selection), Doubleday, 1988.

SCREENPLAYS

"Battle Cry," Warner Brothers, 1955.
"Gunfight at the O.K. Corral," Paramount Pictures, 1957.

OTHER

(With Dimitrios Haussiadis) *Exodus Revisited* (photo-essay), Doubleday, 1959 (published in England as *In the Steps of Exodus,* Heinemann, 1962).
The Third Temple (essay), bound with William Stevenson's *Strike Zion,* Bantam, 1967.
(With Walt Smith) "Ari" (musical version of *Exodus*), first produced on Broadway at the Mark Hellinger Theater, January 15, 1971.
(With wife, Jill Uris) *Ireland, a Terrible Beauty: The Story of Ireland Today* (photo-essay), Doubleday, 1975.
(With J. Uris) *Jerusalem: Song of Songs* (photo-essay), Doubleday, 1984.

Contributor to several anthologies. Contributor to periodicals.

SIDELIGHTS: American writer Leon Uris is the author of several bestselling novels based upon details and events of contemporary history. Among his titles are the landmark *Exodus* (1957), concerning the Jewish settlement of modern Israel, the espionage thriller *Topaz* (1967), *QB VII* (1970), about the libel suit trial of a German doctor, and *Trinity* (1976), about the turmoil in Ireland. Panoramic stories that have become huge commercial successes, Uris's novels have garnered him a dedicated readership, yet throughout his career, critical opinion on his work has been mixed. While Uris is noted for his storytelling abilities—the appeal of his novels has been sometimes described as cinematic in nature—he is frequently criticized for problems with technique, cardboard characters and dialogue, and taking liberties with historical facts. Sharon D. Downey and Richard A. Kallan, noting both Uris's immense popular appeal and his flaws in regards to traditional literary standards, point out in *Communications Monographs,* "in short, Uris remains a reader's writer and a critic's nightmare."

However, according to Pete Hamill in the *New York Times Book Review,* "Leon Uris is a storyteller, in a direct line from those men who sat around fires in the days before history and made the tribe more human. The subject is man, not words; story is all, the form it takes is secondary." Hamill further explains: "It is a simple thing to point out that Uris often writes crudely, that his dialogue can be wooden, that his structure occasionally groans under the excess baggage of exposition and information. Simple, but irrelevant. None of that matters as you are swept along in the narrative. Uris is certainly not as good a writer as Pynchon or Barthelme or Nabokov; but he is a better storyteller." Likewise, as Dan Wakefield notes in *Nation* regarding the novel *Exodus:* "The plot is so exciting that the characters become exciting too; not because of their individuality or depth, but because of the historic drama they are involved in." He continues, "The real achievement . . . lies not so much in its virtues as a novel as in its skillful rendering of the furiously complex history of modern Israel in a palatable, popular form that is usually faithful to the spirit of the complicated realities."

In order to write *Exodus,* which became one of the largest selling books in publishing history, Uris read about 300 books, traveled 12,000 miles inside Israel, and interviewed more than 1,200 people. Similar efforts have gone into his other books, including *Trinity,* which arose out of the people and places Uris and his wife Jill experienced in Ireland. At times, Uris's books have been alternately called "non-fiction" novels, "propaganda" novels, or just plain "journalism." A reviewer for *Christian Science Moni-*

tor comments, "Few readers are expert enough to be 100 percent certain where Mr. Uris's imagination has taken over the record." Nevertheless, as Maxwell Geismar points out in the *Saturday Review:* "If Mr. Uris sometimes lacks tone as a novelist, if his central figures are social types rather than individual portraits, there is also a kind of 'underground power' in his writing. No other novel I have read recently has had the same capacity [as *Exodus*] to refresh our memory, inform our intelligence, and to stir the heart." In the same vein, Hamill writes of *Trinity:* "The novel sprawls, occasionally bores, meanders like a river. . . . But when the story is finished the reader has been to places where he or she has never been before. The news items . . . will never seem quite the same again."

Webster Scott in the *Washington Post Book World,* offers an assessment that novelists with mass audiences like Uris, in addition to James Michener and James Clavell, "may tell us relatively little about our inner weather, but they report on storms and setting suns outside. They read the environment we must function in. Occasionally they replicate our social structures. They sift the history that brought us to the present. They give us the briefing papers necessary to convert news stories into human stories. All of which serve our emotional need to make order out of confusion, to explain the inexplicable, to simplify the complex and find solutions to conundrums."

AVOCATIONAL INTERESTS: Skiing, bowling, and tennis.

MEDIA ADAPTATIONS: Other motion pictures from Uris's novels include "The Angry Hills," Metro-Goldwyn-Mayer, 1959, "Exodus," directed by Otto Preminger, United Artists, 1960, and "Topaz," directed by Alfred Hitchcock, United Artists, 1969; in addition, Paramount Pictures bought the film rights to *Mila 18;* a television movie, "QB VII," based on Uris's novel of the same title, was presented by ABC-TV, April, 1974.

BIOGRAPHICAL/CRITICAL SOURCES:

BOOKS

Authors in the News, Gale, Volume 1, 1976, Volume 2, 1976.
Bestsellers 89, Issue 2, Gale, 1989.
Contemporary Literary Criticism, Gale, Volume 7, 1977, Volume 32, 1985.
Contemporary Novelists, 4th edition, St. James Press/St. Martin's, 1986.

PERIODICALS

Atlantic, July, 1964.
Chicago Tribune, November 24, 1988.
Chicago Tribune Book World, April 29, 1984.
Christian Science Monitor, December 4, 1958, November 16, 1967.
Commentary, October, 1961.
Communication Monographs, September, 1982.
Detroit News, June 3, 1984.
Globe and Mail (Toronto), January 7, 1989.
Inside Books, November, 1988.
Los Angeles Times Book Review, October 30, 1988.
Nation, April 11, 1959.
Newsweek, May 21, 1984.
New York Herald Tribune Book Review, September 28, 1958.
New York Review of Books, April 16, 1964.
New York Times, October 12, 1958, April 27, 1984.
New York Times Book Review, June 4, 1961, June 28, 1964, October 15, 1967, March 14, 1976, April 22, 1984, January 1, 1989.
Philadelphia Bulletin, March 31, 1976.
Publishers Weekly, March 29, 1976.
Saturday Review, April 25, 1953, September 27, 1958.
Time, December 8, 1958, June 2, 1961.
Times Literary Supplement, October 27, 1961.
Washington Post Book World, April 1, 1984, October 30, 1988.

V

VALERY, (Ambroise) Paul (Toussaint Jules) 1871-1945

PERSONAL: Born October 30, 1871, in Cette (now Sete), France; died of a heart ailment, July (some sources say August) 20, 1945, in Paris, France; buried in Cimetiere Marin, Sete, France; son of Barthelemy (a customs officer) and Fanny (Grassi) Valery; married Jeannie (some sources spell given name Jeanne) Gobillard, 1900; children: Francois, Agathe (some sources say three). *Education:* University of Montpellier, licence en droit, 1892.

CAREER: Poet, philosopher, essayist, critic, and dramatist. Ministry of War, Artillery Munitions Bureau, Paris, France, clerk, 1897-1900; Havas News Agency, Paris, private secretary to agency director, 1900-22; co-editor of literary review *Commerce,* 1924-32; Centre Universitaire Mediterraneen, Nice, France, administrator, beginning in 1933; College de France, Paris, professor of poetry, 1937-45. President of League of Nations Committee for Intellectual Cooperation, 1936. *Military service:* French Army, 1889-90; stationed in Montpellier.

AWARDS, HONORS: Legion of Honor (France), Chevalier, 1923, Officer, 1926, Commander, 1931; elected to the French Academy, 1925; numerous honorary doctorates, including Oxford University, 1931, and foreign decorations; street where Valery lived was renamed rue de Paul Valery; at his death Valery was given a full state funeral.

WRITINGS:

POETRY

La Jeune Parque (title means "The Young Fate"), Editions de la Nouvelle Revue Francaise, 1917, with commentary by Alain, Gallimard, 1936, reprinted, 1958, enlarged edition with critical document study by Octave Nadal published as *La Jeune Parque: Manuscrit autographe, texte de l'edition 1942, etats successifs et brouillons inedits du poem,* Club du Meilleur Livre, 1957.

Album de vers anciens, 1890-1900 (collection; title means "Album of Old Verse"), A. Monnier, 1920, Editions de la Nouvelle Revue Francaise, 1927.

Charmes; ou, Poemes (collection; title means "Songs; or, Poems"), Editions de la Nouvelle Revue Francaise, 1922, French text edited by Charles G. Whiting with English introduction and notes, Athlone Press, 1973, reprinted, 1985, translation by James L. Brown published as *Charms,* Forsan Books, 1983.

Melange (collection), Gallimard, 1941.

L'Ange, Gallimard, 1946.

Le Cimetiere marin (first published in *Nouvelle Revue Francaise,* June 1, 1920), preface by Henri Mondor, Roissard, 1954, introduction by Sylvio Samama, illustrations by Abram Krol, A. Krol (Paris), 1964, dual-language edition translated by C. Day Lewis as *Le Cimetiere marin/The Graveyard by the Sea,* Secker & Warburg, 1946, dual-language edition edited and translated by Graham Dunstan Martin as *Le Cimetiere marin/The Graveyard by the Sea,* University of Texas Press, 1971.

Abeille spirituelle (previously unpublished poem), privately printed, 1968.

First drafts of Valery's poem *La Jeune Parque* are included in *Rompre le silence: Les Premiers Etats de La Jeune Parque,* by Bruce Pratt, J. Corti (Paris), 1976, and in *Chant du cygne: Edition critique des premiers etats de La Jeune Parque,* by Pratt, J. Corti, 1979.

PROSE

La Conquete allemande (first published in *New Review* [London], January 1, 1897), Extrait du Mercure de France, 1915, revised edition published as *Une Conquete methodique,* Champion, 1924.

Introduction a la methode de Leonard de Vinci (first published in *Nouvelle Revue,* August 15, 1894 [some sources say 1895]), Editions de la Nouvelle Revue Francaise, 1919, Gallimard, 1964, translation by Thomas McGreevy published as *Introduction to the Method of Leonardo da Vinci,* J. Rodker, 1929.

La Soiree avec M. Teste (short story; first published in *Centaure,* September, 1896), Editions de la Nouvelle Revue Francaise, 1919, translation by Ronald Davis published as *An Evening with Mr. Teste,* R. Davis (Paris), 1925, new and enlarged edition published as *Monsieur Teste,* Gallimard, 1946, revised edition, 1969, translation with notes by Jackson Mathews published as *Monsieur Teste,* Knopf, 1947, McGraw, 1964.

Eupalinos; ou, L'Architecte, precede de L'Ame et la danse (two dialogues; *Eupalinos* first published as "Paradoxe sur l'architecte" in *Ermitage,* March, 1891, translation by William McCausland Stewart published as *Eupalinos; or, The*

Architect, Oxford University Press/H. Milford, 1932; *L'Ame et la danse* first published in *Revue Musicale,* December, 1920, translation by Dorothy Busay published as *Dance and the Soul,* John Lehmann, 1951), Gallimard, 1923, reprinted, 1938, translated and edited with introduction and notes by Vera J. Daniel as *Eupalinos, and, L'Ame et la danse,* Oxford University Press, 1967.

Fragments sur Mallarme, R. Davis (Paris), 1924.

Situation de Baude la ire, Madame Lesafe (Paris), 1924.

Variete (essays), five volumes, Gallimard, 1924-44, reprinted, 1956-60, translation by Malcolm Cowley, William Aspenwall Bradley, and others published as *Variety,* Harcourt, 1927-38.

Durtal, Champion, 1925.

Etudes et fragments sur le reve, Claude Aveline (Paris), 1925.

Petit recueil de paroles de circonstance, Plaisir de Bibliophile, 1926.

Discours de la diction des vers, Le Livre, 1926, revised edition published as *De la diction des vers,* Emile Chamontin (Paris), 1933.

Durtal; ou, Les Points d'une conversion (criticism), M. Senac (Paris), 1927.

Maitres et amis (title means "Masters and Friends"), Beltrand, 1927.

Discours sur Emile Verhaeren (lecture), Champion, 1927.

Discours de reception a l'Academie francaise, Gallimard, 1927.

Odes: Compositions de D. Galanis (criticism), Aux Aldes, 1927.

Poesie: Essais sur la poetique et le poete (essays), Bertrand Guegan (Paris), 1928.

Remarques exterieures, illustrations by L. J. Soulas, Editions des Cahiers Libres, 1929.

Variation sur une "Pensee," annotee par l'auteur, Balancier, 1930.

Litterature (notes; first published in *Commerce,* 1929), Gallimard, 1930.

Regards sur le monde actuel (essays), Stock (Paris), 1931, introduction by Jean Danielou, Vlaletay, 1973, revised and enlarged edition published as *Regards sur le monde actuel et autres essais,* Gallimard, 1945, reprinted, 1963, translation by Francis Scarfe published as *Reflections on the World Today,* Pantheon, 1948, Thames & Hudson, 1951.

L'Idee fixe (dialogue), les Laboratoires Martinet (Paris), 1932, new revised and corrected edition published as *L'Idee fixe;, ou, Deux Hommes a la mer,* Gallimard, 1933, reprinted, 1966.

Choses tues, Gallimard, 1932.

Moralites, Gallimard, 1932.

Suite, Gallimard, 1934.

Etat de la vertu: Rapport a l'academie, L. Pichon (Paris), 1935.

Analecta (extracts from *Notebooks* and other personal records), Gallimard, 1935.

L'Homme et la coquille, illustrations by Henri Mondor, Gallimard, 1937.

Discours aux chirurgiens (lecture), Gallimard, 1938.

Introduction a la poetique, Gallimard, 1938.

Degas, danse, dessin (fragments first published in *Nouvelle Revue Francaise,* October, 1935, April, 1938), Gallimard, 1938, reprinted, 1965, translation by Helen Burlin published as *Degas, Dance, Drawing,* Lear (New York), 1948.

Poesie et pensee abstraite (lecture), Clarendon Press (Oxford), 1939.

Tel quel (extracts), two volumes, Gallimard, 1941-43.

La Politique de l'esprit, notre souverain bien (address), introduction by Lucy Leveaux, *Editions de l'Universite de Manchester,* 1941.

Mauvaises pensees et autres (extracts), Gallimard, 1942.

Dialogues de l'arbre, Firmin-Didot (Paris), 1943.

Au sujet de Nerval, Textes Pretextes (Paris), 1944.

Un Poete inconnu (contains two interviews with Valery), Lettres Francaises, 1944.

(With Paul Eluard, Renee Moutard-Uldry, Georges Blaizot, and Louis-Marie Michon) *Paul Bonet,* A. Blaizot (Paris), 1945.

Discours sur Voltaire (lecture), Domat-Montchrestien (Paris), 1945.

Henri Bergson, Domat-Montchrestien (Paris), 1945.

Souvenirs poetiques, Le Prat (Paris), 1947.

Vues, illustrations by Gilbert Poilliot, Table Ronde, 1948.

Histoires brisees, Gallimard, 1950.

Ecrits divers sur Stephane Mallarme, Editions de la Nouvelle Revue Francaise, 1950.

Propos sur le livre, Bibliophiles Francais, 1956.

The Outlook for Intelligence, edited by Jackson Mathews, translation from original French manuscript by Denise Folliot and Mathews, preface by Francois Valery, Harper, 1963.

Reflexions simples sur le corps, de Paul Valery, ayant inspire des lithographies originales a Hans Erni, E. A. D. (Paris), 1967.

(With Francois Valery) *Les Principes d'anarchie pure et appliquee* [and] *Paul Valery et la politique* (the former by P. Valery, the latter by F. Valery), Gallimard, 1984.

NOTEBOOKS

Rhumbs (notes et autres) par Paul Valery (extracts), Divan, 1926.

Autres rhumbs de Paul Valery (extracts), Editions de France, 1927.

Cahier B 1910 (extracts), Gallimard, 1930.

Autres rhumbs (extracts), Gallimard, 1934.

Cahiers (title means "Notebooks"), twenty-nine volumes, Centre National de Recherche Scientifique, 1957-61, two volume edition presented and annotated by Judith Robinson-Valery, Gallimard, 1973-74, new two volume edition of early notebooks published as *Cahiers 1894-1914,* edited by Robinson-Valery and Nicole Celeyrette-Pietri, Gallimard, 1989.

CORRESPONDENCE

Lettres a quelques-uns, Gallimard, 1952.

Gaston Poulain, Paul Valery, tel quel (includes unpublished letters), illustrations by P. Valery, Licorne, 1955.

(With Andre Gide) *Andre Gide—Paul Valery: Correspondance, 1890-1942,* preface and notes by Robert Mallet, Gallimard, 1955, reprinted as *Correspondance Andre Gide—Paul Valery, 1890-1942,* 1973, abridged and translated edition by June Guicharnaud published as *Self Portraits: The Gide/ Valery Letters, 1890-1942,* edited by Mallet, University of Chicago Press, 1966.

(With Gustave Fourment) *Paul Valery—Gustave Fourment: Correspondance, 1887-1933,* introduction, notes, and documents by Octave Nadal, Gallimard, 1957.

COLLECTIONS

Morceaux choisis: Prose et poesie (anthology), Gallimard, 1930, reprinted, 1957, abridged translation published as *Selected Writings,* New Directions, 1950, reprinted, 1964.

Poesies, Gallimard, 1931, 2nd edition, 1942, reprinted as *Poesies: Album de vers anciens, La Jeune Parque, Charmes, Pieces diverses, Cantate du Narcisse, Amphion, Semiramis,* Gallimard, 1966, Bibliotheque des Chefs-d'Oeuvre, 1979.

Les Divers Essais sur Leonard de Vinci, Editions du Sagittaire, 1931.

Eupalinos, L'Ame et la Danse, Dialogue de l'arbre, Gallimard, 1944, reprinted, 1970.

Oeuvres choisis, introduction by Daniel Simond, Abbaye du Livre, 1947.

Souvenirs poetiques, G. Le Prat (Paris), 1947.

Paul Valery: Prose et vers, compiled by Henri Payre, Blaisdell (Paris), 1968.

La Jeune Parque; L'Ange; Agathe; Histoires brisees, edited with preface and notes by Jean Levaillant, Gallimard, 1974.

Paul Valery: An Anthology (excerpts from *Collected Works*), selected with introduction by James R. Lawler, Princeton University Press, 1976.

Une Chambre conjecturale: Poemes ou proses de jeunesse (juvenalia), Bibliotheque Artistique & Litterature, 1981.

Paul Valery secret, 1937-1945: Lettres intimes, poemes inedits, Ader, Picard, Tajan Commissaires-priseurs Associes (Monaco), 1982.

COMPLETE WORKS

Oeuvres de Paul Valery, twelve volumes, Volumes 1-2, Sagittaire, 1931, Volumes 3-12, Gallimard, 1933-50.

The Collected Works of Paul Valery (fifteen-part collection), edited by Jackson Mathews, Pantheon/Princeton University Press; Part 1: *Poems,* translation by David Paul, [and] *On Poets and Poetry,* selected with translation from the *Notebooks* by James R. Lawler, 1971; Part 2: *Poems in the Rough,* translation by Hilary Corke, introduction by Octave Nadal, 1969; Part 3: *Plays* (some text in French and English), translation by D. Paul and Robert Fitzgerald, introduction by Francis Fergusson, memoir by Igor Stravinsky, 1960; Part 4: *Dialogues,* translation by W. M. Stewart, prefaces by W. Stevens, 1956; Part 5: *Idee fixe,* translation by D. Paul, preface by J. Mathews, introduction by Philip Wheelwright, 1965; Part 6: *Monsieur Teste,* translation and introduction by J. Mathews, 1973; Part 7: *The Art of Poetry,* translation by Denise Folliot, introduction by T. S. Eliot, 1958, Random House, 1961; Part 8: *Leonardo, Poe, Mallarme,* translation by Malcolm Cowley and Lawler, 1972; Part 9: *Masters and Friends,* translation by Martin Turnell, introduction by Joseph Frank, 1968; Part 10: *History and Politics,* translation by Folliot and I. Mathews, preface by Francois Valery, introduction by Salvador de Madariaga, 1962; Part 11: *Occasions,* translation by Roger Shattuck and Frederick Brown, introduction by Shattuck, 1970; Part 12: *Degas, Manet, Morisont,* translation by D. Paul, introduction by D. Cooper, 1960; Part 13: *Aesthetics,* translation by Ralph Manheim, introduction by Herbert Read, 1964; Part 14: *Analecta,* translation by Stuart Gilbert, introduction by W. H. Auden, 1970; Part 15: *Moi,* translation by Marthiel Mathews and I. Mathews, 1975.

Oeuvres, two volumes, edited and annotated by Jean Hytier, Gallimard, 1957-60, reprinted, 1968-71.

OTHER

(Contributor to text) *Tableaux de Paris* (volume of illustrations), Editions Emile-Paul Freres (Paris), 1927.

Amphion (ballet; first produced at The Opera, Paris, France, 1931; music by Arthur Honegger), Rouart Lerolle (Paris), 1931.

Semiramis (three-act ballet; first produced at The Opera, 1934; music by Honegger), Gallimard, 1934.

(Editor and contributor) *Problemes nationaux vus par des francaises,* Editions du Sagittaire, 1934.

(Author of text) *Paraboles* (collection of twelve watercolors), Editions du Raisin, 1935.

(Contributor) *Maillol,* Publications Techniques, 1943.

(Author of preface) E. A. van Moe, *Les Fouquet de la Bibliotheque nationale,* Editions de la Revue Verve, 1943.

(Librettist) Germaine Tailleferre, *Cantate du Narcisse* (opera; first produced in 1939), Gallimard, 1944, Centraux Bibliophiles, 1956.

Mon Faust (unfinished play), Gallimard, 1946, reprinted, 1962.

(Author of prefaces with Stephane Mallarme) *Seize Aquarelles* (title means "Sixteen Watercolors"), Editions des Quatres Chemins, 1946.

(Illustrator) Paul de Man, *Les Dessins de Paul Valery* (anthology of drawings), Editions Universelles, 1948.

(Contributor) *Leonardo da Vinci, 1452-1519* (collection of paintings), Nouvelle Revue Francaise, 1950.

(Author of introduction) Martin Huerlimann, photographer, *La France* (photographs), Braun (Paris), 1951, reprinted, 1967, translation published with historical notes by Valery as *Eternal France: 216 Pictures in Photogravure,* Thames & Hudson (New York), 1952, revised and enlarged edition published as *France: 217 Pictures in Photogravure,* Studio Publications, 1957, new and enlarged edition published as *France,* Studio Publications, 1968.

(Translator) Publius Vergilius Maro, *Les Bucoliques de Virgile* (verse), illustrations by Jacques Villon, Scripta & Pica (Paris), 1953, enlarged edition published as *Bucoliques de Virgile,* Gallimard, 1956.

(Author of preface) *Anthologie des poetes de la Nouvelle revue francaise,* 3rd edition, Gallimard, 1958.

(Compiler and author of explanatory notes) Rene Descartes, *Les Pages immortelles de Descartes,* Buchet/Chastel, 1961.

(Translator and author of commentary) *Fragments des Marginalia* (selections from *Marginalia* by Edgar Allan Poe), Fata Morgana (France), 1980.

MEDIA ADAPTATIONS: Valery's short story *Monsieur Teste* was adapted as "Monsieur Teste," a play by Pierre Franck, L'Avantscene (Paris), 1975.

SIDELIGHTS: Paul Valery occupies a position in the history of French letters that is at once strategic and highly problematic. Critics have affixed to him various labels, all of them partially correct. He has been called the last French symbolist, the first post-symbolist, a masterful classical prosodist, an advocate of logical positivism, and a cerebral narcissist.

Clearly Valery was heir to the symbolist tradition of another French poet, Stephane Mallarme, whom he knew and venerated, who encouraged his early work, and whose other young disciples—Pierre Louis in particular—got Valery's work published. On the other hand, he is understood as having broken away from symbolism, as having rejected the cult of poetry for its own sake in favor of a cult of the mind. These views need not be contradictory.

In the highly formal, mannered musicality of Valery's verse, the influence of Mallarme is unmistakable. Valery's *Notebooks (Cahiers)* record his conviction that the subject of a poem was far less important than its "program": "A sort of program would consist of a gathering of words (among which conjunctives are just as important as substantives) and of types of syntactical moments, and above all a table of verbal tonalities, etc." Mallarme had said something very similar in "Music and Letters" ("La Musique et les lettres"): "I assert, at my own aesthetic risk, this conclusion: . . . that Music and Letters are the alternate face here widened towards the obscure; scintillating there, with certainty of a phenomenon, the only one, I have named it Idea."

For Mallarme, as for his younger disciple, Idea was not a theme that could be formulated in a sentence or two; it was not a thought but rather the ongoing process of thought within the mind. Yet although Mallarme believed that the end product of thought had to be a poem, Valery disagreed. In his view, thought—the mirror-like refraction of the human mind—was always an end in itself; poetry was simply a more or less desirable by-product, to be pursued as long as it stimulated the mental processes. As he put it in his *Notebooks,* "In sum, Mallarme and I, this in common—poem is problem. And this, very important." But Valery also declared: "For him: the work. For me, the self. . . . Poetry has never been an objective for me, but an instrument, an exercise." Responding to seventeenth-century poet and critic Nicolas Boileau's time-honored dictum that "my verse, good or bad, always says something," Valery asserted in the *Notebooks,* "There is the principle and the germ of an infinity of horrors."

A corollary of these convictions was the idea that no pure literature was possible as long as the writer thought of himself as addressing a public. As long as the audience for a text was kept in mind, Valery wrote in his *Notebooks,* "there are always reserves in one's thoughts, a hidden intention in which is to be found a whole stock of charlatanism. Therefore every literary product is an impure product." The relative purity of Mallarme, "the Master," as Valery called him, was thus entirely congruent with and dependent on both Mallarme's total disregard for—indeed, ignorance of—the public taste and his consequent obscurity (no one outside of a very small Parisian circle had read his poems or knew of his existence until well into the twentieth century). For Valery, as he reported in his *Notebooks,* "if a poet is allowed to use crude means, if a mosaic of images is a poem, then damn poetry."

A brief comparison of Valery's famous poem "The Young Fate" ("La Jeune Parque") to Mallarme's "Herodiade" concretely illustrates the nature of the older writer's influence on the young one. Both poems depict a young woman engaged in narcissistic introspection, both embody a severely formal, musical prosody, and both deliberately reject any identifiable "content," or theme. Valery's poem is, in fact, more obscure and less musical than Mallarme's simply because it is more purely metaphysical (one is compelled to use the term despite Valery's abhorrence of it as connoting a certain intellectual frivolity).

Valery's passion for "scientific speculation," which is how he preferred to label his metaphysical writing and that of others, was the reason for his lifelong fascination with American writer Edgar Allan Poe. In *The Tell-Tale Heart: The Life and Works of Edgar Allan Poe,* Julian Symons has described Poe as divided between two obsessive tendencies in his writings, a visionary one and a logical one. Although Mallarme and French poet Charles Baudelaire had celebrated the visionary qualities in Poe, Valery most fully admired his powers of reason, as revealed through Poe's pseudo-scientific meditation on the nature of human knowledge, "Eureka," and through his brilliant practical logician, Auguste Dupin, the detective of "The Murders in the Rue Morgue" and "The Purloined Letter." Valery's unyielding positivism (rationalism) is thus another characteristic setting him apart from other French writers. In an early letter to Andre Gide, Valery wrote: "Poe, and I shouldn't talk about it for I promised myself I wouldn't, is the only writer with no sins. Never was he mistaken—not led instinctively—but lucidly and successfully, he made a synthesis of all the vertigoes."

James Lawler, probably the most prominent and reliable American critic of Valery's work, has, in *The Poet as Analyst: Essays*

on *Paul Valery,* convincingly explained Valery's interest in "Eureka": "Quite apart from Poe's poetics, here was a work that fascinated [Valery] by its scientific theories, by its poetic subject . . . ['the expression of a generalized will to relativity'] and, significantly, by the form adopted, which coincides, one may say, with Valery's own literary practice in *La Jeune Parque* [*The Young Fate*] and *Charmes* [*Charms*] . . . ['example and enactment of the reciprocity of appropriation']." In "Eureka" Poe described knowledge and being as part of an interconnected system: "In the original unity of the first thing lies the secondary cause of all things, with the germ of their inevitable annihilation." From Poe's theory Valery extracted his own, odd fusion of the visionary and the logical, the mystical and the rational, which he however refused to admit as anything but pure science and logic. "The cosmogonic form," he wrote in his essay on "Eureka," "comprises sacred books, admirable poems, excessively bizarre stories, full of beauty and nonsense, physico-mathematical researches of a profundity sometimes worthy of an object less insignificant than the universe. But it is the glory of man to be able to spend himself on the void; and it is not only his glory. Lunatic researches are akin to unforeseen discoveries. The role of the nonexistent exists; the function of the imaginary is real; and pure logic teaches us that *the false implies the true.* It seems then that the history of the mind can be resumed in these terms: it is absurd by what it seeks, great by what it finds. . . . As for the idea of a beginning,—I mean of an absolute beginning—it is necessarily a myth. Every beginning is a coincidence; we would have to conceive it as I don't know what sort of contact between all and nothing. Trying to think of it one finds that all beginning is a consequence—every beginning completes something."

In the face of such statements, Valery's scorn for the mystical may seem incongruous, but this attitude is nevertheless a prominent feature of his thought, evident most of all in his contempt for the seventeenth-century mathematician and philosopher Blaise Pascal. One might say that he projected the visionary aspect, usually recognized in Poe, onto Pascal, while making Rene Descartes, Pascal's contemporary, a figure of what he admired in Poe, a logician and scientist. His recurrent, even obsessive, denigration of Pascal may reflect Valery's fear that his own distinction between science and metaphysics, rationalism and mysticism, might not hold up, that in fact—as is so evident in Valery's own "scientific" musings—there might be some mutual contamination of the categories. This suspicion is also borne out by Valery's response to the Jewish philosopher Henri Bergson during the German occupation of France during World War II; Valery publicly admired Bergson but added that he could not accept Bergson's belief that scientific knowledge was antithetical to the human spirit.

Valery conceived himself as an anti-philosopher, and he despised the new discipline of psychology as it was emerging in the work of neurologist and psychoanalytical pioneer Sigmund Freud, because both philosophy and psychology sought to do precisely what he wished to avoid: to *interpret,* to *reduce* the form of thought, event, and act to a content. He criticized French novelist Marcel Proust for this very tendency, though in doing so he misread Proust. Valery, it must be admitted, was blinded to a great deal in literature by his obsessive commitment to purity of thought. In *Margins of Philosophy* Jacques Derrida has discussed Valery's aversion to Freud: "We will not ask what the meaning of this resistance is before pointing out that what Valery intends to resist is meaning itself. What he reproaches psychoanalysis for is not that it interprets in such or such a fashion, but quite simply that it interprets at all, that it is an interpretation, that it is interested above all in signification, in meaning, and in some principal unity—here, a sexual unity—of meaning."

Derrida sees Valery's formalism as both reflection and instrument of his "repression" of meaning, and indeed, Valery's rigid adherence to classical prosody is another trait that sets him very much apart from other twentieth-century French poets. He is undoubtedly the last French poet to write such intensely regular verse; to this extent at least his influence on later French poetry has been nil. Yet his reasons for remaining faithful to form—more so, in many instances, than Baudelaire and Mallarme who were formalists but innovative ones—were much more interesting than a mindless traditionalism. "To write regular verses," he declared in the *Notebooks,* "is without a doubt to submit oneself to a law which is strange, rather meaningless, always difficult, and sometimes atrocious. . . . Let us however try to find a matter for rejoicing in this. . . . The exigencies of a strict prosody are the artifice which confers upon natural language the qualities of a resistant matter."

Perhaps the most salient characteristic of Valery's work and person, and certainly the one to which he himself would have attached greatest importance, was his cult of the intellectual self. His fascination and personal identification with the Narcissus myth is well documented. Of an early poem on this subject, "Narcissus Speaks" ("Narcisse Parle"), he wrote (quoted in volume 1 of *Oeuvres* [*Works*]): "The theme of Narcissus, which I have chosen, is a sort of poetic autobiography which requires a few explanations and indications. There exists in Montpellier a botanical garden where I used to go very often when I was nineteen. In a rather secluded corner of this garden, which formerly was much wilder and prettier, there is an arch and in it a kind of crevice containing a slab of marble, which bears three words: PLACANDIS NARCISSAE MANIBUS (to placate the spirit of Narcissa). That inscription had brought on reveries in me, and here, in two words, is its story. In 1820, at this place, a skeleton was discovered, and according to local traditions, it was thought to be the tomb of the poet [Edward] Young. This girl, who died in Montpellier toward the end of the eighteenth century, couldn't be buried in the cemetery, since she was a Protestant. Her father is supposed to have buried her, on a moonlit night. The dead girl's name was Narcissa. The remains that had been found were identified as hers. For me the name Narcissa suggested Narcissus. Then I developed the idea of the myth of this young man, perfectly handsome or who found himself so in his reflection. I wrote at the time the very first *Narcissus,* an irregular sonnet. . . ."

Why the young man should have been so inspired by this circumstantial evocation of the Narcissus story is perhaps suggested by a line—"I endlessly delight in my own brain"—appearing in a poem written in 1887. Indeed, Valery's poetic output slowed to the merest trickle from 1892 to 1912 because at that time he apparently judged literature not the best medium for "enjoying his brain."

The events of Valery's life clearly influenced the development of his poetic theories and practices. He was born in the small western Mediterranean village of Cette, now spelled Sete, in the same year as Proust, the year of the Paris Commune and the Franco-Prussian War: 1871. Because his mother was Italian and his father was Corsican, Valery was probably as comfortable speaking Italian as French. He attended school at the College de Sete, now renamed in his honor, and at the lycee of the nearby city of Montpellier. In 1888, he passed the *baccalaureat* and entered law school, where literature first began to strike a responsive chord in him and he began to make contacts with the Parisian literary

group surrounding Mallarme. In 1889 he read Joris Karl Huysmans's novelistic manifesto of decadence, *Against the Grain (A rebours),* in which Mallarme's poem "Herodiade" is discussed admiringly, and the following year he met the young writers Pierre Louis and Andre Gide. It was the former, editor of a small literary magazine called *La Conque,* who first showed Valery's work to Mallarme and got several of his early poems into print, including "Narcissus Speaks."

Valery's introduction to Gide, by Louis, began a friendship that lasted throughout Valery's life and that has been documented in Robert Mallet's *Self-Portraits: The Gide/Valery Letters, 1890-1942.* Mallarme's ambiguously positive response to Valery's early work was reported by Gide: [Gide to Valery, July 1, 1892] "My friend, Mallarme has given me your poems; since he criticized them, he must esteem them. I was delighted by a few that I didn't know; some of them are much less good—that is, in comparison with others of your own. On reading them, I imagined them published, but Mallarme, when I saw him, didn't seem to think it desirable." [Valery to Gide, July 13, 1892] "[Louis] and You are beastly Semites: one of you, for having underhandedly and covered with a cloak of distance, dared to present my vague alchemies to Mallarme, the other of you, for having dared even more, in not repeating to me textually the precious and pure panning I deserved from the Master. [Louis] is completely mute. Whereas you merely hint. Whom shall I kill? All joking apart, you are loathsome. If I knew [Gide's friend, writer Maurice] Quillot better, I should have you poisoned. Speak then, with no fear of stating every lamentable word." [Gide to Valery, July 25, 1892] "Here is what he said about your poems and don't have me poisoned: 'I'm surprised that with the tact and knowledge of poetry he sometimes shows, he leaves, here and there, some that would seem to me *facile.*' The remark surprised me. And that's about it."

Despite Mallarme's reservations, several of the poems were published. "Narcissus Speaks" was immediately celebrated by the Paris literary establishment and selected by Adolphe Van Bever and Paul Leautaud for their important anthology *Poets of Today (Poetes d'aujourd'hui).* In fact, if not for Van Bever and Leautaud's recognition of the merit of his early work, Valery might have been completely forgotten during the long period when he wrote almost no poetry.

In 1892, Valery completed work on his law degree and embarked upon an unrequited and, by his own admission, "ludicrous" love affair. Similar more or less debilitating infatuations symptomatic of Valery's extreme but repressed emotionalism and sensitivity occurred throughout his life. This first love probably had something to do with the intellectual and spiritual crisis of 1892 that caused him to renounce poetry for twenty years. He took up poetry again, of course, but even as an old man he would continue to be profoundly troubled by what he regarded as the unsolvable equation of love.

One of his last works, a two-part dramatic work called *My Faust (Mon Faust),* attempted to deal with the issue and was never completed. As Charles G. Whiting has written in *Paul Valery,* "The unfinished play 'Lust' . . . remains as a testimony of his longing for a perfect communion he never found." In "Lust" and "The Solitary" ("Le Solitaire"), which together comprise *My Faust,* one finds the most frank treatment by Valery of his profound fear of sensuality. This fear probably accounts more than any other factor for his emotional crisis and twenty-year renunciation of poetry, since poetry, despite his attempts to purify or sterilize it, emblemized for Valery a certain sensuality of mind. His fear of sensuality may also explain his violent intellectual prejudices—against Freud, for instance, or against philosophy. According to Derrida, Valery rejected psychoanalysis and metaphysics because they focused upon meaning, and for Valery meaning was associated with the elevation of the physical, the sensual, over the formal properties of "pure" intellect. Furthermore, Freud offered the obvious explanation of why Valery might so vociferously vilify a belief in and search for meaning: the mind's repressed contents are always sexual. "Lust" allegorizes this profound conflict, never resolved by Valery.

Whiting's brief account of the play may thus help explain Valery's twenty-year refusal to embrace poetry as a career: "Before Faust's conclusion by exhaustion of possibilities, liberation, and death, there is in 'Lust' a remarkable apotheosis of *life* in the garden-scene of the second act. Here the magical, musical spell of a beautiful evening brings Faust rapidly to a high point of pure enjoyment of being. . . . 'Lust' . . . attempts to synthesize extreme existence of mind and body with the extreme experience of love, even if in a very incomplete fashion. Almost from the beginning of the garden-scene Lust shows her love for Faust, and immediately after Faust's great monologue, she unconsciously places her hand upon his shoulder. Faust addresses her as 'tu' and there is a brief moment of emotional communion with a birth of intimacy and tenderness, those beginnings of love which Valery prized above all other joys. Immediately, however, Faust retreats, and the apotheosis of the garden-scene comes to an end as he turns again to the dictation of his memoirs."

This "dictation of memoirs" appears to represent Valery's own intellectual narcissism, the self-directed literary activity of the *Notebooks;* Lust with her other-directed emotion seems to symbolize poetry that is meant to be read. Since Valery castigated all such audience-directed writing, he clearly must have felt comfortable with Faust's activities and motivations and anxious about Lust's. Indeed, his anxiety about Lust's appeal must have been extreme, for he was unable to finish the work. As Whiting explains, "Valery planned a fourth act for 'Lust' which would have developed the love theme but he found the project too difficult for theatrical creation, perhaps in large part because of his own defensive attitudes. Already in the first act, Faust tells Mephistopheles that he wants only tenderness, not love, from Lust. . . . Love is a danger because [it is] so closely related to instincts, to the cyclical and repetitive functions of life. . . . And so the intimacy of Lust and Faust is only a fleeting moment in the second act, and the too difficult fourth act was never written."

Valery himself wrote in his *Notebooks* that "Lust and Faust are *me*—and nothing but me. Experience has shown me that what I wanted most is not to be found in another—and cannot find the other capable of trying without reserve to go to the end of the will to . . . *take love where it has never been.*" Neither the period of relative silence from 1892 to 1912 nor the resumption of a poetic vocation resolved this crisis, the dilemma of all Valery's life and work: he was never able to bring himself to embrace Lust, though at the end of his life he admitted that she was as integral to him as was the austere, argumentative, and intellectually prudish Faust.

Valery's crisis occurred during an October, 1892, stay in Genoa, Italy. During a stormy and sleepless night, he decided that poetry was not the loftiest and purest expression of the mind's activity. From then until 1912, he wrote little poetry, instead devoting most of his creative energies to the *Notebooks.* Every morning he would get up at around five o'clock and write meditations, notes, and speculations in small volumes that he intended for no one but himself. There were more than 250 of these

notebooks at the end of his life, and they are not only now available in published form, but are, ironically, among the most important and most read—most *public*—of his writings.

During the years from 1892 to 1922, Valery first worked as a bureaucrat in the French War Office and then as secretary to Edouard Lebey, director of the French Press Association; he attended the Tuesday evening gatherings of artists, writers, and intellectuals at the home of Mallarme, and he married Jeannie Gobillard, a friend of Mallarme's daughter. He continued writing his *Notebooks* and began to publish essays—"Introduction to the Method of Leonardo da Vinci" ("Introduction a la methode de Leonard de Vinci"), and his inquiry into dreams, "Studies" ("Etudes"). He also wrote and published "The Evening with Monsieur Teste" ("La Soiree avec Monsieur Teste"), in which he created the fictional character of Edouard Teste, a paragon of intellectual austerity and self-absorption, an "ideal" thinker, and therefore a role model for Valery himself. Teste might be thought of as a precursor of the figure Faust, but without the opposing figure of Lust. What Valery admired so much in Teste was that, as "The Evening With Monsieur Teste" reveals, he had "*killed his puppet.*" That is, he did nothing conventional, "never smiled, nor said good morning or good night, . . . seemed not to hear a 'How are you?' " In "Letter from Madame Emilie Teste" ("Lettre de Madame Emilie Teste"), Valery's narrator imagined in him "incomparable intellectual gymnastics. This was not, in him, an excessive trait but rather a trained and transformed faculty. Here are his own words: 'I gave up books twenty years ago. I have burned my papers also. I scrape the quick. . . . I keep what I want.' "

In 1912, Valery was persuaded to break his poetical fast by undertaking a major revision of his earlier poems, which would be published under the title *Album of Old Verses (Album de vers anciens)* in 1920. Suzanne Nash, in *Paul Valery's Album de vers anciens: A Past Transfigured,* writes, "Valery seems to have understood that any reconsideration of his own work would perforce lead him to a deeper understanding of problems fundamental to the creative process itself. . . . This potentially self-constitutive dimension of the *Album* was certainly for Valery its ultimate justification. . . . [Its somewhat dated tone is] the result of his intention to mount a critical engagement with his literary heritage, to offer a portrait gallery of predecessors whose faces emerge transfigured and transvalued according to the exigencies of a new poetics." Thus, Nash continues, "The *Album de vers anciens* . . . is a particularly precious and innovative poetic document, one which holds, inscribed within its structure, the poet's interpretation of his creative confrontation with his past. It represents a kind of chronicle in which the older poet seeks to recreate the intellectual crisis which led him to reject a nineteenth-century concept of poetry founded on an ethics of Symbolist idealism in favor of a poetry which claims autonomy through critical self-reference."

By 1920, Valery had already published *The Young Fate,* a long, very difficult poem, to great critical and popular acclaim. He followed the *Album of Old Verses* with *Charms* ("songs" or "incantations") in 1922, and had written his first quasi-Platonic dialogues, *Eupalinos; or, The Architect (Eupalinos; ou, L'architecte)* and *The Soul and the Dance (L'Ame et la danse)* in 1921. The former dialogue treats much the same topics as "The Seaside Cemetery" ("Le Cimetiere marin"), probably Valery's best-known poem: the relationships of life and death, light and darkness, movement and stasis, which compose life itself. Phaedrus proclaims in this dialogue that "nothing beautiful can be separated from life, and life is that which dies." *The Soul and the*

Dance deals with the power of art to transcend individuality and the body and to reach toward the Absolute.

In 1922, Edouard Lebey, Valery's employer at the French Press Association, died, and the necessity of finding a new source of income further confirmed his revived sense of a literary—a publicly literary—vocation. From this point until the end of his life, Valery was known as the French poet. In 1924, *Variety (Variete),* a collection of his essays, appeared. It contained the essay on Leonardo first published in 1895, the important article on Poe's "Eureka," and "Variations on a Thought" ("Variations sur une pensee"), in which he attacked Pascal as a thinker. Valery would publish four more volumes of *Variety* in his lifetime. In 1925, he was elected to the French Academy, and in his 1927 inaugural speech he made the unprecedented gesture of attacking his predecessor, novelist Anatole France, probably because France, as co-editor of a literary magazine, had rejected the poetry of Mallarme. In 1937 Valery was appointed to the new chair in poetry at the College de France, a position he held until his death in 1945.

Some facts about Valery might predict a less than faultless comportment on Valery's part during World War II and France's occupation by Germany: first, he had been quietly but strongly "anti-Dreyfusard" during the famous Dreyfus affair, in which Emile Zola and others accused the French army and government of anti-Semitism in making a scapegoat of Captain Alfred Dreyfus during his 1894 trial for treason. Among the celebrities who, along with Zola, took up Dreyfus's case were Proust, the painter Claude Monet, and Anatole France. Valery in fact went so far as to donate money to aid the widow of Colonel Henry, who in 1898 killed himself when it became known that he had forged the documents used to incriminate Dreyfus. "There is evidence," writes Henry Grubbs in *Paul Valery,* "to show that Valery was annoyed at the propaganda of his liberal friends . . . and personally, at least at that moment, decidedly hostile to democracy. His preoccupation with the intellectual superman had led him to a great interest in the man wielding extreme power, the dictator, the tyrant. Examples of this are the sonnet 'Cesar' . . . and the references in the *cahiers* to the Emperor Tiberius, to Napoleon, and to Caesar. A cahier written late in 1898 contains the following multilingual slogans: 'Le Cesar de soi-meme/El Cesar de su mismo/Il Cesare di se stesso/The Cesar (sic) of himself.' " Furthermore, Valery was also friendly with Marshal Philippe Petain, one of the leaders of France's pro-German Vichy government.

However, the poet did prove sympathetic to the Free French Movement led by General Charles de Gaulle, and of the Nazis he wrote in "War Economy for the Mind": "As for our enemies, we, and the whole world, know that their politics with regard to the mind has been reduced or limited for ten years to repressing the developments of intelligence, to depreciating the value of pure research, to taking often atrocious measures against those who consecrated themselves to these things, to favoring, even as far as endowed chairs and laboratories, worshippers of the idol to the detriment of independent creators of spiritual richness, and they have imposed on the arts as on the sciences the utilitarian ends which a power founded on declamations and terror pursues." Moreover, his praise of Bergson was regarded as a courageous act.

Valery died on July 20, 1945, at the close of France's last twentieth-century war with Germany, having been born at the conclusion of its last nineteenth-century one. He was given a state funeral in Paris and buried at the cemetery at Sete, his birthplace and the setting for "The Seaside Cemetery."

Valery passed on an important legacy of influence in American letters, perhaps much greater than his influence on later French poets. Yves Bonnefoy, who now holds Valery's chair in poetry at the College de France and has succeeded him as the most prominent contemporary French poet, has said in *L'Improbable* that Valery had no real influence on his own poetic development. However, the American poet Allen Tate, a well-known member of the Southern Agrarian movement that flourished particularly during the 1920's and 1930's, has recorded in his *Memoirs and Opinions, 1926-1974* that "Here, in [Valery's] 'Pages Inedites' ['Unpublished Pages'], was a man educated in the French classical tradition and fired imaginatively by his early entretiens with Mallarme: whose apparently casual utterances gave me something more than the shock of recognition. It was rather the sense of my own identity, of a sameness within vast, elusive differences." It may be in the enduring classicism of Southern letters, passed from Tate to such contemporary Southern writers as Reynolds Price, Fred Chappell, and James Applewhite, that Valery's voice, through the veil of translation, can be heard most clearly today.

BIOGRAPHICAL/CRITICAL SOURCES:

BOOKS

Berne-Joffroy, Andre, *Valery,* Gallimard, 1960.

Blanchot, Maurice, *La Part du feu,* Gallimard, 1949.

Bonnefoy, Yves, *L'Improbable,* Mercure de France, 1959.

Carlson, Eric W., editor, *The Recognition of Edgar Allan Poe: Selected Criticism Since 1829,* University of Michigan Press, 1966.

Charpier, Jacques, *Valery,* Editions Pierre Seghers (Paris), 1962.

Cioran, E. M., *Valery face a ses idoles,* L'Heme (Paris), 1970.

Derrida, Jacques, *Margins of Philosophy,* translated with notes by Alan Bass, University of Chicago Press, 1982.

Dragonetti, Roger, *Aux frontieres du langage poetique: Etudes sur Dante, Mallarme, Valery,* Romanica Gandensia (Gent), 1961.

Grubbs, Henry A., *Paul Valery,* Twayne (New York), 1968.

Harari, Josue V., editor, *Textual Strategies,* Cornell University Press, 1979.

Hartman, Geoffrey, *The Unmediated Vision: An Interpretation of Wordsworth, Hopkins, Rilke, and Valery,* Yale University Press, 1954.

Henry, Albert, *Langage et poesie chez Paul Valery,* Mercure de France, 1952.

Hytier, Jean, *La Poetique de Valery,* 2nd edition, Armand Colin (Paris), 1970.

Ince, W. N., *The Poetic Theory of Valery,* University Press, 1961.

Lawler, James, *Lectures de Valery: Une Etude de "Charmes,"* Presses Universitaires de France, 1963.

Lawler, James, *The Poet as Analyst: Essays on Paul Valery,* University of California Press, 1974.

Mackay, Agnes E., *The Universal Self: A Study of Paul Valery,* University of Toronto Press, 1961.

Mallet, Robert, editor, *Self-Portraits: The Gide/Valery Letters, 1890-1942,* abridged and translated by June Guicharnaud, University of Chicago Press, 1966.

Mondor, Henri, *Precocite de Valery,* Gallimard, 1957.

Mondor, Henri, *Propos familiers de Paul Valery,* Grasset (Paris), 1957.

Nash, Suzanne, *Paul Valery's Album de vers anciens: A Past Transfigured,* Princeton University Press, 1983.

Parisier-Plottel, Jeaninne, *Les Dialogues de Paul Valery,* Presses Universitaires de France, 1960.

Raymond, Marcel, *Paul Valery et la tentation de l'esprit,* A La Baconniere, 1964.

Rouart-Valery, Agathe, editor, *Paul Valery,* Gallimard, 1966.
Symons, Julian, *The Tell-Tale Heart: The Life and Works of Edgar Allan Poe,* Harper, 1978.
Tate, Allen, *Memoirs and Opinions, 1926-1974,* Swallow, 1975.
Whiting, Charles G., *Paul Valery,* Athlone Press/University of London, 1978.

PERIODICALS

Georgia Review, Volume 30, 1976.
Lettres nouvelles, September, 1958.
Renaissance, Volume 2-3, 1944-45.
Yale French Studies, Number 44, 1970.

* * *

VALLEJO, Antonio Buero
  See BUERO VALLEJO, Antonio

* * *

Van CAMPEN, Karl
  See CAMPBELL, John W(ood, Jr.)

* * *

VANCE, Gerald
  See SILVERBERG, Robert

* * *

VANCE, Jack
  See VANCE, John Holbrook

* * *

VANCE, John Holbrook 1916-
  (Jack Vance; pseudonyms: Peter Held, John Holbrook, Ellery Queen, John Van See, Alan Wade)

PERSONAL: Born August 28, 1916, in San Francisco, Calif.; son of Charles Albert (a rancher) and Edith (Hoefler) Vance; married Norma Ingold, August 24, 1946; children: John Holbrook II. *Education:* University of California, Berkeley, B.A., 1942. *Politics:* "Above and between Left and Right." *Religion:* None.

ADDRESSES: Home—6383 Valley View Rd., Oakland, Calif. 94611. *Agent*—Kirby McCauley, 432 Park Ave. S., Suite 1509, New York, N.Y. 10016.

CAREER: Writer. Worked briefly for Twentieth Century-Fox.

AWARDS, HONORS: Edgar Allan Poe Award, Mystery Writers of America, 1961, for *The Man in the Cage;* Hugo Award, World Science Fiction Convention, 1964, for *The Dragon Masters,* and 1967, for *The Last Castle;* Nebula Award, Science Fiction Writers of America, 1966, for *The Last Castle;* Jupiter Award for best novelette, 1975, for "The Seventeen Virgins"; nominated for Gandalf Life Award, 1979; World Fantasy Life Achievement Award, 1984.

WRITINGS:

(Under pseudonym Alan Wade) *Isle of Peril,* Mystery House, 1957.
(Under pseudonym Peter Held) *Take My Face,* Mystery House, 1957.
The Man in the Cage, Random House, 1960.

The For Valley Murders, Bobbs-Merrill, 1966.
The Pleasant Grove Murders, Bobbs-Merrill, 1967.
The Deadly Isles, Bobbs-Merrill, 1969.
Bad Ronald, Ballantine, 1973.
The View from Chickweed's Window, Underwood-Miller, 1978.
The House on Lily Street, Underwood-Miller, 1979.
The Dark Ocean, Underwood-Miller, 1985.
Strange Notions, Underwood-Miller, 1985.

UNDER NAME JACK VANCE

Vandals of the Void, Winston, 1953.
The Space Pirate, Toby Press, 1953, published as *The Five Gold Bands,* Ace Books, 1962 (bound with *The Drag Masters,* Ace Books, 1962, Berkley Publishing, 1985).
To Live Forever, Ballantine, 1956.
Big Planet, Ace Books, 1957.
Slaves of the Klau, Ace Books, 1958.
The Languages of Pao, Avalon, 1958.
The Houses of Iszm [and] *Son of the Tree* (also see below), Ace Books, 1964.
Future Tense, Ballantine, 1964.
Space Opera, Pyramid Publications, 1965, reprinted Underwood-Miller, 1984.
Monsters in Orbit [and] *The World Between and Other Stories,* Ace Books, 1965.
The Brains of Earth [and] *The Many Worlds of Magnus Ridolph,* Ace Books, 1966.
The Blue World, Ballantine, 1966.
The Last Castle (bound with *World of the Sleeper,* by Tony R. Wayman), Ace Books, 1967.
Eight Fantasies and Magics: A Science Fiction Adventure Macmillan, 1969 (published in England as *Fantasms and Magics,* Mayflower, 1978).
Emphyrio, Doubleday, 1969.
The Worlds of Jack Vance, Ace Books, 1973.
(Contributor) *Three Trips in Time and Space: Original Novellas of Science Fiction,* Hawthorn Books, 1973.
The Gray Prince, Bobbs-Merrill, 1974.
Showboat World, Pyramid Publications, 1975.
The Best of Jack Vance, Pocket Books, 1976.
Maske: Thaery, Berkley Publications, 1976.
Nopalgarth (includes *The Houses of Iszm* and *Son of the Tree*), DAW Books, 1980.
Galactic Effectuator, Underwood-Miller, 1980.
The Complete Magnus Ridolph, Underwood-Miller, 1984.
Green Magic: The Fantasy Realms of Jack Vance, Tor Books, 1988.

Also author of *The Dragon Masters,* c. 1964, recent edition, Berkley Publishing, 1985.

UNDER NAME JACK VANCE; "DYING EARTH" SERIES

The Dying Earth, Hillman, 1950.
The Eyes of the Overworld, Ace Books, 1966.
Cugel's Saga, Pocket Books, 1983.
Rhialto the Marvellous, Baen Books, 1984.

UNDER NAME JACK VANCE; "DEMON PRINCE" SERIES

The Star King, Berkley Publishing, 1964.
The Killing Machine, Berkley Publishing, 1964.
The Palace of Love, Berkley Publishing, 1967.
The Face, DAW Books, 1979.
The Book of Dreams, DAW Books, 1981.

*UNDER NAME JACK VANCE; "PLANET OF ADVENTURE"
SERIES*

City of the Chasch, Ace Books, 1968, reprinted, Bluejay Books,
     1985.
Servants of the Wankh, Ace Books, 1969.
The Dirdir, Ace Books, 1969.
The Pnume, Ace Books, 1970.

UNDER NAME JACK VANCE; "DURDANE" SERIES

The Anome, Dell, 1973.
The Brave Free Men, Dell, 1973.
The Asutra, Dell, 1974.

UNDER NAME JACK VANCE; "ALASTOR" SERIES

Trullion: Alastor 2262, Ballantine, 1973, reprinted Underwood-
     Miller, 1984.
Maruen: Alastor 933, Ballantine, 1975.
Wyst: Alastor 1716, DAW Books, 1978.

UNDER NAME JACK VANCE; "LYONESSE" SERIES

Lyonesse I: Suldrun's Garden, Underwood-Miller, 1983.
Lyonesse II: The Green Pearl, Underwood-Miller, 1985.
Lyonesse III: Madouc, Underwood-Miller, 1990.

OTHER

Also author of works under pseudonyms John Holbrook, Ellery
Queen, and John Van See. Author of television scripts for "Captain Video." Contributor of fiction to periodicals.

SIDELIGHTS: A prolific author who has published more than
sixty books, John Holbrook Vance, known to most readers as
Jack Vance, started off writing short stories for magazines and
eventually progressed to novels, many of which have evolved
into series. "I'm not one of these chaps who was an instant success," he told Charles Platt in a rare interview for *Dream Makers.* "There was a long period in which I wrote a lot of junk, as
an apprentice, learning my trade. I found out I was no good at
gadget stories, or at least they were very boring to me, and I
found out that I didn't enjoy writing whimsy, and I finally blun-
dered into this thing which I keep on doing, which is essentially
a history of the human future." *Washington Post* reviewer Michael Dirda believes that whether Vance is writing "science fiction, high fantasy, or mysteries . . . his delicious sentences linger
as the chief pleasure of his inventive books." *Village Voice* contributor Baird Searles calls him "science fiction's most elegant
stylist."

Vance's "sensuous, elevated style, at times reminiscent of the art-
prose of Ruskin or Huysmans, can easily cloy or become mere
bejeweled description, gaudy but insubstantial," according to a
Washington Post Book World reviewer. "Vance skirts this danger
by fixing on traditional adventure plots: the revenge saga, the picaresque journey or marvel-filled odyssey, the murder mystery,
the novel of education (his most common form), sword-and-laser
battle epics. . . . All these strong story lines prevent the novels
from bogging down in the merely evocative."

Many of these elements are present in Vance's first book, *The
Dying Earth,* a collection of stories in which different characters
inhabit the same futuristic setting. These characters "seek power
or knowledge, and they compete fiercely for it," according to
Russell Letson in the *Dictionary of Literary Biography.* He believes that here, "as in much of Vance's work, it is less the characters or actions than the settings, atmosphere, and above all the
language that make these stories in *The Dying Earth* memorable."

In the sixties, Vance began to specialize in science fiction series,
and he returned to the milieu of *The Dying Earth* in 1966 with
The Eyes of the Overworld. Cugel the Clever, a picaresque rogue
and Vance's favorite character, dominates this tale, and his journey across the treacherous planet to retrieve a magic cusp forms
the heart of the novel. Letson believes that while "the characters
are no less amoral and self interested and the world no less savage and dangerous," this story is "less elegiac than the earlier
ones, and the atmosphere is lightened by picaresque escapades
and by the avoidance of the serious themes of love and loyalty."
The Eyes of the Overworld ends with Cugel, who has acquired the
magic cusp and completed his hazardous journey, outwitting
himself at the last moment and being thrust back to where he
began.

In *Cugel's Saga,* the next installment, Cugel must again complete
the journey, by a different but equally dangerous route. In his
Washington Post review of the book, Michael Dirda says, "any
reader who has ever enjoyed the voyages of Sinbad, the club stories of Mr. Joseph Jorkens or the tales of Tarzan will hardly find
a more diverting literary entertainment . . . than 'Cugel's Saga.'
Mellower, softer, less rich in texture and invention than 'The
Eyes of the Overworld,' it nonetheless possesses that distinctive
winey tang that is Vance's alone."

BIOGRAPHICAL/CRITICAL SOURCES:

BOOKS

Contemporary Literary Criticism, Volume 35, Gale, 1985.
Dictionary of Literary Biography, Volume 8: *Twentieth-Century
     American Science Fiction Writers,* Gale, 1981.
Platt, Charles, *Dream Makers,* Volume 2: *The Uncommon Men
     and Women Who Write Science Fiction,* Berkley Books,
     1983.

PERIODICALS

Village Voice, July 7, 1975.
Washington Post, December 13, 1983, October 27, 1985, April
     7, 1986.
Washington Post Book World, April 26, 1981, April 24, 1983,
     January 27, 1985.

*   *   *

Van DOREN, Mark   1894-1972

PERSONAL: Born June 13, 1894, in Hope, Ill.; died December
10, 1972, in Torrington, Conn.; buried in Cornwall Hollow,
Conn.; son of Charles Lucius (a physician) and Dora (Butz) Van
Doren; married Dorothy Graffe (a writer), September 1, 1922;
children: Charles, John. *Education:* University of Illinois at Ur-
bana-Champaign, A.B., 1914, A.M., 1915; Columbia University,
Ph.D., 1920.

ADDRESSES: Home—Falls Village, Conn. 06031.

CAREER: Columbia University, New York, N.Y., instructor,
1920-24, assistant professor, 1924-35, associate professor,
1935-42, professor of English, 1942-59. Lecturer at St. John's
College (Maryland), 1937-57; visiting professor of English at
Harvard University, 1963. Participant in "Invitation to Learning," CBS radio talk show, 1940-42. *Military service:* Served in
U.S. Army, Infantry, during World War I.

MEMBER: National Institute of Arts and Letters, American
Academy of Arts and Letters.

AWARDS, HONORS: Pulitzer Prize for poetry, 1940, for *Collected Poems;* Litt.D. from Bowdoin College, 1944, University

of Illinois, 1958, Columbia University, 1960, Knox College, 1966, Harvard University, 1966, and Jewish Theological Seminary of America, 1970; L.H.D. from Adelphi University, 1957, and Mount Mary College, 1965; St. John's College fellowship, 1959; Alexander Hamilton Medal, Columbia College, 1959; Sarah Josepha Hale Award, Richards Free Library (Newport, New Hampshire), 1960; Golden Rose Award, New England Poetry Society, 1960; brotherhood award, National Conference of Christians and Jews, 1960; creativity award, Huntington Hartford Foundation, 1962; Emerson-Thoreau Award, American Academy of Arts and Sciences, 1963; M.D., Connecticut State Medical Society, 1966; Academy of American Poets fellowship, 1967.

WRITINGS:

POEMS

Spring Thunder and Other Poems, Seltzer, 1924.
7 P.M. and Other Poems, Boni, 1926.
Now the Sky and Other Poems, Boni, 1928.
Jonathan Gentry, Boni, 1931.
A Winter Diary and Other Poems, Macmillan, 1935.
The Last Look and Other Poems, Holt, 1937.
Collected Poems, 1922-1928, Holt, 1939.
The Mayfield Deer, Holt, 1941.
Our Lady Peace and Other War Poems, New Directions, 1942.
The Seven Sleepers and Other Poems, Holt, 1942.
The Country Year, Morrow, 1946.
The Careless Clock: Poems about Children in the Family, Sloane, 1947.
New Poems, Sloane, 1948.
Humanity Unlimited: Twelve Sonnets, College of William and Mary Press, 1950.
In That Far Land, Prairie Press, 1951.
Mortal Summer, Prairie Press, 1953.
Spring Birth and Other Poems, Holt, 1953.
Selected Poems, Holt, 1954.
Morning Worship and Other Poems, Harcourt, 1960.
Collected and New Poems, 1924-1963, Hill & Wang, 1963.
(With Archibald MacLeish) *Narrative Poems,* Hill & Wang, 1964.
John Bradford, Hayloft Press, 1966.
100 Poems, Hill & Wang, 1967.
The Stove I Worship, Hayloft Press, 1967.
Winter Calligraphy, Hill & Wang, 1968.
That Shining Place, Hill & Wang, 1969.
In Winter Sing Summer, Bridge & Bryon, Inc., 1970.
Good Morning: Last Poems, Hill & Wang, 1973.

Also author of *Parents' Recompense,* 1965.

FICTION

Dick and Tom: Tales of Two Ponies (juvenile), Macmillan, 1931.
Dick and Tom in Town (juvenile), Macmillan, 1932.
The Transients, Morrow, 1935.
Windless Cabins, Holt, 1940.
The Transparent Tree (juvenile), Holt, 1940.
Tilda, Holt, 1943.
The Witch of Ramoth and Other Tales, Maple Press, 1950.
The Short Stories of Mark Van Doren, Abelard, 1950.
Nobody Say a Word and Other Stories, Holt, 1953.
Home with Hazel and Other Stories, Harcourt, 1957.
Collected Stories, Hill & Wang, Volume I, 1962, Volume II, 1965, Volume III, 1968.
(Author of introduction) Richard Henry Dana, *Two Years before the Mast,* Bantam, 1963.

Somebody Came (juvenile), Quist, 1966.

NONFICTION

Henry David Thoreau, Houghton, 1916, reprinted, Russell & Russell, 1961.
The Poetry of John Dryden, Harcourt, 1920, revised edition, Minority Press, 1931, published as *John Dryden: A Study of His Poetry,* Holt, 1946, first edition reprinted, Haskell House, 1969.
(With brother, Carl Van Doren) *American and British Literature since 1890,* Century Co., 1925, 2nd revised edition, Appleton, 1967.
Edwin Arlington Robinson, Literary Guild, 1927, reprinted, Norwood, 1976.
Shakespeare, Holt, 1939.
(With Theodore Spencer) *Studies in Metaphysical Poetry,* Columbia University Press, 1939, reprinted, Kennikat Press, 1964.
(With Huntington Cairns and Allen Tate) *Invitation to Learning,* Random House, 1941.
(With others) *The New Invitation to Learning,* Random House, 1942.
The Private Reader, Holt, 1942, reprinted, Kraus Reprint, 1968.
Liberal Education, Holt, 1943, published with new introduction, Beacon Press, 1959.
The Noble Voice: A Study of Ten Great Poems, Holt, 1946, published as *Great Poems of Western Literature,* Collier Books, 1962.
Nathaniel Hawthorne, Sloane, 1949, reprinted, Greenwood Press, 1972.
Man's Right to Knowledge and the Free Use Thereof, Columbia University Press, 1954.
The Autobiography of Mark Van Doren, Harcourt, 1958.
Don Quixote's Profession, Columbia University Press, 1958.
(Author of introduction) Francis Parkman, *The Oregon Trail,* Holt, 1959.
The Happy Critic, Hill & Wang, 1961.
The Dialogues of Archibald MacLeish and Mark Van Doren, edited by Warren V. Bush, Dutton, 1964.
(With others) *Insights into Literature,* Houghton, 1965.
Carl Sandburg, U.S. Government Printing Office, 1969.
(With Maurice Samuel) *In the Beginning, Love: Dialogues on the Bible,* edited by Edith Samuel, John Day, 1973.

Also contributor to *The Letters of Robinson Jeffers,* Ann N. Ridgeway, editor, 1966.

EDITOR

An American Bookshelf, five volumes, Macy Masius, 1927-28.
Samuel Sewell's Diary, Macy Masius, 1927.
Mason Locke Weems, *A History of Life and Death, Virtues and Exploits of General George Washington,* Macy Masius, 1927.
The Travels of William Bartram, Macy Masius, 1928.
Robert Montgomery Bird, *Nick of the Woods, or, Jibbenainosay: A Tale of Kentucky,* Macy Masius, 1928.
William Byrd, *A Journey to the Land of Eden and Other Papers,* Macy Masius, 1928.
An Anthology of World Poetry, Boni, 1928, 2nd revised edition, Harcourt, 1963.
(With Garibaldi M. Lapolla) *A Junior Anthology of World Poetry,* Boni, 1929.
An Autobiography of America, Boni, 1929.
Correspondence of Aaron Burr and His Daughter Theodosia, Covici-Friede, 1929.

Cotton Mather, *The Life of Sir William Phips,* Covici-Friede, 1930, reprinted, AMS Press, 1971.

American Poets, 1630-1930, Little, Brown, 1932.

The Oxford Book of American Prose, Oxford University Press, 1932.

(With Lapolla) *The World's Best Poems,* Boni, 1932.

(With John W. Cunliffe and Karl Young) *Century Readings in English Literature,* 5th edition (Van Doren was not associated with earlier editions), Appleton-Century-Crofts, 1940.

A Listener's Guide to "Invitation to Learning," Columbia Broadcasting System, Volume I: *1940-41,* 1940, Volume II: *1941-42,* 1942.

The Night of the Summer Solstice and Other Stories of the Russian War, Holt, 1943.

Walt Whitman, Viking, 1945, revised edition by Malcolm Cowley, 1973.

The Portable Emerson, Viking, 1946, reprinted, Penguin, 1977.

William Wordsworth, Selected Poetry, Random House, 1950.

The Best of Hawthorne, Ronald, 1951.

Introduction to Poetry, Sloane, 1951, also published as *Enjoying Poetry,* Sloane, 1951.

Selected Letters of William Cowper, Farrar, Straus, 1951.

(With others) *Riverside Poetry: 48 New Poems by 27 Poets,* Twayne, 1956.

PLAYS

The Last Days of Lincoln (produced in Tallahassee at Florida State University, October 18, 1961), Hill & Wang, 1959.

"Never, Never Ask His Name" (also see below), produced in Tallahassee at Florida State University, 1965.

Three Plays (contains "Never, Never Ask His Name," "A Little Night Music," and "The Weekend That Was"), Hill & Wang, 1966.

SIDELIGHTS: Mark Van Doren's interest in poetry began with his introduction to Wordsworth. "No poetry had made any great difference to me," he told Archibald MacLeish, "until suddenly I found myself reading Wordsworth. . . . It was music."

During his 39 years of teaching at Columbia University, Van Doren had many opportunities to advise students interested in becoming writers. "My advice to an ambitious young writer," he told Roy Newquist, "is to get the best education he can. . . . And never should he get too far from the soul of man, which is the basic concern of all art." He considered the question of a student's eventual success as a writer to be an impossible one to answer and recalled: "One day when I was talking to such a student, I said, 'Oh dear, let's see. Do you like coffee?' And he said, 'I'm crazy about coffee.' Well, he got the point right away. That's all the point I had." Included among Van Doren's former students are Thomas Merton, Lionel Trilling, Louis Zukofsky, Whittaker Chambers, Jack Kerouac, and Allen Ginsberg.

Van Doren's work is a studied application of his theories of knowledge, poetry, and teaching. He told MacLeish: "The subject [of a poem] is something that has struck you very deeply just because it's there, and because it's beautiful and important." Philip Booth found that "Van Doren's poems are seemingly simply talk made music; he deals with universal themes in the most specific terms, but he risks abstractions where nothing else will reach, and love is a word he is unafraid to write out." Although Paul Engle thought that "now and then one wishes that [Van Doren] would commit some wildness to the page," Theodore Roethke saw him as "a careful craftsman with a sharp eye for the homely and a mind aware of the profound implications of the casual."

Van Doren never considered himself a part of New York's literary world, nor did he establish friendships with writers simply because they were such. As Van Doren himself remained outside of literary circles, so his work stands apart from the mainstream of contemporary American letters. *Poetry* editors commented: "Van Doren has not received, nor will he evoke, applause from the avant garde; he is solidly entrenched in the tradition of definite purpose framed in strict patterns. There is nothing spectacular about his style. . . . He avoids either extreme of the obsessively confessional and the unemotionally unaffected. . . . Van Doren has never been a slave to a vogue, and never having been in fashion will never be out of it."

Van Doren's place among the critics is also characterized by non-extremism. "Among good critics," wrote Alfred Kazin, "Mr. Van Doren has always stood out as The Great Neutral, and that neutrality is the secret and condition of his quality. For if he has an ardent mind, it is also a tidy one; and if it is never aloof, it always lives on its own track; a mind exact and generous and often piercing in its intuitions, but very careful never to overreach, to say too much; ambitious only to stop on the necessary point made, the observation perfectly seen."

In an interview with Melvin Maddocks, Van Doren stated: "The job of the poet is to render the world—to see it and report it without loss, without perversion. No poet ever talks about feelings. Only sentimental people do. Feelings aren't pleasant. No one ever enjoyed real feelings—fear, pity, jealousy, all the feelings connected with love. Feelings mean suffering. Writing poems is a way of getting rid of feelings. You have to think to do anything well. . . . You finally express what you have to express in cold blood."

Van Doren did not turn his talents to writing plays until the middle 1950's, when he composed *The Last Days of Lincoln.* Of this work he told MacLeish: "Having become utterly enthralled by this person, I just had to do something about it. I had to get him talking." The play is wholly in verse except for Lincoln's speeches. "This play scores high as poetic drama," noted critic John Holmes, "and as a distinguished addition to Civil War literature."

BIOGRAPHICAL/CRITICAL SOURCES:

BOOKS

Bush, Warren V., editor, *The Dialogues of Archibald MacLeish and Mark Van Doren,* Dutton, 1964.

Contemporary Literary Criticism, Gale, Volume VI, 1976, Volume X, 1979.

Kreymbourg, Alfred, *Our Singing Strength,* Coward, 1924.

Newquist, Roy, *Counterpoint,* Rand McNally, 1964.

Nyren, Dorothy, editor, *Library of Literary Criticism,* 2nd edition, Ungar, 1961.

Van Doren, D. *The Professor and I,* Appleton, 1959.

Van Doren, Dorothy, *The Country Wife,* Morrow, 1950.

Van Doren, Mark, *The Autobiography of Mark Van Doren,* Harcourt, 1958.

PERIODICALS

Christian Science Monitor, February 25, 1960.

Library Journal, October 15, 1958.

Life, June 30, 1969.

Newsweek, February 23, 1959.

New York Herald Tribune, March 29, 1942.

New York Herald Tribune Book Review, February 15, 1959.

New York Times, October 26, 1958, January 31, 1965, January 11, 1969, June 13, 1969.

New York Times Book Review, November 10, 1968.
Poetry, November, 1960, March, 1964.
Saturday Review, November 17, 1937.
Washington Post, June 11, 1969.

*   *   *

Van DYNE, Edith
See BAUM, L(yman) Frank

*   *   *

van LAWICK-GOODALL, Jane
See GOODALL, Jane

*   *   *

van LHIN, Erik
See del REY, Lester

*   *   *

Van SEE, John
See VANCE, John Holbrook

*   *   *

VARGAS LLOSA, (Jorge) Mario (Pedro)   1936-

PERSONAL: Born March 28, 1936, in Arequipa, Peru; son of Ernesto Vargas Maldonaldo and Dora Llosa Ureta; married Julia Urquidi, 1955 (divorced); married Patricia Llosa, 1965; children: (second marriage) Gonzalo, Alvaro, Morgana. *Education:* Attended University of San Marcos; University of Madrid, Ph.D., 1959. *Politics:* Member of Fredemo, a center-right political party which is part of the Liberty Movement coalition.

CAREER: Writer. Journalist with *La Industria,* Piura, Peru, and with La Radio Panamericana and *La Cronica,* both in Lima, Peru, during 1960s; worked in Paris, France, as a journalist with Agence France-Presse, as a broadcaster with the radio-television network URTF, and as a language teacher; University of London, Queen Mary College and Kings College, London, England, faculty member, 1966-68; University of Washington, Seattle, writer in residence, 1968; University of Puerto Rico, Rio Piedras, visiting professor, 1969; *Libre,* Paris, co-founder, 1971; Columbia University, New York, N.Y., Edward Laroque Tinker Visiting Professor, 1975; former fellow, Woodrow Wilson Center, Washington, D.C.; former host of Peruvian television program "The Tower of Babel"; Peruvian presidential candidate, Liberty Movement, 1990.

AWARDS, HONORS: Premio Leopoldo Alas, 1959, for *Los jefes;* Barral Prix Biblioteca Breve, 1962, for *La ciudad y los perros;* Premio de la Critica Espanola, 1963, for *La ciudad y los perros,* and 1967, for *La casa verde;* Premio Nacional de la Novela, 1967, for *La casa verde;* Ritz Paris Hemingway Award, 1985, for *The War of the End of the World;* Premio Internacional Literatura Romulo Gallegos, for *La casa verde.*

WRITINGS:

Los jefes (story collection; title means "The Leaders"), Editorial Roca, 1959.
Los cachorros (novella), Editorial Lumen, 1967, translation by Ronald Christ and Gregory Kolovakos published, with six short stories, as *The Cubs and Other Stories,* Harper, 1979.
La novela, Fundacion de Cultura Universitaria, 1968.

Lletra de batalla per "Tirant lo Blanc," Edicions 62, 1969.
Antologia minima de M. Vargas Llosa, Editorial Tiempo Contemporaneo, 1969.
La literatura en la revolucion y la revolucion en la literatura, Vientiuno Editores, 1970.
Dia domingo, Ediciones Amadis, 1971.
Garcia Marquez: Historia de un deicidio, Seix Barral, 1971.
La historia secreta de una novela, Tusquets, 1971.
Obras escogidas, Aguilar, 1973.
La orgia perpetua: Flaubert y "Madame Bovary," Seix Barral, 1975, translation by Helen Lane published as *The Perpetual Orgy: Flaubert and Madame Bovary,* Farrar, Straus, 1986.
Art, Authenticity and Latin American Culture, Wilson Center (Washington, D.C.), 1981.
La senorita de Tacna, Seix Barral, 1982, first produced under title "Senorita from Tacna" in New York at INTAR Hispanic American Arts Center, 1983; produced under title "The Young Lady from Tacna" in Los Angeles at the Bilingual Foundation of the Arts, May, 1985.
Kathie y el hipopotamo: Comedia en dos actos, Seix Barral, 1983, translation by Kerry McKenny and Anthony Oliver-Smith produced as "Kathie and the Hippopotamus" in Edinburgh, Scotland, at the Traverse Theatre, August, 1986.
La cultura de la libertad, la libertad de la cultura, Fundacioj Eduardo Frei, 1985.
La chunga, Seix Barral, 1986, translation by Joanne Pottlitzer first produced in New York at INTAR Hispanic American Arts Center, February 9, 1986.
Elogio de la madrastra, Tusquets (Barcelona), 1988.

Also author of play "La Huida" (title means "The Escape"), produced in Piura, Peru; contributor to *The Eye of the Heart,* 1973.

NOVELS

La ciudad y los perros, Seix Bartal, 1963, translation by Lysander Kemp published as *The Time of the Hero,* Grove, 1966.
La casa verde, Seix Barral, 1966, translation by Gregory Rabassa published as *The Green House,* Harper, 1968.
Conversacion en la catedral, Seix Barral, 1969, translation by Rabassa published as *Conversation in the Cathedral,* Harper, 1975.
Pantaleon y las visitadoras, Seix Barral, 1973, translation by Christ and Kolovakos published as *Captain Pantoja and the Special Service,* Harper, 1978.
Aunt Julia and the Scriptwriter, Farrar, Straus, 1982 (published in the original Spanish as *La tia Julia y el escribidor,* 1977).
The War of the End of the World, translation by Lane, Farrar, Straus, 1984 (published in the original Spanish as *Guerra*).
Historia de Mayta, Seix Barral, 1985, translation by Alfred MacAdam published as *The Real Life of Alejandro Mayta,* Farrar, Straus, 1986.
Who Killed Palomino Molero?, translation by MacAdam, Farrar, Straus, 1987 (published in the original Spanish as *¿Quien mato a Palomino Molero?*).
El hablador, Seix Barral, 1988, translation by Lane published as *The Storyteller,* Farrar, Straus, 1989.
In Praise of the Stepmother, translation by Lane, Farrar, Straus, 1990.

SIDELIGHTS: Peruvian writer Mario Vargas Llosa often draws from his personal experiences to write of the injustices and corruption of contemporary Latin America. At one time an admirer of communist Cuba, since the early 1970s Vargas Llosa has been opposed to tyrannies of both the political left and right. He now advocates democracy, a free market, and individual liberty, and he cautions against extreme or violent political action, instead calling for peaceful democratic reforms. In 1989 he was chosen to be the presidential candidate of Fredemo, a political coalition in Peru; he later withdrew from the race. Through his novels—marked by complex structures and an innovative merging of dialogue and description in an attempt to recreate the actual feeling of life—Vargas Llosa has established himself as one of the most important of contemporary writers in the Spanish language. His novels, a London *Times* writer comments, "are among the finest coming out of Latin America."

As a young man, Vargas Llosa spent two years at the Leoncio Prado Military Academy. Sent there by his father, who had discovered that his son wrote poetry and was therefore fearful for the boy's masculinity, Vargas Llosa found the school, with its "restrictions, the military discipline and the brutal, bullying atmosphere, unbearable," he writes in the *New York Times Magazine.* His years at the school inspired his first novel, *The Time of the Hero* (first published in Spanish as *La ciudad y los perros*). The book is, R. Z. Sheppard states in *Time,* "a brutal slab of naturalism about life and violent death." The novel's success was ensured when the school's officials objected to Vargas Llosa's portrayal of their institution. "One thousand copies were ceremoniously burned in the patio of the school and several generals attacked it bitterly. One of them said that the book was the work of a 'degenerate mind,' and another, who was more imaginative, claimed that I had undoubtedly been paid by Ecuador to undermine the prestige of the Peruvian Army," Vargas Llosa recalls in his *New York Times Magazine* article.

In the award-winning *The Green House* (*La casa verde* in the Spanish edition), Vargas Llosa draws upon another period from his childhood for inspiration. For several years his family lived in the Peruvian jungle town of Piura, and his memories of the gaudy local brothel, known to everyone as the Green House, form the basis of his novel. The book's several stories are interwoven in a nonlinear narrative revolving around the brothel and the family that owns it, the military that runs the town, a dealer in stolen rubber in the nearby jungle, and a prostitute who was raised in a convent. "Scenes overlap, different times and places overrun each other . . . echoes precede voices, and disembodied consciences dissolve almost before they can be identified," Luis Harss and Barbara Dohmann write in *Into the Mainstream: Conversations with Latin-American Writers.* Gregory Rabassa, writing in *World Literature Today,* notes that the novel's title "is the connective theme that links the primitive world of the jungle to the primal lusts of 'civilization' which are enclosed by the green walls of the whorehouse." Rabassa sees, too, that Vargas Llosa's narrative style "has not reduced time to a device of measurement or location, a practical tool, but has conjoined it with space, so that the characters carry their space with them too . . . inseparable from their time." Harss and Dohmann find that *The Green House* "is probably the most accomplished work of fiction ever to come out of Latin America. It has sweep, beauty, imaginative scope, and a sustained eruptive power that carries the reader from first page to last like a fish in a bloodstream."

With *Conversation in the Cathedral* (first published in Spanish as *Conversacion en la catedral*), Vargas Llosa widened his scope. Whereas in previous novels he had sought to recreate the repression and corruption of a particular place, in *Conversation in the Cathedral* he attempts to provide a panoramic view of his native country. As John M. Kirk states in *International Fiction Review,* this novel "presents a wider, more encompassing view of Peruvian society. [Vargas Llosa's] gaze extends further afield in a determined effort to incorporate as many representative regions of Peru as possible." Set during the dictatorship of Manuel Udria

in the late 1940s and 1950s, the society depicted in the novel "is one of corruption in virtually all the shapes and spheres you can imagine," Wolfgang A. Luchting writes in the *Review of the Center for Inter-American Relations.* Penny Leroux, in a review of the book for *Nation,* calls it "one of the most scathing denunciations ever written on the corruption and immorality of Latin America's ruling classes."

The nonlinear writing of *Conversation in the Cathedral* is seen by several critics to be the culmination of Vargas Llosa's narrative experimentation. Writing in the *Review of the Center for Inter-American Relations,* Ronald Christ calls the novel "a masterpiece of montage" and "a massive assault on simultaneity." Christ argues that Vargas Llosa links fragments of prose together to achieve a montage effect that "promotes a linking of actions and words, speech and description, image and image, point of view and point of view." Kirk explains that in *Conversation in the Cathedral,* Vargas Llosa is "attempting the ambitious and obviously impossible plan of conveying to the reader all aspects of the reality of [Peruvian] society, of writing the 'total' novel." By interweaving five different narratives, Vargas Llosa forces the reader to study the text closely, making the reader an "accomplice of the writer [which] undoubtedly helps the reader to a more profound understanding of the work." Kirk concludes that *Conversation in the Cathedral* is "both a perfect showcase for all the structural techniques and thematic obsessions found in [Vargas Llosa's] other work, as well as being the true culmination of his personal anguish for Peru."

Speaking of these early novels in *Modern Latin American Literature,* D. P. Gallagher argues that one intention of their complex nonlinear structures is to "re-enact the complexity of the situations described in them." By juxtaposing unrelated elements, cutting off dialogue at critical moments, and breaking the narration, Vargas Llosa suggests the disparate geological conditions of Peru, recreates the difficulties involved in living in that country, and re-enacts "the very nature of conversation and of communication in general, particularly in a society devoted to the concealment of truth and to the flaunting of deceptive images," Gallagher believes. Ronald de Feo points out in the *New Republic* that these early novels all explore "with a near-savage seriousness and single-mindedness themes of social and political corruption." But in *Captain Pantoja and the Special Service* (*Pantaleon y las visitadoras* in its Spanish edition), "a new unexpected element entered Vargas Llosa's work: an unrestrained sense of humor," de Feo reports.

A farcical novel involving a military officer's assignment to provide prostitutes for troops in the Peruvian jungle, *Captain Pantoja and the Special Service* is "told through an artful combination of dry military dispatches, juicy personal letters, verbose radio rhetoric, and lurid sensationalist news reports," Gene Bell-Villada writes in *Commonweal.* Vargas Llosa also mixes conversations from different places and times, as he has in previous novels. And like these earlier works, *Captain Pantoja and the Special Service* "sniffs out corruption in high places, but it also presents something of a break, Vargas Llosa here shedding his high seriousness and adopting a humorous ribald tone," Bell-Villada concludes. The novel's satirical attack is aimed not at the military, a *Times Literary Supplement* reviewer writes, but at "any institution which channels instincts into a socially acceptable ritual. The humor of the narrative derives less from this serious underlying motive, however, than from the various linguistic codes into which people channel the darker forces."

The humorous tone of *Captain Pantoja and the Special Service* is also found in *Aunt Julia and the Scriptwriter* (*La tia Julia y el escribidor* in the original Spanish edition). The novel concerns two characters based on people in Vargas Llosa's own life: his first wife, Julia, who was his aunt by marriage, and a writer of radio soap opera who Vargas Llosa names Pedro Camacho in the novel. The 18-year-old narrator, Mario, has a love affair with the 32-year-old Julia. Their story is interrupted in alternate chapters by Camacho's wildly complicated soap opera scripts. As Camacho goes mad, his daily scripts for ten different soap operas become more and more entangled, with characters from one serial appearing in others and all of his plots converging into a single unlikely story. The scripts display "fissures through which are revealed secret obsessions, aversions and perversions that allow us to view his soap operas as the story of his disturbed mind," Jose Miguel Oviedo writes in *World Literature Today.* "The result," explains Nicholas Shakespeare in the *Times Literary Supplement,* "is that Camacho ends up in an asylum, while Mario concludes his real-life soap opera by running off to marry Aunt Julia."

Although *Aunt Julia and the Scriptwriter* is as humorous as the previous novel, *Captain Pantoja and the Special Service,* "it has a thematic richness and density the other book lacked," de Feo believes. This richness is found in the novel's exploration of the writer's life and of the relationship between a creative work and its inspiration. In the contrasting of soap opera plots with the real-life romance of Mario and Julia, the novel raises questions about the distinctions between fiction and fact. In a review for *New York,* Carolyn Clay calls *Aunt Julia and the Scriptwriter* "a treatise on the art of writing, on the relationship of stimuli to imagination." It is, de Feo observes, "a multilayered, high-spirited, and in the end terribly affecting text about the interplay of fiction and reality, the transformation of life into art, and life seen and sometimes even lived as fiction."

In *The War of the End of the World,* Vargas Llosa for the first time sets his story outside of his native Peru. He turns instead to Brazil of the 19th century and bases his story on an apocalyptic religious movement which gained momentum towards the end of the century. Convinced that the year 1900 marked the end of the world, these zealots, led by a man named the Counselor, set up the community of Canudos. Because of the Counselor's continued denunciations of the Brazilian government, which he called the "antichrist" for its legal separation of church and state, the national government sent in troops to break up this religious community. The first military assault was repulsed, as were the second and third, but the fourth expedition involved a force of some 4,000 soldiers. They laid waste to the entire area and killed nearly 40,000 people.

Vargas Llosa tells Wendy Smith in *Publishers Weekly* that he was drawn to write of this bloody episode because he felt the fanaticism of both sides in this conflict was exemplary of present-day Latin America. "Fanaticism is the root of violence in Latin America," he explains. In the Brazilian war, he believes, is a microcosm of Latin America. "Canudos presents a limited situation in which you can see clearly. Everything is there: a society in which on the one hand people are living a very old-fashioned life and have an archaic way of thinking, and on the other hand progressives want to impose modernism on society with guns. This creates a total lack of communication, of dialogue, and when there is no communication, war or repression or upheaval comes immediately," he tells Smith. In an article for the *Washington Post,* Vargas Llosa explains to Curt Suplee that "in the history of the Canudos war you could really see something that has been happening in Latin American history over the 19th and 20th centuries—the total lack of communication between two sections of a society which kill each other fighting *ghosts,* no?

Fighting fictional enemies who are invented out of fanaticism. This kind of reciprocal incapacity of understanding is probably the main problem we have to overcome in Latin America."

Not only is *The War of the End of the World* set in the 19th century, but its length and approach are also of that time. A writer for the London *Times* calls it "a massive novel in the l9th century tradition: massive in content, in its ambitions, in its technical achievement." Gordon Brotherston of the *Times Literary Supplement* describes the book as being "on the grand scale of the nineteenth century," while Salman Rushdie of *New Republic* similarly defines the novel as "a modern tragedy on the grand scale." Richard Locke of the *Washington Post Book World* believes that *The War of the End of the World* "overshadows the majority of novels published here in the past few years. Indeed, it makes most recent American fiction seem very small, very private, very gray, and very timid."

Vargas Llosa's political perspective in *The War of the End of the World* shows a marked change from his earlier works. He does not attack a corrupt society in this novel. Instead he treats both sides in the Canudos war ironically. The novel ends with a character from either side locked in a fight to the death. As Rushdie observes, "this image would seem to crystallize Vargas Llosa's political vision." This condemnation of both sides in the Canudos conflict reflects Vargas Llosa's view of the contemporary Latin American scene, where rightist dictatorships often battle communist guerrillas. Suplee describes Vargas Llosa as "a humanist who reviles with equal vigor tyrannies of the right or left (is there really a difference, he asks, between 'good tortures and bad tortures'?)."

Although his political views have changed during the course of his career, taking him from a leftist supporter of communist Cuba to a strong advocate of democracy, Vargas Llosa's abhorrence of dictatorship, violence, and corruption has remained constant. And he sees Latin American intellectuals as part of a continuing cycle of "repression, chaos, and subversion," he tells Philip Bennett in the *Washington Post.* Many of these intellectuals, Vargas Llosa explains further, "are seduced by rigidly dogmatic stands. Although they are not accustomed to pick up a rifle or throw bombs from their studies, they foment and defend the violence." Speaking of the ongoing conflict in Peru between the military government and a Maoist guerrilla movement, Vargas Llosa clarifies to Suplee that "the struggle between the guerrillas and the armed forces is really a settling of accounts between privileged sectors of society, and the peasant masses are used cynically and brutally by those who say they want to 'liberate' them."

Vargas Llosa believes that a Latin American writer is obligated to speak out on political matters. "If you're a writer in a country like Peru," he tells Suplee, "you're a privileged person because you know how to read and write, you have an audience, you are respected. It is a moral obligation of a writer in Latin America to be involved in civic activities." This belief led Vargas Llosa in 1987 to speak out when the Peruvian government proposed to nationalize the country's banks. His protest quickly led to a mass movement in opposition to the plan, and the government was forced to back down. Vargas Llosa's supporters went on to create Fredemo, a political party calling for democracy, a free market, and individual liberty. Together with two other political parties, Fredemo established a coalition group called the Liberty Movement. In June of 1989, Vargas Llosa was chosen to be the coalition's presidential candidate for Peru's 1990 elections. Visiting small rural towns, the urban strongholds of his Marxist opponents, and the jungle villages of the country's Indians, Vargas

Llosa campaigned on what he believes is Peru's foremost problem: "We have to defend democracy against the military and against the extreme Left." Opinion polls in late summer of 1988 showed him to be the leading contender for the presidency, with a 44 to 19 percent lead over his nearest opponent.

"A major figure in contemporary Latin American letters," as Locke explains, and "the man whom many describe as the national conscience of his native Peru," as George de Lama writes in the *Chicago Tribune,* Vargas Llosa is usually ranked with Jorge Luis Borges, Gabriel Garcia Marquez, and other writers of what has been called the Latin American "Boom" of the 1960s. His body of work set in his native Peru, Suzanne Jill Levine writes in the *New York Times Book Review,* is "one of the largest narrative efforts in contemporary Latin American letters. . . . [He] has begun a complete inventory of the political, social, economic and cultural reality of Peru. . . . Very deliberately, Vargas Llosa has chosen to be his country's conscience." But Vargas Llosa warns that a writer's role is limited. "Even great writers can be totally blind on political matters and can put their prestige and their imagination and fantasy at the service of a policy, which, if it materialized, would be destruction of what they do . . . ," Sheppard quotes Vargas Llosa as telling a PEN conference. "To be in the situation of Poland is no better than to be in the situation of Chile. I feel perplexed by these questions. I want to fight for societies where perplexity is still permitted."

MEDIA ADAPTATIONS: "The Cubs" was filmed in 1971; *Captain Pantoja and the Special Service* was filmed in 1976 (Vargas Llosa directed the film, which was banned in Peru); *Aunt Julia and the Scriptwriter* was adapted as a television series in Peru and as a screenplay written by William Boyd and directed by Jon Amiel in 1989.

AVOCATIONAL INTERESTS: Tennis, gymnastics, waterskiing, movies.

BIOGRAPHICAL/CRITICAL SOURCES:

BOOKS

Contemporary Literary Criticism, Gale, Volume 3, 1975, Volume 6, 1976, Volume 9, 1978, Volume 10, 1979, Volume 15, 1980, Volume 31, 1985, Volume 42, 1987.
Feal, Rosemary Geisdorfer, *Novel Lives: The Fictional Autobiographies of Guillermo Cabrera Infante and Mario Vargas Llosa,* University of North Carolina Press, 1986.
Gallagher, D. P., *Modern Latin American Literature,* Oxford University Press, 1973.
Harss, Luis, and Barbara Dohmann, *Into the Mainstream: Conversations with Latin-American Writers,* Harper, 1967.
Rossmann, Charles, and Alan Warren Friedman, editors, *Mario Vargas Llosa: A Collection of Critical Essays,* University of Texas Press, 1978.
Williams, Raymond Leslie, *Mario Vargas Llosa,* Ungar, 1986.

PERIODICALS

Bookletter, April 28, 1975.
Bulletin of Bibliography, December, 1986.
Chicago Tribune, January 3, 1989, June 23, 1989, August 3, 1989.
Chicago Tribune Book World, October 7, 1979, January 12, 1986.
Commonweal, June 8, 1979.
Hispania, March, 1976.
Hudson Review, winter, 1976.
International Fiction Review, January, 1977.
Los Angeles Times, May 20, 1985, December 18, 1988.
Los Angeles Times Book Review, February 2, 1986.
Nation, November 22, 1975.
National Review, December 10, 1982.
New Leader, March 17, 1975, November 15, 1982.
New Republic, August 16-23, 1982, October 8, 1984.
Newsweek, February 10, 1986.
New York, August 23, 1982.
New York Review of Books, March 20, 1975, January 24, 1980.
New York Times, March 30, 1985, January 8, 1986, February 9, 1986, February 12, 1986, September 10, 1989.
New York Times Book Review, March 23, 1975, April 9, 1978, September 23, 1979, August 1, 1982, December 2, 1984, February 2, 1986, October 29, 1989.
New York Times Magazine, November 20, 1983.
Partisan Review, Volume 46, number 4, 1979.
Publishers Weekly, October 5, 1984.
Review of the Center for Inter-American Relations, spring, 1975.
Saturday Review, January 11, 1975.
Spectator, May 14, 1983.
Time, February 17, 1975, August 9, 1982, January 27, 1986, March 10, 1986, September 7, 1987.
Times (London), May 13, 1985, August 5, 1986.
Times Literary Supplement, October 12, 1973, May 20, 1983, March 8, 1985, May 17, 1985, July 1, 1988.
Tribune Books (Chicago), October 29, 1989.
Washington Post, August 29, 1983, October 1, 1984, March 26, 1989.
Washington Post Book World, August 26, 1984, February 9, 1986.
World Literature Today, winter, 1978, spring, 1978.

*   *   *

VELTMAN, Vera
See PANOVA, Vera (Fedorovna)

*   *   *

VENDLER, Helen (Hennessy) 1933-

PERSONAL: Born April 30, 1933, in Boston, Mass.; daughter of George (a teacher) and Helen (a teacher; maiden name, Conway) Hennessy; divorced; children: David. *Education:* Emmanuel College, A.B. (summa cum laude), 1954; attended University of Louvain, 1954-55, and Boston University, 1955-56; Harvard University, Ph.D., 1960.

ADDRESSES: Home—16A Still St., Brookline, Mass. 02146. *Office*—Department of English, Warren House, Harvard University, Cambridge, Mass. 02138.

CAREER: Cornell University, Ithaca, N.Y., instructor in English, 1960-63; Haverford College, Haverford, Pa., lecturer in English, and Swarthmore College, Swarthmore, Pa., lecturer in English, both 1963-64; Smith College, Northampton, Mass., assistant professor of English, 1964-66; Boston University, Boston, Mass., associate professor, 1966-68, professor of English, 1968-85, director of graduate studies, department of English, 1970-75 and 1978-79; Harvard University, Cambridge, Mass., visiting professor, 1981-85, professor of English, 1985—, William R. Kenan Professor of English and American Literature and Language, 1986—, associate dean of arts and sciences, 1987—. Fulbright lecturer in American literature, University of Bordeaux, 1968-69; Fanny Hurst Visiting Professor, Washington University, St. Louis, fall, 1975. Judge for National Book Award in poetry, 1972, and Pulitzer Prize in poetry, 1974, 1976,

1978, and 1986. Member of subcommittee on literary criticism awards, Guggenheim Foundation, 1974, 1976, 1977, and 1978; jury member for Mellon fellowships and Rockefeller fellowships, both 1979. Member, Rockefeller Commission on the Humanities, 1978-79, and Board of Educational Consultants, National Endowment for the Humanities.

MEMBER: Modern Language Association of America (member of executive council, 1971-75; second vice-president, 1978; first vice-president, 1979; president, 1980), American Academy of Arts and Sciences (councillor, 1976-80), English Institute (member of supervisory board, 1970-73; trustee, 1977-86), PEN Society of Fellows—Harvard University, Phi Beta Kappa.

AWARDS, HONORS: Fulbright fellowship, 1954-55; American Association of University Women fellowship, 1959-60; American Council of Learned Societies, grant-in-aid, 1963, fellowship, 1971; James Russell Lowell Prize, Modern Language Association, and *Explicator* Literary Foundation Award, 1969, both for *On Extended Wings: Wallace Stevens' Longer Poems;* Guggenheim fellowship, 1971; National Institute of Arts and Letters Award, 1975; Metcalf Teaching Award, Boston University, 1975; National Endowment for the Humanities fellowship, 1977-78 and 1986-87; Graduate Society Medal, Radcliffe College, 1978; National Book Critics Circle Award in criticism, and "Notable Book" citation from American Library Association, 1980, both for *Part of Nature, Part of Us: Modern American Poets;* nomination for National Book Critics Circle Award in criticism, 1983, for *The Odes of John Keats;* honorary degrees from Smith College, University of Oslo, Kenyon College, University of Hartford, Union College, and Columbia University.

WRITINGS:

Yeats's Vision and the Later Plays, Harvard University Press, 1963.
On Extended Wings: Wallace Stevens' Longer Poems, Harvard University Press, 1969.
(Editor with Reuben Brower and John Hollander; also contributor) *I. A. Richards: Essays in His Honor,* Oxford University Press, 1973.
The Poetry of George Herbert, Harvard University Press, 1975.
Part of Nature, Part of Us: Modern American Poets, Harvard University Press, 1980.
The Odes of John Keats, Harvard University Press, 1983.
Wallace Stevens: Words Chosen Out of Desire, University of Tennessee Press, 1984.
(Editor and author of introduction) *The Harvard Book of Contemporary American Poetry,* Harvard University Press, 1985 (published in England as *The Faber Book of Contemporary American Poetry,* Faber, 1987).
(Contributing editor and author of introduction to contemporary poetry section) Donald McQuade, general editor, *The Harper American Literature,* two volumes, Harper, 1987.
(Editor, author of introduction, and contributor) *Voices and Vision: The Poet in America* (companion to "Voices and Vision," broadcast on PBS-TV, January 26-April 19, 1988), Random House, 1987.
The Music of What Happens: Poems, Poets, Critics, Harvard University Press, 1988.

CONTRIBUTOR

Roy Harvey Pearce and Hillis Miller, editors, *The Act of the Mind,* Johns Hopkins Press, 1964.
Reuben Brower, editor, *Forms of Lyric,* Columbia University Press, 1970.
Irvin Ehrenpreis, editor, *Wallace Stevens,* Penguin, 1972.

William H. Pritchard, editor, *William Butler Yeats,* Penguin, 1972.
W. K. Wimsatt, editor, *Literary Criticism: Idea and Act,* University of California Press, 1974.
Frank Doggett and Robert Buttel, editors, *Wallace Stevens: A Celebration,* Princeton University Press, 1980.
Lloyd Schwartz and Sybil P. Estess, editors, *Elizabeth Bishop and Her Art,* University of Michigan Press, 1983.

Also contributor to "Modern Critical Views" series, edited by Harold Bloom, Chelsea House. Contributor of numerous articles to periodicals, including *Atlantic, Mademoiselle, Massachusetts Review, New Republic, New Yorker, New York Times Book Review, Parnassus: Poetry in Review, Salmagundi,* and *Southern Review;* contributor of numerous reviews to periodicals, including *American Scholar, Nation,* and *Yale Review.*

OTHER

Member of advisory board, *Studies in Romanticism;* consulting poetry editor, *New York Times Book Review,* 1971-74; member of editorial board, *American Scholar,* 1978-81; poetry critic, *New Yorker,* 1978.

WORK IN PROGRESS: A commentary on William Shakespeare's *Sonnets.*

SIDELIGHTS: Helen Vendler is regarded by many as one of America's foremost critics of poetry. Since the mid-1960s she has contributed numerous reviews and articles on poetry to prominent literary publications, in particular the *New York Times Book Review,* and since 1978 has served as poetry critic for the *New Yorker.* In addition to her reviews and articles, Vendler is the author of acclaimed book-length studies of poets W. B. Yeats, George Herbert, Wallace Stevens, and John Keats. Her most noted work, the award-winning collection of criticism *Part of Nature, Part of Us: Modern American Poets,* is recognized as an extensive and informed view of contemporary American poetry. A second collection, *The Music of What Happens: Poems, Poets, Critics,* further explores the diversities and issues that surround contemporary British and American poetry. Regarding Vendler's accomplishments, William H. Pritchard once remarked in the *New Republic:* "To begin with a judgment widely shared, if not a truth universally acknowledged: Helen Vendler is the best poetry reviewer in America."

Vendler is often cited as one of poetry's best "close readers," her criticism frequently praised for its insightful explication of individual poems and its comprehension of individual aesthetic principles. Furthermore, she is known as a devout disciple of poetry, the literary art which, she states in the foreword to *Part of Nature, Part of Us,* is "the one form of writing that is to me the most immediate, natural, and accessible." "Poetry, clearly, is Vendler's passion," writes Phoebe Pettingell in the *New Leader.* "She directs her observations straight at the heart of the matter, so that her readers may recognize at once what she finds so marvelous in a poem." Vendler's critical writings have been recognized as assured and illuminating discussions of poetry. Pritchard cites "the pressure of an appetite" and an "unreticent forcefulness" at work in Vendler's poetry criticism, adding that "her virtues are a rigorous attending to verbal structure and texture; the ability to quote appositely and economically; a sure though not a too-exclusive taste; above all, the ability to do the poem one better by putting into words the relevant responses we might have had if we'd been smarter and more feeling." In a review of *Part of Nature, Part of Us* for the *New York Times,* Anatole Broyard describes a respect for poetry that becomes apparent in Vendler's criticism: "Unlike some critics, Helen Vendler puts herself entirely at the service of the poets she is talking about. Although she writes too well to be invisible, she does not compete or pontificate either. . . . What she does is to offer the poetry to you and somehow push and pull you into shape until you can accept it."

Part of Nature, Part of Us was a resounding accomplishment for Vendler, a collection of her reviews and essays published between 1966 and 1979 which "provides a sweeping overview of contemporary American poetry," writes John C. Hawley in *America*. During the time span that these reviews and essays appeared, Vendler's reputation as a formidable literary critic was also bolstered by her extended studies of Stevens and Herbert. *On Extended Wings: Wallace Stevens' Longer Poems* "ought to be read, with care and gratitude, by every reader of Stevens, for no critic before her has understood so well his major poems," says Harold Bloom in the *New York Times Book Review*, adding: "Helen Vendler . . . has written a superb and badly needed book, giving us readings unlikely to be surpassed of Stevens's longer poems, which tend to be his best." Likewise, Vendler's *The Poetry of George Herbert* was praised as an in-depth study of the early seventeenth-century English metaphysical poet. "Vendler is undoubtedly a finely trained and extraordinarily resourceful reader, and I cannot imagine that anybody who cares for Herbert, or more generally for poetry, will fail to learn something from this book," comments Frank Kermode in the *New York Times Book Review*. Kermode adds that although Vendler displays a "willfulness" by examining those of Herbert's poems which most closely "fit her model," she lays the foundations of her study in the works themselves: "Her meditations are nearly always faithful to their texts—she very rarely succumbs to the vice of the 'close reader,' which is to speak more wonders than the poem he is considering; and she has brought off a quite notable feat of construction in making a collection of disparate commentaries stand up as a book."

Vendler achieves a similar effect in *Part of Nature, Part of Us* where, instead of extensively treating various aspects of a single poet, she examines diversity among a number of contemporary American poets—in the process giving testament to an entire artistic movement. "The effect of the book is to give a comprehensive and highly authoritative picture of the American poetry scene today," writes John Bayley in the *Times Literary Supplement*. "There is nothing bitty about the technique: the whole sweep of her survey is sure and purposive, and coming to the end of the book one feels that a number of really significant generalizations have been made about the nature of the American poetic phenomenon, and the way it relates to the American consciousness." Forty-five different poets are discussed in Vendler's survey, including Wallace Stevens, Robert Lowell, Elizabeth Bishop, James Merrill, and Adrienne Rich. Vendler's remarks in the foreword to the collection both describe her approach and offer insight into its objectives: "My own preference is to focus on poets one by one, to find in each the idiosyncratic voice wonderfully different from any other. . . . All the poets of the century become part of a common music, but the voices of genius live vividly in their oddness and their intensity. Still, if they had nothing in common with us—if they were not, as Stevens says, part of nature and part of us, their rarities would not be ours, and we could not hear them speak. To write about them is to try to explain, first to oneself and then to others, what common note they strike and how they make it new." Monroe K. Spears in the *Washington Post Book World* comments that "in a time when much criticism seems increasingly academic and autotelic, self-generating and self-absorbed and perhaps self-destructive, it is a relief to find a critic who conceives of her work as having a defi-

nite and humane purpose." *Part of Nature, Part of Us* was the unanimous choice of the National Book Critics Circle for its 1980 award in criticism.

Vendler's critical perspective and writing style are central to the impact of *Part of Nature, Part of Us* and emerge as overall strengths of her literary criticism. Irvin Ehrenpreis writes in the *New York Review of Books* that Vendler's critical stance is distinguished in that it does not start with the "poem as a completed object"; rather, "Vendler starts with the act of creation. She stands beside the poet and watches him compose. Reading her essays, one acquires a sense of works of art not laid out in an operating theater but just coming into being." Similarly, Harold Beaver notes in *Parnassus: Poetry in Review* that Vendler's "strategy is not so much to center on the poem, or on the poet, but on the problem of writing such and such a poem." Thus, he explains, "the act of writing is itself treated as a critical act: the critic's role is to ponder and assess that act." Bayley contends that Vendler "is certainly the most thoughtful and humane, as she is the least system-bound, critic of poetry now writing. . . . Her examination of a poet is always as absolutely business-like and thorough as it is sympathetic, like that of a really good doctor."

Vendler's writing style in *Part of Nature, Part of Us* particularly earned praise from a number of reviewers. Denis Donoghue writes in the *New York Times Book Review* that "when she likes a poem and sways to its music, she pays it the tribute of paraphrase in terms that are often just as memorable as the poem itself." Ehrenpreis elaborates: "Vendler sparkles with brisk metaphors, colloquial rhythms, newborn phrases, [and] a syntax that evokes a mind endlessly responsive to the article before it. . . . The impression one gets of a wonderfully adaptable sensibility moving in company with the poet's genius is due not only to the wisdom and penetration of her judgement but to the unforeseeable, satisfying notions of her language and phrasing." Beaver describes Vendler's technique as "less a method than an endlessly alert, protracted hesitancy, a hummingbird-like hovering and darting from possibility to possibility."

Vendler attracted much attention with her next book of criticism, *The Odes of John Keats,* a groundbreaking—in some circles, controversial—study of the nineteenth-century English Romantic poet. In the book, Vendler examines several of Keats's most famous odes, not only in regards to their often praised rich language, but, as Ehrenpreis notes, "find[ing] . . . a special relation, dealing progressively with a common theme, the creative imagination." Pettingell explains that "Vendler presents the sequential progression of the odes as a series of tentative solutions, proposed, rejected, then used as building blocks toward the next." A number of reviewers, although impressed with Vendler's reading of the individual odes, point out problems in organizing them as a progressive larger structure. Ehrenpreis writes that "Vendler takes for granted both an order and a progression, with each principle supporting the other. To some readers, therefore, her demonstrations will appear circular." *New Republic* contributor David Bromwich claims that by examining the odes as a progressive development, Vendler "is obliged to discover a fair amount of shortcomings in the earlier odes which readers not attuned to her story have either passed over or refused to consider as faults." And, Frank Kermode comments in the *New York Times Book Review* that Vendler's "overriding need to show development from ode to ode imposes some constraints, perhaps exquisite, on the expositor. It imposes orders, and these orders replace what might be rewarding in a different way, an acceptance of fortuity." Vendler's approach, however, also bears witness to a respect for the strength of Keats's writing, contends Maureen Corrigan in the *Voice Literary Supplement:* "By adopting close reading as her critical technique, she pays Keats the highest compliment of viewing his work as a crystallization of language and culture that anticipates, within its own structures, all the myriad 'outside' frameworks that could be imposed upon it."

While some reviewers take issue with Vendler's thesis in *The Odes of John Keats,* many are quick to point out typical strengths of her literary criticism. "She is a materialist—and in a noble sense of the word," writes Nicholas Bromell in the *Boston Review.* "Vendler roots her discussion of the odes in her deeply felt response to Keats's language. Her ability to *present* what Keats is doing and to describe the effects, registered in our minds, of Keats's verbal facility, is breathtaking." Ehrenpreis concurs, commenting that although "reading the odes as a group is less likely to be successful than individual readings[,] . . . the most appealing feature of Vendler's work remains; and that is her desire to follow the poet in his labor of creation." Ehrenpreis explains that "Vendler's fundamental method is to enter intuitively into the decisions and changes of mind which lie behind the finished work, so that she gives us a dramatic sense of how the poem reached the state in which we know it." Kermode calls Vendler a "virtuoso," adding that "readers should not expect that the task of feeling along her line will be less than arduous for them. Their reward is a renewed sense of what it might be to perform, or even write, these great poems." Similarly, R. Baird Schuman in *English Journal* praises *The Odes of John Keats* as a skillful illumination of the magnitude of Keats's poetic achievement: "To read this book or any major portion of it is to show readers ways of controlling complex detail, of infusing it with sensitivity and imagination, and of bringing forth epiphanies so profound and encompassing as to make one feel a pride in literary accomplishment greater than any that readers have felt before."

In *The Music of What Happens: Poems, Poets, Critics,* Vendler returns to her study of contemporary poetry and, in addition to presenting new studies of poets such as Seamus Heaney, John Ashbery, and A. R. Ammons, offers further insight into the foundations of her critical work. Aligning her methods with what she terms "aesthetic criticism," Vendler is first concerned with approaching a particular poem as a distinct artistic expression, understandable within its own context. She writes in the book's introduction that her aim "is to describe the art work in such a way that it cannot be confused with any other art work (not an easy task), and to infer from its elements the aesthetic that might generate this unique configuration." Vendler distinguishes her approach from "both ideological and hermeneutic (or interpretation-centered) critics [who] want to place the literary work principally within the sphere of history and philosophy." An "aesthetic critic," she explains, "would rather place it in the mimetic, expressive, and constructivist sphere of the fine arts—theater, painting, music, sculpture, dance—where it may more properly belong." Outside of such theoretical bearings, however, *The Music of What Happens* is primarily devoted to offering new insights into a range of contemporary poetry. "These essays confirm Vendler's authority as a subtle, shrewd and demanding critic of recent American poetry," writes James E. B. Breslin in the *Los Angeles Times Book Review,* while Anthony Thwaite comments in the *Washington Post Book World* that "some of Vendler's most incisive, balanced, and sometimes astringent pieces are on poets who are not Americans: Ted Hughes, Stephen Spender, [Donald] Davie." The essays in *The Music of What Happens,* according to Breslin, "aim not to display the cleverness of the critic but to make poetry a habitable place."

BIOGRAPHICAL/CRITICAL SOURCES:

BOOKS

Vendler, Helen, *Part of Nature, Part of Us: Modern American Poets,* Harvard University Press, 1980.
Vendler, Helen, *The Music of What Happens: Poems, Poets, Critics,* Harvard University Press, 1988.

PERIODICALS

America, July 25, 1981.
Boston Review, April, 1984.
Chicago Tribune, May 18, 1988.
English Journal, October, 1984.
Globe and Mail (Toronto), December 14, 1985.
Hudson Review, winter, 1980.
London Review of Books, June 21-July 4, 1984.
Los Angeles Times Book Review, December 22, 1985, February 7, 1988, February 21, 1988.
Nation, March 9, 1970.
New Leader, June 2, 1980, January 9, 1984.
New Republic, March 29, 1980, December 5, 1983.
New York Review of Books, May 29, 1980, April 12, 1984.
New York Times, March 29, 1980.
New York Times Book Review, October 5, 1969, July 6, 1975, March 23, 1980, November 27, 1983.
Parnassus: Poetry in Review, Volume 8, number 2, 1980.
South Atlantic Quarterly, summer, 1976.
Times (London), January 29, 1987.
Times Literary Supplement, August 22, 1980, March 2, 1984, May 24, 1985, May 1, 1987, May 22, 1987.
Virginia Quarterly Review, summer, 1976, autumn, 1980, spring, 1985.
Voice Literary Supplement, December, 1983.
Washington Post Book World, April 6, 1980, January 31, 1988.
World Literature Today, spring, 1981.
Yale Review, summer, 1984.

*   *   *

VENISON, Alfred
    See POUND, Ezra (Weston Loomis)

*   *   *

VERDI, Marie de
    See MENCKEN, H(enry) L(ouis)

*   *   *

VERDU, Matilde
    See CELA, Camilo Jose

*   *   *

VIALIS, Gaston
    See SIMENON, Georges (Jacques Christian)

*   *   *

VIDAL, Gore   1925-
    (Edgar Box)

PERSONAL: Original name Eugene Luther Gore Vidal; born October 3, 1925, at the U.S. Military Academy, West Point, N.Y.; son of Eugene Luther (Director of Air Commerce under

President Franklin Roosevelt) and Nina (Gore) Vidal. *Politics:* Democrat.

ADDRESSES: Home—Rome, Italy, and Ravello, Italy. *Office*— c/o Random House, 201 East 50th St., New York, NY 10022.

CAREER: Writer. E. P. Dutton, New York City, editor, 1946; lived in Antigua, Guatemala, 1947-49; Democratic Party candidate for Congress in the Twenty-ninth District of New York, 1960; member of President's Advisory Committee on the Arts, 1961-63; host of "Hot Line" television program, 1964; co-founder of New Party, 1968-71; co-chairman of People's Party, 1970-72; ran for nomination as Democratic Party senatorial candidate in California, 1982. Lecturer; frequently appears on television and radio talk shows.

AWARDS, HONORS: Edgar Allan Poe Award, Mystery Writers of America, 1955, for television drama; Screen Writers Annual Award nomination and Cannes Critics Prize, both 1964, both for screenplay "The Best Man"; National Book Critics Circle Award, for criticism, 1982, for *The Second American Revolution and Other Essays;* named honorary citizen, Ravello, Italy, 1983; Prix Deauville, 1983, for *Creation.*

WRITINGS:

NOVELS

Williwaw (also see below), Dutton, 1946, reprinted, Ballantine, 1986.
In a Yellow Wood, Dutton, 1947.
The City and the Pillar, Dutton, 1948, revised edition published as *The City and the Pillar Revised,* 1965, reprinted under original title, Ballantine, 1986.
The Season of Comfort, Dutton, 1949.
A Search for the King: A Twelfth Century Legend, Dutton, 1950, reprinted, Random House, 1986.
Dark Green, Bright Red, Dutton, 1950, reprinted, Ballantine, 1986.
The Judgment of Paris, Dutton, 1952, revised edition, Little, Brown, 1965, reprinted, Ballantine, 1986.
Messiah, Dutton, 1954, revised edition, Little, Brown, 1965, reprinted, Ballantine, 1987.
Julian (also see below; two chapters first printed as *Julian the Apostate*), Little, Brown, 1964, reprinted, Ballantine, 1986.
Washington, D.C., Little, Brown, 1967, reprinted, Ballantine, 1988.
Myra Breckinridge (also see below), Little, Brown, 1968.
Two Sisters: A Novel in the Form of a Memoir, Little, Brown, 1970, Ballantine, 1987.
Burr (also see below), Random House, 1973, reprinted, Ballantine, 1988.
Myron (also see below), Random House, 1974.
1876, Random House, 1976.
Kalki (also see below), Random House, 1978.
Creation, Random House, 1981.
Duluth, Random House, 1983.
Lincoln, Random House, 1984.
Myra Breckinridge [and] *Myron,* Random House, 1986.
Empire, Random House, 1987.
Hollywood: A Novel of America in the 1920s, Random House, 1990.

UNDER PSEUDONYM EDGAR BOX; MYSTERIES

Death in the Fifth Position (also see below), Dutton, 1952.
Death before Bedtime . . . (also see below), Dutton, 1953.
Death Likes It Hot (also see below), Dutton, 1954.

Three by Box: The Complete Mysteries of Edgar Box (contains *Death in the Fifth Position, Death before Bedtime . . .* and *Death Likes It Hot*), Random House, 1978.

TELEVISION PLAYS

Visit to a Small Planet and Other Television Plays (contains "Visit to a Small Planet" [also see below; first aired on "Goodyear Playhouse," May 8, 1955], "Barn Burning" [1954], "Dark Possession" [1954], "The Death of Billy the Kid" [1955], "A Sense of Justice" [1955], "Smoke" [1954], "Summer Pavilion" [1955], and "The Turn of the Screw" [1955]), Little, Brown, 1956.

Also author of "The Best Man" (also see below); also author, or adaptor, of "Dr. Jekyll and Mr. Hyde," 1955, "Stage Door," 1955, "A Farewell to Arms," 1955, "Honor" (also see below), 1956, "Portrait of a Ballerina," 1956, "The Indestructible Mr. Gore," 1959, and "Dear Arthur," 1960.

SCREENPLAYS

"The Catered Affair," Metro-Goldwyn-Mayer, 1956.
"I Accuse," Metro-Goldwyn-Mayer, 1958.
(With Robert Hamer) "The Scapegoat," Metro-Goldwyn-Mayer, 1959.
(With Tennessee Williams) "Suddenly Last Summer," Columbia, 1959.
"The Best Man" (also see below; adapted from television play "The Best Man"), United Artists, 1964.
(With Francis Ford Coppola) "Is Paris Burning?," Paramount, 1966.
"The Last of the Mobile Hotshots," Warner Bros., 1970.
The Best Man: A Screen Adaptation of the Original Play, Directed by Franklin Schaffner, edited by George P. Garrett, Irvington, 1989.

Also author of screenplay adaptations of his novels *Kalki* and *Burr;* also author of screenplay adaptation of Lucien Truscott's *Dress Gray.*

PLAYS

Visit to a Small Planet: A Comedy Akin to a Vaudeville (also see below; adapted from television play "Visit to a Small Planet"; first produced on Broadway at the Booth Theater, February 7, 1957), Little, Brown, 1957, revised edition, Dramatists Play Service, 1959.
The Best Man: A Play of Politics (also see below; adapted from television play, "The Best Man"; first produced on Broadway at the Morosco Theater, March 31, 1960), Little, Brown, 1960, revised edition, Dramatists Play Service, 1977.
"On the March to the Sea: A Southron Comedy" (also see below; adapted from television play, "Honor"), first produced in Bonn, West Germany, 1961.
Three Plays (contains "Visit to a Small Planet: A Comedy Akin to a Vaudeville," "The Best Man: A Play of Politics," and "On the March to the Sea: A Southron Comedy"), Heinemann, 1962.
(Adaptor) Freidrich Duerrenmatt, *Romulus: A New Comedy* (first produced on Broadway at the Music Box Theater, January 10, 1962), Dramatists Play Service, 1962.
Weekend (first produced in New Haven, Conn., February 14, 1968; produced on Broadway at the Broadhurst Theater, March 16, 1968), Dramatists Play Service, 1968.
An Evening with Richard Nixon (first produced in New York City, April 30, 1972), Random House, 1972.

ESSAYS

Rocking the Boat, Little, Brown, 1962.
Sex, Death, and Money, Bantam, 1968.
Reflections upon a Sinking Ship, Little, Brown, 1969.
Homage to Daniel Shays: Collected Essays, 1952-1972, Random House, 1972, (published in England as *Collected Essays, 1952-1972,* Heinemann, 1974; published as *On Our Own Now,* Panther, 1976).
Matters of Fact and of Fiction: Essays, 1973-1976, Random House, 1977.
The Second American Revolution and Other Essays, Random House, 1982.
At Home: Essays, Random House, 1989.

OTHER

A Thirsty Evil: Seven Short Stories (also see below), Zero Press, 1956, reprinted, 1981.
Three: Williwaw [and] *A Thirsty Evil: Seven Short Stories* [and] *Julian the Apostate,* New American Library, 1962.
(Editor) *Best Television Plays,* Ballantine, 1965.
"An Evening with Richard" (recording), Ode Records, 1973.
(With others) *Great American Families,* Norton, 1977.
(With Robert J. Stanton) *Views from a Window: Conversations with Gore Vidal,* Lyle Stuart, 1980.
(Editor) Henry James, *The Golden Bowl,* Penguin, 1985.
Vidal in Venice, Summit Books, 1987.

Contributor to periodicals, including *New York Review of Books, Esquire, Partisan Review.* Member of advisory board, *Partisan Review,* 1960-71.

SIDELIGHTS: Gore Vidal is one of the best known literary figures in America. Familiar to millions as a witty and wicked talk show guest, two-time political candidate, and the creator of the outrageous Myra Breckinridge, Vidal has been called "one of the more alert and favoured writers of our time" by a critic in the *Observer* and "the Gentleman Bitch of American Letters" by Stefan Kanfer of the *New Republic.* Vidal has been in the public eye for four decades. His work is noted for its eloquence, intelligence, urbane humor, and biting satire, as well as for its attacks on cultural and political sacred cows. "Gore Vidal's novels, plays, and essays can be divided roughly into three areas of animosity," remarks *Time*'s R. Z. Sheppard. "The first is the author's belief that Western civilization erred, when it abandoned pagan humanism for the stern, heterosexual authority of the Judaeo-Christian patriarchy. . . . The second area that draws Vidal's scorn is American politics, which he dramatizes as a circus of opportunism and hypocrisy. . . . The most freewheeling disdain is directed at popular culture, macho sexuality and social pretensions."

Vidal, as John V. Lindsay points out in the *New York Times Book Review,* "says that he is a novelist first and a playwright last," but classifying him at all is a complex task. His genres run the gamut from historical fiction to autobiographical essays to political commentary, his styles from witty and cultured to sarcastic and acidic. "Vidal is a difficult writer to categorize because he is a man of several voices," writes Robert F. Kiernan in the book *Gore Vidal.* "He has brooded over ancient empires in several novels, as though he were possessed by the spirit of Gibbon, yet he has also written about the American *crise de virilite* and managed to sound a good deal like Hemingway. He has sent young Americans in search of old Europe, as a dutiful son of Henry James, but he has also written novels about the American political system and acknowledged a debt to Henry Adams. In his essays he often seems like Lord Macaulay, magisterial and

urbane, while in the Breckinridge novels he evokes Ronald Firbank, irrepressible and playful." The *Washington Post Book World*'s William McPherson states that Vidal's style "is characterized by urbanity and wit, elegance and polish, and more than occasionally by the venom of a scorpion. It is about as far removed from terminal grunt as Rome, where he lives, from Ethiopia. He emerges from the Eternal City now and then to titillate and castigate the rest of us with further examples of the decline of the West. Then he returns to chart the barbarians' advance and to work on the next novel, the next essay."

With the publication of *Williwaw* in 1946, Vidal joined the ranks of the literary *enfants terribles* who dominated the American cultural scene just after World War II. His name was often linked with other post-War prodigies such as Truman Capote, John Horn Burns, James Jones, and—several years later—Norman Mailer. By 1948, with two fairly successful novels to his credit, Vidal became impatient with the work he was doing and wanted to try something different. "I was bored with playing it safe," Vidal remembered in the 1965 revision of *The City and the Pillar.* "I wanted to take risks, to try something no American had done before." He published the original *The City and the Pillar*—a book that immediately went to the bestseller lists and raised conflicts in the New York publishing world that would reverberate for years afterwards. The subject of *The City and the Pillar*—homosexuality—was not a topic new to American literature (Burns and Vance Bourjaily, among others of Vidal's contemporaries, had both written about it). What was new, however, was the way in which Vidal treated his subject: the novel's young homosexual protagonist, Jim Willard, was presented as a perfectly average, athletic, handsome boy-next-door type. "[Vidal] wrote what had never been published by a reputable American writer: an unreserved novel about the homosexual demimonde and the 'naturalness' of homosexual relations," writes Kiernan.

The City and the Pillar achieved its fame as a *succes de scandale* rather than a work of outstanding artistic merit. Due to the findings of the then-recently-released Kinsey report on sexuality, Americans were just beginning to realize the prevalence of homosexual activity and Vidal's novel seemed to confirm their worst suspicions. *The City and the Pillar* became a bestseller—despite mixed reviews. For instance, although *Library Journal* reviewer R. E. Kingery calls the book a "serious, discerning, and obviously courageous novel having no counterpart in the recent rash of similarly concerned novels," the *New York Times*'s C. V. Terry declares that *The City and the Pillar,* "presented as the case history of a standard homosexual, . . . adds little that is new to a groaning shelf." A writer for the *New Yorker* observes that "artistically, it represents the latest, and possibly ultimate, stage in the decline of the literature of homosexuality to the level of unadorned tabloid writing." R. B. Gehman in the *New York Herald Tribune Weekly Book Review* calls *The City and the Pillar* "frank, shocking, sensational and often embarrassing," as well as poorly written in places, but in addition, he says the book "is also extremely sympathetic, penetrating, and exhortive. It might have been a much better book if it had been written with more care, edited with more taste, cut with more discretion and perhaps allowed to age to maturity. . . . The ideas [Vidal] presents are big enough, fortunately, to surmount the handicap of his style, but they struggle into the reader's consciousness only with considerable heaving and tugging." And, while *Saturday Review of Literature* contributor Richard McLaughlin recognizes the stylistic faults of *The City and the Pillar,* he also understands that Vidal has chosen "to sacrifice . . . any possibility of his novel being hailed as a distinguished literary work in order to put over his message, [so] perhaps it would be wise to judge Mr. Vidal's novel mostly on its merits as a social tract. On this score Vidal is quite successful."

While an inquisitive public put *The City and the Pillar* on the bestseller lists, the more conservative press helped dampen the career of its author. The *New York Times* gave the book a very negative review, refused to accept any advertising for it, and then either did not review or gave extremely harsh reviews of Vidal's next five novels or books of short stories. (At one point Vidal resorted to publishing a series of mystery novels under the pseudonym Edgar Box in order to get them reviewed.) According to Vidal in his annotation to the revised version of *The City and the Pillar,* the *New York Times*'s judgment continued to "[pop] up to haunt that book, and all my writing ever since: 'clinical' and 'sterile.' 'Clinical' is used whenever one writes of relationships which are not familiar—I dare say that if the story had dealt with a boy and a girl instead of two boys the book would have been characterized as 'lyrical.' 'Sterile' is an even deadlier curse upon the house, and comes from a dark syllogism in the American *Zeitgeist:* the homosexual act does not produce children therefore it is sterile; Mr. X's book is concerned with the homosexual act therefore the book is sterile."

The five novels published after *The City and the Pillar* were commercial failures. His financial resources dwindling, unable to support himself and Edgewater, his Hudson Valley estate, Vidal turned from writing fiction and embarked on what he termed his "five-year plan": he went to Hollywood to write screenplays for films and television, determined to earn enough money to last him the rest of his life.

Television was in its heyday in the mid-1950s when Vidal was writing scripts for such highly acclaimed programs as "Philco-Goodyear Playhouse," "Studio One," and "Omnibus Theater." As a screenwriter for the movies he made contributions to the scripts of "Ben Hur" (for which his chief addition was the underlying homosexual motif), "I Accuse," "Suddenly Last Summer," "The Catered Affair," "The Scapegoat," and "The Left-Handed Gun," among others. A self-proclaimed "writer for hire," Vidal eventually met his goal of financial independence, although it took him closer to ten years than to five.

During his Hollywood years Vidal also began to write plays. His first theater script, "Visit to a Small Planet," grew out of a television play by the same title. The story of a visitor from another planet who comes to earth to watch the Civil War battle at Manassas but instead ends up in present-day Virginia, "Visit to a Small Planet" had a Broadway run of 338 performances and an extended national and international tour, and was later produced as a motion picture starring Jerry Lewis.

A hit with critics as well as theatergoers, "Visit to a Small Planet" received largely enthusiastic reviews. *New York Times* critic Brooks Atkinson finds the play "uproarious" and maintains that "in both the writing and the playing, 'Visit to a Small Planet' is a topsy-turvy lark that has a lot of humorous vitality. The tone is low; the entertainment is highly enjoyable." While the *New Yorker*'s Wolcott Gibbs believes that too much "stuffing" has been added to the original television screenplay, he concludes that "it isn't really calamitous. . . . Within its limitations . . . [Vidal's] play is a remarkably lively and agreeable piece of work." And *Saturday Review* critic Henry Hewes expresses a similar view: "There are times when 'Visit to a Small Planet' becomes tedious, because there is little progress that is not merely a further demonstration of the one same joke. But . . . the fun keeps simmering, and, happily, the thirty-two-year-old novelist-playwright has seen to it that his play is usually at least one dimension beyond mere stage foolery."

In 1964 Vidal published *Julian,* his first novel in ten years and his first historical novel written in the style that has become his trademark. Written as the journal of the eccentric fourth-century Roman emperor Julian, framed by a commentary in the form of margin notes and letters by two of Julian's aging contemporaries, the novel is full of cutting remarks, catty asides, ribald jokes, fourth-century gossip, and references to the state of the commentators' health, careers, and sexual performance. It is this humorous interjection of the trivial and the personal into an impeccably researched historical documentary for which Vidal has become famous.

In writing historical fiction, "the interpreter is everything," says Dudley Fitts in the *New York Times Book Review,* and "if, like Gore Vidal in this evocation of Julian the Apostate, he is able to penetrate to depths of human meaning, to the chromatic play of personalities and events, his vision may create a design not wholly remote from parable or allegory." Like Fitts, a number of other reviewers also appreciate that Vidal "is attempting something other than the recreation of the past for its own sake," as Walter Allen puts it in the *New York Review of Books.* "While it would be absurd to see the novel as a parable for our time or to look for any close parallels between Julian's situation and our own, it is impossible to escape the conclusion that Vidal intends the book to have some direct relevance to the world today. The brilliance of his portrayal of Julian persuades us that it has. How accurate this is in terms of historical scholarship, I certainly cannot pretend to know. . . . But all this is beside the point: the novel must stand or fall by the success of his version of the character of Julian, and here it seems to me he has brought off a considerable imaginative achievement." However, other critics find Vidal's Julian a less compelling figure; *Saturday Review*'s Granville Hicks, for instance, finds that he "is a very human mixture of good and bad, and on that score he is quite acceptable. He doesn't, however, really grasp the imagination. Looking at him simply as a character in a novel, one wonders whether he is worth writing about at such great length."

As a novelist, Vidal has enjoyed considerable success. Following his return to fiction writing with *Julian,* he published a string of best-selling novels. Like *Julian,* these novels combine Vidal's gifts for mimicry and satire, his savage sense of humor, his passion for personal and political intrigue, and his jaundiced view of the ruling classes. His post-*Julian* novels have had such diverse settings as fifth-century Greece and Asia, nineteenth-century America, twentieth-century Washington, D.C., a post-apocalypse United States, and a surrealistic Duluth, Minnesota (bordered by Mexico on one side and by Lake Erie on the other). "The fact is that Vidal Novelist had an unusually long apprenticeship," writes Gerald Weale in the *Atlantic Monthly.* "The early books, the eight that preceded *Julian,* are workmanlike enough, but they are curiously flat and undefined, without any of the zest and bitchy vitality Vidal shows in even the most ordinary conversations. But when he did return [from screenwriting] to the novel a decade later in *Julian,* he brought to it the flavor and energy of his own person. He is still an overly intellectual novelist, but now his subjects are more in keeping with his particular novelistic shtik."

The *New York Times*'s John Leonard points out that Vidal has a tendency to "twin" his novels, following one book sometime later with another one using either the same characters, subject, or milieu. Kiernan observes that "*Messiah* and *Kalki* are twin novels about the coming apocalypse, whereas *Burr* and *1876* are paired novels about American history. *Myra Breckinridge* and *Myron* are unmistakable twins, enjoying virtually Siamese attachment. The second novels in these pairs never seem to represent a rethinking or reworking of the material in the first." *Julian*'s twin is *Creation*, an epic of the ancient world as told by Cyrus Spitama, son of a Persian prince and a Greek sorceress, grandson of the prophet Zoroaster, uncle of the philosopher-to-be Democritus, ambassador to the courts of India, China, and Greece, and inveterate name-dropper and shameless gossip. " 'Creation' is obviously a twin of 'Julian,' " says Leonard. " 'Julian' was wonderful; 'Creation,' I am happy to report, is even better."

The theme of *Creation* is just that—the creation of the world as Cyrus Spitama knows it. Contemptuous of the Greeks and their philosophical concepts, Cyrus is an avid defender of the Zoroastrian doctrine of dualism. Yet he also seeks to confirm his understanding of the world, and in his travels he speaks with the great prophets and philosophers of the East. "As a grandson and the last descendant in the male line of the prophet Zoroaster, Cyrus feels obliged to argue theology, to devise an acceptable theory for the creation of the universe and to account for the existence of evil within it," explains *Time*'s Paul Gray. Despite this motive for telling his story, Cyrus pays scant attention to it in his narrative, says I. D. O'Hara in the *Nation*. "Creation, says Cyrus, is 'the only important subject there is,' " notes O'Hara. "The novel spends about twenty-five pages on the subject, total. Usually it is given a mere mention in passing, but most of the Wisdom Figures speak about it. Unfortunately, Cyrus 'cannot follow any of this,' as he says about Democritus' observations. 'It is hard to take seriously another world's wise man, particularly at second hand,' Cyrus remarks."

Kanfer considers Cyrus's message about creation to be revealed through the telling of his life's story rather than stated explicitly. "Though the dualism of his faith made sense throughout the long search, he cannot quite see the Western meaning of existence expressed simply as a line proceeding from birth . . . to what?" says Kanfer. "He cannot say. But he knows that the Eastern notion of life as a circle, unending, infinitely renewed, is also unacceptable. Perhaps, then, life is movement, change, the ceaseless whirl of first things into vast structures and then on to new forms. Flux. This [Spitama's] legacy to his nephew; it became part of the first atomic theory. Nothing remains; nothing dies."

Creation's allure for many critics lies in its richness of fact and detail. Leonard asks, "What is it like to sail from the delta of the Tigris and Euphrates in a trireme? Mr. Vidal knows. Describe the protocol at the courts of Darius, Xerxes, Bimbisara and 'the sun of heaven,' he does. Sit in on the harem intrigues of Atossa with her white-enameled face. He has listened. Ask how the Egyptians thought they could remedy breast cancer. He tells. . . . There isn't a page of 'Creation' that doesn't inform, and very few pages that do not delight. Scholars will fuss . . . ; let them, please, delight as much as *they* inform. Brahma, we are told, is not the only god; 'he's just the most conceited.' " Rex Warner in the *Washington Post Book World* also admires Vidal's facile handling of miscellaneous information and calls Cyrus "the greatest name-dropper who ever lived." "What Cyrus Spitama is really good at is gossip-writing," says Warner. "He can tell you of all the intrigues of the Persian court and knows most of the secrets of the harem. With Xerxes he visits all the best brothels in Babylon. He has inside information on the big banks."

For other reviewers, Vidal's presentation of the ancient world is unnerving, his attention to the minutiae of history rather than to its broader scope, tedious. Although *Creation* sweeps the expanse of the fifth century, Vidal dismisses many of its events and

extraordinary personalities with a few summary sentences. "The crippling discouragement of the novel is Cyrus's prevailing dryness," states *Newsweek*'s Walter Clemons. "His world-weary disdain reduces Pericles, Thucydides, Themistocles, Sophocles, Xerxes and the Buddha to name-tag walk-ons or passing mention. His eastern journeyings are blankly unspecific—he says he can't remember exactly what route he took to Cathay. It was just a long, hard trip. If the Buddha is 'the most-nearly-released of all men' from worldly attachments, Vidal is here the most-nearly-released of all novelists from the busyness and glamorous incidental detail of the usual historical novelist who attempts to bring vanished worlds to life. In 'Creation,' the narrative pulse is feeble." *Los Angeles Times* reviewer Elaine Kendall concurs, saying, "This elliptical approach to history concentrates upon the personalities behind the legends at the expense of the legends themselves. The author's knowledge of his period is so extensive that he often becomes cavalier about essentials. A few readers may be inspired to do further research on their own; others will be dazed by a welter of characters and a confusion of hierarchies, few of them familiar." Writing in the *Nation*, O'Hara declares that Vidal "has contrived a questioner with so anemic a private life and character that he is always free to memorize answers and to notice the scenery. Such a figure can be contrived out of research and used to communicate oodles of facts. But in effect, we go to marriages with a fashion editor and to burials with a geologist; in place of imaginative involvement we get reports." Gray acknowledges the book's shortcomings but then adds, "Whatever its flaws, *Creation* offers a leisurely guided stroll through a complex era. The book is encyclopedic enough to be short on intrinsic pattern; it is also filled with information, oddities and wonder."

With *Washington, D.C.*, Vidal moves from ancient Greece to twentieth-century America. Although *Washington, D.C.* itself has no twin, it helps form a trilogy about American politics in conjunction with *Burr* and *1876*. The book begins in 1937 and follows the paths of two families—that of a prominent senator and of a powerful newspaper publisher—that are joined together when the senator's protege marries the publisher's daughter. The book intends to expose the seamier side of American politics, to give insights into the United States' power structure, as well as to provide a good, dramatic read.

Washington, D.C. "is a lounge-lizard look at American politics," says Peter Ackroyd in the *Spectator*, and it is that intimate but sleazy view of life in the United States capital that appeals to some reviewers. Kiernan, for example, acknowledges that the book is "giddily melodramatic at the same time it is soberly historical" and delights in Vidal's ability to combine the two elements. Calling the novel "a superb story," John Kenneth Galbraith writes in *Book Week*: "Vidal's people are persuasive—their sex life did astonish me a trifle—and he handles the interplay of personality and power with rare skill. . . . [*Washington, D.C.*] sustains constant interest and more than a little suspense. It is resourceful in scene and episode. In fact, it is in every respect the work of a professional, and as such, a pleasure." Other reviewers, such as a *Times Literary Supplement* critic, may consider it "a prodigiously skilled and clever performance" but find its perspective disturbing. "What is a little surprising in this novel is the ferocity of its disbelief in any human, let alone political, good," says the reviewer. "The private and public worlds are pictured in terms of jungle war. . . . Life is warfare, no holds barred, and Mr. Vidal piles nastiness on nastiness to make his point, and also, no doubt, to give his public the kind of *frissons* they have come to expect of him."

Burr and *1876* were published six and nine years, respectively, after *Washington, D.C.,* but are its fictional predecessors. Burr is told as the memoirs of American founding father-turned-renegade Aaron Burr, and *1876* is an account of the United States' centennial year. Both are narrated by the character Charles Schemerhorn Schuyler, who first appears as the young, opportunistic illegitimate son of Aaron Burr, and in the second novel is seen forty years later, a jaded expatriate come home to recoup his lost fortunes. These novels are told in the style familiar to readers of *Julian* and *Creation;* as *Time*'s Paul Gray remarks, "Not only does Vidal do his homework, but he can make old facts look like contemporary gossip. And he takes wicked pleasure in turning accepted notions about the past upside down." Reviewing *Burr,* Christopher Lehmann-Haupt of the *New York Times* comments: "Just at this most disillusioning moment in American history, when all the old verities are beginning to seem hollow, Mr. Vidal gives us an interpretation of our early history that says in effect that all the old verities were never much to begin with. . . . And how thoroughly enjoyable is the entire process of disillusionment!"

Burr "is an extraordinarily intelligent and entertaining novel," says Peter S. Prescott of *Newsweek,* who praises Vidal for making Aaron Burr "more than a political cartoon." Julian Moynahan in *New York Times Book Review* concurs, declaring, "Through Vidal's portrait of Burr as a sort of incarnated pleasure principle with brains and a political vocation, the history of the founding fathers ceases to be a show of marionettes wearing boring costumes, emerges from the school assembly and the hot clutches of the D.A.R., becomes lively and contestable." *New Leader*'s John Simon suggests that the novel's "ultimate wit lies in the satirical, debunking, irreverent notions of the work as a whole. Our Revolutionary myths are [demythologized], our heroes put into, indeed spanked with, slippers."

1876 also takes demythologizing the American past as its task and, as many critics point out, the events recounted in the novel are startlingly similar to those taking place near the time of the book's publication in 1976. Parallels abound: the corrupt Ulysses S. Grant with Richard Nixon, the Whiskey Ring scandal with Watergate, the Hayes-Tilden presidential race with the election of 1972 and the administration of Gerald Ford. *1876* is, according to Paul Levy in *Books and Bookmen,* "an historical contribution of large importance. . . . [Vidal] has written a book with an implicit but chilling prophecy that must be heeded if America is to have the chance of celebrating her tercentenary. . . . What Vidal has done by investigating the scandals leading up to the 1876 election and the election itself is to show that nothing much has changed in America's last hundred years."

A major criticism of *1876* is that, unlike *Burr,* it lacks a strong central character to carry it; whereas Burr was extraordinarily compelling—for himself and as the rival and critic of Thomas Jefferson, Alexander Hamilton, and other Revolutionary heroes—*1876*'s protagonist, Charlie Schuyler, is not as interesting, serving merely as a mouthpiece for Vidal's observations rather than coming to life himself. Also, the Reconstruction does not hold nearly the fascination for Americans as does the Revolutionary War. Explains Philip French in *New Statesman:* "Unlike *Washington, D.C., 1876* has a totally unfamiliar political context and an inflexible *dramatis personae.* Unlike *Burr,* it has no charismatic central character to seize our imagination, no broad historical sweep, and no immediately identifiable public figures such as Washington and Jefferson to be Stracheyfied. . . . So all of Vidal's considerable craft, wit, political insight, elegance and irony is called into play. Unfortunately some of the material here is intractable and many readers will feel that he has overesti-

mated their potential interest in American history of a century ago. They will notice, of course, obvious parallels between past and present, but often they will react as the bewildered Schuyler does when trying to follow a conversation between political insiders: 'I tried to look intelligent but had no idea what they were talking about.' At such sticky points one should press on because, for all its occasional longueurs and feeling of strain, *1876* is a rewarding and accomplished book." Michael Wood calls *1876* a "less vivid" book than its predecessor but adds that "it is in one sense a more serious book. It asks us to believe, not in a rogue hero like Burr, and not even in a man like [failed presidential candidate Samuel] Tilden, who might have been a hero but wasn't, but in politics itself, that grimy and intricate activity we can't afford to give up."

Lincoln is also concerned with the history of the United States. Released in 1984 with an extraordinary 200,000 copy first printing and preview excerpts in the *Atlantic* and *Gentleman's Quarterly,* Lincoln is called "a momentous fictional biography" and a "masterpiece" by Stephen Rubin in the *Chicago Tribune Book World.* "The intelligence, the wit, the humor, the outrageousness are omnipresent," says the critic. "If Vidal is impatient with novelistic techniques such as transitions, he allows himself the luxury to marvelously plot a true political novel of breadth and rich texture. The pace he sets for himself is a noble andante that gives him the time for a spectacular array of detail work, the element that ultimately makes 'Lincoln' unforgettable."

Vidal has since published two other installments in his American history series, 1987's *Empire* and 1990's *Hollywood: A Novel of America in the 1920s.* Set in the late 1890s to early 1900s, *Empire* portrays, according to Lehmann-Haupt, "America's decision to become a world power, and to establish its presence more forcefully in the Caribbean, Latin America and the Eastern Pacific." Lehmann-Haupt considers *Empire* the best of Vidal's series, stating that Vidal tells "a dramatically compelling story without sacrificing either his complex view of American history of his unusual ability to caricature its major players." "Like the rest of Vidal's series," writes David Gates in *Newsweek,* ". . . 'Empire' reanimates the moribund genre of historical fiction with a few modernist jots—and still stays within the conventions of the Good Read," adding that even critics of the novel "won't be able to deny that they've been elegantly entertained."

Hollywood takes up where *Empire* leaves off, with America's entrance into World War I, and covers the presidencies of Woodrow Wilson and Warren Harding, in addition to the rise of the film industry of Hollywood. "Like the earlier books, the new novel is an imaginative re-creation, a heady mix of fact and fancy, wisdom and nonsense," writes Joel Conarroe in the *New York Times Book Review,* noting Vidal's colorful portrayals of Wilson, his wife Edith, the actors Charlie Chaplin and Douglas Fairbanks, in addition to the witty Alice Roosevelt Longworth. Three fictional characters from *Empire,* Caroline Sanford Sanford, Blaise Delacroix Sanford, and James Burden Day, reappear in *Hollywood.* The novel suffers, according to Lehmann-Haupt, in that these recurring characters "have no foreground drama of their own and . . . merge with all the other characters, both fictional and historical, in a middle ground that fills the novel's entire canvas." David Walton in the *Detroit News* likewise comments that while "there are a number of effective scenes and sharply rendered lines in this book . . . , *Hollywood* is too sprawling, too diffused and uncentered, and in most ways too much concerned with what's behind the scenes ever to establish a consistent foreground." Conarroe notes, nonetheless, that "without relinquishing the novelistic pleasures of an essentially comic narrative, Mr. Vidal manages to convey an enormous amount of information, partly factual, partly speculative."

Popular as Vidal's historical novels have been, his greatest coup was *Myra Breckinridge,* a camp, satiric look at the United States today. An instant smash (even though Vidal and his publishers permitted no review copies or advance publicity), *Myra Breckinridge* takes shots at almost everything in America today, from uptight heterosexuality to the burgeoning population (Myra is a fanatic advocate of zero population growth), the New American Novel to 1940s movie stars, American youth to the American dream. Above all, *Myra Breckinridge* is about breaking the barriers of sexuality. "Vidal slides into an elegant nasty commentary on The Young, California, Popular Culture, Psychoanalytic Thought, Overpopulation, and Power. After which he gets down to the real business at hand, his vision of sexuality in America," comments Margo Hentoff in the *New York Review of Books.*

"To say Mr. Vidal's new novel is queer would be an understatement; it is a queer, queer book, a virtuoso exercise in kinkiness, a draught of fizzy hemlock, a strikingly intelligent attempt to go as far as possible in outrageousness," declares John Weightman in *Observer Review.* "Literature about sex is so often soggy and embarrassing or clinical and sick-making. Mr. Vidal pitches his narrative in a key of slightly demented funniness, and sustains this note right to the end." Indeed, the irrepressible Myra is an odd character: a homosexual male turned female by a sex change operation, she comes to California to claim her share in a drama academy and to write a book about the films of the 1940s. Teaching Empathy and Posture at the academy, Myra expounds her views on every possible subject—yet in the end, according to her logic, it all leads back to sex and power. "Myra Breckinridge herself sees all life as a naming of parts, an equating of groins, a pleasing and/or painful forcing of orifices. Which is the essence, after all, of pornography. All is referred to the phallic point, the reductio ad absurdum of the genitalia. Nor is the response spiked, but silkily sensuous to male buttocks, nipples, pubic hair, and the whole repertory of male adornment from jockey briefs to T-shirt and jeans," explains a *Times Literary Supplement* critic. Myra, says Eliot Fremont-Smith in the *New York Times,* "intends to destroy 'the last vestigial traces of traditional manhood in the race' and set the stage for a truly polymorphous society, 'thus reducing population while increasing human happiness.' For Myra, love is power, and where there's a will there's a way—which she demonstrates hideously and, I'm afraid, with all too familiar expertease."

The book is sexually graphic, and most reviewers at the time recognized it as a satire on pornography that had at the same time become what it was satirizing. Hentoff notes that Vidal, "walking on the waters of polymorphous perversity and sexual revolution, . . . has written the first popular book of perverse pornography—a book for which one does not need even the slightest special taste." *Newsweek*'s Joseph Morgenstern refers to it as "dirty . . . but . . . gleefully dirty, wittily dirty, gracefully and intricately dirty in its creation and development of a genuine film freak."

Vidal's other novels about the decline of civilization in the United States have not fared as well as *Myra Breckinridge.* For example, *Myra Breckinridge*'s sequel, *Myron*—in which Myra is returned to her male form and transported to the set of a 1940's B-movie—is called "surprisingly colorless and lumpish" by James Boatright in the *New Republic.* With *Duluth,* Vidal delivers a biting examination of Everytown, U.S.A.—the city "is the whole of America collapsed into its essential nonsense like a constellation of humanity into a crippled white dwarf," states Leh-

mann-Haupt. Writing in *New Statesman,* Angela McRobbie calls the book "one of the most brilliant, most radical and most subversive pieces of writing to emerge from America in recent years." Larry McCaffery concurs in the *Los Angeles Times Book Review,* calling *Duluth* "a book so radical in approach (even for Vidal) that it is certain to delight and surprise some readers while boring or disgusting others. . . . Vidal demonstrates a keen eye for the trivialities and absurdities on which Americans spend so much of their emotional (and literal) currency. In particular, his portrait of the upper class—forever fussing over tax shelters, face lifts, nose jobs and the latest chic fashions—is wonderfully nasty." And in *Punch,* Anthony Burgess comments that *Duluth*'s "scurrility and wit are a large joy." Not all reviewers liked the book; Pearl K. Bell, for example, writes in *Times Literary Supplement:* "Since every joke in *Duluth* lays an egg, it is tempting to think it was written by an imposter. . . . Yet the sour obsessions are all too familiar, as is the carelessly generalized contempt for the United States, that nation of Yahoos. What is new in *Duluth*—and the only genuinely shocking thing about the book—is the unalleviated banality of its satire."

Many critics believe that Vidal, despite his success as a novelist, truly excels as an essayist and critic. "It is not that Vidal's essays are better than his novels," explains Gerald Clarke in the *Atlantic Monthly.* "It is rather that his essays are more consistently good and that the qualities that limit him as a novelist are precisely those that a good essayist needs: a forceful intelligence, a cool detachment, an unpretentious, graceful style, and a sense of perspective that distinguished the big from the little. If most of his fictional characters seem unbelievable, his judgements on real people are both original and irrefutable." His essays display the same incisive wit and characteristic elan that make him such a popular talk show guest and interview subject; his nonfiction is full of autobiographical asides, personal references to the famous and the infamous, allusions to ancient and modern history. His style is irreverent; for instance, he insists on referring to Dwight Eisenhower as the "Great Golfer" and the Kennedy clan as "The Holy Family." He mimics Carson McCullers and pokes fun at Norman Mailer.

"In those journals in which they appear, Gore Vidal's essays are the intellectual equivalent of the comics," declares Joseph Epstein in a *Commentary* study of Vidal. "Intellectual journals are not noted for providing many laughs, but laughter is Gore Vidal's specialty—what he plays for and what he is about. The chief play in a Vidal essay is to point out that the emperor has no clothes and then go a step further and remove the poor man's skin. The spectacle can be most amusing, assuming of course that it is not one's own carcass that is being stripped." Vidal's "formidable powers are most steadily apparent in his essays," writes *Newsweek*'s Walter Clemons. "The energy of his best essays has perhaps not been praised enough. He engages attention, trails his cape in autobiographical asides, dares to administer a '[sic]' to Edmund Wilson's syntax, executes a Henry James parody mid-paragraph with the audacity of the Dantesque opening of 'Myra Breckinridge' and pursues his arguments to their conclusions with a determination that looks like perfect relaxed ease."

Wit alone, though, could not make Vidal the respected essayist that he is. His essays and reviews reveal an erudition and knowledge that are impressive and insight that is often remarkable. In a review of the essay collection *Matters of Fact and of Fiction,* John Simon writes in *Esquire:* "I think that Gore Vidal's greatest service to this society could be in the proper packaging of his style and language. I do not see fiction as being his true medium. . . . Vidal is an essayist of talent . . . [and *Matters of Fact and of Fiction*] contains some very good pieces, as weighty as anything in Oscar Wilde and easily as witty as the best of Matthew Arnold. The learning may not be as encyclopedic as Edmund Wilson's, certainly, the approach is less lofty—but it is considerable all the same."

Although many critics take issue with Vidal's point of view—according to Cosmo Landesman in *Books and Bookmen,* "Vidal's critical judgment has been impaired by his own radical fundamentalism which is every bit as simplistic and narrow as the Christian fundamentalism of the Born-Again-Right-Wingers Vidal so despises"—few challenge the grace and elegance with which he expresses it. "No one else in what he calls 'the land of the tin ear' can combine better sentences into more elegantly sustained demolition derbies than Vidal does in some of his best essays," observes Thomas Mallon in the *National Review.* Quoting Vidal, the *Washington Post Book World*'s William McPherson writes in his review of *Matters of Fact and of Fiction:* " 'One interesting result of today's passion for the immediate and the casual . . . has been the decline, in all the arts, of the idea of technical virtuosity as being in any way desirable.' Technical virtuosity is what Vidal possesses to an extraordinary degree; and intelligence and erudition, irreverence, and an ability to cut through cant. I used to think of him as the brightest rhinestone around. I've revised my opinion though; he's the genuine article."

Asked by *Newsweek* interviewer Arthur Cooper if it is fun being Gore Vidal, the author answered: "Gore Vidal isn't what I set out to be. Early on I wanted to be Franklin Roosevelt, and then as I realized I had to make a choice I saw myself more in the great tradition, somebody like Thomas Mann, going on and on into my old age turning everything into literature like a bivalve collecting sea water. But I don't mind what I've become. My God, what a lucky life. I do exactly what I want to do and I've made a living—which you're not supposed to do if you write the way you want to. I've had really great luck."

MEDIA ADAPTATIONS: "The Death of Billy the Kid" was the basis for the movie, "The Left-Handed Gun," filmed by Warner Bros., 1958; "Gore Vidal's Billy the Kid" aired on Turner Network Television, May 10, 1989. *Visit to a Small Planet* was filmed by Paramount, 1960. *Myra Breckinridge* was filmed by Twentieth Century-Fox, 1970.

BIOGRAPHICAL/CRITICAL SOURCES:

BOOKS

Authors in the News, Volume 1, Gale, 1976.
Bestsellers 90, Issue 2, Gale, 1990.
Contemporary Literary Criticism, Gale, Volume 2, 1974, Volume 4, 1975, Volume 6, 1976, Volume 8, 1978, Volume 10, 1979, Volume 22, 1982, Volume 33, 1985.
Dictionary of Literary Biography, Volume 6: *American Novelists since World War II,* Gale, 1980.
Kiernan, Robert F., *Gore Vidal,* Ungar, 1982.
Vidal, Gore, *Messiah,* Dutton, 1954.
Vidal, Gore, *Three: Williwaw* [and] *A Thirsty Evil: Seven Short Stories* [and] *Julian the Apostate,* New American Library, 1962.
Vidal, Gore, *The City and the Pillar Revised,* Dutton, 1965.
Weightman, John, *The Concept of the Avant Garde: Explorations in Modernism,* Alcove, 1973.
White, Ray Lewis, *Gore Vidal,* Twayne, 1968.

PERIODICALS

America, September 5, 1970, May 20, 1978.
American Film, November, 1987.
American Spectator, June, 1982.
Atlantic Monthly, February, 1949, March, 1972, December, 1973, April, 1976, April, 1981.
Books, April, 1970.
Books and Bookmen, August, 1967, May, 1974, June, 1976, October, 1977, October, 1982.
Book Week, June 7, 1964, April 30, 1967, March 3, 1969, April 13, 1969.
Chicago Tribune Book World, April 26, 1981, April 22, 1984, June 3, 1984.
Commentary, March, 1974, June, 1977.
Critic, June 1968.
Critique, December, 1980.
Detroit News, May 31, 1981, June 19, 1983, June 17, 1984.
Encounter, September, 1978, November, 1981.
Esquire, August, 1977, April, 1981.
Harper's, September, 1970, March, 1976, May, 1977.
Interview, June, 1987, June, 1988.
Library Journal, December 1, 1947.
Los Angeles Times, March 24, 1981, December 5, 1988, August 4, 1989.
Los Angeles Times Book Review, July 3, 1983.
Nation, April 1, 1968, May 25, 1974, April 17, 1976, March 21, 1981, June 16, 1984.
National Observer, March 11, 1968.
National Review, May 20, 1969, March 1, 1974, May 12, 1978, September 18, 1981, August 20, 1982.
New Leader, September 21, 1970, December 10, 1973.
New Republic, February 25, 1957, July 18, 1970, May 27, 1972, April 24, 1976, May 12, 1978, April 25, 1981.
New Statesman, July 14, 1967, September 20, 1968, March 22, 1974, March 19, 1976, August 19, 1977, April 14, 1978, April 6, 1979, May 8, 1981, August 20, 1982, May 6, 1983.
Newsweek, June 15, 1964, February 26, 1968, March 31, 1969, July 6, 1970, November 5, 1973, November 18, 1974, March 8, 1976, May 9, 1977, April 20, 1981, June 11, 1984, June 15, 1987.
New York, May 15, 1972, October 21, 1974.
New Yorker, March 22, 1947, January 10, 1948, February 16, 1957, April 23, 1960, May 6, 1972, April 5, 1976, April 17, 1978.
New York Herald Tribune Weekly Book Review, March 16, 1947, January 18, 1949.
New York Review of Books, July 30, 1964, June 15, 1967, May 9, 1968, June 19, 1969, March 22, 1973, November 15, 1973, November 14, 1974, April 29, 1976, May 26, 1977, April 20, 1978, May 14, 1981.
New York Times, June 23, 1946, March 16, 1947, June 11, 1948, February 6, 1949, January 27, 1957, February 8, 1957, February 3, 1968, March 25, 1969, July 7, 1970, April 28, 1972, May 1, 1972, October 25, 1973, March 2, 1976, April 20, 1977, March 30, 1978, March 10, 1981, April 27, 1982, May 30, 1984, June 11, 1987, November 14, 1988, January 18, 1990.
New York Times Book Review, August 12, 1962, May 31, 1964, April 30, 1967, January 28, 1968, February 1, 1968, February 15, 1968, September 1, 1968, April 6, 1969, July 12, 1970, December 31, 1972, October 28, 1973, March 7, 1976, April 17, 1977, April 2, 1978, December 21, 1980, March 29, 1981, May 2, 1982, June 5, 1983, June 3, 1984, June 14, 1987, January 21, 1990.
Observer, September 13, 1970, August 15, 1982.
Observer Review, September 15, 1968, July 6, 1969, February 7, 1971.

Punch, August 9, 1967, September 18, 1968, May 27, 1981, April 27, 1983.

Reporter, June 29, 1967, April 4, 1968.

Saturday Review, February 23, 1957, August 4, 1962, June 6, 1964, June 24, 1967, May 20, 1972, December 16, 1972, February 8, 1975, March 6, 1976, April 29, 1978, March, 1981, May, 1982.

Saturday Review of Literature, July 6, 1946, May 31, 1947, January 10, 1948, January 15, 1949, October 14, 1950.

Saturday Review/World, December 18, 1973.

Spectator, October 4, 1968, August 2, 1969, March 23, 1974, August 24, 1974, March 27, 1976, September 3, 1977, April 22, 1978, May 2, 1981, August, 1982.

Statesman, August 23, 1968, September 20, 1968, July 4, 1969.

Time, July 27, 1962, June 12, 1964, March 28, 1969, August 22, 1969, July 13, 1970, December 11, 1972, October 21, 1974, March 1, 1976, March 27, 1978, March 30, 1981, June 13, 1983, June 22, 1987.

Times (London), April 30, 1981, September 28, 1983, June 19, 1987.

Times Literary Supplement, November 12, 1964, July 27, 1967, October 10, 1968, July 24, 1969, September 18, 1970, February 21, 1975, March 26, 1976, September 30, 1977, April 14, 1978, May 29, 1981, August 27, 1982, May 13, 1983, November 10-16, 1989.

Tribune Books, January 28, 1990.

Washington Post, July 4, 1984, June 21, 1987.

Washington Post Book World, October 28, 1973, May 1, 1977, April 16, 1978, January 18, 1981, March 22, 1981, April 25, 1982, May 15, 1983, January 14, 1990.

World, December 19, 1972.

*   *   *

VINE, Barbara
See RENDELL, Ruth (Barbara)

*   *   *

VIOLIS, G.
See SIMENON, Georges (Jacques Christian)

*   *   *

VOINOVICH, Vladimir (Nikolaevich) 1932-

PERSONAL: Some sources transliterate middle name as Nikolayevich; born September 26, 1932, in Dushanbe, Tadzhik, U.S.S.R.; immigrated to West Germany, December 25, 1980; son of Nikolai Pavlovich (a journalist) and Rosa (a teacher; maiden name, Goichman) Voinovich; married wife, Valentina, 1957 (marriage ended, 1965); married Irina Braude (a teacher), 1965; children: (first marriage) Marina, Pavel; (second marriage) Olga. *Education:* Attended Moscow Pedagogical Institute, 1957-59.

ADDRESSES: Home—Hans Carossa Strasse 5, 8035 Stockdorf, Federal Republic of Germany. *Agent*—Leonard W. Schroeter, 540 Central Bldg., Seattle, Wash. 98104.

CAREER: Worked as a herdsman on a collective farm when a youth; held a variety of jobs, including factory hand, locksmith, construction worker, railroad laborer, carpenter, aircraft mechanic, and editor of radio programs; went to Moscow and became a writer, 1956. Member of faculty at Institute of Fine Arts, Munich, West Germany. Visiting fellow at Princeton University,

1982-83; writer in residence at University of Southern California. *Military service:* Soviet Army, 1951-55.

MEMBER: Union of Soviet Writers (expelled, 1974), P.E.N. (French division), Mark Twain Society (honorary member), Bavarian Academy of Fine Arts.

WRITINGS:

My zdes' zhivem (short story; title means "We Live Here"), published in *Novy Mir,* 1961, published in book form, [Moscow], 1963.

"Khochu byt' chestnym" (novella; title means "I Want to be Honest"), published in *Novy Mir,* 1963.

"Dva tovarishcha" (novella; title means "Two Friends"), published in *Novy Mir,* 1964.

Vladychitsa (title means "The Sovereign Mistress"), [Moscow], 1969.

Stepen' doveriia (historical novel; title means "A Degree of Trust"), [Moscow], 1972.

Povesti (title means "Novellas"), [Moscow], 1972.

Zhizn' neobychainye prikliucheniia soldata Ivana Chonkina (novel), YMCA Press (Paris), 1975, translation by Richard Lourie published as *The Life and Extraordinary Adventures of Private Ivan Chonkin,* Farrar, Straus, 1977.

Ivan'kiada, ili rasskaz o vselenii pisatelia Voinovicha v novuiu kvartiru (autobiography), Ardis, 1976, translation by David Lapeza published as *The Ivankiad: The Tale of the Writer Voinovich's Installation in His New Apartment,* Farrar, Straus, 1977.

In Plain Russian: Stories, translated by Lourie, Farrar, Straus, 1979.

Pretender to the Throne: The Further Adventures of Private Ivan Chonkin, translated by Lourie, Farrar, Straus, 1981.

Anti Sovietskii Sovietski Soyuz, Ardis, 1985, translation by Lourie published as *The Anti-Soviet Soviet Union,* Harcourt, 1986.

Moscow 2042, translated by Lourie, Harcourt, 1987.

The Fur Hat, translated by Susan Brownsberger, Harcourt, 1989.

Also author of poems, feuilletons, six movie scripts, and two plays, produced in the U.S.S.R., based on his novellas "Khochu byt' chestnym" and "Dva tovarishcha." Contributor of short stories to *Novy Mir* and of articles to journals.

WORK IN PROGRESS: "Many future plans, but I fear to speak of them."

SIDELIGHTS: "I have been enraged and moved to tears by contemporary Russian prose and poetry, but Vladimir Voinovich is the only Russian writer who makes me laugh out loud," declared Susan Jacoby in *Saturday Review.* Other critics have also relished Voinovich's sense of humor. A *New York Times Book Review* contributor called Voinovich "the first genuine comic writer entirely produced by the Soviet system," while a *Newsweek* critic proclaimed him "the most drolly entertaining of the new Soviet dissident writers." Voinovich's reputation as a comic writer began with his first two books published in the United States, *The Life and Extraordinary Adventures of Private Ivan Chonkin* and *The Ivankiad.*

Suppressed in Russia, *The Life and Extraordinary Adventures of Ivan Chonkin* was circulated secretly and became an underground success. Peter Prescott speculated that Soviet officials found the novel subversive because "it suggests that amiable sloth and native cunning will prevail against bureaucracy," and "it illustrates what [Karl] Marx never understood: that even under socialism human nature remains an unregenerate constant." The book recounts the tale of a good-natured bumpkin, Private Chonkin, who is ordered by his army officer to remain on a remote collective farm and guard a downed airplane. Headquarters soon forgets him, and Chonkin amuses himself by puttering in the collective's garden and making love to the local postmistress. Despite his simple and placid exterior, Chonkin can be shrewd and even valiant, as his last-ditch effort to prevent himself from being reclaimed by the army demonstrates. Voinovich told an interviewer that Chonkin is not so dull as he appears: "The stupidity that everyone laughs at is not really stupidity when you examine it. My heroes, not only Chonkin but others, too, are very natural people who fall into unnatural situations."

Reflecting on Voinovich's use of satire in *The Life and Extraordinary Adventures of Ivan Chonkin*, Theodore Solotaroff observed, "The choice of a satirical mode was inspired, for it unearthed a first-rate comic talent that had been lurking beneath the sober gritty surface of his early realism and a new and powerful gift for rendering the transactions between reality and fantasy, the ordinary life haunted by the phantoms and phantasmagoria of the police state." In the same vein, Richard R. Lingeman remarked, "This is a very funny book, its humor making a sly and rueful point, as the best satire does, without being grim or heavy-handed." A reviewer for the *New Yorker* disagreed, however, with such assessments of the book, maintaining that "as satire, it is a bit lame and obvious."

Having written a fictional story about one man's war against bureaucracy, Voinovich then proceeded to write a nonfiction account of his own battles with the "phantasmagoria of the police state." The result was *The Ivankiad*, which *Newsweek* described as a "mock epic account of the author's struggle with a powerful publishing bureaucrat over possession of a two-room apartment in the Writers' Housing Cooperative." The theme of this struggle, Anatole Shub explained, is "the contrast between Soviet pretense and reality, theory and practice . . . but the book's delight lies in the human-scale merriment with which Voinovich tells the tale. As in all great satires, the situation is both thoroughly real and utterly preposterous."

Voinovich's battle to gain a larger apartment was only one of many struggles with Soviet bureaucrats. Although his writings were initially well received in the Soviet Union, he fell into official disfavor in the late 1960s. After writing a letter defending Aleksandr Solzhenitsyn in 1974, Voinovich was ousted from the Union of Soviet Writers and forbidden to earn his living as a writer. "I was expelled for trying to write with talent and to live with conscience," Voinovich told *CA.* He explained that his name could no longer be mentioned in Russian encyclopedias and newspapers.

In retaliation, Voinovich saw fit to lampoon Soviet officialdom with satirical letters. When his telephone service was abruptly severed, Voinovich composed an open letter to the Minister of Communications which began: "It is with deep concern that I bring to your attention the fact that an enemy of the Relaxation of International Tension, the head of the Moscow telephone system, is in hiding somewhere in the field of national economy headed by you." He went on to note, "After all, not even the notorious George Meany has managed to disconnect a single telephone." On another occasion he penned a hilarious epistle to the director of the new Soviet copyright agency. In order to shield Russian authors from Western influences, Voinovich recommended to the director that Moscow's prisons "with the necessary guards and police dogs [be] placed at your disposal."

"There is humor in Soviet life. You only have to have a sense of humor so you can recognize it," Voinovich once assured an inquirer. Voinovich and his family left the Soviet Union in December of 1980 and settled in West Germany. The books he has written since leaving his native country, including *In Plain Russian, Moscow 2042,* and *The Fur Hat,* continue to reveal his gift for provoking humor.

Some of Voinovich's poems were set to music and became popular songs in the U.S.S.R. His books have been translated into more than twenty languages.

BIOGRAPHICAL/CRITICAL SOURCES:

BOOKS

Contemporary Authors Autobiography Series, Volume 12, Gale, 1990.
Contemporary Literary Criticism, Gale, Volume 10, 1979, Volume 49, 1988.
Voinovich, Vladimir, *The Ivankiad,* Farrar, Straus, 1977.

PERIODICALS

Chicago Tribune Book World, August 2, 1981.
Los Angeles Times Book Review, August 23, 1981, August 17, 1986.
Newsweek, February 14, 1977, August 1, 1977, August 31, 1981.
New Yorker, March 7, 1977.
New York Times, March 26, 1977, April 27, 1977, December 4, 1980, September 4, 1981, June 2, 1987, July 11, 1987, November 28, 1989.
New York Times Book Review, January 23, 1977, August 7, 1977, October 7, 1979, September 20, 1981, August 31, 1986, June 7, 1987, November 5, 1989.
Saturday Review, September 17, 1977.
Time, January 3, 1977.
Times Literary Supplement, February 20, 1981, October 9, 1981, April 22, 1988.
Tribune Books (Chicago), May 31, 1987.
Washington Post, May 18, 1981, November 18, 1986, June 3, 1987.
Washington Post Book World, August 19, 1979, August 30, 1981, May 24, 1987.

*   *   *

von HAYEK, Friedrich August
    See HAYEK, F(riedrich) A(ugust von)

*   *   *

VONNEGUT, Kurt, Jr. 1922-

PERSONAL: Born November 11, 1922, in Indianapolis, IN; son of Kurt (an architect) and Edith (Lieber) Vonnegut; married Jane Marie Cox, September 1, 1945 (divorced, 1979); married Jill Krementz (a photographer), November, 1979; children: (first marriage) Mark, Edith, Nanette; (adopted deceased sister's children) James, Steven, and Kurt Adams. *Education:* Attended Cornell University, 1940-42, and Carnegie Institute of Technology (now Carnegie-Mellon University), 1943; University of Chicago, student, 1945-47, M.A. (anthropology), 1971. *Avocational interests:* Painting, wood carving, welded sculpture.

ADDRESSES: Home—New York, NY. *Attorney/Agent*—Donald C. Farber, of Tanner, Propp, Fersko & Sterner, 99 Park Ave., 25th Floor, New York, NY. 10016.

CAREER: Chicago City News Bureau, Chicago, IL, police reporter, 1947; General Electric Co., Schenectady, NY, employed in public relations, 1947-50; free-lance writer, 1950—. Teacher at Hopefield School, Sandwich, MA, 1965—; lecturer at University of Iowa Writers Workshop, 1965-67, and at Harvard University, 1970-71; Distinguished Professor of English Prose, City College of the City University of New York, 1973-74. Speaker, National Coalition against Censorship briefing for the Attorney General's Commission on Pornography hearing, 1986. One-man exhibition of drawings, 1980. *Military service:* U.S. Army, Infantry, 1942-45; was POW; received Purple Heart.

MEMBER: Authors League of America, PEN (American Center; vice-president, 1974), National Institute of Arts and Letters, Delta Upsilon, Barnstable Yacht Club, Barnstable Comedy Club.

AWARDS, HONORS: Guggenheim fellow, Germany, 1967; National Institute of Arts and Letters grant, 1970; Litt.D., Hobart and William Smith Colleges, 1974; Outstanding Children's Program of 1985 Emmy Award, for "Displaced Person," a television version of the story "D.P."; Bronze Medallion, Guild Hall, 1986.

WRITINGS:

NOVELS

Player Piano, Scribner, 1952, published as *Utopia 14,* Bantam, 1954, hardback edition under original title with new preface, 1966, Holt, reprinted, Dell, 1981.
The Sirens of Titan, Dell, 1959, reprinted, Delacourte, 1981.
Mother Night, Fawcett, 1962, Harper, 1967, reprinted, Dell, 1988.
Cat's Cradle, Holt, 1963.
God Bless You, Mr. Rosewater, or Pearls before Swine, Holt, 1965.
Slaughterhouse Five, or the Children's Crusade: A Duty-Dance with Death, by Kurt Vonnegut, Jr., a Fourth-Generation German-American Now Living in Easy Circumstances on Cape Cod (and Smoking Too Much) Who, as an American Infantry Scout Hors de Combat, as a Prisoner of War, Witnessed the Fire-Bombing of Dresden, Germany, the Florence of the Elbe, a Long Time Ago, and Survived to Tell the Tale: This Is a Novel Somewhat in the Telegraphic Schizophrenic Manner of Tales of the Planet Tralfamadore, Where the Flying Saucers Come From, Seymour Lawrence/Delacorte, 1969, reprinted, Barron, 1985.
Breakfast of Champions, or Goodbye Blue Monday, Seymour Lawrence/Delacorte, 1973.
Slapstick, or Lonesome No More, Seymour Lawrence/Delacorte, 1976.
Jailbird, Seymour Lawrence/Delacorte, 1979.
Dead-Eye Dick, Seymour Lawrence/Delacorte, 1982.
Galapagos: A Novel, Seymour Lawrence/Delacorte, 1985.
Bluebeard, Delacorte, 1987.
Hocus Pocus; or, What's the Hurry, Son?, Putnam, 1990.

SHORT FICTION

Canary in a Cathouse, Fawcett, 1961.
Welcome to the Monkey House: A Collection of Short Works, Seymour Lawrence/Delacorte, 1968.

PLAYS

Penelope, first produced on Cape Cod, Mass., 1960, revised version published as *Happy Birthday, Wanda June* (first produced Off-Broadway at the Theater De Lys, October 7, 1970), Seymour Lawrence/Delacorte, 1971, revised edition, Samuel French, 1971.

Between Time and Timbuktu, or Prometheus Five: A Space Fantasy (television play; first produced on National Educational Television Network, 1972), Seymour Lawrence/Delacorte, 1972.
Make Up Your Mind, first performed as an author reading in East Hampton, NY, at the John Drew Theater, August 28, 1989.

Also author of "Something Borrowed," 1958, "The Very First Christmas Morning," 1962, "EPICAC," 1963, "My Name Is Everyone," 1964, and "Fortitude," 1968, all produced Off-Broadway or in summer stock.

OTHER

Wampeters, Foma, and Granfalloons: Opinions (essays), Seymour Lawrence/Delacorte, 1974.
(With Ivan Chermayeff) *Suit, Moon, Star* (juvenile), Harper, 1980.
Palm Sunday: An Autobiographical Collage, Seymour Lawrence/Delacorte, 1981.
(Contributor) *Bob and Ray: A Retrospective, June 15-July 10, 1982,* Museum of Broadcasting, 1982.
(Contributor) W. E. Block and M. A. Walker, editors, *Discrimination, Affirmative Action, and Equal Opportunity: An Economic and Social Perspective,* Fraser Institute, 1982.
Nothing Is Lost Save Honor: Two Essays (contains The Worst Addiction of Them All and Fates Worth Than Death: Lecture at St. John the Divine, New York City, May 23, 1982), Toothpaste Press, 1984.

Contributor of fiction to numerous publications, including *Saturday Evening Post, Cosmopolitan, McCall's, Playboy,* and *Ladies' Home Journal.* Editor and contributor, *Cornell Daily Sun,* 1941-42.

MEDIA ADAPTATIONS: The play *Happy Birthday, Wanda June* was produced as a film in 1971; *Slaughterhouse Five* was produced as a film by Universal in 1972. "Between Time and Timbuktu," adapted from short stories, was broadcast on public television in 1972. *God Bless You, Mr. Rosewater* was adapted for the stage by Howard Ashman and produced by Vonnegut's daughter, Edith, in 1979; *Slapstick of Another Kind,* a film version of *Slapstick,* was released in 1984; *Player Piano, The Sirens of Titan,* and *Cat's Cradle* have also been produced as plays; option to film *The Sirens of Titan* belongs to members of The Grateful Dead through Universal Studios.

SIDELIGHTS: Although he is now one of America's most widely-read and well-respected novelists, Kurt Vonnegut, Jr., was virtually ignored by critics from the beginning of his writing career until the 1963 publication of *Cat's Cradle.* While this may have been the result of his early classification as a science fiction writer, and it is true that technology and the future have played an important part in much of his work, it is generally agreed that his books go far beyond the realm of most pure science fiction. In a *Commonweal* review, Ernest W. Ranly explains: "Vonnegut at times adds fantasy to his stories, whereas pure sci-fi permits only what is possible within a given scientific hypothesis. Vonnegut adds humor, a wild black humor, while most sci-fi is serious to the point of boredom. Vonnegut, generally, adds a distinctive sense and literary class. And, finally, Vonnegut seems preoccupied with genuine human questions, about war, peace, technology, human happiness. He is even bitterly anti-machine, anti-technology, anti-science."

The science fiction aspect of Vonnegut's work is explored by Karen and Charles Wood, who refer to the author's first novel, *Player Piano,* as "one of the best science fiction novels ever written," but point out that "it rests uneasily in the science fiction genre precisely because it is such a good novel—a novel, that is, in the Jamesian sense, a detailed examination of human experience. The devotee of science fiction comes away from *Player Piano* with the uneasy feeling that somehow this isn't science fiction at all, that there is something wrong here. What is wrong here is that someone finally wrote a science fiction novel that puts the emphasis on characters—upon human experience and actions." According to their essay in *The Vonnegut Statement,* edited by Klinkowitz and John Somer, Vonnegut admits that "science exists and has become vastly important to our lives. The communication of such an idea would not be easy to accomplish without the techniques of science fiction. Therefore Vonnegut both philosophizes and characterizes, and when a statement is made, it draws as much importance from who says it, and how, as from the idea itself."

Kurt Vonnegut, Jr. author Peter J. Reed, who sees *Player Piano* as an important social commentary, finds that it is the most difficult of Vonnegut's novels to analyze. He writes: "Initially it may strike us as another socio-moral analysis of the present through the future in the tradition of *The Time Machine, Brave New World,* or *1984.* But then the resemblance shows shifts in the direction of the more immediate kinds of social criticism, like *Babbitt, Main Street,* or even *The Grapes of Wrath.* Furthermore, comic episodes become frequent, sometimes roughly in the social-satiric vein of Aldous Huxley or Evelyn Waugh, sometimes as pure slapstick, sometimes almost of the comic strip guffaw-inducing variety. These references to other works and writers should not be taken to imply that Vonnegut is highly derivative, but simply to suggest the mixture present in the novel." The satiric and humorous qualities which Reed mentions are significant in that they are common to much of Vonnegut's work. Like many writers, he uses satire as a means of emphasizing serious points. However, Vonnegut has the ability to temper biting satire with warmth and concern for his characters and to direct much of the humor toward himself. The result is that Vonnegut, even when he is at his most critical and fatalistic, does not tend to alienate readers; we are able to identify with the writer because he is just as much the object of satire as the rest of society. As Reed concludes, "the attacks on social ills obviously grow out of a deep compassion, and we sense the gentleness of this writer who so often portrays violence."

The Sirens of Titan is sometimes lumped together with *Player Piano* and several short stories as Vonnegut's "science fiction period." However, in a *Journal of Popular Culture* review, G. K. Wolfe argues that *Sirens* is more closely related, thematically and stylistically, to his later fiction; Wolfe calls the book the "seminal work" in Vonnegut's development as a writer. He writes: "It is not possible to read *Sirens* as mere escapist fiction, for we are constantly drawn back to the individual human element and the harsh realities of meaningless cruelty and death, whether on Mars, Titan, Mercury, or earth. Vonnegut suggests that these realities will follow man wherever he goes, whatever he does, not because of a failure in man's vision of himself (though this is certainly involved), but because, fortunately or unfortunately, they are a part of what makes him human." *Sirens* marks the introduction of several themes that continue throughout much of Vonnegut's later work: the futility of trying to change the world and, as a result, the necessity of change within the individual; the fatality of searching for meaning outside of the self when the answer is really a part of human nature; and the elevation of the main character to new levels of understanding through his quest for meaning in human existence.

Mother Night, Vonnegut's third novel, is the story of Howard W. Campbell, Jr., an American playwright living in Germany at the outbreak of World War II, who is persuaded by the Allies to remain in Germany as a spy while posing as a radio propagandist. After the war he fades into obscurity in the United States until, with his wartime cover still intact, he is kidnapped by Israeli agents to stand trial for his crime. Eventually Campbell's American bosses reveal his true identity, but before he can be released he commits suicide in an Israeli jail cell. Richard Schickel expected the tone of such a novel to be dark. "But *Mother Night* . . . is on the contrary, a wonderful splash of bright, primary colors, an artful, zestful cartoon that lets us see despair without forcing us to surrender to it," he writes in a *Harper's* review. Though all reviewers do not share this opinion, Schickel claims, "There is no self-pity at the core of Vonnegut's work, only the purifying laughter of a man who has survived that stage."

Cat's Cradle, published in hardcover in 1963, marked what many critics believe to be the beginning of a turn-around in Vonnegut's career. Although some see the book as the point at which his work gained acceptance, it might more properly be viewed as the first in a series of books through which Vonnegut came to the attention of the general public. However, if one single point must be chosen for the transition of Vonnegut from "cult figure" to "popular author" it would most probably be a statement by Graham Greene calling *Cat's Cradle* "one of the three best novels of the year by one of the most able living writers." The book is held in high regard by most critics, including *Hollins Critic* contributor Robert Scholes who writes: "The life of [*Cat's Cradle*] is in its movement, the turns of plot, of character, and of phrase which give it vitality. Vonnegut's prose has the same virtues as his characterization and plotting. It is deceptively simple, suggestive of the ordinary, but capable of startling and illuminating twists and turns."

Reed believes that *Cat's Cradle* may be the novel that best exemplifies Vonnegut's style. He says that the book "illustrates almost every device, technique, attitude, and subject we encounter in Vonnegut, and is filled with particulars which echo other novels." As an example, *Cat's Cradle* is as autobiographical as any of his work up to that time. The Hoenikker family of the novel closely parallels Vonnegut's own family, consisting of an elder son who is a scientist, a tall middle daughter, and a younger son who joins Delta Upsilon. The narrator is again a writer who, in this case, is working on a book called *The Day the World Ended,* about the bombing of Hiroshima. (This may be the beginning of Vonnegut's preoccupation with apocalyptic endings or an early attempt to deal with the bombing of Dresden later detailed in *Slaughterhouse Five.*) And once again, as in *Mother Night,* Vonnegut introduces the idea that writers are deceivers whose fictional worlds are false depictions of reality.

In *God Bless You, Mr. Rosewater, or Pearls before Swine* we see the introduction of a theme which crops up repeatedly in the later novels and which many believe to be the essence of all of Vonnegut's writing. It is expressed by the main character, Eliot Rosewater, in the motto "Goddamn it, you've got to be kind." John R. May calls the book "Kurt Vonnegut's finest novel to date," and comments in a *Twentieth Century Literature* review that it is the author's "most positive and humane work. . . . We may not be able, Vonnegut is saying, to undo the harm that has been done, but we can certainly love, simply because there are people, those who have been made useless by our past stupidity and greed, our previous crimes against our brothers. And if that seems insane, then the better the world for such folly."

In addition to the familiar theme of human frailty as man's greatest asset, another attempt to deal with the Dresden experience (this time the protagonist hallucinates that Indianapolis is engulfed in a firestorm), and a satire on writers in the character of Kilgore Trout, Vonnegut once again suggests the inability of the individual to conquer his environment. As Raymond M. Olderman, author of *Beyond the Wasteland: A Study of the American Novel in the Nineteen-Sixties,* sees it, "Although Vonnegut's tone, spirit, and overall response to man are very different from Jonathan Swift's, his idea of the universe and man's role in it is somewhat Swiftian, for he pictures us as modern Lilliputians, claiming big things for ourselves in a universe too immense to be anything but indifferent. . . . [According to Vonnegut] men are 'the listless playthings of enormous forces.' " Rosewater's struggle for kindness in an unkind world and the difficulty he experiences in attempting to realize his motto illustrate what Robert W. Uphaus calls "individual action reduced to sham theatricality—to gestures without ultimate significance." However, as Uphaus points out in his *Novel: A Forum on Fiction* essay, even though individual action may be of little consequence to the universe as a whole, it is still "desperately laden with personal meaning." And it is toward this personal meaning that much of Vonnegut's prose is directed.

In *Slaughterhouse Five,* after touching on the subject in several earlier works, Vonnegut finally delivers a complete treatise on Dresden. The main character, Billy Pilgrim, is a very young infantry scout who is captured in the Battle of the Bulge and quartered in a Dresden slaughterhouse where he and other prisoners are employed in the production of a vitamin supplement for pregnant women. During the February 13, 1945, firebombing by Allied aircraft, the prisoners take shelter in an underground meat locker. When they emerge, the city has been levelled and they are forced to dig corpses out of the rubble. The story of Billy Pilgrim is the story of Kurt Vonnegut who was captured and survived the firestorm in which 135,000 German civilians perished, more than the number of deaths in the bombings of Hiroshima and Nagasaki combined.

Writing in the *New York Times Book Review,* Robert Scholes relates that "for twenty years Vonnegut has been trying to do fictional justice to that historical event. Now he has finished, and he calls his book a failure. Speaking of the Biblical destruction of Sodom and Gomorrah (like Dresden, subjected to a firestorm), Vonnegut writes: 'Those were vile people in both of those cities, as is well known. The world is better off without them. And Lot's wife, of course, was told not to look back where all those people and their homes had been. But she looked back, and I love her for that, because it was so human. So she was turned to a pillar of salt. So it goes. People aren't supposed to look back. I'm certainly not going to do it any more. I've finished my war book now. The next one I write is going to be fun. This one is a failure, and had to be, since it was written by a pillar of salt.' " Scholes sums up the theme of *Slaughterhouse Five:* "Be kind. Don't hurt. Death is coming for all of us anyway, and it is better to be Lot's wife looking back through salty eyes than the Deity that destroyed those cities of the plain in order to save them." The reviewer concludes that "far from being a 'failure,' 'Slaughterhouse Five' is an extraordinary success. It is a book we need to read, and to reread. It has the same virtues as Vonnegut's best previous work."

After the publication of *Slaughterhouse Five,* Vonnegut entered a period of depression during which he vowed, at one point, never to write another novel. He concentrated, instead, on lecturing, teaching, and finishing a play, "Happy Birthday, Wanda June," that he had begun several years earlier. The play, which ran Off-Broadway from October, 1970 to March, 1971, received mixed reviews. *Newsweek*'s Jack Kroll wrote that "almost every time an American novelist writes a play he shows up most of our thumb-tongued playwrights, who lack the melody of mind, the wit, dash and accuracy of Saul Bellow and Bruce Jay Friedman. And the same thing must be said of the writing in 'Happy Birthday, Wanda June.'. . . Vonnegut's dialogue is not only fast and funny, with a palpable taste and crackle, but it also means something. And his comic sense is a superior one; 'Wanda June' has as many laughs as anything by Neil Simon." On the other hand, in the *New Republic* Stanley Kauffmann called it "a disaster, full of callow wit, rheumatic invention, and dormitory profundity. . . . The height of its imagination is exemplified by a scene in Heaven between a golden-haired little girl and a Nazi Gauleiter in which they discuss the way Jesus plays shuffleboard."

Whether or not the play was totally successful, however, is less important than the opportunity it gave the author to create solid characters portrayed by real people, a quality which he felt was lacking in the novel. "Most Vonnegut characters represent specific ideas, ideals, or attitudes," explains David Bianculli in a *Film Comment* interview with the author. Though *Slaughterhouse Five* was made into a successful film, his other novels have been harder to adapt for this reason, said Vonnegut: "My books are essentially rational, built more around ideas I want to discuss than characters I want to analyze. I can't turn characters loose and see what they're going to do. For one thing, I'm not that interested in individual lives." The movie version of "Happy Birthday, Wanda June" failed because "the actors took their roles too seriously," Bianculli relates. Vonnegut said of his characters, "They're not real people. . . . It would take a very shrewd director to tell these actors: 'Please be convincing, be sincere, but don't be real.' "

There are several factors which could be interpreted as the cause of Vonnegut's period of depression, including, as he has admitted, the approach of his fiftieth birthday and the fact that his children had begun to leave home. Many critics believe that, having at last come to terms with Dresden, he lost the major impetus for much of his work; others feel that *Slaughterhouse Five* may have been the single great novel that Vonnegut was capable of writing. Whatever the cause, *Breakfast of Champions* marked the end of his depression and a return to the novel. In honor of this event, Vonnegut subtitled the work, *Goodbye Blue Monday. Washington Post Book World* contributor S. K. Oberbeck calls the book "the author's fiftieth birthday present to his swollen ego. . . . From its pop cartoons [Vonnegut includes drawings or doodles on almost every page] . . . to its blithe Radiclib (or 'Radglib,' a word coined by one of those big, black, useless machines), the book is Lit-Pop politics, as if Richard Brautigan were feyly fictionalizing Tom Hayden and wife Jane. From capitalism, imperialism, racism, ecology, overpopulation and Fem Lib to handguns and Holiday Inns, Vonnegut doesn't miss touching a base." Nora Sayre writes in the *New York Times Book Review* that "in this novel Vonnegut is treating himself to a giant brain-flush, clearing his head by throwing out acquired ideas, and also liberating some of the characters from his previous books. Thus, he has celebrated his fiftieth birthday in the same spirit that made Tolstoy release his serfs and Thomas Jefferson free his slaves. Once again, we're back on the people-grid; major and minor personae from other novels resurface in this one, their lives ridiculously entangled. . . . This explosive meditation ranks with Vonnegut's best."

In *Breakfast of Champions,* as in most of Vonnegut's work, there are very clear autobiographical tendencies. In this novel however, the author seems to be even more wrapped up in his characters than usual. He appears as Philboyd Sludge, the writer of the book which stars Dwayne Hoover, a Pontiac dealer (Vonnegut once ran a Saab dealership) who goes berserk after reading a novel by Kilgore Trout, who also represents Vonnegut. Toward the end of the book, Vonnegut arranges a meeting between himself and Trout, whom Robert Merrill calls his "most famous creation," in which he casts the character loose forever; by this time the previously unsuccessful Trout has become rich and famous and is finally able to stand on his own. In *Critique*, Merrill says that Vonnegut "insists on his role as master puppeteer. . . . [The author] allows no pretense about the status of his fictional creations; toward the end, Vonnegut even seats himself at the same bar with his characters. While sipping his favorite drink, he proceeds to explain why he has decided to have these characters act as they do." The result, according to Merrill, is the emphasis of the fact that the novel really has only one character: Vonnegut himself. The reviewer concludes that *Breakfast of Champions* "is about its author's triumph over a great temptation. Saint Anthony's temptation was of the flesh, and Vonnegut's is of the spirit; we should know by now that the spirit both kills and dies. At the end of the novel, Vonnegut's spirit refuses to die. . . . His hope is that we might all become 'better'; his message is that to become so we must resist the seductions of fatalism."

With his next book, *Slapstick*, Vonnegut undertakes the theme that the wane of the extended family has caused loneliness for most Americans, and he proposes a system for providing everyone with such a family (hence the subtitle, *Lonesome No More*). In *National Review*, Charles Nicol notes that the first sentence of the book is, "This is the closest I will ever come to writing an autobiography," and says that "we are then supposed to extrapolate from a few family reminiscences to the action of the novel and marvel at something or other." Vonnegut's sister, Alice, died of cancer at the age of forty-one; she described her impending death as "soap opera" and "slapstick." As Nicol puts it, "a Vonnegut through and through. So *Slapstick* is 'really' about Kurt and Alice. . . . Alice's husband died in a grotesque accident two days before she did; he was a passenger on 'the only train in American railroading history to hurl itself off an open drawbridge.' Consequently *Slapstick* is 'grotesque, situational poetry'; it is supposedly about 'what life *feels* like' to Vonnegut." Nicol goes on to say that the idea of giving everyone an extended family "was supposed to be earthshakingly delightful, the hopeful vision of *Slapstick*, but it doesn't work. . . . What's gone wrong? Simply, as Vonnegut rather circumspectly admits, he has lost the inspiration of the Muse. His sister 'was the person I had always written for.' He felt her 'presence' for a number of years after she died, 'but then she began to fade away, perhaps because she had more important business elsewhere.' Now Vonnegut is without his own 'audience of one,' and it shows. This grotesque tribute to their growing up together hasn't brought back his sister's presence, and *Slapstick* is dedicated not to her, but to Laurel and Hardy. It doesn't live up to their memory, or Vonnegut's either."

Reviewing *Jailbird*, John Leonard of the *New York Times* says that in previous novels Vonnegut has told us "that he believed in the Bill of Rights, Robert's Rules of Order and the principles of Alcoholics Anonymyous. In his new novel, *Jailbird*—his best in my opinion since *Mother Night* and *Cat's Cradle*—he adds another sacred document. It is the Sermon on the Mount." In this novel the main character, Walter F. Starbuck, is asked by Congressman Richard M. Nixon at a 1949 hearing why he has joined the Communist Party; Starbuck replies: "Why? The Sermon on the Mount, sir." And Leonard says, "When you think about it, the Sermon on the Mount is a radical document, promising that

the meek shall inherit the earth. Shall they, indeed? Mr. Vonnegut has his doubts." Jean Strouse, writing in *Newsweek*, agrees that this is his best book "since *Cat's Cradle*. Using the laid-back, ironic voice that has become his trademark, Vonnegut this time combines fiction and fact to construct an ingenious, wry morality play about the capitalist U.S. of A. . . . Vonnegut makes it delightful not to wonder what is really going on."

Leonard perceives Vonnegut's obsessions in *Jailbird* to be "Harvard and Mr. Nixon, the Holocaust and Watergate, Sacco and Vanzetti, Alger Hiss and Whittaker Chambers, trade unionism and conglomerate capitalism, not to mention Roy M. Cohn." The reviewer finds that "not once in *Jailbird* does Mr. Vonnegut nod off, go vague. His people bite into their lives. Kindnesses, as inexplicable as history, are collected, like saving remnants. New York, with catacombs under Grand Central Terminal and harps on top of the Chrysler Building, is wonderfully evoked. The prose has sinew. Mr. Nixon's 'unhappy little smile,' for instance 'looked to me like a rosebud that had just been smashed by a hammer.' Or: 'There was a withered old man . . . hunched over his food, hiding it with his arms. Sarah whispered that he ate as though his meal were a royal flush.' "

Even though Leonard makes a point of identifying *Jailbird* as a "fable of evil and inadvertence," *New York Times Book Review* contributor Michael Wood criticizes Vonnegut for his inability to "see evil at all. He sees only weakness, and in these long, flattened perspectives, everything—Watergate, Auschwitz, Goering and yesterday's news—comes to belong simply to a blurred, generalized representation of damage and error. There is a real subject here, and it is one of Vonnegut's subjects: What are we to do when we cannot perceive the reality of evil, or distinguish it from other forms of human failure?" Wood arrives at the conclusion that "Vonnegut's work is so likable that its shallowness may seem to be a part of its appeal." Leonard's opinion on this is that "it is the fashion these days . . . to dismiss Mr. Vonnegut as simplistic. He is insufficiently obscure; he is not loud enough about the ambiguities. Well, as he would say, listen. The simple—courtesy and decency—is hardest."

Catastrophe comes more easily, Vonnegut says in *Deadeye Dick*: "That is my principal objection to life, I think: It is too easy, when alive, to make perfectly horrible mistakes." The title character's father, for instance, saves the life of a starving artist, the young Hitler, when they are in school together; the narrator, Rudy Waltz, gains his cruel nickname at age twelve when a shot he fires from his father's rifle accidentally kills a pregnant woman; and later, a neutron bomb detonates, either by accident, or by the government's covert design, in Waltz's home town, killing everyone, but leaving the machines and buildings unharmed. Interspersed with these horrors are recipes, provided by Rudy, who has become a chef and co-partner with his brother in a restaurant in Haiti. Throughout, "the grand old Vonnegutian comedy of causelessness still holds center stage. . . . Why does the child of a gun safety specialist, using a rifle from his father's collection, emerge as a double murderer? A tough question. Why do human beings take satisfaction in creating a neutron bomb that destroys 'only' human beings, not their accoutrements? Another toughie. Why should grief-struck Rudy Waltz, headed for a presumably moving moment at his parents' graveside, allow his train of thought to light on a certain cookie, whereupon . . . instead of grief we're provided with a recipe for almond macaroons? . . . Sentence on sentence, paragraph on paragraph, chapter on chapter, so it goes: a tissue of unanswerables," reports Benjamin DeMott in the *New York Times Book Review*.

If catastrophe comes more easily to man than courtesy and decency, man's large brain is to blame, Vonnegut asserts in his next novel. "*Galapagos* brings Vonnegut's lifelong belief in the imperfectibility of human nature to its logical conclusion," observes a *London Times* reviewer. "It covers the evolution of humanity over a million years in a narration by the ghost of Vietnam veteran Leon Trout," Smith says in *Publishers Weekly*. She continues, "The million-year time span was necessary in order to show human beings evolving, in the aftermath of a nuclear war, from destructive 'big brains' into furry, flippered fisher-folk who can successfully survive in the hostile environment of the Galapagos Islands." Trout's story tells how a group of tourists are shipwrecked in the islands where Darwin formulated the notion of progressive adaptation; over time, their oversized brains diminish, sexual interests atrophy, and their hands become flippers, all to the benefit of the race and the ecosystem. "This will eliminate war, starvation, and nuclear terror—that is, many of the things Mr. Vonnegut likes to complain about in his novels," remarks *New York Times* reviewer Michiko Kakutani. It would also eliminate literature, Vonnegut conceded to Jeffrey S. Unger in the *Detroit News:* "Yeah, you wouldn't have my novel, except I would gladly take everything in the Library of Congress and trade all of it in if we could prevent our killing the whole damn planet, which is what we're on the verge of doing now. That's a fair enough trade-off." But for all the seriousness of its message, the book contains sufficient humor to make it satisfying as "a well-crafted comic strip," Kakutani feels. Vonnegut's statement to John Blades of *Chicago Tribune Books* explains this blend: "This wonderful brain of ours . . . has gotten us to the point where we have these extraordinary bombs all over the world, where we're destroying a lot of the Earth's surface, where our leaders aren't interested in the survival of mankind. This has to be a joke. What else is there to do but laugh?"

Though some reviewers find Vonnegut's jokes an easy target for criticism, Thomas M. Disch of the *Times Literary Supplement* sees in the humor a secondary purpose, "which is moral instruction. Indeed, the interest of the Vonnegut voice is not in what it reveals of the author but in the audience that it hypothesizes, an audience that must have the most basic facts of life explained to it in the simplest terms, an audience that will crack up at the sound of a fart, an audience that has the best of intentions even as it paves the road to hell, an audience of children who know they need to be scolded. Vonnegut is unusual among novelists who dramatize the conflict (ever recurring in his work) between fathers and sons in that his sympathies always lie on the sadder-but-wiser side of the generation gap. In an era that has institutionalized adolescent rebellion, here is a father for foundlings of all ages. Small wonder that he is so popular."

In *Bluebeard*, Vonnegut comments again on the horrors of wartime holocaust through the voice of painter Rabo Karabekian, a contemporary of abstract expressionists Mark Rothko and Jackson Pollack. Descended from survivors of the Turkish holocaust in which a million Armenians died, Rabo witnesses the horrors of World War II. The book is a "delicate . . . and clever reprise of the themes that have preoccupied [Vonnegut] all his life: the existential notion that men are wholly responsible for their own lives; that God does not exist or, if he does, God is some cosmic joke; that the best intentions are usually not enough; that the Holocaust is never very far away, and that humankind is both wonderful and terrible," notes Clive Doucet in the Toronto *Globe and Mail.* When compared to *Cat's Cradle* and *Slaughterhouse Five,* says *New York Times Book Review* contributor Julian Moynahan, the novel *Bluebeard* seems to be "a minor achievement." Doucet, however, finds it "a solid success."

Bluebeard represents some significant breakthroughs for Vonnegut, believes John W. Aldridge, who sees a "creative decline" in the novels since *Breakfast of Champions.* This decline, he feels, is reversed in *Bluebeard:* "Gone are the cute refrains, the cartoonographic characters" that, in his opinion, marred the earlier novels, he states in *Chicago Tribune Books.* In Vonnegut's depiction of the painter who can produce only perfect replications of real life that will not last because of the kind of paint he uses, Aldridge hears the author "telling us with as much honesty as he can muster that he has reservations about the kind of writer he has become and the work he has accomplished. . . . It may well be not only the most personal fiction he has written but also the most authentic in tone and substance. . . . What was almost always wrong with his work in the past was that he seemed to be speaking through a ventriloquist's dummy. Now he has found the courage to speak in a voice that sounds as if it is truly his own, and it is a considerable excitement to hear it for the first time." Beyond this, the reviewer feels that *Bluebeard* "clearly shows promise of carrying Vonnegut into a new vital phase of his career, and in view of the quality of his recent novels, it appears to be the product of a remarkable renewal of his energy."

Surveying Vonnegut's career, Curt Suplee of the *Washington Post* comments, "His efforts have earned him fame and indignities. His books have been banned or burned for suspected obscenity in some communities, but he has topped the bestseller lists repeatedly, all of his work is still in print, and he was made a member of the National Institute of Arts and Letters. Critics have praised him as a satirical genius or patronized him as a cult figure for the young, a purveyor of Cynical Chic. 'I'm finally sick of this,' he says of the youth-market charge. 'It's a lazy way for critics to say that something is wrong with me without having to describe it in detail. So they say that I'm just the kind of person that immature readers enjoy. But children don't buy hardcover books. "Jailbird" . . . was number one on the best-seller list in hardcover practically as long as "Sophie's Choice" was. Those weren't children stepping up buying the books.'"

Vonnegut's work has been likened to that of numerous literary figures, including Dickens, Swift, Orwell, Huxley, Richard Stern, Bruce Jay Friedman, Thomas Pynchon, Joseph Heller, and Donald Barthelme, to name only a few. With so many critics arguing for their personal favorites, it is difficult to decide exactly who has influenced whom. What is more important, and more realistic, is to analyze Vonnegut's style, his recurring themes, and, ultimately, his impact on contemporary literature. Charles Thomas Samuels says that Vonnegut "absorbed what preceded him. Like most advanced novelists in the modern period, Vonnegut deemphasizes plot and character while working for effects of emotional contradiction and intellectual ambiguity. He borrows the debased formulas of science fiction and comic books as a serious travesty of our present condition, whose silliness is also represented by one-dimensional grotesques impersonating people. Random structure facilitates digressions, which also preclude the emotional satisfactions of climax, denouement and uniformity of tone. As in his forebears, such technical features express a conviction: the world is incoherent and therefore can't be imitated through closed or univocal forms. Nothing so declares the modernity of Vonnegut as the shortness of his books, chapters and sentences. Jabs to the intellectual and emotional solar plexus are intended; if we judge by his admirers, the intention is achieved." In the same *New Republic* review, Samuels mentions that Vonnegut's admirers include young people, which "isn't difficult to understand. His own spiritual age is late adolescence. . . . That Vonnegut is beloved by critics (and presumably adult readers) is more disconcerting. For them, he provides an easy bridge from an age of skepticism and baffled hope to one of faith in any nostrum that bears the certifications of novelty and youth."

Vonnegut has stated that the two main themes of all his work were best expressed by his brother, who soon after the birth of his first child, wrote, "Here I am cleaning shit off of practically everything," and by his sister, whose last words were, "no pain." In an essay in *The Critic as Artist: Essays on Books, 1920-1970*, J. Michael Crichton calls this analysis "as true as anything a writer has said of his work." Crichton thinks that Vonnegut's novels "have attacked our deepest fears of automation and the bomb, our deepest political guilts, our fiercest hatreds and loves. Nobody else writes books on these subjects; they are inaccessible to normal novelistic approaches. But Vonnegut, armed with his schizophrenia, takes an absurd, distorted, wildly funny framework which is ultimately anaesthetic. . . . And as he proceeds, from his anaesthetic framework, to clean the shit off, we are able to cheer him on—at least for a while. But eventually we stop cheering, and stop laughing." Crichton calls this "a classic sequence of reactions to any Vonnegut book. One begins smugly, enjoying the sharp wit of a compatriot as he carves up Common Foes. But the sharp wit does not stop, and sooner or later it is directed against the Wrong Targets. . . . He becomes an offensive writer, because he will not choose sides, ascribing blame and penalty, identifying good guys and bad." This same idea is expressed by Vonnegut himself when, in *Slaughterhouse Five*, he quotes his father saying to him, "you know—you never wrote a story with a villain in it." Likewise, as numerous critics have pointed out, he has never created a hero. A comment to Unger credits these facts to Vonnegut's background in anthropology: "What seems original in my work is only the attitude of a social scientist. . . . I have society as a villain or the culture as a villain. I do think we have an evil culture, in many ways. And a social scientist is more used to treating it as a separate entity, as a gadget, than most writers are."

In the final analysis, perhaps it is best to look to Vonnegut's first novel, *Player Piano* in which he creates a world where machines not only do manual labor, but also do all of man's thinking; in protest, a renegade group called the Ghost Shirt Society is formed to sabotage all machines. The credo of the group, as Ernest W. Ranly says, can be taken to be Vonnegut's own: "That there must be virtue in imperfection, for Man is imperfect, and Man is a creation of God. That there must be virtue in frailty, for Man is frail and Man is a creation of God. That there must be virtue in inefficiency, for Man is inefficient and Man is a creation of God. That there must be virtue in brilliance followed by stupidity, for Man is alternately brilliant and stupid and Man is a creation of God." Ranly concludes that Vonnegut embraces the principles of the religion of Bokonism in *Cat's Cradle*, namely that "the one thing sacred is not the mountain, is not the ocean, is not the sun, is not even God. The one thing sacred is man. That's all. Just man. Man is that lucky mud from among all the mud which can sit up and see what a nice job God has done."

BIOGRAPHICAL/CRITICAL SOURCES:

BOOKS

Authors in the News, Volume 1, Gale, 1976.

Bellamy, Joe David, editor, *The New Fiction: Interviews with Innovative American Writers*, University of Illinois Press, 1974.

Bryant, Jerry H., *The Open Decision*, Free Press, 1970.

Chernuchin, Michael, editor, *Vonnegut Talks!*, Pylon, 1977.

Clareson, Thomas D., editor, *Voices for the Future: Essays on Major Science Fiction Writers*, Volume 1, Bowling Green University Popular Press, 1976.

Concise Dictionary of American Literary Biography: Broadening Views, 1968-1988, Gale, 1989.

Contemporary Literary Criticism, Gale, Volume 1, 1973, Volume 2, 1974, Volume 3, 1975, Volume 4, 1975, Volume 5, 1976, Volume 8, 1978, Volume 12, 1980, Volume 22, 1982, Volume 40, 1986.

Dictionary of Literary Biography, Gale, Volume 2: *American Novelists since World War II*, 1978, Volume 8: *Twentieth Century American Science Fiction Writers*, Part 2, 1981.

Dictionary of Literary Biography Documentary Series, Volume 3, Gale, 1983.

Dictionary of Literary Biography Yearbook 1980, Gale, 1981.

Dillard, R. H. W., George Garrett, and John Rees Moore, editors, *The Sounder Few: Essays from the "Hollins Critic,"* University of Georgia Press, 1971.

Giannone, Richard, *Vonnegut: A Preface to His Novels*, Kennikat, 1977.

Goldsmith, David H., *Kurt Vonnegut: Fantasist of Fire and Ice*, Bowling Green University Popular Press, 1972.

Harris, Charles B., *Contemporary American Novelists of the Absurd*, College and University Press, 1971.

Harrison, Gilbert A., editor, *The Critic as Artist: Essays on Books, 1920-1970*, Liveright, 1972.

Hassan, Ihab, *Contemporary American Literature 1942-1972*, Ungar, 1973.

Holland, Thomas R., *Vonnegut's Major Works*, Cliff's Notes, 1973.

Hudgens, Betty Lenhardt, *Kurt Vonnegut, Jr.: A Checklist*, Gale, 1972.

Karl, Frederick R., *American Fictions: 1940-1980*, Harper, 1983.

Kazin, Alfred, *Bright Book of Life: American Novelists and Storytellers from Hemingway to Mailer*, Little, Brown, 1973.

Kennard, Jean E., *Number and Nightmare: Forms of Fantasy in Contemporary Fiction*, Archon Books, 1975.

Klinkowitz, Jerome, and John Somer, editors, *The Vonnegut Statement: Original Essays on the Life and Work of Kurt Vonnegut*, Delacorte, 1973.

Klinkowitz, Jerome, and Asa B. Pieratt, *Kurt Vonnegut, Jr.: A Descriptive Bibliography and Secondary Checklist*, Shoe String, 1974.

Klinkowitz, Jerome, *Literary Disruptions: The Making of a Post-Contemporary American Fiction*, University of Illinois Press, 1975.

Klinkowitz, Jerome, and Donald L. Lawler, editors, *Vonnegut in America: An Introduction to the Life and Work of Kurt Vonnegut*, Delacorte, 1977.

Klinkowitz, Jerome, *The American 1960s: Imaginative Acts in a Decade of Change*, Iowa State University Press, 1980.

Klinkowitz, Jerome, *Kurt Vonnegut*, Methuen, 1982.

Klinkowitz, Jerome, *Literary Subversions: New American Fiction and the Practice of Criticism*, Southern Illinois University Press, 1985.

Krementz, Jill, editor, *Happy Birthday, Kurt Vonnegut: A Festschrift for Kurt Vonnegut on His Sixtieth Birthday*, Delacorte, 1982.

Lundquist, James, *Kurt Vonnegut*, Ungar, 1977.

Mayo, Clark, *Kurt Vonnegut: The Gospel from Outer Space, or Yes, We Have No Nirvanas*, Borgo Press, 1973.

Olderman, Raymond M., *Beyond the Wasteland: A Study of the American Novel in the 1960s*, Yale University Press, 1973.

Platt, Charles, *Dream Makers: The Uncommon People Who Write Science Fiction*, Berkley Books, 1980.

Plimpton, George, editor, *Writers at Work: The Paris Review Interviews,* sixth series, Penguin, 1984.

Reed, Peter J., *Kurt Vonnegut, Jr.,* Warner Paperback, 1972.

Schatt, Stanley, *Kurt Vonnegut,* Twayne, 1976.

Short, Robert, *Something to Believe In: Is Kurt Vonnegut Exorcist of Jesus Christ Superstar?,* Harper, 1976.

Tanner, Tony, *City of Words: American Fiction 1950-1970,* Harper, 1971.

Tilton, John W., *Cosmic Satire in the Contemporary Novel,* Bucknell University Press, 1977.

Vonnegut, Kurt, Jr., *Player Piano,* Scribner, 1952, Dell, 1981.

Vonnegut, Kurt, Jr., *Mother Night,* Fawcett, 1962, Harper, 1967.

Vonnegut, Kurt, Jr., *Cat's Cradle,* Holt, 1963.

Vonnegut, Kurt, Jr., *God Bless You, Mr. Rosewater,* Holt, 1965.

Vonnegut, Kurt, Jr., *Slaughterhouse Five,* Seymour Lawrence/Delacorte, 1969.

Vonnegut, Kurt, Jr., *Wampeters, Foma, and Granfalloons,* Seymour Lawrence/Delacorte, 1974.

Vonnegut, Kurt, Jr., *Slapstick,* Seymour Lawrence/Delacorte, 1976.

Vonnegut, Kurt, Jr., *Jailbird,* Seymour Lawrence/Delacorte, 1979.

Vonnegut, Kurt, Jr., *Palm Sunday,* Seymour Lawrence/Delacorte, 1981.

Vonnegut, Kurt, Jr., *Deadeye Dick,* Seymour Lawrence/Delacorte, 1981.

Wohlheim, Donald A., *The Universe Makers,* Harper, 1971.

PERIODICALS

Algol, winter, 1978-79.

America, September 5, 1970, December 8, 1979.

American Literature, May, 1974.

American Poetry Review, January 2, 1973.

Antioch Review, winter, 1983.

Atlantic, September, 1968, May, 1973, October, 1979, April, 1987.

Best Sellers, April 15, 1969, November, 1979.

Books and Bookmen, February, 1969, February, 1973, November, 1973.

Book Week, April 11, 1965.

Book World, August 18, 1968, March 2, 1975, September 2, 1979.

Chicago Tribune, November 15, 1970, January 29, 1982.

Chicago Tribune Book World, August 26, 1979, November 2, 1980, March 1, 1981, October 10, 1982, November 13, 1983, September 22, 1985, October 4, 1985.

Christian Century, August 13, 1969.

Christian Science Monitor, May, 1965, December 5, 1968, September 10, 1979, December 3, 1982.

Cleveland Press, July 10, 1974, July 12, 1974.

Commentary, July, 1974, November, 1975.

Commonweal, September 16, 1966, June 6, 1969, November 27, 1970, May 7, 1971, December 7, 1973.

Critic, September 10, 1973.

Critical Quarterly, winter, 1969.

Critique: Studies in Modern Fiction, Volume 12, number 3, 1971, Volume 14, number 3, 1973, Volume 15, number 2, 1973, Volume 17, number 1, 1975, Volume 18, number 3, 1977, Volume 26, number 2, 1985.

Detroit News, June 18, 1972, September 16, 1979, October 3, 1982, November 10, 1985, January 5, 1986.

Esquire, June, 1968, September, 1970.

Extrapolation, December, 1973.

Film Comment, November/December, 1985.

Globe and Mail (Toronto), March 17, 1984, February 8, 1986, October 17, 1987.

Harper's, May, 1973, July, 1974.

Hollins Critic, October, 1980.

Horizon, October, 1980.

Hudson Review, autumn, 1969.

International Fiction Review, summer, 1980.

Journal of Popular Culture, spring, 1972, winter, 1973.

Library Journal, April 15, 1973.

Life, April 9, 1965, August 16, 1968, September 12, 1969, November 20, 1970.

London Magazine, July, 1981.

Los Angeles Times, February 7, 1983.

Los Angeles Times Book Review, September 23, 1979, October 31, 1982, March 3, 1984, April 18, 1984, September 29, 1985.

Media & Methods, January, 1971.

Modern Fiction Studies, spring, 1973, summer, 1975, winter, 1980-81.

Nation, September 23, 1968, June 9, 1969, September 15, 1979, March 21, 1981, November 13, 1982.

National Observer, June 29, 1974.

National Review, September 28, 1973, November 26, 1976, November 23, 1979, December 10, 1982.

New Republic, August 18, 1952, October 8, 1966, April 26, 1969, November 7, 1970, June 12, 1971, May 12, 1973, September 28, 1973, June 1, 1974, July 5, 1974, September 25, 1976, November 26, 1976.

Newsletter of the Conference on Christianity and Literature, fall, 1972.

New Statesman, April 4, 1975, November 5, 1976.

Newsweek, August 19, 1968, March 3, 1969, April 14, 1969, October 19, 1970, December 20, 1971, May 14, 1973, October 1, 1979.

New York, December 13, 1971.

New Yorker, August 16, 1952, May 15, 1965, May 17, 1969, October 17, 1970, October 25, 1976, November 8, 1982.

New York Review of Books, July 2, 1970, May 31, 1973, November 25, 1976, November 22, 1979.

New York Times, August 18, 1968, September 13, 1969, October 6, 1970, October 18, 1970, May 27, 1971, May 13, 1973, October 3, 1975, September 7, 1979, September 24, 1979, October 15, 1979, March 27, 1981, November 5, 1982, February 4, 1983, February 17, 1983, September 25, 1985, January 27, 1987, April 4, 1987, August 11, 1989.

New York Times Book Review, June 2, 1963, April 25, 1965, August 6, 1967, September 1, 1968, April 6, 1969, February 4, 1973, May 13, 1973, October 3, 1976, September 9, 1979, March 15, 1981, October 17, 1982, October 6, 1985, October 18, 1987.

New York Times Magazine, January 24, 1971.

North American Review, December, 1985.

Novel: A Forum on Fiction, winter, 1975.

Observer, March 22, 1970, November 3, 1985.

Observer Review, March 15, 1970.

Paris Review, spring, 1977.

Partisan Review, Number 1, 1970, Volume 41, number 2, 1974.

People, October 19, 1987.

Progressive, August, 1981.

Publishers Weekly, October 25 1985, January 31, 1986.

Punch, December 4, 1968.

Queen's Quarterly, spring, 1981.

Saturday Review, April 3, 1965, March 29, 1969, February 6, 1971, May 1, 1971, September 15, 1979.

South Atlantic Quarterly, winter, 1979.

Southwest Review, winter, 1971.

Spectator, November 9, 1968.

THOUGHT, March, 1981.

Time, August 30, 1968, April 11, 1969, June 29, 1970, June 3, 1974, October 25, 1976, September 10, 1979, October 21, 1985, October 25, 1982, October 21, 1985, September 28, 1987.

Times (London), July 8, 1981, February 17, 1983, May 17, 1986, May 30, 1987.

Times Literary Supplement, November 11, 1965, December 12, 1968, July 17, 1969, November 5, 1976, December 7, 1979, June 19, 1981, September 26. 1980, February 25, 1983, November 8, 1985.

Tribune Books (Chicago), September 27, 1987.

Twentieth Century Literature, January, 1972.

Village Voice, February 22, 1983.

Virginia Quarterly Review, summer, 1981.

Washington Post, October 12, 1970, May 13, 1973, May 15, 1981, February 2, 1982.

Washington Post Book World, March 8, 1981, October 17, 1982, September 22, 1985, October 4, 1987.

Western Humanities Review, summer, 1974.

World, June 19, 1973.

World Literature Today, winter, 1981.

*   *   *

VOSCE, Trudie
See OZICK, Cynthia

*   *   *

VOZNESENSKY, Andrei (Andreievich) 1933-

PERSONAL: Born May 12, 1933, in Moscow, U.S.S.R.; son of Andrei (an engineer and professor) and Antonina (a teacher; maiden name, Pastuschichina) Voznesensky; married Zoya Boguslavskaya (an author and literary critic); children: Leonid. *Education:* Received degree from Institute of Architecture (Moscow), 1957.

ADDRESSES: Home—Kotelnicheskaya, nab. 1/15, Block W, Apt. 62, Moscow, U.S.S.R. *Agent*—c/o U.S.S.R. Union of Writers, Ulitsa Vorovskogo, 52, Moscow, U.S.S.R.

CAREER: Poet.

MEMBER: Union of Soviet Writers, American Academy of Arts and Letters, Bayerischen Kunst Acad., French Academy Merime.

AWARDS, HONORS: Nomination for Lenin Prize in literature, 1966, for *Antimiry* ("Anti-worlds"); nomination for Books Abroad/Neustadt International Prize for literature, 1975; State Literature Prize, 1978, for *Vitrazhnykh del master;* International award for distinguished achievement in poetry, 1978, for *Nostalgia for the Present.*

WRITINGS:

IN ENGLISH

Selected Poems, translated and introduction by Anselm Hollo, Grove, 1964.

Antimiry, [Moscow], 1964, translation by W. H. Auden, Richard Wilbur, Stanley Kunitz, William Jay Smith, and others published as *Antiworlds,* Basic Books, 1966, enlarged edition published as *Antiworlds and the Fifth Ace,* text in English and Russian, 1967.

Voznesensky: Selected Poems, translation and introduction by Herbert Marshall, Hill & Wang, 1966 (published in England as *Selected Poems,* Methuen, 1966).

Dogalypse (translations from San Francisco poetry reading), City Lights, 1972.

Little Woods: Recent Poems by Andrei Voznesensky (includes poems from *Ten'zvuka;* also see below), translated by Geoffrey Dutton and Igor Mezbakov-Koriakin, introduction by Yevgeny Yevtushenko translated by Eleanor Jacka, Sun Books (Melbourne), 1972.

Avos, translation by Kunitz and others published as *Story Under Full Sail,* Doubleday, 1974.

Nostalgia for the Present, translated by Wilbur, Smith, Lawrence Ferlinghetti, Robert Bly, Allen Ginsburg, and others, forewords by Edward Kennedy and Arthur Miller, Doubleday, 1978.

An Arrow in the Wall: Selected Poetry and Prose, edited and translated by William Jay Smith and Frank D. Reeve, Holt, 1987.

(With others) *Chagall Discovered: From Russian and Private Collections,* H. L. Levin, 1988.

OTHER

Mozaika (title means "Mosaic"), [Vladimir], 1960.

Parabola, [Moscow], 1960.

Pishetsya kak lyubitsya (title means "I Write as I Love"), text in Russian and Italian, Feltrinelli (Milan), 1962.

Treugol'naya grusha (title means "The Triangular Pear"), [Moscow], 1962.

Menya pugayutformalizmom, Flegon Press, 1963.

Akhillesovo serdtse (title means "An Achilles Heart"), [Moscow], 1966.

Moi lybovnyi dnevnik (title means "My Diary of Love"), Flegon Press, 1966.

Stikhi, [Moscow], 1967.

Ten'zvuka (title means "The Shadow of Sound"), [Moscow], 1970.

Vzglyad (title means "The Glance"), [Moscow], 1972.

Vypustiptitsu! (title means "Let the Bird Free"), [Moscow], 1974.

Dubovyi list violonchel'nyi (title means "Violoncello Oak Leaf "),[Moscow], 1975.

Vitrazhnykh del master (title means "The Stained Glass Panel Master"), [Moscow], 1976.

Soblazn (title means "Temptation"), [Moscow], 1978.

Also author of *The Eternal Flesh,* 1978, *Andrey Polisadov,* 1980, and, with others, of *Metropol* (poetry and prose), 1979.

SIDELIGHTS: "The name of Voznesensky in Soviet poetry often becomes the centre of heated discussion," observed Vladimir Ognev. "The young poet leaves nobody indifferent. Widely differing estimations are given to his poetry-some call him a daring innovator, others a cold rhymester." Regardless of the more critical views of his work, Voznesensky warmed the hearts of his followers—and heated the tempers of Soviet officials—during his rise to international prominence in the 1960's. His swift, uncluttered, and often bold verse differed radically from the restricted poetry the Soviet Union had known in the Stalin years; and Russian audiences responded enthusiastically to the young poet's work. Though often compared to the verse of Yevgeny Yevtushenko, Voznesensky's poetry is considered more complex and more intellectual than that of his peer. The public acclaim he enjoyed early in the 1960's dwindled considerably at the end of the decade, largely because of recurrent Soviet crack-downs on authors who failed to promote the country's cause. But Voznesensky continues to write, maintaining the respect of American audiences and a core of American writers in the meantime.

As a child, Voznesensky was introduced to Russia's great literary tradition by his mother, who surrounded him with books by great authors—Blok, Dostoevsky, Pasternak—and read poetry to him as well. Voznesensky experimented a bit with writing when he was young, but devoted himself mainly to painting and drawing. After receiving his degree from the Moscow Architectural Institute, however, his interest in architecture dropped. "Architecture was burned out in me," he recollected. "I became a poet." Some of his poems appeared in magazines at that time and two years later, in 1960, he published his first book, *Mosaika.*

Despite having a tremendously rich Russian poetic tradition to follow, "the only poet who influenced me," Voznesensky once declared, "was Pasternak, who was my god, my father, and for a long time, my university." Strangely, however, Voznesensky feels no similarity between his own poetry and that of his mentor. As a teenager he had sent some of his poems to Pasternak, who consequently invited Vosnesensky to visit. The poems were obvious Pasternak imitations. Later, though, Voznesensky sent some of his post-graduate poems to Pasternak, revealing an entirely different poet. "Yes, this is no longer Pasternak," an admiring Pasternak reportedly said. "This is Voznesensky, a poet in his own right." The compliment encouraged Voznesensky: "I felt I had finally made it." In the 1980s, Voznesensky participated in the drive to reinstate Pasternak into the Soviet Writers' Union, giving the writer official status in the Soviet Union for the first time since 1958.

Several factors contributed to Voznesensky' s "meteoric" rise from a developing poet to one of the Soviet Union's most prominent literary figures. To begin with, poetry is Russia's "national art," contends Voznesensky. This natural interest in poetry combined with a Soviet generation which had "finally achieved sufficient material well-being to afford an interest in spiritual and philosophical matters," reported Peter Young. Thus, when artists like Yevtushenko and Voznesensky began giving poetry readings, these "semipolitical acts," wrote *Newsweek,* "gave voice to the dissatisfaction and exuberance of Soviet youth and created a huge audience" for poetry. By American standards, the audiences were stupendous. Typical crowds for readings by Yevtushenko and Voznesensky numbered more than fourteen thousand. Enthusiasm for the printed word matched the enthusiasm for the spoken. Voznesensky's *Akhillesovo serdtse* ("An Achilles Heart"), for example, had a printing of 100,000 to meet public demand for more than a half-million orders. Such statistics alone support Stanley Kunitz' contention that "the Russian appetite for poetry is simply enormous." Even today, reports say, Voznesensky's new books sell out within hours of publication.

The popularity of Yevtushenko and Vosnesensky brought inevitable comparisons between the two. As Olga Carlisle pointed out, while "Voznesensky's popularity among young Russians is second only to Yevtushenko's . . . he often rates first with the connoisseurs. His verse is full of youthfulness and talent—youth is his main theme as it is Yevtushenko's; in Voznesensky, however, it is never coquettish." David Burg offered another comparison between the two poets: "Voznesensky, a friend and initially a protege of Yevtushenko's, is a poet of an entirely different type. Being more bookish and more clearly conscious of his literary forbears, Voznesensky perpetuates (probably consciously) one specific trend in Russian poetry—the school of futurism, represented by Khlebnikov and Mayakovsky, Tsvetayeva, and Pasternak." According to Robin Milner-Gulland, however, their

shared significance overshadows their differences: "Yevtushenko and Voznesensky: their work is certainly different enough," he declared. "The one rhetorical, the other cerebral; but their melodious names are inseparable, used (not only in the West but in their own country) to typify modem Russian poetry."

For a poet with such a popular audience, Voznesensky can be surprisingly complex; but he has continually defended himself against those who feel he is unnecessarily oblique. "The poet is not the one to supply the answers for mankind," he once contended. "All he can do is pose the questions. And if the poems are complicated, why then so is life. The problem of the poet as a human being is not to become standardized, [but] to be individual, and in this effort the poet provides the reader with the material and way of thinking to achieve it."

To Soviet government officials and heads of the Soviet Writers Union, Voznesensky has been somewhat more of an individual than they would like: many times during his career he has been at the center of controversy. Charges of obscurantism were among the several hurled at Voznesensky in the early 1960's. One especially noteworthy denunciation took place in 1963, when Nikita Khrushchev reprimanded Voznesensky and other Western-oriented intellectuals, accusing them of straying from the paths of "Soviet realism." Attacks continued in 1965 when the government-controlled Communist youth newspaper accused him of obscurity of content and experimenting with complicated poetic forms. Three years later the Soviet press again stood against him, including Voznesensky in a group of "so-called intellectuals [who] continue to display ideological immaturity," reported the *Washington Post.* By 1969, government suppression had erased Voznesensky's name from Soviet literary journals. And, early in 1979, Voznesensky and several other writers were chastised for their roles in the publication of *Metropol,* a new literary magazine which challenged the government's strict control of the arts.

One much publicized incident involving Soviet restrictions occurred in 1967, when a New York City reading had to be canceled. Two days before the scheduled reading, rumors that Voznesensky had been the target of attempts to contain him were confirmed when he wired an uncharacteristically terse message, "Can't come." The powerful and conservative Soviet Writers Union apparently objected to Voznesensky's pro-American attitudes and his refusal to propogate Soviet politics during a previous American tour. (Voznesensky has always avoided political discussions on his U.S. visits.) At first, messages from Moscow said Vosnesensky was sick; later reports revealed that his passport had been sent to the U.S. Embassy with a request for a visa. But renewed hope for Voznesensky's appearance faded when the poet himself phoned New York and canceled his visit. One of the program's participants, Stanley Kunitz, remained unconvinced by the Writers Union's apparent change of heart. "This was a ruse to get off the hook," he charged. "It's very clear what they did. We are not fooled by the last minute reversal [by the Soviet authorities]." Voznesensky himself attacked the Writers Union in a letter addressed to the Communist party newspaper, *Pravda.* "Clearly," he wrote, "the leadership of the union does not regard writers as human beings. This lying, prevarication and knocking people's heads together is standard practice." *Pravda* refused to publish the letter; weeks later it appeared in the *New York Times.*

Despite his conflicts with Soviet authorities, Voznesensky maintains an intense love for his own country. In one poem, for example, "he exalted the ancient idea that it is Russia's mission to save the world from darkness," reported the *New York Times.* He simply believes that artists should enjoy a far more relaxed atmosphere than they do now. Voznesensky has also admired the United States and, particularly, Robert Kennedy. The poet and the senator met together in 1967 and discussed, among other topics, the youth of their respective countries. After Kennedy's death, Voznesensky published a poem paying tribute to his assassinated friend.

Besides earning the attention of U.S. audiences, Voznesensky has become a favorite of several distinguished U.S. literary figures. Among the poets who have translated his work into English are Kunitz, Richard Wilbur, William Jay Smith, Robert Bly, W. H. Auden, Allen Ginsburg, and Lawrence Ferlinghetti. In his introduction to *Nostalgia for the Present,* playwright Arthur Miller assessed Voznesensky's efforts: "He has tried to speak, in these poems, as though he alone had a tongue, as though he alone had learned the news of today and tomorrow, as though the space taken up by his poem were precious and must not be used by counterfeit words." Another Voznesensky admirer, Auden, once gave these reasons for appreciating the poet: "As a fellow maker, I am struck first and foremost by his craftmanship. . . . Obvious, too, at a glance is the wide range of subject matter by which Mr. Voznesensky is imaginatively excited . . . and the variety of tones, eleglac, rebellious, etc., he can command. Lastly, every word he writes, even when he is criticizing, reveals a profound love for his native land and its traditions."

One particular theme in Voznesensky's work is that of the individual lost in a technological society. In his review of *Antiworlds,* Graham Martin noted "Voznesensky's main bogy is 'the cyclotron,' symbol of all the dehumanising pressures in the modern world, and in 'Oza,' a long difficult poem, he deploys all his satiric force against 'the scientist,' damn his eyes." Similarly, M. L. Rosenthal found in Vosnesensky "a satirist . . . who is against the computerization of the soul." As Auden pointed out, however, Voznesensky's focus can vary considerably. Miller Williams explained: "Voznesensky is an exciting writer who bangs and tumbles through his poems, knocking over icons and knocking down walls, talking with curiosity, anguish, and joy—in sharp and startling metaphor—about love and technology, science and art, the self and the soul and Andrei Voznesensky and people." Another admirer, A. Alvarez, praised Voznesensky too, for "whatever direct, passionate thrust launches them [his poems in *Antiworlds*], they curve obliquely and brilliantly through layer after layer of experience before they land again." "They also burst effortlessly through conventions: he mixes slang with formal diction, anger with tenderness, the comic with the serious, and uses every trick of assonance and stress in the book; 'his metrical effects,' W. H. Auden writes, 'must make any translator despair.'"

Translations have been a difficulty with reviewers of Voznesensky's work, especially in some of the earlier volumes. Anselm Hollo's translations in *Selected Poems* (1964), for example, disappointed Gibbons Ruark. Voznesensky's "work is clearly superior to Yevtushenko's," Ruark wrote in comparing the two poets. "Unfortunately, his excellence seldom shows through Anselm Hollo's translations." Critics agreed that Herbert Marshall's translations in *Voznesensky: Selected Poems* surpassed Hollo's. "The volume of selections by Herbert Marshall is, on the whole, an improvement over Anselm Hollo," wrote the Hudson Review. "But it is still an awkward and in places a careless performance." Other translations of Voznesensky's work have received considerably more praise. M. L. Rosenthal compared the translations in *Antiworlds* to those of Marshall and concluded "We are better off with the seven translators of . . . [*Antiworlds*]. They adapt themselves, often superbly, to his tempera-

ment. They help us, through purely poetic means as well as through their attempt to render his sense both literally and connotatively, to feel his compassion, his pain, his hilarity, his buffoonery, his delicacy and calculated coarseness." Meanwhile, Alvarez offered this unequivocal praise for *Antiworlds:* "The translations . . . are immaculate; they simply couldn't have been better done." *Nostalgia for the Present* also featured seven translators, but according to Stefan Kanfer "they are not of equal worth. . . . The best work is the least obtrusive: working with Voznesensky's supple and difficult lines, Max Hayward, Vera Durham and William Jay Smith have given the Russian, both man and language, a new voice."

Voznesensky himself has spoken with a new voice in his later poetry. He has become more introspective; his poems more complex. He explained some changes to William Jay Smith while on his 1977 U.S. reading tour: "When I came before, I was like a rock and roll star. I read poems like 'Goya' and 'Moscow Bells' that were perhaps more dramatic than my recent work. My new poems are more delicate maybe, but I was happy that my audiences liked them too." Voznesensky also detected a change in U.S. audiences, finding them more serious and more conservative than in the past, prompting Smith to wonder if "the poet himself was more mature, probing farther beneath the surface in his search for reality. If so, he had in the process of maturing lost none of the exuberance, humor, and vitality that make him one of the world's finest poets as well as one of the most enjoyable."

BIOGRAPHICAL/CRITICAL SOURCES:

BOOKS

Carlisle, Olga, *Voices in the Snow,* Random, 1962.
Carlisle, Olga, *Poets on Street Corners,* Random, 1969.
Contemporary Literary Criticism, Gale, Volume 1, 1973, Volume 15, 1980.
Voznesensky, Andrei, *Nostalgia for the Present,* Doubleday, 1978.

PERIODICALS

Atlantic, July, 1966.
Christian Science Monitor, April 7, 1966, June 30, 1967, November 13, 1978.
Encounter, July, 1968.
Hudson Review, spring, 1967, autumn, 1968.
Life, April 1, 1966.
Listener, September 7, 1967.
London Magazine, June, 1967.
Los Angeles Times, January 8, 1984, April 8, 1987.
Los Angeles Times Book Review, March 29, 1987.
Nation, November 11, 1968.
New Republic, July 1, 1967, November 18, 1972.
Newsweek, May 15, 1967, July 3, 1967, August 21, 1967.
New Yorker, August 26, 1967.
New York Review of Books, April 14, 1966.
New York Times, August 23, 1965, August 29, 1965, March 24, 1966, March 26, 1966, June 19, 1966, April 1, 1967, April 22, 1967, May 6, 1967, June 19, 1967, June 20, 1967, June 21, 1967, June 22, 1967, August 3, 1967, August 11, 1967, September 7, 1967, June 17, 1968, June 20, 1968, May 27, 1969, May 22, 1978, June 9, 1985, June 18, 1985, October 20, 1986, February 24, 1987, March 16, 1987, June 2, 1987, April 25, 1988.
New York Times Biographical Edition, October 21, 1971.
New York Times Book Review, May 14, 1967, April 16, 1972, December 17, 1978, July 8, 1979, March 29, 1987.
New York Times Magazine, August 20, 1967.

Observer Review, July 9, 1967.

Partisan Review, winter, 1968.

Poetry, April, 1967, November, 1967.

Problems of Communism, September-October, 1962.

Saturday Review, February 4,1978.

Shenandoah, winter, 1968.

Spectator, July 5, 1966.

Time, August 16, 1967, March 9, 1970, May 18, 1970, January 15, 1979.

Times Literary Supplement, November 2, 1967, November 27, 1970, October 11, 1974.

Vogue, February 1, 1972.

Washington Post, June 15, 1968, February 25, 1969, February 4, 1979, May 9, 1987, May 17, 1987.

Washington Post Book World, June 14, 1987.

W

WADE, Alan
See VANCE, John Holbrook

*   *   *

WAIN, John (Barrington) 1925-

PERSONAL: Born March 14, 1925, in Stoke-on-Trent, Staffordshire, England; son of Arnold A. (a dentist) and Anne Wain; married Marianne Urmston, 1947 (divorced, 1956); married Eirian James, 1960; children: William, Ianto, Tobias. *Education:* St. John's College, Oxford, B.A., 1946, M.A., 1950.

ADDRESSES: Home—17 Wolvercote Green, Oxford OX2 8BD, England. *Office*—Century Hutchinson Ltd., 62-65 Chandos Pl., London WC2, England.

CAREER: St. John's College, Oxford University, Oxford, England, Fereday Fellow, 1946-47; University of Reading, Reading, England, lecturer in English literature, 1947-55; writer and critic, 1955—. Churchill Visiting Professor at University of Bristol, 1967; visiting professor at Centre Experimental de Vincennes, University of Paris, 1969; George Elliston Lecturer on Poetry at University of Cincinnati; Professor of Poetry at Oxford University, 1973-78. Director of Poetry Book Society's festival, London, 1961.

MEMBER: Oxford Union Society.

AWARDS, HONORS: Somerset Maugham Award, 1958, for *Preliminary Essays;* Royal Society of Literature fellow, 1960; Brasenose College creative arts fellowship from Oxford University, 1971-72; James Tait Black Memorial Prize and Heinemann Award from Royal Society of Literature, both 1975, both for *Samuel Johnson;* Whitbread Literary Award, 1985, for *The Free Zone Starts Here;* honorary fellow of St. John's College, Oxford, 1985—; companion of the Order of the British Empire.

WRITINGS:

FICTION

Hurry on Down (novel), Secker & Warburg, 1953, published as *Born in Captivity*, Knopf, 1954, published as *Hurry on Down*, Viking, 1965, reprinted with a new introduction by the author, Secker & Warburg, 1978.
Living in the Present (novel), Secker & Warburg, 1955, Putnam, 1960.
The Contenders (novel), St. Martin's, 1958.

A Travelling Woman (novel), St. Martin's, 1959.
Nuncle and Other Stories (short stories), Macmillan (London), 1960, St. Martin's, 1961.
Strike the Father Dead (novel), St. Martin's, 1962.
The Young Visitors (novel), Viking, 1965.
Death of the Hind Legs and Other Stories (short stories), Viking, 1966.
The Smaller Sky (novel), Macmillan, 1967.
A Winter in the Hills (novel; also see below), Viking, 1970.
The Life Guard (short stories), Macmillan, 1971, Viking, 1972.
King Caliban and Other Stories (short stories), Macmillan, 1978.
The Pardoner's Tale (novel), Macmillan, 1978, Viking, 1979.
Lizzie's Floating Shop (juvenile), Bodley Head, 1981.
Young Shoulders (juvenile), Macmillan, 1982, published as *The Free Zone Starts Here*, Delacorte, 1982.
Where the Rivers Meet (novel), Century Hutchinson, 1988.

POETRY

Mixed Feelings, University of Reading, 1951.
(Contributor) D. J. Enright, editor, *Poets of the Fifties,* [London], 1955.
A Word Carved on a Sill, St. Martin's, 1956.
(Contributor) Robert Conquest, editor, *New Lines,* [London], 1956.
Weep before God, St. Martin's, 1961.
A Song about Major Eatherly, Qara Press (Iowa City), 1961.
(Contributor) Chad Walsh, editor, *Today's Poets,* Scribner, 1964.
Wildtrack, Macmillan, 1965, Viking, 1966.
Letters to Five Artists, Macmillan, 1969, Viking, 1970.
The Shape of Feng, Covent Garden Press, 1972.
Feng, Viking, 1975.
Poems for the Zodiac (limited edition), Pisces Press, 1980.
Thinking about Mr. Person, Chimaera Press (Kent), 1980.
Poems, 1949-1979, Macmillan, 1981.
The Twofold, Hunting Raven Press (Somerset), 1981.
Mid-week Period Return: Home Thoughts of a Native, Celandine Press (Stratford-upon-Avon), 1982.

PLAYS

"Harry in the Night," first produced in Stoke-on-Trent, England, 1975.
"You Wouldn't Remember" (radio play), first produced by British Broadcasting Corporation (BBC), 1978.

Frank (radio play; first produced by BBC), Amber Lane Press, 1984.

"Good Morning Blues" (radio play), first produced by BBC, 1986.

Also author of the radio adaptation of *A Winter in the Hills,* 1981.

NONFICTION

Preliminary Essays, St. Martin's, 1957.
Gerard Manley Hopkins: An Idiom of Desperation, Oxford University Press, 1959, reprinted, Folcroft Editions, 1974.
(Contributor) Tom Maschler, editor, *Declaration,* MacGibbon & Kee, 1959.
Sprightly Running: Part of an Autobiography, Macmillan, 1962, St. Martin's, 1963.
Essays on Literature and Ideas, St. Martin's, 1963.
The Living World of Shakespeare: A Playgoer's Guide, St. Martin's, 1964.
Arnold Bennett, Columbia University Press, 1967.
A House for the Truth: Critical Essays, Macmillan, 1972, Viking, 1973.
Samuel Johnson (biography; Book-of-the-Month Club selection), Macmillan, 1974, Viking, 1975.
Professing Poetry, Macmillan, 1977, Viking, 1978.
Dear Shadows: Portraits from Memory, J. Murray, 1986.

EDITOR

Contemporary Reviews of Romantic Poetry, Barnes & Noble, 1953.
Interpretations: Essays on Twelve English Poems, Routledge & Kegan Paul, 1955, Hillary, 1957, 2nd edition, Routledge & Kegan Paul, 1972.
International Literary Annual, two volumes, J. Calder, 1958, 1959, Criterion, 1959, 1960.
Frances Burney d'Arblay, *Fanny Burney's Diary,* Folio Society, 1961.
Anthology of Modern Poetry, Hutchinson, 1963.
(Author of introduction and notes) *Pope,* Dell, 1963.
(Author of introduction) Thomas Hardy, *The Dynasts,* St. Martin's, 1966.
Selected Shorter Poems of Thomas Hardy, Macmillan, 1966.
Selected Stories of Thomas Hardy, St. Martin's, 1966.
Shakespeare: Macbeth; a Casebook, Macmillan, 1968, Aurora Publications, 1970.
Shakespeare: Othello; a Casebook, Macmillan, 1971.
Johnson as Critic, Routledge & Kegan Paul, 1973.
Samuel Johnson, *Lives of the English Poets,* Dent, 1975, Dutton, 1976.
Johnson on Johnson: A Selection of the Personal and Autobiographical Writings of Samuel Johnson, Dutton, 1976.
Edmund Wilson: The Man and His Work, New York University Press, 1978 (published in England as *An Edmund Wilson Celebration,* Phaidon Press, 1978).
Personal Choice: A Poetry Anthology, David & Charles, 1978.
(With wife, Eirian Wain) *The New Wessex Selection of Thomas Hardy's Poetry,* Macmillan, 1978.
Anthology of Contemporary Poetry: Post-War to the Present, Hutchinson, 1979.
Everyman's Book of English Verse, Dent, 1981.
Arnold Bennett, *The Old Wives' Tales,* Penguin, 1983.
James Hogg, *The Private Memoirs and Confessions of a Justified Sinner,* Penguin, 1983.

OTHER

(With Ted Walker) *Modern Poetry* (sound recording), BFA Educational Media, 1972.
The Poetry of John Wain (sound recording), Jeffrey Norton, 1976.
Geoffrey Halson, editor, *A John Wain Selection,* Longman, 1977.
(Translator from Anglo-Saxon) *The Seafarer,* Grenville Press, 1982.

Contributor to numerous periodicals, including *New Republic, Observer, New Yorker, Times Literary Supplement, Saturday Evening Post, Harper's Bazaar,* and *Ladies' Home Journal.* Founding editor of *Mandrake,* 1944.

SIDELIGHTS: For more than thirty years, John Wain, a British man of letters, has devoted his energies primarily to writing. The diversity of his output demonstrates his commitment to his craft—since 1951 he has penned novels, short stories, poetry, critical essays, and a highly acclaimed biography, *Samuel Johnson.* According to *Dictionary of Literary Biography* contributor A. T. Tolley, Wain's novels and stories "make up one of the more substantial bodies of contemporary fiction in English," while his poetry "stands as an important contribution to his total achievement and displays that concern with the life of literature in our day that has permeated his work." Wain is likewise commended for his critical judgments that prove him "adamantly committed to the mystery of literary truths that can advance the universal human experience," in the words of *Dictionary of Literary Biography* essayist Augustus M. Kolich. Kolich calls Wain "an iconoclast who is uncompromising in his dedication to the belief that in a world where 'destruction and disintegration' are the norm, only the artist's creative language can clear the ruins and establish a foundation for heroic individualism." Wain's writings pursue this high ideal in an unpretentious and readable style; Susan Wood notes in the *Washington Post Book World* that the author, while an Oxford graduate, "is no dour Oxford don. . . . Instead, he typifies the very best of what one might call 'Englishness'— good sense, moderation, a feeling for language, erudition without pretension, and wit."

Addressing Wain's fiction specifically, *Esquire* critic Geoffrey Wolff comments: "From his first novel, *Hurry on Down* (1953), Wain has concerned himself with contemporary English manners, with the small choices that comprise a program of values. . . . Wain writes about boredom, the killing regularity of diminished, stunted lives; because he is so skilled a writer, he creates an accurate evocation of the awful coziness and regularity of English conventions." Wain is also preoccupied, in much of his work, with the survival of individual dignity and purpose in a world where bullying and domination often prevail. Kolich states: "In Wain's criticism of contemporary English society, his target is clearly the totalitarian consciousness which has as its object the manipulation and domination of the small child in all of us—that part of our self-concept that naturally sees through folly and pretense and always expects to be left uncontrolled and free. Hence, Wain's fiction is above all morally pledged to a set of values that aim at offending the status quo, when it seems either silly, absurd, or oppressive, and championing commonsense individualism, whenever it can be championed in a world of antiheroes."

This theme of individual rebellion is particularly prevalent in *Hurry on Down,* the novel that established Wain among the clan of writers known as "angry young men" in postwar Great Britain. Set in a provincial town similar to the one in which Wain himself was raised, *Hurry on Down* describes the picaresque adventures of Charles Lumley, a cynical youth who contrives to avoid the respectable middle class lifestyle expected of him by his education and upbringing. *Times Literary Supplement* reviewer Blake Morrison suggests that Lumley could be seen "as representative of a 'less deceived' post-war generation hostile to old values and intent upon radical political change. He and other new heroes in fiction were the subject of much journalistic discussion—discussion which ensured *Hurry on Down*'s success." According to Kolich, Wain came to be identified with his alienated protagonist, even though the author was never comfortable with the way most critics associated him with the "angry decade" movement. Morrison even suggests that the true political significance of the Lumley character "lies in his concern to avoid commitments and his willingness to adapt himself—both features of an era when not anger and rebellion but 'Butskellism' and 'the End of Ideology' were dominant ideals." In any case, *Hurry on Down* was a commercial and critical success for Wain. *South Atlantic Quarterly* contributor Elgin W. Mellown claims that the work "holds the reader by its verisimilitude and artfully contrived though seemingly unposed candid-camera shots of English life in the late forties and early fifties." In his book *Tradition and Dream: The English and American Novel from the Twenties to Our Time,* Walter Allen concludes that *Hurry on Down* made Wain "the satirist of this period of social change."

Disillusioned Englishmen figure in many of Wain's subsequent novels, including *Strike the Father Dead, The Contenders,* and *The Smaller Sky.* Kolich writes: "In the process of breaking away from the confines of economic and social success and the seductive powers of competitive capitalism, Wain's heroes still must face the unsettling business of reordering their lives outside the conventional set plans that either religion or business might offer. . . . Very often, . . . they seem lost and unable to cope with the shifting emotional currents generated by those toward whom they feel drawn." In general, critics have found Wain's novels of the late 1950s and 1960s less successful than his debut fiction work. As Mellown describes it, Wain "commands an almost flawless technique and can write in a truthful, accurate, and revealing way about human beings interacting on the personal level; but when he looks beyond these individuals and attempts to put them into a larger focus or to give them a wider significance, their thoughts and beliefs condemn them as second-rate." In his book entitled *Postwar British Fiction: New Accents and Attitudes,* James Gindin contends: "For the kind of point Wain is making about the contemporary world that he depicts with such specificity, force, and intelligence, he does require some tangible expression of the value of the personal and the humane. But the form of expression often lacks a comic richness that would avoid both the brittle gimmick and the heavy sediment of emotion." Undaunted by the sometimes harsh criticism, Wain has continued to produce fiction. His more recent works have found favor with reviewers, and, in retrospect, his seriousness of purpose and sheer productivity have led Mellown to suggest that "these [early] novels are the most impressive output of any of the postwar British writers."

Kolich describes *A Winter in the Hills,* Wain's 1970 novel, as "perhaps the most typical . . . in terms of themes and characters." The story concerns a philologist who moves to North Wales and becomes involved in a local bus driver's efforts to thwart a business takeover. *Newsweek* contributor Raymond A. Sokolov finds the work "an unashamedly romantic, heroic, plot-heavy, character-ridden, warm piece of narration with a beginning, a middle and an end. . . . Wain proves there is still much life in the old tricks." A *Times Literary Supplement* reviewer asserts that *A Winter in the Hills* "goes farther, perhaps, in defining

and developing Mr. Wain's basic concerns as a writer than most of his earlier works; and does it with a growing maturity and conviction." The reviewer notes Wain's continuing interest in the quality of individual living, and adds, "Observing social situations, catching hints of character and motive in conversational habits, contriving elaborate and efficient plots—these continue to be [Wain's] strengths."

The Pardoner's Tale, published in 1978, has proven even more popular than *A Winter in the Hills.* In *Time,* R. Z. Sheppard calls the work a "thoughtful treatment of two middle-aged men joyfully making fools of themselves over younger women." The book is a novel-within-a-novel; an author, Giles Hermitage, seeks to resolve his own romantic misadventures by writing about a fictitious businessman and his encounter with a woman. The resulting pastiche of stories evokes "a steady sensuous glow that warms the brain," according to Sheppard. *Saturday Review* correspondent Carole Cook contends that it is Wain himself who "shines as the hero" in *The Pardoner's Tale.* "He has beaten the clock," Cook writes, "enticed us into the game, and held us so captivated by his voice of a man desperate for a second chance at life that it becomes, word by word, our own." Amy Wilentz argues a different viewpoint in the *Nation.* She finds *The Pardoner's Tale* a "well-intentioned book," but subsequently declares that there is "so little true atmosphere in Wain's book that his characters, who are sporadically well drawn, also seem shadowy and displaced." Conversely, D. A. N. Jones praises the novel in the *Times Literary Supplement.* "The lineaments of gratified desire are persuasively drawn," Jones asserts. "Precise details of plot and character dissolve into an amorous haze, spreading delight. . . . John Wain's novel is written in a warmly forgiving spirit; and this, together with its engaging riggishness, contributes to the reader's delight."

In an essay for the *Contemporary Authors Autobiography Series,* Wain claims that his book about Samuel Johnson was "the most successful work of my middle life." *Samuel Johnson* provides a comprehensive biography of one of England's leading literary figures, written expressly for the general reader. Most critics praise the account not only for its accessibility to the non-academic public, but also for its subtle reflections on the literary life in any age. *Harper's* reviewer Jack Richardson writes: "To John Wain, Johnson is not only a great figure in literature, he is also a magnificent companion, someone who brings with him a feeling of good company when met for the first time or recalled for the hundredth; and it is this feeling which Wain wishes to celebrate, and which makes *Samuel Johnson* more than anything else a narrative of friendship." In the *Nation,* Robert L. Chapman states: "John Wain's own stature as a literary-academic person assures us a voice both authoritative and eloquent" in *Samuel Johnson,* but the author is still "less interested in the precise delineation of a dead man than in the appraisal of an immortal colleague. . . . I cherish the lively, novelistic quality of [Wain's] book, where I can see an idea being born, growing, and at last enforcing itself as the prime focus of meaning."

Anatole Broyard offers further commendations for *Samuel Johnson* in the *New York Times:* "A good biography of a great man is one of the best ways to define the society he concentrated in himself. Mr. Wain's 'Samuel Johnson' is a brilliant picture of 18th-century England, too." *New York Times Book Review* contributor Christopher Ricks calls the work "vividly humane" and suggests that it "does justice to the range and depth of this just and merciful man. . . . It is a noble story nobly told." Ricks adds: "Johnson's was essentially a commemorative spirit, and Mr. Wain's biography is a dignified achievement because it too is undertaken in a commemorative spirit. Not 'let me tell you about this man,' but 'let us remember together this man.' " As George Gale concludes in the *Spectator,* Wain's biography "is at the end seen to be a very substantial work of synthesis, intuitive understanding and intellectual grasp. . . . We are left with . . . a work which, by persuading us of the stature of its subject, establishes at the same time a very considerable stature of its own."

Wain's poetry is also seen as a significant contribution to the body of English letters since 1945. Tolley explains that, in his early poems, Wain is "affronting the whole modernist poetic, where the emphasis had been on the image, on the maximization of sensory impact, and where generalizations had been seen as the enemies of the poetic. Wain . . . is comfortable with a poetry of statement. However, these [early] poems are far from being doctrinaire literary stunts. Many stand out as simple and passionate statements on what have proved to be some of Wain's abiding themes: love, isolation, honesty, and sympathy for the deprived. . . . Poems . . . seemingly artificial . . . survive as expressions of tenderness." Wain is perhaps better known for his long poems such as *Wildtrack, Feng,* and *Letters to Five Artists.* "Wain's devotion to the long poem," writes Tolley, "is at once courageous and surprising in view of his steady adherence to the realistic tradition in his novels. Whatever may be said about his attainment in his longer poems, he has not been content with the diminished ambitions that have often led to diminished poetry in Britain the last quarter of a century." According to Philip Gardner in the *Times Literary Supplement,* Wain, "concerned with the communication both of humane values and of an imaginative response to experience, . . . sometimes errs on the side of too much clarity: over-insistent, he button-holes the reader or goes on too long." Derek Stanford expresses a different opinion in *Books:* "Wain's unitary theme is the relationship between art and life particularly that between the individual work and the individual producer. . . . All in all, *Letters to Five Artists* is full of vigorous poetry, written in sinewy masculine language but without any of that paraded toughness sometimes indulged in by the New Movement." A *Times Literary Supplement* reviewer concludes that there is "no deliberate order or consistency in Mr. Wain's reflections, except for the unity given by an underlying compassion."

In 1973 Wain was elected to the prestigious Professor of Poetry chair at Oxford. He held the chair for five years, giving lectures on subjects that reflected his critical concerns. These lectures are collected in *Professing Poetry,* his most recent volume of criticism. Kolich contends that, as a literary critic, Wain projects an iconoclasm "derived from a privately felt moral sense of self-determination, a concept that he hopes can be shared by a community of equals, scholars and artists, working toward 'the establishment of a hierarchy of quality.' " According to Herbert Leibowitz in the *New York Times Book Review,* Wain "detests the art chatter and sensationalism of the modern age, with its denial of complexity and the rich diapason of language. For Wain, the imagination is under siege by an 'insistence on explicitness,' 'intellectual slapstick' replaces thought, and our art 'abandons the search for standards' by stupidly rejecting the past." As might be expected of one educated at and honored by Oxford, Wain's critical judgments reside "in his devotion to the idea that the study of the best literature that has been written can provide the criteria for the best judgments," Kolich concludes.

"As a writer I have regarded my basic material as the word rather than as this or that literary form," Wain states in the *Contemporary Authors Autobiography Series.* Wain refuses to be classified as "primarily" one specific sort of writer novelist, poet, or essayist. "I am always primarily what I am doing at the moment," he explains. The author also claims that he knew from an early age that he intended to write, the career being "not a profession but a condition." He offers these thoughts on literature: "The books I most admire are those that take human life as I know it and live it from day to day and describe it honestly and lovingly, and illuminate it fearlessly. As a novelist I have always seen myself as contributing to the central tradition of the novel, the tradition that grew up in the eighteenth century, which means recognisable human beings in familiar settings, doing the kind of things that you and I do, with all the usual consequences. . . . Everything important, everything lyrical and tragic and horrifying and uplifting and miraculous, is there in our ordinary lives if we can open our eyes and see it."

Mellown observes that Wain, who labors "within a tradition sustained by the living presence of earlier literature," is a writer who has consciously developed his skills over three decades. Of all the so-called former "angry young men," according to Mellown, Wain "represents perhaps better than any other the traditional British novelist. His output (in both quantity and versatility) and its quality cause him to be reckoned an outstanding figure of his generation." In *Atlantic,* Benjamin DeMott concludes that in his sober manner, Wain has avoided gags, touched on hard subjects, celebrated classic authors, and produced, on occasion, "an elevated, unironic, unself-protective case for Art-in-the-large." The author, who now divides his time between homes in Oxford and Wales, continues to work—as he puts it in his memoir *Dear Shadows: Portraits from Memory*—"entirely at my own pace and my own sweet will."

AVOCATIONAL INTERESTS: Walking, canoeing.

BIOGRAPHICAL/CRITICAL SOURCES:

BOOKS

Allen, Walter, *Tradition and Dream: The English and American Novel from the Twenties to Our Time,* Phoenix House, 1964.

Allen, Walter, *The Modern Novel,* Dutton, 1965.

Allsop, Kenneth, *The Angry Decade,* P. Owen, 1958.

Burgess, Anthony, *The Novel Now: A Guide to Contemporary Fiction,* Norton, 1967.

Contemporary Authors Autobiography Series, Volume 4, Gale, 1986.

Contemporary Fiction in America and England, 1950-1970, Gale, 1976.

Contemporary Literary Criticism, Gale, Volume 2, 1974, Volume 11, 1979, Volume 15, 1980, Volume 46, 1988.

Dictionary of Literary Biography, Gale, Volume 15: *British Novelists, 1930-1959,* 1983, Volume 27: *Poets of Great Britain and Ireland, 1945-1960,* 1984.

Enright, D. J., *Conspirators and Poets,* Dufour, 1966.

Fraser, G. S. *The Modern Writer and His World,* Penguin, 1964.

Gerard, David, *My Work as a Novelist: John Wain,* Drake Educational Associates (Cardiff, Wales), 1978.

Gindin, James J., *Postwar British Fiction: New Accents and Attitudes,* University of California Press, 1962.

Karl, Frederick R., *The Contemporary English Novel,* Farrar, Straus, 1962.

Maschler, Tom, editor, *Declaration,* MacGibbon & Kee, 1959.

O'Connor, William Van, *The New University Wits and the End of Modernism,* Southern Illinois University Press, 1963.

Ries, Lawrence R., *Wolf Masks: Violence in Contemporary Poetry,* Kennikat, 1977.

Salwak, Dale, *John Braine and John Wain: A Reference Guide,* G. K. Hall, 1980.

Salwak, Dale, *John Wain,* G. K. Hall, 1981.

Wain, John, *Sprightly Running: Part of an Autobiography,* Macmillan, 1962, St. Martin's, 1963,

Wain, John, *Dear Shadows: Portraits from Memory,* John Murray, 1986.

PERIODICALS

Atlantic, May, 1979.
Best Sellers, October 15, 1971.
Books Abroad, summer, 1967.
Books and Bookmen, October, 1967.
Commonweal, February 10, 1967.
Contemporary Review, October, 1978, January, 1979.
Esquire, April 10, 1979.
Globe and Mail (Toronto), June 16, 1984.
Harper's, July, 1975, July, 1979.
Listener, October 12, 1967, October 26, 1978.
London Magazine, November, 1956, October, 1967.
Los Angeles Times, May 17, 1970.
Los Angeles Times Book Review, August 6, 1978.
Nation, October 5, 1970, April 19, 1975, April 7, 1979.
New Leader, July 3, 1978.
New Republic, March 15, 1975.
New Statesman, October 6, 1967, May 19, 1978.
Newsweek, September 14, 1970, February 17, 1975.
New Yorker, April 28, 1975, May 7, 1979.
New York Review of Books, April 14, 1966, March 23, 1967, February 20, 1975.
New York Times, February 13, 1975, December 26, 1978, April 6, 1979.
New York Times Book Review, January 25,' 1959, October 24, 1965, December 18, 1966, September 13, 1970, March 19, 1972, July 29, 1973, March 16, 1975, March 25, 1979.
Observer, October 8, 1967, May 3, 1970, December 20, 1970.
Poetry, February, 1978.
Punch, October 11, 1967.
Saturday Review, May 7, 1955, July 27, 1957, October 16, 1965, December 3, 1966, February 8, 1975, April 28, 1979.
South Atlantic Quarterly, summer, 1969, autumn, 1979.
Spectator, May 16, 1970, November 30, 1974, May 3, 1986.
Stand, Volume XVII, number 1, 1975-76.
Time, April 2, 1979.
Times (London), January 7, 1984, April 24, 1986.
Times Educational Supplement, July 20, 1956.
Times Literary Supplement, July 26, 1963, July 29, 1965, September 30, 1965, October 3, 1966, October 5, 1967, July 3, 1969, February 12, 1970, April 30, 1971, November 19, 1971, March 8, 1974, November 22, 1974, September 26, 1975, February 24, 1978, May 19, 1978, October 13, 1978, November 17, 1978, February 27, 1981, July 10, 1981, October 15, 1982, April 25, 1986.
Washington Post Book World, February 23, 1975, October 8, 1978, April 22, 1979, May 13, 1984.
Wilson Library Bulletin, May, 1963.
World Literature Today, spring, 1979.
Yale Review, winter, 1967.

*   *   *

WALCOTT, Derek (Alton) 1930-

PERSONAL: Born January 23, 1930, in Castries, St. Lucia, West Indies; son of Warwick (a civil servant) and Alix (a teacher) Walcott; married Fay Moston, 1954 (divorced, 1959); married Margaret Ruth Maillard, 1962 (divorced); married Norline Metivier (actress and dancer); children: (first marriage) one son; (second marriage) two daughters. *Education:* St. Mary's College, St. Lucia, B.A., 1953; attended University of the West Indies, Kingston, Jamaica.

ADDRESSES: Home—165 Duke of Edinburgh Ave., Diego Martin, Trinidad and Tobago, (summers); 71 St. Mary's, Brookline, Mass. 02146 (winters). *Office*—Creative Writing Department, Boston University, 236 Bay State Rd., Boston, Mass. 02215. *Agent*—Bridget Aschenberg, International Famous Agency, 1301 Avenue of the Americas, New York, N.Y. 10019.

CAREER: Poet and playwright. Teacher at St. Mary's College, St. Lucia, at Boys' Secondary School, Grenada, and at Kingston College, Jamaica. Founding director of Trinidad Theatre Workshop, 1959—. Visiting professor at Columbia University, 1981, and Harvard University, 1982; visiting professor in Creative Writing Department of Boston University, 1985—. Also lecturer at Rutgers and Yale Universities.

AWARDS, HONORS: Rockefeller fellowship, 1957; Jamaica Drama Festival prize, 1958, for "Drums and Colours"; Guinness Award, 1961; Heinemann Award, Royal Society of Literature, 1966, for *The Castaway,* and, 1983, for *The Fortunate Traveller;* Cholmondeley Award, 1969, for *The Gulf;* Eugene O'Neill Foundation-Wesleyan University fellowship, 1969; Order of the Humming Bird, Trinidad and Tobago, 1969; Obie Award, 1971, for "Dream On Monkey Mountain"; D.H.L., University of the West Indies, 1972; Jock Campbell/*New Statesman* Prize, 1974, for *Another Life;* National Writer's Council Prize, Welsh Arts Council, 1979; John D. and Catherine T. MacArthur Foundation grant, 1981; Los Angeles Times Book Review Prize in poetry, 1986, for *Collected Poems, 1948-1984;* Queen Elizabeth II Gold Medal for Poetry, 1988.

WRITINGS:

POETRY

Twenty-Five Poems, Guardian Commercial Printery, 1948.
Epitaph for the Young: A Poem in XII Cantos, Advocate (Bridgetown, Barbados), 1949.
Poems, Kingston City Printery (Jamaica), 1953.
In a Green Night: Poems, 1948-1960 (also see below), J. Cape, 1962.
Selected Poems (includes poems from *In a Green Night: Poems, 1948-1960*), Farrar, Straus, 1964.
The Castaway and Other Poems (also see below), J. Cape, 1965.
The Gulf and Other Poems, J. Cape, 1969, published with selections from *The Castaway and Other Poems* as *The Gulf: Poems,* Farrar, Straus, 1970.
Another Life (long poem), Farrar, Straus, 1973, 2nd edition published with introduction, chronology and selected bibliography by Robert D. Hammer, Three Continents Press, 1982.
Sea Grapes, J. Cape, 1976, slightly revised edition, Farrar, Straus, 1976.
Selected Verse, Heinemann, 1976.
The Star-Apple Kingdom, Farrar, Straus, 1979.
The Fortunate Traveller, Farrar, Straus, 1981.
Selected Poetry, selected, annotated and introduced by Wayne Brown, Heinemann, 1981.
The Caribbean Poetry of Derek Walcott, and the Art of Romare Beardon, Limited Editions Club (New York), 1983.
Midsummer, Farrar, Straus, 1984.
Collected Poems, 1948-1984, Farrar, Straus, 1986.
The Arkansas Testament, Farrar, Straus, 1987.
Omeros, Farrar, Straus, 1989.

PLAYS

Henri Christophe: A Chronicle in Seven Scenes (first produced in Castries, St. Lucia, West Indies, 1950, produced in London, England, 1951), Advocate (Bridgetown, Barbados), 1950.
Harry Dernier: A Play for Radio Production, Advocate, 1951.

Wine of the Country, University College of the West Indies (Mona, Jamaica), 1953.

The Sea at Dauphin: A Play in One Act (first produced in Mona, Jamaica, 1953, produced in London, 1960; also see below), Extra-Mural Department, University College of the West Indies, 1954.

Ione: A Play with Music (first produced in Port of Spain, Trinidad, 1957), Extra-Mural Department, University College of the West Indies, 1957.

"Drums and Colours: An Epic Drama" (published in *Caribbean Quarterly,* March-June, 1961), first produced in Kingston, Trinidad, April 23, 1958.

"In a Fine Castle," first produced in Jamaica, 1970, produced in Los Angeles, Calif., 1972.

"Ti-Jean and His Brothers" (also see below), first produced in Port of Spain, Trinidad, 1958, produced Off-Broadway at Delacorte Theatre, July 20, 1972.

Malcochon; or, Six in the Rain (one-act; first produced as "Malcochon" in Castries, St. Lucia, 1959, produced in London under title "Six in the Rain," 1960, produced Off-Broadway at St. Mark's Playhouse, March 25, 1969; also see below), Extra-Mural Department, University of West Indies, 1966.

"Dream on Monkey Mountain" (also see below), first produced in Toronto, Ontario, Canada, 1967, produced Off-Broadway at St. Mark's Playhouse, March 9, 1971.

Dream on Monkey Mountain and Other Plays (contains "Dream on Monkey Mountain," "Sea at Dauphin," "Malcochon; or, Six in the Rain," "Ti-Jean and His Brothers," and the essay "What the Twilight Says: An Overture"; also see below), Farrar, Straus, 1970.

"The Joker of Seville" (musical; also see below), first produced in Port of Spain, Trinidad, 1974.

"The Charlatan," first produced in Los Angeles, 1974.

"O Babylon!" (also see below), first produced in Port of Spain, Trinidad, 1976.

"Remembrance" (three-act; also see below), first produced in St. Croix, Virgin Islands, December, 1977, produced Off-Broadway at The Other Stage, May 9, 1979.

"Pantomime" (also see below), Port of Spain, Trinidad, 1978, produced at the Hudson Guild Theater, 1986.

The Joker of Seville & O Babylon!: Two Plays, Farrar, Straus, 1978.

Remembrance & Pantomime: Two Plays, Farrar, Straus, 1980.

"The Isle Is Full of Noises," first produced at the John W. Huntington Theater, in Hartford, Conn., April, 1982.

Three Plays: The Last Carnival; Beef, No Chicken; A Branch of the Blue Nile, Farrar, Straus, 1986.

Also author of "Franklin, a Tale of the Islands," "Jourmard," and "To Die for Grenada."

CONTRIBUTOR

John Figueroa, editor, *Caribbean Voices,* Evans, 1966.

Barbara Howes, editor, *From the Green Antilles,* Macmillan, 1966.

Howard Sergeant, editor, *Commonwealth Poems of Today,* Murray, 1967.

O. R. Dathorne, editor, *Caribbean Verse,* Heinemann, 1968.

Anne Walmsley, compiler, *The Sun's Eye: West Indian Writing for Young Readers,* Longmans, 1968.

Orde Coombs, editor, *Is Massa Day Dead?,* Doubleday, 1974.

D. J. Enright, editor, *Oxford Book of Contemporary Verse, 1945-80,* Oxford University Press, 1980.

Errol Hill, editor, *Plays for Today,* Longman, 1985.

Also contributor to *Caribbean Literature,* edited by George Robert Coulthard; *New Voices of the Commonwealth,* edited by Sergeant; and, *Young Commonwealth Poetry,* edited by Peter Ludwig Brent.

OTHER

Art and literature critic for *Trinidad Guardian;* feature writer for *Public Opinion* (Jamaica). Contributor of poems to numerous periodicals, including *New Statesman, London Magazine, Encounter, Evergreen Review, Caribbean Quarterly, Tamarack Review,* and *Bim.*

SIDELIGHTS: Although born of mixed racial and ethnic heritage on St. Lucia, a West Indian island where a French/English patois is spoken, poet and playwright Derek Walcott was educated as a British subject. Taught to speak English as a second language, he grew to be a skilled craftsman in his adopted tongue. His use of the language has drawn praise from critics including British poet and novelist Robert Graves who, according to *Times Literary Supplement* contributor Vicki Feaver, "has gone as far to state that [Walcott] handles English with a closer understanding of its inner magic than most (if not all) of his English-born contemporaries."

Walcott's major theme is the dichotomy between black and white, subject and ruler, Caribbean and Western civilization present in his culture and ancestry. In "What the Twilight Says," the introduction to *Dream on Monkey Mountain and Other Plays,* Walcott refers to his "schizophrenic boyhood" in which he led "two lives: the interior life of poetry [and] the outward life of action and dialect." In *Derek Walcott* Robert D. Hamner notes that this schizophrenia is common among West Indians and comments further that "since [Walcott] is descended from a white grandfather and a black grandmother on both paternal and maternal sides, he is a living example of the divided loyalties and hatreds that keep his society suspended between two worlds."

"As a West Indian . . . writing in English, with Africa and England in his blood," Alan Shapiro writes in the *Chicago Tribune Book World,* "Walcott is inescapably the victim and beneficiary of the colonial society in which he was reared. He is a kind of a Caribbean Orestes . . . unable to satisfy his allegiance to one side of his nature without at the same time betraying the other." Caryl Phillips describes Walcott's work in much the same way in her *Los Angeles Times Book Review* essay. The critic notes that Walcott's poetry is "steeped in an ambivalence toward the outside world and its relationship to his own native land of St. Lucia."

One often-quoted poem, "A Far Cry from Africa," from *In a Green Night,* deals directly with Walcott's sense of cultural confusion. "Where shall I turn, divided to the vein? / I who have cursed / the drunken officer of British rule, how choose / Between this Africa and the English tongue I love? / Betray them both, or give back what they give?"

In another poem, "The Schooner Flight," from his second collection, *The Star-Apple Kingdom,* the poet uses a Trinidad sailor named Shabine to appraise his own place as a person of mixed blood in a world divided into whites and blacks. According to the mariner: "The first chain my hands and apologize, 'History'; / the next said I wasn't black enough for their pride." Not white enough for whites, not black enough for blacks, Shabine sums up the complexity of his situation near the beginning of the poem saying: "I had a sound colonial education, / I have Dutch, nigger and English in me, / and either I'm nobody or I'm a nation."

It is Walcott, of course, who is speaking, and *New York Review of Books* contributor Thomas R. Edwards notes how the poet suffers the same fate as his poetic alter-ego, Shabine. Edwards writes, "Walcott is a cultivated cosmopolitan poet who is black, and as such he risks irrelevant praise as well as blame, whites finding it clever of him to be able to sound so much like other sophisticated poets, blacks feeling that he's sold his soul by practicing white arts."

Although pained by the contrasts in his background, Walcott has chosen to embrace both his island and colonial heritage. His love of both sides of his psyche is apparent in an analysis of his work. As Hamner notes: "Nurtured on oral tales of gods, devils, and cunning tricksters passed down by generations of slaves, Walcott should retell folk stories; and he does. On the other hand, since he has an affinity for and is educated in Western classics, he should retell the traditional themes of European experience; and he does. As inheritor of two vitally rich cultures, he utilizes one, then the other, and finally creates out of the two his own personalized style."

Walcott seems closest to his island roots in his plays. For the most part, he has reserved his native language—patois or creole—to them. They also feature Caribbean settings and themes. According to *Literary Review* contributor David Mason, through Walcott's plays he hopes to create a "catalytic theater responsible for social change or at least social identity."

Although a volume of poems was his first published work, Walcott originally concentrated his efforts on the theater. In the fifties, he wrote a series of plays in verse, including *Henri Christophe: A Chronicle, The Sea at Dauphin,* and *Ione.* The first play deals with an episode in Caribbean history: ex-slave Henri Christophe's rise to kingship of Haiti in the early 1800s. The second marks Walcott's first use of the mixed French/English language of his native island in a play.

In *Dictionary of Literary Biography Yearbook: 1981* Dennis Jones notes that while Walcott uses the folk idiom of the islands in the play, the speech of the characters is not strictly imitative. It is instead "made eloquent, as the common folk represented in the work are made noble, by the magic of the artist."

In "What the Twilight Says" Walcott describes his use of language in his plays. In particular, he expresses the desire to mold "a language that went beyond mimicry, . . . one which finally settled on its own mode of inflection, and which begins to create an oral culture, of chants, jokes, folk-songs, and fables."

The presence of "chants, jokes, and fables" in Walcott's plays causes critics such as Jones and the *Los Angeles Times*'s Juana Duty Kennedy to call the playwright's best pieces for theater folk dramas. In *Books and Bookmen* Romilly Cavan observes the numerous folk elements in Walcott's plays: "The laments of superstitious fishermen, charcoal-burners and prisoners are quickly counter-pointed by talking crickets, frogs, and birds. Demons are raised, dreams take actual shape, [and] supernatural voices mingle with the natural lilting elliptical speech rhythms of downtrodden natives." Animals who speak and a folk-representation of the devil are characters, for example, in the play, "Ti-Jean and His Brothers."

Walcott's most highly praised play, *Dream on Monkey Mountain,* is also a folk drama. It was awarded a 1971 Obie Award and deemed "a poem in dramatic form" by Edith Oliver in the *New Yorker.* The play's title is itself enough to immediately transport the viewer into the superstitious legend-filled world of the Caribbean backcountry.

In the play, Walcott draws a parallel between the hallucinations of an old charcoal vendor and the colonial reality of the Caribbean. Islanders subjected to the imposition of a colonial culture over their own eventually question the validity of both cultures. Ultimately, they may determine that their island culture—because it has no official status other than as an enticement for tourists—is nothing but a sterile hallucination. Or, as Jones notes, they may reach the conclusion at which Walcott wishes his audience to arrive: the charcoal vendor's "dreams connect to the past, and that it is in that past kept alive in the dreams of the folk that an element of freedom is maintained in the colonized world."

Perhaps because of critics' unfamiliarity with the Caribbean reality which Walcott describes in his plays, the author's work for theater has received only mixed reviews in this country. For example, while Walter Goodman writes in the *New York Times* that Walcott's "Pantomime" "stays with you as a fresh and funny work filled with thoughtful insights and illuminated by bright performances," the *New York Times*'s Frank Rich's comments on the same play are not as favorable. "Walcott's best writing has always been as a poet . . . ," Rich observes, "and that judgment remains unaltered by 'Pantomime.' For some reason, [he] refuses to bring the same esthetic rigor to his playwriting that he does to his powerfully dense verse."

In James Atlas's *New York Times Magazine* biographical/critical essay on Walcott, the critic confronts Rich's remarks head on, asserting that the poet would respond to Rich by commenting "that he doesn't conceive of his plays as finished works but as provisional effects to address his own people. 'The great challenge to me,' he says, 'was to write as powerfully as I could without writing down to the audience, so that the large emotions could be taken in by a fisherman or a guy on the street, even if he didn't understand every line.' "

If Walcott's plays reveal what is most Caribbean about him, his poetry reveals what is most English. If he hopes to reach the common man in his plays, the same cannot be said of his poetry. His poems are based on the traditional forms of English poetry, filled with classical allusions, elaborate metaphors, complex rhyme schemes, and other poetic devices.

In the *New York Times Book Review,* Selden Rodman calls Walcott's poems "almost Elizabethan in their richness." The *New York Times*'s Michiko Kakutani agrees, noting that "from England, [Walcott] appropriated an old-fashioned love of eloquence, an Elizabethan richness of words and a penchant for complicated, formal rhymes. In fact, in a day when more and more poets have adopted a grudging, minimalist style, [his] verse remains dense and elaborate, filled with dazzling complexities of style."

Some critics object that Walcott's attention to style sometimes detracts from his poetry, either by being unsuitable for his Caribbean themes or by becoming more important than the poems' content. Denis Donoghue, for example, remarks in the *New York Times Book Review,* "It is my impression that his standard English style [is] dangerously high for nearly every purpose except that of Jacobean tragedy." In Steve Ratiner's *Christian Science Monitor* review of *Midsummer,* the critic observes that "after a time, we are so awash in sparkling language and intricate metaphor, the subject of the poem is all but obscured." In her *New York Review of Books* essay, Helen Vendler finds an "unhappy disjunction between [Walcott's] explosive subject . . . and his harmonious pentameters, his lyrical allusions, his stately rhymes, [and] his Yeatsian meditations."

More criticism comes from those who maintain that the influence of other poets on Walcott's work have drowned out his authentic voice. While Vendler, for instance, describes Walcott as a "man of great sensibility and talent," she dismisses much of his poetry as "ventriloquism" and maintains that in Walcott's 1982 collection of poems, *The Fortunate Traveller,* he seems "at the mercy of influence, this time the influence of Robert Lowell."

Poet J. D. McClatchy also notices Lowell's influence in *The Fortunate Traveller* as well as two other Walcott poetry collections: *The Star-Apple Kingdom* and *Midsummer.* In his *New Republic* review McClatchy not only finds similarities in the two men's styles but also a similar pattern of development in their poetry. "Like Lowell," the critic notes, "Walcott's mode has . . . shifted from the mythological to the historical, from fictions to facts, and his voice has gotten more clipped and severe. There are times when the influence is almost too direct, as in 'Old New England,' [a poem from *The Fortunate Traveller,*] where he paces off Lowell's own territory."

Both major criticisms of Walcott's poetry are answered in Sven Birkerts's *New Republic* essay. Birkerts observes: "Walcott writes a strongly accented, densely packed line that seldom slackens and yet never loses conversational intimacy. He works in form, but he is not formal. His agitated phonetic surfaces can at times recall Lowell's, but the two are quite different. In Lowell, one feels the torque of mind; in Walcott, the senses predominate. And Walcott's lines ring with a spontaneity that Lowell's often lack."

Other critics defend the integrity of Walcott's poems. Poet James Dickey notes in the *New York Times Book Review,* "Fortunately, for him and for us, . . . Walcott has the energy and the exuberant strength to break through his literary influences into a highly colored, pulsating realm of his own." In his *Poetry* review of *Midsummer* Paul Breslin writes: "For the most part, . . . Walcott's voice remains as distinctive as ever, and the occasional echoes of Lowell register as homage rather than unwitting imitation."

Hamner maintains that when dealing with Walcott's poetry the term assimilation rather than imitation should be used. The critic observes: "Walcott passed through his youthful apprenticeship phase wherein he consciously traced the models of established masters. He was humble enough to learn from example and honest enough to disclose his intention to appropriate whatever stores he found useful in the canon of world literature. . . . But Walcott does not stop with imitation. Assimilation means to ingest into the mind and thoroughly comprehend; it also means to merge into or become one with a cultural tradition."

The uniqueness of Walcott's work stems from his ability to interweave British and island influences, to express what McClatchy calls "his mixed state" and do so "without indulging in either ethnic chic or imperial drag." His plays offer pictures of the common Caribbean folk and comment on the ills bred by colonialism. His poetry combines native patois and English rhetorical devices in a constant struggle to force an allegiance between the two halves of his split heritage.

According to *Los Angeles Times Book Review* contributor Arthur Vogelsang, "These continuing polarities shoot an electricity to each other which is questioning and beautiful and which helps form a vision all together Caribbean and international, personal (him to you, you to him), independent, and essential for readers of contemporary literature on all the continents."

BIOGRAPHICAL/CRITICAL SOURCES:

BOOKS

Contemporary Literary Criticism, Gale, Volume 2, 1974, Volume 4, 1975, Volume 9, 1978, Volume 14, 1980, Volume 25, 1983, Volume 42, 1987.
Dictionary of Literary Biography Yearbook: 1981, Gale, 1982.
Goldstraw, Irma, *Derek Walcott: An Annotated Bibliography of His Works,* Garland Publishing, 1984.
Hamner, Robert D., *Derek Walcott,* Twayne, 1981.
Walcott, Derek, *Collected Poems, 1948-1984,* Farrar, Straus, 1986.
Walcott, Derek, *Dream on Monkey Mountain and Other Plays,* Farrar, Straus, 1970.

PERIODICALS

Books and Bookmen, April, 1972.
Book World, December 13, 1970.
Chicago Tribune Book World, May 2, 1982, September 9, 1984, March 9, 1986.
Christian Science Monitor, March 19, 1982, April 6, 1984.
Georgia Review, summer, 1984.
Hudson Review, summer, 1984.
Literary Review, spring, 1986.
London Magazine, December, 1973-January, 1974, February-March, 1977.
Los Angeles Times, November 12, 1986.
Los Angeles Times Book Review, April 4, 1982, May 21, 1985, April 6, 1986, October 26, 1986, September 6, 1987.
Nation, February 12, 1977, May 19, 1979, February 27, 1982.
National Review, November 3, 1970, June 20, 1986.
New Republic, November 20, 1976, March 17, 1982, January 23, 1984, March 24, 1986.
New Statesman, March 19, 1982.
New Yorker, March 27, 1971, June 26, 1971.
New York Magazine, August 14, 1972.
New York Review of Books, December 31,1964, May 6, 1971, June 13, 1974, October 14, 1976, May 31, 1979, March 4, 1982.
New York Times, March 21, 1979, August 21, 1979, May 30, 1981, May 2, 1982, January 15, 1986, December 17, 1986.
New York Times Book Review, September 13, 1964, October 11, 1970, May 6, 1973, October 31, 1976, May 13, 1979, January 3, 1982, April 8, 1984, February 2, 1986, December 20, 1987.
New York Times Magazine, May 23, 1982.
Poetry, February, 1972, December, 1973, July, 1977, December, 1984, June, 1986.
Review, winter, 1974. Spectator, May 10, 1980.
Time, March 15, 1982.
Times (London), March 24, 1990.
Times Literary Supplement, December 25, 1969, August 3, 1973, July 23, 1976, August 8, 1980, September 8, 1980, September 24, 1982, November 9, 1984, October 24, 1986.
Tribune Books (Chicago), November 8, 1987.
TriQuarterly, winter, 1986.
Village Voice, April 11, 1974.
Virginia Quarterly Review, winter, 1974, summer, 1984.
Washington Post Book World, February 21, 1982, April 13, 1986.
Western Humanities Review, spring, 1977.
World Literature Today, spring, 1977, summer, 1979, summer, 1981, winter, 1985, summer, 1986, winter, 1987.
Yale Review, October, 1973.

WALDO, E. Hunter
    See STURGEON, Theodore (Hamilton)

*   *   *

WALDO, Edward Hamilton
    See STURGEON, Theodore (Hamilton)

*   *   *

WALKER, Alice (Malsenior) 1944-

PERSONAL: Born February 9, 1944, in Eatonton, Ga.; daughter of Willie Lee and Minnie Tallulah (Grant) Walker; married Melvyn Rosenman Leventhal (a civil rights lawyer), March 17, 1967 (divorced, 1976); children: Rebecca Grant. *Education:* Attended Spelman College, 1961-63; Sarah Lawrence College, B.A., 1965.

ADDRESSES: Home—San Francisco, Calif. *Office*—Wild Trees Press, P.O. Box 378, Navarro, Calif. 95463.

CAREER: Writer. Wild Trees Press, Navarro, Calif., co-founder and publisher, 1984-88. Has been a voter registration worker in Georgia, a worker in Head Start program in Mississippi, and on staff of New York City welfare department. Writer in residence and teacher of black studies at Jackson State College, 1968-69, and Tougaloo College, 1970-71; lecturer in literature, Wellesley College and University of Massachusetts—Boston, both 1972-73; distinguished writer in Afro-American studies department, University of California, Berkeley, spring, 1982; Fannie Hurst Professor of Literature, Brandeis University, Waltham, Mass., fall, 1982. Lecturer and reader of own poetry at universities and conferences. Member of board of trustees of Sarah Lawrence College. Consultant on black history to Friends of the Children of Mississippi, 1967.

AWARDS, HONORS: Bread Loaf Writer's Conference, scholar, 1966; first prize, American Scholar essay contest, 1967; Merrill writing fellowship, 1967; McDowell Colony fellowship, 1967, 1977-78; National Endowment for the Arts grant, 1969, 1977; Radcliffe Institute fellowship, 1971-73; Ph.D., Russell Sage College, 1972; National Book Award nomination, 1973, for *Revolutionary Petunias and Other Poems;* Lillian Smith Award, Southern Regional Council, 1973, for *Revolutionary Petunias;* Richard and Hinda Rosenthal Foundation Award, American Academy and Institute of Arts and Letters, 1974, for *In Love and Trouble;* Guggenheim Award, 1977-78; National Book Critics Circle Award nomination, 1982, Pulitzer Prize, 1983, and American Book Award, 1983, all for *The Color Purple;* D.H.L., University of Massachusetts, 1983; O. Henry Award, 1986, for "Kindred Spirits."

WRITINGS:

POETRY

Once: Poems (also see below), Harcourt, 1968, reprinted, Women's Press, 1988.
Five Poems, Broadside Press, 1972.
Revolutionary Petunias and Other Poems (also see below), Harcourt, 1973.
Goodnight, Willie Lee, I'll See You in the Morning (also see below), Dial, 1979.
Horses Make a Landscape Look More Beautiful, Harcourt, 1984.
Alice Walker Boxed Set—Poetry: Good Night, Willie Lee, I'll See You in the Morning; Revolutionary Petunias and Other Poems; Once, Poems, Harcourt, 1985.

FICTION

The Third Life of Grange Copeland (novel; also see below), Harcourt, 1970.
In Love and Trouble: Stories of Black Women (also see below), Harcourt, 1973.
Meridian (novel), Harcourt, 1976.
You Can't Keep a Good Woman Down (short stories; also see below), Harcourt, 1981.
The Color Purple (novel), Harcourt, 1982.
Alice Walker Boxed Set—Fiction: The Third Life of Grange Copeland, You Can't Keep a Good Woman Down, and In Love and Trouble, Harcourt, 1985.
To Hell with Dying (juvenile), illustrations by Catherine Deeter, Harcourt, 1988.
The Temple of My Familiar (novel), Harcourt, 1989.

CONTRIBUTOR TO ANTHOLOGIES

Helen Haynes, editor, *Voices of the Revolution,* E. & J. Kaplan (Philadelphia), 1967.
Langston Hughes, editor, *The Best Short Stories by Negro Writers from 1899 to the Present: An Anthology,* Little, Brown, 1967.
Robert Hayden, David J. Burrows, and Frederick R. Lapides, compilers, *Afro-American Literature: An Introduction,* Harcourt, 1971.
Toni Cade Bambara, compiler, *Tales and Stories for Black Folks,* Zenith Books, 1971.
Woodie King, compiler, *Black Short Story Anthology,* New American Library, 1972.
Arnold Adoff, compiler, *The Poetry of Black America: An Anthology of the Twentieth Century,* Harper, 1973.
Lindsay Patterson, editor, *A Rock against the Wind: Black Love Poems,* Dodd, 1973.
Sonia Sanchez, editor, *We Be Word Sorcerers: Twenty-five Stories by Black Americans,* Bantam, 1973.
Mary Anne Ferguson, compiler, *Images of Women in Literature,* Houghton, 1973.
Margaret Foley, editor, *Best American Short Stories: 1973,* Hart-Davis, 1973.
Foley, editor, *Best American Short Stories, 1974,* Houghton, 1974.
Michael S. Harper and Robert B. Stepto, editors, *Chants of Saints: A Gathering of Afro-American Literature, Art and Scholarship,* University of Illinois Press, 1980.
Mary Helen Washington, editor, *Midnight Birds: Stories of Contemporary Black Women Authors,* Anchor Press, 1980.
Dexter Fisher, editor, *The Third Woman: Minority Women Writers of the United States,* 1980.

OTHER

Langston Hughes: American Poet (children's biography), Crowell, 1973.
(Editor) *I Love Myself When I'm Laughing . . . and Then Again When I Am Looking Mean and Impressive: A Zora Neale Hurston Reader,* introduction by Mary Helen Washington, Feminist Press, 1979.
In Search of Our Mothers' Gardens: Womanist Prose, Harcourt, 1983.
Living by the Word: Selected Writings, 1973-1987, Harcourt, 1988.

Contributor to periodicals, including *Negro Digest, Denver Quarterly, Harper's, Black World,* and *Essence.* Contributing editor, *Southern Voices, Freedomways,* and *Ms.*

WORK IN PROGRESS: Finding the Green Stone, "a fable," with Catherine Deeter.

SIDELIGHTS: "*The Color Purple,* Alice Walker's third [novel,] could be the kind of popular and literary event that transforms an intense reputation into a national one," according to Gloria Steinem of *Ms.* Judging from the critical enthusiasm for *The Color Purple,* Steinem's words have proved prophetic. Walker "has succeeded," as Andrea Ford notes in the *Detroit Free Press,* "in creating a jewel of a novel." Peter S. Prescott presents a similar opinion in a *Newsweek* review. "I want to say," he comments, "that *The Color Purple* is an American novel of permanent importance, that rare sort of book which (in Norman Mailer's felicitous phrase) amounts to 'a diversion in the fields of dread.'"

Although Walker's other books—novels, volumes of short stories, and poems—have not been completely ignored, they have not received the amount of attention that many critics feel they deserve. For example, William Peden, writing about *In Love and Trouble: Stories of Black Women* in *The American Short Story: Continuity and Change, 1940-1975,* calls the collection of stories "a remarkable book that deserves to be much better known and more widely read." And while Steinem points out that *Meridian,* Walker's second novel, "is often cited as the best novel of the civil rights movement, and is taught as part of some American history as well as literature courses," Steinem maintains that Walker's "visibility as a major American talent has been obscured by a familiar bias that assumes white male writers, and the literature they create, to be the norm. That puts black women (and all women of color) at a double remove."

Jeanne Fox-Alston and Mel Watkins both feel that the appeal of *The Color Purple* is that the novel, as a synthesis of characters and themes found in Walker's earlier works, brings together the best of the author's literary production in one volume. Fox-Alston, in the *Chicago Tribune Book World,* remarks: "Celie, the main character in Walker's third . . . novel, *The Color Purple,* is an amalgam of all those women [characters in Walker's previous books]; she embodies both their desperation and, later, their faith." Watkins states in the *New York Times Book Review:* "Her previous books . . . have elicited praise for Miss Walker as a lavishly gifted writer. *The Color Purple,* while easily satisfying that claim, brings into sharper focus many of the diverse themes that threaded their way through her past work."

Walker's central characters are almost always black women; the themes of sexism and racism are predominant in her work, but her impact is felt across both racial and sexual boundaries. Walker, according to Steinem, "comes at universality through the path of an American black woman's experience. . . . She speaks the female experience more powerfully for being able to pursue it across boundaries of race and class." This universality is also noted by Fox-Alston, who remarks that Walker has a "reputation as a provocative writer who writes about blacks in particular, but all humanity in general."

However, many critics see a definite black and female focus in Walker's writings. For example, in her review of *The Color Purple,* Ford suggests that the novel transcends "culture and gender" lines but also refers to Walker's "unabashedly feminist viewpoint" and the novel's "black . . . texture." Walker does not deny this dual bias; the task of revealing the condition of the black woman is particularly important to her. Thadious M. Davis, in his *Dictionary of Literary Biography* essay, comments: "Walker writes best of the social and personal drama in the lives of familiar people who struggle for survival of self in hostile environments. She has expressed a special concern with 'exploring the oppressions, the insanities, the loyalties and the triumph of

black women.'" Walker explains in a *Publishers Weekly* interview: "The black woman is one of America's greatest heroes. . . . Not enough credit has been given to the black woman who has been oppressed beyond recognition."

Critics reviewing Walker's first collection of short stories, *In Love and Trouble: Stories of Black Women,* respond favorably to the author's rendering of the black experience. In *Ms.* Barbara Smith observes: "This collection would be an extraordinary literary work, if its only virtue were the fact that the author sets out consciously to explore with honesty the textures and terror of black women's lives. Attempts to penetrate the myths surrounding black women's experiences are so pitifully rare in black, feminist, or American writing that each shred of truth about these experiences constitutes a breakthrough. The fact that Walker's perceptions, style, and artistry are also consistently high makes her work a treasure." Mary Helen Washington remarks in a *Black World* review: "The stories in *In Love and Trouble . . .* constitute a painfully honest, searching examination of the experiences of thirteen Black women." The critic continues: "The broad range of these characters is indication of the depth and complexity with which Alice Walker treats a much-abused subject: the Black woman."

Walker bases her description of black women on what Washington refers to as her "unique vision and philosophy of the Black woman." According to Barbara A. Bannon of *Publishers Weekly,* this philosophy stems from the "theme of the poor black man's oppression of his family and the unconscious reasons for it." Walker, in her interview with the same magazine, asserts: "The cruelty of the black man to his wife and family is one of the greatest [American] tragedies. It has mutilated the spirit and body of the black family and of most black mothers." Through her fiction, Walker describes this tragedy. For instance, Smith notes: "Even as a black woman, I found the cumulative impact of these stories [contained *In Love and Trouble*] devastating. . . . Women love their men, but are neither loved nor understood in return. The affective relationships are [only] between mother and child or between black woman and black woman." David Guy's commentary on *The Color Purple* in the *Washington Post Book World* includes this evaluation: "Accepting themselves for what they are, the women [in the novel] are able to extricate themselves from oppression; they leave their men, find useful work to support themselves." Watkins further explains: "In *The Color Purple* the role of male domination in the frustration of black women's struggle for independence is clearly the focus."

Some reviewers criticize Walker's fiction for portraying an overly negative view of black men. Katha Pollitt, for example, in the *New York Times Book Review,* calls the stories in *You Can't Keep a Good Woman Down* "too partisan." The critic adds: "The black woman is *always* the most sympathetic character." Guy notes: "Some readers . . . will object to her overall perspective. Men in [*The Color Purple*] are generally pathetic, weak and stupid, when they are not heartlessly cruel, and the white race is universally bumbling and inept." Charles Larson, in his *Detroit News* review of *The Color Purple,* points out: "I wouldn't go as far as to say that all the male characters [in the novel] are villains, but the truth is fairly close to that." However, neither Guy nor Larson feel that this emphasis on women is a major fault in the novel. Guy, for example, while conceding that "white men . . . are invisible in Celie's world," observes: "This really is Celie's perspective, however—it is psychologically accurate to her—and Alice Walker might argue that it is only a neat inversion of the view that has prevailed in western culture for centuries." Larson also notes that by the end of the novel, "several of [Walker's] masculine characters have reformed."

This idea of reformation, this sense of hope even in despair, is at the core of Walker's vision, even though, as John F. Callahan states in *New Republic*, "There is often nothing but pain, violence, and death for black women [in her fiction]." In spite of the brutal effects of sexism and racism suffered by the characters of her short stories and novels, critics note what Art Seidenbaum of the *Los Angeles Times* calls Walker's sense of "affirmation . . . [that] overcomes her anger." This is particularly evident in *The Color Purple*, according to reviewers. Ford, for example, asserts that the author's "polemics on . . . political and economic issues finally give way to what can only be described as a joyful celebration of human spirit—exulting, uplifting and eminently universal." Prescott discovers a similar progression in the novel. He writes: "[Walker's] story begins at about the point that most Greek tragedies reserve for the climax, then . . . by immeasurable small steps . . . works its way toward acceptance, serenity and joy." Walker, according to Ray Anello, who quotes the author in *Newsweek*, agrees with this evaluation. Questioned about the novel's importance, Walker explains: "Let's hope people can hear Celie's voice. There are so many people like Celie who make it, who come out of nothing. People who triumph."

Davis refers to this idea as Walker's "vision of survival" and offers a summary of its significance in Walker's work. "At whatever cost, human beings have the capacity to live in spiritual health and beauty; they may be poor, black, and uneducated, but their inner selves can blossom." This vision, extended to all humanity, is evident in Walker's collection *Living by the Word: Selected Writings 1973-1987*. Although "her original interests centered on black women, and especially on the ways they were abused or underrated," *New York Times Book Review* contributor Noel Perrin believes that "now those interests encompass all creation." Judith Paterson similarly observes in Chicago *Tribune Books* that in *Living by the Word*, "Walker casts her abiding obsession with the oneness of the universe in a question: Do creativity, love and spiritual wholeness still have a chance of winning the human heart amid political forces bent on destroying the universe with poisonous chemicals and nuclear weapons?" Walker explores this question through journal entries and essays that deal with Native Americans, racism in China, a lonely horse, smoking, and response to the criticism leveled against both the novel and film version of *The Color Purple*. Many of these treatments are personal in approach, and Jill Nelson finds many of them trivial. Writing in the *Washington Post Book World*, Nelson comments that "*Living by the Word* is fraught with . . . reaches for commonality, analogy and universality. Most of the time all Walker achieves is banality." But Derrick Bell differs, noting in his *Los Angeles Times Book Review* critique that Walker "uses carefully crafted images that provide a universality to unique events." The critic further asserts that *Living by the Word* "is not only vintage Alice Walker: passionate, political, personal, and poetic, it also provides a panoramic view of a fine human being saving her soul through good deeds and extraordinary writing."

MEDIA ADAPTATIONS: The Color Purple was made into a feature film by Warner Brothers in 1985; the film was directed by Steven Spielberg, and received several Academy Award nominations.

BIOGRAPHICAL/CRITICAL SOURCES:

BOOKS

Bestsellers 89, Issue 4, Gale, 1989.

Contemporary Literary Criticism, Gale, Volume 5, 1976, Volume 6, 1976, Volume 9, 1978, Volume 19, 1981, Volume 27, 1984, Volume 46, 1988.
Dictionary of Literary Biography, Gale, Volume 6: *American Novelists since World War II, 2nd series,* 1980, Volume 33: *Afro-American Fiction Writers after 1955,* 1984.
Evans, Mari, editor, *Black Women Writers (1950-1980): A Critical Evaluation,* Anchor, 1984.
O'Brien, John, *Interviews with Black Writers,* Liveright, 1973.
Peden, William, *The American Short Story: Continuity and Change, 1940-1975,* 2nd edition, revised and enlarged, Houghton, 1975.
Prenshaw, Peggy W., editor, *Women Writers of the Contemporary South,* University Press of Mississippi, 1984.

PERIODICALS

American Scholar, winter, 1970-71, summer, 1973.
Ann Arbor News, October 3, 1982.
Atlantic, June, 1976.
Black Scholar, April, 1976.
Black World, September, 1973, October, 1974.
Chicago Tribune, December 20, 1985, September 10, 1989.
Chicago Tribune Book World, August 1, 1982, September 15, 1985.
Commonweal, April 29, 1977.
Detroit Free Press, August 8, 1982, July 10, 1988, January 4, 1989.
Detroit News, September 15, 1982, October 23, 1983, March 31, 1985.
Freedomways, winter, 1973.
Globe and Mail (Toronto), December 21, 1985.
Jet, February 10, 1986.
Los Angeles Times, April 29, 1981, June 8, 1983.
Los Angeles Times Book Review, August 8, 1982, May 29, 1988, May 21, 1989.
Ms., February, 1974, July, 1977, July, 1978, June, 1982, September, 1986.
Nation, November 12, 1973, December 17, 1983.
Negro Digest, September-October, 1968.
New Leader, January 25, 1971.
New Republic, September 14, 1974, December 21, 1974.
Newsweek, May 31, 1976, June 21, 1982.
New Yorker, February 27, 1971, June 7, 1976.
New York Review of Books, January 29, 1987.
New York Times, December 18, 1985, January 5, 1986.
New York Times Book Review, March 17, 1974, May 23, 1976, May 29, 1977, December 30, 1979, May 24, 1981, July 25, 1982, April 7, 1985, June 5, 1988, April 30, 1989.
New York Times Magazine, January 8, 1984.
Oakland Tribune, November 11, 1984.
Parnassus: Poetry in Review, spring-summer, 1976.
Poetry, February, 1971, March, 1980.
Publishers Weekly, August 31, 1970, February 26, 1988.
Saturday Review, August 22, 1970.
Southern Review, spring, 1973.
Times Literary Supplement, August 19, 1977, June 18, 1982, July 20, 1984, September 27, 1985, April 15, 1988, September 22, 1989.
Tribune Books (Chicago), July 17, 1988.
Washington Post, October 15, 1982, April 15, 1983, October 17, 1983.
Washington Post Book World, November 18, 1973, October 30, 1979, December 30, 1979, May 31, 1981, July 25, 1982, December 30, 1984, May 29, 1988.
World Literature Today, winter, 1985, winter, 1986.

Yale Review, autumn, 1976.

* * *

WALKER, Margaret (Abigail) 1915-

PERSONAL: Born July 7, 1915, in Birmingham, Ala.; daughter of Sigismund C. (a Methodist minister) and Marion (Dozier) Walker (a music teacher); married Firnist James Alexander, June 13, 1943 (deceased); children: Marion Elizabeth, Firnist James, Sigismund Walker, Margaret Elvira. *Education:* Northwestern University, A.B., 1935; University of Iowa, M.A., 1940, Ph.D., 1965. *Religion:* Methodist.

ADDRESSES: Home—2205 Guynes St., Jackson, Miss. 39213. *Office*—Department of English, Jackson State College, Jackson, Miss. 39217.

CAREER: Worked as a social worker, newspaper reporter, and magazine editor; Livingstone College, Salisbury, N.C., member of faculty, 1941-42; West Virginia State College, Institute, W.Va., instructor in English, 1942-43; Livingstone College, professor of English, 1945-46; Jackson State College, Jackson, Miss., professor of English, 1949—, director of Institute for the Study of the History, Life, and Culture of Black Peoples, 1968—. Lecturer, National Concert and Artists Corp. Lecture Bureau, 1943-48. Visiting professor in creative writing, Northwestern University, spring, 1969. Staff member, Cape Cod Writers Conference, Craigville, Mass., 1967 and 1969. Participant, Library of Congress Conference on the Teaching of Creative Writing, 1973.

MEMBER: National Council of Teachers of English, Modern Language Association, Poetry Society of America, American Association of University Professors, National Education Association, Alpha Kappa Alpha.

AWARDS, HONORS: Yale Series of Younger Poets Award, 1942, for *For My People;* named to Honor Roll of Race Relations, a national poll conducted by the New York Public Library, 1942; Rosenthal fellowship, 1944; Ford fellowship for study at Yale University, 1954; Houghton Mifflin Literary Fellowship, 1966; Fulbright fellowship, 1971; National Endowment for the Humanities, 1972; Doctor of Literature, Northwestern University, 1974; Doctor of Letters, Rust College, 1974; Doctor of Fine Arts, Dennison University, 1974; Doctor of Humane Letters, Morgan State University, 1976.

WRITINGS:

POETRY

For My People, Yale University Press, 1942, reprinted, Ayer Co., 1969.
Ballad of the Free, Broadside Press, 1966.
Prophets for a New Day, Broadside Press, 1970.
October Journey, Broadside Press, 1973.
For Farish Street Green, [Jackson, Miss.], 1986.
(With John Warner) *Apparitions,* Jamestown Pubs., 1987.
This Is My Century: New and Collected Poems, University of Georgia Press, 1988.

PROSE

Jubilee (novel), Houghton, 1965, Bantam, 1981.
How I Wrote "Jubilee," Third World Press, 1972 (also see below).
(With Nikki Giovanni) *A Poetic Equation: Conversations between Nikki Giovanni and Margaret Walker,* Howard University Press, 1974, reprinted with new postscript, 1983.

(Author of introduction) *Black Women and Liberation Movements,* edited by Virginia A. Blansford, Institute for the Arts and Humanities, Howard University, 1981.
Richard Wright: Daemonic Genius, Dodd, 1987.
How I Wrote Jubilee and Other Essays on Life and Literature, edited by Maryemma Graham, Feminist Press, 1989.

CONTRIBUTOR

Addison Gayle, editor, *Black Expression,* Weybright & Tally, 1969.
Stanton L. Wormley and Lewis H. Fenderson, editors, *Many Shades of Black,* Morrow, 1969.
Henderson, Stephen, *Understanding the New Black Poetry: Black Speech and Black Music as Poetic References,* Morrow, 1973.

Also contributor to numerous anthologies, including Adoff's *Black Out Loud,* Weisman and Wright's *Black Poetry for All Americans,* and Williams's *Beyond the Angry Black.*

OTHER

Contributor to *Yale Review, Negro Digest, Poetry, Opportunity, Phylon, Saturday Review,* and *Virginia Quarterly.*

WORK IN PROGRESS: Minna and Jim, a sequel to *Jubilee; Mother Broyer,* a novel; an autobiography, for Howard University Press.

SIDELIGHTS: When *For My People* by Margaret Walker won the Yale Younger Poets Series Award in 1942, "she became one of the youngest Black writers ever to have published a volume of poetry in this century," as well as "the first Black woman in American literary history to be so honored in a prestigious national competition," notes Richard K. Barksdale in *Black American Poets between Worlds, 1940-1960.* Walker's first novel, *Jubilee,* is notable for being "the first truly historical black American novel," according to University of Maryland professor Joyce Anne Joyce, reports *Washington Post* contributor Crispin Y. Campbell. It was also the first work by a black writer to speak out for the liberation of the black woman. The cornerstones of a literature that affirms the African folk roots of black American life, these two books have also been called visionary for looking toward a new cultural unity for black Americans that will be built on that foundation.

The title of Walker's first book, *For My People,* denotes the subject matter of "poems in which the body and spirit of a great group of people are revealed with vigor and undeviating integrity," says Louis Untermeyer in the *Yale Review.* Here, in long ballads, Walker draws sympathetic portraits of characters such as the New Orleans sorceress Molly Means; Kissie Lee, a tough young woman who dies "with her boots on switching blades;" and Poppa Chicken, an urban drug dealer and pimp. Other ballads give a new dignity to John Henry, killed by a ten-pound hammer, and Stagolee, who kills a white officer but eludes a lynch mob. In an essay for *Black Women Writers (1950-1980): A Critical Evaluation,* Eugenia Collier notes, "Using . . . the language of the grass-roots people, Walker spins yarns of folk heroes and heroines: those who, faced with the terrible obstacles which haunt Black people's very existence, not only survive but prevail—with style." Soon after it appeared, the book of ballads, sonnets and free verse found a surprisingly large number of readers, requiring publishers to authorize three printings to satisfy popular demand.

Some critics found fault with the sonnets in the book, but others deemed it generally impressive, R. Baxter Miller summarizes in *Black American Poets between Worlds.* "The title poem is itself a singular and unique literary achievement," Barksdale claims. In *Black American Literature: A Critical History,* Roger Whitlow elaborates, "The poem, written in free verse, rhythmically catalogues the progress of black American experience, from the rural folkways, religious practices, and exhausting labor of the South, through the cramped and confusing conditions of the northern urban centers, to what she hopes will be a racial awakening, blacks militantly rising up to take control of their own destinies." Collier relates, "The final stanza is a reverberating cry for redress. It demands a new beginning. Our music then will be martial music; our peace will be hard-won, but it will be 'written in the sky.' And after the agony, the people whose misery spawned strength will control our world. This poem is the hallmark of Margaret Walker's works. It echoes in her subsequent poetry and even in her monumental novel *Jubilee.* It speaks to us, in our words and rhythms, of our history, and it radiates the promise of our future. It is the quintessential example of myth and ritual shaped by artistic genius."

Reviewers especially praise Walker's control of poetic technique in the poem. Dudley Randall writes in Addison Gayle's *The Black Aesthetic,* "The poem gains its force . . . by the sheer overpowering accumulation of a mass of details delivered in rhythmical parallel phrases." To cite Barksdale, "it is magnificently wrought oral poetry. . . . In reading it aloud, one must be able to breathe and pause, pause and breathe preacher-style. One must be able to sense the ebb and flow of the intonations. . . . This is the kind of verbal music found in a well-delivered downhome folk sermon." By giving the poem a musical rhythm, Walker underscores the poem's message, observes Barksdale: "The poet here is writing about the source of the Black peoples' blues, for out of their troubled past and turbulent present came the Black peoples' song." In this case, Walker steps forward to remind her people of the strength to he found in their cultural tradition as she calls for a new, hopeful literature that can inspire social action.

"If the test of a great poem is the universality of statement, then 'For My People' is a great poem," remarks Barksdale. The critic explains in Donald B. Gibson's *Modern Black Poets: A Collection of Critical Essays* that the poem was written when "world-wide pain, sorrow, and affliction were tangibly evident, and few could isolate the Black man's dilemma from humanity's dilemma during the depression years or during the war years." Thus, the power of resilience presented in the poem is a hope Walker holds out not only to black people, but to all people, to "all the adams and eves." As she once remarked, "Writers should not write exclusively for black or white audiences, but most inclusively. After all, it is the business of all writers to write about the human condition, and all humanity must be involved in both the writing and in the reading."

Jubilee, a historical novel, is the second book on which Walker's literary reputation rests. It is the story of a slave family during and after the civil war, and took her thirty years to write. During these years, she married a disabled veteran, raised four children, taught full time at Jackson State College in Mississippi, and earned a Ph.D. from the University of Iowa. The lengthy gestation, she believes, partly accounts for the book's quality. As she told Claudia Tate in *Black Women Writers at Work,* "Living with the book over a long period of time was agonizing. Despite all of that, *Jubilee* is the product of a mature person," one whose own difficult pregnancies and economic struggles could lend authenticity to the lives of her characters. "There's a difference between writing about something and living through it," she said in the interview; "I did both."

The story of *Jubilee*'s main characters Vyry and Randall Ware was an important part of Walker's life even before she began to write it down. As she explains in *How I Wrote "Jubilee,"* she first heard about the "slavery time" in bedtime stories told by her maternal grandmother. When old enough to recognize the value of her family history, Walker took initiative, "prodding" her grandmother for more details, and promising to set down on paper the story that had taken shape in her mind. Later on, she completed extensive research on every aspect of the black experience touching the Civil War, from obscure birth records to information on the history of tin cans. "Most of my life I have been involved with writing this story about my great-grandmother, and even if *Jubilee* were never considered an artistic or commercial success I would still be happy just to have finished it," she claims.

Soon after *Jubilee* was published in 1966, Walker was given a Fellowship award from Houghton-Mifflin, and a mixed reception from critics. Granting that the novel is "ambitious," *New York Times Book Review* contributor Wilma Dykeman deemed it "uneven." Arthur P. Davis, writing in *From the Dark Tower: Afro-American Writers, 1900-1960,* suggests that the author "has crowded too much into her novel." Even so, say reviewers, the novel merits praise. Abraham Chapman of the *Saturday Review* appreciates the author's "fidelity to fact and detail" as she "presents the little-known everyday life of the slaves," their music, and their folkways. In the *Christian Science Monitor,* Henrietta Buckmaster comments, "In Vyry, Miss Walker has found a remarkable woman who suffered one outrage after the other and yet emerged with a humility and a mortal fortitude that reflected a spiritual wholeness." Dykeman concurs, "In its best episodes, and in Vyry, 'Jubilee' chronicles the triumph of a free spirit over many kinds of bondages." Later critical studies of the book emphasize the importance of its themes and its position as the prototype for novels that present black history from a black perspective. Claims Whitlow, "It serves especially well as a response to white 'nostalgia' fiction about the antebellum and Reconstruction South."

Walker's next book to be highly acclaimed was *Prophets for a New Day,* a slim volume of poems. Unlike the poems in *For My People,* which, in a Marxist fashion, names religion an enemy of revolution, says Collier, *Prophets for a New Day* "reflects a profound religious faith. The heroes of the sixties are named for the prophets of the Bible: Martin Luther King is Amos, Medgar Evars is Micah, and so on. The people and events of the sixties are paralleled with Biblical characters and occurrences. . . . The religious references are important. Whether one espouses the Christianity in which they are couched is not the issue. For the fact is that Black people from ancient Africa to now have always been a spiritual people, believing in an existence beyond the flesh." One poem in *Prophets* that harks back to African spiritism is "Ballad of Hoppy Toad" with its hexes that turn a murderous conjurer into a toad. Though Collier feels that Walker's "vision of the African past is fairly dim and romantic," the critic goes on to say that this poetry "emanates from a deeper area of the psyche, one which touches the mythic area of a collective being and reenacts the rituals which define a Black collective self." Perhaps more importantly, in all the poems, says Collier, Walker depicts "a people striking back at oppression and emerging triumphant."

Walker disclosed in *A Poetic Equation: Conversations between Nikki Giovanni and Margaret Walker* that the poem "Ballad of the Free" in *Prophets* articulates "better than even 'For My People' so much of what I [feel] about black people and the whole movement toward freedom." Davis calls the book "the best poetical comment to come from the civil rights movement—the movement which came to a climax with the march on Washington and which began thereafter to change into a more militant type of liberation effort." Barksdale shares this view; as he comments in *Black American Poets between Worlds,* "Because of her experience, background, and training—her familial gift of word power, her intensive apprenticeship in Chicago's literary workshop in the 1930s, and her mastery of Black orature—her *Prophets . . .* stands out as the premier poetic statement of the death-riddled decade of the 1960s. The poems of this small volume reflect the full range of the Black protest during the time—the sit-ins, the jailings, the snarling dogs, the . . . lynching of the three Civil Rights workers in Mississippi. All of the poems in the volume touch the sensitive nerve of racial memory and bring back, in sharply etched detail, the trauma and tension and triumphs of that period."

In the same essay, Barksdale relates that Walker's books owe little to her academic life and much to a rich cultural sensibility gained in her youth. "There was . . . New Orleans with its . . . folk mythology, its music, . . . and its assortment of racial experiences to be remembered and recalled." And there was the shaping influence of Walker's parents. Born in Jamaica but educated at Atlanta's Gammon Theological Institute, her father was a Methodist preacher. Her mother, Marion (nee Dozier), was a musician. "So [the poet] grew up in a household ruled by the power of the word, for undoubtedly few have a greater gift for articulate word power than an educated Jamaican trained to preach the doctrine of salvation in the Black South," Barksdale remarks. In such a home, survival "without mastery of words and language was impossible," he adds, citing Walker's comment. And, given her family background, Walker felt destined for an academic career.

That career was characterized by opposition and difficulty. In the interview with Tate, Walker reflects, "I'm a third-generation college graduate. Society doesn't want to recognize that there's this kind of black writer. I'm the Ph.D. black woman. That's horrible. That is to be despised. I didn't know how bad it was until I went back to school [to teaching] and found out." With her older children nearing college age, Walker had taken leave from her position at Jackson State University to earn an advanced degree in hope that afterward she would be given more pay. She returned only to be slighted by the administration. Eventually, she developed the school's black studies program, attaining personal fulfillment only during the last years of her career as an educator.

Discouragements of many kinds have not kept Walker from producing works that have encouraged many. *For My People, Jubilee,* and *Prophets for a New Day* are valued for their relation to social movements of twentieth century America. In 1937, the poem "For My People" called for a new generation to gather strength from a militant literature, and the black literature of the 1960s—including the autobiographies of Malcolm X, Eldridge Cleaver, Huey Newton, and Angela Davis, to name just a few—answered that challenge, suggests C.W.E. Bigsby in *The Second Black Renaissance: Essays in Black Literature.* Her example over the years has also proved to be instructive. This summary of Walker's achievement closes the epilogue of *How I Wrote "Jubilee":* "She has revealed the creative ways in which methods and materials of the social science scholar may be joined with the craft and viewpoint of the poet/novelist to create authentic black literature. She has reaffirmed for us the critical importance of oral tradition in the creation of our history. . . . Finally, she has made awesomely clear to us the tremendous costs which must be paid in stubborn, persistent work and commitment if we are indeed to write our own history and create our own literature."

BIOGRAPHICAL/CRITICAL SOURCES:

BOOKS

Bankier, Joanna and Dierdre Lashgari, editors, *Women Poets of the World,* Macmillan, 1983.

Baraka, Amiri, *The Black Nation,* Getting Together Publications, 1982.

Bigsby, C.W.E., editor, *The Second Black Renaissance: Essays in Black Literature,* Greenwood Press, 1980.

Contemporary Literary Criticism, Gale, Volume 1, 1973, Volume 2, 1976.

Dictionary of Literary Biography, Volume 76: *Afro-American Writers, 1940-1955,* Gale, 1988.

Davis, Arthur P., *From the Dark Tower: Afro-American Writers, 1900 to 1960,* Howard University Press, 1974.

Emanuel, James A., and Theodore L. Gross, editors, *Dark Symphony: Negro Literature in America,* Free Press, 1968.

Evans, Mari, editor, *Black Women Writers (1950-1980): A Critical Evaluation,* Anchor/Doubleday, 1982.

Gayle, Addison, editor, *The Black Aesthetic,* Doubleday, 1971.

Gibson, Donald B., editor, *Modern Black Poets: A Collection of Critical Essays,* Prentice-Hall, 1983.

Jackson, Blyden and Louis D. Rubin, Jr., *Black Poetry in America: Two Essays in Historical Interpretation,* Louisiana State University Press, 1974.

Jones, John Griffith, in *Mississippi Writers Talking,* Volume II, University of Mississippi Press, 1983.

Kent, George E., *Blackness and the Adventure of Western Culture,* Third World Press, 1972.

Lee, Don L., *Dynamite Voices I: Black Poets of the 1960s,* Broadside Press, 1971.

Miller, R. Baxter, editor, *Black American Poets between Worlds, 1940-1960,* University of Tennessee Press, 1986.

Redmond, Eugene B., *Drumvoices: The Mission of Afro-American Poetry—A Critical Evaluation,* Doubleday, 1976.

Tate, Claudia, editor, *Black Women Writers at Work,* Continuum, 1983.

Walker, Margaret, *For My People,* Yale University Press, 1942, reprinted, Ayer Co., 1969.

Walker, Margaret, *How I Wrote "Jubilee,"* Third World Press, 1972.

Walker, Margaret, and Nikki Giovanni, *A Poetic Equation: Conversations between Nikki Giovanni and Margaret Walker,* Howard University Press, 1974, reprinted with a new postscript, 1983.

Walker, Margaret, *Prophets for a New Day,* Broadside Press, 1970.

Whitlow, Roger, *Black American Literature: A Critical History,* Nelson Hall, 1973.

PERIODICALS

Atlantic, December, 1942.

Best Sellers, October 1, 1966.

Black World, December, 1971, December, 1975.

Books, January 3, 1973.

Book Week, October 2, 1966.

Callaloo, May, 1979.

Christian Science Monitor, November 14, 1942, September 29, 1966, June 19, 1974.

Common Ground, autumn, 1943.

Ebony, February, 1949.

Freedomways, Volume 2, number 3, summer, 1967.

National Review, October 4, 1966.

Negro Digest, February, 1967, January, 1968.
New Republic, November 23, 1942.
New York Times, November 4, 1942.
New York Times Book Review, August 2, 1942, September 25, 1966.
Opportunity, December, 1942.
Publishers Weekly, April 15, 1944, March 24, 1945.
Saturday Review, September 24, 1966.
Times Literary Supplement, June 29, 1967.
Washington Post, February 9, 1983.
Yale Review, winter, 1943.

*   *   *

WALLACE, Dexter
See MASTERS, Edgar Lee

*   *   *

WALLACE, Irving 1916-1990

PERSONAL: Born March 19, 1916, in Chicago, Ill.; died of pancreatic cancer, June 29, 1990, in Los Angeles, Calif.; son of Alexander and Bessie (Liss) Wallace; married Sylvia Kahn (a writer), June 3, 1941; children: David Wallechinsky, Amy Wallace. *Education:* Attended Williams Institute, Berkeley, Calif., and Los Angeles City College.

ADDRESSES: Home and office—P.O. Box 49328, Los Angeles, Calif. 90049.

CAREER: Free-lance magazine writer and interviewer, 1931-53; screenwriter, 1949-58, for Columbia, Warner Bros., Twentieth Century-Fox, Universal, RKO, Metro-Goldwyn-Mayer, and Paramount. Reporter for the Chicago Daily News/Sun Times Wire Service at the Democratic and Republican national conventions, 1972. *Military service:* U.S. Army Air Forces, writer in the First Motion Picture Unit and Signal Corps Photographic Center, 1942-46; became staff sergeant.

MEMBER: Authors Guild, Authors League of America, PEN, Writers Guild of America, Manuscript Society, Society of Authors (London).

AWARDS, HONORS: Supreme Award of Merit and honorary fellowship from George Washington Carver Memorial Institute, 1964, for writing *The Man* and for contributing "to the betterment of race relations and human welfare"; Commonwealth Club silver medal, 1965; Bestsellers magazine award, 1965, for *The Man;* Paperback of the Year citation, National Bestsellers Institute, 1970, for *The Seven Minutes;* Popular Culture Association award of excellence, 1974, for distinguished achievements in the popular arts; Venice Rosa d'Oro Award, 1975, for contributions to American letters.

WRITINGS:

The Fabulous Originals: Lives of Extraordinary People Who Inspired Memorable Characters in Fiction, Knopf, 1955, reprinted, Kraus, 1972.
The Square Pegs, Knopf, 1957.
The Fabulous Showman: The Life and Times of P. T. Barnum, Knopf, 1959.
The Sins of Philip Fleming (novel), Fell, 1959, reprinted, New American Library, 1985.
The Chapman Report (novel), Simon & Schuster, 1960, reprinted, New American Library, 1985.
The Twenty-seventh Wife (biography), Simon & Schuster, 1960, reprinted, New American Library, 1985.

The Prize (novel), Simon & Schuster, 1962, reprinted, New American Library, 1985.
The Three Sirens (novel), Simon & Schuster, 1963.
The Man (novel), Simon & Schuster, 1964.
The Sunday Gentleman (collected writings), Simon & Schuster, 1965.
The Plot (novel), Simon & Schuster, 1967, reprinted, Pocket Books, 1984.
The Writing of One Novel (nonfiction), Simon & Schuster, 1968, reprinted, Dutton, 1986.
The Seven Minutes (novel), Simon & Schuster, 1969, reprinted, Pocket Books, 1983.
The Nympho and Other Maniacs, Simon & Schuster, 1971.
The Word (novel), Simon & Schuster, 1972.
The Fan Club (novel), Simon & Schuster, 1974.
(Editor with son, David Wallechinsky) *The People's Almanac,* Doubleday, 1975.
The R Document (novel), Simon & Schuster, 1976.
(Editor with D. Wallechinsky and daughter, Amy Wallace) *The People's Almanac Presents the Book of Lists,* Morrow, 1977.
(Editor with D. Wallechinsky) *The People's Almanac #2,* Morrow, 1978.
(With A. Wallace) *The Two: A Biography,* Simon & Schuster, 1978.
The Pigeon Project (novel), Simon & Schuster, 1979.
(Editor with wife, Sylvia Wallace, A. Wallace, and D. Wallechinsky,) *The People's Almanac Presents the Book of Lists #2,* Morrow, 1980.
The Second Lady (novel), New American Library, 1980.
(Editor with A. Wallace and D. Wallechinsky) *The People's Almanac Presents the Book of Predictions,* Morrow, 1980.
(Editor with A. Wallace, S. Wallace, and D. Wallechinsky) *The Intimate Sex Lives of Famous People,* Delacorte, 1981.
(Editor with D. Wallechinsky) *The People's Almanac #3,* Morrow, 1981.
The Almighty (novel), Doubleday, 1982.
(Editor with A. Wallace and D. Wallechinsky) *The People's Almanac Presents the Book of Lists #3,* Morrow, 1983.
(Editor with A. Wallace and D. Wallechinsky) *Significa,* Dutton, 1983.
The Miracle (novel), Dutton, 1984.
The Seventh Secret (novel), Dutton, 1986.
The Celestial Bed (novel), Delacorte, 1987.
The Guest of Honor (novel), Delacorte, 1989.
The Golden Room (young adult), Dell, 1989.

SCREENPLAYS

(With John Monks, Jr., and Charles Hoffman) "The West Point Story," Warner Bros., 1950.
"Meet Me at the Fair," Universal, 1953.
(With Lewis Meltzer) "Desert Legion," Universal, 1953.
(With William Bowers) "Split Second," RKO, 1953.
(With Roy Huggins) "Gun Fury," Columbia, 1953.
(With Horace McCoy) "Bad for Each Other," Columbia, 1954.
(With Gerald Adams) "The Gambler from Natchez," Twentieth Century-Fox, 1954.
"Jump into Hell," Warner Bros., 1955.
"Sincerely Yours," Warner Bros., 1955.
"The Burning Hills," United Artists, 1956.
"Bombers B-52," Warner Bros., 1957.
(With Irwin Allen and Charles Bennett) "The Big Circus," Allied Artists, 1959.

OTHER

Author of plays "And Then Goodnight," "Because of Sex," "Hotel Behemoth," "Speak of the Devil," "Murder by Morning," and, with Jerome Weidman, "Pantheon." Also author of biographies for *Collier's Encyclopedia,* 1960, *American Oxford Encyclopedia,* and *Encyclopedia Britannica.* Contributor of over 500 articles and short stories to magazines, including *Saturday Evening Post, Reader's Digest, Esquire, Parade,* and *Cosmopolitan.*

SIDELIGHTS: One of America's most popular writers (and one of its chief literary exports with volumes printed in 31 languages worldwide), Irving Wallace began his career while still in his teens, contributing stories and articles to magazines. He reports that he was amazed when, at that young age, he discovered that the periodicals actually paid people to write for them, and from that moment on, he knew how he would spend his life. Romance combined with career when Wallace married fellow writer Sylvia Kahn in 1941; they would collaborate on two books and two children. The Wallaces saw their writing dynasty continue when their offspring, Amy Wallace and David Wallechinsky (the latter having adopted his paternal grandfather's original surname) became successful authors on their own.

Best known for his novels, Wallace has through the years developed an unusual forte in his fiction. He takes a highly complicated subject—a Kinsey-type survey or the Nobel Prize selection, for instance—and weaves it into a plot designed to hook readers with characters who have much at stake. In this way, Wallace's novels are notable for the amount of research that goes into them. As the author elaborates in John Leverence's study *Irving Wallace: A Writer's Profile,* when he begins a book he's "always curious to investigate what psychological motives bring a certain person into his field or profession. Why is a surgeon a surgeon? Why does he enjoy cutting flesh? Why does he like to tune in on patients' private lives? Why does that woman like to teach, and why does this man like to dig into the earth?"

Among Wallace's early fiction, *The Chapman Report* and *The Prize* (all of the author's novels begin with "The," a trait he attributes to superstition), dealing respectively with the Kinsey plot and the Nobel Prize story, are the most popular. Both works, according to *New York Times Book Review* critic Lawrence Lafore, "skillfully combine the most alluring features of the headline, the expose, the editorial and the mystery story." *The Chapman Report* in particular proved a highly controversial book when it first appeared in 1960, mainly because its sexual *roman a clef* elements were based on discussions Wallace had conducted with his actual neighbors at the time.

"Let me tell you how [*The Chapman Report*] came about," says Wallace in his *Contemporary Authors Autobiography Series* piece. "For years I had wanted to write a novel about the married or once-married young women who lived in my community. . . . I had a friendly face, and I was a good listener, and often at parties other men's wives confided their marital difficulties and sexual problems to me. Yet, my author's instinct told me to refrain from writing a novel about unhappy and restless young wives." One day during research for an article, he continues, "I came across [a study] about some sociologists who were taking a survey of women, on college campuses, I think. . . . I asked myself—what if a team of male sociologists arrived in my community to make a sex survey and interviewed the women I knew? How would these personal interviews affect the women? And how would the interviews affect members of the sex survey team?"

Controversy and its ensuing publicity combined to help make *The Chapman Report* a bestseller, and such fictions are rarely greeted with critical hosannas. But no one could deny that the author could reach an audience that might not otherwise investigate such subject matter. In Lafore's article, the critic remarks that a reader might learn almost nothing about the novel's main characters "except their sexual maladjustments. While a unique fascination with mass rape may create problems, it does not in itself create a personality." Yet at the same time, notes Lafore, Wallace "is refreshingly free of the pedantries and complexities to which novelists are too often prey. He uses few words (aside from anatomical ones), and introduces few ideas, that would be unfamiliar to a high-school sophomore."

On the heels of *The Chapman Report* came *The Prize,* a novel born of the fact that no fictional work had ever been published about the Nobel Prize. After extensive research that included trips to Stockholm and unprecedented interviews with subjects involved in the Nobel selection committee, Wallace released the book to praise for its unique theme and pans for what some saw as stylistic faults. In the Leverence work, Ray B. Browne includes *The Prize* in his critique of Wallace's sense of continuity. While the author's plots "are rich and complex," and each contains an important message, writes Browne, "once this message has been developed, . . . and after the puzzle has been solved, Wallace seems to lose most of his interest in the book. [He] is actually mostly gripped by the themes themselves. Little wonder then that after the questions and answers have been demonstrated and worked out, the author rushes to close the book, apparently content to erase the characters once they have illustrated his point." Still, finds Brown, Wallace, with his "direct, carefully chosen and clear" style, has produced in *The Prize* "a kind of high-water mark in subject and accomplishment. Since that novel Wallace has continued to explore new areas of investigation and to provide rich entertainment."

Such rich entertainment came in the form of two subsequent novels, *The Man* and *The Word,* another pair of bestsellers. Each contains a provocative theme. In *The Man,* the author speculates on what might happen should a black man, alone in the white bastion of American politics, suddenly find himself appointed president. Protagonist Douglass Dilman, a midlevel congressman who becomes chief of state when circumstances eliminate those ahead of him, came about as a Wallace-style reaction to the controversy then brewing over the integration of public schools. As the author himself reveals in his *Contemporary Authors Autobiography Series* article, *The Man* "was an immediate success, . . . [drawing] heavy mail, much of it from readers who admitted it had changed their attitude toward blacks completely."

In a *Best Sellers* review, Eugene J. Linehan sees merit in Wallace's presentation of an emotional theme: "The test of a novel is its people. You will find the men and women of these events singularly real. It is not easy to write well of current events; to walk us around the White House and maintain balance and sense. The danger is that such a choice of subject may lead the author into gross sentimentality or sensationalism. It seems to me that Irving Wallace has succeeded [in *The Man*] in bringing a thrilling story to the end of his book and kept his people alive and real."

Wallace tackled no less a subject than the Bible in *The Word.* Fabricating the discovery of a new set of New Testaments written by James, brother of Jesus, was challenging scholarship, the author acknowledges. But the sense of realism he developed in *The Word* resulted in "endless letters . . . asking me if The Gospel *According to James*, which I had invented, really had been dug up by archeologists, translated, and where copies might be purchased," as Wallace notes in the Leverence book. "While creating my gospel," he adds, "I drew upon the best research, archeological discoveries, theories and speculations of the finest Biblical scholars."

The Word, published in 1972, quickly attained international bestseller status. Its commercial acceptance, however, didn't stop some reviewers from accusing the author of concocting a potboiler. "The Irving Wallace formula for a best seller seems to be: put everything in, make a goulash," as a *New Republic* critic states, adding that besides the Biblical plot, the novel traffics in "spies, international police, two miracles (one gets tentatively canceled out) and a proposed Protestant Vatican. . . . It also has doses of sex, drugs, tragic irony, [and] scholarly hokum."

To Steven Kroll, in a *New York Times Book Review* piece, *The Word* presents an uncomfortable attitude toward women. "Even well-educated women end up as assistants and secretaries," he says. "If they're not capable of real love, they tend to go in for 'geisha acrobatics.' No doubt about it. Wallace women serve." But Kroll further goes on to say that whatever reservations he has about the author's tone, Wallace does have "a flair for controversial, topical subjects and a good liberal's serious respect for honesty, justice and nonconformity. He's also very adept at those unlikely coincidences that keep a reader wondering. But when you've been made to wonder, you feel cheated if you don't get answers, and 'The Word' bypasses those answers for a sweeping message of faith."

Not all Wallace novels center on lofty themes of sexual research, Nobel Prizes, integration, or religion. Many of his other fictional works fall into the category of hard-driving entertainments. Chief among them is *The Fan Club,* a suspense tale in which a Marilyn Monroe-type movie star is kidnapped by a group of men who had made her the object of their long-running fantasies. "The group hassles about how they deserve the actress, since 'the fat cats' get everything in life, including tax write-offs," *New York Times Book Review* writer Joe Flaherty finds. Flaherty, while pointing out that *The Fan Club*'s implicit appeal "is not sexual but [in] our passion to consummate with consumerism," sees in this point that Wallace's "genius comes to the fore. Every brand name is right; and the jet set life style, as decadent as it may be, is the stuff that makes a closet queen of every straphanger."

The 1980s brought a steady stream of fiction from Wallace, including *The Almighty, The Miracle, The Seventh Secret,* and *The Celestial Bed.* None of these novels was hailed as a masterpiece, though in Anatole Broyard's opinion, "a novel like 'The Miracle' is beyond criticism because it has no literary pretensions." As Broyard continues in a *New York Times* feature, this tale of a purported series of healing miracles in Lourdes, where the Virgin Mary was said to have appeared on several occasions in the past, employs "a timely theme that will interest a wide readership." Further, "There is a kind of crossword-puzzle suspense in reading 'The Miracle,' what might be called a mechanical curiosity. The main trouble with the book is not that it has renounced literary ambition in favor of a more ordinary appeal, but that it doesn't do justice to the ordinary. The language, for example, is not conversational, but a strange dialect of pidgin English used by some popular novelists."

One such popular novelist, the Catholic priest Andrew M. Greeley, reviewed *The Miracle* for *Washington Post Book World* and pronounced himself "frankly envious" of Wallace's ability to tell

a religious story that is "witty, ingenious, brilliant" and, "with its irony within ironies, . . . persuasive and even true on a number of different levels." The novel, Greeley concludes, is not "profound [like] *Song of Bernadette* from so long ago. It is, however, a marvelously told tale which, oddly enough, may, for all its slick, quick-flowing style, tell us more about the meaning of Lourdes than did Franz Werfel's classic."

"Across the years the plots and themes of Wallace's numerous books have varied widely, but the body of his work is traceable largely to a characteristic he identifies as 'my desire to listen, to let the imagination run wild, and then to write,' " as *Los Angeles Times* reporter Marshall Berges states. Still quoting Wallace, the article concludes, "I love to tell stories, to create people and worlds half real, half imaginary. Even if I could not earn a penny from my writing, I would earn my livelihood at something else and continue to write at night."

Nonfiction readers can find the Wallace name on a number of volumes he characterizes in *Contemporary Authors Autobiography Series* as "our family books." These include *The People's Almanac* series and its popular spinoff, *The People's Almanac Presents the Book of Lists.* "It all began with my son," Wallace remarks in the autobiographical essay. "From the age of eight, David had always been an almanac buff. . . . Then, one day in 1971, he began to question the infallibility of the almanacs and other reference books he had been reading. He began to see that a good deal of history and current events was distorted by reference books—not necessarily deliberately, but for various reasons." And worst of all, adds Wallace, "most [almanacs] were unforgivably dull."

And so it was David Wallechinsky who embarked on a new sort of reference work, with the enthusiastic input of his father and the assistance of 169 free-lance writers, among them Charles Schulz, "who wrote the definitive biography of Snoopy for us," continues Wallace. As for working alongside his son, the author finds that "David's ego was strong enough to accept me, and we became collaborators—and before it was over we became friends."

The People's Almanac debuted in 1975 to warm reviews and high-ranking bestseller status. Critics and public alike seemed to respond to a reference work that covered topics of history and trivia that no one had ever studied. When research showed that readers especially enjoyed the various lists contained within the series, the result was *The People's Almanac Presents the Book of Lists* (known popularly as just *The Book of Lists*), which would join its predecessor in multiple volumes throughout the 1970s and 1980s. Eventually, each member of the Wallace family would have a hand in the browser's delights. "We aren't a conglomerate," the patriarch tells Joseph McLellan in a *Washington Post* interview. "We're four very autonomous individuals having fun together. We enjoy sitting around and talking about book ideas and it's good for me. Writing fiction is a lonely kind of work. These [nonfictions] are more relaxing than a novel, and your research isn't far from your writing."

MEDIA ADAPTATIONS: Feature-film productions—Columbia Pictures bought *The Fabulous Showman* and *The Fan Club;* Warner Bros. filmed *The Chapman Report* in 1962; Metro-Goldwyn-Mayer filmed *The Prize* in 1963; Brenco Pictures and Stanley Meyer bought *The Three Sirens;* ABC Circle Films bought and filmed *The Man,* which was released by Paramount in 1972; Twentieth Century-Fox bought *The Plot,* and filmed *The Seven Minutes* in 1971, then bought film rights to *The Intimate Sex Lives of Famous People;* United Artists bought *The R Document.* Television productions—Columbia Broadcasting

System (CBS) bought *The Word* and broadcast an eight-hour miniseries in 1978; Lindsay Wagner's independent production company bought rights to *The Second Lady.*

AVOCATIONAL INTERESTS: Travel, collecting autographed letters, inscribed first-edition books, and impressionist paintings.

BIOGRAPHICAL/CRITICAL SOURCES:

BOOKS

Authors in the News, Volume 1, Gale, 1976.
Cawelti, John G., *Adventure, Mystery, and Romance,* University of Chicago Press, 1976.
Contemporary Authors Autobiography Series, Volume 1, Gale, 1984.
Contemporary Literary Criticism, Gale, Volume 7, 1977, Volume 13, 1980.
Leverence, John, *Irving Wallace: A Writer's Profile,* Popular Press, 1974.
Newquist, Roy, *Conversations,* Rand McNally, 1967.
Wallace, Irving, *The Sunday Gentleman,* Simon & Schuster, 1965.
Wallace, Irving, *The Writing of One Novel,* Simon & Schuster, 1968, reprinted, Dutton, 1986.

PERIODICALS

Best Sellers, September 15, 1964.
Chicago Tribune, January 17, 1988.
Chicago Tribune Book World, April 29, 1977.
Detroit News, September 23, 1984.
Journal of Popular Culture, summer, 1973.
Los Angeles Times, June 4, 1981, December 19, 1982, January 27, 1985, April 27, 1987.
Los Angeles Times Book Review, May 15, 1977, September 23, 1984, March 2, 1986.
New Republic, March 25, 1972.
Newsweek, November 1, 1982.
New York, April 1, 1974.
New York Times, August 31, 1984.
New York Times Book Review, September 22, 1963, December 12, 1965, October 2, 1969, March 21, 1971, March 19, 1972, June 16, 1974, March 14, 1976, March 19, 1978, October 12, 1980, October 31, 1982, September 13, 1984.
Philadelphia Bulletin, April 28, 1974.
Saturday Review, March 18, 1978.
Time, April 15, 1974.
Times (London), August 23, 1974, April 30, 1987.
Times Literary Supplement, May 13, 1965, September 10, 1971, October 25, 1974.
Washington Post, April 11, 1976, February 28, 1980, September 23, 1980, October 22, 1980, November 17, 1982.
Washington Post Book World, March 19, 1978, August 12, 1984.
Writer, January, 1965, November, 1968.

*　　*　　*

WALLANT, Edward Lewis 1926-1962

PERSONAL: Born October 19, 1926, in New Haven, Conn.; died December 5, 1962, in Norwalk, Conn.; son of Sol Ellis and Ann (Mendel) Wallant; married Joyce Fromkin, 1948; children: Scott Ellis, Leslie Ann, Kim Robin. *Education:* Attended Pratt Institute, 1947-50, and New School for Social Research, 1954-55.

CAREER: Worked as a graphic artist for various advertising agencies, 1950-62. *Military service:* U.S. Navy, 1944-46; gunner's mate on U.S.S. *Glennon.*

AWARDS, HONORS: Bread Loaf Writers' Conference fellow, 1960; Harry and Ethel Daroff Memorial Fiction Award, Jewish Book Council of America, 1961, for *The Human Season;* Guggenheim fellow, 1962; National Book Award nomination, 1962, for *The Pawnbroker.*

WRITINGS:

NOVELS

The Human Scene, Harcourt, 1960.
The Pawnbroker, Harcourt, 1961, reprinted, 1978.
The Tenants of Moonbloom, Harcourt, 1963.
The Children at the Gate, Harcourt, 1964, reprinted, 1980.

OTHER

(Contributor) Don M. Wolfe, editor, *New Voices 2: American Writing Today,* Hendricks House, 1955.
(Contributor) Charles I. Glicksberg, editor, *New Voices 3: American Writing Today,* Hendricks House, 1958.
(Contributor) D. M. Wolfe, editor, *American Scene: New Voices,* Lyle Stuart, 1963.

SIDELIGHTS: Although Edward Lewis Wallant published only two novels during his life, and two more appeared posthumously, he achieved a reputation as "one of the most important figures among postwar Jewish writers in the United States," as David R. Mesher wrote in the *Dictionary of Literary Biography.* "Despite his small output," Thomas M. Lorch stated in the *Chicago Review,* "Wallant merits recognition as one of our outstanding contemporary novelists."

After working for several years as an advertising artist, Wallant turned to writing seriously at the age of thirty. From that time until his death at the age of thirty-six, Wallant produced the small body of work for which he is remembered. Speaking to *Library Journal* of his turn to literature, Wallant explained: "To say I *enjoy* writing would be less a mistake of degree than of species. I sweat and ache and writhe in my chair; it is decidedly *not* in the nature of a relaxing hobby. . . . I do not write to entertain myself or others (although there may sometimes happily *be* entertainment in my writing). I write to share my views and feelings of the lives of human beings. . . . However a writer can illuminate the human condition, so must he do it."

Wallant's first novel, *The Human Season,* appeared in 1960 and won the Harry and Ethel Daroff Memorial Fiction Award, an award since renamed in honor of Wallant himself. Telling the story of middle-aged plumber Joe Berman as he seeks to recover from his wife's recent death, *The Human Season* presents Berman's transition from bitterness and apathy to a renewed faith in God and humanity. Berman begins the novel cut off from the rest of the world and questioning God, but he ends the book by rejoining society and regaining his faith. Lorch found the book a suitable showcase for Wallant's abilities. "Wallant," he wrote, "immediately reveals himself as a highly skilled craftsman in *The Human Season.* He brings his characters alive, and by his selection of the most ordinary concrete details, gestures and actions he evokes a deeply moving human situation."

Several critics noted the similarity between Berman's story and that of the biblical tale of Job, who also doubted God's wisdom. The *Kirkus* reviewer called the novel "an absorbing portrait of a modern man and a compelling, compassionate retelling of the story of Job." Mesher saw the story of Job as "a parallel which Wallant skillfully develops into an underlying resonance, at times specifically referring to the biblical book." "Wallant's book," the *Time* critic believed, "is a tour de force: what might seem a hopeless tale impresses by the clarity of its compassion."

Lorch concluded that "Wallant's fusion of memory, imagery and style renders *The Human Season* a beautifully poetic yet richly human novel."

It was with his second novel, *The Pawnbroker,* that Wallant established himself as a major new writer. The novel is set in a pawnshop in Harlem owned by Sol Nazerman, a concentration camp survivor. Nazerman survived the camp by suppressing his emotions and cutting himself off from others as much as possible. "The figure of the Pawnbroker looms through the work, a colossus of despair," Jonathan Baumbach stated in his *The Landscape of Nightmare: Studies in the Contemporary American Novel,* "carrying the burden of the world's horror in the dull pain of his spirit. He is an amazing characterization, one of the memorably dark heroes of our fiction."

Nazerman undergoes an emotional reawakening when his young assistant is accidentally killed during a robbery attempt. "In crying for his assistant," Baumbach wrote, "[Nazerman] is able at last to mourn for the death of his family, for all his losses, for all his dead. In discovering the shock of loss, he discovers the redemptive and agonizing wonder of love." David Boroff of the *Saturday Review* found that "the pawnbroker's return to the emotionally-living is not entirely convincing, nor is the somewhat ambiguous sacrifice of his assistant. But there can be no gainsaying the power of this remorselessly honest book. . . . Wallant is a gifted writer who probes with a kind of troubled tenderness into pools of human darkness."

Critical praise for *The Pawnbroker* often spoke of its great emotional power and stirring testimony to the importance and dignity of human life. "Nazerman's emotional resurrection, limited as it seems to be, is a powerful expression of the author's ultimate faith in humanity," Mesher maintained. Boroff described *The Pawnbroker* as "an ambitious, unparochial novel that says something about man's responsibility to man. . . . It is consistently absorbing, highly serious, and often moving." The *Kirkus* reviewer found it "an unforgettable, raw, horrifying portrait of man's inhumanity to man." The *Time* critic was especially drawn to Nazerman, "a creature of fascinating complexity. As the centerpiece of a flawed book, he is that literary rarity—the character whose sorrows seem as real as the reader's own."

With the success of *The Pawnbroker,* Wallant was able to leave his position at an advertising agency. He and his family spent most of 1962 traveling in Europe, where Wallant worked on his two final novels, *The Tenants of Moonbloom* and *The Children at the Gate.* Upon his return to the United States in the fall of 1962, Wallant submitted *The Tenants of Moonbloom* to his publisher and was working on the last rewrite of *The Children at the Gate.* This planned revision was never completed. On December 5, 1962, Wallant died of a ruptured aneurysm at the age of thirty-six.

The Tenants of Moonbloom was published in 1963. Described as a "comic masterpiece" by Leo Gurko in *Twentieth Century Literature,* the novel revolves around landlord Norman Moonbloom and his quixotic attempts to make the necessary repairs to the tenement buildings he manages. Moonbloom imagines that these repairs will somehow change the lives of his poor tenants as well. As do the characters in Wallant's previous novels, Moonbloom undergoes an emotional transformation. "In the tenements," Lorch explained, "Moonbloom is brought face to face with humanity. His awakening develops almost naturally, even inevitably, from this confrontation." Moonbloom's moment of revelation leads him to embrace "Love, Courage and Delusion." S. P. Ryan of *Best Sellers* called *The Tenants of Moonbloom* "a novel of power and strength" which displays "a genuine respect for the human condition." The *Time* critic believed that "no one since Nathanael West has written better of the rootlessness of metropolitan life."

Wallant's final novel, *The Children at the Gate,* appeared in 1964. It tells the story of nineteen-year-old Angelo De Marco, who works at his uncle's drugstore and makes the deliveries to a local hospital. At the hospital he meets Sammy, an orderly whose ultimate suicide leads Angelo to break out of his emotional isolation. The book is, R. K. Burns wrote in *Library Journal,* "a fine story, unpretentious and courageous, a small masterpiece." Baumbach, writing for the *Saturday Review,* called it "a beautifully written short novel of almost unbearable impact." But not all critics were so generous in their appraisal. Mesher believed that *The Children at the Gate* was "Wallant's weakest" novel, while Lorch thought it "an interesting but inferior reworking of *The Pawnbroker.*"

"Each of Wallant's novels," Lorch explained, "describes a form of rebirth, the process of returning to or achieving an affirmation of life." Joe Berman of *The Human Season* regains his faith; Sol Nazerman in *The Pawnbroker* undergoes a rebirth of his emotions; Norman Moonbloom in *The Tenants of Moonbloom* experiences a revelation about humanity; and Angelo De Marco of *The Children at the Gate* breaks out of his isolation. "All of Wallant's novels," Baumbach stated, "have a similar, ritual structure: a man cut off from the source of himself, in a delicate truce with the nightmare of survival, slowly, terrifyingly, at the risk of everything, rediscovers the possibility of feeling." Charles Alva Hoyt, in his study *Minor American Novelists,* concluded that all of Wallant's characters "initiate or take part in certain symbolic acts which eventually result in freeing them for the kind of deep human relationship which their author demands for all men."

This recurring portrayal of an emotional resurrection amid a usually squalid urban landscape makes Wallant's novels important, David W. Pitre wrote in the *Dictionary of Literary Biography,* "because they defiantly affirm that modern man need not and must not despair, for life, with all its vicissitudes, offers so much." Similarly, Gurko found that "dominating the field of [Wallant's] art is his vision of the great city, at once sickeningly ugly and disintegrative, yet in its swarming vitality holding forth the promise of some soul-stirring, spellbinding rejuvenation." M. F. Schulz of *Critique* claimed that "in all four of Wallant's novels, the dead are resurrected, the sleeping awakened, the unborn born. . . . [Wallant's novels] are *bildungsroman* of a special sort. Wallant deals with the coming of age, not in years, not in conventional education and acceptance of society's manners and rules, but in sensibility. It is the terrors of growth and change in the human heart . . . that are all important to him."

Despite his modest output, Wallant has achieved a considerable reputation. His work has, Mesher stated, "a stature and significance far beyond what might be expected of the four slim volumes to which it was limited." Hoyt thought that Wallant's reputation would surely increase with time. "I shall not be surprised," Hoyt wrote, "if future critics award him a high place in our literature."

MEDIA ADAPTATIONS: The Pawnbroker was filmed by Paramount in 1964.

BIOGRAPHICAL/CRITICAL SOURCES:

BOOKS

Baumbach, Jonathan, *The Landscape of Nightmare: Studies in the Contemporary American Novel,* New York University Press, 1965.

Contemporary Literary Criticism, Gale, Volume 5, 1976, Volume 10, 1979.

Dictionary of Literary Biography, Gale, Volume 2: *American Novelists since World War II,* 1978, Volume 28: *Twentieth Century American-Jewish Fiction Writers,* 1984.

Galloway, David, *Edward Lewis Wallant,* Twayne, 1979.

Hoyt, Charles Alva, *Minor American Novelists,* Southern Illinois University Press, 1970.

Malin, Max F., editor, *Radical Sophistication: Studies in Contemporary Jewish American Novelists,* Ohio University Press, 1969.

PERIODICALS

America, September 14, 1963.
Best Sellers, August 15, 1963, March 15, 1964.
Bulletin of Bibliography, Number 28, 1971.
Chicago Review, Volume 19, number 2, 1967.
Cithara, Volume 8, number 1, 1968.
Cresset, Number 31, 1968.
Critique, Volume X, number 3, 1968, Volume XII, number 2, 1970.
Kansas Quarterly, Number 7, 1975.
Kirkus, June 15, 1960, June 1, 1961.
Library Journal, June 1, 1960, August, 1960, February 15, 1964.
Literary Review, winter, 1974.
New York Times Book Review, September 11, 1960, September 3, 1961, August 18, 1963, March 8, 1964.
Renascence, winter, 1972.
Research Studies, Number 40, 1972.
Saturday Review, August 26, 1961, February 29, 1964.
Teacher's Notebook in English, fall, 1963.
Time, September 5, 1960, August 18, 1961, August 16, 1963.
Twentieth Century Literature, October, 1974.
Yale University Library Gazette, Volume 56, numbers 1-2, 1981.

*   *   *

WAMBAUGH, Joseph (Aloysius, Jr.) 1937-

PERSONAL: Born January 22, 1937, in East Pittsburgh, Pa.; son of Joseph A. (a police officer) and Anne (Malloy) Wambaugh; married Dee Allsup, November 26, 1955; children: Mark, David. *Education:* Chaffey College, A.A., 1958; California State College (now University), Los Angeles, B.A., 1960, M.A., 1968. *Religion:* Roman Catholic.

ADDRESSES: Home—72 Mayfair Dr., Rancho Mirage, Calif. 92270.

CAREER: Los Angeles (Calif.) Police Department, 1960-74, became detective sergeant; writer. Creator and consultant, "Police Story" series for National Broadcasting Co. and "The Blue Knight" series for Columbia Broadcasting System. *Military service:* U.S. Marine Corps, 1954-57.

AWARDS, HONORS: Edgar Allan Poe award for best motion picture from Mystery Writers of America, 1981, for "The Black Marble."

WRITINGS:

The New Centurions (fiction), Atlantic-Little Brown, 1971.
The Blue Knight (fiction), Atlantic-Little Brown, 1972.

The Onion Field (nonfiction), Delacorte, 1973.
The Choirboys (fiction), Delacorte, 1975.
The Black Marble (fiction), Delacorte, 1978.
The Glitter Dome (fiction), Morrow, 1981.
The Delta Star (fiction), Morrow, 1983.
Lines and Shadows (nonfiction), Morrow, 1984.
The Secrets of Harry Bright (fiction), Morrow, 1985.
Echoes in the Darkness (nonfiction), Morrow, 1987.
The Blooding (nonfiction), Morrow, 1989.

Wambaugh adapted three of his books into movies: "The Onion Field," released by Avco Embassy in 1979; "The Black Marble," released by Avco Embassy in 1980; and "The Glitter Dome," released by Home Box Office in 1984.

SIDELIGHTS: Thomas Fleming feels that *The New Centurions,* Wambaugh's first book, "performs one of those essential and enduring functions the novel—and the novel alone—can perform. It takes us into the minds and hearts, into the nerves and (sometimes literally) into the guts of other human beings—and, in the hands of a good writer, it achieves a mixture of empathy and objectivity that creates genuine understanding. . . . [Wambaugh] stands outside it all, seemingly as indifferent as the ideal Joycean novelist, calmly letting his characters tell their stories. One can see, to some extent, where his sympathies lie. But he achieves more than enough objectivity to give the reader a picture of everyday police work more revealing than a thousand hours of 'Dragnet' or 'The Mod Squad.'" After describing some of the violent scenes depicted in *The New Centurions,* Jose M. Ferrer III states: "Such incidents have been written about before as well as dramatized for TV audiences. In such cases they are usually presented for thrills, or to sharpen the pace of a story. In *Centurions,* they are encountered as a policeman would encounter them, matter-of-factly, almost at random, and all the more real for it." Ferrer makes the point that Wambaugh "has been admonished by L.A. Police Chief Edward M. Davis, officially, because he failed to get permission to publish *The New Centurions.* Presumably, though, the department also was not pleased by Wambaugh's literary lapse of organizational loyalty. Of course, it is those very displays of unblurred vision that keep Wambaugh's book unpreachy, believable, and out of trouble with the reader."

John J. Fried, however, finds that the book "is not without flaws, the most conspicuous of which is its style. . . . [Wambaugh's] writing is frequently awkward, a kind of low-grade Irving Wallace, especially when he tries to teach the reader a lesson or two in Constitutional Law. He is at his best when writing about the everyday life of the cop on the beat, and this is the real strength of the novel."

Eric Pace found *The Blue Knight* to be "fascinating reading for anyone whose curiosity was whetted by what the Knapp Commission showed of the dark side of police life. Once again, the author gives a cop's-eye-view of police brutality and free-loading as well as police courage and compassion." But he feels that Bumper Morgan, police officer and main character in the novel, "has attributes that seem unlikely in a man his age. He digs hard rock. He dates a black chick. He gets involved with a 19-year-old belly dancer. Perhaps things are different on the Coast. Or it could be argued that these are particularizing details meant to keep Bumper from being a stock figure. This reader was left with the impression that Bumper's character was incomplete in the young author's mind—and has been fleshed out with bits and pieces of Wambaugh's own experiences and tastes." Pace concludes: "*The Blue Knight* abounds in vivid vignettes of police life and the Los Angeles streets. It effectively conveys the loneliness of an aging man who puts too much of himself into his work. Its warty portrayal of the police will make it controversial in some quarters." A reviewer for *Publishers Weekly* calls the book a "hard-hitting, tough talking, utterly realistic novel about an average cop on the beat. . . . If this particular 'blue knight' is no cardboard hero, he is very real, occasionally pitiable, and Wambaugh understands him inside out and makes us do so, too."

In a review of *The Onion Field,* Frank Paul Le Veness says that the book "presents an extremely skillful portrayal of one of California's most notorious crimes and its 'longest, most intricate court case.' . . . [Wambaugh] has not merely presented a disturbing crime story and dramatic court case but has undertaken a psychological study of the major characters: two convicted killers, their policeman victim, and the latter's partner. . . . [The book] offers a penetrating character study, delving into the backgrounds that helped bring all four men to that onion field. It is a study of poverty, broken homes and criminality, as well as of dedication, strength and sincerity. The style is suspenseful and should hold the reader in its grip from start to finish." A *Publishers Weekly* writer calls *The Onion Field* "powerful reading— precisely what one anticipates from this smashing storyteller. . . . Wambaugh's spare, vivid documentary style draws the marrow out of police, court and psychiatric records while shaping a strong case for the reform of American criminal justice." James Conaway writes: "Wambaugh is obviously indebted to Truman Capote—who, in 1965, demonstrated his skill in applying a novelist's techniques to a true-crime narrative. Both *In Cold Blood* and *The Onion Field* involved a prodigious amount of research, and are equally compelling. Wambaugh takes greater liberties with his characters and he lacks Capote's neatness. But in terms of scope, revealed depth of character, and dramatic coherence, this is the more ambitious book. . . . Wambaugh convincingly demonstrates that he belongs to the tradition of Dreiser and Farrell—constructing from a glut of well-observed detail, unspectacular and often squalid lives lived among the concrete freeways, the bright, tawdry strips, the transience, brutality and beleaguered decency of a society set on the edge of America."

John Leonard believes that "very little in Wambaugh's first two novels prepares one for the scabrous humor and ferocity of *The Choirboys. The New Centurions* and *The Blue Knight* were bittersweet slices of naturalism, unlikely Hamlets on wry crisp, as if to elaborate the extenuating circumstance that cops, too, have feelings and may often be the victims of their particularity. In *The Choirboys* Wambaugh comes on like a Celine derailed along the laugh-track. His characters are a brutalized 'M.A.S.H.' unit. . . . Wambaugh proposes an anarchy that lusts for accidents to happen and assigns blame randomly; a uniformed proletariat to mop up our bloody mess—a kind of Drano for dissolving sludge in society's clogged plumbing—which, at the same time, is unable to save itself from being wasted; a necessary alienation, an 'ordinary' brutishness, a lethal banality, an imponderable . . . what? We aren't dignified enough to be evil. . . . Wambaugh is as specific, as visceral, as the strangled child who happens to be one's own son. His is a funny book that makes one gag. He is on his way to rediscovering original sin." According to a reviewer for *Atlantic Monthly,* "Mr. Wambaugh appears to have thrown into this novel everything that loyalty and discretion deleted from his work while he remained a member of the Los Angeles Police Department. The action is constant and the dialogue is tough. The writing has a careless barbarity that may be deliberate, for Mr. Wambaugh is explaining that police work is a one-way ticket to hell."

Reviewing *The Black Marble,* Jerome Charyn says: "Joseph Wambaugh, a former policeman who writes about cops on the planet of Los Angeles has created a detective, Andrei Mikhailovich Valnikov, who is almost as touching, variable, and bravely idiotic as Nabokov's Professor Pnin. . . . As the misadventures of a sad, unlikely cop, *The Black Marble* is a very funny book. The problem with the novel is that it strays from Valnikov much too often. Joseph Wambaugh hasn't found a story that can contain his fat, haunted detective. The plot seems silly next to Valnikov's 'sad runny eyes.' . . . The characters around Valnikov are a pile of weak grotesques. Most of them seem to come out of a simpler and much blunter novel. It's as if all of Wambaugh's energy and love have gone into the creation of Detective Sergeant Valnikov." John Leonard declares: "Somebody should get a grip on Joseph Wambaugh with one hand, and slap him back into shape with the other. He ought not to be allowed to be cute. In *The Choirboys* he looked as though he had lapped Celine and might even be gaining on the young Dostoyevsky: human beings were the pits, and Los Angeles cops had pitched their tent in a septic tank—'The Big Sewer,' he now calls it—and everybody was either going to drown or 'eat his gun.' After too many battered children and severed heads, the soul itself became a mean street. There was nothing cute about *The Choirboys. . . . The Black Marble* is, in part, both sentimental and cute. . . . There are many, many good things about [the book] because Mr. Wambaugh is too talented to be cute full-time. The opening scene, with Valnikov drunk at a Russian Christmas vesper service, having lost his handcuffs, is splendid. . . . Equally good are the depictions of shabby gentility in Pasadena, big-time dog show lunacy in the Los Angeles Memorial Sports Arena, sniper fire, life in the kennels and in the station house. Nobody handles such material as well as Mr. Wambaugh."

Joseph Wambaugh told an interviewer: "Cops want people to like them, and that's why a lot of them don't like [*The New Centurions*]. They want people to have that stereotyped TV image of a cop—which is awfully wholesome and terribly tiresome. The cops in my book have been called brutal, racist, cheating, fornicating bastards. . . . All they are, in the end, is people. What the hell does anybody expect?"

Wambaugh has continued his string of best-selling books with both fiction and nonfiction works. In novels such as *The Glitter Dome, The Delta Star,* and *The Secrets of Harry Bright,* Wambaugh again reveals his enduring fascination with the police and their complicated, dangerous world. As with his earlier works, Wambaugh portrays the police as three-dimensional human beings torn by conflicting ideals of right and wrong. Critics praised the author's intricate plots and complex characters. J. D. Reed of *Time* noted that "Wambaugh's characters have altered America's view of its police. His Los Angeles officers are neither the lone-eagle heroes of reactionary fantasy nor fascist mercenaries cracking the skulls of the innocent. They are, instead, ordinary, besieged working men and women whose lives are presented with war-zone humor, lively plots and a refreshing lack of night-school sociology." And *Los Angeles Times Book Review* contributor John Sutherland commented that "if there's a better writer than Wambaugh working in (and on) Southern California, I can't think who it is."

Reviewers also continue to laud his nonfiction works, including *Lines and Shadows, Echoes in the Darkness,* and *The Blooding.* Whether examining the chaotic relations between the police and illegal aliens along the California-Mexico border, as he does in *Lines and Shadows,* or tracing the search for a brutal English killer, as in *The Blooding,* Wambaugh has proven his ability to create suspense and drama with accounts of actual events. While some critics suggest that Wambaugh excels in writing fiction rather than nonfiction, most agree that Wambaugh's books make for absorbing reading. Writing in the *New York Times Book Review,* Walter Walker called *The Blooding* "a well-written, meticulously researched, nontechnical tour de force." *Los Angeles Times Book Review* contributor Tom Nolan called *Echoes in the Darkness* a "stark and eventually engrossing tale of crime and punishment."

MEDIA ADAPTATIONS: Two of Wambaugh's novels have been made into films: "The New Centurions," directed by Richard Fleischer and released by Columbia Pictures in 1972, and "The Choirboys," directed by Robert Aldrich and released by Universal Studios in 1977. *The Blue Knight* was produced as a miniseries that starred William Holden, and then as a regular series with George Kennedy in the title role; both versions were released by the National Broadcasting Company.

BIOGRAPHICAL/CRITICAL SOURCES:

BOOKS

Bestsellers 89, Issue 3, Gale, 1989.
Contemporary Literary Criticism, Gale, Volume 3, 1975, Volume 18, 1981.
Dictionary of Literary Biography, Volume 6: *American Novelists Since World War II, Second Series,* Gale, 1980.
Dictionary of Literary Biography Yearbook: 1983, Gale, 1984.

PERIODICALS

America, January 19, 1974.
Atlantic Monthly, October, 1973, November, 1975.
Best Sellers, January 15, 1971, February 15, 1972, October 15, 1973, February, 1976.
Bookviews, January, 1978.
Chicago Tribune, September 28, 1979, March 10, 1980, June 17, 1981.
Chicago Tribune Book World, June 13, 1982, March 27, 1983, October 6, 1985, February 8, 1987, February 5, 1989.
Globe and Mail (Toronto), March 10, 1984, February 14, 1987, March 4, 1989.
Los Angeles Times, March 9, 1983, August 5, 1987.
Los Angeles Times Book Review, March 6, 1983, February 19, 1984, November 10, 1985, March 1, 1987, February 5, 1989.
Los Angeles Times Magazine, February 26, 1989.
National Review, March 9, 1971, April 2, 1976.
New Republic, March 13, 1971.
Newsweek, May 2, 1983, February 6, 1984, March 2, 1987.
New York, April 1, 1972.
New York Times, January 22, 1971, September 7, 1973, January 8, 1978, September 19, 1979, September 24, 1979, October 9, 1979, March 7, 1980, June 22, 1981, February 23, 1987.
New York Times Book Review, January 31, 1971, February 13, 1972, September 2, 1973, December 3, 1973, November 2, 1975, January 11, 1978, June 28, 1981, March 20, 1983, October 6, 1985, March 1, 1987, February 19, 1989.
Publishers Weekly, January 3, 1972, July 23, 1973, September 1, 1975, July 12, 1976.
Time, February 15, 1971, February 28, 1972, September 24, 1973, June 8, 1981, March 5, 1984, October 28, 1985.
Times (London), June 6, 1987, February 18, 1989.
Times Literary Supplement, March 16, 1973, November 1, 1974, April 9, 1976.
Washington Post, February 19, 1979, October 19, 1979, June 30, 1981, April 1, 1983, March 6, 1984, September 30, 1985, February 12, 1987.

Washington Post Book World, March 5, 1972, September 2, 1973, October 20, 1974, January 24, 1978, March 22, 1987, March 19, 1989.

*   *   *

WARNER, Sylvia (Constance) Ashton
See ASHTON-WARNER, Sylvia (Constance)

*   *   *

WARNER, Sylvia Townsend   1893-1978

PERSONAL: Born December 6, 1893, in Harrow, Middlesex, England; died May 1, 1978, in Maiden Newton, Dorsetshire, England; daughter of George Townsend (a schoolmaster) and Eleanor Mary (Hudleston) Warner. *Education:* Privately educated in England.

CAREER: Writer.

MEMBER: Royal Society of Literature (fellow), American Academy of Arts and Letters (honorary member), Rachel Carson Trust (sponsor).

AWARDS, HONORS: Prix Menton, 1968.

WRITINGS:

NOVELS

Lolly Willowes; or, The Loving Huntsman (Book-of-the-Month Club selection; also see below), Viking, 1926, reprinted, Academy Chicago, 1979.
Mr. Fortune's Maggot (Literary Guild selection; also see below), Viking, 1927, reprinted, Virago, 1978.
The True Heart, Viking, 1929, reprinted, Virago, 1978.
Summer Will Show, Viking, 1936.
The Corner That Held Them, Viking, 1948, reprinted, Chatto & Windus, 1968.
The Flint Anchor, Viking, 1954.
Lolly Willowes, and Mr. Fortune's Maggot, Viking, 1966.

STORY COLLECTIONS

"*Some World Far from Ours*" and "*Stay, Corydon, Thou Swain,*" Mathews, 1929.
Elinor Barley, Cresset Press, 1930.
A Moral Ending and Other Stories, Joiner & Steele, 1931.
The Salutation, Viking, 1932.
More Joy in Heaven and Other Stories, Cresset Press, 1935.
(With Graham Greene and James Laver) *Twenty-four Stories,* Cresset Press, 1939.
The Cat's Cradle Book, Viking, 1940.
A Garland of Straw: Twenty-eight Stories, Viking, 1943 (published in England as *A Garland of Straw and Other Stories,* Chatto & Windus, 1943).
The Museum of Cheats: Stories, Viking, 1947.
Winter in the Air and Other Stories, Chatto & Windus, 1955, Viking, 1956.
A Spirit Rises: Short Stories, Viking, 1962.
Swans on an Autumn River: Stories, Viking, 1966 (published in England as *A Stranger with a Bag and Other Stories,* Chatto & Windus, 1966).
The Innocent and the Guilty, Viking, 1971.
Kingdoms of Elfin, Viking, 1977.
One Thing Leading to Another: And Other Stories, edited by Susanna Pinney, Viking, 1984.
Selected Stories of Sylvia Townsend Warner, Viking, 1988.

POEMS

The Espalier, Viking, 1925.
Time Importuned, Viking, 1928.
Opus 7: A Poem, Viking, 1931.
Rainbow, Knopf, 1932.
(With Valentine Ackland) *Whether a Dove or Seagull,* Viking, 1933.
(With Reynolds Stone) *Boxwood,* Monotype Corp., 1958, edition, Chatto & Windus, 1960.
King Duffus and Other Poems, Clare, 1968.
Twelve Poems, Chatto & Windus, 1980.
Collected Poems, edited by Claire Harman, Viking, 1983.

NONFICTION

The Portrait of a Tortoise: Extracted from the Journals of Gilbert White, Chatto & Windus, 1946.
Somerset, Elek, 1949.
Jane Austen: 1775-1817, Longmans, Green, 1951, revised edition, 1957.
Sketches from Nature, Clare, 1963.
T. H. White: A Biography, J. Cape, 1967, Viking, 1968.
Scenes of Childhood, Viking, 1982.
Letters, edited by William Maxwell, Viking, 1983.

TRANSLATOR

Marcel Proust, *By Way of Saint-Beuve,* Chatto & Windus, 1958, published as *On Art and Literature: 1896-1917,* Dell, 1964, published as *Marcel Proust on Art and Literature, 1896-1919,* Carroll & Graf, 1984.
Jeane Rene Huguenin, *A Place of Shipwreck,* Chatto & Windus, 1963.

EDITOR

(With others) *Tudor Church Music,* ten volumes, Oxford University Press, c. 1925-30.
The Weekend Dickens, MacLehose, 1932.

OTHER

Contributor of stories and sketches to *New Yorker* and *Spectator.* Contributor to *Grove's Dictionary of Music.*

SIDELIGHTS: Sylvia Townsend Warner had what she once described as an "accidental career" as a writer. She began writing poetry, *Publishers Weekly* quoted her as claiming, because she was given some paper with a "particularly tempting surface," and only wrote her first novel, *Lolly Willowes; or, The Loving Huntsman,* because she "happened to find some very agreeable thin lined paper in a job lot." However she came by her career, once embarked on it Warner was quite prolific. She published some thirty-five books of fiction, nonfiction, and poetry.

There is a special quality that marks all of Warner's writing. She was, as Joseph McClellan stated in the *Washington Post,* "one of that magic and sadly dwindling class: people who write beautifully." John Updike, writing in the *New Yorker,* echoed this assessment. Warner had begun as a poet, Updike noted, and always "did retain magic and music in her prose." He also believed that Warner's "more than half century of brilliantly varied and superbly self-possessed literary production never won her the flaming place in the heavens of reputation that she deserved."

Lolly Willowes, Mr. Fortune's Maggot, and *The True Heart*—Warner's first three novels—established her reputation as a fine prose stylist. "These three short novels, taken together," J. I. M. Stewart wrote in the *Times Literary Supplement,* "surely constitute one of the most notable achievements of English fiction in

the 1920s." *Lolly Willowes,* a novel W. J. Strachan of *London Magazine* called Warner's "first masterpiece," has particularly garnered critical attention. It is the story of Laura Willowes, an English spinster who is unable to accept the conventional demands of her life and so makes a pact with the devil and becomes a witch. Willowes explained her unusual decision as a way "to have a life of one's own, not an existence doled out to you by others." This wish for independence stems from her awareness that "women have such vivid imaginations, and lead such dull lives." The novel is, Updike maintained, "witty, eerie, tender but firm." Stewart found it "a moral fable, fully realized but sparely told." Warner's "sly and almost subdued comedy" reminded Edwin Clark of the *New York Times* of Jane Austen, while L. P. Hartley of *Saturday Review* thought the book "owes something to [David] Garnett in its conception and to [Daniel] Defoe in its execution." "It is quite simply and charmingly written," the *New Republic* critic believed, "with here and there stabs of genuine beauty and happy phrase." *Lolly Willowes* was the first selection of the newly formed Book-of-the-Month Club in 1926.

In her next two novels, Warner "moved from fantasy to realism," Thomas Lask of the *New York Times* noted, "and subtle social criticism could be found between the lines." This trend can be seen in *Mr. Fortune's Maggot,* the story of a homosexual relationship between an English missionary and a South Seas native. During his attempts to convert the humorous and naive people of a remote island, Reverend Timothy Fortune becomes more heathen himself. In the end, he decides to forego the chance to convert his lover and instead leaves the island. "When Mr. Fortune returns to 'the real world,' " Judith Gies wrote in the *New York Times Book Review,* "we grieve for him." The *Spectator* reviewer saw the possibility for a "good many interpretations of this book; one reader will say that it is an attack on foreign missions and conventional religion, another that it is a skit on the church's methods of salvation, a third that it is pure nonsense and a fourth that it is a sad story of man's disillusionment." Critics generally praised the book, however they interpreted it. "The story," Christopher Morley commented in the *Saturday Review of Literature,* "is written with tranquil grace and a most dainty humor." Naomi Royde-Smith of *New Statesman* judged it a "witty, penetrating little tragedy."

In *The True Heart,* an orphan girl is put to work as a farmer's drudge. She falls in love with an idiot and, when he is taken away, goes in search for him. Her faithfulness is eventually rewarded when she is reunited with her love. Although the story has a rustic, fairy tale quality, it is essentially realistic. Katherine Anne Porter described the book for the *New York Herald Tribune* as "not whimsical . . . not fantastic. . . . It might be called fantasy [because it is set] in a world of symbolic truths. . . . [The novel] is like the changing landscape of a dream where figures move on some ageless errand." The *Times Literary Supplement* critic saw the novel in similar terms. "Though the author," the critic wrote, "does not shrink from the ugly and the violent this very charming tale does not belong to the actual world at all, but to the ever-imagined youth of the world when a true and innocent heart could go unscathed through every danger, unspoiled by any contact, to find its love at the last." The book has a "nameless and unusual combination of imp and cherub," Grace Frank wrote in the *Saturday Review of Literature,* "of humor and a lyric tenderness, that makes the story so delectable." Similarly, the *Outlook* reviewer believed *The True Heart* to be "more ambitious" than Warner's previous novels "but no less delicate in its blend of humor and pathos."

Subsequent Warner novels were based on historical events. *Summer Will Show,* set at the time of the French Revolution, was described by L. A. MacKay of *Canadian Forum* as "an excellent novel. The delicate and distinctive style of Miss Warner's earlier work, the deft irony and subtle characterization, reappear in a work of broader scope and more serious feeling." Written during Warner's brief involvement with the British Communist Party, the novel has serious political undertones. Mary McCarthy, in her review for the *Nation*, called *Summer Will Show* "the most skilful, the most sure-footed, sensitive, witty piece of prose yet to have been colored by left-wing ideology." Writing in the *Spectator*, William Plomer praised Warner's style. The book, he said, was "written with great care, it is well constructed and with rare skill—particularly in the choice and arrangement of descriptive detail—it builds up a picture in the reader's mind so that afterwards it seems almost like some old memory revived, some personal experience recalled."

In *The Corner That Held Them* Warner again writes an historical novel, setting her story in a fourteenth-century English convent. Surveying a thirty-three-year period in the convent's history, from the Black Death to the Peasant Uprising, the book focuses on the daily life of the cloistered nuns and not on the historical events of the time. It has been cited for its vivid recreation of medieval life. R. G. Davis of the *New York Times* believed the novel to be "a remarkable feat of living into another period, of making it immediately present to all the physical senses and to common sense as well." This authenticity was also noted by Richard McLaughlin in the *Saturday Review of Literature*. "Much of the appeal of the novel," McLaughlin asserted, "may be traced to Miss Warner's masterful resuscitation of medieval times, for she has not only recaptured the gusty full-bloodedness of that age but has positively drawn life-size figures which might have sprung from the pages of [Honore de] Balzac's 'Droll Stories.'"

The Flint Anchor, a chronicle of family life over a fifty-year period, distinguishes itself from other historical novels, Anthony West wrote in the *New Yorker,* "by being both beautifully written and psychologically profound about family relationships." Dealing with the life story of a family tyrant in nineteenth-century England, the novel unfolds in a deceptive manner, "as a piece of newsy family gossip," according to West. But at book's end a larger theme becomes apparent, "the idea that much more suffering and pain come from blind good will than from wickedness." While complimenting Warner's "witty, precise, unhurried" style, Paul Pickrel of the *Yale Review* nonetheless believed that "the waste of love, the unfulfilled capacity for affection, might have been treated with less sprightliness and more sympathy." Pickrel concluded that *The Flint Anchor* was not among the best of family chronicles, but "it is nevertheless the best example of that kind of fiction in some time."

Although her early reputation was made as a novelist, Warner also published many short stories—144 of them in the *New Yorker* alone—and these stories constitute an important part of her life's work. Warner's stories examine, with wit and charm, the motives and actions of often-eccentric characters. She wrote of a debutante who became a looter during World War II, of a brother and sister who cultivated their dullness to divert attention from their incestuous relationship, and of a clergyman stung to death by insects. "The knowledge that human beings are dangerous, incalculable, and extraordinary," Gies maintained, "is the animating spark at the center of her work." Warner's fiction, Michiko Kakutani wrote in the *New York Times Book Review,* is "peopled by eccentrics, and it is often animated by a gift for mischievous irony that lends the stories a charming, fable-like quality." Benedict Kiely, also writing in the *New York Times Book Review,* believed that whatever her subject matter, Warner

"displays always that irony, that ruthless coolness, that clear sight, that style."

"The strength of [Warner's] stories lies," John L. Abbott wrote in *Studies in Short Fiction,* "not in their range or philosophical depth—she tells us nothing new—but in her extraordinary capacity to depict with astringency of style aspects of the human condition. Her fiction concerns itself less with actions or events and more with states of mind, malaises of the soul." This analysis is echoed by Maybelle Lacey. In her review of the collection *Swans on an Autumn River* for *Library Journal,* Lacey emphasized that Warner's "perception, compassion and command build [these stories] into subtly powerful presentations. Her characters are moved by truly human emotions, and she analyzes the motives which result in actions which are, for example, comic, kind, self-serving, or tyrannical."

Although many of her stories are of a fantastic or whimsical nature, it is only in *Kingdoms of Elfin* that Warner crosses the line into pure fantasy. Set in a fairyland of elf kingdoms, these sixteen stories form an imaginary saga which, in occasional asides, offers ironic observations on the world of men. "It has," William Jay Smith observed in the *New York Times Book Review,* "all the freshness, wit, originality of perception and clarity of insight that have won for [Warner's] rhythmical prose so many admirers. . . . It offers us an unforgettable journey through time and space, a cast of truly fantastic characters and an impressive and seemingly unending display of verbal fireworks." Gabriele Annan pointed out in the *Times Literary Supplement* that Warner's humor in this book is aimed "against religion, against superstition, gullibility, clericalism and priggishness." She also judged the collection to be "poetic, and the poetry comes not only from the fastidious elfin magic of [Warner's] prose, but also from a feeling for nature which could, perhaps, be called mystical."

When writing of her own life in *Scenes of Childhood,* Warner mixed reminiscence with fiction to create a series of sketches loosely based on the characters and events of her turn-of-the-century childhood. Many of the sketches provide autobiographical insights into Warner's early life. Her schoolmaster father, for example, doubted the value of literacy because it encouraged children not to observe, remember, and think for themselves, and so Warner learned to read much later than did her contemporaries. "Warner airs the glamorous and charming eccentricities of her upper middle-class background with a telling irony," Carol Rumens reported in the *Times Literary Supplement.* "With wit and an elegant exactitude of language," Peter S. Prescott wrote in *Newsweek,* "[Warner] develops a garden, a few rooms in a house, a church interior; she then populates her small spaces with amiable eccentrics and leaves to those who will the impulse to infer the larger society. Beside her gentle stories, a tempest in a teapot would appear a life-threatening event." These sketches, however, moved Melvin Maddocks to warn in *Time* that "the too-casual reader . . . who thinks he is strolling down the garden path of English whimsy will soon find his heels being nipped by demons. . . . The Warner world is haunted." Maddocks cites the sketch about a dismissed butler who got his revenge when he returned to the Warner house as leader of a volunteer fire brigade that carefully failed to extinguish the fire. Another sketch concerns a holiday when Warner and a friend came close to burying another child in the sand. Warner, Maddocks claimed, "taught herself how to describe the ordinary with precision and wonder and a certain elegance, until [one] could see that absolutely nothing, in the end, is ordinary."

More details of Warner's life can be found in *Letters,* a collection of her correspondence. Although the collection does not include her love letters to Valentine Ackland, the woman with whom she lived for many years, it does provide an insight into Warner's domestic routine. "The two women," Kakutani stated, "led an essentially quiet, bourgeois life, deep in the countryside of England. What Miss Warner's letters do best is convey, with lots of chatty facts, the texture of that life." Visiting friends, gardening, travel abroad, cooking, her own thoughts on other authors—these are the subjects of Warner's correspondence. The letters, Vicki Feaver wrote in the *Times Literary Supplement,* "form the record of what was ostensibly a retired and uneventful life in the country. . . . What really makes these letters come alive is Warner's capacity to turn the stuff of ordinary existence into a stream of perceptive, witty, compassionate, and sometimes tart observation."

Looking back on Warner's career, Kakutani found that she may have been a minor artist, "but an artist blessed with poised, felicitous command of language and the ability to portray both the ordinary and the odd with charming, compassionate wit." "Warner's contribution to literature," Strachan observed, "has been an enlargement of that peculiarly English world of the imagination, exemplified in [her] works of fantasy." Lask judged Warner as "one of the most stylish, one of the most civilized and cultivated of writers."

BIOGRAPHICAL/CRITICAL SOURCES:

BOOKS

Contemporary Literary Criticism, Gale, Volume VII, 1977, Volume XIX, 1981.
Dictionary of Literary Biography, Volume 34: *British Novelists, 1890-1929: Traditionalists,* Gale, 1985.
Updike, John, *Picked-Up Pieces,* Knopf, 1976.
Warner, Sylvia Townsend, *Letters,* edited by William Maxwell, Viking, 1983.
Warner, Sylvia Townsend, *Scenes of Childhood,* Viking, 1982.

PERIODICALS

British Book News, June, 1980.
Canadian Forum, November, 1936, March, 1948.
Chicago Tribune Book World, February 7, 1982.
Christian Science Monitor, December 31, 1932.
Library Journal, January 5, 1966.
London Magazine, November, 1979.
Los Angeles Times, April 7, 1989.
Nation, May 25, 1927, November 9, 1932, August 15, 1936, April 11, 1966.
New Republic, February 17, 1926, March 5, 1966.
New Statesman, May 21, 1927.
Newsweek, January 11, 1982.
New Yorker, August 28, 1943, October 9, 1954, August 20, 1979.
New York Herald Tribune, February 17, 1929.
New York Herald Tribune Book Review, February 26, 1956.
New York Times, February 7, 1926, February 17, 1929, September 5, 1943, October 31, 1948, December 30, 1981.
New York Times Book Review, February 6, 1966, March 27, 1977, January 17, 1982, April 17, 1983, November 11, 1984.
Outlook, February 27, 1929.
PN Review, Number 23, 1981.
Saturday Review, February 6, 1926.
Saturday Review of Literature, April 16, 1927, March 9, 1929, June 27, 1936, December 4, 1948.
Spectator, April 30, 1927, September 25, 1936, December 3, 1948, December 23, 1955.

Studies in Short Fiction, winter, 1973.
Time, February 4, 1966, February 21, 1977, February 1, 1982.
Times Literary Supplement, February 28, 1929, September 22, 1932, July 31, 1943, January 14, 1977, March 10, 1978, May 23, 1980, November 6, 1981, March 18, 1983.
Washington Post, February 6, 1982.
Washington Post Book World, December 18, 1988.
Yale Review, autumn, 1954.

OBITUARIES:

PERIODICALS

New York Times, May 10, 1978.
Publishers Weekly, May 29, 1978.

*   *   *

WARREN, Robert Penn   1905-1989

PERSONAL: Born April 24, 1905, in Guthrie, Ky.; died September 15, 1989, in Stratton, Vt., of cancer; son of Robert Franklin (a businessman) and Anna Ruth (Penn) Warren; married Emma Brescia, September 12, 1930 (divorced, 1950); married Eleanor Clark (a writer), December 7, 1952; children: (second marriage) Rosanna Phelps, Gabriel Penn. *Education:* Vanderbilt University, B.A. (summa cum laude), 1925; University of California, Berkeley, M.A., 1927; Yale University, graduate study, 1927-28; Oxford University, B.Litt., 1930. *Politics:* Democrat.

ADDRESSES: Home—2495 Redding Rd., Fairfield, Conn. 06430; and Vermont. *Office*—Yale University, New Haven, Conn. 06520. *Agent*—Owen Laster, William Morris Agency, 1350 Avenue of the Americas, New York, N.Y. 10019.

CAREER: Poet, novelist, essayist, playwright, educator, literary critic, and editor. Southwestern Presbyterian University (now Southwestern at Memphis), Memphis, Tenn., assistant professor of English, 1930-31; Vanderbilt University, Nashville, Tenn., acting assistant professor, 1931-34; Louisiana State University, Baton Rouge, assistant professor, 1934-36, associate professor, 1936-42; University of Minnesota, Minneapolis, professor of English, 1942-50; Yale University, New Haven, Conn., professor of playwrighting in School of Drama, 1950-56, professor of English, 1961-73, professor emeritus, 1973-89. Visiting lecturer, State University of Iowa, 1941; Jefferson Lecturer, National Endowment for the Humanities, 1974. Staff member of writers conferences, University of Colorado, 1936, 1937, and 1940, and Olivet College, 1940. Consultant in poetry, Library of Congress, 1944-45.

MEMBER: American Academy of Arts and Letters (member of board), Academy of American Poets (chancellor), American Academy of Arts and Sciences, American Philosophical Society, Modern Language Association (honorary fellow), Century Club (New York).

AWARDS, HONORS: Rhodes Scholar, Oxford University, 1928-30; Caroline Sinkler Prize, Poetry Society of South Carolina, 1936, 1937, and 1938; Levinson Prize, *Poetry* magazine, 1936; Houghton Mifflin literary fellowship, 1936; Guggenheim fellowship, 1939-40 and 1947-48; Shelley Memorial Prize, 1942, for *Eleven Poems on the Same Theme;* Pulitzer Prize for fiction, 1947, for *All the King's Men;* Southern Prize, 1947; Robert Meltzer Award, Screenwriters Guild, 1949; Union League Civic and Arts Foundation Prize, *Poetry* magazine, 1953; Sidney Hillman Award, 1957, Edna St. Vincent Millay Memorial Award, American Poetry Society, 1958, National Book Award, 1958, and Pulitzer Prize for poetry, 1958, all for *Promises: Poems,*

1954-1956; Irita Van Doren Award, *New York Herald Tribune,* 1965, for *Who Speaks for the Negro?;* Bollingen Prize in poetry, Yale University, 1967, for *Selected Poems: New and Old, 1923-1966;* National Endowment for the Arts grant, 1968.

Van Wyck Brooks Award for poetry, National Medal for Literature, and Henry A. Bellaman Prize, all 1970, all for *Audubon: A Vision;* award for literature, University of Southern California, 1973; Golden Rose Trophy, New England Poetry Club, 1975; Emerson-Thoreau Medal, American Academy of Arts and Sciences, 1975; Copernicus Prize, American Academy of Poets, 1976; Wilma and Robert Messing Award, 1977; Pulitzer Prize for poetry, 1979, for *Now and Then: Poems, 1976-1978;* Harriet Monroe Award for poetry, 1979, for *Selected Poems: 1923-1975;* MacArthur Foundation fellowship, 1980; Commonwealth Award for Literature, 1980; Hubbell Memorial Award, Modern Language Association, 1980; Connecticut Arts Council award, 1980; Presidential Medal of Freedom, 1980; National Book Critics Circle Award nomination, 1980, and American Book Award nomination, 1981, both for *Being Here: Poetry, 1977-1980;* poetry prize nomination, *Los Angeles Times,* 1982, for *Rumor Verified: Poems, 1979-1980;* creative arts award, Brandeis University, 1984; named first Poet Laureate of the United States, 1986; National Medal of Arts, 1987.

Honorary degrees from University of Louisville, 1949, Kenyon College, 1952, University of Kentucky, 1955, Colby College, 1956, Swarthmore College, 1958, Yale University, 1959, Bridgeport University, 1965, Fairfield University, 1969, Wesleyan University, 1970, Harvard University, 1973, Southwestern at Memphis, 1974, University of the South, 1974, University of New Haven, 1974, Johns Hopkins University, 1977, Monmouth College, 1979, New York University, 1983, Oxford University, 1983, and Arizona State University.

WRITINGS:

POETRY

Thirty-Six Poems, Alcestis Press, 1935.
Eleven Poems on the Same Theme, New Directions, 1942.
Selected Poems: 1923-1943, Harcourt, 1944.
Brother to Dragons: A Tale in Verse and Voices, Random House, 1953, revised edition published as *Brother to Dragons: A Tale in Verse and Voices—A New Version,* 1979.
Promises: Poems, 1954-1956, Random House, 1957.
You, Emperors and Others: Poems, 1957-1960, Random House, 1960.
Selected Poems: New and Old, 1923-1966, Random House, 1966.
Incarnations: Poems, 1966-1968, Random House, 1968.
Audubon: A Vision, Random House, 1969.
Or Else: Poems, 1968-1974, Random House, 1974.
Selected Poems, 1923-1975, Random House, 1976.
Now and Then: Poems, 1976-1978, Random House, 1978.
Being Here: Poetry, 1977-1980, Random House, 1980.
Rumor Verified: Poems, 1979-1980, Random House, 1981.
Chief Joseph of the Nez Perce, Random House, 1983.
New and Selected Poems, 1923-1985, Random House, 1985.

FICTION

Night Rider (novel), Houghton, 1939, reprinted, Vintage Books, 1979, abridged edition, edited and introduced by George Mayberry, New American Library, 1950.
At Heaven's Gate (novel), Harcourt, 1943, reprinted, New Directions, 1985, abridged edition, edited and introduced by Mayberry, New American Library, 1949.
All the King's Men (also see below; novel), Harcourt, 1946, reprinted, Barron, 1985.

Blackberry Winter (novelette), Cummington Press, 1946.
The Circus in the Attic, and Other Stories (short stories), Harcourt, 1947, reprinted, 1968.
World Enough and Time (novel), Random House, 1950, reprinted, Vintage Books, 1979.
Band of Angels (novel), Random House, 1955.
The Cave (novel), Random House, 1959.
The Gods of Mount Olympus (adaptations of Greek myths for young readers), Random House, 1959.
Wilderness: A Tale of the Civil War (novel), Random House, 1961.
Flood: A Romance of Our Time (novel), Random House, 1964.
Meet Me in the Green Glen (novel), Random House, 1971.
A Place to Come To (novel), Random House, 1977.

NONFICTION

John Brown: The Making of a Martyr, Payson & Clarke, 1929, reprinted, Scholarly Press, 1970.
(With others) *I'll Take My Stand: The South and the Agrarian Tradition,* Harper, 1930.
(Contributor) Herbert Agar and Allen Tate, editors, *Who Owns America?: A New Declaration of Independence,* Houghton, 1936.
(Author of critical essay) Samuel Taylor Coleridge, *The Rime of the Ancient Mariner,* illustrated by Alexander Calder, Reynal & Hitchcock, 1946, reprinted, Folcroft, 1971.
Segregation: The Inner Conflict in the South, Random House, 1956.
Remember the Alamo!, Random House, 1958.
Selected Essays, Random House, 1958.
How Texas Won Her Freedom: The Story of Sam Houston and the Battle of San Jacinto (booklet), San Jacinto Museum of History, 1959.
The Legacy of the Civil War: Meditations on the Centennial, Random House, 1961, reprinted, Harvard University Press, 1983.
Who Speaks for the Negro?, Random House, 1965.
A Plea in Mitigation: Modern Poetry and the End of an Era (lecture), Wesleyan College, 1966.
Homage to Theodore Dreiser (criticism), Random House, 1971.
Democracy and Poetry, Harvard University Press, 1975.
(Contributor) *A Time to Hear and Answer: Essays for the Bicentennial Season,* University of Alabama Press, 1977.
Jefferson Davis Gets His Citizenship Back (essay), University of Kentucky Press, 1980.
New and Selected Essays, Random House, 1989.

WITH CLEANTH BROOKS

(Editors with John T. Purser) *An Approach to Literature,* Louisiana State University Press, 1936, 5th edition, Prentice-Hall, 1975.
(Editors) *Understanding Poetry: An Anthology for College Students,* Holt, 1938, 4th edition, 1976.
(Editors) *Understanding Fiction,* Crofts, 1943, 2nd edition, Appleton-Century-Crofts, 1959, shortened version of 2nd edition published as *Scope of Fiction,* 1960, 3rd edition published under original title, Prentice-Hall, 1979.
Modern Rhetoric, Harcourt, 1949, published as *Fundamentals of Good Writing: A Handbook of Modern Rhetoric,* 1950, 2nd edition published under original title, 1958, 4th edition, 1979.
(Editors) *An Anthology of Stories from the Southern Review,* Louisiana State University Press, 1953.
(And R. W. B. Lewis) *American Literature: The Makers and the Making* (criticism), two volumes, St. Martin's, 1974.

EDITOR

A Southern Harvest: Short Stories by Southern Writers, Houghton, 1937, reprinted, N. S. Berg, 1972.
(With Albert Erskine) *Short Story Masterpieces,* Dell, 1954, 2nd edition, 1958, reprinted, Dell, 1989.
(With Erskine) *Six Centuries of Great Poetry,* Dell, 1955.
(With Erskine) *A New Southern Harvest,* Bantam, 1957.
(With Allen Tate) Denis Devlin, *Selected Poems,* Holt, 1963.
Faulkner: A Collection of Critical Essays, Prentice-Hall, 1966.
Randall Jarrell, 1914-1965, Farrar, Straus, 1967.
John Greenleaf Whittier's Poetry: An Appraisal and a Selection, University of Minnesota Press, 1971.
Selected Poems of Herman Melville, Random House, 1971.
Katherine Anne Porter: A Collection of Critical Essays, Prentice-Hall, 1979.
The Essential Melville, Ecco Press, 1987.

PLAYS

"Proud Flesh" (in verse), produced in Minneapolis, Minn., 1947, revised prose version produced in New York City, 1948.
(With Erwin Piscator) *Blut auf dem Mond: Ein Schauspiel in drei Akten* (adaptation of Warren's novel *All the King's Men;* produced in 1947; produced in Dallas, Tex., as "Willie Stark: His Rise and Fall," 1958; produced on Broadway, 1959), Lechte, 1956.
All the King's Men (adaptation of Warren's novel of same title; produced Off-Broadway at East 74th St. Theatre), Random House, 1960.
Ballad of a Sweet Dream of Piece: An Easter Charade (produced in New York City at Cathedral of St. John the Divine), music by Alexei Haieff, Pressworks, 1981.

OTHER

A Robert Penn Warren Reader, Random House, 1987.
Portrait of a Father, University Press of Kentucky, 1988.

Contributor to numerous publications, including *Virginia Quarterly Review, Southern Review, Mademoiselle, Sewanee Review, New Republic, Poetry, American Review, Harvard Advocate, Nation, American Scholar, New York Times Book Review, Holiday, Fugitive, Botteghe Oscure, Yale Review,* and *Saturday Review.* Co-founding editor, *Fugitive,* 1922-25; founder and editor, with Cleanth Brooks, *Southern Review,* 1935-42; advisory editor, *Kenyon Review,* 1938-61.

The complete papers of Robert Penn Warren are collected at Yale University's Beinecke Rare Book and Manuscript Library.

SIDELIGHTS: Described by *Newsweek* reviewer Annalyn Swan as "America's dean of letters and, in all but name, poet laureate," Robert Penn Warren was among the last surviving members of a major literary movement that emerged in the South shortly after World War I. A distinguished poet, novelist, critic, and teacher, he won virtually every major award given to writers in the United States and was the only person to receive a Pulitzer Prize in both fiction (once) and poetry (twice). He also achieved a measure of commercial success that eludes many other serious artists. In short, as Hilton Kramer once observed in the *New York Times Book Review,* Warren "has enjoyed the best of both worlds. . . . Few other writers in our history have labored with such consistent distinction and such unflagging energy in so many separate branches of the literary profession. He is a man of letters on the old-fashioned, outsize scale, and everything he writes is stamped with the passion and the embattled intelligence of a man for whom the art of literature is inseparable from the most fundamental imperatives of life."

Literature did not always play a central role in Warren's life, however. As he recalled in an interview with John Baker published in *Conversations with Writers:* "I didn't expect to become a writer. My ambition was to be a naval officer and I got an appointment to Annapolis. . . . Then I had an accident. I couldn't go—an accident to my eyes—and then I went to [Vanderbilt University] instead, and I started out in life there as a chemical engineer. That didn't last but three weeks or so, because I found the English courses so much more interesting. History courses were also interesting, but the chemistry was taught without imagination."

The freshman English teacher Warren found so fascinating was fellow Southerner John Crowe Ransom, "a real, live poet, in pants and vest, who had published a book and also fought in the war. . . . As a man, he made no effort to charm his students, but everything he said was interesting." Ransom, recognizing that Warren was no ordinary English student, encouraged the young man to enroll in one of his more advanced courses. He also invited Warren to join the "Fugitives," a group of Vanderbilt teachers and students as well as several local businessmen who had been meeting informally since around 1915 to discuss trends in American life and literature. By 1922, the year Warren joined, many of the Fugitives' discussions focused on poetry and critical theory, Warren's favorite subjects at the time. "In a very important way," says Warren in retrospect, "that group was my education."

The Fugitives drifted apart in the mid-1920s, about the same time Warren graduated from Vanderbilt and headed west to continue his education at the University of California in Berkeley. After receiving his M.A. from there in 1927, Warren attended Yale University and then England's Oxford University where, as he described, he "stumbled on" writing fiction. Homesick and weary of devoting his days and nights to working on his dissertation, Warren, at the request of one of the editors of the literary annual *American Caravan,* agreed to compose a novelette based on the folk tales he had heard as a boy in Kentucky. As he later remarked to Baker, his contribution to the annual received "some pleasant notices in the press," and soon publishers were asking him to write novels.

Though Warren did indeed write several novels during the next decade (only one of which, *Night Rider,* was published), most of his time and effort was spent trying to earn a living. Returning to Tennessee in 1930 after completing his studies at Oxford, he briefly served on the faculty of Southwestern Presbyterian University (now Southwestern at Memphis) before obtaining a teaching position at Vanderbilt. From there Warren went to Louisiana State University in 1934, teaming up with friend and fellow faculty member Cleanth Brooks to write a series of immensely successful and influential textbooks, including *An Approach to Literature and Understanding Poetry.* Based on the authors' class notes and conversations, these books have been largely responsible for disseminating the theories of the New Criticism to several generations of college students and teachers. According to Helen McNeil in the *Times Literary Supplement,* Warren and Brooks helped to establish the New Criticism as "an orthodoxy so powerful that contemporary American fiction and poetry are most easily defined by their rebellion against it."

The New Criticism—a method of analyzing a work of art that focuses attention on the work's intrinsic value as an object in and of itself, more or less independent of outside influences (such as the circumstances of its composition, the reality it creates, the effect it has on readers, and the author's intention) grew out of discussions Warren had participated in first as a member of the

Fugitives, then as an Agrarian. (The Agrarians were former Fugitives who banded together again in the late 1920s to extoll the virtues of the rural South and to promote an agrarian as opposed to an industrial economy). Despite his close association with the Agrarians and his key role in publicizing their theories, Warren did not consider himself to be a professional critic. As he explained to Baker: "I have only two roles, essentially: poetry and fiction—and only a certain kind of fiction. . . . A real critic, like Cleanth Brooks or I. A. Richards, has a system. . . . He's concerned with that, primarily. I'm not. I'm interested in trying to understand this poem or that poem, but I'm not interested in trying to create a system. I'm interested in a different kind of understanding, you might say, a more limited kind of understanding. I'm interested in my enjoyment, put it that way, more than anything else. I've certainly written some criticism, but I usually take it from my class notes. I'm just not a professional critic. That business is just something that happens. . . . But writing fiction, poetry, that's serious—that's for keeps."

Poetry and fiction were thus Warren's main concerns throughout his long career, with poetry having edged out fiction as the author's preferred genre since the mid-1950s. He saw nothing unusual in the fact that he made notable contributions to both, remarking to Baker that "a poem for me and a novel are not so different. They start much the same way, on the same emotional journey, and can go either way. . . . At a certain level an idea takes hold. Now it doesn't necessarily come with a form; it comes as an idea or an impulse. . . . I've started many things in one form and shifted to another. . . . The interesting topics, the basic ideas in the poems and the basic ideas in the novels are the same."

For the most part, these "basic ideas" in Warren's poetry and fiction sprang from his Southern Agrarian heritage. Observes Marshall Walker in *London Magazine:* "Warren began as an enlightened conservative Southerner. Like his close associates, John Crowe Ransom, Donald Davidson, Allen Tate, Andrew Lytle, he was acutely aware of the gulf widening between an America that moved further into slavery to material progress and a minority of artists and intellectuals, self-appointed custodians of traditional values. . . . Agrarians, with Ransom in the lead, were determined to re-endow nature with an element of horror and inscrutability and to bring back a God who permitted evil as well as good—in short, to give God back his thunder."

In Warren's work, especially his novels, there is a strong emphasis on what Walker refers to as "the vitality of Southern history." Continues the critic: "[Warren displays] a sense of . . . history as a continuum in which he was himself involved. . . . [He] has long since left Guthrie, Kentucky and the South, to live in the North. He has, nonetheless, remained a Southerner, and the eternal return has been as much a part of his own life as it is of the lives of his characters." Warren's subject matter, for example, is markedly regional; he drew much of his inspiration from personal reminiscences as well as from narratives, ballads, and folk legends he heard as a child in Kentucky and Tennessee.

Despite his reliance on history for material, Warren balked at being labeled a "historical novelist." "I just happened to encounter stories that had the right germ of an idea for a novel," he once stated in a *Saturday Review* article. "I should hope that the historical novel would be a way of saying something about the present." To this end, he often changes the actual historical focus of a story to concentrate on peripheral characters whose behavior reveals more about the ethical or dramatic issues *behind* the facts. Therefore, maintain Everett Wilkie and Josephine Helterman in the *Dictionary of Literary Biography,* Warren's "main ob-

session is knowledge," not history. Explain the critics: "His works reflect the many forms in which he himself has found knowledge. . . . [His] wisdom is the wisdom of interpretation; his main question, 'How is one to look at life?' From an elaboration of the complex forces which shape both our lives and our perceptions, he shows us history as a living force which can yet tell us something about ourselves."

For Warren, this process of self-discovery was painful, yet the opposite state—ignorance—was brutish. In his book *The Poetic Vision of Robert Penn Warren,* Victor Strandberg declares that the contemplation of this passage from innocence to maturity is "the crucial center" of Warren's career. With this theme in mind, writes Strandberg, Warren typically divides his characters into two groups: "those who refuse passage into a polluted and compromised adult environment" (whom Strandberg refers to as the "Clean" people) and "those who accept passage into the world's stew" (the "Dirty" people). The Clean people prefer to think of themselves as being separate from the filth and corruption of the world, while the Dirty people are willing to face life as it is in order "to proceed to the subsequent stages of spiritual development." In Warren's view, the Clean people can either be relatively harmless, reclusive fundamentalist types, or they can be almost psychopathic in their determination to purify the world and punish sinners (i.e., the Dirty people). In all Warren's writing, the "most negative characters are those who reject the osmosis of being, while his spiritual guides are those who accept it," Strandberg observes.

The "action" in most of Warren's work thus consists primarily of an idealistic narrator's search for his or her identity in an atmosphere of confusion and/or corruption. This search eventually leads to recognition of the world's fallen state and, consequently, of the self's "innate depravity," to use Strandberg's phrase. In an attempt to overcome the sense of alienation caused by these "warring parts of the psyche," a typical Warren character undergoes a period of intense self-examination that ideally results in a near-religious experience of conversion, rebirth, and a mystical feeling of oneness with God. This in turn opens the door to further knowledge, not only about the self but about the world as well. Though the search for identity may not always end in success, notes Strandberg, "the craving to recreate that original felicity [that existed before the Fall] is one of mankind's deepest obsessions, in Warren's judgment."

Therefore, as Wilkie interprets it, Warren's goal is "to provide an overview of the human condition and to explicate, or mirror, the perplexities of existence in a world in which belief in God has faded. [He] characterizes himself as a 'yearner,' suggesting that although he does not believe in God, he does believe that man must work out his own code by which to interpret his life and the things around him. . . . In his view, man must come face to face with a reality stripped of both God's benign or malevolent intentions and the Romantic's pathetic fallacy. Despite whatever difficulties man may face in his existence, Warren does not counsel despair or state that life is not worth living. . . . It is essential, [he] asserts, to learn whatever answers one can. . . . Though being alive may not always be easy and fun, Warren believes it is well worth the effort."

Most observers find Warren's language, style, and tone to be perfectly suited to his subject matter. His language, for example, is a lyrical mixture of earthiness and elegance, of the folk speech of Kentucky and Tennessee and what James Dickey refers to in the *Saturday Review* as a "rather quaintly old-fangled scholastic vocabulary." Richard Jackson offers a similar description in the *Michigan Quarterly Review:* "[Warren's] idiom . . . is at once conversational and lyric, contemporary and historic, profane and sacred. It is a language in which he can slip easily from necessary precept to casual observation, cosmic vision to particular sighting." According to a *Sewanee Review* article by Calvin Bedient, Warren's poetry is written "in a genuinely expansive, passionate style. Look at its prose ease and rapidity oddly qualified by log-piling compounds, alliteration, successive stresses, and an occasional inversion something rough and serviceable as a horse-blanket yet fancy to—and you wonder how he ever came up with it. It is excitingly massive and moulded and full of momentum. Echoes of Yeats and Auden still persist, but it is wonderfully peculiar, homemade."

Charles H. Bohner is equally impressed by Warren's forceful and exuberant style. "There is about his art the prodigality of the writer who exercises his verbal gifts for the sheer magic of the effects he can produce," notes the critic in his book-length study of Warren. "[His] language is robust and rhetorical. He likes his adjectives and nouns to go in pairs, reinforcing one another, begetting rhythm and resonance. When a comparison catches his fancy, his first metaphor is likely to suggest another, and he piles image on image as he warms to his task. . . . About all of Warren's work there is a gusto and masculine force, a willingness to risk bathos and absurdity, reminiscent of the writer who, Warren has said, has had the greatest influence on his own work—Shakespeare. . . . He has always seemed driven to explore the boundaries of his art, to push the possibilities of his form to its outer limits."

Though Warren drew extensively from his own past for the language, settings, and themes that appear in both his fiction and poetry, he approached all of this familiar material somewhat objectively and analytically, as if he were contemplating them from a distance, either far from home or, more frequently, much later in time. Warren's preoccupation with time and how the passage of years affects memory reveals itself in his extensive use of flashbacks to illustrate the often ironic nature of the relationship between the past and the present. Critics also find the abundance of background detail in his work to be evidence of his near-obsession with time. According to James H. Justus in the *Sewanee Review,* for instance, one of the hallmarks of Warren's prose is his practice of including "periods of closely observed details strung out in an evocative rhetoric which invites nostalgia for a specific time and place or which invokes awe for a mythic history that seems to explain national and even human urges." And as Paul West asserts in his book *Robert Penn Warren:* "[No] writer has worked harder than Warren to substantiate narrative through close, doting observation of the physical, emotional world. He sees it, makes the page tremble with it. . . . His 'texture of relations'—to his past, to his work, to familiars and strangers—is something he fingers endlessly; and in the long run it is the feel, not the feel's meaning, that he communicates."

Despite the fact that Warren is popularly known as the author of *All the King's Men,* a novel loosely based on the life of Louisianan politician Huey "Kingfish" Long, he thought of himself primarily as a poet. "I started as a poet and I will probably end as a poet," he once commented in the *Sewanee Review.* "If I had to choose between my novels and my *Selected Poems,* I would keep the *Selected Poems* as representing me more fully, my vision and my self."

After emerging from a ten-year-long period of "poet's block" in 1954, Warren devoted most of his creative energies to writing verse. Unlike his early (pre-1944) poetry, which sprang from either the contemplation of complex metaphysical concepts or the ballads and narratives native to his region, Warren's later poetry was inspired by a mood, a natural event, or a memory that often takes shape as "a moralized anecdote," to use Warren's own words. It is a highly personal and often autobiographical (but by no means confessional) form of poetry. In fact, maintains Kramer, "[Warren's] poetry is so unlike that of most other poets claiming our attention . . . that it requires a certain adjustment of the eye and the ear, and of that other faculty—call it the moral imagination—to which Mr. Warren's verse speaks with so much urgency and that of so many other poets nowadays does not. We are a long way, in this poetry, from the verse snapshot and the campy valentine—a long way, too, from the verse diaries, confessions and dirty laundry lists that have come to occupy such a large place in our poetic literature. . . . [His] is a poetry haunted by the lusts and loves of the flesh, filled with dramatic incident, vivid landscapes and philosophical reflection—a poetry of passion recollected in the tragic mode. It teems with experience, and with the lessons and losses of experience."

"Warren sees . . . what few of us have seen," states David Bromwich in the *Hudson Review.* "His poems draw their sustenance from a world of buzzards and swamps and forests almost unscarred; of iron loyalties and sudden betrayals; of the aimless talk of old men, interrupted by a rifle shot, and followed by silence. It is a world in which everything may depend on a rattlesnake heard scuttling for its hole, or a hawk seen obliquely among the shadows."

As Bromwich and other critics make clear, the natural world plays a prominent role in Warren's poetry, providing him with much of his inspiration and imagery. But according to Wilkie in his *Dictionary of Literary Biography* essay, the poet's fascination with nature does not mean he believes man can turn to nature for answers to age-old questions about life and death. "Warren argues repeatedly that the natural world is not a sympathetic or reliable guide to interpreting human life and that man's affairs are a matter of indifference to the rest of creation," asserts the critic. "Only man's pride or ignorance allows him to impute to the natural world any concern with his comings and goings."

Though Warren did not deny that man is an integral part of nature, what he celebrated in his poetry was the trait that sets man apart from nature—namely, his ability (and desire) to seek knowledge in his quest "to make sense out of life." As a result, reports Peter Stitt in the *Southern Review,* "Warren's poems are a resounding testament to man, to nature, and to poetry itself. . . . Among contemporary poets, it has been Robert Penn Warren's task to discover how the void at man's heart may be filled. Though revolutionary for our age, Warren's answer places him at the heart of the great tradition in English and American poetry."

In a strictly artistic sense, too, Warren worked within this great tradition in English and American poetry. Explains Strandberg: "Through a career that reaches back over a half century, encompassing schools of pre-Modern, Modern, and post-Modern aesthetics, [Warren] has displayed both growth and consistency in technical resources. With respect to the ageless elements of poetic technique—command of metaphor, control of tone and diction, powers of organization, mastery of sound effects, and the like—each phase of Warren's career has evinced a 'morality of style' that is true to the classic standard." As Harold Bloom observes in the *New Leader:* "[Warren] alone among living writers ranks with the foremost American poets of the century: Frost, Stevens, Hart Crane, Williams, Pound, Eliot. . . . [He] is that rarest kind of major poet: he has never stopped developing from his origins up to his work-in-progress." Swan agrees, adding, "The progression is striking—from the impersonal tone, inspired by Eliot, of the early poems . . . to the more personal, more intense free-verse style that began with *Promises: Poems, 1954-1956* . . . to the majestic reverie of the late poems."

Warren's later poetry is noted for its rambling conversational rhythm, due in part to what Edward L. Stewart refers to in the *Washington Post Book World* as its "wide range of conventional but loose-limbed, free but masterfully controlled verse patterns." Warren favored very long and very short lines, the use of which creates an irregular meter and sentences that seem to wind down the page, "run[ning] forward, as it were, into experience," says Bedient in *Parnassus.* The overall tone is one of reflection and meditation, though not in a passive sense, writes Alan Williamson, another *Washington Post Book World* critic. "In the whiplash of [Warren's] long line, the most ordinary syntax becomes tense, muscular, searching," comments Williamson. "His ear is formidable, though given to strong effects rather than graceful ones." The *Times Literary Supplement*'s Jay Parini also finds that "power is the word that comes to mind" when reading Warren's work—power that is expressed in the "raw-boned, jagged quality" of his verse.

According to John Rees Moore of the *Sewanee Review,* these are the same features that make Warren's poetry stand out "in sharp contrast to the jittery rhythms and fragmented images—the reaching out for a style—that are characteristic of much recent poetry. Not that wit, boldness, and even a certain nervous energy are missing but that Warren's poetic quest for identity has reached a stage where he is freer to disregard whatever is not of central interest to him and mull over with increased concentration whatever is." In short, notes Peter Clothier in the *Los Angeles Times Book Review,* "in an age when the quick gratification of surface glitter often replaces slower pleasures of craft and care, Robert Penn Warren's poetry reminds us that the work of a master craftsman is literally irreplaceable. . . . [His] is work of absolute formal and intellectual integrity."

Not all reviewers agree that Warren's work deserves such unqualified praise. The focus of most of their criticism is on the author's attitude toward his material; though they acknowledge that Warren tackles unquestionably important themes, they believe his treatment of those themes borders on the bombastic. As Leslie Fiedler explains in a volume of his collected essays, a Warren poem can be "bombastic in the technical sense of the word: [there is] a straining of language and tone toward a scream which can no longer be heard, the absolute cry of bafflement and pain. Such a tone becomes in Warren . . . ridiculous on occasion, ridiculous whenever we lapse from total conviction."

In his book *Contemporaries,* Alfred Kazin points out that "all [of Warren's] work seems to deal with the Fall of Man. And if in reading [him] I have come to be more wary of his handling of this theme, it is because of the nostalgia it conveys, the strident impatient language with which it is expressed, the abstract use to which it is put. . . . Warren tends to make rhetoric of his philosophy." Bedient expresses a similar thought in the *Sewanee Review,* commenting that Warren "seems bitten by the Enormity of it all. He *will* have mystery." As a result, concludes Bedient, his philosophical musings are "sometimes truly awkward and sometimes pseudo-profound."

A few reviewers attribute Warren's occasional awkwardness to the very quality that has made him such a noteworthy figure in American literature: his versatility. Eric Bentley, for one, speculates that Warren's dual role as both artist *and* critic hinders his ability to "submerge himself in the artist." Continues Bentley in a *Kenyon Review* article: "Trite as it is nowadays to stigmatize an author as a dual personality, I cannot help pointing to a dual-

ity in Warren that may well constitute his major problem: it is his combination of critical and creative power. I am far from suggesting that the critical and the creative are of their nature antithetic and I am fully ready to grant that what makes Warren remarkable among American writers is his double endowment. The problem lies precisely in his being so two-sidedly gifted; he evidently finds it endlessly difficult to combine his two sorts of awareness."

Noting in the *Virginia Quarterly Review* that "Warren has dedicated his career to proving the indivisibility of the critical and the creative imaginations," David M. Wyatt goes on to state: "Such a habit of mind stations Warren on the border between . . . the artist who works from experience and the critic who works toward meaning. . . . His works constantly talk about themselves. . . . His characters are placed out of themselves, the bemused or obsessive spectators of their own wayward acts. . . . [Warren] thus joins that central American tradition of speakers—Emerson, Thoreau, Henry Adams, Norman Mailer—who are not only the builders but the interpreters of their own designs."

Parnassus reviewer Rachel Hadas maintains that Warren's difficulties stem from "nothing as simple as a lack of talent." Explains Hadas: "Part of the problem seems to be an inordinate ambition for grandeur; part is what feels to me like haste. If Warren were in less of a hurry to chronicle each dawn dream, birdsong, and memory as it occurred, a process of distillation just might be allowed to take place. Mostly, though, it's a matter of the poet's judgment of his own work. . . . [Warren exhibits an] inability or unwillingness to recognize and settle for the nature of his particular genius. . . . [He], has an imagination of generous proportions. It embraces history, human drama, perhaps above all the beauty of the natural world; it is capable at times of both beauty of form *and* splendor of color. . . . But Warren cannot do everything well. He is *not* an original thinker or a visionary poet; in his handling of condensed lyric, as well as of abstraction, he can be embarrassingly inept." In effect, declares Bedient, also writing in *Parnassus,* "[Warren] has failed to be ruthless toward himself, and his weaknesses loom oppressively in the reflected brilliance of his accomplishments."

Many critics, of course, disagree with these evaluations of Warren's poetry. In another *Parnassus* article, for instance, Paul Mariani writes: "I could quarrel with certain things in Warren I find alien to my own sense of poetics: a sometimes loose, rambling line, a nostalgia verging on obsession, a veering towards philosophical attitudinizing, the mask of the redneck that outrednecks the redneck. But I would rather leave such critical caveats for others. There is enough [in his poetry] to praise, and I am thankful to have been given to drink, if not out of those too rare 'great depths,' then at least from a spring sufficiently deep, sufficiently clear."

Monroe K. Spears reports in the *Sewanee Review* that Warren's failings "are hard for me to specify; I find his attitudes and themes—moral, psychological, and religious—so congenial that it is difficult for me to regard the poetry with proper detachment. Sometimes the themes are perhaps a little too explicit, not very fully dramatized; and there is a danger in the fact that they are basically few, though combined and varied in many ways." Nevertheless, continues Spears, "Warren's later poetry seems to me to embody most of the special virtues of 'open' poetry—accessibility, immediate emotional involvement, wide appeal—and to resist the temptations to formlessness and to moral exhibitionism, self-absorption, and sentimentality that are the chief liabilities of that school."

Even Bentley admits that Warren, despite his faults, "is worth a dozen petty perfectionists." And as poet and critic James Dickey observes in his book *Babel to Byzantium:* "Opening a book of poems by Robert Penn Warren is like putting out the light of the sun, or like plunging into the labyrinth and feeling the thread break after the first corner is passed. One will never come out in the same Self as that in which one entered. When he is good, and often even when he is bad, you had as soon read Warren as live. He gives you the sense of poetry as a thing of final importance to life: as a way or *form* of life. . . . Warren's verse is so deeply and compellingly linked to man's ageless, age-old drive toward self-discovery, self-determination, that it makes all discussion of line endings, metrical variants, and the rest of poetry's paraphernalia appear hopelessly beside the point."

One point critics do agree on, however, is the extraordinary nature of Warren's contribution to literature. In his critical study of the author, Bohner declares that "no other American literary figure of the twentieth century has exhibited greater versatility than Robert Penn Warren. . . . While arguments about his preeminence in any one field would be ultimately inconclusive, his total accomplishment . . . surpasses that of any other living writer." Marshall Walker has similar words of praise for Warren in the *London Magazine,* calling him "America's most distinguished man of letters in the European sense of a writer involved with books and human kind and at ease in a variety of genres. . . . The range of his achievement testifies to the scope and commitment of Warren's human sympathies. Each intellectual act, whether formally poem, novel, or one of the interviews with black leaders in *Who Speaks for the Negro?* is of the nature of a poem, according to his own definition of the poem as 'a way of getting your reality shaped a little better'. . . . Underlying the energy, even the violence that is part of Warren's metaphor of the world as well as of the world itself, is a concern to visualize the meaning of common experience and, without artistic concessions, to make this meaning available in a body of work which, with astonishing success, unites metaphysical and social themes in a single vision."

Writing in the *Saturday Review,* Dickey suggests Warren's depth rather than his range should be celebrated. "[Warren] is direct, scathingly honest, and totally serious about what he feels," Dickey begins. "He plunges as though compulsively into the largest of subjects: those that seem to cry out for capitalization and afflatus and, more often than not in the work of many poets, achieve only the former. . . . He is a poet of enormous courage, with a highly individual intelligence." But above all, concludes Dickey, Robert Penn Warren "looks, and refuses to look away. . . . [He] wounds deeply; he strikes in at blood-level and gut-level, with all the force and authority of time, darkness, and distance themselves, and of the Nothingness beyond nothingness, which may even be God."

MEDIA ADAPTATIONS: Two of Robert Penn Warren's novels have been made into films: "All the King's Men" (winner of an Academy Award for "Best Picture"), released by Columbia Pictures, 1949, and "Band of Angels," released by Warner Brothers, 1956. *All the King's Men* also served as the basis for an opera by Carlisle Floyd, "Willie Stark," broadcast on television, and was adapted as a play by Adrian Hall, "All the King's Men," presented by Trinity Repertory Company, Providence, R.I., April, 1987.

BIOGRAPHICAL/CRITICAL SOURCES:

BOOKS

Authors in the News, Volume 1, Gale, 1976.

Bohner, Charles H., *Robert Penn Warren,* Twayne, 1964.
Bradbury, John, *The Fugitives,* University of North Carolina Press, 1958.
Brooks, Cleanth, *The Hidden God,* Yale University Press, 1963.
Casper, Leonard, *Robert Penn Warren: The Dark and Bloody Ground,* University of Washington Press, 1960.
Contemporary Literary Criticism, Gale, Volume 1, 1973, Volume 4, 1975, Volume 6, 1976, Volume 8, 1978, Volume 10, 1979, Volume 13, 1980, Volume 18, 1981, Volume 39, 1986, Volume 53, 1989.
Conversations with Writers, Gale, 1977.
Cowan, Louise, *The Fugitive Group,* Louisiana State University Press, 1959.
Cowley, Malcolm, editor, *Writers at Work: The Paris Review Interviews,* Viking, 1959.
Dickey, James, *Babel to Byzantium,* Farrar, Straus, 1968.
Dictionary of Literary Biography, Gale, Volume 2: *American Novelists since World War II,* 1978, Volume 48: *American Poets, 1880-1945, Second Series,* 1986.
Dictionary of Literary Biography Yearbook: 1980, Gale, 1981.
Fiedler, Leslie, *The Collected Essays of Leslie Fiedler,* Volume 1, Stein & Day, 1971.
Gray, Richard, *The Literature of Memory: Modern Writers of the American South,* Johns Hopkins University Press, 1977.
Gray, Richard, editor, *Robert Penn Warren: A Collection of Critical Essays,* Prentice-Hall, 1980.
Kazin, Alfred, *Contemporaries,* Atlantic-Little, Brown, 1962.
Litz, A. Walton, editor, *Modern American Fiction: Essays in Criticism,* Oxford University Press, 1963.
Longley, John L., Jr., editor, *Robert Penn Warren: A Collection of Critical Essays,* New York University Press, 1965.
Newquist, Roy, editor, *Conversations,* Rand McNally, 1967.
Rubin, Louis D., Jr., *Writers of the Modern South: The Faraway Country,* University of Washington Press, 1963.
Strandberg, Victor H., *The Poetic Vision of Robert Penn Warren,* University Press of Kentucky, 1977.
Van O'Connor, William, editor, *Forms of Modern Fiction,* Indiana University Press, 1959.
Watkins, Floyd C., and John T. Hiers, editors, *Robert Penn Warren Talking: Interviews 1950-1978,* Random House, 1980.
West, Paul, *Robert Penn Warren,* University of Minnesota Press, 1964.

PERIODICALS

Chicago Tribune, September 10, 1978, April 7, 1985, June 1, 1987.
Chicago Tribune Book Review, October 14, 1979, September 7, 1980, February 28, 1982.
Christian Science Monitor, September 4, 1946.
Commonweal, October 4, 1946.
Detroit News, February 15, 1981.
Hudson Review, summer, 1977.
Kenyon Review, summer, 1948.
London Magazine, December, 1975/January, 1976.
Los Angeles Times, March 19, 1981.
Los Angeles Times Book Review, September 7, 1980, October 19, 1980, January 17, 1982, July 30, 1986.
Michigan Quarterly Review, fall, 1978.
Nation, August 24, 1946.
New Leader, January 31, 1977.
New Republic, September 2, 1946.
Newsweek, August 25, 1980, March 10, 1986.
New Yorker, August 24, 1946, December 29, 1980.

New York Times, August 18, 1946, December 16, 1969, March 2, 1977, June 2, 1981, March 27, 1983, April 24, 1985, October 6, 1986.

New York Times Book Review, June 25, 1950, January 9, 1977, November 2, 1980, May 12, 1985.

Parnassus: Poetry in Review, fall/winter, 1975, summer, 1977, spring/summer, 1979.

People, March 17, 1986.

San Francisco Chronicle, August 18, 1946.

Saturday Review, June 24, 1950, August 20, 1955, August, 1980.

Saturday Review of Literature, August 17, 1946.

Sewanee Review, spring, 1970, spring, 1974, spring, 1975, summer, 1977, spring, 1979, summer, 1980.

Southern Review, spring, 1976.

Time, August 18, 1975.

Times Literary Supplement, November 28, 1980, January 29, 1982, February 17-23, 1989.

Virginia Quarterly Review, summer, 1977.

Washington Post, May 2, 1980, September 23, 1989.

Washington Post Book World, March 6, 1977, October 22, 1978, September 30, 1979, August 31, 1980, October 4, 1981, June 26, 1983, April 30, 1989.

Yale Review, autumn, 1946.

OBITUARIES:

PERIODICALS

Chicago Tribune, September 16, 1989, September 17, 1989.

Globe and Mail (Toronto), September 16, 1989.

Los Angeles Times, September 16, 1989.

New York Times, September 16, 1989.

Washington Post, September 16, 1989.

*   *   *

WARSHOFSKY, Isaac
See SINGER, Isaac Bashevis

*   *   *

WARUK, Kona
See HARRIS, (Theodore) Wilson

*   *   *

WATERHOUSE, Keith (Spencer) 1929-
(Lee Gibb, a joint pseudonym)

PERSONAL: Born February 6, 1929, in Leeds, England; son of Ernest and Elsie Waterhouse; married Joan Foster, October 21, 1950 (divorced, 1968); children: Penelope, Sarah, Robert. *Education:* Attended Osmondthorpe Council School, Leeds.

ADDRESSES: Home—29 Kenway Rd., London SW5 0RP, England. *Agent*—David Hughes Associates, 5-8 Lower John Rd., London W.1, England.

CAREER: Journalist, screenwriter, playwright, novelist.

WRITINGS:

(With Guy Deghy) *Cafe Royal: Ninety Years of Bohemia,* Hutchinson, 1955.

There Is a Happy Land (novel), M Joseph, 1957.

(With Paul Cave) *Britain's Voice Abroad,* Daily Mirror Newspapers (London), 1957.

The Future of Television, Daily Mirror Newspapers, 1958.

(With Herald Froy [pseudonym of Guy Deghy]) *How to Avoid Matrimony,* Muller, 1958, Day, 1959.

(With Deghy, under joint pseudonym Lee Gibb) *The Joneses: How to Keep Up with Them,* Muller, 1959.

Billy Liar (novel), M. Joseph, 1959, Norton, 1960.

(With Willis Hall) *Billy Liar: A Play in Three Acts* (based on the novel; first produced in London at the Cambridge Theatre, September 13, 1960; first produced in Los Angeles at the Stage Society Theatre, January, 1963), M. Joseph, 1960, Norton, 1961.

(With Deghy, under joint pseudonym Lee Gibb) *The Higher Jones,* Muller, 1961.

(With Hall) *Celebration* (play; first produced in Nottingham, England, at the Nottingham Playhouse, March, 1961; first produced in London at the Duchess Theatre, June 8, 1961), M. Joseph, 1961.

(With Hall) *England, Our England* (play, first produced in London at the Green Hippodrome, April 9, 1962; produced in London at the Prince's Theatre, May 7, 1962), Evans Brothers, 1964.

(With Hall) *All Things Bright and Beautiful* (play; first produced in Bristol, England, at the Bristol Old Vic, October 23, 1962; first produced in London at the Phoenix Theatre, December 13, 1962), M. Joseph, 1963.

(With Hall) *The Sponge Room* and *Squat Betty* (plays; first produced in Nottingham, England, at the Nottingham Playhouse, November 13, 1962; first produced in London at the Royal Court Theatre, December 18, 1962), Evans Brothers, 1963.

(With Hall) *Joey, Joey* (play), first produced in Bristol, England, at the Bristol Old Vic, December 26, 1962; first produced in London at the Saville Theatre, November, 1966.

Jubb (novel), M. Joseph, 1963, Putnam, 1964.

(With Hall) *They Called the Bastard Stephen* (play; first produced in Bristol at the Bristol Old Vic, 1964; first produced in London at the Wimbledon Theatre as *Come Laughing Home,* March 29, 1965), published as *Come Laughing Home,* Evans Brothers, 1966.

(With Hall) *Say Who You Are* (play; first produced in Guildford, England, at the Yvonne Arnaud Theatre, August 3, 1965; first produced in London at the Haymarket Theatre, October 14, 1965; first produced on Broadway at the Booth Theatre as *Help Stamp Out Marriage,* September 29, 1966), Evans Brothers, 1966.

(Editor with Hall) *Writers' Theatre,* Heinemann, 1967.

(With Hall) *Whoops-a-Daisy* (play; first produced in Nottingham at the Nottingham Playhouse, December, 1968), Evans Brothers, 1978.

The Bucket Shop (novel), M. Joseph, 1968, published in America as *Everything Must Go,* Putnam, 1969.

(With Hall) *Children's Day* (play; first produced in Nottingham at the Nottingham Playhouse, July, 1969), Samuel French, 1975.

The Warmongers (television script), British Broadcasting Corp., 1970.

(With Hall) *Who's Who* (play; first produced in Coventry, England, at the Belgrade Theatre, July 6, 1971; first produced in London at the Fortune Theatre, June 27, 1973), Samuel French, 1974.

(With Hall) *The Card* (play; adaptation of novel by Arnold Bennett), first produced in Bristol at the Bristol Old Vic, 1973; first produced in London at the Queen's Theatre, July 23, 1973.

(With Hall) *Saturday, Sunday, Monday* (play; adaptation of play by Eduardo de Filippo; first produced in London at the National Theatre, October 31, 1973), Heinemann, 1974.

The Passing of the Third Floor Buck, M. Joseph, 1974.

Billy Liar on the Moon, M. Joseph, 1975, Putnam, 1976.
Mondays, Thursdays, M. Joseph, 1976.
Office Life, M. Joseph, 1978.
(With Hall) *Filumena* (adaptation of the play by Filippo), Samuel French, 1978.
The Upchat Line (television script), Thames Television, 1978.
The Upchat Connection (television script), Thames Television, 1979.
(With Hall) *The Television Adventures of Worzel Gummidge,* Penguin, 1979.
Rhubarb, Rhubarb, and Other Noises, M. Joseph, 1979.
(With Hall) *Worzel Gummidge* (play), first produced in Birmingham, England, at the Birmingham Repertory Theatre, December 12, 1980.
(With Hall) *More Television Adventures of Worzel Gummidge,* Penguin, 1980.
(With Hall) *Worzel Gummidge at the Fair,* Penguin, 1980.
(With Hall) *Worzel Gummidge Goes to the Seaside,* Penguin, 1980.
(With Hall) *The Trials of Worzel Gummidge,* Penguin, 1981.
Maggie Muggins; or, Spring in Earl's Court, M. Joseph, 1981.
"Daily Mirror" Style, Mirror Books, 1981.
West End Tales (television script), Thames Television, 1981.
In the Mood, M. Joseph, 1983.
Mrs. Pooter's Diary, Corgi, 1984.
Thinks, M. Joseph, 1984.
(With Hall) *Irish Adventures of Worzel Gummidge,* Severn House Publishers, 1984.
Theory and Practice of Lunch, M. Joseph, 1986.
The Collected Letters of a Nobody, M. Joseph, 1986.
(With Hall) *Worzel Gummidge Down Under,* Grafton Books, 1987.
Waterhouse at Large, Grafton Books, 1987.
Our Song, Hodder, 1988.
Jeffrey Bernard Is Unwell (play), first produced in London at the Apollo Theatre, October, 1989.

Contributor to *New Statesman, Cosmopolitan, Punch, Observer, Daily Mirror,* and *Queen.*

SCREENPLAYS; WITH WILLIS HALL

Whistle Down the Wind (adaptation of novel by Mary Hayley Bell), AFM-Beaver, 1961.
A Kind of Loving (adaptation of novel by Stan Barstow), BHP-Euro-International, 1962.
The Valiant, BHP-Euro-International, 1963.
Billy Liar, Vic-Waterhall, 1963.
West Eleven (adaptation of novel by Laura del Rivo), Dial Films, 1963.
Man in the Middle (adaptation of novel by Howard Fast), Pennebaker-Belmont, 1964.
Pretty Polly (adaptation of story by Noel Coward), George-Granat-Universal, 1967.
Lock Up Your Daughters (adaptation of play by Bernard Miles), Domino, 1969.

TELEVISION SCRIPTS; WITH WILLIS HALL

Inside George Webley (series), Yorkshire Television, 1968.
Queenie's Castle (series), Yorkshire Television, 1970.
Budgie (series), Weekend Television, 1971-72.
The Upper Crusts (series), London Weekend Television, 1973.
Three's Company (series), BBC, 1973.
Billy Liar (series), London Weekend Television, 1973-74.

RADIO SCRIPTS

The Town That Wouldn't Vote, BBC, 1951.

There Is a Happy Land, BBC, 1962.
The Woollen Bank Forgeries, BBC, 1964.
The Last Phone-In, BBC, 1976.
The Big Broadcast of 1922, BBC, 1979.

SIDELIGHTS: Keith Waterhouse's brilliant satire and caricatures have been cited in discussions of the "Angry Young Men" school of writing, while his heroes have been compared with those of Alan Sillitoe and John Osborne. But he defies classification. Burling Lowrey writes: "He is not visibly anti-Establishmentarian, nor pro-Red Brick, nor a prole. He is himself an original with a talent for exposing hypocrisy, stupidity, and corruption with comic detachment." Waterhouse's novels and plays are marked by what Paul Schlueter in the *Dictionary of Literary Biography* calls "a sardonic, even cynical perspective, in which seemingly doomed characters flounder as they attempt to discover who they are and what they have to offer the world. Waterhouse uses humor, especially exaggeration and wit, as a calculated, objective means of showing his characters to be both psychically and ethically empty."

Billy Liar, a novel about a daydreaming undertaker's assistant who has trouble distinguishing his fantasies from reality, established Waterhouse as a novelist of distinction, and most critics agree with Hubert Saal of *Saturday Review,* who called the book "a brilliant novel, in language fresh and sweet, with characters vivid and singular in an inventive and dynamic story. It teems, it bursts with originality." Judith Thompson notes in the *Dictionary of Literary Biography* that "the combination of humor and pathos in Billy's adolescent fantasies about life in London and his absurd and painful relationship with his social and domestic context was readily translatable onto the stage." The stage version of the story ran for 600 performances in London; a television series based on the book ran on London Weekend Television in 1973-74.

Later Waterhouse works range from the North Country realism of *All Things Bright and Beautiful* to the black comedy of *Jubb.* In his best work, he manages to present characters "on the fringes of society, finely drawing out the pathos and dignity," as Carol Rumens observes in the *Times Literary Supplement.* Alan Hollinghurst, writing in *New Statesman,* finds that Waterhouse "has compacted two kinds of comedy: a relentlessly observant ridicule of the world, and a private systematisation of things carried out by the characters to protect themselves from their uncharitable and ridiculous circumstances." Thompson believes that Waterhouse's versatility may have "denied him some rightful acclaim," but concludes: "He is a man of exceptionally varied talents: his wit, intelligence, and capacity to entertain are fired by an acute and compassionate observation of society and human behavior, a modest humanitarianism which cares deeply that people should have access to beauty—and to laughter."

BIOGRAPHICAL/CRITICAL SOURCES:

BOOKS

Armstrong, W. A. and others, *Experimental Drama,* G. Bell, 1963.
Contemporary Fiction in America and England, 1950-1970, Gale, 1976.
Contemporary Literary Criticism, Volume 47, Gale, 1988.
Dictionary of Literary Biography, Gale, Volume 13: *British Dramatists since World War II,* 1982, Volume 15: *British Novelists, 1930-1959,* 1983.
Gindin, James, *Postwar British Fiction: New Accents and Attitudes,* University of California Press, 1962.

Gray, Nigel, *The Silent Majority: A Study of the Working Class in Post-War British Fiction,* Barnes & Noble, 1973.

Handley, Graham, *Brodie's Notes on Billy Liar,* Pan Books, 1977.

Karl, Frederick R., *The Contemporary English Novel,* Farrar, Straus, 1962.

O'Connor, William Van, *The New University Wits,* Southern Illinois University Press, 1963.

PERIODICALS

Books and Bookmen, January, 1979; July, 1983.
British Book News, December, 1983; October, 1984.
Chicago Sunday Tribune, June 10, 1960.
Critique, Volume 10, number 3, 1968.
Drama, summer, 1966.
Hudson Review, spring, 1961.
Illustrated London News, December 29, 1962.
Listener, November 6, 1975; June 30, 1983; September 6, 1984.
New Statesman, September 12, 1959; September 17, 1960; December 28, 1962; October 4, 1968; June 12, 1981.
Newsweek, April 6, 1964.
New Yorker, March 7, 1964.
New York Times, September 30, 1966; December 13, 1968; December 1, 1989; December 3, 1989.
New York Times Book Review, January 3, 1960; April 5, 1964; January 26, 1969; February 8, 1976.
Observer, November 5, 1978; October 2, 1983; April 13, 1986.
Saturday Review, February 27, 1960; April 4, 1964.
Spectator, September 11, 1959; December 28, 1962; October 25, 1975; October 21, 1989.
Times (London), February 21, 1961; May 8, 1962; October 15, 1965; September 4, 1969; September 6, 1984; April 17, 1986; March 15, 1990.
Times Literary Supplement, September 4, 1959; September 27, 1963; October 25, 1974; May 29, 1981; May 13, 1983; April 18, 1986.
Yale Review, March, 1960.

*   *   *

WATSON, Irving S.
See MENCKEN, H(enry) L(ouis)

*   *   *

WATSON, Richard F.
See SILVERBERG, Robert

*   *   *

WAUGH, Evelyn (Arthur St. John) 1903-1966

PERSONAL: Born October 28, 1903, in Hampstead, London, England; died April 10, 1966, in Combe Florey, Somerset, England; son of Arthur (an editor and publisher) and Catherine Charlotte (Raban) Waugh; married Evelyn Gardner, 1928 (divorced, 1930; marriage annulled, 1936); married Laura Herbert, 1937; children: (second marriage) Auberon, Margaret, Teresa, Harriet, James, Septimus. *Education:* Attended Hertford College, Oxford, 1921-24, and Heatherley's Art School, 1924. *Religion:* Roman Catholic.

CAREER: Writer. Worked as a school teacher, a journalist for the London *Daily Express,* and as war correspondent in Abyssinia (now Ethiopia). *Military service:* Royal Marines, 1939-40,

Commandos, 1940-43, and the Royal Horse Guards, 1943-45; served in Crete, North Africa, and Yugoslavia; became major.

AWARDS, HONORS: Hawthornden Prize, 1936, for *Edmund Campion: Scholar, Priest, Hero, and Martyr;* Black Memorial Prize, 1953; Royal Society of Literature fellow and companion of literature, 1963; honorary degree from Loyola College; refused to accept Commander of the British Empire award.

WRITINGS:

NOVELS

Decline and Fall, Chapman & Hall, 1928, Doran, 1929, reprinted, Little, Brown, 1977.

Vile Bodies, J. Cape & H. Smith, 1930, reprinted, Little, Brown, 1977.

Black Mischief, Farrar & Rinehart, 1932, reprinted, Little, Brown, 1977.

A Handful of Dust, Farrar & Rinehart, 1934, reprinted, Little, Brown, 1977.

Scoop, Little, Brown, 1938, reprinted, 1977 (published in England as *Scoop: A Novel About Journalists,* Chapman Hall, 1938).

Put Out More Flags, Little, Brown, 1942, reprinted, 1977.

Brideshead Revisited: The Sacred and Profane Memories of Captain Charles Ryder, Little, Brown, 1945, reprinted, 1982, revised edition, Chapman & Hall, 1960.

Scott-King's Modern Europe, Chapman & Hall, 1947, Little, Brown, 1949.

The Loved One: An Anglo-American Tragedy, Little, Brown, 1948, reprinted, 1977.

Helena, Little, Brown, 1950.

Men at Arms (also see below), Little, Brown, 1952, reprinted, 1979.

Love among the Ruins: A Romance of the Near Future, Chapman & Hall, 1953.

Officers and Gentlemen (also see below), Little, Brown, 1955, reprinted, 1979.

The Ordeal of Gilbert Pinfold: A Conversation Piece, Little, Brown, 1957, reprinted, 1979.

Unconditional Surrender (also see below), Chapman & Hall, 1961, published as *The End of the Battle,* Little, Brown, 1962, reprinted, 1979.

Basil Seal Rides Again; or, The Rake's Regress, Little, Brown, 1963.

Sword of Honour (contains *Men at Arms, Officers and Gentlemen,* and *Unconditional Surrender*), Chapman & Hall, 1965, Little, Brown, 1966.

STORY COLLECTIONS

Mr. Loveday's Little Outing and Other Sad Stories, Little, Brown, 1936, expanded edition published as *Charles Ryder's Schooldays and Other Stories,* 1982.

Work Suspended: Two Chapters of an Unfinished Novel, Chapman & Hall, 1942, expanded edition published as *Work Suspended and Other Stories Written before the Second World War,* Chapman & Hall, 1949, reprinted, Penguin, 1982.

Tactical Exercise, Little, Brown, 1954.

OTHER

The World to Come (poems), Westminster Press, 1916.

P.R.B.: An Essay on the Pre-Raphaelite Brotherhood, 1847-1854, Graham, 1926, reprinted, Dalrymple Press, 1982.

Rosetti: His Life and Works, Dodd, 1928, reprinted, Norwood, 1978.

A Bachelor Abroad, J. Cape & H. Smith, 1930 (published in England as *Labels: A Mediterranean Journal,* Duckworth, 1930, reprinted, 1974).

Remote People, Duckworth, 1931, published as *They Were Still Dancing,* Farrar & Rinehart, 1932.

An Open Letter to His Eminence, the Cardinal Archbishop of Westminster, Whitefriars, 1933.

Ninety-Two Days: The Account of a Tropical Journey through British Guinea and Part of Brazil, Farrar & Rinehart, 1934 (published in England as *Ninety-Two Days: A Journey in Guinea and Brazil,* Duckworth, 1986).

Edmund Campion : Scholar, Priest, Hero, and Martyr, Sheed, 1935, reprinted, Oxford University Press, 1980.

Waugh in Abyssinia, Longmans, 1936.

Mexico: An Object Lesson, Little, Brown, 1939 (published in England as *Robbery Under Law: The Mexican Object Lesson,* Chapman & Hall, 1939).

When the Going Was Good, Little, Brown, 1946, reprinted, Greenwood Press, 1976.

Wine in Peace and War, Saccone & Speed, 1947.

The Holy Places (essays), Queen Anne, 1952, Queen Anne British Book Centre, 1953.

The World of Evelyn Waugh, edited by Charles J. Rolo, Little, Brown, 1958.

Monsignor Ronald Knox, Fellow of Trinity College, Oxford, and Protonotary Apostolic to His Holiness Pope Pius XII, Little, Brown, 1959 (published in England as *The Life of the Right Reverend Ronald Knox, Fellow of Trinity College, Oxford, and Protonotary Apostolic to His Holiness Pope Pius XII,* Chapman & Hall, 1959).

Tourist in Africa, Little, Brown, 1960, reprinted, 1986.

A Little Learning: An Autobiography, the Early Years, Little, Brown, 1964, reprinted, 1984 (published in England as *A Little Learning: The First Volume of an Autobiography,* Chapman & Hall, 1964).

The Diaries of Evelyn Waugh, edited by Michael Davie, Weidenfeld & Nicolson, 1976, Little, Brown, 1977.

A Little Order: A Selection from the Journalism of Evelyn Waugh, edited by Donat Gallagher, Eyre Methuen, 1977.

The Letters of Evelyn Waugh, edited by Mark Amory, Ticknor & Fields, 1980.

The Essays, Articles and Reviews of Evelyn Waugh, edited by Donat Gallagher, Little, Brown, 1984.

Evelyn Waugh, Apprentice: The Early Writings, 1910-1927, edited and with an introduction by Robert Murray Davis, Pilgrim Books (Norman, Okla.), 1985.

Also editor of *A Selection from the Occasional Sermons of Ronald Knox,* 1949.

SIDELIGHTS: During a career lasting four decades, Evelyn Waugh was considered to be England's most prominent man of letters. He published highly regarded travel books, short stories, essays, and literary criticism. But it is as a novelist that Waugh is most remembered. Such early novels as *Decline and Fall, Vile Bodies,* and *Black Mischief* established his literary reputation as a fine satirist, while such later works as *Brideshead Revisited* brought him popular acclaim from an international audience. He was "one of the most devastating and effective satirists in the history of English letters," Paul A. Doyle of the *Dictionary of Literary Biography* declared, "and one of its greatest stylists." In an article for the *American Spectator,* George McCartney described Waugh as a "superbly gifted entertainer [who] was also one of our century's most important novelists."

Waugh's father was an editor with the English publishing house of Chapman & Hall. His older brother, Alec, was a novelist and travel writer. But Evelyn at first rebelled against the family's literary tradition. While attending Oxford in the early 1920s, he was more interested in the decorative arts than in literature, and he designed stained glass windows. But he was forced to leave school because of his poor grades. Waugh attended an art school, then worked as a schoolmaster. His career in teaching ended after he was fired from three schools in two years. As Waugh explained in *A Little Learning: An Autobiography, the Early Years,* "I was from the first an obvious dud." Reluctantly, Waugh began to write.

Decline and Fall, written by Waugh at the age of twenty-five, is a satiric novel in which young Paul Pennyfeather is dismissed from Oxford and must make his own way in the world. Pennyfeather is a Candide-like innocent who passively watches the disturbing and corrupt events he finds himself in. The evil prosper, the good are punished, and no standards of behavior are operable. Pennyfeather lives in "a world as remote from moral considerations as a fairy story or a Marx Brothers film," Walter Allen wrote in *The Modern Novel.* Like many of Waugh's narrators, Pennyfeather "stands at the centre of [Waugh's] comedy, omniscient yet evasively neutral, surrounded by outrage and absurdity," as Malcolm Bradbury stated in *Possibilities: Essays on the State of the Novel.*

Because of the scandalous nature of *Decline and Fall,* Waugh was forced by his publisher to remove certain scenes from the novel and to preface the book with a disclaimer. On a first reading, it may seem as if Waugh were "allowing all seven deadly sins to hold sway and was enjoying the triumph of evil and decadence . . . with the most carefree insouciance possible," as Doyle stated. But a more careful examination of the text, Doyle continued, showed that "underneath the surface of absurdity and seeming indifference, there lies a basic standard of decency and fair play against which human aberrations are sharply contrasted." Anthony Burgess argued in his *Urgent Copy: Literary Studies* that the novel's continuing power is due to its underlying moral purpose. "Waugh's humour," Burgess wrote, "is never flippant. *Decline and Fall* would not have maintained its freshness for nearly forty years if it had not been based on one of the big themes of our Western literature—the right of the decent man to find decency in the world."

"*Decline and Fall,*" Stephen Jay Greenblatt stated in *Three Modern Satirists: Waugh, Orwell, and Huxley,* "was characterized by its wild audacity, but *Vile Bodies* [Waugh's second novel] is a comedy haunted by an inexplicable sadness. . . . One of the curious qualities of *Vile Bodies* is the reader's inability to discriminate between guilt and innocence." Because he has lost his belief in traditional values, Adam Symes of *Vile Bodies* is an innocent who innocently commits the most loathsome of crimes. The world he inhabits is unstable and in constant flux, symbolized in one scene in which a wild party is held in a dirigible. This instability is reflected in the narrative, which leaps randomly from scene to scene and has little coherent plot. Because Adam's instability is symbolic of his generation of postwar English youth, "*Vile Bodies* is one of those rare novels, like *The Great Gatsby,* that seem to define and sum up a period. It can stand for one aspect of life in the England of the twenties," Allen believed. "It is a triumph of style and the comic spirit." Writing of the novel for the *New York Review of Books* in 1980, Clive James found that it "remains one of the funniest books in the world."

Black Mischief, Waugh's third novel, is set in Africa and concerns the attempted modernization of the country of Azania. "The abortive attempt to modernize Azania," Greenblatt explained, "is not a statement of the African nation's inability to share in the glories of civilization but a sly and satiric examination of modernity itself." The Emperor Seth of Azania enlists the aid of the Englishman Basil Seal to bring his backward country into the twentieth century. But Seal's understanding of modern civilization is sadly shallow, and Seth's fervent efforts to follow Seal's guidelines result in tragedy for his people. Doyle called *Black Mischief* a "wild, rollicking comedy . . . with a more savage note of satire" than was found in Waugh's earlier books. Greenblatt saw *Black Mischief* as being concerned with the same themes as Waugh's earlier novels: "the shabbiness of Western culture, the decline and fall of institutions, the savagery underlying society."

Waugh's early novels established his reputation as a satirist of the first order. But Edmund Wilson, in his *Classics and Commercials: A Literary Chronicle of the Forties,* believed these books to be more than good satire. Wilson ranked them among the best novels written during the 1920s. Waugh's novels are, he wrote, "the only things written in England that are comparable to Fitzgerald and Hemingway. They are not so poetic; they are perhaps less intense; they belong to a more classical tradition. But I think that they are likely to last and that Waugh, in fact, is likely to figure as the only first-rate comic genius that has appeared in England since Bernard Shaw." Gene Kellogg, writing in *The Vital Tradition: The Catholic Novel in a Period of Convergence,* also praised Waugh's early novels. "The books which assure Waugh his place in literature," Kellogg wrote, "are his satires. Their vitality is such that when one reads them the 'lost generation' and all the tragic emptiness that beset England after the First World War live again in startling immediacy."

Several critics saw the nihilistic chaos of Waugh's early novels as an attack on modern society and its lack of permanent values. As Alvin B. Kernan wrote in the *Yale Review:* "Leave man, individual man, to decide on his own values, throw him into a relativistic world in which nothing is certain, corrupt the traditional institutions and ways of doing things so that no honest man can believe in them, and the result will be, as Waugh regularly shows, confusion, self-defeat, the grotesque distortion of human nature, and frantic but meaningless activity." Steven Marcus, in his *Representations: Essays on Literature and Society,* explained that in Waugh's early novels, he "was able to sustain a tone of bemused mournfulness over a society bent on smashing itself to pieces, while at the same time depicting the feckless innocence of both those who were most active in the smashing and those most hurt by it." And Patricia Corr, writing in *Studies: An Irish Quarterly Review,* thought that "the world depicted in [these] novels is one of seemingly irreparable futility. It is a sham world of hypocrisy and dishonesty, of irresponsibility and license, a world from which all spiritual values have been eliminated."

Because of his portrayal of the modern world as chaotic and without purpose, Waugh was often characterized as a social conservative. He clarified his stance in an interview with Julian Jebb of the *Partisan Review.* Waugh was asked: "Do you think it just to describe you as a reactionary?" He replied: "An artist must be a reactionary. He has to stand out against the tenor of the age and not go flopping along; he must offer some little opposition."

Waugh's disenchantment with modern society led in 1930 to his conversion to Catholicism, an act which Rita Dallas of the *Washington Post* called "the most important event in his life." The conversion was spurred by the breakup of Waugh's first marriage. As Doyle explained it, "he was searching for a focus of order and stability where marriage vows were taken seriously and moral values were constantly emphasized."

This newfound religious purpose is first reflected in *A Handful of Dust,* published in 1934. Here, Waugh presents three-dimensional characters in "a seemingly simple story of the failure of a marriage," Greenblatt stated. But the novel, Greenblatt continued, becomes "a terrifying and bitter examination of humanism and modern society." Gone is the wild satire of Waugh's previous novels. "Waugh turned with this novel to more subtle satire and biting irony," Doyle wrote. "His comic satire [became] more embittered."

Largely autobiographical, the novel traces the collapse of Tony and Brenda Last's marriage after Brenda has an affair with John Beaver. Brenda's affair is encouraged by her sophisticated London friends. "The adultery of Lady Brenda Last and her parasite John Beaver," Brigid Brophy wrote in *Don't Never Forget: Collected Views and Reviews,* "catches a particular cold lust in action—in the very action of cold-sweating; theirs is a sado-masochistic relation which is expressed and enjoyed in social terms, in the actual mental vocabulary of snobbism." The novel ends in tragicomedy. A despairing Tony travels to the Brazilian jungle to forget his troubles but is taken prisoner by a Mr. Todd. Todd, a devotee of Charles Dickens, forces Tony into reading to him from Dickens' novels, presumably for the rest of his life.

The title of the novel is taken from a line in "The Wasteland" by T. S. Eliot, "I will show you fear in a handful of dust." The novel does convey, according to Wilson, "the impression of a terror, of a feeling that the bottom is just about to drop out of things." Doyle also saw this horrific element in *A Handful of Dust,* commenting that the novel was concerned with "the horror of twentieth-century amorality" and calling it "a classic portrayal of contemporary savagery." Robert Murray Davis, in *Papers on Literature and Language,* argued that *Decline and Fall, Black Mischief,* and *A Handful of Dust* were Waugh's "most successful novels." In each, Davis wrote, Waugh "presents the madness of the outer world as inevitable and therefore beyond judgment and the refuge as desirable and necessary but not fully secure or satisfying." Speaking of *A Handful of Dust* in relation to other Waugh novels, Davis found that "because it confronts directly the ills of modern civilization and embodies them in characters rather than in a series of intellectual fads and because it traces more vividly and uncompromisingly the effects of seeking refuge from the world without adequate resources for the retreat or an ordered, enduring place of withdrawal, *A Handful of Dust* is the most penetrating of Waugh's novels."

This high regard for *A Handful of Dust* was shared by several critics, including Wilson, who believed it to be "the author's masterpiece. Here he has perfected his method. . . . The author creates by implication an atmosphere and a set of relations upon which almost any other novelist would spend pages of description and analysis." Speaking of the same novel, Greenblatt called it "the culmination of [Waugh's] art. By the accumulation of a great many seemingly irrelevant details, Waugh evokes a whole world, a philosophy, and a way of life as well as an architecture and a landscape." Allen believed that "at once comic and grim, *A Handful of Dust* is one of the best novels of our time."

While *A Handful of Dust* was strongly Catholic in tone, it was not until *Brideshead Revisited: The Sacred and Profane Memories of Captain Charles Ryder,* published in 1945, that Waugh wrote an overtly Catholic novel. "With *Brideshead Revisited,*" Christopher Hollis explained in his *Evelyn Waugh,* "we enter upon . . . the explicitly and consciously Catholic novels [of Waugh's career]." Although the story revolves around a religious conversion, it is not "a work of apologetics," as Hollis wrote. "All that Waugh . . . is concerned to do is to show the strength of [the Church's] claims on those who have ever come under their influence.''

Brideshead Revisited chronicles twenty years in the lives of the Marchmains, a wealthy English Catholic family. It is narrated by Charles Ryder, who befriends Sebastian Marchmain while attending Oxford in the 1920s and is later engaged to Sebastian's sister, Julia. Sebastian is an alcoholic; Julia has her first marriage annulled; and their father, long separated from his wife, returns to the Church only on his deathbed. "The lives of the Marchmains and of Charles Ryder are not pretty ones," James F. Carens admitted in *The Satiric Art of Evelyn Waugh*, "and their Catholicism is no easy consolation." Despite their trials, the "Marchmain family, in their various fashions, all yield, ultimately, to the promptings of their faith and bear witness to its enduring virtue," Wilson noted. Upon witnessing Lord Marchmain's deathbed return to the Church, Charles, too, accepts Catholicism as his faith.

Because of its essentially Catholic message and its alleged idealizing of the English upper classes, *Brideshead Revisited* proved to be the most controversial of Waugh's novels. "Its sentimentality and its apparent obeisance to the old siren attractions of both the English gentry and the Church," L. E. Sissman wrote in the *New Yorker*, "made [*Brideshead Revisited*] unswallowable to critics." One such critic is Bernard Bergonzi. Writing in *Critical Quarterly*, Bergonzi maintained that in *Brideshead Revisited*, "the aristocracy—particularly the Catholic aristocracy—were seen as the unique custodians of the traditional values in a world increasingly threatened by the barbarians." Wilson claimed that "Waugh's snobbery, hitherto held in check by his satirical point of view, has here emerged shameless and rampant."

Marcus thought that the novel's religious ambitions were undermined by Waugh's inherent class bias. "Waugh's snobbery and growing biliousness," Marcus wrote, "could not accommodate themselves to humane, religious impulses. . . . Even Catholicism, most hierarchic of religious dispensations, is too democratic for Waugh. . . . The unpleasant atmosphere of *Brideshead Revisited* was directly a result of the far-reaching disagreement between Waugh and his religion." But Brad Leithauser of the *New Republic* argued that Waugh's Catholicism "gives *Brideshead Revisited,* the most unfairly denigrated of his novels, its submerged power. *Brideshead* was . . . the book in which Waugh invested the most of himself: in some ways, it was the book of his life."

Other critics noted a lush romanticism in Waugh's prose. Carens complained that Waugh tended in *Brideshead Revisited* "so to romanticize experience that his tone degenerates into sentimentality" and found the section of the book dealing with the affair between Julia and Charles to be filled with "one purple passage after another." Doyle explained in his book Evelyn Waugh that "the only serious mistake for which Waugh blamed himself was to write *Brideshead Revisited* in a romantic style, which has been called lush and lavish by several critics. . . . Waugh had committed an offense against his own canons of stylistic purity and restraint." In 1960 Waugh revised *Brideshead Revisited* in an attempt to curb the lush excesses of the original edition.

Still, *Brideshead Revisited* was Waugh's most successful novel. It was a best-seller in England and the United States and helped to make him internationally known. One reason for the book's success was the timing of its initial appearance. Written during the Second World War and published at the war's end, *Brideshead Revisited,* with its romantic evocation of upper class life in the 1920s, seemed exotic and sensuous to a war-weary audience accustomed to rationing. "In 1945," Dallas wrote, " 'Brideshead

Revisited' was a splash of color in a gray postwar world: Oxford in the 20s, parties at great country houses and beautiful people languishing on luxury liners." Waugh told Jebb that "the fact [*Brideshead Revisited*] is rich in evocative description—in gluttonous writing—is a direct result of the privations and austerity of the times."

And yet, part of the novel's success lies in the power of its prose, despite the critical attacks on its merits. Sissman admitted that the first half of *Brideshead Revisited* "is so beautifully written that it may eclipse much of Waugh's other work." Doyle, writing in the *Dictionary of Literary Biography,* thought that the novel "had so many brilliant scenes and fascinating characters that its supporters can make a strong case for its special achievement. The fact, too, that the novel has aroused such passionate attack and such passionate defense indicates that it possesses a force moving it well beyond the range of a run-of-the-mill work." Writing in his *Twentieth-Century English Literature, 1901-1960,* A. C. Ward allowed that *Brideshead Revisited* "may well become [Waugh's] longest-remembered book, for its sense of period, the firmness of its character-drawing, and its convincing record of a Roman Catholic family."

In the trilogy composed of *Men at Arms, Officers and Gentlemen,* and *The End of the Battle*—later published in a single volume as *Sword of Honour*—Waugh wrote of another religious conversion, that of Guy Crouchback, who is transformed "from an unloving 'loner' to a man of compassion," as Doyle explained in the *Dictionary of Literary Biography.* Tracing Crouchback's military career during the Second World War, the trilogy combines Waugh's usual satire with an emotional depth not found in his previous works. The success of the trilogy moved Patrick O'Donovan of the *New Republic* to call it "the one genuine masterpiece to come out of the war."

The first novel of the trilogy, *Men at Arms,* relates Crouchback's attempts to join the British war effort, his acceptance by the Royal Corps of Halberdiers, and his military career until 1940. Crouchback is one of the last remaining members of an old and distinguished English family. Because he has been deserted by his wife, and his Catholic religious convictions do not permit him to remarry, Crouchback is a lonely and emotionally distant man. He sees the outbreak of the war, with its clear-cut moral distinctions, as a way to give his life meaning and purpose. But few of the other soldiers share his conviction. As Waugh explained to Jebb, "*Men at Arms* was a kind of uncelebration, a history of Guy Crouchback's disillusion with the army. Guy has old-fashioned ideas of honor and illusions of chivalry; we see these being used up and destroyed by his encounters with the realities of army life." Most of the novel's satire is directed at the cynicism and inefficiency of the military. The novel ends with Crouchback facing a court-martial for his role in a successful but unauthorized raid on enemy territory.

Reviewers especially praised *Men at War* for its satire of British military life. Edward Weeks of the *Atlantic* called it "a highly entertaining novel about some of the 'preposterous' experiences of the Second World War. . . . Waugh's sharp wit and sure touch of satire are always at work." James Hilton of the *New York Herald Tribune Book Review* judged *Men at War* to be "the wittiest of the war novels." And the *Times Literary Supplement* critic thought that "the novel contains comic passages as funny as anything since [*Decline and Fall*]."

In the next novel of the trilogy, *Officers and Gentlemen,* the satire is again dominant, although combined with more serious overtones. "The book," Hollis explained, "is mainly concerned, as the title implies, with a study of how gentlemen behave before the challenge of modern war." "Because it verifies a deepening seriousness and charity in Mr. Waugh's art," R. T. Horchler said of the novel in *Commonweal*, "it extends and renews the promise of his brilliant talent." Speaking of the "blend of unlike ingredients" to be found in *Officers and Gentlemen*, James Gray of *Saturday Review* thought that the book "stimulates laughter again and again but its aftertaste is as bitter as the author meant it to be. . . . With it Waugh takes a higher place than he seemed previously to occupy."

The pivotal scene of *Officers and Gentlemen* is set on the Mediterranean island of Crete. Crouchback's unit is called upon to assist the beleaguered English forces fighting on the island. But the battle ends in total defeat as the Germans drive the English troops into the sea. The English officer Ivor Claire, "in whom Guy had thought that he recognized the perfect example of the type," Hollis wrote, "behaves badly at the evacuation, deserting his men in order to save himself."

Officers and Gentlemen is "satire, surely," Richard Sullivan wrote in the *New York Herald Tribune Book Review*. "But behind the mockery there is insight, sympathy and understanding that goes deep." Although disapproving of Waugh's political and social values as expressed in this novel, C. J. Rolo of the *Atlantic* admitted that *Officers and Gentlemen* "is a highly polished piece of work." Similarly, Maurice Richardson of the *New Statesman and Nation* marveled at "how consistently well [Waugh] writes, how much more conscientious he is about his words than most established novelists." Speaking of *Officers and Gentlemen* in the *New York Times,* Anatole Broyard called it "undoubtedly the best novel by an Englishman about [World War II]."

In the final volume of the trilogy, *The End of the Battle,* Crouchback is given a leave from the army to attend his father's funeral. The event serves to reacquaint him with the family religion, and he comes to embrace Catholicism with renewed vigor. His newfound sense of purpose contrasts sharply with his directionless companions. Crouchback "finds himself everywhere in the company of people with no roots, no understanding of what life is about, no sense of the dignity of its purpose," Hollis wrote. Because of his own moral stance, however, Crouchback can now take selfless actions on behalf of others. When his wife returns to him pregnant by a man she no longer loves, Crouchback takes her in to give the child a name and family, explaining that the war has created enough abandoned children. Sent to Yugoslavia to assist the underground, Crouchback helps a group of Jewish refugees to leave the country, despite efforts by the communist partisans to prevent it.

Because of his religious faith, Crouchback ends the trilogy transformed from an isolated, emotionally cold man into an open and giving man. This transformation is underlined by the valueless society of wartime England. As Carens explained, "the essential theme of these three volumes is the total collapse of civilized values which is the concomitant of war." The trilogy, Hollis maintained, "leaves us with a picture of the world in which one institution alone—the Catholic Church—remains in protest against the nihilistic pointlessness of the modern age." Burling Lowrey of the *Saturday Review* found Waugh's Catholicism to be "used admirably on both a symbolic and literal level, and woven beautifully into character and theme."

Evaluations of the *Sword of Honour* trilogy were sharply divided, with some reviewers generous in their appraisal while others disparaged Waugh's accomplishment. Melvin Maddocks of the *Christian Science Monitor* took exception to Waugh's disillusionment with the modern age, calling it "patently indefensible. . . .

The real problem is that Mr. Waugh refuses to believe that human goodness can appear in more than one particular kind of period costume, and this narrows him inevitably, as an artist as well as a thinker." But other critics praised the trilogy. Thomas P. McDonnell of *Catholic World* found it to be "Waugh's masterpiece." Calling the trilogy "Mr. Waugh's main achievement to date," a critic for the *Times Literary Supplement* predicted that it was "the one piece of English fiction about the 1939-45 War which is certain to survive."

Shortly before his death Waugh published *A Little Learning: An Autobiography, the Early Years,* the first volume in a projected multi-volume autobiography. Because this projected work was never completed, and because Waugh's carefully nurtured public persona as an irascible reactionary distorted his true character, the public knew little about Waugh's actual life. This lack of knowledge was remedied with the posthumous publication of several volumes, including *The Diaries of Evelyn Waugh, The Letters of Evelyn Waugh,* and *The Essays, Articles and Reviews of Evelyn Waugh.* Waugh's diaries, letters, and collected articles revealed three levels of his character, as Paul Gray argued in *Time.* "First came the *Diaries,*" Gray wrote, "a revealing look at Waugh's private, sometimes drunken and usually unflattering thoughts about his contemporaries. Next arrived the *Letters . . . ,* in which the writer appeared in the less scathing demeanor he put on for his correspondents. Now this massive selection of Waugh's journalism [*The Essays, Articles and Reviews of Evelyn Waugh*] displays him fully dressed for his reading public."

The Diaries of Evelyn Waugh covers the years from 1911, when he was a young boy, to 1965, the year before his death. Omitted from the collection are Waugh's diaries for his years at Oxford, those written during his first marriage, and those from the period of his nervous breakdown in the 1950s. "The whole Oxford period was destroyed by Waugh," Nigel Dennis revealed in the *New York Review of Books.* During his college years Waugh had gone through a homosexual phase, later renounced, and did not want the record of that period preserved. Similarly, his first marriage and his breakdown were painful memories that Waugh preferred to omit.

But despite the omissions, Waugh's diaries possess an honesty that several critics admired, although some of the traits Waugh revealed were less than exemplary. As Keith Cushman of *Library Journal* noted, "the diaries add up to an invaluable portrait of the life and times of a fascinating if not altogether appealing personality." Waugh's heavy drinking, his often nasty temperament, and his many prejudices are revealed in the diaries. Wilfrid Sheed found in his *New York Times Book Review* analysis that "vile thoughts are shown to have lurked behind the repulsive exterior, [yet Waugh] seems like one of us. . . . Why? The prose, of course, with its simplicity and lack of display, not a cad's prose at all. And then, the self-loathing, strong and dolorous, with the force and genius behind it." "The great diarists," Anthony Powell wrote in the *London Magazine,* "do not care what people think, provided they have made their own point. They write for themselves. By this test, Waugh comes through with flying colours. He is totally uninterested in showing himself in a favourable light, and does not care in the least what other people think."

A more favorable side of Waugh's personality is revealed in *The Letters of Evelyn Waugh.* "This is a far more amusing book than the hefty selection from Waugh's 'Diaries,'" Walter Clemons wrote in *Newsweek.* "Waugh reveals unexpected capacities for friendship: generosity, loyalty, delicacy and concern."

Leithauser thought that "the Evelyn Waugh who emerges [in the letters] is far more humane and interesting than the man who was presented a few years ago with the publication of his diaries." Waugh's letters to his family were especially revealing. "The letters to his children," Geoffrey Wheatcroft wrote in the *Spectator*, "are delightful and if he describes them to others with ironic resignation there is also a gleaming humorous affection." "His love letters to his second wife during their courtship," Michael Howard of the *Times Literary Supplement* commented, "are as tender and moving as any in the English language."

One explanation for this difference in tone between the diaries and the letters was offered by editor Mark Amory in his introduction to the collected letters. Waugh, Amory recounted, wrote his letters in the morning, "when he was sober. He wrote his diary at night when he was drunk." Although Waugh's letters reveal his better qualities, James allowed that "people who want to emphasize his repellent aspects will find plenty to help them." Waugh admitted in one letter: "I am by nature a bully and a scold. I am a bigot and a philistine." In the letter proposing marriage to Laura Herbert, who became his second wife, Waugh warned her of "the awfulness of my character."

But V. S. Pritchett argued in the *New Yorker* that the letters primarily show Waugh to be "a born actor and impersonator, with a bent for exaggeration and caricature and a delight in the inadmissible. . . . Waugh's many selves and persistent impersonations are candidly and divertingly projected in his letters." Similarly, Howard found that Waugh played the part of the cantankerous reactionary even to his correspondents. "He created his persona with dedicated care. . . . These letters, on the whole, show how consistently and effectively he played that part," Howard commented.

But regardless of how much they reveal about Waugh's character, the collected letters are a literary work and as such they contain some of Waugh's best prose. Paul Fussell, writing in the *New York Times Book Review*, recommended *The Letters of Evelyn Waugh*, "because Waugh is much needed as an antidote to the current solemnity, earnestness, literal-mindedness and verbal sloppiness." James complained that because many contemporary writers now preferred to use the telephone, *The Letters of Evelyn Waugh* "will probably be the last collection of letters by a great writer to be also a great collection of letters."

Evaluations of Waugh's career often focus on the reactionary persona which he enjoyed presenting to the world. "Waugh was The Great Literary Snob," Karl Keller maintained in the *Los Angeles Times Book Review*. "Most of the time this was natural enough, for he was high-bred, smart-setted and sharp-eyed. At other times it was a grand pose, for he found the world a great bore and himself a needed performer in it. . . . He gained his notoriety from his snobbery and so he played it to the hilt." Marcus observed that Waugh has been called "nasty, hateful, snobbish, trivial, reactionary, vindictive, fawning, immature, pompous, and rude, ascriptions which are substantially true yet somehow beside the point." McCartney found that Waugh's critics could not agree on a label that properly described him. "In their frustration," McCartney commented, "their labels anxiously proliferate: dandy, curmudgeon, wit, moralist, conservative, anarchist, Tory satirist, Catholic romancer, gentleman, snob, loyal friend, and, off the record, one mean son of a bitch. Well, which is it?" Because of Waugh's "contradictions, paradoxes, biases, and unpredictability," Doyle allowed in the *Dictionary of Literary Biography* that "in the notable history of British character oddities and great eccentrics, he must occupy a prominent place."

But, Michael Dirda argued in the *Washington Post Book World*, "it would be wrong to leave the impression that Evelyn Waugh made himself into a reactionary buffoon and snob. Rather, . . . he was a truly committed man, one for whom literature, civilized values, the private life, and personal salvation deeply, crucially mattered." McCartney saw Waugh as a man who "was convinced, as have been many others, that civilization in the twentieth century was imperiled by a decline in respect for reason and a concomitant rise in mindless self-assertion. This is why he was so disturbed by decent, well-educated people who seemed perfectly comfortable to carry on their lives without any deeply held convictions. He knew mere decency could never stand up to the civilized savagery of modern life." Waugh explained his position in an essay in *The Essays, Articles and Reviews* of Evelyn Waugh. "It is better," he wrote, "to be narrow-minded than to have no mind, to hold limited and rigid principles than to have none at all. That is the danger which faces so many people today—to have no considered opinions on any subject, to put up with what is wasteful and harmful with the excuse that there is 'good in everything'—which in most cases means an inability to distinguish between good and bad."

Because of his strong opposition to the anarchic modern world, Waugh placed great importance on the proper use of language, which he saw as the foundation for rational thought. "Grammar is one of Mr. Waugh's obsessions," Broyard wrote. "He sees it, not altogether incorrectly, as the structure of our morality. It is the logic not only of our speech, he feels, but of our behavior as well. Without it, we hardly know what we are doing." "I regard writing," Waugh told Jebb, "as an exercise in the use of language, and with this I am obsessed."

Fussell believed that Waugh's continued importance as a writer rests in large part on his meticulous use of language. "Waugh," Fussell wrote, "is indispensable today, . . . because he is that rarity, a writer who cares about language. He knows that writing is an affair of words rather than soul, impulse, 'sincerity' or an instinct for the significant. . . . And in our atmosphere where verbal accuracy and elegance and wit seem almost to have disappeared, Waugh is one of the heroes, perhaps one of the saints, of verbal culture." "To read a page of Waugh's prose," Burgess stated in his *Novel Now: A Guide to Contemporary Fiction*, "is to revel in a cool, patrician, Augustan craftsmanship." McDonnell saw the elegance of Waugh's prose to be always combined with a consistent seriousness of purpose. "Waugh," McDonnell stated in the *National Review*, "was the writer who, of all contemporary writers, has given us the most subtle and exquisite balance between substance and elegance. His profoundest observations always had about them the saving grace of elegance; and that elegance, its wit and eternal intelligence, were seldom lacking in the profoundest kind of substance."

Waugh enjoys a considerable reputation in contemporary literature, particularly for his satirical novels. In his evaluation of these satires for the *New York Times Book Review*, James Traub ranked Waugh "in the select company of Swift and Twain and a very few others." But Sissman argued that Waugh's novels were more than excellent satires. He claimed that Waugh "appears to be rising to the highest place in the pantheon of twentieth-century English novelists—a place shared only, perhaps, by Virginia Woolf, Joseph Conrad, and D. H. Lawrence." Doyle claimed in his *Evelyn Waugh* that Waugh's satires and his more serious writings form a continuous whole. "In reviewing Waugh's literary career," Doyle wrote, "a clearly defined pattern presents itself. The early satirist . . . evolved through his religious conversion to Christianity to more serious probing of the limitations of humanism. . . . Critics should not view

Waugh as two different authors—a writer of comic novels and a writer of serious novels. . . . Waugh can be understood fully and enjoyed most completely only when he is viewed as a writer of tragicomedy." Leithauser also saw an intrinsic relationship between Waugh's humorous and serious writing. "That Waugh could surmount his shortcomings to become such a masterful and irreplaceable novelist," Leithauser wrote, "was due in large part to his comic powers." Allen discovered that upon rereading all of Waugh's novels, "one is struck not so much by the differences as by the underlying similarity."

"Ultimately," Davis wrote, "questions about the value of Waugh's work can be reduced to one crucial question of whether or not he gives in his art a vision not of the truth but of a truth. It seems clear that he does." Waugh's novels, Davis explained, argue that "the individual, to be saved as an individual, must retreat from modern society; institutions are finally not worthy of loyalty, though ideals and people are; power in the world inevitably corrupts, but renunciation of the world and of power involves a real cost; the pressure of events is toward greater confusion, increasing drabness, and vitiation of energy; and private salvation cannot be shared."

This vision is enacted by a host of characters who are among the most recognized in modern literature. "Waugh's characters," James observed, "have inexorably established themselves among the enduring fictions to which his countrymen traditionally refer as if they were living beings. In this respect Waugh is in a direct line with Shakespeare and Dickens." Writing in the *Dictionary of Literary Biography,* Doyle agreed with this assessment. Waugh, Doyle wrote, "has created, in true Dickensian fashion, a gallery of characters . . . who appear capable of surviving the test of time."

Calvin W. Lane also believed that Waugh's work will last. "Years from now," Lane wrote in his *Evelyn Waugh,* "readers may encounter Waugh for the first time with the same sense of shocked delight that the uninitiated often discover in a first reading of Twain, Swift, or Pope." Evaluating Waugh's career for the *Dictionary of Literary Biography,* Doyle concluded that his "overall literary achievement is considerable."

MEDIA ADAPTATIONS: The Loved One was filmed by Metro-Goldwyn-Mayer in 1965; *Decline and Fall* was filmed as "Decline and Fall of a Bird Watcher" by Twentieth Century-Fox in 1969; film rights to *Brideshead Revisited* were sold in the late 1940s, but Waugh did not give final approval to the script and the film was never made; *Brideshead Revisited* was filmed for television as an eleven-and-one-half hour series by Granada Television in 1981; *A Handful of Dust* was adapted into a 1988 film by screenwriters Tim Sullivan and Derek Granger and director Charles Sturridge.

BIOGRAPHICAL/CRITICAL SOURCES:

BOOKS

Acton, Harold, *Memoirs of an Aesthete,* Methuen, 1948.

Acton, Harold, *Memories of an Aesthete, 1934-1968,* Viking, 1970 (published in England as *More Memoirs of an Aesthete,* Methuen, 1970).

Allen, Walter, *The Modern Novel,* Dutton, 1964.

Bergonzi, Bernard, *The Situation of the Novel,* University of Pittsburgh Press, 1970.

Bradbury, Malcolm, *Evelyn Waugh,* Oliver & Boyd, 1964.

Bradbury, Malcolm, *Possibilities: Essays on the State of the Novel,* Oxford University Press, 1973.

Brophy, Brigid, *Don't Never Forget: Collected Views and Reviews,* Holt, 1966.

Burgess, Anthony, *The Novel Now: A Guide to Contemporary Fiction,* Norton, 1967.

Burgess, Anthony, *Urgent Copy: Literary Studies,* Norton, 1969.

Carens, James F., *The Satiric Art of Evelyn Waugh,* University of Washington Press, 1966.

Contemporary Literary Criticism, Gale, Volume 1, 1973, Volume 3, 1975, Volume 8, 1978, Volume 13, 1980, Volume 19, 1981, Volume 27, 1984, Volume 44, 1987.

Daiches, David, *The Present Age in British Literature,* Indiana University Press, 1958.

Davis, Robert Murray and others, editors, *Evelyn Waugh: A Checklist of Primary and Secondary Materials,* Whitston, 1972.

Davis, Robert Murray, *Evelyn Waugh, Writer,* Pilgrim Books (Norman, Okla.), 1981.

Davis, Robert Murray, *A Catalogue of the Evelyn Waugh Collection at the Humanities Research Center,* The University of Texas at Austin, Whitston, 1981.

DeVitis, A. A., *Roman Holiday: The Catholic Novels of Evelyn Waugh,* Bookman Associates, 1956.

Dictionary of Literary Biography, Volume 15: *British Novelists, 1930-1959,* Gale, 1983.

Donaldson, Frances, *Evelyn Waugh: Portrait of a Country Neighbor,* Weidenfeld & Nicolson, 1967, Chilton, 1968.

Doyle, Paul A., *Evelyn Waugh,* Eerdmans, 1969.

Doyle, Paul A. and others, editors, *A Bibliography of Evelyn Waugh,* Whitston, 1986.

Green, Martin, *Children of the Sun,* Basic Books, 1976.

Greenblatt, Stephen Jay, *Three Modern Satirists: Waugh, Orwell, and Huxley,* Yale University Press, 1965.

Heath, Jeffrey, *The Picturesque Prison: Evelyn Waugh and His Writing,* McGill-Queens University Press, 1982.

Hollis, Christopher, *Evelyn Waugh,* Longmans, Green, 1954.

Karl, Frederick R., *A Reader's Guide to the Contemporary English Novel,* Farrar, Straus, 1962.

Kellogg, Gene, *The Vital Tradition: The Catholic Novel in a Period of Convergence,* Loyola University Press, 1970.

Littlewood, Ian, *The Writings of Evelyn Waugh,* Basil Blackwell, 1983.

Lodge, David, *Evelyn Waugh,* Columbia University Press, 1971.

Mack, Maynard and Ian Gregor, editors, *Imagined Worlds: Essays on Some English Novels and Novelists in Honour of John Butt,* Methuen, 1968.

Marcus, Steven, *Representations: Essays on Literature and Society,* Random House, 1975.

Morriss, Margaret and D. J. Dooley, *Evelyn Waugh: A Reference Guide,* G. K. Hall, 1984.

O'Faolain, Sean, *The Vanishing Hero: Studies in Novelists of the Twenties,* Little, Brown, 1957.

Phillips, Gene D., *Evelyn Waugh's Officers, Gentlemen and Rogues: The Fact Behind His Fiction,* Nelson-Hall, 1975.

Plimpton, George, editor, *Writers at Work: The "Paris Review" Interviews,* third series, Viking, 1967.

Pryce-Jones, David, editor, *Evelyn Waugh and His World,* Little, Brown, 1973.

Stannard, Martin, editor, *Evelyn Waugh: The Critical Heritage,* Routledge & Kegan Paul, 1984.

Stopp, Frederick J., *Evelyn Waugh: Portrait of an Artist,* Little, Brown, 1958.

Sykes, Christopher, *Evelyn Waugh: A Biography,* Little, Brown, 1975.

Ward, A. C., *Twentieth-Century English Literature, 1901-1960,* Methuen, 1960.

Waugh, Alec, *My Brother Evelyn and Other Profiles,* Farrar, Straus, 1967.

Waugh, Evelyn, *A Little Learning: An Autobiography, the Early Years,* Little, Brown, 1964, reprinted, 1984 (published in England as *A Little Learning: The First Volume of an Autobiography,* Chapman & Hall, 1964).

Waugh, Evelyn, *The Diaries of Evelyn Waugh ,* edited by Michael Davie, Weidenfeld & Nicolson, 1976, Little, Brown, 1977.

Waugh, Evelyn, *The Letters of Evelyn Waugh,* edited by Mark Amory, Ticknor & Fields, 1980.

Waugh, Evelyn, *The Essays, Articles and Reviews of Evelyn Waugh,* edited by Donat Gallagher, Little, Brown, 1984.

Wilson, Edmund, *Classics and Commercials,* Farrar, Straus, 1950.

PERIODICALS

American Spectator, January, 1985.
Antigonish Review, winter, 1978.
Atlantic, December, 1952, August, 1955, November, 1980.
Book Collector, spring, 1976.
Catholic World, March, 1962.
Christian Science Monitor, January 11, 1962.
Commonweal, October 24, 1952, August 12, 1955, February 2, 1962.
Connecticut Review, April, 1975.
Contemporary Literature, winter, 1979.
Critic, fall, 1976.
Critical Quarterly, spring, 1963.
Criticism, winter, 1972.
English Studies in Canada, fall, 1976.
Esquire, September, 1973.
Essays in Criticism, October, 1978.
Evelyn Waugh Newsletter, 1967.
Georgia Review, summer, 1973.
Guardian, October 27, 1961.
Journal of Modern Literature, April, 1976.
Library Journal, October 1, 1977.
London Magazine, August/September, 1973.
Los Angeles Times, July 14, 1988.
Los Angeles Times Book Review, February 15, 1981, October 3, 1982.
Midwest Quarterly, winter, 1977.
Modern Fiction Studies, summer, 1965.
Nation, January 20, 1962.
National Review, June 10, 1983, December 28, 1984.
New Republic, July 11, 1955, February 12, 1962, May 12, 1979, October 18, 1980, December 6, 1982.
New Statesman, October 27, 1961.
New Statesman and Nation, July 9, 1955.
Newsweek, January 22, 1968, May 7, 1973, November 24, 1975, October 27, 1980.
New Yorker, February 4, 1974, January 16, 1978, December 22, 1980.
New York Herald Tribune Book Review, October 19, 1952, July 10, 1955, January 7, 1962.
New York Review of Books, December 8, 1977, December 4, 1980.
New York Times, July 10, 1955, December 28, 1977, March 23, 1979, April 7, 1984, August 15, 1984.
New York Times Book Review, January 7, 1962, July 1, 1973, February 10, 1974, October 16, 1977, November 2, 1980, January 25, 1981.
Novel: A Forum on Fiction, winter, 1980.
Papers of the Bibliographical Society of America, Number 72, 1978.
Papers on Literature and Language, summer, 1967, spring, 1976.

Philological Quarterly, April, 1972.
Saturday Review, July 9, 1955, January 6, 1962, November 12, 1977.
South Atlantic Quarterly, summer, 1967.
Spectator, May 5, 1959, October 11, 1980, February 4, 1984.
Studies: An Irish Quarterly Review, Number 51, 1962.
Texas Studies in Literature and Language, spring, 1965.
Time, July 11, 1955, January 19, 1962, December 8, 1975, October 17, 1977, February 12, 1979, November 12, 1984.
Times Literary Supplement, May 16, 1960, October 27, 1961, September 3, 1976, February 3, 1978, October 17, 1980, October 5, 1984.
Twentieth Century Literature, April, 1964.
Washington Post, January 27, 1981.
Washington Post Book World, December 5, 1982, September 23, 1984.
Yale Review, December, 1963.

OBITUARIES:

PERIODICALS

Antiquarian Bookman, May 2, 1966.
Books Abroad, spring, 1967.
Illustrated London News, April 16, 1966.
National Review, May 3, 1966.
Newsweek, April 25, 1966.
New York Herald Tribune, April 11, 1966.
New York Times, April 11, 1966.
Publishers Weekly, April 18, 1966.
Time, April 25, 1966.

*   *   *

WAYS, C. R.
See BLOUNT, Roy (Alton), Jr.

*   *   *

WEDGWOOD, C(icely) V(eronica)   1910-

PERSONAL: Born July 20, 1910, in Stocksfield, Northumberland, England; daughter of Sir Ralph Lewis (a railway chairman) and Iris Veronica (Pawson) Wedgwood. *Education:* Received degree with first class honors from Lady Margaret Hall, Oxford, 1931. *Religion:* Anglican.

ADDRESSES: Home—Whitegate, Alciston, near Polegate, Sussex, BN26 6UN England. *Office*—c/o William Collins, Sons & Co. Ltd., 14 St. James's Place, London SW1A IPS, England.

CAREER: Historian, translator, and writer. Literary adviser at Jonathan Cape Ltd. (publishers), 1941-44; literary editor of *Time and Tide* (weekly newspaper), 1944-50, and director, 1948-58. Member of Royal Commission on Historical Manuscripts, 1952-78, Institute for Advanced Study, Princeton, N.J., 1953-68, advisory council of Victoria and Albert Museum, 1959-69, and Arts Council Literature Panel, 1965-67. Clark Lecturer at Cambridge University, 1957-58; Northcliffe Lecturer at University of London, 1959; special lecturer at University College, London, 1962-85, and honorary fellow, 1965; honorary fellow of Lady Margaret Hall, Oxford University, 1962. Trustee of National Gallery, London, England, 1960-76. Honorary bencher, Middle Temple, London, 1978.

MEMBER: International PEN (president of English center, 1951-57), British Academy (fellow), Royal Historical Society (fellow), English Association (president, 1955-56), Society of

Authors (president, 1972-77), Royal Society of Literature of the United Kingdom (fellow), Scottish Historical Society, American Academy of Arts and Letters (honorary member), American Academy of Arts and Sciences (honorary member).

AWARDS, HONORS: James Tait Black Memorial Prize, 1944, for *William the Silent;* Officer, Order of Orange-Nassau, 1946; LL.D. from University of Glasgow, 1955; Member of the Order of the British Empire, 1956, Dame, 1968; Goethe Medal from Goethe Institute for the Cultivation of the German Language and Culture in Foreign Lands, 1958; D.Litt. from University of Sheffield, 1958, University of Keele, 1959, Smith College, 1960, Harvard University, 1964, Oxford University, 1965, University of Sussex, 1974, and University of Liverpool, 1975; Order of Merit (British), 1969.

WRITINGS:

Strafford, 1593-1641, J. Cape, 1935, reprinted, Greenwood Press, 1970, revised edition published as *Thomas Wentworth: First Earl of Strafford, 1593-1641; A Revaluation,* J. Cape, 1961, Macmillan, 1962.

The Thirty Years War, J. Cape, 1938, Yale University Press, 1939, reprinted, Methuen, 1981.

(Translator) Carl Brandi, *The Emperor Charles V: The Growth and Destiny of a Man and of a World-Empire,* J. Cape, 1939.

Oliver Cromwell, Duckworth, 1939, Macmillan, 1956, 2nd revised edition, Longwood Publishing Group, 1973, original edition also published as *The Life of Cromwell,* Collier, 1966.

William the Silent: William of Nassau, Prince of Orange, 1533-1584, Yale University Press, 1944.

Battlefields in Britain (photographs, with commentary by Wedgwood), Hastings House, 1945.

(Translator from the German) Elias Canetti, *Auto-da-Fe,* J. Cape, 1946, reprinted, Pan Books, 1978, published as *The Tower of Babel,* Knopf, 1947.

Velvet Studies: Essays on Historical and Other Subjects, J. Cape, 1946, reprinted, Darby, 1980.

Richelieu and the French Monarchy, Hodder & Stoughton, 1949, Macmillan, 1950, reprinted, 1974.

Seventeenth-Century English Literature, Oxford University Press, 1950, revised edition, 1977.

(Contributor) *Reading History,* Cambridge University Press, 1950.

The Last of the Radicals: Josiah Wedgwood, M.P., J. Cape, 1951, reprinted, 1974.

Montrose, Collins, 1952, Archon Books, 1966.

The Great Rebellion, Volume 1: The King's Peace, 1637-1641, Macmillan, 1955, *Volume 2: The King's War, 1641-1647,* Collins, 1958, Macmillan, 1959.

Edward Gibbon, Longmans, Green, 1955.

The Common Man in the Great Civil War, Leicester University Press, 1957.

(Author of introduction) *The Author and the Public: Problems of Communication,* Hutchinson, 1957.

Truth and Opinion: Historical Essays, Macmillan, 1960, published as *The Sense of the Past: Thirteen Studies in the Theory and Practice of History,* Collier, 1967.

Poetry and Politics under the Stuarts, Cambridge University Press, 1960, University of Michigan Press, 1964.

(Contributor) *The Restoration of the Stuarts: Blessing or Disaster?,* Folger Shakespeare Library, 1961.

History and Hope: The Foundation Lecture, Birkbeck College, Birkbeck College, 1963.

A Coffin for King Charles: The Trial and Execution of Charles I, Macmillan, 1964 (published in England as *The Trial of Charles I,* Collins, 1964, new edition, Penguin, 1983).

(Contributor) James Sutherland and Joel Hurtsfield, editors, *Shakespeare's World,* Edward Arnold, 1964.

(Contributor) *Shakespeare Celebrated* (lectures), Cornell University Press, 1966.

(Editor) *New Poems, 1965: A P.E.N. Anthology of Contemporary Poetry,* Nelson, Foster & Scott, 1966.

(With the editors of Time-Life Books) *The World of Rubens, 1577-1640,* Time-Life, 1967.

Milton and His World, Lutterworth, 1969.

Oliver Cromwell and the Elizabethan Inheritance, J. Cape, 1970.

The Political Career of Peter Paul Rubens, Thames & Hudson, 1975.

The Spoils of Time: A Short History of the World, Volume I: From Earliest Times to the Sixteenth Century, Collins, 1984, published as *The Spoils of Time: A World History from the Dawn of Civilization through the Early Renaissance,* Doubleday, 1985.

Contributor of articles and reviews to newspapers, magazines, and journals, including *Saturday Review, Daily Telegraph, Times Literary Supplement, History Today,* and *Horizon.*

WORK IN PROGRESS: The second volume of *The Spoils of Time,* a world history in two volumes.

SIDELIGHTS: Hailed as "one of Britain's most celebrated historians" in the London *Times,* C. V. Wedgwood has earned acclaim for her entertaining and lucidly written histories and biographies. Her books on the English civil war have enjoyed enormous success and inspired Queen Elizabeth II to award her the Order of Merit—a rare distinction for a writer," the article in the *Times* explains. Numerous honors, including the title Dame Commander of the Order of the British Empire, have been conferred upon Wedgwood, who has also held many prestigious civic and academic posts; among them are a fifteen-year membership at the Institute for Advanced Study in Princeton, New Jersey, and twenty-five years of service as a member of the Royal Commission on Historical Manuscripts. An opponent of academic specialization, Wedgwood augments her many studies of seventeenth-century British history with a biography of her ancestor, Josiah Wedgwood; *Auto-da-Fe,* a translation of *Die Blendung,* the Nobel Prize winner by German novelist Elias Canetti; and a two-volume history of the world.

"If I was not born a historian I was an aspirant at six and a practitioner at twelve," Wedgwood reveals in *Velvet Studies: Essays on Historical and Other Subjects.* She returned from school remembering Caradoc, Caesar, and other "complicated names" better than the names of her classmates, and soon began to organize names and dates on a hand-written time line. She wrote incessantly and was advised by her father to write history, which, for Wedgwood, "never lost its enchantment." Her "unorthodox education," as it is described in the *Times,* included travels to Russia, India, Sweden, Turkey, Poland, Italy, and France, and was conducted partly in Switzerland, the home of her mother's maid. While there, Wedgwood began to learn German, the language she would later use in research for books such as *The Thirty Years War,* published when she was twenty-eight, and *William the Silent,* her most acclaimed biography and winner of the James Tait Black Memorial Prize.

Wedgwood's methods as a historian have been compared to those of her mentors G. M. Trevelyan and A. L. Rowse. Their "narrative" approach tells how events occurred instead of analyzing why, and Wedgwood has defended her method by insisting one must know how things happened before they can be understood. "I have tried," she wrote in *The King's Peace, 1637-1641,* "to describe the variety, vitality and imperfections as well as the religion and government of the British Isles in the seventeenth century, deliberately avoiding analysis and seeking rather to give an impression of its vigorous and vivid confusion." Commenting on this statement, Rowse wrote in *Time and Tide:* "How right she is, as against the fashionable analytical historians who are so determined to show how clever they are at the expense of history. Her beguilingly modest attitude is really cleverer and more subtle."

Wedgwood's historical narratives are spiced by a writing style that has been praised throughout her career. Her second book, *The Thirty Years War,* was written with "a clarity and vividness of style," remarked W. K. Ferguson of *Books.* Similar attention came with *William the Silent* (1944), which has, as *Commonweal's* H. G. J. Beck pointed out, "an English style that is crystal clear and a scholarship beyond reproach." Fifteen years later Leo Gerchoy of the *New York Herald Tribune Book Review* said that if *The King's War, 1641-1647* were "fiction, no reader could fail to admire the masterly skill, the symphonic sense with which she brings together the actors and the events." Wedgwood's reputation as a gifted writer was reinforced again when in 1964 Lawrence Stone of the *New York Review of Books* declared her "the best narrative historian writing in the English language. She is a superb stylist."

Within Wedgwood's specialty, seventeenth-century Britain, it is the English civil war that has captured most of her attention. She has written biographies of the premier political figures of the era, *King Charles I* and *Oliver Cromwell,* as well as a two-volume history of the war, *The Great Rebellion.* The *Spectator's* W. K. Hancock remarked upon reading the first volume, *The King's Peace, 1637-1641,* that "there is no more exciting period in the history of the British Isles. The time is ripe for telling the story again and Miss Wedgwood is the perfect storyteller."

Some of the objections to the second volume, *The King's War, 1641-1647,* centered on Wedgwood's use of narrative over interpretative history. "We are left with a masterful political and military narrative," commented George Dangerfield of the *Nation,* "in which we flounder helplessly in search of the 'underlying causes' which set it in motion." The *Spectator's* Christopher Hill reflected this attitude when he said that "Wedgwood does extract explanation from narrative. But the trick is not always successful. . . . We badly need a new synthesis which will bring home to us why our seventeenth-century forefathers fought and killed and died. Granted her limited aim in telling us merely how they did these things, Miss Wedgwood's book could hardly be better."

Wedgwood's comments to *CA* emphasize that her avoidance of the interpretative method is deliberate: "I am by nature an optimist. I continue stubbornly to believe that if an intelligent reader is given all the facts (or should I say all the available facts), he should be able to work out his own conclusions about the underlying causes. There is after all an organic relation between what happened (the facts) and why it happened (the causes). I have a very deep suspicion of the modern habit of analyzing causes without a close attention to facts. Our twentieth-century minds inevitably introduce ideas and theories belonging to the twentieth century which may be either irrelevant or misleading when applied to the remoter past."

In the 1960s, Wedgwood began to prepare a world history because, as the *Times* article relates, she supposed that continued study of seventeenth-century Britain would prevent her from

learning " 'anything else.' " The first volume of *The Spoils of Time: A Short History of the World* appeared twenty years later. Writing in the *New York Times Book Review,* historian Paul Johnson notes that this first volume covers "events and cultures [such as China and India] not normally covered by Western accounts of how the world evolved," and that it offers a superior summary of pre-Columbian history as well. The absence of analytical comment between descriptions of persons and events moved C. Warren Hollister, who reviewed *The Spoils of Time* for the *Los Angeles Times Book Review,* to remark, "Like a two week tour of the capitals of Europe, Wedgwood's survey leaves the reader breathless." As in previous works, Wedgwood "eschews broad interpretations and relies almost exclusively on her very considerable narrative gifts," and "livens her narrative with countless personal verdicts . . . with dextrous turns of phrase," Hollister observes citing for example her comment that Holy Roman Emperor Sigismund "had a fine presence, a weak will and an empty head." Johnson comments, "The book is always a pleasure to read, and one has complete confidence in the author's fairmindedness. She is scrupulous in her handling of the facts and never heightens the truth for effect." Johnson, who "was gently prodded into thinking afresh about many familiar [historic] episodes" also believes that all "professional historian[s] . . . will . . . profit from [Wedgwood's] account."

In 1986, Wedgwood was honored by the festschrift *For Veronica Wedgwood These: Studies in Seventeenth-Century History.* Elizabeth Longford's introduction describes Wedgwood as "a rare spirit, sometimes reticent, always strong. Above all she makes the reading of history an experience not to be missed."

Works by Wedgwood have been translated into Swedish, Dutch, French, Italian and German.

BIOGRAPHICAL/CRITICAL SOURCES:

BOOKS

Kenyon, John, *History Men,* Weidenfeld & Nicolson, 1983, new edition, 1984.
Mehta, Ved, *The Fly and the Fly Bottle: Encounters with British Intellectuals* (interview with Wedgwood), Atlantic-Little, Brown, 1963.
Ollard, Richard, and Pamela Tudor-Craig, editors, *For Veronica Wedgwood These: Studies in Seventeenth-Century History,* Collins, 1986.
Wedgwood, C. V., *Velvet Studies: Essays on Historical and Other Subjects,* J. Cape, 1946, reprinted, Darby, 1980.
Wedgwood, *The Great Rebellion, Volume I: The King's Peace, 1637-1641,* Macmillan, 1955.
Wedgwood, *Truth and Opinion: Historical Essays,* Macmillan, 1960, published as *The Sense of the Past: Thirteen Studies in the Theory and Practice of History,* Collier, 1967.
Wedgwood, *The Spoils of Time: A Short History of the World, Volume I: From Earliest Times to the Sixteenth Century,* Collins, 1984, published as *The Spoils of Time: A World History from the Dawn of Civilization through the Early Renaissance,* Doubleday, 1985.

PERIODICALS

American History Review, October, 1959, July, 1963.
Books, June 11, 1939.
Christian Science Monitor, May 19, 1960.
Commonweal, December 15, 1944.
Los Angeles Times Book Review, April 7, 1985.
Nation, December 10, 1955, June 20, 1959.
New Statesman, December 16, 1961, August 28, 1964.

New York Herald Tribune Book Review, September 25, 1955, April 5, 1959, August 28, 1960, October 28, 1962.
New York Review of Books, September 10, 1964.
New York Times, October 2, 1955, April 19, 1959.
New York Times Book Review, September 20, 1964, April 7, 1985.
Saturday Review, May 6, 1939, December 9, 1944, September 24, 1955, April 4, 1959, May 28, 1960, September 19, 1964.
Spectator, October 28, 1938, May 26, 1944, October 6, 1950, January 14, 1955, December 12, 1958, February 19, 1960.
Time, April 13, 1959, September 4, 1964.
Time and Tide, January 8, 1955, March 10, 1988.
Times (London), July 4, 1984, July 5, 1985.
Times Literary Supplement, November 19, 1938, May 6, 1944, February 3, 1945, October 6, 1950, January 7, 1955, November 28, 1958, January 29, 1960, November 17, 1961, August 27, 1964, February 19, 1988.

*   *   *

WEINSTEIN, Nathan
See WEST, Nathanael

*   *   *

WEINSTEIN, Nathan von Wallenstein
See WEST, Nathanael

*   *   *

WELDON, Fay 1933(?)-

PERSONAL: Born September 22, 1933 (some sources say February 22, 1931), in Alvechurch, Worcestershire, England; daughter of Frank Thornton (a physician) and Margaret (a writer; maiden name Jepson) Birkinshaw; married a schoolmaster, c. 1958 (divorced after six months); married Ronald Weldon (a jazz musician and antique dealer), 1960; children: (first marriage) Nicholas; (second marriage) Daniel, Thomas, Samuel. *Education:* University of St. Andrews, M.A., 1954.

ADDRESSES: Home—23 Ryland Rd., London NW5 3EA, England. *Agent*—Phil Kelvin, Goodwin Associates, 12 Rabbit Row, Kensington Church St., London W8 4DX, England.

CAREER: Novelist, playwright, television and radio scriptwriter. Worked as a propaganda writer for the British Foreign Office and as a market researcher for the *Daily Mirror,* London, England. Advertising copywriter for various firms in London; creator of the slogan, "Go to work on an egg." Former member of the Art Council of Great Britain's literary panel and of the GLA's film and video panel; chairperson of the judges' panel for the Booker McConnell Prize, 1983.

AWARDS, HONORS: Society of Film and Television award for best series, 1971, for "On Trial" episode in "Upstairs, Downstairs" television series; Writer's Guild award for best radio play, 1973, for "Spider"; Giles Cooper Award for best radio play, 1978, for "Polaris"; Booker McConnell Prize nomination, National Book League, 1979, for *Praxis;* Society of Authors' travelling scholarship, 1981; *Los Angeles Times* Book Prize for fiction, 1989, for *The Heart of the Country.*

WRITINGS:

NOVELS

The Fat Woman's Joke (also see below), MacGibbon & Kee, 1967, reprinted, Hodder & Stoughton, 1982, published as *. . . And the Wife Ran Away,* McKay, 1968.

Down Among the Women, Heinemann, 1971, St. Martin's, 1972.
Female Friends, St. Martin's, 1974.
Remember Me, Random House, 1976.
Words of Advice, Random House, 1977 (published in England as *Little Sisters,* Hodder & Stoughton, 1978).
Praxis, Summit Books, 1978.
Puffball, Hodder & Stoughton, 1979, Summit Books, 1980.
The President's Child, Hodder & Stoughton, 1982, Doubleday, 1983.
The Life and Loves of a She-Devil, Hodder & Stoughton, 1983, Pantheon, 1984.
The Shrapnel Academy, Viking, 1987.
The Heart of the Country, Hutchinson, 1987, Viking, 1988.
The Hearts and Lives of Men (Book-of-the-Month Club selection), Heinemann, 1987, Viking, 1988.
The Leader of the Band, Hodder & Stoughton, 1988, Viking, 1989.
The Cloning of Joanna May, Viking, 1990.

PLAYS

"Permanence," first produced on the West End at Comedy Theatre, April 9, 1969, published in *Mixed Blessings: An Entertainment on Marriage,* Methuen, 1970.
"Time Hurries On," published in Scene Scripts, edited by Michael Marland, Longman, 1972.
Words of Advice (one-act; first produced in Richmond, England, at Orange Tree Theatre, March 1974), Samuel French, 1974.
"Friends," first produced in Richmond at Orange Tree Theatre, April, 1975.
"Moving House," first produced in Farnham, England, at Redgrave Theatre, 1976.
"Mr. Director," first produced in Richmond at Orange Tree Theatre, March 24, 1978.
Action Replay (first produced in Birmingham, England, at Birmingham Repertory Studio Theatre, February 24, 1979; produced as "Love Among the Women" in Vancouver, British Columbia, at City Stage, July, 1982), Samuel French, 1980.
"I Love My Love," first produced in Exeter, England, at Northcott Theatre, February, 1981.
"Woodworm," first produced as "After the Prize" Off-Broadway at Phoenix Theatre, November, 1981; produced in Melbourne, Australia, at Playbox Theatre, March, 1983.
"The Western Women," produced in Lyme Regis, Dorset, England, 1984.

Also author of "The Hole in the Top of the World" and "Watching Me, Watching You," a stage adaptation of four of her short stories.

TELEVISION PLAYS

"The Fat Woman's Tale," Granada Television, 1966.
"Wife in a Blond Wig," British Broadcasting Corp. (BBC-TV), 1966.
"Office Party," Thames Television, 1970.
"On Trial" (episode in "Upstairs, Downstairs" series), London Weekend Television, 1971.
"Hands," BBC-TV, 1972.
"Poor Baby," ATV Network, 1975.
"The Terrible Tale of Timothy Bagshott," BBC-TV, 1975.
"Aunt Tatty" (dramatization based on an Elizabeth Bowen short story), BBC-TV, 1975.
"Married Love" (film on the Marie Stopes "Six Women" series), BBC-TV, 1977.

"Pride and Prejudice" (five-part dramatization based on the novel by Jane Austen), BBC-TV, 1980.

"Watching Me, Watching You" (episode in "Leap in the Dark" series), BBC-TV, 1980.

"Life for Christine," Granada Television, 1980.

"Little Miss Perkins," London Weekend Television, 1982.

"Loving Women," Granada Television, 1983.

"The Wife's Revenge," BBC-TV, 1983.

Also author of "Time for Murder," 1985, "Balkan Trilogy," an eight-part dramatization of the Olivia Manning trilogy, BBC-TV, "Fanny," a teleplay of the novel by Erica Jong, "For Love Alone," a teleplay of the novel by Christina Stead, and over twenty-five other teleplays for BBC-TV and independent television networks.

RADIO PLAYS

"Housebreaker," BBC Radio 3, 1973.

"Mr. Fox and Mr. First," BBC Radio 3, 1974.

"The Doctor's Wife," BBC Radio 4, 1975.

"Polaris," American Broadcasting Co. (ABC Radio), 1980, published in *Best Radio Plays of 1978: The Giles Cooper Award Winners,* Eyre Methuen, 1979.

"Weekend" (episode in "Just Before Midnight" series), BBC Radio 4, 1979.

"All the Bells of Paradise," BBC Radio 4, 1979.

Also author of "Spider," 1972, and "If Only I Could Find the Words," BBC.

OTHER

(Editor with Elaine Feinstein) *New Stories 4: An Arts Council Anthology,* Hutchinson, 1979.

Watching Me, Watching You (short stories; also includes the novel *The Fat Woman's Joke*), Summit Books, 1981, large print edition, Chivers, 1983.

Letters to Alice on First Reading Jane Austen (nonfiction), Michael Joseph, 1984, Taplinger, 1985.

Polaris and Other Stories, Hodder & Stoughton, 1985.

Rebecca West (biography), Viking, 1985.

The Rules of Life, Harper, 1987.

Wolf the Mechanical Dog (for children), illustrations by Pat Leyshun, Collins, 1989.

SIDELIGHTS: In her novels, short stories, and plays for the theater, television, and radio, Fay Weldon's "major subject is the experience of women," writes Agate Nesaule Krouse in *Critique.* "Sexual initiation, marriage, infidelity, divorce, contraception, abortion, motherhood, housework, and thwarted careers . . . all receive attention." Products of a keen mind concerned with women's issues, Weldon's novels have been labeled "feminist" by many reviewers. Yet, Weldon's views are her own and are not easily classified. In fact, feminists have at times taken exception to her portrayal of women, accusing the author of perpetuating traditional stereotypes.

Fay Weldon's fiction fosters disparate interpretations because its author sees the complexity of the woman's experience. As Susan Hill notes in *Books and Bookmen,* Weldon has "the sharpest eyes for revealing details which, appearing like bubbles on the surface, are clues to the state of things lying far, far below." Weldon accepts feminist ideology as a liberating force, but she also understands its limitations. Thus, what emerges from Weldon's writing is more than an understanding of women's issues; she appreciates the plight of the individual woman. She told Sybil Steinberg in an interview in *Publishers Weekly,* "Women must

ask themselves: What is it that will give me fulfillment? That's the serious question I'm attempting to answer."

At the heart of Fay Weldon's novels is the battle between the sexes, but it is examined at close range, focusing on its effect upon each individual woman (men play secondary roles in Weldon's fiction). Though concerned with the individual, Weldon does not confine her novel to the condition of one woman. "Instead of relying on a single minutely analyzed protagonist," observes Agate Nesaule Krouse, "she creates numerous vividly individualized women within the same work whose lives intertwine. . . . Her multiple female characters function particularly well to make convincing a fictional world which indirectly questions many traditional assumptions." Of love, marriage, family, and friendship, Weldon paints an unflattering picture. Her characters marry often, but the marriages are seldom a success. Extramarital affairs are common and as unsatisfying as the marriages. Single mothers receive little support in raising their children. Even friendships between women often bring frustration.

Weldon's writing career began in the mid-1960s after an earlier failed attempt to write novels. She first established herself as an advertising copywriter; her success in advertising encouraged her to take up writing scripts for the theater, television, and radio. When Weldon found that one of her television scripts lent itself to further development, she wrote her first published novel, *The Fat Woman's Joke* (published in the United States as *. . . And the Wife Ran Away*).

Weldon's early novels, especially *Down Among the Women, Female Friends,* and *Remember Me,* gained recognition both for their artistry and their social concerns. "Vivid imagery, a strong sense of time and place, memorable dialogue, complex events, and multiple characters that are neither confusing nor superficially observed," characterize these novels, comments Krouse, making them "a rich rendering of life with brevity and wit." In her writing, John Braine adds in *Books and Bookmen,* Weldon "is never vague. . . . She understands what few novelists understand, that physical details are not embellishments on the story, but the bricks from which the story is made." And, like few other novelists, especially those who deal with women's issues, observes Braine, "She possesses that very rare quality, a sardonic, earthy, disenchanted, slightly bitter but never cruel sense of humour."

Although each of these books possesses elements typical of a Weldon novel, they focus on different aspects of the female experience and the forces that influence women. *Down Among the Women* reflects how three generations of women, each the product of a different social climate, react to the same dilemma. Krouse finds that in this book Weldon creates "a work whose very structure is feminist." She adds in her *Critique* review, "The whole novel could profitably be analyzed as a definition of womanhood: passages describing how one has to live 'down among the women' contrast with anecdotes of male behavior." The image of womanhood offered here is not ideal, but as Krouse comments, Weldon's ability to blend "the terrible and the ridiculous is one of the major reasons why a novel filled with the pain endured by women . . . is neither painfully depressing nor cheerfully sentimental."

As its title suggests, *Female Friends* examines relationships among women, how the companionship of other women can be comforting to a woman wearied by the battle of the sexes. "The most radical feminist could not possibly equal the picture of injustice [Weldon] paints with wry, cool, concise words," writes L. E. Sissman in the *New Yorker.* Sissman finds that "the real triumph of 'Female Friends' is the gritty replication of the gross texture of everyday life, placed in perspective and made universal; the perfectly recorded dialogue, precisely differentiated for each character; the shocking progression of events that, however rude, seem real." Weldon does not overlook the injustices committed by women in this day-to-day struggle, however. Ultimately, her characters suggest, women are responsible for their own lives. As Arthur Cooper concludes in *Newsweek,* Weldon "has penetrated the semidarkness of the semiliberated and shown that only truth and self-awareness can set them free."

Remember Me is the story of one man's impact on the lives of three women and how the resentment of one of those women becomes a disruptive force even after her death. This novel suggests that elements beyond the control of the individual often dictate her actions. "Scores of . . . coincidences . . . emphasize the theme that chance, misunderstanding, and necessarily limited knowledge play a significant part in human life," observes Krouse. Human frailties, Krouse adds, body functions, pain, sickness "and death are recurrent images underscoring human mortality." Phyllis Birnbaum, writing in the *Saturday Review,* states, "Precise satire, impassioned monologue, and a sense of limited human possibility make this novel a daring examination of twentieth-century discontent."

By the time she had written her sixth novel, *Praxis* (the fifth, *Words of Advice,* appeared in 1977), Fay Weldon was considered, as Susan Hill puts it, "an expert chronicler of the minutiae of women's lives, good at putting their case and pleading their cause." Kelley Cherry points out in the *Chicago Tribune Book World* that *Praxis* is a novel about endurance. The central character, Praxis Duveen, must endure in a world filled with "just about every kind of manipulation and aggression that men use to get women where they want them," observes Katha Pollitt in the *New York Times Book Review,* "and just about every nuance of guilt and passivity that keeps women there." Struggling against most of the catastrophes that befall a woman, Praxis does emerge, revealing according to Hill, that even though "Weldon's women are victims, they do have many compensatory qualities—toughness, resilience, flexibility, inventiveness, patience, nerve."

A novel in which so many misfortunes plague one character runs the risk of becoming unbelievable. Yet, Kelley Cherty writes, "The writing throughout is brisk and ever so slightly off the wall—sufficiently askew to convey the oddness of events, sufficiently no-nonsense to make that oddness credible." And, concludes Katha Pollitt, "As a narrative it is perhaps too ambitious, but as a collection of vignettes, polemics, epigrams, it is often dazzling, pointing up the mad underside of our sexual politics with a venomous accuracy for which wit is far too mild a word."

In her next novel, *Puffball,* "Weldon mixes gynecology and witchcraft to concoct an unusual brew," Joan Reardon notes in the *Los Angeles Times Book Review.* Here, more than before, Weldon confronts the woman's condition on a physical level, focusing on pregnancy. "Weldon has the audacity to include technical information on fertility, conception, and fetal development as an integral part of the story," comments Lorallee MacPike in *Best Sellers.* "She makes the physical process preceding and during pregnancy not only interesting but essential to the development of both story and character."

In the eyes of some reviewers such as Joan Reardon, however, the technical information weakens the novel. She writes that in *Puffball,* "perspicacity has given way to whimsy and 'the pain in my soul, my heart, and my mind' has become a detailed analysis of the pituitary system." Moreover, some feminists fault this book for its old-fashioned images of women; as Anita Brookner points out in the *Times Literary Supplement,* "superficially, it is

a great leap backwards for the stereotype feminist. It argues in favour of the old myths of earth and motherhood and universal harmony: a fantasy for the tired businesswoman." Yet a reviewer for the *Atlantic* finds that "the assertion of the primacy of physical destiny that lies at the center of *Puffball* gives the book a surprising seriousness and an impressive optimism."

In *The President's Child,* Weldon breaks new ground, exploring the impact of political intrigue on individual lives. Her next novel, however, is reminiscent of *Praxis.* Like Praxis, the protagonist of Fay Weldon's ninth novel, *The Life and Loves of a She-Devil*—which was made into a 1989 film starring Roseanne Barr and Meryl Streep—is buffeted by the injustice of her world. Yet, whereas Praxis endures, Ruth gets revenge. Losing her husband to a beautiful romance novelist, tall, unattractive Ruth turns against husband, novelist, and anyone else who gets in her way. Unleashing the vengeance of a she-devil, she ruins them all; the novelist dies and the husband becomes a broken man. In the end, having undergone extensive surgery to make her the very image of her former competitor, she begins a new life with her former husband. "What makes this a powerfully funny and oddly powerful book is the energy that vibrates off the pages," writes Carol E. Rinzler in the *Washington Post Book World.* Weldon has created in *She-Devil,* Sybil Steinberg notes in *Publishers Weekly,* a "biting satire of the war between the sexes, indicting not only the male establishment's standards of beauty and feminine worthiness, but also women's own willingness . . . to subscribe to these standards."

Seeing Ruth's revenge as a positive response to the injustice of the male establishment, some reviewers are disappointed by her turnaround at the novel's end. As Michiko Kakutani points out in the *New York Times,* "Her final act—having extensive plastic surgery that makes her irresistible to men—actually seems like a capitulation to the male values she says she despises." Weldon is aware of the contradictions suggested by her story; she discussed this issue in her interview with Sybil Steinberg: "The first half of the book is an exercise in feminist thought. . . . It's the feminist manifesto really: a woman must be free, independent and rich. But I found myself asking, what then? . . . I think women are discovering that liberation isn't enough. The companionship of women is not enough. The other side of their nature is unfulfilled."

Fay Weldon's understanding of the individual woman, living in a world somewhere between the nightmare of male chauvinism and the feminist ideal, has allowed her to achieve a balance in her writing. "She has succeeded in uniting the negative feminism, necessarily evident in novels portraying the problems of women, with a positive feminism, evident in the belief that change or equilibrium is possible," writes Agate Nesaule Krouse. For this reason, "[Weldon] speaks for the female experience without becoming doctrinaire," notes *New York Times Book Review* contributor Mary Cantwell, "and without the dogged humorlessness that has characterized so much feminist writing." Having found an audience for her writing—insights into the condition of woman, shaped by her intelligence and humor—Fay Weldon has risen to prominence in literary circles. Writing in the *Times Literary Supplement,* Anita Brookner calls Weldon "one of the most astute and distinctive women writing fiction today."

Weldon continued to explore a wide variety of issues associated with feminism and gender roles in her more recent novels, which include *The Heart of the Country, The Hearts and Lives of Men, The Leader of the Band,* and *The Cloning of Joanna May.* In a 1984 interview with Jean W. Ross of *Contemporary Authors,*

Weldon responded to how she feels about being labeled a feminist: "It's not a label I would ever disown, because it would seem as if I were disowning it for the wrong reasons. Many feminists wouldn't consider me a feminist at all. Many nonfeminists would think I was. I flicker in and out of the feminist mainstream. I just look forward to a time when the word will be meaningless. I think it practically is now."

MEDIA ADAPTATIONS: The Life and Loves of a She-Devil was made into the 1989 Orion film "She-Devil," starring Meryl Streep, Roseanne Barr, and Ed Begely, Jr.

BIOGRAPHICAL/CRITICAL SOURCES:

BOOKS

Contemporary Literary Criticism, Gale, Volume 6, 1976, Volume 9, 1978, Volume 11, 1979, Volume 19, 1981.
Dictionary of Literary Biography, Volume 14: *British Novelists Since 1960,* Gale, 1983.

PERIODICALS

Atlantic, August, 1980.
Best Sellers, October, 1980.
Books and Bookmen, January, 1977, March, 1979, May, 1979.
Chicago Tribune Book World, November 12, 1978, September 28, 1980, February 14, 1982.
Critique, December, 1978.
Detroit News, March 21, 1982, September 23, 1984.
Globe and Mail (Toronto), April 11, 1987, July 23, 1988.
Listener, September 9, 1971, February 22, 1979.
London Review of Books, October 7, 1982, February 2, 1984.
Los Angeles Times, August 31, 1984, March 22, 1990.
Los Angeles Times Book Review, September 7, 1980, April 19, 1987, April 10, 1988, December 18, 1988, June 4, 1989.
New Statesman, September 24, 1982.
Newsweek, November 1974, December 4, 1978.
New Yorker, March 3, 1975, November 1978.
New York Review of Books, February 8, 1979.
New York Times, November 24, 1981, December 21, 1981, August 21, 1984, October 29, 1988, May 31, 1989, March 16, 1990.
New York Times Book Review, February 1973, November 10, 1974, November 21, 1976, December 17, 1978, August 24, 1980, December 27, 1981, September 30, 1984, June 30, 1985, April 26, 1987, March 13, 1988, December 11, 1988, June 4, 1989, March 25, 1990.
Observer (London), February 8, 1987.
Publishers Weekly, January 13, 1984, August 24, 1984.
Saturday Review, December 1976.
Spectator, March 1, 1980, July 1, 1981, October 2, 1982.
Time, February 26, 1973.
Times (London), December 4, 1980, January 14, 1984, January 19, 1984, October 10, 1984, February 5, 1987, September 2, 1987, September 10, 1987, February 13, 1988.
Times Literary Supplement, September 10, 1971, February 22, 1980, May 22, 1981, September 24, 1982, January 20, 1984, July 6, 1984, August 9, 1985, February 13, 1987, July 15, 1988.
Tribune Books, March 13, 1988, November 20, 1988, June 18, 1989, March 18, 1990.
Village Voice, January 3, 1977, July 19, 1983.
Washington Post, December 12, 1978, December 22, 1981, June 11, 1983, April 24, 1988, June 1, 1989.
Washington Post Book World, November 3, 1974, September 30, 1984, July 14, 1985, May 10, 1987, April 24, 1988, November 13, 1988, April 1, 1990.

WELLS, H(erbert) G(eorge) 1866-1946
(Reginald Bliss, D. P.)

PERSONAL: Born September 21, 1866, in Bromley, England; died August 13, 1946, in London, England; cremated and ashes scattered over English Channel; son of Joseph (a gardener, cricket player, and shopkeeper) and Sarah (a housekeeper; maiden name, Neal) Wells; married Isabel Mary Wells, October 31, 1891 (divorced January, 1895); married Amy Catherine Robbins (a writer), October 27, 1895 (died, 1927); children: (second marriage) George Philip, Frank Richard; (with Amber Reeves) Anna-Jane White; (with Rebecca West) Anthony West. *Education:* Attended Normal School of Science (now Imperial College of Science and Technology), 1884-87; University of London, B.S. (with honors), c. 1889, D.Sc., 1943. *Politics:* Liberal democrat.

ADDRESSES: Home—13 Hanover Terrace, Regent's Park, London NW1, England.

CAREER: Rodgers & Denyer, Windsor, England, apprentice draper, 1880; pupil-teacher at school in Wookey, England, 1880; apprentice pharmacist in Midhurst, England, 1880-81; Hyde's Southsea Drapery Emporium, Hampshire, England, apprentice draper, 1881-83; student-assistant at grammar school in Midhurst, 1883-84; teacher at schools in Wrexham, Wales, 1887-88, and London, England, 1889; University Correspondence College, London, tutor, 1890-93; writer, 1893-1946. Member of Research Committee for the League of Nations, 1917; affiliated with British Ministry of Information, 1918; director of Policy Committee for Propaganda in Enemy Countries, 1918.

MEMBER: International P.E.N. (international president, 1934-46), British Association for the Advancement of Science (president of educational science section, 1937), British Diabetic Association (founding president), Abortion Law Reform Society (vice-president, 1936), Film Society (co-founder), Savile Club.

AWARDS, HONORS: D.Litt. from University of London, 1936; honorary fellow of Imperial College of Science and Technology.

WRITINGS:

NOVELS

The Time Machine: An Invention (science fiction; first published in *Science Schools Journal* as "The Chronic Argonauts," 1888), Holt, 1895.
The Wonderful Visit (science fiction), Macmillan, 1895.
The Wheels of Chance: A Bicycling Idyll (first published serially in *Today,* 1896), illustrations by J. Ayton Symington, Macmillan, 1896, published as *The Wheels of Chance: A Holiday Adventure,* Dent, 1896.
The Island of Doctor Moreau: A Possibility (science fiction), Stone & Kimball, 1896.
The Invisible Man: A Grotesque Romance (science fiction; first published serially in *Pearson's Weekly,* June-July, 1897), Arnold, 1897, published as *The Invisible Man: A Fantastic Sensation,* Robert Bentley, 1981.
The War of the Worlds (science fiction; first published serially in *Pearson's Magazine,* April-December, 1897), Harper & Brothers, 1898.
When the Sleeper Wakes (science fiction; first published serially in *The Graphic,* 1898-99), Harper & Brothers, 1899, revised as *The Sleeper Awakes,* Thomas Nelson, 1910.
Love and Mr. Lewisham: The Story of a Very Young Couple, George H. Doran, 1899.
The First Men in the Moon (science fiction; first published serially in *Strand Magazine,* December, 1900-August, 1901), Bowen-Merrill, 1901.

The Sea Lady (first published serially in *Pearson's Magazine,* July-December, 1901), D. Appleton, 1902 (published in England as *The Sea Lady: A Tissue of Moonshine,* Methuen, 1902).

The Food of the Gods, and How It Came to Earth (science fiction; first published serially in *Pearson's Magazine,* December, 1903-June, 1904), Scribner, 1904.

A Modern Utopia (first published serially in *Fortnightly Review,* October, 1904-April, 1905), illustrations by E. J. Sullivan, Scribner, 1905.

Kipps: A Monograph (first published serially in *Pall Mall,* 1905), Scribner, 1905, published as *Kipps: The Story of a Simple Soul,* 1905.

In the Days of the Comet (science fiction; first published serially in *Daily Chronicle,* 1905-06), Century, 1906.

The War in the Air, and Particularly How Mr. Bert Smallways Fared While It Lasted (first published serially in *Pall Mall*), Macmillan, 1908.

Tono-Bungay, Duffield, 1908.

Ann Veronica: A Modern Love Story, Harper & Brothers, 1909.

The History of Mr. Polly, Duffield, 1909.

The New Machiavelli (first published serially in *English Review,* May-October, 1910), Duffield, 1910.

Marriage, Duffield, 1912.

The Passionate Friends: A Novel (first published serially in *Grand Magazine,* March-November, 1913), Harper & Brothers, 1913.

The Wife of Sir Isaac Harman, Macmillan, 1914.

The World Set Free: A Story of Mankind (science fiction; first published serially in *English Review,* December, 1913-May, 1914), E. P. Dutton, 1914.

Bealby: A Holiday (first published serially in *Grand Magazine,* August, 1914-March, 1915), Macmillan, 1915.

(Under name Reginald Bliss) *Boon, The Mind of the Race, The Wild Asses of the Devil, and The Last Trump: Being a First Selection From the Literary Remains of George Boon, Appropriate to the Times, Prepared for Publication by Reginald Bliss With an Ambiguous Introduction by H. G. Wells,* George H. Doran, 1915, published under name H. G. Wells, Unwin, 1920.

The Research Magnificent, Macmillan, 1915.

Mr. Britling Sees It Through (first published serially in *Nation,* May-October, 1916), Macmillan, 1916.

The Soul of a Bishop (first published serially in *Collier's Weekly,* 1917), Macmillan, 1917 (published in England as *The Soul of a Bishop: A Novel—With Just a Little Love in It—About Conscience and Religion and the Real Troubles of Life,* Cassell, 1917).

Joan and Peter: The Story of an Education, Macmillan, 1918.

The Undying Fire: A Contemporary Novel (first published serially in *International Review,* March-June, 1919), Macmillan, 1919.

The Secret Places of the Heart (first published serially in *Nash's* and *Pall Mall,* December, 1921-July, 1922), Macmillan, 1922.

Men Like Gods: A Novel (science fiction; first published serially in *Westminster Gazette,* December, 1922-February, 1923), Macmillan, 1923.

The Dream: A Novel (first published serially in *Nash's* and *Pall Mall,* October, 1923-May, 1924), Macmillan, 1924.

Christina Alberta's Father, Macmillan, 1925.

The World of William Clissold: A Novel at a New Angle, George H. Doran, 1926.

Meanwhile: The Picture of a Lady, George H. Doran, 1927.

Mr. Blettsworthy on Rampole Island, Doubleday, Doran, 1928.

The King Who Was a King: An Unconventional Novel, Doubleday, Doran, 1929 (published in England as *The King Who Was a King: The Book of a Film,* E. Benn, 1929).

The Autocracy of Mr. Parham: His Remarkable Adventures in This Changing World, Doubleday, Doran, 1930.

The Bulpington of Blup: Adventures, Poses, Stresses, Conflicts, and Disaster in a Contemporary Brain, Hutchinson, 1932, Macmillan, 1933.

The Shape of Things to Come: The Ultimate Revolution, Macmillan, 1933.

The Croquet Player, Chatto & Windus, 1936, Viking, 1937.

Star-Begotten: A Biological Fantasia (science fiction), Viking, 1937.

Brynhild; or, The Show of Things, Scribner, 1937 (published in England as *Brynhild,* Methuen, 1937).

The Camford Visitation, Methuen, 1937.

Apropos of Dolores, Scribner, 1938.

The Brothers: A Story, Viking, 1938.

The Holy Terror, Simon & Schuster, 1939.

Babes in the Darkling Wood, Alliance Book, 1940.

All Aboard for Ararat (science fiction), Secker & Warburg, 1940, Alliance Book, 1941.

You Can't Be Too Careful: A Sample of Life, 1901-1951, Secker & Warburg, 1941, G. P. Putnam's Sons, 1942.

The Wealth of Mr. Waddy: A Novel (early draft of *Kipps*), edited with introduction by Harris Wilson, preface by Harry T. Moore, Southern Illinois University Press, 1969.

A Story of the Days to Come (science fiction), Corgi, 1976.

SHORT STORIES

Select Conversations With an Uncle, Now Extinct, and Two Other Reminiscences, Merriam, 1895.

The Stolen Bacillus and Other Incidents (science fiction), Methuen, 1895.

The Red Room, Stone & Kimball, 1896.

"A Perfect Gentleman on Wheels" (first published as "A Perfect Gentleman on Wheels; or, The Humours of Cycling" in *Woman at Home,* April, 1897), published in *The Humours of Cycling,* James Bowden, 1897.

Thirty Strange Stories (science fiction), Arnold, 1897.

The Plattner Story, and Others (science fiction), Methuen, 1897.

A Cure for Love, E. Scott, 1899.

Tales of Space and Time (science fiction), Doubleday & McClure, 1899.

The Vacant Country, A. E. Kent, 1899.

Twelve Stories and a Dream (science fiction), Macmillan, 1903.

The Door in the Wall, and Other Stories (science fiction), M. Kennerley, 1911.

The Country of the Blind, and Other Stories (science fiction), Thomas Nelson, 1911.

The Star (in simplified spelling), Sir Isaac Pitman & Sons, 1913.

The Country of the Blind (science fiction), privately printed, 1915, Golden Cockerel Press, 1939.

The Short Stories of H. G. Wells (science fiction), E. Benn, 1927, Doubleday, Doran, 1929, published as *The Complete Short Stories of H. G. Wells,* E. Benn, 1966, St. Martin's, 1970.

The Adventures of Tommy (for children), self-illustrated, Frederick A. Stokes, 1929.

The Valley of Spiders, London Book, 1930.

The Stolen Body, and Other Tales of the Unexpected, London Book, 1931.

The Favorite Short Stories of H. G. Wells, Doubleday, Doran, 1937, published as *The Famous Short Stories of H. G. Wells,* Garden City Publishing, 1938.

Short Stories by H. G. Wells, notes and questions by A. J. J. Ratcliff, T. Nelson, 1940.

The Land Ironclads, Todd Publishing, 1943.

The New Accelerator (science fiction), Todd Publishing, 1943.

The Empire of the Ants, Todd Publishing, 1943.

The Inexperienced Ghost, Todd Publishing, 1943.

The Truth About Pyecraft, and Other Short Stories, Todd Publishing, 1943.

The Inexperienced Ghost and The New Accelerator, Vallancey Press, 1944.

Twenty-eight Science Fiction Stories, Dover, 1952.

Seven Stories, Oxford University Press, 1953.

Tales of Life and Adventure, introduction by Frank Wells, Collins, 1953.

Tales of the Unexpected, introduction by Frank Wells, Collins, 1954.

Tales of Wonder, introduction by Frank Wells, Collins, 1954.

The Desert Daisy (for children), introduction by Gordon N. Ray, Beta Phi Mu, 1957.

Selected Short Stories, Penguin Books, 1958.

The Inexperienced Ghost, and Nine Other Stories, Bantam, 1965.

Best Science Fiction Stories of H. G. Wells, Dover, 1966.

The Man With a Nose: And the Other Uncollected Short Stories of H. G. Wells, edited with an introduction by J. R. Hammond, Athlone Press, 1984.

NONFICTION

Text-Book of Biology, two volumes, introduction by G. B. Howes, W. B. Clive, Volume I, 1892, Volume II, 1893, revision by A. M. Davies published as *Text-Book of Zoology,* 1898, 7th edition, revised and rewritten by J. T. Cunningham and W. H. Leigh-Sharpe, 1929.

(With R. A. Gregory) *Honours Physiography,* Joseph Hughes, 1893.

Certain Personal Matters: A Collection of Material, Mainly Autobiographical, Lawrence & Bullen, 1898.

Anticipations of the Reaction of Mechanical and Scientific Progress Upon Human Life and Thought (first published serially as "Anticipations: An Experiment in Prophecy" in *Fortnightly Review,* April-December, 1901), Harper & Brothers, 1902, with new introduction, Chapman & Hall, 1914.

Mankind in the Making (first published serially in *Fortnightly Review,* September, 1902-September, 1903), Chapman & Hall, 1903, Scribner, 1904, with new introduction, Chapman & Hall, 1914.

The Future in America: A Search After Realities (first published serially in *Harper's Weekly,* July 14-October 6, 1906), Harper & Brothers, 1906.

First and Last Things: A Confession of Faith and a Rule of Life, G. P. Putnam's Sons, 1908, definitive edition, Watts, 1929.

New Worlds for Old, Macmillan, 1908, revised edition, Constable, 1914.

Floor Games (for children; first published in *Strand Magazine,* December, 1911), self-illustrated, Frank Palmer, 1911, Small, Maynard, 1912.

(Editor with G. R. S. Taylor and Frances Evelyn Warwick, and contributor) *The Great State: Essays in Construction* (first published as "Socialism and the Great State" in *Harper's,* 1911), Harper & Brothers, 1912, published as *Socialism and the Great State: Essays in Construction,* 1914.

Little Wars: A Game for Boys From Twelve Years of Age to One Hundred and Fifty and for That More Intelligent Sort of Girls Who Like Boys' Games and Books With an Appendix on Kriegspiel (first published serially in *Windsor Magazine,* December, 1912, and January, 1913), Small, Maynard, 1913.

Social Forces in England and America (essays), Harper & Brothers, 1914 (published in England as *An Englishman Looks at the World: Being a Series of Unrestrained Remarks Upon Contemporary Matters,* Cassell, 1914).

The War That Will End War (essays), Duffield, 1914.

The War and Socialism, Clarion Press, 1915.

What Is Coming? A European Forecast, Macmillan, 1916 (published in England as *What Is Coming? A Forecast of Things After the War,* Cassell, 1916).

Introduction to Nocturne, G. H. Doran, 1917.

God, the Invisible King, Macmillan, 1917.

Italy, France, and Britain at War, Macmillan, 1917 (published in England as *War and the Future: Italy, France, and Britain at War,* Cassell, 1917).

In the Fourth Year: Anticipations of a World Peace, Macmillan, 1918 (abridged edition published in England as *Anticipations of a World Peace,* Chatto & Windus, 1918).

(With Viscount Grey, Lionel Curtis, William Archer, H. Wickham Steed, A. E. Zimmern, J. A. Spender, Viscount Bryce, and Gilbert Murray) *The Idea of a League of Nations: Prolegomena to the Study of World-Organisation,* Atlantic Monthly Press, 1919.

(With Viscount Grey, Gilbert Murray, J. A. Spender, A. E. Zimmern, H. Wickham Steed, Lionel Curtis, William Archer, Ernest Barker, G. Lowes Dickinson, John Hilton, and L. S. Woolf) *The Way to the League of Nations: A Brief Sketch of the Practical Steps Needed for the Formation of a League,* Oxford University Press, 1919.

(With Arnold Bennett and Grant Overton) *Frank Swinnerton: Personal Sketches; Together With Notes and Comments on the Novels of Frank Swinnerton,* G. H. Doran, 1920.

(With advice and editorial help of Ernest Barker, H. H. Johnston, E. Ray Lankester, and Gilbert Murray) *The Outline of History: Being a Plain History of Life and Mankind,* illustrations by J. F. Horrabin, Macmillan, 1920, published as *The New and Revised Outline of History: Being a Plain History of Life and Mankind,* Garden City Publishing, 1931, published as *The Enlarged and Revised Outline of History: Being a Plain History of Life and Mankind,* Triangle Books, 1940, under original title revised and brought up to the end of World War II by Raymond Postgate, Garden City Publishing, 1949, published as *The Outline of History: Being a Plain History of Life and Mankind From Primordial Life to Nineteen-sixty,* Cassell, 1961, under original title revised and brought up to date by Postgate and G. P. Wells, Doubleday, 1971.

Russia in the Shadows (first published serially in *Sunday Express,* October 31-November 28, 1920), Hodder & Stoughton, 1920, George H. Doran, 1921.

The Salvaging of Civilization: The Probable Future of Mankind, Macmillan, 1921.

A Short History of the World, Macmillan, 1922.

Washington and the Riddle of Peace (first published in *New York World,* November-December, 1921), Macmillan, 1922 (published in England as *Washington and the Hope of Peace,* Collins, 1922).

The Story of a Great Schoolmaster: Being a Plain Account of the Life and Ideas of Sanderson of Oundle (biography; first published serially in *New Leader,* September 14-October 26, 1923), Macmillan, 1924.

A Year of Prophesying (articles), Unwin, 1924, Macmillan, 1925.

A Short History of Mankind, adapted from *A Short History of the World* by E. H. Carter, Macmillan, 1925.

Mr. Belloc Objects to "The Outline of History," George H. Doran, 1926.

Wells' Social Anticipations, edited with introduction by Harry W. Laidler, Vanguard Press, 1927.

(Editor and author of introduction) *The Book of Catherine Wells,* Chatto & Windus, 1928.

The Way the World Is Going: Guesses and Forecasts of the Years Ahead; Twenty-six Articles and a Lecture, E. Benn, 1928, Doubleday, Doran, 1929.

The Open Conspiracy: Blue Prints for a World Revolution, Doubleday, Doran, 1928, published as *The Open Conspiracy: Blue Prints for a World Revolution; a Second Version of This Faith of a Modern Man Made More Explicit and Plain,* Hogarth Press, 1930, revised edition published as *What Are We to Do With Our Lives?,* Doubleday, Doran, 1931, published as *The Open Conspiracy,* Gordon Press, 1979.

(With Bertrand Russell, Fannie Hurst, Theodore Dreiser, Warwick Deeping, Rebecca West, Andre Maurois, and Lionel Feuchtwanger) *Divorce as I See It,* Douglas, 1930.

(With G. Lowes Dickinson, Dean Inge, J. B. S. Haldane, Sir Oliver Lodge, and Sir Walford Davis) *Points of View: A Series of Broadcast Addresses,* Allen & Unwin, 1930.

(With H. R. Knickerbocker, Sir John Russell, Sir Bernard Pares, Margaret S. Miller, B. Mouat-Jones, Stafford Talbot, and Frank Owen) *The New Russia: Eight Talks Broadcast,* Faber & Faber, 1931.

(With Julian S. Huxley and G. P. Wells) *The Science of Life: A Summary of Contemporary Knowledge About Life and Its Possibilities,* Amalgamated Press, 1930, Doubleday, Doran, 1931 (portions published severally as "The Science of Life" series, Doubleday, Doran, 1932; various volumes published in England by Cassell, 1937).

Selections From the Early Prose Works of H. G. Wells, University of London Press, 1931.

The Work, Wealth, and Happiness of Mankind, Doubleday, Doran, 1931, published as *The Outline of Man's Work and Wealth,* Garden City Publishing, 1936.

After Democracy: Addresses and Papers on the Present World Situation, Watts, 1932.

Experiment in Autobiography: Discoveries and Conclusions of a Very Ordinary Brain (Since 1866), self-illustrated, Macmillan, 1934.

The New America: The New World, Macmillan, 1935.

The Anatomy of Frustration: A Modern Synthesis, Macmillan, 1936.

World Brain (essays and addresses), Doubleday, Doran, 1938.

The Fate of Man: An Unemotional Statement of the Things That Are Happening to Him Now, and of the Immediate Possibilities Confronting Him, Longmans, Green, 1939 (published in England as *The Fate of Homo Sapiens: An Unemotional Statement of the Things That Are Happening to Him Now, and of the Immediate Possibilities Confronting Him,* Secker & Warburg, 1939).

Travels of a Republican Radical in Search of Hot Water, Penguin Books, 1939.

The Common Sense of War and Peace: World Revolution or War Unending, Penguin Books, 1940.

H. G. Wells, S. de Madariaga, J. Middleton Murry, C. E. M. Joad on the New World Order, National Peace Council, 1940.

The New World Order: Whether It Is Attainable, How It Can Be Attained, and What Sort of World a World at Peace Will Have to Be, Secker & Warburg, 1939, Knopf, 1940.

The Rights of Man; or, What Are We Fighting For?, Penguin Books, 1940.

Guide to the New World: A Handbook of Constructive World Revolution, Gollancz, 1941.

The Pocket History of the World, Pocket Books, 1941.

Modern Russian and English Revolutionaries: A Frank Exchange of Ideas Between Commander Lev Uspensky, Soviet Writer, and H. G. Wells, privately printed, 1942.

The Conquest of Time (written to replace his *First and Last Things*), Watts, 1942.

The Outlook for Homo Sapiens: An Unemotional Statement of the Things That Are Happening to Him Now, and of the Immediate Possibilities Confronting Him (an amalgamation and modernization of *The Fate of Homo Sapiens* and *The New World Order*), Secker & Warburg, 1942.

Phoenix: A Summary of the Inescapable Conditions of World Reorganisation, Secker & Warburg, 1942.

Crux Ansata: An Indictment of the Roman Catholic Church, Penguin Books, 1943.

'42 to '44: A Contemporary Memoir Upon Human Behaviour During the Crisis of the World Revolution, Secker & Warburg, 1944.

(With J. S. Huxley and J. B. S. Haldane) *Reshaping Man's Heritage: Biology in the Service of Man,* Allen & Unwin, 1944.

The Happy Turning: A Dream of Life, Heinemann, 1945.

(With Joseph Stalin) *Marxism vs. Liberalism: An Interview,* New Century, 1945, published as *H. G. Wells' Interview With J. V. Stalin (Marxism v. Liberalism),* Current Book Distributors (Sydney), 1950.

Mind at the End of Its Tether (first published in *Sunday Express*), Heinemann, 1945.

Henry James and H. G. Wells: A Record of Their Friendship, Their Debate on the Art of Fiction, and Their Quarrel (correspondence), edited with introduction by Leon Edel and Gordon N. Ray, University of Illinois Press, 1958.

Arnold Bennett and H. G. Wells: A Record of a Personal and a Literary Friendship (correspondence), edited with introduction by Harris Wilson, University of Illinois Press, 1960.

George Gissing and H. G. Wells: Their Friendship and Correspondence, edited with introduction by Royal A. Gettmann, University of Illinois Press, 1961.

Journalism and Prophecy, 1893-1946: An Anthology (addresses, essays, and lectures), compiled and edited by W. Warren Wagar, Houghton, 1964.

H. G. Wells's Literary Criticism, edited by Patrick Parrinder and Robert M. Philmus, Harvester Press, 1980.

H. G. Wells in Love: Postscript to an Experiment in Autobiography, edited by G. P. Wells, Little, Brown, 1984.

Treasury of H. G. Wells, Octopus Books, 1985.

OTHER

Socialism and the Family (pamphlet; contains "Socialism and the Middle Classes" and "Modern Socialism and the Family"), A. C. Fifield, 1906.

This Misery of Boots (pamphlet; first published in *Independent Review,* December, 1905), Fabian Society, 1907, Ball Publishing, 1908.

The H. G. Wells Calendar: A Quotation From the Works of H. G. Wells for Every Day in the Year, selected by Rosamund Marriott Watson, Frank Palmer, 1911.

Great Thoughts From H. G. Wells, selected by Rosamund Marriott Watson, Dodge, 1912.

Thoughts From H. G. Wells, selected by Elsie E. Morton, Harrap, 1913.

The Works of H. G. Wells: Atlantic Edition, 28 volumes, Scribner, 1924-27.

The Essex Thin-Paper Edition of the Works of H. G. Wells, 24 volumes, E. Benn, 1926-27.

Democracy Under Revision: A Lecture Delivered at the Sorbonne, March 15th, 1927 (pamphlet), George H. Doran, 1927.

Things to Come: A Film Story Based on the Material Contained in His History of the Future "The Shape of Things to Come" (science fiction), Macmillan, 1935.

Man Who Could Work Miracles: A Film by H. G. Wells, Based on the Short Story Entitled "The Man Who Could Work Miracles," Macmillan, 1936 (published in England as *Man Who Could Work Miracles: A Film Story Based on the Material Contained in His Short Story "Man Who Could Work Miracles,"* Cresset Press, 1936).

The H. G. Wells Papers at the University of Illinois, edited by Gordon N. Ray, University of Illinois Press, 1958.

Hoopdriver's Holiday (dramatization of his novel *The Wheels of Chance*), edited with notes and introduction by Michael Timko, English Department, Purdue University, 1964.

H. G. Wells: Early Writings in Science and Science Fiction, edited with critical commentary and notes by Robert M. Philmus and David Y. Hughes, University of California Press, 1975.

H. G. Wells Science Fiction Treasury, Crown, 1987.

Also author of *Two Hemispheres or One World?,* 1940, and many pamphlets. Author of film scripts, including "Bluebottles," "Daydreams," and "The Tonic." Contributor of introductions and prefaces to numerous books.

Work represented in anthologies, including *Thirty-one Stories by Thirty and One Authors,* edited by Ernest Rhys and C. A. Dawson Scott, Butterworth, 1923, and *Masterpieces of Science Fiction,* edited by Sam Moskowitz, World Publishing, 1967.

Contributor of reviews, letters, essays, and stories to periodicals, including *Clarion, English Review, Fortnightly Review, Independent Review, Labour Leader,* London *Daily Mail,* London *Times, Nation, New Age, Times Literary Supplement,* and *Saturday Review.*

MEDIA ADAPTATIONS: Numerous works by Wells have been adapted as comic books, films, plays, sound recordings, and radio and television productions, including *The Shape of Things to Come,* adapted as the film "Things to Come," 1936, and *The War of the Worlds,* adapted by Orson Welles and broadcast by Columbia Broadcasting System (CBS-Radio) on October 30, 1938; the broadcast sparked a widespread panic by listeners who thought a real alien invasion had taken place.

SIDELIGHTS: H. G. Wells, best remembered for imaginative novels such as *The Invisible Man* and *The War of the Worlds,* prototypes for modern science fiction, was a prolific writer and one of the most versatile in the history of English letters. He produced an average of nearly three books a year for more than fifty years, in addition to hundreds of newspaper and magazine articles. His works ranged from fiction to history, science, social activism, literary criticism, biography, and film. Altogether, Wells penned more words than William Shakespeare and Charles Dickens combined.

Born of lower-middle-class parents—they were, in fact, servants to the gentry—he escaped a servile life by winning a scholarship to the Normal School of Science at South Kensington, a London parliamentary borough, in 1884. Britain's first college to offer a science education for teachers, the Normal School of Science was founded by T. H. Huxley, who also served as its first dean. Wells regarded Huxley as the greatest man he ever met (although they never engaged in actual conversation). Recalling studying biology under Huxley, Wells in *The Fate of Man: An Unemotional Statement of the Things That Are Happening to Him Now, and of the Immediate Possibilities Confronting Him* (1939) declared he had then come to see the world "as I see it today. . . . There has been a lot of expansion and supplementing since, but nothing like fundamental reconstruction." He later summed up his life's work in *'42 to '44: A Contemporary Memoir Upon Human Behaviour During the Crisis of the World Revolution* (1944) by saying, "My role has always been that of a propagandist, direct or indirect, for world socialism." He labeled this ideology "Wellsism," a kind of "political religion," as he described it in *God, the Invisible King* (1917), that informs everything from his novels of social criticism to his utopian pictures of the world as it might be.

The connection between Wellsism and the writer's worship of Huxley may be explained as follows. Before founding the school, Huxley became famous for defending naturalist Charles Darwin in the great Oxford Debate of 1860, doing battle with the Church over the issue of evolution raised in Darwin's *Origin of Species by Means of Natural Selection* (1859). Huxley's merciless victory over Bishop Wilberforce at Oxford, at a time when one did not lightly insult leaders of the established religion, impressed on science students that theirs was more than a harmless academic discipline. With Huxley, science, especially biology, was radical, even revolutionary—at the expense of theology. It inspired Wells from the start, as he said in *The Anatomy of Frustration: A Modern Synthesis* (1936), to cast himself as "a sort of one-man Royal Commission of enquiry into the significance of the universe, as it had been understood and stated heretofore."

For Huxley, biology took in not only the study of man as an animal species but also as a social and cultural animal; biology covered his institutional life as well, a subject currently assigned to sociology and anthropology. It made a bid to replace the idea of man's unity under God with man's unity as a global species. Man was one species, yet his ways were many; for Wells, the world socialist revolution was to unify and pacify the human race, still divided by competing nationalisms, and thereby to reassert its essential oneness. According to Wells, when science proved theology a fiction, the God of the Above was replaced by the God of the Ahead, the evolutionary pull of the future toward a world socialist state.

Small wonder, then, that Wells should make a combination of science and statism—the exertion of economic controls by a centralized government—the basis for his vision of social justice. "The drift of things is in the direction of state ownership and control," he wrote in *God, the Invisible King,* with God being the idea of human purpose, directing itself in the course of racial progress toward its evolutionary fulfillment in a world socialist state. "God is Red, and Red he always has been," he said in *All Aboard for Ararat* (1940). But Wellsism was a very personalized scientific socialism, owing nothing to Marx, as Wells always insisted: "The World-State—c'est moi," he wrote in his *Experiment in Autobiography.*

As it happened, however, Wells lost his scholarship after his third year. Only Huxley, who taught Wells his first year, interested him. Thereafter he failed to keep up with his studies, preoccupied with activities such as debating and the college magazine, which he founded and edited. Wells had no intention of becoming a man of letters, though he showed an early interest in writing, as revealed by *The Desert Daisy,* a narrative written when he was about twelve years old. He began as a professional by producing journalistic sketches, some of which were collected in *Select Conversations With an Uncle, Now Extinct, and Two Other Reminiscences* (1895) and *Certain Personal Matters: A Collection of Material, Mainly Autobiographical* (1898). These essays were bright and informed enough to win the attention of the English *Saturday Review,* which then assigned him to carry the main burden of its fiction reviewing. From 1895 to 1897 he passed judgment on almost every new novel published in English. Sifting out those books deserving of review, as exemplars either of artistic excellence or of instructive failure, he made a distinguished career of producing thoughtful and intelligent literary criticism on a weekly basis.

Wells's term as a book reviewer set new standards of precision in literary criticism, especially with his careful distinction between novels of romance and of realism. He helped define these categories to the benefit of both writers and critics. In addition, he brought public attention to authors Joseph Conrad and James Joyce, writing for their first novels the perceptive review articles that helped launch their distinguished careers.

He would not limit himself to reviewing, however. All along, Wells had nurtured a single promising idea, first introduced in "The Chronic Argonauts," published in his college magazine two years after he dropped out of school—an idea that he hoped would establish him as a novelist in his own right. Developed after many false starts, it finally appeared as *The Time Machine* in 1895. This first novel was hailed as a work of genius, and it is regarded by today's critics as the one great Victorian epic dramatizing the Darwinian vision of cosmic time outside historical time. Wells was on his way to winning fame with a series of similar novels, the scientific romances, as he called them. These are Wells's only works to have remained continuously in print since his death. The best of them are *The Time Machine, The Island of Doctor Moreau* (1896), *The Invisible Man* (1897), *The War of the Worlds* (1898), and *The First Men in the Moon* (1901).

To the end of his life, Wells himself regarded the scientific romances as inconsequential. So did the critical establishment until Bernard Bergonzi, in his 1961 study *The Early H. G. Wells: A Study of the Scientific Romances,* argued to great effect that these works deserved to be ranked among the classics of the English language. Until then, it was thought that Wells's enduring literary fame would come to rest on the so-called Dickensesque novels of social comedy, like *Kipps* (1905) and *The History of Mr. Polly* (1909), together with his novels of social criticism, like *Tono-Bungay* (1908), all from the middle period of Wells's career. These works have not lived up to this expectation, however; the range of comic types in the former genre is narrower by far than anything portrayed by Dickens, and the social criticism in the latter condition-of-England genre no longer seems pointed following the advent of the welfare state in Britain. All the same, these titles established Wells as the preeminent Edwardian novelist. Thereafter, Wells turned to crusading for the world socialist state in numerous titles that failed to enjoy any literary repute even in their own time. This assessment leaves Wells's early works as the only ones of lasting merit; and Bergonzi's estimation of the scientific romances is now the critical consensus: "Wells, at the beginning of his career, was a genuine imaginative artist, who wrote several books of considerable literary importance, before dissipating his talents in directions which now seem more or less irrelevant."

Critics Robert Bloom and Richard Hauer Costa almost alone dissent. In his *Anatomies of Egotism: A Reading of the Last Novels of H. G. Wells* (1977), Bloom argues that among Wells's finest novels are *Brynhild* (1937) and *Apropos of Dolores* (1938) from his late period. Writer Henry James had complained that Wells recklessly sacrificed aesthetic merit in his post-Victorian novels—so far as James lived to read them until his death in 1916—

for the sake of doctrinal considerations. Wells replied that social purpose was more important than refined artiness. Yet Bloom finds that the best of Wells's last novels meet every standard of Jamesian aestheticism. Costa argues in his *H. G. Wells* (1985) that certain of the middle novels deserve reappraisal, notably *Mr. Britling Sees It Through* (1916) for its resolution of the Jamesian problem of artistic unity with a complexity undreamed of by James himself. More especially, Costa singles out *The Undying Fire* (1919) for its masterly handling of the dialogue novel, claiming Wells gave the genre a novelistic integrity never before achieved.

Nevertheless, however deserving of attention these novels have proved in recent years, their initial publication had no influence on the development of English fiction. The works Costa selected for praise were evidently too subtle for critical appreciation at the time, although *Mr. Britling* succeeded as a voguish bestseller. The latter books praised by Bloom came too late to garner any critical attention at all. They do indeed show the aging Wells in a phase of renewed creative vigor, combining a delicacy of artistic form (learned from James) with the usual substantive content—an amazing feat. But by the mid-1920s, Wells's reputation as a novelist had already slipped. It declined decidedly after the publication of *The World of William Clissold* (1926), the last of his novels to be received with enthusiasm on both sides of the Atlantic.

With the scientific romances, Wells defined a new department of twentieth-century literature, not only for science fiction authors but for a number of great mainstream writers who lent their talents to the genre. Notables who have acknowledged this debt include Evgeny Zamyatin, Aldous Huxley, C. S. Lewis, George Orwell, William Golding, Vladimir Nabokov, and Jorge Luis Borges. Wells's scientific romances were accepted by Victorian critics as masterful works of art. But later critics took a different view. When the scientific romances were reprinted in the first issues of *Amazing Stories,* which from 1926 established science fiction as a publisher's category among the many other forms of topical fiction dominating the American pulp magazine industry, Wells was proclaimed "the father of modern science fiction." Critics of the day associated Wells's scientific romances with lowbrow literature belonging to popular culture. Eventually the science fiction genre won critical attention, while Bergonzi rediscovered Wells's scientific romances for quality literature.

More than empty fantasies artistically done, they contain such a heavy load of doctrinal matter that Parrinder in *H. G. Wells* (1977) has called them "ideological fables." Wells himself said in his autobiography that his purpose in them was "to discuss sociology in fable." He might have substituted "socialism" for "sociology."

Wells's influence endures in many ways apart from the narrowed stream of readership devoted to the scientific romances. The measure of this influence may be seen in his lasting achievements as the invisible presence behind some of the most obvious features of the present-day intellectual, social, and political landscape.

Between 1903 and 1908, Wells was a member of the Fabian Society, a group of upper-middle-class intellectuals that promoted socialism. Wells wrote a number of attention-getting Fabian pamphlets, most notably *Socialism and the Family* (1906) and *This Misery of Boots* (1907). Some of the ideas advanced in the pamphlets were later adopted by British Parliament, measures now basic to the British welfare state.

Shortly after leaving the Fabian Society, Wells in 1909 wrote the novel *Ann Veronica,* considered scandalous in its time for presenting the theme of woman's emancipation. That movement traces its ideological ancestry in large part to the transatlantic influence of this novel, together with other Wells books like it, such as *Marriage* (1912), *The Passionate Friends* (1913), *The Wife of Sir Isaac Harman* (1914), and *Christina Alberta's Father* (1925). Wells was also an outspoken advocate of sexual liberation, and his testimony in another author's obscenity trial helped establish the freedom in England to publish explicit books about contraception. Earlier, Wells had lent his name to Margaret Sanger's crusade for family planning in the United States by writing the introduction to her *Pivot of Civilization* (1923).

At the same time, Wells influenced the course of the novel itself. As he says in his autobiography, "After *Ann Veronica,* things were never quite the same again in the world of English fiction." Within a few years other novelists followed the example of this *succes de scandale,* which sold out in a number of editions despite the abuse heaped upon it by press and pulpit. The marketplace became more open to a new kind of fiction, free to explore all aspects of morality. Wells's boldness helped clear the way for such writers as D. H. Lawrence and the mature James Joyce.

Furthermore, the commercial success of packaged war games owes directly to Wells's invention in this field, with his publication of *Little Wars* (1913). Based on a floor game he devised for his children, this book also led to the improvement of the war games played by the military staff colleges of the British Army. Even here, Wells could not resist scoring a political point. He observed that real war was so childish and yet so horrible that the only proper place for uniformed patriots was in the Little Wars toybox; or else the militarism of independent sovereign nation-states would lead, sooner or later, to a ruinous world conflict. If man doesn't end war, war will end man was the message added to this not-so-playful children's book, published just before the onset of World War I.

This idea, in fact, was the central one of his most successful book, *The Outline of History,* which sold more than two million copies during his lifetime. In it Wells wrote, "History is more and more a race between education and catastrophe." The book was intended to help avert that catastrophe, forming as it did the first title of his educational trilogy, which also included *The Science of Life: A Summary of Contemporary Knowledge About Life and Its Possibilities* (1930) and *The Work, Wealth, and Happiness of Mankind* (1931), called by Wells his Bible of World Civilization. Wells believed that if only this new and secular Bible were taught in schools worldwide, mankind would learn the survival values of world citizenship and socialism and unlearn the doom-laden falsities of nationalism and patriotic schooling. With *The Outline of History,* Wells was the first to write the planetary story of mankind, using the insights of the Darwinian biologists and of the early anthropologists in the field of sociocultural evolution.

History for Wells was not only a story about the past. He presumed to write a history of the future as well, as in *The Shape of Things to Come.* A motion picture based on this book was made in 1936. Wells was then seventy years old but still influential enough to stimulate the most expensive production ever mounted by a British studio to that date. One of the first science fiction films, it was the direct ancestor of such big-budget cinematic space operas as "2001: A Space Odyssey" and "Star Wars." But "Things to Come" was no mere entertainment. He meant it to be a "propagandist film" for Wellsism, a plug for the world socialist state. As such it was yet another statement, looking ahead to the coming of World War II, of his war-to-end-war

theme. But the audience of the time found his fears concerning yet another world war unconvincing (this only three short years before war actually broke out), and the film was a box office failure. As a result its message was lost, and the movie circulates today among science fiction film clubs only as a nostalgic predecessor to the big blockbusters.

During the actual course of the war he so accurately predicted, Wells published *The Rights of Man; or, What Are We Fighting For?* (1940). Based on the work of the Sankey Commission, on which he was invited to serve, it declared a list of about a dozen human rights, proposed as the basis for a lasting world peace should the Germans be defeated. As the subtitle indicates, Wells believed that these human rights were what the Allies should be fighting for. He later enlarged the scope of the commission's work, in *Phoenix* and in *'42 to '44,* to read as a declaration of the rights of the world citizen. In this form, it was intended to serve as the legal charter for the world state of his dream. His tireless efforts on its behalf did have one important practical effect. As James Dilloway documents in *Human Rights and World Order* (1983), Wells's contribution to the Sankey Commission directly shaped the language of the charter of the United Nations Organization in its Declaration of Human Rights, adopted December 10, 1948.

This contribution may turn out to be Wells's most important service to humanity, a service he was always ambitious to provide in some way. Yet Wells himself, it seems, thought of human rights not as individual but as collective rights, to be defined to the benefit of socialist planning under his idealized world state. The direction the world will take in the future depends entirely upon which definition prevails. In any event, perhaps no man of letters had more influence than did H. G. Wells in shaping the world's agenda for the days to come.

BIOGRAPHICAL/CRITICAL SOURCES:

BOOKS

Batchelor, John, *H. G. Wells,* Cambridge University Press, 1985.

Belloc, Hilaire, *A Companion to Mr. Wells's "Outline of History,"* Sheed & Ward, 1926.

Belloc, Hilaire, *Mr. Belloc Still Objects,* Sheed & Ward, 1926.

Beresford, John Davys, *H. G. Wells,* Nisbet, 1915, reprinted, Haskell House, 1972.

Bergonzi, Bernard, *The Early H. G. Wells: A Study of the Scientific Romances,* Manchester University Press, 1961.

Bergonzi, Bernard, editor, *H. G. Wells: A Collection of Critical Essays,* Prentice-Hall, 1976.

Bloom, Robert, *Anatomies of Egotism: A Reading of the Last Novels of H. G. Wells,* University of Nebraska Press, 1977.

Brooks, Van Wyck, *The World of H. G. Wells,* Unwin, 1914, M. Kennerley, 1915, reprinted, Gordon Press, 1973.

Costa, Richard Hauer, *H. G. Wells,* Twayne, 1966, revised edition, 1985.

Dictionary of Literary Biography, Gale, Volume 34: *British Novelists, 1890-1929: Traditionalists,* 1985, Volume 70: *British Mystery Writers, 1860-1919,* 1988.

Dilloway, James, *Human Rights and World Order,* H. G. Wells Society, 1983.

Edel, Leon and Gordon N. Ray, editors, *Henry James and H. G. Wells: A Record of Their Friendship, Their Debate on the Art of Fiction, and Their Quarrel,* University of Illinois Press, 1958, reprinted, Greenwood Press, 1979.

Gill, Stephen, *The Scientific Romances of H. G. Wells,* Vesta, 1975.

H. G. Wells: A Comprehensive Bibliography, H. G. Wells Society, 1972.

Haining, Peter, *The H. G. Wells Scrapbook,* New English Library, 1978.

Hammond, J. R., *Herbert George Wells: An Annotated Bibliography of His Works,* Garland Publishing, 1977.

Hammond, J. R., *An H. G. Wells Companion: A Guide to the Novels, Romances, and Short Stories,* Macmillan, 1979.

Hammond, J. R., editor, *H. G. Wells: Interviews and Recollections,* Macmillan, 1980.

Hawley, Elizabeth and Columbia Rossi, *Bertie: The Life After Death of H. G. Wells,* New English Library, 1973.

Huntington, John, *The Logic of Fantasy: H. G. Wells and Science Fiction,* Columbia University Press, 1982.

MacKenzie, Norman and Jeanne MacKenzie, *H. G. Wells: A Biography,* Simon & Schuster, 1973.

MacKenzie, Norman and Jeanne MacKenzie, *The Time Traveller: The Life of H. G. Wells,* Simon & Schuster, 1973.

McConnell, Frank, *The Science Fiction of H. G. Wells,* Oxford University Press, 1981.

Meyer, Mathilde Marie, *H. G. Wells and His Family, As I Have Known Them,* International Publishing, 1956.

Niles, P. H., *The Science Fiction of H. G. Wells: A Concise Guide,* Auriga, 1980.

Parrinder, Patrick, *H. G. Wells,* Oliver & Boyd, 1970, Putnam's, 1977.

Parrinder, Patrick, editor, *H. G. Wells: The Critical Heritage,* Routledge & Kegan Paul, 1972.

Raknem, Ingvald, *H. G. Wells and His Critics,* Allen & Unwin, 1962.

Ray, Gordon N., *H. G. Wells and Rebecca West,* Macmillan, 1974.

Suvin, Darko and Robert M. Philmus, editors, *H. G. Wells and Modern Science Fiction,* Bucknell University Press, 1977.

Twentieth-Century Literary Criticism, Gale, Volume 6, 1982, Volume 12, 1984, Volume 19, 1986.

Wells, Frank, *H. G. Wells: A Pictorial Biography,* Jupiter, 1977.

Wells, Geoffrey H., *The Works of H. G. Wells, 1887-1925: A Bibliography, Dictionary, and Subject-Index,* George Routledge & Sons, 1926.

Wells, H. G., *Experiment in Autobiography: Discoveries and Conclusions of a Very Ordinary Brain (Since 1866),* Macmillan, 1934.

Wells, H. G., *H. G. Wells in Love: Postscript to an Experiment in Autobiography,* edited by G. P. Wells, Little, Brown, 1984.

West, Anthony, *H. G. Wells: Aspects of a Life,* Random House, 1984.

West, Geoffrey H. (formerly Geoffrey H. Wells), *H. G. Wells: A Sketch for a Portrait,* Howe, 1930.

Wood, James Playsted, *I Told You So! A Life of H. G. Wells,* Pantheon, 1969.

Wykes, Alan, *H. G. Wells in the Cinema,* Jupiter, 1977.

PERIODICALS

Los Angeles Times Book Review, December 9, 1984.

Newsweek, May 28, 1984.

New York Times Book Review, March 3, 1985, September 21, 1986.

Times (London), October 4, 1984.

Times Literary Supplement, January 25, 1985, February 7, 1986, September 18-24, 1987.

Washington Post Book World, January 6, 1985.

OBITUARIES:

PERIODICALS

Christian Century, August 28, 1946.

New York Times, August 14, 1946.

Publishers Weekly, August 24, 1946.

Wilson Library Bulletin, October, 1946.

*   *   *

WELTY, Eudora 1909-

PERSONAL: Born April 13, 1909, in Jackson, MS; daughter of Christian Webb (an insurance company president) and Chestina (Andrews) Welty. *Education:* Attended Mississippi State College for Women (now Mississippi University for Women), 1926-27; University of Wisconsin, B.A., 1929; attended Columbia University Graduate School of Business, 1930-31.

ADDRESSES: Home—1119 Pinehurst St., Jackson, MS 39202.

CAREER: Worked for newspapers and radio stations in Mississippi during early depression years, and as a publicity agent for the state office of the Works Progress Administration (WPA). Was briefly a member of the *New York Times Book Review* staff, in New York City. Honorary consultant in American letters, Library of Congress, 1958—.

MEMBER: American Academy and Institute of Arts and Letters.

AWARDS, HONORS: Guggenheim fellowship, 1942; O. Henry Award, 1942, 1943, 1968; National Institute of Arts and Letters, 1944, grant in literature, 1972, Gold Medal for fiction writing; William Dean Howells Medal from American Academy of Arts and Letters, 1955, for *The Ponder Heart;* Edward McDowell Medal, 1970; National Book Award nomination in fiction, 1971, for *Losing Battles;* Christopher Book Award, 1972, for *One Time, One Place: Mississippi in the Depression; A Snapshot;* Pulitzer Prize in fiction, 1973, for *The Optimist's Daughter;* National Medal for Literature, 1980; *The Collected Stories of Eudora Welty* was named an American Library Association notable book for 1980; Presidential Medal of Freedom, 1980; American Book Award, 1981, for *The Collected Stories of Eudora Welty,* 1984, for *One Writer's Beginnings;* Common Wealth Award for Distinguished Service in Literature from Modern Language Association of America, 1984; National Book Critics Circle Award and *Los Angeles Times* Book Prize nominations, both 1984, for *One Writer's Beginnings;* Reader of the Year Award from Mystery Writers of America, 1985; National Medal of Arts, 1987.

WRITINGS:

A Curtain of Green (short stories; also see below) with a preface by Katherine Anne Porter, Doubleday, 1941, published as *A Curtain of Green, and Other Stories,* Harcourt, 1964.

The Robber Bridegroom (novella), Doubleday, 1942.

The Wide Net, and Other Stories (also see below), Harcourt, 1943.

Delta Wedding (novel), Harcourt, 1946.

Music from Spain, Levee Press, 1948.

Short Stories (address delivered at University of Washington), Harcourt, 1949.

The Golden Apples (connected stories; also see below), Harcourt, 1949.

Selected Stories (contains all of the short stories in *A Curtain of Green,* and *The Wide Net, and Other Stories*) introduction by Porter, Modern Library, 1953.

The Ponder Heart (novel), Harcourt, 1954.

The Bride of the Innisfallen, and Other Stories, Harcourt, 1955.

Place in Fiction (lectures for Conference on American Studies in Cambridge, England), House of Books, 1957.

John Rood (catalog of sculpture exhibition), [New York], 1958.

Three Papers on Fiction (addresses), Smith College, 1962.

The Shoe Bird (juvenile), Harcourt, 1964.

Thirteen Stories, edited and introduction by Ruth M. Vande Kieft, Harcourt, 1965.

A Sweet Devouring (nonfiction), Albondocani Press, 1969.

Losing Battles (novel), Random House, 1970.

A Flock of Guinea Hens Seen from a Car (poem), Albondocani Press, 1970.

One Time, One Place: Mississippi in the Depression; A Snapshot Album, illustrated with photographs by Welty, Random House, 1971.

The Optimist's Daughter (novelette), Random House, 1972.

The Eye of the Story (selected essays and reviews), Random House, 1978.

Miracles of Perception, The Library (Charlottesville), 1980.

The Collected Stories of Eudora Welty, Harcourt, 1980.

One Writer's Beginnings (lectures), Harvard University Press, 1984.

Morgana: Two Stories from 'The Golden Apples,' University Press of Mississippi, 1988.

Contributor to *Southern Review, Atlantic, Harper's Bazaar, Manuscript, New Yorker,* and other periodicals. Also contributor of articles under pseudonym, Michael Ravenna, to *New York Times Book Review.*

SIDELIGHTS: With the publication of *The Eye of the Story* and *The Collected Stories,* Eudora Welty achieved the recognition she has long deserved as an important contemporary American fiction writer. Her position was confirmed in 1984 when her autobiographical *One Writer's Beginnings* made the best-seller lists with sales exceeding 100,000 copies. During the early decades of her career, she was respected by fellow writers but often dismissed by critics as a regionalist, a miniaturist, or an oversensitive "feminine" writer. The late 1970s and 1980s, however, saw a critical reevaluation of her work demonstrating, as Michael Kreyling declares in *Eudora Welty's Achievement of Order,* "that it is not primarily regional writing, or even excellent regional writing, but is the vision of a certain artist who must be considered with her peers—[Virginia] Woolf, [Elizabeth] Bowen, and [E. M.] Forster. . . ."

Marked by a subtle, lyrical narrative state, Welty's work typically explores the intricacies of the interior life and the small heroisms of ordinary people. In an article appearing in *Eudora Welty: Critical Essays,* Chester E. Eisinger describes the writer's unique combination of realistic and modernist traditions: "Her work reflects the careful disorder of Chekhovian fiction and the accurate yet spontaneous rendering of detail that belonged to [Anton Checkhov's] slice of life technique. It reflects the modernism, . . . that characterized Woolf's fiction: The door she opened for Welty, she herself had passed through with [James] Joyce, [Franz] Kafka, [Marcel] Proust, [Robert] Musil, and the other twentieth-century makers of experimental, avant-garde fiction." Eisinger has in mind Woolf's rejection of the clear plot structure of the traditional novel, her internalization of experience, her careful rendering of the minutiae of ordinary life, her poetic use of language, and her fragmented point-of-view. Woolf opened another door for Welty as well, demonstrating in *To the Lighthouse* how to center a serious novel in the experiences of women.

Although Welty has always distanced herself from the women's movement, feminist critical interest in the works of women writers also stimulated renewed attention to her fiction in the 1970s and 1980s. In an article collected in *Eudora Welty: Critical Essays,* Margaret Jones Bolsterli expresses some of the major assumptions of the feminist approach when she argues that "Un-

derstanding women's views of themselves and of men is necessary if we are ever going to get at the truth, and the vision Eudora Welty presents of the women's worlds in [her] novels illuminates not only half of the great world which we do not often see, but also touches gently sometimes on the terrible state of affairs on this darkling plain when men and women do not see each other clearly at all." The reading public and the scholarly establishment began to realize that a major body of American fiction had been produced by Southern women writers, as Anne Goodwyn Jones has documented in *Tomorrow Is Another Day: The Woman Writer in the South, 1859-1936.* Moreover, critics perceived that Welty, the most prolific and versatile of these writers, was producing works of an astonishing range: from folktale to historical romance, grotesque farce to novel of manners; from dramatizations of lives contained by sharecropping cabins of the Depression to portraits of relationships in Delta plantations and upper-middle-class suburbs. And all these modes and subject matters are complemented by the distinguished essays, reviews, and reminiscences collected in *The Eye of the Story* and *One Writer's Beginnings.*

The oldest of her family's three children and the only girl, Welty grew up in Jackson, Mississippi. That neither of her parents came from the Deep South may have given her some detachment from her culture and helped her become an astute observer of its manners. Her father, Christian Welty, had been raised on a farm in Ohio and had become a country school teacher in West Virginia. Marrying a fellow teacher, Chestina Andrews, he had moved to Jackson to improve his fortunes by entering business. From bookkeeper in an insurance company, he eventually advanced to president.

Chestina Andrews, the daughter of transplanted Virginians, had grown up on a mountain in West Virginia. At fifteen, she had taken her critically ill father down an icy river on a raft to the railroad and then to a hospital in Baltimore where he died on the operating table of a ruptured appendix. In later years she took her young daughter on memorable summer visits "up home"; Welty's formidable grandmother and five bachelor uncles make a poignant fictional appearance in their mountaintop world as Laurel Hand's grandmother and uncles in *The Optimist's Daughter.*

Welty's reminiscences describe a happy childhood in a close-knit, bookish family. One of her earliest memories was the sound of her parents' voices reading favorite books to one another in the evenings. The Welty children were provided with fairy tales and mythology, dictionaries and encyclopedias, and library cards that allowed young Eudora to practice what she later called, in an essay employing the phrase as a title, "a sweet devouring" of the riches in the Jackson public library. Her delight in the gossip and storytelling that were such a vital part of traditional small-town Southern life was as great as her passion for books. Welty has often said that when her mother's friends would come to visit, she would demand, "Now start talking!" Her experiences of listening established a lifelong pleasure in folktale, mythology, tall tales, humorous anecdote, and comic idiom, which are special marks of her fiction.

Welty's education in the Jackson schools was followed by two years at Mississippi State College for Women between 1925 and 1927, and then by two more years at the University of Wisconsin and a B.A. in 1929. Her father, who believed that she could never earn a living by writing stories, encouraged her to study advertising at the Columbia University Graduate School of Business in New York during 1930-1931. The years in Wisconsin and New York broadened Welty's horizons, and the time she spent in New

York City was especially meaningful. The Harlem Renaissance was at its height, and Welty and her friends went to dances in Harlem clubs and to musical and theatrical performances all over the city. "Everybody that was wonderful was then at their peak," the writer told Jan Norby Gretlund in an interview collected in *Conversations with Eudora Welty.* "For somebody who had never, in a sustained manner, been to the theater or to the Metropolitan Museum, where I went every Sunday, it was just a cornucopia."

Her father's sudden death in 1931 brought an end to Welty's northern sojourn. She went home to help her mother and brothers, and she has essentially remained in Jackson ever since. To support herself, Welty first tried various small jobs with local newspapers and with radio station WJDX, which her father had started in the tower of his insurance building. Then, in 1933, she was offered a position as a publicity agent for the Works Progress Administration (WPA). "I did reporting, interviewing," she explained to Jean Todd Freeman in an interview collected in *Conversations with Eudora Welty.* "It took me all over Mississippi, which is the most important thing to me, because I'd never seen it. . . . [The experience] was the real germ of my wanting to become a real writer, a true writer."

In her travels around Mississippi, Welty was learning the art of seeing and capturing significant moments in the lives of ordinary people, an art she first practiced with a camera. She took hundreds of photographs of Mississippians of all social classes, capturing them at work and at leisure with their friends and families. Although her camera was not much better than a Brownie, the results were so effective that she took them to New York and tried to interest a publisher. The majority of the pictures are of blacks, providing a rare documentation that celebrates lives of quiet dignity and joy in the midst of hardship. But publishers felt Welty's photographs would not be able to compete with *Roll, Jordon, Roll,* a sentimental "Old South" collection by Dorothy Peterkin and Doris Ullman, and Welty could only arrange a one-woman show in 1936 in a small gallery on Madison Avenue. In 1971, however, the best of these pictures were published as *One Time, One Place: Mississippi in the Depression; A Snapshot Album.*

Welty's WPA work of the mid-1930s provided her with far more than visual training. Seeing at first hand the Depression-struck lives of rural and small-town people in a state that had always been the poorest in the nation, she was stimulated to capture their struggles and triumphs in stories, beginning with "Death of a Traveling Salesman," which was published in the literary magazine *Manuscript* in 1936. Other stories followed during the next five years, including some of her most famous—"Why I Live at the P.O.," "Powerhouse," "A Worn Path," "Petrified Man," "Lily Daw and the Three Ladies." Six stories were accepted by *Southern Review* between 1937 and 1939 and earned her the friendship and admiration of writers Albert Erskine, Robert Penn Warren, Katherine Anne Porter, and Ford Madox Ford. In a 1949 *Kenyon Review* essay Warren commented on the contrast between "the said, or violent, or warped" subjects of the stories and a tone that is "exhilarating, even gay, as though the author were innocently delighted . . . with the variety of things that stories could be and still be stories." These early works established Welty's characteristic comic genius with dialogue and with recording the incongruous developments of everyday life. Here she also developed a way of treating poverty, loss, and pain with a lightness that amounts to exquisite respect and discretion. In 1941 a collection of these stories was published as *A Curtain of Green* with a preface by Katherine Anne Porter. As Ruth Vande Kieft explains in *Eudora Welty,* the stories "are largely

concerned with the mysteries of the inner life," "the enigma of man's being—his relation to the universe; what is secret, concealed, inviolable in any human being, resulting in distance or separation between human beings; the puzzles and difficulties we have about our own feelings, our meaning and our identity."

Welty's first sustained experiment with folk materials appeared in 1942 as *The Robber Bridegroom,* a bold fusing of Mississippi history, tall tale, and fairytales of mysterious seducers drawn from British and Germanic sources as well as from the Greek story of Cupid and Psyche. Here, as Carol Manning explains in *With Ears Opening Like Morning Glories: Eudora Welty and the Love of Storytelling,* the innocent tone of the narrative counteracts the dire stuff of robberies, murders, and the depredations of a cruel stepmother. To many early reviewers the result seemed pure magic. Alfred Kazin claimed in a review for the *New York Herald Tribune Books* that Welty had captured "the lost fabulous innocence of our departed frontier, the easy carelessness, the fond bragging and colossal buckskin strut." In the *New York Times Book Review,* Marianne Hauser called it "a modern fairy tale, where irony and humor, outright nonsense, deep wisdom and surrealistic extravaganzas become a poetic unity through the power of a pure, exquisite style." Although some other commentators found it lacking in substance, Kreyling has defended *The Robber Bridegroom* as a valuable addition to the pastoral tradition in American literature: "Welty seems to be saying that the dream of a pastoral paradise on earth is always one step ahead of the dreamers; it is, sadly, only possible in a dream world removed from contact with human flesh and imperfections. But still worth dreaming."

Welty continued to experiment with such materials in her next collection, *The Wide Net, and Other Stories.* Here she explored the interrelationships of everyday Mississippi life with the timeless themes and patterns of myth, creating for her apparently ordinary characters a universality that links them with all times and cultures. The title story, for instance, places a domestic quarrel within the context of fertility tales; the work climaxes with a descent into a watery underworld where the hero encounters "the King of the Snakes" and proves worthy to return to his pregnant wife. In an essay appearing in *Eudora Welty: Critical Essays,* Garvin Davenport sees each of the stories in *The Wide Net* as presenting "at least one character who confronts or encounters a situation which is in some way dark, mysterious or dreamlike. Each such encounter contributes to an awakening or renewal—sometimes only temporarily—of that character's potential for emotional enrichment and experiential meaning. If the nature of the encounter often suggests a kind of regression to a more primitive or fundamental level of consciousness, the overall structures of the stories make clear that it is regression as a phase in problem-solving. . . ."

Welty's first novel, *Delta Wedding,* marks a significant change in her focus. Fertility myth still runs as an undercurrent through the daily affairs described in the book, but Welty has shifted from the dreamlike atmosphere of *The Wide Net* to the ordinary milieu of family life in the Mississippi Delta. Many of the circumstances of the Fairchild family in *Delta Wedding* recall those of the Ramsay family in Woolf's *To the Lighthouse.* The center of the Fairchild family is a mother of eight who continually ministers to her husband, her children, and a wider circle of relatives and friends. The novel is organized around domestic imagery of cooking and eating, wedding preparations, and diplomatic maneuvers to avert conflicts and soothe hurt feelings so that the wedding, on which the work centers, can occur. Both Woolf's and Welty's novels admirably explore the experience and values of women characters and celebrate the community, harmony, and renewal created by mothers for their families.

The narrative technique is similar to Woolf's in its use of multiple perspectives. In Welty's case the observers are all female, from nine-year-old Laura McRaven, a visiting cousin, to the mother, Ellen Fairchild, and her many daughters. In an interview collected in *Conversations with Eudora Welty,* the writer told Jo Brans that the world of *Delta Wedding* is a matriarchy but that it is not at all hostile to men. Men, instead, are the objects of loving attention and perform the occasional acts of heroism that are necessary to protect the charmed and fertile pastoral world of the plantation. Chief among these men is Uncle George Fairchild, who reenacts in modern form the mythic rescue of a maiden from a dragon by St. George. In this case, the dragon is an approaching train, and George Fairchild's rush to pull his niece from the track symbolically expresses his function for the whole Fairchild family.

Welty's allusion to the St. George myth is part of a more complex fabric of myth that bolsters the novel's celebration of human fertility and community. Underlying the story of Dabney Fairchild's wedding to the overseer of the Fairchild family's plantation is the ancient Greek myth of Demeter and Persephone, archetypal mother and daughter.

In the myth, the earth opens up at the feet of the maiden daughter of the goddess Demeter, and Hades (or Pluto) snatches her away to become his bride in his underworld kingdom. In grief, Demeter causes sterility to plague the earth until her daughter is restored, and Persephone's return comes to symbolize the return of vegetation in the spring. In Welty's novel, although the mother loses her daughter to a frightening bridegroom, the loss is only temporary and actually necessary to the initiation of a new cycle of fertility in the family. *Delta Wedding* ends in a picnic feast celebrating the return of bride and groom from their honeymoon and the reunion of the family.

Manning argues that with *Delta Wedding* "the Southern family and community replace the isolated individual and the abnormal one as Welty's favorite focus." Certainly this first novel initiates the period of the writer's creative maturity and her mastery of complex casts of characters. Themes that accompany the emphasis on community include the precariousness of marriage and the intimate suffering it involves, the weight of family tradition and the accompanying tension caused by the need of the young to break out and affirm their individuality, and the stark and hopeless loss that the living must accommodate after the death of parents and mates.

Delta Wedding was followed in 1949 by *The Golden Apples,* a closely related group of stories that functions almost as a novel. *The Golden Apples* depicts several families in the little town of Morgana, Mississippi, during the 1930s or early 1940s, focusing particularly on the defiant and talented Virgie Rainey, who rejects the conventional life of a Southern lady and creates an independent existence for herself while helping her widowed mother run her dairy farm. Fertility myths weave through these stories with particular attention given to the Pan-like figure of King Maclain, who wanders in and out of town seducing maidens like a mythical satyr and then disappearing in almost a twinkling of cloven hooves. But the main emphasis remains on the lives of the townspeople—the growing pains of children, the tragicomic disappointment of the fierce German music teacher Miss Eckhart, the near-drowning of an orphan girl at summer camp, and then the aging of the community and blighting of the lives of many characters who began as children full of possibility in the early stories.

In a 1984 *PMLA* essay Patricia Yeager emphasizes Welty's subversive exploration to traditional gender distinctions in these stories, arguing that she deliberately transgresses masculine and feminine symbolic boundaries in order to call them into question. For Yeager, "the most interesting and persistent rhetorical strategy Welty employs in *The Golden Apples* is to continually shift the figure and ground of her story, allowing 'male' discourse and female desire to contrast with, to comment on, and to influence each other as each becomes the ground on which the figure of the other begins to interact."

Welty's next book, *The Ponder Heart,* is a comic tour de force that concentrates many of her favorite themes in the dramatic events of an eccentric Southern gentleman's life. Set in the small town of Clay, Mississippi, *The Ponder Heart* is ostensibly an examination of the "heart" or character of Uncle Daniel Ponder, narrated by his spinster niece Edna Earle. Uncle Daniel is one of Welty's typical make heroes who unaccountably marries a selfish and brassy lower-class girl. (George Fairchild of *Delta Wedding* and Judge McKelva of *The Optimist's Daughter* are two more serious versions of the type.) In a tone combining sympathy and outrage, Edna Earle describes her uncle's wooing of seventeen-year-old Bonnie Dee Peacock in a dime store, their elopement, her desertion, return, death and burial, and Uncle Daniel's trial for murder.

Playful use of cliche, giddy inversion of social conventions, and the juxtaposition of kindly motives and silly disasters prevent the story from every moving outside the realm of farce. When Uncle Daniel literally tickles his wife to death in an attempt to distract her from her fear of a thunderstorm, readers can only laugh and recognize the ridiculous dimensions of the most painful human experiences. *The Ponder Heart* can also be seen as a satire on the ideal of the Southern gentleman, a satire which is quite horrifying beneath its humor. The old husband does in fact murder his estranged wife during an attempted reconciliation; family and friends side with him, as does the tone of the novella, so that the death of the young wife is a joke at best and only an inconvenience at worst. Welty received the William Dean Howells Medal of the American Academy of Arts and Letters for *The Ponder Heart* in 1955; and the work was successfully translated into a Broadway play in 1956 and adapted as an *opera bouffe* in 1982.

In 1955, Welty published another collected of short stories, *The Bride of Innisfallen, and Other Stories,* experimenting with a more allusive style. Three of the stories—"Circe," "Going to Naples," and "The Bride of Innisfallen"—are set in Europe and lack the vivid sense of place that gives solidity to most of Welty's fiction. The other four stories operate in familiar Mississippi settings. With the exception of "The Burning," a cryptic account of the burning of a plantation by Yankee soldiers during the Civil War, most continue Welty's comedy of small-town manners: adulterous trysts are foiled by rain and curious children ("Ladies in Spring") or by heat and spiritual fatigue ("No Place for You, My Love"), and a visiting niece offers bemused observations on and childhood memories of her Mississippi relatives' social milieu ("Kin").

In the years between 1955 and 1970, Welty published only a few occasional pieces and a children's story, *The Shoe Bird.* These were years of personal difficulty, as she nursed her mother through a long final illness and lost both of her brothers. She was nevertheless at work on long projects, notably *Losing Battles,* which she continued to shape for a decade. This ambitious, rollicking novel of a family reunion in the Mississippi hill country initiated a second flowering of Welty's career. In an interview collected in *Conversations with Eudora Welty,* she explained to Charles Bunting that a major purpose of the novel was to show indomitability in the tireless though losing battles of a spinster schoolteacher to educate her community, and in the strong ties of the Renfro clan who are celebrating the ninetieth birthday of the family matriarch and awaiting the return from jail of a reckless favorite son. The Renfro family picnic becomes the focal point for the examination of family tensions, the settling of old scores, and the celebration of resulting harmony.

One Time, One Place, the collection of photographs from Welty's 1930s WPA travels, appeared in 1971, followed in 1972 by Pulitzer Prize-winning novel, *The Optimist's Daughter.* The sparest of her novels, it recounts an adult daughter's return to Mississippi to be with her elderly father during an eye operation and then to preside over his funeral a few weeks later. As Laurel Hand confronts her memories of both parents, she comes to understand the pain of her mother's dying years and their effect on her father. Laurel is reconciled to her father's unwise second marriage to a ruthless young woman, and at the same time finally recognizes her own grief for the husband she has lost many years before. Welty's exploration of grief in *The Optimist's Daughter* which was in part a working-out of her own losses during the 1960s, contains many autobiographical elements, particularly in the portrait of Laurel's mother. But the novel is also a close fictional examination of the interdependence of child and parents. In an interview collected in *Conversations with Eudora Welty,* Welty told Martha van Noppen that she "tried to give that feeling of support and dependence that just ran in an endless line among the three of them [mother, father, and daughter]." Finally, Laurel Hand works through her grief to achieve a calmer and more practical accommodation with the past.

Losing Battles and *The Optimist's Daughter* brought renewed attention to Welty's writing and consequently an increasingly heavy burden of requests for interviews and speaking engagements. She continued to protect the essential privacy of her daily life, however, by discouraging biographic inquiries, carefully screening interviews, and devoting most of her energies to her work. During the later 1970s this work consisted largely of collecting her nonfiction writings for publication as *The Eye of the Story* and of assembling her short stories as *The Collected Stories of Eudora Welty.* With these two important collections she rounded out the shape of her life's work in literary commentary and fiction.

An invitation to give a series of lectures at Harvard in 1983 resulted in the three autobiographical pieces published as *One Writer's Beginnings* the next year. Perhaps because she wished to forestall potential biographers or because she came to accept public interest in a writer's early experiences in shaping her vision, Welty provided in *One Writer's Beginnings* a recreation of the world that nourished her own imagination. Characteristically, however, she omitted family difficulties and intimate matters, focusing instead on the family love of books and storytelling, the values and examples her parents provided, and the physical sensations of life in Jackson that influenced her literary sensitivities.

Welty's fictional chronicle of Mississippi life adds a major comic vision to American literature, a vision that affirms the sustaining power of community and family life and at the same time explores the need for solitude. In his 1944 essay, Robert Penn Warren aptly identifies these twin themes in Welty's work as love and separateness. While much of modern American fiction has emphasized alienation and the failure of love, Welty's stories show how tolerance and generosity allow people to adapt to each other's foibles and to painful change. Welty's fiction particularly celebrates the love of men and women, the fleeting joys of childhood, and the many dimensions and stages of women's lives.

MEDIA ADAPTATIONS: The Ponder House was adapted for the stage and first produced on Broadway in 1956, and was adapted as an *opera bouffe* and produced in 1982; *The Robber Bridegroom* was adapted for the stage as a musical and first produced in 1978; "The Hitch-hikers" was adapted for the stage in 1986; "Lily Daw and the Three Ladies" was adapted for the stage and produced.

BIOGRAPHICAL/CRITICAL SOURCES:

BOOKS

Appel, Alfred, Jr., *A Season of Dreams: The Fiction of Eudora Welty,* Louisiana State University Press, 1965.
Balakian, Nona and Charles Simmons, editors, *The Creative Present,* Doubleday, 1963.
Concise Dictionary of American Literary Biography, Volume 5: *The New Consciousness, 1941-1968,* Gale, 1987.
Contemporary Authors Bibliographical Series, Volume 1, Gale, 1986.
Contemporary Literary Criticism, Gale, Volume 1, 1973, Volume 2, 1974, Volume 5, 1976, Volume 14, 1980, Volume 22, 1982, Volume 33, 1985.
Conversations with Writers II, Gale, 1978.
Cowie, Alexander, *American Writers Today,* Radiojaenst, 1956.
Dictionary of Literary Biography, Volume 2: *American Novelists Since World War II,* Gale, 1978.
Dictionary of Literary Biography Yearbook: 1987, Gale, 1988.
Evans, Elizabeth, *Eudora Welty,* Ungar, 1981.
Jones, Anne Goodwyn, *Tomorrow Is Another Day: The Woman Writer in the South, 1859-1936,* Louisiana State University Press, 1981.
Kreyling, Michael, *Eudora Welty's Achievement of Order,* Louisiana State University Press, 1980.
Manning, Carol, *With Ears Opening Like Morning Glories: Eudora Welty and the Love of Storytelling,* Greenwood Press, 1985.
Prenshaw, Peggy Whitman, editor, *Eudora Welty: Critical Essays,* University Press of Mississippi, 1979.
Prenshaw, Peggy Whitman, editor, *Conversations with Eudora Welty,* University Press of Mississippi, 1984.
Ruas, Charles, *Conversations with American Writers,* Knopf, 1985.
Short Story Criticism, Volume 1, Gale, 1988.
Vande Kieft, Ruth, *Eudora Welty,* Twayne, 1962.
Westling, Louise, *Sacred Groves and Ravaged Gardens: The Fiction of Eudora Welty, Carson McCullers, and Flannery O'Connor,* University of Georgia Press, 1985.

PERIODICALS

American Book Collector, January/February, 1981.
Bulletin of Bibliography, January, 1956, January, 1960, January, 1963, September, 1963.
Chicago Tribune, December 20, 1984.
Chicago Tribune Book World, April 1, 1982.
Critique, winter, 1964-65.
Globe and Mail (Toronto), March 24, 1984.
Kenyon Review, spring, 1944.
Los Angeles Times, November 13, 1987.
Mississippi Quarterly, fall, 1973, fall, 1984.
New York Herald Tribune Books, October 25, 1942.
New York Times, February 18, 1984, March 1, 1985.

New York Times Book Review, November 1, 1942, April 12, 1970, February 19, 1984.
Notes on Mississippi Writers, Number 2, 1985.

PMLA, October, 1984.

Saturday Review, December, 1984.
Sewanee Review, July-September, 1952.
Shenandoah, spring, 1969.
Southern Humanities Review, summer, 1980.
Southern Review, autumn, 1972.
Southwest Review, summer, 1981.
Twentieth Century Literature, winter, 1982.
U.S. News and World Report, August 18, 1986.

*   *   *

WESKER, Arnold 1932-

PERSONAL: Born May 24, 1932, in London, England; son of Joseph (a tailor) and Leah (Perlmutter) Wesker; married Doreen Cecile Bicker, November 14, 1958; children: Lindsay Joe, Tanya Jo, Daniel. *Education:* Attended London School of Film Technique, 1955-56. *Politics:* Humanist. *Religion:* Jewish.

ADDRESSES: Home—37 Ashley Rd., London N19 3AG, England.

CAREER: Started working at sixteen as furniture maker's apprentice and tried half-a-dozen jobs, mainly along manual lines, before receiving Arts Council of Great Britain grant in 1958. Worked as carpenter's mate, bookseller's assistant, plumber's mate, seed sorter, kitchen porter, 1948-50, 1952-54, and as pastry cook in Norwich and London, England, and in Paris, France, 1954-58; playwright, 1958—; director, 1968—. Centre 42 Ltd., London, co-founder, 1961, and artistic director, 1961-70. *Military service:* Royal Air Force, 1950-52.

AWARDS, HONORS: Arts Council of Great Britain grant, 1958; *Evening Standard* award as most promising British playwright, 1959; co-winner of *Encyclopaedia Britannica* play prize, 1959, for "Chicken Soup with Barley"; Italian Premio Marzotto drama award, 1964, for "Their Very Own and Golden City"; gold medal for best foreign play, "El espectador y la critica" (Madrid), 1973, for "The Kitchen," and 1979, for "Chicken Soup with Barley."

WRITINGS:

PLAYS

Chicken Soup with Barley (also see below; first play of trilogy; first produced in Coventry, England, at Belgrade Theatre, July 7, 1958, produced in London at Royal Court Theatre, July 14, 1958, produced in Cleveland, Ohio, 1962; included in *New English Dramatists,* Penguin, 1959), Evans Brothers, 1961.
Roots (also see below; second play of trilogy; first produced in Coventry, England, at Belgrade Theatre, May 25, 1959, produced at Royal Court Theatre, June 30, 1959, produced off-Broadway at Mayfair Theater, March 6, 1961, produced in New York City by Jewish Repertory Theater, November, 1986), Penguin, 1959, published with introduction and notes by A. H. M. Best and Mark Cohen, Longmans, Green, 1967.
The Kitchen: A Play in Two Parts with an Interlude (also see below; first produced at Royal Court Theatre, September 6, 1959, expanded version produced at Royal Court Theatre, 1961, produced off-Broadway at Eighty-First Street Theatre, June 13, 1966; included in *New English Dramatists 2,*

Penguin, 1960), expanded version, J. Cape, 1961, Random House, 1962.
I'm Talking about Jerusalem (also see below; third play of trilogy; first produced in Coventry, England, at Belgrade Theatre, March 28, 1960, produced in London at Royal Court Theatre, July 27, 1960), Penguin, 1960.
The Wesker Trilogy (also see below; contains "Chicken Soup with Barley, Roots," and "I'm Talking about Jerusalem"), J. Cape, 1960, Random House, 1961, reprinted, Penguin, 1976.
Chips with Everything: A Play in Two Acts (also see below; first produced at Royal Court Theatre, April 27, 1962, produced on the West End at Vaudeville Theatre, 1962, produced on Broadway at Plymouth Theatre, October 1, 1963), J. Cape, 1962, Random House, 1963, critical edition edited by Michael Marland, with introduction by Wesker, Blackie, 1966.
"The Nottingham Captain: A Moral for Narrator, Voices and Orchestra" (also see below; included in *Six Sundays in January*), first produced in Wellingborough, England, at Centre 42 Trades Union Festival, 1962.
Their Very Own and Golden City: A Play in Two Acts and Twenty-Nine Scenes (also see below; first produced in Brussels at Belgium National Theater, 1964, produced at Royal Court Theatre, May 19, 1966), J. Cape, 1966.
The Four Seasons: A Play in Two Parts (also see below; first produced at Belgrade Theatre, 1965, produced on the West End at Saville Theatre, September 21, 1965, produced off-Broadway at Theatre Four, March 14, 1968), J. Cape, 1966.
The Friends: A Play in Two Acts (also see below; first produced in Stockholm at Stadsteatern, January, 1970, produced in London at Roundhouse, May 19, 1970), J. Cape, 1970.
The Old Ones (also see below; first produced at Royal Court Theatre, August 8, 1972, produced in New York at Theatre at the Lambs Club, December 6, 1974), J. Cape, 1973, revised edition edited by Michael Marland, Blackie, 1974.
The Journalists (also see below; first produced in Wilhelmshaven, West Germany, at Municipal Theatre, October 10, 1981, Writers and Readers Publishing Cooperative, 1975, published as *The Journalists: A Triptych,* J. Cape, 1979.
The Merchant (also see below; based on three stories Shakespeare used for "The Merchant of Venice"; produced in Stockholm, Sweden, at Stockholm Royal Dramaten, October 8, 1976, produced on Broadway at Plymouth Theatre, November 16, 1977), first published in German, Henschel Verlag, 1977, revised edition, with commentary and notes by Glenda Leeming, Methuen, 1983.
Three Plays (contains "The Kitchen," "The Four Seasons," and "Their Very Own and Golden City"), Penguin, 1976.
The Plays of Arnold Wesker, Harper, Volume 1 (contains "The Kitchen," "Chicken Soup with Barley," "Roots," "I'm Talking about Jerusalem," and "Chips with Everything"), 1976, Volume 2 (contains "The Four Seasons," "Their Very Own and Golden City," "Menace," "The Friends," and "The Old Ones"), 1977.
Love Letters on Blue Paper (also see below; adapted from Wesker's short story of the same title; first produced in Syracuse, N.Y., 1977, produced in London at Cottlesloe Theatre, February 15, 1978, produced in New York City by Hudson Guild Theatre, April 11, 1984), Writers and Readers Publishing Cooperative, 1978.
Chips with Everything [and] *The Friends* [and] *The Old Ones* [and] *Love Letters on Blue Paper,* Penguin, 1980.
The Journalist [and] *The Wedding Feast* (adapted from Dostoyevsky's short story; produced in Stockholm, 1972, pro-

duced at Leeds Playhouse, January 20, 1977) [and] *The Merchant,* Penguin, 1980.

"Caritas," produced in London at Cottesloe Theatre, October 7, 1981.

"Four Portraits of Mothers," produced in Tokyo, Japan, at Mitzukoshi Royal Theatre, July 2, 1982.

"Annie Wobbler" (first performed as radio play "Annie, Anna, Annabella," 1983), produced in Birmingham, England, by Birmingham Rep Studio, June 27, 1983, produced on the West End at Fortune Theatre, November 14, 1984, produced in New York City by Coota Woota Productions at Westbeth Theater Center, November, 1986.

"The Sullied Hand," produced in Edinburgh, Scotland, by Theatre N.A.C. at Netherbow Arts Centre, August 10, 1984.

"One More Ride on the Merry-Go Round" (comedy), produced in Leicester, England, at Phoenix Arts Theatre, April 25, 1985.

"Yardsale" (also see below) [and] "Whatever Happened to Betty Lemon" (two one-acts), produced in Hammersmith, England, at Lyric Studio, February, 1987.

Also author of "Master," 1966, "The New Play," 1969, "Cinders" (adapted from Paul Bailey's *An English Madam*), 1982, "The Mistress," 1988, "Little Old Lady and Shoeshine" (one-act for young people), and "Stand Up, Stand Up."

TELEVISION PLAYS

"Menace" (also see below), aired on "First Night" series, British Broadcasting Corp. (BBC-TV), December 8, 1963.

"Love Letters on Blue Paper" (also see below; adapted from short story by Wesker), aired on BBC-TV, March 2, 1976.

Also author of "Whitsun" (adapated from Wesker's story, "The Visit"), 1980, "Breakfast," 1981, "Thieves in the Night," (adapted from a novel by Arthur Koestler), 1984, "When God Wanted a Son," 1986, "Badenheim 1939" (adapted from a novel by Aharon Appelfeld), 1987, and "Lady Othello" (adapted from Wesker's filmscript, "Lady Othello"); also author of an adaptation of "The Four Seasons."

OTHER

Labour and the Arts: II, or What, Then, Is to Be Done?, Gemini, 1960.

The Modern Playwright; or, "O Mother, Is It Worth It?," Gemini, 1961.

"The Kitchen" (screenplay adaptation of Wesker's play), produced by Kingsley, 1962.

(Author of introduction) Roger Frith, *The Serving Boy,* Colchester, 1968.

Fears of Fragmentation (essays), J. Cape, 1970.

Six Sundays in January (short stories and television play; includes "The Nottingham Captain: A Moral for Narrator, Voices and Orchestra"), J. Cape, 1971.

Love Letters on Blue Paper: Three Stories (also see below), J. Cape, 1974, Harper, 1975.

(Contributor of text) *Say Goodbye, You May Never See Them Again: Scenes from Two East-End Backgrounds,* paintings by John Allin, J. Cape, 1974.

Words as Definitions of Experience, Writers and Readers Publishing Cooperative, 1976.

Journey into Journalism: A Very Personal Account in Four Parts, Writers and Readers Publishing Cooperative, 1977.

Fatlips: A Story for Children, Harper, 1978.

Said the Old Man to the Young Man: Three Stories (short stories), J. Cape, 1978.

Love Letters on Blue Paper (short stories; includes "Love Letters on Blue Paper," "Six Sundays in January," "The Man Who Became Afraid," and "The Visit"), Penguin, 1980.

"Yardsale" (radio play), aired on BBC-Radio, October 6, 1984.

"Bluey" (radio play), aired on Cologne Radio, May 16, 1985.

Distinctions (essays, lectures, and journalism), J. Cape, 1985.

Also author of filmscript, "Madame Solario," 1968, and "Lady Othello," 1981; also author of filmscript adaptation of *The Wesker Trilogy,* 1979, commissioned by National Film Development Fund.

WORK IN PROGRESS: Musical adaptation of "The Kitchen"; a play entitled "Toys."

SIDELIGHTS: Arnold Wesker's original reknown came from his trilogy of plays, "Chicken Soup with Barley," "Roots," and "I'm Talking about Jerusalem," which traces the attitudes of a family of Jewish Socialist intellectuals from 1936 through 1959. Geoffrey Grigson calls it "a Forsyte Saga of the Left." Wesker, describing his trilogy, writes: "A number of themes bind the trilogy together. Basically it is [about] a family; on another level it is a play about human relationships; and on a third, and most important level, it is a story of people moved by political ideas in a particular social time. There are many theories about Socialism. 'Chicken Soup with Barley' handles the Communist aspect. 'Roots' handles the personal aspect. . . . 'I'm Talking about Jerusalem' is a sort of study in a William Morris kind of Socialism."

Wesker has been described as a "committed" playwright and in his early plays embraced the ideals of Socialism. He was identified with a group of English playwrights who emerged after the dramatic revival in England in 1956 and who were dubbed "the angry young men." A writer for the *Christian Science Monitor* comments that of this group, which included John Osborne, Brendan Behan, and David Storey, "Wesker is certainly—and this is something to admire when most people are busy keeping up their defenses in all directions—the most unafraid, the most naive, the most vulnerable. He is the least technically expert, the most self-indulgent. . . . Yet . . . in all his plays he has striven not to exploit the disintegration of individuals and society, but the possibility of their self-redemption—and this again is not ignoble when the opposite is the fashion, and artists in every medium go all out for easy hysteria."

Beginning with "Chips with Everything," Wesker's work during the 1960s "became less documentary and immediate in impact," according to Glenda Leeming. His more recent plays are not as didactic or political in tone as his earlier Socialist realism. Disillusioned with his earlier political beliefs, Wesker told Richard Skloot that the paradox of Socialism "is that it is producing people who are socially selfish and indifferent. The State has taken on all responsibility and people don't care about each other and they don't care about what happens outside their own country, outside their own community. There's this terrible social listlessness that has been created." Turning from socialistic didacticism in "The Four Seasons," which depicts the allegorical seasons of a love affair from its spring budding through its winter disintegration, Wesker begins to explore what he has called the theme of "private pain." With this play and "The Friends" Wesker is, according to Leeming, "breaking new ground, not in techniques of presentation, but in his increasingly introspective subject matter."

The critical reception to "The Friends" was, for the most part, unfavorable. Benedict Nightingale finds that it "isn't a very good play. The characters, though naturalistically presented, have little objective, individual life. Except when they drop into north-country dialect, they speak much the same ardent, lilting prose. They speak a great deal, too. . . . They don't define themselves by action. . . . One misses, as always in Wesker, any sense of the obstinacy of unreason and the destructive power of human evil." A *Plays and Players* reviewer writes: "The fault of 'The Friends' is that Mr. Wesker is like a man who does not know when to stop. The play is the verbal vomit of his ideas, as if he is suffering from some kind of literary indigestion." Ronald Bryden calls the play "a kind of secular Yom Kippur for his generation of the fifties. In it their faults are confessed, their insincerities admitted, their frittered and waning energies rededicated to the achievement of social justice. . . . I wish I could say the play was as impressive as the intention which churns woolilly behind its almost total lack of action. . . . [Wesker's] real betrayal has been to abandon the role of our most precise social realist for that of a cloudy prophet of uplift."

Michael Kustow believes that Wesker "has suffered unduly from the weight of an undeserved legend [that of a leftist crusader], which has led to superficial readings of his plays, obscuring their real advances of technique and content. The sense of suspension and withdrawal, of inward-turning, in his latest plays and stories is both the natural reassessment of a writer in mid-route, and the enforced, defensiveness . . . of a playwright who seems to have been left out by a head-strong and often mindless theatre, and also made a scapegoat for its unfulfilled promise." Wesker addresses himself to the criticism of his abandonment of his original themes: "There's an argument which says that individual or private pain can have no relevance in a society where man's real tragedies abound inextricably with his social environment. . . . To which I make this reply: if compassion and teaching the possibility of change are two of the many effects of art, a third is this. To remind and reassure people that they're not alone. Not only in their attempt to make a better world, but in their private pains and confusions also."

Several reviewers expressed ambivalent feelings about "The Old Ones," Wesker's play about aging Jewish pensioners. J. W. Lambert writes that the play "has like its predecessor 'The Friends' been given a pretty rough reception, in tones varying from weary contempt to stertorous irritation—and despite all its shortcomings, its loose ends, its repeated losses of dramatic focus, I can't really see why this should have been so. . . . Wesker has written scenes of humanity and understanding I should think any playgoer would be grateful for." Jacob Sonntag believes that "Wesker's achievement is that his characters are accepted, not as some eccentrics arousing one's curiosity, but as real people—unusual perhaps, but real nevertheless. . . . Some critics may find faults in the play's construction, others may consider it too sentimental and vague. . . . Wesker retains his fine sense of dialogue, his compassion, his social involvement, adding to it a newly acquired insight into Jewishness."

Wesker wrote "The Merchant" because he was dissatisfied with the blatant anti-Semitism and what he feels was the unrealistic character portrayal of the original Shakespearean play. "The Merchant" received reviews which ranged from very positive to absolute pans. Colin Chambers calls the play "quite out of character with most contemporary drama but full of the dense argumentation inspired by a critical caring love of people, of their knowledge and of their language." Brendan Gill finds it "an ambitious and very intelligent play." Clive Barnes thinks it is "perhaps Wesker's finest play. . . . Most of the writing is briltiant, with masterly sensibility. . . . The play raises issues and risks arguments and it teems with life as a consequence." Conversely, Martin Gottfried calls it "a theoretical and argumentative play

with little life force of its own. Its own definitions of anti-Semitism are superficial. Its characters and events exist only to disagree with Shakespeare." John Simon is even more sharp in his attack on the play: " 'The Merchant,' I am afraid, is to 'The Merchant of Venice' what lumpfish is to caviar, or a hot-water bottle to the Gulf Stream." Richard Eder feels comparison of Wesker's play to the original Shakespeare to be invalid. "Wesker has used the same rough elements of plot and the same principal characters—all of them with a widely different human weight and meaning—for a totally original play," Eder writes. He describes his mixed reaction to the play: "It is provocative, generally intelligent and sometimes strained or confused. Its writing has moments of ferocious brilliance and wit; on the other hand, its dramatic structure is weak and its dramatic impact fitful and uncertain. It starts and stops; it repeatedly takes off with a thrill and repeatedly disappears into a cloud bank. There is a general effect of a vision that aims for more than it achieves."

Despite so much negative criticism to Wesker's plays, Leeming feels that he is still developing as a playwright and growing in scope. "Unlike many of his erratic contemporaries, Wesker has steadily improved his mastery of theme and techniques, as the brightness of the early plays give way to a more subtle shading of richer colours," Leeming writes. "The very steadiness of his development so far suggests that he will not waste energy on uncharacteristic dead-end experiments, but will evolve within his own line of continuity. He has always had an ear for dialogue and an assured sense of form; this has been reinforced by a new dramatic poetry while the more awkward moments of exposition and occasional didacticism of the trilogy have been eliminated. The level of simple social dramatist that was initially hung like a millstone round Wesker's neck has necessarily hindered assessment of his far-from-simple plays, but . . . the sheer persuasive quality of his writing must elicit recognition of his stature as dramatist."

The stage play and television versions of "Love Letters on Blue Paper" drew the favorable reviews that Leeming feels Wesker deserves. Jack Tinker calls the play "a towering love story" and Micheline Victor comments that "Wesker is remarkably, and un-Englishably daring [in] his representation of emotion." Michael Billington writes that "what is interesting is the way the emotion of the play bursts through with this very tight rigid form. It's a play, simply, it seems to me, about a kind of human desperation. . . . I thought the pulse and intensity of that emotion worked against the artificiality of the form in a very moving way." Alan Hulme comments that "plays as intensely moving as Arnold Wesker's 'Love Letters on Blue Paper' are very rare. It is a play you will have to learn to live with because once experienced it won't go away." Stephen Biscoe goes even further in his praise of the play: "Apart from anything else 'Love Letters on Blue Paper' proved that great plays are still being written; the quality of a masterpiece was unmistakeable. . . . His play was profound and very moving and set a standard that one hopes other playwrights will attempt to emulate if they can."

BIOGRAPHICAL/CRITICAL SOURCES:

BOOKS

Armstrong, W. A., editor, *Experimental Drama*, G. Bell, 1963.
Contemporary Authors Autobiography Series, Volume 7, Gale, 1988.
Contemporary Literary Criticism, Gale, Volume 3, 1975, Volume 5, 1976, Volume 42, 1987.
Contemporary Theatre, Edward Arnold, 1962.
Dictionary of Literary Biography, Volume 13: *British Dramatists since World War II*, Gale, 1982.

Gindin, James, *Postwar British Fiction,* University of California Press, 1962.

Kitchin, Laurence, *Mid-Century Drama,* Faber, 1960.

Leeming, Glenda, and Simon Trussler, *The Plays of Arnold Wesker,* Gollancz, 1971.

Leeming, Glenda, *Arnold Wesker,* Longman, 1972.

Leeming, Glenda, *Wesker on File,* Methuen, 1985.

Lumley, Frederick, *New Trends in Twentieth Century Drama,* Oxford University Press, 1967.

Ribalow, Harold U., *Arnold Wesker,* Twayne, 1966.

Taylor, John Russell, *Anger and After,* Methuen, 1962.

Wager, Walter, editor, *The Playwrights Speak,* Delacorte, 1967.

Ward, A. C., *Twentieth-Century English Literature, 1901-1960,* Methuen, 1964.

Wellworth, G., *Theatre of Protest and Paradox,* New York University Press, 1965.

PERIODICALS

Antioch Review, winter, 1964-65.
BBC Kaleidoscope, March 3, 1976.
Canadian Forum, July, 1961.
Chicago Tribune, November 15, 1988.
Christian Science Monitor, March 22, 1968, June 6, 1970.
Daily Mail, February 16, 1978.
Drama, winter, 1972.
Globe and Mail (Toronto), November 23, 1985.
Jewish Chronicle, October 20, 1978.
Jewish Quarterly, autumn, 1972.
Listener, May 28, 1970.
Los Angeles Times, January 28, 1979.
Manchester Evening News, December 6, 1978.
Morning Star, October 20, 1978.
Nation, November 19, 1960.
New Review, March, 1975.
New Statesman, August 6, 1965, September 17, 1965, May 29, 1970, August 30, 1974.
New York, December 5, 1977.
New Yorker, March 23, 1968, June 9, 1975, November 14, 1977.
New York Post, November 17, 1977.
New York Times, May 22, 1970, July 14, 1970, August 20, 1970, August 26, 1972, November 8, 1977, November 17, 1977, April 12, 1984, November 12, 1986, November 17, 1986.
Observer Review, May 24, 1970.
Performing Arts Journal, winter, 1978.
Plays and Players, May, 1970, July, 1970, August, 1970, October, 1973, February, 1977, December, 1978.
Saturday Review, May 17, 1975.
Spectator, October 21, 1960, August 10, 1962, August 24, 1974.
Theatre Quarterly, Volume 7, number 28, 1977.
Time, March 22, 1968.
Time Out, March 3, 1978.
Times (London), December 3, 1977, October 17, 1978, July 7, 1983, November 10, 1984, November 14, 1984, November 15, 1984, April 27, 1985, February 19, 1987.
Times Educational Supplement, October 20, 1978.
Times Literary Supplement, November 25, 1960, May 3, 1985, September 6, 1985.
Twentieth Century, February, 1961.
Variety, August 23, 1972, November 23, 1977.
Village Voice, March 21, 1968.
Washington Post, June 1, 1975, February 11, 1980.
Yorkshire Post, March 3, 1976.

WESLEY, Mary 1912-

PERSONAL: Born June 24, 1912, in Englefield Green, England; daughter of Mynors (a colonel) and Violet (Dalby) Farmar; married Lord Swinfen, January, 1937 (divorced, 1944); married Eric Siepmann (a journalist), April 22, 1951 (died, 1970); children: (first marriage) Roger Eady, Toby Eady; (second marriage) William. *Education:* Attended Queens College, London, 1928-30, and London School of Economics and Political Science, 1931-32. *Politics:* "Left-wing/Catholic." *Religion:* Roman Catholic.

ADDRESSES: Home—Cullaford, Buckfastleigh, Devon, England. *Agent*—Lekesche & Sayle, 11 Jubilee Place, London SW3, England.

CAREER: War Office, England, staff member, 1939-41.

MEMBER: London Library.

AWARDS, HONORS: Carnegie Prize nomination for *Haphazard House.*

WRITINGS:

CHILDREN'S BOOKS

The Sixth Seal, MacDonald, 1969, revised edition, Dent, 1984.
Speaking Terms, Faber, 1969, Gambit, 1971.
Haphazard House, Dent, 1983.

NOVELS

Jumping the Queue, Macmillan (London), 1983, Penguin, 1988.
The Camomile Lawn, Macmillan, 1984.
Harnessing Peacocks, Macmillan, 1985.
The Vacillations of Poppy Carew, Macmillan, 1986, Penguin, 1988.
Not That Sort of Girl, Macmillan, 1987, Penguin, 1988.
Second Fiddle, Macmillan, 1988, Penguin, 1989.
A Sensible Life, Bantam, 1990.

MEDIA ADAPTATIONS: Jumping the Queue was adapted as a two-part film by the British Broadcasting Corp. in 1988.

SIDELIGHTS: Since her debut as a novelist at the age of seventy, British writer Mary Wesley has produced a string of critically-acclaimed and bestselling works that make her, according to Philip Howard in the London *Times,* "one of the most distinctive voices in English fiction." In her first novel, *Jumping the Queue,* written during the period following the death of her husband Eric's death, Wesley depicts a middle-aged widow on the brink of suicide who reevaluates her life after a chance encounter with a fugitive also contemplating suicide. Praised by critics for its original characterizations, playful depictions of sex, and comic seriousness, *Jumping the Queue* marked, according to John Nicholson in the *Times* "a virtuoso performance of guileful plotting, deft characterization and malicious wit." "Both funny and sexy," according to Caroline Moorehead in the *Times, Jumping the Queue* earn merits, Nicholson comments, for its "extraordinary entertainment value."

In subsequent novels, Wesley, as Jessica Baldwin is quoted in the *Ann Arbor News,* specializes in depicting "gutsy women from privileged backgrounds, unafraid to defy convention." In addition, Wesley is noted for her original and lively portrayals of historical periods; World War II, according to Keith Wheatley in the London *Sunday Times Magazine,* provides the setting for "much of her best and most sensuously exciting writing." Wheatley distinguishes Wesley's literary treatment of the era: "Whereas the characters in Anthony Powell's series *A Dance to the Music of Time* live through the war with grim determination to survive, often making useful future alliances, Wesley's young women (men tend to take the supporting roles in her writing) flit through the blackout enjoying the bomb-induced adrenalin and the unprecedented lack of accountability to husbands or families." Douglas Hill in the Toronto *Globe and Mail* comments that while Wesley's *The Camomile Lawn,* which takes place in the summer before World War II, "has echoes of other works of art, its vitality and scope and, above all, its pressure of theme and delicacy of feeling, make it a unique record of an epoch."

Nicholas Shakespeare writes in the *Times* that Wesley is a writer who "cannot resist trying to shock." Howard similarly comments in a review of *Not That Sort of Girl* that Wesley "has reached an age when she can say dangerous or naughty things without shocking." According to Howard, Wesley demonstrates in *Not That Sort of Girl,* how "people behave just as badly as they do in life." He cites: "Widows take a heretical pleasure in being properly alone for the first time since 1930. Wife, finding valetudinarian husband at last dead in bed as she brings him lightly boiled egg during war, thinks what a waste when eggs are so scarce. Rose's private tonic [in *Not That Sort of Girl*] after severe illness is the recommendation of a quick dip in bed with someone you like but are not in love with." In a review of *Harnessing Peacocks,* Shakespeare cites a quote, "Old people still have feelings," as "the key to Mary Wesley's work." Like Wesley, her characters' "innocent dimples plumb deep wells of experience."

Critics have commented on the overall impressions created by Wesley work. Doris Grumbach in the *Washington Post* notes that "nothing Mary Wesley writes amounts to much more than amusing involvement of comic figures in entangling social configurations. If there is no depth or high seriousness, there is always entertainment. We may take her airy view of British manners as jaunty satire with no intent to instruct or chastise." According to Michiko Kakutani in the *New York Times,* Wesley creates "an idiosyncratic fictional world, a middle-class English world, whose bright comic surface belies a dark subtext of sin, incest, murder and betrayal. Cuckoldry and sexual gamesmanship thrive in her novels, and a chilly air of malice (or at the very least manipulation) that's reminiscent of Muriel Spark's work hovers over her characters." Howard contends that Wesley "has gently and suddenly become one of [Britain's] first-division novelists."

BIOGRAPHICAL/CRITICAL SOURCES:

PERIODICALS

Ann Arbor News, June 4, 1990.
Globe and Mail (Toronto), May 31, 1986.
Los Angeles Times, December 6, 1989.
New York Times, June 27, 1989.
New York Times Book Review, July 8, 1984, July 30, 1989.
Sunday Times Magazine (London), September 25, 1988.
Times (London), May 5, 1983, March 28, 1984, March 29, 1984, June 27, 1985, June 29, 1985, June 25, 1987, July 9, 1987.
Times Literary Supplement, June 17, 1983, September 30, 1983, March 28, 1984, April 13, 1984, June 28, 1985.
Washington Post, May 12, 1988.
Washington Post Book World, July 23, 1989.

*   *   *

WEST, C. P.
   See WODEHOUSE, P(elham) G(renville)

WEST, (Mary) Jessamyn 1902-1984

PERSONAL: Born July 18, 1902, in Jennings County, Ind.; died of a stroke February 23 (some sources say February 22), 1984 in Napa, Calif.; daughter of Eldo Ray (a citrus farmer) and Grace Anna (Milhous) West; married Harry Maxwell McPherson (a school superintendent) August 16, 1923; children: Ann Cash (adopted daughter). *Education:* Whittier College, A.B., 1923; attended University of California at Berkeley; studied at Oxford University, 1929. *Religion:* Society of Friends (Quaker).

ADDRESSES: Home and office—2480 3rd Ave., Napa, Calif. 94558.

CAREER: Writer, 1935-84. Taught at writers' conferences at Breadloaf, Indiana University, University of Notre Dame, University of Colorado, Squaw Valley University of Utah, University of Washington, Stanford University, University of Montana, Portland University, University of Kentucky, and Loyola Marymount University. Visiting professor at Wellesley College, University of California at Irvine, Mills College, and Whittier College. Visiting lecturer at numerous colleges.

MEMBER: American Civil Liberties Union, National Association for the Advancement of Colored People.

AWARDS, HONORS: Indiana Authors' Day Award, 1956, for *Love, Death, and the Ladies' Drill Team;* Thermod Monsen Award, 1958, for *To See the Dream;* California Commonwealth Club award, 1970, and California Literature Medal, 1971, both for *Crimson Ramblers of the World, Farewell;* Janet Kafke prize for fiction, 1976; Indiana Arts Commission Award for Literature, 1977, for body of work. Honorary doctorates from Whittier College, Mills College, Swarthmore College, Indiana University, University of Indiana—Terre Haute, Western College for Women, Wheaton College, Juniata College, and Wilmington College.

WRITINGS:

FICTION

The Friendly Persuasion (short stories), Harcourt, 1945, reprinted, Buccaneer Books, 1982.
The Witch Diggers (novel), Harcourt, 1951.
Cress Delahanty (short stories; Book-of-the-Month Club selection), Harcourt, 1953.
Little Men (novel), Ballantine, 1954, republished as *The Chile Kings,* 1967.
Love, Death, and the Ladies' Drill Team (short stories), Harcourt, 1955 (published in England as *Learn To Say Goodbye,* Hodder & Stoughton, 1960).
South of the Angels (novel), Harcourt, 1960.
A Matter of Time (novel), Harcourt, 1966.
Leafy Rivers (novel), Harcourt, 1967.
Except for Me and Thee: A Companion to "The Friendly Persuasion" (short stories), Harcourt, 1969.
Crimson Ramblers of the World, Farewell (short stories), Harcourt, 1970.
The Massacre at Fall Creek (novel; Literary Guild main selection), Harcourt, 1975.
The Life I Really Lived (novel), Harcourt, 1979.
The State of Stony Lonesome (novel), Harcourt, 1984.
The Collected Stories of Jessamyn West, Harcourt, 1986.

NONFICTION

To See the Dream, Harcourt, 1957.
Love Is Not What You Think, Harcourt, 1959 (published in England as *A Woman's Love,* Hodder & Stoughton, 1960).

Hide and Seek: A Continuing Journey, Harcourt, 1973.

The Woman Said Yes: Encounters with Death and Life (Book-of-the-Month Club alternate selection), Harcourt, 1976 (published in England as *Encounters with Death and Life: Memoirs,* Gollancz, 1978).

Double Discovery: A Journey, Harcourt, 1980.

PLAYS

A Mirror for the Sky (opera libretto; first performed at the University of Oregon at Eugene, May 24, 1957), Harcourt, 1948.

"The Friendly Persuasion" (screenplay; based on story collection of same title), produced by Allied Artists, 1956.

"The Big Country" (screenplay), produced by United Artists, 1958.

"Stolen Hours" (screenplay), produced by United Artists, 1963.

OTHER

(Contributor) *Cross Section 1948: A Collection of New American Writing,* Simon & Schuster, 1948.

(Editor) *A Quaker Reader,* Viking, 1962.

The Secret Look: Poems, Harcourt, 1974.

Contributor to *0. Henry Memorial Award Prize Stories of 1946,* and to *The Living Novel,* 1957. Also contributor of fiction and nonfiction articles to numerous periodicals, including *Town and Country, Mademoiselle, Collier's, Ladies' Home Journal, New Mexico Quarterly, Yale Review, Kenyon Review, Good Housekeeping, McCall's, Harper's, New Yorker, Redbook,* and *Saturday Evening Post.* West's collected papers are stored at Whittier College.

SIDELIGHTS: The late Jessamyn West was a prolific and varied writer whose works include fiction, nonfiction, poetry, screenplays, and even an opera libretto. She is remembered, however, for her numerous short stories that plumb rural American life without sentiment or oversimplicity. Much of West's fiction reflects her involvement with the Society of Friends (Quakers), the religion of her ancestors who farmed in southern Indiana. Her popular story collections *The Friendly Persuasion* and *Except for Me and Thee: A Companion to "The Friendly Persuasion"* recreate Quaker lives in a nineteenth century farming community; these and her tales of adolescence, *Cress Delahanty* and *The State of Stony Lonesome,* remain her best known works. *New York Times Book Review* contributor Nancy Hale called West's stories "homespun but with an exceedingly subtle warp and woof," and explained that West used "small-town life to convey human events that warm the heart and evoke instant sympathy." According to Bill Crider in the *Dictionary of Literary Biography,* West's many volumes were "well-received, even acclaimed, by reviewers" for their "vivid, vigorous, and eloquent style and the compassion and humanity with which she treats . . . serious themes." In his book-length study entitled *Jessamyn West,* Alfred S. Shivers concluded that the author's work retains its "high merit with respect to sensitivity of characterizations, restraint, genuineness of feeling, psychology, and delightful humor."

Los Angeles Times correspondent Kay Mills noted that West wrote "from memory. Her own. Her mother's. That of her Quaker religion and of the two regions she [called] home—southern Indiana, where she was born, and Southern California, where she was raised." Both regions from which West drew her inspiration were rugged and sparsely populated when she first encountered them, so her focus of concern was almost always the country. "Much of Jessamyn West's better writing ignores the ugliness and artificiality of mid-twentieth-century urban life and ensconces itself amid the bucolic back country America of previous eras," Shivers commented. "Her personal love for solitude as a housewife among her chores; her unusual predilection for the writings of [Henry David] Thoreau; her girlhood spent on ranches without (it seems) any important regrets; her dislike of, or at least uneasiness with, highway commercialism—all are consistent with the withdrawal and the idyllic tone found in [her work]." Most critics agreed that West used local color to great effect in her fiction. John T. Flanagan claimed in the *Indiana Magazine of History* that West's success in realizing scenes derived from "her control of the physical locale and her use of authentic and specific colors and objects. . . . Nor is this local color obtrusive. The Indiana and California backgrounds fit naturally into the story, providing both a backdrop and a proscenium for the narrative action."

West's chronicles of rural life are hardly mere idyllic tales of simpler times, however. She strove to create realistic characters, especially teenagers and women, with personalities well-grounded in human nature. Flanagan found West's people "a constant delight, freshly conceived, individual, even a bit eccentric. . . . Generally commonsensical but often endowed with a quirky humor or an ironical point of view, her characters enter the reader's presence in full stature and linger there like old acquaintances." Her Quaker background notwithstanding, West tackled the subject of sexual passion, generally but not always celebrating the stability of marriage over the momentary attraction of a liaison. According to *New York Times Book Review* contributor Webster Schott, West dominated among women novelists as "an advocate of human respect, reason over emotions, and a tough, all-purpose femininity that can face and solve most situations on its own terms." Shivers similarly observed that the author made "no claim that fiction should be morally improving" even though many of her books "exude a subtle moral atmosphere." Within the parameters of domestic drama, West explored universal themes such as values, sexuality, and maturity; to quote *Dictionary of Literary Biography Yearbook* essayist Ann Dahlstrom Farmer, her characters "are complex, not because they represent several ideas but because they are realistic, many-faceted individuals."

Critics also cited West's work for a consistency and quality of style. *Washington Post* reviewer Suzanne Fields maintained that the author wrote "gracefully, occasionally poetically, in a voice both innocent and brave." Flanagan called West's prose "vivid and original . . . often exemplified by surprising similes taken from ordinary life and observation." In the *New York Herald Tribune Book Review,* Virgilia Peterson related style to substance, explaining that West was "not tuned to the high-strung, nervous, angry pitch that, perhaps more than any other, characterizes the writing of our time. Nor [was] she afraid of sentiment. So much tenderness [welled] up and [spilled] out of her that some would say she [was] not leery enough of it. But none of her tenderness [was] blind. . . . What [established] her certainly as one of the most trustworthy and endearing among current American novelists is that, knowing the evil, she [persisted] in countervailing it with the good." Likewise, *New York Times Book Review* correspondent Laurence Lafore found West's work to be grounded "in a classic tradition that imposes a discipline almost as rigid, and as fecund, as the sonnet form. And her ideas [were] as consistent as her methods. Some readers may feel a want of variety; more will welcome the cumulative, and coherent, revelation of her view of the world and of art."

West was born in Indiana on July 18, 1902, to a farming family of modest circumstances. She was related to Richard Nixon through her mother's family, and she became a close and lifelong friend of his, sometimes even travelling with the presidential entourage. When West was still young, her father decided to seek his fortune in California. Eventually the family moved to an undeveloped wilderness area near Yorba Linda, where they began a successful citrus orchard. West and her brother and sister were allowed to roam freely through the arid Orange County lands, and the young girl was able to cultivate her solitary, observant nature. Adolescence brought an interest in reading as well as a fascination with the life and work of Thoreau. Dahlstrom Farmer observed that Thoreau's writings prized two things that West herself prized, namely "solitude and journal-keeping as enhancers of observation and introspection." Although she admired many writers, West quelled her own authorial ambitions and studied to become a school teacher. After graduating from Whittier College, she married Harry Maxwell McPherson and set to work in a one-room school. She soon discovered a great desire to further her education, however, and in 1929 she embarked for a summer session at Oxford University. Upon her return to the United States, she enrolled in a graduate program at the University of California at Berkeley.

Just before taking her doctoral orals, West suffered a severe lung hemorrhage and was diagnosed as having an advanced case of tuberculosis. She was placed in the terminal ward of a Los Angeles sanitorium, and her doctors gave her little hope of survival. After two years in the hospital, West was sent home so that she could "die amongst her loved ones." West's mother refused to accept the inevitability of her daughter's untimely death, however. She went to great lengths to provide favorite foods, and just as important for the depressed patient, entertainment. Reaching into her own past, West's mother recalled her Quaker forebears and told West about them. According to Angela Wigan in *Time* magazine, the elder West recounted "stories about courtship and farming, blizzards and Quaker meetings." As West slowly recovered, she "turned her mother's gift into her own response to extinction—her writing." While still an invalid she began to create sketches about an Indiana Quaker farm couple raising a family during the civil War era. Her husband encouraged her to submit the stories to magazines, and by the time she had regained her health—early in 1940—her work was being accepted by such publications as the *Atlantic Monthly, Harper's,* and the *Ladies' Home Journal.* In retrospect, West was quoted in *Women Writers of the West Coast* as crediting her near-fatal illness with giving her the courage to begin writing. "I thought my life was over," she said of those hopeless days. "Instead, for me, it was the beginning of my life."

The Friendly Persuasion, published in 1945, collects a number of West's stories about Jess and Eliza Birdwell, the Quaker farmers in rural Indiana. Crider described the book thus: "The stories carry the family from the ten years preceding the Civil War to Jess's old age, around the turn of the century. A remarkable feeling of familial love and understanding permeates the book, which is also notable for its warmth and humor." Crider added that the collection "was an immediate success," with critics and general readers alike. *Saturday Review* commentator William Hogan called *The Friendly Persuasion* "a warm, winning tale" that established West's reputation for "style, characterization, humor, and impetuosity." In *Book Week,* Flora Henderson wrote that the work "makes a delightful addition to American literature. There is poetry here, but so subtly woven into the fabric of story and character that it never intrudes." Ernestine Evans made similar observations in the *New York Herald Tribune Book Review.* "Miss West's style is full of surprises, vivid metaphors, odd turns of plot, yet she is never disconcerting, over-ingenious or repetitive," Evans contended. "Though distilled from family legends of the Irish Quaker community into

which she was born, the tales are less nostalgic than provocative. One feels not that loveliness used to be and is no more but that life could be. . . . even quieter and funnier than currently advertised."

According to Shivers, West was able to reconcile her religious tradition with the demands of artistic truth in *The Friendly Persuasion* and its sequel, *Except for Me and Thee.* West "resisted the moralizing impulse," Shivers noted, even though her stories revolve around characters with traditional values. In the *Saturday Review,* Nathan L. Rothman commented: "If we do not get any definitive sense of the world outside [West's Quaker community,] we do get something at least as precious, an intimate knowledge of their inner life. . . . While the tales are slight . . . each of them permits Miss West the full expression of her central theme, the lovely, gentle, ethical essence of the . . . Quaker. The mood is nostalgic, primitive, like a dream of vanished innocence." Another *Saturday Review* critic pointed out that although West was writing of a pioneer family, she depicted them "with loving sympathy rather than sentimentality." Flanagan concluded in the *Great Lakes Review* that both story collections reveal "a fine understanding of the operations of the folk mind." West wrote a screenplay based on *The Friendly Persuasion,* and it was produced as a feature film in 1956. The movie won the Golden Palm Award at the Cannes Film Festival and was nominated for an Academy Award for best picture of the year.

Some of West's early short stories explore the life of a young girl growing up on the California desert. These were collected in a volume entitled *Cress Delahanty,* published in 1953. Acclaimed as a work for teens and adults alike, *Cress Delahanty* follows the heroine of the title through the years of her adolescence, showing moments that advance her maturity. *English Journal* essayist Frederic I. Carpenter called Cress "the typical adolescent American girl," portrayed with "complete success." *New York Times* reviewer Frances Gaither likewise described the character as "no guileless sprite, but a warm-blooded morsel of humanity." In a *Commonweal* review, T. E. Cassidy wrote: "Anyone who knows adolescence, and especially that of young girls, will love [*Cress Delahanty.*] It is beautifully written, with the most extraordinary insight and delicacy." West continued to be fascinated by the transitional years between youth and womanhood; her books *The Witch Diggers, Leafy Rivers, Crimson Ramblers of the World, Farewell,* and *The State of Stony Lonesome* all contain one or more young characters who are determined to establish their identities through a positive affirmation of maturity. Flanagan noted: "Miss West's most engaging portraits . . . are the adolescent girls, the young women reaching out for emotional and economic security, whose lives are strange juxtapositions of embarrassment, humiliation, surprise, and minor triumph." Addressing his comments to the adult audience, Shivers concluded: "In Miss West's detailed sketches of pert, intelligent, and nearly always engaging little people, she attains a success enviable in any literature and in any period."

West was always conscious of death due to her own ill health, but her involvement with the theme of mortality intensified when her sister was stricken with a painful—and fatal—form of cancer. West wrote about her sister's ordeal in two controversial books, the novel *A Matter of Time* and the nonfiction memoir *The Woman Said Yes: Encounters with Death and Life.* The latter volume revealed that West cooperated with her sister and helped her commit suicide when her pain became unendurable. Some reviewers objected to both works on ethical grounds; others, including Crider, saw a deeper point to the author's confession. In his assessment of *The Woman Said Yes,* Crider wrote: "Though for many readers West's complicity in her sister's suicide will seem the center of the story, the life enhancement theme should not be ignored; and though many readers may doubt the morality of the sister's final decision for euthanasia, it is an unforgettable statement." Dahlstrom Farmer also observed that, true to West's belief in the individual, "she considered both the fictional and the factual accounting [of her sister's death] to be about personal choice, not about a general recommendation." Dahlstrom Farmer further explained that West felt "the most important search anyone could make is the search for self, to learn what 'feelings, beliefs, and convictions' he holds, and once having found them, to have the courage and integrity to be true to them." This, Dahlstrom Farmer concluded, is the abiding message of West's writings on euthanasia—the individual's prerogative to act on conviction.

In 1975 West published *The Massacre at Fall Creek,* a historical novel based on the first American trial of white men for the slaying of Indians. Most critics praised the work for its sensitive delineation of complex issues such as the difference between murder and an act of war and the definition of basic humanity. *Newsweek* reviewer Peter S. Prescott called *The Massacre at Fall Creek* "an honorable, affecting piece of work that grapples plainly with what I take to be the principal concerns of good fiction: who we are and why, how we live and what we think of our condition." Elizabeth Fisher offered even more favorable comments in the *New York Times Book Review,* writing that West took "a little-known incident . . . and fashioned from it a rousing adventure story solidly informed with philosophical and moral content. . . . Working at the height of her powers, with wisdom and maturity, ofttimes a quiet irony, close observation and well-researched detail, West has written a novel of character and incident. Believable women and men are caught in a train of events that make the reader turn the pages. . . . This is a fine piece of work, effective fiction and entertainment, and more besides."

Jessamyn West died in 1984, the same year her final novel, *The State of Stony Lonesome,* was published. By the time she died, West had documented her long life in several nonfiction memoirs, spanning all her years save her infancy. The earliest of these biographies is *To See the Dream,* the 1957 chronicle of her adventures during the filming of "The Friendly Persuasion" in Hollywood. The 1973 title *Hide and Seek: A Continuing Journey* contains reminiscences about her childhood in California as well as some philosophical reflections that form the basis for her fiction. *The Woman Said Yes* explores her mother's courageous decision to nurse her back to health when she was tubercular and then details West's decision to aid her sister in suicide. *Double Discovery,* released in 1980, is composed of both her youthful letters and journals from her first trip abroad in 1929 and her mature reflections on the rediscovery of that long-lost youthful self. In a *Dictionary of Literary Biography Yearbook* eulogy, Jacqueline Koenig concluded that West "accomplished things when she'd never actually known anyone else who did them. She must have been fearless. In her life and in her work, she perfected a combination of intelligence, toughness, determination, compassion, talent, beauty, kindness, and love that is inspirational. She truly lived the life she really wanted." That life ended suddenly, in a massive stroke.

"The works of Jessamyn West provide the literary record of a remarkable career," Crider maintained in his essay. Indeed, West's reputation for realistic character studies and careful use of local detail has attracted the attention of regional scholars in the Midwest as well as in California. Crider noted, however, that West's "talents as a storyteller" have accounted for her "large popular success." Shivers also observed that West wove "some

stories of incomparable beauty; and she has made richer the imagination of millions of now loyal readers throughout the world." Flanagan offered the most cogent praise of West's contribution to national letters in his *Indiana Magazine of History* retrospective on her work. "Certainly few contemporary writers evince the ability to create people with the idiosyncracies, homeliness, honesty, wit and simple humanity of those in whose portraiture Jessamyn West [excelled]," Flanagan wrote. "A reader must be grateful for her precision, her authenticity, and her charm. She is a writer to be treasured."

West once told *CA* that the four cornerstones of her life were "family, words on paper (this means books and writing), the world of nature (weeds, wind, buzzards, clouds), and privacy."

BIOGRAPHICAL/CRITICAL SOURCES:

BOOKS

Contemporary Literary Criticism, Gale, Volume 7, 1977, Volume 17, 1981.
Dictionary of Literary Biography, Volume 6: *American Novelists since World War II Second Series,* Gale, 1980.
Dictionary of Literary Biography Yearbook 1984, Gale, 1985.
Gleasner, Diana, *Breakthrough: Women in Writing,* Dodd, 1959.
Muir, Jane, *Famous Modern American Women Writers,* Dodd, 1959.
Shivers, Alfred S., *Jessamyn West,* Twayne, 1972.
West, Jessamyn, *To See the Dream,* Harcourt, 1957.
West, Jessamyn, *Hide and Seek: A Continuing Journey,* Harcourt, 1973.
West, Jessamyn, *The Woman Said Yes: Encounters with Death and Life,* Harcourt, 1976.
West, Jessamyn, *Double Discovery: A Journey,* Harcourt, 1980.
Women Writers of the West Coast, Capra, 1983.

PERIODICALS

Atlantic, January, 1954, December, 1955, May, 1975.
Book Week, November 18, 1945.
Chicago Sun Tribune, January 14, 1951, January 3, 1954.
Chicago Tribune Book Week, November 6, 1966.
Christian Science Monitor, January 13, 1951.
Commonweal, February 16, 1951, January 15, 1954, March 8, 1957.
Critic, winter, 1976.
English Journal, September, 1957.
Explicator, December, 1964.
Great Lakes Review, winter, 1975.
Harper's, July, 1969.
Indiana Magazine of History, December, 1971.
Los Angeles Times, July 24, 1983, February 26, 1987.
Los Angeles Times Book Review, December 23, 1984.
Nation, March, 1957.
Newsweek, April 14, 1975, November 12, 1979.
New York Herald Tribune Book Review, November 25, 1945, January 14, 1951, January 3, 1954, October 16, 1955, February 10, 1957, April 24, 1960.
New York Post, October 5, 1970.
New York Times, November 25, 1945, January 14, 1951, October 17, 1963, October 27, 1966, October 5, 1967, November 2, 1980.
New York Times Book Review, January 14, 1951, January 3, 1954, October 16, 1955, February 10, 1957, April 24, 1960, October 1, 1967, May 11, 1969, January 10, 1971, May 13, 1973, April 27, 1975, May 2, 1976, December 16, 1979, October 19, 1980, January 6, 1985.
Publishers Weekly, April 28, 1969.

San Francisco Chronicle, January 15, 1951, January 10, 1954, April 28, 1960.
Saturday Review, November 17, 1945, January 9, 1954, December 3, 1955, February 23, 1957, September 21, 1957, April 23, 1960, October 7, 1967, May 10, 1969, September 26, 1980.
Time, May 24, 1976.
Times Literary Supplement, April 8, 1977.
Washington Post, January 5, 1980.
Washington Post Book World, April 1, 1973, May 18, 1975, January 6, 1985.
Weekly Book Review, November 25, 1945.
Writer's Digest, May, 1967, January, 1976.

OBITUARIES:

PERIODICALS

Newsweek, March 5, 1984.
New York Times, February 24, 1984.
Publishers Weekly, March 9, 1984.
Time, March 5, 1984.
Variety, February 29, 1984.

*   *   *

WEST, Morris L(anglo) 1916-
(Michael East, Julian Morris)

PERSONAL: Born April 26, 1916, in Melbourne, Australia; son of Charles Langlo and Florence Guilfoyle (Hanlon) West; married Joyce Lawford, August 14, 1952; children: Christopher, Paul, Melanie, Michael. *Education:* Studied with Christian Brothers Order, 1933, leaving before final vows, 1939; University of Melbourne, Australia, B.A., 1937.

ADDRESSES: Home and office—310 Hudson Parade, Clareville, New South Wales, Australia 2107. *Agent*—Maurice Greenbaum, Rosenman Colin, Freund Lewis & Cohen, 587 Madison Ave., New York, N.Y. 10022.

CAREER: Teacher of modern languages and mathematics in New South Wales, Australia, and Tasmania, 1933-39; secretary to William Morris Hughes, former prime minister of Australia, 1943; Australasian Radio Productions, managing director, 1943-53; film and dramatic writer for Shell Co. and Australian Broadcasting Network, 1954—; commentator and writer, 1954—. Publicity manager, Murdoch newspaper chain, Melbourne, 1945-46; chairman, National Book Council; chairman, Council of the National Library of Australia; fellow, World Academy of Art and Science. *Military service:* Australian Imperial Forces, 1939-43; became lieutenant.

MEMBER: Royal Society of Literature (fellow), Royal Prince Alfred Yacht Club (Sydney).

AWARDS, HONORS: William Heinemann Award of the Royal Society, 1959, National Brotherhood Award of the National Council of Christians and Jews, 1960, and James Tait Black Memorial Award, 1960, all for *The Devil's Advocate;* Bestsellers Paperback of the Year Award, 1965, for *The Shoes of the Fisherman;* D.Litt., University of Santa Clara, 1969; Dag Hammarskjoeld International Prize, Pax Mundi, Diplomatic Academy of Peace, 1978; Universe Literary Prize, 1981, for *The Clowns of God;* D.Litt., Mercy College, 1982; invested as member of Order of Australia, 1985 Honours List.

WRITINGS:

(Under pseudonym Julian Morris) *Moon in My Pocket,* Australasian Publishing, 1945.

Gallows on the Sand (also see below), Angus & Robertson, 1956, large print edition, Ulverscroft, 1971.
Kundu (also see below), Dell, 1956.
The Crooked Road, Morrow, 1957 (published in England as *The Big Story,* Heinemann, 1957).
Children of the Shadows: The True Story of the Street Urchins of Naples, Doubleday, 1957 (published in England as *Children of the Sun,* Heinemann, 1957, reprinted, Fontana, 1977).
Backlash, Morrow, 1958 (published in England as *The Second Victory* [also see below], Heinemann, 1958, second edition, Hodder & Stoughton, 1985).
(Under pseudonym Michael East) *McCreary Moves In,* Heinemann, 1958, published as *The Concubine* (also see below), New English Library, 1967, reprinted under real name and original title, Coronet Books, 1983.
The Devil's Advocate (also see below), Morrow, 1959.
(Under pseudonym Michael East) *The Naked Country* (also see below), Heinemann, 1960, reprinted, Coronet, 1983.
Daughter of Silence (novel; also see below), Morrow, 1961.
Daughter of Silence: A Dramatization of the Novel (play; first produced on Broadway by Richard Halliday, November, 1961), Morrow, 1962.
The Shoes of the Fisherman (also see below), Morrow, 1963, limited edition, Franklin Library, 1980.
The Ambassador, Morrow, 1965.
The Tower of Babel (Book-of-the-Month Club selection), Morrow, 1967, large print edition, Ulverscroft, 1986.
The Heretic: A Play in Three Acts, Morrow, 1969.
(With Robert Francis) *Scandal in the Assembly: The Matrimonial Laws and Tribunals of the Roman Catholic Church, 1970,* Morrow, 1970.
Summer of the Red Wolf, Morrow, 1971.
The Salamander (also see below), Morrow, 1973.
Harlequin, Morrow, 1974.
The Navigator, Morrow, 1976.
Selected Works, Heinemann Octopus, 1977.
The Devil's Advocate; [and] *The Second Victory;* [and] *Daughter of Silence;* [and] *The Salamander;* [and] *The Shoes of the Fisherman,* Heinemann, 1977.
Proteus, limited first edition, Franklin Library, 1979, Morrow, 1979.
The Clowns of God, Morrow, 1981.
A West Quartet: Four Novels of Intrigue and High Adventure (includes *The Naked Country, Gallows on the Sand, The Concubine,* and *Kundu*), Morrow, 1981.
The World Is Made of Glass, Avon, 1983.
Cassidy, Doubleday, 1986.
Masterclass (novel), Hutchinson, 1988.
Lazarus (novel), St. Martin's, 1990.

Also author of play "The World Is Made of Glass," 1984, adapted from his novel of the same title.

SIDELIGHTS: Since the mid-1950s, Australian novelist Morris L. West has written suspense novels that plunge the reader into political turmoil, worldwide governmental corruption, and the internal workings of the Catholic Church. West spent several years in a Roman Catholic monastery and worked for six months as the Vatican correspondent for the London *Daily Mail;* his experiences have contributed to a moral and ethical outlook on current events that permeates all his work. According to *New York Times Book Review* contributor Herbert Mitgang, "West is known for his theological thrillers that pose hard, frequently unanswerable questions about today's turbulent world— including the constraints on liberty imposed by democratic societies." West is also known for his high output. Having written over twenty novels, "Morris West invents stories as though the world were running out of them," comments Webster Schott in the *New York Times Book Review*. Says Diane Casselberry Manuel in the *Christian Science Monitor,* "at his best, author West is a skillful storyteller who knows how to build suspense into every twist of the plot."

Three of West's better known works—*The Devil's Advocate, The Shoes of the Fisherman,* and *The Clowns of God*—feature protagonists who are representatives of the Church. *The Devil's Advocate* concerns a dying Catholic priest who is sent to an Italian village to investigate the life of a proposed saint and who ends up making an important self-discovery: "He had kept the rules all his life: all the rules—except one; that sooner or later he must step beyond the forms and conventions and enter into a direct, personal relationship with his fellows and with his God." According to *Renascence* contributor Arnold L. Goldsmith, *The Devil's Advocate* is "a richly textured, finely constructed story with all of the ingredients of a literary classic. . . . West is able to blend the personal with the local and the universal, giving us not only the memorable portrait of a deeply disturbed theologian, but also a wider view of the troubled soul of a church, a country, and the world."

In *The Shoes of the Fisherman,* a humble Ukrainian pope finds himself the central negotiator in an attempt to prevent the United States and the Soviet Union from starting World War III. During the negotiations, the pope must confront the Russian who once tortured him. The work, a popular and critical success, demonstrates West's concern with modern man's inability to communicate with his brother. "We're not using the same words. We don't understand each other. We are not selecting, we aren't balancing . . . simply because life is too risky, too tormenting. . . . I've been trying, therefore, to use what is a very old manner of story telling. To make this conflict of legitimate points of view *clear,* through the medium of the novel," West told Shari Steiner in an interview for *Writer's Digest.* "In *The Shoes of the Fisherman,* the idea of the central character was a man who believed that he was—and publicly claimed to be—the Vicar of Christ," West continued. "Now, theoretically, this is the man who must look at the world through the eye of God, and try to make some sense out of its complexity. He was therefore a natural character medium through which this hopeless attempt had to be made."

Eighteen years later, West again used a pope as a central character, this time in *The Clowns of God.* Pope Gregory is forced by the Church to abdicate his seat when he receives a vision of the Second Coming of Christ and decides to communicate this apocalyptic message to the rest of the world. *The Clowns of God* shows the Church in a harsher light than West's previous theological novels and reflects West's ambivalence with the institution as a governing unit. "West has great faith in the power of faith, but little tolerance for the bureaucratic wranglings that often seem to accompany organized religion," states Manuel. The ambivalence may have originated in West's experiences with the Christian Brothers monastery where he studied for six years. Intending to become a priest, he left before taking his final vows. "My education with the Christian Brothers . . . was very strongly tinged with Jansenism, a restrictive, puritanical attitude to religion," West explained to Steiner. "This has probably produced in me an attitude of extreme tolerance and the desire to find out what the other man thinks first before we make any judgments."

Critics had varying responses to *The Clowns of God.* Walter Shapiro in the *Washington Post* dislikes West's description of Christ,

who appears at the book's conclusion, "a handsome fellow in his early 30s." Robert Kaftan writes in the *Christian Century* that "the characters become so many pieces to be manipulated to propel the story forward." He applauds the novel's setting, however, saying that West's "portrait of the world at the edge is chilling and disquieting." Edmund Fuller agrees. "As a melodrama it is tautly absorbing in its doom-threat genre. Yet the book far transcends that aspect, for Mr. West is an intelligent, thoughtful writer with knowledge of the ecclesiastical and theological issues that are the essence of his tale," he states in the *Wall Street Journal.* And Richard A. Blake writes in *America* that "West has succeeded . . . in raising the most significant questions of human survival in a very human and religious context."

A turning point in West's career came with the publication of *The World Is Made of Glass,* the imaginative expansion of a brief entry in Carl Jung's diary, where he records meeting with a woman: "A lady came to my office. She refused to give her name. . . . What she wanted to communicate to me was a confession." The lady, according to West, is Magda Liliane Kardoss von Gamsfeld, a horse breeder, physician, and the illegitimate offspring of an English duchess and a Hungarian nobleman. Raised by her father, Magda was seduced by him at sixteen, which started her on a path of lesbianism, sadomasochism, and, finally, murder. She comes to Jung in a state of suicidal depression.

The story deviates from West's usual fare in that it contains only two characters, Jung and Magda, who relate the plot in monologue form. "Within the course of a single day Jung has become the recipient of confessions that it would probably take the average psychoanalyst weeks, months or even years to elicit from a patient," writes Francis King in the *Spectator.* But Magda's confessions produce an unexpected reaction in the psychiatrist. "Jung himself is constantly and disturbingly aware of the parallel between his own situation, in which he is poised to attempt the symbolic murder of his beloved father-figure Freud, and that of this siren, who is guilty of real murder," King continues. Magda's honesty also leads Jung to more closely examine his broken marriage and affair with a former student, plus his suddenly remembered, unsavory memories from childhood. The impact of this forces him to conclude, "we are both imprisoned in a transparent world." And finally Magda asks, "Is it possible that Jung, not I, is the clown in this absurd circus? . . . Who here is the crazy one?"

Detroit News contributor Andrew Greeley believes that *The World Is Made of Glass* is one of West's finest works. "Morris West has done for Carl Gustav Jung what D. M. Thomas did for Sigmund Freud—written a novel which brings Jung and his milieu alive. In the process he has produced a story which is very unlike most of his previous work. . . . Jung's chaotic personal life is vividly portrayed." *New York Times Book Review* contributor Philippe Van Rjndt says, "Magda von Gamsfeld is Mr. West's most impressive creation." And Patricia Olson comments in the *Christian Century* that while West is generally "known for his realistic narration, his sensitive character portrayal and his concern for modern religion, [he] has never before presented such melodrama, such passionate characters, or such a critique of conventional Christianity as he does here."

Some critics dislike the book's conclusion, in which the physician who initially sent Magda to Jung provides her with a solution by giving her a job as director of a refuge for fallen women. Mayo Mohs notes in *Time* that "the author kisses off this denouement in a scant few pages, barely hinting at the thoughts and feelings of the new Magda. Having built the novel on the spectacle of her corruption, West might have reflected a bit more on the drama of her return to grace." Beryl Lieff Benderly indicates in the *Washington Post* that "Magda functions not as a person but as a plot device to permit West's exploration of certain themes—the line between good and evil, the nature of guilt and obsession, the curative power of redemption. . . . But to touch deeply, a story about sin and redemption or madness and cure must involve real people in a palpable world, not made-to-order abstractions in a universe of concepts." Van Rjndt, however, finds Magda's new life believable. "For all the cruelty Magda inflicts and receives, her struggle towards redemption demands our respect and compels our fascination," she writes.

Greeley concludes that "so sharp is the departure from earlier stories that one wonders if West . . . has not reached an important and extremely fruitful turning point in his career as a storyteller." But West primarily sees himself as a communicator, and his stories as vehicles for his messages. He told Steiner he wants to be "the type of person who . . . causes other people to examine their lives . . . the kind of man who turns the world upside down and says, lookit, it looks different, doesn't it?"

MEDIA ADAPTATIONS: The Devil's Advocate, as dramatized by Dore Schary, was produced by the Theatre Guild at the Billy Rose Theatre in March, 1961; *The Shoes of the Fisherman* was filmed by Metro-Goldwyn-Mayer in 1968.

BIOGRAPHICAL/CRITICAL SOURCES:

BOOKS

Contemporary Literary Criticism, Gale, Volume 6, 1976, Volume 33, 1985.
West, Morris L., *The Devil's Advocate,* Morrow, 1959.
West, *The World Is Made of Glass,* Avon, 1983.

PERIODICALS

America, August 29-September 5, 1981.
Atlantic, April, 1968.
Best Sellers, March 1, 1968, April 1, 1970, June 1, 1970.
Books and Bookmen, April, 1968, April, 1979, August, 1983.
Catholic World, September, 1961, February, 1962.
Chicago Tribune Book World, December 25, 1983.
Christian Century, May 20, 1981, October 12, 1983.
Christian Science Monitor, August 10, 1981.
Detroit News, July 10, 1983.
International Fiction Review, January, 1975.
Jewish Quarterly, autumn, 1968.
Life, February 23, 1968.
Look, August 1, 1961.
Los Angeles Times Book Review, February 18, 1979, July 17, 1983, October 19, 1986, April 15, 1990.
Nation, December 16, 1961, May 17, 1965.
National Observer, March 11, 1968.
National Review, February 14, 1975.
Newsweek, December 11, 1961.
New Yorker, December 9, 1961.
New York Times, May 27, 1987.
New York Times Book Review, April 25, 1965, February 22, 1968, April 7, 1968, September 19, 1971, October 21, 1973, October 27, 1974, August 29, 1976, March 4, 1979, March 11, 1979, August 9, 1981, November 26, 1981, July 3, 1983, November 9, 1986, May 27, 1987.
Observer Review, March 3, 1968.
Plays and Players, September, 1970.
Punch, March 6, 1968.
Renascence, summer, 1962.
Reporter, January 4, 1962.

Saturday Review, April 24, 1965, February 24, 1968.
Spectator, March 8, 1968, October 5, 1974, July 23, 1983.
Stage, July 23, 1970.
Theatre Arts, February, 1962.
This Week, December 4, 1966.
Time, December 8, 1961, July 6, 1970, November 4, 1974, October 4, 1976, January 22, 1979, July 25, 1983.
Times (London), May 6, 1965, July 14, 1983, February 5, 1987.
Times Literary Supplement, May 6, 1965, July 16, 1970, August 3, 1973.
Wall Street Journal, August 24, 1981.
Washington Post, June 8, 1981, July 8, 1983, November 15, 1986.
Writer's Digest, February, 1971.

*   *   *

WEST, Nathanael 1903-1940
(Nathan Weinstein, Nathan von Wallenstein Weinstein)

PERSONAL: Name originally Nathan Weinstein; name legally changed, August 16, 1926; born October 17, 1903, in New York, N.Y.; died following an automobile accident, December 22, 1940, near El Centro, Calif.; buried in Mount Zion Cemetery, Queens, N.Y.; son of Max (a building contractor) and Anna (Wallenstein) Weinstein; married Eileen McKenney, April 19, 1940. *Education:* Attended Tufts College (now University), 1921; Brown University, Ph.B., 1924.

CAREER: Writer. Worked for father's construction firm during early 1920s; Kenmore Hall (residence hotel), New York City, assistant manager, 1927-1930; Sutton Club Hotel, New York City, manager, 1930-1933; screenwriter for film studios in California, including Columbia, 1933 and 1938, Republic, 1936-38, RKO, 1938 and 1939-40, and Universal, 1938-39.

MEMBER: League of American Writers (member of Hollywood committee), Screen Writers Guild (member of executive board, beginning 1939), Motion Picture Guild (member of executive board), Motion Picture Artists Committee (member of executive board), Motion Picture Democratic Committee, Hollywood Anti-Nazi League.

WRITINGS:

NOVELS

The Dream Life of Balso Snell, Contact Editions, 1931.
Miss Lonelyhearts, Liveright, 1933.
A Cool Million: The Dismantling of Lemuel Pitkin, Covici, Friede, 1934.
The Day of the Locust, Random House, 1939, recent edition, Buccaneer, 1981.
The Complete Works of Nathanael West (omnibus volume of four novels), introduction by Alan Ross, Farrar, Straus, 1957.

Novels also published in dual editions.

SCREENPLAYS

(With Jack Natteford) "Ticket to Paradise," Republic, 1936.
(With Lester Cole) "The President's Mystery," Republic, 1936.
(With Cole and Samuel Ornitz) "Follow Your Heart," Republic, 1936.
"Rhythm in the Clouds," Republic, 1937.
(With Ornitz) "It Could Happen to You," Republic, 1937.
"Born to Be Wild," Republic, 1938.
"I Stole a Million," Universal, 1939.

(With Jerry Cady and Dalton Trumbo) "Five Came Back,"
    RKO, 1939.
(With Whitney Bolton) "The Spirit of Culver," Universal, 1939.
"Men Against the Sky," RKO, 1940.
"Let's Make Music," RKO, 1940.

Also author of unproduced screenplays.

OTHER

(With Joseph Schrank) "Good Hunting" (play), first produced
    on Broadway, 1938.
(Under name Nathan Weinstein) *My Island Os Sonnets* (poems),
    Exposition, 1974.

Also author, with S. J. Perelman, of the unproduced play "Even
Stephen." Contributor of articles, short stories, and poems to periodicals, including *Casements* (under name Nathan von Wallenstein Weinstein), *Americana, Contact, Contempo,* and *Pacific
Weekly.* Associate editor of *Contact,* 1931-32, and *Americana,*
1933.

SIDELIGHTS: An American novelist who wrote primarily during the Great Depression of the 1930s, Nathanael West was
called "the chief neglected talent of [his] age" by Leslie Fiedler
in *Love and Death in the American Novel.* While many of his contemporaries composed straightforward novels about social and
economic injustice, West produced an idiosyncratic blend of pathos and comedy, realism and wild unreality. "He too deplored
the emptiness of twentieth-century life in the United States," declared Richard B. Gehman in *Atlantic Monthly,* "but he chose
to depict that life in terms not of people who were consciously
involved in a struggle, but of those who were unconsciously
trapped—people who were, in their blindness, so tragic as to be
comic figures." Little-known to the American public for years
after his death, West's work maintained a select following in literary circles. As popular tastes in the novel changed, West's fiction gained a broader audience, and he was widely hailed as a
precursor of the "black humor" novelists who wrote in the
1950s, 1960s, and beyond.

Born in 1903 in New York City, West was the son of Jewish immigrants Max Weinstein, a prosperous building contractor, and
Anna Wallenstein, who fancied herself a descendant of a German nobleman of the same last name. West's parents were more
concerned with status and money than art. His father expected
him to enter the family business, and he gave West several Horatio Alger novels—highly popular tales in which honest young
men work their way to financial success. But West was a high-
school dropout whose friends called him "Pep" because he
showed so little energy.

To enroll in Tufts College, West lied about his grades, and when
Tufts asked him to leave because of laziness, another student's
transcript gained him admission to Brown. There West read
widely, but he was better known for his enthusiastic socializing
and a biting intellectual wit. When classmate and future journalist Quentin Reynolds pressed him for a graduation speech, West
created the story of St. Puce, a flea who lives in the armpit of
Christ. During the 1920s West wove St. Puce and similar anecdotes into *The Dream Life of Balso Snell,* a broad parody of the
ideals of Western civilization that became his first published
novel.

Unsure of his future after his graduation from Brown in 1924,
West convinced relatives to fund a trip to Paris, where he could
join other Americans on the city's literary scene. But in 1927,
only a few months after he arrived in Europe, the family construction business began to decline—an economic downturn that

presaged the Great Depression. West's family recalled him to
America, and through their influence he obtained a succession
of jobs managing inexpensive residential hotels. Outside the social mainstream West gained an education far different from his
college years, and the experience would inspire his most successful novels.

By providing rent-free lodgings to struggling writers, West remained close to the New York literary world. His charity aided
the literary critic Edmund Wilson; novelists Robert M. Coates,
Erskine Caldwell, and Dashiell Hammett; and playwright Lillian Hellman. West also housed his newlywed sister and her husband, S. J. Perelman, a renowned satirist and a lifelong friend.
West became fascinated with the desperate lives of his other tenants: a onetime actress worked as a prostitute; young men
headed for work at businesses failing under the impact of the Depression; lonely residents killed time in the lobby reading magazines. At the Sutton Club Hotel six people committed suicide by
jumping from the same terrace. When West was especially curious about a lodger, he would steam open the person's mail, sometimes with Hellman's assistance.

One evening Perelman introduced West to an advice columnist
for the *Brooklyn Eagle.* She showed the two men a sample of her
mail, wondering if it might inspire Perelman to write a comedy.
West was deeply moved by the pain and helplessness the letters
displayed, and he soon began work on *Miss Lonelyhearts,* the tale
of a young advice columnist who destroys himself by becoming
personally involved in the miserable lives of his readers. Considered a major advance over *Balso Snell, Miss Lonelyhearts* was
lauded in the *New Yorker* and the *New York Times Book Review*
when it was published in 1933. But sales of the book faltered
when its publisher, Liveright, declared bankruptcy.

As the 1930s wore on West became increasingly concerned about
his failure to gain either artistic recognition or a steady income
from his writing. He joined the staffs of two literary magazines—
including *Contact,* where he joined poet William Carlos Williams—but the journals soon folded. When Columbia Pictures
offered West a screenwriting job, he eagerly accepted, only to be
laid off within a year. Supported by friends he wrote a third
novel, *A Cool Million,* which vented his bitterness about the
Great Depression by satirizing the myth of success portrayed in
Horatio Alger novels. Commentators have since contended that
the strength of West's anger damaged the book, which received
largely unenthusiastic reviews and sold poorly.

A major Hollywood studio bought the rights to *A Cool Million,*
however, and the sale encouraged West to move to California in
1935 for a second try at screenwriting. Several months passed
and he was unable to find work, even with the aid of an agent.
Hammett had become successful in the movie business, and West
repeatedly approached him for help with a job but was greeted
with taunts. Moreover, at a time when the major studios were
trying to keep unions out of the film industry, West's membership in the Screen Writers Guild hurt his prospects. Depressed
and poor, West became desperately afraid that he would always
be a failure. Money from Perelman sustained him.

As in New York, West occupied a succession of shabby lodgings,
and he began to meet the marginal people of Southern California. He became a confidant of prostitutes and considered compiling their slang into a dictionary. His circle of acquaintances
gradually grew to include midgets, petty criminals, and murder
investigators. Long before West felt accepted as a Hollywood
screenwriter, he was familiar with the industry's stuntmen and
laborers.

After a year West found a screenwriting job at Republic, a minor studio known as a factory for formulaic, low-budget films. He adapted readily to this commercial atmosphere, for he saw screenwriting as merely a craft that could support him while he wrote novels and plays. For extra money he eventually teamed with writer Boris Ingster, developing scripts and script ideas that producers purchased eagerly. As biographer Jay Martin explained, Ingster generated conventional story lines and gave them to West, who contributed his flair for distinctive characters and twists of plot.

Immersed in the unglamorous side of Hollywood, West wrote *The Day of the Locust,* his fourth and final book. Unusual among Hollywood novels, it ignores film stars and financiers to concentrate on the obscure, disheartened people who inhabit the town's social fringes. Like *Miss Lonelyhearts, Day of the Locust* was praised in literary circles but ignored by the larger public. Over the course of his lifetime, West earned less than thirteen hundred dollars from his books.

By contrast, the commercial film industry that West scorned in *Day of the Locust* began to appreciate his screenwriting. He continued to write undistinguished films, but now he worked for the higher-paying major studios, particularly Universal and RKO. While his friend F. Scott Fitzgerald, a highly popular novelist during the 1920s, struggled to survive as a screenwriter, West earned a comfortable income for the first time in his life. He bought a pleasant house in the Hollywood hills and married Eileen McKenney, immortalized as the vivacious title character of Ruth McKenney's book *My Sister Eileen.* Eight months later the couple died in a traffic accident when West ran a stop sign.

Near the end of his life West recognized that his writing had always been too unusual to appeal to a broad audience. As Martin quoted him in a letter to Fitzgerald, "Somehow or other I seem to have slipped in between all the 'schools.' My books meet no needs except my own, their circulation is practically private and I'm lucky to be published. And yet I only have a desire to remedy that *before* sitting down to write, once I begin I do it my way. I forget the broad sweep, the big canvas, the shot-gun adjectives, the important people, the significant ideas, the lessons to be taught . . . and go on making what one critic called 'private and unfunny jokes.' "

As James F. Light noted in *Nathanael West: An Interpretative Study,* if "there is any constant pattern in the novels of West, it is the pilgrimage around which each novel centers." He continued: "In each the hero is in search of something in which he can believe and to which he can belong . . . but the result is always the same: tragic disillusionment." In *The Dream Life of Balso Snell,* the title character pursues cultural enlightenment by journeying to the site of ancient Troy, where Trojans and Greeks had clashed thousands of years earlier in a war that inspired the earliest classic of Western literature, Homer's *Iliad.* Snell finds the wooden horse that the Greeks used to invade and conquer Troy. Entering the horse through its anus, he begins a dreamlike journey through Western culture. The artists and philosophers Snell meets, however, are frauds and fools—one is the devoted chronicler of St. Puce. West derides the characters by making them blatantly repulsive, often associating them with excrement.

Commentators have generally agreed that West has a serious point to make in *Balso Snell*—that art and ideas have become too removed from human reality—but they disagreed substantially about the merits of his technique. Admirers observed that West's vivid imagery and his concern with human dreams and delusions anticipate his later works. Detractors, however, said that *Balso Snell* is overstated and contains too many scholarly allusions—

mistakes, some suggested, that a recent college graduate might make. In the *New York Times Book Review,* Malcolm Cowley called the book "an elaborate joke . . . that doesn't quite come off."

But West soon transcended his penchant for "gratuitous and perverse humour," as V. S. Pritchett observed in *New Statesman.* In his second novel, *Miss Lonelyhearts,* West "became [both] comic and humane." The title character, whose real name West never reveals, is a young newspaperman assigned to write an advice column. At first Miss Lonelyhearts agrees with his friends that the job is a joke, but the letters he receives are a wrenching mixture of inane comedy and undeniable sorrow. A teenage girl, for instance, laments that no one will ask her on dates because she "was born without a nose"; at the end of her letter, she asks for advice—"ought I to commit suicide?" Miss Lonelyhearts finds himself tangled in a moral dilemma: how can he reconcile himself to the existence of such meaningless suffering?

West depicts the plight of the columnist with "ironic and bitter humor," as T. C. Wilson wrote in the *Saturday Review.* The characters around Miss Lonelyhearts offer him solutions that are too simple for him to accept. While his girlfriend ignores the world's troubles by remaining silly and naive, his editor, Shrike, presents an air of worldly disillusionment edged with sadism. When Miss Lonelyhearts becomes physically ill with anxiety, Shrike visits his bedside to belittle him. Shrike lists the columnist's hopes of escape—art, a place in the country, suave indifference—and dismisses them all with a sneer. Miss Lonelyhearts, Shrike declares, is a "leper-licker." The columnist becomes convinced that he can heal his readers with Christian love, but his efforts are ludicrous and futile. Visiting one troubled couple, he holds hands with the husband and is seduced by the wife. The husband, in a jealous rage, seizes a gun and kills Miss Lonelyhearts—by accident. As Wilson concluded, "the tragic lives of [West's] characters impress us even more powerfully because they are made to seem stupid and comic."

Miss Lonelyhearts has repeatedly garnered praise for its adept language and its tight dramatic focus. In fifteen short chapters, West chronicles progressive stages of the columnist's emotional disintegration. Pritchett called the book "a selection of hard, diamond-fine miniatures" and noted the "precision" of the author's "poetic images." As Brad Darrach noted in *Time,* "Nothing else in American fiction radiates the compacted fury of this little parable."

West's third novel, *A Cool Million,* is a political satire directed against America's image as a land of prosperity—a predictable target during the Great Depression. Subtitled *The Dismantling of Lemuel Pitkin,* the book chronicles the misadventures of a well-intentioned fool who is physically torn apart as he quests for financial success. As the novel opens, Pitkin gets a loan from Shagpoke Whipple, a dishonest banker who advises him to venture forth from their small town to pursue his fortune. After Pitkin loses his teeth, an eye, his leg, a thumb, and his scalp, he becomes a performing freak in a vaudeville show, entertaining the audience by being beaten on stage. Shot dead by a Communist agent, Pitkin is turned into a martyr by Whipple's Fascist party. Though *A Cool Million* displays West's gift for a colorful plot, most commentators agree that the book is hampered by a heavy-handed use of mock-heroic prose. West seems uninvolved with his characters, biographer Robert Emmet Long averred, and the book "seems surprisingly crude and rambling," especially "in comparison with *Miss Lonelyhearts.*"

By contrast, as Pritchett observed, "*The Day of the Locust* is an advance from fable and from fragments of people, to the courageous full statement of the novel." This novel, he continued, "is mature because the compassion has no theatrical pressure; because now West is now blocking in a sizeable society, and because his gift for inventing extraordinary scenes has expanded." *Day of the Locust* centers on Tod Hackett, a recent Yale art-school graduate who designs sets in Hollywood. Lacking funds, awaiting the inspiration for a painting, he haunts the underside of California life much as West had done. Tod meets Homer Simpson, a timid bookkeeper from Iowa; Adore Loomis, a snide child actor; Abe Kusich, an angry dwarf; and Faye Greener, a flirtatious aspiring actress who arouses the unfulfilled desires of many men she meets, including Tod and Homer.

Frustration becomes the motif of the novel, for as many critics note, West sees California as a deceptive land of promise inhabited by Americans whose dreams have failed to come true. Feeling bored and deceived, these masses occupy their time with idle thrill-seeking. In the climactic episode of the novel, which reviewers found particularly compelling, a crowd assembles outside a movie house to see the pageantry of a Hollywood premiere. Taunted once too often by Adore, the long-suffering Homer erupts in anger and kills him. The crowd becomes a lynch mob, tearing Homer to pieces, and Tod—nearly crushed in the riot—envisions his completed painting. It will be a portrait of apocalypse entitled "The Burning of Los Angeles."

The Day of the Locust has repeatedly been called the best Hollywood novel ever written. "Mr. West has caught the emptiness of Hollywood," wrote Edmund Wilson in *New Republic,* "and he is, as far as I know, the first writer to make this emptiness horrible." And in *Hudson Review,* Daniel Aaron praised West for turning the movie capital into a powerful symbol. "Not an isolated piece of dreamland or a national joke," Aaron wrote, West's Hollywood "is America carried out to its logical conclusion."

Literary critics have generally agreed that West's work is difficult to categorize. Many have linked him to surrealism, a French aesthetic movement of the 1920s and 1930s that stressed the imagery of dreams; others, citing his interest in America's downtrodden, have linked him to naturalism, a more political movement that stressed an individual's helplessness in a hostile society. In an article titled "West's Disease," which appeared in *The Dyer's Hand and Other Essays,* poet W. H. Auden declared that West "is not, strictly speaking, a novelist" because he portrays neither dreams nor society in an accurate fashion. Fiedler praised this characteristic of West's work, calling the author "the inventor of a peculiar kind of book . . . the neo-gothic novel," which derived from West's understanding that "literary truth is not synonymous with fact." Fiedler wrote that such a style, unburdened by the minutiae of factual and psychological detail, "opened up possibilities . . . of capturing the quality of experience in a mass society." He concluded: "Putting down a book by West, a reader is not sure whether he has been presented with a nightmare endowed with the conviction of actuality or with actuality distorted into the semblance of a nightmare; but in either case, he has the sense that he has been presented with a view of a world in which, incredibly, he lives."

As West himself observed, the world he presents is unrelieved by hope. "There is nothing to root for in my books," Martin quotes him. Reviewers have been particularly troubled by West's portrayal of human relationships. In his books friendship and sexual love appear repulsive, inadequate, or ridiculous, for such ideals are overwhelmed by loneliness, despair, and brutality. Some critics call West's world-view a sign of his limitations as a writer, and some suggest that it reflects deep-seated psycholog-ical problems. In West's books, wrote biographer Kingsley Widmer, "Female sexuality tends to be fascinatingly horrific, women destructive powers demanding hostile responses. . . . West's sex-violence obsessions in his fiction may suggest erotic difficulties in [his] life."

West, however, found nothing abnormal about centering his fiction on brutality. In an essay titled "Some Notes on Violence," he told readers of *Contact* that manuscripts submitted to the magazine generally had this same obsession. "In America," he declared, "violence is idiomatic," so much so that only great violence can attract any attention. As Martin observed, "West's notion of how to express the 'American grain' was to 'do it obviously—cruelly, irresponsible torture, simply, obviously, casually told.'" Sexuality in West's novels was a literary device, according to Victor Comerchero in *Nathanael West: The Ironic Prophet.* "The disorder of the individual mirrors the disorder of the society," Comerchero declared. "Sexual inadequacy is ineffectualness at its most primitive biological level. Tied up in one vivid image are man's social, biological, psychological, and 'metaphysical' inadequacies—man's inadequacy before the 'laws of life.'" West remained true to his artistic vision, but the price he paid was unpopularity. Critics speculated that West's pessimism, coming at a time when America faced the twin burdens of the Great Depression and an impending world war, was simply too painful for his audience to bear.

After West's death his literary reputation languished for many years. But prominent old friends such as Coates and Williams continued to praise him, and in 1947 Daniel Aaron helped begin a broad reassessment of West's work when he praised the novelist in the literary magazine *Partisan Review.* The West revival became extensive in 1957, when the four novels were published in one volume for the first time. Known somewhat inaccurately as the *Complete Works,* the collection received lengthy positive reviews in a wide variety of publications in the United States and England. The first book-length studies of West appeared in the early 1960s, followed by many more works of literary criticism and biography, including Martin's highly detailed *Nathanael West: The Art of His Life.*

As many commentators have observed, West's vivid, brooding humor, so unusual in his own time, became a widespread trend in American literature after World War II. By "the middle decades of the twentieth century," Widmer averred, West had become "one of *the* authors to read." West's followers included Flannery O'Connor, whose novel *Wise Blood* centers on a tormented young Southerner who preaches a new religion called "The First Church Without God." Literary critics found echoes of West in the works of many postwar American novelists, whose writings often blend comedy, chaos, and pessimism. As Stanley Edgar Hyman wrote in his book *Nathanael West,* the author "was a true pioneer and culture hero, making it possible for the younger symbolists and fantasists who came after him, and who include our best writers, to do with relative ease what he did in defiance of the temper of his time, for so little reward, in isolation and in pain."

MEDIA ADAPTATIONS: Miss Lonelyhearts was adapted by Leonard Praskins for the film "Advice to the Lovelorn," Fox/United Artists, 1933; by Howard Teichmann for a play of the original title, 1957; by Dore Schary for the film "Lonelyhearts," United Artists, 1958; and by Michael Dinner and others for a television play of the original title, Public Broadcasting Service, 1983. *The Day of the Locust* was adapted by Waldo Salt for a film of the same title, Paramount, 1975.

BIOGRAPHICAL/CRITICAL SOURCES:

BOOKS

Auden, W. H., *The Dyer's Hand and Other Essays,* Random House, 1962.

Bloom, Harold, editor, *Nathanael West: Modern Critical Views,* Chelsea House, 1986.

Comerchero, Victor, *Nathanael West: The Ironic Prophet,* Syracuse University Press, 1964.

Concise Dictionary of Literary Biography: The Age of Maturity, 1929-1941, Gale, 1989.

Dictionary of Literary Biography, Gale, Volume 4: *American Writers in Paris, 1920-1939,* 1980, Volume 9: *American Novelists, 1910-1945,* 1981, Volume 28: *Twentieth-Century American Jewish Fiction Writers,* 1984.

Fiedler, Leslie A., *Love and Death in the American Novel,* revised edition, Stein & Day, 1966.

Hyman, Stanley Edgar, *Nathanael West,* University of Minnesota Press, 1962.

Light, James F., *Nathanael West: An Interpretive Study,* second edition, Northwestern University Press, 1971.

Long, Robert Emmet, *Nathanael West,* Ungar, 1985.

Madden, David, editor, *Nathanael West; The Cheaters and the Cheated: A Collection of Critical Essays,* Everett/Edwards, 1973.

Martin, Jay, *Nathanael West: The Art of His Life,* Farrar, Straus, 1970.

Martin, Jay, editor, *Nathanael West: A Collection of Critical Essays,* Prentice-Hall, 1971.

Twentieth-Century Literary Criticism, Gale, Volume 1, 1978, Volume 14, 1984.

West, Nathanael, *Miss Lonelyhearts,* introduction by Robert M. Coates, New Directions, 1946.

West, Nathanael, *The Day of the Locust,* introduction by Richard B. Gehman, New Directions, 1950.

West, Nathanael, *The Complete Works of Nathanael West,* introduction by Alan Ross, Farrar, Straus, 1957.

White, William, *Nathanael West: A Comprehensive Bibliography,* Kent State University Press, 1975.

Widmer, Kingsley, *Nathanael West,* Twayne, 1982.

PERIODICALS

Atlantic Monthly, September, 1950, October, 1970.
Commonweal, May 10, 1957, October 23, 1970.
Contact, Volume 1, number 3, 1932.
Hudson Review, winter, 1951.
Nation, July 25, 1934, July 15, 1939, May 4, 1957, August 17, 1970.
New Republic, July 26, 1939, May 23, 1970.
New Statesman, December 7, 1957, October 11, 1968.
Newsweek, September 4, 1950, May 13, 1957, June 29, 1970.
New Yorker, April 15, 1933, May 18, 1957, October 10, 1970.
New York Times, June 2, 1974, February 2, 1987, February 8, 1987.
New York Times Book Review, April 23, 1933, July 1, 1934, May 21, 1939, May 12, 1957.
Saturday Review, May 13, 1933, May 20, 1939, May 11, 1957, June 27, 1970.
Spectator, July 19, 1968.
Time, June 17, 1957, August 17, 1970.
Times Literary Supplement, January 24, 1958, April 11, 1958.
Washington Post, January 25, 1983.

WEST, Owen
See KOONTZ, Dean R(ay)

* * *

WEST, Rebecca 1892-1983
(Lynx)

PERSONAL: Name originally Cicily Isabel Fairfield; adopted name Rebecca West c. 1911; born December 21, 1892, in County Kerry, Ireland; died March 15, 1983 of pneumonia in London, England; daughter of Charles (an army officer, editor, and writer) and Isabella (a musician; maiden name, Mackenzie) Fairfield; married Henry Maxwell Andrews (a banker and investment counselor), November 1, 1930 (died, 1968); children: (with H. G. Wells) Anthony (Panther) West. *Education:* George Watson's Ladies' College, Edinburgh, Scotland, graduate; attended Royal Academy of Dramatic Art, London.

ADDRESSES: c/o Macmillan, 4 Little Essex St., London WC2R 3LF, England. *Agent*—A. D. Peters & Co. Ltd., 10 Buckingham St., London WC2N 6BU, England.

CAREER: Journalist, novelist, biographer, and critic. Began journalist career in 1911 as reviewer for *Freewoman,* a feminist magazine; joined *Clarion* as a political writer in 1912, contributing from then on to British, and later American, newspapers and magazines; during the years following World War I she was the book critic of the *New Statesman and Nation* and regularly contributed to the *New Republic.* Became an advocate of Socialism and was active, for a while, in the Fabian Society. During World War II, supervised British Broadcasting Corp. talks to Yugoslavia; covered postwar treason trials of William Joyce (Lord Haw-Haw) and others, for the *New Yorker.* Fellow of Saybrook College, Yale University. Made cameo appearance in film "Reds," 1981.

MEMBER: Royal Society of Literature (fellow), American Academy of Arts and Sciences, (honorary member), Oxford and Cambridge Club, Lansdowne Club.

AWARDS, HONORS: Order of St. Sava, 1937; Women's Press Club Award for Journalism, 1948; named Commander of the British Empire, 1949; Chevalier of the Legion of Honor, 1957; named Dame Commander of the British Empire, 1959; D.Litt. from New York University, 1965, and Edinburgh University, 1980; Benson Medal from Royal Society of Literature, 1966; Book of the Year Award from *Yorkshire Post,* 1966, for *The Birds Fall Down.*

WRITINGS:

Henry James, Holt, 1916, reprinted, Norwood, 1978.
The Return of the Soldier (novel), Century, 1918, reprinted, Dial, 1982.
The Judge (novel), Doran, 1922, reprinted, Dial, 1981.
(Editor) Carl Sandburg, *Selected Poems,* Harcourt, 1926, reprinted, 1960.
The Strange Necessity (literary essays), Doubleday, 1928, reprinted, Scholarly Press, 1974.
(Author of text under pseudonym Lynx) *Lions and Lambs,* illustrated by David Low, Harcourt, 1929.
Harriet Hume: A London Fantasy (novel), Doubleday, 1929, reprinted, Dial, 1982.
D. H. Lawrence, Martin Secker, 1930, reprinted, Folcroft, 1973, limited autographed edition published as *Elegy,* Phoenix Book Shop, 1930.
Arnold Bennett Himself (monograph), John Day, 1931, reprinted, Folcroft 1973.

Ending in Earnest: A Literary Log (collection of essays), Doubleday, 1931, reprinted, Books for Libraries, 1967.

St. Augustine (biography), Appleton, 1933, reprinted, Darby, 1979.

A Letter to a Grandfather (monograph), Hogarth, 1933.

The Modern "Rake's Progress," illustrated by Low, Hutchinson, 1934, reprinted, Folcroft, 1978.

The Harsh Voice: Four Short Novels (includes "Life Sentence," "There Is No Conversation," "The Salt of the Earth," and "The Abiding Vision"), Doubleday, 1935, reprinted, Virago, 1982.

The Thinking Reed (novel), Viking, 1936, reprinted, Penguin, 1982.

Black Lamb and Grey Falcon: The Record of a Journey through Yugoslavia, two volumes, Macmillan, 1937, published as *Black Lamb and Grey Falcon: A Journey through Yugoslavia,* Viking, 1941, revised edition, 1977.

The Meaning of Treason (Book-of-the-Month Club selection), Viking, 1947, revised edition, 1964, also published as *The New Meaning of Treason,* 1964, reprinted under original title, Virago, 1982.

A Train of Powder (political and social essays), Viking, 1955.

The Fountain Overflows (first novel in a trilogy; Literary Guild selection; Book Club choice in England), Viking, 1956, reprinted, Pan Books, 1979.

The Court and the Castle: Some Treatments of a Recurrent Theme, Yale University Press, 1957 (published in England as *The Court and the Castle: A Study of the Interactions of Political and Religious Ideas in Imaginative Literature,* Macmillan, 1957).

The Vassall Affair, Sunday Telegraph (London), 1963.

The Birds Fall Down (novel; Book-of-the-Month Club selection), Viking, 1966.

McLuhan and the Future of Literature, Oxford University Press, 1969.

Rebecca West: A Celebration, introduction by Samuel Hynes, Viking, 1977.

The Young Rebecca: Writings of Rebecca West, 1911-1917, edited by Jane Marcus, Viking, 1982.

1900, Viking, 1982.

This Real Night (second novel in a trilogy), Viking, 1984.

Cousin Rosamund (third novel in a trilogy), Viking, 1986.

Sunflower, Viking, 1987.

Family Memories, Viking, 1988.

Contributor to numerous books. Regular reviewer for *Sunday Telegraph* (London), beginning in 1931. Contributor to British and American periodicals, including *Harper's, New York Herald Tribune, New Yorker, Vogue,* and *Times* (London).

SIDELIGHTS: Rebecca West was best known as a journalist, but to designate her so is both to diminish and to distort her achievement as a writer. She was a great journalist; she was also a feminist, a book reviewer and literary critic, a novelist, a biographer, a social satirist, and a travel writer. She was eclectic in her interests, and her writing reflects this eclecticism. Though varied, her work is characterized by a literary style of remarkable clarity and vigor, a constant interest in what it means to be a woman, and, as Samuel Hynes quotes in his introduction to *Rebecca West: A Celebration,* a desire to "celebrate communion with reality," whether that reality is the immediate physicality of existence or the more difficult problem of the human continuum and how one fits into it.

Christened Cicily Fairfield, the youngest of three daughters born to Charles and Isabella Fairfield, she had a childhood filled with intellectual stimulation but marred by poverty and instability,

the death of her father, and her own attacks of tuberculosis. Both her parents were gifted, her father with words and ideas, particularly those relating to politics, and her mother with music. Cicily was born and spent her early childhood in London, then accompanied her mother and sisters to Edinburgh where Cicily finished her education. Her father died alone in Liverpool, and a few years later the family moved back to London. There Cicily entered the Royal Academy of Dramatic Art. Her talents proved ill suited to acting, but she stayed long enough to play the part of Rebecca West in Ibsen's *Rosmersholm,* a play she later characterized as "the 'Hamlet' of the revolutionary intellectual movement," in a 1919 London *Daily News* article. Thus she found the name she made her own.

West began her career as an author very much in the spirit of the name she had adopted. She joined the staff of the *Freewoman,* a militantly feminist publication, as a reviewer of books. This was not a matter of happenstance. She was committed already to the Suffragist movement, and she was aware of her talent with language. As she stated in a 1955 *Saturday Review* interview with Bernard Kalb, "I write because all my family do, it is in the blood." The books she reviewed were heterogeneous, but she tested whatever came to hand both as a literary statement and as a comment about women. Since she held strong opinions on both topics and had no fear of expressing them in often witty and memorable language, she quickly was recognized as a new literary personality. Mrs. Humphrey Ward, a formidable member of the literary establishment and a foe of the Suffragists, was one of her first targets. H. G. Wells was another, but he was so intrigued by her clever audacity that he sought her out. Thus began the liaison that resulted in the birth of their son Anthony West in August 1914.

In 1912, West moved to the *Clarion,* a popular socialist newspaper that she found compatible to her feminist interests. There she published essays that rank "among the finest" produced by anyone in this turbulent period of the British feminist movement, according to Jane Marcus in *The Young Rebecca.* These essays are graphic, filled with urgency and brash frankness. Many recount West's reactions to the sometimes violent strategies of the Suffragists and the even more violent reactions of the government. Others contain her equally sharp reactions to publications on topics West thought had feminist significance: women's suffrage foremost, but also economic, legal, professional, and social equality for women. Her ideas were often unorthodox, but they were always rational and cogent.

When World War I began, the pattern of West's life changed. She had a child to care for. Her relationship with Wells continued, but it was hidden from the public. With the issue of women's suffrage submerged by the British war effort, West shifted to literary criticism. Her book review column became a biweekly feature of the London *Daily News and Leader,* and in time her work also began to appear in *Time and Tide, New Statesman,* and *Outlook.* Her book reviews reflected her omnivorous reading, which centered in fiction but also included a large sampling of drama, criticism, biography, history, and sociology. West's association with *Time and Tide* began when that periodical was still a new profeminist, leftist journal: it was created by Lady Rhondda, also an activist in the Suffragist movement, who controlled and subsidized the publication for many years. West's connection with this journal was closer and more enduring than with any other. Her reviews in the *New Statesman* under the general heading "Notes on Novels" (1920-1922) were of such quality that Frank Swinnerton described them as models of excellence. He singled them out in *The Georgian Scene:* "I doubt whether any such brilliant reviews of novels were ever seen before; they certainly have not been seen since. . . ." Later, in *Ending in Earnest,* West characterized this decade of her most active book reviewing (1915-1925) as one in which little fiction of lasting worth was produced, a statement that makes Swinnerton's estimate of her achievement that much more remarkable. Her remark could also help explain why she earned the reputation of being a demanding, acerbic reviewer. An anonymous writer in the *Atheneum* described that reputation as follows: "It is said that some otherwise courageous novelists either blench or are struck into inarticulate fury at the mention of her name." Hugh Walpole was one of her targets, and he feared her. She also found larger targets, including Strindberg and Tolstoy, who were attacked for feminist reasons. But all was not negative; D. H. Lawrence and Virginia Woolf were among those she admired.

It was not long before West's name became known in the United States, her first essay there appearing in the premier issue of the *New Republic.* Later in that same journal, she published a series of essays with the composite title "World's Worst Failure," in which she attacked the timidity and incompetence of British women; she soon followed this series with "Women in England" in the *Atlantic Monthly.* In 1923 and 1924 West made a lecture tour to the United States, speaking on the topic "Woman's View of Life's Problems." That tour was almost aborted before it began because she heard that her relationship with Wells had activated an effort to hold her at Ellis Island. Her tour, however, was a success, resulting in more opportunities for publication in the United States. The most important offer came from the *New York Herald Tribune,* which, from 1926 to 1932, published a series of critical essays that are among the best of West's work of this kind. Characteristically, these essays are not so much reactions to something just read as they are thoughtful portraits of authors she had been contemplating for a long time. Of these writers, the most provocative are a group from the previous generation that she called her "uncles": George Bernard Shaw, Arnold Bennett, John Galsworthy, and H. G. Wells. They were an interesting amalgam both of what she had inherited and what she was rebelling against. Like her, they represented change, but they were still "uncles" and thus less responsive to the changes that she, a woman, desired.

In this period when West was most active as a reviewer (1916-1931), she also produced three books and a monograph of criticism, three novels, and, in collaboration with David Low, a volume of satiric portrayals of contemporary personalities. The first of the critical studies, *Henry James* (1916), was West's first book. Published in the year of James's death, it is unusual for several reasons. In her work for the *Freewoman* and the *Clarion,* West had not indicated any strong interest in the fiction of James; for her to choose his work for her first book thus seems a departure from her primary interests. Also, in 1915 H. G. Wells's *Boon* had featured a violent attack on James and his concept of art. For West to have published in the following year a study basically supportive of James suggested an anomaly in her relationship with Wells. Whatever its purpose, the book contrasted with the generally indifferent temper of Jamesian criticism of that period and still remains a study scholars consider. In *1900,* West reaffirmed her respect for James as an artist, and those, like Peter Wolfe, who have studied her fiction have found there evidence of James's influence, both in theme and technique.

The other two books of criticism, *The Strange Necessity* (1928) and *Ending in Earnest* (1931), are mostly distillations of her decade and one-half of reviewing books, reprints of what she considered her best critical work. The final item of literary criticism, her monograph *D. H. Lawrence: An Elegy* (1930), recounts a meeting with the author in Florence. In it, she celebrates those

qualities of his she admired: his literary genius, his attacks on sexual taboos, his joy of life.

The three novels West published in this period, like the rest of her fiction, differ markedly each from the other. As a writer of fiction West has elicited widely differing responses. Peter Wolfe in *Rebecca West: Artist and Thinker* found most lacking "the yarn spinner's or raconteur's gift for fresh, crisp narrative" and concluded that although in some parts her novels may be brilliant, they fail in their overall effect. In contrast, *Critique: Studies in Modern Fiction* contributor Turner Kobler judged her novels "fascinating in comparison to each other but each a work of art complete and beautiful in itself." Mollie Panter-Downes expressed reservations in her 1977 *New Yorker* article but gave West the benefit of the doubt, noting "it seems possible that this is too large an imagination to be contained in a tidy, conventional frame of fiction."

The first of West's novels, *The Return of the Soldier* (1916), employs what for the time was an original device, amnesia from shell shock, and an unusual perspective on the war, that of those who waited at home. These elements permit West to explore the reactions of three women to a returning soldier who, though married, remembers only an earlier, idyllic love for another woman. The novel describes the women's efforts to bring him back to reality, an act which would mean his return to war and possible death. This is the shortest of West's novels, and although it may be "composed entirely of the fictional cliches of its time," as Martin Green declared in a 1977 *Saturday Review* essay, it remains her most frequently reprinted novel.

The Judge (1922) is a much larger, more ambitious work. Kobler labels it "a long, untidy novel raw with power and pain" and compares it with Hardy's fiction. Its epigraph—"Every mother is a judge who sentences the children for the sins of the father"—expresses the dour theme of the novel and provides evidence of West's conviction that women may nurture love and life but that the nature of men is to frustrate both. Committed to her theme, West permits no happy outcome for her central character, Ellen Melville, who, though more confident of the value of reason than of feeling, is drawn into the destructive vortex created by the man she loves. In *The Novels of Rebecca West: A Complex Unity,* Sister Mary Orlich found the novel flawed by a melodramatic murder and lapses in dialogue, but offered a generally favorable estimate. Patrick Braybrooke's judgment in *Novelists We Are Seven* was less favorable. He disliked "the solid blocks of very close print in which Miss West indulges," which he thought were "not only extremely irritating but tend to obscure the meaning." A strength of West's essays, her ability to explain and comment, becomes a fault in most of her fiction.

Harriet Hume: A London Fantasy (1929) represents a radical departure for West. In this narrative she tries to move away from the somber realism of her first two novels toward a more fanciful, more imaginative embodiment of idea. As in her previous fiction, however, the female and male principles are pitted in contest against each other. The female is allied with music, the male with politics. The female can love with a single-minded, direct purpose that the male, caught between his personal love and his public commitment, lacks; he thus can betray his personal avowal. H. G. Wells's praise of this novel, in a letter to West, seems extravagant. Although she often pursued the intricacies of abstraction as well as anyone, West failed to breathe fictive life into these abstractions in *Harriet Hume.*

In David Low, her collaborator on *Lions and Lambs* (1929), West found someone with a mischievous impiety that she, who tended to look more soberly at the world, was hard pressed to match, sharp-tongued as she may have been. Low makes one laugh; West is more apt to wound. The book is a series of pictorial and verbal portraits of contemporaries, some important, some less important, but all recognizable. For what the book reveals about West, the most important item is probably her comment on Clemence Dane, who to West characterized that fault in female novelists she considered most common and deadly—their tendency to be what the public thinks they should be instead of being true to themselves. Looking at Low's sketch of Clemence Dane, one may read West's comment as satiric, but it is too basic to West's fundamental feminist convictions to be dismissed so lightly. Yet, on the whole, West and Low worked so well together they later created a second book, *The Modern "Rake's Progress"* (1934).

The shift from the 1920s to the 1930s seemed to mark an ending and a beginning in West's professional life; so too did this break affect her private life. From the early 1920s her relationship with Wells had deteriorated. Both Gordon Ray in *H. G. Wells and Rebecca West* and Anthony West in *H. G. Wells: Aspects of a Life* have detailed that deterioration, though they are not in agreement as to its cause. A central issue was the custody and education of young Anthony West, and the acrimony aroused had lasting effects on all three of them. According to Anthony West, the basic incompatibility of his parents doomed their relationship from the beginning. His mother, however, saw her first trip to the United States as the turning point, claiming that her constant motive, from about 1923 on, was to establish her independence from Wells. Through the rest of the 1920s West's writing reflected the increasingly cosmopolitan nature of her life. Her series in the *New York Herald Tribune* required her frequent absence from Britain, and the essays she wrote for the newspaper touch equally on American and English topics. Moreover, her series of "letters" in the *Bookman* (1929-30) are written as often from the Continent as they are from London. All this activity and travel meant new situations and relationships, more public recognition, and a greater assurance in her literary craft. In 1930 she married Henry Maxwell Andrews, a banker, who, judging from the portrait she drew of him in *Black Lamb and Grey Falcon,* provided West order and contentment. The couple lived in Ibstone House, near High Wycombe and led a relatively quiet life.

During the early 1930s West was active preparing a series of book reviews for the London *Daily Telegraph* and a series of anecdotal essays for Hearst's New York *American.* The fact that she was hired by the Hearst newspaper to boost its sagging subscription list is evidence of her growing fame as a journalist. By early 1934 she had completed both of these projects, and from then until the end of World War II she published fewer periodical pieces than in any previous period of her career. When she did publish it was mostly in *Time and Tide.* For that journal she prepared in 1935 a short series of articles on political life in Washington, one of which contains a memorable sketch of Huey Long that catches his feral energy.

If she was less active in the journals and newspapers, she made up for it in books. Her name appeared frequently as a contributor of chapters and introductions to books, and the subjects she wrote on are as varied as the titles. Her tribute to Mrs. Emmeline Pankhurst, a well-known English suffragist, in *The Post Victorians* is memorable, as is her contribution to *I Believe,* edited by Clifton Fadiman. The most consistent element in her writing of this period is a shift of interest to political questions activated by the disturbing rise of dictators in Italy and Germany. This focus is apparent, for example, in her discussions of the Spanish Civil War. She was seeking answers to problems more pressing and

general than those related to feminism, problems that seemed to her to threaten the world she knew. She thought the answers might lie in history.

She began her exploration of history with a short, popular biography, *St. Augustine* (1933), which only begins to suggest the absorbing interest this fourth-century bishop held for her. "Every phrase I read of his," she wrote in *Black Lamb and Grey Falcon,* "sounds in my ears like the sentence of my doom and the doom of my age." West saw Augustine's perception of human nature as still alive in her world, even in herself. It was something primitive, an element in man that had, as she wrote in her comment on Kipling's work, "crawled out of the dark uncharted sea of our common humanity." Or stated differently in one of her comments on St. Augustine, "It seemed to him as if humanity was saturated with the obscene, not by reason of what it did but of what it was." Such a view of human nature provides nothing secure on which to build; whatever man's achievements, they are realized in defiance of rather than as a result of his nature. West also saw historical parallels between Augustine's age and her own; both were sliding into chaos. History was pointed towards disaster. It is doubtful that many readers of *St. Augustine* would have seen West's larger purpose in writing it, but when read in the context of *A Letter to a Grandfather* (1933), *The Thinking Reed* (1936), and that hard-to-characterize masterwork *Black Lamb and Grey Falcon* (1941), the darker theme running through it emerges more clearly.

The monograph *A Letter to a Grandfather,* which in *The Itinerant Ivory Tower* Hutchinson described as "terrifying and marvelous," is West's effort to understand her era better through an examination of England's spiritual history. In method it is, like *Harriet Hume,* a fantasy, though much darker than that novel; the monograph ends with an image of Christ stretched on the cross of existence, attempting to know and feel all but unable to find any ultimate answers. *The Thinking Reed,* a novel about an American woman married to a French industrialist, was West's attempt to portray in realistic fiction the decadence and disintegration apparent in the world she knew, including its obtuseness to the heightening menace of the dictatorships in Germany and Italy. The political and social realities of the time are more explicitly stated in this work than in any of her other fiction except, perhaps, *The Harsh Voice* (1935), a collection of West's short stories previously published in magazines. She approached her topic in *The Thinking Reed* from what Hutchinson defined as a "necessary condition of [her] work," the "antinomy of Innocence and Experience." More specifically, she used here the pattern Henry James made central to much of his fiction, the innocent American trying to come to terms with a European society West described as "wild boars and pythons." The society she portrayed was intent on its own pleasures and oblivious to the anarchic forces that finally would destroy it. Devotion to those one loved and adherence to those modes of civilization that brought order, harmony, and joy were the only possible bulwarks against chaos. Containing as pessimistic a conclusion as the final image in *A Letter to a Grandfather,* the novel suggested hope only through its allusion to the passage from Pascal from which West derived her title: "Man is but a reed, the most feeble thing in nature; but he is a thinking reed."

Near the end of *Black Lamb and Grey Falcon* West stated her reasons for writing this work, the last of her efforts to understand pre-World-War-II Europe: "I resolved to put on paper what a typical Englishwoman felt and thought in the late nineteen-thirties when, already convinced of the inevitability of the second Anglo-German war, she had been able to follow the dark waters of that event back to its source." For this most ambitious effort, two volumes in length, West chose as her subject Yugoslavia, a country she found one of the most diverse and culturally complex in Europe. It brought together the two Catholic traditions St. Augustine had seen falling into chaos. It was European, yet not a part of the advanced industrial development that West believed had spawned many of Europe's problems. In Yugoslavia she found history with continuity. However, she also found a study in contradictions. And to readers in Western Europe, Yugoslavia was largely unknown, a backwash of old empires. Here West could try to weave together all those threads she saw running in a crazy pattern through the rest of Europe.

The book is held together by pivotal events and the places in which they occurred: an assassination in Sarajevo, an ancient ritual near Skolpje, another assassination in Belgrade, a battle at Kossovo. Walking about these places, West contemplated the buildings and streets, the contour of the countryside, the memorials; she simultaneously made the historical events that occurred there spring to life. She presented history as experienced by those who still lived in Yugoslavia and as felt by her.

Hynes considered *Black Lamb and Grey Falcon* to be conclusive in two senses. "It stands at the end of the 1930s like a massive baroque cenotaph" and also provides "in its majestic scale an answer to the notion that the proper scale of a woman's imagination should be 'a little bit (two inches wide) of Ivory' [in Jane Austen's famous phrase]". As Louis Namier recognized in *Facing East,* it is a book difficult to summarize or evaluate: "its merit is in its totality, in which blemishes vanish and the human element conquers." In West's *New York Times* obituary, Diana Trilling judged it as "surely one of the very greatest books of the last 50 years."

One conclusion West drew from her experience in Yugoslavia was that "the nationalism which the intellectuals of my age agreed to consider a vice" was not a vice at all. For these South Slavs, their consciousness of being Serbs or Bosnians or Croats had been their wellspring of survival. Central to the positive side of West's thought was her statement: "Every human being is of sublime value, because his experience, which must be in some measure unique, gives him a unique view of reality, and the sum of such views should go far to giving us the complete picture of reality, which the human race must attain if it is ever to comprehend its destiny." As with the individual, so with the nation. For her, then, Yugoslavia was a lesson in the iniquity of empire and in the virtue of a nationalistic ideal. It was a lesson, too, in what the individual's participation in a larger association of human beings, with their own language and customs, contributed to his sense of well being, his unique view of reality.

This insight from *Black Lamb and Grey Falcon* is central to West's next book, *The Meaning of Treason* (1947). Six years intervened between the two books. At the end of the war, when British courts began to bring to trial those men who had betrayed their country, West realized that they exemplified the opposite side of what she had admired in Yugoslavia. She drew the title of her book from her earlier *Harper's* essay of the same name, in which she defined her own understanding of treason. Using this essay as the prefatory statement for her book, she then presented the case histories of the traitors she had observed in the courts. West realized that allegiance—what it is and how and to what or whom it is given—is a topic of particular significance in the twentieth century. She sat through the trials and wrote her book because she feared that otherwise these court cases would not get the attention they deserved. Her studies concentrated on the psychological characteristics of the traitors; she asked herself what caused these people to do what they did. Her long examina-

tion of William Joyce, better known as Lord Haw Haw, is an example of her method at its best. When the book was published, it became a Book-of-the-Month Club selection. In his *Saturday Review of Literature* assessment, Struthers Burt described it as "the most admirable and important book Miss West has written."

However, soon after this first version of *The Meaning of Treason* appeared, its author realized that all the facts were not in. New traitors were uncovered, but this time they were not making propaganda for an alien Nazi Germany, they were spying for an alien Communist Soviet Union. So West revised her book, deleting old material and adding new, until finally it emerged in 1964 as *The New Meaning of Treason.* Since the end of World War II the scandal of Communist spies in high places has caused recurrent shocks in the British government, and the literature written about it is extensive. It is a tribute to West's acumen that she recognized the importance of the topic so early.

West wrote much more on treason and related topics in various periodicals. Some of this material she collected in two books, *A Train of Powder* (1955) and *The Vassall Affair* (1963). The courtroom atmosphere of *The Meaning of Treason* is present again in *A Train of Powder.* Although it contains two essays on the development of political awareness in postwar Germany, the book focuses primarily on trials: for war crimes at Nuremberg, for a racially motivated murder in South Carolina, for a greed-inspired killing in London, and—again—for treason of various kinds. West's ability to bring these courtroom dramas to life, to make their participants live on the page, enhanced her reputation as one of the greatest journalists of her period. Telford Taylor, U.S. Chief Counsel at the Nuremberg trials, began his *Saturday Review* appraisal of this book with the statement, "If words can paint, Rebecca West's do." As a lawyer, he paid her as well a professional compliment: "With all her literary attainments Miss West is also an exceedingly good lawyer." *The Vassall Affair,* her report of a young Englishman who spied for the Soviets, can be read as an addendum to *The New Meaning of Treason.* The report primarily illustrates how demoralizing the discovery of these spies was to the British government's confidence in its own integrity and its ability to function in the country's best interests.

A final example of West's interest in treason's many faces is her novel *The Birds Fall Down* (1966). Instead of using an example from the gallery of traitors she had observed in the British courtrooms, she drew upon the story of a double agent from czarist Russia, Ievno Azeff, who was both an informant for the secret police and a leader of a terrorist band. The novel West creates out of this double betrayal concludes with the deaths of both the traitor and a friend he betrayed. Told through the consciousness of a young girl, the story is as much about how her innocent involvement in events affects her as it is about the entanglement of loyalties and betrayals among the adults. If West is making here a final comment on treason, it would seem to be twofold: that ours is a century that fosters deception and betrayal and that we are all involved—including the innocents, who may be in more mortal danger than the rest of us. In *Book Week* Emile Capouya praised the novel as "a fascinating story, so contracted in time and focus as to resemble a thriller rather than a conventional novel, but a thriller infinitely superior in style and imaginative power to most of the breed"; *New York Times* contributor Charles Poore called it "a superb novel in the grand manner."

During the 1950s and 1960s West was not entirely absorbed, however, in the topic of treason. When asked to present the Terry Lectures at Yale University, she returned to an earlier interest, literary criticism. For her topic she took as her cue a statement by Paul Valery: "Our greatest authors have nearly always written only about the court." Her lectures were later amplified and published as *The Court and the Castle* (1957). As West used the term *court,* in its narrowest sense it is the seat of government, more broadly it is society. The castle is the castle of God. Beginning with Shakespeare and ending with Kafka, she traced the evolving relationship of the courtier, the individual, to these external forces.

West also published a novel during this period, *The Fountain Overflows* (1956). In her interview with Bernard Kalb, she expressed a peculiarly obsessed attitude toward this work. She had sat down, she said, to write a long short story, but she had not been able to keep it within those bounds: "It is now 400,000 words long, and it takes a family from the cradle to what I sometimes fear will be my grave." West was referring here to the larger, three-part work of which *The Fountain Overflows* is only the first volume. The reason for West's inability to control the growth of her story would appear to lie in its autobiographical content. Much of *The Fountain Overflows* parallels the events and characters of her own childhood. Her father had died when she was a child, her mother when West was twenty-eight, so the normal relations between the generations were cut short. She always expressed admiration for her mother, but early in her career she wrote "I Regard Marriage with Fear and Loathing," an essay about her father that is a bitter statement of what she saw then as his failure both as a husband and father. When she was seventy years old she wrote a second essay about her father for the *Sunday Telegraph,* an essay that is much more charitable, more understanding, an expression of both the affection and admiration she had come to feel for him. The emotional reevaluation of her childhood evident in this second essay is present as well in her novel.

The parents of this novel are the overflowing fountain in which their children, a son and three daughters, are immersed. One of the daughters, Rose, narrates the story, which is basically about the mother's struggle to rear and educate her children. The father gives lavishly of his affection but is little help financially. Towards the end of the novel he deserts his family, and his wife struggles on without him. Music is the art celebrated in this novel; the mother is its source and the children try to emulate her. Their success or failure as musicians becomes the basis for judging them. On the dust jacket of the Viking Press book club edition, West described the book's theme as "the way that human beings look at each other inquisitively, trying to make out what is inside the opaque human frame." She then went on to comment that she had merely written the book, which did not signify that she was the best authority on its meaning. Both the way she composed it and the material she used suggest that she, then past sixty years of age, was making fiction of sensitive realities she would not or could not have used earlier. The sequel to *The Fountain Overflows,* titled *This Real Night,* was a subject Rebecca West often spoke of when interviewed in later years, and a part of it appeared in *Rebecca West: A Celebration,* but the novel was not published in its entirety until the fall of 1984, a year and a half after her death. (She did not finish the third and concluding volume.) A popular success when it appeared, *The Fountain Overflows* was the choice of a book club and *Saturday Review*'s Book of the Week. In his *Saturday Review* assessment, James Gray characterized it as a novel of nostalgia and thought its chief triumph to be that "it looks with a steady, unintimidated eye at the huge, humorous, disturbing spectacle of human experience." Recognizing the autobiographical element in the book, Harvey Curtis Webster commented in his *Saturday Review* inter-

view with West: "Facts may be the basis but they are transformed, distilled, distorted aesthetically."

For West these postwar years were as professionally fruitful as one could expect, considering that during the whole period, her husband suffered from a painful disease that required their remaining at Ibstone House until his death in 1968. The marriage was a happy one, full of mutual affection, and West did what she could to comfort her husband and alleviate his suffering. After Henry Maxwell Andrews's death she moved back to London.

Back in London, West remained busy, but her interests became increasingly retrospective. She oversaw the preparation of *H. G. Wells and Rebecca West* (1974) by Gordon N. Ray. She helped select the work included in *Rebecca West: a Celebration* (1977). She worked closely with Jane Marcus in the preparation of *The Young Rebecca* (1982). She tried also to bring her fictional trilogy to completion, and, moving further back in memory, prepared a memoir of her mother and father. Her last book published while she was still living, *1900* (1982), appeared when she was ninety years old. It is a miscellany of topics pertinent to the year 1900, with pictures and a text by her. Some of her comments are personal reminiscences, but most of them fully reflect the strengths of her best writing: a sharp wit, striking images, an ability to reduce complexities to a comprehensible form.

Holding the mass and variety of West's work together is her passion to experience and understand life fully. When she was a young, ardent feminist she fought for the right to do with her life what she wished, a right she thought was being denied her because she was a woman. Later, when she felt that that battle had lost its urgency, she sought to understand what had caused her world to be as anarchic as it was and found answers in her reading of history and her probing of human nature. Finally, her gaze turned introspective. Characteristically, in this long search, she looked first at the real world, recorded it and tried to reduce it to understandable formulae, then judged it, then let it lie in her mind until she could transform it into fiction.

West's literary production was so varied and at times so unorthodox that attempting to restrain her within any conventional category would do her an injustice. It would be better to ask such questions as "Was she widely read in her lifetime?" and "Did her writing influence significantly those who read it?" and "Will her books continue to be read?" She did have a large reading audience, though its composition shifted from book to book. The readers attracted to *The Fountain Overflows* were not the same as those who sought out *The Meaning of Treason.* As a consequence, she might be thought of by most readers as a one or possibly two-book author. As a novelist she was popular, but her influence was minimal, if for no other reason than that she was not technically innovative. As a book reviewer West had great impact. Since her major targets were shoddy writing and sloppy thinking, her influence was generally beneficial, as painful as it may have been for her victims. Her unorthodoxy, her unwillingness to work within any particular critical method, and her failure to attract imitators makes her criticism singular. She thus will be read for her evaluations of particular authors, not for any critical theory she advanced.

West's wider influence was sociological and political. In her day her opinions on feminism were sought, but most modern feminists seem either uninterested in or unaware of her. The beginnings of a resurgence may have begun with the collection of her early feminist writings made by Jane Marcus who, in urging contemporary feminists to read the essays, stated that "they will be surprised to discover how much of what she wrote . . . remains up-to-date, relevant to our own aspirations." West's efforts in the

1930s to raise British awareness to the growing menace in Central Europe did not change British government policy, but hindsight shows that she was right. Her attempt to create public awareness of treason had more effect. She arrived early at fundamental conclusions that would have saved the British Establishment great embarrassment and anguish if it had taken her advice. She valued allegiance as much as anyone, but her reading of human nature made her suspicious of misplaced or unexamined loyalties, whether they were to an ideology or to an individual.

The ability to recognize what is important at the moment is a characteristic of a great journalist, which is a reason why the term *journalist* so often is attached to West. Victoria Glendinning noted this quality when she wrote in the *New Republic:* "Rebecca West's vision, as it always has, picks out the facts that are really important." But the term *journalist* also has an ephemeral quality that West often transcends. Thus William Shawn could comment in the *New York Times:* "No one in this century . . . looked at the intricacies of human character and the ways of the world more intelligently." She may be remembered, like Robert Burton and T. E. Lawrence, as a writer of eminence *sui generis,* but she also may serve as that "ideal model for any study of twentieth-century woman" Glendinning considered her to be.

MEDIA ADAPTATIONS: The Return of the Soldier was produced as a motion picture starring Alan Bates, Julie Christie, Glenda Jackson, and Ann-Margaret by Brent Walker-Barry R. Cooper Productions in association with Skreba Films and released in 1985; an adaptation of West's *The Birds Fall Down* was broadcast on the BBC.

BIOGRAPHICAL/CRITICAL SOURCES:

BOOKS

Allen, Walter, *The Modern Novel in Britain and the United States,* Dutton, 1964.
Beaton, Cecil and Kenneth Tynan, *Persona Grata,* Putnam, 1954.
Braybrooke, Patrick, *Novelists We Are Seven,* C. E. Daniel, 1926.
Collins, Joseph, *The Doctor Looks at Literature,* Doran, 1923.
Contemporary Literary Criticism, Gale, Volume 7, 1977, Volume 9, 1978, Volume 31, 1985, Volume 50, 1988.
Deakin, Motley F., *Rebecca West,* Twayne, 1980.
Dickinson, Lovat, *H. G. Wells: His Turbulent Life and Times,* Atheneum, 1969.
Dictionary of Literary Biography, Volume 36: *British Novelists, 1890-1929: Modernists,* Gale, 1985.
Dictionary of Literary Biography Yearbook: 1983, Gale, 1984.
Hutchinson, G. Evelyn, *The Itinerant Ivory Tower,* Yale University Press, 1953.
Hutchinson, G. Evelyn, *A Preliminary List of the Writings of Rebecca West, 1912-1951,* Yale University Press, 1957.
Mackenzie, Norman and Jeanne Mackenzie, *H. G. Wells,* Simon & Schuster, 1973.
Marcus, Jane, *The Young Rebecca,* Viking, 1982.
Murrow, Edward E., *This I Believe,* Simon & Schuster, 1952.
Namier, Lewis, *Facing East,* Harper, 1966.
Orlich, Sister Mary Margarita, *The Novels of Rebecca West: A Complex Unity,* University Microfilms, 1967.
Ray, Gordon N., *H. G. Wells and Rebecca West,* Yale University Press, 1974.
Redd, Tony, *Rebecca West: Master of Reality,* University of South Carolina Press, 1972.
Swinnerton, Frank, *The Georgian Scene,* Farrar & Rinehart, 1934.

Tindall, William York, *Forces in Modern British Literature: 1885-1956,* Random House, 1956.
West, Anthony, *H. G. Wells: Aspects of a Life,* Random House, 1984.
West, Rebecca, *D. H. Lawrence: An Elegy,* Adelphi, 1930.
West, Rebecca, *Black Lamb and Grey Falcon: The Record of a Journey through Yugoslavia,* two volumes, Macmillan, 1937, published as *Black Lamb and Grey Falcon: A Journey through Yugoslavia,* Viking, 1941.
West, Rebecca, *The Fountain Overflows,* Viking, 1956.
West, Rebecca, *Rebecca West: A Celebration,* introduction by Samuel Hynes, Viking, 1977.
Williams, William Carlos, *Selected Essays of William Carlos Williams,* Random House, 1954.
Wolfe, Peter, *Rebecca West: Artist and Thinker,* Southern Illinois University Press, 1971.
Wolfer, Verena Elsbeth, *Rebecca West: Kunsttheorie und Romanschaffen,* Francke, 1972.
Writers on Themselves, BBC Publications, 1964.

PERIODICALS

Atheneum, July 29, 1922.
Atlantic Monthly, December, 1966.
Bookman, August, 1930.
Book Week, October 2, 1966.
Bulletin of Bibliography, June, 1982.
Chicago Tribune, April 21, 1985.
Chicago Tribune Book World, May 23, 1982, April 20, 1986.
Critique: Studies in Modern Fiction, Volume XIII, number 2, 1971.
Daily Express (London), October 16, 1956.
Daily News (London), August 11, 1919.
Daily Telegraph (London), December 18, 1931, March 7, 1933.
Dial, March 28, 1918.
Encounter, March, 1961.
Hearst's International Cosmopolitan Magazine, November, 1925.
Los Angeles Times, July 24, 1986, April 3, 1987.
Los Angeles Times Book Review, May 2, 1982, April 14, 1985.
Nation, January 4, 1958.
New Republic, November 18, 1916, September 13, 1922, December 10, 1924, June 8, 1953, November 25, 1957, April 22, 1985.
New Statesman, November 4, 1966.
Newsweek, May 17, 1982.
New York, April 3, 1982.
New Yorker, October 25, 1941, October 3, 1977.
New York Herald Tribune Weekly Book Review, April 22, 1956.
New York Review of Books, August 12, 1982.
New York Times, July 8, 1981, May 28, 1982, March 16, 1983, February 15, 1985, March 23, 1985.
New York Times Book Review, August 20, 1922, November 3, 1929, December 14, 1947, December 9, 1956, October 2, 1977, August 18, 1985, February 15, 1987, July 31, 1988.
Partisan Review, July, 1949.
Redbook, March, 1964.
St. Petersburg Times, October 30, 1966.
Saturday Review, March 19, 1955, December 8, 1956, November 12, 1966, October 15, 1977.
Saturday Review of Literature, April 29, 1933, December 7, 1947.
Southern Review, Volume II, 1936-37.
Sunday Telegraph (London), December 30, 1962.
Sunday Times (London), July 19, 1956.
Time, December 8, 1947.

Times (London), September 1, 1975, February 18, 1982, March 4, 1982, December 6, 1982, October 3, 1985.
Times Literary Supplement, February 8, 1957, December 21, 1973, November 22, 1974, October 18, 1985, July 25, 1986, November 20, 1987.
Tribune Books (Chicago), February 8, 1987, April 10, 1988.
Washington Post, March 31, 1987.
Washington Post Book World, May 2, 1982, April 7, 1985.

OBITUARIES:

PERIODICALS

Chicago Tribune, March 16, 1983, March 20, 1983.
Los Angeles Times, March 16, 1983.
Newsweek, March 28, 1983.
New York Times, March 16, 1983.
Time, March 28, 1983.

*   *   *

WESTMACOTT, Mary
See CHRISTIE, Agatha (Mary Clarissa)

*   *   *

WESTON, Allen
See NORTON, Andre

*   *   *

WHARTON, Edith (Newbold Jones) 1862-1937

PERSONAL: Born January 24 (some sources say 23), 1862 (some sources say 1861), in New York, N.Y.; died of a cardiac attack, August 11, 1937, in St. Brice-sous-Foret, France; buried in Versailles, France, next to Walter Berry; daughter of George Frederic (heir to merchant-ship fortune) and Lucretia Stevens (Rhinelander) Jones; married Edward Robbins Wharton (a banker), 1885 (divorced, 1912). *Education:* Educated privately in New York and Europe.

CAREER: American novelist, poet, and short story writer. *War-time service:* Organized American committee of Red Cross in Paris, France, and worked on behalf of Belgian refugees during World War I.

MEMBER: National Institute of Arts and Letters, 1930-37; American Academy of Arts and Letters, 1934-37.

AWARDS, HONORS: Pulitzer Prize, 1921, for *The Age of Innocence;* D. Litt., Yale University, 1923; Nobel Prize nomination, 1927; Gold Medal, National Institute of Arts and Letters; Cross of the Legion of Honor (France); Chevalier of the Order of Leopold (Belgium); Montyon Prize, French Academy.

WRITINGS:

NOVELS

The Valley of Decision, Scribner, 1902.
Sanctuary, Scribner, 1903.
The House of Mirth (also see below), Scribner, 1905, new edition with forward by Marcia Davenport, 1951, reprinted, Macmillan, 1987.
Madame de Treymes, Scribner, 1907.
The Fruit of the Tree, Scribner, 1907, reprinted, Virago, 1988.
Ethan Frome (also see below), Scribner, 1911, new edition, 1938, reprinted with author's introduction, 1960, reprinted, Penguin, 1988.
The Custom of the Country, Scribner, 1913.

The Reef, Scribner, 1913, reprinted, 1985.
Summer (also see below), Scribner, 1917.
The Marne, Appleton, 1918.
The Age of Innocence, Meredith, 1920.
The Glimpses of the Moon, Appleton, 1922.
A Son at the Front, Scribner, 1923.
Old New York: False Dawn (The 'Forties), The Old Maid (The 'Fifties), The Spark (The 'Sixties), New Year's Day (The 'Seventies) (four short novels), Scribner, 1924, reprinted, Virago, 1988.
The Mother's Recompense, Appleton, 1925, reprinted, Virago, 1988.
Twilight Sleep, Appleton, 1927.
The Children, Meredith, 1928, reprinted, Virago, 1988, published as *The Marriage Playground,* 1930.
Hudson River Bracketed, Meredith, 1929, reprinted, Virago, 1988.
The Gods Arrive (sequel to *Hudson River Bracketed*), Meredith, 1932, reprinted, Virago, 1988.
The Buccaneers (unfinished), Appleton-Century, 1938.
Ethan Frome [and] *Summer,* with introduction by Michael Millgate, Constable, 1965.
The Edith Wharton Omnibus (includes *The Age of Innocence, Ethan Frome,* and *Old New York*), Scribners, 1978.
The House of Mirth; The Reef; The Custom of the Country; The Age of Innocence, edited by R. W. B. Lewis, Cambridge University Press, 1988.
Madame de Treymes and Others, Virago, 1988.

SHORT STORIES

The Greater Inclination (includes "The Muse's Tragedy," "A Journey," "The Pelican," "Souls Belated," "A Coward," "The Twilight of the God," "A Cup of Cold Water," and "The Portrait"), Scribner, 1899.
Crucial Instances (includes "The Duchess at Prayer," "The Angel at the Grave," "The Recovery," " 'Copy:' A Dialogue," "The Rembrandt," "The Moving Finger," and "The Confessional"), Scribner, 1901.
The Descent of Man, and Other Stories (includes "The Mission of Jane," "The Other Two," "The Quicksand," "The Dilletante," "The Reckoning," "Expiation," "The Lady's Maid's Bell," and "A Venetian Lady's Entertainment"), Scribner, 1904.
The Hermit and the Wild Woman and Other Stories (includes "The Last Asset," "In Trust," "The Pretext," "The Verdict," "The Potboiler," and "The Best Man"), Scribner, 1908.
Xingu and Other Stories (includes "Xingu," "Coming Home," "Autres temps . . .," "Kerfol," "The Long Run," "The Triumph of Night," "The Choice," and "The Bunner Sisters"), Scribner, 1916.
Here and Beyond (includes "Miss Mary Pask," "The Young Gentleman," "Bewitched," "The Seed of the Faith," "The Temperate Zone," and "Velvet Ear-Pads"), Appleton, 1926.
Certain People ("Atrophy," "A Bottle of Perrier," "After Holbein," "Dieu d'Amour," "The Refugees," and "Mr. Jones"), Appleton, 1930.
Human Nature (includes "Her Son," "The Day of the Funeral," "A Glimpse," "Joy in the House," and "Diagnosis"), Appleton, 1933.
The World Over (includes "Charm Incorporated," "Pomegranate Seed," "Permanent Wave," "Confession," "Roman Fever," "The Looking-glass," and "Duration"), Appleton-Century, 1936.

Ghosts (includes "All Souls," "The Eyes," "Afterward," "The Lady's Maid's Bell," "Reform," "The Triumph of Night," "Mrs. Mary Pask," "Bewitched," "Mr. Jones," "Pomegranate Seed," and "A Bottle of Perrier"), Appleton-Century, 1937.

An Edith Wharton Treasury (includes *The Age of Innocence, The Old Maid*, "After Holbein," "A Bottle of Perrier," "The Lady's Maid's Bell," "Roman Fever," "The Other Two," *Madame de Treymes*, "The Moving Finger," "Xingu," "Autres temps," and "Bunner Sisters"), edited by A. H. Quinn, Appleton-Century-Crofts, 1950.

The Best Short Stories of Edith Wharton, edited by Wayne Andrews, 1958.

Stories (includes "The Other Two," "The Lady's Maid's Bell," and "The View"), adapted with notes and exercises by Kenneth Croft and E. F. Croft, Prentice-Hall International, 1962.

Roman Fever and Other Stories (includes "Roman Fever," "Xingu," "The Other Two," "Souls Belated," "The Angel at the Grave," "The Last Asset," "After Holbein," and "Autre temps"), Scribner, 1964.

The Edith Wharton Reader (includes *Ethan Frome, The Bunner Sisters*, selections from *The House of Mirth* and *The Age of Innocence*, and short stories), compiled by Louis Auchincloss, Scribner, 1965.

Collected Short Stories (two volumes; includes stories from the ten volume edition and thirteen additional stories), edited by R. W. B. Lewis, Scribner, 1967.

The Ghost Stories of Edith Wharton (includes "The Lady's Maid's Bell," "The Eyes," "Afterward," "Kerfol," "The Triumph of Night," "Miss Mary Pask," "Bewitched," "Mr. Jones," "Pomegranate Seed," "The Looking-Glass," and "All Souls' "), [New York], 1973.

Quartet: Four Stories (includes "Roman Fever," "The Other Two," "The Last Asset," and "Afterward"), Allen Press, 1975.

The Stories of Edith Wharton, edited by Anita Brookner, Simon & Schuster, 1988.

Contributed stories to numerous anthologies and magazines.

OTHER

Verses, C. E. Hammett, Jr. (Rhode Island), 1878.

(With Ogden Codman) *The Decoration of Houses* (nonfiction), Scribner, 1897, reprinted, Arno Press, 1975.

The Touchstone (novelette), Scribner, 1900 (published in England as *A Gift from the Grave: A Tale*).

(Translator) Hermann Sudermann, *The Joy of Living*, Scribner, 1902.

Italian Villas and their Gardens (nonfiction), Century, 1904, reprinted, Da Capo Press, 1976.

Italian Backgrounds (memoirs), Scribner, 1905.

A Motor-Flight through France (nonfiction), Scribner, 1908.

Artemis to Actaeon and Other Verse, Scribner, 1909, reprinted, Folcroft Library Editions, 1974.

Tales of Men and Ghosts, Scribner, 1910.

Fighting France, from Dunkerque to Belfort (nonfiction), Scribner, 1915.

(Compiler) *The Book of the Homeless*, Scribner, 1916.

French Ways and Their Meaning (essays), Appleton, 1919.

In Morocco, Scribner, 1920, reprinted, Century, 1988.

The Writing of Fiction (criticism), 1925, reprinted, Octagon, 1967.

Twelve Poems, The Medici Society (London), 1926.

A Backward Glance (autobiography), Appleton-Century, 1934, reprinted, 1988.

(Compiler with Robert Norton and Gaillard Lapsley) *Eternal Passion in English Poetry*, Appleton-Century, 1939, reprinted, Books for Libraries Press, 1969.

The Old Maid (play based on the novel of the same title), French (New York), 1951.

(Under name David Olivieri) *Fast and Loose: A Novelette by David Olivieri*, edited by Viola Hopkins Winner, University Press of Virginia, 1977.

Also adaptor, with Clyde Fitch, of a play version of *The House of Mirth*. Contributor of poems and stories to literary journals and women's magazines, including *Scribner's, Harper's*, and *Century*.

SIDELIGHTS: American novelist Edith Wharton was the first woman to receive some of the country's most distinguished literary awards—the Gold Medal of the National Institute of Arts and Letters and an honorary degree from Yale—and the most celebrated American female author of her times. The friend of novelist and fellow American expatriate Henry James, Wharton shared with him many of the same themes and values. Wharton is generally perceived as preserving more of the details of her character's lives and less of the Jamesian analysis of their personalities, yet her works show a concentrated interest in personality; her first book, *The Decoration of Houses*, introduced the notion that furnishings should express the homeowner's personal tastes; her novels show the conflict between her characters' individual values and social expectations. Though her characters seek to escape from the pressure to conform, they often find themselves bound by it. Wharton experienced this conflict first-hand, sometimes as the defender of the social establishment, and sometimes as an individualist who paid a high price for her personal freedom. Best known for her novels *The House of Mirth, Ethan Frome*, and *The Age of Innocence*, she also published poetry, criticism, nonfiction about the First World War, travel writing, and several collections of short stories. Her books suffered a period of critical neglect because of their similarity to the works of James. But a revived interest in what they reveal about women's roles in society brought them back into discussion. Her books have been translated into Italian, German, and French.

Edith Wharton was the daughter of George Frederic Jones, a descendent of the merchant ship-owners the Schermerhorns and the Rhinelanders. Her mother descended from Gen. Ebenezer Stevens, who took part in the Boston tea party, the expedition against Quebec, and the battle at Yorktown. Their sensibility, in part determined by their Dutch Reformed and Episcopalian beliefs, did not include a high regard for the world of art. Thus, when the teenager began to write verse and short stories, her family did not encourage it, and later seldom mentioned her literary success. The New York social circuit was also increasingly made up of the *nouveaux riches*, whose appreciation for culture lagged somewhat behind their knack for gaining wealth. Understandably shy in this environment, Edith happily traveled Europe with her parents. There she met Henry James, who became her mentor and admiring critic. When not traveling, she spent most of her time in her father's library, only entering the social milieu when her parents insisted.

In those hours alone, Edith read voraciously and made her first attempts at writing. Some of her first poems were published in the *Atlantic*; other poems and stories appeared in *Scribner's, Harper's*, and *Century* magazines. She had a volume of her poems privately printed when she was sixteen. Walter Berry, a friend of the family, was one of the first to see her early attempts at writing fiction, and helped her to make the necessary improvements. Berry became a life-long confidante, sharing with her the intellectual pursuits that few others cared to share.

In 1885, Edith married Boston banker Edward Robbins Wharton, known to the family because of his membership in her mother's social circle. He was more than ten years older than Edith and suffered ill health, which, combined with Edith's dissatisfactions with their social life, encouraged her to devote more of her time to writing. They owned a house in Newport, Rhode Island, which she redecorated with the help of the architect Ogden Codman. The book they wrote about the project, *The Decoration of Houses,* explained that a house's decor ought to express the owners' personalities instead of merely aping aristocratic tastes. The book sold well, to the dismay of her family; confirmed in her pursuit of a writing career by its success, she moved to Lenox, Massachusetts and enjoyed her association with other writers who lived nearby. Her next book was a volume of short stories, *The Greater Inclination,* published in 1899, followed by another collection and a novelette, *The Touchstone,* published in 1901 and 1902, respectively. She published, on the average, a book each year for the rest of her life.

As Edward's mental illness progressed, her writing and her trips to Europe took on new importance. They were divorced in 1913. Wharton came to prefer life in Europe, where she was esteemed as a writer. In France, she owned two estates, one on the Riviera and the other just outside Paris. She befriended the French writers Paul Bourget, Charles du Bos, Paul Valery, Andre Maurois, Auguste Rodin, Andre Gide, Rainer Maria Rilke, and Jean Cocteau. Also admired by American authors such as William Dean Howells, Thomas Hardy, and George Meredith, she often entertained them as guests. Berry, by this time an international judge and head of the American Chamber of Commerce in Paris, remained her closest friend, advisor, and traveling companion. On friendly terms with notable American families such as the Tafts and the Vanderbilts since childhood, she was also hostess to many distinguished men, including Charles E. Norton, Bernard Berenson, and Theodore Roosevelt. Her home in France was one of the stops on Roosevelt's world tour in 1909-10.

Because Wharton was a perfectionist in everything, she was sometimes seen as a charming person and other times was described as snobbish; the same comments were made about her writings. As Louis Auchincloss remarks in *American Writers,* "As some of Mrs. Wharton's acquaintances complained that her taste in furnishing was too good, her French too precisely idiomatic, so have some of her critics found her heroes and heroines too exquisite, too apt to exclaim in rapt unison over little known beauties in art and literature with which the majority of her readers may not be equally familiar. The glittering structure of her cultivation sits on her novels like a rather showy icing that detracts from the cake beneath. That same majority may be put off by descriptions, however vivid, of physical objects and backgrounds that obtrude on the action, by being made to notice, even in scenes of tensest drama, a bit of red damask on a wall, a Jacqueminot rose, a small, dark Italian primitive."

Other critics recognized Wharton's eye for details as an essential facet of masterful technique. In *The Greater Inclination* and *Crucial Instances,* for example, "Mrs. Wharton shows herself already in full command of the style that was to make her prose as lucid and as polished as any in American fiction. It is a firm, crisp, smooth, direct, easily flowing style, the perfect instrument of a clear, undazzled eye, an analytic mind, and a sense of humor alert to the least pretentiousness," Auchincloss related in *Edith Wharton.*

These first stories were also praised for their cleverness, Henry Dwight Sedgwick noted in an *Atlantic* piece on the novelist's work. "To most people," Sedgwick summarized, "the point she plays most brilliantly is the episode. . . . In Mrs. Wharton, this aptitude is not single, but a combination. It includes the sense of proportion, and markedly that elementary proportion of allotting the proper space for the introduction of the story,—so much to bring the *dramatis personae* into the ring, so much for the preliminary bouts, so much for the climax, and, finally, the proper length for the recessional. It includes the subordination of one character to another, of one picture to another, the arrangement of details in proper hierarchy to produce the desired effect." John Bayley wrote in the *Times Literary Supplement* that "her fiction, like her life, was built on rules and concealments. Neither, she must have felt, was worth much without them." *Bookman* critic Harry Thurston Peck commented in 1899, "In the way of fiction we have seen nothing this year that has impressed us so much as [*The Greater Inclination*]. . . . There is a finish, an assurance, and a tenacity of grasp about her work that show her to be already an accomplished literary artist."

The Writing of Fiction explained what Wharton had learned about the craft from her fellow novelist Henry James. Noticeable similarities in their works are based on a common interest in the rules of society as they encroach upon the freedom of individuals from several social strata, in particular the wealthy and the American abroad. Like characters drawn by James, Wharton's characters met with two kinds of tragedy, Calvin Winter explained in a *Bookman* review. Their problems were due "on the one hand, to the complications arising from not understanding, from the impossibility of ever wholly getting inside another person's mind; and on the other, from the realisation that one cannot escape from one's environment, that one's whole family and race have for generations been relentlessly weaving a network of custom and precedent too strong for the individual to break."

Fred Lewis Pattee, writing in *The New American Literature: 1890-1930* noted other similarities: "Edged with satire, pointed with wit, [Wharton's works] are French rather than American or English. To compare them to the work of Henry James is conventional, but it is also unavoidable. The tap-roots of the art of both pierce through the Anglo-Saxon into Gallic strata. Only in her materials is she American. . . . Both James and Mrs. Wharton must be classed as virtuosi trained in the school of [French novelists] Stendhal [Marie-Henri Beyle], [Honore de] Balzac, [Gustave] Flaubert, and [Ivan] Turgeniev. Both must be classed as intellectuals, concerned fundamentally with form, with manners, with art."

Even so, Wharton's works were significantly different from the works of James. "In technique and finish all [Mrs. Wharton] has touched is distinctive," wrote Pattee. In *Edith Wharton,* Auchincloss observed, "She dealt with definite psychological and social problems and handled them in her own definite way. Her sentences never have to be read and reread, like James's, for richer and deeper disclosures." In contrast to the gradual accumulation of subtle effects for which James is known, Wharton's vivid depictions of people and objects led readers through a series of impacts. As Peck commented, "Mr. James himself has nothing to teach her in those half-elusive but exquisitely effective strokes that reveal in an instant a whole mental attitude or the hidden meaning of a profound emotion."

Wharton was sometimes harshly critical of society. Irving Howe commented in *Encounter,* "In *The Custom of the Country* . . . she turned to—I think it fair to say, she was largely the innovator of—a tough-spirited, fierce and abrasive satire of the barbaric philistinism she felt to be settling upon American society and the source of which she was inclined to locate, not with complete accuracy, in the new raw towns of the Midwest." A member of New York's elite having "old money," Wharton was keenly aware of the relative lack of gentility among those whose fortunes were gained in industry instead of real estate. The corrupting power of wealth was particularly evident among the *nouveaux riches* and the rising middle class. Howe added, "Endless numbers of American novels would later be written on this theme, and Sinclair Lewis would commonly be mentioned as a writer particularly indebted to *The Custom of the Country;* but the truth is that no American novelist of our time—with the single exception of Nathaniel West—has been so ruthless, so bitingly cold as Mrs. Wharton in assaulting the vulgarities and failures of our society."

Wharton was especially effective at piercing the veil of moral respectibility that sometimes masked a lack of integrity among the rich. In *House of Mirth,* for example, an intelligent and lovely girl must lose her status as a member of the leisure class if she is to avoid moral ruin. Lily Bart rebels against the standards of her social group enough to smoke, gamble, and be seen in public with married men; however, her sense of decency keeps her from marrying a wealthy but vulgar suitor merely to secure her fortunes. Her other opportunity consists of a young lawyer who makes fun of the "high society" his modest but adequate means entitle him to observe. When the first proposes, she turns him down; when the second proposes, it is too late—he finds the distraught Lily dead of an overdose of sleeping pills. Publication of this best seller in 1905 provoked much discussion in the United States, where it was hailed as one of the best novels the country had ever produced.

Wharton believed that good faith among the rich was not to be taken for granted, since it was grounded not in conformity to social standards but in an individual's commitment to respond to the needs of the less fortunate. She also understood that social pressure among the poor could be just as confining. In her novel *Ethan Frome,* she shows how the title character suffers when he is caught between two women—his wife, on whom he depends for economic survival, and his true love, a younger relative of his wife's who has come to the farm to help with the work. Ethan and his love see no way out except suicide, but their attempt fails, and they become invalids waited on by Zeena. Edwin Bjoerkman commented in *Voices of Tomorrow: Critical Studies of the New Spirit in Literature* that Ethan lives "between those two spectres of his lost hopes: the woman he needed and the woman he loved. All other tragedies that I can think of seem mild and bearable beside this one." Though often regarded by reviewers as a departure from Wharton's usual subject matter, Bjoerkman suggested, "after all, the tragedy unveiled to us is social rather than personal. . . . 'Ethan Frome' is to me above all else a judgment on that system which fails to redeem such villages as Mrs. Wharton's Starkfield. Those who dwell in our thousand and one Starkfields are [as] wrecked mariners, fallen into their hapless positions through no fault of their own. And though helpless now, they need by no means prove useless under different conditions."

Some critics felt that Wharton's portraits of men were unfairly negative. "Men especially have a hard time of it in Mrs. Wharton's novels," Howe commented in *Encounter.* He continued, "In their notorious vanity and faithlessness, they seldom 'come through'; they fail Mrs. Wharton's heroines less from bad faith than weak imagination, a laziness of spirit that keeps them from a true grasp of suffering; and in a number of her novels one finds a suppressed feminine bitterness, a profound impatience with the claims of the ruling sex." *New York Times Book Review* contrib-

utor Janet Malcolm, however, looking back on *The House of Mirth, The Reef, The Custom of the Country,* and *The Age of Innocence,* remarked that in Wharton's fiction, "the callousness and heartlessness by which this universe is ruled is the callousness and heartlessness of women. There are no bad men in Wharton's fiction. There are weak men and there are foolish men and there are vulgar New Rich men, but no man ever deliberately causes harm to another person; that role is exclusively reserved for women." While not accusing Wharton of misanthropy or misogyny, other critics have spoken of her pervasive pessimism. Howe related Wharton's "feminist resentment" to "a more radical and galling inequity at the heart of the human scheme. The inability of human beings to achieve self-sufficiency drives them to seek relationships with other people, and these relationships necessarily compromise their freedom by subjecting them to the pain of a desire either too great or too small. Things, in Mrs. Wharton's world, do not work out."

Other critics, however, stressed the positive values that infused Wharton's novels. Howe pointed out, "In books like *The House of Mirth* and *The Age of Innocence* she could work on the assumption, so valuable to a writer who prizes economy of structure, that moral values can be tested in a novel by dramatizing the relationships between fixed social groups and mobile characters." The results of this testing were not always negative. As Frances Theresa Russell related in the *Sewanee Review,* in Wharton's characters, for the most part, "the moral failures are offset reasonably enough by the successes." Though far from idealistic, her novels argued the importance of living with a sense of duty to others. James W. Gargano explains in *American Literature,* "Faith, as Edith Wharton defines it, is no generalized and temperamental optimism; it is, instead, an almost mystical assurance that only moral action can save the ever-threatened community of human existence. Beset by dangers inherent in social arrangements, man clings to survival by the thread of his moral instincts; he is, at his best, motivated by what Mrs. Wharton calls, in *Sanctuary,* 'this passion of charity for the race.' In other words, goodness is useful, and men and women must, under pain of extinction, bequeath it to their children."

Wharton produced a body of work that affirmed the need to conserve certain fundamental values that were quickly losing ground in the twentieth century. *The Valley of Decision,* her first long novel, depicted the moral decline in Italy during the eighteenth century, and was deemed a successful work of history recreated in exquisitely-crafted fiction. James W. Tuttleton explained in the *Yale Review,* "She continually argued the necessity of the individual's commitment to the cultural tradition; . . . the catastrophe which ensues when social upheavals like revolution, anarchy, and war destroy the slowly and delicately spun web of that tradition; and the necessity of imaginatively preserving . . . the precious values of the past." By showing in her fiction what becomes of people when culture ceases to be a moral force, and by recording her memories of a time when it was, Wharton "hoped to revive the memory of a set of slowly evolved cultural values suddenly wiped out by a succession of destructive changes in American life beginning in the 1880's—including the rise of the industrial plutocracy ('the lords of Pittsburgh,' as she called them); massive immigration which totally altered the ethnic character of New York City; the First World War, the depression, and the New Deal; and the nationalistic hatreds, at the close of her life in 1937, building toward the Second World War." Wharton seems to have "felt that the universe—which for her is virtually to say, organised society—was profoundly inhospitable to human need and desire," Howe commented in *Encounter.* Q. D. Leavis wrote in *Scrutiny,* "Mrs. Wharton, if unfortunate in her environment, had a strength of character that made her superior to it. She was a remarkable novelist if not a large-sized one, and while there are few great novelists there are not even so many remarkable ones that we can afford to let her be overlooked."

In addition to writing about the importance of values, Wharton validated them in her service to the less fortunate during and after the First World War. An energetic fund-raiser, she was aided by "Edith Wharton" committees in New York, Boston, Philadelphia, Washington, and Providence. With her financial support, an ambulance unit, a workroom for female garment workers, and a sanatorium for women and children with tuberculosis were established in France. She also compiled *Le livre des sans-foyer* (*The Book of the Homeless*), sold to raise money for American hostels for refugees and the Children of Flanders rescue committee. France recognized her philanthropy by awarding her the Cross of the Legion of Honor; she also was made Chevalier of the Order of Leopold in Belgium.

Books informed by her war experience, however, were not regarded as her best. Auchincloss explained that she saw the war "from a simple but consistent point of view: France, virtually singlehanded, was fighting the battle of civilization against the powers of darkness. It was the spirit that made men fight and die, but it has never, unfortunately, been the spirit of fiction. Reading *The Marne* . . . and *A Son at the Front* . . . today gives one the feeling of taking an old enlistment poster out of an attic trunk. . . . Mrs. Wharton knew that the war was terrible; she had visited hospitals and even the front itself. But the exhilaration of the noncombatant, no matter how dedicated and useful her services, has a shrill sound to postwar ears."

After the First World War, *The Age of Innocence,* another novel about Old New York society, again showed passionate characters hemmed in by their desire to keep their membership in a dispassionate social group. Newland Archer is engaged to marry an acceptable and attractive girl, but falls in love with Ellen Olenska, a European divorcee. Olenska had married a Polish Count, a villain from whom she escaped with the eager aid of his secretary. Equally passionate but seeking to reestablish her honor in New York society (which is not sure she is acceptable), Olenska encourages Archer to keep his commitment. To make it easier for him, she returns to Europe. Thirty years later Archer's son is free to live the life of feeling Archer could not bring himself to embrace. "Archer, with his insecurity, his sensitivity, and his passion has obeyed the moral imperatives of his class and time and has given up Ellen and love for the furtherance of the shallow-seeming aims, all amorphous as they are, of his [New York] world," observed Louis O. Coxe in *New Republic.* Wharton allowed Archer to confess that a life of duty had its rewards—and yet it was a lonely life, since the next generation, represented by Archer's son, enjoyed a freedom from social pressure that made them unable to understand this kind of sacrifice, Coxe added. The novel was highly acclaimed as one of Wharton's best novels, and, according to *New York Times* writer W. L. Phelps, as "one of the best novels of the twentieth century" in 1920, and "a permanent addition to literature." *The Age of Innocence* won the Pulitzer Prize in 1921. Wharton believed the honor should have gone to Sinclair Lewis, who dedicated his next novel, *Babbitt,* to her in 1922.

Commenting on Wharton's place in literary history, Louise Bogan wrote in *Selected Criticism,* "Mrs. Wharton's work formed a bridge from the nineteenth-century novel to the magazine fiction of the present. . . . She contained in herself, as it were, the whole transitional period of American fiction, begin-

ning in the bibelot and imported-European-culture era of the late nineties, and ending in the woman's-magazine dream of suburban smartness." Malcolm suggested, "Her strongest work . . . has a stylization and abstraction, a quality of 'madeness,' that propels it out of the sphere of 19th-century realism and nudges it toward the self-reflexive literary experimentation of [the 20th] century." In addition, Alfred Kazan noted in the *Virginia Quarterly Review,* Wharton "could speak out plainly with a force [James] never could muster; and her own alienation and loneliness gave her a sympathy for erratic spirits and illicit emotions that was unique in its time. It has been forgotten how much Edith Wharton contributed to the plain-speaking traditions of American realism." Ten years before her death in 1937, Wharton was nominated to receive the Nobel Prize in recognition that she had become the most distinguished American writer of her generation. That she did not receive the award does not diminish either her achievement in letters or the high esteem granted to her by her contemporaries in both America and Europe. Percy Lubbock maintained in *Portrait of Edith Wharton* in 1947, "The sagest and sternest of the craftsmen must admit that she meets them on their ground."

MEDIA ADAPTATIONS: A play based on *The Old Maid* adapted by Zoe Akins won a Pulitzer Prize for Drama in 1935; a dramatization of *Ethan Frome* by Owen and Donald Davis was produced in New York in 1936; a stage version of *The Custom of the Country* by Jane Stanton Hitchcock was produced On Broadway at McGinn/Cazale Theater, in 1985; "Old New York," adapted from Wharton's story by Donald Sanders, was produced in the parlor of the Old Merchant's House Museum in New York in 1987; "Two By Wharton," a play based on the stories "The Other Two" and "Autres temps" adapted by Dennis Krausnick was produced at The Mount (Wharton's restored estate) in Lenox, Mass., in 1987.

BIOGRAPHICAL/CRITICAL SOURCES:

BOOKS

American Writers: A Collection of Literary Biographies, Scribner, 1981.

Auchincloss, Louis, *Edith Wharton,* University of Minnesota Press, 1961.

Bell, Millicent, *Edith Wharton and Henry James: A Story of their Friendship,* Braziller, 1965.

Bjoerkman, Edwin, *Voices of Tomorrow: Critical Studies of the New Spirit in Literature,* Kennerly, 1913.

Bogan, Louise, *Selected Criticism,* Noonday, 1955.

Dictionary of Literary Biography, Gale, Volume 4: *American Writers in Paris,* 1980, Volume 9: *American Novelists, 1910-1945,* 1981, Volume 12: *American Realists and Naturalists,* 1982.

Grace, Kellogg, *Two Lives of Edith Wharton: The Woman and Her Work,* Appleton, 1965.

Howe, Irving, editor, *Edith Wharton: A Collection of Critical Essays,* Prentice-Hall, 1963.

Howe, *A World More Attractive: A View of Modern Literature and Politics,* Horizon Press, 1963.

Howe, *Decline of the New,* Gollancz, 1971.

James, Henry, *Letters to Walter Berry,* Black Sun Press, 1928.

Kellogg, Grace, *The Two Lives of Edith Wharton,* Meredith, 1965.

Lawson, Richard H., *Edith Wharton,* Ungar, 1977.

Lubbock, Percy, *Portrait of Edith Wharton,* Appleton-Century, 1947.

Lyde, M. J., *Edith Wharton: Convention and Morality in the Work of a Novelist,* University of Oklahoma Press, 1959.

McDowell, Margaret B., *Edith Wharton*, Twayne, 1976.
Nevius, B. R., *Edith Wharton: A Study of Her Fiction*, University of California Press, 1953.
Pattee, Fred Lewis, *The New American Literature: 1890-1930*, Century, 1930.
Twentieth-Century Literary Criticism, Gale, Volume 3, 1980, Volume 9, 1982.
Walton, G., *Edith Wharton: A Critical Interpretation*, Fairleigh Dickinson University Press, 1971.
Wharton, Edith, *A Backward Glance* (autobiography), Scribner, 1934.
Wharton, *Sanctuary*, Scribner, 1903.
Wolff, Cynthia Griffin, *A Feast of Words: The Triumph of Edith Wharton*, Oxford University Press, 1977.

PERIODICALS

American Literature, March, 1972.
American Quarterly, fall, 1957.
Atlantic, August, 1906, February, 1978.
Bookman, volume 9, June, 1899, volume 33, 1911.
Colophon, number 4, 1932.
Encounter, July, 1962.
Films in Review, February, 1977.
Nation, November 3, 1920.
New Republic, June 27, 1955.
Newsweek, September 22, 1975.
New Yorker, September 4, 1978.
New York Review of Books, February 23, 1978.
New York Times, October 17, 1920, October 25, 1986.
New York Times Book Review, November 16, 1986.
Saturday Review, August 9, 1975.
Scrutiny, December, 1938.
Sewanee Review, autumn, 1932.
South Atlantic Quarterly, winter, 1970.
Times (London), July 13, 1984.
Times Literary Supplement, April 1, 1988.
Twentieth Century Literature, January, 1973.
Virginia Quarterly Review, winter, 1941.
Yale Review, summer, 1972.

*   *   *

WHARTON, James
See MENCKEN, H(enry) L(ouis)

*   *   *

WHEATLEY, Dennis (Yeats)   1897-1977

PERSONAL: Born January 8, 1897, in London, England; died November 11, 1977, in London, England; son of Albert David and Florence Baker (Lady Newton) Wheatley; married Nancy Madelaine Leslie Robinson, 1923; married Joan Gwendoline Johnstone, August 8, 1931; children: (first marriage) Anthony Marius. *Education:* Educated at Dulwich College, 1908, aboard H.M.S. *Worcester*, 1909-13, and privately in Germany, 1913. *Politics:* Conservative.

ADDRESSES: Home and office—60 Cadogan Sq., London SW1, England. *Agent*—A. P. Watt Ltd., 26/28 Bedford Row, London WC1R 4HL, England.

CAREER: Wheatley & Son (wine merchants), London, England, 1919-31, became sole owner upon father's death in 1926; free-lance writer, 1932-77. *Wartime service:* British Army, 1914-19; became lieutenant. Member of National Service Re-

cruiting Panel, 1940-41; member of Joint Planning Staff of War Cabinet, 1941-44; wing commander on Sir Winston Churchill's staff, 1945; decorated, awarded U.S. Bronze Star.

MEMBER: Royal Society of Literature (fellow), Royal Society of Arts (fellow), Old Comrades Association (president, 1960), St. James' Club, Paternoster Club.

WRITINGS:

PUBLISHED BY HUTCHINSON, EXCEPT AS INDICATED

The Forbidden Territory (also see below), 1933, reprinted, Arrow Books, 1978.
Such Power Is Dangerous, 1933, reprinted, Merrimack Book Service, 1979.
"Old Rowley": A Private Life of Charles II, 1933, Dutton, 1934, reprinted, Arrow Books, 1969, published as *A Private Life of Charles II*, Hutchinson, 1938, published as *"Old Rowley": A Very Private Life of Charles II*, Arrow Books, 1977.
Black August (also see below), 1934, reprinted, Edito-Service, 1974.
The Fabulous Valley, 1934, reprinted, Edito-Service, 1973.
The Devil Rides Out (also see below), 1935, reprinted, Arrow Books, 1979.
The Eunuch of Stamboul, Little, Brown, 1935, reprinted, Merrimack Book Service, 1979.
(Editor) *A Century of Horror Stories*, 1935, reprinted, Books for Libraries, 1971.
They Found Atlantis (also see below), 1936, reprinted, Merrimack Book Service, 1979.
(With J. G. Links) *Crimefile Number One: File on Bolitho Blane*, Morrow, 1936 (published in England as *Murder off Miami*, Hutchinson, 1936, reprinted, Mayflower Books, 1979).
Contraband (also see below), 1936, reprinted, Edito-Service, 1974.
The Secret War, 1937, reprinted, Arrow Books, 1975.
(With Links) *File on Robert Prentice*, Greenberg, 1937 (published in England as *Who Killed Robert Prentice?*, Hutchinson, 1937, reprinted, Mayflower Books, 1980).
Red Eagle: The Story of the Russian Revolution and of Klementy Efremovitch Voroshilov, Marshal and Commissar for Defence of the Union of Socialist Soviet Republics, 1938, published as *Red Eagle: A Story of the Russian Revolution and of Klementy Efremovitch Voroschilov*, Arrow Books, 1964, Hutchinson, 1967.
Uncharted Seas (also see below), 1938, reprinted, Arrow Books, 1968.
(With Links) *The Malinsay Massacre*, 1938, reprinted, Mayflower Books, 1981.
The Golden Spaniard (also see below), 1938, reprinted, Edito-Service, 1973.
(Editor) *A Century of Spy Stories*, 1938.
The Quest of Julian Day, 1939, reprinted, Heron Books, 1972.
(With Links) *Herewith the Clues*, 1939.
Sixty Days to Live, 1939, reprinted, Arrow Books, 1972.
Those Modern Musketeers (contains *Three Inquisitive People, The Forbidden Territory*, and *The Golden Spaniard*), 1939, reprinted, 1954.
Three Inquisitive People (previously published in *Those Modern Musketeers*), 1940, reprinted, Edito-Service, 1973.
The Scarlet Impostor, 1940, reprinted, Heron Books, 1972.
Faked Passports, 1940, Macmillan (New York), 1943, reprinted, Ballantine, 1973.
The Black Baroness, 1940, Ryerson Press, 1941, reprinted, Arrow Books, 1978.

Strange Conflict (also see below), 1941, reprinted, Merrimack Book Service, 1978.

The Sword of Fate, 1941, reprinted, Edito-Service, 1973.

Total War: A Paper, 1941.

V for Vengeance, 1942, reprinted, 1972.

Mediterranean Nights (short stories), 1942, revised edition, 1965.

Gunmen, Gallants, and Ghosts (short stories), 1943, reprinted, 1965, revised edition, Arrow Books, 1968.

The Man Who Missed the War (also see below), 1946, reprinted, Arrow Books, 1973.

Codeword: Golden Fleece, 1946, reprinted, Edito-Service, 1974.

Come into My Parlor, 1946, reprinted, Arrow Books, 1975.

The Launching of Roger Brook (also see below), 1947, reprinted, Heron Books, 1972.

The Shadow of Tyburn Tree (also see below), 1948, reprinted, Arrow Books, 1979.

The Haunting of Toby Jugg, 1948, reprinted, Merrimack Book Service, 1976.

The Rising Storm (also see below), 1949, reprinted, Arrow Books, 1970.

The Seven Ages of Justerini's: 1749-1949, Riddle Books, 1949, revised edition published as *1749-1965, The Eight Ages of Justerini's,* Dolphin Publishing, 1965.

The Second Seal, 1950, reprinted, 1964.

Early Adventures of Roger Brook (contains *The Launching of Roger Brook* and *The Shadow of Tyburn Tree*), 1951.

The Man Who Killed the King (also see below), 1951, Putnam, 1965, reprinted, Arrow Books, 1979.

The Star of Ill-Omen, 1952, reprinted, Arrow Books, 1979.

Worlds Far from Here (contains *Uncharted Seas, The Man Who Missed the War,* and *They Found Atlantis*), 1952.

To the Devil—a Daughter (also see below), 1953, reprinted, Arrow Books, 1974.

Curtain of Fear, 1953, reprinted, Arrow Books, 1975.

The Island Where Time Stands Still (also see below), 1954, reprinted, Arrow Books, 1975.

The Dark Secret of Josephine, 1955, reprinted, Arrow Books 1974.

Secret Missions of Gregory Sallust, 1955.

Black Magic Omnibus (contains *The Devil Rides Out, Strange Conflict,* and *To the Devil—a Daughter*), 1956.

The Ka of Gifford Hillary, 1956, reprinted, Arrow Books, 1974.

The Prisoner in the Mask, 1957, reprinted, Heron Books, 1972.

Roger Brook in the French Revolution (contains *The Rising Storm* and *The Man Who Killed the King*), 1957.

Death in the Sunshine, 1958.

Traitor's Gate, 1958, reprinted, Edito-Service, 1973.

Plot and Counterplot: Three Adventures of Gregory Sallust (contains *Black August, Contraband,* and *The Island Where Time Stands Still*), 1959.

Stranger than Fiction, 1959, reprinted, Arrow Books, 1977.

The Rape of Venice, 1959, reprinted, Edito-Service, 1974.

The Satanist, 1960, reprinted, Arrow Books, 1979.

Into the Unknown, 1960.

Selected Works, 1961.

Saturdays with Bricks, and Other Days under Shell-Fire, 1961.

Vendetta in Spain, 1961.

Mayhem in Greece, 1962.

The Sultan's Daughter, 1963.

Bill for the Use of a Body, 1964, new edition, Arrow Books, 1972.

They Used Dark Forces, 1964.

Dangerous Inheritance, 1965, published as *Dangerous Inheritance: A Duke de Richleau Story,* 1971.

(Compiler) *Shafts of Fear,* Arrow Books, 1965, published as *Dennis Wheatley's First Book of Horror Stories: Tales of Strange Doings,* Hutchinson, 1968.

(Compiler) *Quiver of Horror,* Arrow Books, 1965, published as *Dennis Wheatley's Second Book of Horror Stories: Tales of Strange Happenings,* Hutchinson, 1968.

The Wanton Princess, 1966, published as *The Wanton Princess: A Roger Brook Story,* 1971.

Unholy Crusade, 1967.

The White Witch of the South Seas, 1968.

Evil in a Mask, 1969.

Gateway to Hell, 1970.

The Devil and All His Works, American Heritage Press, 1971.

The Ravishing of Lady Mary Ware, 1971.

The Strange Story of Linda Lee, 1972.

The Irish Witch, 1973.

Desperate Measures, 1974.

Uncanny Tales, Sphere Books, Volumes I-II, 1974, Volume III, 1977.

Satanism and Witches: Essays and Stories, Sphere Books, 1975.

The Time Has Come: The Memoirs of Dennis Wheatley, Volume I: *The Young Man Said, 1897-1914,* 1977, Volume II: *Officer and Temporary Gentleman, 1914-1919,* 1978, Volume III: *Drink and Ink, 1919-1977,* 1979.

The Deception Planners: My Secret War, edited by Anthony Lejeune, 1980.

Editor of "Dennis Wheatley's Library of the Occult" series, Sphere Books, 1974-77. Author of personalities page column, *Sunday Graphic,* 1939. Contributor to periodicals, including London *Times, Daily Mail, Daily Express,* and *Cosmopolitan.*

MEDIA ADAPTATIONS: J. H. Hoffberg filmed *Forbidden Territory* in 1938 and *The Eunuch of Stamboul*—released as "The Secret of Stamboul"—in 1941. In 1968 Warner Bros. produced "The Lost Continent," a filmed version of *Uncharted Seas,* and Twentieth Century-Fox produced "The Devil's Bride," a filmed version of *The Devil Rides Out.*

SIDELIGHTS: Dennis Wheatley was a best-selling author of historical thrillers, spy stories, and works on the occult. A writer in the *Washington Post* called him "one of the twentieth century's most prolific and best-selling authors" because his more than sixty books have sold over forty-five million copies and have been translated into twenty-nine languages. His *The Devil and All His Works,* a comprehensive survey of the black arts, "is considered a modern textbook on satanism," according to a *New York Times* writer.

Wheatley once related in the *Writer:* "Numerous distinguished critics said of my first novel, *The Forbidden Territory,* and of its successors, that I had broken every rule in the game, that my punctuation was lamentable and my English appalling—but they praised the story. It was reprinted seven times in seven weeks and within a year translated into a dozen foreign languages." Urging novice authors to be conscientious and persistent, Wheatley wrote that anyone "who is prepared to face hard, hard work can achieve—and maintain—success. In my case it has meant writing two books for each one published: a factual, accurate account of a war or period of history or travel, which will interest the better-educated reader, and a thriller with plenty of throat-cutting and boy jumping into bed with girl, then dovetailing the two. But don't let any pedantic idiot tell you that because, like myself, you haven't the faintest idea what the word 'syntax' means, you can't write a best seller."

AVOCATIONAL INTERESTS: Travel; books; building (Wheatley once estimated he had laid more than sixty thousand bricks in his garden); collecting Georgian furniture, Persian rugs, stamps, and fine wines.

BIOGRAPHICAL/CRITICAL SOURCES:

BOOKS

Dictionary of Literary Biography, Volume 77: *British Mystery Writers, 1920-1939,* Gale, 1989.

PERIODICALS

Books and Bookmen, September, 1965.
Los Angeles Times, November 13, 1980.
Writer, October, 1969.

OBITUARIES:

PERIODICALS

AB Bookman's Weekly, February 6, 1978.
New York Times, November 12, 1977.
Washington Post, November 12, 1977.

* * *

WHITE, E(lwyn) B(rooks) 1899-1985

PERSONAL: Born July 11, 1899, in Mount Vernon, N.Y.; died after suffering from Alzheimer's disease, October 1, 1985, in North Brooklin, Me.; son of Samuel Tilly (a piano manufacturer) and Jessie (Hart) White; married Katharine Sergeant Angell (a *New Yorker* editor), November 13, 1929 (died, July 20, 1977); children: Joel McCoun; stepchildren: Nancy Angell Stableford, Roger Angell. *Education:* Cornell University, A.B., 1921.

ADDRESSES: Home—North Brooklin, Me. 04661. *Office*—*New Yorker,* 25 West 43rd St., New York, N.Y. 10036.

CAREER: Reporter with United Press and the American Legion News Service, 1921; *Seattle Times,* Seattle, Wash., reporter, 1922-23; copywriter with Frank Seaman, Inc., and Newmark, Inc., New York, N.Y., 1924-25; *New Yorker,* New York City, writer and contributing editor, beginning 1926. *Military service:* U.S. Army, 1918.

MEMBER: National Institute of Arts and Letters, American Academy of Arts and Sciences (fellow), American Academy of Arts and Letters, Phi Beta Kappa, Phi Gamma Delta.

AWARDS, HONORS: Limited Editions Club gold medal, 1945, for *One Man's Meat;* Litt.D., Dartmouth College, University of Maine, and Yale University, all 1948, Bowdoin College, 1950, Hamilton College, 1952, and Harvard University, 1954; Newbery Honor Book, 1953, Lewis Carroll Shelf Award, 1958, George C. Stone Center for Children's Books Recognition of Merit Award, 1970, and the New England Round Table of Children's Libraries Award, 1973, all for *Charlotte's Web;* Page One Award, New York Newspaper Guild, 1954, and National Association of Independent Schools Award, 1955, both for *The Second Tree from the Corner;* L.H.D., Colby College, 1954.

National Institute of Arts and Letters gold medal, 1960, for his contribution to literature; Presidential Medal of Freedom, 1963; Laura Ingalls Wilder Award, American Library Association, 1970, for "a lasting contribution to children's literature"; National Medal for Literature, National Institute of Arts and Letters, 1971; *The Trumpet of the Swan* was nominated for a National Book Award, 1971, was included on the International Board on Books for Young People Honor List, 1972, and received the Children's Book Award from the William Allen

White Library at Emporia State University, 1973, the Sequoyah Children's Book Award from the Oklahoma Library Association, 1973, the Sue Hefley Award from the Louisiana Association of School Librarians, 1974, and the Young Hoosier Award from the Indiana School Librarians Association, 1975; Pulitzer Prize special citation, 1978, for the body of his work.

WRITINGS:

The Lady Is Cold (poems), Harper, 1929.
(With James Thurber) *Is Sex Necessary?; or, Why You Feel the Way You Do,* Harper, 1929, reprinted, Queens House, 1977.
(Author of introduction) James Thurber, *The Owl in the Attic,* Harper, 1931.
(Editor) *Ho-Hum: Newsbreaks from the "New Yorker,"* Farrar & Rinehart, 1931.
(Editor) *Another Ho-Hum: More Newsbreaks from the "New Yorker,"* Farrar & Rinehart, 1932.
Alice through the Cellophane (pamphlet), John Day, 1933.
Every Day Is Saturday, Harper, 1934.
Farewell to Model T, Putnam, 1936.
The Fox of Peapack and Other Poems, Harper, 1938.
Quo Vadimus?; or, The Case for the Bicycle, Harper, 1939.
(Editor with wife, Katharine Sergeant White, and author of introduction) *A Subtreasury of American Humor,* Coward, 1941, reprinted, Capricorn Books, 1962.
One Man's Meat (also see below; essays previously published in *Harper's*), Harper, 1942, enlarged edition, 1944, reprinted with new introduction, 1982.
(Author of introduction) Roy E. Jones, *A Basic Chicken Guide for the Small Flock Owner,* Morrow, 1944.
World Government and Peace: Selected Notes and Comment, 1943-1945, F. R. Publishing, 1945.
Stuart Little (also see below; juvenile), Harper, 1945.
The Wild Flag: Editorials from the "New Yorker" on Federal World Government and Other Matters, Houghton, 1946.
Here Is New York, Harper, 1949.
(Author of introduction) Don Marquis, *the lives and times of archy and mehitabel,* Doubleday, 1950.
Charlotte's Web (also see below; juvenile), Harper, 1952.
The Second Tree from the Corner, Harper, 1954, new edition, with new introduction, 1984.
(Editorial supervisor and contributor) William Strunk, Jr., *The Elements of Style,* Macmillan, 2nd edition (White not associated with previous edition), 1959, 3rd edition, 1979.
The Points of My Compass: Letters from the East, the West, the North, the South, Harper, 1962.
An E. B. White Reader, edited by William W. Watt and Robert W. Bradford, Harper, 1966.
Topics: Our New Countryman at the U.N. (pamphlet), Congressional Press, 1968.
The Trumpet of the Swan (also see below; juvenile), Harper, 1970.
E. B. White Boxed Set (contains *Charlotte's Web, Stuart Little,* and *The Trumpet of the Swan*), Harper, 1975.
Letters of E. B. White, edited by Dorothy Lobrano Guth, Harper, 1976.
Essays of E. B. White, Harper, 1977.
(Editor) K. S. White, *Onward and Upward in the Garden,* Farrar, Straus, 1979.
Poems and Sketches of E. B. White, Harper, 1981.
(With others) *A Gift from Maine,* Guy Gannett, 1984.

Author of column, "One Man's Meat," *Harper's,* 1938-43. Contributor to periodicals.

RECORDINGS

"Stuart Little," Dell, 1973.
"Charlotte's Web" (narrated by White), RCA, 1976.

SIDELIGHTS: Few writers have achieved recognition in as many fields as has E. B. White. He was regarded as one of the finest essayists of the twentieth century; he was the author of two classics of children's literature, *Charlotte's Web* and *Stuart Little;* and his extensive contributions to the *New Yorker* were instrumental in making that magazine a success.

White began his writing career in 1921 after graduating from Cornell University, where he served as editor of the school newspaper. He worked for a time as a reporter with two news services in New York City, then drove a Model T cross country with his friend Howard Cushman. "When they ran out of money," the late James Thurber recounted in an article for the *Saturday Review of Literature,* "they played for their supper—and their gasoline—on a fascinating musical instrument that White had made out of some pieces of wire and an old shoe or something." Ending up in Seattle, White took a job as a reporter for the *Seattle Times.* He lasted less than a year. White explains in *The Points of My Compass: Letters from the East, the West, the North, the South:* "As a newspaper reporter I was almost useless." He worked for a short time as a mess boy on a ship bound for Alaska but soon returned to New York, where he spent two years as an advertising copywriter.

It was while working as a copywriter that White began to submit short pieces to the fledgling *New Yorker* magazine, barely a few months old at the time. Editor Harold Ross "was so taken by the pieces White submitted to The New Yorker," John Ciardi writes in the *Washington Post Book World,* "that he hired White to write the 'Talk of the Town' section with which the magazine still opens." Both Ross and Katharine Angell, the magazine's literary editor who later became White's wife, found White's style ideal for the *New Yorker.* They "were not slow to perceive that here were the perfect eye and ear, the authentic voice and accent for their struggling magazine," Thurber stated. Over the next forty years, White contributed poems, essays, sketches, stories, and even photo captions to the *New Yorker.* He wrote the "Talk of the Town" section for eleven years. For many years, too, he wrote the "Newsbreak" fillers, short items taken from magazines and newspapers and reprinted with a humorous comment. White, Thurber explained, "had a hand in everything: he even painted a cover and wrote a few advertisements."

Russell Maloney, in an article for the *Saturday Review of Literature,* credits White with "setting *The New Yorker*'s editorial style" in his "Talk of the Town" section. This style, Maloney goes on, is "modest, sly, elliptical, allusive, prim, slightly countrified, wistful, and (God help us) whimsical." Thurber credited White with changing the *New Yorker.* "It is not too much to say that . . . White was the most valuable person on the magazine," Thurber wrote. "His delicate tinkering with the works of *The New Yorker* caused it to move with a new ease and grace." Another "one of E. B. White's great contributions to *The New Yorker,*" Maloney believes, was his insistence, against almost overwhelming opposition, that Thurber was a funny artist whose pictures should appear in the magazine." Thurber had long been a staff writer for the *New Yorker,* having attained the position after White arranged an interview for him. To amuse his co-workers, Thurber sketched humorous cartoons at the office. White urged him to submit these cartoons to the magazine, but Thurber had little faith in them and refused to try. One day White collected some of Thurber's pencil drawings from his wastebasket, inked them in, and submitted them to the *New Yorker*'s art editor. They were accepted. Thurber went on to become a very popular cartoonist as well as writer.

In 1929 White collaborated with Thurber on *Is Sex Necessary?; or, Why You Feel the Way You Do,* a spoof of sex manuals. The book made "both White and Thurber well known," according to Edward C. Sampson in the *Dictionary of Literary Biography.* The two authors, Sampson explains, "parody the serious writers on the subject, making light of complexities, taking a mock-serious attitude toward the obvious, delighting in reducing the case-history technique to an absurdity, and making fun of those writers who proceeded by definition." They expound on such crucial topics as "Osculatory Justification," "Schmalhausen Trouble" (when couples live in small apartments), and "The Nature of the American Male: A Study of Pedestalism." Will Cuppy of the *New York Herald Tribune Book Review* calls *Is Sex Necessary?* "a minor classic—and one uses the term 'minor' only because it is gorgeously funny and not quite ponderous enough to be major. Let's compromise and just call it a classic." Thurber's drawings, turned out in a few hours, illustrate the book, which has gone through more than twenty-five printings since it first appeared. White's share of the royalties enabled him to marry Katharine Angell on November 13, 1929.

Over the years, it has been White's essays for the *New Yorker*—many of which are collected in 1977's *Essays of E. B. White*—that have done the most to build his literary reputation. White's essays are personal and informal, seem to happen upon their subject as they ramble along, and have a gentle humor about them. New York City, where the *New Yorker* has its offices, and the Maine countryside, where White owned a farm, are the two most common settings. White often begins with a small incident in his own life and then extrapolates larger implications from it. One of his first pieces for the *New Yorker,* for example, was a recounting of an accident at a Manhattan restaurant in which a glass of buttermilk was spilled on his suit. The waitress, White relates, "was a little girl, so I let her blot me. In my ear she whispered a million apologies, hopelessly garbled, infinitely forlorn. And I whispered that the suit was four years old, and that I hated dark clothes anyway. One has, in life, so few chances to lie heroically." In other pieces, Christopher Lehmann-Haupt of the *New York Times* notes, White has arrived "at the subject of disarmament by way of Mary Martin's furniture, or at the prospects of American democracy by the route of a dachshund named Fred." This idea is echoed by the late Joseph Wood Krutch, writing in the *Saturday Review,* who maintained that White is "generally concerned less with the Queen than with the little mouse under her chair." William Howarth of the *Washington Post Book World* argues that, for White, "connecting small moments to big issues is a literary impulse." Howarth goes on to say that White "can capture moments of rare evanescence—a small tree, second from the corner and backlit by the sun, 'each gilt-edged leaf perfectly drunk with excellence and delicacy.' "

In all of his essays, White's style is clear, personal, and unaffected. It is, Louis Hasley writes in the *Connecticut Review,* "transparent and unobtrusive. With him, more than with most writers, the style is the man: careful, steady, sure, resourceful, concrete without flourish, capable of fun and even surrealistic fancy, and as often as not, expressing a deadly seriousness that may be richly compounded with humor." Similarly, Webster Schott writes in the *New Republic* that "White has such a subtly-developed literary technique it's almost impossible to know when the words are running the writing, when Mr. White's head is in command, or when the central nervous system has taken over to pick up subliminal signals. That's style for you: marriage of idea, language, sensibility."

Although White's essays cover a wide range of topics—from observations of nature to the problems of city living and from political commentary to literary parody—they invariably display a gentle humor. White sees humor as a necessary counterbalance to everyday life. As he states in his introduction to *A Subtreasury of American Humor,* "there is a deep vein of melancholy running through everyone's life and . . . a humorist, perhaps more sensible of it than some others, compensates for it actively and positively." In the early days of his career, White was, Sampson writes, "considered to be primarily a humorist." An example of White's humor can be found in one of the essays collected in *One Man's Meat* in which White speaks of his dog. "For a number of years," he writes, "I have been agreeably encumbered by a very large and dissolute dachshund named Fred. Of all the dogs whom I have served I've never known one who understood so much of what I say or held it in such deep contempt. When I address Fred I never have to raise either my voice or my hopes. He even disobeys me when I instruct him in something that he wants to do. And when I answer his peremptory scratch at the door and hold the door open for him to walk through, he stops in the middle and lights a cigarette, just to hold me up."

When White turns his attention to political matters, he often focuses on the arms race and the tensions between the world's nations. His approach to politics is typically oblique. In one essay published in *The Second Tree from the Corner,* for example, White tells of participating in a routine air raid drill in his office building. As his elevator passes the thirteenth floor on its way to the basement, he notices that it is numbered "14." Nuclear scientists had successfully looked "into the core of the sun," White observes, "but it might have been a good idea if they had waited to do that until the rest of us could look the number 13 square in the face. Such is the true nature of our peculiar dilemma." White is known as a forceful advocate of world government, which he recommends for democratic nations only, and as a defender of individual privacy.

A concern for the environment, inspired by Henry David Thoreau's *Walden,* is also evident in White's life and work. White describes Thoreau, in one of the essays collected in *The Points of My Compass,* as being the companion and chider for the "fellows who hate compromise and have compromised, fellows who love wildness and have lived tamely," and as the man "who long ago gave corroboration to impulses they perceived were right and issued warnings against things they instinctively knew to be their enemies." In common with Thoreau, White is skeptical about the benefits of material progress and suspects that perhaps what has been left behind is more valuable than what has replaced it. He is, Hasley comments, "a cautious critic of progress, fearing the loss of the precious sense for basic things." Following the example of Thoreau, who lived close to the land, White in 1934 bought a salt water farm in North Brooklin, Maine. He and his wife moved there permanently in 1938 and took to raising geese, chickens, and sheep. The essays collected in *One Man's Meat,* originally written as monthly columns for *Harper's* magazine, are set on White's farm and chronicle his daily life in the country.

Most critics praise White for his work as an essayist. Lehmann-Haupt calls him "an essayist's essayist," while Hasley labels White "our best living personal essayist." Writing in the *New York Times,* Irwin Edman remarks that "White is the finest essayist in the United States. He says wise things gracefully; he is the master of an idiom at once exact and suggestive, distinguished yet familiar." White is, Sampson concludes, "generally recognized as one of the best essayists of the twentieth century."

Although White's essays have won him overwhelming critical acclaim, he is more popularly known as the author of *Charlotte's Web* and *Stuart Little,* two classics of American children's literature. White has written only three books for children in all, but many observers rank him with such notables in the field of children's literature as Lewis Carroll, the author of *Alice in Wonderland.* Sampson acknowledges that *Charlotte's Web* "may well turn out to be the longest remembered of his works." "What makes White's three books outstanding," Sampson continues, "is that he has written them in the classical tradition of children's stories. . . . What the child [learns from White's books]—and what children learn from the other fine children's books—is a great deal about loyalty, honesty, love, sadness, and happiness."

Inspired by a vivid dream, White began in 1939 to write a children's story about a small, mouse-like character. Whenever one of his eighteen nieces and nephews wanted to be told a story, White improvised new adventures for his hero, whom he named Stuart Little. In 1945, he gathered these adventures together into a book-length manuscript which he sent to Harper & Row for consideration. Children's book editor Ursula Nordstrom found it "marvelously well-written, and funny, and touching," she recalls in an article for the *New York Times Book Review,* and accepted *Stuart Little* for publication.

White worked closely with artist Garth Williams on the illustrations for the book. Williams brought his drawings to Nordstrom's office in New York, she mailed them to White in Maine, and White wrote down his suggestions and ideas and mailed them back to her with the drawings. In this way the illustrations for *Stuart Little* were completed to the satisfaction of both author and artist. Williams's illustrations, John Gillespie and Diana Lembo write in *Introducing Books: A Guide for the Middle Grades,* "complement the text beautifully."

Publication of *Stuart Little* met with opposition from Anne Carroll Moore, head of children's literature at the New York Public Library and the most influential person in juvenile publishing at the time. After reading the book in galleys, Moore thought it "was nonaffirmative, inconclusive, unfit for children, and she felt that it would harm its author if published," Nordstrom relates. Nonetheless, Harper went ahead with publication, convinced that *Stuart Little* showed merit. "It is unnerving," Nordstrom quotes White as saying, "to be told you're bad for children; but I detected in Miss Moore's letter an assumption that there are rules governing the writing of juvenile literature. . . . And this I was not sure of. I had followed my instincts in writing about Stuart, and following one's instincts seemed to be the way a writer should operate."

The book tells the story of the Little family's second child, Stuart, who happens to be two inches tall and looks like a mouse, although the Littles themselves are normal-sized and human. Because of his modest stature and adventurous nature, Stuart finds himself in a series of wild situations: he is hoisted aloft by a window shade, attacked by a housecat, dropped into a bathtub drain to retrieve a lost ring, and even put into a piano to free some stuck keys. Stuart's "somewhat random adventures show him to be brave, ingenious, enterprising, and of romantic inclination," Peter M. Neumeyer writes in the *Dictionary of Literary Biography.* Neumeyer also believes that White "has imaginatively extrapolated [Stuart's adventures] with all the ingenuity of Jonathan Swift plotting Gulliver's stay in Lilliput."

When Stuart's newfound love Margalo, a bird, flies away to escape the Littles' housecat, Stuart follows. The remainder of the book concerns his unsuccessful quest for her. "Like any knight errant," Neumeyer writes, "Stuart is tempted and distracted during this pursuit." These distractions include wooing a girl during a canoe ride and teaching a class of fifth-graders when their regular teacher is sick. But the book ends with Stuart driving away in his toy car, continuing his search for Margalo. Calling *Stuart Little* "a lively and, at times, tender book that is a delight to both the imagination and the emotions," Gillespie and Lembo nevertheless find that "the rather inconclusive ending has somewhat marred its appeal for a few readers." Speaking of the book's ending in his *Letters of E. B. White,* White reveals: "Quite a number of children have written me to ask about Stuart. They want to know whether he got back home and whether he found Margalo. They are good questions, but I did not answer them in the book because, in a way, Stuart's journey symbolizes the continuing journey that everybody takes—in search of what is perfect and unattainable. This is perhaps too elusive an idea to put into a book for children, but I put it in anyway." John Rowe Townsend, in his *Written for Children: An Outline of English Language Children's Literature,* muses that "perhaps the ending is right; Stuart's is a quest for freedom and beauty, and such a quest is never completed."

Several reviewers believe that *Stuart Little* has the same wide appeal as do the classics of children's literature. Writing in the *Saturday Review of Literature,* R. C. Benet believes readers of all ages will enjoy the book. "The exact number of years of the reader," he states, "won't matter here any more than it does with 'Alice,' 'The Wind in the Willows,' some of [A. A.] Milne, or indeed the work of Walt Disney, who created that other popular mouse." The *Springfield Republican* critic agrees, finding that "readers of [Ernest] Hemingway as well as six-year-olds will find the book worth their while, much as grown-up readers of 'Alice in Wonderland' . . . find that classic. 'Stuart Little,' indeed, is in the school of 'Alice,' though by no means an imitation." It is a "memorable *Wanderjahr* for children," Timothy Foote writes in *Time,* "loaded with longing and nostalgia." Foote goes on to note that *Stuart Little* "still sells and sells." On its way to becoming "one of the classics of American children's literature," as Neumeyer describes it, *Stuart Little* has sold more than two million copies in English and has been translated into twenty other languages.

White's next children's book, *Charlotte's Web,* was published in 1952. Without fanfare, or even a previous mention that he was working on another children's book, White dropped by his publisher's office with the manuscript. He took Nordstrom by surprise. "He gave me the only copy in existence of 'Charlotte's Web,' " she remembers, "got back on the elevator and left." Nordstrom read only a few chapters before deciding to publish the book. "I couldn't believe that it was so good!" she comments.

Called by Roger Sale in his *Fairy Tales and After: From Snow White to E. B. White* "probably *the* classic American children's book of the last thirty years," *Charlotte's Web* is set on a farm much like the one White owns in Maine. The story "seems to have developed," Neumeyer observes, "directly and exclusively out of White's joy in his own rural existence." White explains to Lee Bennett Hopkins in *More Books by More People:* "I like animals and my barn is a very pleasant place to be. . . . One day when I was on my way to feed the pig, I began feeling sorry for the pig because, like most pigs, he was doomed to die. This made me sad. So I started thinking of ways to save a pig's life. I had been watching a big, gray spider at her work and was impressed by how clever she was at weaving. Gradually I worked the spider into the story, . . . a story of friendship and salvation on a farm." Sale notes that White has referred to *Charlotte's Web* as a "hymn to the barn." "It is the word 'hymn,' " Sale writes, "and

the sense of celebration and praise, that is important here. . . . The essential celebration is of the beautiful things change brings or can bring."

Charlotte's Web tells the story of Wilbur, a small pig destined for slaughter, who is saved by his friend Charlotte, a spider, when she weaves the words "Some Pig" into a web above Wilbur's pen. People who see this miraculous message are so impressed by it that Wilbur is spared and even put on display at the local fair. But during their stay at the fair, Charlotte dies. In the final lines of the book, Wilbur remembers her as being "in a class by herself. It is not often that someone comes along who is a true friend and a good writer. Charlotte was both." David Rees, writing in *The Marble in the Water: Essays on Contemporary Writers of Fiction for Children and Young Adults,* calls *Charlotte's Web* "the one great modern classic about death." Speaking of the book's closing lines, Rees believes them to be "comforting, not depressing. White is telling the child that he is allowed to mourn; that he is allowed to remember with a certain sadness." "The profound themes of selfless love and acceptance of death are found in this story," Gillespie and Lembo write, "and are significantly although delicately explored."

Charlotte's death is shown to be a natural part of the cycle of existence. It is "made bearable," Townsend believes, "by the continuance of life through her offspring." Rees points out that immediately following the passage about Charlotte's death comes another passage about the birth of her children and of small animals on the farm. White's idea "that death is an inevitable and necessary part of the whole scheme of things," Rees states, "is made acceptable by the emphasis he puts, after Charlotte dies, on the joy and happiness of birth." Townsend sees, too, that "the passage of seasons, the round of nature, are unobtrusively indicated" throughout the story.

One indication of this cycle is to be found in the passage of the young girl Fern from childhood. Fern was responsible for saving Wilbur when he was the runt of the litter. She later nursed him until he reached a healthy size, and she visited him in his barn as well. But as she grows older, Fern is less attentive to Wilbur and the other animals. Her attention instead centers on the upcoming fair and a certain boy who will be there. Fern begins the book as one of the central characters, but ends by being only peripheral to the story. "Fern has begun the saving of Wilbur," Townsend notes, "but by the end she has forgotten him; that is life, too. Childhood ends."

Charlotte's Web is written in a style that reminds Neumeyer of "an eighteenth-century definition of poetry: 'proper words in proper places'—the *mot juste.*" This quality is also noted by Eleanor Cameron in her study *The Green and Burning Bush: On the Writing and Enjoyment of Children's Books.* "The artistry of [*Charlotte's Web*]," Cameron writes, "lies not at all in the use of unusual words but, as in all of Mr. White's prose for adults and children alike, in the way he combines words, creates intimations." In *A Critical History of Children's Literature,* Ruth Hill Viguers argues that the story of *Charlotte's Web* is thin and nonsensical, but that White, partly through his style, manages to overcome this weakness. "Mr. White has triumphed," Viguers states. "The style and wit of his writing, his wisdom and his remembrance of a child's rapt concern with the things he loves strengthened the slender thread of story."

Critical evaluation of *Charlotte's Web* places it among the very best of its genre. It is "outstanding among post-war American children's fiction," Townsend believes. "As a piece of work," Eudora Welty writes in the *New York Times,* "[*Charlotte's Web*] is just about perfect, and just about magical in the way it is done." The reviewer for the *Chicago Sunday Tribune* judges *Charlotte's Web* to be a "rare story of a beautiful friendship," as well as "witty and wise, lively and tender." Since its initial publication in 1952, *Charlotte's Web* has become a classic of American children's literature and has sold well over three million copies. Among books for children, Neumeyer sums up, *Charlotte's Web* "must surely be one of the most widely read and best beloved of this century."

It wasn't until 1970 that White published his next children's book, *The Trumpet of the Swan*. It has much in common with his earlier efforts. As in *Stuart Little* and *Charlotte's Web*, the characters in *The Trumpet of the Swan* are animals who participate in the human world and overcome great obstacles to achieve their desires. And like the previous two books, *Trumpet of the Swan* grew out of an experience in White's own life. His fascination with the trumpeter swans at the Philadelphia Zoo, initiated by a story in the *New York Times*, led White to tell the story of Louis, a voiceless trumpeter swan. Because he cannot speak, his human friend Sam Beaver takes Louis to school with him to learn to read and write. Thereafter, Louis carries a chalkboard and chalk with him to write out his messages. His father, wanting him to be able to communicate with other swans as well, steals a trumpet for him to play. Soon Louis's trumpet playing leads to nightclub work and to a meeting with Serena, a female swan with whom he falls in love.

Writing in the *New York Times Book Review*, John Updike expresses his opinion that *The Trumpet of the Swan* joins *Stuart Little* and *Charlotte's Web* "on the shelf of classics." Although it differs from the previous books, Updike finds that *Trumpet* "has superior qualities of its own; it is the most spacious and serene of the three, the one most imbued with the author's sense of the precious instinctual heritage represented by wild nature, . . . yet [the book] does not lack the inimitable tone of the two earlier works—the simplicity that never condescends, the straight and earnest telling that happens upon, rather than veers into, comedy." Neumeyer believes that although it does not compare favorably with *Stuart Little* and *Charlotte's Web*, *Trumpet of the Swan* "is adventurous, imaginative, and it has some touching moments."

White tells Justin Wintle and Emma Fisher in *The Pied Pipers: Interviews with the Influential Creators of Children's Literature* the difference he sees between writing for children and writing for adults. "In my experience, the only difference (save for a very slight modification of vocabulary) is in one's state of mind," he explains. "Children are a wonderful audience—they are so eager, so receptive, so quick. I have great respect for their powers of observation and reasoning. But like any good writer, I write to amuse myself, not some imaginary audience."

Critical evaluations of White's career show that although he may write only to amuse himself, he has in the process entertained many others as well. Hasley defines White as "a kind of national housekeeper and caretaker. He has gone on steadily and quietly, looking around and ahead, poking into public and domestic corners, . . . and hardly any literate American has not benefited from his humor, his nonsense, his creativity, and his engaging wisdom." Calling him "the humble, kindly senior guru of delicate American humor," Jay Scriba of the *Milwaukee Journal* points out that White, "a master wordsmith, . . . is probably in more college literary anthologies than any other" writer. "The pleasures of reading White's prose," Jonathan Yardley writes in the *Washington Post*, "are many and great." Speaking of *One Man's Meat*, a collection of magazine columns, Yardley sees White as "one of the few writers of this or any other century who

has succeeded in transforming the ephemera of journalism into something that demands to be called literature." Edward Hoagland, writing in the *New York Times Book Review*, muses that "there are times, reading an E. B. White book of essays, when you think he must be the most likable man of letters alive. This is as it should be in a collection of personal pieces; and if you are some kind of writer yourself, you probably want to imitate him."

Upon receiving the National Medal for Literature in 1971, White wrote an article for *Publishers Weekly* in which he thanked the National Institute of Arts and Letters for the award. In this article he defines the role of the writer. "I have always felt," White states, "that the first duty of a writer was to ascend—to make flights, carrying others along if he could manage it. To do this takes courage. . . . Today, with so much of earth damaged and endangered, with so much of life dispiriting or joyless, a writer's courage can easily fail him. I feel this daily. . . . But despair is not good—for the writer, for anyone. Only hope can carry us aloft. . . . Only hope, and a certain faith. . . . This faith is a writer's faith, for writing itself is an act of faith, nothing else. And it must be the writer, above all others, who keeps it alive—choked with laughter, or with pain."

MEDIA ADAPTATIONS: Stuart Little was filmed for television by the National Broadcasting Company in 1966; *Charlotte's Web* was adapted as an animated film by Paramount in 1972 and adapted as a filmstrip by Stephen Bosustow Productions, 1974, and by Films Incorporated, 1976; the short story "the Family That Dwelt Apart" was adapted as an animated film by Learning Corporation of America in 1974.

BIOGRAPHICAL/CRITICAL SOURCES:

BOOKS

Anderson, A. J., *E. B. White: A Bibliography*, Scarecrow, 1978.
Authors in the News, Volume 2, Gale, 1976.
Benet, Laura, *Famous English and American Essayists*, Dodd, 1966.
Cameron, Eleanor, *The Green and Burning Bush: On the Writing and Enjoyment of Children's Books*, Atlantic-Little, Brown, 1969.
Children's Literature Review, Volume 1, Gale, 1976.
Contemporary Literary Criticism, Gale, Volume 10, 1979, Volume 34, 1985, Volume 39, 1986.
Dictionary of Literary Biography, Gale, Volume 11: *American Humorists, 1800-1950*, Part 2, 1982, Volume 22: *American Writers for Children, 1900-1960*, 1983.
Elledge, Scott, *E. B. White: A Biography*, Norton, 1984.
Fadiman, Clifton, *Party of One*, World Publishing, 1955.
Georgiou, Constantine, *Children and Their Literature*, Prentice-Hall, 1969.
Gillespie, John and Diana Lembo, *Introducing Books: A Guide for the Middle Grades*, Bowker, 1970.
Gillespie, John and Diana Lembo, *Juniorplots: A Book Talk Manual for Teachers and Librarians*, Bowker, 1967.
Hall, Katherine Romans, *E. B. White: A Bibliographic Catalogue of Printed Materials in the Department of Rare Books, Cornell University Library*, Garland Publishing, 1979.
Hoffmann, Miriam and Eva Samuels, editors, *Authors and Illustrators of Children's Books: Writings on Their Lives and Works*, Bowker, 1972.
Hopkins, Lee Bennett, *More Books by More People*, Citation, 1974.
Kramer, Dale, *Ross and the "New Yorker,"* Doubleday, 1951.
Lanes, Selma G., *Down the Rabbit Hole: Adventures and Misadventures in the Realm of Children's Literature*, Atheneum, 1972.

Meigs, Cornelia, editor, *A Critical History of Children's Literature,* revised edition, Macmillan, 1969.

Rees, David, *The Marble in the Water: Essays on Contemporary Writers of Fiction for Children and Young Adults,* Horn Book, 1980.

Rogers, Barbara J., *E. B. White,* Scribner, 1979.

Sale, Roger, *Fairy Tales and After: From Snow White to E. B. White,* Harvard University Press, 1978.

Sampson, Edward C., *E. B. White,* Twayne, 1974.

Smith, James Steel, *A Critical Approach to Children's Literature,* McGraw, 1967.

Thurber, James, *The Years with Ross,* Little, Brown, 1959.

Townsend, John Rowe, *Written for Children: An Outline of English Language Children's Literature,* revised edition, Lippincott, 1974.

Unger, Leonard, editor, *American Writers: A Collection of Literary Biographies,* Volume 4, Scribner, 1974.

Van Gelder, Robert, *Writers and Writing,* Scribner, 1946.

White, E. B., *Charlotte's Web,* Harper, 1952.

White, E. B., *Letters of E. B. White,* Harper, 1976.

White, E. B., *One Man's Meat,* Harper, 1942, enlarged edition, 1944, reprinted, 1982.

White, E. B., *The Points of My Compass: Letters from the East, the West, the North, the South,* Harper, 1962.

White, E. B., *The Second Tree from the Corner,* Harper, 1954, reprinted, 1984.

White, E. B. and Katharine Sergeant White, editors, *A Subtreasury of American Humor,* Coward, 1941, reprinted, Capricorn Books, 1962.

Wintle, Justin and Emma Fisher, *The Pied Pipers: Interviews with the Influential Creators of Children's Literature,* Paddington Press, 1975.

Yates, Norris W., *American Humorists,* Iowa State University Press, 1964.

PERIODICALS

Chicago Sunday Tribune, November 16, 1952, October 21, 1962.
Children's Literature in Education, May, 1973.
College English, April, 1946, December, 1961.
Connecticut Review, October, 1971.
Los Angeles Times Book Review, August 22, 1982.
Milwaukee Journal, October 13, 1975.
Nation, August 14, 1929.
National Review, June 10, 1977.
New Republic, February 15, 1954, November 24, 1962.
New York Herald Tribune Book Review, May 26, 1929, December 28, 1929, January 17, 1954, October 21, 1962.
New York Review of Books, October 27, 1977.
New York Times, October 7, 1934, October 28, 1945, October 19, 1952, January 17, 1954, July 11, 1969, January 23, 1970, November 17, 1976, September 19, 1977, November 20, 1981.
New York Times Book Review, October 28, 1962, May 24, 1970, June 28, 1970, May 12, 1974, November 8, 1981.
Publishers Weekly, December 6, 1971, December 13, 1976.
Saturday Review, January 30, 1954, November 24, 1962, June 27, 1970.
Saturday Review of Literature, December 7, 1929, October 27, 1934, October 15, 1938, December 8, 1945, August 30, 1947.
Springfield Republican, October 21, 1945.
Time, December 20, 1976, January 25, 1982.
Washington Post, December 1, 1982.
Washington Post Book World, November 8, 1981, October 14, 1984.

Wilson Library Bulletin, February, 1972.

OBITUARIES:

PERIODICALS

Chicago Tribune, October 2, 1985.
Detroit Free Press, October 2, 1985.
Detroit News, October 2, 1985.
Los Angeles Times, October 2, 1985.
Newsweek, October 14, 1985.
New York Times, October 2, 1985.
Publishers Weekly, October 11, 1985.
Time, October 14, 1985.
Washington Post, October 2, 1985.

[Sketch reviewed by son, Joel McCoun White]

*   *   *

WHITE, Edmund (Valentine III) 1940-

PERSONAL: Born January 13, 1940, in Cincinnati, Ohio; son of Edmund Valentine II (an engineer) and Delilah (a psychologist; maiden name, Teddlie) White. *Education:* University of Michigan, B.A., 1962.

ADDRESSES: Home—434 Lafayette St., New York, N.Y. 10003; 8 rue Poulletier, 75004 Paris, France. *Agent*—Maxine Groffsky, Maxine Groffsky Literary Agency, 2 Fifth Ave., New York, N.Y. 10011.

CAREER: Time, Inc., Book Division, New York, N.Y., staff writer, 1962-70; *Saturday Review,* New York City, senior editor, 1972-73; writer. Assistant professor of creative writing at Johns Hopkins University, 1977-79; adjunct professor of creative writing at Columbia University School of the Arts, 1981-83; instructor in creative writing at Yale University and New York University. Executive director of New York Institute for the Humanities, 1981-82.

AWARDS, HONORS: Hopwood Awards, 1961 and 1962, for fiction and drama; Ingram Merrill grants, 1973 and 1978; Guggenheim fellow, 1983; American Academy and Institute of Arts and Letters award for fiction, 1983.

WRITINGS:

NONFICTION

(With Peter Wood) *When Zeppelins Flew,* Time-Life, 1969.
(With Dale Browne) *The First Men,* Time-Life, 1973.
(With Charles Silverstein) *The Joy of Gay Sex: An Intimate Guide for Gay Men to the Pleasures of a Gay Lifestyle,* Crown, 1977.
States of Desire: Travels in Gay America, Dutton, 1980.

FICTION

Forgetting Elena (novel), Random House, 1973.
Nocturnes for the King of Naples (novel), St. Martin's, 1978.
A Boy's Own Story (novel), Dutton, 1982.
Caracole (novel), Dutton, 1985.
(With Adam Mars-Jones) *The Darker Proof: Stories From a Crisis,* Plume, 1988.
The Beautiful Room Is Empty (novel), Knopf, 1988.

OTHER

Also author of *Argument for a Myth* and "The Blue Boy in Black," a play, first performed in New York City at Masque Theater, April, 1963. Contributor of articles and reviews to periodicals.

SIDELIGHTS: Edmund White has often labored under the catchphrase "gay writer," but his literary reputation transcends such simplistic qualification. As William Goldstein notes in *Publishers Weekly,* "To call Edmund White merely a gay writer is to oversimplify his work and his intentions. Although that two-word label . . . aptly sums up White's status, the first word no doubt helps obscure the fact that the second applies just as fittingly." White's fiction in particular has garnered high critical acclaim; the author has received grants from the Ingram Merrill Foundation, the Guggenheim Foundation, and the American Academy and Institute of Arts and Letters. Though his nonfiction deals specifically with aspects of male homosexuality, White offers insights into human behavior in general, according to reviewers. In a piece for the *Nation,* Carter Wilson writes: "Edmund White is to be envied not only for his productivity, . . . but because he is a gifted writer who has staked himself a distinguished claim in the rocky territory called desire."

While stating in *Publishers Weekly* that he is "happy to be considered a gay writer," White nevertheless described the difficulties he encounters as a result of that classification. "Since gay people have very little political representation, we have no gay spokespeople," he said. "What happens is that there is an enormous pressure placed on gay novelists because they are virtually the *only* spokespeople. The problem is that the novelist's first obligation is to be true to his own vision, not to be some sort of common denominator of public relations man to all gay people. . . . Everything is read as though it's a sort of allegory about the political dimensions of homosexuality as a general topic, rather than as a specific story about a specific person. That's understandable, because there are so few gay books, but it is regrettable because it is really an Early Stalinist view of art as propaganda." White expressed the hope that his books, fiction and nonfiction alike, will someday pass out of the narrow "gay writing" context "into a more general literary one." He remarked: "I would hope that eventually my books would be good enough to be read simply as works of literature, as stories."

White's wish seems to have been granted from the outset of his fiction-writing career. His first novel, *Forgetting Elena,* has been cited for its satiric and insightful look at social interaction as well as for its elegant prose. A first-person narrative of an amnesia victim struggling to determine his identity and the identities of those around him, *Forgetting Elena* exposes the subtle entrapments of social hierarchy and etiquette. White told the *Library Journal* that the novel's premise illustrates the "sinister" aspects of life in an artistically obsessed society. He explained: "Every word and gesture would . . . convey a symbolic meaning. Ordinary morality would be obscured or forgotten. People would seek the beautiful and not the good—and, perhaps, cut free from the ethics, the beautiful would turn out to be merely pretty." Setting the novel's action at a fictitious resort reminiscent of New York's Fire Island, White creates, in the words of *Nation* contributor Simon Karlinsky, "a semiology of snobbery, its complete sign system." Karlinsky feels that "what might at first seem to be merely a witty parody of a particular subculture's foibles and vagaries actually turns out to be something far more serious and profound. . . . He has produced a parable about the nature of social interaction that transcends any given period and applies to the human predicament at large."

Most critics consider *Forgetting Elena* a highly accomplished first novel. Karlinsky calls the work "an astounding piece of writing—profound, totally convincing and memorable." Alan Friedman likewise praises the book in the *New York Times Book Review,* though not without qualifications. Friedman writes: "There is something so unfailingly petty about the narrator's ap-

prehensions . . . and something so oppressive about his preoccupations . . . that it is often difficult to be receptive to the book's genuine wonders." Friedman nevertheless concludes that this "tale of a sleuth who strives to detect the mystery of the self " is "an astonishing first novel, obsessively fussy, yet uncannily beautiful."

Nocturnes for the King of Naples, White's second novel, has won similar acclaim for its discerning treatment of human values and relationships. As John Yohalem explains in the *New York Times Book Review,* "*Nocturnes* is a series of apostrophes to a nameless, evidently famous dead lover, a man who awakened the much younger, also nameless narrator . . . to the possibility of sexual friendship. It was an experience that the narrator feels he did not justly appreciate," Yohalem continues, "and that he has long and passionately—and fruitlessly—sought to replace on his own terms." David Shields of the *Chicago Tribune* offers this assessment of the novel's impact: "Because of the speaker's final realization of the impossibility of ever finding a ground for satisfaction, a home, this book is more than a chronicle of sorrow and regret. It becomes, rather, a true elegy in which sorrow and self-knowledge combine and transform into a higher form of insight. This higher insight is the artistic intuition of the mortality of human things and ways."

Reviewers stress that the homosexual theme of *Nocturnes for the King of Naples* serves to create a more universal contemporary myth. As J. D. McClatchy notes in *Shenandoah,* White is "a superior stylist of both erotic theology and plangent contrition. And his special gift is his ability to empty out our stale expectations from genres . . . and types . . . and to reimagine them in a wholly intriguing and convincing manner." While Doris Grumbach suggests in the *Washington Post Book World* that White "will seem to the careful reader to be the poet of the burgeoning homosexual literature," she also notes: "The music of White's prose is seductive. It is of course possible that a tone-deaf, a melody-indifferent reader might turn his back on White's homo-erotic narrative. But the lover of good fictional writing who is open to this most subtle exploration of the many ways of love, desertion, loss, and regret, will read: 'You are the song I wanted to sing, the god I wanted to celebrate or conjure' and inevitably follow the piper-White wherever he leads."

In 1980 White published his second nonfiction work dealing with the male homosexual lifestyle, *States of Desire: Travels in Gay America.* *Village Voice* contributor Richard Goldstein feels that the best aspect of the work "is White's attempt to explain the most tangible aspects of gay culture to homosexuals, who may be more confused by what they do than heterosexuals are by what they see. . . . In its demure way, this is as didactic a treatise on homosexual experience as has ever been written." A documentary on segments of homosexual life in fifteen major American cities, White's book contains interviews, autobiographical reminiscences, and accounts of cultural and entertainment centers for gays. According to Ned Rorem in the *Washington Post Book World,* *States of Desire* "poses as a documentary . . . on our national gay bourgeoisie. Actually it's an artist's selective vision . . . of human comportment which is and is not his own, mulled over, distilled, then spilled onto the page with a melancholy joy."

Some critics have expressed disappointment with White's scope and objectivity in *States of Desire.* Goldstein writes: "Nowhere in [the book] is there any sense of how different life is for a working-class homosexual, for a lesbian, or for a black." *New York Times Book Review* contributor Paul Cowan suggests that White is never able to make "the promiscuous America he portrays

. . . even remotely attractive to an outsider." Cowan elaborates: "Though his book is partly autobiographical, [White] never tries to help readers who don't share his sexual preference to understand his assumptions or the assumptions of the people he describes." According to Rorem, the reader hears "the risky whisper of generality, the undifferentiation common to documentaries where there is no 'building toward,' no climax, only comparisons, and where 10 examples seem better than one. . . . [White's] treatise is more a diary than a Baedeker, being at once too special and too general for reliability."

Despite these qualifications, critics generally praise *States of Desire.* Rorem remarks that despite its flaws, "this book tenders its subject without apology and with the cultured clarity of an address to peers." Former *New York Times* columnist John Leonard concludes: "Mr. White comes out of the closet with a brass band and a Moog synthesizer. He acquaints us with terror and qualm. Simply as anthropology, *States of Desire* commands attention and respect." *Newsweek*'s Walter Clemons feels that White's "novelistic gifts—curiosity about character (his own as well as others'), an alert ear and eye for revelatory detail—make this book absorbing." Goldstein, too, has praise for White: "The author's persona, as open and appreciative as the ever-young men of San Francisco he describes, is a particularly attractive bonus to his intelligence. . . . His passion is evident throughout the trek, and so is his compassion for those who mediate less gracefully between affection and fantasy."

A Boy's Own Story, White's semi-autobiographical novel, was published to high acclaim in 1982. The book concerns the difficult adolescence of a gay youth growing up in the 1950s. *New York Times Book Review* contributor Catherine R. Stimpson believes, however, that the subject of the work is "less a particular boy than the bodies and souls of American men: the teachers and masters; the lovers, brothers, hustlers and friends; the flawed fathers who would be kings to sons who should be princes. . . . Like so many American novels about coming to maturity, 'A Boy's Own Story' asserts that growing up is a descent into painful knowledge, indecency and repression." Christopher Lehmann-Haupt of the *New York Times* likewise writes: "This is not exclusively a homosexual boy's story. It is any boy's story, to the marvelous degree that it evokes the inchoate longing of late childhood and adolescence."

More than one reviewer has called *A Boy's Own Story* a "classic" work. Comparing White to James Baldwin, Herman Wouk, and Mary McCarthy, Thomas M. Disch writes in the *Washington Post Book World* that the novel in question "represents the strongest bid to date by a gay writer to do for his minority experience what the writers above did for theirs—offer it as a representative, all-American instance." Stimpson notes: "This book is as artful as [White's] earlier novels but more explicit and grounded in detail, far less fanciful and elusive. . . . Balancing the banal and the savage, the funny and the lovely, he achieves a wonderfully poised fiction." *Village Voice Literary Supplement* columnist Eliot Fremont-Smith concludes: "*A Boy's Own Story* seems intended to be liberating, as well as touching and clever and smart. It is something else as well: unsettling to the willing heart. This makes it a problem, with no happy solution guaranteed, which defines what's wrong with the book. But also what's right, what intrigues." Lehmann-Haupt calls the work "superior fiction," adding: "Somehow . . . Mr. White does succeed in almost simultaneously elevating and demeaning his self-history. And these extremes of epiphany and emptiness are what is most universal about this haunting Bildungsroman."

Caracole, White's 1985 novel, has been described by *New York Times Book Review* contributor David R. Slavitt as "a grand fantasy—an oddly distancing and, at the same time, intensely intimate form of fiction. . . . Shrewdness and self-awareness ooze from every intricate sentence, every linguistic arabesque and hothouse epigram." Though appreciative of the work, Slavitt suggests that one result of "the artificed quality of the book is the distance at which it puts its characters, who are . . . pastoral figures, vivid and cute, as if seen from the wrong end of a telescope. They can endure pleasure and pain that would be intolerable if they were more plausible and persuasive." In a *Washington Post Book World* review, Julian Barnes expresses a similar opinion: "The characters, despite their opinions being transcribed at great length, remain heavy-hipped and unrealized on the page." Lehmann-Haupt observes in his *New York Times* column that White "has certainly conceived a 19th century plot steeped in the conventions of romanticism" when he writes of two country lovers forcibly separated who turn to sexual escapades in a large city. Lehmann-Haupt finds, however, that the resulting story is a "puzzling melange of comic opera and sleek sensuality," tedious in its "absence of a story or any significant action to engage our interest." Slavitt concludes: "This book is, provokingly, a challenge to taste, which is likely to vary from one reader to another or even from moment to moment in the same reader. . . . But high and dry . . . Mr. White reigns and deigns, impishly looking down and loving the kind of delicious outrage he has worked so hard for in this book and has so richly earned."

Concurrent with his career as an author, White has taught creative writing at several eastern universities, including Johns Hopkins, Columbia, and Yale. He told *Publishers Weekly* that he considers his own creative work "literary fiction," but he added: "I think 'literary' is not necessarily a word of praise. It's a word of description; there's almost a category of literary or serious fiction. . . . The market I'm going for, the kind of reader I'm looking for, is one who is not simply looking for entertainment, but is looking for whatever we look for from art." White, who once had a novel rejected by twenty-two different publishers, admits to being thrilled by the recognition his writing has received. "I know I'll always be doing this," he said, "and I know that I'll never make a living from my writing; but that's fine. It's enough to be published. . . . I don't have very exalted notions of what a writer's life should be like."

BIOGRAPHICAL/CRITICAL SOURCES:

BOOKS

Contemporary Literary Criticism, Volume 27, Gale, 1984.
White, Edmund, *States of Desire: Travels in Gay America,* Dutton, 1980.

PERIODICALS

Chicago Tribune, December 10, 1978, April 6, 1980.
Globe and Mail (Toronto), May 14, 1988.
Harper's, March, 1979, October, 1982.
Library Journal, February 15, 1973.
Los Angeles Times, March 31, 1988.
Los Angeles Times Book Review, May 4, 1980, April 3, 1988.
Nation, January 5, 1974, March 1, 1980, November 13, 1982.
Newsweek, April 30, 1973, February 11, 1980, January 17, 1983.
New York Times, January 21, 1980, December 17, 1982, September 8, 1985, March 17, 1988.
New York Times Book Review, March 25, 1973, February 3, 1980, October 10, 1982, September 15, 1985, March 20, 1988.
Shenandoah, Volume XXX, number 1, fall, 1978.

Times Literary Supplement, September 5, 1980, August 19, 1983, January 22, 1988.
Village Voice, January 28, 1980.
Village Voice Literary Supplement, December, 1982.
Washington Post Book World, November 12, 1978, December 10, 1978, January 27, 1980, October 17, 1982, October 6, 1985, April 3, 1988, May 30, 1988.

*   *   *

WHITE, Patrick (Victor Martindale) 1912-

PERSONAL: Born May 28, 1912, in London, England; son of Victor Martindale and Ruth (Withycombe) White. *Education:* King's College, Cambridge, B, A., 1935.

ADDRESSES: Home—20 Martin Rd., Centennial Park, Sydney, New South Wales 2021, Australia.

CAREER: Writer. *Military service:* Royal Air Force, 1940-45; intelligence officer.

AWARDS, HONORS: Australian Literary Society gold medal for *Happy Valley,* and for *The Tree of Man,* 1956; Miles Franklin Award for *Voss,* 1958, and for *Riders in the Chariot,* 1962; W. H. Smith & Son literary award for *Voss,* 1959; brotherhood award from National Conference of Christians and Jews, 1962, for *Riders in the Chariot;* Nobel Prize for Literature, 1973.

WRITINGS:

The Ploughman and Other Poems, Beacon Press, 1935.
Happy Valley (novel), Harrap, 1939, Viking, 1940.
The Living and the Dead (novel), Viking, 1941.
The Aunt's Story (novel), Viking, 1948.
The Tree of Man (novel), Viking, 1955.
Voss (novel), Viking, 1957.
Riders in the Chariot (novel), Viking, 1961.
The Burnt Ones (short stories), Viking, 1964.
The Solid Mandala (novel), Viking, 1966.
The Vivisector (novel), Viking, 1970.
The Eye of the Storm (novel), J. Cape, 1973, Viking, 1974.
Poems, Soft Press, 1974.
The Cockatoos: Shorter Novels and Stories, J. Cape, 1974, Viking, 1975.
A Fringe of Leaves, J. Cape, 1976, Viking, 1977.
The Twyborn Affair (novel), Viking, 1979.
Flaws in the Grass: A Self-Portrait (autobiography), Viking, 1981.
Memoirs of Many in One, by Alex Xenophon Demirjian Gray (novel), Viking, 1986.
Three Uneasy Pieces (short stories), J. Cape, 1988, Random House, c. 1989.

White adapted one of his short stories, "The Night of the Prowler," into a film, released by Chariot/International Harmony in 1979. Contributor to *Australian Letters,* Volume 1, 1958.

PLAYS

"Return to Abyssinia," produced in London, 1947.
Four Plays (contains "The Ham Funeral," produced in Adelaide, 1961; "The Season at Sarsaparilla," produced in Adelaide, 1962; "A Cheery Soul," produced in Melbourne, 1963; and "Night on Bald Mountain," produced in Adelaide, 1964), Eyre & Spottiswoode, 1965, Viking, 1966.

Also author of "Big Toys," 1977, "Signal Driver," 1981, and "Netherwood," 1983.

SIDELIGHTS: The works of English-born Patrick White are probably the most complex, structurally and thematically, in present-day Australia, the country where White grew up and which he has adopted as his own. Although most critics acknowledge White's talent and genius, several have written of the difficulty in reading his novels because of the multiplicity of symbols, myths, and allegories: William Walsh discussed White's "choking thickets of imagery"; Robert Phillips called reading White "a bit like over-indulgence in chocolate mousse"; Bruce Allen wrote of White's "stylistic crudeness."

White's basic orientation is religious and he takes from a variety of religious attitudes the philosophies he needs to explore his overriding concern: man's search for meaning in an apparently meaningless society. Inherent in White's consideration of spirituality in a mechanical and materialistic world is the concept of man's isolation in a crowded society. He asks, Peter S. Prescott wrote, as a pathologist might, "What pox, what gangrene have we here? What rot will be extruded from this pustule?" Even within the most basic societal structures, man is alienated, alone; man's need for meaning is ultimately to be found in the interior world, the world of the imagination and the soul. Robert Phillips said, "White's thesis . . . is simply this: We are all alone in a chaotic world and only we ourselves can help ourselves during our brief tenure." Often White's theory of the duality of man is exhibited through characters decayed in body but spiritually whole. George Steiner wrote, "Incontinence, the worn skin, the sour odors of senility, the toothless appetites and spasms of the old . . . lay bare the ignoble, perhaps accidental fact that the spirit is so meanly housed."

White's frequent use of the isolation theme in his fiction is rooted in his personal feelings of alienation and non-acceptance by his fellow countrymen. Several periods of expatriation preceded his ultimate return to Australia, as he explained to Ingmar Bjorksten in 1962: "It was eighteen years before I dared to come back to Australia for the third time. . . . I couldn't do without the countryside out here. I don't believe in a final break with the place one originates from. Only in a temporary break . . . to get perspective. You are shaped by the place you have your roots in; it has become part of you. Outside places don't shape you in the same way. This has nothing to do with nationalism. People are always the same. This is what my compatriots find so difficult to understand." Bjorksten explored another possible cause of White's feelings of alienation: "For a long time he was dismissed as peculiar, pretentious, and irrelevant by his countrymen, whose restricted vision and whose limited experience of what human life has to offer he exposes time after time, while simultaneously attacking the holy cow that they so deeply revere: an uncritical materialism that never questions itself." White's 1973 Nobel Prize has gained him greater acceptance among the Australians, although he is still more widely read in other countries.

In expressing his theories of alienation and individual spirituality, White often uses Jungian archetypes of the collective unconscious and symbols of religions such as Buddhism and Christianity. A recurring concept involves the mandala, a motif of Buddhist origin. Mandala is the "Sanskrit word for 'magic ring,'" according to Bjorksten, who also explained that "the mandala represents the Buddhist concept of the universe, of completeness in the form of a square with circles inside or outside it." White most often uses the Jungian explanation of the mandala motif to express man's own divinity, with man at the circle's center rather than God, according to Bjorksten. In a 1973 letter, White himself acknowledged both his early indebtedness to Jung and his more recent belief in the possibility of the existence of God: "I have great admiration for [Jung] and his findings, but I also have

a belief in a supernatural power of which I have been given inklings from time to time: there have been incidents and coincidences which have shown me that there is a design behind the
haphazardness." Peter Beatson discussed White's recent affirmation of God's existence in terms of his recurrent metaphors
expressing the cycles of life, death, and ultimate rebirth.

Although the obscurity of White's novels has resulted in some
critics' labeling him "unreadable," a majority have received his
efforts with warm acceptance. A. Alvarez called White's isolation "an image of great beauty." Shirley Hazzard spoke of his
"rich, distinctive language, now stately, now mercurial, always
borne on the civilizing tide of irony." Pearl K. Bell wrote of
White's "strange and somber poetic truth." And D. Keith Mano
remarked: "It's as easy to be irked or bloody bored by Patrick
White as it is to be astonished by him. If you cooperate, magnificence can be tedious, or tedium magnificent. White is, without
conditional clause, brilliant. And exasperating. . . ."

Harry M. Miller bought the movie rights to *Voss,* and *Variety*
reported in 1970 that the film "should be the biggest attempt in
the history of Aussie film-making to pitch a quality product at
the international market."

AVOCATIONAL INTERESTS: Cooking, gardening, music.

BIOGRAPHICAL/CRITICAL SOURCES:

BOOKS

Alvarez, A., *Beyond All This Fiddle: Essays 1955-1967,* Random
     House, 1969.
Beatson, Peter, *The Eye in the Mandala,* Paul Elek, 1976.
Bjorksten, Ingmar, *Patrick White,* University of Queensland
     Press, 1976.
Contemporary Literary Criticism, Gale, Volume 3, 1975, Volume
     4, 1975, Volume 5, 1976, Volume 7, 1977, Volume 9, 1978,
     Volume 18, 1981.
Dyce, J. R., *Patrick White as Playwright,* University of Queens-
     land Press, 1974.
Finch, Janette, *A Bibliography of Patrick White,* Libraries Board
     of South Australia, 1966.
Morley, Patricia A., *The Mystery of Unity: Theme and Tech-
     nique in the Novels of Patrick White,* McGill-Queen's Uni-
     versity Press, 1972.
White, Patrick, *Flaws in the Grass,* Viking, 1981.

PERIODICALS

Books Abroad, summer, 1974.
Chicago Tribune, April 6, 1980.
Chicago Tribune Book World, February 26, 1984.
Commonweal, May 17, 1974.
Globe and Mail (Toronto), October 25, 1986, March 18, 1989.
Harper's, September, 1970.
Hudson Review, summer, 1974.
Listener, November 5, 1970.
Los Angeles Times, February 4, 1982, December 18, 1986.
Los Angeles Times Book Review, May 18, 1980.
National Review, February 15, 1974.
New Leader, September 7, 1970, January 21, 1974.
New Republic, January 5, 1974, January 12, 1974, March 22,
     1975.
New Statesman, September 7, 1973, July 5, 1974.
Newsweek, January 21, 1974, March 1, 1982.
New York, January 21, 1974.
New Yorker, March 4, 1974.
New York Review of Books, April 4, 1974.
New York Times, April 11, 1980.

New York Times Book Review, January 6, 1974, January 19,
     1975, April 27, 1980, February 7, 1982, October 26, 1986.
Prairie Schooner, fall, 1974.
Saturday Review, January 25,
Sewanee Review, spring, 1974, summer, 1975.
Spectator, June 22, 1974.
Time, January 14, 1974.
Times (London), October 29, 1981, April 3, 1986.
Times Literary Supplement, September 21, 1973, November 20,
     1981, April 4, 1986, December 2, 1988.
Tribune Books (Chicago), December 21, 1986.
Variety, July 22, 1970.
Village Voice, February 7, 1974.
Washington Post Book World, May 18, 1980, May 2, 1982, No-
     vember 16, 1986.

*   *   *

WHITE, Phyllis Dorothy James 1920- (P. D. James)

PERSONAL: Born August 3, 1920, in Oxford, England; daughter of Sidney Victor (a tax officer) and Dorothy May (Hone)
James; married Ernest Conner Bantry White (a medical practitioner), August 8, 1941 (died, 1964); children: Claire, Jane. *Politics:* "I belong to no political party." *Religion:* Church of England.

ADDRESSES: Agent—Elaine Greene Ltd., 31 Newington
Green, Islington, London N16 9PU, England.

CAREER: Former assistant stage manager, Festival Theatre,
Cambridge, England; worked as a Red Cross nurse and at the
Ministry of Food during World War II; North West Regional
Hospital Board, London, England, administrative assistant,
1949-68; Department of Home Affairs, London, civil servant,
1968-72, senior civil servant in crime department, 1972-79, full-
time writer, 1977—.

MEMBER: Institute of Hospital Administration (fellow).

AWARDS, HONORS: Crime Writers Association prize, 1967.

WRITINGS:

MYSTERY NOVELS, UNDER NAME P. D. JAMES

Cover Her Face, Faber, 1962, Scribner, 1966.
A Mind to Murder, Faber, 1963, Scribner, 1967.
Unnatural Causes, Scribner, 1967.
Shroud for a Nightingale, Scribner, 1971.
An Unsuitable Job for a Woman, Faber, 1972, Scribner, 1973.
The Black Tower, Scribner, 1975.
Death of an Expert Witness, Scribner, 1977.
Innocent Blood (Book-of-the-Month Club selection), Scribner,
     1980.
The Skull Beneath the Skin, Scribner, 1982.
A Taste for Death, Knopf, 1986.
Devices and Desires, Random House, 1990.

OMNIBUS VOLUMES, UNDER NAME P. D. JAMES

Crime Times Three, Scribner, 1979.
Murder in Triplicate, Scribner, 1982.
Trilogy of Death, Scribner, 1984.
P. D. James: Three Complete Novels, Crown, 1987.

Also author of *A Case of Classic Whodunits,* Warner Books.

CONTRIBUTOR, UNDER NAME P. D. JAMES

Ellery Queen's Murder Menu, World Publishing, 1969.

Winter's Crimes #5, Macmillan (London), 1973.
Ellery Queen's Masters of Mystery, Davis Publications, 1975.
Winter's Crimes #8, Macmillan (London), 1976.
Dilys Wynn, editor, *Murder Ink: The Mystery Reader's Companion,* Workman Publishing, 1977.
Crime Writers, BBC Publications, 1978.

OTHER, UNDER NAME P. D. JAMES

(With Thomas A. Critchley) *The Maul and the Pear Tree: The Ratcliffe Highway Murders, 1811,* Constable, 1971.
"A Private Treason" (play), first produced in the West End at the Palace Theatre, March 12, 1985.
P. D. James in Murderous Company, Crown, 1988.

SIDELIGHTS: As P. D. James, a name she chose because it is short and sexually neutral, Phyllis Dorothy James White has established herself as one of England's most prominent mystery writers. Often ranked with such masters of the genre as Agatha Christie, Dorothy L. Sayers, and Margery Allingham, James is critically acclaimed for her ability to combine complex and puzzling plots with psychologically believable characters, particularly in her novels featuring Commander Adam Dalgleish of Scotland Yard. Her "keen, cunning mind and a positively bloody imagination" make her "one of the finest and most successful mystery writers in the world," Peter Gorner writes in the *Chicago Tribune.*

When her husband returned from World War II suffering from severe schizophrenia, James needed to support her family on her own. For nineteen years she worked as a hospital administrator and then, following her husband's death, entered the British Department of Home Affairs as a civil servant in the criminal department. Her work there brought her into daily contact with police officials, judges, and magistrates. In her mystery novels, James draws upon these experiences, setting her stories in such places as a police forensic laboratory, a nurses' training school, and a home for the disabled.

Although she had wanted to write for many years, James was not able to devote time to this pursuit until the late 1950s. At that time, while working in a hospital, she began her first novel, *Cover Her Face.* Over a three-year period James wrote for two hours every morning before going to work, composing her story in longhand on notepaper, a method she still prefers. Once completed, the novel was accepted by the first publisher to whom it was sent and James's career as a mystery writer was launched. Since then she has published seven more novels. She has been a full-time writer since her retirement from government service in 1979.

There is an old-fashioned quality to James's novels that puts them squarely in the tradition of classic English detective fiction as practiced by Agatha Christie and similar writers. The character of Adam Dalgleish, Scotland Yard detective and published poet, for example, follows the familiar pattern of the gentleman detective popularized by such earlier writers as Dorothy L. Sayers and Ngaio Marsh. James's plots are puzzles which, she tells Wayne Warga of the *Los Angeles Times,* follow the traditional formula. "You have a murder, which is a mystery," she explains. "There is a closed circle of suspects. . . . You have, in my case, a professional detective. He finds clues and information which, as he discovers them, are also available to the reader. And at the end of the story there is a credible and satisfactory resolution that the reader could have arrived at as well." James's style, too, writes Thomas Lask in the *New York Times,* "is what we think of as typically British. Her writing is ample, leisurely, and full of loving description of house and countryside." And in common

with a number of other writers of mysteries, Norma Siebenheller states in her study *P. D. James,* James's "work is literate, tightly constructed, and civilized. Her people are genteel and polite."

Yet, while conforming to many of the expectations of the genre, James goes beyond its limitations. For instance, where other writers have concentrated almost entirely on the puzzles in their books to the detriment of such things as characterization, James has not. Although she creates a puzzle for her readers, she focuses her attention on writing realistic mysteries with fully rounded characters. "The classic English mystery, as practiced by many of its female creators," Siebenheller explains, "is basically a puzzle-solving exercise. . . . One never gets over the feeling, when reading these books, that they are all make-believe. . . . James departs from that tradition. . . . The worlds she creates are peopled with varied and interesting characters whose actions spring from believable motivations and whose reactions are true to their complex personalities." As James tells Carla Heffner in the *Washington Post,* her frequent comparison to Agatha Christie "amazes me. . . . Hers are the stereotype English crime novel which is set in the small English village where everyone knows their place. . . . I don't set my novels in that never-never land."

James's concern for realism is reflected in her creation of Adam Dalgleish, a complex character who is, Siebenheller believes, "a far cry from the almost comical characters who served Christie and Sayers as sleuths." Dalgleish is an introspective, serious figure—intensely devoted to solving the case at hand—who suppresses his personal feelings. His personality was shaped by one tragic event many years before: the death of his wife and son during childbirth. It is this painful memory, and the essential chaos it implies, that has formed Dalgleish's "vision of the world," as Erlene Hubly states in *Clues: A Journal of Detection.* Because of this memory, Dalgleish is a "Byronic hero," Hubly argues, unable "to adjust to or accept society." Yet, because of his fear of chaos and death, he enforces the rules of society, convinced that they are all humanity has with which to create order. Dalgleish tries, writes Hubly, "to bring order out of chaos: if he cannot stop death he can at least catch and punish those who inflict it on others."

While Dalgleish is her most popular character, James's secondary characters are equally realistic. All of her books, Julian Symons notes in the *New York Times Book Review,* "are marked by powerful and sympathetic characterizations." Perhaps her most fully realized character after Dalgleish is Cordelia Gray, a female private detective who appears in *An Unsuitable Job for a Woman* and *The Skull Beneath the Skin.* As James relates in the first of these two novels, Gray was raised in a series of foster homes she found "very interesting." Despite her past misfortunes, Gray is "a totally positive person," Siebenheller relates. "Not only is she optimistic, capable, and clever, she is good-natured as well. . . . This is not to say Cordelia is a Pollyanna. She fully acknowledges the rougher edges of life." She and Dalgleish enjoy a cordial rivalry whenever they meet on a murder case.

Many of James's other characters are from the respectable English middle class—educated and humanistic, they find themselves "consumed by jealousy, hatred, lust, sexual fears, and ambition," Gorner states. James explores her characters' labyrinthine emotional and psychological states with a penetrating and compassionate eye. Heffner, for example, sees James as someone "passionately curious about people and their peculiarities." Lask believes that James's work, despite its veneer of traditional English fiction, "is modern in the ambiguous makeup of her characters, their complex motives and the shrewd psychological touches of the relationship between the police and the criminals they pursue."

Moved by a deep moral concern, James sees mystery writing as an important expression of basic human values. Mystery novels, she tells Heffner, "are like 20th-century morality plays; the values are basic and unambiguous. Murder is wrong. In an age in which gratuitous violence and arbitrary death have become common, these values need no apology." The "corrosive, destructive aspect of crime," Siebenheller maintains, is one of James's major themes. She traces the effects of crime not only on the victim and criminal, but on their family and friends as well. James's concern is obvious, too, in the values she gives her characters. Comparing Adam Dalgleish with James, Warga describes him as "a man who is a realistic moralist much like his creator."

The success of James's novels can be attributed to their popularity among two different audiences, Heffner argues, "the lovers of a good 'whodunit' who read her novels for their action and intricate plots; and the literary world that admires the books for their character and motivation." In the words of Christopher Lehmann-Haupt, this wide acceptance has made James "one of the most esteemed practitioners of the [mystery] genre in the English-speaking world."

BIOGRAPHICAL/CRITICAL SOURCES:

BOOKS

Contemporary Literary Criticism, Gale, Volume 18, 1981, Volume 46, 1988.
James, P. D., *An Unsuitable Job for a Woman,* Faber, 1972, Scribner, 1973.
Siebenheller, Norma, *P. D. James,* Ungar, 1981.
Wynn, Dilys, editor, *Murder Ink,* Workman Publishing, 1977.
Wynn, Dilys, editor, *Murderess Ink,* Workman Publishing, 1977.

PERIODICALS

Atlantic, June, 1980.
Chicago Tribune, June 10, 1980, November 6, 1986, November 16, 1986.
Chicago Tribune Book World, May 18, 1980, September 19, 1982.
Christian Science Monitor, June 25, 1980.
Clues: A Journal of Detection, fall/winter, 1982, spring/summer, 1985.
Globe and Mail (Toronto), May 10, 1986, November 8, 1986, February 3, 1990.
Listener, June 5, 1975.
Los Angeles Times, June 6, 1980, November 6, 1986, January 21, 1987.
Los Angeles Times Book Review, June 22, 1980, November 30, 1986, February 25, 1990.
Maclean's, June 30, 1980.
Ms., April, 1974, August, 1979.
New Republic, July 31, 1976, November 26, 1977.
Newsweek, January 23, 1978, May 12, 1980, September 13, 1982, October 20, 1986.
New Yorker, March 11, 1976, March 6, 1978, June 23, 1980.
New York Review of Books, July 17, 1980.
New York Times, December 11, 1977, July 18, 1979, February 8, 1980, May 7, 1980, March 11, 1986, October 23, 1986.
New York Times Book Review, July 24, 1966, January 16, 1972, April 22, 1973, November 23, 1975, April 27, 1980, September 12, 1982, April 6, 1986, November 2, 1986, January 28, 1990.

New York Times Magazine, October 5, 1986.
People, December 8, 1986.
Publishers Weekly, January 5, 1976, October 25, 1985.
Spectator, December 23, 1972, June 12, 1976.
Time, April 17, 1978, May 26, 1980, March 31, 1986, October 27, 1986.
Times (London), March 27, 1980, May 14, 1982, March 9, 1985, March 22, 1985.
Times Literary Supplement, October 22, 1971, December 13, 1974, March 21, 1980, October 29, 1982.
Tribune Books (Chicago), February 4, 1990.
Village Voice, December 15, 1975, December 18, 1978.
Voice Literary Supplement, October, 1982.
Washington Post, April 30, 1980, November 10, 1986.
Washington Post Book World, April 15, 1977, April 27, 1980, September 19, 1982, April 20, 1986, November 9, 1986, January 21, 1990.

*   *   *

WHITE, Theodore H(arold)   1915-1986

PERSONAL: Born May 6, 1915, in Boston, Mass.; died after a stroke, May 9, 1986; son of David and Mary (Winkeller) White; married Nancy Ariana Van Der Heyden Bean, March 29, 1947 (divorced, 1971); married Beatrice Kevitt Hofstadter, March, 1974; children: (first marriage) Ariana Van Der Heyden, David Fairbank. *Education:* Harvard University, A.B. (summa cum laude), 1938.

ADDRESSES: Home—Old Route 67, Bridgewater, Conn. 06752. *Office*—168 East 64th St., New York, N.Y. 10021. *Agent*—Julian Bach Literary Agency, Inc., 747 3rd Ave., New York, N.Y. 10017.

CAREER: Time magazine, New York City, Far East correspondent and chief of China bureau, 1939-45; *New Republic* magazine, New York City, editor, 1947; Overseas News Agency, New York City, chief European correspondent, 1948-50; *Reporter* magazine, New York City, chief European correspondent, 1950-53; *Collier's* magazine, national correspondent, 1955-56; free-lance writer and correspondent, 1956-86. Covered China war front, Indian uprising, and Honan famine during World War II; present at Japanese surrender aboard U.S.S. Missouri, 1945; covered post-World War II European events, including administration of Marshall Plan and North Atlantic Treaty Organization. Member of board of overseers, Harvard University, 1968-74.

MEMBER: Council on Foreign Relations, Foreign Correspondents Club (president, 1944-45), Phi Beta Kappa, Century Club, Harvard Club.

AWARDS, HONORS: Sidney Hillman Foundation Award, 1954, and National Association of Independent Schools Award, 1954, both for *Fire in the Ashes;* Benjamin Franklin Magazine Award, 1956, for article in *Collier's,* "Germany—Friend or Foe?"; Ted V. Rodgers Award, 1956; Pulitzer Prize for general nonfiction, 1962, and National Association of Independent Schools Award, 1962, both for *The Making of the President: 1960;* Emmy Awards, National Academy of Television Arts and Sciences, 1964, for best television film in all categories, for "The Making of the President: 1960," 1967, for best documentary television writing, for "China: The Roots of Madness," and 1985, for best documentary television writing, for "Television and the Presidency"; Fourth Estate Award, National Press Club; Journalist of the Year Award, Columbia School of Journalism; English-Speaking Union Books-Across-the-Sea Ambassador of

Honor Books, 1984, for *America in Search of Itself;* honorary doctor of humane letters, Hebrew Union College, 1985; .

WRITINGS:

(With Annalee Jacoby) *Thunder Out of China* (Book-of-the-Month Club selection), Sloane, 1946, reprinted, Da Capo Press, 1980.

(Editor) Joseph Warren Stilwell, *The Stilwell Papers,* Sloane, 1948, reprinted, Schocken, 1972.

Fire in the Ashes (Book-of-the-Month Club selection), Sloane, 1953, reprinted, 1968.

The Mountain Road (Book-of-the-Month Club selection), Sloane, 1958.

The View from the Fortieth Floor (Literary Guild selection), Sloane, 1960.

The Making of the President: 1960, Atheneum, 1961, reprinted as *The Making of the President, 1960: A Narrative History of American Politics in Action,* Macmillan, 1988.

The Making of the President: 1964, Atheneum, 1965.

Caesar at the Rubicon: A Play about Politics, Atheneum, 1968, published as *Caesar at the Rubicon: A Play in Three Acts,* Samuel French, 1971.

China: The Roots of Madness (also see below; revision of television documentary script), Norton, 1968.

The Making of the President: 1968, Atheneum, 1969.

The Making of the President: 1972 (Literary Guild selection), Atheneum, 1973.

Breach of Faith: The Fall of Richard Nixon (Book-of-the-Month Club selection), Atheneum, 1975.

In Search of History: A Personal Adventure (autobiography), Harper, 1978.

America in Search of Itself: The Making of the President 1956-1980, Harper, 1982.

Also author of television documentary scripts, including "The Making of the President: 1960," "China: The Roots of Madness," "The Making of the President: 1968," and "Television and the Presidency," 1985. Contributor to *Life, Time, Fortune, Reporter, Holiday, Harper's, Saturday Review, Collier's, New York, New York Times Magazine,* and other magazines and newspapers.

SIDELIGHTS: With the publication of *The Making of the President: 1960,* his Pulitzer Prize-winning report on the 1960 presidential campaign and election, Theodore White established a tradition of excellence that not only himself but others have found difficult to live up to. Considered by many to be a classic in political journalism, it was, as a *National Observer* critic notes, "a ground-breaking achievement," for "no one before had thought to bring a whole presidential campaign together in a single, lucid, anecdotal, and timely volume." A *San Francisco Chronicle* reviewer called it "the most exhilarating non-fiction of the season. . . . It is both exciting and revealing Americana. . . . A familiar story . . . appears to be new and fresh as White reconstructs it. He does so with brilliance, intelligence and for the most part scrupulous objectivity." Bernard Levin of *Spectator* commented: "Not since Mencken has there been American political reporting of this quality, and Mencken had little of Mr. White's thoroughness and none of his stunningly persuasive objectivity. . . . He produces one of the most exciting and significant pieces of socio-political analysis for years. . . . As journalism [the book] is unsurpassed; as a record and textbook it is invaluable."

James MacGregor Burns, writing in the *New York Times Book Review,* stated: "No book that I know of has caught the heartbeat of a campaign as strikingly as Theodore White has done in *The*

Making of the President: 1960. . . . By artistic rearrangement of his materials he has gained space for long, hard appraisals of American politics. . . . If this book were merely a campaign report, it could be recommended glowingly on its own terms. But it is more than this." A *Saturday Review* critic saw it as "an extraordinary performance by a shrewd interpreter of the American scene. . . . It launches what I hope will be a new genre in American political literature. It is sensitive and brilliant reporting, and an invaluable document for history."

Several other critics, however, questioned White's objectivity. Though most had high praise for his overall achievement in reporting on such a complex chain of events, they felt that his partiality towards certain political figures (as well as an accompanying touch of sentimentality about American politics in general) detracted from the book's impact. "Author White strives for objectivity," reported *Time,* "but there is no question whose campaign button adorned his. . . . His coverage of Kennedy is more complete, more successful than his picture of Nixon. . . . A complete analysis of the 1960 campaign will have to await a later day and more penetrating research. As reporting, the book is a notable achievement. White has written a fascinating story of a fascinating campaign." A *Christian Science Monitor* critic agreed that "never has there been as competent, penetrating, and complete account of an American presidential election as this." But, after noting that White was "warmly received" by the Kennedy group while Nixon's "held [him] at arm's length," the reviewer concluded: "[White] struggles manfully to clarify the Nixon character and only partly succeeds. . . . The book is written in the emotional mood of the correspondents traveling with Mr. Kennedy in the last weeks of the campaign, when they expected a landslide. This is a serious flaw, since the meaning of the outcome is greatly overstated."

The Making of the President: 1964 was not as successful as its predecessor, perhaps, as a *National Observer* critic pointed out, "because the campaign itself was less interesting. . . . [White] found no heroes in 1964; like so many others, he saw no romance in Lyndon Johnson or Barry Goldwater." In the *New York Review of Books,* I. F. Stone admitted that "Theodore H. White has become the poet laureate of American presidential campaigns." Nevertheless, he concluded, *The Making of the President: 1964* "is on a lower level" than its predecessor. "The wonder and zest of the first often decline into a schoolgirlish gushiness in the second. The first is muscular, the second mawkish. . . . [Yet] no one could feel a candidate's pulse more sympathetically [than White]." The *New Yorker* noted that "[Mr. White] does quite a good job of it. . . . His method is a compound of diary-keeping, daily journalism, weekly journalism, editorial writing, and extra-sensory perception. It is an entertaining mixture, and some of the microscopic details are priceless, but on the whole, it is more White than history." A *Times Literary Supplement* reviewer wrote: "Alas, the 1964 version has all and much more than all the faults of the first book and hardly any of its merits. It is a depressing failure. . . . The *aficionados* of American politics will find a little new information here, some, if too infrequent, patches of Mr. White at his brilliant reporter's best . . . and a good deal of unimpressive political cogitation."

On the other hand, an *Atlantic* reviewer noted: "In *The Making of the President: 1960* Theodore H. White had almost a classical plot with a single action and a single hero. . . . By comparison, 1964 presented a more diffuse and less focused drama. Yet *The Making of the President: 1964* is in many ways a more exciting book, if only because his earlier triumph has sharpened Mr. White's skill at a style of reporting that he seems to have made all his own. . . . His politicians . . . emerge as three-dimensional characters in a way not usual in political reporting."

It was not, however, until the appearance of *The Making of the President: 1968* that critics began to take a long, hard look at White's approach. What had only been mentioned more or less in passing by a few reviewers in 1960 and 1964—namely, White's occasional lack of objectivity as well as his patriotic sentimentality about America and the American political system—became a major problem in the eyes of the 1968 reviewers. A *Commonweal* critic wrote: "Like Harold Stassen, T. H. White is ruining a good thing with his quadrennial lustings after the presidency. . . . This third *Making* book is the plain *reductio ad absurdum* of the first, which—for all its fascination and birth of genre—was conspicuously sanguine on issues and soft on politicians. . . . While White's coziness with the candidates may not have hurt his books all that much in 1960 and 1964 when the old politics still had some kick, he is terribly guilty by his associations in *Making 1968*. . . . The unhappiest feature of *Making 1968* is the reporter's undisguised sympathy for the establishment. . . . Except for the Wallace campaign and the peace movement, basely equated in their extremism, White is all heroes and worship. . . . [But] apart from internal criticism, *Making 1968* fails for large reasons. A single reporter is simply incommensurate with a presidential campaign. . . . 'This is the most dramatic confrontation of America and its problems in over 100 years,' White mused in *Newsweek* before publication. 'It's just a question of whether I'm good enough to write the story for what it's really worth.' He wasn't."

Bill Moyers, writing in *Saturday Review,* noted: "If Theodore White did not exist, the Ford Foundation would have to award Harvard University a grant to create him. How else would the Establishment tell its story? *The Making of the President: 1968* is essentially that: the authorized version, the view through the official keyhole. For Teddy White, the most successful entrepreneur of political detail and perception in American journalism today, tells the story of 1968 as he did four and eight years. . . . But times have changed. . . . 1968 was the Year of Decay. . . . Under such circumstances no single author, not even a Teddy White, could chart the shifting boundaries of our political terrain. That he has tried, against impossible odds, is a tribute to the man's intrepid will. Certainly his is the most coherent and the most eloquent account we are likely to get from any reporter's notes. . . . But there is a tone in it that we are not accustomed to hearing in Teddy White."

"Most of what [he] reports is interesting," continued Moyers, "much of what he does not report is significant. Something is missing because interpreting politics at the top so completely and so officially for eight years had finally caught up with Theodore White. . . . He could not, in honest loyalty as well as by instinct, completely separate himself from the besieged. . . . He could never achieve total freedom from his prejudices. . . . And so White is left with this splendid story, not wholly true. . . . [He] told us what happened at the top, and told it as no one else can. But the top was no longer that important."

A *Time* reviewer wrote: "In two previous chronicles of President-making, Theodore H. White's talents were more than equal to the task. . . . This time the odds were against him. White's best reportage delineates character; portraiture is his forte. In 1968, events overshadowed individuals. . . . White's reconstruction of these events often bears the paste-pot smell of newspaper clippings. . . . His reaction is detached and too concerned with the pattern of the old politics. . . . There are nuggets of anecdotage along the way. . . . [But] after eight years and three

elections, White has established his own political system. He has a vast network of friendly power brokers, government aides, trend watchers, reporters, poll takers and precinct vigilantes. This book is almost overwhelmed by his efforts to preserve—and not to offend—this intricate organization."

White's *The Making of the President: 1972* was criticized for virtually the same excesses and deficiencies as the 1968 version. "The rambling chronicle offers few new insights into either the Nixon victory or the McGovern defeat," wrote a *New Republic* reviewer. "Watergate aside, White willingly accepts most of the Nixon rationale—even on the war. . . . But if the analysis is disappointing, the level of characterization is more gratifying, reflecting the legwork, extensive interviews and careful research involved." Garry Wills of the *New York Review of Books,* noting the author's "indiscriminate celebration of the ruler" (Nixon), concluded that "the 'Whitiad,' now in its second decade, gets worse stanza by stanza. . . . White conducts his old civics lesson without having learned a thing." Finally, Anthony Lewis of the *New York Times* commented: "Theodore H. White is so awesomely diligent a reporter, so accomplished a political analyst, so engaging a person that criticizing him seems like sacrilege. . . . But . . . it is time for someone to say that White has written a bad book. *The Making of the President: 1972* is as impressive as its predecessors in its eye for both the revealing detail and the sweep of events. But White naturally does more than describe. He gives his own judgment on larger historical issues, and there I think he has gone profoundly wrong. . . . Alas, one [also] detects in Theodore White some of that unfortunate pleasure in curling up with the powerful. . . . [As a result,] winners take all in the White universe; and losers get no mercy."

In 1976, restless and unable to apply himself to the task of preparing for and writing *The Making of the President: 1976,* White broke with tradition and turned to writing about himself instead. The result, *In Search of History,* was called "a minor classic of American biography" by the *New Leader.* "It vibrates with the themes most characteristic of national self-discovery," continued the reviewer, "recording the passage from obscurity and poverty to the close observation of power; from facts to ideas, from promise to fulfillment and then to perplexity." But even in his autobiography White came under fire for his lack of objectivity. "The special insignia of White's writing has long been the evocation of sympathy," reported the *New Leader.* "The autobiography is similarly free of rancor. Almost everyone . . . is washed in authorial good will." Furthermore, the reviewer wrote, White's "own sense of politics remains rooted in camaraderie rather than causes, and in attributing to politicians ideas that are really only mental gestures, White once again exaggerates the importance of the men he has covered."

Richard Rovere of the *New York Times Book Review* called *In Search of History* "by far [White's] finest, most affecting work. . . . It has all the pace and energy of the earlier work and more of many other things; more insight, more reflection, more candor, more intimacy, more humor, more humility, surer and sharper judgments of those he writes about, including himself." On the other hand, Christopher Lehmann-Haupt felt that "somewhere in this public autobiography Mr. White seems to lose his way. The first half is extremely strong—the sections covering his youth, his education, and his adventures in China. Here personal experience very nearly equals history. . . . But somehow in the second half, the momentum of White's narrative falters. This isn't to say that vivid close-up portraits of historical figures don't continue to appear. . . . It is simply that when White moves on from China to Europe to witness that continent's post-war recovery, and then back to the United States to report on domestic politics, the center of the action moves away from him. He is no longer really part of the story he is covering, as he was in China. So when he writes about himself he neglects history, and vice versa." Lehmann-Haupt, in addition to several other reviewers, found White's occasional use of the third person when referring to himself to be somewhat distracting. "Nowhere do these passages stop reminding us by their lack of irony and humor how much more successfully this device fares in the hands of Norman Mailer," he concluded.

William Greider of *Book World* stated that, as a reflective memoir, *In Search of History* simply "doesn't work. [White] begins bravely, announcing self-doubts and confusion, but after traveling through many continents and interesting events, glimpsing famous men from Mao to Eisenhower, one is left at the conclusion with the same questions. Readers who loved the powerful narrative line of White's other books will find this one strangely disjointed and unthematic. . . . The memoir ends lamely, acknowledging that he has not really sorted out the fundamental confusions about politics and the nation." Unlike other reviewers, however, Greider did not particularly find the first part of the book to be much better than the last half, noting that "even [White's] memories of wartime China and *Time* are seen through a murky lens," as if he is "unable to address them directly."

Finally, Eric F. Goldman of *Saturday Review* wrote that *In Search of History* "has its less than felicitous moments. It has long been noted that White is a man much given to heroes. . . . Moreover, White, like a number of journalists, throws a special aura around 'history.' . . . In this volume, [the author], anxious to escape what he considers the confines of journalism, at times pauses for a passage that can be disconcerting. . . . Happily, neither White's search for history, nor his proneness for heroes—nor his occasional splashes of neon prose—are major aspects of the book. For the most part, it is a work in the high tradition of American memoirs, written with power and grace of style, many an astute perception, and an attitude toward his country that is at once deeply affectionate, unhesitatingly critical, and engagingly quizzical. . . . White's treatment of his Chinese and European years in this book of memoirs is mellower, [and] more balanced, [than his earlier *Thunder out of China* and *Fire in the Ashes*] and it provides a constant flow of absorbing personal material. More strikingly, *In Search of History* includes frequent incisive, richly human vignettes of the great and not-so-great figures White came to know. . . . White indicates that a second and perhaps third volume of memoirs will follow. . . . If the future volume or volumes maintain the vivid, probing, questing 'storytelling' of the first, and White does not search too hard for 'history,' his total memoirs may well prove one the bench-mark books . . . of our generation."

White's last book, *America in Search of Itself: The Making of the President, 1956-1980,* examines the administrations of Eisenhower through Jimmy Carter, up to the election of Ronald Reagan as president in 1980. The book received comments similar to those for White's other books on presidential elections. "This is a somewhat disjointed volume, because of its dual purpose—to philosophize over recent history and to map a particular moment. White is a better mapmaker than philosopher," noted Paul Barker in the London *Times.* "Mr. White demurs, 'I could not present myself as a historian,' but from the start his tone is something other than reportorial," commented Susan Bolotin in the *New York Times,* adding that White "tends to speak in aphorisms . . ., to categorize in terms of big themes . . ., [and] to look back from a vantage point more opinionated than analytic." Despite these criticisms, Bolotin conceded that White "deserves

full credit for his talent as a storyteller" and that "his campaign remembrances are winning."

Upon his death in 1986, White was remembered by Clifton Daniel in the *New York Times* as having "taught the American people more about politics than any writer of his generation." Daniel singled out White's particular talents as being a very good reporter, a historian and scholar, and finally, a storyteller. "The first two qualities made his work sound and unassailable; the third one made it immensely popular," noted Daniel. Suzanne Garment in the *Wall Street Journal* stated that, in addition to his "bringing presidential politics alive with color and personality for his audience of millions," White "told us that American politics was a romantic, glamorous thing and that the glamour lay precisely in the small, pragmatic, grubby details of the professional politician's craft. . . . He made poetry out of the advance work and the delegate counts."

AVOCATIONAL INTERESTS: Woodworking, gardening, and painting.

BIOGRAPHICAL/CRITICAL SOURCES:

BOOKS

White, Theodore H., *In Search of History* (autobiography), Harper, 1978.

PERIODICALS

America, July 17, 1965.
American Heritage, April/May, 1982.
Atlantic, June, 1958, August, 1961, August, 1965, May, 1968.
Best Sellers, May 15, 1968, September 15, 1969, January, 1979.
Books of the Times, August, 1978.
Book Week, July 11, 1965.
Book World, July 14, 1968, July 27, 1969, October 12, 1969, August 27, 1978.
Christian Century, October 1, 1969.
Christian Science Monitor, July 6, 1961, September 4, 1969.
Chicago Tribune Book World, May 16, 1982.
Commentary, September, 1982.
Commonweal, December 8, 1961, August 22, 1969.
Harper's, August, 1965.
Life, June 18, 1965.
Los Angeles Times Book Review, October 15, 1978, May 30, 1982, December 29, 1985.
Maclean's, October 24, 1983.
Nation, October 14, 1978.
National Observer, July 12, 1965, August 18, 1969.
New Leader, October 23, 1978.
New Republic, July 10, 1961, July 10, 1965, August 16, 1969, August 11, 1973, September 9, 1978.
Newsday, June 6, 1978.
New Statesman, April 6, 1962.
Newsweek, January 13, 1969, July 28, 1969, August 13, 1973, August 14, 1978.
New York, September 8, 1969.
New Yorker, June 4, 1960, July 22, 1961, August 7, 1965, September 20, 1969.
New York Herald Tribune Book Review, May 11, 1958, May 22, 1960, July 9, 1961.
New York Post, July 22, 1969.
New York Review of Books, August 5, 1965, October 4, 1973, November 9, 1978.
New York Times, January 2, 1969, July 9, 1969, July 23, 1969, February 21, 1971, August 30, 1973, June 1, 1982.

New York Times Book Review, May 11, 1958, May 22, 1960, July
    9, 1961, July 11, 1965, April 14, 1968, September 22, 1968,
    August 6, 1978, December 24, 1978, May 9, 1982.
Observer, November 23, 1969.
People, July 31, 1978.
Playboy, May, 1968.
San Francisco Chronicle, July 5, 1961, July 6, 1961.
Saturday Review, May 10, 1958, May 21, 1960, July 8, 1961, July
    10, 1965, August 9, 1969, October 9, 1973, September 2,
    1978.
Spectator, April 6, 1962, December 6, 1969, May 2, 1970.
Time, May 23, 1960, July 21, 1961, March 29, 1968, August 1,
    1969, July 3, 1978, May 17, 1982.
Times (London), May 19, 1983.
Times Literary Supplement, December 2, 1960, November 4,
    1965, June 10, 1983.
Us, October 17, 1978.
Virginia Quarterly Review, autumn, 1969.
Washington Post, August 11, 1969.
Washington Post Book World, May 9, 1982, January 5, 1986.

OBITUARIES:

PERIODICALS

Chicago Sun Times, May 17, 1986.
Chicago Tribune, May 17, 1986, May 22, 1986.
Globe and Mail (Toronto), May 17, 1986.
Newsweek, May 26, 1986.
New York Times, May 17, 1986, May 21, 1986.
Time, May 26, 1986.
Times (London), May 17, 1986.
Wall Street Journal, May 26, 1986.
Washington Post, May 17, 1986.

*   *   *

WHITTLEBOT, Hernia
    See COWARD, Noel (Peirce)

*   *   *

WIESEL, Elie(zer)   1928-

PERSONAL: Born September 30, 1928, in Sighet, Romania;
came to the United States, 1956, naturalized U.S. citizen, 1963;
son of Shlomo (a grocer) and Sarah (Feig) Wiesel; married Marion Erster Rose, 1969; children: Shlomo Elisha. *Education:* Attended Sorbonne, University of Paris, 1948-51. *Religion:* Jewish.

ADDRESSES: Office—University Professors, Boston University, 745 Commonwealth Ave., Boston, Mass. 02215. *Agent*—
Georges Borchardt, 136 East 57th St., New York, N.Y. 10022.

CAREER: Foreign correspondent at various times for *Yedioth
Ahronoth,* Tel Aviv, Israel, *L'Arche,* Paris, France, and *Jewish
Daily Forward,* New York City, 1949—; City College of the City
University of New York, New York City, Distinguished Profes-
sor, beginning 1972; Boston University, Boston, Mass., Andrew
Mellon Professor in the Humanities, 1976—. Chairman, U.S.
Holocaust Memorial Council.

MEMBER: Authors League, Foreign Correspondents Association, U.N. Correspondents Association.

AWARDS, HONORS: Prix Rivarol, 1963; Remembrance
Award, 1965, for *The Town beyond the Wall* and all other writ-
ings; William and Janice Epstein Fiction Award, Jewish Book
Council, 1965, for *The Town beyond the Wall;* Jewish Heritage

Award, 1966, for excellence in literature; Litt.D., Jewish Theological Seminary, 1967, Marquette University, 1975, Simmons
College, 1976, St. Scholastica College, 1978, Yale University,
1981, and Hobart and William Smith Colleges, 1982; D.H.L.,
Hebrew Union College, 1968, Manhattanville College, 1972, Ye-
shiva University, 1973, Boston University, 1974, Wesleyan Uni-
versity, 1979, Notre Dame University, 1980, Anna Maria Col-
lege, 1980, Brandeis University, 1980, and Kenyon College,
1982; Prix Medicis, 1969, for *Le Mendiant de Jerusalem;* Prix
Bordin, French Academy, 1972; Eleanor Roosevelt Memorial
Award, 1972; American Liberties Medallion, American Jewish
Committee, 1972; Doctor of Hebrew Letters, Spertus College of
Judaica, 1973; Frank and Ethel S. Cohen Award, Jewish Book
Council, 1973, for *Souls on Fire;* Martin Luther King, Jr.,
Award, City College of the City University of New York, 1973;
Doctor of Philosophy, Bar-Ilan University, 1973; Faculty Dis-
tinguished Scholar Award, 1973-74, and LL.D., 1975, both from
Hofstra University; LL.D., Talmudic University, 1979; Prix
Livre-International, 1980, and Prix des Bibliothecaires, 1981,
both for *Le Testament d'un poete juif assassine;* Nobel Peace
Prize, 1986; Special Christopher Book Award, 1987; Joseph
Prize for Human Rights, Anti-Defamation League of B'nai
B'rith; S. Y. Agnon Gold Medal; Jabotinsky Award; Shazar
Award.

WRITINGS:

Un Di Velt Hot Geshvign (title means "And the World Has Re-
    mained Silent"), [Buenos Aires], 1956, abridged French
    translation published as *La Nuit* (also see below), foreword
    by Francois Mauriac, Editions de Minuit, 1958, translation
    by Stella Rodway published as *Night* (also see below), Hill
    & Wang, 1960, reprinted, Bantam, 1982.
L'Aube (also see below), Editions du Seuil, 1961, translation by
    Frances Frenaye published as *Dawn* (also see below), Hill
    & Wang, 1961, reprinted, Bantam, 1982.
Le Jour (also see below), Editions du Seuil, 1961, translation by
    Anne Borchardt published as *The Accident* (also see below),
    Hill & Wang, 1962.
La Ville de la chance, Editions du Seuil, 1962, translation by Ste-
    phen Becker published as *The Town beyond the Wall,* Athe-
    neum, 1964, new edition, Holt, 1967, reprinted, Schocken,
    1982.
Les Portes de la foret, Editions du Seuil, 1964, translation by
    Frenaye published as *The Gates of the Forest,* Holt, 1966,
    reprinted, Schocken, 1989.
Le Chant des morts, Editions du Seuil, 1966, translation pub-
    lished as *Legends of Our Time,* Holt, 1968.
The Jews of Silence: A Personal Report on Soviet Jewry (originally
    published in Hebrew as a series of articles for newspaper
    Yedioth Ahronoth), translation and with an afterword by
    Neal Kozodoy, Holt, 1966, 2nd edition, Vallentine, Mitch-
    ell, 1973.
Zalmen; ou, La Folie de Dieu (play), 1966, translation by Lily
    Edelman and Nathan Edelman published as *Zalmen; or,
    The Madness of God,* Holt, 1968.
Le Mendiant de Jerusalem, 1968, translation by the author and
    L. Edelman published as *A Beggar in Jerusalem,* Random
    House, 1970, reprinted, Schocken, 1989.
La Nuit, L'Aube, [and] *Le Jour,* Editions du Seuil, 1969, transla-
    tion published as *Night, Dawn,* [and] *The Accident: Three
    Tales,* Hill & Wang, 1972, reprinted as *The Night Trilogy:
    Night, Dawn, The Accident,* Farrar, Straus, 1987, transla-
    tion by Rodway published as *Night, Dawn, Day,* Aronson,
    1985.

Entre Deux Soleils, Editions du Seuil, 1970, translation by the author and L. Edelman published as *One Generation After,* Random House, 1970.

Celebration hassidique: Portraits et legendes, Editions du Seuil, 1972, translation by wife, Marion Wiesel, published as *Souls on Fire: Portraits and Legends of Hasidic Masters,* Random House, 1972.

Le Serment de Kolvillag, Editions du Seuil, 1973, translation by M. Wiesel published as *The Oath,* Random House, 1973.

Ani maamin: A Song Lost and Found Again (cantata), music composed by Darius Milhaud, Random House, 1974.

Celebration biblique: Portraits et legendes, Editions du Seuil, 1975, translation by M. Wiesel published as *Messengers of God: Biblical Portraits and Legends,* Random House, 1976.

Un Juif aujourd'hui: Recits, essais, dialogues, Editions du Seuil, 1977, translation by M. Wiesel published as *A Jew Today,* Random House, 1978.

(With others) *Dimensions of the Holocaust,* Indiana University Press, 1977.

Four Hasidic Masters and Their Struggle against Melancholy, University of Notre Dame Press, 1978.

Le Proces de Shamgorod tel qu'il se deroula le 25 fevrier 1649: Piece en trois actes, Editions du Seuil, 1979, translation by M. Wiesel published as *The Trial of God (as It Was Held on February 25, 1649, in Shamgorod): A Play in Three Acts,* Random House, 1979.

Images from the Bible, illustrated with paintings by Shalom of Safed, Overlook Press, 1980.

Le Testament d'un poete juif assassine, Editions du Seuil, 1980, translation by M. Wiesel published as *The Testament,* Simon & Schuster, 1981.

Five Biblical Portraits, University of Notre Dame Press, 1981.

Somewhere a Master, Simon & Schuster, 1982, reprinted as *Somewhere a Master: Further Tales of the Hasidic Masters,* Summit Books, 1984.

Paroles d'etranger, Editions du Seuil, 1982.

The Golem: The Story of a Legend as Told by Elie Wiesel (fiction), illustrations by Mark Podwal, Summit Books, 1983.

Le Cinquieme Fils, Grasset (Paris), 1983, translation by M. Wiesel published as *The Fifth Son,* Summit Books, 1985.

Against Silence: The Voice and Vision of Elie Wiesel, three volumes, edited by Irving Abrahamson, Holocaust Library, 1985.

Signes d'Exode, Grasset & Fasquelle (Paris), 1985.

Job ou Dieu dans la tempete, Grasset & Fasquelle, 1986.

Le Crepuscule au loin, Grasset & Fasquelle, 1987, translation by M. Wiesel published as *Twilight,* Summit Books, 1988.

(With Albert H. Friedlander) *The Six Days of Destruction,* Paulist Press, 1989.

Contributor to numerous periodicals.

SIDELIGHTS: In the spring of 1944, the Nazis entered the Transylvanian village of Sighet, Romania, until then a relatively safe and peaceful enclave in the middle of a war-torn continent. Arriving with orders to exterminate an estimated 600,000 Jews in six weeks or less, Adolf Eichmann, chief of the Gestapo's Jewish section, began making arrangements for a mass deportation program. Among those forced to leave their homes was fifteen-year-old Elie Wiesel, the only son of a grocer and his wife. A serious and devoted student of the Talmud and the mystical teachings of Hasidism and the Cabala, the young man had always assumed he would spend his entire life in Sighet, quietly contemplating the religious texts and helping out in the family's store from time to time. Instead, along with his father, mother, and

three sisters, Wiesel was herded onto a train bound for Birkenau, the reception center for the infamous death camp Auschwitz.

For reasons he still finds impossible to comprehend, Wiesel survived Birkenau and later Auschwitz and Buna and Buchenwald; his father, mother, and youngest sister did not (he did not learn until after the war that his older sisters also survived). With nothing and no one in Sighet for him to go back to, Wiesel boarded a train for Belgium with four hundred other orphans who, like him, had no reason or desire to return to their former homes. On orders of General Charles de Gaulle, the train was diverted to France, where border officials asked the children to raise their hands if they wanted to become French citizens. As Wiesel (who at that time neither spoke nor understood French) recalls in the *Washington Post,* "A lot of them did. They thought they were going to get bread or something; they would reach out for anything. I didn't, so I remained stateless."

Wiesel chose to stay in France for a while, settling first in Normandy and later in Paris, doing whatever he could to earn a living: tutoring, directing a choir, translating. Eventually he began working as a reporter for various French and Jewish publications. But he could not quite bring himself to write about what he had seen and felt at Auschwitz and Buchenwald. Doubtful of his—or of anyone's—ability to convey the horrible truth without diminishing it, Wiesel vowed never to make the attempt.

The young journalist's self-imposed silence came to an end in the mid-1950s, however, after he met and interviewed the Nobel Prize-winning novelist Francois Mauriac. Deeply moved upon learning of Wiesel's tragic youth, Mauriac urged him to speak out and tell the world of his experiences, to "bear witness" for the millions of men, women, and children whom death, and not despair, had silenced. The result was *Night,* the story of a teenage boy plagued with guilt for having survived the camps and devastated by the realization that the God he had once worshipped so devoutly allowed his people to be destroyed. For the most part autobiographical, it was, says Richard M. Elman in the *New Republic,* "a document as well as a work of literature—journalism which emerged, coincidentally, as a work of art."

Described by the *Nation*'s Daniel Stern as "undoubtedly the single most powerful literary relic of the holocaust," *Night* is the first in a series of nonfiction books and autobiographical novels this "lyricist of lamentation" has written that deal, either directly or indirectly, with the Holocaust. "He sees the present always refracted through the prism of these earlier days," comments James Finn in the *New Republic.* The *New York Times*'s Thomas Lask agrees, stating: "For [more than] twenty-five years, Elie Wiesel has been in one form or another a witness to the range, bestiality and completeness of the destruction of European Jewry by the Germans. . . . Auschwitz informs everything he writes—novels, legends, dialogues. He is not belligerent about it, only unyielding. Nothing he can say measures up to the enormity of what he saw, what others endured. The implications these experiences have for mankind terrify him. . . . He is part conscience, part quivering needle of response and part warning signal. His writing is singular in the disparate elements it has unified, in the peculiar effect of remoteness and immediacy it conveys. He is his own mold."

Other novels by Wiesel about the Jewish experience during and after the Holocaust include *Dawn* and *The Accident,* which were later published together with *Night* in *The Night Trilogy: Night, Dawn, The Accident.* Like *Night,* the other two books in the trilogy have concentration camp survivors as their central characters. *Dawn* concerns the experiences of one survivor just after World War II who joins the Jewish underground efforts to form an independent Israeli state; and *The Accident* is about a man who discovers that his collision with an automobile was actually caused by his subconscious, guilt-ridden desire to commit suicide. In two of Wiesel's later novels, *The Testament* and *The Fifth Son,* the author also explores the effects of the Holocaust on the next generation of Jews. Some critics such as *Globe and Mail* contributor Bronwyn Drainie have questioned the validity of the author's belief that children of Holocaust survivors would be "as morally galvanized by the Nazi nightmare as the survivors themselves." But, asserts Richard F. Shepard in the *New York Times,* even if the feelings of these children cannot be generalized, "the author does make all of us 'children' of that generation, all of us who were not there, in the sense that he outlines for us the burdens of guilt, of revenge, of despair."

Indeed, the Holocaust and the Jewish religious and philosophical tradition involve experiences and beliefs shared by a great many people, including other writers. But as Kenneth Turan declares in the *Washington Post Book World,* Elie Wiesel has become "much more than just a writer. He is a symbol, a banner, and a beacon, perhaps the survivor of the Holocaust. . . . He seems to own the horror of the death camps, or, rather, the horror owns him." But it is a moral and spiritual, not a physical, horror that obsesses Wiesel and obliges him to compose what Dan Isaac of the *Nation* calls "an angry message to God, filled with both insane rage and stoical acceptance; calculated to stir God's wrath, but careful not to trigger an apocalypse." Explains Isaac's *Nation* colleague Laurence Goldstein: "For Elie Wiesel memory is an instrument of revelation. Each word he uses to document the past transforms both the work and the memory into an act of faith. The writings of Elie Wiesel are a journey into the past blackened by the Nazi death camps where the charred souls of its victims possess the sum of guilt and endurance that mark the progress of man. It is a compulsive, fevered, single-minded search among the ashes for a spark that can be thrust before the silent eyes of God himself."

Unlike those who dwell primarily on the physical horror, then, Wiesel writes from the perspective of a passionately religious man whose faith has been profoundly shaken by what he has witnessed. As Goldstein remarks, "He must rediscover himself. . . . Although he has not lost God, he must create out of the pain and numbness a new experience that will keep his God from vanishing among the unforgettable faces of the thousands whose bodies he saw." According to Maurice Friedman of *Commonweal,* Wiesel is, in fact, "the most moving embodiment of the Modern Job": a man who questions—in books that "form one unified outcry, one sustained protest, one sobbing and singing prayer" why the just must suffer while the wicked flourish. This debate with God is one of the central themes of what a *Newsweek* critic refers to as Wiesel's "God-tormented, God-intoxicated" fiction.

In addition to his intense preoccupation with ancient Jewish philosophy, mythology, and history, Wiesel displays a certain affinity with modern French existentialists, an affinity Josephine Knopp believes is a direct consequence of the Holocaust. Writes Knopp in *Contemporary Literature:* "To the young Wiesel the notion of an 'absurd' universe would have been a completely alien one. . . . The traditional Jewish view holds that life's structure and meaning are fully explained and indeed derive from the divinely granted Torah. . . . Against this background the reality of Auschwitz confronts the Jew with a dilemma, an 'absurdity' which cannot be dismissed easily and which stubbornly refuses to dissipate of its own accord. . . . The only possible response that remains within the framework of Judaism is denunciation of God and a demand that He fulfill His contrac-

tual obligation [to protect those who worship Him]. This is the religious and moral context within which Wiesel attempts to apprehend and assimilate the events of the Holocaust. [He seeks] to reconcile Auschwitz with Judaism, to confront and perhaps wring meaning from the absurd." In a more recent novel, *Twilight,* Wiesel explores this absurdity—in this case, he goes so far as to call it madness—of the universe. Again, the protagonist is a Jew, who begins to wonder, as *New York Times* reviewer John Gross explains, whether "it is mad to go on believing in God. Or perhaps . . . it is God who is mad: who else but a mad God could have created such a world?"

The strong emphasis on Jewish tradition and Jewish suffering in Wiesel's works does not mean that he speaks only to and for Jews. In fact, maintains Robert McAfee Brown in *Christian Century,* "writing out of the particularity of his own Jewishness . . . is how [Wiesel] touches universal chords. He does not write about 'the human condition,' but about 'the Jewish condition.' Correction: in writing about the Jewish condition, he thereby writes about the human condition. For the human condition is not generalized existence; it is a huge, crazy-quilt sum of particularized existences all woven together."

To Stern, this time commenting in the *Washington Post Book World,* it seems that "Wiesel has taken the Jew as his metaphor—and his reality—in order to unite a moral and aesthetic vision in terms of all men." Manes Sperber of the *New York Times Book Review* expresses a similar view, stating that "Wiesel is one of the few writers who, without any plaintiveness, has succeeded in revealing in the Jewish tragedy those features by which it has become again and again a paradigm of the human condition."

According to Michael J. Bandler in the *Christian Science Monitor,* Wiesel conveys his angry message to God "with a force and stylistic drive that leaves the reader stunned." Concise and uncluttered, yet infused with a highly emotional biblical mysticism, the author's prose "gleams again and again with the metaphor of the poet," writes Clifford A. Ridley in the *National Observer.* Though it "never abandons its tender intimacy," reports Sperber, "[Wiesel's] voice comes from far away in space and time. It is the voice of the Talmudic teachers of Jerusalem and Babylon; of medieval mystics; of Rabbi Nachman of Bratzlav whose tales have inspired generations of Hasidim and so many writers." As Lask observes, "[Wiesel] has made the form of the telling his own. The surreal and the supernatural combine abrasively with the harsh fact; the parable, the rabbinic tale support and sometimes substitute for narrative. The written law and oral tradition support, explain and expand the twentieth-century event." Goldstein, noting the author's "remarkably compassionate tone," declares that "he writes with that possessive reverence for language that celebrates, as much as describes, experience. The written word becomes a powerful assertion, the triumph of life over death and indifference. . . . Words carved on gravestones, legend torn from the pit where millions of broken bodies lie. This is the inheritance which Elie Wiesel brings to us. His voice claims us with its urgency. His vision lights the mystery of human endurance."

Several critics, however, feel Wiesel's prose does not quite live up to the demands of his subject. Commenting in the *New York Times Book Review,* for example, Jeffrey Burke states that the author occasionally "slips into triteness or purple prose or redundancy," and a reviewer for the *New Yorker* finds that Wiesel becomes "nearly delirious" in his intensity. *Newsweek*'s Geoffrey Wolff believes that Wiesel's work at times "suffers from unnecessary confusions, linguistic cliches, dense and purple thickets, and false mystifications. Ideas tend to hobble about . . . on stilts. . . . The language, seeking to transport us to another world, collapses beneath the weight of its burden much too often." Concludes Burke: "No one can or would deny the seriousness and necessity of Elie Wiesel's role as witness. . . . It is natural that such a mission would remain uppermost in the writer's mind, but that the requirements of art should proportionately diminish in significance is not an acceptable corollary. [Wiesel tends] to sacrifice the demands of craft to those of conscience."

In defense of Wiesel, Turan states that "his is a deliberate, elegant style, consciously elevated and poetic, and if he occasionally tries to pack too much into a sentence, to jam it too full of significance and meaning, it is an error easy to forgive." Elman, this time writing in the *New York Times Book Review,* also finds that "some of Wiesel's existentialist parables are deeply flawed by an opacity of language and construction, which may confirm that 'the event was so heavy with horror . . . that words could not really contain it.' But Wiesel's work is not diminished by his failure to make his shattering theme—God's betrayal of man—consistently explicit." Thus, according to Jonathan Brent in the *Chicago Tribune Book World,* Wiesel is "the type of writer distinguished by his subject rather than his handling of it. . . . Such writers must be read not for themselves but for the knowledge they transmit of events, personalities, and social conditions outside their fiction itself. They do not master their material esthetically, but remain faithful to it; and this constitutes the principle value of their work."

Few would agree with these assessments of Wiesel's stylistic abilities, but many would support Brent's conclusion that the author is almost compulsively faithful to his subject. As Lawrence L. Langer observes in the *Washington Post Book World:* "Although Elie Wiesel has announced many times in recent years that he is finished with the Holocaust as a subject for public discourse, it is clear . . . that the Holocaust has not yet finished with him. Almost from his first volume to his last, his writing has been an act of homage, a ritual of remembrance in response to a dreadful challenge 'to unite the language of man with the silence of the dead.'. . . If Elie Wiesel returns compulsively to the ruins of the Holocaust world, it is not because he has nothing new to say. . . . [It is simply that] the man he did not become besieges his imagination and compels him to confirm his appointments with the past that holds him prisoner."

Wiesel expresses what *Commonweal*'s Irving Halpern calls "the anguish of a survivor who is unable to exorcise the past or to live with lucidity and grace in the present" in the book *Night,* his first attempt to bear witness for the dead. Wiesel writes: "Never shall I forget that night, the first night in camp, which has turned my life into one long night, seven times cursed and seven times sealed. Never shall I forget that smoke. Never shall I forget the little faces of the children, whose bodies I saw turned into wreaths of smoke beneath a silent blue sky. Never shall I forget those flames which consumed my Faith forever. Never shall I forget that nocturnal silence which deprived me, for all eternity, of the desire to live. Never shall I forget those moments which murdered my God and my soul and turned my dreams to dust. Never shall I forget these things, even if I am condemned to live as long as God Himself. Never."

Many years after this painful passage was first written, Wiesel is still torn between words and silence. "You must speak," he told a *People* magazine interviewer, "but how can you, when the full story is beyond language?" Furthermore, he once remarked in the *Washington Post,* "there is the fear of not being

believed, . . . the fear that the experience will be reduced, made into something acceptable, perhaps forgotten." But as he went on to explain in *People:* "We [survivors] believe that if we survived, we must do something with our lives. The first task is to tell the tale." In short, concluded Wiesel, "The only way to stop the next holocaust—the nuclear holocaust—is to remember the last one. If the Jews were singled out then, in the next one we are all victims." For his enduring efforts to keep the memory of the Holocaust alive so that such a tragedy would not repeat itself ever again, Wiesel was awarded the Nobel Peace Prize in 1986. In a *New York Times* article on the event, James M. Markham quotes Egil Aarvik, chairman of the Norwegian Nobel Committee: "Wiesel is a messenger to mankind. . . . His message is one of peace, atonement and human dignity. His belief that the forces fighting evil in the world can be victorious is a hard-won belief . . . repeated and deepened through the works of a great author."

BIOGRAPHICAL/CRITICAL SOURCES:

BOOKS

Authors in the News, Volume 1, Gale, 1976.
Contemporary Authors Autobiography Series, Volume 4, Gale, 1986.
Contemporary Issues Criticism, Volume 1, Gale, 1982.
Contemporary Literary Criticism, Gale, Volume 3, 1975, Volume 5, 1976, Volume 11, 1979, Volume 37, 1986.
Dictionary of Literary Biography, Volume 83: *French Novelists since 1960,* Gale, 1989.
Dictionary of Literary Biography Yearbook: 1987, Gale, 1988.
Rosenfeld, Alvin, *Confronting the Holocaust,* Indiana University Press, 1978.
Wiesel, Elie, *Night,* translated by Stella Rodway, Hill & Wang, 1960.

PERIODICALS

Atlantic, November, 1968.
Best Sellers, March 15, 1970, May, 1981.
Book Week, May 29, 1966.
Chicago Tribune Book World, October 29, 1978, March 29, 1981.
Christian Century, January 18, 1961, June 17, 1970, June 3, 1981.
Christian Science Monitor, November 21, 1968, February 19, 1970, November 22, 1978.
Commonweal, December 9, 1960, January 6, 1961, March 13, 1964, October 14, 1966.
Contemporary Literature, spring, 1974.
Globe and Mail (Toronto), April 20, 1985, August 6, 1988.
London Times, September 3, 1981.
Los Angeles Times Book Review, June 19, 1988.
Nation, October 17, 1966, February 24, 1969, March 16, 1970, January 5, 1974.
National Observer, February 2, 1970.
National Review, June 12, 1981.
New Leader, December 30, 1968, June 15, 1981.
New Republic, July 5, 1964, December 14, 1968.
Newsweek, May 25, 1964, February 9, 1970.
New Yorker, March 18, 1961, January 9, 1965, August 20, 1966, July 6, 1970, July 12, 1976.
New York Herald Tribune Lively Arts, January 1, 1961, April 30, 1961.
New York Review of Books, July 28, 1966, January 2, 1969, May 7, 1970.

New York Times, December 15, 1970, March 10, 1972, April 3, 1981, April 16, 1984, March 21, 1985, October 15, 1986, June 10, 1988.
New York Times Book Review, July 16, 1961, April 15, 1962, July 5, 1964, January 21, 1979, April 12, 1981, August 15, 1982, April 30, 1989.
People, October 22, 1979.
Saturday Review, December 17, 1960, July 8, 1961, July 25, 1964, May 28, 1966, October 19, 1968, January 31, 1970, November 21, 1970.
Time, March 16, 1970, May 8, 1972, July 12, 1976, December 25, 1978, April 20, 1981.
Times Literary Supplement, August 19, 1960, November 20, 1981, June 6, 1986.
TV Guide, February 15, 1969.
Washington Post, October 26, 1968, February 6, 1970, November 15, 1986, November 4, 1989.
Washington Post Book World, October 20, 1968, January 18, 1970, August 8, 1976, October 29, 1978, April 12, 1981, May 29, 1988.

*   *   *

WILBUR, Richard (Purdy)   1921-

PERSONAL: Born March 1, 1921, in New York, N.Y.; son of Lawrence Lazear (a portrait artist) and Helen Ruth (Purdy) Wilbur; married Mary Charlotte Hayes Ward, June 20, 1942; children: Ellen Dickinson, Christopher Hayes, Nathan Lord, Aaron Hammond. *Education:* Amherst College, A.B., 1942; Harvard University, A.M., 1947. *Politics:* Independent. *Religion:* Episcopal.

ADDRESSES: Home—Dodwells Rd., Cummington, Mass. 01026. *Office*—Department of English, Smith College, Northampton, Mass. 01063. *Agent*—(Theatrical) Gilbert Parker, William Morris Agency, 1350 Avenue of the Americas, New York, N.Y. 10019.

CAREER: Harvard University, Cambridge, Mass., Society of Fellows, junior fellow, 1947-50, assistant professor of English, 1950-54; Wellesley College, Wellesley, Mass., associate professor of English, 1955-57; Wesleyan University, Middletown, Conn., professor of English, 1957-77; Smith College, Northampton, Mass., writer in residence, 1977-86; Library of Congress, Washington, D.C., Poet Laureate of the United States, 1987-88. Lecturer at colleges, universities, and Library of Congress. U.S. State Department cultural exchange representative to the U.S.S.R., 1961. *Military service:* U.S. Army, Infantry, 1943-45; became staff sergeant.

MEMBER: American Academy and Institute of Arts and Letters (president, 1974-76; chancellor, 1976-78), American Academy of Arts and Sciences, PEN, Academy of American Poets (chancellor), Dramatists' Guild, Authors League of America, Century Club, Chi Psi.

AWARDS, HONORS: Harriet Monroe Memorial Prize, *Poetry* magazine, 1948, 1978; Oscar Blumenthal Prize, *Poetry* magazine, 1950; M.A., Amherst College, 1952; Guggenheim fellowships, 1952-53, 1963; Prix de Roma fellowship, American Academy of Arts and Letters, 1954; Edna St. Vincent Millay Memorial Award, 1957; Pulitzer Prize for poetry and National Book Award for poetry, both 1957, for *Things of This World;* Boston Festival Award, 1959; Ford Foundation fellowship for drama, 1960; Melville Cane Award, 1962; co-recipient, Bollingen Prize for translation, Yale University Library, 1963, for *Tartuffe,* and for poetry, 1971, for *Walking to Sleep;* Sarah Josepha Hale

Award, 1968; Creative Arts Award, Brandeis University, 1971; Prix Henri Desfeuilles, 1971; Shelley Memorial Award, 1973; *Book World*'s Children's Spring Book Festival award, 1973, for *Opposites: Poems and Drawings;* PEN translation Prize, 1983, for *Moliere: Four Comedies;* St. Botolph's Club Foundation Award, 1983; Drama Desk Award, 1983; Chevalier, Ordre des Palmes Academiques, 1983; named Poet Laureate of the United States, Library of Congress, 1987-88; *Los Angeles Times* Book Prize, 1988, for *New and Collected Poems;* Taylor Poetry Award, *Sewanee Review* and University of the South, 1988. L.H.D., Lawrence College (now Lawrence University of Wisconsin), 1960, Washington University, 1964, Williams College, 1975, University of Rochester, 1976, and Carnegie-Mellon University, 1980; Litt.D., Amherst College, 1967, Clark University, 1970, American International College, 1974, Marquette University, 1977, Wesleyan University, 1977, and Lake Forest College, 1982.

WRITINGS:

The Beautiful Changes and Other Poems, Reynal, 1947.
Ceremony and Other Poems, Harcourt, 1950.
Things of This World: Poems (also see below), Harcourt, 1956.
Poems, 1943-1956, Faber, 1957.
(With Robert Hillyer and Cleanth Brooks) *Anniversary Lectures,* U.S. Government Printing Office, 1959.
(With Louise Bogan and Archibald MacLeish) *Emily Dickinson: Three Views* (criticism), Amherst College Press, 1960.
Advice to a Prophet, and Other Poems, Harcourt, 1961.
Loudmouse (juvenile), illustrated by Don Almquist, Collier, 1963, Harcourt, 1982.
The Poems of Richard Wilbur, Harcourt, 1963.
(Translator) Philippe de Thaun, *The Pelican from a Bestiary of 1120* (poem), privately printed, 1963.
Prince Souvanna Phouma: An Exchange between Richard Wilbur and William Jay Smith (poem), limited edition, Phoenix Book Shop, 1968.
Walking to Sleep: New Poems and Translations, Harcourt, 1969.
Digging to China: Poem (Child Study Association book list; first published in *Things of This World*), Doubleday, 1970.
(Self-illustrated) *Opposites: Poems and Drawings* (children's poems), Harcourt, 1973.
Seed Leaves: Homage to R. F. (poem), limited edition, David R. Godine, 1974.
Responses: Prose Pieces, 1953-1976, Harcourt, 1976.
The Mind-Reader: New Poems, Harcourt, 1976.
Seven Poems, Abbatoir Editions, 1981.
(Translator) *The Whale and Other Uncollected Translations,* Boa Editions, 1982.
Richard Wilbur's Creation, University of Michigan Press, 1983.
New and Collected Poems, Harcourt, 1988.

PLAYS

(Translator) Jean Baptiste Poquelin Moliere, *The Misanthrope: Comedy in Five Acts, 1666* (also see below; first produced in Cambridge, Mass., by the Poet's Theatre, October 25, 1955; produced Off-Broadway at Theatre East, November 12, 1956), Harcourt, 1955.
(Lyricist with John Latouche, Dorothy Parker, Lillian Hellman, and Leonard Bernstein) Voltaire, *Candide: A Comic Operetta Based on Voltaire's Satire* (musical; based on adaptation by Lillian Hellman; music by Leonard Bernstein; first produced on Broadway at Martin Beck Theatre, December 1, 1956; produced on the West End at Saville Theatre, April 30, 1959), Random House, 1957.
(Translator) Moliere, *Tartuffe: Comedy in Five Acts, 1669* (also see below; first produced in Milwaukee, Wis., at Fred Miller

Theatre, January, 1964; produced on Broadway at ANTA Theatre, January 14, 1965), Harcourt, 1963.

(Translator) Moliere, *The Misanthrope* [and] *Tartuffe,* Harcourt, 1965.

(Translator) Moliere, *The School for Wives: Comedy in Five Acts, 1662* (first produced on Broadway at Lyceum Theatre, February 16, 1971), Harcourt, 1971.

(Translator) Moliere, *The Learned Ladies: Comedy in Five Acts, 1672* (first produced in Williamstown, Mass., at the Williamstown Festival Theatre, 1977), Harcourt, 1978.

(Translator) Jean Racine, *Andromanche: Tragedy in Five Acts, 1667,* Harcourt, 1982.

(Translator) *Moliere: Four Comedies,* Harcourt, 1982.

(Translator) Racine, *Phaedra,* Harcourt, 1986.

EDITOR

(With Louis Untermeyer and Karl Shapiro) *Modern American and Modern British Poetry,* revised abridged edition, Harcourt, 1955.

A Bestiary (anthology), Pantheon, 1955.

(And author of introduction and notes) Edgar Allan Poe, *Poe: Complete Poems,* Dell, 1959.

(Editor of section on Poe) *Major Writers of America,* Harcourt, 1962.

(With Alfred Harbage, and author of introduction) William Shakespeare, *Poems,* Penguin, 1966, revised edition published as *Shakespeare, the Narrative Poems and Poems of Doubtful Authenticity,* 1974.

(And author of introduction) Poe, *The Narrative of Arthur Gordon Pym,* David R. Godine, 1974.

(And author of introduction) Witter Bynner, *Selected Poems,* Farrar, Straus, 1978.

OTHER

(Contributor) Gygory Kepes, editor, *The New Landscape in Art and Science,* Paul Theobald, 1955.

"Poems" (recording), Spoken Arts, 1959.

(Contributor) Don C. Allen, editor, *The Moment of Poetry,* Johns Hopkins Press, 1962.

(Lyricist) "On Freedom's Ground" (cantata; music by William Schuman), first produced in New York City at the Lincoln Center for the Statue of Liberty Centennial, October, 1986.

Also recorded "Richard Wilbur Reading His Own Poems," for Caedmon. Translator of *The Funeral of Bobo,* by Joseph Brodsky, for Ardis. Work represented in anthologies. Contributor of critical reviews to periodicals. General editor, "Laurel Poets" series, for Dell; former member of poetry board, Wesleyan University Press.

SIDELIGHTS: Richard Wilbur "is a poet for all of us, whose elegant words brim with wit and paradox," announced Librarian of Congress Daniel J. Boorstin when the poet succeeded Robert Penn Warren to become the second Poet Laureate of the United States. Elizabeth Kastor further quotes Boorstin in her *Washington Post* article: "He is also a poet's poet, at home in the long tradition of the traveled ways of the great poets of our language. . . . His poems are among the best our country has to offer." The new poet laureate has won the Pulitzer Prize and National Book Award for his collection *Things of This World: Poems,* among other numerous awards for his poetry. His translations of French verse, especially Voltaire's *Candide* and the plays of Jean-Baptiste Moliere and Jean Racine, are also highly regarded by critics; his translation of Moliere's *Tartuffe* won the 1971 Bollingen Prize. But because of Wilbur's dedication to the traditional forms of rhyme and meter, and his unwillingness to

compose experimental poetry, his work has in the past stirred controversy among critics.

The son of a commercial artist, Wilbur was interested in painting as a youth; but he eventually opted to pursue writing as his avocation, a decision he attributes to the influence of his mother's father and grandfather, both of whom were editors. As a student, Wilbur wrote stories, editorials, and poems for his college newspaper and magazine, but, as the poet comments in *Twentieth Century Authors: A Biographical Dictionary of Modern Literature:* "It was not until World War II took me to Cassino, Anzio, and the Siegfried Line that I began to versify in earnest. One does not use poetry for its major purposes, as a means to organize oneself and the world, until one's world somehow gets out of hand." Witnessing war firsthand has had a major effect on Wilbur's poetry. "Many of his first poems had a common motive," writes Richard L. Calhoun in the *Dictionary of Literary Biography,* "the desire to stress the importance of finding order in a world where war had served as a reminder of disorder and destruction."

Because of this motivation, Wilbur's first collection, *The Beautiful Changes and Other Poems,* contains "more poetic exercises on how to face the problems of disorder and destruction than laments over the losses occasioned by the war," notes Calhoun. The poems in this book, according to Donald L. Hill in his *Richard Wilbur,* also demonstrate "a pervasive good humor, a sweetness of spirit, unusual among the major poets of the century." This generally light-hearted approach that Wilbur uses in his poetry has caused some critics to charge the poet with avoiding tragic themes by covering them with purely aesthetic verse. James Dickey, for example, writes in his book, *Babel to Byzantium,* that one has "the feeling that the cleverness of phrase and the delicious aptness of Wilbur's poems sometimes mask an unwillingness or inability to think or feel deeply; that the poems tend to lapse toward highly sophisticated play." John Reibetanz speculates in *Modern Poetry Studies* that this is because "for Richard Wilbur, the sights offered by World War II contradict and threaten his most basic beliefs, as we can infer them from his writings: that love is more powerful than hatred; that nature is a source of values and of reassurance; and that there is a strong creative urge in both man and nature which constantly seeks and finds expression in images of graceful plenitude." "But in the 1940's," Reibetanz concludes, "the utter disparity between what he saw and what he wished to see made him run for cover."

The explanation for his choice of subjects and preference for a light-hearted tone in his poetry is, in Wilbur's view, not so much a matter of running from reality as it is a matter of affirming a philosophical conviction. "I feel that the universe is full of glorious energy," he explains in an interview with Peter Stitt in the *Paris Review,* "that the energy tends to take pattern and shape, and that the ultimate character of things is comely and good. I am perfectly aware that I say this in the teeth of all sorts of contrary evidence, and that I must be basing it partly on temperament and partly on faith, but that's my attitude." Still, the poet does not completely refuse to address serious issues. Robert B. Shaw comments in *Parnassus: Poetry in Review* that while "it is true that some of Wilbur's earlier poems veer with disconcerting abruptness from the naturalistic to the esthetic. . . . He has never, in fact, avoided negative subject matter as completely as some critics have charged." The critic later asserts that several poems in his third collection, *Things of This World,* deal directly with humane and political issues.

Certain reviewers have persisted in their arguments that it is necessary for a poet to occasionally use a tragic tone of voice in order to capture all the aspects of life in his poetry. Hill maintains: "A bitter or anguished poet, if he is equally skillful and equally just in his response to his experience, may strike even more deeply into our feelings." Echoing this sentiment, *Sewanee Review* contributor Paul Ramsey feels that Wilbur's tone tends to mar his work. The critic declares in an article on *The Mind-Reader: New Poems* that "the calm precision of touch, the middle-distanced eye, the self-awareness of technique, which make for a comfortably joyful light verse, tend to undercut more serious occasions." But even though Wilbur's is not the tragic mind that many readers sometimes expect to see in poets, Dickey retorts that the poems "are as true and heartening a picture as we are ever likely to have of the best that the twentieth-century American can say of himself or have said about him." Commenting on his 1988 book, *New and Collected Poems,* Robert Richman also reminds critics in his *New York Times Book Review* article: "If it were not for writers like [Wilbur], future students might wonder if there were no poets in the late 20th century who championed beauty . . . or who were capable of rising above all the despair and doubt."

But changes in attitudes toward poetry in the 1960s alienated the future laureate from his fellow poets, as David H. Van Biema's *People* article explains: "American poetry appeared to be moving away from the style at which [Wilbur] excelled. Younger poets such as Allen Ginsberg, Gregory Corso and Robert Creeley were tossing away the traces of metric form completely or engaging in an uncooked, violently confessional poetry that Wilbur would not emulate." The new approaches did not appeal to Wilbur, who comments on the subject in an interview collected in William Packard's *The Craft of Poetry: Interviews from the New York Quarterly:* "I don't like, I can't adjust to, simplistic political poetry, the crowd-pleasing sort of anti-Vietnam poem. I can't adjust to the kind of Black poetry that simply cusses and hollers artlessly. And most of all I can't adjust to the sort of poem, which is mechanically, prosaically 'irrational,' which is often self-pitying, which starts all its sentences with 'I,' and which writes constantly out of a limply subjective world."

While Wilbur obdurately composed reflective, optimistic poetry, using traditional patterns of rhyme and meter, the changing poetic movements that flowed by him caused his image to change over the years. "His poetry was judged too impersonal for the early 1960s," testifies Calhoun; "it was not politically involved enough during the literary protests against the war in Vietnam in the later 1960s, and, in the 1970s, not sufficiently postmodernist." Calhoun does note that Wilbur's poems of the 1960s show some experimentation, "but in comparison with what other poets, Robert Lowell and John Berryman for example, were doing by 1961, the experimentation is comparatively minor." His skill at using rhyme and meter, however, is generally acknowledged among critics like *London Magazine* reviewer Roy Fuller, who believes that "Wilbur is excellent at inventing stanza forms, and his stanzas rhyming in pairs are particularly effective." "His intricately patterned poems reflect the discovery of patterns of natural beauty," adds Shaw.

"I think that critics of Wilbur's urbane formalism have often failed to appreciate the deep emotional needs met by it, and so have overlooked the seriousness of his commitment to it," opines Reibetanz. Indeed, according to Wilbur in a *Paris Review* interview with Ellesa Clay High and Helen McCloy Ellison, his poetic style and need for order in the world are related. The poet remarks: "One of the jobs of poetry is to make the unbearable bearable, not by falsehood but by clear, precise confrontation." Because his formal technique is a matter of personal preference, Wilbur emphasizes that he is not against others using free verse.

"I'm thought to have a quarrel with free-verse poets," he tells David Dillon in the *Southwest Review.* "I really don't at all. I just choose to write free verse that happens to rhyme or to fall into a stanza pattern." "We must recognize that meter in itself is not rigid—," he remarks to Stitt, "it depends on how you use it."

Wilbur's insistence on formalism, critics soon found, was naturally suited to his work in translating French poetry and plays. Speaking of his "tactful, metrical and speakable translation of verse drama," *Hudson Review* critic Alan Shaw comments: "Wilbur's [translations] are almost the solitary example of this kind in English. And it is precisely, I think, because he has stood somewhat apart from the tradition on English-language poetry in this century . . . that he has been able to achieve this." He concludes that "Richard Wilbur's translations of classic French drama are among the undiscovered treasure of our recent literature." The expertise and importance of the poet's translations of plays by Moliere, Voltaire, and Racine has been little questioned by reviewers. "The rendition [of Moliere's *The Misanthrope*], delightful and literate, made Moliere accessible for the first time to a wide American audience and was the start of a lucrative sideline for the poet," writes Van Biema. Compared to other translators, *Saturday Review* contributor John Ciardi believes that "instead of cognate-snapping, as the academic dullards invariably do, [in his translation of *The Misanthrope*] Wilbur has found English equivalents for the turn and nuance of the French, and the fact that he has managed to do so in rhymed couplets that not only respect themselves as English poetry but allow the play to be staged . . . with great success is testament enough."

Contrary to the view that Wilbur's poems have not evolved over the years, several critics feel that the translations have had a noticeable effect on his verse. X. J. Kennedy avers in the *Los Angeles Times Book Review* that "his recent poems are more easily speakable—a result, I suspect, of his translating so much Moliere. More often now, the poems tell stories." And Wilbur admits in a *Time* article by Patricia Blake: "The experience of translating Moliere has enlarged the voice of my own poems. . . . Sometimes I have the illusion that I speak for him." In an article he wrote, which appears in *Shenandoah,* Wilbur says that his "writing is now plainer and more straightforward than it used to be." "Another change in my work has been a partial shift from the ironic meditative lyric toward the dramatic poem," he adds.

Analyzing the laureate's book *New and Collected Poems, Los Angeles Times Book Review* contributor Joshua Odell believes these newer poems "clearly show a continued evolution in style from an ornate elegance found particularly in Wilbur's first collection, 'The Beautiful Changes,' toward a simple, direct and crisp verse." Still, poems like those in *The Mind Reader* manage "to stand up against every kind of poetic chic," according to Bruce Michelson in *Southern Review.* And as some critics have noted, the changes in Wilbur's poetry have not affected the basic philosophy his verses have always shown. "He seems to be seeking even firmer and more affirmative statements of the need for order and responsibility; and his tone in the later poems is more confident, more self-assured," asserts Calhoun. This is a need that Wilbur feels all poets should attempt to meet in their work. In his book, *Responses: Prose Pieces, 1953-1976,* the laureate declares: "Every poet is impelled to utter the whole of the world that is real to him, to respond to that world in some spirit, and to draw all its parts toward some *coherence.*"

Through his efforts to illustrate an optimistic viewpoint, while using traditional techniques on meter and rhyme, Wilbur is able to show considerable depth in his poems, according to William

Heyen in *Southern Review.* "There is for me in the poetry of Richard Wilbur something just past the threshold of realization," writes Heyen, "something elusive, something toward which his formal structures edge and with which they bump shoulders, something that criticism can only hope to graze. This something, I think, is feeling, passion." *P.N. Review* contributor J. D. McClatchy also sees that there is more to Wilbur's poetry than is readily apparent. "Scrupulous questioning and elegant rhetoric, in such skilful hands," he maintains, "can better contour the chaos than the wildest poem; can make us feel the tension between the light touch and the darkness it holds back. One has to watch carefully, beneath the performance that would convince us otherwise, for the harsher realities on which these poems are founded."

AVOCATIONAL INTERESTS: Tennis, herb gardening, walking.

BIOGRAPHICAL/CRITICAL SOURCES:

BOOKS

Contemporary Literary Criticism, Gale, Volume 3, 1975, Volume 6, 1976, Volume 9, 1978, Volume 14, 1980, Volume 53, 1989.
Cummins, Paul F., *Richard Wilbur,* Eerdmans, 1971.
Dickey, James, *Babel to Byzantium,* Farrar, Straus, 1968.
Dictionary of Literary Biography, Volume 5: *American Poets since World War II,* Gale, 1980.
Field, John, *Richard Wilbur: A Biographical Checklist,* Kent State University Press, 1971.
French, Warren, editor, *The Fifties: Fiction, Poetry, Drama,* Everett/ Edwards, 1970.
Hill, Donald L., *Richard Wilbur,* Twayne, 1967.
Hungerford, Edward, editor, *Poets in Progress,* Northwestern University Press, 1962, new edition, 1967.
Jarrell, Randall, *Poetry and the Age,* Knopf, 1953.
Jarrell, Randall, *The Third Book of Criticism,* Farrar, Straus, 1969.
Kunitz, Stanley, and Vineta Colby, *Twentieth Century Authors: A Biographical Dictionary of Modern Literature,* H. W. Wilson, 1955.
Packard, William, editor, *The Craft of Poetry: Interviews from the New York Quarterly,* Doubleday, 1974.
Nemerov, Howard, editor, *Poets on Poetry,* Basic Books, 1966.
Rosenthal, M. L., *The Modern Poets,* Oxford University Press, 1965.
Stepanchev, Stephen, *American Poetry since 1945,* Harper, 1965.
Wilbur, Richard, *Responses: Prose Pieces, 1953-1976,* Harcourt, 1976.

PERIODICALS

Bulletin of Bibliography, January-March, 1980.
Christian Century, March 19, 1958.
Hollins Critic, April, 1977.
Hudson Review, summer, 1969, summer, 1987.
London Magazine, July, 1957.
Los Angeles Times, March 17, 1983, April 18, 1987, October 13, 1987.
Los Angeles Times Book Review, July 31, 1988, October 9, 1988.
Modern Poetry Studies, Volume 2, numbers 1 and 2, 1982.
Nation, November 3, 1956.
National Review, September 2, 1988.
New Republic, June 5, 1976.
New York Times, January 28, 1983.
New York Times Book Review, December 14, 1969, December 26, 1982, April 18, 1987, May 29, 1988.

Paris Review, winter, 1977.
Parnassus: Poetry in Review, spring/summer, 1977.
People, October 5, 1987.
P.N. Review, Volume 13, number 5, 1987.
Saturday Review, August 18, 1956.
Sewanee Review, spring, 1978.
Shenandoah, fall, 1965.
Southern Review, summer, 1973, July, 1979.
Southwest Review, summer, 1973.
Time, November 19, 1984.
Times Literary Supplement, May 20, 1977.
Tribune Books (Chicago), July 24, 1988.
Washington Post, July 25, 1976, October 6, 1987.

*　　*　　*

WILDER, Thornton (Niven) 1897-1975

PERSONAL: Born April 17, 1897, in Madison, Wis.; died of a heart attack, December 7, 1975, in Hamden, Conn.; son of Amos Parker (a newspaper editor and U.S. Consul to China) and Isabella Thornton (Niven) Wilder. *Education:* Attended public and private schools in the United States and in Chefoo, China; attended Oberlin College, 1915-17; Yale University, A.B., 1920; attended American Academy in Rome 1920-21; Princeton University, A.M., 1926. *Politics:* Democrat. *Religion:* Congregationalist.

ADDRESSES: Home—50 Deepwood Dr., Hamden, CT 06517.

CAREER: Lawrenceville School, Lawrenceville, N.J., French teacher and assistant master of Davis House, 1921-25; tutor and writer in the United States and abroad, 1925-27; Davis House, master, 1927-28; writer and cross-country lecturer, 1928-29; University of Chicago, Chicago, Ill., lecturer in comparative literature, 1930-36; writer for several motion picture studios, 1930-36; University of Hawaii, Honolulu, visiting professor, 1935; American delegate to Institut de Cooperation Intellectuelle, Paris, France, 1937; goodwill representative to Latin America for U.S. Department of State, 1941; International PEN Club Congress delegate with John Dos Passos, 1941; Harvard University, Cambridge, Mass., Charles Eliot Norton Professor of poetry, 1950-51; chief of U.S. delegation to UNESCO Conference of Arts, Venice, 1952. Actor in *Our Town,* New York City and summer stock, beginning 1939, in *The Skin of Our Teeth,* stock and summer theaters. *Military service:* Coast Artillery Corps, Fort Adams, R.I., 1918; became corporal; commissioned captain in U.S. Army Air Intelligence, and served 1942-45, advancing to lieutenant colonel; awarded Legion of Merit, Bronze Star; Legion d'Honneur, Honorary Member of the Order of the British Empire (M.B.E.).

MEMBER: American Academy of Arts and Letters, Modern Language Association of America (honorary member), Authors Guild, Actors Equity Association, Hispanic Society of America, Bayerische Akademie (corresponding member), Akademie der Wissenschaften und der Literatur (Mainz, West Germany), Bavarian Academy of Fine Arts (honorary member), Century Association (New York), Players (honorary member), Graduate Club, Elizabethan Club, Alpha Delta Phi.

AWARDS, HONORS: Pulitzer Prize, 1928, for *The Bridge of San Luis Rey,* 1938, for *Our Town,* and 1943, for *The Skin of Our Teeth;* Chevalier, Legion of Honor, 1951; Gold Medal for Fiction, American Academy of Arts and Letters, 1952; Friedenspreis des Deutschen Buchhandels (Frankfurt on the Main, West Germany), 1957; Sonderpreis des Oesterreichischen Staatspreises, 1959, Goethe-Plakette, 1959; Brandeis University Creative

Arts Award, 1959-60, for theater and film; Edward MacDowell Medal (first time presented), 1960; Century Association Art Medal; Medal of the Order of Merit (Peru); Order Pour le Merite (Bonn, West Germany); invited by President Kennedy's cabinet to present reading, 1962; Presidential Medal of Freedom, 1963; National Book Committee's National Medal for Literature (first time presented), 1965; National Book Award, 1968, for *The Eighth Day;* honorary degrees from New York University, Yale University, Kenyon College, College of Wooster, Harvard University, Northeastern University, Oberlin College, University of New Hampshire, University of Zurich.

WRITINGS:

NOVELS

The Cabala (excerpt published in *Double Dealer,* September, 1922; also see below), Boni, 1926, Avon, 1975.

The Bridge of San Luis Rey (also see below), Boni, 1927, reprinted, Avon, 1976, limited edition with illustrations by William Kaughan, Franklin Library, 1976.

The Woman of Andros (based on *Andria* by Terence; also see below), Boni, 1930, reprinted, Avon, 1975.

Heaven's My Destination (Book-of-the-Month Club selection), Longmans, Green, 1934, Harper, 1935, reprinted, Popular Library, 1969.

The Ides of March (Book-of-the-Month Club selection), Harper, 1948, reprinted, Avon, 1975.

The Eighth Day, Harper, 1967.

Theophilus North, Harper, 1973.

Adaptor, with Jerome Kilty, of stage version of *The Ides of March.*

PLAYS

The Trumpet Shall Sound (first published in *Yale Literary Magazine,* 1919-20), produced by the American Laboratory Theater, December 10, 1926.

(Adaptor and translator) *Lucrece* (based on *The Rape of Lucrece* by Andre Obey; first produced on Broadway at the Belasco Theatre, December 20 1932), Houghton, 1933.

Our Town (three-act play; first produced in Princeton, N.J., January 22, 1938; produced in New York at the Henry Miller Theatre, February 4, 1938; produced on Broadway at the Lyceum Theater, December 5, 1988; also see below), Coward, 1938, reprinted, Avon, 1975, acting edition, Coward, 1965, limited edition with introduction by Brooks Atkinson and illustrations by Robert J. Lee, Limited Editions Club, 1974.

(Adaptor and translator) Henrik Ibsen, *A Doll's House,* first produced on Broadway at the Morosco Theatre, December 27, 1938.

The Merchant of Yonkers: A Farce in Four Acts (based on *Einen Jux will er sich Machen* by Johann Nestroy; first produced on Broadway December 28, 1938), Harper, 1939, revised version renamed *The Matchmaker* (first produced in 1954 for Edinburgh Festival; produced on Broadway at the Royale Theatre, December 5, 1955; also see below), Samuel French, 1957.

The Skin of Our Teeth (three-act play; first produced in New Haven, Conn., October 15, 1942; produced on Broadway at the Plymouth Theatre, November 18, 1942; produced in New York City by Classic Stage Company, November 24, 1986; also see below), Harper, 1942, Longmans, Green, 1958.

Our Century (three-scene burlesque; first produced April 26, 1947, in New York City at the Century Association), Century Association, 1947.

The Happy Journey to Trenton and Camden, produced with *The Respectful Prostitute* by Jean Paul Sartre, on Broadway at the Cort Theatre, February 9, 1948.

(Translator) Jean-Paul Sartre, *The Victors,* produced Off-Broadway, 1949.

The Alcestiad (based by *Alcestis* by Euripides), first produced as *A Life in the Sun,* at Assembly Hall, Edinburgh, Scotland, August 25, 1955.

The Wreck of the 5:25 and *Bernice,* first performed at Congresshalle Theater in West Berlin, West Germany, September 20, 1957.

The Drunken Sisters (satyr play; first appeared in centennial issue of *Atlantic Monthly,* 1957; first produced as fourth act of *Die Alkestiade* [also see below], produced in Brooklyn Heights, N.Y., at Spencer Memorial Church, June 28, 1970), Samuel French, 1957.

Childhood (one-act; first appeared in *Atlantic Monthly,* November, 1960; also see below), Samuel French, 1960.

The Long Christmas Dinner (also see below), revised edition, Samuel French, 1960.

(Author of libretto) *Das Lange Weihnachtsmal* (opera; adapted from play, *The Long Christmas Dinner;* first produced at National Theatre in Mannheim, Germany, December 17, 1961), music by Paul Hindemith, translated into German by Hindemith, libretto published by Schott Music, 1961.

Infancy, A Comedy in One Act (also see below), Samuel French, 1961.

Plays for Bleecker Street (three volumes; includes *Infancy, Childhood,* and *Someone from Assisi;* first produced Off-Broadway at Circle in the Square, January 11, 1962), Samuel French, 1960-61.

(Author of libretto) *Die Alkestiade* (opera; adaptation of *A Life in the Sun*), music by Louise Talma, first produced at Stadische Buhnen in Frankfurt, West Germany, March 1, 1962.

Pullman Car Hiawatha (also see below), produced Off-Broadway at Circle in the Square, December 3, 1964.

Thornton Wilder's Triple Bill (includes *The Long Christmas Dinner, The Queens of France* [also see below], and *The Happy Journey to Trenton and Camden* [also see below]), produced Off-Broadway at Cherry Lane Theatre, September 6, 1966.

OMNIBUS VOLUMES

The Angel That Troubled the Waters, and Other Plays (includes *Nascunter Poetae, Proserpina and the Devil, Fanny Otcott, Brother Fire, The Penny That Beauty Spent, The Angel on the Ship, The Message and Jehanne, Childe Roland to the Dark Tower Came, Centaurs, Leviathan, And the Sea Shall Give Up Its Dead, Now the Servant's Name Was Malchus, Mozart and the Gray Steward, Hast Thou Considered My Servant Job?, The Flight into Egypt,* and *The Angel That Troubled the Waters*), Coward, 1928.

The Long Christmas Dinner and Other Plays in One Act (includes *The Long Christmas Dinner, Pullman Car Hiawatha, Such Things Only Happen in Books, The Happy Journey to Trenton and Camden, Love and How to Cure It,* and *The Queens of France*), Yale University Press, 1931, reprinted, Avon, 1980.

(Author of preface) *Three Plays: Our Town, The Skin of Our Teeth, The Matchmaker,* Harper, 1938, reprinted, 1957, published as *Our Town; The Skin of Our Teeth; The Match-*

maker, Penguin Books, 1962, limited edition with illustrations by Dick Brown, Franklin Library, 1979.

A Thornton Wilder Trio: The Cabala, The Bridge of San Luis Rey, The Woman of Andros, Criterion, 1956.

The Cabala and The Woman of Andros, Harper, 1968.

The Alcestiad: or, A Life in the Sun: A Play in Three Acts, with a Satyr Play, The Drunken Sisters, Harper, 1977, limited edition published as *The Alcestiad: or, A Life in the Sun; The Drunken Sisters,* illustrations by Daniel Maffia, Franklin Library, 1977.

OTHER

(Author of preface) Gertrude Stein, *Narration,* University of Chicago Press, 1935.

We Live Again (screenplay; based on *Resurrection* by Leo Tolstoy), Metro-Goldwyn-Mayer, 1936.

(Author of preface) *The Geographical History of America,* Random House, 1936.

(Contributor) *The Intent of the Artist,* edited by Augusto Centeno, Princeton University Press, 1941.

(Author of preface) *Four in America,* Yale University Press, 1947.

An Evening with Thornton Wilder, April thirtieth, 1962, Washington, D.C. (consists of third act of *Our Town*), Harper, 1962.

American Characteristics and Other Essays, edited by Donald Gallup, foreword by Isabel Wilder, Harper, 1979.

Author of screenplay, *Shadow of a Doubt,* 1942. Contributor to periodicals, including *Harper's, Hudson Review, Poetry, Atlantic,* and *Yale Review.* Theatre reviewer for *Theatre Arts Monthly,* 1925.

WORK IN PROGRESS: Two cycles of plays, *The Seven Ages of Man* and *The Seven Deadly Sins.*

MEDIA ADAPTATIONS: The Bridge of San Luis Rey was filmed three times, initially in 1929; also filmed were *Our Town,* 1940, and *The Matchmaker,* 1958. *The Matchmaker* was adapted by Michael Stewart made into a musical, *Hello, Dolly!,* with words and music by Jerry Herman, and opened in 1964, with an initial run of almost 3,000 performances; in 1964, *Hello Dolly!* became the longest running musical on Broadway; *Hello, Dolly!* subsequently became a popular film. *Our Town* was made into the musical *Grover's Corners,* by Harvey Schmidt and Tom Jones, in 1987. *Theophilus North* was made into the movie *Mr. North* by John Huston, starring Danny Huston, Anjelica Huston, and Robert Mitchum. There have also been radio and television versions of many of Wilder's works.

SIDELIGHTS: Thornton Wilder occupied, wrote Edmund Wilson, "a unique position, between the Great Books and Parisian sophistication one way, and the entertainment industry the other way, and in our culture this region, though central, is a dark and almost uninhabited no man's land." Louis Broussard noted that "In such company as O'Neill, Eliot, Anouilh, and many other post-war pessimists, Wilder emerges as a lone dissenter. Not because he was an optimist . . . but because his optimism grows out of an indifference to his own period. . . . No other writer begins with so hopeful a premise: that this age is essentially no different from any other, that its problems, whatever they may be . . . will resolve themselves in change which can only be better than the past. His is not the search for an exit from dilemma; there is no dilemma."

Wilder himself believed the theater consists of presenting experience for its own sake. "I regard the theater as the greatest of all

art forms," he told the *Paris Review,* "the most immediate way in which a human being can share with another the sense of what it is to be a human being. This supremacy of the theater derives from the fact that it is always 'now' on the stage." Ignoring conflict, preferring comedy to tragedy, extolling traditional ideas, Wilder was "the artist of the anachronism," wrote Malcolm Cowley. In commenting on *Our Town,* Broussard said Wilder could "present the cycle of life without conflict because the foundations upon which his ideals rest have not yet been shaken. Romantic love, marriage, the concept of the 'Mind of God'. . . . These remain safe behind the barrier of isolated time." *The Skin of Our Teeth,* which portrays a five thousand-year history of man which some critics think has some basis in James Joyce's *Finnegans Wake,* "is really a way of trying to make sense out of the multiplicity of the human race and its affections," remarked Wilder.

Harold Clurman found Wilder's plays particularly American in "their benign humor, their old-fashioned optimism, their use of the charmingly homely detail, the sophisticated employment of the commonplace, their avuncular celebration of the humdrum, their common sense, popular moralism, and the simplicity—one might almost say simplemindedness—behind a shrewdly captivating manipulation of a large selection of classic elements." Edmund Wilson believed "all of this works very well in the theater. . . . But if one happens to be feeling a little morose . . . or if one tries the experiment of reading [*The Skin of Our Teeth*] in cold blood, the marriage of Plato and Groucho Marx may fail to appeal." Wilder, however, concluded that the theater addresses itself to the group and "partakes of the nature of festival." A play "presupposes a crowd." He once said: "I would love to be the poet laureate of Coney Island."

Originally Wilder had been somewhat ignored by serious critics. In fact, *Our Town* closed after one week in Boston in 1938, because of bad notices. But in time, Wilder was praised for his experimentation and innovation, and *The Skin of Our Teeth* has become a modern classic. Travis Bogard called Wilder "a man who, along with O'Neill, freed the American theater from its traditional forms through his experiments in *Our Town* and *The Skin of Our Teeth. . . .* In a sense, perhaps, all of Wilder's plays are about the Day of Judgment, imaging human character as a bubble rising to burst on the surface of eternity. There undoubtedly were influences on his experimental style, but, in the last analysis, Wilder's innovations are important consequences of his point of view and of his way of commenting on experience." Wilder may have taken himself less seriously; as he once told the *Paris Review:* "I'm the kind of man whom timid old ladies stop on the street to ask about the nearest subway station."

The manuscript of *The Bridge of San Luis Rey* is held in Yale University's American Literature Collection of the Beinecke Rare Book and Manuscript Library.

BIOGRAPHICAL/CRITICAL SOURCES:

BOOKS

Allen, Walter, *The Modern Novel,* Dutton, 1965.

Authors in the News, Volume 2, Gale, 1976.

Bogard, Travis, and William I. Oliver, editors, *Modern Drama: Essays in Criticism,* Oxford University Press, 1965.

Broussard, Louis, *American Drama,* University of Oklahoma Press, 1962.

Burbank, R., *Thornton Wilder,* Twayne, 1961.

Cohn, Ruby, *Dialogue in American Drama,* Indiana University Press, 1971.

Cole, Toby, editor, *Playwrights on Playwriting,* Hill & Wang, 1961.

Contemporary Literary Criticism, Gale, Volume 1, 1973, Volume 5, 1976, Volume 6, 1976, Volume 10, 1979, Volume 15, 1980, Volume 35, 1985.

Cowley, Malcolm, editor, *Writers at Work: The Paris Review Interviews,* Viking, 1957.

Dictionary of Literary Biography, Gale, Volume 4: *American Writers in Paris, 1920-1939,* 1980, Volume 7: *Twentieth-Century American Dramatists,* 1981, Volume 9: *American Novelists, 1910-1945,* 1981.

Edelstein, J. M., compiler, *Bibliographical Checklist of the Writings of Thornton Wilder,* Yale University Press, 1959.

Fergusson, Francis, *The Human Image in Dramatic Literature,* Doubleday, 1957.

Goldstein, Malcolm, *The Art of Thornton Wilder,* University of Nebraska Press, 1965.

Haberman, Donald, *The Plays of Thornton Wilder,* Wesleyan University Press, 1967.

Kuner, M. C., *Thornton Wilder: The Bright and the Dark,* Crowell, 1972.

Papajewski, Helmut, *Thornton Wilder,* translated by John Conway, Unger, 1969.

Stresau, Herman, *Thornton Wilder,* translated by Frieda Schultze, Unger, Thornton Wilder, Yale University Press, 1959.

Wagenknecht, Edward, *Cavalcade of the English Novel,* Holt, 1943.

Wilson, Edmund, *A Literary Chronicle: 1920-1950,* Anchor Books, 1956.

PERIODICALS

A B Bookman's Weekly, January 5, 1976.
Modern Drama, September, 1972.
Nation, September 3, 1955.
New Republic, August 8, 1928.
New York Times, November 24, 1986, December 20, 1987, December 5, 1988, December 11, 1988.
New York Times Book Review, December 30, 1979.
Philadelphia Inquirer, December 14, 1975.
Saturday Review, October 6, 1956.

OBITUARIES:

PERIODICALS

Detroit Free Press, December 8, 1975.
Detroit News, December 8, 1975.
Newsweek, December 22, 1975.
New York Times, December 8, 1975.
Washington Post, December 8, 1975.

*   *   *

WILHELM, Kate
 See WILHELM, Katie Gertrude

*   *   *

WILHELM, Katie Gertrude   1928-
 (Kate Wilhelm)

PERSONAL: Born June 8, 1928, in Toledo, Ohio; daughter of Jesse Thomas and Ann (McDowell) Meredith; married Joseph B. Wilhelm, May 24, 1947 (divorced, 1962); married Damon Knight (a writer and editor), February 23, 1963; children: (first marriage) Douglas, Richard; (second marriage) Jonathan. *Education:* Attended high school in Louisville, Ky.

ADDRESSES: Home—1645 Horn Lane, Eugene, Ore. 97404. *Agent*—Brandt & Brandt, 101 Park Ave., New York, N.Y. 10017.

CAREER: Employed as a model, telephone operator, sales clerk, switchboard operator, and insurance company underwriter; full-time writer, 1956—. Co-director, Milford Science Fiction Writers Conference, 1963-76; lecturer at Clarion Fantasy Workshop, Michigan State University, beginning 1968.

MEMBER: Science Fiction Writers of America, Authors Guild, Authors League of America, P.E.N.

AWARDS, HONORS: Nebula Award of Science Fiction Writers of America, 1968, for best short story, "The Planners"; Hugo Award of World Science Fiction Convention, 1977, Jupiter Award, 1977, and second place for the John W. Campbell Memorial Award, 1977, all for *Where Late the Sweet Birds Sang;* American Book Award nomination, 1980, for *Juniper Time: A Novel.*

WRITINGS:

UNDER NAME KATE WILHELM

More Bitter Than Death, Simon & Schuster, 1962.
The Mile-Long Spaceship (short stories), Berkley Publishing, 1963 (published in England as *Andover and the Android,* Dobson, 1966).
(With Theodore L. Thomas) *The Clone,* Berkley, 1965.
The Nevermore Affair, Doubleday, 1966.
The Killer Thing, Doubleday, 1967 (published in England as *The Killing Thing,* Jenkins, 1967).
The Downstairs Room, and Other Speculative Fiction (short stories), Doubleday, 1968.
Let the Fire Fall, Doubleday, 1969.
(With Thomas) *The Year of the Cloud,* Doubleday, 1970.
Abyss: Two Novellas, Doubleday, 1971.
Margaret and I, Little, Brown, 1971.
City of Cain, Little, Brown, 1973.
(Editor) *Nebula Award Stories,* Number 9, Gollancz, 1974, Harper, 1975.
The Clewiston Test, Farrar, Straus, 1976.
Where Late the Sweet Birds Sang, Harper, 1976.
The Infinity Box: A Collection of Speculative Fiction (short stories), Harper, 1976.
Fault Lines: A Novel, Harper, 1976.
(Editor) *Clarion SF,* Berkley Publishing, 1976.
Somerset Dreams and Other Fictions, Harper, 1978.
"Axoltl" (multimedia science fantasy), first produced in Eugene, Ore., at University of Oregon Art Museum, April 6, 1979.
Juniper Time: A Novel, Harper, 1979.
(With husband, Damon Knight) *Better Than One,* New England Science Fiction Association, 1980.
A Sense of Shadow, Houghton, 1981.
Listen, Listen, Houghton, 1981.
Oh, Susannah!: A Novel, Houghton, 1982.
Welcome Chaos, Houghton, 1983.
"The Hindenberg Effect" (radio play), first broadcast by KSOR (Ashland, Ore.), 1985.
Huysman's Pets, Bluejay Books, 1986.
(With Richard Wilhelm) *The Hills Are Dancing,* Corroborree Press, 1986.
The Dark Door, St. Martin's, 1988.
Crazy Time, St. Martin's, 1989.
Smart House, St. Martin's, 1989.
Children of the Wind, St. Martin's, 1989.

CONTRIBUTOR; UNDER NAME KATE WILHELM

Samuel R. Delany and Marilyn Hacker, editors, *Quark No. 3,* Popular Library, 1971.

Harlan Ellison, editor, *Again, Dangerous Visions: 46 Original Stories,* Doubleday, 1972.

Thomas M. Disch, editor, *Bad Moon Rising: An Anthology of Political Foreboding,* Harper, 1973.

Knight, editor, *A Shocking Thing,* Pocket Books, 1974.

Roger Elwood and Robert Silverberg, editors, *Epoch,* Berkley Publishing, 1975.

Femmes au futur: Anthologie de nouvelles de science-fiction feminine (short stories), Marabout, 1976.

CONTRIBUTOR TO "ORBIT" ANTHOLOGY SERIES, EDITED BY KNIGHT; UNDER NAME KATE WILHELM

Orbit 1, Putnam, 1966.
Orbit 2, Putnam, 1967.
Orbit 3, Putnam, 1968.
Orbit 4, Putnam, 1968.
Orbit 5, Putnam, 1969.
Orbit 6, Putnam, 1970.
Orbit 7, Putnam, 1970.
Orbit 8, Putnam, 1970.
Orbit 9, Putnam, 1971.
Orbit 10, Putnam, 1972.
Orbit 11, Putnam, 1972.
Orbit 12, Putnam, 1973.
Orbit 13, Putnam, 1974.
Orbit 14, Harper, 1974.
Orbit 15, Harper, 1974.
Orbit 18, Harper, 1976.
Orbit 19, Harper, 1977.
Orbit 20, Harper, 1978.

OTHER; UNDER NAME KATE WILHELM

Contributor to periodicals, including *Fantastic, Future, Magazine of Fantasy and Science Fiction, Amazing, Cosmopolitan,* and *Strange Fantasy.*

SIDELIGHTS: A versatile author praised for the psychic reality in her fiction, Katie Gertrude Wilhelm—better known as Kate Wilhelm—has been called a "serene and powerful talent" by Michael Bishop in the *Magazine of Fantasy and Science Fiction.* Wilhelm feels strongly about the political and social forces shaping the modern world and examines them in her novels, writing about such issues as women's roles in society and the threat of environmental collapse. Commenting on the combination of her writing goals and social concerns in a letter to *CA,* Wilhelm wrote: "If could sum up my philosophies and compulsions in a few paragraphs, there would be no need to write books, and there is a need. I believe we are living in an age of cataclysmic changes; we are living in an age that is the end of an era. My work is my attempt to understand how we got here, why we stay, and what lies ahead if anything does."

Wilhelm's Hugo and Jupiter award-winning novel, *Where Late the Sweet Birds Sang,* explores cloning and its consequences for humanity. In this book, the Sumner family survives a nuclear disaster on earth. With scientific equipment, they produce clones intended to eventually breed in a natural way. But the clones, born with telepathic powers, believe they are superior and plot to transform the earth into a clone utopia. Human individuality eventually triumphs; the clones are too dependent on each other to take chances necessary for survival, and in the end, a human escapes the colony to form a new society.

New York Times Book Review contributor Gerald Jonas praises Wilhelm for her technique in this novel. While noting that "at times, her prose strains for 'poetic effects,' " he maintains that for the most part, her writing is powerful and effective: "Her cautionary message comes through loud and clear: giving up our humanity to save our skins is a bad bargain no matter how you look at it." Anne Hudson Jones adds in the *Dictionary of Literary Biography* that the novel "offers a poignant reminder that human strengths and weaknesses are inextricably bound together. It also serves as a timely warning that altering human reproduction may alter the species itself."

Wilhelm focuses on the issues of environmental disaster and alien contact in *Juniper Time.* During a prolonged drought in the United States, an alien message is discovered in space that many believe will contain information to end the drought. Jean Brighton, a young linguist, is the only one capable of decoding it. But instead of relying on the cryptic sign, Jean turns to members of an American Indian tribe who show her how to survive by utilizing the environment carefully. In another *New York Times Book Review* article, Jonas says Wilhelm draws a parallel between *Juniper Time*'s plot and similar events in history where contact between cultures totally ignorant of each other has caused the decimation of one of them. "As Montezuma and the Incas learned," he observes, "gods in machines can kill as well as succor. If this fine novel has a moral, it is a cautionary one, not often found in science fiction: Choose your myths with care; the culture you save may be your own."

Wilhelm writes this novel in a style that is muted and evocative, notes Bishop, who claims that many science fiction novels are written with "clumsy prose, threadbare plotting, comic-book characterization, . . . and out-and-out dumbness in the service of high and honorable ideals." But strong characterization and plot are Wilhelm's tools, according to Bishop. He believes that *Juniper Time* is written by "completely overstepping the most tenacious and annoying bugaboos of [the science fiction] genre."

In *The Clewiston Test* Wilhelm departs from conventional science fiction to explore a woman's alienation from her husband. Anne Clewiston Symons is a brilliant scientist, married to a scientist of lesser ability who underestimates her personally as well as professionally. Anne has isolated a serum in blood that stifles all pain but also causes personality disorders in test chimpanzees, who become violent and then withdrawn. After Anne is in a car accident, she begins to withdraw emotionally from her husband, Clark. Suspecting that she has taken the serum, Clark takes over her research in the lab. As tensions in their relationship mount, it is unclear whether Anne's problems are caused by her marriage or by taking the serum. Anne eventually leaves her husband in order to feel complete as a person.

Several critics praise *The Clewiston Test* for its powerful theme and strong technique. Jones calls the book a "compelling feminist" novel, and Christopher Lehmann-Haupt commends Wilhelm's portrayal of the sexual dynamics of a relationship, observing in the *New York Times* that "whatever is bothering Anne serves as a nice little litmus test for the chauvinism of the male ego." In the *New York Times Book Review,* Jerome Charyn points out that Wilhelm's craftsmanship in this piece of mainstream fiction is as solid as that of her science-fiction works. "Written in a style that never calls attention to itself," Charyn continues, " 'The Clewiston Test' is a horror story that avoids the usual trappings of its genre. Kate Wilhelm isn't interested in futuristic nightmares."

In discussing the variety in Wilhelm's writing, Jones concludes that "whatever the external settings of [Wilhelm's] works, the psychic landscapes in them are very real." Furthermore, she states, "the body of Wilhelm's fiction shows a steady progression in technical control and thematic complexity, and her reputation as a writer has risen with each new work. . . . As Wilhelm continues to develop, her readers have much to look forward to in the future."

BIOGRAPHICAL/CRITICAL SOURCES:

BOOKS

Contemporary Authors Autobiography Series, Volume 8, Gale, 1989.
Contemporary Literary Criticism, Volume 7, Gale, 1977.
Dictionary of Literary Biography, Volume 8: *Twentieth-Century American Science Fiction Writers,* Gale, 1981.
Platt, Charles, *Dream Makers: The Uncommon People Who Write Science Fiction,* Volume 1, Berkley Publishing, 1980.

PERIODICALS

Chicago Tribune Book World, February 16, 1986.
Globe and Mail (Toronto), March 4, 1989.
Los Angeles Times, May 8, 1981, November 15, 1983.
Los Angeles Times Book Review, December 19, 1982.
Magazine of Fantasy and Science Fiction, November, 1971, April, 1979, January, 1980.
Newsweek, November 29, 1971, February 9, 1976.
New York Times, May 13, 1976.
New York Times Book Review, March 10, 1974, January 18, 1976, February 22, 1976, August 26, 1979, March 9, 1986.
Psychology Today, October, 1975.
Saturday Review, April 30, 1977.
Washington Post, September 21, 1982.

*   *   *

WILL, George F(rederick) 1941-

PERSONAL: Born May 4, 1941, in Champaign, Ill.; son of Frederick L. (a professor emeritus of philosophy at the University of Illinois) and Louise Will. *Education:* Trinity College, B.A., 1962; attended Magdalen College, Oxford, 1962-64; Princeton University, Ph.D., 1967. *Politics:* Conservative.

ADDRESSES: Office—ABC-TV Public Relations, 1330 Avenue of the Americas, New York, N.Y. 10019.

CAREER: Michigan State University, East Lansing, professor of politics, 1967-68; University of Toronto, Toronto, Ontario, professor of politics, 1968-69; U.S. Senate, Washington, D.C., congressional aide to Senator Alcott of Colorado, 1970-72; *National Review,* New York City, Washington editor, 1972-76; writer. Panelist, "Agronsky and Company," Post-Newsweek Stations, 1979-84; participant, "This Week with David Brinkley," American Broadcasting Co. (ABC-TV), 1981—; commentator, "World News Tonight," ABC-TV, 1984—.

AWARDS, HONORS: Named Young Leader of America, *Time* magazine, 1974; Pulitzer Prize, 1977, for distinguished commentary.

WRITINGS:

The Pursuit of Happiness, and Other Sobering Thoughts, Harper, 1978.
The Pursuit of Virtue, and Other Tory Notions, Simon & Schuster, 1982.
Statecraft as Soulcraft: What Government Does, Simon & Schuster, 1983.
The Morning After: American Successes and Excesses, 1981-1986, Free Press, 1986.

The New Season: A Spectator's Guide to the 1988 Election, Simon & Schuster, 1987.
Men at Work, Macmillan, 1990.
Suddenly: The American Idea Abroad and at Home, 1986-1990, Free Press, 1990.

Author of a syndicated column for the *Washington Post,* 1974—, and for *Newsweek;* columnist for the *New York Daily News.* Contributor to *London Daily Telegraph* and other periodicals. Contributing editor, *Newsweek,* 1976—.

SIDELIGHTS: George F. Will, author of bi-weekly columns for the *Washington Post* and *Newsweek* and a regular commentator on ABC-TV's "This Week with David Brinkley" and "World News Tonight," is "the most widely read and heard political commentator in America," according to Sally Bedell Smith in the *New York Times.* "Mr. Will's arrival," continues Smith, "has been hailed by conservatives as the first opportunity for a bona fide thinker from among their ranks to have what William F. Buckley calls 'a presence in the room' after years of dominance by what they regard as liberal opinion." A winner of the Pulitzer Prize in 1977 for distinguished commentary, Will writes conservative essays and articles "with a rhythmic cadence that combines logic and literary allusion in concise proportion," says *Christian Science Monitor* contributor Alan L. Miller. These views, however, deviate considerably from what is usually considered to be mainline conservatism. "I trace the pedigree of my philosophy to [Edmund] Burke, [John Henry] Newman, [Benjamin] Disraeli, and others who were more skeptical, even pessimistic, about the modern world than most people who call themselves conservatives," Will tells Miller. Nelson W. Polsby phrases the journalist's beliefs this way in a *Fortune* article: "Will's political philosophy presupposes the primacy of the social order itself and is concerned with the means by which citizens can be encouraged to place civic responsibilities above their own interests."

The Pursuit of Happiness, and Other Sobering Thoughts, Will's first book, is a collection of 138 previously-published essays that express his philosophy while discussing subjects ranging from politics to the author's personal life. Behind this diverse variety of topics lies the consistent opinion in the columnist's essays that American society has degenerated in the last few decades. Will "thinks Americans have become materialistic, selfish, pretentious, and morally flabby, with barely any private, let alone public, sense of what is genuinely important and excellent," writes *New York Review of Books* critic Ronald Dworkin. This is also the attitude that permeates the author's second book, *The Pursuit of Virtue, and Other Tory Notions,* which *New Republic* contributor Charles Krauthammer calls a "textbook of American cultural conservatism" that is "pithy, epigrammatic, and often elegant." "Mr. Will's only noticeable less-than-respectable passion in life appears to be a rock-ribbed loyalty to the Chicago Cubs," notes Neal Johnston in the *New York Times Book Review;* in fact, Will's more recent book, *Men at Work,* is devoted to the subject of baseball, a sport he sometimes alludes to as an example of one of the few virtuous pursuits left in today's society.

Several critics have praised Will for his wit, but Joseph Sobran asserts in the *National Review* that what is important is the journalist's "larger gift of *knowing what needs to be said,* of summoning up a truth whose absence others hadn't even felt." A number of other reviewers, however, have strongly disagreed with Will's views, since, as Dworkin notes, his definition of conservatism "is not . . . how conservative politicians define conservatism. . . . Will thinks they are hopelessly wrong about what conservatism is: he means to define 'true' conservatism, not what passes for political rhetoric." In *Statecraft as Soulcraft: What Government Does,* Will attempts to clarify his beliefs in an extensive treatise on the role of government. The "book has received a mixed, generally unenthusiastic reception," remarks James Nuechterlein in *Commentary.* "The fullest expression of Will's philosophy yet— there is nothing new here for regular readers of his columns—it has encountered far more intellectual resistance than Will's ideas had earlier run into."

Unlike Will's essay collections, which often use specific examples of political cases in order to illustrate his general ideas about society, *Statecraft as Soulcraft* does not deal in particulars. A number of critics complain, therefore, that the book's general thesis that government should instill virtue within its citizens is never fully elucidated. "Will never really tells us 'what government does,' " says *National Review* contributor M. E. Bradford. "We hear of a noble 'ethic of common provision,' meaning, concretely, the welfare state. . . . But we are left to speculate for ourselves" what this entails. However, this lack of a definite outline as to how a government should be run is not a drawback for the book, according to *New York Time Book Review* critic Michael J. Sandel. The "purpose is less to promote particular programs than to change the character and tone of the debate," says Sandel. As the author himself says in *Statecraft as Soulcraft,* "My aim is to recast conservatism."

Discussing *Statecraft as Soulcraft,* Nuechterlein relates that in Will's opinion "what is wrong with American conservatism . . . traces back to flawed philosophic assumptions on the part of the nation's founders." Sobran goes on to explain how the author believes that "America was conceived in coarseness. Its Founders . . . sought to organize American society on the sovereign principle of self-interest," rather than on the promotion of public virtue. This latter view of the proper role of government, which goes back to Aristotle's time, has been called "aristocratic" by reviewers like Sobran, because it is founded on the assumption that there exists in society a natural order in which some people were meant to govern, while others were meant to be governed. Bruce R. Sievers warns in the *Los Angeles Times Book Review* that this Burkeian idea to which Will adheres has a "dark side" in its potential to encourage the "uncritical acceptance of privilege for its own sake under the guise of 'tradition.' "

Despite these reservations about *Statecraft as Soulcraft,* several critics view the book to be a significant commentary on politics. "Will has written a fascinating, and profoundly important, work of contemporary political philosophy," claims Sievers. And Nuechterlein adds that "even those who deplore Will's politics express admiration for the subtlety and sophistication of his arguments as well as the elegance of his prose." Nuechterlein also notes, however, that the author's "columns, taken together, offer a richer and more satisfactory (if less systematic) public philosophy than does his book."

Will's next works, *The Morning After* and *The New Season: A Spectator's Guide to the 1988 Election,* return to his original essay collection format. Like the author's other publications, they have been lauded for their entertaining and skillful style. For example, *Tribune Books* reviewer Clarence Petersen calls Will's essays in *The Morning After* "superbly crafted, witty and skeptical." But although Ronald Steel admits in his *Los Angeles Times Book Review* article that "there is considerable skill at ridicule" in *The Morning After,* he alleges that there is "little effort to understand, much less sympathize" with those who hold different philosophical positions. In *The New Season,* however, Will's steadfast views offer a certain advantage, according to *Washington Post Book World* critic William V. Shannon, because "there

is no gross partisanship in Will's comments" about the 1988 election. But there is, Shannon attests, "much good sense and even wisdom."

Even though Will's positions have stirred controversy among mainstream conservatives, he has remained "one of the strongest and most constructive conservative voices addressing contemporary issues, from abortion to impeachment," says Polsby. "His opinions," the reviewer continues, "grounded in serious consideration of basic philosophical questions, are almost always of the greatest interest." With his weekly appearances on television and regularly published columns in widely-read magazines, Will's views reach some twenty million people, estimates Smith in the *New York Times.* The journalist is also "generally credited with exerting influence among policy-makers in Washington," Smith adds. Nevertheless, Will recognizes his limitations. "The idea that multitudes will be driven to their knees by the force of my words is silly," he tells Smith. Yet he also says in a *Newsweek* article that commentaries such as those he offers are indispensable. "There is a scarcity of reasoned, civilized discourses in the world," he insists. "With such discourse we can stand anything. Without it we are doomed."

BIOGRAPHICAL/CRITICAL SOURCES:

BOOKS

Will, George F., *Statecraft as Soulcraft: What Government Does,* Simon & Schuster, 1983.

PERIODICALS

Atlantic, May, 1983.
Chicago Tribune, May 12, 1988.
Christian Science Monitor, April 21, 1982, May 18, 1983, February 13, 1986.
Commentary, October, 1983.
Fortune, July 25, 1983.
Harvard Law Review, January, 1984.
Los Angeles Times, April 6, 1982.
Los Angeles Times Book Review, June 26, 1983, November 30, 1986, December 6, 1987.
Nation, October 14, 1978, March 27, 1982, July 23, 1983.
National Review, June 9, 1978, June 25, 1982, June 10, 1983.
New Republic, June 10, 1978, June 16, 1982.
Newsweek, September 30, 1974.
New York Review of Books, October 12, 1978.
New York Times, May 16, 1983, May 19, 1985.
New York Times Book Review, June 11, 1978, March 28, 1982, July 17, 1983, November 2, 1986, January 3, 1988.
People, September 19, 1983.
Saturday Review, March, 1982.
Time, August 8, 1983, April 1, 1985.
Times Literary Supplement, May 25, 1984.
Tribune Books (Chicago), November 8, 1987.
Washington Post Book World, June 11, 1978, March 21, 1982, June 5, 1983, November 30, 1986, November 29, 1987.

—*Sketch by Kevin S. Hile*

* * *

WILLARD, Nancy 1936-

PERSONAL: Born June 26, 1936, in Ann Arbor, Mich.; daughter of Hobart Hurd (a chemistry professor) and Margaret (Sheppard) Willard; married Eric Lindbloom (a photographer), August 15, 1964; children: James Anatole. *Education:* University of

Michigan, B.A., 1958, Ph.D., 1963; Stanford University, M.A., 1960; additional study in Paris and Oslo.

ADDRESSES: Home—133 College Ave., Poughkeepsie, N.Y. 12603. *Office*— Department of English, Vassar College, Raymond Ave., Poughkeepsie, N.Y. 12601. *Agent*—Jean V. Naggar Literary Agency, 336 East 73rd St., Suite C, N.Y. 10021.

CAREER: Poet, author of children's literature, literary critic, and short-story writer. Vassar College, Poughkeepsie, N.Y., lecturer in English, 1965—. Instructor at Bread Loaf Writers' Conference, 1975.

MEMBER: Children's Literature Association, The Lewis Carroll Society, The George MacDonald Society.

AWARDS, HONORS: Avery Hopwood Award, 1958; Woodrow Wilson fellowship, 1960; Devins Memorial Award, 1967, for *Skin of Grace;* 0. Henry Award for best short story, 1970; *Sailing to Cythera and Other Anatole Stories* was selected as one of the fifty books of the year by the American Institute of Graphic Arts, 1973; Lewis Carroll Shelf Award, 1974, for *Sailing to Cythera and Other Anatole Stories,* and 1979, for *The Island of the Grass King: The Further Adventures of Anatole;* National Endowment for the Arts grant, 1976; Special Honor Book Plaque from the Society of Children's Book Writers, 1981, John Newbery Medal, Caldecott Honor Book award from American Library Association, and American Book Award nomination, all 1982, for *A Visit to William Blake's Inn: Poems for Innocent and Experienced Travelers;* Creative Artist Service Award; National Endowment for the Arts fellowship (fiction), 1987-88; National Book Critics Circle award nomination (poetry), 1990, for *Water Walker.*

WRITINGS:

POETRY

In His Country: Poems, Generation (Ann Arbor, Mich.), 1966.
Skin of Grace, University of Missouri Press, 1967.
A New Herball: Poems, Ferdinand-Roter Gallerias, 1968.
Nineteen Masks for the Naked Poet: Poems, Kayak, 1971.
The Carpenter of the Sun: Poems, Liveright, 1974.
Household Tales of Moon and Water, Harcourt, 1983.

CHILDREN'S BOOKS

The Merry History of a Christmas Pie: With a Delicious Description of a Christmas Soup, Putnam, 1975.
Sailing to Cythera and Other Anatole Stories, Harcourt, 1974.
All on a May Morning, Putnam, 1975.
The Snow Rabbit, Putnam, 1975.
Shoes without Leather, Putnam, 1976.
The Well-Mannered Balloon, Harcourt, 1976.
Simple Pictures Are Best, Harcourt, 1977.
Strangers' Bread, Harcourt, 1977.
The Highest Hit, Harcourt, 1978.
The Island of the Grass King: The Further Adventures of Anatole, Harcourt, 1979.
Papa's Panda, Harcourt, 1979.
A Visit to William Blake's Inn: Poems for Innocent and Experienced Travelers, Harcourt, 1981.
The Marzipan Moon, Harcourt, 1981.
Uncle Terrible: More Adventures of Anatole, Harcourt, 1982.
Household Tales of Moon and Water, Harcourt, 1982.
The Nightgown of the Sullen Moon, Harcourt, 1983.
Night Story, Harcourt, 1986.
The Voyage of the Ludgate Hill: A Journey with Robert Louis Stevenson, Harcourt, 1987.
The Mountains of Quilt, Harcourt, 1987.

Firebrat, Random House, 1988.
The Ballad of Biddy Early, Knopf, 1989.
Water Walker, Knopf, 1990.

OTHER

The Lively Anatomy of God (short stories), Eakins, 1968.
Testimony of the Invisible Man: William Carlos Williams, Francis Ponge, Rainer Maria Rilke, Pablo Neruda (criticism), University of Missouri Press, 1970.
Childhood of the Magician (short stories), Liveright, 1973.
Angel in the Parlor: Five Stories and Eight Essays, Harcourt, 1983.
Things Invisible to See (novel), Knopf, 1984.
East of the Sun amd West of the Moon: A Play, Harcourt, 1989.

ILLUSTRATOR

John Kater, *The Letter of John to James,* Seabury, 1981.
Kater, *Another Letter of John to James,* Seabury, 1982.

Work represented in anthologies, including *Rising Tides.* Contributor to periodicals, including *Esquire, Field, Massachusetts Review, Redbook, New Yorker,* and *New Directions.*

SIDELIGHTS: Loved by her readers, well-respected by critics, and admired by her students, Nancy Willard is an accomplished author of poetry, children's literature, and adult fiction. Although her first published works were books of poetry followed by two collections of short stories and a volume of literary criticism, most of Willard's recent writings have been aimed at young readers.

Several reviewers have speculated on the reasons for her success. For example, Hilda Gregory points out in *Prairie Schooner* that "Nancy Willard is a teacher, a storyteller. . . . She speaks to the child in us, the student, the wonderer." Donald Hall states in the *New York Times Book Review:* "Willard's imagination—in verse or prose, for children or adults—builds castles stranger than any mad King of Bavaria ever built. She imagines with a wonderful concreteness. But also, she takes real language and by literal-mindedness turns it into the structure of dream."

Critics have also responded enthusiastically to the pleasant and heartwarming nature of Willard's poetry. "[Willard] seems very much at home with herself and her world," comments Stanley Poss in *Western Humanities Review.* "Her poems don't draw blood or blow your head off. . . . Her subjects are cooking, food, sports headlines, marriages that're doing OK, pregnancy, kids, animals, unwashed feet, plants, flea circuses, but her domestic is not merely cozy, and she's not merely domestic. . . . What I think I'm saying is that I like her because her poems are poised, assured, calm, they bid us not to be too hard on ourselves." In agreement, Francine Dranis writes in *Modern Poetry Studies,* "Willard's poetry, bright, graceful, and often playfully radiates womanly fullness, contentment, and reverence."

Writing in *Hudson Review,* John N. Morris calls Willard's poetry collection *The Carpenter of the Sun* "a book full of poems about flowers and vegetables and animals and her son . . . and with not a single hard word to say about her husband and the difficulty of being a poet and a wife." Morris continues: "Since the skill is considerable, since it makes poems, it would be a piece of impertinence to tell her that it is her duty to go out and suffer more so that she might entertain us with the tally of her sorrows. Surely we are right to believe that nowadays no subject is foreign to poetry—not even good luck and decent contentment." Joseph M. Flora also finds this quality of contentment and good humor in Willard's short-story collection *Childhood of the Magician.* He writes in *Michigan Quarterly Review:* "There is an abundance of good humor in these stories. At the same time, Nancy Willard excellently evokes the pathos of life. . . . Life is sad and wonderful and ultimately incomprehensible. There is no self-pity in these stories, no fatigue over the weariness or absurdity of life. Nancy Willard gives us something closer to blessing and benediction."

While reviewers such as Poss and Flora point out that Willard's writing is optimistic in nature and is concerned with many of life's simpler and more basic pleasures, critics do not find her writing to be simple-minded or shallow. "If the writer's voice is not angry nor desperately troubled, neither is it complacent nor trite," states Judith S. Baughman in the *Dictionary of Literary Biography*. Other reviewers acknowledge Willard's commitment to nature and to the basic order that unites us all. Willard is aware and appreciative of her surroundings and in tune with nature; she is also dedicated to the precise representation of her feelings and thoughts. Dabney Stuart explains in *Library Journal:* "[Willard] is a creature among creatures and sees her nature everywhere: as she turns she marvels, variously, at the flea . . . or praises unwashed feet. . . . Willard knows where she is and has invented a way to speak of it so we know, too. . . . She writes, as proud and humble before creation."

In an *Open Places* review of *The Carpenter of the Sun*, Jonathan Holden remarks that, like many of Willard's other works, these poems "are filled with a shy wonderment, a tenderness toward Creation that is rare in contemporary poetry. They celebrate; but they're not effusive, they're not wrung from the spirit by any mechanical operation; they are inspired. Their quiet is the stillness of rapt attention. They are exquisite miniatures, each filled with the luminosity and reverence for detail of a Vermeer painting."

Also characteristic of Willard's work is the caring, compassionate manner in which she tells her story and portrays her characters. "Nancy Willard has . . . a sensitive, almost delicate feeling for tender childhood relationships, and real skill in shaping and bringing off a story," Doris Grumbach remarks in *New Republic*. And Bill Katz points out in *Library Journal* that Willard "shows a strong feeling for individuals—grandmothers, old soldiers, hunters—and the things of nature."

Offering *Childhood of the Magician* as an excellent example of her sensitivity, a critic writing in *Publishers Weekly* praises Willard for "the special texture of her [characters]" coupled with her "vivid remembrance of what it was like to believe literally in the homilies of adults." And in a review of Willard's *The Island of the Grass King*, Natalie Babbitt comments in the *New York Times Book Review* that this book is "loving and gentle, its images and characters [are] all attractive. . . . You seldom find language so lovingly and creatively used these days."

Willard's outlook on writing, especially poetry, is similar to that of the authors she examines in her critical study *Testimony of the Invisible Man: William Carlos Williams, Francis Ponge, Rainer Maria Rilke, Pablo Neruda*. Willard observes that although these authors were born in different countries and wrote in four different languages, they are united by their philosophy of poetic creation or, as Willard herself suggests, "the rhetoric of things." Willard explains in *Testimony of the Invisible Man:* "Art is not a [mere] selection from the world but a transformation of it into something that praises existence."

Baughman comments in *Dictionary of Literary Biography:* "These four writers . . . are united, [Willard] says, by their scrupulous examinations of concrete things. For these poets, Willard contends, the truth of the world resides in particular objects themselves, not in the conventional ideas that men impose upon these things." And Priscilla Whitmore writes in *Library Journal:* "Each [poet] rooted his poetic ideas in observation of things—of the outside world—as opposed to the exclusive self-scrutiny found in confessional poets." It is this association with the art of living and the observation of things of nature that students of Willard's work believe she shares with these great authors.

Another poet Willard has admired since her childhood is William Blake. According to Barbara Karlin writing in the *Los Angeles Times*, "Blake not only inspired author/poet Nancy Willard to write *A Visit to William Blake's Inn: Poems for Innocent and Experienced Travelers*, he is an integral part of many of the poems." "The title should not suggest that this picture book is merely a chronicle of the mystical English poet-painter," Michael Patrick Hearn explains in the *Washington Post Book World*. "Instead, it is a collection of lyrical nonsense poems inspired by a reading of [Blake's] *Songs of Innocence* when Willard was a little girl." And Donald Hall comments in the *New York Times Book Review* that "in this book, William Blake, poet and engraver, is transformed into an innkeeper. . . . These new poems, made with adult skill, successfully embody a 7-year-old's imagining of the poet who keeps an inn for the imagination. Color and verve are everything; import is nothing."

Willard's first adult novel, *Things Invisible to See*, is set in the late 1930s and early 1940s and tells the story of a pair of twin brothers, Ben and Willie—one gregarious, intuitive, sentimental, the other shy, reserved, methodical. The story is also about a girl named Clare, who becomes accidentally paralyzed when Ben hits her on the head with a baseball. Clare later falls in love with Ben. "The point of this luminous first novel," writes Ann Tyler in the *Detroit News*, "is that the miraculous and the everyday often co-exist, or overlap, or even that they're one and the same." While the novel is filled with out-of-the-ordinary events, "what makes this book so moving," according to Tyler, "is not the presence of the magical in the ordinary, but the presenece of the ordinary in the magical." Michiko Kakutani comments in the *New York Times* that Willard "writes of small-town life during World War II with a genuine nostalgia—neither sentimental nor contrived—for the innocence Americans once possessed; and she makes a teen-age love story . . . reverberate, gently, with larger, darker questions about the human condition." The reviewer praises Willard's "pictures of daily life so precisely observed that they leave after-images in the reader's mind," and notes that "in the end, the novel probably most resembles an old-fashioned crazy quilt—eclectic and a little over-embroidered, but all in all a charming work of improvisation, held together by the radiance of its creator's sensibility."

MEDIA ADAPTATIONS: A filmstrip based on *A Visit to William Blake's Inn: Poems for Innocent and Experienced Travelers* was produced by Random House/Miller Brody.

BIOGRAPHICAL/CRITICAL SOURCES:

BOOKS

Children's Literature Review, Volume 5, Gale, 1983.
Contemporary Literary Criticism, Volume 12, Gale, 1977.
Dictionary of Literary Biography, Gale, Volume 5: *American Poets since World War II*, 1980, Volume 52: *Americn Writers for Children since 1960: Fiction*, 1986.
Willard, Nancy, *Testimony of the Invisible Man: William Carlos Williams, Francis Ponge, Rainer Maria Rilke, Pablo Neruda*, University of Missouri Press, 1970.

PERIODICALS

Choice, October, 1968, January, 1971.

Detroit News, January 20, 1985.
Horn Book, August, 1982.
Hudson Review, autumn, 1975.
Library Journal, May 1, 1968, December 15, 1970, February 15, 1975, September 15, 1975.
Los Angeles Times, November 29, 1981.
Los Angeles Times Book Review, January 20, 1985.
Michigan Quarterly Review, winter, 1975.
Modern Poetry Studies, spring, 1978.
New Republic, May 25, 1974, January 4, 1975, January 11, 1975.
New York, October 4, 1982.
New Yorker, December 7, 1981.
New York Times, January 12, 1985.
New York Times Book Review, September 25, 1977, May 21, 1978, May 27, 1979, July 12, 1981, November 15, 1981, October 23, 1983, February 3, 1985, July 12, 1987, November 8, 1987, September 25, 1988, July 7, 1989.
Open Places, fall/winter, 1975-76.
Prairie Schooner, summer, 1976.
Publishers Weekly, October 1, 1973, June 18, 1979, December 14, 1984.
Times Literary Supplement, March 26, 1982.
Washington Post, January 9, 1984.
Washington Post Book World, November 8, 1981.
Western Humanities Review, autumn, 1975.

*   *   *

WILLIAMS, (George) Emlyn   1905-1987

PERSONAL: Born November 26, 1905, in Mostyn, Wales; died of cancer, September 25, 1987, in London, England; son of Richard (a foreman at a steelworks) and Mary Williams; married Molly O'Shann, 1935 (died, 1970); children: two sons. *Education:* Christ Church, Oxford, M.A., 1927.

CAREER: Actor, director, and writer. Actor in stage productions, including "And So to Bed," 1927, "Man Overboard," 1932, "Othello," 1956, "A Month in the Country," 1965, and "Forty Years On," 1969; in motion pictures, including, "Major Barbara," 1941, "Ivanhoe," 1952, "I Accuse!," 1958, "The L-Shaped Room," 1963, and "The Walking Stick," 1969; and in television productions, including "Every Picture Tells a Story," 1949. Actor in one-man shows from the works of Charles Dickens and Dylan Thomas. Director of stage productions, including "A Murder Has Been Arranged," 1930, "The Corn Is Green," 1938, "The Little Foxes," 1942, and "Beth," 1958.

AWARDS, HONORS: New York Drama Critics Circle Award, 1941; LL. D., from University College of North, Wales, Bangor, 1949; Commander of Order of the British Empire, 1962.

WRITINGS:

George: An Early Autobiography, Hamish Hamilton, 1961, Random House, 1962. *Beyond Belief: A Chronicle of Murder and Its Detection,* Hamish Hamilton, 1967, Random House, 1968.
Emlyn: An Early Autobiography, 1927-1935 (also see below), Bodley Head, 1973, Viking, 1974.
Headlong, Heinemann, 1980, Viking, 1981.
Cuckoo, Samuel French, 1986.
Dr. Crippen's Diary: An Invention, Macdonald, 1988.

PLAYS

Vigil (one-act; first produced at the Playhouse in Oxford, England, November, 1925), anthologized in *The Second Book of One-Act Plays,* Heinemann, 1954.

Full Moon, first produced in Oxford at the Playhouse, February 28, 1927; produced in London at the Arts Theatre, January 30, 1929.
Glamour, first produced in London at the Embassy Theatre, December 10, 1928.
A Murder Has Been Arranged: A Ghost Story (first produced in London at the Strand Theatre, November 9, 1930), Collins, 1930, Samuel French, 1931.
Port Said, first produced in London at the Wyndam's Theatre, November 1, 1931; revised edition produced as "Vessels Departing," in London at the Embassy Theatre, July 3, 1933.
The Late Christopher Bean (first produced in London at the St. James Theatre, May 16, 1933; adapted from the play by Sidney Howard), Gollancz, 1933.
Spring 1600 (first produced in London at the Shaftesbury Theatre, January 31, 1934; revised version produced in Hammersmith, England, at the Lyric Theatre, December 6, 1945), Heinemann, 1946.
Josephine (adapted from the work by Herman Bahr), first produced in London at His Majesty's Theatre, September 25, 1934.
Night Must Fall (also see below; first produced in London at the Duchess Theatre, May 31, 1935), Gollancz, 1935, Random House, 1936.
He Was Born Gay: A Romance (also see below; first produced in London at the Queen's Theatre, May 26, 1937), Heinemann, 1937.
The Corn Is Green (also see below; first produced in London at the Duchess Theatre, September 20, 1938), Heinemann, 1938, Random House, 1941.
The Light of Heart (also see below; first produced in London at the Apollo Theatre, February 21, 1940; produced as "Yesterday's Magic," in New York City at the Guild Theatre, April 14, 1942), Heinemann, 1940.
The Morning Star (first produced in London at the Globe Theatre, December 10, 1941), Heinemann, 1942.
A Month in the Country (also see below; first produced in London at the St. James Theatre, February 11, 1943; produced in Chicago, Ill., 1956; adapted from the play by Ivan Turgenev), Heinemann, 1943, Samuel French, 1957.
Pen Don, first produced in Blackpool, England, at the Grand Theatre, December, 1943.
The Druid's Rest (also see below; first produced in London at the St. Martin's Theatre, January 26, 1944), Heinemann, 1944.
The Wind of Heaven (also see below; first produced in London at the St. James Theatre, April 12, 1945; produced in Westport, Conn., 1945), Heinemann, 1945.
Thinking Aloud: A Dramatic Sketch (first produced in London at the Stage Door Canteen, July, 1945; produced in New York City, 1975), Samuel French, 1946.
Guest in the House (adapted from the play by Hagar Wilde and Dale Eunson), first produced in London at the Embassy Theatre, May 21, 1946.
Trespass: A Ghost Story (first produced in London at the Globe Theatre, July 16, 1947), Heinemann, 1947.
Pepper and Sand: A Duologue (first broadcast on radio in 1947), Deane, 1948.
Dear Evelyn (first produced in Rutherglen, Scotland, 1948), Samuel French, c. 1949.
The Corn Is Green, with Two Other Plays (also contains "The Wind of Heaven" and "The Druid's Rest"), Pan, 1950.
Accolade (first produced in London at the Aldwych Theatre, September 7, 1950), Heinemann, 1951.

Readings from Dickens (first produced as "Emlyn Williams as Charles Dickens" in London, 1951; produced in New York City, 1952), Folio Society, 1953.

Someone Waiting (first produced in London at the Globe Theatre, November 25, 1953; produced in New York City, 1956) Heinemann, 1954, Dramatists Play Service, 1956.

A Boy Growing Up, first produced in London, 1955; first produced in New York City, 1957.

Beth (first produced in London at the Apollo Theatre, March 20, 1958), Heinemann, 1959.

The Collected Plays (contains "The Corn Is Green," "He Was Born Gay," "The Light of Heart," and "Night Must Fall"), Random House, 1961.

The Master Builder (first produced in London at the National Theatre, June 9, 1964; adapted from the play by Henrik Ibsen), Theatre Arts Books, 1967.

(With Joshua Logan and Albert Hague) *Miss Moffat,* first produced in Philadelphia at the Shubert Theatre, October 7, 1974.

SCREENPLAYS

"Friday the Thirteenth," 1933.

"Evergreen," 1934.

(Author of additional dialogue; with Ian Dalrymple, Frank Wead, and Elizabeth Hill), "The Citadel" (adapted from the novel by A. J. Cronin), Metro-Goldwyn-Mayer, 1938.

(Author of dialogue; with A. R. Rawlinson and Bridget Boland), "This England," World, 1941.

TELEVISION SCRIPTS

"A Month in the Country" (based on his play of the same title), 1947.

"Every Picture Tells a Story," 1949.

"In Town Tonight," 1954.

"A Blue Movie of My Own True Love," 1968.

"The Power of Dawn," 1975.

OTHER

Also author and narrator of radio script "Emlyn" (based on *Emlyn: An Early Autobiography, 1927-1935*), 1974.

SIDELIGHTS: Emlyn Williams was the writer and actor for the popular British productions of *Night Must Fall* and *The Corn Is Green* during the 1930s. In *Night Must Fall,* he terrified London audiences with his chilling portrayal of a homicidal psychopath stalking an elderly woman and her young niece in a huge old home. "In comparison with this play," wrote Derek Verschoyle in *Spectator,* "all other modern plays with murder as their theme . . . seem in retrospect as flat as the proverbial pancake." When *Night Must Fall* was staged in New York City, critics there were similarly impressed. "When he is at his best," contended a reviewer for the *New York Times,* "as author and actor, Mr. Williams can be morbidly terrifying, and enough of *Night Must Fall* is just that." According to Richard B. Gidez in the *Dictionary of Literary Biography, Night Must Fall* "is one of the most successful and chilling psychological thrillers of the modern stage."

The Corn Is Green concerns the efforts of a spinsterish schoolteacher to found a school for the children of Welsh miners in the late nineteenth century. In the original productions, Williams played Evans, an extremely intelligent older boy coaxed by the schoolteacher into competing for a scholarship to Oxford University. Evans eventually rejects the school teacher's guidance for the affections of a local harlot. After winning the scholarship, he learns of the harlot's pregnancy. He decides to marry the woman and abandon his hopes of further education. The school-

teacher, however, persuades Evans that his hope lies in improving himself, and she adopts his child.

Reviewers were impressed with *The Corn Is Green.* "The simplicity of the story can be relied on to throw the spectator into a mood of acceptance of make-believe," declared James Agate in *The Amazing Theatre,* "from which he need make very occasional sorties to admire this bit of pathos pressed home but not too far home." Agate also praised Williams's "sense of wit and humour." Erik Johns wrote, "In the entire history of Wales [Williams] is the one solitary figure on the plane of first-rate dramatists to write a play in English that is essentially Welch in essence." He added that "Williams brought Wales to the stage most effectively in *The Corn Is Green.*"

Williams enjoyed further popularity for his plays after World War II, such as *Trespass* and *Accolade,* and his performances in stage productions and motion pictures. Perhaps his best known performances are his one-man shows from the works of Charles Dickens and Dylan Thomas. "I got the idea from Charles Dickens in 1951," Williams told the *Washington Post.* "I was reading his autobiography, and I suddenly thought I'll dress up as Dickens and do what he did—tell a story from one of his books." Williams's readings from Dickens were enormously successful, and he estimated in 1979 that he'd performed that show two thousand times. Williams began performing as Dylan Thomas after reading the poet's works at a benefit for the latter's widow and children. "The irony of it is that if [Thomas had] lived," noted Williams, "he almost certainly would have gone into the theater."

BIOGRAPHICAL/CRITICAL SOURCES:

BOOKS

Agate, James, *The Amazing Theatre,* Harrap, 1939.

Contemporary Literary Criticism, Volume 15, Gale, 1980.

Dale-Jones, Don, *Emlyn Williams,* University of Wales Press, 1979.

Dictionary of Literary Biography, Gale, Volume 10: *Modern British Dramatists, 1900-1945,* 1982, Volume 77: *British Mystery Writers, 1920-1939,* 1988.

Findlater, Richard, *Emlyn Williams,* Macmillan, 1956.

Kerr, Walter, *The Theatre in Spite of Itself,* Simon & Schuster, 1963.

PERIODICALS

Commonweal, May 1, 1942, October 2, 1942.

Los Angeles Times Book Review, March 15, 1981.

Nation, December 7, 1940, September 26, 1942.

New Republic, December 9, 1940, September 28, 1942.

New Yorker, December 7, 1940, Febrnary 16, 1952, October 27, 1962, June 24, 1974.

New York Times, September 29, 1936, January 12, 1981.

Spectator, June 7, 1935.

Time, February 18, 1952, May 4, 1953.

Times Literary Supplement, October 3, 1980.

Washington Post, August 21, 1979, February 24, 1981.

OBITUARIES:

PERIODICALS

Chicago Tribune, September 27, 1987.

Globe and Mail (Toronto), September 26, 1987.

Los Angeles Times, September 26, 1987.

Manchester Guardian, October 4, 1987.

New York Times, September 26, 1987.

Time, October 5, 1987.

Times (London), September 26, 1987.
Washington Post, September 26, 1987.

* * *

WILLIAMS, J. Walker
See WODEHOUSE, P(elham) G(renville)

* * *

WILLIAMS, Raymond (Henry) 1921-1988

PERSONAL: Born August 31, 1921, in Abergavenny, Wales; son of Henry Joseph and Gwendolen (Bird) Williams; married Joyce Mary Dalling, June 19, 1942; children: Merryn, Ederyn, Gwydion Madawc. *Education:* Trinity College, Cambridge, M.A., 1946. *Politics:* Socialist. *Religion:* None.

ADDRESSES: Home—White Cottage, Hardwick, Cambridge, England. *Office*—Jesus College, Cambridge University, Cambridge, England.

CAREER: Oxford University Delegacy for Extra-Mural Studies, Oxford, England, staff tutor in literature, 1946-61; Cambridge University, Jesus College, Cambridge, England, 1961-83, fellow, lecturer in English studies, director of English studies, became professor of drama, 1974-83. Visiting professor at Stanford and Open universities. *Military service:* British Army, Guards Armoured Division, 1941-45; became captain.

MEMBER: Welsh Academy, Welsh Arts Council.

AWARDS, HONORS: Welsh Arts Council Prize for Fiction, 1979, for *The Fight for Manod;* D.Litt. from the University of Wales, 1980.

WRITINGS:

Reading and Criticism, Muller, 1950.
Drama from Ibsen to Eliot, Chatto & Windus, 1952, Columbia University Press, 1954, revised edition, Penguin, 1964, new edition published as *Drama from Ibsen to Brecht,* Chatto & Windus, 1968, Oxford University Press, 1969.
Drama in Performance, Muller, 1954, 3rd edition, Penguin, 1973.
Culture and Society, 1780-1950, Chatto & Windus, 1958, Harper, 1966.
Border Country, Chatto & Windus, 1960, Horizon, 1961.
The Long Revolution, Chatto & Windus, 1961, Harper, 1966.
Communications, Penguin, 1961.
Second Generation, Chatto & Windus, 1964.
Modern Tragedy, Stanford University Press, 1966.
(Editor) *Pelican Book of Prose,* Volume II: *From 1780 to the Present Day,* Penguin, 1970.
The English Novel from Dickens to Lawrence, Chatto & Windus, 1970.
(Editor) *George Orwell,* Viking, 1971.
The Country and the City, Oxford University Press, 1973.
Television: Technology and Cultural Form, Fontana, 1973.
Keywords: A Vocabulary of Culture and Society, Oxford University Press, 1976.
Marxism and Literatuure, Oxford University Press, 1977.
The Volunteers, Methuen, 1978.
(With Marie Axton) *English Drama: Forms and Development,* 1978.
The Fight for Manod, Chatto & Windus, 1979.
Politics and Letters, Verso, 1979.
Problems in Materialism and Culture, Verso, 1980.
Writing in Society, Verso, 1983.

Towards 2000, Chatto & Windus, 1983.
Loyalties, Chatto & Windus, 1985.
Resources of Hope, edited by Robin Gable, Verso, 1989.
The Politics of Modernism, edited by Tony Pinkney, Verso, 1989.
What I Came to Say, Century Hutchinson, 1989.

Also author of *Culture,* 1981; editor of *Contact: The History of Human Communications,* 1981. Television plays produced by British Broadcasting Corp. (BBC) include "Letter from the Country," 1966, and "Public Inquiry," 1967. General editor, "New Thinkers' Library," 1961-70.

AVOCATIONAL INTERESTS: Gardening.

BIOGRAPHICAL/CRITICAL SOURCES:

BOOKS

Dictionary of Literary Biography, Volume 14: *British Novelists Since 1960,* Gale, 1983.

PERIODICALS

Times (London), October 20, 1983, February 23, 1989.
Times Literary Supplement, November 4, 1983, November 3-9, 1989.
Voice Literary Supplement, April, 1985.

OBITUARIES:

PERIODICALS

New York Times, January 29, 1988.
Times (London), January 27, 1988.

* * *

WILLIAMS, Tennessee 1911-1983

PERSONAL: Name originally Thomas Lanier Williams; born March 26, 1911, in Columbus, Miss.; choked to death February 24, 1983, in his suite at Hotel Elysee, New York, N.Y.; buried in St. Louis, Mo.; son of Cornelius Coffin (a traveling salesman) and Edwina (Dakin) Williams. *Education:* Attended University of Missouri, 1931-33, and Washington University, St. Louis, Mo., 1936-37; University of Iowa, A.B., 1938. *Religion:* Originally Episcopalian; converted to Roman Catholicism, 1969.

ADDRESSES: Home—1431 Duncan St., Key West, Fla.; also maintained residences in New York, N.Y., and New Orleans, La. *Agent*—Mitch Douglas, ICM, 40 West 57th St., New York, N.Y. 10019.

CAREER: Playwright, novelist, short story writer, and poet; full-time writer, 1944-1983; first published in 1927, winning third prize in an essay contest sponsored by *Smart Set* magazine; first published story in *Weird Tales,* August, 1928; first published under name Tennessee Williams in *Story,* summer, 1939. International Shoe Co., St. Louis, Mo., clerical worker and manual laborer, 1934-36; worked various jobs, including waiter and hotel elevator operator, New Orleans, La., 1939; worked as teletype operator, Jacksonville, Fla., 1940; worked various jobs, including waiter and theater usher, New York, N.Y., 1942; worked as screenwriter for M-G-M, 1943.

MEMBER: Dramatists Guild, National Institute of Arts and Letters, American Society of Composers, Authors, and Publishers (ASCAP), American Automatic Control Council (president, 1965-67), Alpha Tau Omega.

AWARDS, HONORS: Group Theatre Award, 1939, for *American Blues;* Rockefeller Foundation fellowship, 1940; grant, American Academy and National Institute of Arts and Letters,

1943; New York Drama Critics Circle Award, Donaldson Award, and Sidney Howard Memorial Award, 1945, all for *The Glass Menagerie;* New York Drama Critics Circle Award, Pulitzer Prize, and Donaldson Award, 1948, all for *A Streetcar Named Desire;* elected to National Institute of Arts and Letters, 1952; New York Drama Critics Circle Award and Pulitzer Prize, 1955, both for *Cat on a Hot Tin Roof; London Evening Standard* Award, 1958, for *Cat on a Hot Tin Roof;* New York Drama Critics Circle Award, 1962, for *The Night of the Iguana;* first place for best new foreign play, London Critics' Poll, 1964-65, for *The Night of the Iguana;* creative arts medal, Brandeis University, 1964-65; National Institute of Arts and Letters Gold Medal, 1969; received first centennial medal of Cathedral of St. John the Divine, 1973; elected to Theatre Hall of Fame, 1979; Kennedy Honors Award, 1979; Common Wealth Award for Distinguished Service in Dramatic Arts, 1981.

WRITINGS:

PLAYS

(Under original name, Thomas Lanier Williams) "Cairo, Shanghai, Bombay!" (comedy), produced in Memphis, Tenn., by Memphis Garden Players, July 12, 1935.

(Under original name) "Headlines," produced in St. Louis, Mo., at Wednesday Club Auditorium, November 11, 1936.

(Under original name) "Candles to the Sun," produced in St. Louis at Wednesday Club Auditorium, 1936.

(Under original name) "The Magic Tower," produced in St. Louis, 1936.

(Under original name) "The Fugitive Kind" (also see below), produced in St. Louis at Wednesday Club Auditorium, 1937.

(Under original name) "Spring Song," produced in Iowa City, Iowa, at the University of Iowa, 1938.

"The Long Goodbye" (also see below), produced in New York City at New School for Social Research, February 9, 1940 (closed after two performances).

(Contributor) Margaret Mayorga, editor, *The Best One-Act Plays of 1940* (contains "Moony's Kids Don't Cry"), Dodd, 1940.

Battle of Angels (also see below; produced in Boston, Mass., at Wilbur Theatre, December 20, 1940, withdrawn, January 1, 1941), New Directions, 1945.

"Stairs to the Roof," produced in Pasadena, Calif., at Playbox, 1944.

The Glass Menagerie (also see below; first produced in Chicago, Ill., at Civic Theatre, December 26, 1944; produced on Broadway at Playhouse, March 31, 1945), Random House, 1945, published as *The Glass Menagerie: Play in Two Acts,* Dramatists Play Service, 1948.

(With Donald Windham) *You Touched Me!: A Romantic Comedy in Three Acts* (produced on Broadway at Booth Theatre, September 25, 1945), Samuel French, 1947.

(Contributor) *The Best One-Act Plays of 1944* (contains "27 Wagons Full of Cotton"; also see below), Dodd, 1945.

"This Property Is Condemned" (also see below), produced Off-Broadway at Hudson Park Theatre, March, 1946.

"Moony's Kids Don't Cry" (also see below), produced in Los Angeles, Calif., at Actor's Laboratory Theatre, 1946.

"Portrait of a Madonna" (also see below), produced in Los Angeles at Actor's Laboratory Theatre, 1946, produced in New York City as part of "Triple Play," April 15, 1959.

"The Last of My Solid Gold Watches" (also see below), produced in Los Angeles at Actor's Laboratory Theatre, 1946.

27 Wagons Full of Cotton, and Other One-Act Plays by Tennessee Williams (includes "The Long Goodbye," "This Property Is Condemned," "Portrait of a Madonna," "The Last of My Solid Gold Watches," "Auto-da-Fe," "The Lady of Larkspur Lotion," "The Purification," "Hello from Bertha," "The Strangest Kind of Romance," and "Lord Byron's Love Letter" [also see below]), New Directions, 1946, 3rd edition with preface by Williams (contains two new plays, "Talk to Me Like the Rain and Let Me Listen" and "Something Unspoken" [also see below]), 1953.

"Lord Byron's Love Letter" (also see below), produced in New York City, 1947, revised version produced in London, England, 1964.

"Auto-da-Fe," produced in New York City, 1947, produced in Bromley, Kent, England, 1961.

"The Lady of Larkspur Lotion," produced in New York City, 1947, produced in London, 1968.

Summer and Smoke (first produced in Dallas, Tex., at Theatre '47, July 11, 1947; produced on Broadway at Music Box, October 6, 1948; revised as "Eccentricities of a Nightingale," produced in Washington, D.C., April 20, 1966, at Washington Theater Club), New Directions, 1948, published as *Summer and Smoke: Play in Two Acts,* Dramatists Play Service, 1950, published as *The Eccentricities of a Nightingale, and Summer and Smoke: Two Plays,* New Directions, 1964.

A Streetcar Named Desire (also see below; first produced on Broadway at Ethel Barrymore Theatre, December 3, 1947), New Directions, 1947, edition with preface by Williams, 1951, revised edition published as *A Streetcar Named Desire: A Play in Three Acts,* Dramatists Play Service, 1953, edition with foreword by Jessica Tandy and introduction by Williams, Limited Editions Club, 1982, edition with introduction by Williams, New American Library, 1984.

American Blues: Five Short Plays (contains "Moony's Kids Don't Cry," "The Dark Room," "The Case of the Crushed Petunias," "The Long Stay Cut Short; or, the Unsatisfactory Supper," and "Ten Blocks on the Camino Real"; also see below), Dramatists Play Service, 1948, reprinted, 1976.

Camino Real: A Play (also see below; expanded version of "Ten Blocks on the Camino Real"; produced in New York City at National Theatre, March 9, 1953), edition with foreword and afterword by Williams, New Directions, 1953.

The Rose Tattoo (also see below; produced in New York City at Martin Beck Theatre, February 3, 1951), edition with preface by Williams, New Directions, 1951.

Cat on a Hot Tin Roof (also see below; first produced on Broadway at Morosco Theatre, March 24, 1955), edition with preface by Williams, New Directions, 1955, published as *Cat on a Hot Tin Roof: A Play in Three Acts,* Dramatists Play Service, 1958.

"27 Wagons Full of Cotton" (also see below; part of triple bill entitled "All in One"), produced on Broadway at Playhouse, April 19, 1955.

Three Players of a Summer Game (first produced in Westport, Conn., at White Barn Theatre, July 19, 1955), Secker & Warburg, 1960.

(Librettist) Raffaello de Banfield, *Lord Byron's Love Letter: Opera in One Act,* Ricordi, 1955.

"The Case of the Crushed Petunias," produced in Cleveland, Ohio, 1957, produced in New York City, 1958.

Orpheus Descending: A Play in Three Acts (also see below; revision of *Battle of Angels;* produced in New York City at Martin Beck Theatre, March 21, 1957; produced Off-Broadway, 1959), New Directions, 1959.

Orpheus Descending, with Battle of Angels: Two Plays, with preface by Williams, New Directions, 1958.

A Perfect Analysis Given by a Parrot: A Comedy in One Act (also see below), Dramatists Play Service, 1958.

The Rose Tattoo, and, Camino Real, introduced and edited by E. Martin Browne, Penguin, 1958.

Garden District: Two Plays; Something Unspoken and Suddenly Last Summer (also see below; produced Off-Broadway at York Playhouse, January 7, 1958), Secker & Warburg, 1959.

Suddenly Last Summer, New Directions, 1958.

"Talk to Me Like the Rain and Let Me Listen," first produced in Westport, Conn., at White Barn Theatre, July 26, 1958, produced in New York City at West Side Actors Workshop, 1967.

I Rise in Flame, Cried the Phoenix: A Play about D. H. Lawrence (first produced Off-Broadway, 1958-59, produced Off-Broadway at Theatre de Lys, April 14, 1959), with a note by Frieda Lawrence, New Directions, 1951.

A Streetcar Named Desire, and, The Glass Menagerie, edited and introduced by E. Martin Browne, Penguin, 1959.

Sweet Bird of Youth (first produced at Martin Beck Theatre, March 10, 1959), edition with foreword by Williams, New Directions, 1959, revised edition, Dramatists Play Service, 1962.

Period of Adjustment; High Point Over a Cavern: A Serious Comedy (first produced in Miami, Fla., at Coconut Grove Playhouse, 1959 [co-directed by Williams], produced on Broadway at Helen Hayes Theatre, November 10, 1960, simultaneously published in *Esquire*), New Directions, 1960, reprinted as *Period of Adjustment; or, High Point is Built on a Cavern: A Serious Comedy,* Dramatists Play Service, 1961.

The Night of the Iguana (also see below; from Williams's short story of the same title; short version first produced in Spoleto, Italy, 1960, expanded version produced on Broadway at Royale Theatre, December 28, 1961), New Directions, 1961.

"The Purification," produced Off-Broadway at Theatre de Lys, December 8, 1959.

"Hello from Bertha," produced in Bromley, Kent, England, 1961.

"To Heaven in a Golden Coach," produced in Bromley, 1961.

The Milk Train Doesn't Stop Here Anymore (also see below; produced as one-act in Spoleto at Festival of Two Worlds, June, 1962, expanded version produced on Broadway at Morosco Theatre, January 16, 1963, revision produced on Broadway at Brooks Atkinson Theatre, January 1, 1964), New Directions, 1964.

"Slapstick Tragedy" (contains "The Mutilated" and "The Gnaediges Fraulein"; also see below), first produced on Broadway at Longacre Theatre, February 22, 1966 (closed after seven performances).

"The Dark Room," produced in London, 1966.

The Mutilated: A Play in One Act, Dramatists Play Service, 1967.

The Gnaediges Fraulein: A Play in One Act, Dramatists Play Service, 1967, revised as "The Latter Days of a Celebrated Soubrette," produced in New York City at Central Arts Theatre, May 16, 1974.

Kingdom of Earth: The Seven Descents of Myrtle (first published in *Esquire* as one-act "Kingdom of Earth," February, 1967, expanded as "The Seven Descents of Myrtle," produced on Broadway at Ethel Barrymore Theatre, March 27, 1968, revised as "Kingdom of Earth," produced in Princeton, N.J., at McCarter Theatre, March 6, 1975), New Directions, 1968, published as *The Kingdom of Earth (The Seven Descents of Myrtle): A Play in Seven Scenes,* Dramatists Play Service, 1969.

The Two-Character Play (first produced in London, at Hampstead Theatre Club, December, 1967), revised as *Out Cry* (produced in Chicago at Ivanhoe Theatre, July 8, 1971, produced on Broadway at Lyceum Theatre, March 1, 1973), New Directions, 1969.

In the Bar of a Tokyo Hotel (first produced Off-Broadway at Eastside Playhouse, May 11, 1969), Dramatists Play Service, 1969.

"The Strangest Kind of Romance," produced in London, 1969.

(Contributor) "Oh! Calcutta!," produced Off-Broadway at Eden Theatre, June 17, 1969.

"The Frosted Glass Coffin" [and] "A Perfect Analysis Given by a Parrot," produced in Key West, Fla., at Waterfront Playhouse, May 1, 1970.

"The Long Stay Cut Short; or, The Unsatisfactory Supper" (also see below), produced in London, 1971.

"I Can't Imagine Tomorrow" [and] "Confessional," produced in Bar Harbor, Me., at Maine Theatre Arts Festival, August 19, 1971.

Small Craft Warnings (produced Off-Broadway at Truck and Warehouse Theatre, April 2, 1972), New Directions, 1972.

The Red Devil Battery Sign (produced in Boston, June 18, 1975, revised version produced in Vienna, Austria, at English Theatre, January 17, 1976), New Directions, 1988.

"Demolition Downtown: Count Ten in Arabic," produced in London, 1976.

"This Is (An Entertainment)," produced in San Francisco at American Conservatory Theatre, January 20, 1976.

Vieux Carre (produced on Broadway at St. James Theatre, May 11, 1977), New Directions, 1979.

A Lovely Sunday for Creve Coeur (first produced under title "Creve Coeur" in Charleston, S.C., at Spoleto Festival, May, 1978, produced Off-Broadway at Hudson Guild Theatre, January 21, 1979), New Directions, 1980.

Clothes for a Summer Hotel: A Ghost Play (produced on Broadway at Cort Theatre, March 26, 1980), Dramatists Play Service, 1981.

Steps Must Be Gentle: A Dramatic Reading for Two Performers, Targ Editions, 1980.

"Something Cloudy, Something Clear," first produced Off-Off-Broadway at Bouwerie Lane Theater, September, 1981.

It Happened the Day the Sun Rose, Sylvester & Orphanos, 1981.

The Remarkable Rooming-House of Mme. Le Monde: A Play, Albondocani Press, 1984.

Also author of "Me, Vashya," "Not about Nightingales," "Kirche, Kutchen und Kinder," "Life Boat Drill," "Will Mr. Merriwether Return from Memphis?," "Of Masks Outrageous and Austere," and "A House Not Meant to Stand." Also author of television play, "I Can't Imagine Tomorrow." Contributor to anthologies. Contributor to periodicals, including *Esquire.*

Williams's plays appear in numerous foreign languages.

COLLECTIONS

Four Plays (contains "The Glass Menagerie," "A Streetcar Named Desire," "Summer and Smoke," and "Camino Real"), Secker & Warburg, 1956.

Five Plays (contains "Cat on a Hot Tin Roof," "The Rose Tattoo," "Something Unspoken," "Suddenly Last Summer," and "Orpheus Descending"), Secker & Warburg, 1962.

Three Plays: The Rose Tattoo, Camino Real, Sweet Bird of Youth, New Directions, 1964.

Baby Doll: The Script for the Film [and] *Something Unspoken* [and] *Suddenly Last Summer,* Penguin, 1968.

The Night of the Iguana [and] *Orpheus Descending,* Penguin, 1968.

The Milk Train Doesn't Stop Here Anymore [and] *Cat on a Hot Tin Roof,* Penguin, 1969.

Dragon Country: A Book of Plays, New Directions, 1970.

Battle of Angels [and] *The Glass Menagerie* [and] *A Streetcar Named Desire,* New Directions, 1971.

Cat on a Hot Tin Roof [and] *Orpheus Descending* [and] *Suddenly Last Summer,* New Directions, 1971.

The Eccentricities of a Nightingale [and] *Summer and Smoke* [and] *The Rose Tattoo* [and] *Camino Real,* New Directions, 1971.

The Theatre of Tennessee Williams, New Directions, Volume 1, 1971, Volume 2, 1971, Volume 3, 1971, Volume 4, 1972, Volume 5, 1976, Volume 6, 1981, Volume 7, 1981.

Three by Tennessee Williams, New American Library, 1976.

Cat on a Hot Tin Roof [and] *The Milk Train Doesn't Stop Here Anymore* [and] *The Night of the Iguana,* Penguin, 1976.

Selected Plays, illustrations by Jerry Pinkney, Franklin Library, 1977.

Tennessee Williams: Eight Plays, introduction by Harold Clurman, Doubleday, 1979.

Selected Plays, illustrations by Herbert Tauss, Franklin Library, 1980.

"Ten by Tennessee" (one-act plays), produced in New York City at Lucille Lortel Theater, May, 1986.

SCREENPLAYS

(With Gore Vidal) "Senso," Luchino Visconti, c. 1949.

(With Oscar Saul) "The Glass Menagerie," Warner Bros., 1950.

"A Streetcar Named Desire," 20th Century-Fox, 1951.

(With Hal Kanter) "The Rose Tattoo," Paramount, 1955.

"Baby Doll," Warner Bros., 1956, published as *Baby Doll: The Script for the Film,* New American Library, 1956, published as *Baby Doll; the Script for the Film, Incorporating the Two One-Act Plays which Suggested It: 27 Wagons Full of Cotton* [and] *The Long Stay Cut Short; or, The Unsatisfactory Supper,* New Directions, 1956.

(With Vidal) "Suddenly Last Summer," Columbia, 1959.

(With Meade Roberts) "The Fugitive Kind" (based on "Orpheus Descending"), United Artists, 1959, published as *The Fugitive Kind,* Signet, 1960.

"Boom" (based on "The Milkman Doesn't Stop Here Anymore"), Universal, 1968.

Stopped Rocking and Other Screenplays (contains "All Gaul Is Divided," "The Loss of a Teardrop Diamond," "One Arm," and "Stopped Rocking"), introduced by Richard Gilman, New Directions, 1984.

Also author, with Paul Bowles, of "The Wanton Countess" (English-language version), filmed in 1954.

NOVELS

The Roman Spring of Mrs. Stone (novel), New Directions, 1950.

Moise and the World of Reason (novel), Simon & Schuster, 1975.

STORIES

One Arm, and Other Stories (includes "The Night of the Iguana"), New Directions, 1948.

Hard Candy: A Book of Stories, New Directions, 1954.

Man Brings This Up Road: A Short Story, Street & Smith, 1959.

Three Players of a Summer Game, and Other Stories, Secker & Warburg, 1960, reprinted, Dent, 1984.

Grand, House of Books, 1964.

The Knightly Quest: A Novella and Four Short Stories, New Directions, 1967.

Eight Mortal Ladies Possessed: A Book of Stories, New Directions, 1974.

Collected Stories, introduction by Gore Vidal, New Directions, 1985.

Contributor of short stories to *Esquire.*

POETRY

(Contributor) James Laughlin, editor, *Five Young American Poets,* New Directions, 1944.

In the Winter of Cities: Poems, New Directions, 1956.

Androgyne, Mon Amour: Poems, New Directions, 1977.

OTHER

(Author of introduction) Carson McCullers, *Reflections in a Golden Eye,* Bantam, 1961.

Memoirs, Doubleday, 1975.

Tennessee Williams' Letters to Donald Windham, 1940-65, edited with commentary by Windham, [Verona], 1976, Holt, 1977.

Where I Live: Selected Essays, edited by Christine R. Day and Bob Woods, introduction by Day, New Directions, 1978.

Conversations with Tennessee Williams, edited by Albert J. Devlin, University Press of Mississippi, 1986.

A collection of Williams's manuscripts and letters is located at the Humanities Research Center of the University of Texas at Austin.

SIDELIGHTS: The production of his first two Broadway plays, *The Glass Menagerie* (1945) and *A Streetcar Named Desire* (1947), secured Tennessee Williams's place, with Eugene O'Neill and Arthur Miller, as one of America's major playwrights of the twentieth century. Critics, playgoers, and fellow dramatists recognized in him a poetic innovator who, refusing to be confined in what Stark Young in the *New Republic* called "the usual sterilities of our playwriting patterns," pushed drama into new fields, stretched the limits of the individual play, and became one of the founders of the so-called "New Drama." Praising *The Glass Menagerie* "as a revelation of what superb theater could be," Brooks Atkinson in *Broadway* asserted that "Williams's remembrance of things past gave the theater distinction as a literary medium." Twenty years later, Joanne Stang wrote in the *New York Times* that "the American theater, indeed theater everywhere, has never been the same" since the premier of *The Glass Menagerie.* Four decades after that first play, C. W. E. Bigsby in *A Critical Introduction to Twentieth-Century American Drama* termed it "one of the best works to have come out of the American theater." *A Streetcar Named Desire* became only the second play in history to win both the Pulitzer Prize and the New York Drama Critics Circle Award. Eric Bentley, in *What Is Theatre?,* called it the "master-drama of the generation." "The inevitability of a great work of art," T. E. Kalem stated in Albert J. Devlin's *Conversations with Tennessee Williams,* "is that you cannot imagine the time when it didn't exist. You can't imagine a time when *Streetcar* didn't exist."

More clearly than with most authors, the facts of Williams's life reveal the origins of the material he crafted into his best works. The Mississippi in which Thomas Lanier Williams was born March 26, 1911, was in many ways a world that no longer exists, "a dark, wide, open world that you can breathe in," as Williams nostalgically described it in Harry Rasky's *Tennessee Williams: A Portrait in Laughter and Lamentation.* The predominantly rural state was dotted with towns such as Columbus, Canton, and Clarksdale, in which he spent his first seven years with his mother, his sister Rose, and his maternal grandmother and grandfather, an Episcopal rector. A sickly child, Tom was pampered by doting elders. In 1918, his father, a traveling salesman who had been often absent—perhaps, like his stage counterpart in *The Glass Menagerie,* "in love with long distances"—moved the family to St. Louis. Something of the trauma they experienced is dramatized in the 1945 play. The contrast between leisurely small-town past and northern big-city present, between protective grandparents and the hard-drinking, gambling father with little patience for the sensitive son he saw as a "sissy," seriously affected both children. While Rose retreated into her own mind until finally beyond the reach even of her loving brother, Tom made use of that adversity. St. Louis remained for him "a city I loathe," but the South, despite his portrayal of its grotesque aspects, proved a rich source to which he returned literally and imaginatively for comfort and inspiration. That background, his homosexuality, and his relationships, painful and joyous, with members of his family were the strongest personal factors shaping Williams's dramas.

During the St. Louis years, Williams found an imaginative release from unpleasant reality in writing essays, stories, poems, and plays. After attending the University of Missouri, Washington University from which he earned a B.A. degree in 1938, and the University of Iowa, he returned to the South, specifically to New Orleans, one of two places where he was for the rest of his life to feel at home. Yet a recurrent motif in his plays involves flight and the fugitive, who, Lord Byron insists in *Camino Real: A Play,* must keep moving, and the flight from St. Louis initiated a nomadic life of brief stays in a variety of places. Williams fled not only uncongenial atmospheres but a turbulent family situation that had culminated in a decision for Rose to have a prefrontal lobotomy in an effort to alleviate her increasing psychological problems. (Williams's works often include absentee fathers, enduring—if aggravating—mothers, and dependent relatives; and the memory of Rose appears in some character, situation, symbol or motif in almost every work after 1938.) He fled as well some part of himself, for he had created a new persona, Tennessee Williams the playwright, who shared the same body as the proper young gentleman named Thomas with whom Tennessee would always be to some degree at odds.

In 1940 Williams's *Battle of Angels* was staged by the Theater Guild in an ill-fated production marred as much by faulty smudge pots in the lynching scene as by Boston censorship. Despite the abrupt out-of-town closing of the play, Williams was now known and admired by powerful theater people. During the next two decades, his most productive period, one play succeeded another, each of them permanent entries in the history of modern theater: *The Glass Menagerie, A Streetcar Named Desire, Summer and Smoke, The Rose Tattoo, Camino Real, Cat on a Hot Tin Roof, Orpheus Descending, Suddenly Last Summer, Sweet Bird of Youth,* and *Night of the Iguana.* Despite increasingly adverse criticism, Williams continued his work for the theater for two more decades, during which he wrote more than a dozen additional plays containing evidence of his virtues as a poetic realist. In the course of his long career he also produced three volumes of short stories, many of them as studies for subsequent dramas; two novels, *The Roman Spring of Mrs. Stone* and *Moise and the World of Reason;* two volumes of poetry; his memoirs; and essays on his life and craft. His dramas made that rare transition from legitimate stage to movies and television, from intellectual acceptance to popular acceptance. Before his death in 1983, he had become the best-known living dramatist; his plays had been translated and performed in many foreign countries, and his name and work had become known even to people

who had never seen a production of any of his plays. The persona named Tennessee Williams had achieved the status of a myth.

Plays, stories, poems, and personal essays were all drawn from the experiences of his persona. Williams saw himself as a shy, sensitive, gifted man trapped in a world where "mendacity" replaced communication, brute violence replaced love, and loneliness was, all too often, the standard human condition. These tensions "at the core of his creation" were identified by Harold Clurman in his introduction to *Tennessee Williams: Eight Plays* as a terror at what Williams saw in himself and in America, a terror that he must "exorcise" with "his poetic vision." In the preface to *The Rose Tattoo,* the playwright declared that "Snatching the eternal out of the desperately fleeting" was "the great magic trick of human existence." In an interview collected in *Conversations with Tennessee Williams,* Williams identified his main theme as a defense of the Old South attitude—"elegance, a love of the beautiful, a romantic attitude toward life"—and "a violent protest against those things that defeat it." An idealist aware of what he called in a *Conversations* interview "the merciless harshness of America's success-oriented society," he was ironically, naturalistic as well, conscious of the inaccessibility of that for which he yearned. He early developed, according to John Gassner in *Theatre at the Crossroads: Plays and Playwrights of the Mid-Century American Stage,* "a precise naturalism" and continued to work toward a "fusion of naturalistic detail with symbolism and poetic sensibility rare in American playwriting." The result was a unique romanticism, as Kenneth Tynan observed in *Curtains,* "which is not pale or scented but earthy and robust, the product of a mind vitally infected with the rhythms of human speech."

Williams's characters, then, endeavor to embrace the ideal, to advance and not "hold back with the brutes," a struggle no less valiant for being vain. In *A Streetcar Named Desire* Blanche's idealization of life at Belle Reve, the DuBois plantation, cannot protect her once, in the words of the brutish Stanley Kowalski, she has come "down off them columns" into the "broken world," the world of sexual desire. Since every human, as Val Xavier observes in *Orpheus Descending,* is sentenced "to solitary confinement inside our own lonely skins for as long as we live on earth," the only hope is to try to communicate, to love, and to live—even beyond despair, as *The Night of the Iguana* teaches. The attempt to communicate often takes the form of sex (and Williams has been accused of obsession with that aspect of human existence), but at other times it becomes a willingness to show compassion, as when in *The Night of the Iguana* Hannah Jelkes accepts the neuroses of her fellow creatures and when in *Cat on a Hot Tin Roof* Big Daddy understands, as his son Brick cannot, the attachment between Brick and Skipper. In his preface to *Cat on a Hot Tin Roof* Williams might have been describing his characters' condition when he spoke of "the outcry of prisoner to prisoner from the cell in solitary where each is confined for the duration of his life." "The marvel is," as Tynan stated, that Williams's "abnormal" view of life, "heightened and spotlighted and slashed with bogey shadows," can be made to touch his audience's more normal views, thus achieving that "miracle of communication" Williams believed to be almost impossible.

Some of his contemporaries—Arthur Miller notably—responded to the modern condition with social protest, but Williams, after a few early attempts at that genre, chose another approach. It is generally characteristic of Southern authors not to comment overtly on social problems because of these writers' Calvinistic distrust of programs and schemes for the perfectibility of man. Thus Williams insisted in a *Conversations* interview that he wrote about the South not as a sociologist: "What I am writing about is human nature." Moreover, as a romantic, Williams sought an ideal unobtainable through social action; recognizing, as he stated in *Conversations,* that "human relations are terrifyingly ambiguous," Williams chose to present characters full of uncertainties, mysteries, and doubts. Yet Arthur Miller himself wrote in *The Theatre Essays of Tennessee Williams* that although Williams might not portray social reality, "the intensity with which he feels whatever he does feel is so deep, is so great" that his audiences glimpse another kind of reality, "the reality in the spirit." Clurman likewise argued that though Williams was no "propagandist," social commentary is "inherent in his portraiture." The inner torment and disintegration of a character like Blanche in *A Streetcar Named Desire* thus symbolize the lost South from which she comes and with which she is inseparably entwined. It was to that lost world and the unpleasant one which succeeded it that Williams turned for the majority of his settings and material.

Like most Southern writers, Williams's work exhibits an abiding concern with time and place and how they affect men and women. "The play is memory," Tom proclaims in *The Glass Menagerie;* and Williams's characters are haunted by a past that they have difficulty accepting or that they valiantly endeavor to transform into myth. Interested in yesterday or tomorrow rather than in today, painfully conscious of the physical and emotional scars the years inflict, they have a static, dream-like quality, and the result, Tynan observed, is "the drama of mood." The Mississippi towns of his childhood continued to haunt Williams's imagination throughout his career, but New Orleans offered him, he told Robert Rice in the 1958 *New York Post* interviews, a new freedom: "the shock of it against the Puritanism of my nature has given me a subject, a theme, which I have never ceased exploiting." (That shabby but charming city became the setting for several stories and one-act plays, and *A Streetcar Named Desire* derives much of its distinction from French Quarter ambience and attitudes; as Stella informs Blanche, "New Orleans isn't like other cities," a view reinforced by Williams's 1977 portrait of the place in *Vieux Carre.*) Atkinson observed, "Only a writer who had survived in the lower depths of a sultry Southern city could know the characters as intimately as Williams did and be so thoroughly steeped in the aimless sprawl of the neighborhood life."

Williams's South provided not only settings but other characteristics of his work: the romanticism that tinges almost every play; a myth of an Arcadian existence now disappeared; a distinctive way of looking at life, including both an inbred Calvinistic belief in the reality of evil eternally at war with good and what Bentley called a "peculiar combination of the comic and the pathetic." The South also inspired Williams's fascination with violence, his drawing upon regional character types, and his skill in recording Southern language—eloquent, flowery, sometimes bombastic. Moreover, Southern history, particularly the lost cause of the Civil War and the devastating Reconstruction period, imprinted on Williams, as on such major Southern fiction writers as William Faulkner, Flannery O'Conner, and Walker Percy, a profound sense of separation and alienation. Williams, as Thomas E. Porter declared in *Myth and Modern American Drama,* explored "the mind of the Southerner caught between an idyllic past and an undesirable present," commemorating the death of a myth even as he continued to examine it. "His broken figures appeal," Bigsby asserted, "because they are victims of history—the lies of the old South no longer being able to sustain the individual in a world whose pragmatics have no place for the fragile spirit." In a *Conversations* interview the playwright commented that "the South once had a way of life that I am just old enough to remember—a culture that had grace, elegance. . . . I write out of regret for that."

Williams's plays are peopled with a large cast that J. L. Styan termed, in *Modern Drama in Theory and Practice,* "Garrulous Grotesques"; these figures include "untouchables whom he touches with frankness and mercy," according to Tynan. They bear the stamp of their place of origin and speak a "humorous, colorful, graphic" language, which Williams in a *Conversations* interview called the "mad music of my characters." "Have you ever known a Southerner who wasn't long-winded?" he asked; "I mean, a Southerner not afflicted with terminal asthma." Among that cast are the romantics who, however suspect their own virtues may be, act out of belief in and commitment to what Faulkner called the "old verities and truths of the heart." They include fallen aristocrats hounded, Gerald Weales observed in *American Drama since World War II,* "by poverty, by age, by frustration," or as Bigsby called them in his 1985 study "martyrs for a world which has already slipped away unmourned"; fading Southern belles such as Amanda Wingate and Blanche DuBois; slightly deranged women, such as Aunt Rose Comfort in an early one-act play and in the film "Baby Doll"; dictatorial patriarchs such as Big Daddy; and the outcasts (or "fugitive kind," the playwright's term later employed as the title of a 1960 motion picture). Many of these characters tend to recreate the scene in which they find themselves—Laura with her glass animals shutting out the alley where cats are brutalized, Blanche trying to subdue the ugliness of the Kowalski apartment with a paper lantern; in their dialogue they frequently poeticize and melodramatize their situations, thereby surrounding themselves with protective illusion, which in later plays becomes "mendacity." For also inhabiting that dramatic world are more powerful individuals, amoral representatives of the new Southern order, Jabe Torrance in *Battle of Angels,* Gooper and Mae in *Cat on a Hot Tin Roof,* Boss Finley in *Sweet Bird of Youth,* enemies of the romantic impulse and as destructive and virtueless as Faulkner's Snopes clan. Southern though all these characters are, they are not mere regional portraits, for through Williams's dramatization of them and their dilemmas and through the audience's empathy, the characters become everyman and everywoman.

Although traumatic experiences plagued his life, Williams was able to press "the nettle of neurosis" to his heart and produce art, as Gassner observed. Williams's family problems, his alienation from the social norm resulting from his homosexuality, his sense of being a romantic in an unromantic, postwar world, and his sensitive reaction when a production proved less than successful all contributed significantly to his work. Through the years he suffered from a variety of ailments, some serious, some surely imaginary, and at certain periods he overindulged in alcohol and prescription drugs. Despite these circumstances, he continued to write with a determination that verged at times almost on desperation, even as his new plays elicited progressively more hostile reviews from critics.

An outgrowth of this suffering is the character type "the fugitive kind," the wanderer who lives outside the pale of society, excluded by his sensitivity, artistic bent, or sexual proclivity from the world of "normal" human beings. Like Faulkner, Williams was troubled by the exclusivity of any society that shuts out certain segments because they are different. First manifested in Val of *Battle of Angels* (later rewritten as *Orpheus Descending*) and then in the character of Tom, the struggling poet of *The Glass Menagerie* and his shy, withdrawn sister, the fugitive kind appears in varying guises in subsequent plays, including Blanche DuBois, Alma Winemiller (*Summer and Smoke*), Kilroy (*Camino Real*), and Hannah and Shannon (*The Night of the*

Iguana). Each is unique but they share common characteristics, which Weales as physical or mental illness, a preoccupation with sex, and a "combination of sensitivity and imagination with corruption." Their abnormality suggests, the critic argued, that the dramatist views the norm of society as being faulty itself. Even characters within the "norm" (Stanley Kowalski for example) are often identified with strong sexual drives. Like D. H. Lawrence, Williams indulged in a kind of phallic romanticism, attributing sexual potency to members of the unintelligent lower classes and sterility to aristocrats. Despite his romanticism, however, Williams's view of humanity was too realistic for him to accept such pat categories. "If you write a character that isn't ambiguous," Williams said in a *Conversations* interview, "you are writing a false character, not a true one." Though he shared Lawrence's view that one should not suppress sexual impulses, Williams recognized that such impulses are at odds with the romantic desire to transcend and that they often lead to suffering like that endured by Blanche DuBois. Those fugitive characters who are destroyed, Bigsby remarked, often perish "because they offer love in a world characterized by impotence and sterility." Thus phallic potency may represent a positive force in a character such as Val or a destructive force in one like Stanley Kowalski; but even in *A Streetcar Named Desire* Williams acknowledges that the life force, represented by Stella's baby, is positive. There are, as Weales pointed out, two divisions in the sexual activity Williams dramatizes: "desperation sex," in which characters such as Val and Blanche "make contact with another only tentatively, momentarily" in order to communicate; and the "consolation and comfort" sex that briefly fulfills Lady in *Orpheus Descending* and saves Serafina in *The Rose Tattoo*. There is, surely, a third kind, sex as a weapon, wielded by those like Stanley; this kind of sex is to be feared, for it is often associated with the violence prevalent in Williams's dramas.

Beginning with *Battle of Angels,* two opposing camps have existed among Williams's critics, and his detractors sometimes have objected most strenuously to the innovations his supporters deemed virtues. His strongest advocates among established drama critics, notably Stark Young, Brooks Atkinson, John Gassner, and Walter Kerr, praised him for realistic clarity; compassion and a strong moral sense; unforgettable characters, especially women, based on his keen perception of human nature; dialogue at once credible and poetic; and a pervasive sense of humor that distinguished him from O'Neill and Miller. Young commended his revolt against archaic dramatic conventions and his "true realism" with all its "variety, suddenness, passion and freedom"; he applauded Williams's relation to a tradition and his "free and true" language and motifs. In 1968, Bentley, commenting on Williams's influence on American drama, suggested that he "bids fair to become, theatrically speaking, the father of his country: the new playwrights derive from him, not from O'Neill, [Clifford] Odets, [Thorton] Wilder or Miller, . . . his only conceivable rivals." Crediting Williams with overcoming "resistance to emotional improvisations that dispensed with the conventional dramatic forms," Atkinson termed Williams and Miller "two natural theater men" who resuscitated a failing art and dominated it in the years after World War II. In them, Frederick Lumley stated in *New Trends in Twentieth Century Drama: A Survey since Ibsen and Shaw,* "the immigrant strain is less conscious," because they learned from the European masters without becoming mere disciples. Miller identified Williams's "greatest value" as "his aesthetic valor," that is, "his very evident determination to unveil and engage the widest range of causation conceivable to him." Even in 1979, when Williams's career, near its end, had survived years of failed productions and bad reviews, Kerr would pronounce him "our finest living playwright," and

Kalem would go further to insist that this "laureate of the violated heart" was "the world's greatest playwright."

Not surprisingly, it was from the conservative establishment that most of the adverse criticism came. Obviously appalled by this "upstart crow," George Jean Nathan, dean of theater commentators when Williams made his revolutionary entrance onto the scene, sounded notes often to be repeated. In *The Theatre Book of the Year, 1947-1948,* he faulted Williams's early triumphs for "mistiness of ideology," "questionable symbolism" "debatable character drawing," "adolescent point of view," "theatrical fabrication," and obsession with sex, fallen women, and "the deranged Dixie damsel." In short, Nathan saw Williams as a melodramatist whose attempts at tragedy were as ludicrous as "a threnody on a zither." Subsequent detractors—notably Richard Gilman, Robert Brustein, Clive Barnes, and John Simon—taxed the playwright for theatricality, repetition, lack of judgment and control, excessive moralizing and philosophizing, and conformity to the demands of the ticket-buying public. His plays, they variously argued, lacked unity of effect, clarity of intention, social content, and variety; these critics saw the plays as burdened with excessive symbolism, violence, sexuality, and attention to the sordid, grotesque elements of life. Additionally, certain commentators charged that Elia Kazan, the director of the early masterpieces, virtually rewrote *A Streetcar Named Desire* and *Cat on a Hot Tin Roof.* A particular kind of negative criticism, often intensely emotional seemed to dominate evaluations of the plays produced in the last twenty years of Williams's life.

Most critics, even his detractors, have praised the dramatist's skillful creation of dialogue. "What we need in the theater is a sense of language, a sense of texture in speech," Young wrote of *The Glass Menagerie,* in which he heard "the echo of great literature, or at least a respect for it." Twenty years later Bentley asserted that "no one in the English-speaking theater" created better dialogue, that Williams's plays were really "*written*—that is to say, set down in living language." Ruby Cohn stated in *Dialogue in American Drama* that Williams gave to American theater "a new vocabulary and rhythm" by expanding dialogue in range and content to embrace "nostalgia, frustration, sadness, gaiety, cruelty, and compassion." Praising Williams's "uncanny ear" for dialogue that was "effortlessly euphonious, rich in subtle gradations of the vernacular," Clurman concluded, "No one in the theater has written more melodiously. Without the least artificial flourish, his writing takes flight from the naturalistic to the poetic." Even Mary McCarthy, no ardent fan, stated in *Theatre Chronicles: 1937-1962* that Williams was the only American realist other than Paddy Chayevsky with an ear for dialogue and that although he sometimes abandoned real speech for "his special poetic long-play prose," he knew speech patterns and really heard his characters. There were, of course, objections to Williams's lyrical dialogue, different as it is from the dialogue of O'Neill, Miller, or any other major American playwright. Bentley admitted to finding his "fake poeticizing" troublesome at times, while Bigsby insisted that Williams was at his best only when he restrained "over-poetic language" and symbolism with "an imagination which if melodramatic is also capable of fine control." However, those long poetic speeches or "arias" in plays of the first twenty-five years of his career, became a hallmark of the dramatist's work.

Another major area of contention among commentators has been Williams's use of symbols, which he called in a *Conversations* interview "the natural language of drama." Laura's glass animals, the paper lantern and cathedral bells in *A Streetcar Named Desire,* the legless birds of *Orpheus Descending,* and the iguana in *The Night of the Iguana,* to name only a few, are integral to the plays in which they appear. Cohn commented on Williams's extensive use of animal images in *Cat on a Hot Tin Roof* to symbolize the fact that all the Pollitts, "grasping, screeching, devouring," are "greedily alive." In that play, Big Daddy's malignancy effectively represents the corruption in the family and in the larger society to which the characters belong. However, Weales objected that Williams, like *The Glass Menagerie*'s Tom, had "a poet's weakness for symbols," which can get out of hand; he argued that in *Suddenly Last Summer,* Violet Venable's garden does not grow out of the situation and enrich the play. Sometimes, Cohn observed, a certain weakness of symbolism "is built into the fabric of the drama."

Critics favorable to Williams have agreed that one of his virtues lay in his characterization. Those "superbly actable parts," Atkinson stated, derived from his ability to find "extraordinary spiritual significance in ordinary people." Cohn admired Williams's "Southern grotesques" and his knack for giving them "dignity," although some critics have been put off by the excessive number of such grotesques, which contributed, they argued, to a distorted view of reality. Commentators generally concurred in their praise of Williams's talent in creating credible female roles. "No one in American drama has written more intuitively of women," Clurman asserted; Gassner spoke of Williams's "uncanny familiarity with the flutterings of the female heart." Walter Kerr in *The Theatre in Spite of Itself* expressed wonder at such roles as that of Hannah in *Night of the Iguana,* "a portrait which owes nothing to calipers, or to any kind of tooling; it is all surprise and presence, anticipated intimacy. It is found gold, not a borrowing against known reserves." Surveying the "steamy zoo" of Williams's characters with their violence, despair, and aberrations, Stang commended him for the "poetry and compassion that comprise his great gift." *Compassion* is the key word in all tributes to Williams's characterization. It is an acknowledgment of the playwright's uncanny talent for making audiences and readers empathize with his people, however grotesque, bizarre, or even sordid they may seem on the surface.

Although they granted him compassion, some of his detractors felt Williams did not exhibit a clear philosophy of life, and they found unacceptable the ambiguity in judging human flaws and frailties that was one of his most distinctive qualities. Bentley chided Williams for his "besetting sin" of "fake philosophizing, a straining after big statements." Noting that Williams had "said that he only feels and does not think," the critic stated that perhaps "he only thinks he feels," since the "Serenity and Truth, of which he *speaks* and *thinks,* tend to remain in the head too— mere abstractions." On the other hand, Arthur Ganz in *Realms of the Self: Variations on a Theme in Modern Drama,* insisted that Williams's best work "derives its force from the strength of his moral temper, which leads him to censure even what he most wishes to exalt." One difficulty, for those concerned about his seeming lack of judgments on characters and their actions, stemmed from the playwright's recognition of and insistence on portraying the ambiguity of human activities and relationships. Moral, even puritanical, though he might be, Williams never seemed ready to condemn any action other than "deliberate cruelty," and even that was sometimes portrayed as resulting from extenuating circumstances.

In terms of dramatic technique, those who acknowledged his genius disagreed as to where it was best expressed. For Jerold Phillips, writing in *Dictionary of Literary Biography Documentary Series,* Williams's major contribution lay in turning from the Ibsenesque social problem plays to "Strindberg-like explorations of what goes on underneath the skin," thereby freeing American theater from "the hold of the so-called well-made play." For

Allan Lewis in *American Plays and Playwrights of the Contemporary Theatre* he was a "brilliant inventor of emotionally intense scenes" whose "greatest gift [lay] in suggesting ideas through emotional relations." His preeminence among dramatists in the United States, Jean Gould wrote in *Modern American Playwrights,* resulted from a combination of poetic sensitivity, theatricality, and "the dedication of the artist." If, from the beginning of his career, there were detractors who charged Williams with overuse of melodramatic, grotesque, and violent elements that produced a distorted view of reality, Kerr, in *The Theatre in Spite of Itself,* termed him "a man unafraid of melodrama, and a man who handles it with extraordinary candor and deftness." Agreeing that Williams's endings were melodramatic, Lewis compared them to Jacobean drama, powerful in that "they reach beyond the immediate locale to wherever brutality and ugliness suppress the cry for beauty." Robert Heilman believed, however, that like O'Neill, Williams himself despaired and thus did not develop "the authentic note of tragic completeness."

Other commentators have been offended by what Bentley termed Williams's "exploitation of the obscene": his choice of characters—outcasts, alcoholics, the violent and deranged and sexually abnormal—and of subject matter—incest, castration, and cannibalism. Robert Brustein, in *Seasons of Discontent: Dramatic Opinions, 1959-1965,* condemned his "Strindbergian identification of the human body with excrement and defilement" and the "obsessively sexual determinism of every character." Williams justified the "sordid" elements of his work in a *Conversations* interview when he asserted that "we must depict the awfulness of the world we live in, but we must do it with a kind of aesthetic" to avoid producing mere horror. Clearly he viewed himself as a realist, even a naturalist in the tradition of Emile Zola, who argued that the artist had a commitment to examine the unpleasant, grotesque elements of life.

Another negative aspect of Williams's art, some critics argued, was his theatricality. Gassner asserted in *Directions in Modern Theatre and Drama* that Kazan, the director, avoided flashy stage effects called for in Williams's text of *The Glass Menagerie,* but that in some plays Kazan collaborated with the playwright to exaggerate these effects, especially in the expressionistic and allegorical drama *Camino Real.* In a *Conversations* interview, Williams addressed this charge, particularly as it involved Kazan, by asserting, "My cornpone melodrama is all my own. I want excitement in the theater. . . . I have a tendency toward romanticism and a taste for the theatrical."

Depending on which critic one happened to be reading, Kazan appeared to be saint or sinner, the greatest blessing to come to Tennessee Williams's career or its greatest liability. No playwright was ever more cognizant than Williams of the fact that the script represented an incomplete play, that until it was mounted by a director, with the contribution of actors, set designers, lighting technicians, and costumers, it was in a sense merely an outline. Repeatedly he paid tribute to all those who managed to materialize the dreams that issued from his imagination. Kazan was a brilliantly innovative but controversial director whose staging of works by both Williams and Miller raised a number of questions as to the extent of his contribution: Did he merely enhance masterpieces, or was he significantly reworking the playwrights' material? Williams was so sensitive to this criticism that there came a point in his career when he saw fit to sever his ties with the director. Atkinson had nothing but praise for Kazan's "sensitive and scrupulous" direction, and Rasky attributed to the collaboration a theatrical revolution and argued that both were "diminished by Kazan's leaving." On the other hand, Bentley complained that through Kazan's insistence on changes in the final act of *Cat on a Hot Tin Roof,* "the professional pessimism" of "an avant-garde writer, is converted into its opposite." The relationship between Williams and Kazan seems destined to remain a part of any serious analysis of the plays with which both were involved.

Late in his career, Williams was increasingly subject to charges that he had outlived his talent. Beginning with *Period of Adjustment,* a comedy generally disliked by critics, there were years of rejection of play after play: *The Milk Train Doesn't Stop Here Any More, Kingdom of Earth, Small Craft Warnings, Out Cry, Vieux Carre, Clothes for a Summer Hotel, The Red Devil Battery Sign.* By the late 1960s, even the longtime advocate Brooks Atkinson observed that in "a melancholy resolution of an illustrious career" the dramatist was producing plays "with a kind of desperation" in which he lost control of content and style. Lewis, accusing Williams of repeating motifs, themes, and characters in play after play, asserted that in failing "to expand and enrich" his theme, he had "dissipated a rare talent." Berating him for "heavy-handed gongorism," John Simon said that Williams's style was becoming as "baroque" as his subject matter; Richard Gilman, in a particularly vituperative review entitled "Mr. Williams, He Dead," included in his *Common and Uncommon Masks: Writings on Theatre, 1961-1970,* charged that the "moralist," subtly present in earlier plays, was "increasingly on stage." Citing the dramatist's growing concern with his own unconscious, Brustein accused him of hypocritically pandering to "the very groups he assaults." Even if one granted a diminution of creative powers, however, the decline in Williams's popularity and position as major playwright in the 1960s and 1970s can be attributed in large part to a marked change in the theater itself. Audiences constantly demanded variety, and although the early creations of the playwright remained popular, theatregoers wanted something different, strange, exotic. One problem, Kerr pointed out, was that Williams was so good, people expected him to continue to get better; judging each play against those which had gone before denied a fair hearing to the new creations. Sadly, the playwright's accidental death came when his career, after almost two decades of bad reviews and of dismissals of his "dwindling talents," was at its lowest ebb since the abortive 1940 production of *Battle of Angels.* Since his death, however, an inevitable reevaluation has begun. Bigsby, for example, has found in a reanalysis of the late plays more than mere vestiges of the strengths of earlier years, especially in *Out Cry,* an experimental drama toward which Williams felt a particular affection.

Whatever the final judgment of literary historians on the works of Tennessee Williams, certain facts are clear. He was, without question, the most controversial American playwright, a situation unlikely to change as the debate over his significant and the relative merits of individual plays continues. Critics, scholars, and theatergoers do not remain neutral in regard to the man or his work. He is also the most quotable of American playwrights, and even those who disparage the highly poetic dialogue admit the uniqueness of the language he brought to modern theater. In addition, he has added to dramatic literature a cast of remarkable, memorable characters and has turned his attention and sympathy toward people and subjects that, before his time, had been considered beneath the concern of serious authors. Amanda, Blanche, Stanley, Big Daddy, Brick, and Maggie—all are established as enduring members of the pantheon of great dramatic creations. With "distinctive dramatic feeling," Gassner said in *Theatre at the Crossroads,* Williams "made pulsating plays out of his visions of a world of terror, confusion, and perverse beauty." As a result, Gassner concluded, Williams "makes indifference to the theater virtually impossible." Following his

death, some of those who had been during his last years his severest critics acknowledged the greatness of his achievement. Even John Simon, who had dismissed play after play as valueless repetitions created by an author who had outlived his talent, acknowledged in a 1983 *New York* essay that he had underestimated the playwright's genius and significance. Tennessee Williams was, finally, a rebel who broke with the rigid conventions of drama that had preceded him, explored new territory in his quest for a distinctive form and style, created characters as unforgettable as those of Charles Dickens, Nathaniel Hawthorne, or William Faulkner, and lifted the language of the modern stage to a poetic level unmatched in his time.

MEDIA ADAPTATIONS: "The Roman Spring of Mrs. Stone" was filmed by Warner Bros. in 1961; "Sweet Bird of Youth" was filmed in 1962; "Period of Adjustment" was filmed in 1962; "This Property Is Condemned" was filmed by Paramount in 1966; "I Can't Imagine Tomorrow" and "Talk to Me Like the Rain and Let Me Listen" were televised together under the title "Dragon Country," December 3, 1970, by New York Television Theatre; an adaptation of "The Seven Descents of Myrtle" was filmed by Warner Bros. in 1970 under the title, "The Last of the Mobile Hot-Shots"; *Summer and Smoke: Opera in Two Acts,* Belwin-Mills, 1972, was adapted from Williams's play, with music by Lee Hoiby and libretto by Lanford Wilson; "The Glass Menagerie" was filmed by Burt Harris for Cineplex Odeon in 1987; "A Streetcar Named Desire" was filmed for television in 1984 and broadcast on ABC-TV; "Cat on a Hot Tin Roof" was filmed for television in 1984 by International TV Group; "Summer and Smoke" was filmed for television in 1989 and broadcast on NBC-TV.

BIOGRAPHICAL/CRITICAL SOURCES:

BOOKS

Atkinson, Brooks, *Broadway,* revised edition, Macmillan, 1974.
Authors in the News, Gale, Volume 1, 1976, Volume 2, 1976.
Bentley, Eric, *What Is Theatre?,* Atheneum, 1968.
Bernstein, Samuel J., *The Strands Entwined: A New Direction in American Drama,* Northeastern University Press, 1980.
Bigsby, C. W. E., *Confrontation and Commitment: A Study of Contemporary American Drama 1959-66,* University of Missouri Press, 1968.
Bigsby, C. W. E., *A Critical Introduction to Twentieth-Century American Drama,* three volumes, Cambridge University Press, 1985.
Broussard, Louis, *American Drama: Contemporary Allegory from Eugene O'Neill to Tennessee Williams,* University of Oklahoma Press, 1962.
Brustein, Robert, *Seasons of Discontent: Dramatic Opinions 1959-1965,* Simon & Schuster, 1965.
Brustein, Robert, *Critical Moments: Reflections on Theatre and Society, 1973 1979,* Random House, 1980.
Cohn, Ruby, *Dialogue in American Drama,* Indiana University Press, 1971.
Concise Dictionary of American Literary Biography, 1941-1968, Gale,
Contemporary Literary Criticism, Gale, Volume 1, 1973, Volume 2, 1974, Volume 5, 1976, Volume 7, 1977, Volume 8, 1978, Volume 11, 1979, Volume 15, 1980, Volume 19, 1981, Volume 30, 1984, Volume 39, 1986, Volume 45, 1987.
Devlin, Albert J., editor, *Conversations with Tennessee Williams,* University Press of Mississippi, 1986.
Dickinson, Hugh, *Myth on the Modern Stage,* University of Illinois Press, 1969.

Dictionary of Literary Biography, Volume 7: *Twentieth-Century American Dramatists,* Gale, 1981.

Dictionary of Literary Biography Documentary Series, Volume 4, Gale, 1984.

Dictionary of Literary Biography Yearbook: 1983, Gale, 1984.

Donahue, Francis, *The Dramatic World of Tennessee Williams,* Ungar, 1964.

Downer, Alan S., *Fifty Years of American Drama 1900-1950,* Regnery, 1951.

Falk, Signi, *Tennessee Williams,* 2nd edition, Twayne, 1978.

Ganz, Arthur, *Realms of the Self: Variations on a Theme in Modern Drama,* New York University Press, 1980.

Gassner, John, *Theatre at the Crossroads: Plays and Playwrights of the Mid-Century American Stage,* Holt, 1960.

Gassner, John, *Directions in Modern Theatre and Drama,* Holt, 1966.

Gilman, Richard, *Common and Uncommon Masks: Writings on Theatre, 1961-1970,* Random House, 1971.

Gould, Jean, *Modern American Playwrights,* Dodd, 1966.

Gunn, Drewey Wayne, *Tennessee Williams: A Bibliography,* Scarecrow, 1980.

Heilman, Robert Bechtold, *Tragedy and Melodrama: Versions of Experience,* University of Washington Press, 1968.

Herron, Ima Honaker, *The Small Town in American Drama,* Southern Methodist University Press, 1969.

Kerr, Walter, *The Theatre in Spite of Itself,* Simon & Schuster, 1963.

Kerr, Walter, *Journey to the Center of Theatre,* Knopf, 1979.

Langer, Lawrence, *The Magic Curtain,* Dutton, 1951.

Laughlin, James, editor, *Five Young American Poets,* New Directions, 1944.

Leavitt, Richard F., editor, *The World of Tennessee Williams,* Putnam, 1978.

Lewis, Allan, *American Plays and Playwrights of the Contemporary Theatre,* Crown, 1965.

Little, Stuart W. and Arthur Cantor, *The Playmakers,* Norton, 1970.

Logan, Joshua, *Josh: My Up and Down, In and Out Life,* Delacorte, 1976.

Londre, Felicia Hardison, *Tennessee Williams,* Ungar, 1979.

Lumley, Frederick, *New Trends in Twentieth Century Drama: A Survey since Ibsen and Shaw,* Oxford University Press, 1967.

Maxwell, Gilbert, *Tennessee Williams and Friends: An Informal Biography,* World, 1965.

McCann, John S., *The Critical Reputation of Tennessee Williams: A Reference Guide,* G. K. Hall, 1983.

McCarthy, Mary, *Theatre Chronicles: 1937-1962,* Farrar, Straus, 1963.

Miller, Arthur, *The Theatre Essays of Tennessee Williams,* edited by Robert A. Martin, Penguin, 1978.

Nathan, George Jean, *The Theatre Book of the Year,* Knopf, *1947-1948,* 1948, *1948-1949,* Knopf, 1949.

Phillips, Gene D., *The Films of Tennessee Williams,* Art Alliance Press, 1980.

Porter, Thomas E., *Myth and Modern American Drama,* Wayne State University Press, 1969.

Rabkin, Gerald, *Drama and Commitment: Politics in the American Theatre of the Thirties,* Indiana University Press, 1964.

Rasky, Harry, *Tennessee Williams: A Portrait in Laughter and Lamentation,* Dodd, 1986.

Simon, John, *Acid Test,* Stein & Day, 1963.

Spoto, Donald, *The Kindness of Strangers: The Life of Tennessee Williams,* Little, Brown, 1985.

Steen, Mike, *A Look at Tennessee Williams,* Hawthorne, 1969.

Styan, J. L., *Modern Drama in Theory and Practice,* Volume 1, Cambridge University Press, 1981.

Tharpe, Jac, editor, *Tennessee Williams: A Tribute,* University Press of Mississippi, 1977.

Tischler, Nancy M., *Tennessee Williams: Rebellious Puritan,* Citadel, 1961.

Tynan, Kenneth, *Curtains,* Atheneum, 1961.

Weales, Gerald, *American Drama since World War II,* Harcourt, 1962.

Williams, Dakin, and Shepherd Mead, *Tennessee Williams: An Intimate Biography,* Arbor, 1983.

Williams, Edwina Dakin, as told to Lucy Freeman, *Remember Me to Tom,* Putnam, 1963.

Williams, Tennessee, *The Glass Menagerie,* Random House, 1945, published as *The Glass Menagerie: Play in Two Acts,* Dramatists Play Service, 1948.

Williams, Tennessee, *The Roman Spring of Mrs. Stone,* New Directions, 1950.

Williams, Tennessee, *Camino Real: A Play,* edition with foreword and afterword by Williams, New Directions, 1953.

Williams, Tennessee, *Cat on a Hot Tin Roof,* edition with preface by Williams, New Directions, 1955, published as *Cat on a Hot Tin Roof: A Play in Three Acts,* Dramatists Play Service, 1958.

Williams, Tennessee, *In the Winter of Cities,* New Directions, 1956.

Williams, Tennessee, *Orpheus Descending: A Play in Three Acts* New Directions, 1959.

Williams, Tennessee, *The Theatre of Tennessee Williams,* New Directions, Volume 1, 1971, Volume 2, 1971, Volume 3, 1971, Volume 4, 1972, Volume 5, 1976, Volume 6, 1981, Volume 7, 1981.

Williams, Tennessee, *Memoirs,* Doubleday, 1975.

Williams, Tennessee, *Moise and the World of Reason,* Simon & Schuster, 1975.

Williams, Tennessee, *Androgyne, Mon Amour: Poems by Tennessee Williams,* New Directions, 1977.

Williams, Tennessee, *Tennessee Williams' Letters to Donald Windham: 1940-1965,* edited by Windham, Holt, 1977.

Williams, Tennessee, *Where I Live: Selected Essays,* edited by C. Day and B. Wood, New Directions, 1978.

Williams, Tennessee, *Tennessee Williams: Eight Plays,* introduction by Harold Clurman, Doubleday, 1979.

Williams, Tennessee, *Stopped Rocking and Other Screenplays,* New Directions, 1984.

Williams, Tennessee, *Collected Stories,* New Directions, 1985.

Windham, Donald, *Lost Friendships: A Memoir of Truman Capote, Tennessee Williams, and Others,* Morrow, 1987.

Yacowar, Maurice, *Tennessee Williams and Film,* Ungar, 1977.

PERIODICALS

After Dark, August, 1971.

Atlantic, November, 1970.

Esquire, November, 1969, September, 1971.

Modern Drama, Volume 2, 1959, Volume 15, 1972.

Nation, Volume 165, 1947.

New Republic, Volume 112, 1945.

New York, March 14, 1983.

New York Post (interviews), April 21-May 4, 1958.

New York Times, May 1, 1960, March 28, 1965, November 3, 1975.

Playboy, April, 1973.

Quarterly Journal of Speech, Volume 61, 1975.

Renascence, Volume 28, 1976.

Reporter, Volume 12, 1955.

Southern Review, summer, 1979.
Tennessee Studies in Literature, Volume 10, 1965.
Theatre Arts, January, 1962.
Washington Post, April 4, 1979.
Western Humanities Review, Volume 18, 1964.

OBITUARIES:

PERIODICALS

Chicago Tribune, February 26, 1983, February 27, 1983.
Los Angeles Times, February 26, 1983.
Newsweek, March 7, 1983.
New York Times, February 26, 1983.
Time, March 7, 1983.
Times (London), February 26, 1983.
Washington Post, February 26, 1983.

* * *

WILLIAMS, William C.
 See WILLIAMS, William Carlos

* * *

WILLIAMS, William Carlos   1883-1963
 (William C. Williams)

PERSONAL: Born September 17, 1883, in Rutherford, N.J.; died March 4, 1963, in Rutherford; son of William George (in business) and Raquel Helene (Hoheb) Williams; married Florence Herman, December 12, 1912; children: William, Eric, Paul Herman. *Education:* University of Pennsylvania, M.D., 1906; postgraduate study at University of Leipzig, 1909-10.

CAREER: Poet, playwright, novelist, essayist, and physician. French Hospital and Nursery and Child's Hospital, New York, N.Y., intern, 1906-09; private medical practice in Rutherford, N.J., 1910-51. Visiting professor of English at University of Washington, Seattle, 1948.

MEMBER: American Academy of Arts and Letters, National Institute of Arts and Letters, Academy of American Poets, Bergen County (N.J.) Medical Association.

AWARDS, HONORS: Dial Award, 1926, for distinguished service to American literature; Guarantors Prize from *Poetry,* 1931; LL.D. from University of Buffalo, 1946, and Fairleigh Dickinson University, 1959; Russell Loines Memorial Award for poetry from National Institute of Arts and Letters, 1948; Litt.D. from Rutgers University, 1948, Bard College, 1948, and University of Pennsylvania, 1952; appointed to chair of poetry at Library of Congress, 1949 (appointment withdrawn, but subsequently renewed); National Book Award for poetry, 1950, for *Selected Poems* and *Paterson,* Book III; Bollingen Prize in poetry from Yale University Library, 1952; Levinson Prize, 1954, and Oscar Blumenthal Prize, 1955, both for poems published in *Poetry;* Academy of American Poets fellowship, 1956; Brandeis University creative arts medal in poetry-fiction-nonfiction, 1957-58, in recognition of a lifetime of distinguished achievement; Pulitzer Prize in poetry for *Pictures From Brueghel* and American Academy of Arts and Letters gold medal for poetry from National Institute of Arts and Letters, both 1963.

WRITINGS:

POEMS

(Under name William C. Williams) *Poems,* privately printed, 1909.

The Tempers, Elkin Matthews, 1913.
Al Que Quiere!, Four Seas, 1917.
Kora in Hell: Improvisations, Four Seas, 1920, reprinted, Kraus Reprint, 1973 (also see below).
Sour Grapes, Four Seas, 1921.
Go Go, Monroe Wheeler, 1923.
Spring and All, Contact Publishing, 1923, reprinted, Frontier Press, 1970 (also see below).
The Cod Head, Harvest Press, 1932.
Collected Poems, 1921-1931, preface by Wallace Stevens, Objectivist Press, 1934.
An Early Martyr and Other Poems, Alcestis Press, 1935.
Adam & Eve & The City, Alcestis Press, 1936.
The Complete Collected Poems of William Carlos Williams, 1906-1938, New Directions, 1938.
The Broken Span, New Directions, 1941.
The Wedge, Cummington Press (Cummington, Mass.), 1944.
Paterson, New Directions, Book I, 1946, Book II, 1948, Book III, 1949, Book IV, 1951, Book V, 1958, Books I-V published in one volume, 1963.
The Clouds, Wells College Press and Cummington Press, 1948.
Selected Poems, introduction by Randall Jarrell, New Directions, 1949, revised edition, 1968.
The Pink Church, Golden Goose Press, 1949.
The Collected Later Poems, New Directions, 1950, revised edition, 1963.
Collected Earlier Poems, New Directions, 1951, revised edition, 1966.
The Desert Music and Other Poems, Random House, 1954 (also see below).
Journey to Love, Random House, 1955.
"The Lost Poems of William Carlos Williams or The Past Recaptured," collected by John C. Thirlwall, published in *New Directions 16,* New Directions, 1957.
Pictures From Brueghel and Other Poems, New Directions, 1962.
Selected Poems, introduction by Charles Tomlinson, Penguin, 1976.
Collected Poems: Volume 1, 1909-1939, edited by A. Walton Litz and Christopher MacGowan, Carcanet, 1988, *Volume 2, 1939-1962,* edited by MacGowan, 1989.

OTHER

The Great American Novel, Three Mountains Press, 1923, reprinted, Folcroft, 1973.
In the American Grain (essays), A. & C. Boni, 1925, reprinted with introduction by Horace Gregory, New Directions, 1967.
A Voyage to Pagany (novel), Macaulay, 1928, reprinted, New Directions, 1970.
(Translator) Philippe Soupault, *Last Nights of Paris,* Macaulay, 1929, reprinted, Full Court Press, 1982.
The Knife of the Times and Other Stories (short stories), Dragon Press, 1932, reprinted, Folcroft, 1974.
A Novelette and Other Prose, TO Publishers, 1932.
"The First President" (three-act libretto for an opera), published in *American Caravan,* 1936.
White Mule (novel), New Directions, 1937, reprinted, 1967.
Life Along the Passaic River (short stories), New Directions, 1938.
In the Money (novel), New Directions, 1940, reprinted, 1967.
A Dream of Love (three-act play), New Directions, 1948.
A Beginning on the Short Story: Notes, Alicat Bookshop Press, 1950, reprinted, Norwood, 1978.
Make Light of It: Collected Stories, Random House, 1950.

Autobiography, Random House, 1951, published as *The Autobiography of William Carlos Williams,* New Directions, 1967.

The Build-Up (novel), Random House, 1952.

(Translator with mother, Raquel Helene Williams) Pedro Espinosa, *A Dog and the Fever* (novella), Shoe String Press, 1954.

Selected Essays, Random House, 1954.

The Selected Letters of William Carlos Williams, edited by John C. Thirlwall, McDowell, Obolensky, 1957.

I Wanted to Write a Poem: The Autobiography of the Works of a Poet, edited by Edith Heal, Beacon Press, 1958.

Yes, Mrs. Williams: A Personal Record of My Mother, McDowell, Obolensky, 1959.

Many Loves and Other Plays: The Collected Plays of William Carlos Williams, New Directions, 1961.

The Farmers' Daughters: Collected Stories, introduction by Van Wyck Brooks, New Directions, 1961.

The William Carlos Williams Reader, edited and introduced by M. L. Rosenthal, New Directions, 1966.

Imaginations, edited by Webster Schott, New Directions, 1970.

The Embodiment of Knowledge (philosophy), edited by Ron Loewinsohn, New Directions, 1974.

Interviews With William Carlos Williams: "Speaking Straight Ahead," edited and introduced by Linda Welshimer Wagner, New Directions, 1976.

A Recognizable Image: William Carlos Williams on Art and Artists, edited by Bram Dijkstra, New Directions, 1978.

William Carlos Williams: The Doctor Stories, compiled with an introduction by Robert Coles, New Directions, 1984.

Contributor to numerous literary magazines and journals, including *Poetry, The Dial, Origin, Blast, Pagany, Little Review, New Masses, Partisan Review,* and *Glebe.* Contributing editor of literary magazines and journals, including *Contact I,* 1920-23, and *Contact II,* 1932.

SIDELIGHTS: William Carlos Williams was an experimenter, an innovator, a revolutionary figure in American poetry. Yet, Williams lived a remarkably conventional life. A doctor for more than forty years serving the New Jersey town of Rutherford, he relied on his patients, the America around him, and his own ebullient imagination to create a distinctively American verse. Often domestic in focus and "remarkable for its empathy, sympathy, its muscular and emotional identification with its subjects," Williams's poetry is also characteristically honest: "There is no optimistic blindness in Williams," wrote Randall Jarrell, "though there is a fresh gaiety, a stubborn or invincible joyousness." It was while a medical student at the University of Pennsylvania that Williams first met fellow student Ezra Pound. Although he loved literature—especially the works of Keats and Whitman—and harbored dreams of becoming a writer himself, Williams' friendship with Pound marked a watershed in the young poet's life: he later insisted, "before meeting Pound is like B.C. and A.D." "Under Pound's influence and other stimuli," reported John Malcolm Brinnin, "Williams was soon ready to close the door on the 'studied elegance of Keats on one hand and the raw vigor of Whitman on the other.' " Pound also introduced Williams to a group of friends, including poet Hilda Doolittle (H.D.) and painter Charles Demuth, "who shared the kinds of feelings that in Rutherford had made him frightened and isolated," Breslin declared. H.D., for example, with her arty dress and her peculiarities—sometimes she'd splash ink onto her clothes "to give her a feeling of freedom and indifference towards the mere means of writing"—fascinated Williams with a "provocative indifference to rule and order which I liked."

In a similar way, it was a reaction against the rigid and ordered poetry of the time that led Williams to join Pound, H.D., and others as the core of what became known as the Imagist movement. The Imagists broke from what they saw as formulaic poetry by stressing a verse of "swift, uncluttered, functional phrasing," wrote David Perkins. In Williams's second book, *The Tempers* (1913), as Bernard Duffey realized, Williams's "style was directed by an Imagist feeling, though it still depended on romantic and poeticized allusiveness." And while Pound drifted towards increased allusiveness in his work, Williams stuck with Pound's tenet to "make it new." By 1917 and the publication of his third book, *Al Que Quiere!,* "Williams began to apply the Imagist principle of 'direct treatment of the thing' fairly rigorously," declared James Guimond. Also at this time, as Perkins demonstrated, Williams was "beginning to stress that poetry must find its 'primary impetus' . . . in 'local conditions.' " "I was determined to use the material I knew," Williams later reflected; and as a doctor, Williams knew intimately the people of Rutherford.

Throughout his forty years of private practice in Rutherford, Williams heard the "inarticulate poems" of his patients. As a doctor, his "medical badge," as he called it, permitted him "to follow the poor defeated body into those gulfs and grottos . . ., to be present at deaths and births, at the tormented battles between daughter and diabolic mother." From these moments, poetry developed: "it has fluttered before me for a moment, a phrase which I quickly write down on anything at hand, any piece of paper I can grab." Some of his poems were born on prescription blanks, others typed in a few spare minutes between patient visits. Williams's work, however, did more than fuel his poetry: it allowed him "to write what he chose, free from any kind of financial or political pressure. From the beginning," disclosed Linda Wagner, "he understood the tradeoffs: he would have less time to write; he would need more physical stamina than people with only one occupation." There is little doubt that he succeeded in both occupations: Richard Ellman and Robert O'Clair called him "the most important literary doctor since Chekov."

Corresponding with Williams's attraction to the locale was his lifelong quest to have poetry mirror the speech of the American people. Williams sought a "language modified by our environment, the American environment." Marc Hofstadter explained: "Thinking of himself as a local poet who possessed neither the high culture nor the old-world manners of an Eliot or Pound, he sought to express his democracy through his way of speaking. . . . His point was to speak on an equal level with the reader, and to use the language and thought materials of America in expressing his point of view."

While Williams continued with his innovations in the American idiom and his experiments in form, he fell out of favor with some of his own contemporaries. *Kora in Hell: Improvisations,* for example, suffered some stinging attacks. For a year Williams had made a habit of recording something—anything—in his notebooks every night, and followed these jottings with a comment. One of "Williams's own favorite books . . ., the prose poetry of *Kora* is an extraordinary combination of aphorism, romanticism, philosophizing, obscurity, obsession, exhortation, reverie, beautiful lines and scary paragraphs," wrote Webster Schott. Yet, as Hugh Fox reported, few peers shared Williams's enthusiasm for the book. Pound called it "incoherent" and "un-American"; H.D. objected to its "flippancies," its "self-mockery," its "unseriousness"; and Wallace Stevens complained about Williams's "tantrums." Surrounded by criticism, Williams became increasingly defensive during this time.

What Williams did not foresee, however, was the "atom bomb" on modern poetry—T. S. Eliot's *The Waste Land.* Williams had no quarrel with Eliot's genius—he said Eliot was writing poems as good as Keats's "Ode to a Nightingale"—but, simply, "we were breaking the rules, whereas he was conforming to the excellencies of classroom English." As he explained in his *Autobiography,* "I felt at once that it had set me back twenty years and I'm sure it did. Critically, Eliot returned us to the classroom just at the moment when I felt we were on a point to escape to matters much closer to the essence of a new art form itself—rooted in the locality which should give it fruit." Not only did Williams feel threatened by Eliot's success, but also by the attention *The Waste Land* received. As Karl Shapiro pointed out, "he was left high and dry: Pound, who was virtually the co-author of Eliot's poems, and Marianne Moore were now polarized to Eliot. Williams felt this and would feel it for another twenty years. His own poetry would have to progress against the growing orthodoxy of Eliot criticism." But while the Eliot wave undoubtedly sunk his spirits, at the same time it buoyed his determination: "It was a shock to me that he was so tremendously successful," Williams admitted. "My contemporaries flocked to him—away from what I wanted. It forced me to be successful."

According to Breslin, *The Waste Land* was one of the "major influence[s] on that remarkable volume," Williams's next book, *Spring and All.* The last in a decade of experimental poetry, *Spring and All* viewed the same American landscape as did Eliot but interpreted it differently. Williams "saw his poetic task was to affirm the self-reliant, sympathetic consciousness of Whitman in a broken industrialized world," Stauffer noted. "But unlike Eliot, who responded negatively to the harsh realities of this world, Williams saw his task as breaking through restrictions and generating new growth."

Just as meeting Pound had measurably affected Williams's early life, the appearance of Eliot's *The Waste Land* marked important changes in his mid-career. Though some of Williams's finest poetry appeared in the 1923 *Spring and All,* he did not release another book of poems for nearly ten years. "One reason," speculated Rod Townley, "was probably Eliot's success. Another may have been his own success, known only to a few, in *Spring and All.* For decades thereafter he could not outdo himself; some think he never did." Instead, Williams wrote prose. And in it he concentrated on one subject in particular: America.

Williams explained his attraction towards America in a 1939 letter to Horace Gregory: "Of mixed ancestry I felt from earliest childhood that America was the only home I could ever possibly call my own. I felt that it was expressedly founded for me, personally, and that it must be my first business in life to possess it." He later echoed this sentiment in his preface to *Selected Essays.* "I loved my father but never forgave him for remaining, in spite of everything, a British subject," Williams admitted. "It had much to do with my sometimes violent partisanship towards America." As a result of such feelings, reasoned Vivienne Koch, "the logic of Williams' allegiance to the quest for a knowledge of localism, for a defining of the American grain, has compelled in his fiction a restriction to American materials."

So, in *In the American Grain,* Williams tried "to find out for myself what the land of my more or less accidental birth might signify" by examining the "original records" of "some of the American founders." In its treatment of the makers of American history, ranging from Columbus to Lincoln, *In the American Grain* has impressed many as Williams's most succinct definition of America and its people. D. H. Lawrence, for example, learned from Williams that "there are two ways of being American, and

the chief . . . is by recoiling into individual smallness and insentience, and gutting the great continent in frenzies of mean fear. It is the Puritan way. The other is by touch; touch America as she is; dare to touch her! And this is the heroic way."

Williams's novel trilogy, *White Mule, In the Money,* and *The Build-Up,* also focused on America, and on his wife's family in particular. He first conceived the idea for *White Mule* because he wanted to write about a baby—he delivered more than two thousand in his career—and had heard stories of Floss's babyhood. But beyond the story of the infant Floss Stecher is the story of her infant American family, immigrants growing toward success in America. Philip Rahv gave this description of Joe and Gurlie Stecher: "Gurlie is so rife with the natural humors of a wife that she emerges as a veritable goddess of the home, but since it is an American home she is constantly urging her husband to get into the game, beat the other fellow, and make money. Joe's principal motivation, however, is his pride of workmanship; he is the pure artisan, the man who has not yet been alienated from the product of his labor and who thinks of money as the reward of labor and nothing else." In *In the Money* Williams follows Joe as he establishes his own printing business and moves to the suburbs, making way for the picture of middle-class life he presents in *The Build-Up.* W. T. Schott gave these examples of Williams's focus: "The stolid admirable Joe, the arrogant Gurlie on her upward march in society, a neighbor woman ranting her spitefulness, . . . Flossie and her sister at their little-girl wrangling over bathroom privileges." Reed Whittemore felt that such moments reveal Williams's fond tolerance of middle-class life. *The Build-Up* does have its "tough sections," Whittemore admitted, but "its placidness is striking for a book written by a long-time literary dissenter. What it is is a book of complacent reflection written from inside apple-pie America. It has not the flavor of the letters of the real young doctor-poet sitting in his emptiness forty years earlier in Leipzig. . . . Between 1909, then, and the time of the writing of *The Build-Up* WCW was *taken* inside, and found that with reservations he liked it there."

During the time the trilogy was being published, Williams also labored over a massive work of poetry, *Paterson,* which was meant to further examine the American way of life. Though some dismiss the "epic" label often attached to the five-book poem, Williams's intentions were certainly beyond the ordinary. His devotion to understanding his country, its people, its language—"the whole knowable world about me"—found expression in the poem's central image, defined by Whittemore as "the image of the city as a man, a man lying on his side peopling the place with his thoughts." With roots in his 1926 poem "Paterson," Williams took the city as "my 'case' to work up. It called for a poetry such as I did not know, it was my duty to discover or make such a context on the 'thought.' "

In his prefatory notes to the original four-book *Paterson,* Williams explained "that a man himself is a city, beginning, seeking, achieving and concluding his life in ways which the various aspects of a city may embody—if imaginatively conceived—any city, all the details of which may be made to voice his most intimate convictions." A. M. Sullivan outlined why Williams chose Paterson, New Jersey: It was once "the prototype of the American industrial community . . . the self-sustaining city of skills with the competitive energy and moral stamina to lift the burdens of the citizen and raise the livelihood with social and cultural benefits." One hundred years later, continued Sullivan, "Williams saw the Hamilton concept [of 'The Society of Useful Manufacturers'] realized, but with mixed results of success and misery. The poet of Paterson understood the validity of the hopes of Hamilton but also recognized that the city slum could be the price of progress in a mechanized society." The world Williams chose to explore in this poem about "the myth of American power," added James Guimond, was one where "this power is almost entirely evil, the destructive producer of an America grown pathetic and tragic, brutalized by inequality, disorganized by industrial chaos, and faced with annihilation."

Williams revealed "the elemental character of the place" in Book I. The time is spring, the season of creativity, and Paterson is struck by the desire to express his "immediate locality" clearly, observed Guimond. The process is a struggle: to know the world about him Paterson must face both the beauty of the Passaic Falls and the poverty of the region. In Book II, said Williams, Paterson moves from a description of "the elemental character" of the city to its "modern replicas." Or, as Guimond pointed out, from the "aesthetic world" to the "real material world where he must accomplish the poet's task as defined in Book I—the invention of a language for his locality. . . . The breakdown of the poet's communication with his world is a disaster," both for himself and for others. Williams himself, on the other hand, made his own advance in communication in Book II, a "milestone" in his development as a poet. A passage in Section 3, beginning "The descent beckons . . .," "brought about—without realizing it at the time—my final conception of what my own poetry should be." The segment is one of the earliest examples of Williams's innovative method of line division, the "variable foot."

To invent the new language, Paterson must first "descend from the erudition and fastidiousness that made him impotent in Book II," summarized Guimond. As Paterson reads—and reflects—in a library, he accepts the destruction in Book II, rejects his learning, and realizes "a winter of 'death' must come before spring." Williams believed that "if you are going to write realistically of the concept of filth in the world it can't be pretty." And so, Book IV is the dead season, symbolized by the "river below the falls," the polluted Passaic. But in this destruction, the poet plants some seeds of renewal: a young virtuous nurse; a Paterson poet, Allen Ginsburg, who has promised to give the local new meaning; Madame Curie, "divorced from neither the male nor knowledge." At the conclusion of Book IV, a man, after a long swim, dresses on shore and heads inland—"toward Camden," Williams said, "where Walt Whitman, much traduced, lived the later years of his life and died." These seeds of hope led Breslin to perceive the basic difference between *Paterson* and Williams's long-time nemesis, Eliot's *Waste Land*. " 'The Waste Land' is a kind of anti-epic," Breslin said, "a poem in which the quest for meaning is entirely thwarted and we are left, at the end, waiting for the collapse of Western civilization. *Paterson* is a pre-epic, showing that the process of disintegration releases forces that can build a new world. It confronts, again and, again, the savagery of contemporary society, but still affirms a creative seed. Eliot's end is Williams's beginning."

Williams scrapped his plans for a four-book *Paterson* when he recognized not only the changes in the world, but "that there can be no end to such a story I have envisioned with the terms which I have laid down for myself." To Babette Deutsch, Book V "is clearly not something added on, like a new wing built to extend a house, but something that grew, as naturally as a green branch stemming from a sturdy ole tree. . . . This is inevitably a work that reviews the past, but it is also one that stands firmly in the present and looks toward the future. . . . 'Paterson Five' is eloquent of a vitality that old age cannot quench. Its finest passages communicate Dr. Williams's perennial delight in walking in the world." Book VI was in the planning stages at the time of Williams's death.

While Williams himself declared that he had received some "gratifying" compliments about *Paterson,* Breslin reported "reception of the poem never exactly realized his hopes for it." *Paterson*'s mosaic structure, its subject matter, and its alternating passages of poetry and prose helped fuel criticism about its difficulty and its looseness of organization. In the process of calling *Paterson* an " 'Ars Poetica' for contemporary America," Dudley Fitts complained, "it is a pity that those who might benefit most from it will inevitably be put off by its obscurities and difficulties." Breslin, meanwhile, accounted for the poem's obliqueness by saying, "*Paterson* has a thickness of texture, a multi-dimensional quality that makes reading it a difficult but intense experience."

Paterson did help bring Williams some of the attention he had been missing for many years. One honor came in 1949 when he was invited to become consultant to the Library of Congress. At first Williams refused the appointment because of poor health, but decided in 1952 that he was ready to assume the post. Unfortunately for Williams, the Library of Congress was told of his "Communist" affiliations and suddenly backed off from the appointment. After several excuses and postponements, some made, ostensibly, out of a concern for Williams's health, Librarian Luther Evans wrote, "I accordingly hereby revoke the offer of appointment heretofore made to you." A few months before the term was to have ended, Williams learned that the appointment had been renewed. The Library of Congress, however, made no offer to extend the appointment through the following year.

While Williams had his troubles with the literary establishment, he fared well with a whole generation of poets who adopted him as their father in poetry. "*Paterson* is our *Leaves of Grass,*" announced Robert Lowell. "The times have changed." And indeed they had. The dominant school of poetry, the academic school of Eliot and Allen Tate, was giving way to what Whittemore called the fifties' "Revolution of the Word." Such poets as Lowell, Allen Ginsburg, Charles Olson, Denise Levertov, Robert Creely, and Cid Corman found in Williams an alternative to the academics. As Bruce Cook explained, Williams "withstood the influence of Eliot, ignored the New Critics and the academic poets who followed their lead, and simply went his own way, his lines growing shorter, more austere, more pointed with each poem." With this style, reported James Dickey, he appealed to many aspiring writers who looked at his work and said, "Well if *that's* poetry, I believe I might be able to write it too!"

Williams's health deteriorated in the late 1940s when he suffered the first of several heart attacks and strokes which would plague him for the rest of his life. And though Williams later complained of the effects of a particularly serious stroke (1952)—"That was the end. I was through with life"—his devotion to poetry did not suffer. Breslin reported that after retiring from medicine in 1951, and after recuperating from a stroke, Williams spoke "optimistically of the 'opportunity for thought' and reading afforded by his new idleness." Hofstadter pointed out that "death was a major focus of this reflectiveness," and explained how Williams reflected his concerns in his poetry: "In the face of death what Williams seeks is renewal—not a liberation toward another world but an intensified return to this one. Revitalization both of one's inner energies and of one's contact with the outside world, renewal is the product of two forces: love and the imagination. . . . Love and imagination are the essence of life. He who loses them is as good as dead."

Williams explored the theme of renewed love in two particular later works, the play, "A Dream of Love," and the poem, "Asphodel, That Greeny Flower." In "A Dream of Love" the protagonist has an affair with his secretary and confesses to his wife that he did it only to "renew our love." The explanation fails to convince her. Thus, Williams dramatizes his belief in the "conflict between the male's need for emotional renewal in love and the female's need for constancy in love," explained Guimond. According to Thomas Whitaker, " 'A Dream of Love' points to an actuality that Williams at this time could not fully face but that he would learn to face—most noticeably in 'Asphodel, That Greeny Flower.' " In this "elegiac epithalamian," Williams confesses his infidelities to his wife and asks for her forgiveness; "he seeks new life on the very edge of death," said Whitaker. While Williams proclaimed his life as a husband in his love poem, his strength as a poet was evident, too: "Asphodel" received some very complimentary reviews, including W. H. Auden's praise as "one of the most beautiful poems in the language."

Williams's weakened physical powers, apparently, strengthened his creative ones. "I think he did much better work after the stroke slowed him down," reflected Flossie. Stanley Koehler agreed. *The Desert Music* and *Journey to Love,* he said, "were written in an unusual period of recovery of creative power after Dr. Williams's first serious illness in 1952." Aside from featuring the variable foot and such outstanding poems as "Asphodel," these two books impressed readers as the mature work of a poet very much in control of his life and craft. *Desert Music* reviewer Kenneth Rexroth called the title poem "an explicit statement of the irreducible humaneness of the human being." The book's ideas are simple, indisputable, presented with calm maturity," continued Rexroth. "I prophesy that from now on, as Williams grows older, he will rise as far above his contemporaries as Yeats did in his later years." The love poems of *Journey to Love* were no less impressive to Babette Deutsch. "The poet gives us vignettes of the daily scene, notations on the arts, affirmations of a faith no less sublime for being secular, in the language, the rhythms, that he has made his own," reported Deutsch. "The pages bear the indelible signature of his honesty, his compassion, his courage." Finally, to highlight a decade of productivity, Williams's last book, *Pictures From Brueghel,* won a Pulitzer Prize in 1963.

Despite his failing health, Williams lived as productively as possible throughout his later years. He traveled, gave lectures, and entertained writers in the same home that had been visited by members of the Imagist movement more than forty years earlier. Williams wrote, too—poetry, of course, as well as essays and short stories. He continued to cooperate with writers interested in him and his work: John Thirlwall worked with him in the publication of *Selected Letters* and a series of discussions with Edith Heal became the "autobiography" of his works, *I Wanted to Write a Poem.* A partially paralyzing stroke in 1958 and a 1959 cancer operation, however, stole much of his remaining energy and capabilities. No longer able to read, by the end of the decade he depended on Floss to read to him, often as long as four hours a day. A particularly painful view of the aging Williams appeared in his 1962 interview with Stanley Koehler for the *Paris Review.* "The effort it took the poet to find and pronounce words can hardly be indicated here," reported Koehler. Continued failing health further slowed Williams until, on March 4, 1963, he died in his sleep.

BIOGRAPHICAL/CRITICAL SOURCES:

BOOKS

Angoff, Charles, editor, *William Carlos Williams* (papers by four critics), Fairleigh Dickinson University Press, 1974.

Breslin, James E., *William Carlos Williams: An American Artist,* Oxford University Press, 1970.

Brinnin, John Malcolm, *William Carlos Williams,* University of Minnesota Press, 1963.

Concise Dictionary of American Literary Biography: The Twenties, 1917-1929, Gale, 1989.

Contemporary Literary Criticism, Gale, Volume 1, 1973, Volume 2, 1974, Volume 5, 1976, Volume 9, 1978, Volume 13, 1980, Volume 22, 1982, Volume 42, 1987.

Cook, Bruce, *The Best Generation,* Scribner's, 1971.

Deutsch, Babette, *Poetry in Our Time,* Holt, 1952.

Dickey, James, *Babel to Byzantium,* Farrar, Straus, 1968.

Dictionary of Literary Biography, Gale, Volume 4: *American Writers in Paris, 1920-1939,* 1980, Volume 16: *The Beats: Literary Bohemians in Postwar America,* 1983, Volume 54: *American Poets, 1880-1945, Third Series,* 1987.

Ellman, Richard and Robert O'Clair, editors, *The Norton Anthology of Modern Poetry,* Norton, 1973.

Guimond, James, *The Art of William Carlos Williams: A Discovery and Possession of America,* University of Illinois Press, 1968.

Jarrell, Randall, *Poetry and the Age,* Knopf-Vintage, 1953.

Jarrell, *The Third Book of Criticism,* Farrar, Straus, 1969.

Koch, Vivienne, *William Carlos Williams,* New Directions, 1950.

Malkoff, Karl, *Escape From the Self: A Study in Contemporary Poetry and Poetics,* Columbia University Press, 1977.

Miller, J. Hillis, editor, *William Carlos Williams: A Collection of Critical Essays,* Prentice-Hall, 1966.

Owen, Guy, editor, *Modern American Poetry: Essays in Criticism,* Everett/Edwards, 1972.

Perkins, David, *A History of Modern Poetry: From the 1890's to the High Modernist Mode,* Harvard University Press, 1976.

Peterson, Walter S., *An Approach to "Paterson,"* Yale University Press, 1967.

Rexroth, Kenneth, *American Poetry in the Twentieth Century,* Herder, 1971.

Rosenthal, M. L., *The Modern Poets: A Critical Introduction,* Oxford University Press, 1960.

Shapiro, Karl, *In Defense of Ignorance,* Random House, 1960.

Simpson, Louis, *Three on the Tower: The Lives and Works of Ezra Pound, T. S. Eliot and William Carlos Williams,* Morrow, 1975.

Stauffer, Donald Barlow, *A Short History of American Poetry,* Dutton, 1974.

Ungar, Leonard, editor, *Seven Modern American Poets: An Introduction,* University of Minnesota Press, 1967.

Wagner, Linda Welshimer, editor, *Interviews With William Carlos Williams: "Speaking Straight Ahead,"* New Directions, 1976.

Wagner, *The Poems of William Carlos Williams,* Wesleyan University Press, 1964.

Wagner, *The Prose of William Carlos Williams,* Wesleyan University Press, 1970.

Wagner, *William Carlos Williams: A Reference Guide,* G. K. Hall, 1978.

Whitaker, Thomas R., *William Carlos Williams,* Twayne, 1968.

Whittemore, Reed, *William Carlos Williams: Poet From New Jersey,* Houghton, 1975.

Williams, William Carlos, *The Autobiography of William Carlos Williams,* New Directions, 1967.

Williams, *Imaginations,* edited by Webster Schott, New Directions, 1970.

Williams, *Paterson,* Books I-V, New Directions, 1963.

Williams, *Selected Essays,* Random House, 1954.

Williams, *Selected Letters,* edited by John C. Thirlwall, McDowell, Obolensky, 1957.
Writers at Work: The Paris Review Interviews, third series, introduction by Alfred Kazin, Viking, 1967.

PERIODICALS

Atlantic Monthly, October, 1951, September, 1957, May, 1958, July, 1959.
Briarcliff Quarterly, October, 1946.
Christian Science Monitor, April 10, 1958, November 14 1970.
Commonweal, October 4, 1946, November 7, 1952, December 10, 1954.
Criticism, winter, 1972.
Encounter, December, 1971.
Explicator, fall, 1976.
Hudson Review, winter, 1961-62.
Illustrated London News, March 16, 1963.
Journal of Modern Literature, September, 1976.
Kenyon Review, summer, 1952, spring, 1959.
London Magazine, June/July, 1974.
Los Angeles Times Book Review, October 17, 1982.
Massachusetts Review, winter, 1962.
Modern Poetry Studies, Volume 1, number 6, 1970.
Nation, April 4, 1926, March 28, 1934, June 26, 1937, November 19, 1938, November 23, 1940, April 14, 1945, August 24, 1946, June 19, 1948, July 9, 1949, April 8, 1950, March 3, 1951, August 25, 1951, November 8, 1952, April 24, 1954, January 22, 1955, October 5, 1957, May 31, 1958, November 23, 1970, December 14, 1970, December 11, 1976.
National Review, March 26, 1963.
New Leader, June 9, 1975.
New Republic, March 24, 1926, April 18, 1934, July 15, 1936, July 7, 1937, December 21, 1938, November 18, 1940, February 12, 1945, February 24, 1951, August 27, 1951, February 7, 1955, November 13, 1961, December 20, 1970.
Newsweek, March 16, 1963.
New York Herald Tribune Book Review, June 27, 1948, March 5, 1950, December 3, 1950, December 17, 1950, July 1, 1951, September 16, 1951, November 2, 1952, March 28, 1954, November 7, 1954, November 13, 1955, September 1, 1957, July 6, 1958, September 28, 1958, June 21, 1959.
New York Review of Books, November 13, 1975.
New York Times, February 7, 1926, September 30, 1928, February 18, 1934, November 15, 1936, June 20, 1937, July 23, 1939, November 7, 1954, December 18, 1955, September 1, 1957, April 13, 1958, September 14, 1958, October 25, 1966, October 20, 1984.
New York Times Book Review, June 28, 1959, December 26, 1971, October 5, 1975, September 18, 1983.
Partisan Review, November-December, 1951.
Perspective, autumn-winter, 1953.
Poetry, May, 1934, May, 1936, November, 1936, September, 1939, April, 1945, February, 1947, April, 1949, May, 1952, April, 1954, March, 1955, March, 1956, June, 1958, May, 1959, February, 1964, October, 1967.
Saturday Review, December 19, 1925, May 7, 1932, June 26, 1937, March 19, 1938, February 11, 1939, November 9, 1940, September 25, 1948, October 9, 1948, August 20, 1949, May 20, 1950, December 9, 1950, September 21, 1951, October 20, 1951, March 15, 1952, October 18, 1952, June 5, 1954, November 20, 1954, February 18, 1956, September 7, 1957, October 11, 1958, July 11, 1959, August 1, 1970, November 14, 1970.
Southwest Review, summer, 1974.
Time, December 4, 1950, March 15, 1963, September 21, 1970.

Times Literary Supplement, November 29, 1928, March 23, 1951, February 1, 1952, January 29, 1954, July 29, 1965, February 10, 1966, April 13, 1967, June 22, 1967, April 27, 1984, May 22, 1987, February 19, 1988, May 19, 1989.
Twentieth Century Literature, October, 1975, December, 1977.
Village Voice Literary Supplement, September, 1982.
Western Review, summer, 1953.
Yale Review, spring, 1939, autumn, 1948, spring, 1950, autumn, 1951, winter, 1952, winter, 1955, December, 1957, December, 1958, May, 1959, December, 1961, June, 1970.*

* * *

WILLIAMSON, Henry 1895-1977

PERSONAL: Born December 1, 1895, in Bedfordshire, England; died August 13, 1977, in Berkshire, England; son of William Williamson; married twice (divorced twice); children: seven.

CAREER: Writer, 1921-74. *Weekly Dispatch,* London, England, reporter, 1920-21; served as a broadcaster on farming life in the 1930's and was a farmer in Norfolk. *Military service:* British Army, 1914-20; infantryman and officer.

MEMBER: National Liberal Club, Savage Club, Chelsea Arts Club.

AWARDS, HONORS: Hawthornden Prize, 1928, for *Tarka the Otter.*

WRITINGS:

The Lone Swallows, Collins, 1922, Dutton, 1926, reprinted, Sutton Publishing, 1984, revised edition published as *The Lone Swallows and Other Essays of Boyhood and Youth,* Putnam, 1933.
The Peregrine's Saga and Other Stories of the Country Green, Collins, 1923, published as *Sun Brothers,* Dutton, 1925.
The Old Stag: Stories, Putnam (London), 1926, Dutton, 1927.
Tarka the Otter: Being His Joyful Water-Life and Death in the Country of the Two Rivers (novel), Dutton, 1927, published as *The Illustrated Tarka the Otter,* Webb & Bower, 1985, Salem House, 1986.
The Linhay on the Downs (short stories), Mathews & Marrot, 1929, reprinted, Sutton Publishing, 1984.
The Wet Flanders Plain (war recollections), Dutton, 1929, revised edition, Faber, 1929, reprinted, Gliddon Books, 1987.
The Ackymals (short stories), Windsor Press, 1929.
The Patriot's Progress: Being the Vicissitudes of Private John Bullock (novel), Dutton, 1930.
The Village Book (short stories), Dutton, 1930.
The Wild Red Deer of Exmoor: A Digression on the Logic and Ethics and Economics of Stag-Hunting in England Today, Faber, 1931.
The Labouring Life (short stories), J. Cape, 1932, published as *As the Sun Shines,* Dutton, 1933.
The Gold Falcon; or, The Haggard of Love: Being the Adventures of Manfred, Airman and Poet of the World War, and Later, Husband and Father, in Search of Freedom and Personal Sunrise, in the City of New York, and of the Consummation of His Life (novel; published anonymously), Smith, 1933, revised edition published under own name, Faber, 1947.
The Star-Born, Faber, 1933, revised edition, 1948, Chivers, 1973.
On Foot in Devon; or, Guidance and Gossip: Being a Monologue in Two Reels (short stories), Maclehose, 1933.
The Linhay on the Downs and Other Adventures in the Old and New World (short stories), J. Cape, 1934.
Salar the Salmon (novel), Faber, 1935, reprinted, Webb & Bower, 1987.

Devon Holiday, J. Cape, 1935.
Goodbye West Country, Putnam (London), 1937, Little, Brown, 1938.
The Children of Shallowford (autobiography), Faber, 1939, revised edition, 1959.
As the Sun Shines: Selections, Faber, 1941.
The Story of a Norfolk Farm (autobiography), Faber, 1941, reprinted, Holloway Books, 1986.
Genius of Friendship: "T. E. Lawrence," Faber, 1941, reprinted, Henry Williamson Society, 1988.
The Sun in the Sands (novel), Faber, 1945.
Life in a Devon Village (short stories), Faber, 1945, reprinted, Breslich & Foss, 1983.
Tales of a Devon Village, Faber, 1945.
The Phasian Bird (novel), Faber, 1948, Little, Brown, 1950.
Scribbling Lark, Faber, 1949.
Tales of Moorland and Estuary (short stories), Macdonald, 1953.
A Clear Water Stream (autobiography), Faber, 1958, Washburn, 1959, revised edition, Macdonald, 1975.
In the Woods (short stories), St. Albert's Press (Wales), 1960.
(Contributor) *A First Adventure with Francis Thompson,* St. Albert's Press, 1966.
Collected Nature Stories, Macdonald, 1970.
The Vanishing Hedgerow (television play), 1972.
The Scandaroon (novel), Macdonald, 1972, Saturday Review Press, 1973.
Animal Saga (short stories), Macdonald and Jones, 1974.
Contributions to "The Weekly Dispatch," Henry Williamson Society, 1983.
Village Tales, Robinson Publishing, 1984.
Days of Wonder, Henry Williamson Society, 1987.
From a Country Hilltop, Henry Williamson Society, 1988.
Some Notes on "The Flax of Dream" and Other Essays, Paupers' Press, 1988.

Also contributor to *Some Nature Writers and Civilization,* 1960.

"THE FLAX OF DREAM" SERIES

The Beautiful Years, Dutton, 1921, revised edition, 1929.
Dandelion Days, Dutton, 1922, revised edition, 1930.
The Dream of Fair Women, Dutton, 1924, revised edition, 1931.
The Pathway, J. Cape, 1928, Dutton, 1929.
The Flax of Dream (contains *The Beautiful Years, Dandelion Days, The Dream of Fair Women,* and *The Pathway*), Faber, 1936.

"A CHRONICLE OF ANCIENT SUNLIGHT" SERIES

The Dark Lantern, Macdonald, 1951.
Donkey Boy, Macdonald, 1952.
Young Phillip Maddison, Macdonald, 1953, revised edition, Hamish Hamilton, 1962.
How Dear Is Life, Macdonald, 1954.
A Fox Under My Cloak, Macdonald, 1955.
The Golden Virgin, Macdonald, 1957, revised edition, Panther, 1963.
Love and the Loveless: A Soldier's Tale, Macdonald, 1958.
A Test to Destruction, Macdonald, 1960, revised edition, Panther, 1964.
The Innocent Moon, Macdonald, 1961.
It Was the Nightingale, Macdonald, 1962.
The Power of the Dead, Macdonald, 1963, revised edition, Panther, 1966.
The Phoenix Generation, Macdonald, 1965.
A Solitary War, Macdonald, 1966.
Lucifer before Sunrise, Macdonald, 1967.
The Gale of the World, Macdonald, 1969.

EDITOR

An Anthology of Modern Nature Writing, Thomas Nelson, 1936.
Richard Jefferies: Selections of His Work, Faber, 1937.
Richard Jefferies, *Hodge and His Masters,* Methuen, 1937.
L. R. Haggard, *Norfolk Life,* Faber, 1943.
My Favourite Country Stories, Lutterworth, 1946.
Unreturning Springs: Being the Poems, Sketches, Stories and Letters of James Farrar, William & Norgate, 1950.

OTHER

Columnist for *Daily Express.*

MEDIA ADAPTATIONS: Tarka the Otter was filmed by Rank in 1979, with Peter Ustinov as narrator.

SIDELIGHTS: Henry Williamson was not a novelist who also wrote short stories, or an essayist who managed to write an autobiography: he was a writer recognized as a talent in each of those genres and more. In the wide range of Williamson's works, however, there does seem to be one underlying theme with which the author was particularly captivated. This theme is nature and its effects on the characters he created as well as on himself. Williamson's own close association with the country provided him with background information and observations for his writings, and lent authenticity and factuality to his "nature stories." His best known books are *Tarka the Otter,* the story of an otter that Williamson raised, and *Salar the Salmon.*

Many of the nature books which Williamson wrote, particularly those he wrote as a younger man, appeal to children, for he gave his animal characters their own unique personalities. *Sun Brothers,* a collection of eighteen sketches, was completed and compiled just after World War I. The stories were described by J. O. Swift in the *New York World* as "vivid, splendidly written and [they] grip the heart. The book is full of poetry in prose, color, and a vague, haunting sadness, so common since the war, but is lightened with hope—the hope of Life."

The Old Stag brought Williamson to public and critical attention. One critic wrote in the *New York Times:* "In literary skill, native equipment and innate interest Henry Williamson is of the elect among nature writers." Another critic said in the *Saturday Review of Literature* that the book was "far from exciting," but added "even in its dullest moments the author's deep knowledge and love of his subject is apparent. Such qualifications as are provided by complete sincerity and an exquisite feeling for the details of what may be termed animal psychology, Mr. Williamson's book possesses."

The author's most critically acclaimed animal book was a novel entitled *Tarka the Otter,* which tells the story of an otter that Williamson raised. A critic for the *New York Times* said of the novel: "In keen, sympathetic, accurate and comprehensive observation of wild life, Mr. Williamson's nature tales, of which this is the fourth, are not excelled by any English or American writer."

The countryside Williamson described so well in *Tarka the Otter* and many other books is Devon, the small country village where he moved in the early 1920's and spent roughly seven years. *A Clear Water Stream* revolves around Devon's stream, which ran alongside Williamson's cottage, and the novel advocates a concern for water conservation. S. B. Bellows wrote in the *Christian Science Monitor:* "This is a book that goes far beyond nature observation, or even nature-sympathy. It is the work of a thinker and an artist, of a man who is trying to understand himself along with the rest of nature, and there are passages of pure literature that will greatly reward the thoughtful seeker for beauty and wisdom."

The Phasian Bird allowed Williamson to point out the necessity of soil conservation in the same manner in which he advocated water conservation in *A Clear Water Stream.* F. F. Van de Water remarked that "if Mr. Williamson is not completely able to make the twin themes of avian biography and soil conservation march in step, I can think of no writer in either field who could have done better." In the *Chicago Sunday Tribune* Bob Becker stated that *The Phasian Bird* "has all the richness of detail, the fast pace and color of [Williamson's] previous outdoor narratives. It's the kind of book that combines authentic natural history with . . . action and suspense."

Goodbye West Country focuses on the last year Williamson lived in Devon. The book also includes fond recollections of his years as a resident in the area and remembers the years of his youth. R. P. Harriss wrote of the book: "To read Henry Williamson is to read nature writing at its best. It is not merely beautiful prose, it is intensely and everlasting factual stuff." In the *New York Times,* Anita Moffett said, "The book is an interesting record, perhaps at its best in its observations of the natural world, in actuality of experience conveyed with light and clarity, a world of infinite beauty, strangeness and variety seen through a temperament of unusual sensitivity, fineness and fidelity."

One of the largest of Williamson's works was "The Flax of Dream" series, a tetralogy of autobiographically-based novels which follow the life of one boy from the English country. Speaking of the first novel in the series, Herschel Brickell wrote: "*The Beautiful Years* is the story of the childhood of Willie Madison. . . . It is not an easy feat to make an adult novel out of the first ten years of a hero's life. But this Mr. Williamson has done. On its own merits, the book is likely to take its place in the enduring literature of boyhood." The second novel in the tetralogy, *Dandelion Days,* continued the story of the hero into his school years. "Mr. Williamson's style has an original and distinguished quality," commented Helen Berlin about the novel. "His profound feeling for nature makes sometimes lush writing, but is effective in creating an atmosphere of languor and sentimentality to which the mood of the young is so responsive." Completing the series was *The Pathway,* about which E. C. Beckwith wrote: "The splendors of Williamson's prose, always brilliant in his novels of the strictly nature genre, here enriched by the power of a poignant human theme rise to heights of magnificence he has never hitherto achieved. An exquisite work of art, this is surely a book that should long endure." A *Springfield Republican* review contained several insights into the novel's strongpoints: "Perhaps the dominant quality of the book is its accurate observation and description. . . . The style is very beautiful. The book's prose is pliant and supple, capable of rising to the heights of sustained intense feeling."

Williamson's own involvement in World War I inspired several of his books, including *The Wet Flanders Plain* and *The Patriot's Progress.* War, in the author's opinion, is the act of man most distant from the "natural"; Williamson's books were written to deglamorize war and encourage peace. Harold King described *The Wet Flanders Plain* in this manner: "The book is a series of vignettes, done with that delicate skill of which Mr. Williamson is master. It is deep and tender and moving, and will probably rank with the few really great books of the war. The style is as beautiful as ever, and its rare power of conveying the charm of the English countryside is as successful with the ruin and the gaudy resurrection of the wet Flanders plain." "The book has a spiritual body as well as a material body," reported the critic for the *New York Times,* "and it is the spiritual body which makes it important, and, one ventures to predict, probably lasting, and this in spite of its modest and self-effacing mien. . . . From it seems to emanate something rather rare, and not easy to classify."

"*The Patriot's Progress* is undoubtedly one of the best of the British War books, and Mr. Williamson has proved that he is a writer of the utmost integrity," declared Vernon Bartlett of Williamson's second war book, which followed the story of one soldier's experiences from his enlistment until the end of the war. Brickell said of this novel: "*Patriot's Progress* . . . shows [Williamson] in a changed mood as well as a changed manner. Here he has apparently suppressed the sensitivity that is so marked a quality of his nature books and of his four-part novel as well; he writes with feelings so deeply harrowed, perhaps, that he has them under complete control, and the effect is all the stronger. Mr. Williamson's book . . . is superior because it is written by a man whose business is writing, who knows his job, and who in this instance was powerfully moved before he sat down to write. . . ."

BIOGRAPHICAL/CRITICAL SOURCES:

BOOKS

Baker, Denys Val, editor, *Modern British Writing,* Vanguard, 1947.
Girvan, I. Waveny, *A Bibliography and a Critical Survey of the Works of Henry Williamson,* Alcuin Press (Gloucestershire), 1931.
Sewell, Brocard, editor, *Henry Williamson, the Man, the Writings: A Symposium,* Tabb House, 1980.
West, Herbert Faulkner, *The Dreamer of Devon: An Essay on Henry Williamson,* Ulysses Press, 1932.
Williamson, Henry, *The Children of Shallowford,* Faber, 1939, revised edition, 1959.
Williamson, Henry, *The Story of a Norfolk Farm,* Faber, 1941.
Williamson, Henry, *A Clear Water Stream,* Faber, 1958, Washburn, 1959.

PERIODICALS

Bookman, January, 1928; September, 1930.
Chicago Sunday Tribune, November 5, 1950.
Christian Science Monitor, November 4, 1950; July 30, 1959.
Mentor, May, 1929.
New York Herald Tribune Book Review, September 8, 1929; July 20, 1930; April 10, 1933.
New York Times, April 17, 1927; March 4, 1928; December 8, 1929; July 13, 1930; March 27, 1938; October 15, 1950.
New York Times Book Review, September 19, 1948.
New York Tribune, June 14, 1925.
New York World, June 21, 1925; March 24, 1928; June 15, 1930.
Saturday Review of Literature, January 3, 1925; May 21, 1927; December 21, 1929; July 19, 1930.
Scholastic, September 26, 1936.
Spectator, July 14, 1930.
Springfield Republican, April 21, 1929.
Times Literary Supplement, June 27, 1958.

OBITUARIES:

PERIODICALS

AB Bookman's Weekly, October 10, 1977.
New York Times, August 14, 1977.

WILLIE, Frederick
See LOVECRAFT, H(oward) P(hillips)

* * *

WILLINGHAM, Calder (Baynard, Jr.) 1922-

PERSONAL: Born December 23, 1922, in Atlanta, Ga.; son of Calder Baynard (a hotel manager) and Eleanor Churchill (Willcox) Willingham; married Helene Rothenberg, 1945; married second wife, Jane Marie Bennett, September 15, 1953; children: (first marriage) Paul Thomas; (second marriage) Frederick Calder, Sara Jane, Mark Osgood, Pamela, Christopher. *Education:* Attended The Citadel, 1940-41, and University of Virginia, 1941-43.

ADDRESSES: Home—1 Shingle Camp Hill Rd., New Hampton, N.H. 03256.

CAREER: Novelist, playwright, and screenwriter.

AWARDS, HONORS: British Film Academy Award for best screenplay, 1969, for "The Graduate."

WRITINGS:

End as a Man, Vanguard, 1947.
Geraldine Bradshaw, Vanguard, 1950.
Reach to the Stars, Vanguard, 1951.
The Gates of Hell (short stories), Vanguard, 1951.
Natural Child, Dial, 1952.
To Eat a Peach, Dial, 1955.
Eternal Fire, Vanguard, 1963.
Providence Island, Vanguard, 1969.
Rambling Rose, Delacorte, 1972.
The Big Nickel, Dial, 1975.
The Building of Venus Four, Manor, 1977.

Also author of a play, "End as a Man," based on his novel of the same title.

SCREENPLAYS

"The Strange One" (based on his novel *End as a Man*), Columbia, 1957.
(With Stanley Kubrick and Tim Thompson) "Paths of Glory" (based on the novel of the same title by Humphrey Cobb), United Artists, 1957.
"The Vikings," United Artists, 1958.
"One-Eyed Jacks," Paramount, 1961.
(With Buck Henry) "The Graduate" (based on the novel of the same title by Charles Webb), Embassy Pictures, 1967.
"Little Big Man" (based on the novel of the same title by Thomas Berger), CBS Films, 1972.
"Thieves Like Us," United Artists, 1975.

SIDELIGHTS: Calder Willingham's work has sparked a good deal of controversy among literary critics. To some he is, as Jack Kroll of *Newsweek* puts it, "perhaps the outstanding talent of that generation" of authors which includes Norman Mailer, William Styron, and James Jones, "the most original, the real, although perhaps subtlest, innovator, and the one writer who has achieved what used to be called mastery over the craft of his art." But to others he is a verbose smut writer. An *Atlantic Monthly* reviewer says that "Willingham has a mind for the hallucinated, the perverse, the psychopathic, and the unillusioned and unlovely in human being and human situation. He also has a fine, clear ear for speech, and some disturbingly independent notions on what is fit for telling and how to tell it. The results are not ingratiating." Willingham responds: "The charge made by some

that I am 'a verbose smut writer' and that my work is 'pornographic' amazes me. I see in my writing virtually none of the sadism of pornography or the nasty and jejune neuroticism of smut. On the contrary, the erotic power of my writing seems to me to derive from love and respect for humanity's better half. My best characters by no coincidence are girls and women. This is a cheap, cowardly, and lying criticism. These people fear the erotic for reasons of their own. Beyond such disgusting cowardice, they reflect and express the spiritual sickness of our time."

Willingham's first novel, *End as a Man,* was written when he was twenty-three years old. Critically, it has remained the best received of his novels, and it is the one to which his later work is most often compared. John Woodburn of the *Saturday Review* calls it "a fearful book, a hard and angry book, filled with a contempt that is close to loathing; but the contempt is made valid and mature because it is balanced with understanding and pity, and the restless, ranging imagination, creative and often brilliant is laid like a montage upon the flat surface of the setting. . . . Calder Willingham is a good and sharply arresting writer, . . . someone to watch steadily." In a *New Yorker* article, J. M. Lalley writes, "With all its technical crudities and philosophic immaturity, this is a novel capable of evoking, even in a seasoned reader, something like cathartic terror." And J. T. Farrell of the *New York Times* says that "this first novel is the work of an artist, written with power, honesty and courage; it carries its own conviction on every page. Its complete realism may shock the tender-minded; yet few of those who read *End as a Man* are ever likely to forget it. . . . I consider it a permanent contribution to American literature."

In a *New York Times* review of *Geraldine Bradshaw,* John Barkham makes the point that "none of the characters in this story is in the least likable, yet," he feels, "even the most subsidiary of them is pinpointed with clarity and economy. . . . In its way the book is a dazzling performance." Barkham concludes that *Geraldine Bradshaw* is "remarkable enough to establish Mr. Willingham among the foremost of our realistic novelists." A *San Francisco Chronicle* writer says that Willingham "does not exercise his undeniable talent sufficiently. It is possible that his reflection of the monotony of single-minded sex-pursuit comes close to the truth. But the four-letter monotone in which it is here related defeats what may have been the author's purpose." Kelsey Guilfoil of the *Chicago Sunday Tribune* states that "this novel will have no serious competitors for the title of the filthiest book of the year."

The mixed reviews continue with *Eternal Fire,* published in 1963. *Library Journal's* J. C. Pine writes that "Willingham has been the *enfant terrible* of American fiction. . . . [Yet] he is a serious and in many ways a talented writer." Saul Maloff, in a *Commonweal* article, expresses contempt for Willingham's work: "Stripped down to what it essentially is, we have nothing but melodrama of the grand guignol variety, advanced soap-opera against a background of Southern Gothic. . . . Obviously, the stage is set for pornography; and if that is what we are looking for, Willingham is not one to disappoint us." But a *Newsweek* writer gives the book high praise: "*Eternal Fire* deserves a place among the dozen or so novels that must be mentioned if one is to speak of greatness in American fiction. . . . Willingham sustains a broad, pitiless, and savagely serious burlesque of all men who presume to call themselves virtuous and civilized."

Providence Island appears to have evoked even more criticism than most of Willingham's novels. There is disapproval of the eroticism in the book. Guy Davenport of the *National Review,* for instance, asks "who reads such trash? A Victorian would have said, 'The Cook.' But there are no more cooks, or very few, and the ones I know are too intelligent to follow the doings of Mr. Willingham's paper-doll characters, even into their fornications, which have the same relation to sex as screaming does to a Rossini aria." Thomas Lask, in a *New York Times* review, criticizes Willingham's use of dialogue in this novel. He writes: "There is enough talk in it to drive a totally deaf man to sign on as a lighthouse keeper off the Cape of Good Hope. . . . If all the blather were pumped out of this novel, it could be reduced to the size of a restaurant menu without a loss of a single vital ingredient." *Life*'s Melvin Maddocks says that *Providence Island* is "a poor book in cruelly obvious ways. The style wanders erratically from New York satirical to Southern pastoral. Scenes ramble on and on, slightly out of focus, like a home movie. Worst of all, the plot seems borrowed from a bad *Playboy* cartoon." Even Jack Kroll, who normally has great praise for Willingham, writes that "it is the sad and deliberate anticlimax of this review to report that his new book will not help him to gain the belated recognition which is more than his due. . . . For the first time in his career this brilliant original sounds old-fashioned—it is as if he were really writing, disguised as the kind of big book that is making it these days, a tract against that kind of book and all the moral and esthetic implications of the culture that produces it."

In his *Best Sellers* review of *Rambling Rose,* Fred Rotondaro writes: "In the hands of a writer less talented than Willingham, Rambling Rose would have become just another girl on the make. In this volume though she becomes much more than that. She is a very uninhibited woman trying to find happiness as she lives her crazy and sometimes tragic life. Eventually, she does find happiness and Willingham, excellent artist that he is, simply touches that portion of her life leaving the reader to draw his own conclusions." But a *Virginia Quarterly Review* writer notes that "the book must be criticized for its change in viewpoint and direction at midpoint, when emphasis is shifted away from a nubile young girl for whom sex is a constant preoccupation to the even younger lad who tells the story, and to his imperceptive family. As a yarn about female concupiscence the volume has some pornographic interest; when it wanders on the other hand into a pseudo-serious analysis of situation and character it becomes tiresome."

Of *The Big Nickel,* published in 1975, *Library Journal*'s Eric Moon writes: "The old, old plot—a novelist whose first book has been a critical success can't get started on opus no. 2—is given a little livelier treatment here than in dozens of other novels which have used it. . . . Willingham is never uninteresting but there's no doubt that he's batting well below his average this time." And Jonathan Yardley of the *New Republic* calls the author "one of the most skilled, observant and purely funny satirists of the post-war generation. . . . Even at his least successful, Willingham is fun to read—which is about all that can be said on behalf of *The Big Nickel.* . . . Nobody, but nobody, writes about sex with such irreverence, such outrageous imagery. The utter astonishment with which man can view woman is rarely depicted so humorously—or so knowingly. That's Willingham at his best." But Yardley concludes that this book is "more tantalizing than satisfying."

Although Willingham has become a very well-known novelist, he has also been extremely successful in the field of screen writing. One of his most famous scripts is "The Graduate," produced in 1967 by Embassy Pictures, starring Dustin Hoffman, Katherine Ross, and Anne Bancroft. Bosley Crowther of the *New York Times* calls it "a film that is not only one of the best of the year,

but also one of the best seriocomic social satires we've had from Hollywood since Preston Sturges was making them. . . . In telling a pungent story of the sudden confusions and dismays of a bland young man fresh out of college who is plunged headlong into the intellectual vacuum of his affluent parents' circle of friends, it fashions a scarifying picture of the raw vulgarity of the swimming-pool rich, and it does so with a lively and exciting expressiveness through vivid cinema." Another well-known screenplay by Willingham is "Little Big Man," a 1972 CBS Films production which also starred Dustin Hoffman. The film proved extremely popular, although critics gave it a rather lukewarm reception. A *Time* reviewer, for instance, says that the author "has provided a scenario that begins with robust rawhide humor, turns to profundity—then collapses into petulant editorial. In the era of occupied Alcatraz, surely it is no news that the white man spoke with forked tongue, that the first Americans were maltreated as the last savages." John Simon says that the film "does not come off as a whole because it is too episodic, which could work better in a book where the author can take his time." Simon does, however, find that "if you look at the film as a series of cavalierly tacked together vignettes, an estimable number of these work, either in part or even as a whole." And the *Newsweek* critic, after denouncing some parts of the movie, decides that it is a "rambunctious triumph" because it "has contrived to lampoon, revere or revile the length and breadth of the entire frontier. . . . [It] accomplishes that rarest achievement, the breathing of life into an ossified art form. . . . Blood brother to the 1903 one-reeler, 'The Great Train Robbery,' 'Little Big Man' is the new western to begin all westerns."

Willingham says that he writes in the dramatic media for money and for recreation, and that his "serious work has been done in the novel." He further notes: "I today regard narrative as the most important quality of the novel; I believe that a good story is more than merely entertaining, that characterization, style, philosophical depth, even poetry flow from the story. I believe a novel should have plot, suspense, dramatic development, and I strive to achieve same."

BIOGRAPHICAL/CRITICAL SOURCES:

BOOKS

Contemporary Literary Criticism, Gale, Volume 5, 1976, Volume 51, 1989.
Dictionary of Literary Biography, Gale, Volume 2: *American Novelists Since World War II,* 1978, Volume 44: *American Screenwriters, Second Series,* 1986.

PERIODICALS

Best Sellers, March 15, 1969, November 1, 1972.
Books and Bookmen, December, 1969.
Chicago Sunday Tribune, March 19, 1950.
Choice, June, 1975.
Commonweal, February 1, 1963, January 22, 1971.
Library Journal, December 1, 1962, February 15, 1975.
Life, February 14, 1969.
Nation, June 4, 1955, March 31, 1969.
National Review, May 20, 1969.
New Leader, December 28, 1971.
New Republic, March 24, 1947, December 26, 1970, April 5, 1975.
Newsweek, March 10, 1969.
New Yorker, March 8, 1947, March 18, 1950.
New York Herald Tribune Book Review, February 16, 1947, June 17, 1951, December 2, 1951, November 30, 1952.

New York Times, February 26, 1950, July 22, 1951, December 16, 1951, November 2, 1952, February 27, 1955, December 22, 1967, April 1, 1969.

New York Times Book Review, February 16, 1947, February 26, 1950, October 29, 1972, March 23, 1975.

San Francisco Chronicle, March 5, 1950.

Saturday Review, April 5, 1947, April 30, 1955.

Time, December 21, 1970.

Times Literary Supplement, July 6, 1973.

Virginia Quarterly Review, winter, 1973.

* * *

WILLIS, Charles
See CLARKE, Arthur C(harles)

* * *

WILLY
See COLETTE, (Sidonie-Gabrielle)

* * *

WILLY, Colette
See COLETTE, (Sidonie-Gabrielle)

* * *

WILSON, Angus (Frank Johnstone) 1913-

PERSONAL: Surname originally Johnstone-Wilson; born August 11, 1913, in Bexhill, Sussex, England; son of William and Maude (Caney) Johnstone-Wilson. *Education:* Merton College, Oxford, B.A. (with honors), 1936.

ADDRESSES: Home—7 Place de la Republique, Apt. 61, 13210 St. Remy de Provence, France.

CAREER: Writer. British Museum, London, England, member of staff of department of printed books, 1936-42, 1946-49, deputy superintendent of the Reading Room, 1949-55; University of East Anglia, Norwich, England, lecturer, 1963-66, professor of English literature, 1966-78, professor emeritus, 1978—. Ewing Lecturer, University of California, Los Angeles, 1960; Bergen Lecturer, Yale University, 1960; William Vaughan Moody Lecturer, University of Chicago, 1960; Northcliffe Lecturer, University College, London, 1961; Leslie Stephen Lecturer, Cambridge University, 1962-63; Beckman Professor, University of California, Berkeley, 1967; John Hinkley Visiting Professor, Johns Hopkins University, 1974; Ida Beam Professor, University of Iowa, 1978 and 1986. Distinguished visiting professor, University of Delaware, 1977, 1980, and 1983, Georgia State University, 1979, University of Michigan, 1979, University of Minnesota, 1980, University of Pittsburgh, 1981, University of Missouri, 1982, and University of Arizona, 1984. Leader of the British jury, Formentor Literary Conference, 1962; member of the committee, Royal Literary Fund, 1966; member of the Arts Council of Great Britain, 1966-69; chairman, National Book League, 1971-74. *Military service:* Foreign Office, intelligence officer, 1942-46.

MEMBER: Society of Authors, PEN, Royal Society of Literature (president, 1982—), Powys Society (president, 1970—), Dickens Fellowship (president, 1974-75), American Academy and Institute of Arts and Letters (honorary member), Athenaeum Club.

AWARDS, HONORS: Royal Society of Literature, fellow, 1958, companion of literature, 1972; James Tait Black Memorial Prize,

1959, for *The Middle Age of Mrs. Eliot;* Prix de Meilleur Roman Etranger, 1960; Commander, Order of the British Empire, 1968, knighted, 1980; honorary fellow, Cowell College, University of California, Santa Cruz, 1968; Yorkshire Post Book of the Year Award, 1970, for *The World of Charles Dickens;* Chevalier de l'Ordre des Arts et des Lettres, 1972; D.Litt., University of Leicester, 1978, University of East Anglia, 1979, University of Liverpool, 1979, and University of Sussex, 1981; honorary doctorate degree, the Sorbonne, 1983; Focus Award, 1985.

WRITINGS:

NOVELS

Hemlock and After, Viking, 1952, reprinted, Academy Chicago, 1983.

Anglo-Saxon Attitudes (Book Society choice), Viking, 1956, reprinted, Granada Publishing, 1983.

The Middle Age of Mrs. Eliot, Secker & Warburg, 1958, Viking, 1959, reprinted, Penguin, 1982.

The Old Men at the Zoo, Viking, 1961, reprinted, Secker Warburg, 1983.

Late Call, Secker & Warburg, 1964, Viking, 1965, reprinted, Academy Chicago, 1983.

No Laughing Matter, Viking, 1967, reprinted, Academy Chicago, 1983.

As If by Magic, Viking, 1973.

Setting the World on Fire, Viking, 1980.

STORY COLLECTIONS

The Wrong Set and Other Stories (Book Society choice), Secker & Warburg, 1949, Morrow, 1950, reprinted, Academy Chicago, 1983.

Such Darling Dodos and Other Stories (Book Society choice), Secker & Warburg, 1950, Morrow, 1951, reprinted, Panther Books, 1980.

A Bit off the Map and Other Stories, Viking, 1957, reprinted, Panther Books, 1982.

Death Dance: Twenty-Five Stories, Viking, 1969.

NONFICTION

Emile Zola: An Introductory Study of His Novels, Morrow, 1952, 2nd edition, Secker & Warburg, 1964.

(With Phillippe Jullian) *For Whom the Cloche Tolls: A Scrapbook of the Twenties,* Methuen, 1953, reprinted, Academy Chicago, 1983.

The Wild Garden; or, Speaking of Writing (lectures), University of California Press, 1963.

Tempo: The Impact of Television on the Arts, Studio Vista, 1964, Dufour, 1966.

The World of Charles Dickens, Viking, 1970, reprinted, Academy Chicago, 1985.

(With Kathleen Tillotson and Sylvere Monad) *Dickens Memorial Lecture, 1970,* Viking, 1970.

The Naughty Nineties, Methuen, 1976.

The Strange Ride of Rudyard Kipling: His Life and Works, Secker & Warburg, 1977, Viking, 1978.

Diversity and Depth in Fiction: Selected Critical Writings of Angus Wilson, Secker & Warburg, 1983, Viking, 1984.

Reflections in a Writer's Eye: Travel Pieces, Penguin, 1986 (published in England as *Reflections in a Writer's Eye: Writings on Travel,* Secker & Warburg, 1986).

EDITOR

(And author of introduction) W. Somerset Maugham, *A Maugham Twelve,* Heinemann, 1966, expanded edition published as *Cakes and Ale, and Twelve Stories,* Doubleday, 1967.

(With Peter Fairclough) Charles Dickens, *Oliver Twist,* Penguin, 1967.

Writers of East Anglia, Secker & Warburg, 1977.

East Anglia in Verse and Prose, Secker & Warburg, 1982.

(And author of introduction) *The Portable Dickens,* Penguin, 1983.

Essays by Divers Hands: The Transactions of the Royal Society of Literature, Boydell & Brewer, 1984, Longwood, 1985.

PLAYS

The Mulberry Bush (three-act; first produced in Bristol, England, at the Bristol Old Vic, September 27, 1955), Secker & Warburg, 1956.

TELEVISION PLAYS

"After the Show," British Broadcasting Corporation (BBC), 1959.

"The Stranger," BBC, 1960.

"The Invasion," BBC, 1963.

CONTRIBUTOR

Seven Deadly Sins, Morrow, 1962.

John Jacob Gross and Gabriel Pearson, editors, *Dickens and the Twentieth Century,* University of Toronto Press, 1966.

John Colmer, editor, *Approaches to the Novel,* Oliver & Boyd, 1967.

B. C. Southam, editor, *Critical Essays on Jane Austen,* Routledge & Kegan Paul, 1968.

Shiv K. Kumar, editor, *British Victorian Literature: Recent Revaluations,* New York University Press, 1969.

Charles Burkhart, editor, *The Art of I. Compton-Burnett: A Collection of Critical Essays,* Gollancz, 1972.

Ann Thwaite, editor, *My Oxford,* Robson Books, 1977.

John Wain, editor, *An Edmund Wilson Celebration,* Phaidon Press, 1978.

Belinda Humfrey, editor, *Recollections of the Powys Brothers: Llewelyn, Theodore and John Cowper,* Owen, 1980.

Jean-Pierre Michaux, editor, *George Gissing: Critical Essays,* Barnes & Noble, 1981.

AUTHOR OF INTRODUCTION

Edwin Smith, *England,* Viking, 1971.

Charles Dickens, *David Copperfield,* F. Watts, 1971.

John Cowper Powys, *Weymouth Sands,* Rivers Press, 1973.

Dickens, *The Mystery of Edwin Drood,* Penguin, 1974.

Arthur Conan Doyle, *The Return of Sherlock Holmes,* J. Murray, 1974.

Elizabeth Bowen, *The Collected Short Stories of Elizabeth Bowen,* Knopf, 1980.

Rudyard Kipling, *Kim,* Macmillan, 1981.

RECORDINGS

"Dickens," BFA Educational Media, 1972.

"Angus Wilson: An Interview by John H. Raleigh," Jeffrey Norton, 1974.

"The Bloomsbury Group," Jeffrey Norton, 1974.

"Charles Dickens," Jeffrey Norton, 1974.

"The English Novel: Dickens to Snow," Jeffrey Norton, 1974.

OTHER

Author of radio play, "Skeletons and Assegais," BBC; compiler, *An Anthology: Green River Review, 1968-73,* Green River. Television critic, *Queen Magazine,* 1962-63. Contributor of short stories, essays, reviews, and articles to *Observer, Sunday Times, Sunday Telegraph, Encounter, New York Times, New Statesman, Atlantic, Holiday, New Yorker, Partisan Review,* and other publications.

SIDELIGHTS: Although British author Angus Wilson has earned an esteemed reputation for his literary criticism, short stories, and biographies, and for editing the works of Charles Dickens, he is most widely acclaimed for his novels. He is, Jay L. Halio maintains in the *Dictionary of Literary Biography,* "one of the leading novelists of the post-World War II period and the only one of his generation so far to be knighted by Queen Elizabeth II for his services to literature and the arts." His ability to successfully combine the techniques of modernist fiction with the traditional novel moves Michael Moorcock, writing in *Books and Bookmen,* to argue that "Wilson better than any novelist of his generation is confronting the problems of writing a fiction which is not stifled by the conventions of the past hundred years, yet avoids obscurity and retains the dramatic elements which, to my mind, are necessary if a book is justifiably to be called a novel." Julian Symons, in a review for the *Washington Post Book World,* describes Wilson as "the most finely and directly ambitious of contemporary British novelists [and] one of the few . . . who confront the modern world head-on, making no attempt to take refuge in rediscovery of their own childhood, or in minute examination of a single class or group." Peter Faulkner, in his book *Angus Wilson: Mimic and Moralist,* finds that "Wilson has established himself as one of the half-dozen most distinguished English writers."

Wilson began his writing career relatively late in life. He spent nearly fifteen years on the staff of the British Museum, and served as deputy superintendent of its renowned Reading Room for six of those years. It was only while undergoing psychotherapy during World War II that Wilson, following the advice of his doctor, began to write for therapeutic reasons. These efforts did not lead to any serious work at the time but after the war, Wilson began to write short stories on weekends as a way to divert himself from his work at the museum. He showed some of these stories to his friend Robin Ironside, who passed them along to the editor of *Horizon* magazine, Cyril Connolly. Connolly published two of the stories, an editor at the publishing house of Secker & Warburg saw them, and Wilson was asked to do a collection. The resulting volume, *The Wrong Set and Other Stories,* appeared in 1949. It was followed in 1950 by *Such Darling Dodos and Other Stories,* and by *A Bit off the Map and Other Stories* in 1957. *Death Dance: Twenty-Five Stories* is a selection of stories from the earlier collections.

These early short stories are noted for their incisive wit and satire, and for their accurate portraits of postwar English society. James Gindin writes in *Postwar British Fiction: New Accents and Attitudes* that Wilson's stories "depict, with precision and detachment, the delusions and the pretense under which people operate." As Faulkner explains, the stories in *The Wrong Set and Other Stories* are concerned with the question, "can there be relationships . . . which allow and help all concerned to grow and develop, or are they necessarily props for some and prisons for others? The sombreness which underlies the wit comes from the fact that the answer suggested is negative." Writing in the *Saturday Review,* Joyce Carol Oates describes Wilson's short stories as "masterful, concise, rather macabre tales of post-war England," and judges Wilson to be "a master of what we now call the Chekhovian short story." These early collections helped to bring Wilson recognition as what Richard Boston of the *New York Times Book Review* calls "one of the most brilliant short-story writers of the century."

But despite this immediate success, Wilson was dissatisfied with the short story, wishing to express his ideas in a longer and more developed form. Before trying his hand at a novel, however, he wrote a study of the great French novelist of the nineteenth century, Emile Zola. In this book, *Emile Zola: An Introductory Study of His Novels,* Wilson examined the relationship between the author's personal life and his fiction. More important, as Halio points out, the study of Zola's writing methods confirmed Wilson's own ideas about how to write a novel: "writing copious notes and sketches until one is ready to draft the entire novel," as Halio states. The critical study received generally favorable reviews, with V. S. Pritchett of the *New Statesman and Nation* calling it "pithy, searching and decided," and Henri Peyre of the *New York Times* finding it "intelligent and lively."

During his annual four-week vacation from the British Museum in 1951, Wilson wrote his first novel, *Hemlock and After,* which appeared in 1952. It tells the story of famous novelist Bernard Sands, who establishes an anarchistic writer's colony. Sands considers this colony a great success but soon comes to doubt the wisdom of what he has done. He wonders if his administration of authority in the writer's colony runs contrary to his humanistic beliefs. In his personal life, Sands finds that he has not fulfilled his ideals about marriage and parenthood. His wife suffers from a neurotic illness, his children are unhappy, and Sands has begun to have homosexual affairs. The realization of his own fallibility—what he considers to be the aspect of evil in every man—brings Sands to a nervous breakdown and a fatal heart attack.

Faulkner sees the novel questioning "the adequacy of liberalism . . . on both the public and the private planes," citing the failure of Sands's beliefs in his professional and personal life. But Halio argues that "if Bernard's humanism finally fails him because it screens off the uglier aspects of human motive and behavior and pretends to qualify acts of altruism with only the most enlightened or innocuous self-interest, it nevertheless contains something of positive value." *Hemlock and After* met with a favorable critical reception and sold well enough for Wilson to leave his British Museum post and become a full-time writer.

It was with his second novel, *Anglo-Saxon Attitudes,* that Wilson established himself among the most important new British writers of the 1950s. While similar to *Hemlock and After* in that the protagonist comes to a self-realization after examining the course of his life, in *Anglo-Saxon Attitudes* "the lines . . . have become finer than in *Hemlock and After,* and the mature wit gives tone and shape to the material," Frederick R. Karl writes in *A Reader's Guide to the Contemporary British Novel.* The book revolves around Gerald Middleton, a professor of history who is alienated from his family and friends. The story delineates the course of events that have led to this impasse. Around this central narrative are a cluster of related stories "and a vast company of characters representing all phases of contemporary life," James Gray recounts in the *Saturday Review.*

Several critics comment on the enormous range of the novel. Bernard Bergonzi notes in his *The Situation of the Novel* that *Anglo-Saxon Attitudes* possesses a "crowded canvas and broad temporal sweep." Karl admits that "the characters of the novel are varied, the range of comment wide, the point of view . . . sophisticated, and the verbal gifts . . . abundant," although he finds that it "fails for several reasons to realize its potential." Gray believes that "covering four decades of English social life, touching every level from those of political and spiritual leader to that of the criminal, exploring every mood from that of high comedy to that of bitter melodrama, Wilson's book seems to be

as boldly conceived and as deftly executed as any novel of the great tradition."

Halio reports that *Anglo-Saxon Attitudes* "secured Wilson's growing reputation as a major English novelist," while Gill claims that with this book Wilson "leaped with astonishing speed into the front rank of contemporary English novelists." Gray calls *Anglo-Saxon Attitudes* "a brilliant novel with a story to tell, an outlook upon human experience to reveal, wit and insight to display. And all this has been accomplished fluently, casually, without intellectual pretension or faking."

With *The Middle Age of Mrs. Eliot,* Wilson wrote a different kind of novel than he had previously attempted. "Whereas *Anglo-Saxon Attitudes* flashed words, events, and thoughts against one another in a complicated pattern," Gindin explains, "*The Middle Age of Mrs. Eliot* unfolds slowly." Faulkner calls it "the most relaxed of Wilson's early novels." The book also narrows its focus to a single character, Meg Eliot, and explores in depth her thoughts and emotions. Meg is an upper-middle-class English woman whose husband is killed in the Far East. His death destroys her stable world, resulting in her nervous breakdown. But Meg eventually recovers and is able to go on with her life. "Her heroism," Halio writes, "consists of an ability to look deeply within herself and, seeing what is there, to accept what she finds and, properly disciplined, move on."

The Middle Age of Mrs. Eliot has been critically well-received and won the James Tait Black Memorial Prize and the Prix du Meilleur Roman Etranger. Gindin judges the book to be "as complete and as totally satisfying as is *Anglo-Saxon Attitudes.*" Robert Kiely of the *New York Times Book Review* finds *Anglo-Saxon Attitudes* and *The Middle Age of Mrs. Eliot* "Wilson's two most acclaimed and best-known works of the 1950's. . . . Both novels contain whole sections of glittering dialogue, wonderfully satiric imitations of academics, politicians, diplomats, artists, [and] scientists. [Wilson] probes the inner lives and especially the disappointments of the 'unheroic' figures who are the central characters in his fiction."

While his first three novels follow traditional approaches to form, Wilson's fourth novel, *The Old Men at the Zoo,* is a political fable set in the near future. Through its story of bickering zoo administrators caught up in a European invasion of England, the novel satirically contrasts the treatment of animals with the treatment of human beings in modern society. The sane management of both man and animal is the novel's primary concern. As Gindin explains, "Man can survive, in terms of the novel, only if he recognizes his own animalism but attempts, as intelligently as he can, to govern this brutality rationally and wisely." Bergonzi, in an article for the *New York Review of Books,* finds *The Old Men at the Zoo* "a dismaying work" in which "Wilson abandoned his natural talent for a portentous essay in fantastic allegory." But Anthony Burgess, writing in his *The Novel Now: A Guide to Contemporary Fiction,* believes that *The Old Men at the Zoo* "seems the best thing that Wilson has ever done."

Wilson returned to the more traditional novel with *Late Call,* a study of a retired woman, Sylvia Calvert, coming to terms with her life. *Late Call* is "a nineteenth-century kind of novel about self and society, commitment and blindness, textured with the barren stuff of contemporary English life," as Jonathan Baumbach describes it in the *Saturday Review.* Retired and married to a compulsive gambler who has spent their savings, Sylvia is obliged to move in with her widowed son. As do the characters in Wilson's earlier novels, she examines the course of her life and is disappointed. But Sylvia weathers her crisis by accepting her past life. And, through a selective process, she finds usable insights in the essentially false depictions of life found in the popular fiction she reads and the stories she sees on television and in films.

Faulkner finds that in *Late Call,* Wilson is examining "the relation between the stereotypes of popular culture and life" and "the relation between fiction and reality." This Wilson accomplishes, Faulkner argues, by introducing "a large variety of inner narratives" and by contrasting Sylvia's experiences with the expectations she has derived from books, television, and film. In *Contemporary British Novelists,* Arthur Edelstein writes that *Anglo-Saxon Attitudes, The Middle Age of Mrs. Eliot,* and *Late Call* constitute a "trilogy on the theme of the wasted life" and are primarily concerned with "the solitary crisis of consciousness."

This focus on individual crisis was abandoned with *No Laughing Matter,* a generations-spanning novel with a host of characters. "Hundreds of characters and incidents crowd the canvas," Liam Lenihan writes in the *Nation,* "yet Wilson manages to juggle them all with consummate skill, and the relationships are all sharply drawn." Wilson follows the eight members of the Matthews family—mother, father, and six children—from 1912 to 1967. The Matthews are an eccentric family, no longer wealthy, whose experiences echo those of 20th century British society at large. Wilson tells their story through their dreams, the playacting of the children, and selected scenes spanning five decades. As a family chronicle, writes Marilyn Gardner in the *Christian Science Monitor,* it is "a *magnum opus* in every sense of the term, a complex, intricate work spanning half a century and crisscrossing nearly a dozen lives. Mr. Wilson's scope is simultaneously intimate and global, his technique varied and highly unconventional." But it is more than a family chronicle, Gardner observes, it is also "a fascinating compendium of recent history." Lenihan describes the book as "a shrewd and compassionate appraisal of social and political England from its sunny, easy days of greatness to its twilight hours." Richard Mayne, writing in the *Reporter,* goes beyond the categories of family chronicle and historical novel to describe the book. *No Laughing Matter,* he maintains, "is in many respects an experimental novel that uses dazzling freehand technique to enter deeply into the nature of personality and perception, revealing more thoroughly than any of Angus Wilson's previous work the complex responses, the image-making, mimesis, parody, and unconscious feedback that inform a family entity."

Wilson's next novel, *As If by Magic,* presents Hamo, a scientist who has developed a hybrid rice to feed the Third World, and his goddaughter Alexandra, a hippie who travels with her two lovers and young child. The two characters leave England and travel to the Far East, Hamo to see the effects of his rice which he calls "magic" rice, and Alexandra to find spiritual enlightenment in first a Moroccan commune and then an Indian ashram. Both are seeking a quick answer to life's major problems. But Hamo finds that his new rice does not solve the Third World's hunger problem. It causes new problems instead. Alexandra discovers that the Indian swami she turns to for guidance is a sham. Both Hamo's rationalism and Alexandra's spiritualism fail.

"None of these 'magics,' or any of the sorts that people put their faith in, can truly solve the problems of human society or human predicaments . . . ," Halio explains. "At the same time, Wilson is also concerned with the magic of art—literature—and the ways it can touch our lives, not transform us or solve our problems, but awaken in us something other than what we have previously known or felt or otherwise experienced." Though acknowledging the novel's humor, Phoebe Adams of the *Atlantic* states

that Wilson's "underlying purpose is serious. He is quite savagely out of patience with the fashion for magic shortcuts to Utopia and Nirvana." Discussing the wide range of characters, classes, and locales found in *No Laughing Manner* and *As If by Magic,* Jonathan Raban writes in the *New Review* that "the two novels form something very close to an encyclopedia of life in society in the 20th century, an inventory of roles and stages."

This broad canvas is also found in *Setting the World on Fire,* a novel that contrasts the lives of two English brothers. Piers Masson is a theatrical director, while brother Tom is a lawyer. The two were raised in Tothill House, an estate in the heart of London built in the classic, symmetrical design of Sir Roger Pratt but with a lush, Baroque dome designed by Sir John Vanbrugh. Within the dome is pictured the story of Phaethon, "the demigod who lost control of the chariot of the Sun and nearly set the world on fire," as Boston writes in *Punch.* The contrasting architectural styles are reflected in the two brothers, who nickname themselves after the great architects: "Van" for Piers and "Pratt" for Tom.

Margaret Drabble reports in the *Listener* that "the complex relationships between art and reality, between the stage-mannered and the spontaneous, the formal and the wild, the wildly aspiring and the solidly based, the amusing and the boring, the private fantasy and the public role, . . . are explored with a mixture of elegance, panache and concern." Citing the novel's dichotomy in his review for the *London Times,* Michael Ratcliffe comments that although *Setting the World on Fire* may have begun as an allegory of Chaos and Society, . . . it triumphs as a macabre cultural comedy of English family life."

The variety found in Wilson's novels and his willingness to experiment with form and technique are cited by several critics in their appraisals of his achievement as a novelist. As Robert Ostermann writes in the *Detroit News,* "although certainly in the tradition of Dickens, Zola and Kipling . . . , Wilson has never ceased experimenting subtly with narrative form, chiefly under the increasing influence of such modernists as Virginia Woolf, and is always capable of surprising the open reader." Kiely believes that in the novels since the 1960s Wilson "not only explores the relationships among very different groups—large families, young children, the very old, bureaucrats, students—but he experiments more and more with narrative form." Remarking on this continual change in Wilson's novels, Malcolm Bradbury writes in *Twentieth Century Literature* that "like most of the best of writers, [Wilson] has seen his work as an ever-developing, ever-changing, ever-questioning *oeuvre* in which repetition is a danger and self-skepticism a necessary rule."

Having begun as a traditionalist and even as an antimodernist, Wilson has evolved into a novelist who combines traditional and modernist forms. He admits in a letter to Rubin Rabinovitz, published in *The Reaction against Experiment in the English Novel, 1950-1960,* that his early dismissal of the modernist writers had since been modified by his "own development as a novelist—my feeling that the traditional form was inhibiting me from saying all I wanted to say." Wilson explains to Israel Shenker of the *New York Times Book Review* the direction he has been taking in his novels: "I'm trying all the time to maintain the narrative form and to give to it those dimensions—which I like so much in Dickens's work—of masque or ballet, theatrical dimensions by which you can read the novel story-wise or narrative-wise, but also as though it were a masque. . . . Since I'm also deeply concerned about a connection between the human being and the external scene, I'm all the time trying to play around with different ways of description, how to interpenetrate description, dialogue, interior thoughts."

"In addition to the works that have established him as a major contemporary novelist," Kerry McSweeney writes in his introduction to *Diversity and Depth in Fiction: Selected Critical Writings of Angus Wilson,* "Wilson has also produced a remarkable amount of critical prose, almost all of it on novels and novelists." As A. N. Wilson notes in the London *Times,* "the skills of the critic and of the novelist are as different as those of the map-maker and the landscape painter; it is a rare thing if the two are combined in a single genius. . . . Wilson, however, as well as being one of the few postwar English novelists to come close to being 'a great writer,' has always been an astutely catholic critic of literature." Although not trained as a literary critic—he studied medieval history while attending Oxford—Wilson provides insights into the works of others by using a biographical approach. He is, Alice Green Fredman writes in *Twentieth Century Literature,* "a critic who scrutinizes the relationship between a writer's life and art in the belief that what transpires in the work of art is illuminated and elucidated by what has been lived in the life."

Perhaps his most successful use of this approach occurs in *The World of Charles Dickens* and *The Strange Ride of Rudyard Kipling,* both of which are critical biographies. *The World of Charles Dickens* compares events in Dickens's life to incidents found in his fiction and is illustrated with engravings and paintings of places and people of the time. It is, Geoffrey Wolff summarizes for *Newsweek,* "at once a biography, a splendidly condensed critical examination by one writer of another's work and a re-creation—through portraits, plates and photographs of artifacts—of the externals of Charles Dickens's mid-nineteenth-century world." K. J. Fielding says in the *New York Times Book Review* that the book's illustrations link "Dickens's life, his writings and the world that lay about him."

Wolff sees a strong similarity between Wilson and Dickens, describing Wilson as "a fellow novelist, whose own fiction, in its attention to social details and the mesh between imagination and active life, moves in the wide groove Dickens cut." Calling Wilson "the most outstanding British novelist today," Fielding also compares him with Dickens, finding that both men "share certain gifts and obsessions: the deepening concern with self-discovery . . . , an understanding of their characters' life-styles and their relation to society, and the power of mimicry aided by a sharp eye and sensitive ear." Because of these similarities Fielding believes that "there has never been a comparable study of how Dickens's imagination fed on his vision of the world about him." Virginia Tiger of the *Washington Post* judges *The World of Charles Dickens* to be "a beautifully measured, gentle study, yet critical and tough about the faults of the man and the flaws in the books." In her review for the *Nation,* Helen Yglesias finds that "Wilson's scholarship is solid and he uses it imaginatively, with the free, clear style of the skilled novelist that he is. . . . Agree with the judgments or not, the reader can only gain by following Wilson's analysis."

Wilson's affinity for Dickens has led him to edit an edition of *Oliver Twist,* to deliver the Dickens Memorial Lecture, to contribute to *Dickens and the Twentieth Century,* a collection of essays, and to compile *The Portable Dickens,* a book of selections from Dickens's oeuvre. In his essay "Charles Dickens: A Haunting," published in *Diversity and Depth in Fiction,* Wilson admits to a "constant and haunting pressure of Dickens's created world upon my imagination." In an interview with Frederick P. W. McDowell in the *Iowa Review,* Wilson comments on the similarities between his work and the work of Dickens. "Apart from the humour of Dickens which lies very close to a good deal of my humour," Wilson states, "what is vital to his approach and to mine is that he sees his central figures always in relation to, first of all, a group and then in relation to the whole of society. Frequently with him the direction in his novels is, rather, outward from society and inwards toward the group and the central figure but always in connection with a great number of other people; he sees the central figures internally and the others are presented externally. On the whole, this has been my method. It has been the only way, I think, in which I can present my sense of man's total isolation, his working out of his problems within himself but also in terms of the other human beings whom he comes across."

In *The Portable Dickens,* a volume meant to be a condensed introduction to Dickens's work, Wilson reprints *Great Expectations* in its entirety and then gathers excerpts from other Dickens's novels under such headings as "Crime, Murder and Pursuit," "Humor," and "Theater." He also provides an introduction that covers Dickens's life and critically examines his books. The result, Frederick Busch writes in the *Washington Post Book World,* is "a full and useful, entertaining and instructive plum pudding of Dickens' work. It is brilliantly introduced and wisely selected."

Diversity and Depth in Fiction: Selected Critical Writings of Angus Wilson is a collection of essays, reviews, introductions, and lectures that Wilson has written on novelists of the last three centuries. The authors covered range from Dostoevsky to Proust and from Zola to Grass. "It's as a novelist—on the job, as it were—that [Wilson] has analyzed the forms of fiction," Loma Sage comments in the *Observer.* This approach allows Wilson to present his personal reactions to books and authors. "He seems to have deliberately displayed a most unprofessional capacity for flexibility, tolerance, and changing his mind," Sage remarks. James Atlas of the *New York Times Book Review* agrees with this assessment, saying that "there is something amateurish about Mr. Wilson's criticism—amateurish in the good sense. Unimpaired by professional envy or ideological bias, he writes about literature with a student's pure enthusiasm. . . . Wilson ranges effortlessly among the whole of English literature, rattling off subplots and minor characters. For all his reiterated insistence on his amateur status, Mr. Wilson is clearly up on contemporary criticism and unafraid to challenge the big boys in the field."

This collection documents, by gathering pieces from over three decades, that Wilson's criticism has undergone a change similar to that found in his novels. David Montrose notes this in *New Statesman:* "This volume demonstrates that Wilson's critical preferences have paralleled his creative style. Reacting against modernism in the early Fifties, he favoured—in his fiction and non-fiction—'a return to the traditional novel.' By the end of the decade, he was commending 'experimental' techniques, having begun to incorporate them into his own work." All of Wilson's criticism, despite the transformation it has undergone over the years, has retained a consistent concern. As J. I. M. Stewart explains in the *London Review of Books,* "nothing is more impressive in these essays than the constancy of [Wilson's] concern for prose fiction as a moral instrument and a vehicle of 'that sense of felt life which is the glory of the traditional English novel.' " A. N. Wilson finds that "each essay is marked by a reverence for the great writers and a sensitive understanding of anyone who has tried his hand at the art in which [Wilson] himself has achieved such eminence."

The moral concern evident in Wilson's literary criticism is crucial to an understanding of his fiction as well. As David Lodge comments in the *New Statesman,* Wilson "has always been obsessed with the theme of evil, and the problems it poses to the liberal humanist and the liberal humanist novel." Wilson explains his perception of evil to Michael Barber of the *New York Times Book Review:* "The sense that there exists something which is very strong and very bad obsesses me. . . . Somewhere in my world is a force of evil. . . . I also believe that some things do become more than what is called Right and Wrong. It was fortified for my generation by our learning of the concentration camps and the Soviet purges. Here was the emergence of wickedness and brutality and evil. . . . All this talking about Right and Wrong without taking into account something stronger and deeper and more horrible wasn't satisfactory." Wilson tells Shenker: "I live and always have lived and always shall live in a world which is cracking ice and walking on eggs, in a world which I see as disintegrating."

Opposed to this apparent pessimism is Wilson's trust in the power of the novel. He writes in his essay "The Dilemma of the Contemporary Novelist," published in *Diversity and Depth in Fiction:* "The novel seems to me to be the most hopeful form of communication in the present age. It is a sort of break-down by corresponding imaginations of the immense isolation that we all feel." Faulkner believes that "the remarkable feature of his . . . career as a writer has been the way in which despite the nihilistic tendencies of the age, Wilson has retained his care for humanity."

Wilson's standing in contemporary British letters is unique because of the range of his writings and his iconoclastic stance. He is, as Busch writes, "a superior novelist, dramatist, storywriter, and critic." Sage, writing in *Twentieth Century Literature,* states that "Wilson has always combined two roles—novelist and man of letters (bohemian and literary statesman, iconoclast and professional, risk-taker and representative)—that are traditionally, tactfully assumed to follow one after the other. It's not particularly surprising, in retrospect, that the authority and vitality of his early fiction 'established' him so quickly. What is extraordinary and distinctive is his having gone on taking risks." Bradbury calls Wilson "unquestionably a leading novelist of his generation and one of Britain's most important literary figures, but there is something in his career and character which is fiercely resistant to all such formulae. He began as a comic writer, a maverick and mimic, and he has continued to be so. He has always written with a strong sense of a tradition, yet in urgent dispute with it. [Critics] have sensed something elusive about him, and often seem unsure in what mode of definition to cast their commentary. This is, I believe, the spirit of a virtuous career, but it is a spirit not always understood."

Among the qualities most often praised by critics of Wilson's work are his gift for mimicry, his mastery of dialogue, and his ability to render a broad social canvas as well as a character's private thoughts. "His novels," Dennis Drabelle writes in the *Washington Post Book World,* "display the careful narration, deft characterization (which draws on his famous skill at mimicry), social acuity and grand scale that we associate with the great Victorians." Anne Tyler, in an article for the *New Republic,* lists some of the qualities of Wilson's fiction. "As a novelist," she writes, "he is tireless in his pursuit of each and every character. He pounces upon the slightest telltale gesture or turn of phrase. . . . He is meticulous, exhaustive in building up his scenes, word by word and clink of china upon clink of china. The result is people so firmly defined that you feel you could count the stitches in their English lawn dresses although, in fact, you

could not, for it is by their speech and movements that he describes them."

Defining Wilson's position in contemporary literature, Lodge maintains that he is "a highly self-conscious, very *literary* novelist, widely and deeply read in the European novel of the last two centuries, and also a very ambitious one, prepared to take risks to earn his own place in that great tradition." Faulkner sees Wilson as "a restless and ambitious novelist who has never repeated himself, and who has used his great powers of observation and mimicry both to illuminate the change of English society and to suggest the epistemological problems posed by all literary texts. Criticism probably fails to do justice to the brilliance of his wit, but it can at least point to the range of relevance of his work. For Wilson has written about many of the main issues of our time: freedom and bondage in human relationships; the dilemmas of liberalism; the limits of language; the relation between public and private life; the appeals of role-playing; the temptations of magic; and, pervasively, the violence of the world." Halio believes that "Angus Wilson's position as a major novelist and, perhaps more important, as a distinguished man of letters—writer, teacher, critic, public servant—for the period after World War II is eminently secure."

MEDIA ADAPTATIONS: The Old Men at the Zoo and *Late Call* were adapted for television by the British Broadcasting Corp.

AVOCATIONAL INTERESTS: Gardening, travel, medieval history.

BIOGRAPHICAL/CRITICAL SOURCES:

BOOKS

Allen, Walter, *The Modern Novel: In Britain and the United States,* Dutton, 1964.

Bergonzi, Bernard, *The Situation of the Novel,* University of Pittsburgh Press, 1970.

Bradbury, Malcolm, *Possibilities: Essays on the State of the Novel,* Oxford University Press, 1973.

Bradbury, Malcolm, editor, *The Novel Today: Contemporary Writers on Modern Fiction,* Manchester University Press, 1977.

Burgess, Anthony, *The Novel Now: A Guide to Contemporary Fiction,* Norton, 1976.

Contemporary Literary Criticism, Gale, Volume 2, 1974, Volume 3, 1975, Volume 5, 1976, Volume 25, 1983, Volume 34, 1985.

Cowley, Malcolm, editor, *Writers at Work: The 'Paris Review' Interviews,* Viking, 1959.

Cox, C. B., *The Free Spirit,* Oxford University Press, 1963.

Dictionary of Literary Biography, Volume 15: *British Novelists, 1930-1959,* Gale, 1983.

Faulkner, Peter, *Angus Wilson: Mimic and Moralist,* Viking, 1980.

Gardner, Averil, *Angus Wilson,* Twayne, 1985.

Gindin, James, *Postwar British Fiction: New Accents and Attitudes,* University of California Press, 1962.

Gindin, James, *Harvest of a Quiet Eye: The Novel of Compassion,* University of Indiana Press, 1971.

Gransden, K. W., *Angus Wilson,* Longman, 1969.

Halio, Jay L., *Angus Wilson,* Oliver & Boyd, 1964.

Halio, Jay L., editor, *Critical Essays on Angus Wilson,* G. K. Hall, 1985.

Karl, Frederick R., *A Reader's Guide to the Contemporary English Novel,* Farrar, Straus, 1962.

McDowell, Frederick P. W., and Sharon Graves, *The Angus Wilson Manuscripts in the University of Iowa Libraries,* University of Iowa Press, 1969.

Rabinovitz, Rubin, *The Reaction against Experiment in the English Novel, 1950-1960,* Columbia University Press, 1967.

Shapiro, Charles, editor, *Contemporary British Novelists,* Southern Illinois University Press, 1965.

Wilson, Angus, *Diversity and Depth in Fiction: Selected Critical Writings of Angus Wilson,* Secker & Warburg, 1983, Viking, 1984.

Wilson, Edmund, *The Bit between My Teeth: A Literary Chronicle, 1950-1965,* Farrar, Straus, 1965.

The Writer's Place: Interviews on the Literary Situation in Contemporary Britain, University of Minnesota Press, 1974.

PERIODICALS

Atlantic, November, 1973, May, 1978, October, 1980, May, 1984.
Best Sellers, January 1, 1968, September 15, 1970.
Book World, May 25, 1969.
Books Abroad, winter, 1966.
Books and Bookmen, May, 1973, July, 1973, July, 1980.
Christian Science Monitor, December 7, 1967, October 1, 1970.
Commentary, January, 1968.
Commonweal, March 26, 1965, March 8, 1968.
Contemporary Literature, Number 21, 1980.
Critical Quarterly, autumn, 1961, spring, 1970.
Detroit News, November 30, 1981.
Dutch Quarterly Review, Number 6, 1976.
Encounter, November, 1980.
Essays in Criticism, Number 9, 1959.
Four Quarters, summer, 1982.
Globe and Mail (Toronto), October 22, 1988.
Guardian, June 2, 1973.
Harper's Bazaar, May, 1970.
Hudson Review, spring, 1968, winter, 1974.
Iowa Review, fall, 1972.
Kenyon Review, March, 1967.
Listener, October 5, 1967, July 10, 1980.
Literary Review, November, 1980.
London Magazine, November, 1967.
London Review of Books, December 1-21, 1983.
Morning Star, May 17, 1968.
Nation, April 15, 1968, November 23, 1970.
National Review, September 13, 1974.
New Leader, January 25, 1971, November 17, 1980.
New Republic, November 8, 1980.
New Review, April, 1974.
New Statesman, October 6, 1967, November 1, 1977, July 18, 1980, September 9, 1983.
New Statesman and Nation, March 29, 1952.
Newsweek, August 31, 1970, December 21, 1970, November 26, 1973.
New Yorker, August 23, 1952, October 6, 1956, January 16, 1965, April 3, 1978.
New York Herald Tribune Book Review, October 5, 1952.
New York Review of Books, February 25, 1965, January 18, 1968, October 8, 1970, November 1, 1973, March 9, 1978, November 20, 1980.
New York Times, May 18, 1952, November 23, 1967, October 14, 1973, March 16, 1978, October 17, 1980.
New York Times Book Review, November 26, 1967, September 13, 1970, March 12, 1978, November 16, 1980, August 19, 1984.
Observer, May 24, 1970, July 6, 1980, August 28, 1983.

Publishers Weekly, March 9, 1984.
Punch, July 9, 1980.
Reporter, February 8, 1968.
Review of English Literature, April, 1960.
Saturday Review, January 16, 1965, November 18, 1967, July 5, 1969, March 4, 1978, October, 1980.
Saturday Review of Literature, February 17, 1951, October 6, 1956.
Spectator, February 29, 1952, September 17, 1954, October 6, 1967, July 12, 1980.
Studies in the Literary Imagination, spring, 1980.
Studies in the Novel, spring, 1970.
Time, December 1, 1967, December 3, 1973, March 13, 1978.
Times (London), July 7, 1980, September 1, 1983.
Times Literary Supplement, April 6, 1967, October 5, 1967, December 23, 1977, July 11, 1980, September 16, 1983, February 7, 1986, November 12, 1987.
Toronto Star, October 25, 1981.
Twentieth Century Literature, summer, 1983.
Washington Post, December 30, 1970.
Washington Post Book World, November 1, 1973, November 2, 1980, July 3, 1983.
Yale Review, spring, 1968, summer, 1974.

*   *   *

WILSON, August   1945-

PERSONAL: Born in 1945 in Pittsburgh, Pa.

ADDRESSES: Home—St. Paul, Minn.

CAREER: Writer. Worked as founder and director of Black Horizons Theatre Company in St. Paul, Minn., beginning in 1968; scriptwriter for Science Museum of Minnesota.

AWARDS, HONORS: Award for best play of 1984-85 from New York Drama Critics' Circle, 1985, Antoinette Perry ("Tony") Award nomination from League of New York Theatres and Producers, 1985, and Whiting Writers' Award from the Whiting Foundation, 1986, all for "Ma Rainey's Black Bottom"; Outstanding Play Award from American Theatre Critics, 1986, Pulitzer Prize for drama, Tony Award for best play, and award for best Broadway play from Outer Critics Circle, all 1987, all for "Fences"; John Gasner Award for best American playwright from Outer Critics Circle, 1987; named Artist of the Year by *Chicago Tribune,* 1987.

WRITINGS:

"Jitney" (two-act play), first produced in Pittsburgh, Pa., at the Allegheny Repertory Theatre, 1982.

Ma Rainey's Black Bottom (play; first produced in New Haven, Conn., at the Yale Repertory Theatre, 1984; produced on Broadway at the Cort Theatre, October, 1984), New American Library, 1985.

Fences (play; first produced in New Haven at the Yale Repertory Theatre, 1985; produced on Broadway at 46th Street Theatre, March, 1987), New American Library, 1986.

Joe Turner's Come and Gone (play; first produced in New Haven at the Yale Repertory Theatre, 1986; produced on Broadway, March, 1988), New American Library, 1988.

"The Piano Lesson" (play), first produced in New Haven at the Yale Repertory Theatre, 1987.

Also author of play "Fullerton Street" and the book for a stage musical about jazz musician Jelly Roll Morton. Poetry anthologized in *The Poetry of Blackamerica,* Adoff. Contributor to periodicals, including *Black Lines* and *Connection.*

WORK IN PROGRESS: "Two Trains Running," a play set in 1968; a screenplay adaptation of "Fences."

SIDELIGHTS: August Wilson has been hailed since the mid-1980s as an important talent in the American theatre. He spent his childhood in poverty in Pittsburgh, Pennsylvania, where he lived with his parents and five siblings. Though he grew up in a poor family, Wilson felt that his parents withheld knowledge of even greater hardships they had endured. "My generation of blacks knew very little about the past of our parents," he told the *New York Times* in 1984. "They shielded us from the indignities they suffered."

At age sixteen Wilson, who had already flunked ninth grade, quit school and began working at menial jobs. But he also pursued a literary career and successfully submitted poems to black publications at the University of Pittsburgh. In 1968 he became active in the theatre by founding—despite lacking prior experience—the Black Horizons Theatre Company in St. Paul, Minnesota. Recalling his early theatre involvement, Wilson described himself to the *New York Times* as "a cultural nationalist . . . trying to raise consciousness through theater."

In St. Paul Wilson wrote his first play, "Jitney," a realistic drama set in a Pittsburgh taxi station. "Jitney" was accepted for workshop production at the O'Neill Theatre Center's National Playwrights Conference in 1982. This brought Wilson into contact with other playwrights. Inspired, he wrote another play, "Fullerton Street," but this work failed to strengthen his reputation.

Wilson then resumed work on an earlier unfinished project, "Ma Rainey's Black Bottom," a play about a black blues singer's exploitation of her fellow musicians. This work, whose title role is named after an actual blues singer from the 1920s, is set in a recording stuido in 1927. In the studio, temperamental Ma Rainey verbally abuses the other musicians and presents herself—without justification—as an important musical figure. But much of the play is also set in a rehearsal room, where Ma Rainey's musicians discuss their abusive employer and the hardships of life in racist America.

Eventually, the musicians are all revealed to have experienced, in varying degrees, racist treatment. The most resigned member is the group's leader, a trombonist who has learned to accept racial discrimination and merely negotiates around it. The bassist's response is to wallow in hedonism and ignore his nation's treatment of blacks, while the pianist takes an intellectual approach to solving racial problems. The group's trumpeter, however, is bitter and cynical. He is haunted by the memory of his mother's rape by four white men. Tensions mount in the play when the sullen trumpeter clashes with Ma Rainey and is fired. The manager of the recording studio then swindles him in a recording rights agreement, and a subsequent and seemingly insignificant incident precipitates a violent act from the trumpeter, who has simply endured too much abuse. The London *Times*'s Holly Hill called the play's climactic moment "a melodramatically violent act."

"Ma Rainey's Black Bottom" earned Wilson a return to the O'Neill Center's playwriting conference in 1983. There Wilson's play impressed director Lloyd Richards from the Yale Repertory Theatre. Richards worked with Wilson to refine the play, and when it was presented at Yale in 1984 it was hailed as the work of an important new playwright. Frank Rich, who reviewed the Yale production in the *New York Times*, acclaimed Wilson as "a major find for the American theater" and cited his ability to write "with compassion, raucous humor and penetrating wisdom."

Wilson enjoyed further success with "Ma Rainey's Black Bottom" after the play came to Broadway later in 1984. The *Chicago Tribune*'s Richard Christiansen reviewed the Broadway production as "a work of intermittent but immense power" and commended the "striking beauty" of the play's "literary and theatrical poetry." Christiansen added that "Wilson's power of language is sensational" and that "Ma Rainey's Black Bottom" was "the work of an impressive writer." The London *Times*'s Hill agreed, calling Wilson "a promising new playwright" and hailing his work as "a remarkable first play."

Wilson's subsequent plays include the Pulitzer Prize-winning "Fences," which is about a former athlete who forbids his son to accept an athletic scholarship, and "Joe Turner's Come and Gone," which concerns an ex-convict's efforts to find his wife. Like "Ma Rainey's Black Bottom," these plays underwent extensive rewriting. Guiding Wilson in this process was Lloyd Richards, dean of Yale's drama school and director of the school's productions of Wilson's plays. "August is a wonderful poet," Richards told the *New York Times* in 1986. "A wonderful poet turning into a playwright." Richards added that his work with Wilson involved "clarifying" each work's main theme and "arranging the material in a dynamic way."

Both "Fences" and "Joe Turner's Come and Gone" were praised when they played on American stages. The *New York Times*'s Frank Rich, in his review of "Fences," wrote that the play "leaves no doubt that Mr. Wilson is a major writer, combining a poet's ear for vernacular with a robust sense of humor (political and sexual), a sure instinct for cracking dramatic incident and passionate commitment to a great subject." And in his critique of "Joe Turner's Come and Gone," Rich speculated that the play "will give a lasting voice to a generation of uprooted black Americans." Rich contended that the work was "potentially its author's finest achievement yet" and described it as "a teeming canvas of black America . . . and a spiritual allegory."

Throughout his career Wilson has stressed that his first objective is in getting his work produced. "All I want is for the most people to get to see this play," he told the *New York Times* while discussing "Joe Turner's Come and Gone." Wilson added, however, that he was not opposed to having his works performed on Broadway. He told the *New York Times* that Broadway "still has the connotation of Mecca" and asked, "Who doesn't want to go to Mecca?"

BIOGRAPHICAL/CRITICAL SOURCES:

BOOKS

Contemporary Literary Criticism, Gale, Volume 39, 1986, Volume 50: *Yearbook 1987,* 1988.

PERIODICALS

Chicago Tribune, October 15, 1984, June 8, 1987, December 17, 1987, December 27, 1987.
Chicago Tribune Book World, February 9, 1986.
Ebony, January, 1985.
Los Angeles Times, November 24, 1984, November 7, 1986, April 17, 1987, June 7, 1987, June 8, 1987, June 9, 1987, February 6, 1988.
Newsweek, April 6, 1987.
New York Times, April 11, 1984, April 13, 1984, October 12, 1984, October 22, 1984, May 6, 1986, May 14, 1986, June 20, 1986, March 27, 1987, April 5, 1987, April 9, 1987, April 17, 1987, May 7, 1987, December 10, 1987, December 11, 1987.
Saturday Review, January/February, 1985.

Time, April 27, 1987.

Times (London), November 6, 1984, April 18, 1987, April 24, 1987.

Washington Post, May 20, 1986, April 15, 1987, June 9, 1987, October 4, 1987, October 9, 1987.

* * *

WILSON, Colin 1931-

PERSONAL: Born June 26, 1931, in Leicester, England; son of Arthur (a factory worker) and Anetta (Jones) Wilson; married Dorothy Betty Troop, 1951 (divorced, 1952); married Pamela Joy Stewart (a librarian), 1960; children: (first marriage) Roderick; (second marriage) Sally, John Damon, Christopher Rowan. *Education:* Attended schools in Leicester until he was sixteen. *Politics:* "Moderate right." *Religion:* "My deepest interest is religion. My deepest need—to create my own."

ADDRESSES: Home and office—Tetherdown, Gorran Haven, Cornwall, England. *Agent*—Georges Borchardt, 136 East 57th St., New York, N.Y. 10022.

CAREER: Writer. Employed by Cranbourne Products Ltd. (wool company), Leicester, England, 1947; laboratory assistant at Gateway Secondary Technical School, 1947-48; tax collector, 1947-49; held various jobs as laborer and office worker; hospital porter in Fulham, England; spent some time in Paris and Strasbourg in the early 1950s, working in Paris on *Merlin* and *Paris Review,* 1954; lecturer in American universities. Writer in residence, Hollins College, 1966-67; visiting professor, University of Washington, 1967-68, Rutgers University, 1974. *Military service:* Royal Air Force, 1949-50; became aircraftman second grade.

MEMBER: Society of Authors, Gentleman's Club (St. Austell, Cornwall), Savage Club (London).

AWARDS, HONORS: Ford Foundation grant, 1961.

WRITINGS:

NONFICTION

The Outsider, Houghton, 1956.

Religion and the Rebel, Houghton, 1957, revised edition, Salem House, 1984.

(Contributor) Tom Maschler, editor, *Declaration,* Dutton, 1958, reprinted, Kennikat, 1972.

The Stature of Man, Houghton, 1959, reprinted, Greenwood Press, 1986 (published in England as *Age of Defeat,* Gollancz, 1959).

The Strength to Dream: Literature and the Imagination, Houghton, 1962, reprinted, Greenwood Press, 1973.

Origins of the Sexual Impulse, Putnam, 1962.

(With Patricia Pitman) *An Encyclopedia of Murder,* Putnam, 1962.

Rasputin and the Fall of the Romanovs, Farrar, Straus, 1964.

The Brandy of the Damned: Discoveries of a Musical Eclectic (essays on music), John Baker, 1964, published as *Chords and Discords: Purely Personal Opinions on Music,* Atheneum, 1966, published as *Colin Wilson on Music,* Pan, 1967.

Beyond the Outsider: The Philosophy of the Future, Houghton, 1965.

Eagle and Earwig (essays on literature), John Baker, 1965.

Introduction to the New Existentialism, Hutchinson, 1966, Houghton, 1967.

Sex and the Intelligent Teenager, Arrow, 1966.

(Author of introduction) James Drought, *Drugoth,* new edition, Skylight Press, 1966.

Voyage to a Beginning: An Intellectual Autobiography, Crown, 1969.

(Contributor) James F. T. Bugental, editor, *Challenges of Humanistic Psychology,* McGraw, 1967.

Bernard Shaw: A Reassessment, Atheneum, 1969.

A Casebook of Murder, Ferwin, 1969, Cowles, 1970.

Poetry and Mysticism, City Lights, 1969, expanded edition, Hutchinson, 1970.

(With J. B. Pick and E. H. Visiak) *The Strange Genius of David Lindsay,* John Baker, 1970, published as *The Haunted Man: The Strange Genius of David Lindsay,* Borgo Press, 1979.

The Occult: A History, Random House, 1971.

(With Piero Rimaldi) *L'Amour: The Ways of Love,* Crown, 1972.

New Pathways in Psychology: Maslow and the Post-Freudian Revolution, Taplinger, 1972.

Order of Assassins: The Psychology of Murder, Hart-Davis, 1972.

(Author of introduction) Alexander Garfield Kelly, *Jack the Ripper: A Bibliography and Review of the Literature,* Association of Assistant Librarians (London), 1973.

Tree by Tolkien, Covent Garden Press, 1973, Capra, 1974.

Strange Powers, Latimer New Dimensions, 1973, Random House, 1975.

A Book of Booze, Gollancz, 1974.

Hesse-Reich-Borges, Leaves of Grass Press, 1974.

The Craft of the Novel, Gollancz, 1975, reprinted, Ashgrove, 1985.

The Unexplained, edited by Robert Durand and Roberta Dyer, Lost Pleiade Press, 1975.

(Editor) Valeri Briussov, *Fiery Angel,* Neville Spearman, 1976.

Men of Strange Powers, Doubleday, 1976, published with *Minds without Boundaries,* by Stuart Holroyd, as *Mysteries of the Mind,* Aldus Books, 1978.

Enigmas and Mysteries, Doubleday, 1976.

The Geller Phenomena, Doubleday, 1976.

(Editor) *Dark Dimensions: A Celebration of the Occult,* Everest House, 1978.

Mysteries: An Investigation into the Occult, the Paranormal, and the Supernatural, Putnam, 1978.

Science Fiction as Existentialism, Bran's Head Books, 1978.

(With George Hay) *Necronomicon,* Spearman, 1978.

Starseekers, Hodder & Stoughton, 1980.

Frankenstein's Castle: The Double Brain-Door to Wisdom, Ashgrove, 1980, published as *Frankenstein's Castle: The Right Brain-Door to Wisdom,* Salem House, 1982.

The War against Sleep: The Philosophy of Gurdjieff, Aquarian Press, 1980, revised edition published as *G. I. Gurdjieff: The War against Sleep,* Newcastle, 1986.

The Quest for Wilheim Reich, Doubleday, 1981.

Anti Sartre: With an Essay on Camus, Borgo, 1981.

(Editor with John Grant) *The Directory of Possibilities,* W. H. Smith, 1981.

Poltergeist!, New English Library, 1981.

Witches, Dragon's World, 1981.

(Editor with Donald Seaman) *Encyclopaedia of Modern Murder,* Barker, 1983, published as *The Encyclopedia of Modern Murder: 1962-1982,* Putnam, 1985.

Access to Inner Worlds, Rider, 1983.

A Criminal History of Mankind, Putnam, 1984.

Janus Murder Case, Granada, 1984.

Psychic Detectives: Story of Psychometry and the Paranormal in Crime Detection, Pan Books, 1984, Mercury House, 1986.

Lord of the Underworld: Jung and the Twentieth Century, Aquarian Press, 1984.

Rudolf Steiner: The Man and His Vision, Aquarian Press, 1984.

Bicameral Critic: Collected Shorter Writings, edited by Howard F. Dossor, Ashgrove, 1985.

Life Force, Warner Books, 1985.

Afterlife, Harrap, 1985, Doubleday, 1987.

The Essential Colin Wilson, Harrap, 1985, Celestial Arts, 1986.

(With Ted Holiday) *The Goblin Universe,* Llewellyn, 1986.

Existentially Speaking: Essays on Philosophy and Literature, Borgo, 1986.

(With Seaman) *Scandal!: An Encyclopedia,* Stein & Day, 1986.

The Laurel and Hardy Theory of Consciousness, Rob Briggs, 1986.

The Encyclopedia of Unsolved Mysteries, State Mutual Books, 1987.

Aleister Crowley: The Nature of the Beast, Sterling, 1988.

The Magician from Siberia, State Mutual Books, 1988.

The Mammoth Book of True Crime, Carroll & Graf, 1988.

(With Damon Wilson) *The Encyclopedia of Unsolved Mysteries,* Contemporary Books, 1988.

Beyond the Occult: A Twenty Year Investigation into the Paranormal, Carroll & Graf, 1989.

The Misfits: A Study of Sexual Outsiders, Carroll & Graf, 1989.

FICTION

Ritual in the Dark, Houghton, 1960, reprinted, Academy Chicago, 1982.

Adrift in Soho, Houghton, 1961.

The Violent World of Hugh Greene, Houghton, 1963 (published in England as *The World of Violence,* Gollancz, 1963).

The Sex Diary of Gerard Sorme, Dial, 1963 (published in England as *Man without a Shadow: The Diary of an Existentialist,* Barker, 1963).

Necessary Doubt, Simon & Schuster, 1964.

The Mind Parasites, Barker, 1966, Arkham, 1967, 3rd edition, Oneiric, 1972.

The Glass Cage: An Unconventional Detective Story, Barker, 1966, Random House, 1967.

The Philosopher's Stone, John Baker, 1969, Crown, 1971.

The Killer, New English Library, 1970, published as *Lingard,* Crown, 1970.

The God of the Labyrinth, Hart-Davis, 1970, published as *The Hedonists,* New American Library, 1971.

The Black Room, Weidenfeld & Nicolson, 1971, Pyramid Publications, 1975.

The Schoolgirl Murder Case, Crown, 1974.

(Contributor) *Tales of the Cthulu Mythos,* Arkham House, 1974.

The Space Vampires, Hart-Davis, 1975, Random House, 1976.

The Personality Surgeon, Mercury House, 1986.

Spider World: The Tower, Grafton, 1987.

The Sex Diary of a Metaphysician, Ronin, 1988.

Spider World: The Desert, Ace Books, 1988.

Spider World: Fortress, Ace Books, 1989.

PLAYS

Strindberg: Playscript 31 (first produced as "Pictures in a Bath of Acid" in Leeds, Yorkshire, 1971; produced as "Strindberg: A Psychological Portrait" in New York City, 1974), J. Calder, 1970, Random House, 1971.

Also author of "Viennese Interlude," produced in Scarborough, Yorkshire, and London, 1960, "The Metal Flower Blossom," 1960, and "The Death of God," 1966.

OTHER

Editor, "Occult" series, Aldus Books, 1975. Contributor to *Encounter, Time and Tide, London Magazine, Chicago Review,* and other periodicals.

Wilson's books have been translated into more than fourteen languages. A collection of Wilson's manuscripts can be found in Austin Texas, at the University of Texas.

WORK IN PROGRESS: Lulu, a novel.

SIDELIGHTS: For more than thirty years author Colin Wilson has concerned himself with a reexamination of modern philosophy and with the amelioration of the human condition. His body of work includes nonfiction, novels, biographies, plays, and encyclopedic investigations of crime and the occult. Wilson has often stirred controversy by imbuing his philosophical works— and his fiction—with a sense of urgency and the strong conviction that human consciousness is slumbering or limited to a "tunnel vision" far short of its potential. In *Colin Wilson: The Outsider and Beyond,* Clifford P. Bendau writes: "The essence of Wilson's position is that man can and must expand the present modes of consciousness. His casebook studies are meant to give people an idea of what can be developed. The phenomenon of man's resignation to littleness is used to show the reader that man is perceptually aware of very little; but moreover, that man is conscious or unconsciously *choosing* not to be aware."

Wilson published his first book, *The Outsider,* at the age of twenty-four. His writings since then have expanded upon the theme he introduced in that work, the premise that "with the development of the Romantic Movement in art, literature, and philosophy, a group of outstanding individuals has developed who are no longer satisfied with the dead-end streets of scientific or existentialist thought," according to Martha Eckman in *The Contemporary Literary Scene 1973.* In his philosophical works subsequent to *The Outsider,* including *Religion and the Rebel, The Stature of Man,* and *Beyond the Outsider: The Philosophy of the Future,* Wilson posits a kind of "optimistic existentialism" that places importance on intuition and visionary experiences. Though Wilson's ideas have met with criticism and derision at times, John A. Weigel, in his book *Colin Wilson,* notes that recent changes in the philosophical climate "have redefined Wilson's significance as a thinker who has persistently challenged pessimism and despair." Weigel also contends that Wilson "is to be credited with the courage to rebel against deterministic philosophies and to insist that man is free to improve himself and his community *if he wants to.* In one sense, Colin Wilson is both heroic and inevitable. As a freedom-espousing philosopher, he chose for himself a big job, . . . to diagnose and to cure mankind's sickness."

As Weigel notes in the *Dictionary of Literary Biography,* Wilson also "firmly believes that fiction is an appropriate vehicle for exploring philosophical concerns." Bendau similarly states: "Wilson's fiction is didactic. It is the nature of his style to make fiction and nonfiction complementary as instructional devices; an unusual, but not illegitimate technique aimed concurrently at different sensibilities in the reader." Indeed, Wilson utilizes a variety of fiction genres to promote his ideas, among them psychological thrillers, science fiction, and murder mysteries. Some of his best-known novels fall into the science fiction/fantasy category, including *The Mind Parasites, The Philosopher's Stone,* and *The Space Vampires.* In *Colin Wilson,* Weigel writes: "For Wilson, fantasy is highly useful as a relatively unblinkered kind of storytelling, for he writes neither to delight nor to solace. He packs his parables with his own experiences and speculations. Since Wilson has a difficult message to communicate he needs all the help he can get in the way of supportive mysteries and heuristic fantasies." Weigel also comments that while none of Wilson's fiction "has that kind of inevitability which awes literary critics" it is nonetheless "honestly adequate to its purpose."

According to Bendau, Wilson's writing "always works well when he chooses subjects that can carry his philosophical weight, when he builds on philosophical foundations that galvanize his fiction with the nonfiction."

On one point Wilson's champions and detractors concur; namely, that his prodigious literary output stands as testament to his seriousness of purpose. He has authored more than eighty books since 1956 and has supported himself primarily by writing for thirty years. During that time he has maintained a high degree of confidence in his talent and ideas, even in the face of severe criticism.

The notion that he was destined for recognition sustained Wilson even before he was published, as he notes in his 1969 autobiography *Voyage to a Beginning*. While still in his early teens he began to feel superior to the "vegetable mediocrity" of his working-class Leicester background. According to Weigel, Wilson "*chose* greatness, feeling rightfully that his choice was limited to that or nothing; and he wasted little time in getting started in his pursuit of it." An early interest in science lasted until Wilson graduated from secondary school. Then he discovered literature and determined that he wanted to be a writer. As he notes in an essay for *Declaration,* however, many impediments stood in the way of his goals. "My problem," he claims, "became simply the problem of how to find leisure to read and think and write, when my circumstances made it necessary to work forty-eight hours a week to live." After drifting through a series of jobs and apartments, Wilson took the desperate measure of sleeping outdoors on London's Hampstead Heath in order to save money. During the day he read and wrote in the British Museum Reading Room, where author Angus Wilson took an interest in his work.

In *Declaration,* Wilson states that he conceived the idea for *The Outsider* when he was nineteen, but work on a novel (later published as *Ritual in the Dark*) postponed his ambitions for the nonfiction. He began writing *The Outsider* in 1955, culling ideas from his diaries and from an eclectic sampling of books he had read. In *Voyage to a Beginning* he describes the central concern of the work as "the misfits in modern civilization, the creative men who feel out of place in the rat race." He adds: "But I took care to state that the Outsider is not necessarily creative. His lack of self-understanding may be so complete that he never even begins to achieve the catharsis of creation." Using case studies from fiction by Hermann Hesse, Ernest Hemingway, and Fedor Dostoevski, as well as exploring the lives of painter Vincent Van Gogh and the dancer Vaslav Nijinski, Wilson delineates the troubles of the "Outsider," an individual at odds with himself and his conventional social environment. Wilson admits that he was so excited about the book he was writing that he noted in his journal: "This book will be the *Waste Land* of the fifties, and should be the most important book of its generation." Victor Gollancz published the work in May of 1956.

Critical reaction to *The Outsider* followed a "spectacular parabola," notes Kenneth Allsop in *The Angry Decade: A Survey of the Cultural Revolt of the 1950s.* As Allsop describes it, Wilson rose "from out of nowhere (or, to be precise, from out of a sleeping bag on Hampstead Heath) up through a dizzying arc of fame and fortune, with a steep nose-dive into disfavour." At first the popular media "enthusiastically endorsed young Colin Wilson as a genius," according to Weigel in his book on the author. For instance, *Observer* contributor Philip Toynbee called *The Outsider* "an exhaustive and luminously intelligent study of a representative theme of our time . . . truly astounding . . . a real contribution to an understanding of our deepest predicament." Other reviewers offered similar praise, and the book became a

bestseller in England and the United States. Wilson, who had long labored in poverty and anonymity, was accorded celebrity status, but the publicity was not always of a positive nature. He was misquoted on several occasions, and a domestic dispute with his fiancee's family provided a scandal that was "of exactly the right palate for the popular Press," in Allsop's words. Within six months of *The Outsider*'s publication, critics began to reevaluate it—and its author—with less-than-flattering results. Wilson was called to task for his excessive quotations from other sources, for his disregard of formal philosophical method, and for the stridency of his assertions. Dismayed by the change in the critical climate, Wilson moved to a cottage in Cornwall and continued to write. By the end of 1956, notes Weigel, the young author "had fully sampled the equivocal flavor of success."

Wilson claims in *Voyage to a Beginning* that after his second book *Religion and the Rebel* was "hatcheted to death" by the critics, his name got mentioned "if someone needed a symbol of intellectual pretentiousness, or unfounded generalization, or an example of how hysteria can make a reputation overnight." He adds: "I must admit that during the 1956-58 period I felt badly treated. On the other hand, I've always had an optimistic temperament, a basic feeling that the gods mean well by me, as well as several years' training in getting on with the work in hand and ignoring other people. . . . I think things worked out well. The feeling that no one much cared about what I was doing led me to give my full attention to the task of creating a new form of existentialism." Martha Eckman breaks Wilson's "new existentialism" down into two components: "(1) that consciousness needs to be expanded by an act of *will*—not through hallucinogens and not through the trance state achieved by a number of religious groups—and (2) that there is *meaning* in the evolving world, as opposed to the popular existential view that planet Earth is a meaningless, accidental, and absurd fiasco." From this viewpoint, notes Weigel, "Wilson prepares the case for the desirability of increasing the duration as well as the frequency of liberating experiences."

The controversy over the viability of Wilson's message continues, though the tone of the criticism is more subdued. In a *Times Literary Supplement* assessment of *Introduction to the New Existentialism,* a reviewer states: "It seems a pity that someone so widely read and so obviously intelligent should not bother to understand something, at least, of what professional philosophers have been doing for the past few decades. If Mr. Wilson could add something of their patience, respect for fact, and dislike of vagueness to his own quite impressive armoury of insight, perceptiveness and enthusiasm, he might write something which would persuade reasonable men rather than merely reflecting the crises of identity, alienation, neurosis, hopelessness or however we care to describe the modern malaise." *Saturday Review* contributor Emile Capouya calls Wilson's philosophical works "a chaos of definite assertions." The critic continues: "It is not so much that [Wilson] is vague, . . . but that he is arbitrary. He will set out premises lucidly enough, and then draw conclusions from other, unmentioned premises, or perhaps arrive at them by parthenogenesis. His examples do not exemplify. His demonstrations are less than conclusive. He abounds in private formulas and talismans. . . . These peculiarities make Mr. Wilson damnably hard to follow, and easy to praise or blame. They account for the fact that his critics have most often been provoked to narrow-minded strictures or else to vaporous enthusiasm." Capouya concludes that the author's "trees are freaks of nature, but his woods have nevertheless a certain comeliness."

While some critics express dissatisfaction with Wilson's writings, others find him a seminal thinker with an innovative form of expression. "Wilson is not a stylist," writes Weigel in *Colin Wilson,* "therefore, his most significant effects are seldom achieved with the delicate nuances or with pastel epiphanies. . . . He has always been concerned about his effectiveness as a writer, but his objective is not to find the irreducible form of an idea, for he is a persuader rather than a poet." Bendau offers the opinion that Wilson has been criticized because his analyses do not follow the formal guidelines of academic writing. "In some respects, the critics are right," Bendau contends. "When subjected to analysis, [Wilson's] arguments often fall short. Isolated from the whole, individual works may appear to be hasty generalizations. But logical analysis and isolated dissection, while valid for criticism, do not justify a complete rejection of Wilson's ideas. These are not the only criteria available. . . . Unlike the scientist or mathematician, he is not interested in discovering universal theoretical truths. He is interested in the particulars of existence, here and now. He is oriented practically to the way reality could and should be. . . . In short, Wilson [is] a pioneer in the interdisciplinary approach to problem solving; he could never justify the separation of philosophy from art or literature." Weigel concludes: "Presenting himself as a prophet of reality, Wilson has always believed that his work has the highest kind of significance. . . . His confidence is usually more reassuring than the demure modesty of more timid candidates for significance." Eckman makes a more succinct statement when she comments: "My contention is that *The Outsider* contains the key idea to understanding the twentieth century."

More recently, much of Wilson's best-known nonfiction concerns the occult and paranormal phenomena, or investigations of violent crimes. Once again, according to *Washington Post* reviewer Christopher Bird, readers of Wilson's works on the occult are called upon "to adjust their thinking to worlds beyond the bleakly materialist and limited version of the cosmos presently expounded by mainstream science." In *Colin Wilson,* Weigel notes that Wilson "emerges as one of the first of the intellectuals interested in the validity of paraintellectual events such as hunches and premonitions." Alan Hull Walton makes a similar observation in *Books and Bookmen,* where he suggests that Wilson fits in "the top rank of serious contemporary investigators of the paranormal." Wilson is also fascinated with murder as a sort of negative art that some desperate people employ in order to escape boredom and triviality. His approach in nonfiction, according to Bendau, "is to splash his readers in the face with enough cold water to rouse them from their passivity, and generate an active interest in their own freedom." *New York Times Book Review* contributor Allen J. Hubin suggests that Wilson's *A Casebook of Murder* "does set murder into quite useful social and historical perspective."

In his essay for *Declaration,* Wilson makes the assertion that the modern artist "must cease to be the limp, impassive observer. He must become actively involved in the task of restoring a metaphysical consciousness to this age." Throughout his ever-growing canon Wilson strives to put this conviction into action, uniting "the truth of religion with the truth of science in a hopeful and progressive manner," according to *Chicago Review* contributor Richard Hack. As Walton notes in *Books and Bookmen,* Wilson "is a controversial writer. Inescapably so; since in an age of talented mediocrity, he is blessed with far more than talent—he is blessed with insight, sincerety, humility [and] extraordinarily wide learning." In *Hollins Critic,* R. H. W. Dillard finds the same strengths in Wilson's fiction. "If doing and being are somehow one," Dillard writes, "[Wilson's] novels, with their developing manner and matter, their movement toward a viable existential realism of inner as well as outer truth, show Colin Wil-

son to be a . . . man of real vision who has never ceased to grow." Kenneth Allsop offers this final assessment of Wilson's accomplishments: "Throughout Wilson's writing, despite its brashness and want of precision, there is a general dynamic synthesis: you know what he is getting at, and although there is an ugly look about some of the methods he seems prepared to use, you can accept the ultimate object, which is, fundamentally, a richer spiritual life for man."

AVOCATIONAL INTERESTS: Collecting opera records, mathematics.

BIOGRAPHICAL/CRITICAL SOURCES:

BOOKS

Aldridge, John W., *Time to Murder and Create: The Contemporary Novel in Crisis,* McKay, 1966.

Allsop, Kenneth, *The Angry Decade: A Survey of the Cultural Revolt of the 1950s,* Peter Owen Ltd., 1958.

Bendau, Clifford P., *Colin Wilson: The Outsider and Beyond,* Borgo, 1979.

Bugental, James F. T., editor, *Challenges of Humanistic Psychology,* McGraw, 1967.

Campion, Sidney R., *The World of Colin Wilson,* Muller, 1962.

Contemporary Authors, Autobiography Series, Volume 5, Gale, 1987.

Contemporary Literary Criticism, Gale, Volume 3, 1975, Volume 14, 1980.

Dictionary of Literary Biography, Volume 14: *British Novelists since 1960,* Gale, 1983.

Gindin, James, *Postwar British Fiction: New Accents and Attitudes,* University of California Press, 1962.

Holroyd, Stuart, *Flight and Pursuit: A Venture into Autobiography,* Gollancz, 1959.

Magill, Frank N., editor, *The Contemporary Literary Scene 1973,* Salem Press, 1974.

Maschler, Tom, editor, *Declaration,* Dutton, 1958, reprinted, Kennikat, 1972.

Weigel, John A., *Colin Wilson,* Twayne, 1975.

Wilson, Colin, *Voyage to a Beginning: An Intellectual Autobiography,* Crown, 1969.

PERIODICALS

American Poetry Journal, January/February, 1973.

American Scholar, fall, 1971.

Antioch Review, summer, 1969.

Atlantic, December, 1959, March, 1960, May, 1967, January, 1972, July, 1974.

Book List, June 1, 1976.

Books and Bookmen, January, 1970, December, 1971, March, 1979.

Book World, July 12, 1970.

Chicago Review, winter, 1972.

Chicago Sunday Tribune, April 10, 1960.

Chicago Sunday Tribune Books Today, August 30, 1964.

Choice, April, 1972.

Christian Century, March 24, 1965, April 5, 1967.

Christian Science Monitor, November 14, 1957, December 24, 1959, September 24, 1964, September 4, 1969.

Commonweal, April 1, 1960.

Critic, October, 1974.

Economist, November 6, 1971.

Encounter, August, 1962.

English Record, October, 1967.

Harper's, November, 1961, October, 1962, November, 1963.

Hollins Critic, October, 1967.

Illustrated London News, October, 1978.
Library Journal, October 15, 1964, October 1, 1966.
Life, October 1, 1956, December 13, 1971.
Listener, September 7, 1961, February 16, 1967, May 21, 1970.
London Evening News, May 24, 1956.
Los Angeles Times, March 12, 1981.
Los Angeles Times Book Review, May 9, 1982.
Magazine of Fantasy and Science Fiction, January, 1968, August, 1972.
Manchester Guardian, February 9, 1967.
Nation, August 25, 1956, April 16, 1960.
National Review, December 2, 1961, November 9, 1979.
New Republic, February 1, 1960, May, 1962, November 22, 1969.
New Statesman, September 5, 1959, March 5, 1960, May 24, 1963, June 14, 1963, March 20, 1964, December 11, 1964, January 15, 1965, June 27, 1966, June 26, 1970, December 22, 1978, December 29, 1978.
Newsweek, December 17, 1956, March 14, 1960, July 21, 1969.
New Yorker, August 20, 1960, June 3, 1967, November 29, 1969, September 16, 1974.
New York Herald Tribune Book Review, November 24, 1957, March 6, 1960.
New York Review of Books, December 31, 1964.
New York Times Book Review, July 1, 1956, November 15, 1959, March 6, 1960, October 15, 1961, December 13, 1964, July 30, 1967, November 9, 1969, June 14, 1970, January 28, 1973, July 21, 1974.
Observer, May 27, 1956, September 18, 1966.
Punch, November 6, 1963, October 5, 1966, February 8, 1967, May 29, 1974.
San Francisco Chronicle, March 13, 1960.
Saturday Review, September 8, 1956, December 19, 1959, March 12, 1960, March 20, 1965, November 15, 1969, January 15, 1972.
Science Fiction Review, February, 1970.
Spectator, June 15, 1956, December 22, 1961, April 27, 1962, January 29, 1965, June 28, 1969, May 30, 1970, June 27, 1970, November 6, 1971.
Temps Modernes (Paris), August 14, 1958.
Time, July 2, 1956, March 7, 1960, May 31, 1963.
Times (London), March 20, 1986.
Times Literary Supplement, June 8, 1956, October 25, 1957, September 4, 1959, June 14, 1963, February 27, 1964, January 28, 1965, November 3, 1966, January 26, 1967, July 10, 1969, November 6, 1969, November 27, 1969, June 18, 1970, February 5, 1971, November 26, 1971, December 8, 1972, April 26, 1974, June 14, 1974.
Twentieth Century (London), June, 1960.
Wall Street Journal, June 17, 1976.
Washington Post, December 24, 1978, January 29, 1981.
Washington Post Book World, March 18, 1973, December 24, 1978, June 24, 1984.

* * *

WILSON, Dirk
See POHL, Frederik

* * *

WILSON, Edmund 1895-1972

PERSONAL: Born May 8, 1895, in Red Bank, N.J.; died June 12, 1972; buried in Wellfleet, Mass.; son of Edmund (a lawyer)

and Helen Mather (Kimball) Wilson; married Mary Blair (an actress), 1923 (divorced, 1929); married Margaret Canby, 1930 (deceased, 1932); married Mary McCarthy (writer and critic), 1938 (divorced, 1946); married Elena Thornton Mumm, 1946; children: Rosalind (first marriage), Reuel (third marriage), Helen (fourth marriage). *Education:* Princeton University, A.B., 1916.

CAREER: Social and literary critic, essayist, editor, poet, novelist, and playwright. *New York Evening Sun,* New York City, reporter, 1916-17; *Vanity Fair* magazine, New York City, managing editor, 1920-21; *New Republic* magazine, New York City, associate editor, 1926-31; *New Yorker* magazine, New York City, book reviewer, 1944-48. *Military service:* U.S. Army, 1917-1919; served as enlisted man at Base Hospital 36, in France, and in the Intelligence Corps.

MEMBER: Charter Club (Princeton), Princeton Club (New York).

AWARDS, HONORS: Guggenheim fellowship, 1935; National Institute of Arts and Letters Gold Medal Award, 1955, for essays and criticism; Presidential Medal of Freedom, 1963; Edward MacDowell Medal, 1964; Emerson-Thoreau Medal, 1966; National Medal for Literature, National Book Committee, 1966; Aspen Award, 1968; Nice Book Festival Golden Eagle Award, 1971.

WRITINGS:

I Thought of Daisy (also see below; novel), Scribner, 1929.
The American Jitters: A Year of the Slump (essay collection), Scribner, 1932, reprinted, Books for Libraries, 1968 (published in England as *Devil Take the Hindmost: A Year of the Slump,* Scribner, 1932).
Travels in Two Democracies (essays and story collection), Harcourt, 1936.
To the Finland Station: A Study in the Writing and Acting of History, Harcourt, 1940, revised edition, Farrar, Straus, 1972.
Memoirs of Hecate County (story collection), Doubleday, 1946, revised edition, W. H. Allen, 1958, Farrar, Straus, 1959, reprinted, Hippocrene Books, 1979.
Europe without Baedeker: Sketches among the Ruins of Italy, Greece, and England, Doubleday, 1947, revised edition published as *Europe without Baedeker: Sketches among the Ruins of Italy, Greece, and England, together with Notes from a European Diary: 1963-64,* Farrar, Straus, 1966.
The Scrolls from the Dead Sea, Oxford University Press, 1955, revised edition published as *The Dead Sea Scrolls: 1947-1969,* 1969.
Red, Black, Blond, and Olive: Studies in Four Civilizations; Zuni, Haiti, Soviet Russia, Israel, Oxford University Press, 1956.
A Piece of My Mind: Reflections at Sixty, Farrar, Straus, 1957.
The American Earthquake: A Documentary of the Twenties and Thirties, Doubleday, 1958.
Apologies to the Iroquois, Farrar, Straus, 1960, reprinted, Octagon, 1978.
(Contributor) Donald Alfred Stauffer, editor, *The Intent of the Critic,* Peter Smith, 1963.
The Cold War and the Income Tax: A Protest, Farrar, Straus, 1963.
O Canada: An American's Notes on Canadian Culture, Farrar, Straus, 1965.
A Prelude: Landscapes, Characters, and Conversations from the Earlier Years of My Life, Farrar, Straus, 1967.
Galahad [and] *I Thought of Daisy* (novels; contains revised edition of *I Thought of Daisy*), Farrar, Straus, 1967.
(With Marianne Moore) *Homage to Henry James,* Appel, 1971.

Upstate: Records and Recollections of Northern New York, Farrar, Straus, 1971.

The Twenties: From Notebooks and Diaries of the Period, edited by Leon Edel, Farrar, Straus, 1975.

Letters on Literature and Politics, 1912-1972, edited by wife, Elena Wilson, Farrar, Straus, 1977.

Israel and the Dead Sea Scrolls, foreword by Edel, Farrar, Straus, 1978.

(With Vladimir Nabokov) *The Nabokov-Wilson Letters: Correspondence between Vladimir Nabokov and Edmund Wilson,* edited by Simon Karlinsky, Harper, 1979.

The Thirties: From Notebooks and Diaries of the Period, edited by Edel, Farrar, Straus, 1980.

The Forties: From Notebooks and Diaries of the Period, edited by Edel, Farrar, Straus, 1983.

The Portable Edmund Wilson, edited by Lewis M. Dabney, Penguin, 1983.

The Fifties: From Notebooks and Diaries of the Period, edited by Edel, Farrar, Straus, 1986.

LITERARY CRITICISM

Axel's Castle: A Study in the Imaginative Literature of 1870-1930, Scribner, 1931, reprinted, Norton, 1984.

The Triple Thinkers: Ten Essays on Literature, Harcourt, 1938, revised edition published as *The Triple Thinkers: Twelve Essays on Literary Subjects* (also see below), Oxford University Press, 1948, reprinted, Octagon, 1976.

The Boys in the Back Room: Notes on California Novelists, Colt Press, 1941.

The Wound and the Bow: Seven Studies in Literature (also see below), Houghton, 1941, revised edition, Oxford University Press, 1965.

Classics and Commercials: A Literary Chronicle of the Forties, Farrar, Straus, 1950, reprinted, 1967.

The Shores of Light: A Literary Chronicle of the Twenties and Thirties, Farrar, Straus, 1952, reprinted, Northeastern University Press, 1985.

Patriotic Gore: Studies in the Literature of the American Civil War, Oxford University Press, 1962, reprinted, Northeastern University Press, 1984.

The Bit between My Teeth: A Literary Chronicle of 1950-1965, Farrar, Straus, 1965.

A Window on Russia for the Use of Foreign Readers, Farrar, Straus, 1972.

The Devils and Canon Barham: Ten Essays on Poets, Novelists, and Monsters, Farrar, Straus, 1973.

The Triple Thinkers [and] *The Wound and the Bow: A Combined Volume,* Northeastern University Press, 1984.

POETRY

(With John Peale Bishop) *The Undertaker's Garland,* Knopf, 1922, reprinted, Haskell House, 1974.

Poets, Farewell! (also includes essays), Scribner, 1929.

Note-Books of Night (also includes essays and stories), Colt Press, 1942.

Wilson's Christmas Stocking: Fun for Young and Old, Thomas Todd, 1953.

A Christmas Delirium, Thomas Todd, 1955.

Night Thoughts, Farrar, Straus, 1961.

Holiday Greetings 1966, Thomas Todd, 1966.

Also author of several poetry pamphlets.

PLAYS

"The Evil Eye," lyrics by F. Scott Fitzgerald, music by P. B. Dickey and F. Warburton Guilbert, produced, 1915.

"The Crime in the Whistler Room" (also see below), produced in New York City, 1924.

Discordant Encounters: Plays and Dialogues, Boni, 1926.

This Room and This Gin and These Sandwiches: Three Plays (also see below; contains "The Crime in the Whistler Room," "Beppo and Beth" [also see below], and "A Winter in Beech Street"), New Republic, 1937.

The Little Blue Light (also see below; produced in Cambridge, Mass., 1950), Farrar, Straus, 1950.

Five Plays: Cyprian's Prayer, The Crime in the Whistler Room, This Room and This Gin and These Sandwiches, Beppo and Beth, This Little Blue Light, Farrar, Straus, 1954.

The Duke of Palermo and Other Plays, with an Open Letter to Mike Nichols (includes "The Duke of Palermo," "Dr. McGrath," and "Osbert's Career; or, The Poet's Progress"), Farrar, Straus, 1969.

EDITOR

Fitzgerald, *The Last Tycoon: An Unfinished Novel by F. Scott Fitzgerald, together with The Great Gatsby and Selected Stories,* Scribner, 1941.

The Shock of Recognition: The Development of Literature in the United States Recorded by the Men Who Made It, Doubleday, 1943, revised edition, Farrar, Straus, 1955, reprinted, Octagon, 1974.

Fitzgerald, *The Crack-Up: With Other Uncollected Pieces, Note-Books, and Unpublished Letters,* New Directions, 1945.

Bishop, *The Collected Essays of John Peale Bishop,* Scribner, 1948.

Anton Chekhov, *Peasants and Other Stories,* Doubleday, 1956.

(With Malcolm Cowley) Fitzgerald, *Three Novels* (contains *The Great Gatsby, Tender Is the Night,* and *The Last Tycoon*), Scribner, 1970.

OTHER

Contributor to numerous periodicals.

Wilson's papers are collected at the Beinecke Rare Book and Manuscript Library, Yale University.

SIDELIGHTS: As one of the nation's foremost literary critics, Edmund Wilson enjoyed a high position in American letters. L. E. Sissman called him "the greatest of our critics of this century, and among the three or four greatest—along with T. S. Eliot, Wallace Stevens, and F. Scott Fitzgerald—of our literary men." Wilson, according to T. S. Matthews, was "the foremost American man of letters of the twentieth century." Norman Podhoretz judged Wilson as "one of the greatest men of letters this country has ever produced."

Wilson's influence upon American literature was substantial. Warner Berthoff said that "for nearly every important development in contemporary writing Edmund Wilson was in some way a spokesman—an arbiter of taste, a supplier of perspective, at the least (to adapt his own phrase for Hemingway) a gauge of intellectual morale." Leonard Kriegel described Wilson's writing as "one of the standards of sanity in this culture." Despite misgivings about some of Wilson's strongly held opinions, Berthoff believed that "all who have to do with literature have played parasite to his writings, his discoveries and revaluations, and are too much in his debt to allow much complaining. He has been one of his time's indispensable teachers and transmitters of important news."

One of Wilson's most important contributions was his role in giving an international perspective to American literature. Speaking of this, Sissman praised Wilson for his "destruction of the literary isolationism of this continent." "No man," Anthony Burgess wrote, "has had a profounder influence on the capacity of a couple of generations (including my own) to form its own judgements on a very large and important sector of European literature." A reviewer for *Times Literary Supplement* cited Wilson's "incontestably important task" as "explaining the world to America and explaining America to itself."

Axel's Castle, Wilson's first book of literary criticism, established his reputation as a critic and still stands as one of his most important works. Sherman Paul explained that the book, a study of the Symbolist literary movement, "established the writers of the *avant garde* in the consciousness of the general reader: not only did it place them in a significant historical development, it taught the uninitiated how to read them." Pointing out the book's lasting value, Taylor stated that "it is that rare work that can never really be dated or superceded." Kriegel agreed, writing that "the book remains one of the truly seminal works of literary criticism published in our century."

Wilson's strongly held opinions were expressed in a manner that drew respect from even those readers who did not agree with him. When reading Wilson, Burgess claimed, one was "enlightened with conclusions that, so well are they stated and so logically arrived at, appear inevitable and hence obvious." George H. Douglas believed that "even when we find [Wilson's] ideas eccentric, perverse, and opinionated, as at times all of his readers must, we cannot but admire his ability to think through all of his problems for himself, his ceaseless endeavor to understand the world that confronts him and bring some order to it." Alfred Kazin wrote that Wilson "fascinates even when he is wrong." Joseph Epstein complained that "the stamp of Wilson's personality was on every sentence he wrote, yet nothing he wrote could by any stretch of the imagination be called 'personable'." Nevertheless, he admired Wilson as "a living embodiment of the belief in literature . . . as a guide to life, and a weapon . . . with which to bring some sort of order to an otherwise possibly quite senseless world."

Wilson's concern with literary values was reflected in his concern for political values as well. "He always retained his strong faith in our American democratic traditions," Douglas wrote, "even though he found the original dream of the founding fathers foundering in a sea of commercial ethics and impersonal, insensate government." After a brief interest in socialism, culminating in *To the Finland Station,* a study of the subject, Wilson grew disillusioned with politics. His writings after the Second World War ignored the contemporary scene. "Having lived through two World Wars in which he did not believe," Robert Emmet Long wrote, "[Wilson could] no longer believe in the power of rationality to create a humane and meaningful world." Despite his disillusionment with politics, Wilson protested the Cold War of the 1950s by not paying his income taxes for nine years on the grounds that the money was used to purchase nuclear and bacteriological weapons.

"Some years before he died," Luckett stated, "[Wilson] attempted an assessment of his own contribution to modern literature, and seemed content to stand on his achievements as an interpreter, explaining the characteristics of the literatures of other nations to readers in the United States. This was absurdly modest." Matthews believed that Wilson's "place in the hall of literary immortals is secure." Summing up Wilson's career, Douglas wrote: "He was not only an imaginative writer of the first rank but a great democratic idealist, and a spokesman for liberal learning in the best sense. And the combination of these virtues produced for us a remarkable body of works which is sure to re-main one of the great contributions to American literature of the 20th century."

BIOGRAPHICAL/CRITICAL SOURCES:

BOOKS

Aaron, Daniel, *Writers on the Left,* Harcourt, 1961.

Aldridge, John W., *Time to Murder and Create: The Contemporary Novel in Crisis,* McKay, 1966.

Berthoff, Warner, *Fiction and Events: Essays in Criticism and Literary History,* Dutton, 1971.

Breit, Harvey, *The Writer Observed,* World Publishing, 1956.

Burgess, Anthony, *Urgent Copy: Literary Studies,* Norton, 1968.

Castronovo, David, *Edmund Wilson,* Ungar, 1984.

Contemporary Literary Criticism, Gale, Volume 1, 1973, Volume 2, 1974, Volume 3, 1975, Volume 8, 1978, Volume 24, 1983.

Costa, Richard Hauer, *Edmund Wilson: Our Neighbor from Talcottville,* Syracuse University Press, 1980.

Dictionary of Literary Biography, Volume 63: *Modern American Critics, 1920-1955,* Gale, 1988.

Douglas, George, *Edmund Wilson's America,* University of Kentucky Press, 1983.

Frailberg, Louis, *Psychoanalysis and American Literary Criticism,* [Detroit, Mich.], 1960.

Frank, Charles P., *Edmund Wilson,* Twayne, 1970.

Glicksberg, C. I., editor, *American Literary Criticism, 1900-1950,* Farrar, Straus, 1952.

Goldhurst, William, *F. Scott Fitzgerald and His Contemporaries,* World Publishing, 1963.

Graves, Robert, *Five Pens in Hand,* Doubleday, 1958.

Highet, Gilbert, *People, Places, and Books,* Oxford University Press, 1953.

Howe, Irving, *A World More Attractive: A View of Modern Literature and Politics,* Horizon, 1963.

Hyman, Stanley Edgar, *The Armed Vision,* Knopf, 1948.

Kazin, Alfred, *On Native Grounds,* Reynal, 1942.

Kazin, Alfred, *The Inmost Leaf,* Harcourt, 1955.

Kazin, Alfred, *Contemporaries,* Little, Brown, 1962.

Kempton, Murray, *Part of Our Time: Some Ruins and Monuments of the Thirties,* Simon & Schuster, 1955.

Kermode, Frank, *Puzzles and Epiphanies,* Routledge & Kegan Paul, 1962.

Kriegel, Leonard, *Edmund Wilson,* Southern Illinois University Press, 1971.

Matthiessen, F. O., *Responsibilities of the Critic,* Oxford University Press, 1952.

Paul, Sherman, *Edmund Wilson: A Study of Literary Vocation in Our Time,* University of Illinois Press, 1965.

Podhoretz, Norman, *Doings and Undoings,* Farrar, Straus, 1964.

Pritchard, John Paul, *Criticism in America: An Account of the Development of Critical Technique,* University of Oklahoma Press, 1956.

Quinn, Kerker, and Charles Shattuck, editors, *Accent Anthology,* Harcourt, 1946.

Ramsey, Richard David, *Edmund Wilson: A Bibliography,* David Lewis, 1971.

Rexroth, Kenneth, *Assays,* New Directions, 1961.

Stoll, Elmer Edgar, *From Shakespeare to Joyce: Authors and Critics, Literature and Life,* Doubleday, 1944.

Trilling, Diana, *Reviewing the Forties,* Harcourt, 1978.

Trilling, Lionel, *The Liberal Imagination,* Doubleday, 1950.

Wain, John, editor, *Edmund Wilson: The Man and His Work,* New York University Press, 1978.

Wilson, Edmund, *A Prelude: Landscapes, Characters, and Conversations from the Earlier Years of My Life,* Farrar, Straus, 1967.

Wilson, Edmund, *The Nabokov-Wilson Letters: Correspondence between Vladimir Nabokov and Edmund Wilson*, edited by Simon Karlinsky, Harper, 1979.

PERIODICALS

America, June 24, 1972.
Antioch Review, December, 1946, summer, 1976.
Atlantic, December, 1961, May, 1962, July, 1967, September, 1972.
Books, May, 1965.
Books & Bookmen, March, 1974.
Book Week, May 9, 1965.
Bulletin of Bibliography, May, 1968.
Chicago Tribune Book World, April 24, 1983.
Christian Science Monitor, April 26, 1962.
Commentary, August, 1962.
Commonweal, July 8, 1938, December 12, 1952, May 13, 1960, November 5, 1971, July 14, 1972.
Detroit News, July 24, 1983.
Encounter, May, 1966.
Esquire, July, 1963, May, 1972.
Furioso, spring, 1948.
Harper's, January, 1971, June, 1975.
Listener, November 29, 1973.
Los Angeles Times Book Review, May 1, 1983, September 21, 1986.
Nation, October 16, 1948, December 8, 1956, June 26, 1972, August 7, 1972, October 2, 1972.
National Review, September 12, 1975.
New Leader, September 4, 1972.
New Republic, December 12, 1934, June 3, 1936, October 7, 1940, March 25, 1946, June 25, 1962, November 30, 1963, May 9, 1970, January 17, 1976.
New Statesman, April 26, 1958, May 21, 1960, June 22, 1962.
Newsweek, March 11, 1946, November 12, 1956, August 30, 1971.
New Yorker, July 5, 1958, June 24, 1972.
New York Herald Tribune Book Review, March 13, 1960, December 24, 1961, April 29, 1962.
New York Review of Books, October 7, 1971.
New York Times, June 13, 1972, October 6, 1977, August 18, 1980, April 13, 1983, August 26, 1986.
New York Times Book Review, February 9, 1958, March 20, 1960, December 10, 1961, July 2, 1972, July 29, 1973, June 5, 1975, June 8, 1980, May 22, 1983, July 20, 1986, August 31, 1986.
Prairie Schooner, summer, 1972.
Progressive, August, 1973, December, 1977.
Saturday Review, June 4, 1960, April 28, 1962, August 28, 1971.
Sewanee Review, April, 1948.
Spectator, April 25, 1958, May 27, 1960, November 17, 1973.
Texas Quarterly, winter, 1974.
Time, November 13, 1939, May 4, 1962, September 13, 1971, September 8, 1986.
Times Literary Supplement, April 25, 1958, June 3, 1960, May 19, 1972, August 5, 1983, December 26, 1986.
Tribune Books (Chicago), September 21, 1986.
Village Voice, August 26, 1965, May 26, 1975.
Virginia Quarterly Review, winter, 1968.
Wall Street Journal, September 16, 1971.
Washington Post Book World, April 17, 1983, September 14, 1986.
World, August 15, 1972.

OBITUARIES:

PERIODICALS

L'Express, June 20-July 2, 1972.
New York Times, June 13, 1972.
Time, June 26, 1972.
Washington Post, June 13, 1972.

*   *   *

WILSON, Edward O(sborne)   1929-

PERSONAL: Born June 10, 1929, in Birmingham, Ala.; son of Edward O., Sr. (an accountant) and Inez (Freeman) Wilson; married Irene Kelley, October 30, 1955; children: Catherine. *Education:* University of Alabama, B.S., 1949, M.S., 1950; Harvard University, Ph.D., 1955.

ADDRESSES: Home—9 Foster Rd., Lexington, Mass. 02173. *Office*—Museum of Comparative Zoology, Harvard University, Cambridge, Mass. 02138.

CAREER: Harvard University, Cambridge, Mass., assistant professor of biology, 1956-58, associate professor of zoology, 1958-64, professor of zoology, 1964-76, Frank B. Baird, Jr., Professor of Science, 1976—, curator of entomology at Museum of Comparative Zoology, 1972—; writer. Member of selection committee, J. S. Guggenheim Foundation. Trustee of Marine Biological Laboratory (Woods Hole).

MEMBER: American Philosophical Society (fellow), American Genetics Association (honorary life member), World Wildlife Fund (member of advisory council, 1977—), National Academy of Sciences, American Academy of Arts and Sciences (fellow), German Academy of Sciences (fellow), Society for the Study of Evolution.

AWARDS, HONORS: Award from American Association for the Advancement of Science, 1969; Mercer Award, Ecological Society of America, 1971; Founders Memorial Award, Entomological Society of America, 1972; Distinguished Service award, American Institute of Biological Sciences, 1976; National Medal of Science, 1977; Leidy Medal, Academy of Natural Sciences, 1979; Pulitzer Prize in general nonfiction, 1979, for *On Human Nature;* Sesquicentennial medal, University of Alabama, 1981; Distinguished Humanist award, American Humanist Association, 1982; Richard M. Weaver Award for Scholarly Letters, Ingersoll Foundation, 1989; also recipient of several honorary degrees.

WRITINGS:

(With R. H. MacArthur) *The Theory of Island Biogeography,* Princeton University Press, 1967.
The Insect Societies, Belknap Press, 1971.
(With W. H. Bossert) *A Primer of Population Biology,* Sinauer Associates, 1971.
(Co-author) *Life on Earth,* Sinauer Associates, 1973.
Sociobiology: The New Synthesis, Belknap Press, 1975.
(Author of introduction with Thomas Eisner) *The Insects: Readings from Scientific American,* Freeman, 1977.
(With George F. Oster) *Caste and Ecology in Social Insects,* Princeton University Press, 1978.
On Human Nature, Harvard University Press, 1978.
(With Charles J. Lumsden) *Genes, Mind, and Culture: The Coevolutionary Process,* Harvard University Press, 1981.
(With Lumsden) *Promethean Fire: Reflections on the Origin of the Mind,* Harvard University Press, 1983.
Biophilia: The Human Bond to Other Species, Harvard University Press, 1984.

(With Bert Holldobler) *The Ants,* Harvard University Press/ Belknap Press, 1990.

Contributor of about two hundred articles to scientific and popular journals. Co-editor, *Theoretical Population Biology,* 1971-74, *Behavioral Ecology and Sociobiology,* 1975—, and *Psyche.*

SIDELIGHTS: Prior to 1975, Edward O. Wilson was primarily known as one of America's foremost experts on the insect world, with his specialty being the study of ants and other social insects. The entomologist produced several books on insect culture and physiology before becoming, as Peter Gwynne describes him in *Newsweek,* "one of the most visible and articulate spokesmen for sociobiology, the controversial scientific discipline whose purpose is to examine the biological bases of behavior."

Wilson's 1975 book on the subject, *Sociobiology: The New Synthesis,* is considered the first detailed study of this emerging science, and made its author a respected, if controversial, figure in the field of human behavior. "The concepts [of sociobiology] are startling—and disturbing," begins a *Time* cover story. "Conflict between parents and children is biologically inevitable. Children are born deceitful. All human acts—even saving a stranger from drowning or donating a million dollars to the poor—may be ultimately selfish. Morality and justice, far from being the triumphant product of human progress, evolved from man's animal past and are securely rooted in the genes."

The most debated tenet of sociobiology is that all human behavior is genetically based, or, as Wilson once put it, that "genes hold culture on a leash." As *Time* elaborates upon the theory: "All forms of life exist solely to serve the purposes of DNA, the coded master molecule that determines the nature of all organisms and is the stuff of genes." Sociobiologists, the article continues, "argue that without consideration of biology, the study of human culture makes no sense." This new discipline has been the focus of heated debate in the scientific and cultural communities since its inception. While some of its critics have merely dismissed the discipline as "so-so biology," others have gone as far as labeling it "dangerously racist," according to *Time,* because "the new science would give comfort to the supporters of psychologist Arthur Jensen, a leading proponent of another controversial theory: that racial differences in IQs have a genetic basis." Still others have accused Wilson and other sociobiologists of advocating the idea of eugenics, the so-called "purifying" of races by genetic control of breeding. Wilson has called such attacks "slander," as *Time* reports, "and even [leading sociobiology opponent Richard] Lewontin came to his defense, conceding that 'sociobiology is not a racist doctrine.' But he added, 'Any kind of genetic determinism can and does feed other kinds, including the belief that some races are superior to others.'"

Sociobiology's explanation of altruism is equally controversial: *Time* notes that some twenty years prior to the science's formal inception, British biologist J. B. S. Haldane "anticipated the gene-based view of sociobiology when, tongue in cheek, he announced that he would lay down his life for two brothers or eight cousins. His reasoning: the survival of two full siblings (each with about half of his genes identical to Haldane's) or the group of cousins (each with about one-eighth of his genes the same as Haldane's) made the decision genetically acceptable."

"According to sociobiologists," *Time* continues, "evolution produces organisms that automatically follow this mathematical logic, as if they were computers, totting up the genetic costs or benefits of helping out relatives who bear many of the same genes." This theory, which undermines the concepts of culture and conscience, angers some sociologists. There is even a socio-

biological exegesis for religion, adding further fuel to the controversy.

And, while *Humanist* published a 1981 article by Nathaniel S. Lehrman decrying sociobiology as "Wilson's Fallacy" (in which Lehrman states that the scientist "is wrong . . . when he claims that complex human behaviors, such as altruism, are caused to any extent by genetic as opposed to cultural factors, other than merely acknowledging the rather obvious fact that human behavior cannot go beyond the limits set by our genetically determined biology"), the magazine went on to name Wilson its 1982 Distinguished Humanist. In doing so, Frederick Edwords, administrator of the American Humanist Association, declared in the journal: "Many challenges have been made to Wilson's sociobiology, particularly as it applies to humans, but it seems that many of the challenges are railings at some of Wilson's *conclusions*—not his evidence or reasons. Wilson has linked humans and human behavior more closely to the genes than many people feel comfortable with. He has compared human social structure to animal societies. He has found selfish roots in altruistic behavior." Edwords indicates that "along with many scientists today, [Wilson] has focused on the survival of the species and not the survival of the individual as the main motivational force behind behavior. He has interpreted human sexual behavior, male and female relationships, aggression, and other actions in terms of evolutionary biology. . . . Because many of Wilson's carefully arrived at conclusions have seemed to burst a few bubbles, or have seemed to threaten a few ideals, Wilson has been persecuted to some extent. But he has stood by his ideas, stood firm on his facts."

In a *New York Review of Books* article about Wilson's book *Sociobiology,* C. H. Waddington cites the author's "extraordinarily ambitious aim" in outlining the synthesis, and adds that Wilson "has been astoundingly successful in achieving [that aim]. This book will undoubtedly be for many years to come a major source of information about all aspects of our knowledge of social behavior in animals, from the most primitive types such as corals, through insects, fishes, birds, to the many varieties of mammals and primitive man. It has also some of the clearest discussions yet written about the recent advances in general population biology and demography." *New York Times Book Review* critic John Pfeiffer, while noting that Wilson "falters somewhat in presenting the human story" of sociobiology in his book, and that the author "can also be faulted for his vision of the future (in which Wilson predicts an 'ecologically steady state,' where mankind will achieve 'total knowledge, right down to the levels of the neutron and gene' by the end of the 21st century)," nevertheless concludes that *Sociobiology* "may be regarded as an evolutionary event in itself, announcing for all who can hear that we are on the verge of breakthroughs in the effort to understand our place in the scheme of things."

Wilson's next book, *On Human Nature,* is one he describes as "not a work *of* science," but rather "a work *about* science, and about how far the natural sciences can penetrate into human behavior before they will be transformed into something new." "As its ambitious title implies," states Nicholas Wade in *New Republic,* the book "is a work of high intellectual daring. [Wilson] attempts to lay out a biological foundation for the social sciences, describe the genetic basis of the mind, sketch out the design of the ideal society, bridge the gap between the two cultures, suggest how existing religions could and should be replaced with a kind of scientific pantheism, and answer [philosopher David] Hume's questions about the nature of human understanding— all within a mere 200 pages."

On Human Nature "takes up in a philosophical way where *Sociobiology* left off," observes William McPherson in a *Washington Post Book World* review. "It is a vastly ambitious attempt to bring the 'two cultures' of science and the humanities together." As with the earlier book, some of Wilson's hypotheses in *On Human Nature* met with skepticism from the scientific community. For instance, a passage from the work reveals Wilson's prediction that a "durable foundation for peace" might be found by creating "a confusion of cross-finding loyalties," according to the *New York Times Book Review*, "to prevent the formation of the kinds of group loyalties that give rise to aggressive behavior," as reviewer Colin Beer, a professor of psychology, describes it. But Beer responds that "it is doubtful whether this solution, in itself, would be sufficient to make human aggression, in all its forms, a thing of the past. But the argument that [the author] uses here is typical of his tactics throughout most of the book: it is quietly persuasive rather than belligerently coercive, and it appeals to plausible possibility rather than logical necessity. At least to readers of good will, most of the conclusions will seem reasonable interpretations of the evidence—so much so that many may be left wondering what all the fuss [about Wilson's theory of sociobiology as a basis for behavior] has been about."

Wilson's "most grandiose and least appealing scheme is to replace conventional religion with a mythology based on scientific materialism and incorporating a more objectively chosen value system," finds Wade. "Gee-whiz wonders from the scientific textbooks—evolution, the Big Bang and so forth—would replace religious awe and the sense of the sacred. This false touch makes the reader wonder if Wilson here hasn't slipped too far afield." However, Wade concludes that *On Human Nature* "is a splendid departure from the dead-hand canons of the scientific 'literature.' Clarity, precision and boldness distinguish Wilson's attempt to complete the Darwinian revolution. He is dealing with matters that lie mostly beyond the reach of present scientific methods, and perhaps for that reason has chosen to present his ideas in a way that makes them accessible to the public at large as well as to his scientific peers." And despite the controversy surrounding its subject matter, *On Human Nature* was awarded the 1979 Pulitzer Prize in general nonfiction, prompting its author to tell Megan Rosenfeld of the *Washington Post:* "The Pulitzer is an affirmation that this is an important new area of thought. It's not necessarily a certification that I'm right, but an affirmation that this is an important thing we should be talking about."

In 1981, Wilson and theoretical physicist Charles J. Lumsden collaborated on a scholarly work, *Genes, Mind, and Culture: The Coevolutionary Process*. Extending the theory of sociobiology, the two scientists described what they labeled the "gene-culture coevolution," a process by which human genetic makeup "helps guide and create culture, while culture in turn operates directly on the genes," as *Harper's* reviewers James L. Gould and Carol Grant Gould write. Two years later, Wilson and Lumsden produced a layman's book on the subject, called *Promethean Fire: Reflections on the Origin of the Mind*.

A case in point of the authors' gene-culture theory lies in their detailed study of the incest taboo in *Promethean Fire*. Historically considered a cultural phenomenon, the incest taboo, Wilson and Lumsden propose, has actually been programmed genetically into humans as a reaction against the mentally and physically deformed offspring that incestuous unions inevitably produce. Thus, the cultural taboo of familial sexual relations is an outgrowth of the genetic rule. "The authors also point out how easily (and in some cases even spontaneously) certain deep, long-lasting phobias appear [to such ancient terrors as snakes,

spiders, and thunderstorms, for instance], while determined attempts on the part of parents to instill fear of the real threats of modern-day life (electrical outlets, knives, and busy streets) rarely succeed, at least at the phobia level," note the *Harper's* critics. "Surely this argues for a type of genetic programming that could have a role in culture."

Sociologist Howard Kaye reviewed *Promethean Fire* for *Commentary* and found fault with the authors' conclusions: "Although Lumsden and Wilson view their theory as orthodox science, certain questionable assumptions about mind and culture and an extreme reductionism mar their thought and inflate their claims. . . . Observers of men in society have always known that no human culture, not even our own, is a supermarket of discrete and competing cultural products—row upon row of hymns, gods, cuisines, clothing styles, styles of life—to which each individual is uniformly exposed, and from which he selects according to genetically prescribed preferences and abhorrences," Kaye continues. "Rather, each culture has done the shopping for us, circumscribing the chaos of possibility and ordering our choices to make our lives possible and meaningful. . . . Only an a-priori reductionism could lead one to conclude that *all* human choices and tendencies [are] governed by epigenetic rules. Not even the few such 'rules' which Lumsden and Wilson do identify are so constraining. We may tend to fear and hate strangers, but we also find them attractive, even seductive. . . . Nor is the example of brother-sister incest avoidance so univocal. We may find the idea abhorrent, but even the authors refer to an undercurrent of 'quiet titillation' at the prospect."

And, while acknowledging that "a moral and social passion is at work in this valuable attempt to integrate the disparate findings of various scientific specialties into a new natural philosophy with which to create a more harmonious and integrated society," Kaye wonders if sociobiology constitutes "the right [passion]. This is not for the authors, but rather for all of us, to say." "Sociobiology is rapidly unraveling many of the mysteries of animal societies," maintain James and Carol Gould in their *Harper's* article. "In doing so, it will give us invaluable insights into why we humans organize ourselves as we do, act as we do, perhaps even think as we do. To the extent that this sort of armchair speculation, bolstered by anthropological anecdote and mathematical calculation of probabilities, can encourage new ways of looking at our own evolution and the genetic constraints on our behavior, Lumsden and Wilson have done a service in making their theories accessible to the thinking public in *Promethean Fire*."

But the *Harper's* critics add this caution: "In proposing any sort of eugenic fallout from sociobiology, [the authors] are opening themselves to the same hysterical criticism from Marxists, creationists, and other anthropocentrics that almost overwhelmed Wilson's original formulation of his brave new synthesis. It is a sad truth that until scientists are able to present their ideas clearly to well-educated and receptive minds, valuable theories like sociobiology will inevitably fall prey to our disproportionate fears and feed our unrealistic hopes."

Wilson's attraction to biology and evolution grew from his fascination, as a young boy, with the natural wonders surrounding his home in rural Alabama (Wilson's family had also lived in Washington, D.C., which afforded the youngster the opportunity to frequently visit the National Zoo and the Smithsonian Institution). The scientist's biophilia—what he describes as "the innate tendency to focus on life and lifelike processes"—is the subject of his 1984 work *Biophilia: The Human Bond to Other Species.*

"No one can doubt [that Wilson] is powerfully drawn to other creatures, but he wants to make some larger points: human attraction to other living things is innate, and this natural affinity should serve as the philosophical basis for a new conservation ethic," finds *New York Times Book Review* critic Sarah Boxer. Boxer, however, feels that while Wilson's "attempt to promote conservation is noble and appealing," the author "loses the thread of his main argument" when he "flits from a reverie about time scales to a reminiscence about his work in biogeography."

Psychology Today writer Wray Herbert cites an example of Wilson's biophilic notions in his review. Pointing to "an appreciation of the 'savanna gestalt,' " Herbert explains that "early humans evolved on the African savannas, presumably because tree-studded open land overlooking water offered the optimal environment for survival; this predisposition became ingrained, Wilson argues, and today is reflected in our esthetics [in designs like] malls, gardens and cemeteries." Herbert also comments that such notions are "incendiary . . . but Wilson is probably used to the heat."

"It's hard not to like this little book . . . and it's hard not to like Wilson after having read it," concludes Herbert, adding that *Biophilia* "is a very personal statement. Mixing bits of autobiography with meditations on nature, he has put together a poetic rather than a scientific argument; he offers biophilia as an article of faith, making only a half-hearted effort to prove it for what he calls his 'determined critics'. . . . Wilson's critics want certain things—like beauty and morality—kept mysterious; they are angered by what they perceive as a reductionist view of human culture. And like Darwin, Wilson has tendered an idea that is shocking in its simplicity, which if correct will demand a basic revision of what it is to be human."

BIOGRAPHICAL/CRITICAL SOURCES:

BOOKS

Wilson, Edward O., *Sociobiology: The New Synthesis,* Belknap Press, 1975.
Wilson, *On Human Nature,* Harvard University Press, 1978.
Wilson and Charles J. Lumsden, *Promethean Fire: Reflections on the Origin of the Mind,* Harvard University Press, 1983.
Wilson, *Biophilia: The Human Bond to Other Species,* Harvard University Press, 1984.

PERIODICALS

Chicago Tribune Book World, November 5, 1978.
Commentary, October, 1983.
Harper's, June, 1983.
Humanist, July/August, 1981, September/October, 1982.
Los Angeles Times, December 17, 1984.
New Republic, November 11, 1983.
Newsweek, October 16, 1978.
New York Review of Books, August 7, 1975, October 12, 1978.
New York Times, December 18, 1978, September 21, 1989.
New York Times Book Review, July 27, 1975, October 18, 1981, November 26, 1981, April 24, 1983, October 7, 1984.
Omni, February, 1979.
Psychology Today, November, 1984.
Saturday Night, September, 1983.
Time, August 1, 1977.
Washington Post, May 4, 1979.
Washington Post Book World, October 8, 1978, October 15, 1978, March 25, 1990.

WILSON, Ethel Davis (Bryant)   1888(?)-1980

PERSONAL: Born January 20, 1888 (listed in some sources as 1890), in Port Elizabeth, South Africa; immigrated to Canada, 1898; died December 22, 1980, in Vancouver, British Columbia, Canada; daughter of Robert William (a missionary) and Lila (Malkin) Bryant; married Wallace Wilson (a physician), January 4, 1921 (died March 12, 1966). *Education:* Educated in England and Canada.

CAREER: Worked as public school teacher in Canada, 1907-1920; writer.

AWARDS, HONORS: D. Litt., from University of British Columbia, 1955; Canada Council medal, 1961; Royal Society of Canada Lorne Pierce gold medal from Learned Societies, 1964; Order of Canada medal of service, 1970.

WRITINGS:

Hetty Dorval, Macmillan, 1947, reprinted, 1967.
The Innocent Traveller, Macmillan, 1949.
The Equations of Love: Tuesday and Wednesday and Lilly's Story (two novellas; also see below), Macmillan, 1952, reprinted, 1974.
Lilly's Story (novella; also see above), Harper, 1953.
Swamp Angel (novel), Harper, 1954.
Love and Salt Water (novel), St. Martin's, 1957.
Mrs. Golightly, and Other Stories (short stories), Macmillan, 1961.
Ethel Wilson: Stories, Essays, and Letters, edited by David Stouck, University of British Columbia Press, 1987.

Work represented in anthologies. Editor of *Red Cross,* 1941-45. Contributor of short stories and essays to periodicals, including *New Statesman and Nation, Canadian Forum,* and *Chatelaine.*

SIDELIGHTS: Born in South Africa, Ethel Davis Wilson was taken to England by her grandparents after the death of her mother. They then moved to Canada, where Wilson remained thereafter. During her marriage to Vancouver physician Wallace Wilson she and her husband took trips to the Middle East, the Mediterranean, and Europe.

Wilson came to writing late in life; her first story appeared when she was forty-nine, and her first novel was published ten years later. Thus as Desmond Pacey noted in *Ethel Wilson,* she was a contemporary of James Joyce and T. S. Eliot, though her novels were not written until after World War II. However, she was much less experimental than either Joyce or Eliot. Pacey wrote: "Her stories are almost always told in straightforward chronological order by an omniscient narrator who is not above commenting occasionally, in a very old-fashioned way, on the persons and events he is narrating. . . . Upon everything she writes is the mark of a fastidious and exigent craftsman: her art is quiet, gentle, controlled, exquisitely fashioned and finished."

Wilson strove to imbue her work with "incandescence." She wrote: "There is a moment, I think, within a novelist of any originality, whatever his country or his scope, when some sort of synthesis takes place over which he has only partial control. There is an incandescence, and from it meaning emerges, words appear, they take shape in their order, a fusion occurs. A minor writer, whose gift is small and canvas limited, stands away at last if he can and regards what he has done, without indulgence. This is a counsel of perfection which I myself am not able to take with skill, but I must try to take it. I am sure that the very best writing in our country will result from such an incandescence which takes place in a prepared mind where forces meet."

Wilson has also been compared to Jane Austen and Daniel Defoe. Her sense of reality as well as her devotion to the details of place and social behavior were similar to those earlier writers. And on a psychological level, Wilson has been compared to Marcel Proust and Virginia Woolf, for she enriched her characterizations by portraying the emotional reverberations of phenomena and the subtleties of human relationships.

Many critics have focused on Wilson's style and symbolism. Pacey listed her strengths as "economy, matter-of-fact-statement, limpid style, lack of pretentiousness, and a combination of involvement and detachment." Other reviewers described the quality of her prose in similar terms. Edith James, reviewing *Hetty Dorval* in the *San Francisco Chronicle,* declared that "Wilson's writing has the precision of Janet Lewis and the singing quality of the early Willa Cather." And V. P. Hass of the *Chicago Tribune* praised the "admirable economy of words" of *Lilly's Story.*

Beneath the finely crafted simplicity, however, is a complexity of meaning. Reviewing *Swamp Angel,* L. A. G. Strong wrote, "From the quiet but powerful opening to the last Excalibur flight of *Swamp Angel* the story troubles the mind with overtones and reticences, as if each chapter were a moon with a hidden side more important than the one which Mrs. Wilson shows us." Similarly, W. H. New wrote that *The Innocent Traveller* "has at its base a kind of symbolic structure." Pacey observed that "Wilson's chief themes are loneliness and love, human vulnerability and tenacity, the juxtaposition in the world of innocence and cruelty, beauty and fear, and she treats these themes in a style that is straightforward but also suggestive, realistic but also poetic and symbolic." He added that Wilson "sees human beings as lonely creatures who forever seek, and occasionally find, the comfort and sustaining power of mutual love, and nature as a setting which is at once beautiful and menacing."

BIOGRAPHICAL/CRITICAL SOURCES:

BOOKS

Contemporary Literary Criticism, Volume 13, Gale, 1980.
Dictionary of Literary Biography, Volume 68: *Canadian Writers, 1920-1959, First Series,* Gale, 1988.
Pacey, Desmond, *Ethel Wilson,* Twayne, 1967.

PERIODICALS

British Columbia Library Quarterly, April 1958.
Canadian Forum, December, 1949.
Canadian Literature, autumn, 1959, autumn, 1965.
Chicago Tribune, May 3, 1953, August 29, 1954.
Christian Science Monitor, October 21, 1949.
Kirkus Review, June 15, 1954.
New York Herald Tribune Book Review, October 19, 1947, January 15, 1950, May 3, 1953, August 29, 1954.
Queen's Quarterly, spring, 1954.
San Francisco Chronicle, August 21, 1947, May 7, 1953.
Saturday Night, July 26, 1952.
Saturday Review of Literature, December 10, 1949, May 16, 1953, September 4, 1954.
Spectator, September 3, 1954.
Times Literary Supplement, July 24, 1948, March 28, 1952.

OBITUARIES:

PERIODICALS

Chicago Tribune, December 24, 1980.

WILSON, John (Anthony) Burgess   1917-
(Anthony Burgess, Joseph Kell)

PERSONAL: Born February 25, 1917, in Manchester, England; son of Joseph and Elizabeth (Burgess) Wilson; married Llewela Isherwood Jones, January 23, 1942 (died, 1968); married Lilliana Macellari (a translator), 1968. *Education:* Attended Bishop Bilsborrow School, Xaverian College; Manchester University, B.A. (honors), 1940.

ADDRESSES: Home—Monte Carlo.

CAREER: Lecturer, Central Advisory Council for Adult Education in the Forces, 1946-48; lecturer in phonetics, Ministry of Education, 1948-50; Banbury Grammar School, Oxfordshire, England, master, 1950-54; Colonial Service, education officer in Malaya and Brunei, 1954-59; composer; writer. Visiting professor, Columbia University, 1970-71, and City University of New York, 1972-73. Visiting fellow, Princeton University, 1970-71. Literary adviser, Guthrie Theatre, 1972—. *Military service:* British Army, Education Corps, 1940-46; became sergeant-major.

MEMBER: Royal Society of Literature (fellow).

AWARDS, HONORS: Prix du Meilleur Livre Etranger, 1981, for *Earthly Powers.*

WRITINGS:

FICTION; UNDER NAME ANTHONY BURGESS, EXCEPT AS INDICATED

Time for a Tiger (first novel in trilogy; also see below), Heinemann, 1956.
The Enemy in the Blanket (second novel in trilogy; also see below), Heinemann, 1958.
Beds in the East (third novel in trilogy; also see below), Heinemann, 1959.
The Right to an Answer, Norton, 1960.
The Doctor Is Sick, Heinemann, 1960, Norton, 1966.
The Worm and the Ring, Heinemann, 1961, revised edition, 1970.
Devil of a State (Book Society selection), Heinemann, 1961, Norton, 1962.
(Under pseudonym Joseph Kell) *One Hand Clapping,* P. Davies, 1961, published under name Anthony Burgess, Knopf, 1972.
A Clockwork Orange, Heinemann, 1962, revised edition, Norton, 1963, reprinted, 1987.
The Wanting Seed, Heinemann, 1962, Norton, 1963.
Honey for the Bears, Heinemann, 1963, Norton, 1964.
(Under pseudonym Joseph Kell) *Inside Mr. Enderby* (also see below), Heinemann, 1963.
Nothing Like the Sun, Norton, 1964.
The Eve of Saint Venus, Sidgwick & Jackson 1964, Norton, 1970.
The Long Day Wanes (trilogy; includes *Time for a Tiger, The Enemy in the Blanket,* and *Beds in the East*), Norton, 1965 (published in England as *Malayan Trilogy,* Penguin, 1972).
A Vision of Battlements, Sidgwick & Jackson, 1965, Norton, 1966.
Tremor of Intent, Norton, 1966.
Enderby Outside (also see below), Heinemann, 1968.
Enderby (contains *Inside Mr. Enderby* and *Enderby Outside*), Norton, 1968.
"A Clockwork Orange" and "Honey for the Bears," Modern Library, 1968.
MF, Knopf, 1971.
Napoleon Symphony, Knopf, 1974.

The Clockwork Testament, or Enderby's End, Hart-Davis, 1974, Knopf, 1975.

Beard's Roman Women, McGraw, 1976.

A Long Trip to Tea Time, Stonehill Publishing, 1976.

Moses (based on his film script of the same title; also see below), Stonehill Publishing, 1976.

Abba, Abba, Faber, 1977.

Nineteen Eighty-Five, Little, Brown, 1978.

Man of Nazareth (based on his film script "Jesus of Nazareth"; also see below), McGraw, 1979.

The Land Where the Ice Cream Grows, Doubleday, 1979.

Earthly Powers, Simon & Schuster, 1980.

On Going to Bed, Abbeville Press, 1982.

The End of the World News: An Entertainment, Hutchinson, 1982, McGraw, 1983.

This Man and Music, McGraw, 1983.

Enderby's Dark Lady, or No End to Enderby, McGraw, 1984.

The Kingdom of the Wicked, Arbor House, 1985.

The Piano Players, Arbor House, 1986.

The Devil's Mode, Random House, 1989.

Any Old Iron, Random House, 1989.

NONFICTION; UNDER NAME ANTHONY BURGESS, EXCEPT AS INDICATED

(Under name John Burgess Wilson) *English Literature: A Survey for Students,* Longmans, Green, 1958, new edition published under name Anthony Burgess, 1974.

The Novel Today, British Council, 1963.

Language Made Plain, English Universities Press, 1964, Crowell, 1965, revised edition, Fontana, 1975.

Re Joyce (critical study of James Joyce), Norton, 1965 (published in England as *Here Comes Everybody,* Faber, 1965).

(Author of commentary) Paul Elek and Elizabeth Elek, editors, *Coaching Days of England,* Time-Life, 1967.

The Novel Now: A Guide to Contemporary Fiction, Norton, 1967 (published in England as *The Novel Now: A Student's Guide to Contemporary Fiction,* Faber, 1967, revised edition, 1971).

Urgent Copy: Literary Studies (collection of essays), J. Cape, 1968, Norton, 1969.

Shakespeare, J. Cape, 1970, Knopf, 1971.

Joysprick: An Introduction to the Language of James Joyce, Deutsch, 1973, Harcourt, 1975.

Ernest Hemingway and His World, Scribner, 1978.

Ninety-nine Novels: The Best in English Since 1939, Summit, 1984.

D. H. Lawrence in Italy, Penguin, 1985.

Flame Into Being: The Life and Work of D. H. Lawrence, Arbor House, 1985.

But Do Gentlemen Prefer Blondes?, McGraw, 1986 (published in England as *Homage to Qwert Yuiop: Selected Journalism, 1978-1985,* Hutchinson, 1986).

Little Wilson and Big God (autobiography), Weidenfeld & Nicolson, 1987.

EDITOR; UNDER NAME ANTHONY BURGESS

Daniel Defoe, *A Journal of the Plague Year,* Penguin, 1966.

James Joyce, *A Shorter Finnegans Wake,* Faber, 1966, Viking, 1967.

New York, Time-Life, 1977.

TRANSLATOR; UNDER NAME ANTHONY BURGESS

(With first wife, Llewela Burgess) Michel de Saint-Pierre, *The New Aristocrats,* Gollancz, 1962.

(With L. Burgess) Jean Pelegri, *The Olive Trees of Justice,* Sidgwick & Jackson, 1962.

Jean Sewin, *The Man Who Robbed Poor Boxes,* Gollancz, 1965.

Also translator of librettos for "Carmen" and "Oberon."

PLAYS; UNDER NAME ANTHONY BURGESS

(Translator and adaptor) Edmond de Rostand, *Cyrano de Bergerac,* Knopf, 1971 (produced on Broadway as "Cyrano," May 13, 1973).

(Translator and adaptor) Sophocles, *Oedipus the King* (produced in Minneapolis, Minn., 1972), University of Minnesota Press, 1972.

"A Clockwork Orange 2004" (adapted from author's novel), produced at Barbican Theater, London, 1990.

Also author of "Morning in His Eyes," 1968.

AUTHOR OF INTRODUCTION; UNDER NAME ANTHONY BURGESS

Francis Haskell, editor, *The Age of the Grand Tour,* Crown, 1967.

G. K. Chesterton, *Autobiography,* Hutchinson, 1969.

G. V. Desani, *All about H. Hatten,* Bodley Head, 1970.

OTHER; UNDER NAME ANTHONY BURGESS

Author of film and television scripts, including "Moses," released by ITC/RAI, 1976, and "Jesus of Nazareth," released by the National Broadcasting Co., 1977; contributor to film script for "Quest for Fire," released by Fox, 1982; author of television program "The Rage of D. H. Lawrence," produced in Canada, 1986.

Contributor to *Partisan Review, Hudson Review, Times Literary Supplement, New York Times Book Review,* and other periodicals.

Author has read several of his own books for audio-cassette recordings, including "A Clockwork Orange," Caedmon, 1973; "Anthony Burgess Reads from *The Eve of Saint Venus* and *Nothing Like the Sun,*" Caedmon, 1974; and "Anthony Burgess Reads from *A Clockwork Orange* and *Enderby,*" Spoken Arts, 1974.

SIDELIGHTS: Anthony Burgess began his writing career while employed as a teacher in the English colony of Malaya. "The impact of a mixed culture," he writes, "opened up my imagination and dissolved a creative block that had persisted since the end of the war. I began to write and publish." His first three novels, a trilogy, are set in Malaya and confront the problems of an aging colonial power.

Burgess's stay in Malaya was suddenly ended in 1959 when he was told by a local doctor that he had a brain tumor, and to live at most another year, he should return to England's more temperate climate. He followed the doctor's advice and, anticipating his imminent death, quickly wrote five novels. A year later he was still alive. After medical tests confirmed his good health, Burgess became suspicious: "I think there may have been a lot of politics in [the original diagnosis]."

Despite the anxiety connected with their creation, Burgess's five novels were published, receiving critical praise and firmly establishing his place in contemporary English literature. With each successive novel, he has gained even more respect for his work. As Ralph McInerny notes: "Anthony Burgess is among the half dozen most important English novelists writing today. He is surely one of the most intelligent." Stephen W. Soule claims that

"[Vladimir] Nabokov and [Anthony] Burgess are our two leading English-language novelists."

Burgess's novels are experimental exercises related in a humorous, linguistically-inventive style. They occupy the gray area between "popular" and "serious" literature. "[Burgess's] novels are a marriage—perhaps a violent and almost profane union—of popular and elitist literature," John J. Stinson writes. "Burgess uses the standard devices of the modernist elitists . . . but uses them to strikingly original purposes, bouncing them incongruously off more 'popular' elements, or even more incongruously, merging them."

Burgess's most popular novel, *A Clockwork Orange*, tells the story of a murderous, Beethoven-loving teenage gang leader in a complacent and conformist society of the near future. It is written in a future slang/dialect of Burgess's own invention. Burgess, however, is not happy with the book's popularity. "It's not my favorite book," he says, "and I really wish they'd think of me in relation to something else."

The movie version of *A Clockwork Orange*, filmed in 1971 by Stanley Kubrick, created a controversy as some of its violent scenes seemed to inspire real-life violence. Burgess found himself defending his work against critical attacks. In *A Clockwork Testament*, he fictionalizes this experience. As Charles Nicol summarizes, Burgess "thought the film was good, but lush in its treatment of sexual brutality; while he recognized his book in it, the film was a separate work for which he was not responsible."

Burgess told *CA:* "I call myself a professional writer in that I must write in order to eat, and I am not ashamed to belong to the 'Grub Street' confraternity which Dr. Johnson honored. But primarily I call myself a serious novelist who is attempting to extend the range of subject matter available to fiction, as also a practitioner who is anxious to exploit words much as a poet does. I acknowledge as masters [Laurence] Sterne, James Joyce, [and] Evelyn Waugh.

"I was brought up a Catholic, became an agnostic, flirted with Islam, and now hold a position which may be termed Manichee—I believe the wrong God is temporarily ruling the world and that the true God has gone under. Thus I am a pessimist but believe the world has much solace to offer—love, food, music, the immense variety of race and language, literature, the pleasure of artistic creation."

MEDIA ADAPTATIONS: *A Clockwork Orange* was adapted into a film of the same name and released by Warner Brothers in 1971.

BIOGRAPHICAL/CRITICAL SOURCES:

BOOKS

Adams, Robert Martin, *After Joyce: Studies in Fiction After "Ulysses,"* Oxford University Press, 1977.
Bergonzi, Bernard, *The Situation of the Novel,* University of Pittsburgh Press, 1970.
Boytinck, Paul W., *Anthony Burgess: An Enumerative Bibliography,* Norwood, 1973.
Burgess, Anthony, *Little Wilson and Big God,* Weidenfeld & Nicolson, 1987.
Contemporary Literary Criticism, Gale, Volume 1, 1973, Volume 2, 1974, Volume 4, 1975, Volume 5, 1976, Volume 8, 1978, Volume 10, 1979, Volume 13, 1980, Volume 15, 1980, Volume 22, 1982, Volume 40, 1986.
Devitis, A. A., *Anthony Burgess,* Twayne, 1972.
Dictionary of Literary Biography, Volume 14: *British Novelists Since 1960,* Gale, 1983.
Dix, Carol M., *Anthony Burgess,* Longman, 1971.
Kennard, Jean E., *Number and Nightmare: Forms of Fantasy in Contemporary Fiction,* Archon Books, 1975.
Kostelanetz, Richard, editor, *On Contemporary Literature,* Avon, 1964.
Mathews, Richard, *The Clockwork Universe of Anthony Burgess,* Borgo Press, 1978.
Morris, Robert K., *Consolations of Ambiguity: An Essay on the Novels of Anthony Burgess,* University of Minnesota Press, 1971.
Morris, *Continuance and Change: The Contemporary British Novel Sequence,* Southern Illinois University Press, 1972.
Schoenbaum, Samuel, *Shakespeare's Lives,* Clarendon Press, 1970.
Solotaroff, Theodore, *The Red Hot Vacuum,* Atheneum, 1970.

PERIODICALS

America, October 22, 1966.
Arizona Quarterly, autumn, 1969.
Atlantic, February, 1975.
Bookletter, March 31, 1975.
Books & Bookmen, December, 1965.
Carleton Miscellany, spring, 1966.
Chicago Tribune, October 29, 1978, April 15, 1979.
Chicago Tribune Book World, November 23, 1980, March 27, 1983, September 8, 1985, October 13, 1985, May 4, 1986.
Christian Science Monitor, May 29, 1974.
Commonweal, May 28, 1971, December 6, 1974.
Contemporary Literature, summer, 1970.
Encounter, November, 1965.
Globe and Mail (Toronto), July 7, 1984, November 23, 1985, April 5, 1986, May 24, 1986, November 29, 1986, February 28, 1987, July 11, 1987, April 29, 1989.
Guardian, October 10, 1964.
Harper's, March, 1966.
Hudson Review, spring, 1967, autumn, 1967.
Journal of Popular Culture, summer, 1973.
Life, October 25, 1968.
Listener, February 10, 1977.
London Magazine, February, 1964.
Los Angeles Times, November 7, 1985, March 27, 1986.
Los Angeles Times Book Review, December 14, 1980, May 30, 1982, May 1, 1983, March 16, 1986, May 10, 1987, February 5, 1989, December 31, 1989.
Malahat Review, April, 1969.
Massachusetts Review, summer, 1966.
National Elementary Principal, May, 1971.
National Review, May 9, 1975.
New Republic, October 15, 1966.
Newsweek, February 21, 1966, June 4, 1974, October 25, 1976.
New Yorker, May 7, 1966.
New York Herald Tribune, February 8, 1965.
New York Review of Books, September 30, 1976.
New York Times, December 1, 1965, November 19, 1980, March 12, 1983, August 8, 1983, April 14, 1984, September 11, 1985, December 31, 1986, February 14, 1987, February 14, 1990.
New York Times Book Review, May 1, 1966, December 4, 1966, November 29, 1970, November 19, 1978, April 15, 1979, December 7, 1980, March 6, 1983, September 22, 1985, March 30, 1986, June 1, 1986, November 2, 1986, February 22, 1987, February 26, 1989, December 10, 1989.
New York Times Magazine, April 2, 1967, November 3, 1968.
Paris Review, spring, 1973.
Publishers Weekly, January 31, 1972.

Punch, June 12, 1968.
Saturday Review, July 15, 1967.
Seventeen, August, 1973.
Spectator, May 31, 1968, August 30, 1968.
Time, March 21, 1983, October 17, 1983, April 23, 1984, November 17, 1986, February 16, 1987.
Times (London), January 16, 1964, October 20, 1980, April 4, 1982, October 28, 1982, March 29, 1984, May 16, 1985, August 12, 1985, March 6, 1986, May 17, 1986, August 28, 1986, February 27, 1987, March 2, 1989.
Times Literary Supplement, November 4, 1965, October 24, 1980, October 8, 1982, November 5, 1982, December 10, 1982, December 24, 1982, March 30, 1984, May 31, 1985, October 18, 1985, November 16, 1985, April 4, 1986, August 29, 1986, February 27, 1987, April 7, 1989.
Times-Picayune (New Orleans), February 18, 1973.
Tribune Books (Chicago), January 12, 1987, February 15, 1987, January 29, 1989.
Variety, May 16, 1973.
Village Voice, April 14, 1966.
Washington Post, October 30, 1978, December 26, 1980, March 8, 1987, December 24, 1989.
Washington Post Book World, March 31, 1968, November 23, 1980, June 13, 1982, March 13, 1983, January 1, 1984, April 8, 1984, March 17, 1985, May 12, 1985, October 6, 1985, January 19, 1986, March 9, 1986, November 16, 1986, March 1, 1987, February 12, 1989.
Wilson Library Bulletin, May, 1965.

                    *   *   *

WILSON, Robert M. 1944-

PERSONAL: Born October 4, 1944, in Waco, Tex.; son of D. M. (a lawyer) and Loree (Hamilton) Wilson. *Education:* Attended University of Texas, 1959-62; studied painting with George Mc-Neil in Paris, 1962; Pratt Institute, B.F.A., 1965; apprentice to architect Paolo Soleri in Phoenix, Ariz., 1966.

ADDRESSES: Home—67 Vestry St., New York, N.Y. 10013. *Office*—Byrd Hoffman Foundation, Inc., 325 Spring St., New York, N.Y. 10013.

CAREER: Playwright, director, designer, painter, teacher, and architect. Artistic director, Byrd Hoffman Foundation, Inc., New York City. Has conducted seminars and workshops at various institutions, including University of California, Berkeley, Newark State College (now Keane College of New Jersey), University of California, Los Angeles, New York University, Harvard University, and Centre de Development du Potential Humain, Paris; lecturer at University of Iowa Center for New Performing Arts, Ohio State University, International School, Paris, University of Torino, Italy, UNESCO International Theater Institute, Durdan, France, and at European theatre festivals; teacher and consultant in body movement and body awareness with numerous colleges, universities, schools, community groups, and government agencies.

Solo exhibitions of work at Paula Cooper Gallery (New York City), Marian Goodman Gallery, (New York City), Galerie le Dessin (Paris), Galerie Annemarie Verna (Zurich), Pavillion des Arts (Paris), Galerie Brinkman (Amsterdam), Gallery Ueda (Tokyo), Otis Art Institute/Parsons School of Design (Los Angeles), Museo di Folklore (Rome), Kolnishcer Kunstverein (Koln), Galleria Franca Mancini (Pesaro, Italy), and Institute of Contemporary Art (Boston); work displayed in group exhibitions, including "Biennal Exhibition," Whitney Museum of American Art (New York City), "The Next Wave Artists," Paula Cooper Gallery (New York City), "Der Hang zum Gesamtkunstwerk," Museum Moderner Kunst (Vienna) and Kunsthaus (Zurich), "Survey of Contemporary Painting and Sculpture," "New Works on Paper 3" and "Spatial Relationships in Video," all Museum of Modern Art (New York City), "Highlights: Selections from the BankAmerica Corporation Art Collection," Giannini Gallery (San Francisco), and "Large Drawings," a traveling exhibit organized by Independent Curators, Inc. (New York City); public collections of work at Australian National Gallery (Canberra), Museum of Modern Art (New York City), Museum of Modern Art (Paris), Rhode Island School of Design (Providence), Bank of America (San Francisco), and Museum of Fine Arts (Boston). Has directed 16-mm films, including "Slant," for NET-TV, 1963, "The House," 1963, and adaptation of own play "Overture for a Deafman," 1971.

MEMBER: Societe des Auteurs et Compositeurs Dramatiques (Paris), PEN American Center, Dramatists Guild.

AWARDS, HONORS: Critics Award for best foreign play, Syndicat de la Critique Musicale (Paris), 1970, for "Deafman Glance"; Vernon Rice Drama Desk Award, 1971, for direction of "Deafman Glance"; Guggenheim fellowship, 1971; Off-Broadway Award (OBIE) special citation for direction, 1974, for "The Life and Times of Joseph Stalin"; Antoinette Perry Award (Tony) nomination for best score and lyrics, and Joseph Maharam Foundation Award for best set design, both 1975, both for "A Letter for Queen Victoria"; Rockefeller Foundation fellowship, 1975 and 1981; Grand Prize, International Festival of Nations (Belgrade), Critics Award for best musical theatre, Le Syndicat de la Critique Musicale, and Lumen Award for design, all 1977, all for "Einstein on the Beach"; citation in "Top Ten Plays," German Critics Award (Berlin) and first prize in playwright category, German Press Award (Berlin), both 1979, both for "Death, Destruction and Detroit"; Der Rosenstrauss Award (Munich) for best play of the year, 1982, for "The Golden Windows"; San Sebastian Film and Video Festival award (San Sebastian, Spain), 1984, for "Stations"; Berlin Festspiele Theatertreffen, 1984, for "the CIVIL warS: a tree is best measured when it is down"/German Section.

WRITINGS:

THEATER WORKS; ALSO DIRECTOR

"Dance Event," produced in New York City, 1965.
"Solo Performance," produced in New York City at Byrd Hoffman Studio, 1966.
"Theater Activity" (one-act), first produced in New York City at Bleecker Street Cinema, 1967.
"Byrd-woMAN" (two-act), first produced in New York City at Byrd Hoffman Studio, 1968.
"The Life and Times of Sigmund Freud" (three-act), first produced Off-Broadway at Brooklyn Academy of Music, 1969.
"The King of Spain" (also see below; one-act), first produced Off-Broadway at Anderson Theater, January 30, 1969.
"Deafman Glance" (one-act), first produced in Iowa City, Iowa, at University Theater, 1970, produced Off-Broadway at Brooklyn Academy of Music, 1971.
"Program Prologue Now, Overture for a Deafman" (three-act), first produced in Paris, France, at Espace Pierre Cardin, 1971, produced in New York City at Byrd Hoffman Studio, 1972.
"Overture" (two-act), first produced in New York City at Byrd Hoffman Studio, 1972, produced as one-act play in Shiraz, Iran, at Khaneh-e Zinatolmolk, 1972, produced as "twenty-

four hour continuous one-act" in Paris at Musee Galliera and Opera Comique, 1972.

"KA MOUNTAIN AND GUARDenia TERRACE: A Story about a Family and Some People Changing" ("seven-day continuous one-act"), produced in Shiraz at Haft Tan Mountain, 1972.

"king lyre and lady in the wasteland" (one-act), first produced in New York City at Byrd Hoffman Studio, 1973.

"The Life and Times of Joseph Stalin" (seven-act), first produced in Copenhagen, Denmark, at Det Ny Teater, 1973, produced Off-Broadway at Brooklyn Academy of Music, December 15, 1973, produced in Sao Paulo, Brazil, as "The Life and Times of Dave Clark," 1974.

A Letter for Queen Victoria (produced in Spoleto, Italy, at Spoleto Festival, June, 1974, produced on Broadway at ANTA Theatre, March 22, 1975), privately printed, 1974.

"A Mad Man a Mad Giant a Mad Dog a Mad Urge a Mad Face," produced in Washington, D.C., 1974.

" 'Prologue' to a Letter for Queen Victoria," produced in Spoleto, 1974.

"The $ Value of Man," produced Off-Broadway at Brooklyn Academy of Music, 1975.

(With Christopher Knowles) "Dia Log," produced Off-Broadway at Public Theatre, 1975, produced as "Dia Log/ Curious George," in New York City at Mitzi E. Newhouse Theater, 1980.

(With Philip Glass) *Einstein on the Beach* (opera; produced in New York City at Metropolitan Opera House, 1976, produced Off-Broadway at Brooklyn Academy of Music, 1984), EOS Enterprises, 1976.

I Was Sitting on My Patio This Guy Appeared I Thought I Was Hallucinating (first produced Off-Broadway at Cherry Lane Theatre, May 22, 1977), privately printed, 1978.

Death, Destruction and Detroit (also see below; first produced in Berlin, West Germany, at Schaubuehne Theatre, 1979), Schaubuehne am Halleschen Ufer, 1979.

"Edison," first produced in Lyon, France, 1979, produced in New York City at Lion Theatre, 1979.

"The Man in the Raincoat," produced in Koln, West Germany, at Theater der Welt, 1981.

(Adaptor with Gavin Bryars) "Medea" (from the opera "Medee" by Marc Antoine Charpentier), produced in Washington, D.C., at Kennedy Center for the Performing Arts, 1981, produced in New York City at City College of New York, 1982, produced in Paris at Theatre des Champs-Elysees, October 23, 1984.

The Golden Windows (produced in Munich at Kammerspiele, 1982, produced Off-Broadway at Brooklyn Academy of Music, October, 1985), Carl Hanser Verlag (Munich), 1982.

(With Jessye Norman) "Great Day in the Morning," produced in Paris at Theatre des Champs-Elysees, 1982.

the CIVIL warS: a tree is best measured when it is down/Dutch Section (produced in Rotterdam, Holland, at Schouwburg Theater, 1983, with subsequent productions throughout France), Meulenhoff/Landshoff (Amsterdam), 1983.

"the CIVIL warS: a tree is best measured when it is down"/ Japan, produced in Tokyo, February 10, 1984.

"the CIVIL warS: a tree is best measured when it is down"/ Marseille, produced in Marseille, France, at Office Regionale de la Culture de Provence-Alpe-Cote d'Azur, 1984.

the CIVIL warS: a tree is best measured when it is down/Rome Section (produced in Rome, Italy, at Teatro dell'Opera di Roma, March 25-31, 1984, concert version [with music by Glass] produced Off-Broadway at Brooklyn Academy of Music, December, 1986), Edizioni del Teatro dell'Opera (Rome), 1984.

(With music by David Byrne) "the CIVIL warS: a tree is best measured when it is down"/American Section, or "The Knee Plays," first produced in Minneapolis, Minn., at Guthrie Theater, Walker Art Center, April 26-28, 1984, produced in New York City at Alice Tully Hall, December, 1986.

the CIVIL warS: a tree is best measured when it is down/German Section (first produced in Koln, West Germany, at Schauspiel Koln, January 19, 1984), Suhrkamp Verlag (Frankfurt), 1984.

(With Heiner Mueller) *the CIVIL warS: a tree is best measured when it is down*/Act III, Scene E, and Act IV, Scene A and Epilogue (produced in Cambridge, Mass., at American Repertory Theatre, February 27, 1985), American Repertory Theatre, 1985.

(Adaptor) "King Lear" (from the play by William Shakespeare), produced as work in progress in Hollywood, Calif., at Stage One by UCLA Extension, Metromedia Square, May, 1985.

(Adaptor with Mueller) "Hamletmachine" (from the play by Mueller), produced in New York City at Mainstage II by New York University Theatre Department, May, 1986.

(Adaptor) "Alceste" (from the opera by Christoph Willibald Gluck), produced in Stuttgart, West Germany, by Stuttgart Opera Company, December, 1986.

(Adaptor) "Salome" (from the opera by Richard Strauss), produced in Milan, Italy, at Teatro alla Scala, January, 1987.

"Death Destruction & Detroit II" (sequel), produced in Berlin at Schaubuehne Theatre, May, 1987.

(With Byrne) "The Forest" (includes parts of "The Knee Plays"), produced Off-Broadway at Brooklyn Academy of Music, December, 1988.

Also author of "Alley Cat," produced in New York City at New York University.

OTHER

(Contributor) William Hoffman, editor, *New American Plays,* Volume 3 (contains "The King of Spain"), Hill & Wang, 1970.

the CIVIL warS: Drawings, Models and Documentation, Otis Institute/Parsons School of Design, 1984.

SIDELIGHTS: One of the most innovative figures in American theatre, playwright, director, and designer Robert M. Wilson is credited with developing a new kind of theatre that combines surrealistic sets and images, music, dance, and what Jack Kroll of *Newsweek* terms "psychodrama." The outcome and effect of this combination, as well as the large-scale productions and length of his plays, are often compared to that of a spectacle. Leo Bersani explains, "The dozens of players in each work, the dizzying number of things going on, the elaborate sets, the hundreds of costumes, the rich colors and symphonies of variegated sounds make Wilson the Cecil B. De Mille of the avant-garde."

Wilson's plays are composed of what Kroll describes as a "shifting collage of images and actions." Frequently taking five or more hours to perform, his work relies on visual elements and experimental "uses of space, silence and sound," according to Judith Searle in the *New York Times.* That is, rather than the conventional theatrical means of plot, language, and character interaction, Wilson employs a variety of acts and scenes that are simultaneously performed on different sets, changing backdrops, pantomime, and little, if any, dialogue. In her article on the performance of "KA MOUNTAIN AND GUARDenia TERRACE" (a seven-day-and-night event that began at the base of

Iran's Haf Tan Mountain and concluded at its summit), Searle comments: "Actors—some on platforms, some in side rooms, some on a kind of low stage at one end—began to perform very slowly actions related to the stated theme of the piece—'a family and some people changing.' But the actors never related to each other in the conventional theatrical way. Their actions took place simultaneously, but with no apparent effect on each other." The *Village Voice*'s Michael Smith offers a similar description of "The Life and Times of Joseph Stalin," Wilson's twelve-hour, seven-act play: "There is always so much going on that . . . the eye never catches up with it. Some of it is always changing, some of it always stays the same. You get interested in watching something on the left side of the stage . . . and when you look back over on the right, everything is different. Or a new backdrop will suddenly slowly fly in and the whole reality be changed."

Time and movement are of major concern to Wilson; his plays frequently explore the effects of slowing down body movements. For example, a character will take hours to peel and slice an onion or to walk from one end of the stage to the other. Searle states that through these methods Wilson is "attempting . . . to explore the gradualness and imperceptibility of change." Stanley Kauffmann notes that the use of slow motion is a basic point of difference between Wilson's theatre and Surrealist theatre: "Wilson's tempo is *largo*. His intent is not the surrealist fracture of our 'defenses' with speedy sequences of illogic. He wants us to savor pictures."

Reviewers have commented that the length, slow motion, and spectacle of Wilson's plays produce a dream or trance-like state. To look for meanings or to form conclusions during a performance, they contend, ruins the intent of his work. In a *New Yorker* profile of Wilson and his work, the playwright tells Calvin Tomkins the "ideal" effect he is striving for: "When you have a group of people together for twelve hours or twenty-four hours, all sorts of things happen. The brain begins to operate on a slower frequency. Ideally, in our work, someone in the audience might reach a point of consciousness where he is on the same frequency as one of the performers—where he receives communications directly."

Because Wilson's chief interests lie in visual imagery and nonverbal communication, his plays contain a minimum of dialogue. Moreover, what little dialogue there is usually amounts to "verbal anarchy," according to T. E. Kalem of *Time*. In a review of "A Letter for Queen Victoria," he writes: "In a typical scene, characters shoutingly reiterate the following word-sounds contrapuntally: 'HAP-HATH-HAP-HAP-HATH—O.K., O.K., A-O.K., O.K., O.K.—SKY-SKY.' This sort of thing is punctuated by screams of primal therapy." And a writer for the *New York Times* reports that the dialogue in "Death, Destruction and Detroit" is made up of "fragmentary snatches of conversation, frequently repeated, and used as a kind of acoustic backdrop."

Tomkins suggests that "language is something [Wilson] uses as another theatrical material, like movement or light; the sense of the words is of minor importance." In the same article, Wilson tells Tomkins that "most of the important things never get communicated in words anyway"; and he outlines the motive behind his experimental approach to language and movement: "The object of a lot of the work we're doing with movement is to break movements down into very small units. Like Balinese dancers, who have something like a hundred and seventy-five eye movements alone. The question becomes 'Can we break down the phrasing of sounds in the same way and work with that?' "

Critical reaction to Wilson's methods and theories has been mixed. While some reviewers consider Wilson's plays truly innovative works of art, others find them boring, sometimes tasteless, exhibitions. As Kroll states, "[His] tactics enrage many critics, but others place Wilson among such modern masters as Beckett." Kauffmann, for example, praises Wilson's skill in presenting a "flowing gallery of pictures," but remarks, "This does not keep the performance from frequently being boring." *New York Magazine*'s John Simon holds a somewhat harsher opinion of Wilson's work. He claims that "A Letter for Queen Victoria" is a "scandal . . . that deadens you with its boredom more surely than Novacain could." He adds that "though the work calls itself an opera, it is merely *tableaux vivants* done to monotonous non-music and accompanied by meaningless verbalizing and gyrations." And "The $ Value of Man," according to Simon in a later review, is no more than "a farrago of meaningless stage images, nonsensical verbal fragments, and purposeless actions endlessly repeated and dribbling into numbing inertia."

Response to one of Wilson's better-known plays, the multimedia stage epic "the CIVIL warS: a tree is best measured when it is down," is likewise divided. Wilson has been quoted that the play—staged in sections around the world and not yet in its entirety—is meant to depict "a civil struggle that has gone on through all times" and provide a "comment on man's long journey to brotherhood." The effect of the work, according to John Rockwell in the *New York Times*, is one of "a sequence of dreamy stage-pictures without overt plot but interweaving a variety of world myths and historical personages." Some of the more striking elements of Wilson's assemblage, as Alan M. Kriegsman recounts in a *Washington Post* review of the play's "Rome Section," include "a giant Abraham Lincoln [which] floats across the stage like a dirigible; a pounding choric dance styled after Hopi rituals . . .; a vision of Robert E. Lee gyrating in the porthole of a spaceship . . .; and the descent of Hercules from the stage ceiling on a golden ladder." Kriegsman finds "throughout the opera, sounds, images and choreographed movements of stunning originality and imaginative reach." Frank Rich of the *New York Times* complains, however, that such elements are "intermingled . . . to the self-aggrandizement of the author rather than the invigoration of the audience," adding that "not even Mr. Wilson's levitating tableaux of figurative or literal trees could prevent a potentially towering theater piece from falling with a thud." The Pulitzer Prize committee was also divided on "the CIVIL warS." While the prize jury unanimously chose the play for the 1986 Pulitzer Prize in drama, the board overruled their decision in light of the fact that the work had never been staged in its entirety, "queasy about honoring work so few had seen or could see," reports Kriegsman.

Most critics—although they may not be able to understand or interpret his work—agree that Wilson is exploring important new concepts in the theatre and arts. Smith believes that Wilson is "reaching back to a deeper level of theatre," and gives this account of his reaction to "The Life and Times of Joseph Stalin": "What is performed and witnessed doesn't translate into anything. . . . I didn't know what to follow; I didn't know if there was anything to follow. I didn't even try to make sense of it. It's in another language, one that has its meaning on another level. . . . It's a slow, heady language, its content accumulated through years of work and elusive as any esoteric communication." And Tomkins offers a similar assessment of Wilson's theatre. He notes that these experimental plays are not "susceptible to rational interpretation. All Wilson's plays," he continues, "come out of his own inner imagery, or that of people who are close to him, and they must be experienced rather than understood."

MEDIA ADAPTATIONS: Audio recordings of Wilson's plays include "The Life and Times of Joseph Stalin," Byrd Hoffman Foundation, 1973, "Einstein on the Beach" (originally released by Tomato Records), CBS Masterworks, 1979, and "the CIVIL warS: Knee Plays," ECM/Warner Brothers, 1985.

BIOGRAPHICAL/CRITICAL SOURCES:

BOOKS

Arrabal, Fernando, editor, *Le Theatre,* 1972, Volume 1, Christian Bourgeois, 1972.
Bersani, Leo, *A Future for Astyanax: Character and Desire in Literature,* Little, Brown, 1976.
Bourgeois, Araball Christian, editor, *Le Theatre,* [Paris], 1972.
Brecht, Stephan, *The Theater of Visions: Robert Wilson,* Suhrkamp Verlag (Frankfurt), 1979.
Contemporary Literary Criticism, Gale, Volume 7, 1977, Volume 9, 1978.
Denby, Edwin, *Two Conversations with Edwin Denby,* Byrd Hoffman Foundation, 1973.
Kauffmann, Stanley, *Persons of the Drama,* Harper, 1976.
Nelson, Craig, editor, *Robert Wilson: The Theater of Images,* Contemporary Arts Center, Cincinnati, 1980, 2nd edition, Harper, 1984.
Quadri, Franco, *Il teatro di Robert Wilson,* Edizioni de La Biennale di Venizia, 1976.
Rose, Bernice, *New Works on Paper 3,* Museum of Modern Art, New York, 1985.
Shank, Theodore, *American Alternative Theater,* Grove Press, 1982.
Tomkins, Calvins, *The Scene,* Viking, 1976.

PERIODICALS

Artforum, February, 1977, February, 1978, October, 1984.
Art in America, November, 1980.
Boston Phoenix, July 18, 1978.
Cahiers, numbers 81-82, 1972.
Connoisseur, April, 1984.
Dallas Morning News, May 20, 1984.
Der Spiegel, July 4, 1983.
Drama Review, June, 1973, June, 1974, September, 1975, March, 1976, December, 1976.
Kansas Quarterly, Volume 12, number 4, 1980.
Le Monde, October 24, 1984.
Los Angeles Times, December 23, 1984, December 21, 1986.
Newsweek, December 6, 1976, April 9, 1984, December 31, 1984.
New York Arts Journal, spring, 1977.
New Yorker, March 27, 1971, January 13, 1975.
New York Magazine, April 7, 1975, May 26, 1975.
New York Post, May 23, 1977.
New York Times, March 7, 1971, July 5, 1971, November 12, 1972, May 23, 1977, February 18, 1979, October 30, 1979, November 1, 1984, December 2, 1984, December 17, 1984, December 23, 1984, October 20, 1985, November 3, 1985, May 25, 1986, December 4, 1986, December 11, 1986, December 16, 1986, December 23, 1986, January 8, 1987, January 10, 1987, May 2, 1987.
Performance Art, Volume 1, number 1, 1979.
Theater, summer/fall, 1981, fall/winter, 1984.
Theater Heute, September, 1980, July, 1982.
Time, December 31, 1973, April 7, 1975, May 21, 1984.
Times Saturday Review (London), June 10, 1978.
Variety, March 3, 1971.

Village Voice, December 20, 1973, November 22, 1976.
Wall Street Journal, December 21, 1984.
Washington Post, December 17, 1984, November 16, 1986, December 16, 1986, December 5, 1988.

*   *   *

WINDHAM, Basil
See WODEHOUSE, P(elham) G(renville)

*   *   *

WINTERS, (Arthur) Yvor   1900-1968

PERSONAL: Born October 17, 1900, in Chicago, Ill.; died of cancer, January 25, 1968, in Palo Alto, Calif.; son of Harry Lewis and Faith Evangeline (Ahnefeldt) Winters; married Janet Lewis (a writer), June 22, 1926; children: Joanna Winters Thompson, Daniel Lewis. *Education:* Attended University of Chicago, 1917-18; University of Colorado, A.B. and A.M., 1925; Stanford University, Ph.D., 1934.

ADDRESSES: Home—143 West Portola Ave., Los Altos, Calif. 94022.

CAREER: Taught in coal camps of Madrid and Los Cerillos, N.M., two years; University of Idaho, Moscow, instructor in French and Spanish, 1925-27; Stanford University, Stanford, Calif., instructor, 1928-37, assistant professor, 1937-41, associate professor, 1941-49, professor of English, 1949-61, Albert Guerard Professor of Literature, 1961-66.

MEMBER: American Association of University Professors, National Association for the Advancement of Colored People (life), American Academy of Arts and Sciences (fellow), American Civil Liberties Union (for Northern California), Phi Beta Kappa (resigned).

AWARDS, HONORS: Oscar Blumenthal Prize of *Poetry* Magazine, 1945; National Institute of Arts and Letters award, 1952; University of Chicago Harriet Monroe Poetry Award, 1960-61; Bollingen Prize, 1960, for *Collected Poems;* Guggenheim grant, 1961-62; Brandeis University Creative Arts award for poetry, 1963; National Endowment for the Arts grant, 1967.

WRITINGS:

POETRY

The Immobile Wind, M. Wheeler, 1921.
The Magpie's Shadow, Musterbookhouse, 1922.
The Bare Hills, Four Seas Co., 1927.
The Proof, Coward, 1930.
The Journey, Dragon Press, 1931.
Before Disaster, Tryon Pamphlets, 1934.
Poems, Gyroscope Press, 1940.
To the Holy Spirit, California Poetry Folios, 1947.
Three Poems, Cummington Press, 1950.
Collected Poems, ·A. Swallow, 1952, revised edition, 1960.
The Early Poems of Yvor Winters, 1920-1928, A. Swallow, 1966.

EDITOR

Twelve Poets of the Pacific, New Directions, 1937.
Elizabeth Daryush, *Selected Poems,* Swallow Press, 1948.
Poets of the Pacific, Second Series, Stanford University Press, 1949.

OTHER

Notes on the Mechanics of the Poetic Image, [Vienna], 1925.
(With Frances Theresa Russell) *The Case of David Lamson: A Summary,* Lamson Defense Committee, 1934.

Primitivism and Decadence: A Study of American Experimental Poetry, Arrow Editions, 1937.

Maule's Curse: Seven Studies in the History of American Obscurantism, New Directions, 1938.

The Anatomy of Nonsense, New Directions, 1943.

Edwin Arlington Robinson, New Directions, 1946.

In Defense of Reason, Swallow Press, 1947, 3rd revised edition, A. Swallow, 1960.

The Function of Criticism: Problems and Exercises, A. Swallow, 1957, 2nd edition, 1966.

(Contributor) Irving Howe, editor, *Modern Literary Criticism,* Beacon Press, 1958.

On Modern Poets: Stevens, Eliot, Ransom, Crane, Hopkins, Frost, Meridian Books, 1959.

The Poetry of W. B. Yeats (pamphlet), A. Swallow, 1960.

The Poetry of J. V. Cunningham (pamphlet), A. Swallow, 1961.

The Brink of Darkness (pamphlet), A. Swallow, c. 1965.

(Contributor) Paul J. Alpers, editor, *Elizabethan Poetry: Modern Essays in Criticism,* Oxford University Press, 1967.

Forms of Discovery: Critical and Historical Essays on the Forms of the Short Poem in English, A. Swallow, 1967.

(Compiler with Kenneth Fields) *Quest for Reality: An Anthology of Short Poems in English,* Swallow Press, 1969.

Work represented in many anthologies, including *Robert Frost: A Collection of Critical Essays,* edited by James Melville Cox, Prentice-Hall, 1962; *A Dial Miscellany,* edited by William Wasserstrom, Syracuse University Press, 1963; and *The Structure of Verse: Modern Essays on Prosody,* edited by Harvey Seymour Gross, Fawcett, 1966. Contributor to *Poetry, New Republic, MS, Hudson Review, Dial, Transition, American Caravan, Modern Verse, New Mexico Quarterly, Southern Review, American Literature, Kenyon Review, Sewanee Review, American Scholar, Arizona Quarterly,* and other publications. Co-editor, *Gyroscope,* 1929-30; western editor, *Hound and Horn,* 1932-34.

SIDELIGHTS: Allen Tate once commented on Yvor Winters the poet thus: "If he has been neglected—when he has not been ignored—the reasons are not hard to find. He has conducted a poetic revolution all his own that owes little or nothing to the earlier revolution of Pound and Eliot, and that goes back to certain great, likewise neglected Tudor poets for metrical and stylistic models." Winters commented to *CA:* "Tate is wrong about this, but in general my admirers have read me as carelessly as my detractors." Winters deals in strict rhymes and formal metrics, maintaining detachment from his subject in the process. If his poetry is cold, it is "that burning cold that belongs to ice," writes Babette Deutsch. In *Poetry in Our Time* she observes: "His small output testifies to the rigor of his craftsmanship and to his belief that a poem, being 'a full and definitive account of a human experience,' is 'an act of moral judgment.' His songs and sonnets, a sheaf of his longer pieces, are fired with the moral passion of this absolutist."

Winters writes, says William Troy, "like a combination of a medieval scholastic and a New England divine." ("Twaddle," said Winters.) Keith F. McKean asserts that "Winters defends reason and warns against certain aspects of romantic philosophy," and explains Winters's approach thus: "First, Winters believes, the critic should record any historical or biographical data necessary to understand the mind and the method of the author; second, he should analyze the literary theories that are relevant to the work; third, he must make a critique of the paraphrasable content; and fourth, he must make a critique of the feelings motivated by the experience; and last of all, he must judge the work."

Though his approach to literature has been called "narrow" and "dogmatic," he has, as Troy admits, sharpened the focus on certain problems and formulated useful distinctions. Poet Hayden Carruth has the highest praise for him: "I admire Winters, and what he has done for American literature; no one else could have done it—I mean aside from his own poems, some of which are superb. There's no one like him for making a simple declarative sentence crackle under your eyes like a burning apple-bough. Such magnificent wrath. . . . Of course, Winters is as insane as the rest of us, but he has made a whole career out of covering it up. . . . Winters is able to *prove*—demonstrate irrefutably with step-by-step arguments and copious illustrations from line and stanza—that our favorite poets are idiots, and in the process show us just why we like them so much."

Winters recorded his poems for the Library of Congress and the Yale Series of Recorded Poets.

BIOGRAPHICAL/CRITICAL SOURCES:

BOOKS

Bogan, Louis, *Selected Criticism: Prose, Poetry,* Noonday, 1955.

Contemporary Literary Criticism, Gale, Volume 4, 1975, Volume 8, 1978, Volume 32, 1985.

Deutsch, Babette, *Poetry in Our Time,* Columbia University Press, 1952.

Dictionary of Literary Biography, Volume 48: *American Poets, 1880-1945, Second Series,* Gale, 1986.

Glicksberg, C. I., *American Literary Criticism, 1900-1950,* Hendricks House, 1951.

Hyman, Stanley Edgar, *The Armed Vision,* Knopf, 1948.

Matthiessen, F. O., *Responsibilities of the Critic,* Oxford University Press, 1952.

McKean, Keith F., *The Moral Measure of Literature,* A. Swallow, 1961.

Moore, H. T., editor, *The World of Lawrence Durrell,* Southern Illinois University Press, 1962.

Nemerov, Howard, *Poetry and Fiction: Essays,* Rutgers University Press, 1963.

Pritchard, John Paul, *Criticism in America,* University of Oklahoma Press, 1956.

Whittemore, Reed, *The Fascination of the Abomination,* Macmillan, 1939,

PERIODICALS

American Quarterly, fall, 1967.

Bookman, June, 1928.

Centennial Review, fall, 1970.

Commonweal, October 20, 1967.

Criticism, fall, 1968.

Hudson Review, summer, 1968.

Nation, February 20, 1937.

New Republic, July 12, 1943, March 2, 1953, March 2, 1968.

New Statesman, September 24, 1960.

New York Review of Books, February 29, 1968.

New York Times Book Review, August 24, 1947.

Partisan Review, summer, 1968.

Poetry, August, 1958.

South Atlantic Quarterly, April, 1951.

Southern Review, winter, 1969.

Spectator, July 1, 1960.

WODEHOUSE, P(elham) G(renville) 1881-1975
(P. Brooke-Haven, Pelham Grenville, J. Plum, C. P. West, J. Walker Williams, Basil Windham)

PERSONAL: Surname is pronounced "*Wood*-house"; born October 15, 1881, in Guildford, Surrey, England; naturalized U.S. citizen, 1955; died of a heart attack, February 14, 1975, in Southampton, N.Y.; son of Henry Ernest (a civil servant and judge) and Eleanor (Deane) Wodehouse; married Ethel Rowley, September 30, 1914; children: Leonora (stepdaughter; deceased). *Education:* Attended Dulwich College, 1894-1900.

CAREER: Novelist, short story writer, and playwright. Hong Kong & Shanghai Bank, London, England, clerk, 1901-03; *London Globe,* London, assistant on "By the Way" column, 1902-03, writer of column, 1903-09; writer, under various pseudonyms, and drama critic for *Vanity Fair,* 1915-19.

MEMBER: Dramatists Guild, Authors League of America, Old Alleynian Association (New York; president), Coffee House (New York).

AWARDS, HONORS: Litt.D., Oxford University, 1939; named Knight Commander, Order of the British Empire, 1975.

WRITINGS:

NOVELS

The Pothunters, A & C Black, 1902, Macmillan, 1924, reprinted, Souvenir Press, 1972, International Scholarly Book, 1977.

A Prefect's Uncle, A & C Black, 1903, Macmillan, 1924, reprinted, Souvenir Press, 1972, International Scholarly Book, 1977.

The Gold Bat, A & C Black, 1904, Macmillan, 1923, reprinted, Souvenir Press, 1974, International Scholarly Book, 1977.

The Head of Kay's, A & C Black, 1905, Macmillan, 1922, reprinted, Souvenir Press, 1974, International Scholarly Book, 1977.

Love among the Chickens, George Newnes, 1906, Circle Publishing, 1909, revised edition, Jenkins, 1921, autograph edition, 1963.

The White Feather, A & C Black, 1907, Macmillan, 1922, reprinted, Souvenir Press, 1972, International Scholarly Book, 1977.

(With A. W. Westbrook) *Not George Washington,* Cassell, 1907.

The Swoop!; or, How Clarence Saved England: A Tale of the Great Invasion, Alston Rivers, 1909.

Mike: A Public School Story, two parts, A & C Black, 1909, Macmillan, 1924, revised edition of second part published as *Enter Psmith,* Macmillan, 1935, entire book published in two volumes as *Mike at Wrykyn,* Jenkins, 1953, reprinted, Barrie & Jenkins, 1976, and *Mike and Psmith,* Jenkins, 1953, reprinted, Meredith Press, 1969.

The Intrusion of Jimmy, W. J. Watt, 1910 (published in England as *A Gentleman of Leisure,* Alston Rivers, 1910, abridged edition, George Newnes, 1920, autograph edition, Jenkins, 1962, reprinted, Star Books, 1978).

Psmith in the City, A & C Black, 1910, reprinted, Penguin, 1970.

The Prince and Betty, W. J. Watt, 1912 (published in England as *Psmith, Journalist,* A & C Black, 1915, reprinted, Penguin, 1970).

The Prince and Betty (different book from above title), Mills & Boon, 1912.

The Little Nugget, Methuen, 1913, W. J. Watt, 1914, reprinted with a new preface by the author, Barrie & Jenkins, 1972, Penguin, 1978.

Something New, Appleton, 1915, reprinted, Beagle Books, 1972 (published in England as *Something Fresh,* Methuen, 1915, reprinted, Jenkins, 1969).

Uneasy Money, Appleton, 1916, reprinted, Penguin, 1978.

Piccadilly Jim, Dodd, 1917, revised edition, 1931, autograph edition, Jenkins, 1966, reprinted, Penguin, 1969.

A Damsel in Distress, Doran, 1919, autograph edition, Jenkins, 1956, reprinted, Star Books, 1978.

Their Mutual Child, Boni & Liveright, 1919 (published in England as *The Coming of Bill,* Jenkins, 1920, autograph edition, 1966, reprinted, Barrie & Jenkins, 1976).

The Little Warrior, Doran, 1920 (published in England as *Jill the Reckless,* Jenkins, 1921, autograph edition, 1958).

Three Men and a Maid, Doran, 1922 (published in England as *The Girl on the Boat,* Jenkins, 1922, autograph edition, 1956).

The Adventures of Sally, Jenkins, 1922, reprinted, Barrie & Jenkins, 1973, published as *Mostly Sally,* Doran, 1923.

Leave It to Psmith, Jenkins, 1923, autograph edition, 1961, reprinted, 1976, Doran, 1924.

Bill the Conqueror: His Invasion of England in the Springtime, Methuen, 1924, Doran, 1925, reprinted, British Book Center, 1975.

Sam in the Suburbs, Doran, 1925 (published in England as *Sam the Sudden,* Methuen, 1925, reprinted with a new preface by the author, Barrie & Jenkins, 1972, Penguin, 1978).

The Small Bachelor (based on his play, "Oh! Lady, Lady!"), Doran, 1927, reprinted, Ballantine, 1977.

Money for Nothing, Doubleday, Doran, 1928, autograph edition, Jenkins, 1959, reprinted, Barrie & Jenkins, 1976.

Fish Preferred, Doubleday, Doran, 1929, reprinted, Simon & Schuster, 1969 (published in England as *Summer Lightning,* Jenkins, 1929, autograph edition, 1964).

Big Money, Doubleday, Doran, 1931, autograph edition, Jenkins, 1965.

If I Were You, Doubleday, Doran, 1931, autograph edition, Jenkins, 1958, reprinted, Barrie & Jenkins, 1976.

Doctor Sally, Methuen, 1932, reprinted, Thomas Nelson, 1966.

Hot Water, Doubleday, Doran, 1932, autograph edition, Jenkins, 1956, reprinted, Penguin, 1978.

Heavy Weather, Little, Brown, 1933, autograph edition, Jenkins, 1960, reprinted, Penguin, 1973.

Thank You, Jeeves, Little, Brown, 1934, autograph edition, Jenkins, 1956, reprinted, Coronet Books, 1977.

Brinkley Manor, Little, Brown, 1934 (published in England as *Right Ho, Jeeves,* Jenkins, 1934, autograph edition, 1957, reprinted, Penguin, 1975).

Trouble Down at Tudsleigh, International Magazine Co., 1935.

The Luck of the Bodkins, Jenkins, 1935, Little, Brown, 1936, autograph edition, Jenkins, 1956, reprinted, Penguin, 1975.

Laughing Gas, Doubleday, Doran, 1936, autograph edition, Jenkins, 1959, reprinted, Ballantine, 1977.

Summer Moonshine, Doubleday, Doran, 1937, autograph edition, Jenkins, 1956, reprinted, Penguin, 1976.

The Code of the Woosters, Doubleday, Doran, 1938, autograph edition, Jenkins, 1962, reprinted, Penguin, 1975.

Uncle Fred in the Springtime, Doubleday, Doran, 1939, autograph edition, Jenkins, 1962, reprinted, Penguin, 1976.

Quick Service, Doubleday, Doran, 1940, autograph edition, Jenkins, 1960, reprinted, Penguin, 1972.

Money in the Bank, Doubleday, Doran, 1942, reprinted, Penguin, 1978.

Joy in the Morning, Doubleday, 1946, reprinted with a new preface by the author, Jenkins, 1974.

Full Moon, Doubleday, 1947.

Spring Fever, Doubleday, 1948, reprinted, Jenkins, 1976.

Uncle Dynamite, Jenkins, 1948, reprinted, Star Books, 1978.

The Mating Season, Didier, 1949, reprinted, Penguin, 1971.

The Old Reliable, Doubleday, 1951, reprinted, Pan Books, 1968.

Angel Cake (based on the play, "The Butter and Egg Man," by George F. Kaufman), Doubleday, 1952 (published in England as *Barmy in Wonderland,* Jenkins, 1952, autograph edition, 1958).

Pigs Have Wings, Doubleday, 1952, reprinted with a new preface by the author, Barrie & Jenkins, 1974, Ballantine, 1977.

Ring for Jeeves, Jenkins, 1953, autograph edition, 1963, reprinted, Sphere Books, 1977, published as *The Return of Jeeves,* Simon & Schuster, 1954.

Jeeves and the Feudal Spirit, Jenkins, 1954, reprinted, Coronet Books, 1977, published as *Bertie Wooster Sees It Through,* Simon & Schuster, 1955.

French Leave, Jenkins, 1956, Simon & Schuster, 1959, reprinted with a new preface by the author, Barrie & Jenkins, 1974.

The Butler Did It, Simon & Schuster, 1957 (published in England as *Something Fishy,* Jenkins, 1957, reprinted, Star Books, 1978).

Cocktail Time, Simon & Schuster, 1958.

How Right You Are, Jeeves, Simon & Schuster, 1960 (published in England as *Jeeves in the Offing,* Jenkins, 1960).

Ice in the Bedroom, Simon & Schuster, 1961.

Service with a Smile, Simon & Schuster, 1961, reprinted, Penguin, 1975.

Stiff Upper Lip, Jeeves, Simon & Schuster, 1963.

Biffen's Millions, Simon & Schuster, 1964 (published in England as *Frozen Assets,* Jenkins, 1964, reprinted, Barrie & Jenkins, 1976).

The Brinkmanship of Galahad Threepwood: A Blandings Castle Novel, Simon & Schuster, 1965 (published in England as *Galahad at Blandings,* Jenkins, 1965).

The Purloined Paperweight, Simon & Schuster, 1967 (published in England as *Company for Henry,* Jenkins, 1967).

Do Butlers Burgle Banks?, Simon & Schuster, 1968.

A Pelican at Blandings, Jenkins, 1969, published as *No Nudes Is Good Nudes,* Simon & Schuster, 1970.

The Girl in Blue, Barrie & Jenkins, 1970, Simon & Schuster, 1971.

Jeeves and the Tie That Binds, Simon & Schuster, 1971 (published in England as *Much Obliged, Jeeves,* autograph edition, Barrie & Jenkins, 1971).

Pearls, Girls, and Monty Bodkins, Barrie & Jenkins, 1972, published as *The Plot That Thickened,* Simon & Schuster, 1973.

Bachelors Anonymous, Barrie & Jenkins, 1973, Simon & Schuster, 1974.

The Cat-Nappers: A Jeeves and Bertie Story, Simon & Schuster, 1974 (published in England as *Aunts Aren't Gentlemen: A Jeeves and Bertie Story,* Barrie & Jenkins, 1974).

Sunset at Blandings, Chatto & Windus, 1977, Simon & Schuster, 1978.

STORIES

Tales of St. Austin's, A & C Black, 1903, Macmillan, 1923, reprinted, Penguin, 1978.

The Man Upstairs and Other Stories, Methuen, 1914, reprinted with a new preface by the author, Barrie & Jenkins, 1971.

The Man with Two Left Feet and Other Stories, Methuen, 1917, A. L. Burt, 1933, reprinted, Penguin, 1978.

My Man Jeeves, George Newnes, 1919, published as *Carry On, Jeeves,* Jenkins, 1925, autograph edition, 1960, reprinted, Penguin, 1975.

The Indiscretions of Archie, Doran, 1921, reprinted, Jenkins, 1965.

The Clicking of Cuthbert, Jenkins, 1922, autograph edition, 1956, published as *Golf without Tears,* Doran, 1924.

Jeeves, Doran, 1923 (published in England as *The Inimitable Jeeves,* Jenkins, 1923, autograph edition, 1956, reprinted, Penguin, 1975).

Ukridge, Jenkins, 1924, autograph edition, 1960, reprinted, Penguin, 1973, published as *He Rather Enjoyed It,* Doran, 1926.

The Heart of a Goof, Jenkins, 1926, autograph edition, 1956, reprinted, Penguin, 1978, published as *Divots,* Doran, 1927.

Meet Mr. Mulliner, Jenkins, 1927, Doubleday, Doran, 1928, autograph edition, Jenkins, 1956.

Mr. Mulliner Speaking, Jenkins, 1929, Doubleday, Doran, 1930, autograph edition, Jenkins, 1961.

Very Good, Jeeves, Doubleday, Doran, 1930, autograph edition, Jenkins, 1958, reprinted, Penguin, 1975.

Mulliner Nights, Doubleday, Doran, 1933, autograph edition, Jenkins, 1966, reprinted, Vintage Books, 1975.

Blandings Castle, Doubleday, Doran, 1935 (published in England as *Blandings Castle and Elsewhere,* Jenkins, 1935, autograph edition, 1957).

Young Men in Spats, Doubleday, Doran, 1936, autograph edition, Jenkins, 1957.

The Crime Wave at Blandings, Doubleday, Doran, 1937 (published in England as *Lord Emsworth and Others,* Jenkins, 1937, autograph edition, 1956, reprinted, 1976).

Eggs, Beans and Crumpets, Doubleday, Doran, 1940, autograph edition, Jenkins, 1963, reprinted, Penguin, 1976.

Dudley Is Back to Normal, Doubleday, Doran, 1940.

Nothing Serious, Jenkins, 1950, Doubleday, 1951, autograph edition, Jenkins, 1964.

Selected Stories, introduction by John W. Aldridge, Modern Library, 1958.

A Few Quick Ones, Simon & Schuster, 1959, reprinted, Coronet Books, 1978.

Plum Pie, Jenkins, 1966, Simon & Schuster, 1967.

Jeeves, Jeeves, Jeeves, Avon, 1976.

David A. Jasen, editor, *The Swoop and Other Stories,* with an appreciation by Malcolm Muggeridge, Seabury, 1979.

OTHER BOOKS

(Adapter) *William Tell Told Again* (based on the classic tale), A & C Black, 1904.

(With H. W. Westbrook) *The Globe "By the Way" Book: A Literary Quick-Lunch for People Who Have Only Got Five Minutes to Spare,* Globe, 1908.

Louder and Funnier (essays), Faber, 1932, autograph edition, Jenkins, 1963, reprinted, Barrie & Jenkins, 1976.

(Editor) *A Century of Humour,* Hutchinson, 1934.

(Editor with Scott Meredith and author of introduction) *The Week-End Book of Humour,* Washburn, 1952, published as *P. G. Wodehouse Selects the Best of Humor,* Grosset, 1965.

(Editor with Meredith and author of introduction) *The Best of Modern Humour,* Metcalf, 1952, reprinted, Books for Libraries, 1971.

Performing Flea: A Self-Portrait in Letters (letters written by Wodehouse to William Townsend), introduction by Townsend, Jenkins, 1953, published as *Author! Author!,* Simon & Schuster, 1962.

(With Guy Bolton) *Bring On the Girls!: The Improbable Story of Our Life in Musical Comedy with Pictures to Prove It,* Simon & Schuster, 1953.

America, I Like You, Simon & Schuster, 1956, revised edition published as *Over Seventy: An Autobiography with Digressions,* Jenkins, 1957.

(Editor with Meredith and author of introduction) *A Carnival of Modern Humor,* Delacorte, 1967.

Wodehouse on Wodehouse (contains *Performing Flea, Bring On the Girls!,* and *Over Seventy*), Hutchinson, 1980.

PLAYS

(With John Stapleton) "A Gentleman of Leisure" (comedy; based on Wodehouse's novel of the same title), first produced on Broadway at Playhouse Theatre, August 24, 1911.

(With Stapleton) "A Thief for the Night," first produced on Broadway at Playhouse Theatre, 1913.

(With H. W. Westbrook) "Brother Alfred," first produced on West End at Savoy Theatre, 1913.

The Play's the Thing (three-act drama; based on *Spiel in Schloss* by Ferenc Molnar; first produced on Broadway at Henry Miller's Theatre, November 3, 1926), Brentano's, 1927.

(With Valerie Wyngate) "Her Cardboard Lover" (based on a play by Jacques Deval), first produced in New York at Empire Theatre, March 21, 1927.

Good Morning, Bill (three-act comedy; based on a play by Ladislaus Fodor; first produced on West End at Duke of York's Theatre, November 28, 1927), Methuen, 1928.

(With Ian Hay) *A Damsel in Distress* (three-act comedy; based on Wodehouse's novel of the same title; first produced Off-Broadway at New Theatre, August 13, 1928), Samuel French, 1930.

(With Hay) *Baa, Baa, Black Sheep* (three-act comedy; first produced Off-Broadway at New Theatre, April 22, 1929), Samuel French, 1930.

Candlelight (three-act drama; based on "Kleine Komodie" by Siegfried Geyer; first produced in New York at Empire Theatre, September 30, 1929), Samuel French, 1934.

(With Hay) *Leave It to Psmith* (three-act comedy; based on Wodehouse's novel of the same title; first produced in London at Shaftesbury Theatre, September 29, 1930), Samuel French, 1932.

(With Guy Bolton) "Who's Who" (three-act comedy), first produced on West End at Duke of York's Theatre, September 20, 1934.

"The Inside Stand" (three-act farce), first produced in London at Saville Theatre, November 20, 1935.

(With Bolton) "Don't Listen, Ladies" (two-act comedy; based on the play "N'ecoutez pas, mesdames," by Sacha Guitry), first produced on Broadway at Booth Theatre, December 28, 1948.

(With Bolton) *Carry On, Jeeves* (three-act comedy; based on Wodehouse's novel of the same title), Evans Brothers, 1956.

Several of the author's novels were adapted by Edward Duke into a play, "Jeeves Takes Charge," c. 1984.

MUSICALS

(Author of lyrics with others) "The Gay Gordons," book by Seymour Hicks, music by Guy Jones, first produced in London at Aldwych Theatre, 1913.

(With C. H. Bovill and F. Tours) "Nuts and Wine," first produced in London at Empire Theatre, 1914.

(With Guy Bolton and H. Reynolds) "Miss Springtime," music by Emmerich Kalman and Jerome Kern, first produced in New York at New Amsterdam Theatre, September 25, 1916.

(With Bolton) "Ringtime," first produced in New York, 1917.

(Author of book and lyrics with Bolton) "Have a Heart," music by Kern, first produced in New York at Liberty Theatre, January 11, 1917.

(Author of book and lyrics with Bolton) "Oh, Boy," first produced in New York at Princess Theatre, February 20, 1917, produced in London as "Oh, Joy," 1919.

(Author of book and lyrics with Bolton) "Leave It to Jane" (musical version of "The College Widow" by George Ade) music by Kern, first produced in Albany, N.Y., July, 1917, produced on Broadway at Longacre Theatre, August 28, 1917.

(Author of book and lyrics with Bolton) "The Riviera Girl," music by Kalman, first produced in New York at New Amsterdam Theatre, September 24, 1917.

(Author of book and lyrics with Bolton) "Miss 1917," music by Victor Herbert and Kern, first produced Off-Broadway at Century Theatre, November 5, 1917.

(With Bolton) "The Second Century Show," first produced in New York, 1917.

(Author of book and lyrics with Bolton) "Oh! Lady, Lady!," music by Kern, first produced in New York at Princess Theatre, February 1, 1918.

(With Bolton) "See You Later," music by J. Szule, first produced in Baltimore at Academy of Music, April 15, 1918.

(Author of book and lyrics with Bolton) "The Girl behind the Gun" (based on play "Madame et son filleul," by Hennequin and Weber), music by Ivan Caryll, first produced in New York at New Amsterdam Theatre, September 16, 1918, produced in London as "Kissing Time" at Winter Garden Theatre, 1918.

(Author of book and lyrics with Bolton) "Oh My Dear," music by Louis Hirsch, first produced in New York at Princess Theatre, November 27, 1918, produced in Toronto as "Ask Dad," 1918.

(With Bolton) "The Rose of China," music by Armand Vecsey, first produced in New York at Lyric Theatre, November 25, 1919.

(Author of lyrics with Clifford Grey) "Sally," music by Kern, first produced in New York by Flo Ziegfeld, 1920.

(Author of book and lyrics with Fred Thompson) "The Golden Moth," music by Ivor Novello, first produced in London at Adelphi Theatre, October 5, 1921.

(Author of book and lyrics with George Grossmith) "The Cabaret Girl," music by Kern, first produced in London at Winter Garden Theatre, 1922.

(Author of book and lyrics with Grossmith) "The Beauty Prize," music by Kern, first produced in London at Aldwych Theatre, September 5, 1923.

(Author of book and lyrics with Bolton) "Sitting Pretty," music by Kern, first produced in New York at Fulton Theatre, April 8, 1924.

(Adapter with Laurie Wylie) *Hearts and Diamonds* (light opera; based on *The Orlov* by Biuno Granichstaedten and Ernest Marischka; first produced in London at Strand Theatre, June 1, 1926), English lyrics by Graham John, Keith Prowse & Co., 1926.

(With others) "Showboat," music by Oscar Hammerstein, first produced on Broadway at Ziegfeld Theatre, December 27, 1927.

(Author of book with Bolton) "Oh Kay!," lyrics by Ira Gershwin, music by George Gershwin, first produced on Broadway at Imperial Theatre, November 8, 1926.

(Author of book and lyrics with Bolton) "The Nightingale," music by Vecsey, first produced on Broadway at Al Jolson's Theatre, January 3, 1927.

(Author of lyrics with Ira Gershwin) "Rosalie," book by Bolton and Bill McGuire, music by George Gershwin and Sigmund Romberg, first produced in New York at New Amsterdam Theatre, January 10, 1928.

(Author of book with Grossmith; author of lyrics with Grey) *The Three Musketeers* (based on the novel by Alexandre Dumas; first produced in New York at Lyric Theatre, March 13, 1928), music by Rudolph Frinil, Harms Inc., 1937.

(Author of book with Bolton, Howard Lindsay, and Russel Crouse) *Anything Goes* (first produced on Broadway at Alvin Theatre, November 21, 1934), music and lyrics by Cole Porter, Samuel French, 1936.

FILMS

Coauthor of "A Damsel in Distress," based on his novel of the same title, released by RKO General, Inc., 1920; author of "Rosalie," based on his play of the same title, released by Metro-Goldwyn-Mayer, Inc., 1930. Also author of "Summer Lightning," based on his novel of the same title, and "Three French Girls."

SIDELIGHTS: Pelham Grenville Wodehouse long entertained thoughts of becoming a writer—he told interviewer Gerald Clarke of the *Paris Review:* "I was writing stories when I was five. I don't remember what I did before that. Just loafed, I suppose." Best known for his stories concerning the young Bertram Wilberforce Wooster ('Bertie') and his valet Jeeves, Wodehouse is considered a master of English humor and a powerful influence on many later writers.

The world P. G. Wodehouse created in his writings may, at times, seem strange and somewhat dated to the modern reader. Wodehouse, it must be remembered, was born in Victorian England. He was a member of the Beefsteak Club while Rudyard Kipling was still a member (he became a correspondent of Kipling's), and as a boy he read the works of many of the great nineteenth-century writers as they were published. Richard Voorhees points out that "since Wodehouse wrote his first fourteen books during the reign of Edward VII, they are bound to date in many ways." But why, then, are his later books, those written in the fifties and sixties, also full of outdated manners and customs? Sometimes, according to Voorhees, the anachronisms are accidental, as when 1948 model cars are equipped with running boards, or when a character is found to be smoking a brand of cigarette that has long since disappeared from the market. But he maintains that, more often, "the anachronisms are clearly deliberate. Wodehouse perpetrates some of them because they deal to his sense of the absurd, because they have an antiquarian smack. . . . Wodehouse commits other anachronisms because they are part of his equipment as a professional novelist, because he has used them successfully for so many years. Thus he continues to write of village concerts at which baritones sing 'The Yeoman's Wedding Song,' of village fetes with bun-eating contests and egg-and-spoon races; thus he writes as though people wore pince-nez and men wore spats." But Voorhees concludes that the most important reason for the anachronisms is that Wodehouse is "repelled by much of the modern world and is taking refuge from it."

The characters in Wodehouse's world are thoroughly unique. Easily his most famous characters are Bertram Wilberforce Wooster and his incredible valet Jeeves. They first appeared in a story entitled "Extricating Young Gussie" which Wodehouse wrote for the *Saturday Evening Post.* While Bertie was a main character in the story, Jeeves was relegated to a minor part. As Wodehouse explained to Clarke: "I only intended to use him once. His first entrance was: 'Mrs. Gregson to see you, Sir'. . . . He only had one other line: 'Very good, Sir. Which suit will you wear?' But then I was writing a story, 'The Artistic Career of Corky,' about two young men, Bertie Wooster and his friend Corky, getting into a lot of trouble. I thought: Well, how can I get them out? And I thought: 'Suppose one of them had an omniscient valet?' I wrote a short story about him, then another short story, then several more short stories and novels." In the introduction to his *Jeeves Omnibus,* Wodehouse wrote, "I still blush to think of the off-hand way I treated him at our first encounter."

Contrary to the assumptions of many readers and critics, Jeeves is no mere butler; he is a valet or, as he puts it, a gentleman's personal gentleman. In addition to the duties normally performed by a butler, a gentleman's gentleman is responsible for the running of the entire household as well as such things as his employer's dress and daily schedule. Jeeves, unlike most valets, is also entrusted with the task of saving the lives of Bertie and his numerous scheming accomplices from time to time.

In his book *The Comic Style of P. G. Wodehouse,* Robert A. Hall calls Jeeves "one of the most memorable characters invented in twentieth-century English-language fiction. His head sticks out at the back, and he eats a great deal of fish, which to Bertie's way of thinking makes him so brainy. His favorite reading is Spinoza, or else the great Russian novelists. His range of knowledge is encyclopaedic, so that he can furnish information or give an extempore lecture on almost every subject. . . . His speech is an exaggeratedly ultra-formal, ultra-standard English. In the stories, his function is to get Bertie (and often others as well) out of jams, through his analysis of the 'psychology of the individual' (one of his favorite expressions) and through the measures he takes, often when Bertie, through his own bungling, is *in extremis.* Jeeves is an intellectual *deus ex machina,* to rescue Bertie from the scrapes the latter gets into through his presumption unsupported by intellectual strength."

Bertie, for his part, may be seen as the most outstanding example of a long line of irresponsible young gentlemen characterized by Wodehouse, or, as Voorhees phrases it, the "crowning achievement in the creation of the silly young ass," and "one of literature's idiots." While there can be little doubt as to Bertie's lack of intelligence (he readily admits it; in one of the stories in *My Man Jeeves,* when Jeeves says, "We must think, sir," Bertie replies, "You do it. I don't have the equipment."), he remains one of Wodehouse's most personable and engaging characters. He is extremely good natured and gregarious, always ready for a dinner party or a weekend at one of his aunts' country houses. Although he is presumably in his late twenties, he persists in childish schemes that invariably backfire leaving his salvation, time and again, in the hands of Jeeves. Bertie lives by the strict "Code of the Woosters" which compels him never to let a pal down. As a result he is at the mercy of an endless supply of old school chums and girl friends who entreat him to rescue them from a variety of sticky situations. French surmises that "if the Duke of Wellington had asked the Wooster of that day to charge the Old Guard, you would not have heard that Wooster saying that he had to run into Brussels for a moment and was afraid he would not be able to manage it. He would have been where Bertie is to be found—in the thick of the grape-shot, or purloining a policeman's helmet to get young Stephanie Byng out of a jam, as the case may be."

In the early short stories featuring Jeeves and Bertie, the young master gets himself into a variety of scrapes from which it becomes necessary for the wise valet to extricate him, including a few accidental engagements to young ladies to whom he is particularly unsuited. But beginning with the first novel in which they are the main characters, Hall points out, "the emphasis changes, and Bertie's efforts to avoid marriage become the main-spring of the plot. Florence Craye appears (in *Joy in the Morning*) as one of the threats to his bachelordom; but there are others as well. In *Right Ho, Jeeves* the droopy, soupy, sentimental Madeline Bassett misunderstands Bertie's pleas on behalf of his newt-fancier friend Gussie Fink-Nottle, and thinks he is pleading his own cause. From then on, every time that she feels disappointed in her love for someone else, she tells Bertie she will marry him; his naive code of being a *preux chevalier* forbids him to spurn her love. . . . This essential situation is repeated in each one of the later Bertie-Jeeves novels, with marriage to either Pauline Stoker (in *Thank You, Jeeves*), Madeline Bassett, or the red-haired hellion Bobbie Wickham (in *Jeeves in the Offing*) as a major threat."

As a result of his distinctive writing style—a style that has served as the inspiration for a number of contemporary humorists—many critics have labeled Wodehouse the dominant force in the establishment of modern humorous fiction technique. But Robert A. Hall, who notes that the author has been hailed as "the greatest master of twentieth-century prose," says that "despite general recognition of Wodehouse's merits as a stylist . . . there has been relatively little detailed analysis of the features that have contributed to his almost unparallelled success in humorous writing." Hall's book *The Comic Style of P. G. Wodehouse* is a thorough study of the stylistic devices Wodehouse used for comic effect. "Humor," says Hall, "has two essential ingredients. For us to laugh at something, it must contain some kind of incongruity, and we must be emotionally neutral, without our personal feelings being involved." He finds that "Wodehouse makes use of just about every resource available in standard English plus a few from non-standard English, to obtain his effects."

Hall mentions Wodehouse's inventive word formations, adding and subtracting prefixes and suffixes, as an example. He writes: "To *de-dog the premises* is not too great a variation on the pattern of *de-louse* or *de-bunk;* but Wodehouse obtains a greater humorous effect by prefixing *de-* to proper names, as when Pongo Twistleton brings the housemaid Elsie Bean out of a cupboard [in *Uncle Dynamite*]: 'His manner as he de-Beaned the cupboard was somewhat distrait,' or when 'Kipper' Herring, after Bobbie Wickham has left his company, is described as 'finding himself de-Wickhamed' [in *Jeeves in the Offing*]. On the analogy of such formations as *homeward, northward, inward,* Wodehouse obtains a special effect when he says of Lord Emsworth [in *Summer Lightning*], 'He pottered off pigward.' " Hall also cites several instances in which Wodehouse stretches the patterns of word formations and meanings beyond their normal limits. In *Heavy Weather* he fashions a verb *to huss* from the noun hussy: "I regard the entire personnel of the ensemble of our musical comedy theatres as—if you will pardon me being Victorian for a moment—painted hussies." "They've got to paint." "Well, they needn't huss." In Wodehouse's parlance, a cowpuncher punches cows and corn-chandler chandles corn. He is also prone to separate some words, such as *hobnob,* into their constituent elements. Thus in *Uncle Dynamite* a character says, "To offer a housemaid a cigarette is not hobbing. Nor, when you light it for her, does that constitute nobbing."

As a master craftsman Wodehouse would never overuse any single stylistic device, but one that comes up, Hall points out, about twice in any given story, is what is called the transferred epithet, "especially an adjective modifying a noun instead of the corresponding adverb modifying the verb of the sentence." In the story "Jeeves and the Impending Doom," this phenomenon is evidenced by the sentence, "He uncovered the fragrant eggs and I pronged a moody forkful." In *Joy in the Morning* we have, "I balanced a thoughtful lump of sugar on the teaspoon." And in *Jeeves and the Feudal Spirit,* "He waved a concerned cigar."

Misunderstandings of many kinds abound in Wodehouse stories. These often are the result of syntactic or lexicographic confusion, as in a scene from "Jeeves and the Yuletide Spirit" in which Sir Roderick Glossop misunderstands Bertie Wooster's use of the nickname Tuppy: " 'Awfully sorry about all this,' I said in a hearty sort of voice. 'The fact is, I thought you were Tuppy.' 'Kindly refrain from inflicting your idiotic slang on me. What do you mean by the adjective "tuppy"?' 'It isn't so much an adjective, don't you know. More of a noun, I should think, if you examine it squarely. What I mean to say is, I thought you were your nephew.' " Hall cites one more case of this type of misunderstanding which occurs in *Uncle Dynamite* when Constable Potter confuses two meanings of the word *by:* " 'I was assaulted by the duck pond.' " " 'By the duck pond?' Sir Aylmer asked, his eyes widening." " 'Yes, sir.' " " 'How the devil can you be assaulted by a duck pond?' Constable Potter saw where the misunderstanding had arisen. The English language is full of these pitfalls. 'When I say "by the duck pond," I didn't mean "by the duck pond," I meant "by the duck pond." That is to say,' proceeded Constable Potter, speaking just in time, 'near or adjacent to, in fact on the edge of.' "

Another good example of Wodehouse's unique use of language to evoke humor can be found running throughout the Jeeves and Bertie stories. Even though Bertie is supposedly a graduate of Eton and Oxford, his vocabulary is extremely limited, and he spends a good deal of time groping for the right word, or, as Wodehouse so often says, the *mot juste.* In *Stiff Upper Lip, Jeeves* he says, "I suppose Stiffy's sore about this . . . what's the word? . . . Not vaseline . . . Vacillation, that's it." In *Jeeves and the Feudal Spirit* Hall finds one of the many instances in which Bertie depends on Jeeves to fill in the blank: "Let a pluggly like young Thos loose in the community with a cosh, and you are inviting disaster and . . . what's the word? Something about cats." Jeeves replies, "Cataclysms, sir?"

Jeeve's vocabulary is, in fact, so broad that Bertie, who is at least somewhat accustomed to it, is often forced to translate for his friends. Hall refers to a scene in "The Artistic Career of Corky" as an example; Jeeves says, "The scheme I would suggest cannot fail of success, but it has what may seem to you a drawback, sir, in that it requires a certain financial outlay." "He means," Bertie explains to Corky, "that he has got a pippin of an idea but it's going to cost a lot."

Puns also make frequent appearances in Wodehouse' work. In *Thank You, Jeeves,* a Mr. Stoker says, "Reminds me of that thing about Lo somebody's name led all the rest." Jeeves refreshes his memory, "Abou ben Adhem, sir." And the puzzled Stoker asks, "Have I *what?*" When, in *Jeeves and the Feudal Spirit,* Bertie is released from jail and is asked, "Are you all right, now?" he replies, "Well, I have a pinched look." And in *The Mating Season* Bertie asks, "I look like something the cat found in Tutankhamen's tomb, do I not?" Jeeves answers, "I would not go as far as that, sir, but I have unquestionably seen you more *soigne.*" Bertie notes that "it crossed my mind for an instant that with a little thought one might throw together something rather clever about 'Way down upon the soigne river,' but I was too listless to follow up."

But Hall identifies Wodehouse's best-known stylistic device as "his imagery involving similes, metaphors, and other types of comparison. The chief characteristic of his imagery is the wide range from which he draws his comparisons, using them in every instance to emphasize resemblances which at first glance seem highly incongruous (and hence provide the reader's laughter), but which at the same time are highly appropriate to the particular person or situation described. His imagery—carefully planned, of course, like all the rest of his writing—is therefore particularly vivid and apposite." An example from *Leave It to Psmith:* "A sound like two or three pigs feeding rather noisily in the middle of a thunderstorm interrupted his meditation." In *The Mating Season* Wodehouse used, "That 'ha, ha,' so like the expiring quack of a duck dying of a broken heart." And finally in *The Code of the Woosters* we find: "Have you ever heard Sir Watkyn Bassett dealing with a bowl of soup? It's not unlike the Scottish express going through a tunnel." As Hall says, "such a list could be continued almost indefinitely; a whole volume could be compiled simply by excerpting all the imagery which Wodehouse uses in his stories."

Wodehouse's brilliance in utilizing these various stylistic devices, his deft handling of the English language, and his humorous observations on human nature combined to make him one of the most popular writers of the twentieth century. David A. Jasen, who calls Wodehouse the "funniest writer in the world," believes that the author built up a large following through the use of repetition. "It is always a delight to welcome an old friend," he writes, "for old friends recall happily shared experiences, and this is the sense of intimacy gotten when reading the works of Wodehouse." Jasen says that Wodehouse "took pieces of his childhood, blended with snatches of the quickly altering world of the Edwardians and the early Georgians, and added his own abundantly creative imagination. His plots fit his people, who are consistent not with reality but with themselves and the world of his conception. He attempted to be realistic only in this way and achieved a timelessness in his world which makes his writings universally appealing. His humor depends mainly on exaggeration and understatement, the incongruous, the inappropriate phrase, and the use of the literal interpretation of an idiomatic expression out of context for effect. He developed a new vocabulary, mixing slang along with classical phrases, and fashioning supremely inventive as well as highly diverting hyperboles. He is extremely serious about his work and took tremendous trouble with its construction. He polished his sentences as meticulously as one of his Drones would choose a tie. His only object in writing was purely and simply to amuse." Wodehouse confirmed this in his autobiographical *Over Seventy* when he wrote: "My books may not be the sort of books the cognoscenti feel justified in blowing the twelve and a half shillings on, but I do work at them. When in due course Charon ferries me across the Styx and everyone is telling everyone else what a rotten writer I was, I hope at least one voice will be heard piping up: 'But he did take trouble.' "

MEDIA ADAPTATIONS: Some of Wodehouse's short stories were produced by the BBC under the title "Wodehouse Playhouse."

BIOGRAPHICAL/CRITICAL SOURCES:

BOOKS

Aldridge, John W., *Time to Murder and Create,* McKay, 1966.
Authors in the News, Volume II, Gale, 1976.
Cazalet-Keir, Thelma, editor, *Homage to P. G. Wodehouse,* Barrie & Jenkins, 1973.
Contemporary Literary Criticism, Gale, Volume I, 1973, Volume II, 1974, Volume V, 1976, Volume X, 1979, Volume XXII, 1982.
Dictionary of Literary Biography, Volume 34: *British Novelists, 1890-1929: Traditionalists,* Gale, 1985.
French, R. B. D., *P. G. Wodehouse,* Oliver & Boyd, 1966, Barnes & Noble, 1967.
Green, Benny, *P. G. Wodehouse: A Literary Biography,* Rutledge Press, 1981.
Hall, Robert A., Jr., *The Comic Style of P. G. Wodehouse,* Archon, 1974.
Heineman, James H. and Donald R. Benson, editors, *P. G. Wodehouse: A Centenary Celebration, 1881-1981,* Pierpoint Morgan Library, 1981.
Jaggard, Geoffrey W., *Wooster's World,* Macdonald & Co., 1967.
Jaggard, *Blandings the Blest and the Blue Blood,* Macdonald & Co., 1968.
Jasen, David A., *A Bibliography and Reader's Guide to the First Editions of P. G. Wodehouse,* Archon, 1970.
Jasen, *P. G. Wodehouse: A Portrait of a Master,* Mason & Lipscomb, 1974.
Orwell, George, *The Orwell Reader,* Harcourt, 1933.
Short Story Criticism, Volume II, Gale, 1989.
Sproat, Iain, *Wodehouse at War,* Ticknor & Fields, 1981.
Usborne, Richard, *Wodehouse at Work,* Jenkins, 1961.
Usborne, *Wodehouse Nuggets,* Hutchinson, 1983.
Voorhees, Richard, *P. G. Wodehouse,* Twayne, 1966.
Wind, H. W., *The World of P. G. Wodehouse,* Praeger, 1972.
Wodehouse, P. G., *Performing Flea: A Self-Portrait in Letters,* Jenkins, 1953.
Wodehouse and Guy Bolton, *Bring On the Girls!: The Improbable Story of Our Life in Musical Comedy with Pictures to Prove It,* Simon & Schuster, 1953.
Wodehouse, *Over Seventy: An Autobiography with Digressions,* Jenkins, 1957.

PERIODICALS

Chicago Tribune, October 15, 1981.
New York Times, February 15, 1975, October 18, 1981, November 12, 1984, November 7, 1985, October 20, 1987, March 23, 1989.
Paris Review, winter, 1975.
Times (London), November 24, 1983, June 21, 1984, June 29, 1985, July 9, 1987.
Washington Post, February 3, 1984.
Washington Post Book World, November 29, 1981.
Writers Digest, October, 1971.

*   *   *

WOLF, Christa 1929-

PERSONAL: Born March 18, 1929, in Landsberg an der Warthe, Germany (now Gorzow Wielkopolski, Poland); daughter of Otto Ihlenfeld (a salesman); married Gerhard Wolf (a Germanist and essayist) in 1951; children: Annette, Katrin. *Education:* Attended University of Jena and University of Leipzig, 1949-53.

ADDRESSES: Office—c/o Aufbau Verlag, Postfach 1217, Franzoesische Strasse 32, DDR-108 Berlin, East Germany.

CAREER: Novelist, short story writer, and essayist. Prior to 1959 worked as technical assistant for East German Writers Union, a reader for Neues Leben (publishing house), East Berlin, and editor of *Neue Deutsche Literatur* (periodical); Mitteldeutscher Verlag (publisher), Halle, East Germany, reader, 1959-62; also worked in a railroad freight car manufacturing company, Halle, 1959-62; full-time writer, 1962—.

MEMBER: P.E.N., German Academy of Arts.

AWARDS, HONORS: Literary prize, City of Halle, 1961; Heinrich Mann Prize, German Academy, 1963, for *Der geteilte Himmel;* National Prize for Art and Literature, German Democratic Republic, 1964; Fontane Prize, 1972; Bremen Literature Prize, 1978; Georg Buechner Prize, 1980.

WRITINGS:

(Editor with husband, Gerhard Wolf) *Wir, unsere Zeit* (title means "We in Our Time"), Aufbau, 1959.

(Editor) *In diesen Jahren: Deutsche Erzaehler der Gegenwart* (title means "In These Years: Contemporary German Short Story Writers"), Reclam, 1957.

(Editor) *Proben junger Erzahler: Ausgewaehlte deutsche Prosa* (title means "A Sampler of Work by Young Short Story Writers: Selected German Prose"), Reclam, 1959.

Moskauer Novelle (novella; title means "Moscow Novella"), Mitteldeutscher, 1961.

Der geteilte Himmel (novel), Mitteldeutscher, 1963, reprinted, EMC, 1980, translation by Joan Becker published as *Divided Heaven: A Novel of Germany Today,* Seven-Seas Press, 1965, Adler's Foreign Books, 1976.

Nachdenken ueber Christa T. (novel), Mitteldeutscher, 1968, translation by Christopher Middleton published as *The Quest for Christa T.,* Farrar, Straus, 1971.

Lesen und Schreiben: Aufsaetze und Betrachtungen (essays), Aufbau, 1972, reprinted as *Lesen und Schreiben: Aufsaetze und Prosastuecke,* Luchterhand, 1972, translation by Becker published as *The Reader and the Writer: Essays, Sketches, Memories,* Signet, 1977.

(With G. Wolf) *Till Eulenspiegel: Erzaehlung fuer den Film* (film script), Aufbau, 1973.

Unter den Linden: Drei unwahrscheinliche Geschichten (short stories; title means "Under the Linden Tree: Three Improbable Stories"), Aufbau, 1974.

Kindheitsmuster (novel), Aufbau, 1976, translation by Ursule Molinaro and Hedwig Rappolt published as *A Model Childhood,* Farrar, Straus, 1980.

J'ecris sur ce qui m'inquiete: debat dans Sinn und Form sur son dernier roman, Centre d'etudes et de recherches marxistes (Paris), 1977.

Kein Ort. Nirgends (novel), Aufbau, 1979, translation by Jan Van Heurck published as *No Place on Earth,* Farrar, Straus, 1982.

Fortgesetzter Versuch: Aufsaetze, Gespraeche, Essays, Reclam, 1979.

(Editor) Karoline von Guenderode, *Der Schatten eines Traumes,* Der Morgen, 1979.

Gesammelte Erzaehlungen (stories, 1960-1972), Luchterhand, 1980.

Neue Lebensansichten eines Katers; Juninachmittag, Reclam, 1981.

Kassandra: Vier Vorlesungen; eine Erzaehlung, Aufbau, 1983, translation by Van Heurck published as *Cassandra: A Novel and Four Essays,* Farrar, Straus, 1984.

(Editor) *Historischer verien fuer Hessen, 1934-1983: Vortraege, Exkursionen, Publikationen,* Verlag des Historischen Veriens fuer Hessen, 1983.

Voraussetzungen einer Erzaehlung: Kassandra (lectures; title means "Genesis of a Story: Kassandra"), Luchterhand, 1983.

(Editor) Anna Seghers, *Ausgewaehlte Erzaehlungen,* Luchterhand, 1983.

Stoerfall (novel), Luchterhand, 1987, translation by Heike Schwarzbauer and Rick Takvarian published as *Accident: A Day's News,* Farrar, Straus, 1989.

Die Dimension des Autors: Essays und Aufsaetze, Reden und Gespraeche 1959-1986 (essays, speeches, and conversations), Luchterhand, 1987.

Ansprachen (speeches and letters), Luchterhand, c. 1989.

Sommerstueck (novel), Luchterhand, c. 1989.

SIDELIGHTS: East German novelist, short story writer, and essayist Christa Wolf is "arguably the most influential figure in contemporary German literature, East or West," writes Peter Graves in the *Times Literary Supplement.* Since the early 1960s, and despite various literary restrictions enacted by East Germany's government, Wolf has produced a substantial body of letters that have made her one of the most widely read writers in either Germany. Anne McElvoy remarks in the London *Times* on Wolf's popularity: "She is a saturnine, cerebral writer whose work resounds with challenges to entrenched attitudes in both East and West. The relationships between past and present, men and women, individual and society, provide the axes round which she weaves her prose. . . . Wolf remains the bright, difficult child of German socialism stubbornly evading political fetters, uniting the antinomies of alliance and effortlessly vaulting the cultural as well as the concrete divide of the Berlin Wall." Wolf's writings have garnered an international reputation as well. Mary Fulbrook in the *Times Literary Supplement* praises Wolf's "directness of approach, her 'subjective authenticity,' " and adds that "in grappling with the specific problems of her generation, her society and her gender—the psychological effects of fascism, the development of socialism, the social roles of women—Wolf's writing reaches a much wider audience."

Wolf gained widespread recognition in both Germanies with her first novel, 1963's *Der geteilte Himmel (The Divided Heaven),* which tells the story of an East German woman who refuses to join her lover who has fled to the West. Published shortly after the building of the Berlin Wall, the novel's popularity, according to Dieter Sevin in *Dictionary of Literary Biography,* was due to its treatment of "the German question" and its portrayal of the "intensification of the cold war and the fear that it might lead to actual war." Sevin adds: "Although the story takes place in the GDR, Wolf addresses general problems and concerns: the anxieties resulting from leaving the idyllic village for the big city—the feeling of being lost, lonely, and scared—are common in any industrialized nation." *The Divided Heaven* received an enthusiastic official reception in East Germany—it was awarded the country's prestigious Heinrich Mann Prize—despite Wolf's portrayal of a suicide attempt in an "accident" which occurs to the female character after she decides to remain in East Berlin. East German critics tended to overlook the suicide possibilities of the woman's actions and instead focused on her decision to remain in East Germany "as a demonstration of her commitment to the socialist state."

Unlike *Divided Heaven,* Wolf's next novel, *Nachdenken ueber Christa T. (The Quest for Christa T.)* caused controversy in East Germany. Publicly attacked at the Sixth East German Writers Congress, where it was condemned as "a pessimistic attempt to replace Marx with Freud," *The Quest for Christa T.* was delayed in its publication for two years by East German censors. It finally appeared in 1968, yet in a limited edition of 4,000 copies and with special orders for booksellers to release it only to "well-known customers professionally involved in literary matters." Sevin comments that much of the controversy surrounding *The Quest for Christa T.* was due to the book meeting "none of the criteria of the prevailing literary doctrine of socialist realism—the demands for a positive hero, for the setting of an example, for an appeal to the masses, and, most of all, for strict adherence to the policies of the party."

The Quest for Christa T. centers around a woman named Christa who graduates from a university, teaches school, marries and bears children, and who dies at the age of thirty-five of leukemia. As the novel opens, the narrator (a friend of Christa's) has come upon Christa's papers and letters and resolves to tell her story. On the surface, as Jack D. Zipes comments in *MOSAIC,* "there is nothing outstanding or remarkable" about Christa, which Zipes concludes is "exactly the point." In describing the life and thoughts of Christa T., Wolf "writes about an average woman in East Germany, and she wants to understand why this woman is 'drained' of her exuberance for life." Christa's writings show a woman who increasingly is forced to the fringes of East German society. As one critic describes it, Christa is "unable to reconcile herself to East Germany's noisy parades, pompous speeches and mass meetings with flags and songs, and she is particularly affected by the general air of servility, the subservience to official precepts. . . . She is convinced . . . that one has the right to question, to doubt, to investigate and to lead a unique and independent life listening to one's inner voice and making personal decisions." Zipes comments that the narrator of *The Quest for Christa T.* "has written about Christa's growing alienation in order to question the conditions which led to her withdrawal and death."

The Quest for Christa T. was either denounced or ignored by many East German critics, yet Western reviewers had much praise for the book. A *New York Times Book Review* critic described it as a "beautifully written, imaginative novel [that] has nothing explicitly to do with politics," while a critic for the *New Leader* commented that Wolf "succeeds in creating that fictional rarity, a character who is ordinary and engaging, complex and credible, and well worth knowing." The *Times Literary Supplement* called it "a remarkable novel, not merely because it deviates from the prescribed ideological pattern, a fact which has earned it an inflated reputation in the West and a difficult passage in the East, but because it respects the delicacy of individual personality despite threatening restraints."

The autobiographical *Kindheitsmuster (A Model Childhood),* which Wolf considers to be her most important and extensive literary contribution, recalls her life under the growing influence of Hitler in Nazi Germany and the experiences of her family during the World War II. Wolf begins *Kindheitsmuster* by stating: "What is past is not dead. It is not even past. We separate ourselves from it and pretend to be strangers." Approaching Germany's recent history in this manner, *Kindheitsmuster* differed from East German official literature in that, as one critic points out, East Germans have "maintained that the establishment of a socialist state created an entirely new order untainted by complicity in Nazi atrocities. . . . To suggest that the citizens of the new Republic might have been scarred so deeply by life under Hitler that not even a profession of faith in Marxism could completely eradicate its effect would be quite unthinkable."

In *A Model Childhood,* Wolf retraces her life under the rule of Hitler: at the age of five his very name brings a lump in her throat, her father joins the Party, she progresses through various Nazi youth organizations, in school she learns of racial purity and begins to fear the alien race—the Jews—and finally, she states that no objections are made "not even at the euthanasia programme, that costs the family their simple-minded aunt Jette." While Wolf recounts these "trivialities," the difficulty emerges, as Fiona MacCarthy points out in the London *Times,* of her "recalling the whole pattern, the whole long horrendous build-up of the incidents she vaguely knew were out of key but somehow did not question."

One section of the book recounts a trip Wolf made with her husband, brother, and daughter, to her birthplace (now a town in Poland) where she must confront her daughter with the truth of what happened. Throughout *Kindheitsmuster,* however, as John Leonard comments in the *New York Times,* Wolf portrays "how hard it is to make literature out of the unknowable, to select and defend and deny, to resist anecdote, to avoid punch lines." Graves calls *Kindheitsmuster* "a courageous book that breaks taboos . . . it is infused with an integrity and a deep moral concern that raise it far above the narrow and self-conscious partisanship of much GDR literature. It speaks equally to East and West Germany—itself a daring accomplishment for an East German author—but also, with its atmospheric depiction of a fateful era and its patent and compelling truthfulness, to wider audiences beyond." MacCarthy calls it "a powerful book, a most extraordinary testament. . . . Her vision of the fundamental strangeness of what seemed at the time a fairly ordinary childhood, in the bosom of a normal Nazi family in Landsberg, which makes Christa Wolf's narrative so moving, so convincing."

In *Kein Ort. Nirgends (No Place on Earth)* Wolf departs from the milieu of modern Germany to write an experimental novel featuring two actual nineteenth-century German literary figures. *No Place on Earth* depicts a fictionalized meeting between poet Karoline von Guenderrode and dramatist Heinrich von Kleist, two young Romantic writers who committed suicide in the early 1800s. "In their mysterious encounter . . . they share a utopian vision of their artistic potential," notes Amity Shlaes in *New Republic,* adding that, like Wolf's earlier works, *No Place on Earth* "is about people trying to reconcile themselves to the difficult worlds they live in." Marilyn French concurs in the *New York Times Book Review,* noting that Wolf focuses on "what it feels like to know oneself utterly unsuited, utterly *wrong* in one's culture, to have no place on earth." While the novel's themes are Romantic in nature, they are also universal, according to French. "Its concerns are ours," she notes: "the difficulties of becoming oneself in a world that demands conformity; of living with others when one is unlike them and refuses to hide that; of juggling inter-dependency and the demands that arise from it; of needing solitude by being oppressed by isolation." While some critics find difficult the novel's complex argumentative nature, French praises it as "very concentrated and intricately woven," calling it "a dramatic meditation on constriction; the freedom the characters lack is felt almost like a lack of air."

Wolf's 1987 novel *Stoerfall (Accident: A Day's News),* written after the nuclear disaster at Chernobyl in the Soviet Union which affected much of Europe, juxtaposes that incident with the occurrence of a brain tumor in the brother of the novel's narrator. According to Eva Hoffman in the *New York Times,* Wolf describes how events such as these "register on our consciousness and imagination, how the deep intrusions of technology into our existence alter the substance of our world, our very sense of what it means to be human, of who and what we are." Hoffman calls Wolf's voice in *Stoerfall* "impassioned, intimate, variable. . . . A voice that allows us poignantly to gauge how the large and abstract forces shaping our world fall upon one vulnerable, perishable entity that we still like to think of as human."

While she is most recognized for her fiction, Wolf is also praised for her critical writings, which include essays, speeches, and letters. In these works, Wolf discusses many of the ideas that abound in her fiction, allowing, as Fulbrook remarks regarding *Die Dimension des Autors: Essays und Aufsaetze, Reden und Gespraeche 1959-1986,* "a sustained engagement with Wolf's reflections on a range of themes." According to Fulbrook, "a key question" that has permeated Wolf's work "is that of the formation and channelling of personality under fascism." Wolf has at times frankly commented on the difficulty of life in East Germany; Graves notes that the speeches and letters collected in *Ansprachen* show "much personal anguish at the strain of exerting a humanizing influence in an increasingly oppressive environment." Graves describes Wolf as "an immensely earnest writer whose ruthlessness in dissecting her own subjectivity is made bearable only by the manifest honesty which informs the enterprise and the lightness of touch with which it is executed."

BIOGRAPHICAL/CRITICAL SOURCES:

BOOKS

Behn, Manfred, editor, *Wirkungsgeschichte von Christa Wolfs "Nachdenken ueber Christa T.,"* Athenaeum, 1978.
Buehler, George, *The Death of Socialist Realism in the Novels of Christa Wolf,* Lang, 1984.
Contemporary Literary Criticism, Gale, Volume 14, 1980, Volume 29, 1984.
Dictionary of Literary Biography, Volume 75: *Contemporary German Fiction Writers, Second Series,* Gale, 1988.
Ezergailis, Inta, *The Divided Self: Analysis of Novels by Christa Wolf, Ingeborg Bachmann, Doris Lessing and Others,* Grundmann, 1982.
Giesen, Winfried, *Christa Wolf,* Universitaetsbibliothek, 1982.
Kuhn, Anna K., *Christa Wolf's Utopian Vision: From Marxism to Feminism,* Cambridge University Press, 1988.
Mannack, Eberhard, *Zwei deutsche Literaturen?: Zu G. Grass, U. Johnson, H. Katn, U. Plenzdorf, und C. Wolf,* Athenaeum, 1977.
Ryan, Judith, *The Uncompleted Past: Postwar German Novels and the Third Reich,* Wayne State University Press, 1983.
Sauer, Klaus, editor, *Christa Wolf: Materialienbuch,* Luchterhand, 1979.
Smith, Brian Keith, editor, *Essays on Contemporary German Literature,* Oswald Wolff, 1966.
Stephen, Alexander, *Christa Wolf,* Edition Text und Kritik, 1976.
Waidson, H. M., *The Modern German Novel,* Oxford University Press, 1971.

PERIODICALS

Books Abroad, winter, 1975, spring, 1975, autumn, 1977.
Los Angeles Times Book Review, September 28, 1980, July 29, 1984, June 4, 1989.
MOSAIC, spring, 1972.
Nation, February 13, 1967.
New Leader, May 31, 1971.
New Republic, April 4, 1983.
New York Review of Books, September 2, 1971.
New York Times, June 3, 1969, July 29, 1980, September 6, 1982, July 31, 1984, April 12, 1989.
New York Times Book Review, October 19, 1969, January 31, 1971, October 10, 1982, September 9, 1984, October 12, 1986, April 23, 1989.
Saturday Review, May 8, 1971.
Times (London), April 29, 1982, January 7, 1989, May 6, 1989.
Times Literary Supplement, July 24, 1969, August 13, 1971, April 7, 1978, October 3, 1980, June 4, 1982, May 13, 1983, November 15, 1985, October 2-8, 1987, April 21-27, 1989.

*   *   *

WOLFE, Thomas (Clayton) 1900-1938

PERSONAL: Born October 3, 1900, in Asheville, N.C.; died of miliary tuberculosis of the brain, September 15, 1938, in Baltimore, Md.; buried in Riverside Cemetery, Asheville, N.C.; son of William Oliver (a stonecutter) and Julia Elizabeth (a boardinghouse proprietor; maiden name, Westall) Wolfe. *Education:* University of North Carolina, Chapel Hill, B.A., 1920; Harvard University, M.A., 1922, post-graduate study, 1923.

ADDRESSES: Home—Brooklyn, N.Y.

CAREER: Writer. New York University, New York City, instructor in English at Washington Square College, intermittently, 1924-30. Worked in naval shipyards, Newport News, Va., 1918.

MEMBER: National Institute of Arts and Letters.

AWARDS, HONORS: Worth Prize, 1919, for essay *The Crisis in Industry;* Guggenheim Fellowship, 1930; *Scribner's Magazine* Prize, 1932, for *A Portrait of Bascom Hawke.*

WRITINGS:

The Crisis in Industry (essay), University of North Carolina, 1919, reprint, 1978.
The Return of Buck Gavin: The Tragedy of a Mountain Outlaw (play; first produced by Carolina Playmakers, March, 1919), published in *Carolina Folk-Plays, Second Series,* edited by Frederick H. Koch, Holt, 1924.
Third Night (play), first produced by Carolina Playmakers, December, 1919.
The Mountains: A Play in One Act (produced by 47 Workshop at Harvard University, Boston, Mass., 1921), edited with an introduction by Pat M. Ryan, University of North Carolina Press, 1970.
Welcome to Our City (play; first produced in 1923), abridged version published in *Esquire,* October, 1957, published as *Welcome to Our City: A Play in Ten Scenes,* edited with an introduction by Richard S. Kennedy, Louisiana State University Press, 1983.
Look Homeward, Angel: A Story of the Buried Life (novel), Scribner, 1929 (published in England under same title with textual variations, Heinemann, 1930), published with introduction by Maxwell E. Perkins, illustrations by Douglas W. Gorsline, Scribner, 1952, recent edition, Southern Living Gallery, 1984.
A Portrait of Bascom Hawke (novella), published in *Scribner's Magazine,* 1932.
Of Time and the River: A Legend of Man's Hunger in His Youth (novel), Scribner, 1935, recent edition, 1971.
From Death to Morning (short stories), Scribner, 1935, recent edition, 1970.
The Story of a Novel (essay), serialized in *Saturday Review of Literature,* December, 1935, published in one volume with certain modifications, Scribner, 1936, published with *Writing and Living* as *The Autobiography of an American Novelist,* edited by Leslie Field, Harvard University Press, 1983 (also see below).
A Note on Experts: Dexter Vespasian Joyner (fragment), House of Books (New York), 1939.
The Web and the Rock (novel), Harper, 1939, recent edition, Perennial Library, 1986.
You Can't Go Home Again (novel), Harper, 1940, recent edition, Perennial Library, 1973.
The Hills Beyond (contains a novel fragment, the play "Gentleman of the Press," and short stories, including "The Lost Boy" and "The Web of Earth"), biographical note by Edward C. Aswell, Harper, 1941, recent edition, New American Library, 1968 (also see below).

Mannerhouse: A Play in a Prologue and Three Acts (produced by the Yale University dramatic association, 1949), Harper, 1948, recent edition, edited by Louis D. Rubin, Jr., and John L. Idol, Jr., Louisiana State University Press, 1985.

A Western Journal: A Daily Log of the Great Parks Trip, June 20-July 2, 1938, University of Pittsburgh Press, 1951, recent edition, 1967.

Thomas Wolfe's Purdue Speech: Writing and Living, edited with an introduction and notes by William Braswell and Field, Purdue University Studies, 1964, published with *The Story of a Novel* as *The Autobiography of an American Novelist,* edited by Field, Harvard University Press, 1983 (also see below).

The Notebooks of Thomas Wolfe, edited by Kennedy and Paschal Reeves, two volumes, University of North Carolina Press, 1970.

The Streets of Durham (play), introduction by Richard Walser, Wolf's Head Press, 1982.

The Autobiography of an American Novelist: The Story of a Novel [and] *Writing and Living,* edited by Field, Harvard University Press, 1983.

The Hound of Darkness (play), edited with foreword by Idol, Thomas Wolfe Society (Akron, Ohio), 1986.

Contributor of short stories, essays, and book reviews to such periodicals as *Scribner's Magazine, New Yorker, New York Evening Post, Saturday Review of Literature, Saturday Evening Post, Harper's Bazaar, Atlantic Monthly, American Mercury, Redbook,* and *Vogue.* Editor of *Tar Heel,* literary magazine of University of North Carolina at Chapel Hill, c. 1917.

CORRESPONDENCE

Thomas Wolfe's Letters to His Mother, Julia Elizabeth Wolfe (facsimile edition), edited with an introduction by John Skally Terry, Scribner, 1943, revised edition newly edited from the original manuscript by C. Hugh Holman and Sue Fields Ross published as *The Letters of Thomas Wolfe to His Mother,* University of North Carolina Press, 1968.

The Correspondence of Thomas Wolfe and Homer Andrew Watt, edited by Oscar Cargill and Thomas Clark Pollock, New York University Press, 1954.

Letters, collected and edited with introduction and explanatory text by Elizabeth Nowell, Scribner, 1956 (abridged version with selection by Daniel George published in England as *Selected Letters of Thomas Wolfe,* Heinemann, 1958).

"Dear Mabel": Letters of Thomas Wolfe to His Sister, Mabel Wolfe Wheaton, edited by Mary Lindsay Thornton, published in *South Atlantic Quarterly,* autumn, 1961, reprinted, [Durham, N.C.], 1961.

Beyond Love and Loyalty: The Letters of Thomas Wolfe and Elizabeth Nowell; Together With "No More Rivers," a Story, edited by Kennedy, University of North Carolina Press, 1983.

My Other Loneliness: Letters of Thomas Wolfe and Aline Bernstein, edited by Suzanne Stutman, University of North Carolina Press, 1983.

Holding On For Heaven: The Cables and Postcards of Thomas Wolfe and Aline Bernstein, edited by Stutman, Thomas Wolfe Society, 1985.

SELECTED WRITINGS

The Face of a Nation: Poetical Passages From the Writings of Thomas Wolfe, selected and edited with introduction by John Hall Wheelock, Scribner, 1939.

A Stone, A Leaf, A Door: Poems by Thomas Wolfe, selected and arranged in verse by John S. Barnes, foreword by Louis Untermeyer, Scribner, 1945, recent edition, 1961.

The Portable Thomas Wolfe, edited by Maxwell Geismar, Viking, 1946 (published in England as *The Portable Thomas Wolfe: Selections From the Works of Thomas Wolfe,* Heinemann, 1952).

Short Novels, edited with an introduction and notes by Holman, Scribner, 1961.

The Thomas Wolfe Reader, edited with an introduction and notes by Holman, Scribner, 1962.

K-19: Salvaged Pieces, edited with an introduction by Idol, Thomas Wolfe Society, 1983.

The Complete Short Stories of Thomas Wolfe, edited by Francis E. Skipp, foreword by James Dickey, Scribner, 1987.

Selected works and excerpts are published in various volumes. Writings translated into French, German, Spanish, Russian, Polish, and Hungarian.

The William B. Wisdom collection of Wolfe's letters, manuscripts, inscribed works, galley and page proofs, notebooks, and school papers is gathered at the Houghton Library at Harvard University. A smaller collection of both printed and manuscript materials is housed at the Library of the University of North Carolina and a collection of printed materials and some letters is gathered at the Pack Memorial Public Library in Asheville, North Carolina.

MEDIA ADAPTATIONS: Look Homeward, Angel was adapted as a three-act comedy-drama by Ketti Frings, first produced in New York at the Ethel Barrymore Theater in 1957, and published by Scribner in 1958; it won the Pulitzer Prize, was made into a motion picture, and was adapted by Frings and Peter Udell as the musical comedy *Angel,* published by S. French in 1979. *Mannerhouse* was translated into French and adapted for the stage by Georges Sion and first produced as *Le manoir* at the Theatre national de Belgique in 1957.

SIDELIGHTS: Thomas Wolfe was an important twentieth-century American writer who will be remembered for his four sprawling novels, *Look Homeward, Angel, Of Time and the River, The Web and the Rock,* and *You Can't Go Home Again,* all of which burst with youthful exuberance and reveal an unquenchable thirst for experience. "I will go everywhere and see everything," Wolfe wrote early in his career to his mother, as cited in the *Dictionary of Literary Biography.* "I will meet all the people I can. I will think all the thoughts, feel all the emotions I am able, and I will write, write, write." Though Wolfe was popular with the reading public during his lifetime, critical reaction to his works was mixed. None, however, could dismiss his contribution to the American literary tradition: two American Nobel laureates, William Faulkner and Sinclair Lewis, even commended him in their acceptance speeches. Yet controversy followed Wolfe all his life. His disclosure that he freely collaborated with his editors cast doubt upon his literary abilities, while his highly autobiographical novels—*Look Homeward, Angel* in particular—angered the residents of his small Southern hometown, who saw themselves in its pages. Shaken but undaunted by adverse criticism, Wolfe declared in a 1935 essay titled *The Story of a Novel:* "A man must use the material and experience of his own life if he is to create anything that has substantial value."

Wolfe's novels read as a fictional chronicle of his life. He was born October 3, 1900, in the Blue Ridge Mountain resort town of Asheville, North Carolina, which he would romanticize as Altamont in *Look Homeward, Angel* and *Of Time and the River* and as Old Catawba in *The Web and the Rock* and *You Can't Go Home Again.* He was the youngest of six surviving children born to Julia Elizabeth Westall, a cold, overprotective, and parsimonious native who avidly purchased property but forced her children to wear shoes they long outgrew, and William Oliver Wolfe, an uproarious Pennsylvania tombstone cutter who recited Shakespeare. From 1906 the couple lived apart, with W. O. and one daughter sharing the apartment behind his shop and Julia and the rest of the children residing at the boardinghouse she owned and operated.

Wolfe portrays himself through *Look Homeward, Angel*'s Eugene Gant as a child who identified with the heroes of his adventure stories and history books. He attended public elementary school in Asheville, but, a promising student, he entered a private school there in 1912 at the request of its supervisors, Mr. and Mrs. J. M. Roberts (the Leonards in *Look Homeward, Angel*). Though basically uninspiring teachers, the Robertses introduced him to the arts and classical literature and encouraged him to write. At his mother's urging—she grudgingly paid his private-school tuition but willingly financed college—Wolfe entered the University of North Carolina at Chapel Hill at age fifteen, intending to pursue a career as a dramatist. As a freshman, while overwrought with anxiety about contracting venereal disease, Wolfe lost his virginity in a brothel, and the next year he had an affair with one of his mother's boarders, who was five years his senior. He would later write about their bittersweet romance in the Laura James episodes in *Look Homeward, Angel*, which critics claimed capture perfectly the passion and angst of adolescent love.

In March, 1919, Wolfe's first play, the melodrama *The Return of Buck Gavin: The Tragedy of a Mountain Outlaw,* was staged by the university's Carolina Playmakers. Encouraged by its success, Wolfe entered Harvard University as a graduate student in 1920 to study play writing under George Pierce Baker at his famous 47 Workshop. The Workshop performed two of Wolfe's plays, *The Mountains* and *Welcome to Our City,* but attempts to secure New York producers for the verbose dramas were unsuccessful. Needing money after graduating with his master's degree, Wolfe taught English at Washington Square College of New York University intermittently between 1924 and 1930.

In the fall of 1924 Wolfe took his first trip to Europe. He spent time in Germany and in France, where he met writers Sinclair Lewis and F. Scott Fitzgerald and a former Harvard classmate, Kenneth Raisbeck. Wolfe would later record their escapades in Parisian bistros and brothels in the Francis Starwick episodes in *Of Time and the River.* After his return to New York, while again seeking a producer for one of his plays, Wolfe met Aline Bernstein, a wealthy set designer with the New York Theatre Guild. Although Bernstein was married, a mother, and nearly twenty years his senior, she and Wolfe carried on a tempestuous affair over the next five years. Wolfe dedicated *Look Homeward Angel* to her, and she was the model for Esther Jack of *The Web and the Rock.*

Wolfe resumed teaching for a short while, then he joined Bernstein in England's Lake District in June, 1926. There she convinced him to forsake drama for novel writing, which she thought was better suited to his sweeping descriptive style. Wolfe began writing *Look Homeward, Angel* in London, and after he returned to the United States he shared a Manhattan apartment with Bernstein, who supported him while he worked full time on his novel. After he finished the book in 1928 he submitted it to several publishing houses, each rejecting it because, according to Wolfe in *The Story of a Novel,* in its original form it "was so amateurish, autobiographical, and unskilful that a publisher could not risk a chance on it." Sensitive to adverse criticism, a despondent Wolfe set sail for Europe. But while in Germany he received word that Scribner's editor Maxwell Perkins, who worked with

Ernest Hemingway and Fitzgerald, was interested in his novel. Perkins recognized Wolfe's genius but also believed that the ponderous manuscript was unmanageable. It is generally maintained that Perkins' judicious editing and cutting shaped the work.

Look Homeward, Angel, which tells the story of Wolfe's coming of age through the character of Eugene Gant, is primarily concerned with Eugene's turbulent relationships with his family during his childhood and later with society in general as a college student at North Carolina. The episodic novel climaxes with his beloved brother's death and Eugene's vowing to seek artistic and spiritual fulfillment within himself. The novel met with an enthusiastic reception and many hailed Wolfe as a writer of great promise. " 'Look Homeward, Angel' is as interesting and powerful a book as has ever been made out of the drab circumstances of provincial American life," Margaret Wallace opined in the *New York Times Book Review.* "It is at once enormously sensuous, full of the joy and gusto of life, and shrinkingly sensitive, torn with revulsion and disgust. Mr. Wolfe's style is sprawling, fecund, subtly rhythmic and amazingly vital." Some detractors, though, complained that the novel lacked structure and was self-indulgent and unabashedly lyric. "Whenever Mr. Wolfe feels like it, which is fairly often, he launches into episodes, descriptions and proclamations of his own that could be cut out without impairing the architectural unity of his book," Geoffrey T. Hellman revealed in a *New Republic* review. "Such deletions, however, would rob it of its gusto, and anyone in favor of making them is the sort of person who thinks that 'Moby Dick' would be a good book if it weren't for Mr. Melville's digressions."

Look Homeward, Angel's autobiographical content angered residents of Asheville. They were provoked by its thinly disguised and often unflattering characterizations, and many Southerners were appalled by passages that indicted Southern society in general. "Years later," Wolfe wrote of Eugene in one such passage, "when he could no longer think of the barren spiritual wilderness, the hostile and murderous entrenchment against all new life—when their cheap mythology, their legend of the charm of their manner, the aristocratic culture of their lives, the quaint sweetness of their drawl, made him writhe—when he could think of no return to their life and its swarming superstition without weariness and horror, so great was his fear of the legend, his fear of their antagonism, that he still pretended the most fantastic devotion to them, excusing his Northern residence on grounds of necessity rather than desire." Shaken by their hostility—one indignant local wrote the author that she longed to see his "big overgoan karkus" dragged across the public square—Wolfe did not return to Asheville for seven years.

The royalties from *Look Homeward, Angel* allowed Wolfe to leave his teaching post in February, 1930. The following month he received a Guggenheim fellowship and sailed to Europe, where he could live relatively cheaply and write uninterrupted. Although in Paris Wolfe associated with many American expatriates—including Lewis, Fitzgerald, and Hemingway—he did not share their political interests and rejection of American society. On the contrary, while there Wolfe "discovered" his America. "During that summer in Paris," Wolfe explained in *The Story of a Novel,* "I think I felt this great homesickness more than ever before, and I really believe that from this emotion, this constant and almost intolerable effort of memory and desire, the material and structure of the books I now began to write were derived." Knowing that European nations possessed long literary traditions and believing that the foundation of American literature was still being laid, Wolfe vowed to leave his mark on the fledgling tradition by capturing the American experience in his subsequent novels.

Thus in 1931 Wolfe began work on his second novel, in which he aimed to describe America's greatness as experienced by one man. After severing his ties with Bernstein when their affair became wearisome, Wolfe found a cheap flat in Brooklyn and lived on canned beans and coffee and cigarettes and sold a few short stories while he wrote his book. Throughout 1934 Wolfe and Perkins edited the immense manuscript, with Perkins generally excising long passages and Wolfe rewriting transitions even longer than the originals. Finally Perkins sent the novel to the typesetter without Wolfe's knowledge, thinking it as complete as it would ever be; an aghast Wolfe insisted that he had needed six more months to make it less episodic. Nervous about the novel's reception, Wolfe set sail for Europe a week before the 912-page *Of Time and the River* was published in March, 1935.

Of Time and the River continues the story of Eugene's growth and development. Covering the years 1920 to 1925 in the author's life, the novel opens with Eugene, now an aspiring novelist, on a northbound train anticipating life in Boston. The book follows him to England, France, and Germany, where his homesickness is apparent in his vivid memories and idyllic descriptions of American life. *Of Time and the River* ends with Eugene returning home on an ocean liner and falling in love with Esther Jack, a stage designer based on Wolfe's former mistress Aline Bernstein.

Again, critical reaction was mixed. *Of Time and the River* was faulted for its episodic nature—whole segments of the story seemed disconnected—and its apparent "formlessness." Some reviewers, however, maintain that the "formlessness" was intentional and that Wolfe, instead of ordering the novel around a sequence of events, unified it around a series of sense impressions, thereby capturing the diversity of the American experience and of life itself. Although various reviewers condemned the book for its lyricism and excessive emotion, others claimed that the rhapsodic, elegiac style complemented the book's loose structure.

Malcolm Cowley's *New Republic* assessment of *Of Time and the River* was representative of general critical opinion. "Thomas Wolfe at his best is the only contemporary American writer who can be mentioned in the same breath with [Charles] Dickens and [Fyodor] Dostoevsky," he wrote. "But the trouble is that the best passages are scattered, that they occur without logic or pattern, except the biographical pattern of the hero's life, and they lack the cumulative effect, the slow tightening of emotions to an intolerable pitch, that one finds in great novels." Cowley also pointed out that "the author's style goes flabby as soon as attention is taken away from the outside world and concentrated on the hero's yearning and hungering soul." William Styron's impressions were similar. He wrote in his *Harper's* review of the novel: "That furrow-browed, earnest sense of discovery in which the reader participates willingly in *Look Homeward, Angel* loses a great deal of its vivacity when the same protagonist has begun to pass into adulthood." Thomas C. Moser simply stated in *The American Novel:* "The older [Eugene] becomes, the less interesting the central character. When Wolfe writes badly, the subject is almost always Eugene."

Many critics were deeply moved by Wolfe's energy, however. *New York Post* contributor Herschel Brickell, for one, announced in his review of *Of Time and the River:* "You can't, if you are of ordinary stature and vitality, believe completely in [Wolfe's] gigantic world of shadow shapes, where everything is magnified and intensified, but you will be fascinated just the same, swept along on the tides of his passions, carried away with the gargantuan appetite of a man who wishes to swallow life whole when most of us are content to chew a tiny fragment in

our frightened and dyspeptic way." Bernard DeVoto was less impressed with Wolfe's passion than exasperated by the author's lack of rhetorical restraint. He complained in his notorious *Saturday Review* critique "Genius Is Not Enough" that all of Eugene's experiences are portrayed with equal intensity: "If the death of one's father comes out emotionally even with a ham-on-rye, then the art of fiction is cockeyed." *Of Time and the River* nonetheless was a best-selling novel, and Wolfe cemented his literary reputation later in 1935 with the publication of his short story volume *From Death to Morning,* which Perkins culled from manuscript discarded from *Look Homeward, Angel* and *Of Time and the River.*

For a writer's conference in July of 1935, Wolfe composed the lecture that was later published as *The Story of a Novel,* in which he discussed his writing theories as well as his close working relationship with Perkins. DeVoto, in his *Saturday Review* article, questioned Wolfe's craftsmanship and editorial judgment, claiming that his writing was only formless autobiography chopped up and rearranged by Perkins. "Works of art cannot be assembled like a carburetor," the critic averred, "they must be grown like a plant." Stung by this criticism, Wolfe broke with Perkins and signed in December, 1937, with Harper's, where his editor would be Edward C. Aswell.

In 1936 Wolfe took his seventh and last trip to Europe. He spent much of his time in Germany, where he was celebrated, his success due in part to fine translations of his works by German writer Hermann Hesse. Wolfe was dismayed, however, at the changes in Germany that had taken place since Adolph Hitler rose to power. Upon returning to the United States Wolfe discussed the new Germany in the *New Republic* essay "I Have a Thing to Tell You." He wrote that the dark forests, with "their legendary sense of magic and time," were replaced by the "dark Messiah" Hitler and his Nazi followers who beat Jews in the streets. The following year Wolfe, no longer vilified, visited his native Asheville. Though he was also disheartened by changes he encountered there—a land boom brought industry and commerce and corruption to the town—he rented a cottage nearby and wrote there during the summer of 1937.

During the first part of 1938 Wolfe wrote in seclusion in Brooklyn before he accepted an invitation to tour the national parks in the West. En route he stopped at Purdue University, where he delivered a speech that would later be published as *Writing and Living.* In this essay he admitted that as a youthful writer he was too egocentric and that he had only recently realized his responsibility to society. In his new novels he planned to address problems common to all men and to integrate his growing knowledge of worldwide political and socioeconomic situations. To symbolize his new literary direction, he changed his protagonist from recognizable alter-ego Eugene Gant to George "Monk" Webber.

Wolfe resumed his trip across America but in July in Seattle he caught pneumonia. When his condition worsened he was taken back east to Baltimore, where doctors diagnosed tuberculosis of the brain. Wolfe unknowingly contracted tuberculosis in his youth, the pneumonia activated old tubercular scars in his lungs, and the tuberculosis found its way to his brain through his bloodstream. After a series of operations Wolfe died on September 15, 1938, only a few weeks before his thirty-eighth birthday.

Before Wolfe traveled out west he had entrusted Aswell with a packing crate of manuscript eight feet high, containing thirty-five notebooks and other papers recording his impressions of America and Europe. He had also provided Aswell with extensive outlines and summaries for his works, and within three years

Aswell edited—many say overedited—much of the manuscript, extracting from it the novels *The Web and the Rock* (1939) and *You Can't Go Home Again* (1940) and the volume *The Hills Beyond* (1941), a collection of short stories, a play, and a novel fragment.

The Web and the Rock carries forward Wolfe's story through protagonist George Webber, a successful novelist whose works resemble Wolfe's own. The first half of *The Web and the Rock* parallels *Look Homeward, Angel*—although it is written in a more detached tone than *Angel*—as the story of a small-town Southern boy arriving in the North eager to experience life. The book's second half, which stands as a sequel to *Of Time and the River,* is devoted to George's affair with his muse, the sophisticated Esther Jack, and features luxuriant passages describing their love-making, feasts, and quarrels and reconciliations.

But George and Esther's love affair ultimately collapses, precipitated by events surrounding a swank dinner party the Jacks host for the New York literati and various socialites at their Park Avenue apartment. Elsewhere in the building a fire breaks out, and as the guests evacuate, the superficial sophisticates mix with elevator operators, fire fighters, and street people in a sharp commentary on the gap between the rich and poor in Depression-era America. Rejecting Esther and the privileged life she represents, George flees to Europe. But he cannot find solace there, for in Germany Hitler had risen to power, dashing Wolfe's romantic image of the nation. Thus at the end of *The Web and the Rock* George learns that time and change can only corrupt.

George is also disappointed when he returns to his native North Carolina in Wolfe's next novel, *You Can't Go Home Again.* Having avoided his hometown throughout much of the burgeoning 1920s, George discovers that new-found wealth has debased many of its natives, including a once-respected judge who has degenerated into a syphilitic loanshark. Regardless of the present corruption, *You Can't Go Home Again* ends with an optimistic cry of faith for all Americans: "I believe that we are lost here in America but I believe we shall be found." Although the Americans cannot recapture the innocence lost during the 1920s, Wolfe maintains, they must have faith in the future, when all Americans will be able to fulfill their potential through honest work, to live—as he professed to be doing—the American dream. "Though he used his life and art interchangeably," wrote Alfred Kazin in *On Native Grounds,* "they were, taken together, a reflection of Wolfe's conviction that he himself was a prime symbol of American experience and of a perpetual American ambition."

The Web and Rock and *You Can't Go Home Again* received mixed reviews. While critics commended Wolfe for passages revealing his heightened sensitivity to the plight of the oppressed, many noticed that Wolfe's more restrained style often fell flat. Most were struck by the disconcerting mixture of brilliant and poor writing in the novels (recent studies of the original texts show that Aswell amalgamated early and late writing in these works). Stephen Vincent Benet, nevertheless, acknowledged Wolfe's growth as a writer and as a social being in his *Saturday Review of Literature* critique of *You Can't Go Home Again:* "There is . . . a mature line. George Webber does grow up."

Aswell also edited Wolfe's posthumous collection *The Hills Beyond,* which contains some of Wolfe's finest short stories, including "The Lost Boy," a moving account of his brother's death, and "The Web of Earth," a monologue in which Wolfe's mother relates her life story. Also collected is a 150-page novel fragment—from which the work takes its title—which was to be a history of George Webber's maternal ancestors. Wolfe planned to tell the story of America through the descendants of one man

and his twenty children, including a lawyer, politician, teacher, and businessman. Although Wolfe asked his mother to send him their family tree as a basis, none of the characters were derived from people he knew. Some critics maintained that *The Hills Beyond* features some of Wolfe's most restrained and controlled writing, as well as some of his least exciting. Others, such as J. Donald Adams, admired Wolfe's more objective, dispassionate style. Critiquing the volume in the *New York Times Book Review,* Adams noted: "It contains some of his best, and certainly his most mature, work. The unfinished novel from which the book takes its title would, I think, have surpassed in creative power those other four on which his reputation must rest."

Fifty years after Wolfe's death critics still debate his merits as a novelist. Although many decry his craftsmanship, none can dismiss his epic, exuberant, and unaffected celebration of American and European life. "[I intend] to use myself to the top of my bent," Wolfe wrote in *You Can't Go Home Again.* "To use everything I have. To milk the udder dry, squeeze out the last drop, until there is nothing left." "My admiration for Wolfe is that he tried his best to get it all said," William Faulkner wrote to Richard Walser, editor of *The Enigma of Thomas Wolfe.* "He was willing to throw away style, coherence, all the rules of preciseness, to try to put all the experience of the human heart on the head of a pin."

BIOGRAPHICAL/CRITICAL SOURCES:

BOOKS

Bernstein, Aline, *The Journey Down,* Knopf, 1938.
Concise Dictionary of American Literary Biography: The Age of Maturity, 1929-1941, Gale, 1989.
Dictionary of Literary Biography, Volume 9: *American Novelists, 1910-1945,* Gale, 1982.
Dictionary of Literary Biography Documentary Series, Volume 2, Gale, 1982.
Dictionary of Literary Biography Yearbook: 1985, Gale, 1986.
Donald, David Herbert, *Look Homeward: A Life of Thomas Wolfe,* Little, Brown, 1987.
Kazin, Alfred, *On Native Grounds: An Interpretation of Modern American Prose Literature,* Harcourt, 1970.
Kennedy, Richard S., *The Window of Memory: The Literary Career of Thomas Wolfe,* University of North Carolina Press, 1962.
Magi, Aldo P. and Richard Walser, editors, *Thomas Wolfe Interviewed: 1929-1938,* Louisiana State University Press, 1985.
Reeves, Paschal, editor, *Thomas Wolfe: The Critical Reception,* David Lewis, 1974.
Rubin, Louis D., Jr., editor, *Thomas Wolfe: A Collection of Critical Essays,* Prentice-Hall, 1973.
Twentieth-Century Literary Criticism, Gale, Volume 4, 1981, Volume 13, 1984, Volume 29, 1988.
Walser, Richard, editor, *The Enigma of Thomas Wolfe: Biographical and Critical Selections,* Harvard University Press, 1953.
Wolfe, Thomas, *Look Homeward, Angel,* Scribner, 1952.
Wolfe, Thomas, *You Can't Go Home Again,* Perennial Library, 1973.
Wolfe, Thomas, *The Autobiography of an American Novelist: The Story of a Novel* [and] *Writing and Living,* edited by Leslie Field, Harvard University Press, 1983.

PERIODICALS

American Review, April, 1935.
Atlantic Monthly, January, 1940.

Harper's, April, 1968.
Harvard Library Bulletin, autumn, 1947.
New Republic, December 18, 1929, March 20, 1935.
New York Post, March 8, 1935, June 22, 1939.
New York Times Book Review, October 27, 1929, October 26, 1941.
Publisher's Weekly, December 24, 1938.
Saturday Review of Literature, April 25, 1936, September 21, 1940.
Times Literary Supplement, January 2, 1969.

OBITUARIES:

PERIODICALS

New Republic, September 28, 1938.
New York Herald Tribune, September 16, 1938.
New York Times, September 16, 1938.
Time, September 26, 1938.

—*Sketch by Carol Lynn DeKane*

*   *   *

WOLFE, Thomas Kennerly, Jr. 1931-
(Tom Wolfe)

PERSONAL: Born March 2, 1931, in Richmond, Va.; son of Thomas Kennerly (a scientist and business executive) and Helen (Hughes) Wolfe; married Sheila Berger (art director of *Harper's* magazine), 1978; children: Alexandra. *Education:* Washington and Lee University, B.A. (cum laude), 1951; Yale University, Ph.D., 1957.

ADDRESSES: Home—New York, N.Y. *Agent*—International Creative Management, 40 West 57th St., New York, N.Y. 10019.

CAREER: Writer, journalist, social commentator, and artist. *Springfield Union,* Springfield, Mass., reporter, 1956-59; *Washington Post,* Washington, D.C., reporter and Latin American correspondent, 1959-62; *New York Herald Tribune,* New York City, reporter and writer for *New York* Sunday magazine (now *New York* magazine), 1962-66; *New York World Journal Tribune,* New York City, writer, 1966-67; *New York* magazine, New York City, contributing editor, 1968-76; *Esquire* magazine, New York City, contributing editor, 1977—; *Harper's* magazine, New York City, contributing artist, 1978-81. Has exhibited drawings in one-man shows at Maynard Walker Gallery, 1965, and Tunnel Gallery, 1974.

AWARDS, HONORS: Washington Newspaper Guild awards for foreign news reporting and for humor, both 1961; Society of Magazine Writers award for excellence, 1970; D.F.A., Minneapolis College of Art, 1971; Frank Luther Mott research award, 1973; D.Litt., Washington and Lee University, 1974; named Virginia Laureate for literature, 1977; American Book Award and National Book Critics Circle Award, both 1980, for *The Right Stuff;* Harold D. Vursell Memorial Award for excellence in literature, American Institute of Arts and Letters, 1980; Columbia Journalism Award, 1980; citation for art history from National Sculpture Society, 1980; L.H.D. from Virginia Commonwealth University, 1983, and Southampton College, 1984; John Dos Passos Award, 1984; Gari Melchers Medal, 1986; Benjamin Pierce Cheney Medal from Eastern Washington University, 1986; Washington Irving Medal for literary excellence from Nicholas Society, 1986.

WRITINGS:

UNDER NAME TOM WOLFE

(Self-illustrated) *The Kandy-Kolored Tangerine-Flake Streamline Baby* (essays), Farrar, Straus, 1965, recent edition, 1987.
(Contributor) Alan Rinzler, editor, *The New York Spy,* David White, 1967.
The Electric Kool-Aid Acid Test, Farrar, Straus, 1968, recent edition, 1987.
The Pump House Gang (essays), Farrar, Straus, 1968 (published in England as *The Mid-Atlantic Man and Other New Breeds in England and America,* Weidenfeld & Nicolson, 1969).
Radical Chic and Mau Mauing the Flak Catchers (two essays), Farrar, Straus, 1970, recent edition, 1987.
(Editor with E. W. Johnson and contributor) *The New Journalism* (anthology), Harper, 1973.
(Self-illustrated) *The Painted Word,* Farrar, Straus, 1975.
(Self-illustrated) *Mauve Gloves & Madmen, Clutter & Vine, and Other Short Stories* (essays), Farrar, Straus, 1976.
(Contributor) Susan Feldman, editor, *Marie Cosindas, Color Photographs,* New York Graphic Society, 1978.
The Right Stuff (Book-of-the-Month-Club selection), Farrar, Straus, 1979.
(Self-illustrated) *In Our Time* (essays), Farrar, Straus, 1980.
From Bauhaus to Our House, Farrar, Straus, 1981.
(Self-illustrated) *The Purple Decades: A Reader* (collection), Farrar, Straus, 1982.
The Bonfire of the Vanities (novel), Farrar, Straus, 1987.

Contributor of numerous articles to periodicals. Co-founder of literary quarterly *Shenandoah.*

SIDELIGHTS: "Those of you who are not aware of Tom Wolfe should—really—do your best to acquaint yourselves with him," writes William F. Buckley in the *National Review.* "He is probably the most skilful writer in America. I mean by that he can do more things with words than anyone else." Satirist, caricaturist, social critic, coiner of phrases ("Radical Chic," "The Me Decade"), Wolfe has become known as a leading chronicler of American trends. His painstaking research and detailed accounts have made him a widely respected reporter; at the same time, his unorthodox style and frequently unpopular opinions have resulted in a great deal of controversy. Leslie Bennetts of the *Philadelphia Bulletin* calls him "a professional rogue," who has "needled and knifed at the mighty of every description, exposing in print the follies and foibles of superstars from Leonard Bernstein to the Hell's Angels. Gleefully ripping off every shred of disguise from anyone's pretensions, Wolfe has performed his dissections in *New York* Magazine, *Esquire,* and *Rolling Stone,* not to mention his earlier years on the *New York Herald Tribune* and the *Washington Post.*"

Wolfe is generally recognized as one of the leaders in the branch of writing known as "New Journalism." Bennetts says that while Wolfe did not invent the movement, "he at least became its stentorian spokesman and most flamboyant practitioner." *Fort Lauderdale Sun-Sentinel* writer Margo Harakas believes that there is "only a handful of standouts among [New Journalists]— Jimmy Breslin, Gay Talese, Hunter Thompson, and of course, Wolfe, with his explosive punctuation, name brand detailing, and kaleidoscopic descriptions." In a *Writer's Digest* article, Wolfe defines New Journalism as "the use by people writing nonfiction of techniques which heretofore had been thought of as confined to the novel or to the short story, to create in one form both the kind of objective reality of journalism and the subjective reality that people have always gone to the novel for."

The techniques employed in New Journalism, then, include a number of devices borrowed from traditional fiction writing: extensive dialogue; shifting point of view; scene-by-scene construction; detailed descriptions of setting, clothes, and other physical features; complex character development; and, depending on the reporter and on the subject, varying degrees of innovation in the use of language and punctuation.

Wolfe's association with New Journalism began in 1963, when he wrote his first magazine article, a piece on custom automobiles. He had become intrigued with the strange subculture of West Coast car customizers and was beginning to see these individuals as folk artists worthy of serious study. He convinced *Esquire* magazine to send him to California, where he researched the story, interviewed a number of subjects, and, says Harakas, "racked up a $750 tab at the Beverly Wilshire Hotel (picked up by *Esquire,* of course)." Then, having returned to New York to write the article, he found that standard journalistic techniques, those he had employed so successfully during his years of newspaper work, could not adequately describe the bizarre people and machines he had encountered in California.

Stymied, he put off writing the story until, finally, he called Byron Dobell, his editor at *Esquire,* and admitted that he was unable to finish the project. Dobell told him to type up his notes so that the magazine could get another writer to do the job. In the introduction to *The Kandy-Kolored Tangerine-Flake Streamline Baby,* Wolfe writes: "About 8 o'clock that night I started typing the notes out in the form of a memorandum that began, 'Dear Byron.' I started typing away, starting right with the first time I saw any custom cars in California." In an attempt to provide every possible detail for the writer who was to finish the piece, he wrote in a stream-of-consciousness style, including even some of his most garbled notes and random thoughts. "I wrapped up the memorandum about 6:15 A.M., and by this time it was 49 pages long. I took it over to *Esquire* as soon as they opened up, about 9:30 A.M. About 4 P.M. I got a call from Byron Dobell. He told me they were striking out the 'Dear Byron' at the top of the memorandum and running the rest of it in the magazine."

It is the style developed during the writing of the custom car article—his unique blend of "pop" language and creative punctuation—that for many years remained Wolfe's trademark. He was a pioneer in the use of what several reviewers refer to as an "aural" style of writing, a technique intended to make the reader come as close as possible to experiencing an event first-hand. Wilfrid Sheed, in the *New York Times Book Review,* says that Wolfe tries to find "a language proper to each subject, a special sound to convey its uniqueness"; and *Newsweek*'s Jack Kroll feels that Wolfe is "a genuine poet" among journalists, who is able "to get under the skin of a phenomenon and transmit its metabolic rhythm. . . . He creates the most vivid, most pertinent possible dimension of his subject." F. N. Jones, in a *Library Journal* article, describes Wolfe's prose as "free-flowing colorful Joycean, quote-slang, repetitive, cult or class jargon with literary and other reverberations."

Wolfe's style, combined with solid reporting and a highly critical eye, quickly gained a large audience for his magazine pieces. When his first book, *The Kandy-Kolored Tangerine-Flake Streamline Baby,* a collection of twenty-two of his best essays, was published in 1965, William James Smith wrote in *Commonweal:* "Two years ago [Tom Wolfe] was unknown and today those who are not mocking him are doing their level best to emulate him. Magazine editors are currently flooded with Zonk! articles written, putatively, in the manner of Wolfe and, by common

account, uniformly impossible. . . . None of his parodists—and even fewer of his emulators—has successfully captured much of the flavor of Wolfe. . . . They miss the spark of personality that is more arresting than the funny punctuation. Wolfe has it, that magical quality that marks prose as distinctively one's own."

In *The Kandy-Kolored Tangerine-Flake Streamline Baby* Wolfe analyzes, caricaturizes, and satirizes a number of early-sixties American trends and pop culture heroes. His essays zero in on the city of Las Vegas, the Peppermint Lounge, demolition derbies, fashion, art galleries, doormen, nannies, and such personalities as Murray the K, Phil Spector, Baby Jane Holzer, and Muhammed Ali (then Cassius Clay). "He knows everything," writes Kurt Vonnegut in the *New York Times Book Review.* "I do not mean he *thinks* he knows everything. He is loaded with facile junk, as all personal journalists have to be—otherwise, how can they write so amusingly and fast?. . . . Verdict: Excellent book by a genius who will do anything to get attention."

What Wolfe has done, according to *Commonweal*'s Smith, "is simply to describe the brave new world of the 'unconscious avant-garde' who are shaping our future, but he has described this world with a vividness and accuracy that makes it something more than real." In a *New Republic* article, Joseph Epstein expresses the opinion that "Wolfe is perhaps most fatiguing when writing about the lower classes. Here he becomes Dr. Wolfe, Department of American Studies, and what he finds attractive about the lower orders, as has many an intellectual slummer before him, is their vitality. At bottom, what is involved here is worship of the Noble Savage. . . . Wolfe is much better when he writes about New York City. Here he drops his studied spontaneity, eases up on the rococo, slips his doctorate, and takes on the tone of the reasonably feeling New Yorker who has not yet been knocked insensate by the clatter of that city." A *Newsweek* writer concludes that "partly, Wolfe belongs to the old noble breed of poet-journalists, like Ben Hecht, and partly he belongs to a new breed of supereducated hip sensibilities like Jonathan Miller and Terry Southern, who see the complete human comedy in everything from a hair-do to a holocaust. Vulgar? A bit. Sentimental? A tick. But this is the nature of journalism, with its crackling short waves transmitting the living moment."

In *The Electric Kool-Aid Acid Test,* Wolfe applies his distinctive brand of journalism to novelist Ken Kesey and his "Merry Pranksters," a West Coast group dedicated to LSD and the pursuit of the psychedelic experience. Joel Lieber of the *Nation* says that in this book Wolfe "has come as close as seems possible, with words, at re-creating the entire mental atmosphere of a scene in which one's understanding is based on feeling rather than verbalization. . . . [The book] is nonfiction told as experimental fiction; it is a genuine feat and a landmark in reporting style." Lawrence Dietz, in a *National Review* article, calls *The Electric Kool-Aid Acid Test* "the best work Wolfe has done, and certainly the most profound and insightful book that has been written about the psychedelic life. . . . [He] has elicited a history of the spread of LSD from 1960 (when Kesey and others got their first jolts in lab experiments) to 1967, when practically any kid with five dollars could buy some kind of trip or other." Dietz feels that Wolfe displays "a willingness to let accuracy take the place of the hysterical imprecations that have passed for reportage in most magazine articles and books" on this subject.

Wolfe's 1970 book, *Radical Chic and Mau Mauing the Flak Catchers,* was made up of two lengthy essays. The first, "Radical Chic," elicited by far the most critical commentary; it deals with a fund-raising party given by Leonard Bernstein in his Park Avenue apartment on January 14, 1970, to raise money for the Black

Panthers. Wolfe was at the party, and he became aware of the incongruity of the scene, distinguished, according to Melvin Maddocks of the *Christian Science Monitor,* by "white liberals nibbling caviar while signing checks for the revolution with their free hand." Thomas R. Edwards writes in the *New York Times Book Review:* "For Wolfe, the scene in the Bernsteins' living room demonstrates his pet sociological thesis, here called *nostalgie de la boue,* the aristocrat's hankering for a proletarian primitivism. He shows us cultivated parvenu Jews, torn between cherished new 'right wing' lifestyles and the 'left wing' politics of their own oppressive history, ludicrously confused about how to take the black revolution. Though there's a touch of ugliness in his determination to let us know, without seeming to do so, that certain socialites with gentile names weren't born that way, 'Radical Chic' is sometimes brilliant and telling in its dramatization of this case."

A *Times Literary Supplement* reviewer says that Wolfe "both defends and exonerates the Bernsteins, that is—their motives were sound, liberal, serious, responsible—while cocking an almighty snook at 'the essential double-track mentality of Radical Chic—*nostalgie de la boue* and high protocol' that can entertain Afro hair-styles with Roquefort cheese savouries in a Park Avenue duplex. . . . The slogan 'Mr. Parlour Panther,' in the end, is inevitably unfurled to flutter in the ironic breeze. Such is this dazzling piece of trapeze work by the most practised social stuntman of them all."

Many readers were not happy with *Radical Chic and Mau Mauing the Flak Catchers.* As William F. Buckley explains in the *National Review,* "[Wolfe] has written a very very controversial book, for which he has been publicly excommunicated from the company of the orthodox by the bishops who preside over the *New York Review of Books.*" Buckley continues: "What Mr. Wolfe did in this book was MAKE FUN of Bernstein et al., and if you have never been told, you MUST NOT MAKE FUN of Bernstein et al., when what hangs in the balance is Bernstein's moral prestige plus the integrity of Black Protest; learn the lesson now." Edwards feels that Wolfe "humiliates and degrades everyone concerned, his pre-potent but child-like and shiftless blacks no less than his gutless, time-serving, sexually-fearful white bureaucrats." Timothy Foote, in a *Time* article, notes: "When a *Time* reporter recently asked a minister of the Panther Party's shadow government about the truthfulness of Wolfe's *Radical Chic* account, the reply was ominous: 'You mean that dirty, blatant, lying, racist dog who wrote that fascist disgusting thing in *New York* magazine?' " Yet, despite the objections to the book, Foote insists, the fact remains that "it is generally so accurate that even some of the irate guests at the Bernsteins later wondered how Wolfe—who in fact used shorthand—managed to smuggle a tape recorder onto the premises."

Christopher Lehmann-Haupt of the *New York Times,* noting that "Radical Chic" first appeared as a magazine article, writes: "When the news got out that it would be published as a book eventually, one began to prepare a mental review of it. One had certain questions—the usual Tom Wolfe questions: Where exactly was Wolfe located when all those things occurred? Just how did he learn Leonard Bernstein's innermost fantasies? At exactly what points did Wolfe's imagination impinge on his inferences, and his inferences on his facts? . . . Still, one was prepared to forget those questions. The vision of the Beautiful People dos-a-dosing with black revolutionaries while white servants passed out 'little Roquefort cheese morsels rolled in crushed nuts' was too outrageous. Shivers of malice ran up and down one's spine. Wolfe's anatomy of radical chic would have to be celebrated." The book, Lehmann-Haupt concludes, "represents

Wolfe at his best, worst, and most. It has his uncanny eye for lifestyles; his obsessive lists of brand names and artifacts; his wicked, frequently cruel, cartoon of people's physical traits; his perfect mimicry of speech patterns. Once again, Wolfe proves himself the complete chameleon, capable of turning any color. He understands the human animal like no sociologist around."

The Painted Word was another of Wolfe's more controversial works. T. O'Hara, in a *Best Sellers* review, sums up the book's thesis: "About 10,000 people constitute the present art world. Artists, doing what they must to survive, obey orders and follow the gospel as written by the monarchs." Among these monarchs, in Wolfe's opinion, are three of our most influential and well-respected art critics: Clement Greenberg, Harold Rosenberg, and Leo Steinberg (the "kings of cultureburg," he calls them). In a *Time* article, Robert Hughes says that "the New York art world, especially in its present decay, is the easiest target a pop sociologist could ask for. Most of it is a wallow of egotism, social climbing and power brokerage, and the only thing that makes it tolerable is the occasional reward of experiencing a good work of art in all its richness, complexity and difficulty. Take the art from the art world, as Wolfe does, and the matrix becomes fit for caricature. Since Wolfe is unable to show any intelligent response to painting, caricature is what we get. . . . Wolfe seems to know virtually nothing about the history of art, American or European."

New York Times art critic John Russell, writing in the *New York Times Book Review,* states: "If someone who is tone-deaf goes to Carnegie Hall every night of the year, he is, of course, entitled to his opinion of what he has listened to, just as a eunuch is entitled to his opinion of sex. But in the one case, as in the other, we on our side are entitled to discount what they say. Given the range, the variety and the degree of accomplishment represented by the names on Mr. Wolfe's list [including artists such as Pollock, de Kooning, Warhol, Newman, Rauschenberg, and Stella], we are entitled to think that if he got no visual reward from any of them, . . . the fault may not lie with the art."

As Ruth Berenson of the *National Review* points out, however, response to the book is generally dependent on the extent to which an individual is involved in the world of modern art. She maintains that *The Painted Word* "will delight those who have long harbored dark suspicions that modern art beginning with Picasso is a put-on, a gigantic hoax perpetrated on a gullible public by a mysterious cabal of artists, critics, dealers, and collectors aided and abetted by *Time* and *Newsweek.* Those who take modern art somewhat more seriously will be disappointed."

In *From Bauhaus to Our House,* published in 1981, Wolfe does to modern architecture what he did to modern art in *The Painted Word,* and the response has been similar: Readers close to the subject tend to resent the intrusion by an "outsider," while those with a more detached point of view often appreciate the author's fresh perspective. *New York Times* architecture critic Paul Goldberger, in a *New York Times Book Review* article, writes: "Mr. Wolfe wants to argue that ideology has gotten in the way of common sense. Beginning half a century ago with the origins of the International Style in Europe, he attempts to trace the development of that style, which for many, including Mr. Wolfe, is a virtual synonym for modern architecture. . . . We are told how the International Style became a 'compound'—a select, private, cult-like group of ideologues [including Walter Gropius, Mies van der Rohe, Marcel Breuer, and Josef Albers] whose great mission, as Mr. Wolfe sees it, was to foist modern design upon an unwilling world. . . . The problem, I think . . . is that Tom Wolfe has no eye. He has a wonderful ear, and he listens hard and long, but he does not seem to see. . . . He does precisely what he warns us against; he has listened to the words, not looked at the architecture."

And in a *Washington Post Book World* review, *Post* architecture critic Benjamin Forgey says that "the book is a case of crying Wolfe for one more time. *Bauhaus* is distinguished by the same total loathing of modern culture that motivated *The Painted Word*. . . . Wolfe's explanation is that modernism has been a conspiracy. In place of the New York critics who foisted abstract art upon us, we have the European giants of architecture . . . and their abject American followers. In Wolfe's view the motivation was pretty much the same, too. They were all playing the hypocritical bohemian game of spitting on the bourgeois." Forgey feels that "there is some truth in this, but it makes for a thin book and a narrow, limited history of architecture in the 20th century."

On the other hand, *New York Times* literary critic Christopher Lehmann-Haupt makes the point that even many architects have been unhappy with the structures created by proponents of the Bauhaus school. This style of architecture (distinguished by what is often referred to as a "glass box" appearance) was, for instance, denigrated by architect Peter Blake in his 1977 book, *Form Follows Fiasco*. According to Lehmann-Haupt, Blake "anathematized modern architecture for being sterile, functionless and ugly"; thus Wolfe "has not really come up with anything very startling when he laments the irony that four-fifths of the way into the American Century, when what we ought to be expressing with our building is 'exuberance, power, empire, grandeur, or even high spirits and playfulness,' what we still see inflicted upon us is the anti-bourgeois, socialist, pro-worker ideas that arose from 'the smoking rubble of Europe after the Great War.' But the explication of this notion is done with such verve and hilarity by Mr. Wolfe that its substance almost doesn't seem to matter. . . . It flows with natural rhetorical rhythm. . . . And often enough it is to laugh right out loud." John Brooks, in a *Chicago Tribune Book World* review, calls the book "a readable polemic on how in our architecture over the past few decades things have gone very much as they have in the other visual arts—a triumph of conformity over true innovation, of timidity over uninhibited expression, of irony over straightforwardness, of posing over real accomplishment. . . . *From Bauhaus to Our House* is lucidly and for the most part gracefully written."

In 1979 Wolfe published the book that many critics consider his finest: *The Right Stuff,* an award-winning study of the early years of the American space program. At one point in the book Wolfe attempts to define the "ineffable quality" from which the title is taken: "It obviously involved bravery. But it was not bravery in the simple sense of being willing to risk your life . . . any fool could do that. . . . No, the idea . . . seemed to be that a man should have the ability to go up in a hurtling piece of machinery and put his hide on the line and then have the moxie, the reflexes, the experience, the coolness, to pull it back in the last yawning moment—and then to go up again *the next day,* and the next day, and every next day."

The main characters in the book are, of course, the first U.S. astronaut team: Scott Carpenter, Gordon Cooper, John Glenn, Gus Grissom, Wally Schirra, Alan Shepard, and Deke Slayton. Wolfe assiduously chronicles their early careers as test pilots, their private lives, their selection for the astronaut program and the subsequent medical processing and training. But, as *Commonweal*'s Thomas Powers points out, *The Right Stuff* "is not a history; it is far too thin in dates, facts and source citations to serve any such pulse. It is a work of literature which must stand or fall as a coherent text, and its subject is not the Mercury program itself but the impulse behind it, the unreflecting competitiveness which drove the original astronauts to the quite extraordinary lengths Wolfe describes so vividly." That the author goes beyond mere reportage of historical fact is confirmed by Mort Sheinman in a *Chicago Tribune* article: "Wolfe tells us what it's like to go 'shooting straight through the top of the sky,' to be 'in a king's solitude, unique and inviolate, above the dome of the world.' He describes what happens when someone is immolated by airplane fuel, and he talks about the nightmares and hallucinations experienced by the wives. . . . [*The Right Stuff*] is a dazzling piece of work, something that reveals much about the nature of bravery and celebrity and—yes—patriotism."

Time writer R. Z. Sheppard says that the book "is crammed with inside poop and racy incident that 19 years ago was ignored by what [Wolfe] terms the 'proper Victorian gents' of the press. The fast cars, booze, astro groupies, the envies and injuries of the military caste system were not part of what Americans would have considered the right stuff. Wolfe lays it all out in brilliantly stated Op Lit scenes: the tacky cocktail lounges of Cocoa Beach where one could hear the *Horst Wessel Song* sung by ex-rocket scientists of the Third Reich; Vice President Lyndon Johnson furiously cooling his heels outside the Glenn house because Annie Glenn would not let him in during her husband's countdown; Alan Shepard losing a struggle with his full bladder moments before lift-off; the overeager press terrifying Ham the chimp after his proficient flight; the astronauts surrounded by thousands of cheering Texans waving hunks of raw meat during an honorary barbecue in the Houston Coliseum."

Christopher Lehmann-Haupt of the *New York Times* writes: "What fun it is to watch Mr. Wolfe put the antiseptic space program into the traces of his inimitable verbal cadenzas. It's a little like hearing the story of Jesus of Nazareth through the lips of the Chicago nightclub comedian Lord Buckley." Lehmann-Haupt says that in this book Wolfe undertakes "the restoration of the zits and rogue cilia of hair to the face of the American space program" and reveals a good deal of the gossip that was denied the public by a hero-worshipping press in the early sixties, gossip "about how the test-pilot fraternity looked down on the early astronauts for being trained monkeys in a capsule ('spam in a can') instead of pilots in control of their craft; about the real feelings of the original seven for one another and the tension that arose between the upright John Glenn and some of the others over their after-hours behavior, particularly with the 'juicy little girls' who materialized wherever they trained; and about what National Aeronautical and Space Administration engineers really felt about the flight of Gus Grissom and Scott Carpenter and the possibility that they had secretly panicked."

Former test pilot and astronaut Michael Collins (a member of the Gemini 10 flight and command module pilot on the Apollo 11 moon flight), writes in a *Washington Post Book World* review: "I lived at Edwards [Air Force Base, site of the Air Force Flight Test Center,] for four years, and, improbable as some of Tom's tales seem, I know he's telling it like it was. He is the first gifted writer to explore the relationship between test pilots and astronauts—the obvious similarities and the subtle differences. He's obviously done a lot of homework—too much in some cases. Some of this stuff could only be interesting to Al Shepard's mother. While the first part of the book is a paean to guts, to the 'right stuff,' it is followed by a chronology—but one that might have profited from a little tighter editing. But it's still light-years ahead of the endless drivel [Norman] Mailer has put out about the Apollo program, and in places the Wolfe genius really shines." Collins feels that at times Wolfe allows himself to get too close to his subject: "He's almost one of the boys—and there's too much to admire and not enough to eviscerate." As a result "*The Right Stuff* is not vintage, psychedelic Tom Wolfe, but if you . . . have ever been curious about what the space program was really all about in those halcyon Kennedy and Mercury years, then this is your book."

In a review of *The Right Stuff* for the *Lone Star Book Review,* Martha Heimberg says that, for the most part, "Wolfe's reporting, while being marvelously entertaining writing, has also represented a telling and trustworthy point of view. His is one of those finely critical intelligences that can detect the slightest pretention or falsification in an official posture or social pose. And, when he does, he goes after the hypocrisy—whether large or small, left or right—with all the zeal of the dedicated reformer." Like Collins, Heimberg feels that *The Right Stuff* "represents a departure for the satirist whose observant eye and caustic pen have impaled on the page a wide range of American social phenomena" in that Wolfe "clearly likes his subjects—none are treated as grist for the satirist's mill, but put down with as great a skill and detail as an observer could possibly muster." She concludes that "the book represents a tremendous accomplishment and a new direction for a writer who figures among the top stylists of his generation."

By the mid-1980s Wolfe had a new ambition for his writing. As he told the *New York Times:* "I was curious, having spouted off so much about fiction and nonfiction, and having said that the novelists weren't doing a good job, to see what would happen if I tried it. Also, I guess I subconsciously had the suspicion that maybe, what if all this to-do I've made about nonfiction is because I really, secretly think I can't do a novel. So I said, well, I've got to prove this to myself." The result was *The Bonfire of the Vanities,* a novel that exposes the greed and hate seething in modern New York City. In the book, a smug Wall Streeter named Sherman McCoy is reduced to a political pawn when he is implicated in the hit-and-run traffic death of a young black man. *Washington Post Book World*'s Jonathan Yardley called *Bonfire* "a superb human comedy and the first novel ever to get contemporary New York, in all its arrogance and shame and heterogeneity and insularity, exactly right." After his novel became a major bestseller, Wolfe issued what he called a "literary manifesto" in *Harper's* magazine. He urged fellow novelists to abandon the esoteric literary experiments that have characterized fiction for much of the twentieth century and use realism to chronicle the bizarre and astounding world around them. The author's peers reacted with both praise and condemnation. "Ever the provocateur," reported *Time,* "Wolfe is enjoying the controversy."

Although there can be no question that Tom Wolfe has achieved a reputation as a superb stylist and skillful reporter, no discussion of Wolfe would be complete without some mention of his famous wardrobe. *Philadelphia Bulletin* writer Leslie Bennetts tells of an encounter with the author when he lectured at Villanova University: "The legendary sartorial splendors were there, of course: the gorgeous three-piece creamy white suit he has been renowned for . . . (how many must he have, do you suppose, to appear in spotless vanilla every day: rows upon rows of them hanging in shadowed closets, a veritable army of Gatsby ghosts waiting to emerge?). Not to mention the navy suede shoes, dark as midnight, or the jaunty matching suede hat, or the sweeping midnight cashmere coat of the exact same hue, or the crisp matching tie on which perched a golden half-moon pin to complement the glittering gold watch chain that swung gracefully from the milky vest. Or the navy silk handkerchief peeking out from the white suit pocket, or the white silk handkerchief peeking out from the navy coat pocket."

Wolfe told Bennetts that he began wearing the white suits in 1962: "That was when I had a white suit made, started wearing it in January, and found it annoyed people tremendously. Even slight departures in dress at that time really spun people out. So I liked it. It's kind of a harmless form of aggression, I guess." But Wolfe's mode of dress has also been an important part of his journalism, serving as a device to distance him from his subject. He told Susan Forrest of the *Fort Lauderdale News:* "A writer can find out more if he doesn't pretend to be hip. . . . If people see you are an outsider, they will come up and tell you things. If you're trying to be hip, you can't ask a lot of naive questions." This technique has been effective for Wolfe in interviewing stock car racers, Hell's Angels, and—particularly—astronauts. He feels that at least part of the success of *The Right Stuff* is due to the fact that he did not try to get too close to that inner circle. Wolfe told Janet Maslin of the *New York Times Book Review:* "I looked like Ruggles of Red Gap to them, I'm sure. . . . But I've long since given up on the idea of going into a situation trying to act like part of it. . . . Besides, it was useless for me to try to fit into the world of pilots, because I didn't know a thing about flying. I also sensed that pilots, like people in the psychedelic life, really dislike people who presume a familiarity with the Lodge."

A writer for *Time* calls Wolfe's form of dress "a splendiferous advertisement for his individuality. The game requires a lot of reverse spin and body English but it boils down to antichic chic. Exclaims Wolfe proudly: 'I own no summer house, no car, I wear tank tops when I swim, long white pants when I play tennis, and I'm probably the last man in America to still do the Royal Canadian Air Force exercises.' "

MEDIA ADAPTATIONS: The Right Stuff was adapted for a film of the same title, Warner Bros., 1983; *Bonfire of the Vanities* was scheduled to be adapted for a film.

AVOCATIONAL INTERESTS: Window shopping.

BIOGRAPHICAL/CRITICAL SOURCES:

BOOKS

Authors in the News, Volume 2, Gale, 1976.
Bellamy, Joe David, editor, *The New Fiction: Interviews With Innovative American Writers,* University of Illinois Press, 1974.
Bestsellers 89, Issue 1, Gale, 1989.
Contemporary Literary Criticism, Gale, Volume 1, 1973, Volume 2, 1974, Volume 9, 1978, Volume 15, 1980, Volume 35, 1985, Volume 51, 1989.

PERIODICALS

America, February 5, 1977, April 2, 1988.
Atlantic, October, 1979, December, 1987.
Best Sellers, August, 1975.
Books and Art, September 28, 1979.
Books in Canada, April, 1988.
Business Week, November 23, 1987.
Chicago Tribune, September 9, 1979, September 15, 1979, January 16, 1983, November 4, 1987.
Chicago Tribune Book World, December 7, 1980, October 25, 1981, January 16, 1983.
Christian Science Monitor, November 17, 1970, November 3, 1987.
Commentary, March, 1971, May, 1977, February, 1980, February, 1988.
Commonweal, September 17, 1965, December 20, 1968, March 3, 1978, October 12, 1979, February 26, 1988.

Detroit News, October 14, 1979, November 9, 1980.

Encounter, September, 1977.

Fort Lauderdale News, April 22, 1975.

Fort Lauderdale Sentinel, April 22, 1975.

Globe and Mail (Toronto), December 5, 1987.

Guardian Weekly, February 21, 1988.

Harper's, February, 1971, November, 1989, January, 1990.

Library Journal, August, 1968.

Listener, February 11, 1988.

London Review of Books, February 18, 1988.

Lone Star Book Review, November, 1979.

Los Angeles Times, October 19, 1979, November 22, 1987, October 12, 1989.

Los Angeles Times Book Review, November 2, 1980, October 25, 1981, October 17, 1982, January 23, 1983, October 25, 1987.

Nation, March 5, 1977, November 3, 1977.

National Review, August 27, 1968, January 26, 1971, August 1, 1975, February 19, 1977, December 18, 1987.

New Leader, January 31, 1977.

New Republic, July 14, 1965, December 19, 1970, November 23, 1987.

New Statesman, February 12, 1988.

Newsweek, June 28, 1965, August 26, 1968, June 9, 1975, September 17, 1979, October 26, 1987.

New York, September 21, 1981, March 21, 1988.

New Yorker, February 1, 1988.

New York Review of Books, August 26, 1965, December 17, 1970, June 26, 1975, January 20, 1977, October 28, 1979, November 4, 1982, February 4, 1988.

New York Times, November 25, 1970, May 27, 1975, November 26, 1976, September 14, 1979, October 9, 1981, December 20, 1981, October 13, 1987, October 22, 1987, November 21, 1987, December 31, 1987, January 3, 1988, March 11, 1988.

New York Times Book Review, June 27, 1965, August 18, 1968, November 29, 1970, December 3, 1972, June 15, 1975, December 26, 1976, October 28, 1979, October 11, 1981, October 10, 1982, November 1, 1987.

Observer (London), February 7, 1988.

Partisan Review, Number 3, 1969, Number 2, 1974.

People, December 24, 1979, November 23, 1987.

Philadelphia Bulletin, February 10, 1975.

Punch, February 12, 1988.

Rolling Stone, August 21, 1980, November 5-December 10, 1987.

Saturday Review, September 15, 1979, April, 1981.

Spectator, February 13, 1988.

Time, September 6, 1968, December 21, 1970, June 23, 1975, December 27, 1976, September 29, 1979, November 9, 1987, February 13, 1989, November 27, 1989.

Times (London), February 11, 1988, February 13, 1989, April 22, 1989.

Times Literary Supplement, October 1, 1971, November 30, 1979, November 26, 1980, March 18, 1988.

Tribune Books, August 2, 1987, October 18, 1987.

U.S. News and World Report, November 23, 1987.

Village Voice, September 10, 1979.

Wall Street Journal, October 29, 1987.

Washington Monthly, March, 1988.

Washington Post, September 4, 1979, October 23, 1980, March 27, 1988, October 17, 1989.

Washington Post Book World, September 9, 1979, November 23, 1980, November 15, 1981, November 7, 1982, October 25, 1987.

Writer's Digest, January, 1970.

*   *   *

WOLFE, Tom
See WOLFE, Thomas Kennerly, Jr.

*   *   *

WOODCOTT, Keith
See BRUNNER, John (Kilian Houston)

*   *   *

WOODIWISS, Kathleen E(rin)   1939-

PERSONAL: Born June 3, 1939, in Alexandria, La.; daughter of Charles Wingrove, Sr., and Gladys (Coker) Hogg; married Ross Woodiwiss (a retired U.S. Air Force major), July 20, 1956 (divorced); children: Sean Alan, Dorren James, Heath Alexander. *Education:* Attended schools in Alexandria, La. *Politics:* Republican.

ADDRESSES: Home—Princeton, Minn. *Office*—Avon Books, Hearst Corporation, 959 Eighth Ave., New York, N.Y. 10019.

CAREER: Writer.

WRITINGS:

NOVELS

The Flame and the Flower, Avon, 1972.
The Wolf and the Dove, Avon, 1974.
Shanna, Avon, 1977.
Ashes in the Wind, Avon, 1979.
A Rose in Winter, Avon, 1982.
Come Love a Stranger, Avon, 1984.
So Worthy My Love, Avon, 1989.

SIDELIGHTS: Kathleen E. Woodiwiss is a pioneering writer of romance fiction whose first novel is generally credited with creating the sub-genre known as "erotic historical" romance. When *The Flame and the Flower* was published in 1972 the field of romance writing was dominated by "contemporary gothics" produced by writers such as Mary Stewart, Victoria Holt, and Phyllis Whitney. *The Flame and the Flower* differed from its predecessors in that it was substantially longer, but also because it contained lengthy, often detailed passages describing the sexual encounters of the hero and heroine. The immediate success of *The Flame and the Flower* cleared the way for writers like Rosemary Rogers and Laura McBain, authors who, along with Woodiwiss, have helped to make the historical romance an enormously popular form.

The novels following *The Flame and the Flower* continued to be ground-breakers and assured Woodiwiss a large and loyal readership. *Shanna,* Woodiwiss's third book, made publishing history by becoming the first historical romance released in a trade paperback edition. *Shanna* went on to sell over three million copies and spent a full year on the *New York Times* best-seller list. In 1979 Avon published *Ashes in the Wind* with a first printing of 1.5 million copies and backed the book with a huge promotional campaign, including full-page advertisements in national women's magazines and commercials on network television. The publicity paid off almost immediately as *Ashes in the Wind* sold over two million copies and went into a third printing within a month of its release. All told, Woodiwiss's books have sold over ten million copies.

In spite of her remarkable success, Woodiwiss's initial motives for writing were rather simple. "I couldn't find anything good to read, a good romantic book to pass a few hours away, so I decided to write one myself," she told Judy Klemesrud in the *New York Times Book Review.* "I just started pecking away at this story set during the American Revolution. It wasn't anything I could get completely absorbed in. I had three boys at home, and there were always dishes to be put in the dishwasher." Woodiwiss finished the book and, following the advice of her husband and friends, submitted it to half a dozen publishers. After they had all rejected it, she sent the book to Avon where an editor, Nancy Coffey, picked it out of a group of submitted manuscripts known as the "slush pile." The book became *The Flame and the Flower* and went on to launch Woodiwiss into a successful writing career.

Historical romances vary in some respects but share fundamental similarities. Settings are typically exotic and frequently change from continent to continent. Heroes are characteristically handsome and commanding while heroines are beautiful and sensitive. Often innocent, the heroine is usually introduced to the hero with whom she falls in love, only to be parted from him for much of the story. The book inevitably ends with the heroine being united with her true love. *The Flame and the Flower* clearly embodies the traditions of its genre. The heroine, Heather, is a teenager throughout a story that begins around 1800 in England and moves to the American Carolinas. A beautiful and proper girl who becomes the ward of a cruel aunt, Heather is raped by a handsome Yankee who in turn is forced to marry her. After many adventures, the pair reunite and their initial hatred for each other turns to love. *The Flame and the Flower* also maintains the traditional structural relationship of males as dominant to and protective of females.

Where *The Flame and the Flower* and other Woodiwiss novels break with tradition is in their frank depiction of the sexual relationship between the hero and the heroine. Yet while her books contain occasional sexual passages, Woodiwiss objects to charges that her books are "erotic." "I'm insulted when my books are called erotic," she told an interviewer in *Cosmopolitan.* "I don't think people who say that have read my books. I believe I write love stories. With a little spice. Some of the other current romances are a bit savage, though. They make sex dirty. It's embarrassing to read them. But women are looking for the love story. I get a lot of fan mail, and they tell me that."

Woodiwiss's enormous success does not seem to have greatly affected her lifestyle. She still spends much of her time with her family at their home in rural Minnesota. As she told Klemesrud, "I enjoy cooking and cleaning, my family and my home." Writing has been something of a family affair for Woodiwiss. In scheduling her books she does her writing primarily during the school year, because, as she explained to Klemesrud, "when the boys are home in the summer, I like to spend time with them." Woodiwiss's former husband, a retired Air Force major, often got involved in the writing process by giving Woodiwiss ideas for her books. In fact, he wrote the poems that begin and end both *Shanna* and *Ashes in the Wind.*

That her books are generally ignored by "serious" reviewers does not seem to bother Woodiwiss, nor does it make her wish to change her approach to writing. As she told Klemesrud: "I never started out to win any prizes for my writing. I wanted to appease a hunger for romantic novels, and that is what I shall continue to do."

BIOGRAPHICAL/CRITICAL SOURCES:

BOOKS

Bestsellers 90, Issue 1, Gale, 1990.

Falk, Kathryn, *Love's Leading Ladies,* Pinnacle Books, 1982.

PERIODICALS

Cosmopolitan, February, 1978.
New York Times Book Review, November 4, 1979.
Publishers Weekly, January 31, 1977, May 30, 1977.
Village Voice, May 9, 1977.
Washington Post Book World, October 7, 1979.
WB, September-October, 1989.

* * *

WOODRUFF, Robert W.
See MENCKEN, H(enry) L(ouis)

* * *

WOODWARD, Bob
See WOODWARD, Robert Upshur

* * *

WOODWARD, Robert Upshur 1943-
(Bob Woodward)

PERSONAL: Born March 26, 1943, in Geneva, Ill.; son of Alfred E. Woodward (a judge) and Jane (Upshur) Woodward Barnes; married, November 29, 1974 (divorced); children: Mary Taliesin. *Education:* Yale University, B.A., 1965.

ADDRESSES: Home—3027 Q St. N.W., Washington, D.C. 20007. *Office—Washington Post,* Washington, D.C. 20007.

CAREER: Montgomery County Sentinel, Rockville, Md., reporter, 1970-71; *Washington Post,* Washington, D.C., reporter, 1971—. *Military service:* U.S. Navy, active duty, 1965-70; became lieutenant.

AWARDS, HONORS: Pulitzer Prize to the *Washington Post,* Drew Pearson Foundation award, Heywood Brun award, George Polk Memorial Award, Sidney Hillman Foundation award, Worth Bingham prize, and Sigma Delta Chi award, all 1973, all for investigative reporting of Watergate scandal; Worth Bingham Prize, 1986.

WRITINGS:

UNDER NAME BOB WOODWARD

(With Carl Bernstein) *All the President's Men,* Simon & Schuster, 1974.
(Contributor) Staff of the Washington Post, *The Fall of a President,* Dell, 1974.
(With Bernstein) *The Final Days,* Simon & Schuster, 1976.
(With Scott Armstrong) *The Brethren: Inside the Supreme Court,* Simon & Schuster, 1979.
Wired: The Short Life and Fast Times of John Belushi, Simon & Schuster, 1984.
Veil: The Secret Wars of the CIA, 1981-1987, Simon & Schuster, 1987.

Also co-writer, with Christopher Williams, of "The Nightmare Years," a screenplay for television based on William Shirer's memoir of the same name, in 1986; co-writer of "Under Seige," a movie made for television by National Broadcasting Corporation in 1986.

WORK IN PROGRESS: Newspaper work.

SIDELIGHTS: Bob Woodward had been with the *Washington Post* nine months on the night police beat when he was called upon to cover the arraignment of five men who had been arrested for breaking into the Democratic National Committee's offices in the Watergate complex. The astonished young reporter learned the burglars had CIA connections and that one of them, James McCord, was an employee of the Committee to Reelect the President. Woodward, teamed with Carl Bernstein, followed the story from a Washington courtroom through a complicated tangle of clandestine political activity into the highest offices of the White House. The affair eventually led, in part due to Woodward and Bernstein's persistent efforts, to the resignation of numerous government officials in the executive branch, including that of President Richard Nixon.

The reporter's first book, *All the President's Men,* was originally planned to be the culmination of their investigative work for their *Washington Post* stories. At the time—October, 1972—Woodward and Bernstein were the only reporters pursuing the story. The result of the scant attention from the rest of the press was a pile of information which they intended to use in a book about the secret activities of White House aides. Two chapters of this never-finished book were already written when Judge Sirica released to the press a letter he had received from James McCord. In the letter, McCord revealed the involvement of higher-ups in the burglary and the perjury and political pressure that had occurred during his trial. Realizing that by the time their book could be finished it would appear merely to be rehashing well-reported events, Woodward then suggested that their book should tell the story of how they reported the Watergate cover-up.

The story was told in a third person narrative style. The authors worried that a different style or more personal point of view might appear to be an "ego trip" when dealing with their successes, or worse, might become a defense or justification when dealing with their failures. The reporters openly acknowledged their mistakes: they approached grand jury members for information; they revealed a confidential source; and they overstepped some guidelines in certain rights to privacy. As reporters and authors, they wanted to be objective and honest. The third person narrative with its advantage of impartiality, it was decided, allowed them the best opportunity to do this. In addition, said Doris Kearns in the *New York Times Book Review,* "it turns Watergate into a fast moving mystery, a whodunit written with ease if not elegance." Critics praised the book wholeheartedly for its ability to sustain reader interest, for its behind-the-scenes explanation of the workings of a large metropolitan newspaper, and for its indispensible historical value. Reviewers commended the co-authors for their frankness and their fascinating, personal portraits of the men surrounding the president.

After the completion of *All the President's Men,* the reporters turned their attention back to the final ranklings of Watergate. They planned to follow six senators around for background for a book about the apparent upcoming impeachment trial of Richard Nixon, a project they dropped when it became obvious that the president was going to resign. They decided their next book would be based on the significant news in the day-to-day operation of the White House that was being overlooked by much of the rest of the press. The authors explained in the foreword to *The Final Days:* "Some of our most reliable sources said that the real story of those final days of the Nixon presidency had not been adequately told; to report that story and sort through the contradictions would require a concentrated effort of perhaps a year or more."

The authors, taking a leave of absence from the *Post,* hired two assistants and quickly fanned out a few days after Nixon's resig-

nation to interview everyone associated with the White House who agreed to talk with them. Many sources demanded they not be identified before they consented to be interviewed, and some suggested that they would publicly deny any cooperation after the book appeared. Three hundred and ninety-four people were interviewed in six months. Many of them gave the authors access to their notes, memos, diaries, and logs.

In allowing the sources complete anonymity, Woodward and Bernstein knew they would have to accept responsibility for the accuracy of every statement made in *The Final Days.* In the foreword, the authors explained: "If we obtained two versions, we resolved disagreements through re-interviewing. If this proved impossible, we left out any material we could not confirm." Woodward added: "Anything in the book has been checked and rechecked. The more sensitive the material, the higher the standard we applied. There are several things being disputed now that we have as many as six sources for." The cross-checking and confirmation of all statements in the book was an enormous task of which the authors were quite proud.

The publication of *The Final Days* developed into a media event. Highlights of the book had been syndicated by *Newsweek* in a two-part, thirty thousand-word excerpt containing many of the most controversial passages. The issue that included the second part was the fastest selling issue in *Newsweek*'s history. Like *All the President's Men, The Final Days* was a sure bet for commercial success. Upon release in 1976, it sold one-half million copies in the first month. Another record was set in the book industry when paperback rights were sold at one and one half million dollars.

The people written about in *The Final Days* were reported to believe the account to be "basically accurate" and without "factual error"; yet most complained that the book's total effect was an exaggeration, an overdramatization, and a distortion. These people and a few critics blamed the book's style. *The Final Days* was a narrative written from the omniscient point of view. In a *Christian Science Monitor* review, John Hughes commented: "Woodward and Bernstein were not inside the heads of the participants at the moment crucial events took place, and yet the book unceasingly gives that impression." On the other hand, *New York Review of Books* contributor Nicholas von Hoffman defended the point of view. "Assuming they have a good base for believing that so-and-so did say or think something close to that at the time, there's no reason to object. Using such devices as 'he thought,' 'it seemed to her,' etc., may make the narrative flow more easily and there's no need to think history has to be dull to be good." In fact, the self-imposed journalistic restraints limit the accuracy of the book, feels Von Hoffman, who concludes that, regarding Nixon's fall from power, "*The Final Days* isn't the last word."

John K. Galbraith, writing in the *Washington Post Book World,* felt that the authors of *The Final Days* could have analyzed flaws in the American political system instead of prolonging the public scrutiny of Nixon's demise. In Woodward's next book—*The Brethren: Inside the Supreme Court*—Woodward and co-author Scott Armstrong also decline to analyze what they uncover about the inner workings of the American government. Reviewers again question the reliability of the reporter's sources, and complain that some of the revelations in the best seller are of a personal nature and made in poor taste. That *The Brethren* has sold so well despite these concerns reflects Woodward's ability to satisfy public curiosity in the United States, a country in which, says Galbraith, "politics . . . has become a major spectator sport."

After John Belushi died of a drug overdose in 1982, his widow asked Woodward to write about the popular actor's death. With characteristic diligence, Woodward interviewed hundreds of people "and conducted a marathon paper chase" for supporting evidence, Matt Beer relates in the *Detroit News*. In Beer's opinion, the scene in which "a friend finds Belushi's bloated body amid the trash of a weeklong binge in a Hollywood hotel" presents, in Beer's words, "the gonzo lifestyle of the 1970s in its harshest, most revealing light ever." Many reviewers found the amount of detail in the book overwhelming and sometimes irrelevant. "John Belushi died of excess. And it is excess that deals a near-fatal blow to investigative reporter Bob Woodward's encyclopedic, intermittently tedious account of the comedian's death," notes Beer. People who had known Belushi also complained "that Woodward concentrated on the dark side of Belushi's life, providing exact details of the drugs, alcohol and tantrums that characterized his final days in Hollywood," reports Eleanor Randolph in the *Washington Post*.

Most notably dissatisfied with Woodward's portrayal of Belushi was his widow Judy Jacklin Belushi, who had hoped that his story might "communicate how 'drugs can ruin your life,'" as Randolph reports in the *Chicago Tribune*. Belushi said that although *Wired* succeeds on this level, it minimizes the positive aspects of her late husband's personality. She tried to block the distribution of the book on the grounds that it contained family pictures she had not authorized for use; however, the real reason, she told the *Chicago Tribune*, was that she wanted the public to know she did not approve of the book as a whole. Randolph records Woodward's response to these and other negative comments: "Read the book. It goes on and on about his talent, going into skit after skit. I think they are reacting to a strong and reasonable wish that it had been different, that it hadn't happened, and I understand they don't want to remember him this way. . . . I believe their distress is directed at what happened to John and not my reporting."

Woodward's next "rhubarb . . . on the ethics (if any) of investigative journalism and the relationship (if any) between its findings and 'history'" is *Veil: The Secret Wars of the CIA, 1981-1987*, notes Edwin M. Yoder, Jr., in the *Los Angeles Times*. Much of the information in *Veil* came from the late William Casey, formerly the director of the Central Intelligence Agency. The result is what has been called a largely sympathetic portrait of the director, who saw the CIA as an active branch of the Reagan administration; it was up to the CIA to make its own foreign policy using covert means when necessary, Casey felt. In *Veil*, "the mumbling, almost comic Casey familiar from TV emerges as a passionate anti-communist and wily strategic thinker, albeit with the cloak-and-dagger mind-set he developed as spymaster for the OSS [Office of Strategic Services] during World War II," relates David M. Alpern in *Newsweek*. Clarence Petersen remarks in the *Chicago Tribune* that "it would be hard to choose a more fascinating central character."

Angered by various parts of the book were Casey's widow, Ronald and Nancy Reagan, other journalists, and critics who felt that the book contained either too much or too little truth. Other reporters questioned Woodward's claim that the usually reticent Casey had granted him dozens of private interviews. Speaking to a "Today" show audience, Woodward said he supposes—as do many of the book's reviewers—that Casey cooperated in order to have some control over what would be said about the CIA. Woodward also felt Casey gave him unprecedented frequent access "as a defensive measure, to learn exactly how much [Woodward] knew about CIA operations," *Time* magazine reports. Yoder maintains that the key to the unusual relationship is the role of secrecy in contemporary political affairs: "The fact is that secrecy, a necessary feature of government, has suffered, in the postwar world of the national-security state, from a terrible elephantiasis: A whole structure of self-importance and self-deception has rooted itself in the culture of secrecy. Unless you understand this addiction, the games that reporters and officials play cannot be understood."

Some readers expressed disappointment that *Veil* revealed so little new information about the diversion of profits from Iran arms sales to the Contras in Central America. At the end of the book, Woodward records a conversation that took place in a hospital room shortly after Casey had undergone brain surgery. When asked if he knew of the diversion, Casey nodded his head to indicate yes; when asked for an explanation, he reportedly replied, "I believed." In the opinion of several reviewers, disputes about whether or not this exchange actually took place sidestep more important issues raised in the book. Writing in the *Chicago Tribune*, Roger Simon contends, "Nobody in this business has greater credibility than Bob Woodward. His devotion to careful fact-checking is not only legendary but also is supposed to border on mania. . . . If he was going to make it up, he could have made up better stuff than a head nod and two words."

More important, the reviewers suggest, are the other CIA activities disclosed in the book, such as a failed assassination attempt in Beirut that left 80 dead and hundreds injured. Woodward apparently agrees. The book's subject, he told *Los Angeles Times* writer Betty Cuniberti, is "Casey and the CIA, six years and one day, how essentially they went unmonitored, where he had in a certain sense a blank check within the executive branch to do what he wanted and that he was able to roll, or frustrate Congress. To a certain extent we all kind of have to face what happened. And it's not a very encouraging story."

Cuniberti reports that "There is a common thread in the criticisms leveled against all the books Woodward has written or co-authored. . . . And that thread, Woodward believes, is not inaccuracy. 'It's contested ground,' said Woodward, 'and it's essentially people living their lives and conducting their business a certain way and projecting a way that is untruthful.'"

MEDIA ADAPTATIONS: All the President's Men was made into a Warner Bros. film starring Dustin Hoffman and Robert Redford in 1976; a film version of *Wired* was produced by Edward S. Feldman for release in 1989.

BIOGRAPHICAL/CRITICAL SOURCES:

BOOKS

Woodward, Bob and Carl Bernstein, *All the President's Men*, Simon & Schuster, 1974.
Woodward, Bob and Carl Bernstein, *The Final Days*, Simon & Schuster, 1976.

PERIODICALS

Atlantic, June, 1976.
Chicago Tribune, December 2, 1979, December 16, 1979, May 27, 1984, June 3, 1984, September 9, 1987, September 30, 1987, October 4, 1987, October 5, 1987, October 9, 1987, October 12, 1987.
Christian Science Monitor, May 19, 1976.
Detroit News, July 1, 1984.
Encounter, October, 1980.
Esquire, December, 1983.
Globe and Mail (Toronto), October 17, 1987.
Harpers, April, 1980.

Los Angeles Times, June 17, 1984, September 27, 1987, September 28, 1987, September 30, 1987, October 1, 1987, October 2, 1987, October 6, 1987.

Los Angeles Times Book Review, June 17, 1984.

Miami Herald, July 17, 1974.

National Review, February 8, 1980, August 6, 1984.

New Republic, April 24, 1976, February 23, 1980.

New Statesman, May 21, 1976.

Newsweek, April 12, 1976, May 3, 1976, October 5, 1987, October 12, 1987.

New York Review of Books, June 10, 1976, February 7, 1980, November 19, 1987.

New York Times, April 7, 1976, December 3, 1977, June 2, 1984, September 19, 1984, January 12, 1986, September 30, 1987, October 3, 1987, April 15, 1989.

New York Times Book Review, June 9, 1974, April 18, 1976, December 16, 1979, January 13, 1980, December 21, 1980, June 10, 1984, September 6, 1987, October 18, 1987, September 4, 1988.

People, October 12, 1987, November 9, 1987.

Philadelphia Bulletin, July 10, 1974.

Publishers Weekly, April 26, 1976, October 14, 1983.

Saturday Review, May 3, 1976, May 29, 1976, March 1, 1980.

Time, April 22, 1974, December 30, 1974, April 12, 1976, May 3, 1976, March 10, 1980, June 11, 1984, October 12, 1987.

Times (London), April 18, 1985.

Times Literary Supplement, April 11, 1980, March 8, 1985, January 22, 1988.

Tribune Books, September 11, 1988.

Washington Post, December 2, 1979, May 30, 1984, May 31, 1984, June 1, 1984, June 4, 1984, June 5, 1984, September 27, 1987, October 4, 1987, October 15, 1987, May 10, 1988.

Washington Post Book World, April 11, 1976, December 16, 1979, September 27, 1987, August 28, 1988.

—*Sketch by Marilyn K. Basel*

*   *   *

WOOLF, (Adeline) Virginia   1882-1941
(Virginia Stephen)

PERSONAL: Born January 25, 1882, in London, England; committed suicide by drowning, March 28, 1941, in the Ouse River, Lewes, Sussex, England; daughter of Sir Leslie (a biographer, critic, and scholar) and Julia Prinsep Jackson Stephen; married Leonard Woolf (an economist, publisher, critic, and writer), August 10, 1912 (died, 1969). *Education:* Self-educated.

CAREER: Writer. Morley College, London, England, instructor in English, c. 1905-1907; founder and operator of Hogarth Press, with husband, Leonard Woolf, beginning in 1917. Founder, with brother Thoby Stephen, of *Hyde Park Gate News* (a weekly paper written and published by the siblings from 1891 through 1895).

AWARDS, HONORS: Prix *Femina* from *Femina* and *Vie Heureuse* reviews, 1928.

WRITINGS:

The Voyage Out (novel), Duckworth, 1915, revised, Doran, 1920 (also see below).

Two Stories Written and Printed by Virginia Woolf and L. S. Woolf, Hogarth, 1917, story by Virginia Woolf published separately as *The Mark on the Wall,* Hogarth, 1919 (also see below).

Kew Gardens (short stories), Hogarth, 1919, reprinted, Folcroft Press, 1969 (also see below).

Night and Day (novel), Duckworth, 1919, Doran, 1920.

Monday or Tuesday (short stories; includes "The Mark on the Wall" and "Kew Gardens"), Harcourt, 1921.

Jacob's Room (novel), Hogarth, 1922, Harcourt, 1923.

Mr. Bennett and Mrs. Brown (criticism), Hogarth, 1924, reprinted, Folcroft Press, 1977.

The Common Reader (criticism), Harcourt, 1925, reprinted, 1984.

Mrs. Dalloway (novel), Harcourt, 1925, reprinted with introduction by Woolf, Modern Library, 1928, reprinted, Harcourt, 1985 (also see below).

To the Lighthouse (novel), Harcourt, 1927, reprinted, University of Toronto Press, 1982.

Orlando (novel), Crosby Gaige, 1928.

A Room of One's Own (essays), Harcourt, 1929, reprinted, 1981.

The Waves (novel), Harcourt, 1931.

The Second Common Reader (criticism), Harcourt, 1932, reprinted, 1986 (published in England as *The Common Reader, Second Series,* Hogarth, 1932).

Flush: A Biography, Harcourt, 1933, reprinted, Hogarth, 1983.

The Years (novel), Harcourt, 1937 (also see below).

Three Guineas (essays), Harcourt, 1938.

Roger Fry (biography), Harcourt, 1940.

Between the Acts (novel), Harcourt, 1941, reprinted, University Publications (New York), 1983.

The Death of the Moth, and Other Essays, Harcourt, 1942, reprinted, Hogarth, 1981.

A Haunted House, and Other Short Stories, Hogarth, 1943, Harcourt, 1944.

The Moment, and Other Essays, Hogarth, 1947, Harcourt, 1948, reprinted, Hogarth, 1981.

The Captain's Death Bed, and Other Essays, Harcourt, 1950, reprinted, Hogarth, 1981.

Granite and Rainbow (essays), Harcourt, 1958.

Contemporary Writers (essays), preface by Jean Guiguet, Hogarth, 1965, Harcourt, 1966.

Collected Essays, four volumes, Hogarth, 1966-67, Harcourt, 1967.

Mrs. Dalloway's Party: A Short Sequence, edited with an introduction by Stella McNichol, Hogarth, 1973, Harcourt, 1975.

Moments of Being (autobiographical essays), edited by Jeanne Schulkind, Chatto & Windus, 1976, Harcourt, 1977.

Freshwater (comedy), edited with a preface by Lucio P. Ruotolo, illustrated by Loretta Trezzo, Harcourt, 1976.

Books and Portraits: Some Further Selections From the Literary and Biographical Writings of Virginia Woolf, edited by Mary Lyon, Hogarth, 1977, Harcourt, 1978.

The Pargiters: The Novel-Essay Portion of The Years, edited with an introduction by Mitchell A. Leaska, New York Public Library, 1977.

Melymbrosia: An Early Version of The Voyage Out, edited with an introduction by Louise A. DeSalvo, New York Public Library, 1982.

The Complete Shorter Fiction of Virginia Woolf, edited by Susan Dick, Harcourt, 1985.

The Essays of Virginia Woolf, edited by Andrew McNeillie, Harcourt, 1986.

Also author of essays under maiden name, Virginia Stephen. Essays, novels, and short stories published in numerous other collections; short stories also published separately. Works represented in anthologies. Contributor of criticism, essays, and short fiction to periodicals, including *Times Literary Supplement,* beginning in 1905, *Guardian, Cornhill, Athenaeum,* and *New Statesman.*

JOURNALS

A Writer's Diary: Being Extracts From the Diary of Virginia Woolf, edited by husband, Leonard Woolf, Hogarth, 1953, Harcourt, 1954.

The Diary of Virginia Woolf, five volumes, edited by Anne Olivier Bell, introductory notes by Quentin Bell, Volume 1: *1915-1919,* Hogarth, 1977, Harcourt, 1979; Volume 2: *1920-1924,* Harcourt, 1978; Volume 3: *1925-1930,* Harcourt, 1980; Volume 4: *1931-1935,* Harcourt, 1982; Volume 5: *1936-1941,* Hogarth, 1984.

CORRESPONDENCE

Letters: Virginia Woolf and Lytton Strachey, edited by Leonard Woolf and James Strachey, Harcourt, 1956.

The Letters of Virginia Woolf, six volumes, edited by Nigel Nicolson and Joanne Trautmann, Volume 1: *The Flight of the Mind, 1888-1912,* Hogarth, 1975, published as *1888-1912,* Harcourt, 1975; Volume 2: *The Question of Things Happening, 1912-1922,* Hogarth, 1976, published as *1912-1922,* Harcourt, 1976; Volume 3: *A Change of Perspective, 1923-1928,* Hogarth, 1977, published as *1923-1928,* Harcourt, 1978; Volume 4: *A Reflection of the Other Person, 1929-1931,* Hogarth, 1978, published as *1929-1931,* Harcourt, 1979; Volume 5: *The Sickle Side of the Moon, 1932-1935,* Hogarth, 1979, published as *1932-1935,* Harcourt, 1979; Volume 6: *Leave the Letters Till We're Dead, 1936-1941,* Hogarth, 1980, published as *1936-1941,* Harcourt, 1980.

Letters also published separately and in additional collections.

OTHER

Translator, with S. S. Koteliansky, of works by Fedor Dostoevsky and Leo Tolstoy.

SIDELIGHTS: English writer Virginia Woolf was one of the most innovative and influential literary figures of the twentieth century. A prolific author of essays, journals, letters, and long and short fiction, she is probably best remembered for her provocative experimental novels. As an early practitioner of stream-of-consciousness writing, Woolf subordinated dramatic action and plot development in her novels, exploring instead the inner thoughts and feelings of her characters. Through her revolutionary writings, she questioned both the nature of reality and the significance of the individual human being in an alienating and dehumanizing world. Her works offer a unique perspective on such topics as sexuality, feminism, life and death, madness and sanity, and the disintegration of society. Deeming Woolf "one of the half-dozen novelists of the present century whom the world will not easily let die," David Daiches, writing in *Virginia Woolf,* asserted: "There can be little question that she was the greatest woman novelist of her time, though she herself would have objected to the separation of her sex implied in such a judgment."

Woolf was born in London in 1882 to a distinguished family that promoted the study and appreciation of literature and the arts. Leading literary and political figures frequented Woolf's childhood home at Hyde Park Gate. Often ill as a child, she was unable to attend school regularly but benefited from the ongoing intellectual exchange occurring in her rich cultural milieu. Woolf's father, noted scholar and biographer Leslie Stephen, further facilitated his daughter's quest for knowledge by opening his private library to her. He also counseled her in the art of effective reading: his advice, as recounted by Woolf in *A Writer's Diary,* was "to read what one liked because one liked it [and] never to pretend to admire what one did not."

Throughout her early years, Woolf saw several members of her family fall victim to insanity and illness. Her half sister's mental illness and her cousin's madness from an accidental head injury both exerted a profound effect on her. And in his 1972 study *Virginia Woolf: A Biography,* Quentin Bell alleged that Woolf's endurance of sexual abuse as a young girl by her older half brother permanently altered her attitude toward sex. In addition to the psychological strain brought on by the abuse, the perverted relationship, according to Bell, may have contributed to Woolf's frigidity as a married woman. Critics have indicated that the combined effect of these childhood experiences drained Woolf of her delicate emotional reserves, heightened her sensitivity to the harsh realities of life, and seriously damaged her ability to cope.

Woolf's first mental breakdown was precipitated by the 1895 death of her mother, Julia Stephen, a warm and loving individual who had worked to achieve an atmosphere of harmony in the Stephen household. Slowly recovering from the trauma after a prolonged period of rest and introspection, Woolf suffered additional trials in rapid succession. Her half sister Stella Duckworth, who had taken over some of the homemaking responsibilities after Julia Stephen's death, became ill and died in 1902. Two years later, Woolf's father also died. Woolf experienced another mental collapse in the months following her father's death, and she attempted suicide that same year. Upon her recovery, she moved with her sister Vanessa and brothers Thoby and Adrian from the family home at Hyde Park Gate to Bloomsbury, a London district with relatively inexpensive housing.

Around the time of her father's illness and death, Woolf began to envision ideas for stories and consequently decided that she wanted to pursue a career in writing. By 1905, she was leading a relatively independent life and had begun a more than thirty-year affiliation with the *Times Literary Supplement,* writing reviews and feature articles. Meanwhile, Woolf's older brother Thoby arranged for gatherings of his friends from Cambridge at the house in Bloomsbury to discuss art, literature, and world affairs. Manly Johnson, writing in *Virginia Woolf,* noted that Woolf thrived in the company of the intellectuals. The "Bloomsburys," as the group was called, came to include Vanessa and her husband, art critic Clive Bell; biographer Lytton Strachey; economist John Maynard Keynes; novelist E. M. Forster; artist Roger Fry; and critic and economist Leonard Woolf, the author's future husband.

In 1906, Thoby Stephen was taken ill with typhoid and died. His death—at the age of twenty-six—devastated Woolf, and her sister Vanessa's marriage to Clive Bell intensified that sense of loss. She moved with her younger brother Adrian to a smaller house in Bloomsbury, maintained her ties with the Bloomsbury group, and concentrated on writing. Although annoyed by suggestions that she should find a husband, Woolf harbored thoughts—revealed in her letters—that she would never marry. Strachey, a known homosexual, proposed to Woolf, but after due consideration they both thought better of such an arrangement. Woolf soon experienced another mental breakdown, and Strachey, still concerned about the author, encouraged Leonard Woolf, a friend from Cambridge, to pursue her. The Woolfs were married in 1912, and for the next three decades, Leonard sought to instill in her a sense of stability, confidence, and worthiness.

Several years after their marriage, the Woolfs founded the Hogarth Press. Leonard engineered the couple's foray into publishing, hoping that the experience of setting type and operating the press might relieve his wife of some of the tension brought on by her writing. The Hogarth Press became an important publisher of experimental and alternative literature, including works by

Woolf, W. H. Auden, Forster, Sigmund Freud, Robert Graves, Katherine Mansfield, H. G. Wells, and many others then perceived as radical.

Critics have suggested that writing, though a physically and psychologically taxing process, served Woolf as an outlet for self-exploration. Her writings reflect an attempt to reconcile the dual nature of her sexuality, her unfulfilled desire to bear a child—she often compared the writing process with childbirth—her consuming fear of failure, and an overwhelming sense that she might lose control over her life. Woolf herself admitted, as quoted by Bell, that she wrote "to prove to myself that there was nothing wrong with me—which I was already beginning to fear there was."

Woolf fought an ongoing battle against depression for most of her life. In adulthood, such bouts were usually precipitated by her insecurities as a writer. Excerpts from the author's copious diary entries indicate that the act of writing both sustained and tortured her. *A Writer's Diary*—selected notes on writing culled from Woolf's diaries and edited by Leonard Woolf—conveys her vacillating attitudes toward her craft: "What a born melancholic I am! The only way I keep afloat is by working," she declared in the summer of 1929; in a later entry, she proclaimed, "Few people can be so tortured by writing as I am." In composing each of her most enduring works of fiction, Woolf went through a predictable, almost ritualistic progression. In a flash of inspiration, she conceived the original ideas for her novels. She would labor over the actual writing of a book, usually for more than a year, alternating between periods of great productivity and utter frustration. Though never completely satisfied with a finished manuscript, even after extensive rewriting, Woolf, working with her husband, readied her texts for distribution. The production cycle culminated in exhaustion—and, periodically, mental collapse—as Woolf awaited the reaction of literary critics. Ironically, these periods of near madness seemed to fuel the author's imagination with ideas for future novels.

Woolf became gravely ill in 1913 after finishing the manuscript for her debut novel, *The Voyage Out,* about a young woman coming of age while traveling in South America. This tragic tale, which offered radical new views on women and education, was generally viewed as the work of a promising author. But according to Bell, Woolf's fears of a negative critical reception had already driven her to despair, causing severe headaches, a profound state of melancholia, and both visual and audio hallucinations, including one in which she was taunted by a mocking crowd. A brief stay at a nursing home proved ineffective therapy, and Woolf returned home anorectic, insomniac, and suicidal. Under her husband's nurturing care, she slowly improved, but, as Bell theorized, "After two years of intermittent lunacy it appeared [thereafter] that her mind and her character were permanently affected."

Woolf wrote her second novel, *Night and Day,* while recuperating from the mental breakdown brought on by the completion of *The Voyage Out.* Published in 1919, the work revolves around a group of poorly matched young couples and the events that lead to their recombining as more suitable duos. Woolf viewed *Night and Day* as a safe project, one less demanding psychologically than its predecessor. But while critics generally commended Woolf for her writing style in *Night and Day,* many—including Mansfield—found the book's subject matter trite and its treatment predictable. Although the book received only mixed reviews, Woolf herself was more satisfied with it than with *The Voyage Out.*

Woolf was less confident in withstanding the critical ambivalence accorded her next book, the 1921 short fiction collection *Monday or Tuesday,* which contains stories usually regarded as precursors to her best experimental long works. Though hailed for their stunning imagery and evocations of characters' inner lives, the stories in *Monday or Tuesday,* according to some critics, are obscured by indirectness. "The reader is left with nothing definite in his mind," a *Springfield Republican* reviewer noted, "no real idea or purpose, no clear-cut thought." Perhaps as a consequence of the book's reception, Woolf underwent another period of extreme self-doubt: "I'm a failure as a writer. I'm out of fashion," she proclaimed in an entry from *A Writer's Diary,* ever sensitive to critical commentary. But at this time Woolf was already writing the experimental *Jacob's Room*—the book that marked a turning point in her career.

The idea for *Jacob's Room* reportedly came to Woolf as she stared into the fireplace at Hogarth House. A powerful depiction of the effects of a harsh world on an individual human being, the novel chronicles the life and wartime death of young Jacob Flanders, who is revealed indirectly through brief glimpses of the contents of his room and scattered impressions from others. Reviewers generally considered *Jacob's Room* a stunning progression that demonstrated a technical mastery lacking in both *The Voyage Out* and *Night and Day.* "For the first time Virginia Woolf caught both her society and her sense of the soul in a unified vision," asserted A. D. Moody in *Virginia Woolf. Jacob's Room* remains a testament to Woolf's achievements as a writer, containing some of her most vivid imagery and polished lyrical prose. As a *Spectator* reviewer commented, "There is no writer who can give the illusion of reality with more certainty and with so complete a concealment of illusionary devices behind a perfection of style which is at once solid and ethereal."

Already known for rendering with precision the thoughts and feelings of her characters, Woolf gained recognition with her next novel, *Mrs. Dalloway,* for evoking the actual thought process. Commenting on the work in an essay included in *Abinger Harvest,* Forster wrote: "It is easy for a novelist to describe what a character thinks of. . . . But to convey the actual process of thinking is a creative feat, and I know of no one except Virginia Woolf who has accomplished it."

Favorably compared to James Joyce's classic *Ulysses, Mrs. Dalloway* ranks among Woolf's greatest triumphs. Following the events of a single day in the life of Clarissa Dalloway, an upper-class English woman, the work is regarded as a stunning document of the state of post-World War I society. The story opens with Mrs. Dalloway making last minute preparations for a party to be held at her home that evening. Utilizing the stream-of-consciousness technique, Woolf exposes Mrs. Dalloway's inner thoughts as the heroine reviews the course her life has taken. Prior to marrying the respectable but passionless Parliament member Richard Dalloway, Mrs. Dalloway had been pursued by sprightly suitor Peter Walsh. But after an emotionally fulfilling encounter with another woman, Mrs. Dalloway rejected Walsh in favor of Mr. Dalloway, thus insulating herself from the true nature of her sexuality. On the day of her party, Walsh reenters Mrs. Dalloway's life.

Mrs. Dalloway never meets the novel's other significant character, World War I veteran Septimus Smith. His sensitive temperament destroyed, Smith leaps to his death from a balcony at the prospect of commitment to a sanatorium. More than merely the culmination of his madness, Septimus's suicide is generally viewed as an expression of freedom, his ultimate assertion of independence at a time when he had lost control over his own future. During her party, Mrs. Dalloway learns of Septimus's suicide. Commenting on the evolution of the story line in her introduction to the 1928 edition of *Mrs. Dalloway,* Woolf noted some of the revisions she had made to the text: "In the first version Septimus, who later is intended to be [Mrs. Dalloway's] double, had no existence; and . . . Mrs. Dalloway was originally to kill herself, or perhaps merely to die at the end of the party."

In an article for *Renascence,* Rene E. Fortin pointed to Mrs. Dalloway's "inconsistent . . . appraisal" of Septimus's death: his suicide is, for Mrs. Dalloway, both "a triumph and a disaster." "Death was defiance. Death was an attempt to communicate. . . . There was an embrace in death," the character initially muses. She then proceeds to agonize over the suicide, viewing it in purely personal, selfish terms: "Somehow it was her disaster—her disgrace. It was her punishment to sink and disappear . . . in this profound darkness, . . . forced to stand here in her evening dress." Referring to the latter statement, Moody implied that Mrs. Dalloway is an embodiment of vapidity—she is a character created by Woolf to disclose the moral degeneration of society. "Clarissa Dalloway isn't set off against her world," Moody asserted; "she is realised at its own valuation as one of its fine products; and by that very fact she exposes its bankruptcy the more absolutely." As quoted by Lyndall Gordon in *Virginia Woolf: A Writer's Life,* Woolf strove through *Mrs. Dalloway* to illuminate one of her chief concerns: "The truth is people scarcely care for each other."

With the publication of her 1927 novel *To the Lighthouse,* Woolf established herself as a leading writer of the twentieth century. Divided into three sections, the lush, poetic narrative offers insights into the processes of decay and renewal and the enduring influence of the past on the present. The story revolves around the Ramsays—a family that occupies a summer house off the coast of Scotland—and several of their guests, including a painter named Lily Briscoe. Mrs. Ramsay functions as a link between the members of the household. In the first of the book's sections, young James Ramsay's hopes of trekking to the island's lighthouse are frustrated by the pessimistic and preoccupied Mr. Ramsay's prediction of rain. Part two of the book begins with the storm's onset. In this section ten years elapse, during which Mrs. Ramsay and two of the Ramsay children die and the summer house falls to ruin. Even after her death, though, Mrs. Ramsay's memory lives on, and in part three the remaining Ramsays return to the house, James and Mr. Ramsay complete the journey to the lighthouse, and Lily Briscoe—also back at the house—finally completes a painting she had begun a decade earlier.

To the Lighthouse has been judged a profound and moving portrait of the human spirit. As Conrad Aiken wrote in a piece from his *Collected Criticism,* "Nothing happens, in this houseful of odd nice people, and yet all of life happens. The tragic futility, the absurdity, the pathetic beauty of life—we experience all of this." Speculating on the symbolism intended in *To the Lighthouse,* James Ginden wrote in his *Harvest of a Quiet Eye:* "The lighthouse itself, distant and ambiguous across the water, stands as the central symbol of meaning and achievement in the novel. . . . Mrs. Woolf's symbolic searcher must suffer, must pass through the tumult of destruction and war, before he can reach the lighthouse." In a diary entry for November 28, 1928, Woolf admitted: "I used to think of [father] and mother daily; but writing the *Lighthouse* laid them in my mind. . . . I was obsessed by them both, unhealthily; and writing of them was a necessary act." But, as quoted by Bell, the author disclaimed any single critical interpretation of the novel: "I meant *nothing* by *The Lighthouse.* . . . [I] trusted that people would make it the

deposit for their own emotions—which they have done, one thinking it means one thing another another. I can't manage Symbolism except in this vague, generalised way. . . . [When] directly I'm told what a thing means, it becomes hateful to me."

Woolf's next novel, the thinner *Orlando,* is a mock biography that transcends the limits of time, mortality, and sexuality. Published in 1928, this fantastic work traces the adventures of young Orlando, a sixteenth-century poet born to a wealthy English family. Having taken Queen Elizabeth as a lover and engaged in a steamy affair with a Russian princess, the charming Orlando falls into a series of deep sleeps, awakening in the eighteenth century as a thirty-six-year-old woman who maintains her youth throughout the twentieth century. Woolf based the character of Orlando on Vita Sackville-West, an English writer and Bloomsbury member with whom Woolf shared an intimate friendship. The book is said to be a mythic reconciliation of Woolf's sexual duality. Critics heralded *Orlando* as a clever and substantial literary document that catalogs English manners and sensibilities over various generations and examines human history from multiple perspectives through the androgynous Orlando.

Woolf reaffirmed her place in contemporary literature with her 1931 publication *The Waves,* a highly experimental novel without dialogue. Widely regarded as the most difficult of Woolf's books, *The Waves* focuses on three men and three women, all of whom reveal themselves through soliloquies and interior monologue. As the characters eulogize their heroic friend Percival, they progress in their understanding of life's mutability. Some reviewers objected to the novel's radical structure and found its premise overly obscure. Others lauded Woolf's revolutionary vision and technical acumen. Alluding to the sense of mystery inherent in *The Waves,* Gerald Bullett, in a review for *New Statesman and Nation,* asserted, "It is impossible to describe, impossible to do more than salute, the richness, the strangeness, the poetic illumination of this book. The characters are not analysed, . . . they are entered into, intuited."

In her 1937 novel *The Years* Woolf again addresses life's mysteries and tragedies, offering insights into the effects of war, the aging process, and modernization on both the individual and society as a whole. Chronicling three generations of the mundane Pargiter family, the novel presents an overview of England's upper middle class from the end of the nineteenth through the beginning of the twentieth century. True to Woolf's style, *The Years* lacks substantial action, but several critics applauded the book as a valuable exploration of both the evolution of modern society and the inner resources of the human personality. "Many people will wonder what on earth Mrs. Woolf is trying to say in so many uneventful pages. [But] the long last chapter plainly tells," surmised Olga Owens in the *Boston Transcript.* George Stevens, writing in *Saturday Review,* commented: "An expression of abstract experience, *The Years* is one of Mrs. Woolf's most brilliant achievements, written with imagination that is luminous and evocative."

Critical reaction to *The Years* was not entirely positive, though. The book was faulted by some for its seemingly slight and haphazard world view. Moody, for instance, deemed it "the least inspired . . . of Virginia Woolf's novels." Woolf herself had her doubts, as revealed in *A Writer's Diary,* about the importance of the work, but upon reading it in its entirety she produced this reassessment: "Seldom have I been more completely miserable than I was . . . reading over the last part of *The Years,*" she began. "Such feeble twaddle—such twilight gossip—it seemed; such a show up of my own decrepitude. . . . I could only plumb it down on the table and rush upstairs with burning cheeks to

L[eonard]. He said 'This always happens.' But I felt, No, it has never been so bad as this. I make this note should I be in the same state after another book. Now this morning, dipping in, it seems to me, on the contrary, a full, bustling live book."

But Woolf's feelings of anguish eventually returned. In an entry for January of 1941, as documented in *A Writer's Diary,* she resolved, "This trough of despair shall not, I swear, engulf me." Two months later, however, fearing that she lacked the stamina needed to recover from any further bouts of depression, Woolf filled her pockets with rocks and waded into the Ouse River. In her last note to Leonard, excerpted in *Virginia Woolf: A Biography,* she explained: "I am doing what seems the best thing to do. . . . If anybody could have saved me it would have been you. Everything has gone from me but the certainty of your goodness. I can't go on spoiling your life any longer. I don't think two people could have been happier than we have been."

Woolf's final novel, *Between the Acts,* was published in 1941, shortly after her death. The slim volume concerns an English family and their guests, all of whom gather one summer day in the country to watch a village pageant. The audience, however, lacks a commonality of spirit: the failure of the viewers to unite symbolizes the fragmentation of society. At the end of the pageant, the members of the audience go their own separate ways, absorbed by their own personal obsessions. *Between the Acts* received mixed reviews, and critics differed in their assessments of its meaning. Though not generally regarded as one of Woolf's major works, the posthumous novel is said to contain several unforgettably disturbing passages. David Cecil's *Spectator* review captured the critical consensus: "Perhaps had she lived to revise [*Between the Acts*], Mrs. Woolf would have brought it into clear pattern and harmony. As it is, it must be counted as in part a failure. But Mrs. Woolf's failures are more precious than most writers' successes."

In addition to her status as a novelist and short story writer, Woolf distinguished herself as both a critic and essayist with several impressive works of nonfiction, including *Mr. Bennett and Mrs. Brown, A Room of One's Own,* and *Three Guineas.* In *Mr. Bennett and Mrs. Brown,* Woolf attacks John Galsworthy, Arnold Bennett, and Wells—leading writers of the day—for their inability to capture a character's individuality in their works. *A Room of One's Own*—which Rebecca West in *Ending in Earnest: A Literary Log* deemed "an uncompromising piece of feminist propaganda: . . . the ablest yet written"—offers witty commentary on women and literature, and *Three Guineas* provides insightful political discourse on women and society. The keenness and precision with which Woolf articulates her opinions has made her nonfiction as valuable and enduring as her fiction.

Some critics have implied that Woolf's literary achievements are overrated and her lasting popularity undeserved. In his *Selected Essays,* for example, William Troy maintained: "What is so often regarded as unique in her fiction is actually less the result of an individual attitude than of the dominant metaphysical bias of a whole generation." A half century after her death, though, most observers maintain that Woolf's contributions to the development of the modern English novel are unrivalled. John Lehmann, in his piece for *English Critical Essays,* concluded: "The dazzling surface radiance of the world and a terror and despair always lurking beneath: nowhere in modern writing have these things found symbols more audacious and memorable than in the novel-poems of Virginia Woolf, so that one can truly say that she enlarged the sensibility of her time, and *changed* English literature."

MEDIA ADAPTATIONS: To the Lighthouse was adapted for a British film of the same title in 1983.

BIOGRAPHICAL/CRITICAL SOURCES:

BOOKS

Aiken, Conrad, *Collected Criticism,* Oxford University Press, 1968.
Bell, Quentin, *Virginia Woolf: A Biography,* Harcourt, 1972.
Blackstone, Bernard, *Virginia Woolf: A Commentary,* Hogarth, 1949.
Daiches, David, *The Novel and the Modern World,* revised edition, University of Chicago Press, 1960.
Daiches, David, *Virginia Woolf,* New Directions, 1963.
Dictionary of Literary Biography, Volume 36: *British Novelists, 1890-1929: Traditionalists,* Gale, 1985.
Forster, E. M., *Abinger Harvest,* Harcourt, 1936.
Forster, E. M., *Virginia Woolf,* Harcourt, 1942.
Ginden, James, *Harvest of a Quiet Eye: The Novel of Compassion,* Indiana University Press, 1971.
Gordon, Lyndall, *Virginia Woolf: A Writer's life,* Norton, 1984.
Hudson, Derek, editor, *English Critical Essays: Twentieth Century, Second Series,* Oxford University Press, 1958.
Johnson, Manly, *Virginia Woolf,* Ungar, 1973.
Majumdar, Robin and Allen McLaurin, editors, *Virginia Woolf: The Critical Heritage,* Routledge & Kegan Paul, 1975.
Moody, A. D., *Virginia Woolf,* Oliver & Boyd, 1963.
Naremore, James, *The World Without a Self: Virginia Woolf and the Novel,* Yale University Press, 1973.
Rosenbaum, S. P., *The Bloomsbury Group: A Collection of Memoirs, Commentary, and Criticism,* University of Toronto Press, 1975.
Seltzer, Alvin J., *Chaos in the Novel: The Novel in Chaos,* Schocken, 1974.
Spater, George and Ian Parsons, *A Marriage of True Minds: An Intimate Portrait of Leonard and Virginia Woolf,* Harcourt, 1978.
Sprague, Claire, *Virginia Woolf: A Collection of Critical Essays,* Prentice-Hall, 1971.
Troy, William, *William Troy: Selected Essays,* edited by Stanley Edgar Hyman, Rutgers University Press, 1967.
Twentieth-Century Literary Criticism, Gale, Volume 1, 1978, Volume 5, 1981, Volume 20, 1986.
West, Rebecca, *Ending in Earnest: A Literary Log,* Doubleday, 1931.
Woolf, Leonard, *Beginning Again: An Autobiography of the Years 1911-1918,* Harcourt, 1964.
Woolf, Leonard, *Downhill All the Way: An Autobiography of the Years 1919-1939,* Harcourt, 1967.
Woolf, Leonard, *The Journey Not the Arrival That Matters: An Autobiography of the Years 1939-1969,* Harcourt, 1970.
Woolf, Virginia, *Mrs. Dalloway,* Modern Library, 1928.
Woolf, Virginia, *A Writer's Diary,* edited by Leonard Woolf, New American Library, 1968.
Woolf, Virginia, *The Diary of Virginia Woolf,* Volume 3: *1925-1930,* Harcourt, 1983.

PERIODICALS

Boston Transcript, April 10, 1937.
Bulletin of the New York Public Library, winter, 1977.
English Studies, June, 1960.
Modern Fiction Studies, autumn, 1972, summer, 1979.
New Republic, January 3, 1981.
New Statesman and Nation, October 10, 1931.
New York Review of Books, April 20, 1978.
Renascence, autumn, 1965.

Saturday Review, April 10, 1937, February, 1982.
Spectator, November 11, 1922, July 18, 1941.
Springfield Republican, December 25, 1921.

OBITUARIES:

PERIODICALS

New York Herald Tribune, April 3, 1941.
Publishers Weekly, April 12, 1941.
Saturday Review of Literature, April 12, 1941.

*   *   *

WOUK, Herman 1915-

PERSONAL: Surname is pronounced "Woke"; born May 27, 1915, in New York, N.Y.; son of Abraham Isaac (an industrialist in the power laundry field who started as an immigrant laundry laborer at $3 a week) and Esther (Levine) Wouk; married Betty Sarah Brown, December 9, 1945; children: Abraham Isaac (deceased), Nathaniel, Joseph. *Education:* Columbia University, B.A. (with honors), 1934. *Religion:* Jewish.

ADDRESSES: Agent—BSW Literary Agency, 3255 N St. N.W., Washington, D.C. 20007.

CAREER: Gag writer for radio comedians, New York, N.Y., 1934-35; scriptwriter for Fred Allen, 1936-41; U.S. Treasury Department, "dollar-a-year-man," writing and producing radio plays to promote war bond sales, 1941; self-employed writer, 1946—. Visiting professor, Yeshiva University, 1953-57; scholar in residence, Aspen Institute of Humanistic Studies, 1973-74; lectured in China, 1982. Trustee, College of the Virgin Islands, 1962-69; member of board of directors, Washington National Symphony, 1969-71, and Kennedy Center Productions, 1974-75; member of advisory council, Center for U.S.-China Arts Exchange, 1981-87. *Military service:* U.S. Navy, 1942-46; served on Pacific Ocean aboard two destroyer-minesweepers, U.S.S. *Zane* and U.S.S. *Southard;* became lieutenant; received four campaign stars and Presidential Unit Citation.

MEMBER: Authors Guild, P.E.N., Dramatists Guild, Reserve Officers Association of the United States, Writers Guild of America East, Century Club (New York City), Bohemian Club (San Francisco); Cosmos Club, Metropolitan Club (both Washington, D.C.).

AWARDS, HONORS: Richard H. Fox Prize, 1934; Pulitzer Prize in fiction, 1952, for *The Caine Mutiny: A Novel of World War II;* Columbia University Medal of Excellence, 1952; L.H.D., Yeshiva University, 1955; LL.D., Clark University, 1960; Litt.D., American International University, 1979; Alexander Hamilton Medal, Columbia College Alumni Association, 1980; American Book Award nomination, 1981, for *War and Remembrance;* Ralph Waldo Emerson Award, International Platform Association, 1981; University of California—Berkeley Medal, 1984; Golden Plate Award, American Academy of Achievement, 1986; *Washingtonian* Book Award, 1986, for *Inside, Outside.*

WRITINGS:

Aurora Dawn; or, The True History of Andrew Reale, Containing a Faithful Account of the Great Riot, Together With the Complete Texts of Michael Wilde's Oration and Father Stanfield's Sermon (novel; Book-of-the-Month Club selection), Simon & Schuster, 1947, reprinted, Pocket Books, 1983.

The City Boy: The Adventures of Herbie Bookbinder and His Cousin, Cliff (novel; Reader's Digest Condensed Book Club selection; Family Book Club selection; Book-of-the-Month Club alternate selection), Simon & Schuster, 1948, published as *The City Boy,* Doubleday, 1952, published as *City Boy: The Adventures of Herbie Bookbinder,* Doubleday, 1969.

The Caine Mutiny: A Novel of World War II (Reader's Digest Condensed Book Club selection; Literary Guild alternate selection), Doubleday, 1951, reprinted, Franklin Library, 1977, published as *The Caine Mutiny,* Dell, 1966.

Marjorie Morningstar (novel; Reader's Digest Condensed Book Club selection; Book-of-the-Month Club selection), Doubleday, 1955, reprinted, Pocket Books, 1977.

This Is My God (nonfiction; Reader's Digest Condensed Book Club selection; Book-of-the-Month Club alternate selection), Doubleday, 1959, published as *This Is My God: The Jewish Way of Life,* 1970, revised edition, Collins, 1973.

Youngblood Hawke (novel; Reader's Digest Condensed Book Club selection; Book-of-the-Month Club selection), Doubleday, 1962.

Don't Stop the Carnival (novel; Book-of-the-Month Club selection), Doubleday, 1965.

The "Lomokome" Papers, Pocket Books, 1968.

The Winds of War (novel; Literary Guild selection; Reader's Digest Condensed Book Club selection), Little, Brown, 1971.

War and Remembrance (novel; sequel to *The Winds of War;* Literary Guild selection; Reader's Digest Condensed Book Club selection), Little, Brown, 1978.

Inside, Outside (novel; Book-of-the-Month Club selection), Little, Brown, 1985.

PLAYS

The Traitor (two-act; first produced on Broadway at Forty-Eighth Street Theater, April 4, 1949), Samuel French, 1949.

The Caine Mutiny Court-Martial (two-act; based on his novel *The Caine Mutiny;* first produced in Santa Barbara, Calif., 1953; produced on Broadway at Plymouth Theater, January 20, 1954), Doubleday, 1954, reprinted, Pocket Books, 1974.

Slattery's Hurricane (screenplay; produced by Twentieth Century-Fox, 1949), Permabooks, 1956.

Nature's Way (two-act comedy; first produced on Broadway at Coronet Theater, October 15, 1957), Doubleday, 1958, reprinted, Samuel French, 1977.

Also author of screenplay "The Winds of War," ABC-TV, 1983, and co-author of screenplay "War and Remembrance," ABC-TV, 1988.

SIDELIGHTS: An American novelist and playwright of Russian-Jewish heritage, Herman Wouk received the 1952 Pulitzer Prize in fiction for *The Caine Mutiny: A Novel of World War II* and has since published several other best-sellers, including *The Winds of War* and *War and Remembrance.* The *Atlantic*'s Edward Weeks calls him a compelling narrator "who uses large canvases and who, without much fuss for style or symbolism, drives his story ahead with an infectious belief in the people he is writing about." According to a reviewer for *Time,* Wouk's chief significance is that "he spearheads a mutiny against the literary stereotypes of rebellion—against three decades of U.S. fiction dominated by skeptical criticism, sexual emancipation, social protest, and psychoanalytic sermonizing." He remains, writes Pearl K. Bell in *Commentary,* "an unembarrassed believer in such 'discredited' forms of commitment as valor, gallantry, leadership, patriotism." Because of the reaffirmation of traditional values in his works, Wouk has enjoyed wide readership but has also been accused by some critics of pandering to popular prejudice.

Wouk began writing fiction in 1943 while on sea duty on the Pacific Ocean, and he later used his Navy experience aboard the U.S.S. *Zane* and U.S.S. *Southard* as background for his third novel, *The Caine Mutiny* (which is not autobiographical). The book is not concerned with battles at sea but with adherence to appointive authority. The conflict centers around Lieutenant Commander Philip Francis Queeg, who, according to W. J. Stuckey in *The Pulitzer Prize Novels,* "manifests a professional incompetence that will probably remain unparalleled in or out of fiction." When it appears that Queeg is too terrified to issue the necessary orders to save the ship during a typhoon, Lieutenant Maryk, the ship's executive officer, is persuaded by Lieutenant Keefer and his followers to seize control. Maryk is subsequently tried for making a mutiny but is acquitted through the efforts of Lieutenant Barney Greenwald, an adept trial lawyer. Ironically, at a party celebrating Maryk's acquittal, Greenwald tells Maryk that it is he, Maryk, (and not Queeg) who is morally guilty, for he deserted a military system that had, despite its flaws, protected America from foreign fascists.

Several critics consider Wouk's treatment of the military affair insightful and carefully constructed. Harry Gilroy, for example, writes in the *New York Times* that Wouk "has a profound understanding of what Navy men should be, and against some who fell short of the mark he has fired a deadly broadside." Edmund Fuller points out in his *Man in Modern Fiction* that the book's ability "to view the problem within the inescapable military premise without oversimplifying it" distinguishes *The Caine Mutiny* from other World War II novels. Discussing the justification of the mutiny in his *In My Opinion,* Orville Prescott says that it is "the crux of [the novel, and] Mr. Wouk develops it extremely well, with racy wit and genial humor, with lively pace and much ingenuity of incident and with unexpected subtlety." Similarly, a reviewer for the *Times Literary Supplement* concludes: "So convincingly has Mr. Wouk created his officers, so subtly has he contrived the series of incidents that culminate in the final drama, that, given both the characters and the situations, the climax is perfectly acceptable."

W. J. Stuckey, however, sees the climax as "the unwarranted whitewash" of Queeg: "Throughout three-fourths of the novel, Captain Queeg is a thoroughly incompetent and badly frightened man. However, toward the close of the book Wouk springs a wholly unprepared-for surprise: Queeg, he tells us, is not really the incompetent everyone thinks him; he is the victim of ambitious and cowardly subordinates. . . . While it is easy to understand the reason for Lieutenant Greenwald's emotional defense of the United States Navy, it is difficult to see why he—an intelligent trial lawyer, we are told—defends an incompetent American ship's captain who had not served in the Atlantic and who, if he had encountered Nazi warships, would have fled in terror. Greenwald's only defense of Queeg is that he was a member of the regular navy. It would make as much sense to defend a doctor guilty of malpractice on the grounds that he engaged in a humane calling. . . . The war in Europe and Hitler's treatment of the Jews had nothing to do with Queeg's or Maryk's innocence or guilt."

Eric Bentley finds the same weakness in "The Caine Mutiny Court Martial," Wouk's play based on the court martial sequence of the novel. Discussing the theme that the important thing is not to save a particular ship but to preserve the authority of commanders, Bentley writes in the *New Republic:* "There is a good point here, and there must surely be a good play in it—a play that would show up the sentimentality of our prejudice against commanders and in favor of mutineers. If, however, Mr. Wouk wanted to write such a play, he chose the wrong story and told it in the wrong way, for we spend three quarters of the evening hoping that Queeg—the commander—will be found insane and the mutineers vindicated. When, in the very last scene, Mr. Wouk explains that this is not the right way to take the story, it is too late. We don't believe him. At best we say that he is preaching at us a notion that ought to have been dramatized. And no amount of shock technique—not even the reiterated image of Jews melted down for soap—can conceal the flaw."

Marjorie Morningstar, Wouk's fourth novel, also focuses on rebellion but in a civilian context. The book traces the life of a beautiful, intelligent girl who renounces the values and authority of her hard-working Jewish parents only to end up, years later, affirming them as a suburban matron and community servant. E. W. Foell notes in the *Christian Science Monitor* that Wouk "has not flinched at what he sees in his characters' thoughts, [but] many of his readers are likely to." A *Time* critic writes that, indeed, "Wouk [sets] teeth on edge by advocating chastity before marriage, suggesting that real happiness for a woman is found in a home and children, cheering loud and long for the American middle class and blasting Bohemia and Bohemians. Wouk is a Sinclair Lewis in reverse." Reviewing the book in the *New York Times,* Maxwell Geismar believes that "here as in *The Caine Mutiny* [the conflict] is settled by a final bow to the red-tape of a bureaucracy or to the properties of a social class, under the impression that these are among the eternal verities. *Marjorie Morningstar* is very good reading indeed. But to this reviewer at least the values of true culture are as remote from its polished orbit as are, at base, the impulses of real life."

Leslie A. Fiedler, however, sees the most popular novel of 1955 as untraditional in one regard. In *Love and Death in the American Novel,* Fiedler calls *Marjorie Morningstar* "the first fictional celebration of the mid-twentieth-century detente between the Jews and middle-class America." He explains: "In the high literature of Europe and, more slowly, in that of the United States, gentile and Jew have joined forces to portray the Jewish character as a figure representing man's fate in . . . an age of rootlessness, alienation, and terror, in which the exiled condition so long thought peculiar to the Jew comes to seem the common human lot. This is neither a cheery nor a reassuring view. . . . Wouk [suggests] a counterview: the contention that the Jew was never (or is, at least, no longer) the rootless dissenter, the stranger which legend has made him, but rather the very paragon of the happy citizen at home, loyal, chaste, thrifty, pious, and moderately successful—in short, Marjorie Morningstar."

After *Marjorie Morningstar,* Wouk interrupted his career as a novelist to write a short, clear account of the Jewish faith from a personal viewpoint—something he had been thinking of doing for years. Dedicated to the memory of his grandfather, Mendel Leib Levine, a rabbi from Minsk, *This Is My God* was published in 1959 and became a best-seller. Then, with *Youngblood Hawke* and *Don't Stop the Carnival,* Wouk returned to writing fiction, but he also began work on a second ambition: a panoramic novel of World War II.

Wouk first considered doing a global war novel in 1944, according to *Time*'s Timothy Foote. Later, *The Caine Mutiny* "threatened to sprawl in that direction," notes Foote, "with more home-front material and a subplot in Europe. Wisely, Wouk cut it back and waited." Having begun reading standard histories in 1962, Wouk moved to Washington two years later to utilize the National Archives and Library of Congress, as well as to interview surviving military leaders. His quest for information also led him to England, France, Italy, Germany, Poland, Czechoslovakia, Israel, Iran, and the Soviet Union. Due to the scope of his task, Wouk ended up writing not one but two novels: *The Winds of War* and a sequel, *War and Remembrance.* "Since both have been best sellers, it is likely that more Americans have learned about, or remembered, the war through Wouk's account than from any other single source in the last decade," claims Michael Mandelbaum in *Political Science Quarterly.*

Generally praised by critics for their depth and accuracy of detail, the two books may be described as the history of the Second World War seen through the eyes of an American family and their immediate friends and contacts. *The Winds of War* takes Commander Victor "Pug" Henry and his family from the invasion of Poland to the attack on Pearl Harbor, Hawaii, and *War and Remembrance* details their experiences from Pearl Harbor to the dropping of the atomic bomb on Hiroshima, Japan. Over the course of the war, Henry serves as a special presidential envoy; meets Hitler, Stalin, Churchill, and Mussolini; is in Hawaii the day after the attack on Pearl Harbor; is present at the summit meetings off Nova Scotia in 1940 and in Tehran in 1943; is in London during the Battle of Britain; accompanies the Harriman-Beaverbrook mission to Moscow in 1941; participates in the battles of Midway, Guadalcanal, and Leyte Gulf; tours the Russian front in 1944; and even comes in contact with people working on the Manhattan Project. What he fails to witness, members of his family see: the invasion of Poland, the war in North Africa, the fall of Singapore, and the horrors of Auschwitz.

In reviewing the two books, critics often point out that this technique of depicting the effects of war on ordinary people (some of whom rub shoulders with the high and mighty) is a familiar one. Timothy Foote, among others, suggests that Wouk's opus is reminiscent of *War and Peace*—though not of the same quality—and that Wouk's aim is "nothing less than to do for the middle-class American vision of World War II pretty much what [Leo] Tolstoy did for the Battle of Borodino." More often, however, reviewers like Granville Hicks of the *New York Times Book Review* cite the resemblance between "Pug" Henry and Upton Sinclair's Lanny Budd: "Like Lanny, Pug becomes a kind of secret Presidential agent. In this role, he turns up at most of the places where history is being made."

Several critics charge that the technique results in characterization that is purely functional. Though Hicks admits that Wouk has "the gift of compelling narrative," he feels that the characters in *The Winds of War,* "even Pug Henry, are never living human beings. Although [Wouk] tries to give these men and women some semblance of reality by involving them in more or less complicated love affairs, they remain essentially observers and reporters." Similarly, Pearl K. Bell, reviewing *War and Remembrance* in *Commentary,* describes the characters as "not merely trivial but offensively so. Time and again, Wouk the student of history writes a brilliantly evocative account of battle—he has mastered every maneuver, knows exactly how submarines, aircraft carriers, battleships, destroyers, dive bombers work, how the vast machinery of war was deployed during a particular operation—only to return with a dismaying thump to his super-Lanny Budd hero, Captain (eventually Admiral) Victor (Pug) Henry." Foote is willing "to forgive Henry, and the author, the narrative necessities that shoot [Henry] hither and yon and miraculously equip him with the Russian and German necessary to do his work for Wouk, F.D.R., and the reader. [But] not so the other Henrys. The wife who would worry about getting her hair done on the day of Armageddon, a wayward daughter caught up in the sleazy radio industry in New York, two

naval-officer sons, all are conventional appurtenances, without the emotional or dynastic depth to support a drama on the scale of World War II."

Nevertheless, Michael Mandelbaum asserts that Wouk's aim was to create something not purely fictional and that his "hybrid literary genre" of historical romance "turns out to be singularly appropriate." Other critics agree. Reviewing *The Winds of War* in the *Midwest Quarterly,* Richard R. Bolton writes: "Critics who have castigated the book for failing in various ways as a *novel* have seemingly overlooked the author's description of it as a romance. That form is older, and adheres to rather different standards, than the novel. Much criticism directed at the book's emphasis of incident and plot over deep character development, or its unfashionably detailed descriptions of people's appearances, becomes immaterial if one accepts Wouk's idea of what *The Winds of War* is—a historical romance, with a didactic purpose. That purpose is to dramatize the author's ideas about his themes—how the 'curse' emerged, how we might constructively understand it, and how 'men of good will' have been involved with it."

A major theme of the two books, according to Mandelbaum, "centers on the German question. Why did the Germans do it? Why did they cause so much trouble? Why, especially, did they behave in such brutal, aggressive fashion? These questions arise again and again, and Wouk has different characters give different answers—[geopolitical, political, cultural, historical]. Together they make for a symposium on the central puzzle of the twentieth century." Mandelbaum suggests that at the heart of the German question is the fate of the Jews under the Third Reich, the description of which "gives the two books their enduring message, a message that neither plain fiction nor standard history could convey as forcefully. It is not, [however,] the only, nor perhaps the primary, message that the author intends."

Wouk widens the scope of the story by presenting a German perspective on the war through excerpts of General Armin von Roon's *World Empire Lost,* an imaginary treatise based on actual writings of German generals. Bolton claims that von Roon's views, "and (in places) Henry's 'later' comments on them, jolt the reader out of enough preconceptions to make him more receptive to Wouk's own explanations of why things turned out as they did, or (more important) *how* they might have been made to turn out better." Bolton surmises that, according to Wouk, World War II was a "natural" disaster in that it arose from fallible human nature: "Human cruelty, of which war is the most massive and spectacular manifestation, occurs not because most people are cruel, but because most people are weak or lazy, or too wishful to perceive in time what truly cruel people like the Nazis are about. . . . Given that fallibility, World War II, and possibly other wars since, probably could not have been avoided." But, he continues, "given also the availability of enough men with the training and virtues of Victor Henry—the truly 'best' in Wouk's view, those who do not lack conviction—that war, and possibly others since, could have been ameliorated, at least. It was not ameliorated, because democratic societies, notably ours, have little stomach for the unpleasant facts that are a military professional's daily fare."

Thus, Bolton discerns a thematic relation to *The Caine Mutiny:* "Captain Henry can be seen as the fulfillment and justification of Lt. Barney Greenwald's unexpected and much discussed encomium to Regular Navy officers in the post-trial scene of *The Caine Mutiny.* Greenwald pays his tributes not so much to the *Caine's* fallen captain as to what-Queeg-could-have-been . . .—the selfless and dedicated guardian of a reckless and unappreciative nation's safety. In Henry, Wouk presents a man who really *is* what Queeg could only try, pretend, or fail to be, the 'compleat' and admirable United States Navy officer." Pearl K. Bell believes that Wouk's traditionalist support of the military career man will strike many "as at best naive, at worst absurdly out of touch with the Catch-22 lunacy of all war, including the war against Hitler. [However,] it is precisely to confute such facile and ahistorical cynicism that Wouk devotes so large and sober a part of his novel to the Final Solution and the ideological poison that overwhelmed the German people during Hitler's twelve years of power."

In Wouk's eyes, men like Victor Henry, writes Bolton, have instincts and habits that "predispose them to be builders and preservers. . . . 'Constructive' rather than creative, they build things that are not particularly original, but are for Wouk the cement of civilization—families, homes, churches, firms, and especially, professional reputations. What repels Capt. Henry first about Nazi racism is that it destroys these things, and judges men on factors other than their accomplishments. Only after learning of the *Einsatzgruppen*'s atrocities does he react to Nazi racism with more visceral rage." Referring to the one-word Hebrew epigraph of *The Winds of War,* "Remember!," Bolton concludes: "Part of remembering, in Wouk's sense, would be to emulate Victor Henry and to listen, early and attentively, to those men who live in his tradition. If we do not, the author suggests, . . . it becomes too easy to look away, to make excuses while the massacres begin, while terrorism becomes pardonable."

Wouk's 1985 novel, *Inside, Outside,* "comes as close to being an outright autobiography as he is likely to write," declares John Eisenhower in the *Chicago Tribune Book World.* It tells of a Jewish man who, like Wouk, was born in New York City in 1915, the son of immigrant parents who established a commercial laundry business. Like Wouk, protagonist Israel David Goodkind—"Yisroelke" to his friends and family on the "inside"—worked as a gag writer, although Goodkind becomes a lawyer rather than a novelist. Goodkind is, however, writing his memoirs, which transforms Wouk's novel into "a paean to the American Jewish experience," according to *Diversion* contributor Sybil S. Steinberg. Unifying the novel, which deals by turns with Goodkind's present reality as a speech writer for U.S. President Richard Nixon and with Goodkind's childhood and relatives, is the tension between the "inside" (which includes Jewish religious life, values, and heritage as well as the search for identity for Jew or gentile) and the "outside" (secular American life).

The novel—Wouk's first in seven years—has received mixed reviews. Critics such as Steinberg praise the "breezy, humorous style" in which it is written and cite its compassion and wisdom. Writes Eisenhower, it is "an easy-to-read, informative tale that . . . provides an enlightening perspective on Jewish attitudes." He singles out one scene in which "Jews of varying persuasions . . . exchange views and insults" and concludes that "that scene alone, which illuminates so much of the current Jewish dilemma, gives this novel the right to be regarded as Wouk's most significant work since 'The Caine Mutiny.' " In contrast, Christopher Lehmann-Haupt of the *New York Times* finds the novel "remarkably predictable" and, "worst of all, . . . smug." Others criticize the book for superficiality and express reservations about what Bill Wine in the *Philadelphia Inquirer* deems "the failure of Wouk's storytelling proclivities to break out. The narrative, though carefully wrought, somehow registers as out of kilter, as if the seemingly appropriate admixture of memories, insights, observations and descriptions were really a convenience embraced by a writer unable to find a handle on his material." Nonetheless, Wine approvingly concludes that, "on the whole,

Inside, Outside is an entertaining X-ray of Being Jewish in America." Novelist James Michener, reviewing the book in the *New York Times Book Review,* judges it "ambitious," lauding its segments as "compact, beautifully focused and often hilarious." Among the critics who acknowledge faults, several, like Steinberg, still maintain that "the universality of [the] theme . . . lifts this novel above the level of inbred American Jewish experience. For *Inside, Outside* is about anyone who must reconcile private and public commitments. It is about living a good life on many levels, and while it makes no pretension of being profound, it is funny, wise, and kind."

MEDIA ADAPTATIONS: The Caine Mutiny was filmed by Columbia in 1954, starring Humphrey Bogart as Captain Queeg; *The City Boy* was made into a motion picture by Columbia in 1950; Warner Bros. filmed *Marjorie Morningstar* and *Youngblood Hawke* in 1958 and 1964, respectively. A television adaptation of "The Caine Mutiny Court Martial," with Barry Sullivan, Lloyd Nolan, and Frank Lovejoy, aired on "Ford Star Jubilee" in 1955; *The Winds of War* and *War and Remembrance* were adapted as television miniseries airing on ABC-TV in 1983 and 1988, respectively.

AVOCATIONAL INTERESTS: Judaic scholarship, Zionist studies, travel (especially in Israel).

BIOGRAPHICAL/CRITICAL SOURCES:

BOOKS

Beichman, Arnold C., *Herman Wouk: The Novelist as Social Historian,* Transaction Books, 1984.
Bentley, Eric, *The Dramatic Event: An American Chronicle,* Horizon Press, 1954.
Contemporary Literary Criticism, Gale, Volume 1, 1973, Volume 9, 1978, Volume 38, 1986.
Dictionary of Literary Biography Yearbook: 1982, Gale, 1983.
Fiedler, Leslie A., *Love and Death in the American Novel,* Stein & Day, 1966.
Fuller, Edmund, *Man in Modern Fiction: Some Minority Opinions on Contemporary American Writing,* Random House, 1958.
Geismar, Maxwell, *American Moderns From Rebellion to Conformity,* Hill & Wang, 1958.
Hyman, Stanley Edgar, *Standards: A Chronicle of Books for Our Time,* Horizon Press, 1966.
Prescott, Orville, *In My Opinion,* Bobbs-Merrill, 1952.
Stuckey, W. J., *The Pulitzer Prize Novels,* University of Oklahoma Press, 1966.

PERIODICALS

Antioch Review, Volume 16, 1956.
Atlantic, August, 1951, October, 1955, December, 1971.
Book Week, March 7, 1965.
Boston Sunday Globe, March 24, 1985.
Chicago Sunday Tribune, March 18, 1951.
Chicago Tribune, February 6, 1983, September 12, 1988.
Chicago Tribune Book World, November 14, 1971, March 24, 1985.
Christian Science Monitor, September 1, 1955, September 24, 1959, May 24, 1962, October 23, 1978.
College English, Volume 17, 1956.
Commentary, December, 1978.
Critic, August, 1965.
Detroit Free Press, February 6, 1983, April 7, 1985.
Detroit News, January 24, 1985.
Diversion, May, 1985.
Economist, November 20, 1971.

Globe and Mail (Toronto), June 15, 1985.
Life, June, 1962, November 19, 1971.
Los Angeles Times Book Review, March 3, 1985, May 8, 1986.
Midwest Quarterly, July, 1975.
New Republic, February 15, 1954, September 3, 1955, June 11, 1962, October 14, 1978.
Newsweek, March 9, 1965, November 29, 1971, October 9, 1978, February 7, 1983.
New York, August 30, 1971.
New York Herald Tribune Book Review, March 18, 1951, September 4, 1955, May 20, 1962.
New York Herald Tribune Weekly Book Review, April 20, 1947, August 29, 1948.
New York Times, April 20, 1947, August 29, 1948, March 18, 1951, September 4, 1955, September 27, 1959, January 2, 1983, January 21, 1983, January 30, 1983, February 5, 1983, February 6, 1983, March 7, 1985.
New York Times Book Review, September 16, 1951, May 20, 1962, November 14, 1971, November 12, 1978, March 10, 1985.
Parade, February 6, 1983.
Partisan Review, Volume 20, 1953.
Philadelphia Inquirer, April 14, 1985.
Publishers Weekly, February 7, 1972.
San Francisco Chronicle, March 24, 1985.
Saturday Review, February 6, 1954, September 3, 1955, September 26, 1959, May 19, 1962, November 27, 1971.
Saturday Review of Literature, April 19, 1947, August 21, 1948, March 31, 1951.
Time, April 9, 1951, September 5, 1955, May 18, 1962, March 5, 1965, November 22, 1971, October 16, 1978, February 7, 1983, February 28, 1983, April 1, 1985.
Times (London), March 2, 1985.
Times Literary Supplement, November 9, 1951.
USA Today, March 22, 1985.
Vogue, February 15, 1952.
Washingtonian, March, 1986.
Washington Post, April 29, 1985, May 31, 1986.
Washington Post Book World, October 8, 1978, March 10, 1985.

* * *

WRIGHT, Charles (Penzel, Jr.) 1935-

PERSONAL: Born August 25, 1935, in Hardin County, Tenn.; son of Charles Penzel and Mary Castleman (Winter) Wright; married Holly McIntire, April 6, 1969; children: Luke Savin Herrick. *Education:* Davidson College, B.A., 1957; University of Iowa, M.F.A., 1963; graduate study, University of Rome, 1963-64.

ADDRESSES: Home—940 Locust Ave., Charlottesville, Va. 22901. *Office*—Department of English, University of Virginia, Charlottesville, Va. 22903.

CAREER: University of California, Irvine, 1966-83, began as assistant professor, became professor of English; affiliated with University of Virginia, Charlottesville, 1983—. Fulbright lecturer in Venice, Italy, 1968-69. *Military service:* U.S. Army, Intelligence Corps, 1957-61.

MEMBER: PEN American Center.

AWARDS, HONORS: Fulbright scholar at University of Rome, 1963-65; Eunice Tietjens Award, *Poetry* magazine, 1969; Guggenheim fellow, 1975; Melville Cane Award, Poetry Society of America, and Edgar Allan Poe Award, Academy of American Poets, both 1976, both for *Bloodlines;* Academy-Institute

Award, American Academy and Institute of the Arts, 1977; PEN translation award, 1978; Ingram Merrill fellow, 1980; runner-up for Pulitzer Prize in poetry, 1982, for *The Southern Cross;* American Book Award in poetry (shared with Galway Kinnell), 1983, for *Country Music/Selected Early Poems;* National Book Critics Circle award nomination in poetry, 1984, for *The Other Side of the River.*

WRITINGS:

POETRY

The Dream Animal (chapbook), House of Anansi (Toronto), 1968.
Private Madrigals, limited edition, Abraxas, 1969.
The Grave of the Right Hand, Wesleyan University Press, 1970.
The Venice Notebook, Barn Dream Press, 1971.
Hard Freight, Wesleyan University Press, 1973.
Bloodlines, Wesleyan University Press, 1975.
China Trace, Wesleyan University Press, 1977.
Colophons, limited edition, Windhover, 1977.
Wright: A Profile, with interview and critical essay by David St. John, Grilled Flowers Press, 1979.
Dead Color, limited edition, Meadow Press (San Francisco, Calif.), 1980.
The Southern Cross, Random House, 1981.
Country Music/Selected Early Poems, Wesleyan University Press, 1982.
Four Poems of Departure, limited edition, Trace Editions, 1983.
The Other Side of the River, Random House, 1984.
Five Journals, limited edition, Red Ozier Press, 1986 (also see below).
Zone Journals (includes *Five Journals*), Farrar, Straus, 1988.

Also author of *Six Poems,* 1965.

OTHER

(Translator) Eugenio Montale, *The Storm,* Field Editions, 1978.
(Translator) Montale, *Motets,* Windhover, 1981.
(Translator) Dino Campana, *Orphic Songs,* Field Editions, 1984.
Halflife: Improvisations and Interviews, 1977-1987, University of Michigan Press, 1988.

Also author of *The Voyage,* 1963, and *Backwater,* 1973.

SIDELIGHTS: Charles Wright's reputation has increased steadily with each poetry collection he has published. Today, he is widely regarded as one of the most important poets living in the United States. From his early collection *The Grave of the Right Hand* to more recent books, such as *The Southern Cross* and *The Other Side of the River,* Wright has worked in a style which creates a feeling of immediacy and concreteness by emphasizing objects and personal perspective. Many critics believe that Wright's youth in rural Tennessee remains a vital force in his writing, for he shows a typically Southern concern for the past and its power. He began writing poetry while serving in Italy with the U.S. Army. While there he "began using Ezra Pound's Italian Cantos first as a guide book to out-of-the-way places, then as a reference book and finally as a 'copy' book," quotes *Dictionary of Literary Biography Yearbook: 1982* essayist George F. Butterick.

Ezra Pound's influence is obvious in *The Grave of the Right Hand,* Wright's first major collection. These poems "have the polished clarity one would expect from a master of the plain style," *Georgia Review* contributor Peter Stitt observes. "They are obviously meant to speak to the reader, to communicate something he can share." At the same time, *The Grave of the Right Hand* is the most symbolic of all Wright's works, with images of gloves, shoes, hands, and hats recurring throughout. Through these images, the poet introduces themes that recur in all his later work, described by Butterick as "mortality, the uses of memory, the irrepressible past, states of being, personal salvation, the correspondence between nature and the spiritual work, and, most broadly, the human condition."

Wright is credited with finding his own voice in *Hard Freight,* which Peter Meinke calls in a *New Republic* review "less Poundian, less hard-edged, than his first book, *The Grave of the Right Hand.*" John L. Carpenter praises Wright for reaching for his own style in a *Poetry* review of *Hard Freight:* "It is less incisive and less deliberate than the first book, but it is more experimental, less ironclad and defensive." It is in this volume that the poet first exhibits his technique of creating poetry by compiling catalogs of fragmented images. It is a device which requires "that the reader assist in the creative activity," finds *Washington Post Book World* contributor Edward Kessler. "[Wright's] almost spastic writing can at times be enlivening and fascinating, like watching the changing fragments of a kaleidoscope." But this technique is not praised by all critics. Some find it excessive, including Sally M. Gall, who protests in *Shenandoah:* "He frantically piles up details, images, similes, and metaphors as if sheer quantity can replace quality of perception. His catalogues can be perniciously boring rather than enlightening." Kessler disagrees: "His senses are awake, and even when he cannot quite bring his *things* of the world into a satisfying shape, his fragments are rife with suggestions. This man is feeling his way toward a personal definition."

Bloodlines continues in the same vein as *Hard Freight,* but many reviewers feel that Wright's voice is even stronger in this volume, including J. D. McClatchy, who writes in *Yale Review,* "Charles Wright has come completely home in *Bloodlines,* a book that confirms and emphasizes his reputation." Carol Muske also notes the power of this collection in *Parnassus: Poetry in Review:* "[Wright] is on the move. His poems fairly explode from the page in hurly-burly refrain, elliptical syntax, and giddy shifts that recall Hopkins." McClatchy adds, "He recreates not aspects but images of his past experiences—prayer meetings, sexual encounters, dreams—mingling memory and fantasy. The poems are suffused with remembered light."

Hard Freight, Bloodlines, and *China Trace* comprise what Wright thinks of as a trilogy of poetry collections. Explains Kathleen Agena in *Partisan Review,* "Like Wallace Stevens, Wright has conceived of his work as a whole. Individual poems are arresting but none of them quite has its meaning alone. The poems elucidate and comment on each other, extending and developing certain key metaphors and images." In *China Trace,* Wright again considers universal connections to the past. According to Butterick, the poet describes this collection as "a book of Chinese poems that don't sound like Chinese poems and aren't Chinese poems but are *like* Chinese poems in the sense that they give you an idea of one man's relationship to the endlessness, the ongoingness, the everlastingness of what's around him, and his relationship to it as he stands in the natural world."

Agena contends that Wright's power comes from his faith in "the mad sense of language" and his willingness to abandon himself to it. She summarizes: "When Charles Wright's poems work, which is most of the time, the poetic energies seem to break the membrane of syntax, exploding the surface, reverberating in multiple directions simultaneously. It is not a linear progression one finds but rather a ricocheting, as if, at the impact of a single cue, all the words bounced into their pockets, rearranged, and displaced themselves in different directions all over again. And it seems to happen by accident, as if Wright simply sets the words in motion and they, playing a game according to their own rules, write the poem."

BIOGRAPHICAL/CRITICAL SOURCES:

BOOKS

Contemporary Authors, Autobiography Series, Volume 7, Gale, 1988.
Contemporary Literary Criticism, Gale, Volume 6, 1976, Volume 13, 1980, Volume 28, 1984.
Dictionary of Literary Biography Yearbook: 1982, Gale, 1983.
Friebert, Stuart and David Young, editors, *A Field Guide to Contemporary Poetry and Poetics,* Longman, 1980.

PERIODICALS

American Poetry Review, September/October, 1982.
Antioch Review, spring, 1982.
Choice, September, 1976.
Georgia Review, summer, 1978, spring, 1982.
Hudson Review, spring, 1974, autumn, 1975.
Los Angeles Times Book Review, February 7, 1982.
Michigan Quarterly Review, fall, 1978.
New Republic, November 24, 1973, November 26, 1977.
New Yorker, October 29, 1979.
New York Times Book Review, February 17, 1974, September 7, 1975, December 12, 1982, July 1, 1984, September 4, 1988.
Parnassus: Poetry in Review, spring-summer, 1976.
Partisan Review, Volume 43, number 4, 1976.
Poetry, December, 1974, December, 1978.
Sewanee Review, spring, 1974.
Shenandoah, fall, 1974.
Times Literary Supplement, March 1, 1985.
Washington Post Book World, May 5, 1974.
Yale Review, autumn, 1975.

*   *   *

WRIGHT, James (Arlington) 1927-1980

PERSONAL: Born December 13, 1927, in Martins Ferry, Ohio; died of cancer, March 25, 1980, in New York, N.Y.; married second wife, Edith Anne Runk, 1967; children: (first marriage) Franz Paul, Marshall John. *Education:* Kenyon College, B.A., 1952; University of Washington, M.A., 1954, Ph.D., 1959; also studied with John Crowe Ransom and Theodore Roethke.

ADDRESSES: Home—466 Lexington Ave., 13th Floor, New York, N.Y. 10017. *Office*—Department of English, Hunter College of the City University of New York, New York, N.Y. 10021.

CAREER: Poet and translator; instructor in English at University of Minnesota, Minneapolis, 1957-64, and Macalester College, St. Paul, Minn., 1963-65; Hunter College of the City University of New York, New York, N.Y., professor of English, 1966-80. Visiting lecturer, State University of New York at Buffalo, 1974. *Military service:* U.S. Army, during World War II.

MEMBER: Academy of American Poets (fellow).

AWARDS, HONORS: Fulbright fellow in Austria, 1952-53; Eunice Tietjens Memorial Prize, 1955, and Oscar Blumenthal Award, 1968, both from *Poetry;* Yale Series of Younger Poets award, 1957, for *The Green Wall; Kenyon Review* fellowship in poetry, 1958; National Institute of Arts and Letters grant in literature, 1959; Ohiona Book Award, 1960, for *Saint Judas;* Guggenheim fellowship, 1964 and 1978; Creative Arts Award, Brandeis University, 1970; Academy of American Poets fellowship,

1971; Melville Cane Award, Poetry Society of America, 1972; Pulitzer Prize in poetry, 1972, for *Collected Poems.*

WRITINGS:

POETRY

The Green Wall, Yale University Press, 1957.
Saint Judas, Wesleyan University Press, 1959.
(With William Duffy and Robert Bly) *The Lion's Tail and Eyes: Poems Written Out of Laziness and Silence,* Sixties Press, 1962.
The Branch Will Not Break, Wesleyan University Press, 1963.
Shall We Gather at the River, Wesleyan University Press, 1968.
Collected Poems, Wesleyan University Press, 1971.
Two Citizens, Farrar, Straus, 1973.
I See the Wind, Brandea, 1974.
Old Booksellers and Other Poems, Cotswold Press, 1976.
Moments of the Italian Summer, Dryad, 1976.
To a Blossoming Pear Tree, Farrar, Straus, 1978.
This Journey, Random House, 1982.
The Temple in Nimes, Metacom Press, 1982.

Also author of *Salt Mines and Such,* 1971, and *The Shape of Light: Prose Poems,* White Pine. Work represented in anthologies, including *Poems on Poetry,* edited by Robert Wallace and J. G. Taaffe, Dutton, 1965; *An Introduction to Poetry,* edited by Louis Simpson, St. Martin's, 1967; *Heartland,* edited by Lucien Stryk, Northern Illinois University Press, 1967; and *Poems of Our Moment,* edited by John Hollander, Pegasus, 1968.

TRANSLATOR, EXCEPT AS NOTED

(With Bly) *Twenty Poems of Georg Trakl,* Sixties Press, 1961.
(With Bly and John Knoepfle) *Twenty Poems of Cesar Vallejo,* Sixties Press, 1962.
Theodor Storm, *The Rider on the White Horse,* New American Library, 1964.
(With Bly) *Twenty Poems of Pablo Neruda,* Sixties Press, 1968.
(And editor) Hermann Hesse, *Poems,* Farrar, Straus, 1970.
(With Bly and Knoepfle) *Neruda and Vallejo: Selected Poems,* Beacon Press, 1971.
Hesse, *Wandering: Notes and Sketches,* Farrar, Straus, 1972.
(Editor) *Winter's Tales Twenty-Two,* St. Martin's, 1977.

OTHER

The Poetry and Voice of James Wright (recording), Caedmon, 1977.
Collected Prose, edited by Anne Wright, University of Michigan Press, 1982.
James Wright: A Profile, limited edition, edited by Frank Graziano and Peter Stitt, Logbridge-Rhodes, 1988.

Also author of *The Summers of James and Annie Wright,* 1980, and *With the Delicacy and Strength of Lace: Letters Between Leslie Marmon Silko and Wright,* edited by Anne Wright, 1986. Also recorded, with others, *Today's Poets Three,* for Folkways. Contributor to *Hudson Review, Kenyon Review, Sewanee Review, Western Review, Yale Review, Harper's, Poetry, Frescoe, New Poets of England and America, Paris Review, London Magazine, Botteghe Obscure, New Yorker, Minnesota Review, Big Table, Audience, Nation,* and other publications.

SIDELIGHTS: James Wright was frequently referred to as one of America's finest contemporary poets. He was admired by critics and fellow poets alike for his willingness and ability to experiment with language and style, as well as for his thematic concerns. In the *Minnesota Review,* Peter A. Stitt wrote that Wright's work both represents and parallels the development of the best modern American poets: "Reading the *Collected Poems* of James Wright from the point of view of style is like reading a history of the best contemporary American poetry. One discovers a development which could be said to parallel the development generally of our finest recent poets. . . . [This development shows] a movement generally away from rhetoric, regular meter and rhyme, towards plainer speech, looser rhythms and few rhymes."

Wright's early poems, especially those in his first two volumes, are "too literary, too subservient to the poems and poets of the past," according to Stitt. Other critics noted the elaborate rhymes, complex rhetoric, and traditional use of imagery in these early efforts. As Wright began to experiment "he loosened his forms" and "whittled rhetoric to a succession of intense perceptions," Laurence Goldstein explained in the *Michigan Quarterly Review.* The result was that his speech became more natural and his settings, Marjorie G. Perloff reported in *Contemporary Literature,* "are dream images rather than actual places." Paul Zweig of the *Partisan Review* outlined the impact of Wright's later style: "Long before [he was awarded the Pulitzer Prize], Wright had been acknowledged by a generation of poets as the artisan of a new language for poetry: A style of pastoral surrealism, built around strong images and a simple spoken rhetoric. Wright's art lay not in complex grammar, but in a stark structure of perceptions which became their own statement."

Although Wright experimented with style and language, his themes—loneliness and alienation—remained constant. "Perhaps the most pervasive general theme in Wright's poetry . . . is that of separation," Stitt suggested. "Separation appears in two guises—as the result of death and as the result of being at odds with one's society." James Seay, writing in the *Georgia Review,* agreed and elaborated: "His most abiding concern has been loneliness. It is the one abstract word that recurs most frequently in his work. In a sense the theme of loneliness gives rise to, or is somehow connected with, most of Wright's other thematic concerns." The critic named death and "Wright's compassion for what Auden . . . called 'social outsiders'—criminals, prostitutes, drunks, and social outcasts in general" as the poet's other concerns. Seay continued, "In Wright's poems these people are almost always lonely and damned."

Eric Pace of the *New York Times* once noted that while "the mood of the poet was sometimes very dark, . . . one of his great strengths . . . was the life-affirming quality of his work." Edward Butscher of the *Georgia Review* contended that a "pattern" of despair followed by celebration ran throughout Wright's work. "Despair and celebration, ritual damnation and ritual salvation," Butscher observed, "the agony of human existence miraculously made bearable by nature's . . . eloquence." In a *Washington Post Book World* review of *Two Citizens,* Perloff further explained Wright's view of nature and salvation, stating that "his poems . . . usually present the poet in a specific midwestern locale, contemplating a landscape which seems wholly alien until a sudden gesture or change in perspective momentarily unites poet and nature, self and other, in a muted epiphany."

For the most part, *The Branch Will Not Break* is considered the watershed of Wright's career. Stitt called it "Wright's happiest book" and noted that "the book's title indicates its major affirmation—the faith that nature will endure and continue to sustain man." Moreover, Cor van den Heuvel in *MOSAIC* praised the "great advance in technical proficiency [and the] dazzling blossoming of images." Zweig termed it "one of the key books of the 1960s." Seay offered a similar appraisal: "I cannot recall experiencing anything like that keen sense of discovery which I felt in reading *The Branch Will Not Break*. . . . What Wright offered in [that book], as far as I could tell, was unlike anything being written in America at the time."

One criticism aimed at Wright's poetry was that it lacks discipline. Roger Hecht of *Nation* identified Wright's "weaknesses" as "self-pity" and "talkiness." And a *Sewanee Review* critic found *Two Citizens* "badly marred by personal indulgence and conversationality." The poet himself seemed aware of these shortcomings. "My chief enemy in poetry is glibness," he told Stitt in an interview published in the *Paris Review*. He continued: "My family background is partly Irish, and this means many things, but linguistically it means that it is too easy for me to talk sometimes. I keep thinking of Horace's idea which Byron so very accurately expressed in a letter . . ., 'Easy writing is damned hard reading.' I suffer from glibness. . . . I have [to struggle] to strip my poems down."

Some critics, however, argued that the talkiness and sentimentality in Wright's verse have been misinterpreted. Alan Williamson of *Shenandoah,* for example, once remarked: "The emotional exclamatoriness that some have called sentimental in Wright is more prominent than ever [in *Two Citizens*]; but I, for one, have been led to a new insight about it. It is a part of the American speech that Wright . . . wants to speak: A vocal violence needed to break the . . . barrier against uttering feeling at all in our culture."

Finally, in discussing Wright's work, critics spoke of the evident craftsmanship, of his skill and gift as a poet. Van den Heuvel found that "there is a universality in Wright's work not only in subject matter but in form and technique as well." The reviewer added that "[he is] a craftsman who can put to use the traditional elements of his art while at the same time exploring new means of expression." Seay voiced a like assessment, stating that "what makes Wright's poetry special is not that he has any new philosophical insights into the problems of existence but that he has the gift of using language in a way that the human spirit is awakened and alerted to its own possibilities."

BIOGRAPHICAL/CRITICAL SOURCES:

BOOKS

Authors in the News, Volume II, Gale, 1976.
Carroll, Paul, *The Poem in Its Skin,* Follett, 1968.
Contemporary Literary Criticism, Gale, Volume 3, 1975, Volume 5, 1976, Volume 10, 1979, Volume 28, 1984.
Dictionary of Literary Biography, Volume 5: *American Poets since World War II,* Gale, 1980.
Stepanchev, Stephen, *American Poetry since 1945,* Harper, 1965.

PERIODICALS

Chicago Review, Volume IXX, number 2, 1967.
Contemporary Literature, winter, 1973.
Georgia Review, spring, 1973, summer, 1974.
Los Angeles Times Book Review, May 16, 1982.
Michigan Quarterly Review, summer, 1972.
Minnesota Review, spring, 1972.

MOSAIC, spring, 1974.

Nation, August, 1971.
New York Times, March 27, 1980.
New York Times Book Review, February 12, 1978, March 18, 1984.
Paris Review, summer, 1975.
Saturday Review, January 21, 1978.
Sewanee Review, spring, 1974.

Shenandoah, winter, 1974.
The Sixties, spring, 1966.
Washington Post Book World, September 16, 1973, June 27, 1982.
Partisan Review, Volume XV, number 2, 1973.

* * *

WRIGHT, Judith (Arandell) 1915-

PERSONAL: Born May 31, 1915, in Armidale, New South Wales, Australia; daughter of Phillip Arundell and Ethel Mabel (Bigg) Wright; married Jack Philip McKinney (a philosophical writer; died, 1966); children: Meredith Anne. *Education:* Attended New South Wales Correspondence School, New England Girls' School, and University of Sydney. *Politics:* "Swing voter."

ADDRESSES: P.O. Box 93, Braidwood, New South Wales 2622, Australia.

CAREER: J. Walter Thompson (advertising agency), Sydney, Australia, secretary, 1938-39; University of Sydney, Sydney, Australia, secretary, 1940-42; Australian Universities Commission, Brisbane, Australia, clerk, 1943-46; University of Queensland, Brisbane, statistician, 1946-49. Part-time lecturer in Australian literature at various Australian universities. President, Wildlife Preservation Society of Queensland, 1962-74; member, Committee of Inquiry into the National Estate, Australia, 1973-74; member, Aboriginal Treaty Committee, 1978-83.

MEMBER: Society of Authors (Australia; council member), Australian Academy of the Humanities (fellow).

AWARDS, HONORS: Grace Leven Prize, 1953; D.Litt., University of New England, Armidale, Australia, 1963, Monash University, 1977, University of Sydney, 1977, Australian National University, 1980, University of New South Wales, 1985, Griffith University, 1988, University of Melbourne, 1988; *Encyclopedia Britannica* Award, 1964; Robert Frost Medallion, Fellowship of Australian Writers, 1975; Asan World Prize, Asan Memorial Association, 1984.

WRITINGS:

Kings of the Dingoes (juvenile), illustrated by Barbara Albiston, Oxford University Press, 1958.
The Generations of Men, illustrated by Alison Forbes, Oxford University Press, 1959, reprinted, 1975.
The Day the Mountains Played (juvenile), Jacaranda, 1960, Boolarong, 1988.
Range the Mountains High (juvenile), Lansdowne Press, 1962, 3rd edition, 1971.
Charles Harpur (biography and criticism), Lansdowne Press, 1963.
Country Towns (juvenile), Oxford University Press, 1963.
Preoccupations in Australian Poetry (history and criticism), Oxford University Press, 1965, new edition, 1966.
The Nature of Love (short stories), Sun Books (Melbourne, Australia), 1966.
The River and the Road (juvenile), Lansdowne Press, 1966, revised edition, 1971.
Henry Lawson, Oxford University Press, 1967.
Because I Was Invited, Oxford University Press, 1975.
The Coral Battleground (documentary), Thomas Nelson (Australia), 1977.
The Cry for the Dead, Oxford University Press, 1981.
We Call for a Treaty, William Collins/John M. Fontana, 1985.

POETRY

The Moving Image, Meanjin, 1946, revised edition, 1953.

Woman to Man, Angus & Robertson, 1949, 2nd edition, 1955.
The Gateway, Angus & Robertson, 1953.
The Two Fires, Angus & Robertson, 1955.
Birds, Angus & Robertson, 1962, 3rd edition, 1978.
Five Senses: Selected Poems, Angus & Robertson, 1963, revised edition, 1972.
City Sunrise, limited edition, Shapcott Press, 1964.
The Other Half, Angus & Robertson, 1966.
Collected Poems, Angus & Robertson, 1971, 2nd edition, 1975.
Alive: Poems 1971-1972, Angus & Robertson, 1973.
Fourth Quarter, and Other Poems, Angus & Robertson, 1976.
The Double Tree: Selected Poems, Houghton, 1978.
(Contributor) Fay Zwicky, editor, *Journeys: Poems,* Sisters (Carleton South, Australia), 1982.
Phantom Dwelling, Angus & Robertson, 1985.

EDITOR

Australian Poetry, Angus & Robertson, 1948.
(And author of introduction) *A Book of Australian Verse,* Oxford University Press, 1956, 2nd revised edition, 1968.
(And author of introduction) *New Land, New Language: An Anthology of Australian Verse,* Oxford University Press, 1957.
Judith Wright (selected poetry), Angus & Robertson, 1963.
Shaw Neilson (biography and selected poetry), Angus & Robertson, 1963.
(With Andrew Thomson) *The Poet's Pen,* Jacaranda, 1965.
John Shaw Neilson, *Witnesses of Spring: Unpublished Poems of Shaw Neilson,* Angus & Robertson, 1970.

SIDELIGHTS: A well-known author and poet in Australia, Judith Wright has been "outrageously neglected" outside of her native land, according to *London Magazine* critic D. M. Thomas. After years of publishing her verses in Australian periodicals, as well as in books in her homeland and abroad, Wright has accumulated much critical attention in Australia for her distinctly endemic poetry. One Australian reviewer, *Meanjin* contributor Elizabeth Vassilieff, considers Wright to be "the most interesting of Australian poets, with no exceptions." "Her poetry has the touch and feel of [Australia]," notes another *Meanjin* reviewer, S. Musgrove, "for she knows that man . . . must not lose that immediate contact" with the land. But although her poetry has gained her the most attention, Ken Goodwin writes in his *A History of Australian Literature,* "Judith Wright, in both poetry and prose, presents a wide panorama of the interests of the socially conscious present-day Australian."

Wright's prose writing includes children's stories, which she originally composed for her daughter, criticism, a biographical novel, *The Generations of Men,* and a historical work, *The Cry for the Dead.* The latter two books concern the author's own ancestors; Wright's grandfather, Albert Wright, figures prominently in both books, and the author takes much of her material for these books from her grandfather's diary. Next to other comparable novels, critics have viewed these retrospects on life in nineteenth-century Australia favorably. One "never has the feeling . . . that he is watching an artificial period-piece or costume melodrama," remarks *Meanjin* contributor Russel Ward. *New Statesman* critic V. S. Pritchett observes, too, that in *The Generations of Men* Wright "is also free of that family complacency which affects so many writers when they are describing their pioneer forebears." In another review of this book, Leonie Kramer writes in *Southerly:* "Judith Wright has shown herself to be a biographer of rare sensitivity." Kramer later concludes that the author's "prose transmits particularly well the atmosphere of the times, and the arid beauty of the country."

Both books not only tell the story of the author's family, but also that of the land itself. Albert Wright's diary becomes a helpful source in this regard, for, as Goodwin describes, "his book tells less of the official story than of the disastrous neglect of proper land-management procedures and the story of the brutal extermination of Aborigines." The tragic waste which these practices have brought to Australia is a concern in much of Wright's poetry as well. As a result, several of the author's poems are meditations "on the problem of how to give meaning to, or discover meaning in, this 'flowing and furious world,' " says *Australian Quarterly* critic R. F. Brissenden, quoting a poem from Wright's *Five Senses: Selected Poems.*

Maintaining a respect for the timelessness of the land throughout her work, Wright expresses in such poetry collections as *Alive: Poems 1971-1972* and *Fourth Quarter, and Other Poems* a horror "at the efficiency with which her fellow countrymen are raping their country," writes Peter Porter in the *London Observer.* Having been raised on a "station," or ranch, as a child, and being active as an adult in the conservation movement in Australia, Wright maintains a strong bond with her surroundings, which is evident in her poetry. She has, asserts Arthur Murphy in *Southerly,* an ability "to merge herself with all natural forces, delving deep into the almost inexpressible in verse of highly wrought formation and full content." But although several critics, such as one *Times Literary Supplement* reviewer, feel that her poems "about people, landscapes, and animals are good when she describes her subjects directly," Val Vallis remarks in the *Times Literary Supplement* that "the most commonly heard objection to her poetry as it progressed was that its author 'had gone too philosophical.' " *Carleton Miscellany* critic Keith Harrison, however, notes that even though one might see some "occasional vagueness" in her sometimes metaphysical poems, "the strengths of her work far outweigh the faults."

Some of these strengths, declares Elyne Mitchell in *Southerly,* include "vivid imagery, lovely songs of creation and of a creator, poems of philosophic journey, of the integration of dark and light, [and] of rebirth." Wright is a poet, who, as S. E. Lee characterizes her in *Southerly,* is "a rare combination of metaphysical thinker . . . and down-to-earth realist." Her "best poems then," concludes Lee, "integrate the intellect, passion, imagination and common sense of the thinker-mystic-poet-country wife." What is evident in both Wright's prose and poetry is "her bond to her native land and its once pastoral wilderness," asserts Margaret Gibson in the *Library Journal.* Goodwin summarizes the author's career this way: "Her lifelong quest [has been] to define Australia as a land, a nation and a metaphysical entity, in language that [shows] awareness of contemporary overseas writing in English but also [recognizes] the unique environment and society of Australia."

AVOCATIONAL INTERESTS: Gardening.

BIOGRAPHICAL/CRITICAL SOURCES:

BOOKS

Contemporary Literary Criticism, Gale, Volume 11, 1979, Volume 53, 1989.
Goodwin, Ken, *A History of Australian Literature,* St. Martin's, 1986.
Hope, A. D., *Judith Wright,* Oxford University Press (Melbourne), 1975.
Kramer, L., editor, *The Oxford History of Australian Literature,* Oxford University Press, 1982.
Walker, Shirley, *The Poetry of Judith Wright,* Edward Arnold, 1980.

Walker, Shirley, *Judith Wright,* Oxford University Press, 1981.

PERIODICALS

American Poetry Review, September/October, 1980.
Australian Quarterly, March, 1964.
Carleton Miscellany, summer, 1980.
Library Journal, June 15, 1978.
London Magazine, May, 1967.
London Observer, May 7, 1978.
Meanjin, September, 1946, March, 1950, June, 1960, December, 1962.
New Statesman, September 5, 1959.
Southerly, Volume 11, number 3, 1950, Volume 16, number 1, 1955, Volume 17, number 2, 1956, Volume 20, number 9, 1959, Volume 23, number 2, 1963, Volume 27, number 1, 1967.
Times Literary Supplement, September 10, 1964, April 9, 1976, October 15, 1982, November 27, 1987.

—*Sketch by Kevin S. Hile*

* * *

WRIGHT, Kenneth
See del REY, Lester

* * *

WRIGHT, Richard (Nathaniel) 1908-1960

PERSONAL: Born September 4, 1908, near Natchez, Miss.; died of a heart attack, November 28, 1960, in Paris, France; buried in Pere Lachaise, Paris, France; son of Nathan (a mill worker) and Ellen (a teacher) Wright; married Rose Dhima Meadman, 1938 (marriage ended); married Ellen Poplar, 1941; children: two daughters. *Education:* Attended school in Jackson, Miss.

CAREER: Novelist, short story writer, poet, and essayist. Worked at odd jobs in Memphis, Tenn., and other cities; clerk at U.S. Post Office in Chicago, Ill., during 1920s; associated with Works Progress Administration Federal Writers' Project, Chicago, and New York, N.Y., 1935-37.

AWARDS, HONORS: Prize from *Story* magazine, 1938, for *Uncle Tom's Children;* Guggenheim fellowship, 1939; Spingarn Medal from National Association for the Advancement of Colored People, 1940, for *Native Son.*

WRITINGS:

Uncle Tom's Children: Four Novellas, Harper, 1938, expanded edition published as *Uncle Tom's Children: Five Long Stories,* 1938, reprinted, 1965.
Native Son (novel; also see below), Harper, 1940, reprinted, 1986.
Twelve Million Black Voices: A Folk History of the Negro in the U.S., Viking, 1941, reprinted, Thunder's Mouth, 1988.
(With Paul Green) *Native Son* (play; adapted from own novel; first produced on Broadway at the St. James Theatre, March 24, 1941), Harper, 1941, revised edition, Samuel French, 1980.
Black Boy: A Record of Childhood and Youth (autobiography), Harper, 1945, reprinted, 1969.
"Native Son" (screenplay; adapted from own novel), Classic Films, 1951.
The Outsider (novel), Harper, 1953.
Savage Holiday (novel), Avon, 1954, reprinted, Chatham Bookseller, 1975.
Black Power: A Record of Reactions in a Land of Pathos, Harper, 1954, reprinted, Greenwood Press, 1974.

The Color Curtain (nonfiction), World, 1956.
Pagan Spain (nonfiction), Harper, 1957.
White Man, Listen! (nonfiction), Doubleday, 1957, reprinted, Greenwood Press, 1978.
The Long Dream (novel), Doubleday, 1958, reprinted, Harper, 1987.
(Editor and contributor) *Quintet* (short stories), Pyramid Books, 1961.
Eight Men (short stories), World, 1961, reprinted, Thunder's Mouth, 1987.
Lawd Today (novel), Avon, 1963, reprinted, Northeastern University Press, 1986.
(With Louis Sapin) "Daddy Goodness" (play), first produced Off-Broadway at St. Mark's Playhouse, June 4, 1968.
The Man Who Lived Underground (novella), Aubier-Flammarion, 1971.
(Contributor) Hiroshi Nagase and Tsutomu Kanashiki, editors, *What the Negro Wants,* Kaitakusha, 1972.
Farthing's Fortunes, Atheneum, 1976.
American Hunger (autobiography), Harper, 1977.
Ellen Wright and Michel Fabre, editors, *The Richard Wright Reader,* Harper, 1978.
David Ray and Robert M. Farnsworth, editors, *The Life and Works of Richard Wright,* University of Missouri, 1979.

Contributor of articles, essays, short stories, and poems to magazines and newspapers, including *Atlantic Monthly, Saturday Review, New Republic, Negro Digest, Daily Worker, New York World Telegram,* and *New Masses.*

SIDELIGHTS: One of the most influential black American authors of the twentieth century, Wright was "the first American Negro writer of large ambitions to win a major reputation in [American] literary life." The southern-born Wright was the first black novelist to write of life in the ghettos of northern cities and of the rage felt by blacks at the white society that excluded them. As James A. Page observed in *English Journal,* Wright was "powerful enough to break out of the narrow compartment previously occupied by Black writers. . . . He made sense, he handled his themes with authority, expressed himself with power and eloquence, and was entitled to the place he had won in the literary firmament of the Depression years. . . . That Wright was the most impressive literary talent yet produced by negro America was rarely disputed in his time. . . . His name was bracketed with the small handful of America's foremost writers."

Wright was largely self-educated. His formal schooling, frequently interrupted as he moved from town to town, ended when he was fifteen. Thereafter, he read widely, beginning with H. L. Mencken, whose books he obtained from Memphis's "whites only" public library by forging a note from a white patron: "Dear Madam: Will you please let this nigger boy have some books by H. L. Mencken?" Wright was strongly affected by the naturalistic fiction of Stephen Crane, Sinclair Lewis, and Theodore Dreiser, and, after he moved to Chicago in the late 1920s, by the Chicago school of sociologists, including Robert Redfield, Louis Wirth, and Robert Park. Wright also read, and was strongly impressed with, Marcel Proust and Gertrude Stein.

His concern with the social roots of racial oppression led Wright to join the Communist party in 1932. He was a party activist in Chicago and New York, and worked at developing a Marxist perspective in the poems and short stories he was writing at that time. But his individualism brought him into conflict with other party members, who labeled him an intellectual and regarded his writing with suspicion. Wright, in turn, found himself repelled by the narrowness and rigidity of his fellow Communists, whose minds he found "sealed against new ideas, new facts, new feelings, new attitudes, new hints at ways to live. They denounced books they could never understand, and doctrines they could not pronounce." In 1944, after witnessing the trial of a party member for ideological "deviationism," Wright resigned from the party.

Until 1938, Wright's work appeared only in left-wing publications such as *New Masses* and *Left Front.* In that year, *Story* magazine offered a $500 prize for the best book-length manuscript by a writer connected with the Federal Writers' Project. Wright's collection of four long stories inspired by the life of a black communist he had known in Chicago won the contest and was published as *Uncle Tom's Children.* Malcolm Cowley, in the *New Republic,* found the book "heartening, as evidence of a vigorous new talent, and terrifying as the expression of a racial hatred that has never ceased to grow and gets no chance to die." All of the stories (a fifth, "Bright and Morning Star," was added to subsequent editions) deal with the oppression of black people in the South, of the violence of whites against blacks, and the violence to which the black characters are driven by their victimization. Some critics have found the stories in *Uncle Tom's Children* too melodramatic and marred by the infusion of communist ideology. But Houston A. Baker, in his *Black Literature in America,* wrote: "Wright showed a mastery of style and a dramatic sense far superior to that of most of black contemporaries and predecessors and on a par with that of his most talented white contemporaries. The violence and the terrible effects of prejudice are perhaps nowhere more skillfully set forth."

Though *Uncle Tom's Children* was well received, Wright was dissatisfied with the response to it. He realized, he wrote later, "that I had written a book which even bankers' daughters could read and weep over and feel good. I swore to myself that if I ever wrote another book, no one would weep over it; that it would be so hard and deep that they would have to face it without the consolation of tears." The book he wrote was *Native Son,* the story of Bigger Thomas, a young black man in Chicago who murders two women and is condemned to death. To depict the dehumanization of blacks in the "hard and deep" manner he wished, Wright avoided making his protagonist a sympathetic character. As reviewer Margaret Marshall wrote in the *Nation,* "Mr. Wright has chosen for his 'hero,' not a sophisticated Negro who at least understands his predicament and can adapt himself to it, but a 'bad nigger,' a 'black ape,' who is only dimly aware of his extra-human status and therefore completely at the mercy of the impulses it generates. . . . One gets a picture of a dark world enclosed by a living white wall. . . . Bigger and his friends are resentful; all feel powerless and afraid of the white world, which exploits, condescends to, and in turn fears the race it has segregated. . . . Mr. Wright has laid bare, with a ruthlessness that spares neither race, the lower depths of the human and social relationship of blacks and whites; and his ruthlessness. . . . clearly springs not from a vindictive desire to shock but from a passionate—and compassionate—concern with a problem obviously lying at the core of his own personal reality. . . . It is not pleasant to feel at the end that one is an accessory to the crimes of Bigger Thomas; but that feeling is impressive evidence of the power of Mr. Wright's indictment with its cutting and accurate title of 'Native Son.' "

Bigger Thomas is a young tough and a petty thief who is hired as a chauffeur by a rich white man. He drives his employer's daughter, Mary, to a political lecture, where he is confused and frightened by the white communists' insistence on treating him as an equal, something he can only interpret as mockery. Mary gets drunk, and Bigger, after driving her home, carries her to her room. When Mary's mother, who is blind, enters the room, Bigger accidentally smothers Mary while trying to keep her from speaking and revealing his presence. He burns Mary's body in a furnace, then conceives a scheme to extort money from her parents by pretending to have kidnapped her and demanding ransom. When Mary's charred bones are discovered, Bigger kills his girlfriend, Bessie, who was his accomplice in the kidnap plot. He is captured by the police and, despite an eloquent defense by his communist lawyer, convicted and condemned. The lawyer, Max, argues that Bigger cannot be held responsible for his crimes, that the greater guilt lies with the society that would not accept him as a full human being, and so drove him to his brutal acts. Bigger feels that he has found a measure of freedom in the act of murder—the only act in his life that seems to him to have been truly creative, to have involved genuine self-assertion.

Some critics have seen in the ending of *Native Son* a clash between two literary and philosophical visions. Much of the book is in the tradition of naturalism, especially of Theodore Dreiser's novel *An American Tragedy.* This deterministic philosophy is made explicit when Max argues, in Marxist terms, that Bigger, as a product of his environment, is not truly guilty of the murders he committed. But Bigger's final sense of violence as a vital act of self-definition is drawn from Fedor Dostoevski's *Crime and Punishment,* and prefigures the existentialist position Wright adopted in his later work. Edward Margolies found the two attitudes incompatible, and their conflict a weakness in the novel: "Wright was probing larger issues than racial injustice and social inequality. He was asking questions regarding the ultimate nature of man. What indeed are man's responsibilities in a world devoid of meaning and purpose? . . . The contradiction is never resolved, and it is precisely for this reason that the novel fails to fulfill itself. For the plot, the structure, even the portrayal of Bigger himself are often at odds with Wright's official determinism. . . . The chief philosophical weakness of *Native Son* is not that Bigger does not surrender his freedom to Max's determinism or that Bigger's Zarathustrian principles do not jibe with Max's socialist visions; it is that Wright himself does not seem able to make up his mind. . . . Wright, though intellectually committed to Max's views, is more emotionally akin to Bigger's. . . . There is an inconsistency of ideologies, an irresolution of philosophical attitudes which prevent Bigger and the other characters from developing properly, which adulterate the structure of the novel, and which occasionally cloud up an otherwise lucid prose style."

Sheldon Brivic, in *Novel: A Forum on Fiction,* defended the apparent contradiction, insisting that the "ambivalence which critics have attacked in *Native Son* is really a complexity that adds to its validity, comprehension and prophetic power." Brivic found that "a conflict of values is skillfully developed and organized throughout. This conflict is embodied in the plot, in American society as Wright sees it, and most centrally in Bigger's mind. . . . Bigger is both the helpless victim of social oppression and the purposeful hero of a racial war. . . . Wright has balanced both sides in a dialectic, and it is because he keeps the book open ended that *Native Son* has the depth of perspective of a major work of modern literature rather than mere propaganda."

James Baldwin, who began his writing career as Wright's protege, called *Native Son* "the most powerful and celebrated statement we have yet had of what it means to be a Negro in America." But for Baldwin, the novel is marred by Wright's use of Bigger as a social symbol. Baldwin noted: "Bigger has no discernible relationship to himself, to his own life, to his own people, nor to any other people—in this respect, perhaps, he is most American—and his force comes not from his significance as a social (or anti-social) unit, but from his significance as the incarnation of a myth. It is remarkable that, though we follow him step by step from the tenement room to the death cells, we know as little about him when this journey is ended as we did when it began; and, what is even more remarkable, we know almost as little about the social dynamic which we are to believe created him. . . . What is missing in this situation and in the representation of his psychology—which makes his situation false and his psychology incapable of development—is any revelatory apprehension of Bigger as one of the Negro's realities or as one of the Negro's roles. This failure is part of the . . . failure to convey any sense of Negro life as a continuing and complex group reality."

Darryl Pinckney, in the *Village Voice,* argued: "*Native Son* is unmatched in its power. The rage, the human misery, seizes the mind and there is no relief. It is not true, as Baldwin claims, that Bigger Thomas, the doomed, frustrated black boy, is just another stereotype. . . . Baldwin criticizes Wright for not giving us black life, black community, the sense of shared experience. But Bigger Thomas is not a social symbol, exactly, and it is precisely his isolation that causes his fury. What Bigger must combat is circumstance, and we know he cannot win. . . . Bigger's black skin is the real object of his scorn and he hates those who make him aware of it—whites. . . . Baldwin feels we do not get any understanding of Bigger's psychology, that we do not know him better in the end any more than we did in the beginning. But Bigger did not know himself. . . . To understand Bigger, the meaning in his crimes, perhaps we should not view them as merely a desire to get revenge on white society. . . . It is wrong to read this novel as a matter of group reality, a matter of race. Bigger had no real relations with other blacks. Everyone was an enemy. . . . [Wright] claimed he valued the 'state of abandonment, aloneness.' In this he was, finally, a true product of Western culture. . . . In *Native Son* he gave us a lasting record of the howl of modern man."

Wright's autobiography, *Black Boy,* published in 1945, is considered by many critics to be his most important work. In it he told of his southern childhood, up to the time when he left Memphis for Chicago. Ralph Ellison, in his essay "Richard Wright's Blues," wrote: "In *Black Boy* Wright has used his own life to probe what qualities of will, imagination, and intellect are required of a Southern Negro in order to possess the meaning of his life in the United States. . . . Imagine Bigger Thomas projecting his own life in lucid prose, guided, say, by the insights of Marx and Freud, and you have an idea of this autobiography. . . . Along with the themes, equivalent descriptions of milieu and the perspectives to be found in Joyce, Nehru, Dostoievsky, George Moore and Rousseau, *Black Boy* is filled with blues-tempered echoes of railroad trains, the names of Southern towns and cities, estrangements, fights and flights, deaths and disappointments, charged with physical and spiritual hungers and pain. And like a blues song by such an artist as Bessie Smith, its lyrical prose evokes the paradoxical, almost surreal image of a black boy singing lustily as he probes his own grievous wound. . . . And while it is true that *Black Boy* presents an almost unrelieved picture of a personality corrupted by brutal environment, it also presents those fresh, human responses brought to its world by the sensitive child."

Along with his accounts of mistreatment by whites, Wright describes the complicity of southern blacks in their own oppression. Wright's family strove to make him conform to the submissive, servile behavior expected of black people, often beating him when he asserted himself too strongly. "In scene after scene," noted Morris Dickstein in *Gates of Eden,* "Wright represents his

younger self as a rebellious misfit, incapable of adapting to ... modes of deference. . . . He makes an intense effort of self-restraint, but try as he will there is always a provocative hint of pride and self-respect, a touch of the uppity nigger about him. A latecomer to the white world, he is unable to quite master the shuffling, degraded, but apparently contented manner that will tell whites he not only knows his place but loves it." Christianity is portrayed as an instrument of white oppression, by which blacks are convinced of their inferiority and convinced to passively accept their position; Wright, like many of his fictional characters, bitterly rejects the black church. *Black Boy* was attacked by some for its one-sided picture of southern life, but David Littlejohn, in *Black on White: A Critical Survey of Writing by American Negroes,* praised it for revealing "the inside dimension of the Negro's experience of prejudice in America: what it feels like to live in the mad prison house of sadistic white obsessions."

Howard Mumford Jones, writing in the *Saturday Review of Literature,* found *Black Boy* a powerful social document and indictment of racism, but a weak literary work. "The total effect of the volume is an effect of passive suffering, punctuated by outbursts of blind emotional rebellion. . . . [Wright] emphasizes an endless array of wrongs, but he minimizes the development of his own personality. . . . In contrast to the passivity of virtue in these pages, the acts of the boy's persecutors, white and black, are presented in dramatic scenes of vivid and even violent writing. . . . In some degree this verbal violence may conceal the central failure of the story, which is the failure to chronicle the growth of a personality under suffering. . . . This either-or formula of passive virtue . . . and active evil is the formula of melodrama; and just as an easy recourse to melodrama was the structural weakness of 'Native Son,' so it is the structural weakness of 'Black Boy.' "

Some critics have seemed unsure whether to consider *Black Boy* as a sociological statement, a true autobiography, or an autobiographical novel. Wright uses many of the techniques of fiction, and it has been suggested that some of the incidents may have been invented. At the time of its publication, *Black Boy* was seen primarily as an attack on southern white supremacist society; critics in the 1960s came to view it as the story of the development of a young writer's sensibility, in which race was only one factor, albeit a central one. As Warren French pointed out in *The Black American Writer: Fiction,* "What few noticed in the hubbub over Wright's powerful apologia is that: (1) a great many Negroes and members of other minority groups had suffered as he had without ever being able to find an adequate vehicle for the articulation of their personal grievances; (2) Wright's account had many similarities to other non-Negro portraits of the artist as a young man, including Joyce's famous novel [*Portrait of the Artist as a Young Man*]. . . . *Black Boy* is an outstanding account of a particularly sensitive type of artistic personality striving for identity, but it is as erroneous to read it as an account of the representative Negro experience as it would be to read Winston Churchill's memoirs as an account of the representative British schoolboy's 'making his way.' "

In 1946, the government of France invited Wright to visit that country. He spent six months in Paris and returned to France in 1947, to live there until his death. In Paris, Wright became acquainted with the circle of existentialist writers of whom the most prominent were Jean-Paul Sartre and Simone de Beauvoir. Existentialism appealed to Wright's deeply felt sense of alienation and rootlessness, and his later work combined racial themes with existentialist metaphysics. Wright's existentialism was as much instinctive as adopted, and similar ideas inform his work as early as *Native Son,* but the first novel he wrote after moving to France, *The Outsider,* was more overtly motivated by philosophical concerns. Granville Hicks, in the *New York Times Book Review,* noted that *The Outsider* was "one of the first consciously existentialist novels to be written by an American."

Cross Damon, the hero of *The Outsider,* is black, but his central problems have nothing to do with race. Harassed by his wife, his mother, and his mistress, he finds an escape from his encumbered life when he is believed killed in a subway accident. Seeking a new identity, Damon joins the Communist party, not out of sympathy with its political goals but out of a fascination with the party's "conviction that it had mastered the art of living; its will that it could define the ends of existence." Damon kills two communists and a fascist, but the district attorney who solves the crimes understands Damon's nihilistic creed and chooses to let him go free: "You are your own law, so you'll be your own judge," the lawyer tells him. Left alone, more an outsider than ever, Damon is executed by the Communist party's hired gunmen.

Hicks concluded: " 'The Outsider' is both melodrama and novel of ideas. . . . If the ideas are sometimes incoherent, that does not detract from the substance and power of the book. . . . [*The Outsider*] is only incidentally a book about Negroes. Being a Negro helps Cross Damon to understand that he is an outsider, . . . but there are . . . many outsiders. 'The Outsider' is, as it was intended to be, a book about modern man, and, because of Mr. Wright's driving force, it challenges the modern mind as it has rarely been challenged in fiction." But *The Outsider* was not generally well received; a number of critics found the melodramatic aspects of the plot too lurid, the philosophy poorly integrated with the story (especially a fourteen-page speech in which Cross Damon explains his philosophy of history), and the style clumsy. Phoebe Adams of the *Atlantic Monthly* called *The Outsider* "a very disappointing novel, for the qualities of sympathy, directness, effective detail, and mordant humor which distinguished Mr. Wright's earlier books seem to operate at cross-purposes in *The Outsider.* . . . Whether Mr. Wright nailed his grim thesis to a plot already in his mind, or concocted his plot, which is full of coincidence, accident, and blind luck, to fit his thesis, the book shows a hiatus between means and ends."

Stanley Edgar Hyman, in his 1970 article "Richard Wright Reappraised," dismissed *The Outsider* as "wretched. . . . A kind of spurious display of French existentialism . . . , a mechanical and rigid parallel to *Crime and Punishment,* with Damon as Raskolnikov and Houston as Porfiry, all frozen in stiff postures by cold drafts of theory from Wright's friend Sartre." But Nathan A. Scott, Jr., in *Graduate Comment,* wrote: "For all its melodramatic sensationalism, [*The Outsider*] is an impressive book. Indeed, it is one of the very few American novels of our time that, in admitting into itself a large body of systematic ideas, makes us think that it wants seriously to compete with the major philosophic intelligence of the contemporary period. . . . [*The Outsider*], though it is a very imperfect work, is yet (after *Black Boy*) [Wright's] finest achievement and, as the one emphatically existentialist novel in contemporary American literature, a book that deserves to have commanded a great deal more attention than it has."

Many critics have felt that Wright made more effective use of existentialist ideas in his novella *The Man Who Lived Underground,* a surreal fable about a black man named Fred Daniels, a fugitive who takes refuge from the police in a sewer system. From his underground hiding place he spies on and robs the soci-

ety from which he is excluded; he comes to understand the absurdity of that society and finds a new identity in his very anonymity and invisibility. When he emerges from his sewer, even though he has been cleared of the crime for which he was originally wanted, he is shot in cold blood by the police. Edward Margolies wrote: "Fred Daniels . . . is not merely the victim of a racist society, . . . he has become by the very nature of his experiences a symbol of all men in that society. . . . The underground man is the essential nature of all men—and is composed of dread, terror, and guilt. . . . Fred Daniels is then Everyman, and his story is very nearly a perfect modern allegory. The Negro who lives in the underground of the city amidst its sewage and slime is not unlike the creature who dwells amidst the sewage of the human heart. And Fred Daniels knows that all of the ways men attempt to persuade themselves that their lives are meaningful and rational are delusions." Hyman declared, " 'The Man Who Lived Underground' is a pioneering work in going beyond realism and naturalism to symbolism and fantasy, and is thus perhaps the single most revolutionary work in American Negro literature."

Much of Wright's energy during his years in Paris was devoted to writing nonfiction and to supporting national independence movements in Africa. In 1953 he traveled to the Gold Coast (now Ghana), one of the first British colonies in Africa to be granted self-government. In *Black Power* Wright describes his experiences in Africa and sets forth his ideas for the political future of the continent under black rule. While critics praised Wright's reporting, his political recommendations sparked controversy, especially his advocacy of a militarized and regimented social structure to provide the coherence that tribal traditions, he believed, could not. Joyce Cary, in the *Nation,* remarked: "The author has rejected the party, but his political thinking still belongs to communism. He imagines that violence, cruelty, injustice, and some clever lying can achieve a new civilization. But this is false. They can only produce new forms of oppression." But Cary found that *Black Power,* as reporting, "is a first-class job and gives the best picture I've seen of an extraordinary situation. . . . Wright . . . writes so honestly, so directly as he feels, that he gives material for another book contradicting his own arguments. . . . There are no easy answers in politics. . . . We are still groping our way, and need, above all, the facts. . . . That is why books like this of Wright's are so valuable—so far, that is, as they give facts, and so far as the facts can be distinguished from the bias. Wright is so honest a reporter, so vivid a writer, that this is easily done."

Wright continued to deal with African and Asian nationalism in *The Color Curtain,* a book about the 1955 Bandung conference of Third World nations. Tillman Durdin of the *New York Times Book Review* found *The Color Curtain* "a vivid and illuminating job of reportage," though he thought the book unbalanced in some respects, especially in what he saw as Wright's overemphasis on race as a source of conflict between the new nations and the former colonial powers. Wright wrote on the same theme in the essays in *White Man, Listen!,* linking colonialism and imperialism to racism in Western civilization. Oscar Handlin, in the *New York Times Book Review,* wrote: "This is an indignant book. It is argumentative, belligerent, and often wrong-headed. But it deserves to be read with the utmost seriousness."

In his last novel (*Lawd Today,* which was written in the 1930s and posthumously published) Wright returned to his earliest subject matter, racial conflict in the South. *The Long Dream* is about Fishbelly, the son of a black vice lord in a southern town. When his father, who was proud of the independence he had won through his illegal enterprises, is destroyed by the equally corrupt white leaders of the town, Fishbelly attempts to take his father's place. He is defeated and framed for a crime he did not commit, and when he is finally released he leaves for France. Charles Shapiro of the *New Republic* called *The Long Dream* "a powerful novel reminiscent of *Native Son,* one that smashes into experience treating it directly, not by analogy. . . . The imperfections are carried away by the power of the story, for the writing sins are of excess and not of cowardice."

Other critics were less pleased, pointing to the same faults that had been found in Wright's earlier work: a tendency toward melodrama and stylistic clumsiness. Granville Hicks of *Saturday Review* noted: "[Wright] displays a preoccupation with scenes of violence that can be understood but cannot be fully defended on literary grounds. His material constantly seems to be getting out of hand, as if he were driven—as I believe he is—by forces beyond his control. I am also troubled by the characterization of Fish Tucker. . . . One ought to feel, as I do not, that the ideas Fish expresses are his ideas and not Richard Wright's. . . . Finally, there is the question of style. Wright has never been a master of polished prose, and 'The Long Dream' is marred by frequent lapses. . . . The characters are likely to talk in a fashion that is hard to accept . . . [and] the prose [sometimes] becomes pretentious." But Hicks acknowledged the novel's power, observing that "alienation is what Wright has from the first been able to render. He is not basically a realist, although he probably thinks that he is; he is a man who uses, and perhaps is used by, certain powerful symbols. . . . There are few signs of development in his work, but if he has not grown, he has never lost his ability to touch both the emotions and the consciences of his readers."

Wright's reputation ebbed during the 1950s as younger black writers such as James Baldwin and Ralph Ellison rejected his naturalistic approach and the ideological preoccupations of his fiction. But in the 1960s, with the growth of the militant black consciousness movement, there was a resurgence of interest in Wright's work. Wright's place in American literature remains controversial: some contend that his writing is of sociological and historical, rather than literary interest; his defenders believe that his books of the early 1940s are as important in the American naturalist tradition as they are in the history of black literature, and that Wright is properly ranked with such writers as Dreiser, James T. Farrell, and John Steinbeck. Warren French wrote that Wright was "a man praised too soon for the wrong reasons and too soon dismissed for more wrong reasons. . . . In death as in life, Wright has been forced to win as a Negro who happened to be a writer the recognition that he desired as a *writer* who happened to be a Negro."

MEDIA ADAPTATIONS: Native Son was adapted for a film of the same title by the author, Classic Films, 1951; and by Richard Wesley, Cinecom, 1986.

BIOGRAPHICAL/CRITICAL SOURCES:

BOOKS

Baker, Houston A., Jr., *Black Literature in America,* McGraw, 1971.
Baldwin, James, *Notes of a Native Son,* Beacon Press, 1955.

Baldwin, James, *Nobody Knows My Name,* Dial, 1961.
Bigsby, C. W. E., editor, *The Black American Writer: Fiction, Volume One,* Everett/Edwards, 1969.
Concise Dictionary of American Literary Biography: The Age of Maturity, 1929-1941, Gale, 1989.
Contemporary Literary Criticism, Gale, Volume 1, 1973, Volume 3, 1975, Volume 4, 1975, Volume 9, 1978, Volume 14, 1980, Volume 21, 1982, Volume 48, 1988.
Dickstein, Morris, *Gates of Eden,* Basic Books, 1977.
Dictionary of Literary Biography, Volume 76: *Afro-American Writers, 1940-1955,* Gale, 1988.
Dictionary of Literary Biography Documentary Series, Volume 2, Gale, 1982.
Ellison, Ralph, *Shadow and Act,* Random House, 1945.
Fabre, Michel, *The Unfinished Quest of Richard Wright,* Morrow, 1973.
Fabre, Michel, and Charles Davis, *Richard Wright: The Primary Sources,* G. K. Hall, 1982.
Gayle, Addison, Jr., *Richard Wright: Ordeal of a Native Son,* Anchor Press, 1980.
Littlejohn, David, *Black on White: A Critical Survey of Writing by American Negroes,* Viking, 1966.
Margolies, Edward, *The Art of Richard Wright,* Southern Illinois University Press, 1969.
Short Story Criticism, Volume 2, Gale, 1989.
Webb, Constance, *Richard Wright: A Biography,* Putnam, 1968.
Wright, Richard, *Black Boy,* Harper, 1945.
Wright, Richard, *American Hunger,* Harper, 1977.

PERIODICALS

Atlantic Monthly, May, 1940, June, 1940, March, 1945, May, 1953, March, 1970.
Ebony, March, 1987.
English Journal, May, 1973.
Los Angeles Times, December 24, 1986.
Nation, March 16, 1940, April 5, 1941, April 7, 1945, October 16, 1954, October 25, 1958.
National Review, February 3, 1978.
New Republic, April 6, 1938, April 7, 1941, March 12, 1945, February 18, 1957, November 24, 1958, February 13, 1961.
New York Times, December 23, 1986, December 24, 1986, December 26, 1986.
New York Times Book Review, March 3, 1940, March 4, 1945, March 22, 1953, September 26, 1954, March 18, 1956, February 24, 1957, October 26, 1958.
Novel: A Forum on Fiction, spring, 1974.
Saturday Review, March 2, 1940, March 3, 1945, March 28, 1953, October 23, 1954, October 18, 1958, March 30, 1963, January 21, 1978.
Village Voice, July 4, 1977.
Washington Post, January 16, 1987.

*   *   *

WYLIE, Laura
See MATTHEWS, Patricia (Anne)

Y

YANEZ, Jose Donoso
See DONOSO (YANEZ), Jose

* * *

YEATS, William Butler   1865-1939

PERSONAL: Born June 13, 1865, in Sandymount, Ireland; died January 28, 1939, in Roquebrune, France; buried in Drumcliffe, Sligo, Ireland; son of John Butler (a lawyer and an artist) and Susan Mary (Pollexfen) Yeats; married Georgiana Hyde-Lees, October 20, 1917; children: Anne Butler, William Michael Butler. *Education:* Attended Metropolitan School of Art, Dublin, 1884-86.

CAREER: Writer. Co-founder of Irish Literary Theatre. Senator of the Irish Free State, 1923-29.

AWARDS, HONORS: D.Litt., Queen's University, Belfast, and Trinity College, Dublin, both 1922, Oxford University, 1931, and Cambridge University, 1933; Nobel Prize for Literature, 1923.

WRITINGS:

Mosada: A Dramatic Poem (first published in *Dublin University Review,* March, 1885), Sealy, Bryers & Walker, 1886.

The Wanderings of Oisin and Other Poems, Kegan Paul, Trench & Company, 1889.

John Sherman [and] *Dhoya* (fiction), Cassell Publishing Company, 1891.

The Countess Kathleen and Various Legends and Lyrics (poetry and plays; includes "The Countess Kathleen," play first produced in Dublin at Antient Concert Rooms, May 8, 1899), Roberts Brothers, 1892, title play revised and published separately as *The Countess Kathleen,* T. Fischer Unwin, 1912.

The Celtic Twilight (nonfiction), Lawrence & Bullen, 1893, Macmillan, 1894, revised and enlarged edition, A. H. Bullen, 1902.

The Land of Heart's Desire (play; first produced in London at Avenue Theatre, March 29, 1894), Stone & Kimball, 1894.

Poems, T. Fischer Unwin, 1895, revised editions, 1899, 1901, 1912, 1927.

The Table of the Law [and] *The Adoration of the Magi* (fiction), privately printed, 1897, Elkin Mathews, 1904.

The Secret Rose (short stories), illustrations by father, John Butler Yeats, Dodd, Mead, 1897.

The Wind among the Reeds (poetry), John Lane/Bodley Head, 1899.

The Shadowy Waters (play; first produced in Dublin at Molesworth Hall, January 14, 1904), Hodder & Stoughton, 1900, Dodd, Mead, 1901.

1899 to 1900, first edition, 1900, reprinted, F. Cass, 1970.

1901 to 1908, seven volumes, first edition, 1901, reprinted, F. Cass, 1970.

Cathleen ni Houlihan (one-act play; first produced in Dublin at St. Teresa's Hall April 2, 1902), A. H. Bullen, 1902.

Where There Is Nothing (five-act play; first produced in London at Royal Court Theatre, June 26, 1904), John Lane, 1902, revised (with Lady Gregory) as "The Unicorn from the Stars" (first produced in Dublin at Abbey Theatre, November 21, 1907) in *The Unicorn from the Stars and Other Plays,* Macmillan, 1908, new edition published as *Where There Is Nothing* [and] *The Unicorn from the Stars,* Catholic University Press, 1987.

On Baile's Strand (play; first produced in Dublin at Abbey Theatre, December 27, 1904), Dun Emer Press, 1903.

In the Seven Woods: Being Poems Chiefly of the Irish Heroic Age, Macmillan, 1903.

The Hour Glass: A Morality (play; first produced in Dublin at Molesworth Hall, March 14, 1903, revised version produced in Dublin at Abbey Theatre, November 21, 1912), Heinemann, 1903.

Ideas of Good and Evil (nonfiction), Macmillan, 1903.

The Hour Glass and Other Plays (includes "The Hour Glass: A Morality" and "The Pot of Broth," first produced in Dublin at Antient Concert Rooms, October 30, 1902), Macmillan, 1904.

The King's Threshold (play; first produced in Dublin at Molesworth Hall, October 8, 1903, revised version produced in Dublin at Abbey Theatre, October 13, 1913), John Quinn, 1904.

The King's Threshold [and] *On Baile's Strand* (plays), A. H. Bullen, 1904.

The Hour-Glass and Other Plays, first edition, 1904, reprinted, Roth, 1976.

Stories of Red Hanrahan (short stories), Dun Emer Press, 1905.

Poems, 1899-1905, A. H. Bullen (London), 1906.

The Poetical Works of William B. Yeats, two volumes, Macmillan, 1906, revised edition, 1912.

Deirdre (play; first produced in Dublin at Abbey Theatre, November 24, 1906), A. H. Bullen, 1907.

Discoveries: A Volume of Essays, Dun Emer Press, 1907.

The Golden Helmet (play; first produced in Dublin at Abbey Theatre, March 19, 1908), John Quinn, 1908, revised as "The Green Helmet" (produced in Dublin at Abbey Theatre, February 10, 1910), published in *The Green Helmet and Other Poems* (also see below).

(With Lionel Johnson) *Poetry and Ireland,* first edition, 1908, reprinted, Cuala Press, 1970.

Poems: Second Series, A. H. Bullen, 1910.

(With Lady Gregory) "The Travelling Man" (play), first produced in Dublin at Abbey Theatre, March 2, 1910.

The Green Helmet and Other Poems (includes poems "Words," "Against Unworthy Praise," and "The Mask"), Cuala Press, 1910, R. Harold Paget, 1911, enlarged edition, Macmillan, 1912.

Synge and the Ireland of His Time (nonfiction), Cuala Press, 1911.

The Cutting of an Agate (nonfiction), Macmillan, 1912, enlarged edition, 1919.

Poems Written in Discouragement, 1912-1913, Cuala Press, 1913.

Stories of Red Hanrahan, The Secret Rose, Rosa Alchemica (fiction), A. H. Bullen, 1913, Macmillan, 1914.

A Selection from the Poetry of W. B. Yeats, Bernard Tauchnitz, 1913.

A Selection from the Love Poetry of W. B. Yeats, Cuala Press, 1913.

Responsibilities (poetry; includes "To a Shade," "The Magi," and "A Coat"), Cuala Press, 1914, enlarged edition, Macmillan, 1916.

The Wild Swans at Coole (poetry and plays; includes play "At the Hawk's Well," first performed privately in London, April 2, 1916, produced in Dublin at Abbey Theatre, July 25, 1933), Cuala Press, 1917, enlarged edition, Macmillan, 1919.

Per Amica Silentia Lunae (nonfiction), Macmillan, 1918.

Two Plays for Dancers (includes "The Only Jealousy of Emer," first produced in foreign language in Amsterdam at Hollandsche Schouwburg, April 2, 1922, produced in English in Dublin at Abbey Theatre, May 9, 1926, revised as "Fighting the Waves" [also see below]; and "The Dreaming of the Bones," first produced in Dublin at Abbey Theatre, December 6, 1931), Cuala Press, 1919.

Four Plays for Dancers (includes "The Only Jealousy of Emer" and "At the Hawk's Well"), Macmillan, 1921.

Selected Poems, Macmillan, 1921.

Michael Robartes and the Dancer (poetry), Cuala Press, 1921.

Plays in Prose and Verse, Written for an Irish Theatre (includes "The Player Queen," first produced in London at King's Hall, May 25, 1919), Macmillan, 1922.

Later Poems, Macmillan (London), 1922, Macmillan (New York), 1924.

Seven Poems and a Fragment, first edition, 1922, reprinted, Cuala Press, 1970.

Plays and Controversies, Macmillan (London), 1923, Macmillan (New York), 1924.

Essays, Macmillan, 1924.

"The Cat and the Moon" and Certain Poems (includes play "The Cat and the Moon," first produced in Dublin at Abbey Theatre, May 9, 1926), Cuala Press, 1924.

The Bounty of Sweden (nonfiction), Cuala Press, 1925.

A Vision: An Explanation of Life Founded upon the Writings of Giraldus and upon Certain Doctrine Attributed to Kusta Ben Luka, T. Werner Laurie, 1925, revised edition published as *A Vision,* Macmillan (London), 1937, Macmillan (New York), 1938, published as *A Critical Edition of "Yeats's A Vision" (1925),* edited by George Mills Harper and Walter Kelly Hood, Macmillan, 1978.

October Blast (poetry), Cuala Press, 1927.

(Translator) "Sophocles' 'Oedipus at Colonus' " (also see below), first produced in Dublin at Abbey Theatre, September 12, 1927.

(Translator) *Sophocles' "King Oedipus"* (play; first produced in Dublin at Abbey Theatre, December 7, 1926), Macmillan, 1928.

The Tower (poetry; includes "The Tower," "Sailing to Byzantium," "Leda and the Swan," "Nineteen Hundred Nineteen," and "Among School Children"), Macmillan, 1928.

A Packet for Ezra Pound (nonfiction), Cuala Press, 1929.

The Winding Stair (poetry), Fountain Press, 1929, enlarged edition, Macmillan, 1933.

Words for Music Perhaps and Other Poems, Cuala Press, 1932.

Stories of Michael Robartes and His Friends (plays and fiction; includes play "The Resurrection," first produced in Dublin at Abbey Theatre, July 30, 1934), Cuala Press, 1932.

Letters to the New Island (essays and reviews), edited by Horace Reynolds, Harvard University Press, 1934, reprinted, Oxford University Press, 1970.

Wheels and Butterflies (plays), Macmillan (London), 1934, Macmillan (New York), 1935.

The King of the Great Clock Tower (play; first produced in Dublin at Abbey Theatre, July 30, 1934), Cuala Press, 1934, Macmillan, 1935.

The Words upon the Window Pane (play; first produced in Dublin at Abbey Theatre, November 17, 1930), Cuala Press, 1934.

Wheels and Butterflies (includes "Fighting the Waves" [revision of "The Only Jealousy of Emer"; also see above]), Macmillan, 1934.

A Full Moon in March, Macmillan, 1935.

Poems, Cuala Press, 1935.

New Poems, Cuala Press, 1938.

The Herne's Egg and Other Plays (includes "The Herne's Egg," first produced in 1950), Macmillan, 1938.

Purgatory (first produced in Dublin at Abbey Theatre, August 10, 1938), critical edition, Cornell University Press, 1985.

Last Poems and Two Plays (includes play "The Death of Cuchulain,"; and poems "The Gyres," "Lapis Lazuli," "The Wicked Old Man," "Crazy Jane on the Mountain," "The Man and the Echo," "Politics," and "Under Ben Bulben"), Cuala Press, 1939.

On the Boiler (nonfiction), Cuala Press, 1939.

Two Plays, Cuala Press, 1939.

Last Poems and Plays, Macmillan, 1940.

If I Were Four-and-Twenty (nonfiction), Cuala Press, 1940.

The Death of Cuchulain (first produced in 1949), critical edition edited by Phillip L. Marcus, Cornell University Press, 1981.

(With George Moore) *Diarmuid and Grania* (play; first produced in Dublin at Gaiety Theatre, October 21, 1901), Becker, 1951.

The Variorum Edition of the Poems of W. B. Yeats, edited by Peter Allt and Russell K. Alspach, Macmillan (New York), 1957, reprinted, 1987.

Mythologies (stories and essays), Macmillan, 1959.

The Senate Speeches of W. B. Yeats, edited by Donald R. Pearce, Indiana University Press, 1960.

Essays and Introductions, Macmillan, 1961.

Explorations (nonfiction), Macmillan, 1962.

The Variorum Edition of the Plays of W. B. Yeats, edited by Russell K. Alspach, Macmillan, 1966.

Uncollected Prose by W. B. Yeats, two volumes, edited by John P. Frayne and Colton Johnson, Columbia University Press, 1970.

(With Thomas Kinsella) *Davis, Mangan, Ferguson* (critical study), Dufour, 1971.

The Speckled Bird (unfinished novel), edited by William H. O'Donnell, Cuala Press, 1974, annotated edition, McClelland & Stewart, 1977.

(With Swami Shree) *The Ten Principal Upanishads,* Macmillan, 1975.

The Secret Rose: Stories by W. B. Yeats: A Variorum Edition, edited by Phillip L. Marcus, Warwick Gould, and Michael J. Sidnell, Cornell University Press, 1981.

Byzantium, Black Swan, 1983.

The Poems: A New Edition, edited by Richard J. Finneran, Macmillan, 1983.

Poems of W. B. Yeats: A New Selection, with an introduction and notes by A. Norman Jeffares, Macmillan, 1984.

A Poet to His Beloved: The Early Love Poems of W. B. Yeats, St. Martin's, 1985.

Treasury of Irish Myth, Legend, and Folklore, Crown, 1986.

Mosada [and] *The Island of Statues: Manuscript Materials,* edited by George Bornstein, Cornell University Press, 1987.

The Early Poems: Manuscript Materials, edited by George Bornstein, Cornell University Press, 1987.

(With others) *The Second Book of the Rhymers Club,* British American Books, 1987.

Also author of *Irish Fairy and Folk Tales,* 1918. Contributor to periodicals.

AUTOBIOGRAPHIES AND DIARIES

Reveries Over Childhood and Youth, Cuala Press, 1915, Macmillan, 1916.

Four Years, Cuala Press, 1921.

The Trembling of the Veil, T. Werner Laurie, 1922.

Autobiographies: "Reveries Over Childhood and Youth" and "The Trembling of the Veil," Macmillan (London), 1926, Macmillan (New York), 1927.

The Death of Synge and Other Passages from an Old Diary, Cuala Press, 1928.

Dramatis Personae, Cuala Press, 1935.

"Dramatis Personae," "Estrangement," "The Death of Synge," "The Bounty of Sweden," Macmillan (London and New York), 1936.

The Autobiography of William Butler Yeats, Consisting of "Reveries Over Childhood and Youth," "The Trembling of the Veil," and "Dramatis Personae," Macmillan, 1938, reprinted, 1987, published with *Estrangement, The Death of Synge,* and *The Bounty of Sweden,* as *Autobiographies,* Macmillan, 1955.

Pages from a Diary Written in Nineteen Hundred and Thirty, Cuala Press, 1944.

Memoirs: Autobiography, edited by Denis Donoghue, Macmillan, 1972.

LETTERS

Letters on Poetry from W. B. Yeats to Dorothy Wellesley, Oxford University Press, 1940.

W. B. Yeats and T. Sturge Moore: Their Correspondence: 1901-1937, edited by Ursula Bridge, Routledge & Kegan Paul, 1953.

Some Letters from W. B. Yeats to John O'Leary and His Sister, edited by Allan Wade, New York Public Library, 1953.

Letters of W. B. Yeats to Katharine Tynan, edited by Roger McHugh, Macmillan, 1953.

The Letters of W. B. Yeats, edited by Allan Wade, Macmillan, 1954.

Ah, Sweet Dancer: W. B. Yeats and Margot Ruddock, a Correspondence, edited by Roger McHugh, Macmillan, 1970.

The Correspondence of Robert Bridges and W. B. Yeats, edited by Richard J. Finneran, Macmillan, 1977.

Theatre Business: The Correspondence of the First Abbey Theatre Directors: William Butler Yeats, Lady Gregory and J. M. Synge, edited by Ann Saddlemyer, Colin Smythe, 1982.

The Collected Letters of W. B. Yeats, Volume 1: *1865-1895,* edited by John Kelly and Eric Domville, Oxford University Press, 1986.

EDITOR

(With Edwin John Ellis) *The Works of William Blake, Poetic, Symbolic, and Critical,* Quaritch, 1893.

The Oxford Book of Modern Verse: 1892-1935, Clarendon Press, 1936.

(And translator, with Shri Purohit Swami) *The Ten Principal Upanishads,* Macmillan, 1937.

Fairy and Folk Tales of Ireland, Colin Smythe, 1973.

Representative Irish Tales, Dufour, 1979.

Also editor of *A Book of Irish Verse,* 1900.

COLLECTED WORKS

The Collected Works in Verse and Prose of William Butler Yeats, eight volumes, Shakespeare Head Press, 1908.

The Collected Poems, Macmillan (London and New York), 1933.

The Collected Plays (includes "Sophocles's 'Oedipus at Colonus' "), Macmillan, 1934.

Nine One-Act Plays, Macmillan, 1937.

The Poems of W. B. Yeats, two volumes, Macmillan, 1949.

The Collected Poems of W. B. Yeats, Macmillan, 1950.

The Collected Plays of W. B. Yeats, Macmillan (London), 1952, Macmillan (New York), 1953.

Eleven Plays of William Butler Yeats, Macmillan, 1967.

Selected Poems and Three Plays, 3rd revised edition edited by M. L. Rosenthal, Macmillan, 1987.

Collected works also published in fourteen volumes by Macmillan, 1989—.

SIDELIGHTS: William Butler Yeats is widely acknowledged as the greatest poet of the twentieth century. He belonged to the Protestant, Anglo-Irish minority that had controlled the economic, political, social, and cultural life of Ireland since at least the end of the seventeenth century. Most members of this minority considered themselves English people who merely happened to have been born in Ireland, but Yeats was staunch in affirming his Irish nationality. Although he lived in London for fourteen years of his childhood (and kept a permanent home there during the first half of his adult life), Yeats maintained his cultural roots, featuring Irish legends and heroes in many of his poems and plays. He was equally firm in adhering to his self-image as an artist. This conviction led many to accuse him of elitism, but it also unquestionably contributed to his greatness. As fellow poet W. H. Auden noted in a 1948 *Kenyon Review* essay entitled "Yeats as an Example," Yeats accepted the modern necessity of having to make a lonely and deliberate "choice of the principles and presuppositions in terms of which [made] sense of his experience." Auden assigned Yeats the high praise of having written "some of the most beautiful poetry" of modern times.

Eighteen eighty-five was an important year in Yeats's early adult life, marking the first publication, in the *Dublin University Review,* of his poetry and the beginning of his important interest in occultism. It was also the year that he met John O'Leary, a famous patriot who had returned to Ireland after totaling twenty years of imprisonment and exile for revolutionary nationalistic activities. O'Leary had a keen enthusiasm for Irish books, music, and ballads, and he encouraged young writers to adopt Irish subjects. Yeats, who had preferred more romantic settings and themes, soon took O'Leary's advice, producing many poems based on Irish legends, Irish folklore, and Irish ballads and songs. As he explained in a note included in the 1908 volume *Collected Works in Verse and Prose of William Butler Yeats:* "When I first wrote I went here and there for my subjects as my reading led me, and preferred to all other countries Arcadia and the India of romance, but presently I convinced myself . . . that I should never go for the scenery of a poem to any country but my own, and I think that I shall hold to that conviction to the end."

As Yeats began concentrating his poetry on Irish subjects, he was compelled to accompany his family in moving to London at the end of 1886. There he continued to devote himself to Irish subjects, writing poems, plays, novels, and short stories—all with Irish characters and scenes. In addition, he produced book reviews, usually on Irish topics. The most important event in Yeats's life during these London years, however, was his acquaintance with Maud Gonne, a tall, beautiful, prominent young woman passionately devoted to Irish nationalism. Yeats soon fell in love with Gonne, and for nearly three decades he courted her; although he eventually learned that she had already borne two children from a long affair, with Gonne's encouragement Yeats redoubled his dedication to Irish nationalism and produced such nationalistic plays as "The Countess Kathleen" (1892), which he dedicated to her, and "Cathleen ni Houlihan" (1902), which featured her as the personification of Ireland in the title role.

Gonne also shared Yeats's interest in occultism and spiritualism. Yeats had been a theosophist, but in 1890 he turned from its sweeping mystical insights and joined the Golden Dawn, a secret society that practiced ritual magic. The society offered instruction and initiation in a series of ten levels, the three highest of which were unattainable except by magi (who were thought to possess the secrets of supernatural wisdom and enjoy magically extended lives). Yeats was fascinated by the possibility of becoming a magi, and he became convinced that the mind was capable of perceiving past the limits of materialistic rationalism. Yeats remained an active member of the Golden Dawn for thirty-two years, becoming involved in its direction at the turn of the century and achieving the coveted sixth grade of membership in 1914, the same year that his future wife, Georgiana Hyde-Lees, also joined the society.

Although Yeats's occult ambitions were a powerful force in his private thoughts, the Golden Dawn's emphasis on the supernatural clashed with his own need—as a poet—for interaction in the physical world, and thus in his public role he preferred to follow the example of John Keats, a Romantic poet who remained—in comparison with Romantics William Blake and Percy Bysshe Shelley—relatively close to the materials of life. Yeats avoided what he considered the obscurity of Blake, whose poetic images came from mystical visions rather than from the familiar physical world. Even so, Yeats's visionary and idealist interests were more closely aligned with those of Blake—and Shelley—than

with those of Keats, and in the 1899 collection *The Wind among the Reeds* he featured several poems employing occult symbolism.

Most of Yeats's poetry, however, used symbols from ordinary life and from familiar traditions, and much of his poetry in the 1890s continued to reflect his interest in Irish subjects. During this decade he also became increasingly interested in poetic techniques. He befriended English decadent poet Lionel Johnson, and in 1890 they helped found the Rhymers' Club, a group of London poets who met to read and discuss their poems. The Rhymers placed a very high value on subjectivity and craftsmanship and preferred sophisticated aestheticism to nationalism. The club's influence is reflected in the lush density of Yeats's poetry of the times, culminating in *The Wind among the Reeds* (1899). Although Yeats was soon to abandon that lush density, he remained permanently committed to the Rhymers' insistence that a poet should labor "at rhythm and cadence, at form and style"—as he reportedly told a Dublin audience in 1893.

The turn of the century marked Yeats's increased interest in theatre, an interest influenced by his father, a famed artist and orator whose love of highly dramatic moments in literature certainly contributed to Yeats's lifelong interest in drama. In the summer of 1897 the author enjoyed his first stay at Coole Park, the County Galway estate of Lady Augusta Gregory. There he devised, with Lady Gregory and her neighbor Edward Martyn, plans for promoting an innovative, native Irish drama. In 1899 they staged the first of three annual productions in Dublin, including Yeats's "The Countess Kathleen," and in 1902 they supported a company of amateur Irish actors in staging both George Russell's Irish legend "Deirdre" and Yeats's "Cathleen ni Houlihan." The success of these productions led to the founding of the Irish National Theatre Society with Yeats as president. With a wealthy sponsor volunteering to pay for the renovation of Dublin's Abbey Theatre as a permanent home for the company, the theatre opened on December 27, 1904, and included plays by the company's three directors: Lady Gregory, John M. Synge (whose 1907 production "The Playboy of the Western World" would spark controversy with its savage comic depiction of Irish rural life), and Yeats, who was represented that night with "On Baile's Strand," the first of his several plays featuring heroic ancient Irish warrior Cuchulain.

During the entire first decade of the twentieth century Yeats was extremely active in the management of the Abbey Theatre company, choosing plays, hiring and firing actors and managers, and arranging tours for the company. At this time he also wrote ten plays, and the simple, direct style of dialogue required for the stage became an important consideration in his poems as well. He abandoned the heavily elaborated style of *The Wind among the Reeds* in favor of conversational rhythms and radically simpler diction. This transformation in his poetic style can be traced in his first three collections of the twentieth century: *In the Seven Woods* (1903), *The Green Helmet and Other Poems* (1910), and *Responsibilities* (1914). Several poems in those collections use style as their subject. For example, in "A Coat," written in 1912, Yeats derided his 1890s poetic style, saying that he had once adorned his poems with a coat "covered with embroideries / Out of old mythologies." The poem concludes with a brash announcement: "There's more enterprise / In walking naked." This departure from a conventional nineteenth-century manner disappointed his contemporary readers, who preferred the pleasant musicality of such familiar poems as "The Lake Isle of Innisfree," which he wrote in 1890.

Simplification was only the first of several major stylistic changes. In "Yeats as an Example?" an essay in *Preoccupations: Selected Prose 1968-1978,* the prominent Irish poet Seamus Heaney commended Yeats for continually altering and refining his poetic craftsmanship. "He is, indeed, the ideal example for a poet approaching middle age," Heaney declared. "He reminds you that revision and slog-work are what you may have to undergo if you seek the satisfaction of finish; he bothers you with the suggestion that if you have managed to do one kind of poem in your own way, you should cast off that way and face into another area of your experience until you have learned a new voice to say that area properly."

Eventually, Yeats began experimenting as a playwright; in 1916, for instance, he adopted a deliberately esoteric, nonrealistic dramatic style based on Japanese Noh plays, a theatrical form to which he had been introduced by poet Ezra Pound. These plays were described by Yeats as "plays for dancers."

While Yeats fulfilled his duties as president of the Abbey Theatre group for the first fifteen years of the twentieth century, his nationalistic fervor, however, was less evident. Maud Gonne, with whom he had shared his Irish enthusiasms, had moved to Paris with her husband, exiled Irish revolutionary John MacBride, and the author was left without her important encouragement. But in 1916 he once again became a staunch exponent of the nationalist cause, inspired by the Easter Rising, an unsuccessful, six-day armed rebellion of Irish republicans against the British in Dublin. MacBride, who was now separated from Gonne, participated in the rebellion and was executed afterwards. Yeats reacted by writing "Easter, 1916," an eloquent expression of his complex feelings of shock, romantic admiration, and a more realistic appraisal.

The Easter Rising contributed to Yeats's eventual decision to reside in Ireland rather than England, and his marriage to Georgie Hyde-Lees in 1917 further strengthened that resolve. Earlier, in an introductory verse to *Responsibilities,* he had asked his ancestors' pardon for not yet having married to continue his Irish lineage: "Although I have come close on forty-nine, / I have no child, I have nothing but a book." Once married, however, Yeats traveled with his bride to Thoor Ballylee, a medieval stone tower where the couple periodically resided. With marriage came another period of exploration into complex and esoteric subjects for Yeats. He had long been fascinated by the contrast between a person's internal and external selves—between the true person and those aspects that the person chooses to present as a representation of the self. Yeats had first mentioned the value of masks in 1910 in a simple poem, "The Mask," where a woman reminds her lover that his interest in her depends on her guise and not on her hidden, inner self. Yeats gave eloquent expression to this idea of the mask in a group of essays, *Per Amica Silentia Lunae* (1918): "I think all happiness depends on the energy to assume the mask of some other life, on a re-birth as something not one's self." This notion can be found in a wide variety of Yeats's poems.

Yeats also continued to explored mysticism. Only four days after the wedding, his bride began what would be a lengthy experiment with the psychic phenomenon called automatic writing, in which her hand and pen presumably served as unconscious instruments for the spirit world to send information. Yeats and his wife held more than four hundred sessions of automatic writing, producing nearly four thousand pages that Yeats avidly and patiently studied and organized. From these sessions Yeats formulated theories about life and history. He believed that certain patterns existed, the most important being what he called *gyres,* in-terpenetrating cones representing mixtures of opposites of both a personal and historical nature. He contended that gyres were initiated by the divine impregnation of a mortal woman—first, the rape of Leda by Zeus; later, the immaculate conception of Mary. Yeats found that within each two-thousand-year era, emblematic moments occurred at the midpoints of the thousand-year halves. At these moments of balance, he believed, a civilization could achieve special excellence, and Yeats cited as examples the splendor of Athens at 500 B.C., Byzantium at A.D. 500, and the Italian Renaissance at A.D. 1500.

Yeats further likened these historical cycles to the twenty-eight day lunar cycle, contending that physical existence grows steadily until it reaches a maximum at the full moon (phase fifteen), which Yeats described as perfect beauty. In the remaining half of the cycle, physical existence gradually falls away, until it disappears completely at the new moon, whereupon the cycle begins again. Applying this pattern both to historical eras and to individuals' lives, Yeats observed that a person completes the phases as he advances from birth to maturity and declines toward death. Yeats further elaborated the scheme by assigning particular phases to specific types of personality, so that although each person passes through phases two through fourteen and sixteen through twenty-eight during a lifetime, one phase provides an overall characterization of the individual's entire life. Yeats published his intricate and not completely systematic theories of personality and history in *A Vision* (1925; substantially revised in 1937), and some of the symbolic patterns (gyres, moon phases) with which he organized these theories provide important background to many of the poems and plays he wrote during the second half of his career.

During these years of Yeats's esoterica Ireland was rife with internal strife. In 1921 bitter controversies erupted within the new Irish Free State over the partition of Northern Ireland and over the wording of a formal oath of allegiance to the British Crown. These issues led to an Irish civil war, which lasted from June, 1922, to May, 1923. In this conflict Yeats emphatically sided with the new Irish government. He accepted a six-year appointment to the senate of the Irish Free State in December, 1922, a time when rebels were kidnapping government figures and burning their homes. In Dublin, where Yeats had assumed permanent residence in 1922 (after maintaining a home for thirty years in London), the government even posted armed sentries at his door. As senator, Yeats considered himself a representative of order amid the chaotic new nation's slow progress toward stability. He was now the "sixty-year-old smiling public man" of his poem "Among School Children," which he wrote after touring an Irish elementary school. But he was also a world renowned artist of impressive stature, having received the Nobel Prize for Literature in 1923.

Yeats's poems and plays produced during his senate term and beyond are, at once, local and general, personal and public, Irish and universal. At night the poet could "sweat with terror" (a phrase in his poem "Nineteen Hundred and Nineteen") because of the surrounding violence, but he could also generalize those terrifying realities by linking them with events in the rest of the world and with all of history. The energy of the poems written in response to these disturbing times gave astonishing power to his collection *The Tower* (1928), which is often considered his best single book, though *The Wild Swans at Coole* (1917; enlarged edition, 1919), *Michael Robartes and the Dancer* (1921), *The Tower, The Winding Stair* (1929); enlarged edition, 1933), and *Words for Music Perhaps and Other Poems* (1932), also possess considerable merit.

Another important element of poems in both these collections and other volumes is Yeats's keen awareness of old age. Even his romantic poems from the late 1890s often mention gray hair and weariness, though those poems were written while he was still a young man. But when Yeats was nearly sixty, his health began to fail and he was faced with real, rather than imaginary, "bodily decrepitude" (a phrase from "After Long Silence") and nearness to death. Nevertheless, despite the author's often keen awareness of his physical decline, the last fifteen years of his life were marked by extraordinary vitality and an appetite for life. He continued to write plays, including "Sophocles' 'King Oedipus' " and "Sophocles' 'Oedipus at Colonus' " (translations performed with masks in 1926 and 1927) and "The Words upon the Window Pane" (1934), a full-length work about spiritualism and the eighteenth-century Irish writer Jonathan Swift. In 1929, as an expression of gaiety after recovering from a serious illness, he also wrote a series of brash, vigorous poems narrated by a fictitious old peasant woman, "Crazy Jane." His pose as "The Wild Old Wicked Man" (the title of one of his poems) and his poetical revitalization was reflected in the title of his 1938 volume *New Poems*.

As Yeats aged, he saw Ireland change in ways that angered him. The Anglo-Irish Protestant minority no longer controlled Irish society and culture, and with Lady Gregory's death in 1932 and the consequent abandonment of the Coole Park estate, Yeats felt detached from the brilliant achievements of the eighteenth-century Anglo-Irish tradition. According to Yeats's unblushingly antidemocratic view, the greatness of Anglo-Irishmen such as Jonathan Swift, philosopher George Berkeley, and statesman Edmund Burke, contrasted sharply with the undistinguished commonness of contemporary Irish society, which seemed preoccupied with the interests of merchants and peasants. He stated his unpopular opinions in late plays such as *Purgatory* (1938) and the essays of *On the Boiler* (1939).

But Yeats offset his frequently brazen manner with the personal conflicts expressed in his last poems. He faced death with a courage that was founded partly on his vague hope for reincarnation and partly on his admiration for the bold heroism that he perceived in Ireland in both ancient times and the eighteenth century. In proud moods he could speak in the stern voice of his famous epitaph, written within six months of his death, which concludes his poem "Under Ben Bulben": *"Cast a cold eye / On life, on death. / Horseman, pass by!"* But the bold sureness of those lines is complicated by the error-stricken cry that "distracts my thought" at the end of another late poem, "The Man and the Echo," and also by the poignantly frivolous lust for life in the last lines of "Politics," the poem that he wanted to close *Last Poems:* "But O that I were young again / And held her in my arms."

Throughout his last years Yeats's creative imagination remained very much his own, isolated to a remarkable degree from the successive fashions of modern poetry despite his extensive contacts with other poets. Literary modernism held no inherent attraction for him except perhaps in its general association with youthful vigor. He admired a wide range of traditional English poetry and drama, and he simply was unconcerned that, during the last two decades of his life, his preference for using rhyme and strict stanza forms would set him apart from the vogue of modern poetry. Yeats's allegiance to poetic tradition did not extend, however, to what he considered an often obscure, overly learned use of literary and cultural traditions by T. S. Eliot and Pound. Yeats deplored the tremendous enthusiasm among younger poets for Eliot's *The Waste Land*, published in 1922. Disdaining Eliot's flat rhythms and cold, dry mood, Yeats wanted all art to be full of energy. He felt that the literary traditions furnishing Eliot with so many allusions and quotations should only be included in a poem if those traditions had so excited the individual poet's imagination that they could become poetic ingredients of the sort Yeats described in "The Tower": "Poet's imaginings / And memories of love, / Memories of the words of women, / All those things whereof / Man makes a superhuman / Mirror-resembling dream."

Yeats wanted poetry to engage the full complexity of life, but only insofar as the individual poet's imagination had direct access to experience or thought and only insofar as those materials were transformed by the energy of artistic articulation. He was, from first to last, a poet who tried to transform the local concerns of his own life by embodying them in the resonantly universal language of his poems. His brilliant rhetorical accomplishments, strengthened by his considerable powers of rhythm and poetic phrase, have earned wide praise from readers and, especially, from fellow poets, including W. H. Auden (who praised Yeats as the savior of English lyric poetry), Stephen Spender, Theodore Roethke, and Philip Larkin. It is not likely that time will diminish his achievements.

BIOGRAPHICAL/CRITICAL SOURCES:

BOOKS

Archibald, Douglas, *Yeats,* Syracuse University Press, 1983.
Bloom, Harold, *Yeats,* Oxford University Press, 1970.
Bradley, Anthony, *William Butler Yeats,* Ungar, 1979.
Dictionary of Literary Biography, Gale, Volume 10: *Modern British Dramatists, 1940-1945,* 1982, Volume 19: *British Poets, 1840-1914,* 1983.
Domville, Eric, *A Concordance to the Plays of W. B. Yeats,* two volumes, Cornell University Press, 1972.
Donoghue, Denis, *William Butler Yeats,* Viking, 1971.
Ellmann, Richard, *The Identity of Yeats,* 2nd edition, Faber, 1964.
Ellmann, Richard, *Yeats: The Man and the Masks,* 2nd edition, Faber, 1961.
Heaney, Seamus, *Preoccupations: Selected Prose 1968-1978,* Faber, 1980.
Henn, Thomas R., *The Lonely Tower,* 2nd edition, Methuen, 1965.
Hone, Joseph W., *W. B. Yeats: 1865-1939,* 2nd edition, Macmillan, 1965.
Jeffares, A. Norman, *W. B. Yeats: Man and Poet,* 2nd edition, Barnes & Noble, 1966.
Jochum, K. P. S., *W. B. Yeats: A Classified Bibliography of Criticism, Including Additions to Allan Wade's Bibliography of the Writings of W. B. Yeats and a Section on the Irish Literary and Dramatic Revival,* University of Illinois Press, 1978.
Parrish, Steven M., *A Concordance to the Poems of W. B. Yeats,* Cornell University Press, 1963.
Peterson, Richard, *William Butler Yeats,* Twayne, 1982.
Ransom, John Crowe, editor, *The Kenyon Critics: Studies in Modern Literature from "The Kenyon Review,"* World Publishing, 1951.
Twentieth-Century Literary Criticism, Gale, Volume 1, 1978, Volume 11, 1983, Volume 18, 1985, Volume 31, 1989.
Vendler, Helen, *Yeats's "Vision" and the Later Plays,* Harvard University Press, 1963.
Yeats Annual, Macmillan (London), 1982—.
Yeats: An Annual of Critical and Textual Studies, Cornell University Press, 1983—.
Yeats, William Butler, *The Collected Poems of W. B. Yeats,* Macmillan, 1950.

Yeats, William Butler, *Memoirs: Autobiography,* edited by Denis Donaghue, Macmillan, 1972.
Yeats, William Butler, *The Autobiography of William Butler Yeats, Consisting of "Reveries Over Childhood and Youth," "The Trembling of the Veil," and "Dramatis Personae,"* Macmillan, 1987.

PERIODICALS

Times (London), January 28, 1989, May 6, 1989.
Tri-Quarterly, winter, 1965.

*   *   *

YERBY, Frank G(arvin) 1916-

PERSONAL: Born September 5, 1916, in Augusta, Ga.; son of Rufus Garvin (a postal clerk) and Wilhelmina (Smythe) Yerby; married Flora Helen Claire Williams, March 1, 1941 (divorced); married Blanca Call-Perez (now her husband's secretary, translator, researcher, and "general manager"), July 27, 1956; children: (first marriage) Jacques Loring, Nikki Ethlyn, Faune Ellena, Jan Keith. *Education:* Paine College, A.B., 1937; Fisk University, M.A., 1938; graduate study, University of Chicago, 1939. *Politics:* Independent. *Religion:* Agnostic.

ADDRESSES: Home and office—Edificio Torres Blancas, Apt. 710, Avenida de America, 37, Madrid 2, Spain. *Agent*—Owen Laster, William Morris Agency, 1350 Avenue of the Americas, New York, N.Y. 10019.

CAREER: Novelist. Florida Agricultural and Mechanical College (now University), Tallahassee, instructor in English, 1939-40; Southern University and Agricultural and Mechanical College, Baton Rouge, La., instructor in English, 1940-41; Ford Motor Co., Dearborn, Mich., laboratory technician, 1941-44; Ranger (Fairchild) Aircraft, Jamaica, N.Y., chief inspector, Magnaflux, 1944-45; resident of Madrid, Spain, since 1955; also lived in France for an extended period earlier in the 1950s.

MEMBER: Authors Guild (New York), Authors League of America, Real Sociedad Hipica Espanola (Madrid), Madrid Country Club.

AWARDS, HONORS: O. Henry Memorial Award, 1944, for best first short story, "Health Card"; Doctor of Letters, Fisk University, 1976, and Doctor of Humane Letters, Paine College, 1977; named honorary citizen of State of Tennessee by Governor's Proclamation, 1977.

WRITINGS:

NOVELS; ORIGINALLY PUBLISHED BY DIAL

The Foxes of Harrow, 1946, reprinted, Dell, 1986.
The Vixens, 1947, reprinted, Dell, 1976.
The Golden Hawk, 1948.
Pride's Castle, 1949.
Floodtide, 1950.
A Woman Called Fancy, 1951.
The Saracen Blade, 1952.
The Devil's Laughter, 1953.
Benton's Row, 1954.
The Treasure of Pleasant Valley, 1955.
Captain Rebel, 1956.
Fairoaks, 1957.
The Serpent and the Staff, 1958.
Jarrett's Jade, 1959.
Gillian, 1960.
The Garfield Honor, 1961.
Griffin's Way, 1962.

The Old Gods Laugh: A Modern Romance, 1964.
An Odor of Sanctity: A Novel of Medieval Moorish Spain, 1965.
Goat Song: A Novel of Ancient Greece, 1968.
Judas My Brother: The Story of the Thirteenth Disciple, 1968.
Speak Now: A Modern Novel, 1969.
The Dahomean: An Historical Novel, 1971 (published in England as *The Man From Dahomey,* Heinemann, 1972).
The Girl from Storyville: A Victorian Novel, 1972.
The Voyage Unplanned, 1974.
Tobias and the Angel, 1975.
A Rose for Ana Maria, 1976.
Hail the Conquering Hero, 1977.
A Darkness at Ingraham's Crest: A Tale of the Slaveholding South, 1979.
Western: A Saga of the Great Plains, 1982.

NOVELS; PUBLISHED BY DOUBLEDAY

Bride of Liberty, 1954.
Devilseed, 1984.
McKenzie's Hundred, 1985.

CONTRIBUTOR

John Fischer and Robert B. Silvers, editors, *Writing in America,* Rutgers University Press, 1960.
Langston Hughes, editor, *The Best Short Stories by Negro Writers: An Anthology from 1899 to the Present,* Little, Brown, 1967.
Darwin T. Turner, editor, *Black American Literature,* C. E. Merrill. 1969.
Gerald Goff, editor, *Voices of Man/This is Just to Say,* Addison-Wesley, 1969.
Arna Bontemps and Hughes, editors, *The Poetry of the Negro, 1746-1970,* Doubleday, 1970.
Stewart H. Benedict, editor, *Blacklash,* Popular Library, 1970.
Elizabeth White, Joan Wofford, and Edward J. Gordon, editors, *Understanding Literature,* Ginn, 1970.
Ramay K. Singh and Peter Fellowes, editors, *Black Literature in America: A Casebook,* Crowell, 1970.
Conn McAuliffe, editor, *Re-Action,* Boyd & Fraser, 1971.

OTHER

Contributor to *Harper's, Liberty, Collier's France Soir, Le Meuse, La Laterne, Berlin Zeitung,* and numerous other periodicals.

SIDELIGHTS: A prolific novelist who has published thirty-two tales of adventure, Frank G. Yerby has sold more than fifty-five million hardback and paperback books in the last forty years. While many of these novels have been best-sellers, their popularity has had little effect on Yerby's critical stature. Since the appearance of his first novel, *The Foxes of Harrow,* in 1946, the author has been routinely—and some say unfairly—slighted by critics. Early in his career, for instance, when Yerby was producing mainstream fiction, black reviewers attacked him for abandoning his race. Those who knew his work, but not his color, accused him of squandering his writing talent on cardboard characters and hackneyed plots. Still others objected to his "overblown" prose and the way he sensationalized his material. Writing in *The Negro Novel in America,* Robert A. Bone dubbed him "the prince of the pulpsters."

In the face of such criticism, Yerby has steadfastly maintained his integrity: "The only excuse for writing is that you love it beyond measure and beyond reason," he once commented, adding that "to make any compromise whatsoever for the sake of sales or popularity is to join the world's oldest profession. I believe that a writer should have the guts to starve; and that if he doesn't come close to it most of the time, he'd better take a long, hard look at what he's doing. . . . I write only because I have to. What I get out of it financially doesn't come under consideration at all. I write exactly what I feel and think . . . but within that framework I try to give pleasure to the reading public."

Yerby's novels are characterized by colorful language, complex plot lines, and a multiplicity of characters. Hugh M. Gloster calls Yerby's formula "the recipe of Southern historical romance," listing the following ingredients in *Crisis* magazine: "a bold, handsome, rakish, but withal somewhat honorable hero; a frigid, respectable wife; a torrid unrespectable mistress; and usually a crafty, fiendish villain." According to the *Washington Post Book World,* "a typical Yerby plot seems to involve a strong man who has to choose between two women and . . . more-than-generous helpings of revenge, madness, suffering and violence." *Time* sums up his writing as "a crude, shrewd combination of sex, violence, sadism, costuming and cliche."

A common criticism of Yerby's fiction is that he habitually solves apparently insoluble problems through a *deus ex machina,* or stroke of fate. "Despite his skillful tangling and untangling of exciting narratives which mesmerize even many sophisticated readers, Yerby too often depends on contrived endings," writes Darwin T. Turner in *The Black Novelist.* Nick Aaron Ford echoes this sentiment in *Phylon,* writing that in all Yerby's books "there are scenes of great literary power, followed by episodes of incredible adventure, with too little preparation for the miraculous results. . . . This is not to say that Yerby is an inferior writer. He has rich imagination, a talent for vivid expression, ability to create pity and terror, and an understanding of the suffering of the poor and the oppressed. In short, he possesses the qualifications that could make of him a great novelist. But it appears that Yerby is satisfied with popularity and greatness. He says emphatically, 'I think the novelist has a professional obligation to please his reading public.' "

A more sensitive arena is Yerby's treatment of racial issues. The second of four children of a racially mixed couple, Yerby encountered his share of discrimination as a boy. "When I was young," he told *People* magazine, "a bunch of us black kids would get in a fight with white kids and then I'd have to fight with a black kid who got on me for being so light." Though he was an excellent student, and, after graduation, secured teaching positions at a number of black universities, Yerby became dissatisfied with what he regarded as the "stifling" atmosphere of these "Uncle Tom factories" and abandoned academia for a wartime factory job in Detroit. His first published fiction, which earned him an O. Henry Memorial Award in 1944, was a bitter story of racial injustice called "Health Card." It was the last black theme he would directly address in his fiction for almost thirty years.

Following "Health Card," Yerby published a string of historical novels with Anglo-Saxon protagonists, leading Hugh M. Gloster to surmise that Yerby "gained his laurels by focusing upon white rather than Negro characters. Performance—and not pigmentation—has been the basis of his success." Yerby staunchly defends his focus, explaining that "the novelist hasn't any right to inflict on the public his private ideas on politics, religion or race. If he wants to preach he should go on the pulpit." Later he stated: "My mother was Scotch-Irish, a grandparent was an Indian; I've far more Irish blood than Negro. I simply insist on remaining a member of the human race. I don't think a writer's output should be dictated by a biological accident. It happens there are many things I know far better than the race problem."

Yerby's personal solution to problems of discrimination was to leave the country. He moved from the United States to Spain in 1955 and has remained there ever since.

Despite his contempt for didactic fiction, Yerby does address racial issues indirectly in several novels, some critics say. "In his earliest novels, the racial problems are employed peripherally, almost perfunctorily, and occupy little space or overt interest in the novel," writes Jack B. Moore in the *Journal of Popular Culture.* "None the less Yerby's racial attitudes pervade these early novels of the South, sometimes in obvious and sometimes in disguised fashion." Darwin T. Turner sees Yerby's position manifested in "the theme of the outcast who, as in existentialist literature, pits his will against a hostile universe. By intelligence and courage, he proves himself superior to a society which rejects him because of his alien, inferior, or illegitimate birth."

This theme surfaces in his first novel, *The Foxes of Harrow,* a lush southern romance which traces the fortunes of the dashing young Stephen Fox in his rise from poverty to great wealth. It is "a good, old-fashioned obese historical novel of the Old South that seems, more than once, to be haunted by the affluent ghost of Scarlett O'Hara," according to the *New York Times.* While acknowledging Yerby's ability to hold the reader captive with his fast-paced plotting and vivid prose, many critics dismiss the book as socially insignificant melodrama. *New Yorker* contributor Edmund Wilson, for instance, notes that Yerby "has packed everything in—passion, politics, creole society, sex, the clash of races, and war—but he never captures the faintest flutter of the breath of life." In N. L. Rothman's view, "the book rings throughout with colorful passions and the words to match. It is not a historical novel—for that must have some reality in it," he continues in the *Saturday Review of Literature,* "but it is a good example of the technicolored fantasies that have been passing as such of late." In recent years, Yerby himself has belittled the work, telling *People* magazine that *The Foxes of Harrow* comprises "every romantic cliche in history."

The novel's literary shortcomings had no effect on its enormous popularity. With sales of over two million copies, *The Foxes of Harrow* became one of the hottest titles of the decade. It was translated into at least twelve languages, reprinted in several national magazines, and made into a lucrative movie starring Rex Harrison and Maureen O'Hara.

Though Yerby despised the film adaptation, he was pleased with his novel's popular acceptance, and he continued to work the vein of historical fiction in future books. His next novel, *The Vixens,* utilized research material he hadn't been able to incorporate into his first book. And he followed *The Vixens* with a string of other southern romances, set for the most part in the nineteenth century. With *The Golden Hawk,* in 1948, Yerby turned to picaresque adventure in other lands and earlier centuries. And his research, which had been admittedly careless in his first novels, became meticulous.

While Yerby's novels of the 1950s and 1960s qualify as popular fiction, they also reflect some serious concerns. In addition to escapism, they "exhibit another dimension, disregarded by the readers who lament Yerby's failure to write an historical novel and by the others who condemn his refusal to write an overtly polemical treatise on the plight of the American Negro," according to Darwin T. Turner in *The Black Novelist.* "Ideas—bitter ironies, caustic debunkings, painful gropings for meaning—writhe behind the soap-facade of his fiction." And, in 1971, after protesting his indifference to racial issues for many years, Yerby addressed the matter directly in *The Dahomean,* his novel of Black Africa.

Set in the nineteenth century, *The Dahomean* traces the life of Nyasanu/Hwesu as he advances in position from a chief's son to governor of an entire province, only to be sold into American slavery by two jealous relatives. "At the same time, his rise and fall illustrates the customs and folkways of his country: the rites of manhood and marriage; the feudal system; war," according to the *New York Times Book Review.* "Virtues of the book," says Turner, writing in *Black World,* "are the presentation of an exciting and illuminating history of Black people and a determined focus of the story on a single Black hero. But there is more. In *The Dahomean,* Yerby's strength reveals itself to best advantage and even his former weaknesses become strengths. . . . Yerby is at his best when he envelops his plot with a history he has unearthed painstakingly and with a serious or satirical but always devastating debunking of historical legends and myths. That achievement is superior in *The Dahomean,* not so much in the presentation of historical facts as in the presentation of a people and a culture."

In a prefatory note to the novel, Yerby explains that part of his reason for writing the book was "to correct, so far as possible, the Anglo-Saxon reader's historical perspective" on black history. By portraying the Dahomean culture in all its rich complexity, Yerby dispels the myth of a totally primitive Africa, even hinting at times that the tribal cultures "sometimes surpassed in their subtlety, their complexity, their dignity the ones to which the slaves were brought," in the *Best Sellers* critic's words. But in depicting the cruelties that certain tribesmen perpetrated on their black brothers, including selling them into slavery, Yerby also shatters the illusion that blacks are inherently superior morally. What Yerby seems to be suggesting, Turner maintains, is that "the differences between people do not stem from a difference of blood, but from a difference of opportunity and power."

Hailed by several reviewers as Yerby's masterpiece, *The Dahomean* also settled an old score for the author, as he explained: "I am much more relaxed about racial matters, that increased tranquility being due in part to the fact that *The Dahomean* received (with one lone exception) rave notices from the critics. Thereafter, reviewers seemed to have waked up to what I was actually writing as distinct from and opposed to 1) what I used to write; and 2) what they thought I was writing. In short, I seem to have succeeded in changing many critics' minds. Pleasantly surprising was the high praise bestowed upon this novel by the critics of the South African papers. Needless to say, black critics immediately removed me from the list of 'non-conductors' and welcomed me back into the fold like a sinner redeemed by faith."

Yerby postulates that critical reaction to his books reflects the reviewers' biases: "Those who confuse literature with sexual morality damn them; those wise enough, emotionally mature enough to realize that the two things have practically nothing to do with each other, generally like them very much indeed." Since the publication of *The Dahomean,* Yerby admits, "two things have been of considerable comfort to me. First is the fact that I am no longer accused of colorful, purplish over-writing. And the second is the dawning realization that fifty-five million readers in eighty-two countries and twenty-three languages (who have bought and paid for my novels) are not necessarily all idiots. Strangely enough (or perhaps not so strangely after all) the degree of appreciation for a novel of mine is directly increased by the degree of knowledge the reader has of the subject. In other words, people who know the themes I've written about either by reason of having lived through them, or deeply and professionally studied them, find no fault with my novels. I am praised by experts, attacked by—well, let's be kind and call them amateurs."

Ultimately, however, critical reaction is incidental. Yerby, who in recent years has turned increasingly to subjects he finds personally—rather than commercially—appealing, works from compulsion. As he told *People* magazine, "I won't stop writing as long as there's breath in me."

MEDIA ADAPTATIONS: The Foxes of Harrow was filmed by Twentieth Century-Fox in 1947.

BIOGRAPHICAL/CRITICAL SOURCES:

BOOKS

Bone, Robert A., *The Negro Novel in America,* Yale University Press, revised edition, 1965.
Breit, Harvey, *The Writer Observed,* World Publishing, 1956.
Contemporary Literary Criticism, Gale, Volume 1, 1973, Volume 7, 1977, Volume 22, 1982.
Dictionary of Literary Biography, Volume 76: *Afro-American Writers, 1940-1955,* Gale, 1988.
Hemenway, Robert, *The Black Novelist,* C. E. Merrill, 1970.
Yerby, Frank G., *The Dahomean: An Historical Novel,* Dial, 1971.

PERIODICALS

Best Sellers, February 15, 1968, January 1, 1969, September 1, 1971, November, 1982.
Black World, February, 1972.
Book Week, February 10, 1946, April 27, 1947.
Crisis, January, 1948.
Journal of Popular Culture, spring, 1975.
Los Angeles Times Book Review, November 7, 1982.
Negro Digest, July, 1968, April, 1969.
Newsweek, November 30, 1959.
New Yorker, February 9, 1946, April 24, 1948.
New York Herald Tribune Book Review, May 4, 1947, June 12, 1949, October 22, 1950, July 15, 1951, September 21, 1952, October 4, 1953, November 14, 1954, December 19, 1954, October 14, 1956, September 22, 1957.
New York Times, February 10, 1946, May 2, 1948, May 15, 1949, September 10, 1950, May 6, 1951, April 6, 1952, November 15, 1953, December 5, 1954, September 23, 1956, September 8, 1957, October 12, 1958.
New York Times Book Review, November 10, 1968, October 17, 1971, September 17, 1972.
People, March 30, 1981.
Phylon: The Atlanta University Review of Race and Culture, Volume XXV, number 1, 1954.
Publishers Weekly, May 10, 1971, June 4, 1982.
Saturday Review, May 10, 1952, October 27, 1956, August 24, 1957.
Saturday Review of Literature, February 23, 1946, May 8, 1948, June 18, 1949, September 30, 1950, June 23, 1951.
Time, May 5, 1947, September 4, 1950, April 7, 1952, November 23, 1953, November 29, 1954.
Times Literary Supplement, March 27, 1959.
Washington Post Book World, August 15, 1982.

*   *   *

YEVTUSHENKO, Yevgeny (Alexandrovich) 1933-

PERSONAL: Name is transliterated in some sources as Evgenii Evtushenko, Yevgeniy Yevtushenko, or Evgeny Evtushenko; born July 18, 1933, in Stanzia Zima, Siberia, U.S.S.R.; son of Gangnus (a geologist) and Zinaida (a geologist and singer) Yevtushenko; married Bella Akhmadulina (a poet), 1954 (divorced); married Galina Semyonovna (a literary translator); children:

one. *Education:* Attended Gorky Literary Institute, 1951-54. *Politics:* Communist. *Religion:* "Revolution."

ADDRESSES: Office—Union of U.S.S.R. Writers, ul Vorovskogo 52, Moscow, U.S.S.R.

CAREER: Poet, filmmaker, actor, and author. Worked on geological expedition in Kazakhstan, U.S.S.R. Appearances in films include "Take-Off," 1979, and "The Kindergarten," 1983.

MEMBER: International PEN (vice-president of Russian center), Gorky Literary Institute, Writer's Union.

AWARDS, HONORS: U.S.S.R. Commission for the Defense of Peace award, 1965; U.S.S.R. state prize, 1984; Order of Red Banner of Labor; finalist for Ritz Paris Hemingway award for best 1984 novel published in English, 1985, for *Wild Berries.*

WRITINGS:

POETRY IN ENGLISH

(With others) *Red Cats,* City Lights, 1961.
Selected Poems, translated from the Russian by Robin Milner-Gulland and Peter Levi, Dutton, 1962.
Yevtushenko (young adult), edited by Milner-Gulland, Penguin, 1962.
Selected Poetry, Pergamon, 1963.
Winter Station, translated from the Russian by Oliver J. Frederiksen, C. Gerber, 1964.
The Poetry of Yevgeny Yevtushenko, 1953-1965, translated from the Russian and edited by George Reavey, October House, 1964.
Bratskaya GES, Russian Language Specialties, 1965, translation by Tina Tupikina-Glaessner, Igor Mezhakoff-Koriakin, and Geoffrey Dutton published as *New Works: The Bratsk Station,* Praeger, 1966, published as *The Bratsk Station and Other New Poems,* Praeger, 1967.
The City of Yes and the City of No and Other Poems, translated from the Russian by Tupikina-Glaessner, Mezhakoff-Koriakin, and Dutton, Sun Books, 1966.
Yevtushenko's Reader: The Spirit of Elbe, A Precocious Autobiography, Poems, Dutton, 1966.
Poems, translated from the Russian by Herbert Marshall, Dutton, 1966.
Poems Chosen by the Author, translated from the Russian by Milner-Gulland and Levi, Collins, 1966, Hill & Wang, 1967.
New Poems, Sun Books, 1968.
Bratsk Station, The City of Yes and the City of No, and Other New Poems, translated from the Russian by Tupikina-Glaessner, Dutton, and Mezhakoff-Koriakin, Sun Books, 1970.
Flowers and Bullets & Freedom to Kill, City Lights, 1970.
Stolen Apples, Doubleday, 1971.
Kazan University and Other New Poems, translated from the Russian by Dutton and Eleanor Jacka, Sun Books, 1973.
From Desire to Desire, Doubleday, 1976.
Invisible Threads, Macmillan, 1982.
Ardabiola, St. Martin's, 1985.
Almost at the End, translated by Antonina W. Bouis, Albert C. Todd, and Yevtushenko, Henry Holt, 1987.

POETRY IN RUSSIAN

Razvedchiki Gryadushchego (title means "The Prospectors of the Future"), Sovietsky Pisatel, 1952.
Tretii Sneg (title means "Third Snow"), Sovietsky Pisatel, 1955.
Shosse Entusiastov (title means "Highway of the Enthusiasts"), Moskovskii Rabochii, 1956.
Obeschanie (title means "Promise"), Sovietsky Pisatel, 1957.

Luk i lira (title means "The Bow and the Lyre"), Zara Vostoka, 1959.
Stikhi Raznykh Let (title means "Poems of Several Years"), Molodaya Gvardia, 1959.
Yabloko (title means "The Apple"), Sovietsky Pisatel, 1960.
Vzmakh Ruki (title means "A Wave of the Hand"), Molodaya Gvardia, 1962.
Nezhnost: Novyii Stikhi (title means "Tenderness: New Poems"), Sovietsky Pisatel, 1962.
Posie Stalina (title means "After Stalin"), Russian Language Specialties, 1962.
Kater Sviazi (title means "Torpedo Boat Signalling"), Molodaya Gvardia, 1966.
Kazanskii universitet (title means "Kazan University"), Tatarskoe knizhnoe izd-vo, 1971.

PLAYS

"Bratsk Power Station," produced in Moscow, 1968.
"Under the Skin of the Statue of Liberty," produced in 1972.

OTHER

A Precocious Autobiography, translated from the Russian by Andrew R. MacAndrew, Dutton, 1963.
Wild Berries (novel; originally published c. 1981 in U.S.S.R.), translated by Antonina W. Bouis, Morrow, 1984.
Divided Twins: Alaska and Siberia, Viking, 1988.

Writer and director of films, including "The Kindergarten," released in the U.S.S.R. in 1983, and "The End of the Musketeers."

SIDELIGHTS: As with few other living poets, Yevtushenko's career sharply illustrates the relationship between poetry and politics. While there exists a long Western tradition of politically engaged poetry, poets in the West have generally remained, as Shelly said in 1840, "the unacknowledged legislators of the world." But in the Soviet Union, the political nature and power of poetry, and literature in general, have been more often recognized. This is evident by the persecution of various writers, including Alexander Solzhenitsyn, who have been considered as subversive or as some political threat.

Yevtushenko has always frankly embraced his political role as a poet by incorporating both public and personal themes in his work as well as by being outspoken on current events. Consequently, his stature among the Soviet literati has fluctuated despite his insistence that he is a loyal, revolutionary Soviet citizen. Following the death of Stalin, the morally outraged tone and revolutionary idealism of Yevtushenko's early poetry were enthusiastically received by young Russians and generally tolerated by the post-Stalin authorities. During the 1950s, Yevtushenko's books were published regularly and in 1960, he was permitted to travel outside the Soviet Union to give poetry readings in Europe and the United States.

Occasionally, however, Yevtushenko overstepped his privileged bounds and found himself caught up in political controversy. One such situation developed upon the publication of "Babi Yar" in 1960. The title of the poem refers to a ravine near Kiev where 96,000 Jews were killed by Nazis during the German occupation; because the poem attributes anti-Semitism to Russians as well as Germans, Yevtushenko was criticized. He was also reprimanded in 1963 for allowing, without official permission from the state, the publication of "Notes for an Autobiography" in the French newspaper, *L'Express.*

On still other occasions, Yevtushenko has been censored because of his political "indiscretions." In 1968, he wrote a letter condemning the Soviet Union's occupation of Czechoslovakia. The negative response provoked by the letter resulted in a cancellation of a performance of "Bratsk Station." In 1974, he sent a telegram to Soviet official Leonid Breshnev expressing concern for the safety of Solzhenitsyn after his arrest. Shortly after Yevtushenko's letter was received, a major recital of his work was canceled.

In the West, Yevtushenko's reputation has also been unstable, though often in inverse relation to his reputation at home. In 1968, when he was nominated for an Oxford professorship, Kingsley Amis denounced him as a pawn of the Communist Party; his defenders, including Arthur Miller and William Styron, affirmed his integrity with evidence of his protests against the Czechoslovakian invasion. Yet, in 1972, he headlined an enormously successful recital in New York City which also featured James Dickey and Stanley Kunitz.

Despite a flair for publicity and occasional successes at recitals, Yevtushenko's popularity has declined in the United States as his poetry becomes more available. When "Bratsk Station" appeared in 1967, Rosemary Neiswender praised his "technical virtuosity" and Andrew Field dubbed him "the best of the political activists writing editorials in verse form." But two of Yevtushenko's most recent collections of poetry have caused some critics to question his writing ability. J. F. Cotter, in a review of *Stolen Apples,* wrote that "Yevtushenko is simply not that great a poet." Gerard Grealish was even less kind in his dismissal of *From Desire to Desire.* "Yevtushenko is the Rod McKuen of Russia," Grealish wrote. "Both men have captured the popular mind and neither man can write poetry. It is sad."

Nevertheless, Yevtushenko remains a major literary figure in the post-Stalinist Soviet Union. Comparisons to past Russian poets, including Voznesensky and early Mayakovsky continue to be made, and Yevtushenko persists in speaking out for his art and his political ideals. "It goes without saying that the dogmatists used, still use, and will go on using every opportunity they can find to arrest the process of democratization in our society," wrote Yevtushenko in *A Precocious Autobiography.* "I have no rosy illusions about that."

During the 1980s, Yevtushenko began to experiment with literary forms outside of poetry. His first novel, *Wild Berries,* was a finalist for the Ritz Paris Hemingway prize in 1985, and his first feature film, "The Kindergarten," played in the Soviet Union, England, and the United States.

BIOGRAPHICAL/CRITICAL SOURCES:

BOOKS

Alexandrova, Vera, *History of Soviet Literature,* Doubleday, 1963.
Blair, Katherine Hunter, *A Review of Soviet Literature,* Ampersand, 1966.
Brown, Edward James, *Russian Literature Since the Revolution,* Collier, 1963.
Carlisle, Olga, *Voices in the Snow,* Random House, 1962.
Contemporary Literary Criticism, Gale, Volume 1, 1973, Volume 3, 1975, Volume 13, 1980, Volume 26, 1983, Volume 51, 1989.
Hayward, Max and Leopold Labedz, editors, *Literature and Revolution in Soviet Russia,* Oxford University Press, 1963.
Yevtushenko, Yevgeny, *A Precocious Autobiography,* Dutton, 1963.

PERIODICALS

America, November 13, 1971.

Book Week, February 26, 1967.
Chicago Tribune Book World, August 19, 1984.
Library Journal, January 15, 1967.
Life, February 17, 1967.
Los Angeles Times, January 27, 1982, October 9, 1984, April 1, 1987, November 12, 1988.
Los Angeles Times Book Review, July 22, 1984, December 7, 1986.
Newsweek, August 27, 1984.
New York Times, June 22, 1984, June 9, 1985, June 18, 1985, February 2, 1986, April 16, 1986, June 20, 1987, January 2, 1988, January 19, 1988.
New York Times Book Review, July 15, 1984, June 23, 1985, June 28, 1987, December 25, 1988.
Paris Review, spring-summer, 1965.
Time, May 25, 1987.
Times (London), July 13, 1983, November 2, 1984, September 27, 1984, January 18, 1986.
Times Literary Supplement, November 6, 1981, August 26, 1988.
Washington Post, February 21, 1987, January 2, 1988, May 17, 1988, July 8, 1989.
Washington Post Book World, June 14, 1987.

* * *

YEZIERSKA, Anzia 1885(?)-1970

PERSONAL: Surname is pronounced "Ye-*zyer*-ska"; born c. October 19, 1885 (some sources say 1880, 1881, or 1883), in Plinsk, Russian Poland; immigrated to United States, c. 1901, naturalized citizen, 1912; died of a stroke, November 21, 1970, in Ontario, Calif.; daughter of Bernard (a Talmudic scholar) and Pearl (a homemaker) Yezierska; married Jacob Gordon (an attorney), 1910 (marriage annulled, 1910); married Arnold Levitas (a teacher and textbook writer), 1911 (marriage ended, 1916); children: (second marriage) Louise. *Education:* Studied domestic science at Columbia University.

CAREER: Writer, 1915-69. Worked as a seamstress in a sweatshop, as a cook and domestic for a wealthy family, and in a factory, all on New York's Lower East Side, c. 1900-03; teacher of domestic science in an elementary school, c. 1908-10; translator for a project among Polish-speaking people in Philadelphia run by John Dewey through Columbia University, 1917-18; screenwriter in Hollywood, 1922; U.S. Government, Works Progress Administration (WPA), Writers' Project, New York City, cataloger of trees in Central Park during the early 1930s.

MEMBER: Authors' League of America.

AWARDS, HONORS: Prize for best short story of the year from Edward J. O'Brien, 1919, for "The Fat of the Land."

WRITINGS:

Hungry Hearts (short stories; contains "Wings," "Hunger," "The Lost Beautifulness," "The Free Vacation House," "The Miracle," "Where Lovers Dream," "Soap and Water," "The Fat of the Land," "My Own People," and "How I Found America"), Houghton, 1920, reprinted, Arno Press, 1975 (also see below).
Salome of the Tenements (novel), Boni & Liveright, c. 1923.
Children of Loneliness (short stories), Funk, 1923.
Bread Givers: A Struggle Between a Father of the Old World and a Daughter of the New (novel), introduction by Alice Kessler Harris, Doubleday, 1925, reprinted, Braziller, 1975.
Arrogant Beggar (novel), Doubleday, 1927.
All I Could Never Be (novel), Putnam, 1932.

Red Ribbon on a White Horse (autobiographical novel), introduction by W. H. Auden, Scribner, 1950, reprinted, Persea Books, 1981.

The Open Cage: An Anzia Yezierska Collection, edited with an introduction by Harris, afterword by Louise Levitas Henriksen, Persea Books, 1979.

Hungry Hearts and Other Stories (contains *Hungry Hearts,* "This Is What $10,000 Did to Me," "Wild Winter Love," and "One Thousand Pages of Research"), preface by Henriksen, Persea Books, 1985.

Short story "The Fat of the Land" also included in *Best Short Stories of 1919,* edited by Edward J. O'Brien. Contributor of short stories to periodicals, including *Forum* and *Chicago Jewish Forum.*

SIDELIGHTS: Through her short stories and novels, Russian-born Jewish writer Anzia Yezierska reanimated her experience as a poor, young immigrant woman living on New York's Lower East Side at the turn of the twentieth century. Although largely drawn from episodes in her own life, Yezierska's prose plots are widely regarded as accurate depictions of the entire Jewish immigrant experience. Her female protagonists struggle against the restrictions of their traditional Judaic values and orthodox religion, striving for autonomy, prosperity, and acceptance in the new world.

Yezierska was born in the village of Plinsk near Warsaw in Russian Poland. Since the author never knew the date of her birth, she chose her own—October 19, 1883. Although the exact date remains unknown, historians and biographers, including Alice Kessler-Harris who recently edited a collection of Yezierska's shorter works, now agree that 1885 was the probable year of the author's birth. According to most sources, Yezierska immigrated to the United States with her impoverished family in 1901. Her father, a Talmudic scholar, was not gainfully employed; he engaged in a tedious, full-time study of the sacred books and authoritative laws of the Jewish faith while his wife and children worked menial jobs and surrendered their meager wages to sustain the household.

Viewing America as a country of unlimited opportunities for determined, intelligent immigrants, Yezierska sought to free herself from the poverty and oppression of her highly conservative, patriarchal roots and begin a new life. Studying English at night and working in a sweatshop by day, she earned a scholarship to Columbia University three years after her arrival in the United States. Discontented with her subsequent role as a teacher of domestic science, she was married briefly in 1910. After an annulment that same year and another failed marriage that produced her only daughter, Yezierska relinquished her familial responsibilities to pursue a career in writing.

The author made her literary debut in 1915 with the publication of "Free Vacation House" in the December issue of *Forum.* The short story details the humiliating and insensitive treatment of the poor by charitable agencies, a subject Yezierska would again address in later writings. Four years after her first piece was published, American anthologist Edward J. O'Brien included her short story "The Fat of the Land" in his volume *Best Short Stories of 1919* and proclaimed it the best of the year. The award-winning tale centers on a newly affluent, elderly Jewish woman who finds herself yearning for the vibrance and kinship of her former East Side ghetto neighborhood.

In 1920, Yezierska published a collection of short works entitled *Hungry Hearts.* Hollywood producer Samuel Goldwyn based a 1922 silent film of the same name on the volume and turned the young writer into a celebrity. She moved to California to pursue a career in fiction and screen writing but, removed from the milieu of the New York ghetto, was uninspired and virtually unable to write. Refusing a one-hundred-thousand-dollar Hollywood writing contract, she returned to New York.

Back in her own neighborhood, Yezierska began her first novel, *Salome of the Tenements.* Its plot revolves around Sonya, a beautiful, headstrong, uneducated immigrant who falls in love with and marries Manning, a rational, upper-class American philanthropist. The marriage fails. In an excerpt of the book cited by Louise Maunsell Field in the *New York Times Book Review,* Yezierska attributed the faded romance to Manning's inherently "paler passions, paler needs; paler capacity—paler fire!" Field remarked, "Resentment . . . breathes through almost every page of the book," but conceded that Yezierska's powerful characterization made Sonya "a living human being" who is "real to [the reader], even when the incidents of her story are far from convincing; real in her ignorances and her crudities, her idealization of Manning and her ardent amorousness, her flaming desires and her complete egotism. . . . Sonya is drawn with strong, sure, vivid, strokes."

The author's subsequent works were, to the chagrin of many reviewers, built around the same themes that made her famous; she treated these themes, however, with a force and vigor that was consistently recognized by critics. The 1923 short story collection *Children of Loneliness* contains pieces similar in content and style to those in the *Hungry Hearts* anthology. A writer for the *New York Times Book Review,* referring to Yezierska's self-conscious and repeated use of familiar characters, noted that "it is almost always about herself that [the author] writes." The critic continued, "Her gift is not creative; she is a reporter and an autobiographist rather than a fiction writer." The title story, "Children of Loneliness," illuminates the gap that widens between immigrant parents of the old world and their Americanized children. An excerpt from the story published in the *New York Times Book Review* depicts young immigrant Rachel Ravinsky's harsh rejection of her unsophisticated parents, and indeed, of her entire culture: "To think I was born of these creatures! It's an insult to my soul." Yet, in keeping with Yezierska's established theme, the girl finds her relationship with an American-born man passionless and unfulfilling because he cannot understand her past. The *New York Times* critic allowed, "[*Children of Loneliness*] has color and a dramatic quality which, if it frequently slips into melodrama, nevertheless gives effectiveness to many of its scenes."

Similarly, Yezierska's 1927 novel *Arrogant Beggar* was censured as an "elaboration of the obvious" by a writer for the *Saturday Review.* The book portrays social service agencies as patronizing institutions run by incompetent members of the upper class. But beyond its "thin" characters and "trite" plot, the *Saturday Review* critic declared, "Surely never was a poor story better told. . . . Both scene and situation are . . . of the most familiar, but like an old room newly decorated they gleam beneath their author's furnishings."

Commenting on the aspirations of the foreign-born personalities that populate the author's works, Richard F. Shepard asserted in the *New York Times* that "Yezierska's people . . . did not want to find themselves. They wanted to lose themselves and find America, to shed Europe and to live the American dream." But a recurring motif of disappointment in success is evidenced by her characters' inability to find contentment as their desires are fulfilled and by the author's own anguished response to wealth and fame in Hollywood. "It was only when Yezierska had achieved . . . relative comforts," wrote Johanna Kaplan in the *New York Times Book Review,* "that she perceived herself as lost and disconnected, and ceased to thrive." For the writer and her characters, the satisfaction gained from becoming Americanized was tainted by an accompanying sense of alienation from the Jewish culture.

Conflict, tension, and a sense of bitter disillusionment inform Yezierska's work as her characters attempt to reconcile their old-world heritage with the promise of a new land. These emotions are vividly captured in *Bread Givers,* the writer's most successful novel. Considered an early piece of feminist literature, *Bread Givers* is Yezierska's first-person indictment of her father, fictionally represented by the character of Reb Smolinsky, for his patriarchal Jewish beliefs. Johan J. Smertenko, writing for the *Saturday Review of Literature,* credited her for the "fierce vitality" that distinguishes the work but went on to call that same vitality, "unharnessed and little directed," the author's "undoing." The *New York Times Book Review,* however, unequivocally hailed the novel as a "colorful, almost barbaric tapestry" of "raw, uncontrollable poetry and a powerful, sweeping design."

In the 1932 novel *All I Could Never Be,* Yezierska expanded on the theme she introduced in *Salome of the Tenements*—that of the doomed romance between a poor, young immigrant woman and a wealthy, established American man. Critics agree that Yezierska imbued the work with the spirit of her own passion and restlessness. *All I Could Never Be* is a fictionalized account of the author's ill-fated romance with American educator and philosopher John Dewey. Yezierska met Dewey in 1917 when she attended a social and political philosophy seminar he was conducting at Columbia University. Dewey became her mentor and encouraged her literary pursuits; Yezierska's idea for a sober, intellectual American male to play against her fiery, uneducated immigrant heroine is said to have been based on her conception of Dewey. Echoing the sentiment of several reviewers, a writer for the *New York Times Book Review* faulted *All I Could Never Be* for its lack of original plot and character development, calling it a "story [Yezierska] has told before."

Over the next twenty years, Yezierska's literary reputation declined. She slipped into virtual obscurity as an author before her fictionalized autobiography, *Red Ribbon on a White Horse,* was published in 1950. The book takes its title from a ghetto proverb which holds that poverty enhances a wise man as does a red ribbon on a white horse. Chronicling the lean years of the depression, her Hollywood and New England sojourns, emotional meetings with her father, and the idealized love affairs of her youth, *Red Ribbon on a White Horse* earned considerable acclaim as a work of great truth and passion. Nathan L. Rothman declared in *Saturday Review,* "Only a madman or a poet or a dreamer, only an artist would pause to ask the questions . . . Yezierska asked herself."

Literary critics generally recognize Yezierska's fiction as a distinctive and valid account of the Jewish immigrant experience from a woman's point of view. The author is remembered more for the honesty and intensity of her narratives than the skill with which she developed her plots and characters. Yezierska's later work of the 1950s and 1960s focused on the problems facing the wave of Puerto Rican immigrants to the mainland states and on the aged in America. "Take Up Your Bed and Walk," her last story to be published, was written from the perspective of an elderly Jewish woman and appeared in the *Chicago Jewish Forum* in 1969. This and several other short stories were compiled in a volume entitled *The Open Cage: An Anzia Yezierska Collection,* which was published in 1979, almost a decade after the author's death.

MEDIA ADAPTATIONS: Hungry Hearts was adapted by Julien Josephson for a silent film of the same title, released by Goldwyn, 1922; Sidney Olcott directed "Salome of the Tenements," a silent film based on the novel of the same name, in 1925.

BIOGRAPHICAL/CRITICAL SOURCES:

BOOKS

Contemporary Literary Criticism, Volume 46, Gale, 1988.
Dictionary of Literary Biography, Volume 28: *Twentieth-Century American Jewish Fiction Writers,* Gale, 1984.
Neidle, Cecyle S., *America's Immigrant Women,* Hippocrene, 1976.
Schoen, Carol B., *Anzia Yezierska,* Twayne, 1982.

PERIODICALS

New York Times, February 21, 1980.
New York Times Book Review, December 24, 1922, October 28, 1923, September 13, 1925, August 21, 1932, September 24, 1950, February 24, 1980.
Saturday Review, October 10, 1925, December 3, 1927, November 4, 1950.

OBITUARIES:

PERIODICALS

New York Times, November 23, 1970.

* * *

YGLESIAS, Helen 1915-

PERSONAL: Born March 29, 1915, in New York, N.Y.; daughter of Solomon and Kate (Goldstein) Bassine; married Bernard Cole (a photographer), 1937; married second husband, Jose Yglesias (a writer), August 20, 1950; children: (first marriage) Tamar (Mrs. Richard Lear), Lewis Cole; (second marriage) Rafael. *Education:* Attended public schools in New York, N.Y.

ADDRESSES: Home—13 West 13th St., New York, N.Y. 10011; and North Brooklin, Me. 04661. *Agent*—Lynn Nesbit, International Creative Management, 40 West 57th St., New York, N.Y. 10019.

CAREER: Nation, New York, N.Y., literary editor, 1965-69; writer, 1969—. Adjunct professor of nonfiction, Columbia University, School of the Arts, spring, 1973; visiting professor of creative writing, Writers Workshop, University of Iowa, 1980.

MEMBER: Brooklin Garden Club.

AWARDS, HONORS: Houghton Mifflin literary fellowship, 1971, for *How She Died.*

WRITINGS:

How She Died (novel), Houghton, 1972.
Family Feeling (novel; Literary Guild selection), Dial, 1976.
Starting: Early, Anew, Over, and Late (nonfiction), Rawson, Wade, 1978.
Sweetsir (novel; Literary Guild selection), Simon & Schuster, 1981.
The Saviors (novel), Houghton, 1987.
Isabel Bishop, Rizzoli International, 1989.

Helen Yglesias's novels have been translated into German, Dutch, Swedish, Danish, Finnish, French, Italian, Spanish, and Norwegian. Contributor to numerous magazines, including *New*

Yorker, Nation, New York Times Book Review, Harper's, Seventeen, and *Parent's Magazine.*

SIDELIGHTS: At age 54, after leaving her position as a literary editor for the *Nation,* Helen Yglesias turned to writing full time. Her first effort as a novelist, the opening pages of *How She Died,* earned for her the Houghton Mifflin literary fellowship. The novel focuses on the dying of Mary Moody Schwartz, a radical activist and the daughter of Isabelle Vance Moody, who had been imprisoned in the 1930s for passing information to the Soviets. "The story is created with rich imaginative specificity," writes Martin Green in the *Nation,* "making us participate in all its themes, personal and impersonal, by an almost meaty, vascular substantiality." Mary suffers from cancer, and when her physical and mental health deteriorate, she is committed to a mental institution. Her closest friend Jean, who has been caring for her at the request of a leftist group, finds herself caught up in Mary's dying while at the same time becoming involved in an affair with Mary's husband. "It is a dense novel," comments Roger Baker in *Books and Bookmen,* "packed with people, events and much hard-hitting examination of the position of women in the fairly well-heeled urban society." Green observes, "What [Yglesias] sees and hears is never a cliche. She catches the characterizing detail which brings the person and the scene to life, and makes it poignant or funny." In her *New York Times Book Review* article, Shirley Schoonover adds, "Although she chivvies her characters from one scene to another, the author never fails in her sensibilities or consistency." Schoonover concludes, "A real craftsman, Helen Yglesias has made her perceptions visible, coherent and moving."

Family Feeling is "an extraordinary family portrait" of the grown children of two Jewish immigrants to America, writes Sandra Salmans in *Times Literary Supplement.* Of the seven children, Salmans notes, "Two stand out from the rest: Anne, marked by her radical politics, literary ambitions, a recent divorce and a gentile lover; and Barry, a ruthless businessman whose multimillion-dollar corporation employs and sustains the rest of the family." Ivan Gold commends Yglesias's writing in the *New York Times Book Review,* noting, "She commands . . . a style of deceptive simplicity, a language pared of all frills and distractions, and as fine an ear for the speech rhythms of her scores of complex characters as I've lately encountered." Gold calls *Family Feeling* "an example of one kind of first-rate fiction" because he feels that Yglesias succeeds in conveying the notion that Anne Goddard "exists chiefly as a member of the family, and this, . . . however much we may sometimes war with the process, is one of the profounder ways in which we see ourselves."

Yglesias's first excursion into nonfiction, *Starting: Early, Anew, Over, and Late,* features an "Autobiographical Fragment" in which Yglesias relates the story of her decision to leave the *Nation* to begin writing books. "I wanted to be on my way as a storyteller," she writes, "even though it was very late. I wanted to make a start on what I had always wanted to do." Christopher Lehmann-Haupt of the *New York Times* writes: "The 'Autobiographical Fragment' is superb. Without a jot of self-pity and without putting the blame on anyone outside herself, Mrs. Yglesias manages to draw an evocative picture of the self, first retreating in the face of disapproval and then finally blossoming." With her own story, Yglesias includes the stories of others who, as the title indicates, started either early, anew, over, or late. Among these are Grandma Moses, Artur Rubinstein, and Alberta Hunter. Of this portion of Yglesias's book Lehmann-Haupt writes, "The stories she tells of other lives have their moments of interest . . . but on the whole, these sketches are perfunctory

and anticlimactic." Even so, as Doris Grumbach explains in a *New York Times Book Review* article, "Perhaps the most intriguing thing about the book is the portrait that emerges of . . . Helen Yglesias: a good listener with an understanding ear and a compassionate intelligence toward her subjects."

From the details of an actual case in which a New England woman was tried for killing her abusive husband, Yglesias fashioned her third novel, *Sweetsir.* In an article in the *Nation* Vivian Gornick calls Yglesias's work "the psychic history of two human beings who come together, thrash wildly about in an attempt to reduce their mutual isolation, fail miserably and are punished brutally for their failure." It is the story of Sally Sweetsir, the battered wife of Morgan Beauchamp Sweetsir, and their turbulent relationship, which grows into a terrible mix of love and violence. Commenting on *Sweetsir* in the *Los Angeles Times,* Elaine Kendall writes, "Yglesias confronts the difficult issue of marital assault, exploring a complex subject with compassion for both victims: the man who dies and the woman who survives."

For some critics, Yglesias's decision to construct a novel whose events closely parallel those of an actual case inhibits the creative process. "Yglesias's intelligence provides sophisticated insights that come in bits and pieces," writes Vivian Gornick in her review, "but they remain separate and unworked, without . . . vivid fullness." Melvyn Bragg, contributing to *Punch,* adds, "Despite her considerable best efforts, the author does not really break free from the case history on which she based the book." Bragg does point out, however, that *Sweetsir*'s "organisation was excellent, the dialogue was convincing, the characters acted true, the social context was well caught."

Dealing, as it does, with the volatile issue of domestic violence, and especially wife abuse, *Sweetsir* lends itself to close scrutiny by those deeply concerned with such problems. Yet as Walter Clemons observes in *Newsweek,* "Yglesias's sense of character is infallible, and what might have been a doctrinaire novel on the timely topic of battered wives contains many surprises." In the novel, feminists try to enlist Sally Sweetsir as a symbol for their cause, but she refuses to see herself in their terms. "This novel is not a feminist tract," notes Merryl Maleska in the *Chicago Tribune Book World.* "It is a human story." Elisabeth Duvall offers a similar view in an *Atlantic* article: "The book's concerns are always for the specific and the personal, which are conveyed with a wonderfully gritty dialogue and the humor of self-deprecation."

For Rosellen Brown, writing in the *New York Times Book Review,* Helen Yglesias's ability to see through the "theoretical questions and polemical answers" generated by controversial issues to the individual struggle "has let us hear a real, anguished voice in the act of self-discovery." At the trial for the murder of her husband, Sally Sweetsir tells each woman in the courtroom, "[I am] a woman much like you, in a marriage much like yours. Ours went over the edge, but what happened to us could have happened to any of you." "In *Sweetsir,*" Brown concludes, "[Yglesias] has given us a vulnerable but sturdy character who takes her first painful steps toward understanding before our eyes. It is a moving sight."

MEDIA ADAPTATIONS: Warner Brothers has acquired the rights to *Sweetsir* for a film to be produced and directed by Robert Redford.

BIOGRAPHICAL/CRITICAL SOURCES:

BOOKS

Contemporary Literary Criticism, Gale, Volume 7, 1977, Volume 22, 1982.

PERIODICALS

Atlantic, May, 1981.
Books and Bookmen, May, 1973.
Chicago Tribune Book World, April 26, 1981.
Detroit News, March 5, 1972.
Hudson Review, summer, 1976.
Los Angeles Times, April 16, 1981.
Nation, June 19, 1972, March 17, 1979, June 20, 1981.
Newsweek, March 6, 1972, April 20, 1981.
New Yorker, February 26, 1972.
New York Review of Books, April 6, 1972.
New York Times, February 8, 1972, February 25, 1976, January 9, 1979, July 20, 1981.
New York Times Book Review, February 13, 1972, February 1, 1976, March 4, 1979, April 5, 1981, August 16, 1987.
Punch, September 9, 1981.
Saturday Review, March 18, 1972.
Times (London), August 6, 1981.
Times Literary Supplement, January 26, 1973, July 1, 1977.
Tribune Books (Chicago), August 9, 1987.
Village Voice, March 15, 1976.
Washington Post, May 7, 1981.
Washington Post Book World, April 16, 1972.

*   *   *

YORK, Jeremy
   See CREASEY, John

*   *   *

YORK, Simon
   See HEINLEIN, Robert A(nson)

*   *   *

YOURCENAR, Marguerite   1903-1987

PERSONAL: Born June 8, 1903, in Brussels, Belgium; French citizen born abroad; immigrated to United States, naturalized U.S. citizen, 1947; name legally changed in 1947; French citizenship restored, 1980; died December 17, 1987, in Maine; daughter of Michel and Fernande (de Cartier de Marchienne) de Crayencour. *Education:* Educated privately.

ADDRESSES: Home—Mount Desert Island, Maine.

CAREER: Writer, 1921-87. Professor of comparative literature at Sarah Lawrence College, 1940-50.

MEMBER: Academie Francaise, Academie Royale de Langue et de Litterature Francaises de Belgique, American Academy and Institute of Arts and Letters, American Civil Rights Association.

AWARDS, HONORS: Prix Femina-Vacaresco, 1951, for *Memoires d'Hadrien;* Page One Award from Newspaper Guild of New York, 1955; L.T.D. from Smith College, 1961; Prix Combat, 1963, for ensemble of work; Prix Femina, 1968, for *L'Oeuvre au noir;* L.T.D. from Bowdoin College, 1968; L.T.D. from Colby College, 1972; Prix Monaco, 1973, for ensemble of work; Grand Prix National des Lettres from French Ministry of Culture, 1975; Grand Prix de la Litterature from Academie Francaise, 1980; L.T.D. from Harvard University, 1981; National Arts Club Medal of Honor for Literature, 1985; commander of Legion of Honor (France).

WRITINGS:

IN ENGLISH TRANSLATION

Alexis; ou, Le Traite du vain combat (novel; title means "Alexis; or, Treatise on Useless Combat"), [Paris], 1929, revised edition, Plon, 1965, translation by Walter Kaiser published as *Alexis,* Farrar, Straus, 1984.
Dernier du reve (novel; title means "Coin of Dreams"), Grasset, 1934, revised edition, 1959, translation by Dori Katz published as *A Coin in Nine Hands,* Farrar, Straus, 1982.
Feux (poems), [Paris], 1936, revised edition, Gallimard, 1974, translation by Katz published as *Fires,* Farrar, Straus, 1981.
Nouvelles Orientales (short stories), Gallimard, 1938, translation by Alberto Manguel published as *Oriental Tales,* Farrar, Straus, 1985.
Le Coup de grace (novel), Gallimard, 1939, translation by Grace Frick published as *Coup de Grace,* Farrar, Straus, 1957, reprinted, 1981.
Memoires d'Hadrien (novel), Plon, 1951, translation by Frick published as *Memoirs of Hadrian,* Farrar, Straus, 1954, reprinted, Modern Library, 1984, published as *"Memoirs of Hadrian" and Reflections on the Composition of "Memoirs of Hadrian,"* Farrar, Straus, 1989.
Les Charites d'Alcippe (poems), [Brussels], 1956, translation published as *The Alms of Alcippe,* Targ Editions, 1982.
Sous benefice d'inventaire (essays; title means "With Reservations"), Gallimard, 1962, revised edition, 1978, translation by Richard Howard published as *The Dark Brain of Piranesi and Other Essays,* Farrar, Straus, 1984.
L'Oeuvre au noir (novel; title means "The Work in Black"), Gallimard, 1968, translation by Frick published as *The Abyss,* Farrar, Straus, 1976.
Theatre, two volumes, Gallimard, 1971, translation by Katz published as *Plays,* Performing Arts Journal Publications, 1985.
Les Yeux ouverts: Entretiens avec Matthieu Galey, Centurion, 1980, translation by Arthur Goldhammer published as *With Open Eyes: Conversations with Matthieu Galey,* Beacon Press, 1986.
Mishima; ou, La Vision du vide (biography), Gallimard, 1981, translation by Manguel published as *Mishima: A Vision of the Void,* Farrar, Straus, 1986.
Comme l'eau qui coule (short stories), Gallimard, 1982, translation by Kaiser published as *Two Lives and a Dream,* Farrar, Straus, 1987.
Le Temps, ce grand sculpture: Essais, Gallimard, 1983, translation by Kaiser published as *That Mighty Sculptor, Time,* Farrar, Straus, 1989.

IN FRENCH

La Jardin des chimeres (verse; title means "The Garden of the Chimeras"), privately printed, 1921.
La Nouvelle Eurydice (novel; title means "The New Eurydice"), Grasset, 1931.
Pindare, Grasset, 1932.
Les Songes et les sorts (essays; title means "Dreams and Spells"), Grasset, 1938.
Electra; ou, La Chute des masques (play), Plon, 1954.
(Author of critique and translator from the Greek with Constantin Dimaras) *Presentation critique de Constantin Cavafy,*

1863-1933 (title means "Critical Presentation of Constantin Cavafy"), Gallimard, 1958, reprinted, 1978.

Le Mystere d'Alceste [and] *Qui n'a pas son minotaure?* (plays), Plon, 1963.

(Translator from the English) *Fleuve profond, sombre riviere: Les Negro spirituals* (title means "Deep, Dark River"), Gallimard, 1964.

(Author of critique and translator from the English) *Presentation critique d'Hortense Flexner*, Gallimard, 1969.

Le Labyrinthe du monde, Gallimard, Volume I: *Souvenirs pieux*, 1974, Volume II: *Archives du nord*, 1977, Volume III: *Quoi?: L'Eternite*, 1990.

(Translator) *La Couronne et la lyre* (classical Greek poems; title means "The Crown and the Lyre"), Gallimard, 1979.

Suite d'estampes pour Kou-Kou-Hai, High Loft, 1980.

Discours de reception de Mme Marguerite Yourcenar a l'Academie Francaise et reponse de M. Jean d'Ormesson, Gallimard, 1981.

Oeuvres romanesques, Gallimard, 1982.

Blues et gospels, Gallimard, 1984.

En pelerin et en etranger (essays and articles), Gallimard, 1990.

Also author of *Les Dieux ne sont pas morts* (verse; title means "The Gods Are Not Dead"), 1922, *La Mort conduit l'attelage* (short stories; title means "Death Drives the Team"), 1934, *Anna Sonor*, 1979, and *Un Homme obscur*, 1982.

OTHER

Translator of works by James Baldwin, Henry James, and Virginia Woolf. Contributor to French periodicals, including *Le Monde*, *Le Figaro*, and *Nouvelle Revue Francaise*.

SIDELIGHTS: When author Marguerite Yourcenar was elected to the Academie Francaise in 1981, she became the first woman to receive the French state's highest literary honor. Throughout its three hundred fifty years of existence, the Academie Francaise had elected only men until the octogenarian novelist was asked to join its ranks. The honor was formidable, and most critics agreed that Yourcenar, long a resident of Mount Desert Island off the coast of Maine, deserved such unprecedented acclaim. She had written fiction, essays, poetry, and a biography, but she was best known for two thought-provoking historical novels, *Memoirs of Hadrian* and *The Abyss*, first published in France as *Memoires d'Hadrien* and *L'Oeuvre au noir*. According to Moses Hadas in the *Saturday Review*, Yourcenar's "highest usefulness and greatest success [was] in a field beyond the range of the orthodox historian, a field to which only the imaginative writer can be adequate." Her example, Hadas adds, "is to be commended to all writers of historical fiction." *Los Angeles Times Book Review* contributor Frances McConnel offered a similar appraisal of the Belgian-born writer: "Whatever magic she is about, Yourcenar crosses barriers of century, discipline, language, myth and history with no sense of impropriety or danger. The path her mind takes through these landscapes is always stepping-stone easy to follow, yet everywhere full of bold jumps and staggering views." In *World Literature Today*, Alexander Coleman concluded that an open-minded reader "will discover in all Yourcenar's writings a luminous and keenly magisterial intelligence."

Yourcenar lived primarily in America after 1939, although she traveled widely, and received United States citizenship in 1947. She always wrote in French, however, having been taken to France by her family shortly after her birth, and her French citizenship was restored to her in 1980. *Saturday Review* essayist Stephen Koch suggested that Yourcenar for many years found herself in "the anomalous—indeed, unique—position of being a major French writer and an American citizen." If her summer domicile was in Maine, critics noted, Yourcenar's style and substance were still clearly French. Writing in the *Times Literary Supplement* before her death, John Weightman contended that her novels "show an extraordinary range of knowledge in various fields, and a quite exceptional awareness of the whole French literary tradition. Although . . . she protests that she has never been a systematic scholar, she must be one of the most learned practitioners of the French novel in her time." Addressing his comments to Yourcenar's style, Hugh Lloyd-Jones claimed in the *New York Times Book Review* that the author "writes an ornamental and mellifluous French prose, studded with the literary allusions which come so easily to such a cultivated writer." *New York Review of Books* contributor Mavis Gallant elaborated: "Writers who choose domicile in a foreign place, for whatever reason, usually treat their native language like a delicate timepiece, making certain it runs exactly and no dust gets inside. Mme. Yourcenar's distinctive and unplaceable voice carries the precise movement of her finest prose, the well-tended watch." Gallant also observed that Yourcenar's "mind, her manner, the quirks and prejudices that enliven her conclusive opinions, the sense of caste that lends her fiction its stern framework, her respect for usages and precedents, belong to a vanished France."

Commentary essayist Joseph Epstein discussed the theme that arises from much of Yourcenar's fiction. "Intricate moral questions are usually not at the center of Marguerite Yourcenar's work," Epstein wrote. "Human destiny, its meaning and even more its mysteries, are. She has a clearer sense than anyone now writing of the tragedy yet also the hope inherent in human lives. . . . The effect of reading her novels is to be reminded of the difficulty of life and of its heroic possibilities—hardly a thing that contemporary literature does best, if at all. Most of us are undone by life. Ours is but to do, then die. Marguerite Yourcenar's novels make us question why. This is what major writers have always done. This is why she is among their number." In the *Times Literary Supplement*, George Steiner reflected on the notion that through strong central characters, Yourcenar "argues her vision of essential human solitude, of the radical incapacity of human beings, particularly and paradoxically when they are most self-conscious and articulate, to communicate to others, even to those they love best, the final quality or truth of their convictions. This, indeed, is the Yourcenar leitmotif." The vision is sometimes bleak; *New York Times Book Review* contributor Michael Wood felt that Yourcenar's characters "make tremendous demands of themselves and generally despair of others," but erudition and estimations of human potential for intellectual and spiritual sovereignty alleviate the solemnity. In a *New York Times Book Review* piece, Koch called Yourcenar "one of the great scholar-artists," who provides "riches for anyone interested in history, humanism or the psychology of power."

Yourcenar "had an ideally vagrant and unsettling youth for a writer of historical fiction," according to John Sturrock in the *New York Times Book Review*. She was born in Brussels in 1903; her father was French and her mother Belgian. Yourcenar lost her mother to a fever shortly after her birth, so her father undertook sole responsibility for her care. Together they traveled extensively in England, France, Italy, and Switzerland, using the family name of de Crayencour that Yourcenar later scrambled to form her unusual nom de plume. As a youngster, Marguerite de Crayencour was educated privately, largely by her father. Weightman wrote of him: "M. de Crayencour must have been a curious mixture of playboy and free-thinking, gentleman-scholar, because it was he who gave [Yourcenar] a grounding in Latin and Greek and read many of the French classics with her;

nor does he seem to have imposed on her any of the conventional restraints of the time. Father and daughter were fairly constant companions until his death in 1929, after which she continued the nomadic life, in undefined circumstances but with apparently adequate financial resources, sharing her time between France, Italy, Greece and other countries." Yourcenar began writing while still in her teens, and she was twenty-six when her first novel, *Alexis; ou, Le Traite du vain combat,* was published. *New Republic* contributor Anne Tyler reflected on how Yourcenar's unsettled youth—interrupted by both World Wars—influenced her writings: "Her physical distance from her Belgian homeland and her psychological distance from the country she has adopted [the United States] combine to give a picture of someone watching the world at one remove—as Marguerite Yourcenar most certainly does. Her concern is man's relationship with history. Her characters are most often tiny, lonely figures in a vortex of political events."

In 1934 Yourcenar made the acquaintance of Grace Frick, an American visiting Paris. They became inseparable companions, and in 1939 Yourcenar moved to the United States because of the outbreak of war. She taught comparative literature at Sarah Lawrence College for ten years and continued to write short stories, novels, essays, and plays. If her life can be said to have had a turning point, it may have occurred shortly after the Second World War, when a friend sent Yourcenar some personal belongings and papers she had left in France. Yourcenar told the *Washington Post* of a discovery she made while burning some of this old correspondence: "As I unfolded and threw mechanically into the fire that exchange of dead thoughts between a Marie and a Francois or a Paul, long since disappeared, I came upon four or five typewritten sheets, the paper of which had turned yellow. The salutation told me nothing: 'My dear Mark. . . .' Mark . . . what friend or love, what distant relative was this? I could not recall the name at all. It was several minutes before I remembered that Mark stood here for Marcus Aurelius, and that I had in hand a fragment of [a] lost manuscript. From that moment there was no question but that this book must be taken up again, whatever the cost."

The book in question was *Memoirs of Hadrian,* hailed in France and America as a classic achievement in postwar fiction. In the *Spectator,* Miranda Seymour called the work "arguably the finest historical novel of this century." Likewise, *New York Herald Tribune Book Review* contributor Geoffrey Bruun noted that *Memoirs of Hadrian* "is an extraordinarily expert performance. . . . It has a quality of authenticity, of verisimilitude, that delights and fascinates." Drawing on her vast knowledge of ancient Rome, Yourcenar recreated the world of the Emperor Hadrian, who, in a series of first-person letters to his nephew Marcus Aurelius, reminisces about his life and times. James Boatwright described the work in the *Washington Post Book World:* "In a prose of exquisite clarity and grace, the Emperor Hadrian . . . reveals himself as both a creator and worshiper of beauty, a man of keen intelligence and strong passion, powerful and magnanimous, a poet, a lover, a prince 'who was *almost* wise.' " According to Epstein, the novel's outlook "is worldly; its tone philosophical; its feeling completely Roman. The book is a triumph of historical ventriloquism; it is impossible to read it and not think that, had Hadrian left memoirs, this is how they would have read. . . . To bring off such a book requires not only artistry and scholarship but intelligence of a very high order."

Other critics were similarly impressed with *Memoirs of Hadrian.* In the *Nation,* Stanley Cooperman called it "historical fiction at its best" and added that Yourcenar "has avoided the usual hack plot and romantic baubles and produced a moving and scholarly

recreation of a fascinating scene and epoch—Hadrian's Rome." Cooperman further commented that *Memoirs of Hadrian* reaches "deeply into the blend of humanism and cruelty, decadence and power, art and economics referred to inadequately as 'pagan Rome.' " Hadas wrote: "Even a reader indifferent to history and historical personages must find the Hadrian here presented a full and sensitive man well worth knowing. . . . Miss Yourcenar breathes life into the enigmatic data concerning the man and communicates a vivid sense of the multifarious empire he ruled." *Washington Post* correspondent Michael Kernan expressed the opinion that it "is hard to find a reader who refuses to love 'Hadrian.' The man comes through so clearly, in the loneliness of his intelligence, in his practiced but wary handling of his own immense power, in his grief over the death of his young lover Antinous, that we feel this is what greatness must be like." *New Yorker* columnist George Steiner went so far as to suggest that *Memoirs of Hadrian* earned Yourcenar her invitation to join the Academie Francaise. "It is in [Hadrian's] eminent glow," Steiner concluded, "that the new Academician took her historic seat."

The Abyss, published in France as *L'Oeuvre au noir,* first appeared in English translation in 1976. Another historical/philosophical novel, the work follows the life of a fictitious Renaissance physician, Zeno of Bruges. In a *New York Times Book Review* assessment of the French edition, Marc Slonim called the book "at the same time a study of the Renaissance and a picture of that turbulent era as seen through the eyes of a poet. . . . What gives this fateful story a singular dimension is its high intellectual content. . . . 'L'Oeuvre au noir,' written in the compact, poetic language so typical of Mme. Yourcenar, is a stirring, unusual and often disturbing experience for the contemporary reader." Once again critics praised *The Abyss* for its authenticity and intellectual content. As Muriel Haynes noted in *Ms.* magazine, Yourcenar's "immense erudition and meticulous scholarship recreate this period of dissolution. . . . Beneath this richly textured surface, the book is a compendium of ideas, a philosophical examination of the abyss in which humankind is plunged still. . . . Like *Memoirs of Hadrian* it is a meditation on history in which the past is seen as both present and eternal." Kernan likewise felt that the work "is a brilliant tapestry of western Europe in the Middle Ages, . . . so rich in smells and sounds and scenes that it seems like superb reporting." Haynes suggested that although Zeno is a fictitious character, "his cast of mind, his convictions and experiences, are a kind of collage of those of actual personages who shared his century," and a *Times Literary Supplement* reviewer offered the compliment that the novel "will delight historians of this period."

One consequence of Yourcenar's inclusion in the Academie Francaise was that more of her work was translated and published in English. Novels such as *Alexis, Coup de Grace,* and *A Coin in Nine Hands* were all issued or reprinted after 1981. These works precede *Memoirs of Hadrian* in a chronological listing of Yourcenar's oeuvre, but the author revised them extensively after their first publications between 1929 and 1939. In these novels, Yourcenar explored the contemporary world through tales of unrequited love, homosexuality, and political assassination. They were generally considered secondary offerings, dwarfed in importance by *Memoirs of Hadrian* and *The Abyss,* but critics nonetheless cited them for interesting characterization and cogent style. Seymour, for instance, claimed that *A Coin in Nine Hands* "is among [Yourcenar's] best work, a testament to her extraordinary ability to turn stereotypes into archetypes, to invoke the past to illuminate the present." *A Coin in Nine Hands* charts the progress of an Italian coin as it passes from person to person in Italy during the dictatorship of Benito Mussolini. *Times Literary Supplement* reviewer Michael Tilby called the work "at heart an ironic and even playful novel. The omniscient narrator, endowed with a roving cinematographic eye, creates a deliberate impression of stylization, as does the mingling of the straightforwardly mimetic and the world of myth, or the abrupt changes of style and tone." In the *Los Angeles Times Book Review,* Doris Grumbach listed the novel's distinctions: "vivid characters, passages that move close to poetry and a story that belongs to both literature and history."

In addition to her novels, Yourcenar published poetry, essays, and stories, and many of these were also made available in English translation. *Fires* is a collection of poetic monologues based on classical Greek and Judeo-Christian stories; Boatwright contended that the pieces "are variations on the theme of absolute love, its terrible price and transcendent rewards, whatever its form." *Times Literary Supplement* contributor Oswyn Murray felt that the poems in *Fires* demonstrate "those qualities which were to make [Yourcenar] a great novelist—empathy, a sense of individuality, and wisdom." *Oriental Tales* offers a series of folktales from various European and Far Eastern cultures. In the *New York Times Book Review,* Koch stated that the stories "are wonderful. . . . [Each] of them seems a small window opened, magically, on some quite real but lost world. For Miss Yourcenar, scholarship is the entryway to the imagination, and, like all her work, these borrowed stories are simultaneously efforts at reconstruction and new creation. . . . At once immemorial and new, they show us the fabulist as mythographer and sage." Yourcenar's first essay collection, *Sous benefice d'inventaire,* published in the United States as *The Dark Brain of Piranesi and Other Essays,* also garnered critical praise. Assessing the work in the *New York Times,* John Gross concluded that Yourcenar's essays "make it clear that she is . . . an outstanding critic. They are forceful, deeply pondered, the record of a full imaginative response."

Marguerite Yourcenar was an intensely private person who preferred to avoid the literary circles in both New York and Paris. For half the year she lived in the cottage on Mount Desert Island that she and the late Grace Frick purchased together; Yourcenar told the *New York Times* that she stayed there both to avoid autograph-seekers and because she liked the "village rhythm" and the beautiful scenery. Although Gross, among others, noted that the author was "reticent about her private life, and . . . more preoccupied with long perspectives than with the fashion of the hour," Yourcenar did publish some books about herself. One ongoing project was *Le Labyrinthe du monde;* its first two components, *Souvenirs pieux* and *Archives du nord,* describe her parents' families in the century before she was born. She also released a series of interviews translated as *With Open Eyes: Conversations with Matthieu Galey.* Gross claimed that the views expressed in that book "are all of a piece—those of a liberal and a humanitarian who believes that 'the social problem is more important than the political problem,' and whose deepest public concerns tend to be cultural and ecological."

Mavis Gallant felt that Yourcenar "stands among a litter of flashier reputations as testimony to the substance and clarity of the French language and the purpose and meaning of a writer's life." Well into her eighties, the author continued to write, travel, and contemplate historical and philosophical issues central to the human condition. "Some novelists pull us more deeply into our own time;" Epstein observed, "she pulls us away from it—or rather above it. Marguerite Yourcenar's subject is human destiny. It was the only serious subject for the Greeks, whom she so much admires. It has always been the great subject of the

novel, and always will be, even though few writers in our day have been able to find the means to take it on, let alone so directly as Marguerite Yourcenar has done." In his *Saturday Review* essay, Koch concluded: "As an artist and thinker—for Yourcenar's novels must be regarded as simultaneously art, scholarship, and profound philosophical meditation—Marguerite Yourcenar writes squarely in defense of the very highest standards and traditions of that enlightened humanism which Hadrian promulgated for an empire and to the agonized rebirth of which her Zeno dies a martyr. It is, to say the least, heartening to find a writer so deeply committed to that humanism who is producing major art at this moment in our own history. It is, in fact, inspiring."

BIOGRAPHICAL/CRITICAL SOURCES:

BOOKS

Contemporary Literary Criticism, Gale, Volume 19, 1981, Volume 38, 1986, Volume 50, 1988.
Dictionary of Literary Biography, Volume 72: *French Novelists, 1930-1960,* Gale, 1988.
Dictionary of Literary Biography Yearbook: 1988, Gale, 1989.
Yourcenar, Marguerite, *Le Labyrinthe du monde,* Gallimard, Volume I: *Souvenirs pieux,* 1974, Volume II: *Archives du nord,* 1977, Volume III: *Quoi?: L'Eternite,* 1990.
Yourcenar, *Les Yeux ouverts: Entretiens avec Matthieu Galey,* Centurion, 1980, translation by Arthur Goldhammer published as *With Open Eyes: Conversations with Matthieu Galey,* Beacon Press, 1986.

PERIODICALS

Chicago Tribune, December 29, 1986.
Chicago Tribune Book World, June 28, 1981, October 27, 1985.
Commentary, August, 1982.
Commonweal, September 6, 1957, October 23, 1981.
Globe and Mail (Toronto), November 16, 1985, November 15, 1986, January 24, 1987, December 19, 1987.
Harper's, October, 1984.
Hudson Review, winter, 1976-77.
Los Angeles Times, November 28, 1986, June 26, 1987.
Los Angeles Times Book Review, October 3, 1982, February 3, 1985, November 3, 1985.
Ms., August, 1976.
Nation, December 25, 1954, October 30, 1976.
New Republic, January 10-17, 1983.
Newsweek, June 28, 1976.
New Yorker, June 14, 1976, August 17, 1981, February 11, 1985.
New York Herald Tribune Book Review, November 21, 1954.
New York Review of Books, October 14, 1976, October 10, 1985, December 5, 1985.
New York Times, December 3, 1979, March 7, 1980, December 27, 1984, April 10, 1987.
New York Times Book Review, August 25, 1968, July 11, 1976, October 4, 1981, January 30, 1983, September 16, 1984, February 24, 1985, September 22, 1985, December 14, 1986, April 19, 1987.
Saturday Review, November 27, 1954, July 20, 1957, June 12, 1976, June, 1981.
Spectator, June 19, 1982, February 19, 1983, November 12, 1983.
Times (London), July 8, 1982, November 17, 1983, May 10, 1984, July 16, 1987.
Times Literary Supplement, October 3, 1968, August 6, 1971, August 23, 1974, March 3, 1978, April 4, 1980, May 29, 1981, August 13, 1982, October 8, 1982, April 1, 1983, July 22, 1983, February 17, 1984, November 30, 1984, November 8, 1985, February 2-8, 1990.

Village Voice, November 4-10, 1981.

Washington Post, August 8, 1983.

Washington Post Book World, July 11, 1976, September 6, 1981, December 19, 1982, September 2, 1984, September 22, 1985, December 28, 1986, June 14, 1987.

World Literature Today, autumn, 1978, autumn, 1979, autumn, 1981, spring, 1982, autumn, 1984, summer, 1985, summer, 1986.

OBITUARIES:

BOOKS

Current Biography, H. W. Wilson, 1988.

PERIODICALS

Los Angeles Times, December 19, 1987.
Newsweek, December 28, 1987.
New York Times, December 19, 1987.
Times (London), December 19, 1987.
Washington Post, December 19, 1987.

Z

ZELAZNY, Roger (Joseph) 1937-
(Harrison Denmark)

PERSONAL: Born May 13, 1937, in Cleveland, Ohio; son of Joseph Frank and Josephine (Sweet) Zelazny; married Sharon Steberl, December 5, 1964 (divorced, June 27, 1966); married Judith Alene Callahan, August 20, 1966; children: (second marriage) Devin, Trent (sons), Shannon (daughter). *Education:* Western Reserve University (now Case Western Reserve University), B.A., 1959; Columbia University, M.A., 1962.

ADDRESSES: Home—Santa Fe, N.M. *Agent*—Kirby McCauley, 432 Park Ave. S., Suite 1509, New York, N.Y. 10016.

CAREER: Writer, 1969—. U.S. Social Security Administration, claims representative in Cleveland, Ohio, 1962-65, claims policy specialist in Baltimore, Md., 1965-69. Lecturer at colleges, universities, and at writing workshops and conferences. *Military service:* U.S. Army Reserve, 1960-66.

MEMBER: Authors Guild, Authors League of America, School of American Research, Science Fiction Oral History Association, Science Fiction Research Association, Science Fiction Writers of America (secretary-treasurer, 1967-68), Ohioana Library Association, Santa Fe Chamber of Commerce.

AWARDS, HONORS: Nebula Award, Science Fiction Writers of America, 1965, for best novella, "He Who Shapes," 1965, for best novelette, "The Doors of His Face, the Lamps of His Mouth," and 1975, for best novella, "Home Is the Hangman"; Hugo Award, World Science Fiction Convention, 1966, for best novel, *This Immortal,* 1968, for best novel, *Lord of Light,* 1975, for best novella, "Home Is the Hangman," 1983, for best novelette, "Unicorn Variations," 1986, for best novella, "Twenty-Four Views of Mount Fuji by Hokusai," and 1987, for best novelette, "Permafrost"; Prix Apollo, 1972, for French edition of *Isle of the Dead;* Guest of Honor, World Science Fiction Convention, 1974, Australian National Science Fiction Convention, 1978, and at numerous regional and local science fiction conventions; *Doorways in the Sand* named one of the best young adult books of the year, 1976, American Library Association; Balrog Award, 1980, for best story, "The Last Defender of Camelot," and 1984, for best collection, *Unicorn Variations; Locus* Award, 1984, for collection *Unicorn Variations,* and 1986, for novel *Trumps of Doom.*

WRITINGS:

SCIENCE FICTION NOVELS

This Immortal, Ace Books, 1966.
The Dream Master, Ace Books, 1966, reprinted, 1982.
Lord of Light, Doubleday, 1967.
Isle of the Dead, Ace Books, 1969, reprinted, 1985.
Creatures of Light and Darkness, Doubleday, 1969.
Damnation Alley, Putnam, 1969, reprinted, Tor Books, 1984.
Jack of Shadows, Walker & Co., 1971.
Today We Choose Faces, Signet, 1973.
To Die in Italbar, Doubleday, 1973.
Doorways in the Sand, Harper, 1976.
Bridge of Ashes, New American Library, 1976.
(With Philip K. Dick) *Deus Irae,* Doubleday, 1976.
Roadmarks, Ballantine, 1979.
Changeling, Ace Books, 1980.
The Changing Land, Ballantine, 1981.
Madwand, Ace Books, 1981.
(With Fred Saberhagen) *Coils,* Simon & Schuster, 1982.
Eye of Cat, Ultramarine, 1982.
Dilvish, the Damned, Ballantine, 1983.
(With others) *Berserker Base,* Tor Books, 1985.
A Dark Traveling, Walker & Co., 1987.
Knight of the Shadows, Morrow, 1989.

"AMBER" SERIES

Nine Princes in Amber (also see below), Doubleday, 1970.
The Guns of Avalon (also see below), Doubleday, 1972.
Sign of the Unicorn (also see below), Doubleday, 1975.
The Hand of Oberon (also see below), Doubleday, 1976.
The Courts of Chaos (also see below), Doubleday, 1978.
The Chronicles of Amber (contains *Nine Princes in Amber, The Guns of Avalon, Sign of the Unicorn, The Hand of Oberon,* and *The Courts of Chaos*), Doubleday, 1979.
A Rhapsody in Amber (chapbook), Cheap Street, 1981.
Trumps of Doom, Arbor House, 1985.
Blood of Amber, Arbor House, 1986.
Sign of Chaos, Arbor House, 1987.
(With Neil Randell) *Roger Zelazny's Visual Guide to Castle Amber,* Avon, 1988.

STORY COLLECTIONS

Four for Tomorrow, Ace Books, 1967 (published in England as *A Rose for Ecclesiastes,* Hart Davis, 1969).
The Doors of His Face, The Lamps of His Mouth, and Other Stories, Doubleday, 1971.
My Name Is Legion, Ballantine, 1976.
The Last Defender of Camelot, Pocket Books, 1980.
Unicorn Variations, Pocket Books, 1983.
Frost and Fire: Fantasy and Science Fiction Stories, Morrow, 1989.

OTHER

(Author of introduction) Harlan Ellison, *From the Land of Fear,* Belmont/Tower, 1967.
(Author of introduction) Philip Jose Farmer, *A Private Cosmos,* Ace Books, 1968.
(Editor) *Nebula Award Stories 3,* Doubleday, 1968.
Poems, Discon, 1974.
(Author of introduction) Bruce Gillespie, editor, *Philip K. Dick: Electric Shepherd,* Norstrilia Press, 1975.
(With Gray Morrow) *The Illustrated Roger Zelazny,* Baronet, 1978.
The Bells of Shoredan (booklet), Underwood/Miller, 1979.
When Pussywillows Last in the Catyard Bloomed (poems), Norstrilia Press, 1980.
For a Breath I Tarry, Underwood/Miller, 1980.
To Spin Is Miracle Cat (poems), Underwood/Miller, 1982.
He Who Shapes: The Infinity Box (novella), Tor Books, 1989.
Wizard World, Baen Books, 1989.

CONTRIBUTOR

Avram Davidson, editor, *The Best from Fantasy and Science Fiction,* Doubleday, 1965.
Harlan Ellison, editor, *Dangerous Visions: 33 Original Stories,* Doubleday, 1967.
Terry Carr, editor, *New Worlds of Fantasy #2,* Ace Books, 1970.
Robert Silverberg, editor, *The Science Fiction Hall of Fame,* Doubleday, 1970.
Robert Silverberg, editor, *Great Short Novels of SF,* Ballantine, 1970.
Ted White, editor, *The Best from Amazing,* Manor Books, 1973.
Ted White, editor, *The Best from Fantastic,* Manor Books, 1973.
Isaac Asimov, Martin Henry Greenberg, and Joseph T. Olander, editors, *100 Great Science Fiction Short Short Stories,* Doubleday, 1978.
Ben Bova, editor, *The Best of Analog,* Baronet, 1978.

Also contributor to other books. Contributor of more than one hundred stories, sometimes under pseudonym Harrison Denmark, to *New Worlds, Omni, Magazine of Fantasy and Science Fiction, Fantastic Stories, Amazing Stories,* and *Galaxy.*

SIDELIGHTS: Known for his colorful prose style and innovative adaptations of ancient myth, Roger Zelazny is one of the most popular of contemporary science fiction writers. His early works, first published in the 1960s, feature characters derived from Egyptian and Hindu mythology, while his more recent "Amber" series concerns a world existing in all times and places at once, and of which the Earth and other worlds are mere reflections. Speaking of the wide range of interests and approaches to be found in his work, Michael Vance of *Fantasy Newsletter* claims that Zelazny is "not easily categorized. He seems at home swimming with or against the main currents of science fiction. . . . [But] Zelazny wins awards and sells books because he weaves wordspells that transport readers into the farthest reaches of space or the darkest mysteries of magic with equal ease."

Zelazny burst on the science fiction scene in the early 1960s. At that time working for the Social Security Administration, a position he was to hold until 1969, Zelazny began to write short stories during his spare time in the evenings and on weekends. "Zelazny's procedure," Joseph L. Sanders explains in his *Roger Zelazny: A Primary and Secondary Bibliography,* ". . . was to write one story an evening and to polish it the following night." He submitted these stories to the major science fiction magazines, working his way down an alphabetical list he compiled. After a short time the editor of *Amazing Stories* began to show an interest in his work, jotting down encouraging comments on Zelazny's manuscripts. "Slightly more than a month after Zelazny began sending stories around," Sanders notes, his first story was accepted for publication in *Amazing.* He published another seventeen stories in his first year as a science fiction writer. And between 1962 and 1969, Zelazny "was nominated for the Hugo and Nebula awards sixteen times," Carl B. Yoke reports in the *Dictionary of Literary Biography.*

Zelazny's most important writings from this period are novellas between 20,000 and 40,000 words in length. "A Rose for Ecclesiastes" and "The Doors of His Face, the Lamps of His Mouth" have been especially cited by critics as among the best of his early work. Zelazny's novellas, George Warren writes in the *Los Angeles Times Book Review,* are "full of fantastic imagery and soaring, even overblown, poetry." Writing in *Voices for the Future: Essays on Major Science Fiction Writers,* Thomas D. Clareson claims that "A Rose for Ecclesiastes" "revitalized science fiction. . . . Zelazny introduced color, poetry, metaphor, and a deeper psychological dimension into science fiction." The story concerns an Earth man, Gallinger, who works on Mars as a translator of ancient religious texts. The Martian race is sterile and dying out. When Gallinger impregnates Braxa, a Martian woman with whom he has fallen in love, it promises a continuance of the Martian race. But Gallinger soon realizes that Braxa has never loved him, has only had his child to fulfill an old religious prophecy, and his ego is shattered. Gallinger attempts suicide. This painful episode leads him to undergo a dramatic personality change. Yoke remarks that "in 'A Rose for Ecclesiastes' Zelazny brilliantly explores man's capability to grow from his experience."

Zelazny again borrows from biblical precedents for the title of "The Doors of His Face, the Lamps of His Mouth," which is taken from the Book of Job. The protagonist of this story, Carlton Davits, is similar to the biblical Job as well. Both are wealthy, self-centered men. Davits is undone when he travels to Venus in quest of a giant sea creature never before caught by Earthlings. The creature wrecks his ship and kills six of his crew, and Davits is reduced to bankruptcy and alcoholism. But during a later trip in search of the creature, this time with his ex-wife, Davits succeeds in capturing and killing the monster. This triumph brings him to a new maturity. Like Gallinger in "A Rose for Ecclesiastes," Davits undergoes a personality change. In an article for *Extrapolation,* Yoke notes that "in the pattern of his development, Davits mirrors the psychological evolution of many Zelazny protagonists." Acknowledging the story's popularity among science fiction readers, Douglas Barbour of *Riverside Quarterly* refers to "The Doors of His Face, the Lamps of His Mouth" as "the now famous" story. Zelazny won a Nebula Award for the work.

Zelazny's early stories, with their dazzling prose style and audacious mix of myth, allusions, and high technology, quickly made him a major figure in the science fiction field. Speaking of these early writings, Sidney Coleman of the *Magazine of Fantasy and Science Fiction* states: "In an important sense Zelazny really was without fear and without blame; he would try the most daring tricks, and bring them off. Zelazny's famous skill as a culture-magpie is an outstanding instance: He would cast a computer as both Faust and Adam, mix grail legend with electric psychotherapy, work a line from the *Cantos* into a story whose basic plot was the old pulp chestnut about the white hunter and Miss Richbitch . . . [and] he made it work." Algis Budrys of the *Magazine of Fantasy and Science Fiction,* writing of Zelazny's early career, claims that those were "the days when each new Zelazny story was like nothing that had been done before."

By 1969, having established himself in the science fiction field, Zelazny left his job with the Social Security Administration to become a full-time writer. The career move entailed one major change in his writing. While employed with the government, Zelazny had been obliged to write relatively short works, stories he could finish in his spare time. But once he relied on science fiction for his livelihood, he relegated the shorter, less profitable works to secondary status and focused his attention on the writing of novels. As George R. R. Martin explains in the *Washington Post Book World,* "it was in the shorter forms that he first made a name for himself. Like many other writers, however, Zelazny was soon seduced away from his first love by the greater glory and riches of the novel."

Zelazny's first novel, *This Immortal,* is inspired in part by the author's experiences while serving in the Army's Arts, Monuments, and Archives unit, a department which preserves important historical and cultural landmarks in occupied foreign countries. In the novel, the alien Myshtigo is on a tour of Earth's cultural monuments, guided by the immortal Earthling Conrad. Myshtigo has bought the planet, long before devastated by nuclear war and conquered by the Vegans, and is now interested in learning something about his property. His unspoken desire is to determine whether Conrad is fit to lead the massive restoration effort Myshtigo plans for the ruined Earth.

The novel's focus is on Conrad's ability to overcome his longstanding antagonism to the aliens and see where both he and Myshtigo share common goals and concerns. His immortality has enabled Conrad to experience widely divergent aspects of life. Through this process he has learned that "things, places, people are real; judgments that might have applied to reality in the past, though, cannot be trusted," as Sanders remarks in *Death and the Serpent: Immortality in Science Fiction and Fantasy.* By suppressing his strong aversion to the aliens and allowing himself to learn about Myshtigo, Conrad is eventually given leadership of the effort to restore the Earth, an effort that even the most persistent opponents of the Vegans support. "Conrad," Joseph V. Francavilla writes in *Extrapolation,* "passes from being a destroyer, disrupter, and fighter to being a creator, restorer, and peacemaker." "The main thing Zelazny shows about immortality in *This Immortal,*" Sanders writes, "is that the successful immortal, such as Conrad, who not only stays alive but does something satisfying with his life, does so by avoiding confinement within a set of rules or preconceptions." Writing in the *Dictionary of Literary Biography,* Yoke maintains that "the striking originality of the story and its characterization make [*This Immortal*] well worth reading." *This Immortal* won a Hugo Award in 1966.

Lord of Light is concerned with many of the same themes introduced in *This Immortal,* including personality growth, immortality, and the renewal of a planet. It is set on a far future world where technologically advanced human beings have set them-

selves up as gods over the less advanced populace. Taking the Hindu deities as their models, they have enhanced their mental powers through neurosurgery, hypnosis, and drugs to achieve a semblance of actual godlike ability. One of their number has succeeded in reaching inner perfection. When it becomes clear to him that his companions have become tyrants, he overthrows their system and frees the native population. *Lord of Light,* Yoke explains in the *Dictionary of Literary Biography,* "was hailed as a science-fiction classic" when it first appeared, and won Zelazny a Hugo Award.

Later Zelazny novels are also fashioned from a blend of ancient myths and futuristic science. *Creatures of Light and Darkness* features the gods of Egyptian mythology, while the plot borrows elements from several different mythologies. As Pauline F. Micciche of *Library Journal* notes, it is "a warp of Christian, Greek, Egyptian and Norse myths spun into one thread." *Isle of the Dead* concerns a battle between a wealthy, sardonic immortal and his enemy, who is a personification of a god. Writing in the *New York Times Book Review,* Gerald Jonas notes that "Zelazny is a playful writer, but there is nothing lighthearted about his play. He plays with myths—archetypes and themes borrowed from the ancestral storehouses of different cultures."

A continuing theme in these novels is the nature of divinity. Often, Zelazny writes of immortal characters with enormous technological powers who must grow to godlike stature to deal with overwhelming situations. "Immortality, or near-immortality, is a persistent theme in Zelazny's writing," Yoke acknowledges in *The Mechanical God: Machines in Science Fiction,* "and it is a key factor in raising man or humanoid to the god level." "To live forever," Francavilla explains, "means simply to have time enough to experience, learn, develop, and to increase one's self-awareness—to define oneself. In his quest for self-definition . . . , the immortal hero in Zelazny's works defines what it means to be human by expanding man's potential and by boldly extending the boundaries of the human into the region of the divine."

Perhaps Zelazny's most ambitious project has been the series of books set in the imaginary world of Amber; the series consists of a five-novel sequence, three novels in a new, ongoing sequence, and a chapbook. The world of Amber transcends normal time and space limitations. It exists in all times at once, and its inhabitants are immortals who can time travel as they please between an endless multitude of alternate worlds. These alternate worlds, one of which is the Earth, are mere reflections of the one true world of Amber. As Edwin Morgan of the *Times Literary Supplement* maintains, "Amber is a place, a city, a state, a 'world'. . . . Amber is the perfect place, the Substance to which everything else is Shadow. It is not in our space and time, and its inhabitants, although they talk and act for the most part in human ways, are not human. Since they have enormous powers, they appear at times like gods."

The series follows the machinations among Amber's ruling family as they vie for power over multiple worlds. The first five novels form one complete story in which Corwin seeks the throne during a demonic invasion that threatens to reduce Amber and her shadow worlds to chaos. He begins the first novel with amnesia, his memory wiped clean by his rivals, and ends the fifth book as the ruler of Amber. "In the Amber series, as Corwin finally comes to understand," Sanders writes in his Zelazny bibliography, "life exists between two poles, Pattern and Chaos. Neither 'wins'. The difficult, creative tension between them continues, just as life continues." Lester Del Rey, writing in *Analog: Science Fiction/Science Fact,* warns that the Amber "books have to be read from first to last. They form a single novel, not a series of novels." He concludes with the comment that the five novels would have been a better story if written as a single book. "Had that been done," Del Rey writes, "this could well have been a genuinely superb piece of fantasy. As it is, it's a good story—no more." But Marshall B. Tymm, Kenneth J. Zoharski, and Robert H. Boyer have a more positive reaction to the five-novel Amber sequence in their *Fantasy Literature: A Core Collection and Reference Guide.* These books are, they claim, "on the whole excellent, both for their unusually original fantasy elements and for their literary qualities," and they judge Amber to be "one of the more ingeniously conceived secondary worlds in fantasy literature."

The three most recent Amber novels concern the adventures of Corwin's son, Merlin, who is being stalked through alternate worlds by an unknown group of assassins. Speaking of *Blood of Amber,* H. J. Kirchhoff of the Toronto *Globe and Mail* states: "As usual in the Amber books, Zelazny parlays hip dialogue, quirky characters and an anything-is-possible multiple universe into a winning swords-and-sorcery adventure." *Trumps of Doom,* the first in the new Amber series won a Locus Award in 1986.

Speaking to Vance about his conception of science fiction, Zelazny explains: "It is, for me, a special way of looking at anything, really—by pulling it out of context and into a different situation. . . . Sometimes you just ask yourself, 'What If?' And you make up something that's considered unlikely to happen, just to take a look at it." When writing science fiction, Zelazny prefers a spontaneous technique. In an article for *Science Fiction Chronicle* about how he writes, Zelazny claims: "Generally, I do not like knowing beforehand how I will end a novel. My ideal method of composition is to begin writing once I know my major character and a few of the situations in which he or she will be functioning—*i.e.,* about thirty percent of the story. . . . I enjoy relying upon a subconscious plotting mechanism and discovering its operation as I work."

Zelazny's work has explored a range of genre types during his career, moving from strict science fiction based on mythological models to an alternate world fantasy of castles, kings, and sword-wielding heroes. Charles Platt of the *Washington Post Book World* notes that "in his early work, . . . closely observed characters interacted with advanced technology; today, Zelazny deals more with sorcery than science, in fanciful mythic landscapes, laconically described. He still writes more fluently and with more authority than nine-tenths of his contemporaries." Lew Wolkoff of *Best Sellers* believes that Zelazny can handle both types of fiction well. "He can take a reader," Wolkoff writes, "on tour across a radiation-scarred America in one story and show him/her a wizards' duel in the next, swinging easily from hard science to dark fantasy."

Not all critics have been satisfied with the changes in Zelazny's writing. Some prefer his earlier, more flamboyantly poetic work. Coleman, for example, complains that Zelazny "put away his magician's tricks and turned his gold into lead. . . . We once had something unique and wonderful, and it is gone, and what we have in its place is only a superior writer of preposterous adventures." Although Nick Totton of the *Observer* calls Zelazny "a skilled and fluent writer with both powerful ideas and a grasp of their broader reference," he also finds that Zelazny "generally prefers playing cosily within a familiar convention to exploring fresh territory." Sanders notes in his Zelazny bibliography that some critics of the author "have voiced irritation when Zelazny has not done exactly *what they expected.*"

Despite such criticism, Zelazny enjoys a prominent position in contemporary science fiction. Martin places the book *The Doors of His Face, the Lamps of His Mouth, and Other Stories* "among the three best story collections of the last decade," and calls Zelazny "one of the most important contemporary science-fiction writers." "There is no question of his stature," Yoke maintains in the *Dictionary of Literary Biography.* "He has contributed major works to the field, and perhaps more than any other writer has brought the techniques, style, and language of serious literature to science fiction. His greatest contribution, however, may be that he has brought to a literature famous for its cardboard figures, characters who are psychologically credible, who are sympathetic, who have scope and dimension." Clareson concludes that "Zelazny has dealt intelligently, lightly, and good-humoredly with a number of serious questions about the ways in which our fantasies mesh with our realities." Although holding some reservations about Zelazny's work, Clareson nevertheless believes he is "a story teller, an entertainer in the best sense," and praises his "exemplary craftsmanship, which has continued with few hiatuses throughout his career."

BIOGRAPHICAL/CRITICAL SOURCES:

BOOKS

Clareson, Thomas D., *Voices for the Future: Essays on Major Science Fiction Writers,* Bowling Green State University, 1979.
Collins, R. A., editor, *Scope of the Fantastic: Culture, Biography, Themes in Children's Literature,* Greenwood Press, 1985.
Contemporary Literary Criticism, Volume 21, Gale, 1982.
Dictionary of Literary Biography, Volume 8: *Twentieth-Century American Science Fiction Writers,* Gale, 1981.
Dunn, Thomas P. and Richard D. Erlich, editors, *The Mechanical God: Machines in Science Fiction,* Greenwood Press, 1982.
Krulik, Theodore, *Roger Zelazny,* Ungar, 1986.
Levack, Daniel J. H., *Amber Dreams: A Roger Zelazny Bibliography,* Underwood/Miller, 1983.
Reilly, Robert, editor, *The Transcendent Adventure,* Greenwood Press, 1984.
Sanders, Joseph L., *Roger Zelazny: A Primary and Secondary Bibliography,* G. K. Hall, 1980.
Science Fiction and Fantasy Authors: A Bibliography of First Printings of Their Science Fiction and Selected Nonfiction, G. K. Hall, 1979.
Staicar, Tom, editor, *Critical Encounters II,* Ungar, 1982.
Tymm, Marshall B., Kenneth J. Zoharski, and Robert H. Boyer, *Fantasy Literature: A Core Collection and Reference Guide,* Bowker, 1979.
Walker, Paul, *Speaking of Science Fiction,* Luna Publications, 1978.
Yoke, Carl B., *Roger Zelazny and Andre Norton: Proponents of Individualism,* State Library of Ohio, 1979.
Yoke, Carl B., *A Reader's Guide to Roger Zelazny,* Starmont, 1979.
Yoke, Carl B., and Donald M. Hassler, editors, *Death and the Serpent: Immortality in Science Fiction and Fantasy,* Greenwood Press, 1985.

PERIODICALS

Algol, summer, 1976.
Amazing Stories, July, 1984.
Analog: Science Fiction/Science Fact, February, 1979, March 2, 1981, March, 1983.
Baltimore Sun, January 29, 1967.
Best Sellers, September, 1976, June, 1978.
Extrapolation, December, 1973, summer, 1980, spring, 1984.

Fantasy Newsletter, October 1980, January 1983, September, 1983.
Foundation, March, 1977.
Future Life, March, 1981.
Globe and Mail (Toronto), February 14, 1987, November 14, 1987.
Journal of American Culture, summer, 1979.
Library Journal, September 15, 1969.
Locus, October, 1983.
Los Angeles Times Book Review, January 11, 1981.
Magazine of Fantasy and Science Fiction, May, 1971, August, 1974, February, 1982.
Media Sight, summer, 1984.
Mosaic, winter, 1981.
New Scientist, February 23, 1978.
New York Review of Books, October 2, 1975.
New York Times Book Review, May 23, 1976, December 19, 1982.
Observer, June 24, 1979.
Riverside Quarterly, June, 1970, August, 1973.
Science Fiction: A Review of Speculative Literature, June, 1978, December, 1979.
Science Fiction Chronicle, January, 1985.
Science Fiction Review, May, 1980, August, 1980.
SF Commentary, November, 1978.
Times Literary Supplement, February 29, 1968, March 28, 1968, February 13, 1981.
Washington Post Book World, December 23, 1979, January 25, 1981, December 25, 1983.

*   *   *

ZINDEL, Paul 1936-

PERSONAL: Born May 15, 1936, in Staten Island, N.Y.; son of Paul (a policeman) and Betty Beatrice Mary (a practical nurse; maiden name, Frank) Zindel; married Bonnie Hildebrand (a writer), October 25, 1973; children: David Jack, Lizabeth Claire. *Education:* Wagner College, B.S., 1958, M.Sc., 1959.

ADDRESSES: Home—New York, N.Y. *Agent*—Curtis Brown, Ltd., Ten Astor Pl., New York, N.Y. 10003.

CAREER: Tottenville High School, Staten Island, N.Y., chemistry teacher, 1959-69; playwright and author of children's books, 1969—. Playwright in residence, Alley Theatre, Houston, Tex., 1967.

MEMBER: Dramatists Guild, Writers Guild of America West, Authors Guild, Actors Studio.

AWARDS, HONORS: Ford Foundation grant, 1967; *New York Times Book Review* Outstanding Books of the Year selection, 1969, for *My Darling, My Hamburger;* Obie Award for best new American play, *Village Voice,* 1970, New York Drama Critics Circle Award for best American play, 1970, *Variety* award for most promising playwright, 1970, Pulitzer Prize in drama, 1971, New York Critics Award, 1971, and Vernon Rice Drama Desk Award for most promising playwright, 1971, all for "The Effect of Gamma Rays on Man-in-the-Moon Marigolds"; American Library Association (ALA) Notable Book selection and Best Books for Young Adults selection, both 1971, both for *The Effect of Gamma Rays on Man-in-the-Moon Marigolds;* D.H.L., Wagner College, 1971; ALA Best Books for Young Adults selection, 1981, for *The Pigman's Legacy;* Los Angeles Drama Critics Award for best American play, for "And Miss Reardon Drinks a Little."

WRITINGS:

NOVELS; FOR YOUNG ADULTS

The Pigman, Harper, 1968, reprinted, Bantam, 1983.
My Darling, My Hamburger, Harper, 1969.
I Never Loved Your Mind, Harper, 1970.
Pardon Me, You're Stepping on My Eyeball, Harper, 1976.
Confessions of a Teenage Baboon (also see below), Harper, 1977.
The Undertaker's Gone Bananas, Harper, 1978.
(With wife, Bonnie Zindel) *A Star for the Latecomer,* Harper, 1980.
The Pigman's Legacy, Harper, 1980.
The Girl Who Wanted a Boy, Harper, 1981.
(With Crescent Dragonwagon) *To Take a Dare,* Harper, 1982.
Harry and Hortense at Hormone High, Harper, 1984.
The Amazing and Death-Defying Diary of Eugene Dingman, Harper, 1987.
A Begonia for Miss Applebaum, Harper, 1989.

PLAYS

"Dimensions of Peacocks," first produced in New York, 1959.
"Euthanasia and the Endless Hearts," first produced in New York City at Take 3, 1960.
"A Dream of Swallows," first produced Off-Broadway at Jan Hus House, April 14, 1964.
The Effects of Gamma Rays on Man-in-the-Moon Marigolds (also see below; first produced in Houston at Alley Theatre, May 12, 1965; produced Off-Broadway at Mercer-O'Casey Theatre, April 7, 1970; produced on Broadway at the New Theatre, August 11, 1970), Harper, 1971.
And Miss Reardon Drinks a Little (first produced in Los Angeles, Calif., at Mark Taper Forum, 1967; revised version produced on Broadway at Morosco Theatre, February 25, 1971), Dramatists Play Service, 1971.
The Secret Affairs of Mildred Wild, (first produced on Broadway at Ambassador Theatre, November 14, 1972), Dramatists Play Service, 1973.
Let Me Hear You Whisper [and] *The Ladies Should Be in Bed* ([the former based on his screenplay of the same title; also see below]; both plays produced Off-Off Broadway at the Nat Horne Musical Theatre as "Zindel X 2," April 29, 1982), Dramatists Play Service, 1973.
Ladies at the Alamo (first produced Off-Off Broadway at Actors Studio, May 29, 1975; produced on Broadway at the Martin Beck Theater, April 7, 1977), Dramatists Play Service, 1977.
"A Destiny with Half Moon Street," first produced in Coconut Grove, Fla., at Players State Theater, March 4, 1983.
"Amulets against the Dragon Forces" (based in part on his novel *Confessions of a Teenage Baboon*), first produced in New York City at the Circle Repertory Theatre, April 5, 1989.

SCREENPLAYS AND TELEPLAYS

"The Effect of Gamma Rays on Man-in-the-Moon Marigolds" (adapted from his play), National Educational Television (NET), 1966.
Let Me Hear You Whisper (produced by NET, 1966), Harper, 1974.
"Up the Sandbox" (adapted from Anne Roiphe's novel), National General, 1972.
"Mame" (adapted from Patrick Dennis's *Auntie Mame*), Warner Brothers, 1973.
(With Gerard Brach, Andrei Konchalovsky, and Marjorie David) "Maria's Lovers," Cannon, 1985.

"Alice in Wonderland" (adapted from Lewis Carroll's *Alice's Adventures in Wonderland* and *Through the Looking Glass*), Columbia Broadcasting Service (CBS-TV), 1985.

(With Djordje Milicevic and Edward Bunker) "Runaway Train," Cannon, 1986.

"Babes in Toyland" (adapted from the Victor Herbert operetta), National Broadcasting Company (NBC-TV), 1986.

"A Connecticut Yankee in King Arthur's Court" (based on Mark Twain's novel), NBC-TV, 1989.

OTHER

I Love My Mother (for children), Harper, 1975.
When a Darkness Falls (adult novel), Bantam, 1984.

Contributor of articles to newspapers and periodicals.

SIDELIGHTS: Paul Zindel was still teaching high school chemistry when he burst onto the literary scene with two powerful works in two different media: "The Effect of Gamma Rays on Man-in-the-Moon Marigolds," which became a Broadway hit and garnered Zindel an Obie Award and a Pulitzer Prize; and *The Pigman,* a novel for young adults which "critics of adolescent literature generally cite . . . as helping this subgenre break its ties with its past romanticism and move dramatically into a much more realistic mode," as Theodore W. Hipple describes it in a *Dictionary of Literary Biography* essay. While they are targeted at different audiences, both Zindel's drama and fiction contain elements in common, such as a strong ear for dialogue, characters that are generally misfits or outsiders, and an honest, realistic approach to life's often overwhelming problems. Frequently based on his own experiences, as Ruth L. Strickland notes in another *Dictionary of Literary Biography* piece, "Zindel's art is one which realistically combines humor and pathos, poetry and terror."

Although Zindel had seen some productions of his work prior to the New York premiere of "Marigolds" in 1970, he was still largely unknown to drama devotees. But when the play opened to rave reviews, "everyone was suddenly aware of 'Marigolds,' a relentless, powerfully drawn portrait of a bitter, frequently brutal mother and her two anguished daughters," relates Guy Flatley in the *New York Times.* The play presents the frequently hostile relationship between sarcastic Beatrice, who supports her family by boarding a semi-comatose old woman, and her two daughters. Ruth, the elder, is mentally unbalanced and becoming as resentful and emotionally crippled as her mother; her sister Tillie, however, is optimistic and interested in life and especially her science project, where gamma radiation has produced marigold blossoms both withered and vigorous. "Zindel, who writes alarmingly well, contrasts the fate of the poor marigolds with the fate of this tortured family," observes *New York Times* drama critic Clive Barnes. "We are all the product of our environment, all the product of our particular 'gamma-rays,' but some survive and some are destroyed." *Christian Science Monitor* contributor Alan Bunce also sees this parallel, and remarks that the flowers' "symbolism for this family is strong enough for meaning without weighting down the play's rampant activity."

While many critics believe the symbolism of "Marigolds" is effective, they particularly praise Zindel's forthright approach to depicting his characters' lives. As Harold Clurman of the *Nation* reports, "The play is 'old-fashioned,' harking back to a slice-of-life realism rarely practiced any more, [and] the clarity of its writing, the health of its spirit, and the touching courage of its basic statement are most sympathetic." The critic adds that "Marigolds" "faces life far more honestly than the muddy stream of playlets which speak gleefully about the world going

to hell." Barnes similarly commends Zindel's realistic strategy: "This is the kind of true-life melodrama that fascinates Arthur Miller, and rather like Mr. Miller it is extremely successful. My heart was held by it," he continues. "And, unlike most of its genre, the ending is unusually satisfying."

Another satisfying aspect of "Marigolds" is the author's ability to create rounded characters; Barnes finds interesting "Zindel's taut regard for the things people say, and his skill at making insights from these things." Contributing to this skill is the dramatist's "sizable talent for writing penetrating dialogue, for probing the intensity of mental anguish, and for supplying strong dramatic moments in lieu of a strong plot," *Cue*'s Marilyn Stasio writes. *Village Voice* contributor John Lahr likewise observes that "there is so much good writing within the melodramatic machinery, so much insight into Beatrice and Tillie . . . that the play gives us intimations of our mortality." While *New York* reviewer John Simon believes that the plot of "Marigolds" is neither very original nor carefully crafted, he acknowledges that the play is "engaging," and notes that "its first strength lies in the sympathy and humor with which Paul Zindel views all its characters." The critic also says that "there are other virtues: an unassuming, leisurely sense of humor, and a pathos under strict surveillance lest it jerk obscuring tears. . . . Best of all, there is the ability to make the barest utterance grow into the stature of poetry." "It is difficult to know where praise of *Marigolds* should begin or end, and how to contain it," concludes T. E. Kalem of *Time.* The critic proposes, however, that "the ultimate accolade must go to Paul Zindel for creating a psychologically perceptive ambience. . . . [It is] one of the honest and intelligent values of this splendid and tormented play."

"Bitterly funny and wrenchingly sad," Zindel's next production, "And Miss Reardon Drinks a Little," "presents a half-dozen shrewdly observed and eminently actable characters," states Richard L. Coe in the *Washington Post.* Chief among these characters are the three teaching Reardon sisters, the two eldest of which, Ceil and Catherine, are gathered to deal with the increasing insanity of the youngest, Anna. *Boston Globe* reviewer Kevin Kelly, who calls the play "funny and fierce and, well, absolutely extraordinary," declares that "within this simple format, with the three sisters stamped as stereotypes almost before we know them, Zindel draws together his drama and then, insight for insight, turns the stereotypes inside out and reveals the complexities of his characters." These characters, comments a *Variety* critic, "pulsate with pain and, in most cases, express themselves in convulsively comic terms. As with real people, they react to each other," the reviewer continues, "hurt and wound each other, and change during the course of an evening of unintentional, inescapable, pointless violence." It is with this violence that "Zindel is stating some hard facts about our increasingly uncomfortable world," Coe points out, adding that "there will be those who will loathe this play, some for its language, some for its ruthlessness."

Some critics were dissatisfied with "Miss Reardon," faulting the playwright for describing instead of developing its situation. Kalem, for example, notes that while Zindel's "wacky humor is present, along with his abrupt pathos, . . . and his frequently well-honed dialogue, . . . under it all, the plot, point, and purpose and direction of the play seem to have been lost." As Stasio explains, Zindel's "talent" for dialogue and character "is insufficient for sustaining the play. The sisters' conflict is a static situation, lacking dramatic action to develop it and a central crisis to resolve it." Nevertheless, as Barnes remarks, "far from all is lost. Zindel . . . is an accomplished writer. A few of his jokes are witty, and better still, some of them are relevant and locked into the character of the play." *Newsweek*'s Jack Kroll, however, finds "Miss Reardon" a "deceptively simple but sharply observed play," and asserts that Zindel is "that rarity—a playwright who can write intelligent, sensitive, entertaining plays for a wide public." " 'And Miss Reardon Drinks a Little' will probably and deservedly turn out to be the best American play of the season," concludes Kelly; the critic maintains that "with it, Paul Zindel more than confirms his early reputation."

Such critical opinion notwithstanding, Zindel did not have another acclaimed play until the success, almost twenty years later, of "Amulets against the Dragon Forces," a play that "illuminates the miracle by which . . . [a child] finds the courage to hold on to his own sweetness and his ability to love," as Laurie Winer describes it in the *Wall Street Journal.* "And in this impassioned new work," the critic continues, "Mr. Zindel gives us a teen-age protagonist who is as original, believable and decent as [J. D.] Salinger's Holden Caulfield." The child in question is Chris Boyd, who follows his mother from job to job as a home nurse; in their current circumstances, Chris is harassed by the patient's son, an alcoholic with a penchant for corrupting young men. "Though they have not all been created with equal depth by Mr. Zindel," Frank Rich remarks in the *New York Times,* "the characters are invariably fascinating—even the ravaged, nearly comatose patient who bites anyone who comes near her." Simon similarly observes that "Zindel writes juicy dialogue" for these characters, "simple yet idiosyncratic." While both Simon and Rich fault the author for overloading his drama with spectacular and strange events and people, they both find "Amulets" effective as a whole. "[When] we see the child at center stage trying to ward off the horrors," Rich concludes, "the child too genuine to dismiss as fiction, . . . 'Amulets' becomes gripping and disturbing despite its Gothic overkill."

While Zindel's stature in the theater community began fading after "Miss Reardon," his prominence as a writer of young adult novels was rapidly gaining tremendous proportions, due to the success of *The Pigman.* The novel is told alternately by two high school outsiders, John and Lorraine, who narrate their "epic" relationship with a lonely old man, Mr. Pignati. The two youths befriend the "Pigman," and after taking advantage of the friendship inadvertently contribute to his death. "Their 'epic' makes a very funny book at one level because Mr. Zindel catches the bright, hyperbolic sheen of teen-age language accurately and with humor," John Weston comments in the *New York Times Book Review,* adding that due to its subject, *The Pigman* is also "a serious book." "It is a somber and chastening story that gets better and better as it goes on," states David Rees in *The Marble in the Water: Essays on Contemporary Writers of Fiction for Children and Young Adults.* The critic explains that *The Pigman* "has coherent shape and direction, and its climax is particularly good: a chilling, sobering, morality-tale conclusion." While the novel may present a moral, Zena Sutherland of the *Bulletin of the Center for Children's Books* notes that "the story is effective because of its candor, its humor, and its skilful construction"; further, the writing "has the casual flavor of adolescence." As Diane Farrell concludes in the *Horn Book Magazine,* Zindel's novel is exceptional because "few books that have been written for young people are as cruelly truthful about the human condition."

Zindel's follow-up novel, *My Darling, My Hamburger,* also presents an honest treatment of a controversial issue. The title refers to a sex education teacher's suggestion that a girl propose going out for a burger when her boyfriend gets too eager, and the novel details the romances of two couples, one of which ends in pregnancy. "Second books are disappointments almost by definition,

but 'My Darling, My Hamburger' . . . seems to me to be a better novel than 'The Pigman,' " asserts John Rowe Townsend in the *New York Times Book Review.* The critic describes the book as "concerned single-mindedly with sex and growing up; more precisely, it's about the predicament—funny, bitter and nervewracking—of men and women who are also children." Zindel once again presents a moral issue for his readers to consider, but does so in an entertaining manner, as *Children's Book Review* contributor Valerie Anderson explains: "The author's development of his theme is wholly sympathetic, engaging the good will of the reader throughout, and yet, so honest is his treatment that no surer way could have been found for underlining the moral issues." In addition, "in the main the reader is left to form his own judgments," as a *Times Literary Supplement* reviewer observes. "[This story] is told with such compassionate and loving awareness that the reader is swept immediately into the illusion that no outsider is recording their story: they are talking it out loud themselves," remarks Lavinia Russ in *Publishers Weekly.* "And that, my friends, is *writing.*"

It is Zindel's ability to recreate adolescent life that distinguishes his novels, as many critics observe; *Times Literary Supplement* writer Isabel Quigly, for example, states that "Zindel's people seem to take over his book entirely and live so vividly you forget there's a narrator at all. . . . The quality of [his work] lies its understanding of the incoherence as well as the precocious intelligence of its young, and its wry reaction to those damaging comics, their elders." Quigly adds in a later review that while Zindel's subjects "[are] not the stuff that teenage novels used to deal with . . . the stuff of teenage life is not what it used to be either, and what counts is the way Paul Zindel handles it, with a delicacy at once funny and heartfelt, outspoken and sensitive." Likewise, Zindel's themes of adolescent loneliness and youthful questioning "are universal and most of them classic," as Beverly A. Haley and Kenneth L. Donelson maintain in *Elementary English,* and the author "makes these primordial themes believable and relevant and significant to young people." The critics elaborate on one of Zindel's prominent themes, that "the protagonists are basically lonely because they are unable to establish communication with their parents. Ironically, the adolescents themselves seem to understand *why* the parents behave as they do and to forgive them," while their parents cannot do either. The result, write Haley and Donelson, is that "the instinctive wisdom of youth seems superior to the learned wisdom of adults."

This message, that adults are distant and even antagonistic, is one Zindel emphasizes throughout his fiction. "Teenagers *have* to rebel," the author told *Publishers Weekly* interviewer Jean F. Mercier. "It's part of the growing process. In effect, I try to show them they aren't alone in condemning parents and teachers as enemies or ciphers. I believe I must convince my readers that I am on their side," the author continued, which explains why "I write always from their own point of view." Zindel also noted to Paul Janeczko in *English Journal* that this sympathy for his teenage readers serves two functions in his work: "Through pathos I can see the world as one of the most hilarious and comic places that there can be to live. Then, by use of pathos again, I can look at another element and see the world as quite ghastly, see it through very morbid eyes and find everything threatening and dangerous."

This seemingly contrary viewpoint is crucial to Zindel's work, as Stanley Hoffman suggests in the *Lion and the Unicorn:* "If there is any one 'message' that runs through Zindel's works, it has to be this: if reality is ugly, in facing it we can prepare ourselves to see beyond the ugliness to something hopeful." In addition, this mix of hope and hostility contributes to the "black comedy" that "[perhaps] is the key to Zindel's adolescent novels," as Judith N. Mitchell proposes in *Voice of Youth Advocates*. It would be "a mistake to chide him for fantastic plot shifts, or a gallery of grotesqueries masquerading as normal people," the critic relates. "His exaggerations pinpoint the absurdities of normalcy, and his novels carry the theme of loving and being loved like contraband with a homing device." "Clearly the body of Zindel's work and its individual parts place him in the forefront of adolescent novelists," notes Hipple, for "few other writers match his awareness of teenagers' problems and attitudes. He even compensates for their dislike of reading by including in his books all manner of graphics," a technique which accommodates the audience Zindel has said he wishes to reach. Hipple concludes that "it is not at all surprising—indeed, it is gratifying—that he is among their most esteemed novelists."

MEDIA ADAPTATIONS: "The Effect of Gamma Rays on Man-in-the-Moon Marigolds" was made into a film by Twentieth Century-Fox in 1973; the rights to *My Darling, My Hamburger* have been sold to Qualis Productions, while producer Jerome Hellman has purchased the rights to *I Never Loved Your Mind; The Pigman* has been adapted for the stage.

BIOGRAPHICAL/CRITICAL SOURCES:

BOOKS

Children's Literature Review, Volume 3, Gale, 1978.
Contemporary Literary Criticism, Gale, Volume 6, 1976, Volume 26, 1983.
Dictionary of Literary Biography, Gale, Volume 7: *Twentieth-Century American Dramatists,* 1981, Volume 52: *American Writers for Children since 1960: Fiction,* 1986.
Rees, David, *The Marble in the Water: Essays on Contemporary Writers of Fiction for Children and Young Adults,* Horn Book, 1980.

PERIODICALS

Boston Globe, February 9, 1971, February 14, 1971.
Bulletin of the Center for Children's Books, April, 1969.
Children's Book Review, February, 1971.
Christian Science Monitor, May 2, 1970, March 1, 1971.
Cue, April 18, 1970, March 6, 1971.
Elementary English, October, 1974.
English Journal, October, 1977.
Horn Book Magazine, February, 1969.
Lion and the Unicorn, fall, 1978.
Nation, April 20, 1970, March 15, 1971.
Newsweek, April 27, 1970, March 8, 1971.
New York, May 4, 1970, March 15, 1971, April 17, 1989.
New Yorker, April 18, 1970.
New York Times, April 8, 1970, April 19, 1970, July 26, 1970, November 22, 1970, February 26, 1971, March 2, 1971, March 7, 1971, April 9, 1971, April 2, 1989, April 6, 1989.
New York Times Book Review, November 3, 1968, November 9, 1969.
Publishers Weekly, September 22, 1969, December 5, 1977.
Saturday Review, May 2, 1970, March 20, 1971.
Time, April 20, 1970, March 8, 1971, May 17, 1971.
Times Literary Supplement, April 16, 1970, December 10, 1976, April 7, 1978.
Variety, March 3, 1971.
Village Voice, April 16, 1970.
Voice of Youth Advocates, October, 1981.
Wall Street Journal, April 12, 1989.
Washington Post, January 27, 1971.

—*Sketch by Diane Telgen*

ZOILUS
See LOVECRAFT, H(oward) P(hillips)

*   *   *

ZUKOFSKY, Louis   1904-1978

PERSONAL: Born January 23, 1904, in New York, N.Y.; died May 12, 1978, in Port Jefferson, N.Y.; son of Paul and Chana (Pruss) Zukofsky; married Celia Thaew (a composer), August 20, 1939; children: Paul. *Education:* Columbia University, M.A., 1924.

CAREER: University of Wisconsin, Madison, instructor in English, 1930-31; Polytechnic Institute of Brooklyn, New York, N.Y., 1947-66, began as assistant, became associate professor of English; writer. Visiting assistant professor, Colgate University, summer, 1947; poet in residence, San Francisco State College (now California State University), 1958.

AWARDS, HONORS: Lola Ridge Memorial Award of Poetry Society of America, 1949; Longview Foundation award, 1961; Union League Civic and Arts Foundation Prize of *Poetry* Magazine, 1964; Oscar Blumenthal/Charles Leviton Prize of *Poetry* Magazine, 1966, and National Endowment for the Arts *American Literary Anthology* awards, 1967 and 1968, all for excerpts from "A" 13-21 in *Poetry* Magazine; nominee, 1968, for National Book Award in poetry; awards from National Institute and American Academy.

WRITINGS:

(Editor) An *"Objectivists" Anthology,* To Publishers (Le Beausset, France), 1932.
(With Rene Taupin) *Le Style Apollinaire* (criticism), [Paris], 1934.
First Half of "A" 9, privately printed, 1934.
55 Poems, Press of J. A. Decker, 1941.
Anew, Press of J. A. Decker, 1946.
A Test of Poetry (criticism), The Objectivist Press, 1948, Routledge & Kegan Paul, 1952, Jargon/Corinth Books, 1964.
Some Time (poetry), Jargon Books, 1956.
Barely & Widely, [New York], 1958.
5 Statements for Poetry, [San Francisco], 1958.
It Was, Origin Press (Kyoto), 1959.
"A" 1-12 (poetry; with an essay by Zukofsky and note by William Carlos Williams), Origin Press, 1959, 2nd edition (with note by Robert Creeley), J. Cape, 1966, Doubleday, 1967.
Louis Zukofsky: 16 Once Published (a selection by his wife, Celia Zukofsky, from *55 Poems, Anew, Some Time,* and *Barely & Widely*), Wild Hawthorn Press (Edinburgh), 1962.
(With wife, Celia Zukofsky) *Bottom: On Shakespeare* (criticism), two volumes (Volume 2 is wife's musical setting of Shakespeare's "Pericles"), University of Texas Press, 1963.
I's, Trobar Books, 1963.
Found Objects: 1962-1926, Blue Grass Books, 1964.
After I's, Boxwood Press, 1964.
Iyyob, Turret Books, 1965.
An Unearthing, [Cambridge, Mass.], 1965.
I Sent Thee Late, [Cambridge, Mass.], 1965.
Finally a Valentine: A Poem, Piccolo Press (London), 1965.
All: The Collected Short Poems, 1956-64, Norton, 1966.
Prepositions: The Collected Critical Essays of Louis Zukofsky, Rapp & Whiting, 1967, Horizon, 1968.
Little: A Fragment for Careenagers, Black Sparrow Press, 1967.
"A"14, Turret Books, 1967.
Ferdinand, Including "It Was," Grossman, 1968.

(Translator with Celia Zukofsky; music by Paul Zukofsky) *Catullus Fragmenta,* Turret Books, 1968.

The Gas Age, Ultima Thule Book, 1969.

"A" 13-21 (excerpts first published serially in *Poetry* Magazine), Doubleday, 1969.

(Translator with Celia Zukofsky) *Catullus,* Grossman, 1969.

Initial, Phoenix Book Shop, 1970.

Autobiography (poems set to music by Celia Zukofsky), Grossman, 1970.

Little (novel), Grossman, 1970.

All the Collected Short Poems, 1923-1964, Norton, 1971.

"A" 24, Grossman, 1972.

Arise, Arise (play; first published in *Kulture,* 1962; first produced Off-Broadway at Cinematheque Theatre, August, 1965), Grossman, 1973.

"A" 22 & 23, Grossman, 1975.

"A," University of California Press, 1978.

80 Flowers, Stinehour Press, 1978.

Work included in *American Literary Anthology,* Volume 1, edited by John Hawkes, Farrar, Strauss, 1966, and Volume 2, edited by George Plimpton and Peter Ardery, Random House, 1968.

SIDELIGHTS: Louis Zukofsky is an important American poet. The son of immigrant Russian Jews, he was born into the Jewish ghetto of the Lower East Side of Manhattan in 1904. His conception of himself as a poet was indebted to Kaballistic Judaism, with both its emphasis on the magically transforming power of language and its division of the world into a tiny circle of initiates and a great mass of ignorant outsiders.

Zukofsky was a *New York* Jewish poet, responsive to the cacophonous voice of the cosmopolitan city and determined to find a place for himself in the world beyond the ghetto. Zukofsky's route out of the ghetto was poetry. In his brief *Autobiography* he reported how he began to appropriate the heritage of Western literature, first in Yiddish and then in English: "My first exposure to letters at the age of four was thru the Yiddish theaters. . . . By the age of nine I had seen a good deal of Shakespeare, Ibsen, Strindberg and Tolstoy performed—all in Yiddish. Even Longfellow's *Hiawatha* was to begin with read by me in Yiddish, as was Aeschylus' *Prometheus Bound.* . . . By eleven I was writing poetry in English, as yet not 'American English.' "

At age sixteen, Zukofsky entered Columbia University, where he wrote for and helped edit various student literary magazines. He identified with the literary *avant garde* (as represented especially by James Joyce, Ezra Pound, and T. S. Eliot) that saw itself as an elite committed to a revolutionary assault upon a dead bourgeois culture. Zukofsky's first major poetic work, "Poem Beginning 'The,' " written in 1926 and published in *Exile* in 1928, demonstrates his commitment to a modernist poetic. "The poem's obvious predecessor," says Barry Ahearn in *Zukofsky's "A": An Introduction,* "is [T. S. Eliot's] 'The Waste Land.' In an attempt to surpass Eliot, Zukofsky pushes formal details to an excessive, but liberating, limit." "Poem Beginning 'The' " cultivates a tone of Eliot-like irony, as the poet tries to mediate between the insistently alien, Jewish particulars of his experience and an aspiration toward a broader American, "English," vaguely Christian culture.

If "Poem Beginning 'The' " resonates with echoes of Eliot, Zukofsky soon abandoned Eliot for Ezra Pound, who was at once more approachable and more overpowering. Pound's warm response to "Poem Beginning 'The' " led to a flurry of letters between the two men, and Zukofsky eventually visited Pound at his home in Rapallo, Italy. Pound gave Zukofsky's poetic career an important boost by urging *Poetry* editor Harriet Monroe to appoint the young New Yorker as guest editor of a special issue devoted to new English and American poets.

For this *Poetry* issue Zukofsky invented the name "objectivists" to describe himself and the other poets—including Charles Reznikoff, George Oppen, Carl Rakosi, and Basil Bunting—whose work he liked. (Zukofsky, however, never used the term "objectivism" and never claimed to be the leader of a movement named "objectivism.") Most of these objectivists also appeared in Zukofsky's An *"Objectivists" Anthology,* where they were joined by Pound and even Eliot. The core group of Zukofsky, Reznikoff, Bunting, Oppen, Rakosi, and Niedecker eventually cohered into something approaching a movement, with Zukofsky established as both the principal theorist and—until World War II—the most diligent critic of and advocate for the poetry of his friends.

Objectivist verse owed a great deal to imagism. Indeed, in his preface to An *"Objectivists" Anthology* Zukofsky quoted Pound's 1912 imagist credo: "direct treatment of the 'thing' whether subjective or objective." But in two respects objectivist poetry went beyond imagism. First, unlike such imagists as Amy Lowell, most of the objectivists were unwilling to treat the poem simply as a transparent window through which one could perceive the objects of the world. Rather the objectivists wanted, as Zukofsky declared in his *Poetry* essay "Sincerity and Objectification," to see the "poem as object," calling attention to itself by, for example, deliberate syntactic fragmentation and by line breaks that disrupt normal speech rhythm. Second, following Pound's poetic practice of the 1920s, the objectivist poets were at least as much interested in historic particulars as they were in immediate sensory images. All the objectivists shared Pound's aspiration to create a "poem containing history"; and Pound's incorporation into his *Cantos* of various historic documents showed these poets a way of incorporating history into their poems without violating the principle of objectivity.

As the Western world slid into the economic and political crisis of the 1930s, a concern with history more and more often translated into some form of political engagement. During the 1930s Zukofsky regularly described himself as a communist. At times in the 1930s, Zukofsky's Leftism took the form of a vague, sentimental admiration for Soviet leader Joseph Stalin, but Zukofsky was also outspokenly critical of the crude dogmatism characteristic of certain Stalinists. During this period Zukofsky did become, however, a serious student of the writings of Karl Marx.

The short poems that Zukofsky wrote in the 1920s and 1930s, ultimately gathered in the opening two sections of *All,* bring together in various complex ways three currents: a Pound-like faith that truth can be achieved through a poetry which stays with the movement of "the particulars;" a neo-formalist concern with the poem as a shaped object; and a Marxist concern with social oppression and class struggle. A case in point is "Mantis" and "Mantis, an Interpretation," written in 1934 and constituting a single two-part poem. The theme of "Mantis" is overtly political: a praying mantis becomes a symbol of "the poor," lost and harried in a harshly mechanical world. Individually the "separate poor," like the solitary mantis, are powerless; but the work ends with a vision of the mantis drawing up the "armies of the poor," which, inspired by this fragile bit of nature that has managed to survive in the stone subway, will "arise like leaves" to "build the new world."

In "Mantis, an Interpretation," which is written in free verse, Zukofsky annotates his own poem; describes his own compositional process (providing, for example, lines from early drafts); and deconstructs the very symbol that he has created within the poem. ("The Mantis," he says, "might have heaped up upon itself a/ Grave of verse,/ But the facts are not a symbol.") As his commentary demonstrates, Zukofsky isn't so much interested in the perfectly shaped created object, the "well-made poem," as he is in the *process* of objectification; and the full text of the mantis sequence demonstrates his conviction that poetry faithful to this process will justify both the particulars of the world (the mantis as fact rather than symbol) and a history in which the poor are struggling to become the masters of their own destiny.

Generally, the poems in *All* seek the condition of song, a distilled lyric quintessence. In *"A,"* Zukofsky allows himself a much looser method. Like Pound's *Cantos, "A,"* is a ragbag: in theory anything can go in, and the sheer heterogeneity of the materials is itself the point. Yet there are thematic continuities in *"A,"* and the opening ten sections return repeatedly to the social and political concerns of "Mantis." Beginning with an image of a young Jewish man (apparently Zukofsky) listening to a Carnegie Hall performance of *The Passion According to St. Matthew,* these opening sections of *"A,"* revolve obsessively around the relationship between insider (economic, artistic, ethnic, religious) and outsider in American society—the young poet at once finds himself identifying with German composer Johann Sebastian Bach's artistic purity and repelled by the capitalist world that has, among other things, built Carnegie Hall and paid the musicians.

Zukofsky composed the first seven sections of *"A"* between 1928 and 1930, and then abandoned the project for five years, returning to it in 1935 with the much longer *"A" 8,* where paraphrases of Henry Adams and Marx interweave in an extended meditation on "Labor as creator/Labor as creature." Here Zukofsky struggles to redefine art itself, still represented chiefly by Bach, as a form of labor in Marx's sense—that is, as the creation of use value. The Marxist concerns of *"A" 8* return in the first half of *"A" 9,* an intricately musical text made up largely of phrases from *Das Kapital*. And in *"A" 10* written in 1940, Zukofsky laments the Nazi violation of Europe and summons the people of the world to fight back.

After *"A" 10,* however, the social and political concerns that dominated Zukofsky's work in the 1930s retreat into the background. The years around 1940 mark a major rupture caused not only by the fading of the revolutionary hopes that had stirred Zukofsky and others during the 1930s but also by a re-centering of Zukofsky's life around home and family. Zukofsky met Celia Thaew, a musician and composer, in 1933, and they married in 1939; their only child, Paul, became a concert violinist in his early teens. (Zukofsky's only novel, *Little,* is a *roman a clef* centered on Paul's musical career.)

The short poems that Zukofsky wrote in the 1940s often record the music of domestic life, as in the delicate "Song for the Year's End" collected in *All:* "Daughter of music/ and her sweet son/ awake/ the starry sky and bird." But in the 1940s Zukofsky both suspended work on *"A"* and wrote considerably fewer short poems than he had written in the previous two decades. He also largely suspended the various entrepreneurial poetic activities to which he had devoted much of his energy through the 1930s. This partial withdrawal from poetry may have been dictated by the need to support his family. At least while Paul was a small child, the combined demands of job and family seem to have left Zukofsky with relatively little time for writing.

In 1950 Zukofsky returned to *"A"* with the brief, dense *"A" 11* and the expansive *"A" 12.* As Ahearn explains in *Zukofsky's "A",* both these new sections "use the family Zukofsky as a foundation." *"A" 12,* which may well be Zukofsky's greatest single poem, is built thematically, like the final section of Bach's *The Art of the Fugue,* on the letters B, A, C, and H. At both the beginning and end of the movement is a repeated sequence of words: Blest, Ardent, Celia, Happy. The sequence dances harmoniously, impelled by a love which is, for Zukofsky as for Dante, "the force that moves the sun and the other stars," and which *is* music—the music of the spheres, of Bach, of Paul practicing his violin. The outside world disrupts this harmony from time to time: in the middle of *"A" 12* a young family friend is drafted and sent off to Korea, and Zukofsky incorporates his wistful letters into the poem. But the harmony here sounded can absorb into itself even such discords, for the poem breathes a confidence that the poet has found a place within a larger order.

Despite the sense of confidence and control pervading *"A" 12,* this poem seems less a new beginning than the finale of the first part—what might be called the neo-Poundian part—of Zukofsky's career. *"A" 12* is still essentially a collage text, layering incidents from domestic life with passages paraphrased from such sources as Spinoza and Aristotle. Zukofsky's line in the first twelve sections of *"A"* is shorter than Pound's, but it too is Poundian in that it attempts "to compose in the sequence of the musical phrase," as Pound declared in "A Retrospect." Thus Zukofsky says, in an often quoted passage from *"A" 12:* "I'll tell you. / About my *poetics*— / music / speech / An integral / Lower limit speech / Upper limit music."

But after *"A" 12* the flexible Poundian line, ranging freely between speech and music, gives way to another kind of line, more artful, perhaps more brittle, certainly further from the cadences of everyday speech; and the musical pattern of organization also gives way to something new, heard in the opening of *"A" 13* and continued through its thirteen-page first section: "What do you want to know / What do you want to do, / In a trice me the gist us; / Don't believe things turn untrue / A sea becomes teacher; / When the son takes his wife / Follows his genius, / Found in search / Come out of mysteries."

Roughly two decade separates *"A" 12* from *"A" 13*—which was written in 1960—and during this period Zukofsky's poetic method underwent an enormous change. Hints of this new method appeared in some of the earlier short poems, where there the intricate, mannered patterns justified themselves as varieties of song—distinctly modern, often jaggedly atonal songs, but songs nonetheless. However, in *"A" 13* and thereafter, Zukofsky began composing long poems organized not by music but by arbitrary, quasi-mathematical patterns. Zukofsky worked out the principles of this new poetics in a monumental prose work titled *Bottom: On Shakespeare,* written between 1947 and 1960 and published in 1963.

If Pound influenced the first half of Zukofsky's career, Shakespeare influenced the second half. To Zukofsky, everything Shakespeare wrote revealed that love is ineffable: The language used to describe it is always too little or too much. Seeing love is no problem, but in speaking of it, love and reason split apart, creating a tragic world. The distance between eye and tongue troubled Zukofsky, as it troubled Shakespeare. This distance in turn meant that a "true" language must constantly reinforce the idea that it is a more or less arbitrary construct, not an infallible vehicle for conveying certainties about the world. Shakespeare's language, Zukofsky proposed, enacts its own arbitrariness by constantly changing the terms of its engagement with the world. But poetic language, at least since William Wordsworth, has sought to validate itself by its claim to embody the felt truth of experience. When this claim becomes untenable, what happens to poetry? This is the question that Zukofsky's later poetry systematically explores.

The new direction in which Zukofsky's poetry moved during the 1950s is perhaps most clearly evident in his English adaptation of all the poetry of Catullus. Zukofsky's versions of Catullus are best described as transliterations rather than as translations, for they seek to reproduce the sound as well as the sense of Catullus's Latin. Or more accurately, it might be said that they reproduce the sound first and the sense only secondarily. He had given himself an insurmountable task. As Davenport noted, "To translate all of Catullus so that the English sounds like the Latin Zukofsky had to pay attention to three things at once: sound, rhythm, and syntax. The choice of each word therefore involved three decisions. This is of course impossible. . . ."

In the later sections of *"A"* Zukofsky also explored language. For example, *"A" 14,* forty-four pages long, is composed entirely of three-line stanzas. In the first sixteen pages almost every line consists of two words; then it shifts to a three-word line, with occasional passages in one-word lines. The poet allows himself dashes, question marks, and quotation marks, but only an occasional period or comma. The resulting sense of syntactic indeterminacy has been described as follows by Bruce Comens in a 1986 *Sagetrieb* article: "Rather than excluding meaning, Zukofsky's increasing suppression of context . . . *expands* meaning. . . . [His] method results in a multiplicity of meanings having no central 'point,' so that, while the poem itself is remarkably assured, the reader is likely to feel considerable insecurity among the rapidly shifting perspectives available in reading any given line. Becoming more or less constantly ironic, the text achieves that . . . skepticism which [in Zukofsky's words] 'doubts its own skepticism and becomes the only kind of skepticism true to itself.'"

The remarkable opacity of Zukofsky's later poetry offended many critics and even some his former friends—for example, Zukofsky quarrelled bitterly with George Oppen, his objectivist comrade from the 1930s, after Oppen accused Zukofsky of using obscurity as a tactic. But the 1960s and 1970s also brought Zukofsky a degree of public recognition that he had never before received. By the late 1960s, critics were also beginning to acknowledge the importance of Zukofsky's work. In particular, the influential scholar Hugh Kenner became a close friend of Zukofsky and an advocate of his work. More important still, the later years brought Zukofsky the warm admiration of many younger poets. Such major poets as Robert Duncan and Robert Creeley have testified to Zukofsky's importance as an example of dedication to the poetic craft and as the creator of daring experimental writing. As Creeley declares in his *Paideuma* tribute to Zukofsky: "For myself and others of my generation, our elders in the art were extraordinary example and resource. Despite a chaos of restrictive generalization, we had nonetheless the active, persistent functioning of example: Ezra Pound, William Carlos Williams, Basil Bunting, Louis Zukofsky—to note those most dear to my own heart."

BIOGRAPHICAL/CRITICAL SOURCES:

BOOKS

Ahearn, Barry, *Zukofsky's "A": An Introduction,* Johns Hopkins University (dissertation), 1978.
Contemporary Literary Criticism, Gale, Volume 1973, Volume 2, 1974, Volume 4, 1975, Volume 7, 1977, Volume 11, 1979, Volume 18, 1981.
Dictionary of Literary Biography, Volume 5: *American Poets Since World War II,* Gale, 1980.
Heller, Michael, *Conviction's Net of Branches: Essays on the Objectivist Poets and Poetry,* Southern Illinois University Press, 1985.
Pound, Ezra, *Polite Essays,* Faber, 1937.
Zukofsky, Celia, *A Bibliography of Louis Zukofsky,* Black Sparrow Press, 1969.
Zukofsky, Louis, *Autobiography,* Grossman, 1970.

PERIODICALS

Agenda, autumn-winter, 1970, autumn-winter, 1971-72.
Black Mountain Review, Number 7.
Chicago Panorama, September 13, 1970.
Critic, February-March, 1967.
Kulchur, Numbers 12 and 14.
National Review, March 25, 1969.
New York Times, September 17, 1970.
New York Times Book Review, July 28, 1957, June 15, 1969, December 6, 1970.
Paideuma, winter, 1978.
Poetry, January, 1958.
Saturday Review, September 5, 1970.

OBITUARIES:

PERIODICALS

New York Times, May 14, 1978.

Nationality Index

This index lists writers alphabetically under their country of origin and/or their country of citizenship.

ARGENTINA
Bioy Casares, Adolfo
Borges, Jorge Luis
Cortazar, Julio
Guiraldes, Ricardo
Sabato, Ernesto

AUSTRALIA
Caldicott, Helen
Carey, Peter
Greer, Germaine
Hazzard, Shirley
Hope, A. D.
James, Clive
Keneally, Thomas
McCullough, Colleen
Prichard, Katharine Susannah
Rodd, Kylie Tennant
Stead, Christina
Stow, Randolph
West, Morris L.
White, Patrick
Wright, Judith

AUSTRIA
Adamson, Joy
Bernhard, Thomas
Buber, Martin
Freud, Anna
Handke, Peter
Hochwaelder, Fritz
Kafka, Franz
Lorenz, Konrad Zacharias
Popper, Karl R.
Rilke, Rainer Maria

BARBADOS
Lamming, George

BELGIUM
de Man, Paul
Simenon, Georges

BRAZIL
Amado, Jorge

BULGARIA
Canetti, Elias

BURMA
Munro, H. H.

CAMEROON
Biyidi, Alexandre

CANADA
Atwood, Margaret
Avison, Margaret
Bellow, Saul
Berne, Eric
Birney, Earle
bissett, bill
Blais, Marie-Claire
Callaghan, Morley Edward
Cameron, Eleanor
Cohen, Leonard
Davies, Robertson
Frye, Northrop
Galbraith, John Kenneth
Gallant, Mavis
Hailey, Arthur
Hebert, Anne
Kinsella, W. P.
Kroetsch, Robert
Laurence, Margaret
Layton, Irving
Livesay, Dorothy
MacLennan, Hugh
McLuhan, Marshall
Merril, Judith
Moore, Brian
Mowat, Farley
Munro, Alice
Page, P. K.
Richler, Mordecai
Roy, Gabrielle
Tremblay, Michel
Wilson, Ethel Davis

CHILE
Allende, Isabel
Donoso, Jose
Godoy Alcayaga, Lucila
Neruda, Pablo
Parra, Nicanor

CHINA
Ch'ien Chung-shu
Mao Tse-tung

COLOMBIA
Garcia Marquez, Gabriel

CUBA
Cabrera Infante, G.
Fornes, Maria Irene

CZECHOSLOVAKIA
Hasek, Jaroslav
Havel, Vaclav
Kundera, Milan
Seifert, Jaroslav
Skvorecky, Josef
Stoppard, Tom

DENMARK
Blixen, Karen
Cixous, Helene
Undset, Sigrid

EGYPT
Lively, Penelope
Mahfouz, Naguib

ENGLAND
Adams, Richard
Aiken, Joan
Aldiss, Brian W.
Allingham, Margery
Ambler, Eric
Amis, Kingsley
Arden, John
Auden, W. H.
Ayckbourn, Alan
Bainbridge, Beryl
Ballard, J. G.
Barker, Clive
Barker, George Granville
Barnes, Peter
Bates, H. E.
Bell, Clive
Bennett, Alan
Betjeman, John
Bishop, Elizabeth
Blair, Eric
Blunden, Edmund
Bolt, Robert
Bond, Edward
Bowen, Elizabeth
Bradbury, Malcolm

Bradford, Barbara Taylor
Braine, John
Brenton, Howard
Brittain, Vera
Brook, Peter
Brooke, Rupert
Brookner, Anita
Brophy, Brigid
Brunner, John
Byatt, A. S.
Cabrera Infante, G.
Calder, Nigel
Carter, Angela
Cartland, Barbara
Causley, Charles
Chesterton, G. K.
Christie, Agatha
Churchill, Caryl
Churchill, Winston
Clark, Kenneth
Clarke, Arthur C.
Cleese, John
Colegate, Isabel
Compton-Burnett, I.
Connolly, Cyril
Conrad, Joseph
Conran, Shirley
Cookson, Catherine
Cornwell, David
Coward, Noel
Creasey, John
Dahl, Roald
Davie, Donald
Day Lewis, C.
de Bono, Edward
Deighton, Leonard Cyril
Delaney, Shelagh
Dennis, Nigel
Drabble, Margaret
Duffy, Maureen
du Maurier, Daphne
Durrell, Gerald
Durrell, Lawrence
Eagleton, Terence
Edgar, David
Empson, William
Esslin, Martin
Ewart, Gavin
Farrell, J. G.
Feinstein, Elaine
Fleming, Ian
Follett, Ken
Ford, Ford Madox
Forster, E. M.
Forsyth, Frederick
Fowles, John
Francis, Dick
Fraser, Antonia
Frayn, Michael
Freud, Anna

Fry, Christopher
Gardam, Jane
Gardner, John
Garner, Alan
Gascoyne, David
Golding, William
Goodall, Jane
Graves, Robert
Gray, Simon
Greene, Graham
Grigson, Geoffrey
Gunn, Thom
Hailey, Arthur
Hall, Willis
Hampton, Christopher
Hardy, Thomas
Hare, David
Harrison, Tony
Hartley, L. P.
Hayek, F. A.
Henri, Adrian
Heyer, Georgette
Hill, Geoffrey
Hill, Susan
Holroyd, Michael
Housman, A. E.
Hoyle, Fred
Hughes, Richard
Hughes, Ted
Huxley, Aldous
Huxley, Julian
Jennings, Elizabeth
Jhabvala, Ruth Prawer
Johnson, Pamela Hansford
Jones, David
Jones, Mervyn
Keating, H. R. F.
King, Francis
Kipling, Rudyard
Larkin, Philip
Lawrence, D. H.
Leavis, F. R.
Lee, Laurie
Leigh Fermor, Patrick
Lessing, Doris
Levertov, Denise
Lewis, Norman
Lively, Penelope
Lodge, David
Lovesey, Peter
Lowry, Malcolm
MacInnes, Colin
MacNeice, Louis
Manning, Olivia
Masefield, John
Maugham, William Somerset
McEwan, Ian
Mercer, David
Milligan, Terence Alan
Milne, A. A.

Mo, Timothy
Moorcock, Michael
Morris, Desmond
Morris, Jan
Mortimer, John
Muggeridge, Malcolm
Munro, H. H.
Murdoch, Iris
Naipaul, Shiva
Naughton, Bill
Newby, P. H.
Nichols, Peter
Nye, Robert
Orton, John Kingsley
Osborne, John
Pargeter, Edith Mary
Patterson, Harry
Peake, Mervyn
Pevsner, Nikolaus
Pinter, Harold
Plomer, William Charles
  Franklin
Potter, Dennis
Potter, Stephen
Powell, Anthony
Powys, John Cowper
Priestley, J. B.
Pritchett, V. S.
Pym, Barbara
Raine, Kathleen
Rattigan, Terence
Rendell, Ruth
Rhys, Jean
Robinson, Joan
Russell, Bertrand
Sacks, Oliver
Sackville-West, V.
Sansom, William
Sassoon, Siegfried
Sayers, Dorothy L.
Scott, Paul
Shaffer, Peter
Sheed, Wilfrid
Sillitoe, Alan
Sinclair, Andrew
Sitwell, Dame Edith
Smith, Florence Margaret
Snow, C. P.
Spender, Stephen
Stewart, J. I. M.
Storey, David
Symons, Julian
Taylor, A. J. P.
Taylor, Elizabeth
Thomas, D. M.
Tolkien, J. R. R.
Townsend, Sue
Wain, John
Warner, Sylvia Townsend
Waterhouse, Keith

Waugh, Evelyn
Wedgwood, C. V.
Weldon, Fay
Wells, H. G.
Wesker, Arnold
Wesley, Mary
West, Rebecca
Wheatley, Dennis
White, Phyllis Dorothy James
Williams, Raymond
Williamson, Henry
Wilson, Angus
Wilson, Colin
Wilson, John Burgess
Wodehouse, P. G.
Woolf, Virginia

FINLAND
Sillanpaa, Frans Eemil

FRANCE
Anouilh, Jean
Aragon, Louis
Barthes, Roland
Beauvoir, Simone de
Biyidi, Alexandre
Bonnefoy, Yves
Breton, Andre
Butor, Michel
Camus, Albert
Char, Rene
Cocteau, Jean M.
Colette
Cortazar, Julio
Cousteau, Jacques-Yves
Destouches, Louis-Ferdinand
Duhamel, Georges
Duras, Marguerite
Foucault, Michel
Genet, Jean
Gide, Andre
Giono, Jean
Green, Julien
Ionesco, Eugene
Kavan, Anna
Leger, Alexis
Levi-Strauss, Claude
Malraux, Andre
Marcel, Gabriel Honore
Mauriac, Francois
Maurois, Andre
Montherlant, Henry de
Nin, Anais
Pagnol, Marcel
Prevert, Jacques
Proust, Marcel
Queneau, Raymond
Quoirez, Francoise
Robbe-Grillet, Alain
Romains, Jules
Rostand, Edmond

Saint-Exupery, Antoine de
Sarraute, Nathalie
Sartre, Jean-Paul
Sauser-Hall, Frederic
Simon, Claude
Thibault, Jacques Anatole
    Francois
Tournier, Michel
Troyat, Henri
Valery, Paul
Yourcenar, Marguerite

GERMANY
Amichai, Yehuda
Andersch, Alfred
Arendt, Hannah
Boell, Heinrich
Brecht, Bertolt
Bultmann, Rudolf Karl
Einstein, Albert
Frank, Anne
Grass, Guenter
Heidegger, Martin
Hesse, Hermann
Hochhuth, Rolf
Jhabvala, Ruth Prawer
Johnson, Uwe
Mann, Thomas
Pevsner, Nikolaus
Remarque, Erich Maria
Traven, B.
Wolf, Christa

GHANA
Armah, Ayi Kwei

GREECE
Elytis, Odysseus
Kazantzakis, Nikos
Ritsos, Yannis
Seferiades, Giorgos Stylianou

GUATEMALA
Asturias, Miguel Angel

GUINEA
Laye, Camara

GUYANA
Harris, Wilson
Heath, Roy A. K.

HONG KONG
Mo, Timothy

HUNGARY
Lukacs, Gyorgy

INDIA
Anand, Mulk Raj

Desai, Anita
Gandhi, Mohandas Karamchand
Kaye, M. M.
Kipling, Rudyard
Mehta, Ved
Mukherjee, Bharati
Narayan, R. K.
Nehru, Jawaharlal
Rao, Raja
Rushdie, Salman
Tagore, Rabindranath

IRELAND
Beckett, Samuel
Behan, Brendan
Cox, William Trevor
Donleavy, J. P.
Friel, Brian
Hanley, James
Heaney, Seamus
Joyce, James
Kavanagh, Patrick
Kinsella, Thomas
Lewis, C. S.
McGahern, John
Montague, John
Murdoch, Iris
O'Brien, Edna
O'Casey, Sean
O'Faolain, Julia
O'Faolain, Sean
O'Flaherty, Liam
Shaw, George Bernard
Yeats, William Butler

ISRAEL
Agnon, S. Y.
Amichai, Yehuda
Buber, Martin
Oz, Amos

ITALY
Bassani, Giorgio
Calvino, Italo
de Filippo, Eduardo
Eco, Umberto
Fallaci, Oriana
Fo, Dario
Ginzburg, Natalia
Levi, Primo
Montale, Eugenio
Morante, Elsa
Pasolini, Pier Paolo
Pincherle, Alberto
Quasimodo, Salvatore
Schmitz, Aron Hector
Sciascia, Leonardo
Silone, Ignazio

JAMAICA
Abrahams, Peter

Hearne, John
Mais, Roger

JAPAN
Abe, Kobo
Endo, Shusaku
Hiraoka, Kimitake
Oe, Kenzaburo
Suzuki, Daisetz Teitaro

KENYA
Kenyatta, Jomo
Leakey, Louis S. B.
Ngugi wa Thiong'o

LITHUANIA
Milosz, Czeslaw

MARTINIQUE
Cesaire, Aime

MEXICO
Azuela, Mariano
Fuentes, Carlos
Paz, Octavio
Rulfo, Juan
Torres Bodet, Jaime

NEW ZEALAND
Ashton-Warner, Sylvia
Clutha, Janet Paterson Frame
Marsh, Ngaio

NICARAGUA
Cardenal, Ernesto
Dario, Ruben

NIGERIA
Achebe, Chinua
Ekwensi, Cyprian
Emecheta, Buchi
Okigbo, Christopher
Soyinka, Wole
Tutuola, Amos

NORTHERN IRELAND
Blackwood, Caroline
Heaney, Seamus

NORWAY
Heyerdahl, Thor
Pedersen, Knut

PAKISTAN
Rushdie, Salman

PANAMA
Fuentes, Carlos

PERU
Vargas Llosa, Mario

POLAND
Conrad, Joseph
Gray, Francine du Plessix
Herbert, Zbigniew
Konwicki, Tadeusz
Lem, Stanislaw
Mrozek, Slawomir
Rozewicz, Tadeusz

ROMANIA
Antschel, Paul
Eliade, Mircea
Ionesco, Eugene

SAINT LUCIA
Walcott, Derek

SCOTLAND
Brown, George Mackay
Doyle, Arthur Conan
Dunn, Douglas
Gray, Alasdair
Grieve, C. M.
Laing, R. D.
MacBeth, George
MacInnes, Helen
MacLean, Alistair
Maxwell, Gavin
Spark, Muriel

SENEGAL
Diop, Birago
Ousmane, Sembene
Senghor, Leopold Sedar

SOUTH AFRICA
Brink, Andre
Coetzee, J. M.
Fugard, Athol
Gordimer, Nadine
Head, Bessie
La Guma, Alex
Paton, Alan
Smith, Wilbur
Wilson, Ethel Davis

SOVIET UNION
Adamov, Arthur
Aitmatov, Chingiz
Akhmatova, Anna
Brodsky, Iosif Alexandrovich
Gorbachev, Mikhail
Grossman, Vasily
Kazakov, Yuri Pavlovich
Leonov, Leonid
Luria, Alexander R.
Nabokov, Vladimir
Panova, Vera
Pasternak, Boris
Sarraute, Nathalie

Sholokhov, Mikhail
Solzhenitsyn, Aleksandr I.
Trifonov, Yuri
Troyat, Henri
Tsvetaeva, Marina
Voinovich, Vladimir
Voznesensky, Andrei
Yevtushenko, Yevgeny

SPAIN
Aleixandre, Vicente
Benavente, Jacinto
Blasco Ibanez, Vicente
Buero Vallejo, Antonio
Cela, Camilo Jose
Delibes Setien, Miguel
Echegaray, Jose
Garcia Lorca, Federico
Goytisolo, Juan
Jimenez, Juan Ramon
Matute, Ana Maria
Ortega y Gasset, Jose
Sender, Ramon
Unamuno, Miguel de

SWEDEN
Lagerkvist, Paer

SWITZERLAND
Duerrenmatt, Friedrich
Frisch, Max
Jung, C. G.
Kueng, Hans
Piaget, Jean

TRINIDAD AND TOBAGO
James, C. L. R.
Lovelace, Earl
Naipaul, V. S.
Selvon, Samuel

UGANDA
p'Bitek, Okot

UNITED STATES
Adams, Alice
Adler, Mortimer J.
Adler, Renata
Aiken, Conrad
Albee, Edward
Alexander, Lloyd
Algren, Nelson
Allen, Woody
Alther, Lisa
Ammons, A. R.
Anaya, Rudolfo A.
Anderson, Poul
Anderson, Sherwood
Andrews, V. C.
Angelou, Maya

Anthony, Piers
Arnow, Harriette Simpson
Ashbery, John
Asimov, Isaac
Auchincloss, Louis
Auden, W. H.
Bach, Richard
Baker, Russell
Baldwin, James
Bambara, Toni Cade
Baraka, Amiri
Barnes, Djuna
Barth, John
Barthelme, Donald
Baum, L. Frank
Baumbach, Jonathan
Beattie, Ann
Bell, Marvin
Bellow, Saul
Benchley, Peter
Berger, Thomas
Berne, Eric
Berryman, John
Bester, Alfred
Bettelheim, Bruno
Blish, James
Blount, Roy, Jr.
Blume, Judy
Bly, Robert
Bogan, Louise
Bombeck, Erma
Bontemps, Arna
Bova, Ben
Bowles, Paul
Boyle, Kay
Bradbury, Ray
Bradley, Marion Zimmer
Brautigan, Richard
Breslin, James
Brodsky, Iosif Alexandrovich
Brooks, Cleanth
Brooks, Gwendolyn
Brown, Dee
Brown, Rita Mae
Brown, Sterling Allen
Brownmiller, Susan
Buchwald, Art
Buck, Pearl S.
Buckley, William F., Jr.
Buechner, Frederick
Bukowski, Charles
Bullins, Ed
Burke, Kenneth
Burroughs, Edgar Rice
Burroughs, William S.
Butler, Octavia E.
Byars, Betsy
Cain, James M.
Caldwell, Erskine
Calisher, Hortense

Campbell, John W.
Campbell, Joseph
Capote, Truman
Card, Orson Scott
Carr, John Dickson
Carruth, Hayden
Carson, Rachel Louise
Carter, James Earl, Jr.
Carver, Raymond
Castaneda, Carlos
Cather, Willa Sibert
Chandler, Raymond
Charyn, Jerome
Cheever, John
Chesnutt, Charles W.
Childress, Alice
Chomsky, Noam
Ciardi, John
Clancy, Thomas L., Jr.
Clark, Mary Higgins
Clavell, James
Cleary, Beverly
Clifton, Lucille
Colum, Padraic
Colwin, Laurie
Commager, Henry Steele
Commoner, Barry
Condon, Richard
Connell, Evan S., Jr.
Conroy, Pat
Coover, Robert
Cormier, Robert
Corso, Gregory
Cousins, Norman
Cowley, Malcolm
Cozzens, James Gould
Crane, Hart
Creeley, Robert
Crews, Harry
Crichton, Michael
Cullen, Countee
Cummings, E. E.
Dahlberg, Edward
Dailey, Janet
Daly, Mary
Dannay, Frederic
Delany, Samuel R.
DeLillo, Don
Deloria, Vine, Jr.
del Rey, Lester
de Man, Paul
De Vries, Peter
Dexter, Pete
Dick, Philip K.
Dickey, James
Didion, Joan
Dillard, Annie
Disch, Thomas M.
Doctorow, E. L.
Donleavy, J. P.

Doolittle, Hilda
Dos Passos, John
Dreiser, Theodore
Du Bois, W. E. B.
Duncan, Robert
Durant, Will
Dworkin, Andrea
Eberhart, Richard
Ehrenreich, Barbara
Einstein, Albert
Eliot, T. S.
Elkin, Stanley L.
Ellin, Stanley
Ellison, Harlan
Ellison, Ralph
Ellmann, Richard
Erdrich, Louise
Erikson, Erik H.
Estleman, Loren D.
Everson, William
Farmer, Philip Jose
Farrell, James T.
Faulkner, William
Feiffer, Jules
Ferber, Edna
Ferlinghetti, Lawrence
Feynman, Richard Phillips
Fiedler, Leslie A.
Fitzgerald, F. Scott
Flanagan, Thomas
Fossey, Dian
Fox, Paula
French, Marilyn
Friday, Nancy
Friedan, Betty
Friedman, Milton
Fromm, Erich
Frost, Robert
Fuller, Charles
Fuller, R. Buckminster
Fussell, Paul
Gaddis, William
Gaines, Ernest J.
Galbraith, John Kenneth
Gardner, Erle Stanley
Gardner, John, Jr.
Gass, William H.
Geisel, Theodor Seuss
Gilbert, Sandra M.
Gilchrist, Ellen
Gill, Brendan
Ginsberg, Allen
Giovanni, Nikki
Godwin, Gail
Goodman, Paul
Gordon, Caroline
Gordon, Mary
Gordone, Charles
Gould, Lois
Gould, Stephen Jay

Gouldner, Alvin W.
Grau, Shirley Ann
Greeley, Andrew M.
Grey, Zane
Grimes, Martha
Grizzard, Lewis
Guare, John
Gubar, Susan
Guest, Judith
Gunn, Thom
Haley, Alex
Hamilton, Virginia
Hammett, Dashiell
Hannah, Barry
Hansberry, Lorraine
Hardwick, Elizabeth
Hawkes, John
Hayden, Robert E.
Heinlein, Robert A.
Heller, Joseph
Hellman, Lillian
Helprin, Mark
Hemingway, Ernest
Henley, Elizabeth Becker
Herbert, Frank
Herr, Michael
Hersey, John
Higgins, George V.
Highsmith, Patricia
Himes, Chester
Hinton, S. E.
Hirsch, E. D., Jr.
Hite, Shere
Hoban, Russell
Hoffman, Abbie
Hoffman, Alice
Hofstadter, Douglas R.
Horgan, Paul
Howard, Maureen
Howe, Irving
Hughes, Langston
Hunter, Evan
Hurston, Zora Neale
Illich, Ivan
Inge, William Motter
Irving, John
Isaacs, Susan
Isherwood, Christopher
James, Henry
Jarrell, Randall
Jeffers, Robinson
Johnson, Diane
Johnson, James Weldon
Jones, Gayl
Jones, James
Jong, Erica
Jordan, June
Kammen, Michael G.
Karnow, Stanley
Keillor, Gary

Keller, Helen
Kennedy, John Fitzgerald
Kennedy, William
Kerouac, Jean-Louis Lebrid de
Kesey, Ken
Kidder, Tracy
Kienzle, William X.
King, Larry L.
King, Martin Luther, Jr.
King, Stephen
Kingston, Maxine Hong
Kinnell, Galway
Kirk, Russell
Kissinger, Henry A.
Knowles, John
Koestler, Arthur
Konigsburg, E. L.
Koontz, Dean R.
Kopit, Arthur
Kosinski, Jerzy
Krantz, Judith
Kumin, Maxine
Kunitz, Stanley
L'Amour, Louis
Langer, Susanne K.
Lardner, Ring W.
Lasch, Christopher
Lavin, Mary
Leary, Timothy
Lebowitz, Fran
Lee, Harper
Le Guin, Ursula K.
Leiber, Fritz
L'Engle, Madeleine
Leonard, Elmore
Levertov, Denise
Levin, Ira
Lewis, Sinclair
Lindbergh, Anne Morrow
Lippmann, Walter
Little, Malcolm
London, John Griffith
Lopez, Barry Holstun
Lorde, Audre
Lovecraft, H. P.
Lowell, Robert
Luce, Henry R.
Ludlum, Robert
Lukas, J. Anthony
Lurie, Alison
MacDonald, John D.
MacLeish, Archibald
Madden, David
Mailer, Norman
Malamud, Bernard
Mamet, David
Manchester, William
Marshall, Paule
Martin, Steve
Maslow, Abraham H.

Mason, Bobbie Ann
Masters, Edgar Lee
Matthews, Patricia
Matthiessen, Peter
McCaffrey, Anne
McCarthy, Mary
McCullers, Carson
McGrath, Thomas
McGuane, Thomas
McIntyre, Vonda N.
McKay, Festus Claudius
McKillip, Patricia A.
McMurtry, Larry
McPhee, John
McPherson, James Alan
McPherson, James M.
Mead, Margaret
Meaker, Marijane
Mencken, H. L.
Menninger, Karl
Merrill, James
Merton, Thomas
Merwin, W. S.
Michaels, Leonard
Michener, James A.
Millar, Kenneth
Millay, Edna St. Vincent
Miller, Arthur
Miller, Henry
Millett, Kate
Milner, Ron
Milosz, Czeslaw
Mitchell, Margaret
Momaday, N. Scott
Moore, Marianne
Morgan, Robin
Morris, Wright
Morrison, Toni
Mukherjee, Bharati
Nabokov, Vladimir
Nash, Ogden
Naylor, Gloria
Nelson, Alice Ruth Moore
    Dunbar
Nemerov, Howard
Nin, Anais
Niven, Laurence Van Cott
Nixon, Richard M.
Norton, Andre
Oates, Joyce Carol
O'Connor, Flannery
Odets, Clifford
O'Hara, Frank
O'Hara, John
Olsen, Tillie
Olson, Charles
O'Neill, Eugene
Oppenheimer, J. Robert
Ozick, Cynthia
Paley, Grace

Parker, Dorothy
Parker, Robert B.
Parsons, Talcott
Patchen, Kenneth
Paterson, Katherine
Pauling, Linus
Peale, Norman Vincent
Pearson, Andrew Russell
Percy, Walker
Perelman, S. J.
Petry, Ann
Phillips, Jayne Anne
Piercy, Marge
Pilcher, Rosamunde
Pirsig, Robert M.
Plante, David
Plath, Sylvia
Plimpton, George
Pohl, Frederik
Pollitt, Katha
Porter, Katherine Anne
Porter, William Sydney
Potok, Chaim
Pound, Ezra
Powers, J. F.
Puzo, Mario
Pynchon, Thomas
Rand, Ayn
Ransom, John Crowe
Ravitch, Diane
Reed, Ishmael
Rexroth, Kenneth
Rice, Elmer
Rich, Adrienne
Richter, Conrad
Robbins, Harold
Robbins, Thomas Eugene
Robinson, Edwin Arlington
Roethke, Theodore
Rogers, Carl R.
Rogers, Rosemary
Rooney, Andrew A.
Rossner, Judith
Roth, Henry
Roth, Philip
Rukeyser, Muriel
Russ, Joanna
Saberhagen, Fred
Sagan, Carl
Salisbury, Harrison E.
Sanchez, Sonia
Sandburg, Carl
Sanders, Lawrence
Sandoz, Mari
Santmyer, Helen Hooven
Saroyan, William
Sarton, May
Schaeffer, Susan Fromberg
Schlafly, Phyllis
Schlesinger, Arthur M., Jr.

Schwartz, Delmore
Segal, Erich
Sendak, Maurice
Sexton, Anne
Shange, Ntozake
Shapiro, Karl
Shaw, Irwin
Sheed, Wilfrid
Sheehy, Gail
Sheen, Fulton J.
Sheldon, Alice Hastings Bradley
Sheldon, Sidney
Shepard, Sam
Shirer, William L.
Siddons, Anne Rivers
Silverberg, Robert
Simak, Clifford D.
Simon, Kate
Simon, Neil
Simpson, George Gaylord
Simpson, Louis
Sinclair, Upton
Singer, Isaac Bashevis
Skinner, B. F.
Snodgrass, William D.
Sontag, Susan
Spencer, Elizabeth
Spillane, Frank Morrison
Spock, Benjamin
Stafford, Jean
Steel, Danielle
Stegner, Wallace
Stein, Gertrude
Steinbeck, John
Steinem, Gloria
Steiner, George
Stevens, Wallace
Stevenson, Anne
Stone, Irving
Stone, Robert
Straub, Peter
Sturgeon, Theodore
Styron, William
Susann, Jacqueline
Swenson, May
Talese, Gay
Tate, Allen
Taylor, Peter
Taylor, Telford
Teller, Edward
Terkel, Louis
Theroux, Paul
Thomas, Audrey
Thomas, Joyce Carol
Thomas, Lewis
Thompson, Hunter S.
Thurber, James
Tillich, Paul
Toffler, Alvin
Toland, John

Toomer, Jean
Trillin, Calvin
Trilling, Diana
Trilling, Lionel
Truman, Margaret
Tryon, Thomas
Tuchman, Barbara W.
Tyler, Anne
Tynan, Kenneth
Uchida, Yoshiko
Updike, John
Uris, Leon
Vance, John Holbrook
Van Doren, Mark
Vendler, Helen
Vidal, Gore
Vonnegut, Kurt, Jr.
Walker, Alice
Walker, Margaret
Wallace, Irving
Wallant, Edward Lewis
Wambaugh, Joseph
Warren, Robert Penn
Welty, Eudora
West, Jessamyn
West, Nathanael
Wharton, Edith
White, E. B.
White, Edmund
White, Theodore H.
Wiesel, Elie
Wilbur, Richard
Wilder, Thornton
Wilhelm, Katie Gertrude
Will, George F.
Willard, Nancy
Williams, Tennessee
Williams, William Carlos
Willingham, Calder
Wilson, August
Wilson, Edmund
Wilson, Edward O.
Wilson, Robert M.
Winters, Yvor
Wolfe, Thomas
Wolfe, Thomas Kennerly, Jr.
Woodiwiss, Kathleen E.
Woodward, Robert Upshur
Wouk, Herman
Wright, Charles
Wright, James
Wright, Richard
Yerby, Frank G.
Yezierska, Anzia
Yglesias, Helen
Zelazny, Roger
Zindel, Paul
Zukofsky, Louis

URUGUAY
Onetti, Juan Carlos
Quiroga, Horacio

VENEZUELA
Gallegos, Romulo

WALES
Rubens, Bernice
Simpson, Dorothy
Thomas, Dylan
Thomas, R. S.
Williams, Emlyn

YUGOSLAVIA
Andric, Ivo
Kis, Danilo

Genre/Subject Index

This index lists writers alphabetically under the genres for which they are known and/or the principal subjects reflected in their work.

ART and ARCHITECTURE
Bell, Clive
Betjeman, John
Breton, Andre
Brookner, Anita
Butor, Michel
Clark, Kenneth
Feiffer, Jules
Grass, Guenter
Malraux, Andre
O'Hara, Frank
Pevsner, Nikolaus
Wilson, Robert M.

BIOGRAPHY and AUTOBIOGRAPHY
Adamson, Joy
Alexander, Lloyd
Angelou, Maya
Anthony, Piers
Ashton-Warner, Sylvia
Baker, Russell
Beauvoir, Simone de
Behan, Brendan
Bell, Clive
Bettelheim, Bruno
Blixen, Karen
Brittain, Vera
Brook, Peter
Buck, Pearl S.
Buckley, William F., Jr.
Buechner, Frederick
Calisher, Hortense
Carter, James Earl, Jr.
Churchill, Winston
Connolly, Cyril
Diop, Birago
Dos Passos, John
Ellmann, Richard
Ford, Ford Madox
Francis, Dick
Frank, Anne
Fraser, Antonia
Gide, Andre
Gill, Brendan
Green, Julien
Greer, Germaine
Haley, Alex
Hellman, Lillian
Himes, Chester

Holroyd, Michael
Horgan, Paul
Ionesco, Eugene
James, Clive
Johnson, Diane
Johnson, James Weldon
Jung, C. G.
Kavanagh, Patrick
Keller, Helen
Kingston, Maxine Hong
Kosinski, Jerzy
Kunitz, Stanley
Laing, R. D.
Laye, Camara
Leary, Timothy
Lee, Laurie
Levi, Primo
Lindbergh, Anne Morrow
Little, Malcolm
Livesay, Dorothy
Mailer, Norman
Maurois, Andre
Mehta, Ved
Merton, Thomas
Millett, Kate
Milosz, Czeslaw
Morris, Wright
Muggeridge, Malcolm
Nelson, Alice Ruth Moore
  Dunbar
Nin, Anais
Nixon, Richard M.
O'Casey, Sean
O'Faolain, Sean
O'Flaherty, Liam
Osborne, John
Pasternak, Boris
Paton, Alan
Perelman, S. J.
Plante, David
Plimpton, George
Powys, John Cowper
Raine, Kathleen
Rexroth, Kenneth
Rodd, Kylie Tennant
Rukeyser, Muriel
Sandburg, Carl
Sandoz, Mari
Sarton, May
Sassoon, Siegfried

Shaw, George Bernard
Sheen, Fulton J.
Shirer, William L.
Simon, Kate
Sinclair, Andrew
Soyinka, Wole
Spark, Muriel
Stafford, Jean
Stegner, Wallace
Stein, Gertrude
Stevenson, Anne
Stone, Irving
Tate, Allen
Taylor, A. J. P.
Terkel, Louis
Trilling, Diana
Troyat, Henri
Truman, Margaret
Uchida, Yoshiko
Walker, Margaret
Waugh, Evelyn
West, Jessamyn
Williamson, Henry
Wilson, Colin
Wilson, Edmund
Woodward, Robert Upshur
Wright, Richard

CHILDREN'S and YOUNG ADULT BOOKS
Adamson, Joy
Aiken, Joan
Alexander, Lloyd
Baum, L. Frank
Blish, James
Blume, Judy
Bova, Ben
Bradbury, Ray
Bradford, Barbara Taylor
Byars, Betsy
Causley, Charles
Cleary, Beverly
Clifton, Lucille
Commager, Henry Steele
Cormier, Robert
Creasey, John
Dahl, Roald
Ekwensi, Cyprian
Emecheta, Buchi
Fleming, Ian

Fox, Paula
Gardam, Jane
Gardner, John, Jr.
Garner, Alan
Geisel, Theodor Seuss
Giovanni, Nikki
Greene, Graham
Hall, Willis
Hamilton, Virginia
Henri, Adrian
Hinton, S. E.
Hoban, Russell
Hughes, Langston
Hughes, Richard
Hughes, Ted
Jarrell, Randall
Jennings, Elizabeth
Jordan, June
Kaye, M. M.
Kesey, Ken
King, Larry L.
Kipling, Rudyard
Konigsburg, E. L.
Kumin, Maxine
Lewis, C. S.
Lively, Penelope
Lurie, Alison
MacBeth, George
Matthews, Patricia
McKillip, Patricia A.
Meaker, Marijane
Milne, A. A.
Morante, Elsa
Mowat, Farley
Norton, Andre
Nye, Robert
Paterson, Katherine
Petry, Ann
Prevert, Jacques
Prichard, Katharine Susannah
Sendak, Maurice
Silverberg, Robert
Singer, Isaac Bashevis
Spillane, Frank Morrison
Steel, Danielle
Thomas, Joyce Carol
Thurber, James
Uchida, Yoshiko
Wesley, Mary
White, E. B.
Willard, Nancy
Williamson, Henry
Wright, Judith
Zindel, Paul

CRITICISM
Aldiss, Brian W.
Amis, Kingsley
Aragon, Louis
Ashbery, John

Auchincloss, Louis
Auden, W. H.
Barthes, Roland
Baumbach, Jonathan
Bell, Clive
Bell, Marvin
Bishop, Elizabeth
Blish, James
Blunden, Edmund
Bogan, Louise
Bonnefoy, Yves
Bradbury, Malcolm
Brookner, Anita
Brooks, Cleanth
Brophy, Brigid
Burke, Kenneth
Byatt, A. S.
Calvino, Italo
Cameron, Eleanor
Campbell, Joseph
Cather, Willa Sibert
Ch'ien Chung-shu
Ciardi, John
Coetzee, J. M.
Connolly, Cyril
Cowley, Malcolm
Creeley, Robert
Cullen, Countee
Dario, Ruben
Davie, Donald
de Man, Paul
Dillard, Annie
Duerrenmatt, Friedrich
Durrell, Lawrence
Eagleton, Terence
Eco, Umberto
Eliot, T. S.
Ellmann, Richard
Empson, William
Esslin, Martin
Fiedler, Leslie A.
Ford, Ford Madox
Forster, E. M.
Foucault, Michel
Frayn, Michael
French, Marilyn
Fry, Christopher
Frye, Northrop
Fussell, Paul
Gardner, John, Jr.
Gass, William H.
Gilbert, Sandra M.
Greene, Graham
Greer, Germaine
Gubar, Susan
Gunn, Thom
Hardwick, Elizabeth
Harris, Wilson
Hartley, L. P.
Hill, Susan

Hirsch, E. D., Jr.
Hope, A. D.
Howard, Maureen
Howe, Irving
James, Clive
James, Henry
Jarrell, Randall
Kavanagh, Patrick
Kinnell, Galway
Leavis, F. R.
Lem, Stanislaw
Lodge, David
Lukacs, Gyorgy
Madden, David
McCarthy, Mary
Mencken, H. L.
Michaels, Leonard
Montale, Eugenio
Morris, Wright
Nemerov, Howard
Potter, Stephen
Pound, Ezra
Powys, John Cowper
Priestley, J. B.
Pritchett, V. S.
Raine, Kathleen
Ransom, John Crowe
Rexroth, Kenneth
Sarraute, Nathalie
Sender, Ramon
Shapiro, Karl
Shaw, George Bernard
Sheed, Wilfrid
Sitwell, Dame Edith
Sontag, Susan
Spender, Stephen
Steiner, George
Stevens, Wallace
Stevenson, Anne
Stewart, J. I. M.
Symons, Julian
Tate, Allen
Thibault, Jacques Anatole
  Francois
Tolkien, J. R. R.
Trilling, Diana
Trilling, Lionel
Tynan, Kenneth
Updike, John
Van Doren, Mark
Vendler, Helen
Wain, John
Warren, Robert Penn
West, Rebecca
Williams, Raymond
Wilson, Angus
Wilson, John Burgess
Winters, Yvor
Wolf, Christa

DRAMA

Abe, Kobo
Adamov, Arthur
Albee, Edward
Anaya, Rudolfo A.
Angelou, Maya
Anouilh, Jean
Arden, John
Asturias, Miguel Angel
Auden, W. H.
Ayckbourn, Alan
Baldwin, James
Baraka, Amiri
Barnes, Djuna
Barnes, Peter
Beckett, Samuel
Behan, Brendan
Benavente, Jacinto
Bennett, Alan
Bernhard, Thomas
Birney, Earle
Blais, Marie-Claire
Boell, Heinrich
Bolt, Robert
Bond, Edward
Bradbury, Malcolm
Braine, John
Brecht, Bertolt
Brenton, Howard
Brook, Peter
Buero Vallejo, Antonio
Bullins, Ed
Canetti, Elias
Cesaire, Aime
Char, Rene
Childress, Alice
Christie, Agatha
Churchill, Caryl
Cixous, Helene
Clavell, James
Cocteau, Jean M.
Colum, Padraic
Conrad, Joseph
Coward, Noel
Cox, William Trevor
Davies, Robertson
de Filippo, Eduardo
Delaney, Shelagh
Dennis, Nigel
Donleavy, J. P.
Dos Passos, John
Duerrenmatt, Friedrich
Duffy, Maureen
Duhamel, Georges
Duras, Marguerite
Echegaray, Jose
Edgar, David
Eliot, T. S.
Endo, Shusaku
Feiffer, Jules

Ferber, Edna
Fitzgerald, F. Scott
Fo, Dario
Fornes, Maria Irene
Frayn, Michael
Friel, Brian
Frisch, Max
Fry, Christopher
Fuentes, Carlos
Fugard, Athol
Fuller, Charles
Garcia Lorca, Federico
Genet, Jean
Gide, Andre
Giono, Jean
Gordone, Charles
Grass, Guenter
Gray, Alasdair
Gray, Simon
Green, Julien
Guare, John
Hall, Willis
Hampton, Christopher
Handke, Peter
Hansberry, Lorraine
Hare, David
Harrison, Tony
Havel, Vaclav
Hawkes, John
Heller, Joseph
Hellman, Lillian
Henley, Elizabeth Becker
Hill, Susan
Hiraoka, Kimitake
Hochhuth, Rolf
Hochwaelder, Fritz
Hughes, Langston
Hughes, Richard
Hughes, Ted
Hurston, Zora Neale
Inge, William Motter
Isherwood, Christopher
Jeffers, Robinson
Johnson, Pamela Hansford
Jordan, June
Keneally, Thomas
King, Larry L.
Kopit, Arthur
Kundera, Milan
Lagerkvist, Paer
Leonov, Leonid
Levin, Ira
Lovelace, Earl
Lowell, Robert
MacLeish, Archibald
MacNeice, Louis
Madden, David
Mamet, David
Marcel, Gabriel Honore
Marsh, Ngaio

Masefield, John
Maugham, William Somerset
Mauriac, Francois
Mercer, David
Millay, Edna St. Vincent
Miller, Arthur
Milne, A. A.
Milner, Ron
Montherlant, Henry de
Mortimer, John
Mrozek, Slawomir
Munro, H. H.
Murdoch, Iris
Nash, Ogden
Naughton, Bill
Ngugi wa Thiong'o
Nichols, Peter
O'Brien, Edna
O'Casey, Sean
Odets, Clifford
O'Neill, Eugene
Orton, John Kingsley
Osborne, John
Pagnol, Marcel
Panova, Vera
Pedersen, Knut
Pincherle, Alberto
Pinter, Harold
Potter, Dennis
Priestley, J. B.
Quoirez, Francoise
Rattigan, Terence
Rice, Elmer
Rodd, Kylie Tennant
Rostand, Edmond
Rozewicz, Tadeusz
Rukeyser, Muriel
Saroyan, William
Sartre, Jean-Paul
Shaffer, Peter
Shange, Ntozake
Shaw, George Bernard
Shaw, Irwin
Shepard, Sam
Silone, Ignazio
Simon, Neil
Sinclair, Andrew
Sinclair, Upton
Soyinka, Wole
Spender, Stephen
Stoppard, Tom
Storey, David
Swenson, May
Tagore, Rabindranath
Taylor, Peter
Thomas, Joyce Carol
Thurber, James
Townsend, Sue
Tremblay, Michel
Tynan, Kenneth

Unamuno, Miguel de
Valery, Paul
Walcott, Derek
Waterhouse, Keith
Weldon, Fay
Wesker, Arnold
White, Patrick
Wilder, Thornton
Williams, Emlyn
Williams, Tennessee
Wilson, August
Wilson, John Burgess
Wodehouse, P. G.
Wouk, Herman
Yeats, William Butler
Zindel, Paul

ECONOMICS
Friedman, Milton
Galbraith, John Kenneth
Hayek, F. A.
Luce, Henry R.
Parsons, Talcott
Robinson, Joan

ESPIONAGE and SUSPENSE
Ambler, Eric
Benchley, Peter
Buckley, William F., Jr.
Clancy, Thomas L., Jr.
Cornwell, David
Crichton, Michael
Deighton, Leonard Cyril
Fleming, Ian
Follett, Ken
Forsyth, Frederick
Francis, Dick
Gardner, John
Johnson, Pamela Hansford
Ludlum, Robert
MacInnes, Helen
MacLean, Alistair
Patterson, Harry
West, Morris L.

FILM
Allen, Woody
Ambler, Eric
Anouilh, Jean
Barker, Clive
Barnes, Peter
Benchley, Peter
Bennett, Alan
Bolt, Robert
Braine, John
Brook, Peter
Bukowski, Charles
Cabrera Infante, G.
Cain, James M.
Chandler, Raymond

Cleese, John
Condon, Richard
Crichton, Michael
de Filippo, Eduardo
Delaney, Shelagh
Duras, Marguerite
Edgar, David
Feiffer, Jules
Fry, Christopher
Garner, Alan
Guare, John
Guest, Judith
Hampton, Christopher
Hare, David
Hartley, L. P.
Hellman, Lillian
Herr, Michael
Hiraoka, Kimitake
Isaacs, Susan
Isherwood, Christopher
Jhabvala, Ruth Prawer
Kennedy, William
King, Stephen
Konwicki, Tadeusz
Kosinski, Jerzy
Leonard, Elmore
Mamet, David
Martin, Steve
McEwan, Ian
McGrath, Thomas
McGuane, Thomas
Miller, Arthur
Moore, Brian
Mortimer, John
Nichols, Peter
Odets, Clifford
Ousmane, Sembene
Pagnol, Marcel
Parker, Dorothy
Pasolini, Pier Paolo
Pinter, Harold
Potter, Dennis
Prevert, Jacques
Puzo, Mario
Rattigan, Terence
Richler, Mordecai
Robbe-Grillet, Alain
Rubens, Bernice
Sheldon, Sidney
Shepard, Sam
Simon, Neil
Stone, Robert
Stoppard, Tom
Tremblay, Michel
Uris, Leon
Wallace, Irving
West, Nathanael
Williams, Tennessee
Willingham, Calder
Yevtushenko, Yevgeny

HISTORICAL FICTION
Brown, Dee
Card, Orson Scott
Clavell, James
Doyle, Arthur Conan
Farrell, J. G.
Haley, Alex
Hearne, John
Heyer, Georgette
Isherwood, Christopher
Kaye, M. M.
Keneally, Thomas
L'Amour, Louis
Michener, James A.
Morris, Jan
Pargeter, Edith Mary
Richter, Conrad
Romains, Jules
Scott, Paul
Sinclair, Upton
Stone, Irving
Styron, William
Toland, John
Undset, Sigrid
Vidal, Gore
Yourcenar, Marguerite

HISTORY
Brown, Dee
Churchill, Winston
Commager, Henry Steele
Connell, Evan S., Jr.
Deighton, Leonard Cyril
Durant, Will
Flanagan, Thomas
Foucault, Michel
Fraser, Antonia
Fussell, Paul
Gray, Francine du Plessix
Head, Bessie
Hochhuth, Rolf
Horgan, Paul
Howe, Irving
James, C. L. R.
Johnson, James Weldon
Jones, James
Karnow, Stanley
Kennedy, John Fitzgerald
Manchester, William
Maurois, Andre
McPherson, James M.
Morris, Jan
O'Faolain, Julia
O'Faolain, Sean
Ravitch, Diane
Salisbury, Harrison E.
Sandburg, Carl
Sandoz, Mari
Schlesinger, Arthur M., Jr.
Shirer, William L.

Solzhenitsyn, Aleksandr I.
Stegner, Wallace
Taylor, A. J. P.
Taylor, Telford
Toland, John
Tuchman, Barbara W.

HORROR and the SUPERNATURAL

Adams, Richard
Aiken, Joan
Barker, Clive
Carter, Angela
King, Stephen
Levin, Ira
Lovecraft, H. P.
Straub, Peter
Tryon, Thomas
Wheatley, Dennis

JOURNALISM

Adler, Renata
Baker, Russell
Blair, Eric
Blount, Roy, Jr.
Breslin, James
Buchwald, Art
Caldwell, Erskine
Chesterton, G. K.
Cousins, Norman
Davies, Robertson
Dexter, Pete
Didion, Joan
Donoso, Jose
Fallaci, Oriana
Grizzard, Lewis
Grossman, Vasily
Herr, Michael
Hersey, John
Jones, Mervyn
Karnow, Stanley
Lardner, Ring W.
Larkin, Philip
Lebowitz, Fran
Lippmann, Walter
Luce, Henry R.
Lukas, J. Anthony
Mailer, Norman
Manchester, William
McPhee, John
Mencken, H. L.
Mitchell, Margaret
Muggeridge, Malcolm
Pearson, Andrew Russell
Rooney, Andrew A.
Salisbury, Harrison E.
Schmitz, Aron Hector
Steinem, Gloria
Talese, Gay
Terkel, Louis

Thompson, Hunter S.
Trillin, Calvin
Trilling, Diana
Vargas Llosa, Mario
White, E. B.
Will, George F.
Wolfe, Thomas Kennerly, Jr.
Woodward, Robert Upshur

LINGUISTICS and SEMIOTICS

Barthes, Roland
Chomsky, Noam
Delany, Samuel R.
Eco, Umberto
Tolkien, J. R. R.

MYSTERY and CRIME

Aiken, Joan
Allingham, Margery
Bates, H. E.
Brunner, John
Cain, James M.
Capote, Truman
Carr, John Dickson
Chandler, Raymond
Chesterton, G. K.
Christie, Agatha
Clark, Mary Higgins
Creasey, John
Dannay, Frederic
Day Lewis, C.
Doyle, Arthur Conan
Ellin, Stanley
Estleman, Loren D.
Fraser, Antonia
Gardner, Erle Stanley
Greene, Graham
Grimes, Martha
Hammett, Dashiell
Heyer, Georgette
Higgins, George V.
Highsmith, Patricia
Himes, Chester
Hunter, Evan
Kaye, M. M.
Keating, H. R. F.
Kennedy, William
Kienzle, William X.
Leonard, Elmore
Levin, Ira
Lovesey, Peter
MacDonald, John D.
Marsh, Ngaio
Millar, Kenneth
Mortimer, John
Pargeter, Edith Mary
Parker, Robert B.
Patterson, Harry
Rendell, Ruth
Sanders, Lawrence

Santmyer, Helen Hooven
Sayers, Dorothy L.
Sciascia, Leonardo
Simenon, Georges
Simpson, Dorothy
Spillane, Frank Morrison
Stewart, J. I. M.
Stow, Randolph
Symons, Julian
Truman, Margaret
Wambaugh, Joseph
White, Phyllis Dorothy James
Williams, Emlyn

NATURE

Adamson, Joy
Carson, Rachel Louise
Cousteau, Jacques-Yves
Durrell, Gerald
Fossey, Dian
Goodall, Jane
Gould, Stephen Jay
Lopez, Barry Holstun
Matthiessen, Peter
McPhee, John
Morris, Desmond
Mowat, Farley

NOVELS

Abe, Kobo
Abrahams, Peter
Achebe, Chinua
Adams, Alice
Adler, Renata
Aiken, Conrad
Aitmatov, Chingiz
Aldiss, Brian W.
Algren, Nelson
Allende, Isabel
Alther, Lisa
Amado, Jorge
Amis, Kingsley
Anand, Mulk Raj
Anaya, Rudolfo A.
Andersch, Alfred
Anderson, Sherwood
Andric, Ivo
Aragon, Louis
Armah, Ayi Kwei
Arnow, Harriette Simpson
Ashton-Warner, Sylvia
Asturias, Miguel Angel
Atwood, Margaret
Auchincloss, Louis
Azuela, Mariano
Bach, Richard
Bainbridge, Beryl
Baldwin, James
Ballard, J. G.
Bambara, Toni Cade

Barnes, Djuna
Barth, John
Barthelme, Donald
Bassani, Giorgio
Baumbach, Jonathan
Beattie, Ann
Beauvoir, Simone de
Beckett, Samuel
Bellow, Saul
Benchley, Peter
Berger, Thomas
Bernhard, Thomas
Bester, Alfred
Bioy Casares, Adolfo
Biyidi, Alexandre
Blackwood, Caroline
Blair, Eric
Blais, Marie-Claire
Blasco Ibanez, Vicente
Blume, Judy
Boell, Heinrich
Bontemps, Arna
Bowen, Elizabeth
Bowles, Paul
Boyle, Kay
Bradbury, Malcolm
Braine, John
Brautigan, Richard
Breslin, James
Brink, Andre
Brittain, Vera
Brookner, Anita
Brophy, Brigid
Brown, George Mackay
Brown, Rita Mae
Brownmiller, Susan
Buck, Pearl S.
Buechner, Frederick
Bukowski, Charles
Bullins, Ed
Burroughs, Edgar Rice
Burroughs, William S.
Butor, Michel
Byatt, A. S.
Cabrera Infante, G.
Caldwell, Erskine
Calisher, Hortense
Callaghan, Morley Edward
Calvino, Italo
Camus, Albert
Canetti, Elias
Capote, Truman
Carey, Peter
Carver, Raymond
Cather, Willa Sibert
Cela, Camilo Jose
Charyn, Jerome
Cheever, John
Chesnutt, Charles W.
Ch'ien Chung-shu

Childress, Alice
Cixous, Helene
Clavell, James
Clutha, Janet Paterson Frame
Cocteau, Jean M.
Coetzee, J. M.
Cohen, Leonard
Colegate, Isabel
Colette
Colum, Padraic
Colwin, Laurie
Compton-Burnett, I.
Condon, Richard
Connell, Evan S., Jr.
Connolly, Cyril
Conrad, Joseph
Conran, Shirley
Conroy, Pat
Cookson, Catherine
Coover, Robert
Cormier, Robert
Cortazar, Julio
Cox, William Trevor
Cozzens, James Gould
Crews, Harry
Dahl, Roald
Dahlberg, Edward
Davies, Robertson
Deighton, Leonard Cyril
Delibes Setien, Miguel
DeLillo, Don
Dennis, Nigel
Desai, Anita
Destouches, Louis-Ferdinand
De Vries, Peter
Dexter, Pete
Dickey, James
Didion, Joan
Dillard, Annie
Doctorow, E. L.
Donleavy, J. P.
Donoso, Jose
Doolittle, Hilda
Dos Passos, John
Drabble, Margaret
Dreiser, Theodore
Du Bois, W. E. B.
Duerrenmatt, Friedrich
Duffy, Maureen
Duhamel, Georges
Duras, Marguerite
Durrell, Gerald
Durrell, Lawrence
Dworkin, Andrea
Eco, Umberto
Ekwensi, Cyprian
Eliade, Mircea
Elkin, Stanley L.
Ellison, Ralph
Emecheta, Buchi

Endo, Shusaku
Erdrich, Louise
Estleman, Loren D.
Farrell, James T.
Faulkner, William
Feinstein, Elaine
Ferber, Edna
Fiedler, Leslie A.
Fitzgerald, F. Scott
Flanagan, Thomas
Ford, Ford Madox
Forster, E. M.
Fowles, John
Fox, Paula
Frayn, Michael
French, Marilyn
Frisch, Max
Fuentes, Carlos
Gaddis, William
Gaines, Ernest J.
Gallant, Mavis
Gallegos, Romulo
Garcia Marquez, Gabriel
Gardam, Jane
Gardner, John, Jr.
Garner, Alan
Gass, William H.
Genet, Jean
Gide, Andre
Gilchrist, Ellen
Ginzburg, Natalia
Giono, Jean
Godwin, Gail
Golding, William
Goodman, Paul
Gordimer, Nadine
Gordon, Caroline
Gordon, Mary
Gould, Lois
Goytisolo, Juan
Grass, Guenter
Grau, Shirley Ann
Graves, Robert
Gray, Alasdair
Gray, Francine du Plessix
Greeley, Andrew M.
Green, Julien
Greene, Graham
Grossman, Vasily
Guest, Judith
Guiraldes, Ricardo
Hailey, Arthur
Handke, Peter
Hanley, James
Hannah, Barry
Hardwick, Elizabeth
Hardy, Thomas
Harris, Wilson
Hartley, L. P.
Hasek, Jaroslav

Hawkes, John
Hazzard, Shirley
Head, Bessie
Hearne, John
Heath, Roy A. K.
Hebert, Anne
Heller, Joseph
Hemingway, Ernest
Henri, Adrian
Herr, Michael
Hersey, John
Hesse, Hermann
Highsmith, Patricia
Hill, Susan
Himes, Chester
Hinton, S. E.
Hiraoka, Kimitake
Hoban, Russell
Hochhuth, Rolf
Hoffman, Alice
Howard, Maureen
Hughes, Richard
Hunter, Evan
Hurston, Zora Neale
Huxley, Aldous
Irving, John
James, Henry
Jhabvala, Ruth Prawer
Johnson, Diane
Johnson, Pamela Hansford
Johnson, Uwe
Jones, Gayl
Jones, James
Jones, Mervyn
Jong, Erica
Joyce, James
Kafka, Franz
Kavan, Anna
Kazantzakis, Nikos
Keneally, Thomas
Kennedy, William
Kerouac, Jean-Louis Lebrid de
Kesey, Ken
King, Francis
Kingston, Maxine Hong
Kis, Danilo
Knowles, John
Koestler, Arthur
Konwicki, Tadeusz
Koontz, Dean R.
Kosinski, Jerzy
Krantz, Judith
Kroetsch, Robert
Kumin, Maxine
Kundera, Milan
Lagerkvist, Paer
La Guma, Alex
Lamming, George
Larkin, Philip
Laurence, Margaret

Lavin, Mary
Lawrence, D. H.
Laye, Camara
Lee, Harper
Leonov, Leonid
Lessing, Doris
Levi, Primo
Lewis, Norman
Lewis, Sinclair
Lindbergh, Anne Morrow
Lively, Penelope
Lodge, David
London, John Griffith
Lovelace, Earl
Lowry, Malcolm
Lurie, Alison
MacBeth, George
MacDonald, John D.
MacInnes, Colin
MacLennan, Hugh
Madden, David
Mahfouz, Naguib
Mailer, Norman
Mais, Roger
Malamud, Bernard
Malraux, Andre
Mann, Thomas
Manning, Olivia
Marshall, Paule
Masefield, John
Mason, Bobbie Ann
Matthiessen, Peter
Matute, Ana Maria
Maugham, William Somerset
Mauriac, Francois
Maurois, Andre
McCaffrey, Anne
McCarthy, Mary
McCullers, Carson
McCullough, Colleen
McEwan, Ian
McGrath, Thomas
McGuane, Thomas
McKay, Festus Claudius
McMurtry, Larry
Meaker, Marijane
Michaels, Leonard
Miller, Henry
Mitchell, Margaret
Mo, Timothy
Momaday, N. Scott
Montherlant, Henry de
Moore, Brian
Morante, Elsa
Morris, Wright
Morrison, Toni
Mukherjee, Bharati
Munro, Alice
Munro, H. H.
Murdoch, Iris

Nabokov, Vladimir
Naipaul, Shiva
Naipaul, V. S.
Narayan, R. K.
Naughton, Bill
Naylor, Gloria
Nemerov, Howard
Newby, P. H.
Ngugi wa Thiong'o
Nin, Anais
Nye, Robert
Oates, Joyce Carol
O'Brien, Edna
O'Connor, Flannery
Oe, Kenzaburo
O'Faolain, Julia
O'Flaherty, Liam
O'Hara, John
Olsen, Tillie
Onetti, Juan Carlos
Oz, Amos
Ozick, Cynthia
Page, P. K.
Pagnol, Marcel
Panova, Vera
Parker, Robert B.
Pasolini, Pier Paolo
Pasternak, Boris
Patchen, Kenneth
Paton, Alan
p'Bitek, Okot
Pearson, Andrew Russell
Pedersen, Knut
Percy, Walker
Petry, Ann
Phillips, Jayne Anne
Piercy, Marge
Pincherle, Alberto
Plante, David
Plath, Sylvia
Plomer, William Charles
    Franklin
Porter, Katherine Anne
Potok, Chaim
Powell, Anthony
Powers, J. F.
Prichard, Katharine Susannah
Priestley, J. B.
Pritchett, V. S.
Proust, Marcel
Puzo, Mario
Pym, Barbara
Pynchon, Thomas
Queneau, Raymond
Quoirez, Francoise
Rand, Ayn
Rao, Raja
Reed, Ishmael
Remarque, Erich Maria
Rhys, Jean
Richler, Mordecai

Robbe-Grillet, Alain
Robbins, Harold
Robbins, Thomas Eugene
Rodd, Kylie Tennant
Rossner, Judith
Roth, Henry
Roth, Philip
Roy, Gabrielle
Rubens, Bernice
Rulfo, Juan
Rushdie, Salman
Sabato, Ernesto
Sackville-West, V.
Saint-Exupery, Antoine de
Sansom, William
Saroyan, William
Sarraute, Nathalie
Sarton, May
Sartre, Jean-Paul
Sassoon, Siegfried
Sauser-Hall, Frederic
Schaeffer, Susan Fromberg
Schmitz, Aron Hector
Sciascia, Leonardo
Scott, Paul
Segal, Erich
Selvon, Samuel
Sender, Ramon
Shaw, Irwin
Sheed, Wilfrid
Sheehy, Gail
Sheldon, Sidney
Shirer, William L.
Sholokhov, Mikhail
Siddons, Anne Rivers
Sillanpaa, Frans Eemil
Sillitoe, Alan
Silone, Ignazio
Simon, Claude
Sinclair, Andrew
Singer, Isaac Bashevis
Skvorecky, Josef
Smith, Florence Margaret
Smith, Wilbur
Snow, C. P.
Solzhenitsyn, Aleksandr I.
Sontag, Susan
Soyinka, Wole
Spark, Muriel
Spencer, Elizabeth
Stafford, Jean
Stead, Christina
Steel, Danielle
Stegner, Wallace
Steinbeck, John
Steiner, George
Stewart, J. I. M.
Stone, Robert
Storey, David
Stow, Randolph

Styron, William
Tagore, Rabindranath
Taylor, Elizabeth
Taylor, Peter
Theroux, Paul
Thibault, Jacques Anatole
    Francois
Thomas, Audrey
Thomas, D. M.
Toomer, Jean
Torres Bodet, Jaime
Tournier, Michel
Townsend, Sue
Traven, B.
Tremblay, Michel
Trifonov, Yuri
Troyat, Henri
Tryon, Thomas
Tutuola, Amos
Tyler, Anne
Unamuno, Miguel de
Undset, Sigrid
Updike, John
Uris, Leon
Vargas Llosa, Mario
Vidal, Gore
Voinovich, Vladimir
Vonnegut, Kurt, Jr.
Wain, John
Walker, Alice
Walker, Margaret
Wallace, Irving
Wallant, Edward Lewis
Warner, Sylvia Townsend
Warren, Robert Penn
Waterhouse, Keith
Waugh, Evelyn
Weldon, Fay
Wells, H. G.
Welty, Eudora
Wesley, Mary
West, Jessamyn
West, Morris L.
West, Nathanael
West, Rebecca
Wharton, Edith
White, Edmund
White, Patrick
Wiesel, Elie
Wilder, Thornton
Willard, Nancy
Williams, Tennessee
Williams, William Carlos
Williamson, Henry
Willingham, Calder
Wilson, Angus
Wilson, Colin
Wilson, Ethel Davis
Wilson, John Burgess
Wodehouse, P. G.

Wolf, Christa
Wolfe, Thomas
Wolfe, Thomas Kennerly, Jr.
Woolf, Virginia
Wouk, Herman
Wright, Richard
Yerby, Frank G.
Yevtushenko, Yevgeny
Yezierska, Anzia
Yglesias, Helen

PHILOSOPHY

Adler, Mortimer J.
Arendt, Hannah
Beauvoir, Simone de
Buber, Martin
Burke, Kenneth
Camus, Albert
Canetti, Elias
Chomsky, Noam
de Bono, Edward
de Man, Paul
Eco, Umberto
Foucault, Michel
Fromm, Erich
Fuller, R. Buckminster
Heidegger, Martin
Hofstadter, Douglas R.
Jeffers, Robinson
Kirk, Russell
Koestler, Arthur
Langer, Susanne K.
Lukacs, Gyorgy
Mann, Thomas
Marcel, Gabriel Honore
Murdoch, Iris
Ortega y Gasset, Jose
Percy, Walker
Pirsig, Robert M.
Popper, Karl R.
Rand, Ayn
Rao, Raja
Russell, Bertrand
Sartre, Jean-Paul
Steiner, George
Suzuki, Daisetz Teitaro
Tillich, Paul
Tuchman, Barbara W.
Valery, Paul
Williams, Raymond
Wilson, Colin

POETRY

Aiken, Conrad
Akhmatova, Anna
Aleixandre, Vicente
Amichai, Yehuda
Amis, Kingsley
Ammons, A. R.
Angelou, Maya

Antschel, Paul
Aragon, Louis
Ashbery, John
Asturias, Miguel Angel
Atwood, Margaret
Auden, W. H.
Avison, Margaret
Baraka, Amiri
Barker, George Granville
Bassani, Giorgio
Beckett, Samuel
Bell, Marvin
Berryman, John
Betjeman, John
Birney, Earle
Bishop, Elizabeth
bissett, bill
Blais, Marie-Claire
Blunden, Edmund
Bly, Robert
Bogan, Louise
Bond, Edward
Bonnefoy, Yves
Bontemps, Arna
Borges, Jorge Luis
Bowles, Paul
Boyle, Kay
Brautigan, Richard
Brecht, Bertolt
Breton, Andre
Brodsky, Iosif Alexandrovich
Brooke, Rupert
Brooks, Gwendolyn
Brown, George Mackay
Brown, Rita Mae
Brown, Sterling Allen
Bukowski, Charles
Butor, Michel
Cardenal, Ernesto
Carruth, Hayden
Carver, Raymond
Causley, Charles
Cesaire, Aime
Chesterton, G. K.
Ciardi, John
Clifton, Lucille
Cocteau, Jean M.
Cohen, Leonard
Colum, Padraic
Coover, Robert
Corso, Gregory
Cowley, Malcolm
Crane, Hart
Creeley, Robert
Cullen, Countee
Cummings, E. E.
Dahlberg, Edward
Dario, Ruben
Davie, Donald
Day Lewis, C.

Dickey, James
Dillard, Annie
Diop, Birago
Disch, Thomas M.
Doolittle, Hilda
Duffy, Maureen
Duhamel, Georges
Duncan, Robert
Dunn, Douglas
Durrell, Lawrence
Eberhart, Richard
Eliot, T. S.
Elytis, Odysseus
Empson, William
Everson, William
Ewart, Gavin
Feinstein, Elaine
Ferlinghetti, Lawrence
Frost, Robert
Garcia Lorca, Federico
Gascoyne, David
Genet, Jean
Gilbert, Sandra M.
Ginsberg, Allen
Giovanni, Nikki
Godoy Alcayaga, Lucila
Goodman, Paul
Graves, Robert
Gray, Alasdair
Grieve, C. M.
Grigson, Geoffrey
Guiraldes, Ricardo
Gunn, Thom
Handke, Peter
Hardy, Thomas
Harris, Wilson
Harrison, Tony
Hayden, Robert E.
Heaney, Seamus
Hebert, Anne
Henri, Adrian
Herbert, Zbigniew
Hesse, Hermann
Hill, Geoffrey
Hope, A. D.
Housman, A. E.
Hughes, Langston
Hughes, Ted
Jarrell, Randall
Jeffers, Robinson
Jennings, Elizabeth
Jimenez, Juan Ramon
Jones, David
Jones, Gayl
Jong, Erica
Jordan, June
Joyce, James
Kavanagh, Patrick
Kazantzakis, Nikos
Kinnell, Galway

Kinsella, Thomas
Kipling, Rudyard
Kroetsch, Robert
Kumin, Maxine
Kunitz, Stanley
Lagerkvist, Paer
Laing, R. D.
Lamming, George
Larkin, Philip
Lawrence, D. H.
Layton, Irving
Lee, Laurie
Leger, Alexis
Levertov, Denise
Livesay, Dorothy
Lorde, Audre
Lowell, Robert
MacBeth, George
MacLeish, Archibald
MacNeice, Louis
Mao Tse-tung
Masefield, John
Masters, Edgar Lee
McGrath, Thomas
McKay, Festus Claudius
Merrill, James
Merwin, W. S.
Millay, Edna St. Vincent
Milne, A. A.
Milosz, Czeslaw
Momaday, N. Scott
Montague, John
Montale, Eugenio
Moore, Marianne
Morgan, Robin
Nash, Ogden
Nelson, Alice Ruth Moore
   Dunbar
Nemerov, Howard
Neruda, Pablo
Nye, Robert
O'Hara, Frank
Okigbo, Christopher
Olson, Charles
Page, P. K.
Parra, Nicanor
Pasolini, Pier Paolo
Pasternak, Boris
Patchen, Kenneth
Paz, Octavio
p'Bitek, Okot
Peake, Mervyn
Piercy, Marge
Plath, Sylvia
Plomer, William Charles
   Franklin
Pollitt, Katha
Pound, Ezra
Prevert, Jacques
Quasimodo, Salvatore

Queneau, Raymond
Raine, Kathleen
Reed, Ishmael
Rexroth, Kenneth
Rich, Adrienne
Rilke, Rainer Maria
Ritsos, Yannis
Robinson, Edwin Arlington
Roethke, Theodore
Romains, Jules
Rostand, Edmond
Rozewicz, Tadeusz
Rukeyser, Muriel
Sanchez, Sonia
Sandburg, Carl
Sarton, May
Sassoon, Siegfried
Sauser-Hall, Frederic
Schaeffer, Susan Fromberg
Schwartz, Delmore
Seferiades, Giorgos Stylianou
Seifert, Jaroslav
Senghor, Leopold Sedar
Sexton, Anne
Shange, Ntozake
Shapiro, Karl
Sillitoe, Alan
Simpson, Louis
Sitwell, Dame Edith
Smith, Florence Margaret
Snodgrass, William D.
Soyinka, Wole
Spender, Stephen
Stein, Gertrude
Stevens, Wallace
Stevenson, Anne
Stow, Randolph
Swenson, May
Tagore, Rabindranath
Tate, Allen
Thomas, D. M.
Thomas, Dylan
Thomas, Joyce Carol
Thomas, R. S.
Toomer, Jean
Torres Bodet, Jaime
Tsvetaeva, Marina
Unamuno, Miguel de
Valery, Paul
Van Doren, Mark
Voznesensky, Andrei
Wain, John
Walcott, Derek
Walker, Alice
Walker, Margaret
Warner, Sylvia Townsend
Warren, Robert Penn
White, E. B.
Wilbur, Richard
Willard, Nancy

Williams, William Carlos
Winters, Yvor
Wright, Charles
Wright, James
Wright, Judith
Yeats, William Butler
Yevtushenko, Yevgeny
Yourcenar, Marguerite
Zelazny, Roger
Zukofsky, Louis

POLITICS and GOVERNMENT
Brink, Andre
Buckley, William F., Jr.
Carter, James Earl, Jr.
Cesaire, Aime
Chomsky, Noam
Churchill, Winston
Commager, Henry Steele
Deloria, Vine, Jr.
Friedman, Milton
Fussell, Paul
Galbraith, John Kenneth
Gandhi, Mohandas Karamchand
Gorbachev, Mikhail
Hayek, F. A.
Higgins, George V.
James, C. L. R.
Kammen, Michael G.
Kennedy, John Fitzgerald
Kenyatta, Jomo
King, Martin Luther, Jr.
Kirk, Russell
Kissinger, Henry A.
Koestler, Arthur
Lasch, Christopher
Malraux, Andre
Mao Tse-tung
Nehru, Jawaharlal
Nixon, Richard M.
Senghor, Leopold Sedar
Shaw, George Bernard
Silone, Ignazio
Thompson, Hunter S.
Vidal, Gore
Wedgwood, C. V.
White, Theodore H.
Will, George F.
Woodward, Robert Upshur

PSYCHOLOGY and EDUCATION
Adler, Mortimer J.
Berne, Eric
Bettelheim, Bruno
Erikson, Erik H.
Freud, Anna
Freud, Sigmund
Friday, Nancy
Fromm, Erich

Goodall, Jane
Hirsch, E. D., Jr.
Jung, C. G.
Laing, R. D.
Leary, Timothy
Lorenz, Konrad Zacharias
Luria, Alexander R.
Maslow, Abraham H.
Mead, Margaret
Menninger, Karl
Piaget, Jean
Ravitch, Diane
Rogers, Carl R.
Sacks, Oliver
Skinner, B. F.
Spock, Benjamin
Wilson, Edward O.

RELIGION and SPIRITUALITY
Agnon, S. Y.
Bach, Richard
Buber, Martin
Buechner, Frederick
Bultmann, Rudolf Karl
Campbell, Joseph
Castaneda, Carlos
Daly, Mary
Eliade, Mircea
Gandhi, Mohandas Karamchand
Greeley, Andrew M.
Hesse, Hermann
King, Martin Luther, Jr.
Kueng, Hans
L'Engle, Madeleine
Lewis, C. S.
Matthiessen, Peter
Mauriac, Francois
Merton, Thomas
Muggeridge, Malcolm
Peale, Norman Vincent
Sheen, Fulton J.
Tillich, Paul
Wiesel, Elie

ROMANCE
Aiken, Joan
Andrews, V. C.
Bates, H. E.
Bradford, Barbara Taylor
Cartland, Barbara
Cookson, Catherine
Dailey, Janet
du Maurier, Daphne
Ferber, Edna
Heyer, Georgette
Isaacs, Susan
Kirk, Russell
Matthews, Patricia
Pargeter, Edith Mary
Pilcher, Rosamunde

Powys, John Cowper
Rogers, Rosemary
Steel, Danielle
Susann, Jacqueline
Woodiwiss, Kathleen E.
Yerby, Frank G.

SCIENCE and TECHNOLOGY
Asimov, Isaac
Bova, Ben
Calder, Nigel
Campbell, John W.
Clarke, Arthur C.
Commoner, Barry
Einstein, Albert
Feynman, Richard Phillips
Fossey, Dian
Fuller, R. Buckminster
Gould, Stephen Jay
Hofstadter, Douglas R.
Hoyle, Fred
Huxley, Julian
Kidder, Tracy
Lorenz, Konrad Zacharias
McLuhan, Marshall
Oppenheimer, J. Robert
Parra, Nicanor
Pauling, Linus
Popper, Karl R.
Russell, Bertrand
Sagan, Carl
Simpson, George Gaylord
Snow, C. P.
Teller, Edward
Thomas, Lewis
Toffler, Alvin
Wilson, Edward O.

SCIENCE FICTION and FANTASY
Adams, Richard
Aldiss, Brian W.
Alexander, Lloyd
Anderson, Poul
Anthony, Piers
Asimov, Isaac
Ballard, J. G.
Baum, L. Frank
Bester, Alfred
Blish, James
Bova, Ben
Bradbury, Ray
Bradley, Marion Zimmer
Brunner, John
Burroughs, Edgar Rice
Butler, Octavia E.
Campbell, John W.
Card, Orson Scott
Clarke, Arthur C.
Crichton, Michael

Delany, Samuel R.
del Rey, Lester
Dick, Philip K.
Disch, Thomas M.
Ellison, Harlan
Farmer, Philip Jose
Heinlein, Robert A.
Herbert, Frank
Hoyle, Fred
Kafka, Franz
Kavan, Anna
Kinsella, W. P.
Koontz, Dean R.
Le Guin, Ursula K.
Leiber, Fritz
Lem, Stanislaw
L'Engle, Madeleine
Lessing, Doris
Lewis, C. S.
London, John Griffith
Lovecraft, H. P.
MacDonald, John D.
McCaffrey, Anne
McIntyre, Vonda N.
McKillip, Patricia A.
Merril, Judith
Moorcock, Michael
Niven, Laurence Van Cott
Norton, Andre
Peake, Mervyn
Pohl, Frederik
Russ, Joanna
Saberhagen, Fred
Saint-Exupery, Antoine de
Sheldon, Alice Hastings Bradley
Silverberg, Robert
Simak, Clifford D.
Sturgeon, Theodore
Tolkien, J. R. R.
Vance, John Holbrook
Vonnegut, Kurt, Jr.
Wells, H. G.
Wilhelm, Katie Gertrude
Zelazny, Roger

SHORT STORIES
Adams, Alice
Agnon, S. Y.
Aiken, Conrad
Aitmatov, Chingiz
Algren, Nelson
Anaya, Rudolfo A.
Anderson, Sherwood
Andric, Ivo
Atwood, Margaret
Auchincloss, Louis
Bambara, Toni Cade
Barker, George Granville
Barnes, Djuna
Barth, John

Barthelme, Donald
Bassani, Giorgio
Bates, H. E.
Baumbach, Jonathan
Beattie, Ann
Berger, Thomas
Bioy Casares, Adolfo
Blackwood, Caroline
Blasco Ibanez, Vicente
Blixen, Karen
Boell, Heinrich
Borges, Jorge Luis
Bowen, Elizabeth
Bowles, Paul
Boyle, Kay
Bradbury, Ray
Brautigan, Richard
Brophy, Brigid
Brown, George Mackay
Burroughs, Edgar Rice
Caldwell, Erskine
Calisher, Hortense
Callaghan, Morley Edward
Calvino, Italo
Capote, Truman
Card, Orson Scott
Carey, Peter
Carter, Angela
Carver, Raymond
Cather, Willa Sibert
Cela, Camilo Jose
Cheever, John
Chesnutt, Charles W.
Ch'ien Chung-shu
Cixous, Helene
Clutha, Janet Paterson Frame
Colegate, Isabel
Colette
Conrad, Joseph
Cortazar, Julio
Cox, William Trevor
Cozzens, James Gould
Creeley, Robert
Crews, Harry
Dahl, Roald
Dario, Ruben
De Vries, Peter
Diop, Birago
Donleavy, J. P.
Donoso, Jose
Dreiser, Theodore
Endo, Shusaku
Farrell, James T.
Fiedler, Leslie A.
Fitzgerald, F. Scott
Flanagan, Thomas
Frank, Anne
Friel, Brian
Fuentes, Carlos
Gaines, Ernest J.

Gallant, Mavis
Gardam, Jane
Gilchrist, Ellen
Giono, Jean
Godwin, Gail
Gordimer, Nadine
Gordon, Mary
Goytisolo, Juan
Grau, Shirley Ann
Greene, Graham
Grossman, Vasily
Guiraldes, Ricardo
Hannah, Barry
Hardy, Thomas
Hasek, Jaroslav
Head, Bessie
Helprin, Mark
Hemingway, Ernest
Hesse, Hermann
Higgins, George V.
Highsmith, Patricia
Hurston, Zora Neale
Huxley, Aldous
James, Henry
Jhabvala, Ruth Prawer
Jones, Gayl
Joyce, James
Kafka, Franz
Kavan, Anna
Kazakov, Yuri Pavlovich
King, Francis
King, Stephen
Kinsella, W. P.
Kipling, Rudyard
Kundera, Milan
Lamming, George
Lardner, Ring W.
Laurence, Margaret
Lavin, Mary
Lawrence, D. H.
Lessing, Doris
Levi, Primo
Livesay, Dorothy
London, John Griffith
Lovelace, Earl
Lowry, Malcolm
MacDonald, John D.
Mahfouz, Naguib
Mais, Roger
Malamud, Bernard
Mann, Thomas
Marshall, Paule
Mason, Bobbie Ann
Matute, Ana Maria
Maugham, William Somerset
McCarthy, Mary
McGahern, John
McPherson, James Alan
Michaels, Leonard
Millay, Edna St. Vincent

Milner, Ron
Morante, Elsa
Mrozek, Slawomir
Mukherjee, Bharati
Munro, Alice
Nabokov, Vladimir
Naipaul, Shiva
Nelson, Alice Ruth Moore
   Dunbar
Oates, Joyce Carol
O'Brien, Edna
O'Connor, Flannery
Oe, Kenzaburo
O'Faolain, Julia
O'Faolain, Sean
O'Flaherty, Liam
Olsen, Tillie
Onetti, Juan Carlos
Oz, Amos
Ozick, Cynthia
Paley, Grace
Panova, Vera
Parker, Dorothy
Pedersen, Knut
Phillips, Jayne Anne
Pincherle, Alberto
Porter, Katherine Anne
Porter, William Sydney
Prichard, Katharine Susannah
Proust, Marcel
Quiroga, Horacio
Rao, Raja
Rhys, Jean
Sansom, William
Saroyan, William
Schaeffer, Susan Fromberg
Schmitz, Aron Hector
Schwartz, Delmore
Selvon, Samuel
Shaw, Irwin
Shepard, Sam
Sillitoe, Alan
Singer, Isaac Bashevis
Skvorecky, Josef
Spark, Muriel
Stafford, Jean
Stead, Christina
Steinbeck, John
Taylor, Elizabeth
Taylor, Peter
Theroux, Paul
Thibault, Jacques Anatole
   Francois
Thomas, Audrey
Thomas, Dylan
Toomer, Jean
Tournier, Michel
Traven, B.
Van Doren, Mark
Voinovich, Vladimir

Walker, Alice
Warner, Sylvia Townsend
Welty, Eudora
Wesker, Arnold
West, Jessamyn
Wharton, Edith
White, Patrick
Williams, William Carlos
Wilson, Ethel Davis
Wodehouse, P. G.
Wolf, Christa
Wolfe, Thomas
Woolf, Virginia
Wright, Judith
Wright, Richard
Yeats, William Butler
Yezierska, Anzia
Yourcenar, Marguerite

SOCIAL ACTIVISM
Achebe, Chinua
Aitmatov, Chingiz
Andersch, Alfred
Baldwin, James
Baraka, Amiri
Blair, Eric
Brink, Andre
Brittain, Vera
Brownmiller, Susan
Calder, Nigel
Caldicott, Helen
Cardenal, Ernesto
Carson, Rachel Louise
Conran, Shirley
Cousins, Norman
Cousteau, Jacques-Yves
Daly, Mary
Du Bois, W. E. B.
Dworkin, Andrea
Ehrenreich, Barbara
Einstein, Albert
Fossey, Dian
Friedan, Betty
Galbraith, John Kenneth
Goodman, Paul
Gordimer, Nadine
Gould, Lois
Gouldner, Alvin W.
Greer, Germaine
Grieve, C. M.
Hazzard, Shirley
Hoffman, Abbie
Huxley, Aldous
Illich, Ivan
James, C. L. R.
Johnson, James Weldon
Kidder, Tracy
King, Larry L.
King, Martin Luther, Jr.
Lasch, Christopher

Leary, Timothy
Little, Malcolm
Lorde, Audre
Lukas, J. Anthony
Mao Tse-tung
Matthiessen, Peter
McLuhan, Marshall
Mead, Margaret
Mehta, Ved
Mencken, H. L.
Millett, Kate
Milosz, Czeslaw
Morgan, Robin
Morrison, Toni
Mowat, Farley
Neruda, Pablo
Ousmane, Sembene
Oz, Amos
Paton, Alan
Pauling, Linus
Pearson, Andrew Russell
Pound, Ezra
Rand, Ayn
Sanchez, Sonia
Schlafly, Phyllis
Schlesinger, Arthur M., Jr.
Senghor, Leopold Sedar
Sheehy, Gail
Sinclair, Upton
Snow, C. P.
Steinem, Gloria
Talese, Gay
Thompson, Hunter S.
Toffler, Alvin
Voznesensky, Andrei
Wambaugh, Joseph
Wells, H. G.
West, Rebecca
Wilson, Edmund

SOCIOLOGY and
ANTHROPOLOGY
Buck, Pearl S.
Campbell, Joseph
Castaneda, Carlos
Eliade, Mircea
Gouldner, Alvin W.
Hite, Shere
Jung, C. G.
Leakey, Louis S. B.
Levi-Strauss, Claude
Mead, Margaret
Morris, Desmond
Parsons, Talcott
Reed, Ishmael
Terkel, Louis

TRAVEL and ADVENTURE
Adamson, Joy
Algren, Nelson

Andersch, Alfred
Anderson, Sherwood
Behan, Brendan
Bowen, Elizabeth
Buck, Pearl S.
Cousteau, Jacques-Yves
Durrell, Lawrence
Gardner, Erle Stanley
Genet, Jean
Golding, William
Gray, Francine du Plessix
Greene, Graham
Grigson, Geoffrey
Heyerdahl, Thor
Kazantzakis, Nikos
King, Francis
Laurence, Margaret
Lawrence, D. H.
Leigh Fermor, Patrick
Lewis, Norman
London, John Griffith
Lopez, Barry Holstun
Matthiessen, Peter
Maxwell, Gavin
McPhee, John
Michener, James A.
Morris, Jan
Naipaul, Shiva
Naipaul, V. S.
Perelman, S. J.
Pritchett, V. S.
Sansom, William
Simon, Kate
Steinbeck, John
Theroux, Paul
Waugh, Evelyn

TELEVISION
Arden, John
Bainbridge, Beryl
Bambara, Toni Cade
Bennett, Alan
Campbell, Joseph
Cleese, John
Cousteau, Jacques-Yves
Delaney, Shelagh
Edgar, David
Ellison, Harlan
Feinstein, Elaine
Gray, Simon
Hailey, Arthur
Hall, Willis
Hare, David
James, Clive
McLuhan, Marshall
Mercer, David
Milligan, Terence Alan
Nichols, Peter
Osborne, John
Richler, Mordecai

Sagan, Carl
Sheldon, Sidney
Simon, Neil
Spillane, Frank Morrison
Stoppard, Tom
Townsend, Sue
Weldon, Fay
Wesker, Arnold
Wouk, Herman

The WEST
Berger, Thomas
Brown, Dee
Cather, Willa Sibert
Creasey, John
Estleman, Loren D.
Grey, Zane
Horgan, Paul
Jakes, John (William)
L'Amour, Louis
Leonard, Elmore
McGuane, Thomas
McMurtry, Larry
Michener, James A.
Momaday, N. Scott
Morris, Wright
Sandoz, Mari
Stegner, Wallace